Springer Commentaries on International
and European Law

The Springer Commentaries on International and European Law Series publishes practice oriented article-by-article commentaries on legal instruments written for researchers and practitioners.

Robert Böttner • Hermann-Josef Blanke
Editors

Treaty on the Functioning of the European Union – A Commentary

Volume II: Articles 90–164

Editors
Robert Böttner
Faculty of Law, Economics and Social Sciences
University of Erfurt
Erfurt, Germany

Hermann-Josef Blanke
Faculty of Law, Economics and Social Sciences
University of Erfurt
Erfurt, Germany

ISSN 2662-9666   ISSN 2662-9674   (electronic)
Springer Commentaries on International and European Law
ISBN 978-3-031-42360-4   ISBN 978-3-031-42361-1   (eBook)
https://doi.org/10.1007/978-3-031-42361-1

© The Editor(s) (if applicable) and The Author(s), under exclusive license to Springer Nature Switzerland AG 2024

This work is subject to copyright. All rights are reserved by the Publisher, whether the whole or part of the material is concerned, specifically the rights of translation, reprinting, reuse of illustrations, recitation, broadcasting, reproduction on microfilms or in any other physical way, and transmission or information storage and retrieval, electronic adaptation, computer software, or by similar or dissimilar methodology now known or hereafter developed.

The use of general descriptive names, registered names, trademarks, service marks, etc. in this publication does not imply, even in the absence of a specific statement, that such names are exempt from the relevant protective laws and regulations and therefore free for general use.

The publisher, the authors, and the editors are safe to assume that the advice and information in this book are believed to be true and accurate at the date of publication. Neither the publisher nor the authors or the editors give a warranty, expressed or implied, with respect to the material contained herein or for any errors or omissions that may have been made. The publisher remains neutral with regard to jurisdictional claims in published maps and institutional affiliations.

This Springer imprint is published by the registered company Springer Nature Switzerland AG
The registered company address is: Gewerbestrasse 11, 6330 Cham, Switzerland

If disposing of this product, please recycle the paper.

*To Jean Monnet (1888-1979)
and Robert Schumann (1886-1963)
architects of the European integration
and creators of the European Community's
intellectual, political and economic
foundations*

Preface

While finalising the second volume of this commentary project, Professor Hermann-Josef Blanke, one of the initiators and a *spiritus rector* of this endeavour, passed away unexpectedly. His death is a painful loss, both personally and academically. All the more reason for me, as co-editor of this volume, to complete the work he co-founded.

The second volume of the TFEU Commentary covers Articles 90 to 164 and focuses on the provisions of Title VIII on the Economic and Monetary Union including analyses concerning the reform of the EMU. This supplement is due to the fact that, as a result of the international treaties which the Member States have concluded to reform the EMU (Treaties on ESM and SCG), but also of the numerous directives and regulations establishing the Banking Union, the Treaty norms and secondary legislation as it existed before have ceased to be the sole basis for policy making within the Economic and Monetary Union.

The institutional reforms carried out in the wake of the sovereign debt crisis and the monetary policy measures taken by the ECB have helped to stabilise the public finances of the EMU Member States and strengthen the resilience of the euro area economy. The Member States which adopted the Euro and together constitute the Eurozone could therefore look towards the future with positive expectations at the beginning of the 70th year of the Schuman Declaration (9 May 1950). The Covid-19 pandemic, however, faced the Union and its Member States with unprecedented challenges. It had serious socio-economic consequences also in the long term and has again put the solidarity within the European multilevel governance under scrutiny. The financial protective walls erected by the Member States and the aid measures of the Union, in particular the Union's post-COVID recovery fund *Next Generation EU* launched in attempt to cushion the fall of the Member State economies in a recession, illustrate the exceptional nature of the pandemic situation. Against this backdrop, a return to a stability-oriented budgetary and monetary policy as soon as possible is essential.

The fact that "reform processes are needed in multiple governance areas" (European Parliament, 15 January 2020) is also reflected in the "Conference on the Future of Europe" which concluded its work in 2022. Even if an amendment to the Lisbon Treaty will not be at the centre of the agenda following up on the Conference, it opens up the opportunity for a closer involvement of EU citizens in a bottom-up approach in which they are listened to and their voices and expectations towards the Union contribute to current debates.

The need to step up the European integration process is also a result of the Covid-19 pandemic, although in political circles there is still uncertainty about how far reform can go. However, deeper integration in policy fields whose challenges can only be mastered together has long since become a precondition that Europe can assert itself in the world of the future.

The war of aggression that the Russian Federation and its President Vladimir Putin have launched on Ukraine has led to a *Zeitenwende* or "turning point" (*Olaf Scholz*) in Europe and the world. Instead of being divided, the members of NATO and the European Union stand closer together than before, despite all the existing disagreements. Further reforms can grow out of this environment.

Erfurt, Germany   Robert Böttner

Structure of the Commentary

The whole Commentary is organised as follows:
The Treaty on the European Union (TEU) – A Commentary
The Treaty on the Functioning of the European Union (TFEU) – A Commentary
  Volume I: Preamble, Articles 1–89
  Volume II: Articles 90–164
  Volume III: Articles 165–358
  Volume IV: Protocols (No 3 CJEU, No 4 ESCB and ECB, No 5 EIB, No 19 Schengen)

Contents

Title VI Transport

Article 90. [Common Transport Policy] (*Bernauw*)   3

Article 91. [Principles] (*Bernauw*)   15

Article 92. [Standstill Obligation] (*Bernauw*)   25

Article 93. [State Aid] (*Bernauw*)   27

Article 94. [Economic Circumstances of Carriers]
(*Eftestøl/Huemer/Wyatt*)   35

Article 95. [Prohibition of Discrimination] (*Eftestøl/Huemer/Wyatt*)   39

Article 96. [Forbidden State Aid and Exceptions]
(*Eftestøl/Huemer/Wyatt*)   45

Article 97. [Reasonable Frontier Crossing Charges]
(*Eftestøl/Huemer/Wyatt*)   51

Article 98. [German Unification] (*Niedobitek*)   55

Article 99. [Advisory Committee] (*Eftestøl/Huemer/Wyatt*)   65

Article 100. [Scope of the Title and Legislative Procedure] (*Eftestøl/
Huemer/Wyatt*)   69

Title VII Common Rules on Competition, Taxation and Approximation of Laws

Chapter 1 Rules on Competition

Section 1 Rules Applying to Undertakings

Article 101. [Prohibition of Agreements That Restrict Competition]
(*Vedder/Herz/Busscher*)   85

Article 102. [Prohibition of Abuses of a Dominant Position] (*Herz/Vedder*) 119

Article 103. [Adoption of Secondary Enforcement Measures for Articles 101 and 102 TFEU] (*Hinds*) 163

Article 104. [Transitional Enforcement Arrangements] (*Hinds*) 195

Article 105. [Role of the Commission] (*Hinds*) 201

Article 106. [Public and Privileged Undertakings and Services of General Economic Interest] (*Hinds*) 209

Section 2 Aids Granted by States

Article 107. [Prohibition of State Aid] (*Aalbers*) 261

Article 108. [Enforcement] (*Aalbers*) 297

Article 109 TFEU. [Implementation] (*Aalbers*) 321

Chapter 2 Tax Provisions

Article 110. [Discriminatory and Protective Internal Taxation] (*Jørgensen/Terkilsen*) 327

Article 111. [Tax Repayments for Exported Products] (*Jørgensen/Terkilsen*) 347

Article 112. [Approval of Reimbursements] (*Jørgensen/Terkilsen*) 349

Article 113. [Harmonisation of Indirect Taxes] (*Jørgensen/Terkilsen*) 351

Chapter 3 Approximation of Laws

Article 114. [Harmonisation in the Internal Market] (*Böttner/Blanke*) 371

Article 115. [Harmonising Laws Directly Affecting the Internal Market] (*Böttner/Blanke*) 411

Article 116. [Distortion of Competition] (*Ćemalović*) 417

Article 117. [National Measures] (*Ćemalović*) 435

Article 118. [European Intellectual Property Rights] (*Carre*) 445

Title VIII Economic and Monetary Policy

Article 119. [Principles of Economic and Monetary Policy] (*Blanke*) 477

Chapter 1 Economic Policy

Article 120. [Conduction of Economic Policies] (*Blanke*) 517

Article 121. [Coordination of Economic Policies] (*Blanke*) 553

Article 122. [Solidarity] (*Weber/Pilz*) 597

Article 123. [Prohibition of Credit Facilities] (*López Escudero*) 617

Article 124. [Prohibition of Privileged Access to Financial Institutions] (*López Escudero*) 643

Article 125. ["No-Bail-Out" Clause] (*Allemand*) 651

Article 126. [Prohibition of Excessive Government Deficits] (*Palmstorfer*) 689

Chapter 2 Monetary Policy

Article 127. [The European System of Central Banks] (*Palmstorfer*) 723

Article 128. [The Euro Currency] (*Palmstorfer*) 743

Article 129. [Statute of the ESCB] (*Tupits*) 749

Article 130. [Independence of Central Banks] (*Lambrinoc-Schanz/Kröger*) 753

Article 131. [Compatibility of National Legislation] (*de Sousa Botelho*) . . . 783

Article 132. [Legal Acts of the ECB] (*Schulte*) 793

Article 133. [Legal Acts Concerning the Euro] (*Palmstorfer*) 835

Chapter 3 Institutional Provisions

Article 134. [Economic and Financial Committee] (*Cafaro*) 843

Article 135. [Initiatives of the Council and the Member States] (*Cafaro*) 857

Chapter 4 Provisions specific to Member States whose Currency is the Euro

Article 136. [Measures Specific to the Member States Whose Currency Is the Euro] (*De Gregorio Merino*) 863

Article 137. [Eurogroup] (*Adalid*) 875

Article 138. [Common Positions] (*Adalid*) 899

Chapter 5 Transitional Provisions

Article 139. [Member States with a Derogation] (*Seyad*) 915

Article 140. [Progress Reports and Abrogation of Derogations] (*Seyad*) 939

Article 141. [General Council of the ECB] (*Seyad*) 957

Article 142. [Exchange-Rate Policy] (*Seyad*) 965

Article 143. [Mutual Assistance] (*Seyad*) 975

Article 144. [Protective Measures] (*Seyad*) 987

Supplement to Title VIII

Reforms and Perspectives of the Economic and Monetary Union: An Introduction (*Pilz*) 995

Treaty Establishing the European Stability Mechanism (TESM) (*Pilz*) 1029

Fiscal Union (*Wutscher*) 1113

The European Banking Union (*Lo Schiavo*) 1175

Title IX Employment

Article 145. [Coordinated Strategy for Employment] (*Dimitriu*) 1263

Article 146. [Promoting Employment] (*Dimitriu*) 1279

Article 147. [High Level of Employment] (*Dimitriu*) 1291

Article 148. [Employment Guidelines] (*Dimitriu*) 1295

Article 149. [Incentive Measures] (*Dimitriu*) 1305

Article 150. [Employment Committee] (*Dimitriu*) 1311

Title X Social Policy

Article 151. [Objectives] (*Jimena Quesada*) 1319

Article 152. [Social Dialogue] (*Jimena Quesada*) 1339

Article 153. [Union Action] (*Jimena Quesada*) 1353

Article 154. [Participation of the Social Partners] (*Jimena Quesada*) 1397

Article 155. [Agreements at Union Level] (*Jimena Quesada*) 1411

Article 156. [Inter-State Cooperation] (*Jimena Quesada*) 1427

Article 157. [Equal Pay Between Men and Women] (*Jimena Quesada*) . . . 1447

Article 158. [Paid Holiday Schemes] (*Kombos*) 1473

Article 159. [Report on the Social and Demographic Situation] (*Kombos*). 1479

Article 160. [Social Protection Committee] (*Kombos*) 1483

Article 161. [Annual Report on Social Development] (*Kombos*) 1487

Title XI   The European Social Fund

Article 162. [Aims of the ESF] (*Nyikos*) 1491

Article 163. [Administration] (*Nyikos*) 1503

Article 164. [Implementation] (*Nyikos*) 1507

Index 1511

Contributors

Maarten Aalbers, LL.M.   Senior Legal Advisor, Dutch Ministry of the Interior and Kingdom Relations, The Hague, The Netherlands
PhD Candidate, Leiden University, Leiden, The Netherlands

Sebastien Adalid, Dr.   Professor of Public Law, Université Rouen Normandie, Rouen, France

Frédéric Allemand, Dr.   Research Fellow, Robert Schuman Institute, Faculty of Law, Economics and Finance, University of Luxembourg, Esch-sur-Alzette, Luxembourg

Kristiaan Bernauw, Dr.   Professor of Transport and Insurance Law, Ghent University, Ghent, Belgium

Hermann-Josef Blanke, Dr.   Professor of Public Law, Public International Law and European Integration, Jean Monnet Chair, University of Erfurt, Erfurt, Germany

Robert Böttner, Dr.   Assistant Professor for German Public Law, Public International Law and European Law, University of Erfurt, Erfurt, Germany

Rick J. Busscher   Authority for Consumers and Markets, The Hague, The Netherlands

Susanna Cafaro, Dr.   Full Professor of EU Law, Jean Monnet Chair, Università del Salento, Lecce, Italy

Stéphanie Carre, Dr.   Maître de Conférences-HDR, Associate Professor, Centre d'Etudes Internationales de la Propriété Intellectuelle (CEIPI), Strasbourg, France

Uroš Ćemalović, Dr.   Professor of EU Law and Intellectual Property Law, Belgrade, Serbia
Senior Research Associate at the Institute of European Studies, Belgrade, Serbia

Alberto De Gregorio Merino Director, Council of the European Union, General Secretariat, Legal Service, Directorate 6 - Economic and Financial Affairs/EU Budget/Structural Funds, Brussels, Belgium

Raluca Dimitriu, Dr. Professor of Labour Law, Faculty of Law, University of Economic Studies, Bucharest, Romania

Ellen Eftestøl, Dr. Professor in Law, Department of Law and Governance, Norwegian Business School, Oslo, Norway

Martin S. E. Herz PhD Candidate in European Competition Law, University of Groningen, Groningen, The Netherlands
Lecturer in European Law, University of Groningen, Groningen, The Netherlands

Anna-Louise Hinds Lecturer in Law, University of Galway, Galway, Ireland

Maximilian Huemer Doctoral Researcher, University of Helsinki, Helsinki, Finland

Luis Jimena Quesada, Dr. Professor of Constitutional and European Law, University of Valencia, Valencia, Spain

Carsten Willemoes Jørgensen, PhD Associate Professor of Law, Department of Law, Aarhus University, Aarhus, Denmark

Constantinos Kombos Formerly Associate Professor of Public Law, Law Department, University of Cyprus, Nicosia, Cyprus
Minister of Foreign Affairs of the Republic of Cyprus, Nicosia, Cyprus

Malte Kröger, LL.M., Dr. Administrative Court Judge, Stade, and Lecturer in Public Law, Hamburg University of Applied Sciences, Hamburg, Germany

Simona Lambrinoc-Schanz Principal Legal Counsel (Institutional Law), European Central Bank, Frankfurt, Germany

Gianni Lo Schiavo, Dr. Senior Supervisor, European Central Bank, Frankfurt, Germany

Manuel López Escudero, Dr. Professor of Public International Law and European Law, University of Granada, Granada, Spain
Legal Secretary, Court of Justice of the European Union, Luxembourg, Luxembourg

Matthias Niedobitek, Dr. Jean Monnet Professor of European Integration, Chemnitz University of Technology, Chemnitz, Germany

Györgyi Nyikos, Dr. Associate Professor, National University of Public Service, Budapest, Hungary

Raimer Palmstorfer, LL.M., MMMag. Dr. Professor of European Law, University of Linz, Linz, Austria

Stefan Pilz, Dr. Advisor at the Thuringian Ministry of Finance, Erfurt, Germany
Lecturer in Administrative Law, Schmalkalden University of Applied Sciences, Schmalkalden, Germany

Martin Schulte, Dr. General Counsel, Bankhaus Scheich Wertpapierspezialist AG, Frankfurt am Main, Germany

Mohamed Sideek Seyad, Dr. Associate Professor for European Union Financial Law, Faculty of Law, University of Stockholm, Stockholm, Sweden

Gustavo de Sousa Botelho, Dr. Vice President, JPMorgan Chase & Co., Senningerberg Luxembourg, Grand Duchy of Luxembourg

Lars Kjærgård Terkilsen, PhD Director, KPMG Acor Tax, Hellerup, Denmark

Andres Tupits, PhD London University, Queen Mary College, London, UK
Visiting Professor at the Estonian Business School, Tallinn, Estonia

Hans H. B. Vedder, Dr. Professor of Economic Law, University of Groningen, Groningen, The Netherlands

Albrecht Weber, Dr. iur. utr. Professor Emeritus, European and Public Law, Faculty of Law, University of Osnabrück, Osnabrück, Germany

Claudia Wutscher, Dr. Associate Professor at the Institute for Austrian and European Public Law, Vienna, Austria
Director WU Legal Tech Center, Vienna University of Economics and Business (WU), Vienna, Austria

Daniel Wyatt LL.D. Candidate, University of Helsinki, Helsinki, Finland

Abbreviations

arg.	argumentum
A.S.	Atto Senato
ABoR	Administrative Board of Review
ABSPP	Asset Backed Securities Purchase Programme
AC	Appeal Cases
ACER	Agency for the Cooperation of Energy Regulators
ACP	African, Caribbean and Pacific States (Group)
AETR	European Agreement on Road Transport
AEUV	Vertrag über die Arbeitsweise der Europäischen Union (Treaty on the Functioning of the European Union—TFEU)
AFSJ	Area of Freedom, Security and Justice
AG	Advocate General
AGS	Annual Growth Survey
al.	alias (other)
AMR	Alert Mechanism Report
APP	Asset Purchase Programme
AQR	Asset Quality Review
ASOR	Agreement on the international occasional carriage of passengers by coach and bus
ASS	Asset Purchase Programme
AT1	Additional Tier 1
ATC	average total costs
AVC	average variable costs
BBA	British Bankers' Association
BCBS	Basel Committee on Banking Supervision
BDI	Bundesverband der Deutschen Industrie (Federation of German Industries)
BGBl.	Bundesgesetzblatt
BGEP	Broad guidelines for the economic policies
BIS	Bank for International Settlements

BIT	bilateral investment treaty
BL	Basic Law (German Constitution = Grundgesetz)
BR-Drs.	Bundesratsdrucksache
BRRD	Bank Recovery and Resolution Directive
BT-Drs.	Bundestagsdrucksache
BVerfG	Bundesverfassungsgericht (German Federal Constitutional Court)
BVerfGE	Entscheidung des Bundesverfassungsgerichts (Decision of the German Federal Constitutional Court)
BV-G	Bundesverfassungsgesetz (Austrian Constitution)
CA(s)	Competent Authority(ies)
CAC(s)	Collective Action Clause(s)
CAP	Common Agricultural Policy
CAT	Capital Acquisition Tax
CBDC	Central Bank Digital Currency
CBPP3	Covered Bond Purchase Programme
CC	Constitutional Court/Council
CCNR	Central Commission for the Navigation of the Rhine
CCP	Common Commercial Policy
CCT	Common Customs Tariff
CEAS	Common European Asylum System
CEBS	Committee on European Banking Supervisors
CEDAW	Committee on the Elimination of Discrimination Against Women
Cedefop	European Centre for the Development of Vocational Training
CEDH	Convention européenne des droits de l'homme Cour européenne des droits de l'homme
CEECs	Central and Eastern European countries
CEFTA	Central European Free Trade Agreement
CEPS	Centre for European Policy Studies
CET1	Common Equity Tier 1
CETA	Comprehensive Economic and Trade Agreement
cf.	confer (compare)
CF	Cohesion Fund
CFA	Franc de la Communauté Financière d'Afrique
CFI	Court of First Instance
CFP	Franc des Colonies françaises du Pacifique
CFSP	Common Foreign and Security Policy
Chap.	chapter
CISA	Convention implementing the Schengen Agreement
cit.	cited
CJEU	Court of Justice of the European Union
CJEU Statute	Protocol (No 3) on the Statue of the Court of Justice of the European Union

CMFB	Committee on monetary, financial and balance of payments statistics
CMO	Common Market Organisation
COA	Court of Auditors
CoC	Code of Conduct
CoE	Council of Europe
COM	Commission
CoR	Committee of the Regions
COREPER	Comité des représentants permanents (= Committee of Permanent Representatives)
COSAC	Conference of Parliamentary Committees for Union Affairs of Parliaments of the European Union
COSI	Standing Committee on Operational Cooperation on Internal Security
COVID-19	Corona Virus Disease 2019
CPC	Convention for the European Patent for the Common Market
CPSS	Committee on Payment and Settlement Systems
CRD	Capital Requirements Directive
CRR	Capital Requirements Regulation
CSD	Central Securities Depositaries
CSDP	Common Security and Defence Policy
CSPP	Corporate Sector Purchase Programme
CSR	country-specific recommendation(s)
CST	European Union Civil Service Tribunal
CUP	Cambridge University Press
DG	Directorate-General
DGS(s)	Deposit Guarantee Scheme(s)
DGSD	Deposit Guarantee Scheme Directive
DLT	Distributed Ledger Technology
DNA	National Anti-Corruption Directorate
Doc.	Document
DPA	Data Protection Authority
DPD	Data Protection Directive
EA	Euro Area
EAEC	European Atomic Energy Community
EAFRD	European Agricultural Fund for Rural Development
EAGF	European Agricultural Guarantee Fund
EAGGF	European Agricultural Guidelines and Guarantee Fund
EAW	European Arrest Warrant
EBA	European Banking Authority
EBU	European Banking Union
EC Treaty	Treaty establishing the European Community
EC	European Community/European Communities

ECB	European Central Bank
ECCL	Enhanced Conditions Credit Line
ECHR	European Convention on Human Rights and Fundamental Freedoms
ECJ	European Court of Justice
ECJ Statute	Protocol (No 3) on the Statue of the Court of Justice of the European Union
ECN	European Competition Network
ECN+	European Competition Network as reformed by Directive 2019/1
ECOFIN	Economic and Financial Affairs Council
ECommHR	European Commission of Human Rights
ECR	European Court Reports
ECSC	European Coal and Steel Community
ECSC Treaty	Treaty establishing the European Coal and Steel Community
ECSR	European Committee of Social Rights
ECtHR	European Court of Human Rights
ECU	European Currency Unit
EDA	European Defence Agency
EDC	European Defence Community
Ed(s).	Editor(s)
EDIS	European Deposit Insurance Scheme
edn.	edition
EDP	Excessive deficit procedure
EDPB	European Data Protection Board
EDP Protocol	Protocol (No. 12) on the Excessive Deficit Procedure
EDPS	European Data Protection Supervisor
EEA	European Economic Area
EEAS	European External Action Service
EEC	European Economic Community
EEC Treaty	Treaty establishing the European Economic Community
EES	European Employment Strategy
EFB	European Fiscal Board
EFC	Economic and Financial Committee
EFSF	European Financial Stability Facility/Europäische Finanzstabilisierungsfazilität
EFSM	European Financial Stability Mechanism/Europäischer Finanzstabilisierungsmechanismus
EFTA	European Free Trade Association
e.g.	exempli gratia (for example)
EGF	European Globalization Adjustment Fund
EGTC	European Grouping of Territorial Cooperation
EIB	European Investment Bank

EIB Statute	Protocol (No 5) on the Statute of the European Investment Bank
EIF	European Investment Fund
EIOPA	European Insurance and Occupational Pensions Authority
EIP	Excessive Imbalances Procedure
EJN	European Judicial Network
ELA	Emergency Liquidity Assistance/European Labour Authority
EMCF	European Monetary Cooperation Fund
EMCO	Employment Committee
EMF	European Monetary Fund
EMFF	European Maritime and Fisheries Fund
EMI	European Monetary Institute
EMS	European Monetary System
EMU	Economic and Monetary Union
ENP	European Neighbourhood Policy
EnzEuR	Enzyklopädie Europarecht
EP	European Parliament
EPC	European Patent Convention
EPO	European Patent Office
EPOrg	European Patent Organisation
EPP	Economic Partnership Programme
EPPO	European Public Prosecutor's Office
EPSO	European Personnel Selection Office
EPSR	European Pillar of Social Rights
ERA	EU Agency for Railways
ERDF	European Regional Development Fund
ERM	(European) Exchange Rate Mechanism
ERM2	(European) Exchange Rate Mechanism 2
ESA(s)	European Supervisory Authority(ies)/European System of Integrated Economic Accountss
(E)ESC	(European) Economic and Social Committee
ESNRA	European system of national and regional accounts
ESCB	European System of Central Banks
ESCB Statute	Protocol (No 4) on the Statute of the European System of Central Banks and of the European Central Bank
ESDP	European Security and Defence Policy
ESF	European Social Fund
ESF+	European Social Fund Plus
ESFS	European System of Financial Supervision/Supervisors
ESI Funds	European Structure and Investment Funds
ESM	European Stability Mechanism
ESMA	European Securities and Markets Authority
ESMV	Vertrag zur Errichtung des Europäischen Stabilitätsmechanismus

ESP	European statistical programme
ESPN	European Social Policy Network
ESRB	European Systemic Risk Board
ESS	European statistical system
et al.	et alii (and others)
eTEN	Trans-European Telecommunication Networks
et seq(q).	et sequens, et sequentes (and the following)
EU	European Union
EUCFR	European Union Charter of Fundamental Rights
EU-OSHA	European Agency for Safety and Health at Work
EUR	Euro (currency)
EURATOM	European Atomic Energy Community
EURIMF	Coordination Group of European Executive Directors in the IMF
Eurofund	European Foundation for the Improvement of Living and Working Conditions
EUROPOL	European Police Office
EUSFTA	EU-Singapore Free Trade Agreement
EUSR	EU Special Representative
EU Treaty	Treaty on European Union—TEU
EUV	Vertrag über die Europäische Union (Treaty on European Union—TEU)
EUZBBG	Gesetz über die Zusammenarbeit von Bundesregierung und Deutschem Bundestag in Angelegenheiten der Europäischen Union (Act on the Cooperation between the Federal Government and the German Bundestag in European matters)
EWG	Eurogroup Working Group
F.A.Z.	Frankfurter Allgemeine Zeitung
FCC	(German) Federal Constitutional Court
FDI	foreign direct investment
FEAD	European Fund for Aid to the Most Deprived
FEU Treaty	Treaty on the Functioning of the European Union—TFEU
FICOD	Financial Conglomerate Directive
fn.	footnote
FPS	freedom to provide services
FR	Financial Rules
FROB	Fondo de Restructuracion Ordendada Bancaria (Spanish Bank Restructuring Fund)
FSA Plan	Financial Services Action Plan
FSB	Financial Stability Board
G10	Group of Ten (consisting of Belgium, Canada, France, Germany, Italy, Japan, the Netherlands, Sweden, the United Kingdom, and the United States)
GATS	General Agreement on Trade in Services

GATT	General Agreement on Tariffs and Trade
GBER	General Block Exemption Regulation
GC	General Court (part of the CJEU)/Grand Chamber
GCC	German Constitutional Court
GDP	Gross Domestic Product
GDPR	General Data Protection Regulation
GDR	German Democratic Republic
GG	Grundgesetz (German Basic Law)
GNI	gross national income
GNP	gross national product
GOBR	Geschäftsordnung des Bundesrats (Rules of Procedure of the German Bundesrat)
GOBT	Geschäftsordnung des Deutschen Bundestags (Rules of Procedure of the German Bundestag)
G-SII(s)	Global Systematically Important Institution(s)
GVBl.	Gesetz- und Verordnungsblatt
HDR	Habilitation à diriger des recherches (authorised to steer researches)
HICP	Harmonized Index of Consumer Prices
HLEG	High Level Expert Group
HQ	headquarters
HR	High Representative (of the Union for Foreign Affairs and Security Policy)
HRA	Human Rights Act
i.a.	inter alia (among other things)
i.e.	id est (that is)
ibid.	ibidem (at the same place)
ICANN	Internet Corporation for Assigned Names and Numbers
ICC	International Criminal Court
ICJ	International Court of Justice
ICR	International Court Reports
id.	idem (the same)
IGA	Intergovernmental Agreement
IGC	Intergovernmental Conference
ILM	International Law Materials
ILO	International Labour Organisation
IMF	International Monetary Fund
IMFC	International Monetary and Financial Committee
INEA	Innovation and Networks Executive Agency
IOSCO	International Organization of Securities Commission
IP	intellectual property
IPU	intermediate EU parent undertaking

IRB	internal ratings based
ISO	International Organization for Standardization
ITS(s)	Implementing Technical Standard(s)
ISS	EU Institute for Security Studies
IWF	Internationaler Währungsfonds (= International Monetary Fonds in German)
JER	Joint Employment Report
JHA	Justice and Home Affairs
JST	Joint Supervisory Team(s)
LCR	Liquidity Coverage Ratio
LfE	Licence for Europe
loc. cit.	loco citato (in the place already cited)
LSI(s)	Less Significant Institution(s)
MEIP	Market Economy Investor Principle
MEO	Market Economy Operator
MEOP	Market Economy Operator Principle
MEP	Member of the European Parliament
MEQR	measure equivalent to quantitative restriction
MIP	Macroeconomic Imbalance Procedure
MLP	Mutual Learning Programme
MoU	Memorandum of Understanding
MP	Member of Parliament
MREL	Minimum Requirement for own funds and Eligible Liabilities
MS	Member State(s)
MSP	Multilateral Surveillance Procedure
MTO	medium-term budgetary objective
NAB	New Arrangements to Borrow
NACE	statistical classifications of economic activities
NATO	North Atlantic Treaty Organisation
N.B.	nota bene (note well)
n.F.	neue Fassung (new Version)
NCA(s)	National Competent Authority(ies)
NCB(s)	National Central Bank(s)
NDICI	Neighbourhood, Development and International Cooperation Instrument "Global Europe"
NGEU	Next Generation EU
NGO	Non-Governmental Organization
No.	Number
NPL(s)	Non-Performing Loan(s)
NRA(s)	National Resolution Authority(ies)
NRP	National Reform Programme
NSFR	Net Stable Funding Ratio
NSI	National Statistical Institute

NSM	Non-Standard Measures
NUTS	Territorial units for statistics (nomenclature des unités territoriales statistiques)
nyr	not yet reported
NZZ	Neue Zürcher Zeitung
O.J.	Official Journal
O.J. C	Official Journal (Communications)
O.J. L	Official Journal (Legislation)
OCTs	Overseas Countries and Territories
OECD	Organisation for Economic Cooperation and Development
OEEC	Organisation for European Economic Cooperation
OLAF	Office européen de lutte anti-fraude (European Anti-Fraud Office)
OMC	Open Method of Coordination
OMRs	Outermost Regions
OMT	Outright Monetary Transactions
OSCE	Organisation for Security and Cooperation in Europe
OUP	Oxford University Press
p.	page(s)
para	paragraph(s)
passim	widely mentioned, at various places
PCCL	Precautionary Conditioned Credit Line
PCIJ	Permanent Court of International Justice
PEPP	Pandemic Emergency Purchase Programme
PESCO	Permanent Structured Cooperation
PIF	Protection of the Financial Interests of Union (protection des intéréts financiers)
PJCC	Police and Judicial Cooperation in Criminal Matters
PMP	Primary Market Purchase
PNR	Passenger Name Record
PRGT	Poverty Reduction and Growth Trust
PRP	Parliamentary Rules of Procedure
PSC	Permanent Structured Cooperation/Political and Security Committee
PSI	Private Sector Involvement
PSO	Public Service Obligation
PSPP	Public Sector Purchase Programme
PUF	Presses Universitaires de France
QM	qualified majority
QMV	qualified majority voting
Racc.	Raccolta della giurisprudenza della Corte di giustizia e del Tribunale di primo grado
RAP	Rules of application

Rass. parl.	Rassegna parlamentare
REACT-EU	Recovery Assistance for Cohesion and the Territories of Europe
REFIT	Regulatory Fitness and Perand Performance Programme
Règ. Ass.Nat.	Règlement de Assemblée Nationale
Règ.Sén.	Règlement du Sénat de la République Française
RMV	reverse majority voting
RP	rules of procedure
RPR	reference(s) for a preliminary ruling
RQMV	reverse qualified majority voting
RTGS	real-time gross settlement
RTS(s)	Regulatory Technical Standard(s)
RWA(s)	Risk Weighted Asset(s)
SBC	Schengen Borders Code
scil.	scilicet (namely)
SCIMF	Sub-Committee on International Monetary Fund
SDR(s)	Special Drawing Right(s)
SE	Societas Europea
SEA	Single European Act
Sec.	section
seq(q).	sequence/sequentes (following)
ser.	series
SFA	Financial Services Action
SGEI(s)	Service(s) of General Economic Interest
SGP	Stability and Growth Pact
SI(s)	Significant Institution(s)
SIFI	Systematically Important Financial Institutions
SIPI	Systematically important payment systems
SIS	Schengen Information System
SMEs	Small and Medium-sized Enterprises
SMP	Securities Markets Programme
SRB	Single Resolution Board
SREP	Supervisory Review and Evaluation Process
SRF	Single Resolution Fund
SRM	Single Resolution Mechanism
SRMR	Single Resolution Mechanism Regulation
SRSP	Structural Reform Support Programme
SSM	Single Supervisory Mechanism
SSMR	Single Supervisory Mechanism Regulation
STC	Sentencia del Tribunal Constitucional (judgment of the Spanish Constitutional Tribunal)
SURE	Support Mitigating Unemployment Risks in Emergency
SZ	Süddeutsche Zeitung
T2S	TARGET2-Securities

TARGET	Trans-European Automated Real-time Gross Settlement Express Transfer
TARGET2	Trans-European Automated Real-time Gross Settlement Express Transfer System
TCE	Treaty establishing a Constitution for Europe/Traité instituant la Communauté européenne
TEC	Treaty establishing the European Community
TECSC	Treaty establishing the European Coal and Steel Community
TEEC	Treaty establishing the European Economic Community
TEN	Trans-European Network
TEN-E	Trans-European Energy Networks
TEN-T	Trans-European Transport Networks
TESM	Treaty Establishing the European Stability Mechanism
TEU	Treaty on European Union (as amended by the Treaty of Lisbon)
TEU-Amsterdam	Treaty on European Union as amended by the Treaty of Amsterdam
TEU-Maastricht	Treaty on European Union as drawn up by the Treaty of Maastricht
TEU-Nice	Treaty on European Union as amended by the Treaty of Nice
TFEU	Treaty on the Functioning of the European Union
TFUE	Trattato sul funzionamento dell'Unione europea/Traité sur le fonctionnement de l'Union européenne (Treaty on the Functioning of the European Union—TFEU)
TLAC	Total-Loss Absorption Capacity
TLTRO	Targeted longer-term refinancing operations
TMCA	Agreement on the transfer and mutualisation of contributions to the single resolution fund
TRIPS	Agreement on Trade-Related Aspects of Intellectual Property Rights
TSCG	Treaty on Stability, Coordination and Governance in the Economic and Monetary Union
TTIP	Transatlantic Trade and Investment Partnership
TUE	Trattato sull'Unione europea/Traité sur l'Union européenne (Treaty on European Union—TEU)
UEF	Union Européenne des Féderalistes
UK	United Kingdom
UNC	Charter of the United Nations
UN(O)	United Nations Organisation
UNCLOS	United Nations Convention on the Law of the Sea
UNFCCC	United Nations Framework Convention on Climate Change
UNTS	United Nations Treaty Series
US	United States

USA	United States of America
v/v.	versus (against)
VAT	Value Added Tax
VCLT	Vienna Convention on the Law of Treaties (1969)
VCLT-IO	Vienna Convention on the Law of Treaties between States and International Organizations and between International Organizations (1986)
VCSST	Vienna Convention on Succession of States in respect of Treaties
Vol.	Volume
VVDStRL	Veröffentlichungen der Vereinigung der Deutschen Staatsrechtslehrer
WD	Working Document
WEAG	Western European Armaments Group
WEU	Western European Union
WFStG	Gesetz zur Übernahme von Gewährleistungen zum Erhalt der für die Finanzstabilität in der Währungsunion erforderlichen Zahlungsfähigkeit der Hellenischen Republik (Law on the giving of guarantees to maintain the Hellenic Republic's ability to pay which is required for financial stability in the monetary union)
WHO	World Health Organization
WTO	World Trade Organisation

Title VI
Transport

Article 90 [Common Transport Policy]
(ex-Article 70 TEC)

The objectives of the Treaties[12] shall, in matters governed by this Title,[18-29] be pursued within the framework of a common transport policy.[8-11]

Contents

1. The Original and Present Treaty Text 1
2. The Distinctive Nature of Transport 2
3. The Derogatory Regime for Transport 6
4. The Common Policy Technique 8
5. The Treaty Objectives Pursued: The Subject Matter 12
   - 5.1. The Creation of the Internal Transport Market 13
   - 5.2. Other Objectives 17
6. The Matters Governed by This Title 18
   - 6.1. Transport, Traffic and Other Business? 18
   - 6.2. Grey Area 22
   - 6.3. Transport Mode 23
   - 6.4. Geographic Scope 27
7. Shared Competence 30
8. Subsidiarity and Proportionality 31
9. The Instrument for Implementation of the Policy 32
10. Treaty-Making Power 36
11. Timing 38

List of Cases
References

1. The Original and Present Treaty Text

The text of the TFEU Part III, Title VI (ex-Title IV TEC) on transport is an **almost identical**, but renumbered,[1] copy of its homologue formulation in the original TEC. The substantive difference between the original and the present wording of the provisions primarily relates to the altered decision-making process (Article 91 TFEU), as interlinked with the standstill provision (Article 92 TFEU) and the transition period (ex-Article 8 TEC) phasing the gradual integration of the EU through transition from national protectionism and public monopolies (in air and rail transport and in road passenger transport) to free trade and free market access.

---

[1] First by the Treaty of Amsterdam 1997 (from Articles 74-84 to Articles 70-80, and then by the TFEU to Articles 90–100).

2. The Distinctive Nature of Transport

2   Transport is of cardinal economic importance, not only in its own right as a **major segment of economic activity** (e.g. it accounts for about 5% of GDP and employment), but to an even greater extent because it provides the indispensable ancillary instrument for other industrial sectors by effecting the movement of persons and goods.

3   Thus, transport also **supports the free movement of persons and goods** (Article 26.2 TFEU), a key objective pursued by the EU for the ultimate goal of the establishment of the European internal market, which is a major factor of European integration. In this interactive capacity, transport is not only a component of but also an instrument for the integration of the European economy and society.

4   Moreover, in some instances it is the **object of a public service obligation** (→ Article 93 TFEU para 17) and is considered crucial for national security and defence. In those capacities, it fulfils a systemic and strategic function of national interest, which explains why its organisation is of particular concern for the public authority, national and regional.

5   These and other differential characteristics, as acknowledged by Article 91 TFEU (→ Article 91 TFEU para 6), **distinguish transport from other sectors of economy** and explain why transport is one of the two (besides agriculture) economic sectors the original TEC endowed with a special chapter and for which it prescribed a specific common policy. While some of these distinctive features have faded since the inception of the Union and merely have an historical interest, others remain relevant.

3. The Derogatory Regime for Transport

6   Because of this specificity, transport services are **excluded from the application** of some general provisions of the Treaty, namely in the field of **freedom to provide services** (Article 58 TFEU) and are governed by a special regime for **some competition aspects** (Article 14,[2] Article 107.1 and Article 93 TFEU). Transport is also governed by a special regime in the TFEU in other respects, such as (i) the residual external (extra-union) competence of the MS in the area of transport (→ Article 91 TFEU para 10) in Article 4.2 point (g) TFEU, (ii) Trans-European Transport Networks (Articles 170 et seq. TFEU) and (iii) the negotiation and conclusion process for international agreements in the field of transport (Article 207.5 TFEU).

7   To achieve the general Treaty objectives, because of the specific features of the transport sector, the common transport policy **may deviate from the general**

---

[2] The general provision of Article 14 TFEU on the regime of services of general economic interest contains an express reservation for the specific regime of transport services in Article 93 TFEU (→ Article 14 TFEU para 8).

Treaty precepts in those instances where the transport activity is excepted from those principles, namely the general regime of freedom to provide services (Article 58 TFEU) and the ban on free competition distorting State aid (Article 93 TFEU). Only in those instances will the derogatory provisions prevail over the general regime. Apart from those express derogations from the general regime, transport is governed by the general rules of the TFEU: see the French merchant seamen case.[3] This derogatory regime does not prevent that also in the field of transport, the general objectives of the Treaty are to be pursued, as expressly instructed by Article 90 TFEU.

4. The Common Policy Technique

In the field of transport, the original lawmakers of the TEC were **confronted with a situation that complicated reaching agreement**, namely: 8

- closed national markets
- diverging positions among the treaty signatories: regional integration and free market on the one hand as opposed to national protectionism and State interference on the other hand
- numerous pre-existing international (bilateral, plurilateral and multilateral) agreements the signatories had to respect according to the *pacta sunt servanda* precept (also Article 351 TFEU)

Only by temporising via referral of the issue to another decision-making level (secondary legislation) and body (the Council) for compromise (cf. the "common" nature of the policy) and gradual transition in this complex matter, could they reach agreement in the TEC. This method resulted in featuring transport as **one of the** (besides agriculture) **first common policy areas** of the EU and before the trade, fisheries, and foreign and security policies. The common transport policy referred to in Article 90 TFEU was already called for in the ex-Article 3 point (e) TEC. 9

For lack of a comprehensive regime on transport in the TFEU itself, the **common transport policy is instrumental** or servile to the establishment and maintenance of the internal transport services market. This common transport policy was the path towards the creation of the internal European transport market and in some instances, it still is: see the ongoing vertical disintegration of the infrastructure management and the transport services provision yet to be fully achieved in rail transport. 10

Thus, in the course of time transport activity was gradually liberalised by progressively aligning its regime to the general rules of the TFEU (ex-TEC), as applicable to all other sectors of economic activity. Consequently, the **derogations** for transport from the general regime have rather become **exceptional**, e.g. the former block exemptions for the transport sector have been abolished. While the 11

---

[3] Case 167/73, *Commission v France* (ECJ 4 April 1974).

creation of the internal transport market is presently virtually accomplished, this process is actually still ongoing in the segment of rail transport.

5. The Treaty Objectives Pursued: The Subject Matter

12 To the extent that these respective Treaty objectives may mutually conflict, the common transport policy is also to elaborate the best possible compromise. Like in other sectors, also in the field of transport, the **general objectives of the Treaty** are to be pursued (Article 90 TFEU).

5.1. The Creation of the Internal Transport Market

13 The primary objective of the Treaty is the creation of an **internal market** (Article 3.2 TEU). This internal market is based on the "four freedoms", namely the free movement of persons, services, goods and capital. The internal transport market creates a single economic area (Article 26 TFEU) establishing free (freedom to provide the transport services)[4] and fair (not distorted by differential operating conditions, creating a level playing field, either geographically or between the transport modes) competition (cf. Article 116 TFEU) among (transport) undertakings.

14 The avoidance of competition distortion for service providers on the internal transport services market implies significant **approximation** (Article 114 TFEU) of the MS' legislation and regulation. This harmonisation creates the required **level playing field** between the transport operators established in different MS. It also allows mutual reciprocal recognition of the MS' certifications, so that transport operators are not subject to double compliance, once in their home State of establishment and once more in the host State of their operation ("**single passport**" principle). While in principle, the compliance control lies with the transport operator's home State (home country or "**flag State**" **control** as it is known in the maritime mode), the host State (cf. the "**port State**" **control** – PSC – in the maritime mode) retains a subsidiary competence for the sake of safety: see, e.g. the "roadside inspection"[5] of motor vehicles. Non-compliance may lead to **blacklisting** of the operator.

15 In this context the distinction must be stressed between, on the one hand, the **access to the transport market** and, on the other hand, the **access to the occupation of transport operator**. While liberalisation implies free market access without quantitative restrictions, without price regulation and without discrimination, it does not necessarily entail complete deregulation. Total reliance on market forces

---

[4] Cieslik and Michalek (2015).
[5] Parliament/Council Directive 2014/47/EU *on the technical roadside inspection of the roadworthiness of commercial vehicles circulating in the Union*, O.J. L 127/134 (2014).

alone will not balance and reconcile in a satisfactory manner the conflicting interests of the stakeholders. Public intervention by accompanying measures is required to correct the dysfunctioning of a liberalised market: protection of users and consumers by quality control of the service providers and from abuses by service providers, safeguarding stability of the transport system by avoiding excessive competition, protection of the general public through (traffic) safety measures, etc.

The **licensing conditions** set for access to the occupation of transport operator intend to guarantee (i) the quality of the transport service offered by the carrier to his customer/user and (ii) the safety of his transport operations vis-à-vis the general public (iii) as well as for the personnel he employs. These licensing conditions traditionally require the transport operator to meet minimum standards in three respects: (i) **professional competence** (through education and/or experience), (ii) **reliability** (absence of infringements) and (iii) financial **solvency** (also via insurance cover).

16

5.2. Other Objectives

While the initial emphasis of the common transport policy was on the creation of the internal transport market via the freedom to provide transport services (liberalisation, ensuring market access by abolishing quantitative restrictions and price regulation, eliminating competition distortions, etc.), in the course of time, the subject matter of the common transport policy was **extended and supplemented** (→ Article 91 TFEU para 18 and para 21) **with additional themes** reflecting the other objectives pursued by the Treaty, e.g. environment protection, safety and security, consumer protection (particularly passenger rights → Article 91 TFEU para 23), social protection, infrastructure development, etc. to co-ordinate it with the common policies in those other fields, under the precept of Article 7 TFEU. Those additional transport related Treaty objectives have considerably extended the scope of the common transport policy and therefore the Council's assignment (Article 91 TFEU). The Commission's "Mobility Package" illustrates this cross-cutting approach (→ para 33).

17

6. The Matters Governed by This Title

6.1. Transport, Traffic and Other Business?

The repeated reference to the position of the transport service providers (the carriers) in the TFEU provisions (Article 91.1 point (b), Article 92 and Article 94 TFEU), clarifies the meaning of the term "transport" as the **commercial movement of persons and goods**, as opposed to the mere private traffic (mobility). Since it may give rise to confusion, it is submitted that the term *"Verkehr"* in the German text of the instrument is also to be understood in this sense.

18

19   As they operate in the same medium, some measures in the area of transport will however indiscriminately also affect **private traffic,** e.g. in the field of safety and environment protection. There will be an automatic "spill over".

20   In this respect, **transport intermediary and auxiliary services** do not come within the ambit of the transport concept.

21   In this sense, the subject matter of "transport" also encompasses the position of the **user** (the transport operator's/carrier's contract partner) and the **traffic infrastructure** (the medium of the transport operation).

6.2. Grey Area

22   Considering the extended field of the common transport policy ($\rightarrow$ Article 91 TFEU para 22), border line discussion may arise whether certain legislative measures can qualify as transport related so as to be governed by the derogatory regime. This may be the case, e.g. for some **transport related enforcement measures** (e.g. police, criminal, fiscal).

6.3. Transport Mode

23   The passage "matters governed by this Title" in Article 90 TFEU raises the question of the scope of this title in terms of transport mode and more particularly the issue of the status of sea and air transport in the context of the formulation of a common transport policy. Article 100.1 TFEU renders this Title VI of Part Three of the TFEU applicable to "transport by rail, road and inland waterway", but Article 100.2 TFEU empowers the European legislators to adopt "appropriate provisions for sea and air transport". Inter alia, because of their particular extra-Union relevance, affecting the relationship with third (non-union) countries, the **air and sea modes** were exempted from the scope of the TFEU title on transport.

24   In the landmark case of the *French merchant seamen*[6] for sea transport, as confirmed later in the *Nouvelles Frontières*[7] case for air transport, the ECJ held that the **general provisions** of the Treaty also **apply in full to the air and sea transport activity**, as long as and to the extent secondary legislation did not provide an appropriate regime.

25   For lack of explicit mention, **space transport** is not within the ambit of the title.

26   In this respect, the status of **energy conveyance** (via gas and fuel pipelines and via electric power lines) and telecommunication and **data transmission** is questionable. Strictly speaking, they may qualify as the performance of a transport contract, though by using fixed instead of mobile means of transfer.

---

[6] Case 167/73, *Commission v France* (ECJ 4 April 1974).
[7] Case C-209-213/84, *Ministère Public v Lucas Asjes* (ECJ 30 April 1986).

Article 170 TFEU on trans-European networks distinguishes transport from telecommunication and energy infrastructures.

6.4. Geographic Scope

In the first place by its very nature this Title applies to **intra-Union cross-border transport operations**. 27

It was controversial whether Article 91.1 TFEU also covers **extra-Union transport** operations. From Article 91.1 point (a) TFEU it flows that transport operations with third (extra-union) countries also come within the ambit of this title. The ECJ held that the EU's internal competence implies its external competence in the field of transport.[8] 28

This Title expressly also applies to **cabotage** (Article 91.1 point (b) TFEU), i.e. transport operations entirely within the territory of one and the same MS, but performed by a transport operator established in another MS. While the cross-border transport is the prime objective of the title, the **purely domestic transport** (i.e. transport operations within the national territory of an MS by an operator established in the territory of that same MS) cannot be dissociated from it, lest creating conflicts, inconsistencies and discriminations. In an integrated transport market, there is a natural "spill over" from the regional into the national level: as foreign and domestic operators encounter each other on the same national market, differential regimes may cause competition distortion; as they operate in the same territory, safety measures should apply equally; environment protection measures should not be constrained by political borders; etc. 29

7. Shared Competence

Under Article 4.2 point (g) TFEU, there is **shared competence** between the EU and the MS in the area of transport. 30

8. Subsidiarity and Proportionality

In terms of "depth", the EU legislative mandate is however nuanced by the subsidiarity and proportionality precepts in respectively Articles 5.3 and 5.4 TEU and Protocol No. 2. As transport does not fall within the EU's exclusive competence, the principle of subsidiarity defines the circumstances in which the EU rather than the MS initiative is preferable as follows: "insofar as the objectives of the 31

---

[8] Case 22/70, *Commission v Council (European Agreement on Road Transport)* (ECJ 31 March 1971); Opinion 1/76, *Draft Agreement establishing a European laying-up fund for inland waterway vessels* (ECJ 26 April 1977). Kuijper (2009), p. 291.

proposed action cannot be sufficiently achieved by the Member States, either at central level or at regional and local level, but can rather, by reason of the scale or effects of the proposed action, be better achieved at Union level".

9. The Instrument for Implementation of the Policy

32   The achievement of the Treaty objectives does not necessarily imply action by the issuance of secondary EU legislation as suggested in Article 91 TFEU. The implementation measures may be legislative/regulatory and binding (directive, regulation, decision), but also **in the nature of guidelines** (recommendations and opinions): the entire gamma of Article 288 TFEU may be used.

33   Under the **ordinary legislative procedure** (→ Article 91 TFEU para 1), the Commission formulates proposals (visions, strategies, master plans, action plans or programmes, agendas, time planning horizons, roadmaps, "(legislative) packages" in the form of "white papers" after consultation in "green papers", "communications" and "memoranda", etc.. The Council may adopt those Commission proposals and act upon them by legislating jointly with the EP via the issuance of directives, regulations or decisions. The Commission may also be entrusted with **delegated legislative competence** in specific areas.

34   The European Commission's most recent policy document on transport, is the White Paper titled "**Roadmap to a Single European Transport Area** —Towards a competitive and resource efficient transport system".[9] It sets out a vision for the future of European transport up to 2050, recommends fundamental changes in policy thinking and is accompanied by a series of concrete targets and initiatives. The Commission Communication "Clean Power for Transport: A European Alternative Fuels Strategy"[10] illustrates the present-day integrated approach in the pursuance of the various objectives of the Treaty (→ Article 91 TFEU para 23).

In 2006 the European Commission issued the communication "**NAIADES**",[11] formulating an action plan to support the inland navigation in the EU.[12]

In 2017-2018 the European Commission launched its three-part **Mobility Package**, a major legislative initiative on the governance of commercial road transport in the EU. It covers, among others, market access, fiscality, road traffic safety, social protection, environment protection, infrastructure, digitalisation, etc.[13]

---

[9] COM(2011) 144.

[10] COM (2013) 17.

[11] Commission Communication *on the promotion of inland waterway transport 'NAIADES' - an integrated European action programme for inland waterway transport*, COM(2006) 6 final.

[12] Sevinga (2006), p. 115.

[13] See the Mobility Package I: Parliament/Council Regulation (EU) 2020/1054 *amending Regulation (EC) No. 561/2006 as regards minimum requirements on maximum daily and weekly driving times, minimum breaks and daily and weekly rest periods and Regulation (EU) No. 165/2014 as regards positioning by means of tachographs*, O.J. L 249/1 (2020); Parliament/Council Regulation (EU) 2020/1055 *amending Regulations (EC) No. 1071/2009, (EC) No. 1072/2009 and (EU) No.*

The EP may also adopt **resolutions** expressing its views on the policy and formulate recommendations. 35

10. Treaty-Making Power

On the occasion of the recast EU architecture, the Treaty of Lisbon codified the controversial (see the "AETR"[14] and "open skies"[15] rulings of the ECJ) transport **"treaty-making power"**, namely the distribution of competence between the EU and its MS in their external relationship with third countries in the field of transport, as **shared but residual**, as opposed to exclusive or concurrent or coordinative (supporting) MS competence. The combined effect of the Article 3.2 TFEU, Article 4.2 point (g) TFEU and Article 216 TFEU results in a **priority competence for the EU** and residual competence for MS in the field of the conclusion of transport treaties with third countries. 36

The EU has already concluded a large number of treaties with third countries in the field of transport. In land transport the EU concluded with third countries, e.g. the **Transit Agreement** with Switzerland,[16] the **Interbus agreement**[17] and others. 37

11. Timing

The **standstill precept** and the transition period express(ed) the **staged integration process** of the Union (ex-Article 8 TEEC). The maximum **transitional period** of 15 years to establish the common market had expired by the late 1960s (more precisely 31 December 1969). 38

For a number of reasons, such as the lack of detailed and concrete definition of its substance, the MS' inertia, the reluctance and aversion (for motives of vested interests and national protectionism) against it and its underrated importance in the creation of the internal market, the formulation and implementation of the common 39

1024/2012 with a view to adapting them to developments in the road transport sector, O.J. L 249/17 (2020); Parliament/Council Regulation (EU) 2020/1056 *on electronic freight transport information*, O.J. L 249/33 (2020); Parliament/Council Directive (EU) 2020/1057 *laying down specific rules with respect to Directive 96/71/EC and Directive 2014/67/EU for posting drivers in the road transport sector and amending Directive 2006/22/EC as regards enforcement requirements and Regulation (EU) No. 1024/2012*, O.J. L 249/49 (2020).

[14] Case 22/70, *Commission v Council - European Agreement on Road Transport* (ECJ 31 March 1971).

[15] Cases C-466/98 et al., *Commission v United Kingdom, Denmark, Sweden, Finland, Belgium, Luxembourg, Austria, Germany* (ECJ 5 November 2002).

[16] Agreement between the European Union and the Swiss Confederation on the Carriage of Goods and Passengers by Rail and Road.

[17] Agreement on the international occasional carriage of passengers by coach and bus (ASOR) (Interbus Agreement), Dublin 26 May 1982.

transport policy was characterised by a **status quo** or at least a very slow pace until the 1980s.

40 The comprehensive formulation and development of the European common transport policy was triggered by the ECJ judgment of 22 May 1985[18] establishing the Council's **omission** to introduce a common transport policy and urging it to take action. The "common market" was not a goal in itself, but a means to establish the "single market", the intermediate step to achieve the ultimate economic integration objective of the "internal market". The Single European Act (1986) set the objective of establishing the single market by 1992 in all economic sectors, including transport. The combined factors of the ECJ omission judgment and the Single European Act sparked significant acceleration in the development of the common transport policy.

41 Except for some aspects in the rail mode, the internal European transport market is presently virtually achieved. However, **transitional rules** may still apply for MS that joined the EU after the establishment of the internal transport market, when their Accession Treaties contain exceptions, particularly on the freedom to provide transport services.[19]

List of Cases

ECJ 31.03.1971, 22/70, *Commission v Council (European Agreement on Road Transport)*, ECLI:EU:C:1971:32 [cit. in para 28, 36]

ECJ 04.04.1974, 167/73, *Commission v France (French merchant seamen)*, ECLI:EU:C:1974:35 [cit. in para 7, 24]

ECJ 22.05.1985, 13/83, *Parliament v Council*, ECLI:EU:C:1985:220 [cit. in para 40]

ECJ 30.04.1986, 209/84 to C-213/84, *Ministère Public v Asjes*, ECLI:EU:C:1986:188 [cit. in para 24]

ECJ 05.11.2002, C-466/98, *Commission v United Kingdom (Open Skies)*, ECLI:EU:C:2002:624

ECJ 05.11.2002, C-467/98, *Commission v Denmark (Open Skies)*, ECLI:EU:C:2002:625 [cit. in para 36]

ECJ 05.11.2002, C-468/98, *Commission v Sweden (Open Skies)*, ECLI:EU:C:2002:626 [cit. in para 36]

ECJ 05.11.2002, C-469/98, *Commission v Finland (Open Skies)*, ECLI:EU:C:2002:627 [cit. in para 36]

ECJ 05.11.2002, C-471/98, *Commission v Belgium (Open Skies)*, ECLI:EU:C:2002:628 [cit. in para 36]

ECJ 05.11.2002, C-472/98, *Commission v Luxembourg (Open Skies)*, ECLI:EU:C:2002:629 [cit. in para 36]

---

[18] Case 13/83, *Parliament v Council* (ECJ 22 May 1985).

[19] Valette (2005), p. 105.

ECJ 05.11.2002, C-475/98, *Commission v Austria (Open Skies)*, ECLI:EU:C:2002:630 [cit. in para 36]

ECJ 05.11.2002, C-476/98, *Commission v Germany (Open Skies)*, ECLI:EU:C:2002:631 [cit. in para 36]

References

Cieslik, A., & Michalek, J. (2015). *Liberalization of transportation services in the EU: the Polish perspective*. Peter Lang.

Kuijper, P. (2009). Re-reading external relations cases in the field of transport: The function of community loyalty. In M. Bulterman et al. (Eds.), *Views of European law from the mountain: liber amicorum Piet Jan Slot (pp. 291 et seqq)*. Wolters Kluwer.

Sevinga, K. (2006). NAIADES: nieuwe vaart in de binnenvaart. *Nederlands Tijdschrift voor Europees Recht*, p. 115.

Valette, C. (2005). Les incidences de l'élargissement et de la future Constitution européenne sur le droit des transports terrestres. In Union des Avocats européens (Ed.), *De Schengen à Mondorf-les-Bains: le citoyen au coeur de l'Europe élargie* (pp. 105 et seqq.). Bruylant.

Article 91 [Principles]
(ex-Article 71 TEC)

1. For the purpose of implementing Article 90,[1] and taking into account the distinctive features of transport,[6] the European Parliament and the Council shall, acting in accordance with the ordinary legislative procedure[3] and after consulting the Economic and Social Committee and the Committee of the Regions,[5] lay down:

   (a) common rules applicable to international transport to or from the territory of a Member State or passing across the territory of one or more Member State;[8-10]
   (b) the conditions under which non-resident carriers may operate transport services within a Member State;[10]
   (c) measures to improve transport safety;[18-20]
   (d) any other appropriate provisions.[21-23]

2. When the measures referred to in paragraph 1 are adopted, account shall be taken of cases where their application might seriously affect the standard of living and level of employment in certain regions, and the operation of transport facilities.[24-25]

Contents

1.	The Ordinary Legislative Procedure	1
2.	The Distinctive Features of Transport	6
3.	The Substance of the Common Transport Policy	7
	3.1. Traffic Rights	8
	3.1.1. Intra- and Extra-Union Transport	11
	3.1.2. Road Transport	14
	3.1.3. Rail Transport	15
	3.1.4. Inland Navigation	17
	3.2. Safety	18
	3.3. Miscellaneous	21
4.	Consideration for Socio-Economic Impact	24

List of Cases
References

1. The Ordinary Legislative Procedure

Article 91 TFEU is one of the **core provisions** of this Title as it creates the concrete basis for legislative action and defines the scope of the tasking. Thus, it issues at the same time a mandate and an order.

Since the signature of the TEC, the decision-making process to formulate the common transport policy underwent several changes in the course of time: (i) from the original unanimity over-qualified majority to the present simple majority in the EP and qualified majority in the Council and (ii) from the initial consultation over co-operation to the present **co-decision** between Council and EP, acting as co-legislators. This development in the decision-making process must be linked to the standstill precept that can only be waived by unanimity and to the transition period towards gradual integration (Article 92 TFEU).

3   The **ordinary legislative procedure** is defined in Article 289 TFEU as the joint adoption by the EP and the Council of a regulation, directive or decision on a proposal from the Commission. Article 294 TFEU further specifies the procedure.

4   Article 218.6 point (a) (v) TFEU requires the prior consent of the EP for the Council's decision authorising the signing of **agreements with third countries** covering fields to which the ordinary legislative procedure applies, as is the case for transport. This requirement amounts to the granting of a **veto right** to the EP.

5   In addition, the consultation of the Economic and Social Committee (Articles 301 and 304 TFEU) and of the Committee of the Regions (Articles 305 and 307 TFEU, and Article 13.4 TEU) is prescribed. In this respect, the other advisory bodies must also be mentioned (Article 99 TFEU).

2. The Distinctive Features of Transport

6   The distinctive features of transport were allegedly related and some of them still relate to:

(i) the geographic differences in the MS' transport markets:
  (a) differential **modal split** (e.g. rail in the big countries, road in the small countries);
  (b) differential but generally high degree of **State intervention,** abstracting transport from market forces based on public policy priorities, often qualifying transport as an **essential and universal service**,[1] effected via **public monopolies, public service obligations** and **State aid.**

(ii) the largely **transboundary** character of transport by its very nature, source of pre-union MS agreements with third countries (Article 351 TFEU on the status of international agreements concluded by MS before the creation of or their accession to the Union).

(iii) the **natural monopoly** transport infrastructure networks (roads, railways, waterways), create because their duplication is either physically impossible or so onerous that it prohibits market access for prospective new entrants.

---

[1] Greaves (2004), pp. 19–20.

3. The Substance of the Common Transport Policy

In contrast with the agricultural policy, the TFEU defines the substance of the common transport policy only in a fragmentary manner in Article 91 TFEU. This reflects the lack of consensus among the original Treaty signatories on the matter. For this reason, point (d) of Article 91.1 TFEU is a very broad **open-ended provision** that allows to further fill in the common transport policy: It may also cover, namely competition, purely domestic transport within the MS, extra-union transport between the EU and third countries.

3.1. Traffic Rights

The points (a) and (b) of Article 91.1 TFEU relate to the concrete establishment of the internal transport services market via the **free cross-border transport market access**, i.e. the freedom to provide services in the transport sector. Concretely, it means the right for a transport service provider to perform commercial transport operations in the territory of a host country, i.e. another country than the transport service provider's home country of establishment.

The freedom to provide services implies the market access without **quantitative restrictions**, without **discrimination** (differential treatment according to nationality, place of establishment, origin, destination etc.), **without price regulation**, without **distortion of competition** (→ Article 90 TFEU para 15).

In public transport law the freedom to provide cross-border transport services is traditionally referred to as the granting of the so-called "**traffic rights**":

(a) **inbound** to (entry), **outbound** from (exit) and **transit** through (traversing) the host country territory; and
(b) **cabotage** (domestic transport performed entirely within the territory of a single host country, i.e. other than the carrier's home country of establishment). Cabotage proved to be the major obstacle for the achievement of the EU internal transport market. As Articles 8 et seq. of Regulation 1072/2009[2] and Articles 14 et seq. of Regulation 1073/2009[3] illustrate, restrictions on cabotage still apply. To give an example, in road cargo transportation, [4] cabotage is allowed only in the course of a cross-border transport operation, with the same vehicle, for a maximum of three operations within seven days after the unloading of the inbound carriage and in road passenger transportation (Article 8.2 of Regulation 1072/2009). The cabotage right may even be temporarily suspended in a given area in case of serious market disturbance due to oversupply

---

[2] Parliament/Council Regulation (EC) No. 1072/2009 *on common rules for access to the international road haulage market*, O.J. L 300/72 (2009).
[3] Parliament/Council Regulation (EC) No. 1073/2009 *on common rules for access to the international market for coach and bus services*, O.J. L 300/88 (2009).
[4] Vicaire (2005), p. 101.

(Article 10 of Regulation 1072/2009). In rail transportation restrictions on cabotage may apply pursuant to exclusive rights granted in domestic passenger transport to fulfil a public service obligation in accordance with Regulation 1370/2007 (Articles 10-11 of Directive 2012/34).

3.1.1. Intra- and Extra-Union Transport

11 It was controversial whether Article 91.1 TFEU also covers **extra-union transport** operations. The European Court of Justice held that the EU's internal competence implies its external competence in the field of transport.[5]

12 The TFEU codified this ruling in its Article 4.2 point (g): **shared (or parallel) competence** between the Union and its MS and **residual competence** for the MS. Article 207.5 TFEU governs the negotiation and conclusion of international agreements in the field of transport.

13 Since the legislative competence of the EU is limited to the EU MS, any arrangements with third countries must be the subject of a treaty.[6]

3.1.2. Road Transport

14 After previous secondary legislation gradually implementing the internal transport market, the regime for the free provision of road transport services is presently contained in the package of Regulations 1071/2009 (access to the occupation: **road transport operator licensing**),[7] 1072/2009 (access to the cargo transport market, including cabotage) and 1073/2009 (access to the passenger transport market). The access to the occupation and the market access is discussed above (→ Article 90 TFEU para 15 and 16). This regime also governs the extra-union transport operations to the extent that a treaty with the third country to that effect is in force.

3.1.3. Rail Transport

15 Although progress has been made in the rail transport mode, especially with Directive 2012/34/EU on the single European railway area,[8] the liberalisation process is still ongoing and the internal market is yet to be fully achieved.[9] Equal non-discriminatory access to the rail network infrastructure is guaranteed at cost-

---

[5] Case C-22/70, *Commission v Council (European Agreement on Road Transport)* (ECJ 31 March 1971); Opinion 1/76, *Draft Agreement establishing a European laying-up fund for inland waterway vessels* (ECJ 26 April 1977).

[6] Knieps (2014).

[7] Parliament/Council Regulation (EC) No. 1071/2009 *establishing common rules concerning the conditions to be complied with to pursue the occupation of road transport operator*, O.J. L 300/51 (2009).

[8] Parliament/Council Directive 2012/34/EU *establishing a single European railway area*, O.J. L 343/31 (2012).

[9] Calme (2008).

based user charges (Article 31 of Directive 2012/34/EU), save restrictions pursuant to **exclusive rights** granted in domestic passenger transport fulfilling a **public service obligation** in accordance with Regulation 1370/2007[10] (Articles 10-11 of Directive 2012/34/EU). The cabotage right in rail cargo transport is guaranteed by Directive 91/440 (Article 10.3).[11] Also, harmonised minimum **rail transport operator licensing conditions** were formulated for this mode of transport (Articles 16 et seq. Directive 2012/34/EU). Like in other transport modes (roads, inland waterways), the rail network infrastructure is characterised by a **natural monopoly** (duplication of the infrastructure is physically impossible or at least economically inefficient) and its management is entrusted to the public authority. In addition, however, besides the infrastructure management, rail transport operation in the EU was/is also traditionally **State owned** and under a **public monopoly**.

For the sake of the completion of the internal rail transport market, the **functional dissociation ("unbundling")**[12] is pursued between the capacities of, on the one hand, the rail network manager (operator of the infrastructure and facilities) and, on the other hand, the rail carrier (provider of transport services). This dissociation aims at opening up the rail transport services market to independent (private) rail carriers without competition distortion between the (private) new market entrants and the vested (public) carriers. To create this level playing field by avoiding conflicts of interests and **cross-subsidization**, the unbundling may range from (Articles 4 et seq. Directive 2012/34/EU):

(i) the accounting level (transparent separate bookkeeping), over
(ii) the organisational level (independent management staff),
(iii) the legal level (vertical disintegration via split up into separate legal entities that may however be owned by the same mother company in a holding structure), up to
(iv) the ownership level (by divesting the transport activity).

---

[10] Parliament/Council Regulation (EC) No. 1370/2007 *on public passenger transport services by rail and by road,* O.J. L 315/1 (2007).
[11] Nougaret (2007), p. 116.
[12] Salque (2006), p. 51.

3.1.4. Inland Navigation

17 The EU regime[13] basically adopted and incorporated the pre-existing liberal regime that also involves third countries.[14] Regulation 3921/91[15] grants the cabotage right to carriers established in the EU, subject to meeting the **genuine link requirement** (based on the criteria of **substantive ownership** and **effective control** by EU nationals) (Article 1) to avoid competition from third country nationals via formal incorporation of a transport operator as a legal person in the EU, thus sidetracking the reciprocity between the countries in the exchange of traffic rights. The **licensing requirements** (access to the occupation condition) were harmonised.[16] **Price regulation** was abolished.[17]

3.2. Safety

18 Point (c) of Article 91.1 TFEU, relating to the safety, was subsequently added by the Maastricht Treaty to the original text of the TEC. Since the insertion of this specific provision, the **transport safety regulation** is no longer to be based on the open-ended point (d) of Article 91.1 TFEU. It is recalled that "**safety**" relates to the prevention of accidental mishaps, as opposed to "**security**" that concerns the avoidance of man-made intentional malicious acts.

19 Safety implies the regulation by the setting of minimum standards for the various aspects of the transport operation:

---

[13] Council Regulation (EC) No. 1356/96 *on common rules applicable to the transport of goods or passengers by inland waterway between Member States with a view to establishing freedom to provide such transport services*, O.J. L 175/7 (1996).

[14] Revised Convention for the Navigation of the Rhine (1868 Mannheim Convention), implemented by the Central Commission for the Navigation of the Rhine (CCNR); Convention on Navigation on the Danube (1948 Belgrade Convention), implemented by the Danube Commission; Haak (1988).

[15] Council Regulation (EEC) No. 3921/91 *laying down the conditions under which non-resident carriers may transport goods or passengers by inland waterway within a Member State*, O.J. L 373/1 (1991).

[16] Council Directive 87/540/EEC *on access to the occupation of carrier of goods by waterway in national and international transport and on the mutual recognition of diplomas, certificates and other evidence of formal qualifications for this occupation*, O.J. L 322/20 (1987).

[17] Council Directive 96/75/EC *on the systems of chartering and pricing in national and international inland waterway transport in the Community*, O.J. L 304/12 (1996).

(i) **technical characteristics** (size, weight, axle load,[18] equipment, emission standards,[19] etc. of the means of transport (primarily vehicles)[20] and infrastructure;[21]
(ii) technical condition of the means of transport (**roadworthiness** inspection);[22]
(iii) besides the professional competence, reliability and solvency requirements as licensing conditions for the transport operator (see the access to the profession or occupation above (→ Article 90 TFEU para 16), also the fitness and qualification of the vehicle crew (**drivers licenses**, pilots certificates, etc.);[23]
(iv) manner of performance of the transport operation (e.g. **driving time limitation**,[24] procedures for the **transportation of dangerous goods**,[25] etc.).

Safety regulation may also include the creation of an advisory authority (e.g. the EU Agency for Railways (ERA)) and the development of an **accident investigation procedure** (e.g. Chapter V of Directive 2016/798[26]).

3.3. Miscellaneous

The **transport market liberalisation**, via guaranteeing free transport market access and safeguarding undistorted competition, was the first and prime objective of the common transport policy. Later the pursuance of **safety** was expressly added

---

[18] Council Directive 96/53/EC *laying down for certain road vehicles circulating within the Community the maximum authorized dimensions in national and international traffic and the maximum authorized weights in international traffic*, O.J. L 235/59 (1996).

[19] Parliament/Council Regulation (EC) No. 595/2009 *on type-approval of motor vehicles and engines with respect to emissions from heavy duty vehicles (Euro VI) and on access to vehicle repair and maintenance information*, O.J. L 188/1 (2009).

[20] Parliament/Council Regulation (EU) 2018/858 *on the approval and market surveillance of motor vehicles and their trailers, and of systems, components and separate technical units intended for such vehicles*, O.J. L 151/1 (2018); Parliament/Council Directive (EU) 2016/1629 *laying down technical requirements for inland waterway vessels*, O.J. L 252/118 (2016).

[21] E.g., Parliament/Council Directive 2004/54/EC *on minimum safety requirements for tunnels in the Trans-European Road Network*, O.J. L 167/39 (2004).

[22] Parliament/Council Directive 2014/45/EU *on periodic roadworthiness tests for motor vehicles and their trailers*, O.J. L 127/51 (2014).

[23] Parliament/Council Directive 2006/126/EC *on driving licences*, O.J. L 403/18 (2006); Parliament/Council Directive 2007/59/EC *on the certification of train drivers operating locomotives and trains on the railway system in the Community*, O.J. L 315/51 (2007).

[24] Parliament/Council Regulation (EC) No. 561/2006 *on the harmonisation of certain social legislation relating to road transport*, O.J. L 102/11 (2006) and Parliament/Council Regulation (EC) No. 1073/2009 *on common rules for access to the international market for coach and bus services*, O.J. L 300/88 (2009).

[25] Parliament/Council Directive 2008/68/EC *on the inland transport of dangerous goods*, O.J. L 260/13 (2008) (covers road, rail and inland navigation transportation).

[26] Parliament/Council Directive (EU) 2016/798 *on railway safety*, O.J. L 138/102 (2016).

to the common transport policy goals (see the insertion of Article 91.1 point (c) TFEU).

22 After transport was addressed as one of the first common policies, subsequently common policies have also been formulated in several other fields to address the other Treaty objectives. The reference in the transport context to those **other Treaty objectives** creates a broad mandate for further legislative action. The mandate is, however, not limitless; under Article 90 TFEU, its implementation is (i) to serve the "objectives of the Treaties" (ii) "in matters governed by this Title".

23 The residual "catch all" point (d) of Article 91.1 TFEU allows the common transport policy to consider those other domains and to pursue a coordinated and integrated approach under the precept of Article 7 TFEU. The following interlinked aspects are presently, among others, also addressed by the common transport policy:[27]

- **Fiscality** (road user charges and tolls) subject to the non-discrimination precept (Article 96 TFEU);
- **Security** (Article 2.4 TFEU on the security policy);
- Social wellbeing (protection of transport workers: working conditions, **driving time restrictions** etc.) and **animal wellbeing**/welfare during transportation (Article 13 TFEU);
- **Consumer (passenger) rights protection** (Article 12 and Article 169 TFEU): guaranteeing service quality, particularly the regulations on delay and cancellation of transport operations,[28] but also minimum carrier liability for death or bodily injury in case of traffic accidents;[29]
- **Environment protection**[30] (Article 11 and Article 191 TFEU): the model of "**sustainable mobility**" minimising or internalising[31] the so-called "**externalities**" or external costs, i.e. social (as opposed to private) costs that are caused by an economic activity, but that are not borne by the private operator causing them, but by the society as a whole: infrastructure wear and tear, traffic congestion, noise, pollution, accidents. It has become a particularly relevant item of the common transport policy, as the transport sector accounts for roughly a quarter of total man-made greenhouse gas emissions in the EU;
- **Technological development**: promotion of innovative solutions;
- Pursuance of efficiency (avoiding **traffic congestion** and bottlenecks);

---

[27] Common Transport Policy Action Programme 1995-2000; see also DG Move Mission Statements (2015), available at http://ec.europa.eu/dgs/transport/doc/2015-10-12-move-mission-statement.pdf.

[28] Speijer (2009), p. 220; Tonner (2007), p. 138; Duintjer Tebbens (2008), p. 653.

[29] Parliament/Council Regulation (EU) No. 181/2011 *concerning the rights of passengers in bus and coach transport*, O.J. L 55/1 (2011); Parliament/Council Regulation (EC) No. 1371/2007 *on rail passengers' rights and obligations*, O.J. L 315/14 (2007); Parliament/Council Regulation (EU) No. 1177/2010 *concerning the rights of passengers when travelling by sea and inland waterway*, O.J. L 334/1 (2012); Hübner (2006), p. 984.

[30] Mainier-Schall Trascu (2005), p. 785.

[31] Humphreys (2001), p. 451 et seq.

- Infrastructure development: Transport infrastructure formed a major lacuna in the original TEC, but was inserted by the Treaty of Maastricht (1992) that introduced the **Trans-European Networks** (TEN) policy (Title XVI, Articles 170 et seqq. TFEU), building the missing cross-border connections for the corridors;
- **Multimodal** approach: promotion of modal integration, **intermodality** (**combined transport**) and **interoperability**.[32]

4. Consideration for Socio-Economic Impact

Paragraph 2 contains a caveat to consider the impact of the measures taken on: **24**
- the **standard of living**;
- the **level of employment** in certain regions;
- the **operation of transport facilities**: the transport infrastructure.

Hence, it instructs the legislators/regulators to adapt their measures accordingly. This provision is to be **linked with the following TFEU provisions**: **25**

- Article 107.3 TFEU on the permissible State aid to certain regions in a disadvantaged economic and social situation in terms of standard of living and employment;
- Article 98 TFEU and Article 107.2 point (c) TFEU on the special situation of Germany caused by its division;
- Article 27 TFEU on the consideration of differences in development of certain economies.

List of Cases

ECJ 31.03.1971, C-22/70, *Commission v Council (European Agreement on Road Transport)*, ECLI:EU:C:1971:32 [cit. in para 11]

ECJ 26.04.1977, Opinion 1/76, *Draft Agreement establishing a European laying-up fund for inland waterway vessels*, ECLI:EU:C:1977:63 [cit. in para 11]

---

[32] Council Directive 92/106/EEC *on the establishment of common rules for certain types of combined transport of goods between Member States*, O.J. L 368/38 (1992); Aubry-Caillaud (2005), p. 419.

References[33]

Aubry-Caillaud, F. (2005). Le transport combiné des marchandises: l'intermodalité, un outil au service de la décongestion routière. In L. Grard (Ed.), *L'Europe des transports* (pp. 419 et seqq.).

Calme, S. (2008). *L'évolution du droit des transports ferroviaires en Europe*. Thesis, P.U.A.M.

Duintjer Tebbens, H. (2008). The European Union and the Athens Convention on Maritime Carriers' Liability for Passengers in case of accidents: An incorporation adventure. *Revue hellénique de droit international*, 653 et seqq.

Greaves, R., (2004). *EC transport in the European Union*. Palgrave Macmillan.

Haak, W. (1988). Experience in the Netherlands regarding the case-law of the chamber of appeal of the Central Commission for Navigation on the Rhine. *Netherlands Yearbook of International Law*, 1–51.

Hübner, C. (2006). Erika III: règlement introduisant le Protocole de 2002 à la Convention d'Athènes en matière de transport fluvial. *Le droit maritime français*, 984 et seqq.

Humphreys, M. (2001). The polluter pays principle in transport policy. *European Law Review, 26*, 451–467.

Knieps, G. (2014). *Competition and third party access in railroads*, Freiburg: Institut für Verkehrswissenschaft und Regionalpolitik, Discussion Paper No. 150.

Mainier-Schall Trascu, L. (2005). Maîtrise écologique ou liberté du transport routier: l'exemple autrichien. In L Grard (Ed.), *L'Europe des transports* (pp. 785 et seqq.). La Documentation Française.

Nougaret, G. (2007). L'achèvement de la libéralisation du transport ferroviaire de fret: revitalisation ou coup de grâce pour le fret ferroviaire?. *Revue Lamy de la concurrence*, 116 et seqq.

Salque, S. (2006). Intégration du marché européen des transports ferroviaires et nouvelle stratégie des entreprises ferroviaires historiques européennes. *Revue du droit de l'Union européenne*, 51–110.

Speijer, E. (2009). Gelijke passagiersrechten voor alle vervoerswijzen? *Nederlands tijdschrift voor Europees recht*, 220 et seqq.

Tonner, K., (2007). Deregulation of transport utilities and reregulation by "Passengers' rights" in the European Union, *Diritto e politiche dell'Unione europea*, 138 et seqq.

Vicaire, V. (2005). Le cabotage routier existe-t-il?: cadastrage statistique du marché du cabotage (acteurs, géographie et croissance). In L. Grard (Ed.). *L'Europe des transports* (pp. 101 et seqq.). La Documentation Française.

---

[33] All cited Internet sources in this comment have been accessed on 6 July 2022.

Article 92 [Standstill Obligation]
(ex-Article 72 TEC)

Until the provisions referred to in Article 91(1) have been laid down,[4] no Member State[2] may, unless the Council has unanimously adopted a measure granting a derogation,[3] make the various provisions governing the subject on 1 January 1958[1] or, for acceding States, the date of their accession less favourable[1] in their direct or indirect effect on carriers of other Member States as compared[1] with carriers who are nationals of that State.

Article 92 TFEU contains a so-called "**standstill provision**" addressed to the MS. It allows MS to maintain the discrimination (differential treatment) existing ("freezing the situation") at the date of their accession to the Union, between their national carriers and the carriers established in other MS, but it forbids any aggravation of such discrimination after this date. It is a specific formulation of the commitment of **loyal compliance** pursuant to the Union goals in **Article 4.3 TEU** and a specific application of the **discrimination ban** in **Article 18 TFEU**. 1

It is clarified that the ban: 2

- is directed at the MS: the EU itself is not bound by it;
- aims at any regulatory act, whether legislative or executive;
- irrespective whether it has a direct or indirect effect;
- is absolute and an infringement is not susceptible for justification;
- can only be invoked by foreign as opposed to domestic transport enterprises: if possible at all in the **non-harmonised field**, a complaint of **reverse discrimination** could not be based on this provision;
- can only be invoked by enterprises (carriers) as opposed to private traffic users;
- applies only to differential as opposed to unjust, but equal, treatment;
- applies only to differential as opposed to stricter regulation that applies equally to foreign and domestic undertakings.

An MS is required to notify the Commission and the other MS of any measure that is likely to interfere substantially with the common transport policy.[1] It may apply to the Council for a derogation from the precept of Article 92 TFEU. Such a derogation is to be granted by express unanimous decision of the Council. So far, no use has been made of this exemption. An **unconditional exemption** would normally not be granted (cf. the WTO GATS Article XXI system of compensatory adjustment for the withdrawal of a MS's earlier commitment). 3

The ban applies as long as no secondary EU harmonisation legislation on the matter is adopted. As the internal transport market was for the most part established 4

---

[1] Parliament/Council Decision No. 357/2009/EC *on a procedure for prior examination and consultation in respect of certain laws, regulations and administrative provisions concerning transport proposed in Member States*, O.J. L 109/37 (2009).

via far reaching harmonisation in the field by secondary EU legislation, there is little margin left for national regulation. Consequently, this provision is largely outdated and fulfils only a residual (default) function where the common transport policy is not yet fully elaborated. For example, secondary EU legislation addressed the issue of the so-called "**Euro-vignettes**": road user charges or tolls on motorways for cargo vehicles.[2] The transitional regimes in the accession treaties for newly joining MS must, however, be recalled (→ Article 90 TFEU para 38 on timing).

---

[2] See Parliament/Council Directive 1999/62/EC *on the charging of heavy goods vehicles for the use of certain infrastructures*, O.J. L 187/42 (1999).

Article 93 [State Aid]
(ex-Article 73 TEC)

Aids[3-11] shall be compatible with the Treaties if they meet the needs of coordination[15-16] of transport or if they represent reimbursement for the discharge of certain obligations inherent in the concept of a public service.[17-20]

Contents

1. The Concept of Aid 1
   1.1. An Advantage 4
   1.2. By a National Public Authority 8
   1.3. To an Undertaking 9
   1.4. Selectively 10
   1.5. Actually or Possibly Distorting Competition 11
2. The State General Aid Prohibition and Its Exemptions 12
3. The Transport Specific Exemptions 15
   3.1. Coordination of Transport 15
   3.2. Public Service Obligation 17

List of Cases
References

1. The Concept of Aid

In an era in which the establishment of the internal transport market is virtually completed, the other provisions of the title may have become less acute, but the **public subsidisation**, as addressed by Article 93 TFEU, remains an ever-current issue.

The **general competition provisions** of the Treaty (Articles 106-109 TFEU) apply to State aid granted in the field of road, rail and inland waterway transport[1] and for that matter also in the field of air and maritime transport. Article 93 TFEU is a *lex specialis* in its relationship with Article 107.1 TFEU.

State aid is defined as: any aid granted by an MS or through State resources in any form whatsoever which distorts or threatens to distort competition by favouring certain undertakings (Article 107.1 TFEU). According to this definition, to qualify as State aid, a measure needs to cumulatively present the following characteristics:

---

[1] See, among others, Article 2 of the (repealed) Council Regulation (EEC) No. 1107/70 *on the granting of aids for transport by rail, road and inland waterway*, O.J. L 130/1 (1970).

1.1. An Advantage

4 An **advantage in any form,** such as, e.g. direct cash grants, soft loans with below-market interest rate or interest-free loans, capital investment, (unlimited) State guarantee or insurance cover, tax reliefs, concession of exclusive rights, provision of services on preferential terms, etc. Two important types of advantages require further explanation.

5 **Public capital investment** in an undertaking may also amount to State aid. However, public investment will not be considered as State aid if the State acted under the same terms and conditions as a commercial investor when providing the funding. This requires the demonstration *ex ante* that the investment is expected to provide an adequate and normal market rate of return in line with the expectations of commercial operators on comparable projects, so that a similar measure would also have been undertaken by a market economy investor (the so-called "**Market Economy Investor Principle**" (MEIP) or "**Market Economy Operator Principle**" (MEOP) test) (→ Article 107 TFEU para 33 et seqq.).

6 The advantage may **compensate the discharge of a service of general economic interest** (SGEI) (public service). According to the ECJ's 2003 "*Altmark*" ruling[2] under Article 107 TFEU (→ Article 107 TFEU para 49 et seqq.), for lack of economic advantage, State funding of SGEI does not amount to State aid, provided the following four conditions are cumulatively met:

(i) clear definition of the public service obligation for those services,
(ii) objective and transparent manner of the compensation calculation parameters,
(iii) compensation not exceeding the real cost plus a reasonable profit, and
(iv) pursuance of least cost through selection of the beneficiary tenderer/bidder via a public procurement procedure.

7 Pursuant to the *Altmark* ruling, the Commission issued a **State Aid Package on Services of General Economic Interest**, also known as the post-*Altmark* Package,[3] comprising the SGEI Decision and the SGEI Framework.

The subsequently recast (new) package comprises:

(i) the Commission Communication on the application of the EU State aid rules to compensation granted for the provision of services of general economic interest;[4]
(ii) the Commission Decision of 20 December 2012 on the application of Article 106(2) TFEU to State aid in the form of **public service compensation** granted to certain undertakings entrusted with the operation of services of general economic interest;[5]

---

[2] Case C-280/00, *Altmark Trans* (ECJ 24 July 2003).
[3] Rusche and Schmidt (2011), p. 249.
[4] O.J. C 8/4 (2012).
[5] Commission Decision 2012/21/EU, O.J. L 7/3 (2012).

(iii) the Commission Communication, **EU framework for State aid in the form of public service compensation** (2011);[6]
(iv) the Commission Regulation on the application of Articles 107 and 108 TFEU to *de minimis* **aid** granted to undertakings providing services of general economic interest.[7]

1.2. By a National Public Authority

On the donor side, to qualify as aid, it is to be granted by a **national public** 8 **authority** (→ Article 107 TFEU para 26 et seqq.): this means an **intervention by the MS or through MS resources, as opposed to EU subsidisation.**

1.3. To an Undertaking

On the recipient side, to qualify as aid, it is to be granted to an **undertaking** 9 (→ Article 101 TFEU para 23 et seqq.): this means an entity engaged in an economic, as opposed to a non-commercial, activity. It does not comprise benefits granted to individuals in their private capacity. The entity may be either **private or public**, since the level playing field is also pursued in the activity segment where public and private undertakings compete with each other.

1.4. Selectively

To qualify as aid, it is to be granted on a **selective basis** to specific undertakings or 10 categories of undertakings, sector-wise or geographically (→ Article 107 TFEU para 54 et seqq.). This means that **general measures**, benefiting to all enterprises, **do not constitute State aid** and consequently are not affected by this prohibition. For example, the public financing of infrastructure that is open to all potential users, does not constitute State aid.

1.5. Actually or Possibly Distorting Competition

The prohibition concerns measures that **distort or** are **susceptible to distort** 11 **competition in the trade between MS** by granting an undertaking such an advantage that it prevents effective competition on the market (→ Article 107 TFEU para 70), e.g. by deterring outside undertakings or new players from entering certain national or regional markets. Support granted may not be regarded as

---

[6] O.J. C 8/15 (2012).
[7] Commission Regulation (EU) No. 360/2012, O.J. L 114/8 (2012).

State aid if it has no effect on competition, e.g. because it does not exceed the *de minimis* **threshold**,[8] or because there is no competition in a transport network infrastructure under statutory monopoly.

2. The State General Aid Prohibition and Its Exemptions

12 Article 93 TFEU in the field of transport[9] confirms the basic ban on State aid as laid down in the general (horizontal) competition regime (Article 107.1 TFEU).[10] However, Article 107.2-3 TFEU list **general exemptions**, i.e. instances in which State aid may escape from the prohibition, all of which also apply to all modes of transport. In the field of transport by **road, rail and inland waterway**, Article 93 TFEU supplements the general list of exceptions of Article 107.2-3 TFEU by adding **specific exemptions**, i.e. two more derogation grounds rendering State aid permissible, namely in relation to (i) the coordination of transport (→ para 15) and (ii) the provision of a public service (→ para 17).

13 Various **secondary legislation** (regulations and decisions) was adopted to better regulate public service obligations and the provision of State aid in the transport sectors of road, rail and inland waterway. The precepts of Article 93 TFEU are subject of a secondary implementation instrument; this came about by Regulation 1370/2007[11] (rail and road transport).

14 In summary,[12] as a rule, a measure creating a selective advantage is forbidden and therefore unlawful, but it **may be exempted** from the ban in either one of the following cases:

(i) It does not qualify as aid because it does not meet the criteria of the definition in Article 107.1 TFEU (e.g., when it does not reach the threshold as defined in the *de minimis* regulation[13] → para 11 on the concept of State aid).

---

[8] Commission Regulation (EU) No. 1407/2013 *on the application of Articles 107 and 108 [TFEU] to* de minimis *aid*, O.J. L 352/1 (2013) implementing Article 2 of the enabling Council Regulation (EU) 2015/1588 *on the application of Articles 107 and 108 [TFEU] to certain categories of horizontal State aid (codification)*, O.J. L 248/1 (2015). Aid under the regime of the general *de minimis* Regulation 1407/2013 may be cumulated with aid under the specific SGEI de minimis Regulation 360/2012 (Article 5 Regulation 1407/2013).

[9] Bovis (2005a), p. 587.

[10] Kekelis and Nicolaides (2008), p. 421.

[11] Parliament/Counil Regulation (EC) No. 1370/2007 *on public passenger transport services by rail and by road*, O.J. L 315/1 (2007); Sousse (2008). See also the Proposal for a Council Regulation *on the application of Articles 93, 107 and 108 [TFEU] to certain categories of State aid in the rail, inland waterway and multimodal transport sector*, COM(2022) 327 final.

[12] See the Commission Staff Working Document, *Guide to the application of the EU rules on State aid, public procurement and the internal market to services of general economic interest, and in particular to social services of general interest*, SWD(2013) 53 final/2.

[13] Commission Regulation (EU) No. 1407/2013 *on the application of Articles 107 and 108 [TFEU] to* de minimis *aid*, O.J. L 352/1 (2013) (*de minimis* Regulation), implementing Article 2 of the enabling Council Regulation (EU) 2015/1588.

(ii) It qualifies as one of the automatic exceptions listed as compatible with the competition rules (Article 107.2 TFEU).
(iii) It constitutes one of the two additional exemption cases in Article 93 TFEU chapter on transport, namely coordination of transport and provision of a public service (→ para 15 and para 17).
(iv) It meets the parameters of a block exemption as defined in the General Block Exemption Regulation (GBER)[14] (under Articles 107.3 point (e) and 108.4 TFEU): **aid with a social character granted for transport** in favour of residents of remote regions and without discrimination as to the identity of the carrier.
(v) Upon notification, it benefits from an individual exemption: a derogation granted by discretionary decision of the Commission, if judged compatible with the common market (Articles 107.3 and 108.2 TFEU).

3. The Transport Specific Exemptions

3.1. Coordination of Transport

State aid meeting the coordination needs of transport is exempt from the prohibition. The concept of "**transport coordination**" in Article 93 TFEU implies an intervention by public authorities that is aimed at guiding the development of the transport sector in the common interest. Permissible aid for coordination of transport may appear in several forms:[15]   **15**

- aid for infrastructure use;
- aid for development of multimodal transport;
- aid for reducing external costs designed to encourage a modal shift from road to rail;
- aid for promoting interoperability, and, to the extent to which it meets the needs of transport coordination, aid for promoting greater safety, the removal of technical barriers and the reduction of noise pollution;
- aid for research and development in response to the needs of transport coordination.

The Commission presents in detail the method to determine eligible **transport**   **16**
coordination costs, as well as the conditions making it possible to ensure that this aid meets the **conditions of compatibility** mentioned in Article 93 TFEU. Aid for rail infrastructure use, reducing external costs and interoperability is considered compatible when it is necessary and proportionate.

---

[14] Section 9 of the General Block Exemption Regulation (GBER), Commission Regulation (EU) No. 651/2014 of *declaring certain categories of aid compatible with the internal market in application of Articles 107 and 108 of the Treaty*, O.J. L 187/1 (2014), implementing Article 1.1.1 point (a) (xii) of the enabling Council Regulation (EU) 2015/1588.

[15] Community Guidelines *on State aid for railway undertakings*, O.J. C 184/13 (2008), Chapter 6.

3.2. Public Service Obligation

17 A "public service" or **Service of General Economic Interest** is a service the provision of which is considered to be in the public interest and which therefore may be regulated and financed by the state.[16] The concept of SGEI appears in Articles 14 and 106.2 TFEU and in Protocol (No 26) to the TFEU, but it is not defined in the TFEU or in secondary legislation. The Commission[17] has clarified in its Quality Framework that SGEIs are economic activities which deliver outcomes in the overall public good that, without public intervention, would not be supplied (or would be supplied under different conditions in terms of objective quality, safety, affordability, equal treatment or universal access) by the market (→ Article 106 TFEU para 54 et seqq.).

Typical examples of SGEI are: postal services, social services and transport services more specifically local and regional transport services, ferry-boat services to small or distant islands and small airports in peripheral areas.

18 A **Public Service Obligation** (PSO)[18] is the duty imposed by the public authority on the provider of the service to ensure the achievement of certain general interest goals (assuring a universal service) which the operator would not assume or not to the same extent or not under the same conditions without reward, if it were considering its own commercial interests.[19]

19 State aid control comes into play when these services are **financed through public resources**, particularly because overcompensation in return for their provision of the service could enable the public service providers to **cross-subsidise** their other commercial activities, and thereby distort competition. Therefore, the discharge of a public service obligation and the concomitant **exclusive right** or compensation via State subsidies is to be performed in the framework of a public service contract awarded via a **public procurement procedure** based on **competitive tendering**.[20]

20 The specific exemption based on public transport service obligation in Article 93 TFEU seems redundant after the ECJ *Altmark* ruling:[21] if a State advantage does not qualify as State aid, it should not require a derogation.

---

[16] Bovis (2005b), p. 1329.

[17] See, among others, the White paper *on Services of General Interest*, COM(2004) 374, the Communication on social services of general interest, *Implementing the Union Lisbon programme: Social services of general interest in the European Union*, COM(2006) 177 and the Communication on *Services of general interest, including social services of general interest: a new European commitment*, COM(2007) 725 final.

[18] Vieu (2010).

[19] Article 2 point (e) of Regulation (EC) No. 1370/2007; Commission Communication, *Interpretative guidelines concerning Regulation (EC) No. 1370/2007 on public passenger transport services by rail and by road*, O.J. C 92/1 (2014).

[20] Article 5 of Regulation (EC) No. 1370/2007.

[21] Case C-280/00, *Altmark Trans* (ECJ 24 July 2003).

List of Cases

ECJ 24.07.2003, C-280/00, *Altmark Trans*, ECLI:EU:C:2003:415 [cit. in para 6, 20]

References

Bovis, C. (2005a). State aid and European Union transport: Reflection on law, policy and practice. *Journal of World Trade*, 587–636.
Bovis, C. (2005b). Public service obligations in the transport sector: The demarcation between State aids and services of general economic interest under EU law. *European Business Law Review, 16*(6), 1329–1347.
Kekelis, M., & Nicolaides, P. (2008). Public financing of urban transport: The application of EC State aid rules. *World Competition*, 421–448.
Rusche, T.M., & Schmidt, S. (2011). The post-Altmark era has started: 15 months of application of Regulation (EC) No. 1370/2007 to public transport services. *European State Aid Law Quarterly*, 249–264.
Sousse, M. (2008). *Le règlement (CE) n° 1370/2007 relatif aux services publics de transport de voyageurs par chemin de fer et par route*. Europe 2008 (n°6).
Vieu, P. (2010). À propos de l'intégration de l'Europe des transports: observations sur l'interprétation et l'application de la norme européenne: le cas du règlement OSP. *Revue trimestrielle de droit européen*, 297–331.

Article 94 [Economic Circumstances of Carriers]
(ex-Article 74 TEC)

Any measures[6] taken within the framework of the Treaties[6] in respect of transport rates[9] and conditions[10] shall take account of the economic circumstances of carriers.[11,12]

Contents

1. Overview 1
2. Any Measures Taken Within the Framework of the Treaties 6
3. Transport Rates and Conditions 8
4. Taking Account of the Economic Circumstances of Carriers 11
5. The Current Relevance of Article 94 TFEU 13

List of Cases
References

1. Overview

Article 94 TFEU provides a qualification upon the manner in which public authorities can introduce measures on transport rates and conditions. The Article 94 TFEU qualification requires the relevant public authorities, which take measures within the framework of the treaties to take **account of the economic circumstances of carriers**.

This special focus afforded to the economic conditions of carriers was not arbitrary. The transport industry has always been viewed as **integral to the proper operation of the internal market** and, as such, was viewed as deserving of this special protection.[1] The article does not, however, offer any specific protection to carriers. The Article 94 TFEU qualification merely exists to ensure that carriers' economic interests are considered in the process of introducing measures within the meaning of the article. The weight to be given to their economic interests in any given case rests entirely with the relevant public authority. In essence, Article 94 TFEU is just a specific example of the general principle espoused in Article 91.1 TFEU, namely that transport has distinctive features that need to be considered when new measures are introduced.

Article 94 TFEU was adopted in the Treaty of Lisbon practically **unchanged from its predecessors**, Article 78 TEEC and Article 74 TEC. Any changes between these articles were purely semantic and have no bearing upon the substantive meaning.

---

[1] Fehling, in von der Groeben et al. (2015), Article 94 AEUV para 1 and 2.

4 The qualification contained within Article 94 TFEU applies *prima facie* only to measures taken on transport rates and conditions which concern **road, rail and inland waterway** modes of transport (→ Article 100 TFEU para 7). The Article 94 TFEU qualification applies to carriers of goods and passengers.[2]

5 Transport rates today are generally subject to **free pricing** within the EU. For instance, measures concerning transport rates between MS in road transport have been abolished by Regulation (EEC) No 4058/89[3] and the market is now liberalised.[4] In air transport, air fares for flights within the EU are to be freely set by the carriers, since the adoption of Regulation (EEC) No. 2409/92.[5] For this reason, the practical importance of Article 94 TFEU has significantly diminished (→ para 13 to 14).

2. Any Measures Taken Within the Framework of the Treaties

6 Article 94 TFEU is **addressed primarily to the Union** and its institutions and aims to restrict the competence of the Union to pass secondary legislation under Article 91 TFEU, and therefore within the framework of the common transport policy, as far as transport rates and conditions are concerned.[6] This part of the provision implies the **principle of conferral** as laid down in Article 5.2 TEU, and supplemented by the explicit competences of the Union as defined in Article 2 to 6 TFEU.[7] According to the principle of conferral, the Union only possesses competence so far as its MS have conferred that competence to the Union. Any measures taken must be within the framework of the Treaties, i.e. any measures falling outside the Treaty framework are outside Union competence and rest solely in the realm of its MS.

7 MS are also bound by Article 94 TFEU as it relates to their introduction of measures on transport rates and conditions within the framework of the Treaties. This conclusion is consistent with the **principle of subsidiarity** elucidated in Article 5.3 TEU. For example, in the implementation of an EU directive, an MS is often left a significant degree of leeway. In the circumstances where such a directive will require the MS to legislate on transport rates or conditions within the scope of the common transport policy, the MS must consider the economic circumstances of the carrier under Article 94 TFEU.

---

[2] Rusche in Kellerbauer et al. (2019), Article 94 TFEU para 7.
[3] O.J. L 390/1 (1989).
[4] Rusche, in Kellerbauer et al. (2019), Article 94 TFEU para 11.
[5] See Council Regulation (EEC) 2409/92 *on fares and rates for air services*, O.J. L 240/15 (1992). The Regulation, as part of the third air transport liberalisation package has been recast, together with other Regulations within that package, as Regulation (EC) 1008/2008 *on common rules for the operation of air services in the Community (Recast)*, O.J. L 293/3 (2008). See also Martinez, in Calliess and Ruffert (2022), Article 94 AEUV para 6.
[6] Fehling, in von der Groeben et al. (2015), Article 94 AEUV para 5.
[7] In the area of transport, the competence is shared, see Article 4.2 point (g) TFEU.

3. Transport Rates and Conditions

Article 94 TFEU governs the political mandate of public authorities when introducing measures on **transport rates and conditions**. The rule is that when transport rates and conditions are subject to a measure introduced within the framework of the Treaties, that measure must consider the economic circumstances of the carrier.

The scope of Article 94 TFEU on **transport rates** is relatively straightforward. This concept clearly entails any direct infringement upon the market price of transport rates. Perhaps the most overt example of such a measure on transport rates is legislative price control.

On the other hand, the concept of **transport conditions** connotes a much wider definition. Conditions of carriage are considered to include all fiscal, technical, environmental and social norms that are applicable to transport, and which have a direct impact upon transport rates.[8] For example, the Directive on the organisation of the working time of persons performing mobile road transport activities[9] was presumed by the Court of Justice to fall within the ambit of this concept.[10]

4. Taking Account of the Economic Circumstances of Carriers

The **carrier,** which benefits from the conceptual protection of Article 94 TFEU, is not defined in the provision. Attention must therefore be paid to Article 91.1 point (b) TFEU, which also applies to 'carriers' (→ Article 91 TFEU para 10). As with Article 94 TFEU generally (→ para 4), the scope of the carrier concept is limited by Article 100.1 TFEU to carriers in the modes of transport of road, rail and inland waterway. Sea and air transport remain to be covered by Article 100.2 TFEU.

The requirement for the public authority introducing measures to '**take account of the economic circumstances of carriers**' is a somewhat light burden to offload. It appears that if evidence can be adduced that the relevant body in some way considered the economic circumstances, then the burden will be discharged.[11] This conclusion is reasonable in the circumstances. Any legislator necessarily must balance numerous often conflicting interests in the introduction of any measures. Article 94 TFEU serves in this instance merely as a reminder of the importance of the transport industry in the operation of a functional European single market. It does not automatically mean that the economic interests of carriers should trump other, perhaps equally or even more, important considerations. However, in the

---

[8] Fehling, in von der Groeben et al. (2015), Article 94 AEUV para 8.

[9] Directive 2002/15/EC *on the organisation of the working time of persons performing mobile road transport activities*, O.J. L 80/35 (2002).

[10] See Joined Cases C-184/02 and C-223/02, *Spain and Finland v Parliament and Council* (ECJ 9 September 2004) para 68.

[11] See, e.g. Joined Cases C-184/02 and C-223/02, *Spain and Finland v Parliament and Council* (ECJ 9 September 2004) para 68.

case of complete ignorance on the part of the measure-taking authority, the measure could then be open to administrative challenge.[12]

5. The Current Relevance of Article 94 TFEU

13 The ability to set transport rates has been practically demolished through EU secondary legislation (→ Article 91 TFEU para 9). This is obviously desirable, given that a primary motivator behind the EU project is the creation of a fully functioning free and competitive single internal market. Since the Common Transport Policy (CTP) has led to the liberalisation and opening of the transport market, any regulation of transport rates has largely disappeared, and Article 94 TFEU holds **little to no practical relevance**.[13]

14 On the other hand, **Article 94 TFEU is still technically relevant with respect to measures in respect of transport conditions**, assuming the broad meaning of the concept as detailed above. However, given the relatively weak obligation to consider contained within Article 94 TFEU, the article is relatively simple to discharge.

List of Cases

ECJ 09.09.2004, C-184/02, C-223/02, *Spain and Finland v Parliament and Council*, ECLI:EU:C:2004:497 [cit. in para 10, 12]

References

Calliess, C., & Ruffert, M. (2022). *EUV/AEUV. Commentary* (6th ed.). C.H. Beck.
Kellerbauer, M., Klamert, M., & Tomkin, J. (Eds.). (2019). *The EU Treaties and the Charter of Fundamental Rights. A commentary*. OUP.
von der Groeben, H., Schwarze, J., & Hatje, A. (Eds.). (2015). *Europäisches Unionsrecht* (7th ed.). Nomos.

---

[12] See, e.g. Article 263 TFEU.
[13] Martinez, in Calliess and Ruffert (2022), Article 94 AEUV para 6; Rusche, in Kellerbauer et al. (2019), Article 94 TFEU para 6.

Article 95 [Prohibition of Discrimination]
(ex-Article 75 TEC)

1. In the case of transport within the Union,[11] discrimination which takes the form of carriers charging different rates[6] and imposing different conditions[6] for the carriage of the same goods over the same transport links[2] on grounds of the country of origin or of destination of the goods[7] in question shall be prohibited.[4]
2. Paragraph 1 shall not prevent the European Parliament and the Council from adopting other measures pursuant to Article 91(1).[13]
3. The Council shall, on a proposal from the Commission and after consulting the European Parliament and the Economic and Social Committee, lay down rules for implementing the provisions of paragraph 1.[14,15]
   The Council may in particular lay down the provisions needed to enable the institutions of the Union to secure compliance with the rule laid down in paragraph 1 and to ensure that users benefit from it to the full.[16]
4. The Commission shall, acting on its own initiative or on application by a Member State, investigate any cases of discrimination falling within paragraph 1 and, after consulting any Member State concerned, shall take the necessary decisions within the framework of the rules laid down in accordance with the provisions of paragraph 3.[17]

Contents

1. Overview 1
2. Prohibited Discrimination (Paragraph 1) 5
3. The Right to Adopt Other Measures Under Article 91.1 TFEU (Paragraph 2) .. 13
4. Implementing the Prohibition (Paragraph 3) 14
5. Commission's Right to Investigate (Paragraph 4) 17
6. Current Relevance of Article 95 TFEU 18
References

1. Overview

Article 95 TFEU creates a **special prohibition against discriminatory carriage rates and conditions** based on the destination or origin of the goods in question. This prohibition is, in essence, a restatement of the general prohibition of discrimination on the ground of nationality under Article 18 TFEU, but with a particular focus on carriage of goods. Article 95 TFEU also provides a specific complement to

Articles 28 to 37 TFEU, which govern the free movement of goods regime within the EU.[1]

2 The first paragraph of Article 95 TFEU lays down the **general prohibition of discrimination in the case of the carriage of goods**. Carriers may not charge different rates or impose different conditions for the carriage of the same goods over the same transport links. For the prohibition to apply, therefore, the **transport link and the goods carried must be practically identical**. The transport modes used in the journey must also be the same.[2]

3 The second to fourth paragraphs of Article 95 TFEU detail the application of the first paragraph. The second paragraph allows the EP and the Council to adopt **other measures** under Article 91.1 TFEU. The third paragraph lays down **rules for implementation** of and securing compliance with the first paragraph. The fourth paragraph lays down the process by which the Commission can deal with a case of **suspected infringement**.

4 Article 95 TFEU is substantially the same as its progenitor articles, Article 75 TEC and Article 79 TEEC. One important change was made however between Article 75.1 TEC and the current Article 95 TFEU. The phrase 'discrimination shall be abolished', found in Article 75 TEC, was amended to read in the current Article 95.1 TFEU 'shall be prohibited'. Therefore, Article 95 TFEU now constitutes a directly applicable prohibition, while the prior versions of the provision merely formed the legal basis for the adoption of secondary legislation.[3] Nonetheless, the provision retains this latter character with regard to Article 95.3 TFEU.[4]

2. Prohibited Discrimination (Paragraph 1)

5 Article 95.1 TFEU creates the **prohibition of discrimination** on transport rates and conditions within the EU. The concept underpinning the prohibition is that carriage of the same goods should be subject to the same rates and conditions when carried within the EU, no matter the origin or destination of the goods. As discussed above, this concept is merely a specific extension of the Treaty's general prohibition of discrimination on the grounds of nationality under Article 18 TFEU.

6 The prohibition is limited to discrimination on **rates and conditions**. Rates of carriage in this context include both rates set by the state as well as those freely agreed to in the market, unlike Article 94 TFEU where transport rates refer only to the first of these meanings.[5] Transport conditions in the context of Article 95.1 TFEU must also be distinguished from the same phrase in Article 94 TFEU. The

---

[1] Greaves (2000), p. 21.

[2] Fehling, in von der Groeben et al. (2015), Article 95 AEUV para 5.

[3] Khan and Henrich, in Geiger et al. (2015), Article 95 TFEU para 4; Rusche, in Kellerbauer et al. (2019), Article 95 TFEU para 1.

[4] Khan and Henrich, in Geiger et al. (2015), Article 95 TFEU para 4.

[5] Fehling, in von der Groeben et al. (2015), Article 95 AEUV, para 3.

reason for this is that while Article 94 TFEU seeks to protect carriers from acts undertaken within the framework of the Treaties—therefore including within the conceptual ambit of transport conditions such things as social norms or environmental regulation—Article 95 TFEU seeks to protect those looking to transport goods from discriminatory actions by carriers. Costs incurred by carriers because of the imposition of transport conditions within the meaning of Article 94 TFEU, for example a piece of environmental legislation, will subsequently be passed on by carriers of goods to all users of their services. On the other hand, transport conditions within the meaning of Article 95.1 TFEU are those imposed by carriers that discriminate between users of their service. These would include such things as discriminatory insurance or load requirements.

Article 95.1 TFEU further stipulates that the discrimination on rates or conditions must be based upon the grounds of the **country of origin or the country of destination of the goods**. 7

Article 95 TFEU applies to all **carriers of goods**. The article must therefore be read in conjunction with Article 91.1 point (b) TFEU, which also applies to 'carriers' (→ Article 91 TFEU para 10). Due to the structure of Article 100 TFEU, carriers in this context refers only to carriers in the fields of road, rail and inland waterway (→ Article 100 TFEU para 1, 7). The prohibition also applies to government-operated railways.[6] Undertakings that set their own rates and which are not subject to government controls will also be covered by the Article 95 TFEU prohibition.[7] 8

In 1960, the Council, pursuant to its authority under Article 95.3 TFEU (ex-Article 79.3 TEEC), laid down rules for the implementation of the Article 95.1 TFEU prohibition in the form of **Council Regulation (EEC) No. 11/1960** (the Regulation) (→ para 14).[8] The Regulation aids in fleshing out the meaning of the Article 95.1 TFEU prohibition. 9

Under the Regulation, the charging of different rates and the imposition of different conditions **will not fall within the meaning** of the Article 95.1 TFEU prohibition if these *prima facie* discriminatory rates and conditions result solely from competition between carriers or are due to the specific operating conditions of the transport link in question.[9] 10

The Regulation provides further that the prohibition applies to the carriage of **all goods by rail, road or inland waterway within the Community**.[10] This means that it applies to the carriage of all types of goods consigned from or to a point 11

---

[6] Greaves (2000), p. 20.
[7] Greaves (2000), p. 20.
[8] Council Regulation (EEC) No. 11/1960 *concerning the abolition of discrimination in transport rates and conditions etc*, O.J. L 52/1121 (1960) as amended by Council Regulation (EC) No. 569/2008, O.J. L 161/1 (2008). The original Council Regulation came into force on 1 July 1961.
[9] Article 12.2 of Regulation 11/1960.
[10] Goods listed in Annexes I and III to the TECSC are exempted from the scope of this regulation, see Article 1 of Regulation 11/1960.

within an MS, including if the carriage is between MS or non-EU countries.[11] Only the parts of the journey, which take place within the EU, however, will be covered by the prohibition.[12] Further, where parts of a journey of carriage are undertaken by the transport modes listed above and parts are undertaken by other modes of transport—air transport for example—then the Article 95.1 TFEU prohibition will apply only to those legs of the journey effected by the listed transport modes.[13]

12 As detailed above, the Regulation governs **only the carriage of goods by rail, road or inland waterway**. It is likely that this is primarily as a result of the fact that, at the time of introduction of the Regulation, unanimity was required on the part of the Council to include **sea and air transport** within the ambit of such legislation (→ Article 100 TFEU para 3 to 6). It is unlikely that the Regulation will be amended to include sea and air transport now, given that any infringement of the Article 95.1 TFEU prohibition in these areas would be dealt with generally by EU competition law.

3. The Right to Adopt Other Measures Under Article 91.1 TFEU (Paragraph 2)

13 Under Article 95.2 TFEU, the EP and Council's **ability to adopt other measures pursuant to Article 91.1 TFEU is not affected by Article 95.1 TFEU**. This paragraph leaves to the EP and Council a degree of flexibility on the ways in which they could choose to pursue this issue within the overarching framework of a common transport policy.

4. Implementing the Prohibition (Paragraph 3)

14 Under Article 95.3 TFEU the Council shall, on proposal from the Commission and after consulting the EP and the Economic and Social Committee, lay down **rules for the implementation** of the Article 95.1 TFEU prohibition. As outlined above (→ para 9), the Regulation is the product of this procedure, although it was introduced under former Article 79.3 TEEC.

15 The creation of implementation rules under Article 95.3 TFEU therefore follows a **special legislative procedure**, whereby the EP is only required to be consulted by the Council.

16 Article 95.3 TFEU further provides that the Council **may, in particular**, lay down rules enabling EU institutions to secure compliance with the prohibition, as well as to enable users to obtain the benefit of the prohibition in full. Given that this part of the provision stipulates that the Council 'may' do so, this section of

---

[11] Article 2.1 of Regulation 11/1960.
[12] Article 2.2 of Regulation 11/1960.
[13] Article 2.3 of Regulation 11/1960.

Article 95.3 TFEU does nothing more than orient the Council as to particularly important pieces that should be included in the implementing rules.

5. Commission's Right to Investigate (Paragraph 4)

Cases of discrimination falling within the scope of the Article 95.1 TFEU prohibition shall be **investigated by the Commission**, upon its own initiative or application by an MS. Rules on investigation and enforcement are provided for in detail in the Regulation.[14] Following its investigation, the Commission must then make a **decision** within the framework of the Regulation regarding the suspected infringement of the prohibition.

17

6. Current Relevance of Article 95 TFEU

The prohibition embodied in Article 95.1 TFEU currently holds **very little practical relevance**. In the face of open markets and free competition with strictly enforced competition rules, Article 95 TFEU is now little more than an antique piece of the now over fifty-year-old puzzle to create a free and open internal European market.

18

References

Geiger, R., Khan, D.-R., & Kotzur, M. (Eds.). (2015). *European Union Treaties*. Hart Publishing.
Greaves, R. (2000). *EC transport law*. Dorset Press.
Kellerbauer, M., Klamert, M., & Tomkin, J. (Eds.). (2019). *The EU Treaties and the Charter of Fundamental Rights. A commentary*. OUP.
von der Groeben, H., Schwarze, J., & Hatje, A. (Eds.). (2015). *Europäisches Unionsrecht* (7th ed.). Nomos.

---

[14] See, in particular, Articles 11 to 25 of Regulation 11/1960.

Article 96 [Forbidden State Aid and Exceptions]
(ex-Article 76 TEC)

1. The imposition by a Member State, in respect of transport operations[8] carried out within the Union,[9] of rates and conditions[8] involving any element of support or protection[10] in the interest of one or more particular undertakings or industries shall be prohibited, unless authorised by the Commission.[12–14]
2. The Commission shall, acting on its own initiative or on application by a Member State, examine the rates and conditions[8] referred to in paragraph 1, taking account in particular[13,14] of the requirements of an appropriate regional economic policy, the needs of underdeveloped areas and the problems of areas seriously affected by political circumstances on the one hand, and of the effects of such rates and conditions on competition between the different modes of transport on the other.
After consulting each Member State concerned, the Commission shall take the necessary decisions.[15]
3. The prohibition provided for in paragraph 1 shall not apply to tariffs fixed to meet competition.[16,17]

Contents

1. Overview 1
2. The General Prohibition (Paragraph 1) 7
3. Prohibited, Unless Authorised by the Commission (Paragraph 2) 12
4. Tariffs Fixed to Meet Competition (Paragraph 3) 16
5. Practical Relevance of Article 96 TFEU 18

List of Cases
References

1. Overview

Article 96.1 TFEU **prohibits MS from imposing rates or conditions** involving any element of support or protection in the interest of one or more undertakings or industries. The prohibition applies to transport operations carried out within the EU and is not absolute as the Commission has the ability to authorise the imposition of such rates or conditions by MS as it sees fit.

The process by which **the Commission determines whether or not to authorise a particular charge or condition** is articulated in Article 96.2 TFEU.

The third paragraph of the article stipulates that **the Article 96.1 TFEU prohibition shall not apply to tariffs fixed to meet competition**, serving as an exception to the general prohibition.

4   The Article 96.1 TFEU prohibition **applies only to transport by road, rail and inland waterway**. This is due to the structure of Article 100.1 TFEU, which provides that the provisions of the transport title of the TFEU, within which Article 96 TFEU falls, only apply to those modes of transport. Sea and air transport, on the other hand, are regulated independently by Article 100.2 TFEU (→ Article 100 TFEU para 9). The imposition of the types of rates prohibited in Article 96 TFEU on sea and air transport would likely instead be caught by the state aids provision found in Articles 107 and 108 TFEU.[1] Air and sea transport are in this area also subject to particular sector guidelines issued by the Commission.[2]

5   The **origin of Article 96 TFEU** can be found in Article 70 TECSC. Paragraph 2 of this article provided that '[f]or traffic among the Member States, discriminations in transport rates and conditions of any kind, based on the country of origin or destination of the products in question, are particularly forbidden.' This prohibition was then subsequently reflected in the direct predecessors of Article 96 TFEU, Article 80 TEEC and then Article 76 TEC.

6   The **evolution of the article** since the inception of the EEC-focused Article 80 TEEC has been one of predominately semantic rather than substantial change. Perhaps the most notable change made since the article's creation has been the wording of what is now Article 96.2 TFEU. The original Article 80.2 TEEC read that the Commission will consult 'any interested Member State', whereas current Article 96.2 TFEU provides that it will consult 'each Member State concerned'. This change can be considered a narrowing of the scope of the paragraph. 'Any interested Member State' covers a potentially larger group of states than 'each Member State concerned'. Other than this somewhat minor change, the article has undergone only minor terminological and word order changes, which do not impact its substantive effect.

2. The General Prohibition (Paragraph 1)

7   The Article 96.1 TFEU prohibition is directed at Member States and is clear and expansive. It applies primarily to the imposition of **rates and conditions.** For this reason, Article 96.1 TFEU must be read in conjunction with Article 94 TFEU, which also applies to rates and conditions (→ Article 94 TFEU para 8 to 10).

8   **Transport operations** is the area of the transport sector at which the prohibition is directed. This term is not defined in the TFEU. However, based on a plain reading of the term as well as by looking at relevant EU secondary legislation,[3] a transport operation can be defined as the operation of carrying goods or passengers.

---

[1] Fehling, in von der Groeben (2015), Article 96 AEUV para 4.
[2] On sea transport, see Commission Communication *Community Guidelines on State aid to maritime transport*, O.J. C 13/3 (2008); on air transport, see Commission Communication, *Guidelines on State Aid to Airports and Airlines*, O.J. C 99/3 (1999).
[3] See Regulation (EC) No. 561/2006 *on the harmonisation of certain social legislation relating to road transport, etc.*, O.J. L 102/1 (2006).

The Article 96.1 TFEU prohibition only applies to transport operations that are **carried out within the Union**. This restriction on the prohibition operates such that, perhaps obviously, the transport operation must be conducted in or between EU MS for the prohibition to be effective. However, the fact that a transport operation conducts part of its journey through, from or into a non-EU MS, does not lead to the inapplicability of Article 96.1.[4]   9

The relevant rates or conditions looking to be imposed by an MS **cannot 'involve any element of support or protection'**. This wording is wide and provides to the Commission a significant breadth in their ability to determine that a rate or condition is contrary to Article 96 TFEU. Other authors on this topic have noted that the word 'support' implies an element of positive action and promotion, whereas 'protection' involves defending the undertaking or undertakings from certain disadvantages.[5]   10

By prohibiting MS from imposing protective or supportive rates or conditions onto one or more undertakings on transport operations carried out within the EU, Article 96.1 TFEU effectively embodies in the field of transport the Treaty's general principle of **non-discrimination on the grounds of nationality** as found in Article 18 TFEU.[6] Further, by being directed at the MS, the article serves as a specific **complement to the general Articles 107 to 109 TFEU rules on State aid**.[7] The general rules on state aid also allow the Commission to authorise particular rates or conditions if they deem it appropriate in the circumstances.   11

3. Prohibited, Unless Authorised by the Commission (Paragraph 2)

The imposition by an MS of a rate or condition within the meaning of Article 96.1 TFEU must be **authorised by the Commission** for that rate or condition to be legally valid. Under Article 96.2 TFEU, the Commission shall consult all of the MS concerned and, while exercising its discretion on whether authorisation may be granted, must consider the **relevant factors of the situation**. These relevant factors are: the requirements of regional policy, the needs of underdeveloped areas and the problems of areas seriously affected by political circumstances and the effect of the rates and conditions on competition between different forms of transport, with the final one being balanced against the first two.[8]   12

The list of factors is not, however, exclusive, as the Commission is only required to consider the factors stated in Article 96.2 TFEU **'in particular'**. Under Article 96.2 TFEU, therefore, the Commission is able to consider any other factors it may deem relevant.   13

---

[4] Fehling, in von der Groeben et al. (2015), Article 96 AEUV para 5.
[5] Fehling, in von der Groeben et al. (2015), Article 96 AEUV para 8.
[6] Greaves (2000), p. 21.
[7] Greaves (2000), p. 21.
[8] Greaves (2000), p. 21.

14   In the case of *Italy v Commission*,[9] the Court elaborated upon the Commission's role as detailed in Article 96.2 TFEU. The case concerned the imposition of a tariff by the Italian government. By a 1969 decision, the Commission authorised the tariff in question under then Article 80.2 TEEC (now Article 96.2 TFEU), but in doing so provided that Italy would need to reduce the tariff by at least 50% by 1 January 1970, and ultimately abolish it entirely by 1 January 1971. The relevant decision also provided that the Commission could amend or revoke the decision if it found that the authorised tariff was no longer justified, or that it was causing distortions in competition. Italy opposed the Commission's decision. They argued that the Commission themselves acknowledged first that the tariff as approved in the relevant decision satisfied the condition found in Article 80.2 TEEC, on the requirements of an appropriate regional economic policy and the needs of underdeveloped areas, and second, that the tariff in question did not affect competition. For these reasons, Italy maintained that the Commission ought to have maintained the tariff's authorisation for as long as the factors which led to its approval continued to exist.[10] On the other hand, the Commission argued that Article 80.2 TEEC provided an exception to the Article 80.1 TEEC prohibition, therefore any authorisations granted thereunder should be temporary and exceptional.[11] In this instance, the Court sided with the Commission, articulating a wide interpretation of Article 80.2 TEEC.

The Court held that the wording of Article 80.2 TEEC confers upon the Commission a wide discretionary power on the examination and authorisation of rates and conditions of the kind prohibited by the first paragraph of the article. This is due in part to the fact that the Commission shall, under this paragraph, particularly consider the requirements, needs, problems and effects in the areas mentioned. To the Court, this implies that the Commission has a very wide discretion on not only the tariffs to be authorised, but also the particular details or requirements attached to the authorisation. The Court held that the paragraph cannot be interpreted to mean that the Commission must grant an authorisation for a rate or condition once particular factors are established, or, as Italy had argued, that it must maintain an authorisation whilst those factors remain the same.[12] Second, the Court held that the wording '**in particular**' means that the Commission is at liberty to consider other factors than those mentioned in the paragraph, even if they might conflict with those stipulated.[13]

15   Under Article 96.2 TFEU, following the consultation with the concerned MS, the Commission shall then take the **necessary decisions** on the relevant rates or conditions. The TFEU does not provide any guidance as to the interpretation of this phrase. It is clear, however, that the Commission is granted a wide discretion in its ability to take a decision regarding the course of action it deems appropriate.

---

[9] Case 1/69, *Italy v Commission* (ECJ 9 July 1969).

[10] Case 1/69, *Italy v Commission* (ECJ 9 July 1969), p. 280.

[11] Case 1/69, *Italy v Commission* (ECJ 9 July 1969), p. 280.

[12] Case 1/69, *Italy v Commission* (ECJ 9 July 1969), p. 284.

[13] Case 1/69, *Italy v Commission* (ECJ 9 July 1969), p. 284.

4. Tariffs Fixed to Meet Competition (Paragraph 3)

Article 96.3 TFEU provides an **exception to the general prohibition** found in Article 96.1 TFEU. This article stipulates that a tariff fixed to meet competition introduced by an MS is not covered by the general prohibition. 16

The TFEU does not provide any assistance in the interpretation of this phrase. The case of *Chambre syndicale*,[14] however, opens up the concept somewhat. This decision was with respect to Article 70 TECSC, which, as detailed above, was the forebear to Article 96 TFEU. In this case, the Court held that a tariff fixed to meet competition is one that enables a carrier to **maintain its own tariff in the face of competition from another mode of transport**.[15] It is unlikely that this is the only meaning of the concept; however, without more litigation on the matter, it is difficult to define the limits of what could actually be covered by such an exception. 17

5. Practical Relevance of Article 96 TFEU

Article 96 TFEU is **rarely applied in practice**.[16] The reason for this is that the prohibition enumerated therein can be subsumed entirely within the general TFEU rules on State aid. It has therefore been argued that Article 96 TFEU is superfluous and any future revision of the TFEU should see it being removed in its entirety.[17] 18

List of Cases

ECJ 15.07.1960, 24/58, 34/58, *Chambre syndicale de la sidérurgie de l'est de la France and others v High Authority*, ECLI:EU:C:1960:32 [cit. in para 17]
ECJ 09.07.1969, 1/69, *Italy v Commission*, ECLI:EU:C:1969:34 [cit. in para 14]

References

Greaves, R. (2000). *EC transport law*. Dorset Press.
Hancher, L., Ottervanger, T., & Slot, P. S. (2012). *EU State aids* (4th ed.). Sweet & Maxwell.
von der Groeben, H., Schwarze, J., & Hatje, A. (Eds.). (2015). *Europäisches Unionsrecht* (7th ed.). Nomos.

---

[14] Joined Cases 24/58 and 34/58, *Chambre syndicale de la sidérurgie de l'est de la France and others v High Authority* (ECJ 15 July 1960).
[15] Greaves (2000), p. 295.
[16] Hancher et al. (2012), p. 502.
[17] Fehling, in von der Groeben et al. (2015), Article 96 AEUV para 22–23.

Article 97 [Reasonable Frontier Crossing Charges]
(ex-Article 77 TEC)

Charges or dues in respect of the crossing of frontiers which are charged by a carrier[3] in addition to the transport rates shall not exceed a reasonable level after taking the costs actually incurred thereby into account.[5]

Member States shall endeavour to reduce these costs progressively.[6]

The Commission may make recommendations to Member States for the application of this Article.[7]

Contents

1. Overview 1
2. Charges or Dues in Respect of the Crossing of Frontiers (Paragraph 1) 2
3. Progressive Reduction of Costs and Commission Recommendations (Paragraphs 2 and 3) 6
4. Current Practical Relevance of Article 97 TFEU 8

References

1. Overview

Article 97 TFEU ensures that **charges levied by carriers due to frontier crossings are not unreasonable**.[1] The focus of this provision is not on the general concept of charging for a frontier crossing, but on the carrier being prevented from overcharging users of their service when they incur costs associated with crossing a frontier. The provision is aimed at both undertakings and MS.[2] The provision supplements Article 30 TFEU, which governs the elimination of customs duties by reason of crossing a frontier. Article 97 TFEU replaces its predecessors of Article 81 TEEC and Article 77 TEC. The changes from TEEC to TEC to TFEU are, however, merely semantic and therefore **altered nothing in substance**.

1

2. Charges or Dues in Respect of the Crossing of Frontiers (Paragraph 1)

Underpinning Article 97 TFEU is, perhaps self-evidently, the concept of reduction of barriers to free trade. Allowing carriers to price gouge in the event of a frontier crossing would be somewhat of a hindrance to the European internal market project.

2

---

[1] Greaves (2000), p. 21.

[2] Stadler, in Schwarze et al. (2019), Article 97 AEUV para 1.

3   The **scope of Article 97 TFEU** is restricted to frontier crossings on road, rail and inland waterway modes of transport (Article 100 TFEU). Article 97 TFEU is also isolated to unreasonable charges levied by **carriers** operating in either the road, rail or inland waterway modes of transport. To understand the meaning of carrier, Article 97 TFEU must be read in conjunction with Article 91.1 point (b) TFEU (→ Article 91 TFEU para 10).

4   The article provides that the amount charged by carriers for the crossing of a frontier, in addition to the transport rates, must **not exceed a reasonable level**. The amount charged by the carrier must therefore be justified by the actual costs incurred by crossing the border as compared to purely domestic carriage.[3]

5   Although the provision was aimed at the creation of a single European market, i.e. focused on frontier crossing between MS, Article 97 TFEU can also be interpreted to include unreasonable frontier crossing charges levied by a carrier in an MS with respect to **external frontier crossings**. The focus of Article 97 TFEU is, however, undoubtedly on internal frontiers.

3. Progressive Reduction of Costs and Commission Recommendations (Paragraphs 2 and 3)

6   The stipulation in Article 97 TFEU that MS should **endeavour to reduce the costs** of frontier crossings is now effectively redundant. This will be discussed below (→ para 8).

7   The Commission has a right to give **recommendations** to the MS regarding the application of Article 97 TFEU. The Commission has not issued any recommendations pursuant to Article 97 TFEU.

4. Current Practical Relevance of Article 97 TFEU

8   With the introduction of the Single European Act,[4] the first major revision of the TEEC, the European Community began to move swiftly towards the establishment of a true single European market with the free movement of goods, persons, services and capital. To achieve this goal, the abolition of internal frontier crossings was to be achieved by 1 January 1993. A single market free of frontier crossings is now the effective reality of the modern European Union.[5] Consequently, the

---

[3] Fehling, in von der Groeben et al. (2015), Article 97 AEUV para 5.

[4] O.J. L 169/1 (1987).

[5] Legislation relevant to Article 97 TFEU in this respect includes Council Regulation (EEC) No. 4060/89 *on the elimination of controls performed at the frontiers of Member States in the field of road and inland waterway transport*, O.J. L 390/21 (1989) as amended and codified by Regulation (EC) No. 1100/2008 *on the elimination of controls performed at the frontiers of Member States in the field of road and inland waterway transport*, O.J. L 304/63 (2008); Council Regulation 3912/92 *on controls carried out within the Community in the field of road and inland waterway transport in*

relevance of Article 97 TFEU is next to negligible. Other commentators have stated that Article 97 TFEU could be deleted in any future revision of the TFEU,[6] a conclusion with which these authors agree.

Further, although not technically within the conceptual scope of Article 97 TFEU, controls and formalities relating to cabin and hold-baggage of persons taking intra-EU flights sea crossing have also been abolished.[7]

9

References

Greaves, R. (2000). *EC transport law*. Dorset Press.
Schwarze, J., Becker, U., Hatje, A., & Schoo, J. (2019). *EU-Kommentar* (4th ed.). Nomos.
von der Groeben, H., Schwarze, J., & Hatje, A. (Eds.). (2015). *Europäisches Unionsrecht* (7th ed.). Nomos.

---

respect of means of transport registered or put into circulation in a third country, O.J. L 395/6 (1992). The concept of free movement of persons, regardless of nationality, within the EU is also embodied in Article 77 TFEU.

[6] Fehling, in von der Groeben et al. (2015), Article 97 AEUV para 10.

[7] Council Regulation (EEC) No. 3925/91 *concerning the elimination of controls and formalities applicable to the cabin and hold baggage of persons taking an intra-Community flight and the baggage of persons making an intra-Community sea crossing*, O.J. L 374/4 (1991).

Article 98 [German Unification]
(ex-Article 78 TEC)

The provisions of this Title[5, 6] shall not form an obstacle[6] to the application of measures taken in the Federal Republic of Germany[7] to the extent that such measures are required[11] in order to compensate for the economic disadvantages caused by the division of Germany to the economy of certain areas of the Federal Republic affected by that division.[8–10] Five years after the entry into force of the Treaty of Lisbon, the Council, acting on a proposal from the Commission, may adopt a decision repealing this Article.[14, 17]

Declaration No 28[3]
on Article 98 of the Treaty on the Functioning of the European Union

The Conference notes that the provisions of Article 98 shall be applied in accordance with the current practice. The terms "such measures are required in order to compensate for the economic disadvantages caused by the division of Germany to the economy of certain areas of the Federal Republic affected by that division" shall be interpreted in accordance with the existing case law of the Court of Justice of the European Union.

Contents

1. Development of the Provision, Treaty Context 1
2. The Scope of Article 98 TFEU as Stipulated in Its First Sentence 5
   2.1. Substantive Scope of Application 5
   2.2. Relevance of the Provision 12
   2.3. Procedural Questions 15
3. The Possibility of Repealing Article 98 TFEU Pursuant to Its Second Sentence 17

List of Cases
References

1. Development of the Provision, Treaty Context

The first sentence of Article 98 TFEU formed part, as Article 82 TEEC, of the original version of the EEC Treaty (1957). At that time, Article 82 TEEC was one of the several treaty provisions which took account of the division of Germany[1] in order not to deepen the division of this nation through the European integration

---

[1] For an overview cf. Erdmenger, in von der Groeben and Schwarze (2003), Article 78 EG para 2.

© Springer Nature Switzerland AG 2022
R. Böttner, H.-J. Blanke (eds.), *Treaty on the Functioning of the European Union – A Commentary*, Springer Commentaries on International and European Law, https://doi.org/10.1007/16559_2022_49

process.² Although Germany was reunited in 1990, **the provision was not repealed**—or replaced³—by the subsequent treaties. The Treaty of Amsterdam (1997) changed the numbering of the article from 82 to 78. The Treaty establishing a Constitution for Europe (2004), the so-called Constitutional Treaty, which did not enter into force, retained the provision in Article III-243 and added a second sentence allowing its repeal five years after the entry into force of the Constitutional Treaty.⁴ The possibility of repealing the provision was adopted by the Lisbon Treaty which accordingly added a second sentence to the later Article 98 TFEU.

2   A provision similar to Article 98 TFEU is contained in **Article 107.2 point (c) TFEU** providing for a derogation from the principle of incompatibility of State aid with the internal market as stated in Article 107.1 TFEU. Not surprisingly, the Lisbon Treaty added a second sentence to Article 107.2 point (c) TFEU, too, providing for the possibility of repealing the provision. Furthermore, the EEA Agreement (1992), in Article 61.2 point (c) in the chapter concerning State aid, provides for the same derogation as Article 107.2 point (c) TFEU. This is remarkable given the fact that the EEA Agreement was concluded after German reunification. No doubt, "[f]ar from being implicitly repealed following German reunification",⁵ that provision—and the same must hold true for Article 98 TFEU—was intentionally retained in primary Union law.⁶

3   In a **declaration on Article 98 TFEU** annexed to the Lisbon Treaty—Declaration No. 28—the Intergovernmental Conference (IGC) has stated that the terms "such measures are required in order to compensate for the economic disadvantages caused by the division of Germany to the economy of certain areas of the Federal Republic affected by that division" shall be interpreted in accordance with the existing case law of the CJEU.⁷ However, since Article 98 TFEU and its predecessors were never, with one less important exception,⁸ dealt with in the jurisprudence of the Court, Declaration No. 28 must be understood as referring to the case

---

² Cf. Martenczuk, in von der Groeben et al. (2015), Article 107 AEUV para 208.

³ In its resolution of 22 November 1990 on the IGC in the context of the EP's strategy for European Union, O.J. C 324/219 (1990), the EP had proposed to replace Article 82 TEC by the following general provision: "The rules of competition of the Treaty shall apply to the areas referred to in Title IV. The Community shall adopt, in accordance with Article 188b, the appropriate proposals with a view to their application taking into account the distinctive features of transport".

⁴ The Draft Constitutional Treaty (2003) was silent in that regard. Cf. Article III-141.

⁵ Joined Cases T-132/96 and T-143/96, *Freistaat Sachsen and others v Commission* (CFI 15 December 1999) para 130.

⁶ In Joined Cases T-132/96 and T-143/96, *Freistaat Sachsen and others v Commission* (CFI 15 December 1999) para 123 the Commission argued that "the retention of the provision in Article 92(2)(c) of the Treaty in the Maastricht and Amsterdam Treaties is explained by the veto put forward by the Federal Republic of Germany against its removal".

⁷ See also Declaration No. 29 on Article 107.2 point (c) TFEU.

⁸ Joined Cases C-57/00 P and C-61/00 P, *Freistaat Sachsen and others v Commission* (ECJ 30 September 2003) para 54 et seq.

law concerning the parallel phrase in Article 107.2 point (c) TFEU. Thus, that case law in question must be applied *mutatis mutandis* to Article 98 TFEU.[9]

Neither the (expired) ECSC Treaty **nor** the EURATOM Treaty **contain provisions like Article 98 TFEU or Article 107.2 point (c) TFEU**. On State aid, the CFI ruled out the possibility to apply Article 107.2 point (c) TFEU (or, more precisely, its predecessor) to State aid falling within the scope of the ECSC Treaty.[10]

4

2. The Scope of Article 98 TFEU as Stipulated in Its First Sentence

2.1. Substantive Scope of Application

Article 98 TFEU provides for a derogation from provisions "of this Title", i.e. Title VI "Transport". Thus, its scope is restricted to prohibitions or constraints imposed upon the MS in the Title "Transport", and it is not applicable to prohibitions or constraints enunciated in other Treaty provisions.[11] Furthermore, given the clear wording of Article 98 TFEU ("The provisions of this Title"), the derogation is not applicable to prohibitions or **constraints arising from secondary law**, particularly from implementing measures under Article 91 TFEU.[12]

5

The **"obstacles"** arising from Title VI are **contained in** Article 92 (standstill clause), Article 95 (prohibition of discrimination), Article 96 (prohibition of supportive or protective measures) and Article 97 (reduction of charges and dues in respect of the crossing of frontiers),[13] notwithstanding their today's lack of practical relevance (→ Article 97 TFEU para 8).[14] No obstacles within the meaning of Article 98 TFEU arise from Article 93 TFEU (admissibility of certain State aids) since that provision aims to mitigate the general prohibition of State aids under Article 107.1 TFEU;[15] moreover, Article 107.2 point (c) TFEU provides for an exception from that prohibition for the same reasons as Article 98 TFEU.

6

---

[9] For a concurring view cf. Schäfer and Kramer, in Streinz (2018), Article 98 AEUV para 2; Fehling, in von der Groeben et al. (2015), Article 98 AEUV para 2. The remaining literature applies the mentioned case law by implication.

[10] Case T-308/00, *Salzgitter AG v Commission* (CFI 1 July 2004) para 64.

[11] Cf. Joined Cases C-57/00 P and C-61/00 P, *Freistaat Sachsen and others v Commission* (ECJ 30 September 2003) para 57, where the ECJ declared that measures under Article 98 TFEU "cannot ... derogate from the rules governing public aid to transport infrastructure". For a concurring view cf. Epiney, in Vedder and Heintschel von Heinegg (2018), Article 98 AEUV para 2.

[12] For a concurring view cf. Epiney, in Vedder and Heintschel von Heinegg (2018), Article 98 AEUV para 2.

[13] More narrowly, Khan, in Geiger et al. (2017), Article 98 TFEU para 1: Article 98 TFEU is considered to be a *lex specialis* to Article 93 and Article 96 TFEU.

[14] Cf., e.g. Schäfer and Kramer, in Streinz (2018), Article 97 AEUV para 3.

[15] For dissenting views cf. Schäfer and Kramer, in Streinz (2018), Article 98 AEUV para 1; Fehling, in von der Groeben et al. (2015), Article 98 AEUV para 2.

7   The **addressee** and beneficiary of Article 98 TFEU is the Federal Republic of Germany[16] although admittedly, the wording of the provision is not unambiguous in that regard ("measures taken *in* the Federal Republic of Germany").

8   **Before German reunification,** Article 98 TFEU (resp. Article 82 TEEC) applied to "certain areas of the Federal Republic" affected by the division of Germany,[17] particularly in the context of the so-called *Zonenrandförderung*, i.e. the support of certain Western German regions (near the borders of what used to be the iron curtain) economically impaired by the division of Germany (→ para 10).[18] Since the provision was retained after German reunification, its field of application near-automatically—"through the effect of the principle of the mobility of the territorial scope of treaties"[19]—extended to reunited Germany. Although, after German unification, the wording of ex-Article 78 TEC (now Article 98 sentence 1 TFEU) did not seem to be accurate anymore,[20] no amendment was enacted.

9   **After German reunification** the purpose of Article 98 TFEU is considered to have changed.[21] This, however, does not seem to be correct. Rather, the factual situation originally envisaged by Article 98 TFEU has changed. Opposed to what the German government claimed in proceedings before the European Courts, namely that Article 98 TFEU is, after German reunification, intended to compensate for the economic backwardness of the new *Länder* resulting "from particular decisions of economic policy taken by the former authorities of the German Democratic Republic",[22] the consequence of such an interpretation would be "that the entire territory of the new *Länder* could benefit from aid of any kind".[23] This interpretation would not be in conformity with the principle of a narrow interpretation of derogations from primary law principles, particularly the principle that State aid is incompatible with the internal market,[24] and it would run contrary to the wording of Article 98 TFEU which refers to "certain areas of the Federal Republic". In fact, "before reunification, it was never considered that all of the areas

---

[16] Cf. Joined Cases C-57/00 P and C-61/00 P, *Freistaat Sachsen and others v Commission* (ECJ 30 September 2003) para 57: "Article 82 [now Article 98 TFEU] permits the German authorities to maintain or introduce national measures".

[17] For an overview cf. Everling, in Wohlfarth et al. (1960), Article 92 EEC Treaty para 10.

[18] Cf. Everling, in Wohlfarth et al. (1960), Article 82 EEC Treaty.

[19] Cf. Joined Cases C-57/00 P and C-61/00 P, *Freistaat Sachsen and others v Commission* (Opinion of AG Mischo of 28 May 2002) para 32.

[20] Cf. in that regard the proposals of the IGC Secretariat of the 2003 IGC, CIG4/1/03, with "Editorial and legal comments on the draft Treaty establishing a Constitution for Europe", pp. 207, 296, 297.

[21] Cf. Epiney, in Vedder and Heintschel von Heinegg (2018), Article 98 AEUV para 1; Fehling, in von der Groeben et al. (2015), Article 98 AEUV para 1.

[22] Joined Cases C-57/00 P and C-61/00 P *Freistaat Sachsen and others v Commission* (Opinion of AG Mischo of 28 May 2002) para 33.

[23] Joined Cases C-57/00 P and C-61/00 P, *Freistaat Sachsen and others v Commission* (ECJ 30 September 2003) para 41.

[24] Cf., e.g. Case C-277/00, *Germany v Commission* (ECJ 29 April 2004) para 20, 47.

or undertakings of West Germany could rely on the division clause" (→ para 8).[25] Thus, the scope and content of Article 98 TFEU cannot be construed as being modified simply through its extension to the new *Länder*.[26] Rather, following the reunification of Germany the application of Article 98 TFEU to the new *Länder* "can only be on the same conditions as those applicable in the old *Länder* during the period preceding the date of that reunification".[27]

In the light of the preceding paragraph, the **ECJ has always adhered to its constant jurisprudence** which was endorsed by the IGC 2007 (→ para 3). According to the Court's case law, the phrase "economic disadvantages caused by the division of Germany to the economy of certain areas of the Federal Republic affected by that division" must, first, be construed narrowly (→ para 9). Second, "the phrase 'division of Germany' refers historically to the dividing line between the two occupied zones in 1948".[28] Thus, the economic disadvantages referred to in Article 98 TFEU cannot be understood to mean the economic backwardness of the new *Länder* as a result of the East German politico-economic system (planned economy)[29] but only those disadvantages caused by the physical inner German frontier "such as breaking of communication links or the loss of markets as a result of the breaking off of commercial relations between the two parts of the German territory".[30] In other words, the ECJ deems necessary a "direct link ... between the economic disadvantage and the geographical division of Germany".[31] Thus, in the course of time and with a growing distance to German reunification those disadvantages fade and will ultimately disappear (→ para 14).

10

Measures under Article 98 TFEU must be "*required* in order to compensate". This phrase is an expression the **principal of proportionality** as generally enshrined in Article 5.4 (1) TEU.

11

---

[25] Joined Cases C-57/00 P and C-61/00 P, *Freistaat Sachsen and others v Commission* (Opinion of AG Mischo of 28 May 2002) para 45.

[26] As rightly stated by AG *Mischo*, Joined Cases C-57/00 P and C-61/00 P, *Freistaat Sachsen and others v Commission* (Opinion of AG Mischo of 28 May 2002) para 32, and the Commission, Joined Cases T-132/96 and T-143/96, *Freistaat Sachsen and others v Commission* (CFI 15 December 1999) para 123, 124.

[27] Case C-277/00, *Germany v Commission* (ECJ 29 April 2004) para 49; Case C-156/98, *Germany v Commission* (ECJ 19 September 2000) para 51.

[28] Case C-277/00, *Germany v Commission* (ECJ 29 April 2004) para 50.

[29] Cf. also, in that regard, Case T-357/02 RENV, *Saxony v Commission* (GC 14 July 2011) para 75: "difficulties caused by the transition, in Saxony, to a market economy" are not covered by the provision.

[30] Case C-277/00, *Germany v Commission* (ECJ 29 April 2004) para 50.

[31] Cf. Case C-301/96, *Germany v Commission* (ECJ 30 September 2003) para 74.

2.2. Relevance of the Provision

12 Apparently, Article 98 TFEU or its predecessors have **never been invoked** by Germany, neither before nor after reunification.[32] This, however, in itself, does not prevent Germany from invoking the provision in the future.

13 Furthermore, some scholars[33] and the Commission[34] say that the provision **became obsolete following German reunification**.[35] This, however, seems to be a premature conclusion since the treaties amending the primary law of the Union retained the provision (→ para 1) which, thus, in the light of the principle of effectiveness, must be interpreted as having (some) legal significance. As AG *Mischo* rightly stated in the *Volkswagen Sachsen* case, the reference to the division of Germany "must now be understood as referring to the *consequences* of that division".[36]

14 With a growing temporal distance to German reunification, the **consequences** of the division of Germany mentioned in para 12 **will fade** and ultimately disappear (→ para 10). Thus, Article 98 TFEU tends to become obsolete.[37] Provision for this is made in Article 98 sentence 2 TFEU (→ para 17).

2.3. Procedural Questions

15 Article 98 TFEU is part of Title VI "Transport", which as the Court stated in Case 167/73[38] **does not establish an exclusive regime** for the EU transport policy but whose aims are subsidiarily pursued by the general norms of the treaty.[39] As a consequence of this relationship between the Title "Transport" and the general Treaty norms (the so-called "principle of additive application"[40]) a number of the provisions of the Title "Transport", particularly Article 98 TFEU, are considered

---

[32] Cf. Maxian Rusche and Kotthaus, in Grabitz et al. (2022), Article 98 AEUV para 1, 2 (released in 2018); unclear *Martinez*' reference to Joined Cases C-57/00 P and C-61/00 P, *Freistaat Sachsen and others v Commission* (ECJ 30 September 2003) para 54, in Calliess and Ruffert (2022), Article 98 AEUV para 2.

[33] Cf. *inter alia* Maxian Rusche and Kotthaus, in Grabitz et al. (2022), Article 98 AEUV para 2 (released in 2018).

[34] Commission Communication, *A Constitution for the Union*, COM(2003) 548 p. 13.

[35] Cf. also The European Convention, *Part Two of the Constitution – Second report by the working party of experts nominated by the Legal Services of the European Parliament, the Council and the Commission*, Doc CONV 729/03, p. 136 fn. 63: "The Convention may wish to consider whether this Article is still relevant".

[36] Joined Cases C-57/00 P and C-61/00 P, *Freistaat Sachsen and others v Commission* (Opinion of AG Mischo of 28 May 2002) para 29.

[37] For a concurring view, cf. Fehling, in von der Groeben et al. (2015), Article 98 AEUV para 7.

[38] Case 167/73, *Commission v France* (ECJ 4 April 1974) para 25 et seq.

[39] Cf. also Erdmenger, in von der Groeben and Schwarze (2003), Vorbem. zu den Artikeln 70 bis 80 AEUV para 16 et seq.

[40] Fehling, in von der Groeben et al. (2015), Article 90 AEUV para 18 et seq.

imperfect.⁴¹ Notwithstanding, notably in the case of Article 98 TFEU it makes sense to claim that the provision is imperfect since it refers to prohibitions or constraints imposed upon the MS in the Title "Transport" (→ para 5) and can thus only be applied in connection with those provisions.

Article 98 sentence 1 TFEU **does not form a legal basis** for secondary EU law as, however, some scholars seem to assume.⁴² It was, thus, legally impossible to adopt Regulation No. 3572/90⁴³ based on Article 82 TEEC (now Article 98 TFEU);⁴⁴ rather, it had to be, and was, adopted based on Article 75 TEEC (now Article 91 TFEU) and contained no reference to Article 82 TEEC. Article 98 TFEU can only be relied on by Germany who is the exclusive addressee of the provision (→ para 7).

16

3. The Possibility of Repealing Article 98 TFEU Pursuant to Its Second Sentence

The Lisbon Treaty added sentence 2 to Article 78 TEC (now Article 98 TFEU), which enables the Council, acting (by a qualified majority; Article 16.3 TEU) on a proposal from the Commission, to adopt a decision repealing the article five years after the entry into force of the Lisbon Treaty, i.e. as of 1 December 2014. Sentence 2 considers the decreasing relevance of the Article (→ para 13). It establishes an "autonomous" Treaty amendment procedure, which among the numerous simplified revision procedures dispersed over the Treaties⁴⁵ is evidently the simplest procedure. Apparently, no initiative has been taken so far to apply sentence 2.⁴⁶

17

---

⁴¹ Cf. Erdmenger, in von der Groeben and Schwarze (2003), Vorbem. zu den Artikeln 70 bis 80 para 19; cf. also Fehling, in von der Groeben et al. (2015), Article 90 AEUV para 18 et seq.

⁴² Cf. Knauff, in Schwarze (2019), Article 98 AEUV para 1; Joined Cases C-57/00 P and C-61/00 P, *Freistaat Sachsen and others v Commission* (Opinion of AG Mischo of 28 May 2002) para 91.

⁴³ Council Regulation (EEC) No. 3572/90 *amending, as a result of German unification, certain Directives, Decisions and Regulations relating to transport by road, rail and inland waterway*, O.J. L 353/12 (1990).

⁴⁴ As AG Mischo, Joined Cases C-57/00 P and C-61/00 P *Freistaat Sachsen and others v Commission* (Opinion of AG Mischo of 28 May 2002) para 91, deemed possible.

⁴⁵ For an overview cf. Niedobitek (2011), pp. 165 et seq.

⁴⁶ In 2017, the Commission answered to a parliamentary question that the "current Commission legislative programme does not include a Commission proposal to the Council to repeal Articles 107(2)(c) and 98 of the Treaty on the Functioning of the European Union (TFEU)"; cf. the EP Website, https://www.europarl.europa.eu/doceo/document/E-8-2017-005568-ASW_EN.html.

List of Cases

ECJ

ECJ 04.04.1974, 167/73, *Commission v France*, ECLI: EU:C:1974:35 [cit. in para 15]

ECJ 19.09.2000, C-156/98, *Germany v Commission*, ECLI:EU:C:2000:467 [cit. in para 9]

ECJ 30.09.2003, C-301/96, *Germany v Commission*, ECLI:EU:C:2003:509 [cit. in para 10]

ECJ 30.09.2003, C-57/00 P, C-61/00 P, *Freistaat Sachsen and others v Commission*, ECLI:EU:C:2003:510 [cit. in para 3, 5, 7, 8, 9, 13, 16]

ECJ 29.04.2004, C-277/00, *Germany v Commission*, ECLI:EU:C:2004:238 [cit. in para 9, 10]

CFI/GC

CFI 15.12.1999, T-132/96, T-143/96, *Freistaat Sachsen and others v Commission*, ECLI:EU:T:1999:326 [cit. in para 2]

CFI 01.07.2004, T-308/00, *Salzgitter AG v Commission*, ECLI:EU:T:2004:199 [cit. in para 4]

GC 14.07.2011, T-357/02 RENV, *Saxony v Commission*, ECLI:EU:T:2011:376 [cit. in para 10]

References[47]

Calliess, C., & Ruffert, M. (Eds.). (2022). *EUV / AEUV* (6th ed.). C.H. Beck.

Geiger, R., Khan, D.-E., & Kotzur, M. (Eds.). (2017). *EUV / AEUV – Kommentar* (6th ed.). C.H. Beck.

Grabitz, E., Hilf, M., & Nettesheim, M. (Eds.). (2022). *Das Recht der Europäischen Union*. looseleaf (last supplement: 75). Beck.

Niedobitek, M. (2011). Die Integrationsverantwortung von Bundestag und Bundesrat nach dem "Lissabon-Urteil" des Bundesverfassungsgerichts. In G. Abels & A. Eppler (Eds.), *Auf dem Weg zum Mehrebenenparlamentarismus?* (pp. 159–176). Nomos.

Schwarze, J., Becker, U., Hatje, A., & Schoo, J. (Eds.). (2019). *EU-Kommentar* (4th ed.). Nomos.

Streinz, R. (Ed.). (2018). *EUV / AEUV* (3rd ed.). C.H. Beck.

Vedder, C., & Heintschel von Heinegg, W. (Eds.). (2018). *Europäisches Unionsrecht* (2nd ed.). Nomos.

---

[47] All Internet sources cited in this comment have been accessed on 20 October 2022.

von der Groeben, H., & Schwarze, J. (Eds.). (2003). *Kommentar zum Vertrag über die Europäische Union und zur Gründung der Europäischen Gemeinschaft* (6th ed.). Nomos.
von der Groeben, H., Schwarze, J., & Hatje, A. (Eds.). (2015). *Europäisches Unionsrecht* (7th ed.). Nomos.
Wohlfarth, E., Everling, U., Glaesner, H. J., & Sprung, R. (1960). *Die Europäische Wirtschaftsgemeinschaft – Kommentar zum Vertrag*. Franz Vahlen.

Article 99 [Advisory Committee]
(ex-Article 79 TEC)

An Advisory Committee consisting of experts designated by the governments of Member States shall be attached to the Commission. The Commission, whenever it considers it desirable, shall consult the Committee on transport matters.

Contents

1. Overview 1
2. The Advisory Committee 2
3. Current Practical Significance of Article 99 TFEU 3
References

1. Overview

This obliges the Commission to set up an **advisory committee that may be consulted with respect to transport matters**. Article 99 TFEU is in substance the same as its predecessor articles, Article 83 TEEC and Article 79 TEC. The advisory committee should be composed of national experts appointed by the MS.

2. The Advisory Committee

Under then Article 83 TEEC (current Article 99 TFEU), a Council Decision was issued which embodied the rules of the new Transport Committee (the Committee).[1] Under the Rules, each MS should propose one or two experts from amongst senior officials of central administration.[2] MS also have the right to designate a maximum of three people who have particular expertise in each of the road, rail and inland waterway modes of transport.[3] The rules also stipulate that the experts should be appointed in their personal capacity and not as an expert subject to national constraints.[4] The opinions of the committee can be presented to the

---

[1] Council Decision No. 94/390/EEC *Rules of the Transport Committee*, O.J. P 25/509 (1958) as amended by Council Decision No. 64/390/EEC *Amending the Rules of the Transport Committee*, O.J. P 102/145 (1964).
[2] *Rules of the Transport Committee*, Article 1.
[3] *Rules of the Transport Committee*, Article 1.
[4] *Rules of the Transport Committee*, Article 3.

Commission in the form of a report or alternatively presented orally.[5] The **Commission however is under no obligation to consult the Committee** on transport related issues, but can merely call upon the Committee at its discretion.[6] Because of this, the Committee has not played a significant role in the development of a Common Transport Policy.[7]

3. Current Practical Significance of Article 99 TFEU

3   The Committee has **little, if any, current practical significance**, as can be witnessed by the fact that it has not been called upon by the Commission since the 1980s.[8] The reason for its irrelevance appears to be that the work of the Committee essentially doubles that undertaken by the Commission's own legislative working groups.[9]

4   The importance of the Transport Committee moving forward also does not appear set to change. In 2001, the Commission opted to set up a joint consultative committee for energy and transport called the **European Energy and Transport Forum** (the Forum).[10] Underpinning the creation of the Forum was the concept that the transport and energy sectors are interdependent, and thus require a single body with which to deal with relevant issues.[11]

5   The Forum is made up of 34 individuals qualified to deal with issues relating to energy and transport and the interaction between these two sectors.[12] The 34 individuals are drawn, in varying numbers specified in the Decision, from the following sub-sections of the transport and energy sector: operators; networks and infrastructures; users and consumers; unions; environmental and safety organisations; and the academic world or think tanks.[13] Similarly to the Committee, the Forum can be consulted at will by the Commission on any EU energy or transport related matter.[14] Unlike the Committee, however, the Forum is also granted the ability to provide reports or opinions to the Commission concerning EU energy or transport matters **'on its own initiative'**.[15] The Forum is also given the responsibility of acting as a 'monitoring centre' on energy and transport policy, meaning

---

[5] *Rules of the Transport Committee*, Article 7.
[6] *Rules of the Transport Committee*, Article 7.
[7] Greaves (2000), p. 22.
[8] Fehling, in von der Groeben et al. (2015), Article 99 AEUV para 5.
[9] Fehling, in von der Groeben et al. (2015), Article 99 AEUV para 6; Greaves (2000), p. 22.
[10] Commission Decision No. 2001/546/EC *setting up a consultative committee, to be known as the "European Energy and Transport Forum"*, O.J. L 195/58 (2001).
[11] Commission Decision No. 2001/546/EC, recital 4.
[12] Commission Decision No. 2001/546/EC, Article 1.2 and 3.1.
[13] Commission Decision No. 2001/546/EC, Article 3.2.
[14] Commission Decision No. 2001/546/EC, Article 2.1.
[15] Commission Decision No. 2001/546/EC, Article 2.3.

that it is to examine topical matters which may arise in these sectors.[16] The Forum is also empowered to set up *ad hoc* working parties, comprising of maximum eleven members, to aid it in its basic functions.[17]

References

Greaves, R. (2000). *EC transport law*. Dorset Press.
von der Groeben, H., Schwarze, J., & Hatje, A. (Eds.). (2015). *Europäisches Unionsrecht* (7th ed.). Nomos.

---

[16] Commission Decision No. 2001/546/EC, Article 2.2.
[17] Commission Decision No. 2001/546/EC, Article 4.

Article 100 [Scope of the Title and Legislative Procedure]
(ex-Article 80 TEC)

1. The provisions of this Title shall apply[11] to transport by rail, road and inland waterway.[7]
2. The European Parliament and the Council, acting in accordance with the ordinary legislative procedure,[6] may[11] lay down appropriate provisions[9, 11] for sea and air transport.[9] They shall act after consulting the Economic and Social Committee and the Committee of the Regions.[6]

Contents

1. Overview and Evolution 1
2. Provisions of the Transport Title Shall Apply to Road, Rail and Inland Waterway (Paragraph 1) 7
3. Parliament and Council May Lay Down Appropriate Provisions for Air and Sea Transport (Paragraph 2) 9
4. Practical Effect of the Article 100.1 and 100.2 TFEU Split 10
5. Article 100 TFEU and the General Rules of the Treaty 12
6. Issues in Transport and European Union Legislation 16
   6.1. Air Transport 17
   6.2. Sea Transport 21
List of Cases
References

1. Overview and Evolution

Article 100 TFEU articulates **the substantive scope of Title VI TFEU** (the Transport Title). The first paragraph of Article 100 TFEU provides that the Transport Title shall apply to transport by rail, road and inland waterway. The second paragraph grants the European Parliament and Council the power to lay down appropriate provisions within the scope of the Transport Title on sea and air transport. The reason for the transport mode split between paragraphs 1 and 2 lies in the historical evolution of Article 100 TFEU.

A well-functioning transport network is an essential element in the functioning of the EU's internal market. Without the effective means to transport services, goods and persons, the goal of the common market can hardly be achieved.[1] The importance of the transport sector within the context of the common market can be evidenced by the fact that transport was one of the first common policy areas of the

---
[1] Greaves (2000), p. 3.

© Springer Nature Switzerland AG 2022
R. Böttner, H.-J. Blanke (eds.), *Treaty on the Functioning of the European Union – A Commentary*, Springer Commentaries on International and European Law,
https://doi.org/10.1007/16559_2022_61

EEC.[2] Indeed, the first draft of a transport policy appears in the 1956 Spaak Report.[3] The manner in which different modes of transport were to be regulated by the original Treaty of Rome, however, proved to be somewhat contentious.

3 From the outset, the ceding of regulatory power by the MS to the then Community over inland modes of transport was relatively uncontroversial. **MS did not however wish to hand over control with respect to sea and air transport** to the fledgling Community's external commercial policy.[4] These modes of transport were generally regarded as too important to national economies[5] and, particularly with respect to aviation, subject to national defence considerations.[6] This concern by MS to retain control over sea and air transport was subsequently directly reflected in Article 84 TEEC, the original incarnation of Article 100 TFEU.

Article 84.2 TEEC (now Article 100.2 TFEU) provided that '[t]he Council, acting by means of a unanimous vote, may decide whether, to what extent and by what procedure appropriate provisions might be adopted for sea and air transport.' As can be seen, **the content of Article 84.2 TEEC was quite different from the current Article 100.2 TFEU**. The wording of this paragraph ensured that the Council was required to take positive action before the Community's Common Transport Policy (CTP), and any measures introduced in furtherance of the CTP, would also apply to sea and air transport.[7] Further, the unanimity requirement dictated that agreements leading to the inclusion of sea and air transport into CTP measures would be few and far between. Article 84.1 TEEC, however, remains unchanged in its current form of Article 100.1 TFEU.

4 The **Single European Act** (SEA) of 1986[8] introduced the **first major change to the Treaty of Rome**, and particularly had a significant impact upon then Article 84 TEEC (current Article 100 TFEU). Article 16.5 SEA amended Article 84.2 TEEC, replacing the unanimity requirement with a mere 'qualified majority'—a substantially easier hurdle for the Council to jump. This change introduced by the SEA was eventually enshrined in Article 80.2 TEC (current Article 100.2 TFEU). The primary motivator for this amendment was the enlargement of the Community. An increased number of MS brought about a desire for greater mobility within the EU as well as introducing a distinct ideological shift towards regulation favouring market mechanisms.[9] The qualified majority mechanism for regulating sea and air transport remained until the introduction of the Treaty of Lisbon in 2009.

---

[2] European Commission, *The European Union Explained: Transport. Resource Document*, 2014, p. 4.

[3] The Unofficial Abridged and Translated Version of the Brussels Report on "The General Common Market", June 1956, Chapter 3, p. 15 (http://aei.pitt.edu/995/1/Spaak_report.pdf).

[4] Greaves (2000), p. 4.

[5] Greaves (2000), p. 4.

[6] Balfour (2008), p. 443.

[7] Greaves (2000), p. 4.

[8] O.J. L 169/1 (1987).

[9] Kaeding (2007), p. 46.

With the introduction of the Treaty of Lisbon, the qualified majority mechanism gave way to the co-decision procedure now found in Article 100.2 TFEU. The change to co-decision did not, however, do away with the article's structural separation of sea and air and inland transport modes. Currently, therefore, the Transport Title—and by extension the CTP and any measures introduced in furtherance of it—continues to apply automatically to road, railway and inland waterway, while the Council and Parliament must still undertake positive action to bring sea and air transport within the scope of the CTP and its associated measures.

Despite this division of Article 100 TFEU, all modes of transport listed in the article are currently subject to the same **legislative procedure**. Legislation governing transport by rail, road and inland waterway must be enacted pursuant to the procedure provided for in Article 91.1 TFEU, while the legislative procedure for sea and air transport is provided for in Article 100.2 TFEU. Both Article 91.1 and Article 100.2 TFEU provide that legislation is to be enacted by the European Parliament and Council in accordance with the ordinary legislative procedure and after consulting the Economic and Social Committee and the Committee of the Regions. The ordinary legislative procedure is governed by Article 294 TFEU.

2. Provisions of the Transport Title Shall Apply to Road, Rail and Inland Waterway (Paragraph 1)

Under Article 100.1 TFEU, the provisions of the Transport Title, that is Articles 90 to 99 TFEU, 'shall'—meaning in this instance will—apply to road, rail and inland waterway modes of transport. What this means in practice is that not only, for example, will the Article 95.1 TFEU prohibition on discriminatory charging only apply to these modes of transport, but also that the EU's CTP—and measures introduced in pursuit of the CTP framework—will only apply to road, rail and inland waterway transport.

Transportation through pipelines is **not included in the scope** of the Title VI TFEU.[10] The electricity sector is also not included within the scope of application of the Transport Title.

3. Parliament and Council May Lay Down Appropriate Provisions for Air and Sea Transport (Paragraph 2)

As detailed above, by separating the inland modes of transport from sea and air transport, Article 100.2 TFEU limits what may best be termed the *automatic* scope of the Transport Title of the TFEU. This effectively means the converse of what was explained above on road, rail and inland waterway transport modes. That is, **sea**

---

[10] Rusche, in Kellerbauer et al. (2019), Article 100 TFEU para 8.

and air transport are excluded from the *automatic* scope of the Transport Title of the TFEU. Sea and air transport cannot, therefore, be inadvertently included in the EU's CTP framework. The Parliament and Council must expressly choose— and indeed it is a choice, because Article 100.2 TFEU provides that they 'may' do so—to 'lay down appropriate provisions' for these modes of transport. This aspect of Article 100.2 TFEU must be read in conjunction with Article 91.1 point (d) TFEU, which provides that the Parliament and Council shall lay down 'any other appropriate provisions' for the purposes of implementing the CTP ($\rightarrow$ Article 91 TFEU para 21).

4. Practical Effect of the Article 100.1 and 100.2 TFEU Split

10   The practical impact of the 'automatic' and 'non-automatic' scope restriction of Article 100 TFEU is negligible. Where once unanimity was required in the Council to introduce measures related to sea or air transport, now only the ordinary legislative procedure applies. Given the importance of sea and air transport generally, it seems unlikely that these would inadvertently be left out by the EU legislator.

11   The important difference implied by the Article 100 TFEU split may now lie solely in the **responsibility of the Parliament and Council as regards legislating with respect to the different transport modes**. Road, rail and inland waterway are legislated under Article 91.1 TFEU. Here it states that, for the purposes of implementing Article 90 TFEU, i.e. the CTP, the Parliament and Council 'shall' lay measures of the kind enumerated in Article 91.1 TFEU. On the other hand, Article 100.2 TFEU provides that the Parliament and Council 'may lay down appropriate provisions'. The implication from the difference in these wordings is that there is an obligation upon the Parliament and Council to introduce measures for the purposes of implementing Article 90 TFEU, which applies automatically only to road, rail and inland waterway modes of transport. No such obligation exists on sea and air transport given that the Parliament and Council 'may' introduce appropriate measures. This point is likely only theoretical given the extensive amount of secondary legislation on all modes of transport.[11]

5. Article 100 TFEU and the General Rules of the Treaty

12   Because of the Articles 100.1 and 100.2 TFEU transport mode split, it was originally unclear whether the **general rules of the Treaty**—e.g., the competition rules enshrined in Articles 101 to 109 TFEU—also applied to sea and air transport. Indeed, commentators made the argument at the time that sea and air transport fell

---

[11] See, e.g. Fehling, in von der Groeben et al. (2015), Article 100 AEUV para 16.

entirely outside of the general scope of the Treaty.[12] Given the MS' initial reluctance to allow Community intervention in their sea and air transport sectors, this line of reasoning could be seen to hold some water. The ECJ, however, did not take a similar view on the matter. In the seminal 1974 *French Seamen* case,[13] the ECJ began a series of cases that had an important impact on the regulatory landscape of the transport sector.

The *French Seamen* **case** concerned the rights of non-French nationals to work on a French merchant vessel. The relevant piece of French legislation provided that the Minister for the Merchant Fleet may lay down an order specifying a specific proportion of staff on French ships who must be French. Such an order was subsequently made which provided that employment on the bridge or the engine room of a French vessel is restricted to only persons of French nationality, and that employment generally on a French ship must be limited to a ratio of three French nationals to one non-French national. The Commission brought proceedings against France, alleging that the French legislation infringed the general Treaty rule on the freedom of movement of workers found in Article 48 TEEC (current Article 45 TFEU). The French government argued that, on the contrary, the general rules of the EEC did not apply to the Transport Title because the Title was exhaustive with respect to transport. Further, they argued that even if the general rules did apply, they could not apply to the transport modes listed under Article 84.2 TEEC because regulating those modes required positive action on the part of the Council, action which had not occurred. The ECJ ultimately agreed with the Commission's arguments.

13

The ECJ held that **the general rules of the Treaty apply to the entire Transport Title of the Treaty**, including sea and air transport, except where a Treaty provision expressly excluded transport.[14] MS were therefore still free to legislate in areas not harmonised by Community legislation, provided that in doing so they did not breach relevant general rules of the Treaty. In their argument, the Court noted that Article 61.1 TEEC (current Article 58.1 TFEU) provided that the freedom to provide services in the field of transport is to be regulated by the Transport Title and not the Treaty provisions on the freedom to provide services generally, found in Article 59 TEEC (current Article 56 TFEU).

To the Court, this article was a confirmation of the above conclusion. Because Article 61.1 TEEC (current Article 100.2 TFEU) explicitly states that services in the field of transport do not fall within the general freedom to provide services regime, this is proof that the so-called general rules of the Treaty will apply unless the Treaty itself excludes them.[15] Further, the existence of Article 84.2 TEEC (current Article 100.2 TFEU) merely excludes sea and air transport from the

---

[12] See, e.g. Bird (1967), p. 24.

[13] Case 167/73, *Commission v France* (ECJ 4 April 1974).

[14] Case 167/73, *Commission v France* (ECJ 4 April 1974) para 28.

[15] Case 167/73, *Commission v France* (ECJ 4 April 1974) para 28.

automatic application of the CTP, not from the general rules of the Treaty.[16] The relevant French legislation was therefore infringing the general Treaty rules on the freedom of movement of workers. With this decision, the ECJ indicated that they would strictly interpret the purpose of Article 84.2 TEEC (current Article 100.2 TFEU) and that it would not therefore become a mechanism for the MS to avoid the application of the Treaty generally to the fields of air and sea transport.

14   The ECJ further developed the *French Seamen* line of reasoning in the case of *Asjes*.[17] This case concerned a French legislation which provided that air transport undertakings must submit their rates to the French Minister for Civil Aviation for approval, creating a system of minimum airline ticket prices. A number of airlines and travel agencies subsequently incurred substantial fines after selling airline tickets at prices that had either not been submitted to the Minister for consideration or were different from the prices originally approved. The question for consideration was whether the French legislation was compliant with the Community law, particularly the provisions of the Treaty relating to competition.

The Commission and others argued that the existence of Article 84 TEEC (current Article 100 TFEU) did not mean that the competition rules of the Treaty—Articles 85 to 90 TEEC (current Article 101 to 106 TFEU)—were inapplicable to transport. Citing the *French Seamen* case, they argued that the Treaty's competition rules were general Treaty rules which were applicable to the air transport sector, regardless of whether the Council had legislated on the issue under Article 84.2 TEEC (current Article 100.2 TFEU). France, however, argued that the *French Seamen* decision referred only to the rules contained in Part Two of the Treaty concerning the foundation of the Community and not the rules in Part Three of the Treaty concerning the policy of the Community, where the competition provisions can be found. The ECJ once again accepted the arguments of the Commission.

Upholding and expanding the *French Seamen* line of reasoning, the ECJ held that **the Treaty rules on competition are applicable to transport**. In support of this view, the ECJ noted that Article 74 TEEC (current Article 90 TFEU) clearly indicates that the objectives of the Treaty—including Article 3 point (f) TEEC which provided that an objective of the Community is the establishment of a system preventing the distortion of competition—are applicable to the transport sector.[18] The general competition rules therefore apply to transport unless there is an express statement to the contrary in a provision of the Treaty.[19] Concurring once again with the *French Seamen* case, the ECJ also held that it is clear that Article 84.2 TEEC (current Article 100.2 TFEU) was merely intended to define the scope of the Transport Title as it relates to different modes of transport. The article therefore

---

[16] Case 167/73, *Commission v France* (ECJ 4 April 1974) para 31 and 32.

[17] Joined Cases 209-213/84, *Ministère public v Lucas Asjes and others* (ECJ 30 April 1986).

[18] Joined Cases 209-213/84, *Ministère public v Lucas Asjes and others* (ECJ 30 April 1986) para 35 and 36.

[19] Joined Cases 209-213/84, *Ministère public v Lucas Asjes and others* (ECJ 30 April 1986) para 40 and 41.

only serves to exclude sea and air transport from the automatic application of measures of the rules of the Transport Title relating to the CTP.[20] By confirming that the Treaty rules on competition were indeed applicable to transport—even without legislative action on the part of the Council—the *Asjes* decision served to reinforce the strict reading of the purpose of Article 84.2 TEEC (current Article 100.2 TFEU) introduced by the Court in the *French Seamen* case.

In addition to the Treaty rules preventing restrictions on the freedom of movement of workers and those preventing anti-competitive practices, the ECJ has held that the **Treaty rules concerning establishment**[21] **and the free movement of goods**[22] **are also to be considered general rules applicable to transport.**

15

6. Issues in Transport and European Union Legislation

Title VI TFEU merely provides a number of general guidelines upon which the EU regulation of transport can be built. Attention must therefore be paid to **relevant secondary legislation**, and the practical transport issues dealt with therein to appreciate the substance and true scope of EU regulation in this field. Due to the extensive amount of EU legislation relating to transport, attention will only briefly be paid below to particular pieces of EU legislation dealing with air and sea transport, particularly air traffic management and port infrastructure.[23]

16

6.1. Air Transport

The EU's involvement in the regulation of air transport was historically limited. This was due in part to the national-centric view of air transport among the MS as well as the constraining Community level regulatory mechanics of the previous incarnations of Article 100.2 TFEU. However, following the enlargements of the European Community, the judgment in the *French Seamen* case which signalled the liberalisation of sea and air transport and the amendment of Article 84.2 TEEC by the SEA, the then Community's ability to legislate on air transport became stronger and the need for them to utilise this ability became apparent.

17

The classic national sovereignty model of airspace control—upon which the original Article 84.2 TEEC was based—was a clear hindrance to the furtherance of a European common single market as well as to increasing the volume of air traffic

---

[20] Joined Cases 209-213/84, *Ministère public v Lucas Asjes and others* (ECJ 30 April 1986) para 43 and 44.

[21] Case C-467/98, *Commission v Denmark* (ECJ 5 November 2002).

[22] Case C-389/96, *Aher-Waggon GmbH v Germany* (ECJ 14 July 1998).

[23] For a comprehensive list of relevant pieces of legislation in the fields of sea and air transport see, e.g. Fehling, in von der Groeben et al. (2015), Article 100 AEUV para 10 to 55.

generally in European airspace.[24] For example, the European Commission noted in a 1999 Communication on this issue that as a result of a nationally fragmented, as opposed to centralised, system of Air Traffic Management (ATM), one third of all flights in Europe were late, with an average delay of 20 minutes, creating obvious burdens to passengers, airlines, the economy and the environment.[25] Against this backdrop, the **Single European Sky** project (SES) began in 2004 with the release of a series of regulations with Article 80.2 TEC (current Article 100.2 TFEU) as their legal base.[26]

18   The aims of the SES were to enhance the safety and general standards of European air traffic while contributing to the sustainable development of air transport and improving the performance of the European ATM system.[27] The SES Regulations also brought European ATM generally within the CTP. Although the first phase of the SES proved somewhat successful as regards the above objectives, it failed to deliver important results in a number of important areas, particularly in the creation of the **Functional Airspace Block** (FAB) system.[28]

19   A major aspect of the SES project was the move towards the creation and use of FABs. The idea of the FAB system is to move away from traditional national ATM fragmentation by splitting European airspace into a number of blocks that ignore national borders and enable the optimal use and management of the airspace within and between FABs.[29] In addition to the drawbacks listed above (→ para 17), the traditional airspace fragmentation based on national borders '...prevents the ATM industry from developing economies of scale, leads to suboptimal size of en route centres and unnecessary duplication of non-standardised systems with their associated maintenance costs, as well as creating economic inefficiencies which amount to approximately EUR 2 billion per year.[30] The proposed FAB system, however, did not materialise after the introduction of the SES 2004 Regulations. A major issue was that the SES legislation left the creation and organisation of FABs

---

[24] Simoncini (2013), p. 211.

[25] Commission Communication, *The creation of the single European sky*, COM(1999) 614 final/2, p. 2.

[26] Regulation (EC) No. 549/2004 *laying down the general principles for the creation of the single European sky (the framework Regulation)*, O.J. L 96/1 (2004); Regulation (EC) No. 550/2004 *on the provision of air navigation services in the single European sky*, O.J. L 96/10 (2004); Regulation (EC) No. 551/2004 *on the organisation and use of the airspace in the single European sky*, O.J. L 96/20 (2004); Regulation (EC) No. 552/2004 *on the interoperability of the European Air Traffic Management network (the interoperability Regulation)*, O.J. L 96/26 (2004).

[27] Regulation (EC) No. 549/2004, Article 1.1.

[28] See, e.g. Commission Communication, *Single European Sky II: towards more sustainable and better performing aviation*, COM(2008) 389 final.

[29] See Regulation (EC) No. 551/2004, Article 5; Commission Communication, *Building the Single European Sky through functional airspace blocks: A mid-term status report*, COM(2007) 101 final.

[30] Commission Communication, *First Report on the Implementation of the Single Sky Legislation: achievements and the way forward*, COM(2007) 845 final, pp. 3–4.

Article 100 [Scope of the Title and Legislative Procedure]

entirely up to the MS with no obligation for them to act or to cooperate with each other.

It became readily apparent that MS were uninterested in moving away from their national-centric ATM system, with the issue of sovereignty remaining a considerable, or at least oft-cited, roadblock.[31] Another notable problem was that the FAB concept as detailed in the SES Regulations was vague and that the objectives were unclear. This led to numerous problems for the MS in implementation.[32] This and other problems led to the introduction of the **SES II package** in 2009 with another series of regulations.[33]

Amongst other changes, the SES II package introduced a more concrete structure upon which the MS were required to create FABs. Most importantly, MS were required to implement FABs by 4 December 2012.[34] The SES II package also introduced the concept of FAB system coordinators, impartial third-party mediators appointed by the Commission to facilitate the establishment of FABs.[35] Although nine FABs were formally established pursuant to SES II,[36] the goal of optimal use and management of airspace has not been achieved.[37] In 2013, the Commission proposed a series of reforms to SES II called **SES II+** that aim, amongst many other reforms, to shift focus onto the performance and efficiency of FABs, rather than on their organisational structure.[38] These reforms were ultimately withdrawn, and subsequently subsumed into the comprehensive update of the European Aviation Safety Agency Regulation that came into force in September 2018.[39]

20

---

[31] COM(2007) 845 final, p. 7.

[32] Performance Review Commission, *Evaluation of the Impact of the Single European Sky Initiative on ATM Performance*, Eurocontrol, 21 December 2006, p. 32.

[33] Regulation (EC) No. 1070/2009 *amending Regulation (EC) No. 549/2004, (EC) No. 550/2004, (EC) No. 551/2004 and (EC) No. 552/2004 in order to improve the performance and sustainability of the European Aviation System*, O.J. L 300/34 (2009); Regulation (EC) No. 1108/2009 *amending Regulation (EC) No. 216/2008 in the field of aerodromes, air traffic management and air navigation services and repealing Directive 2006/23/EC*, O.J. L 309/51 (2009); Commission Regulation (EU) No. 691/2010 *laying down a performance scheme for air navigation services and network functions and amending Regulation (EC) No. 2096/2005 laying down common requirements for the provision of air navigation services*, O.J. L 201/1 (2010), as well as numerous other implementing rules.

[34] Regulation (EC) No. 550/2004, Article 9a.

[35] Regulation (EC) No. 550/2004, Article 9b.

[36] For more information on the established FABs see, e.g. Commission website on FABs: https://transport.ec.europa.eu/transport-modes/air/single-european-sky/functional-airspace-blocks-fabs_en.

[37] Commission Report *on the implementation and progress of the Single European Sky during the 2012-2014 period*, COM(2015) 663 final, pp. 4–5.

[38] See Commission *Proposal for a Regulation of the European Parliament and of the Council on the implementation of the Single European Sky (recast)*, COM(2013) 410 final.

[39] Regulation (EU) 2018/1139 *on common rules in the field of civil aviation and establishing a European Union Aviation Safety Agency*, O.J. L 212/1 (2018).

6.2. Sea Transport

21 A Commission Green Paper released in 1997[40] aimed to start a conversation regarding **European ports and maritime infrastructure,** particularly on improving their efficiency and quality. The importance of ports within the context of European transport generally was (and still is) substantial: at the time of release of the Green Paper, the European port sector handled more than 90% of the Union's external trade and approximately 30% of intra-EU trade, in addition to the carriage of 200 million passengers every year.[41] The Green Paper highlighted a number of key issues facing the European port sector from the perspective of European integration.

The financing of ports and maritime infrastructure, as well as issues relating to the charging of users, presented substantial problems to the sector. Because ownership models were not consistent between MS—that is, ports were owned by either the state, other level governments or by private enterprises—policies on financing and charging varied drastically from MS to MS.[42] These issues were also reflected in concerns on the financial transparency of port operations and, consequently, the effective and fair application of state aid.[43] The Green Paper also called for a **greater systematic liberalisation** of European port services, levels of which also varied greatly between MS.[44] Another issue highlighted in the Green Paper was the importance of fully integrating European ports into the wider Trans-European Transport Network (TEN-T).[45]

22 Despite the acknowledgement in the Green Paper of the vital importance of ports and maritime infrastructure and the need for substantial reform, successful legislative action in the area was not forthcoming.[46] Not until 2007 and the release by the Commission of its Communication on a European Ports Policy[47] did steam appear to pick up again for European port and maritime infrastructure regulatory reform. In the 2007 Communication, the Commission identified a number of horizontal or soft

---

[40] Commission *Green Paper on Sea Ports and Maritime Infrastructure*, COM(1997) 678 final.

[41] COM(1997) 678 final, p. 6.

[42] COM(1997) 678 final, p. 14.

[43] COM(1997) 678 final, pp. 14–18.

[44] COM(1997) 678 final, pp. 26–27.

[45] COM(1997) 678 final, pp. 9–12. For more information about TEN-T generally, see, e.g. the Commission website on the topic: http://ec.europa.eu/transport/themes/infrastructure/index_en.htm.

[46] This was not, however, due to lack of trying. The Commission twice attempted to introduce European port liberalisation measures, but was ultimately unsuccessful both times. Although major legislative reform was unsuccessful, in 2001 the maps of ports relevant to the TEN-T were added to the general TEN-T maps, see Decision No. 1346/2001/EC *amending Decision No. 1692/96/EC as regards seaports, inland ports and intermodal terminals as well as project No. 8 in Annex III*, O.J. L 185/1 (2001). A ports security directive was also introduced in 2005, see Directive 2005/65/EC *on enhancing port security*, O.J. L 310/28 (2005).

[47] Commission Communication *on a European Ports Policy*, COM(2007) 616 final.

measures to be taken, particularly in financing, transparency and fair market access to port services. These soft proposals were unsuccessful in achieving reform, and indeed some national measures taken actually served to further fragment the internal market.[48] After more than fifteen years of political failure, the Commission in May 2013 introduced a **proposal for a regulation on market access to port services and financial transparency of ports**[49] accompanied by a parallel Communication.[50] The Commission adopted Article 100.2 TFEU as the legal basis for this particular legislative proposal. Following lengthy debate and substantial amendments proposed by the European Parliament, the Regulation ultimately came into force on 4 March 2017 and applies since 24 March 2019.[51]

Rather than achieving the liberalisation of European port services—as was encouraged in the 1997 Green Paper and as was the Commission's intention in the original proposed regulation—the Regulation merely purports to create a **framework** for the provision of port services as well as for the financial transparency of ports. The Regulation applies to all 329 ports identified as part of the TEN-T.[52] MS will have the option to not apply the regulation to TEN-T ports located in the outermost regions,[53] and conversely to apply the regulation to ports not designated as part of the TEN-T.[54] 23

Chapter II of the Regulation contains the **rules relating to the provision of port services**. The Regulation allows MS to subject port services providers to certain minimum requirements, to limit the number of service providers at ports, to impose public service obligations on service providers and to create restrictions regarding internal operators.[55] The Regulation contains an exhaustive list of requirements that may be imposed by MS on the provision of port services. These requirements include, *inter alia*, the professional qualifications of the provider, the financial capacity of the provider, the good repute of the port service provider and the availability of the port services to all users.[56] The requirements imposed need to be transparent, objective, non-discriminatory, proportionate and relevant.[57] Likewise, the Regulation contains requirements relating to the limitations on the number of service providers. Most notably, a tender procedure is required in cases where the 24

---

[48] See Commission Communication, *Ports: an engine for growth*, COM(2013) 295 final, p. 4.

[49] Commission *Proposal for a Regulation establishing a framework on market access to port services and financial transparency of ports*, COM(2013) 296 final.

[50] Commission Communication, *Ports: an engine for growth*, COM(2013) 295 final.

[51] Regulation (EU) No. 2017/352 *establishing a framework for the provision of port services and common rules on the financial transparency of ports*, O.J. L 57/1 (2017).

[52] Regulation (EU) No. 2017/352, Article 1.4.

[53] Regulation (EU) No. 2017/352, Article 1.5.

[54] Regulation (EU) No. 2017/352, Article 1.6.

[55] Regulation (EU) No. 2017/352, Article 3.

[56] Regulation (EU) No. 2017/352, Article 4.2.

[57] Regulation (EU) No. 2017/352, Article 4a.

25   Interestingly, Chapter II of the Regulation **does not apply to cargo handling, passenger services or pilotage**.[60] However, MS may opt to apply Chapter II to pilotage.[61] By limiting the application of Chapter II to the port services of bunkering, mooring, towing and the collection of ship-generated waste and cargo residues, in addition to not requiring a call for tenders in situations where an internal operator provides the service, it is clear that the original intention of the Commission to create a free market for the provision of port services has all but dissipated.

26   Chapter III of the Regulation contains the provisions relating to the **transparency of financial relations** of ports. This chapter also regulates port service charges in certain circumstances[62] as well as the levying of port infrastructure charges.[63]

number of port services providers are limited.[58] Interestingly, however, the tender procedure is not required in circumstances where an internal operator provides the service—that is, where the managing body of the port or the competent authority provide the service in question.[59]

List of Cases

ECJ 04.04.1974, 167/73, *Commission v France*, ECLI:EU:C:1974:35 [cit. in para 12]

ECJ 30.04.1986, 209/84, 210/84, 211/84, 212/84, 213/84, *Ministère public v Lucas Asjes and others*, ECLI:EU:C:1986:188 [cit. in para 14]

ECJ 14.07.1998, C-389/96, *Aher-Waggon GmbH v Germany*, ECLI:EU:C:1998:357 [cit. in para 15]

ECJ 05.11.2002, C-467/98, *Commission v Denmark*, ECLI:EU:C:2002:625 [cit. in para 15]

References[64]

Balfour, J. (2008). EC external aviation relations: The Community's increasing role, and the new EC/US Agreement. *Common Market Law Review, 45*(2), 443–463.

Bird, J. (1967). Further debate on the Treaty of Rome, Article 84, paragraph 2 as it may affect maritime transport. *European Transport Law, 2*(1), 24–47.

Greaves, R. (2000). *EC transport law*. Dorset Press.

---

[58] Regulation (EU) No. 2017/352, Article 6.4.
[59] Regulation (EU) No. 2017/352, Article 8.
[60] Regulation (EU) No. 2017/352, Article 10.1.
[61] Regulation (EU) No. 2017/352, Article 10.2.
[62] Regulation (EU) No. 2017/352, Article 13.
[63] Regulation (EU) No. 2017/352, Article 14.
[64] All Internet sources cited in this comment have been accessed on 23 July 2022.

Kaeding, M. (2007). *Better regulation in the European Union: Lost in translation or full steam ahead? The transposition of EU transport directives across member States.* Leiden University Press.

Kellerbauer, M., Klamert, M., & Tomkin, J. (Eds.). (2019). *The EU Treaties and the Charter of Fundamental Rights. A commentary.* OUP.

Simoncini, M. (2013). Governing air traffic management in the Single European Sky: The search for possible solutions to safety issues. *European Law Review, 38*(2), 209–228.

von der Groeben, H., Schwarze, J., & Hatje, A. (Eds.). (2015). *Europäisches Unionsrecht* (7th ed.). Nomos.

Title VII
Common Rules on Competition, Taxation and Approximation of Laws

Chapter 1
Rules on Competition

Section 1
Rules Applying to Undertakings

Article 101 [Prohibition of Agreements That Restrict Competition]
(ex-Article 81 TEC)

1. The following shall be prohibited as incompatible with the internal market: all agreements[12–15] between undertakings[22–25], decisions by associations[16] of undertakings and concerted practices[17–21] which may affect trade between Member States[58, 59] and which have as their object[26–28, 51–57] or effect[26–50] the prevention, restriction[47–50] or distortion of competition within the internal market, and in particular[61] those which:

   (a) directly or indirectly fix purchase or selling prices or any other trading conditions;
   (b) limit or control production, markets, technical development, or investment;
   (c) share markets or sources of supply;
   (d) apply dissimilar conditions to equivalent transactions with other trading parties, thereby placing them at a competitive disadvantage;
   (e) make the conclusion of contracts subject to acceptance by the other parties of supplementary obligations which, by their nature or according to commercial usage, have no connection with the subject of such contracts.

2. Any agreements or decisions prohibited pursuant to this Article shall be automatically void.[67]

3. The provisions of paragraph 1 may, however, be declared inapplicable[61–66] in the case of:

   - any agreement or category of agreements between undertakings,
   - any decision or category of decisions by associations of undertakings,
   - any concerted practice or category of concerted practices,

   which contributes to improving the production or distribution of goods or to promoting technical or economic progress, while allowing consumers a fair share of the resulting benefit,[61] and which does not:

   (a) impose on the undertakings concerned restrictions which are not indispensable to the attainment of these objectives;
   (b) afford such undertakings the possibility of eliminating competition in respect of a substantial part of the products in question.

Contents

1. Introduction 1
2. An Overview of Article 101 TFEU Within the Treaty Framework 4
3. Prohibited Action Incompatible with the Internal Market (Article 101.1 TFEU) 12
   3.1. Agreements, Decisions and Concerted Practices 13

3.2.	Undertakings	23
3.3.	Object or Effect of Restricting Competition	27
	3.3.1. Establishing Effects on Competition: Market Definition and the Counterfactual Analysis	30
	3.3.2. The Object Category	52
3.4.	Effect on Trade Between Member States	59
4.	Justifications (Article 101.3 TFEU)	67
5.	Automatic Nullity (Article 101.2 TFEU) and the Enforcement of Article 101 TFEU	72

List of Cases
References

1. Introduction

1   Article 101 TFEU is one of the **most prominent Treaty provisions on competition** in view of the fact that it is quite frequently applied and tends to result in high-profile decisions that often involve the imposition of significant fines.[1] These fines are used to punish those involved in hard-core restrictions, more colloquially referred to as cartels. At the same time, it is a provision that concerns a practice that is the lifeblood of any company in any market: the conclusion of agreements. All agreements seek to coordinate the behaviour of the parties to that agreement. This reduction of the commercial independence or freedom of these parties can be construed as a restriction of competition. Furthermore, these agreements may impact the output, prices or innovation of the products and parties involved, impacting consumer welfare. Ultimately, therefore, competition is a primarily economic phenomenon that can be understood, measured and appraised in myriad ways.[2] However, it is also a concept of law, thus requiring a legal definition. This gnomic nature of competition is compounded by the different conceptions within economics and law and between economics and the legal discipline. By and large, conceptions of competition are the remit of the debate concerning the "more economic" or more "effects-based" approach to Article 101 TFEU and the more legalistic interpretation of this provision.

2   This debate centres on the biggest challenge for the application of Article 101 TFEU. This is to ensure sufficient legal certainty and ease of application in a structure that encompasses undercover cartels as much as innocent cooperation agreements. This **two-pronged structure** coincides largely with the distinction in the text of Article 101 TFEU between the agreements that have the *object* of restricting competition and those that have this *effect*. This approach and its effects on the legal and economic appraisal involved will be central to this commentary.

---

[1] According to cartel statistics published on DG Competition's website at ec.europa.eu/competition/cartels/statistics/statistics.pdf the total fine imposed since 2011 amounts to well over EUR 6 billion.

[2] For a discussion, see Bishop and Walker (2010), pp. 16–21.

Article 101   [Prohibition of Agreements That Restrict Competition]

In this chapter, we will first discuss the general framework of Article 101 TFEU **3** and the preliminaries of its application. After that, the first and third paragraphs of Article 101 TFEU will be discussed on the basis of the Court's interpretation as well as the decisional practice of and guidance by the Commission. Finally, Article 101.2 TFEU will be discussed. In doing so, we will also engage in a succinct **comparison with US antitrust law**, given that many of the issues surrounding Article 101 TFEU can be found in other jurisdictions and that a comparative approach may provide valuable insights.[3] A quick look at the structure of the provision reveals an indicative list of restrictions in Article 101.1 TFEU. Given that this is a purely indicative list, we shall not pay any further attention to the items listed other than mention that these restrictions are often seen as particularly onerous and therefore most probably incompatible with Article 101 TFEU.

2. An Overview of Article 101 TFEU Within the Treaty Framework

Article 101 TFEU features in the Treaties in unchanged form since 1957 **4** (Article 85 TEEC and then Article 81 TEC).[4] The provision itself consists of a **broadly formulated** prohibition enshrined in the first paragraph and a justification contained in the third paragraph. The latter is equally broadly construed using ill-defined terms such as "improving the production or distribution of goods" and "economic and technological progress". These two paragraphs can be seen as the substantive parts of Article 101 TFEU as they contain the rule and exception to it. They are compounded by the second paragraph, which provides for automatic nullity as an incentive not to violate Article 101 TFEU (→ para 66 et seqq.).

The Treaty framework for Article 101 TFEU is the **chapter containing the** **5** **rules on competition** and more specifically those addressed to undertakings. These Treaty provisions essentially implement the old Article 3.1 point (g) TEC that envisaged a Community "system ensuring that competition in the internal market is not distorted". This provision, however, was removed from the Treaty itself with the implementation of the Treaty of Lisbon, only to find its way in Protocol No. 27. For all practical means and purposes, this move has no implications.[5]

In the context of Article 102 TFEU, the prohibition of the abuse of a dominant **6** position, it has been invoked by the Court to include considerations related to the market structure in the appraisal of what constitutes abuse, but in *Continental Can*, the Court clearly cast the net much wider to substantiate the central importance of the

---

[3] Such an approach exists from early on in EU competition law, cf. Joliet (1967).

[4] The Treaty of Lisbon replaced the words 'common market' with 'internal market'. This does not entail any substantial change.

[5] The Commission and Court, for example, never referred to this provision in any case other than the cases on the *effet utile* of (then) Article 81 TEC, e.g. Case 267/86, *Van Eycke v ASPA* (ECJ 21 September 1988) para 20.

competition rules.⁶ Indeed, in *Courage/Crehan*, we also see a reference to Article 3.1 point (g) TEC to substantiate the fundamental nature of Article 101 TFEU and its essential nature for the **fulfilment of the tasks of the Union** and in particular those relating to the **internal market**.⁷ As a result, Article 3.1 point (g) TEC appears to have had predominantly symbolic and constitutional importance rather than substantive impact. This confirms that the removal of "the competition principle" enshrined in Article 3.1 point (g) TEC by the Treaty of Lisbon affected neither the Commission's enforcement policy⁸ nor the Court's approach.⁹

7 Article 101 TFEU is also connected to the rest of the Treaty provisions through the **principle of EU loyalty** (Article 4.3 TEU). This provision has been used to expand the scope of Article 101 TFEU to the actions of the MS in relation to restrictions of competition by private parties. In a nutshell, applying Article 4.3 TEU in connection with Article 101 TFEU entails a duty for the MS not to enact any measures that could detract from the full effect of Article 101 TFEU. Such measures exist where the MS action requires cooperation contrary to Article 101 TFEU or reinforces the effects of such cooperation or delegates the powers of economic intervention to the undertakings involved.¹⁰

8 The Article must also be understood in the wider context of the Treaties and notably the TFEU. Being part of the provisions concerning the **internal market**, it has meant that parallels exist between this provision and—for example—the provisions concerning the free movement of goods. We see this where the Court explains the scope of Article 101 TFEU by virtue of the fact that undertakings could not be allowed to reconstruct the **barriers to free trade** that are, insofar as they emanate from the MS, abolished by the free movement provisions.¹¹

9 The importance of the **Treaty context** of Article 101 TFEU can furthermore be seen in relation to collective agreements in the social sphere. In *Albany*, the Court used a contextual interpretation, in which it relied on the Treaty provisions relating to social policy to exclude collective agreements from the scope of Article 101 TFEU.¹² Later cases have refined and restricted this exclusion.¹³ On

---

⁶ Case 6/72, *Continental Can v Commission* (ECJ 21 February 1973) para 24, cf. notably: "This requirement [of a system ensuring that competition is not distorted] is so essential that without it numerous provisions of the treaty would be pointless."

⁷ Case C-453/99, *Courage and Crehan* (ECJ 20 September 2001) para 20.

⁸ See Memo 07/250 of 23 June 2007 concerning the Commission's unwavering approach to competition law.

⁹ Case C-52/09, *TeliaSonera Sverige* (CJEU 17 February 2011) para 20, for a reference by the Court to Protocol No 27 that effectively confirms the continued existence of Article 3.1 point (g) TEC post-Lisbon.

¹⁰ Case C-35/96, *Commission v Italy* (CNSD) (ECJ 18 June 1998).

¹¹ Joined Cases 56 and 58/64, *Consten and Grundig v Commission* (ECJ 13 July 1966) p. 340.

¹² Case C-67/96, *Albany* (ECJ 21 September 1999) para 60 and Case C-413/13, *FNV Kunsten Informatie en Media* (CJEU 4 December 2014) para 22, 23.

¹³ E.g. Joined Cases C-180/98 to C-184/98, *Pavlov and Others* (ECJ 12 September 2000) para 67–69.

a similar note, Article 101 TFEU must be interpreted in the light of the integration clauses, such as Article 11 TFEU, which require other interests to be taken into account in applying the competition provisions.[14] Another case to show the context within which Article 101 TFEU operates is *APVE*, dealing with the applicability of that provision to cooperation in the agricultural sector.[15] Under the Common Agricultural Policy, agricultural undertakings are allowed to fix minimum prices and agree on production quota as producer organisations. Insofar as such actions are strictly necessary to attain the objectives set for the producer organisations, these actions fall outside Article 101 TFEU.[16]

The Treaty framework of Article 101 TFEU relies on its enforcement in part by means of direct actions and in part by means of the adoption of acts that enable the Commission to operationalise this provision (Articles 103–105 TFEU). Such **direct enforcement** actions follow largely from the direct effect of this provision,[17] whereas the enforcement by the Commission was enabled by the adoption of Regulation 1/2003 on the basis of Article 103 TFEU (→ Article 103 TFEU para 19).[18] Concerning the enforcement of Article 101 TFEU, the open-worded nature of this provision results in its interpretation and application playing a major role. This can be seen in the very significant number of judgments that concern this provision as well as the many Commission decisions that apply it. Apart from these cases that entail an individual application of Article 101 TFEU to a specific case, there is a considerable body of secondary EU law and soft law pertaining to Article 101 TFEU. In this regard, we refer to the block exemption regulations[19] and the Commission's guidance.[20] All three layers, despite the clear hierarchy

10

---

[14] Note that Article 11 TFEU has not been applied in connection with Article 101 TFEU, although the Commission has referred to Article 192 TFEU (ex-Article 174 TEC) to take environmental benefits into account in Decision 2000/475, *CECED*, O.J. L 187/47 (2000) para 55. For a discussion of this policy to take other than competition/efficiency reasons into account see Townley (2009), p. 72 et seq.

[15] Case C-671/15, *APVE and Others* (CJEU 14 November 2017).

[16] Case C-671/15, *APVE and Others* (CJEU14 November 2017) para 50–66.

[17] Confirmed in Case 127/73, *BRT v SABAM* (ECJ 27 March 1974) para 2 for Articles 101.1 and 102 TFEU. Note that the direct effect of Article 101.3 TFEU was confirmed in Case C-439/09, *Pierre Fabre Dermo-Cosmétique* (CJEU13 October 2011) para 49.

[18] Council Regulation (EC) No 1/2003 *on the implementation of the rules on competition laid down in Articles 81 and 82 of the Treaty*, O.J. L 1/1 (2003).

[19] Such regulations are adopted on the basis of a Council delegating regulation, currently Regulation No 19/65/EEC *on application of Article 85 (3) of the Treaty to certain categories of agreements and concerted practices*, O.J. 36/533 (1965) and Regulation (EEC) No 2821/71 *on application of Article 85 (3) of the Treaty to categories of agreements, decisions and concerted practices*, both as amended by Regulation 1/2003, O.J. L 1/1 (2003), adopted on the basis of Article 103 TFEU.

[20] E.g. Commission Communication, *Guidelines on the applicability of Article 101 [TFEU] to horizontal co-operation agreements*, O.J. C 11/1 (2011).

between them,[21] are important to understand this provision. This follows from the fact that the Commission is still the most important institution to apply and enforce Article 101 TFEU, and in many respects, it stands at the helm of the policy changes involved in this provision. The Commission, for example, has changed the way Article 101.3 TFEU is applied by introducing new block exemption regulations. Moreover, in many national cases, judges and national competition authorities often use the Commission's guidance for the interpretation of Article 101 TFEU. This central role for the Commission is all the more noticeable for Article 101.3 TFEU in view of the relative dearth of Court cases on that provision.

11 The identification of the **institutional Treaty framework** for the interpretation of Article 101 TFEU is important in view of the open-worded, fundamentally undefined nature of this provision and the functional approach to EU (competition) law of the Court. Prohibiting preventions, restrictions and distortions of competition automatically raises the question of what competition is. Legally speaking, the answer is clear because the Court has stated that EU competition rules seek workable[22] or effective competition.[23] Both terms are interchangeable in that they signify the fact that the degree or intensity of competition sought by the Treaty is that which is "necessary to ensure the observance of the basic requirements and the attainment of the objectives of the treaty, in particular the creation of a single market achieving conditions similar to those of a domestic market".[24] This means that the exact definition of what constitutes a restriction of competition takes place in the economic, social and political framework set by the Treaty and the objective of market integration in particular. The objective of market integration can be at odds with the economic objective of optimising consumer welfare, which is currently widely accepted as an important goal of EU competition law.[25] As a result, applying Article 101 TFEU involves a value judgment on what is the right balance or hierarchy between these objectives and thus what the restriction of competition seems to be that triggers the prohibition. This value judgment may well differ between the institutions that apply Article 101 TFEU.[26]

---

[21] In Case C-226/11, *Expedia Inc. v Autorité de la concurrence* (CJEU 13 December 2012), for example, the Court stated that Commission Guidelines are not binding upon the MS, whereas decisions and regulations are. Moreover, such regulations and decisions, being secondary to EU law, can never detract from the Treaty itself and its interpretation by the Court.

[22] Case 26/76, *Metro v Commission* (ECJ 25 October 1977) para 20.

[23] Case 27/76, *United Brands v Commission* (ECJ 14 February 1978) para 65.

[24] Case 26/76, *Metro v Commission* (ECJ 25 October 1977) para 20.

[25] See in general: Bishop and Walker (2010), pp. 7, 8 and, with regard to recent antitrust cases in the energy sector: Sadowska and Willems (2013).

[26] In this regard we refer to the *GlaxoSmithKline* saga, where the Commission, CFI and ECJ all came to different value judgments as can be seen in Joined Cases C-501/06 P et al., *GlaxoSmithKline Services Unlimited v Commission* (ECJ 6 October 2009) para 62–64.

3. Prohibited Action Incompatible with the Internal Market (Article 101.1 TFEU)

Article 101.1 TFEU contains a prohibition of all forms of coordination between undertakings that have as an object or effect the restriction of competition. Below we will analyse the various elements of Article 101.1 TFEU.

3.1. Agreements, Decisions and Concerted Practices

Article 101 TFEU touches upon **coordinated behaviour** (between undertakings), whereas Article 102 TFEU concerns the unilateral action of one or more undertakings. This coordination may take several forms, but the most important aspect in this regard is that the specific form hardly matters for the purpose of applying this provision, whereas two or more independent undertakings must be involved.[27] This is in line with the functional approach to competition law that focuses on the effects of the behaviour and not on form.[28] It does, however, highlight the importance of deciding on a good balance between this functional approach that greatly aids enforceability on the one hand and setting the evidence standard that provides parties with adequate legal certainty as to what triggers competition liability on the other. In order to prove the existence of an agreement, for example, all that matters is evidence of the concurrence of wills, irrespective of the form, insofar as this form constitutes the faithful representation of the parties' intentions.[29] Evidence of a shift in the balance between the functional approach and the need to provide legal certainty can be seen when comparing the jurisprudence on vertical relations with that concerning single continuous infringements in horizontal relations.

In relation to **vertical cooperation**, i.e. between a producer, distributor and retailer, the Court requires the express or tacit acquiescence of the (mostly downstream) partners to an agreement. This has most recently been confirmed in the *Bayer* case, concerning a change in the standard terms by Bayer of the agreement concerning the distribution of Adalat in Spain.[30] Bayer essentially sought to limit parallel exports by Spanish wholesalers, but this policy failed because the

---

[27] This means that there cannot be a restrictive agreement between undertakings that are connected to the extent that they are not independent, Case C-279/06, *CEPSA* (ECJ 11 September 2008) para 33–44.

[28] Cf. Gallo (2020).

[29] Joined Cases C-2/01 P and C-3/01 P, *BAI and Commission v Bayer AG* (ECJ 6 January 2004) para 97.

[30] Joined Cases C-2/01 P and C-3/01 P, *BAI and Commission v Bayer AG* (ECJ 6 January 2004) para 141.

wholesalers by and largely kept on parallel exporting.[31] In that case, it is for the person relying on Article 101 TFEU to adduce evidence of express or tacit acquiescence, raising the standard for the evidence required.[32] The other side of the coin is that the "parties" to the agreement avoid being held responsible for any infringement of competition that could attract significant penalties without even being aware of this. In *Bayer*, the alternative approach for the one sought by the Commission is to classify Bayer's actions as abuse within the meaning of Article 102 TFEU. Given that this provision requires the Commission to establish dominance, which is rather more difficult to prove than the existence of an agreement, this would have made the Commission's case even less successful.

15 Concerning **horizontal restrictions**, i.e. coordination between undertakings in the same market, the standard is considerably lower and lowered even more in cases of a single continuous infringement. In these classic cartel cases, evidence of just one meeting suffices to prove an agreement between those who attended the meeting, even if only information was divulged and no (express) concurrence of the wills as to the other participants' reaction to this information was sought or obtained.[33] This makes it significantly easier for the competition authorities to prove such an infringement. In fact, the Court of Justice held that even an exchange of information between competitors may be regarded as a concerted practice restricting competition. In *T-Mobile Netherlands*, the Court stated that an exchange of information between competitors is tainted with an anti-competitive object if the exchange is capable of removing uncertainties concerning the intended conduct of the participating undertakings.[34]

16 The same focus on effective enforcement is also visible in the Commission's practice and the Court's approval of the inclusion of **cartel facilitators** in Article 101 TFEU. The seminal case in this regard is *AC-Treuhand*, where Swiss consultancy AC-Treuhand was fined for facilitating the collusion of a number of chemical producers in several cartels.[35] AC-Treuhand appealed, essentially arguing that as a facilitator not active on the markets affected by the cartel, it could not be expected to know that it infringed Article 101 TFEU, resulting in an infringement of the principle of *nullum crimen, nulla poena sine lege*. The Court rejected this argument, holding that the full effectiveness of Article 101 TFEU would be negated if the narrow interpretation of Article 101 TFEU, as confined to cartelists active on

---

[31] Joined Cases C-2/01 P and C-3/01 P, *BAI and Commission v Bayer AG* (ECJ 6 January 2004) para 121, 122, revealing the "genuine wishes" on the part of the distributors to keep on parallel exporting.

[32] See also Case T-208/01, *Volkswagen v Commission* (CFI 3 December 2003) para 30 et seq.

[33] Case T-202/98, *Tate & Lyle and others v Commission* (CFI 12 July 2001) para 54–61. See further: Case T-141/94, *Thyssen Stahl AG v Commission* (CFI 11 March 1999) para 177.

[34] Case C-8/08, T-*Mobile Netherlands and Others* (ECJ 4 June 2009) para 43.

[35] Case C-194/14 P, *AC-Treuhand AG v Commission* (CJEU 22 October 2015). Note that the symbolic fine imposed on AC-Treuhand in an earlier case was also unsuccessfully challenged in Case T-99/04, *AC-Treuhand v Commission* (CFI 8 July 2008). See further on cartel facilitators Case T-180/15, *Icap plc v Commission* (GC 10 November 2017).

the markets affected by the cartel, would be followed.[36] In addition, the Court found the Commission's interpretation of Article 101 TFEU to be sufficiently predictable.[37]

This effectiveness-focused and functional approach can also be seen in relation to the coordination that takes the form of a **decision of an association of undertakings**. In this regard, again, all that matters is that the decision is a faithful representation of the wills of the member undertakings.[38] This also makes sense in view of the fact that both the agreement and the decision are forms of coordination that are relatively apparent and easily identifiable because they will often take a written and formalised form.

17

In this regard, most problems arise in relation to the least well-defined and most openly ended form of coordination: **concerted practice**. A concerted practice is understood by the ECJ as the result of a desire to be able to address "less formalised" forms of coordination.[39] This means that the Commission and Court have had to sail a delicate course between the Scylla of construing the concept sufficiently wide so as to enable EU competition law not to be circumvented and the Charybdis of finding cartels where there are none. This tension is less apparent where the concerted practice forms part of a single continuous infringement and represents little more than a less structured period in the cartel's existence.[40]

18

The tension is most clearly visible where the market involved shows traits of an oligopoly. In a nutshell, **oligopolistic markets** show a high degree of concentration, homogeneous products and production processes, and market transparency. The more these circumstances are present, the more likely is a situation of **oligopolistic interdependence**. This refers to the economic thinking according to which competition, resulting eventually in low prices, will be different in such markets. A situation of supra-competitive prices could arise in a market where the few participants follow the price set by the company that is perceived to be the market leader, so-called barometric price leadership.[41] The outcome of such a market could show a remarkable resemblance to that of a successful cartel: parallel price increases to a supra-competitive level. Competition law scrutiny could easily be triggered by evidence of such parallel price increases, and in this respect, the Court has held the parallelism to be a strong indicator of a concerted practice, but it does

19

---

[36] Case C-194/14 P, *AC-Treuhand AG v Commission* (CJEU 22 October 2015) para 36.

[37] Case C-194/14 P, *AC-Treuhand AG v Commission* (CJEU 22 October 2015) para 40–44.

[38] Case 45/85, *Verband der Sachversicherer e.V. v Commission* (ECJ 27 January 1987) para 29–32.

[39] Joined Cases 40/73 et al., *Suiker Unie and Others v Commission* (ECJ 16 December 1975) para 26.

[40] Case C-49/92 P, *Commission v Anic Partecipazioni SpA* (ECJ 8 July 1999) para 131.

[41] Note that this has been accepted by the Commission in Decision 84/405, *Zinc Producers Group*, para 75, 76.

not constitute evidence.[42] It is thus for the Commission to adduce evidence that rules out any alternative explanation for these price increases. If the Commission succeeds in this, a concerted practice is proven. If, however, the Commission fails or the parties produce an alternative explanation for the parallel behaviour, no concerted practice will be found.[43]

20   In the absence of evidence of parallel actions on the market, the Commission may have **evidence of concertation**: a meeting between the undertakings involved. If such a meeting can be proven and the matters discussed during that meeting are relevant to the competitive process, such as the parties' future pricing or output strategy, this essentially suffices to prove a concerted practice.[44] The reasoning in this regard is that in these circumstances, the parties will invariably align their decisions to the matters discussed during the meeting.[45] In such cases, the only escape clause is to immediately openly distance oneself from the meeting or—of course—prove that the company in question was not represented during the meeting where the concertation took place.[46] Finally, it may be noted that it can also be assumed that the information that was exchanged in a meeting influenced the actions of the companies involved in the concerted practice where the persons representing these companies in the concertation only took part in their companies' decisions on pricing strategies and could not determine this themselves.[47]

21   Whereas most cases involving a concerted practice concern horizontal cases and the logic underlying them is most easily **applied between competitors**, it is **equally relevant to vertical relations**.[48]

22   Concerning vertical relations, there is an important line of cases touching upon the question of whether and to what extent vertically related undertakings can be seen as independent or rather as emanations of one undertaking. This is important in relation to the instructions by parent companies to their daughter undertakings (→ para 25). It is also important as regards the liability of a specific legal entity

---

[42] Case 48/69, *Imperial Chemical Industries Ltd. v Commission* (Dyestuffs) (ECJ 14 July 1972) para 66.

[43] Joined Cases C-89/85 et al., *A. Ahlström Osakeyhtiö and others v Commission* (ECJ 31 March 1993) para 73–120. See also Case T-442/08, *CISAC v Commission* (GC 12 April 2013), where there was an alternative explanation for the absence of market entry by the national collecting societies.

[44] In cases where the concertation has a restrictive object, effects need not be proven (→ para 26 et seqq.), and a causal connection between the concertation and the practice is assumed to exist, Case C-8/08, *T-Mobile Netherlands and Others* (ECJ 4 June 2009) para 61, even if only one meeting took place.

[45] Case C-199/92 P, *Hüls v Commission* (ECJ 8 July 1999) para 167.

[46] Case C-49/92 P, *Commission v Anic Partecipazioni SpA* (ECJ 8 July 1999) para 96.

[47] Case C-286/13 P, *Dole Food Company Inc. and Dole Fresh Fruit Europe v Commission* (CJEU 19 March 2015) para 129–133.

[48] Joined Cases 100 to 103/80, *SA Musique Diffusion française and others v Commission* (ECJ 7 June 1983) para 72–80.

for the sanctions that can be imposed as well as the civil liability for damages arising from the infringement of Article 101 TFEU.[49]

3.2. Undertakings

Article 101 TFEU, as well as the other competition provisions, only applies to **undertakings and associations of undertakings**. This is construed broadly as encompassing any entity "engaged in an economic activity regardless of the legal status of the entity and the way in which it is financed".[50] As a result, formal requirements are largely irrelevant, and what matters is the activity concerned and the circumstances under which this activity is performed. This has resulted in essentially two exceptions to the concept of an undertaking. **23**

Firstly, so-called **solidarity activities** are taken outside the scope of the competition provisions for lack of economic activity. The case law in this respect hinges heavily on the specific facts of the individual cases, but the following factors are generally of importance: **24**

- The presence or absence of a for-profit objective or social objective[51]
- The degree to which the solidarity principle is implemented[52]
- The level of state control over the performance of the activity[53]

Secondly, in some cases, the Court has referred to the essential **State prerogatives** to exclude certain activities from the scope of the competition rules. In this regard, airspace control and preventive environmental surveillance have been excluded.[54] Both exceptions have been defined most prominently in relation to the entities likely to be characterised as public undertakings in the meaning of Article 106 TFEU (→ Article 106 TFEU para 11–12). **25**

The **functional concept** of an undertaking also takes into account the fact that companies may belong to a group of undertakings. In that regard, the Court has held that there is no room for a restriction of competition between undertakings belonging to one group where, for example, a subsidiary enjoys no economic independence from its parent company.[55] Competition (→ para 29 et seqq.) requires a certain degree of **autonomy**[56] on the part of the undertakings that are alleged to be **26**

---

[49] Case C-724/17, *Skanska Industrial Solutions* (CJEU 14 March 2019) para 36–47.

[50] Case C-41/90, *Höfner & Elser v Macrotron* (ECJ 23 April 1991) para 21. See further Case 118/85, *Commission v Italy (AAMS)* (ECJ 16 June 1987) para 7.

[51] E.g. Case C-350/07, *Kattner Stahlbau* (ECJ 5 March 2009) para 35, 41, 42.

[52] E.g. Case C-437/09, *AG2R Prévoyance* (CJEU 3 March 2011) para 47–52.

[53] E.g. Case C-437/09, *AG2R Prévoyance* (CJEU 3 March 2011) para 53–65.

[54] Case C-364/92, *SAT Fluggesellschaft mbH v Eurocontrol* (ECJ 19 January 1994), and Case C-343/95, *Diego Calì & Figli Srl v Servizi ecologici porto di Genova SpA* (ECJ 18 March 1997).

[55] Case 22/71, *Béguelin Import v S.A.G.L. Import Export* (ECJ 25 November 1971) para 8.

[56] Autonomy may also be absent or limited as a result of government interference, see Case C-198/01, *CIF* (ECJ 9 September 2003) para 51–58.

involved in restrictive cooperation.[57] This again works on the basis of an assumption that entails a degree of abstraction from economic reality. In this case, the assumption is that a parent company and its 100% subsidiary share the same economic objective and that the parent can control the subsidiary to attain this objective.[58] They are, as a result, to be treated as a single economic entity, unless one of the companies can rebut this presumption.[59]

3.3. Object or Effect of Restricting Competition

27   In the wording of Article 101 TFEU, the coordination, i.e. the agreement, concerted practice or decision, is connected to that which is regulated—competition that is not restricted or distorted—by means of the **object or effect**. This element of Article 101 TFEU thus has two functions. Firstly, it connects the real-world and tangible element of coordination to the more enigmatic or even intangible[60] element of competition. Secondly, it qualifies the degree to which the competition affected by the cooperation has to be specified and quantified in a concrete case. With cooperation that falls in the object category, no such specification and quantification are required as competition is assumed to be affected. In the alternative, the effects on competition must be identified and specified, again greatly raising the bar for the application of Article 101.1 TFEU.

28   The object and effect are **alternatives** in the text of Article 101 TFEU.[61] This means that once cooperation is classified as having a restrictive object, actual effects on competition need no longer be proven.[62] In the Court's recent jurisprudence, the criterion for distinguishing between the object category and the effect category is explained as follows:

> [...] certain collusive behaviour, such as that leading to horizontal price-fixing by cartels, may be considered so likely to have negative effects, in particular on the price, quantity or quality of the goods and services, that it may be considered redundant, for the purposes of applying Article 81(1) EC, to prove that they have actual effects on the market. Experience

---

[57] Case C-73/95 P, *Viho Europe BV v Commission* (ECJ 24 October 1996) para 15–18.

[58] Note that nearly 100% ownership will also result in the applicability of this assumption: Case T-299/08, *Elf Aquitaine v Commission* (GC 17 May 2011) para 55, 56 (concerning 97% ownership), confirmed in Case C-404/11 P and Case C-508/11, *Eni v Commission* (ECJ 2 February 2012) para 47–51.

[59] Case C-97/08 P, *Akzo Nobel NV and Others v Commission* (ECJ 10 September 2009) para 59–61.

[60] The metaphysical nature of competition is further evidenced in the presence of several "schools of thought" on competition whose proponents often exhibit almost religious zeal in defending and furthering the ideas of their school. Bork (1978) can be taken as a zealous furthering of the Chicago school. For a more disentangled analysis of these schools and their influence on EU competition policy, see Hildebrand (2002).

[61] Joined Cases 56 and 58/64, *Consten and Grundig v Commission* (ECJ 13 July 1966) p. 342.

[62] This is standard case law since *Consten and Grundig*, e.g. Case C-286/13 P, *Dole Food Company Inc. and Dole Fresh Fruit Europe v Commission* (CJEU 19 March 2015) para 113.

shows that such behaviour leads to falls in production and price increases, resulting in poor allocation of resources to the detriment, in particular, of consumers.[63]

Essentially, the **object category** contains cooperation where the effects on competition are so likely that they can be presumed, obviating the need to prove such effects. To understand why and when this presumption applies, competition and its restriction or distortion must first be analysed. An understanding of the analysis involved in proving effects on competition on the market is therefore essential. 29

3.3.1. Establishing Effects on Competition: Market Definition and the Counterfactual Analysis

An effects analysis involves a **counterfactual analysis**. In the words of the Court, what must be established is the "impact of the agreement on existing and potential competition and the competition situation in the absence of the agreement".[64] This raises the question of what (existing and potential) competition is and how, using what indicators, it can be measured to determine the impact of the agreement on it. By and large, the indicators used below can be divided into three categories: those pertaining to the market structure, those concerning the conduct on the market and, finally, the indicators concerning the efficiencies derived from a market.[65] 30

Market Definition

The analysis of competition invariably starts with a definition of the relevant market.[66] The exercise of identifying a relevant market encompasses the **identification and delimitation of the arena in which competition takes place** and is helpful to identify what competition is. Market definition requires the definition of the relevant product market as well as the relevant geographical market. In this regard, it must be taken into account that market definition is not an end in itself but rather serves a purpose in the identification of effects on competition. In the context of Article 102 TFEU (→ Article 102 TFEU para 10 et seqq.) or the Merger Regulation,[67] it functions to establish the existence of market power or, to use the 31

---

[63] Case C-286/13 P, *Dole Food Company Inc. and Dole Fresh Fruit Europe v Commission* (CJEU 19 March 2015) para 115, citing Case C-67/13 P, *Groupement des Cartes Bancaires v Commission* (CJEU 11 September 2014) para 51.

[64] Case 56/65, *Société minière et technique v Maschinenbau Ulm* (ECJ 30 June 1966) pp. 249–250 as cited in Case T-328/03, *O2 (Germany) v Commission* (CFI 2 May 2006) para 67 and in Case C-382/12spiepr132 P, *MasterCard v Commission* (CJEU 11 September 2014) para 161.

[65] These factors comprise the three elements of the S-C-P-paradigm (→ para 39).

[66] Note, however, that the definition is functional to the identification of the restriction or distortion of competition that is investigated, potentially negating extensive market definitions. See Case T-62/98, *Volkswagen AG v Commission* (CFI 6 July 2000), upheld in appeal in Case C-338/00 P, *Volkswagen AG v Commission* (ECJ 18 September 2003). Cf. Ortiz Blanco (2012), pp. 1–3.

[67] Regulation 139/2004, O.J. L 24/1 (2004).

legal terminology, dominance. In the context of Article 101 TFEU, it is necessary to determine whether the agreement has an **effect on trade** and competition.[68]

32   To determine the relevant market, however, in both cases of Articles 101 and 102 TFEU, the same basic methodology applies. In both cases, the essential question is the degree to which products form substitutes for the products under investigation, i.e. the products where a restriction of competition is suspected. This **substitution** can be identified with regard to the demand and supply sides of the market. As regards the demand side, what matters are the preferences of consumers. One way of identifying such preferences is by using a **SSNIP test or hypothetical monopolist test**.[69] This requires an identification of consumer responses to a small but significant non-transitory increase in the price of the product under investigation. What matters is whether it would be profitable to increase the price of this product by 5 to 10%. If this is not profitable because sufficient consumption would switch away to an alternative product, this product forms part of the same relevant product market.

33   In line with what has already been observed above, defining **demand-side substitution** invariably requires treading a very fine line between the infinite complexity of actual consumer preferences and the need to come to predictable and reproducible outcomes. The *cause célèbre* in this regard is *United Brands*, which involved the definition of the relevant market for bananas. The pressing issue was whether this constituted part of a general market for fruit or rather formed a separate product market. The Court discussed several issues, such as the reduction of banana prices in periods where other seasonal fruits were available, but ultimately took into account the banana's shape and ease of consumption in reaching the conclusion that the constant needs of the young, elderly and sick are satisfied by the "privileged fruit" that a banana is, making it a market "sufficiently distinct from other fresh fruit markets".[70] This shows the difficulty of the basic exercise to be performed in defining the relevant market.

34   Determining demand-side substitutability involves myriad customers whose, at times very personal, **preferences** need to be turned into an abstract appraisal on what can only be a *degree of* **substitutability**. This makes any definition of the market a judgement call that may or may not be replicated in another case or by another authority.[71] In that regard, reducing substitution to the criterion of price alone represents an abstraction from reality that aids the feasibility of this appraisal but at the same time limits the degree to which it corresponds to economic reality. Moreover, even with this abstraction, there is the issue of weighing the marginal

---

[68] Joined Cases T-259/02 et al., *Raiffeisen Zentralbank Österreich v Commission* (CFI 14 December 2006) para 172. Upheld in appeal in Joined Cases C-125/07 P et al., *Erste Group Bank AG and Others v Commission* (ECJ 24 September 2009) para 60.

[69] See Commission Notice *on the definition of the relevant market*, O.J. C 372/5 (1997) para 17.

[70] Case 27/76, *United Brands v Commission* (ECJ 14 February 1978) para 25–35.

[71] This has been held by the General Court to mean that—in an Article 102 TFEU case, but this principle holds for an Article 101 TFEU case as well—the market must be defined anew in every case Joined Cases T-125/97 and T-127/97, *Coca-Cola v Commission* (CFI 22 March 2000).

consumers, i.e. those that would change to another product in the light of a small but significant price increase, in relation to the infra-marginal consumers as well as determining the degree to which the latter are infra-marginal. This potential failure of a competition law appraisal to reflect economic reality may, in turn, affect the effectiveness of the decision taken on the basis of this appraisal, potentially resulting in over- or under-enforcement.[72] In relation to zero-price goods, such as those often found in digital platform markets, market definition being even more challenging, in particular as there may be multi-sided markets involved, raising the question of whether one platform market or several markets for each side of the platform must be defined.[73]

Many of these findings can also be employed in the definition of **supply-side** **substitution**. In this regard, matters are further complicated by the asymmetry of information between the regulator and the regulated entity. Even if demand-side substitution could be reduced to an analysis of the profitability of market entry, determining the relevant costs and thus profitability involves the appraisal of data and facts that are only—if at all—known with a predictable degree of certainty by the companies involved. This means that the authorities in charge of defining supply-side substitution will ultimately have to rely on facts brought forward by the economic actor(s) under scrutiny. 35

Moreover, the Commission will only take supply-side substitution into account insofar as the effects are equivalent to those of demand-side substitution in terms of **effectiveness and immediacy**.[74] This essentially means that the magnitude and speed of market entry by new companies must be appraised and play a role in deciding whether factors relating to what is often called the contestability of a market are taken into account. 36

In addition to the relevant product market, the relevant **geographical market** must also be defined. In the words of the Court, this comprises the area in which the "conditions of competition are sufficiently homogeneous" while being "appreciably different" in other areas.[75] The words "sufficiently" and "appreciably" again indicate the presence of discretion, but more fundamentally challenging is the seemingly simple concept of "conditions of competition". Again, this could be reduced to a matter of price or (transport and distribution) costs, but it is obvious 37

---

[72] The *locus classicus* for such under-enforcement, often referred to as the cellophane fallacy, is the 1956 USC decision in *DuPont*, 351 U.S. 377, 76, where the Supreme Court failed to take into account that prices were already inflated. In that case, raising the price by another 5–10% will result in relatively more switching behaviour and thus an unrealistically wide market definition and reduced probability of finding market power.

[73] For a discussion see Franck and Peitz (2021). The Commission has taken a multi-market approach and defined markets for each side of the platform. The judgment in Case C-67/13 P, *Groupement des cartes bancaires v Commission* (CJEU 11 September 2014) para 77–79, seems to point in the direction that the multi-market approach is required under EU law.

[74] Commission Notice *on the definition of the relevant market*, O.J. C 372/5 (1997) para 20.

[75] Case 27/76, *United Brands v Commission* (ECJ 14 February 1978) para 11. See also Commission Notice *on the definition of the relevant market*, O.J. C 372/5 (1997), para 8.

that many factors impact geographical market definition, such as local consumption preferences or differences in language.

38 In many instances, the ultimate abstraction from economic reality takes place where it is observed that a further refined (broader or narrower) definition of the market is unnecessary in the light of the **economic effects irrespective of this market definition**. As a result, the Commission may refrain from further defining (limiting or expanding) the relevant market if, for example, market power can be ruled out anyway even on the most narrowly defined markets.[76]

Market Structure, Conduct and Performance

39 Following an adequate definition of the relevant market, the structure of that market may be identified. This refers to the barriers to entry (*inter alia*, sunk costs identified as part of the supply-side substitution and local consumption specificities or market entry regulations) but also to the number and relative market shares of the undertakings active on the market.[77] These factors form essential indicators of the degree of concentration on a market, which, in turn, can be used to predict possible behaviours of the undertakings on the market. If we take the hypothetical monopolist test and assume that prices are the only competitive parameter, we may observe that even an undertaking with a 100% market share is unable to sustainably raise prices above the level where these prices elicit market entry. Even in the absence of actual market entry, the prospect of this happening (often referred to as potential competition) is enough to exert competitive pressure and may result in the incumbent monopolist to lower its prices to avoid potential competition from turning into real competitors.[78] This is not fundamentally different for a successful cartel that has conspired to raise prices. Moreover, it shows the complex relation between **market structure**, behaviour on the market, performance and what competition is.

40 It is the behaviour, or **conduct**, to use the S-C-P-paradigm's terminology,[79] to which Article 101 TFEU attaches.[80] Essentially, the coordination, agreement or concertation is a **form of behaviour that triggers the applicability of Article 101 TFEU**. The subject of this behaviour then determines whether these qualify as restrictions by object or by effect. This, however, leaves open to what extent the performance should also influence the finding of a restriction of competition. This follows from the fact that the restriction of competition is something that follows from the action of agreeing or engaging in concertation.

---

[76] As happened in the decision at stake in Case T-62/98, *Volkswagen AG v Commission* (CFI 6 July 2000).

[77] Note that the volatility of market shares is dependent on, inter alia, the barriers to entry.

[78] This could take the form of limit pricing. See, inter alia, Milgrom and Roberts (1982).

[79] S-C-P stands for Structure-Conduct-Performance, Bishop and Walker (2010), pp. 65–67. Note that we do not refer to the (extended) S-C-P paradigm as a prescriptive tool, as the Harvard School did, but only as an analytical framework to describe what competition is and what factors impact its regulation.

[80] See further Mestmäcker and Schweitzer (2014), § 11 para 3–12.

41 In an Article 101 TFEU case, the market structure is generally not the cause of the lack of competition. Apart from markets that exhibit significant oligopolistic traits, most markets take a specific form of conduct, the agreement, concertation or decision, to restrict competition. In the words of the Court, this conduct is "designed to **replace the risks of competition and the hazards of competitors' spontaneous reactions by cooperation**".[81] The risks of competition in this regard refers to competitors endlessly trying to outcompete each other by seeking to lower production costs, by raising quality and by innovating. In doing so, these undertakings respond to the price cuts, innovations and efforts of the others, so some degree of market transparency is required. Moreover, the competitors as well as consumers should be able to adapt their decisions to the latest information on the best offers on that market.[82] The central element to which Article 101 TFEU could attach this perception of competition is the competitive behaviour on the market. This, intuitively as it may be, raises the question of to what extent any contract that binds parties and thus limits their freedom to adapt their (re)actions,[83] and/or the "free play of competition",[84] should qualify as a restriction of competition. In this regard, the Court has held that not all restrictions on rivalry or the freedom to compete are to be equated to restrictions of competition.[85]

42 In coming to this conclusion, the Court often looks at the (**economic**) **effects of such coordination**. In this regard, for example, the Court has held that selective distribution agreements limit rivalry while making obvious economic sense because of the positive effects on efficiency in the distribution of the products.[86] As a result, the Court finds the restrictions of rivalry that do not go beyond what is necessary to achieve the economic benefits, not to constitute restrictions of competition.[87]

43 Economic efficiency is therefore an indicator of what constitutes competition and thus informs what in the Court's approach constitutes a restriction of competition. This has prompted the question of whether and to what extent effects on

---

[81] Case 48/69, *Imperial Chemical Industries Ltd. v Commission* (Dyestuffs) (ECJ 14 July 1972) para 119.

[82] Together with an atomistic market structure with no barriers to entry these two conditions form the core requirements for the textbook model of perfect competition Bishop and Walker (2010), pp. 22, 23.

[83] See, e.g., Case C-399/93, *H. G. Oude Luttikhuis and others v Verenigde Coöperatieve Melkindustrie Coberco BA* (ECJ 12 December 1995) para 15.

[84] Case 22/71, *Béguelin Import v S.A.G.L. Import Export* (ECJ 25 November 1971) para 16 and Case C-231/14 P, *InnoLux Corp. v Commission* (Opinion of AG *Wathelet* of 30 April 2015) para 54.

[85] Case 161/84, *Pronuptia* (ECJ 28 January 1986) para 14–21.

[86] Case 26/76, *Metro v Commission* (ECJ 25 October 1977) para 20, 21.

[87] Case 161/84, *Pronuptia* (ECJ 28 January 1986) para 27 and Case C-250/92, *Gøttrup-Klim and Others Grovvareforeninger v Dansk Landbrugs Grovvareselskab AmbA* (ECJ 15 December 1994) para 32–45.

consumer welfare must be demonstrated before a restriction of competition can be found. Again, the Court has given an unequivocal answer. In *GlaxoSmithKline*, the Court held that "like other competition rules laid down in the Treaty, [Article 101 TFEU] aims to protect not only the interests of competitors or of consumers, but also the structure of the market and, in so doing, competition as such".[88] In this regard, the Court appears to understand competition broadly, encompassing a market structure that will enable conduct resulting in consumer welfare. As a result, the harm that triggers the applicability of competition law can arise in relation to the market structure, conduct as well as consumer welfare, with neither category being decisive. This means that the counterfactual analysis needs to take into account and relate to all changes in any of these categories. Effects on consumers or consumer welfare feature prominently but do not act as a litmus test in this regard.[89] Needless to say, this amounts to a task of considerable complexity potentially resulting in less predictable outcomes. In this regard, the Court and Commission have formulated two doctrines in which certain elements of the counterfactual analysis are expedited or streamlined: appreciability and ancillary restraints.[90]

The Effects Category and Appreciability

44   **Appreciability** is often referred to as a *de minimis* analysis to exclude anti-competitive actions that do not warrant intervention for want of sufficient effects. In this regard, two perspectives on appreciability can be distinguished, namely a quantitative and a qualitative one.

45   In the **quantitative analysis** of appreciability, market shares are used to exclude effects on competition. We see this in the Court's case law[91] and, very prominently, in the Commission's *de minimis* Notice.[92] The latter holds that agreements between competitors with a market share not exceeding 10% are considered not to have appreciable effects. For coordination between non-competitors, the bar is put at 15% unless the market exhibits cumulative effects, in which case the threshold is lowered to 5% (→ para 47). It may be noted that the mere fact that these thresholds are exceeded does not automatically mean that appreciability can be ruled out; it

---

[88] Joined Cases C-501/06 P et al., *GlaxoSmithKline Services Unlimited v Commission* (ECJ 6 October 2009) para 63.

[89] We can also see this in the quote from Case C-67/13 P, *Groupement des Cartes Bancaires v Commission* (CJEU 11 September 2014), where the Court refers to effects to the "detriment, *in particular*, of consumers" [emphasis added]. See Case C-286/13 P, *Dole Food Company Inc. and Dole Fresh Fruit Europe v Commission* (CJEU 19 March 2015) para 125.

[90] In particular, with regard to the latter, a considerable debate exists in the literature as to the characterisation and more particularly whether this can be likened to the US doctrine of the Rule of Reason, cf. Jones (2006).

[91] E.g. Case 5/69, *Franz Völk v S.P.R.L. Ets J. Vervaecke* (ECJ 9 July 1969) para 5/7 and Case 132C-238/05, *Asnef-Equifax* (ECJ 23 November 2006) para 50.

[92] O.J. C 291/1 (2014). For an analysis see Mestmäcker and Schweitzer (2014), § 11 para 69–86.

only means that the shorthand route to exclude appreciable effects does not apply, necessitating further analysis.[93]

In the **qualitative analysis** of appreciability, the effects on competition are determined by appraising the importance of the subject of the restriction in relation to all other factors on which competition is possible. Elements of this can be seen in *Metro I*, where the Court held that in the selective distribution system at hand, "price competition is not generally emphasized either as an exclusive or even as a principal factor".[94] Obviously, competition could be envisaged on myriad other factors, such as pre- and after-sales services, the availability of stocks or the quality of the products. We see similar reasoning in Commission decisions[95] and more recent Court judgments.[96] It is obvious that this kind of analysis is more complex compared to that under the quantitative appreciability test, if only because of the difficulty in coming to an objective weighing of the relative importance of the various elements on which competition has taken and can take place. The infinite complexity of competition and the need to ensure adequate legal certainty argue in favour of interpreting this rule to mean that only manifestly inappreciable restrictions qualify and thus escape scrutiny on the basis of Article 101 TFEU.

46

The final strand of the appreciability doctrine applies to the **cumulative effect** that may arise from the existence of bundles of similar contracts. This doctrine has been developed most prominently in relation to beer distribution agreements,[97] *inter alia* in *Delimitis*.[98] This involved a beer tie agreement between a German brewery and a publican in Frankfurt. The Court analysed this case from the perspective of the effect such beer ties would have on the possibility for foreign players to become active on the market for beer distribution in Germany, adopting what is called a contestability approach to competition in which barriers to entry are what matters.[99] In this regard, the Court suggests a two-step approach in which first the contribution of all contracts to reducing market access must be identified.[100] This would involve an analysis of the means to enter such a market, for example by taking over or merging with an incumbent brewery or creating a new distribution network. If such a cumulative effect is observed, the contribution of the individual

47

---

[93] Case T-374/94, *European Night Services Ltd (ENS) a.o. v Commission* (CFI 15 September 1998) para 102.

[94] Case 26/76, *Metro v Commission* (ECJ 25 October 1977) para 21.

[95] Decision 86/507, *Irish Banks' Standing Committee*, O.J. L 295/28 (1986) para 16 in relation to opening hours of banks.

[96] Joined Cases C-180/98 to C-184/98, *Pavlov and Others* (ECJ 12 September 2000) para 94, 95, where the Court finds that the subject, supplementary pension funds, forms only an insignificant element of all aspects with regard to which the undertakings in question competed on.

[97] Note that it also informs the competition law appraisal in automotive fuel distribution cases, e.g. Case C-214/99, *Neste* (ECJ 7 December 2000), as well as the retail sale of ice creams Case C-344/98, *Masterfoods and HB* (ECJ 14 December 2000).

[98] Case C-234/89, *Stergios Delimitis v Henninger Bräu AG* (ECJ 28 February 1991).

[99] For a discussion see Baumol et al. (1982).

[100] Case C-234/89, *Stergios Delimitis v Henninger Bräu AG* (ECJ 28 February 1991) para 20–23.

contracts to this cumulative barrier to entry must be established by reference to the market share of the brewery and the tied pubs, as well as the degree to which the individual contract forecloses market access.[101] The latter involves an appraisal of the degree of exclusivity following from the duration, percentage of output covered and conditions for termination of the contract. This analysis is likely to be fraught with many practical difficulties relating to the required intricate understanding of the market involved as well as the complexity of weighing the many factors that must be taken into account[102] Still, an appreciability test goes some way to ensuring that only those restrictions that warrant intervention because they have a (potential) impact are caught.

Effects and Ancillary Restraints

48   The full potential breadth of the effect appraisal can be seen in the line of cases that are often subsumed under the heading of **ancillary restraints**. By and large, they exempt all agreements that do not result in a (net) restriction of competition from the scope of Article 101.1 TFEU. In relation to verticals, it has been used to balance restrictions of **intra-brand competition** with increases of **inter-brand competition**. This means that, provided certain conditions are met, for example, the restrictive effects on competition between franchise takers are considered to be outweighed by the increases in competition between the various franchise systems.[103] A similar balancing exercise has been performed in relation to selective distribution agreements,[104] membership and the regulation of agricultural cooperatives,[105] exclusive licences for plant-breeding rights[106] and non-compete agreements as part of mergers and take-overs.[107]

49   The likeness of this line of cases to what is considered the **rule of reason** in US Antitrust law (→para 41, 42) has triggered a debate on whether or not the EU has or should have such a rule of reason. In this regard, we must first point out that the formal legal structure of Article 101 TFEU is incomparable to that of **Section 1 of**

---

[101] Case C-234/89, *Stergios Delimitis v Henninger Bräu AG* (ECJ 28 February 1991) para 24–26.

[102] Mr. Crehan, for example, was refused damages initially by the High Court that considered the Delimitis criteria not to be met, despite the Commission's assessment in this regard; *Crehan v Inntrepreneur Pub Company*, [2003] E.W.H.C. 1510, for an account of the entire saga see Whelan (2007), pp. 93–98. See further, for an application to shopping centre tenancy agreements, Case C-345/14, *SIA 'Maxima Latvija'v Konkurences padome* (CJEU 26 November 2015) para 26–30.

[103] Case 161/84, *Pronuptia* (ECJ 28 January 1986) para 15.

[104] Case 26/76, *Metro v Commission* (ECJ 25 October 1977) para 20, 21.

[105] Case C-250/92, *Gøttrup-Klim and Others Grovvareforeningen v Dansk Landbrugs Grovvareselskab AmbA* (ECJ 15 December 1994) para 34.

[106] Case 258/78, *Nungesser v Commission* (8 June 1982) para 54–85 and Case 27/87, *SPRL Louis Erauw-Jacquery v La Hesbignonne SC* (ECJ 19 April 1988) para 10.

[107] Case 42/84, *Remia BV and others v Commission* (ECJ 11 July 1985) para 17–20.

the **Sherman Act**, if only because the latter does not contain the equivalent of Article 101.3 TFEU. This means that, irrespective of the procedures for applying the third paragraph (→ para 67 et seqq.),[108] agreements with some form of beneficial effects can only escape the Section 1 prohibition if that provision is interpreted reasonably. Leaving aside the formal structure of both provisions, the reasoning underlying and applied in the ancillary restraint doctrine and by the "rule of reason" shows a remarkable similarity in the sense that restrictive effects are balanced with pro-competitive and efficiency-enhancing effects. The similarity ends, however, when we observe that the Supreme Court[109] in its decisions explicitly refers to an appraisal of the transaction costs involved in deciding on whether a certain category of restrictions should be dealt with under the rule of reason or treated as a *per se* restriction.[110] The Court does not include such reasoning and confines itself to defining the object and effect categories on an *ad hoc* basis with succinct economic argumentation only. Transaction costs, however, do seem to be relevant in the Court's case law on the object-effect dichotomy and notably the role played in this regard by the degree of clarity with which certain forms of collusion can be assumed to be harmful (→ para 28, 29).

A final difference between the rule of reason and the European ancillary restraint doctrine relates to the fact that the latter can also save restrictive agreements from Article 101.1 TFEU if these restrictions do not go beyond what is necessary to ensure public interest.[111] This so-called ***Wouters* exception** is grounded on a case that concerned self-regulation by the Netherlands bar association, which precluded structural cooperation between members of the bar and accountancy firms.[112] Following this, many authors doubted the authority of this ruling.[113] However, it has since then also been applied to public interests involved in the (self-)regulation of the professional education of accountants,[114] anti-doping rules,[115] tariffs for

50

---

[108] The exclusive right, up until 2004, for the Commission to apply the third paragraph has resulted in a considerable backlog of agreements that had notified so that the Commission could apply this provision. The Court's more liberal interpretation of the first paragraph can be seen as a response to this.

[109] E.g., *Leegin Creative Leather Products, Inc. v. PSKS, Inc.*, 551 U.S. 877 (2007), at pp. 25–28 and p. 20 of the dissenting opinion.

[110] The per se category can be likened to the object category in the terminology of EU competition law (→para 52). Again, the formal legal structure makes this comparison difficult, given that under Article 101 TFEU, restrictions by object could benefit from an exemption on the basis of Article 101.3 TFEU, whereas *per se* restrictions under paragraph 1 are invariably prohibited.

[111] In the context of US antitrust law, this is dealt with under the heading of the state action defence. See, on such considerations and the role that these may play in a rule of reason analysis, US Supreme Court, *National Collegiate Athletic Assn. v. Alston et al.*, 594 U. S. (2021), case nos. 20-512 and 20-520 (21 June 2021).

[112] Case C-309/99, *Wouters and Others* (ECJ 19 February 2002).

[113] E.g., the discussion on p. 238 of the second edition of Faull and Nikpay (2007) and notably the unsubstantiated claim in fn. 367. For a fuller discussion see Wendt (2013).

[114] Case C-1/12, *Ordem dos Técnicos Oficiais de Contas* (CJEU 28 February 2013).

[115] Case C-519/04, *David Meca-Medina and Igor Majcen v Commissie* (ECJ 18 July 2006).

geologists[116] and minimum haulage tariffs.[117] What can be seen in these cases is the perhaps increasingly strict review of the proportionality of the (self-)regulation. Whereas the rule in *Wouters* met with only a marginal review by the Court, the rules in *OTOC* and notably *API* received a considerably more in-depth review, resulting in a negative opinion of the Court.[118]

51   The broad analysis that takes into account the market structure, behavioural freedom and efficiencies as well as public interest benefits may well reflect the actual pros and cons of a particular agreement. At the same time, it is likely to be an unwieldy instrument leading to results that may be hard to predict, offering limited legal certainty and significant enforcement and compliance costs. In this regard, EU competition law may be compared to **US antitrust** law in that both seek to provide very high predictability and limited enforcement costs for a category of particularly damaging forms of cooperation. Both systems do this by means of an enforcement shortcut, in US terminology often referred to as the *per se* restriction.[119] These fall under the heading of the object category in the framework of Article 101.1 TFEU. For other forms of cooperation, establishing restrictive effects involves a more complex and potentially uncertain appraisal with potentially higher costs for the Commission and undertakings involved, proving an infringement of Article 101.1 TFEU.

3.3.2. The Object Category

52   The Court has consistently held that the object and effect are alternatives in the text of Article 101 TFEU, leading to the conclusion that effects need not be established for actions that fall in the object category. This object category is often referred to as a list of **hard-core restrictions**.[120] In view of the (potential) difficulty of conducting a full-fledged effects analysis it should not come as a surprise that the Commission has been keen to categorise restrictions as by object. The first question, however, that has only fairly recently been given a clear answer is on what grounds and reasoning a certain form of conduct falls in the object category. In other words, what test determines whether cooperation classifies as a restriction by object?

53   In this regard, we first reiterate the findings of the Court in *Cartes Bancaires*, where it was asked to rule on the statement by the General Court that the object

---

[116] Case C-136/12, *Consiglio nazionale dei geologi* (CJEU 18 July 2013).

[117] Joined Cases C-184/13 et al., *API and others* (CJEU 11 September 2014).

[118] Case C-1/12, *Ordem dos Técnicos Oficiais de Contas* (CJEU 28 February 2013) para 96–100 and Joined Cases C-184/13 et al., *API and others* (CJEU 11 September 2014) para 51–57.

[119] Case C-413/14 P, *Intel Corporation Inc. v Commission* (Opinion of AG *Wahl* of 6 September 2017) para 42.

[120] Case C-439/09, *Pierre Fabre Dermo-Cosmétique* (CJEU 13 October 2011) para 32, 33, where the Court equates these terms. Note that this terminology may be part of an analogy between EU competition law and US antitrust law.

category should not be interpreted strictly.[121] The Court clearly disagreed and held that the **object category is to be interpreted restrictively**.[122] The criterion for determining whether a restriction qualifies as by object is the likelihood of a sufficient degree of harm to competition. Where experience shows that a form of coordination leads to inefficiency, there is no need to actually prove such effects.[123] This experience must be 'sufficiently reliable and robust', meaning that—for example—one enforcement decision by a single competition authority does not constitute such experience.[124]

The *test* to determine whether or not the *criterion* is satisfied requires taking into account, inter alia, the objectives of the cooperation and the **economic and legal context** of which it forms a part. As part of determining that context, it is also necessary to take into consideration the nature of the goods or services affected, as well as the real conditions of the functioning and structure of the market or markets in question.[125] This will be referred to as the **context test**. In view of its central role in determining which of the two routes that make up the bifurcation in Article 101 TFEU is to be followed, it merits further attention. 54

Starting with the **legal context** and the objectives of the cooperation, the Court's consistent case law holds that the intention of the parties is not a necessary factor for the applicability of Article 101 TFEU, but it can be taken into account.[126] In the most obviously harmful forms of cooperation, horizontal price-fixing cartels, the parties' intention will often be to eliminate the competition between the parties with the aim of increasing prices. This can be seen clearly in *Hoffmann-La Roche*, where two pharmaceutical companies were found to have colluded on the market for the sale of a drug that one of them had developed and licensed for a specific medical application to the other. When doctors started prescribing the version of the drug that retailed at a lower price, the licensing company, Hoffmann-La Roche, disseminated misleading information to disincentivise such off-label prescriptions. The purpose of this scheme was to increase the sales of the more expensive drug and thus increase income for the licence holder as well as licence fee income for Hoffmann-La Roche, which the Court classifies as a restriction by object.[127] 55

---

[121] Case C-67/13 P, *Groupement des Cartes Bancaires v Commission* (CJEU 11 September 2014) para 55.

[122] Case C-67/13 P, *Groupement des Cartes Bancaires v Commission* (CJEU 11 September 2014) para 58.

[123] Case C-286/13 P, *Dole Food Company Inc. and Dole Fresh Fruit Europe v Commission* (CJEU 19 March 2015) para 115.

[124] Case C-228/18, *Budapest Bank and Others* (CJEU 2 April 2020) para 76, in connection with Case C-228/18, *Budapest Bank and Others* (Opinion of AG *Bobek* of 5 September 2019) para 63–73.

[125] Case C-286/13 P, *Dole Food Company Inc. and Dole Fresh Fruit Europe v Commission* (CJEU 19 March 2015) para 117.

[126] Joined Cases C-501/06 P et al., *GlaxoSmithKline Services Unlimited v Commission* (ECJ 6 October 2009) para 58.

[127] C-179/16, *F. Hoffmann-La Roche* (CJEU 23 January 2018).

56 As regards the **economic context**, the starting point is often the characterisation of the relation between the parties as horizontal or vertical. In this regard, the Court has held that, although vertical agreements are often less damaging to competition compared to horizontal forms of cooperation, this does not exclude a restrictive object.[128] Following on from that, the Court appears to engage in what we call a manifest inappreciability test. In this test, which serves to exclude manifestly inappreciable restrictions, a short-form appreciability test is undertaken. This can be seen in *BIDS*, where the Court placed particular emphasis on the fact that the coordinated 25% reduction in capacity and 75% decrease in excess capacity at hand had the object to appreciably change the market structure.[129] This approach further ties in with the (earlier) case law, according to which coordination between undertakings with only a minimal market share fell outside the scope of Article 101.1 TFEU, irrespective of the fact that the agreement entailed market partitioning.[130]

57 One problem with the **context analysis** is that in some cases, the analysis employed by the Court shows a remarkable similarity to the analysis of restrictive effects, raising the question of what role is left for the latter if an effect analysis is to be undertaken as part of answering the question of whether there is a restriction by object or by effect. A prominent example of such a case is *Allianz*, where the Court was asked how to qualify a contract between insurance companies and car repair shops acting as intermediaries where the remuneration creates an incentive for the repair shops to promote the insurances provided by the companies they had a contract with. One of the methods suggested by the Court was to identify whether these contracts foreclosed market access in view of the structure of that market, the existence of alternative distribution channels and their respective importance, and the market power of the companies concerned.[131] It suffices to say that even a simple analysis of market power of one company entails an actually complex analysis as it involves a market definition and an analysis of the barriers to entry and of price elasticity.[132] The same holds for the Court's appraisal of selective distribution systems, where the prohibition of online retailing by a producer was qualified as a restriction by object, unless this prohibition could be objectively justified.[133] In this regard, the most prominent one concerns the trade-off between

---

[128] Case C-32/11, *Allianz Hungária Biztosító* (CJEU 14 March 2013) para 43.

[129] Case C-209/07, *Beef Industry Development Society and Barry Brothers* (CJEU 20 November 2008) para 31–33.

[130] Case 5/69, *Franz Völk v S.P.R.L. Ets J. Vervaecke* (ECJ 9 July 1969) para 7.

[131] Case C-32/11, *Allianz Hungária Biztosító* (CJEU 14 March 2013) para 48.

[132] The analysis in Case C-345/14, *Maxima Latvija* (CJEU 26 November 2015) para 22, 23, appears also to involve an appraisal of the foreclosure effect and/or the effects on downstream prices. Any sensible analysis of the effect on downstream prices requires an analysis of the competitive situation on that market together with an analysis of price elasticities.

[133] Case C-439/09, *Pierre Fabre Dermo-Cosmétique* (CJEU 13 October 2011) para 39–47.

price rigidity in selective distribution systems and combatting free riding in (pre-sales) advice.[134] Again, this type of balancing appraisal is invariably complex, difficult to reproduce and ill-suited for the framework of Article 101.1 TFEU. This is exemplified by *Coty*, which builds on *Pierre Fabre* to find that an online marketplace ban could be objectively justified in light of the luxurious nature of the products in question.[135] The assessment concerned the proportionality of the restrictive effects of a blanket online sales ban (*Pierre Fabre*) or a marketplace ban (*Coty*) in the light of the value presented by a prestigious image (*Pierre Fabre*) or a luxurious image (*Coty*).

To summarise, the Court is **narrowing the scope of the object category** to the obvious candidates where harm to competition, in particular in the form of inefficiencies to the detriment of consumers, can be assumed without a significant risk of false positives. In this regard, the Court's approach can be likened to that under Article 102 TFEU, where a prominent question is whether actual effects must be proven for certain types of abuse. The Commission attempts to provide more **legal certainty** under Article 101 TFEU by compiling lists of hard-core restrictions as the blacklists that form part of the block exemption regulations (→ para 71) or the exclusions to the *de minimis* Notice (→ para 45). These documents contain lists of what can be called the usual suspects: horizontal and vertical price fixing, output limitation and market sharing. Interestingly, the Commission's initially harsh stance on vertical price fixing is mitigated slightly in the Verticals Guidelines[136] but again narrowed in the Guidance on restrictions by object.[137] All in all, restrictions that are likely to be categorised under the object heading are generally caught by Article 101.1 TFEU, requiring an open and transparent procedure for legalisation pursuant to Article 101.3 TFEU or under the *Wouters* exception as regards the pursuance of certain public interests. The open and transparent nature of this procedure will then separate the restrictive chaff from the economically justified wheat.

3.4. Effect on Trade Between Member States

Article 101 TFEU, or any of the Treaty rules on competition for that matter, will only apply if there is an **effect on trade** between MS. The Court's approach in this regard was first set in *Consten & Grundig*, where the parties argued that their agreement had actually increased trade in the products concerned between Germany and France. This builds on the text of Article 101.1 TFEU, which requires

---

[134] This is what the Court refers to in para 40 of *Pierre Fabre*. See further Commission Guidelines *on Vertical Agreements*, O.J. C 130/16 (2010) para 64.

[135] Case C-230/16, *Coty Germany* (CJEU 6 December 2017), notably para 29–36 where the Court distinguishes *Coty* from the facts in *Pierre Fabre* and connects this to a proportionality assessment.

[136] Commission Guidelines *on Vertical Agreements*, O.J. C 130/16 (2010) para 223–229.

[137] Commission Staff Working Document, SWD(2014) 198 final, p. 16.

that trade must be affected, i.e. suggesting a negative effect. The Court gave short shrift to this argument and held that such positive effects do not exclude the applicability of Article 101.1 TFEU, in particular in view of the fact that the agreement concerned the import and parallel trade in goods between two MS.[138] This line of reasoning has been continued to include agreements involving a large percentage of the trade in a MS and covering its entire territory,[139] as well as agreements between companies in third countries insofar as these agreements had an effect on competition and trade in the internal market.[140] The bottom line is that, as a jurisdictional criterion, the requirement of an effect on trade between MS has functioned overwhelmingly in a way to bring cases within the European jurisdiction.

60   In this regard, a remarkable distinction can be seen when the Court's position is compared to that of the Commission. Whereas the Court has consistently kept to its wide and unclear definition,[141] the **Commission has sought to clarify and restrict this criterion in its guidelines.**[142] This can probably be explained by the fact that the Commission cooperates with the competition authorities of the MS in the European Competition Network when the latter enforce their national competition laws that are spontaneously harmonised with the European competition rules. As a result, the Commission is less hard-pressed to ensure uniformity in the interpretation of Article 101 (and Article 102) TFEU by means of claiming jurisdiction.

4. Justifications (Article 101.3 TFEU)

61   All conduct falling under the first paragraph is open to be **justified** under the third paragraph of Article 101 TFEU.[143] This means that four cumulative conditions must be satisfied: firstly, the cooperation must result in technical or economic progress or lead to better production or distribution. Basically, it entails objective efficiency gains arising from the cooperation.[144] In order to ensure that economic efficiencies that only benefit the parties to the agreement do not qualify, the Treaty requires, secondly, a fair share for consumers in the benefit identified under the first criterion. The third criterion intends to ensure the proportionality of the restrictions

---

[138] Joined Cases 56 and 58/64, *Consten and Grundig v Commission* (ECJ 13 July 1966) p. 341.

[139] Case 8/72, *Vereeniging van Cementhandelaren v Commission* (ECJ 17 October 1972) para 29.

[140] Joined Cases 89/85 et al., *A. Ahlström Osakeyhtiö and others v Commission* (Woodpulp) (ECJ 20 January 1994) para 13–16.

[141] Joined Cases C-295/04 to C-298/04, *Vincenzo Manfredi* (ECJ 13 July 2006) para 41–51.

[142] O.J. C 101/81 (2004).

[143] Case T-17/93, *Matra Hachette SA v Commission* (CFI 15 July 1994) para 85.

[144] Joined Cases 56 and 58/64, *Consten and Grundig v Commission* (ECJ 13 July 1966) p. 348. This can, for example, be interpreted to include environmental benefits, see Commission Decision 2000/475 *CECED*, O.J. L 187/47 (2000). The Court has furthermore condoned that employment considerations are taken into account, Case T-17/93, *Matra Hachette SA v Commission* (CFI 15 July 1994) para 139.

in view of the objectives set out under the first criterion. The fourth requirement ensures that sufficient residual competition remains.[145]

The application of Article 101.3 TFEU raises several difficulties that are of a fundamental nature. Firstly, the question arises of how exact and certain the **benefits** taken into account under the first paragraph must be. Imperfect information underlies many business decisions, and as a result, the "technical and economic progress" may be difficult to substantiate *ex ante*, whereas the (effects of) the restriction of competition may be more readily accepted on the basis of past experiences.[146] Secondly, the application of this provision may entail a transfer of welfare between groups of persons, where the costs arising from a restriction of competition accrue in another group than that which benefits from the fair share. The General Court's approach in *Asnef* suggests a consumer welfare standard where negative effects for some consumers can be balanced with positive effects for others and thus still guarantee a fair share for consumers.[147] Finally, the open wording of the **proportionality test** raises the question of which specific sub-test or tests (suitability (i.e. causality), necessity or proportionality *stricto sensu*[148]) apply. 62

The Commission possessed the exclusive right to apply Article 101.3 TFEU until 1 May 2004, at which time Regulation 1/2003 entered into application. The exemption decisions adopted pursuant to the predecessor of that Regulation (Regulation 17 of 1962) have **limited precedential value** nowadays. Coupled with the fact that there is **hardly any recent decision** applying the third paragraph, as well as the fact that the Commission arguably has limited the scope of this provision compared to its earlier decision-making,[149] this means that there is very limited guidance on the boundaries of policy under this provision.[150] 63

This sits uneasily with the Court's acknowledgement that this provision is directly effective, i.e. to be applied by the parties to an agreement and by a (national) court asked for a ruling on the compatibility of an agreement with Article 101 TFEU.[151] 64

In practice, this means that Article 101.3 TFEU has its most prominent and practically relevant application in the form of **block exemption regulations**. These are the regulations that declare this provision applicable to entire categories of agreements, subject to conditions. By and large, these conditions concern a market 65

---

[145] Note that this is a narrower concept than that of dominance, e.g. Case T-395/94, *Atlantic Container Line AB and Others v Commission* (CFI 28 February 2002) para 330.

[146] See on this Case T-168/01, *GlaxoSmithKline Services Unlimited v Commission* (CFI 27 September 2006) para 247–249, upheld on appeal in Joined Cases C-501/06 P et al., *Glaxo-Smith-Kline Services Unlimited v Commission* (ECJ 6 October 2009).

[147] Case C-238/05, *Asnef-Equifax* (ECJ 23 November 2006) para 68–71.

[148] Case C-331/88, *The Queen v Minister of Agriculture, Fisheries and Food and Secretary of State for Health, ex parte: Fedesa and others* (ECJ 13 November 1990) para 13.

[149] Cf. Hancher and Lugard (2004).

[150] The Commission has, however, issued various notices providing guidance on the Commission's assessment, e.g. O.J. C 101/97 (2004).

[151] Case C-439/09, *Pierre Fabre Dermo-Cosmétique* (CJEU 13 October 2011) para 49.

share cap (often referred to as the safe haven) and a blacklist of clauses that remove the block exemption benefit for the entire agreement or the specific clause. In view of the difficulty of applying Article 101.3 TFEU in individual cases, the Court has indicated that the practice of first checking compliance with a block exemption regulation complies with EU law.[152] Given that a block exemption constitutes an exception to the general rule that restrictions of competition are prohibited, it requires a narrow interpretation.[153]

5. Automatic Nullity (Article 101.2 TFEU) and the Enforcement of Article 101 TFEU

66 Article 101.2 TFEU provides for the **automatic nullity** of all agreements that fall under the first paragraph without meeting the conditions set out in the third paragraph. The Court has consistently held that the civil law effects of this sanction, such as deciding on the severability of certain clauses, are a matter for the national civil law of the MS,[154] provided that this law complies with the principles of equivalence and effectiveness.[155] Notably, the latter principle has had a profound effect in relation to the national law consequences of both public law[156] and private law enforcement of Article 101 TFEU.[157]

67 It is precisely this enforcement that drives much of the substance of Article 101 TFEU, such as the need to define and confine a category of restrictions by object that does not require a cumbersome appraisal of effects. At the same time, an overly broadly construed prohibition may well result in **over-enforcement**, potentially triggering an overly cautious self-assessment by the undertakings that seek to cooperate, for example in order to attain efficiencies.

68 A close corollary to the nullity is the **liability for damages**. Though not confined to the parties to the agreement, the liability of parties to an agreement that is illegal under Article 101 TFEU is also construed as a **civil law sanction** designed to incentivise compliance with that provision. It was originally encouraged by the European Commission in the form of a small paragraph at the end of the press release issued at the publication of an infringement decision, but it is now the subject of the Damages Directive as well as considerable judicial activity.[158] Preliminary references have already been made on various issues arising mostly from the interaction between the national procedural rules and the EU law

---

[152] Case C-260/07, *Pedro IV Servicios SL v Total España* (ECJ 2 April 2009) para 36.

[153] Case C-70/93, *Bayerische Motorenwerke v ALD* (ECJ 24 October 1995) para 28.

[154] Case 319/82, *Société de vente de ciments v Kerpen & Kerpen* (ECJ 14 December 1983) para 11.

[155] Case C-453/99, *Courage and Crehan* (ECJ 20 September 2001) para 21–27.

[156] This is primarily done by the European Commission on the basis of Regulation 1/2003, O.J. L 1/1 (2003).

[157] For a fuller overview and discussion see Bovis and Clarke (2015), pp. 49–71.

[158] For a succinct overview see Jones et al. (2019), pp. 1021–1022.

centred on maximising the effectiveness of Article 101 TFEU by means of civil liability.[159]

List of Cases

ECJ/CJEU

ECJ 30.06.1966, 56/65, *Société minière et technique v Maschinenbau Ulm*, ECLI:EU:C:1966:38 [cit. in para 30]

ECJ 13.07.1966, 56 and 58/64, *Consten and Grundig*, ECLI:EU:C:1966:41 [cit. in para 8, 28, 59, 61]

ECJ 09.07.1969, 5/69, *Franz Völk v S.P.R.L. Ets J. Vervaecke*, ECLI:EU:C:1969:35 [cit. in para 45, 56]

ECJ 25.11.1971, 22/71, *Béguelin Import v S.A.G.L. Import Export*, ECLI:EU:C:1971:113 [cit. in para 26, 41]

ECJ 14.07.1972, 48/69, *Imperial Chemical Industries Ltd. (Dyestuffs)*, ECLI:EU:C:1972:70 [cit. in para 19, 41]

ECJ 17.10.1972, Case 8/7, *Vereeniging van Cementhandelaren*, ECLI:EU:C:1972:84 [cit. in para 59]

ECJ 21.02.1973, 6/72, *Continental Can v Commission*, ECLI:EU:C:1973:22 [cit. in para 7]

ECJ 27.03.1974, 127/73, *BRT v SABAM*, ECLI:EU:C:1974:6 [cit. in para 10]

ECJ 16.12.1975, 40/73 et al., *Suiker Unie and Others*, ECLI:EU:C:1975:174 [cit. in para 18]

ECJ 25.10.1977, 26/76, *Metro v Commission*, ECLI:EU:C:1977:167 [cit. in para 11, 42, 46, 48]

ECJ 14.02.1978, 27/76, *United Brands*, ECLI:EU:C:1978:22 [cit. in para 11, 33, 37]

ECJ 08.06.1982, 258/78, *Nungesser*, ECLI:EU:C:1982:211 [cit. in para 48]

ECJ 07.06.1983, 100 to 103/80, *SA Musique Diffusion française and others*, ECLI:EU:C:1983:158 [cit. in para 21]

ECJ 14.12.1983, 319/82, *Société de vente de ciments v Kerpen & Kerpen*, ECLI:EU:C:1983:374 [cit. in para 66]

ECJ 11.07.1985, 42/84, *Remia BV and others*, ECLI:EU:C:1985:327 [cit. in para 48]

---

[159] E.g. Joined Cases C-295-298/04, *Vincenzo Manfredi v Lloyd Adriatico Assicurazioni SpA, Antonio Cannito v Fondiaria Sai SpA and Nicolò Tricarico and Pasqualina Murgolo v Assitalia SpA.* (ECJ 13 July 2006), Case C-360/09, *Pfleiderer AG v Bundeskartellamt* (CJEU 14 June 2011), Case C-199/11, *Europese Gemeenschap v Otis et al.* (CJEU 6 November 2012), Case C-536/11, *Bundeswettbewerbsbehörde v Donau Chemie et al.* (CJEU 6 June 2013), Case C-557/12, *Kone AG et al. v ÖBB-Infrastruktur AG* (CJEU 5 June 2014) and Case C-724/17, *Skanska Industrial Solutions* (CJEU 13 March 2019). Several other cases concerning these matters have just been ruled on, e.g., Case C-882/19, *Sumal* (CJEU 6 October 2021).

ECJ 28.01.1986, 161/84, *Pronuptia*, ECLI:EU:C:1986:41 [cit. in para 41, 42, 48]
ECJ 27.01.1987, 45/85, *Verband der Sachversicherer e.V.*, ECLI:EU:C:1987:34 [cit. in para 17]
ECJ 16.06.1987, 118/85, *Commission v Italy (AAMS)*, ECLI:EU:C:1987:283 [cit. in para 23]
ECJ 19.04.1988, 27/87, *SPRL Louis Erauw-Jacquery*, ECLI:EU:C:1988:183 [cit. in para 48]
ECJ 21.9.1988, 267/86, *Van Eycke v ASPA*, ECLI:EU:C:1988:427 [cit. in para 6]
ECJ 13.11.1990, C-331/88, *The Queen v Minister of Agriculture, Fisheries and Food and Secretary of State for Health, ex parte: Fedesa and others*, ECLI:EU:C:1990:391 [cit. in para 62]
ECJ 28.02.1991, C-234/89, *Stergios Delimitis v Henninger Bräu AG*, ECLI:EU:C:1991:91 [cit. in para 47]
ECJ 23.04.1991, C-41/90, *Höfner & Elser*, ECLI:EU:C:1991:161 [cit. in para 23]
ECJ 31.03.1993, C-89/85, C-104/85 et al., *A. Ahlström Osakeyhtiö and others*, ECLI:EU:C:1993:120 [cit. in para 19]
ECJ 19.01.1994, C-364/92, *SAT Fluggesellschaft mbH*, ECLI:EU:C:1994:7 [cit. in para 25]
ECJ 20.01.1994, C-89/85 et al., *A. Ahlström Osakeyhtiö and others* (Woodpulp), ECLI:EU:C:1988:447 [cit. in para 59]
ECJ 15.12.1994, C-250/92, *Gøttrup-Klim and Others Grovvareforeninger*, ECLI:EU:C:1994:413 [cit. in para 42, 48]
ECJ 24.10.1995, C-70/93, *Bayerische Motorenwerke*, ECLI:EU:C:1995:344 [cit. in para 66]
ECJ 12.12.1995, C-399/93, *H. G. Oude Luttikhuis and others*, ECLI:EU:C:1995:434 [cit. in para 41]
ECJ 24.10.1996, C-73/95 P, *Viho Europe BV*, ECLI:EU:C:1996:405 [cit. in para 26]
ECJ 18.03.1997, C-343/95, *Diego Calì & Figli Srl v Servizi ecologici porto di Genova SpA*, ECLI:EU:C:1997:160 [cit. in para 25]
ECJ 08.07.1999, C-49/92 P, *Commission v Anic Partecipazioni SpA*, ECLI:EU:C:1999:356 [cit. in para 18, 20]
ECJ 08.07.1999, C-199/92 P, *Hüls*, ECLI:EU:C:1999:358 [cit. in para 20]
ECJ 21.09.1999, C-67/96, *Albany*, EU:C:1999:430 [cit. in para 9]
ECJ 12.09.2000, C-180/98 to C-184/98, *Pavlov and Others*, ECLI:EU:C:2000:428 [cit. in para 9, 46]
ECJ 14.12.2000, C-344/98, *Masterfoods and HB*, ECLI:EU:C:2000:689 [cit. in para 47]
ECJ 07.12.2000, C-214/99, *Neste*, ECLI:EU:C:2000:679 [cit. in para 47]
ECJ 20.09.2001, C-453/99, *Courage and Crehan*, ECLI:EU:C:2001:465 [cit. in para 7, 66]
ECJ 19.02.2002, C-309/99, *Wouters and Others*, ECLI:EU:C:2002:98 [cit. in para 50]
ECJ 09.09.2003, C-198/01, *CIF*, ECLI:EU:C:2003:430 [cit. in para 26]

ECJ 18.09.2003, C-338/00 P, *Volkswagen AG*, ECLI:EU:C:2003:473 [cit. in para 31]
ECJ 06.01.2004, C-2/01 P and C-3/01 P, *BAI and Commission v Bayer AG*, ECLI:EU:C:2004:2 [cit. in para 13]
ECJ 13.07.2006, C-295/04 to C-298/04, *Vincenzo Manfredi*, ECLI:EU:C:2006:461 [cit. in para 60]
ECJ 18.07.2006, C-519/04, *David Meca-Medina and Igor Majcen*, ECLI:EU:C:2006:492 [cit. in para 50]
ECJ 23.11.2006, C-238/05, *Asnef-Equifax*, ECLI:EU:C:2006:734 [cit. in para 45, 68]
ECJ 11.09.2008, C-279/06, *CEPSA*, ECLI:EU:C:2008:485 [cit. in para 13]
ECJ 20.11.2008, C-209/07, *Beef Industry Development Society and Barry Brothers*, EU:C:2008:643 [cit. in para 56]
ECJ 05.03.2009, C-350/07, *Kattner Stahlbau*, ECLI:EU:C:2009:127 [cit. in para 24]
ECJ 04.06.2009, C-8/08, *T-Mobile Netherlands and Others*, ECLI:EU:C:2009:343 [cit. in para 15, 20]
ECJ 10.09.2009, C-97/08, P *Akzo Nobel NV and Others*, ECLI:EU:C:2009:536 [cit. in para 26]
ECJ 24.09.2009, C-125/07 P et al., *Erste Group Bank AG and Others*, ECLI:EU:C:2009:576 [cit. in para 31].
ECJ 06.10.2009, C-501/06 P et al., *GlaxoSmithKline Services Unlimited*, ECLI:EU:C:2009:610 [cit. in para 11, 43, 55, 62]
CJEU 17.02.2011, C-52/09, *TeliaSonera Sverige*, ECLI:EU:C:2011:83 [cit. in para 7]
CJEU 03.03.2011, C-437/09, *AG2R Prévoyance*, ECLI:EU:C:2011:112 [cit. in para 24]
CJEU 13.10.2011, C-439/09, *Pierre Fabre Dermo-Cosmétique*, ECLI:EU:C:2011:649 [cit. in para 64]
CJEU 13.12.2012, C-226/11, *Expedia Inc. v Autorité de la concurrence*, ECLI:EU:C:2012:795 [cit. in para 10]
CJEU 28.02.2013, C-1/12, *Ordem dos Técnicos Oficiais de Contas*, ECLI:EU:C:2013:127 [cit. in para 50]
CJEU 14.03.2013, C-32/11, *Allianz Hungária Biztosító*, ECLI:EU:C:2013:160 [cit. in para 56, 57]
CJEU 18.07.2013, C-136/12, *Consiglio nazionale dei geologi v Autorità garante della concorrenza e del mercato*, ECLI:EU:C:2013:489 [cit. in para 50]
CJEU 06.09.2014, C-413/14 P, Opinion of AG Wahl, *Intel Corporation Inc. v Commission*, ECLI:EU:C:2016:788 [cit. in para 51]
CJEU 11.09.2014, C-382/12 P, *MasterCard,* ECLI:EU:C:2014:2201 [cit. in para 30]
CJEU 11.09.2014, C-67/13 P, *Groupement des Cartes Bancaires*, EU:C:2014:2204 [cit. in para 28, 53]
CJEU 11.09.2014, C-184/13 et al., *API and others*, ECLI:EU:C:2014:2147 [cit. in para 50]

CJEU 04.12.2014, C-413/13, *FNV Kunsten Informatie en Media*, ECLI:EU:C:2014:2411 [cit. in para 9]
CJEU 19.03.2015, C-286/13 P, *Dole Food Company Inc. and Dole Fresh Fruit*, ECLI:EU:C:2015:184 [cit. in para 20]
CJEU 30.04.2015, C-231/14 P, Opinion of AG Wathelet, *InnoLux Corp.*, ECLI:EU:C:2015:292 [cit. in para 41]
CJEU 22.10.2015, C-194/14 P, *AC-Treuhand AG*, ECLI:EU:C:2015:717 [cit. in para 16]
CJEU 26.11.2015, C-345/14, *Maxima Latvija*, ECLI:EU:C:2015:784 [cit. in para 57]
CJEU 06.09.2017, C-413/14 P, *Intel Corporation Inc.*, ECLI:EU:C:2016:788 [cit. in para 51]
CJEU 14.11.2017, C-671/15, *APVE and Others*, ECLI:EU:C:2017:860 [cit. in para 9]
CJEU 06.12.2017, C-230/16, *Coty Germany*, ECLI:EU:C:2017:941 [cit. in para 57]
CJEU 23.01.2018, C-179/16, *F. Hoffmann-La Roche*, ECLI:EU:C:2018:25 [cit. in para 55]
CJEU 14.03.2019, C-724/17, *Skanska Industrial Solutions*, ECLI:EU:C:2019:204 [cit. in para 22, 68]
CJEU 05.09.2019, C-228/18, Opinion of AG Bobek, *Budapest Bank and Others*, ECLI:EU:C:2019:678 [cit. in para 53]
CJEU 02.04.2020, C-228/18, *Budapest Bank and Others*, ECLI:EU:C:2020:265 [cit. in para 53]
CJEU 06.10.2021, C-882/19, *Sumal*, ECLI:EU:C:2021:800 [cit. in para 68]

CFI/GC
CFI 15.07.1994, T-17/93, *Matra Hachette SA*, ECLI:EU:T:1994:89 [cit. in para 67]
CFI 11.03.1999, T-141/94, *Thyssen Stahl AG*, ECLI:EU:T:1999:48 [cit. in para 1]
CFI 15.09.1998, T-374/94, *European Night Services Ltd (ENS) and Others*, ECLI:EU:T:1998:198 [cit. in para 45]
CFI 28.02.2002, T-395/94, *Atlantic Container Line AB and Others*, ECLI:EU:T:2002:49 [cit. in para 67]
CFI 22.03.2000, T-125/97 and T-127/97, *Coca-Cola*, ECLI:EU:T:2000:84 [cit. in para 34]
CFI 12.07.2001, T-202/98, *Tate & Lyle and Others*, ECLI:EU:T:2001:185 [cit. in para 15]
CFI 03.12.2003, T-208/01, *Volkswagen*, ECLI:EU:T:2003:326 [cit. in para 14]
CFI 02.05.2006, T-328/03, *O2 (Germany) v Commission*, ECLI:EU:T:2006:116 [cit. in para 30]
CFI 27.09.2006, T-168/01, *GlaxoSmithKline Services Unlimited*, ECLI:EU:T:2006:265 [cit. in para 62]
CFI 14.12.2006, T-259/02 to T-264/02 and T-271/02, *Raiffeisen Zentralbank Österreich*, ECLI:EU:T:2006:396 [cit. in para 31]

CFI 08.07.2008, T-99/04, *AC-Treuhand*, ECLI:EU:T:2008:256 [cit. in para 16]
GC 12.04.2013, T-442/08, *CISAC*, ECLI:EU:T:2013:188 [cit. in para 19]
GC 10.11.2017, T-180/15, *Icap plc*, ECLI:EU:T:2017:795 [cit. in para 16]

U.S. Supreme Court

US Supreme Court, 11.06.1956, *United States v. E. I. du Pont de Nemours & Co.*, 351 U.S. 377 [cit. in para 34]
US Supreme Court, 28.06.2007, *Leegin Creative Leather Products, Inc. v. PSKS, Inc.*, 551 U.S. 877 [cit. in para 49]
US Supreme Court, 21.06.2021, *National Collegiate Athletic Assn. v. Alston et al.*, 594 U. S. (2021) [cit. in para 50]

References[160]

Baumol, W. J., Panzar, J. C., & Willig, R. D. (1982). *Contestable markets and the theory of industry structure*. Harcourt Brace Jovanovich.
Bishop, S., & Walker, M. (2010). *The economics of EC competition law*. Sweet & Maxwell.
Bork, R. (1978). *The antitrust paradox*. Free Press.
Bovis, C. H., & Clarke, C. M. (2015). Private enforcement of EU competition law. *Liverpool Law Review, 36*, 49–71.
Faull, J., & Nikpay, A. (2007). *The EU law of competition*. OUP.
Franck, J.-U., & Peitz, M. (2021). Market definition in the platform economy, CRC TR 224 Discussion Paper Series 2021. Retrieved from SSRN: https://ssrn.com/abstract=3773774 / https://doi.org/10.2139/ssrn.3773774
Gallo, D. (2020). Functional approach and economic activity in EU competition law, today: The case of social security and healthcare. *European Public Law*, 569–586.
Hancher, L., & Lugard, P. (2004). Honey, I shrunk the article! A critical assessment of the Commission's notice on Article 81 (3) of the EC Treaty. *European Competition Law Review*, 410–420.
Hildebrand, D. (2002). The European school in EC competition law. *World Competition, 25*(1), 3–23.
Joliet, R. (1967). *The rule of reason in antitrust law, American, German and Common Market laws in comparative perspective*. Nijhoff.
Jones, A. (2006). Analysis of agreements under U.S. and EC antitrust law – convergence or divergence? *Antitrust Bulletin*, 691–811.
Jones, A., Sufrin, B. E., & Dunne, N. (2019). *Jones and Sufrin's EU competition law - text, cases, and materials* (7th ed.). OUP.
Mestmäcker, E. J., & Schweitzer, H. (Eds.). (2014). *Europäisches Wettbewerbsrecht*. C.H. Beck.
Milgrom, P., & Roberts, J. (1982). Limit pricing and entry under incomplete information: An equilibrium analysis. *Econometrica, 50*(2), 443–459.
Ortiz Blanco, L. (2012). *Market power in EU antitrust law*. Hart Publishing.

---

[160] All Internet sources cited in this comment have been accessed on 13 August 2022.

Sadowska, M., & Willems, B. (2013). Market integration and economic efficiency at conflict? Commitments in the Swedish interconnectors case. *World Competition*, 99–132.

Townley, C. (2009). *Article 81 EC and public policy*. Hart Publishing.

Wendt, E. (2013). *EU competition law and liberal professions: An uneasy relationship?* Nijhoff.

Whelan, P. (2007). Private enforcement and Commission decisions: The Crehan case. *Cambridge Student Law Review*, 108.

Article 102 [Prohibition of Abuses of a Dominant Position]
(ex-Article 82 TEC)

Any abuse[40–88] by one or more undertakings of a dominant position[10–36] within the internal market or in a substantial part of it[2] shall be prohibited as incompatible with the internal market[6] in so far as it may affect trade between Member States.

Such abuse may, in particular, consist in:

(a) directly or indirectly imposing unfair purchase or selling prices or other unfair trading conditions;[55–61]
(b) limiting production, markets or technical development to the prejudice of consumers;[59]
(c) applying dissimilar conditions to equivalent transactions with other trading parties, thereby placing them at a competitive disadvantage;[60]
(d) making the conclusion of contracts subject to acceptance by the other parties of supplementary obligations which, by their nature or according to commercial usage, have no connection with the subject of such contracts.[75–78]

Contents

1.	Introduction		1
2.	Treaty Framework		5
3.	Dominance		10
	3.1.	Market Shares	14
	3.2.	Other Factors	16
		3.2.1. Legal Factors	19
		3.2.2. Factors Relating to the Undertaking	21
		3.2.3. Market Factors	25
		3.2.4. Independence from Customers and Consumers: Countervailing Powers	31
	3.3.	Collective Dominance	33
4.	Special Responsibility		37
5.	Abuse		40
	5.1.	General Definition	43
	5.2.	The Test and Required Evidence for Proving Abuse	49
	5.3.	Exploitative Abuses	53
		5.3.1. Unfair Excessive Prices	54
		5.3.2. Other Unfair Trading Conditions	59
	5.4.	Exclusionary Abuses	60
		5.4.1. Price Discrimination	61
		5.4.2. Predatory Pricing	62
		5.4.3. Margin Squeezes	65
		5.4.4. Refusals to Deal and Essential Facilities	68
		5.4.5. Tying and Bundling	74
		5.4.6. Exclusive Dealing	78
		5.4.7. Rebates	81
		5.4.8. Other Forms of Abuse	88

List of Cases
References

1. Introduction

1   Article 102 TFEU **prohibits the anti-competitive behaviour of dominant undertakings**.[1] It restricts the autonomy of economic actors that qualify as dominant, forcing them to adapt their actions to the lessened degree of competition on the dominated market.[2] Alongside Article 101 TFEU and Regulation 139/2004, it is another tool in the shed of EU and national competition authorities so as to ensure competitive markets within the internal market.

2   The text of Article 102 TFEU can be deconstructed into **five relevant textual elements**: abuse, one or more undertakings, dominance, a substantial part of the internal market[3] and effect on inter-State trade. The concepts of an undertaking, and of the effect on inter-State trade, have been addressed in the chapter on Article 101 TFEU, and their applications are equal to the eponyms in Article 102 TFEU.[4]

3   The provision, however, revolves around **two central concepts**: dominance and abuse.[5] These concepts form the core challenge in Article 102 TFEU's administration, namely striking the right balance between legal certainty and foreseeability on the one hand and adaptation to new legal and economic insights as well as changes in markets, notably digital markets, on the other. At the same time, the administration of Article 102 TFEU requires a balance between freedom of contract and right

---

[1] Where 'undertaking' is used in this contribution, 'group of undertakings' can be read as Article 102 TFEU prohibits abusive conduct by 'one or more undertakings in a dominant position' (→ para 33–36).

[2] Schröter and Bartl, in von der Groeben et al. (2015), Article 102 AEUV para 35–36. The creation of dominance may be subject to competition law by means of the Merger Control Regulation, Council Regulation (EC) No. 139/2004 *on the control of concentrations between undertakings*, O.J. L 24/1 (2004).

[3] This concept is not found in Article 101 TFEU and basically coincides with the required effect on trade between MS in that it entails a threshold below which EU competition law no longer applies, whereas national equivalents of Article 102 TFEU may apply. The territory of one MS, Case T-228/97, *Irish Sugar v Commission* (CFI 7 October 1999), para 99, a region (*Bundesland*), Case C-475/99, *Ambulanz Glöckner* (ECJ 25 October 2001), para 38, and a significant (air)port facility, Case C-179/90, *Merci convenzionali porto di Genova SpA v Siderurgica Gabrielli SpA* (ECJ 10 December 1991), para 15, and Commission Decision No. 95/364/EC, *Zaventem*, O.J. L 216/8 (1995), para 9, have been found substantial parts. As regards the relevant test, see Joined Cases 40/73 et al., *Suiker Unie and Others v Commission* (ECJ 16 December 1975), para 371.

[4] See for their mutual applicability, for the concept of undertaking, Case C-41/90, *Höfner and Elser v Macrotron* (ECJ 23 April 1991), para 21, for the substantial part of the internal market, Case 322/81, *Michelin v Commission* (ECJ 9 November 1983), para 28, or Case 7/82, *GVL v Commission* (ECJ 2 March 1983), para 44, and for the effect on inter-state trade Joined Cases 56 and 58/64, *Consten and Grundig v Commission* (ECJ 13 July 1966) p. 341.

[5] Note that these have remained unchanged since their introduction as Article 86 TEEC. At its core, however, the Article can even be traced back further, to Article 66.7 TECSC, handing the High Authority a right to recommend changes of dominant undertakings' behaviour contrary to the then goals of the ECSC Treaty. See also Schröter and Bartl, in von der Groeben et al. (2015), Article 102 AEUV para 2.

to property, on the one hand, and the need for well-functioning markets, at both shorter and longer terms, on the other.[6]

This chapter focuses on the two central elements of Article 102 TFEU. In the parts that follow, the first part analyses Article 102 TFEU as part of the structure of the Treaties; the second part analyses the concept of dominance, followed by a third part on special responsibility and, last, a part on the elements constituting abuse.[7]

2. Treaty Framework

Article 102 TFEU forms **part of primary EU competition law**. It falls within the title governing common rules on competition, taxation and approximation of laws, in the chapter on competition, the section on rules applying to undertakings. No specific secondary law has been issued by the Union legislature for Article 102 TFEU.[8] The Commission has recently published a proposal for a Digital Markets Act, which contains some rules to complement the existing competition rules and notably Article 102 TFEU.[9]

Abuse by dominant undertakings is 'prohibited as incompatible with the internal market', which shows the function of Article 102 TFEU, similar to Article 101 TFEU, of **creating and maintaining the internal market**.[10]

---

[6] Case C-152/19 P, *Deutsche Telekom AG v Commission* (CJEU 25 March 2021), para 46–47.

[7] It is a legal practice to first establish dominance following which abuse may be investigated, Commission Communication, *Guidance on the Commission's enforcement priorities in applying Article 82 of the EC Treaty to abusive exclusionary conduct by dominant undertakings*, O.J. C 45/7 (2009) p. 8, point 9.

[8] It may be noted the Merger Control Regulation (EC) No. 139/2004 establishes the creation or strengthening of dominance as part of its substantive test, Article 2.2 of the Regulation. In recital 32 of the preamble to the Merger Control Regulation, market problems are not expected when the market share of the firms involved in a concentration remains below 25%. A comparison could further be made with secondary law for Articles 101.1 and 101.3 TFEU. The Commission exempts vertical restraints between suppliers and customers from Article 101.1 TFEU if both parties have a 30% or lower individual market share, see Articles 2.1 and 3 of Regulation 330/2010. As the preamble indicates, such agreements are presumed to have pro-competitive consequences: above the 30% threshold, this presumption is removed. The legislature appears to filter in some sort of *de minimis* for undertakings in a vertical relationship here. Below 30% market share, the Commission does not deem it necessary to enforce the competition rules. Cf. Case 66/86, *Ahmed Saeed Flugreisen and Silver Line Reisebüro GmbH v Zentrale zur Bekämpfung unlauteren Wettbewerbs e.V.* (ECJ 11 April 1989), para 37.

[9] See Proposal *for a regulation of the European Parliament and of the Council on contestable and fair markets in the digital sector*, COM(2020) 842 final (Digital Markets Act).

[10] Case 85/76, *Hoffmann-La Roche v Commission* (ECJ 13 February 1979), para 132, and Case 6/72, *Europemballage Corporation and Continental Can Company Inc. v Commission* (ECJ 21 February 1973), para 25.

Furthermore, in accordance with Protocol No. 27 on the internal market and competition,[11] the competition rules, and thus Article 102 TFEU, have as their aim to ensure a system of undistorted competition in the internal market.[12]

7 The **relationship between Articles 101 and 102 TFEU** is one of **complementarity**. Articles 101 and 102 TFEU can apply to the same set of facts, as the Court already stressed in *Consten & Grundig*.[13] Furthermore, in *Hoffmann-La Roche*, the Court clarified that agreements that are eligible for exemption under Article 101.3 TFEU might still face enforcement under Article 102 TFEU.[14] Therefore, a full legal assessment should incorporate a check for the application of both provisions. In addition, Article 102 TFEU can be applied to situations of coordinated behaviour between two or more undertakings insofar as these qualify as collectively dominant.[15]

8 Structurally, **the clauses differ**. For instance, contrary to Article 101 TFEU, Article 102 TFEU neither has a nullity sanction[16] nor a justification clause.[17] However, conduct amounting to a *prima facie* abuse of dominance can be objectively justified.[18] This integrates into Article 102 TFEU elements of what in the framework of Article 101 TFEU are called ancillary restraints (→ Article 101 TFEU para 47).

---

[11] With the change introduced by the Treaty of Lisbon, the explicit reference to the 'system ensuring that competition in the internal market is not distorted' (see Article 3.1. point (g) TEC) was supplanted by Protocol (No 27) *on the internal market and competition*, and was replaced in substance by Article 3.1 point (b) TFEU. Also, Case C-52/09, *TeliaSonera Sverige* (CJEU 15 January 2011), para 20–22 (→ Article 101 TFEU para 5). See also Buendia Sierra (2014), para 6.05–6.06.

[12] This is also shown by the location of Article 102 in Section 1 of Chapter 1 of Title VII, concerning the *common* competition rules applying to undertakings.

[13] Joined Cases 56 and 58/64, *Consten and Grundig* (ECJ 13 July 1966) p. 339. Reiterated recently in Case C-307/18, *Generics UK v Competition and Markets Authority* (CJEU 30 January 2020), para 146. See also de la Mano et al. (2014), pp. 331–332.

[14] Case 85/76, *Hoffmann-La Roche v Commission* (ECJ 13 February 1979), para 116.

[15] See further, on collective dominance → para 33–36.

[16] In MS' competition laws, only Article 9.2 of the Polish Act on Competition and Consumer Protection, contains a nullity clause, stating: '[I]egal transactions which constitute abuse of a dominant position shall be in their entirety or in the respective part void'. Cf. Burrichter (2008), p. 243. See also Schröter and Bartl, in von der Groeben et al. (2015), Article 102 AEUV para 3–16, and Jung, in Grabitz et al. (2022), Article 102 AEUV para 22–27 (released in 2015).

[17] Furthermore, whereas Article 101.3 TFEU historically had been governed by an exemption regime governed by the European Commission, Article 102 TFEU never contained such exemption possibilities. See Case 66/86, *Ahmed Saeed Flugreisen and Silver Line Reisebüro GmbH v Zentrale zur Bekämpfung unlauteren Wettbewerbs e.V.* (ECJ 11 April 1989), para 32, and Joined Cases C-395 and C-396/96 P, *Compagnie maritime belge transports and others v Commission* (ECJ 16 March 2000), para 135.

[18] The objective justification possibility was introduced by the Court in Case 27/76, *United Brands v Commission* (ECJ 14 February 1978), para 236. A more specific indication was given in, for instance, Case C-333/94 P, *Tetra Pak v Commission* (ECJ 14 November 1996), para 37. Cf. Rousseva (2010), p. 259. Also Mestmäcker and Schweitzer (2014), § 2 para 50–60. See also Van der Vijver (2012).

Article 102 TFEU can only be applied to undertakings. Nevertheless, MS are obliged to ensure the full effectiveness of the Treaty provisions, in accordance with the **duty of sincere cooperation**, as enshrined in Article 4.3 TEU.[19] This duty includes the competition rules.[20] As such, the Treaty obliges MS not to take measures that would result in abuses of dominant positions by undertakings. In a direct manner, Articles 37 and 106 TFEU provide for *leges speciales* for MS concerning measures related to **State monopolies**, other public undertakings or undertakings with exclusive rights.[21] Indirectly, the Court stated in *INNO v ATAB* that the MS' duty of sincere or loyal cooperation extends to private undertakings as well.[22] Hence, theoretically, the Commission could start Article 258 TFEU infringement proceedings *vis-à-vis* MS for allowing a private firm to infringe Article 102 TFEU. However, no specific case has risen dealing with the issue, also because most cases are subsumed under Article 106 TFEU.[23]

3. Dominance

The point of departure for any substantive assessment of Article 102 TFEU is the requirement to establish **dominance**. The main interpretation of dominance was given in the *United Brands* case, entailing 'a position of economic strength', enabling the undertaking to prevent effective competition on a market and to act in appreciable independence from competitors, customers and consumers.[24]

Hence, the ruling concerns a **structural element**, regarding the position of strength; a **behavioural element**, relating to the ability to act to an appreciable extent independently; and an **element that connects** these two in terms of the

---

[19] For instance, Joined Cases C-140 to C-142/94, *DIP and Others v Comune di Bassano del Grappa and Others* (ECJ 17 October 1995), para 14 et seq.

[20] Whish and Bailey (2018), p. 224 et seq.; see also → Article 4 TEU para 82 and 90.

[21] At its fringes, Article 102 TFEU also has relations with the fundamental freedoms. See, e.g., Case 155/73, *Giuseppe Sacchi* (ECJ 30 April 1974), para 7, and Case 402/85, *Basset v SACEM* (ECJ 12 March 1987), para 18.

[22] Case 13/77, *INNO v ATAB* (ECJ 16 November 1977), para 31–34.

[23] Cf. Case 66/86, *Ahmed Saeed Flugreisen and Silver Line Reisebüro GmbH v Zentrale zur Bekämpfung unlauteren Wettbewerbs e.V.* (ECJ 11 April 1989), para 52 and 58, 'as the case may be'; → para 19–20.

[24] Case 27/76, *United Brands v Commission* (ECJ 14 February 1978), para 65. In earlier case law, this was described as the 'power to impede the maintenance of effective competition over a considerable part of the relevant market, having regard in particular to the existence and position of any producers or distributors who may be marketing similar goods or goods which may be substituted for them', see Case 40/70, *Sirena v Eda* (ECJ 18 February 1971), para 16, as applied, for example, in Joined Cases 40/73 et al., *Suiker Unie and Others v Commission* (ECJ 16 December 1975), para 376–382.

ability to prevent effective competition.[25] The Court reiterated this ruling in *Hoffmann-La Roche*, adding a paragraph on the appreciable influence the undertaking has to have on the conditions for the development of competition in a market.[26] Despite these interpretations, dominance is regarded as 'nebulous',[27] 'not self-explanatory',[28] and even interpreted as impossible to prove with a reasonable degree of certainty.[29]

12 Whereas absolute rules on dominance or market power have not been given by the Court, establishing dominance relies on a **case-specific**[30] **test** that takes several factors into account and starts with a definition of the relevant market[31] (→ Article 101 TFEU para 31 et seqq.) and an assessment of the particular undertaking within the competitive situation on that market.[32] The list of factors to be taken into account is quite open-ended. Depending on the type of market and its conditions, different factors could have different weights; also, new factors could be introduced with the emergence of new markets that exhibit new economic dynamics.

13 Nevertheless, this part will explain the following **three-step assessment**. Firstly, an assessment of the undertaking's position on the relevant market is undertaken. Secondly, barriers to entry or expansion are ascertained. Thirdly, potential countervailing buyer power is taken into account. This part identifies the now known relevant factors. As market definition was already explained in relation to Article 101 TFEU, our commentary is confined to the general observation that more narrowly defined markets make it more likely to find dominance, whereas broader defined markets make it less so.

---

[25] The reference to structure and behaviour in this analysis refers to the Structure-Conduct-Performance paradigm, by means of which a market can be assessed (→ Article 101 TFEU para 39).

[26] Case 85/76, *Hoffmann-La Roche v Commission* (ECJ 13 February 1979), para 38–39.

[27] Jones and Sufrin (2012), p. 286.

[28] Nazzini (2013), p. 329.

[29] Bishop and Walker (2010), p. 233. Cf. Elhauge and Geradin (2007), p. 237 et seq.

[30] Case 6/72, *Europemballage Corporation and Continental Can Company Inc. v Commission* (ECJ 21 February 1973), para 32, repeated in Case 31/80, *L'Oréal v De Nieuwe AMCK* (ECJ 11 December 1980), para 25. Case 27/76, *United Brands v Commission* (ECJ 14 February 1978), para 66; Case 322/81, *Michelin v Commission* (ECJ 9 November 1983), para 37.

[31] Case 27/76, *United Brands v Commission* (ECJ 14 February 1978), para 10. See also Case C-49/07, *MOTOE* (ECJ 1 July 2008), para 31; Case C-242/95, *GT-Link A/S v De Danske Statsbaner (DSB)* (ECJ 17 July 1997), para 36; Case C-7/97, *Bronner* (ECJ 26 November 1998), para 32.

[32] Case 27/76, *United Brands v Commission* (ECJ 14 February 1978), para 66–67.

3.1. Market Shares

In most markets, **market share calculations** are a useful first step to assessing dominance.[33] However, as there is no objective way to proving that the market exists, the allocation of market-shares is also subjective, providing the one assessing with the freedom to choose the most relevant factors on the basis of which to assign the market shares.[34] In this regard, the legislature has also not defined a uniform evidence standard on which basis market shares should be allocated, or what evidence counts as conclusive in this regard.[35] 14

Regardless, the Court ruled that **large market shares give a clear indication of market power**.[36] It must be stressed that market shares are indicatory, not definite proof, considering a substantial market share is 'not a constant factor and its importance varies from market to market',[37] yet 'very large market shares are in themselves, and save in exceptional circumstances, evidence of the existence of a dominant position'.[38] The question of what 'very large' exactly entails was 15

---

[33] Only in markets with a single supplier, market share calculations are redundant. Such an undertaking would occupy 100% of the market and would *de facto* be a monopoly. Cf. Case 7/82, *GVL v Commission* (ECJ 2 March 1983), where GVL was considered to be the only supplier of managing performers' rights of secondary exploitation. Even though the copyright law of Germany at the time allowed for more organisations to engage in such management, the GVL had been the only one and, as such, was regarded to maintain a *de facto* monopoly. See also Case C-52/07, *Kanal 5 and TV 4* (ECJ 11 December 2008), para 21, and Case T-321/05, *AstraZeneca v Commission* (GC 1 July 2010), para 260, where it was designated as the 'first-mover status'. Cf. Mestmäcker and Schweitzer (2014), § 17 para 39, and Schröter and Bartl, in von der Groeben et al. (2015), Article 102 AEUV para 93.

[34] O'Donoghue and Padilla (2013), p. 144: 'There is no single correct approach to assigning market shares.' Also, de la Mano et al. (2014), para 4.141.

[35] For example, the European Commission uses, as a rule of thumb, volume sales and value sales, see Commission Notice *on the definition of relevant market for the purposes of Community competition law*, O.J. C 372/5 (1997) p. 12 point 53.

[36] For example, Case 27/76, *United Brands v Commission* (ECJ 14 February 1978), para 107.

[37] Case 85/76, *Hoffmann-La Roche v Commission* (ECJ 13 February 1979), para 40 and 44, in which the Court rejected retention of market shares as a factor for dominance: market shares by themselves cannot confirm indubitably that the undertaking is in a dominant position on its market; it could still be in a fiercely competitive market.

[38] Case 85/76, *Hoffmann-La Roche v Commission* (ECJ 13 February 1979), para 41. For the opposite, i.e. an absence of dominance as a result of insignificant market shares, see Case 75/84, *Metro v Commission* (ECJ 22 October 1986), para 85–86, where SABA possessed a market share of 'lower than 10%', a share 'too small to be regarded as evidence of a dominant position on the market'. See, in that regard, also Case 26/76, *Metro SB v Commission* (ECJ 25 October 1977), para 17, stating that without exceptional circumstances, very low market shares cannot lead to dominance. The lowest market share to have led to a dominance ruling was Case T-219/99, *British Airways plc v Commission* (CFI 17 December 2003), where BA held a declining market share of at the least 39.7% over a period of more than 7 years. In Case C-250/92, *Gøttrup-Klim e.a. Grovvareforeninger v Dansk Landbrugs Grovvareselskab AmbA* (ECJ 15 December 1994), para 48, the Court even stated that undertakings having shares of 32–36% can be dominant, having regard to the power and number of competitors.

answered by the Court in *AKZO*, stating that '[t]hat is the situation where there is a market share of 50%'.[39] Hence, after proving that the undertaking or group of undertakings has a market share of 50% or larger, the burden of proof will shift to the undertaking or group of undertakings.

3.2. Other Factors

16 Despite the *AKZO* legal presumption, the Court and the Commission have been very reluctant to rule on dominance solely based on evidence of a (very high) market share.[40] Often, additional factors are used. One of these is the **market share of close competitors**; if the difference in shares with competitors is large, then a conclusion for dominance will be stronger.[41]

17 Furthermore, most rulings on dominance are determined by the existence of **additional characteristics**, related either to the market or to the undertaking, which strengthen or weaken its position.[42] Dominant positions raise 'almost insuperable practical and financial obstacles' for actual and potential competitors.[43] Hence, it is in defining and valuing these obstacles on a case-by-case basis that an undertaking can be held dominant. If those elements are not convincing, the undertaking is not

---

[39] Case C-62/86, *AKZO v Commission* (ECJ 3 July 1991), para 60. It may be noted that this included a temporal element, as AKZO's market share consistently exceeded 50% over a period of three years (para 59). For more on market shares, see Schröter and Bartl, in von der Groeben et al. (2015), Article 102 AEUV para 93 et seq.

[40] See Case C-62/86, *AKZO v Commission* (ECJ 22 May 1991), para 61. Furthermore, see, e.g., Case 85/76, *Hoffmann-La Roche v Commission* (ECJ 13 February 1979), para 40–42; Case T-30/89, *Hilti v Commission* (CFI 12 December 1991), para 92–93, and Case C-333/94 P, *Tetra Pak v Commission* (ECJ 14 November 1996), para 109–110. With regard to *Hoffmann-La Roche*, the market for which the Court relied only on evidence of market shares was the relevant market for Vitamin H, intended both for bionutritive and for technological uses, para 67, referring to La Roche's factual monopoly on this market. Also, de la Mano et al. (2014), para 4.163.

[41] Case 85/76, *Hoffmann-La Roche v Commission* (ECJ 13 February 1979), para 60, 63 and 66. Competitors with a larger share can exercise stronger competitive pressure on the undertaking under scrutiny.

[42] Even in Case C-62/86, *AKZO v Commission* (ECJ 22 May 1991), para 61, the Commission and the Court utilised such factors. Also, Commission Communication, *Guidance on the Commission's enforcement priorities in applying Article 82 of the EC Treaty to abusive exclusionary conduct by dominant undertakings*, O.J. C 45/7 (2009), para 15.

[43] Case 27/76, *United Brands v Commission* (ECJ 14 February 1978), para 123. In literature, they have become known as barriers to entry and expansion, e.g., O'Donoghue and Padilla (2013), p. 151 et seq.; Whish (2015), p. 179 et seq.; Whish and Bailey (2018), p. 184 et seq.; European Commission's DG Competition discussion paper on the application of Article 82 of the Treaty to exclusionary abuses, December 2005, para 34 et seq. See also Case 27/76, *United Brands v Commission* (ECJ 14 February 1978), para 122.

dominant. The list of these case-specific factors was expanded through later case law, but does not form a fully defined set.[44]

The Court has been reluctant to accept these additional characteristics. On the one hand, in *Continental Can*, the Court emphasised the importance of proving the possibilities of other competitors to enter the market, before ascertaining the existence of dominance.[45] On the other, in *Hoffmann-La Roche*, it gave a caveat for listing the factors because, individually, certain factors could indicate a perfectly competitive market situation and not a dominant position *per se*.[46] The following paragraphs give an account of the various factors taken into account by the Court.[47]

18

3.2.1. Legal Factors

The first factor is the **applicable legal regime and/or exclusive rights** to the market and/or undertaking. Some markets are governed by public law, by a system of public licensing, that only allows for one[48] or a few undertakings to offer their

19

---

[44] Most factors were defined in Case 27/76, *United Brands v Commission* (ECJ 14 February 1978); Case 85/76, *Hoffmann-La Roche v Commission* (ECJ 13 February 1979); and Case 322/81, *Michelin v Commission* (ECJ 9 November 1983). The list does not appear to be exhaustive, and several are often used in the supply-side substitutability analysis of the definition of the relevant product market.

[45] Case 6/72, *Europemballage Corporation and Continental Can Company Inc. v Commission* (ECJ 21 February 1973), para 33. The phrase forms part of what has later been designated as the supply-side substitutability of the relevant market analysis.

[46] Case 85/76, *Hoffmann-La Roche v Commission* (ECJ 13 February 1979), para 39: '[t]he existence of a dominant position may derive from several factors which, taken separately, are not necessarily determinative'. The Court struck down the factors the Commission had used. Whereas evidence for a large market share held over a certain period of time can be seen as evidence for dominance, an argument in favour of retaining market shares alone is not *per se* an indicative factor for dominance, since such retention could also have come from effective competition (→ para 44); subsequently, the ability to supply a range of different products, for which separate market definitions can be made, does not necessarily make a firm dominant on any of them (→ para 46); cf. Case 322/81, *Michelin v Commission* (ECJ 5 October 1983), para 55, in which the Court concluded that the 'certain types of tyre' of the Michelin group to which the Dutch subsidiary belonged, and for which Michelin was the sole supplier, were advantages for Michelin over its competitors. As the relevant market was held to be the retail market for new replacement tyres for lorries buses and similar vehicles, the different qualities, treads and sizes Michelin provided were considered to be a factor for dominance); lastly, the factors of having a position as the world's largest producer, with turnovers exceeding that of one's competitors, and of heading the largest product group in the world, do not in themselves result in dominance, as these arguments do not confer any competitive advantage to the alleged dominant undertaking (→ para 47).

[47] We use a similar order as other scholars, cf. Mestmäcker and Schweitzer (2014), Article 102 AEUV; O'Donoghue and Padilla (2013); Whish and Bailey (2018).

[48] Case C-260/89, *ERT v DEP* (ECJ 18 June 1991), para 31; Case C-18/93, *Corsica Ferries Italia Srl v Corpo dei Piloti del Porto di Genova* (ECJ 17 May 1994), para 40.

services.⁴⁹ A legal monopoly in that regard will depend on the ambit of the law, the extent of the licence and the number of licences granted.⁵⁰ If an undertaking has a licence or exclusive public right, such a position will generally equate with dominance as long as the extent of the licence coincides with the market definition.⁵¹ Companies acting under a legal monopoly have competition law immunity for their actions under a *State action defence*,⁵² meaning the MS is liable for the restriction of competition.⁵³

20   Regarding **intellectual property** (IP) **rights**, the case law states clearly that having an IP right does not directly equate with dominance.⁵⁴ The CFI clarified that competitors need to be barred from developing substitutes,⁵⁵ or from entering the market, in order to add to the undertaking's strength.⁵⁶ Other circumstances may obscure a ruling on dominance, such as the extent of the IP or the ambit of the relevant market. In relation to contractual settlements of patent disputes, the Court has distinguished between the legitimate exercise of IP rights and actions that are

---

⁴⁹ E.g., Case C-209/98, *Sydhavnens Sten & Grus* (ECJ 23 May 2000), para 62. See also, e.g., Commission Communication, *Guidance on the Commission's enforcement priorities in applying Article 82 of the EC Treaty to abusive exclusionary conduct by dominant undertakings*, O.J. C 45/7 (2009), para 17, referring to tariffs and quotas as potential legal barriers to expansion and entry.

⁵⁰ E.g., Case 26/75, *General Motors v Commission* (ECJ 13 November 1975), para 9.

⁵¹ See Case C-260/89, *ERT v DEP* (ECJ 18 June 1991), para 31; Case C-18/93, *Corsica Ferries Italia Srl v Corpo dei Piloti del Porto di Genova* (ECJ 17 May 1994), para 40. Cf. Case 30/87, *Corinne Bodson v SA Pompes funèbres des régions libérées* (ECJ 4 May 1988), para 28, where only a particular share was governed by a public concession. See also Case C-23/14, *Post Danmark* (CJEU 6 October 2015), para 39, indicating that the company enjoyed a statutory monopoly on a sub-market.

⁵² Case C-52/09, *TeliaSonera Sverige* (CJEU 17 February 2011), para 49; Joined Cases C-359 and C-379/95 P, *Commission and France v Ladbroke Racing* (ECJ 11 November 1997), para 33–35 and mentioned case law.

⁵³ Such procedures are generally followed under Article 106.1 and Article 106.2 TFEU (→ Article 106 TFEU para 22). However, a company under public licensing remains liable under Article 102 TFEU for autonomous actions, which are not governed by the licence; see Case 402/85, *Basset v SACEM* (ECJ 9 April 1987), para 18–20, and Case T-271/03, *Deutsche Telekom v Commission* (CFI 10 April 2008), para 80.

⁵⁴ Case 40/70, *Sirena v Eda* (ECJ 18 February 1971), para 16; Case 78/70, *Deutsche Grammophon v Metro-SB* (ECJ 8 June 1971), para 16; Case 53/87, *CICRA and Others v Renault* (ECJ 5 October 1988), para 14–16; Case 238/87, *Volvo v Veng* (ECJ 5 October 1988) para 7–9; and Joined Cases C-241 and C-242/91 P, *RTE and ITP v Commission* (ECJ 6 April 1995), para 46. See also Case T-321/05, *AstraZeneca v Commission* (GC 1 July 2010), para 270, stating that an IP right can contribute to the establishment of a dominant position.

⁵⁵ Or, in the case of recording artists, other record manufacturers should not be able to obtain services from comparable performers, see Case 78/70, *Deutsche Grammophon v Metro-SB* (ECJ 8 June 1971), para 18.

⁵⁶ E.g., Case T-30/89, *Hilti v Commission* (CFI 12 December 1991), para 93.

3.2.2. Factors Relating to the Undertaking

The second set of factors relates to the undertaking itself. First, if a firm regards itself, and/or admits in court, that it is the world leader in the market, that **statement** will point towards dominance.[58] Also, admitting that it is the sole supplier of a particular good/service will not work favourably in court.[59]

21

The second factor is the **degree of vertical integration**. If an undertaking owns more elements of the supply chain, it will be able to control a larger part of the market.[60] Hence, possessing a highly developed sales network,[61] or marketing organisation,[62] provides an undertaking with 'technical and commercial advantages' over actual and potential competitors.[63] In that regard, possessing an input for which no alternative exists can also be held in favour of dominance.[64]

22

The third factor is the **technological lead of the undertaking concerned**.[65] In order to ascertain this, a dominance analysis should include the research opportunities of newcomers to match that of the undertaking under scrutiny.[66] This may overlap with existing legal barriers because the undertaking might possess several patents to which it may deny competitors' access.

23

Another factor on the part of the company in question is the **potential of the undertaking to expand its maximum production capacity**. In other words, if the company is able to meet the general demand in the market where others cannot, it will have an advantage over competitors.[67]

24

---

[57] Case C-307/18, *Generics UK v Competition and Markets Authority* (CJEU 30 January 2020), para 151–152.
[58] Case C-62/86, *AKZO v Commission* (ECJ 3 July 1991), para 61.
[59] Case 22/78, *Hugin v Commission* (ECJ 31 May 1979), para 9.
[60] Case 27/76, *United Brands v Commission* (ECJ 14 February 1978), para 70–94.
[61] Case 27/76, *United Brands v Commission* (ECJ 14 February 1978), para 90; Case 85/76, *Hoffmann-La Roche v Commission* (ECJ 13 February 1979), para 48.
[62] Case C-62/86, *AKZO v Commission* (ECJ 3 July 1991), para 61.
[63] See also Case 322/81, *Michelin v Commission* (ECJ 9 November 1983), para 58.
[64] Case C-7/97, *Bronner* (ECJ 26 November 1998), para 33–36.
[65] Case 27/76, *United Brands v Commission* (ECJ 14 February 1978), para 82. See also Case 85/76, *Hoffmann-La Roche v Commission* (ECJ 13 February 1979), para 48; Case C-62/86, *AKZO v Commission* (ECJ 3 July 1991), para 61; and Case 322/81, *Michelin v Commission* (ECJ 9 November 1983), para 55.
[66] Case 27/76, *United Brands v Commission* (ECJ 14 February 1978), para 84.
[67] E.g., Case 85/76, *Hoffmann-La Roche v Commission* (ECJ 13 February 1979), para 48.

3.2.3. Market Factors

25 The third type of factors concerns the degree of competition in the market. In essence, these factors look at **market characteristics** and at the degree of competitive pressure on the entity in question.[68] Each factor in this regard has to be verified for conferring competitive advantages to the undertaking concerned.[69]

26 The first barrier to entry for undertakings is formed by **large *sunk cost* investments**.[70] The Court exemplified this with regard to the costs of setting up a proper sales network or mounting large-scale advertising campaigns.[71] Without these elements in place, a competitor cannot reach customers and consumers and cannot compete equally with the undertaking under scrutiny.

27 The second barrier is the **investment required for running the operation** concerned. The larger the investments, the higher the barrier to entry or expansion and the more it confirms the dominance of an existing player. In this regard, market-specific circumstances play a role. For example, the Court in *United Brands* ruled that the requirement to increase the sources of supply and the introduction of an essential system of logistics raised barriers to entry for newcomers into the banana market.[72] In *Hugin*, an alternative manner for producing spare Hugin cash register parts was not regarded feasible by the ECJ.[73]

28 Third, **economies of scale of production** can promulgate dominance.[74] A firm might lower its overall production costs and establish a more competitive price per product than (potential) competitors after having invested significantly in upgrading its production capabilities. New entrants to the market might not be able to achieve such efficiencies immediately and might have difficulty gaining ground in a particular market.

29 As a specific corollary for (digital) platform markets, over the last two decades, **network effects** have become more important.[75] According to the economic theory, this effect expresses the value change of particular products as consumption

---

[68] Case 85/76, *Hoffmann-La Roche v Commission* (ECJ 13 February 1979), para 48: 'the absence of potential competition [is a] relevant factor [...] because it is the consequence of the existence of obstacles preventing new competitors from having access to the market'.

[69] Case 27/76, *United Brands v Commission* (ECJ 14 February 1978), para 123.

[70] Case 27/76, *United Brands v Commission* (ECJ 14 February 1978), para 122.

[71] See also Case T-139/98, *AAMS v Commission* (CFI 22 November 2001), para 52.

[72] Case 27/76, *United Brands v Commission* (ECJ 14 February 1978), para 122. The Court drew a link here with the products' characteristics: bananas are perishable products, whose cultivation strongly depends on climate and weather conditions.

[73] Hence, the lack of sufficient alternative sources of supply may also lead to a dominant position, Case 22/78, *Hugin v Commission* (ECJ 31 May 1979), para 9.

[74] Case 27/76, *United Brands v Commission* (ECJ 14 February 1978), para 122.

[75] See how the factor is used by the EU Commission in Case T-201/04, *Microsoft v Commission* (CFI 17 September 2007), para 31 and 33, for the client PC and work group server OS markets, respectively, more specifically addressed in para 1061–1067.

changes.[76] Insofar as relevant for competition law, a company that sells a product that experiences strong positive network effects (when the experienced value rises after a consumption increase) is more likely to be considered dominant. Whereas direct network effects relate to the value generated by and for a particular group of consumers itself, indirect effects relate to the value generated for a different group of customers, which a platform undertaking may wish to balance out with one another.[77] The Commission seems to take a case-by-case approach with respect to these externalities.[78]

Another and controversial factor concerns the **financial capabilities of the undertaking**. On the one hand, (temporary un)profitability of the undertaking was held irrelevant in relation to dominance.[79] Firms might lower prices below rational standards in order to drive out competitors. Also, high profits can still be evidence of a competitive market. On the other, in *AstraZeneca*, the leading financial position of AstraZeneca was taken into account by the General Court (GC).[80] In *Corinne Bodson*, the Court of Justice drew up specific assessment rules for a group of undertakings that had a large share in the market for funerals due to an exclusive concession. Besides its market share, the financial strength of the group was also held to be a factor contributing to dominance.[81] Furthermore, with regard to competitors, the Court seems willing to take into account their financial strength. Lastly, evidence of the display of non-abusive behaviour does not disprove the existence of a dominant position.[82]

30

---

[76] Katz and Shapiro (1985), p. 424; Economides (1996), p. 678 et seq.

[77] Cf. Case T-79/12, *Cisco Systems and Messagenet v Commission* (GC 11 December 2013), para 79–80, regarding alleged dominance created from the merger of Microsoft Windows Live Messenger and Skype (Commission Decision of 7 October 2011 *declaring a concentration to be compatible with the common market (Case No COMP/M.6281 - Microsoft/Skype)*). Furthermore, the General Court held that an analysis of technical or economic constraints or obstacles was required, preventing users of a product to switch to an alternative supplier.

[78] Commission Communication, *Guidance on the Commission's enforcement priorities in applying Article 82 of the EC Treaty to abusive exclusionary conduct by dominant undertakings*, O.J. C 45/7 (2009), para 17. Commission Decision of 24 March 2004 *relating to a proceeding under Article 82 of the EC Treaty (Case COMP/C-3/37.792 Microsoft)*, para 420; Commission Decision of 27 June 2017, *AT.39740 – Google Search (Shopping)*, para 270; Commission Decision of 18 July 2018, *AT.40099 – Google Android*, para 438, leaning heavily on the 'actual cost of entry' factor mentioned in Case 27/76, *United Brands v Commission* (ECJ 14 February 1978), para 122.

[79] Case 27/76, *United Brands v Commission* (ECJ 14 February 1978), para 126; Case 322/81, *Michelin v Commission* (ECJ 9 November 1983), para 59. Also, Case 85/76, *Hoffmann-La Roche v Commission* (ECJ 13 February 1979), para 47, where the combination of being the largest vitamin producer, having turnover exceeding that of its competitors, and heading the largest pharmaceutical group in the world was not considered to amount to dominance.

[80] Case T-321/05, *AstraZeneca v Commission* (GC 1 July 2010), para 284–285.

[81] Case 30/87, *Corinne Bodson v SA Pompes funèbres des régions libérées* (ECJ 4 May 1988), para 29.

[82] Case 322/81, *Michelin v Commission* (ECJ 9 November 1983), para 59.

3.2.4. Independence from Customers and Consumers: Countervailing Powers

31 It follows from the definition of dominance that an undertaking should be independent not only of its competitors but also of its customers and of its consumers.[83] Hence, part of the firm's independence is given by the **control** it can have **over its clients** and *vice versa*.[84]

32 Most Article 102 TFEU cases involve supply-side dominance over demand, but *BA/Virgin* shows how British Airways was **dominant on the purchasing market** for air travel agency services.[85]

3.3. Collective Dominance

33 The phrase 'one or more undertakings' in Article 102 TFEU clarifies that more than one entity can be captured by that provision.[86] **Collective dominance** refers to two or more independent activities that are linked by economic, legal or factual ties to the extent that these enable uniform conduct on a particular market,[87] independent of external competitors, customers and consumers.[88] After such links are

---

[83] Case 27/76, *United Brands v Commission* (ECJ 14 February 1978), para 65.

[84] See, *inter alia*, Joined Cases T-68/89, T-77/89 and T-78/89, *SIV and Others v Commission* (CFI 10 March 1992), para 367, where the Commission was censured for not having verified the influence of Fiat, being the only large purchaser of flat glass among the three producers, on the degree of competition between them. See, in more couched terms, Case 78/70, *Deutsche Grammophon v Metro-SB* (ECJ 8 June 1971), para 18, referring to taking into account the popularity of recording artists, when assessing their exclusivity contracts.

[85] Case T-219/99, *British Airways plc v Commission* (CFI 17 December 2003), para 101 and 191. The relevant criterion in this context was considered the number of tickets BA had been able to sell via travel agents to and from British airports (para 192). Hence, it is questionable to what extent BA actually was dominant (only) on the purchasing side of the air travel market as it was also the supplier of tickets/seats to air travel agents. See, e.g., Jones and Sufrin (2012), p. 312 et seq., and O'Donoghue and Padilla (2013), pp. 205–206. See Case T-219/99, *British Airways plc v Commission* (CFI 17 December 2003), para 195, where the Court literally applied the *United Brands* conditions for independence to BA's competitors on all routes to and from British airports, to travel agents and to travellers. Hence, customers and suppliers might therefore be seen as interchangeable according to this ruling.

[86] It does not solely apply to a collective abuse by two separate dominant positions; see Joined Cases T-24/93 et al., *Compagnie Maritime Belge Transports and Others v Commission* (CFI 8 October 1996), para 60. This has been the prevailing interpretation since Case 85/76, *Hoffmann-La Roche v Commission* (ECJ 13 February 1979), para 39, second sentence, where the ECJ maintained that a dominant position should be distinguished from 'parallel courses of conduct' in oligopoly markets.

[87] Joined Cases C-395 and C-396/96 P, *Compagnie maritime belge transports and others v Commission* (ECJ 16 March 2000), para 42–45.

[88] Case 30/87, *Corinne Bodson v SA Pompes funèbres des régions libérées* (ECJ 4 May 1988), para 19; reiterated in Case C-393/92, *Municipality of Almelo and others v NV Energiebedrijf IJsselmij* (ECJ 27 April 1994), para 41; Case C-96/94, *Centro Servizi Spediporto Srl v Spedizioni*

established, their joint dominant position can be assessed.[89] Simultaneously, Article 101.1 TFEU could apply to such links.[90] However, for Article 102 TFEU, proof of agreements or of other structural links between undertakings alone is insufficient: an economic assessment of the links is required.[91] Furthermore, *Italian Flat Glass* exemplifies that agreements or licences among multiple firms that ensure a technological lead may entail a collective dominant position.[92]

For **tight oligopolies**, meaning markets that are characterised by a homogeneous product, a small number of large suppliers and high barriers to entry, the Courts created specific collective dominance rules.[93] In merger judgments, the economic interdependence of undertakings created by those markets was held to form a sufficiently strong economic link: a decision allowing a structural change would reinforce such circumstances.[94] The CFI applied this ruling to Article 102 TFEU situations as well.[95]

34

In those situations, the **three *Airtours* conditions** have to be met: the market has to be sufficiently transparent so each competitor can know what the others do; adequate deterrents have to exist for all undertakings not to deviate from the common policy; and competitors and consumers should be unable to alter the common policy of the individual suppliers.[96] If those criteria are met, then the undertakings are to be held in a collective dominant position as the market structure enables them to adopt a common policy that is unassailable by competitive pressure.

35

Marittima del Golfo Srl (ECJ 5 October 1995), para 33; and Case C-70/95, *Sodemare and Others v Regione Lombardia* (ECJ 17 June 1997), para 46. Also, Joined Cases C-395 and C-396/96 P, *Compagnie maritime belge transports and others v Commission* (ECJ 16 March 2000), para 35–36. Also, Joined Cases C-68/94 and C-30/95, *France and SCPA and EMC v Commission* (ECJ 31 March 1998), para 221.

[89] See Joined Cases C-395 and C-396/96 P, *Compagnie maritime belge transports and others v Commission* (ECJ 16 March 2000), para 39. Also, Joined Cases C-68/94 and C-30/95, *France and SCPA and EMC v Commission* (ECJ 31 March 1998), para 221, and Case T-17/93, *Matra Hachette v Commission* (CFI 15 July 1994), para 153.

[90] Note that this overlaps with the appraisal of oligopolistic interdependence under Article 101 TFEU (→ Article 101 TFEU para 18), as well as the application of the concept of non-coordinated effects in the context of the EU Merger Regulation, see Commission Guidelines *on the assessment of horizontal mergers under the Council Regulation on the control of concentrations between undertakings*, O.J. C 31/5 (2004).

[91] Joined Cases C-395 and C-396/96 P, *Compagnie maritime belge transports and others v Commission* (ECJ 16 March 2000), para 43 and 45.

[92] Joined Cases T-68/89, T-77/89 and T-78/89, *SIV and Others v Commission* (CFI 10 March 1992), para 358.

[93] Case T-102/96, *Gencor v Commission* (CFI 25 March 1999), para 276.

[94] Case T-102/96, *Gencor v Commission* (CFI 8 February 1999), para 277, and Case T-342/99, *Airtours v Commission* (CFI 6 June 2002), para 61; later confirmed in Case C-413/06 P, *Bertelsmann and Sony Corporation of America v Impala* (ECJ 10 July 2008), para 123–124.

[95] Case T-374/00, *Verband der freien Rohrwerke and Others v Commission* (CFI 8 July 2003), para 121. Case T-193/02, *Piau v Commission* (CFI 27 January 2005), para 111.

[96] Case T-193/02, *Piau v Commission* (CFI 27 January 2005), para 111.

36   In vertical relationships, between suppliers and their direct customers, **dominance may emanate from links between undertakings**.[97] In such situations, *Irish Sugar* stipulates the following relevant factors to amount to dominance: holding shares in the customer undertaking, representing part of its board, having influence on its policy-making structure, and the facilitating communication process, financing downstream consumer promotions and rebates, and having direct economic ties through an exclusive supply commitment.[98]

4. Special Responsibility

37   Once an undertaking is dominant, Article 102 TFEU bestows upon it a special responsibility, obliging it **not to further restrict or distort the already weakened competition in the market**.[99] From a public interest point of view, the dominant company is obliged to put its conduct in the perspective of the entire market and assess its competitive impact on consumers and competitors.[100] Since *Michelin I*, this formula has been established as standing law.[101]

38   Furthermore, an undertaking's relative strength is attached to the **conduct**, not to the assessment of dominance as such. In *TeliaSonera*, the Court closed arguments on the tendency to assess dominance in terms of degrees.[102] If a market share approaches 100%, some consider the market participant to have a more than dominant position and would therefore have a higher *Michelin* responsibility. However, the Court ruled that no such degree in dominance exists.[103] It is

---

[97] Case T-228/97, *Irish Sugar v Commission* (CFI 7 October 1999), para 63.

[98] Case T-228/97, *Irish Sugar v Commission* (CFI 7 October 1999), para 51 et seq., upheld in Case C-497/99 P, *Irish Sugar v Commission* (ECJ 10 July 2001), para 46–47.

[99] Case 322/81, *Michelin v Commission* (ECJ 9 November 1983), para 57. Also, Joined Cases C-395/96 P and C-396/96 P, *Compagnie maritime belge transports and others v Commission* (ECJ 16 March 2000), para 37.

[100] Cf. Case 136/79, *National Panasonic v Commission* (ECJ 26 June 1980), para 20, and Case C-94/00, *Roquette Frères* (ECJ 22 October 2002), para 42.

[101] E.g., Case C-209/10, *Post Danmark* (CJEU 27 March 2012), para 21–24.

[102] See Case C-52/09, *TeliaSonera Sverige* (CJEU 17 February 2011), para 81, in which the Court refers to Case C-333/94 P, *Tetra Pak v Commission* (ECJ 14 November 1996), para 31, and Joined Cases C-395 and C-396/96 P, *Compagnie maritime belge transports and others v Commission* (ECJ 16 March 2000), para 119.

[103] Case C-52/09, *TeliaSonera Sverige* (CJEU 17 February 2011), para 80. A position may have 'extraordinary features', such as Microsoft's market share exceeding 90% in the work group servers operating systems market, and its status as the 'quasi-standard', Case T-201/04, *Microsoft v Commission* (CFI 17 September 2007), para 387. See also Schröter and Bartl, in von der Groeben et al. (2015), Article 102 AEUV para 94–95.

binary:[104] an undertaking on a market is dominant, or it is not.[105] Consequently, potentially abusive behaviour is fully legal when the undertaking is regarded not to have a dominant position.[106]

Furthermore, the Court decided in *CMB* and in *Tetra Pak II* that the 'actual **scope of the special responsibility** [...] must be considered in the light of the specific circumstances in each case'.[107] Hence, depending on the specificities of each case, the responsibility requires the undertaking to abstain from certain conduct, although it might be considered legitimate market behaviour for non-dominant competitors. Considering that the special responsibility is a corollary of a dominant position, theoretically it would apply to any type of conduct. However, thus far, the Court has not given judgment connecting the responsibility to exploitative practices. Furthermore, the *Michelin* responsibility is often situated in a debate on whether or not there is an effect-based or a rule-based approach in Article 102 TFEU. In this regard, we note that in taking into account the specific circumstances, the Court requires a likelihood of exclusionary effects, as part of which the degree of market power is taken into account.[108] Therefore, a pre-established abuse may be exacerbated by a stronger position of the undertaking. In sum, there is a sliding scale neither as to dominance nor as to the *Michelin* responsibility.[109]

39

---

[104] Case C-52/09, *TeliaSonera Sverige* (CJEU 17 February 2011), para 79–80. See also Appeldoorn (2005), pp. 653–658, and Whish and Bailey (2018), p. 198 et seq.

[105] Cf. Joined Cases C-395 and C-396/96 P, *Compagnie maritime belge transports and others v Commission* (Opinion of AG *Fennelly* of 29 October 1998), para 137, referring to 'super dominance'; Case T-201/04, *Microsoft v Commission* (CFI 17 September 2007), para 775, referring to 'quasi-monopoly'; or, *in abstracto*, Case 85/76, *Hoffmann-La Roche v Commission* (ECJ 13 February 1979), para 39, and Case C-333/94 P, *Tetra Pak v Commission* (ECJ 14 November 1996), para 31, and Case C-52/09, *TeliaSonera Sverige* (CJEU 17 February 2011), para 81, indicating that, generally, the power degree only matters in relation to the assessment of effects of conduct, not in relation to a finding of abuse (or dominance) itself; Cf. Case T-228/97, *Irish Sugar v Commission* (CFI 7 October 1999), para 185. As such, there is legally no super dominance. See, e.g., O'Donoghue and Padilla (2013), pp. 206–208.

[106] E.g., Joined Cases T-191 and T-212 to T-214/98, *Atlantic Container Line AB and Others v Commission* (CFI 30 September 2003), para 1460; Case 27/76, *United Brands v Commission* (ECJ 14 February 1978), para 189–191.

[107] Joined Cases C-395 and C-396/96 P, *Compagnie maritime belge transports and others v Commission* (ECJ 16 March 2000), para 114; Case C-333/94 P, *Tetra Pak v Commission* (ECJ 14 November 1996), para 24.

[108] Case C-52/09, *TeliaSonera Sverige* (CJEU 17 February 2011), para 81–82; confirmed in Case C-549/10 P, *Tomra Systems ASA and Others v Commission* (CJEU 19 April 2012), para 39. See also Case C-23/14, *Post Danmark* (CJEU 6 October 2015), para 30, and, e.g., Commission Communication, *Guidance on the Commission's enforcement priorities in applying Article 82 of the EC Treaty to abusive exclusionary conduct by dominant undertakings*, O.J. C 45/7 (2009), para 20.

[109] Cf. Bailey and John (2018), para 10.019.

5. Abuse

40   In accordance with the Court's standing case law, **only the abusive conduct of dominant positions is prohibited**.[110] Therefore, firms are allowed to hold a dominant position; hence, in theory, monopolies are allowed. In terms of compliance, this means that as soon as an undertaking passes the dominance threshold, it might not be able to continue regular business practices and needs to be aware of the possible qualification of such practices as abuse.

41   As a general remark, **since 2009**, the Commission has adopted a **new enforcement approach** to abuse.[111] In its practice, it will only target exclusionary conduct that does not achieve efficiencies and, thus, impedes consumer welfare.[112] This approach means that the Commission will test that the effects of the conduct are or can be anti-competitive, whereby this anti-competitiveness exists in reductions of consumer welfare. In addition, such effects on consumer welfare are to be established on a case-by-case basis, rather than to be assumed for a more broadly applicable rule. This will have an impact on the administrability and predictability of Article 102 TFEU enforcement practice.

42   This part focuses on the definition of abuse and the methods for establishing it. It will start with a general introduction, followed by a more detailed analysis of the distinction between exclusionary and exploitative abuses.[113] In this regard, we point out that, in general, this distinction is artificial to the extent that the Court never explicitly endorsed it.[114] Nevertheless, this distinction might support the understanding of the concept, providing a framework for the theories of harm that underlie a type of abuse.[115]

---

[110] Cf. Case 322/81, *Michelin v Commission* (ECJ 9 November 1983), para 57; Joined Cases T-125 and 127/97, *Coca-Cola v Commission* (CFI 22 March 2000), para 53; Case T-65/98, *Van den Bergh Foods v Commission* (CFI 23 October 2003), para 158; Case C-52/09, *TeliaSonera Sverige* (CJEU 17 February 2011), para 24; Case C-209/10, *Post Danmark* (CJEU 27 March 2012), para 21. This reflects the choice made by the drafters of the Treaties, see Amato (1997), p. 65.

[111] Commission Communication *on the Commission's enforcement priorities in applying Article 82 of the EC Treaty to abusive exclusionary conduct by dominant undertakings*, O.J. C 45/7 (2009); preceded by European Commission (2009). In academic practice, the persistent phrase in this sense is 'the more economic approach to competition law', e.g., Wils (2014), Witt (2016).

[112] Commission Communication *on the Commission's enforcement priorities in applying Article 82 of the EC Treaty to abusive exclusionary conduct by dominant undertakings*, O.J. C 35/7 (2009), para 19. See also Ehlermann and Laudati, in Ehlermann and Laudati (1997), p. ix; Kellerbauer (2010); Wils (2014); Witt (2016); Daly (2016), p. 9. Monti (2007), p. 52; → Article 101 TFEU para 43.

[113] de la Mano et al. (2014), para 4.253.

[114] Cf. the 'exclusionary effect', as referred to in, e.g., Case C-280/08 P, *Deutsche Telekom AG v Commission* (CJEU 14 October 2010), para 177.

[115] A theory of harm refers to economic theory that explains the harm to the economic process resulting from certain behaviour that may constitute abuse. E.g., Zenger and Walker (2012), pp. 185–209.

5.1. General Definition

Much of the scene for understanding abuse is set by the **special responsibility** mentioned above.[116] The special responsibility is most relevant in relation to abuses that are construed as directed against (potential) competitors (exclusionary abuses). 43

Like Article 101.1 TFEU, Article 102 TFEU contains an **open list of four broadly phrased examples of abuse**.[117] Furthermore, the Court provided for a general definition of abuse, containing three open-worded elements.[118] 44

First of all, **abuse is objective** and can be proven regardless of the intent of the undertaking.[119] However, as all circumstances surrounding the conduct should be considered, any anti-competitive intent can be taken into account in the analysis of the conduct.[120] Also, certain categories require proof of an intention, such as a plan to destroy competition in certain predatory pricing situations (→ para 62). 45

Second, abuse consists of methods that run counter to **normal competition**.[121] It is often compared to its counterpart, **competition on/for the merits**, although the meaning and ambit of the latter concept have not been further clarified.[122] Considering the *ex post* nature of Articles 101 and 102 TFEU, normal competition or competition on the merits depends on the specificities of each case. It may be 46

---

[116] Case C-333/94 P, *Tetra Pak v Commission* (ECJ 14 November 1996), para 24.

[117] Cf. O'Donoghue and Padilla (2013), and Schröter and Bartl, in von der Groeben et al. (2015), Article 102 AEUV para 174–182.

[118] Case 85/76, *Hoffmann-La Roche v Commission* (ECJ 13 February 1979), para 91; reiterated and rephrased, inter alia, in Case 322/81, *Michelin v Commission* (ECJ 9 November 1983), para 70; Case C-280/08 P, *Deutsche Telekom AG v Commission* (CJEU 14 October 2010), para 174; Case C-52/09, *TeliaSonera Sverige* (CJEU 17 February 2011) para 27; and Case C-549/10 P, *Tomra Systems ASA and Others v Commission* (CJEU 19 April 2012), para 17.

[119] Case 85/76, *Hoffmann-La Roche v Commission* (ECJ 13 February 1979), para 91. See also Case C-549/10 P, *Tomra Systems ASA and Others v Commission* (CJEU 19 April 2012), para 22.

[120] Case C-549/10 P, *Tomra Systems ASA and Others v Commission* (CJEU 19 April 2012), para 18–21, in effect referring back to Case C-95/04 P, *British Airways v Commission* (ECJ 15 March 2007), para 67. See also Case T-321/05, *AstraZeneca v Commission* (GC 1 July 2010), para 349.

[121] Case 85/76, *Hoffmann-La Roche v Commission* (ECJ 13 February 1979), para 91. See also Case C-457/10 P, *AstraZeneca v Commission* (CJEU 6 December 2012), para 129; de la Mano et al. (2014), para 4.256.

[122] E.g., Case T-321/05, *AstraZeneca v Commission* (GC 1 July 2010), referring to 'legitimate protection of an investment designed to contribute to competition on the merits' as a form of justification in para 830, and 'use of regulatory procedures without any basis in competition on the merits' as a form of abuse in, e.g., para 845. On appeal, in Case C-457/10 P, *AstraZeneca v Commission* (CJEU 6 December 2012), para 75–76—referring to Case C-62/86, *AKZO v Commission* (ECJ 3 July 1991), para 70 (competition on the basis of quality)—the Court applied the concept as is, and ruled that AstraZeneca had manifestly not conformed to it, by misleading public authorities, para 98. Also, Case C-280/08 P, *Deutsche Telekom AG v Commission* (CJEU 14 October 2010), para 177. In Case T-201/04, *Microsoft v Commission* (CFI 17 September 2007), the CFI expanded on this, ruling Microsoft's conduct had secured a competitive advantage unrelated to the *intrinsic merits* of its tied product, the media player software. Cf. OECD (2006). Lastly, Case C-413/14 P, *Intel v Commission* (CJEU 6 September 2017), para 133–135.

argued that this implies the efficiency defence, enabling the justification of *prima facie* abusive conduct on the basis of efficiencies.

47   Third, the effect of the conduct has to be a **restriction to the (growth of the) remaining degree of competition**.[123] A deterioration of the position of consumers can be seen as such a restriction.[124] The effects have to be neither actual nor concrete. Evidence of potential effects or capabilities to restrict competition will suffice.[125] Also, effects do not have to pass a *de minimis* threshold: any potential anti-competitive effect can support a conclusion for abuse. These potential effects have to be probable.[126] Therefore, it appears that conduct, the anti-competitive effects of which are likely to occur, will amount to an abuse of a dominant position.[127] Depending on the situation (i.e. the type of conduct, market conditions etc.), the likelihood of potential anti-competitive effects differs. As of yet, no particular guidance exists regarding likelihood. The Court held that this capability and likelihood may be assumed on the basis of the nature of certain forms of abuse.[128] If, however, the undertaking under investigation challenges this assumed capability, it is for those invoking Article 102 TFEU to adduce evidence of the capacity to restrict competition.[129]

48   **A link between abuse and pre-existing dominance is generally presupposed**.[130] Conduct by a dominant undertaking in another market than the one in which it is dominant will only constitute abuse if there are special circumstances, such as evidence of leveraging the dominance to the non-dominated market.[131] Whereas the concept of dominance is strictly limited to a specific market, abuse is not.[132]

---

[123] Cf. Case 6/72, *Europemballage Corporation and Continental Can Company Inc. v Commission* (ECJ 21 February 1973), para 26, 'substantially fetters competition'.

[124] Case C-209/10, *Post Danmark* (CJEU 27 March 2012), para 24. Note that this detriment was in both direct and indirect ways, for instance through exclusionary practices aimed against competitors, decreasing choice for consumers. Cf. Case C-62/86, *AKZO v Commission* (ECJ 3 July 1991), para 69; Case C-202/07 P, *France Télécom v Commission* (CJEU 2 April 2009), para 104–105; and Case C-280/08 P, *Deutsche Telekom AG v Commission* (CJEU 14 October 2010), para 174, 176, and 180.

[125] Case C-23/14, *Post Danmark* (CJEU 6 October 2015), para 66.

[126] Case C-23/14, *Post Danmark* (CJEU 6 October 2015), para 72–73.

[127] Note that the Commission apparently considers 'capable' and 'likely' as interchangeable, Case T-814/17, *Lietuvos geležinkeliai v Commission* (GC 18 November 2020), para 239.

[128] Case C-413/14 P, *Intel v Commission* (CJEU 6 September 2017), para 142–147.

[129] Case C-413/14 P, *Intel v Commission* (CJEU 6 September 2017), para 138.

[130] Case C-333/94 P, *Tetra Pak v Commission* (ECJ 14 November 1996), para 27; See also Case C-52/09, *TeliaSonera Sverige* (CJEU 17 February 2011), para 86.

[131] Case C-52/09, *TeliaSonera Sverige* (CJEU 17 February 2011), para 86.

[132] Joined Cases 6 and 7/73, *Istituto Chemioterapico Italiano S.p.A. and Commercial Solvents Corporation v Commission* (ECJ 6 March 1974), para 22. See also Case 22/79, *Greenwich Film v SACEM* (ECJ 25 October 1979), para 13.

5.2. The Test and Required Evidence for Proving Abuse

Depending on the type of abusive practice, a different **methodology** is used. At the core of these methodologies for indicating anti-competitive effects, reliance is put on economic analyses. However, such effect analyses may be complex and difficult to measure in a reproducible manner, placing them at odds with predictability.

49

To take just one example, a controversial part of the discussion surrounding the test for predatory pricing, whereby a dominant company sells below costs, centres on whether or not recoupment is a constituent part of that test (→ para 63–65). Whereas the below cost-pricing benchmark for predatory pricing is clear, whether or not such loss-leading prices also qualify as an infringement of the competition rules depends on the jurisdiction. Under the US equivalent of Article 102 TFEU, Section 2 of the Sherman Act, evidence of recoupment is required.[133] This means that it must be proven that post-predation prices are raised to the supra-competitive level to recoup the losses incurred during the predation.[134] In the EU, no such requirement exists.[135] This difference can be taken as an example of the **approach under EU competition law** that attached **less weight to economic analysis in general and the effects on consumer welfare in particular**. It can also be understood as an attempt to reduce the enforcement costs of Article 102 TFEU. This follows from the fact that ascertaining a certain price-cost ratio is difficult; the substantive test applicable already presents several methodological difficulties in the absence of a universally applicable method for assigning costs.[136]

50

Moreover, the underlying question is how we **understand and measure competition**: narrowly as an outcome centred on low prices (optimal consumer welfare) or broadly as a combination of competitors, certain behaviour and outcome. Obviously, the latter increases the possibilities for intervention, but it also includes factors that are measured at lower costs with potentially higher levels of reproducibility. This is also what is at the heart of the introduction of the as-efficient competitor test as part of the more economic approach. It basically entails the introduction of the requirement that only the disappearance of competitors that are as efficient as the dominant company will trigger an intervention on the basis of Article 102 TFEU. This reduces the formalism used to identify abuses to essentially one question: is there short-term harm to consumer welfare? The questions involved in these issues largely coincide with the issues that underlie the object-

51

---

[133] See the change in the US Supreme Court jurisprudence in *Standard Oil co. v. United States*, 221 U.S. 1 (1911), to *Matsushita Electric Industrial Co. v. Zenith Radio Corp*, 475 U.S. 574 (1986). See also Areeda and Turner (1975) and Leslie (2013).

[134] In this regard, the high prices can be compared with the cartel mark-up price, whereby the difficulty of measuring such price increases is widely accepted: Commission Communication *on quantifying harm in actions for damages based on breaches of Article 101 or 102 [TFEU]*, O.J. C 167/19 (2013), where the Commission acknowledges the 'challenge' and 'major difficulty' (heading 1 and para 3).

[135] Case C-202/07 P, *France Télécom v Commission* (ECJ 2 April 2009), para 32–37.

[136] For a discussion see: Königsgruber (2014), Whittington (2014), and Bromwich (2014).

effect dichotomy in Article 101.1 TFEU (→ Article 101 TFEU para 27 et seqq.). This will be explored in greater detail below when the specific forms of abuse are discussed.

52   In several jurisdictions, this general attitude resulted in the control over exploitative abuses primarily taking the shape of *ex ante* **regulation of statutory monopolies**, meaning those instances of market power that result from legal barriers to entry or expansion that are often associated with natural monopolies.[137] This raises the question of to what extent *ex post* enforcement of general antitrust rules to instances of exploitation is warranted in addition to the *ex ante* regulation.[138] All in all, the application of competition law to exploitative abuses raises a number of fundamental economic and legal issues.[139]

5.3. Exploitative Abuses

53   The general reticence mentioned above underlies the approach to **exploitative abuses**. The winner in a market would be able to charge a supra-competitive price, and it might be said that for certain undertakings, this rationale underlies competition. The significant enforcement costs and risk of chilling competition mean that competition law enforcement should take place with reticence[140] and, above all, with awareness of potential over- and under-enforcement and the effects thereof.[141]

5.3.1. Unfair Excessive Prices

54   Article 102 (2) point (a) TFEU prohibits 'imposing unfair purchase or selling prices or other unfair trading conditions' as a form of abuse. The seminal case dealing with unfair prices is *United Brands*, in which the European Commission had found that United Brands, the producer of Chiquita bananas, had abused its dominant position by, *inter alia*, charging excessive prices to consumers for its bananas. The Commission reached this conclusion by **comparing prices charged in several MS** to those charged in Ireland as well as **comparing them with** the banana **prices**

---

[137] Dunne (2015), p. 41 et seq.

[138] Discussed at length in *Verizon Communications v. Law Office of Curtis V. Trinko*, 540 U.S. 398 (2004). Cf. the opposite conclusion reached by the CJEU in Case C-280/08 P, *Deutsche Telekom AG v Commission* (CJEU 14 October 2010).

[139] Eloquently brought forward by the Judge Learned Hand in the *Alcoa* case, *United States v. Aluminum Co of America*, 148 F 2d 416, (2nd Circuit 1945), pp. 426–433.

[140] This is also clearly voiced in the comments by EU Competition Commissioner *Vestager* during the Chillin' Competition Conference, Brussels, 21 November 2016.

[141] Cf. Case C-177/16, *Biedrība 'Autortiesību un komunicēšanās konsultāciju aģentūra – Latvijas Autoru apvienība' v Konkurences padome* (Opinion of AG *Wahl* of 6 April 2017), para 42.

charged by competitors.[142] The Court upheld the appeal on the ground that prices are only excessive when they have no reasonable relation to the economic value of the product.[143] This results in a two-stage test, whereby the first question is whether the difference between the costs actually incurred and the price actually charged is excessive and, if so, whether this price is either unfair in itself or unfair compared to competing products.[144]

This test has been consistently applied since *United Brands*[145] and, thus, first requires a **comparison between the costs and prices to reveal an excess.**[146] This is fraught with difficulties, given that no guidance was given as to the costs to be taken into account,[147] nor has a standard for 'excessiveness' been defined.[148] In addition to the cost-based approach to the first test, the Court has also allowed a comparative approach to determine the excessive nature of prices. In that regard, comparisons can be made with other companies selling similar products[149] and with comparable products from the same company.[150] Such comparisons must, of course, take into account the **objective differences** that may well exist between

55

---

[142] Commission Decision *relating to a procedure under Article 86 of the EEC Treaty (IV/26699 - Chiquita)*, O.J. L 95/1 (1975), under heading 3.

[143] Case 27/76, *United Brands v Commission* (ECJ 14 February 1978), para 250.

[144] Case 27/76, *United Brands v Commission* (ECJ 14 February 1978), para 252.

[145] E.g., Case T-699/14, *Topps Europe Ltd v Commission* (GC 11 January 2017), para 49, and Case C-242/95, *GT-Link A/S v De Danske Statsbaner (DSB)* (ECJ 17 July 1997), para 39.

[146] Cf. in this regard the discussion on whether or not passing on carbon costs in electricity prices ('windfall profits') constitutes abusive pricing precisely because of the unclear nature of the costs involved in these costs, Friederiszick and Röller (2008), pp. 929–940.

[147] This is acknowledged by the Court itself in Case 27/76, *United Brands v Commission* (ECJ 14 February 1978), para 254. See also Ezrachi and Gilo (2009), pp. 175–177.

[148] It is unlikely that the experiences gained in the related area of the regulation of statutory (natural) monopolies, for example as part of determining what constitutes a reasonable profit in applying the third *Altmark* criterion; Case C-280/00, *Altmark Trans* (ECJ 24 July 2003), para 92, Commission Communication *on the application of the European Union State aid rules to compensation granted for the provision of services of general economic interest*, O.J. C 8/4 (2012), para 61, can be used sensibly in the context of Article 102 TFEU given the fundamentally different market circumstances.

[149] Case 395/87, *Tournier* (ECJ 13 July 1989), para 38, and Joined Cases 110, 241 and 242/88, *Lucazeau and Others v SACEM and Others* (ECJ 13 July 1989), para 25–32, where the comparison involved different MS. See Case 30/87, *Corinne Bodson v SA Pompes funèbres des régions libérées* (ECJ 4 May 1988), para 31, where the comparison was made within an MS between companies holding a concession to provide certain services and companies lacking such exclusive rights.

[150] A fitting example can be found in *British Leyland*, where the Court compared the activities relating to the issuing of certificates of conformity for the conversion of left- and right-hand drive vehicles (which it found to be almost identical) with the costs (which were six times higher), Case 226/84, *British Leyland v Commission* (ECJ 11 November 1986), para 28. Note further that the mere fact that prices are higher in one MS does not automatically lead to abuse, Case 24/67, *Parke, Davis and Co. v Probel and Others* (ECJ 29 February 1968), p. 72, and Case 53/87, *CICRA and Others v Renault* (ECJ 5 October 1988), para 17.

the products or (geographic) markets that are compared.[151] In the more recent *AKKA/LAA* case, the Court added that factors such as consumption habits, gross domestic product per capita or cultural and historical heritage can be taken into account, and where price levels differ greatly between countries, adjustments on the basis of purchasing power parity indices should be made.[152]

56   The second step involves **determining whether the excessive price is unfair**. The nature of this second step is not entirely clear. In *AKKA/LAA*, the Court explained that differences in rates must be significant, persistent and not temporary in order to be 'indicative of abuse'.[153] *Port of Helsingborg* involved the allegedly unfair port fees that were found not to be abusive, inter alia, because of the non-cost economic value of that port's location and the connection brought to its users. With this increased value, prices could be higher without being unfair.[154] Similar reasoning was employed in *Kanal 5*, where the Court suggested a 'balance between the interest of composers of music protected by copyright to receive remuneration for the television broadcast of those works and those of the television broadcasting companies to be able to broadcast those workers under reasonable conditions'.[155] This boils down to balancing the value for the copyright owners against the value of the broadcasters that had to pay the royalties. In the recent *Gazprom* decision, the Commission reached a preliminary conclusion that Gazprom's prices were unfair, firstly, by identifying the profit margin at 170% and, secondly, by finding that Gazprom prices were roughly 20% higher than those on comparable sufficiently liquid markets.[156]

57   In other cases, the unfair prices were found to be the result of an **ulterior motive** on the part of the dominant undertaking.[157] In *General Motors*, for example, the high prices charged also served to limit parallel imports of cars.[158] More recently, the decision and judgment in *Duales System Deutschland* are evidence of how the

---

[151] Case C-177/16, *Biedrība 'Autortiesību un komunicēšanās konsultāciju aģentūra – Latvijas Autoru apvienība' v Konkurences padome* (CJEU 14 September 2017), para 37–38.

[152] Case C-177/16, *Biedrība 'Autortiesību un komunicēšanās konsultāciju aģentūra – Latvijas Autoru apvienība' v Konkurences padome* (CJEU 14 September 2017), para 42.

[153] Case C-177/16, *Biedrība 'Autortiesību un komunicēšanās konsultāciju aģentūra – Latvijas Autoru apvienība' v Konkurences padome* (CJEU 14 September 2017), para 56–57.

[154] Commission Decision of 23 July 2004 in Case COMP/36.568, *Scandlines Sverige AB v Port of Helsingborg*, para 241–248.

[155] Case C-52/07, *Kanal 5 and TV 4* (ECJ 11 December 2008), para 31.

[156] Commission Decision 24 May 2018 in case AT.39816, *Upstream gas supplies in Central and Eastern Europe (Gazprom)*, para 69–78.

[157] In the context of Article 106 TFEU in connection with Article 102 TFEU, instances of excessive unfair prices are more prolific, see chapter (→ Article 106 TFEU para 24).

[158] Case 26/75, *General Motors v Commission* (ECJ 13 November 1975), para 11. This also underlay Case 226/84, *British Leyland v Commission* (ECJ 11 November 1986). See further Wahl (2007), p. 53.

excessive price had the effect of keeping potential competitors at bay.[159] The dominant company in question, Duales System Deutschland (DSD), operated a packaging waste management system that is funded through licence fees payable by companies that print the green dot logo on their packaging. Even when such packaging waste would be managed outside the DSD system, the fee was payable. This meant that companies bringing packaging on the market were forced to pay for services never actually used, thus making entry for companies seeking to manage such special waste streams less attractive.

Restricting output can also qualify as a form of exploitative abuse, as follows **58** from the Commission's thinking in the *German Electricity Wholesale Market* case.[160] This concerned the alleged strategic withdrawal of electricity generation capacity from the market. The resultant scarcity translated itself into higher wholesale prices, which the Commission considered abusive in an initial appraisal as part of a commitment decision.[161]

5.3.2. Other Unfair Trading Conditions

As price is only one, albeit perhaps the most important, of the trading conditions, **59** exploitative abuse can also be envisaged with regard to **other trading conditions**. Intuitively, we could expect a dominant undertaking to charge a supra-competitive price or deliver infra-competitive quality, for example, by imposing unfair conditions. Again, we witness a relative dearth of cases, with quite a few cases arising in the context of Article 106 TFEU. By and large, the Court's approach entails a review of the necessity and proportionality of the clauses or conditions imposed in the light of the objectives pursued by these clauses.[162] In this regard, the Court will consider the economic impact of a certain clause on the counterparty of the dominant undertaking as well as the duration of such contracts.[163]

5.4. Exclusionary Abuses

In *Continental Can*, the Court of Justice confirmed that abuse does not have to be **60** aimed at consumers directly but also concerns actions impacting the structure of a

---

[159] Case C-385/07 P, *Der Grüne Punkt - Duales System Deutschland GmbH v Commission* (ECJ 24 May 2009), para 141–143, and Commission Decision, *Case COMP D3/34493 — DSD*, O.J. L 166/1 (2001), where the Commission classified this as exploitative and obstructive abuse (point 2.2).
[160] Commission Decision of 26 November 2008, *Case COMP/39.388, German Electricity Wholesale Market*. See also Case 77/77, *B.P. v Commission* (ECJ 29 June 1978), para 18 et seq.
[161] For a fuller discussion see Vedder et al. (2016), p. 233.
[162] E.g., Case 127/73, *Belgische Radio en Televisie v SV SABAM* (ECJ 30 January 1974), para 8–12.
[163] Case 247/86, *Alsatel v Novasam* (ECJ 25 August 1988), para 10, and Case T-83/91, *Tetra Pak v Commission* (CFI 6 October 1994).

market.¹⁶⁴ In later cases, the Court specifically referred to the exclusionary effect that conduct (e.g. a pricing policy) can have.¹⁶⁵ It put in place specific tests in order to rule on the legitimacy of a dominant undertaking's conduct vis-à-vis its competitors.¹⁶⁶ In addition to the Court's case law, account must be taken of the Commission's policy change that basically entails a reduced scope for the enforcement of Article 102 TFEU to **exclusionary abuses**, broadly functioning under the heading of the more economic approach.¹⁶⁷ In line with what has been shortly set out above, one of the current issues is the degree to which exclusionary effects need to be proven and whether these are confined to as-efficient competitors. Concerning price-based abuses, the Commission's current enforcement priorities require evidence of a capability to foreclose market access to as-efficient competitors,¹⁶⁸ and the Court also regularly refers to the fact that the competition rules are not intended to protect inefficient companies on a market.¹⁶⁹

5.4.1. Price Discrimination

61 Regarding **discriminatory prices**, in *MEO*, aside from being discriminatory, conduct also has to tend to lead to a distortion of competition on the downstream market. Merely establishing that an entity had to pay more for the equivalent service, therefore suffering an immediate disadvantage, does not fulfil this requirement. It should appear from all circumstances of the case (e.g. the dominant position, bargaining power regarding price, duration and amount of the price and a strategy aiming to exclude an as-efficient competitor downstream) that

---

[164] This involved the acquisition of a competitor by Continental Can, the dominant undertaking. The specific aggressive takeover abuse has been largely rendered obsolete since the adoption of Council Regulation (EEC) 4064/89 *on the control of concentrations between undertakings*, O.J. L 395/1 (1989), as replaced by Council Regulation (EC) No 139/2004 *on the control of concentrations between undertakings (EU Merger Regulation)*, O.J. L 24/1 (2004) (→ Article 103 TFEU para 47). The exclusionary abuse had already been acknowledged in the US, e.g. by the US Supreme Court in *Standard Oil Co. v. United States*, 221 U.S. 1, 1911, para 75.

[165] Case C-280/08 P, *Deutsche Telekom AG v Commission* (CJEU 14 October 2010), para 177, and Case C-209/10, *Post Danmark* (CJEU 27 March 2012), para 25.

[166] The manner in which the Court of Justice subsequently tackles each individual type of abuse is comparable to the difference between object and effect restrictions under Article 101 TFEU matters (→ Article 101 TFEU para 26 et seq.).

[167] See Commission Communication, *Guidance on the Commission's enforcement priorities in applying Article 82 of the EC Treaty to abusive exclusionary conduct by dominant undertakings*, O.J. C 45/7 (2009).

[168] Commission Communication, *Guidance on the Commission's enforcement priorities in applying Article 82 of the EC Treaty to abusive exclusionary conduct by dominant undertakings*, O.J. C 45/7 (2009), para 23.

[169] Case C-525/16, *MEO — Serviços de Comunicações e Multimédia SA v Autoridade da Concorrência* (CJEU 19 April 2018), para 31.

the entity is at a competitive disadvantage.[170] No appreciability is, however, required.[171]

5.4.2. Predatory Pricing

The first exclusionary category is predatory pricing, or predation. This is a price-related abuse that occurs when a **dominant undertaking charges a price that does not cover certain costs**. The idea behind it is that such loss-leading prices will force competitors out of the market. The counter-intuitive element in this doctrine is that such price wars can be regarded as cut-throat competition and, therefore, contributory to consumer welfare. The Court, however, states that not all competition by price is legitimate.[172] The test in this regard requires a comparison of the price, costs and potential anti-competitive strategy of the dominant undertaking.[173] The material test was given in *AKZO* and corresponds to the broadly used Areeda-Turner test.[174] Prices below average variable costs (AVC) are said to be abusive because each individual sale will generate a loss for the dominant undertaking, against which a competitor is unable to compete.[175] Prices above AVC yet below average total costs (ATC) are abusive if these are part of a plan to eliminate the competition.[176] Competitors that operate as efficiently as the dominant undertaking are able to compete with such prices, but not for long, due to their restricted financial resources.[177] It may be noted that both tests do not require evidence of market exit by as-efficient competitors. 62

A variation on this theme arose in *Post Danmark I*, in which postal incumbent Post Danmark used the same infrastructure to operate two distinct markets (for addressed and unaddressed mail).[178] Post Danmark was held to have charged prices below ATC but above average *incremental* costs[179] on the market for the 63

---

[170] Because of this test, discriminatory prices would belong more in the category of exclusionary abuses than the exploitative abuse category.

[171] Case C-525/16, *MEO — Serviços de Comunicações e Multimédia SA v Autoridade da Concorrência* (CJEU 19 April 2018), para 25–31.

[172] Case C-62/86, *AKZO v Commission* (ECJ 3 July 1991), para 70.

[173] Case C-62/86, *AKZO v Commission* (ECJ 3 July 1991), para 74, and Case C-202/07 P, *France Télécom v Commission* (ECJ 7 March 2009), para 108. Only in case of higher prices than the variable costs per product (Average Variable Costs, AVC), consideration of the strategy of the dominant undertaking is required, see Case C-333/94 P, *Tetra Pak v Commission* (ECJ 14 November 1996), para 41–42.

[174] Areeda and Turner (1975), p. 703 et seq.

[175] Case C-62/86, *AKZO v Commission* (ECJ 3 July 1991), para 71.

[176] Case C-62/86, *AKZO v Commission* (ECJ 3 July 1991), para 72; reiterated in Case C-333/94 P, *Tetra Pak v Commission* (ECJ 4 October 1996), para 41.

[177] Case C-62/86, *AKZO v Commission* (ECJ 3 July 1991), para 72.

[178] 'Incumbent' is frequently used to describe a former monopolist in a liberalised market.

[179] Incremental costs are those costs specific for one of the activities that would no longer have to be borne once it is no longer performed, see also Case C-209/10, *Post Danmark* (Opinion of AG Mengozzi of 24 May 2011), para 37.

distribution of unaddressed mail, for which it competed with Forbruger-Kontakt. The Court held, firstly, that **prices above ATC** cannot be considered to have anti-competitive effects.[180] Secondly, **prices below ATC but above the average incremental costs**, 'covering the great bulk of costs attributable to the supply of good or services in question', will allow for an as-efficient competitor to compete effectively.[181]

64 The abuse tests for predation centre on **presumptions of foreclosure**, not on the exploitation of dominance, meaning that recoupment of the losses incurred as a result of the predatory price setting is not required.[182] However, evidence for predation can be utilised against potential objective justifications for the price setting or in favour of an anti-competitive plan.[183] Even without recoupment, predation strengthens a dominant position because a competitor is forced to exit the market,[184] which will of course also impact potential competition.

5.4.3. Margin Squeezes

65 A second exclusionary, also price-related, abuse is margin squeeze.[185] Here, an upstream supplier, often an incumbent (e.g. telephone network operator), not only **offers services to consumers** but also **sells upstream services** (such as access to its network infrastructure) **to a competitor on the downstream consumer market**. The position of the vertically integrated incumbent operating an essential facility, to which access is required for effective competition on the downstream market, enables it to set a price squeeze. This is possible because the incumbent controls both the price for the essential[186] input for the competitor and the downstream price of its own services.[187]

66 The **test for an abusive margin squeeze** involves comparing the price that competitors pay for access to the retail market with the retail price that end users

---

[180] Case C-209/10, *Post Danmark* (CJEU 27 March 2012), para 36.

[181] Case C-209/10, *Post Danmark* (CJEU 27 March 2012), para 37–38. For a discussion and recent application of the *AKZO* formula and Long-Run Average Incremental Costs benchmark the Commission uses, see e.g. Commission Decision of 18 July 2019, *Case AT.39711 – Qualcomm (predation)*, para 780–796.

[182] Case C-333/94 P, *Tetra Pak v Commission* (ECJ 4 October 1996), para 44. See also → para 54 et seqq.

[183] Case C-202/07 P, *France Télécom v Commission* (ECJ 2 April 2009), para 111.

[184] Case C-202/07 P, *France Télécom v Commission* (ECJ 2 April 2009), para 112.

[185] The Court also linked this abuse to Article 102 point (a) TFEU, unfair pricing practices, in Case C-280/08 P, *Deutsche Telekom AG v Commission* (CJEU 14 October 2010), para 172, and Case C-52/09, *TeliaSonera Sverige* (CJEU 17 February 2011), para 25.

[186] Note that for a margin squeeze, evidence of indispensability (within the meaning of the first requirement for an abusive refusal to supply (→ para 72) is not required, Case C-152/19 P, *Deutsche Telekom AG v Commission* (CJEU 25 March 2021), para 50.

[187] Such input will often involve regulated prices. The involvement of a national regulatory authority in setting such prices does not preclude the *ex post* application of competition law, Case C-280/08 P, *Deutsche Telekom AG v Commission* (CJEU 14 October 2010), para 77–96.

pay to the dominant undertaking.[188] The question to be answered is whether the dominant undertaking is able to offer its retail services profitably, given the upstream price charged to its competitors. If this is not the case, an exclusionary effect *vis-à-vis* as-efficient competitors is assumed.[189]

With regard to the **evidence for effects of a squeeze**, the Court makes a distinction between the ability, capability and likeliness of the abusive conduct. In general, the conduct has to hinder the *ability* of as-efficient competitors to trade with consumers.[190] This means that no actual exclusionary effects have to be proven.[191] In case of a negative spread, the conduct should be *capable* of excluding competitors as these would be forced to sell at a loss.[192] Moreover, if access to the wholesale product is indispensable, the anti-competitive effects of a negative spread are probable.[193] In case of a positive spread, evidence for *likely* exclusionary effects as a result of reduced profitability of the squeeze must be provided,[194] enabling competitors to rely on Article 102 TFEU in a preventive manner.[195]

67

5.4.4. Refusals to Deal and Essential Facilities

The third exclusionary abuse is the **refusal to deal**. It is subjected to a high standard because it may put a severe restriction on the freedom to contract of a business

68

---

[188] The test also involves scrutiny of the costs and strategy of the dominant undertaking, Case C-280/08 P, *Deutsche Telekom AG v Commission* (CJEU 14 October 2010), para 198. In *Deutsche Telekom*, the costs were designated as product-specific costs for the provision of its own services (para 197) and, in *TeliaSonera*, as wholesale prices for intermediary services.

[189] Case C-280/08 P, *Deutsche Telekom AG v Commission* (CJEU 14 October 2010), para 169 and 177, and Case C-52/09, *TeliaSonera Sverige* (CJEU 17 February 2011), para 40. Neither the excessiveness of the wholesale price, nor the predatory nature of the retail price needs to be proven. See e.g., Case C-280/08 P, *Deutsche Telekom AG v Commission* (CJEU 14 October 2010), para 48–49 and 159. Cf. Case T-5/97, *Industrie des poudres sphériques SA v Commission* (CFI 30 November 2000), para 179. Note that a comparison with competitors' wholesale and retail prices is required only where it is not possible to take account of the incumbent's own costs and charges, Case C-52/09, *TeliaSonera Sverige* (CJEU 17 February 2011), para 46.

[190] Case C-280/08 P, *Deutsche Telekom AG v Commission* (CJEU 14 October 2010), para 254; Case C-52/09, *TeliaSonera Sverige* (CJEU 17 February 2011), para 66.

[191] Case C-280/08 P, *Deutsche Telekom AG v Commission* (CJEU 14 October 2010), para 254.

[192] Case C-280/08 P, *Deutsche Telekom AG v Commission* (CJEU 14 October 2010), para 198, and Case C-52/09, *TeliaSonera Sverige* (CJEU 17 February 2011), para 73.

[193] Case C-280/08 P, *Deutsche Telekom AG v Commission* (CJEU 14 October 2010), para 234; Case C-52/09, *TeliaSonera Sverige* (CJEU 17 February 2011), para 70–71; and Case C-152/19 P, *Deutsche Telekom AG v Commission* (CJEU 25 March 2021), para 50.

[194] Case C-52/09, *TeliaSonera Sverige* (CJEU 17 February 2011), para 74.

[195] Case C-52/09, *TeliaSonera Sverige* (CJEU 17 February 2011), para 108: 'Article 102 TFEU requires action as quickly as possible, to prevent the formation and consolidation in that market of a competitive structure distorted by the abusive strategy of an undertaking which has a dominant position on that market or on a closely linked neighbouring market, in other words it requires action before the anticompetitive effects of that strategy are realised.'

operator.[196] Depending on the object of the request for access, refusal-to-deal situations are subjected to different legal tests. These situations require finding a balance between the freedom of contract and of property rights on the one hand (→ Article 36 TFEU para 8; → Article 345 TFEU para 8 et seqq.) and free competition on the other.[197]

69   First of all, a dominant undertaking that **refuses to supply a customer with raw material** or reserves it to itself (for instance, by way of a vertically integrated downstream undertaking) commits an abuse if the refusal has the risk of eliminating all competition for the customer entirely.[198]

70   A second type of abuse in this regard is the **refusal to supply services that are indispensable in order for an undertaking to become active on a market separate from the dominated one**.[199] Such refusals are, however, susceptible to objective justification.[200]

71   The third and fourth categories concern **refusals to grant access to so-called essential facilities**, amenities that are legally[201] or economically[202] nigh impossible to duplicate. Refusing access to or refusing licences for intellectual property rights,[203] such as for copyright-protected material, may lead to a third refusal-to-deal situation, but only if the following four cumulative conditions are fulfilled.[204] Firstly, access or supply has to be indispensable.[205] This means that the refusal

---

[196] See Case C-7/97, *Bronner* (Opinion of AG *Jacobs* of 28 May 1998), and Cases C-152/19 P and C-165/19 P, *Deutsche Telekom AG and Slovak Telekom v Commission* (Opinion of AG *Saugmandsgaard Øe* of 9 September 2020), para 66 et seq.

[197] Case C-418/01, *IMS Health* (ECJ 29 April 2004), para 48.

[198] Joined Cases 6 and 7/73, *Istituto Chemioterapico Italiano S.p.A. and Commercial Solvents Corporation v Commission* (ECJ 6 March 1974), para 25. Case 27/76, *United Brands v Commission* (ECJ 14 February 1978), para 182.

[199] Case 311/84, *CBEM v CLT and IPB* (ECJ 3 October 1985), para 26.

[200] Case 311/84, *CBEM v CLT and IPB* (ECJ 3 October 1985), para 26–27. See also Case T-83/91, *Tetra Pak v Commission* (CFI 6 October 1994), para 115.

[201] Legal barriers could arise from exclusive rights, such as those covered by Article 106 TFEU (→ Article 106 TFEU para 13 et seq.).

[202] This situation is often characterised as a natural monopoly.

[203] Note that the application of competition law to the licensing of IP rights, and so-called standard essential patents, has evolved into a separate doctrine; see, e.g., Case C-170/13, *Huawei Technologies* (CJEU 16 July 2015). See Picht (2017).

[204] Case C-418/01, *IMS Health* (ECJ 29 April 2004), para 38. Hence, a refusal to grant a license by a dominant undertaking is not *per se* abusive, Joined Cases C-241 and C-242/91 P, *RTE and ITP v Commission* (ECJ 6 April 1995), para 49. See also Case 24/67, *Parke, Davis and Co. v Probel and Others* (ECJ 29 February 1968) p. 72, Case 238/87, *Volvo v Veng* (ECJ 5 October 1988), para 8. Also, acquiring an exclusive right does not equate with abuse, Case 53/87, *CICRA and Others v Renault* (ECJ 5 October 1988), para 15. Abuse in earlier case law was exemplified as the arbitrary refusal to supply spare parts, unfair price-fixing, or termination of spare parts production, Case 238/87, *Volvo v Veng* (ECJ 5 October 1988), para 9, and Case 53/87, *CICRA and Others v Renault* (ECJ 5 October 1988), para 16.

[205] Joined Cases C-241 and C-242/91 P, *RTE and ITP v Commission* (ECJ 6 April 1995), para 50, and Case C-7/97, *Bronner* (ECJ 26 November 1998), para 41.

concerns a product for which there are no alternatives.[206] Indicators in this regard are the degree to which end users have become dependent on, for instance, the technology of the dominant undertaking and the additional investments required for developing alternatives.[207] Secondly, the refusal should bar the creation of a new product, for which there is consumer demand.[208] The third condition is that the refusal eliminates all competition on the secondary market.[209] The last condition for an abusive refusal to license IP rights is that the dominant undertaking cannot objectively justify its refusal to grant access.[210]

With respect to **refusals to grant access to any other facility**, for instance to certain infrastructure owned by the dominant undertaking, the aforementioned criteria are used to assess such a situation, apart from the so-called new product rule.[211]

72

As regards effects, **the refusal should be likely to eliminate all competition on the market**. All in all, the bar for using an essential facility doctrine to force a dominant undertaking into granting access or providing a certain service is placed rather high, which makes sense in view of the incentive that should be available to the dominant undertaking as a reward for developing or constructing the facility.[212] Where such facilities are not the result of the dominant undertaking's investments and/or business acumen, Article 102 TFEU may be used to obtain access more easily.[213]

73

---

[206] Case C-7/97, *Bronner* (ECJ 26 November 1998), para 43–44, and Case C-418/01, *IMS Health* (ECJ 29 April 2004), para 28.

[207] Case C-418/01, *IMS Health* (ECJ 29 April 2004), para 29.

[208] Joined Cases C-241 and C-242/91 P, *RTE and ITP v Commission* (ECJ 6 April 1995), para 54. See also Case C-7/97, *Bronner* (ECJ 26 November 1998), para 40. Note that this requires market research, Case C-418/01, *IMS Health* (ECJ 29 April 2004), para 49.

[209] Joined Cases C-241 and C-242/91 P, *RTE and ITP v Commission* (ECJ 6 April 1995), para 53 and 56. See also Case C-7/97, *Bronner* (ECJ 26 November 1998), para 40. Note that this could mean the creation of a new market, see Case T-201/04, *Microsoft v Commission* (CFI 17 September 2007), para 291–721.

[210] Joined Cases C-241 and C-242/91 P, *RTE and ITP v Commission* (ECJ 6 April 1995), para 55. See also Case C-7/97, *Bronner* (ECJ 8 November 1998), para 40.

[211] In *Bronner*, Oscar Bronner GmbH wished to utilise the home-delivery infrastructure for newspapers owned by Mediaprint Zeitungs- und Zeitschriftenverlag GmbH & Co. KG in order to compete with the latter on the daily newspaper market, but Mediaprint refused. Case C-7/97, *Bronner* (ECJ 26 November 1998), para 38 and 41.

[212] Cf. Renda (2010), esp. pp. 31–34.

[213] E.g. Commission Decision 94/119/EC *concerning a refusal to grant access to the facilities of the port of Rødby (Denmark)*, O.J. L 55/52 (1994). Note that certain jurisdictions, like Germany, may have special regimes for such networks, cf. Section 19(4) of the Act against restrictions of competition (GWB).

5.4.5. Tying and Bundling

74 The fourth category in exclusionary abuses is tying or bundling abuse. Different situations can be distinguished. In tying situations, a dominant undertaking makes the **availability of one product conditional on the acquisition of another**, generally a product in which the undertaking is not dominant. Hence, customers are not able to buy the dominated product without the non-dominated product.[214] In bundling situations, neither the dominated nor the non-dominated product is sold separately.

75 **Examples of tying** were the tying by Hilti GmbH of its patented cartridge strips to nails for Hilti nail guns,[215] by Microsoft of its Windows Operating System to its Media Player software[216] and by Tetra Pak of its carton machines with the cartons and maintenance and repair services.[217]

76 Article 102 (2) point (d) TFEU **expressly prohibits tying**. The test in jurisprudence, however, has not neatly followed this phrase. Older examples in the case law follow a *per se* abuse approach: when a dominant undertaking jointly offered products belonging to different product markets, then that conduct would deprive consumers of choice, by its very nature have a foreclosure effect on competitors and therefore be prohibited.[218]

77 Subsequent case law by the CFI/GC embraced a **more effect-based test with four conditions**.[219] First, the conduct should consist of an obligation to purchase the tying (i.e. dominant) product with the tied product.[220] This means that the undertaking cannot also offer the products separately. Second, the tied product has to be distinct from the tying product, requiring a separate market definition. Third,

---

[214] Tying excludes competitors and can thus be classified as exclusionary, but it may also reduce the quality of services for consumers and thus be characterised as an unfair trading condition.

[215] Commission Decision 88/138/EEC, *IV/30.787 and 31.488 - Eurofix-Bauco v. Hilti*, O.J. L 65/19 (1988). As Hilti had admitted the abuses as referred to in the Decision, the Court did not go into the details of tying rules, see Case T-30/89, *Hilti v Commission* (CFI 12 December 1991), para 101.

[216] Case T-201/04, *Microsoft v Commission* (CFI 17 September 2007).

[217] Case T-83/91, *Tetra Pak v Commission* (CFI 6 October 1994), and Case C-333/94 P, *Tetra Pak v Commission* (ECJ 14 November 1996).

[218] Case 85/76, *Hoffmann-La Roche v Commission* (ECJ 13 February 1979), para 111; Case T-201/04, *Microsoft v Commission* (CFI 17 September 2007), para 862, 868 and 1034–1035. Cf. O'Donoghue and Padilla (2013), p. 612; see also Rousseva (2010), p. 221 et seq., esp at. p. 225. Cf. Case T-83/91, *Tetra Pak v Commission* (CFI 6 October 1994), para 82 et seq., and Case C-333/94 P, *Tetra Pak v Commission* (ECJ 14 November 1996), para 34 et seq., where the Court of Justice interpreted the element 'commercial usage' in Article 102 point (d) TFEU as meaning that there is a natural link, or indivisibility between the products concerned, yet ruled that this did not apply to Tetra Pak: other manufacturers were able to separately produce cartons which could be used in Tetra Pak machinery.

[219] Case T-201/04, *Microsoft v Commission* (CFI 17 September 2007), para 842–843 and 869.

[220] Case T-201/04, *Microsoft v Commission* (CFI 17 September 2007), para 961.

the conduct should have a foreclosure effect on competition.[221] In *Microsoft*, the Commission compared advantages of the conduct for the dominant undertaking with methods used by competitors to access the market or to expand market share.[222] Fourth, the conduct should not be objectively justified.[223]

5.4.6. Exclusive Dealing

The fifth abuse situation concerns exclusive dealing. Here, a **dominant supplier binds its customers to purchase all or most of their required quantities of products with the former.**[224] The exclusivity does not have to be restricted to contractual clauses or obligations but can also arise from factual circumstances that incentivise customers into exclusivity, requiring an appraisal of all the circumstances.[225]

The **initial test** stems from *Hoffmann-La Roche* and **followed a *per se* abuse approach.**[226] If the supplier was dominant, then an exclusivity clause in a contract would be abusive because such clauses would be designed to restrict the

---

[221] The foreclosure effect does not immediately follow from the bundling itself, but must be proven separately, Case T-201/04, *Microsoft v Commission* (CFI 17 September 2007), para 859–860, Cf. Rousseva (2010), p. 252 et seq.

[222] As the Commission had reasons to believe consumers were installing other media players from other sources, it reasoned there was no foreclosure by nature, and had to examine the actual effects of the behaviour, Case T-201/04, *Microsoft v Commission* (CFI 17 September 2007), para 846, and, for the substantive review, para 1036 et seq.

[223] Case T-201/04, *Microsoft v Commission* (CFI 17 September 2007), para 1144. See further Case C-333/94 P, *Tetra Pak v Commission* (ECJ 14 November 1996), para 36.

[224] The extent to which exclusivity should exist is not entirely clear. Cf. O'Donoghue and Padilla (2013), p. 434.

[225] Case T-65/98, *Van den Bergh Foods v Commission* (CFI 23 October 2003), para 158–160, supported on appeal in Case C-552/03 P, *Unilever Bestfoods (Ireland) Ltd v Commission* (ECJ 28 September 2006), ECLI:EU:C:2006:607 para 136 also (→ para 72 et seq.). E.g., Case 85/76, *Hoffmann-La Roche v Commission* (ECJ 13 February 1979), para 104–107, where the Court analysed so-called English clauses in Hoffmann-La Roche's contracts. Such clauses stipulate that the exclusivity obligation shall not be breached if a better offer can be found with another supplier, which, after notification, is not equalled by the dominant undertaking. In theory, this could mitigate the exclusivity, by providing customers with the opportunity to switch to other suppliers. However, the English clauses in *Hoffmann-La Roche* were very limited in scope, and were subject to conditions, which seriously strengthened the exclusivity. See also Case T-155/06, *Tomra Systems ASA and Others v Commission* (GC 9 September 2010), para 58–66 and 88–197, and Case C-549/10 P, *Tomra Systems ASA and Others v Commission* (CJEU 19 April 2012), para 91–92.

[226] Case 85/76, *Hoffmann-La Roche v Commission* (ECJ 13 February 1979), para 89. See also Case C-62/86, *AKZO v Commission* (ECJ 3 July 1991), para 149, and Case C-393/92, *Municipality of Almelo and others v NV Energiebedrijf IJsselmij* (ECJ 27 April 1994), para 44. *Hoffmann-La Roche* concerned the abusive assessment of contractual clauses, concluded between Hoffmann-La Roche and 22 customers, binding customers of vitamins by ways of rebates. Cf. Whish and Bailey (2018). Even if the contract is concluded at the request of the customers, it is perceived as abuse, as reiterated in Case C-552/03 P, *Unilever Bestfoods (Ireland) Ltd v Commission* (ECJ 28 September 2006), para 129.

purchasers' choice for other dealing partners and cause 'additional interference with the structure of competition in a market'.[227]

80   A **more effect-based** course seems to have been taken in *Vandenbergh Foods*, where the CFI applied a type of **foreclosure reasoning to *de facto* exclusivities**.[228] Hence, for non-contractual exclusivities, foreclosure has to be proven.[229] This more effect-based approach is particularly relevant where the exclusivity results from a financial incentive in the form of a rebate.

5.4.7. Rebates

81   The sixth and final category of exclusionary abuses is formed by rebates. Anticompetitive rebates grant **cost advantages to customers, which incentivise them to continue dealing only with the dominant supplier**. Due to this incentive, dominant suppliers bind their customers, preventing them from purchasing from direct competitors and, thus, foreclosing the market. Rebates connect to Article 102 points (b) and (c) TFEU[230] but are generally assessed under the broader concept of abuse.[231] Furthermore, they can be seen as a specific type of price-based *de facto* exclusive dealing.[232]

---

[227] Case 85/76, *Hoffmann-La Roche v Commission* (ECJ 13 February 1979), para 90. Overlap exists with Articles 101.1 and 101.3 TFEU where the anti-competitive elements are weighed against pro-competitive efficiencies of the exclusivities. Hence, the agreements themselves may escape the application of competition law under Article 101.3 TFEU. See Case 85/76, *Hoffmann-La Roche v Commission* (ECJ 13 February 1979), para 90 and 120: 'unless there are exceptional circumstances which may make an agreement between undertakings in the context of Article [101] [...] (3) [...], permissible'. The difference with Article 102 TFEU is the existence of a dominant undertaking. In that regard, see Case C-310/93 P, *BPB Industries plc and British Gypsum Ltd v Commission* (ECJ 6 April 1995), para 11, and Opinion of AG *Léger* of 13 December 1994 para 44–45, stating that the existence of a dominant position naturally weakens competition in a market *ex hypothesi* and that an exclusivity obligation would entail additional interference with the structure of the market.

[228] Case T-65/98, *Van den Bergh Foods v Commission* (CFI 23 October 2003), para 160. The *de facto* exclusivity arose from offers to retailers to supply freezer cabinets exclusively with impulse ice cream from HB, the dominant undertaking, and to maintain those cabinets free of charge. Consequently, retailers were prevented from opting for other ice suppliers, who were then barred from accessing the market. On appeal, the Court dismissed the objections raised against the CFI analysis as either manifestly inadmissible or manifestly unfounded, Case C-552/03 P, *Unilever Bestfoods (Ireland) Ltd v Commission* (ECJ 28 September 2006), para 136. Cf. O'Donoghue and Padilla (2013), p. 429 et seq.

[229] Cf. Commission Communication, *Guidance on the Commission's enforcement priorities in applying Article 82 of the EC Treaty to abusive exclusionary conduct by dominant undertakings*, O.J. C 45/7 (2009), para 33–36.

[230] Joined Cases 40/73 et al., *Suiker Unie and Others v Commission* (ECJ 16 December 1975), para 526–527 and 522–523, respectively.

[231] Case C-95/04 P, *British Airways v Commission* (ECJ 15 March 2007), para 58.

[232] Cf. Commission Communication, *Guidance on the Commission's enforcement priorities in applying Article 82 of the EC Treaty to abusive exclusionary conduct by dominant undertakings*, O.J. C 45/7 (2009), para 37 et seq.; see also OECD (2008), p. 26.

Case law exemplified **numerous types of rebates**: from individualised contractual rebates in *Hoffmann-La Roche*, targets in *Michelin I* and retroactive rebates in *Tomra* to bonuses or discounts on overall turnover in *British Airways* and standardised conditional retroactive rebates in *Post Danmark II*. Depending on the conditions under which discounts are granted, a rebate scheme is either held lawful or unlawful. This makes it important to look at all the relevant conditions.[233]

82

The approach taken by the Court has not gone without resistance. A vivid debate has risen with regard to the number of categories and **which test should apply to them individually or to all of them**.[234]

83

As regards the jurisprudence, first, **rebates that are solely connected to volumes of purchases are presumed lawful**.[235] Such 'simple' quantity rebates represent economies of scale, the advantages of which can be transferred to consumers. It is held that they are based on an economic transaction that justifies the anti-competitive advantage that a dominant undertaking receives.[236] However, a dominant undertaking should not discriminate when applying a quantity rebate scheme, for instance by applying it only to very large customers or by having a greater than linear discount increase for large orders, unless it can objectively justify doing so.[237]

84

Second, **rebates that are granted only when a customer is obliged to purchase all or most of its requirements over a certain period with the dominant undertaking are presumed unlawful**.[238] These so-called loyalty or exclusivity rebates overlap with the former abuse category of exclusive contractual dealing, for which *per se* unlawfulness is also the applicable norm.[239]

85

---

[233] The Court emphasises the same wording for the tests for all price-related abuses, such as margin squeezes, e.g. Case C-280/08 P, *Deutsche Telekom AG v Commission* (CJEU 14 October 2010), para 175, and Case C-52/09, *TeliaSonera Sverige* (CJEU 17 February 2011), para 28. Cf. Case 322/81, *Michelin v Commission* (ECJ 9 November 1983), para 73; Case C-549/10 P, *Tomra Systems ASA and Others v Commission* (CJEU 19 April 2012), para 71; and Case C-23/14, *Post Danmark* (CJEU 6 October 2015), para 29, 50 and 68. Cf. Case T-57/01, *Solvay v Commission* (GC 17 December 2009), para 320, referring to quantity rebates (in the authoritative French: '[...] d'un système de rabais quantitatifs [...]').

[234] E.g. Case C-413/14 P, *Intel v Commission* (Opinion of AG *Wahl* of 20 October 2016), para 80 et seq.; see also, among many others, Wils (2014) and Ibáñez Colomo (2016).

[235] Joined Cases 40/73 et al., *Suiker Unie and Others v Commission* (ECJ 16 December 1975), para 518; Case 322/81, *Michelin v Commission* (ECJ 9 November 1983), para 71; Case 85/76, *Hoffmann-La Roche v Commission* (ECJ 13 February 1979), para 89, 90 second subparagraph, and Case C-163/99, *Portugal v Commission* (ECJ 29 March 2001), para 50. Stating that a rebate is a 'normal price reduction' in that regard is insufficient, Joined Cases 40/73 et al., *Suiker Unie and others v Commission* (ECJ 16 December 1975), para 517–518.

[236] See Case 85/76, *Hoffmann-La Roche v Commission* (ECJ 13 February 1979), para 90.

[237] Case C-163/99, *Portugal v Commission* (ECJ 29 March 2001), para 51–53.

[238] Case 85/76, *Hoffmann-La Roche v Commission* (ECJ 13 February 1979), para 89–90.

[239] In this regard, designating a rebate clause in a contract as a fidelity rebate clause emphasises the link between exclusivity and the rebate, see Case 85/76, *Hoffmann-La Roche v Commission* (ECJ 13 February 1979), para 95.

86   In general, **a *prima facie* scrutiny of the discount system of the dominant undertaking can reveal into which of the two former categories a rebate falls**. However, if a rebate by a dominant undertaking is based neither purely on volume nor on contractual exclusivity obligations, an assessment will be more difficult. That third category of rebates requires more thorough scrutiny of all the circumstances and is subjected to a more effect-oriented test. This test assesses the loyalty-inducing effect of the rebates, namely whether they tend to restrict choices regarding suppliers, raise entry barriers, discriminate or distort competition by strengthening the existing dominant position.[240] The appeal in *Intel* upheld the earlier case law set out above and clarified that the Commission is required to research all relevant circumstances in case a company indicates during the administrative phase that its pricing practice was not capable of restricting competition.[241]

87   An **as-efficient competitor test is not required for rebates**. In some cases, it might even be of no relevance whatsoever.[242] Furthermore, as regards effects, actual anti-competitive effects do not have to be indicated.[243] Also, there is no specific appreciability requirement for abusive rebates.[244] The conduct has to be capable of producing exclusionary effects. Hence, providing evidence for potential anti-competitive effects in the abstract is sufficient.[245]

5.4.8. Other Forms of Abuse

88   As was noted above, Article 102 TFEU needs to be sufficiently flexible to deal with **new forms of behaviour** that may also be classified as abuse. Such a novel form of abuse arose in the *Baltic Rail* case, in which the abuse consisted of the **non-repair and ultimately demolition of a railway track** by the incumbent railway operator, to the effect that a downstream competitor was forced to offer more expensive railway transportation services to a third party. This was found to be abusive by the GC.[246] In addition, the advent of so-called digital markets has resulted in new theories of harm whereby, for example, **self-preferencing** was found to harm competition.[247] In self-preferencing, the dominant provider of an online service

---

[240] Case 322/81, *Michelin v Commission* (ECJ 9 November 1983), para 73, as repeated in Case C-23/14, *Post Danmark* (CJEU 6 October 2015), para 64.

[241] Case C-413/14 P, *Intel v Commission* (CJEU 6 September 2017), para 138–141.

[242] Case C-23/14, *Post Danmark* (CJEU 6 October 2015), para 59–62.

[243] Case C-23/14, *Post Danmark* (CJEU 6 October 2015), para 66.

[244] Case 85/76, *Hoffmann-La Roche v Commission* (ECJ 13 February 1979), para 123; Case C-23/14, *Post Danmark* (CJEU 6 October 2015), para 72. See also Case C-549/10 P, *Tomra Systems ASA and Others v Commission* (CJEU 19 April 2012), para 68. Cf. Whish (2015), p. 2.

[245] Case C-457/10 P, *AstraZeneca v Commission* (CJEU 6 December 2012), para 112, referring to Case C-52/09, *TeliaSonera Sverige* (CJEU 17 February 2011), para 64.

[246] Case T-814/17, *Lietuvos geležinkeliai v Commission* (GC 18 November 2020).

[247] Crémer et al. (2019) provide an interesting overview and analysis of the policy challenges.

will shape the service in such a manner that consumers will be more inclined to use another service offered by that provider.[248]

List of Cases

ECJ/ CJEU

ECJ 13.07.1966, 56 and 58/64, *Consten and Grundig v Commission*, ECLI:EU:C:1966:41 [cit. in para 3, 7]

ECJ 29.02.1968, 24/67, *Parke, Davis and Co. v Probel and Others*, ECLI:EU:C:1968:11 [cit. in para 56, 72]

ECJ 18.02.1971, 40/70, *Sirena v Eda*, ECLI:EU:C:1971:18 [cit. in para 10, 20]

ECJ 08.06.1971, 78/70, *Deutsche Grammophon v Metro-SB*, ECLI:EU:C:1971:59 [cit. in para 20, 31]

ECJ 21.02.1973, 6/72, *Europemballage Corporation and Continental Can Company Inc. v Commission*, ECLI:EU:C:1973:22 [cit. in para 6, 12, 18, 47 62]

ECJ 06.03.1974, 6 and 7/73, *Istituto Chemioterapico Italiano S.p.A. and Commercial Solvents Corporation v Commission*, ECLI:EU:C:1974:18 [cit. in para 48, 70]

ECJ 30.04.1974, 155/73, *Giuseppe Sacchi*, ECLI:EU:C:1974:40 [cit. in para 9]

ECJ 13.11.1975, 26/75, *General Motors v Commission*, ECLI:EU:C:1975:150 [cit. in para 19, 58]

ECJ 16.12.1975, 40/73 et al., *Suiker Unie and Others v Commission*, ECLI:EU:C:1975:174 [cit. in para 2, 10, 82, 85]

ECJ 25.10.1977, 26/76, *Metro SB v Commission*, ECLI:EU:C:1977:167 [cit. in para 15]

ECJ 16.11.1977, 13/77, *INNO v ATAB*, ECLI:EU:C:1977:185 [cit. in para 9]

ECJ 14.02.1978, 27/76, *United Brands v Commission*, ECLI:EU:C:1978:22 [cit. in para 8, 10, 12, 15, 17, 22–23, 25–28, 30, 43, 55–56, 70]

ECJ 29.06.1978, 77/77, *B.P. v Commission*, ECLI:EU:C:1978:141 [cit. in para 59]

ECJ 13.02.1979, 85/76, *Hoffmann-La Roche v Commission*, ECLI:EU:C:1979:36 [cit. in para 6, 7, 11, 15–18, 22–25, 30, 33, 38, 44, 45, 46, 77, 79, 80, 85, 86, 88]

ECJ 31.05.1979, 22/78, *Hugin v Commission*, ECLI:EU:C:1979:138 [cit. in para 21, 27]

ECJ 25.10.1979, 22/79, *Greenwich Film v SACEM*, ECLI:EU:C:1979:245 [cit. in para 48]

ECJ 26.06.1980, 136/79, *National Panasonic v Commission*, ECLI:EU:C:1980:169 [cit. in para 37]

ECJ 11.12.1980, 31/80, *L'Oréal v De Nieuwe AMCK*, ECLI:EU:C:1980:289 [cit. in para 12]

ECJ 02.03.1983, 7/82, *GVL v Commission*, ECLI:EU:C:1983:52 [cit. in para 2, 14]

---

[248] E.g., Commission Decision of 27 June 2017, *Case AT.39740, Google Search (Shopping)*.

ECJ 09.11.1983, 322/81, *Michelin v Commission*, ECLI:EU:C:1983:313 [cit. in para 2, 12, 17, 18, 21, 23, 30, 37, 44, 83, 85, 87]

ECJ 03.10.1985, 311/84, *CBEM v CLT and IPB*, ECLI:EU:C:1985:394 [cit. in para 71]

ECJ 22.10.1986, 75/84, *Metro v Commission*, ECLI:EU:C:1986:399 [cit. in para 15]

ECJ 11.11.1986, 226/84, *British Leyland v Commission*, ECLI:EU:C:1986:421 [cit. in para 56, 58]

ECJ 09.04.1987, 402/85, *Basset v SACEM*, ECLI:EU:C:1987:197 [cit. in para 9, 19]

ECJ 04.05.1988, 30/87, *Corinne Bodson v SA Pompes funèbres des régions libérées*, ECLI:EU:C:1988:225 [cit. in para 19, 30, 33, 56]

ECJ 05.10.1988, 238/87, *Volvo v Veng*, ECLI:EU:C:1988:477 [cit. in para 20, 72]

ECJ 05.10.1988, 247/86, *Alsatel v Novasam*, ECLI:EU:C:1988:469 [cit. in para 61]

ECJ 05.10.1988, 53/87, *CICRA and Others v Renault*, ECLI:EU:C:1988:472 [cit. in para 20, 56, 72]

ECJ 11.04.1989, 66/86, *Ahmed Saeed Flugreisen and Silver Line Reisebüro GmbH v Zentrale zur Bekämpfung unlauteren Wettbewerbs e.V.*, ECLI:EU:C:1989:140 [cit. in para 5, 8, 9]

ECJ 13.07.1989, 395/87, *Tournier*, ECLI:EU:C:1989:319 [cit. in para 56]

ECJ 13.07.1989, 110, 241 and 242/88, *Lucazeau and Others v SACEM and Others*, ECLI:EU:C:1989:326 [cit. in para 56]

ECJ 23.04.1991, C-41/90, *Höfner and Elser v Macrotron*, ECLI:EU:C:1991:161 [cit. in para 2]

ECJ 18.06.1991, C-260/89, *ERT v DEP*, ECLI:EU:C:1991:254 [cit. in para 19]

ECJ 03.07.1991, C-62/86, *AKZO v Commission*, ECLI:EU:C:1991:286 [cit. in para 15–17, 21–23, 46–47, 63, 80]

ECJ 10.12.1991, C-179/90, *Merci convenzionali porto di Genova SpA v Siderurgica Gabrielli SpA*, ECLI:EU:C:1991:464 [cit. in para 2]

ECJ 27.04.1994, C-393/92, *Municipality of Almelo and others v NV Energiebedrijf IJsselmij*, ECLI:EU:C:1994:171 [cit. in para 33, 80]

ECJ 17.05.1994, C-18/93, *Corsica Ferries Italia Srl v Corpo dei Piloti del Porto di Genova*, ECLI:EU:C:1994:195 [cit. in para 19]

ECJ 13.12.1994, C-310/93 P, Opinion of AG Léger, *BPB Industries plc and British Gypsum Ltd v Commission*, ECLI:EU:C:1995:101 [cit. in para 79]

ECJ 15.12.1994, C-250/92, *Gøttrup-Klim e.a. Grovvareforeninger v Dansk Landbrugs Grovvareselskab AmbA*, ECLI:EU:C:1994:413 [cit. in para 15]

ECJ 06.04.1995, C-310/93 P, *BPB Industries plc and British Gypsum Ltd v Commission*, ECLI:EU:C:1995:101 [cit. in para 80]

ECJ 06.04.1995, C-241 and C-242/91 P, *RTE and ITP v Commission*, ECLI:EU:C:1995:98 [cit. in para 20, 72]

ECJ 05.10.1995, C-96/94, *Centro Servizi Spediporto Srl v Spedizioni Marittima del Golfo Srl*, ECLI:EU:C:1995:308 [cit. in para 33]

ECJ 17.10.1995, C-140, 141 and C-142/94, *DIP and Others v Comune di Bassano del Grappa and Others*, ECLI:EU:C:1995:330 [cit. in para 9]

ECJ 14.11.1996, C-333/94 P, *Tetra Pak v Commission*, ECLI:EU:C:1996:436 [cit. in para 8, 16, 38, 39, 48, 63-65, 76-77]
ECJ 17.06.1997, C-70/95, *Sodemare and Others v Regione Lombardia*, ECLI:EU:C:1997:301 [cit. in para 33]
ECJ 17.07.1997, C-242/95, *GT-Link A/S v De Danske Statsbaner (DSB)*, ECLI:EU:C:1997:376 [cit. in para 12, 56]
ECJ 11.11.1997, C-359 and C-379/95 P, *Commission and France v Ladbroke Racing*, ECLI:EU:C:1997:531 [cit. in para 19]
ECJ 31.03.1998, C-68/94 and C-30/95, *France and SCPA and EMC v Commission*, ECLI:EU:C:1998:148 [cit. in para 33]
ECJ 29.10.1998, C-395/96 P and C-396/96 P, Opinion of AG Fennelly, *Compagnie maritime belge transports and others v Commission*, ECLI:EU:C:1998:518 [cit. in para 38]
ECJ 26.11.1998, C-7/97, *Bronner*, ECLI:EU:C:1998:569 [cit. in para 12, 22, 72–73]
ECJ 16.03.2000, C-395 and C-396/96 P, *Compagnie maritime belge transports and others v Commission*, ECLI:EU:C:2000:132 [cit. in para 8, 33, 38–39]
ECJ 23.05.2000, C-209/98, *Sydhavnens Sten & Grus*, ECLI:EU:C:2000:279 [cit. in para 19]
ECJ 29.03.2001, C-163/99, *Portugal v Commission*, ECLI:EU:C:2001:189 [cit. in para 85]
ECJ 10.07.2001, C-497/99 P, *Irish Sugar v Commission*, ECLI:EU:C:2001:393 [cit. in para 36]
ECJ 22.10.2002, C-94/00, *Roquette Frères*, ECLI:EU:C:2002:603 [cit. in para 37]
ECJ 24.07.2003, C-280/00, *Altmark Trans*, ECLI:EU:C:2003:415 [cit. in para 55]
ECJ 29.04.2004, C-418/01, *IMS Health*, ECLI:EU:C:2004:257 [cit. in para 69, 72]
ECJ 28.09.2006, C-552/03 P, *Unilever Bestfoods (Ireland) Ltd v Commission*, ECLI:EU:C:2006:607 [cit. in para 79–81]
ECJ 15.03.2007, C-95/04 P, *British Airways v Commission*, ECLI:EU:C:2007:166 [cit. in para 44, 82]
ECJ 01.07.2008, C-49/07, *MOTOE*, ECLI:EU:C:2008:376 [cit. in para 12]
ECJ 10.07.2008, C-413/06 P, *Bertelsmann and Sony Corporation of America v Impala*, ECLI:EU:C:2008:392 [cit. in para 34]
ECJ 11.12.2008, C-52/07, *Kanal 5 and TV 4*, ECLI:EU:C:2008:703 [cit. in para 14, 57]
ECJ 02.04.2009, C-202/07 P, *France Télécom v Commission*, ECLI:EU:C:2009:214 [cit. in para 47, 51, 63, 65]
ECJ 16.06.2009, C-385/07 P, *Der Grüne Punkt - Duales System Deutschland GmbH v Commission*, ECLI:EU:C:2009:456 [cit. in para 58]
CJEU 14.10.2010, C-280/08 P, *Deutsche Telekom AG v Commission*, ECLI:EU:C:2010:603 [cit. in para 41, 42, 44, 46–47, 53, 62, 66–68, 83]
CJEU 17.02.2011, C-52/09, *TeliaSonera Sverige*, ECLI:EU:C:2011:83 [cit. in para 6, 19, 38–40, 44, 48, 66–68, 83, 88]
CJEU 27.03.2012, C-209/10, *Post Danmark*, ECLI:EU:C:2012:172 [cit. in para 37, 40, 47, 62, 64]

CJEU 19.04.2012, C-549/10 P, *Tomra Systems ASA and Others v Commission*, ECLI:EU:C:2012:221 [cit. in para 39, 44, 79, 83, 88]
CJEU 06.12.2012, C-457/10 P, *AstraZeneca v Commission*, ECLI:EU:C:2012:770 [cit. in para 46, 88]
CJEU 16.06.2015, C-170/13, *Huawei Technologies*, ECLI:EU:C:2015:477 [cit. in para 72]
CJEU 06.10.2015, C-23/14, *Post Danmark*, ECLI:EU:C:2015:651 [cit. in para 39, 45, 47, 83, 87–88]
CJEU 20.10.2016, C-413/14 P, Opinion of AG Wahl, *Intel v Commission*, ECLI:EU:C:2016:788 [cit. in para 83]
CJEU 06.04.2017, C-177/16, Opinion of AG Wahl, *Autortiesību un komunicēšanās konsultāciju aģentūra - Latvijas Autoru apvienība v Konkurences padome*, ECLI:EU:C:2017:286 [cit. in para 53]
CJEU 06.09.2017, C-413/14 P, *Intel v Commission*, ECLI:EU:C:2017:632 [cit. in para 47, 84, 87]
CJEU 14.09.2017, C-177/16, *Autortiesību un komunicēšanās konsultāciju aģentūra / Latvijas Autoru apvienība tegen Konkurences padome*, ECLI:EU:C:2017:689 [cit. in para 56–57]
CJEU 19.04.2018, C-525/16, *MEO - Serviços de Comunicações e Multimédia*, ECLI:EU:C:2018:270 [cit. in para 60, 62]
CJEU 30.01.2020, C-307/18, *Generics UK v Competition and Markets Authority*, ECLI:EU:C:2020:52 [cit. in para 7, 20]
CJEU 09.09.2020, C-152/19 P, Opinion of AG Saugmandsgaard Øe, *Deutsche Telekom AG v Commission*, ECLI:EU:C:2020:678 [cit. in para 68]
CJEU 09.09.2020, C-165/19 P, Opinion of AG Saugmandsgaard Øe, *Slovak Telekom v Commission*, ECLI:EU:C:2020:678 [cit. in para 68]
CJEU 25.03.2021, C-152/19 P, *Deutsche Telekom AG v Commission*, ECLI:EU:C:2021:238 [cit. in para 3]

CFI/GC

CFI 12.12.1991, T-30/89, *Hilti v Commission*, ECLI:EU:T:1991:70 [cit. in para 16, 20, 76]
CFI 10.03.1992, T-68/89, T-77/89 and T-78/89, *SIV and Others v Commission*, ECLI:EU:T:1992:38 [cit. in para 31, 33]
CFI 15.07.1994, T-17/93, *Matra Hachette v Commission*, ECLI:EU:T:1994:89 [cit. in para 33]
CFI 06.10.1994, T-83/91, *Tetra Pak v Commission*, ECLI:EU:T:1994:246 [cit. in para 61, 71, 76–77]
CFI 08.10.1996, T-24/93 et al., *Compagnie maritime belge transports and Others v Commission*, ECLI:EU:T:1996:139 [cit. in para 33]
CFI 25.03.1999, T-102/96, *Gencor v Commission*, ECLI:EU:T:1999:65 [cit. in para 34]

CFI 07.10.1999, T-228/97, *Irish Sugar v Commission*, ECLI:EU:T:1999:246 [cit. in para 2, 36, 38]
CFI 22.03.2000, T-125 and T-127/97, *Coca-Cola v Commission*, ECLI:EU:T:2000:84 [cit. in para 40]
CFI 30.11.2000, T-5/97, *Industrie des poudres sphériques SA v Commission*, ECLI:EU:T:2000:278 [cit. in para 67]
CFI 22.11.2001, T-139/98, *AAMS v Commission*, ECLI:EU:T:2001:272 [cit. in para 26]
CFI 06.06.2002, T-342/99, *Airtours v Commission*, ECLI:EU:T:2002:146 [cit. in para 34]
CFI 08.07.2003, T-374/00, *Verband der freien Rohrwerke and Others v Commission*, ECLI:EU:T:2003:188 [cit. in para 34]
CFI 30.09.2003, T-191 and T-212 to T-213/98, *Atlantic Container Line AB and Others v Commission*, ECLI:EU:T:2003:245 [cit. in para 43]
CFI 23.10.2003, T-65/98, *Van den Bergh Foods v Commission*, ECLI:EU:T:2003:281 [cit. in para 40, 79, 81]
CFI 17.12.2003, T-219/99, *British Airways plc v Commission*, ECLI:EU:T:2003:343 [cit. in para 15, 32]
CFI 26.01.2005, T-193/02, *Piau v Commission*, ECLI:EU:T:2005:22 [cit. in para 34]
CFI 17.09.2007, T-201/04, *Microsoft v Commission*, ECLI:EU:T:2007:289 [cit. in para 29, 38, 46, 72, 76–78]
CFI 10.04.2008, T-271/03, *Deutsche Telekom v Commission*, ECLI:EU:T:2008:101 [cit. in para 19]
GC 17.12.2009, T-57/01, *Solvay v Commission*, ECLI:EU:T:2009:519 [cit. in para 83]
GC 01.07.2010, T-321/05, *AstraZeneca v Commission*, ECLI:EU:T:2010:266 [cit. in para 14, 20, 30, 44, 46]
GC 09.09.2010, T-155/06, *Tomra Systems and Others v Commission*, ECLI:EU:T:2010:370 [cit. in para 78]
GC 11.12.2013, T-79/12, *Cisco Systems and Messagenet v Commission*, ECLI:EU:T:2013:635 [cit. in para 29]
GC 11.01.2017, T-699/14, *Topps Europe Ltd v Commission*, ECLI:EU:T:2017:2 [cit. in para 56]
GC 18.11.2020, T-814/17, *Lietuvos geležinkeliai v Commission*, ECLI:EU:T:2020:545 [cit. in para 47, 88]

US Supreme Court
SCOTUS 15.05.1911, *The Standard Oil Company of New Jersey, et al. v. The United States*, 221 U.S. 1 [cit. in para 52, 62]
SCOTUS 12.03.1945, *United States v. Alcoa*, 148 F.2d 416 (2d Cir. 1945) [cit. in para 52]

SCOTUS 26.03.1986, *Matsushita Electric Industrial Co., Ltd. v. Zenith Radio Corp.*, 475 U.S. 574 [cit. in para 51]
SCOTUS 13.01.2004, *Verizon Communications, Petitioner v. Law Offices of Curtis V. Trinko, LLP*, 540 U.S. 398 [cit. in para 53]

References[249]

Amato, G. (1997). *Antitrust and the bounds of power. The dilemma of liberal democracy in the history of the market.* Hart Publishing.
Appeldoorn, J. (2005). He who spareth his roth, hateth his son? Microsoft, super-dominance and Article 82 EC. *European Competition Law Review, 26*(12), 653–658.
Areeda, P., & Turner, D. F. (1975). Predatory pricing and related practices under section 2 of the Sherman Act. *Harvard Law Review, 88*(4), 697–733.
Bailey, D., & John, L. E. (Eds.). (2018). *Bellamy & child: European Union law of competition* (8th ed.). OUP.
Bishop, S., & Walker, M. (2010). *The economics of EC competition law: Concepts, application and measurement.* Sweet & Maxwell.
Bromwich, M. (2014). A comparison of historical cost and fair value accounting systems: General and some regulatory concerns. In R. Di Pietra, S. McLeay, & J. Ronen (Eds.), *Accounting and regulation: New insights on governance, markets and institutions* (pp. 269–290). Springer.
Buendia Sierra, J. L. (2014). Chapter 6 Article 106. In J. Faull & A. Nikpay (Eds.), *The EU law of competition* (3rd ed.). OUP.
Burrichter, J. (2008). A reformed approach to Article 82: The impact on private enforcement. In C. Ehlermann & M. Marquis (Eds.), *European competition law annual 2007. A reformed approach to Article 82 EC* (pp. 243–253). Hart Publishing.
Crémer, J., de Montjoye, Y.-A., & Schweitzer, H. (2019). *Competition policy for the digital era*, Final Report. Publications Office of the European Union.
Daly, A. (2016). *Private power, online information flows and EU law: Mind the gap.* Hart Publishing.
de la Mano, M., Nazzini, R., & Zenger, H. (2014). Chapter 4 Article 102. In J. Faull & A. Nikpay (Eds.), *The EU law of competition* (3rd ed.). OUP.
Dunne, N. (2015). *Competition law and economic regulation.* CUP.
Economides, N. (1996). The economics of networks. *International Journal of Industrial Organization, 14*, 673–699.
Ehlermann, C.-D., & Laudati, L. L. (Eds.). (1997). *Competition law annual 1997: Objectives of competition policy.* Hart Publishing.
Elhauge, E., & Geradin, D. (2007). *Global competition law and economics.* Hart Publishing.
Ezrachi, A., & Gilo, D. (2009). The darker side of the moon: Assessment of excessive pricing. In A. Ezrachi (Ed.), *Article 82 EC: Reflections on its recent evolution* (pp. 225–248). Hart Publishing.
Friederiszick, H. W., & Röller, L.-H. (2008). Überwälzungen der Opportunitätskosten von CO2-Zertifikaten als Ausbeutungsmissbrauch – eine ökonomische Analyse. *Wirtschaft und Wettbewerb, 58*(9), 929–940.
Grabitz, E., Hilf, M., & Nettesheim, M. (Eds.). (2022). *Das Recht der Europäische Union. EUV/AEUV.* C.H. Beck. Loose leaf (last supplement: 75).
Ibáñez Colomo, P. (2016). Post Danmark II: The emergence of a distinct 'effects-based' approach to Article 102 TFEU. *Journal of European Competition Law & Practice, 7*(2), 113–115.
Jones, A., & Sufrin, B. (Eds.). (2012). *EU competition law* (4th ed.). OUP.

---

[249] All cited internet sources in this comment have been accessed on 20 July 2022.

Katz, M. L., & Shapiro, C. (1985). Network externalities, competition, and compatibility. *AER, 75*(3), 424–440.

Kellerbauer, M. (2010). The Commission's new enforcement priorities in applying Article 82 EC to dominant companies' exclusionary conduct: A shift towards a more economic approach? *European Competition Law Review, 31*(5), 175–186.

Königsgruber, R. (2014). Accounting standard setting in two political contexts. In R. Di Pietra, S. McLeay, & J. Ronen (Eds.), *Accounting and regulation: New insights on governance, markets and institutions* (pp. 59–79). Springer.

Leslie, C. R. (2013). Predatory pricing and recoupment. *Columbia Law Review, 113*(7), 1695–1771.

Mestmäcker, E.-J., & Schweitzer, H. (2014). *Europäisches Wettbewerbsrecht*. C.H.Beck.

Monti, G. (Ed.). (2007). *EC competition law*. CUP.

Nazzini, R. (2013). *The foundations of European Union competition law: The objective and principles of Article 102*. OUP.

O'Donoghue, R., & Padilla, J. A. (2013). *The law and economics of Article 102 TFEU*. Hart Publishing.

OECD. (2006). *What is competition on the merits?*. Policy Brief. Retrieved from oecd.org/competition/mergers/37082099.pdf

OECD Policy Roundtables. (2008). Fidelity and Bundled Rebates and Discounts. DAF/COMP (2008)29. Retrieved from oecd.org/daf/competition/abuse/41772877.pdf

Picht, P. G. (2017). "FRAND wars 2.0" – Rechtsprechung im Anschluss an die Huawei/ZTE-Entscheidung des EuGH. *Wirtschaft und Wettbewerb, 68*(5), 234–241.

Renda, A. (2010). Competition–regulation interface in telecommunications: What's left of the essential facility doctrine. *Telecommunications Policy, 34*, 23–35.

Rousseva, E. (2010). *Rethinking exclusionary abuses in EU competition law*. Hart Publishing.

Van der Vijver, T. (2012). Objective justification and Article 102 TFEU. *World Competition, 35*(1), 55–76.

Vedder, H., Roggenkamp, M., Ronne, A., & Del Guayo, I. (2016). EU energy law. In M. Roggenkamp, C. Redgwell, A. Ronne, & I. Del Guayo (Eds.), *Energy law in Europe* (pp. 187–366). OUP.

Vestager, M. (2016). Protecting consumers from exploitation. Speech delivered at Chillin' Competition Conference, Brussels, 21 November 2016.

von der Groeben, H., Schwarze, J., & Hatje, A. (Eds.). (2015). *Europäisches Unionsrecht* (8th ed.). Nomos.

Wahl, N. (2007). Exploitative high prices and European competition law – A personal reflection. In Konkurrensverket (Ed.), *The pros and cons of high prices* (pp. 47–64). Retrieved from konkurrensverket.se/globalassets/english/research/the-pros-and-cons-of-high-prices-14mb.pdf

Whish, R. (2015). Intel v Commission: Keep calm and carry on! *Journal of European Competition Law & Practice, 6*(1), 2.

Whish, R., & Bailey, D. (Eds.). (2018). *Competition law* (9th ed.). OUP.

Whittington, G. (2014). Fair value and the IASB/FASB conceptual framework project: An alternative view. In R. Di Pietra, S. McLeay, & J. Ronen (Eds.), *Accounting and regulation: New insights on governance, markets and institutions* (pp. 229–269). Springer.

Wils, W. (2014). The judgment of the EU General Court in Intel and the so-called 'more economic approach' to abuse of dominance. *World Competition: Law and Economics Review, 37*(4), 405–434.

Witt, A. C. (2016). *The more economic approach to EU antitrust law*. Hart Publishing.

Zenger, H., & Walker, M. (2012). Theories of harm in European competition law: A progress report. In J. Bourgeois & D. Waelbroeck (Eds.), *Ten years of effects: Based approach in EU competition law* (pp. 185–209). Bruylant.

Article 103 [Adoption of Secondary Enforcement Measures for Articles 101 and 102 TFEU]
(ex-Article 83 TEC)

1. The appropriate regulations or directives[2, 4] to give effect to the principles set out in Articles 101 and 102 shall be laid down by the Council,[2, 3] on a proposal from the Commission[2] and after consulting the European Parliament.[2]
2. The regulations[1, 3, 5–47] or directives[1, 3, 15, 34, 35, 41] referred to in paragraph 1 shall be designed in particular:

    (a) to ensure compliance with the prohibitions laid down in Article 101(1) and in Article 102 by making provision for fines[7, 9, 23, 24, 37] and periodic penalty payments;[7, 9, 23, 37]
    (b) to lay down detailed rules for the application of Article 101(3),[6, 7, 19, 20] taking into account the need to ensure effective supervision on the one hand, and to simplify administration to the greatest possible extent on the other;[16–18]
    (c) to define, if need be, in the various branches of the economy, the scope of the provisions of Articles 101 and 102;[45–47]
    (d) to define the respective functions of the Commission[6–8, 12, 19–26, 29–31, 36] and of the Court of Justice of the European Union[9, 19, 37] in applying the provisions laid down in this paragraph;
    (e) to determine the relationship between national laws and the provisions contained in this Section or adopted pursuant to this Article.[10, 38, 47]

Contents

1. Overview 1
2. Secondary Law Measures Under Article 103 TFEU 2
3. General Enforcement Regime 5
    3.1. General Enforcement Regulations 5
    3.2. Block Exemption Regulations 42
4. Special Enforcement Regimes 45
List of Cases
References

1. Overview

Articles 101 and 102 TFEU put in place the **substantive competition law rules** of the Treaty. The Treaty does not, however, lay down detailed **enforcement rules** for these provisions. Rather, Article 103, Article 104 and Article 105 TFEU, operating together, lay down the bare framework for their enforcement. Article 103 TFEU 1 requires the Council to enact **secondary enforcement measures** (→ para 2–47) to ensure the effective enforcement of Articles 101 and 102 TFEU. Pending the enactment of appropriate Article 103 TFEU measures, Article 104 TFEU and Article 105 TFEU provide for **transitional enforcement arrangements** by the MS authorities and the Commission (→ Article 104 TFEU para 1–4, → Article 105 TFEU para 1–2, 4–5). The omission of enforcement rules in the Treaty stems predominantly from a negotiation impasse between Germany and France and other MS at the time of the Treaty of Rome negotiations (→ para 2). Whereas the French were keen to adopt an abuse model prohibiting only "bad" anti-competitive agreements with harmful effects and allowing "good" anti-competitive agreements with pro-competitive benefits under a legal exception system (→ para 20), the Germans were keen on a prohibition model based on notification and authorisation.[1] Compromise was eventually reached on a prohibition of anti-competitive agreements subject to exemption upon the satisfaction of certain conditions, but to avoid further impasse, the decision on how the exemption system was to operate in practice was postponed to a later time, hence the inclusion of Article 103 TFEU.[2]

However, **Article 103 TFEU has not been the sole legal basis for secondary enforcement measures**. Some secondary legislation has required a joint legal basis, such as the Merger Regulation[3] (→ para 3, 10, 37, 47), which was enacted on the **joint legal basis of** Article 103 TFEU and Article 352 TFEU, the latter providing a general legal basis where legislation is required to attain an objective of the Treaties and the Treaties do not provide the requisite powers to do so (Article 352.1 TFEU), and both the Private Action Directive[4] (also known as the Damages Directive) (→ para 3, 15, 34, 35) and the ECN+ Directive[5] (→ para 3, 13, 28, 41), which were enacted on the joint legal basis of Article 103 TFEU and Article 114 TFEU, the latter providing a legislative base for legislation relating to the approximation of MS law for the achievement of the internal market.

2. Secondary Law Measures Under Article 103 TFEU

2   Article 103 TFEU provides the **basis for the adoption of detailed enforcement rules** for Articles 101 and 102 TFEU. Article 103.1 TFEU obliges the Council to adopt **appropriate regulations** (Article 288.2 TFEU) **or directives** (Article 288.3

---

[1] McGowan (2010), p. 109; Ehlermann (2000), pp. 553–554; Wils (2013), p. 294.
[2] Akman and Kassim (2010), p. 114; Pace and Seidel (2013), pp. 62–63, 71–73, 77.
[3] Council Regulation (EC) No 139/2004 *on the control of concentrations between undertakings*, O.J. L 24/1 (2004).
[4] Parliament/Council Directive No 2014/104/EU *on certain rules governing actions for damages under national law for infringements of the competition law provisions of the Member States and of the European Union*, O.J. L 349/1 (2014).
[5] Parliament/Council Directive No 2019/1/EU *to empower the competition authorities of the Member States to be more effective enforcers and to ensure the proper functioning of the internal market*, O.J. L 11/3 (2019).

TFEU) to give effect to Articles 101 and 102 TFEU (→ para 3–33, 36–38, 41–47). The choice between the two types of secondary legislative measures remains with the Council under Article 101.3 TFEU, allowing it therefore to exercise its power of discretion as to the type of appropriate secondary enforcement measure. Rather than being understood in the strict sense of proportionality, the use of the term "appropriate" suggests objectively suitable legislation to give effect to Articles 101 and 102 TFEU. The original wording of Article 103.1 TFEU (Article 87.1 TEEC) required unanimity in the Council to enact appropriate legislation for the first three years of the Treaty of Rome, after which qualified majority voting applied. Due to considerable debate and differences in MS opinion (→ para 1) surrounding the nature and enforcement of the substantive competition law provisions,[6] there was no legislative proposal from the Commission for appropriate legislation during this initial three-year period, thus avoiding the need for unanimity in the Council. Negotiations on the draft proposal endured for over two years, and it was not until 1962 that the first enforcement Regulation was enacted (→ para 5–16).

In line with Article 16.3 TEU, the use of **qualified majority voting** in the Council is currently the norm for legislation in this area as Article 103 TFEU does not specify otherwise. Whilst the voting requirements in the Council have changed, the Treaty has not, however, been amended regarding the role of the EP in the legislative process in this area. The ordinary legislative procedure (Article 294 TFEU) is not applicable, meaning that legislation in this area is not subject to the joint adoption of the Council and the EP; rather, a **special legislative procedure** applies, with the **EP having a purely consultative role**. This limited role for the EP stems from a political decision by the MS to keep control in the Council, although ultimately, the Council largely relinquished its legislative role in the area of competition law by delegating law-making powers to the Commission (→ para 8, 26, 43, 44). The role of the EP is extended, however, in cases where legislation is enacted on a joint legal basis, combining Article 103 TFEU with some other Treaty provision that envisages a more prominent role for the EP. For example, in the case of the Merger Regulation (→ para 1, 10, 37, 47), where the joint legal basis of Article 103 TFEU and Article 352 TFEU was employed (→ para 1), the law-making requirements of Article 352 TFEU prevailed over Article 103 TFEU, and this legislation was thus adopted on the basis of the consent, rather than the mere consultation, of the EP. In the case of the Damages Directive (→ para 1, 15, 34, 35), at the insistence of the EP, the law-making requirements of Article 114 TFEU prevailed (→ para 1), and this Directive was thus adopted according to the ordinary legislative procedure (marking the first occasion this procedure was utilised in competition legislation),[7] making the EP co-legislator with the Council. Likewise, the more recent ECN+ Directive was adopted jointly by the EP and the Council according to the ordinary legislative procedure (→ para 1, 13, 28, 41).

3

---

[6] Gerber (2004), pp. 103–105; Akman (2009), pp. 283–285; Akman and Kassim (2010), p. 115; McGowan (2010), pp. 8, 93, 97–101, 106; Pace and Seidel (2013), pp. 66–71.
[7] Doherty and Fitzpatrick (2015), p. 26.

In the event that the Council adopts **legislation solely on the basis of Article 103.1 TFEU**, it is **not obligated by the principle of subsidiarity** in Article 5.3 (1) TEU because according to Article 3.1 point (b) TFEU (→ Article 3 TFEU para 38–46), the Union has exclusive competence in establishing the competition rules necessary for the functioning of the internal market, and the principle of subsidiarity does not apply in areas of exclusive Union competence. However, the Council may be obligated by the principle of subsidiarity where a secondary legislative measure requires a joint legal basis and the second legal basis falls within the scope of a mixed or shared Union-MS competence under Article 4.1 TFEU (→ Article 4 TFEU para 10 et seqq.).

4   Article 103.2 TFEU envisages **"appropriate" legislative measures** in five instances, some general and some specific,[8] but this list of measures is not exhaustive, as denoted by the words "in particular". The specific legislative measures (→ para 45–47) include those outlined in Article 103.2 point (a) and point (b) TFEU, and the general legislative measures (→ para 5–34, 36–44) envisaged are those outlined in Article 103.2 point (c) to point (e) TFEU.

3. General Enforcement Regime

3.1. General Enforcement Regulations

5   As required under Article 103.1 TFEU, the Council has put in place a series of regulations governing the procedures applicable in the enforcement of EU competition law. The initial transitional enforcement system of Article 104 TFEU (→ Article 104 TFEU para 1–4) and Article 105 TFEU (→ Article 105 TFEU para 1–2, 4–5) was in place for a number of years but was eventually overhauled with the advent of the **first general enforcement regulation**, Regulation **17/62**[9] (→ para 6–16), and **specific legislation** setting up special enforcement regimes in certain sectors in keeping with Article 103.2 point (c) TFEU (→ para 45–47). Together, this general and sector-specific enforcement legislation legislated for many of the "appropriate" measures envisaged by Article 103.2 points (a) through (e) TFEU (→ para 2, 4).

6   Largely inspired by German influence and tradition,[10] Regulation 17/62 created a comprehensive enforcement and procedural regime and moulded the landscape of the public enforcement of Community (now EU) competition law by **centralising the application and enforcement** of Articles 101 and 102 TFEU **in the Commission**. In satisfaction of Article 103.2 point (b) TFEU, the Commission gained exclusive competence to apply Article 101.3 TFEU by granting exemptions

---

[8] Goyder and Albors-Llorens (2009), p. 51.
[9] Council Regulation (EEC) No 17/62 *implementing Article 85 and 86 of the Treaty*, O.J. Special Edition Series 1/87 (1959–1962).
[10] Pace and Seidel (2013), pp. 55, 63, 65, 67.

(→ Article 101 TFEU para 62) upon the notification of agreements under Article 9.1 of the Regulation. Notification resulted in immunity from fines (→ para 7, 9, 23, 24, 37) until the Commission decided if an agreement merited exemption, and if the Commission eventually granted authorisation, undertakings benefitted from immunity from sanction by the Commission and from findings of infringement by national authorities at the national level. Notification and authorisation, combined with the general centrality of enforcement vested in the Commission and a strict prohibition regime (until this time largely unfamiliar to most MS,[11] where cartels with a cross-border nature had prevailed in the first half of the twentieth century[12] and where national champions were supported), ensured the **uniform application** of Articles 101 and 102 TFEU throughout the Community and the "merging of the common market".[13] Moreover, centralised enforcement contributed to the **creation of a competition culture** in Europe[14] in an era when competition policy was a novelty,[15] with competition law regimes absent in many MS.[16] However, the creation of an impartial supranational enforcer for competition law was not without its initial opponents.[17] France, in particular, was eager for decisions to be made jointly by the Commission and representatives of the MS and had advocated a strong role for a body of national representatives (→ para 12),[18] but this was ultimately rejected in favour of a completely impartial supranational enforcer (the Commission) to promote and ensure compliance with the rules.

In addition to creating a centralised enforcement system and establishing an *ex ante* authorisation regime for the application of Article 101.3 TFEU, Regulation 17/62 established other key elements of the Commission's enforcement and procedural regime, as required by Article 103.2 point (d) TFEU. It conferred extensive **powers of investigation and enforcement** on the Commission (→ para 21–26), including the powers to: 7

– Request information (Article 11)
– Conduct inspections, comprising the power to examine books and other business records and to take copies of such materials, to demand oral explanations on the spot from the undertakings under investigation and to enter premises, land or vehicles owned by the undertaking (Article 14)
– Terminate infringements (Article 3)

---

[11] Wils (2001), pp. 1673–1674.

[12] McGowan (2010), pp. 8, 44–67. See Pech (2008), p. 175 on the importance of uniformity and an impartial enforcer of competition law.

[13] Deringer (1963), p. 31.

[14] Commission White Paper *on Modernisation of the Rules Implementing Articles 85 and 86 of the EC Treaty*, O.J. C 132/1 (1999) p. 4 para 4.

[15] Akman and Kassim (2010), p. 113.

[16] See further Ehlermann (2000), p. 540.

[17] McGowan (2010), pp. 1, 14.

[18] McGowan (2010), p. 107.

- Impose sanctioning fines (→ para 23), as required by Article 103.2 point (a) TFEU, of up to 10% of an undertaking's turnover in the preceding year for substantive infringements (Article 15.2) or lesser fines for procedural infringements, such as supplying incorrect, incomplete or misleading information during investigations or failing to submit to investigations (Article 15.1)
- Impose periodic penalty payments (daily fines which endure until the undertaking complies) (→ para 23), as required by Article 103.2 point (a) TFEU, to achieve future compliance with Article 3 termination orders, the terms of an Article 101.3 TFEU exemption, information requests and investigations sanctioned by decision (Article 16)
- Grant negative clearance (→ para 25) (essentially a declaration from the Commission) where it believed there were no grounds for action on its behalf under Articles 101.1 or 102 TFEU on the basis of the facts in its possession (Article 2); and
- Carry out sector enquiries (Article 12)

8   Under Article 24 of Regulation 17/62, the Council also **delegated power to the Commission to adopt supplementary enforcement or procedural rules**, necessary for the implementation of Regulation 17/62. For example, the Commission introduced a Regulation on the form and content of applications and notifications for exemption[19] and on hearings.[20] In essence therefore, Regulation 17/62 instituted a very powerful enforcer for competition law, not just in terms of enforcement and sanctioning powers but also in terms of developing policy (→ para 3, 26, 43, 44).

9   In addition to setting out the functions of the Commission in applying Articles 101 and 102 TFEU, in line with Article 103.2 point (d) TFEU, Article 17 of Regulation 17/62 defined the **judicial review function of the ECJ** (→ para 37), declaring it to have unlimited jurisdiction to review Commission infringement decisions, to impose fines (→ para 7, 23) or periodic penalty payments (→ para 7, 23) and to cancel, reduce or increase the penalty imposed.

10   Regulation 17/62 failed, however, to directly determine the **relationship between national competition law and Articles 101 and 102 TFEU**, as required by Article 103.2 point (e) TFEU. Its preamble referred to securing the "uniform application of Articles 85 [now 101] and 86 [now 102] in the common market", but there was no substantive provision in the Regulation on the demarcation of national

---

[19] Commission Regulation (EEC) No 27/62 *implementing Council Regulation 17/62 of 6 February 1962*, O.J. Special Edition 132 (1959–1962), repealed by Commission Regulation (EC) No 3385/94, O.J. L 377/28 (1994), which was in turn repealed by Commission Regulation (EC) No 773/2004 *relating to the conduct of proceedings by the Commission pursuant to Articles 81 and 82 of the EC Treaty*, O.J. L 123/18 (2004).

[20] Commission Regulation (EEC) No 99/63 *on the hearing provided for in Article 19(1) and (2) of Council Regulation No. 17*, O.J. Special Edition 47 (1963–1964), repealed by Commission Regulation (EC) No 2842/98, O.J. L 354/18 (1998), which was in turn repealed by Commission Regulation (EC) No 773/2004, O.J. L 123/18 (2004).

and Community (now EU) competition law. In the late 1960s, in *Walt Wilhelm*,[21] the ECJ ruled that the application of national competition law should "not prejudice the uniform application throughout the common market of the Community rules on cartels and of the full effect of the measures adopted in the implementation of those rules" and that Community (now EU) competition law takes precedence over national competition law.[22] This was elaborated on in the Commission's 1993 Notice on cooperation with the national courts (→ para 15) and its 1997 Notice on cooperation with national competition authorities (→ para 13), but it was not until Regulation 1/2003[23] that definitive legislative provision was made on the demarcation of national and EU competition law (→ para 38) in the general enforcement regime. The first Merger Regulation of 1989[24] (→ para 1, 3, 37, 47), however, clearly delineated the application of national and EU competition law in the field of merger control law (→ para 47).

Regulation 17/62's centralised enforcement regime maintained a residual **role for national competition authorities** (→ para 27–32), even though Article 104 TFEU was intended to be transitional only until such time as Article 103 TFEU legislation was enacted (→ Article 104 TFEU para 1–4). By virtue of Article 9.3 of Regulation 17/62, however, Article 104 TFEU continued to play a role, allowing the MS authorities to apply Articles 101.1 and 102 TFEU, where they are empowered to do so by national laws. Therefore, the MS authorities were not completely deprived of their powers under Article 104 TFEU, bar the application of Article 101.3 TFEU. The role of the national competition authorities was residual because it was only insofar as the Commission had not formally opened proceedings under Regulation 17/62 that national competition authorities could pursue infringements in accordance with Article 104 TFEU (→ Article 104 TFEU para 3). **11**

Notwithstanding the residual role of national competition authorities, Regulation 17/62 did facilitate **cooperation between the Commission and national competition authorities** (→ para 30). It allowed for an exchange of information between the Commission and national competition authorities by requiring the Commission to make available notification and negative clearance applications to them and to otherwise liaise with them during its administrative procedures (Article 10 of the Regulation). It also required national competition authorities to submit all necessary information concerning pending cases to the Commission, to conduct investigations on its behalf and to escort and assist the Commission in its investigations in accordance with national procedural requirements (Articles 11, 13 and 14). Any materials or information gathered as evidence by national competition authorities in the course of such investigations on behalf of the Commission could not **12**

---

[21] Case 14/68, *Walt Wilhelm and Others v Bundeskartellamt* (ECJ 13 February 1969) para 4.

[22] Case 14/68, *Walt Wilhelm and Others v Bundeskartellamt* (ECJ 13 February 1969) para 6.

[23] Council Regulation (EC) No 1/2003 *on the implementation of the rules on competition laid down in Articles 81 and 82 of the Treaty*, O.J .L 1/1 (2003).

[24] Council Regulation (EEC) No 4064/89/EEC *on the control of concentrations between undertakings*, O.J. L 395/1 (1989).

subsequently be used by the national competition authorities in proceedings under national competition law (→ para 30).[25] National competition authorities were also involved in enforcement through their participation in the **Advisory Committee on Restrictive Practices and Monopolies** (now the Advisory Committee on Restrictive Practices and Dominant Positions → para 31), which the Commission was obligated to consult prior to adopting infringement decisions, negative clearance decisions or exemption decisions (Article 10.3). Although France had initially wanted a body of national representatives to be joint decision-makers with the Commission (→ para 8), ultimately under Regulation 17/62, the Advisory Committee was purely a consultative body and had no power to veto Commission decisions.[26] Indeed, the Commission was not even obligated by the opinion of the Advisory Committee.

13   In the 1990s, with an increasing enforcement workload and a considerable body of law on the application of Articles 101 and 102 TFEU, as well as the greater capacity of national competition authorities, the Commission grew keen on their more active involvement in competition law enforcement. It issued its **Notice on cooperation with national competition authorities** in 1997 (→ para 10).[27] Although a significant number of cases would remain in the Commission's jurisdiction because the political, legal or economic issues at stake were vital to the "Community" interest, the Notice recognised the competence of the national competition authorities to apply Articles 101 and 102 TFEU, and it established a framework for case allocation between the Commission and national competition authorities. The Notice was, however, relatively unsuccessful in augmenting the role of national competition authorities in the enforcement of Articles 101 and 102 TFEU,[28] and it was not until Regulation 1/2003 that their role was dramatically increased (→ para 27–32), strengthened more recently by Directive 2019/1 on the enforcement powers of the national competition authorities (ECN+; → para 1, 3, 28, 41).

14   Regulation 17/62 did not make any reference to or regulate the **role of national courts in the enforcement of the substantive competition law provisions** of the Treaty (→ para 33, 34, 36). Nor did it provide for cooperation between the national courts and the Commission or national competition authorities. However, in 1974, the ECJ ruled that Articles 101 and 102 TFEU produced a direct effect,[29] thereby ensuring their enforceability before the national courts. This did not, however, apply to Article 101.3 TFEU, which remained within the exclusive remit of the Commission under Regulation 17/62 (→ para 6–7) until Regulation 1/2003

---

[25] Case C-67/91, *Asociación Española de Banca Privada and others* (ECJ 16 July 1992).

[26] McGowan (2010), p. 118.

[27] Commission Notice *on cooperation between national competition authorities and the Commission in handling cases falling within the scope of Articles 85 or 86*, O.J. C 313/3 (1997).

[28] Rodger (1999), p. 659.

[29] Case 127/73, *BRT v SABAM* (ECJ 27 March 1974).

(→ para 19–20). The role of national courts was further defined by the Court in *Delimitis*,[30] identifying a number of operational principles under Regulation 17/62, including that:

1. National courts could interpret and apply block exemption regulations
2. The Commission and national courts shared competence to apply Articles 101.1 and 102 TFEU and national courts could apply Article 101.2 TFEU to declare anti-competitive agreements void in the absence of a Commission Article 101.3 TFEU exemption decision
3. National courts had no jurisdiction to apply Article 101.3 TFEU; and
4. National courts should stay proceedings before them or adopt interim measures where they believed that an Article 101.3 TFEU exemption might be merited and seek Commission assistance or a preliminary ruling from the ECJ.

The Commission subsequently introduced a **Notice on cooperation between national courts and the Commission** (→ para 10),[31] detailing these principles in the application of Articles 101 and 102 TFEU. However, notwithstanding the direct effect of Articles 101 and 102 TFEU and the Commission's endeavours at developing cooperation between it and the national courts, private enforcement of EU competition law before national courts did not flourish to the same extent as private litigation in the US. Nonetheless, the Commission remained eager to develop **private enforcement**, and in 2014, the Council and Parliament issued a directive to facilitate private competition law actions before national courts (→ para 1, 3, 34, 35).[32]

15

Regulation 17/62 remained in operation largely unchanged for over four decades, at which stage, however, it was proving **incapable of ensuring the balance between effective supervision and simplifying administration** required under Article 103.2 point (b) TFEU.[33] Considerable changes brought about by the completion of the internal market in 1992 and increased membership of the Community consequently **increased the demands being put on the Commission's competition enforcement regime** in terms of the scope and number of notifications and cases that the Commission was faced with. This undoubtedly also impacted the **effectiveness of the regime**. The Commission's attempts to reduce the high number of notifications by means of block exemption regulations (→ para 42–44) and its attempts to increasingly involve national competition authorities (→ para 11–13) and national courts (→ para 14) were insufficient to deal with the strain it was under. Nor did the use of so-called comfort letters alleviate the workload facing the Commission. Comfort letters were administrative letters issued by the Commission

16

---

[30] Case C-234/89, *Delimitis v Henninger Bräu* (ECJ 28 February 1991).

[31] Commission Notice *on cooperation between national courts and the Commission in applying Articles 85 and 86 of the EEC Treaty*, O.J. C 39/6 (1993).

[32] Parliament/Council Directive No 2014/104/EU *on certain rules governing actions for damages under national law for infringements of the competition law provisions of the Member States and of the European Union*, O.J. L 349/1 (2014).

[33] Mathijsen (2007), p. 307.

at the early stage of the notification process, stating that the Commission regarded notified agreements to escape the application of Article 101.1 TFEU or to fall (or not, as the case may be) within the scope of an Article 101.3 TFEU or block exemption, but they were of little utility to notifying parties as they lacked a legally binding effect.

17   Likewise, the *de minimis* doctrine,[34] whereby agreements of minor importance (determined according to market share thresholds of the parties involved) escaped the application of Article 101.1 TFEU once they did not pertain to hard-core anti-competitive behaviour, did little to relieve the Commission of its overall burden. At the start of the 1990s, the **notification backlog was considerable**, with the Commission facing in the region of 1000 cases[35] (although just how backlogged the notification system was and the general overload on the Commission has been queried).[36] Moreover, the notification system had caused the Commission to be a **reactive enforcer** from the start,[37] had prevented it from pursuing hard-core infringements due to the resources it consumed and was **inefficient**.[38] Although the number of agreements notified was dropping in the 1990s, many more agreements, particularly those with serious anti-competitive effects, were clearly not being notified to the Commission.[39] Indeed, most notified agreements were innocuous. Authorisation from the Commission could take considerable time. All of this indicated that the notification and authorisation system was "more pretence than reality".[40]

18   Although "throwing out" Regulation 17/62 may have been a "largely heretical notion" until the 1990s,[41] the untenable workload and resulting strain on the Commission's enforcement regime eventually led it to propose a complete **decentralisation** of competition law enforcement in its 1999 **White Paper on the modernisation of the implementing rules of Articles 85 and 86 of the EC Treaty**. This White Paper was described as "the most important policy paper ... in more than 40 years of EC Competition policy ... suggest[ing] a legal and cultural revolution"[42] in the division of responsibilities between the Commission, the national competition authorities and the national courts.

---

[34] Currently contained in Commission Notice *on agreements of minor importance which do not appreciably restrict competition under Article 101(1) of the Treaty on the Functioning of the European Union*, O.J. C 291/01 (2014).

[35] McGowan (2010), p. 154.

[36] Möschel (2000), pp. 495–496; Riley (2003), pp. 604, 615.

[37] Wilks (2005), p. 436.

[38] McGowan (2010), pp. 153–154.

[39] Ehlermann (2000), p. 546; Temple Lang (1981), p. 336.

[40] Wils (2001), p. 1663. See also p. 1655.

[41] Maher (2007), p. 1716.

[42] Ehlermann (2000), p. 537.

Article 103 [Adoption of Secondary Enforcement Measures for Articles 101 ... 173

Broadly supported by all the MS and "taking place against the background of enlargement",[43] the White Paper resulted in the **enactment of Regulation 1/2003**, which came into effect on 1 May 2004. This date deliberately **coincided with the enlargement of the EU** by ten new MS, and the Regulation thus became applicable immediately in all of the then 25 MS. Marking a "sizeable shift in the administering of policy"[44] and heralding "an appreciably progressive policy-making attitude",[45] the Regulation establishes new rules for the application of Article 101.3 TFEU in line with Article 103.2 point (b) TFEU, indeed simplifying administration by abolishing the notification system and fully decentralising enforcement powers to national competition authorities and courts (→ para 27, 33). It also provides for fines and periodic penalty payments, as required by Article 103.2 point (a) TFEU (→ para 23); defines the functions of the Commission in line with Article 103.2 point (d) TFEU by confirming and augmenting its enforcement powers (→ para 21–27); defines the functions of the Court of Justice in line with Article 103.2 point (d) TFEU (→ para 37); and specifically deals with the relationship between EU and national competition law, as required by Article 103.2 point (e) TFEU (→ para 38). **19**

Regarding the application of Article 101.3 TFEU, Regulation 1/2003 facilitated a "radical change"[46] through the decentralisation of EU competition law enforcement, envisaging a **parallel enforcement competence for the Commission and national competition authorities**. In particular, the Commission's *ex ante* control and authorisation over Article 101.3 TFEU exemptions (→ para 6) were done away with as a result of Regulation 1/2003's directly applicable legal exception regime (→ para 19). This greatly simplifies the overall application of Article 101 TFEU as it renders the notification of agreements redundant and facilitates automatic exemptions on the satisfaction of the Article 101.3 TFEU conditions, with no prior authorisation to this effect required from either the Commission or the national competition authorities (Article 1.2 of the Regulation). The abolishment of the notification system and its *ex ante* control by the Commission has largely brought the Commission's enforcement regime into alignment with the French model originally proposed in the late 1950s (→ para 1).[47] Consequently, undertakings and their legal advisers are expected to be fully cognisant of the rules and comply with them. **20**

As demanded by Article 103.2 point (d) TFEU, Regulation 1/2003 sets out the functions of the Commission, and many of the Commission's previous **powers of investigation and enforcement** (→ para 7–8) are retained and strengthened by it. Its investigative powers include the powers to: **21**

– Request information (Article 18)
– Take statements (Article 19); and

---

[43] Cseres (2010a), p. 145; see also pp. 146–147.
[44] McGowan (2010), p. 153.
[45] Todino (2000), p. 348.
[46] Wils (2013), p. 1.
[47] Wilks (2005), p. 435.

– Conduct inspections or unannounced dawn raids by entering premises, land or vehicles; examining physical and electronic records and taking copies thereof (and given that legal professional privilege only extends to advice from independent counsel,[48] the Commission has considerable unlimited access to business records);[49] sealing off business premises and records; and seeking on-the-spot explanations from any representative or staff member of the undertaking (Article 20).

Significantly, under this Regulation, unlike Regulation 17/62, inspections now extend to private dwellings and means of transport when there is reasonable suspicion that records are being kept there (Article 21).

22 Regarding its **broader enforcement powers**, subsequent to a finding of infringement, the Commission can order undertakings to terminate infringements (Article 7) and can now impose not only behavioural but also structural remedies under Regulation 1/2003 where there is a substantial risk of a lasting or repeated infringement that derives from the very structure of the undertaking(s) and there is no equally effective or less burdensome behavioural remedy (Article 7). Further, the Commission launched a New Competition Tool initiative in early June 2020,[50] which would have equipped it with the power of intervention to impose behavioural and structural remedies in markets where it identified competition concerns. This New Competition Tool stemmed from the Commission's experience in dealing with competition in certain markets and particularly with digital markets, and its goal was to ensure that competition and policy are fit for purpose for the modern economy. Where the Commission identified structural problems in a market, the tool would have enabled it to impose behavioural and structural remedies without the necessity of a finding of infringement or the imposition of fines.

Following a three-month public consultation in June 2020, a Commission legislative proposal was expected in **late 2020**, but instead, the **Commission seemingly incorporated the New Competition Tool as part of its broader Digital Markets Act** proposal,[51] which establishes rules for large online platforms that control digital ecosystems (so-called "gatekeepers") preventing them from engaging in unfair practices and allowing the Commission to impose *ex ante* control measures. Together with the Digital Services Act proposal,[52] the Digital Market Act makes up the **Digital Service Act Package**, which has as its goal the establishment of a level playing field for businesses to foster innovation, growth and

---

[48] Case 155/79, *AM and S Europe v Commission* (ECJ 18 May 1982), confirmed in Case C-550/07 P, *Akzo Nobel Chemicals and Akcros Chemicals v Commission* (CJEU 14 September 2010).

[49] Stephan (2010), p. 139.

[50] See https://ec.europa.eu/info/law/better-regulation/have-your-say/initiatives/12416-Single-Market-new-complementary-tool-to-strengthen-competition-enforcement_en.

[51] Proposal *for a Regulation of the European Parliament and of the Council on contestable and fair markets in the digital sector (Digital Markets Act)*, COM(2020) 842 final.

[52] Proposal *for a Regulation of the European Parliament and of the Council on a Single Market For Digital Services (Digital Services Act)*, COM(2020) 825 final.

competitiveness both in the internal market and globally *and* the creation of a safer digital space where the fundamental rights of users are protected.[53]

Regulation 1/2003 reserves the power of the Commission to impose **sanctioning fines** (→ para 7) and **periodic penalty payments** (→ para 7), as specified by Article 103.2 point (a) TFEU. Under Article 23 of the Regulation, sanctioning fines (→ para 7) of up to 10% of total turnover in the preceding year apply to substantive infringements. Sanctioning fines can also be imposed of up to 1% of total turnover in the preceding year for procedural infringements, such as supplying incorrect, incomplete or misleading information during investigations (→ para 7), and, new to Regulation 1/2003, for breaking seals during inspections[54] (Article 23). Periodic penalty payments of up to 5% of average daily turnover (a significant increase from Regulation 17/62) (→ para 7) can be imposed for failing to comply with termination orders, interim measure orders, commitment decisions[55] and information requests and for failing to submit to investigations sanctioned by a decision (Article 24). A **Fining Notice** is in place to enhance objectivity and transparency in the setting of fines for substantive breaches of Articles 101 and 102 TFEU.[56]

23

In terms of its **enforcement tools**, firstly, the Commission operates a **leniency policy** for undertakings that blow the whistle on cartels, and under certain conditions, undertakings can benefit from full immunity from sanctioning fines (→ para 7, 23) or reduced sanctioning fines for substantive breaches of Article 101 TFEU, where they reveal their cartel activity to the Commission.[57] Since March 2017, in addition to the undertakings themselves blowing the whistle on their cartel activity under the leniency policy, it has also been possible for individuals to inform the Commission of suspected cartel behaviour (and indeed other anti-competitive behaviours) under the Commission's new Whistleblower Communication Tool, which can protect the anonymity of the whistle-blower where they do not wish to reveal their identity.[58] Moreover, the new EU **Whistleblowing Directive**[59] (to be transposed by 17 December 2021) offers its protection to whistle-blowers who report information about infringements of EU competition law obtained in the course of their employment.

24

---

[53] For more, see https://digital-strategy.ec.europa.eu/en/policies/digital-services-act-package.

[54] The Commission imposed such a fine of EUR 38 million for the first time on E.ON in 2008 in Commission Decision, *Case COMP/B-1/39.326 — E.ON Energie AG*, O.J. C 240/6 (2008).

[55] The Commission imposed such a fine of EUR 561 million for the first time on Microsoft in 2013 in Commission Decision, *Case COMP/C-3/37.792 — Microsoft*, O.J. C 138/10 (2013).

[56] Commission Guidelines *on the method of setting fines imposed pursuant to Article 23(2)(a) of Regulation No 1/2003*, O.J. C 210/02 (2006).

[57] Commission Notice *on Immunity from fines and reduction of fines in cartel cases*, O.J. C 298/11 (2006).

[58] *See* https://ec.europa.eu/competition/cartels/whistleblower/index.html.

[59] Parliament/Council Directive No 2019/1937/EU *on the protection of persons who report breaches of Union law (EU Whistleblowing Directive)*, O.J. L 305/17 (2019).

Secondly, **cartel settlement**,[60] introduced by the so-called **settlement package** in 2008,[61] also provides the possibility of reduced fines whereby cartelists, having seen the evidence in the Commission's file after its initial investigation, can settle the case with the Commission by admitting their cartel participation and accepting their liability, thereby allowing the Commission to streamline and expedite its post-investigation enforcement process. The benefit of participating in this simplified procedure for cartelists is a set fine reduction of 10%. The broader purpose of cartel settlement is to free up Commission resources, granting it more time and manpower to dedicate to its detection and investigation functions. Thirdly, the Commission also retains the power to carry out **sector enquiries** (Article 17),[62] and it may order interim measures in the case of irreparable damage to competition on the basis of a *prima facie* finding of infringement (Article 8). Finally, under the Regulation, the Commission can now formally enter into settlements with undertakings in the form of **commitment decisions** (Article 9), which are largely akin to consent decrees in US antitrust law and used mostly in the case of potential Article 102 TFEU abuse.[63]

25   Negative clearance (→ para 7) is no longer provided for in Regulation 1/2003, but the Commission has the power to make a **finding or declaration of inapplicability** of Articles 101 or 102 TFEU where the public interest requires it (Article 10). A finding of inapplicability is available in exceptional circumstances only "to clarif[y] the law and ensur[e] its consistent application throughout the [EU], in particular with regard to new types of agreements or practices [...]" (Recital 14 of the Regulation).

26   As with Regulation 17/62 (→ para 5, 8), the Council has also conferred a **delegated legislative power** on the Commission under Article 33 of Regulation 1/2003 to introduce supplementary enforcement measures in order to apply Regulation 1/2003. On this basis, the Commission has introduced a Regulation on the conduct of proceedings by the Commission.[64]

27   Decentralisation has fully endorsed the **power and responsibilities of national competition authorities** (→ para 11–12) and national courts (→ para 14–15) to

---

[60] On cartel settlement, see https://ec.europa.eu/commission/presscorner/detail/en/IP_08_1056.

[61] Commission Regulation (EC) No 622/ 2008 *amending Regulation (EC) No 773/2004, as regards the conduct of settlement procedures in cartel cases*, O.J. L 171/3 (2008), accompanied by Commission Notice *on the conduct of settlement procedures in view of the adoption of Decisions pursuant to Article 7 and Article 23 of Council Regulation (EC) No 1/2003*, O.J. C 167/01 (2008), as amended by Commission Communication *Amendments to the Commission Notice on the conduct of settlement procedures in view of the adoption of Decisions pursuant to Article 7 and Article 23 of Council Regulation (EC) No 1/2003 in cartel cases*, O.J. C 256/02 (2015).

[62] The Commission has conducted five sector enquiries pursuant to Article 17 of Regulation 1/2003: Consumer Internet of Things (2020), E-commerce (2015), Pharmaceuticals (2008), Financial Services (2005), and 3G (2004).

[63] Stephan (2010), p. 140.

[64] Commission Regulation (EC) No. 773/2004 *relating to the conduct of proceedings by the Commission pursuant to Articles 81 and 82 of the EC Treaty*, O.J. L 123/18 (2004).

Article 103   [Adoption of Secondary Enforcement Measures for Articles 101 ...   177

enforce EU competition law. It eliminates the "procedural complexities"[65] that resulted under the previous regime as Regulation 1/2003 allows the national competition authorities and courts to apply Article 101 TFEU in its entirety,[66] as well as Article 102 TFEU (Article 1.2, Articles 5 and 6 of the Regulation). The Article 5 powers and responsibilities of the national competition authorities to order the termination of infringements and interim measures, to accept commitments, to impose sanctions (including criminal sanctions) envisaged by national law and to decide that there are no grounds for action on their behalf operate in parallel to the Commission's and transform the national competition authorities into "cartel-like agencies" of the Commission.[67] National competition authorities also have the power to withdraw the benefit of a block exemption Regulation for their respective territories where such effects are experienced in their territory, or part thereof, which has all the characteristics of a distinct geographic market (Article 29.2) (→ para 44).

Whilst the Regulation sets out these broad powers of national competition authorities, the **procedures deployed by national competition authorities in the application of EU competition law are entirely governed by national procedural rules.** This is because Regulation 1/2003 only regulates the enforcement powers of the Commission and remains silent on the procedures, enforcement methods and institutional frameworks of national competition regimes. Nonetheless, even prior to Directive 2019/1, the EU enforcement regime had already indirectly exercised influence on enforcement methods and institutional frameworks at the national level, where some level of convergence emerged,[68] for example regarding structural remedies, interim measures, commitment decisions, sealing off premises and records during inspections, inspections of private properties, the level of fines and leniency policies.[69] Since Directive 2019/1, national procedural rules have been updated, where necessary, to comply with its requirements on various enforcement powers of national competition authorities, resulting in further harmonisation vis-à-vis some procedural matters (→ para 1, 3, 13, 41).   **28**

Regulation 1/2003 does not deal with **case allocation** amongst the various enforcers of EU competition law, but according to the Notice on Cooperation within the Network of Competition Authorities, cases will generally be allocated on the basis of a single authority objective, with the authority best placed to handle   **29**

---

[65] Venit (2003), pp. 558–559.

[66] The Commission introduced a series of notices to accompany Council Regulation (EC) No 1/2003 *on the implementation of the rules on competition laid down in Articles 81 and 82 of the Treaty*, O.J. L 1/1 (2003), including Commission Notice *Guidelines on the application of Article 81(3) of the Treaty*, O.J. C 101/97 (2004), to assist in the application of Article 101.3 TFEU.

[67] McGowan (2010), p. 155.

[68] Commission Communication, *Report on the Functioning of Regulation 1/2003*, COM(2009) 206 final, para 31 and 32.

[69] Cseres (2010a), pp. 146, 155–161; Cseres (2010b), pp. 17–20.

the investigation and terminate the infringement dealing with the case.[70] This is determined on the basis of discussions in the **European Competition Network** (ECN). However, if the Commission initiates proceedings in a case already under investigation at the MS level, the Commission thereby appropriates the power to deal with the case from the national authority, **relieving it of its competence** to apply Articles 101 and 102 TFEU (Article 11.6 of Regulation 1/2003). In keeping with the earlier judgment in *Walt Wilhelm*, this does not prevent the application of national competition law in parallel national proceedings.[71] A national competition authority can, however, refuse to handle a complaint or suspend proceedings if another national competition authority or the Commission is already dealing with the matter (Article 13).

30 In the application of Articles 101 and 102 TFEU, the national competition authorities continue to have a **duty to cooperate with the Commission** under Regulation 1/2003 (→ para 12). Article 11 imposes a general duty to cooperate and requires the provision of information on proceedings between the Commission and the national competition authorities and vice versa, as well as amongst the national competition authorities (→ para 31). It also provides that the national competition authorities may consult with the Commission during the course of proceedings at the national level.

Article 12 facilitates the **exchange of information** for **use in evidence**, subject to the rules on professional secrecy (Article 28) and subject also to the qualifications that such evidence may only be used to impose sanctions on natural persons where the transmitting MS imposes similar sanctions and where the rights of defence are awarded the same level of protection in the transmitting and receiving authority as regards the collection of evidence. In essence, this means that receiving authorities cannot impose criminal sanctions where the law of the transmitting MS does not similarly envisage the imposition of criminal sanctions. Cooperation extends to the carrying out of inspections on behalf of other competition authorities or the Commission under Article 22. It seems that the earlier restriction imposed by the ECJ in *Asociación Española de Banca Privada* (→ para 12) no longer applies, and the collecting authority may use the evidence collected during such investigations in the application of national competition law in parallel proceedings (Article 12.2). All of this is further fleshed out in the Notice on cooperation within the Network of Competition Authorities accompanying Regulation 1/2003. MS authorities can also be called upon by the Commission, with the consent of the national courts where required under national law, to provide the Commission with assistance in conjunction with the police or equivalent enforcement authority where an undertaking is refusing to submit to a Commission inspection (Article 20.6).

31 Representatives of the national competition authorities continue to form the **Advisory Committee on Restrictive Agreements and Dominant Positions**

---

[70] Commission Notice *on cooperation within the Network of Competition Authorities*, O.J. C 101/42 (2004), para 5–15.

[71] Case 14/68, *Walt Wilhelm and Others v Bundeskartellamt* (ECJ 13 February 1969) para 3 and 9.

(→ para 12), which the Commission is obliged to consult before taking any decision on infringements, interim measures, commitments, inapplicability, fines, periodic penalty payments, or the withdrawal of a block exemption Regulation (Article 14). In addition, together with the Commission, the national competition authorities make up the **ECN**, described as a dual powerbase transnational and multi-level enforcement network with a horizontal dimension (the membership of national competition authorities from all the MS) and a vertical dimension (the membership of the Commission).[72] This network was envisaged by Regulation 1/2003, although there are no specific provisions on it in the Regulation other than the provisions on cooperation. The Commission fleshed out the purpose and operation of the ECN in its Notice on cooperation within the Network of Competition Authorities.[73] The ECN was established to foster the relationship between the Commission and the national competition authorities and amongst the national authorities themselves. It aims to facilitate cooperation through dialogue and information exchanges (→ para 30) and to ensure effectiveness, efficiency and consistency in the application of competition law throughout the EU.

Notwithstanding an early claim that a huge devolution of cases from the Commission to national competition authorities should not be expected,[74] the **national competition authorities have been very active** (and some, notably the French and German authorities, as active as the Commission)[75] in investigating breaches of Articles 101 and 102 TFEU and finding infringements. Of some 2800 investigations from 2004 to 2020, the national competition authorities have been responsible for 2388 investigations and the Commission for 412, and the national competition authorities have envisaged a total of 1263 decisions during the same period.[76] In this regard, the enforcement regime established under Regulation 1/2003 has been a "major success, beyond expectations".[77] Increased enforcement at the national level has led the Commission to conclude that decentralisation has made "a single legal standard a reality on a very large scale".[78] 32

Article 6 of Regulation 1/2003 augments the **role of national courts** (→ para 14), placing them on an **equal footing** with the Commission and national enforcement authorities[79] by conferring on them the power to apply Articles 101 and 102 TFEU. 33

---

[72] Maher (2007), p. 1731.

[73] Recitals 15–18. See further Commission Notice *on cooperation within the Network of Competition Authorities*, O.J. C 101/43 (2004), para 1.

[74] Todino (2000), p. 357.

[75] Wils (2013), p. 296. See also Commission Communication, *Ten Years of Antitrust Enforcement under Regulation 1/2003: Achievements and Future Perspectives*, COM(2014) 453, para 8.

[76] Statistics available at http://ec.europa.eu/competition/ecn/statistics.html.

[77] Wils (2013), p. 295. See also p. 301.

[78] Commission Staff Working Paper accompanying Commission Communication, *Report on the Functioning of Regulation 1/2003*, COM(2009)206 final, p. 6 para 20 and para 23–24. See similarly Commission Communication, *Ten Years of Antitrust Enforcement under Regulation 1/2003: Achievements and Future Perspectives*, COM(2014) 453 final, para 8.

[79] Komninos (2007), p. 666.

In some jurisdictions, the national courts act as national competition authorities where national law provides for a separation of powers between the investigatory body and the decision-maker, with national courts having the power to make the final decision on the infringement of competition law in these jurisdictions (→ para 41). In other jurisdictions, national courts act as review bodies before which the decisions of the national competition authorities can be appealed.

34   In all jurisdictions, national courts hear actions on competition law brought by private parties. However, in spite of removing the exclusive competence of the Commission to apply Article 101.3 TFEU (→ para 19–20) and the obstacle that this posed to **private enforcement** and in spite of the ECJ establishing the right to full compensation for harm caused by infringements of Articles 101 and 102 TFEU,[80] the impact of Regulation 1/2003 on the enforcement of Articles 101 and 102 TFEU by private parties before national courts has not been overly significant, although the number of follow-on actions for damages did increase in its aftermath.[81] Undeterred, and inspired by the level of private enforcement in the US, after a decade of negotiation, the Commission finally introduced its **Private Action Directive** (or **Damages Directive**) in 2014[82] (→ para 1, 3, 15, 35), which was to be transposed into national law by 27 December 2016 (Article 21 of the Directive) with no retrospective effect (Article 22).

The purpose of the Directive is to **encourage increased private actions** by overcoming some of the perceived obstacles to private enforcement and to **guarantee a minimum level of protection for citizens and businesses** across the EU. The Directive, applicable to individual and collective actions (where the latter are provided for in EU or national law),[83] essentially seeks to harmonise national rules, differences in which had made it difficult and expensive to bring private damages actions; ensure a more level playing field for the victims of infringements of Articles 101 and 102 TFEU; and render it more straightforward for private parties to pursue infringers, particularly in cross-border cases.[84] The key features of the Directive include:[85]

- The right to full compensation (Article 3)
- The application of the principles of effectiveness and equivalence (Article 4)
- The disclosure of evidence (Article 5–8)

---

[80] Case C-453/99, *Courage Ltd v Crehan* (ECJ 20 September 2001).

[81] Wils (2013), pp. 297–298.

[82] Accompanied by a Commission Communication *on quantifying harm in actions for damages based on breaches of Article 101 or 102 [TFEU]*, O.J. C 167/07 (2013) and the accompanying Commission Staff Working Document, *Practical Guide: Quantifying Harm in Actions for Damages Based on Breaches of Article 101 or 102 [TFEU]*, SWD (2013) 205.

[83] Article 2.4 of Council Directive 2014/104/EU *on certain rules governing actions for damages under national law for infringements of the competition law provisions of the Member States and of the European Union*, O.J. L 349/1 (2014).

[84] Doherty and Fitzpatrick (2015), p. 25.

[85] See further Doherty and Fitzpatrick (2015), p. 29.

- The binding effect of national competition authority infringement decisions for the purpose of follow-on actions and evidence of liability (Article 9)
- Limitation periods of at least five years (Article 10)
- Joint and severable liability (Article 11)
- Passing on and the rights of indirect purchasers to compensation (Article 12, Article 14 and Article 16)
- The requisite burden and standard of proof for the quantification of harm (Article 17); and
- The use of consensual dispute resolution (Articles 18 and 19)

The issue of collective redress had featured in early discussions and proposed policy documents (the Green and White Papers)[86] leading to the Private Action Directive (→ para 1, 3, 15, 34), but was not in fact legislated for as a requirement in the Directive. Instead, and because the issue of collective redress is one that extends beyond competition law, the Commission issued a generic non-binding **recommendation on injunctive and compensatory collective redress.**[87] This Recommendation set out common principles for the development of collective redress mechanisms and invited MS to introduce such mechanisms for the enforcement of all EU law rights, including the right to damages for antitrust harm, by 26 July 2015. Given its optional nature, doubt was expressed as to the ability of the Recommendation to achieve the aim of procedural coherence for collective redress across the EU,[88] and it was thought that this would likely lead the Commission to propose further measures after assessing the implementation of the Recommendation, as required in 2017. 35

The Commission issued its **assessment report** on the Recommendation in early **2018.**[89] In the report, the Commission examined the extent to which national developments since the Recommendation had resulted in a widespread and coherent application of its principles, and the extent to which its implementation had thereby contributed to the objectives of enhancing access to justice and preventing abusive litigation. At the time of the report, nine MS had yet to put in place compensatory collective redress mechanisms,[90] with others limiting the scope of

---

[86] Commission Green Paper *on Damages Actions for Breach of the EC antitrust Rules*, COM(2005) 672 final and the subsequent White Paper, COM(2008) 165 final.

[87] Commission Recommendation 2013/396/EU *on common principles for injunctive and compensatory redress mechanisms in the Member States concerning violations of the rights granted under Union law*, O.J. L 201/60 (2013). On the Recommendation, see further Sorabji (2014).

[88] Sorabji (2014), p. 75.

[89] COM(2018) 40 final.

[90] Injunctive collective redress mechanisms ensuring consumer protection were already required for matters falling within the scope of Parliament/Council Directive No 2009/22/EC *on injunctions for the protection of consumers' interests*, O.J. L 110/30 (2009), repealing the original Parliament/Council Directive No 98/27/EC *on injunctions for the protection of consumers' interests*, O.J. L 166/51 (1998) (the Injunctions Directive). Directive 2009/22/EC has recently been repealed by Parliament/Council Directive No 2020/1828/EU of the *on representative actions for the protection of the collective interests of consumers*, O.J. L 409/1 (2020).

such mechanisms, specifically instituting compensatory collective redress in the field of competition law, amongst other areas.[91] Given the diversity in the implementation of the Recommendation, the Commission's conclusion was that the availability and nature of collective redress mechanisms continued to vary greatly across the MS. The 2018 report therefore called for further measures in the area, specifically in terms of the availability of collective redress actions in national legislation, protection against abusive litigation and the strengthening of the Injunctions Directive.[92] In April 2018, the Commission issued a proposal for a new directive for representative actions for collective injunctive and compensatory relief,[93] essentially proposing the extension of the current Injunctions Directive to collective compensatory redress.

Subsequently, **Directive 2020/1828 on representative actions for the protection of the collective interests of consumers**[94] was enacted in November 2020, to be transposed by the MS by 25 December 2022 and to be applicable six months thereafter, with collective address mechanisms available therefore by 25 June 2023. The Directive puts in place rules for designated collective entities (such as consumer organisations or independent public bodies) to pursue representative actions to protect the collective interests of consumers by means of injunction, damages and other forms of redress for infringements of some 66 EU law measures, specifically listed in Annex 1 to the Directive. Whereas infringements of EU competition law are featured in the 2013 Recommendation, infringements of EU competition law are not included in Annex 1 to Directive 2020/1828. It is unclear how exactly this legislation is related to the Recommendation; certainly, the initial legislative proposal suggested that it took account of the 2013 Recommendation and suggested that the principles of the Recommendation are in fact self-standing, but there is no reference to the 2013 Recommendation in the subsequent Directive 2020/1828.

36 Under Regulation 1/2003, a **duty of cooperation exists between the national courts and the Commission**.[95] Under Article 15.1, national courts have the right to seek information and advice from the Commission on issues relating to the application of Articles 101 and 102 TFEU, and they have availed of this opportunity.[96] National courts are obliged under Article 15.2 of Regulation 1/2003 to transmit copies of their Article 101 and 102 TFEU judgments to the Commission. It seems that this has not worked smoothly, with the Commission receiving very few

---

[91] COM(2018) 40 final, pp. 2–4.
[92] COM(2018) 40 final, pp. 20–21.
[93] COM(2018) 184 final.
[94] Parliament/Council Directive No 2020/1828/EU of the *on representative actions for the protection of the collective interests of consumers*, O.J. L 409/1 (2020).
[95] Elaborated further in Commission Notice *on the co-operation between the Commission and the courts of the EU Member States in the application of Articles 81 and 82 EC*, O.J. C 101/54 (2004).
[96] The Commission reports in *Ten Years of Antitrust Enforcement under Regulation 1/2003: Achievements and Future Perspectives*, COM(2014) 453 final, para 22 that it delivered 26 opinions to national courts between 2004 and 2013.

national court judgments.[97] Under Article 15.3 of that Regulation, the Commission and the national competition authorities have the power to submit *amicus curiae* briefs to the national courts. Whereas, in this regard, the Commission's intervention is limited to ensuring the coherent application of Article 101 or 102 TFEU, the national competition authorities have a general right of intervention before the national courts on any issue relating to Articles 101 and 102 TFEU.

Regulation 1/2003, like its predecessor, defines not just the role and functions of the Commission but also the **role of the CJEU** (→ para 9), as is stipulated by Article 103.2 point (d) TFEU, once again declaring it to have unlimited jurisdiction to review Commission infringement decisions imposing fines or periodic penalty payments (→ para 23) and to cancel, reduce or increase the penalty imposed (Article 31). Article 16 of Regulation 139/2004, the Merger Regulation[98] (→ para 1, 3, 10, 47), similarly provides for the unlimited jurisdiction of the CJEU over Commission decisions imposing fines or periodic penalty payments and to likewise cancel, reduce or increase the penalty imposed.

37

Unlike Regulation 17/62 (→ para 10), however, Regulation 1/2003 specifies the **relationship between national and EU competition laws**, as necessitated by Article 103.2 point (e) TFEU, thereby resolving any ambiguity surrounding the relationship between the two.[99] Article 3 of Regulation 1/2003 facilitates the simultaneous application of national and EU competition laws by national competition authorities. Where national competition authorities apply national competition law, they must also apply Articles 101 and 102 TFEU to activity that has an effect on trade between MS. Furthermore, Article 3 of Regulation 1/2003 provides for the supremacy of EU competition law over national competition law, but national competition authorities are entitled to apply stricter national laws to unilateral conduct.

38

In keeping with the doctrine of supremacy and the Court's ruling in *Masterfoods*,[100] under Article 16 of Regulation 1/2003, **national competition authorities and courts cannot take decisions that run counter to a Commission decision** where the Commission has already dealt with the matter. National courts must also avoid decisions that run counter to decisions contemplated by the Commission where it has initiated proceedings, and in that regard national courts may have to stay proceedings pending the outcome of the Commission proceedings. If there is any doubt in the mind of the national court judge regarding the application of Articles 101 and 102 TFEU, a preliminary reference request can be submitted to the CJEU (→ Article 267 TFEU). Whilst the doctrine of supremacy reigns in the application of EU and national competition laws, Regulation 1/2003 has not

---

[97] Commission Communication, *Ten Years of Antitrust Enforcement under Regulation 1/2003: Achievements and Future Perspectives*, COM(2014) 453 final, para 22.
[98] Council Regulation (EC) No 139/2004 *on the control of concentrations between undertakings*, O.J. L 24/1 (2004).
[99] Venit (2003), p. 557.
[100] Case C-344/98, *Masterfoods v HB* (ECJ 14 December 2000).

prevented MS from enacting competition rules that differ from Articles 101 and 102 TFEU. Nonetheless, the Regulation and cooperation amongst enforcement authorities have indirectly resulted in the convergence of national substantive rules with these two Treaty articles, furthering the parallel application of national and EU competition laws and contributing to both uniformity and consistency throughout the decentralised enforcement system.[101]

39 Article 44 of Regulation 1/2003 provided for a **review** of its operation and for its possible amendment if the review necessitates this. The Commission submitted a report on the functioning of the Regulation to the EP and the Council in 2009,[102] suggesting some areas for improvement, for example imposing penalties on legal and natural persons for making misleading and false replies during interviews (para 12), creating a procedure for imposing periodic penalty payments (para 18), removing the uncertainty surrounding the application of stricter national rules for unilateral conduct (para 22), improving the ability to exchange information between national competition authorities where the receiving authority imposes different sanctions on individuals (para 27), the convergence of national procedural rules and sanctions (para 33) and improved transfer of judgments from national courts to the Commission (para 26). No subsequent amendment to the Regulation was proposed at this stage, however. Since then, the ECN+ Directive[103] has been enacted and implemented with regard to the convergence of national procedural rules and sanctions.

40 The Commission reported positively on the change over from the notification and authorisation system under Regulation 17/62 to the legal exception system of Regulation 1/2003, noting that there had been no major difficulties in this regard.[104] The overall idea behind decentralisation was to release Commission resources and allow the **Commission to focus its attention on hard-core breaches of competition law**,[105] in particular on cartel activity. The increased enforcement powers conferred on the Commission were intended to further support this mission. The 2009 Report suggests that the new system under Regulation 1/2003 allowed the Commission to become more proactive and refocus its enforcement priorities on

---

[101] Cseres (2010a), p. 161. Whilst *Cseres* makes this comment in relation to the new Central and Eastern European MS, the same is equally true in relation to the older MS, many of whose national competition law provisions now mirror Articles 101 and 102 TFEU. See also Venit (2003), pp. 557–558.

[102] Commission Communication, *Report on the Functioning of Regulation 1/2003*, COM(2009) 206 final.

[103] Parliament/Council Directive No 2019/1/EU *to empower the competition authorities of the Member States to be more effective enforcers and to ensure the proper functioning of the internal market*, O.J. L 11/3 (2019).

[104] COM(2009) 206 final, para 7.

[105] White Paper, p. 5 para 13 and p. 19 para 42. See also Recital 3 of Council Regulation (EC) No 1/2003.

sector enquiries, a more economics-based approach to infringements and increased enforcement.[106] However, based on case statistics, it is arguable that **increased Commission enforcement** has not generally materialised to the extent originally envisaged in the White Paper.[107]

The **resources released by the abandonment of the notification and authorisation system have not resulted in a dramatic increase in infringement decisions** (and certainly not as regards hard-core cartel activity, for which recent figures show there has been an average of 4.6 cases per year from 2017 to 2021, with an average of 7.1 cases between 2005 and 2021, albeit multiple undertakings may be involved in each cartel case)[108] nor indeed in a dramatic increase in commitment decisions, although this is a tool that the Commission is resorting to more frequently for abuse of dominance cases. The reasons for this are unclear, although it has been suggested that 1) the level of overall resources devoted to competition enforcement may have been reduced; 2) more resources may be going to the coordination function of the Commission under Regulation 1/2003; 3) the cases being prioritised may be more resource intensive, given their level of complexity; and 4) cases may be more resource intensive due to increased levels of internal quality control or increased analysis of economic effects in abuse of dominance cases.[109] Another considerable factor may be that the Commission's leniency policy ($\rightarrow$ para 24) has become a victim of its own success and the Commission is inundated with leniency applications, which consume a lot of resources.

The Commission further reviewed the operation of Regulation 1/2003 after ten years of enforcement in 2014. Once again, it generally reported positively on the overall experience and level of enforcement but suggested some **areas for improvement**, particularly as regards the institutional position, independence and resourcing of national competition authorities; the convergence of their investigative, decision-making and fining powers; and the further convergence of national leniency programmes ($\rightarrow$ para 41).[110]

In early 2017, the Commission proposed a directive on the harmonisation and strengthening of the enforcement powers of national competition authorities.[111] Subsequently, **Directive 2019/1 on the enforcement power of national competition authorities**[112] ($\rightarrow$ para 1, 3, 13, 28), the ECN+ Directive, was implemented in

41

---

[106] COM(2009) 206 final, para 8.

[107] White Paper, p. 31 para 87.

[108] Figure generated from Commission statistics at https://ec.europa.eu/competition-policy/cartels/statistics_en.

[109] Wils (2013), pp. 299–300.

[110] COM(2014) 453 final para 46. These issues were further elaborated on in a Commission Staff Working Document, *Enhancing competition enforcement by the Member States' competition authorities: institutional and procedural issues*, SWD(2014) 231/2.

[111] COM(2017) 142 final.

[112] Parliament/Council Directive No 2019/1/EU *to empower the competition authorities of the Member States to be more effective enforcers and to ensure the proper functioning of the internal market*, O.J. L 11/3 (2019).

early 2019, to come into force by 4 February 2021 (Article 34.1). The purpose of Directive 2019/1 is to further **empower the national competition authorities** by ensuring that they have the appropriate public enforcement tools and operational independence in the application of EU competition law, with the aim of contributing to a "truly common competition enforcement area" in the EU (Recital 8). With this purpose in mind, Directive 2019/1 establishes, *inter alia*, **minimum harmonisation rules** on the institutional set-up of national competition authorities, on their enforcement and fining powers and on mutual assistance amongst national competition authorities. It also provides for **strict rules in relation to leniency** beyond minimum harmonisation rules. The reason for tighter rules in the area of leniency is to create a level playing field and minimise differences in the various leniency policies of the individual MS, differences that are thought to have weakened the incentives for cartelists to apply for leniency (Recital 11).

As regards the **institutional set-up of national competition authorities**, and in line with Article 35 of Regulation 1/2003, the Directive recognises that the MS can opt for an administrative system (a "single-tier system")[113] entailing a national competition authority both investigating and deciding on the outcome of a case) or an administrative-judicial system (a "two-tier system")[114] entailing a national competition authority investigating the case and a national court of law deciding the final outcome of the case) (→ para 33).[115] Article 4 of the Directive is aimed at ensuring the **independence** of national administrative competition authorities. Amongst other things, this provision requires **impartiality** in the exercise of the duties and powers of national competition authorities (Article 4.1) and specifies that the staff of national competition authorities can act independently of political and other external influences or instructions without any conflict of interest (Article 4.2) or fear of reprisal in the form of dismissal (Article 4.3). National competition authorities are all now empowered by the Directive to **set their priorities** (Article 4.5), meaning that they do not have to investigate every complaint and can prioritise the cases that they deal with. The Directive also requires the **adequate resourcing of national competition authorities** for the exercise of their functions (Article 5.1).

The Directive **enhances the existing enforcement powers of some national competition authorities** (→ para 28) by facilitating, amongst other things, their inspection of non-business premises (Article 7.1) in addition to business premises (Article 6), their collection of digital evidence during investigations (Article 6.1 point (b)), their adoption of interim measures (Article 11), their ability to find that an infringement has occurred and their imposition of any behavioural and structural remedy (Article 10) and their imposition of commitments (Article 12). The Directive provides that national competition authorities shall be empowered to impose "effective, proportionate and dissuasive" **fines** (Article 13.1), with a maximum amount of not less than 10% of the total worldwide turnover of the undertaking

---

[113] Botta (2017), p. 476.
[114] Botta (2017), p. 476.
[115] Directive No 2019/1/EU, Recital 13.

(s) in the preceding business year (Article 15.1). The Directive also legislates for joint **parent-subsidiary liability** as well as **successive liability** at the national level (Article 13.5). Broadly speaking, the enhanced enforcement powers of the national competition authorities mirror many of the Commission's own enforcement powers under Regulation 1/2003. However, a comment has been made (albeit in the context of the Commission's recommendations in its report on "Ten Years of Antitrust Enforcement" → para 40) that "these tools do not fit so neatly" in a two-tier administrative-judicial system and that the objectives of the Commission in seeking the convergence of the national enforcement of EU competition law have failed to take into account deeply rooted divergent systems.[116]

The Directive's provisions on **mutual assistance** are an innovation from the Commission's 2014 suggestions. The Directive essentially reinforces **cooperation between national competition authorities** under Regulation 1/2003 (→ para 30) as regards assistance in the carrying out of inspections and interviews (Article 24). In cross-border cases, the Directive requires the national competition authorities to notify addressees of documents concerning preliminary objections, decisions applying Articles 101 and 102 TFEU, procedural acts in enforcement proceedings required in national law and documents relating to the application of Articles 101 and 102 TFEU (such as decisions imposing fines or periodic penalty payments) on behalf of other national competition authorities (Article 25). The Directive further requires that the national competition authorities enforce the fining and periodic penalty payment decisions of another national competition authority against an undertaking based in their jurisdictions where the undertaking does not have sufficient assets or legal presence in the jurisdiction adopting the decision (Article 26). The Directive effectively thereby elevates the principle of mutual assistance by initiating a *de facto* mutual recognition of national administrative decisions.[117]

Finally, Directive 2019/1 requires all MS to adopt a **leniency policy** (Article 17.1), and it sets out rules on the conditions to obtain immunity or fine reductions (Article 19); the form of leniency applications, including summary applications (Article 20); and markers for immunity applications (Article 21). The creation of a **system of summary leniency applications** (for cartels affecting more than three MS) under Article 22, whereby on application to the Commission a leniency applicant can then submit separate summary applications to the national competition authorities responsible for the case, is significant. Most MS already have leniency policies premised on the ECN's Leniency Model, but this system of summary applications is new for some MS, which had not, until now, been obliged to recognise leniency applications submitted to the Commission. Although falling short of one-stop-shop leniency, this system of summary applications is thought to nonetheless incentivise leniency applications. The Directive also sets out rules regarding the **protection of natural persons** against criminal and administrative sanctions (Article 24) in order to improve legal certainty.

---

[116] Lucy (2016), p. 13.
[117] Botta (2017), p. 471.

Overall, given the extensive nature of the Directive, it is considered to be a step in the right direction[118] in terms of meeting the goal of a more "resource-efficient, uniform, coherent and forceful enforcement" of EU competition law in a common competition enforcement area throughout the MS.[119]

3.2. Block Exemption Regulations

42   The Article 101.3 TFEU *ex ante* control regime of Regulation 17/62 (→ para 6) inevitably brought with it a high volume of notifications, contributing to an extensive workload for the Commission. Many notifications pertained to exclusive distribution agreements and to patent licences. After acquiring some experience in treating exclusive distribution agreements, the Commission was able to distinguish between innocuous distribution agreements and those that had pernicious effects on competition in the internal market. This experience led the Commission to request the Council to introduce **enabling regulations** in 1963 under Article 103.2 point (b) TFEU to empower the Commission to subsequently adopt **block exemption regulations** for certain categories of agreements and concerted practices and to define the scope of application of Article 101 TFEU to these categories of agreement or sectors of the economy, in line with Article 105.3 TFEU (→ Article 105 TFEU para 6). However, the Council declined to introduce enabling legislation in the immediate aftermath of the enactment of Regulation 17/62 as the Commission had not yet acquired adequate experience, and it was not until 1965 that the Council agreed to allow the Commission to introduce block exemption regulations.[120]

43   **Enabling Regulation 19/65**[121] mandated the Commission to grant Article 101.3 TFEU exemptions on a block or group basis to vertical bilateral exclusive distribution and patent licence agreements subject to certain conditions, which were to be established by the Commission. **Enabling Regulation 2821/71**[122] provided the Commission with the same mandate regarding certain horizontal cooperation agreements, namely research and development and specialisation agreements. On the basis of these enabling regulations, several Commission block exemption regulations were introduced under the Regulation 17/62 enforcement regime as a tool for reducing the number of notifications, but their impact was to be much more far-reaching. By delegating power to the Commission to enact legislation pertaining to Article 101.3 TFEU, the Council, perhaps unwittingly, facilitated the

---

[118] See further, Rusu (2018) regarding the Draft Directive.

[119] Rusu (2018), p. 27, commenting on the Draft Directive.

[120] Akman and Kassim (2010), p. 122.

[121] Council Regulation (EEC) No 19/65 *on the application of Article 85(3) of the Treaty to certain categories of agreements and concerted practices*, O.J. Special Edition Series 1/35 (1965–1966).

[122] Council Regulation (EEC) No 2821/71 *on the application of Article 85(3) of the Treaty to categories of agreements, decisions and concerted practices*, O.J. Special Edition Series 1/1032 (1971).

Commission's becoming a very powerful actor in not just enforcement but moreover policy development (→ para 3, 8).[123]

Although there have been question marks raised over the **necessity of block** **44** **exemption regulations in the directly applicable legal exception regime** and the consequent move to self-assessment by undertakings and decentralised enforcement by national competition authorities,[124] block exemption regulations remain important in the new enforcement regime of Regulation 1/2003, thus further strengthening the powers of the Commission in developing policies to the exclusion of the Council (→ para 3). The block exemption regulations currently in force, which set out the application of Article 101.3 TFEU in specific areas, include:

1. The Vertical Restraints Regulation (Regulation 330/2010)[125]
2. The Technology Transfer Regulation (Regulation 316/2014)[126]
3. The Research and Development Block Exemption Regulation (Regulation 1217/2010)[127]
4. The Specialisation Block Exemption Regulation (Regulation 1218/2010)[128]
5. The Motor Vehicle Block Exemption (Regulation 461/2010) (which currently applies to vertical agreements in the motor vehicle aftermarket as under Article 3 of the Regulation, the vertical restraints regulation, Regulation 330/2010, has applied to vertical agreements relating to the purchase, sale or resale of new motor vehicles since 1 June 2013).[129]

Once the conditions of these block exemption regulations are satisfied, **agreements falling within their scope benefit from an exemption** from the application of the Article 101.1 TFEU prohibition. However, where an agreement has effects incompatible with the requirements of Article 101.3 TFEU, the

---

[123] McGowan (2010), p. 129.

[124] See in general Marcos and Sánchez Graells (2010). See also Riley (2003), p. 605; Wesseling (2001), p. 361; Wissman (2000), p. 142.

[125] Commission Regulation (EU) No 330/2010 *on the application of Article 101(3) of the Treaty on the Functioning of the European Union to categories of vertical agreements and concerted practices*, O.J. L 102/1 (2010). This Regulation is due to expire in May 2022, and the Commission issued a proposal for its replacement in July 2021. See https://ec.europa.eu/commission/presscorner/detail/en/ip_21_3561.

[126] Commission Regulation (EU) No 316/2014 *on the application of Article 101(3) of the Treaty on the Functioning of the European Union to categories of technology transfer agreements*, O.J. L 93/17 (2014).

[127] Commission Regulation (EU) No 1217/2010 *on the application of Article 101(3) of the Treaty on the Functioning of the European Union to certain categories of research and development agreements*, O.J. L 335/36 (2010).

[128] Commission Regulation (EU) No 1218/2010 *on the application of Article 101(3) [TFEU] to certain categories of specialisation agreements*, O.J. L 335/43 (2010).

[129] Commission Regulation (EU) No 461/2010 *on the application of Article 101(3) [TFEU] to categories of vertical agreements and concerted practices in the motor vehicle sector*, O.J. L 129/52 (2010).

Commission can retract the benefit of a block exemption Regulation (Article 29.1 of Regulation 1/2003), as can national competition authorities (→ para 27).

4. Special Enforcement Regimes

45 A number of **special enforcement regimes** were introduced in certain sectors (regulating in some instances both procedural and substantive issues) in line with Article 103.2 point (c) TFEU, starting with the **transport sector**, for which the Council initially set aside the application of Regulation 17/62 by Regulation 141/62.[130] The Council subsequently enacted specific legislation for the application of Articles 101 and 102 TFEU to rail, road and inland waterway transport,[131] as well as to maritime[132] and air transport.[133] These three regulations covered all transport with the exception of certain types of transport, including tramp shipping,[134] cabotage[135] and air transport between the Community and third countries. These areas of transport therefore remained subject to the transitional arrangements of Articles 104 and 105 TFEU for some time (→ Article 104 TFEU para 4, → Article 105 TFEU para 1–2, 4–5). The procedures applicable to competition law in the transport sector have since been brought within the general regime of Regulation 1/2003, although Article 32 of Regulation 1/2003 initially continued to omit tramp shipping, cabotage and air transport between the EU and third countries from the application of its general enforcement regime. However, these transport areas have since been brought within the remit of Regulation 1/2003 as a result of Regulation 1419/2006[136] and Regulation 411/2004.[137]

46 Another area entailing specific enforcement legislation is agriculture. The establishment of a common agricultural policy (CAP) is provided for in Articles 38 through 44 TFEU. Article 38.2 TFEU establishes that the internal market extends to agricultural products as defined by the Treaty, save as otherwise provided (→ Article 38 TFEU para 1, 6). Article 42 TFEU otherwise provides that the

---

[130] Council Regulation (EEC) No 141/62 *exempting transport from the application of Council Regulation No. 17*, O.J. Special Edition Series 1/291 (1959–1962).

[131] Council Regulation (EEC) No 1017/68 *applying rules of competition to transport by rail, road and inland waterway*, O.J. Special Edition Series 1/302 (1968), repealed by Council Regulation (EC) No 169/2009, O.J. L 61/1 (2009).

[132] Council Regulation (EEC) No 4056/86 *laying down detailed rules for the application of Arts 85 and 86 to maritime transport*, O.J. L 378/4 (1986), repealed by Council Regulation (EC) No 1419/2006, O.J. L 269/1 (2006).

[133] Council Regulation (EEC) No 3975/87 *laying down the procedure for the application of the rules on competition to undertakings in the air transport sector*, O.J. L 374/1 (1987), repealed by Council Regulation (EC) No 411/2004, O.J. L 68/1 (2004).

[134] A type of shipping operation where the vessel follows the work.

[135] A maritime transport service that takes place internally in one MS.

[136] O.J. L 269/1 (2006).

[137] O.J. L 68/1 (2004).

application of competition law to agriculture depends on a determination of the EP and Council within the framework of Article 43.2 TFEU (→ Article 42 TFEU para 2), taking into account CAP objectives (→ Article 39 TFEU para 12). Article 43.2 TFEU is linked to Article 40.1 TFEU, which provides for a common organisation of agricultural markets, which can take the form of common rules on competition (→ Article 40 TFEU para 11). Article 43.2 TFEU allows the EP and Council to enact legislation to establish the common organisation of agricultural markets and legislation necessary for the pursuit of CAP objectives on the basis of the ordinary legislative procedure (→ Article 43 TFEU para 40). On the basis of Articles 42 and 43 TFEU, Regulation 26/62[138] put in place a **special regime for competition rules in the agricultural sector**, applying Articles 101 through 106 TFEU to agriculture but exempting anti-competitive activity in agricultural products from the scope of Article 101.1 TFEU. Regulation 17/62 otherwise applied in the application of competition law to this sector. Regulation 26/62 basically recognised the need to balance competition and agricultural policy, and the exemption operated on the understanding that a stable agricultural market may necessitate anti-competitive practices, such as price fixing, in order to stabilise markets, increase productivity in agricultural production, sustain agricultural producers in a reasonable standard of living and allow for predictable and reasonable prices, as well as guarantee supplies for consumers in keeping with CAP objectives (Article 39.1 point (a) TFEU; → Article 39 TFEU para 17).[139] This area is now governed by Regulation 1308/2013,[140] the "Common Market Organisation (CMO) Regulation" (as amended by the "Omnibus Regulation"[141]), which provides in its Article 206 that standard competition rules apply to agricultural products except for some specific derogations as set out in the CMO Regulation regarding certain agricultural sectors. In its Article 152, the Omnibus Regulation offers a safe harbour from the application of competition law to recognised producer organisations.

Finally, there is a specific enforcement regime in operation on the **control of mergers** in EU competition law. This specific merger control regime was first introduced by Regulation 4064/89 on the control of concentrations between undertakings[142] and is now governed by Regulation 139/2004 (→ para 1, 3, 10, 37).[143] With a clear jurisdictional delineation between national and EU competition laws (→ para 10), the merger control regime requires the Commission's *ex ante* approval 47

---

[138] Council Regulation No 26/62 *applying certain rules of competition to production of and trade in agricultural products*, O.J. Special Edition Series 1/129 (1959–1962), repealed by Council Regulation (EC) No 1184/2006, O.J. L 214/7 (2006).

[139] Power (2001), p. 1160.

[140] Parliament/Council Regulation (EU) No 1308/2013 *establishing a common organisation of the markets in agricultural products*, O.J. L 347/671 (2013).

[141] Parliament/Council Regulation (EU) 2017/2393, O.J. L 350/15 (2017).

[142] Council Regulation (EEC) No 4064/89 *on the control of concentrations between undertakings*, O.J. L 395/1 (1989).

[143] Council Regulation (EC) No 139/2004 *on the control of concentrations between undertakings*, O.J. L 24/1 (2004).

of mergers with an EU dimension (determined by turnover) and lays down a tight procedural framework and deadlines to be observed by the Commission for approving mergers.

List of Cases

ECJ/CJEU

ECJ 13.02.1969, 14/68, *Walt Wilhelm and Others v Bundeskartellamt,* ECLI:EU:C:1969:4 [cit. in para 10, 29]

E ECJ 30.01.1974, 127/73, *BRT v SABAM,* ECLI:EU:C:1974:25 [cit. in para 14]

ECJ 04.02.1981, 155/79, *AM and S Europe v Commission,* ECLI:EU:C:1982:157 [cit. in para 21]

ECJ 28.02.1991, C-234/89, *Delimitis v Henninger Bräu,* ECLI:EU:C:1991:91 [cit. in para 14]

ECJ 16.07.1992, C-67/91, *Asociación Española de Banca Privada and others,* ECLI:EU:C:1992:330 [cit. in para 12, 30]

ECJ 14.12.2000, C-344/98, *Masterfoods v HB,* ECLI:EU:C:2000:689 [cit. in para 38]

ECJ 20.09.2001, C-453/99, *Courage Ltd v Crehan,* ECLI:EU:C:2001:465 [cit. in para 34]

CJEU 14.09.2010, C-550/07 P, *Akzo Nobel Chemicals and Akcros Chemicals v Commission,* ECLI:EU:C:2010:512 [cit. in para 21]

References[144]

Akman, P. (2009). Searching for the long lost soul of Article 82 EC. *Oxford Journal of Legal Studies, 29*(2), 267–303.

Akman, P., & Kassim, H. (2010). Myths and myth-making in the European Union: The institutionalization and interpretation of EU competition policy. *Journal of Common Market Studies, 48*(1), 111–132.

Botta, M. (2017). The draft directive of the powers of national competition authorities: The glass half empty half full. *European Competition Law Review, 38*(10), 470–477.

Cseres, K. J. (2010a). The impact of Regulation 1/2003 in the new member States. *Competition Law Review, 6*(2), 145–182.

Cseres, K. J. (2010b). Comparing laws in the enforcement of EU and national competition laws. *European Journal of Legal Studies, 3*(1), 7–44.

Deringer, A. (1963). The distribution of powers in the enforcement of the rules of competition under the Rome Treaty. *Common Market Law Review, 1*(1), 30–40.

---

[144] All cited Internet sources have last been consulted on 28 August 2022.

Doherty, B., & Fitzpatrick, A. (2015). Courage to change? The rocky road to Directive 2014/104/EU and the future of private competition law enforcement in Ireland. *Irish Journal of European Law, 18*(2), 15–42.

Ehlermann, C. D. (2000). The modernization of EC anti-trust policy: A legal and cultural revolution. *Common Market Law Review, 37*(3), 537–590.

Gerber, D. J. (2004). The transformation of European Community competition law? *Harvard International Law Journal, 35*(1), 97–147.

Goyder, J., & Albors-Llorens, A. (2009). *Goyder's EC competition law* (5th ed.). OUP.

Komninos, A. P. (2007). Modernisation and decentralisation: Retrospective and prospective. In G. Amato & C. D. Ehlermann (Eds.), *EC competition law: A critical assessment* (pp. 629–673). Hart Publishing.

Lucy, M. C. (2016). Public enforcement of EU competition law in Ireland: Appraising divergence. *Competition Law Review, 12*(1), 9–17.

Maher, I. (2007). Regulation and modes of governance in EC competition law: What's new in enforcement. *Fordham International Law Journal, 31*(6), 1713–1740.

Marcos, F., & Sánchez Graells, A. (2010). A missing step in the modernisation stairway of EU competition law – Any role for block exemption Regulation in the realm of Regulation 1/2003. *Competition Law Review, 6*(2), 183–201.

Mathijsen, P. S. R. F. (2007). *A guide to European Union law* (2nd ed.). Sweet & Maxwell.

McGowan, L. (2010). *The antitrust revolution in Europe, exploring the European Commission's cartel policy*. Edward Elgar.

Möschel, W. (2000). Guest editorial: Change of policy in European competition law. *Common market Law Review, 37*(3), 495–499.

Pace, L. F., & Seidel, K. (2013). The drafting and role of Regulation 17: A hard fought compromise. In K. K. Patel & H. Schweitzer (Eds.), *The historical foundations of EU competition law* (pp. 54–88). OUP.

Pech, L. (2008). *The European Union and its constitution*. Clarus Press.

Power, V. (2001). *Competition law and practice*. Butterworths.

Riley, A. (2003). EC antitrust modernisation: The Commission does very nicely – Thank you! Part 1: Regulation 1 and the notification burden. *European Competition Law Review, 24*(11), 604–615.

Rodger, B. (1999). The Commission white paper on modernisation of the rules Implementing Articles 81 and 82 of the E.C. Treaty. *European Law Review, 24*(6), 653–663.

Rusu, C. (2018). The real challenge of boosting the EU competition law enforcement powers of NCAs: In need of a reframed formula? *Competition Law Review, 13*(1), 27–55.

Sorabji, J. (2014). Reflections on the Commission communication on collective redress. *Irish Journal of European Law, 17*(1), 62–76.

Stephan, W. (2010). Editorial – Reforming EU competition law. *Competition Law Review, 6*(2), 139–143.

Temple Lang, J. (1981). Community antitrust law – Compliance and enforcement. *Common Market Law Review, 18*(3), 335–362.

Todino, M. (2000). Modernisation from the perspective of national competition authorities: Impact of the reform on the decentralised application of E.C. competition law. *European Competition Law Review, 21*(8), 348–358.

Venit, J. S. (2003). Brave new world: The modernization and decentralization of enforcement under Articles 81 and 82 of the EC Treaty. *Common Market Law Review, 40*(3), 545–580.

Wesseling, R. (2001). The draft-regulation modernising the competition rules: The Commission is married to one idea. *European Law Review, 26*(4), 357–378.

Wilks, S. (2005). Agency escape: Decentralisation or dominance of the European Commission in the modernization of competition policy. *Governance, 18*(3), 431–452.

Wils, W. (2001). The modernization of the enforcement of Articles 81 and 82 EC: A legal and economic analysis of the Commission's proposal for a new Council Regulation replacing Regulation No. 17. *Fordham International Law Journal, 24*, 1655–1717.

Wils, W. (2013). Ten years of Regulation 1/2003 – A retrospective. *Journal of European Competition Law and Practice, 4*(4), 293–301.

Wissman, T. (2000). Decentralised enforcement of EC competition law and the new policy on cartels; the Commission white paper of 28th of April 1999. *World Competition, 23*(2), 123–154.

Article 104 [Transitional Enforcement Arrangements]
(ex-Article 84 TEC)

Until the entry into force of the provisions adopted in pursuance of Article 103,[1–4, 6] the authorities[5] in Member States shall rule[1] on the admissibility of agreements, decisions and concerted practices and on abuse of a dominant position in the internal market[1–2] in accordance with the law of their country[6–7] and with the provisions of Article 101, in particular paragraph 3,[1] and of Article 102.

Contents

1. Overview 1
2. Transitional Arrangements Under Article 104 TFEU 3
   2.1. "Authorities" 5
   2.2. The Application of National Law and Articles 101 and 102 TFEU 6
3. The Interaction Between Articles 104 and Article 105 TFEU 8

List of Cases
References

1. Overview

Whereas Articles 101 and 102 TFEU govern substantive EU competition law rules, the TFEU does not cater for their enforcement beyond providing a **broad enforcement framework** in Articles 103, 104 and 105 TFEU combined. Until such time as the Council enacts appropriate Article 103 TFEU legislation to ensure the effective enforcement of Articles 101 and 102 TFEU (→ Article 103 TFEU para 2, 4), the opening words of Article 104 TFEU provide for the **provisional or transitional enforcement** of national law and Article 101 TFEU, particularly the Article 101.3 TFEU exemption (→ Article 101 TFEU para 60), and Article 102 TFEU by MS authorities in conjunction with the Commission under Article 105 TFEU (→ Article 105 TFEU para 1, 4). The power of MS authorities to rule on Article 101.3 TFEU exemptions in transitional arrangements is important as it suggests that the Commission does not have the authority to do so. Moreover, Article 104 TFEU suggests that a *ruling* is necessary, meaning that Article 101.3 TFEU does not operate as a directly applicable exception system during transitional arrangements. That the MS authorities have the power to so rule in transitional arrangements, coupled with the fact that only they have powers of compulsion and sanctions during such arrangements (→ para 8), arguably means that the real

1

enforcement power lies with national competition authorities in transitional enforcement arrangements.[1]

2   Although the opening words of the provision indicate that it is a transitional rule, Article 104 TFEU should not simply be understood as transitional in nature because, in fact, **decentralised enforcement by MS authorities is the default rule** in situations where Article 103 TFEU legislation has not been introduced, has expired without being repealed or replaced or has been annulled by the CJEU. In general, however, as a result of the coverage of the general enforcement regime of Regulation 1/2003[2] and the numerous appropriate legislative measures that have been adopted under Article 103 TFEU (→ Article 103 TFEU para 5–16, 19–31, 33, 36, 38, 42–47), recourse is rarely made to Article 104 TFEU, and it currently plays a **marginal role** only in the enforcement of Articles 101 and 102 TFEU. However, any area that may be excluded from the general and sector-specific enforcement regimes provided for in Article 103 TFEU legislation remains under the scope of Article 104 TFEU and is subject to the jurisdiction of national competition authorities.

2. Transitional Arrangements Under Article 104 TFEU

3   Pending appropriate Article 103 TFEU legislation, **MS authorities are empowered by Article 104 TFEU** to apply national law and Articles 101 and 102 TFEU. The first enforcement regulation introduced by the Council, namely Regulation 17/62[3] (→ Article 103 TFEU para 5–16), had expansive coverage, excluding only several sectors of the economy from the application of Articles 101 and 102 TFEU (→ Article 103 TFEU para 45–47). Moreover, Regulation 17/62 centralised enforcement in the Commission and left a **residual role only for national competition authorities**, as it was only insofar as the Commission had not formally opened Regulation 17/62 proceedings that national authorities could pursue infringements in accordance with Article 104 TFEU (Article 9.3 of Regulation 17/62). Given that Article 104 TFEU was only supposed to be transitional in application, it was interesting that the Council expressly provided a role for national authorities in Regulation 17/62 (→ Article 103 TFEU para 11). The role of the national competition authorities has since been considerably strengthened, particularly by Regulation 1/2003, under which the national competition authorities expressly share enforcement responsibility with the Commission (→ Article 103 TFEU para 19–20, 27–31).

---

[1] Lane (2000). See also Kerse and Khan (2005), pp. 2–3.
[2] Council Regulation (EC) No 1/2003 *on the implementation of the rules on competition laid down in Articles 81 and 82 of the Treaty*, O.J.L 1/1 (2003).
[3] Council Regulation (EEC) No 17/62 *implementing Articles 85 and 86 of the Treaty*, O.J. Special Edition Series 1/87 (1959–1962).

A number of **special enforcement regimes** were introduced in certain sectors of 4
the economy, including the transport sector, in which the Council legislated for the
application of Articles 101 and 102 TFEU to rail, road and inland waterway
transport,[4] as well as to maritime[5] and air transport[6] (→ Article 103 TFEU para
44). This legislation initially contained a number of exclusions (→ Article 103
TFEU para 45), **which therefore remained subject to the transitional arrangements of Article 104 TFEU** and the jurisdiction of the MS authorities. These areas
continued to be excluded from the general enforcement regime of Regulation
1/2003 (Article 32) but were subsequently brought within its scope,[7] thus terminating the Article 104 TFEU jurisdiction of the national authorities in these domains.

2.1. "Authorities"

The Treaty does not identify the **relevant national "authorities"** that are empowered to provisionally enforce the competition law provisions under Article 104 5
TFEU. In *Bilger v Jehle*, the ECJ first adopted a functional approach to the concept
of "authorities", ruling that national courts fell within the concept.[8] This was
reiterated in *BRT v SABAM*, in which the ECJ ruled that Article 104 TFEU covered
all authorities competent to apply Articles 101 and 102 TFEU, including in certain
MS "courts especially entrusted with the task of applying domestic legislation on
competition or that of ensuring the legality of that application by the administrative
authorities".[9] Article 5 of the current enforcement regulation, Regulation 1/2003,
expressly provides that it is the "competition" authorities of the MS that are
empowered to apply Articles 101 and 102 TFEU. Article 6 of Regulation 1/2003
provides that the national courts also have the power to apply these articles.

---

[4] Council Regulation (EEC) No 1017/68 *applying rules of competition to transport by rail, road and inland waterway*, O.J. Special Edition Series 1/302 (1968). This was repealed by Council Regulation (EC) No 169/2009 *applying rules of competition to transport by rail, road and inland waterway*, O.J. L 61/1 (2009).

[5] Council Regulation (EEC) No 4056/86 *laying down detailed rules for the application of Articles 85 and 86 to maritime transport*, O.J. L 378/4 (1986). This was repealed by Council Regulation (EC) No 1419/2006 *repealing Regulation (EEC) No 4056/86 [. . .] and amending Regulation (EC) No 1/2003 as regards the extension of its scope to include cabotage and international tramp services*, O.J. L 269/1 (2006).

[6] Council Regulation (EEC) No 3975/87 *laying down the procedure for the application of the rules on competition to undertakings in the air transport sector*, O.J. L 374/1 (1987). This was repealed by Council Regulation (EC) No 411/2004 *repealing Regulation (EEC) No 3975/87 and amending Regulations (EEC) No 3976/87 and (EC) No 1/2003, in connection with air transport between the Community and third countries*, O.J. L 68/1 (2004).

[7] Council Regulation (EC) No 1419/2006, O.J. L 269/1 (2006); Council Regulation No 411/2004/EC, O.J. L 68/1 (2004).

[8] Case 43/69, *Bilger v Jehle* (ECJ 18 March 1970) para 9.

[9] Case 127/73, *BRT v SABAM* (ECJ 30 January 1974) para 19; confirmed in Joined Cases 209-213/84, *Ministère Public v Asjes and others (Nouvelles Frontières)* (ECJ 30 April 1986) para 55.

Article 35 of Regulation 1/2003 stipulates that the MS should designate competition authorities, including courts responsible for the application of Articles 101 and 102 TFEU, and the MS were required to do so by 1 May 2004.

2.2. The Application of National Law and Articles 101 and 102 TFEU

6 Article 104 TFEU refers to national authorities ruling on the admissibility of agreements, decisions and concerted practices and on abuse of dominance in the internal market **in accordance with the law of their country and with Article 101 and Article 102 TFEU**. Article 103.2 point (e) TFEU (→ Article 103 TFEU para 10, 38) requires the Council to specify the exact nature of the relationship between national and EU competition laws, but this was not actually articulated until the enactment of Regulation 1/2003 (→ Article 103 TFEU para 38). In the interim, Article 104 TFEU suggested a co-existence of national competition law and EU competition law and that **national and EU competition law could be applied simultaneously**. As Article 104 TFEU advances the coexistence of national law and Articles 101 and 102 TFEU, it was understood that undertakings therefore had to comply with both sets of law.[10] However, EU competition law takes precedence over national competition law in line with the doctrine of supremacy, and therefore, national competition law cannot be applied in a manner that undermines Articles 101 and 102 TFEU and the measures adopted to give them effect.[11] The Commission further explained this in its 1993 Notice on cooperation with the national courts[12] and its 1997 Notice on cooperation with national competition authorities.[13] Eventually, the relationship between national competition law and Articles 101 and 102 TFEU was concretised by Regulation 1/2003, which allows for the parallel application of EU and national competition laws subject to the doctrine of supremacy (→ Article 103 TFEU para 38).

7 It was also understood that the term "in accordance with the law of their country and with the provisions of Articles 101 and 102 TFEU" meant that national authorities were to be governed by **national procedural law** in the application of Articles 101 and 102 TFEU.[14] It was only therefore to the extent that national law provided for appropriate authorities (→ para 5) and appropriate procedures that national authorities could in fact apply Articles 101 and 102 TFEU.[15] At the time of

---

[10] Deringer (1963), p. 31.

[11] Case 14/68, *Walt Wilhelm and Others v Bundeskartellamt* (ECJ 13 February 1969) para 4–6.

[12] Commission Notice *on cooperation between national courts and the Commission in applying Articles 85 and 86 of the EEC Treaty*, O.J. C 39/6 (1993) para 12 and 18–32.

[13] Commission Notice *on cooperation between national competition authorities and the Commission in handling cases falling within the scope of Articles 85 or 86 of the EC Treaty*, O.J. C 313/3 (1997) para 16–22.

[14] Kerse (1997), p. 19.

[15] Deringer (1963), pp. 32–33. For a detailed overview of the historical evolution of competition law in Europe, see Gerber (1998).

the inception of the Treaty of Rome, not all of the six original MS had substantive competition law rules or procedures governing the application of competition law rules in place. Only one had substantive and procedural rules and administrative authority in place (Germany), and another (France) had sufficient substantive and procedural law governing unfair competition to cover Article 104 TFEU responsibilities; some (Belgium, Netherlands and Italy) implemented special enforcement rules, but others (Luxembourg) did not.[16] In any case, Regulation 17/62 came into force in 1962, and the Commission largely assumed enforcement responsibilities. Of course, nowadays, all MS operate sophisticated national competition law regimes, with substantive competition law provisions that mirror those of Articles 101 and 102 TFEU *and* procedures governing the application of both national and EU competition laws.

3. The Interaction Between Articles 104 and Article 105 TFEU

Although the national competition authorities can act independently of Article 105 TFEU,[17] their jurisdiction during transitional arrangements is not entirely an exclusive jurisdiction as the **Commission has the power to investigate alleged competition law infringements** under Article 105.1 TFEU **in transitional enforcement arrangements** (→ Article 105 TFEU para 2). However, the Commission cannot compel the termination of the infringements, nor can it sanction undertakings for breaches of competition law in transitional enforcement arrangements (→ Article 105 TFEU para 1, 2, 4). If the infringement continues, the Commission must mandate the relevant MS authorities to take appropriate remedial action (→ Article 105 TFEU para 3). Thus, the Commission's powers are limited in transitional enforcement arrangements as it has no power of compulsion or sanction (→ para 1).

8

List of Cases

ECJ
ECJ 13.02.1969, 14/68, *Walt Wilhelm and Others v Bundeskartellamt*, ECLI:EU:C:1969:4 [cit. in para 6]
ECJ 18.03.1970, 43/69, *Bilger v Jehle*, ECLI:EU:C:1970:20 [cit.in para 5]
ECJ 30.01.1974, 127/73, *BRT v SABAM*, ECLI:EU:C:1974:25 [cit. in para 5]
ECJ 30.04.1986, 209-213/84, *Ministère Public v Asjes and others (Nouvelles Frontières)*, ECLI:EU:C:1986:188 [cit. in para 5]

---

[16] See further Deringer (1963), p. 33.
[17] Kerse (2007), p. 19.

References

Deringer, A. (1963). The distribution of powers in the enforcement of the rules of competition under the Rome Treaty. *Common Market Law Review, 1*(1), 30–40.

Gerber, D. (1998). *Law and competition in twentieth century Europe: Protecting Prometheus.* OUP.

Kerse, C. S. (2007). Enforcing Community competition policy under Articles 88 and 89 of the E.C. Treaty – New powers for UK competition authorities. *European Competition Law Review, 18* (1), 17–23.

Kerse, C. S., & Khan, N. (2005). *EC antitrust procedure* (5th ed.). Sweet & Maxwell.

Lane, R. (2000). *EC competition law*. Longman Pearson.

Article 105 [Role of the Commission]
(ex-Article 85 TEC)

1. Without prejudice to Article 104, the Commission shall ensure the application of the principles laid down in Articles 101 and 102.[1–4] On application by a Member State or on its own initiative, and in cooperation with the competent authorities in the Member States, which shall give it their assistance,[2] the Commission shall investigate cases of suspected infringement of these principles.[2] If it finds that there has been an infringement, it shall propose appropriate measures to bring it to an end.[2–3]
2. If the infringement is not brought to an end, the Commission shall record such infringement of the principles in a reasoned decision.[2–3] The Commission may publish its decision and authorise Member States to take the measures, the conditions and details of which it shall determine, needed to remedy the situation.[3–4]
3. The Commission may adopt regulations relating to the categories of agreement in respect of which the Council has adopted a regulation or a directive pursuant to Article 103(2)(b).[6–7]

Contents

1. Overview 1
2. Transitional Enforcement Arrangements Under Article 105 TFEU 2
3. The Current Scope of Application of Paragraphs 1 and 2 5
4. Legislating Powers Under Paragraph 3 6

List of Cases
References

1. Overview

The Treaty does not provide detailed enforcement rules for Articles 101 and 102 TFEU (→ Article 101 TFEU para 9, → Article 102 TFEU para 3). Instead, it establishes a **broad enforcement framework** in Article 103 TFEU (→ Article 103 TFEU para 1–2), Article 104 TFEU (→ Article 104 TFEU) and Article 105 TFEU. Detailed enforcement rules are to be legislated by the Council under Article 103 TFEU (→ Article 103 TFEU para 1–4), and until such time as this legislation is enacted, the MS authorities under Article 104 TFEU (→ Article 104 TFEU para 1–5), along with the Commission under Article 105 TFEU, are responsible for the **provisional or transitional enforcement of Articles 101 and 102 TFEU**. In the original wording of the 1957 Treaty of Rome, then Article 89 TEEC specified: 'Without prejudice to Article 88 the Commission shall *as soon as it takes up its* *duties* ensure the application of the principles laid down in Articles 85 and 86.'[1] The words 'as soon as it takes up its duties' are considered to be suggestive that this provision was of a temporal nature, allowing the Commission to enforce the competition law provisions of the Treaty until such time as the Council implemented the Article 103 TFEU enforcement legislation (→ Article 103 TFEU para 1–2).[2] The words 'as soon as it takes up its duties' were removed by the amending Treaty of Amsterdam 1997, indicating that albeit a temporary or transitory power, the Commission has in fact a 'permanent residual power to intervene'[3] (→ para 5).

In combination with Article 104 TFEU, Article 105.1–2 TFEU (→ para 2–4) envisages a **largely decentralised application of Articles 101 and 102 TFEU during transitional enforcement arrangements**. This is due to the limited role of the Commission during such arrangements (→ para 2–4), with the power of compulsion and sanction resting with the MS authorities (→ para 3–4). The term '[w]ithout prejudice to Article 104' in Article 105.1 TFEU indicates that the Commission nonetheless retains a certain centralised supervisory function in ensuring the application of the principles set out in Articles 101 and 102 TFEU. Indeed, the CFI has acknowledged that Article 105.1 TFEU is a specific expression of the general supervisory role conferred on the Commission by old Article 115 TEEC as regards Articles 101 and 102 TFEU.[4] Broadly speaking, this supervisory function has been carried over to the current Article 17.1 TEU (→ Article 17.1 TEU para 16). While initially this made the Commission the main agent responsible for ensuring the application of Articles 101 and 102 TFEU, the advent of Regulation 1/2003[5] (→ Article 103 TFEU para 5–40) marked the decentralisation of enforcement, enabling the national competition authorities and national courts to apply these provisions to competition issues. Nonetheless, deriving from Article 105.1 TFEU, the Commission is entrusted with the responsibility for 'defining and implementing the orientation of [Union] competition policy'.[6]

As Article 104 and Article 105.1, together with Article 105.2, TFEU operate in tandem with each other and as the enforcement of Articles 101 and 102 TFEU has been comprehensively legislated (→ Article 103 TFEU para 5–47), Article 105.1–2 TFEU currently plays a **mostly residual and default role only in the EU competition law enforcement regime** (→ Article 104 TFEU para 1). Article 105.1 TFEU, however, has more than a residual or transitory significance as regards the Commission's supervisory function, and also **Article 105.3 TFEU**, introduced by the Lisbon Treaty 2009, has more than a residual or transitory significance

---

[1] Emphasis added.

[2] Jones et al. (2019), p. 93.

[3] Jones et al. (2019), p. 93.

[4] Case T-24/90, *Automec v Commission (Automec II)* (CFI 18 September 1992) para 74 and Case T-77/92, *Parker Pen Ltd v Commission* (CFI 14 July 1994) para 63.

[5] Council Regulation (EC) No 1/2003 *on the implementation of the rules on competition laid down in Articles 81 and 82 of the Treaty*, O.J. L 1/1 (2003).

[6] Case C-344/98, *Masterfoods and HB* (ECJ 14 December 2000) para 46.

(→ para 6). The legislative authority the latter confers on the Commission gives the Commission considerable law- and policy-making powers in the field of competition law.

2. Transitional Enforcement Arrangements Under Article 105 TFEU

Article 105.1–2 TFEU specifies the **role of the Commission** in transitional enforcement arrangements. Under Article 105.1 TFEU, the Commission is to 'ensure the application of the principles laid down in Articles 101 and 102'. However, Article 105.1 TFEU provides the Commission with **limited enforcement powers** only, requiring it (in combination with Article 105.2 TFEU) to work closely with the MS authorities due to the lack of implementing legislation during transitional enforcement arrangements.[7] It is empowered, on the application of an MS or of its own motion (or, indeed, on the basis of a complaint by a private individual), to investigate alleged competition law infringements, and its investigation is to be conducted 'in cooperation with the competent authorities in the Member States' and with their investigative assistance.

So at its inception, Article 105 TFEU introduced a principle of **'close and constant liaison' between the Commission and the MS authorities**.[8] This can be viewed as a specific application of the Article 4.3 TEU duty of sincere cooperation, according to which, at a vertical level,[9] the Union and MS are required to assist each other in carrying out tasks that flow from the Treaties (→ Article 4 TEU para 86). Article 105.1 TFEU specifies that the Commission 'shall' investigate suspected infringements of Articles 101 and 102 TFEU on application by an MS, thereby imposing an obligation on it to do so. Failure to perform this obligation could result in the applicant MS pursuing the Commission in a failure to act case under Article 265 TFEU. This Article 265 TFEU failure to act possibility, however, does not extend to private individuals who complain to the Commission about Articles 101 and 102 TFEU infringements[10] under Article 7(2) of Regulation 1/2003[11] because there is no obligation on the Commission to investigate such complaints from individuals under Article 105.1 TFEU, and moreover, the Commission is not under any duty to adopt a legal decision as regards the existence or otherwise of the alleged infringements vis-à-vis such complainants.[12] Rather, infringement decisions are directed to the perpetrators of anti-competitive

---

[7] Wesseling (2000), p. 16.
[8] Pace and Seidel (2013), p. 82.
[9] Lafarge (2010), p. 602.
[10] Case 246/81, *Lord Bethell v Commission* (ECJ 10 June 1982) para 15–16.
[11] Council Regulation (EC) No 1/2003 *on the implementation of the rules on competition laid down in Articles 81 and 82 of the Treaty*, O.J. L 1/1 (2003).
[12] Case 125/78, *GEMA v Commission* (ECJ 18 October 1979) para 17; T-24/90, *Automec v Commission (Automec II)* (CFI 18 September 1992) para 75–76.

behaviour. For this reason, individual complainants do not therefore qualify for standing under Article 265 TFEU.

Nonetheless, the **Commission is under a duty to consider complaints submitted to it by private individuals**.[13] This duty means that the Commission must carefully examine 'the factual and legal particulars brought to its notice by the [individual] complainant in order to decide whether they disclose conduct of such a kind as to distort competition in the common market and affect trade between Member States'.[14] Indeed, following an initial investigation, the Commission can, under Article 2(4) of Regulation 773/2004,[15] reject complaints from private individuals because it deems that no infringement has occurred. Article 7(1) of Regulation 773/2004, however, obliges the Commission to substantiate any such rejection, and the individual complainant then has a right to submit observations in this regard. If there is no change to the Commission's stance following these observations, the Commission must issue a decision rejecting the complaint under Article 7(2) of Regulation 773/2004. The Commission can also reject a complaint on the ground of lack of Union interest in the case[16] or if a national competition authority is already dealing or has dealt with the case under Article 13 of Regulation 1/2003 or if a national competition authority would be better placed to deal with the case.[17] As for Article 105.1 TFEU investigations, the Commission has the power under Article 105.1 TFEU to propose measures to end infringements on the completion of its investigation. It cannot compel the infringer(s) to terminate the infringement, nor can it impose sanctions for the infringement; it can simply record the continued infringement in a reasoned opinion under Article 105.2 TFEU but take no further action itself.

3   Having recorded a continued infringement following its initial investigation and proposals for termination, the Commission is obliged by Article 105.2 TFEU to **mandate the MS to take appropriate remedial action** against the infringer(s), although it is thought to be unlikely that it could instruct the MS to impose criminal sanctions envisaged by national law.[18] While the Commission cannot impose remedies or cannot sanction the infringer(s) (→ para 2), Article 105.2 TFEU nonetheless allows it to determine the 'conditions and details' of the MS' remedial action.

---

[13] Case 210/81, *Demo-Studio Schmidt v Commission* (ECJ 11 October 1983) para 19.

[14] Case T-24/90, *Automec v Commission (Automec II)* (CFI 18 September 1992) para 79.

[15] Commission Regulation (EC) No 773/2004 *relating to the conduct of proceedings by the Commission pursuant to Articles 81 and 82 of the EC Treaty*, O.J. L 123/18 (2004).

[16] Case T-24/90, *Automec v Commission (Automec II)* (CFI 18 September 1992) para 77 and 85, confirmed in Recital 18 of Regulation 1/2003. See also Commission Notice *on the handling of complaints by the Commission under Articles 81 and 82 of the EC Treaty*, O.J. C 101/05 (2004) points 41–45.

[17] Commission Notice *on cooperation within the Network of Competition Authorities*, O.J. C 101/43 (2004) points 8–15.

[18] Buxbaum (1961), p. 422 note 80.

So under transitional enforcement arrangements, effectively the Commission 4
can investigate, find infringement and make recommendations for the termination
of the infringement, but it has **no power of compulsion or sanction**, which remains
with the MS. **Nor does the Commission have the power to rule on the exemption
under Article 101.3 TFEU** (→ Article 101 TFEU para 60) in transitional enforcement arrangements, which also remains with the MS under Article 104 TFEU
(→ Article 104 TFEU para 1). Arguably, therefore, during transitional enforcement
arrangements, the powers of the Commission are quite limited vis-à-vis those of the
MS authorities,[19] with its investigatory powers in alignment with the Commission's
Article 337 TFEU powers to collect information and carry out any checks required
for the performance of tasks entrusted to it (subject to limitations and conditions
imposed by the Council) and its decision-making powers limited to finding infringements and making recommendations to terminate infringements.

3. The Current Scope of Application of Paragraphs 1 and 2

As the Council has legislated extensively for the enforcement of Articles 101 and 5
102 TFEU (→ Article 103 TFEU para 5–47), **Article 105.1–2 TFEU currently
plays a marginal role** only in the enforcement of these provisions, with the
exception of the Commission's broader ongoing supervisory role. Most areas
were brought within the general enforcement regime of Regulation 17/62[20] and
were therefore covered by its replacement, Regulation 1/2003,[21] with the exception
of a number of areas in the transport sector (→ Article 103 TFEU para 45). While
these transport areas continued to fall under the transitional arrangements of
Article 104 TFEU and Article 105 TFEU (→ Article 103 TFEU para 45,
→ Article 104 TFEU para 4) even after the enactment of Regulation 1/2003
because its Article 32 specifically omitted them from its scope of application,
they have since been brought within the remit of Regulation 1/2003 as a result of
amending legislation.[22] Therefore, the temporary or transitory procedural rules set

---

[19] Lane (2000), p. 164. Kerse and Khan (2005), pp. 2–3.

[20] Council Regulation (EEC) No 17/62 *implementing Articles 85 and 86 of the Treaty*, O.J. Special Edition Series 1/87 (1959–1962).

[21] Council Regulation (EC) No 1/2003 *on the implementation of the rules on competition laid down in Articles 81 and 82 of the Treaty*, O.J. L 1/1 (2003).

[22] Council Regulation (EC) No 1419/2006 *repealing Regulation (EEC) No 4056/86 [...] and amending Regulation (EC) No 1/2003 as regards the extension of its scope to include cabotage and international tramp services*, O.J. L 269/1 (2006); Council Regulation (EC) No 411/2004 *repealing Regulation (EEC) No 3975/87 and amending Regulations (EEC) No 3976/87 and (EC) No 1/2003 in connection with air transport between the Community and third countries*, O.J. L 68/1 (2004).

out in Article 104 TFEU and Article 105 TFEU are 'largely of historic interest',[23] even if they confer the Commission with a 'permanent residual power to intervene'[24] (→ para 1).

4. Legislating Powers Under Paragraph 3

6   Although Articles 105.1 and 105.2 TFEU pertain to transitional enforcement arrangements, Article 105.3 TFEU, which was introduced by the Lisbon Treaty 2009 and grants 'broad regulatory competence' to the Commission,[25] seemingly has a more permanent and constant application (→ para 1). Article 105.3 TFEU essentially **allows the Commission to adopt regulations for certain categories of agreement** once the Council has enacted enabling legislation under Article 103.2 point (b) TFEU (→ Article 103 TFEU para 42–44), empowering the Commission to do so. This provision therefore simply provides a Treaty base for the already existing practice of Council regulations delegating legislative powers to the Commission (→ Article 103 TFEU para 42–44).[26]

7   The Council has introduced various enabling regulations under Article 103.2 point (b) TFEU (→ Article 103 TFEU para 42–43),[27] facilitating the **Commission's Article 105.3 TFEU legislating power**. Resulting from these enabling regulations, the Commission has adopted exemption regulations for certain categories of agreements and concerted practices (→ Article 103 TFEU para 44), exempting them on a block basis from the application of the Article 101.1 TFEU prohibition on anti-competitive agreements once certain conditions are met in line with the Article 101.3 TFEU exemption clause (→Article 101.3 TFEU para 60).

List of Cases

ECJ
ECJ 18.10.1979, 125/78, *GEMA v Commission*, ECLI:EU:C:1979:237 [cit. in para 2]
ECJ 10.06.1982, 246/81, *Lord Bethell v Commission*, ECLI:EU:C:1982:224 [cit. in para 2]

---

[23] Lasok (2001), p. 617.
[24] Jones et al. (2019), p. 93.
[25] Lianos et al. (2019), p. 31.
[26] Lianos et al. (2019), p. 31.
[27] Council Regulation (EEC) No 19/65 *on application of Article 85(3) of the Treaty to certain categories of agreements and concerted practices*, O.J. Special Edition Series 1/35 (1965–1966); Council Regulation (EEC) No 2821/71 *on application of Article 85 (3) of the Treaty to categories of agreements, decisions and concerted practices*, O.J. Special Edition Series 1/1032 (1971).

ECJ 11.10.1983, 210/81, *Demo-Studio Schmidt v Commission*, ECLI:EU:C:1983:277 [cit. in para 2]

ECJ 14.12.2000, 344/98, *Masterfoods and HB*, ECLI:EU:C:2000:689 [cit. in para 1]

CFI

CFI 14.07.1992, T-77/92, *Parker Pen Ltd v Commission*, ECLI:EU:T:1994:85 [cit. in para 1]

CFI 19.09.1992, T-24/90, *Automec v Commission (Automec II)*, ECLI:EU:T:1992:97 [cit. in para 1; 2]

References

Buxbaum, R. M. (1961). Antitrust regulation within the European Economic Community. *Columbia Law Review, 61*, 402–429.

Jones, A., Sufrin, B., & Dunne, N. (2019). *Jones and Sufrin's EU competition law: Text, cases and materials* (7th ed.).

Kerse, C. S., & Khan, N. (2005). *EC antitrust procedure* (5th ed.). Thomson Sweet & Maxwell.

Lafarge, F. (2010). Administrative cooperation between member states and implementation of EU law. *European Public Law, 16*(4), 597–616.

Lane, R. (2000). *EC competition law*. Longman Pearson.

Lasok, K. P. E. (2001). *Law and institutions of the European Union* (7th ed.). Butterworths.

Lianos, I., Korah, V., & Siciliani, P. (2019). *Competition law: Analysis, cases & materials*. OUP.

Pace, L. F., & Seidel, K. (2013). The drafting and role of Regulation 17: A hard fought compromise. In K. K. Patel & H. Schweitzer (Eds.), *The historical foundations of EU competition law* (pp. 54–88). OUP.

Wesseling, R. (2000). *The modernisation of EC antitrust law*. Hart Publishing.

Article 106 [Public and Privileged Undertakings and Services of General Economic Interest]
(ex-Article 86 TEC)

1. In the case of public undertakings[11, 12] and undertakings to which Member States grant special or exclusive rights,[13–15] Member States shall neither enact nor maintain in force any measure contrary to the rules contained in the Treaties,[16–38] in particular to those rules provided for in Article 18[6, 18] and Articles 101 to 109.[3, 6, 11, 18–32, 34–38, 42, 66, 67, 74, 75, 81, 83, 85, 87]
2. Undertakings entrusted with the operation of services of general economic interest[51–60] or having the character of a revenue-producing monopoly[61] shall be subject to the rules contained in the Treaties, in particular to the rules on competition, in so far as the application of such rules does not obstruct the performance, in law or in fact, of the particular tasks assigned to them.[62–70] The development of trade must not be affected to such an extent as would be contrary to the interests of the Union.[71–74]
3. The Commission shall ensure the application of the provisions of this Article[39, 40, 76] and shall, where necessary, address appropriate directives[78–85] or decisions[87–89] to Member States.

Contents

1. Overview 1
   1.1. Introduction 1
   1.2. The Broader Context of Article 106 TFEU 4
   1.3. The Role of Article 106 TFEU 5
2. Member State Obligations Under Paragraph 1 8
   2.1. The Broader Context 9
   2.2. Elements 10
      2.2.1. Public Undertakings 11
      2.2.2. Undertakings Granted Special or Exclusive Rights 13
      2.2.3. Measures Contrary to the Treaty Rules 16
   2.3. Enforcement 39
3. Exceptions Under Paragraph 2 41
   3.1. The Broader Context 43
   3.2. Elements 49
      3.2.1. Beneficiaries 50
      3.2.2. Obstruction of the Performance of Services of General Economic Interest Tasks 62
      3.2.3. Development of Trade Contrary to Union Interest 71
   3.3. Services of General Economic Interest and State Aid 75
   3.4. Enforcement 76
4. Commission's Law-Making Competence Under Paragraph 3 77
   4.1. Directives 78
   4.2. Decisions 87
List of Cases
References

1. Overview

1.1. Introduction

1   Article 106 TFEU is concerned with public undertakings and undertakings granted special or exclusive rights by the MS (**privileged undertakings**). It consists of three paragraphs. Article 106.1 TFEU (→ para 8–40) specifies the application of the Treaty rules to public undertakings (→ para 11–12) and to undertakings granted special or exclusive rights (→ para 13–15). Article 106.2 TFEU (→ para 41–76) subjects the application of the Treaty rules to public undertakings and privileged undertakings to a limited exception for services of general economic interest (SGEI) (→ para 51–60) and for revenue-producing monopolies (→ para 61). Its final paragraph, Article 106.3 TFEU (→ para 77–89), provides for expedited enforcement of the provision by the Commission by allowing the Commission to address decisions to the MS applying Article 106 TFEU (→ para 87–89), thus by-passing the standard enforcement mechanism procedure of Article 258 TFEU. In addition, Article 106.3 TFEU provides the Commission with specific and autonomous law-making powers (→ para 81–84) to ensure the effective application of Article 106 TFEU, in this case by-passing the standard ordinary legislative procedure of Article 294 TFEU.

2   The full scope of Article 106 TFEU has undergone a **gradual development**. It was not until the 1990s that the provision came to the fore with four major cases[1] (→ para 22–25) and with the introduction of legislation (→ para 79–82) in the area. Article 106 TFEU is a complex area of law, partly due to inconsistent and at times confusing case law, and it is an area of law that continues to be developed. Its gradual application and development can be explained on the basis of significant changes in economic and social policy, including the **move from nationalisation to liberalisation** and the dynamics of **technological advances**, as well as the **trajectory of the internal market** and its market integration goal.[2]

3   This trajectory has been marked by an initial focus on removing tariff barriers to trade in the form of customs duties and charges with equivalent effect (Article 30 TFEU) and in the form of discriminatory and protectionist internal taxation (Article 110 TFEU), shifting to a focus on non-tariff barriers to trade in the form of quantitative restrictions and measures with equivalent effect (Articles 34, 35 TFEU) and eventually progressing to a focus on "the most intransigent"[3] barriers to market integration in the form of State intervention in the market directly through public undertakings or indirectly through the conferral of privilege on undertakings, and in the form of State aid (Article 107 TFEU).

---

[1] Case C-41/90, *Höfner & Elser v Macrotron* (ECJ 23 April 1991); Case C-260/89, *ERT v DEP* (ECJ 18 June 1991); Case C-179/90, *Merci Convenzionali Porto di Genova v Siderurgica Gabrielli* (ECJ 10 December 1991); Case C-18/88, *RTT v GB-Inno-BM* (ECJ 13 December 1991).

[2] Hancher (1999), pp. 724–725.

[3] Hancher (1999), p. 724.

1.2. The Broader Context of Article 106 TFEU

The state can exercise considerable influence in the market either directly or indirectly through legislation, regulation and subsidisation and through participation in the market of public undertakings and privileged undertakings on which it has conferred special or exclusive rights. Neither the TEU nor the TFEU interferes with **property ownership**, with Article 345 TFEU providing that nothing in the Treaties shall prejudice MS rules governing the system of property ownership. As the Treaties are neutral regarding **public and private ownership**,[4] they leave it to the MS to decide on the extent to which they own undertakings or otherwise confer privileged status on either public undertakings or private undertakings. In the past, there was a strong tradition of **State ownership** and **nationalisation of certain industries** (particularly in the utilities), as well as a tradition of State conferral of privileged status on some undertakings. The **process of liberalisation or privatisation** has, however, marked a move away from State ownership and opened up competition in sectors previously nationalised. This process has been complemented by the imposition of **public service obligations** (→ para 51, 54, 59), including **universal service obligations** (→ para 54), on some undertakings in liberalised markets in order to ensure the availability of certain services to all consumers in a particular territory at an affordable price and at a certain level of quality, thereby ensuring consumer and user rights.[5]

1.3. The Role of Article 106 TFEU

Notwithstanding the liberalisation or "marketisation"[6] of certain sectors, both **public ownership** and the **practice of States conferring privileges** on undertakings persist. This is not prohibited by the TFEU; indeed, Article 106.1 TFEU recognises and tolerates the practice of public and privileged undertakings. This does not mean, however, that MS have absolute discretion when it comes to public and privileged undertakings. Article 106 TFEU also recognises that **Treaty infringements** can arise as a result of State intervention in the market or State involvement in economic activities.

To control State action and intervention, **Article 106.1 TFEU prohibits the MS from introducing or maintaining measures concerning public or privileged undertakings that conflict with the obligations contained in other Treaty provisions**. Article 106.1 TFEU highlights in particular that the principle of non-discrimination (Article 18 TFEU) must be adhered to, as must the competition law rules (Articles 101 through 106 TFEU) and State aid rules (Articles 107 through

---

[4] On the absolute neutrality of the Treaty regarding property ownership, see Van Cleynenbreugel (2014).
[5] Jones et al. (2019), p. 583.
[6] Jones et al. (2019), p. 583.

109 TFEU) (→ para 18). This is subject to the limited **Article 106.2 TFEU exception** for SGEI and revenue-producing monopolies (→ para 51–61). Under this exception, the circumvention of Treaty rules is permissible to the extent that this is necessary and proportionate for the performance of SGEI tasks and to the extent that the development of trade is not affected contrary to EU interests (→ para 71–74).

Although it highlights the principle of non-discrimination and the competition law rules, in line with its wording, Article 106 TFEU is applicable in conjunction with *all* Treaty rules. Nonetheless, **Article 106 TFEU is situated within the Treaty rules on competition law**,[7] and it has been most frequently invoked in conjunction with them. This undoubtedly reflects the fact that the drafters of the Treaty were especially cognisant of the possibility of MS distorting competition by favouring public and privileged undertakings.[8] As a result, Article 106 TFEU has had a certain bearing on the application of the competition law rules to public and privileged undertakings, notably the Article 102 TFEU prohibition on abuse of dominance, given that public and privileged undertakings typically enjoy a dominant position in the market.

Essentially, however, public and privileged undertakings are subject to all of the Treaty rules and obligations on the same basis as private undertakings, not just competition law rules. The general purpose and indeed the rationale of Article 106 TFEU is therefore to provide a mechanism ensuring a **level playing field** or **competitive neutrality for the application of all Treaty rules** to public, private, and privileged undertakings alike and to safeguard against the unfair treatment of private undertakings vis-à-vis public or privileged undertakings.

7   Article 106 TFEU is, to a certain extent, a **middle ground between an "absolute sovereignty approach" and an "absolute competition approach"**. According to the absolute sovereignty approach, MS have free reign regarding public ownership and privileged undertakings and the organisation and provision of public goods with immunity from the Treaty rules, whereas according to the absolute competition approach, the creation or existence of privileged undertakings is prohibited due to their inherent anti-competitive nature.[9] **Article 106 TFEU thereby reconciles two different interests**: those of the MS in determining the organisation and provision of public goods, and indeed in supporting certain national interests and more broadly shaping their broader economic and social policies, and those of the EU in the pursuit of its objectives. This was highlighted by the ECJ, for example, in *Spain v Commission* when it stated that "paragraph (2) of Article [106 TFEU], read with paragraph (1) thereof, seeks to reconcile the Member States' interests in using certain undertakings, in particular in the public sector, as an instrument of economic and social policy with the [EU's] interest in

---

[7] Chapter 1 Rules on Competition in Title VII Common Rules on Competition, Taxation and Approximation of Laws of the TFEU.

[8] Whish and Bailey (2021), p. 232.

[9] See further Lane (2000), pp. 224–225; Hancher (1999), pp. 727–728.

ensuring compliance with the rules on competition and the preservation of the unity of the [internal] market".[10]

2. Member State Obligations Under Paragraph 1

Article 106.1 TFEU is addressed directly to the MS, and it seeks to ensure that the **MS do not breach the Treaty provisions in their treatment of public and privileged undertakings**. As it is addressed to MS, they alone are responsible for any breaches of the provision. Undertakings are immune from any finding of infringement of Article 106.1 TFEU, where through legislation or regulation the MS have facilitated a breach of the Treaty provisions by them. However, in the absence of a State measure setting aside the full rigours of the Treaty, the undertakings themselves will be responsible for the breach.

8

2.1. The Broader Context

By requiring the MS to ensure compliance with all Treaty provisions in the treatment of public and privileged undertakings, Article 106.1 TFEU embodies a specific instance of the Article 4.3 TEU **obligation of sincere cooperation**.[11] Article 4.3 TEU requires the MS to ensure the fulfilment of their EU law obligations, to facilitate the achievement of the EU's tasks and to refrain from any measure that would jeopardise the attainment of the EU's objectives. Such obligations, tasks and objectives are specified in Article 3.3 TEU and involve, *inter alia*, the establishment of the internal market, which by virtue of Protocol No 27 on the internal market and competition includes a system ensuring that competition is not distorted,[12] and a highly competitive social market economy, as well as the promotion of economic, social and territorial cohesion (→ Article 3 TEU para 31 et seqq.). So while the Treaties might be neutral on the issue of property ownership, this is qualified somewhat by the internal market and competition ethos which run through the Treaties, and which permeate Article 106.1 TFEU.

9

This ethos extends beyond internal market and competition law rules and sweeps across numerous other Treaty provisions concerning the EU's **open market economy** and **competitive markets**. Article 3.3 TEU also provides, for example, that the EU shall work for the sustainable development of Europe based on a highly

---

[10] Case C-463/00, *Spain v Commission* (ECJ 13 May 2003) para 82. The Court had previously issued similar statements, e.g., in Case 202/88, *France v Commission* (ECJ 19 March 1991) para 12.

[11] For a detailed examination of the relationship between Article 4.3 TEU and Article 106 TFEU, see Davies (2009), pp. 551–558.

[12] See Szyszczak (2011), pp. 1748–1749 for a discussion on the replacement of Article 3.1 point (g) TEC by Protocol (No 27). See also Pech (2008), p. 176; Fiedziuk (2011), p. 227 and pp. 230–232.

competitive social market economy (→ Article 3 TEU para 33). Furthermore, Article 119 TFEU, introduced originally by the 1992 Maastricht Treaty,[13] provides that the activities of the MS and the EU shall be conducted in accordance with the principle of an open market economy with free competition (→ Article 119 TFEU para 40–41). Article 173.1 TFEU further stipulates that the EU and the MS shall ensure that the conditions necessary for the competitiveness of the EU's industry exist and that their action in this regard shall be in accordance with a system of open and competitive markets (→ Article 173 TFEU para 22).

There is much to suggest therefore, beyond the actual wording of Article 106.1 TFEU, that in tolerating public ownership and the conferral of special or exclusive rights on public or privileged undertakings under Article 106.1 TFEU, the Treaties nonetheless oblige the **MS to ensure** in particular the principles of **free competition and competitiveness** in the internal market, to facilitate the achievement of a highly competitive social market economy and the competitiveness of the EU's industry and, ultimately, to prevent impediments to the internal market objectives.

2.2. Elements

10 There are a number of **key elements** that need to be considered under Article 106.1 TFEU: firstly, the concept of a "public undertaking" (→ para 11–12); secondly, undertakings "granted special or exclusive rights" (→ para 13–15); and, thirdly, "measures contrary to the Treaty rules" (→ para 16–38).

2.2.1. Public Undertakings

11 There are two steps involved in defining a "public undertaking". It is necessary to ascertain, firstly, if an entity is an "undertaking" and, secondly, if the entity is a "public" undertaking. There is no Treaty **definition of an "undertaking"**, but the concept has been accorded an EU law meaning by the CJEU, which, adopting a functional approach, ruled in *Höfner & Elser* (→ para 22, 23, and 63) that "the concept of an undertaking encompasses every **entity engaged in an economic activity**, regardless of the legal status of the entity and the way in which it is financed"[14] (→ Article 101 TFEU para 22 et seqq.). Entities that fulfil social functions premised on the principle of solidarity do not constitute undertakings.[15]

---

[13] This was initially introduced as ex-Article 4 TEC. It has been suggested that the shift from nationalisation to liberalisation is partly attributable to the insertion of ex-Article 4 TEC. See Jones et al. (2019), p. 583.

[14] Case C-41/90, *Höfner & Elser v Macrotron* (ECJ 23 April 1991) para 21. For an analysis of the concept of economic activity, see further Hatzopoulos (2011).

[15] Case T-319/99, *FENIN v Commission* (CFI 4 March 2003) para 37–40. Upheld on appeal in Case C-205/03 P *FENIN v Commission* (ECJ 11 July 2006).

So, for example, in *Poucet et Pistre*,[16] two entities charged with the management of special social security schemes by French legislation were not undertakings as the social security system fulfilled an entirely social function premised on the principle of solidarity, with no distinction between those in good and ill health.

The **State itself is not an undertaking** when exercising true public law functions, including the provision of public services or functions,[17] but State-owned undertakings can fall within the *Höfner & Elser* definition when involved in economic activities of a commercial nature.[18] In this way, the State can constitute an "undertaking" subject to the prohibitions in Articles 101 and 102 TFEU (→ Article 101 TFEU para 11 et seqq., → Article 102 TFEU para 8 et seqq.) and can therefore fall under the consideration of Article 106.1 TFEU coupled with these provisions.

The **"public" undertaking** concept is likewise undefined by the Treaty, but to ensure uniformity across the MS, it has been accorded an EU law meaning. This meaning is a broad one, encompassing the various ways that the State can be involved in an undertaking. The Commission definition of a public undertaking is to be found in Article 2 point (b) of the 2006 Transparency Directive (→ para 13, 14, 15, 81),[19] which specifies that a public undertaking is:

12

> any undertaking over which the public authorities may exercise directly or indirectly a dominant influence by virtue of their ownership of it, their financial participation therein or the rules which govern it.

A dominant influence on the part of the public authorities shall be presumed when these authorities, directly or indirectly in relation to an undertaking:

(i) hold the major part of an undertaking's subscribed capital; or
(ii) control the majority of votes attached to the shares issued by the undertakings; or
(iii) can appoint more than half of the members of the undertaking's administrative, managerial or supervisory body.[20]

---

[16] Joined Cases C-159 and 160/91, *Poucet und Pistre v AGF and Cancava* (ECJ 17 February 1993).

[17] Case 30/87, *Bodson v Pompes Funèbres des Régions Libérées* (ECJ 4 May 1988) para 18 and 35; Case C-364/92, *SAT Fluggesellschaft mbH v Eurocontrol* (ECJ 19 January 1994) para 30; Case C-309/99, *Wouters and others* (ECJ 19 February 2002) para 57–58.

[18] Case C-41/90, *Höfner & Elser v Macrotron* (ECJ 23 April 1991) para 21–23.

[19] Commission Directive 2006/111/EC *on the transparency of financial relations between Member States and public undertakings as well as on financial transparency within certain undertakings*, O.J. L 318/17 (2006).

[20] This definition was contained in the original Transparency Directive (Commission Directive 80/723/EEC *on the transparency of financial relations between Member States and public undertakings*, O.J. L 195/35 (1980)), which was challenged but upheld in Joined Cases 188-190/80, *France, Italy and United Kingdom v Commission* (ECJ 6 July 1982), with the ECJ endorsing the "public undertaking" definition in this case.

Public authorities are deemed to encompass "all public authorities, including the State and regional, local and all other territorial authorities" by virtue of Article 2 point (a) of the 2006 Transparency Directive (→ para 13, 14, 15, 81).

The legal form of the undertaking is therefore not decisive; what matters is whether the State exercises control by means of a **dominant influence** over the undertaking. So, for example, in the *Greek Lignite* case (→ para 33–36),[21] where the Greek State held 51.12% of the voting stock of the former legal monopoly electricity company, the Commission found that the State exercised a dominant influence on the company. The company was effectively therefore under State control, and as a result, it was a public undertaking, in addition to being one granted exclusive rights (→ para 14).

2.2.2. Undertakings Granted Special or Exclusive Rights

13 Article 106.1 TFEU also applies to undertakings "granted special or exclusive rights", which include both public and private undertakings. Such rights are **awarded for a variety of reasons**, including the continuity of supply, universal service provision, efficiency in avoiding the costly duplication of networks and effectiveness. They are **typically awarded in the utility sectors**, including postal, telecommunications, transport, energy and water services. While Article 106.1 TFEU does not prohibit the actual grant of special or exclusive rights as such, often such rights can threaten the internal market in the sectors where they are granted, and the line between the legitimate and illegitimate grant of such rights can be a fine one.

There are two distinct rights in the concept of "special *or* exclusive rights"[22] as **"special rights" do not mean the same thing as "exclusive rights"**. However, the Court has not always differentiated between the two, and there have been some curious **inconsistencies in the case law**. For example, in *ERT* (→ para 18, 23, 60 and 76), the rights granted to the television duopoly in Greece were labelled as "special or exclusive" rights and not as one or the other;[23] *three* entities granted rights to collect recycling waste in just one area, Copenhagen, were described as holding "exclusive" rights in *FFAD*,[24] with the Court failing to explain why these were exclusive rather than special rights; and some *eight* undertakings and a district authority were held to have been granted "exclusive" rights for waste management in *Dusseldorp*,[25] but at least in this case, there was a limited partnership between the

---

[21] Commission Decision, *Case COMP/B-1/38.700, Greek Lignite and Electricity Markets*, O.J. C 93/3 (2008) para 5. This Commission decision was annulled on other grounds by the GC in Case T-169/08, *DEI v Commission* (GC 20 September 2012), which was overturned on appeal in Case C-553/12spiepr132 P, *Commission v DEI* (CJEU 17 July 2014).

[22] Case C-202/88, *France v Commission* (ECJ 19 March 1991) para 32.

[23] Case C-260/89, *ERT v DEP* (ECJ 18 June 1991).

[24] Case C-209/98, *Sydhavnens Sten & Grus* (ECJ 23 May 2000).

[25] Case C-203/96, *Chemische Afvalstoffen Dusseldorp and others v Minister van Volkshuisvesting, Ruimtelijke Ordening en Milieubeheer* (ECJ 25 June 1998).

eight undertakings and the district authority in question, and therefore this was more akin to exclusive rights being granted to *one* undertaking rather than to some *nine* separate entities.

There is no Treaty **definition of "special" or "exclusive" rights**, but it has been accepted that the concepts are EU concepts, meaning that their "content must be shaped independently and uniformly"[26] at the EU level. Definitions are offered in Article 2 point (f) and point (g) of the 2006 Transparency Directive (→ para 12, 14, 15, 81). Although this legislation is context specific, it is understood to have a broader application in terms of its definitions of special and exclusive rights.[27]

Article 2 point (f) of the 2006 Transparency Directive (→ para 12, 13, 15, 81) **14** defines **exclusive rights** as rights that are granted by an MS to *one* undertaking through any legislative, regulatory or administrative instrument, *reserving it the right to provide a service or undertake an activity within a given geographical area*.

Exclusive rights therefore entail rights granted by the State by a variety of different means to a **single beneficiary** to **engage in a particular economic activity on an exclusive basis** in a particular area. They are consequently akin to monopoly rights[28] as the beneficiary is shielded from competition in a certain area. Examples of exclusive rights include State television and broadcasting monopolies,[29] exclusive rights to provide voice telephony services and to approve telephone equipment,[30] exclusive rights to provide employment recruitment services,[31] exclusive rights to operate air routes,[32] exclusive rights to provide port unloading services,[33] exclusive rights to provide temporary labour in a port,[34] exclusive rights to provide bovine insemination services,[35] exclusive rights to receive social security contributions and to manage a compulsory social insurance scheme,[36] monopoly over basic and advanced postal services,[37] quasi-monopoly rights to explore and exploit lignite deposits amounting to 91% of the total State deposits for which such

---

[26] Szydło (2011), p. 1412, albeit his discussion at this point is limited to exclusive rights.

[27] See further Szydło (2011), pp. 1413–1414.

[28] Szydło (2011), p. 1412.

[29] Case 127/73, *BRT v SABAM* (ECJ 30 January 1974); Case 155/73, *Giuseppe Sacchi* (ECJ 30 April 1974); Case C-260/89, *ERT v DEP* (ECJ 18 June 1991).

[30] Case C-18/88, *RTT v GB-Inno-BM* (ECJ 13 December 1991).

[31] Case C-41/90, *Höfner & Elser v Macrotron* (ECJ 23 April 1991); Case C-258/98, *Carra and Others* (ECJ 8 June 2000).

[32] Case 66/86, *Ahmed Saeed Flugreisen and others v Zentrale zur Bekämpfung unlauteren Wettbewerbs* (ECJ 11 April 1989).

[33] Case C-179/90, *Merci Convenzionali Porto di Genova v Siderurgica Gabrielli* (ECJ 10 December 1991).

[34] Case C-163/96, *Raso and Others* (ECJ 12 February 1998).

[35] Case C-323/93, *Centre d'insémination de la Crespelle v Coopérative de la Mayenne* (ECJ 5 October 1994).

[36] Case C-437/09, *AG2R Prévoyance* (CJEU 3 March 2011).

[37] Case C-320/91, *Corbeau* (ECJ 19 May 1993).

rights were granted,[38] and exclusive rights to provide hybrid mail services that entail the electronic transfer of mail content from the sender to the postal service operator, which prints it out, envelopes it and then sorts and delivers it.[39]

15   Article 2 point (g) of the 2006 Transparency Directive (→ para 12, 13, 14, 81) defines **special rights** as rights granted by an MS to a limited number of undertakings, through any legislative, regulatory or administrative instrument, which, within a given geographical area:

(i) limits to two or more the number of such undertakings, authorised to provide a service or undertake an activity, otherwise than according to objective, proportional and non-discriminatory criteria; or

(ii) designates, otherwise than according to such criteria, several competing undertakings, as being authorised to provide a service or undertake an activity; or

(iii) confers on any undertaking or undertakings, otherwise than according to such criteria, any legal or regulatory advantages which substantially affect the ability of any other undertaking to provide the same service or to operate the same activity in the same geographical area under substantially equivalent conditions.[40]

This Transparency Directive definition essentially therefore distinguishes special rights as **rights granted by the State** to a limited number of undertakings according to discretionary and subjective criteria, **which may substantially affect the ability of other undertakings to exercise the economic activity in question in the same geographical area under substantially equivalent conditions**. The ECJ has defined special rights similarly in *Ambulanz Glöckner* (→ para 31 and 67) as rights involving "protection [...] conferred by a legislative measure on a limited number of undertakings which may substantially affect the ability of other undertakings to exercise the economic activity in question in the same geographical area under substantially equivalent conditions",[41] albeit in this case, the Court referred to special *or* exclusive rights involving such protection rather than just special rights to do so. Special rights were involved in *MOTOE* (→ para 32 and 42), where the ECJ found that the power granted to ELPA, the Greek Motorcycling Federation, to authorise and thereby regulate the organisation of motorcycling events was a special right.[42]

---

[38] Case C-553/12 P, *Commission v DEI* (CJEU 17 July 2014).

[39] Case T-556/08, *Slovenská pošta v Commission* (GC 25 March 2015). Upheld in Case C-293/15 *Slovenská pošta v Commission* (CJEU 30 June 2016).

[40] A broadly similar definition can be found in Article 1.4 of Commission Directive 2008/63/EC *on competition in the markets in telecommunications terminal equipment*, O.J. L 162/20 (2008).

[41] Case C-475/99, *Ambulanz Glöckner* (ECJ 25 October 2001) para 24.

[42] Case C-49/07, *MOTOE* (ECJ 1 July 2008) para 43.

2.2.3. Measures Contrary to the Treaty Rules

In order for MS to breach Article 106.1 TFEU, they are required to adopt a "measure" contrary to the rules contained in the Treaties. The term "measure" was identified in an early Commission Directive 70/50[43] on the free movement of goods to include "**laws, regulations, administrative provisions, administrative practices, and all instruments issued from a public authority**, including recommendations", and it is understood that this meaning is equally applicable in the area of Article 106.1 TFEU.

The measure in question must be "**contrary to the Treaty rules**" in order to breach Article 106.1 TFEU. It is important to note that Article 106.1 TFEU does not and cannot apply in a vacuum because it contains no substantive rule or prohibition of its own; it can only operate alongside other Treaty provisions. In *Commission v Netherlands*, the ECJ posited that Article 106.1 TFEU "must be interpreted as being intended to ensure that the Member States do not take advantage of their relations with those undertakings in order to evade the prohibitions laid down by other *Treaty* rules *addressed* directly to them [...] by obliging or encouraging those undertakings to engage in conduct which, if engaged in by the Member States, would be contrary to those rules".[44]

While Article 106.1 TFEU specifies the rules on non-discrimination of Article 18 TFEU, and on competition law and State aid of Articles 101–109 TFEU (→ para 6), its use is not confined to these Treaty provisions. It can be and has been employed regarding **infringements of the free movement rules**. Article 106.1 TFEU was invoked in conjunction with Article 34 TFEU, which prohibits quantitative restrictions and measures with equivalent effect in *RTT v GB-Inno* (→ para 25, 60 and 62).[45] It was invoked in combination with Article 45 TFEU on the prohibition on discrimination on grounds of nationality in the free movement of workers in *Merci Convenzionali* (→ para 24 and 63),[46] with Article 49 TFEU governing the freedom of establishment in *Greek Insurance*[47] and with Article 56 TFEU governing the freedom of services in *ERT*[48] (→ para 13, 23, 60 and 76) and *Deutsche Post* (→ para 30 and 67).[49]

---

[43] Commission Directive 70/50/EEC *based on the provisions of Article 33(7) on the abolition of measures which have an effect equivalent to quantitative restrictions on imports and which are not covered by other provisions adopted in pursuance of the EEC Treaty*, O.J. L 13/29 (1970).

[44] Case C-157/94, *Commission v Netherlands* (ECJ 23 October 1997) para 30 (emphasis added).

[45] Case C-18/88, *RTT v GB-Inno-BM* (ECJ 13 December 1991).

[46] Case C-179/90, *Merci Convenzionali Porto di Genova v Siderurgica Gabrielli* (ECJ 10 December 1991).

[47] Commission Decision (EEC) No 85/276 *concerning the insurance in Greece of public property and loans granted by Greek State-owned banks*, O.J. L 152/25 (1985). Greece failed to comply with this Commission decision, and the Commission subsequently and successfully took an enforcement action against it in Case 226/87, *Commission v Greece* (ECJ 30 June 1988).

[48] Case C-260/89, *ERT v DEP* (ECJ 18 June 1991).

[49] Joined Cases C-147 and 148/97, *Deutsche Post AG* (ECJ 10 February 2000).

19   The effect of Article 106.1 TFEU is therefore that MS do not have invincible rights to create legal monopolies or confer privileged status on undertakings under any conditions they choose.[50] The ECJ posited as much in *France v Commission*, in which France sought the annulment of the Telecommunications Equipment Directive[51] (→ para 82–83), stating that "even though Article [106] presupposes the existence of undertakings which have certain special or exclusive rights, it does not follow that all special or exclusive rights are necessarily compatible with the Treaty. *That depends on different rules, to which Article [106.1] refers*"[52] The Court held in this case that **the grant of special or exclusive rights does not infringe Article 106.1 TFEU *per se*,** but it examined them in light of the Treaty system of undistorted competition and the prohibition on the abuse of dominance in Article 102 TFEU. In assessing the compatibility of State measures granting special and exclusive rights provided for by the Telecommunications Equipment Directive with the Treaty system of undistorted competition and in particular with Article 102 TFEU, the ECJ premised its **test of compatibility** on the concept of "**equality of opportunity**". It noted that equality of opportunity could not be guaranteed where an undertaking that markets telephone terminal equipment would also be mandated to control product specifications, to monitor their application and to grant approval certificates to its competitors in the equipment market.[53]

20   While the Court held in and since this case that measures granting special or exclusive rights do not infringe Article 106.1 TFEU *per se*, since according to case law an infringement of Article 106.1 TFEU occurs where the **conferral of such rights leads to or induces an undertaking to commit an infringement of the Treaty rules,** particularly Article 102 TFEU.[54] Moreover, there is case law to suggest that where the conferral of special or exclusive rights results in **anticompetitive consequences similar to those resulting from an abuse of dominance,** an infringement of Article 106.1 TFEU in combination with Article 102 TFEU occurs (→ para 26 and 33–38).[55] This brings the actual conferral of special or exclusive rights close to an infringement of the Treaty rules in and of itself and blurs the line between lawful and unlawful conferrals of such rights.

21   A **causal link between an MS measure and the breach of Article 102 TFEU is nevertheless required** to show that Article 106.1 TFEU has been infringed.[56] MS

---

[50] Jones et al. (2019), p. 593.

[51] Commission Directive 88/301/EEC *on competition in the markets in telecommunications terminal equipment*, O.J. L 131/73 (1988), replaced by Commission Directive 2008/63/EC *on competition in the markets in telecommunications terminal equipment*, O.J. L 162/20 (2008).

[52] Case C-202/88, *France v Commission* (ECJ 19 March 1991) para 22 (emphasis added).

[53] Case C-202/88, *France v Commission* (ECJ 19 March 1991) para 51.

[54] E.g. Case C-260/89, *ERT v DEP* (ECJ 18 June 1991); Case C-18/88, *RTT v GB-Inno-BM* (ECJ 13 December 1991); Joined Cases C-147 and 148/97, *Deutsche Post AG* (ECJ 10 February 2000).

[55] Case C-320/91, *Corbeau* (ECJ 19 May 1993); Case C-553/12 P, *Commission v DEI* (CJEU 17 July 2014); Case T-556/08, *Slovenská pošta v Commission* (GC 25 March 2015). See further Davies (2009), pp. 554–558; Zevgolis (2012), pp. 85–87.

[56] See further Davies (2009), pp. 551–562.

are not liable under Article 106.1 TFEU for autonomous breaches of Article 102 TFEU by undertakings.[57] The exact nature and standard of the causal link between Article 106.1 TFEU and Article 102 TFEU have varied in case law,[58] and State measures have been found to be in breach of Article 106.1 TFEU where they **lead to an inevitable or unavoidable abuse** or where they **induce or enable an infringement of Article 102 TFEU or where they create a risk of abuse under Article 102 TFEU**. It has been suggested that some of the formulations of the causal link impose a higher threshold than others, but this might be explained on the basis of the specific context of different cases and the likelihood that abuse will result from a particular State measure.[59] Notwithstanding contextual differences, the various formulations further contribute to blurring the distinction between lawful and unlawful conferrals of special or exclusive rights.

There have been various attempts at **classifying State measures that are contrary to Article 102 TFEU**, given that the conferral of special or exclusive rights can especially result in the creation of a dominant position.[60] With considerable overlap, as well several different abuses occurring in one and the same case, there is no definitive classification. State measures contrary to Article 102 TFEU that have consequently infringed Article 106.1 TFEU have included those that cause **inability to meet demand**,[61] **accumulate rights** in an undertaking or **extend monopoly**,[62] create a **conflict of interest** between regulatory responsibilities and commercial activities,[63] result in **discrimination** or **inequality of opportunity**,[64]

---

[57] As highlighted in Case C-323/93, *Centre d'insémination de la Crespelle v Coopérative de la Mayenne* (ECJ 5 October 1994).

[58] Vermeersch (2009), p. 1337.

[59] Whish and Bailey (2021), pp. 238–239; on a similar but somewhat different note, see Lane (2000), p. 229.

[60] As confirmed by the ECJ, e.g., in Case C-18/88, *RTT v GB-Inno-BM* (ECJ 13 December 1991) para 17; Case C-320/91, *Corbeau* (ECJ 19 May 1993) para 11; Case C-323/93, *Centre d'insémination de la Crespelle v Coopérative de la Mayenne* (ECJ 5 October 1994) para 18; Joined Cases C-147 and 148/97, *Deutsche Post AG* (ECJ 10 February 2000) para 38. See further Jones et al. (2019), pp. 613–615; Whish and Bailey (2021), pp. 239–244.

[61] E.g. Case C-41/90, *Höfner & Elser v Macrotron* (ECJ 23 April 1991); Case C-179/90, *Merci Convenzionali Porto di Genova v Siderurgica Gabrielli* (ECJ 10 December 1991); Case C-55/96, *Job Centre* (ECJ 11 December 1997); Case C-437/09, *AG2R Prévoyance* (CJEU 3 March 2011).

[62] E.g. Case C-202/88, *France v Commission* (ECJ 19 March 1991); Case C-18/88, *RTT v GB-Inno-BM* (ECJ 13 December 1991); Case C-320/91, *Corbeau* (ECJ 19 May 1993); Case C-475/99, *Ambulanz Glöckner* (ECJ 25 October 2001); Case T-556/08, *Slovenská pošta v Commission* (GC 25 March 2015).

[63] E.g. Case C-18/88, *RTT v GB-Inno-BM* (ECJ 13 December 1991); Case C-49/07, *MOTOE* (ECJ 1 July 2008).

[64] E.g. Case C-260/89, *ERT v DEP* (ECJ 18 June 1991); Case C-163/96, *Raso and Others* (ECJ 12 February 1998); Case C-462/99, *Connect Austria* (ECJ 22 May 2003); Case C-553/12 P, *Commission v DEI* (CJEU 17 July 2014).

result in **pricing abuses**[65] and result in a **refusal to supply**.[66] It is useful and insightful to examine some of the key case law of the CJEU to illustrate its reasoning and illuminate the various tests deployed in ascertaining if State measures are contrary to Article 102 TFEU and therefore in breach of Article 106.1 TFEU.

22   In *Höfner & Elser* (→ para 11, 23, and 63),[67] the German Federal Employment Office was granted **exclusive rights** over recruitment services. However, it proved **incapable of meeting the demand** for executive recruitment. As a result, private undertakings had entered the executive recruitment service market and were competing with it. The client of one such private recruiter refused to pay for its services on the ground that the private undertaking was operating illegally in contravention of the exclusive rights granted to the German Federal Employment Office. On preliminary reference, the ECJ ruled that the limitation of the service offered to customers resulting from the legal monopoly's inability to meet the demand was an abuse under Article 102 TFEU. The Court deployed a test of "unavoidable infringement" in ascertaining whether the State measure granting the exclusive right was contrary to Article 102 TFEU. It stressed that creating a dominant position by granting exclusive rights is not as such incompatible with the Treaty but that an MS will infringe the Treaty if the undertaking in question **cannot avoid abusing its dominant position merely by exercising the rights granted to it**.[68] Germany, in granting exclusive rights to an undertaking that could not meet the demand, had created such a situation.

23   As well as the inability to meet demands, State measures granting exclusive rights that result in the **accumulation of rights** in an undertaking and create a potential **conflict of interest** are similarly contrary to Article 102 TFEU and consequently in breach of Article 106 TFEU. In *ERT* (→ para 13, 18, 60 and 76), the Greek Government granted exclusive rights to ERT, a Greek radio and television undertaking, to broadcast and retransmit television programmes in Greece. ERT sought to prevent DEP, a municipal undertaking, and the Mayor of Thessaloniki from subsequently setting up a local television station in violation of its exclusive rights. In a similar but somewhat different approach to *Höfner & Elser* (→ para 11, 22, and 63), the ECJ ruled that the grant of an exclusive right to an undertaking would infringe Article 106 TFEU where "those rights *are liable* **to create a situation in which that undertaking** *is led to infringe* **Article [102 TFEU]** by virtue of a discriminatory broadcasting policy which favours its own

---

[65] E.g. Case C-179/90, *Merci Convenzionali Porto di Genova v Siderurgica Gabrielli* (ECJ 10 December 1991); Case C-163/96, *Raso and Others* (ECJ 12 February 1998); Case C-242/95, *GT-Link A/S v Danske Staatsbaner (DSB)* (ECJ 17 July 1997); Case C-266/96, *Corsica Ferries France v Gruppo Antichi Ormeggiatori del porto di Genova and others* (ECJ 18 June 1998).

[66] E.g. Joined Cases C-147 and 148/97, *Deutsche Post AG* (ECJ 10 February 2000).

[67] Case C-41/90, *Höfner & Elser v Macrotron* (ECJ 23 April 1991).

[68] Case C-41/90, *Höfner & Elser v Macrotron* (ECJ 23 April 1991) para 29.

programmes, unless the application of Article [102 TFEU] obstructs the performance of the particular tasks entrusted to it".[69] In *ERT* (→ para 13, 18, 60 and 76), unlike *Höfner & Elser* (→ para 11, 22, and 63), the conferral of exclusive rights did not result in an unavoidable infringement of Article 102 TFEU but rather resulted in a situation where the exclusive right holder is being led to infringe Article 102 TFEU. This was due to an obvious conflict of interest that could potentially result in discriminatory treatment. Significantly, the **potential for abuse** is sufficient for Article 106.1 TFEU to be infringed in combination with Article 102 TFEU, **without the necessity of the abuse actually manifesting itself**, as had in fact occurred in *Höfner & Elser*.

In *Merci Convenzionali* (→ para 18 and 63), the test of **unavoidable abuse** or **induced abuse** was embraced by the ECJ.[70] Italian law reserved stevedoring services in Italian ports to certain dock-working companies, whose employees were required to be of Italian nationality. Merci Convenzionali was granted such exclusive stevedoring rights in the Port of Genoa. The defendant, Siderurgica Gabrielli, argued that the exclusive rights granted to Merci Convenzionali were contrary to the free movement of workers under Article 45 TFEU on grounds of discrimination and also contrary to Article 102 TFEU on the following grounds: 1) causing delays due to the strike action by its dock workers at the Port of Genoa, 2) charging excessive fees for services it did not avail of, 3) charging different service fees to different customers and 4) refusing to have recourse to modern technology. The defendant's grievance was exacerbated by the fact that its own crew could have unloaded its ship more efficiently. The Court agreed and ruled that Article 106.1 TFEU was infringed as the exclusive rights were contrary to both Article 45 TFEU and Article 102 TFEU. As regards the latter, the Court determined that the exclusive rights were **liable to induce** Merci Convenzionali to commit a breach by resulting in inability to meet demand, in charging unfair and discriminatory prices and by enabling it to behave inefficiently.[71]

The **potential for abuse** contrary to Article 102 TFEU likewise arose in *RTT v GB-Inno-BM* (→ para 18, 60 and 62), where there were issues surrounding a **conflict of interest** and the **extension of a dominant position**. RTT, a Belgian telecom company, was granted a **monopoly over the Belgian public telephone network**. It was also granted **exclusive rights to approve telephone equipment** to be connected to its network. In addition to these monopoly and exclusive rights, RTT operated at the sales level of the market, selling telephones and competing with private undertakings on this front. One such competitor, GB-Inno, offered for sale non-approved telephones to be connected to RTT's network. RTT subsequently invoked proceedings to prevent GB-Inno from selling these non-approved

---

[69] Case C-260/89, *ERT v DEP* (ECJ 18 June 1991) para 37 (emphasis added).
[70] Case C-179/90, *Merci Convenzionali Porto di Genova v Siderurgica Gabrielli* (ECJ 10 December 1991) para 17.
[71] Case C-179/90, *Merci Convenzionali Porto di Genova v Siderurgica Gabrielli* (ECJ 10 December 1991) para 19.

telephones without informing consumers of the fact that they were not RTT approved. In response, GB-Inno claimed that the measure granting RTT exclusive rights was contrary to Article 102 TFEU as RTT was abusing its dominant position.

The ECJ found that an Article 102 TFEU infringement resulted from "the fact that an undertaking holding a monopoly in the market for the establishment and operation of the network, without any objective necessity, reserves to itself a neighbouring but separate market, in this case the market for the importation, marketing, connection, commissioning and maintenance of equipment for connection to the said network, thereby eliminating all competition from other undertakings". As this abuse stemmed from a State measure granting exclusive rights, there was a breach of Article 106.1 TFEU.[72]

RTT had tried unsuccessfully to argue that an infringement of Article 106.1 TFEU could only be found if the MS measure had favoured an **abuse that had *actually* been committed**. RTT maintained that there was no such actually committed abuse and that the mere fact that it had been designated as the authority for granting approval while competing in the equipment markets with equipment undertakings that must obtain its approval could not be tantamount to abuse. The Court, rejecting this argument, ruled that a system of undistorted competition is only guaranteed if **equality of opportunity** exists between the various economic operators. When a "**regulatory function**" is accorded to the telephone network monopoly, enabling it to determine which telephone equipment may be connected to the public network, its competitors in the downstream sales market are disadvantaged.[73] This could lead to the **extension of a dominant position from one market to another**, and this potentiality was sufficient to breach Article 106.1 TFEU, even though no abuse had actually occurred.

26   In *Corbeau*, the Régie des Postes was conferred a **monopoly in Belgium for the collection, carrying, distribution and delivery of all post**. Corbeau launched an express personal delivery service in and around Liège, collecting and delivering mail from the sender's address, although for deliveries beyond the Liège area, he placed postal items in the ordinary post. Although Corbeau's express personal service was not offered by the Belgian post office, he was charged with an offence under the Belgian legislation conferring exclusive rights on Régie des Postes. In his defence, he challenged these exclusive powers as contrary to Article 102 TFEU even though there was no instance of abuse. Corbeau's objection therefore centred on the very **creation and existence of the exclusive rights**.

On preliminary reference, the ECJ reiterated that the Treaty "requires the Member States **not to adopt or maintain in force any measure which might deprive Articles [102 and 106.1 TFEU] of their effectiveness**", subject to the Article 106.2 TFEU exception (→ para 64).[74] The Court determined that the grant of exclusive rights and the consequent prohibition on other economic operators

---

[72] Case C-18/88, *RTT v GB-Inno-BM* (ECJ 13 December 1991) para 19, 21.

[73] Case C-18/88, *RTT v GB-Inno-BM* (ECJ 13 December 1991) para 23–25.

[74] Case C-320/91, *Corbeau* (ECJ 19 May 1993) para 11, 14.

from offering certain services in the postal market under threat of criminal penalties were contrary Article 102 TFEU and therefore in breach of Article 106.1 TFEU but without ascertaining how an infringement of Article 102 TFEU had or could manifest itself.

Arguably, therefore, in omitting to clearly identify any actual breach of Article 102 TFEU or to identify how Régie des Postes might be led to such abuse or to identify how the conferral of its exclusive right would be otherwise liable to result in abuse, the Court seemingly **condemns the mere creation of a monopoly resulting from a State measure** for undermining the effectiveness of Articles 106.1 and 102 TFEU,[75] unless permissible by Article 106.2 TFEU.

It has been suggested that such an approach **changes the burden of proof**, moving the focus from Article 106.1 TFEU to Article 106.2 TFEU,[76] because it means that special or exclusive rights are no longer legal under Article 106.1 TFEU but rather illegal unless they fall under Article 106.2 TFEU. Any resulting harshness of Article 106.1 TFEU might have subsequently occasioned a widening of the protection offered under Article 106.2 TFEU.[77] However, following this *Corbeau* judgment, the Court withdrew from this line of reasoning, reverting to its requirement that Article 106.1 TFEU will only be infringed if in exercising its exclusive rights an undertaking cannot avoid or is led to a breach of Article 102 TFEU.

So, for example in *La Crespelle*, the ECJ reiterated that Article 106.1 TFEU and Article 102 TFEU combined do not prevent MS from granting exclusive rights. This case entailed French legislation, under which some 50 bovine insemination centres had been **granted exclusive rights to provide their services in particular areas of France**. An unauthorised competitor, La Crespelle, started to operate in one area and was sued by the official centre in that area for breaching its exclusive rights. La Crespelle argued that the French measure granting the exclusive rights to the official insemination centres was contrary to Article 102 TFEU as the official centres were charging breeders **excessive prices** to cover additional costs involved when a breeder requested semen from an official insemination centre of their choice rather than the local area centre. The responsibility for calculating these additional costs was that of the official centres.

The ECJ, upholding the exclusive rights granted under French law, ruled that the creation of a dominant position is not itself incompatible with Article 106.1 TFEU combined with Article 102 TFEU and reiterated that Article 106.1 TFEU is only breached if in the exercise of its rights **an undertaking cannot avoid abusing its dominant position**. Article 106.1 TFEU had not been infringed as the French legislation allowing the centres to provide semen to breeders from other areas and to charge them for the additional cost involved did not lead the centres to

27

---

[75] See further Hancher (1994), p. 111.
[76] Ezrachi (2014), p. 319.
[77] Ezrachi (2014), p. 319.

charge excessive prices.⁷⁸ In other words, **charging excessive prices was not a direct consequence of the exclusive rights**. As a result, there was an **insufficient causal link** between the State measure granting the exclusive rights and the charging of excessive prices by the dominant undertakings to prove a breach of Article 106.1 TFEU by France.

28   A similar approach was taken in *Corsica Ferries*, involving Italian legislation granting exclusive rights to local mooring companies to provide port mooring services. Corsica Ferries claimed that the fees it had paid for such mooring services were contrary to Article 102 TFEU for being excessive and discriminatory, given that different service fees were charged in different ports. Without any elaboration, the Court ruled that the Italian measure was not in breach of Article 106.1 TFEU because the mooring companies **did not abuse or were not necessarily led to abuse their dominant position as a result of the exclusive rights granted by the Italian measure**.⁷⁹ In any case, the Court focused on the mooring services in question as **SGEI under Article 106.2 TFEU**, rather than dealing with the issue under Article 106.1 TFEU (→ para 66).

29   In *Albany*, a decision of the Dutch public authorities rendering sectoral pension fund affiliation compulsory was challenged as contrary to Article 102 TFEU. The ECJ accepted that this decision entailed the granting of an exclusive right to collect and administer the sectoral pension fund contributions and that it resulted in a dominant position.⁸⁰ It reiterated, however, that in order for a finding of infringement of Article 106.1 TFEU in combination with Article 102 TFEU, **an undertaking must be led to abuse its dominant position or its exclusive rights must be liable to lead to such an abuse contrary to Article 102 TFEU as a result of the State measure**. In this case, the Court did in fact find a restriction of competition deriving directly from the exclusive rights. This arose because undertakings in a particular sector that wanted to offer superior pension schemes to that offered by the sectoral pension fund were prevented from doing so due to the latter's exclusive rights.⁸¹ The Court did not explain how exactly the exercise of the sectoral pension fund's exclusive rights led it to abuse its dominance. Rather, as in *Corsica* Ferries, the Court swiftly moved on to **justify the measure under Article 106.2 TFEU** (→ para 67).⁸²

30   The Court took a comparable approach in *Deutsche Post* (→ para 18 and 67), finding that the exclusive rights were contrary to Article 102 TFEU and therefore that **Article 106.1 TFEU was breached in combination with Article 102 TFEU** but admitting justification under Article 106.2 TFEU (→ para 67). The case

---

⁷⁸ Case C-323/93, *Centre d'insémination de la Crespelle v Coopérative de la Mayenne* (ECJ 5 October 1994) para 18, 20.

⁷⁹ Case C-266/96, *Corsica Ferries France v Gruppo Antichi Ormeggiatori del porto di Genova and others* (ECJ 18 June 1998) para 40–41.

⁸⁰ Case C-67/96, *Albany* (ECJ 21 September 1999) para 90–92.

⁸¹ Case C-67/96, *Albany* (ECJ 21 September 1999) para 93–97.

⁸² Case C-49/07, *MOTOE* (ECJ 1 July 2008).

concerned the delivery of mail from Germany via Denmark to Germany. Under the Universal Postal Convention 1989, a receiving State is entitled to charge terminal dues for the cost of delivering international mail passed to it by the postal service of another contracting State. In addition, for bulk mail from senders based in one country to addressees in that country posted in a second country, the receiving State is entitled to either charge internal rates or return the mail to its origin. A dispute arose between Deutsche Post, the State monopoly with the exclusive right to collect, carry and deliver certain post in Germany, and two German-based credit card companies over the delivery of their credit card bills. Deutsche Post charged internal postage rates for the delivery of their credit card bills as the bills, having been electronically transmitted to the Danish processing centres of the two credit card companies, were posted from Denmark, where the rate for international mail is lower than the German internal postage rate. The two credit card companies argued that Deutsche Post's exercise of its exclusive rights under the Universal Postal Code in this way was contrary to Article 102 TFEU and therefore that the State measure granting exclusive rights to Deutsche Post infringed Article 106.1 TFEU.

On preliminary ruling, the ECJ reiterated that the mere creation of a dominant position by the grant of exclusive rights is not in breach of Article 106.1 TFEU for being contrary to Article 102 TFEU but that **MS must not adopt or maintain in force any measure depriving Article 106.1 TFEU of its effectiveness**.[83] Accordingto the Court, the right of Deutsche Post to treat international mail as internal mail resulting from the exclusive right granted to it to forward and deliver international mail created a situation where Deutsche Post may be **led to abuse** its dominant position.[84] Without elaborating on what this abuse might entail, the Court moved on to justify Deutsche Post's exclusive rights under Article 106.2 TFEU (→ para 67).

Ambulanz Glöckner marks a similar approach by the ECJ. The case concerned a German law that conferred the **exclusive provision of emergency public ambulance services** to medical aid organisations in various German territories (→ para 15). The two exclusive right holders in the Rheinland-Pfalz district also provided **non-emergency ambulance services**. A regional law allowed the district administration to refuse licences for non-emergency transport services to private operators where this would negatively impact the operation of an effective public ambulance service. Ambulanz Glöckner had been providing licensed non-emergency transport services, but its application for licence renewal was refused on the objection of the two exclusive right holders. They claimed that renewed **competition in non-emergency services would negatively impact their ability to effectively provide public emergency ambulance services**.

The ECJ repeated that an MS will only breach Article 106.1 TFEU in combination with Article 102 TFEU if the undertaking conferred with exclusive rights is **led**

31

---

[83] Joined Cases C-147 and 148/97, *Deutsche Post AG* (ECJ 10 February 2000) para 38–40. See further Bartosch (2001).

[84] Joined Cases C-147 and 148/97, *Deutsche Post AG* (ECJ 10 February 2000) para 48.

to abuse its dominant position by merely exercising its rights or where such rights are **liable to result in an abuse** contrary to Article 102 TFEU.[85] In line with previous Article 102 TFEU case law, the ECJ acknowledged that it was an abuse for an undertaking dominant in one market to **reserve to itself ancillary activities in a neighbouring market**, with the possibility of eliminating competition in that neighbouring market. Where this results from a State measure, that measure is in breach of Article 106.1 TFEU in combination with Article 102 TFEU.[86] In this case, extending the exclusivity of the two medical aid organisations in the emergency ambulance service to non-emergency services had the effect of **limiting markets**, and according to the Court, the State measure was consequently contrary to Article 102 TFEU, but the Court then went on to justify the measure under Article 106.2 TFEU (→ para 67).

32   The **accumulation of regulatory and commercial activities** exercised by an undertaking creating a potential **conflict of interest** and disadvantaging competitors, which we came across in *RTT v GB Inno* (→ para 18, 25, 60 and 62),[87] arose again in *MOTOE* (→ para 15 and 42). In this case, the Greek Road Traffic Code required approval from the Minister for Public Order to hold motor cycling competitions and events. The legislation stipulated that the approval could only be given with the consent of the Greece Motorcycling Federation, ELPA. ELPA also organised such competitions itself and arranged sponsorship, advertising and insurance for its own competitions. When MOTOE, another organiser of motorcycling competitions in Greece, failed to obtain ELPA consent for various competitions, it instigated proceedings at the national level, challenging the dual role of ELPA as regulator and competitor in the market, as contrary to Article 102 TFEU.

On preliminary reference, the ECJ recollected that where special or exclusive rights **lead an undertaking to abuse its dominant position** "or where such rights are *liable* **to create a situation in which the undertaking is led to commit such abuses**", a breach of Article 106.1 TFEU in combination with Article 102 TFEU occurs, *without* the necessity of such abuse *actually* occurring.[88] The Court ruled that the conferral of special approval rights for competitions on an entity that also organised such competitions itself amounted to an infringement of Article 106.1 TFEU because it gave rise to a **risk of abuse** contrary to Article 102 TFEU.[89] The risk of abuse lied in the possibility that the conferral of the special right may "lead the undertaking which possesses it to deny other operators access to the relevant market" and result in **inequality of opportunity**.[90]

---

[85] Case C-475/99, *Ambulanz Glöckner* (ECJ 25 October 2001) para 39.

[86] Case C-475/99, *Ambulanz Glöckner* (ECJ 25 October 2001) para 40.

[87] Case C-18/88, *RTT v GB-Inno-BM* (ECJ 13 December 1991).

[88] Case C-49/07, *MOTOE* (ECJ 1 July 2008) para 49 (emphasis added). See further, Vermeersch (2009).

[89] Case C-49/07, *MOTOE* (ECJ 1 July 2008) para 50.

[90] Case C-49/07, *MOTOE* (ECJ 1 July 2008) para 51 and 52.

In *Greek Lignite* (→ para 12 and 14),[91] the CJEU ostensibly took its reasoning a step further. DEI, the former Greek electricity monopoly with exclusive rights to produce, transport and supply electricity, was transformed into a limited liability company in 2001[92] but remained a public undertaking due to the State's shareholding of 51.12%. This was in line with Greek law which requires that for an undertaking to be a public undertaking, the State's shareholding cannot be lower than 51% of the shares with voting rights, even after an increase of capital. DEI, which owned all Greek power stations operating on lignite,[93] was subsequently granted a right to explore and extract State-owned lignite deposits of some 2200 million tonnes without any financial consideration. A further 85 million tonnes of lignite deposits were privately owned, and some 220 million State-owned tonnes were exploited by private third parties for financial consideration, which partially supplied DEI's power stations. No exploitation rights had been allocated for the remaining State deposits, amounting to a further 2000 million tonnes.

In an Article 106.3 TFEU decision,[94] the Commission noted that DEI had been granted exploitation rights for some 91% of State-owned lignite deposits for which such rights had been granted, thereby conferring a quasi-monopolistic right on it (→ para 14). The Commission found a breach of Article 106.1 TFEU as the State measure in favour of DEI **led or could potentially lead to an abuse of its dominant position** contrary to Article 102 TFEU. This stemmed from DEI's quasi-monopolistic right offering it **privileged access** to lignite, resulting in **inequality of opportunity** between it and other economic operators regarding access to primary fuel for the production of electricity. This in turn allowed DEI **to maintain or reinforce its dominant position** on the Greek wholesale electricity market, in which DEI held an 85% market share, by excluding or hindering market entry in spite of liberalisation.[95]

33

34

---

[91] Case C-553/12 P, *Commission v DEI* (CJEU 17 July 2014). For a discussion of the case, see Babirad (2014).

[92] Pursuant to liberalisation measures in the electricity market under Parliament/Council Directive 96/92/EC *concerning common rules for the internal market in electricity*, O.J. L 27/20 (1997).

[93] Lignite is the cheapest combustible material from which electricity can be produced and it accounted for some 60% of electricity production in Greece.

[94] Commission Decision of 5 March 2008, *Case COMP/B-1/38.700, Greek lignite and electricity markets*, O.J. C 93/3 (2008). This 2008 decision led to a second decision, a 2009 commitment decision establishing the specific measures to correct the anti-competitive effects identified in the 2008 decision, Summary of Commission Decision of 4 August 2009, *Case COMP/B-1/38.700, Greek lignite and electricity markets*, O.J. C 243/4 (2009). The 2009 decision was appealed to the GC on grounds of lack of necessity to impose a remedy and was annulled by the GC in Case T-421/09, *DEI v Commission* (GC 20 September 2012). The Commission subsequently appealed its annulment to the CJEU in Case C-554/12 P, *Commission v DEI* (CJEU 17 July 2014), which remanded the case back to GC. On remand, the GC dismissed the action in Case T-421/09 RENV, *DEI v Commission* (GC 15 December 2016).

[95] Commission Decision of 5 March 2008, *Case COMP/B-1/38.700, Greek Lignite and Electricity Markets*, O.J. C 93/3 (2008) para 190 and 238.

35   The GC, invoking previous ECJ case law, stressed that the fact that an undertaking finds itself in **an advantageous position** in comparison with its competitors as a result of a State measure is not sufficient to amount to abuse of a dominant position.[96] The GC therefore annulled the Commission decision because, in its view, the **Commission had failed to identify or establish, to a sufficient legal standard, any actual or potential abuse** that the State measure led to or could lead to.[97] The lack of extraction rights for other operators could not be attributable to DEI as it was the Greek State that was responsible for granting licences to explore and exploit lignite.[98] Essentially, and due to the fact Article 106.1 TFEU has no independent application of its own, the GC required the Commission to provide separate proof of an Article 102 TFEU breach because an infringement of Article 106.1 TFEU cannot be established where the State measure is not contrary to the Treaty rules. For the GC, **inequality of opportunity** was insufficient to demonstrate abuse contrary to Article 102 TFEU. So, according to the GC, the State measure from which DEI's advantageous situation arose was not therefore in breach of Article 106.1 TFEU.

36   On appeal, the **CJEU overturned the ruling of the GC** and agreed with the Commission that the State measure conferring quasi-exclusive lignite access rights on DEI amounted to an infringement of Article 106.1 TFEU combined with Article 102 TFEU.[99] The CJEU repeated its previous reasoning that a State measure conferring **special or exclusive rights that leads an undertaking to abuse its dominant position as a result of exercising those rights** or when those rights are **liable to lead to an abuse** is in breach of Article 106.1 TFEU.[100] It emphasised that a system of undistorted competition can only be guaranteed if **equality of opportunity** between market operators is secured. A State measure that results in inequality of opportunity and thereby distorts competition is an infringement of Article 106 TFEU in combination with Article 102 TFEU,[101] irrespective of whether an actual abuse exists, because it **suffices to establish an actual or potential anti-competitive *consequence*.**[102] In other words, anti-competitive

---

[96] Case T-169/08, *DEI v Commission* (GC 20 September 2012) para 102.

[97] Case T-169/08, *DEI v Commission* (GC 20 September 2012) para 91, 92, 105 and 118.

[98] Case T-169/08, *DEI v Commission* (GC 20 September 2012) para 89.

[99] Case C-553/12 P, *Commission v DEI* (CJEU 17 July 2014). The CJEU, however, referred the case back to the GC to rule on the various other pleas raised concerning infringements by the Commission of the duty to state reasons; of the principles of legal certainty, legitimate expectations, private property and misuse of powers; and of the principle of proportionality. The GC had dismissed these pleas at first instance. On remand, the GC once again dismissed these pleas in Case T-169/08 RENV, *DEI v Commission* (GC 15 December 2016), rendering the Commission Decision of 5 March 2008 final and binding. The Commission recently endorsed the Greek measures to ensure fair access to lignite-fired electricity generation in its commitment decision, Commission Decision of 17 April 2018, *Case AT.38700 — Greek lignite and electricity markets*, C(2018) 2104 final.

[100] Case C-553/12 P, *Commission v DEI* (CJEU 17 July 2014) para 41.

[101] Case C-553/12 P, *Commission v DEI* (CJEU 17 July 2014) para 43 and 44; reiterated at para 57.

[102] Case C-553/12 P, *Commission v DEI* (CJEU 17 July 2014) para 46.

effects similar to those arising from an abuse of dominance are sufficient. This is satisfied where the State measure affects the actual structure of the market by creating **unequal conditions of competition** and allowing an undertaking to **maintain, strengthen or extend its dominant position over another market** without the need to prove the existence of actual abuse.[103] Arguably, the reasoning of the CJEU in *Greek Lignite* considerably realigns this judgment with that of *Corbeau*,[104] where the Court hinted that the **mere granting of special or exclusive rights could breach Article 106.1 TFEU** (→ para 26).

The GC applied the *Greek Lignite* (→ para 36) reasoning of the CJEU in *Slovakian Hybrid Mail*,[105] a case concerning **hybrid mail services** (→ para 14) in Slovakia. Hybrid mail services in Slovakia had previously been liberalised pursuant to the Postal Directive[106] and were subject to strong competition among private undertakings. A subsequent amendment to the Slovakian Postal Law in 2008 **reserved the hybrid mail service to the postal universal service operator** in Slovakia, Slovenská pošta, which was wholly owned by the Slovak State. This 2008 legislation effectively therefore **re-monopolised the delivery of hybrid mail**, preventing private hybrid mail competitors from continuing their activity and endangering their economic viability. In addition, Slovenská pošta's hybrid mail service lacked many of the features that had been offered by the private undertakings, including tracking services and seven-days-a-week service, both of which were under demand and valued by customers, and therefore the State measure also resulted in **consumer harm**.

37

The Commission found that granting an exclusive right to an undertaking that **extended its monopoly in the traditional postal service**[107] **to the hybrid mail service** and **limited hybrid mail services** available to consumers infringed Article 106 TFEU because it was contrary to Article 102 TFEU.[108] Neither the Slovak Republic nor Slovenská pošta was successful in showing that the restriction of competition was necessary for the provision of the postal universal service under Article 106.2 TFEU (→ para 68).[109]

---

[103] Case C-553/12 P, *Commission v DEI* (CJEU 17 July 2014) para 46; reiterated at para 66–68.

[104] Case C-320/91, *Corbeau* (ECJ 19 May 1993).

[105] Case T-556/08, *Slovenská pošta v Commission* (GC 25 March 2015).

[106] Parliament/Council Directive 97/67/EC *on common rules for the development of the internal market of Community postal services and the improvement of quality of service*, O.J. L 15/14 (1998). This was amended by the second Postal Directive, Parliament/Council Directive 2002/39/EC, O.J. L 176/ 21 (2002), and further amended by the third Postal Directive, Parliament/Council Directive 2008/6/EC, O.J. L 52/3 (2008).

[107] The traditional postal service entails the physical clearance, sorting, transport and distribution of mail items.

[108] Commission Decision No. 39562 *on the Slovakian postal legislation relating to hybrid mail services*, C(2008) 5912 final para 149–155.

[109] Commission Decision No. 39562 *on the Slovakian postal legislation relating to hybrid mail services*, C(2008) 5912 final para 165–167, 192 and 199.

The GC upheld the Commission decision on appeal, reiterating that Article 106.1 TFEU is breached if an MS adopts any law, regulation or administrative provision that creates a situation in which a public undertaking or an undertaking conferred with special or exclusive rights is **led, merely by exercising the special or exclusive rights conferred upon it, to abuse its dominant position** or where such rights are **liable to create a situation in which that undertaking is led to commit an abuse** contrary to Article 102 TFEU.[110] Referring to the **risk of abuse**, a **system of undistorted competition** and **inequality of opportunity**,[111] in keeping with the CJEU judgment in *Greek Lignite* (→ para 36), the GC confirmed that an infringement of Article 106.1 TFEU combined with Article 102 TFEU may be established irrespective of whether an actual abuse exists. All that the Commission is required to identify is a **potential or actual anti-competitive *consequence*** liable to result from the State measure at issue.[112] The GC ruled that an infringement of Article 106.1 TFEU combined with Article 102 TFEU can result where the State measure at issue affects the **structure of the market** by creating **unequal conditions of competition** between companies and allowing the privileged undertaking to **maintain, strengthen or extend its dominant position** over another market without the necessity of proving the existence of an actual abuse.[113] The judgment of the GC was upheld by the CJEU, reiterating that a breach of Article 106.1 TFEU occurs where an undertaking with exclusive right is led, merely by exercising those rights, to abuse its dominant position or where such rights are liable to create a situation in which that undertaking is led to commit such abuses.[114] This can occur in particular, according to the CJEU, where an undertaking is manifestly unable to satisfy particular demand in a market.[115]

38 These recent rulings in *Greek Lignite* (→ para 36) and *Slovakian Hybrid Mail* (→ para 37), finding that the creation or existence of **inequality of opportunity** in favour of a public or privileged undertaking suffices to find an infringement of Article 106.1 TFEU combined with Article 102 TFEU because it brings about **anti-competitive *consequences* akin to those resulting from the abuse of dominance**, effectively confirm that a low threshold for competitive distortion is adequate to prove a breach.

2.3. Enforcement

39 Article 106.1 TFEU is **enforceable by the Commission**, which can adopt decisions under Article 106.3 TFEU (→ para 77 and 87–89). They compel MS to repeal or

---

[110] Case T-556/08, *Slovenská pošta v Commission* (GC 25 March 2015) para 97.
[111] Case T-556/08, *Slovenská pošta v Commission* (GC 25 March 2015) para 98–100.
[112] Case T-556/08, *Slovenská pošta v Commission* (GC 25 March 2015) para 102.
[113] Case T-556/08, *Slovenská pošta v Commission* (GC 25 March 2015) para 102–103.
[114] Case C-293/15 P *Slovenská pošta v Commission* (CJEU 30 June 2016) para 34.
[115] Case C-293/15 P *Slovenská pošta v Commission* (CJEU 30 June 2016) para 35.

amend any offending measure and indicate what they must do in order to comply with their EU law obligations. The Commission can do so of its own volition or on the basis of a complaint. However, as Article 106.3 TFEU only requires the Commission to issue decisions "where necessary", the Commission is not obliged to act under Article 106.3 TFEU when it receives complaints about alleged Article 106.1 TFEU infringements. Indeed, in *max.mobil*, the ECJ ruled that the refusal by the Commission to pursue an Article 106.1 TFEU complaint and bring proceedings against a State is not a challengeable act under the Article 263 TFEU annulment action procedure.[116]

In addition to the Commission acting as the public enforcer of Article 106.1, **Article 106.1 TFEU is directly effective** in conjunction with other Treaty provisions,[117] meaning that it is enforceable by means of private litigation where the other Treaty provision(s) being relied on meet the conditions of direct effect. Private enforcement of Article 106.1 TFEU is in fact the norm over public enforcement, with many cases instigated by private parties at the national level and reaching the CJEU on preliminary reference, rather than being pursued by the Commission under Article 106.3 TFEU. **40**

3. Exceptions Under Paragraph 2

Although Article 106.1 TFEU prohibits State measures that are contrary to the Treaty rules, **undertakings entrusted with the provision of SGEI or revenue-producing monopolies** can **plead the circumstances of Article 106.2 TFEU in their defence**. This is only possible where the application of the Treaty rules obstructs the performance of the tasks assigned to them (→ para 62–68), and it is subject to the qualification that the development of trade must not be affected in a manner contrary to EU interests (→ para 71–74). Article 106.2 TFEU provides a **limited exception** only to the normal application of Treaty rules as it is confined *rationae personae* to undertakings that provide SGEI or to revenue-producing monopolies. **41**

In facilitating this limited exception, Article 106.2 TFEU recognises that the **public interest** in the provision of SGEI may require the Treaty rules, particularly the competition law rules, to be set aside. The application of this exception is very much a balancing exercise, meaning that the public interest must be balanced against respect for Treaty articles and the overall objectives of the EU.[118]

Unlike Article 106.1 TFEU, **Article 106.2 TFEU is directed to undertakings entrusted with SGEI and to revenue-producing monopolies** rather than to the **42**

---

[116] Case C-141/02, *Commission v max.mobil* (ECJ 22 February 2005).

[117] As found in, e.g., Case C-41/90, *Höfner & Elser v Macrotron* (ECJ 23 April 1991); Case C-260/89, *ERT v DEP* (ECJ 18 June 1991); Case C-179/90, *Merci Convenzionali Porto di Genova v Siderurgica Gabrielli* (ECJ 10 December 1991).

[118] Case 202/88, *France v Commission* (ECJ 19 March 1991) para 12; Case C-463/00, *Spain v Commission* (ECJ 13 May 2003) para 82.

MS. Even though it is directed to these undertakings, Article **106.2 TFEU can also be relied on by the MS**. In *Italy v Commission*, the ECJ ruled that "Article [106] (2) of the Treaty ranks among those provisions whose infringement may be pleaded by any Member State in support of an [annulment] action to have a [Commission] measure[119] declared void".[120]

T. Bekkedal, relying on the judgment in *MOTOE*[121] (→ para 15 and 32), advocates that according to a strict interpretation, Article 106.2 TFEU should only be available to entities that conduct activities as "undertakings" (→ para 11).[122] In *MOTOE*, the Greek State had conferred regulatory powers on an entity to authorise the organisation of motorcycling events. *T. Bekkedal* argues that such regulatory powers cannot be equated to the economic activities of an "undertaking", and because, in his view, Article 106.2 TFEU is a justification for objectives of an economic nature only, the ECJ correctly ruled that Article 106.2 TFEU could not be relied on to justify the regulatory powers in question.[123] However, *T. Bekkedal* posits that the fact that Article 106.2 TFEU can only be invoked by *undertakings* does not mark a departure from the occasional reliance by the *Member States* on Article 106.2 TFEU. MS reliance on Article 106.2 TFEU has occurred where national regulatory frameworks have been challenged pursuant to Article 106.1 TFEU combined with Article 102 TFEU where the abuse of a dominant position by a private undertaking is attributable to the regulatory act of the State. Where an MS is responsible for the act of abuse by a private undertaking, *Bekkedal* maintains that the MS must have available the same exceptions that would apply to a private undertaking under the circumstances, thereby allowing the MS to rely on Article 106.2 TFEU.[124] In any case, where an undertaking or an MS invokes Article 106.2 TFEU, it is incumbent on it to show that the conditions of Article 106.2 TFEU are satisfied.[125]

3.1. The Broader Context

43 Undertakings entrusted with the provision of **SGEI** (→ para 51–60) and revenue-producing monopolies (→ para 61) merit special treatment under Article 106.2

---

[119] For example, an Article 106.3 TFEU Commission decision or Article 106.3 TFEU Commission legislation.

[120] Case 41/83, *Italy v Commission* (ECJ 20 March 1985) para 30.

[121] Case C-49/07, *MOTOE* (ECJ 1 July 2008) para 46, in which the ECJ stated: "As regards the power to give consent to applications for authorisation to organise motorcycling events, that does indeed stem from an act of public authority, namely Article 49 of the Greek Road Traffic Code, but it cannot be classified as an economic activity."

[122] Bekkedal (2011), p. 63, pp. 71–72, and pp. 76–77.

[123] Bekkedal (2011), p. 64 and pp. 71–72.

[124] Bekkedal (2011), p. 72 and pp. 76–77.

[125] Case C-157/94, *Commission v Netherlands* (ECJ 23 October 1997) para 58, repeated most recently in Case T-556/08, *Slovenská pošta v Commission* (GC 25 March 2015) para 358.

TFEU. The broader context of Article 106.2 TFEU is important in terms of understanding its interpretation and application to SGEI-entrusted undertakings.

The **importance of SGEI and the value of these services** was first asserted by the inclusion of a new provision, ex-Article 16 TEC by the Treaty of Amsterdam 1997, which is now Article 14 TFEU (→ para 46, 47, 70 and 79).[126] Their importance was reinforced by Article 36 EUCFR (→ para 45) and more recently by Protocol No 26 on services of general interest[127] (→ para 46, 48, 53 and 57).

44

Article 14 TFEU emphasises the place occupied by SGEI in the shared values of the Union (→ Article 14 TFEU para 2 et seqq.), which according to Article 2 TEU contains respect for human dignity, freedom, democracy, equality, the rule of law and respect for human rights, including the rights of persons belonging to minorities. It also highlights the role of SGEI in promoting social and territorial cohesion (→ Article 14 TFEU para 13). Against this backdrop, Article 14 TFEU stipulates that the EU and the MS must take care that such services operate on the basis of principles and conditions, particularly economic and financial conditions, which enable them to fulfil their missions (→ Article 14 TFEU para 8). Finally, Article 14 TFEU requires the EP and the Council to legislate in order to establish these principles and set these conditions without prejudice to the competence of the MS to provide, commission and fund such services (→ Article 14 TFEU para 16), but no such legislation has been enacted as yet.

Significantly, **Article 36 EUCFR** affords a fundamental right status to SGEI access, which it considers to contribute to the social and territorial cohesion of the EU. The Commission's view, in keeping with the tenet of Article 36 EUCFR, is that such access is "an essential component of European citizenship" and is "necessary in order to allow [citizens] to fully enjoy their fundamental rights".[128]

45

In December 2009, the Lisbon Treaty introduced **Protocol No 26 on services of general interest** (→ para 44, 48, 53 and 57), annexed to the TEU and TFEU. Expanding on Article 14 TFEU (→ para 44, 47, 70, and 79), the Protocol emphasises "the essential role and the wide discretion of national, regional and local authorities in providing, commissioning and organising SGEI as closely as possible to the needs of the users" (Article 1 of the Protocol) (→ Article 14 TFEU para 18).[129] It also identifies the values underpinning SGEI as including quality, safety, affordability, equal treatment and the promotion of universal services and universal rights (→ Article 14 TFEU para 3). Notwithstanding this, it seems that the Protocol does not add much to the substance of SGEI, although it has been

46

---

[126] See further Ross (2000); Flynn (1999); Pech (2008), p. 172 and pp. 181–185.

[127] Protocol (No 26) on services of general interest, O.J. C 115/308 (2008).

[128] Commission Communication *White Paper on services of general interest*, COM(2004) 374 final p. 4.

[129] Article 2 of Protocol (No. 26) also reiterates that "the Treaties do not affect in any way the competence of Member States to provide, commission and organise non-economic services of general interest."

suggested that the values it identifies will be further substantiated as basic SGEI principles as regards universal services.[130]

47 While signifying the increased recognition of SGEI importance, **Article 14 TFEU, Article 36 EUCFR and Protocol No 26 do not alter the nature or scope of Article 106.2 TFEU in any way, or indeed the case law of the CJEU**.[131] *W. Sauter* suggests that this is a convenient solution from the Commission's perspective because it has diffused the political tension concerning MS' interests involved in SGEI while at the same time ensures that the EU does not become crippled with an extensive public service exception to the competition law rules.[132] Nevertheless, he acknowledges that this solution also has certain disadvantages, particularly a looseness or haziness regarding basic definitions (→ para 52–53), the purpose of SGEI and the proportionality test applicable to balance MS' interests in ensuring the provision of SGEI with the Treaty rules (→ para 62–69).[133] While it may be the case that the nature and scope of Article 106.2 TFEU are not altered as a result of Article 14 TFEU, Article 36 EUCFR and Protocol No 26, in *ANODE*, the CJEU ruled that Article 106.2 TFEU must be set in this new broader context of the Treaty of Lisbon, and it emphasised, in this regard, the recognition of the essential role of SGEI and the wide discretion of the MS in providing, commissioning and organising SGEI.[134]

48 In addition to Article 14 TFEU, Article 36 EUCFR and Protocol No 26, the Commission has introduced a **body of soft law on services of general interest**,[135]

---

[130] Sauter (2008), p. 173.

[131] See Fiedziuk (2011) for a more detailed discussion.

[132] Sauter (2008), p. 174.

[133] Sauter (2008), p. 174.

[134] Case C-121/15, *ANODE* (CJEU 7 September 2016) para 40 and 41.

[135] Commission Communication *on Services of General Interest in Europe*, O.J. C 281/03 (1996); Commission Communication *on Services of General Interest in Europe*, O.J. C 17/4 (2001); Commission Communication *on Services of General Interest, including Social Services of General Interest: A New European Commitment, accompanying Communication on 'A Single Market for 21st Century Europe'*, COM(2007) 725 final (this followed the Commission *Green Paper on services of general interest*, COM(2003) 270 final and Commission Communication *White Paper on services of general interest*, COM(2004) 374 final); Commission Communication *on A Quality Framework for Services of General Interest in Europe of December*, COM(2011) 900 final, accompanied by a Commission Staff Working Document, *Guide to the application of the European Union rules on state aid, public procurement and the internal market to services of general economic interest, and in particular to social services of general interest*, SEC(2010) 1545 final. The Communication *on A Quality Framework for Services of General Interest in Europe* was issued at the same time as a package of measures on SGEIs and state aid. The SGEI state aid package consists of Commission Decision 2012/21/EU *on the application of Article 106(2) [TFEU] to State aid in the form of public service compensation granted to certain undertakings entrusted with the operation of services of general economic interest*, O.J. L 7/3 (2012), two Communications, Commission Communication *on the application of the European Union State aid rules to compensation granted for the provision of services of general economic interest*, O.J. C 8/4 (2012) and Commission Communication *European Union framework for State aid in the form of public service compensation (2011)*, O.J. C 8/15 (2012), and a *de minimis* regulation, Commission Regulation (EU) No 360/2012 *on the application of Articles 107 and 108 [TFEU] to de minimis aid granted to undertakings providing services of general economic interest*, O.J. L 114/

including SGEI (→ para 52–53 and 57). The Commission initially introduced this soft law partly in response to MS' concern for the need to define SGEI broadly in consideration of their important economic and social function.[136] This body of soft law seeks to clarify the application of internal market and competition law rules to all services of general interest, but it is marked by particular flexibility to the definition of SGEI, allowing MS to determine their exact scope (→ para 52).

3.2. Elements

There are three **key elements** to Article 106.2 TFEU. First, an undertaking must be "entrusted with the provision of services of general economic interest", or it must be a "revenue-producing monopoly". Second, it must be determined if the application of the Treaty rules would "obstruct the performance of the tasks assigned" to the SGEI provider or revenue-producing monopoly. If so, the Treaty rules can be set aside where this is proportionate to the public interest and where it is necessary to allow the fulfilment of SGEI tasks, but this is subject to the third element of Article 106.2 TFEU, the proviso that stipulates that the development of trade must not be affected to an extent that is contrary to EU interests. 49

3.2.1. Beneficiaries

Whereas Article 106.1 TFEU is addressed to MS and only they can be found in breach of this provision, **Article 106.2 TFEU is addressed to two types of undertakings**: private and public undertakings entrusted with the provision of SGEI *and* revenue-producing monopolies. 50

Undertakings Entrusted with the Provision of Services of General Economic Interest

The first requirement concerning undertakings entrusted with the provision of SGEI is a **concrete act** by an MS **"entrusting" or assigning an SGEI mission** and imposing public service obligations in the general economic interest on specific 51

---

8 (2012). A Staff Working Document, *Guide to the application of the European Union rules on state aid, public procurement and the internal market to services of general economic interest, and in particular to social services of general interest*, SWD (2013) 53/final/2, was subsequently issued to provide guidance on the package to public authorities, service users and providers, and other stakeholders. This package replaces the 2005 package which was introduced to deal with the consequences of Case C-280/00, *Altmark Trans* (ECJ 24 July 2003) on SGEIs and public procurement. Commission Directive 2006/111/EC *on the transparency of financial relations between Member States and public undertakings as well as on financial transparency within certain undertakings*, O.J. L 318/17 (2006) continues to apply. On the Commission's soft law in the area of SGEIs, see further Neergard (2011).

[136] Goyder and Alborens-Llorens (2009), p. 569.

undertakings.[137] The mere acceptance or endorsement of an undertaking's activities by an MS is insufficient.[138] The entrustment of an SGEI mission by an MS is also to be differentiated from the imposition of general regulatory rules by an MS. For example, the GC stated in *BUPA* that "[t]he mere fact that the national legislature, acting in the general interest in the broad sense, imposes certain rules of authorisation, of functioning or of control on all the operators in a particular sector does not in principle mean that there is an SGEI mission".[139] Nonetheless, an SGEI mission can be assigned to more than a single incumbent. The assignment of the mission to several incumbents does not, however, require several individual acts of entrustment; one overall act is sufficient.[140] The act assigning the SGEI must specify the **content and duration of the public service obligation**; the undertaking on which it imposed and the relevant territory, where applicable; the nature of the exclusive or special rights assigned; the parameters for calculating, controlling and reviewing compensation for the provision of the SGEI; and arrangements for avoiding and recovering over-compensation.[141]

52   The second requirement concerning undertakings entrusted with SGEI provision is that the services actually entail a **general economic interest**. SGEI are not defined by the Treaty, and the **MS have considerable autonomy in defining them**. This autonomy is endorsed by the Commission's soft law (→ para 48, 53 and 57), which facilitates a broad definition of SGEI. The autonomy of the MS in defining SGEI has nevertheless been curtailed somewhat by the CJEU in an effort to ensure that the scope of Article 106.2 TFEU is restricted, given its inherent nature as a derogation to Treaty rules. In *BUPA*, for example, the GC held that while the MS have broad competence in determining the nature and scope of SGEI and broad discretion in defining them, this discretion should not be exercised in a way that arbitrarily removes certain sectors from the scope of the competition law rules.[142]

W. *Sauter* posits that there are a number of **plausible explanations as to why there is no concrete definition of SGEI at the EU level**. First, he posits that the Treaty itself allows the MS a wide discretion to define SGEI missions and to set the organisational principles to accomplish these missions. Second, he posits that the

---

[137] Case C-203/96, *Chemische Afvalstoffen Dusseldorp and others v Minister van Volkshuisvesting, Ruimtelijke Ordening en Milieubeheer* (Opinion of AG *Jacobs* of 23 October 1997) para 103; Case C-49/07, *MOTOE* (ECJ 1 July 2008) para 45–47.

[138] Jones et al. (2019), p. 620.

[139] Case T-289/03, *BUPA and Others v Commission* (CFI 4 March 2005) para 178. See also para 179–184.

[140] Case T-289/03, *BUPA and Others v Commission* (CFI 4 March 2005) para 183.

[141] Commission Decision of 20 Dec 2011 *on the application of Article 106(2) [TFEU] to State aid in the form of public service compensation granted to certain undertakings entrusted with the operation of services of general economic interest*, O.J. L 7/3 (2012) para 52.

[142] Case T-289/03, *BUPA and Others v Commission* (CFI 4 March 2005) para 166–168. See further Ross (2009), pp. 132–135.

concept of SGEI is understood to be dynamic, which is important in terms of accommodating changes in time and place.[143]

While there is no Treaty definition of SGEI, Protocol No 26 on services of general interest (→ para 44, 46, 47 and 57) includes them as a **subset of the broader services of general interest**.[144] This is in keeping with the Commission's body of soft law (→ para 48, 52 and 57),[145] among which the Commission's 2011 Communication on a Quality Framework for Services of General Interest in Europe[146] acknowledges certain obscurity surrounding the definition of SGEI, compounded by an interchangeable and oftentimes inaccurate use of terminology.[147] The 2011 Communication seeks therefore to provide clarity by delineating certain basic concepts concerning services of general interest. 53

Accordingly, it contains the following definitions and explanations: 54

- **Services of general interest** are defined as "services that public authorities of the Member States classify as being of general interest and, therefore, subject to specific public service obligations (PSO). The term covers both economic activities [...] and non-economic services. The latter are not subject to specific EU legislation and are not covered by the internal market and competition rules of the Treaty."[148]
- **Services of general economic interest** are defined as "economic activities which deliver outcomes in the overall public good that would not be supplied (or would be supplied under different conditions in terms of quality, safety, affordability, equal treatment or universal access) by the market without public intervention. The PSO is imposed on the provider by way of an entrustment and on the basis of a general interest criterion which ensures that the service is provided under conditions allowing it to fulfil its mission."[149]
- **Social services of general interest** are defined as including "social security schemes covering the main risks of life and a range of other essential services provided directly to the person that play a preventive and socially cohesive/inclusive role. While some social services (such as statutory social security schemes) are not considered by the European Court as being economic activities, the jurisprudence of the Court makes clear that the social nature of a service is not sufficient in itself to classify it as non-economic. The term social

---

[143] Sauter (2008), pp. 174–175.

[144] The term "services of general interest" does not feature otherwise in the Treaties. It is however used in the Services Directive, Parliament/Council Directive 2006/123/EC *on services in the internal market*, O.J. L 376/36 (2006).

[145] Commission Communication *on Services of General Interest in Europe*, O.J. C 17/4 (2001). For a discussion on the definition of services of general interest, see Lenaerts (2012).

[146] Commission Communication *on A Quality Framework for Services of General Interest in Europe* COM(2011) 900 final, pp. 3–4.

[147] COM(2011) 900 final, p. 3.

[148] COM(2011) 900 final, p. 3.

[149] COM(2011) 900 final, p. 3.

service of general interest consequently covers both economic and non-economic activities".[150]

- **Universal service obligation** (→ para 4) is defined as "a type of PSO which sets the requirements designed to ensure that certain services are made available to all consumers and users in a Member State, regardless of their geographical location, at a specified quality and, taking account of specific national circumstances, at an affordable price".[151]

55 SGEI, the focus of Article 106.2 TFEU, are therefore **essential market services of an economic nature generally provided in the public interest**. The reason that they may be entrusted to undertakings is that private market operators may not be inclined to provide them.[152] As *J. L. Buendia Sierra* points out, the essential nature of a service and its underlying public interest characteristics are what "justifies a degree of intervention of the public authorities", ensuring that the "given service is actually provided" and controlling "the conditions under which it is provided".[153]

56 As market services, SGEI belong to the market and are subject to internal market and competition law rules, whereas non-market services are not subject to internal market and competition law rules. Indeed, State entities that provide non-market services escape the definition of an "undertaking" as an entity engaged in economic activity in the market place, irrespective of the way in which they are financed[154] (→ para 11), and are not within the scope of the competition law rules or indeed of Article 106 TFEU (→ para 11).

57 The nature of the activity or service involved and its characteristics are therefore critical in determining whether it is of general economic interest, distinguishable from the general interest and from non-economic activities. Case law, the Commission's body of soft law (→ para 48, 52 and 53)[155] and Protocol No 26 on services of general interest (→ para 44, 46, 47 and 53) have pinpointed **SGEI characteristics** to include **universality, continuity, equal treatment, affordability, quality of service, safety, accessibility, efficiency, transparency, consumer protection and user rights**.

58 The ECJ has established **various conditions** to be met before a service can be considered an SGEI premised on these characteristics: 1) the service must be *essential* in terms of the needs of the public, 2) the service must be *provided within*

---

[150] COM(2011) 900 final, pp. 3–4.

[151] COM(2011) 900 final, p. 4.

[152] Case C-203/96, *Chemische Afvalstoffen Dusseldorp and others v Minister van Volkshuisvesting, Ruimtelijke Ordening en Milieubeheer* (Opinion of AG *Jacobs* of 23 October 1997) para 105. On this type of market failure and the need to ensure public service obligations, and in particular universal service obligations, see Fiedziuk (2011), p. 226; Sauter (2008), pp. 179–181.

[153] Buendia Sierra (1999), p. 277.

[154] Case C-41/90, *Höfner & Elser v Macrotron* (ECJ 23 April 1991) para 21.

[155] See similarly, Commission Communication, *White Paper on services of general interest*, COM(2004) 374 final para 2.1. See also Neergard (2011), p. 44.

a defined territory, 3) the service must be *available to all consumers* in this territory and 4) the service must be provided *under affordable conditions*.[156] AG *Colomer* reiterated in 2009 that to be of **general** *economic* **interest**, a service should be uninterrupted and available at a uniform rate for the benefit of all consumers in the relevant market.[157]

In *BUPA*, the CFI stipulated that SGEI must satisfy the **minimum criteria** established in the case law, most critically that the service mission has to be both compulsory and universal in nature.[158] The **compulsory nature of the mission** means that the operator of the service is "required to offer the service in question on the market in compliance with the SGEI obligations which govern the supply of that service";[159] in other words, the operator of the service is subject to a public service obligation in line with the mission entrusted to it. As concerns **universality**, the CFI pointed out in *BUPA* that although a classic SGEI element, universality "does not mean that the service in question must respond to a need common to the whole population or be supplied throughout a territory"; rather, the CFI seemed to accept that partial universality is sufficient.[160] This means, therefore, that SGEI that are 1) restricted as to their scope of application *rationae personae* because they do not meet a universal need as such or 2) that are territorially restricted can still satisfy the universality criterion.[161] *M. Ross* postulates that this approach is caught up in the primary compulsory character of SGEI, requiring their operators to provide their service to whosoever may request it.[162] 59

Services recognised as SGEI in Article 106.2 TFEU case law have included utility services, comprising water,[163] gas,[164] electricity[165] and basic or traditional postal services.[166] SGEI have moreover extended beyond these traditional utilities to include public telecommunication networks[167] and services,[168] public broadcast- 60

---

[156] Case C-320/91, *Corbeau* (ECJ 19 May 1993) para 15.

[157] Case C-265/08, *Federutility and Others* (Opinion of AG *Colomer* of 20 October 2009) para 54–55.

[158] Case T-289/03, *BUPA and Others v Commission* (CFI 4 March 2005) para 172.

[159] Case T-289/03, *BUPA and Others v Commission* (CFI 4 March 2005) para 188.

[160] Case T-289/03, *BUPA and Others v Commission* (CFI 4 March 2005) para 186–187.

[161] See Ross (2009), pp. 134–135.

[162] Ross (2009), p. 135.

[163] Joined Cases 96/82 et al., *IAZ v Commission* (ECJ 8 November 1983).

[164] Case C-159/94, *Commission v France* (ECJ 23 October 1997).

[165] Case C-393/92, *Gemeente Almelo and Others v Energiebedriff Ijsselmij NV* (ECJ 27 April 1994); Case C-157/94, *Commission v Netherlands* (ECJ 23 October 1997).

[166] Case C-320/91, *Corbeau* (ECJ 19 May 1993); Joined Cases C-147 and 148/97, *Deutsche Post AG* (ECJ 10 February 2000); Case T-556/08, *Slovenská pošta v Commission* (GC 25 March 2015).

[167] Case C-18/88, *RTT v GB-Inno-BM* (ECJ 13 December 1991).

[168] Case 41/83, *Italy v Commission* (ECJ 20 March 1985).

ing services,[169] ambulance services,[170] port-mooring services,[171] funeral services,[172] recruitment services,[173] the operation of air services on uneconomical routes,[174] the administration and management of waterways,[175] the management of supplementary pension schemes,[176] the collection and treatment of waste[177] and the provision of private medical health insurance.[178]

Revenue-Producing Monopolies

61 In addition to SGEI-entrusted undertakings, Article 106.2 TFEU applies to revenue-producing monopolies. The Treaty does not provide a definition of revenue-producing monopolies, but the term is understood to apply to **monopolies created with the purpose of raising revenue for the State**. This ordinarily involves monopolies conferred on public undertakings whose profits go to the State, but it can also include private undertakings conferred with such monopolies by the State in return for revenue. Article 37 TFEU, which deals with State monopolies of a commercial character in the context of the free movement of goods, is applicable to such revenue-producing monopolies, but Article 106.2 TFEU can be invoked to seek immunity from the application of Article 37 TFEU (→ Article 37 TFEU para 16).[179]

3.2.2. Obstruction of the Performance of Services of General Economic Interest Tasks

62 Under Article 106.2 TFEU, undertakings entrusted with an SGEI mission and revenue-producing monopolies are subject to the Treaty rules only in so far as their application **does not obstruct the performance, in law or in fact, of the**

---

[169] Case C-260/89, *ERT v DEP* (ECJ 18 June 1991).

[170] Case C-475/99, *Ambulanz Glöckner* (ECJ 25 October 2001).

[171] Case C-266/96, *Corsica Ferries France v Gruppo Antichi Ormeggiatori del porto di Genova and others* (ECJ 18 June 1998).

[172] Case 30/87, *Bodson v Pompes Funèbres des Régions Libérées* (ECJ 4 May 1988).

[173] Case C-41/90, *Höfner & Elser v Macrotron* (ECJ 23 April 1991); Case C-55/96, *Job Centre* (ECJ 11 December 1997).

[174] Case 66/86, *Ahmed Saeed Flugreisen and others v Zentrale zur Bekämpfung unlauteren Wettbewerbs* (ECJ 11 April 1989).

[175] Case 10/71, *Muller* (ECJ 14 July 1971).

[176] Case C-67/96, *Albany* (ECJ 21 September 1999).

[177] Case C-203/96, *Chemische Afvalstoffen Dusseldorp and others v Minister van Volkshuisvesting, Ruimtelijke Ordening en Milieubeheer* (ECJ 25 June 1998).

[178] Case T-289/03, *BUPA and Others v Commission* (CFI 4 March 2005).

[179] It was invoked to justify restrictions to the prohibition on commercial monopolies and the free movement of goods in, e.g., Case C-157/94, *Commission v Netherlands* (ECJ 23 October 1997); C-158/94, *Commission v Italy* (ECJ 23 October 1997), Case C-159/94, *Commission v France* (ECJ 23 October 1997), Case C-160/94, *Commission v Spain* (ECJ 23 October 1997).

particular tasks assigned to them. As the application of this provision can result in Treaty rules being avoided, it was initially interpreted restrictively, with the Commission and ECJ proving to be unreceptive to arguments that the application of Treaty rules, particularly those concerning competition law, was such as to obstruct the SGEI task assigned to undertakings. So, for example, in the early days of the application of Article 106.2 TFEU, the Court ruled in *BRT v Sabam*[180] that since Article 106.2 TFEU entails derogation from the application of the Treaty's competition law rules, it should be narrowly construed. The Commission also proclaimed in *Anseau/Navewa*:[181] "It is not sufficient [. . .] that compliance with the provisions of the Treaty makes the performance of the particular task more complicated. A possible limitation of the application of the rules on competition can be envisaged only in the event that the undertaking concerned has no *other technically or economically feasible means* of performing its particular task."[182] This suggested that the appropriate test to determine whether the application of Treaty rules resulted in the obstruction of the performance of SGEI tasks was a proportionality test premised on the **less restrictive alternative** standard, and this was upheld on appeal by the ECJ.[183] The result of this restrictive interpretation meant that for some time, the ECJ was reluctant to find that the conditions of Article 106.2 TFEU were satisfied. So, for example, shortly after its *IAZ* judgment, in *British Telecom*,[184] the Court found that the application of competition law rules to British Telecom's prohibition on private forward transmission agencies using its network did not put the performance of its SGEI tasks in operating the UK's telecommunication system into *economic jeopardy*.[185]

The ECJ's restrictive approach was diluted somewhat in the *Höfner & Elser* judgment (→ para 11, 22, and 23), where the ECJ ruled that a privileged undertaking is subject to competition rules "unless and to the extent to which it is shown that their application is ***incompatible* with the discharge of its duties**", albeit this was not so in this case.[186] In spite of this dilution, the Court continued to find that the application of Treaty rules was not such as to obstruct the performance of SGEI tasks. So, in *Merci Convenzionali* (→ para 18 and 24),[187] the Court ruled that even if dock work was an SGEI, this did not necessitate the setting aside of the Treaty rules, in particular those relating to competition and freedom of movement, as these rules did not obstruct the performance of the undertaking's tasks. In *RTT v GB-Inno* (→ para 18, 25 and 60), the Court found that an undertaking entrusted with the

63

---

[180] Case 127/73, *BRT v SABAM* (ECJ 30 January 1974).
[181] Commission Decision No. 82/371/EEC *Anseau/Navewa*, O.J. L 167/39 (1982).
[182] Commission Decision No. 82/371/EEC *Anseau/Navewa*, O.J. L 167/39 (1982) para 66.
[183] Joined Cases 96/82 et al., *IAZ v Commission* (ECJ 8 November 1983).
[184] Case 41/83, *Italy v Commission* (ECJ 20 March 1985).
[185] Case 41/83, *Italy v Commission* (ECJ 20 March 1985) para 33.
[186] Case C-41/90, *Höfner & Elser v Macrotron* (ECJ 23 April 1991) para 24 (emphasis added).
[187] Case C-179/90, *Merci Convenzionali Porto di Genova v Siderurgica Gabrielli* (ECJ 10 December 1991).

public telephone network did not need the power to lay down the standards for telephone equipment and that the resulting restriction of competition in the telephone equipment market was not justified by a public SGEI task.[188]

64 The ECJ further **significantly diluted its restrictive approach** in *Corbeau*,[189] reading a **lower standard principle of proportionality** into Article 106.2 TFEU than the less restrictive alternative standard.[190] It ruled that the test to apply under Article 106.2 TFEU was "the extent to which a restriction on competition or even the exclusion of all competition from other economic operators is **necessary in order to allow the holder of the exclusive right to perform its task** of general interest and in particular to have the benefit of **economically acceptable conditions**".[191] The conferral and maintenance of exclusive rights (→ para 26) on the Belgian post office, Régie des Postes, therefore had to be necessary for that undertaking to perform the SGEI tasks assigned to it under economically acceptable conditions. The ECJ ruled that while it was acceptable to protect the Belgian post office's exclusive rights to collect, transport and deliver mail in Belgium due to its universal service obligation (→ para 4 and 54) and the need to prevent competitors "creaming off" its more profitable activities, it was not justifiable for Régie des Postes to prevent competition in special services dissociable from the SGEI which were not offered by the traditional postal service where such special services did not compromise the **economic equilibrium** of the SGEI.[192]

65 The ECJ provided further clarification in the four *Electricity Supply* cases.[193] In these cases, national law had granted monopoly rights for the importation of electricity for public distribution. The Commission challenged these monopoly rights as breaching Articles 34 and 37 TFEU. The ECJ ruled that the nationwide distribution of electricity to all consumers at a uniform tariff was an SGEI. It then appraised the justification of the monopoly rights. By means of illustration, in *Commission v Netherlands*, the ECJ ruled that for Article 106.2 TFEU to justify setting aside the Treaty rules, "[i]t is not necessary that the survival of the undertaking itself be threatened".[194] The **financial balance or economic viability of the undertaking therefore does not need to be under threat** from the application of the Treaty rules. Rather, repeating what it had said in *Corbeau*,[195] the Court ruled that "[i]t is sufficient that, in the absence of the rights at issue, it would not be possible for the undertaking to perform the particular tasks entrusted to it, defined

---

[188] Case C-18/88, *RTT v GB-Inno-BM* (ECJ 13 December 1991) para 22.

[189] Case C-320/91, *Corbeau* (ECJ 19 May 1993).

[190] See also Case C-393/92, *Gemeente Almelo and Others v Energiebedriff Ijsselmij NV* (ECJ 27 April 1994).

[191] Case C-320/91, *Corbeau* (ECJ 19 May 1993) para 16 (emphasis added).

[192] Case C-320/91, *Corbeau* (ECJ 19 May 1993) para 19.

[193] Case C-157/94, *Commission v Netherlands* (ECJ 23 October 1997); C-158/94, *Commission v Italy* (ECJ 23 October 1997), Case C-159/94, *Commission v France* (ECJ 23 October 1997), Case C-160/94, *Commission v Spain* (ECJ 23 October 1997).

[194] Case C-157/94, *Commission v Netherlands* (ECJ 23 October 1997) para 43.

[195] Case C-320/91, *Corbeau* (ECJ 19 May 1993).

by reference to the obligations and constraints to which it is subject",[196] and that the rights are necessary to allow their holder to perform the SGEI tasks under **economically acceptable conditions**.[197] Moreover, the ECJ emphasised that the MS are not required to demonstrate that there were no other conceivable means to allow the tasks to be performed under the same economically acceptable conditions.[198]

In *Corsica Ferries*, an Italian law requiring the use of local mooring services, was challenged on the basis that various mooring service providers were abusing their dominant position by charging **excessive and differentiated prices to different consumers** (→ para 28). The mooring service providers argued that the prices were justified as indispensable to the maintenance of a universal mooring service and that price differences arose due to different local conditions in various ports. The ECJ found that the mooring services amounted to SGEI under Article 106.2 TFEU because the mooring companies were obliged to provide universal service at any time under any conditions to any user for reasons of safety in port waters.[199] Moreover, the Court found that the exclusive rights enjoyed by the mooring companies were **justified in terms of safety in port waters and public security**. This being so, it was not contrary to Article 102 TFEU to include an amount to cover the cost of maintaining a universal mooring service in the mooring fee once this amount corresponded with the special characteristics of that universal service. Nor was it contrary to Article 102 TFEU for this amount to be different in different ports, given the particular characteristics of each port.[200] For these reasons, the State measure conferring the exclusive rights was not incompatible with Article 106.1 TFEU.

66

In *Albany* (→ para 29 and 60), where a Dutch law-making compulsory affiliation to a sectoral supplementary pension scheme was challenged, the Court ruled that an exclusive right to manage the scheme and to collect and administer the contributions paid to the pension fund was similarly justified. In the absence of such rights, it would not be possible for the provider of the SGEI to perform the tasks assigned to it, and the maintenance of the rights was necessary to ensure the performance of its SGEI tasks under **economically acceptable conditions**.[201] Without these rights, it would be difficult to cover the spread of risk, and the performance of the SGEI tasks in managing the sectoral supplementary pension scheme under economically acceptable conditions might be imperilled due to "**creaming off**", threatening the financial equilibrium of the service provider.[202] The ECJ adopted the same

67

---

[196] Case C-157/94, *Commission v Netherlands* (ECJ 23 October 1997) para 52.

[197] Case C-157/94, *Commission v Netherlands* (ECJ 23 October 1997) para 53.

[198] Case C-157/94, *Commission v Netherlands* (ECJ 23 October 1997) para 58.

[199] Case C-266/96, *Corsica Ferries France v Gruppo Antichi Ormeggiatori del porto di Genova and others* (ECJ 18 June 1998) para 45.

[200] Case C-266/96, *Corsica Ferries France v Gruppo Antichi Ormeggiatori del porto di Genova and others* (ECJ 18 June 1998) para 46–47.

[201] Case C-67/96, *Albany* (ECJ 21 September 1999) para 107.

[202] Case C-67/96, *Albany* (ECJ 21 September 1999) para 108–111.

reasoning in accepting that the conditions of Article 106.2 TFEU were satisfied in *Deutsche Post* (→ para 18 and 30), in which it granted immunity from the application of Article 102 TFEU to Deutsche Post for the manner in which it charged for international post as if it were internal mail. Deutsche Post was justified in doing so because otherwise the performance of its obligations in economically balanced conditions would be jeopardised if it were obliged to forward and deliver mail to German-based addressees that had been posted by German-based senders using the postal services of other MS without any financial compensation for the cost involved in fulfilling this obligation.[203]

A similarly generous stance was taken by the Court in *Ambulanz Glöckner* (→ para 15 and 31), where the Court accepted that protection from competition in the non-emergency ambulance service market was necessary for the universal emergency ambulance service incumbent to ensure **economically acceptable conditions** and to **prevent the quality and reliability of its services from being jeopardised.**[204] In other words, extending protection from competition in the emergency transport to the non-emergency transport market was justified so that the incumbent could subsidise the emergency ambulance service.[205]

68 The approach of the GC has not, however, been as generous in the recent *Slovakian Hybrid Mail* case (→ para 37).[206] The Slovak State and Slovenská pošta argued that the exclusive rights granted to Slovenská pošta to provide hybrid mail services were justified under Article 106.2 TFEU. The Postal Directive allows certain postal services to be reserved to the universal service operator if this is **necessary for the maintenance of the universal service**. The **Postal Notice**[207] **establishes a rebuttable presumption of *prima facie* justification** under Article 106.2 TFEU to the extent that special or exclusive rights fall within reserved areas as defined by the Postal Directive.[208] The GC ruled that this presumption of *prima facie* justification is not applicable if the service in question has been liberalised and the functioning of the universal service has not been endangered by liberalisation.[209] Having been previously liberalised without endangering the universal postal service, the hybrid mail market could not benefit from the presumption. The Slovak Republic and Slovenská pošta had to otherwise justify the exclusive right conferred on Slovenská pošta, but they were unable to produce satisfactory evidence that the liberalisation of the hybrid market had negatively impacted Slovenská pošta's universal postal service obligations. Nor were they able

---

[203] Joined Cases C-147 and 148/97, *Deutsche Post AG* (ECJ 10 February 2000) para 50.

[204] Case C-475/99, *Ambulanz Glöckner* (ECJ 25 October 2001) para 61.

[205] Case C-475/99, *Ambulanz Glöckner* (ECJ 25 October 2001) para 57.

[206] Case T-556/08, *Slovenská pošta v Commission* (GC 25 March 2015). Upheld in Case C-293/15 *Slovenská pošta v Commission* (CJEU 30 June 2016).

[207] Commission Notice *on the application of the competition rules to the postal sector and on the assessment of certain State measures relating to postal services*, O.J. C 39/2 (1998).

[208] Commission Notice *on the application of the competition rules to the postal sector and on the assessment of certain State measures relating to postal services*, O.J. C 39/2 (1998) para 8.3.

[209] Case T-556/08, *Slovenská pošta v Commission* (GC 25 March 2015) para 361.

to prove that liberalisation would have prevented Slovenská pošta from carrying out its universal postal service obligations under economically acceptable conditions. In particular, they were unable to prove that the reservation of hybrid mail services to Slovenská pošta was necessary to finance the universal service obligation (→ para 4 and 54) reserved to it and to provide or maintain it under economically acceptable conditions.[210] Therefore, the re-monopolisation of the hybrid mail market was not necessary or justifiable under Article 106.2 TFEU.[211]

Notwithstanding the outcome of the *Slovakian Hybrid Mail* case[212] and some of the other cases,[213] all of the judgments since *Corbeau*[214] speak of jeopardising the SGEI operation and of justification for setting aside Treaty rules in terms of ensuring "economically acceptable conditions" and the "economic equilibrium" for the SGEI provider. The Court's approach has clearly moved on from the approach in *IAZ*,[215] in which the test of proportionality was premised on the less restrictive alternative standard, to a distilled test[216] of **proportionality based on necessity**. By virtue of this distilled test, the Article 106.2 TFEU exception is applicable where setting aside the Treaty rules is *reasonably* necessary for the performance of SGEI tasks, particularly those involving a universal service obligation (→ para 4 and 54).[217] **69**

The change in the Court's approach has corresponded to a change in the Treaty, marked by the inclusion of **Article 14 TFEU** (→ para 44, 46, 47, and 79) by the Amsterdam Treaty, which recognises the place of SGEI in the shared values of the EU. Article 14 TFEU emphasises the importance of conditions, notably economic and financial conditions, that enable undertakings entrusted with the provision of SGEI to fulfil their mission. It is understood that Article 106.2 TFEU must be read in light of Article 14 TFEU. Although Article 14 TFEU has yet to be addressed by the CJEU, it is arguable that in emphasising the importance of economic and financial conditions enabling the provision of SGEI, Article 14 TFEU will continue to facilitate a generous approach to the interpretation of Article 106.2 TFEU. **70**

---

[210] Case T-556/08, *Slovenská pošta v Commission* (GC 25 March 2015) para 363–424.

[211] This issue did not arise on appeal in Case C-293/15 *Slovenská pošta v Commission* (CJEU 30 June 2016).

[212] Case T-556/08, *Slovenská pošta v Commission* (GC 25 March 2015).

[213] Case C-41/90, *Höfner & Elser v Macrotron* (ECJ 23 April 1991); Case C-179/90, *Merci Convenzionali Porto di Genova v Siderurgica Gabrielli* (ECJ 10 December 1991); Case C-18/88, *RTT v GB-Inno-BM* (ECJ 13 December 1991); Case C-320/91, *Corbeau* (ECJ 19 May 1993).

[214] Case C-320/91, *Corbeau* (ECJ 19 May 1993).

[215] Joined Cases 96/82 et al., *IAZ v Commission* (ECJ 8 November 1983).

[216] See similarly Lenaerts (2012), p. 1259, who describes this as a "soft" version of the principle of proportionality. For an alternative view, see Davies (2009), pp. 572–574, who argues that a less intense standard of proportionality under Article 106.2 TFEU is "illusionary". For a more detailed discussion, and somewhat different view, comprising the thick and thin aspects of proportionality, see Sauter (2008), pp. 185–188. See also Fiedziuk (2011), pp. 229–230; Bekkedal (2011), pp. 67–70.

[217] Korah (2007), p. 225.

3.2.3. Development of Trade Contrary to Union Interest

71 Article 106.2 TFEU specifies that in order to avail of the Article 106.2 TFEU exception, **the development of trade must not be affected in a manner that is contrary to the interests of the EU**. This proviso has been reinforced by the ECJ, stating, for example, in *Commission v Netherlands* that "Article [106.2] provides that undertakings entrusted with the operation of services of general economic interest are to be subject to the rules contained in the Treaty, in particular the rules on competition, in so far as the application of such rules does not obstruct the performance, in law or in fact, of the particular tasks assigned to them, subject to the proviso, however, that the development of trade must not be affected to such an extent as would be contrary to the interests of the Community".[218]

72 AG *Cosmas* had suggested in this case that to exclude the Article 106.2 TFEU exception, it would be necessary that trade in the EU was actually or potentially affected to the extent of "the restrictive effects being so great that intra-Community trade in the sector in question is practically non-existent".[219] The Court did not go this far and merely held that for an exclusive right to escape the application of Treaty rules by virtue of Article 106.2 TFEU, the Commission is required to identify the EU interest at stake and to prove that the EU interest has been and would continue to be adversely affected.[220]

73 In spite of the Court's endorsement, **the Article 106.2 TFEU proviso has in practice been applied fleetingly and has often been overlooked**.[221] In *Corsica Ferries*, for example, the ECJ indicated that it was one of two applicable tests under Article 106.2 TFEU (the other test being that of the obstruction of the SGEI task assigned to an undertaking) but did not consider the proviso beyond this, nor in fact did it specifically apply it.[222] The result of its fleeting application has led to some confusion as to the exact content and scope of the test involved.

74 A. *Jones*, B. *Sufrin* and N. *Dunne* posit that it entails something different from the jurisdictional clause (the effect on trade between MS clause) of Articles 101 and 102 TFEU and suggest that it may in fact be an extension of the proportionality requirement.[223] This would not be out of line with the nature of the proviso as a qualification to the exception. In other words, Article 106.2 TFEU may be inapplicable where setting aside the Treaty rules affects the development of trade to an extent that disproportionately undermines the interests of the EU, even where the

---

[218] Case C-157/94, *Commission v Netherlands* (ECJ 23 October 1997) para 28.
[219] Case C-157/94, *Commission v Netherlands* (Opinion of AG *Cosmas* of 26 November 1996) para 126.
[220] Case C-157/94, *Commission v Netherlands* (ECJ 23 October 1997) para 65–68.
[221] Lane (2000), p. 240.
[222] Case C-266/96, *Corsica Ferries France v Gruppo Antichi Ormeggiatori del porto di Genova and others* (ECJ 18 June 1998) para 42 and 44.
[223] Jones et al. (2019), p. 634. See similarly Whish and Bailey (2021), p. 249.

setting aside of the Treaty rules is proportionate and necessary for the performance of the SGEI.

3.3. Services of General Economic Interest and State Aid

Financing SGEI can result in State aid (Article 107 TFEU). However, in *Altmark*,[224] the ECJ determined that compensation for SGEI providers is not State aid where certain conditions are met. There are four conditions in total to satisfy as part of the **Altmark compensation test**: 1) the SGEI task and its obligations must be clearly articulated, 2) the level of compensation must be set out in advance, 3) the level of compensation must not be excessive but can include a reasonable amount of profit and 4) there must be a proper and transparent tender procedure or a benchmarking efficiency test.[225] If these conditions are not satisfied, an obligation to notify the Commission of State aid arises, but it may be that Article 106.2 TFEU comes into play, and if the State aid is proportionate and necessary to carry out the SGEI task at issue, the aid is compatible with the internal market. Subsequent to this *Altmark* judgment, the Commission introduced a number of measures to deal with its consequences (→ para 48).[226]

3.4. Enforcement

As with Article 106.1 TFEU (→ para 39), the **Commission is responsible for the application of Article 106.2 TFEU** by virtue of Article 106.3 TFEU (→ para 77 and 87–89). Also, similar to the enforcement of Article 106.1 TFEU (→ para 40), **Article 106.2 TFEU is directly effective** and can be invoked by private litigants before national courts. The ECJ ruled in *ERT* (→ para 13, 18, 23 and 60) that the national courts can determine whether the application of Treaty rules would obstruct the performance of SGEI tasks entrusted to an undertaking. Article 106.2 TFEU is therefore directly effective without the need for Commission action under Article 106.3 TFEU.[227] However, determining whether the EU interest proviso of Article 106.2 TFEU is satisfied might prove challenging for national courts as they may not have the necessary information to determine what the EU interest at stake is and whether trade is affected contrary to that interest.

The ECJ suggested in *Commission v Netherlands* that it is **incumbent on the Commission to define the EU interest according to which the development of trade is to be assessed** and that this might necessitate a Commission decision or

---

[224] Case C-280/00, *Altmark Trans* (ECJ 24 July 2003). See further Hancher and Sauter (2014).
[225] On the application of the *Altmark* criteria, see further Ross (2009), pp. 138–139.
[226] See further Sauter (2014); Sauter (2008), pp. 191–193.
[227] Case C-260/89, *ERT v DEP* (ECJ 18 June 1991) para 33–34.

directive under Article 106.3 TFEU (→ para 77).[228] If so, the Article 106.2 TFEU proviso does not in fact meet the conditions of direct effect, primarily because it depends on further action by the Commission. *A. Jones*, *B. Sufrin* and *N. Dunne* theorise that even if this is the case, if, as indeed they posit (→ para 74), this proviso is part of the broader proportionality test to which the obstruction of SGEI tasks resulting from the application of Treaty rules is subject, then Article 106.2 TFEU as a whole has direct effect.[229] In the absence of any case law on the issue, they also acknowledge, however, the possibility that only the first sentence of Article 106.2 TFEU has direct effect and that its second sentence depends on the Commission declaring infringement of the EU and thereby lacks direct effect.[230]

4. Commission's Law-Making Competence Under Paragraph 3

77 Article 106.3 TFEU galvanises the role of the **Commission** as guardian of the Treaties by **empowering** it **to adopt directives or decisions** addressed to the MS to ensure the application of Article 106 TFEU. Article 106.3 TFEU thus enables the Commission to specify the scope of Article 106 TFEU obligations and to ensure compliance with Article 106 TFEU.

4.1. Directives

78 Article 106.3 TFEU provides an **independent and direct legal basis** for the Commission to adopt directives obviating the ordinary legislative procedure, and thereby by-passing the legislative involvement of the Council and the EP. In practice, the Commission nonetheless engages in extensive consultation with the other EU institutions, and indeed with the MS and other stakeholders, before legislating under Article 106.3 TFEU. The Commission's Article 106.3 TFEU legislative power is a limited one, confined to determining MS obligations under Article 106 TFEU. It does not therefore confer a general legislative power on the Commission, and its power is much more limited than the legislative power of the EP and the Council.

79 Notwithstanding the Article 106.3 TFEU legislative power of the Commission, **Article 14 TFEU** (→ para 44, 46, 47, and 70), as amended by the Lisbon Treaty, confers a specific legislative power on the EP and the Council to establish the principles and conditions, particularly the economic and financial conditions, to enable SGEI providers to fulfil the tasks assigned to them (→ Article 14 TFEU para 8). Article 14 TFEU does acknowledge that it is without prejudice to Article 106 TFEU, but there is a potential for conflict between the Commission's Article 106.3 TFEU

---

[228] Case C-157/94, *Commission v Netherlands* (ECJ 23 October 1997) para 69.
[229] Jones et al. (2019), p. 637.
[230] Jones et al. (2019), p. 637.

legislative powers and those of the EP and the Council under Article 14 TFEU (→Article 14 TFEU para 15). As yet, Article 14 TFEU has not been relied on to enact legislation, and therefore this potential conflict has not materialised.

The **Commission's exercise of Article 106.3 TFEU legislative powers has** 80 **been contentious** and has been challenged by the MS. The MS have argued, for example, that the Commission has acted *ultra vires* in enacting legislation under Article 106.3 TFEU because the issue legislated for is beyond the scope of Article 106.3 TFEU and requires an alternative legal base.[231] Given its contentious nature, the Commission has infrequently used its Article 106.3 TFEU legislative powers, generally confining its use to circumstances involving many instances of similar and concurrent Treaty infringements by the MS in a particular sector where it is more pragmatic to issue Article 106.3 TFEU legislation rather than to pursue individual infringement decisions against the MS.

The Commission first invoked its **Article 106.3 TFEU legislative power** in 81 enacting the first **Transparency Directive**.[232] This Directive concerned the application of the State aid rules to public undertakings and required transparency from the MS in this regard. It was challenged in *France, Italy and the UK v Commission*,[233] with the MS arguing that Article 106.3 TFEU should be limited to addressing particular circumstances entailing breaches in one or more MS and also that Article 109 TFEU governing the introduction of legislation by the EP and the Council to regulate State aid was the correct legal base for the legislation. The ECJ upheld the right of the Commission to legislate under Article 106.3 TFEU to ensure greater transparency in financial relations between the MS and their privileged undertakings, as this was part of its policing or surveillance functions under Article 106.3 TFEU.

The Commission subsequently issued a number of **directives for the liberal-** 82 **isation of the telecommunications sector**, the Telecommunications Equipment Directive[234] (→ para 19 and 83) and the Telecommunications Services Directive (→ para 84).[235] The Telecommunications Equipment Directive required the withdrawal of certain special or exclusive rights to privileged undertakings for terminal

---

[231] Joined Cases 188-190/80, *France, Italy and United Kingdom v Commission* (ECJ 6 July 1982) (Transparency Directive Case); Cases C-271, 281 and 289/90, *Spain, Belgium and Italy v Commission* (ECJ 17 November 1992) (Telecommunications Services Case); Case 202/88, *France v Commission* (ECJ 19 March 1991) (Telecommunications Equipment Case).

[232] Commission Directive 80/723/EEC, O.J. L 195/35 (1980), which has been replaced by Commission Directive 2006/111/EC *on the transparency of financial relations between Member States and public undertakings as well as on financial transparency within certain undertakings*, O.J. L 318/17 (2006).

[233] Joined Cases 188-190/80, *France, Italy and United Kingdom v Commission* (ECJ 6 July 1982) (Transparency Directive Case).

[234] Commission Directive 88/301/EEC, O.J. L 131/73 (1988), replaced by Commission Directive 2008/63/EC *on competition in the markets in telecommunications terminal equipment*, O.J. L 162/20 (2008).

[235] Commission Directive 90/388/EEC, O.J. L 192/10 (1990). This Telecommunications Services Directive was amended on several occasions and eventually replaced by a consolidating directive,

equipment; the opening of competition regarding the importation, marketing, connection and maintenance of terminal equipment; the creation of independent bodies to draw up approval specifications; and the establishment of rules on the duration of leasing and maintenance for such equipment to prevent long-term contracts.

83 The **Telecommunications Equipment Directive** (→ para 19 and 82) was challenged in *France v Commission*,[236] in which France argued that Article 106.3 TFEU was only intended to enable the Commission to inform the MS on how compliance with the Treaty is to be achieved in cases where this was unclear, rather than to confer a more extensive legislative power on the Commission to elaborate general rules concerning Article 106 TFEU obligations. The ECJ upheld the specific legislative power of the Commission to deal with State measures concerning privileged undertakings by laying down general rules specifying Article 106 TFEU obligations by means of directives. The Directive was nevertheless partially annulled as regards the withdrawal of special rights because the Commission failed to specify the nature of special rights and how their existence would be contrary to the Treaty. The Commission subsequently amended the Directive[237] to include a definition of special rights (→ para 15). The Directive was also partially annulled in this case concerning the rules on the avoidance of long-term contracts. This was because Article 106.3 TFEU confines the Commission's legislative powers to dealing with State measures only. As long-term contracts result from private agreements rather than State measures, the Commission is required to tackle them individually under Article 101 TFEU or Article 102 TFEU and not by means of Article 106.3 TFEU legislation.

84 The **Telecommunications Services Directive**, which stipulated the abolition of monopoly rights in telecommunications services to liberalise this sector, was also challenged by three MS, with a similar outcome.[238] The ECJ once again upheld the right of the Commission to legislate under Article 106.3 TFEU in order to ensure its policing and monitoring functions under the provision. However, the Court annulled the Directive's provisions on special rights and on the avoidance of long-term contracts on the same basis as in *France v Commission* (→ para 83).[239]

85 Although these Article 106.3 TFEU telecommunications directives served an important function in the **liberalisation of the telecommunications sector**, the Commission has deployed other means to achieve such liberalisation, including the individual pursuit of undertakings under Articles 101 and 102 TFEU, individual

---

Commission Directive 2002/77/EC *on competition in the markets for electronic communications networks and services*, O.J. L 249/21 (2002).

[236] Case 202/88, *France v Commission* (ECJ 19 March 1991) (Telecommunications Equipment Case).

[237] Commission Directive 94/46/EC, O.J. L 268/15 (1994).

[238] Joined Cases C-271, 281 and 289/90, *Spain, Belgium and Italy v Commission* (ECJ 17 November 1992) (Telecommunications Services Case).

[239] Case 202/88, *France v Commission* (ECJ 19 March 1991) (Telecommunications Equipment Case).

enforcement actions against MS under Article 258 TFEU, sector enquiries under Regulation 17/62[240] and Regulation 1/2003[241] and merger control under Regulation 139/2004.[242] The Commission has not, however, been a sole actor in liberalising this sector, with the EP and the Council having also enacted liberalisation legislation governing the regulatory framework for telecommunications.[243]

As for liberalisation in other sectors, such as the **energy and postal sectors**, it has been the EP and the Council that have enacted liberalisation legislation. 86

4.2. Decisions

The Commission is also empowered by Article 106.3 TFEU to address **infringement decisions** to the MS for breaches of Article 106 TFEU resulting from State measures concerning public and privileged undertakings, ordering them to rectify the breach. By empowering the Commission to issue such decisions, Article 106.3 TFEU bypasses the normal enforcement action procedure of Article 258 TFEU, although the Article 258 TFEU mechanism can subsequently be invoked by the Commission where an MS fails to comply with an Article 106.3 TFEU decision. Article 106.3 TFEU decisions can only be addressed to MS; they cannot be 87

---

[240] Council Regulation (EEC) No 17/62 *implementing Articles 85 and 86 of the Treaty*, O.J. Special Edition Series 1/87 (1959–1962).

[241] Council Regulation (EC) No 1/2003 *on the implementation of the rules on competition laid down in Articles 81 and 82 of the Treaty*, O.J. L 1/1 (2003).

[242] Council Regulation (EC) No 139/2004 *on the control of concentrations between undertakings*, O.J. L 24/1 (2004).

[243] Parliament/Council Directive 2002/21/EC *on a common regulatory framework for electronic communications networks and services* (Framework Directive), O.J. L 108/33 (2002); Parliament/Council Directive 2002/20/EC *on the authorisation of electronic communications networks and services* (Authorisation Directive), O.J. L 108/21 (2002); Parliament/Council Directive 2002/19/EC *on access to, and interconnection of, electronic communications networks and associated facilities* (Access Directive), O.J. L 108/7 (2002); Parliament/Council Directive 2002/22/EC *on universal service and users' rights relating to electronic communications networks and services* (Universal Service Directive), O.J. L 108/51 (2002); Parliament/Council Directive 2002/58/EC *concerning the processing of personal data and the protection of privacy in the electronic communications sector* (Directive on Privacy and Electronic Communications), O.J. L 201/37 (2002). This 2002 Telecoms Package was amended by the 2009 Telecoms Package entailing Parliament/Council Directive 2009/140/EC, O.J. L 337/37 (2009); Parliament/Council Directive 2009/136/EC, O.J. L 337/11 (2009); Parliament/Council Regulation (EC) No 1211/2009, O.J. L 337/1 (2009) (this Regulation expired at the end of 2018 and has been replaced by Parliament/Council Regulation (EU) No 2018/1971 *establishing the Body of European Regulators for Electronic Communications (BEREC) and the Agency for Support for BEREC (BEREC Office)*, O.J. L 321/1 (2018)); and by Parliament/ Council Regulation (EU) No 2015/2120 *laying down measures concerning open internet access*, O.J. L 310/1 (2015), amended by the aforementioned Parliament/Council Regulation (EU) No 2015/1971. More recently, the 2002 Telecoms Package (with the exception of the 2002 Directive on Privacy and Electronic Communications) has been repealed by Parliament/Council Directive 2018/1972/EU *establishing the European Electronic Communications Code (Recast)*, O.J. L 321/ 36 (2018).

addressed to undertakings. Infringements of competition law by private undertakings must be addressed to them under the procedures governing the enforcement of Articles 101 and 102 TFEU contained in Regulation 1/2003 (→ Article 103 TFEU para 19–33, 36–40).[244]

88 In issuing Article 106.3 TFEU decisions to MS, the Commission is obliged to comply with the **general principles of EU law**, including the rights of due process. This means that MS have the right to be heard prior to the adoption of an Article 106.3 TFEU decision.[245] Failure to facilitate a hearing and ensure other rights of due process can result in an Article 106.3 TFEU decision being annulled under Article 263 TFEU (→ Article 263 TFEU).

89 **Article 106.3 TFEU decisions** are more common than directives. The Commission has issued many decisions to MS concerning breaches of Article 106 TFEU and ordered compliance in the postal, telecommunications, airport, transport and broadcasting sectors, for example. It has also issued general decisions under Article 106.3 TFEU, including that on State aid and public service compensation,[246] dealing with the aftermath of the *Altmark* judgment (→ para 75).[247]

List of Cases

ECJ/CJEU
ECJ 14.07.1971, 10/71, *Muller*, ECLI:EU:C:1971:85 [cit. in para 60]
ECJ 30.01.1974, 127/73, *BRT v SABAM*, ECLI:EU:C:1974:25 [cit. in para 14 and 62]
ECJ 30.04.1974, 155/73, *Giuseppe Sacchi*, ECLI:EU:C:1974:40 [cit. in para 14]
ECJ 06.07.1982, 188/80 to 190/80, *France, Italy and United Kingdom v Commission*, ECLI:EU:C:1982:257 [cit. in para 12, 80 and 81]
ECJ 08.11.1983, 96/82 et al., *IAZ v Commission*, ECLI:EU:C:1983:310 [cit. in para 60, 62 and 69]
ECJ 20.03.1985, 41/83, *Italy v Commission*, ECLI:EU:C:1985:120 [cit. in para 42, 60 and 62]
ECJ 04.05.1988, 30/87, *Bodson v Pompes Funèbres des Régions Libérées*, ECLI:EU:C:1988:225 [cit. in para 11 and 60]

---

[244] Council Regulation (EC) No 1/2003 *on the implementation of the rules on competition laid down in Articles 81 and 82 of the Treaty*, O.J. L 1/1 (2003).

[245] Cases C-48 and 66/90, *Netherlands and PTT Nederland v Commission* (ECJ 12 February 1992).

[246] Commission Decision No. 2005/842/EC, O.J. L 312/67 (2005), introduced on the foot of the ruling of Case C-280/00, *Altmark Trans* (ECJ 24 July 2003). This decision was replaced by Commission Decision 2012/21/EU *on the application of Article 106(2) [TFEU] to State aid in the form of public service compensation granted to certain undertakings entrusted with the operation of services of general economic interest*, O.J. L 7/3 (2012).

[247] Case C-280/00, *Altmark Trans* (ECJ 24 July 2003).

ECJ 30.06.1988, 226/87, *Commission v Greece*, ECLI:EU:C:1988:354 [cit. in para 18]
ECJ 11.04.1989, 66/86, *Ahmed Saeed Flugreisen and others v Zentrale zur Bekämpfung unlauteren Wettbewerbs*, ECLI:EU:C:1989:140 [cit. in para 14 and 60]
ECJ 19.03.1991, 202/88, *France v Commission*, ECLI:EU:C:1991:120 [cit. in para 7, 13, 19, 21, 41, 80, 83 and 84]
ECJ 23.04.1991, C-41/90, *Höfner & Elser v Macrotron*, ECLI:EU:C:1991:161 [cit. in para 2, 11, 14, 21, 22, 23, 40, 56, 60, 63, and 69]
ECJ 18.06.1991, C-260/89, *ERT v DEP*, ECLI:EU:C:1991:254 [cit. in para 2, 13, 14, 18, 20, 21, 23, 40, 60 and 76]
ECJ 10.12.1991, C-179/90, *Merci Convenzionali Porto di Genova v Siderurgica Gabrielli*, ECLI:EU:C:1991:464 [cit. in para 2, 14, 18, 21, 24, 40, 63 and 69]
ECJ 13.12.1991, 18/88, *RTT v GB-Inno-BM*, ECLI:EU:C:1991:474 [cit. in para 2, 14, 18, 20, 21, 25, 32, 60, 63, and 69]
ECJ 12.02.1992, C-48/90 and C-66/90, *Netherlands and PTT Nederland v Commission*, ECLI:EU:C:1992:63 [cit. in para 88]
ECJ 17.11.1992, C-271/90, C-281/90 and C-289/90, *Spain, Belgium and Italy v Commission*, ECLI:EU:C:1992:440 [cit. in para 80 and 84]
ECJ 17.02.1993, C-159/91 and C-160/91, *Poucet und Pistre v AGF and Cancava*, ECLI:EU:C:1993:63 [cit. in para 11]
ECJ 19.05.1993, C-320/91, *Corbeau*, ECLI:EU:C:1993:198 [cit. in para 14, 20, 21, 26, 36, 58, 60, 64, 65 and 69]
ECJ 19.01.1994, C-364/92, *SAT Fluggesellschaft mbH v Eurocontrol*, ECLI:EU:C:1994:7 [cit. in para 11]
ECJ 27.04.1994, C-393/92, *Gemeente Almelo and Others v Energiebedriff Ijsselmij NV*, ECLI:EU:C:1994:171 [cit. in para 60 and 64]
ECJ 05.10.1994, C-323/93, *Centre d'insémination de la Crespelle v Coopérative de la Mayenne*, ECLI:EU:C:1994:368 [cit. in para 14, 21, and 27]
ECJ 26.11.1996, C-157/94, Opinion of AG Cosmas, *Commission v Netherlands*, ECLI:EU:C:1996:449 [cit. in para 72]
ECJ 17.07.1997, C-242/95, *GT-Link A/S v Danske Staatsbaner (DSB)*, ECLI:EU:C:1997:376 [cit. in para 21]
ECJ 23.10.1997, C-157/94, *Commission v Netherlands*, ECLI:EU:C:1997:499 [cit. in para 17, 42, 60, 61, 65, 71, 72 and 76]
ECJ 23.10.1997, C-158/94, *Commission v Italy*, ECLI:EU:C:1997:500 [cit. in para 61 and 65]
ECJ 23.10.1997, C-159/94, *Commission v France*, ECLI:EU:C:1997:501 [cit. in para 60, 61, and 65]
ECJ 23.10.1997, C-203/96, Opinion of AG Jacobs, *Chemische Afvalstoffen Dusseldorp and others v Minister van Volkshuisvesting, Ruimtelijke Ordening en Milieubeheer*, ECLI:EU:C:1997:508 [cit. in para 103; 105]
ECJ 23.11.1997, C-160/94, *Commission v Spain*, ECLI:EU:C:1997:502 [cit. in para 61 and 65]

ECJ 11.12.1997, C-55/96, *Job Centre*, ECLI:EU:C:1997:603 [cit. in para 21 and 60]

ECJ 12.02.1998, C-163/96, *Raso and Others*, ECLI:EU:C:1998:54 [cit. in para 14 and 21]

ECJ 18.06.1998, C-266/96, *Corsica Ferries France v Gruppo Antichi Ormeggiatori del porto di Genova and others*, ECLI:EU:C:1998:306 [cit. in para 21, 28, 29, 60, 66 and 73]

ECJ 25.06.1998, C-203/96, *Chemische Afvalstoffen Dusseldorp and others v Minister van Volkshuisvesting, Ruimtelijke Ordening en Milieubeheer*, ECLI:EU:C:1998:316 [cit. in para 13, 51, 55 and 60]

ECJ 21.09.1999, C-67/96, *Albany*, ECLI:EU:C:1999:430 [cit. in para 29, 60 and 67]

ECJ 10.02.2000, C-147/97 and C-148/97, *Deutsche Post AG*, ECLI:EU:C:2000:74 [cit. in para 18, 20, 21, 30, 60 and 67]

ECJ 23.05.2000, C-209/98, *Sydhavnens Sten & Grus*, ECLI:EU:C:2000:279 [cit. in para 13]

ECJ 08.06.2000, C-258/98, *Carra and Others*, ECLI:EU:C:2000:301 [cit. in para 14]

ECJ 25.10.2001, C-475/99, *Ambulanz Glöckner*, ECLI:EU:C:2001:577 [cit. in para 15, 21, 31, 60 and 67]

ECJ 19.02.2002, C-309/99, *Wouters and others*, ECLI:EU:C:2002:98 [cit. in para 11]

ECJ 13.05.2003, C-463/00, *Spain v Commission*, ECLI:EU:C:2003:272 [cit. in para 7 and 41]

ECJ 22.05.2003, C-462/99, *Connect Austria*, ECLI:EU:C:2003:297 [cit. in para 21]

ECJ 24.07.2003, C-280/00, *Altmark Trans*, ECLI:EU:C:2003:415 [cit. in para 48, 75 and 89]

ECJ 22.02.2005, C-141/02, *Commission v max.mobil*, ECLI:EU:C:2005:98 [cit. in para 39]

ECJ 11.07.2006, C-205/03 P, *FENIN v Commission*, ECLI:EU:C:2006:453 [cit. in para 11]

ECJ 01.07.2008, C-49/07, *MOTOE*, ECLI:EU:C:2008:376 [cit. in para 15, 21, 29, 32, 42, and 51]

ECJ 20.10.2009, C-265/08, Opinion of AG Colomer, *Federutility and Others*, ECLI:EU:C:2009:640 [cit. in para 58]

CJEU 03.03.2011, C-437/09, *AG2R Prévoyance*, ECLI:EU:C:2011:112 [cit. in para 14 and 21]

CJEU 17.07.2014, C-553/12 P, *Commission v DEI*, ECLI:EU:C:2014:2083 [cit. in para 12, 14, 20, 21, 33 and 36]

CJEU 17.07.2014, C-554/12 P, *Commission v DEI*, ECLI:EU:C:2014:2085 [cit. in para 34]

CJEU 30.06.2016, spiepr132C-293/15, spiepr132 *Slovenská pošta v Commission*, ECLI:EU:C:2016:51 [cit. in para 14, 37 and 68]
CJEU 07.08.2016, C-121/15, *ANODE*, ECLI:EU:C:2016:637 51 [cit. in para 47]

GC/CFI

CFI 04.03.2003, T-319/99, *FENIN v Commission*, ECLI:EU:T:2003:50 [cit. in para 11]
CFI 04.03.2005, T-289/03, *BUPA and others v Commission*, ECLI:EU:T:2008:29 [cit. in para 51, 52, 59 and 60]
GC 20.09.2012, T-169/08, *DEI v Commission*, ECLI:EU:T:2012:448 [cit. in para 12 and 35]
GC 20.09.2012, T-421/09, *DEI v Commission*, nyr [cit. in para 34]
GC 25.03.2015, T-556/08, *Slovenská pošta v Commission*, ECLI:EU:T:2009:443 [cit. in para 14, 20, 21, 37, 42, 60, 68 and 69]
GC 15.12.2016, T-169/08 RENV, *DEI v Commission*, ECLI:EU:T:2016:733 [cit. in para 36]
GC 15.12.2016, T-421/09 RENV, *DEI v Commission* ECLI:EU:T:2016:748 [cit. in para 34]

References

Babirad, R. (2014). European Commission v Dimosia Epicheirisi Ilektrismou AE (DEI). *European Competition Law Review, 35*(12), 613–616.
Bartosch, A. (2001). Joined Cases C-147/97 and C-148/97, Deutsche Post AG v. Gesellschaft für Zahlungssysteme mbH (GZS) and Citicop Kartenservice GmbH CKG. Judgment of the Full Court of 10 February 2000. *Common Market Law Review, 38*(1), 195–210.
Bekkedal, T. (2011). Article 106 TFEU is dead. Long live Article 106 TFEU! In E. Szyszczak, J. Davies, M. Andenæs, & T. Bekkedal (Eds.), *Developments in services of general interest* (pp. 61–102). T.M.C. Asser Press.
Buendia Sierra, J. L. (1999). *Exclusive rights and State monopolies under EC law: Article 86 (former Article 90) of the EC Treaty*. OUP.
Davies, G. (2009). Article 86 EC, the EC's economic approach to competition law and the general interest. *European Competition Journal, 5*(2), 549–584.
Ezrachi, A. (2014). *EU competition law, an analytical guide to the leading cases*. Hart Publishing.
Fiedziuk, N. (2011). Services of general economic interest and the Treaty of Lisbon: Opening doors to a whole new approach or maintaining the "status quo". *European Law Review, 36*(2), 226–242.
Flynn, L. (1999). Competition policy and public services in EC law after the Maastricht and Amsterdam Treaties. In D. O'Keefe & P. Twomey (Eds.), *Legal issues of the Amsterdam Treaty* (pp. 185–201). Hart Publishing.
Goyder, J., & Alborens-Llorens, A. (2009). *Goyder's EC competition law*. OUP.
Hancher, L. (1994). Case C-320/91 P, *Procureur du Roi v. Paul Corbeau*, Judgment of the full Court, 19 May 1993. *Common Market Law Review, 31*(1), 105–122.
Hancher, L. (1999). Community, State and market. In P. Craig & G. de Búrca (Eds.), *The evolution of EU law* (pp. 721–743). OUP.

Hancher, L., & Sauter, W. (2014). Public services and EU law. In C. Barnard & S. Peers (Eds.), *European Union law* (pp. 539–567). OUP.

Hatzopoulos, V. (2011). The concept of 'economic activity' in the EU treaty: From ideological dead-ends to workable judicial concepts. *College of Europe European Legal Studies Research Paper in Law*.

Jones, A., Sufrin, B., & Dunne, N. (2019). *Jones and Sufrin's EU competition law: Text, cases and materials* (7th ed.).

Korah, V. (2007). *An introductory guide to EC competition law and practice*. Hart Publishing.

Lane, R. (2000). *EC competition law*. Pearson.

Lenaerts, K. (2012). Defining the concept of 'services of general interest' in light of the 'checks and balances' set out in the EU treaties. *Jurisprudence, 19*(14), 1247–1267.

Neergard, U. (2011). The Commission's soft law in the area of services of general economic interest. In E. Szyszczak, J. Davies, M. Andenaes, & T. Bekkedal (Eds.), *Developments in services of general economic interest* (pp. 37–59). Springer.

Pech, P. (2008). *The European Union and its constitution, from Rome to Lisbon*. Clarus Press.

Ross, M. (2000). Article 16 EC and services of general interest: From derogation to obligation. *European Law Review, 25*(1), 22–38.

Ross, M. (2009). A healthy approach to services of general economic interest? The BUPA judgment of the Court of First Instance. *European Law Review, 34*(1), 127–140.

Sauter, W. (2008). Services of general economic interest and universal service in EU law. *European Law Review, 33*(2), 167–193.

Sauter, W. (2014). The Altmark package mark II: New rules for State aid and the compensation of services of general economic interest. *European Competition Law Review, 33*(7), 307–313.

Szydło, M. (2011). The process of granting exclusive rights in the light of treaty rules on free movement. *German Law Journal, 12*(7), 1408–1445.

Szyszczak, E. (2011). Controlling dominance in European markets. *Fordham International Law Journal, 33*(6), 1738–1775.

Van Cleynenbreugel, P. (2014). No privatisation in the service of fair competition? Article 345 TFEU and the EU market-state balance after Essent. *European Law Review, 39*(2), 264–275.

Vermeersch, A. (2009). Case C-49/07, Motosykletistiki Omospondia Ellados NPID (MOTOE) v Elliniko Dimosio, judgment of the Court of Justice (Grand Chamber) of 1 July 2008, not yet reported. *Common Market Law Review, 46*(4), 1327–1341.

Whish, R., & Bailey, D. (2021). *Competition law* (10th ed.). OUP.

Zevgolis, N. (2012). Anti-competitive conduct from public or privileged enterprises: Towards a per se abuse of dominant position? Applicability of the provision of TFEU Article 106(2) by national competition authorities. *European Competition Law Review, 33*(2), 84–90.

Section 2
Aids Granted by States

Article 107 [Prohibition of State Aid]
(ex-Article 87 TEC)

1. Save as otherwise provided in the Treaties, any aid[1–19] granted by a Member State[20–25] or through State resources in any form whatsoever[26–32] which distorts or threatens to distort competition[70,71] by favouring certain undertakings or the production of certain goods[33–53, 54–66] shall, in so far as it affects trade between Member States,[67–69] be incompatible with the internal market.
2. The following shall be compatible with the internal market:

   (a) aid having a social character, granted to individual consumers, provided that such aid is granted without discrimination related to the origin of the products concerned;[74]

   (b) aid to make good the damage caused by natural disasters or exceptional occurrences;[75]

   (c) aid granted to the economy of certain areas of the Federal Republic of Germany affected by the division of Germany, in so far as such aid is required in order to compensate for the economic disadvantages caused by that division. Five years after the entry into force of the Treaty of Lisbon, the Council, acting on a proposal from the Commission, may adopt a decision repealing this point.[76]

3. The following may be considered to be compatible with the internal market:[77–86]

   (a) aid to promote the economic development of areas where the standard of living is abnormally low or where there is serious underemployment, and of the regions referred to in Article 349, in view of their structural, economic and social situation;[80]

   (b) aid to promote the execution of an important project of common European interest or to remedy a serious disturbance in the economy of a Member State;[81]

   (c) aid to facilitate the development of certain economic activities or of certain economic areas, where such aid does not adversely affect trading conditions to an extent contrary to the common interest;[82]

   (d) aid to promote culture and heritage conservation where such aid does not affect trading conditions and competition in the Union to an extent that is contrary to the common interest;[83]

   (e) such other categories of aid as may be specified by decision of the Council on a proposal from the Commission.[84]

Contents

1. The Concept of State Aid 1
2. The Involvement of State Resources 20
   2.1. Transfer of State Resources 20
   2.2. Through the State in Any Form Whatsoever: The Criterion of Imputability to the State 26
3. Advantage 33
   3.1. The Concept of an Economic Advantage 33
   3.2. The Market Economy Operator Test: The Standard Test for Assessing an Advantage 36
   3.3. Market Economy Investor Test: The MEO Test Applied to Investments 39
   3.4. The Private Creditor Test: The MEO Test Applied to Obtain Payment of Debtors 42
   3.5. The Private Vendor Test: The MEO Test Applied to the Vending of Goods 46
   3.6. The *Altmark* Test: Specific Test to Assess Whether a Measure Constitutes Compensation for a Public Service 49
4. Selectivity 54
5. Effect on Inter-State Trade 67
6. Distortion of Competition 70
7. Exemptions to the State Aid Prohibition of Article 107.1 TFEU 72
   7.1. De jure Exemptions: Article 107.2 TFEU 73
   7.2. Discretionary Exemptions 77
      7.2.1. Exemptions Under Article 107.3 TFEU 77
      7.2.2. Exemption Under Article 106.2 TFEU for Services of General Economic Interest 87
      7.2.3. Exemption Under Article 93 TFEU for the Coordination of Transport ... 92
List of Cases
References

1. The Concept of State Aid

1 Article 107.1 TFEU provides that, save as otherwise provided in the Treaties, any **aid** granted by an MS or through State resources in any form whatsoever which distorts or threatens to distort competition by favouring certain undertakings or the production of certain goods shall, in so far as it affects trade between MS, be **incompatible with the common market**.

2 The **notion of State aid** was developed by the Court as an objective legal concept.[1] According to the Court's settled case law a measure constitutes 'State aid' if all the conditions of Article 107.1 TFEU are fulfilled.[2] Accordingly, Article 107.1 TFEU prohibits State aids to undertakings or productions if **five conditions** are fulfilled. First, an aid must be granted by the State or granted through

---

[1] Case C-362/19 P, *Commission v Fútbol Club Barcelona* (CJEU 4 March 2021) para 61.
[2] Case C-522/13, *Ministerio de Defensa and Navantia* (CJEU 9 October 2014); Case C-399/08 P, *Commission v Deutsche Post* (CJEU 2 September 2010) para 38.

State resources (→ para 20 et seqq.). Second, an aid must confer an advantage to one or more undertakings (→ para 33 et seqq.). Third, the aid must be selective, favouring an undertaking or a specific group of undertakings (→ para 4 et seqq.). Fourth, the aid must be liable to affect trade between MS (→ para 67 et seqq.). Finally, the aid must distort or threaten to distort competition (→ para 70 et seqq.).[3] Article 107.1 TFEU requires that all these conditions be cumulatively fulfilled.[4]

Since State aid is an **objective concept**, all types of State measures which favour certain undertakings directly or indirectly are regarded as State aid.[5] That is the case when an advantage is obtained under **conditions that deviate from normal market circumstances** (→ para 35 et seqq.).[6]

3

Clear examples of State aids are financial transactions such as **subsidies or measures with an equivalent effect to a subsidy**. Such measures may include financial instruments such as loans and guarantees at below market rates.[7] Other forms of State intervention on the market which may be considered as State aid are: the lowering costs of capital,[8] distribution,[9] labour,[10] production[11] and energy.[12] Also the reduction of direct or indirect taxation[13] or social security contributions;[14] export aid,[15] lower charges for goods or services delivered by public undertakings;[16] rescue- and restructuring aid;[17] land sales at below market rates;[18] and financial incentives for privatisation[19] or research and development[20] can be considered to be types of State aid.

4

---

[3] Case C-74/16, *Congregación de Escuelas Pías Provincia de Betania* (CJEU 27 June 2017) para 78.

[4] Case C-74/16, *Congregación de Escuelas Pías Provincia de Betania* (CJEU 27 June 2017) para 38; Cyndecka (2016), p. 150.

[5] Case C-362/19 P, *Commission v Fútbol Club Barcelona* (CJEU 4 March 2021) para 61; Case C-399/08 P, *Commission v Deutsche Post* (CJEU 2 September 2010) para 40.

[6] Case C-270/15 P, *Belgium v Commission* (CJEU 30 June 2016) para 34.

[7] Case C-518/13, *Eventech* (CJEU 14 January 2015) para 33.

[8] Case C-20/15 P, *World Duty Free* (CJEU 21 December 2016).

[9] Case C-233/16, *ANGED* (CJEU 26 April 2018); Case C-526/04, *Labotoires Boiron* (ECJ 7 September 2006).

[10] Case T-89/09, *Pollmeier Massivholz* (GC 17 March 2015).

[11] Case C-329/15, *ENEA* (CJEU 13 September 2017).

[12] Case C-329/15, *ENEA* (CJEU 13 September 2017).

[13] Case C-374/17, *A-Brauerei* (CJEU 19 December 2018) para 53.

[14] Case C-211/15 P, *Orange v Commission* (CJEU 26 October 2016).

[15] Case C-20/15 P, *World Duty Free* (CJEU 21 December 2016).

[16] Case C-446/14 P, *Germany v Commission* (CJEU 18 February 2016).

[17] Joined Cases C-533/12 P and C-536/12 P, *SNCM and Corsica Ferries* (CJEU 4 September 2014).

[18] Case C-39/14, *BVVG v Jerichower Land* (CJEU 16 July 2015); Case C-239/09, *Seydaland* (CJEU 16 December 2010).

[19] Case C-214/12 P, *Land Burgenland v Commission* (CJEU 24 October 2013).

[20] Case C-677/11, *Doux Élevage v Ministère de l'Agriculture* (CJEU 30 May 2015).

5   Article 107.1 TFEU is **not restricted to subsidising measures**. State measures that reduce or absolve charges that under normal market conditions would have to be paid by undertakings also constitute State aid.[21] Measures that mitigate the charges which are normally included in the budget of an undertaking, and which thus, without being subsidies in the strict sense of the word, are similar in character and have a comparable effect to subsidies.[22] The Court, for example, ruled that the costs linked to remuneration of employees naturally place a burden on the budgets of undertakings, irrespective of whether or not those costs stem from legal obligations or collective agreements.[23]

6   These types of measures are similar to subsidies and have the same character and effect.[24] Consequently, to determining the existence of State aid, a **clear link** must be established **between State intervention**, by the State or through State resources and **an advantage conferred to an undertaking**.[25] A reduction of the budget of an MS or a sufficiently concrete economic risk on that budget is, however, a clear indication for an existing type of aid and must be examined under Article 107.1 TFEU.[26]

7   Type of aids granted through resources other than those of the State do not fall within the scope of Article 107.1 TFEU.[27] Accordingly, Article 107.1 TFEU exclusively refers to **State resources** or aid granted through State resources, whereas so-called **Union aid** does not fall within the scope of the EU State aid regime because MS enjoy no discretion in the allocation of Union aid funds.[28]

8   Similar to **Articles 101 and 102 TFEU**, Article 107.1 TFEU applies exclusively to the **functional concept of undertakings**, which includes all entities that provide economic activities by offering goods and/or services on a market ($\rightarrow$ Article 101 TFEU para 23 et seqq.).[29] Consequently, both private undertakings and public owned undertakings fall within the scope of Article 107.1 TFEU.[30]

9   The Court has interpreted the concept of State aid **as broad as possible**.[31] The reason for this is that the prohibition of Article 107.1 TFEU and the concepts of this provision cannot be easily circumvented by the MS. In addition to the Court, the

---

[21] Case T-47/15, *Germany v Commission* (GC 10 May 2016) para 112; Joined Cases C-164/15 P and C-165/15 P, *Aer Lingus* (CJEU 21 December 2016) para 104–105.

[22] Case C-518/13, *Eventech* (CJEU 14 January 2015) para 33; Case C-81/10 P, *France Télécom v Commission* (CJEU 8 December 2011) para 16.

[23] Case C-211/15 P, *Orange v Commission* (CJEU 26 October 2016).

[24] Case C-73/11 P, *Frucona Košice v Commission* (CJEU 24 January 2013) para 69.

[25] Case C-518/13, *Eventech* (CJEU 14 January 2015) para 34.

[26] Hancher et al. (2021), p. 64. See also Case C-596/19 P, *Commission v Hungary* (CJEU 16 March 2021) para 36.

[27] Case C-649/15 P, *TV2/Danmark v Commission* (CJEU 9 November 2017).

[28] Hancher et al. (2021), p. 76.

[29] Case C-437/09, *AG2R Prévoyance* (CJEU 3 March 2011) para 42; Joined Cases C-262/18 P and C-271/18 P, *Commission v Dôvera zdravotná poist'ovňa* (CJEU 11 June 2020) para 29.

[30] Hancher et al. (2021), pp. 48–49.

[31] Aalbers and Ottervanger (2019), pp. 779–780.

Commission has asserted an important role in explaining the application of these concepts by adopting a Communication on the notion of State aid.[32] Article 107.1 TFEU leaves only a very limited discretion for the MS to derogate from this prohibition in cases of taxes and public service obligations (→ para 49 et seqq.).

To be considered as State aid, a measure must be imputable to the State for it to fall within the scope of Article 107.1 TFEU. The concept of **aid imputable to the State** is closely connected with the concept of an aid granted through State resources. Both concepts have a broad application range.

10

The concept of **selectivity**, which is a constituent factor for the application of Article 107.1 TFEU, can be determined by the assessment whether a national measure favours 'certain undertakings or the production of certain goods' over other undertakings which, in the light of the objective pursued by that regime, are in a comparable factual and legal situation and who accordingly are treated differently without an objective justification.[33]

11

The central assessment of Article 107.1 TFEU is to determine whether a State measure confers an **economic advantage** upon one or more undertakings. In addition to the concept of selectivity, the concept of an economic advantage must be interpreted also very broadly.[34] According to the Court's settled case law, measures which are likely to favour certain undertakings directly or indirectly, qualify as an economic advantage by the State in case the recipient undertaking would not have obtained this advantage under normal market conditions.[35] In case the State concludes a financial transaction with one or more undertaking under conditions and circumstances which correspond to **normal market conditions**, an economic advantage—within the notion of State aid of Article 107.1 TFEU—may be precluded.[36]

12

Whether or not aid measures are intentionally designed to provide economic advantages to undertakings is not relevant for the application of Article 107.1 TFEU.[37] The decisive factor is not the objective of the aid but rather the *potential* **adverse effects on trade and competition**.[38] Conferring an advantage leads in most cases to a potential effect on trade and competition.

13

---

[32] Commission, *Notice on the notion of State aid in Article 107.1 TFEU*, O.J. C 262 (2016); See also Biondi and Stefan (2018).

[33] Case C-20/15 P, *World Duty Free* (CJEU 21 December 2016); Case C-403/10 P, *Mediaset v Commission* (CJEU 28 July 2011) para 36; Joined Cases C-106/09 P and C-107/09 P, *Gibraltar* (CJEU 15 November 2011) para 75 and 101; Case C-518/13, *Eventech* (CJEU 14 January 2015) para 53–55; Case C-15/14 P, *Commission v MOL* (CJEU 4 June 2015) para 59.

[34] Buendía Sierra (2018).

[35] Joined Cases C-197/11 and C-203/11, *Libert* (CJEU 8 May 2013) para 83; Case C-164/15 P, *Aer Lingus* (CJEU 21 December 2016) para 36–41. Werner and Verouden (2017), pp. 17–19.

[36] Case C-73/11 P, *Frucona Košice* (CJEU 24 January 2013) para 70; Case C-131/15 P, *Club Hotel Loutraki* (CJEU 21 December 2016) para 72–73.

[37] Case C-164/15 P, *Aer Lingus* (CJEU 21 December 2016) para 99–100.

[38] Zelger (2018); Case C-524/14 P, *Hansestadt Lübeck* (CJEU 21 December 2016) para 48–49; Case C-20/15 P, *World Duty Free* (CJEU 21 December 2016) para 74.

The assessment of Article 107.1 TFEU therefore does not require that a real effect on trade is established, nor does it require that competition be distorted.[39] The Court applies a very broad interpretation.[40] In *Banco Privado Português*, it made clear that it is not necessary to proof whether an aid measure had an actual adverse effect on the internal market. A causal link between financial aid and the strengthening of the position of an undertaking on the market can be considered to have a potential effect on the internal market.[41] The Court only determines whether an aid is *liable* to have an adverse effect on trade and a potential effect on competition.[42] Accordingly, the Commission is not required to carry out an economic analysis of the actual situation on the relevant markets, nor does it need to take the market share of the recipient undertakings or the actual trade flows between MS into consideration for applying the concept of State aid.[43]

14   The concept of State aid is in principle applied by the Court to **every imaginable economic sector**, including economic sectors that have not been (fully) harmonised by EU legislation.[44] Excluding certain economic sectors from the notion of State aid would lead to a circumvention of the conditions of Article 107.1 TFEU and would strengthen the financial position of certain undertakings or productions, and to the detriment of other operators.[45] The concept of State aid applies to every economic activity performed by an undertaking.

15   Article 107.1 TFEU makes **no distinction between the causes or the objectives of State aid** but defines aid measures in relation to their effects.[46] Therefore, the Court has ruled out that economic or social policy goals of the MS can override the State aid prohibition of Article 107.1 TFEU.[47] Social unrest, dangers to public order, unemployment, and the disruption of normal economic life cannot be considered as grounds for derogation within Article 107.1 TFEU.[48] But such objectives can play an important role in the application of the **compatibility tests**

---

[39] Case C-74/16, *Congregación de Escuelas Pías Provincia de Betania* (CJEU 27 June 2017) para 78; Case C-659/17, *Azienda Napoletana Mobilità* (CJEU 29 July 2019) para 29.

[40] Werner and Verouden (2017), pp. 2, 16–25.

[41] Case C-667/13, *Banco Privado Português* (CJEU 5 March 2015); Case C-518/13, *Eventech* (CJEU 14 January 2015) para 65; Case 197/11, *Libert* (CJEU 8 May 2013) para 76.

[42] Case C-74/16, *Congregación de Escuelas Pías Provincia de Betania* (CJEU 27 June 2017) para 78; Case C-659/17, *Azienda Napoletana Mobilità* (CJEU 29 July 2019) para 29.

[43] Case C-164/15 P, *Aer Lingus* (CJEU 21 December 2016); Case C-131/15, *Club Hotel Loutraki* (CJEU 21 December 2016); Case C-69/13, *Mediaset v Commission* (CJEU 13 February 2014) para 145; Case C-197/11 *Libert* (CJEU 8 May 2013) para 76.

[44] Quigley (2015), p. 14; see also Case T-538/11, *Belgium v Commission* (GC 25 March 2015) para 65.

[45] Bacon (2017), pp. 12–13.

[46] Case C-362/19 P, *Commission v Fútbol Club Barcelona* (CJEU 4 March 2021) para 61.

[47] Case C-431/14 P, *Greece v Commission* (CJEU 8 March 2016) para 59; Case C-63/14, *Commission v France* (CJEU 9 June 2015) para 52–53.

[48] Case C-63/14, *Commission v France* (CJEU 9 July 2015) para 52–53.

under Articles 107.2, 107.3, and 106.2 TFEU. Under Article 107.2 TFEU, MS must notify with the Commission, however, the aid categories under Article 107.2 TFEU apply automatically.[49] Under Articles 107.3 and 106.2 TFEU, the Commission has exclusive powers to determine whether aid is compatible with the internal market. Such exemptions can also be found in Article 43 TFEU for the agricultural sector and in Articles 93 and 98 TFEU for the transport sector.[50] As a result, the MS are not allowed to deviate from Article 107.1 TFEU, without the distinct permission of the Commission.[51]

In addition, Article 107.1 TFEU applies to **all the various State authorities** within an MS. The concept of the 'State' includes therefore not only centralised or federal authorities but also autonomous or fully or semi-dependant local and regional authorities,[52] public undertakings,[53] and private bodies established or appointed by the State to administer certain state resources.[54]

16

The concept of State aid is based on the existence of a financial or economic relationship between the State and undertakings.[55] Consequently, this concept **does not include advantages** for a particular undertaking or branch of industry that may result from legal or administrative measures which are **not directly quantifiable in pecuniary terms**.[56] For example certain employment conditions[57] and income transfers between undertakings to promote the use of 'green' electricity do not fall within the scope of Article 107.1 TFEU.[58]

17

Although the effect of aid measures takes preference over the objectives of the MS, the Court has ruled that the concept of State aid does not per definition apply to measures which may **differentiate between undertakings** if this differentiation arises from the general structure of the national legal system of which these measures are part of.[59] For the determination whether differentiation between undertakings results into State aid, the Court developed a **non-discrimination** doctrine which enables it and the Commission to assess whether prima facie selective measures discriminate or can be justified.[60]

18

---

[49] Hancher et al. (2021), pp. 135–142.

[50] Hancher et al. (2021), pp. 123, 512, 705.

[51] Aalbers and Ottervanger (2019).

[52] Hofmann (2016), p. 65. See for example Case C-233/16, *ANGED* (CJEU 26 April 2018) para 41.

[53] Hancher et al. (2021), p. 47. See also Case C-329/15, *ENEA* (CJEU 13 September 2017) para 23.

[54] Case C-329/15, *ENEA* (CJEU 13 September 2017) para 23, 25.

[55] Piernas López (2015), pp. 20–25.

[56] Hancher et al. (2021), p. 62.

[57] Joined Cases C-533/12 P and C-536/12 P, *SNCM and Corsica Ferries* (CJEU 4 September 2014) para 24.

[58] Case C-329/15, *ENEA* (CJEU 13 September 2017) para 24–26; Case C-379/98, *PreussenElektra* (ECJ 13 March 2001) para 58.

[59] Case C-78/08, *Paint Graphos* (CJEU 8 September 2011); Joined Cases C-106/09 P and C-107/09 P, *Gibraltar* (CJEU 15 November 2011) para 45.

[60] Case C-233/16, *ANGED* (CJEU 26 April 2018) para 42.

19 Especially in tax cases, the Court has applied this non-discrimination '**material selectivity test**' to ascertain whether prima facie selective measures were objectively justified within the scope of Article 107.1 TFEU (→ para 54 et seqq.).[61] The Court's case law requires that the authorities of the MS, but also the Commission have to carry out a comprehensive review of alleged infringements of Article 107.1 TFEU by tax schemes and should take into account both the objectives and the effects of State measures.[62] Above all, the exemption of tax schemes based on external objectives which are not intrinsic to the national tax system are prohibited under Article 107.1 TFEU, since such schemes would circumvent the conditions of this provision (further → para 55 et seqq.).[63]

2. The Involvement of State Resources

2.1. Transfer of State Resources

20 Article 107.1 TFEU applies to **State intervention** by means of providing an **advantage granted by the State or through State resources**. The Court has interpreted the concept of State resources very broadly by covering both direct payments to undertakings and indirect transfers from the State budget.[64] Therefore, positive benefits, but also the mitigation of charges, can be considered as including State resources.[65] As a rule of thumb, the Court assesses whether State measures may result in a reduction of the State budget.[66] If there is an effect on the budget, then the condition of intervention through State resources is met.[67] State resources are also involved in case a financial transaction poses a sufficiently concrete economic burden on the State budget.[68] For the Commission, it is sufficient to demonstrate that there is a potential risk that the budget of an MS will be affected by the measure.[69]

---

[61] Hancher et al. (2021), pp. 85–86; Hofmann (2016), p. 129.

[62] See Buendía Sierra (2018); see also Panci (2018). See also for an overview Lovhdahl Gormsen (2019); Case C-337/19 P, *Commission v Belgium (Magnetrol International)* (CJEU 16 September 2021).

[63] See Rapp (2018); Joined Cases C-78/08 to C-80/08, *Paint Graphos* (CJEU 8 September 2011) para 70 and 91.

[64] Case C-657/15 P, *TV2 Danmark* (CJEU 9 November 2017).

[65] Case C-81/10 P, *France Télécom v Commission* (CJEU 8 December 2011) para 16; Case C-518/13, *Eventech* (CJEU 14 January 2015) para 33.

[66] Case C-39/14, *BVVG v Jerichower Land* (CJEU 16 July 2015) para 26.

[67] Hofmann (2016), p. 65.

[68] Joined Cases C-399/10 P and C-401/10 P, *Bouygues Télécom v Commission* (CJEU 19 March 2013) para 109.

[69] Hancher et al. (2021), pp. 64–65.

The **State budget** encompasses the budget of all public and private entities that fall under the control by the State.[70] For determining the degree of control by the State, the objectives of those entities are of no concern.[71] Almost every financial transfer between public companies or private holdings and recipient undertakings is covered by Article 107.1 TFEU.[72] Accordingly even private sources, may qualify as State resources if they fall under **State control**.[73]

An exception to the concept of State resources concerns the so-called **self-financed aid**.[74] This type of aid can be described as charges to undertakings in a certain sector which are entirely re-distributed within that same sector.[75]

In some situations, the **distribution of funds** cannot be qualified as State resources due to the lack of sufficient State control. In *Pearle* and *Doux Elévages*, the Court ruled that resources, which are reserved by a private trade organisation cannot be considered as 'State recourses' if the State only plays an instrumental role by declaring a financial contribution to a trade organisation compulsory.[76] Even if the distribution of funds has the effect of conferring an advantage to undertakings, a sufficient degree of State control is the measurement for determining whether State resources are involved.[77] In *PreussenElektra*, the Court considered that an obligation imposed by a statutory measure on private electricity suppliers to purchase electricity produced from renewable energy sources at fixed minimum prices did not involve any State resources.[78] The Court ruled that the private electricity suppliers were not appointed by the State to manage the aid scheme. On the contrary, they were obliged to purchase a renewable energy from their own resources. Accordingly, the producers of renewable energy received **funding through private entities**, which were not under the control of the State.[79]

However, the *PreussenElektra* judgment may not be relied upon by undertakings too easily.[80] In *Austria v Commission*, the GC held that an aid mechanism for green energy and an exemption mechanism for energy-intensive businesses were established under national law and therefore were attributable to the Austria.[81] A measure does not include State resources, if financial resources flow directly from one private undertaking to another, without any interference from a public or

---

[70] Hancher et al. (2021), pp. 64–65.
[71] Case C-262/12, *Vent de Colère* (CJEU 19 December 2013).
[72] See Nicolaides (2018).
[73] Case C-329/15, *ENEA* (13 September 2017).
[74] Case C-329/15, *ENEA* (13 September 2017).
[75] Case C-379/98, *PreussenElektra* (ECJ 13 March 2001).
[76] Hancher (2017), p. 152. Case C-677/11, *Doux Élevage v Ministère de l'Agriculture* (CJEU 30 May 2015).
[77] Joined Cases C-72/91 and C-73/91, *Sloman Neptune* (ECJ 17 March 1993).
[78] Case C-379/98, *PreussenElektra* (ECJ 13 March 2001) para 59–60.
[79] Case C-379/98, *PreussenElektra* (ECJ 13 March 2001) para 63–65.
[80] Hancher et al. (2021), pp. 65–69.
[81] Case T-251/11, *Austria v Commission* (GC 11 December 2014).

private entity designated by the State.[82] In the Austrian scheme, as opposed to the situation in *PreussenElektra*, the required amount of charges for energy-intensive businesses was reduced. As a result, the measure had the *effect* **of a reduction of the State revenues**.

25 In *Vent de Colère*, the Court ruled that compulsory payments by private bodies must be considered as the transfer of State resources, in case the **State appoints private entities to manage the provision of given advantages**.[83] Moreover, the *PreussenElektra* judgment focuses on the concept of State resources and not on the aid granted through State resources in any form whatsoever.[84] State control can take various forms, by appointment of public tasks but also in other ways.[85] The General Court and Court of Justice have dismissed several cases in which recipients or the State claimed that the State lacked control over sectoral distribution funds. In the following, the nexus between State resources and the degree of control of State regulation will be explained in the light of the concept of imputability to the State (→ para 26 et seqq.).

2.2. Through the State in Any Form Whatsoever: The Criterion of Imputability to the State

26 The distinction between '**aid granted by an MS**' and **aid granted 'through State resources'** does not signify that all advantages granted by a State, whether financed through State resources or not, constitute State aid. This distinction is merely intended to bring both advantages, which are granted directly by the State and those granted by a public or private body designated or established by the State.[86]

27 In addition to the involvement of measures that affect the State budget, a measure must also be **imputable to the State** to be classified as State aid under Article 107.1 TFEU.[87] The wording of 'through the State in any form whatsoever' has been construed by the Court as a condition of imputability. The imputability requirement is essentially based on the assessment of the degree of influence of the State over the distribution of resources with a pecuniary value.[88] Influence of the State over the distribution of funding can take the form of control and beyond.[89]

28 Especially in situations in which public or private undertakings are transferring financial resources the requirement of imputability can be important for the assessment of whether a measure constitutes State aid. Clear examples of imputability

---

[82] Case T-57/15, *Trajektna luka Split* (GC 14 September 2016).
[83] Case C-262/12, *Vent de Colère* (CJEU 19 December 2013).
[84] Hancher et al. (2021), p. 64.
[85] Quigley (2015), pp. 153–186.
[86] Case T-47/15, *Germany v Commission* (GC 10 May 2016).
[87] Case C-128/16 P, *Bankia* (CJEU 25 July 2018).
[88] Hancher et al. (2021), pp. 71–73.
[89] Case C-482/99, *France v Commission (Stardust Marine)* (ECJ 16 March 2002) para 37–38.

arise when the **State designates a private or public entity** to administer the provision of aids.[90] When public authorities designate a private or public entity to administer aid to undertakings, the transfer of State resources is considered to be imputable to the State.[91] The imputability requirement is not easily met if the aid is granted through one or more intermediate public or private entities which are *not* directly designated by the State to provide such aids.[92]

To determine whether the transfer of State resources through public or private entities is imputable to the State depends on the **degree of influence** over these undertakings.[93] One type of influence is State control.[94] In *Commerz v Havenbedrijf Rotterdam*, the Court cleared that the mere fact that a public undertaking is influenced or under control by the State does not automatically lead to the conclusion that the public undertaking cannot act autonomously.[95] The Court ruled that even if the State is in a position to control a public undertaking and to exercise a decisive influence over it that the actual exercise of that control in a particular case cannot be automatically presumed.[96] Accordingly, it is also necessary to examine whether public authorities were actually involved in the adoption an aid measure.[97]

The mere fact that a private entity is a concession holder and is bound to provide services against remuneration rates established by the State, does not suffice to determine whether such an entity falls under State control. In *Trajektna Luka Split*, the GC ruled that in such a case it cannot be assumed that the **concession holder** actually transfers State resources.[98] Acting upon national legislation on services tariffs does therefore not automatically result in a financial transfer imputable to the State.[99]

Whether a measure is imputable depends on the specific facts of the individual case. Specific **indicators for imputability** may include: the degree of integration of the public undertaking; the nature of the undertaking's activities; the degree of autonomy a legal body enjoys with regard to following directives from the State, and the extent to which the undertaking in question operates in the relevant market under normal conditions of competition.[100]

---

[90] Hancher et al. (2021), p. 71.
[91] Hancher et al. (2021), pp. 71–73.
[92] Nicolaides (2017c).
[93] Case C-329/15, *ENEA* (CJEU 13 September 2017) para 25–26.
[94] Case C-482/99, *Stardust Marine* (ECJ 16 May 2002) para 34.
[95] Case C-242/13, *Commerz Nederland v Havenbedrijf Rotterdam* (CJEU 23 October 2014).
[96] Case C-242/13, *Commerz Nederland v Havenbedrijf Rotterdam* (CJEU 23 October 2014) para 31.
[97] Case C-482/99, *Stardust Marine* (ECJ 16 May 2002) para 50–52.
[98] Case T-57/15, *Trajektna Luka Split* (GC 14 September 2016).
[99] Case T-57/15, *Trajektna Luka Split* (GC 14 September 2016).
[100] Hancher et al. (2021), pp. 71–73.

32 In *ENEA*, the Court stated that the State can also be imputed for funds distributed by private undertakings that fall outside State control.[101] In *Stardust Marine* it ruled that a measure is imputable if the transfer of State resources can be **attributed to some form of government decision**.[102] Moreover, even unauthorised guarantees, deliberately and secretly granted by officials of public undertakings, may result in aid that can be imputed to the State, unless the State can demonstrate that the aid would have been opposed by the responsible public authority had it been aware of such conduct.[103]

3. Advantage

3.1. The Concept of an Economic Advantage

33 Article 107.1 TFEU is applicable to the advantages granted by a State to one or more undertakings. The concept of an advantage can be considered as the most important objective concept of Article 107.1 TFEU to be determined. This concept has been developed by the Court as any **economic benefit which an undertaking would not have obtained** under normal market conditions.[104] Measures that may directly or indirectly favour certain undertakings are to be regarded as an economic advantage, which the recipient undertaking would not have obtained under normal market conditions.[105] To establish whether an undertaking would have obtained such an advantage from the State under normal market conditions, the objectives and their grounds for justification have no bearing whatsoever.[106]

34 Article 107.1 TFEU makes no distinction according to the causes or aims of the State measures but characterises them based on their effects.[107] For the fulfilment of the criterion of an advantage, the single fact that a **recipient financially benefits** from an aid measure can be considered as sufficient.[108] For example, a subsidy resembles a clear financial benefit to an undertaking. Without State intervention, the recipient undertaking would not have obtained this benefit. The Court developed a general framework for determining an advantage, since State intervention—other than subsidies—does not always immediately show that an undertaking benefits from a State measure.

---

[101] Case C-329/15, *ENEA* (CJEU 13 September 2017).

[102] Case C-482/99, *Stardust Marine* (ECJ 16 May 2002).

[103] Case C-242/13, *Commerz Nederland v Havenbedrijf Rotterdam* (CJEU 23 October 2014) para 34–35.

[104] Joined Cases C-533/12 P and C-536/12 P, *SNCM and Corsica Ferries* (CJEU 4 September 2014); Case C-522/13, *Ministerio de Defensa and Navantia* (CJEU 9 October 2014).

[105] Case C-690/13, *Trapeza Eurobank* (CJEU 16 April 2015) para 20.

[106] Case C-362/19 P, *Commission v Fútbol Club Barcelona* (CJEU 4 March 2021) para 61.

[107] Case C-81/10 P, *France Télécom v Commission* (CJEU 8 December 2011) para 17.

[108] Säcker and Montag (2016), p. 88.

The Court has developed **two tests** to establish an economic advantage. The first test is the market economy investor principle. This test examines whether the State concluded a financial transaction with one or more undertakings based on comparable conditions as a market economy operator would agree to (→ para 36 et seqq.). The second is called the '*Altmark* test'. In the *Altmark* judgment, the Court created a 'compensation approach', containing of four cumulative criteria to ascertain whether a measure constitutes a compensation for operating public service obligations (→ para 49 et seqq.). 35

3.2. The Market Economy Operator Test: The Standard Test for Assessing an Advantage

The central test for assessing whether an aid measure qualifies as an advantage is the so-called test of a market economy operator (MEO).[109] The Court has developed this principle, in case law previously referred to as the 'market economy investor test', to determine whether public investments, for example capital injections, are made under normal market conditions.[110] In more recent case law the Court applies this test also to other types of State intervention to determine whether the State acted in the capacity of a public authority or as a diligent market operator would act. If **investments by the State are conducted under conditions comparable to those a private investor would choose**, the State is acting as a market economy investor.[111] Hence, such conduct does qualify as an advantage ruling out State aid within the meaning of Article 107.1 TFEU.[112] 36

The MEO test applies to **State intervention by means of ownership or control of certain assets or in decisions to purchase certain goods and services**. Therefore it must be distinguished from public prerogative powers.[113] National authorities may not invoke public policy goals, such as full employment and access to social security, as a justification for financial risks that market operators normally would not take.[114] In such a case a national authority does not act as market economy investor.[115] In *FIH*, the Court ruled that the Commission and the General 37

---

[109] Case C-579/16 P, *FIH* (CJEU 6 March 2018). See for a comprehensive study on the MEO test Cyndecka (2016).

[110] Case C-142/87, *Belgium v Commission (Tubemeuse)* (ECJ 21 March 1990) para 29; Case C-305/89, *Italy v Commission (Alfa Romeo)* (ECJ 21 March 1991) para 18–19.

[111] Cyndecka (2016), pp. 163–165.

[112] Säcker and Montag (2016), pp. 88–90.

[113] Hancher et al. (2021), pp. 48–51; Case C-74/16, *Congregación de Escuelas Pías Provincia de Betania* (CJEU 27 June 2017) para 50.

[114] Joined Cases C-533/12 P and C-536/12 P, *SNCM and Corsica Ferries* (CJEU 4 September 2014) para 42.

[115] Case C-124/10 P, *Commission v EDF* (5 June 2012) para 83–85 and 105.

Court must investigate all available economic and financial information to determine whether an MS has acted as a market economy operator.[116]

38 The MEO test applies not only to investments or capital participations by public authorities but also to **other financial transactions**, such as land sales,[117] public crediting,[118] public vending, guarantee schemes[119] and debt renegotiations.[120]

3.3. Market Economy Investor Test: The MEO Test Applied to Investments

39 The test of the market economy investor (MEIO) determines whether, in similar circumstances, a **private investor operating under normal conditions** could have been involved. This principle has been developed by the General Court and the Court and has been applied in accordance with the MEO test. As the MEIO test is further explained in the Commission notice on the notion of State aid, the MEO test is now applied to multiple instruments for public investments, such as participation in equity, capital injections and guarantee schemes. For other financial transactions, such as public vending and public crediting, the Court has developed comparable criteria, which can all be deduced to the MEO test.[121]

40 The private investor test, also referred to as the **market economy investor principle** (MEIP), applies also to situations of privatisation. To act as a private investor a State-owned company must be sold to the highest bidder, based on an open and transparent procedure.[122]

41 When the State conducts economic activities it must act under the same conditions as a private market investor would do.[123] For example, the State acts as a buyer on the market it has to conclude transactions under **normal competitive conditions**, that is to say at the highest price which a private investor acting under normal competitive conditions would have been to pay for the goods, services or capital involved.[124] In such a case there is no economic advantage granted, and therefore Article 107.1 TFEU does not apply.

---

[116] Case C-579/16 P, *FIH* (CJEU 6 March 2018) para 47.

[117] Case C-39/14, *BVVG v Jerichower Land* (CJEU 16 July 2015).

[118] Case C-73/11 P, *Frucona Košice v Commission*, (CJEU 24 January 2013).

[119] Case C-214/12 P, *Land Burgenland v Commission* (CJEU 24 October 2013).

[120] Case C-150/16, *Fondul Proprietatea* (CJEU 18 May 2017).

[121] Hancher et al. (2021), pp. 96–114.

[122] Hancher et al. (2021), pp. 101–104.

[123] Case T-375/15, *Germanwings v Commission* (GC 27 April 2017) para 64.

[124] Hancher et al. (2021), pp. 101–104.

3.4. The Private Creditor Test: The MEO Test Applied to Obtain Payment of Debtors

The private creditor test depends on the State, acting not as a public authority, but in the capacity of a private creditor seeking to obtain payment of sums owed to it by a debtor.[125] In *Frucona*, the Court described the private creditor test as a test to determine whether the payment by an MS would also have been granted by a **private creditor** or whether it is clear that such a creditor would not have offered comparable facilities. In *EDF*, the Court ruled that the private creditor test applies to the conduct of the State that is acting as a private operator which has the incentive of making a profit.[126]

In *FIH*, the GC specified the private creditor test as opposed to the private investor test.[127] According to the GC, the goal of the State is to conduct investments on market conditions, the latter test must be applied. If the goal is to obtain payment of sums the State owes in the capacity of a debtor, the GC ruled that the private creditor test must always be applied as a separate test.[128] However, the Court annulled the GC's judgment and ruled that **both the private creditor and the private investor test derive from the MEO test.**[129] Therefore the MEO test is the overriding and guiding principle on determining normal market conditions, and therefore the Court ruled that the Commission may apply the general private investor test instead of the private creditor principle.[130]

To determine whether the private creditor test applies, the Commission but also the General Court and the Court of Justice rely on the existence of **certain factors**.[131] Those factors include the creditor's status as the holder of a secured, preferential or ordinary claim, the nature and extent of any security it may hold, its assessment of the chances of restoring the firm to viability, as well as the amount it would receive in the event of liquidation[132]

To identify whether a State acts as a normally prudent and diligent private creditor would have, the Commission is required to **compare the behaviour of the State with possible more advantageous alternatives**, namely financial arrangements which allow a private creditor to obtain a greater profit from the sums owed.[133]

---

[125] Case C-73/11 P, *Frucona Košice v Commission* (CJEU 24 January 2013) para 72.

[126] Cyndecka (2017); Case C-124/10 P, *Commission v EDF* (CJEU 5 June 2012).

[127] Case T-386/14, *FIH* (GC 15 September 2016); Cyndecka (2017).

[128] Case T-386/14, *FIH* (GC 15 September 2016).

[129] See for a critical comment, Cyndecka (2017).

[130] Case C-579/16 P, *FIH* (CJEU 6 March 2018).

[131] Cyndecka (2017).

[132] Case T-103/14, *Frucona Košice* (GC 16 March 2016).

[133] Case T-103/14, *Frucona Košice* (GC 16 March 2016) para 137.

3.5. The Private Vendor Test: The MEO Test Applied to the Vending of Goods

46 In addition to the private creditor test, the Court has developed a private vendor test. This test is suitable to determine **whether the State acts as a rational private vendor** in a situation as close as possible to that of private undertakings in comparable economic circumstances.[134]

47 Offering goods or services on a not-for-profit basis does not prevent entities to fall under the **MEO principle**, since that offer exists in competition with that of other operators which do seek to make a profit.[135]

48 An important factor for determining whether a public authority acts as a private investor is the **profitability of the transaction in the future**.[136] In the Court's case law the private vendor test has been applied to the vending of formerly State-owned public undertakings, such as regional banks.[137] The test is also frequently applied to assess whether land sale arrangement constitute an advantage. In *BVVG v Jerichower Land*, the Court held that the application of the private vendor test requires a public authority to agree to a price which is as close as possible to the market value of the land concerned.[138]

3.6. The *Altmark* Test: Specific Test to Assess Whether a Measure Constitutes Compensation for a Public Service

49 In addition to the test for a market economy operator, the Court has created a specific legal test to determine whether undertakings discharged with public service obligations receive an advantage.[139] According to this so-called '**compensation test**', compensations for public service obligations do not necessarily constitute an advantage.[140] Based on the landmark *Altmark* judgment, a compensation for a public service obligation does *not* constitute an advantage, on condition that **four cumulative criteria** are met.[141] Control by the Commission and the GC and Court on the application of the *Altmark* criteria is limited to ascertaining whether there is a manifest error of assessment.[142]

---

[134] Joined Cases C-214/12 P, C-215/12 P and C-223/12, *Land Burgenland and Others v Commission* (CJEU 24 October 2013).

[135] Case C-74/16, *Congregación de Escuelas Pías Provincia de Betania* (CJEU 27 June 2017) para 46.

[136] Case C-124/10 P, *Commission v EDF* (CJEU 5 June 2012) para 84.

[137] Case C-214/12 P, *Land Burgenland v Commission* (CJEU 24 October 2013).

[138] Case C-39/14, *BVVG v Jerichower Land* (CJEU 16 July 2015).

[139] Jaeger (2021), pp. 271–273.

[140] de Cecco (2013), pp. 140–143.

[141] Case C-280/00, *Altmark Trans* (ECJ 24 July 2003).

[142] Fiedziuk (2013), pp. 387–390.

First, there must be a **clear public service obligation**. There must be an **50** economic activity which can clearly distinguish itself from normal market activities, on account of a genuine general interest. The GC applied in several cases a market failure test to distinguish services of a general economic interest (SGEI) from normal market activities.[143] Second, prior to the entrustment, **objective and transparent criteria** must be determined **to calculate the total net costs** that the compensation must cover. Thirdly, the compensation may not exceed the total net cost incurred by the SGEI provider, including a reasonable profit. The second and third conditions exclude the risk of retroactive compensation and require that national authorities create a **control mechanism that precludes overcompensation**.[144] The fourth criterion requires that if the public service provider is not selected pursuant to a public tender, the compensation will need to be calculated based on the **total net costs**, which a well-run **average undertaking** would incur in carrying out the services. To clarify the application of the *Altmark* judgment the Commission has adopted specific guidance notices on State aid, public procurement and SGEI–compensations.[145]

The *Altmark* test can be regarded as the '**problem child**' of the State aid **51** provision of Article 107.1 TFEU.[146] In applying the *Altmark* test, the GC has navigated between a very lenient approach to the four cumulative conditions in *BUPA* and a more strict interpretation afterwards.[147] In *TV2/Danmark v Commission II* Denmark invoked the *BUPA* judgment and claimed that the Court should apply a more lenient approach towards the second and fourth *Altmark* conditions.[148] In the *BUPA* case, the GC applied the principle of proportionality for assessment of the *Altmark* conditions, noting that a compensation fulfils these criteria when it was designed in accordance with the 'spirit and the purpose of *Altmark*'.[149] The Court stipulates that in *BUPA* the circumstances were of a special nature given the private insurance equalisation scheme in the healthcare sector.[150] In the case of *TV2/Danmark* there were no comparable special circumstances. Accordingly, the Court distanced itself from the *BUPA* ruling, stating that solely examining the goals of *Altmark* does not make any sense without actually applying the Altmark conditions.[151]

---

[143] Case T-289/03, *BUPA v Commission* (CFI 12 February 2008).

[144] Case 66/16 P, *Comunidad Autónoma del País Vasco* (CJEU 20 December 2017).

[145] Commission Communication *on the application of the European Union State aid rules to compensation granted for the provision of services of general economic interest*, O.J. C 8/4 (2012); Commission Guide *on the application of the EU rules on state aid, public procurement and the internal market on SGEI*, SWD (2013) 53 final/2.

[146] Nicolaides (2017b), pp. 96–100.

[147] Case T-289/03, *BUPA v Commission* (GC 12 February 2008). See Szyszczak (2012).

[148] Nicolaides (2017b).

[149] Ross (2009) and Sauter (2013).

[150] Case C-649/15 P, *TV2/Danmark v Commission* (CJEU 9 November 2017).

[151] Case C-660/15 P, *Viasat* (CJEU 8 March 2017); Case C-649/15 P, *TV2/Danmark v Commission* (Opinion AG Wathelet 30 May 2017) para 47–49.

52   In *Viasat v Commission*, the Court ruled that the second *Altmark* criterion does not require MS to incorporate efficiency incentives for the calculation of the cost parameters.[152] However, the selection of a **well-run undertaking** does require the introduction of **an ex-ante efficiency framework**.

53   The Court also clarified the scope of the **compatibility test of Article 106.2 TFEU** in *TV2/Danmark* and *Viasat*.[153] Referring to the Commission's soft law on Article 106.2 TFEU, Viasat claimed that the second and fourth *Altmark* conditions are part of the compatibility test of State aid with the internal market. The Court dismissed this claim and referred to the *BUPA* case as an incidental case in which the proportionality condition of Article 106.2 TFEU was applied in the assessment of the *Altmark* conditions. According to the Court, the *Altmark* test is the applicable test for establishing a breach of Article 107.1 TFEU, whilst Article 106.2 TFEU must be applied when investigating the compatibility under State aid with the internal market → para 87 et seqq.).[154]

4. Selectivity

54   To fall within the scope of Article 107.1 TFEU, a measure must confer a selective advantage favouring certain products or certain undertakings. In accordance with the objectivity of the concept of State aid, the selectivity of a measure must be assessed by its effects.[155] In its case law, the Court held that measures have a selective nature when they **effectively favour a particular undertaking or group of undertakings**.[156]

55   The concept of selectivity implies **discrimination or unequal treatment**: an advantage is available only to some undertakings within a given sector or to a certain branch within the market.[157] Both in cases of *individual* differentiation (for example an advantage given to undertaking X, but not to undertakings Y and Z) and *sectoral* differentiation (for example an advantage awarded to all undertakings producing A but not to those producing B), State measures may have a selective effect.[158]

56   **General measures of economic policy** which apply *a priori* to all undertakings operating in an MS are in principle not selective.[159] Accordingly, general tax

---

[152] Case C-660/15 P, *Viasat* (CJEU 8 March 2017).

[153] Case C-649/15 P, *TV2/Danmark v Commission* (CJEU 9 November 2017).

[154] Case C-660/15 P, *Viasat* (CJEU 8 March 2017).

[155] Hancher et al. (2021), pp. 77–84.

[156] Joined Cases C-106/09 P and C-107/09 P, *Gibraltar* (CJEU 15 November 2011) para 101.

[157] Case C-270/15 P, *Belgium v Commission* (Opinion of AG Bobek of 21 April 2016); Case C-270/15 P, *Belgium v Commission* (CJEU 30 June 2016).

[158] Case C-270/15 P, *Belgium v Commission* (Opinion of AG Bobek of 21 April 2016).

[159] Case C-20/15 P, *World Duty Free v Commission* (CJEU 21 December 2016).

schemes fall outside of the scope of Article 107.1 TFEU.[160] However, measures tailored for a selected group of undertakings, or undertakings representing a specific economic sector, remain selective and do not fall within the notion of general measures.[161]

In some cases, the Court considers aid schemes to be **de facto selective**. It ruled in the case of the *Gibraltar tax scheme* that a tax reduction, although a priori available for undertakings in Gibraltar, de facto favoured offshore companies, since this group of undertakings was preferentially treated 'on account of the specific features characteristic of that group'.[162]

57

In other cases, the Court assesses whether *a priori* advantages have a selective effect. In the *Nox* case it ruled that a measure can be considered to be a selective advantage if a scheme **potentially strengthens the position** of 'a specific group of large industrial undertakings which are active in trade between Member States'.[163] Accordingly, the assessment of selectivity and the existence of an advantage overlap to some extend in the case law of the Court.[164]

58

In general, when assessing selectivity, this case law requires the determination of undertakings which are in a '**comparable legal and factual situation**'.[165] The concrete application of this requirement depends nonetheless on the complexity of the case and the number of undertakings concerned.[166] In cases of individual selectivity, the Court can easily establish that a measure has the aim or effect of benefiting a single undertaking.[167] For instance in *Trapeza Eurobank Ergasias,* the Court ruled that if a State does not disclose whether other banks would benefit from a measure, the measure can be considered as '**de facto selective**'.[168] In *Ministero dell'Economia v 3M Italia*, the Court held that it is only necessary to conduct a selectivity test when dealing with a general measure 'which effects a differentiation between undertakings that does not result from the nature or scheme of the system of which it forms part'.[169] In cases of sectoral selectivity, in which advantages are awarded to certain undertakings on a sectoral basis, the Court has developed several approaches to selectivity.[170]

59

---

[160] Werner and Verouden (2017), p. 120.

[161] Case C-143/99, *Adria-Wien Pipeline* (ECJ 8 November 2001) para 48.

[162] Werner and Verouden (2017), pp. 144–145; Joined Cases C-106/09 P and C-107/09 P, *Gibraltar* (CJEU 15 November 2011) para 107.

[163] Werner and Stoican (2018).

[164] Nicolaides (2017d) and Bousin and Piernas (2008).

[165] Case C-15/14 P, *Commission v MOL* (CJEU 4 June 2015) para 59–61. Werner and Verouden (2017), pp. 133–134.

[166] Säcker and Montag (2016), pp. 189–191.

[167] Case C-270/15 P, *Belgium v Commission* (CJEU 30 June 2016) para 49.

[168] Case C - 690/13, *Trapeza Eurobank* (CJEU 16 April 2015) para 28.

[169] Case C-417/10, *3M Italia* (CJEU 29 March 2012) para 40–43.

[170] See Romariz (2014) and Bousin and Piernas (2008).

60 Under the **two-step approach**, the first step consists of determining whether the measure is **prima facie selective**, that is, whether some undertakings enjoy an advantage in relation to other undertakings that are in a comparable legal and factual situation in the light of the objective pursued by the measure. If the answer to the first step is in the affirmative, a presumption of selectivity is established. It might still be **possible to justify** the measure in the second step if the differentiation arose from the nature or general scheme of the system to which the measure is part of. Although the Commission will have to demonstrate that the measure is prima facie selective in the first step, it is for the MS to rebut this presumption in the second step.[171]

61 Under the **three-step approach**, the first step is to define the **reference framework**, which is sometimes referred to by the Court as the 'common' or the 'normal' regime.[172] The following steps of this approach are essentially the same as those outlined above for the two-step approach. Therefore, the second step consists of assessing whether the measure treats undertakings in a similar **legal and factual situation** differently. The third and last step assesses whether the MS has provided an **objective justification** for this **different treatment**. This **objectively justification** must be invoked in accordance with the nature of the general scheme of the system of which it forms part.[173]

62 Under both approaches, it is necessary to first establish a reference framework. However, within the two-step approach, the assessment of different treatment and objective justification are somewhat blurred.[174] As a result, the **three-step approach** might be **better suited** in terms of clarity and predictability.[175] In addition it provides a more structured analysis of the inherent objectives and effects of a general measure.[176] In *World Duty Free*, the Court opted definitely for three-step test for material selectivity, thereby refining the concept of selectivity, after several attempts from the GC to adopt a more flexible approach.[177]

63 By applying the principle of **non-discrimination** to the selectivity test, the Court has developed the selectivity criterion further in *Hansestadt Lübeck* and *World Duty Free*.[178] In the case of *World Duty Free*, the Court held that if a tax measure forms an exception from the general tax system, such a measure is not necessarily 'selective' as long as it is open to any undertaking.[179] In this case, the Commission, to classify the measure at issue as a selective measure, relied on the fact that a tax

---

[171] Case C-279/08 P, *Commission v Netherlands (Nox)* (CJEU 8 September 2011).

[172] Säcker and Montag (2016), pp. 194–196.

[173] Case C-233/16, *ANGED v Catalunya* (CJEU 26 April 2018).

[174] Case C-270/15 P, *Belgium v Commission* (Opinion of AG Bobek of 21 April 2016) para 26. Nicolaides and Rusu (2012).

[175] Nicolaides (2017a).

[176] Case C-270/15 P, *Belgium v Commission* (Opinion of AG Bobek of 21 April 2016) para 27–28.

[177] Case C-20/15 P, *World Duty Free* (21 December 2016).

[178] Buendía Sierra (2018); Case C-20/15 P, *World Duty Free* (CJEU 21 December 2016).

[179] Nicolaides (2015).

advantage conferred by a general measure did not indiscriminately benefit all economic operators who were objectively in a comparable situation, in the light of the objective pursued by the ordinary Spanish tax system, since resident undertakings acquiring shareholdings of the same kind in companies resident for tax purposes in Spain could not obtain that advantage. The Commission then considered that the justification put forward by Spain for this distinction between operators, based on the nature or general structure of the system of which that measure formed part, could not be accepted. The GC rejected the argument of the Commission that a national tax regime is selective in that it favours only groups of undertakings which were making certain investments abroad. To counter this argument the GC ruled that the fact that the measure favours undertakings taxable in one MS, as compared to undertakings taxable in other MS, did not constitute a selective measure. The reasoning behind this argument is that determining the selectivity of a measure must be based on a different treatment between categories of undertakings under the legislation of the same MS as opposed to a different treatment between companies with branches in different MS. However, in 2017 the Court annulled the judgment of the GC. The Court ruled that in assessing whether a derogation of a general rule constitutes a selective or a general measure, the principle of non-discrimination plays a central role.[180] An MS can only **justify differentiation** of a group of undertakings **based on a legitimate aim**. Moreover such differentiation may not result in discriminatory treatment. Accordingly, the Court cleared in *World Duty Free* under which conditions a general tax scheme cannot be considered selective.[181]

If a measure is conceived as an **aid scheme** and not as individual aid, it is for the Commission to establish that the measure in question, while conferring an advantage of general application, confers the benefit of that advantage exclusively on certain undertakings or certain sectors of economic activity.[182] On the other hand, a tax advantage resulting from a general measure applicable without distinction to all economic operators does not constitute such aid.[183]

64

To classify a **national tax measure** as 'selective', the Commission must begin by identifying the ordinary or 'normal' tax system applicable in the MS concerned, and thereafter demonstrate that a tax measure at issue is a derogation from that ordinary system, in so far as it differentiates between operators who, in the light of the objective pursued by that ordinary tax system, are in a comparable factual and legal situation.[184] In determining the selectivity of the measure at issue, it is necessary to ascertain whether that measure introduces a distinction between

65

---

[180] Case C-20/15 P, *World Duty Free* (CJEU 21 December 2016) para 54, 92–95.

[181] See Aalbers (2017).

[182] Case C-270/15 P, *Belgium v Commission* (CJEU 30 June 2016) para 49–50.

[183] Case C-100/15 P, *NMTA v Commission* (CJEU 4 April 2016) para 80.

[184] Säcker and Montag (2016), pp. 200–203. Case C-20/15 P, *World Duty Free* (CJEU 21 December 2016).

66 From a general perspective the Court's **non-discrimination approach** towards material selectivity in relation to general tax schemes also **applies to general aid schemes**. In *Hansestadt Lübeck*, the Court upheld the GC's judgment, ruling that the fact that a State measure prima facie differentiates between certain groups of undertakings is sufficient to prove its selectivity. The Court ruled that in such a case the Commission must assess whether a measure introduces distinctions between operators who are, in the light of the objective pursued, in a comparable factual and legal situation.[186] In *Eventech*, the Court applied this assessment to ascertain whether national authorities may limit access to public infrastructure to a specific category of companies. The Court ruled that the selectivity criterion is not met if the companies concerned are not in a comparable factual and legal situation to other companies, in view of the legitimate policy objective pursued by the State.[187] In this case, the Court ruled that a State does not necessarily confer a selective economic advantage when it grants a right of privileged access to public infrastructure which is not operated commercially by the public authorities to some users of that infrastructure to pursue a legitimate objective. In *Eventech*, local legislation fulfilled this criterion since it pursued a safe and efficient transport system; as a result, the measure was not considered by the Court to be selective.[188]

5. Effect on Inter-State Trade

67 Article 107.1 TFEU applies to measures which are liable to affect trade between the MS. According to the Court, the Commission is not required to establish an actual effect on cross-border trade, but may investigate whether an advantage **potentially strengthens the market position of beneficiaries**.[189] Such an advantage may namely hinder or influence goods and service providers, or capital investors, from other MS.[190]

68 In *World Duty Free*, the Court ruled that for this analysis it does not matter whether the beneficiaries of the aid are directly or indirectly involved in intra EU trade.[191] Accordingly, the concept of an effect on inter-State trade must be **interpreted broadly**. The exception to this concept are measures which the Commission

---

[185] Case C-15/14 P, *Commission v MOL* (CJEU June 2015) para 61.
[186] See Case C-524/14 P, *Hansestadt Lübeck* (CJEU 21 December 2016).
[187] Case C-518/13, *Eventech* (CJEU 14 January 2015) para 47.
[188] Parret and van Heezik (2018).
[189] Case C-74/16, *Congregación de Escuelas Pías Provincia de Betania* (CJEU 27 June 2017); Zelger (2018).
[190] Case C-280/00, *Altmark Trans* (ECJ 24 July 2003) para 77 and 78.
[191] Case C-20/15 P, *World Duty Free* (CJEU 21 December 2016).

declares to have a so-called local effect.[192] In 2015, the Commission drafted non-binding guidance on local investment measures which were considered to be of a purely local nature by the Commission.[193] This guidance consist out of seven best practices in the Commission's decision practice, in which the Commission decided that the advantages have a merely marginal effect on trading undertakings in other MS.[194] Examples of the activities concern, *inter alia*, local sport activities, local harbours, local hospitals with only marginal foreseeable effects on intra-EU trade investments.

Moreover, the Commission adopted a so-called Exemption Regulation for *de minimis* aid.[195] Under Article 107.1 TFEU, this '*de minimis* Regulation' exempts aid measures not exceeding the total amount of EUR 200,000 (over a period of three years) from the concept of State aid because according to the Commission, this relatively small amount does not affect inter-State trade.[196]

69

6. Distortion of Competition

An advantage must distort or threaten to distort competition within the internal market. Usually this is the case when an aid potentially makes it more difficult for undertakings established in other MS to access the market in which beneficiaries of aid operate in.[197] Accordingly, an advantage distorts competition when it **possibly strengthens the competitive position of an undertaking compared to other undertakings**.[198] Inherent to a State intervention on the market is that the involvement of State resources may create selective advantages which deviate from normal market conditions. The circumstance that this advantage allows beneficiary undertakings to operate under unilaterally strengthened market conditions, is sufficient for the Commission to conclude that there is a possible distortion of competition at play.[199] According to the Court's case law, it is not necessary to determine in detail

70

---

[192] Dekker (2017), p. 154.

[193] Commission Guidance *on local public support measures that can be granted without prior Commission approval*, 29 April 2015, Press Release IP/15/4889; Dekker (2017), p. 154.

[194] Commission Decisions: *United Kingdom - Member-owned golf clubs*, SA.38208, O.J. C 277 (2015); *United Kingdom - Glenmore Lodge*, SA. 37963, O.J. C 277 (2015); *The Netherlands – Investment aid for Lauwersoog port*, SA.39403, O.J. C 259 (2015); *Germany - Städtische Projektgesellschaft "Wirtschaftsbüro Gaarden - Kiel"*, SA.33149, O.J. C 188 (2015); *Germany – Medical centre in Durmersheim*, SA.37904, O.J. C 188 (2015); *Czech Republic - Hradec Králové public hospitals*, SA.37432. O.J. C 203 (2015).

[195] Commission Regulation (EU) No 1407/2013 *on the application of Articles 107 and 108 of the Treaty on the Functioning of the European Union to de minimis aid*, O.J. L 352/1 (2013).

[196] Case C-74/16, *Congregación de Escuelas Pías Provincia de Betania* (CJEU 27 June 2017) para 84.

[197] Bacon (2017), pp. 12–13.

[198] Joined Cases C-197/11 and C-203/11, *Libert* (CJEU 8 May 2013).

[199] Joined Cases C-197/11 and C-203/11, *Libert* (CJEU 8 May 2013).

the market position of the beneficiary and its competitors. As a result, the Commission is not obligated to make a relevant market analysis comparable to its duties under Articles 101.1 TFEU and 102 TFEU (→ Article 101 TFEU para 30 et seqq.).[200]

71 Since intervention by means of preferential treatment imputable to the State creates competitive advantage, a **potential distortion of competition** can be quite easily established by the Commission.[201] Accordingly, the Court has created a low threshold for the Commission to prove a distortion of completion, as no conditions of 'significance' or 'appreciability' are required.[202]

7. Exemptions to the State Aid Prohibition of Article 107.1 TFEU

72 State aid is prohibited under Article 107.1 TFEU. However, State aid can also be compatible with the internal market. Concerning compatibility there are two types of exemptions which can be invoked to justify State aids under Article 107.1 TFEU. all, MS may rely on the special categories listed in Article 107.2 TFEU, which are de jure, or **automatically, compatible** (→ para 73 et seqq.).[203] Second, MS may ask the Commission to use its exclusive powers to **declare** categories of aid measures **compatible** with the internal market according to the provisions laid down in Article 107.3 TFEU, Article 106.2 TFEU or Article 93 TFEU (→ para 77 et seqq.). Under these provisions, the Commission has a wide discretion to decide if the invoked general interests outweigh negative effects for the functioning of the internal market.[204]

7.1. De jure Exemptions: Article 107.2 TFEU

73 Article 107.2 TFEU **allows the MS to exempt** certain categories of aid de jure without prior approval of the Commission.[205] Although MS still may be required to notify their intention to grant aid under this provision, the Commission has no discretion to decide whether the aid is compatible.[206] In practice, the legal exceptions under paragraph 2 are of little significance.

---

[200] Säcker and Montag (2016), pp. 230–236. Hancher et al. (2021), p. 120. Joined Cases C-164/15 P and C-165/15 P, *Ryanair and Aer Lingus* (CJEU 21 December 2016).
[201] Säcker and Montag (2016), pp. 229–231.
[202] Hancher et al. (2021), p. 95.
[203] Hancher and Salerno (2021), pp. 139–140; Stuart and Roginska-Green (2018), pp. 53–59.
[204] Säcker and Montag (2016), pp. 268–271. See Case T-356/15, *Hinkley Point* (GC 12 July 2018).
[205] Säcker and Montag (2016), p. 244.
[206] Quigley (2015), p. 197.

The first category concerns **aid of a social character** as listed in Article 107.2 point (a) TFEU.[207] Article 107.2 TFEU strictly applies to aid granted in a non-discriminatory fashion to individuals, and therefore prohibits granting aid directly or indirectly to undertakings.[208] Aid to consumers may, however, constitute incompatible aid to undertakings if it promotes the purchase of goods that selectively benefit certain undertakings.[209]

74

The second category for exemption is Article 107.2 point (b) TFEU as specified by Article 50 of the General Block Exemption Regulation (GBER). This exemption allows for **aid to compensate the damage** caused by natural disasters or exceptional occurrences. **Natural disasters** are earthquakes, avalanches, landslides, floods, tornadoes, hurricanes, volcanic eruptions and wild fires (of natural origin), as well as tornadoes, hurricanes, volcanic eruptions and wild fires (of natural origin) (Article 50.1 GBER).[210] Damage caused by adverse weather conditions such as frost, hail, ice, rain or drought, which occur on a more regular basis, should not be considered a natural disaster (Recital 69 GBER). Aid can only be granted if the competent authorities of the MS have formally classified the event as a natural disaster and the damage to the enterprises is causally linked to it (Article 50.2 GBER). The aid schemes must be introduced within three years of the event. Aid to enterprises must be granted within four years of the natural disaster (Article 50.3 GBER).

75

Exceptional occurrences may comprise a variety of aspects such as unusual weather fluctuations if they are particularly significant in comparison to the usual weather conditions[211] or, most recently, the economic crisis resulting from the **COVID-19** pandemic.[212] Under Article 107.2 point (b) TFEU, MS have been instructed by the Commission to notify compensation schemes for undertakings in sectors that have been particularly hit by the outbreak.[213] The notifications under Article 107.2 point (b) TFEU were examined by the Commission in accordance with the Temporary Framework for State Aid Measures to support the Economy in the current COVID-19 outbreak.[214]

The third exemption is listed in Article 107.2 point (c) TFEU. This provision exempts aid granted to combat the **division in Germany** between the States on both sides of the Berlin wall.[215] Since the re-unification process of the Federal Republic of Germany has been completed, Article 107.2 point (c) TFEU has **lost most of its**

76

---

[207] See for example Case C-672/13, *OTP Bank* (CJEU 19 March 2015).

[208] Säcker and Montag (2016), p. 245.

[209] Cf. Case C-403/10 P, *Mediaset v Commission* (CJEU 28 July 2011) para 81.

[210] Hancher and Salerno (2021), pp. 139–140.

[211] Cf., for example, Joined Cases C-346/03 and C-529/03, *Atzeni* (ECJ 23 February 2006) para 81.

[212] Commission Communication *on the Temporary Framework for State Aid Measures to support the Economy in the current COVID-19 Outbreak*, O.J. C 91 I/1 (2020) and its amendments. Hancher and Salerno (2021), pp. 161–162.

[213] See Riedel et al. (2020).

[214] Commission Communication *on the Temporary Framework for State Aid Measures to support the Economy in the current COVID-19 Outbreak*, O.J. C 91 I/1 (2020) and its amendments. Hancher and Salerno (2021), pp. 161–162. See also Robbins et al. (2020).

[215] Säcker and Montag (2016), p. 247.

practical application.[216] Therefore, the Lisbon Treaty amended the provision stating that five years after the entry into force of the Treaty of Lisbon (i.e. as of 1 December 2014), the Council, acting on a proposal from the Commission, may adopt a decision repealing this point.

7.2. Discretionary Exemptions

7.2.1. Exemptions Under Article 107.3 TFEU

77 In contrast to Article 107.2 TFEU, the invocation of one of the exemptions under Article 107.3 TFEU falls within the **exclusive discretion of the Commission**. According to the wording of Article 107.3 TFEU, the Commission is the exclusive supervisory body which is competent to decide upon the compatibility of aid with the internal market, save for the categories under Article 107.2 TFEU.

78 In its assessment, the Commission must weigh all the relevant social, fiscal and economic interests involved, and determine to what extend the invocation of general interests affects intra-EU trade and competition.[217] According to the principles of **transparency, non-discrimination and proportionality** the Commission conducts a balancing test between national interests and EU interests on the internal market.[218]

79 To improve the **predictability** and the transparency of compatibility decisions under Article 107.3 TFEU, the Commission has adopted an extensive set of guidance, consisting out of various instruments such as guidelines and communications. Examples of these guidelines concern a framework for research and development aid;[219] guidelines for environmental aid;[220] and aid for rescuing and restructuring non-financial undertakings in difficulty;[221] aid for the banking sector[222] and aid for public broadcasting.[223]

---

[216] Hancher and Salerno (2021), pp. 141–142.

[217] See for instance Case T-356/15, *Hinkley Point* (GC 12 July 2018).

[218] Hancher and Salerno (2021), pp. 143–164.

[219] Commission, *Framework for State aid for research, development and innovation*, O.J. C 198/1 (2014), revised in 2022.

[220] Commission, *Guidelines on State aid for climate, environmental protection and energy 2022*, O.J. C 80/1 (2022).

[221] Commission, *Guidelines on State aid for rescuing and restructuring non-financial undertakings in difficulty*, O.J. C 249/1 (2014).

[222] Commission Communication, *State aid rules to support measures in favour of banks in the context of the financial crisis ('Banking Communication')*, O.J. C 216/1 (2013).

[223] Commission Communication *on the application of State aid rules to public service broadcasting*, O.J. C 257/1 (2009).

The first category of potentially compatible aid under point (a) is **aid for particular underdeveloped areas** in the EU where living standards are abnormally low or where there is serious underemployment.[224]

80

Point (b) concerns the **promotion and execution of an important project of common EU interest** or to **remedy a serious disturbance in the economy of an MS**. The Commission has drafted a specific set of rules for projects with an EU common interest in the Communication on the compatibility of State aid for important projects of common European interest.[225] During the **COVID-19** outbreak the Temporary Framework (→ para 74) was adopted to the compatibility category of Article 107.3 point (b) TFEU for 'measures directly dealing with the liquidity of undertakings and ensuring employment preservation, and in addition measuring dealing with the outbreak itself'.[226] These measures included: direct grants, selective tax advantages and advance payments up to EUR 800,000 to a company to address its urgent liquidity needs; State guarantees for loans taken by companies from banks; subsidised public loans to companies; safeguards for banks that channel State aid to the real economy, and short-term export credit insurance.

81

Article 107.3 point (c) TFEU is one of the most frequently applied horizontal exemptions as it covers very broad range of regional and sectoral interests.[227] It applies to **economic projects** within a national context and requires the Commission to balance regional and sectoral interest against the effects on the internal market.[228] Due to its wide range, the Commission applies Article 107.3 point (c) TFEU as a 'residual' or 'generic' category for State aid measures which pursue national policies.[229]

82

Article 107.3 point (d) TFEU provides for an exemption for **cultural interests**. The Commission attaches a broad scope to this provision by applying this provision also to infrastructural projects in the sports sector.[230]

83

Article 107.3 point (e) TFEU empowers the Council with the exclusive power to create additional categories for compatibility. As a result, point (e) allows for the creation of **'other discretionary exceptions'** as an exemption category. In practice additional exempted categories of aid by the Council do not occur very often since

84

---

[224] Hancher and Salerno (2021), pp. 150–151.
[225] Commission Communication *on the compatibility of State aid to promote the execution of important projects of common European interest*, O.J.C 528/104 (2021).
[226] Commission Communication *on the Temporary Framework for State Aid Measures to support the Economy in the current COVID-19 Outbreak*, O.J. C 91 I/1 (2020) and its amendments. Hancher and Salerno (2021), pp. 161–162.
[227] Hancher and Salerno (2021), pp. 162–163.
[228] See Nowak (2018).
[229] Aalbers and Ottervanger (2019), pp. 789–790.
[230] Craven (2014).

85 the Council must decide on the extension of compatible aid by means of a qualified majority in a proposal from the Commission.[231]

85 Since the Commission's policy is to focus on the biggest distortions on the internal market it has adopted a tailored block exemption for the MS. Under the **General Block Exemption Regulation** the Commission exempts particular categories of aid, which fall within the scope of Article 107.3 TFEU from notification under Article 108.3 TFEU.[232] The GBER has a broad substantive range and applies to regional aid, social aids, culture and sports, investments in infrastructural projects, research & development, environmental protection, sustainable energy and training aid from notification.[233] If the MS fail to comply with the procedural and substantive conditions, the aid is considered by the Court to be unlawful.[234]

86 The application of the GBER is bound to specific procedural and substantive conditions. Therefore the GBER contains specific conditions on the status of beneficiaries, the nature of exempted activities, incentive effects, cost methodology and transparency. Moreover the GBER sets out thresholds for notification, monitoring and reporting. From a substantive point of view the MS may exempt specific **horizontal aid categories** under the GBER. Sector specific block exempted aid categories exist inter alia for agriculture and fisheries.[235] Aid which does not meet the criteria of the block exemptions must be notified under Article 107.3 TFEU.[236]

7.2.2. Exemption Under Article 106.2 TFEU for Services of General Economic Interest

87 Articles 14 and 106.2 TFEU refer to services of general economic interest.[237] Under these Treaty provisions, the MS have a wide discretionary power to define SGEI on a national, regional and local level.[238] As a result, **public service obligations** can be qualified as an SGEI and **entrusted to undertakings**, on condition that the

---

[231] Hancher et al. (2021), p. 172.

[232] Commission Regulation (EU) No 651/2014 *declaring certain categories of aid compatible with the internal market*, O.J. L 187/1 (2014), last amended by Commission Regulation (EU) 2021/1237, O.J. L 270/39 (2021); Säcker and Montag (2016), pp. 474–492.

[233] Casteele (2021).

[234] Case C-493/14, *Dilly's Wellnesshotel v Finanzamt Linz* (CJEU 21 July 2016); Case C-349/17, *Eesti Pagar* (CJEU 5 March 2019) para 90–95.

[235] Commission Regulation (EU) No 702/2014 *declaring certain categories of aid in the agricultural and forestry sectors and in rural areas compatible with the internal market*, O.J. L 193/1 (2014); Commission Regulation (EU) No 1388/2014 *declaring certain categories of aid to undertakings active in the production, processing and marketing of fishery and aquaculture products compatible with the internal market*, O.J. L 369/37 (2014).

[236] Commission, *Guidelines for State aid in the agricultural and forestry sectors and in rural areas 2014 to 2020*, O.J. C 204/1 (2014); *Guidelines for the examination of State aid to the fishery and aquaculture sector*, O.J. C 217/1 (2015).

[237] See also Protocol No 26 to the TFEU. See Neergaard (2011) and Jaeger (2021).

[238] Joined Cases C-66/16 P through C-69/16 P, *Comunidad Autónoma del País Vasco* (CJEU 20 December 2017).

entrustment, and subsequent financial transactions, do not breach EU law, in particular State aid law. Examples of SGEI can be found in the healthcare sector,[239] public transport services,[240] social housing,[241] public broadcasting[242] and postal services.[243] Within its investigative powers, the Commission may only investigate whether an SGEI-entrustment contains a manifest error.[244]

Although SGEI are a concept of EU law, the Union has no powers to define SGEI, the Court and the Commission may set **minimum conditions** for its application in condition to EU substantive law.[245] Examples of such conditions are the *Altmark* test and the secondary legislation on the application of Articles 107.1 and 106.2 TFEU. In case financial compensations to undertakings entrusted with an SGEI do not satisfy the *Altmark* conditions, and therefore constitute an advantage and possibly State aid, **MS can invoke public interests and notify under Article 106.2 TFEU**. In that case, the Commission has a discretionary power to determine whether or not an SGEI is compatible with the internal market. According to the principles of proportionality and necessity, the Commission must determine whether the undertaking which is entrusted with the SGEI, can perform the particular tasks which have been assigned to it under economically acceptable conditions. Concerning the concept of 'economically acceptable conditions', the Court has held that MS enjoy discretion to proof that without State aid the economic continuity is in danger.[246] **88**

As of 2012, the Commission has adopted secondary legislation, the so-called 'Almunia package', to **exempt certain categories of SGEIs from notification** under Articles 106.2, 107.1 and 108.3 TFEU.[247] To allow more leeway for small and local SGEI compensations, the Commission adopted a special Regulation on *de minimis* **aid for SGEI**.[248] The SGEI *de minimis* Regulation excludes compensation not exceeding EUR 500,000 (over a period of three years) for SGEI's from notification. **89**

---

[239] Case T-137/10, *CBI* (GC 7 November 2012).
[240] Case C-303/13 P, *Commission v Jørgen Andersen* (6 October 2015).
[241] Case C-132/12 P, *Woonpunt* (CJEU 27 February 2014).
[242] Case C-660/15 P, *Viasat* (CJEU 8 March 2017).
[243] Case C-559/12 P, *France v Commission (La Poste)* (CJEU 3 April 2014).
[244] Szyszczak (2012).
[245] Jaeger (2021); Case C-66/16 P, *Comunidad Autónoma del País Vasco* (CJEU 20 December 2017).
[246] Jaeger (2021), pp. 288–290.
[247] Jaeger (2021), pp. 291–299; Buendía Sierra and Panero Rivas (2013); Gallo and Mariotti (2021).
[248] Commission Regulation (EU) No 360/2012 *on de minimis aid granted to undertakings providing services of general economic interest*, O.J. L 114/8 (2012).

90 In addition to the special *de minimis* aid, the Commission also adopted a SGEI Exemption Decision in 2012,[249] allowing especially SGEI compensations in social and passenger transport sectors to be exempted from notification. The **SGEI Exemption Decision** exempts compensation for average SGEI from notification up to a threshold of EUR 15 million per year in areas other than transport and transport infrastructure, e.g. compensations for social housing, childcare and hospitals.[250] Moreover, specific thresholds apply to public service obligations to ports, airports and air and maritime links to islands.[251]

91 The substantive application of the SGEI *de minimis* Regulation and the SGEI Exemption Decision **still require** SGEI compensations to meet the **first, second and third** *Altmark* **conditions**.[252] If these conditions are not met, an MS is still obligated to notify the aid for SGEIs to the Commission according to substantive conditions of Article 106.2 TFEU.[253]

7.2.3. Exemption Under Article 93 TFEU for the Coordination of Transport

92 Article 93 TFEU can be considered as the *lex specialis* for Article 106.2 TFEU concerning the compatibility of State aids for public services in the transport sector.[254] Regulation (EC) No. 1370/2007 (PSO-Regulation) lays down rules for public service obligations for the road and rail sectors.[255] Comparable to the *Altmark* judgment, these rules concern parameters for the calculation of the costs incurred, provisions on overcompensation and tendering conditions according to the principles of transparency and non-discrimination.[256] Moreover the PSO-Regulation provides sets specific rules for granting exclusive rights to public service providers.[257]

---

[249] Commission Decision 2012/21/EU *on State aid in the form of public service compensation granted to certain undertakings entrusted with the operation of services of general economic interest*, O.J. L7/3 (2011).

[250] Article 2.1 point (a) of Commission Decision 2012/21/EU. Baquero Cruz (2013).

[251] Article 2.1 points (d) and (e) of Commission Decision 2012/21/EU.

[252] Gallo and Mariotti (2021) and Szyszczak (2017).

[253] Case C-66/16 P, *Comunidad Autónoma del País Vasco* (CJEU 20 December 2017) para 54–56. See also European Union *framework for State aid in the form of public service compensation* (2011), *O.J. C 8/15 (2012)*.

[254] Säcker and Montag (2016), pp. 1372–1373. See Case C-280/00, *Altmark Trans* (ECJ 24 July 2003) para 106–108.

[255] Scharf (2021), pp. 654–657.

[256] Parliament/Council Regulation (EC) No 1370/2007 *on public passenger transport services by rail and by road*, O.J. L 315/1 (2007); Scharf (2021), pp. 654–657. Case C-303/13 P, *Commission v Jørgen Andersen* (CJEU 6 October 2015) para 52.

[257] Commission Communication *on interpretative guidelines concerning Regulation (EC) No 1370/2007 on public passenger transport services by rail and by road*, O.J. C 92/1 (2014).

In addition, Article 93 TFEU also allows for an exemption for aids aimed at the **93** coordination of transport.[258] Article 93 TFEU is especially aimed to coordinate activities concerning the need for open access transport infrastructure on a non-discriminatory basis.[259] Accordingly, the Commission has drafted **guidelines** for the application of Article 93 TFEU as exemption to Article 107.1 TFEU in the airport sector[260] and railway sector.[261]

List of Cases

ECJ/CJEU

ECJ 21.03.1990, 142/87, *Belgium v Commission (Tubemeuse)*, ECLI:EU:C:1990:125 [cit. in para 36]

ECJ 21.03.1991, 305/89, *Italy v Commission (Alfa Romeo)*, ECLI:EU:C:1991:142 [cit. in para 36]

ECJ 17.03.1993, C-72/91 and C-73/91, *Sloman Neptun*, ECLI:EU:C:1993:97 [cit. in para 23]

ECJ 13.03.2001, C-379/98, *PreussenElektra*, ECLI:EU:C:2001:160 [cit. in para 17, 23]

ECJ 08.11.2001, C-143/99, *Adria-Wien Pipeline*, ECLI:EU:C:2001:598 [cit. in para 56]

ECJ 16.05.2002, C-482/99, *France v Commission (Stardust Marine)*, ECLI:EU:C:2002:294 [cit. in para 27, 29, 32]

ECJ 24.07.2003, C-280/00, *Altmark Trans*, ECLI:EU:C:2003:415 [cit. in para 49, 67, 92]

ECJ 23.02.2006, C-346/03 and C-529/03, *Atzeni*, ECLI:EU:C:2006:130 [cit. in para 75]

ECJ 07.09.2006, C-526/04, *Laboratoires Boiron*, ECLI:EU:C:2006:528 [cit. in para 4]

CJEU 02.09.2010, C-399/08 P, *Commission v Deutsche Post*, ECLI:EU:C:2010:481 [cit. in para 2, 3]

CJEU 16.12.2010, C-239/09, *Seydaland Vereinigte Agrarbetriebe*, ECLI:EU:C:2010:778 [cit. in para 4]

CJEU 03.03.2011, C-437/09, *AG2R Prévoyance*, ECLI:EU:C:2011:112 [cit. in para 8]

---

[258] Säcker and Montag (2016), pp. 1383–1393.

[259] Case C-303/13 P, *Commission v Jørgen Andersen* (CJEU 6 October 2015); Scharf (2021).

[260] Commission, *Guidelines on State aid to airports and airlines*, O.J. C 99/3 (2014). Guillamond (2021).

[261] Commission, *Guidelines on State aid for railway undertakings*, O.J. C 184/13 (2008). Säcker and Montag (2016), pp. 1382–1387.

CJEU 28.07.2011, C-403/10 P, *Mediaset v Commission*, ECLI:EU:C:2011:533 [cit. in para 11, 74]

CJEU 08.09.2011, C-78/08 to C-80/08, *Paint Graphos*, ECLI:EU:C:2011:550 [cit. in para 18, 19]

CJEU 08.09.2011, C-279/08 P, *Commission v Netherlands (Nox)*, ECLI:EU:C:2011:551 [cit. in para 60]

CJEU 15.11.2011, C-106/09 P and C-107/09 P, *Gibraltar*, ECLI:EU:C:2011:732 [cit. in para 11, 17, 54]

CJEU 08.12.2011, C-81/10 P, *France Télécom v Commission*, ECLI:EU:C:2011:811 [cit. in para 5, 20, 34]

CJEU 29.03.2012, C-417/10, *3M Italia*, ECLI:EU:C:2012:184 [cit. in para 59]

CJEU 05.06.2012, C-124/10 P, *Commission v EDF*, ECLI:EU:C:2012:318 [cit. in para 37, 42, 48]

CJEU 24.01.2013, C-73/11 P, *Frucona Košice*, ECLI:EU:C:2013:32 [cit. in para 6, 12, 38, 42]

CJEU 19.03.2013, C-399/10 P and C-401/10 P, *Bouygues Télécom*, ECLI:EU:C:2013:175 [cit. in para 20]

CJEU 08.05.2013, C-197/11 and C-203/11, *Eric Libert*, ECLI:EU:C:2013:288 [cit. in para 12, 13, 70]

CJEU 24.10.2013, C-214/12 P, C-215/12 P and C-223/12 P, *Land Burgenland v Commission*, ECLI:EU:C:2013:682 [cit. in para 4, 38, 46, 48]

CJEU 19.12.2013, C-262/12, *Vent de Colère*, ECLI:EU:C:2013:851 [cit. in para 20, 25]

CJEU 27.02.2014, C-132/12 P, *Stichting Woonpunt v Commission*, ECLI:EU:C:2014:100 [cit. in para 87]

CJEU 04.09.2014, C-533/12 P and C-536/12 P, *SNCM and Corsica Ferries*, ECLI:EU:C:2014:2142 [cit. in para 4, 17, 33, 37]

CJEU 09.10.2014, C-522/13, *Ministerio de Defensa and Navantia*, ECLI:EU:C:2014:2262 [cit. in para 2, 33]

CJEU 23.10.2014, C-242/13, *Commerz Nederland*, ECLI:EU:C:2014:2326 [cit. in para 29, 32]

CJEU 14.01.2015, C-518/13, *Eventech*, ECLI:EU:C:2015:9 [cit. in para 4-6, 11, 13, 20, 66]

CJEU 19.03.2015, C-672/13, *OTP Bank*, ECLI:EU:C:2015:185 [cit. in para 74]

CJEU 16.04.2015, C-690/13, *Trapeza Eurobank*, ECLI:EU:C:2015:235 [cit. in para 33, 59]

CJEU 30.05.2015, C-677/11, *Doux Élevage v Ministère de l'Agriculture*, ECLI:EU:C:2013:348 [cit. in para 4, 23]

CJEU 04.06.2015, C-15/14 P, *Commission v MOL*, ECLI:EU:C:2015:362 [cit. in para 11, 59, 65]

CJEU 09.06.2015, C-63/14, *Commission v France*, ECLI:EU:C:2015:458 [cit. in para 15]

CJEU 16.07.2015, C-39/14, *BVVG v Jerichower Land*, ECLI:EU:C:2015:470 [cit. in para 4, 20, 38, 48]

CJEU 06.10.2015, C-303/13 P, *Commission v Jørgen Andersen*, ECLI:EU:C:2015:647 [cit. in para 87, 92, 93]

CJEU 15.10.2015, C-677/13, *Banco Privado Português v Commission*, ECLI:EU:C:2015:703 [cit. in para 13]

CJEU 18.02.2016, C-446/14 P, *Germany v Commission*, ECLI:EU:C:2016:97 [cit. in para 4]

CJEU 08.03.2016, C-431/14 P, *Greece v Commission*, ECLI:EU:C:2016:145 [cit. in para 15]

CJEU 14.04.2016, C-100/15 P, *NMTA v Commission*, ECLI:EU:C:2016:254 [cit. in para 64]

CJEU 30.06.2016, C-270/15 P, *Belgium v Commission*, ECLI:EU:C:2016:489 [cit. in para 3, 55, 59, 62, 64]

CJEU 21.07.2016, C-493/14, *Dilly's Wellnesshotel*, ECLI:EU:C:2016:577 [cit. in para 85]

CJEU 26.10.2016, C-211/15 P, *Orange v Commission*, ECLI:EU:C:2016:798 [cit. in para 4, 5]

CJEU 21.12.2016, C-164/15 P and C-165/15 P, *Commission v Ryanair and Aer Lingus*, ECLI:EU:C:2016:990 [cit. in para 5, 12, 13, 70]

CJEU 21.12.2016, C-131/15 P, *Club Hotel Loutraki v Commission*, ECLI:EU:C:2016:989 [cit. in para 12, 13]

CJEU 21.12.2016, C-524/14 P, *Commission v Hansestadt Lübeck*, ECLI:EU:C:2016:971 [cit. in para 13, 66]

CJEU 21.12.2016, C-20/15 P, *World Duty Free*, ECLI:EU:C:2016:981 [cit. in para 4, 11, 13, 56, 62, 63, 65, 68]

CJEU 08.03.2017, C-660/15 P, *Viasat*, ECLI:EU:C:2017:178 [cit. in para 51-53, 87]

CJEU 18.05.2017, C-150/16, *Fondul Proprietatea*, ECLI:EU:C:2017:388 [cit. in para 38]

CJEU 27.06.2017, C-74/16, *Congregación de Escuelas Pías Provincia de Betania*, ECLI:EU:C:2017:496 [cit. in para 2, 13, 37, 47, 67, 69]

CJEU 13.09.2017, C-329/15, *ENEA*, ECLI:EU:C:2017:671 [cit. in para 4, 16, 17, 21, 22, 29, 32]

CJEU 30.05.2017, C-649/15 P, Opinion of AG Wathelet, *TV2/Danmark v Commission*, ECLI:EU:C:2017:403 [cit. in para 51]

CJEU 09.11.2017, C-649/15 P, *TV2/Danmark v Commission*, ECLI:EU:C:2017:835 [cit. in para 7, 51, 53]

CJEU 20.12.2017, C-66/16 P to C-69/16 P, *Comunidad Autónoma del País Vasco v Commission*, ECLI:EU:C:2017:999 [cit. in para 50, 87, 88, 91]

CJEU 06.03.2018, C-579/16 P, *Commission v FIH*, ECLI:EU:C:2018:159 [cit. in para 36, 37, 43]

CJEU 26.04.2018, C-233/16, *ANGED*, ECLI:EU:C:2018:280 [cit. in para 4, 16, 18, 61]

CJEU 25.07.2018, C-128/16 P, *Commission v Spain (Bankia)*, ECLI:EU:C:2018:591 [cit. in para 27]

CJEU 19.12.2018, C-374/17, *A-Brauerei*, ECLI:EU:C:2018:1024 [cit. in para 4]

CJEU 05.03.2019, C-349/17, *Eesti Pagar*, ECLI:EU:C:2019:172 [cit. in para 85]
CJEU 29.07.2019, C-659/17, *Azienda Napoletana Mobilità*, ECLI:EU:C:2019:633 [cit. in para 13]
CJEU 11.06.2020, C-262/18 P and C-271/18 P, *Commission v Dôvera zdravotná poist'ovňa*, ECLI:EU:C:2020:450 [cit. in para 8]
CJEU 04.03.2021, C-362/19 P, *Commission v Fútbol Club Barcelona*, ECLI:EU:C:2021:169 [cit. in para 2, 3, 15, 33]
CJEU 16.03.2021, C-596/19 P, *Commission v Hungary*, ECLI:EU:C:2021:202 [cit. in para 6]
CJEU 16.09.2021, C-337/19 P, *Commission v Belgium (Magnetrol International)*, ECLI:EU:C:2021:741 [cit. in para 19]

CFI/GC

CFI 12.02.2008, T-289/03, *BUPA v Commission*, ECLI:EU:T:2008:29 [cit. in para 50, 51]
GC 07.11.2012, T-137/10, *CBI v Commission*, ECLI:EU:T:2012:584 [cit. in para 87]
GC 11.12.2014, T-251/11, *Austria v Commission*, ECLI:EU:T:2014:1060 [cit. in para 24]
GC 17.03.2015, T-89/09, *Pollmeier Massivholz v Commission*, ECLI:EU:T:2015:153 [cit. in para 4]
GC 25.03.2015, T-538/11, *Belgium v Commission*, ECLI:EU:T:2015:188 [cit. in para 14]
GC 16.03.2016, T-103/14, *Frucona Košice v Commission*, ECLI:EU:T:2016:152 [cit. in para 44, 45]
GC 10.05.2016, T-47/15, *Germany v Commission*, ECLI:EU:T:2016:281 [cit. in para 5, 26]
GC 14.09.2016, T-57/15, *Trajektna luka Split*, ECLI:EU:T:2016:470 [cit. in para 24, 30]
GC 15.09.2016, T-386/14, *FIH v Commission*, ECLI:EU:T:2019:623 [cit. in para 43]
GC 27.04.2017, T-375/15, *Germanwings v Commission*, ECLI:EU:T:2017:289 [cit. in para 41]
GC 12.07.2018, T-356/15, *Austria v Commission (Hinkley Point)*, ECLI:EU:T:2018:439 [cit. in para 72, 78]

References

Aalbers, M. (2017). Gibraltar: A rock solid interpretation of the selectivity criterion. *European State Aid Law Quarterly, 16*(3), 496–499.
Aalbers, M., & Ottervanger, T. (2019). State aid law. In P. Kuijper et al. (Eds.), *The law of the European Union* (pp. 779–797). Kluwer.
Bacon, K. (2017). *European Union law of State aid*. OUP.

Baquero Cruz, J. (2013). Social services of general interest and the State aid rules. In E. Szyszczak (Ed.), *Social services of general interest in the EU* (pp. 303–329). Springer.

Biondi, A., & Stefan, O. (2018). The notice on the notion of State aid: Every light has its shadow. In B. Nascimbene & A. Di Piscale (Eds.), *The modernisation of State aid for economic and social development* (pp. 43–60). Springer.

Bousin, J., & Piernas, J. (2008). Developments in the notion of selectivity. *European State Aid Law Quarterly, 7*(4), 640–642.

Buendía Sierra, J. (2018). Finding selectivity or the art of comparison. *European State Aid Law Quarterly, 17*(1), 85–98.

Buendía Sierra, J., & Panero Rivas, J. (2013). The Almunia package: State aid and SGEI. In J. van den Gronden (Ed.), *Financing services of general economic interest* (pp. 125–142). Springer.

Casteele, K. (2021). General Block Exemption Regulation. In L. Hancher, T. Ottervanger, & P. Slot (Eds.), *EU State aids* (pp. 217–250). Sweet and Maxwell.

Craven, R. (2014). State aid and sports stadiums: EU sports policy or deference to professional football. *European Competition Law Review, 9*, 453–460.

Cyndecka, M. (2016). *The MEI test in EU State aid law*. Kluwer.

Cyndecka, M. (2017). The FIH-Case and the MEIP - A step forward or a step in the wrong direction? *European State Aid Law Quarterly, 16*(1), 86–92.

de Cecco, F. (2013). *State aid and the European economic constitution*. Hart.

Dekker, C. (2017). The 'effect on trade between the Member States' criterion: Is it the right criterion by which the Commission's workload can be managed? *European State Aid Law Quarterly, 16*(2), 154–163.

Fiedziuk, N. (2013). Towards decentralization of State aid control: The case of services of general economic interest. *World Competition: Law and Economic Review, 36*, 387–408.

Gallo, D., & Mariotti, C. (2021). Social services of general economic interest. In L. Hancher, T. Ottervanger, & P. Slot (Eds.), *EU State aids* (pp. 307–386). Sweet and Maxwell.

Guillamond, M. (2021). Aviation. In L. Hancher, T. Ottervanger, & P. Slot (Eds.), *EU State aids* (pp. 683–714). Sweet and Maxwell.

Hancher, L. (2017). Pearle revisited, or does our State aid vision really improve with hindsight? In C. Buts & J. Buendía Sierra (Eds.), *Milestones in State aid case law* (pp. 152–159). Lexxicon.

Hancher, L., & Salerno, F. (2021). Article 107(2) and Article 107(3). In L. Hancher, T. Ottervanger, & P. Slot (Eds.), *EU State aids* (pp. 131–182). Sweet and Maxwell.

Hancher, L., Ottervanger, T., & Slot, P. (2021). *EU State aids*. Sweet and Maxwell.

Hofmann, H. (2016). *State aid law of the European Union*. OUP.

Jaeger, T. (2021). Services of general economic interest. In L. Hancher, T. Ottervanger, & P. Slot (Eds.), *EU State aids* (pp. 255–306). Sweet and Maxwell.

Lovdahl Gormsen, L. (2019). *European State aid and tax rulings*. Edward Elgar.

Neergaard, U. (2011). Services of general economic interest under EU law constraints. In D. Schiek, U. Liebert, & H. Schenider (Eds.), *European economic and social constitutionalism after the Treaty of Lisbon* (pp. 174–195). CUP.

Nicolaides, P. (2015). New limits to the concept of selectivity: The birth of 'general exception' to the prohibition of State aid in EU competition law. *Journal of European Competition Law & Practice, 6*(5), 315–323.

Nicolaides, P. (2017a). Excessive widening of the concept of selectivity. *European State Aid Law Quarterly, 16*(1), 62–72.

Nicolaides, P. (2017b). Altmark: The Mount Everest of State aid. In C. Buts & J. Buendía Sierra (Eds.), *Milestones in State aid case law* (pp. 96–112). Lexxicon.

Nicolaides, P. (2017c). Imputability to the State. *State Aid Uncovered*, blogpost 4 July 2017, https://www.lexxion.eu/en/stateaidpost/imputability-to-the-state

Nicolaides, P. (2017d). Developments on the concepts of advantage and selectivity. *State Aid Uncovered*, blogpost 17 January 2017, https://www.lexxion.eu/stateaidpost/part-ii-developments-on-the-concepts-of-advantage-and-selectivity/

Nicolaides, P. (2018). Do Member States grant State aid when they act as regulators? *European State Aid Law Quarterly, 17*(1), 2–18.

Nicolaides, P., & Rusu, I. (2012). The concept of selectivity: An ever wider scope. *European State Aid Law Quarterly, 11*(4), 796–797.

Nowak, A. (2018). Evidence requirements for State aid compatibility assessment. *European State Aid Law Quarterly, 17*(2), 212–221.

Panci, L. (2018). Latest developments on the interpretation of the concept of selectivity in the field of corporate taxation. *European State Aid Law Quarterly, 17*(3), 353–367.

Parret, L., & van Heezik, G. (2018). Eventech, the selectivity of a bus lines policy. *European State Aid Law Quarterly, 17*(1), 93–100.

Piernas López, J. (2015). *The concept of State aid under EU law*. OUP.

Quigley, C. (2015). *European State aid law and policy*. Hart.

Rapp, J. (2018). Taxation, State aid and distortions of competition. In J. L. da Cruz Villaça et al. (Eds.), *Institutional rapport FIDE Conference Estoril 2018*. FIDE.

Riedel, P., Wilson, T., & Cranly, S. (2020). Learnings from the Commission's initial State aid response to the COVID-19 outbreak. *European State Aid Law Quarterly, 19*(2), 115–126.

Robbins, N., Puglissi, L., & Yang, L. (2020). State aid tools to tackle the impact of COVID-19: What is the role of economic and financial analysis? *European State Aid Law Quarterly, 19*(2), 137–149.

Romariz, C. (2014). Revisiting material selectivity in EU State aid law–Or the ghost of yet-to-come. *European State Aid Law Quarterly, 13*(1), 41–42.

Ross, M. (2009). A Healthy approach to services of general economic interest? The BUPA judgment of the Court of First Instance. *European Law Review, 34*(1), 27–140.

Säcker, F., & Montag, F. (2016). *European State Aid Law: A commentary*. C.H. Beck.

Sauter, W. (2013). The impact of EU competition law on national healthcare systems. *European Law Review, 38*(4), 457–478.

Scharf, T. (2021). Transport. In L. Hancher, T. Ottervanger, & P. Slot (Eds.), *EU State aids* (pp. 643–682). Sweet and Maxwell.

Stuart, E., & Roginska-Green, I. (2018). *Sixty years of EU State aid law and policy*. Kluwer.

Szyszczak, E. (2012). Modernising State aid and the financing of SGEI. *Journal of European Competition Law & Practice, 3*(4), 332–343.

Szyszczak, E. (2017). The Altmark case revisited: Local and regional subsidies to public services. *European State Aid Law Quarterly, 16*(3), 395–407.

Werner, P., & Stoican, L. (2018). The Nox case - Still trying to fit in a system. *European State Aid Law Quarterly, 17*(1), 101–109.

Werner, P., & Verouden, V. (2017). *EU State Aid Control: Law and economics*. Kluwer.

Zelger, B. (2018). The effect on trade criterion in European Union State aid law: A critical approach. *European State Aid Law Quarterly, 17*(1), 28–42.

Article 108 [Enforcement]
(ex-Article 88 TEC)

1. The Commission shall, in cooperation with Member States, keep under constant review all systems of aid existing in those States. It shall propose to the latter any appropriate measures required by the progressive development or by the functioning of the internal market.[1–11]
2. If, after giving notice to the parties concerned to submit their comments, the Commission finds that aid granted by a State or through State resources is not compatible with the internal market having regard to Article 107, or that such aid is being misused, it shall decide that the State concerned shall abolish or alter such aid within a period of time to be determined by the Commission.[21]

   If the State concerned does not comply with this decision within the prescribed time, the Commission or any other interested State may, in derogation from the provisions of Articles 258 and 259, refer the matter to the Court of Justice of the European Union direct.[52–62]

   On application by a Member State, the Council may, acting unanimously, decide that aid which that State is granting or intends to grant shall be considered to be compatible with the internal market, in derogation from the provisions of Article 107 or from the regulations provided for in Article 109, if such a decision is justified by exceptional circumstances. If, as regards the aid in question, the Commission has already initiated the procedure provided for in the first subparagraph of this paragraph, the fact that the State concerned has made its application to the Council shall have the effect of suspending that procedure until the Council has made its attitude known.

   If, however, the Council has not made its attitude known within three months of the said application being made, the Commission shall give its decision on the case.
3. The Commission shall be informed, in sufficient time to enable it to submit its comments, of any plans to grant or alter aid. If it considers that any such plan is not compatible with the internal market having regard to Article 107, it shall without delay initiate the procedure provided for in paragraph 2. The Member State concerned shall not put its proposed measures into effect until this procedure has resulted in a final decision.[22–32]
4. The Commission may adopt regulations relating to the categories of State aid that the Council has, pursuant to Article 109, determined may be exempted from the procedure provided for by paragraph 3 of this Article.[33,34]

Contents

1. The Procedural Framework for State Aid Control 1
2. Existing Aid Versus New Aid 12
   2.1. Control of Existing Aid Under Article 108.1 TFEU and Article 108.2 TFEU 21
   2.2. Control of New Aid: Notification and Investigation 22
   2.3. Deviations to the Notification Duty of Article 108.3 TFEU 33
   2.4. Recovery of Unlawful Aid 35
3. Legal Remedies 44
   3.1. The Application of Article 108.3 TFEU Before the National Courts 44
   3.2. Review of State Aid by the Union Courts 52
List of Cases
References

1. The Procedural Framework for State Aid Control

1 The **central provision** for the enforcement of EU State aid law is Article 108 TFEU. Article 108.1 TFEU provides the Commission with the power to review all systems of aid. Article 108.2 TFEU confers the Commission with a discretionary power to declare aid granted by the MS compatible with the internal market. Article 108.2 TFEU also enables the Commission to open a formal investigation (→ para 24 et seqq.), in case it has serious doubts about the compatibility of State aid measures.[1]

2 While Articles 107.1, 107.2 and 107.3 TFEU (→ Article 107 para 76 et seqq.) respectfully concern the notion of State aid and the prohibition of State aid, as well as the substantive grounds for compatibility with the internal market, Article 108 TFEU contains the **procedural framework to enforce** these provisions.[2]

3 Central to the enforcement of the substantive State aid provisions is Article 108.3 TFEU. This provision contains a **standstill obligation** (→ para 21 et seqq.) for the MS. The standstill obligation requires the MS to **notify** all proposed State aid measures to the Commission, prior to implementation, except for aid measure that may fall under the scope of the block exemption regulations.[3] Consequently, this provision precludes the MS to implement aid measures until the Commission has made a final decision on whether the measure constitutes State aid, and if so, whether the measure is **compatible with the internal market**.[4] Article 108.3 TFEU has direct effect and can be enforced by the Commission (public enforcement of Article 108.3 TFEU; → para 21 et seqq.) and before the national courts (private enforcement; → para 45 et seqq.).

---

[1] Loewenthal and Ziegler (2021), pp. 1048–1050.
[2] Loewenthal and Ziegler (2021), p. 1034.
[3] Werner and Verouden (2017), pp. 221–228.
[4] See Hancher and Salerno (2021), pp. 124, 133–135.

Article 108.4 TFEU in conjunction with Article 109 TFEU allow the Commission to adopt **regulations** on the compatibility of certain categories of **State aid** that are **exempted from notification**. The functioning of Article 108 TFEU is outlined and specified in regulations by the Council.

The procedural conditions of Article 108 TFEU are specified by **Council Regulation (EU) 2015/1589** (the **Procedural Regulation**) (→ Article 109 TFEU para 9).[5] This procedural regulation provides the legal framework for State aid enforcement by the Commission under secondary law. It also defines important legal concepts for the enforcement of State aid law such as 'existing aid' (→ para 21), 'new aid' (→ para 22 et seqq.) and 'unlawful aid' (→ para 36 et seqq.). Furthermore, the Procedural Regulation sets up a legal framework for the several stages of the administrative procedure (→ para 26 et seqq.) and the Commission's investigative powers. Moreover, the procedural regulation further clarifies the Commission's specific investigative powers and the decisions and remedies at its exposal.

Another important mechanism for the function of Article 108 TFEU is the **Commission Regulation (EU) 2015/2282**.[6] This regulation contains a procedural framework for the MS to notify aid measures correctly. In essence, the regulation sets out four different procedures: for duly notified aid, for unlawful aid, for so-called 'misuse of aid', and for existing aid schemes.[7]

Next to the Procedural Regulation the **Council Regulation (EU) 2015/1588 (the Enabling Regulation)**[8] (→ Article 109 TFEU para 5 et seqq.) attributes to the Commission the powers to declare specified **exempted categories of aid** to be compatible with the internal market. The Enabling Regulation is of particular importance against the backdrop of Article 109 TFEU, which enables the Council to adopt all appropriate regulations for the application of the Articles 107 and 108 TFEU (→ Article 109 TFEU para 1). Based on the Enabling Regulation, the Commission can exempt categories of aid from the notification requirement of Article 108.3 TFEU and Article 2 of the Procedural Regulation (→ para 9 et seqq.). In addition, this regulation allows the Commission to adopt regulations, such as the General Block Exemption Regulation (GBER) (→ para 33 et seqq.), which set out specified procedural and substantive provisions for exemption.[9]

Attributing the Commission with the relevant powers, Article 108 TFEU and the Procedural Regulation, grant the Commission with an exclusive competence to

---

[5] Council Regulation 2015/1589/EU *on detailed procedural rules for the application of Article 108 TFEU*, O.J. L 248 (2015).

[6] Commission Regulation (EU) 2015/2282 *amending Regulation (EC) No. 794/2004 as regards the notification forms and information sheets*, O.J. L 325/1 (2015).

[7] Hofmann (2016), pp. 368–377.

[8] Council Regulation 2015/1588/EU *on certain categories of horizontal State aid*, O.J. L 248 (2015); Hancher and Salerno (2021), pp. 218–221.

[9] Commission Regulation (EU) No. 651/2014 *declaring certain categories of aid compatible with the internal market*, O.J. L 187/1 (2014), as amended by Commission Regulation (EU) 2021/1237, O.J. L 270/39 (2021).

decide upon the compatibility of State aid measure with the internal market.[10] This exclusive power is only subject to **judicial review** by the GC and Court (→ para 52 et seqq.).[11]

9   From a point of private enforcement it is important to note that the **standstill obligation** of Article 108.3 TFEU, in addition to Article 3 of the Procedural Regulation, **has direct effect**.[12] Therefore, Article 108.3 TFEU can be relied upon by individuals before the national courts.[13] The application of Article 108.3 TFEU before national courts must protect the rights of individuals concerned.[14] In national proceedings the national court has to apply both Article 107.1 TFEU and uphold Article 108.3. TFEU when determining whether a State measure constitutes State aid and has been implemented in contravention with Article 108.3 TFEU.[15] Moreover, national courts (→ para 44 et seqq.) have jurisdiction when it comes to the implementation of negative Commission decisions, especially concerning the ordering of recovery of aid (→ para 36 et seqq.).[16] In addition, national courts may also be required to give effect to the application of block exemptions. In accordance with the principle of procedural autonomy, national courts can be required to enforce the application of the General Block Exemption Regulation (GBER) (→ para 33).[17] Accordingly, the provisions of block exceptions, such as the GBER, are directly applicable before national courts.[18]

10   However, there is an important limit for litigation before the national courts as they are not allowed to rule on the **compatibility of aid** with the internal market, since this competence is **exclusive reserved for the Commission**.[19]

11   As to provide guidance to the MS, the Commission has published a detailed **'State aid manual of procedures'**.[20] This non-binding, internal working document

---

[10] Hancher and Salerno (2021), pp. 132–133.

[11] Flynn and Gilliams (2021), pp. 1118–1120; Case C-574/14, *PGE* (CJEU 15 September 2016) para 32 and 36; Case C-284/12, *Deutsche Lufthansa* (CJEU 21 November 2013) para 41; Case C-119/05, *Lucchini* (ECJ 18 July 2007) para 28, 51–52.

[12] Case C-284/12, *Deutsche Lufthansa* (CJEU 21 November 2013) para 28; Case C-199/06, *CELF* (ECJ 12 February 2008) para 45, 47; Case 120/73, *Lorenz v Germany* (CJEU 11 December 1973).

[13] Case C-33/14, *Mory* (CJEU 17 September 2015) para 59; Case C-505/14, *Klausner Holz Niedersachsen* (CJEU 11 November 2015) para 21, 24. See also Flynn and Gilliams (2021), pp. 1118–1120 and Säcker and Montag (2016), p. 1548.

[14] See Case C-284/12, *Deutsche Lufthansa* (CJEU 21 November 2013) para 28.

[15] Case C-119/05 *Lucchini* (ECJ 18 July 2007) para 50; see also Nicolaides (2014), pp. 409–413.

[16] See Kreuschitz and Bermejo (2017), pp. 221–252; see also Adriaanse and den Ouden (2009), pp. 15–26.

[17] Case C-349/17, *Eesti Pagar* (CJEU 5 March 2019) para 91, 130; Van de Casteele (2021), pp. 248–251.

[18] Case C-349/17, *Eesti Pagar* (CJEU 5 March 2019) para 142; see also Rusu and Looijestijn (2017), p. 22; Hofmann (2016), p. 463.

[19] Hancher and Salerno (2021), p. 133. Case 6/64, *Costa v ENEL* (ECJ 15 July 1964); Case C-275/10, *Residex* (CJEU 8 December 2011); Case C-284/12, *Deutsche Lufthansa* (CJEU 21 November 2013).

[20] European Commission (2013), *State Aid Manual of Procedures. Internal DG Competition working documents on procedures for the application of Articles 107 and 108 TFEU*.

provides guidance in the application of the procedures of Article 108 TFEU. Moreover, the MS are required to apply substantive guidelines on horizontal and sectoral type of aids.[21] In addition, national authorities may consult Commission guidance on the application of the GBER.[22] Furthermore, the Commission also provided **guidelines for the enforcement** of the Articles 107 and 108 TFEU **by national courts** (→ para 44 et seqq.).[23]

2. Existing Aid Versus New Aid

Article 108.1.TFEU States that the Commission shall, in cooperation with MS, keep under constant **review all systems of aid existing in the MS** and shall propose to the MS any appropriate measures required by the progressive development or by the functioning of the internal market. Detailed rules are laid down in the Procedural Regulation (Council Regulation 2015/1589), whereby the Commission's competence to continuously monitor all existing aid schemes in cooperation with the MS is specified in particular in Articles 21 to 23.[24] Article 108.1 TFEU provides the **Commission** with the **exclusive competence** to review all existing aids under the notion of aid of Article 107.1 TFEU, and also to declare existing aids compatible with the internal market.[25]

12

Article 1 point (b) of the Procedural Regulation describes **existing aid** as (i) all aid which **existed prior to the entry into force of the TFEU** in the respective MS, that is to say, aid schemes and individual aid which were put into effect before, and are still applicable after, the entry into force of the TFEU in the respective MS; (ii) authorised aid (aid which have been authorised by the Commission or by the Council); (iii) aid which is deemed to have been authorised pursuant to specified provisions; (iv) aid which is deemed to be existing aid under Article 17 of the Procedural Regulation; (v) aid which is deemed to be an existing aid because it can be established that at the time it was put into effect it did not constitute an aid, and subsequently became an aid due to the evolution of the internal market and without having been altered by the MS.

13

Article 1 point (c) of the Procedural Regulation describes **new aid** as 'all aid, that is to say, aid schemes and individual **aid, which is not existing aid**, including alterations to existing aid'. Therefore the distinction between these two concepts

14

---

[21] See for an encompassing overview Säcker and Montag (2016), pp. 440–450.

[22] See the Practical Guide to the GBER - Frequently Asked Questions, available at https://ec.europa.eu/regional_policy/sources/conferences/state-aid/rdi/8gber_practical_quite_faq.pdf. See Van de Casteele (2021), p. 222.

[23] Commission, *Notice on the enforcement of state aid law by national courts*, O.J. C 85/1 (2009). See also Van den Gronden (2017), p. 143.

[24] Loewenthal and Ziegler (2021), pp. 1046–1047.

[25] Article 21 of the Procedural Regulation (EU) 2015/1589. Loewenthal and Ziegler (2021), pp. 1042–1043.

depends on the moment of the MS' accession to the EU, or its legal predecessors such as the EC.[26]

15 The distinction between the concepts of existing aid and new aid is very important from a procedural point of view, as **different procedures apply to existing aid and new aid**, respectively.[27] New aid must be notified in advance to the Commission under Article 108.3 TFEU.[28] It is important to note that the obligation to notify (and the prohibition to implement aid prior to notification) only applies to aid measures that do not fall under the scope of block exempted aid categories as are listed in Article 1 of the Empowering Regulation under Article 109 TFEU (→ Article 109 TFEU para 5).[29] Hence, under Article 2.1 of the Procedural Regulation and Article 1 of the Enabling Regulation, MS may deviate from the notification requirement of Article 108.3 TFEU. These deviations are specified in individual block exemption regulations such as the GBER. Consequently, this deviation is conditional on the correct application of the procedural and substantive conditions specified in the block exemption regulations (→ para 33) and *de minimis* regulations (→ Article 107 TFEU para 69, 89–91).[30] If these conditions are not met, implemented aid may still be considered as unlawful.[31]

16 **New aid** cannot be implemented prior to the moment that the Commission has rendered a final decision on its **compatibility with the internal market**. In case new aids are implemented in breach with Article 108.3 TFEU or declared as incompatible aid under Article 108.2 TFEU, they must be recovered.[32]

17 **Existing aid** may, under Article 108.1. TFEU, be duly implemented in accordance with the **cooperation procedure** set out in the Article 21 of the Procedural Regulation, on the condition that the Commission has not found it to be incompatible with the internal market (→ para 21).[33] In such instances, the Commission may, under Articles 22 and 23 of the Procedural Regulation, propose recommendations for appropriate measures which are necessary to restore the level playing field on the internal market.[34]

18 The procedures on existing aid and new aid differ and also entail different remedies. In contrast to new aid, **existing aid does not have to be recovered by the MS**. However, if the existing aid is found incompatible with the internal market,

---

[26] Loewenthal and Ziegler (2021), pp. 1043–1044.

[27] Loewenthal and Ziegler (2021), pp. 1043–1044.

[28] Metaxas (2017), pp. 73–77; Loewenthal and Ziegler (2021), p. 1040.

[29] Werner and Verouden (2017), p. 216.

[30] Commission Regulation (EU) No. 651/2014, O.J. L 187 (2014) (GBER); Commission Regulation (EC) No. 1407/2013 *on de minimis aid*, O.J. L 352 (2013); Commission Regulation (EU) No. 360/2012 *on de minimis aid granted to undertakings providing services of general economic interest*, O.J. L 114/8 (2012).

[31] Case C-349/17, *Eesti Pagar* (CJEU 5 March 2019) para 87. Van de Casteele (2021), pp. 248–251.

[32] Szyszczak (2011), p. 336.

[33] Loewenthal and Ziegler (2021), pp. 1046–1047.

[34] Loewenthal and Ziegler (2021), p. 1047.

the Commission may decide according to the proceedings of the Articles 4.4, 6 and 9 of the Procedural Regulation (→ para 24–30) that the MS must alter or terminate the existing aid measure by means of appropriate measures. However, prior to initiating such investigative proceedings, the Commission relies on the cooperation procedure as set out in Articles 21 through 23 of the Procedural Regulation.[35] Only in the event of rejection of proposed appropriate measures will the formal investigation procedure be initiated under Article 108.2 TFEU in conjunction with Articles 4.4, 6 and 9 of Procedural Regulation 2015/1589.

'**Unlawful aid**' is defined in Article 1 point (f) of the Procedural Regulation as 'new aid' put into effect in contravention of Article 108.3. TFEU. This definition covers situations in which aid is implemented without prior notification. In addition, implementing measures, pending the notification phase are unlawful according to the standstill clause of Article 108.3 TFEU.[36] **19**

In case of unlawful implementation, affected parties may start litigation before national courts to remedy the implementation of unlawful aid.[37] National courts are required to provide a **national remedy for breaches of the standstill clause** of Article 108.3 TFEU and may under national procedural law suspend the implementation of unlawful aid and order the recovery of payments already made to safeguard the interests of the parties concerned and to give effect to Commission decisions concerning unlawful aid.[38] **20**

2.1. Control of Existing Aid Under Article 108.1 TFEU and Article 108.2 TFEU

Under Article 108.1 TFEU existing aid is only subject to **ex-post control**. The Commission's constant review of existing aid schemes under Article 108.1 TFEU, which are prior to initiating the procedure under Article 108.2 TFEU, includes the gathering of all necessary information by the Commission in cooperation with the MS concerned (Article 21.1 of Procedural Regulation 2015/1589). This procedure is founded on the principle of sincere cooperation (Art. 4.3 TEU). Under Article 21.2 of the Procedural Regulation, the Commission may consider that an existing aid scheme is not, or is no longer, compatible with the internal market. In such instance, the Commission shall inform the MS concerned of its preliminary view and give the MS concerned the opportunity to submit its comments within a period of one month, which may be extended by the Commission. After the exchange of information between the Commission and the MS, the Commission may conclude under Article 21 of the Procedural Regulation that an existing aid **21**

---

[35] Loewenthal and Ziegler (2021), pp. 1046–1047.
[36] Loewenthal and Ziegler (2021), pp. 1063–1064. Adriaanse and Aalbers (2021), pp. 1090–1092.
[37] Case C 505/14 *Klausner Holz Niedersachsen* (CJEU 11 November 2015) para 24.
[38] Case C-284/12, *Deutsche Lufthansa* (CJEU 21 November 2013) para 43. See Adriaanse and Aalbers (2021), pp. 1110–1113; Case C-505/14 *Klausner Holz Niedersachsen* (CJEU 11 November 2015) para 25.

scheme is not compatible with the internal market and consequently issue a recommendation proposing appropriate measures to the MS. Under Article 22, the Commission may propose substantive amendments of the existing aid scheme; or the introduction of procedural requirements; or abolition of the existing aid scheme. It is important to note that the appropriate measures under Article 22.2. of Regulation 2015/1589 are not exhaustive.[39] If the MS concerned accepts the proposed measures, it its bound by its acceptance to implement the appropriate measures and must also inform the Commission of the implementation stage (Article 23.1 of the Procedural Regulation). In case the MS does not accept the Commission's recommendations, the Commission may decide to initiate proceedings for formal investigation under Article 108.2 TFEU and Articles 4.4, 6 and 9 of the Procedural Regulation.[40] The outcome of this procedure may be that, when the Commissions finds that the aid is incompatible, it shall require the MS to alter or altogether abolish an existing aid scheme.[41]

2.2. Control of New Aid: Notification and Investigation

22 Save for block exempted aid categories—which are listed in the Article 1 of the Empowering Regulation of the Council (and specified in Commission block exemption regulations such as the GBER)—**any plans to grant new aid shall be notified to the Commission**. Article 108.3 TFEU, read in conjunction with the Procedural Regulation, constitutes the legal framework for two important administrative procedures: the notification phase under Article 2 of the Procedural Regulation, which includes a preliminary assessment (→ para 24) of the aid (Article 4 of the Procedural Regulation) and the investigation phase (Article 6 of the Procedural Regulation; → para 28), which concerns the formal investigation of the notified aid measure.

23 Article 108.3 TFEU establishes a **prior control of alterations to existing aid** (which can be considered as new aid) and of plans to grant new aid.[42] MS must notify these changes to the Commission, save for the possibility of the application of a block exemption regulation. The goal of the prior control mechanism of Article 108.3 TFEU is that only aid which is compatible with the internal market may be implemented by the MS.[43] New aid which has not been notified is unlawful and its implementation by an MS may result in public enforcement actions by the Commission (→ para 24–32) or private enforcement injunctions before national courts by third parties (→ para 45–52).

---

[39] Loewenthal and Ziegler (2021), pp. 1048–1049.

[40] See Article 22 of the Procedural Regulation 2015/1589; Hofmann (2016), pp. 371–377.

[41] Loewenthal and Ziegler (2021), pp. 1046–1049.

[42] Joined Cases C-630/11 P to C-633/11 P, *HGA v Commission* (CJEU 13 June 2013) para 90.

[43] Case C-284/12, *Deutsche Lufthansa* (CJEU 21 November 2013) para 25–26.

Article 108   [Enforcement]   305

24 After the Commission has received all relevant information concerning the notified aid measure, it will start to **examine the notification**.[44] Article 4 of the Procedural Regulation enables the Commission to conduct a **preliminary examination** of the notified aid.[45] This preliminary examination will result in a decision on the status of the notification (Article 4.2 of the Procedural Regulation).[46] This procedure includes the examinations of possible State aid and a preliminary assessment of the measure's compatibility. The notification system enables the Commission to examine the proposed aid measure's compatibility with Article 107.2 TFEU, Article 107.3 TFEU, Article 106.2 TFEU or Article 93 TFEU (→ Article 107 TFEU para 77–93).

25 In principle, the Commission shall **take a decision** under Article 4 of the Procedural Regulation **within two months** from the moment that the notification was complete (meaning: all the relevant information for assessing the notification was provided by the MS).[47] The Commission must be informed on time and provided with all the facts and figures of an new aid measure. The period can be extended with the consent of both the Commission and the MS concerned.

26 During the administrative procedure, the Commission may require MS to send **additional information**. Under Article 5 of the Procedural Regulation, the notification shall be deemed to be withdrawn if the requested information is not provided within the prescribed period, save for extension with the consent of both the Commission and the MS.

27 The Commission will usually make **one of the following decisions**: 1) Under Article 4.2 of the Procedural Regulation, the Commission may decide that the notified measure does not constitute State aid under Article 107.1 TFEU. 2) The Commission may, under Article 4.3 of the Procedural Regulation, find that there are no doubts regarding the compatibility with the internal market of the notified measure, which is referred to as a decision not to raise objections.[48] 3) In case the Commission has doubts concerning the compatibility with the internal market of a notified measure, i.e. when a preliminary investigation shows that the measure *prima facie* constitutes State aid in the sense of Article 107.1 TFEU, it shall decide to initiate the formal investigation procedure (→ para 28–30) under Article 108.2 TFEU (Article 4.4 of the Procedural Regulation).[49]

28 Under Article 6.1 of the Procedural Regulation, the decision to initiate the **formal investigation procedure** shall summarise the relevant issues of fact and law; shall include a preliminary assessment of the Commission as to the aid character of the proposed measure, and shall set out the doubts as to its compatibility with the internal market. Accordingly, the Commission will allow the MS

---

[44] Säcker and Montag (2016), pp. 1568–1569.
[45] Loewenthal and Ziegler (2021), pp. 1060–1061.
[46] Case C-590/14 P, *DEI v Commission* (CJEU 26 October 2016) para 98.
[47] Loewenthal and Ziegler (2021), pp. 1060–1061.
[48] See Case C-131/15 P, *Club Hotel Loutraki* (CJEU 21 December 2016) para 35.
[49] Case C-131/15 P, *Club Hotel Loutraki* (CJEU 21 December 2016) para 32.

29 concerned, but also interested parties to submit comments on the aid measure. During the formal investigation, the Commission may order **suspension of the implementation** of the aid or **order interim orders for its recovery**.[50]

29 After the initiation of the formal investigation procedure provided for in Article 6 of the Procedural Regulation, the Commission may under Article 7 of the Procedural Regulation—for substantively determining technically complex cases—**request undertakings** or associations of undertakings (→ Article 101 TFEU para 23 et seqq.) **to provide relevant market information** to enable the Commission to complete its substantive analysis of a notified aid measure. Under Article 7.1 of the Procedural Regulation, the Commission may only initiate this request in case the information provided by the MS proofs insufficient and ineffective (Article 7.2 poin (a)). In so far as aid beneficiaries are concerned, the MS must agree to the request (Article 7.2 poin (b)).

30 Article 9 of the Procedural Regulation provides the legal basis for the **closure of the formal investigation proceedings by means of a decision**.[51] The Commission may find that—after appropriate modification of the aid measure by the MS concerned—the notified aid does not constitute State aid (and thereby rendering a decision declaring that the notified **aid does not constitute State aid** under Article 9.2 Procedural Regulation). Alternatively, the Commission may decide that the doubts raised by the notified aid concerning the compatibility have been removed by the MS, allowing the Commission to declare the aid as compatible with the internal market (and thereby rendering a **positive decision** under Article 9.3 of the Procedural Regulation). To provide guidance for the MS, the Commission has adopted various guidelines for determining the compatibility of specific types of State aid. Furthermore, the Commission may decide that the notified aid is compatible with the internal market on condition that certain obligations are complied with by the MS (and thereby rendering a **conditional decision** under Article 9.4 of the Procedural Regulation). Such decision occur for instance in case of restructuring aid, in which case MS may be required to provide monitoring information on the implementation of the restructuring activities.[52] Lastly, the Commission may also find that the notified aid is not compatible with the internal market and prohibit the implementation of the aid scheme by means of a so-called **negative decision** (Article 9.5 of the Procedural Regulation). A negative decision has the effect that notified aid, which was not put in effect, must be cancelled. In case the aid was already implemented—in breach with the standstill obligation of Article 108.3 TFEU—the aid is unlawful and the Commission will be able to render a recovery decision within the meaning of Article 16 of Regulation 2015/1589.

31 The Commission shall take a decision under Article 108.2 TFEU on the notified aid as soon as all the doubts on the notified aid are removed. In practice, the Commission tries to adopt a decision within a period of 18 months after the opening

---

[50] Adriaanse and Aalbers (2021), pp. 1092–1099; Hofmann (2016), pp. 368–369.
[51] Loewenthal and Ziegler (2021), p. 1062.
[52] Bourgeois (2021), pp. 1011–1014.

of the formal investigation procedure (Article 9.6 of the Procedural Regulation). However, this limit may be extended after agreement between the Commission and the MS concerned. From the moment the Commission has received all the relevant information by the MS concerned for rendering a decision, it shall take a decision within two months. Before adopting a decision, the Commission will give the MS concerned the opportunity of making comments within the time-limit of 1 month. Moreover, the Commission will request the MS and interested parties concerned to State whether the provided information has a **confidentiality status** (Article 9.9 of the Procedural Regulation), for instance in case of legitimate interests such as the protection of business information (Article 9.10 of the Procedural Regulation).

The **Commission's decisions under Article 108.2 TFEU are legally binding acts** within the meaning of Article 288.4 TFEU, and are among the acts which may be challenged in an action for annulment under Article 263 TFEU. 32

2.3. Deviations to the Notification Duty of Article 108.3 TFEU

Aid under the **General Block Exemption Regulation** is exempted from notification.[53] However, there are some important requirements, such specific transparency—and proportionality conditions. Article 6 GBER requires for instance an incentive effect and Article 7 GBER requires that only proportionate aid intensities apply to the eligible costs.[54] When applying the GBER, MS are required to inform the Commission within 20 working days after an aid measure is adopted. Moreover, aid must not exceed the individual thresholds for notification (Article 4 GBER) and fulfil cumulation requirements (Article 8 GBER). In principle aid categories under the GBER are exempted from the standstill clause. Article 1 of the GBER has a very broad scope including: regional aid, aid to SME's, aid for environmental protection, aid for research and development and innovation, training aid, aid for several types of infrastructure (including sports infrastructure, regional airport and harbours) and aid for culture. These aid categories are only block exempted from notification on condition that the relevant procedural and substantive conditions are met.[55] Consequently, Article 3 GBER stipulates that aid which does not fulfil these conditions will be considered unlawful.[56] 33

Under Article 108.2 (3) TFEU **the Council**, on application by an MS, may, by acting unanimously, **decide that aid** which that State is granting or intends to grant is to be **considered to be compatible with the internal market**, in derogation from the provisions of Article 107 TFEU or from the regulations provided under Article 109 TFEU, if such a decision is justified by exceptional circumstances. The 34

---

[53] Recital 1 and Article 3 of Commission Regulation (EU) No. 651/2014, O.J. L 187 (2014).
[54] Van de Casteele (2021), pp. 217–231.
[55] Van de Casteele (2021), p. 228.
[56] Case C-349/17, *Eesti Pagar* (CJEU 5 March 2019) para 87; Case C-493/14, *Dilly's Wellnesshotel v Finanzamt Linz* (CJEU 21 July 2016) para 33–34.

Court ruled that the Articles 107 and 108 TFEU reserve a central role for the Commission in determining whether aid is incompatible and that the power conferred upon the Council in the area of State aid by the third subparagraph of Article 108.2 TFEU is exceptional in character, which means that it must necessarily be interpreted strictly.[57] Consequently, the Court held in *Eurallumina* that a Council decision authorising an MS to introduce an exemption of excise duties could not have the effect of preventing the Commission from exercising the powers to review whether that exemption constituted State aid, and on the conclusion of that procedure, if appropriate, to adopt a decision such as the contested decision.[58]

2.4. Recovery of Unlawful Aid

35 The recovery requirements of Article 108 TFEU and the Procedural Regulation apply to the concepts of **unlawful aid** and cases of **misuse of aid**.[59] 'Unlawful aid' is defined in Article 1 point (f) of the Procedural Regulation as 'new aid' put into effect in contravention of Article 108.3 TFEU. Unlawful aid can be considered aid which is implemented without notification (→ para 19). Moreover, the term unlawful aid also applies to notified aid which is, despite the standstill clause, implemented by the MS before the Commission has decided whether or not the aid is compatible with the internal market. Misuse of aid concerns aid which was used by the recipient in contrast with a Commission decision under Articles 4, 7 and 9 of the Procedural Regulation (→ para 24–30).[60] Lastly, aid may be considered to be **illegal aid** if it is granted despite of the fact that the Commission decided that the aid was incompatible.[61]

36 The recovering of unlawful aid is a legal instrument to **restore the level playing field** of competition by requiring the recipient of aid to repay the received aid and thus end the distortion of competition created by an unlawful intervention of the State.[62] The recovery of unlawful aid is therefore necessary to re-establish the market situation prior to the moment of granting State aid to an undertaking.[63] The level playing field will be restored from the moment unlawful aid has been repaid by the undertaking which actually benefited from it.[64]

---

[57] Cf. Quigley (2015), pp. 508–509; also Bach (2017), pp. 667–674.

[58] Case C-272/12 P *Commission v Ireland and Others* (CJEU 10 December 2013) para 49; Joined Cases C-369/16 P, C-373/16, C-323/16 P, *Eurallumina, Aughinish et al. v Commission* (CJEU 7 December 2017) para 47.

[59] Hofmann (2016), pp. 368–369, 382–385.

[60] See Article 1 point (g) of the Procedural Regulation.

[61] Case C-37/14, *Commission v France ("Plan de Campagne")* (CJEU 12 February 2015) para 87.

[62] Case C-672/13, *OTP Bank v Magyar Állam* (CJEU 19 March 2015) para 71.

[63] Adriaanse and Aalbers (2021), pp. 1109–1121.

[64] Case C-357/14 P, *Electrabel* (CJEU 1 October 2015) para 110.

Article 108 [Enforcement]

After concluding a formal investigation, the **Commission may order for recovery** after a decision under Article 9 of the Procedural Regulation. By deciding that aid is unlawful and incompatible with the internal market the Commission may in addition order the total amount of aid, including interest, to be recovered from the recipient undertaking.[65] Article 16.1 of the Procedural Regulation enables the Commission to decide that the MS that granted aid must take all necessary measures to recover the aid. Under Article 16.2 of the Procedural Regulation, the Commission will also require interest to be paid from the date on which the unlawful aid was at the disposal of the beneficiary until the moment of recovery.[66] Under Article 16.3 of the Procedural Regulation, MS must initiate immediately a recovery action under the procedures of national law. Effectively the implementation of recovery procedures is a matter to be settled for the national courts alone.[67]

When rendering a recovery decision, the Commission is not required to calculate the exact amount to be recovered.[68] According to the principles of procedural autonomy and loyal cooperation, the national authorities of **MS themselves must order recovery from the recipient** under close judicial review by the national courts.[69] In the absence of a recovery the national authorities of the MS themselves, under review of national proceeding before national courts, are responsible to determine the exact amount for recovered, although they may ask the Commission for guidance.[70]

As to the temporal aspects of the recovery of the aid found to be unlawful and incompatible with the internal market, first, it should be recalled that **delayed recovery**, namely, after the period prescribed, **breaches Articles 107 and 108 TFEU**.[71] In case of failure to implement a Commission decision on recovery, Article 108.2 TFEU proceedings allow the Commission to set a specified to date to recalculate the total amount for recovery including interests.[72] However, as long as the MS has not requested extension of the period specified by the decision ordering the recovery of the unlawful aid, the relevant date for the application of Article 108.2 TFEU and, in particular, for the registration of the debt relating to the

---

[65] Adriaanse and Aalbers (2021), p. 1109.

[66] Commission Notice o*n the recovery of unlawful and incompatible State aid*, O.J. C 247 (2019), para 110–111.

[67] Case C-33/14, *Mory v Commission* (CJEU 17 September 2015) para 68, 76. Commission Notice on the *recovery of unlawful and incompatible State aid*, O.J. C 247 (2019), para 20.

[68] Adriaanse and Aalbers (2021), pp. 1109–1110. Case C-69/13, *Mediaset* (CJEU 13 February 2014).

[69] See for example Case C-69/13, *Mediaset* (CJEU 13 February 2014) para 21; Hofmann (2016), p. 386.

[70] Case T-468/08, *Dunamenti Erömü v Commission* (CFI 30 April 2014) para 28, 38.

[71] Case C-363/16, *Commission v Greece* (CJEU 17 January 2018) para 40.

[72] Adriaanse and Aalbers (2021), pp. 1109–1100; Case C-37/14, *Commission v France* (CJEU 12 February 2015).

recovery of the aid remains the date specified in the Commission's recovery decision.[73]

40 The Court trusts that the Commission and MS work together in good faith to overcome the difficulties in full compliance with the provisions of the TFEU, and in particular those on aid, in keeping with loyal cooperation.[74] For practical guidance purposes, the Commission has adopted a **Notice on Recovery**.[75] In *Larco*, the Court underlined that the only defence available for the MS is the objective and absolute impossiblity to properly implement a recovery decision.[76] The circumstance that the beneficiary undertakings is insolvent or bankrupt does therefore not diminish the obligation to repay unlawful received aid. In *Société Nationale Corse Méditerranée*, the Court ruled that removal of this obligation in the event of liquidation would render the State aid rules ineffective.[77]

41 Under Article 108 TFEU, **undertakings** to which aid has been granted **may not, in principle, entertain a legitimate expectation that the aid is lawful**, unless it has been granted in compliance with the procedure laid down in Article 16.1 of the Procedural Regulation.[78] Furthermore, the Court requires that an average economic operator exercising due care should normally be able to determine whether that procedure has been followed.[79] In particular, if aid is implemented without prior notification to the Commission, with the result that it is unlawful under Article 108.3 TFEU, the recipient of the aid cannot have at that time a legitimate expectation that its grant is lawful.[80] Moreover, the Court ruled in *Scuola Elementare Maria Montessori* that the Commission is not obligated to attach an order for recovery to every decision declaring aid to be unlawful and incompatible with the internal market.[81] The judges have ruled out the defence of exceptional circumstances in many occasions. For instance in *Greece v Commission*, the Court dismissed arguments relating to national legislation which precluded timely recovery proceedings.[82] In *Ryan Air & Aer Lingus*, the Court underpinned that a so-called 'passing on defence', although beneficial for consumers, could not be justified

---

[73] Case C-363/16, *Commission v Greece* (CJEU 17 January 2018) para 47.

[74] Case C-672/13, *OTP Bank v Magyar Állam and Magyar Államkincstár* (CJEU 19 March 2015) para 28.

[75] Commission Notice *on the recovery of unlawful and incompatible State aid*, O.J. C 247/1 (2019).

[76] Case C-481/16, *Commission v Greece (Larco)* (CJEU 9 November 2017) para 28–29.

[77] Case C-63/14, *Commission v France (Société Nationale Corse Méditerranée)* (CJEU 9 July 2015) para 52.

[78] Case C-493/14, *Dilly's Wellneshotel v Finanzamt Linz* (CJEU 21 July 2016).

[79] Joined Cases C-622/16 P and C-624/16 P, *Scuola Elementare Maria Montessori* (CJEU 6 November 2018) para 80, 82.

[80] Commission Notice *on the recovery of unlawful and incompatible State aid*, O.J. C 247 (2019), para 39–42.

[81] Joined Cases C-622/16 P and C-624/16 P, *Scuola Elementare Maria Montessori* (CJEU 6 November 2018) para 84.

[82] Case C-263/12, *Commission v Greece* (CJEU 17 November 2013).

under Article 108 TFEU. As a result, the tax advantages for the Irish airlines had to be recovered in full.[83]

If an undertaking is not able to repay the MS, the provision of Article 108.2 TFEU allows **national courts** to **declare a definitive cessation of the activities of the recipient undertaking** receiving, on condition that the recovery of the entire amount of the aid remains impossible throughout the insolvency proceedings.[84] **42**

In case an MS has failed to fulfil its obligation to recover, the Commission may request the **Court,** under **Article 260 TFEU,** to take the **necessary measures** to comply with the duty to recover.[85] If the Commission then considers that the MS concerned still has not taken the necessary measures to comply, it may bring the case directly before the Court under Article 108.2 TFEU or Article 258 TFEU. If the Court agrees with the Commission and finds that the MS did not comply with its judgment, it may ultimately impose a penalty payment.[86] The Commission may apply directly to the Court if the MS does not comply with these orders or in case there is a misuse of aid.[87] **43**

3. Legal Remedies

3.1. The Application of Article 108.3 TFEU Before the National Courts

National courts fulfil an important role in the **private enforcement** of Article 108.3 TFEU, which is complementary to the Commission's public enforcement functions and powers.[88] Individuals may invoke the standstill obligation of Article 108.3 TFEU before the national courts, since this provision has direct effect.[89] As a result, national courts may be asked in national proceedings by parties to determine a breach of Article 108.3 TFEU to protect the interests of individuals affected by potential unlawful aid.[90] **44**

In their duties the **national courts** are bound to **cooperate loyally with the Commission** when applying Article 108.3 TFEU.[91] As a consequence, national **45**

---

[83] Joined Cases C-164/15 P and C-165/15 P, *Ryanair and Aer Lingus* (CJEU 21 December 2016) para 99; see also Olykke (2017a), pp. 93–97.

[84] Case C-363/16, *Commission v Greece* (CJEU 17 January 2018) para 39.

[85] Commission Notice *on the recovery of unlawful and incompatible State aid*, O.J. C 247 (2019), para 149; Adriaanse and Aalbers (2021), p. 1104. See also Case C-184/11, *Commission v Spain* (CJEU 13 May 2014) para 35, 58–60.

[86] Flynn and Gilliams (2021), p. 1179.

[87] See the Articles 16 and 20 of the Procedural Regulation 2015/1589/EU. See Säcker and Montag (2016), p. 1619.

[88] Case C-284/12, *Deutsche Lufthansa v Flughafen Frankfurt-Hahn GmbH* (CJEU 21 November 2013) para 27.

[89] See Metselaar (2017), pp. 106–110.

[90] Case C-505/14, *Klausner Holz Niedersachsen* (CJEU 11 November 2015) para 26.

[91] Case C-574/14, *PGE t URE* (CJEU 15 September 2016) para 33.

courts must order unlawful aid for recovery, in case Article 108.3 TFEU is breached. The national courts must guard the rights of individuals that are possibly affected by unlawful implementation of notified aids which are under the examination of the Commission until the Commission renders a final decision (→ para 30).[92] Accordingly, even if the Commission is likely to declare aid compatible in a future final decision, the national courts may be required to preserve the direct effect of Article 108.3 TFEU.[93] A breach of this provision obliges the national court to declare the implementation as unlawful and order its recovery.[94] According to the Court, any other interpretation of Article 108.3 TFEU would deprive this TFEU provision of its effectiveness.[95]

46 In the application of Article 108.3 TFEU, the national courts do not possess the exclusive powers the Commission enjoys when it comes to investigating the compatibility of aid measures.[96] Therefore, the **national courts may not determine whether or not State aid is compatible with the internal market**.[97]

47 National courts can on the request of interested parties apply the concept of aid, under Article 107.1 TFEU, in national proceedings to determine whether a State measure constitutes as State aid, and if so, whether this measure had to be notified under Article 108.3 TFEU, or **whether the aid measure was exempted under an de minimis or block exemption regulation** (→ para 15).[98] Within the limits of procedural autonomy the national courts may apply Commission decisions, for instance recovery decisions. However, they must refrain from interpreting their validity, which must be left to the Court by means of referring for a preliminary ruling.[99] National interpretation would undermine an effective State aid control, especially when State aid is already declared incompatible with the internal market by the Commission and is required to be recovered by an MS.[100]

48 Individuals may also claim **damages** from the recipient of unlawful State aid before the national court.[101] The Court held in *Mory* that competitors must have a legitimate interest in these damages proceedings, but that is up to the national courts and national procedural law to determine whether such interests exist in national

---

[92] Joined Cases C-352/14 and C-353/14, *Iglesias Gutiérrez* (CJEU 15 October 2015) para 27–30.
[93] Case C-515/16, *Enedis v Aza* (CJEU 15 March 2017) para 19.
[94] See Kreuschitz and Bermejo (2017), pp. 221–252; see also Adriaanse and den Ouden (2009), pp. 15–26.
[95] Case C-505/14, *Klausner Holz Niedersachsen* (CJEU 11 November 2015) para 40–45.
[96] Case C-690/13, *Trapeza Eurobank v ATE* (CJEU 16 April 2015) para 38–41; Case C-598/17, *A-fonds v Inspecteur Belastingdienst* (CJEU 2 May 2019) para 46–47.
[97] Case C-598/17, *A-fonds v Inspecteur Belastingdienst* (CJEU 2 May 2019) para 46–47.
[98] Adriaanse and den Ouden (2009); Case C-349/17, *Eesti Pagar* (CJEU 5 March 2019) para 73.
[99] Case C-212/19, *Compagnie des pêches de Saint-Malo* (CJEU 17 September 2020) para 26–28.
[100] Case C-33/14, *Mory v Commission* (CJEU 17 September 2015) para 50.
[101] Flynn and Gilliams (2021), pp. 1192–1196; Almeida (2019), pp. 169–179.

proceedings.[102] National courts must therefore rule on the merits of the action for damages within the context of national procedural autonomy.[103]

National courts may be required to take interim relief measures in national **49** proceedings.[104] This may result in conflicts between national procedural law and the duties of national courts under Article 108.3 TFEU.[105] In *Klausner Holz Niedersachsen* the Regional Court Münster asked the CJEU whether a national judgment in *res judicata*, in which a national court had omitted to determine a breach with Article 108.3 TFEU, must be set aside on the principle of effectiveness.[106] The CJEU answered affirmative, ruling that a judgment in *res judicata* may not diminish the **effectiveness** of both Article 107.1 and 108.3 TFEU, nor the useful effect of the Commission's exclusive power to start a formal investigation (→ para 28).[107]

Although the **cooperation between the Commission and national courts** is **50** founded on the applicable standards, the Court established in its case law, the Commission has also adopted formal rules for cooperation in the procedural regulation. Article 29.2 of Regulation No. 2015/1589 enables the Commission to act as an *amicus curiae* by submitting (non-binding) written observations or making oral statements on the application of the Articles 107 and 108 TFEU.[108] In the follow-up of a preliminary reference procedure under Article 267 TFEU, national courts may be encouraged by the Court to involve the Commission in a national procedure.[109] When ordering provisional measures, pending a formal investigation by the Commission, national courts must either verify with the Commission, or ask a preliminary question to the Court, as to whether such measures do not obstruct the outcome of a formal investigation.[110] In practice, especially during proceedings for interim measures, a national court might opt to cooperate with the Commission.[111]

However, there may be **exceptional circumstances in which the recovery of** **51** **unlawful State aid would not be appropriate**.[112] The details, as confirmed and

---

[102] Case C-33/14, *Mory* (CJEU 17 September 2015) para 57–62.

[103] Case C-387/17, *Fallimento Traghetti del Mediterraneo* (CJEU 23 January 2019) para 36.

[104] Commission Notice *on the enforcement of State aid rules by national courts*, O.J. C 305/1 (2021).

[105] See Szyszczak (2011), p. 390.

[106] Olykke (2017b), pp. 718–726; Case C-505/14, *Klausner Holz Niedersachsen* (CJEU 11 November 2015).

[107] Case C-505/14, *Klausner Holz Niedersachsen* (CJEU 11 November 2015) para 45.

[108] Article 29.2 of Regulation No. 2015/1589/EU.

[109] Scott (2017), pp. 354–366; see also Szyszczak (2011), p. 390.

[110] Case C-284/12, *Deutsche Lufthansa AG v Flughafen Frankfurt-Hahn* (CJEU 21 November 2013) para 45. See also De Bandt (2014), pp. 206–207; Colombo (2015).

[111] Commission Notice *on the enforcement of State aid rules by national courts*, O.J. C 305/1 (2021) para 144–145.

[112] Adriaanse and Aalbers (2021), pp. 1104–1105.

elaborated in later case law,[113] have been detailed and expanded by the Commission in its Notice on the enforcement of State aid law by national courts. As is explained in this Notice, the State may also, and independently of any obligation to recover the aid, be subject to claims for damages brought in the national courts based on the EU law by competitors who incur loss or damage as a result of unlawfully implementing the aid.[114] Other remedies include preventing the payment of unlawful aid, recovery of illegality interest, and interim measures against unlawful aid.[115] The Court ruled in *CELF* that a national court is no longer obligated to order full recovery once the Commission renders a final positive Commission decision.[116] However, in such circumstances the national court must order the aid recipient to pay interest in respect of the period of unlawfulness.[117]

3.2. Review of State Aid by the Union Courts

52   MS may appeal against decisions for annulment under the Article 263 TFEU or against a failure to act under Article 265 TFEU.[118] The Commission may directly start an action before the Court under Article 108.2 TFEU against an MS which fails to comply with a decision issued under Article 108.2 TFEU or the Procedural Regulation 2015/1589.[119] Consequently, **Article 108.2 TFEU deviates from the administrative infraction procedure set out in Article 258 TFEU**. Such an action falls entirely within the discretion of the Commission.[120]

53   In *Scuola Elementare Maria Montessori*, the Court considered that the concept of '**regulatory act**' within the meaning of Article 263.4. TFEU extends to all non-legislative acts of general application, including State aid decisions by the Commission which authorise or prohibit a general applicable national aid scheme.[121]

54   **Individuals** who are affected by the aid should demonstrate that they are **directly and individually concerned** by the decision addressed to the MS, as set

---

[113] Case C-275/10, *Residex* (CJEU 8 December 2011) para 42; Case C-672/13, *OTP Bank v Magyar Állam* (CJEU 19 March 2015) para 71–73.

[114] Commission Notice *on the enforcement of State aid rules by national courts*, O.J. C 305/1 (2021) para 87–99.

[115] Säcker and Montag (2016), p. 1596.

[116] Case C-199/06, *CELF* (ECJ 12 February 2008) para 54. See Derenne (2018b), pp. 342–355.

[117] Case C-199/06, *CELF* (ECJ 12 February 2008) para 52; Case C-445/19, *Viasat Broadcasting UK v TV2/Danmark A/S* (CJEU 24 November 2020) para 25–27; Säcker and Montag (2016), p. 1548; see also Derenne (2018b), pp. 342–355.

[118] Quigley (2015), pp. 675–685; Hofmann (2016), p. 447.

[119] Säcker and Montag (2016), pp. 1597–1598.

[120] Case T-676/13 *Italian International Film* (CFI 4 February 2016) para 26. See also Szyszczak (2011), p. 354; Flynn and Gilliams (2021), pp. 1178–1180.

[121] Joined Cases C-622/16 P and C - 624/16 P, *Scuola Elementare Maria Montessori* (CJEU 6 November 2018) para 21, 31–33.

forth in paragraph 4 of Article 263 TFEU.[122] According to the Court's settled case law, undertakings have to show that an **aid is liable to affect its market position 'substantially'**.[123] As regards that 'substantial effect' a mere influence on the competitiveness of undertakings, compared to the recipient(s) of aid is not enough.[124] On the contrary, it should be demonstrated that the applicant was particularly affected by the aid in relation to its competitors.[125] If an undertaking calls into question the merits of the decision appraising the aid taken under Article 108.3 TFEU, or after the formal investigation procedure, the mere fact that it may be regarded as concerned within the meaning of Article 108.2 TFEU cannot suffice to render the action admissible.[126] The affected third party concerned must demonstrate that it has a particular status within the meaning of Article 263.4. TFEU.[127]

Regarding the status of concerned parties, not only the beneficiary but also the **undertakings competing with the beneficiary**, which have been recognised as having an individual concern by the Commission in its decision after ending the formal investigation procedure, may request the GC to annul a Commission decision, provided that they are substantially affected by the aid which is the subject of the contested decision and have played an active role during the Commission's investigation.[128] In *Netflix*, the GC declared Netflix' motion inadmissible, since Netflix had failed to fulfil the test of an individually concerned party.[129] Netflix objected to a Commission decision in which the Commission declared an aid and levy scheme on German language video and cinematic productions compatible with Article 107.3 point (c) TFEU. With concern to Netflix' status, the GC ruled that Netflix did not distinguish itself from other economic operators, since all film and video producers were eligible for distribution aid. Moreover, Netflix had not achieved to convince the GC that its market position was affected. This stringent application of the *Plaumann* test is not very common in State aid and competition cases since competitors of aid beneficiaries are usually awarded the status of an individually concerned party.[130] 55

Once a concerned party is declared admissible before the Court under Article 263.4 TFEU, the GC will conduct a **full review of the Commission's** 56

---

[122] Flynn and Gilliams (2021), pp. 1160–1166.

[123] Joined Cases C-164/15 P and C-165/15 P, *Ryanair and Aer Lingus* (CJEU 21 December 2016) para 105,127; Case T-79/14, *Secop v Commission* (CFI 1 March 2016) para 78.

[124] See Quigley (2015), p. 688.

[125] Flynn and Gilliams (2021), pp. 1160–1167.

[126] Hofmann (2016), p. 424.

[127] See for instance Case T-162/13, *Magic Mountain Kletterhallen v Commission* (CFI 9 June 2016); Staviczky (2017), pp. 77–81.

[128] Derenne (2018a), p. 280. Case C-33/14, *Mory v Commission* (CJEU 17 September 2015) para 97–98.

[129] Case T-818/16, *Netflix v Commission* (CFI 16 May 2018) para 63–65.

[130] See for instance Case T-693/14, *Hamr Sport v Commission* (CFI 12 May 2016).

decision, taking into consideration the Commission's **soft law as a source of secondary legislation**.[131] And although the Court also applies the Commission's guidelines and guidance sometimes as guiding principles, it does not consider itself bound to it.[132] Therefore, the Court reviews Commission decisions in accordance with the general EU principles of equal treatment, non-discrimination, transparency and proportionality.[133]

List of Cases

ECJ/CJEU
ECJ 15.07.1964, 6/64, *Costa v ENEL*, ECLI:EU:C:1964:66 [cit. in para 10]
ECJ 11.12.1973, 120/73, *Lorenz v Germany*, ECLI:EU:C:1973:152 [cit. in para 9]
ECJ 18.07.2007, C-119/05, *Lucchini*, ECLI:EU:C:2007:434 [cit. in para 8, 9]
ECJ 12.02.2008, C-199/06, *CELF*, ECLI:EU:C:2008:79 [cit. in para 9, 51]
CJEU 08.12.2011, C-275/10, *Residex Capital v Gemeente Rotterdam*, ECLI:EU:C:2011:814 [cit. in para 10, 51]
CJEU 13.06.2013, C-630/11 P to C-633/11 P, *Hotel Industry Sardinia v Commission*, ECLI:EU:C:2013:387 [cit. in para 23]
CJEU 21.11.2013, C-284/12, *Deutsche Lufthansa*, ECLI:EU:C:2013:755 [cit. in para 8–10, 20, 23, 40]
CJEU 10.12.2013, C-272/12 P, *Commission v Ireland*, ECLI:EU:C:2013:812 [cit. in para 34]
CJEU 13.02.2014, C-69/13, *Mediaset v Ministero dello Sviluppo economico*, ECLI:EU:C:2014:71 [cit. in para 38]
CJEU 12.02.2015, C-37/14, *Commission v France*, ECLI:EU:C:2015:90 [cit. in para 35, 39]
CJEU 19.03.2015, C-672/13, *OTP Bank v Magyar Állam*, ECLI:EU:C:2015:185 [cit. in para 36, 40, 51]
CJEU 17.09.2015, C-33/14, *Mory v Commission*, ECLI:EU:C:2015:609 [cit. in para 9, 37, 47, 48, 55]
CJEU 01.10.2015, C-357/14 P, *Electrabel v Commission*, ECLI:EU:C:2015:642 [cit. in para 36]
CJEU 15.10.2015, C-352/14 and C-353/14, *Iglesias Gutiérrez*, ECLI:EU:C:2015:69 [cit. in para 45]
CJEU 11.11.2015, C-505/14, *Klausner Holz Niedersachsen*, ECLI:EU:C:2015:742 [cit. in para 920, 44, 45, 49]
CJEU 21.07.2016, C-493/14, *Dilly's Wellnesshotel v Finanzamt Linz*, ECLI:EU:C:2016:577 [cit. in para 33, 41]

---

[131] Case T-289/03, *BUPA v Commission* (CFI 12 February 2008) para 118, 221.
[132] Case C-349/17, *Eesti Pagar* (CJEU 5 March 2019) para 73.
[133] See for an overview Stefan (2013).

CJEU 15.09.2016, C-574/14, *PGE v URE*, ECLI:EU:C:2016:686 [cit. in para 8, 45]
CJEU 26.10.2016, C-590/14 P, *DEI v Commission*, ECLI:EU:C:2016:797 [cit. in para 24]
CJEU 21.12.2016, C-164/15 P to C-165/15 P, *Commission v Ryanair and Aer Lingus*, ECLI:EU:C:2016:99 [cit. in para 41, 54]
CJEU 15.03.2017,C-515/16, *Enedis v Axa Corporate Solutions*, ECLI:EU:C:2017:217 [cit. in para 45]
CJEU 09.11.2017, C-481/16, *Commission v Greece (Larco)*, ECLI:EU:C:2017:845 [cit. in para 40]
CJEU, 17.01.2018, C-363/16, *Commission v Greece (United Textiles)*, ECLI:EU:C:2018:12 [cit. in para 39, 42]
CJEU 06.11.2018, C-622/16 P to C-624/16 P, *Scuola Elementare Maria Montessori v Commission*, ECLI:EU:C:2018:873 [cit. in para 41, 53]
CJEU 23.01.2019, C-387/17, *Fallimento Traghetti del Mediterraneo*, ECLI:EU:C:2019:51 [cit. in para 48]
CJEU 02.05.2019, C-598/17, *A-fonds v Inspecteur Belastingdienst*, ECLI:EU:C:2019:352 [cit. in para 46]
CJEU 05.03.2019, C-349/17, *Eesti Pagar*, ECLI:EU:C:2019:172 [cit. in para 9, 15, 33, 47, 56]
CJEU 17.11.2020, C-212/19, *Compagnie des pêches de Saint-Malo*, ECLI:EU:C:2020:726 [cit. in para 47]
CJEU 24.11.2020, C-445/19, *Viasat Broadcasting UK v TV2/Danmark*, ECLI:EU:C:2020:952 [cit. in para 51]

GC

GC 30.04.2014, T-468/08, *Dunamenti Erömü v Commission*, ECLI:EU:T:2014:235 [cit. in para 38]
GC 04.02.2016, T-676/13, *Italian International Film*, ECLI:EU:T:2016:62 [cit. in para 52]
GC 01.03.2016, T-79/14, *Secop v Commission*, ECLI:EU:T:2016:118 [cit. in para 54]
GC 12.05.2016, T-693/14, *Hamr Sport v Commission*, ECLI:EU:T:2016:292 [cit. in para 55]
GC 09.06.2016, T-162/13, *Magic Mountain Kletterhallen v Commission*, ECLI:EU:T:2016:341 [cit. in para 54]
GC 16.05.2018, T-818/16, *Netflix v Commission*, ECLI:EU:T:2018:274 [cit. in para 55]

References

Adriaanse, P., & Aalbers, M. (2021). Recovery of unlawful aid. In L. Hancher, T. Ottervanger, & P. Slot (Eds.), *EU State aids* (pp. 1089–1116). Sweet and Maxwell.

Adriaanse, P., & den Ouden, W. (2009). *Enforcement of State aid law in the Netherlands. Legislative initiative for effective recovery procedures in Dutch law* (pp. 15–26). European State Aid Law Quarterly.

Almeida, A. (2019). Private enforcement of EU State aid law through damages claims. *European State Aid Law Quarterly, 18*(2), 169–179.

Bach, K. (2017). A small step towards stricter practice in cases of breach of the Treaty under Article 108(2) TFEU? *European State Aid Law Quarterly, 16*(3), 667–674.

Bourgeois, K. (2021). Rescue and restructuring aid. In L. Hancher, T. Ottervanger, & P. Slot (Eds.), *EU State aids* (pp. 993–1029). Sweet and Maxwell.

Buts, C., & Buendia Sierra, J. (2017). *Milestones in State aid case law*. Lexxion.

Colombo, C. (2015). Lufthansa and the coherent application of State aid law: What is the role of national judges in concurrent proceedings? *Review of European Administrative Law, 8*(2), 319–345.

De Bandt, P. (2014). Lufthansa: A new era for State aid enforcement? *Journal of European Competition Law and Practice, 5*(4), 206–207.

Derenne, J. (2018a). Article 108 TFEU - Procedure before the Commission: Notification of aid (2018). In W. Verloren van Themaat & B. Reuder (Eds.), *European competition law: A case commentary* (pp. 279–318). Edward Elgar.

Derenne, J. (2018b). The powers and obligations of national courts with regard to unlawful State aid: Lessons from CELF I and CELF II. In C. Buts & J. L. Buendía Sierra (Eds.), *Milestones in State aid case law* (pp. 348–357). Lexxicon.

Flynn, L., & Gilliams, H. (2021). Judicial protection. In L. Hancher, T. Ottervanger, & P. Slot (Eds.), *EU State aids* (pp. 1117–1197). Sweet and Maxwell.

Hancher, L., & Salerno, F. (2021). The general framework. In L. Hancher, T. Ottervanger & P. Slot (Eds.), *EU State aids* (pp. 124–218). Sweet and Maxwell.

Hofmann, H. (2016). *State aid law of the European Union*. OUP.

Kreuschitz, V., & Bermejo, N. (2017). The role of national courts in the enforcement of the European State aid rules. In V. Tomljenovic et al. (Eds.), *EU competition and State aid rules* (pp. 221–252). Springer.

Loewenthal, P., & Ziegler, C. (2021). Administrative procedure. In L. Hancher, T. Ottervanger, & P. Slot (Eds.), *EU State aids* (pp. 1033–1087). Sweet and Maxwell.

Metaxas, A. (2017). Alteration of existing State aid and new aid: On the criteria of this legal categorisation. *European State Aid Law Quarterly*, 73–77.

Metselaar, A. (2017). The enforcement of the EU State aid rules by the Dutch courts. In S. Rusu & A. Looijestijn (Eds.), *Boosting the enforcement of EU competition law at the domestic level* (pp. 109–128). CUP.

Nicolaides, P. (2014). Are national courts becoming an extension of the Commission? *European State Aid Law Quarterly, 13*(3), 409–413.

Olykke, G. (2017a). The passing-on defence catapulted out of State aid law. *European State Aid Law Quarterly, 16*(1), 93–97.

Olykke, G. (2017b). State aid as a defence for public authorities? In C. Buts & J. L. Buendía Sierra (Eds.), *Milestones in State aid case law* (pp. 718–726). Lexxicon.

Quigley, C. (2015). *European State aid law and policy*. Hart.

Rusu, C., & Looijestijn, A. (2017). Domestic enforcement of EU antitrust and State aid rules: Status quo and foreseen developments. In S. Rusu & A. Looijestijn (Eds.), *Boosting the enforcement of EU competition law at the domestic level* (pp. 2–25). CUP.

Säcker, F., & Montag, F. (2016). *European State aid law: A commentary*. C.H. Beck.

Scott, A. (2017). Co-operation and good faith: State aid rules and national courts - Procedural and interpretive consequences. *European State Aid Law Quarterly, 16*(3), 354–366.

Staviczky, P. (2017). Difficulties to prove direct concern for competitors of State aid beneficiaries. *European State Aid Law Quarterly, 16*(1), 77–81.

Stefan, O. (2013). *Soft law in court, competition law, State aid and the Court of Justice in the European Union*. Kluwer.

Szyszczak, E. (2011). *Research handbook on EU State aid law*. Edward Elgar.
Van de Casteele, H. (2021). General block exemption regulation. In L. Hancher, T. Ottervanger, & P. Slot (Eds.), *EU State aids* (pp. 217–251). Sweet and Maxwell.
Van den Gronden, J. (2017). The enforcement of the State aid rules by national (judicial) authorities. In S. Rusu & A. Looijestijn (Eds.), *Boosting the enforcement of EU competition law at the domestic level* (pp. 143–160). CUP.
Werner, P. & Verouden, V. (2017). *EU State aid control: Law and economics*. Kluwer.

Article 109 TFEU [Implementation]
(ex-Article 89 TEC)

The Council, on a proposal from the Commission and after consulting the European Parliament, may make any appropriate regulations[2] for the application of Articles 107 and 108 and may in particular determine the conditions in which Article 108.3 TFEU shall apply and the categories of aid exempted from this procedure.[4-7]

Contents

1. Functioning of Article 109 TFEU 1
List of Cases
References

1. Functioning of Article 109 TFEU

Article 109 TFEU allows the Council to enact implementing regulations. This provision requires the **Council** to **adopt regulations** acting by a qualified majority on a proposal from the Commission and by consulting the European Parliament. In practice, Article 109 TFEU allows for the adoption of regulations which allow certain measures may be exempted from the obligation to notify. Although the Council has discretionary powers, it does not often use this power.[1]

Article 109 TFEU lays down that the Council may make '**any appropriate regulations**' for the application of Articles 107 and 108 TFEU. The provision lists 'the conditions in which Article 108.3 TFEU shall apply' and 'the categories of aid exempted from this procedure' as examples, but the Council has a certain degree of discretion as to regulate other issues it deems necessary. However, it may only *specify* the application of those provisions as long as it does not lead to a shift in decision-making powers between the Council and the Commission (Article 13.2 TEU).

In addition, as provided in **Article 108.4 TFEU**, the **Commission may adopt regulations** relating to the categories of State aid that the Council has, under Article 109 TFEU, determined may be exempt from the procedure provided under Article 108.3 TFEU.[2]

---

[1] Säcker and Montag (2016), p. 1650.
[2] Case C-493/14, *Dilly's Wellnesshotel v Finanzamt Linz* (CJEU 21 July 2016) para 33.

4 An example of an adopted regulation under Article 109 TFEU is the **Enabling Regulation** 2015/1588 (→ Article 108 TFEU para 7) declaring certain types of horizontal aid compatible with the internal market.[3] The Enabling Regulation constitutes the legal basis for Commission Regulations on exempted aid categories, such as the General Block Exemption Regulation, and the *de minimis* Regulations (→ Article 107 TFEU para 69, 89–91).[4]

5 Article 1 of the Enabling Regulation allows for **block exempted aid categories** such as small and medium-sized enterprises; research, development and innovation; regional aids, environmental protection; employment and training; culture and heritage conservation; making good the damage caused by natural disasters; sports; broadband infrastructure, and other types of infrastructure.

6 Article 2 of the Enabling Regulation allows the Commission to adopt *de minimis* **regulations**, which exempt 'aid that does not meet all the criteria of Article 107.1 TFEU' from notification 'provided that aid granted to the same undertaking over a given period of time does not exceed a certain fixed amount'. Accordingly, the Enabling Regulation constitutes the legal basis for *de minimis* aid.[5]

7 Another important regulation which was adopted according to the procedure of Article 109 TFEU is the **Procedural Regulation 2015/1589** (→ Article 108 TFEU para 5).[6] Article 2 of the Procedural Regulations states that 'save as otherwise provided in regulations made pursuant to Article 109 TFEU or to other relevant provisions thereof, any plans to grant new aid shall be notified to the Commission in sufficient time by the Member State concerned. The Commission shall inform the Member State concerned without delay of the receipt of a notification'. The Procedural Regulation lays down detailed rules on the procedure concerning Article 108 TFEU (→ Article 108 TFEU para 21 et seqq.), including: procedure regarding notified aid (Articles 2–11); procedure regarding unlawful aid (Articles 12–16); procedures concerning misuse of aid (Article 20); procedure concerning existing aid; investigations into sectors of the economy and into aid instruments (Article 25) and monitoring (Articles 26–28).[7]

List of Cases

CJEU 21.07.2016, C-493/14, *Dilly's Wellnesshotel v Finanzamt Linz*, ECLI:EU:C:2016:577 [cit. in para 3]

---

[3] Council Regulation 2015/1588/EU *on certain categories of horizontal State aid*, O.J. L 248 (2015); Hancher et al. (2021), pp. 115–116.

[4] Säcker and Montag (2016), pp. 322–325.

[5] See Säcker and Montag (2016), p. 1652.

[6] Council Regulation 2015/1589/EU *on detailed procedural rules for the application of Article 108 TFEU*, O.J. L 248 (2015).

[7] See Säcker and Montag (2016), p. 1652.

References

Hancher, L., Ottervanger, T., & Slot, P. (2021). *EU State aids*. Sweet and Maxwell.
Säcker, F. J., & Montag, F. (2016). *European State aid law: a commentary*. C.H. Beck/Hart/Nomos.

Chapter 2
Tax Provisions

Article 110 [Discriminatory and Protective Internal Taxation]
(ex-Article 90 TEC)

No Member State shall impose,[5–7] directly or indirectly, on the products[8] of other Member States[9–14] any internal taxation[15–20] of any kind in excess[21] of that imposed directly[28–32] or indirectly[33–36] on similar[22–27] domestic products.[37–40]

Furthermore,[41,42] no Member State shall impose[5–7] on the products[8] of other Member States[9–14] any internal taxation[15–20] of such a nature as to afford indirect protection[46–53] to other products.[43–45]

Contents

1. Overview: Origin and Rationale 1
2. Common Parts of the Provision 5
   2.1. Imposed by Member States 5
   2.2. Protected Products 8
   2.3. Products of Other States 9
      2.3.1. Products from Third Countries 10
      2.3.2. Products for Export 13
      2.3.3. Domestic Products 14
   2.4. Any Internal Taxation of Any Kind 15
      2.4.1. Internal Tax or Customs Duty 15
      2.4.2. Internal Tax 18
3. Discriminatory Internal Taxation of Similar Products (Paragraph 1) 21
   3.1. Similar Products 22
   3.2. Direct Discrimination 28
   3.3. Indirect Discrimination 33
   3.4. Consequences of Discriminatory Internal Taxation of Similar Products 37
4. Discriminatory Internal Taxation of Other Products (Paragraph 2) 41
   4.1. Competing Products 42
      4.1.1. Other Products or Similar Products 42
      4.1.2. Competing Products 43
   4.2. Indirect Protection 46
      4.2.1. Differences in the Tax System 48
      4.2.2. Market Effect 50
   4.3. Consequences of Protective Internal Taxation of Other Products 53

List of Cases
References

1. Overview: Origin and Rationale

Article 110 TFEU prohibits Member States (MS) from **imposing discriminatory** 1
or protective internal taxation on products from other MS. The provision is

closely linked to and must be understood in connection with: the prohibition of internal customs duties in Article 30 TFEU (→ Article 30 TFEU para 3–5); the principle of the free movement of goods in Articles 26 and 28 TFEU; and the prohibition in Article 34 TFEU of quantitative restrictions between MS and all charges having equivalent effect (→ Article 34 TFEU para 4 et seqq.).[1] These provisions aim to ensure the free movement of goods between MS under **normal conditions of competition**.[2] The function of Article 110 TFEU is to prevent MS circumventing these provisions by imposing internal taxation.[3]

2   The Court has interpreted Article 110 TFEU widely to cover *all* internal taxation measures which **directly or indirectly undermine the equal treatment of domestic products and imported products**, particularly those which discriminate against products from other MS. The prohibition in Article 110 TFEU must therefore apply whenever a fiscal charge is likely to discourage imports of goods originating in other MS to the benefit of domestic production.[4]

3   Accordingly, Article 110 TFEU can be characterised as a **special provision prohibiting discrimination**, elaborating the general prohibition of discrimination in Article 18 TFEU (→ Article 18 TFEU para 11 et seqq.).[5]

4   The first paragraph of Article 110 TFEU prohibits all MS from imposing on the products of other MS **internal taxation in excess of that imposed on similar domestic products**. The first paragraph seeks to guarantee the complete neutrality of internal taxation as regards competition between products already on the domestic market and imported products.[6]

The second paragraph of Article 110 TFEU prohibits MS from using internal **taxes to protect other (non-similar) domestic products**. Where the first paragraph seeks complete neutrality, the second paragraph seeks to remove all protective taxes, without requiring the complete equalisation of taxes.[7]

---

[1] Article 110 TFEU (i.e. its predecessor) was also one of the first provisions in the Treaty that was given direct effect. See the first paragraph in Case 57/65, *Lütticke* (ECJ 16 June 1966); and the second paragraph in Case 27/67, *Firma Fink-Frucht* (ECJ 4 April 1968).

[2] Case C-586/14, *Budişan* (CJEU 9 June 2016) para 19.

[3] Case 24/68, *Commission v Italy* (ECJ 1 July 1969) para 11; Case C-640/17, *dos Santos* (CJEU 17 April 2018) para 12.

[4] Case C-221/06, *Stadtgemeinde Frohnleiten* (ECJ 8 November 2007) para 40.

[5] Waldhoff, in Calliess and Ruffert (2022), Article 110 AEUV para 5.

[6] See Craig and de Búrca (2011), p. 621; Fairhurst (2016), p. 569.

[7] See Barnard and Peers (2017), p. 360.

2. Common Parts of the Provision

2.1. Imposed by Member States

Article 110 TFEU concerns taxes imposed by an MS. "Member State" includes not only State authorities but **all authorities administering, collecting or enforcing taxes**.[8]

Article 110 TFEU prohibits MS from introducing discriminatory or protective internal taxes. The objective is to guarantee the **complete neutrality of internal taxation** as regards competition between products already on the domestic market and imported products.[9] On the one hand, the provision prohibits discriminatory internal taxation, but on the other hand, the provision does not prohibit any specific tax system, level of tax, or even **reverse discrimination**.[10] As long as their tax system is free from any discriminatory or protective effect, MS are free to choose any system of taxation. MS may establish a system whereby tax is increased progressively according to objective criteria,[11] they may impose **new internal taxes, or raise or lower existing tax rates**.[12]

Article 110 TFEU does not specify any **method for imposing an internal tax**. A tax will often be imposed by a formal regulation, but the discriminatory administration of tax regulations will also conflict with the provision.[13]

MS have to transpose EU directives into national law in a manner that is consistent with the requirements of the Treaties.[14] The prohibition of discriminatory and protective internal taxes under Article 110 TFEU also applies when **MS implement EU directives**,[15] thus ensuring that the implementing legislation does not result in the different treatment of products from the other MS.[16]

2.2. Protected Products

Article 110 TFEU only refers to "products", but the provision is to be interpreted widely and covers all **taxation measures which, directly or indirectly,**

---

[8] Case 74/76, *Iannelli v Meroni* (ECJ 22 March 1977) para 19.
[9] Case C-402/09, *Ioan Tatu* (CJEU 7 April 2011) para 35.
[10] See Barnard and Peers (2017), p. 364.
[11] Case C-132/88, *Commission v Greece* (ECJ 5 April 1990) para 17; Case 252/86, *Gabriel Bergandi v Directeur général des impôts* (ECJ 3 March 1988) para 31.
[12] Case C-402/09, *Ioan Tatu* (CJEU 7 April 2011) para 50.
[13] Case C-45/94, *Cámara de Comercio, Industria y Navegación de Ceuta v Ayuntamiento de Ceuta* (ECJ 7 December 1995) para 34, 35.
[14] Case C-166/98, *Socridis* (ECJ 17 June 1999) para 19.
[15] E.g. Council Directive 2008/118/EC *concerning the general arrangements for excise duty*, O.J. L 9/12 (2009).
[16] Case 21/79, *Commission v Italy* (ECJ 8 January 1980) para 26; Case C-221/06, *Stadtgemeinde Frohnleiten* (ECJ 8 November 2007) para 67.

undermine the equal treatment of domestic products and imported products. To that end, the Court has ruled that Article 110 TFEU also applies to internal taxation that is imposed on the *use* of imported products where those products are essentially intended for such use and have been imported solely for that purpose.[17]

2.3. Products of Other States

9   Article 110 TFEU only refers to discrimination against products from other MS and the **protection of domestic products**. If a national provision does not affect products from other MS more than domestic products, clearly Article 110 TFEU does not apply.[18] As the provision only refers to products from other MS, it seems to exclude products from third countries, products for export and domestic products from the treaty protection of the free movement of goods.

2.3.1. Products from Third Countries

10   It is settled case law that Article 110 TFEU **does not apply** to products from third countries,[19] but there are **two exceptions** to this.

11   The first exception follows from the principle of the free movement of goods in Articles 26 and 28 TFEU.[20] **Goods** originating from third countries which have been **put into free circulation** in one MS are covered by the Treaty provisions on freedom of movement (Article 28.2 TFEU; → Article 28 TFEU para 14, 27, 30), including Article 110 TFEU, meaning that the goods can move freely within the internal market.[21]

12   The second exception concerns products imported from a **third country that has an agreement with the EU**. Such products are not discriminated against if the agreement contains a provision similar to Article 110 TFEU.[22] In this case, the article in the agreement that is similar to Article 110 TFEU should be interpreted in the same way as Article 110 TFEU and treated as part of the EU law.[23]

The **General Agreement on Tariffs and Trade** (GATT) contains a provision similar to Article 110 TFEU. Article III, paragraph 2, of the GATT states that "[t]he

---

[17] Case 252/86, *Gabriel Bergandi v Directeur général des impôts* (ECJ 3 March 1988) para 27.

[18] Case C-385/12, *Hervis Sport v Nemzeti Adó* (CJEU 5 February 2014) para 27.

[19] Case C-284/96, *Didier Tabouillot v Directeur des services fiscaux de Meurthe-et-Moselle* (ECJ 18 December 1997) para 25; Case C-130/92, *OTO SpA v Ministero delle Finanze* (ECJ 13 July 1994) para 19.

[20] Case C-130/92, *OTO SpA v Ministero delle Finanze* (ECJ 13 July 1994) para 16.

[21] Case C-284/96, *Didier Tabouillot v Directeur des services fiscaux de Meurthe-et-Moselle* (ECJ 18 December 1997) para 21.

[22] Joined Cases C-228/90 et al., *Simba SpA and others v Ministero delle finanze* (ECJ 9 June 1992) para 19.

[23] Joined Cases C-114/95 and C-115/95, *Texaco v Middelfart Havn and others* (ECJ 17 July 1997) para 31–33.

products of the territory of any contracting party imported into the territory of any other contracting party shall not be subject, directly or indirectly, to internal taxes or other internal charges of any kind in excess of those applied, directly or indirectly, to like domestic products". In the Council Decision acceding to the Agreement Establishing the WTO, including its Annexes, it is emphasised that the Agreement "is not susceptible to being directly invoked in Community or Member State courts".[24] Thus, discriminatory internal taxation of third country products will be in breach of the WTO Agreement[25] but not of Article 110 TFEU.

2.3.2. Products for Export

Article 110 TFEU only refers to the discriminatory or protective application of systems of internal taxation to products imported from other MS. The CJEU has applied an analogous interpretation of the provision, finding that, taken in conjunction with the other tax provisions in the Treaty, it must be interpreted as also **prohibiting any tax discrimination against products intended for export to other MS.**[26]

13

2.3.3. Domestic Products

The Court has retained that Article 110 TFEU cannot be relied on by **domestic producers** of the MS imposing the internal tax.[27]

14

2.4. Any Internal Taxation of Any Kind

2.4.1. Internal Tax or Customs Duty

Article 110 TFEU regulates discriminatory or protective **internal taxation**. The provision cannot be applied together with the provisions in Articles 30 and 34 TFEU relating to **customs duties and charges on importation having equivalent effect to customs duties.**[28] Only if a tax is not a customs duty or a charge having

15

---

[24] See Council Decision of 22 December 1994 *concerning the conclusion on behalf of the European Community, as regards matters within its competence, of the agreements reached in the Uruguay Round multilateral negotiations (1986–1994)*, O.J. L 336/1 (1994).

[25] See Cottier and Oesch (2012), p. 161.

[26] Case 51/74, *van der Hulst v Produktschap voor Siergewassen* (ECJ 23 January 1975) para 35; Case 142/77, *Statens Kontrol* (ECJ 29 June 1978) para 27; Case C-234/99, *Niels Nygård v Svineafgiftsfonden* (ECJ 23 April 2002) para 41; Case C-305/17, *FENS* (CJEU 6 December 2018) para 30.

[27] Case 68/79, *Just* (ECJ 27 February 1980) para 15.

[28] Case C-101/00, *Tulliasiamies and Antti Siilin* (ECJ 19 September 2002) para 115; Case C-254/13, *Orgacom* (CJEU 2 October 2014) para 20; Case C-305/17, *FENS* (CJEU 6 December 2018) para 30.

equivalent effect to a customs duty will it be necessary to determine whether that tax constitutes discriminatory or protective internal taxation prohibited by Article 110 TFEU.[29]

The essential feature of a charge having equivalent effect to a customs duty, which distinguishes it from an internal tax, is that a customs duty is borne solely by a product which crosses a frontier, while an internal tax is borne by imported, exported and domestic products.[30]

16   A charge that is imposed on goods by reason of their crossing a frontier may escape classification as a charge having equivalent effect to a customs duty if it relates to a **general system of internal taxation** that is applied systematically and in accordance with the same criteria to domestic products and imported or exported products alike.[31]

17   A **charge that is intended to offset the effect of internal taxation** thereby takes on the character of the internal taxation which it is intended to offset.[32] If domestic products in general are exempted from an internal tax, the charge will lose its characteristic as an internal tax.[33]

2.4.2. Internal Tax

18   **Internal taxation covers all general taxes** in an MS where the tax revenue helps to finance the MS's expenditure in general.[34] The Court has characterised a general internal tax as a tax governed by common tax rules, charged on categories of products irrespective of their origin and in accordance with an objective criterion.[35]

19   It is clearly the intention that the concept of internal taxation in Article 110 TFEU should be understood broadly.[36] Tax obviously covers all sorts of payments on goods.[37] Even internal **taxation imposed on the use of imported products**, where those products are essentially intended for such use and are imported solely for that purpose, is in breach of Article 110 TFEU.[38]

---

[29] C-254/13, *Orgacom* (CJEU 2 October 2014) para 21.

[30] Joined Cases C-441/98 and C-442/98, *Michaïlidis* (ECJ 21 September 2000) para 22.

[31] Case C-130/93, *Lamaire v Nationale Dienst voor Afzet van Land- en Tuinbouwprodukten* (ECJ 7 July 1994) para 14; Case C-39/17, *Lubrizol France* (CJEU 14 June 2018) para 39.

[32] Case 57/65, *Lütticke* (ECJ 16 June 1966), Grounds of judgment part 2; third question, 2nd para.

[33] Case C-163/90, *Administration des Douanes et Droits Indirects v Léopold Legros and others* (ECJ 16 July 1992) para 12; Case C-517/04, *Koornstra* (ECJ 8 June 2006) para 28.

[34] Case C-130/92, *OTO SpA v Ministero delle Finanze* (ECJ 13 July 1994) para 12.

[35] Joined Cases C-228/90 et al., *Simba SpA and others v Ministero delle finanze* (ECJ 9 June 1992) para 8.

[36] Case 252/86, *Gabriel Bergandi v Directeur général des impôts* (ECJ 3 March 1988) para 25.

[37] Bahns et al., in von der Groeben et al. (2015), Article 110 AEUV para 19.

[38] Case 252/86, *Gabriel Bergandi v Directeur général des impôts* (ECJ 3 March 1988) para 26.

Article 110 TFEU also covers **taxation on an activity necessarily connected with a product**.[39] Thus a surcharge imposed on the price of transmitted electricity is an internal tax.[40] Likewise, a tax on the management of a waste disposal site is an internal tax, although it is paid by the operator of the waste disposal site.[41] The tax must be charged on an activity related to the products and must be at least partly calculated based on the quantity of the products, and have an immediate effect on the cost of the products.[42]

Internal taxation also covers **tax advantages** such as tax exemptions[43] and reductions.[44]

3. Discriminatory Internal Taxation of Similar Products (Paragraph 1)

According to settled case law, the first paragraph of Article 110 TFEU will be infringed where the tax charged on an imported product and the tax charged on a similar domestic product are calculated differently based on different criteria which leads to a higher tax being imposed on the imported product, even if this occurs only in certain cases.[45]

3.1. Similar Products

The prohibition of discriminatory internal taxation in Article 110.1 TFEU only applies where the **domestic and imported products are similar**. The provision presupposes a market or production of similar products in the importing MS. As a consequence, the provision cannot be invoked against internal taxation imposed on imported products where there is no similar domestic product or production.[46] Likewise, if there are no imports of the products in question from other MS to the taxing MS, Article 110 TFEU will not be applicable.[47]

---

[39] Case C-221/06, *Stadtgemeinde Frohnleiten* (ECJ 8 November 2007) para 43; Case C-206/06, *Essent Netwerk Noord v Aluminium Delfzijl* (ECJ 17 July 2008) para 44.

[40] Case C-206/06, *Essent Netwerk Noord v Aluminium Delfzijl* (ECJ 17 July 2008) para 43.

[41] Case C-221/06, *Stadtgemeinde Frohnleiten* (ECJ 8 November 2007) para 47.

[42] Case C-39/17, *Lubrizol France* (CJEU 14 June 2018) para 30.

[43] Case C-221/06, *Stadtgemeinde Frohnleiten* (ECJ 8 November 2007) para 73.

[44] Case 21/79, *Commission v Italy* (ECJ 8 January 1980) para 15.

[45] Case C-393/98, *Gomes Valente* (ECJ 22 February 2001) para 21; Case C-387/01, *Weigel* (ECJ 29 April 2004) para 67; Case C-313/05, *Brzeziński* (ECJ 18 January 2007) para 29; Case C-74/06, *Commission v Greece* (ECJ 20 September 2007) para 25; Case C-104/17, *Cali Esprou* (CJEU 15 March 2018) para 41.

[46] Case C-47/88, *Commission v Denmark* (ECJ 11 December 1990) para 10; Case C-402/14, *Viamar* (CJEU 17 December 2015) para 36.

[47] Case C-76/14, *Manea* (CJEU 14 April 2015) para 32.

23 In an MS where there is no production of a product, there can still be a **market for that product**, based on products imported and traded in that MS. A product becomes a domestic product as soon as it has been imported and placed on the market. Thus, imported second-hand photocopiers and those bought locally constitute similar or competing products in an MS which does not have domestic production of photocopiers.[48] In the *car taxation* cases[49] the CJEU consistently ruled that in an MS without any car production, a car tax on imported used cars should be measured against **the market for similar used cars** already in that country.[50] According to recent cases, the used car market seems to be an independent market, distinct from the market for new cars for the purposes of Article 110.1 TFEU.[51]

24 In its early cases, the CJEU took the view that products are similar when they are identical or almost identical and fall within **the same fiscal, customs or statistical classification**.[52]

25 In the *John Walker* case, the Court had to decide whether fruit wine and Scotch whisky were similar products. It found that to determine whether the products are similar it was first necessary to consider **certain objective characteristics** of both categories of beverage, such as their origin, method of manufacture and organoleptic properties, particularly taste and alcohol content. Second, it was necessary to consider whether or not both categories of beverage are capable of **meeting the same needs from the point of view of consumers**.[53] In this case, the characteristics of the two beverages were fundamentally different and therefore not similar.[54]

26 In subsequent cases, the CJEU has endorsed this broad interpretation of the concept of similarity and assessed the similarity of products, not according to whether they were strictly identical, but according to whether their use was **similar and comparable**.[55] In the *dark and light cigarettes* case, the Court noted that dark tobacco cigarettes and light tobacco cigarettes were manufactured from different types of the same basic product, tobacco, using comparable processes. The **organoleptic characteristics** of the dark and light tobacco cigarettes, such as their taste

---

[48] Case C-228/98, *Dounias* (ECJ 3 February 2000) para 42. On used cars, see Case C-47/88, *Commission v Denmark* (ECJ 11 December 1990) para 17.

[49] E.g., Case C-437/12, *X* (CJEU 19 December 2013); Case C-402/09, *Ioan Tatu* (CJEU 7 April 2011); Case C-2/09, *Kalinchev* (CJEU 3 June 2010); Case C-426/07, *Krawczyński* (ECJ 17 July 2008); Case C-74/06, *Commission v Greece* (ECJ 20 September 2007).

[50] Case C-2/09, *Kalinchev* (CJEU 3 June 2010) para 33.

[51] Case C-76/14, *Manea* (CJEU 14 February 2015) para 31; Case C-640/17, *dos Santos* (CJEU 17 April 2018) para 17.

[52] Case 27/67, *Firma Fink-Frucht* (ECJ 4 April 1968), Ruling of the Court, 3(a).

[53] Case 243/84, *Walker v Ministeriet for Skatter og Afgifter* (ECJ 4 March 1986) para 11.

[54] Case 243/84, *Walker v Ministeriet for Skatter og Afgifter* (ECJ 4 March 1986) para 14.

[55] Joined Cases C-367/93 to C-377/93, *F. G. Roders BV and others v Inspecteur der Invoerrechten en Accijnzen* (ECJ 11 August 1995) para 27; Case C-102/09, *Camar* (CJEU 29 April 2010) para 29.

and smell, were not identical. Although there were differences, the Court ruled that the cigarettes were nevertheless similar.[56]

This broad interpretation of similarity seems to emphasise the "**needs from the point of view of consumers**".[57] While the physical characteristics of products are important, they do not have the same decisive significance. The CJEU has examined the question of similar products repeatedly in the *car taxation* cases.[58] To decide whether cars are similar it is first necessary to decide whether their characteristics and the needs which they serve place them in a competitive relationship and, second, whether the degree of competition between two models depends on the extent to which they meet various requirements including price, size, comfort, performance, fuel consumption, durability, reliability etc.[59] Since there is an independent market for used cars, the same criteria apply to internal taxation on used cars.[60] The tests of similarity developed in case law do not relate exclusively to the technical equipment of vehicles, and other characteristics may also be considered. For example, the Court has found that it is clear that in the eyes of consumers, whether or not they are fitted with a six-speed manual gearbox or five-speed automatic transmission, vehicles of different makes may constitute similar vehicles.[61]

27

3.2. Direct Discrimination

Direct discrimination arises where **differing tax is charged on similar products of different origins**. This is obviously the case when imported products are taxed at a higher rate than domestic products.[62] But it is also the case if one product is taxed at a flat rate while another is taxed at a differentiated rate,[63] or when imported products do not benefit from the same tax exemptions as domestic products.[64]

28

It is not only the tax actually charged that can be discriminatory. Under Article 110 TFEU, in addition to considering the rate of tax, it is also necessary to take into consideration **provisions on the basis of assessment and the detailed rules**

29

---

[56] Case C-302/00, *Commission v France* (ECJ 27 February 2002) para 24.

[57] Bahns et al., in von der Groeben et al. (2015), Article 110 AEUV para 45.

[58] Case C-437/12, *X* (CJEU 19 December 2013) para 25; Case C-402/09, *Ioan Tatu* (CJEU 7 April 2011) para 55; Case C-2/09, *Kalinchev* (CJEU 3 June 2010) para 33; Case C-426/07, *Krawczyński* (ECJ 17 July 2008) para 33.

[59] Case C-421/97, *Tarantik* (ECJ 15 June 1999) para 28.

[60] Case C-437/12, *X* (CJEU 19 December 2013) para 23.

[61] Case C-265/99, *Commission v France* (ECJ 15 March 2001) para 44.

[62] Case 21/79, *Commission v Italy* (ECJ 8 January 1980) para 27; Case C-640/17, *dos Santos* (CJEU 17 April 2018) para 22.

[63] Case 127/75, *Bobie Getränkevertrieb v Hauptzollamt Aachen-Nord* (ECJ 22 June 1976) para 4; Case C-213/96, *Outokumpu Oy* (ECJ 2 April 1998) para 35.

[64] Case 148/77, *Hansen v Hauptzollamt Flensburg* (ECJ 10 October 1978) para 20; Case C-91/18, *Commission v Greece* (CJEU 11 July 2019) para 52.

for levying the various duties.⁶⁵ The Court has found that there is direct discrimination when domestic products benefit from having a longer period within which to pay a tax,⁶⁶ or if national legislation systematically penalises the non-payment of tax on imports more severely than the non-payment of tax on domestic goods.⁶⁷

30   The **administration of national regulations** can result in discriminatory internal taxation. Internal taxation can be directly discriminatory either by reason of the wording of the provisions imposing it or by reason of the manner in which the administrative authorities apply it, for example if it is levied on imported products or certain categories of those products but not on local products in the same category.⁶⁸

31   Differences in **assessments of the values of taxable products** will also be discriminatory.⁶⁹ Assessments of the values of taxable products have been at issue in several of the car taxation cases. The problem occurs because car tax is charged only once, when the vehicle is first registered. Part of the lump sum-tax remains incorporated in the value of second-hand vehicles, which have already been registered and purchased in an MS.⁷⁰ If, each time a used car is imported to another MS, car tax is charged on it, while a similar used car already in that MS is not charged because the car tax is inherent in its price, there will be different treatment. Thus the car tax on used cars must reflect the depreciated value of the car. A system of taxation in which the depreciation in the value of a vehicle is calculated in a general and abstract manner based on fixed criteria is therefore prohibited.⁷¹

In other words, if the tax on an imported used car is higher than the calculated residual tax on a domestic used car, the import tax will be directly discriminatory, because one must presume that the residual value of the tax on domestic used cars decreases in line with the depreciation of the value of the car.⁷²

32   On the other hand, Article 110 TFEU does not prohibit the use of **different systems of taxation**.⁷³ Goods from another MS may be charged in a different way or by a different system, as long as the tax charged on the imported product remains at all times equal to or less than the tax charged on similar domestic products.⁷⁴

---

⁶⁵ Case C-76/14, *Manea* (CJEU 14 April 2015) para 34.

⁶⁶ Case 55/79, *Commission v Ireland* (ECJ 27 February 1980) para 14; Case C-349/13, *Oil Trading Poland* (CJEU 12 February 2015) para 48; Case C-68/96, *Grundig Italiana v Ministero delle Finanze* (ECJ 17 June 1998) para 23.

⁶⁷ Case 299/86, *Rainer Drexl* (ECJ 25 February 1988) para 25.

⁶⁸ Case C-45/94, *Cámara de Comercio, Industria y Navegación de Ceuta v Ayuntamiento de Ceuta* (ECJ 12 December 1995) para 34, 35.

⁶⁹ Case 74/76, *Iannelli v Meroni* (ECJ 22 March 1977) para 21.

⁷⁰ Case C-437/12, *X* (CJEU 19 December 2013) para 30.

⁷¹ Case C-393/98, *Gomes Valente* (ECJ 22 February 2001) para 44.

⁷² Joined Cases C-290/05 and C-333/05, *Nádasdi* (ECJ 5 October 2006) para 55.

⁷³ De Sadeleer (2014), p. 259.

⁷⁴ Case 127/75, *Bobie Getränkevertrieb v Hauptzollamt Aachen-Nord* (ECJ 22 June 1976) para 3; Case C-393/98, *Gomes Valente* (ECJ 22 February 2001) para 44.

3.3. Indirect Discrimination

Indirect discrimination occurs when national regulations appear neutral, without any explicit distinction between domestic and imported products,[75] but where **a greater burden is nonetheless placed on products from other MS**.[76] The CJEU does not make a clear distinction between direct and indirect discrimination in all cases, but only establishes that the national tax is discriminatory contrary to Article 110 TFEU.[77] 33

If domestic and imported goods are assessed by the same rules, using the same price and cost factors, there will be no direct discrimination.[78] But if **the same price and cost factors** are not used and as a result imported products are taxed more heavily, this will constitute indirect discrimination contrary to Article 110.2 TFEU.[79] 34

If legislation sets **objective criteria for assessing** the depreciation of motor vehicles, such as a vehicle's age, mileage, general condition, propulsion method, make or model, the assessment will come close to the vehicle's actual value,[80] there will be no discrimination. On the other hand, if an assessment is based on a single criterion of depreciation, such as the age of the vehicle[81] or its engine output,[82] this will not guarantee that the assessment will reflect the actual depreciation of the vehicle.

Even where products are similar, MS may lay down tax arrangements that differentiate between certain products based on the objective criteria, such as the nature of the raw materials used, the production processes employed[83] or the quantity of packaging waste being recovered or recycled.[84] 35

If a **tax system** is **progressive** and the highest rates only apply to products from other MS, this could indicate that the system is indirectly discriminatory.[85] The Court has underlined that a system of taxation cannot be regarded as discriminatory 36

---

[75] Case C-402/09, *Ioan Tatu* (CJEU 7 April 2011) para 37.

[76] See Barnard and Peers (2017), p. 362; Craig and de Búrca (2011), p. 621.

[77] E.g., Case C-228/98, *Dounias* (ECJ 3 February 2000) para 51; Case C-39/17, *Lubrizol France* (CJEU 14 June 2018) para 49.

[78] Kamann, in Streinz (2018), Article 110 AEUV para 25.

[79] Case C-228/98, *Dounias* (ECJ 3 February 2000) para 47.

[80] Case C-402/09, *Ioan Tatu* (CJEU 7 April 2011) para 41; Case C-586/14, *Budişan* (CJEU 9 June 2016) para 29.

[81] Case C-402/09, *Ioan Tatu* (CJEU 7 April 2011) para 42. See similarly Case C-393/98, *Gomes Valente* (ECJ 22 February 2001) para 28–29; Case C-74/06, *Commission v Greece* (ECJ 20 September 2007) para 38–42.

[82] Case C-402/09, *Ioan Tatu* (CJEU 7 April 2011) para 45.

[83] Case 196/85, *Commission v France* (ECJ 7 April 1987) para 6.

[84] Case C-198/14, *Visnapuu* (CJEU 12 November 2015) para 76; Case C-104/17, *Cali Esprou* (CJEU 15 March 2018) para 43.

[85] Seiler, in Grabitz et al. (2022), Article 110 AEUV para 33 (released in 2016).

solely because only imported products fall within the most heavily taxed category, particularly products imported from other MS.[86]

3.4. Consequences of Discriminatory Internal Taxation of Similar Products

37   The first consequence of an internal tax being found to be in breach of Article 110.1 TFEU is that the MS must **equalise the tax on domestic products and similar products** from other MS. Until there is equalisation of the internal tax, the national courts and administration must disregard any national laws or regulations contrary to Article 110 TFEU, and **individuals are not obliged to pay any taxes contrary to Article 110 TFEU**.[87]

38   Second, internal taxes collected contrary to Article 110.1 TFEU must be repaid.[88] The **repayment** to the taxpayer must include interest for the period from the date of the undue levy of the tax until its repayment.[89]

39   The repayment must also be in accordance with Article 110 TFEU. If the system for repayment does not enable individuals to effectively exercise their rights under the EU law to seek repayment, for example because the system sets off the repayment, the repayment itself will be in breach of Article 110 TFEU.[90]

40   The Court has acknowledged that there are **practical difficulties in assessing the real market value of goods**, e.g. second-hand vehicles, for the purposes of calculating tax. However, even if the existence of such difficulties were proved, they cannot justify the application of internal taxes which discriminate against products from other MS in breach of Article 110 TFEU.[91]

4. Discriminatory Internal Taxation of Other Products (Paragraph 2)

41   Internal taxation may also affect the free movement of goods in situations where there are no similar domestic goods. To **prevent protection of any kind**, Article 110.2 TFEU, supplementing Article 110.1 TFEU, prohibits discriminatory internal taxation of other products. The application of Article 110.2 TFEU requires two conditions to be met.[92] First, the subject of the internal tax must be "other

---

[86] Case C-132/88, *Commission v Greece* (ECJ 5 April 1990) para 18; see also Case 140/79, *Chemial Farmaceutici* (ECJ 14 January 1981) para 18.

[87] Joined Cases C-228/90 et al., *Simba SpA and others v Ministero delle finanze* (ECJ 9 June 1992) para 28.

[88] Case C-565/11, *Irimie* (CJEU 18 April 2013) para 20; Case C-76/17, *Petrotel-Lukoil and Georgescu* (CJEU 1 March 2018) para 32.

[89] Case C-565/11, *Irimie* (CJEU 18 April 2013) para 21; Case C-69/14, *Târşia* (CJEU 6 October 2015) para 25.

[90] Case C-331/13, *Nicula* (CJEU 15 October 2014) para 39.

[91] Case C-345/93, *Fazenda Pública v Nunes Tadeu* (ECJ 9 March 1995) para 19.

[92] See Barnard and Peers (2017), p. 362; Fairhurst (2016), p. 579.

products". "Other products" means products that are not similar products in competition with domestic products. Second, the internal tax must be discriminatory, i.e. protecting domestic products against products from other MS.

4.1. Competing Products

4.1.1. Other Products or Similar Products

Since the second paragraph starts with the word **"furthermore"**, the provision only applies to cases which do not involve internal taxation of similar products under the first paragraph. In some older cases the Court seemed to pay little attention to the distinction between the first and second paragraph,[93] even refusing to give judgment on the question, arguing that it did not seem necessary.[94] By not distinguishing between the two paragraphs, the Court created problems for the MS, since the consequences of the two paragraphs are not the same.[95] In its more recent judgments the Court has seemed more interested in identifying the correct paragraph of Article 110 TFEU,[96] so now the second paragraph will only be applied in cases other than where the first paragraph of Article 110 TFEU applies.

42

4.1.2. Competing Products

When it is established that a tax is not imposed on similar products, the Court will try to determine whether the tax is imposed on other products that compete with domestic products.[97] To establish whether products compete, it is sufficient for an imported product to compete with a protected domestic product by reason of one or more economic uses to which it may be put.[98] It is settled case law that if **products are substitutable by consumers or are capable of meeting identical needs,**[99] **there will be competition between them.**

43

In assessing whether products compete, it is not only necessary to consider the present state of the market but also **possible developments in the free movement of goods within the Union** and the further potential for the substitution of products.[100]

44

---

[93] Case C-230/89, *Commission v Greece* (ECJ 18 April 1991) para 10.
[94] Case 168/78, *Commission v France* (ECJ 27 February 1980) para 39.
[95] See Fairhurst (2016), p. 577; Barnard and Peers (2017), p. 364; Horspool et al. (2018), p. 309.
[96] Case C-198/14, *Visnapuu* (CJEU 12 November 2015) para 57–58; Case C-586/14, *Budişan* (CJEU 9 June 2016) para 23.
[97] Case C-167/05, *Commission v Sweden* (ECJ 8 April 2008) para 42.
[98] Case 168/78, *Commission v France* (ECJ 27 February 1980) para 6.
[99] Case 170/78, *Commission v United Kingdom* (ECJ 12 July 1983) para 8.
[100] Case 170/78, *Commission v United Kingdom* (ECJ 12 July 1983) para 7–8.

45   In the *wine and beer* cases, the Court had to decide whether wine and beer were competing products.[101] First, the Court found that there were substantial **differences in quality and price**. For this reason, the Court decided that the competitive relationship between beer, a popular and widely consumed beverage, and wine had to be based on those wines that are the most accessible to the public at large, i.e. generally the lightest and cheapest varieties.[102] This approach has been repeated in subsequent cases.[103]

In the *spirits cases* the Court has found that, as products obtained by distillation, spirits obtained from cereals have sufficient characteristics in common with spirits obtained from wine and fruit to constitute an **alternative choice for consumers**, at least in certain circumstances. Thus, the two categories of spirits were competing products.[104] The Court generally seems to find that, if they are not similar products, different spirits will be competing products.[105]

In the *bananas - fruits* case, bananas and domestic fruit such as apple and pears were found not to be similar products, but bananas were an alternative choice of fruit for consumers. As a result, bananas must be regarded as being in **partial competition** with the domestic fruit.[106] The competition only relates to fresh bananas; dried bananas and banana flour are not in competition with domestic fruits.[107]

4.2. Indirect Protection

46   If an **internal tax protects domestic products partially, indirectly or potentially**, Article 110.2 TFEU is applicable.[108] Article 110.2 TFEU prohibits the protective element of the internal tax, but "does not restrict the freedom of each Member State to lay down tax arrangements which differentiate between certain products on the basis of objective criteria, such as the nature of the raw materials used or the production processes employed. Such differentiation is compatible with Community law if it pursues objectives of economic policy which are themselves compatible with the requirements of the Treaty and its secondary legislation, and if the detailed rules are such as to avoid any form of discrimination, direct or indirect, in

---

[101] Case C-167/05, *Commission v Sweden* (ECJ 8 April 2008) para 43.

[102] Case 170/78, *Commission v United Kingdom* (ECJ 12 July 1983) para 12.

[103] Case 356/85, *Commission v Belgium* (ECJ 9 July 1987) para 11; Case C-166/98, *Socridis* (ECJ 17 June 1999) para 18.

[104] Case 168/78, *Commission v France* (ECJ 27 February 1980) para 40.

[105] Case 319/81, *Commission v Italy* (ECJ 15 March 1983) para 16; Joined Cases C-367/93 to C-377/93, *F. G. Roders BV and others v Inspecteur der Invoerrechten en Accijnzen* (ECJ 11 August 1995) para 31; Case C-230/89v *Commission v Greece* (ECJ 18 April 1991) para 8.

[106] Case 184/85, *Commission v Italy* (ECJ 7 May 1987) para 12.

[107] Case 184/85, *Commission v Italy* (ECJ 7 May 1987) para 14.

[108] Case 168/78, *Commission v France* (ECJ 27 February 1980) para 6.

regard to imports from other Member States or any form of protection of competing domestic products."[109]

Since a tax system may differentiate between products that are not similar, it is difficult to compare competing products; this must be done by a general criterion— **the protective nature of the system of internal taxation.**[110]   47

4.2.1. Differences in the Tax System

First, the Court will compare the **tax arrangements for the competing products** to determine whether there is any difference in their tax treatment and, if so, the extent of that difference.[111] The Court has underlined that the methods used should be based on objective criteria which reflect the characteristics of the products in question.[112] In *spirits cases* and *wine and beer cases* the Court often uses the criterion of alcoholic strength by volume. In some cases only products from other MS have been taxed, which obviously demonstrates differences in the tax system.[113] Likewise, there will be an obvious difference if all domestic products benefit from a reduced tax rate.[114]   48

If an analysis shows that the **tax system treats competing products differently**, the differences must be analysed to determine their market effect. On the other hand, if the analysis reveals that there are no differences in the internal tax system, there will be no protection and Article 110.2 TFEU will not be applicable.   49

4.2.2. Market Effect

If there are differences in the tax system, the Court must then examine whether, in the market in question, the differences have **the effect of reducing the potential consumption of imported products** to the advantage of competing domestic products.[115] To establish the protective nature of a system of internal taxation, the Court compares the tax burdens of the products in question. Ultimately, the comparison will be based on the effect of the internal tax on the market price of the competing products. If the internal tax has no effect or only very little effect on the market price, the internal tax will not be found to be protective.[116]   50

---

[109] Case 243/84, *Walker v Ministeriet for Skatter og Afgifter* (ECJ 4 March 1986) para 22; Case 319/81, *Commission v Italy* (ECJ 15 March 1983) para 21 regarding differentiated rates in the VAT system.

[110] Case 168/78, *Commission v France* (ECJ 27 February 1980) para 7.

[111] Case C-167/05, *Commission v Sweden* (ECJ 8 April 2008) para 45.

[112] Case C-167/05, *Commission v Sweden* (ECJ 8 April 2008) para 48.

[113] Case 184/85, *Commission v Italy* (ECJ 7 May 1987) para 13.

[114] Case 319/81, *Commission v Italy* (ECJ 15 March 1983) para 17.

[115] Case C-132/88, *Commission v Greece* (ECJ 5 April 1990) para 19; Case C-167/05, *Commission v Sweden* (ECJ 8 April 2008) para 52.

[116] Case C-167/05, *Commission v Sweden* (ECJ 8 April 2008) para 57.

51   If the burden of an internal tax can be established in more than one way, the Court will consider all the alternatives.[117] And if **the tax on domestic products is substantially below the tax on competing products** from other MS and all market analyses point in the same direction, the Court will conclude that the internal tax system is protective.[118] In the *banana case*, the amount of the tax was as much as half the price of the imported product, and there was no similar tax on domestic fruits. The difference in taxation obviously influenced the market for the products in question by reducing the potential consumption of the imported products. The tax was therefore protective.[119]

On the other hand, a **minor difference in tax rates** that only leads to a minor difference in the prices of the products will not be capable of influencing consumer behaviour in all cases. In such cases, the internal taxes will not protect the domestic product, and the tax system will not be found to be protective.[120]

52   In some cases, the Court has found that a tax system is protective without closely analysing the market effect. This is so in cases where an MS only taxes a product from other MS[121] and where all or most of domestic production falls within favourable tax categories whereas the kinds of product which are mostly imported from other MS are subject to higher taxation.[122]

4.3. Consequences of Protective Internal Taxation of Other Products

53   If an MS is found to impose an indirectly discriminatory internal tax, it **must remove the protective effect of the tax**, but it does not have to equalise the tax on domestic products and on products from other MS. If a national system of taxation has different tax rates and is found to be incompatible with Union law, the MS in question must apply a rate of tax to imported products that eliminates the margin of protection prohibited by Article 110.2 TFEU.[123]

List of Cases

ECJ 16.06.1966, 57/65, *Lütticke*, ECLI:EU:C:1966:34 [cit. in para 1 and 17]
ECJ 04.04.1968, 27/67, *Firma Fink-Frucht GmbH v Hauptzollamt München*, ECLI: EU:C:1968:22 [cit. in para 1 and 24]

---

[117] Case 170/78, *Commission v United Kingdom* (ECJ 12 July 1983) para 18.
[118] Case 170/78, *Commission v United Kingdom* (ECJ 12 July 1983) para 27.
[119] Case 184/85, *Commission v Italy* (ECJ 7 May 1987) para 13.
[120] Case 356/85, *Commission v Belgium* (ECJ 9 July 1987) para 18.
[121] Case 184/85, *Commission v Italy* (ECJ 7 May 1987) para 13.
[122] Case 168/78, *Commission v France* (ECJ 27 February 1980) para 41; Case 319/81, *Commission v Italy* (ECJ 15 March 1983) para 18.
[123] Case 68/79, *Just* (ECJ 27 February 1980) para 16.

Article 110 [Discriminatory and Protective Internal Taxation] 343

ECJ 01.07.1969, 24/68, *Commission v Italy*, ECLI:EU:C:1969:29 [cit. in para 2]
ECJ 23.01.1975, 51/74, *van der Hulst v Produktschap voor Siergewassen*, ECLI: EU:C:1975:9 [cit. in para 13]
ECJ 22.06.1976, 127/75, *Bobie Getränkevertrieb GmbH v Hauptzollamt Aachen-Nord*, ECLI:EU:C:1976:95 [cit. in para 28 and 32]
ECJ 22.03.1977, 74/76, *Iannelli v Meroni*, ECLI:EU:C:1977:51 [cit. in para 5 and 31]
ECJ 29.06.1978, 142/77, *Statens Kontrol*, ECLI:EU:C:1978:144 [cit. in para 13]
ECJ 10.10.1978, 148/77, *Hansen v Hauptzollamt Flensburg*, ECLI:EU:C:1978:173 [cit. in para 28]
ECJ 08.01.1980, 21/79, *Commission v Italy*, ECLI:EU:C:1980:1 [cit. in para 7, 20 and 28]
ECJ 27.02.1980, 168/78, *Commission v France*, ECLI:EU:C:1980:51 [cit. in para 42, 43, 45, 46, 47 and 52]
ECJ 27.02.1980, 55/79, *Commission v Ireland*, ECLI:EU:C:1980:56 [cit. in para 29]
ECJ 27.02.1980, 68/79, *Just*, ECLI:EU:C:1980:57 [cit. in para 14 and 56]
ECJ 14.01.1981, 140/79, *Chemial Farmaceutici*, ECLI:EU:C:1981:1 [cit. in para 36]
ECJ 15.03.1983, 319/81, *Commission v Italy*, ECLI:EU:C:1983:71 [cit. in para 45, 46, 48 and 52]
ECJ 12.07.1983, 170/78, *Commission v United Kingdom*, ECLI:EU:C:1983:202 [cit. in para 43, 44, 45 and 51]
ECJ 04.03.1986, 243/84, *Walker v Ministeriet for Skatter og Afgifter*, ECLI:EU: C:1986:100 [cit. in para 25 and 46]
ECJ 07.04.1987, 196/85, *Commission v France*, ECLI:EU:C:1987:182 [cit. in para 35]
ECJ 07.05.1987, 184/85, *Commission v Italy*, ECLI:EU:C:1987:207 [cit. in para 45, 48, 51 and 52]
ECJ 09.07.1987, 356/85, *Commission v Belgium*, ECLI:EU:C:1987:353 [cit. in para 45 and 51]
ECJ 25.02.1988, 299/86, *Rainer Drexl*, ECLI:EU:C:1988:103 [cit. in para 29]
ECJ 03.03.1988, 252/86, *Gabriel Bergandi v Directeur général des impôts*, ECLI: EU:C:1988:112 [cit. in para 6, 8 and 19]
ECJ 05.04.1990, C-132/88, *Commission v Greece*, ECLI:EU:C:1990:165 [cit. in para 6, 36 and 50]
ECJ 11.12.1990, C-47/88, *Commission v Denmark*, ECLI:EU:C:1990:449 [cit. in para 22 and 23]
ECJ 18.04.1991, C-230/89, *Commission v Greece*, ECLI:EU:C:1991:156 [cit. in para 42 and 45]
ECJ 09.06.1992, C-228/90 to C-234/90, C-339/90 and C-353/90, *Simba SpA and others v Ministero delle finanze*, ECLI:EU:C:1992:251 [cit. in para 12, 18 and 37]
ECJ 16.07.1992, C-163/90, *Administration des Douanes et Droits Indirects v Léopold Legros and others*, ECLI:EU:C:1992:326 [cit. in para 17]

ECJ 07.07.1994, C-130/93, *Lamaire NV v Nationale Dienst voor Afzet van Land- en Tuinbouwprodukten*, ECLI:EU:C:1994:281 [cit. in para 16]

ECJ 13.07.1994, C-130/92, *OTO SpA v Ministero delle Finanze*, ECLI:EU:C:1994:288 [cit. in para 10, 11 and 18]

ECJ 09.03.1995, C-345/93, *Fazenda Pública v Nunes Tadeu*, ECLI:EU:C:1995:66 [cit. in para 40]

ECJ 11.08.1995, C-367/93 to C-377/93, *F. G. Roders BV and others v Inspecteur der Invoerrechten en Accijnzen*, ECLI:EU:C:1995:261 [cit. in para 25 and 45]

ECJ 07.12.1995, C-45/94, *Cámara de Comercio, Industria y Navegación de Ceuta v Ayuntamiento de Ceuta*, ECLI:EU:C:1995:425 [cit. in para 7 and 30]

ECJ 17.07.1997, C-114/95 and C-115/95, *Texaco v Middelfart Havn and others*, ECLI:EU:C:1997:371 [cit. in para 12]

ECJ 18.12.1997, C-284/96, *Didier Tabouillot v Directeur des services fiscaux de Meurthe-et-Moselle*, ECLI:EU:C:1997:630 [cit. in para 10 and 11]

ECJ 02.04.1998, C-213/96, *Outokumpu Oy*, ECLI:EU:C:1998:155 [cit. in para 28]

ECJ 17.06.1998, C-68/96, *Grundig Italiana SpA v Ministero delle Finanze*, ECLI:EU:C:1998:299 [cit. in para 29]

ECJ 15.06.1999, C-421/97, *Tarantik*, ECLI:EU:C:1999:309 [cit. in para 27]

ECJ 17.06.1999, C-166/98, *Socridis*, ECLI:EU:C:1999:316 [cit. in para 7 and 45]

ECJ 03.02.2000, C-228/98, *Dounias*, ECLI:EU:C:2000:65 [cit. in para 23, 33 and 34]

ECJ 21.09.2000, C-441/98 and C-442/98, *Michaïlidis*, ECLI:EU:C:2000:479 [cit. in para 15]

ECJ 22.02.2001, C-393/98, *Gomes Valente*, ECLI:EU:C:2001:109 [cit. in para 21, 31, 32 and 34]

ECJ 15.03.2001, C-265/99, *Commission v France*, ECLI:EU:C:2001:169 [cit. in para 27]

ECJ 27.02.2002, C-302/00, *Commission v France*, ECLI:EU:C:2002:123 [cit. in para 23]

ECJ 23.04.2002, C-234/99, *Niels Nygård v Svineafgiftsfonden*, ECLI:EU:C:2002:244 [cit. in para 13]

ECJ 19.09.2002, C-101/00, *Tulliasiamies and Antti Siilin*, ECLI:EU:C:2002:505 [cit. in para 15]

ECJ 29.04.2004, C-387/01, *Weigel*, ECLI:EU:C:2004:256 [cit. in para 21]

ECJ 08.06.2006, C-517/04, *Koornstra*, ECLI:EU:C:2006:375 [cit. in para 17]

ECJ 05.10.2006, C-290/05 and C-333/05, *Nádasdi*, ECLI:EU:C:2006:652 [cit. in para 31]

ECJ 18.01.2007, C-313/05, *Brzeziński*, ECLI:EU:C:2007:33 [cit. in para 21]

ECJ 20.09.2007, C-74/06, *Commission v Greece*, ECLI:EU:C:2007:534 [cit. in para 21, 23 and 34]

ECJ 08.11.2007, C-221/06, *Stadtgemeinde Frohnleiten and Gemeindebetriebe Frohnleiten*, ECLI:EU:C:2007:657 [cit. in para 2, 7 and 20]

ECJ 08.04.2008, C-167/05, *Commission v Sweden*, ECLI:EU:C:2008:202 [cit. in para 43, 45, 48 and 50]

ECJ 17.07.2008, C-206/06, *Essent Netwerk Noord v Aluminium Delfzijl*, ECLI:EU:C:2008:413 [cit. in para 20]
ECJ 17.07.2008, C-426/07, *Krawczyński*, ECLI:EU:C:2008:434 [cit. in para 23 and 27]
CJEU 29.04.2010, C-102/09, *Camar*, ECLI:EU:C:2010:236 [cit. in para 25]
CJEU 03.06.2010, C-2/09, *Kalinchev*, ECLI:EU:C:2010:312 [cit. in para 23 and 27]
CJEU 07.04.2011, C-402/09, *Ioan Tatu*, ECLI:EU:C:2011:219 [cit. in para 6, 23, 27, 33 and 34]
CJEU 18.04.2013, C-565/11, *Irimie*, ECLI:EU:C:2013:250 [cit. in para 38]
CJEU 19.12.2013, Case C-437/12, *X*, ECLI:EU:C:2013:857 [cit. in para 23. 27 and 31]
CJEU 05.02.2014, C-385/12, *Hervis Sport v Nemzeti Adó*, ECLI:EU:C:2014:47 [cit. in para 9]
CJEU 02.10.2014, C-254/13, *Orgacom*, ECLI:EU:C:2014:2251 [cit. in para 15]
CJEU 15.10.2014, C-331/13, *Nicula*, ECLI:EU:C:2014:2285 [cit. in para 39]
CJEU 12.02.2015, C-349/13, *Oil Trading Poland sp. z o.o.*, ECLI:EU:C:2015:84 [cit. in para 29]
CJEU 14.04.2015, C-76/14, *Manea*, ECLI:EU:C:2015:216 [cit. in para 22, 23 and 29]
CJEU 06.10.2015, C-69/14, *Târşia*, ECLI:EU:C:2015:662 [cit. in para 38]
CJEU 12.11.2015, C-198/14, *Visnapuu*, ECLI:EU:C:2015:751 [cit. in para 35 and 42]
CJEU 17.12.2015, C-402/14, *Viamar*, ECLI:EU:C:2015:830 [cit. in para 22]
CJEU 09.06.2016, C-586/14, *Budişan*, ECLI:EU:C:2016:421 [cit. in para 1, 34 and 42]
CJEU 01.03.2018, C-76/17, *Petrotel-Lukoil and Georgescu*, ECLI:EU:C:2018:139 [cit. in para 38]
CJEU 15.03.2018, C-104/17, *Cali Esprou*, ECLI:EU:C:2018:188 [cit. in para 21 and 35]
CJEU 17.04.2018, C-640/17, *dos Santos*, ECLI:EU:C:2018:275 [cit. in para 1, 23 and 28]
CJEU 14.06.2018, C-39/17, *Lubrizol France*, ECLI:EU:C:2018:438 [cit. in para 16, 20 and 33]
CJEU 06.12.2018, C-305/17, *FENS*, ECLI:EU:C:2018:986 [cit. in para 13 and 15]
CJEU 11.07.2019, C-91/18, *Commission v Greece*, ECLI:EU:C:2019:600 [cit. in para 28]

References

Barnard, C., & Peers, S. (2017). *European Union law*. OUP.
Calliess, C., & Ruffert, M. (Eds.). (2022). *EUV/AEUV mit Europäischer Grundrechtecharta. Kommentar* (6th ed.). C.H. Beck.
Cottier, T., & Oesch, M. (2012). Direct and indirect discrimination in WTO and EU law. In S. E. Gaines, B. E. Olsen, & K. E. Sørensen (Eds.), *Liberalising trade in the EU and the WTO* (pp. 141–175). CUP.

Craig, P., & de Búrca, G. (2011). *EU law. Text, cases and materials*. OUP.
De Sadeleer, N. (2014). *EU environmental law and the internal market*. OUP.
Fairhurst, J. (2016). *Law of the European Union*. Pearson.
Grabitz, E., Hilf, M., & Nettesheim, M. (Eds.). (2022). *Das Recht der Europäischen Union. EUV/AEUV*. loose-leaf (last supplement: 75). C.H. Beck.
Horspool, M., Humphreys, M., & Wells-Greco, M. (2018). *European Union law*. OUP.
Streinz, R. (Ed.). (2018). *EUV/AEUV*. C.H. Beck.
von der Groeben, H., Schwarze, J., & Hatje, A. (Eds.). (2015). *Europäisches Unionsrecht. Commentary* (7th ed.). Nomos.

Article 111 [Tax Repayments for Exported Products]
(ex-Article 91 TEC)

Where products are exported to the territory of any Member State,[1, 5] any repayment of internal[3] taxation shall not exceed[4] the internal taxation imposed on them whether directly or indirectly.[6]

Contents

1. Overview: Origin and Rationale 1
2. Restrictions on Repayments 3

List of Cases
References

1. Overview: Origin and Rationale

Article 111 TFEU is the counterpart to Article 110 TFEU. It concerns **exports of products** to other MS whereas Article 110 TFEU concerns imports from other MS (→ Article 110 TFEU para 1–4). Article 111 TFEU is aimed at preventing MS from using the **repayment of internal taxes** to **distort competition** in the internal market, by repaying more than what was initially levied. Thus, Article 111 TFEU is linked not only to the rules on the free movement of goods, but also to the State aid rules in Article 107 TFEU (→ Article 107 TFEU).[1]   1

Article 111 TFEU is **directly applicable** in the MS.[2]   2

2. Restrictions on Repayments

The repayment of internal taxes when goods are exported is also referred to as a *border adjustment*. The prohibition in Article 111 TFEU of excessive repayment of internal taxes or border adjustments is absolute. On the other hand, MS may decide to repay less than the amount of internal tax paid, or to make no border adjustment at all.[3] MS may use any system of repayment, as long as the system guarantees that, in all cases, such payments remain within the limits of Article 111 TFEU.[4]   3

---

[1] Bahns et al., in von der Groeben et al. (2015), Article 111AEUV para 2.
[2] Khan and Lichtblau, in Geiger et al. (2015), Article 111 AEUV para 2.
[3] Case 27/74, *Demag v Finanzamt Duisburg-Süd* (ECJ 22 October 1974) para 7.
[4] Case 45/64, *Commission v Italy*, second judgment (ECJ 19 November 1969) para 10, 11.

4   An MS making a border adjustment must provide evidence that, in all cases, the **repayment does not exceed the tax levied.**[5]

5   Article 111 TFEU only applies to **products exported to other MS** and not to third countries. However, similarly to Article 110 TFEU (→ Article 110 TFEU para 12), it is possible that an agreement with a third country that includes a provision similar to Article 111 TFEU could be part of the EU law. Exports to such a third country would have to comply with Article 111 TFEU.

6   The expression "directly" must be understood as referring to taxation imposed on a finished product, while "indirectly" refers to taxation imposed at various stages of production, on the raw materials or on semi-finished products used in the manufacture of the product.[6] The internal tax must be **on the product and not on the producer**. Charges on the producer such as registration, stamp and mortgage duties, charges on licences and concessions, car and advertising, cannot be repaid under Article 111 TFEU.[7] It follows that the repayment of internal taxes *on products* can be made pursuant to Article 111 TFEU. However, direct taxation or general taxes imposed upon the producer of the products cannot be repaid.[8]

List of Cases

ECJ 01.12.1965, 45/64, *Commission v Italy*, first judgment, ECLI:EU:C:1965:116 [cit. in para 6]

ECJ 19.11.1969, 45/64, *Commission v Italy,* second judgment, ECLI:EU:C:1969:58 [cit. in para 3]

ECJ 22.10.1974, 27/74, *Demag AG v Finanzamt Duisburg-Süd*, ECLI:EU:C:1974:104 [cit. in para 3]

ECJ 26.06.1991, C-152/89, *Commission v Luxembourg*, ECLI:EU:C:1991:272 [cit. in para 4]

ECJ 26.06.1991, C-153/89, *Commission v Belgium*, ECLI:EU:C:1991:273 [cit. in para 4]

References

Geiger, R., Khan, D.-E., & Kotzur, M. (Eds.). (2015). *European Union Treaties. A commentary.* Hart Publishing/C.H. Beck.

von der Groeben, H., Schwarze, J., & Hatje, A. (Eds.). (2015a). *Europäisches Unionsrecht. Commentary* (7th ed.). Nomos.

---

[5] Case C-152/89, *Commission v Luxembourg,* (ECJ 26 June 1991) para 36; Case C-153/89, *Commission v Belgium* (ECJ 26 June 1991) para 27.

[6] Case 45/64, *Commission v Italy*, first judgment (ECJ 1 December 1965), p. 866.

[7] Case 45/64, *Commission v Italy*, first judgment (ECJ 1 December 1965), p. 866.

[8] Bahns et al., in von der Groeben et al. (2015), Article 111 AEUV para 5.

Article 112 [Approval of Reimbursements]
(ex-Article 92 TEC)

In the case of charges other than[1] turnover taxes, excise duties and other forms of indirect taxation, remissions and repayments in respect of exports to other Member States may not be granted and countervailing charges in respect of imports from Member States may not be imposed[3] unless the measures contemplated have been previously approved for a limited period[4] by the Council[2] on a proposal from the Commission.

Contents

References

1   Article 112 TFEU is to be seen as a **supplement to Articles 110 and 111 TFEU**. While Articles 110 and 111 TFEU prohibit discriminatory indirect taxes, Article 112 TFEU prohibits the use of **direct taxes** to discriminate against products from other MS. Article 112 TFEU has not prompted extensive case law, but its purpose is to play a role in the internal market by preventing MS from circumventing the requirements of Articles 110 and 111 TFEU by simply introducing charges in the form of direct taxation rather than indirect taxes. Without Article 112 TFEU, this could be done by imposing charges on companies that import goods or by remitting or repaying charges paid by companies that export goods.

2   The wording of the provision was changed by the Lisbon Treaty, as it previously stated that the approval of the Council required a **qualified majority**. This still applies but has been removed from Article 112 TFEU since qualified majority is now the default voting rule under Article 16.3 TEU (→ Article 16 TEU para 86 et seqq.).

3   The prohibition is twofold, as in the case of Article 110 TFEU. Both the **remission and repayment of charges in the event of exports** and the **imposition of charges in the event of imports** are prohibited. Thus, the MS are prohibited from both supporting exporters and penalising importers.

4   However, unlike the other fiscal provisions, Article 112 TFEU can be set aside if there is a previous approval for doing so from the Council. This approval may be

granted based on a proposal from the Commission and it must be for a **limited time**. Until now, no such approval has been granted.[1]

References

Geiger, R., Khan, D.-E., & Kotzur, M. (Eds.). (2015). *European Union Treaties. A Commentary*. Hart Publishing/C.H. Beck.

von der Groeben, H., Schwarze, J., & Hatje, A. (Eds.). (2015). *Europäisches Unionsrecht. Commentary* (7th ed.). Nomos.

Lenz, C. O., & Borchardt, K.-D. (Eds.). (2013). *EU-Verträge. Kommentar* (6th ed.). Bundesanzeiger.

---

[1] Khan and Lichtblau, in Geiger et al. (2015), Article 112 AEUV para 2; Bahns et al., in von der Groeben et al. (2015), Article 112 AEUV para 2; Wolffgang and Gellert, in Lenz and Borchardt (2013), Article 112 AEUV para 3.

Article 113 [Harmonisation of Indirect Taxes]
(ex-Article 93 TEC)

The Council shall, acting unanimously in accordance with a special legislative procedure[1–9] and after consulting the European Parliament and the Economic and Social Committee, adopt provisions for the harmonisation of legislation[15–21] concerning turnover taxes[22–28], excise duties[29–31] and other forms of indirect taxation[32–36] to the extent that such harmonisation is necessary to ensure the establishment and the functioning of the internal market[10–13] and to avoid distortion of competition.[14]

Contents

1. Overview: Origin and Rationale 1
2. Basis for Harmonisation: Internal Market 10
   2.1. Establishment and Functioning of the Internal Market 12
   2.2. Avoiding Distortion of Competition 14
3. Relationship to Other Harmonisation Provisions 15
   3.1. Ordinary Legislative Procedure in Articles 114 and 192 TFEU 15
   3.2. Direct and Indirect Taxes 18
   3.3. Ordinary Legislative Procedure in Article 116 TFEU 20
4. Harmonisation of Indirect Taxes 21
   4.1. Turnover Taxes 22
   4.2. Excise Duties 29
   4.3. Other Forms of Indirect Taxation 32
List of Cases
References

1. Overview: Origin and Rationale

Articles 110 to 113 TFEU are some of the few provisions in the TFEU that deal explicitly with **fiscal regulation**. However, this does not mean that no other parts of the TFEU influence the tax measures of the MS. Since tax measures cannot be viewed in isolation in a legal system, as they both heavily influence and are influenced by other areas of law, it is appropriate to consider several other provisions of the TFEU when dealing with the EU tax law.[1]

While the fiscal provisions in Articles 110 to 112 TFEU deal with the prohibition of fiscal discrimination, Article 113 TFEU is a **harmonisation provision,** laying down the legal basis for harmonising **indirect taxes.** Thus, Article 113 TFEU is not

---

[1] On the concept of the EU tax law, see Helminen (2018), p. 2 and on European tax law, Terra and Wattel (2012), p. 35.

© Springer Nature Switzerland AG 2022
R. Böttner, H.-J. Blanke (eds.), *Treaty on the Functioning of the European Union – A Commentary,* Springer Commentaries on International and European Law, https://doi.org/10.1007/16559_2022_43

intended to influence domestic legislation, but rather to determine when the European institutions should apply the unanimity rule for approving harmonisation.[2]

2   Harmonisation based on Article 113 TFEU **can be adopted as "provisions"**. This broad scope for harmonisation means that all the types of legislation referred to in Article 288 TFEU can form the basis for the harmonisation of indirect taxes, i.e. regulations, directives, decisions, recommendations and opinions.

This is **notably different to the harmonisation of direct taxes** based on Article 115 TFEU, for which only directives can be used (→ Article 115 TFEU para 6, 9, 12 et seqq.). However, directives are the most frequently used tool for harmonising indirect taxation. In contrast to decisions, recommendations and opinions, directives involve full discussion in the Council, the EP and the Economic and Social Committee, as well as it being possible to refer disputes to the CJEU.

3   The procedure for harmonising indirect taxes involves a **special legislative procedure** requiring unanimity. Legislation is adopted from proposals made by the Commission and adopted by the Council. The procedure requires the Parliament and the Economic and Social Committee to be consulted. This means that the Parliament does not function as a co-legislator as in the co-decision procedure (for ordinary legislation) under Article 294 TFEU. Harmonisation based on Article 113 TFEU is discussed below (→ para 21 et seqq.).

4   Article 113 TFEU strikes a balance between, on the one hand, **national tax sovereignty**[3] and the interests of the MS in protecting their tax bases and, on the other hand, the objectives of the internal market.[4] As there is a **close connection between the internal market and indirect taxation**, the harmonisation of indirect taxes is more evident than the harmonisation of direct taxes. From an early stage in EU's development, the MS acknowledged that some form of harmonisation was required if a properly functioning internal market was to be achieved.[5] An internal market, as referred to in Article 26.2 TFEU, is to be understood as "an area without internal frontiers in which the free movement of goods, persons, services and capital is ensured in accordance with the provisions of the Treaties" (→ Article 26 TFEU para 20 et seqq.). An internal market could not be achieved if the MS were allowed to introduce non-harmonised indirect taxes, as national provisions would hinder the free movement of goods and services within the EU.

5   Nevertheless, the harmonisation of tax regulations is still a **sensitive area for the MS**, as is evident from the requirement for unanimity to achieve harmonisation.[6] This is because the tax system is the basis for financing the public sector, as well as one of the most effective regulatory tools a State can have.

---

[2] Herrera (2005a), p. 209.

[3] As expressed by the ECJ in Case 270/83, *Commission v France* (ECJ 28 January 1986) and pretty much every direct tax case since.

[4] Khan and Lichtblau, in Geiger et al. (2015), Article 110 AEUV para 1 and Terra and Wattel (2012), p. 37.

[5] Terra and Wattel (2012), p. 11.

[6] Khan and Lichtblau, in Geiger et al. (2015), Article 110 AEUV para 1.

The requirement for unanimity for harmonisation has been challenged by **6**
the Commission. In its Communication "Tax policy in the European Union - priorities for the years ahead",[7] the Commission raised the question of whether other legislative procedures should be considered. The Commission concluded that, in the areas of mutual assistance and administrative cooperation for combatting tax fraud, it would be better if there were harmonisation by a qualified majority (→ Article 114 TFEU para 55, 66)[8] and that a clear VAT strategy would be better implemented if legislation could be passed with a **qualified majority**.[9] The Commission's arguments were repeated in a communication in 2003,[10] where it was argued that the requirement for unanimity in tax matters should be dispensed with for harmonisation of tax legislation connected with the functioning of the internal market.[11]

The Commission's proposed solutions range from a qualified majority to a period of deliberation after which objections of one or two MS would not be enough to stop the Council in adopting a measure.[12] In January 2019, the Commission published the Communication "Towards a more efficient and democratic decision making in EU tax policy".[13] In the Communication, the Commission argues that Article 116 TFEU on elimination of distortions of competition and Article 325 TFEU on measures to tackle fraud affecting the financial interests of the Union could serve as the legal basis for harmonisation of certain tax measures without requiring amendments to the TFEU. These provisions only require a qualified majority. The Commission points to the **passerelle procedures** in Article 48.7 TFEU and Article 192.2 TFEU as tools to introduce adoption of tax measures under the ordinary legislative procedure.[14] In sections 4 and 5 of the Communication, the Commission provides its view on the steps to be taken to be able to adopt tax measures under the ordinary legislative procedure.

The Commission suggests a **four-step approach**. The first step is to employ the qualified majority voting for measures with no direct impact on MS' taxing rights, bases or rates, but which are critical for combatting tax fraud, evasion and avoidance and in facilitating tax compliance for businesses in the single market—such as legislation on administrative cooperation and mutual assistance between MS. The second step would be to apply qualified majority voting on measures of a fiscal

---

[7] Commission Communication, *Tax policy in the European Union - priorities for the years ahead*, COM(2001) 260 final.

[8] COM(2001) 260 final, section 2.2.

[9] COM(2001) 260 final, section 2.3.

[10] Commission Communication, *A Constitution for the Union - Opinion of the Commission, pursuant to Article 48 of the Treaty on European Union, on the Conference of representatives of the Member States' governments convened to revise the Treaties*, COM(2003) 548 final.

[11] COM(2001) 260 final, section 7.

[12] COM(2001) 260 final, section 8.

[13] Commission Communication *Towards a more efficient and democratic decision making in EU tax policy*, COM(2019) 8 final. See on this, Böttner (2020), pp. 487–488.

[14] Böttner (2020), pp. 492 et seqq.

nature, but designed to support other policy goals such as environmental protection, improvement of public health etc. The third step mentioned by the Commission is to focus on areas of taxation that are already largely harmonised, and which must evolve and adapt to new circumstances, such as the VAT system. The fourth and final step would be to introduce qualified majority voting on other initiatives in the taxation area, which are necessary for the single market and for fair and competitive taxation in Europe. So far, the Commission's views on the harmonisation procedure in Article 113 TFEU have not yet led to any changes to the Treaty.[15]

7   The Commission's communication also points to the **enhanced cooperation** procedure in Article 20 TEU, introduced by the Amsterdam Treaty, as a useful tool for tax harmonisation.[16] The procedure allows for a number of at least nine MS to agree to harmonise their national legislation. This dilutes the requirement of unanimity, as only the MS that wish to harmonise are required to support the harmonisation (Article 330 TFEU). The financial transaction tax (FTT) proposed by the Commission[17] is a result of enhanced cooperation between a number of MS (→ para 36).

8   The **genesis** of the provision existed in **Article 99 TEEC**, which obliged the Commission to "consider how the legislation of the various Member States concerning turnover taxes, excise duties and other forms of indirect taxation, including countervailing measures applicable to trade between Member States, can be harmonised in the interest of the common market." Such proposals were to be adopted by the Council unanimously.

With the **Maastricht Treaty** in 1992, the wording of Article 99 TEEC was changed to a version similar to the current Article 113 TFEU. It followed from ex-Article 99 TEC that the Council was to adopt harmonisation of indirect taxes to ensure the establishment and functioning of the internal market. The provision contained a reference to the time limit in ex-Article 7a TEC.

The introduction of the **single market** in 1992 intensified the focus on the harmonisation of tax regulations as the fiscal boundaries between MS were abolished. This meant that the crossing of a border by a product or a service within the EU did not equal a tax triggering factor.

In 2007 the provision was changed to its current wording and moved to Article 113 TFEU. Compared to the previous wording in ex-Article 93 TEC-Amsterdam, the reference to the time limit was omitted and the requirement for the necessity of harmonisation was changed so as to include avoidance of distortion of competition. In its Communication on a Single Market Act from 2011,[18] the Commission identified tax harmonisation as one of twelve levers of importance to boosting

---

[15] In a draft of the European Constitution, it was proposed to introduce a provision in Article III-62 stating that legislation on administrative cooperation or to combat tax fraud and tax evasion was to be adopted by a qualified majority.

[16] Böttner (2020), p. 498. On enhanced cooperation, see in detail Böttner (2021).

[17] COM(2011) 594 final.

[18] Commission Communication, *Single Market Act - Twelve levers to boost growth and strengthen confidence; Working together to create new growth*, COM(2011) 206 final.

growth and strengthening confidence. In the communication the Commission called for increased harmonisation of both direct[19] and indirect taxation.[20]

As the historical basis of the EU is a customs union, some of the first rules harmonised within the former EC were customs and other indirect taxes.[21] It follows from Article 3.1 point (a) TFEU that the customs union is an exclusive competence of the Union, meaning that no MS may adopt its own legislation in the area (→ Article 3 TFEU para 34–37). **Indirect taxes** that are not customs are covered by the **shared competence with pre-emption** in Article 4 TFEU, as the internal market is referred to in Article 4.2 point (a): TFEU. "Shared competence with pre-emption" means that when the Union harmonises an area, the area is not to be regulated by national legislation (→ Article 4 TFEU para 2–3).

The difference between Union competence and the scope for the MS to regulate makes it essential to distinguish between custom duties, as referred to in Article 30 TFEU, which are harmonised with reference to Article 207 TFEU, and indirect taxes covered by Article 113 TFEU. Basically, a customs duty is a tax on border crossing, whereas the indirect taxes covered by Article 113 TFEU are general taxes on products or services (→ Article 110 TFEU para 15 et seqq.).

2. Basis for Harmonisation: Internal Market

If the harmonisation of indirect taxes is to be adopted, it must be based on **necessity to secure the establishment and functioning of the internal market** or the **avoidance of distortion of competition**. There is a similar requirement in Article 115 TFEU which authorises harmonisation of "such laws, regulations or administrative provisions of the Member States as directly affect the establishment or functioning of the internal market" (→ Article 115 TFEU para 4, 7).

This requirement illustrates that **tax harmonisation is not a goal in itself**,[22] but a tool for securing the internal market. If the internal market is not affected there will be no need or possibility for harmonisation. It is unclear to what extent indirect taxes will need to be harmonised to satisfy the requirements of Article 113 TFEU.[23]

2.1. Establishment and Functioning of the Internal Market

The reference to the establishment and functioning of the internal market is to be understood as a **prerequisite for legislation** to be adopted under Article 113 TFEU.

---

[19] The Common Consolidated Corporate Tax Base proposal, COM(2011) 121/4 was particularly emphasised.
[20] The Commission focused on energy taxation and the VAT system.
[21] Terra and Wattel (2012), p. 10.
[22] Bahns et al., in von der Groeben et al. (2015), Article 110 AEUV para 30 with notes.
[23] Bahns et al., in von der Groeben et al. (2015), Article 110 AEUV para 21.

If a proposal for regulation does not benefit the internal market, then harmonisation will have to be introduced based on some other harmonisation provision. The CJEU has not ruled on how this requirement is to be understood. This is probably to be seen as a consequence of the difficulties in achieving unanimity on tax matters, so it is unlikely that Union institutions will want to push for adoption of harmonisation based on this provision.

13   However, **Article 114 TFEU**, on the **approximation of laws**, contains a similar wording. This provision has been the subject of several cases referred to the CJEU. In Case C-376/98, the CJEU stated that "a measure adopted on the basis of [Article 114 TFEU] must genuinely have as its object the improvement of the conditions for the establishment and functioning of the internal market. If a mere finding of disparities between national rules and of the abstract risk of obstacles to the exercise of fundamental freedoms or of distortions of competition liable to result therefrom were sufficient to justify the choice of [Article 114 TFEU] as a legal basis, judicial review of compliance with the proper legal basis might be rendered nugatory. The Court would then be prevented from discharging the function entrusted to it by [Article 19 TEU] of ensuring that the law is observed in the interpretation and application of the Treaty."[24] Later, the CJEU summarised this view as referring to situations where there are "obstacles to trade or it is likely that such obstacles will emerge in future because the Member States have taken or are about to take divergent measures with respect to a product or a class of products such as to ensure different levels of protection and thereby prevent the product or products concerned from moving freely within the Community".[25] The requirement that harmonisation should affect the establishment and functioning of the internal market is thus to be understood as a real pre-condition for adopting harmonised indirect tax legislation.

2.2. Avoiding Distortion of Competition

14   The reference to the avoidance of distortion of competition was introduced by the Lisbon Treaty ($\rightarrow$ para 10). It is unclear whether this change to Article 113 TFEU is meant to change the circumstances under which indirect taxes can be harmonised or if it just a codification of the CJEU's case law.[26]

At present, indirect tax harmonisation in the Union is based on the principle of **destination-State taxation**. However, there exists an objective of State-of-origin taxation[27] as this would ease the administrative burdens of indirect taxation on undertakings operating in the internal market. If there were **State-of-origin**

---

[24] Case C-376/98, *Germany v Parliament and Council* (ECJ 5 October 2000) para 84.

[25] Case C-434/02, *Arnold André* (ECJ 14 December 2004) para 34.

[26] Khan and Lichtblau, in Geiger et al. (2015), Article 110 AEUV para 3.

[27] Article 402 of Directive 2006/112/EC stipulates that at some point a definitive VAT system based on the origin principle is to be introduced.

taxation, undertakings would only have to comply with the rules of a single tax administration.[28] To have State-of-origin taxation, the level of harmonisation of indirect taxes would have to be extensive enough to ensure that the change of principle would not lead to distortion of competition. In this way, the changed wording of Article 113 TFEU can be seen as necessary for moving from the destination-State principle to the State-of-origin principle.[29]

3. Relationship to Other Harmonisation Provisions

3.1. Ordinary Legislative Procedure in Articles 114 and 192 TFEU

While harmonisation under Article 113 TFEU must follow a special legislative procedure, Article 114 TFEU provides for the use of the ordinary legislative procedure (→ Article 114 TFEU para 39). Harmonisation of fiscal legislation is explicitly excluded in Article 114.2 TFEU (→ Article 114 TFEU para 59 et seqq.). This means that the **ordinary legislative procedure does not apply to harmonisation of either direct or indirect taxes** because of the requirement of unanimity. The term "fiscal provisions" referred to in these provisions is to be understood more broadly than the term "indirect taxes" referred to in Article 114 TFEU.[30] Harmonisation of other fiscal provisions is to be made under the procedure referred to in Article 115 TFEU (→ Article 115 TFEU para 2). 15

The exclusion of the use of the ordinary legislative procedure for fiscal provisions is also apparent from Article 192 TFEU, which provides the legal basis for harmonising environmental regulations. The main rule in Article 192 TFEU is that the ordinary legislative procedure applies to the harmonisation of environmental regulations, but under Article 192.2 point (a) TFEU, harmonisation of a primarily fiscal nature must be adopted under a special legislative procedure.

The wording of Article 192.2 point (a) TFEU means that **environmental taxes** can be harmonised based on the **ordinary legislative procedure** as long as the nature of the **measure is primarily environmental** (→ Article 192 TFEU para 13). For example, Article 11 of Directive 2000/60/EC[31] contains a programme of measures which the MS are obliged to introduce to achieve the objectives of the Directive. Part B of Annex IV of the Directive sets out some of the measures that the MS are to use. This list includes economic or fiscal instruments.[32] It is thus evident that the harmonisation of charges can be made based on a qualified majority 16

---

[28] Bahns et al., in von der Groeben et al. (2015), Article 110 AEUV para 26.
[29] Bahns et al., in von der Groeben et al. (2015), Article 110 AEUV para 30.
[30] Case C-533/03, *Commission v Council* (ECJ 26 January 2006) para 47.
[31] Parliament/Council Directive 2000/60/EC *establishing a framework for Community action in the field of water policy*, O.J. L 327/1.
[32] Directive 2000/60/EC Annex IV, Part B, no. iii.

under Article 192 TFEU, meaning that the term "fiscal provisions" in Article 114.2 and Articles 110 to 113 TFEU does not cover all charges and levies.[33]

17   The **relationship between the different harmonisation provisions** has been the **subject of several cases referred to the CJEU**. In Case C-300/89, the CJEU stated that the use of harmonisation provisions depends on the purpose of the harmonised legislation. If harmonised legislation has a dual purpose, leading to two mutually exclusive legislative procedures, it must be decided which purpose must give way to the other.[34] In Case C-338/01, the Court ruled on how [Article 113 TFEU] functions as a *lex specialis* in relation to the other Treaty provisions on harmonisation. As the CJEU put it, "[i]t follows that, if the Treaty contains a more specific provision that is capable of constituting the legal basis for the measure in question, that measure must be founded on such provision. That is, in particular, the case with regard to Article 113 TFEU so far as concerns the harmonisation of legislation concerning turnover taxes, excise duties and other forms of indirect taxation."[35]

3.2. Direct and Indirect Taxes

18   To harmonise the MS' direct or indirect tax legislation, there is a requirement for **unanimity**. Article 114 TFEU provides the legal basis for the approximation of laws, applying the ordinary legislative procedure. However, under Article 114.2 TFEU, fiscal measures are explicitly excluded from this provision (→ Article 114 TFEU para 59 et seqq.). This means that legislation on direct or indirect taxes must be harmonised based on the special legislative procedure in Article 115 TFEU. The wording of the provision was changed with the Nice Treaty from "The Council shall, acting unanimously on a proposal from the Commission and after consulting the European Parliament and the Economic and Social Committee" to the reference to the special legislative procedure. This change does not affect that under Article 115 TFEU, it is the Council that adopts harmonising measures based on a proposal from the Commission (Article 17.2 TEU in conjunction with Article 289.3 TFEU).

However, there is a difference between the harmonisation of the two different types of taxes. The legal basis for harmonising direct taxes is in Article 115 TFEU, which states that only directives can be used for harmonising direct taxes (→ Article 115 TFEU para 12). This makes it **necessary to distinguish between direct and indirect taxes**. While a direct tax is an income tax imposed on a tax subject, indirect taxes are taxes on sales of goods or services.[36] There are examples

---

[33] Herrera (2005b), p. 217.

[34] Case C-300/89, *Commission v Council* (ECJ 11 June 1991) esp. para 13–18.

[35] Case C-338/01, *Commission v Council* (ECJ 29 April 2004) para 60.

[36] Craig and de Búrca (2015), p. 658.

of directives harmonising legislation regarding both direct and indirect taxation. This is possible as long as the harmonisation is done through directives.[37]

As the harmonisation of direct taxes requires unanimity, only a limited number of directives have been adopted (→ Article 114 TFEU para 4; → Article 115 TFEU para 12–14).[38] However, on several occasions the Court has dealt with national tax provisions and their compliance with treaty provisions.[39] This means that the harmonisation of direct tax law in the Union can be described as having been done primarily through negative integration.[40]

19

3.3. Ordinary Legislative Procedure in Article 116 TFEU

Article 116.1 TFEU provides for the possibility of **harmonisation by a qualified majority** in cases where difference between the provisions in the MS are "distorting the conditions of competition in the internal market and that the resultant distortion needs to be eliminated." This provision does not exclude fiscal provisions, so that if a national tax provision fulfils the criteria in Article 116.1 TFEU, harmonisation can be adopted by the ordinary legislative procedure. Harmonisation based on Article 116 TFEU requires the Commission to consult the MS with the national regulation that is distorting competition before harmonisation measures are adopted (→ Article 116 TFEU para 16–18).

20

---

[37] See, for instance Council Directive 2011/16/EU *on administrative cooperation in the field of taxation*, O.J. L 64/1 (2011).

[38] Hitherto the harmonisation in force comprises Council Directive 2011/96/EU *on the common system of taxation applicable in the case of parent companies and subsidiaries of different Member States*, O.J. L 345/8 (2011), amended by Council Directive 2015/121/EU, O.J. L 21/1 (2015), in which an anti-abuse rule was introduced; Council Directive 2009/133/EC *on the common system of taxation applicable to mergers, divisions, partial divisions, transfers of assets and exchanges of shares concerning companies of different Member States and to the transfer of the registered office of an SE or SCE between Member States (codified)*, O.J. L 310/34 (2009); Council Directive 2003/49/EC *on a common system of taxation applicable to interest and royalty payments made between associated companies of different Member States*, O.J. L 157/49 (2003), amended by Directive 2004/66/EC, 2004/76/EC and 2006/98/EC; Council Directive 2014/48/EU *amending Directive 2003/48/EC on taxation of savings income in the form of interest payments*, O.J. L 111/50; Council Directive 2011/16/EU *on administrative cooperation in the field of taxation and repealing Directive 77/799/EEC*, O.J. L 64/1; and Council Directive 2010/24/EU *concerning mutual assistance for the recovery of claims relating to taxes, duties and other measures*, O.J. L 84/1.

[39] See, e.g. the extensive case law on the influence of the fundamental freedoms in Articles 28–30 TFEU on the free movement of goods, Articles 44–48 TFEU on the free movement for workers, Articles 49–55 TFEU on freedom of establishment, Articles 56–62 TFEU on the free movement of services and Articles 63–66 TFEU on the free movement of capital and payments, as well as Article 107 TFEU prohibiting State aid in the national tax laws of the MS.

[40] Terra and Wattel (2012), p. 37.

4. Harmonisation of Indirect Taxes

21 Article 113 TFEU mentions the **types of taxes** to be harmonised under its provisions. Three types are referred to: turnover taxes, excise duties and other indirect taxes. As these taxes are not defined in any treaty provision, other sources of law must be used to determine their content. If a tax measure is covered by one of the types of taxes referred to in Article 113 TFEU, then any harmonisation must be adopted based on unanimity.

4.1. Turnover Taxes

22 At an early stage in its development, the EU adopted the system of a **value added tax (VAT) with the deduction of input VAT**. The earliest adoption of a common turnover tax was the First VAT Directive in 1967.[41] It obliged the MS to introduce a VAT system as defined in Article 2 of the Directive.

Of the founding MS, only France used a system similar to the current one where input VAT is deductible. The other five MS used a system of cumulative turnover tax.[42] However, such a system is not feasible for an internal market, as it favours insourcing and the internalisation of undertakings to have as few taxed transactions as possible. A system where input VAT is deducted can achieve a higher level of neutrality, thus equalising taxation between the use of external and internal suppliers.

23 VAT in the EU is currently primarily regulated by **Directive 2006/112/EC**.[43] The Directive is also known as the "**Recast VAT Directive**"; it repeals the earlier Sixth Directive as well as the First Directive.[44] The Recast VAT Directive has been amended several times[45] and is supplemented by a number of other directives and regulations regulating different aspects of VAT. The most significant other legislation regarding VAT is the following:

- Directive 2017/2455 amending Directive 2006/112/EC and Directive 2009/132/EC as regards certain value added tax obligations for supplies of services and distance sales of goods;[46]
- Implementing Regulation 282/2011 laying down implementing measures for Directive 2006/112/EC on the common system of value added tax (recast);[47]

---

[41] First Council Directive 67/227/EEC *on the harmonisation of legislation of Member States concerning turnover taxes*, O.J. 71/1301 (1967).

[42] Terra and Wattel (2012), p. 12.

[43] O.J. L 347/1 (2006).

[44] Terra and Wattel (2012), p. 305.

[45] There have been more than 20 amendments. The most recent amendment was through Council Directive (EU) 2022/5429, O.J. L 107/1 (2022).

[46] O.J. L 348/7 (2017).

[47] O.J. L 77/1 (2011).

- Regulation 904/2010 on administrative cooperation and combating fraud in the field of value added tax (recast);[48]
- Directive 2007/74 on the exemption from value added tax and excise duty of goods imported by persons travelling from third countries;[49]
- Directive 2008/9/EC laying down detailed rules for the refund of value added tax, provided for in Directive 2006/112/EC, to taxable persons not established in the Member State of refund but established in another Member State.[50]

Harmonisation adopted on the basis of Article 113 TFEU is based on shared competence with pre-emption, meaning that when harmonisation has been adopted the MS are no longer allowed to introduce national legislation for the same area (→ para 9). In the case of turnover taxes this rule has been implemented in the Recast VAT Directive, Article 401. The provision specifies that "[w]ithout prejudice to other provisions of Community law, this Directive shall not prevent a Member State from maintaining or introducing taxes on insurance contracts, taxes on betting and gambling, excise duties, stamp duties or, more generally, any taxes, duties or charges which cannot be characterised as turnover taxes, provided that the collecting of those taxes, duties or charges does not give rise, in trade between Member States, to formalities connected with the crossing of frontiers." This means that the **MS are free to introduce other indirect taxes as long as they are not characterised as turnover taxes** (or any other harmonised tax based on Article 113 TFEU). 24

Over the years the prohibition of national regulations on turnover taxes has given rise to a number of cases being referred to the CJEU.[51] In *Banco Popolare di Cremona*, the CJEU identified **four characteristics of turnover taxes**.[52] First, they apply generally to transactions relating to goods or services. Second, the tax is proportional to the price charged by the taxable person in return for the goods or services they supply. Third, the tax is charged at each stage of production and distribution, including upon retail sale, irrespective of the number of previous transactions. Fourth, the tax paid during the preceding stages is deducted from the tax payable by a taxable person, so that, at any given stage, the tax applies only to the value added at that stage and the final burden of the tax rests ultimately on the consumer. 25

---

[48] O.J. L 268/1 (2010).
[49] O.J. L 346/6 (2007).
[50] O.J. L 44/23 (2008).
[51] Terra and Wattel (2012), p. 461.
[52] Case C-475/03, *Banca Popolare di Cremona* (ECJ 3 October 2006) para 28. The CJEU has identified the characteristics on the distinguishing between turnover taxes and other indirect taxes in other earlier cases but in the *Banco Popolare di Cremona* case, the ECJ for the first time formalises the characteristics into four points.

26   As the harmonisation of indirect taxes is aimed at the establishment and functioning of the internal market, the harmonised VAT system is based on a principle of **neutrality**.[53] This means that taxes must not affect where a good or service is purchased.[54] Neutrality can be of two different kinds; internal and external neutrality.[55] Internal neutrality is neutrality within a single tax jurisdiction where the aim is to make sure that taxation is neutral, based on whether production is integrated in a buyer's company or not. External neutrality refers to cases involving cross-border transactions. The purpose of external neutrality is to equalise the use of domestic and foreign trading partners. However, the principle of neutrality is to be understood as a broad principle overarching the entire VAT system with its goal that VAT should not be a factor influencing business decisions.

27   Under Article 402 of the Recast VAT Directive, the VAT system is intended to use the State-of-origin principle, so that VAT is to be paid in the country from where the goods or services depart. This principle is already evident when goods or services do not cross borders. However, hitherto this has not been possible in cases of cross-border sales of good or services as the harmonisation of VAT has not been extensive enough. At the current level of harmonisation, a State-of-origin based VAT system would make it more favourable to use suppliers in low tax countries by making tax rates part of the costs compared.

The principle of neutrality would not be achieved by this means. By using a **destination-State based VAT system**, neutrality is achieved because the VAT rate for the buyer is the same whether the supplier is from the same or a different MS. However, the ideal of using a State-of-origin based VAT system could be an effective harmonisation tool as it will encourage MS to equalise their VAT rates. The current system applying the destination-State principle for cross-border transactions is referred to as a "transitional" system, which is to be replaced at some point. However, regardless of what is stated in Article 402 of the Recast VAT Directive, there have been discussions about whether the definitive system should apply the State-of-origin or the destination-State principle.[56]

At present, the Commission is working on a major **revision of the existing VAT system**, labelled "the definitive VAT system." The revision includes several proposed directives and was originally expected to be fully implemented in 2022, resulting in a **Single VAT area** within the EU. The revision consists of a series of fundamental principles, "Cornerstones", as well as "Quick Fixes" to improve the functioning of the current system. Based on the proposed directives, the Commission has moved away from the ideal of an origin principle and instead maintain the

---

[53] Cnossen et al. (1994), p. 7.

[54] Tutu (2014), p. 118.

[55] Tutu (2014), p. 122.

[56] European Parliament Directorate-General for Parliamentary Research Services – Working papers: Options for a definitive VAT system, Economic affairs series E – 5 09 – 1995.

destination principle.⁵⁷ Apart from the destination principle, the corner stones of the proposed major revision is confirmation that the vendor as a general rule is liable in case of an intra-EU supply of goods and extension of the One Stop Shop principle, rendering it possible for businesses to make declarations, payments and deductions for cross-border supplies through a single online portal. However, the initiative may be overhauled by the Commission's initiative on "VAT in the digital era" announced in its 2020 Action Plan on fair and simple taxation.⁵⁸

In the Recast VAT Directive, the MS agreed on **minimum rates for VAT**. Under Article 97 of the Directive, the standard rate for the period 1 January 2006 to 31 December 2010 must not be less than 15%. The expiration date for this minimum standard rate has been extended several times and was made permanent by Directive 2018/912/EU. Apart from the standard rate, the Directive allows the possibility of introducing reduced rates down to 5%. Under Article 98, each MS may have up to two reduced rates. The reduced rate can only be applied to goods or services listed in Annex III to the Directive. A reduced rate must not be lower than 5% (Article 99 of the Directive). **28**

4.2. Excise Duties

Excise duties are **taxes on specific categories of products**. There is not a widespread harmonisation of this kind of indirect taxes within the Union, so the primary concern in Union law is that MS should comply with the fundamental freedoms when introducing excise duties. This does not mean that excise duties are a neglected area. The first step towards harmonisation was taken in 1972 with Directive 72/464/EEC.⁵⁹ **29**

The general arrangements of excise duties were harmonised with Directive 92/12/EEC,⁶⁰ which was replaced with Directive 2008/118.⁶¹ The purpose of the directive is to harmonise the conditions for charging excise duties to ensure the functioning of the internal market.⁶² **30**

---

⁵⁷ The revision includes several proposed directives, where one of the core proposals is Proposal for a Council Directive amending Directive 2006/112/EC as regards the introduction of the detailed technical measures for the operation of the definitive VAT system for the taxation of trade between Member States, COM(2018) 329.

⁵⁸ COM(2020) 312 final.

⁵⁹ Council Directive 72/464/EEC *on taxes other than turnover taxes which affect the consumption of manufactured tobacco*, O.J. L 303/3 (1972). The Directive was repealed by Council Directive 95/59/EC, O.J. L 291/40 (1995), which in turn was codified by Council Directive 2011/64/EU *on the structure and rates of excise duty applied to manufactured tobacco*.

⁶⁰ Directive 92/12/EEC *on the general arrangements for products subject to excise duty and on the holding, movement and monitoring of such products*, O.J. L 76/1 (1992).

⁶¹ Directive 2008/118 *concerning the general arrangements for excise duty*, O.J. L 9/12 (2008).

⁶² Directive 2008/118, preamble, second indent.

31 So far, **three areas** have been **covered by harmonising measures**: alcohol, energy products (especially mineral oils) and tobacco. However, neither the tax base nor the tax rate have undergone extensive harmonisation.

Excise duties on cigarettes and other **tobacco** products are harmonised with Directive 2011/64/EU on the structure and rates of excise duty applied to manufactured tobacco.[63] Under Article 7 of the Directive, excise duties on cigarettes must consist of both an *ad valorum* component calculated on the maximum retail selling price and a specific component calculated per unit. As for other tobacco products, the MS are free to choose between to two components (cf. Article 14 of the Directive).

As for **alcohol**, the harmonised legislation consists of Directive 92/83/EEC[64] and Directive 92/84/EEC.[65]

Finally the taxation of **energy** has been harmonised with Directive 2003/96/EC[66] and Directive 95/60/EC.[67]

Part of Directive 2008/118 was Excise Movement and Control System (EMCS). To implement this system, two regulations have been passed:

- Commission Regulation (EC) No 684/2009 implementing provisions as regards the computerised procedures for the movement of excise goods under suspension of excise duty;[68]
- Council Regulation 389/2012/EU on administrative cooperation in the field of excise duties.[69]

In December 2013, a report on the functioning of ECMS was published, which led to discussions on further administrative cooperation—including exchange of information and statistics.

4.3. Other Forms of Indirect Taxation

32 Apart from the above-mentioned types of indirect taxation, Article 113 TFEU contains a general wording regarding "other forms of indirect taxation." In the following, a short presentation of legislation harmonised based on this part of Article 113 TFEU will be given.

---

[63] O.J. L 176/24 (2011).

[64] Directive 92/83/EEC *on the harmonization of the structures of excise duties on alcohol and alcoholic beverages*, O.J. L 317/21 (1992).

[65] Directive 92/84/EEC *on the approximation of the rates of excise duty on alcohol and alcoholic beverages*, O.J. L 316/29 (1992).

[66] Directive 2002/96/EC *restructuring the Community framework for the taxation of energy products and electricity*, O.J. L 283/51 (2009).

[67] Directive 95/60 *on fiscal marking of gas oils and kerosene*, O.J. L 291/46 (1995).

[68] O.J. L 197/24 (2009).

[69] O.J. L 121/1 (2012).

In 1969, the **capital duty** directive was introduced.[70] The aim of the directive was to harmonise the structures and rates of indirect taxation on the raising of capital. The directive was amended several times until the capital duty was abolished in 2008.[71]

Since 1983, **indirect taxation on temporary imports of motor-driven road vehicles and their trailers** have been exempt on a harmonised basis.[72]

Administrative cooperation in tax matters is a key issue in European tax law. In 1977, the first harmonised legislation in the matter was introduced.[73] This directive only covered direct taxation. Administrative cooperation on VAT was added to the directive in 1979.[74] In 2003, VAT was excluded from the directive once again.[75] At the same time, a regulation on exchange of VAT information was passed.[76]

In 2011 a new directive on administrative cooperation in tax matters was passed.[77] This Directive does not cover exchange of information on VAT matters. However, the directive has an impact on indirect taxes, as indirect taxes that are not covered by harmonised legislation are covered by the directive. The directive has been amended several times through the years, increasing the level of administrative cooperation between the MS.[78] The most recent amendments include technical changes to the existing provisions on exchanges of information and administrative cooperation as well as an extension of the scope to cover automatic exchange of information with respect to the information reported by digital platform operators. The recent amendment is part of a package for fair and simple taxation supporting the recovery of the EU, which also includes a Communication for an Action Plan

33

34

35

---

[70] Directive 69/335/EEC *concerning indirect taxes on the raising of capital*, O.J. L 249/25 (1969).

[71] Directive 2008/7 *concerning indirect taxes on the raising of capital*, O.J. L 46/11 (2008).

[72] Council Directive 83/182/EEC *on tax exemptions within the Community for certain means of transport temporarily imported into one Member State from another*, O.J. L 105/59 (1983).

[73] Council Directive 77/799/EEC *concerning mutual assistance by the competent authorities of the Member States in the field of direct taxation*, O.J. L 336/15 (1977).

[74] Directive 79/1070/EEC, O.J. L 331/8 (1979).

[75] Directive 2003/93/EC, O.J. L 264/23 (2003).

[76] Regulation (EC) No. 1798/2003, O.J. L 264/1 (2003), replaced by Council Regulation (EU) No 904/2010 *on administrative cooperation and combating fraud in the field of value added tax*, O.J. L 268/1 (2010).

[77] Directive 2011/16/EU *on administrative cooperation in the field of taxation*, O.J. L 64/1 (2011).

[78] Council Directive 2014/107/EU (DAC2) *as regards the automatic exchange of financial account information between Member States based on the OECD Common Reporting Standard (CRS) which prescribes the automatic exchange of information on financial accounts held by non-residents*; Council Directive (EU) 2015/2376 (DAC3) *as regards the mandatory automatic exchange of information on advance cross-border tax rulings*; Council Directive (EU) 2016/881 (DAC4) *as regards the mandatory automatic exchange of information on country-by-country reporting (CbCR) amongst tax authorities*; Council Directive (EU) 2016/2258 (DAC5) *as regards access to anti-money-laundering information by tax authorities*; Council Directive (EU) 2018/822 (DAC6) *as regards mandatory automatic exchange of information in the field of taxation in relation to reportable cross-border arrangements*; Council Directive (EU) 2021/514, O.J. L 104/1 (2021).

36   presenting a number of upcoming initiatives for fair and simple taxation supporting the recovery strategy.[79]

36   Since the financial crisis of 2008, several MS have pushed for measures requiring a larger contribution to the public finances from the financial sector, partly due to the fact that most financial institutions are exempt from VAT. As a step towards achieving that goal, there was a discussion about introducing a **tax on financial transactions**. Since unilateral national measures could lead to distortion and the fragmentation of the single market, in September 2011 the Commission proposed the adoption of a harmonised financial transaction tax (FTT) based on Article 113 TFEU.[80] The proposed directive would tax financial transactions between financial institutions at the rate of 0.1% on transactions for shares and bonds and 0.01% on transactions for derivatives. This should result in revenue of EUR 57 billion per year.

In 2012, the European finance ministers concluded that unanimity on the proposal could not be reached. Since a number of MS still argued in favour of an FTT, the Commission proposed to use the enhanced cooperation procedure under Article 20 TEU (→ Article 20 TEU para 56) to let those MS pushing for an FTT adopt it. The Council and the Parliament gave their consent to this and in February 2013 a new proposal was submitted by the Commission[81] but no legal act has been adopted thus far.[82]

37   In June 2018, the Commission issued a proposal for two new directives to ensure that digital business activities are taxed in a fair and growth-friendly way in the EU.[83] As an interim measure, the Commission proposed a **digital services tax** (DST).[84] The purpose of the DST was to ensure a level playing field between highly digitalised companies (HDBs) and traditional bricks and mortar companies as well as make sure that companies relying heavily on user participation as a driver for value creation are taxed, although they do not have any physical presence in an MS. The purpose was to be achieved by levying a 3% tax on turnover from certain digital services. The second proposal for a directive contains a new type of permanent establishment (PE) based on digital presence.[85] The DST is meant to be an interim measure until international agreement on a PE based on **digital presence** is adopted.

---

[79] Commission Communication, *An action plan for fair and simple taxation supporting the recovery strategy*, COM(2020) 312 final.

[80] IP/11/85 The financial transaction tax (FTT), COM(2011) 594 final.

[81] Commission, *Proposal for a Council Directive implementing enhanced cooperation in the area of financial transaction tax*, COM(2013) 71 final.

[82] See also Böttner (2021), pp. 54 et seqq.

[83] On the proposals, see Niemenen (2018).

[84] Commission, *Proposal for a Council Directive on the common system of a digital services tax on revenues resulting from the provision of certain digital services*, COM(2018) 148.

[85] Commission, *Proposal for a Council Directive laying down rules relating to the corporate taxation of a significant digital presence*, COM(2018) 147.

Since there is no present international agreement on the digital PE, the DST was proposed as a levy to make sure that it does not infringe existing double taxation treaties. This view has been criticised extensively afterwards.[86] To this date, no agreement has been reached on the directive.

List of Cases

ECJ 28.01.1986, 270/83, *Commission v France*, ECLI:EU:C:1986:37 [cit. in para 4]
ECJ 11.06.1991, C-300/89, *Commission v Council*, ECLI:EU:C:1991:244 [cit. in para 17]
ECJ 05.10.2000, C-376/98, *Germany v Parliament and Council*, ECLI:EU:C:2000:544 [cit. in para 13]
ECJ 29.04.2004, C-338/01, *Commission v Council*, ECLI:EU:C:2004:253 [cit. in para 17]
ECJ 14.12.2004, C-434/02, *Arnold André*, ECLI:EU:C:2004:800 [cit. in para 13]
ECJ 03.10.2006, C-475/03, *Banca popolare di Cremona*, ECLI:EU:C:2006:629 [cit. in para 25]
ECJ 26.01.2006, C-533/03, *Commission v Council*, ECLI:EU:C:2006:64 [cit. in para 15]

References

Böttner, R. (2020). The Commission's initiative on the passerelle clauses. Exploring the unused potential of the Lisbon Treaty. *Zeitschrift für europarechtliche Studien*, 483–503.
Böttner, R. (2021). *The constitutional framework for enhanced cooperation in EU law*. Brill Nijhoff.
Cnossen, C., Vogel, K., Brands, J., & van Raad, K. (1994). *Taxation of cross-border income, harmonization, and tax neutrality under European Community law: An institutional approach*. Kluwer Law International.
Craig, P., & de Búrca, G. (2015). *EU law. Text, cases and materials* (6th ed.). OUP.
Geiger, R., Khan, D.-E., & Kotzur, M. (Eds.). (2015). *European Union Treaties. A commentary*. Hart Publishing/C.H. Beck.
Helminen, M. (2018). *EU tax law – Direct taxation*. IBFD.
Herrera, P. M. (2005a). The restrictive impact of the principles of EU law on tax sovereignty and the concept of tax in the EU Member States. In B. Peeters (Ed.), *The concept of tax* (pp. 209–213). EATLP.
Herrera, P. M. (2005b). The concept of tax in the EC Treaty and in the failed European Constitution: (1) Fiscal and tax provisions. In B. Peeters (Ed.), *The concept of tax* (pp. 215–220). EATLP.
Niemenen, M. (2018). International/European Union/OECD – The scope of the Commission's digital tax proposals. *Bulletin for International Taxation, 72*(11).

---

[86] van Horzen and van Esdonk (2018) consider the DST a direct tax and Nogueira (2019) considers the DST an infringement of both EU and WTO law.

Nogueira, J. F. (2019). The compatibility of the EU digital services tax with EU and WTO law. In P. Pistone & D. Weber (Eds.), *Taxing the digital economy* (pp. 247–287). IBFD.

Terra, B. J. M., & Wattel, P. J. (2012). *European tax law*. Wolters Kluwer Law and Business.

Tutu, R. (2014). Designing VAT systems for the 21st century: neutrality. In R. Petruzzi & K. Spies (Eds.), *Tax policy challenges in the 21st century* (pp. 117–138). Linde.

van Horzen, F., & van Esdonk, A. (2018). European Union - Proposed 3% digital services tax. *International Transfer Pricing Journal, 25*(4), 267–272.

von der Groeben, H., Schwarze, J., & Hatje, A. (Eds.). (2015b). *Europäisches Unionsrecht. Commentary* (7th ed.). Nomos.

Chapter 3
Approximation of Laws

Article 114 [Harmonisation in the Internal Market]
(ex-Article 95 TEC)

1. Save where otherwise provided in the Treaties, the following provisions shall apply for the achievement of the objectives set out in Article 26.[30–32] The European Parliament and the Council shall, acting in accordance with the ordinary legislative procedure[45] and after consulting the Economic and Social Committee, adopt the measures[46–50] for the approximation[18–23] of the provisions laid down by law, regulation or administrative action in Member States[33–36] which have as their object the establishment and functioning of the internal market.[24–29]
2. Paragraph 1 shall not apply to fiscal provisions, to those relating to the free movement of persons nor to those relating to the rights and interests of employed persons.[41–44]
3. The Commission, in its proposals envisaged in paragraph 1 concerning health, safety, environmental protection and consumer protection, will take as a base a high level of protection, taking account in particular of any new development based on scientific facts. Within their respective powers, the European Parliament and the Council will also seek to achieve this objective.[37–40]
4. If, after the adoption of a harmonisation measure by the European Parliament and the Council, by the Council or by the Commission, a Member State deems it necessary to maintain national provisions on grounds of major needs referred to in Article 36, or relating to the protection of the environment or the working environment, it shall notify the Commission of these provisions as well as the grounds for maintaining them.[53–58]
5. Moreover, without prejudice to paragraph 4, if, after the adoption of a harmonisation measure by the European Parliament and the Council, by the Council or by the Commission, a Member State deems it necessary to introduce national provisions based on new scientific evidence relating to the protection of the environment or the working environment on grounds of a problem specific to that Member State arising after the adoption of the harmonisation measure, it shall notify the Commission of the envisaged provisions as well as the grounds for introducing them.[59–65]
6. The Commission shall, within six months of the notifications as referred to in paragraphs 4 and 5, approve or reject the national provisions involved after having verified whether or not they are a means of arbitrary discrimination or a disguised restriction on trade between Member States and whether or not they shall constitute an obstacle to the functioning of the internal market.[66–69]
   In the absence of a decision by the Commission within this period the national provisions referred to in paragraphs 4 and 5 shall be deemed to have been approved.[72]

When justified by the complexity of the matter and in the absence of danger for human health, the Commission may notify the Member State concerned that the period referred to in this paragraph may be extended for a further period of up to six months.[70–71]

7. When, pursuant to paragraph 6, a Member State is authorised to maintain or introduce national provisions derogating from a harmonisation measure, the Commission shall immediately examine whether to propose an adaptation to that measure.[73]

8. When a Member State raises a specific problem on public health in a field which has been the subject of prior harmonisation measures, it shall bring it to the attention of the Commission which shall immediately examine whether to propose appropriate measures to the Council.[62]

9. By way of derogation from the procedure laid down in Articles 258 and 259, the Commission and any Member State may bring the matter directly before the Court of Justice of the European Union if it considers that another Member State is making improper use of the powers provided for in this Article.[74–76]

10. The harmonisation measures referred to above shall, in appropriate cases, include a safeguard clause authorising the Member States to take, for one or more of the non-economic reasons referred to in Article 36, provisional measures subject to a Union control procedure.[77–79]

Contents

1. Genesis, Systematic Reading and Rationale 1
    1.1. Genesis 4
    1.2. Systematic Reading 8
    1.3. Harmonisation vs. Mutual Recognition 14
2. Conditions for the Approximation of Laws 18
    2.1. Terminology 18
    2.2. Connection to the Internal Market 24
    2.3. Achieving the Objectives Set Out in Article 26 TFEU 30
    2.4. Provisions Laid Down by Domestic Law, Regulation or Administrative Action 33
    2.5. Ensuring a High Level of Protection 37
    2.6. Areas Exempted from Harmonisation 41
    2.7. Procedure and Instruments 45
3. National Opt-Outs and Exceptions 51
    3.1. Maintaining National Provisions 53
    3.2. Introducing New National Provisions 59
    3.3. Assessment by the European Commission 66
4. Simplified Infringement Procedure Before the CJEU 74
5. Safeguard Clauses for the Adoption of Provisional Measures by a Member State 77
6. Recent Practice of Internal Market Harmonisation 80
List of Cases
References

1. Genesis, Systematic Reading and Rationale

Article 114 TFEU authorises the Union legislator to adopt measures harmonising national laws and regulations that have as their object the **establishment and functioning of the internal market**. It is supplemented by Article 115 TFEU, which allows for the approximation of national provisions directly affecting the internal market. It tries to strike a balance between the establishment of an internal market with uniform law and the regulatory autonomy of the MS and their specific legal orders. Approximation therefore leads to converging rules in the MS but allows for certain specificities. To this end, national derogations are admissible under strict circumstances and under the strict control of the Union.

Harmonisation is not an end in itself but rather a means for the preservation and functioning of the internal market as objectives of Article 3.3 TEU and Article 26 TFEU.[1] However, integration is a dynamic process, and thus the harmonisation of laws is both a **"realisation of objectives"** and a **"determination of objectives"**.[2] The Union must always determine the measures necessary for the development of the internal market on the basis of the development already achieved.[3] At the same time, it faces the problem of observing the requirement of coherence (Article 7 TFEU) in the harmonised legal matters since harmonisation has often taken place in a multitude of legal acts.[4]

Since **divergent national laws are the greatest obstacles to European integration**, it can be particularly advanced through the approximation of laws. At the same time, positive integration can be achieved through common rules. This is in contrast to mere negative integration[5] by using the market freedoms and the principle of mutual recognition,[6] where only certain measures of the MS can be prevented. This entails the danger of a "race to the bottom", in which more and more national laws may not be applied because they violate the fundamental freedoms or the principle of mutual recognition. However, the Union can now set positive rules through the approximation of laws and is not limited to objecting to MS measures that are contrary to the fundamental freedoms. Which principle—competition of national systems or harmonisation of laws[7]—makes more sense is an economic question, which is also the question of the application of Article 34 or

---

[1] Reich and Burkhardt, in Smit and Herzog (2017), Article 114 TFEU para 3.

[2] von der Groeben (1970), p. 360.

[3] See Tietje, in Grabitz et al. (2022), Artikel 114 AEUV para 7 (released in 2016), who argues that the dynamic aspect is very present within the sphere of the EU while the MS focus more on the static aspect; see C-376/98, *Germany v Parliament and Council* (ECJ 5 October 2000) para 23 seq., 36 seq.

[4] Oppermann et al. (2021), § 32 para 4.

[5] This difference between negative and positive integration was developed by *Tinbergen*, see Tinbergen (1954), p. 122.

[6] See for the different objects of fundamental freedoms and harmonisation Case 193/80, *Commission v Italy* (ECJ 9 December 1981) para 17.

[7] Tiebout (1956).

Article 114 TFEU.[8] However, these two poles do not necessarily contradict one another, so that it is more a question of the respective degree of harmonisation or, conversely, of system competition.[9]

1.1. Genesis

4   The foreign ministers of the six States founding the future European Coal and Steel Community (ECSC) decided on 3 June 1955 at the Messina Conference that "the further progress must be towards the setting up of a united Europe by [...] the **gradual merging of national economies** [and] the **creation of a common market**".[10] In order to establish this, various means were to be used. These are, on the one hand, the market freedoms, which make negative integration possible by prohibiting MS from engaging in conduct that is contrary to economic free movement. On the other hand, the so-called Spaak Committee already recognised the importance of legal harmonisation as a possibility of positive integration (→ para 3).[11] The aim of this is to improve the internal market and prevent distortions of competition through common legal standards.[12] Consequently, the possibility for harmonisation measures was already created in the EEC Treaty in the form of **Article 100 TEEC** (now Article 115 TFEU) and other special provisions.[13] However, this provision required unanimity in the Council for the adoption of legal harmonisations. For this reason, it was difficult, not to say impossible, to adopt measures against the will of even a single MS.[14] Moreover, it was only possible to adopt directives, which meant that it was not possible to adopt measures with a high degree of harmonisation.

5   Thus, in 1985, the Commission stated in its **White Paper "Completing the Internal Market"** that a "new strategy" was needed to create "a genuine common

---

[8] See Weatherill (2010), para 13.24.

[9] Bätge (2009), p. 65, for criteria to decide on these degrees, see p. 65–75. See in general Blanke and Böttner (2020), para 15-25; Tietje, in Grabitz et al. (2022), Artikel 114 AEUV para 25–31 (released in 2016); von Danwitz (2018), B. II. para 87–90; in-depth Ludwigs (2004), pp. 35–58; cf. also Schweitzer (2010), pp. 1–3 who argues that there could be a conflict between the "State's responsibility for the common good" and competition.

[10] Resolution adopted by the Ministers of Foreign Affairs of the Member States of the ECSC at their meeting at Messina, 1-3 June 1955.

[11] Report of the Heads of Delegation to the Foreign Ministers ('Spaak Report'), Brussels, 21 April 1956, p. 60 seq.

[12] Oppermann et al. (2021), § 32 para 1; cf. Case 32/65, *Italy v Council and Commission* (ECJ 13 July 1966), p. 405.

[13] Ipsen (1972), § 39 para 2–5.

[14] Cf. Commission White Paper, *Completing the Internal Market*, COM(85) 310 final of 14 June 1985, para 68.

market"[15] by simplifying the harmonisation procedure[16] and by strengthening the principle of mutual recognition or country-of-origin principle[17] (→ para 14–17) and applying it whenever harmonisation measures did not seem absolutely necessary.[18] These two suggestions were then implemented in 1987 in the **Single European Act** (SEA). Firstly, a new Article 100a TEEC was inserted, which made harmonisation measures possible with a qualified majority in the Council. Secondly, **Article 100b TEEC** was added, which was intended to strengthen the principle of mutual recognition by enabling the Council to prescribe the application of the principle in individual cases.[19]

The problem with the amendment by the SEA was that it was only inserted "at the last minute" and as a result "was not only unfortunate in terms of language but also imprecisely formulated in terms of content".[20] It took until 1997 to correct these editorial problems through the **Amsterdam Treaty**. Paragraph 3 now obliges not only the Commission but also the EP and the Council to ensure a high level of protection (→ para 37). Paragraphs 4 and 5 were adapted and now regulate in a more differentiated manner the maintaining and subsequent introduction of divergent national regulations (→ para 51 et seqq.). Furthermore, the so-called "confirmation procedure" (paragraph 6) was put into more specific terms (→ para 66 et seqq.): on the one hand, the Commission is granted greater discretion (it no longer "confirms" but "shall [...] approve or reject"); on the other hand, it is given a deadline of six months to do so. In addition, paragraphs 7 and 8 are added, according to which the adaptation of harmonisation measures is examined (→ para 73). Finally, the treaty also changed the numbering, with Articles 100 and 100a becoming Articles 94 and 95, respectively.[21]

The **Lisbon Treaty** introduces some minor editorial changes concerning the amended legislative procedures. In addition, Article 95 TEC (= Article 114 TFEU) and Article 94 TEC (= Article 115 TFEU) switched places, so that the importance of Article 114 TFEU is clearly emphasised, and it becomes clear that this is the primarily relevant provision. The Treaty of Lisbon also consolidated the wording by abolishing the distinction between the terms "common market" (Article 100

6

7

---

[15] COM(85) 310 final, para 61 seq.

[16] COM(85) 310 final, para 61, 67 seq.

[17] Established by the ECJ in Case 120/78, *REWE v Bundesmonopolverwaltung für Branntwein* (ECJ 20 February 1979) para 14; for the wording and interpretation of the Commission see COM (85) 310 final, para 58. See also Blanke and Böttner (2020), para 115 et seq. with further references.

[18] COM(85) 310 final, para 77 seq.

[19] Article 19 SEA, O.J. L 169/8 (1987); cf. Ehlermann (1995), p. 13; Ehlermann (1987), pp. 399–402; this norm has never been used and has therefore been denounced by the Treaty of Amsterdam cf. Blanke and Böttner (2020), para 116.

[20] Schröder, in Streinz (2018), Artikel 114 AEUV para 2 (our translation).

[21] Cf. Schröder, in Streinz (2018), Artikel 114 AEUV para 2.

TEEC) and "internal market" (Article 100a TEEC), which had led to debates on potential differences between the two concepts.[22]

1.2. Systematic Reading

8   Article 114 TFEU is in Part Three of the TFEU on "Union Policies and Internal Actions" in its Title VII on "Common Rules on Competition, Taxation and Approximation of Laws", Chapter 3 ("Approximation of Laws", Articles 114–118 TFEU).[23] Articles 116 and 117 TFEU deal with specific distortions of competition, which Article 116 TFEU aims to eliminate repressively, Article 117 TFEU preventively.[24] Article 118 TFEU was inserted by the Treaty of Lisbon and allows the creation of separate legal titles in the field of intellectual property. Finally, Articles 114 and 115 TFEU contain competences concerning "the functioning and establishment of the internal market". They have a **horizontal character**"[25] and give the Union a great deal of room for manoeuvre.[26] Article 114 TFEU serves as the general competence for the adoption of legal acts. Its significance is now underlined by its position at the head of the chapter.[27] This, however, makes it fundamentally different from sector-specific legal bases authorising legal action in a carefully defined area, whereas the general competence for approximation can cover nearly everything as long as it has an internal market connection (→ para 24).[28]

9   The approximation of laws under Chapter 3 in general and on the basis of Article 114 TFEU in particular belongs to the area of **shared competences** in accordance with Article 4.2 point (a) TFEU. It concerns the "internal market", which comprises measures with the aim of establishing or ensuring the functioning of the "area without internal frontiers in which the free movement of goods, persons, services and capital is ensured" in accordance with Article 26 TFEU.[29] This categorisation was contested with regard to Article 118 TFEU based on the argument that the creation of European intellectual property rights concerns the preservation of undistorted competition and thus belongs to the Union's exclusive

---

[22] On this issue see Barents (1993), p. 102–105. Using this as a criterion of differentiation Ihns (2005), pp. 107–110, 115.

[23] For the reasons for this placement see Tietje, in Grabitz et al. (2022), Artikel 114 AEUV para 4 (released in 2016); Terhechte and Kübek, in Pechstein et al. (2023), Artikel 114 AEUV para 12.

[24] Cf. inter alia Blanke and Böttner (2020), para 121.

[25] Case C-376/98, *Germany v Parliament and Council* (Opinion of AG Finnelly of 15 June 2000) para 62.

[26] Cf. Khan and Eisenhut, in Geiger et al. (2015), Article 114 TFEU para 6.

[27] Khan and Eisenhut, in Geiger et al. (2015), Article 114 TFEU para 4; see in-depth Blanke and Böttner (2020), para 139 et seqq.

[28] Weatherill (2017), p. 84.

[29] Cf. Joined Cases C-274/11 and C-295/11, *Spain and Italy v Council* (CJEU 16 April 2013) para 20.

competence to set rules for "the establishing of the competition rules necessary for the functioning of the internal market" in the sense of Article 3.1 point (b). The CJEU rejected this claim with reference to the wording and systematic reading of the provision.[30]

Of particular interest is the **distinction between the scopes of application of Articles 114 and 115 TFEU**. Both are characterised by a reference to the internal market and thus a very wide area of application. In principle, **Article 114 TFEU has priority** over Article 115 TFEU. On the one hand, this is already evident from its position; on the other hand, Article 114 TFEU is also a (albeit marginally) more specific norm. It also follows from the fact that Article 115 TFEU is only applicable "without prejudice to Article 114". Moreover, Article 115 TFEU concerns those measures that "*directly affect* the establishment or functioning of the internal market", whereas Article 114 TFEU refers to measures "which have as their *object* the establishment and functioning of the internal market".[31] One must bear in mind, however, that the wording of Article 115 TFEU dates back to the time before the existence of today's Article 114 TFEU[32] and that their wording remained almost unchanged. When it was decided in the SEA not to amend the then Article 100 TEEC but to insert a new article with a simpler procedure (Article 100a), this new article was to replace the current Article 115 TFEU in its scope of application.[33] In the delimitation, Article 115 TFEU is relevant especially when the application of Article 114 TFEU is excluded according to its paragraph 2 (→ para 41–44).[34] However, since there are more specific rules on the indirect fiscal provisions (Article 113 TFEU), the free movement of persons, and those relating to the rights and interests of employed persons (→ para 17), in practice only the area of direct taxation remains for the application of Article 115 TFEU (→ Article 115 TFEU para 3).[35]

10

Apart from general competence, there is a whole series of **special provisions** scattered around the Treaties for the harmonisation of laws, **which take**

11

---

[30] Joined Cases C-274/11 and C-295/11, *Spain and Italy v Council* (CJEU 16 April 2013) para 16 et seqq.; cf. also Case C-58/08, *Vodafone and Others* (ECJ 8 June 2010) para 75; Case C-376/98, *Germany v Parliament and Council* (ECJ 9 October 2001) para 83; Case C-491/01, *British American Tobacco (Investments) and Imperial Tobacco* (ECJ 10 December 2002) para 179.

[31] Emphasis added.

[32] Tietje, in Grabitz et al. (2022), Artikel 115 AEUV para 6 (released in 2016); with the same result also Weatherill (2010), para 13.10.

[33] Bardenheuer and Pipkorn, in von der Groeben (1999), Artikel 100a EGV para 3.

[34] Khan and Eisenhut, in Geiger et al. (2015), Article 114 TFEU para 5; Weatherill (2010), para 13.07.

[35] Recent examples of legal acts based on that provision are Council Directive 2011/16/EU *on administrative cooperation in the field of taxation*, O.J. L 64/1 (2011) (also based on Article 113 TFEU); Council Directive (EU) 2016/1164 *laying down rules against tax avoidance practices that directly affect the functioning of the internal market*, O.J. L 193/1 (2016); Council Directive (EU) 2017/1852 *on tax dispute resolution mechanisms in the European Union*, O.J. L 265/1 (2017); and Council Directive (EU) 2022/2523 *on ensuring a global minimum level of taxation for multinational enterprise groups and large-scale domestic groups in the Union*, O.J. L 328/1 (2022).

precedence over Article 114 TFEU as *leges speciales*. This is emphasised by the provision's wording ("safe where otherwise provided in the Treaties"). These special provisions are Article 43.2 (agriculture),[36] Article 46 (free movement of workers), Article 50 (freedom of establishment),[37] Article 52.2 (justified special arrangements for foreigners with regard to freedom of movement), Article 53 (mutual recognition of diplomas),[38] Article 59 (liberalisation of services), Article 62 in conjunction with Articles 52.2 and 53 (services), Article 64.2 (movement of capital with third countries), Article 81.2 (judicial cooperation in civil matters), Articles 82.2 and 83.2 (judicial cooperation in criminal matters), Articles 91 and 100.2 (transport), Article 171 (trans-European networks)[39] and Article 194 (energy policy).

12   However, the situation is different in **cases where the Treaties do not contain specific rules on approximation** with the aim of improving the functioning of the internal market, i.e. cases where a measure is to be adopted on the basis of Article 114 TFEU, which, although it affects another policy area for which there are special provisions, also pursues the internal market objective. It thus needs to be determined which provision the EU legislator has to rely on in this case. According to the so-called **centre of gravity approach**, the relevant provision is the one that most closely corresponds to the (main) objective of the legal act.[40] With regard to Article 114 TFEU, however, the ECJ seems to regard the internal market as a high good that may prevail over other objectives. This applies, inter alia, in cases regarding health protection (Article 168 TFEU).[41] The prevalence of Article 114 TFEU is justified by the fact that paragraph 3 explicitly prescribes a high level of protection also with regard to health[42] and that health protection must be taken into account in all measures of the Union according to Article 168.1 TFEU.[43] Consequently, measures of legal harmonisation that at least *also* aim to improve the internal market can almost always be based on Article 114, even if this is not the *main* purpose of the measure. Ultimately, however, the Union legislator has a

---

[36] Case 83/78, *Pigs Marketing Board v Raymond Redmond* (ECJ 29 November 1978) para 37; Case C-180/96, *United Kingdom v Commission* (ECJ 5 May 1998) para 133; Case C-269/97, *Commission v Council* (ECJ 4 April 2000) para 47.

[37] Cf. Case C-97/96, *Verband deutscher Daihatsu-Händler eV v Daihatsu Deutschland GmbH* (ECJ 4 December 1997) para 18.

[38] C-233/94, *Germany v Parliament and Council* (ECJ 13 May 1997) para 14, 17, 20.

[39] Case C-271/94, *Parliament v Council* (ECJ 26 March 1996) para 32 seq.

[40] See Case C-411/06, *Commission v Parliament and Council* (ECJ 8 September 2009) para 46; Case C-36/98, *Spain v Council* (ECJ 30 January 2001) para 59; Case C-42/97, *Parliament v Council* (ECJ 23 February 1999) para 39 seq.

[41] Case C-300/89, *Commission v Council* (ECJ 11 June 1991) para 21–23; Case C-376/98, *Germany v Parliament and Council* (ECJ 5 October 2000) para 76, 88.

[42] Cf. Case 380/03, *Germany v Parliament and Council* (ECJ 12 December 2006) para 39, 92; Case C-491/01, *British American Tobacco (Investments) and Imperial Tobacco* (Opinion of AG Geelhoed of 10 September 2002) para 96.

[43] Case C-376/98, *Germany v Parliament and Council* (ECJ 5 October 2000) para 78; Case C-380/03, *Germany v Parliament and Council* (ECJ 12 December 2006) para 94.

margin of discretion and can base a measure alternatively on other competences, unless it is obviously intended to improve the internal market.[44] The measure can also be based on multiple legal bases if the legislative procedures do not contradict each other.[45]

Finally, the **flexibility clause of Article 352 TFEU** can be used for the purpose of harmonisation. Since it is subsidiary to other treaty provisions, it can only be used for harmonisation in cases where no other legal basis in the treaties provides for such competence. In practice, this is only the case if the EU wants to set its own harmonised law alongside national law.[46]

13

1.3. Harmonisation vs. Mutual Recognition

The principle of mutual recognition was **developed by the ECJ** in *Cassis de Dijon*. It states that products that have been lawfully produced and marketed in one MS may be introduced into and traded in every other MS. A restriction or prohibition constitutes a measure having an equivalent effect as a quantitative restriction within the meaning of Article 34 TFEU.[47]

14

As part of a "new strategy" (→ para 5), mutual recognition was to be used much more than before and partly replace the need for harmonisation of laws. When national rules are recognised, no harmonisation measures are necessary to ensure the free movement (of goods). For this reason, the principle of mutual recognition can serve as an **alternative to harmonisation**. The advantage of this is that the legal systems of the MS are spared as they retain full control over their national legislation.

15

In order for this principle to apply, **national regulations** to be recognised must be roughly **equivalent**. Otherwise, more far-reaching regulations in one State will almost inevitably lead to higher production costs.[48] This represents a distortion of competition and is thus an impairment of the internal market. Mutual recognition cannot of itself create equivalent standards. However, the MS are encouraged to adapt their national regulations voluntarily.[49] There is a danger of a "race to the bottom", which, however, should not be overestimated.[50] A deviation from the principle of mutual recognition remains possible on the basis of Article 36 TFEU and the "mandatory requirements" developed in the *Cassis* decision.

16

---

[44] Bock (2005), p. 246 seq.
[45] See on this Böttner (2022), p. 29 et seqq.
[46] Oppermann et al. (2021), § 32 para 32; Terhechte and Kübek, in Pechstein et al. (2023), Artikel 114 AEUV para 50.
[47] Case 120/78, *REWE v Bundesmonopolverwaltung für Branntwein* (ECJ 20 February 1979) para 14. See also Ćemalović (2015), p. 256 et seq.
[48] Ihns (2005), p. 198 seq.
[49] There can even be a duty of the MS deduced from Article 34 TFEU to change their national provisions, see Case C-184/96, *Commission v France* (ECJ 22 October 1998) para 28.
[50] Ihns (2005), p. 199; Blanke and Böttner (2020), para 173.

17 If the Union wants to adopt an approximation measure, it must check whether the measure is really necessary or whether an application of the principle of mutual recognition is sufficient. If, on the other hand, the MS can adopt conflicting national rules on the basis of Article 36 TFEU or "mandatory requirements" in the sense of the *Cassis* case law, approximation becomes possible. It should be noted, however, that the **recognition of common standards does not in itself improve the internal market**;[51] it only reduces the obstacle. Ultimately, the question of whether to harmonise legislation or apply the principle of mutual recognition boils down to the question of system competition or harmonisation ($\rightarrow$ para 3). On the basis of Article 114 TFEU, the Union may establish procedures to promote mutual recognition between MS. It may also, in respect of certain products, require MS to apply this principle.[52]

2. Conditions for the Approximation of Laws

2.1. Terminology

18 The Treaties use the terms **"approximation" and "harmonisation" interchangeably**.[53] The Treaties also use the term "coordination", which may be different and is more difficult to assess. As a category of competences, Article 2.5 (1) TFEU stipulates that, in certain cases, "the Union shall have competence to carry out actions to support, coordinate or supplement the actions of the Member States, without thereby superseding their competence in these areas". As the second subparagraph stipulates, this may not entail any "harmonisation of Member States' laws or regulations". Thus, there is a difference between "harmonisation" and "coordination". Nevertheless, the term **"coordination"** is often understood as a synonym for harmonisation measures.[54] In some provisions, the term "coordination" is also found in connection with an approximation of laws (e.g. Article 53 TFEU). "Coordination" could thus be understood as somewhat weaker than "harmonisation". However, the different language versions of the Treaties, which are all equally binding (Article 55 TEU), reveal diverging uses of the terms.[55] It must be

---

[51] Ihns (2005), p. 199.

[52] Tietje, in Grabitz et al. (2022), Artikel 114 AEUV para 45 (released in 2016), argues that this is a harmonisation of the "lowest intensity"; see, e.g., Regulation (EC) No 764/2008, O.J. L 218/21 (2008).

[53] Weatherill (2017), p. 83; Pernice (1996), p. 10 seq. who shows that in Article 100a TEEC the two terms are used synonymously; in-depth Lohse (2017), pp. 26–29; but the ECJ decided differently in 1986 Case 41/84, *Pietro Pinna v Caisse d'allocations familiales de la Savoie* (ECJ 15 January 1986) para 20. With a different view also Ćemalović (2015).

[54] Korte, in Calliess and Ruffert (2022), Artikel 114 AEUV para 23; Tietje, in Grabitz et al. (2022), Artikel 114 AEUV para 2 (released in 2016); Bock (2005), p. 53 seq.

[55] A very early argument at Lochner (1962), pp. 37–48; there is no reason to think that the situation has become less confusing considering today's quantity of official EU languages.

assumed, therefore, that the terms "approximation", "harmonisation", "coordination" and others may sometimes be used synonymously and that the differences in their concrete meaning result from the policy area and the provision that uses the term.[56]

The purpose of an approximation measure is to set a certain framework to be followed in all MS. However, the implementation is to be left to the individual States, leaving them a certain room for manoeuvre. The harmonisation of laws is not about the creation of uniform European law by the Union's institutions.[57] Rather, **the EU creates requirements that must be implemented by the MS** within the defined limits by means of national transposition acts.[58] This can lead to differences in the actual implementation. **19**

Depending on the harmonisation technique, the Union can adopt widely or narrowly formulated rules on the approximation of laws, which do or do not leave the MS much room for manoeuvre in transposition.[59] In fact, the Union legislator can use **different modalities of approximation**. These are partial harmonisation and full harmonisation. Partial harmonisation can in turn be divided into optional harmonisation and minimum harmonisation.[60] This distinction concerns the intensity of the harmonisation. **20**

Optional harmonisation is an approach whereby the Union creates certain standards to ensure the free movement of goods and services that comply with these standards.[61] Goods or services that do not comply with these standards can be traded subject to the national provisions of the MS concerned.[62] In principle, MS may adopt national provisions that deviate from these standards, but these must not restrict free movement.[63] In special cases, producers or suppliers are given the choice of applying EU standards or the national regulations of the importing State. This option is provided for in the harmonisation act itself.[64] An example of the manifold cases of optional harmonisation can be found in Article 5.3 of the Consumer Rights Directive,[65] which allows MS not to apply the provisions on certain information requirements for contracts which involve day-to-day transactions and are performed immediately at the time of their conclusion. **21**

---

[56] See especially Lochner (1962), p. 61.

[57] On the aspect of the different languages in the MS, which make it more or less impossible to create a "single" European law, see Lohse (2017), p. 32.

[58] Schröder, in Streinz (2018), Artikel 114 AEUV para 36.

[59] Case C-66/04, *United Kingdom v Parliament and Council* (ECJ 6 December 2005) para 45 seq.; Case C-380/03, *Germany v Parliament and Council* (ECJ 12 December 2006) para 42; Case C-270/12, *United Kingdom v Parliament and Council* (ECJ 22 January 2014) para 102 seq.

[60] See Blanke and Böttner (2020), para 154 et seqq.

[61] Schröder, in Streinz (2018), Artikel 114 AEUV para 54.

[62] Schütze (2021), p. 578.

[63] Blanke and Böttner (2020), para 159; Schröder, in Streinz (2018), Artikel 114 AEUV para 54.

[64] Blanke and Böttner (2020), para 160.

[65] Parliament/Council Directive 2011/83/EU *on consumer rights*, O.J. L 304/64 (2011).

22 In the case of **minimum harmonisation**, the Union legislator sets a level of protection which the MS may not fall below. The mode of minimum harmonisation is explicitly provided for in other provisions of the Treaties, such as Article 153.2 point (b) TFEU on employment policy, Article 168.4 point (a) TFEU on health policy or Article 169.4 TFEU on consumer policy. Minimum harmonisation does not mean a minimal level of common standards.[66] The Union sets its own, possibly already high, level of protection (→ para 37),[67] but the MS may very well adopt stricter regulations with an (even) higher level of protection, as long as these are in line with the primary law requirements (→ para 51 et seqq.).[68] The MS may also adopt provisions which further promote the implementation of the legal act[69] or which have not yet been regulated by the Union.[70] The Consumer Rights Directive 2011/83 provides that the minimum period for consumers to withdraw from a distance or off-premise contract contained in the Directive (14 days) may be extended up to 30 days for specific circumstances (Article 9.1a).

23 Finally, the Union legislator can, by way of **full harmonisation**, make detailed regulations, which are to be applied equally in all MS. Thus, a uniform European standard is created which does not allow any deviations; i.e., there is no room for manoeuvre in the implementation of such a legal act. If the EU legislator lays down an exhaustive set of rules governing a specific area, it does not leave the MS any scope to introduce other measures in their national legislation.[71] National opt-outs are possible only within the strict limits of paragraphs 4 and 5 (→ para 51 et seqq.). In the case of full harmonisation, fully harmonised secondary law supersedes the provisions of primary law.[72] The above-mentioned Consumer Rights Directive 2011/83 contains large areas of full harmonisation. It provides in its Article 4 that MS shall not maintain or introduce provisions diverging from those laid down in the Directive, including more or less stringent provisions, to ensure a different level of consumer protection, unless otherwise provided for in the Directive.

2.2. Connection to the Internal Market

24 Harmonising measures under Article 114 TFEU require a connection to the internal market. The internal market is defined in Article 26.2 TFEU as "an **area without internal frontiers in which the free movement of goods, persons, services and capital is ensured**". Despite this definition, the *concept* of the internal market for

---

[66] Terhechte and Kübek, in Pechstein et al. (2023), Artikel 114 AEUV para 26.

[67] Cf. Case C-84/94, *United Kingdom v Council* (ECJ 12 November 1996) para 17, 56; Schütze (2021), p. 579.

[68] Dougan (2000), p. 855.

[69] Case C-315/05, *Lidl Italia* (ECJ 23 November 2006) para 48.

[70] Case C-446/08, *Solgar Vitamin's France and Others* (ECJ 29 April 2010) para 20–24.

[71] Case 278/85, *Commission v Denmark* (ECJ 14 October 1987) para 12.

[72] Case C-322/01, *Deutscher Apothekenverband* (ECJ 11 December 2003) para 64.

the purpose of the approximation of laws is broad.[73] However, the mere regulation of the internal market is not sufficient. Instead, the functioning of the internal market must be objectively improved; i.e., there must be a contribution to the better functioning of the internal market (→ para 30 et seqq.).[74] The Union legislator can achieve this by removing obstacles to the exercise of market freedoms ("establishment of the internal market") or noticeable distortions of competition ("functioning of the internal market").[75] The presence of one of these two characteristics is sufficient.[76] However, since the free movement of persons does not fall within the scope of application of Article 114 TFEU (→ para 43) and there are special competences for harmonisation in the other freedoms, approximation under Article 114 TFEU focuses on the free movement of goods.[77] Article 114 TFEU can be relied upon in conjunction with other legal bases (→ para 12) or as a sole legal basis even if another aspect (such as public health or safety) "is a decisive factor in the choices to be made".[78]

The German language version of Article 26.1 TFEU provides that "[t]he Union shall adopt the *necessary* measures" ("*die erforderlichen Maßnahmen*"), aiming at establishing or ensuring the functioning of the internal market. The English version merely provides that "[t]he Union shall adopt measures" with the same aim.[79] However, the ECJ underlined "that the measures referred to in Article [114.1 TFEU] are intended to improve the conditions for the establishment and the functioning of the internal market". The wording and the Court's interpretation insinuate a limited, purpose-bound scope of the measures. There can therefore be no absolute regulatory competence for the internal market. This is underlined by the principle of conferral, which warrants a limited scope of conferred competences.[80]

25

---

[73] See Weatherill (2017), p. 92.

[74] Case C-376/98, *Germany v Parliament and Council* (ECJ 5 October 2000) para 83; Case C-491/01, *British American Tobacco (Investments) and Imperial Tobacco* (ECJ 10 December 2002) para 60; Joined Cases C-465/00, C-138/01, C-139/01, *Österreichischer Rundfunk and Others* (ECJ 20 May 2003) para 41. See also Weatherill (2017), p. 93 et seqq.

[75] Case C-376/98, *Germany v Parliament and Council* (ECJ 5 October 2000) para 84; Case C-491/01, *British American Tobacco (Investments) and Imperial Tobacco* (ECJ 10 December 2002) para 60; see also Schütze (2021), p. 563.

[76] Case C-491/01, *British American Tobacco (Investments) and Imperial Tobacco* (ECJ 10 December 2002) para 60; emphasised in Case C-380/03, *Germany v Parliament and Council* (ECJ 12 December 2006) para 67; von Danwitz (2018), B. II. para 119.

[77] Blanke and Böttner (2020), para 208; Tietje, in Grabitz et al. (2022), Artikel 114 AEUV para 82 (released in 2016).

[78] Case C-491/01, *British American Tobacco (Investments) and Imperial Tobacco* (ECJ 10 December 2002) para 62; C-358/14, *Poland v Parliament and Council* (ECJ 4 May 2016) para 34; C-482/17, *Czech Republic v Parliament and Council* (ECJ 3 December 2019) para 36.

[79] Similarly the French ("*L'Union adopte les mesures destinées à ...*") or Italian ("*L'Unione adotta le misure destinate all' ...*") language version.

[80] Case C-376/98, *Germany v Parliament and Council* (ECJ 5 October 2000) para 83; see in this sense also Defalque et al. (2006), para 423.

26   On the other hand, there is no requirement for a current, existing problem or distortion in the internal market. Instead, sufficient for harmonisation measures is already the **likely danger** of different developments in the MS that will lead to obstacles to fundamental freedoms or noticeable distortions of competition, the so-called preventive harmonisation.[81] This corresponds to the settled case law of the ECJ.[82]

27   Distortions in the internal market may also occur in relation to **obligations arising from international treaties**.[83] International treaties concluded by the Union in the area of its exclusive competences are considered to be an "integral part" of EU law[84] and therefore do not require approximation; they are directly applicable. In the case of treaties concluded by the MS, it may well be necessary for the EU to take legal action in order to remove obstacles to fundamental freedoms or to eliminate significant distortions of competition. In doing so, however, only the interpretation of international treaties may be regulated.[85] No measures may be taken that conflict with the obligations of the MS under international law.[86] In the case of mixed agreements, the Union has a harmonisation competence.[87]

28   Obstacles to fundamental freedoms may be justified. MS may restrict the free movement of goods by applying Article 36 TFEU and the other "mandatory requirements" developed by the Court of Justice.[88] However, these **restrictions, even if justified, create obstacles to the internal market**. For this reason, approximations of laws should be used in this area of justified obstacles to fundamental freedoms.[89] Whether such an obstacle exists is determined in accordance with the case law of the ECJ, according to which "all trading rules enacted by Member

---

[81] In this sense already, Case C-350/92, *Spain v Council* (ECJ 13 July 1995) para 35; more clearly in Case C-376/98, *Germany v Parliament and Council* (ECJ 5 October 2000) para 86; Case C-377/98, *Netherlands v Parliament and Council* (ECJ 9 October 2001) para 15; Case 491/01, *British American Tobacco (Investments) and Imperial Tobacco* (ECJ 10 December 2002) para 61; C-434/02, *Arnold André* (ECJ 14 December 2004) para 31; Case C-210/03, *Swedish Match* (ECJ 14 December 2004) para 34; Case C-58/08, *Vodafone and Others* (ECJ 8 June 2010) para 47; Chalmers et al. (2019), p. 638; early argumentation at Vogelaar (1975), p. 213; see also Weatherill (2017), p. 90 et seq.; critically Schütze (2021), p. 562 et seq.

[82] Case C-380/03, *Germany v Parliament and Council* (ECJ 12 December 2006) para 38; prior to this judgment, it was argued that the possibility of preventive harmonisation was uttered by the ECJ in mere *obiter dicta* in cases before, see Seidel (2006), pp. 29–31, 45.

[83] In depth, Tietje, in Grabitz et al. (2022), Artikel 114 AEUV para 107–111 (released in 2016).

[84] See Case 104/81, *Hauptzollamt Mainz v Kupferberg & Cie* (ECJ 26 October 1982) para 13.

[85] Case C-377/98, *Netherlands v Parliament and Council* (ECJ 9 October 2001) para 20 seq.

[86] Tietje, in Grabitz et al. (2022), Artikel 114 AEUV para 109 (released in 2016).

[87] Opinion 1/94, *International agreements concerning services and the protection of intellectual property* (ECJ 15 November 1994) para 104.

[88] Case 120/78, *REWE v Bundesmonopolverwaltung für Branntwein* (ECJ 20 February 1979) para 8.

[89] COM(85) 310 final, para 65; Case C-128/89, *Commission v Italy* (ECJ 12 July 1990) para 16; Case C-491/01, *British American Tobacco (Investments) and Imperial Tobacco* (Opinion of AG Geelhoed of 10 September 2002) para 103–109.

States which are capable of hindering, directly or indirectly, actually or potentially, intra-Community trade" constitute a restriction of fundamental freedoms,[90] as long as not only sales modalities are regulated which bind all economic operators to the same extent.[91] Furthermore, there is no obstacle to the internal market if the national measures are "too uncertain and too indirect" to constitute a real obstacle.[92] In contrast to distortions of competition, this obstacle does not have to be "appreciable".[93]

In accordance with Protocol No. 27 annexed to the Treaties, the internal market, as set out in Article 3 TEU, includes a system **ensuring that competition is not distorted** (→ Article 26 TFEU para 25, 27). Distortions of competition allow the Union legislator to enact harmonising measures. However, it is necessary that these distortions are "appreciable".[94] The ECJ justifies this with the fact that, otherwise, practically any matter could be the subject of harmonisation of laws since a large number of national regulations can create a distortion of competition, at least indirectly.[95] In other words, the provision prohibits any implementing measure that adversely affects the level of internal market integration only if it is disproportionate.[96]

29

2.3. Achieving the Objectives Set Out in Article 26 TFEU

Not only must an approximation measure be related to the internal market, but the Union legislator, when adopting approximation measures, must also subjectively

30

---

[90] Case 8/74, *Dassonville* (ECJ 11 July 1974) para 5.
[91] Joined Cases C-267/91 and C-268/91, *Keck and Mithouard* (ECJ 24 November 1993) para 16; for the applicability of these rules as a condition for the approximation of laws, see Case C-491/01, *British American Tobacco (Investments) and Imperial Tobacco* (ECJ 10 December 2002) para 64; Case C-434/02, *Arnold André* (ECJ 14 December 2004) para 39; Case C-210/03, *Swedish Match* (ECJ 14 December 2004) para 38.
[92] Case C-69/88, *Krantz v Ontvanger der Directe Belastingen* (ECJ 7 March 1990) para 11; Case C-93/92, *CMC Motorradcenter v Baskiciogullari* (ECJ 13 October 1993) para 12; Case C-379/92, *Peralta* (ECJ 14 July 1994) para 24; Case C-96/94, *Centro Servizi Spediporto Srl v Spedizioni Marittima del Golfo Srl* (ECJ 5 October 1995) para 41; Joined Cases C-140/94 et al., *DIP and Others v Comune di Bassano del Grappa and Others* (ECJ 17 October 1995) para 29; Case C-134/94, *Esso Español SA v Comunidad Autónoma de Canarias* (ECJ 30 November 1995) para 24; Case C-266/96, *Corsica Ferris France v Gruppo Antichi Ormeggiatori del porto di Genova* (ECJ 18 June 1998) para 31.
[93] Chalmers et al. (2019), p. 638; Korte, in Calliess and Ruffert (2022), Artikel 114 AEUV para 41; Terhechte and Kübek, in Pechstein et al. (2023), Artikel 114 AEUV para 65; in this sense Case C-350/92, *Spain v Council* (ECJ 13 July 1995) para 33, 35.
[94] Case C-300/89, *Commission v Council* (ECJ 11 June 1991) para 23; Case C-376/98, *Germany v Parliament and Council* (ECJ 5 October 2000) para 106; critical on the vagueness of this requirement Chalmers et al. (2019), p. 643.
[95] Case C-376/98, *Germany v Parliament and Council* (ECJ 5 October 2000) para 107.
[96] Böttner (2021), p. 190.

pursue the objective of improving the internal market.[97] The achievement of this objective "must be based on objective factors which are amenable to judicial review"[98] in order to evaluate the legislator's intention. Accordingly, the act must be reasoned (Article 296 (2) TFEU),[99] which is reflected in particular in the recitals but may also result from the circumstances of the proceedings (→ Article 296 TFEU para 17 et seqq.).

31 The aim or intention of a positive development of the internal market is not sufficient in itself. Rather, the achievement of this goal **must also objectively lead to a measurable improvement**.[100] This is achieved by eliminating the divergences between the national rules. Depending on the circumstances of the case, this may entail that all the MS are required to authorise the marketing of a certain product or even, on the other hand, that the marketing of a certain product is provisionally or definitively prohibited.[101] The Court of Justice first examines whether there are differences between the regulations in the MS or whether they are likely to arise.[102] Then it examines whether the measure actually removes obstacles to fundamental freedoms[103] or reduce appreciable distortions of competition.[104] If this is affirmed, there is an improvement of the internal market, and the measure is permissible. The Union legislator has discretion as to the pace at which approximation is implemented.[105] Nonetheless, there must still be an improvement in the internal market. The EU cannot therefore make internal market improvements in such small steps that no measurable positive effect is actually achieved.

---

[97] Case C-376/98, *Germany v Parliament and Council* (ECJ 5 October 2000) para 83; Case C-491/01, *British American Tobacco (Investments) Ltd and Imperial Tobacco Ltd* (ECJ 10 December 2002) para 60; Case C-58/08, *Vodafone and Others* (ECJ 8 June 2010) para 32; von Danwitz (2018), B. II. para 118; Tietje, in Grabitz et al. (2022), Artikel 114 AEUV para 95 (released in 2016).

[98] Case 45/86, *Commission v Council* (ECJ 26 March 1987) para 11; for the later use of this formula see Case C-301/06, *Ireland v Parliament and Council* (ECJ 10 February 2009) para 60; Case C-233/94, *Germany v Parliament and Council* (ECJ 13 May 1997) para 12; Case 300/89, *Commission v Council* (ECJ 11 June 1991) para 10.

[99] E.g. Case 376/98, *Germany v Parliament and Council* (ECJ 5 October 2000) para 90 seq.

[100] Case C-376/98, *Germany v Parliament and Council* (ECJ 5 October 2000) para 85, 95; the formula of "measurable improvements" is found in Korte, in Calliess and Ruffert (2022), Artikel 114 AEUV para 50.

[101] Case C-434/02, *Arnold André* (ECJ 14 December 2004) para 35; C-210/03, *Swedish Match* (ECJ 14 December 2004) para 34; C-380/03, *Germany v Parliament and Council* (ECJ 12 December 2006) para 43; C-358/14, *Poland v Parliament and Council* (ECJ 4 May 2016) para 38.

[102] Cf. e.g. Case C-376/98, *Germany v Parliament and Council* (ECJ 5 October 2000) para 97.

[103] Cf. Case C-376/98, *Germany v Parliament and Council* (ECJ 5 October 2000) para 99–105.

[104] Cf. Case C-376/98, *Germany v Parliament and Council* (ECJ 5 October 2000) para 108–114.

[105] See Case 37/83, *Rewe-Zentral* (ECJ 29 February 1984) para 20; C-63/89, *Les Assurances du Crédit SA and Compagnie Belge d'Assurance Crédit SA v Council and Commission* (ECJ 18 April 1991) para 11; C-547/14, *Philip Morris Brands and Others* (ECJ 4 May 2016) para 63; C-549/15, *E.ON Biofor Sverige* (ECJ 22 June 2017) para 30.

Article 114. TFEU [Harmonisation in the Internal Market]

The measures taken at the EU level must also comply with the principle of **proportionality** (Article 5.4 TEU), which requires that the harmonisation measure is appropriate for eliminating obstacles to the internal market and does not exceed the limits of what is necessary in order to achieve this objective. In addition, the disadvantages caused must not be disproportionate to the aim pursued. In this context, Article 27 TFEU should be mentioned, which requires the Commission, when drawing up proposals with a view to achieving the objectives set out in Article 26 TFEU, to **consider the position of "economies showing differences in development"**, taking into account the extent of the effort that these economies will have to sustain for the establishment of the internal market. Since harmonisation based on a high level of protection in all MS may require specific political, economic and social choices and complex assessments, the Union legislator has broad discretion. In this context, it should be noted that the establishment of the **internal market is one of several objectives** laid down in Article 3 TEU that guide the Union's functioning. The establishment of the internal market is mentioned there in the context of "sustainable development ... based on balanced economic growth and price stability" and "a highly competitive social market economy" (Article 3.3 (1) TEU). The ECJ reviews if the measure is manifestly inappropriate with regard to the aims pursued.[106]

32

2.4. Provisions Laid Down by Domestic Law, Regulation or Administrative Action

Article 114 TFEU can only be used to approximate the laws, regulations or administrative actions in the MS. This means, in other words, that **national regulations must exist**[107] and be amended in order to be able to base measures on Article 114 TFEU.[108] The term "law, regulation or administrative action" must be understood comprehensively. It refers to all "abstract-general rules issued by sovereign bodies or at least endowed with sovereign authority".[109] In particular, it also includes administrative regulations and practice,[110] customary law and precedent jurisdiction,[111] as well as private norms that the State has adopted as its own.[112] It is not required, on the other hand, that rules exist in *all* MS since the existence of provisions in only some MS may lead to the distortions that Article 114

33

---

[106] Case C-491/01, *British American Tobacco (Investments) and Imperial Tobacco* (ECJ 10 December 2002) para 122–123; C-358/14, *Poland v Parliament and Council* (ECJ 4 May 2016) para 78–79.

[107] Weatherill (2017), p. 96.

[108] Case C-436/03, *Parliament v Council* (ECJ 2 May 2006) para 44, 46.

[109] Korte, in Calliess and Ruffert (2022), Artikel 114 AEUV para 35 (our translation).

[110] Cf. Eiden (1997), para 2107.

[111] Classen, in von der Groeben et al. (2015), Artikel 114 AEUV para 114.

[112] Cf. Case C-171/11, *Fra.bo* (ECJ 12 July 2012) para 31 seq.

TFEU envisages to overcome. Thus, approximation can lead to the introduction of rules on a subject in some MS where no rules previously existed.

34   The existence of a mere difference in national provisions is not sufficient. Rather, these regulations must have an **adverse effect on the internal market**.[113] This already follows from the principle of proportionality (Article 5.4 TEU), as an approximating measure must be suitable to achieve its aim, i.e. reduce impairments of the internal market. The decisive factor is the effect on the internal market and not the content of the national regulation.[114] This impairment can also be caused by identical national provisions, as a comparison of the wording with Article 116 TFEU shows (→ Article 116 TFEU para 4).[115] Harmonising measures may be adopted already if there is only a "likely danger" that national provisions would be detrimental to the internal market.[116] It is not necessary that national provisions exist in all MS; the existence of (diverging) rules in some States or a different level of protection in the MS may also be "likely" to impair the internal market and thus justifies preventive harmonisation.[117]

35   One may wonder whether **common procedures or institutions** of the EU can be based on Article 114 TFEU. This is problematic if EU law is placed alongside national law without superseding it. However, it should also be possible to base such measures on Article 114 TFEU, which provide for procedures to implement the approximation.[118] Although these procedures do not themselves change national regulations, they are a necessary part of the harmonisation measure as a whole. The ECJ justifies this with the discretion that the Union legislator has with regard to the approximation technique, particularly complex technical issues.[119] The same should apply to bodies, offices and agencies with a separate legal

---

[113] Case C-376/98, *Germany v Parliament and Council* (ECJ 5 October 2000) para 84 and 95; C-491/01, *British American Tobacco (Investments) and Imperial Tobacco* (ECJ 10 December 2002) para 59 and 60; C-434/02, *Arnold André* (ECJ 14 December 2004) para 30; C-210/03, *Swedish Match* (ECJ 14 December 2004) para 29; C-380/03, *Germany v Parliament and Council* (ECJ 12 December 2006) para 37; C-58/08, *Vodafone and Others* (ECJ 8 June 2010) para 32; C-358/14, *Poland v Parliament and Council* (ECJ 4 May 2016) para 32.

[114] Oppermann et al. (2021), § 32 para 10.

[115] Vogelaar (1975), p. 213 seq.; Korte, in Calliess and Ruffert (2022), Artikel 114 AEUV para 36.

[116] Case C-350/92, *Spain v Council* (ECJ 13 July 1995) para 35; Case C-376/98, *Germany v Parliament and Council*, (ECJ 5 October 2000) para 86; Case C-434/02, *Arnold André* (ECJ 14 December 2004) para 31; Case C-58/08, *Vodafone and Others* (ECJ 8 June 2010) para 33; critically Schütze (2021), p. 563.

[117] Case C-434/02, *Arnold André* (ECJ 14 December 2004) para 34.

[118] Case C-41/93, *France v Commission* (ECJ 17 May 1994) para 22; Case C-359/92, *Germany v Council* (ECJ 9 August 1994) para 32–37; Case C-66/04, *United Kingdom v Parliament and Council* (ECJ 6 December 2005) para 62 seq.

[119] Case C-66/04, *United Kingdom v Parliament and Council* (ECJ 6 December 2005) para 45 seq.; Case C-270/12, *United Kingdom v Parliament and Council* (ECJ 22 January 2014) para 102–105.

personality.[120] This only applies as long as there is no specific competence on which they can be based.[121]

If, in contrast, the Union wants to **create new legal titles** to be added to the law of the MS, it cannot rely on Article 114 TFEU because there is no change in national rules, and they are not mere "appendices" to an actual approximation measure.[122] This is the reason for the creation of Article 118 TFEU, which explicitly authorises the creation of new titles in the field of intellectual property rights. Otherwise, the Union must base legal acts aimed at creating new titles on Article 352 TFEU (→ para 13).[123]

36

2.5. Ensuring a High Level of Protection

Paragraph 3 obliges the Commission in the areas of "health, safety, environmental protection and consumer protection" to "take as a base a high level of protection, taking account in particular of any new development based on scientific facts". As clearly stated in the second sentence, this obligation applies also to Parliament and the Council, which are involved in the legislative process. The areas mentioned are to be understood **in parallel with other provisions of the Treaty**.[124] The term health has the same meaning as in Article 168 TFEU.[125] The term safety refers primarily to product safety, as mentioned in Article 153.1 point (a) or Article 169.1 TFEU, but it appears that the legislator and the Court of Justice extend the term to reasons of public security.[126] The term environmental protection corresponds to Articles 191–193 TFEU, as well as to the horizontal provision of Article 11

37

---

[120] Case C-217/04, *United Kingdom v Parliament and Council* (ECJ 2 May 2005) para 43–45. See, for example, the creation of the ESRB, the EBA, the EIOPA and the ESMA as supervisory authorities for the financial markets: Parliament/Council Regulations (EU) No 1092/2010, No 1093/2010, No 1094/2010 and No 1095/2010, O.J. L 331 (2010). On the EBA as part of the ESFS see critically Fahey (2011).

[121] See, for example, Parliament/Council Regulation (EC) No 1907/2006 *concerning the Registration, Evaluation, Authorisation and Restriction of Chemicals (REACH), establishing a European Chemicals Agency*, O.J. L 396/1 (2006), whose amendments are still based on Article 114 TFEU. In contrast, Parliament/Council Regulation (EC) No 713/2009 *establishing an Agency for the Cooperation of Energy Regulators*, O.J. L 211/1 (2009) was based on then Article 95 TEC, whereas the recast, Parliament/Council Regulation (EU) 2019/942, O.J. L 158/1 (2019) was based on Article 194.2 TFEU which had been introduced by the Lisbon Treaty.

[122] Case C-436/03, *Parliament v Council* (ECJ 2 May 2006) para 40, 44.

[123] Opinion 1/94, *International agreements concerning services and the protection of intellectual property* (ECJ 15 November 1994) para 59; Case C-377/98, *Netherlands v Parliament and Council* (ECJ 9 October 2001) para 24; in this sense regarding the EBA Fahey (2011), p. 539 seq.

[124] Weatherill (2010), para 13.26, 13.64.

[125] Cf. Case C-547/14, *Philip Morris Brands and Others* (ECJ 4 May 2016) para 61.

[126] Cf. Case C-267/16, *Buhagiar* (ECJ 23 January 2018) para 56; Terhechte and Kübek, in Pechstein et al. (2023), Artikel 114 AEUV para 85.

TFEU.[127] Consumer protection is to be understood in the sense of Article 169 TFEU and the horizontal provision of Article 12 TFEU.[128] The high level of protection in the areas mentioned in paragraph 3 thus corresponds to the EU's objectives in the public interest.[129]

38 The obligation on the part of the EU to achieve a high level of protection is intended to take account of the MS' concern about a deterioration in the level of protection in the areas of health, safety and environmental and consumer protection. Since the Union is at the same time committed to other objectives, **conflicting objectives must be balanced** according to the principle of practical concordance.[130] This means that the EU must be guided by its *own* level of protection and is not obliged to take the highest possible level,[131] the highest level achieved in an MS[132] or the average level of protection of the MS[133] as a yardstick.[134] The institutions have a margin of discretion to determine the Union's level of protection.[135] Moreover, the Commission must take due account of the position and potential effort of weaker economies when proposing measures for achieving the objectives in Article 26 TFEU (see Article 27 TFEU).

39 For the determination of the high level of protection, the Commission has to take into account, in particular, new developments **based on scientific facts**. This means, first of all, that all available and scientifically proven data must be used to check whether an adequate level of protection is being achieved. In addition, the Union is committed to the so-called **precautionary principle**.[136] This has long been found in the case law of the ECJ[137] and explicitly in Article 191 TFEU. It states that protective measures can be taken even if there is no imminent danger of

---

[127] See Case C-549/15, *E.ON Biofor Sverige* (ECJ 22 June 2017) para 48.

[128] Tietje, in Grabitz et al. (2022), Artikel 114 AEUV para 146 (released in 2016).

[129] See for the Union's responsibility for the common good Schweitzer (2010), pp. 3–11.

[130] Tietje, in Grabitz et al. (2022), Artikel 114 AEUV para 142 (released in 2016); cf. Herresthal (2011), p. 329.

[131] Cf. with regard to the similar clause in Article 191.2 TFEU Case C-284/95, *Safety Hi-Tech Srl v S. & T. Srl* (ECJ 14 July 1998) para 49; Case C-341/95, *Bettati v Safety Hi-Tech Srl* (ECJ 14 July 1998) para 47.

[132] Case C-233/94, *Germany v Parliament and Council* (ECJ 13 May 1997) para 48.

[133] Case C-376/98, *Germany v Parliament and Council* (Opinion of Advocate General Fennelly of 15 June 2000) para 85.

[134] Schroeder (2002), p. 215 seq.

[135] Khan and Eisenhut, in Geiger et al. (2015), Article 114 TFEU para 21; cf. also Reich and Burkhardt, in Smit and Herzog (2017), Article 114 TFEU para 5.

[136] See in-depth da Cruz Vilaça (2004), pp. 380–399.

[137] Case C-2/90, *Commission v Belgium* (ECJ 9 May 1992) para 30; Case C-355/90, *Commission v Spain* (ECJ 2 August 1993) para 15; Case C-157/96, *National Farmers' Union and Others* (ECJ 5 May 1998) para 63; Case C-180/96, *United Kingdom v Commission* (ECJ 5 May 1998) para 61 seq., 98 seq.; with it being named as such T-13/99, *Pfizer Animal Health SA v Council* (CFI 11 September 2002) para 114, 139–148; Case T-70/99, *Alpharma Inc. v Council* (CFI 11 September 2002) para 153.

damage occurring, but only a sufficiently clear risk.[138] This is justified by the fact that in the areas relevant here, damage can very easily be irreparable, and it is therefore justified to minimise the risk in advance. This is always the case when the scientific data are insufficient, inconclusive or uncertain and where there are indications that the possible effects on the environment or health may be potentially dangerous.[139]

The reference to "**new developments**" implies a certain dynamic element. The Union can (and should) regularly bring legislative measures up to date with the current state of science.[140] If necessary, the measures taken are then to be amended in the legislative process. **40**

2.6. Areas Exempted from Harmonisation

Paragraph 2 explicitly identifies three areas excluded from the scope of Article 114 TFEU. These are the approximation of fiscal provisions, the free movement of persons and the rights and interests of employed persons. These three areas are excluded because they are considered to be **politically sensitive** and therefore should not be regulated by a qualified majority voting in the Council.[141] However, since majority voting has become the rule in the meantime and there are also special provisions in some of these matters where a qualified majority is also sufficient, this list of exceptions could well be shortened.[142] Nevertheless, harmonisation in these three areas is still possible on the basis of Article 115 TFEU or other provisions. **41**

The ECJ interprets the term "**fiscal provision**" broadly to include "all areas of taxation, without drawing any distinction between the types of duties or taxes concerned", including all aspects, comprising both material and procedural rules.[143] Indirect taxes can be approximated on the basis of Article 113 TFEU and direct taxes on the basis of Article 115 TFEU. However, both provisions provide for a special legislative procedure with unanimity in the Council, which again shows their political sensitivity. **42**

In the area of **free movement of persons**, harmonisation no longer plays a major role as Article 21.1 TFEU provides for the general freedom of movement for EU citizens (→ Article 21 TFEU para 18 et seqq.). If it seems necessary to take harmonisation measures in this area, paragraphs 2 and 3 of Article 21 TFEU provide the necessary competences. General rules on free movement shall be **43**

---

[138] Cf. Commission Communication *on the precautionary principle*, COM(2000) 1 final with the explicit mentioning of Article 95.3 TEC (= Article 114.3 TFEU)] at p. 22.
[139] COM(2000) 1 final, p. 7.
[140] Korte, in Calliess and Ruffert (2022), Artikel 114 AEUV para 65.
[141] Tietje, in Grabitz et al. (2022), Artikel 114 AEUV para 88 (released in 2016).
[142] Khan and Eisenhut, in Geiger et al. (2015), Article 114 TFEU para 16.
[143] Case C-338/01, *Commission v Council* (ECJ 29 April 2004) para 66; C-533/03, *Commission v Council* (ECJ 26 January 2006) para 47; C-674/20, *Airbnb Ireland* (ECJ 27 April 2022) para 27; differing opinion Tietje, in Grabitz et al. (2022), Artikel 114 AEUV para 90 (released in 2016).

adopted through the ordinary legislative procedure (→ Article 21 TFEU para 18–23), whereas measures concerning social security or social protection shall be subject to a special legislative procedure with unanimity in the Council (→ Article 21 TFEU para 5–6). The exemption under Article 114.2 TFEU does not apply to the free movement of workers, self-employed persons or service providers as the rules on the fundamental freedoms take precedence over harmonisation measures.[144]

44 The "**rights and interests of employed persons**" are somewhat more difficult to define. It does not include the working environment as this is explicitly mentioned in paragraph 4. On the other hand, a demarcation to the field of employment policy (Articles 145 et seqq. TFEU) or social policy (Articles 151 et seqq. TFEU) seems obvious. However, since Article 148 and Article 153.2 (2) TFEU also provide for the ordinary legislative procedure for harmonisation in most areas, the subjects mentioned there are practically not excluded from harmonisation by Article 114.2 TFEU either. Instead, the exclusion of workers' rights and interests only refers to a few, limited areas. These are social security, collective labour law, the protection of employment relationships and the employment conditions of third-country nationals.[145]

2.7. Procedure and Instruments

45 In contrast to Article 115 TFEU, Article 114.1 TFEU provides for the **ordinary legislative procedure** (Articles 289 and 294 TFEU) as the procedure for adopting a measure on the approximation of laws. Parliament and Council are thus equal legislators. The Economic and Social Committee is consulted in the procedure (Article 304(1) TFEU) and can give an opinion on the economic aspects of approximation. The Committee of the Regions is informed of the consultation and can give an opinion if specific regional interests are affected (Article 307(3) TFEU).

46 Article 114.1 TFEU, unlike Article 115 TFEU, does not specify a particular type of measure that can be adopted. Any "measure" can be chosen. These are primarily the forms of action mentioned in Article 288 TFEU.[146] Classically, harmonisation takes place through the use of **directives**, as is also provided for in Article 115 TFEU (→ Article 115 TFEU para 10). When concluding the SEA, the MS made a declaration on Article 100a TEEC, according to which "the Commission shall give precedence to the use of the instrument of a directive if harmonisation involves the amendment of legislative provisions in one or more Member States".[147] In

---

[144] Terhechte and Kübek, in Pechstein et al. (2023), Artikel 114 AEUV para 34.
[145] Tietje, in Grabitz et al. (2022), Artikel 114 AEUV para 93 (released in 2016).
[146] See in this sense Case C-319/97, *Kortas* (Opinion of AG Saggio of 28 January 1999) para 14.
[147] O.J. L 169/24 (1987).

connection with the principle of proportionality (Article 5.4 TEU, Article 296(1) TFEU), this declaration argues for the preferred use of directives over other types of acts.

Nevertheless, the ECJ has ruled that "in particular in fields which are characterised by complex technical features", the Union legislator has broad discretion also with regard to the choice of legal acts.[148] Thus, harmonisation measures on the basis of Article 114.1 TFEU can also be adopted as **regulations**. In fact, the Commission has expressed the view that regulations should be used more frequently instead of directives for harmonisation as this would eliminate differences in the timing of national legislation entering into force across the Union and reduce the risk of divergent transposition, interpretation and application.[149] Another advantage of using regulations is that they directly generate rights (and obligations) for the individual citizen.[150] If the regulation is used, however, there must not be a unification of the law because in such a case, it would no longer be an *approximation* of laws. This is particularly the case when new legal elements are placed alongside national law.[151]

47

It is questionable whether the instrument of a **decision** can also be used for legal harmonisation measures. Decisions are always addressed to concrete addressees and are thus not general in nature. However, in certain cases, decisions can also be considered for the harmonisation of laws. The ECJ has ruled that, particularly in the area of product safety, the approximation of general laws may not be sufficient to ensure the unity of the market.[152] Therefore, individual decisions can also be adopted, if necessary.[153] There must of course be a reason why it is necessary to take concrete measures in a certain case. In practice, however, decisions do not play a major role.[154]

48

Article 288 TFEU also mentions **recommendations and opinions** as legal acts of the Union. In conjunction with Article 292 TFEU, it is only the Council that may adopt recommendations (on a proposal from the Commission) under Article 114 TFEU. As Article 288 TFEU specifies, recommendations and opinions shall not have binding force, but it is generally accepted that they can nevertheless exert a degree of bindingness (**soft law**).[155] As approximation measures, recommendations

49

---

[148] Case C-66/04, *United Kingdom v Parliament and Council* (ECJ 6 December 2005) para 45; C-217/04, *United Kingdom v Parliament and Council* (ECJ 2 May 2006) para 43; C-58/08, *Vodafone and Others* (ECJ 8 June 2006) para 35.

[149] Commision Communication, *A vision for the internal market for industrial products*, COM (2014) 25 final, p. 8.

[150] In this sense Mattera (1990), p. 185.

[151] Korte, in Calliess and Ruffert (2022), Artikel 114 AEUV para 76.

[152] Case C-359/92, *Germany v Council* (ECJ 9 August 1994) para 37; differently Lohse (2017), p. 61; though arguing the possibility of using decisions in particular cases Bock (2005), p. 55.

[153] See, e.g., Parliament/Council Decision (EU) 2020/263 *on computerising the movement and surveillance of excise goods (recast)*, O.J. L 58/43 (2020).

[154] See e.g. Ihns (2005), pp. 19–24.

[155] See, generally, Senden (2004); von Graevenitz (2013); Lancos (2019).

do not seem suitable, but in fact, they can develop a "compliance pull", leading to a *de facto* harmonising effect. This may be further enhanced through guidelines by the Commission on the basis of the harmonisation act.[156] Finally, EU conduct and non-binding measures can lead to voluntary compliance in MS, leading to so-called spontaneous approximation.

50 According to Article 290 TFEU, a legislative act can endow the Commission with the power to adopt **delegated acts** to supplement or amend certain non-essential elements of the legislative act. Article 291 TFEU provides that a legal act may confer on the Commission (or the Council) the power to adopt so-called **implementing acts** laying down the uniform conditions for the implementation of legally binding Union acts. As general powers, this authorisation may also be included in harmonisation acts under Article 114 TFEU.[157]

3. National Opt-Outs and Exceptions

51 When the SEA introduced approximation by a qualified majority in the Council, the MS feared a loss of sovereignty since harmonisation measures could now be adopted against their will.[158] For this reason, the so-called opt-out clauses were introduced, which allow the MS under certain conditions to **maintain or even introduce national measures contrary to the harmonising EU act**. However, these clauses are subject to a specific procedure designed to limit their use. If harmonisation is incomplete and primary law remains applicable to trade in a certain good, the MS must base restrictive measures on Article 36 TFEU.[159]

52 Paragraphs 4 and 5 mention "the adoption of a harmonisation measure by the European Parliament and the Council, by the Council or by the Commission". Since harmonisation measures are adopted under paragraph 1 in the ordinary legislative procedure (i.e., "by the European Parliament and the Council"), the wording of the opt-out clauses could imply that they apply also to harmonisation measures beyond Article 114 TFEU. On the other hand, the reference to the adoption of a measure "by the Council or by the Commission" could point solely towards the adoption of delegated or implementing acts under Articles 290 and 291 TFEU (→ para 49). While it seems incomprehensible, for systematic reasons, to apply these

---

[156] See, for example, Article 47 of Parliament/Council Regulation (EU) 2022/1925, O.J. L 265/1 (2022).

[157] See, for example, Article 87 (delegated acts) and Article 88 (implementing acts) of Parliament/Council Regulation (EU) 2022/2065 *on a Single Market for Digital Services (Digital Services Act)*, O.J. L 277/1 (2022) or Article 49 (delegated acts) and Article 50 (implementing acts) of Parliament/Council Regulation (EU) 2022/1925 *on contestable and fair markets in the digital sector (Digital Markets Act)*, O.J. L 265/1 (2022).

[158] Cf. Case C-41/93, *France v Commission* (Opinion of AG Tesauro of 26 January 1994) para 4 with further references.

[159] Case 215/87, *Heinz Schumacher v Hauptzollamt Frankfurt am Main-Ost* (ECJ 7 March 1989) para 15; Khan and Eisenhut, in Geiger et al. (2015), Article 114 TFEU para 25.

derogations to *all* cases in which the Treaties provide for harmonisation, the genesis of the provision and its connection to Article 115 TFEU argue for the application of paragraphs 4 and 5 to **harmonisation measures adopted under paragraph 1 of Article 114 TFEU or under Article 115 TFEU**.[160]

3.1. Maintaining National Provisions

Paragraph 4 allows MS to maintain a national rule that contradicts the harmonising act. The provision states that the relevant national rules must exist before the adoption of the EU act. More precisely, the national rule must be **in force prior to the adoption of the EU act** (or the entry into force of the accession treaty) and must have been communicated to the Union legislator.[161] This applies also to directives as their entry into force leads to a ban on conflicting national provisions even before the expiry of the transposition period. If the MS wishes to adopt divergent regulations after this date, this is governed by paragraph 5 ($\rightarrow$ para 59 et seqq.). 53

As a provision allowing the MS to derogate from the objective of European integration, it is to be **interpreted narrowly** according to the settled case law of the ECJ.[162] A systematic reading with paragraph 3 insinuates that the MS may not deviate "downwards". The national regulations that an MS wishes to maintain must therefore necessarily have a **higher level of protection** than the harmonisation measure.[163] This may be because the MS makes a different risk assessment than the Commission.[164] This provision can be invoked by all MS, even if they voted in favour of the approximation measure in the Council.[165] Purely economic reasons 54

---

[160] Van Rijn (2016), p. 258; with a differing view Korte, in Calliess and Ruffert (2022), Artikel 114 AEUV para 94, 97.

[161] Cf. Case C-3/00, *Denmark v Commission* (ECJ 20 March 2003) para 58.

[162] See with regard to the free movement of goods Case 46/76, *W. J. G. Bauhuis v Netherlands* (ECJ 25 January 1977) para 12; Case 103/84, *Commission v Italy* (ECJ 5 June 1986) para 22; Joined Cases C-267/95, C-268/95, *Merck & Co. Inc. and Others v Primecrown Ltd and Others and Beecham Group plc v Europharm of Worthing Ltd* (ECJ 5 December 1996) para 23; with regard to the right of establishment Case 2/74, *Reyners* (ECJ 21 June 1974) para 42–45; with regard to the equal treatment of men and women Case 222/84, *Marguerite Johnston v Chief Constable of the Royal Ulster Constabulary* (ECJ 15 May 1986) para 36; Case C-285/98, *Kreil* (ECJ 11 January 2000) para 20.

[163] Cf. Case C-3/00, *Denmark v Commission* (ECJ 20 March 2003) para 64; Case C-41/93, *France v Commission* (Opinion of AG Tesauro of 26 January 1994) para 4; Case C-319/97, *Kortas* (Opinion of AG Saggio of 28 January 1999) para 24; Tietje, in Grabitz et al. (2022), Artikel 114 AEUV para 165 (released in 2016); Jans (2000), p. 122 seq.

[164] Case C-360/14 P, *Germany v Commission* (ECJ 9 July 2015) para 33 seq.; Case C-3/00, *Denmark v Commission* (ECJ 20 March 2003) para 63 seq.

[165] Case C-3/00, *Denmark v Commission* (Opinion of AG Tizzano of 30 May 2002) para 78; Van Rijn (2016), p. 257.

are excluded.[166] The burden of proof for relying on a justification lies with the MS.[167] In practice, however, the maintaining of national provisions does not play a major role[168] because it is difficult to invoke this justification if a high level of protection is already observed in the drafting of the measure (→ para 37).

55 Maintaining a national provision is possible, first, if there is an important reason within the meaning of **Article 36 TFEU** ("**major need**"). This includes grounds of public morality, public policy or public security; the protection of health and life of humans, animals or plants; the protection of national treasures possessing artistic, historic or archaeological value; or the protection of industrial and commercial property (→ Article 36 TFEU para 3–8). As a narrow exception, it does not, however, cover the "overriding reasons based on the general interest", as developed in *Cassis*.[169]

56 Paragraph 4 also mentions environmental protection and the protection of the working environment as further grounds for justification. The concept of **environmental protection** corresponds to that in Article 191 TFEU, which includes the entire "natural environment". This includes both the "natural" or "untouched" environment and the "artificial" environment influenced by man.[170] The term "**working environment**" corresponds to that in Article 152.1 point (a) TFEU. It includes "all factors, physical or otherwise, capable of affecting the health and safety of the worker in his working environment, including in particular certain aspects of the organisation of working time".[171]

57 An important area that is not explicitly mentioned is the area of **consumer protection**. The ECJ recognises consumer protection as an "overriding reason" of general interest,[172] but these justifications do not apply under Article 114.4 TFEU. Some authors therefore conclude that consumer protection cannot be considered a reason for maintaining national rules.[173] However, a closer look at the Union's competence in consumer policy reveals that it is not an end in itself. Rather, as Article 169.1 TFEU provides, it shall aim to protect the health, safety and economic interests of consumers and promote their right to information, to education and to organise themselves. Reasons of consumer protection that aim to protect their health and safety can be considered as grounds for "the protection of health . . . of humans" in the sense of Article 36 TFEU and thus justify the maintaining of more

---

[166] de Sadeleer (2002), p. 62.

[167] Case C-3/00, *Denmark v Commission* (ECJ 20 March 2003) para 84; Weatherill (2010), para 13.33.

[168] Schütze (2021), p. 569.

[169] Case C-41/93, *France v Commission* (Opinion of AG Tesauro of 26 Janurary 1994) para 5; Classen, in von der Groeben et al. (2015), Artikel 114 AEUV para 226; Van Rijn (2016), p. 260.

[170] Epiney (2020), para 10.

[171] Case C-84/94, *United Kingdom v Council* (ECJ 12 November 1996) para 15; cf. also Mattera (1990), p. 172; Van Rijn (2016), p. 261.

[172] See already Case 178/84, *Commission v Germany* (ECJ 12 March 1987) para 28.

[173] Classen, in von der Groeben et al. (2015), Artikel 114 AEUV para 226.

stringent national provisions. The protection of their economic interests, as mentioned in Article 169.1 TFEU, is not covered.

Unlike paragraph 4, paragraph 5 stipulates that the derogations permitted there by the MS are only possible in the case of a "**problem specific to that Member State**" (→ para 65). It is questionable whether maintaining national provisions on the basis of paragraph 4 also requires such a specific problem. Although this is required in certain parts of the literature[174] and sometimes also by the Advocate General,[175] the ECJ underlined that this requirement **does not apply to paragraph 4**.[176] However, when a problem is in fact specific to the applicant MS, that circumstance can be highly relevant in guiding the Commission as to whether to approve or reject the notified national provisions.[177] In the Commission's practice, i.e. the aforementioned assessment, the question of the specificity of the problem plays a significant role.[178]

58

3.2. Introducing New National Provisions

Paragraph 5 stipulates that MS may introduce diverging regulations **after the adoption of a harmonisation measure**. This means that they can introduce national provisions that derogate from the approximation even after discussions and negotiations on the harmonisation (and thus on the common European standard) have taken place at EU level.

59

Since the MS decides under paragraph 5 to adopt a measure after the discussions on a common European level of protection, it is more likely to jeopardise harmonisation. The Union institutions could not, by definition, have taken account of the national text when drawing up the harmonisation measure.[179] Therefore, the possible justifications are limited compared to paragraph 4.[180] New provisions may be introduced by the MS only for reasons of **environmental protection** or the **protection of the working environment**. This has the same scope as under paragraph 4 (→ para 56).

60

In comparison to existing derogations, the scope for derogations under paragraph 5 is narrower as **justifications under Article 36 TFEU do not apply**. The protection of industrial and commercial property can thus be no reason for new derogating national provisions.

61

---

[174] Tietje, in Grabitz et al. (2022), Artikel 114 AEUV para 171–176 (released in 2016).
[175] Case C-3/00, *Denmark v Commission* (Opinion of AG Tizzano of 30 May 2002) para 74.
[176] Case C-3/00, *Denmark v Commission* (ECJ 20 March 2003) para 59–61; see Korte, in Calliess and Ruffert (2022), Artikel 114 AEUV para 108; de Sadeleer (2002), p. 63.
[177] Case C-3/00, *Denmark v Commission* (ECJ 20 March 2003) para 60.
[178] Tietje, in Grabitz et al. (2022), Artikel 114 AEUV para 172 (released in 2016); cf. Albin and Bär (1999), p. 189.
[179] Case C-3/00, *Denmark v Commission* (ECJ 20 March 2003) para 58.
[180] Cf. also Van Rijn (2016), p. 259 et seq.

62   By excluding Article 36 TFEU, health protection is *prima facie* no justification for the introduction of new national regulations either. Only those aspects of health protection that result from the protection of the environment or the working environment can be considered under paragraph 5.[181] However, this does not mean that health protection cannot be considered *ex post* once harmonising measures have been adopted. Instead, **public health** issues can be subject to amended European rules under paragraph 8 and can thus also be assessed by the Commission (→ para 66 et seqq.). They may not, however, be used as grounds for the introduction of a measure by that MS.

63   Moreover, **consumer protection**, which may justify maintaining more stringent national provisions for grounds of health and safety (→ para 57), **cannot serve as a reason** to introduce new national derogations. Articles 169.1 and 169.2 point (a) TFEU require the Union "to ensure a high level of consumer protection" when adopting measures under Article 114 TFEU. This high level of protection shall be the common European standard.

64   The national provisions must be **based on new scientific evidence**. Even though strict requirements must be met for this exception,[182] the term "scientific evidence" cannot be interpreted as "proof" in the narrow scientific sense.[183] This is supported by the precautionary principle already mentioned (→ para 57).[184] However, the situation must have changed to a considerable degree compared to the time of the adoption of the harmonisation measure (*new* evidence).[185] A mere reassessment of known facts is not by itself sufficient.[186]

65   There must also be a **specific problem** due to which the MS makes the derogation. This is to be seen not in the sense of a unique problem[187] but one of such a nature that it has a particularly serious impact on the MS concerned due to local circumstances.[188] The problem may well affect several MS at the same time due to the same considerations. For example, Germany, Denmark and the Netherlands were allowed to derogate from Directive 91/173/EEC[189] with regard to the ban on pentachlorophenol (PCP) because they were all particularly affected.[190] If the

---

[181] Tietje, in Grabitz et al. (2022), Artikel 114 AEUV para 191 (released in 2016).

[182] Tietje, in Grabitz et al. (2022), Artikel 114 AEUV para 192–194 (released in 2016).

[183] Albin and Bär (1999), p. 187 seq.; de Sadeleer (2002), p. 65 seq.

[184] Albin and Bär (1999), p. 188.

[185] Cf. Case C-512/99, *Germany v Commission* (ECJ 21 January 2003) para 82.

[186] Weatherill (2010), para 13.33.

[187] Joined Cases C-439/05 P and C-454/05 P, *Land Oberösterreich and Austria v Commission* (ECJ 13 September 2007) para 65; Albin and Bär (1999), p. 189.

[188] Case T-182/06, *Netherland v Commission* (CFI 27 June 2007) para 61–64; Korte, in Calliess and Ruffert (2022), Artikel 114 AEUV para 113; cf. de Sadeleer (2002), p. 64 seq. for an even broader interpretation.

[189] O.J. L 85/34 (1991).

[190] For Germany see Commission Decision 94/783/EC, O.J. L 316/43 (1994); for Denmark see Commission Decision 96/211/EC, O.J. L 68/32 (1996); for the Netherlands see Commission Decision 99/831/EC, O.J. L 329/15 (1999).

provision required a unique problem, the possibility in paragraph 7 for the Commission to adopt the harmonisation measure across the Union would not make sense.[191] In any event, the problem must have arisen after the adoption of the harmonisation measure.

3.3. Assessment by the European Commission

The MS must **notify the Commission** of a deviation according to paragraph 4 or 5.[192] The MS should submit the text of the national derogation as well as all factual and legal information and, where appropriate, scientific evidence that may serve to justify the requested derogation.[193] For reliance on a derogation, the burden of proof lies with the MS in question; the Commission has a wide discretion in assessing this evidence.[194] The Commission usually transfers the notification (alongside the scientific evidence presented under paragraph 5) to external experts, such as the European Food Safety Authority (EFSA) or the Scientific Committee on Health, Environmental and Emerging Risks (SCHEER).[195]

66

In addition, the Commission examines whether the deviation constitutes arbitrary discrimination, a disguised restriction on trade or an obstacle to the functioning of the internal market. **Arbitrary discrimination** and **disguised restriction on trade** are already mentioned in Article 36 sentence 2 TFEU, whose interpretation (→ Article 36 TFEU para 18–19) applies also in the context of Article 114.6 TFEU.

67

The last element, the **obstacle to the functioning of the internal market**, is more difficult to assess. It cannot mean any impairment of the internal market as this would make paragraphs 4 and 5 *ad absurdum*[196] and exclude any national derogation. Therefore, the derogation must lead to an appreciable and severe impairment of the internal market in order to constitute an obstacle to its functioning. The Commission understands this as a disproportionate effect in relation to the pursued objective.[197]

68

In accordance with paragraph 6, the Commission examines the national measure to determine whether the facts and justifications put forward are valid.[198] The Commission assesses the national measures and the information contained in the notification but takes into consideration all new scientific evidence available, not

69

---

[191] Tietje, in Grabitz et al. (2022), Artikel 114 AEUV para 195 (released in 2016).
[192] See Commission Communication *concerning Article 95 (paragraphs 4, 5 and 6)*, COM(2002) 760.
[193] COM(2002) 760, para 6, 13.
[194] Case C-360/14 P, *Germany v Commission* (9 July 2015) para 36.
[195] Van Rijn (2016), p. 261 et seq.
[196] Cf. Tietje, in Grabitz et al. (2022), Artikel 114 AEUV para 214 (released in 2016).
[197] See, for example, Commission Decision (EU) 2020/1205, O.J. L 270/7 (2020), recital 93 with reference to previous decisions.
[198] Commission Decision of 26 October 1999, O.J. L 329/25 (1999) para 34.

only those presented by the MS.[199] Depending on its assessment, the Commission **confirms or rejects the national measure**. The authorisation is generally not temporary,[200] but the Commission may choose to approve measures for a limited period of time[201] or until the Union legislator has adopted a relevant revision of the harmonisation measure.[202] These restrictions may be required in order to ensure that the notified national provisions, and the potential obstacle to the functioning of the internal market, are limited to what is strictly necessary to achieve the objectives pursued by them.

70 The Commission has **six months** from the date of notification by the MS in question to confirm or reject the national rule. However, if the MS has not provided sufficient information, the Commission may request further documentation. The time limit only starts to run from the moment when all documents are available.[203]

71 This period can be **extended by a further six months**, but only "when justified by the complexity of the matter and in the absence of danger for human health".[204] With regard to the question of whether these conditions are met, the Commission bears the burden of proof but has a margin of discretion.[205] The Commission must provide sufficient legal and factual justification for its decision.[206]

72 If the Commission does not reply within this period, the MS's derogation is deemed to be approved (**fictitious approval**). Since the national measure may only be applied after confirmation by the Commission, the Commission could prevent or at least significantly delay the application of protective measures deemed necessary by failing to take a decision as the (positive) decision of the Commission has a constitutive effect.[207] Before that, the national measure may not be applied. The fictitious approval creates a legally secure situation after the expiry of the deadline and at the same time acts as a means of pressure on the Commission to bring about its decision quickly.

73 When an MS notifies a derogation under paragraph 6 or raises a specific problem on public health under paragraph 8, the Commission is required to **examine an existing harmonisation measure** and, if necessary, **propose a revision**. This concretises and reinforces the already existing duty of the Commission to periodically review such a measure with regard to "any new development based on

---

[199] Van Rijn (2016), p. 262.

[200] Van Rijn (2016), p. 265.

[201] For a differentiated assessment of notified derogations (approving, approving for a limited time or rejecting parts of the notified measures), see Commission Decision 2012/160/EU, O.J. L 80/19 (2012).

[202] See, for example, Commission Decision (EU) 2020/1178, O.J. L 259/14 (2020).

[203] de Sadeleer (2002), p. 67 seq.

[204] Regarding the periods in this case see Case T-69/08, *Poland v Commission* (CFI 6 December 2010) para 67, 69. See, inter alia, Commission Decision 2012/230/EU, O.J. L 116/29 (2012).

[205] Albin and Bär (1999), p. 191.

[206] Case C-41/93, *France v Commission* (ECJ 17 May 1994) para 34–37.

[207] Case C-41/93, *France v Commission* (ECJ 17 May 1994) para 30; C-319/97, *Kortas* (ECJ 1 June 1999) para 28.

scientific facts" (→ para 37) in case a situation arises where this seems necessary.[208] The Commission is obliged to state the reasons why it does or does not propose a revision of the Union measure.[209]

4. Simplified Infringement Procedure Before the CJEU

Paragraph 9 allows the Commission or an MS to bring an action before the ECJ against another MS which is alleged to have **misused any of its powers** under Article 114 TFEU. Misuse of powers occurs when an MS applies divergent national provisions without the Commission's approval or when these provisions go further than approved by the Commission.[210]

The reference to Articles 258 and 259 TFEU shows that it is an **infringement procedure**. However, this is considerably shortened as the preliminary proceedings are omitted; the **ECJ is seized "directly"**. If an MS wants to challenge an authorisation already granted by the Commission according to paragraph 6, only an action on the basis of Article 263 TFEU is admissible.[211] The ECJ is also free to deal with the question of whether an MS has misused its powers under Article 114 TFEU in the context of a preliminary ruling procedure (Article 267 TFEU).[212]

The simplified procedure **does not apply to paragraph 10**.[213] This follows from the systematic position of paragraph 9, which "concludes" the derogation procedure, but is listed before the provision on safeguard clauses in paragraph 10.[214] Also, paragraph 10 does not confer rights on an MS directly, but only by way of the safeguard clauses adopted "in appropriate cases".[215] In addition, the safeguard clauses in paragraph 10 should contain their own control procedure.

74

75

76

5. Safeguard Clauses for the Adoption of Provisional Measures by a Member State

According to paragraph 10, the Union legislator[216] may include in a harmonisation act a safeguard clause "**in appropriate cases**". It is also the Union legislator who decides when there is an appropriate case. This is without prejudice to the

77

---

[208] Korte, in Calliess and Ruffert (2022), Artikel 114 AEUV para 111.
[209] Albin and Bär (1999), p. 190.
[210] Schröder, in Streinz (2018), Artikel 114 AEUV para 119.
[211] Tietje, in Grabitz et al. (2022), Artikel 114 AEUV para 226 (released in 2016); see as an example Case C-41/93, *France v Commission* (ECJ 17 May 1994).
[212] Korte, in Calliess and Ruffert (2022), Artikel 114 AEUV para 133.
[213] With a different opinion Schröder, in Streinz (2018), Artikel 114 AEUV para 119.
[214] Tietje, in Grabitz et al. (2022), Artikel 114 AEUV para 227 (released in 2016).
[215] Classen, in von der Groeben et al. (2015), Artikel 114 AEUV para 259.
[216] Cf. de Sadeleer (2002), p. 56.

maintaining or introduction of more stringent national measures under paragraphs 4 and 5. However, measures under paragraph 10 shall only be of a temporary nature.[217] In this way, the Union aims to achieve a high level of protection by means of harmonisation but allows, in individual cases, temporary derogations by individual MS.[218]

78   A safeguard clause empowers MS to take provisional measures for one or more of the **non-economic reasons listed in Article 36 TFEU** (→ para 55).[219] Especially in the area of product safety, safeguard clauses are a component of harmonisation measures. If an MS has concerns about the authorisation of a product, it can thus take temporary measures derogating from the provisions of the harmonisation act.[220] Furthermore, in line with Article 36 TFEU, the safeguard clauses may not lead to arbitrary discrimination[221] or disguised restrictions on trade (→ para 67), which also applies to the use of safeguard clauses by MS.[222]

79   However, the national application of the safeguard clause must be interpreted narrowly and limited to "emergencies" in the MS.[223] The national measures taken within this framework are subject to **Union control mechanism**, which is primarily the responsibility of the Commission.[224] On the one hand, it is to be examined whether the measure of the MS is in line with the principle of proportionality, i.e. in particular whether it does not go beyond what is necessary to achieve the objective. In doing so, the MS will be granted a margin of discretion. In addition, the Union control mechanism, similar to paragraph 7, will examine whether adjustments to the harmonisation act are necessary because the underlying situation goes beyond the claimed individual case.

6. Recent Practice of Internal Market Harmonisation

80   Over the decades, Article 114 TFEU and its predecessors have been used for a number of harmonisation projects. A comprehensive list would be out of the scope of this contribution, but a few, especially recent, examples should be mentioned. Harmonisation measures adopted under Article 114 TFEU shall aim for a high level of consumer protection (→ para 37). This insinuates that, of course, the legislator

---

[217] Terhechte and Kübek, in Pechstein et al. (2023), Artikel 114 AEUV para 112.

[218] Case C-359/92, *Germany v Council* (Opinion of AG Jacobs of 8 June 1994) para 23.

[219] Cf. Case C-120/95, *Nicolas Decker v Caisse de maladies des employés privés* (ECJ 28 April 1998) para 39.

[220] Löwer (2012), p. 86.

[221] Case 5/77, *Tedeschi v Denkavit* (ECJ 5 October 1977) para 40, this is with regard to Article 100 TEEC but the principle remains, as discussed above, the same.

[222] de Sadeleer (2002), p. 56.

[223] Case 11/82, *SA Piraiki-Patraiki and Others v Commission* (ECJ 17 Janurary 1985) para 26; Case C-359/92, *Germany v Council* (Opinion of AG Jacobs of 8 June 1994) para 23; cf. de Sadeleer (2002), p. 56 seq.

[224] Case 148/78, *Ratti* (ECJ 5 April 1979) para 37.

may adopt genuine consumer protection measures as long as they improve the functioning of the internal market. Indeed, a number of consumer protection measures have been adopted on the basis of Article 114 TFEU. In the 1980s and 1990s, for example, the Community legislator adopted measures regarding off-premise and distance contracts.[225] They have been replaced by the more comprehensive **Consumer Rights Directive** in 2011.[226] It covers not only distance or off-premise contracts but more generally all consumer contracts as regards information requirements.

In 1994, the Community legislator adopted a regulation on the Community trademark and established the **Office for Harmonization in the Internal Market** (OHIM), but contrary to what the name suggests, the founding act was based not on Article 114 TFEU's predecessor but on what is now Article 352 TFEU.[227] Over time, tasks were entrusted on the agency on the basis of Article 114 TFEU. In 2017, a new regulation[228] was adopted pursuant to Article 118 TFEU, a legal basis introduced by the Lisbon Treaty for intellectual property rights, and the agency was renamed European Union Intellectual Property Office (EUIPO). 81

In response to the economic and financial crisis in the 2010s, the system of financial supervision in the EU was reformed. To this end, new agencies—the so-called **European Supervisory Authorities** (ESAs)—were established, among them the European Banking Authority (EBA),[229] the European Insurance and Occupational Pensions Authority (EIOPA)[230] and the European Securities and Markets Authority (ESMA).[231] The system was complemented by the establishment of a European Systemic Risk Board (ESRB) for macroprudential oversight.[232] The establishment of EBA was an important step towards the creation of the so-called banking union (→ Supplement to Title VIII: Banking Union para 1 et seqq.). 82

In the last decade, the creation of a **digital single market** was a priority project of the Commission. One of the first aspects was the field of cross-border electronic communication. In this field, a major achievement of harmonisation is the reduction 83

---

[225] Council Directive 85/577/EEC *to protect the consumer in respect of contracts negotiated away from business premises*, O.J. L 372/31 (1985) (based on what is now Article 115 TFEU) and Parliament/Council Directive 97/7/EC *on the protection of consumers in respect of distance contracts*, O.J. L 144/19 (1997).

[226] Parliament/Council Directive 2011/83/EU *on consumer rights*, O.J. L 304/64 (2011).

[227] Council Regulation (EC) No 40/94 *on the Community trade mark*, O.J. L 11/1 (1994).

[228] Parliament/Council Regulation (EU) 2017/1001 *on the European Union trade mark (codification)*, O.J. L 154/1 (2017).

[229] Parliament/Council Regulation (EU) No 1093/2010, O.J. L 331/12 (2010).

[230] Parliament/Council Regulation (EU) No 1094/2010, O.J. L 331/48 (2010).

[231] Parliament/Council Regulation (EU) No 1095/2010, O.J. L 331/84 (2010).

[232] Parliament/Council Regulation (EU) No 1092/2010 *on European Union macro-prudential oversight of the financial system and establishing a European Systemic Risk Board*, O.J. L 331/1 (2010).

and abolition of roaming costs for cross-border mobile communication.[233] In 2020, the Commission presented a Communication on "Shaping Europe's digital future".[234] Based on Article 114 TFEU, the Union legislator adopted the **Digital Markets Act**[235] and the **Digital Services Act**.[236] They aim to create a safer digital space in which the fundamental rights of all users of digital services are protected and to establish a level playing field to foster innovation, growth and competitiveness in the single market and internationally. They are complemented by rules on cybersecurity.[237] In connection with the digal single market, the Commission recently submitted a proposal for an **Artificial Intelligence Act**.[238]

84 Finally, in late 2022, the European Commission presented its plans for legislative action to tackle problems in the functioning of the internal market for media services and the operation of media service providers. The proposed **European Media Freedom Act**[239] aims to abolish interference in the editorial decisions of media service providers and to promote pluralism and independence in the media market. In replacement of the European Regulators Group for Audiovisual Media Services (ERGA), the Commission proposes the establishment of a European Board for Media Services composed of representatives from national regulatory authorities and with broader competences.

List of Cases

ECJ

ECJ 13.07.1966, 32/65, *Italy v Council and Commission*, ECLI:EU:C:1966:42 [cit. in para 4]
ECJ 21.06.1974, 2/74, *Reyners*, ECLI:EU:C:1974:68 [cit. in para 54]
ECJ 11.07.1974, 8/74, *Dassonville*, ECLI:EU:C:1974:82 [cit. in para 28]
ECJ 25.01.1977, 46/76, *Bauhuis*, ECLI:EU:C:1977:6 [cit. in para 54]
ECJ 05.10.1977, 5/77, *Tedeschi v Denkavit*, ECLI:EU:C:1977:144 [cit. in para 78]
ECJ 29.11.1978, 83/78, *Redmond*, ECLI:EU:C:1978:214 [cit. in para 11]
ECJ 20.02.1979, 120/78, *REWE v Bundesmonopolverwaltung für Branntwein*, ECLI:EU:C:1979:42 [cit. in para 5, 14, 28]

---

[233] See the recast Parliament/Council Regulation (EU) 2022/612 *on roaming on public mobile communications networks within the Union*, O.J. L 115/1 (2022).

[234] COM(2020) 67 final.

[235] Parliament/Council Regulation (EU) 2022/1925, O.J. L 265/1 (2022).

[236] Parliament/Council Regulation (EU) 2022/2065, O.J. L 277/1 (2022).

[237] See Parliament/Council Regulation (EU) 2019/881 *on ENISA (the European Union Agency for Cybersecurity) and on information and communications technology cybersecurity certification*, O.J. L 151/1 (2019) and Parliament/Council Directive (EU) 2022/2555 *on measures for a high common level of cybersecurity across the Union (NIS 2 Directive)*, O.J L 333/80 (2022).

[238] COM(2021) 206 final.

[239] COM(2022) 457 final.

ECJ 05.04.1979, 148/78, *Ratti*, ECLI:EU:C:1979:110 [cit. in para 79]
ECJ 09.12.1981, 193/80, *Commission v Italy*, ECLI:EU:C:1981:298 [cit. in para 3]
ECJ 26.10.1982, 104/81, *Hauptzollamt Mainz v Kupferberg & Cie*, ECLI:EU:C:1982:362 [cit. in para 27]
ECJ 29.02.1984, 37/83, *Rewe-Zentral*, ECLI:EU:C:1984:89 [cit. in para 31]
ECJ 17.01.1985, 11/82, *Piraiki-Patraiki v Commission*, ECLI:EU:C:1985:18 [cit. in para 79]
ECJ 15.01.1986, 41/84, *Pietro Pinna v Caisse d'allocations familiales de la Savoie*, ECLI:EU:C:1986:1 [cit. in para 18]
ECJ 15.05.1986, 222/84, *Marguerite Johnston v Chief Constable of the Royal Ulster Constabulary*, ECLI:EU:C:1986:206 [cit. in para 54]
ECJ 05.06.1986, 103/84, *Commission v Italy*, ECLI:EU:C:1986:229 [cit. in para 54]
ECJ 26.03.1987, 45/86, *Commission v Council*, ECLI:EU:C:1987:163 [cit. in para 30]
ECJ 14.10.1987, 278/85, *Commission v Denmark*, ECLI:EU:C:1987:439 [cit. in para 23]
ECJ 07.03.1989, 215/87, *Heinz Schumacher v Hauptzollamt Frankfurt am Main-Ost*, ECLI:EU:C:1989:111 [cit. in para 51]
ECJ 07.03.1990, C-69/88, *Krantz v Ontvanger der Directe Belastingen*, ECLI:EU:C:1990:97 [cit. in para 28]
ECJ 12.07.1990, C-128/89, *Commission v Italy*, ECLI:EU:C:1990:311 [cit. in para 28]
ECJ 18.04.1991, C-63/89, *Assurances du Crédit v Council and Commission*, ECLI:EU:C:1991:152 [cit. in para 31]
ECJ 11.06.1991, C-300/89, *Commission v Council*, ECLI:EU:C:1991:244 [cit. in para 12, 29, 30]
ECJ 09.05.1992, C-2/90, *Commission v Belgium*, ECLI:EU:C:1992:310 [cit. in para 39]
ECJ 24.11.1993, C-267/91 and C-268/91, *Keck and Mithouard*, ECLI:EU:C:1993:905 [cit. in para 28]
ECJ 02.08.1993, C-355/90, *Commission v Spain*, ECLI:EU:C:1993:331 [cit. in para 39]
ECJ 13.10.1993, C-93/92, *CMC Motorradcenter v Baskiciogullari*, ECLI:EU:C:1993:838 [cit. in para 28]
ECJ 26.01.1994, C-41/93, Opinion of AG Tesauro, *France v Commission*, ECLI:EU:C:1994:23 [cit. in para 51, 54, 55]
ECJ 17.05.1994, C-41/93, *France v Commission*, ECLI:EU:C:1994:196 [cit. in para 35, 66, 72, 75]
ECJ 08.06.1994, C-359/92, Opinion of AG Jacobs, *Germany v Council*, ECLI:EU:C:1994:231 [cit. in para 77, 79]
ECJ 14.07.1994, C-379/92, *Peralta*, ECLI:EU:C:1994:296 [cit. in para 28]
ECJ 09.08.1994, C-359/92, *Germany v Council*, ECLI:EU:C:1994:306 [cit. in para 35, 48]
ECJ 15.11.1994, Opinion 1/94, *International agreements concerning services and the protection of intellectual property*, ECLI:EU:C:1994:384 [cit. in para 27, 36]

ECJ 13.07.1995, C-350/92, *Spain v Council*, ECLI:EU:C:1995:237 [cit. in para 26, 28, 34]

ECJ 05.10.1995, C-96/94, *Centro Servizi Spediporto Srl v Spedizioni Marittima del Golfo Srl*, ECLI:EU:C:1995:308 [cit. in para 28]

ECJ 17.10.1995, C-140/94, C-141/94, C-142/94, *DIP and Others v Comune di Bassano del Grappa and Others*, ECLI:EU:C:1995:330 [cit. in para 28]

ECJ 30.11.1995, C-134/94, *Esso Español SA v Comunidad Autónoma de Canarias*, ECLI:EU:C:1995:414 [cit. in para 28]

ECJ 26.03.1996, C-271/94, *Parliament v Council*, ECLI:EU:C:1996:133 [cit. in para 11]

ECJ 12.11.1996, C-84/94, *United Kingdom v Council*, ECLI:EU:C:1996:431 [cit. in para 21, 56]

ECJ 05.12.1996, C-267/95, C-268/95, *Merck v Primecrown and Beecham v Europharm*, ECLI:EU:C:1996:468 [cit. in para 54]

ECJ 13.05.1997, C-233/94, *Germany v Parliament and Council*, ECLI:EU:C:1997:231 [cit. in para 11, 30, 38]

ECJ 04.12.1997, C-97/96, *Verband deutscher Daihatsu-Händler eV v Daihatsu Deutschland GmbH*, ECLI:EU:C:1997:581 [cit. in para 11]

ECJ 28.04.1998, C-120/95, *Nicolas Decker v Caisse de maladies des employés privés*, ECLI:EU:C:1998:167 [cit. in para 78]

ECJ 05.05.1998, C-157/96, *National Farmers' Union and Others*, ECLI:EU:C:1998:191 [cit. in para 39]

ECJ 05.05.1998, C-180/96, *United Kingdom v Commission*, ECLI:EU:C:1998:192 [cit. in para 11, 39]

ECJ 18.06.1998, C-266/96, *Corsica Ferris France v Gruppo Antichi Ormeggiatori del porto di Genova and Others*, ECLI:EU:C:1998:306 [cit. in para 28]

ECJ 14.07.1998, C-284/95, *Safety Hi-Tech Srl v S. & T. Srl*, ECLI:EU:C:1998:352 [cit. in para 38]

ECJ 14.07.1998, C-341/95, *Bettati v Safety Hi-Tech Srl*, ECLI:EU:C:1998:353 [cit. in para 38]

ECJ 22.10.1998, C-184/96, *Commission v France*, ECLI:EU:C:1998:495 [cit. in para 16]

ECJ 28.01.1999, C-319/97, Opinion of AG Saggio, *Kortas*, ECLI:EU:C:1999:37 [cit. in para 46, 54]

ECJ 23.02.1999, C-42/97, *Parliament v Council*, ECLI:EU:C:1999:81 [cit. in para 12]

ECJ 01.06.1999, C-319/97, *Kortas*, ECLI:EU:C:1999:272 [cit. in para 72]

ECJ 11.01.2000, C-285/98, *Kreil*, ECLI:EU:C:2000:2 [cit. in para 54]

ECJ 04.04.2000, C-269/97, *Commission v Council*, ECLI:EU:C:2000:183 [cit. in para 11]

ECJ 15.06.2000, C-376/98, Opinion of AG Finnelly, *Germany v Parliament and Council*, ECLI:EU:C:2000:324 [cit. in para 8]

ECJ 05.10.2000, C-376/98, *Germany v Parliament and Council*, ECLI:EU:C:2000:544 [cit. in para 2, 9, 12, 24, 25, 26, 29, 30, 31, 34]

ECJ 30.01.2001, C-36/98, *Spain v Council*, ECLI:EU:C:2001:64 [cit. in para 12]

ECJ 10.09.2002, C-491/01, Opinion of AG Geelhoed, *British American Tobacco (Investments) and Imperial Tobacco*, ECLI:EU:C:2002:476 [cit. in para 12, 28, 32]
ECJ 09.10.2001, C-377/98, *Netherlands v Parliament and Council*, ECLI:EU:C:2001:523 [cit. in para 26, 27, 36]
ECJ 30.05.2002, C-3/00, Opinion of AG Tizzano, *Denmark v Commission*, ECLI:EU:C:2002:314 [cit. in para 54, 58]
ECJ 10.12.2002, C-491/01, *British American Tobacco (Investments) and Imperial Tobacco*, ECLI:EU:C:2002:741 [cit. in para 9, 24, 26, 28]
ECJ 21.01.2003, C-512/99, *Germany v Commission*, ECLI:EU:C:2003:40 [cit. in para 64]
ECJ 20.03.2003, C-3/00, *Denmark v Commission*, ECLI:EU:C:2003:167 [cit. in para 53, 54, 58, 60]
ECJ 20.05.2003, C-465/00, C-138/01, C-139/01, *Österreichischer Rundfunk and Others*, ECLI:EU:C:2003:294 [cit. in para 24]
ECJ 11.12.2003, C-322/01, *Deutscher Apothekenverband*, ECLI:EU:C:2003:664 [cit. in para 23]
ECJ 29.04.2004, C-338/01, *Commission v Council*, ECLI:EU:C:2004:253 [cit. in para 41]
ECJ 14.12.2004, C-434/02, *Arnold André*, ECLI:EU:C:2004:800 [cit. in para 26, 28, 31, 34]
ECJ 14.12.2004, C-210/03, *Swedish Match*, ECLI:EU:C:2004:802 [cit. in para 26, 28, 31, 34]
ECJ 06.12.2005, C-66/04, *United Kingdom v Parliament and Council*, ECLI:EU:C:2005:743 [cit. in para 19, 35, 47]
ECJ 26.01.2006, C-533/03, *Commission v Council*, ECLI:EU:C:2006:64 [cit. in para 41]
ECJ 02.05.2006, C-436/03, *Parliament v Council*, ECLI:EU:C:2006:277 [cit. in para 33, 36]
ECJ 23.11.2006, C-315/05, *Lidl Italia*, ECLI:EU:C:2006:736 [cit. in para 21]
ECJ 12.12.2006, C-380/03, *Germany v Parliament and Council*, ECLI:EU:C:2006:772 [cit. in para 12, 19, 24, 26, 31, 34]
ECJ 13.09.2007, C-439/05 P, C-454/05 P, *Land Oberösterreich and Austria v Commission*, ECLI:EU:C:2007:510 [cit. in para 65]
ECJ 10.02.2009, C-301/06, *Ireland v Parliament and Council*, ECLI:EU:C:2009:68 [cit. in para 30]
ECJ 08.09.2009, C-411/06, *Commission v Parliament and Council*, ECLI:EU:C:2009:518 [cit. in para 12]
ECJ 29.04.2010, C-446/08, *Solgar Vitamin's France and Others*, ECLI:EU:C:2010:233 [cit. in para 21]
ECJ 08.06.2010, C-58/08, *Vodafone and Others*, ECLI:EU:C:2010:321 [cit. in para 9, 26, 30, 34, 47]
ECJ 12.07.2012, C-171/11, *Fra.bo*, ECLI:EU:C:2012:453 [cit. in para 33]
ECJ 16.04.2013, C-274/11 and C-295/11, *Spain and Italy v Council*, ECLI:EU:C:2013:240[cit. in para 9]

ECJ 22.01.2014, C-270/12, *United Kingdom v Parliament and Council*, ECLI:EU:C:2014:18 [cit. in para 19, 35]

ECJ 09.07.2015, C-360/14 P, *Germany v Commission*, ECLI:EU:C:2015:457 [cit. in para 54, 66]

ECJ 04.05.2016, C-358/14, *Poland v Parliament and Council*, ECLI:EU:C:2016:323 [cit. in para 24, 31, 34]

ECJ 04.05.2016, C-547/14, *Philip Morris Brands and Others*, ECLI:EU:C:2016:325 [cit. in para 31, 37]

ECJ 22.06.2017, C-549/15, *E.ON Biofor Sverige*, ECLI:EU:C:2017:490 [cit. in para 31, 37]

ECJ 23.01.2018, C-267/16, *Buhagiar*, ECLI:EU:C:2018:26 [cit. in para 37]

ECJ 03.12.2019, C-482/17, *Czech Republic v Parliament and Council*, ECLI:EU:C:2019:1035 [cit. in para 24]

ECJ 27.04.2022, C-674/20, *Airbnb Ireland*, ECLI:EU:C:2022:303 [cit. in para 42]

CFI

CFI 11.09.2002, T-13/99, *Pfizer Animal Health SA v Council*, ECLI:EU:T:2002:209 [cit. in para 39]

CFI 11.09.2002, T-70/99, *Alpharma Inc. v Council*, ECLI:EU:T:2002:210 [cit. in para 39]

CFI 27.06.2007, T-182/06, *Netherland v Commission*, ECLI:EU:T:2007:191 [cit. in para 65]

CFI 06.12.2010, T-69/08, *Poland v Commission*, ECLI:EU:T:2010:504 [cit. in para 71]

References[240]

Albin, S., & Bär, S. (1999). Nationale Alleingänge nach dem Vertrag von Amsterdam. Der neue Art. 95 EGV: Fortschritt oder Rückschritt für den Umweltschutz? *Natur und Recht, 21*(4), 185–192.

Barents, R. (1993). The internal market unlimited: Some observations on the legal basis of Community legislation. *Common Market Law Review, 30*(1), 85–109.

Bätge, J. (2009). *Wettbewerb der Wettbewerbsordnungen? Überlegungen zum richtigen Grad von Dezentralität und Harmonisierung im Recht gegen Wettbewerbsbeschränkungen*. Nomos.

Blanke, H.-J., & Böttner, R. (2020). § 13: Binnenmarkt, Rechtsangleichung, Grundfreiheiten. In M. Niedobitek (Ed.), *Europarecht – Grundlagen und Politiken der Union* (pp. 887–1114). DeGruyter.

Bock, Y. (2005). *Rechtsangleichung und Regulierung im Binnenmarkt*. Nomos.

Böttner, R. (2021). *The constitutional framework for enhanced cooperation in EU law*. Brill Nijhoff.

Böttner, R. (2022). *Special legislative procedures in the Treaties - institutional balance and sincere cooperation*. Study for the Policy Department for Citizens' Rights and Constitutional

---

[240] All cited internet sources have last been accessed on 31 January 2022.

Affairs of the European Parliament. PE 738.331. https://www.europarl.europa.eu/RegData/etudes/STUD/2022/738331/IPOL_STU(2022)738331_EN.pdf

Calliess, C., & Ruffert, M. (2022). *EUV/AEUV. Kommentar* (6th ed.). C.H. Beck.

Ćemalović, U. (2015). Framework for the approximation of national legal systems within the European Uinon's acquis. *Croatian Yearbook of European Law & Policy, 11*(1), 241–258.

Chalmers, D., Davies, G., & Monti, G. (2019). *European Union Law* (4th ed.). Cambridge University Press.

da Cruz Vilaça, J. L. (2004). The precautionary principle in EU law. *Common Market Law Review, 10*(2), 369–406.

de Sadeleer, N. (2002). Les clauses de sauvegarde prévues à l'article 95 du Traité CE. L'efficacité du marché intérieur en porte-à-faux avec les intérêts nationaux dignes de protection. *Revue Trimestrielle de Droit Européen, 38*(1), 53–73.

Defalque, L., Pertek, J., Steinfeld, P., & Vigneron, P. (2006). *Libre circulation des personnes et des capitaux. Rapprochement des législations* (3rd ed.). Editions de l'Université de Bruxelles.

Dougan, M. (2000). Minimum harmonization and the internal market. *Common Market Law Review, 37*(4), 853–885.

Ehlermann, C.-D. (1987). The internal market following the Single European Act. *Common Market Law Review, 24*(3), 361–409.

Ehlermann, C.-D. (1995). Ökonomische Aspekte des Subsidiaritätsprinzips: Harmonisierung versus Wettbewerb der Systeme. *Integration, 18*(1), 11–21.

Eiden, H. C. (1997). § 26: Die Angleichung von Rechtsvorschriften. In A. Bleckmann (Ed.), *Europarecht* (6th ed.). Carl Heymanns Verlag.

Epiney, A. (2020). § 19: Die Umweltpolitik der Union. In M. Niedobitek (Ed.), *Europarecht – Grundlagen und Politiken der Union* (pp. 1569–1648). DeGruyter.

Fahey, E. (2011). Does the emperor have financial crisis clothes? Reflections on the legal basis of the European Banking Authority. *Modern Law Review, 74*(4), 581–595.

Geiger, R., Khan, D.-E., & Kotzur, M. (Eds.). (2015). *European Union Treaties*. C.H. Beck/Hart.

Grabitz, E., Hilf, M., & Nettesheim, M. (Eds.). (2022). *Das Recht der Europäischen Union: EUV/AEUV. Commentary, looseleaf*. C.H. Beck.

Herresthal, C. (2011). Die Ablehnung einer primärrechtlichen Perpetuierung des sekundärrechtlichen Verbraucherschutzniveaus. *Europäische Zeitschrift für Wirtschaftsrecht, 22*(9), 328–333.

Ihns, A. (2005). *Entwicklung und Grundlagen der europäischen Rechtsangleichung*. Peter Lang.

Ipsen, H. P. (1972). *Europäisches Gemeinschaftsrecht*. Mohr Siebeck.

Jans, J. H. (2000). *European environmental law* (2nd ed.). Europa Law Publishing.

Lancos, P. (2019). The power of soft law: Spontaneous approximation of fining policies for anti-competitive conduct. *European Competition Law Review, 40*(11), 538–546.

Lochner, N. (1962). Was bedeuten die Begriffe Harmonisierung, Koordinierung und gemeinsame Politik in den Europäischen Verträgen? *Zeitschrift für das gesamte Staatsrecht, 118*(1), 35–61.

Lohse, E. J. (2017). *Rechtsangleichungsprozesse in der Europäischen Union. Instrumente, Funktionsmechanismen und Wirkparameter effektiver Harmonisierung*. Mohr Siebeck.

Löwer, W. (2012). *Tierversuchsrichtlinie und nationales Recht*. Mohr Siebeck.

Ludwigs, M. (2004). *Rechtsangleichung nach Art. 94, 95 EG-Vertrag*. Nomos.

Mattera, A. (1990). *Le marché unique européen: ses règles, son fonctionnement* (2nd ed.) Editions Jupiter.

Oppermann, T., Classen, C. D., & Nettesheim, M. (2021). *Europarecht* (9th ed.). C. H. Beck.

Pechstein, M., Nowak, C., & Häde, U. (Eds.). (2023). *Frankfurter Kommentar zu EUV, GRC und AEUV* (2nd ed.). Mohr Siebeck.

Pernice, I. (1996). Harmonization of legislation in federal systems: Constitutional, federal and subsidiary aspects. In I. Pernice (Ed.), *Harmonization of legislation in federal systems*. Nomos.

Schroeder, W. (2002). Die Sicherung eines hohen Schutzniveaus für Gesundheits-, Umwelt- und Verbraucherschutz im Europäischen Binnenmarkt. *Deutsches Verwaltungsblatt, 117*(4), 213–221.

Schütze, R. (2021). *European Union law* (3rd ed.). Cambridge University Press.

Schweitzer, H. (2010). Staatliche Gemeinwohlverantwortung und Wettbewerb. In U. Becker & J. Schwarze (Eds.), *Gemeinwohlverantwortung im Binnenmarkt*. Mohr Siebeck.

Seidel, M. (2006). Präventive Rechtsangleichung im Bereich des Gemeinsamen Marktes. *Europarecht, 41*(1), 26–45.

Senden, L. (2004). *Soft law in European Community law*. Hart.

Smit, H., & Herzog, E. (Eds.) (2017). *Smit & Herzog on the Law oft he European Union, looseleaf*. LexisNexis.

Streinz, R. (Ed.). (2018). *EUV/AEUV* (3nd ed.). C. H. Beck.

Tiebout, C. M. (1956). A pure theorie of local expenditures. *Journal of Political Economy, 64*(5), 416–424.

Tinbergen, J. (1954). *International economic integration* (2nd ed.). Elsevier.

Van Rijn, T. (2016). Dérogations en matière d'harmonisation de législation. In F. Picod (Ed.), *Le principe majoritaire en droit de l'Union européenne* (pp. 255–269). Bruylant.

Vogelaar, T. W. (1975). The approximation of the laws of the member states under the Treaty of Rome. *Common Market Law Review, 12*(2), 211–230.

von Danwitz, T. (2018). Rechtsetzung und Rechtsangleichung. In M. Dauses & M. Ludwigs (Eds.), *Handbuch des EU-Wirtschaftsrechts, looseleaf*. C.H. Beck.

von der Groeben, H. (1970). Die Politik der europäischen Kommission auf dem Gebiet der Rechtsangleichungen. *Neue Juristische Wochenschrift, 23*(9), 359–364.

von der Groeben, H. (1999). *Kommentar zum EU-, EG-Vertrag* (5th ed.). Nomos.

von der Groeben, H., Schwarze, J., & Hatje, A. (Eds.). (2015). *Europäisches Unionsrecht. Commentary* (7th ed.). Nomos.

von Graevenitz, A. (2013). Mitteilungen, Leitlinien, Stellungnahmen – Soft Law der EU mit Lenkungswirkung. *Europäische Zeitschrift für Wirtschaftsrecht*, 169–173.

Weatherill, S. (2010). Union legislation relating to the free movement of goods. In P. Oliver (Ed.), *Oliver on free movement of goods in the European Union* (5th ed.). Hart.

Weatherill, S. (2017). The competence to harmonise and its limits. In P. Koutrakos & J. Snell (Eds.), *Research handbook on the law of the EU's internal market* (pp. 82–101). Edward Elgar.

Article 115 [Harmonising Laws Directly Affecting the Internal Market]
(ex-Article 94 TEC)

Without prejudice to Article 114,[3] the Council shall, acting unanimously in accordance with a special legislative procedure and after consulting the European Parliament and the Economic and Social Committee,[10] issue directives[9] for the approximation[5] of such laws, regulations or administrative provisions of the Member States[8] as directly affect the establishment or functioning of the internal market.[6]

Contents

1.	Overview and Genesis	1
2.	Scope of Application	5
3.	Form and Procedure	9
4.	Derogations and Safeguard Clauses	11

List of Cases
References

1. Overview and Genesis

As with Article 114 TFEU, Article 115 TFEU is a norm of a **horizontal nature**[1] that allows Union action as long as the internal market is concerned (→ Article 114 TFEU para 8). This harmonisation competence also belongs to the shared competence of the Union (→ Article 114 TFEU para 9). In particular, both provisions have as their object the harmonisation of legislation for the establishment or functioning of the internal market.

Article 115 TFEU, almost identical in wording, **has been a part of the Treaties since 1957** as Article 100 TEEC (→ Article 114 TFEU para 4). Until its revision by the Single European Act (SEA), it was the basic norm for the approximation of national laws and regulations. In 1985, the Commission in its "White Paper on Completing the Internal Market" put forward proposals to simplify the harmonisation of legislation[2] and to strengthen the principle of mutual recognition[3]

1

2

---

[1] Cf. Case C-376/98, *Germany v Parliament and Council* (Opinion of AG Finnelly of 15 June 2000) para 62.

[2] Commission White Paper, *Completing the Internal Market*, COM(85) 310 final of 14 June 1985, para 61, 67 seq.

[3] Established by the ECJ in Case 120/78, *REWE v Bundesmonopolverwaltung für Branntwein* (ECJ 20 February 1979) para 14; for the wording and interpretation of the Commission see COM(85) 310 final, para 58. See also Blanke and Böttner (2020), para 115 et seq. with further references.

(→ Article 114 TFEU para 5), which were essentially implemented in the SEA of 1987. A new Article 100a TEEC was introduced (now Article 114 TFEU), which allowed for the approximation of laws even with a qualified majority in the Council. This new provision increasingly replaced the old Article 100 TEEC. The wording of the old Article 100, which later became Article 94 TEC, was first changed by the Lisbon Treaty. As in all other Treaty provisions, the term "common market" was replaced by "internal market". Furthermore, the reference "[w]ithout prejudice to Article 114…" was inserted. Finally, Article 114 (ex-Article 95 TEC) and Article 115 (ex-Article 94 TEC) switched places.

3   It should be noted that **Article 114 TFEU takes precedence** over Article 115 TFEU (→ Article 114 TFEU para 10). Due to the broad scope of application of Article 114 TFEU, Article 115 TFEU is of little importance in the approximation of laws for the realisation of the internal market. Only in those areas in which Article 114.2 TFEU excludes from its scope of application and for which no more specific provisions are mentioned in the Treaties that the Union legislator can and must have recourse to Article 115 TFEU for the approximation of laws and regulations. This is the case in particular with the **approximation of direct taxes**.[4] In fact, since the entry into force of the Lisbon Treaty, the Union legislator adopted a number of directives on minimum or common taxation[5] as well as rules on administrative cooperation in the field of taxation[6] and tax dispute resolution[7] or against tax avoidance.[8]

4   Harmonisation according to Article 114 or 115 TFEU is in principle the same.[9] The different wording (Article 114 TFEU mentions measures "which *have as their object* the establishment and functioning of the internal market", whereas Article 115 TFEU states that the harmonisation measures must "*directly affect* the establishment or functioning of the internal market") is without particular importance (→ Article 114 TFEU para 4). The **differing formal and procedural requirements** of Article 115 (→ para 9–10), on the other hand, are significant. However, since both provisions treat the issue of approximation of national laws and regulations with the aim of achieving the internal market, the case law of the ECJ on Article 114 TFEU can be applied *mutatis mutandis* to Article 115 TFEU.

---

[4] See e.g. Khan and Eisenhut, in Geiger et al. (2015), Article 115 TFEU para 2. An example of this application of Article 115 is Council Directive (EU) 2015/2060, O.J. L 301/1 (2015).

[5] Council Directive 2011/96/EU *on the common system of taxation applicable in the case of parent companies and subsidiaries of different Member States (recast)*, O.J. L 345/8 (2011); Council Directive (EU) 2022/2523 *on ensuring a global minimum level of taxation for multinational enterprise groups and large-scale domestic groups in the Union*, O.J. L 328/1 (2022).

[6] Council Directive 2011/16/EU *on administrative cooperation in the field of taxation*, O.J. L 64/1 (2011) (also based on Article 113 TFEU).

[7] Council Directive (EU) 2017/1852 *on tax dispute resolution mechanisms in the European Union*, O.J. L 265/1 (2017).

[8] Council Directive (EU) 2016/1164 *laying down rules against tax avoidance practices that directly affect the functioning of the internal market*, O.J. L 193/1 (2016).

[9] Tietje, in Grabitz et al. (2022), Artikel 115 AEUV para 5 (released in 2016).

2. Scope of Application

Approximation of laws is about **harmonising national provisions**, not about 5 creating a uniform European law (→ Article 114 TFEU para 19). This is underlined in Article 115 TFEU by the fact that the Union legislator may only use directives as instruments (→ para 9). However, the Union retains discretion as to the intensity of harmonisation and thus the MS' scope for implementation (→ Article 114 TFEU para 20 et seqq.). Directives can also contain very detailed specifications.

The prerequisite for harmonisation is a connection to the **internal market**. The 6 internal market is defined in Article 26.2 TFEU as "an area without internal frontiers in which the free movement of goods, persons, services and capital is ensured". Apart from a mere connection to the internal market, there must be an actual improvement through harmonisation (→ Article 114 TFEU para 30 et seqq.). An interpretation in the sense of a general internal market competence would violate the principle of conferral.[10] However, preventive harmonisation is possible if there is a "likely danger" that the MS will adopt national regulations that impair the internal market (→ Article 114 TFEU para 26).[11]

Although Article 115 TFEU, in contrast to Article 114 TFEU, does not mention 7 "**the objectives set out in Article 26**", these objectives consist precisely in the improvement of the internal market. It can therefore be assumed that this aspect must also be taken into account when applying Article 115 TFEU.[12] This means that the Union legislator must, on the one hand, subjectively want to bring about an improvement of the internal market in the approximation of laws. In order to verify this subjective element, the recitals and the explanatory memorandum of the legislative act must be consulted (→ Article 114 TFEU para 30). On the other hand, the measure must also objectively and measurably lead to an improvement in the internal market (→ Article 114 TFEU para 31).

Article 115 TFEU can be used for the approximation of **national laws, regula-** 8 **tions or administrative provisions** (→ Article 114 TFEU para 33). The (divergent) national rules must have a negative effect on or jeopardise ("preventive harmonisation"; → Article 114 TFEU para 26) the internal market.

3. Form and Procedure

Harmonisation measures according to Article 115 TFEU may be adopted only in 9 the form of a **directive**. Unlike in Article 114 TFEU, regulations are not permitted as harmonising acts. To a certain extent, this corresponds to the idea of harmonisation, which is about the adaptation of national legislation and not its substitution by

---

[10] Case C-376/98, *Germany v Parliament and Council* (ECJ 5 October 2000) para 83.
[11] See inter alia Case C-380/03, *Germany v Parliament and Council* (ECJ 12 December 2006) para 38.
[12] Cf. Tietje, in Grabitz et al. (2022), Artikel 115 AEUV para 25 (released in 2016).

directly applicable EU provisions. However, this does not mean that full harmonisation (→ Article 114 TFEU para 23) is not possible. Directives can also contain very detailed provisions that leave very little room for national implementation.

10 Directives based on Article 115 TFEU are adopted in accordance with a **special legislative procedure** by the Council, acting unanimously after consulting the EP. The Economic and Social Committee is also consulted in the procedure (Article 304(1) TFEU) and can give an opinion on the economic aspects of approximation. The Committee of the Regions is informed of the consultation and can give an opinion if specific regional interests are affected (Article 307(3) TFEU).

4. Derogations and Safeguard Clauses

11 In comparison to Article 114 TFEU, the provision of Article 115 TFEU is rather short and does not include express authorisation for the **maintaining or introduction of derogations by the MS** (→ Article 114 TFEU para 51 et seqq.). However, paragraphs 4 and 5 of Article 114 refer to harmonisation measures adopted "by the European Parliament and the Council, by the Council or by the Commission". Harmonisation measures under Article 114.1 TFEU are adopted in the ordinary legislative procedure and thus by Parliament and the Council. The reference to acts adopted "by the Council" is to be understood as referring to acts adopted under Article 115 TFEU (→ Article 114 TFEU para 52).[13]

12 Article 115 TFEU does not contain any express authorisation to include safeguard clauses in the harmonisation act (cf. Article 114.10 TFEU). It is rightly held, however, that this right exists independently of an explicit authorisation.[14] Accordingly, the **legislator's right to enact safeguard clauses** exists simply **by virtue of its legislative competence**. The Council or the European Parliament in the legislative procedure or the Commission in its proposal can include safeguard clauses in the harmonisation measure, without requiring any further authorisation. This corresponds to the Council's practice on Article 115 (or Article 100 TEEC/ Article 94 TEC).[15] The application of the safeguard clauses does not differ from Article 114.10 TFEU (→ Article 114 TFEU para 77 et seqq.).

List of Cases

ECJ

ECJ 20.02.1979, 120/78, *REWE v Bundesmonopolverwaltung für Branntwein*, ECLI:EU:C:1979:42 [cit. in para 2]

---

[13] Van Rijn (2016), p. 258.
[14] Cf. Case C-359/92, *Germany v Council* (Opinion of AG Jacobs 8 June 1994) para 20.
[15] Ehlermann (1987), p. 398 seq.

ECJ 08.06.1994, C-359/92, Opinion of AG Jacobs, *Germany v Council*, ECLI:EU:C:1994:231 [cit. in para 11]

ECJ 15.06.2000, C-376/98, Opinion of AG Finnelly, *Germany v Parliament and Council*, ECLI:EU:C:2000:324 [cit. in para 1]

ECJ 05.10.2000, C-376/98, *Germany v Parliament and Council*, ECLI:EU:C:2000:544 [cit. in para 6]

ECJ 12.12.2006, C-380/03, *Germany v Parliament and Council*, ECLI:EU:C:2006:772 [cit. in para 6]

References

Blanke, H.-J., & Böttner, R. (2020). § 13: Binnenmarkt, Rechtsangleichung, Grundfreiheiten. In M. Niedobitek (Ed.), *Europarecht – Grundlagen und Politiken der Union* (pp. 887–1114). DeGruyter.

Ehlermann, C.-D. (1987). The internal market following the Single European Act. *Common Market Law Review, 24*(3), 361–409.

Geiger, R., Khan, D.-E., & Kotzur, M. (Eds.). (2015). *European Union Treaties*. C.H. Beck.

Grabitz, E., Hilf, M., & Nettesheim, M. (Eds.). (2022). *Das Recht der Europäischen Union: EUV/AEUV. Commentary, looseleaf*. C.H. Beck.

Van Rijn, T. (2016). Dérogations en matière d'harmonisation de législation. In F. Picod (Ed.), *Le principe majoritaire en droit de l'Union européenne* (pp. 255–269). Bruylant.

Article 116 [Distortion of Competition]

(ex-Article 96 TEC)

Where the Commission[7] finds that a difference[8] between the provisions[9–11] laid down by law, regulation or administrative action in Member States is distorting[12–13] the conditions of competition in the internal market and that the resultant distortion needs to be eliminated,[14–15] it shall consult[16–17] the Member States concerned.[18]

If such consultation does not result in an agreement eliminating the distortion in question,[19–20] the European, Parliament and the Council, acting in accordance with the ordinary legislative procedure, shall issue the necessary directives.[21–29] Any other appropriate measures provided for in the Treaties may be adopted.[30–32]

Contents

1. Article 116 TFEU in the Global Context of the Law Approximation Policy 1
2. Elimination of Distortion: Two Possible Phases of the Union's Response 5
   2.1. Phase One: Consultation, Leading to an Agreement 7
      2.1.1. Role of the Commission 7
      2.1.2. Three Conditions for the Union's Action 8
      2.1.3. Procedure of Consultation 16
      2.1.4. Agreement Eliminating the Distortion 19
   2.2. Phase Two: Legislative Action of the Union 21
      2.2.1. Procedure for the Adoption of the "Necessary Directives" 22
      2.2.2. Why Have the Directives Provided for in Article 116 TFEU Still Not Been "Necessary"? 25
3. Residual Mechanism of "Other Appropriate Measures" 30
4. Partial Derogation of Article 116 TFEU Introduced by Article 117.2 TFEU 33

List of Cases
References

1. Article 116 TFEU in the Global Context of the Law Approximation Policy

The existence of divergent national legislation in the EU MS is neither forbidden *per se* nor necessarily undesirable. This is a direct consequence of the **principle of conferral**, which governs "the limits of Union competences" (sentence 1 of Article 5.1 TEU). Moreover, the principle of conferral is significantly reinforced by the Lisbon Treaty for at least two reasons: on the one hand, it is—for the first time—mentioned *expressis verbis* by Article 5.1 TEU, while, on the other, the provision of Article 5.2 TEU goes even further than the TEC in the definition of its content. Whereas the Community was allowed to "act within the limits of the

1

powers conferred upon it by this Treaty" (ex-Article 5.2 sentence 1 TEC), the Union can "act *only* within the limits of the competences conferred upon it by the Member States in the Treaties" (Article 5.2 sentence 1 TEU).[1] Even if it may seem that this semantic reinforcement is devoid of practical consequences, it represents an undeniable tendency,[2] supporting the assumption of competence in favour of the MS established by Article 4.1 TEU. The strengthening of the principle of conferral may also be seen as a counterpart of an undeniable extension of EU competences, given that "the overt integration of the Lisbon Treaty [...] has also been flanked with covert integration".[3] It is, however, clear that striking a balance between Union's and national legal orders requires permanent efforts and "should not rely upon simple casuistic conflict avoiding".[4]

2 Divergent national legislation in a field covered by an exclusive EU competence, such as the establishment of competition rules necessary for the functioning of the internal market (Article 3.1 point (b) TFEU), is forbidden and would represent an open threat to the Union's legal order. On the other hand, the differences between the MS' provisions in the field covered by a shared competence (Article 4 TFEU), such as the internal market (Article 4.2 point (a) and Article 26 TFEU), are commonly undesirable and subject to law approximation measures. Those measures taken together can also be seen "as a genuine policy"[5] of a cross-cutting nature since the **provisions conferring competence to approximate national provisions** can be found in the chapter of the TFEU dedicated to the approximation of laws (Articles 114 et seqq. TFEU) and also in a specific provision dedicated to a common policy, "which may include directly or indirectly the use of law approximation measures, when objectives defined by these policies make it necessary".[6]

3 The overall objective of Article 116 TFEU is to introduce the rules devised to tackle the problem of divergent national legal, regulatory or administrative provisions causing the distortion of the conditions of competition in the internal market. Consequently, it is important to underline the difference[7] between the **unified legislation on competition**[8] (exclusive EU competence) and the **national**

---

[1] Emphasis added.

[2] For a more extensive overview of the consequences of the changing structure of European law on national constitutional systems and on their relations with the Union's legal order, see Schütze (2009), pp. 129–188.

[3] De Bièvre and Bursens (2016), p. 9.

[4] Ćemalović (2021), p. 72.

[5] Ćemalović (2015), p. 245.

[6] Michel (2003), pp. 20–21.

[7] E.g. in Case C-174/02, *Streekgewest* (ECJ 13 January 2005) para 24, where the Court's reasoning is particularly explicit: "It must be observed [...] that the Treaty makes a clear distinction between, on the one hand, the regime [...] concerning State aid and, on the other, that [...] concerning the distortions which arise from differences between the laws, regulations or administrative provisions of the Member States". → see also para 9.

[8] The notion of "competition" is here to be taken in the broader sense, in order to include the State aid; see Case C-174/02, *Streekgewest* (ECJ 13 January 2005) para 24.

legislation potentially distorting competition (shared competence, subject to harmonisation[9] measures). As the ECJ has clearly pointed out in its early case *IGAV v ENCC*, "apart from the rules on competition applicable to undertakings [...] the Treaty includes various provisions relating to **infringements of the normal functioning of the competition system** by actions on the part of the States. This in particular is the purpose of [...] Articles 101 and 102 [now Articles 116 and 117 TFEU] on distortions resulting from provisions of public law capable of distorting competitive conditions on the Common Market".[10] Therefore, *ratione materiae*, the jurisprudence of the ECJ and the legal doctrine in the field of competition law can be applied to Article 116 TFEU nothing but residually, only when it comes to the definition of the notion of "distortion of the conditions of competition" (→ para 14).

Finally, the place of Article 116 TFEU in the global context of the law approximation policy should also be defined on the basis of its relations with other provisions belonging to the same chapter of the TFEU. A systematic-teleological method of interpretation shows that Articles 114 and 115 TFEU, on the one hand, and Articles 116–118 TFEU, on the other, are clearly in a rule-exception relationship for at least two reasons: first, the former can be used by the EU as a legal ground for the adoption of goal-driven[11] approximation measures aiming to **establish or ensure the functioning of the internal market** (→ Article 114 TFEU para 24 et seqq.) or can be invoked preventively in order to eliminate the disparities of national provisions in MS that **affect the establishment or functioning of the internal market** (→ Article 115 TFEU para 4), while the latter concerns only the distortion of competition (Articles 116 and 117 TFEU) or the establishment of measures in order to provide uniform protection of intellectual property rights throughout the Union (→ Article 118 TFEU para 18 et seqq.); second, the specific two-phased procedure of Article 116 TFEU indicates that the approximation *stricto sensu* may only occur in the absence of an agreement eliminating the distortion of competition, while the goal-driven and preventive approximation of Articles 114 and 115 TFEU have the approximation of laws as their exclusive objective. **4**

2. Elimination of Distortion: Two Possible Phases of the Union's Response

Divergent national legislation, as such, cannot represent a valid legal ground for the adoption of approximation measures pursuant to Article 116 TFEU. The Union's action is legitimate only if a difference between national (legal, regulatory or administrative) provisions causes the distortion of the conditions of competition **5**

---

[9] For the differences between the notions of harmonisation and approximation, see Ćemalović (2015), pp. 242–244.
[10] Case 94/74, *IGAV v ENCC* (ECJ 18 June 1975) para 33–34.
[11] See Lohse (2011), p. 295; Ćemalović (2015), p. 247; Case C-217/04, *United Kingdom v Parliament and Council* (Opinion of AG Kokott of 22 September 2005) para 24.

in the internal market. Moreover, the EU can legislate only if a prior consultation did not result in an agreement eliminating the distortion in question. Consequently, the notion of the **Union's action** should be understood as a broader concept, comprising the **phase of consultation** (→ para 16–20) and the **phase of legislative action** (→ para 21–24). Therefore, an EU directive harmonising national legislation may be issued only if the four following conditions are met:

(1) The existence of a difference (→ para 8) between the provisions in MS observed by the Commission (→ para 7)
(2) The distortive effect of such a provision on the condition of competition in the internal market (→ para 12–13)
(3) The need to eliminate such a distortion (→ para 14–15)
(4) The absence of an agreement eliminating the distortion (→ para 19–20)

6   Since the adoption of the E(E)C Treaty, Article 116 TFEU (initially Article 101 TEEC, then Article 96 TEC in the consolidated version) has globally[12] remained unaffected. The only substantial change concerns the **majority necessary for the adoption of directives** (→ para 23) bringing about the law approximation in the case of distortion of the conditions of competition.

2.1. Phase One: Consultation, Leading to an Agreement

2.1.1. Role of the Commission

7   The multifaceted and pivotal role of the European Commission in the enforcement of the EU rules on competition (Articles 101 and 105 TFEU)—despite its relative weakening after the adoption of **Regulation** 1/2003[13]—is beyond any doubt. In such a context, the Commission's investigative prerogatives in the case of suspected infringement of the principles "laid down in Articles 101 and 102" (Article 105.1 sentence 1 TFEU) provide an outstanding example. On the other hand, in the global context of the law approximation policy (→ para 1–4), the Commission's main role is substantially different, and it stems from its "near monopoly of legislative initiative".[14] In comparison with the general rules of goal-driven and preventive law approximation, the specificity of the **Commission's prerogatives related to law approximation** in the case of distortion of the

---

[12] The minor differences in the wording of the initial Article 101 TEEC and Article 96 TEC (consolidated version) are generally due to the fact that the Treaty of Rome was not signed in the English language but was translated into English from the languages of six initial contracting parties; see Rossini (1998), pp. 191–199.

[13] Council Regulation (EC) No 1/2003 *on the implementation of the rules on competition laid down in Articles 81 and 82 of the Treaty*, O.J L 1/1 (2003). For an extensive overview of the Commission's role in the network of competition authorities, known as the "European Competition Network", see Rodger and MacCulloch (2009), pp. 36–42.

[14] Jacqué (2016), p. 33.

conditions of competition unequivocally appears already in the first words of Article 116 TFEU. The role of the Commission is much closer here to its investigative prerogatives in the field of competition than to its role as an institution entitled to propose EU legal acts.[15] Therefore, even if Article 116 TFEU belongs to the chapter dedicated to law approximation, its inextricable connection to the rules on competition (→ para 3) has left an important mark. Whereas in the latter the Commission is competent "to investigate cases of suspected infringement" (Article 105.1 sentence 2 TFEU) and, if there has been an infringement, to "propose appropriate measures to bring it to an end" (Article 105.1 sentence 2 TFEU), in the former, if the national provisions are distorting the conditions of competition, the Commission is entitled to establish this fact ("Commission finds") and to independently assess whether this distortion "needs to be eliminated". Therefore, only an unacceptable difference between the national provisions—a difference which, in a regular, non-distortive context for the conditions of competition would not require any approximation measure on the EU level—triggers the Commission's action. It is, therefore, necessary to focus on the nature of the MS' legislative intervention that is likely to represent a threat to the "free play of competition"[16] in the internal market.

2.1.2. Three Conditions for the Union's Action

Apart from indicating that a national provision introducing a difference that causes the distortion of free competition can be "laid down by law, regulation or administrative action", the provision of Article 116 TFEU does not specify neither the nature of the national provision in question nor the particularities of "a difference" between the national legal solutions. It is important to underline that a national provision in itself should not be considered a genuine origin of distortion. It is the difference between two or more national provisions—potentially having certain cross-border effects and, consequently, **actually distorting** (→ para 12) **the conditions of competition** in the internal market—that gives rise to the action of the Union. However, this is still not enough; the third element that actually triggers the Union's action is **a need for the elimination** (→ paras 13–14) of such a distortion. Therefore, the focus will first be on the nature of national provisions distorting the conditions of competition (→ para 9 et seqq.), before examining the existence of an actual distortion (→ para 12) and the need for its elimination (→ para 14). 8

Nature of National Provisions

Given that the Treaty does not provide any explicit specification concerning the nature of national laws, regulations or administrative provisions whose difference 9

---

[15] This conclusion has recently been indirectly corroborated by the General Court, see Case T-508/19, *Mead Johnson Nutrition (Asia Pacific) and Others v Commission* (GC 6 April 2022) para 73.

[16] Case 22/71, *Béguelin Import Co. v S.A.G.L. Import Export* (ECJ 25 November 1971) para 16.

from one MS to another is distorting the conditions of competition in the internal market, nothing opposes the conclusion that the notion "provision" is here to be understood in the broadest possible sense. The Court's interpretation has not significantly contributed to the detection of possible types or forms of national normative activities that might trigger the application of the mechanism of Article 116 TFEU. In *IGAV v ENCC*, the Court gave a general specification according to which ex-Articles 101 and 102 TEEC (now Articles 116 and 117 TFEU, respectively) are applicable "on distortions resulting from provisions of *public law* capable of distorting competitive conditions on the Common Market".[17] However, certain categories of national legislation belonging to public law have a "natural" predisposition to represent a **threat to the free competition**; this is clearly the case of **tax provisions**, which are "in particular"[18] likely to cause distortions. In this specific case, the reasoning of the Court explicitly relies on the distinction between the two sets of provisions of the TFEU (Articles 107–109 TFEU on the one hand and Articles 116–117 TFEU on the other) and includes a direct mention of Articles 116 and 117 TFEU.

10   In order to define which type of national provisions can potentially be detrimental to competition, the analysis of the ECJ's case law has to go beyond the limits of the judicial interpretation of the rules laid down in Article 116 TFEU. In other words, the Court's interpretation of the secondary legislation adopted in the context of a **goal-driven approximation** (→ para 4 and 24) could also be valuable for the detection of possible national provisions containing undesirable disparities. The case of Directive 2014/40/EU[19]—and of the case law it gave rise to—provides a sound example of wider applicability. Notwithstanding the fact that this Directive was adopted on the basis of, among others, Article 114 TFEU, its jurisprudential analysis has offered some insights into competition-related "national laws and practices", whose disparities, "in the absence of measures adopted at Union level [...] are likely to increase over the coming years".[20] The above-mentioned disparities clearly "present an obstacle to the free movement of goods and the freedom to provide services", but they also "create an appreciable risk of distortion of competition".[21] It is particularly important to underline the subtle distinction in the Court's reasoning: while the disparities between national provisions on advertising and sponsorship undoubtedly *present an obstacle* to the free movement of goods and the freedom to provide services, there is only an **appreciable risk of distortion of competition**. The absence of an actual distortion (→ para 12) could not justify the application of the mechanism of Article 116 TFEU, but any rise in the disparities

---

[17] Case 94/74, *IGAV v ENCC* (ECJ 18 June 1975) para 33-34 (emphasis added).

[18] Case T-533/10, *DTS Distribuidora de Televisión Digital, SA v Commission* (GC 11 July 2014) para 48; Case C-174/02, *Streekgewest* (ECJ 13 January 2005) para 24.

[19] Parliament/Council Directive 2014/40/EU *on the approximation of the laws, regulations and administrative provisions of the Member States concerning the manufacture, presentation and sale of tobacco and related products* O.J. L 127/1 (2014).

[20] Case C-477/14, *Pillbox 38* (ECJ 4 May 2016) para 112.

[21] Case C-477/14, *Pillbox 38* (ECJ 4 May 2016) para 112.

over time might transform an appreciable risk into an actual distortion of competition.

Finally, even a total absence of action on the part of one or several States—in the case of the participation of all other MS in certain measures adopted in the context of a Union policy *unrelated to the internal market*—may lead to a **difference between national provisions potentially distorting the conditions of competition** in the internal market. This is clearly the case of Treaty provisions concerning the area of freedom, security and justice (AFSJ), given that Declaration No. 26 on non-participation by an MS in a measure based on Title V of Part Three of the TFEU annexed to the Treaty specifies that any MS "may ask the Commission to examine the situation on the basis of Article 116" (→ para 7). Notwithstanding the fact that, *prima facie*, the seemingly narrow formulation of Article 116 TFEU concerns only the distortions caused by *national lawmaking activities* ("provisions laid down by law, regulation or administrative action"), from the perspective of a MS, a difference between its legislation and provisions existing in other States may distort the conditions of competition even if it did not legislate.

11

Existence of an Actual Distortion

Unlike in the field of competition law *stricto sensu*[22] (→ para 9)—for which the stable[23] and long-lasting case law has established that when "certain types of coordination between undertakings reveal a sufficient degree of harm to competition that it may be found that there is no need to examine their effects"[24]—the action at the Union level pursuant to Article 116 TFEU can be triggered only if the distortion is actual. In other words, a sufficient degree of harm to competition, foreseeable with a sufficient degree of probability,[25] is already enough to consider that a concerted practice of undertakings, by its object,[26] falls under the prohibition of Article 101 TFEU. On the other hand, a difference between two or more MS' national provisions must be the cause of a real, **actually existing distortion**, in

12

---

[22] The situation is similar in state aid law; see Joined Cases C-71/09 P, C-73/09 P and C-76/09 P, *Comitato 'Venezia vuole vivere' and Others v Commission* (ECJ 9 June 2011) para 134: "the Commission is not required to establish the existence of a real impact of the aid on trade between Member States and *an actual distortion of competition*, but is required only to examine whether that aid *is capable of affecting such trade and distorting competition*" (emphasis added).

[23] The same line of the Court's reasoning can be traced back to its judgment in Case 56/65, *LTM* (ECJ 30 June 1966).

[24] Case C-67/13 P, *CB v Commission* (ECJ 11 September 2014) para 49.

[25] E.g. in Case 56/65, *LTM* (ECJ 30 June 1966) para 249.

[26] It is established in the case law that "an anti-competitive *object* and anti-competitive *effects* constitute not cumulative but alternative conditions in determining whether a practice falls within the prohibition in Article 81(1) EC", which means that "it is necessary, first, to consider the precise purpose of the concerted practice, in the economic context in which it is to be pursued. Where, however, an analysis of the terms of the concerted practice does not reveal the effect on competition to be sufficiently deleterious, its consequences should then be considered", Case C-8/08, *T-Mobile Netherlands and others* (ECJ 4 June 2009) para 28 (emphasis added).

order to bring into play the mechanism of Article 116 TFEU. The Commission should, therefore, find that a discrepancy "by actions on the part of the States"[27] has had an actual effect "on the competition system"[28] established by the Treaty.

13   Interestingly, what at first glance may appear as a mere nuance of judicial interpretation actually is a cornerstone of the Court's understanding of an important part of the Union's legal order. There are, on the one hand, rules on competition applicable to undertakings, which constitute the narrow notion of the EU competition law. On the other hand, **various national normative activities** can cause infringements on the normal functioning of a more general set of provisions, which could be covered by a broader notion of "competition system" in the internal market. Consequently, some specific rules, like in the case concerning the existence of an actual distortion, may legitimately vary from one to another.

Need for the Elimination of a Distortion

14   As the wording of Article 116.1 TFEU implicitly indicates, it is conceivable that a difference between national provisions effectively distorting competition is still not of such a scope and/or importance that it requires to be eliminated[29] by an action on the Union level. It is in this particular requirement that the difference fully appears between the rules on competition *stricto sensu* and the rules related to law approximation in the case of distortion of the conditions of competition (→ para 3). More precisely, "*all* agreements between undertakings [. . .] which *have as their object or effect* the prevention, restriction or distortion of competition within the internal market" are prohibited by Article 101 TFEU. There is absolutely no requirement related to the **need for the elimination of distortion**, given that every agreement between undertakings—harming competition by its very object or by the appreciable extent of its effects—is *ipso facto* considered to be incompatible with the internal market. In other words, as underlined in *Allianz Hungária Biztosító*, where "the analysis of the content of the agreement does not reveal a sufficient degree of harm to competition, the effects of the agreement should then be considered and, for it to be caught by the prohibition, it is necessary to find that factors are present which show *that competition has in fact been prevented, restricted or distorted* to an appreciable extent".[30] On the other hand, in order to trigger the mechanism of Article 116 TFEU—on top of the actual ("in fact") prevention, restriction or distortion of competition—it is also necessary that the distortion already observed is considered to be of such a nature that it needs to be eliminated. Consequently, it is not only the **extent of a distortion** that is decisive in

---

[27] Case 94/74, *IGAV v ENCC* (ECJ 18 June 1975) para 33–34.

[28] Case 94/74, *IGAV v ENCC* (ECJ 18 June 1975) para 33–34.

[29] For an analysis of the elimination of distortion in one market and in several markets, see Evans (1996), pp. 33–34.

[30] Case C-32/11, *Allianz Hungária Biztosító and others* (ECJ 14 March 2013) para 34 (emphasis added).

the Commission's assessment but, more generally, its need for elimination, which should also include a dynamic perspective of certain disparities between the national provisions that are likely to appear or increase over the years.[31]

While the assessment of an existing agreement (and of its effects) potentially distorting competition is carried out only by taking into account the actual coordination/concertation between undertakings, the appreciation of the need for the elimination of distortion in the context of Article 116 TFEU has to take into consideration the comparative and progressive dimension of national provisions distorting competition. Unlike it is the case of the threshold of "appreciable extent" of the effects of distortion, the notion of the need for the elimination of distortion in the context of law approximation still awaits further judicial clarification. However, the case law interpreting Article 101 TFEU may—to some extent—be applied, *mutatis mutandis*, to distortions caused by lawmaking activities on the part of the MS in the context of Article 116 TFEU. While interpreting Article 101 TFEU, the Court has established the difference between **the object and the effect of a concerted practice**, underlining that "there is no need to consider the effects of a concerted practice where its anti-competitive object is established".[32] Even if it is difficult to compare a concerted practice of economic operators, on the one hand, and a difference between provisions in different MS, on the other, it is evident that they both might have a detrimental effect to competition. If it is clear that the distortion of competition triggering law approximation measures has, firstly, to be effective (→ para 12) and, secondly, to be such that it has to be eliminated (→ para 14), there is no specification whatsoever concerning the object of national legislation. Given that, in its interpretation of Article 101 TFEU, the Court emphasised that the analysis of concerted practices having an anti-competitive object primarily requires "to consider the precise *purpose* of the concerted practice, in the *economic context* in which it is to be pursued",[33] the systematic interpretation of Article 116 TFEU would suggest a **purposive and economic analysis** of the differences between national legislation. Even if it is reasonable to assume that an MS would not deliberately adopt legislation distorting competition, it seems appropriate to suggest a subject-matter approach in the analysis of national provisions whose differences may cause a distortion that requires elimination. The recent case law implies a conclusion that the Court has made some steps in this direction, singling out national tax legislation (→ para 9) as particularly likely to cause distortions.

2.1.3. Procedure of Consultation

Notwithstanding the fact that Article 116 TFEU belongs to the chapter dedicated to law approximation, legislative action by the EU is far from being its primary

---

[31] E.g. in Case C-477/14, *Pillbox 38* (ECJ 4 May 2016) para 43.
[32] Case C-8/08, *T-Mobile Netherlands and others* (ECJ 4 June 2009) para 30 (emphasis added).
[33] Case C-8/08, *T-Mobile Netherlands and others* (ECJ 4 June 2009) para 28 (emphasis added).

objective. On the contrary, the main goal of the Union's action is the elimination of the distortion of the conditions of competition in the internal market, while the principal tool to achieve this elimination is **consultation with the MS**. In addition, the legislative action phase (phase two), leading to the adoption of a directive harmonising[34] national legislation, can take place only if prior consultation (phase one) has not resulted in an agreement putting an end to the distortion of competition. In other words, phase two can occur *only after* phase one and *only if* it was unsuccessful. The conditions to be fulfilled in order to launch the phase of consultation with the MS are globally set by Article 116.1 TFEU (→ paras 8–15). It is, nonetheless, the Commission's exclusive competence to determine whether the procedure of consultation—potentially leading to the Union's legal action—will be engaged.

17 Unlike in the case of some other provisions of the TFEU (→ Article 126 TFEU paras 29–31), there is no protocol or declaration annexed to the Treaty setting out the provisions relating to the implementation of the procedure, the framework of which is vaguely defined by Article 116 TFEU. While it is indubitable that the Commission conducts the procedure of consultation, the involvement of the MS is far from being clear, apart from their passive role of the parties that should be consulted. However, some clarifications regarding this issue are made by a provision unexpectedly unrelated to either competition law *stricto sensu* or the rules on law approximation. In the "Declaration on non-participation by a Member State in a measure based on Title V of Part Three of the TFEU annexed to the Treaty" (Annex 26), it is provided that if an MS opts not to participate in a measure based on the Treaty provision concerning the AFSJ (Articles 67–89 TFEU), "the Council will hold a full discussion on the possible implications and effects of that Member State's non-participation in the measure". It is in the second paragraph of the Declaration where its cross-cutting nature appears, given that it introduces a provision the applicability of which is much wider than its title would appear to suggest. It stipulates that "in addition, any Member State may ask the Commission to examine the situation on the basis of Article 116 [TFEU]". The systematic-teleological interpretation of this provision allows three conclusions related to the approximation of laws in the case of distortion of the conditions of competition. First, it corroborates the assertion that even an MS's passive behaviour might have a detrimental effect on competition (→ para 11) because it is **a difference between national provisions**—and not those national provisions *as such*—that is potentially harmful. Second, it shows that a passive or active behaviour of an MS in the Union's policy unrelated to the internal market—such as the one on border checks, asylum and immigration; on judicial cooperation in civil or criminal matters; or on police cooperation—may also be relevant for "the competition system"[35] established on the Union level (→ paras 3 and 12). Third, it offers valuable clarifications

---

[34] For differences between the notions of harmonisation and approximation, see Ćemalović (2015), pp. 242–244; for specificities of law harmonisation in EU candidate countries and its possible interconnections with positive and negative conditionality, see Ćemalović (2020), pp. 288–289.

[35] Case 94/74, *IGAV v ENCC* (ECJ 18 June 1975) para 33–34.

concerning the position of Member States in the procedure of consultation provided for in Article 116 TFEU. Here, the focus will be put on the third aspect.

The specificity of the Commission's prerogatives related to law approximation in the case of distortion of the conditions of competition has been already discussed (→ para 7). The wording of Article 116 TFEU is clear when it comes to the fact that the Commission conducts **the procedure of consultation** and determines whether it will be engaged. However, the issue of the scope of consultation remains unresolved, given that Article 116 TFEU only vaguely defines that the Commission is entitled to consult the MS "concerned". Taken *lato sensu*, this provision could be interpreted in such a way to allow the widest possible consultation, given that, at least theoretically, every distortion that includes at least two MS is potentially detrimental to competition on the entire internal market. This conclusion is corroborated by a combined reading of Articles 116 TFEU and 117.2 TFEU; given that the provisions of Article 116 TFEU shall not apply "if the Member State which has ignored the recommendation of the Commission causes distortion detrimental only to itself" (→ Article 117 TFEU para 18), it is, *a contrario*, allowed to conclude that every distortion of competition with a cross-border effect might trigger the procedure of consultation, which potentially involves all MS. What is more, the interpretation of paragraph 2 of Declaration No. 26 (→ para 17) validates this conclusion. If, in the context of measures based on Title V of Part Three of the TFEU, "*any Member State* may ask the Commission to examine the situation on the basis of Article 116 [TFEU]",[36] it is *a fortiori* the case for a "regular" application of Article 116 TFEU. The differences arising from the non-participation of an MS in a measure related to the AFSJ are certainly not more likely to distort the conditions of competition than the differences in national legislation concerning an issue related to the internal market.

2.1.4. Agreement Eliminating the Distortion

Neither the Treaties nor the Court's case law provided more details concerning the parties, the content, the structure and **the procedure for the adoption of an agreement eliminating the distortion of competition** in the internal market caused by a difference in the national provisions of the MS. More generally, the fact that the mechanism of Article 116 TFEU is used rarely,[37] if at all,[38] is very

---

[36] Emphasis added.

[37] Some authors underline that Articles 116 and 117 TFEU have "rarely been used", see Jones and Sufrin (2011), p. 114. On the other hand, in some more recent studies, other authors consider that "the Commission does not use Articles 116 and 117 TFEU to tackle harmful tax competition", see Wattel (2016), p. 71. The European Parliament's Resolution (2015/2066 (INI)) of 25 November 2015 seems to corroborate the second opinion.

[38] E.g. Helminen (2011), referring to Article 116 TFEU, concluded that „in practice, directives on direct taxes on a majority decision do not exist", while "the possibility of a majority directive [...] has been discussed, for example, in connection with the preparation of the common consolidated tax base for the EU Member States", p. 20.

clearly pointed out in the EP's Resolution of 25 November 2015 *on tax rulings and other measures similar in nature or effect*.[39] Paragraph 172 of this Resolution "calls on the Commission not to refrain from making use, where appropriate, of Article 116 TFEU", given that "unless the procedure laid down [in it] is used, Treaty change would be required to change the unanimity requirement in matters of direct taxation".[40] It is clear that the formulation "making use of Article 116 TFEU" includes not only the adoption of directives but, especially and above all, the consultation procedure (→ paras 16–18) leading to the agreement eliminating the distortion.

20   A systematic and teleological interpretation of the two paragraphs of Article 116 TFEU can only lead to the conclusion that the **parties to the agreement** eliminating the distortion of competition are the Commission and the very same "Member States concerned" mentioned in paragraph 1 *in fine*, with whom the consultation was conducted. The **content of the agreement** should include the mention of necessary changes to the provisions "laid down by law, regulation or administrative action" which every concerned MS accepts to carry out. When it comes to the **procedure for the adoption** of the agreement, it is undoubted that all concerned (→ para 18) MS should unanimously agree upon the concrete changes in their respective internal provisions that would bring an end to the distortion. This conclusion is corroborated by the fact that the adoption of the directives provided for in Article 116.2 TFEU requires a qualified majority in the Council. If there is no unanimous agreement in the context of the consultation procedure, legislative action on the Union level can take place without the unanimity requirement.

2.2. Phase Two: Legislative Action of the Union

21   The adoption of the directives that would approximate national legislation in order to eliminate the distortion of competition, as has already been discussed elsewhere (→ para 5 and 16), is far from being the main objective of Article 116 TFEU. Apart from the fact that **the EU can legislate only in the absence of an agreement eliminating the distortion**, even the internal structure of Article 116 TFEU indicates that the adoption of a directive (second paragraph) can take place only if the procedure of consultation between the Commission and the concerned MS (first paragraph) did not result in an agreement. In the following discussion, the focus will first be on the procedure for the adoption of a directive pursuant to Article 116 TFEU (→ paras 22–24), before turning to the question of the possible reasons for the absence of the Union's legislative action (→ paras 25–29).

---

[39] European Parliament Resolution 2015/2066 (INI) of 25 November 2015 on tax rulings and other measures similar in nature or effect, P8_TA(2015)0408.
[40] European Parliament Resolution 2015/2066 (INI), Recital F *in fine*.

Article 116. [Distortion of Competition]

2.2.1. Procedure for the Adoption of the "Necessary Directives"

From 1957, the only substantial change that Article 116 TFEU (initially Article 101 TEEC, then Article 96 EC) has undergone (→ para 6) concerns the procedure and the majority necessary for the adoption of the directives approximating national provisions in the case of distortion of the conditions of competition. Article 101 TEEC provided that if the consultation procedure fails, "the Council, acting during the first stage by means of a unanimous vote and subsequently by means of a qualified majority vote on a proposal of the Commission, shall issue the directives". This two-stage procedure, first requiring unanimity and then a qualified majority, corroborates the conclusion (→ para 20) that the overall dynamics of the two paragraphs of Article 116 TFEU (both from a historical and a positive legal perspective) goes **from unanimous** (now necessary only for the conclusion of an agreement eliminating the distortion) **to decision-making based on qualified majority**. In other words, the initial version of this article showed the intention of the contracting parties to search for a consensus both for the conclusion of an interstate agreement and for the first stage of the Community's legislative action.

Apart from the fact that a new article was introduced (→ Article 118 TFEU para 2 et seqq.), the adoption of the Lisbon Treaty has not made any significant changes regarding the pre-existing substantive provisions[41] conferring competence for law approximation. Articles 94–97 EC became Articles 114–117 TFEU, while the EP became co-legislator with the Council for the majority[42] of legislative actions based on the provisions of the chapter entitled "Approximation of laws". It is outside the scope of this entry to provide a comprehensive commentary on the differences between ordinary and special legislative procedures (→ Article 289 TFEU). However, a **comparative analysis of the procedures** for the adoption of directives under Articles 114, 115 and 116 TFEU can be valuable for a better understanding of the specificity of law approximation in the case of distortion of the conditions of competition.

If a consultation procedure, as an obligatory preliminary phase (→ paras 16–18), did not result in an agreement eliminating the distortion (→ para 19 and 20), "the necessary directives" under Article 116 TFEU can be issued in accordance with the ordinary legislative procedure. The same procedure is also provided for in the process of **goal-driven approximation**, for the adoption of "the measures for the approximation of the provisions laid down by law, regulation or administrative action in Member States which *have as their object* the establishment and functioning of the internal market" (Article 114.1 sentence 1 (*in fine*) TFEU).[43] On the other

---

[41] Ćemalović (2015), p. 248 et seqq.

[42] The only exceptions are the procedure of preventive approximation (→ Article 115 TFEU para 6 and 8) and the procedure for language arrangements for the European intellectual property rights (→ Article 118 TFEU para 49 et seqq.); preventive approximation is to be analysed in relation to the one designated as goal driven (→ para 4).

[43] Emphasis added.

hand, the directives adopted in the context of preventive approximation[44] (→ Article 115 TFEU para 6 and 8), whose objective is to approximate "such laws, regulations or administrative provisions of the Member States *as directly affect* the establishment or functioning of the internal market", are issued by the Council, acting unanimously in accordance with a special legislative procedure and after consulting the EP and the Economic and Social Committee (ESC) (Article 115 TFEU).[45] Regardless of the question—which will be discussed further on (→ paras 25–29)—of the actual use of the mechanisms of Articles 114 and 115 TFEU, on the one hand, and Article 116 TFEU, on the other, for the adoption of various law-approximation directives, it is noteworthy that Article 116 TFEU has the narrowest scope of all three provisions. While the former can be invoked in order to approximate *all national provisions whose finality* (Article 114 TFEU) *or effect* (Article 115 TFEU) is in connection with "the establishment and functioning of the internal market", the latter can serve as a legal basis for the adoption of a directive *only if national provisions are effectively distorting the conditions of competition* in the internal market and only if the above distortion was not eliminated before the adoption of a directive. The fact that Articles 116 and 114 TFEU require the same (ordinary) legislative procedure should not obfuscate the undeniable difference in their scopes.

2.2.2. Why Have the Directives Provided for in Article 116 TFEU Still Not Been "Necessary"?

25 The approximation of laws of the MS is one of the Union's policies the impact of which on the good functioning of the internal market cannot be overestimated. Due to the changes it has introduced and by virtue of its new systematisation of the "categories and areas of Union competence" (Title I), the TFEU does not mention *expressis verbis* the role of law approximation for the functioning of the internal market. On the other hand, ex-Article 3.1 (h) EC, in order to provide the Community with the necessary competences and procedures to carry out its mission, specified that "the activities of the Community shall include [...] the approximation of the laws of Member States to the extent required for the functioning of the common market". Nevertheless, the scope of Article 116 TFEU and, respectively, Articles 114 and 115 TFEU, has globally remained unchanged by the adoption of the Lisbon Treaty, as is the case concerning the importance of law approximation for the **establishment and functioning of the internal market**. Another observation that is equally valid for the period before and after December 2009 is the one concerning the actual use of Article 116 TFEU (ex-Article 96 EC) for the legislative action of the Union: there are no directives adopted under this legal basis.

---

[44] For a more extensive overview of the complex relations between preventive and goal-driven approximation, see Ćemalović (2015), pp. 246–251.

[45] Emphasis added.

The overall mechanism of Article 116 TFEU may lead to the adoption of the directives only *ultima ratio* if it is necessary to legislate **in the absence of a successful consultation procedure**. Therefore, in order to determine why it has, for now, remained unused to its full potential, a teleological examination of Article 116 TFEU should be added to the comparative and historical analysis initiated above.

Undistorted "free play"[46] of competition is certainly a very important, but far from being a unique, precondition for "the accomplishment of the internal market".[47] Moreover, the parallel use, in various provisions of the TEU and TFEU, of the terms "accomplishment", "establishment" and "functioning" clearly indicates that the internal market is somewhat a moving target, a constantly mutating and maturing concept of **economic cohesion**, having different levels of realisation in different areas of EU competence. In such a context, Articles 114 and 115 TFEU can be invoked whenever the provisions in the MS, by their finality or effect (→ para 24), affect "the establishment and functioning of the internal market", thus almost entirely covering the narrow scope of Article 116 TFEU, which entails law approximation only in the case of distortion of the conditions of competition.

One recent proposal for a directive provides a good example of the very limited invokability of Article 116 TFEU. As it has already been discussed elsewhere (→ paras 9 and 19), **national tax provisions** are "in particular"[48] likely to cause distortions of competition in the internal market. Nevertheless, the Commission's Proposal for a Council Directive on a Common Consolidated Corporate Tax Base (CCCTB)[49] "falls within the ambit of Article 115",[50] given that the Commission's objective is to harmonise "the corporate tax base, which is a prerequisite for curbing identified obstacles that distort the internal market".[51] Despite the fact that Article 115 TFEU requires unanimity and—as the EP had underlined in its Resolution of 25 November 2015 *on tax rulings and other measures similar in nature or effect*—by "giving each Member State a veto right, reduces the incentive to move from the status quo towards a more cooperative solution",[52] the Commission has chosen not to invoke Article 116 TFEU. It has apparently been concluded that a wider legislative action justifies a resort to the heavier mechanism of a unanimous vote within the Council. If the problem of disparate national corporate tax systems had been regarded exclusively in the light of their detrimental effects on

---

[46] Case 22/71, *Béguelin Import Co. v S.A.G.L. Import Export* (ECJ 25 November 1971) para 16.

[47] Paragraph 10 of the preamble of the TEU.

[48] Case T-533/10, *DTS Distribuidora de Televisión Digital, SA v European Commission* (GC 11 July 2014) para 48; Case C-174/02, *Streekgewest* (ECJ 13 January 2005) para 24.

[49] Proposal for a Council Directive on a Common Consolidated Corporate Tax Base (CCCTB), COM(2016) 683 final. On 15 March 2018, the EP adopted a legislative resolution on the CCCTB. As of 1 February 2023, the act is still awaiting final adoption.

[50] Proposal for a Council Directive on CCCTB, p. 5.

[51] Proposal for a Council Directive on CCCTB, p. 5.

[52] European Parliament Resolution 2015/2066 (INI), para 172.

competition, a resort to Article 116 TFEU might have led to the adoption of a directive without falling foul of the unanimity rule. On the other hand, the scope of such a directive would certainly be limited, given that the distortion of the internal market comprises, but is not limited to, the distortion of competition.

29 Finally, when both Articles 114/115 TFEU and Article 116 TFEU can be used as a legal basis for the adoption of a directive, the former has been systematically invoked not only because of its larger scope but also since it does not require a prior consultation procedure. The *telos* of Article 116 TFEU is the elimination of distortions of competition caused by the **difference in the national provisions** in MS; the main tool for such elimination is, primarily, the agreement reached in the consultation and, only subsequently, the Union's legislative action. Moreover, as *P.J. Wattel* pertinently pointed out, "even though Articles 116 and 117 TFEU allow harmful tax competitive national measures to be outlawed by a qualified majority, they make the Commission dependent on changing political coalitions of member States which may not be interested at all in binding measures at EU level encroaching upon their (perceived) tax sovereignty".[53] In the context of the unprecedented COVID-19 crisis, in July 2020, the European Commission proposed "An Action Plan for Fair and Simple Taxation Supporting the Recovery Strategy", which also includes the possibility to adopt proposals on taxation "by ordinary legislative procedure, including article 116 TFEU".[54]

3. Residual Mechanism of "Other Appropriate Measures"

30 Article 116 TFEU is a unique provision of the TFEU, which, *expressis verbis*, allows the adoption of "**any other appropriate measures** provided for in the Treaties". Even if it may seem both indubitably unnecessary and extremely general, it is paradigmatic of the entire Article 116 TFEU and merits a closer examination. The focus will first be on its general nature (→ para 31), before turning to the question of its rationale (→ para 32).

31 The "measures" mentioned in the second sentence of Article 116.2 TFEU are not to be understood only as measures leading to the adoption of EU legislation. The intent seemed to be to include, on the one hand, the possibility of the Union's legislative action under the TFEU's **residual clause**,[55] allowing to fill gaps in the Treaty if "action by the Union should prove necessary [...] to attain one of the objectives set out in the Treaties, and the Treaties have not provided the necessary powers" (→ Article 352 TFEU). On the other hand, this provision also appears to indicate the possibility to initiate the infringement procedure (Article 258 TFEU and Article 260 TFEU). The use of the passive form "may be adopted" corroborates the above interpretation.

---

[53] Wattel (2016), p. 70.
[54] Communication from the Commission COM(2020) 312 final.
[55] Michel (2003), p. 32.

If the conditions for the adoption of any "measure" provided for in one of the provisions of the Treaties are fulfilled, it can be lawfully taken, without any particular mention in its other provisions. If this is not the case, then almost every article of the TFEU conferring competence to the EU in the context of its policies (Part Three) could have ended with a provision allowing the adoption of "other appropriate measures". However, **the rationale for the introduction of this residual mechanism** seems to have more to do with the very nature of Article 116 TFEU, endeavouring to compensate for its narrow scope and limited mission.

32

4. Partial Derogation of Article 116 TFEU Introduced by Article 117.2 TFEU

Finally, it should be noted that Article 117.2 TFEU has introduced a **partial derogation** from Article 116 TFEU. If an MS adopted or modified certain national provisions despite the recommendation the Commission had addressed pursuant to Article 117.1 TFEU, all other MS are released from the obligation to apply Article 116 TFEU (→ Article 117 TFEU para 17). It remains unclear why the disrespect of one MS for the EU's legal order should allow its further deterioration by keeping certain zones of potentially distorted competition out of the reach of approximation measures.

33

List of Cases

ECJ

ECJ 25.11.1971, 22/71, *Béguelin Import Co. v S.A.G.L. Import Export*, ECLI:EU: C:1971:113 [cit. in para 7; 27]
ECJ 18.06.1975, 94/74, *IGAV v ENCC*, ECLI:EU:C:1975:81 [cit. in para 9; 12; 17]
ECJ 13.01.2005, C-174/02, *Streekgewest*, ECLI:EU:C:2005:10 [cit. in para 3; 9; 28]
ECJ 02.05.2006, C-217/04, Opinion of AG Kokott, *United Kingdom v Parliament and Council*, ECLI:EU:C:2005:574 [cit. in para 4]
ECJ 04.06.2009, C-8/08, *T-Mobile Netherlands and others*, ECLI:EU:C:2009:343 [cit. in para 15]
ECJ 09.06.2011, C-71/09 P, C-73/09 P and C-76/09 P, *Comitato 'Venezia vuole vivere' and Others v Commission*, ECLI:EU:C:2011:368 [cit. in para 12]
ECJ 14.03.2013, C-32/11, *Allianz Hungária Biztosító and Others*, ECLI:EU: C:2013:160 [cit. in para 15]
ECJ 11.09.2014, C-67/13 P, *CB v Commission*, ECLI:EU:C:2014:2204 [cit. in para 12]
ECJ 04.05.2016, C-477/14, *Pillbox 38*, ECLI:EU:C:2016:324 [cit. in para 10]

CFI/GC

GC 06.04.2022, T-508/19, *Mead Johnson Nutrition (Asia Pacific) and Others v Commission*, ECLI:EU:T:2022:217 [cit. in para 7]

GC 11.07.2014, T-533/10, *DTS Distribuidora de Televisión Digital, SA v Commission*, ECLI:EU:T:2014:629 [cit. in para 9, 28]

References

Ćemalović, U. (2015). Framework for the approximation of national legal systems with the European Union's acquis: From a vague definition to jurisprudential implementation. *Croatian Yearbook of European Law and Policy, 11*, 241–258.

Ćemalović, U. (2020). Towards a new strategy for EU enlargement – between the wish for an encouragement, the reality of the fatigue and the threat of a dead end. In D. Duić (Ed.), *Book of Proceedings of the 4th ECLIC International Scientific Conference* (pp. 281–298). University of Osijek, Faculty of Law.

Ćemalović, U. (2021). Supremacy of EU law over national legislation and supreme jurisdictions of the member states – a quest for a new balance. In K. Zakić & B. Demirtaş (Eds.), *Europe in changes: The old continent at a new crossroads* (pp. 63–78). Institute of International Politics and Economics, Faculty of Security Studies.

De Bièvre, D., & Bursens, P. (2016). Patterns of covert integration in EU governance. A response to Héritier. In P. Bursens et al. (Eds.), *Complex political decision-making: Leadership, legitimacy, and communication* (pp. 31–39). Routledge.

Evans, A. (1996). *The integration of the European Community and third states in Europe – a legal analysis*. OUP.

Helminen, M. (2011). *EU tax law – direct taxation*. IBFD.

Jacqué, J. P. (2016). Lost in transition: The European Commission between intergovernmentalism and integration. In D. Ritleng (Ed.), *Independence and legitimacy in the institutional system of the European Union* (pp. 15–56). OUP.

Jones, A., & Sufrin, B. (2011). *EU competition law* (4th ed.). OUP.

Lohse, E. J. (2011). The meaning of harmonisation in the context of European Union law – a process in need of definition. In M. Andenas & C. Baasch Andersen (Eds.), *Theory and practice of harmonisation* (pp. 282–313). Edward Elgar.

Michel, V. (2003). *Recherches sur les compétences de la Communauté européenne*. L'Harmattan.

Rodger, B., & MacCulloch, A. (2009). *Competition law and policy in the EC and UK* (4th ed.). Routledge.

Rossini, C. (1998). *English as a legal language*. Kluwer Law International.

Schütze, R. (2009). *From dual to cooperative federalism: The changing structure of European law*. OUP.

Wattel, P. J. (2016). State aid, free movement, harmful tax competition and disparities. In I. Richelle, W. Schön, & E. Traversa (Eds.), *State aid law and business taxation* (pp. 59–71). Springer.

Article 117 [National Measures]
(ex-Article 97 TEC)

1. Where there is a reason to fear[6] that the adoption or amendment[7] of a provision laid down by law, regulation or administrative action may cause distortion within the meaning of Article 116,[8] a Member State desiring to proceed therewith[9] shall consult the Commission. After consulting[10-11] the Member States, the Commission shall recommend to the States concerned[12] such measures as may be appropriate[13-14] to avoid the distortion in question.
2. If a State desiring to introduce or amend its own provisions does not comply[15-16] with the recommendation addressed to it by the Commission, other Member States shall not be required, pursuant to Article 116, to amend their own provisions in order to eliminate such distortion.[17] If the Member State which has ignored the recommendation of the Commission causes distortion detrimental only to itself, the provisions of Article 116 shall not apply.[18]

Contents

1. Article 117 TFEU in the Global Context of the Law Approximation Policy 1
   1.1. Indirect Approximation of Article 117 TFEU 2
   1.2. Interdependence of Articles 117 and 116 TFEU 3
2. Distortion of Competition Caused by the Adoption or Amendment of a National Provision: Two Possible Outcomes 4
   2.1. Procedure Aiming to Avoid Distortion 5
      2.1.1. Four Conditions for the Union's Action 6
      2.1.2. Procedure of Consultation 10
      2.1.3. Recommendation Aiming to Avoid Distortion 13
   2.2. Rules Applicable in the Case of the Emergence of Distortion 15
      2.2.1. Non-compliance with the Recommendation of the Commission 16
      2.2.2. Rules Applicable to the "Other Member States" 17
      2.2.3. Rules Applicable in the Case of the Limited Effect of Distortion 18
List of Cases
References

1. Article 117 TFEU in the Global Context of the Law Approximation Policy

Article 117 TFEU belongs to the chapter of the Treaty dedicated to law approximation, but—unlike all other four articles (Articles 114, 115, 116 and 118 TFEU) of the same chapter—it **does not include any prerogatives whatsoever that would allow the adoption of approximation legislation** on the EU level (→ para 2). Moreover, a combined reading of Articles 116 and 117 TFEU (→ Article 116

1

TFEU para 18) reveals that the latter—even if only by double reference (in both paragraphs) to it – is, in various aspects, subsidiary[1] to the former and, more generally, interdependent with it (→ para 3).

1.1. Indirect Approximation of Article 117 TFEU

2   The very essence of the EU policy of law approximation[2] is the adoption of legislation on the Union level, while the notion of "approximation" refers to the "process, the objective of which is to eliminate differences, to varying degrees, between national laws with a view to bringing such laws closer together".[3] However, the TFEU provisions dedicated to this policy either expressly mention EU legislative acts ("directives for the approximation" or "the necessary directives", as is the case of, respectively, Articles 115 and 116 TFEU) or, more generally, refer to "the measures for the approximation" (Article 114 TFEU) or "measures [...] to provide uniform protection of intellectual property rights" (Article 118 TFEU). In both cases, those provisions confer competence to adopt genuinely European legal acts, belonging to the Union's legal order. The overall rationale of Article 117 TFEU clearly deviates from this pattern of **direct approximation**, introducing the possibility for a recommendation to the "States concerned" of "such measures as may be appropriate to avoid the distortion". The potential and—especially in light of its second paragraph—legally not binding (→ para 13), thus highly improbable, law approximation that might result from Article 117.1 TFEU is, therefore, **indirect**, given that the elimination or reduction of national differences can only occur as a result of a measure taken solely on the MS level. While, for example, an unsuccessful consultation led in the context of Article 116 TFEU triggers the Union's competence to legislate (→ Article 116 TFEU para 21–29), the non-compliance of an MS with the Commission's recommendation pursuant to Article 117.1 TFEU entitles all other MS not to amend their legislation (→ para 17).

1.2. Interdependence of Articles 117 and 116 TFEU

3   The application of Article 117 TFEU—but also its mere understanding – would not be possible without the prior consideration of Article 116 TFEU. Even if the latter can be applied when a difference in the existing provisions between the national provisions distorts competition, while the former concerns the introduction of a new

---

[1] For a more detailed review of other examples of subsidiarity between different provisions of the EU primary law, see Klamert (2014).

[2] For more details concerning the cross-cutting nature of the Union's law approximation policy, see Ćemalović (2015), pp. 246–251.

[3] Gutman (2014), p. 25. The overall objective of the law approximation policy is additionally complexified by the fact that the adoption of the Lisbon Treaty has not brought an end to "some fundamental, value-based discrepancies"; see Ćemalović (2022), p. 174 et seqq.

provision ("the adoption or amendment") having the same effect, the wording "within the meaning of Article 116" could not represent a more direct reference. Moreover, the second paragraph of Article 117 TFEU mentions Article 116 twice, but, interestingly, both times in order to introduce an exoneration of one MS (→ para 17) or all the other MS (→ para 18) from the application of Article 116 TFEU.

2. Distortion of Competition Caused by the Adoption or Amendment of a National Provision: Two Possible Outcomes

As already observed (→ para 2 and 3), in comparison with Article 116 TFEU, the two main *differentiae specificae* of Article 117 TFEU lie in the fact that, on the one hand, it **does not include any prerogatives allowing the adoption of EU legislation** and, on the other hand, it concerns the introduction or modification, by an MS, of a provision that potentially may cause the distortion of the conditions of competition in the internal market. In a similar vein, the competence of the EU and the resulting prerogatives of the Commission are also different. While the elimination of distortion caused by divergent national legislation (→ Article 116 TFEU para 5–29) can consist of two phases (consultation and legislative action), the Commission's recommendation pursuant to Article 117 TFEU can have two possible outcomes. In the following discussion, the focus will first be on the procedure aiming to avoid distortion (→ para 5 et seqq.), before turning to the rules applicable in the case of the emergence of distortion (→ para 15 et seqq.).

4

2.1. Procedure Aiming to Avoid Distortion

The mechanism of indirect law approximation provided for in Article 117.1 TFEU is intended to lead to the **avoidance of distortion**. Given that the elimination of the differences between national provisions realised by such (if successful) avoidance of distortion does not include the legislative action of the EU, it can, to some extent, be compared to the mechanism of consultation introduced by Article 116.1 TFEU. However, as has been already pointed out (→ Article 116 TFEU para 21), the failure of the consultation procedure pursuant to Article 116.1 TFEU can only lead to the EU's legislative action, while an unsuccessful avoidance of distortion pursuant to Article 117.1 TFEU justifies the inaction on the national level, potentially leading to the maintenance of "infringements of the normal functioning of the competition system by actions on the part of the States".[4] Further analysis of the procedure aiming to avoid distortion will include the examination of the following three points: (1) conditions for the Union's action (→ para 6–9), (2) the procedure of consultation (→ para 10–12) and (3) the recommendation aiming to avoid distortion (→ para 13–14).

5

---

[4] Case 94/74, *IGAV v ENCC* (ECJ 18 June 1975) para 33–34.

2.1.1. Four Conditions for the Union's Action

6   Unlike in the case of Article 116 TFEU (→ Article 116 TFEU para 12), even a **potential distortion** ("a reason to fear") can trigger the procedure under Article 117.1 TFEU. Moreover, a systematic interpretation suggests that the only moment when the mechanism of Article 117 TFEU can be initiated is before the potential distortion takes place, given that an MS is invited to consult with the Commission during the period that starts from the time an intention to introduce or modify the national provision is clearly expressed ("desiring to proceed therewith") and ends before the moment of its definitive adoption. Consequently, the possible distortive effects of a planned revision of national legislation can only be estimated with a reasonable[5] level of predictability.

7   Article 117.1 TFEU is applicable only when an MS intends to introduce a new provision or modify an existing one. On the other hand, in the context of Article 116 TFEU, the "free play of competition"[6] in the internal market can only be distorted by a difference (→ Article 116 TFEU para 8) between the national provisions already in force. It is, therefore, the **potential change**[7] **of national legislation** that might trigger the application of Article 117.1 TFEU, indicating the **preventive (*ex ante*) nature** of approximation that it may bring about. In other words, only the intention of an MS to introduce certain changes—potentially distortive for competition in the internal market—can bring into play the mechanism of Article 117.1 TFEU, given that all other actual (→ Article 116 TFEU para 12) distortions caused by existing national provisions are covered by the *ex post* **approximation** of Article 116 TFEU.

8   An intended modification of national legislation (→ para 7) can fall into the scope of Article 117 TFEU only if it represents **a reasonable risk** (→ para 6) **of distortion** "within the meaning of Article 116 [TFEU]". Therefore, all observations regarding the notion of distortion and the relations of Articles 116 and 101 TFEU made elsewhere (→ Article 116 TFEU para 3, 7, 12, 14 and 15; → Article 101 TFEU para 48) are also applicable to Article 117 TFEU.

9   As has already been pointed out (→ para 6), the need to launch the consultation procedure pursuant to Article 117.1 TFEU appears only after an MS clearly expressed its intention to introduce or modify a national provision potentially detrimental to competition in the internal market. What is, however, uncertain is **who assesses the risk of distortion** and, consequently, whether there is an obligation to consult the Commission. At least three reasons indicate that it can only be an MS: first, an MS is undoubtedly better able to know both its legislative intentions and its desire "to proceed therewith", especially given that the systematic

---

[5] For an analysis of the risk of competition distortion in the legislative negotiation related to the services of general economic interest, see Wehlander (2016), pp. 228–240.

[6] Case 22/71, *Béguelin Import Co. v S.A.G.L. Import Export* (ECJ 25 November 1971) para 16.

[7] The notion of "change" is to be understood here in a broader sense, in order to encompass both the introduction of a new provision and the modification of an existing one.

interpretation indirectly indicates that mere draft legislation with no serious prospect of adoption should not give rise to the application of Article 117.1 TFEU. Second, a combined reading of Articles 116.1 and 117.1 TFEU shows that the former supposes the proactive approach of the Commission (→ Article 116 TFEU para 7), while the latter depends on the estimation on the part of an MS. Third, if national legislation passes the "filter" of the preventive law approximation of Article 117.1 TFEU, it immediately becomes possible to apply the mechanism of ex post law approximation in Article 116 TFEU (→ Article 116 TFEU para 5–29). In conclusion, even if it is – most probably – initially intended to rest upon the MS' responsibility and not upon their estimation of the possible distortive effect of their own legislative intentions, the consultative and practically optional mechanism of Article 117.1 TFEU reduced it to a weak complement of Article 116 TFEU.

2.1.2. Procedure of Consultation

As is the case for Article 116 TFEU (→ Article 116 TFEU para 17–19), the **procedure of consultation** set out in Article 117 TFEU, as well as the **role of the parties involved in it**, are far from being precisely defined. However, the teleological analysis of Article 117 TFEU and the combined reading of Articles 116.1 and 117.1 TFEU can provide some valuable conclusions concerning the prerogatives of the Commission (→ para 11), the involvement of the MS and the notion of "States concerned" (→ para 12). **10**

The main objective of the procedure of consultation provided for in Article 117.1 TFEU is to avoid the distortion of competition in the internal market before the above-mentioned distortion actually occurs. Therefore, the procedure is led by the Commission, but it is initiated by an MS, whose **assessment of the potential risk** that the change of its legislation may create for competition (→ para 6) triggers the mechanism of Article 117.1 TFEU. Its wording corroborates this conclusion because the terms "consult" (end of the first sentence) and "consulting" (beginning of the second sentence) describe two clearly different and separate activities. While the first "consultation" practically refers to the information that an MS gives to the Commission regarding its intention to introduce certain changes in its legislation, the second one specifies the actual consultation process between the Commission and the MS. This consultation *stricto sensu* is conducted by the Commission, and it is intended to end with a recommendation comprising measures to avoid the potential distortion. **11**

Another incertitude concerning the consultation procedure is related to its scope. As has already been underlined (→ Article 116 TFEU para 18), this provision should be interpreted in such a way to allow the **widest possible consultation**, given that, at least theoretically, every distortion that includes at least two MS is potentially detrimental to competition in the entire internal market. Moreover, one important difference between Article 116.1 and 117.1 TFEU provides another argument in favour of such an interpretation. While the former mentions consultation with "the Member States concerned", the latter suggests the existence of two different degrees of involvement on the MS' side, given that, "after **12** consulting the Member States, the Commission shall recommend to the *States concerned*" (emphasis added) measures aiming to avoid the distortion. If the consultation with the Member States "concerned" is to be interpreted *lato sensu*, then, *a fortiori*, the consultation of "the Member States" should be as broad as possible.

2.1.3. Recommendation Aiming to Avoid Distortion

13 The overall objective of Article 117.1 TFEU is to avoid the potential distortion of competition in the internal market by a preventive, **ex ante approximation of national provisions** that still have not produced any distortive effect. Concerning the types or forms of potential national normative activities[8] that might trigger the application of the mechanism of Article 117.1 TFEU, everything that has been already observed for *ex post* approximation (→ Article 116 TFEU para 9–11) is applicable here as well. The measures recommended to the MS by the Commission in the context of Article 117.1 TFEU are not legally binding.[9] However, according to settled case law, "the national courts are bound to take recommendations into consideration [...] in particular where they cast light *on the interpretation of national measures adopted in order to implement them* or where they are designed to supplement binding Community provisions".[10]

14 Neither the provision of Article 117.1 TFEU nor the Court's case law has given any indication concerning the possible content of the Commission's recommendation. The broad, overarching formulation "such measures as may be appropriate" allows the Commission to recommend **various legislative, regulatory or administrative measures** to the MS and/or abstain from certain such measures. It should be noted, though, that there is a certain parallelism between the Commission's recommendation and the agreement eliminating the distortion (→ Article 116 TFEU para 5–29) in the context of *ex post* law approximation of Article 116 TFEU.

---

[8] E.g., in Case C-524/14 P, *Commission v Hansestadt Lübeck* (Opinion of AG Wahl of 15 September 2016) para 64: "As the Commission has pointed out, it is apparent from the scheme and origin of the Treaties that a distinction must be drawn between *general* measures of fiscal or economic policy (which now fall within the scope of Articles 113 and 115 to 117 TFEU) and *specific* measures which lead to the acquisition of *advantages* by means of State resources (which are, for their part, now covered by Articles 107 to 109 TFEU)."

[9] In the EU competition law *stricto sensu*, "although Article 288(5) TFEU states that soft law does not have any binding force, it still may have an effect on the application of the EU competition rules by national competition authorities and courts", Lorenz (2013), p. 33; for further analysis, see Sauter (2016), Patel and Schweitzer (2013).

[10] Case C-207/01, *Altair Chimica v ENEL Distribuzione* (ECJ 11 September 2003) para 41 (emphasis added).

Article 117. [National Measures] 441

2.2. Rules Applicable in the Case of the Emergence of Distortion

As has already been pointed out (→ para 2 and 13), the **recommendation** of the Commission, addressed pursuant to Article 117 TFEU, is **not legally binding**. Thus, the Treaty had to provide the rules applicable when – in spite of the attempt to prevent the distortion by the measures recommended by the Commission—an MS does not comply with the Commission's recommendation. It is, therefore, necessary to examine the legal nature of such non-compliance by an MS (→ para 16) before turning to the question of the rules applicable to the "other Member States" (→ para 17) and the rules applicable in the case of the limited effect of distortion (→ para 18).

15

2.2.1. Non-compliance with the Recommendation of the Commission

Every application of Article 117.2 TFEU first requires the removal of the uncertainty that may arise regarding the effects of non-compliance, by an MS, with the recommendation of the Commission.[11] The systematic interpretation seems to indicate that the application of the rules of Article 117.2 TFEU necessitates **an effective distortion of competition**. In other words, not only that "appropriate measures" recommended by the Commission have not been taken, but the reasonable risk ("a reason to fear") of distortion (→ para 6) mentioned by Article 117.1 TFEU must have become an actual, effective distortion. At least three arguments in favour of such an interpretation can be found in the somewhat unclear wording of Article 117.2 TFEU. First, its first sentence *in fine* mentions "such distortion", allowing the conclusion that an MS persisted in its desire to introduce or amend its provisions in a way that actually distorts competition. Second, the non-application, to the other MS, of Article 116 TFEU indicates that the distortion did effectively take place (→ Article 116 TFEU para 12–13), given that, otherwise, reference to the previous article of the TFEU would be devoid of sense. Third, the second sentence of Article 117.2 TFEU—mentioning the distortion detrimental only to the MS that caused it—proves *a contrario* that the distortion mentioned in the first sentence is effective and detrimental to more than one State.

16

2.2.2. Rules Applicable to the "Other Member States"

Given that Article 117.1 TFEU introduces the rules intended to realise a preventive law approximation (→ para 7), if national legislation passed the "filter" of *ex ante* approximation of Article 117.1 TFEU, it immediately becomes possible to apply the mechanism of *ex post* approximation of Article 116 TFEU (→ Article 116 TFEU para 17). However, if a MS adopted or modified certain national provisions despite the recommendation the Commission addressed it pursuant to Article 117.1

17

---

[11] For a comprehensive overview of the complex and mutating role of the Commission in the EU's legal order, see Jacqué (2016).

TFEU, all other MS are released from the obligation to apply Article 116 TFEU (→ Article 116 TFEU para 33). Not only that Article 117 is a *lex imperfecta*, but it also **partially undermines the purpose of Article 116 TFEU**. The fact that a disregard of the Commission's recommendation by one MS can have as a consequence the right of all other MS to invoke the non-applicability, to that case, of Article 116 TFEU can be harmful to the law approximation policy of the Union and, more generally, to its entire legal order, as well as to its relations with potential new MS.[12]

2.2.3. Rules Applicable in the Case of the Limited Effect of Distortion

18 Finally, if the effect of distortion caused by the legal action of one MS remains limited to its own borders—while the same State ignored the recommendation that the Commission had addressed to it pursuant to Article 117.1 TFEU—the Treaty allows the non-application of approximation measures pursuant to Article 116 TFEU. Moreover, not even the **cross-border effect** of such **distortion of competition** can trigger the procedure of Article 116 TFEU, given that all other MS can invoke its non-applicability (→ para 17). In other words, if the Commission's recommendation was ignored by an MS, the application of Article 116 TFEU is almost totally blocked. Only the absence of the Commission's recommendation pursuant to Article 117.1 TFEU can open the way to the *ex post* approximation of Article 116 TFEU. In case Article 117 TFEU was introduced with the intention to complete and fortify Article 116 TFEU, what it actually achieved was to open a way to undermine it. In the present state of legislation, law approximation in the case of distortion of the conditions of competition in the internal market significantly depends on the MS' goodwill and their respect for the Union's legal order.

List of Cases

ECJ 25.11.1971, 22/71, *Béguelin Import Co. v S.A.G.L. Import Export*, ECLI:EU:C:1971:113 [cit. in para 7]
ECJ 18.06.1975, 94/74, *IGAV v ENCC*, ECLI:EU:C:1975:81 [cit. in para 5]
ECJ 11.09.2003, C-207/01, *Altair Chimica v ENEL Distribuzione*, ECLI:EU:C:2003:451 [cit. in para 13]

References

Ćemalović, U. (2015). Framework for the approximation of national legal systems with the European Union's acquis: From a vague definition to jurisprudential implementation. *Croatian Yearbook of European Law and Policy, 11*, 241–258.

---

[12] For interplay between the law approximation policy and the conditionality in the EU enlargement process, see Ćemalović (2020), p. 186 et seqq.

Ćemalović, U. (2020). One step forward, two steps back: the EU and the Western Balkans after the adoption of the new enlargement methodology and the conclusions of the Zagreb Summit. *Croatian Yearbook of European Law and Policy, 16*, 179–196.

Ćemalović, U. (2022). *Between European Union's aptitude for enlargement and 'a clearer prospect' of accession - some lessons of the French presidency of the Council of the EU* (pp. 173–184). Lazarski University.

Gutman, K. (2014). *Foundations of European contract law*. OUP.

Jacqué, J. P. (2016). Lost in transition: The European Commission between intergovernmentalism and integration. In D. Ritleng (Ed.), *Independence and legitimacy in the institutional system of the European Union* (pp. 15–56). OUP.

Klamert, M. (2014). *The principle of loyalty in EU law*. OUP.

Lorenz, M. (2013). *An introduction to EU competition law*. CUP.

Patel, K. K., & Schweitzer, H. (2013). *The historical foundations of EU competition law*. OUP.

Sauter, W. (2016). *Coherence in EU competition law*. OUP.

Wehlander, C. (2016). *Services of general economic interest as a constitutional concept of EU law*. Asser Press-Springer.

Article 118 [European Intellectual Property Rights]

In the context of the establishment and functioning of the internal market,[3–10, 19–22, 28–30] the European Parliament and the Council, acting in accordance with the ordinary legislative procedure,[17, 47–48] shall establish measures for the creation of European intellectual property rights to provide uniform protection of intellectual property rights throughout the Union[33–38] and for the setting up of centralised Union-wide authorisation, coordination and supervision arrangements.[39–41]

The Council, acting in accordance with a special legislative procedure,[49–51] shall by means of regulations establish language arrangements for the European intellectual property rights.[42–43] The Council shall act unanimously after consulting the European Parliament.

Contents

1. Genesis and Justification 1
    1.1. Intellectual Property in the EU Before the Lisbon Treaty 3
        1.1.1. Intellectual Property and the Treaties: No Reserved Domain of Member States 3
        1.1.2. "Acquis Communautaire" in Intellectual Property 7
    1.2. Rationale for Adopting Article 118 TFEU 11
2. Nature of the Competence 18
    2.1. Shared Competence of the European Union 19
    2.2. A Specific Competence to Be Articulated with Other EU Competences 22
        2.2.1. The Residual Competence of Article 352 TFEU 24
        2.2.2. The "General" Competences to Harmonise of Articles 114 and 115 TFEU 27
3. Scope of Competence 31
    3.1. The Nature of the "Measures" 32
    3.2. Creation of European IP Rights to Provide Uniform Protection Throughout the Union 33
    3.3. Centralised Union-Wide Authorisation, Coordination and Supervision Arrangements 39
    3.4. Regulation to Establish Language Arrangements for European IP Rights 42
    3.5. Intellectual Property 44
    3.6. Subsidiarity and Proportionality 45
4. Procedure 47
    4.1. Ordinary Legislative Procedure Under Article 118 (1) TFEU 47
    4.2. Special Legislative Procedure Under Article 118 (2) TFEU 49

List of Cases
References

1. Genesis and Justification

1 The **Treaty of Lisbon introduced** for the first time an express and **specific competence** of the Union for the creation of European intellectual property (IP) rights.[1] Article 118 TFEU confers a double competence upon the Union to create European uniform and unitary IP rights and to adopt language arrangements for these rights. In order to understand the reason for the adoption of Article 118 TFEU, it is necessary to consider its genesis from a historical and political perspective.

2 Before the introduction of Article 118 TFEU, even though no provision of the founding treaties granted the EU special and express competence or specific powers to act in the field of IP, the Community acted to **harmonise national laws** on the basis of ex-Articles 94 and 95 TEC (now Articles 115 and 114 TFEU, respectively) and to create industrial property rights essentially on the basis of ex-Article 308 TEC (Article 352 TFEU).

1.1. Intellectual Property in the EU Before the Lisbon Treaty

1.1.1. Intellectual Property and the Treaties: No Reserved Domain of Member States

3 As the trade in products and services involving IP rights has been significant in the Community, issues relating to IP rights have come before the Court of Justice from an early stage in its history. From an economic point of view, IP rights are **territorial monopolies**. The Court had to consider how best to reconcile these monopolies with those **liberties that are essential for the achievement of the common market** (free movement of goods, services and competition). However, the legitimacy of the Court's jurisdiction in dealing with IP rights issues has been questioned particularly with regard to Article 222 TEEC (now Article 345 TFEU), which states that "the Treaties shall in no way prejudice the rules in Member States governing the system of property ownership", and Article 36 TEEC (now Article 36 TFEU), which provides MS with the possibility of justifying limitations or restrictions on the free movement of goods in the interest of protecting industrial and commercial property.

4 In the *Grundig* case,[2] the **Court of Justice** clearly explained, first, that neither Article 222 nor Article 36 TEEC excludes any Community law influence whatsoever on the exercise of national industrial property rights and, second, that Article 222 TEEC states only that the founding treaty *does not prejudice the rules governing property ownership* in MS. This position has been confirmed about ten years later in

---

[1] See regarding the evolution of the wording of the provision in the preliminary documents since the draft TCE: Gaster, in von der Groeben et al. (2015), Artikel 118 AEUV para 8 et seq.; Stieper, in Grabitz et al. (2022), Artikel 118 AEUV para 1 et seq. (released in 2022).

[2] Joined Cases 56 and 58/64, *Consten and Grundig* (ECJ 13 July 1966) p. 345, para 6.

the well-known *Simmenthal* case. According to the Court, Article 36 TEEC "is not designed to reserve certain matters to the exclusive jurisdiction of Member States but permits national law to derogate from the principle of the free movement of goods to the extent to which such derogation is and continues to be justified for the attainment of the objectives referred to in that article".[3]

Following the *Grundig* case, and in a constant subsequent case law concerning IP,[4] the Court of Justice has drawn a **fundamental distinction between the existence and the exercise of IP rights** and has developed some reasoning that permits the reconciliation of Community essential economic liberties within the Community and national protection for IP rights. This reasoning is based on the interpretation of Article 36 TFEU (ex-Article 36 TEEC). The latter permits only prohibitions or restrictions on the freedom of movement which are justified for the purpose of protecting industrial and commercial property (→ Article 36 TFEU para 8) and which do not constitute a means for arbitrary discrimination or a disguised restriction on trade between MS (→ Article 36 TFEU para 18–19). According to the ECJ, this article "only admits derogations to the extent to which they are justified for the purpose of safeguarding rights which constitute the specific subject-matter of such property".[5]

The **"specific subject-matter"** of an IP right is determined by the Court regarding its essential function, which is determined itself with regard to the purpose of the IP right. The Court has been concerned to establish whether the holder of an IP right has exercised it in accordance with its purpose. As a consequence, it developed the **"exhaustion doctrine"** to reconcile fundamental economic freedoms with IP rights. Under this doctrine, when a product has been put on the market in the territory of an MS by the IP right owner or with his consent, then the right to control its further circulation is exhausted. Even though Article 36 TEEC only expressly mentioned industrial and commercial property, the Court has accepted since the *GEMA* case that it also applies to artistic and literary property rights, observing that the "commercial exploitation of copyright raises the same issues as that of any other industrial or commercial property right".[6]

This case law provided the basis for the activity of the Commission in the domain of IP rights. Firstly, and paradoxically, given that the exhaustion principle was founded on the fundamental distinction between the existence and exercise of IP rights, the Court laid the foundation for intervention in the definition of IP rights. Indeed, the instruments of this principle (as the "essential function" and "specific subject-matter") deal inevitably with the definition of these rights. Secondly, there is no doubt that there is a very **strong link between the Court's case law in IP**

---

[3] Case 35/76, *Simmenthal* (ECJ 15 December 1976) para 24.

[4] Notably Case 24/67, *Parke, Davis and Co v Probel and Others* (ECJ 29 February 1968) and Case 78/70, *Deutsche Grammophon* (ECJ 8 June 1971) para 11.

[5] See especially Case 78/70, *Deutsche Grammophon* (ECJ 8 June 1971) para 11.

[6] Case 55 and 57/80, *Musik-Vertrieb Membran v GEMA* (ECJ 20 January 1981) para 13, and before, less explicitly, in Case 62/79, *Coditel v Ciné Vog Films* (ECJ 18 March 1980) para 15.

rights and the subsequent work of legislative harmonisation in this field.[7] The fact that there was a disparity between national laws, which was capable of both creating an obstacle to the freedom of movement of goods and services and distorting competition between MS, did not, according to the Court, justify MS in giving legal protection to the practices of a private body that are incompatible with the rules concerning the fundamental economic freedoms.[8] Furthermore, in demonstrating the fact that the main problem was the disparity between national laws, the Court underlined the need for harmonisation. The need to eliminate such disparity is one of the main reasons for legislating, which is asserted in the recitals of the directives in IP law. Finally, the Court dealt with IP rights essentially from an economic perspective, a point of view shared by the Commission and the Council when they have undertaken to approximate national IP laws.

1.1.2. "Acquis Communautaire" in Intellectual Property

7 The "acquis communautaire" in IP before the adoption of the Treaty of Lisbon is important. The Community legislator initiated legislation to repair various types of **impediments to the free movement of goods or services and to free competition**, resulting from the fact that the Treaty of Rome allowed for the existence of **diverging national rules on IP rights** and their territorial application. The Community action in the field of IP focused mainly on the harmonisation of substantive national law through the adoption of directives and maintaining the territorial character of IP rights. The approximation of national legislation contributed also to the creation of a Community IP law and therefore prepared and facilitated the creation, in the 1990s, of autonomous Community-wide industrial property rights.

8 As far as harmonisation is concerned, numerous directives were adopted on the general legal basis of Articles 100 and 100a TEEC (ex-Articles 94 and 95 TEC = Articles 115 and 114 TFEU). In the area of industrial property, a significant degree of **harmonisation** has been achieved in trademark law[9] and in industrial design law.[10] By contrast, patent law remains a special case. Harmonisation directives have not achieved a general legal approximation covering the definition of the protectable objects, the protective conditions, the conferred rights and the term of protection. **In relation to patents, legal approximation** has been **limited**. This state of affairs may reveal the lobbying power of affected undertakings,

---

[7] Würfel (2005), p. 129.

[8] See, among a constant case-law, Case 55 and 57/80, *Musik-Vertrieb Membran v GEMA* (ECJ 20 January 1981) para 24.

[9] Council Directive 89/104/EEC, O.J. L 40/1 (1989), replaced by Parliament/Council Directive 2008/95/EC, O.J. L 299/25 (2008), and now Parliament/Council Directive (EU) 2015/2436 *to approximate the laws of the Member States relating to trade marks (recast)*, O.J. L 336/23 (2015).

[10] Parliament/Council Directive 98/71/EC *on the legal protection of designs*, O.J. L 289/28 (1998). The revision of that Directive is pending and the proposal has been published in November 2022 (COM(2022) 667 final).

particularly pharmaceutical lobbies.[11] A directive had been adopted in order to harmonise the topic of the patentability of biotechnological inventions,[12] and a further directive concerning software patentability was considered but not adopted as a result of the Parliament's intervention.[13] Two directives have also been adopted to create "special" national protections—supplementary protection certificates.[14] They correspond to a very particular form of harmonisation of the (extended) term of protection for inventions relating to medicinal or plant products. In the area of literary and artistic property, the harmonisation came later and was particularly fragmentary and limited before 2001. In this way, some rights,[15] some legal frameworks concerning specific objects,[16] the term of economic rights,[17] and their collective management[18] were subject to harmonisation. Directive 2001/29 is the first to ensure a more general, horizontal harmonisation of the law relating to copyright and neighbouring rights.[19] It has been modified by Directive 2019/790 on copyright and related rights in the Digital Single Market, which deals mainly with exceptions, the specific regime of online content sharing platform

---

[11] See Kingston (2008), p. 439 sq.

[12] Parliament/Council Directive 98/44/EC *on the legal protection of biotechnological inventions*, O.J. L 213/13 (1998).

[13] Proposal for a Parliament/Council Directive *on the patentability of computer-implemented inventions*, COM(2002) 92 final.

[14] Council Regulation (EEC) No. 1768/92, O.J. L 182/1 (1992), consolidated by Parliament/Council Regulation (EC) No. 469/2009 *concerning the supplementary protection certificate for medicinal products*, O.J. L 152/1 (2009), and the Parliament/Council Regulation (EC) No. 1610/96 *concerning the creation of a supplementary protection certificate for plant protection products*, O.J. L 198/30 (1996).

[15] Council Directive 92/100/EEC, O.J. L 346/61 (1992) repealed and replaced by Parliament/Council Directive 2006/115/EC *on rental right and lending right and on certain rights related to copyright in the field of intellectual property (codified version)*, O.J. L 376/28 (2006); Council Directive 93/83/EEC *on the coordination of certain rules concerning copyright and rights related to copyright applicable to satellite broadcasting and cable retransmission*, O.J. L 248/15 (1993) and later the Parliament/Council Directive 2001/84/EC *on the resale right for the benefit of the author of an original work of art*, O.J. L 272/32 (2001).

[16] For computer programmes: Council Directive 91/250/EEC, O.J. L 122/42 (1991) replaced by Parliament/Council Directive 2009/24/EC *on the legal protection of computer programs (codified version)*, O.J. L 111/16 (2009); for databases: Parliament/Council Directive 96/9/EC *on the legal protection of databases*, O.J. L 77/20 (1996); and, later, for orphan works: Parliament/Council Directive 2012/28/EU *on certain permitted uses of orphan works*, O.J. L 299/5 (2012).

[17] Council Directive 93/98/EEC, O.J. L 290/9 (1993), replaced by Parliament/Council Directive 2006/116/EC *on the term of protection of copyright and certain related rights (codified version)*, O.J. L 372/12 (2006).

[18] Parliament/Council Directive 2014/26/EU *on collective management copyright and related right and multi-territorial licensing of rights in musical works for online use in the internal market*, O.J. L 84/72 (2014).

[19] Parliament/Council Directive 2001/29/EC *on the harmonisation of certain aspects of copyright and related rights in the information society*, O.J. L 167/10 (2001).

responsibility and also, for the first time, contracts.[20] The Community legislator has also adopted a harmonisation directive on the enforcement of intellectual property, dealing with this issue for all intellectual property rights.[21] In the past, the competence attributed now by Article 83.2 TFEU (→ Article 83 TFEU para 35 et seqq.) has been recognised as an implied competence (*a priori* less extended because it did not encompass the nature and scope of criminal law sanctions).

9   As far as the creation of **IP rights** is concerned, two **Community titles** were created in the 1990s on the basis of the general clause of ex-Article 308 TEC (Article 352 TFEU): the Community trademark[22] and the Community plant variety protection.[23] As an integral part of the common agricultural policy (CAP), Community protection for geographical indications and appellations of origin has been established by a Regulation based on ex-Article 37 TEC (Article 43 TFEU).[24] About ten years later, the Community design was created.[25]

10   If we consider the two pillars of IP—patent and copyright—we see that, in both cases, **harmonisation is incomplete** and has not been followed by the creation of Community titles. However, while the creation of a Community-wide unitary patent has been foreseen for long (by different means from an act of the Union or a convention under the auspices of the EU), this has not been the case for copyright (which has, however, experienced a more extended and audacious legislative and jurisdictional harmonisation of copyright since 2001).

1.2. Rationale for Adopting Article 118 TFEU

11   In fact, one reason, if indeed not the main one, for the integration of Article 118 TFEU was that the EU needed **clear and indisputable competence and legitimacy to create European IP rights**. When considering the rationale for the adoption of Article 118 TFEU, a historical and political perspective is relevant. The project of

---

[20] Parliament/Council Directive 2019/790/EC *on copyright and related rights in the Digital Single Market*, O.J. L 130/92 (2019). A second Directive has been adopted in 2019: Parliament/Council Directive 2019/789/EC *laying down rules on the exercise of copyright and related rights applicable to certain online transmissions of broadcasting organisations and retransmissions of television and radio programmes*, O.J. L 130/82 (2019).

[21] Parliament/Council Directive 2004/48/EC *on the enforcement of intellectual property rights*, O.J. L 195/16 (2004).

[22] Council Regulation (EC) No. 40/94, O.J. L 11/1 (1994), repealed by Council Regulation (EC) No. 207/2009, O.J. L 78/1 (2009), and eventually codified by Parliament/Council Regulation (EU) No 2017/1001 *on the European Union trade mark (codification)*, O.J. L 154/16 (2017).

[23] Council Regulation (EC) No. 2100/94 *on Community plant variety rights*, O.J. L 227/1 (1994).

[24] Council Regulation (EEC) No. 2081/92, O.J. L 208/1 (1992), replaced by Council Regulation (EC) No. 510/2006, O.J. L 93/1 (2006), and eventually replaced by Parliament/Council Regulation (EU) No 2015/2424 *on quality schemes for agricultural products and foodstuffs* O.J. L 343/1 (2015).

[25] Council Regulation (EC) No. 6/2002 *on Community designs*, O.J. L 3/1 (2002), currently under revision (see the proposal of the Commission, COM(2022) 666 final).

creating a Community patent was born in the 1960s, whereas the idea of integrating a specific clause in the Treaties to confer the Union an undisputable competence to create autonomous European IP rights dates back only to the 1990s. However, both issues are linked.

In the 1960s, six MS, encouraged by IP professionals, undertook a first effort to establish common rules relating to IP.[26] However, at that time, IP issues were essentially the concern of a "little world" populated by IP professionals, who were familiar with national IP law but were not very confident with the Community system. These professionals, as the representatives of States, generally thought IP to be a matter of national sovereignty. They chose a negotiated and "mastered" solution, that of an **intergovernmental approach**. Two twin conventional projects arose: the **Convention on the Grant of European Patents** (EPC)[27] and its twin, the **Convention for the European Patent for the Common Market** (CPC).[28] However, for reasons of political opportunity, they were separated, and only the EPC was signed and entered into force. 12

In the 1980s, the Union institutions, more and more conscious of the growing importance of IP rights, notably for economic development and the establishment of a common market, undertook the **approximation of national IP law**, and even **Community titles** were created on the basis of ex-Article 308 TEC (Article 352 TFEU). However, the multiple, fragmented and non-specific legal foundations for Community action were controversial because they were uncertain, especially as regards the competence to create a Community title. As a result, Community action was fragmented and the legal framework in IP lacked coherence. 13

In the 1990s, IP and in particular patents and copyright had become a trade issue, especially due to the **WTO** TRIPS negotiations and the ensuing **TRIPS Agreement**. It had also become a question of internal economic policy. Besides, patent and copyright law had been rediscovered as instruments of innovation policy. There was a need for a clear response relating to the **internal and external competence of the Community** regarding IP, and the Court of Justice undertook to provide it. The Court affirmed the internal (and, according to the implied competence theory, the external; → Article 3 TFEU para 23) Community competence in IP in very clear words: "neither Article 222 nor Article 36 of the Treaty reserves a power to regulate substantive patent law to the national legislature, to the exclusion of any Community action in the matter. [At] the level of internal legislation, the Community is competent, in the field of intellectual property, to harmonize national laws pursuant 14

---

[26] Scordamaglia (2013), p. 62 et seqq.; Ullrich (2007), p. 65 et seqq.

[27] Convention on the Grant of European Patents (EPC), signed in Munich on 5 October 1973 and entered into force in 1976, published now by the European Patent Office, 15th ed., 2013.

[28] Convention for the European Patent for the Common Market (Community Patent Convention) of 15 December 1975, O.J. L 17/1 (1976); Agreement Relating to Community Patents, 15 December 1989, O.J. L 401/1 (incorporating inter alia the Convention for the European Patent for the Common Market and the Protocol on the settlement of Litigation Concerning the Infringement and Validity of Community Patents).

to Articles 100 and 100a and may use Article 235 as the basis for creating new rights super-imposed on national rights [...]."[29]

15   The Commission also undertook two important tasks in the areas of copyright and patent law. In the case of copyright, the **European Commission** initiated a first horizontal directive in 1996.[30] In the case of patent, in 1997, the Commission produced a Green Paper designed to boost the old project of a Community patent.[31] Following the first action plan for innovation,[32] the Commission presented in 1999 a Communication entitled "Promoting innovation through patents".[33] A year later, in March 2000, at a meeting of the European Council in Lisbon, the EU set itself the strategic goal of becoming the most competitive and dynamic knowledge-based economy in the world by 2010.[34] The Commission, the main engine room of EU policymaking, was charged with the task of acting upon the Lisbon's objectives and putting into place appropriate measures to ensure that those objectives were met. In establishing a legal framework to foster new products and services, the Commission has recognised the importance of the protection of knowledge, creativity and invention. Furthermore, it should also be noted that, in December 2000, IP protection was expressly recognised in Article 17.2 EUCFR.[35]

16   Outside the EU framework, the **European Patent Organisation** (EPOrg), which had striven to enhance the European patent system and which had, in fact, become used to taking a lead in European patent matters, was a "rival" of the Community. Just before the official publication of the first Commission proposal for a Council Regulation on the Community Patent,[36] the MS of the EPOrg took the initiative to set up a Working Party on Litigation during the Intergovernmental Conference (IGC) of Paris in 1999.[37] Almost concurrently, this Working Party

---

[29] Case C-350/92, *Spain v Council* (ECJ 13 July 1995) para 22 and 23, recalling the Case C-30/90, *Commission v United Kingdom* (ECJ 18 February 1992) para 18–19 where the Court rejected the argument that the Community had no competence with regard to Article 222 TEEC to regulate the substantive law of patent and can only harmonise aspects relative to the industrial exercise of the property right rights susceptible to influence the realisation of the general objectives planned in the treaty.

[30] Proposal for a Parliament/Council Directive *on the harmonisation of certain aspects of copyright and related rights in the Information Society*, COM(97) 628.

[31] Commission, *Green Paper on the Community patent and the patent system in Europe*, COM(97) 314 final.

[32] Commission, *Innovation for growth and employment*, COM(1996) 589.

[33] Commission, *Promoting innovation through patents*, COM (1999) 42 final (the follow-up to the Green Paper on the Community Patent and the Patent System in Europe).

[34] See notably document IP/00/714, Council document 6874/03 issued from the 2490th Council meeting Competitiveness (Internal Market, Industry and Research) of 3 March 2003.

[35] See Note from the Praesidium, Charte 4473/00, Brussels, 11 October 2000, p. 20 (explaining this adjunction and separate mentioning of IP rights by its growing importance).

[36] COM(2000) 412.

[37] The second IGC in London in 2000 sought to address another issue at core of the Community discussion relating to patent: the cost of translation.

succeeded in drafting an optional European Patent Litigation Agreement (EPLA),[38] and the Community published several propositions designed to establish **a European judicial patent system**, especially a proposal for a Regulation on the Community Patent[39] and two proposals for decisions establishing a European Patent Court and conferring jurisdiction on the Court of Justice in disputes relating to Community patent.[40] The rivalry between the two organisations primarily arose from their different conceptions of the patent system, its function and the fundamental question of enforcement and litigation. What is clear is that if an efficient judicial system had been established within the European patent system (under the EPC), the chances of creating a Community patent would have decreased significantly.

The ensuing history of drafts and changes is long and winding,[41] marked by the **persistent disagreement** on the language regime for the Community patent and by the development of positions concerning the type of jurisdictional system to be established. Debate took place within a broader context of discussions, activities and negotiations undertaken with the aim of making the EU more democratic, more efficient and better able to address the problems linked to its objectives. The protection of IP has been integrated as one of the major levers of a policy based on the promotion and encouragement of research, of innovation and of a knowledge economy.[42]

17

As IP rights came to be viewed as at the core of economic activity, as a fundamental driver of growth and even as an important social lever, the legitimacy of EU intervention in the sphere of IP increased. As a result, it was decided to **introduce clear competence for the EU to create European IP titles**, that is uniform protection of IP rights throughout the Union, and to provide that the ordinary legislative procedure would apply to the creation of such titles. It was envisaged to adopt a voting rule facilitating the EU's legislative action and making the legislative process more democratic (ex-Article 308 TEC = Article 352 TFEU requires unanimity in the Council and only the EP's consent; → para 50). However, the drafting of Article 118 TFEU bears the stigma of its history and, in particular, of its relationship with the history of the Community patent project. This is visible in

---

[38] Working Party on Litigation, *Draft Agreement on the establishment of a European Patent Litigation System* of 16 February 2004 (https://www.biicl.org/files/2465_european_patent_litigation_agreement.pdf) and *Draft statute of the European Patent Court* of 16 February 2004 (https://www.uaipit.com/uploads/legislacion/files/1259753423_3_EPLA-20040216-Draft_Statute_of_EPCourt.pdf).

[39] Council Document No 7119/04 PI 28, 8 March 2004.

[40] Commission, *Proposal for a Council Decision establishing the Community Patent Court and concerning appeals before the Court of First Instance*, COM(2003) 828 final and Commission, *Proposal for a Council Decision conferring jurisdiction on the Court of Justice in disputes relating to the Community patent*, COM(2003) 827 final.

[41] Jaeger (2010), Pagenberg (2007), Pila (2015) and Plomer (2017, 2020).

[42] This assertion is more or less present and often underlined in all the Community documents and proposals and can be traced back to the very roots of the Community IP plans. See especially, as far as Community Patent plans are concerned: Beier (1969), p. 147 et seqq.

the fact that while the ordinary legislative procedure is foreseen for the creation of European titles, Article 118 (2) TFEU requires unanimity regarding the adoption of the language regimes of the European IP titles (→ para 51).

2. Nature of the Competence

18   The nature of the competence conferred by Article 118 TFEU has been widely discussed, both by scholars and by the CJEU. Indeed, the legal characterisation of this competence is a major issue when MS consider resorting to enhanced cooperation as enhanced cooperation cannot apply to areas that fall within the EU's exclusive competence according to Article 20 TEU. Considering that the EU competence under Article 118 TFEU was a shared competence, 12 MS requested to establish enhanced cooperation for the first exercise of this competence in 2010.[43] Recognising the "impossibility" of obtaining the agreement of all the MS and while unanimity was necessary as translation arrangements are indispensable for the creation of a unitary patent, the Council authorised **enhanced cooperation in the area of the creation of unitary patent protection**.[44] This decision was contested by the two non-participating MS, Spain and Italy, while the Commission presented a proposal for a Regulation implementing enhanced cooperation in the area of the creation of unitary patent protection based on Article 118 TFEU.[45] Before the ECJ's decision, the "patent package"[46] was adopted and again challenged by Spain before the Court. As a result, the Court of Justice has had two opportunities to specify the nature of the competence granted to the Union by Article 118 TFEU.[47]

---

[43] See the response to this request in the proposal for a Council Decision *authorising enhanced cooperation in the area of the creation of unitary patent protection*, COM(2010) 790 final.

[44] Council Decision 2011/167/EU *authorising enhanced cooperation in the area of the creation of unitary patent protection*, O.J. L 76/53 (2011). On the development see Böttner (2021), p. 50 et seqq.

[45] Proposal for a Parliament/Council Regulation *implementing enhanced cooperation in the area of the creation of unitary patent protection*, COM(2011) 215 final.

[46] Parliament/Council Regulation (EU) No. 1257/2012 *implementing enhanced cooperation in the area of the creation of unitary patent protection*, O.J. L 361/1 (2012); Council Regulation (EU) No. 1260/2012 *implementing enhanced cooperation in the area of the creation of unitary patent protection with regard to the applicable translation arrangements*, O.J. L 361/89 (2012) and the Agreement on a Unified Patent Court, signed on 19 February 2013, O.J. C 175/1 (2013).

[47] One Opinion and three decisions of the Court are dealing with the "patent package", only the rulings specified the nature of the specific competence: Opinion 1/09, *unified patent litigation system* (ECJ 8 March 2011); Joined Cases C-274/11 and C-295/11, *Spain and Italy v Council* (ECJ 16 April 2013); Case C-146/13, *Spain v Parliament and Council* (ECJ 5 May 2015) and Case C-147/13, *Spain v Council* (ECJ 5 May 2015).

Article 118. [European Intellectual Property Rights]

2.1. Shared Competence of the European Union

The Treaty of Lisbon introduces a precise classification of the division of competences between the EU and the MS, distinguishing between three main types of competence and identifying their respective domain: exclusive competences (Articles 2.1 and 3 TFEU), shared competences (Article 2.2 and 4 TFEU) and supporting competences (Article 2.5 and Article 6 TFEU). To determine the nature of the competence granted by Article 118 TFEU, the domain concerned must be identified. This is a relatively easy task as a result of the **formal place** of the provision within the rules relating to the harmonisation of laws with a view to the realisation of the internal market and because its wording is clear in attributing the competence to the EU "in the context of the **establishment and functioning of the internal market**". Thus, according to Article 4.2 point (a) TFEU, shared competence should be retained.

19

However, the specific nature of European IP rights (the **object of the competence**) implies, for some,[48] the exclusivity of EU competence because European IP rights cannot, by nature, be created by MS and, when created, must be a part of the "acquis", which is not the case if enhanced cooperation is used according to Article 20.4 TEU.

20

The application of **exclusive competence** was defended by Spain and Italy in their challenge to the decision authorising enhanced cooperation under Article 329.1 TFEU on the grounds of lack of competence, misuse of powers, infringement of the Treaties and misunderstanding of the judicial system of the Union. The applicants argued that the competence conferred by Article 118 TFEU was within the ambit of the "**competition rules necessary for the functioning of the internal market**" referred to in Article 3.1 point (b) TFEU and, therefore, fell within the Union's exclusive competence.

The Grand Chamber, in a decision of great constitutional importance, delivered a rich and thorough analysis of the wording of the Treaties, making Article 118 TFEU fall within the area of shared competence. The Court demonstrated that both paragraphs of Article 118 TFEU confer a competence falling within the ambit of the functioning of the internal market.[49] The internal market is defined in Article 26.2 TFEU, and Article 26.1 TFEU states that the Union shall "adopt measures with the aim of establishing or ensuring the functioning of the internal market, in accordance with the relevant provisions of the Treaties". According to the Court, these provisions make it clear that competences falling within the sphere of the internal market are not confined to those conferred by Articles 114 and 115 TFEU relating to the adoption of harmonisation measures but cover also any competence attaching to the objectives set out in Article 26 TFEU.[50] In adopting a systematic and teleological

21

---

[48] Lamping (2011), pp. 911–912; Ullrich (2012), pp. 270–275.
[49] Joined Cases C-274/11 and C-295/11, *Spain v Council* (ECJ 16 April 2013) para 17–18.
[50] Joined Cases C-274/11 and C-295/11, *Spain v Council* (ECJ 16 April 2013) para 20.

interpretation of the provisions at issue, the Court noted that competences conferred by Article 118 TFEU are attached to the objectives set out in Article 26 TFEU. Although it is true, according to the Grand Chamber, that rules on intellectual property are essential in order to maintain undistorted competition, they do not, as noted by the AG, constitute "competition rules" for the purpose of Article 3.1 point (b) TFEU, unless extending unduly the scope of this Article and misjudging Article 2.6 TFEU.[51] The Court therefore concluded that the specific competences conferred by Article 118 TFEU fall within an area of **shared competences** in accordance with Article 4.2 TFEU. This was confirmed in the second decision brought by Spain against the regulations implementing the enhanced cooperation project.[52] As the competence conferred by Article 118 TFEU falls within an area of shared competences, it is, in consequence, non-exclusive for the purpose of Article 20.1 TEU and thus **susceptible of enhanced cooperation**.

2.2. A Specific Competence to Be Articulated with Other EU Competences

22   The competence conferred by Article 118 TFEU is linked to the completion of the internal market and thus focuses on **economic rather than the cultural, social and other non-economic aspects of IP**. However, some changes made by the Treaty of Lisbon are significant from this point of view. The Parliament was accorded greater significance in the lawmaking process. The positions adopted by the Parliament reveal that it does not have a purely economic vision of IP rights. The non-economic aspects of IP linked to culture (Article 167 TFEU) and research (Article 179 TFEU) are also recognised explicitly; furthermore, Article 3.3 (3) TEU aims to promote cultural diversity, the safeguarding of European heritage and its development. Finally, from a material point of view, Article 17.2 EUCFR (which has the same primary law value as the Treaties, Article 6.1 TEU) provides for the fundamental rights protection of intellectual property.[53]

23   Moreover, the identification of the legal basis is important. Article 296 (2) TFEU requires every measure with intended legal effect to refer expressly to its **legal basis**. The Court of Justice nevertheless considers that this requirement is sufficiently fulfilled if the legal basis follows unmistakeably from the statement of reasons accompanying the directive or regulation.[54] The Court further demands that the application of the relevant legal basis should be well **founded on objective grounds**—particularly as regards the aim and content of the measure—in the statement of reasons.[55]

---

[51] Joined Cases C-274/11 and C-295/11, *Spain v Council* (ECJ 16 April 2013) para 22–24.
[52] Case C-146/13, *Spain v Parliament and Council* (ECJ 5 May 2015) para 40.
[53] See in particular Geiger (2013), p. 113 et seqq.
[54] Case 45/86, *Commission v Council* (ECJ 26 March 1987).
[55] Case C-300/89, *Commission v Council* (ECJ 11 June 1991).

2.2.1. The Residual Competence of Article 352 TFEU

The **flexibility clause** of Article 352 TFEU allows the Council, with the EP's consent, to unanimously adjust the Union's competences to the objectives laid down by the Treaty when the specific or explicit powers of action necessary to attain them have not been provided and if the action envisaged is "necessary, within the framework of the policies defined in the Treaties [except the CFSP], to attain one of the objectives set out in the Treaties" and so long as no measures based on this article shall entail the harmonisation of MS' laws or regulations in cases in which the Treaties exclude such harmonisation. 24

Prior to the Treaty of Lisbon, the legislator used **ex-Article 308 TEC** to create Community titles, given that no explicit power to create such Community titles existed. It was in fact the only available option for the **establishment of Community IP rights**. Article 308 TEC was the legal basis employed to create the Community trademark, Community plant variety protection and Community designs (→ para 9). However, the recourse to this general clause had the huge disadvantage that it required unanimity in the Council and consultation with the Parliament. Besides, the possibility for the Community to act on this basis was debated because of Article 345 TFEU (ex-Article 295 TEC, ex-Article 222 TEEC), according to which the Treaties shall not prejudice the rules in MS governing the system of property ownership and the exact meaning and scope of which has been, and still is, controversial (→ Article 345 TFEU para 1 et seqq.). The main reason for this is that its wording is so broad that the meaning becomes difficult to determine.[56] However, since the *Grundig* case,[57] the Court has always rejected this argument and notably did so in the case brought before the Court by Spain (→ para 14). 25

This interpretation took place in a special context, in the absence of any specific and express EU competence to create a new European IP right and especially in relation to the need for the Union to justify an external competence in IP (now Article 207 TFEU). Since the Union has now been granted a specific competence to create European IP rights under Article 118 (1) TFEU, **Article 352 TFEU can no longer serve as a legal basis** for the creation of such rights **when the main objective** is dealing with issues related to the **internal market** insofar as Article 118 TFEU is *lex specialis* in relation to Article 352 TFEU. Whenever the main objectives of a measure foreseen in the field of IP do not relate to the internal market, the flexibility clause, as a subsidiary competence mechanism, may still provide a legal basis, where another article conferring specific EU competence is not applicable, e. g. culture (Article 167.5 TFEU) or agriculture (Article 43 TFEU), to name but a few.[58] 26

---

[56] Akkermans and Ramaekers (2010), p. 292.

[57] Joined Cases 56 and 58/64, *Consten and Grundig* (ECJ 13 July 1966) p. 345, para 6.

[58] See on this point the Declarations annexed to the Final Act of the Intergovernmental Conference which adopted the Treaty of Lisbon, (§41; §42) O.J. C 83/350 (2010).

2.2.2. The "General" Competences to Harmonise of Articles 114 and 115 TFEU

27 Historically, **Article 115 TFEU**'s predecessors (→ Article 115 TFEU para 2) provided the **legal basis for the first legislative act** in the area of IP.[59] This first Directive was the only one based on this provision because six months after its adoption, the Single European Act (SEA) came into effect and established a new legal basis likely to be used for the harmonisation of national IP legislation (Article 100a TEEC, now Article 114 TFEU; → Article 114 TFEU para 5) as this new provision required a qualified majority, whereas Article 100 TEEC required unanimity.

28 As soon as it was introduced, Article 100a TEEC became the main instrument for the approximation of national legislation. Since the Maastricht Treaty of 1992, the EP is invested with a real legislative function, with the Council as part of the co-decision procedure. If **Article 114 TFEU** is employed as the **main legal basis for a harmonisation directive**, sometimes complemented by reference to further provisions, its scope of application remains limited as harmonisation measures must materially be focused on "the establishment and functioning on the internal market" (→ Article 114 TFEU para 26 et seqq.). The Lisbon Treaty leaves materially unchanged the competence concerning the approximation of laws adopted with a view to the internal market within Article 114 TFEU; this approach to approximation will always necessitate an economic conception and vision for IP rights. A second limitation arises as a result of the function and purpose of these provisions, which relate to legal approximation of national provisions (→ Article 114 TFEU para 33 et seqq.). It cannot provide the legal basis for the creation of European IP right as such, as has been specified by the Court of Justice.[60]

29 However, while Article 114 TFEU grants power to harmonise the laws of the MS to the extent required for the functioning of the internal market, speaking of "measures for the approximation of the provisions" of national laws, this does not mean that directives or regulations cannot introduce rights that are new for certain MS (→ Article 114 TFEU para 33). It is a large-scale power permitting the legislator to make existing provisions of national law substantively similar (harmonisation in a narrow sense), to introduce new rights and to extend the term of protection of these rights. The patent cases in which the **ECJ ruled that ex-Article 95 TEC is an appropriate legal basis** for the extension of the term of protection for certain patents (by supplementary certificates)[61] and for the introduction of protection for biotechnological inventions (formerly excluded from protection in a

---

[59] Council Directive 87/54/EC *on the legal protection of topographies of semiconductor products*, O.J. L 24/36 (1987).

[60] Opinion 1/94, *WTO Agreement* (ECJ 15 November 1994) para 59 and also Case C-350/92, *Spain v Council* (ECJ 13 July 1995) para 23.

[61] See on that point Case C-350/92, *Spain v Council* (ECJ 13 July 1995).

number of MS)[62] are illustrative. There are now also numerous examples relating to copyright, which establish autonomous concepts defining key notions about copyright law.[63]

However, these competences have been distinguished since the Treaty of Lisbon. The Union is competent to approximate IP laws in order to harmonise differing legislations, mainly on the basis of Article 114 TFEU, and to **create new autonomous intellectual property titles** (or to modify existing rights) under the specific and express provision of **Article 118 TFEU**.

3. Scope of Competence

The competence attributed by Article 118 (1) TFEU may be implemented through the adoption of "measures" submitted to the ordinary legislative procedure. The nature of these "measures" is not specified in Article 118 (1) TFEU, although Article 118 (2) TFEU requires the EU to employ a regulation where it acts to establish language arrangements for European IP rights. As for content under Article 118 (1) TFEU, such measures may either be "for the creation of European intellectual property rights" or "for the setting up of centralised Union-wide authorisation, coordination and supervision arrangements".

3.1. The Nature of the "Measures"

In the absence of further precision concerning the type of acts that can be adopted in accordance with **Article 118 (1) TFEU**, the term employed ("measures") *a priori* refers to **different legal acts** that can be adopted by the Union's institutions and more precisely by the EP and the Council.[64] A classification of these acts can be found in Article 288 TFEU, which distinguishes regulations, directives, decisions, recommendations and opinions and specifies the legal scope of each. According to Article 296 (1) TFEU, when the type of act to be adopted is not specified in the Treaties, the choice is open on a case-by-case basis, in compliance with the applicable procedures and with the principle of proportionality. It would appear that measures provided for under Article 118 TFEU must be of general scope, of a mandatory nature and directly applicable in any MS. These measures would *a priori* be regulations, and in fact, current IP legislation has been adopted in the

---

[62] See Case C-377/98, *Netherlands v Parliament and Council* (ECJ 9 October 2001).

[63] Since Case C-5/08, *Infopaq International* (ECJ 16 July 2009) for the "originality" or "communication to the public" concepts especially, see on the subsequent case-law on copyright: Rosati (2019); Griffith (2014), p. 1098 et seqq.; Leistner (2014), p. 559 et seqq.; Carre (2013), p. 19 et seqq.; Benabou (2012).

[64] See Holzmüller, in Schwarze et al. (2018), p. 1385.

form of regulations.[65] The Commission itself explained that the form chosen for the instrument in its proposal (a regulation) is warranted by a number of considerations: "The Member States cannot be left with any discretion either to determine the Community law applicable to the Community patent or to decide on the effects and administration of the patent once it has been granted. The unity of the patent could not be guaranteed by less 'binding' measures."[66] **Article 118 (2) TFEU** specifies that the language regime of European IP rights will be established through **regulations**.

3.2. Creation of European IP Rights to Provide Uniform Protection Throughout the Union

33 Such wording of the English version of Article 118 (1) TFEU as "measures for the creation of European IP rights" is rather redundant. When an interpreter takes a look at the French (*"mesures relatives à la création de titres européens"*) and German (*"Maßnahmen zur Schaffung europäischer Rechtstitel"*) versions, the meaning appears not so clear. One might wonder if the competence assigned to the Union concerns the creation of "rights" or "titles". The term "rights" used in the English version is more readily understood than the German expression *Rechtstitel* or the French *titres*. It seems that to give a sense to the chosen word "right" rather than "title", the more comprehensive interpretation of the wording of Article 118 (1) TFEU should be retained. The rationale for adopting this provision was to provide the EU with **efficient tools and powers to provide uniform protection** of IP throughout the Union in creating autonomous and unitary rights. It was motivated by the need to give the Union the necessary competence to implement strong European IP rights (in order to achieve its objectives).

34 The competence is specifically conferred for the creation of these IP rights "to provide uniform protection of intellectual property rights throughout the Union". The fundamental characteristic of these rights is that they ought to be **Union-wide** rights, submitted to a uniform, unitary and autonomous EU regime in the Union.

35 These European IP rights, like the Community industrial property rights previously adopted on the basis of Article 308 TEC, would be *a priori* rights **"in addition" to national IP rights**. National and existing Community IP rights are intended to exist "side by side", and it seems that no change has been foreseen with regard to this characteristic. Union IP rights are not intended to replace national rights; to date, they remain **"optional"**. They are identified by scholars as

---

[65] Parliament/Council Regulation No. 1257/2012 *implementing enhanced cooperation in the area of the creation of unitary patent protection*, O.J. L 361/1 (2012); Council Regulation No. 1260/2012 *implementing enhanced cooperation in the area of the creation of unitary patent protection with regard to the applicable translation arrangements*, O.J. L 361/89 (2012) and Parliament/Council Regulation (EU) No 2017/1001 *on the European Union trade mark*, O.J. L 154/16 (2017).

[66] Explanatory Memorandum of the Proposal for a Council Regulation on the Community patent, COM(2000) 412, para 2.2 §2.

corresponding to "optional instruments",[67] that is EU legislative acts, usually in the form of a regulation, which creates a parallel and optional EU-wide legal regime for a given legal issue. Such optional regimes do not replace national regimes but coexist alongside them. To take the example of the Community trademark or Community design, the applicant can, as a matter of principle, choose between a Community trademark or design (through the registration of the mark or the model at the European Union Intellectual Property Office (EUIPO)),[68] on the one hand, and several parallel national property rights, on the other. The applicant may also obtain both.[69]

In this regard, one particularity exists in the case of the Regulation on **geographical indications and appellations of origin**,[70] which partly pre-empts the protection of geographical indications at the national level and still exists within the different Regulations in force.[71] As the Court states very clear in one of the "Bud" cases, "The aim of Regulation No 510/2006 is not to establish, alongside national rules which may continue to exist, an additional system of protection for qualified geographical indications, like, for example, that introduced by Council Regulation No 40/94 [...] on the Community trade mark,[72] but to provide a uniform and exhaustive system of protection for such indications".[73] It should be noted, however, that this Regulation is based on ex-Article 43 TEC (Article 47 TFEU) on agricultural policy[74] and that geographical indications are quite different in nature

36

---

[67] See notably for a comprehensive overview of the study for the EP by Fauvarque-Cosson and Behar-Touchais (2002) and also Smits (2010).

[68] The EUIPO is an agency of the Union and the successor of the Office for Harmonization in the Internal Market (OHIM), which was founded in 1994. The EUIPO was established by the Parliament/Council Regulation (EU) No 2015/2424; → Article 114 TFEU para 81.

[69] See especially on the issue of territorial overlaps: Dinwoodie (2017). On the impact of Brexit, see notably d'Erme (2020) and Basire et al. (2017).

[70] Council Regulation (EC) No. 510/2006, O.J. L 93/12 (2006).

[71] Parliament/Council Regulation (EU) No 2015/2424 *on quality schemes for agricultural products and foodstuffs* O.J. L 343/1 (2015), O.J. L 93/12 (2006) (repealing Regulations (EC) No. 510/2006 and No. 509/2006); Parliament/Council Regulation (EU) No 1308/2013 *establishing a common organisation of the markets in agricultural products*, O.J. L347/671 (2013); Parliament/Council Regulation (EU) No 2019/787 *on the definition, description, presentation and labelling of spirit drinks, the use of the names of spirit drinks in the presentation and labelling of other foodstuffs, the protection of geographical indications for spirit drinks, the use of ethyl alcohol and distillates of agricultural origin in alcoholic beverages*, O.J. L 130/1 (2019).

[72] Now Parliament/Council Regulation (EU) No 2017/1001, O.J. L 154/16 (2017).

[73] Case C-478/07, *Budějovický Budvar* (ECJ 8 September 2009) para 114, see also Case C-56/16 P, *EUIPO v Instituto dos Vinhos do Douro e do Porto IP* (ECJ 14 September 2017).

[74] Parliament/Council Regulation (EU) No 2019/787 is based on Articles 43.2 and 114.1 TFEU. This specificity is not called into question by the accession of the EU to the Geneva Act of the Lisbon Agreement regarding Council Decision (EU) 2019/1754 *on the accession of the European Union to the Geneva Act of the Lisbon Agreement on Appellations of Origin and Geographical Indications* O.J. L 271/12 (2019) and Parliament/Council Regulation (EU) No 2019/1753 *on the action of the Union following its accession to the Geneva Act of the Lisbon Agreement on Appellations of Origin and Geographical Indications* O.J. L 271/1 (2019).

from classic intellectual property rights as they are not transferable property interests. Therefore, one might consider that European IP rights are as a general rule designed to exist alongside national ones. However, it cannot be excluded that in the future, a political choice might be made to prohibit the coexistence or even to replace national IP rights with a European right.

37 The Commission has expressly envisaged the creation of an **optional unitary copyright title** on the basis of Article 118 TFEU.[75] Yet the situation is particular insofar as European copyright is concerned because European copyright without the need for registration is foreseen (as the international legal obligations of MS under international conventions have to be considered, especially the Berne Convention (Article 5.2), which prohibits formal acts as a precondition for the existence of copyright).[76] If copyright therefore comes into existence by the mere creation of a work, the creator will (in principle) be entitled to the property right once the conditions of protection are fulfilled. Under these circumstances, the coexistence of parallel legal systems of national and Union law, without being impossible, would be complicated and, for some, "would involve barely solvable problems",[77] which may explain the very daring and interventionist jurisprudence of the ECJ (→ para 29).[78] Even when registration is required, the EU legislature may prefer to avoid competition between national and Union rights, and it should be noted that the draft regulation for a Community patent prohibited simultaneous protection.[79] The Regulation finally adopted created, as mentioned, not an EU patent but a European patent with a unitary effect.

38 To conclude, two points have to be made with regard to the **current Regulations** adopted on the basis of Article 118 TFEU. The first addresses the question of the **territorial extent of European IP rights**. Article 118 TFEU mentions uniform protection "throughout the Union". This is the case with the EU trademark. In the field of European patent, the Court of Justice acknowledged, since this competence

---

[75] Commission Green Paper *on the online distribution of audiovisual works in the European Union: opportunities and challenges towards a digital single market*, COM(2011) 427 final, p. 13, n° 3: "It could also provide the opportunity to examine whether the exceptions and limitations to copyright allowed under the Information Society Directive need to be updated. In addition to such a Code, the feasibility of creating an optional unitary copyright title on the basis of Article 118 TFEU could be examined. An optional title could be made available on a voluntary basis and co-exist with national titles. Future authors or producers of audiovisual works would have the option to register their works and then obtain a single title that would be valid throughout the EU. The feasibility, actual demand for, and the tangible advantages of, such a title, together with the consequences of its application alongside existing territorial protection must be thoroughly examined."

[76] This question of registration is not the sole specificity regarding copyright, see notably for further developments: Stieper, in Grabitz et al. (2022), Artikel 118 AEUV para 37 et seqq. (released in 2022).

[77] Hilty (2004), p. 769.

[78] Rosati (2019).

[79] Article 54 of the Commission Proposal for a Council Regulation on the Community patent, O.J. C 337/278 (2000).

is exercised through enhanced cooperation, "that the European intellectual property right so created, the uniform protection given by it and the arrangements attaching to it will be in force, *not in the Union in its entirety, but only in the territory of the participating Member States*".[80] For the Court, far from amounting to the infringement of Article 118 TFEU, that consequence necessarily follows from the implementation of enhanced cooperation as Article 20.4 TEU states that "acts adopted in the framework of enhanced cooperation shall bind only participating Member States".[81]

The second point deals with the fact that Regulation No. 1257/2012, which is a special agreement within the meaning of Article 142 EPC,[82] has created not an EU patent but, according to its title, a **unitary patent protection**.[83] The terminological elision in the different versions of the text aimed at establishing the title in question is interesting and implies a real shift in meaning. In 2000, the Commission proposal mentioned a **Community patent**,[84] then the expression of "Community unitary patent" appeared in the following discussions and proposed texts, to be replaced by the wording "unitary patent" or "unitary patent protection" in the decision authorising enhanced cooperation.[85] It became a "**European patent with a unitary effect**" in Regulation No. 1257/2012 (Article 3). The Council decision authorised enhanced cooperation in the area of the *creation of unitary patent protection*. The title created is in fact *an effect*, a unitary effect, given to a European patent according to the EPC, so one may say that the title created is a "European patent with unitary effect". However, the grant, validity and effect of such a European patent are not subject to EU law. The European patent at issue is granted by the European Patent Office (EPO) and is subject to the conditions of the EPC. Recital 7 of the regulation proclaims that "the unitary effect attributed to a European patent should have an accessory nature and should be deemed not to have arisen to the extent that the basic European patent has been revoked or limited". As far as the unitary effect is concerned, the European patent with a unitary effect will provide uniform protection, but this protection is not defined by EU law. It will have almost an equal effect in all the participating MS, but that effect will be defined by a national law designated by the application of a private international law rule provided for in Article 7 of the Regulation. Numerous critical voices have

---

[80] Joined Cases C-274/11 & C-295/11, *Spain v Council* (ECJ 16 April 2013) para 68 (emphasis added).

[81] Joined Cases C-274/11 & C-295/11, *Spain v Council* (ECJ, 16 April 2013) para 68.

[82] As recalled in Case C-146/13, *Spain v Parliament and Council* (ECJ 5 May 2015) para 28.

[83] Parliament/Council Regulation (EU) No. 1257/2012 *implementing enhanced cooperation in the area of the creation of unitary patent protection*, O.J. L 361/1 (2012).

[84] COM(2000) 412.

[85] Council Decision 2011/167/EU *authorising enhanced cooperation in the area of the creation of unitary patent protection*, O.J. L 76/53 (2011).

denounced the failure to create a new European Union IP right[86] because the "title" provided by the regulation does not arise from a specific deliverance procedure.[87] There is no specific duration nor specific cancellation and revocation conditions. Regulation No. 1257/2012 does not include indeed a definition of an EU regime with the deletion of Articles 6 to 8 of the Commission proposal of 2000.[88] Absent any specific provision in the Regulation, rules to be applied result of the EPC and national legislations but not of EU law.[89] However, the Court stated that the European patent with a unitary effect has a unitary character and provides uniform protection in all the participating MS within the meaning of the first paragraph of Article 118 TFEU.[90]

3.3. Centralised Union-Wide Authorisation, Coordination and Supervision Arrangements

39   The competence assigned to the Union under Article 118 TFEU allows the EP and the Council to adopt measures relating to the implementation of centralized authorisation, coordination and control arrangements at the Union level. It seemed to be obvious that such a regime should be related to IP rights. Within this perspective, authorisation and coordination regimes on a European level correspond to those already existing in Europe, notably for European patents. The **European Patent Office** grants patents after a common and centralized application procedure. The examination of the conditions for patentability described by the Munich Convention is conducted by the EPO, which also manages the payment of annual taxes needed for title validity.

40   When the Commission re-established its leadership on the Community patent project, it was necessary to build on the existing European system and on the expertise acquired by the EPO. **Regulation No. 1257/2012** nowadays provides that unitary effect occurs from the registration (in the Register for unitary patent protection administered by the EPO) of a European patent (granted by the EPO

---

[86] See notably Galloux (2013), p. 67; Ullrich (2014), p. 12 et seqq.; Warusfel (2013), p. 101. It should also be recalled that in Recital 4 of Council Regulation (EC) No. 207/2009 on the Community trade mark, the necessity of trademarks submitted to Community law was expressly mentioned.

[87] On the contrary, EU trademark is issued by EUIPO as provided by Parliament/Council Regulation (EU) No 2017/1001.

[88] COM(2000) 412. However Article 5.3 of Regulation (EU) No. 1257/2012, by a cross-reference to the national law as determined in accordance with Article 7, is seen by some as escaping, at least formally, to the reproach to create a title without content nor own effect. See in that sense also Case C-146/13, *Spain v Parliament and Council* (ECJ 5 May 2015) para 47–48.

[89] See notably the critical position expressed in the Max Planck Working Papers in general and especially, Hilty et al. (2012); Ullrich (2013), and for a discussion about the legality of Council decision authorising enhanced cooperation: Lamping (2011), p. 899 et seqq.

[90] Case C-146/13, *Spain v Parliament and Council* (ECJ 5 May 2015) para 47–52. The Court relied notably on Articles 3.1 and 3.2 of the regulation combined with its Articles 5.3 and 7.

according to the EPC with the same set of claims for every participating MS according to Article 3.1 of the Regulation). This Regulation authorises the EPO to carry out important administrative tasks, notably the management of fees and statements related to operating licenses (Article 9 of the Regulation).[91] Through this Regulation, the EPO has responsibility for important centralised functions.

There are two types of centralised control: administrative and jurisdictional control. The centralised control referred to in Article 118 TFEU corresponds to the **administrative control** conducted nowadays by the **EPO** concerning the granting of titles or oppositions. It should be noted that the opposition procedures before the EPO and the decisions rendered in such cases are "quasi-judicial". Issues relating to the compatibility of such procedures with the requirements of Article 6 ECHR have arisen.[92] Regulation No. 1257/2012 provides a key role for the EPO regarding that centralised control.

As for **judicial review**, it is essential to note that Article 118 TFEU does not empower the Union to create a unified jurisdiction to regulate the application and interpretation of the European title. In this regard, Article 262 TFEU expressly provides that the Court of Justice's competence could be extended to cover litigation between individuals in the field of IP. Nevertheless, States can decide together, through a convention, to assign litigation regarding national or non-Community titles to an international jurisdiction.[93] It has to be noted that what is often described as a "patent package" includes not only the two Regulations No. 1257/2012 (related to the creation of the European patent with unitary effect) and No. 1260/2012 (related to the language regime) but also an Agreement on a **Unified Patent Court**, signed on 19 February 2013.[94] The purpose of this Agreement is to assign the litigation of European patents with a unitary effect to a unified jurisdiction (→ Article 262 TFEU para 10). The Agreement is also the reason why neither Regulation No. 1257/2012 nor Regulation No. 1260/2012 has started to apply yet: according to Article 18.2 of Regulation No. 1257/2012 and Article 7.2 of Regulation No. 1260/2012, both only start applying once the Agreement on a Unified Patent Court enters into force. This process, however, has first been slowed down by Brexit[95] and then halted by a decision of the German Federal Constitutional Court, which declared the act ratifying the Agreement unconstitutional.[96] Whether and when the unitary patent system will ever start functioning was therefore unclear.[97] The Protocol to the Agreement on a Unified Patent Court on

41

---

[91] On the role of the EPO, see notably: Luginbuehl (2015), p. 45 et seqq.

[92] The questioning even led to a structural reform proposal of the EPO Boards of Appeal, EPO doc. CA/16/15, 6 March 2015.

[93] Opinion 1/09, *unified patent litigation system* (ECJ 8 March 2011) para 61 et seq.

[94] Agreement on a Unified Patent Court, signed on 19 February 2013, O.J. C 175/1 (2013).

[95] Jaeger (2017), p. 266 et seqq.

[96] German Federal Constitutional Court (Bundesverfassungsgericht), 2 BvR 739/17 (Decision of 13 February 2020).

[97] Tilmann (2020).

3.4. Regulation to Establish Language Arrangements for European IP Rights

42   Article 118 TFEU confers two competences in fact. The first paragraph confers the power to create European IP rights and to set up centralised Union-wide authorisation, coordination and supervision arrangements. The second confers competence to establish language arrangements. The provision relating to this latter competence is very clear and precise. The competence has to be exercised **by means of regulations**. It is clear that the language arrangements referred to are those aimed at dealing with the language regime of European IP rights created under paragraph 1.

43   A first Regulation, implementing the enhanced cooperation, has been adopted on the basis of Article 118 (2) TFEU[99] after long and highly political discussions.[100] Indeed, one major issue regarding the unitary patent has been the determination of **official languages**. The Regulation provides that the request for a unitary effect has to be submitted in the language of the proceedings before the EPO, as defined in Article 14.3 of EPC (Articles 2 and Article 3.2 of Regulation No. 1260/2012), i.e. **English, French and German**. According to Article 3, no further translations are required for a European patent with a unitary effect, which has been granted by the EPO, according to EPC conditions, and has been published in accordance with Article 14.6 of the EPC. While further provisions foresee the need for a translation in the event of a dispute (Article 4) and an issue of compensation for the cost of translation (Article 5), the language arrangements adopted are far from the common political approach to the Community patent adopted by the Council in March 2003, which provided that patent proprietors would have to supply translations of claims into all the official languages of the MS.[101]

3.5. Intellectual Property

44   Article 118 TFEU establishes the Union's competence to create *intellectual property* rights. IP rights embrace both **industrial property right** (patent, trademark, industrial designs, plant variety protection etc.) and **artistic and literary property**

---

[98] Besides, a final version of the Rules of Procedure applicable before the UPC was adopted by the Administrative Committee and published (in the three languages: English, French and German), the entry into force of the text comprising 382 rules has been set for 1 September 2022.

[99] Council Regulation (EU) No. 1260/2012 *implementing enhanced cooperation in the area of the creation of unitary patent protection with regard to the applicable translation arrangements*, O.J. L 361/89 (2012).

[100] See, for further discussion on this issue notably: Jaeger (2012), p. 287 et seqq.; Ullrich (2014), espec. p. 46 et seqq.

[101] Council document 7159/03, Common political approach on the Community patent, para 2.3.

Article 118. [European Intellectual Property Rights] 467

rights (copyright, neighbouring rights, database protection). The text does not limit itself to the protection of industrial property rights. However, some have argued that the provision in its conception is aimed at protecting industrial property rather than copyright. Two main reasons explain this observation. The French version of Article 118 TFEU mentions a European *title*, while copyright protection needs no registration. However, this opinion is open to criticism as the expression *titres européens* and its equivalents in the German (*europäischer Rechtstitel*) and English (European intellectual property rights) versions should be understood in the sense of "rights", regardless of the need for registration (→ para 33).

The other reason is that the reference to the internal market covers the economic aspects of copyright but not its cultural dimension and, in particular, questions of the author's moral rights. However, and despite the fact that some may regret the **economic approach** implied by Article 118 TFEU, on a literal reading of the clear wording of this article, there is no reason to exclude copyright as a whole from its scope of application. This conception is reinforced if we consider Article 36 TFEU or Article 262 TFEU. Article 36 TFEU has been interpreted as permitting justified limitations on the free movement of goods relating to copyright (→ Article 36 TFEU para 8) even though the clear wording of the provision appears to exclude its application to copyright by mentioning only industrial and commercial property. Furthermore, it is worth mentioning that, since the Lisbon Treaty, Article 262 TFEU has covered not only industrial property, as before, but also intellectual property in general, establishing in this sphere the possibility of adopting provisions to confer jurisdiction on the ECJ in disputes between private parties.

3.6. Subsidiarity and Proportionality

According to the **subsidiarity principle** (Article 5.3 TEU), "the Union shall act only if and insofar as the objectives of the proposed action cannot be sufficiently achieved by the Member States, either at central level or at regional and local level, but can rather, by reason of the scale or effects of the proposed action, be better achieved at Union level". National parliaments in the Union have an allocated role in ensuring that this principle is respected (Protocol Nos. 1 and 2). All legislative proposals must be directly transmitted to them for consultation (→ Protocol No. 2 para 171 and 215). The legal act may also be subject to judicial review by the ECJ (→ Protocol No. 2 para 184 et seqq.). 45

Under the **proportionality principle** (Article 5.4 TEU), the content and form of Union action shall not exceed what is necessary to achieve the objectives of the Treaties. This principle requires that the measures adopted to achieve EU objectives are appropriate for attaining the objective pursued and do not go beyond what is necessary. However, the Court's control is limited as, according to a settled case law, the EU legislature must be allowed broad discretion in areas that involve political, economic and social choices on its part and in which it is called on to 46 undertake complex assessments.[102] Jurisdictional control is then limited to manifestly inappropriate measures, having regard to the objective pursued. In the first regulations based on Article 118 TFEU, the EU legislator took care to specify that both of those principles had been respected.[103]

4. Procedure

4.1. Ordinary Legislative Procedure Under Article 118 (1) TFEU

47 With the Treaty of Lisbon, the ordinary legislative procedure (Article 294 TFEU) has become the main legislative procedure of the EU decision-making system. The ordinary legislative procedure could *a priori* ease the Union's action within the IP area and strengthen the legitimacy of its interventions (→ para 17). The **qualified majority voting** rule is a necessity in an enlarged Union to act in the politically sensitive field of IP. In any case, this rule will facilitate the adoption of acts (creating IP rights or modifying the existing European title regime). It should be recalled that the Regulation that creates the Community trademark was adopted only after 13 years of hard work.

48 However, the fact that the question of the language arrangements for new European IP rights continues to be subject to the rule of unanimity (→ para 49) obliges us to keep a sense of proportion about the previous observation. Some authors consider that MS did not "fulfil the work". After all, it was precisely the sensitive question of languages that has in the past proved to be an important obstacle to the adoption of a Regulation on this issue, even though additional **political reasons** relating predominantly to lobbying explain the failure of preceding attempts to adopt a European patent system. In fact, even though the ordinary legislative procedure is retained for the creation of European IP rights, as rights that need to be registered can hardly be created without simultaneously providing for the language of the register and also that of legal proceedings in the case of dispute, the creation of such IP rights will require a **consensus within the Council**. Therefore, if one might have thought that Article 118 TFEU will promote decision-making on language arrangements by virtue of enhanced political pressure, as a decision by a qualified majority will already have been taken regardless of language arrangements, the history of the European patent tells us another story. An enhanced cooperation process has been preferred, and ultimately, no European patent but a patent with a unitary effect has been adopted (→ para 28). In fact, Article 118

---

[102] See in particular Joined Cases C-453/03 et al., *ABNA and Others* (ECJ 6 December 2005) para 68–69.

[103] Parliament/Council Regulation (EU) No. 1257/2012, Recital 27; Parliament/Council Regulation (EU) No 2015/2424, Recital 46; Parliament/Council Regulation (EU) No 2017/1001, Recital 48.

TFEU could have been helpful in creating one if it were not for the influence of powerful lobbies.[104]

4.2. Special Legislative Procedure Under Article 118 (2) TFEU

Under Article 118 (2) TFEU, the adoption of regulations to establish language arrangements for the European IP rights requires a special legislative procedure under which **unanimity in the Council** is required after **consulting the European Parliament**. Some scholars have denounced Article 118 (2) TFEU as a sign of a failure to take responsibility at the EU level. Language arrangements are certainly sensitive and have been designated officially as being the cause of the failure to adopt a European patent. Then requiring the unanimity vote of the Council is not facilitating the adoption of such arrangements. 49

However, the ECJ has had the opportunity in a case dealing with the application of Article 118 TFEU to specify that nothing in Article 20 TEU or Article 326 to 334 TFEU forbids MS from establishing enhanced cooperation between them (and nothing forbids the Council from authorising such cooperation) within the ambit of those competences that must, according to the Treaties, be exercised unanimously.[105] Spain contested the recourse to the mechanism of enhanced cooperation as an indirect means of avoiding and circumventing the unanimity condition. The Court added that when the conditions provided by those articles are satisfied and when enhanced cooperation has been authorised for the exercise of a competence requiring unanimity, the votes of only those MS taking part constitute unanimity, provided that the Council has not decided to act by qualified majority.[106] One may even consider, like AG *Bot*, that "the **enhanced cooperation** mechanism was established in order to enable a group of Member States to **deal with a deadlock in a specific matter**" and that "it is self-evident that deadlock is especially likely to occur in matters which require unanimity in the Council" (→ Article 20 TEU para 53).[107] Moreover, Article 333 TFEU expressly provides for the application of enhanced cooperation in a situation in which unanimity is required in the Council or in which special legislative procedure applies. 50

The Court underlined the particular importance of the last resort condition provided by Article 20.2 TEU (→ Article 20 TEU para 37 and 38). On this point, the Grand Chamber considered that Article 20 TEU and Articles 326 to 334 TFEU do not circumscribe the right to resort to enhanced cooperation solely to the case, as argued by applicants, in which at least one MS declares that it is not yet ready to 51

---

[104] See notably Kingston (2008), p. 442.
[105] Joined Cases C-274/11 & C-295/11, *Spain v Council* (ECJ 16 April 2013) para 35.
[106] Joined Cases C-274/11 & C-295/11, *Spain v Council* (ECJ 16 April 2013) para 35.
[107] Joined Cases C-274/11 & C-295/11, *Spain v Council* (Opinion of AG Bot of 11 December 2012) para 85.

take part in a legislative action of the Union in its entirety.[108] In a thorough control, the Court, while recognising that the Council is in the best place to determine whether the MS have demonstrated any willingness to compromise and are in a position to put forward proposals capable of leading to the adoption of legislation for the Union as a whole in the foreseeable future,[109] validated the Council decision authorising enhanced cooperation[110] and the regulations implementing it.[111]

List of Cases

ECJ 13.07.1966, 56/64 and 58/64, *Consten and Grundig*, ECLI:EU:C:1966:41 [cit. in para 4, 24]

ECJ 29.02.1968, 24/67, *Parke, Davis and Co v Probel and Others*, ECLI:EU:C:1968:11 [cit. in para 4]

ECJ 08.06.1971, 78/70, *Deutsche Grammophon*, ECLI:EU:C:1971:59 [cit. in para 4, 5]

ECJ 15.12.1976, 35/76, *Simmenthal*, ECLI:EU:C:1976:180 [cit. in para 4]

ECJ 18.03.1980, 62/79, *Coditel v Ciné Vog Films*, ECLI:EU:C:1980:84 [cit. in para 5]

ECJ 20.01.1981, 55/80 and 57/80, *Musik-Vertrieb Membran GmbH v GEMA*, ECLI:EU:C:1981:10 [cit. in para 5, 7]

ECJ 26.03.1987, 45/86, *Commission v Council*, ECLI:EU:C:1987:163 [cit. in para 23]

ECJ 11.06.1991, C-300/89, *Commission v Council (Titanium dioxide)*, ECLI:EU:C:1991:244 [cit. in para 23]

ECJ 18.02.1992, C-30/90, *Commission v United Kingdom*, ECLI:EU:C:1992:74 [cit. in para 14]

ECJ 13.07.1995, C-350/92, *Spain v Council*, ECLI:EU:C:1995:237 [cit. in para 14, 28, 29]

ECJ 09.10.2001, C-377/98, *Netherlands v Parliament and Council*, ECLI:EU:C:2001:523 [cit. in para 29]

ECJ 6.12.2005, C-453/03 et al., *ABNA and Others*, ECLI:EU:C:2005:74 [cit. in para 47]

ECJ 16.07.2009, C-5/08, *Infopaq International*, ECLI:EU:C:2009:465 [cit. in para 29]

ECJ 08.09.2009, C-478/07, *Budějovický Budvar*, ECLI:EU:C:2009:521 [cit. in para 36]

---

[108] Joined Cases C-274/11 & C-295/11, *Spain v Council* (ECJ 16 April 2013) para 36, 37.

[109] Joined Cases C-274/11 & C-295/11, *Spain v Council* (ECJ 16 April 2013) para 53.

[110] Joined Cases C-274/11 & C-295/11, *Spain v Council* (ECJ 16 April 2013).

[111] Case C-146/13, *Spain v Parliament and Council* (ECJ 5 May 2015) and Case C-147/13, *Spain v Council* (ECJ 5 May 2015).

ECJ 08.03.2011, Opinion 1/09, *Unified patent litigation system*, ECLI:EU: C:2011:123 [cit. in para 18, 41]
ECJ 16.04.2013, C-274/11 and C-295/11, *Spain v Council*, ECLI:EU:C:2013:240 [cit. in para 18, 21, 38, 51]
ECJ 05.05.2015, C-146/13, *Spain v Parliament and Council*, ECLI:EU:C:2015:298 [cit. in para 18, 21, 39, 52]
ECJ 05.05.2015, C-147/13, *Spain v Council*, ECLI:EU:C:2015:299 [cit. in para 18, 52]
ECJ 14.09.17, C-56/16 P, *EUIPO v Instituto dos Vinhos do Douro e do Porto IP*, ECLI:EU:C:2017:693 [cit. in para 36]

References[112]

Akkermans, B., & Ramaekers, E. (2010). Article 345 TFEU (ex. 295 EC), its meanings and interpretations. *European Law Journal*, 292–314.
Basire, Y., Roda, J.-C., Kiesel Le Cosquer, G., Favreau, A., & Treppoz, E. (2017). The impact of Brexit on the unitary rights of the European Union. *Centre for International Intellectual Property Studies (CEIPI) Research Paper No. 2017-18*. Retrieved from: https://ssrn.com/abstract=3260487
Beier, F.-K. (1969). Stand und Aussichten der europäischen Rechtsvereinheitlichung auf dem Gebiete des gewerblichen Rechtsschutzes. *GRUR International: Journal of European and International IP Law*, 145–153.
Benabou, V.-L. (2012). Retour sur dix ans de jurisprudence de la Cour de justice de l'Union européenne en matière de propriété littéraire et artistique : les méthodes. *Propriétés intellectuelles, 44*, 140–153.
Böttner, R. (2021). *The constitutional framework for enhanced cooperation in EU law*. Brill Nijhoff.
Carre, S. (2013). Le rôle de la Cour de Justice dans la construction du droit d'auteur de l'Union. In C. Geiger (Ed.), *La contribution de la jurisprudence à la construction de la propriété intellectuelle en Europe* (pp. 1–71). LexisNexis/Université de Strasbourg.
d'Erme, R. (2020). L'impact du Brexit sur les droits de propriété intellectuelle. *Revue Francophone de la Propriété intellectuelle de l'UE, 10*, 83–93.
Dinwoodie, G. B. (2017). Territorial overlaps in trademark law: The evolving European model. *Notre Dame Law Review, 92*(4), 1670–1744.
Fauvarque-Cosson, B., & Behar-Touchais, M. (2002). *Implementation of optional instruments within European civil law*. Study for the European Parliament, PE 462.425.
Galloux, J.-C. (2013). The unitary effect: From transplant to capture. In C. Geiger (Ed.), *What patent law for the European Union?* (pp. 55–74). LexisNexis/Université de Strasbourg.
Geiger, C. (2013). Intellectual property shall be protected!? Article 17 (2) of the Charter of Fundamental Rights of the European Union: A mysterious provision with an unclear scope. *European Intellectual Property Review*, 113–117.
Grabitz, E., Hilf, M., & Nettesheim, M. (Eds.). (2022). *Das Recht der Europäischen Union. Kommentar*. (Loose leaf). C.H. Beck.
Griffith, J. (2014). The role of the Court of Justice in the development of European Union copyright law. In I. Stamatoudi & P. Torremans (Eds.), *EU copyright law, a commentary*. Edward Elgar.

---

[112] All cited Internet sources in this comment have been accessed on 6 February 2023.

Hilty, R. (2004). Copyright in the internal market. *International Review of Intellectual Property and Competition Law, 35*(7), 760–775.

Hilty, R., Jaeger, T., Lamping, M., & Ullrich, H. (2012). The unitary patent package: Twelve reasons for concern. *Max Planck Institute for Intellectual Property and Competition Law Research Paper Series*, No. 12-12.

Jaeger, T. (2010). The EU patent: cui bono et quo vadit? *Common Market Law Review, 47*, 63–115.

Jaeger, T. (2012). Back to square one? An assessment of the latest proposals for a patent and court for the internal market and possible alternative. *International Review of Intellectual Property and Competition Law, 43*, 286–308.

Jaeger, T. (2017). Reset and go: The unitary patent system post-Brexit. *International Review of Intellectual Property and Competition Law, 48*, 254–285.

Kingston, W. (2008). Intellectual property in the Lisbon Treaty. *European Intellectual Property Review, 30*(11), 439–443.

Lamping, M. (2011). Enhanced cooperation – A proper approach to market integration in the field of unitary patent protection? *International Review of Intellectual Property and Competition Law, 42*(8), 879–925.

Leistner, M. (2014). Europe's copyright law decade: Recent case law of the European Court of Justice and policy perspectives. *Common Market Law Review, 51*, 559–600.

Luginbuehl, S. (2015). An institutional perspective I: The role of the EPO in the unitary (EU) patent system. In J. Pila & C. Wadlow (Eds.), *The unitary EU patent system* (pp. 45–56). Hart Publishing.

Pagenberg, J. (2007). Another year of debates on patent jurisdiction in Europe and no end in sight? *International Review of Intellectual Property and Competition Law, 38*(7), 805–833.

Pila, J. (2015). An historical perspective I: The unitary patent package. In J. Pila & C. Wadlow (Eds.), *The unitary EU patent system* (pp. 9–32). Hart Publishing.

Plomer, A. (2017). The unified patent court: Past, present and future. In M. Cremona, A. Thies, & R. Wessel (Eds.), *The European Union and international dispute settlement* (pp. 275–292). Hart Publishing.

Plomer, A. (2020). The unified patent court and the transformation of the European patent system. *International Review of Intellectual Property and Competition Law*, 791–796.

Rosati, E. (2019). *Copyright and the Court of Justice of the European Union*. OUP.

Schwarze, J., Becker, U., Hatje, A., & Schoo, J. (Eds.). (2018). *EU-Kommentar* (4th ed.). Nomos.

Scordamaglia, V. (2013). The legal framework of the legislative activity concerning intellectual property rights at European regional level. In C. Geiger (Ed.), *Constructing European intellectual property. Achievements and new perspectives* (pp. 61–74). Edward Elgar.

Smits, J. (2010). Optional law: A plea for multiple choice in private law. *Maastricht Journal of European and Comparative Law, 17*, 347–352.

Tilmann, W. (2020). The UPC without the UK: Consequences and alternatives. *GRUR -International: Journal of European and International IP law*, 847–851.

Ullrich, H. (2007). National, European and Community patent protection: Time for reconsideration. In A. Ohly & D. Klippel (Eds.), *Eigentum und Gemeinfreiheit* (pp. 61–106). Mohr Siebeck.

Ullrich, H. (2012). Harmonizing patent law: The untameable Union patent. In M.-C. Janssens & G. Van Overwalle (Eds.), *Harmonisation of European IP law: From European rules to Belgian law and practice. Contribution in honor of Frank Gotzen* (pp. 243–294). Bruylant.

Ullrich, H. (2013). The property aspects of the European Patent with unitary effect: A national perspective for a European prospect?. *Max Planck Institute for Intellectual Property and Competition Law Research Paper Series*, Working Paper No 13-17.

Ullrich, H. (2014). Le futur système de protection des inventions par brevets dans l'Union européenne: un exemple d'intégration (re-)poussée?, *Discussion Paper No 1*. Retrieved from: https://www.irpi.fr/upload/pdf/etude_UPP_RTDE.pdf

von der Groeben, H., Schwarze, J., & Hatje, A. (Eds.). (2015). *Europäisches Unionsrecht. Commentary*. 7th ed. Nomos.

Warusfel, B. (2013). European Court for Intellectual Property Rights: Between desirable and attainable. In C. Geiger (Ed.), *What patent law for the European Union?* (pp. 95–106). LexisNexis/Université de Strasbourg.

Würfel, C. E. (2005). *Europarechtliche Möglichkeiten einer Gesamtharmonisierung des Urheberrechts*. Universitätsverlag Karlsruhe.

Title VIII
Economic and Monetary Policy

Article 119 [Principles of Economic and Monetary Policy]
(ex-Article 4 TEC)

1. For the purposes set out in Article 3 of the Treaty on European Union,[42–45] the activities of the Member States and the Union shall include, as provided in the Treaties, the adoption of an economic policy which is based on the close coordination of Member States' economic policies,[11–12] on the internal market and on the definition of,[11, 39] and conducted in accordance with the principle of an open market economy with free competition.[12, 40–41]
2. Concurrently with the foregoing, and as provided in the Treaties and in accordance with the procedures set out therein, these activities shall include a single currency, the euro, and the definition and conduct of a single monetary policy and exchange-rate policy the primary objective of both of which shall be to maintain price stability and, without prejudice to this objective, to support the general economic policies in the Union, in accordance with the principle of an open market economy with free competition.[13–27]
3. These activities of the Member States and the Union shall entail compliance with the following guiding principles: stable prices, sound public finances and monetary conditions and a sustainable balance of payments.[16–18, 39, 42–45]

Contents

1.	Genesis, Context and Systematic Position of Article 119 TFEU	1
2.	Some Remarks on the Beginnings of EMU and Its Openness for a Multi-Speed Europe	2
2.1.	Three Stages in the History of EMU	2
2.2.	Differentiated Integration Within the EMU	6
3.	Developing an Imperfect Parallelism Between Monetary Union and Convergence of National Economic Policies (Paragraphs 1 and 2)	7
3.1.	Two-Pillar Structure and Resulting Reforms of EMU	7
3.2.	A Closely Coordinated Economic Policy	11
3.3.	Monetary Policy and Exchange-Rate Policy	13
3.3.1.	Price Stability	16
3.3.2.	The Relationship Between Price Stability and Independence of the ESCB	19
3.4.	Secondary Objectives of the ESCB Mandate	28
3.4.1.	The ESCB's Secondary Mandate to Support the EU General Economic Policies	28
3.4.2.	Contribution to Financial Stability as an Objective Related to Price Stability	32
4.	A Principle-Oriented Pursuit of the EMU Objectives (Paragraphs 1 to 3)	39
4.1.	Principle of an Open Market Economy with Free Competition (Paragraphs 1 and 2)	40
4.2.	Guiding Principles for Economic and Monetary Policy Activities in the EMU (Paragraph 3)	42

List of Cases
References

© Springer Nature Switzerland AG 2022
R. Böttner, H.-J. Blanke (eds.), *Treaty on the Functioning of the European Union – A Commentary*, Springer Commentaries on International and European Law, https://doi.org/10.1007/16559_2022_34

1. Genesis, Context and Systematic Position of Article 119 TFEU

1   Article 119 TFEU, right at the beginning of Title VIII of the third part of the TFEU, is a provision on the very essence of the European Economic and Monetary Union (EMU) and its guiding principles. It corresponds at its core to Article 4 TEC, which was introduced by the Treaty of Maastricht (1993). After the euro became the Union's single currency on 1 January 1999, the successor provision to Article 4 TEC was placed at the beginning of Title VIII in the Treaty of Lisbon and cleared of those formulations that had become obsolete. Similar but not nearly as far-reaching rules were previously spelt out in Article 102a TEEC (introduced by the Single European Act) and Article 103 TEEC on cooperation in economic and monetary policy and on short-term economic policy. With the Treaty of Lisbon, Article 119 TFEU was systematically placed at the beginning of Title VIII on economic and monetary policy as a **basic norm** and adapted merely terminologically to the level of integration already achieved (existence of the euro, completion of the Stages Two and Three of EMU).[1] This provision puts the **objective enunciated in Article 3.4 TEU** into more concrete terms, in particular, despite the lack of a substantial degree of economic union, with regard to "the parallel advancement in monetary and economic integration"[2] (paragraphs 1 and 2), the creation of a single currency in pursuance of the objective of price stability (paragraph 2) and the alignment of the economic and monetary policies of the Union and the MS to further economic and financial principles (paragraph 3).

2. Some Remarks on the Beginnings of EMU and Its Openness for a Multi-Speed Europe

2.1. Three Stages in the History of EMU

2   In an **approach to realise EMU in three stages**,[3] the competences for **"inner monetary policy"** have been transferred to the Union level (Article 3.1 point (c) TFEU) in order to be executed within the ESCB is independent of the political

---

[1] Herrmann, in Pechstein et al. (2017), Article 119 AEUV para 45.

[2] This expression is taken from the "Delors Report" of 17 April 1989, point 42: "parallelism" (available at https://ec.europa.eu/economy_finance/publications/pages/publication6161_en.pdf). Pursuant to Herrmann, in Pechstein et al. (2017), Article 119 AEUV para 58, the constituent element "concurrently with the foregoing" in paragraph 2 has "practically no [more] normative content" neither from a temporal nor from a substantive point of view.

[3] The so-called Werner Report of 8 October 1970, p. 14 et seqq., contained programmatic phrased "principles of realization of the [EMU] plan by stages" (available at https://ec.europa.eu/economy_finance/publications/pages/publication6142_en.pdf); the Delors Report of 17 April 1989 took up this approach (p. 27 et seqq.) and outlined in detail "the final stage of economic and monetary union" (p. 13 et seqq.). Finally, the Maastricht Treaty has laid down the three-stage approach, see e.g. Article 109g TEC-Maastricht. See also Gramlich (2020), para 15 et seqq.; Scheinert (2021).

influence of the MS. As a further step within the monetary union, a **"single and stable currency"** area (Recital 6 of the Preamble to TEU-Maastricht) has been created "in which policies are managed jointly with a view to attaining common macroeconomic objectives".[4] The economic and monetary union form two integral parts of a single whole, with the continued responsibility of the MS for their national economic policy. The economic union combines the characteristics of an **unrestricted common market based on the same market-oriented principles and rules that underlie the economic order of its MS**, namely a large degree of freedom for market behaviour and private economic initiative.

In **Stage One** (from 1 July 1990 to 31 December 1993), the **free movement of capital** between MS was established. While the freedom of payments is already a prerequisite for the free movement of goods and services, only the free cross-border flow of capital creates the necessary, if not sufficient, conditions for a single financial market. For its part, it is indispensable for the monetary policy impulse transmission and thus the effective use of monetary policy instruments to achieve common monetary policy goals throughout the entire currency area.[5] The free movement of capital in the EU was initially implemented independently of monetary policy developments as part of the "Single Market Programme" introduced into the Treaties by the Single European Act through the adoption of the Capital Movements Directive, the implementation period of which ended for the MS on 1 July 1990. With the entry into force of the Maastricht Treaty, the free movement of capital was then also enshrined in primary law (now Articles 63 to 66 TFEU) and has since enjoyed the same status as the other fundamental freedoms. In particular, it is directly applicable and takes precedence over national law.

Stage Two (from 1 January 1994 to 31 December 1998) aimed at the **convergence of MS' economic policies** and the strengthening of cooperation between MS' national central banks (NCBs). The coordination of monetary policies was institutionalised by the establishment of the **European Monetary Institute** (EMI), which was tasked with strengthening cooperation between the national central banks and carrying out the necessary preparations for the introduction of the single currency. The national central banks were to become independent during this stage.

Stage Three began for 11 EU MS on 1 January 1999 (Article 121.4 TEC-Maastricht) in accordance with a recommendation of the Commission of 25 March 1998 (Article 121.1 TEC) and a decision of the European Council at the beginning of May 1998. Replacing the previous European Monetary System (EMS

---

[4] On this and the following features of a monetary and economic union, cf. the Delors Report of 17 April 1989, p. 14 et seqq., 16 et seqq.

[5] Herrmann, in Pechstein et al. (2017), Article 119 AEUV para 21. With regard to the guidelines, methods and measures to be taken for achieving an Economic and Monetary Union, see: first the *Report to the Council and the Commission on the realisation by stages of Economic and Monetary Union in the Community* ("Werner Report" of 8 October 1970), p. 10, 20 et seq.; then Committee for the Study of Economic and Monetary Union, *Report of economic and monetary Union in the European Community* ("Delors Report" of 17 April 1989), points 22, 24, 25; Hatje, in Schwarze et al. (2019), Article 119 AEUV para 5.

I – 1979 to 1998), a mechanism for fixed but adjustable exchange rates of the currencies participating in the ECU basket and with the European Monetary Cooperation Fund (1973–1993) and a system of credit facilities for mutual payment support,[6] the **single monetary policy was established** under the aegis of the Eurosystem. The Eurosystem comprises the ECB and the national central banks of the euro area. Euro banknotes and coins were introduced in all participating euro area MS on 1 January 2002. Transition to Stage Three was subject to the achievement of a high degree of durable convergence measured against a number of criteria laid down by the Treaties (Article 104c TEC-Maastricht; see now Article 126 TFEU, Protocol No 12 and Declaration No 30; → para 2, 11 et seq. and 23). When the euro was first introduced in 1999 – as 'book' money –, the euro area was made up of 11 of the then 15 EU MS. On 1 January 2001, **Greece** became the 12th MS to join the Eurosystem, having remained "undetected" the falsifications of its public deficit data (**use of creative accounting**) since 1997.[7] It was followed by Slovenia in 2007, Cyprus and Malta in 2008, Slovakia in 2009, Estonia in 2011, Latvia in 2014 and Lithuania in 2015. In 2022, the euro area numbered 19 EU MS. On 1 June 2022, the Commission assessed in its 2022 **Convergence Report** that Croatia fulfils all the criteria for joining the euro area and proposed to the Council that **Croatia** adopt the euro on 1 January 2023.

With the entry into the Stage Three of EMU, the budgetary rules were to become binding, and any MS failing to comply could face penalties. The conversion rates between the MS participating in the single currency were "irrevocably fixed", and the "ecu" (euro) thus became a "currency in its own right" (ex-Article 1091.4 sentence 1 TEC-Maastricht; → Article 133 TFEU para 1). Since then, the euro has been the **"single currency of the Union"** for the members of the euro area (Article 3.4 TEU; Article 140.3 TFEU). In order to establish the euro by issuing euro banknotes and coins as "the only [...] legal tender within the Union"[8] (Article 128.1 sentence 3 TFEU; → Article 128 TFEU para 1, 3 et seqq.), it was necessary to establish a legal framework at the level of the Union (Article 133 TFEU; → Article 128 TFEU para 12)[9] and the MS. This was achieved in the MS in particular through the national accompanying legislation. The sole right to issue euro banknotes and coins, which are the sole legal tender, lies with the ECB and, respectively, the national central banks of the MS, with the right to authorise the issue of banknotes vested exclusively in the ECB (Article 128.1 TFEU; Article 282.3 sentence 2 TFEU).[10]

---

[6] Cohen (1981), p. 2; Köster (1990).

[7] Galanos et al. (2011), p. 263 et seqq.

[8] For a definition of the term legal tender see Joined Cases C-422/19 and C-423/19, *Hessischer Rundfunk* (CJEU 26 January 2021) para 49 referring to Commission Recommendation 2010/191/EU, point 1.

[9] See, in particular, Council Regulation (EC) No 1103/97 *on certain provisions relating to the introduction of the euro*, O.J. L 162/1 (1997); Council Regulation (EC) No 974/98 *on the introduction of the euro*, O.J. L. 139/1 (1998).

[10] Herrmann, in Pechstein et al. (2017), Article 119 AEUV para 22.

2.2. Differentiated Integration Within the EMU

In principle, by adhering to the Treaties, all EU MS agreed to adopt the euro (Article 3.4 TEU and Article 119.2 TFEU). However, no deadline has been set, and some MS have yet to fulfil all the convergence criteria (2022). These MS benefit from a **provisional derogation** (Articles 139 et seqq. TFEU). Furthermore, Denmark and the United Kingdom had given notification of their intention not to participate in Stage Three of EMU and therefore not to adopt the euro. Since the United Kingdom has left the EU in 2020, only **Denmark** currently benefits from an **exemption** with regard to its participation in EMU's Stage Three, but it maintains an option to end its exemption. The exemption arrangements are detailed in a protocol annexed to the EU Treaties (Protocol No 16 on certain provisions relating to Denmark; → Article 139 TFEU para 7 et seqq., 11 et seqq.). At the time of writing, 19 of the 27 MS have adopted the euro. The Treaty provisions on "Member States with a derogation" are evidence of **differentiated integration** in EU primary law.[11] In EMU, these elements are particularly pronounced since lasting economic convergence as a prerequisite for joining the euro area could not be fulfilled by all MS at the same time. The rules on EMU therefore distinguish between MS that have already adopted the euro as their currency and those that have a "derogation" (Articles 139.1 and 282.4 sentence 2 TFEU). The MS (2021: 22) that have opted to join, e.g., the Fiscal Compact (Bulgaria, Denmark and Romania) or those (Bulgaria and Croatia) that have established close cooperation, e.g., with the Single Supervisory Mechanism (SSM) also point to the phenomenon of flexible integration within the EMU.[12]

3. Developing an Imperfect Parallelism Between Monetary Union and Convergence of National Economic Policies (Paragraphs 1 and 2)

3.1. Two-Pillar Structure and Resulting Reforms of EMU

As European law in its original design did not impose any specific obligation on the national governments, economic policy (along with regional, budgetary and revenue policies) remained with the MS; meanwhile, their creative scope is partly restricted by EU secondary legislation and international law. EMU therefore essentially rests on a **two-pillar structure**, splitting competences between the Union and its members. Due to different traditions and historical experiences, the national concepts, measures and aims tend to diverge with regard to economic policy.[13] The process of sustaining a monetary union is only conceivable if a high degree of

---

[11] Böttner (2021), p. 296 et seqq.
[12] Böttner (2021), p. 299 et seqq.
[13] Lastra (2006), p. 245 et seq.

economic convergence is attained.[14] Within the institutional balance established by the provisions of Title VIII of the TFEU, which includes the independence of the ESCB (→ para 19 et seqq.), the authors of the Treaties did not intend to make an absolute separation between economic and monetary policies (→ para 29).[15]

8   Against this background, the **core concept** that is supposed to hold the imperfect EMU together **is aimed at avoiding excessive deficits in the national budgets at different levels**. The factual criteria to be applied to realise the basic concept of the monetary union as **a "community committed to long-term stability"**[16] are explained in Article 126.2 (1) TFEU and are quantified in greater detail in Protocol No 12 on the excessive deficit procedure (Article 126.2 (2) TFEU). As a consequence, the role of the Union is focused on coordination measures (Article 5.1 TFEU; → Article 5 TFEU para 6 et seqq.; → Article 120 TFEU para 9, 11 et seqq.; → Article 121 TFEU para 8 et seqq.) in order to respond to the **need for** interaction and **reciprocity between economic and monetary policies** (intermediate target), "thereby supporting the achievement of the European Union's objectives for sustainable growth, employment, competitiveness and social cohesion" (Article 1.1 TSCG – ultimate objective).[17]

9   Given that **Articles 119.1 and 119.2 TFEU do not constitute a legal basis for economic and monetary policy measures**, competences cannot be derived from them, nor can the scope of the relevant responsibilities in this field be measured according to them.[18] Instead, measures in the area of the EMU must be taken **"as provided in the Treaties"**, i.e. solely on the basis of the enabling and procedural rules enshrined in the five chapters following Article 119 TFEU.[19] So far, the Union's powers in the area of the EMU are characterised by an **asymmetric**[20] or

---

[14] From the situation of that time with a mere perspective of "achieving monetary union", also based on "parallel advancement in monetary and economic integration" ("parallelism") including "a substantial degree of economic union", see the ambitious proposals of the Committee for the Study of Economic and Monetary Union, *Report of economic and monetary Union in the European Community* (1989), p. 14, 28. They have not materialised neither in the Treaties nor in political practice (→ para 3); see also Richter, in Geiger et al. (2015), Article 119 TFEU para 4.

[15] Case C-493/17, *Weiss et al.* (CJEU 11 December 2018) para 60; German Federal Constitutional Court, 2 BvR 859/15 and others, *PSPP* (Judgment of 5 May 2020) para 121.

[16] German Federal Constitutional Court, 2 BvR 2134/92 and 2 BvR 2159/922 BvE 2/08 (Judgment of 12 October 1993) para 147.

[17] Case C-370/12, *Pringle* (CJEU 27 November 2012) para 64; Case T-450/12, *Anagnostakis v Commission* (GC 30 September 2015) para 6; Häde, in Calliess and Ruffert (2022), Article 120 AEUV para 2.

[18] Hatje, in Schwarze et al. (2019), Article 119 AEUV para 1.

[19] Herrmann, in Pechstein et al. (2017), Article 119 AEUV para 42; Bandilla, in Grabitz et al. (2022), Article 119 AEUV para 17 (released in 2021); Müller, in Jaeger and Stöger (2021), Article 119 AEUV para 35 (released in 2020); Richter, in Geiger et al. (2015), Article 119 TFEU para 11.

[20] Müller, in Jaeger and Stöger (2021), Article 119 AEUV para 2 (released in 2020); Hatje, in Schwarze et al. (2019), Article 119 AEUV para 4.

binary²¹ **and therefore vulnerable structure**: while economic policy falls into the category of coordinating competences of the Union (Article 5.1 TFEU; → Article 5 TFEU para 6 et seqq.), the single monetary policy belongs to its exclusive competences (→ Article 3 TFEU para 47 et seqq.).²²

In response to the **structural defects of the EMU**, the EU Heads of State and Government, in particular those of the euro area, have adopted a number of reforms that partly have been implemented outside the Treaties. The **Euro Plus Pact** and the agreements within the framework of the so-called **Six-Pack** introduced for the first time coordination mechanisms in the field of economic policy (→ Supplement to Title VIII: Fiscal Union para 5 et seq.). As another consequence of the sovereign debt crisis, the TESM (2012, as amended in 2021) was conceived as a permanent source of financial assistance for MS in financial crisis with a view to ensuring financial stability and thus stabilising the euro area (→ Supplement to Title VIII: TESM para 1 et seqq.). The **Stability and Growth Pact**, revised several times;²³ the **TSCG** (2012/2013 – with the Fiscal Compact in Title III²⁴), which aims at more binding rules for budgetary discipline for achieving better economic governance for the Union (→ Supplement to Title VIII: Fiscal Union para 16 et seqq.);²⁵ and, finally, resulting from the banking crisis, the **Banking Union** (→ Supplement to Title VIII: Banking Union) are (complementing) elements of the EMU and the single market. A characteristic feature of the **Transfer and Fiscal Union** is its codification by means of **international law instruments** (→ Supplement to Title VIII: Introduction para 2 et seq.),²⁶ thus escaping from Union law to international law.²⁷ The **Banking Union**, on the other hand, which is largely based on European regulatory law, contains only one element of international law: the **Single Resolution Fund** regulated in Article 67 of the SRM Regulation was established by the Intergovernmental Agreement (IGA) on the transfer and mutualisation of contributions to the Single Resolution Fund (SRF; → Supplement to Title VIII: Banking

10

---

²¹ Blanke (2011), p. 407 et seq.

²² See Richter, in Geiger et al. (2015), Article 119 TFEU para 14, who elucidates that the exclusive competence comprises internal and external aspects of monetary reserves.

²³ Cf. Borchardt (2020), para 854 et seqq.

²⁴ The Fiscal Compact (Title III of the TSCG) binds 22 MS of the EU: the 19 MS of the euro area (2022) plus Bulgaria, Denmark and Romania who have decided to opt in.

²⁵ Cf. Craig (2012), p. 231 et seqq.

²⁶ Schorkopf (2012), p. 209 et seq., speaks of an "intergovernmental transformation"; cf. Dimopoulos (2014), p. 41 et seqq; de Witte (2015), p. 437 et seqq., 448 et seqq.

²⁷ Pursuant to Article 16 TSCG, "[w]ithin five years, at most, of the date of entry into force of this Treaty, on the basis of an assessment of the experience with its implementation, the necessary steps shall be taken [...] with the aim of incorporating the substance of this Treaty into the legal framework of the European Union." The TESM lacks such a clause, but since 2017 the Commission has been pursuing the plan to transform the ESM into a European Monetary Fund based on Article 352 TFEU (COM(2017) 827 final); → Article 352 TFEU para sub 4...; see further Manger-Nestler and Böttner (2019).

Union para 174 et seqq.).[28] The fact that the TESM and the Fiscal Treaty are placed outside the primary law of the Union is characteristic for the limited willingness of some MS to reform the Treaties, which, following on from the Treaty of Lisbon, could take the Union to a **new level of fiscal integration**. For the first time since the ratification of the Lisbon Treaties, the unanimity requirement for treaty amendments (Article 48 TEU) is being circumvented by means of concluding international treaties between the MS (TSCG, TESM and IGA on the SRF).[29]

3.2. A Closely Coordinated Economic Policy

11 In order to pursue the objective of the economic and monetary union (Article 3.4 TEU) even after the entry into Stage Three, Article 119.1 TFEU provides for the "adoption of an economic policy". The **concept of economic policy (of the Union)**, which is to be distinguished from the subsequently mentioned "economic policies of the Member States", **includes** in a targeted manner (→ Article 120 TFEU para 32 et seqq., 37 et seqq.) **the internal market and encompasses all economic policy tasks of the Union, including the competition policy**. The only exception is the monetary policy, which is regulated by the special provision in Article 119.2 TFEU. The economic policy of the Union is based on the **coordination of** the **national economic policies within the Eurogroup and ECOFIN Council** (→ Article 121 TFEU para 8). **Cross-sectoral economic policy**, related to all areas of the national economy (e.g. employment and structural policy,

---

[28] Cf. the Intergovernmental Agreement *on the Transfer and Mutualisation of Contributions to the Single Resolution Fund* of 21 May 2014 (IGA on the SRF, available at https://data.consilium.europa.eu/doc/document/ST-8457-2014-INIT/en/pdf) as amended by the Agreement amending the Agreement *on the transfer and mutualisation of contributions to the Single Resolution Fund* of 27 January 2021 (available at https://www.consilium.europa.eu/media/48068/agreement-amending-the-intergovernmental-agreement-on-the-transfer-and-mutualisation-of-contributions-to-the-single-resolution-fund-27-january-2021_en.pdf). The objective of the SRF is to minimise the overall cost of resolution of financial institutions to taxpayers and to establish a joint liability of the financial institutions in the participating MS, which can ensure the financing of a resolution even in cases where the use of the owners and creditors is not sufficient (Recital 11 of the IGA on the SRF). The content of this Agreement is limited to those specific elements concerning the Fund that remain within the competence of the MS (Recital 10 of the IGA on the SRF), in particular their obligation to transfer the contributions raised at the national level towards the Fund. The participating MS chose this arrangement because they did not consider Article 114.1 TFEU to be a sufficient legal basis in this respect; see German Federal Constitutional Court, 2 BvR 2134/92 and 2 BvR 2159/92 (Judgment of 30 July 2019) para 307. The Contracting Parties have manifested the objective "to incorporate the substance provisions of this Agreement, in accordance with the TEU and the TFEU, as soon as possible into the legal framework of the Union" (Recital 25 of the IGA on the SRF).

[29] At the time of the application of the EC Treaty, the Schengen Convention of 19 June 1990 *Implementing the Schengen Agreement of 14 June 1985* has been concluded by means of an international treaty.

wage and income policy), falls within the economic policy competence of the MS (→ Article 120 TFEU para 16, 31).[30]

Union economic policy, based on the coordination of the MS' economic policies, shall be conducted in accordance with the **principle of an open market economy with free competition** (→ para 40 et seq.; → Article 120 TFEU para 37 et seqq.). In an open or free market economy, the interplay between supply and demand determines which goods and services are exchanged and at what price and quality. Competition means that several companies compete with one another for the favour of customers. In a competitive environment, customers or suppliers can switch to another company. Consequently, companies endeavour to offer their goods or services at a price in line with the market and to improve their quality. Competition therefore encourages companies to be **innovative**. Effective competition also prevents the creation or strengthening of power positions that are too influential in society and politics. *Adam Smith*, the founder of classical economics, coined the term "invisible hand" for this process. Each company aiming to maximise its profits has to respond to the wishes and preferences of the opposite side of the market. Competition can therefore rightly be described as the driving force of the market economy. The principle is underpinned by the pursuit of the objectives of achieving **economic growth and employment**. Even if it has a legally binding effect on the MS, it does not constitute a general prohibition of interventions[31] that are inconsistent with the market, given the MS' **margin of appreciation** in choosing the measures of action (→ Article 120 TFEU para 32). This principle, however, does not give rise to individual rights.[32] **12**

3.3. Monetary Policy and Exchange-Rate Policy

"Concurrently", the activities of the Union and the MS "shall include a single currency, the euro, and the definition and conduct of a **single monetary policy and exchange-rate policy**". The significant step to political integration through the Maastricht Treaty, which was partly criticised by economists in the fields of academia, finance and banking exactly for this reason,[33] was the establishment of a monetary union by **transferring** monetary policy from State competence **to the** **13**

---

[30] Häde, in Calliess and Ruffert (2022), Article 119 AEUV para 3 et seq., Richter, in Geiger et al. (2015), Article 119 TFEU para 12 states that "[e]conomic policy in terms of fiscal policy, taxation, regional economic policy or infrastructure" remains with the MS.

[31] Nevertheless, it does prohibit an introduction of other economic systems; see Hatje, in Schwarze et al. (2019), Article 119 AEUV para 9.

[32] Häde, in Calliess and Ruffert (2022), Article 119 AEUV para 9.

[33] Bofinger (1996), p. 30 et seqq.; Seiler (1996), p. 587 et seqq; de Grauwe (2020), p. 27 et seq.; Vaubel (1998), p. 85 et seqq.; Weinert (1998), p. 254 et seqq.; cf. also the contributions in Caesar and Scharrer (1994) and Caesar and Scharrer (1998); see further Terlau (2004); Hatje, in Schwarze et al. (2019), Article 119 AEUV para 8.

ESCB and the ECB.[34] The transfer of this basic element of statehood is an expression of a far-reaching denationalisation and depoliticisation of monetary policy and therefore **of epochal importance**. Monetary policy decisions have been removed from the directly and democratically legitimated representatives' authority on the MS level[35] and transferred to the exclusive competence of the Union (Article 3.1 point (c) TFEU).[36] Its starting point is the principle of the "singleness" of monetary policy (Article 119.2 TFEU), which sets out that the monetary policy applied in a currency area can only be controlled by a central bank. Initially, the ECB was conceived not as a new organ of the European Community but rather – by separating it from the institutions normally responsible for day-to-day political decisions[37] – as an **autonomous special body with legal personality** under Community law (Article 4a TEU-Maastricht read together with Article 9.1 of the ESCB Statute-Maastricht).[38] Thus, the successful method of "integration through law", spelt out in the case law of the CJEU, also gained validity in the area of the EMU.[39] Whereas in the Draft Constitutional Treaty (2004) the ECB was still distinguished from the Union´s institutional framework (Article I-19.1 TCE) as one of the "other institutions of the Union" (Article I-30.3 TCE), it **has become an equal organ** through the Treaty reform of Lisbon (Article 13.1 TEU).[40]

14 A primary task of the ESCB is to **define and implement the single monetary policy** of the Union (Article 127.2 TFEU in conjunction with Article 3.1, first indent, of the ESCB Statute), which is the responsibility of the **Governing Council**, which "shall formulate the monetary policy of the Union, including, as appropriate, decisions relating to intermediate monetary objectives, key interest rates and the supply of reserves in the ESCB" (Article 12.1 (1) of the ESCB Statute). The **Executive Board** shall implement monetary policy in accordance with the guidelines and decisions laid down by the Governing Council (Article 12.1 (1) and (2) of the ESCB Statute) and pursuant to the **operational rules**[41] laid down in Chapter IV of the ESCB Statute. In order to achieve its monetary policy objectives, the Eurosystem has at its disposal a **set of monetary policy instruments**. These include liquidity-providing and liquidity-absorbing **open market operations**, through which the central banks of the Eurosystem give money to commercial

---

[34] Hatje, in Schwarze et al. (2019), Article 119 AEUV para 13.

[35] See also German Federal Constitutional Court, 2 BvR 2728/13 and others, *OMT* (Judgment of 21 June 2016) para 188.

[36] Richter, in Geiger et al. (2015), Article 119 TFEU para 14.

[37] Selmayr (1999), p. 372.

[38] Selmayr (1999), p. 372; see now Article 9 of the ESCB Statute; Richter, in Geiger et al. (2015), Article 119 TFEU para 14.

[39] Selmayr (1999).

[40] Louis (2004), p. 599 et seqq.; Manger-Nestler (2008), p. 153.

[41] See ECB (May 1999), *The operational framework of the Eurosystem: description and first assessment, Monthly Bulletin* (available at https://www.ecb.europa.eu/pub/pdf/other/p.29_43_mb199905en.pdf).

banks for a certain period of time in return of the collateral. The key interest rate, which determines the monetary policy stance, applies to these operations.

The **Council of the EU** plays an important role in **exchange-rate policy**, i.e. the relationship between the euro currency and the currencies of third States (**external monetary policy**). Article 219.1 TFEU empowers the Council, taking into account the objective of price stability, to conclude formal agreements relating to an **exchange-rate system** for the euro in relation to the currencies of third States (outside the Union).[42] The **implementation** of an exchange-rate policy, however, is in principle **a matter for the ESCB** under Article 127.2, second indent, TFEU. For this purpose, Article 127.2 TFEU, read together with Article 3.1, second indent, of the ESCB Statute, provides the necessary instrument. Therefore, the ESCB shall be responsible "to conduct foreign-exchange operations [...]" on its own (i.e. unilaterally) or as part of a coordinated intervention involving other central banks (i.e. concerted action), in a centralised or decentralised manner, and to carry out operations such as the sale of interest income derived from foreign reserve assets and "commercial transactions". The euro is one of the most traded currencies, along with the US dollar, the Japanese yen and the pound sterling. These reference rates are meant for information purposes only. The ECB also publishes a nominal effective exchange rate of the euro based on weighted averages of bilateral euro exchange rates against the currencies of 19 trading partners of the euro area. This rate indicates whether it is getting more or less expensive on average to exchange foreign currency for euro.

15

Due to the responsibility of the Council, fixing the **exchange rate against the currency of third (non-EU) States is not a policy target of the ESCB**. The ECB also does not try to influence the exchange rate with its monetary policy operations. The G20 group of major economies has committed to refraining from competitive devaluations and from targeting exchange rates for competitive purposes while resisting all forms of protectionism. Exchange rates do have implications for price stability and growth. The ECB needs to watch such developments carefully when setting monetary policy to fulfil its mandate to maintain price stability in the euro area (→ para 16 et seqq.).[43]

3.3.1. Price Stability

Under Articles 127.1 sentence 1 and 282.2 sentence 2 TFEU, the "primary objective" of the ESCB "shall be to maintain price stability". Article 3.3 (1) TEU places **price stability right next to "economic growth"** at the top of the seven objectives that are to determine the work of the Union "for the sustainable development of Europe". Price stability refers to the internal value, to the internal stability and thus to the purchasing power of a currency (→ Article 127 TFEU para 5 to 9).

16

---

[42] Cf. Gramlich (2020), § 15 para 13.
[43] See ECB, *What is the role of exchange rates?* (available at https://www.ecb.europa.eu/explainers/tell-me-more/html/role_of_exchange_rates.en.html).

Understood not as a convergence criterion but as monetary policy control of the money creation process,[44] the ECB chose to adopt in its **monetary policy strategy of 8 May 2003** the objective of maintaining price stability in terms of maintaining **inflation rates at levels below but close to 2% over the medium term**.[45] Thereby, in substance, it confirmed the target set forth on **13 October 1998**, which was considered to be achieved when **"a year-on-year increase in the Harmonised Index of Consumer Prices** (HICP) **for the euro area [is] of below 2%.** Price stability according to this definition 'is to be maintained over the medium term'".[46] Price stability also plays a role for the adoption of the euro. Article 1 of Protocol No 13 specifies the relevant convergence criterion in Article 140 TFEU as an average rate of inflation of an MS (with a derogation) which shall not exceed by more than 1.5 percentage points that of, at most, the three best performing MS in terms of price stability (→ Article 140 TFEU para 17 et seqq.).

17 In fact, **money can only fulfil its role as an "individual instrument of freedom"** (e.g. Article 17.1 EUCFR) **if prices are stable** ("money is coined freedom").[47] The genesis, the wording and the systematic position of the concept of price stability under EU law and national constitutional law require it to be understood as an absolute value.[48] Market interventions that affect price stability may be used to guarantee but may also affect this freedom. On the occasion of the monetary policy strategy statement in 2021 (→ para 18), the Governing Council also confirmed that the **set of interest rates remains "the primary monetary policy instrument" of the ECB**. Other instruments, such as "forward guidance, asset purchases and longer-term refinancing operations", will remain an integral part of the ECB's toolkit, to be used "as appropriate".[49] However, the ECB should

---

[44] Hatje, in Schwarze et al. (2019), Article 119 AEUV para 15.

[45] Cf. the ECB's monetary policy strategy of 8 May 2003. Available at https://www.ecb.europa.eu/home/search/review/html/ecb.strategyreview_monpol_strategy_statement.en.html https://www.ecb.europa.eu/press/pr/date/2003/html/pr030508_2.en.html; later on, see e.g. ECB (April 2009), *Price Stability: Why is it Important for You?*, p. 61 (available at https://www.ecb.europa.eu/pub/pdf/other/whypricestabilityen.pdf).

[46] Cf. ECB (January 1999), Monthly Bulletin, p. 46. On 8 May 2003, after a thorough evaluation of the ECB's monetary policy strategy, the Governing Council of the ECB concluded: "Today, the Governing Council confirmed this definition (which it announced in 1998). At the same time, the Governing Council agreed that in the pursuit of price stability it will aim to maintain inflation rates close to 2% over the medium term. This clarification underlines the ECB's commitment to provide a sufficient safety margin to guard against the risks of deflation." With regard to the development of the Eurosystem'sstability-oriented monetary policy strategy over the years, cf. Blanke and Pilz, in Huber and Voßkuhle (2023), Article 88 GG para 83 et seqq.; Herrmann, in Pechstein et al. (2017), Article 119 AEUV para 55.

[47] Hasse (1989), p. 126. The term was coined by Dostoevsky, *The House of the Dead* (1862).

[48] Cf. Herdegen, in Dürig et al. (2022), Article 88 GG para 32 et seq. (released in 2010); Nicolaysen (1993), p. 39; Janzen (1996), p. 159 et seq., who considers the definition of a ceiling with regard to "price stability" as legally impracticable.

[49] See No 8 of the ECB's Governing Council's monetary policy strategy statement of 8 July 2021. Available at https://www.ecb.europa.eu/home/search/review/html/ecb.strategyreview_monpol_strategy_statement.en.html.

make it clear that **negative interest rates (2014–2022),** as a consequence of ultra-loose monetary policy, are a crisis management tool to combat the risk of deflation. A clear **exit scenario** should always be presented when a tool of this kind is deployed. As a first step in a **turnaround in interest rates**, the ECB **on 21 July 2022** raised its three key interest rates for the first time in over a decade. The move was aimed to combat inflation as consumer prices in the eurozone rose at an 8.6% annual pace in June 2022. At the same time the ECB raised its negative benchmark deposit rate by 50 basis points from minus 0.5% to 0%, lifting the bank's deposit facility out of negative territory for the first time in eight years.[50]

In **July 2021**, more than 18 years after its reflections on the future monetary policy strategy 2003 and due to "profound structural changes", in particular "declining trend growth, which can be linked to slower productivity growth and demographic factors, and the legacy of the global financial crisis", but also in view of "globalisation, digitalisation, the threat to environmental sustainability[51] and changes in the financial system", the Governing Council of the ECB has **published a new monetary policy strategy, which it has set out in a** statement of 8 July 2021:[52] "The Governing Council considers that price stability is best maintained by **aiming for two per cent inflation over the medium term**." Thereby, the ECB relinquished the previous target of "below, but close to, 2%". Continuing the ECB policy under *Draghi*, the Governing Council's commitment to the updated **target is symmetric**. "Symmetry means that the Governing Council considers negative and positive deviations from this target as equally undesirable. The two per cent inflation target provides a clear anchor for inflation expectations, which is essential for maintaining price stability."[53] Hence, the symmetric approach aims at incorporating hysteresis effects into its monetary policy deliberations.[54] Although "the immediate implications [for the path of monetary policy] are modest", the decision is partly seen as **"a historic shift for the ECB"**,[55] which marks an important break with the conservative monetary doctrine of Germany's *Bundesbank*, which formed the bedrock of the euro's creation.[56] Others see the new strategy "in the **good tradition of the Bundesbank** and its successful focus on price stability".[57] Critics

18

---

[50] The ECB press release of 21 July 2022 "on its its policy rate normalisation path" is available at https://www.ecb.europa.eu/press/pr/date/2022/html/ecb.mp220721~53e5bdd317.en.html.

[51] See the ECB's action plan of 8 July 2021 to include climate change considerations in its monetary policy strategy (→ para 18). The ECB "roadmap to greening monetary policy" is available at https://www.ecb.europa.eu/ecb/climate/roadmap/html/index.en.html.

[52] Available at https://www.ecb.europa.eu/home/search/review/html/ecb.strategyreview_monpol_strategy_statement.en.html.

[53] See No 5 of the Governing Council´s monetary policy strategy statement of 8 July 2021.

[54] Cf. Dullien and Tober (2021), p. 2, 4 et seqq.

[55] See Kenningham, an economist at Capital Economics, cited in Arnold (2021, July 12).

[56] Arnold (2021, July 12).

[57] Fratzscher (2021). *J. Weidmann*, the president of the Bundesbank, has acknowledged the new strategy with his consent: "The new strategy helps monetary policy to ensure price stability for the people of the euro area [. . .]", cited in Handelsblatt of 9 July 2021. See for the former impact of the

found that the ECB had defined this new inflation target regardless of the rising inflation rate in the euro area in order to be able to maintain its (former) **loose monetary policy**.[58] The ECB nevertheless did not go as far as the US Federal Reserve, which in 2020 formally committed to a flexible average inflation target, which means it will aim for price growth to exceed its target to make up for a period of running below it.

3.3.2. The Relationship Between Price Stability and Independence of the ESCB

19 The primary objective of the ESCB, regulating the money supply and thus having an impact on public finance as well as the areas of policy dependent on it, is to **secure price stability through depoliticised and thus independent decisions** (→ para 13, 21). The "principle" of independence, spelt out in Article 130 TFEU, enshrines the **permanent guarantee of the ECB's freedom from instructions from Union and national authorities in the context of monetary policy decisions** (→ Article 130 TFEU para 7 et seqq.). This independence is primarily based on institutional safeguards to ensure that decisions are made on the basis of expert knowledge. An independent central bank is more likely than State bodies to safeguard the monetary value and, thus, the general economic basis for governmental budgetary policies as well as for private plans and transactions in the exercise of economic freedoms.[59] Instead, politically independent experts make macroeconomic decisions. The *exemptio partialis* opened up by the national legislatures in favour of the ESCB, i.e. the need to exempt this institution from political influence,[60] allows their bodies to govern effectively beyond the parliamentary control of the EP or the national assemblies[61] and disconnects the exercise of the powers for monetary policy also from direct governmental responsibility in order to free the monetary system from access by interest groups and holders of political office who are concerned about their re-election.[62]

Bundesbank on the inflation policy of past decades, Starck (1998), p. 9 et seqq.; Apel (2003), p. 64 et seqq., 117 et seqq.; Kleinheyer (2014), p. 34.

[58] Heinemann (2021a, b).

[59] Cf. German Federal Constitutional Court, 2 BvR 2134/92, 2 BvR 2159/92, *Maastricht* (Judgment of 12 October 1993) para 154 (BVerfGE 89, 155, 208).

[60] See Case C-518/07, *Commission v Germany* (CJEU9 March 2010) para 42; with regard to the transferability of this functional approach to other authorities, beyond those responsible for data protection, cf. Manger-Nester and Gentzsch (2021), p. 23, within their analysis of "Central Bank Independence and Democracy".

[61] German Federal Constitutional Court, 2 BvR 2728/13 and others, *OMT* (Judgment of 21 June 2016) para 188: "The independence of the European Central Bank as well as of the national central banks releases the public authority exercised by them from direct national or supranational parliamentary responsibility."

[62] Cf. German Federal Constitutional Court, 2 BvR 2134/92, 2 BvR 2159/92, *Maastricht* (Judgment of 12 October 1993) para 155 (BVerfGE 89, 155, 208), where the Court refers to the Government Draft on the Bundesbank Act, BT-Drs. 2/2781, p. 24 et seq.

The TFEU guarantees the independence of the ECB, the national central banks **20** and the members of their decision-making bodies in the exercise of their competences and duties under the Treaty (Article 130 sentence 1 TFEU and Article 282.3 sentences 3 and 4 TFEU) through (a) **institutional-functional as well as** (b) **personal and substantial autonomy and**, last but not least, through (c) **financial autonomy** (→ Article 130 TFEU para 16 et seqq., 22 et seqq., 25 et seqq., 32 et seqq.).[63] (a) Giving the ECB its **own legal personality** is an effective means of underlining the independent fulfilment of the tasks entrusted to it within a discretionary scope of action (Article 282.3 sentence 1 TFEU, Article 9.1 of the ESCB Statute). The functional aspect of independence is further taken into account by the prohibition of monetary budget financing without exception (Articles 123, 124 TFEU). (b) The **personal independence of the members of the Executive Board** is ensured by long terms of office without the possibility of reappointment (Article 283.2 (3) TFEU; Article 11.2 (2) of the ESCB Statute), a restrictive regulation of the conditions for dismissal (Article 11.4 of the ESCB Statute) as well as the power to determine the conditions of employment largely independently (Articles 11.3, 36 of the ESCB Statute). Relatively weak are the Treaty provisions on the safeguarding of the independence of the governors of national central banks, given that these conditions are basically subject to national regulations. So far, the ESCB Statute only contains a few provisions regarding the term of office (Article 14.2 (1)) and grounds for dismissal (Article 14.2 (2)). (c) In financial terms, the autonomy of the ESCB is guaranteed by provisions on the financial accounts of the ECB, which draw **a clear line between the budget of the EU and the "annual accounts" of the ECB** (Article 129.2 TFEU read together with Article 26 of the ESCB Statute). The ECB currently has a **total capital** (Article 28 of the ESCB Statute) of approximately EUR 10.825 billion, which includes the paid-up subscriptions of euro area NCBs to the ECB's capital in accordance with the percentage share of each NCB amounting to **EUR 7.584 billion**, Article 29 of the ESCB Statute and the paid-in capital of non-euro area NCBs of around EUR 75 million.[64]

At the core of the **substantial independence** of the ECB is the prohibition **21** addressed to the ECB, the national central banks and any member of their decision-making bodies to "seek or accept instructions from Union institutions, bodies, offices or agencies, from any government of a Member State or from any other body" (Article 130 sentence 1 TFEU). Pursuant to Article 130 sentence 2 TFEU, this includes the prohibition addressed to the Union institutions, bodies, offices or agencies and the governments of the MS "to seek to influence the members of the decision-making bodies of the European Central Bank or of the national central banks in the performance of their tasks". In essence, this provision is intended **to shield the ESCB from external influences or even political**

---

[63] See Manger-Nester and Gentzsch (2021), p. 8 et seqq.
[64] See, with regard to the capital subscription, the ECB information updated on 29 December 2020 (available at https://www.ecb.europa.eu/ecb/orga/capital/html/index.de.html).

pressure in order to enable it effectively to pursue the objectives attributed to its tasks, through the independent exercise of the specific powers conferred on it for that purpose by primary law.[65] The ECB's independence does not preclude judicial review with regard to the delineation of its mandate (Article 263 (1) and (2) and Article 267 TFEU).[66] On the other hand, its legal personality also allows the ECB to refer matters to the CJEU, if necessary, in order to assert its independence (Article 263 (3) TFEU). This principle also does not exclude dialogues and discussions between the ECB and national central banks integrated into the ESCB or between the ECB and other Union institutions or the national governments. Therefore, it is apparent from Article 130 TFEU that the **ESCB is to be independent when carrying out its task of formulating and implementing the Union's monetary policy** (arg. Article 282.4 TFEU).[67] In its judgment on the PSPP programme, the German Federal Constitutional Court (FCC) rightly observed that "the independence afforded the ECB relates only to the powers conferred upon it in the Treaties and the substantive exercise of such powers but is not applicable with regard to defining the extent and scope of the ECB's mandate".[68] This brings into focus the distinction between monetary policy and economic policy measures (→ Article 120 TFEU para 21 et seqq.).

22   It is mainly the ECB's task to ensure continuous compliance with these requirements. The legitimation of this political process depends on whether the standardised political performance is promoted in an effective manner and whether the highly complex decisions taken by experts to achieve it are recognised by those who are affected by them (**output legitimation**).[69] The focus of interest is solely on the effectiveness and efficiency of the tasks performed by independent experts.[70] The growing importance of regulatory institutions within international organisations, such as the ESM or the IMF, shows that trust in qualities such as competence, discretion, coherence, fairness and independence is more important than trust in the original political decisions themselves. The legitimation in substance depends on

---

[65] Case C-62/14, *Gauweiler et al.* (CJEU 16 June 2015) para 40; German Federal Constitutional Court, 2 BvR 2728/13 and others, *OMT* (Judgment of 21 June 2016) para 40.

[66] Case C-11/00, *Commission v ECB* (ECJ 10 July 2003) para 135 et seq.; German Federal Constitutional Court, 2 BvR 2728/13 and others, *OMT* (Reference for preliminary ruling) (Order of 14 January 2014) para 60. In contrast to the CJEU, the German FCC maintains the "imperative that the mandate of the ESCB be subject to strict limitations given that the ECB and the national central banks are independent institutions"; see, most recently, German Federal Constitutional Court, 2 BvR 859/15 and others, *PSPP* (Judgment of 5 May 2020) para 143; critical of this position Nettesheim (2020), p. 1633.

[67] See Case C-62/14, *Gauweiler et al.* (CJEU 16 June 2015) para 40.

[68] German Federal Constitutional Court, 2 BvR 859/15 and others, *PSPP* (Judgment of 5 May 2020) para 143.

[69] On output legitimation in general, see Scharpf (2005), p. 709; Trute (2012), para 53; Unger (2008), pp. 52–53; rejected by von Bogdandy (2003), p. 873; on output legitimation in the ESM, the ECB and the IMF, see Pilz (2016), p. 115 et seqq.

[70] Unger (2016), p. 61; Falcon (2016), p. 110.

how precisely the institutional purposes are defined. This is decisive because the **operational objectives** the ECB is accountable for can only be achieved if they are **not vague or formulated too broadly**.[71]

At the time of the German FCC's decision on the Maastricht Treaty,[72] the substantial-political independence of the ECB and the national central banks may still have been sufficiently contained by the Maastricht criteria and the objective of maintaining price stability. Meanwhile, however, at the latest, since the rise of the ECB under its former President, *M. Draghi*, as a crisis manager and the unconventional monetary policy measures the Bank has taken for more than a decade (2011-2022), **the question of the democratic legitimacy of the ECB has been raised in a new light**. The emerging doubts about the legitimacy of the ECB's measures manifest themselves in the **OMT preliminary ruling proceedings** initiated by the German FCC, which find their point of departure in the disputed decisions of the ECB Governing Council of 6 September 2012 for undertaking Outright Monetary Transactions (OMTs) in secondary markets for sovereign bonds in the euro area.[73] The subject of the German Constitutional Court's reference for preliminary ruling pursuant to Article 267 TFEU was in particular the question of whether the OMT decisions are incompatible with Article 119 and Articles 127.1 and 2 TFEU and with Articles 17 to 24 of the ESCB Statute "because it exceeds the European Central Bank's monetary policy mandate, which is regulated in the above-mentioned provisions, and infringes the powers of the Member States".[74] Finally, in its Judgment of 21 June 2016, the FCC, notwithstanding "serious objections [...] [in particular] in respect of [...] the principle of conferral [...], and the judicial review of acts of the European Central Bank that relate to the definition of its mandate",[75] followed the EU Court's preliminary ruling and did not rule out the purchases of government bonds by the ESCB (OMT decisions) as exceeding the

---

[71] Pilz (2016), p. 116.
[72] German Federal Constitutional Court, 2 BvR 2134/92, 2 BvR 2159/92, *Maastricht* (Judgment of 12 October 1993) para 109, 112 (BVerfGE 89, 155).
[73] For a more detailed foundation of the OMT decisions of 6 September 2012 on Technical Features of Outright Monetary Transactions, i.e. the main parameters approved by the Governing Council of the ECB on 5 and 6 September 2012, see ECB, Monthly Bulletin (October 2012), p. 9: Compliance of Outright Monetary Transactions with the prohibition on monetary financing (available at https://www.ecb.europa.eu/pub/pdf/other/mb201210_focus01.en.pdf). The last issue addressed in this short analysis from the perspective of the ECB refers to "Central bank independence". It points out: "The operational modalities for OMTs have been designed by the Governing Council, in full independence, from the perspective of what is necessary, proportional and effective for monetary policy purposes. The Governing Council will have full discretion in deciding on the start, continuation and suspension of OMTs in accordance with its monetary policy mandate."
[74] German Federal Constitutional Court, 2 BvR 2728/13 and others, *OMT* (Reference for preliminary ruling) (Order of 14 January 2014) sub II of the decision.
[75] German Federal Constitutional Court, 2 BvR 2728/13 and others, *OMT* (Judgment of 21 June 2016) para 181 et seqq.

EU's competences nor recognise any violation of the constitutional identity within the meaning of Articles 20.1–2 and 79.3 of the German Basic Law. But under Articles 119 and 127 TFEU, the Court considered the OMT decisions justifiable "only" if the ECB uses it "to secure price stability".[76] It has held "that the independence granted to the European Central Bank (Article 130 TFEU) leads to a **noticeable reduction in the level of democratic legitimation of its actions and should thus lead to a restrictive interpretation**, as well as to a particularly strict judicial review, **of the mandate of the European Central Bank**".[77]

24   The **judicial dispute** between the FCC and CJEU culminated on the occasion of the **proceedings on the ECB's PSPP**,[78] which essentially concerned the question of whether this programme is to be classified as an economic or monetary policy measure (→ Article 120 TFEU para 27 et seqq.). The FCC concluded in its judgment that the PSPP has **"economic policy effects"**, which both the CJEU and the ESCB "completely disregarded", and therefore the application of the principle of proportionality by the CJEU could not fulfil its purpose.[79] The CJEU, on the other hand, in the case of *Weiss*, had clearly stated: "[…] it does not appear that the ESCB's economic analysis – according to which the **PSPP was appropriate**, in the monetary and financial conditions of the euro area, **for contributing to** achieving the objective of maintaining **price stability** – is vitiated by a manifest error of assessment".[80]

25   Hence, the FCC qualified this ESCB programme and its judicial assessment by the CJEU as **ultra vires acts**[81] and called upon the German Federal Government and the *Bundestag* to renegotiate. Referring to their responsibility with regard to European integration (*Integrationsverantwortung*), the FCC obliged "the Federal Government and the *Bundestag* to take steps seeking to ensure that the ECB conducts a proportionality assessment in relation the PSPP, […] given the ECB's

---

[76] German Federal Constitutional Court, 2 BvR 2728/13 and others, *OMT* (Judgment of 21 June 2016) para 194; this requirement was affirmed by the CJEU, also with regard to the holding of bonds by the ECB, in Case C-62/14, *Gauweiler et al.* (CJEU 16 June 2015) para 51; later than in Case C-493/17, *Weiss et al.* (CJEU 11 December 2018), with regard to (1) Article 123 TFEU and (2) the holding of bonds by the ECB (para 134, 152).

[77] German Federal Constitutional Court, 2 BvR 2728/13 and others, *OMT* (Judgment of 21 June 2016) para 187.

[78] ECB Decision (EU) 2015/774 *on a secondary markets public sector asset purchase programme*, O.J. L 121/20 (2015), as last amended by Decision (EU) 2017/100 of the ECB of 11 January 2017, O.J. L 16/51 (2017), now replaced by ECB Decision (EU) 2020/188 *on a secondary markets public sector asset purchase programme* (ECB/2020/9), O.J. L 39/12 (2020).

[79] German Federal Constitutional Court, 2 BvR 859/15 and others, *PSPP* (Judgment of 5 May 2020) para 138 et seqq. (relating to the CJEU), and 164 et seqq. (relating to the ESCB).

[80] Case C-493/17, *Weiss et al.* (CJEU 11 December 2018) para 78.

[81] German Federal Constitutional Court, 2 BvR 859/15 and others, *PSPP* (Judgment of 5 May 2020) para 119, 154, 163 (relating to the CJEU), and 165, 178, 232 (relating to the ESCB).

Article 119   [Principles of Economic and Monetary Policy]

failure to substantiate that the programme is proportionate".[82] In the opinion of the FCC, the independence afforded to both the ECB and the *Bundesbank* does not conflict with this "specific obligation to act".[83] On 2 July 2020, the **German Bundestag adopted a joint motion** on the FCC's ruling on the ECB's bond purchase programme, PSPP. According to that motion, the majority of the members of the *Bundestag* consider the ECB's explanation for conducting a proportionality test to be comprehensible and the requirements of the Federal Constitutional Court's ruling to be fulfilled. Irrespective of this, the German *Bundestag* emphasises that it permanently fulfils its responsibility for integration with regard to the monetary policy decisions of the ECB Governing Council.[84]

But, in fact, the **independence of the ESCB system** (Article 130 sentence 1 TFEU) **is being limited** in favour of the responsibility of the German constitutional bodies with regard to European integration. Judicial review, as important as it is for the delimitation of competences between the Union and the MS in accordance with the principle of conferral, must not become a means to substitute ESCB decisions in matters of monetary policy with judges' assessment. Even the FCC has acknowledged "that the ECB is afforded a margin of appreciation as regards the assessment and appraisal of the *consequences* of its actions and the weighing of such *consequences* in relation to the objectives pursued by the asset purchase programme".[85] Against this backdrop, it is not convincing that the constitutional judges assessed the *measures* selected by the ECB to be disproportionate to the economic and fiscal policy effects resulting from the programme.[86] As a result, referring to the principle of proportionality, which is a highly disputed standard in the context of an *ultra vires* review and thus for delimiting spheres of competence,[87] the **ECB's scope for**

26

---

[82] German Federal Constitutional Court, 2 BvR 859/15 and others, *PSPP* (Judgment of 5 May 2020) para 232: "The Federal Government and the *Bundestag* must clearly communicate their legal view to the ECB or take other steps to ensure that conformity with the Treaties is restored."

[83] German Federal Constitutional Court, 2 BvR 859/15 and others, *PSPP* (Judgment of 5 May 2020) para 232 read together with para 231.

[84] See Bundestags-Drucksache 19/20621 (available at https://dserver.bundestag.de/btd/19/206/1920621.pdf).

[85] German Federal Constitutional Court, 2 BvR 859/15 and others, *PSPP* (Judgment of 5 May 2020) para 141 (emphasis added). The FCC criticises in this context "that the CJEU attaches no legal relevance whatsoever to the effects of the asset purchase programme, neither in determining the objectives pursued by the ESCB nor in reviewing the proportionality of the programme."

[86] See German Federal Constitutional Court, 2 BvR 859/15 and others, *PSPP* (Judgment of 5 May 2020) para 138 to 141.

[87] See, relating to the controversy of the applicability of the proportionality principle in the case of public sector asset purchase by the ECB, Ziller (2020), p. 93 et seq., who criticises the judges of the Second Senate about interpreting this principle, in disregard of Article 5.1 TEU, as a delimitation of EU competences, although it is a boundary to the *exercise* of these competences; similarly, Müller, in Jaeger and Stöger (2021), Article 119 AEUV para 29 (released in 2020) and Kratzmann (2022), p. 408 et seq. Ohler (2021), p. 325 et seq., 335, on the other hand, considers the principle of proportionality "as a general legal principle in Union law [...] applicable at the various decision-making levels of monetary policy" (my translation). In a clear distinction between the principle of proportionality, as it is enshrined Article 5.1 and Article 5.4 TEU on the one hand and as a general

monetary policy assessment is completely negated by the FCC.[88] But the Court's view that a **clear exit scenario** should always be presented when a tool of this kind is deployed[89] can be fully endorsed. This needs better communication by the ECB vis-à-vis the market operators and the public.

27   The **explosive nature of the FCC decision** lies in the fact that it excludes Decision (EU) 2015/774 and subsequent ECB decisions from the precedence of the application of EU law[90] and thus ignores the CJEU's monopoly on the interpretation of Union law as a whole (Article 19.1 (1) sentence 2 TEU) but at the same time

---

legal principle on the other hand, he comes to the conclusion that it seems problematic to apply Article 5.4 TEU to the decision of the ECB on PSPP. From an economic perspective, cf. Feld and Wieland (2020), p. 32, who hold that the proportionality principle has already been influential in shaping key aspects of the ECB strategy in the past and propose "to develop quantitative benchmarks for a regular proportionality check". In headnotes 6a and 6b and para 119 of the PSPP Judgment, the Second Senate of the FCC observes: "In its Judgment of 11 December 2018, the CJEU held that the Decision of the ECB Governing Council on the PSPP and its subsequent amendments were still within the ambit of the ECB's competences [...]. This view manifestly fails to give consideration to the importance and scope of the principle of proportionality (Art. 5 (1) second sentence and Art. 5 (4) TEU), *which also applies to the division of competences* [...]" (emphasis is mine). In para 133, the Senate continues: "When applied in this manner, as undertaken by the CJEU, the principle of proportionality enshrined in Art. 5(1) second sentence and Art. 5(4) TEU cannot fulfil its corrective function for the purposes of safeguarding the competences of the Member States."

[88] See also Kainer (2020), p. 535 et seq.; Calliess (2020), p. 901, 903, who points out: "The Second Senate's assessment of the ECJ's proportionality test is all the more astonishing as the FCC, even after the reform of the federal system in 2006, has not referred to the principle of proportionality set out in the 'necessity clause' of Article 72 (2) GG [as amended in 2006] for the delimitation of competences between the Federation and the *Länder*" (my translation). The following judgment can serve as proof for this: German Federal Constitutional Court, 1 BvF 2/13, *Social benefits of public assistance* (Judgment of 21 July 2015) para 67. See also the sharp criticism of Ziller (2020), p., 94 et seq., towards the FCC's interpretation of the proportionality principle: "[...] only a manifest error of methodology on the part of the CJEU could be censured by the *BVerfG*. What the judges of the majority of the Second *Senat* do is what the administrative judge or the constitutional judge in the other Member States do: they decide themselves what is a manifest error, and they do not apply a transcendental legal methodology to do so"; also Galetta 2020, p. 3 et seqq. criticises that this interpretation deviates from CJEU case law and criticises the Karlsruhe Judges of the Second Senate about "cultural dominance" ("dominanza culturale"). Similarly, Montoro Chiner and Rodríguez Pontón (2021), p. 24, 31 t seq. with footnote 37, criticise the Karlsruhe constitutional judges about interpreting the principle of proportionality "in their own [German] way" ("[...] que el TCFA interpreta según su propio modo de entenderlo [...] a la alemana"). Very harsh in his criticism of this part of the judgment, Kratzmann (2022), p. 408 et seq., points out (my translation): "[The Federal Constitutional Court] has bypassed Article 5.1 sentence 1 and sentence 2 TEU, and created a principle of proportionality on the German model, which the CJEU is unable to cope with. [....] The CJEU's proportionality test may in itself be a failure in balancing the interests involved [....]. However, this is due to Article 5.4 TEU, which defines the European proportionality principle."

[89] German Federal Constitutional Court, 2 BvR 859/15 and others, *PSPP* (Judgment of 5 May 2020) para 194, 212, 214.

[90] German Federal Constitutional Court, 2 BvR 859/15 and others, *PSPP* (Judgment of 5 May 2020) para 234.

Article 119   [Principles of Economic and Monetary Policy]   497

also rejects as a second "ultra vires" act the preliminary ruling of the CJEU on the legal questions about the PSPP referred to by the FCC.[91] By Order of 29 April 2021, the FCC rejected two requests seeking an order of execution for the Judgment of 5 May 2020.[92] But on 9 June 2021, the European Commission announced that it is bringing an **infringement procedure against Germany** for breach of the fundamental principles of EU law, in particular the principles of autonomy, primacy, effectiveness and uniform application of Union law, as well as respect for the jurisdiction of the European Court of Justice under Article 267 TFEU.[93] Due to Germany's commitments, the infringement procedure was closed by the Commission in December 2021 before reaching the CJEU ($\rightarrow$ Article 127 TFEU para 23 et seq.).[94]

3.4. Secondary Objectives of the ESCB Mandate

3.4.1. The ESCB's Secondary Mandate to Support the EU General Economic Policies

In fact, since it follows from Articles 119.2, 127.1 and 282.2 TFEU that, without prejudice to the objective of price stability, the **ESCB is to support the general economic policies in the Union**, the action taken by the ESCB on the basis of Article 123 TFEU cannot be such as to contravene the effectiveness of those policies by lessening the impetus of the MS concerned to follow a sound budgetary policy.[95] The ESCB shall *support*, without prejudice to the objective of maintaining

28

---

[91] German Federal Constitutional Court, 2 BvR 859/15 and others, *PSPP* (Judgment of 5 May 2020) para 119, 154, 163.

[92] German Federal Constitutional Court, 2 BvR 1651/15 and 2 BvR 2006/15 (Order of 29 April 2021) with a documentation on eight "ECB-confidential" documents in para 6 et seqq. In para 109 the FCC has held: "Ultimately, and even though not all individual steps might necessarily be documented in detail, the numerous activities undertaken by the Federal Government and the *Bundestag* in response to the Judgment of 5 May 2020, which were in part carried out via or with the assistance of the *Bundesbank*, have led to the ECB Governing Council demonstrating, in its decisions nos. 4 and 5 adopted 3–4 June 2020 and in the preceding discussions, that it conducted a proportionality assessment in accordance with Art. 5(1) second sentence and Art. 5(4) TEU in conjunction with Art. 119 ff. and Art. 127 ff. TFEU – the lack of which had been objected to by the Second Senate in its Judgment. It is not for the Court to decide in the present case whether this proportionality assessment satisfies the substantive requirements deriving from Art. 5(1) second sentence and Art. 5(4) TFEU in every respect."

[93] See already before the opening of the procedure, Poli and Cisotta (2020) with a comparative examination of ECJ case law (Cases C-129/00, C-154/08 and C-416/17). Nguyen (2021).

[94] With regard to the three commitments Germany had to make in relation to the EU, cf. Commission, *December infringements package: key decisions*, INF/21/6201. In view of these consequences Kratzmann (2022), p. 410, speaks of a "phyrrhic victory" of the FCC; Germany has, in the author's choice of words, "capitulated".

[95] German Federal Constitutional Court, 2 BvR 2728/13 and others, *OMT* (Judgment of 21 June 2016) para 109.

price stability, the general economic policies in the Union. Without any formal amendment to the TFEU, the ESCB's reaction to the ongoing crisis situation has at least changed the perception of this priority in its range of tasks. Hence, the polycrisis has reversed the prevailing monetary policy paradigm as the supposedly "exclusive" task of the ESCB. Especially in view of the "Transmission Protection Instrument" (→ Article 127 TFEU para 21, 25), this remains the case also after the end of the net asset purchases under the ECB asset purchase programme (APP) as of 1 July 2022,[96] and the interest rate turnaround initiated by the ECB on 21 July 2022 (→ para 17). But the **Treaty does not empower the ESCB to gear an own economic policy**. Developing an independent economic policy with no relation to monetary policy and not oriented to the primary objective of price stability is prohibited for the ESCB.[97]

29 The **dispute between the FCC and CJEU**, ultimately evoked through the different assessments of the powers, competences and tasks of the ESCB against the background of the level of democratic legitimacy of its bodies,[98] **also captures the interpretation of the clause** on the "support of the general economic policies in the Union". Whereas the CJEU, referring to the principle of institutional balance established by the Treaties, regards this clause as proof that "the authors of the Treaty did not intend to make an absolute separation between economic and monetary policies" (→ Article 120 TFEU para 28 et seqq.),[99] the FCC finds that "the *Weiss* Judgment of the CJEU essentially affords the ECB the competence to pursue its own economic policy agenda".[100] Leaving the "balancing of the economic and fiscal policy effects of the PSPP" to the appraisal of the ECB instead of subjecting its actions to an effective review, also in view of the order of competences, means for the FCC exceeding the judicial mandate given to the CJEU (Article 19.1 sentence 2 TEU).[101]

30 Beyond the support of the general economic policies, taken up in Article 127.1 sentences 2 and 3 TFEU, the Treaty sets forth further (secondary) objectives of the ESCB's action in terms of tasks relating to the **prudential supervision of credit institutions** and other financial institutions and its **contribution to the stability of the financial system** (Article 127.5 and Article 127.6 TFEU; → para 32 et seqq.).

---

[96] See the ECB press release of 9 June 2022, available at https://www.ecb.europa.eu/press/pr/date/2022/html/ecb.mp220609~122666c272.en.html.

[97] See Müller, in Jaeger and Stöger (2021), Article 119 AEUV para 10, 23 (released in 2020).

[98] Manger-Nester and Gentzsch (2021), p. 14 et seqq., 133 et seqq.

[99] Case C-493/17, *Weiss et al.* (CJEU 11 December 2018) para 60. Insofar as the CJEU speaks in this context of "institutional balance", Kratzmann (2022), p. 406 et seq., reproaches it with loosing in "pure rhetoric" (*Wortgeklingel*).

[100] German Federal Constitutional Court, 2 BvR 859/15 and others, *PSPP* (Judgment of 5 May 2020) para 163.

[101] German Federal Constitutional Court, 2 BvR 859/15 and others, *PSPP* (Judgment of 5 May 2020) para 163.

Following the conclusion of the strategy review of 2020–21, the Governing Council of the **ECB** decided on a comprehensive **action plan to further incorporate climate change considerations into its policy framework**. Thus, it plans to tackle climate change risks by tilting its asset purchases and collateral rules away from heavy carbon-emitting companies. Referring to "its obligations under the EU Treaties",[102] the Governing Council has argued that "climate change and the transition towards a more sustainable economy affect the **outlook for price stability** through their impact on macroeconomic indicators [...]. Moreover, climate change and the carbon transition affect the value and the risk profile of the assets held on the Eurosystem's balance sheet, potentially leading to an **undesirable accumulation of climate-related financial risks**." In this context, reference is also made to the **cross-sectional clause of Article 11 TFEU**, according to which "environmental protection requirements must be integrated into the definition and implementation of the Union's policies and activities, in particular with a view to promoting sustainable development". Although not conferring a specific mandate for ESCB climate change action, it requires consistency between EU policies.[103] According to the ECB statement, the design of these measures within a risk-based supervisory approach "will be consistent with the price stability objective".[104]

There is nevertheless a **risk** of overburdening monetary policymakers with general policy objectives that will expose the central bank to greater political pressure. The desire of certain social groups and politicians to see the monetary policy used to influence further socio-political goals will be likely to increase with all the **negative effects on the substantial-political independence of the E(S)CB**

31

---

[102] See also Elderson (Member of the Executive Board of the ECB) (2021) who refers primarily to the ECB mandate "to support the general economic policies in the Union".

[103] See the reference the ECB's Governing Council makes in its statements to the principles set out in Article 3 TEU, namely in its monetary policy strategy statement of 8 July 2021, No 2: "Without prejudice to the price stability objective, the Eurosystem shall support the general economic policies in the EU with a view to contributing to the achievement of the Union's objectives as laid down in Article 3 of the Treaty on European Union. These objectives include balanced economic growth, a highly competitive social market economy aiming at full employment and social progress, and a high level of protection and improvement of the quality of the environment. [...]." Elderson (2021); with regard to the need for broader political action in the area of economic policy, including environmental protection, also Kauppi, in Herzog et al. (2019), Article 119 TFEU para 119-4-5, in very general terms points out that "Article 2 TEC [Principles] cannot be achieved simply by an orthodoxy economic policy. These aims include a high level of employment and social protection, protection of the environment, the raising of standards of living quality of life and economic and social cohesion and solidarity among Member States. They clearly require some form of official intervention, whether at Community or Member States level." See further Association of German Banks (2020): "The European Central Bank could pursue climate change mitigation policies under its 'secondary' mandate, which authorises it to support general economic policies in the European Union."

[104] See ECB, Press release of 8 July 2021 (available at https://www.ecb.europa.eu/press/pr/date/2021/html/ecb.pr210708_1~f104919225.en.html); see already ECB (Banking Supervision), Ramping up climate-related and environmental risk supervision, Supervision Newsletter of 18 November 2020 (available at https://www.bankingsupervision.europa.eu/press/publications/newsletter/2020/html/ssm.nl201118_4.en.html).

(→ para 21).[105] A similar situation threatens to arise if the ECB abandons the principle of market neutrality in its monetary policy measures. If the ECB gave preferential treatment to climate-friendly companies in its bond-buying programme, for example, the **distinction between monetary policy and active industrial or structural policy would become blurred**.

3.4.2. Contribution to Financial Stability as an Objective Related to Price Stability

32 The polycrisis revealed that a monetary policy geared to price stability alone is no guarantee for avoiding undesirable developments on the financial markets. Distortions on the capital markets can also affect the real economy and thus ultimately endanger price stability.[106] Since 2007, the **importance of financial stability for monetary policy** has become apparent, especially in the fact that the risk appetite of financial market players can be influenced by means of monetary policy management.[107] Since distortions on the financial markets not only cause high economic costs but can also significantly influence price developments, the "task" of securing the stability of the financial system increasingly determines the ECB's actions. The Governing Council of the ECB considers it part of its mandate to ensure that "the Eurosystem [...] contribute[s] to the smooth conduct of policies pursued by the competent authorities relating to the prudential supervision of credit institutions and the stability of the financial system".[108] One institutional example is the **European Systemic Risk Board** (ESRB), whose establishment in 2010 was accompanied by an increase in the ECB's tasks.[109] Its macro-prudential powers were expanded again in the context of the establishment of a Banking Union.[110] The Banking Union includes a **Single Supervisory Mechanism** attached to the ECB,[111] which is to identify and correct undesirable developments in the national banking sectors at an early stage in order to prevent interactions between the

---

[105] See Association of German Banks (2020).

[106] Pilz (2016), p. 14 et seqq.

[107] Deutsche Bundesbank, Monthly report March 2015, p. 41; International Monetary Fund, Global Financial Stability Report. Financial Market Turbulence: Causes, Consequences, and Policies, October 2007, p. 116. See also Michler and Smeets (2011), p. 3 et seqq.

[108] See e.g. No 2 of the ECB's Governing Council's monetary policy strategy statement of 8 July 2021.

[109] Parliament/Council Regulation (EU) No 1092/2010 *on European Union macro-prudential oversight of the financial system and establishing a European Systemic Risk Board*, O.J. L 331/1 (2010) and Council Regulation (EU) No 1096/2010 *conferring specific tasks upon the European Central Bank concerning the functioning of the European Systemic Risk Board*, O.J. L 331/162 (2010). See in detail Kohtamäki (2011), p. 115 et seqq.; Thiele (2014), p. 500 et seqq.

[110] Manger-Nestler (2014), p. 299 et seqq.

[111] Council Regulation (EU) No 1024/2013 *conferring specific tasks on the European Central Bank concerning policies relating to the prudential supervision of credit institutions*, O.J. L 287/63 (2013).

national banking systems and the public finances. Within the framework of this macro-prudential policy, the ECB is given extensive supervisory and investigative powers (Articles 4, 9, 16 of the SSM Regulation) in order to be able to counter the risks to the financial system as a whole.[112]

However, it is not at all clear **what** the term **"financial stability"**, stipulated in particular in Article 127.5 TFEU, exactly **means and how it relates to the maintenance of price stability**.[113] "Defining financial stability is as difficult as it is important."[114] In the *Pringle* case, the CJEU merely stated that "an economic policy measure cannot be treated as equivalent to a monetary policy measure for the sole reason that it may have indirect effects on the stability of the euro".[115] In other words, such a measure goes beyond the objective of price stability. Financial stability is thus an **implicit prerequisite of price stability** since the latter can only be secured in an environment in which the transmission of monetary policy signals runs smoothly. This, in turn, presupposes a stable financial system.[116] The main objective of financial stability is updating and strengthening international standards for core (systemically important) financial market infrastructures, including payment systems, securities settlement systems and central counterparties to reduce moral hazard risks.[117] According to the **ECB**, "financial stability is a state whereby the build-up of systemic risk is prevented. Systemic risk can best be described as the risk that the provision of necessary financial products and services by the financial system will be impaired to a point where economic growth and welfare may be materially affected".[118] The *Deutsche Bundesbank* defines financial stability as the ability of the financial system to fulfil its central macroeconomic functions smoothly at all times, especially in stressful situations and phases of transition.[119] Based on the use and scope of financial stability and "stability of the financial system" (Article 127.5 TFEU), the term refers to **a state in which the financial system fulfils its economic functions and market players continuously**

33

---

[112] Manger-Nestler (2014), p. 313 et seqq.; Manger-Nestler and Böttner (2014), p. 624; Manger-Nestler, in Pechstein et al. (2017) Article 127 AEUV para 54 et seqq.

[113] The FSB recommendations of 20 October 2010 for addressing the systemic and moral hazard risks associated with systemically important financial institutions do not even mention the concept of price stability. Also, Donges et al. (2011) make no statement about this connection; with regard to German constitutional law, Thiele (2014), p. 256 et seq., cannot identify any normative basis ("The term financial (market) stability is not used at all in the Basic Law (...)."); on the term financial stability cf. Pilz (2016), p. 65 et seqq.

[114] Issing (2003).

[115] Case C-370/12, *Pringle* (CJEU 27 November 2012) para 56. Neither of the AGs in the cases of *Pringle* and *Gauweiler* defines the term "financial stability", cf. Case C-370/12, *Pringle* (Opinion of AG Kokott of 26 October 2012) and Case C-62/14, *Gauweiler* (Opinion of AG Cruz Villalón of 14 January 2015).

[116] Selmayr, in von der Groeben et al. (2015), Article 282 AEUV para 61.

[117] Cf. FSB Recommendations, p. 1, 8 et seq.

[118] European Central Bank, Financial Stability Review, May 2016, p. 3; see also Danzmann (2015), p. 94; Freedman and Goodlet (2007), p. 3; Padoa-Schioppa (2002), p. 20.

[119] Deutsche Bundesbank, Financial Stability Review 2012, p. 5.

adapt to changing framework conditions – if necessary, also by leaving the market. The financial system comprises the various financial intermediaries, the financial markets, payment transactions and market infrastructures. Threats to financial stability, which can be addressed through **the macro-prudential supervision** of the financial system, arise from an interplay between vulnerabilities that build up in the financial system, shocks and unexpected developments that hit the system and the reactions of market actors to them.[120]

34   A **stable financial system is a prerequisite for direct financing** through the capital markets and indirect financing through financial intermediaries to channel funds between suppliers and demanders in a reasonable manner.[121] In this sense, the stability of the financial system is understood as **a more comprehensive concept**[122] that, aiming at the stability of the banking system, takes both States and private financial institutions into consideration and strives for a cross-border integration of the financial markets. The actors on both sides are only disregarded in this concept if the actions of MS and banks do not have (financial) systemic consequences.[123]

35   This interpretation of the concept of financial stability is in line with the principles of EMU as laid down in Article 119.3 TFEU. Due to the systematic position of Article 136.3 TFEU, "financial stability" is to be understood in the sense of economic and monetary policy and follows the principles and systematics of this area. Accordingly, **financial stability is to be classified in the stability principles according to Article 119.3 TFEU** (→ para 42 et seqq.) and cannot be reduced to a single indicator.[124] These are, in particular, the objective of stable prices but also the maintenance of sound public finances and monetary conditions as well as the safeguarding of a sustainable balance of payments that can be financed in the long term. They are sub-goals of financial stability, the cumulative realisation of which is a prerequisite for a stable financial system. **Financial stability is thus also conceptually much more complex than price stability**, which can be measured by a single index, namely the consumer price index.

36   Since the monetary policy has to guarantee both price and financial stability during the crisis, this can lead to **conflicting goals**. In principle, the two objectives are not mutually exclusive. Financial stability benefits from price stability, and at

---

[120] Cf. Ausschuss für Finanstabilität (2020), p. 1 which defines this term with regard to the German Financial Stability Oversight Act. See also Tuori and Tuori (2014), p. 58; similarly, Selmayr, in von der Groeben et al. (2015), Article 127 AEUV para 38.

[121] However, "transfer payments [...] can serve as a stabilizing instrument" as well; see Richter, in Geiger et al. (2015), Article 119 TFEU para 6.

[122] Tuori and Tuori (2014), p. 58.

[123] According to Tuori and Tuori (2014), p. 133, the openness of the term marks that the institutions can take deliberate action to avoid moral hazard on the part of the recipient states in the case of financial rescue measures. Otherwise, in order to receive financial assistance, an MS could make fiscal policy decisions that endanger the financial stability of the euro area as a whole.

[124] Palm, in Grabitz et al. (2022), Article 136 AEUV para 55 et seq. (released in 2022).

the same time financial stability facilitates the maintenance of price stability.[125] However, there is also a risk that measures taken to preserve financial stability can undermine the credibility of monetary policy measures necessary to ensure price stability.[126] Given that a central bank may have an incentive to deviate from the socially optimal inflation ex post, in a monetary policy that aims for both price stability and financial stability, a time inconsistency problem can arise.[127] Hence, at least temporary conflicts between these objectives are inevitable if monetary policy is exposed to a situation that requires a looser stance in accordance with the objective of price stability but a tighter one in the case of an orientation towards financial stability. In this case, a deviation from one of the objectives must be accepted, at least temporarily.[128]

In the wake of the financial and sovereign debt crisis, the ECB had to realise that the two areas are inextricably linked. In safeguarding financial stability, the ECB claims an annex competence since **an exclusive orientation towards the goal of price stability is no longer sufficient** to cope with the multiple crises that the Union is experiencing since 2007. A scenario of this scale was not foreseeable for the MS when the Maastricht TEU was signed and ratified.[129] However, a consensus has not yet emerged on the assessment of the relationship between financial stability and price stability. Advocates of an integral approach propagate a "dual mandate" of the ECB,[130] which places financial stability as an equally important objective alongside price stability.[131] However, Article 127.1 TFEU and Article 2 of the ESCB Statute set forth that price stability is the **"primary objective"** of the monetary policy of the ESCB. It can only be considered a **secondary ("supporting") task of the ESCB** to ensure the stability of the financial systems.[132] This follows from Article 127.5 TFEU, which states that "the ESCB shall contribute to the smooth conduct of policies pursued by the competent authorities relating to [...] the stability of the financial system". It follows that the **primary responsibility for ensuring financial stability lies with the MS.** They must coordinate the content of their financial stability policies at least in the form of a basic orientation of financial stability policy through (common) basic policy guidelines. Hence, the **contribution**

37

---

[125] Weidmann (2015). See also Weidmann (2018): "Thus a stringent macroprudential reaction to financial stability risks is also a means to protect monetary policy. [...] In the long term, price stability and financial stability can complement each other."

[126] Deutsche Bundesbank, Monthly report March 2015, p. 52, 65 et seqq.; Görgens et al. (2013), p. 87; Shin (2012), passim.

[127] Ueda and Valencia (2014), p. 327 et seqq.

[128] Deutsche Bundesbank, Monthly report March 2015, p. 73.

[129] Waldhoff, in Siekmann (2013), Article 127 AEUV para 32; Danzmann (2015), p. 98; Kohtamäki (2011), p. 91 et seqq.; Scherf (2014), p. 48.

[130] Weidmann (2015).

[131] Leeper and Nason (2014), p. 44 et seq.; Brunnermeier and Sannikov (2014).

[132] Manger-Nestler, in Pechstein et al. (2017), Article 127 AEUV para 58; Griller, in Grabitz et al. (2022), Article 127 AEUV para 57 (released in 2022); Waldhoff, in Siekmann (2013), Article 127 AEUV para 78.

of the ESCB to the stability of the financial system is not a component of its monetary policy.[133]

38   The constituent element **"shall contribute"** (Article 127.5 TFEU) is characterised by the power to take action on its own and by the lack of an EU exclusive competence in the field of financial stability.[134] The different scope of tasks within the ESCB becomes clear when comparing the wording of Article 127.1 TFEU on the one hand and Article 127.5 TFEU on the other. The maintenance of financial stability is only a **supporting task of the ESCB vis-à-vis the MS**, which is why it has no decision-making rights on its own (→ para 29). Like all other secondary objectives pursued by the ESCB (→ para 28 et seqq.), **it may not be pursued in violation of its primary mandate (price stability)**.[135] The lack of nearly any concretising provisions on the ESCB's powers in this policy area, at least outside the provisions of the SSM Regulation on banking supervision, confirms this finding. Insofar as the national central banks perform banking supervisory functions, they do so outside the ESCB framework on their own responsibility and for their own account (Article 14.4 of the ESCB Statute). In the future, the increased importance of financial stability could be taken into account through an additional objective in Article 127 TFEU, backed up by a **special set of instruments**,[136] as well as through a corresponding amendment to the ESCB Statute.[137] It must remain, however, a **limited power** explicitly assigned to the ESCB **to support** the national governments in fulfilling their tasks in ensuring financial stability.

---

[133] See in this sense also Weidmann (2018): "There can be little doubt [...] that monetary policy is able to influence financial stability. What follows from that? Should financial stability become an additional objective of monetary policy? Maybe even on a par with price stability? To me, this would be a perilous proposition. For one thing, aiming for more than one objective risks complicating communication with the general public, thereby jeopardising accountability. [...] Taking on financial stability as an additional objective for monetary policy would likely do more harm than good. Nevertheless, central banks can play a productive role in safeguarding financial stability. It certainly makes sense to harness central banks' high level of expertise with regard to financial stability risks. However, the 'weapon of choice' for combatting these risks is not monetary policy – it is macroprudential policy."

[134] With a different view, Waldhoff, in Siekmann (2013), Article 127 AEUV para 78, who interprets the English wording of Article 127.5 TFEU ("shall contribute") to mean that the ESCB may act without the competent national authorities in the MS having taken prior measures. However, for this interpretation, he cannot cite any considerations of the Contracting States. Waldhoff's interpretation results in the ESCB not only being able to act in a supportive manner within an impending crisis situation, but also being allowed to actively take the initiative. This may have been in line with the monetary policy of the E(S)CB under former President Draghi, but it does not arise as an exclusive power from the Treaties.

[135] Cf. Thiele (2013), pp. 26–27; Association of German Banks (2020).

[136] ESRB Recommendation ESRB/2013/1 *on intermediate objectives and instruments of macroprudential policy*, O.J. C 170/1 (2013).

[137] See also Häde, in Calliess and Ruffert (2022), Article 127 AEUV para 25; Rodi, in Vedder and Heintschel von Heinegg (2018), Article 127 AEUV para 15.

4. A Principle-Oriented Pursuit of the EMU Objectives (Paragraphs 1 to 3)

Given the purpose of Article 119 within Title VIII of the TFEU to serve as a "chapeau" of the provisions on EMU, the **EMU policies**, sketched here in its **basic lines**, are **oriented towards principles**. These principles (Article 3 TEU, the principle of an open market economy and the principles set out in Article 119.3 TFEU) are taken up again in some other provisions of this title (→ Article 120 TFEU para 33 et seq., 37 et seqq., 41).[138] In Article 119.1 TFEU, and in the provisions outlined in parallel, the Union's overarching constitutional principles, as expressed namely in the standard for its **objectives (Article 3 TEU)**,[139] serve as a primary **reference for legitimising and at the same time limiting the scope of its activities** *also* **in the area of economic and monetary policy** while **emphasising the unity of action**.[140] The following objectives enshrined in **Articles 3.3 and 3.4 TEU** are of particular importance for EMU policies (→ Article 120 TFEU para 33 et seq.): the **internal market** as well as other goals like **price stability**, the **social market economy** and full employment and social progress (see also Recital 9 of the Preamble to TEU); the strengthening and convergence of their economies; and the **establishment of an economic and monetary union, including a single and stable currency** (Recital 8 of the Preamble to TEU).

39

4.1. Principle of an Open Market Economy with Free Competition (Paragraphs 1 and 2)

A second point of reference for carving out an economic (→ para 11) and monetary policy is the principle of an open market economy with free competition (paragraphs 1 and 2), which corresponds to the notion of "a system of open and competitive markets" in Article 173.1 (2) TFEU. Hence, an **economic policy model** has been anchored in the TFEU, and at the same time, a **self-obligation of the Union for its future action** has been standardised. They are characterised by private autonomy, decentralised activity of the economy's subjects and therefore private incentives, and, last but not least, coordination through trade and competition, including multilateralism (→ Article 120 TFEU para 37).[141] However, this

40

---

[138] See Article 120 sentence 2 TFEU; Article 127.1 sentence 3 TFEU; Article 2 sentence 3 of the ESCB Statute. However, it is controversial if these principles are applicable to other spheres of the Treaty; see Hatje, in Schwarze et al. (2019), Article 119 AEUV para 16.

[139] As *Sommermann* (→ Article 3 TEU para 1) has spelt out, with the formulation "For the purposes set out in Article 3 of the Treaty on European Union" Article 119 TFEU is one of the provisions of the Treaties which refers *generally* to the objectives of the Union. This fact already hints at the special relevance of Article 3 TEU, here in the context of EMU.

[140] See Sommermann (→ Article 3 TEU para 2, 4); Kempen, in Streinz (2018), Article 119 AEUV para 27 underscores with regard to Article 119.3 TFEU its purpose of limiting the Union's powers in the field of economic and monetary policies.

[141] For details see Blanke (2012), p. 374 et seqq.

only applies without prejudice to the primary objective of price stability. Although the MS are obliged to actively contribute to the achievement of the Union's objectives by consciously formulating and implementing their policies, the "open market economy" clause, like the principles set out in paragraph 3, **does not impose on the MS clear and unconditional legal obligations** (→ Article 120 TFEU para 32). This model **neither constitutes an independent legal yardstick for the Union's lawmaking**. Concrete measures of Union organs and institutions are to be assessed solely on the basis of the concrete rules for determining the Union's powers and the prohibitions and requirements provided for in other (special) provisions of the Treaties and in the EUCFR.[142]

41   The principle **refuses protectionist policies**, including obstacles to foreign direct investment or to foreign ownership of shares (→ TFEU Preamble para 59 et seqq.; → Article 34 TFEU para 5; → Article 120 TFEU para 37), but it does not prohibit all interferences with competition,[143] and it neither restricts nor extends specific competences for EU sectoral policies and principles for policymaking.[144] Nonetheless, it can serve as *one* **tool for interpretation** intended to clarify the Treaty provisions on EMU.[145] Therefore, also due to commitment to the principle of an open market economy with free competition, **open market operations** are the ESCB's most important monetary policy instrument. The requirement to keep markets open might have as well a warning function in front of quantitative credit restrictions if they become a means of monetary policy.[146]

4.2. Guiding Principles for Economic and Monetary Policy Activities in the EMU (Paragraph 3)

42   As **prerequisites for "these activities of the Member States and the Union"**, paragraph 3 mentions **stable prices, sound public finances and monetary conditions and a sustainable balance of payments**. These principles of **economic and financial soundness as well as monetary stability** are indispensable conditions for the functioning of the EMU and have to be monitored in a strict manner.[147] Articles 120 sentence 2 and 127.1 sentence 2 TFEU and Article 2 sentence 3 of the ESCB Statute take them up ("and in compliance with the principles set out in Article 119" TFEU). It is to be assumed that these principles encompass only the activities in the fields of economic and monetary policy, mentioned in the preceding

---

[142] Bandilla, in Grabitz et al. (2022), Article 119 AEUV para 23 (released in 2021); Hatje, in Schwarze et al. (2019), Article 119 AEUV para 10 et seqq.

[143] Cf. Häde, in Calliess and Ruffert (2022), Article 119 AEUV para 9; Kempen in Streinz (2018), Article 119 AEUV para 16 who in this context points to Articles 101 et seqq., 107 et seq. and 110 et seqq. TFEU.

[144] Bandilla, in Grabitz et al. (2022), Article 119 AEUV para 24 (released in 2021).

[145] See also Bandilla, in Grabitz et al. (2022), Article 119 AEUV para 23 (released in 2021).

[146] Häde, in Calliess and Ruffert (2022), Article 119 AEUV para 8 et seq.

[147] Cf. Richter, in Geiger et al. (2015), Article 119 TFEU para 18.

paragraphs, but not for other Union policies (such as trade or competition policy).[148] Against this background, paragraph 3 refers to **all – but only – the activities of the MS and the Union to exercise in these areas and in accordance with their respective powers**.[149] They are addressed to the **MS inside and outside the euro area** and also oblige the latter to ensure sound monetary and economic conditions. These commandments should be read not as binding legal requirements but rather as **optimisation rules**, as **principles of interpretation and for guiding the implementation of the following EMU standards** (in particular, Articles 121 through 133 TFEU),[150] which reflect a close connection between the EMU and other activities of the MS and the Union.[151] They are not to be understood as a concrete mandate for action directed at very specific political measures.[152] However, an **evident non-compliance** with the EMU objectives and rules and **obvious errors of assessment**, such as the adoption of objectively unsuitable measures by the responsible institutions on the supranational or national level, constitute a breach of law.[153]

The principle of price stability, established in paragraph 3, has the same meaning as the price stability requirement of paragraph 2 (→ para 16 et seqq.). The reiteration of that principle in the legal context on EMU emphasises the **priority of price stability for monetary policy**. Price stability is an **essential criterion for interpretation**. In case of doubt, the interpretation that serves price stability is to be preferred.[154] It is "apparent from a rate of inflation which is close to that of, at most, the three best performing Member States in terms of price stability" (Article 140.1 sentence 3, first indent, TFEU, Protocol No 13) and **specified strategically by the ECB** (→ para 17 et seqq.). As Article 127.1 sentence 1 TFEU, Article 282.2 sentence 2 TFEU and Article 2 of the ESCB Statute reveal, the price stability requirement **takes precedence over other economic policy principles** when Eurosystem monetary policy decisions are taken. In contrast, although price stability is, among other objectives, *also* an important goal of EU economic policy

43

---

[148] Kempen, in Streinz (2018), Article 119 AEUV para 27; Müller, in Jaeger and Stöger (2021), Article 119 AEUV para 32 (released in 2020); likewise, albeit doubtfully, Häde, in Calliess and Ruffert (2022), Article 119 AEUV para 25; Herrmann, in Pechstein et al. (2017), Article 119 AEUV para 44.

[149] Häde, in Calliess and Ruffert (2022), Article 119 AEUV para 26; Kempen, in Streinz (2018), Article 119 AEUV para 27.

[150] Kempen, in Streinz (2018), Article 119 AEUV para 29; Müller, in Jaeger and Stöger (2021), Article 119 AEUV para 32 (released in 2020); Hatje, in Schwarze et al. (2019), Article 119 AEUV para 16; Richter, in Geiger et al. (2015), Article 119 TFEU para 15, 18 expresses a different view and states that Article 119 TFEU and its objectives "are binding" but only of "complementary nature".

[151] Häde, in Calliess and Ruffert (2), Article 119 AEUV para 27; Herrmann, in Pechstein et al. (2017), Article 119 AEUV para 59.

[152] Müller, in Jaeger and Stöger (2021), Article 119 AEUV para 35 (released in 2020).

[153] Müller (2014), p. 154; Müller, in Jaeger and Stöger (2021), Article 119 AEUV para 35.

[154] Häde, in Calliess and Ruffert (2022), Article 119 AEUV para 23, Article 120 AEUV para 23 and Article 126 AEUV para 5.

(→ para 11), economic policy is not primarily committed to price stability. Within this area, MS and the Union have to observe to the same extent also all other economic principles enshrined in paragraph 3 and simultaneously enjoy a considerable margin of political discretion (→ Article 120 TFEU para 12, 23, 32).[155]

44 The term "sound public finances" refers to the convergence criterion, laid down in Article 140.1 sentence 3, second indent, TFEU (→ Article 140 TFEU para 17), of "the sustainability of the government financial position [...] [that is] apparent from having achieved a government budgetary position without a deficit that is excessive".[156] Hence, sound public finances are given when a sustainable financial position of the public sector is ensured without an excessive deficit within the meaning of Article 126.2 TFEU and Protocol No 12. However, just as in the case of the principle of price stability, it should be noted that the standard specified in Article 2 of the Convergence Protocol No 13 (absence of a Council decision pursuant to Article 126.6 TFEU) only concerns admission to the circle of participants in the monetary union, whereas the fundamental **requirement of sound and sustainable public finances**, further decreed in the Stability and Growth Pact and in the Fiscal Compact (→ Supplement to Title VIII: Fiscal Union para 5), **constitutes a permanent legal obligation**. Compliance with this requirement is assessed on the basis of a reference value for the government deficit-to-GDP ratio of 3% and a reference value for the government debt-to-GDP ratio of 60% (Protocol No 12). Softening or even replacing these Maastricht criteria through individually negotiated and country-specific "realistic targets" relating to a total debt reduction to be achieved within a fixed period of time would entail **an assumption of liability under the TESM for decisions on revenue and expenditure taken by other MS**. Due to their national creditworthiness, the taxpayers of MS meeting the restrictions of the debt brake or pursuing austerity policies would then have to stand in "solidarity" with the debtor countries (in particular, Italy). The condition that "stability support [may be provided] on the basis of a strict conditionality [...] in the form of a macro-economic adjustment programme" (Recitals 6 and 12 of the Preamble to TESM) would be relinquished.

45 The same applies to the requirement of **entailing "compliance with [...] sound monetary conditions"**. "Monetary conditions", which influence the economic cycle by controlling the money supply, are ensured by the NCBs or the ECB.[157] These framework conditions are "sound" if monetary policy promotes growth on the one hand and keeps the price level stable on the other.[158] The aim of an "overall balance of payments" is a guiding principle that was already contained in Article

---

[155] Kempen, in Streinz (2018), Article 119 AEUV para 28; Häde, in Calliess and Ruffert (2022), Article 120 AEUV para 24 and Article 126 AEUV para 4; Kauppi, in Herzog et al. (2019), Article 119 TFEU para 119-6.

[156] See also Hatje, in Schwarze et al. (2019), Article 119 AEUV para 17.

[157] Richter, in Geiger et al. (2015), Article 119 TFEU para 16.

[158] Hatje, in Schwarze et al. (2019), Article 119 AEUV para 18.

104 TEEC.[159] The **sustainable balance of payments** refers to the **record of all international trade and financial transactions** and is defined as the external balance of payments of the euro area. It is "sustainable" if there is not a permanent current account deficit that cannot be balanced by capital imports or from foreign exchange reserves. The valuation is based on market prices prevailing on the date of the transaction. Compliance with the principle can be ensured by both economic policy (**attractive investment and export conditions**) and monetary policy (**low exchange rates or high interest rates to attract capital**).[160] From the beginning of the third stage, the organs of the ESCB (Article 127 TFEU) as well as, in matters of exchange rate policy, the Commission and the Council (Articles 219, 138 TFEU) are addressees of the obligation. Given that the national economic policies have an impact on the balance of payment sheet of the euro area as a whole, in addition to the Union institutions, the MS are bound to this principle.[161]

List of Cases

ECJ/CJEU
ECJ 14.12.1991, Opinion 1/91, *European Economic Area,* ECLI:EU:C:1991:490 [cit. in para 34]
ECJ 02.06.2005, C-266/03, *Commission v Luxembourg,* ECLI:EU:C:2005:341 [cit. in para 6]
CJEU 09.03.2010, C-518/07, *Commission v Germany,* ECLI:EU:C:2010:125 [cit. in para 19]
CJEU 03.06.2010, *Caja de Ahorros,* ECLI:EU:C:2010:309 [cit. in para 32]
CJEU 03.10.2010, C-9/99, *Échirolles Distribution SA,* ECLI:EU:C:2000:532 [cit. in para 32, 43, 44, 50]
CJEU 26.10.2012, C-370/12, Opinion of AG Kokott, *Pringle,* ECLI:EU:C:2012:675 [cit. in para 29]
CJEU 27.11.2012, C-370/12, *Pringle,* ECLI:EU:C:2012:756 [cit. in para 4, 7, 14, 15, 19, 21-23, 26]
CJEU 14.01.2015, C-62/14, Opinion of AG Cruz Villalón, *Gauweiler et al.*, ECLI:EU:C:2015:7 [cit. in para 33]
CJEU 16.06.2015, C-62/14, *Gauweiler et al.*, ECLI:EU:C:2015:400 [cit. in para 21, 23]
CJEU 11.12.2018, C-493/17, *Weiss et al.*, ECLI:EU:C:2018:1000 [cit. in para 7, 23, 24, 29]

---

[159] Article 104 TEEC read as follows: "Each Member State shall pursue the economic policy necessary to ensure the equilibrium of its overall balance of payments and to maintain confidence in its currency, while ensuring a high level of employment and the stability of the level of prices...."
[160] Herrmann, in Pechstein et al. (2017), Article 119 AEUV para 63.
[161] Kempen, in Streinz (2018), Article 119 AEUV para 30.

CJEU 26.01.2021, C-422/19 and C-423/19, 26.6.2021, *Hessischer Rundfunk*, ECLI:EU:C:2021:63 [cit. in para 5]

CFI/GC
GC 30.09.2015, T-450/12, *Anagnostakis*, ECLI:EU:T:2015:739 [cit. in para 8]

German Federal Constitutional Court
German FCC 12.10.1993, 2 BvR 2134/92, 2 BvR 2159/92, *Maastricht* [cit. in para 8, 10, 19, 23]
German FCC 14.01.2014, 2 BvR 2728/13 et al., *OMT (Reference for preliminary ruling)*, ECLI:DE:BVerfG:2014:rs20140114.2bvr272813 [cit. in para 21, 23]
German FCC 21.06.2016, 2 BvR 2728/13 et al., *OMT*, ECLI:DE:BVerfG:2016:rs20160621.2bvr272813 [cit. in para 13, 19, 21, 23]
German FCC 05.05.2020, 2 BvR 859/15 et al., *PSPP*, ECLI:DE:BVerfG:2020:rs20200505.2bvr085915 [cit. in para 7, 21, 24-29]

References[162]

Apel, E. (2003). *Central banking systems compared*. Routledge.
Arnold, M. (2021, July 12). ECB changes inflation target, leaving extra room to keep rates low. First strategy review for nearly two decades amends key elements of monetary policy. *The Financial Times*. Retrieved from https://www.ft.com/content/ab3b8c36-2199-4230-b9b3-b9e12c09d44b
Association of German Banks. (2020, January 13). *Strategy Review of the European Central Bank*. Retrieved from https://en.bankenverband.de/newsroom/comments/strategy-review-european-central-bank/
Ausschuss für Finanstabilität. (2020). *Die makroprudenzielle Strategie des Ausschusses für Finanzstabilität*. Bundesministerium für Finanzen. Retrieved from https://afs-bund.de/afs/Content/DE/Downloads/Strategie-Geschaeftsordnung/afs-strategie.pdf?__blob=publicationFile&v=6
Blanke, H.-J. (2011). The European economic and Monetary Union – Between vulnerability and reform. *International Journal of Public Law and Policy, 1*(4), 402–433.
Blanke, H.-J. (2012). The economic constitution of the European Union. In H.-J. Blanke & S. Mangiameli (Eds.), *The European Union after Lisbon. Constitutional basis, economic order and external action* (pp. 369–420). Springer.
Bofinger, P. (1996). Die Krise der europäischen Währungsintegration: Ursachen und Lösungsansätze. *Wirtschaftsdienst*, 30–36.
Borchardt, K.-D. (2020). *Die rechtlichen Grundlagen der Europäischen Union* (7th ed.). Facultas.
Böttner, R. (2021). *The constitutional framework for enhanced cooperation in EU Law*. Brill Nijhoff.
Brunnermeier, M. K., & Sannikov, Y. (2014). *The I Theory of Money*. National Bureau of Economic Research.
Caesar, R., & Scharrer, H.-E. (Eds.). (1994). *Maastricht: Königsweg oder Irrweg zur Wirtschafts- und Währungsunion*. Europa-Union-Verlag.
Caesar, R., & Scharrer, H.-E. (Eds.). (1998). *Die Europäische Wirtschafts- und Währungsunion. Regionale und globale Herausforderungen*. Europa-Union-Verlag.

---

[162] All cited internet sources of this comment have been accessed on 20 June 2022.

Calliess, C. (2020). Konfrontation statt Kooperation zwischen BVerfG und EuGH? Zu den Folgen des Karlsruher PSPP-Urteils. *Neue Zeitschrift für Verwaltungsrecht*, 897–904.

Calliess, C., & Ruffert, M. (Eds.). (2022). *EUV/AEUV. Kommentar* (6th ed.). C. H. Beck.

Cohen, B. J. (1981). The European Monetary system: An outsider's view. In *Essays in international finance* (Vol. 142). Princeton University Press.

Craig, P. (2012). The stability, coordination and governance treaty: Principle, politics and pragmatism. *European Law Review, 37*(3), 231–248.

Danzmann, M. (2015). *Das Verhältnis von Geldpolitik, Fiskalpolitik und Finanzstabilitätspolitik*. Duncker & Humblot.

de Grauwe, P. (2020). *The economics of Monetary Union* (13th ed.). OUP.

de Witte, B. (2015). Euro crisis responses and the EU legal order: Increased institutional variation or constitutional mutation? *European Constitutional Law Review*, 434–457.

Dimopoulos, A. (2014). The use of international law as a tool for enhancing governance in the Eurozone and its impact on EU institutional integrity. In M. Adams, F. Fabbrini, & P. Larouche (Eds.), *The constitutionalization of European budgetary constraints* (pp. 41–63) Hart.

Donges, J. B., Feld, L. P., Möschel, W., Neumann, M. J. M., & Wieland, V. (2011). *Systemstabilität für die Finanzmärkte*. Stiftung Marktwirtschaft.

Dullien, S., & Tober, S. (2021). ECB strategy: Best practice and new frontiers. In *IMK Policy Brief No 105*. Macroeconomic Policy Institute (IMK) of Hans-Böckler-Foundation. Retrieved from https://www.imk-boeckler.de/de/imk-policy-brief-15382.htm

Dürig, G., Herzog, R., & Scholz, R. (Eds.). (2022). *Grundgesetz. Kommentar*, loose-leaf (last supplement: 96). C.H. Beck.

Elderson, F. (2021). Greening monetary policy. *The ECB Blog* of 13 February 2021. Retrieved from https://www.ecb.europa.eu/press/blog/date/2021/html/ecb.blog210213~7e26af8606.en.html

Falcon, G. (2016). People, peoples, democratic deficit and "output legitimation" in the European Union. In F. Wollenschläger & L. De Lucia (Eds.), *Staat und Demokratie. Beiträge zum XVII. Deutsch-Italienischen Verfassungskolloquium* (pp. 103–112). Mohr Siebeck.

Feld, L. P., & Wieland, V. (2020). The German Federal Constitutional Court ruling and the European Central Bank's strategy. *Freiburger Diskussionspapiere zur Ordnungsökonomik*, No 20/05.

Financial Stability Board (FSB). (2010). *Reducing the moral hazard posed by systemically important financial institutions. FSB Recommendations and Time Lines*. Retrieved from https://www.fsb.org/wp-content/uploads/r_101111a.pdf?page_moved=1

Fratzscher, M. (2021). *"Neues EZB-Inflationsziel ist kein Bruch mit der Bundesbank". Statement of 8 July 2021*. Deutsches Institut für Wirtschaftsforschung e.V. Retrieved from https://www.diw.de/de/diw_01.c.821251.de/neues_ezb-inflationsziel_ist_kein_bruch_mit_der_bundesbank.html

Freedman, C., & Goodlet, C. (2007). *Financial stability*. C. D. Howe Institute.

Galanos, G., Kotios, A., & Pavlidis, G. (2011). Greece and the Euro: The chronicle of an expected collapse. *Intereconomics, 46*(5), 263–269.

Galetta, D.-U. (2020). Karlsruhe über alles? Il ragionamento sul principio di proporzionalità nella pronunzia del 5 maggio 2020 del BVerfG tedesco e le sue conseguenze, *Federalismi.it, 14*, 13/05/2020. 1-8 (Retrieved from https://www.federalismi.it/nv14/articolo-documento.cfm?Artid=42380)

Geiger, R., Khan, D.-E., & Kotzur, M. (Eds.). (2015). *European Union Treaties*. C. H. Beck.

Görgens, E., Ruckriegel, K., & Seitz, F. (2013). *Europäische Geldpolitik* (6th ed.). UVK.

Grabitz, E., Hilf, M., & Nettesheim, M. (Eds.). (2022). *Das Recht der Europäischen Union: EUV/AEUV. Kommentar*, loose leaf (last supplement: 75). C. H. Beck.

Gramlich, M. (2020). Die Wirtschafts- und Währungspolitik der Union. In M. Niedobitek (Ed.), *Europarecht, Grundlagen und Politiken der Union* (2nd ed., pp. 1239–1331). de Gruyter.

Hasse, R. (1989). *Die Europäische Zentralbank: Perspektiven für eine Weiterentwicklung des Europäischen Währungssystems*. Bertelsmann-Stiftung.

Heinemann, F. (2021a). "Fortdauer der extrem lockeren Geldpolitik jetzt leichter zu rechtfertigen". *Press release of ZEW*, 8 July 2021. Leibniz-Zenrum für Europäische Wirtschaftsforschung: Mannheim. Retrieved from https://www.zew.de/presse/pressearchiv/zew-oekonom-friedrich-heinemann-zum-neuen-ezb-inflationsziel

Heinemann, F. (2021b). Die Inflation hat in der Zielfunktion der EZB an Gewicht verloren. *Press release of ZEW*, 22 July 2021. Leibniz-Zentrum für Europäische Wirtschaftsforschung: Mannheim. Retrieved from https://www.zew.de/presse/pressearchiv/zew-oekonom-friedrich-heinemann-zur-ezb-entscheidung-1

Herzog, P., Campbell, C., & Zagel, G. (Eds.). (2019). *Smit & Herzog on the law of the European Union*, loose-leaf. LexisNexis.

Huber, P. M., & Voßkuhle, A. (Eds.). (2023). *Kommentar zum Grundgesetz: GG. Vol. 3: Art. 83-146* (8th ed.). C.H. Beck.

Issing, O. (2003). *Monetary and financial stability – is there a trade-off? Speech at the Conference on "Monetary Stability, Financial Stability and the Business Cycle"*. Bank for International Settlements.

Jaeger, T., & Stöger, K. (Eds.) (2021). *Kommentar zu EUV und AEUV*, loose-leaf (last supplement: 266). Manz.

Janzen, D. (1996). *Der neue Artikel 88 Satz 2 des Grundgesetzes*. Duncker & Humblot.

Kainer, F. (2020). Aus der nationalen Brille: Das PSPP-Urteil des BVerfG. *Zeitschrift für Europäisches Wirtschaftsrecht*, 533–536.

Kleinheyer, N. (2014). Die Rolle der EZB in einer Europäischen Wirtschaftsregierung. In H.-J. Blanke & S. Pilz (Eds.), *Die "Fiskalunion"* (pp. 25–38). Mohr Siebeck.

Kohtamäki, N. (2011). *Die Reform der Bankenaufsicht in der Europäischen Union*. Mohr Siebeck.

Köster, C. (1990). *Das Recht der europäischen Währungspolitiken*. Carl Heymanns Verlag.

Kratzmann, H. (2022). Licht und Schatten im PSPP-Urteil des Bundesverfassungsgerichts. *Die Öffentliche Verwaltung*, 75/10, 400–410.

Lastra, R. M. (2006). *Legal foundations of international monetary stability*. OUP.

Leeper, E. M., & Nason, J. M. (2014). *Bringing financial stability into monetary policy*. Centre for Applied Macroeconomic Analysis.

Louis, J.-V. (2004). The economic and Monetary Union: Law and institutions. *Common Market Law Review*, 41(2), 575–608.

Manger-Nester, C., & Gentzsch, M. (2021). *Democratic legitimation of central bank independence in the European Union*. Springer.

Manger-Nestler, C. (2008). *Par(s) inter pares?: Die Bundesbank als nationale Zentralbank im europäischen System der Zentralbanken*. Duncker & Humblot.

Manger-Nestler, C. (2014). Die Bankenunion: Gemeinsame Mechanismen zur Bankensicherung und –überwachung. In H.-J. Blanke & S. Pilz (Eds.), *Die "Fiskalunion"* (pp. 299–345). Mohr Siebeck.

Manger-Nestler, C., & Böttner, R. (2014). Ménage à trois? Zur gewandelten Rolle der EZB im Spannungsfeld zwischen Geldpolitik, Finanzaufsicht und Fiskalpolitik. *Europarecht*, 621–637.

Manger-Nestler, C., & Böttner, R. (2019). Der Europäische Währungsfonds nach den Plänen der Kommission. *Zeitschrift für ausländisches öffentliches Recht und Völkerrecht*, 43–84.

Michler, A. F., & Smeets, H.-D. (2011). *Die aktuelle Finanzkrise: Bestandsaufnahmen und Lehren für die Zukunft*. Lucius & Lucius.

Montoro Chiner, M. J., & Rodríguez Pontón, F. J. (2021). ¿Un intersticio en el diálogo nunca interrumpido? (A propósito de la sentencia del Tribunal Constitucional Federal de Alemania, de 5 de mayo de 2020). *Revista española de Derecho Administrativo*, 210, 11–44.

Müller, T. (2014). *Wettbewerb und Unionsverfassung. Begründung und Begrenzung des Wettbewerbsprinzips in der europäischen Verfassung*. Mohr Siebeck.

Nettesheim, M. (2020). Das PSPP-Urteil des BVerfG – ein Angriff auf die EU? *Neue Juristische Wochenschrift*, 1631–1634.

Nguyen, T. *(2021)*. *A matter of principle: The Commission's decision to bring an infringement procedure against Germany. Verfassungsblog.* 6/11. Retrieved from https://verfassungsblog.de/a-matter-of-principle/
Ohler, C. (2021). *Unkonventionelle Geldpolitik.* Mohr Siebeck.
Padoa-Schioppa, T. (2002). *Central banks and financial stability.* Policy Panel Introductory Paper, Second ECB Central Banking Conference, "The transformation of the European financial system", 24 and 25 October 2002. Retrieved from https://www.ecb.europa.eu/events/pdf/conferences/tps.pdf
Pechstein, M., Nowak, C., & Häde, U. (2017). *Frankfurter Kommentar zu EUV, GRC und AEUV.* Mohr Siebeck.
Pilz, S. (2016). *Der Europäische Stabilitätsmechanismus: eine neue Stufe der Integration.* Mohr Siebeck.
Poli, S., & Cisotta, R. (2020). The German Federal Constitutional Court's exercise of ultra vires review and the possibility to open an infringement action for the Commission. *German Law Journal*, 1078–1089.
Scharpf, F. W. (2005). Legitimationskonzepte jenseits des Nationalstaats. In G. F. Schuppert, I. Pernice, & U. Haltern (Eds.), *Europawissenschaft* (pp. 705–741). Nomos.
Scheinert, C. (2021). *History of economic and monetary union.* Retrieved from https://www.europarl.europa.eu/factsheets/en/sheet/79/history-of-economic-and-monetary-union
Scherf, G. (2014). *Financial stability policy in the euro-zone. The political economy of national bnking regulation in an integrating monetary union.* Springer Gabler.
Schorkopf, F. (2012). Finanzkrisen als Herausforderung der internationalen, europäischen und nationalen Rechtsetzung. In G. Lienbacher, B. Grzeszick, & C. Calliess (Eds.), *Grundsatzfragen der Rechtsetzung und Rechtsfindung* (pp. 183–220). de Gruyter.
Schwarze, J., Becker, U., Hatje, A., & Schoo, J. (Eds.). (2019). *EU-Kommentar* (4th ed.). Nomos.
Seiler, H.-W. (1996). EWU: Sind die Konvergenzkriterien wirklich ernstzunehmen? *Wirtschaftsdienst*, 587–589.
Selmayr, M. (1999). Die Wirtschafts- und Währungsunion als Rechtsgemeinschaft. *Archiv des öffentlichen Rechts*, 357–399.
Shin, H.-S. (2012). Global banking glut and loan risk premium. *IMF Economic Review*, 155–192.
Siekmann, H. (Ed.). (2013). *EWU. Kommentar zur Europäischen Währungsunion.* Mohr-Siebeck.
Starck, J. (1998). Europa an der Schwelle zur einheitlichen Währung. *Zentrum für Europäisches Wirtschaftsrecht, Vorträge und Berichte*, No. 96.
Streinz, R., & (Ed.). (2018). *EUV/AEUV. Kommentar* (3rd ed.). C.H. Beck.
Terlau, W. (2004). Theorie optimaler Währungsräume. EWU und USA im Vergleich. *Das Wirtschaftsstudium*, 104–109.
Thiele, A. (2013). *Das Mandat der EZB und die Krise des Euro.* Mohr Siebeck.
Thiele, A. (2014). *Finanzmarktaufsicht.* Mohr Siebeck.
Trute, H.-H. (2012). § 6: Die demokratische Legitimation der Verwaltung. In W. Hoffmann-Riem, E. Schmidt-Aßmann, & A. Voßkuhle (Eds.), *Grundlagen des Verwaltungsrechts. Vol. I: Methoden, Maßstäbe, Aufgaben, Organisation* (2nd ed., pp. 341–435). C.H. Beck.
Tuori, K., & Tuori, K. (2014). *The eurozone crisis: A constitutional analysis.* CUP.
Ueda, K., & Valencia, F. (2014). Central bank independence and macro-prudential regulation. *Economics Letters, 125*, 327–330.
Unger, S. (2008). *Das Verfassungsprinzip der Demokratie.* Mohr Siebeck.
Unger, S. (2016). Verwaltungslegitimation in der Europäischen Union. In F. Wollenschläger & L. De Lucia (Eds.), *Staat und Demokratie. Beiträge zum XVII. Deutsch-Italienischen Verfassungskolloquium* (pp. 41–77). Mohr Siebeck.
Vaubel, R. (1998). Europäische Währungsunion: Wer darf an den Euro-Start? *Wirtschaftsdienst*, 85–89.
Vedder, C., & Heintschel von Heinegg, W. (Eds.). (2018). *Europäisches Unionsrecht.* Nomos.
von Bogdandy, A. (2003). Demokratie, Globalisierung, Zukunft des Völkerrechts – eine Bestandsaufnahme. *Heidelberg Journal of International Law, 63*(4), 853–877.

Blanke

von der Groeben, H., Schwarze, J., & Hatje, A. (Eds.). (2015). *Europäisches Unionsrecht. Kommentar* (7th ed.). Nomos.

Weidmann, J. (2015). *Zur Rolle der Finanzstabilität für die Geldpolitik*. Speech given at the "Münchner Seminare" on 25 March 2015. Retrieved from https://www.bundesbank.de/de/presse/reden/zur-rolle-der-finanzstabilitaet-fuer-die-geldpolitik-710820

Weidmann, J. (2018). *The relationship between monetary and macroprudential policies – black and white or shades of grey?* Dinner Speech at the Annual Meeting of the Central Bank Research Association (20.08.2018). Retrieved from https://www.bundesbank.de/en/press/speeches/the-relationship-between-monetary-and-macroprudential-policies-black-and-white-or-shades-of-grey%2D%2D757724

Weinert, G. (1998). EWU-Start: Konflikte institutionell angelegt. *Wirtschaftsdienst*, 254–255.

Ziller, J. (2020). The unbearable heaviness of the German constitutional judge. On the judgment of the Second Chamber of the German Federal Constitutional Court of 5 May 2020 concerning the European Central Bank's PSPP programme. *Rivista Interdisciplinare sul Diritto delle Amministrazioni Pubbliche*, 2, 87–99.

Chapter 1
Economic Policy

Article 120 [Conduction of Economic Policies]
(ex-Article 98 TEC)

Member States shall conduct their economic policies[6–20, 21–30] with a view to contributing to the achievement of the objectives of the Union, as defined in Article 3 of the Treaty on European Union,[10, 32–36] and in the context of the broad guidelines referred to in Article 121(2).[11, 14, 42] The Member States and the Union shall act in accordance with the principle of an open market economy with free competition,[37–38] favouring an efficient allocation of resources,[39–40] and in compliance with the principles set out in Article 119.[41]

Contents

1. Overview ... 1
   1.1. Genesis and Ratio ... 1
   1.2. National Economic Policies as the Subject of Coordination ... 6
   1.3. Embedding Article 120 TFEU in the Provisions on EMU ... 8
   1.4. Coordination as a Substitute for a Lack of Union Power ... 11
2. Constituent Elements of Article 120 TFEU ... 15
   2.1. Economic Policy ... 15
      2.1.1. Meaning and Relation to Other Policies ... 15
      2.1.2. Distinguishing Economic Policy from Monetary Policy ... 21
      2.1.3. Scope of Application ... 31
   2.2. Fundamental Objectives ... 32
      2.2.1. Reference to Article 3 TEU ... 33
      2.2.2. Principle of an Open Market Economy with Free Competition ... 37
      2.2.3. Favouring an Efficient Allocation of Resources ... 39
   2.3. In Compliance with the Principles Set Out in Article 119 TFEU ... 41
   2.4. Broad Guidelines Referred to in Article 121.2 TFEU ... 42
3. Legal Effects ... 43
4. Territorial Scope of Application ... 45

List of Cases
References

1. Overview

1.1. Genesis and Ratio

Article 120 TFEU provides a **principle-oriented framework** for the coordination of the MS' economic policies in accordance with the procedure regulated in Article

1

121 TFEU.[1] In its turn, Article 120 TFEU builds on Article 119 TFEU, which covers "the adoption of an economic policy [...] based on the close coordination of the Member States' economic policies" by the Union and the MS for the purposes set out in Article 3 TEU. According to the original Article 104 TEEC, each MS was obliged to pursue the economic policy needed to ensure the equilibrium of its overall balance of payments and to maintain confidence in its currency while taking care to ensure a high level of employment and a stable level of prices. In order to facilitate the attainment of the objectives set out in Article 104 TEEC, MS should **coordinate their economic policies**. Whereas the original Rome Treaty focused on the creation of the customs union and the common agricultural policy (CAP), a mechanism for the "soft coordination" of economic policies was first created in the early 1960s through the Conjunctural Policy Committee and in 1964 through the Medium-Term Economic Policy Committee and the Committee of Central Bank Governors.[2]

2 Unlike the monetary, credit and interest rate policy, the harmonisation of economic policy was neither intended nor feasible when a political agreement was reached on the Treaty of Maastricht (1992) between the then MS.[3] The competences of "inner monetary policy" have been transferred to the Union level in order to be executed within the ESCB, which is independent of the political influence of the MS. The independence of the ECB and its obligation to have price stability as its paramount objective should be considered the "first and foremost [...] pillar" of the euro's stability.[4] On the other hand, economic policy (along with regional, budgetary and revenue policy) remains with the MS, but their creative scope is partly restricted by EU secondary legislation, "instruments of intergovernmental cooperation"[5] and international law (→ para 5, 12). Thus, the construction of the so-called European "Economic and Monetary Union" (EMU) is significantly different from the monetary union of a nation State. It is **a monetary union without economic union**.[6]

Hence, pursuant to the theory of optimum currency areas,[7] the convergence of national economic policies is one of the institutional and political frameworks that can act as a shock absorber.[8] An economic union is seen as the indispensable basis for keeping the common currency stable and for balancing economic imbalances in

---

[1] Hattenberger, in Schwarze et al. (2019), Article 120 AEUV para 4.

[2] Mortensen (2013), p. 1. See also Schwarze (2007), para 391 et seq.

[3] Regarding the following explanations, cf. Häde, in Kahl et al. (2022), Article 88 para 312–352, 368 (released in 2012).

[4] Cf. Hentschelmann (2011), p. 282.

[5] Hattenberger, in Schwarze et al. (2019), Article 120 AEUV para 3.

[6] Horn (2011), p. 1399: "cardinal sin" of the EMU.

[7] Cf. Mundell (1961), p. 657 et seqq; McKinnon (1963), p. 717 et seqq.; Kenen (1969), p. 41 et seqq.

[8] De Grauwe (2016), p. 217.

the event of a loss of the exchange rate buffer.[9] If this requirement is used as a measure for the EMU's susceptibility to crises, it can be seen that one characteristic of the euro area lies in the **different economic policy traditions of the MS**. Economic policy priorities and strategies differ from one MS to another. They do not follow one consistent economic policy model and the same set of objectives. Against this background, in the process of developing the Union's economic policy, it has been more and more recognised that the EU's functioning requires a well-developed mechanism of economic policy coordination. The coordination of MS' economic policies takes place at three separate operational levels, i.e. at the national, Union and intergovernmental levels. Within the meaning of Articles 120 and 121 TFEU it concerns **coordination at the Union level**.[10]

The **Delors Report** of 17 April 1989 laid down the necessary preconditions for the establishment of an EMU in a three-step process,[11] yet could not achieve with its claim for decisions in the economic field "to be placed within an agreed macroeconomic framework and to be subject of *binding procedures and rules*". Based on a French proposal, according to which the integration process demands "more intensive and effective policy coordination [...] not only in the monetary field but also in areas of national economic management affecting aggregate demand, prices and costs of production",[12] this concept has not been followed by the IGC of the early 1990s when it drafted the provision on economic policies (Article 103.1 TEC-Maastricht).[13] The historical events at that time, and mainly the

3

---

[9] This view is an expression of the so-called "coronation theory" advocated by Germany and the Netherlands, which presupposes an advanced economic integration process for the establishment of a monetary union. See on this Lipp and Reichert (1991), p. 40; Bonn (2007a), p. 20, 28; Seidel (2000), p. 863. The opposite view is taken by proponents of the so-called "vehicle theory", namely Italy, Belgium and France. According to this theory, monetary integration promotes the convergence of national economic policies. Cf. Bonn (2007a), p. 23; Bonn (2007b), p. 234. On the "primordial conflict" between the two conceptions cf. Müller-Franken (2014), p. 230 et seq.; Schoenfleisch (2018), p. 60 et seqq. who analyses the coordination of economic policy as a consequence of the "asymmetric compromise" of the Economic and Monetary Union.

[10] Joined Cases C-597/18 P, *Chrysostomides et al.*, (Opinion of AG Pitruzzella of 28 May 2020) para 46; Müller, in Jaeger and Stöger (2021), Article 121 AEUV para 8 (released in 2020).

[11] Cf. Committee for the Study of Economic and Monetary Union, *Report of economic and monetary Union in the European Community* (1989), p. 13 et seqq. (available at https://ec.europa.eu/economy_finance/publications/pages/publication6161_en.pdf) – emphasis is mine. In Chap. II about "The final stage of economic and monetary union", this Report points out: "The existence and preservation of [individual nations with differing economic, social, cultural and political characteristics] would require a degree of autonomy in economic decision-making to remain with individual member countries and a balance to be struck between national and Community competences. For this reason, it would not be possible simply to follow the example of existing federal States; it would be necessary to develop an innovative and unique approach." In detail on this, Kortz (1996), p. 39 et seqq.

[12] Cf. Baum-Ceisig (2002), p. 34; Wendt (2002), p. 112.

[13] Article 103.1 TEC-Maastricht (now Article 121.1 TFEU) reads as follows: "Member States shall regard their economic policies as a matter of common concern and shall coordinate them within the Council, in accordance with the provisions of Article 102a." See also Article III-179.1 TCE. In the wake of the financial crisis (2010), the discussion on the establishment of a

4 The formulation of economic policy by the EU would require **a "dominant budget" in the sense of comprehensive Union competences for revenue and expenditure**.[14] This would entail an enormous transfer of sovereign rights to the Union since such a budget as a regulating instrument of a central economic policy would require that the MS confer upon the Union large-scale authority in expenditure-related policy areas, such as defence, social, educational or infrastructural policy, combined with the respective competence to create revenue.[15] Accordingly, the Union would need to have the competence to raise taxes, while the EP would need to have budgetary sovereignty, as was once conferred upon national assemblies in the wake of emerging parliamentarism at the domestic level. As a result, this would imply the transformation of the Union from an "association of sovereign States" to a true federal State.[16] According to the current status, "the Union does not have exclusive competence in (the) area ... of economic policy".[17]

5 However, such a transfer of powers for economic policy (especially fiscal and income policy) to the Union, to a *gouvernement économique*, which would transform the supranational organisation into a quasi-State entity, does not match the **political will of the MS**, which want to remain "masters of the Treaties", namely in tax and fiscal policy. The call for stronger centralisation of national economic and financial policies within the EU was thus yet to be realised. The Eurogroup's "Euro Plus Pact" of 24 March 2011 was the first step on the **way to restructuring the EMU**.[18] It was followed by adjustments to the Stability and Growth Pact (SGP), through the so-called Six Pack (2011)[19] and Two Pack (2013),[20] by the Pact for

---

"gouvernement économique" was revived by German Chancellor *A. Merkel* and French President *N. Sarkozy*. However, not in terms of a new institution of the euro countries or a counterpart to the ECB, but as a coordination and cooperation obligation between all MS of the Union; cf. Pilz (2016), p. 43 et seq.

[14] Seidel (1994), p. 94.

[15] Seidel (1992), p. 134; Weber (1994), p. 54.

[16] Cf. Seidel (1995), p. 793, 796.

[17] Case C-370/12, *Pringle* (CJEU 27 November 2012) para 160.

[18] European Council, 24-25 March 2011, Conclusions, EUCO 10/11, p. 5. See in detail Pilz (2016), p. 51 et seqq and also Hattenberger, in Schwarze et al. (2019), Article 120 AEUV para 9.

[19] Regulation (EU) No 1173/2011 *on the effective enforcement of budgetary surveillance in the euro area*, O.J. L 306/1 (2011); Regulation (EU) No 1174/2011 *on enforcement measures to correct excessive macroeconomic imbalances in the euro area*, O.J. L 306/8 (2011); Regulation (EU) No 1175/2011 amending Council Regulation (EC) No 1466/97 *on the strengthening of the surveillance of budgetary positions and the surveillance and coordination of economic policies*, O.J. L 306/12 (2011); Regulation (EU) No 1176/2011 *on the prevention and correction of macroeconomic imbalances*, O.J. L 306/25 (2011); Council Regulation (EU) No 1177/2011 amending Regulation (EC) No 1467/97 *on speeding up and clarifying the implementation of the excessive deficit procedure*, O.J. L 306/33 (2011); and Council Directive 2011/85/EU *on requirements for budgetary frameworks of the Member States*, O.J. L 306/41 (2011).

[20] Regulation (EU) No 472/2013 *on the strengthening of economic and budgetary surveillance of Member States in the euro area experiencing or threatened with serious difficulties with respect to*

Growth and Employment (2012)[21] and the Treaty on Stability, Coordination and Governance (TSCG, so-called "Fiscal Compact" – 2012/2013) (→ para 13; → Article 121 TFEU para 4; → Supplement to Title VIII: Fiscal Union para 5).

1.2. National Economic Policies as the Subject of Coordination

Article 120 TFEU establishes the principles regarding the policy coordination of the MS in the field of economic policy, which remains part of their competences and, therefore, is primarily **a matter for coordination** (Article 5.1 TFEU) within the institutions of the Union. Coordination procedures mark an abandonment of the paradigm of "integration through law". In place of negative integration, coordination as a **form of positive integration** (→ Article 26 TFEU para 35–36) does not use law, but politics as a medium of integration. These procedures involve, in a formal sense, mutual information and consultation between MS in order to achieve common objectives.[22] Coordination of economic policies therefore requires the States to act with a view to contributing to the achievement of the EMU objectives and in line with the broad guidelines on economic policy. Thus, the **national economic policies** are declared to be **a matter of common concern**.[23] MS shall consider the coordination of their national economic policies as a **shared responsibility**.[24] The development of prices, the level of interest rates and the general economic development of an economic area depend to a large extent on both government budgetary policy and general economic policy decisions, e.g. the promotion of investments, the social security systems or wage policy, etc. If these policies of different countries and their economic development differ considerably in this respect, the resulting divergences are usually cushioned by the currencies' exchange rates. This possibility, however, no longer exists within the euro area (→ Article 119 TFEU para 13 et seqq.).[25]

6

The TFEU provisions on EMU are guided by the objective of bringing the MS' economic, fiscal and budgetary policies under an **efficient assessment by the financial markets**. The lack of sound (budgetary) policies is to be sanctioned by an increase in financing costs. The sanction mechanism presupposes that MS accept responsibility for their own national economies and do not assume obligations of other MS. With regard to financial aid from MS to those countries of the Union

7

---

their financial stability, O.J. L 140/1 (2013) and Regulation (EU) No 473/2013 *on common provisions for monitoring and assessing draft budgetary plans and ensuring the correction of excessive deficit of the Member States in the euro area*, O.J. L 140/11 (2013).

[21] European Council, 28-29 June 2012, Conclusions, EUCO 76/12, Annex; cf. Pilz (2016), p. 53 et seq.

[22] Schoenfleisch (2018), p. 250.

[23] Richter, in Geiger et al. (2015), Article 120 TFEU para 3.

[24] Yoo, in von der Groeben et al. (2015), Article 119 AEUV para 7; cf. Yábar Sterling (2004), p. 666.

[25] Herrmann, in Pechstein et al. (2017), Article 119 AEUV para 26.

having a national debt that endangers the European monetary system, it is disputed whether the **prohibition of bailout** (Article 125 TFEU) is to be interpreted as an **absolute ban on financial aid**,[26] where aid can be granted only in exceptional circumstances (emergency right),[27] **or** whether Article 125 TFEU, providing that the EMU does not constitute a "joint liability community", is addressed to potential creditors. According to this latter interpretation, Article 125 TFEU **does not restrict the MS' sovereign right to voluntarily assume liability**.[28]

1.3. Embedding Article 120 TFEU in the Provisions on EMU

8   Due to different traditions and historical experiences, the national concepts, measures and aims tend to diverge with regard to economic policy.[29] As a consequence, the process of sustaining monetary union is only conceivable if a high degree of economic convergence is attained.[30] In view of the sovereignty of the MS in the area of their economic policies (→ para 4 to 5), Article 120 TFEU **intends to commit** them **to common objectives**, first and foremost those enshrined in Article 3 TEU and, referring to the broad economic guidelines (Article 121.2 TFEU), this provision sets a **framework that allows for coordination** of their national economic policies. Against this background, the **concept** that is supposed to hold the imperfect EMU together **is aimed mainly at avoiding excessive deficits in the national budgets at different levels**. The factual criteria to be applied to realise the basic concept of the monetary union as **a "community committed to long-term stability"**[31] are spelt out in Article 126.2 (1) TFEU and are quantified in greater

---

[26] Cf. Blanke (2011), p. 417 seq.; Kirchhof (2012), p. 87, calls for a "return to the law" with regard to the sovereign debt crisis, by which is meant that, in view of the debt and financial crisis, the States involved should move as quickly and steadily as possible towards the legally required state of affairs (p. 79).

[27] Cf. Hufeld (2011), p. 122, 130 et seq., who seeks to justify the EFSF as emergency assistance *praeter legem*.

[28] Cf. Herrmann (2010), p. 215; Blanke (2011), p. 417; von Arnauld (2013), p. 513; different view Häde, in Kahl et al. (2022), Article 88 para 385 with references also for the opposite view (released in 2012).

[29] Lastra (2006), p. 245 seq.

[30] From the situation of that time with a mere perspective of "achieving monetary union", also based on "parallel advancement in monetary and economic integration" ("parallelism") including "a substantial degree of economic union", see the ambitious proposals of the Committee for the Study of Economic and Monetary Union, *Report of economic and monetary Union in the European Community* (1989), p. 14, 28. They have not materialised neither in the Treaties nor in political practice (→ para 3); see also Hattenberger, in Schwarze et al. (2019), Article 120 AEUV para 1 who stresses that adequate economic conditions as well as disciplined fiscal policies are also needed to maintain a stable single currency.

[31] German Federal Constitutional Court, 2 BvR 2134/92 and 2 BvR 2159/922 BvE 2/08 (Judgment of 12 October 1993) para 147; c.f. Amtenbrink (2008), p. 907, considers why "neither Article 98 EC nor any of the following provisions on economic policy include any reference to short-term economic policy."

detail in the Protocol (No 12) on the excessive deficit procedure (Article 126.2 (2) TFEU; → Article 126 TFEU para 12 et seqq.). In addition to this peer review procedure, sanctioning by means of the financial markets is established in accordance with the provisions of Articles 123 et seqq. TFEU[32]

Hence, the diverging interests of the Union and the MS or between the MS are (partly) reconciled by means of coordination, thus aiming at a functioning economy. Coordination includes budgetary, labour market, social (health, pensions etc.), wage and income, investment and infrastructure policies.[33] With regard to **economic and employment policy** (Articles 145 et seqq. TFEU), the MS are primarily obliged by Article 2.3 TFEU to practise **self-coordination**. The Union contributes to that process by supporting the coordination between the MS in order to achieve the "**durability of convergence**" required for the single currency (Article 140.1, 4th indent, TFEU).[34] In the area of economic policy, Article 5.1 TFEU limits the Union's competences in favour of the MS ("*The Member States* shall coordinate their economic policies within the Union"). A "European Economic Government" (→ Article 137 TFEU para 4) would be hardly compatible with this provision. Article 5.2 TFEU, on the other hand, provides that "*the Union* shall take measures to ensure coordination of the employment policies of the Member States". Similarly, Article 5.3 TFEU allows *the Union* to "take initiatives to coordinate the social policies of the Member States".[35]

Conducting the national economic policies with a view to contributing to the achievement of the **objectives of the Union**, including in particular "balanced economic growth [...], price stability, a highly competitive social market economy, [and the aim of] full employment and social progress" (Article 3.3 (1) sentence 2 TEU),[36] Article 120 TFEU dovetails the measures of the Union with those of the MS, mainly by reference to the "broad guidelines" set out in Article 121.2 TFEU (→ Article 121 TFEU para 13 et seqq.). In order to support the **magical triangle of price stability, economic growth and full employment**, the MS shall regard their economic policies as a matter of common European interest (Article 121.1 TFEU) (→ Article 3 TEU para 48 et seqq.).[37] The provision systematically builds a **bridge between the principles** set out for the EMU (Article 119 TFEU) and their concrete application in the economic policies of the Union and the MS (Articles 121 to 126 TFEU). Overall, however, Article 120 TFEU has **only limited independent regulatory content** due to its referential and repetitive normative character. For the

---

[32] Schoenfleisch (2018), p. 59, 63 et seq.

[33] Herrmann, in Pechstein et al. (2017), Article 119 AEUV para 46.

[34] With regard to the "Member States with a derogation" (Article 139.1 TFEU), cf. the concept of convergence set out in Article 140 TFEU and the Protocol (No 13) on the convergence criteria.

[35] Cf. Martucci, in Pingel (2010), Article 98 CE para 4; Richter, in Geiger et al. (2015), Article 120 TFEU para 3; Scharf (2009), p. 23.

[36] Cf. Richter, in Geiger et al. (2015), Article 120 TFEU para 4 et seq.

[37] Cf. Blanke (2012a), p. 408.

purposes of fair competition between MS, the provisions of Articles 123 to 126 TFEU take **precautions to prevent** individual MS from gaining unjustified advantages in their budgetary policies by resorting to costly **steering measures**.[38]

1.4. Coordination as a Substitute for a Lack of Union Power

11   The **necessary coordination methods** include, i.a., policy dialogue, exchange of information, identification of best practices through peer review and common economic measures within a multilateral surveillance procedure (→ Article 121 TFEU para 23 et seqq.). Like the economic policy decisions of the MS, the coordinating measures of the Union (Article 5.1 TFEU) are governed by "the principle of an open market economy with free competition, favouring an efficient allocation of resources and in compliance with the principles set out in Article 119". The Council, on a recommendation from the Commission, shall "formulate a draft for the broad guidelines of the economic policies of the Member States and of the Union and [...] report its findings to the European Council" (Article 121.2 (1) TFEU). On the basis of a European Council conclusion on the initial draft (Article 121.2 (2) TFEU), the Council adopts a recommendation setting out the **broad economic policy guidelines** (Article 121.2 (3) TFEU). Without a legally binding nature, the guidelines spell out orientation points and possible directions with regard to the annual economic policy in both the MS and the EU as a whole, taking into account the particular circumstances of each MS. The procedure for their adoption (→ Article 121 TFEU para 14 et seqq.) as well as their non-binding and thus non-enforceable character confirm the rather **intergovernmental method of coordinating the Union's economic policy** as a whole with the effect that the Union may not act in this area through legislative means.[39]

The lack of an active role on the part of the European Parliament in the adoption of the guidelines, in particular by limiting its "involvement" to a mere right to information on the Council's recommendation (Article 121.2 (3) sentence 2 TFEU), marks a **democratic deficit within the EMU** already inherent in primary Union law. It reveals economic policy as part of the MS' national sovereignty, from which follows the intergovernmental coordination procedure (→ Article 121 TFEU para 13 et seqq.). This deficit has been further deepened, in particular by the introduction of the European Semester through secondary Union law.[40]

---

[38] Borchardt (2020), para 851.

[39] Cf. Herrmann and Rosenfeld, in Pechstein et al. (2017), Article 120 AEUV para 6; Lenaerts (2014), p. 763; Müller-Graff (2009), p. 173.

[40] Cf. Calliess (2012), p. 163, who speaks of the "impasse of coordination"; with regard to the "normativity" in European financial and economic policy matters, see also Schorkopf (2012), p. 209, who speaks of an "intergovernmental transformation"; Blanke and Böttner (2015), p. 263 et seqq., analyse "the democratic dilemma of the Union in the crisis"; Schoenfleisch (2018), p. 196 et seq., 220 et seq.

The guidelines shall also include the **employment guidelines**, i.e. common priorities and targets for employment policies, which, in accordance with Article 5.2 TFEU in conjunction with Article 148 TFEU, shall be adopted by the Council on a proposal from the Commission after consulting the EP, the Economic and Social Committee, the Committee of the Regions and the Employment Committee (Article 150 TFEU). Also, these employment guidelines, which are likewise politically attributable to the European Council conclusions (Article 148.1 TFEU), must be **consistent with broad economic policy guidelines**.[41]

Economic coordination between the European and national levels is beset by the fact that the effectiveness of national policies can be increased without reducing the MS' scope for action.[42] It is expected that such **soft "economic governance"**, if possible without the adoption of legally binding measures or at the very least with only limited legally binding force, will lead to more harmonised standards in national economic policies. In order to achieve the "**balanced budgetary rule**", coordination takes place in **"soft" and "hard" forms** (→ para 13).

One example of the former is the **Fiscal Compact** (→ Article 121 TFEU para 66 et seqq.).[43] According to this Treaty, the stability criteria set out in Article 3.1 TSCG "shall take effect in the national law of the Contracting Parties [...] through provisions of binding force and permanent character, preferably constitutional, or otherwise guaranteed to be fully respected and adhered to throughout the national budgetary processes" (Article 3.2 TSCG). Hence, the national legislators have a margin of discretion in implementing the rules intended to foster budgetary discipline.[44] However, in substance, the TSCG provides for "hard" economic and budgetary surveillance coordination to avoid excessive deficit and debt issuance by the MS. In the event of significant deviations from the medium-term objective or the adjustment path towards it, a "correction mechanism shall be triggered automatically" (Article 3.1 point (e) TSCG). The European Commission is to assess whether the MS have complied with their obligation under Article 3.2 TSCG to introduce "**debt brakes**" in the national legal order. If a Contracting Party has failed to comply with Article 3.2 TSCG, the matter will be brought to the CJEU by one or more Contracting Parties (Article 8.1 TSCG; → Supplement to Title VIII: Fiscal Union para 36, 53, 56).[45]

Another example for "hard" economic policy coordination is Article 126.11 TFEU: if a euro area MS fails to comply with the Council's decision on deficit

---

[41] Cf. Obwexer, in von der Groeben et al. (2015), Article 5 AEUV para 17; Richter, in Geiger et al. (2015), Article 120 TFEU para 6.

[42] Schoenfleisch (2018), p. 2, therefore rightly speaks with regard to coordination of a "competence-preserving alternative to the transfer of legislative powers to the Union whose results [...] are similiar."

[43] Cf. Keppenne (2021), p. 813 et seqq.

[44] Kauppi, in Herzog et al. (2019), Article 119 para 119-6, states that the "Member States have considerable leeway in terms of their fiscal policy".

[45] Cf. Blanke (2012b), p. 95 et seq.; Pilz (2012), p. 460; Pilz (2016), p. 62.

13 The coordination of the national economic policies is carried out by means of "**measures**", among which ("in particular") are the above-mentioned broad economic policy guidelines (Article 5.1 second sentence TFEU).[47] The coordination, developed in its procedural aspects in Article 121 TFEU, was further underpinned by the secondary legislation reform packages in the wake of the economic and financial crisis to prevent and redress macroeconomic imbalances (→ para 5; → Article 121 TFEU para 54 et seqq., 63 et seqq.; → Supplement to Title VIII: Fiscal Union para 5).[48]

reduction (Article 126.9 TFEU), the Council can impose on that MS "a non-interest-bearing deposit of an appropriate size with the Union" or "fines of an appropriate size".[46]

14 As a result, the role of the Union is limited to coordination;[49] however, if the MS take action in the area of economic policy, they must commit themselves to Union objectives (Article 3 TEU),[50] including the **functioning of the internal market** (Article 119.1 TFEU), and, as far as they are members of the euro area (arg. *e contrario*: Article 139.2 point (a) TFEU), to the legally non-binding broad guidelines (Article 121.2 TFEU) referred to in Article 120 TFEU and to the criteria established by the Union within the framework of its coordination.[51] The responsibility for economic policy, however, remains an unshared competence of the MS (Article 5.1 TFEU). Nevertheless, the performance of all related tasks in the network of the national economies requires the involvement of the Union since there is an **interdependence of economic policies** at the national level, especially with regard to those MS whose currency is the euro and which are therefore fatefully bound to each other within the political project of the "**monetary union**". Consequently, pursuant to Article 5.1 (2) TFEU, "specific provisions" shall apply to those MS whose currency is the euro, which are in fact the default rules that do not (yet) apply to non-euro countries in accordance with Article 139.2 TFEU. Nevertheless, the coordination of economic policies by the Union must leave the MS with enough leeway to take substantial decisions in the field of their economic policies.[52] So far, Articles 119 and 120 TFEU also put forward the idea of

---

[46] See on this also Pilz and Dittmann (2012), p. 65 et seqq.

[47] Cf. Calliess, in Calliess and Ruffert (2022), Article 5 EUV para 7.

[48] Cf. Pilz and Dittmann (2012), p. 53 et seqq.; Flynn (2021), p. 858 et seqq.; cf. Richter, in Geiger et al. (2015), Article 120 TFEU para 7, who sees a "final responsibility of the political decision makers to define the framework for macroeconomic development with a view to the *bonum commune*."

[49] However, in exceptional situations, the Union may adopt measures that bind the MS (Article 122 TFEU); see Hattenberger, in Schwarze et al. (2019), Article 120 AEUV para 4.

[50] Hattenberger, in Schwarze et al. (2019), Article 120 AEUV para 6.

[51] Cf. Case C-370/12, *Pringle* (CJEU 27 November 2012) para 69; see also Obwexer, in von der Groeben et al. (2015), Article 5 AEUV para 11.

[52] Cf. Schulte, in von der Groeben et al. (2015), Article 121 AEUV para 4; Yábar Sterling (2004), p. 666 et seq.

economic competition between the MS.[53] Similar to constitutional constraints that bind MS domestically (e.g. Articles 2 and 3 of the Italian Constitution; Articles 20.1 and 28.1 sentence 1 of the Basic Law), the Union must **take appropriate account of social aspects** in coordinating measures on economic policy (Article 9 TFEU).

2. Constituent Elements of Article 120 TFEU

2.1. Economic Policy

2.1.1. Meaning and Relation to Other Policies

Under Article 119.1 TFEU, the activities of the MS and the Union include "the adoption of an economic policy based on the close coordination of Member States' economic policies, on the internal market and on the definition of common objectives, conducted in accordance with the principles of an open market economy with free competition". Although this provision is general and thus ambiguous, it nonetheless provides the basic, defining elements of those aspects of economic policy that fall within the Union's competence (→ Article 119 TFEU para 7 et seqq.).[54] The Union economic policy is regulated by Articles 2.3 and 5.1 TFEU and Articles 120 to 126 TFEU. Article 120 TFEU is intended to strengthen the economic pillar of the EMU as a whole, which in its **fragile construction**[55] needs stabilisation through coordination (→ para 6–7). According to the CJEU, an "economic policy measure cannot be treated as equivalent to a monetary policy measure for the sole reason that it may have indirect effects on the stability of the euro".[56] By analogy, "a monetary policy measure cannot be treated as equivalent to an economic policy measure for the sole reason that it may have indirect effects that can also be sought in the context of economic policy".[57] **Indirect effects** are, according to the Court, "effects which, even at the time of adoption of the measures, were foreseeable consequences of those measures, which must therefore have been knowingly accepted at that time".[58] This distinction between direct and indirect effects is highly controversial, given that, according to the German FCC, effects can

15

---

[53] Ohler, in Siekmann (2013), Article 120 AEUV para 4; Müller, in Jaeger and Stöger (2021), Article 119 AEUV para 14 (released in 2020); Müller (2014), p. 188 et seqq., who underlines the vagueness of this principle.

[54] Cf., literally, Case C-62/14, *Gauweiler et al.* (Opinion of AG Cruz Villalón of 14 January 2015) para 126.

[55] Hattenberger, in Schwarze et al. (2019), Article 120 AEUV para 9, holds the "asymmetric architecture" of a centralised monetary policy and a decentralised economic policy responsible for the fragility of EMU.

[56] Case C-370/12, *Pringle* (CJEU 27 November 2012) para 56.

[57] Case C-493/17, *Weiss et al.* (CJEU 11 December 2018) para 61; Case C-62/14, *Gauweiler et al.* (CJEU 16 June 2015) para 52.

[58] Case C-493/17, *Weiss et al.* (CJEU 11 December 2018) para 63.

no longer be qualified "to be indirect in nature if the economic policy effects of a measure are intended or deliberately [knowingly] accepted, and these effects are at least comparable in weight to the monetary policy objective pursued".[59] It illustrates that the **delimitation of economic and monetary policy** against the background of the various asset purchase programmes of the ECB is **one of the most controversial issues in EU law** (→ para 21 et seqq.). Indeed, preserving national decision-making powers and constitutional prerogatives are at stake. The principle of conferral of powers (Article 5.1 TEU in conjunction with Articles 119 and 127 et seq. TFEU) is a key determinant in this debate.

16   In that regard, it should be noted that the **TFEU does not define economic policy** but refers to the objectives of Article 3 TEU and to one principle that has relevance to economic policy, i.e. "an open market economy with free competition" (→ para 37; → Article 119 TFEU para 40–41). "Economic policy" is a **broad term**[60] used to describe government actions that are intended to influence the economy of a nation. They include (cross-sectoral) measures that influence macroeconomic variables such as economic growth, unemployment rate, export surpluses or the domestic investment climate (→ Article 119 TFEU para 11).[61] Following a universal understanding of the term, economic policy contains all State measures affecting the organisation, formation and implementation of the national economic system. This includes economic reforms in the goods, capital and labour markets to raise productivity and employment. Economic policy therefore influences the behaviour and interactions of economic agents and has an impact on how economies work. This understanding indicates that the term economic policy comprises two areas: microeconomics and macroeconomics.[62]

17   While **microeconomics** analyses the behaviour of basic elements in the economic system, including individual agents and markets, their interactions and the outcomes of their interactions, **macroeconomics** examines the whole economic system. Aggregate indicators involve national income, production, consumption, savings, and investment and issues affecting it, including the unemployment of resources, inflation, economic growth and public policies that address these issues. Two main regulatory macroeconomic policies are fiscal policy and monetary policy. Structural, property, social, environmental or regional policies are also a part of the scope of Article 120 TFEU. In a nutshell, **Article 120 TFEU refers to all economic activities and legislative measures.**[63]

---

[59] See German Federal Constitutional Court, 2 BvR 859/15 and others (Order of 18 July 2017) para 119 – *PSPP* (reference for preliminary ruling); reiterated in German Federal Constitutional Court, 2 BvR 859/15 and others (Judgment of 5 May 2020) para 135 – *PSPP*.

[60] Hattenberger, in Schwarze et al. (2019), Article 120 AEUV para 5.

[61] Herrmann and Rosenfeldt, in Pechstein et al. (2017), Article 120 AEUV para 11.

[62] Ohler, in Siekmann (2013), Article 120 AEUV para 8; cf. also Amtenbrink (2008), p. 903. Hattenberger, in Schwarze et al. (2019), Article 120 AEUV para 5 sees in "Articles 120 et seqq. a set of instruments for influencing macroeconomic variables".

[63] Cf. Amtenbrink (2008), p. 903; Rodi, in Vedder and Heintschel von Heinegg (2018), Article 120 AEUV para 3.

There are **several instruments to drive economic development**. These include **18**
all actions and measures that may be taken in view of the economic process, the
economic structure and the economic order.[64] The basic macroeconomic framework,
stability-oriented macropolicies, cost-reducing measures on the supply side to
increase flexibility and sustainability are decisive factors for the general thrust of
the economic policy. The means of economic governance differ from one MS to
another. All industrialised countries with a market economy strive to manage the
economic processes in their territory with a view to achieving a **"macroeconomic
equilibrium"**. The "magic square" of price stability, full employment, balance in
foreign trade relations and balanced economic growth is considered to be the set of
objectives to prosper on a long-term basis. Only rarely can a national economy
achieve these objectives simultaneously.[65]

With regard to the EU, the term "economic policy" stands for **the medium-term 19
economic and budgetary position of the MS**, their fulfilment of the criteria for
compliance with budgetary discipline and their fiscal policies, including the relationship between government deficit and government investment expenditure.[66]
Also with regard to Article 119.1 TFEU, the concept of economic policy is
extensive (→ Article 119 TFEU para 11). So far, it is necessary to take into account
the **relationship between economic policy and other policies**, such as social or
competition policy. According to some scholars, this relationship is to be determined by the **principle of subsidiarity**. Following this principle, "economic
policy" is regarded as being a "residual variable", which is to be defined by
deducting the more specific regulations for individual policy areas that are significant in terms of economic policy, such as social or labour market policy.[67] Opponents of this view[68] prefer to decide if a matter belongs to economic policy on the
basis of the primary objective of a measure and the chosen instruments. According
to them, the **aim of a policy measure is crucial**. If the (primary) objective is
maintaining price stability, it will be a matter of monetary policy. It is in this sense
that the CJEU has decided in the **Pringle case** on the distinction between economic
and monetary policy.[69] But the Union has no competence to define what "economic

---

[64] Cf. Bieber and Haag, in Bieber et al. (2020), § 24 para 3.

[65] Cf. Bieber and Haag, in Bieber et al. (2020), § 24 para 3; Gramlich (2020), para 53 et seqq.

[66] Lastra (2006), p. 246.

[67] Schulze-Steinen (1997), p. 37; for further information, see also Hattenberger, in Schwarze et al. (2019), Article 120 AEUV para 5.

[68] See Hattenberger, in Schwarze et al. (2019), Article 120 AEUV para 5; in a differentiated manner Häde, in Calliess and Ruffert (2022), Article 119 AEUV para 13 outlines: "The fact that monetary policy can be understood as a sub-area of economic policy does not exclude drawing the borderline between them, but argues against an overly strict either-or."

[69] Case C-370/12, *Pringle* (CJEU 27 November 2012) para 56: "As regards, first, the objective pursued by that mechanism, which is to safeguard the stability of the euro area as a whole, that is clearly distinct from the objective of maintaining price stability, which is the primary objective of the Union's monetary policy. Even though the stability of the euro area may have repercussions on the stability of the currency used within that area, an economic policy measure cannot be treated as

policy" means, not only due to the lack of a relevant competence but also in view of the fact that the Union economic model, laid down in Article 120 TFEU "with the principle of an open market economy with free competition", is rooted in various national economic or even legal[70] orders of the MS as holders of the competence for economic policy.[71]

20 **Economic governance** can be described as **a two-stage procedure**. Failure during the first stage, the multilateral surveillance phase, results in the introduction of the second phase, which is the excessive deficit procedure (SGP). While the multilateral surveillance procedure, which is shaped by the voluntary observance of the broad economic guidelines by the MS and the orientation effect of the corresponding criteria for compliance with budgetary discipline and their fiscal policies, is part of the open method of coordination, the excessive deficit procedure leading to obligations for the MS and also the European institutions brings into the system of economic coordination an element of "closed method of coordination".[72] This procedure even allows imposing ("symbolic") sanctions on MS in the case of a breach of the rules to avoid continuous excessive deficit in an MS.[73] Obviously, as a result of the debt crisis and other severe problems within the euro area, the **nature of the European economic policy coordination has changed over the last years**.

2.1.2. Distinguishing Economic Policy from Monetary Policy

21 The distinction provided for in Article 119 TFEU between the objectives regarding economic policy (paragraph 1) and monetary policy (paragraph 2) clearly indicates that **monetary policy and economic policy are fundamentally two distinct fields**.[74] However, economic policy measures will affect the fiscal policy of the MS. The Union's monetary policy provisions (Articles 127.1 and 282.2 TFEU) stipulate that the ESCB is to support the general economic policies of the Union, with a view to contributing to the achievement of its objectives, as enunciated in

---

equivalent to a monetary policy measure for the sole reason that it may have indirect effects on the stability of the euro."

[70] See, for example, the Constitution of Poland (1997) which in Article 20 sets forth: "A social market economy, based on the freedom of economic activity, private ownership, and solidarity, dialogue and cooperation between social partners, shall be the basis of the economic system of the Republic of Poland."

[71] See also Lasa López (2013), p. 990.

[72] Amtenbrink and De Haan (2003), p. 1079, 1086; for more information see Nettesheim (2012), p. 31 et seqq.; Herrmann (2012a), p. 79 et seqq.

[73] With regard to MS under a European Deficit Procedure, the provisions of Article 126 TFEU and Regulation 1467/97 replace the usual infringement procedure before the CJEU with a system of financial sanctions. Regulation 1173/2011, as part of the "Six Pack", provides for financial sanctions both in the preventive arm and in the corrective arm of SGP. This system has been used twice so far – in the case of Spain and Portugal (2016) – but the gesture remains symbolic. See Keppenne (2021), para 28.83 et seqq.

[74] Hattenberger, in Schwarze et al. (2019), Article 120 AEUV para 5.

Article 3 TEU.[75] The TFEU does not define the meaning of either economic policy (→ para 16) or monetary policy.[76] Of course, there is a functional distinction between the two policy fields, which, in formal terms, is also reflected in the division into "Economic Policy" (Chapter 1) and "Monetary Policy" (Chapter 2) within Title VIII.[77] However, there is no list defining the actions to take within the respective subject areas. The MS' responsibility for their economic policies implies their parallel responsibility for budgetary policy and thus, at the same time, for economic, social, labour market and fiscal policies.[78] In other words, a common monetary policy is confronted with a wide range of economic policy concepts, which, without coordination, tend to diverge irreconcilably. The asymmetric structure of the economic and monetary union as a result of the different competences for economic policy on the one hand and monetary policy on the other makes it **essential to distinguish, as far as possible, between the responsibility for the national economic policies and that for the monetary policy,** which lies in the hands of the ECB.[79] Hence, it is crucial to find out first whether an act directly pursues economic or monetary policy objectives.

The CJEU has decided in *Pringle* that the TFEU "refers, in its provisions relating to [monetary] policy, to the objectives, rather than to the instruments of monetary policy".[80] This makes the distinction between economic policy (instruments) and monetary policy (instruments) even more complicated. Interpretative notes on the **provisions** relating to the objectives and instruments of these policies should bear in mind that they **are at the interface between two politically overlapping fields** (→ para 15),[81] which, however, does not make impossible a clear delimitation of competences *per se*. The difficulty here lies in identifying the underlying policy areas linked to **"exceptional" Eurosystem programmes for the purchase of**

22

---

[75] Case C-370/12, *Pringle* (CJEU 27 November 2012) para 54; cf. Schütze (2015), p. 800, who mentions that following the "economist school" a functioning monetary union requires a substantial degree of macroeconomic unity.

[76] With regard to monetary policy, see Case C-370/12, *Pringle* (CJEU 27 November 2012) para 53; Case C-493/17, *Weiss et al.* (CJEU 11 December 2018) para 50.

[77] Ohler, in Siekmann (2013), Article 120 AEUV para 8.

[78] Seidel (1998), p. 374; Seidel (2000), p. 867.

[79] Cf. Häde (2012), p. 37.

[80] Case C-370/12, *Pringle* (CJEU 27 November 2012) para 53. In para 55, the Court then addresses also the instruments available to the ESCB for the purpose of implementing monetary policy: "It is necessary therefore to examine whether or not the objectives to be attained by the stability mechanism whose establishment is envisaged by Article 1 of Decision 2011/199 and the instruments provided to that end fall within monetary policy for the purposes of Articles 3(1)(c) TFEU and 127 TFEU." Slightly different, although referring to its *Pringle* judgment, the CJEU points out in Case C-62/14, *Gauweiler et al.* (CJEU 16 June 2015) para 42, that the TFEU "defines both the objectives of monetary policy and the instruments which are available to the ESCB for the purpose of implementing that policy".

[81] See also Dietze et al. (2020), p. 527; Hattenberger, in Schwarze et al. (2019), Article 120 AEUV para 1 states that the economic union is a prerequisite as well as a complement to the monetary union.

public debt (→ para 24 et seqq., 27 et seqq.) since they "[fall] between the traditional lines of monetary and fiscal policy".[82] So far, the cases of *Pringle*, *Gauweiler* and *Weiss* are instructive. Referring to the principle of conferral of powers set out in Article 5.2 TEU, the Court of Justice declares: "It is appropriate to refer *principally* to the objectives" of the measure in question.[83] And the Court adds: "The instruments which the measure employs in order to attain those objectives are *also relevant*."[84] The **decisive factor** for identifying the specific competence of the Union within a policy area is **the objective pursued by a measure**, be it in economic or in monetary matters.[85] Under Articles 127.1 and 282.2 TFEU, the primary objective of the Union's monetary policy is to maintain **price stability**[86] (→ Article 119 para 16 et seqq.), followed by the ESCB's obligation "to **support the general economic policies in the Union**, with a view to contributing to the achievement of its objectives, as laid down in Article 3 TEU" (→ Article 119 para 28 et seqq.).[87]

23   The direct aim and the effects of a Union act, with regard to the question of whether it is to be understood as economic or monetary policy measure, is to be defined objectively, whereas the **choice of the instruments or means**, envisaged to achieve the objective, is the **result of the decision-making body and its margin of assessment**, and thereby often linked to further provisions. According to Article 119.1 TFEU, the MS and the Union have to pursue an economic policy "based on the close coordination of Member States' economic policies, on the internal market and on the definition of the common objectives, conducted in accordance with the principle of an open market economy with free competition". Are the objectives and instruments set forth in Articles 119 through 123 TFEU and Articles 125 through 127 TFEU compatible with measures of financial assistance towards MS currently in an excessive deficit situation when agreed upon in an international treaty between MS on the establishment of an international financial institution? With regard to the **European Stability Mechanism** (ESM), the CJEU has assumed that such **activities** of the ESM do not fall within the scope of monetary policy, as governed by Articles 127 through 133 TFEU. Instead, they **have an economic policy purpose**: "Under Articles 3 and 12(1)1 of the ESM Treaty, it is not the purpose of the ESM to maintain price stability, but rather to meet the financing requirements of ESM Members, namely Member States whose currency is the euro, who are experiencing or are threatened by severe financing problems, if indispensable to safeguard the financial stability of the euro area as a whole and of its

---

[82] Cf. Tuori (2021), para 22.178, who looks at the bond purchase programmes (OMT, PSPP) "from the perspective of a potential euro area breakup" (para 22.228).

[83] Case C-62/14, *Gauweiler et al.* (CJEU 16 June 2015) para 46 (my emphasis).

[84] Case C-62/14, *Gauweiler et al.* (CJEU 16 June 2015) para 46, with reference to para 53 and 55 of the *Pringle* judgment (my emphasis).

[85] For a more detailed discussion of the link between economic and monetary policy and the resulting problems of demarcation, cf. Pilz (2016), p. 197 et seqq.; Städter (2013), p. 148 et seqq.

[86] Amtenbrink (2008), p. 901.

[87] Case C-493/17, *Weiss et al.* (CJEU 11 December 2018) para 51.

Article 120 [Conduction of Economic Policies]

Member States [...]. [T]he activities of the ESM fall under economic policy. The Union does not have exclusive competence in that area [...]."[88] The above-mentioned rules and objectives of the TFEU "do not preclude the conclusion between the Member States whose currency is the euro of an agreement such as the [ESM] Treaty".[89] Furthermore, the **ESM is not concerned with the coordination of the economic policies of the MS** but rather constitutes a financing mechanism.

In the *Outright Monetary Transactions* (OMT) case,[90] the CJEU has ruled that the competence to set up a programme for the **purchase of government bonds** on the secondary market is **part of the Union's monetary policy** and, therefore, has assigned responsibility for the decision on the programme to the ESCB. The programme "is intended to rectify the disruption to the monetary policy transmission mechanism caused by the specific situation of government bonds issued by certain MS. In those circumstances, the mere fact that the programme is specifically limited to those government bonds is thus not of a nature to imply, of itself, that the instruments used by the ESCB fall outside the realm of monetary policy."[91] The Eurosystem was given large discretion to define its own mandate, and it was also assigned a major role in defining economic policies in the MS that face economic problems.[92]

24

The **German Federal Constitutional Court** has addressed in its jurisprudence the criteria underlying the case law of the CJEU for making a clear distinction between the competences of the Union and **the competences of** the MS (**"aims" and "means"**). Sharing the view on the significance of the aims of a Union act when delimiting competences between the EU and the MS in the field of EMU policy, the Second Senate of the Karlsruhe Court has quoted passages from the CJEU's *Gauweiler* ruling.[93] **Criticising the distinction drawn in the European Court's case law between the (relevant) direct effects and the (irrelevant) indirect effects of such a Union measure**, the Constitutional Court spells out in its reasoning that the CJEU "has held that in order to determine whether a measure falls within the area of monetary policy it is appropriate to refer principally to the objectives of that measure. The instruments which the measure employs in order to attain those objectives are also relevant [...]. [It] can be seen from the press release [issued by the ECB] that the aim of the programme is to safeguard both 'an

25

---

[88] Cf. Case C-370/12, *Pringle* (CJEU 27 November 2012) para 95 et seq., 160; Case C-62/14, *Gauweiler et al.* (CJEU 16 June 2015) para 46; see also German Federal Constitutional Court, 2 BvR 2728/13 (Order of 14 January 2014) para 39 – *OMT* (reference for preliminary ruling), BVerfGE 134, 366; see also German Federal Constitutional Court, 2 BvR 1390/12 and others (Judgment of 18 March 2014) para 180 seq. – *European Stability Mechanism (*BVerfGE 135, 317).
[89] Cf. Case C-370/12, *Pringle* (CJEU 27 November 2012) ruling 2.
[90] On the launch of this programme and for economic analysis, cf. Tuori (2021), para 22.148 et seqq., 22.153 et seqq., 22.156 et seqq.
[91] Case C-62/14, *Gauweiler et al.* (CJEU 16 June 2015) para 55.
[92] Cf. Tuori (2021), para 22.178.
[93] Case C-62/14, *Gauweiler et al.* (CJEU 16 June 2015) inter alia para 46-49 and para 52.

appropriate monetary policy transmission and the singleness of the monetary policy'. First, the objective of safeguarding the singleness of monetary policy contributes to achieving the objectives of that policy inasmuch as, under Article 119(2) TFEU, monetary policy must be 'single'. Secondly, the objective of safeguarding an appropriate transmission of monetary policy is likely both to preserve the singleness of monetary policy and to contribute to its primary objective, which is to maintain price stability. [...] Indeed, a monetary policy measure cannot be treated as equivalent to an economic policy measure merely because it may have indirect effects on the stability of the euro area."[94]

26 Moreover, the German Constitutional Court points out that the CJEU generally looks into the aims of the act in question when delimiting competences between the EU and the MS, but when delimiting economic and monetary policy, it also looks into the means employed[95] and that the Court of Justice considers irrelevant the merely indirect effects an act may have on other areas for the delimitation of competences.[96] The Senate expresses **doubts regarding the Court's approach to simply accept the monetary policy objective asserted by the ECB** without questioning the underlying factual assumptions or at least reviewing whether the respective reasoning was comprehensible and without testing these assumptions against other indications that evidently argue against its **qualification as a monetary policy measure**. This "does not sufficiently take into account the constitutional dimension of the principle of conferral", which the Constitutional Court considers as "the predominant justification for the decrease in the level of democratic legitimation of the public authority exercised by the European Union". Despite these concerns, the Karlsruhe judges do not find the policy decision on the OMT programme, as interpreted by the Court of Justice, as exceeding "manifestly" the competences attributed to the ECB "within the meaning of the competence retained by the Federal Constitutional Court to review *ultra vires* acts".[97] Others have argued that the OMT programme "could even be seen as the Eurosystem contributing to the economic policies in the EU, and as such mainly pushing the boundaries of prohibition of Article 123 TFEU".[98]

27 The conflict over the classification of the purchase of government-issued bonds by the ESCB peaked in a **judicial dispute** on the occasion of the constitutional

---

[94] See German Federal Constitutional Court, 2 BvR 2728/13 (Judgment of 21 June 2016) para 69 – *Gauweiler*. So far, the FCC makes reference to its prior Order of 14 January 2014, in which it referred two questions for preliminary ruling to the CJEU, 2 BvR 2728/13 and others, para 33 et seqq. – *OMT*.

[95] Cf. Case C-370/12, *Pringle* (CJEU 27 November 2012) para 55, 60.

[96] German Federal Constitutional Court, 2 BvR 2728/13 (Judgment of 21 June 2016) para 178 – *OMT*.

[97] German Federal Constitutional Court, 2 BvR 2728/13 (Judgment of 21 June 2016) para 182 et seqq. (184 et seq.) – *OMT*; see also German Federal Constitutional Court, 2 BvR 859/15 and others (Judgment of 5 May 2020) para 134 – *PSPP*.

[98] Cf. Tuori (2021), para 22.178.

complaints **against the ECB's PSPP Decision**.[99] In its reference for preliminary ruling on the Decision's conformity with EU law, the Constitutional Court had reiterated that determining whether an act like the Secondary Markets Public Sector Purchase Programme constitutes a measure of monetary policy or economic policy should not be limited to assessing the objective pursued and the means employed but should also give consideration to relevant effects resulting from the measure in question. In its view, effects can no longer be qualified as being indirect in nature if the economic policy effects of a measure are intended or knowingly accepted and these effects are at least comparable in weight to the monetary policy objective pursued.[100] It further had hold that if the purchasing of government bonds by the ESCB essentially amounted to granting financial assistance to MS, it would qualify as an economic policy measure for which the EU has no competence.[101] In essence, responding to the questions referred for a preliminary ruling, the **CJEU stated that "taking account of its objective and of the means provided for achieving that objective, a decision such as [PSPP] Decision 2015/774 falls within the sphere of monetary policy"**.[102] The Luxemburg Court has argued that the authors of the Treaties did not intend to make an absolute separation between economic and monetary policies, considering (i) the primacy of maintaining price stability when supporting the general economic policies in the Union (Article 127.1 TFEU), (ii) the ESCB's obligation to act in accordance with the principles laid down in Article 119 TFEU and (iii) the independence of the ESCB guaranteed by Article 130 and Article 282.3 TFEU.[103] The CJEU limits its review to "**a manifest error of assessment**" made in the context of "the ESCB's economic analysis" on the appropriateness of purchases of government debt "for contributing to achieving the objective of maintaining price stability".[104] Hence, the Court **restrains the intensity of its judicial control** with regard to monetary policy decisions.

In its subsequent **PSPP judgment of 5 May 2020**, the **FCC sharply criticised the Court's decision** in that "**the CJEU essentially affords the ECB the competence to pursue its own economic policy agenda by means of an asset purchase programme**, and refrains from subjecting the ECB's actions to an effective review as to conformity with the order of competences on the basis of the principle of proportionality, including a balancing of the economic and fiscal policy effects of the PSPP against its monetary policy objective". As a result, the CJEU's judgment

28

---

[99] ECB Decision (EU) 2015/774 *on the secondary markets public sector asset purchase programme* (ECB/2015/10), O.J. L 121/20 (2015). On the launch of this programme and its economic logic, cf. Tuori (2021), para 22.179 et seqq., 22.192 et seqq.

[100] See German Federal Constitutional Court, 2 BvR 859/15 and others (Order of 18 July 2017) para 119 et seqq. – *Weiss et al.* (reference for preliminary ruling).

[101] See German Federal Constitutional Court, 2 BvR 859/15 and others (Order of 18 July 2017) para 108 et seq. – *Weiss et al.* (reference for preliminary ruling).

[102] Case C-493/17, *Weiss et al.* (CJEU 11 December 2018) para 70.

[103] Case C-493/17, *Weiss et al.* (CJEU 11 December 2018) para 60.

[104] Case C-62/14, *Gauweiler et al.* (CJEU 16 June 2015) para 68, 74, 81 and 91; Case C-493/17, *Weiss et al.* (CJEU 11 December 2018) para 24, 56, 78, 91.

"exceeds the judicial mandate deriving from Art. 19(1) second sentence TEU [...]. The CJEU thus acted *ultra vires,* which is why, in that respect, its Judgment has no binding force in Germany."[105]

29   AG *Cruz Villalón*, in his **Opinion** in the **Gauweiler case**, had already criticised as unsuitable the attempt to achieve strict substantive separation and thus distinctiveness between economic policy on the one side and monetary policy on the other: "Although it may appear self-evident, it is important to make the point that monetary policy forms part of general economic policy. The division that EU law makes between those policies is a requirement imposed by the structure of the Treaties and by the horizontal and vertical distribution of powers within the Union, **but in economic terms it may be stated that any monetary policy measure is ultimately encompassed by the broader category of general economic policy.**"[106] Referring to the Court's judgment and AG *Kokott*'s Opinion in the *Pringle* case[107] that "an economic policy measure cannot be treated as equivalent to a monetary policy measure for the sole reason that it may have indirect effects on the euro" (→ para 15, 19), AG *Cruz Villalón* turned this reasoning around: "[...] a monetary policy measure does not become an economic policy measure merely because it may have indirect effects on the economic policy of the Union and the Member States".

30   According to this view, there is no monetary policy without an impact on factors that can also be the subject of economic policy, of course, for other purposes and with other means. **Monetary policy** has an impact on the real economy, just as economic policy does, so it **is economic policy with a specific, primary objective: price stability.**[108] Rightly so, Article 127.1 sentence 2 TFEU in conjunction with Article 2 sentence 1 of the ESCB Statute emphasise that "[w]ithout prejudice to the objective of price stability, the ESCB shall support the general economic policies in the Union" (i.e. of the Union and the MS) "with a view to contributing to the achievement of the objectives of the Union".[109] In the opposite view, it is hardly comprehensible to classify the purchase of bonds by the ESM as economic policy and the same purchase by the ESCB as monetary policy merely because it pursues a price stability objective. These critics assert that it is exceedingly questionable whether the purchase of public sector bonds from individual decentralised units of a

---

[105] German Federal Constitutional Court, 2 BvR 859/15 and others (Judgment of 5 May 2020) para 163 –*PSPP*.

[106] Case C-62/14, *Gauweiler et al.* (Opinion of AG Cruz Villalón of 14 January 2015) para 129.

[107] Case C-370/12, *Pringle* (Opinion of AG Kokott of 26 October 2012) para 85: "Finally, it must be observed that – as the German Government to an extent correctly submitted – not every form of economic policy can be treated as equivalent to monetary policy solely because it may indirectly affect the price stability of the euro. If it were otherwise, the entire economic policy would be reserved to the ESCB and the rules of the Treaty on the coordination of economic policy within the Union would be devoid of meaning."

[108] Cf. Pernice (2020), p. 514 et seq. who shares the views of AG *Cruz Villalón*; Müller, in Jaeger and Stöger (2021), Article 119 AEUV para 30 (released in 2020); Hilpold (2021), sub III. D.

[109] Cf. Hellwig (2020), p. 2500; Tuori (2021), para 22.231.

currency area can still be considered monetary policy. For them, **such measures are clearly economic policy and**, depending on the form it takes, **also fiscal policy** as a sub-category of general economic policy.[110] A diametrically opposed position to that of AG *Cruz Villalón* underlines that particularly in a federal system, respect for the distribution of powers once established must remain the basis of all political action. Therefore, **the EU MS** would be **obliged to amend and adapt primary law in order to assign to the ECB a central role in crisis management.**[111]

However, the German Constitutional Court did not deny that the **PSPP programme falls within the ECB's monetary policy competence**. This cannot be seriously doubted in view of the monetary policy objective and the means used (secondary market operations under Article 18.1 ESCB Statute).[112] Whenever the ECB makes use of **one of the instruments explicitly listed in Articles 18 and 19 of the ESCB Statute**, whose direct impact on the money supply from the ECB is evident, a **presumption in favour of** a specific measure as **monetary policy** must apply.[113] Moreover, when preparing and implementing an open market operation programme of the same kind as the PSPP programme, **the ESCB is given a broad margin of discretion** – "to make choices of a technical nature and to undertake complex forecasts and assessment".[114]

2.1.3. Scope of Application

Policy areas subject to special regulation in the Treaties are exempted from the coordination of the MS' economic policies by the Union institutions. It is disputed, however, whether there are economic sectors that, *by their very nature*, are exempted from coordination under Union law and thus from the scope of Article 120 TFEU. Some argue that Article 120 TFEU applies to all economic policy areas that are not otherwise subject to special Treaty rules. **Economic policy coordination**, as a necessary condition for the success of the EMU, can only be achieved by continuously aligning it with the objectives of Article 3.3 TEU.[115] Others argue that, although the obligations set out in Article 120 TFEU refer to economic policy as a whole, a **distinction** must be made between measures aimed at influencing the economy as a whole, even if they depart from individual sectors

31

---

[110] Cf. Siekmann (2020), p. 495 et seq.

[111] Cf. Nettesheim (2020), p. 1634.

[112] Cf. Hellwig (2020), p. 2499; this position is supported by Herrmann, in Pechstein et al. (2017), Article 119 AEUV para 54 with regard to the OMT programme.

[113] Cf. Herrmann, in Pechstein et al. (2017), Article 119 AEUV para 54.

[114] Case C-62/14, *Gauweiler et al.* (CJEU 16 June 2015) para 68; Case C-493/17, *Weiss et al.* (CJEU 11 December 2018) para 73. See the consenting appraisal of Müller, in Jaeger and Stöger (2021), Article 119 AEUV para 31 (released in 2020).

[115] Kempen, in Streinz (2018), Article 120 AEUV para 3. For a broad understanding of economic policy see also Wittelsberger, in von der Groeben et al. (2015), Article 120 AEUV para 10.

and measures aimed at regulating individual sectors, which follow their own specific Treaty rules.[116] As a result, the main objective of European economic policy is the close coordination of cross-sectoral economic policies in order to promote a **lasting convergence of economic performance**. Only through the convergent development of national economies that a support base for achieving the functioning of the internal European market can be retained and the making of the monetary union as a long-term stability project can be possible (→ para 7).

2.2. Fundamental Objectives

32 The **mandate** addressed to the MS to "conduct their economic policies with a view to contributing to the achievement of the objectives of the Union, as defined in Article 3 [TEU] [...]", and the **further imperative addressed to the MS *and* the Union** to "act in accordance with the principle of an open market economy with free competition [...]" have **a legally binding effect**, but national governments have a **margin of appreciation** in choosing the measures of action.[117] National decisions contrary to the objectives of the Union constitute infringements of Union law.[118] The MS are obliged not only to comply with the Union's objectives but also to actively contribute to their achievement by consciously formulating and implementing their policies. However, those provisions **do not impose on the MS clear and unconditional obligations** which may be relied on by individuals before the national courts. What is involved is a general principle whose application calls for complex economic assessments which are a matter for the legislature or the national administration.[119] The economic policy targets are too vague to derive justiciable parameters for concrete decisions by the EU institutions and the MS. The MS shall carve out their national economic policies, embedding them "in the context of the broad guidelines referred to in Article 121(2)" (→ para 11). Their competence to formulate the national economic policies thus remains unchanged (→ para 14), which in turn proves that **the Treaty defines binding objectives but does not authorise the Union to harmonise in pursuit of these goals the national economic policies with binding effect**.[120] Nevertheless, those **guidelines are the key factor for coordinating national economic policies**.[121]

---

[116] Bandilla, in Grabitz et al. (2022), Article 120 AEUV para 10 (released in 2011).

[117] Richter, in Geiger et al. (2015), Article 120 TFEU para 3, 7.

[118] See also Bandilla, in Grabitz et al. (2022), Article 121 AEUV para 6 (released in 2011); Ohler, in Siekmann (2013), Article 120 AEUV para 10; Richter, in Geiger et al. (2015), Article 120 TFEU para 7.

[119] Case C-9/99, *Échirolles Distribution SA* (CJEU 1 October 2010) para 25 (emphasis added); Case C-484/08, *Caja de Ahorros* (CJEU 3 June 2010) para 46 et seqq.

[120] Bandilla, in Grabitz et al. (2022), Article 120 AEUV para 8 (released in 2011); Martucci, in Pingel (2010), Article 98 CE para 4.

[121] Herrmann in Pechstein et al. (2017), Article 119 AEUV para 59; Herrmann and Rosenfeldt (2017), Article 120 AEUV para 6.

Article 120 [Conduction of Economic Policies]

2.2.1. Reference to Article 3 TEU

Article 3.3 (1) TEU places **price stability right next to "economic growth"** at the top of the seven objectives that are to determine the work of the Union "for the sustainable development of Europe". "Price stability" refers to the internal value of a currency, including its purchasing power.[122] It is guaranteed when the average of all prices of goods and services, i.e. the price level, remains stable overall,[123] which the ECB measures by using a harmonised index of consumer prices (→ Article 119 TFEU para 16, 18). Price stability is achieved when a year-on-year increase in consumer prices in the "euro area" as a whole is **"below 2%" over the medium term** (relative price stability).[124] This objective is inextricably linked to the aim of "economic growth" and thus, at the same time, to the goal "to establish an internal market". From the latter, the economic policy of the Union draws its key principles (→ Article 26 TFEU para 6 et seqq.). To a large extent, economic growth and the internal market are fed by the **idea of "free competition"**. In **Protocol No 27** on the internal market and competition, adopted on a British initiative after the expression "free and undistorted competition" had been excised in the Treaty of Lisbon (Article 3 TEU) due to the pressure of former French President *Sarkozy*, the Contracting States acknowledge in a compensatory way that "the internal market as set out in Article 3 of the Treaty on European Union includes a system ensuring that competition is not distorted". Furthermore, they have agreed that "[t]o this end, the Union shall, if necessary, take action under the provisions of the Treaties, including under Article 352 [TFEU]". Indirectly, this emphasises the crucial role of the rules on competition and state aid policy in the economic policy approach of the Treaties. 33

Among the objectives enshrined in Article 3.3 (1) TEU, the **social market economy**,[125] which has been marked in the Treaty of Lisbon with the mere additional attribute "**highly competitive**" (→ para 33),[126] is of particular importance for the economic policies of the MS and the Union. The commitment to an open market economy, a fundamental decision under primary law, supersedes conflicting options for another economic order, which may be taken by the MS. In view of the interpretation of the German Constitution, the dogma of the 34

---

[122] Wutscher, in Schwarze et al. (2019), Article 127 AEUV para 4.

[123] Häde, in Calliess and Ruffert (2022), Article 119 AEUV para 21; Häde, in Calliess and Ruffert (2022), Article 127 AEUV para 3.

[124] Cf. ECB (January 1999), Monthly Bulletin, p. 46; Cf. Blanke and Pilz, in Huber and Voßkuhle (2023), Article 88 GG para 83 et seqq.; Herrmann in Pechstein et al. (2017), Article 119 AEUV para 55.

[125] Ohler, in Siekmann (2013), Article 120 AEUV para 18; to the term "market economy", → Article 26 TFEU para 27 with footnote 90.

[126] On the background of this wording, see Blanke (2012a) p. 377 et seq. who asks about a "paradigm change"; Hattenberger, in Schwarze (2019), Article 120 para 7 doubts normative consequences as a result of this "shift in emphasis".

"neutrality of the Basic Law with regard to the economic order"[127] also loses relevance.[128] The core of a social market economy is competition – based on achievements of output and efficiency (*Leistungswettbewerb*). Since real competition does not automatically result from the free play of forces, the policy of the MS and the Union has the responsibility to enable, establish and promote competition, as well as to safeguard it from restrictions by powerful individuals or collective amalgamations. However, **no concrete normative consequences can be derived from this basic decision**. In the ensemble of the MS and the Union, legislators and governments must therefore create the legal framework for every economic activity, business, trade and industry.[129] The law of competition **protects** the openness of the market **against distortions through governmental or private actors**. This needs also intervention by the Union in order to ensure that competition in the internal market is not distorted and trade and competition are not affected (Articles 101-106 TFEU).[130] Free trade and competition are not an end in themselves but "merely means of achieving [the economic and monetary] objectives" set out in the Treaties,[131] and thus are ultimately intended to **strengthen also the economic, social and territorial cohesion of the Union** (Article 175.1 TFEU in conjunction with Article 174 TFEU).

35 The **key drivers of** this **liberal order** are private autonomy, including contractual freedom as guaranteed by Article 6.3 TEU in terms of a fundamental Union right and, at the same time, as a general principle of law under the private law of the Union;[132] decentralised activity of the economy's subjects; the fundamental freedom of economic activity, in particular the right to engage in work and to pursue a freely chosen or accepted occupation (Article 15 EUCFR), the freedom to conduct a business (Article 16 EUCFR) and the right to property (Article 17 EUCFR);

---

[127] For this established case law of the German Federal Constitutional Court, see e.g. decisions 1 BvR 459/52 and others, (Judgment of 20 July 1954) – *Investitionshilfe* (BVerfGE 4, 7); 1 BvR 532, 533/77 and others (Judgment of 1 March 1979) para 139 seqq. – *Mitbestimmung* (BVerfGE 50, 290-340).

[128] Cf. Badura, in Burmeister (1997), p. 409; Herrmann (2012b), p. 53; Ohler, in Siekmann (2013), Article 120 AEUV para 15; Ruffert (2009), p. 202; Richter, in Geiger et al. (2015), Article 120 TFEU para 4.

[129] Müller-Armack (1956), p. 390 et seq.; Müller-Armack (1966); Ruffert, in Calliess and Ruffert (2022), Article 3 EUV para 38, calls for prudence in assuming that the EC's economic order has simply taken from the social market economy model as developed in Germany by A. *Müller-Armack* and implemented namely by L. *Erhard*. However, the ordoliberal character of the internal market in its principles cannot be ignored; cf. Blanke (2012a), p. 370 et seqq., 373 et seqq.

[130] Hatje (2010), p. 596 seq.; see also Martucci, in Pingel (2010), Article 98 CE para 6; see also Richter, in Geiger et al. (2015), Article 120 TFEU para 6 who stresses that "Article 120 TFEU does not prevent the Union from implementing interventionist measures".

[131] Opinion 1/91, *European Economic Area* (ECJ 14 December 1991) para 50. In this context, the ECJ refers in particular to Articles 2, 8a and 102a TEEC (as amended in 1987 by the SEA).

[132] Cf. Lüttringhaus (2018), p. 150 et seqq., 202 et seqq. Rightly so, Lüttringhaus (2018), p. 94 et seqq., points out that the principle of open market economy with free competition (Article 119.1 TFEU) aims to create, maintain and strengthen the functional conditions of the contractual freedom, but does not establish an individual freedom right (→ para 32).

coordination through trade and competition; and the balance between supply and demand of scarce goods and services.[133] As already spelt out in its "label", the **social dimension** is an essential part of the concept to bring about a fair and level playing field in the economic arena (→ Article 3 TEU para 34). It is an inseparable element of the "competitiveness" of the "market economy" since it prohibits economic growth and competition to increase whatever the price is, at the cost of social protection.[134] The aim of a social market economy is, according to neoliberal thought, to combine the free initiative of individuals in the marketplace with a social welfare development that is based and safeguarded by market economy achievements.

There is also at least an indirect reference to the **ecological market economy**, which, in view of **climate change**, is becoming an increasingly important objective in the policies of the Union and the MS.[135] The fact that in economic policies there is still talk of an **open market economy** (→ para 37) points to the achievement of social market economy set forth in Article 3.3 (2) TEU through "social justice and protection".[136] Although economic policy must primarily be viewed in terms of a market economy, the general-objective-oriented provision of Article 3.3 TEU as a whole should not be overlooked.[137] While this rule does not call for a turn away from an open market economy, it does cite **"social progress" as important for balanced economic growth and full employment** (Article 3.3 (1) sentence 2 TEU). Thus, it also serves social progress by guaranteeing the economic and financial basis for such advances. An open market and a social market therefore do not exclude each other. However, the social dimension prohibits exaggerations at the expense of the socially vulnerable groups, e.g. through dumping wages or a lack of social security.[138] It becomes also visible in the harmonisation and improvement of living and working conditions as well as in the implementation of the European Social Charter.[139] Due to a **lack of direct legal effect**, the **individual sub-goals** of the social market economy and the objective of an ecological market economy **need to be specified in secondary legislation** in order to achieve a balance between environmental protection and welfare and also between competition goals and the objectives of the social and ecological market economy.

36

---

[133] Müller-Graff (1987), p. 27.

[134] Frenz and Ehlenz (2010), p. 330; Blanke (2012a), p. 373.

[135] Ohler, in Siekmann (2013), Article 120 AEUV para 18.

[136] Cf. Blanke and Böttner (2020), para 8, 17, 19, 21 et seq., 24 et seq.

[137] Hattenberger, in Schwarze et al. (2019), Article 120 AEUV para 6; Richter, in Geiger et al. (2015), Article 120 TFEU para 5.

[138] Frenz and Ehlenz (2010), p. 330; Blanke (2012a), p. 373.

[139] Ruffert, in Calliess and Ruffert (2022), Article 3 EUV para 38.

2.2.2. Principle of an Open Market Economy with Free Competition

37   The principle enshrined in Article 120 sentence 2 TFEU, which requires the **MS and Union institutions** to act in compliance with the principles of an open market economy with free competition is a repeated commitment (Article 119.1 and 2 TFEU; → Article 119 TFEU para 40 et seq.) to a type of **economy** that **is "open"** not only for domestic activities but also for **trade with third countries both inside and outside the single market**.[140] Within the framework of its supportive-coordinating economic policy, necessary interventions of the Union are limited to those that are in line with the market principle.[141] That demands, in particular, **equal treatment of all market participants**.[142] An "open market economy" also requires that, without legal grounds for justification, neither the MS nor the institutions of the Union may interfere with the **free market access and exit of private enterprises**. Such measures must be subjected to a **proportionality test**.[143] With regard to the single market, this stems from the fact that the completion of the four fundamental freedoms (Article 26.2 TFEU) builds also the basis for the EMU. Trade can take the form of technology transfers, all kinds of goods and services and managerial exchange. Even before the Treaty of Lisbon, which made trade policy an exclusive Union competence (Article 3.1 point (e) in conjunction with Article 207 TFEU), there could be no doubt that **foreign trade** was also covered by the "open market economy" concept. The free movement of capital equally extends to foreign trade. This characterises the open market economy as an **anti-protectionist directive**.[144] Hence, the concept is based on the wish to promote the sound development of the single market *and* the world economy based on free and open market principles. Paralleling the standards that are set out in Article 119.2 TFEU with regard to the **monetary union**, this principle is also couched in Article 127.1 sentence 3 TFEU and Article 2 sentence 3 of the ESCB Statute for orienting actions and decisions carried out by the ESCB/ECB.

38   The **principle of an open market economy** with free competition, **like the principle of price stability** (Article 3.3 (1) TEU), is **subject to restrictions** in the form of the relevant limitations and justifications under EU law (written justifications), mandatory requirements relating to the public interest (including Union interests) and cross-sectoral clauses, as well as encroachments provided for in various provisions on EU policies, such as export, agricultural and environmental policies.[145] Thus, **Regulation (EU) 2015/479 on common rules for exports**, based in particular on Article 207.2 TFEU, commits to freedom of "exportation of

---

[140] See Article 3.5 TEU: "In its relations with the wider world, the Union [...] shall contribute to [...] free and fair trade [...]." Cf. Hatje (2010), p. 594 et seq.; Amtenbrink (2008), p. 903.

[141] Cf. Siekmann, in Siekmann (2013), Article 119 AEUV para 33, 106.

[142] Herrmann, in Pechstein et al. (2017), Article 119 AEUV para 57.

[143] Müller, in Jaeger and Stöger (2021), Article 119 AEUV para 14 (released in 2020).

[144] Bandilla, in Grabitz et al. (2022), Article 119 AEUV para 24 (released in 2021).

[145] Herrmann (2012b), p. 54; Richter, in Geiger et al. (2015), Article 120 TFEU para 6.

products from the Union to third countries" but allows "restrictions" (Article 1).[146] According to this Regulation, such restriction is required "in order to prevent a critical situation from arising on account of a shortage of essential products, or to remedy such a situation, and where Union interests call for immediate intervention". In these circumstances, "the Commission may make the export of a product subject to the production of an export authorisation" (Article 3). Referring to Regulation (EU) 2015/479, the European Commission adopted **Implementing Regulation (EU) 2021/111**,[147] which requires authorisation for the export of goods from the Union to third countries concerning vaccines against SARS-related coronaviruses (export mechanism). Then in March 2021, at the request of the Italian government, rather dubiously an export ban on 250,000 doses of AstraZeneca vaccine was imposed at the expense of Australia. If, however, the flow of the Union's economic lifeblood, which means free trade, shall not dry up, the "interests of the Union" must be interpreted *narrowly* also "with due regard for existing international obligations" (eighth Recital to the Preamble of Regulation 2015/479).[148] Otherwise, the Union will run the risk of "tearing up the rule book" (*S. Birmingham*).

2.2.3. Favouring an Efficient Allocation of Resources

Allocative efficiency is concerned with spending limited resources in the areas that are best able to maximise public value, e.g. in health economics. The meaning of the element "favoring an efficient allocation of resources" in the context of economic policy coordination is unclear, in particular the question of whether this criterion represents a description of an aspect of the open market economy or is to be understood normatively in the sense of a binding principle to be observed. This raises the question of whether this element is to be interpreted in dependence of the objective of an "open market economy with free competition" or as a separate principle within Article 119 TFEU. In view of the vague wording within a relative clause and the fact that the use of resources is regularly a matter for the economic operators, which the EU institutions can at best influence through appropriate framework conditions, it cannot be assumed that this element was intended by the Contracting Parties to establish a further economic policy principle; rather, it is **to be understood purely descriptively**. Hence, it is **not a concrete action directive**.[149]

39

---

[146] Regulation (EU) 2015/479, O.J. L 83/34 (2015).

[147] Implementing Regulation (EU) 2021/111 *making the exportation of certain products subject to the production of an export authorisation*, O.J.LI 31/1.

[148] According to Recital 5 of Implementing Regulation (EU) 2021/111, a prohibition of export is reasoned with a Union's "vital demand, but without impacting on the Union's international commitments in this respect".

[149] Bandilla, in Grabitz et al. (2022), Article 120 AEUV para 13 (released in 2011). With a similar view Herrmann and Rosenfeldt, in Pechstein et al. (2017), Article 120 AEUV para 13; Wittelsberger, in von der Groeben et al. (2015), Article 120 AEUV para 14; Richter, in Geiger et al.

40   It would be problematic to recognize the legal relevance of this criterion, from which concrete consequences could then be derived. Moreover, it would be **incompatible** with the principle of an open market economy with free competition if the Union institutions and national bodies acted in such a way as to "control" the allocation of resources in the private sector and its achievement. The **institutions, bodies, offices and agencies, neither national nor European, are not called upon to become**, with a view to the economic policy objectives of the Union, **"arbiters" of efficiency and deficiencies in the use of resources in the private sector.**[150]

2.3. In Compliance with the Principles Set Out in Article 119 TFEU

41   Article 120 TFEU as part of the Treaty framework on economic policy is linked not only to the provision on the EU's objectives (Article 3 TEU)[151] but also to the broad guidelines referred to in Article 121.2 and to "the principles set out in Article 119" TFEU.[152] Article 119 TFEU refers in its paragraphs 1 and 2, **in a very general manner** (the "activities [...] shall include [...] [conducted] in accordance with [...]"), to an **"open market economy with free competition"** (→ para 37; → Article 119 TFEU para 40–41), which as an overarching principle determines the activities of the MS and the Union in **economic policy** as well those of the Union in **monetary policy**. Although the competences for both areas fall apart (→ para 2, 7), the alignment of both with this principle underlines their **common and central role in an economic system with little to no barriers to free-market activity.** The **"guiding principles"** set out in Article 119.3 TFEU – stable prices, sound public finances and monetary conditions and a sustainable balance of payments – are binding[153] and of particular importance to the supporting role that national economic policies must play with regard to the common monetary policy (→ para 2, 7, 9; → Article 119 TFEU para 42 et seqq.). These principles shall be

---

(2015), Article 120 TFEU para 4 who considers the efficient allocation of resources as "an (automatic) result of the openness of the market economy"; with a different view Häde, in Calliess and Ruffert (2022), Article 120 AEUV para 4 (who regards this clause as a "mandate"), and Hattenberger, in Schwarze et al. (2019), Article 120 AEUV para 7. Cf. also Amtenbrink (2008), p. 904.

[150] Ohler, in Siekmann (2013), Article 120 AEUV para 17.

[151] Kauppi's comment on Article 119 TFEU (Kauppi, in Herzog et al. (2019), para 119.02 et seqq.) focuses mainly on Article 4 TEC-Nice (i.e. former Article 3a TEC-Maastricht) which, in Part I of that Treaty on "Principles" and in the context of Articles 2 (Task) and 3 (Activities/Objectives) TEC-Nice, provided for "the adoption of an economic policy which is based on the close coordination of Member States' economic policies, on the internal market and on the definition of common objectives, and conducted in accordance with the principle of an open market economy with free competition".

[152] See also → Article 3 TEU para 48 et seqq.

[153] Hattenberger, in Schwarze et al. (2019), Article 120 AEUV para 8.

followed by market-compatible control mechanisms and incentives, i.e. in accordance with the principle of an open market economy with free competition.

2.4. Broad Guidelines Referred to in Article 121.2 TFEU

Article 121.2 TFEU refers to the broad economic guidelines, which are adopted by the Council in terms of recommendations.[154] In a "broad" structure, they specify the framework of the economic policies of the MS (Article 120 sentence 1 TFEU) and, in turn, constitute the main coordination instrument for medium-term EU economic policy (→ para 11; → Article 121 TFEU para 13 et seqq.).[155] They deal with macroeconomic and structural policies for both the EU as a whole and the individual EU countries. Although the recommendations are not legally binding (Article 288.5 TFEU), they **have a high political relevance vis-à-vis the MS through the involvement of the European Council and the Council.**[156] Even though these guidelines do not harmonise the economic policies of the MS, they have an **orientation function**, and, together with the coordination and control mechanisms pursuant to Articles 121 to 126 TFEU, they make possible **certain synchronisation** of the national economic policies – at least in terms of the basic issues.[157] They are subject to a multilateral surveillance mechanism, which aims to ensure that EU countries comply with them (→ Article 121 TFEU para 23 et seqq.). Much depends on the **readiness of the national governments**.

42

3. Legal Effects

On the whole, Article 120 TFEU is **a political guideline** to be used in carving out economic policy measures in the Union. Consequently, this provision does not have any legally binding consequences but serves as a basic standard for the MS and the EU institutions when conducting and coordinating economic policies within an intergovernmental procedure. Since the norm serves only for orientation, the concrete implementation of the Union's economic policy objectives has to be assessed with a particular sector-by-sector focus, in accordance with the relevant rules regarding competences and the requirements and prohibitions of the Treaties,

43

---

[154] The current Council Recommendation (EU) 2015/1184 *on broad guidelines for the economic policies of EU countries and of the EU as a whole* dates back to 14 July 2015, O.J. L 192/27 (2015).

[155] Richter, in Geiger et al. (2015), Article 120 TFEU para 3.

[156] Bandilla, in Grabitz et al. (2022), Article 120 AEUV para 8 (released in 2011); Wittelsberger, in von der Groeben et al. (2015), Article 120 AEUV para 2.

[157] Cf. also Kempen, in Streinz (2018), Article 120 AEUV para 2 et seq.; with the same result Häde, in Calliess and Ruffert (2022), Article 120 AEUV para 2 ("key role within the coordination of economic policies").

namely provisions on the internal market as well as on the Union's competition law and fundamental rights.[158]

44 Article 120 TFEU reiterates and confirms the existing division of competences between the Union and the MS in the field of economic policy and thus **does not constitute a legal basis for pursuing rights and claims** (such as compliance with).[159] However, Article 120 TFEU **prohibits – in a legally binding way – the transition to a planned economy** at the national **subjective** or even European level.[160] Such an economic system would obviously run counter to the principle of an open economy with free competition. However, mixed economic systems that permit deviations from the pure market economy are sporadically regarded as being compatible with the European economic constitution.[161]

4. Territorial Scope of Application

45 The territorial scope of Article 120 TFEU primarily **covers the MS**, where the national economic policies are conducted, but its **applicability also extends to some sub-markets, such as the internal market and trade with third countries** (→ para 37). In view of the objectives set out for the functioning of the internal market, this means that Article 120 TFEU also has a guiding effect on the free movement of goods, persons, services and capital. However, the provision may not be interpreted to exclusively refer to the economic policy of a special MS. If the Union intervenes in national markets through secondary legislation, it is also bound by Article 120 TFEU (→ para 37). As long as it respects the principle of equality of the MS before the Treaties (→ Article 4 TEU para 11 seqq.), the Union may, however, in accordance with Article 4.2 TEU, override the limits of national jurisprudence under international law.[162]

---

[158] Case C-9/99, *Échirolles Distribution SA* (CJEU 1 October 2010), para 25; with the same view Hatje (2010), p. 594 et seqq.; Bandilla, in Grabitz et al. (2022), Article 119 AEUV para 23 (released in 2011); Schwarze (2007), para 22; in a more general approach, with regard to the constituent element "adoption of an economic policy" (Article 119.1 TFEU), see Müller, in Jaeger and Stöger (2021), Article 119 AEUV para 9 (released in 2020).

[159] Case C-9/99, *Échirolles Distribution SA* (CJEU 1 October 2010) para 25; affirmed, inter alia, by Hatje (2010), p. 595; Bandilla, in Grabitz et al. (2022), Article 119 AEUV para 24 (released in 2011); Herrmann (2012b), p. 54; Herrmann and Rosenfeldt, in Pechstein et al. (2017), Article 120 AEUV para 10; Ohler, in Siekmann (2013), Article 120 AEUV para 19 seqq.; cf. also Hatje (2010), p. 595.

[160] Cf. Brömmelmeyer, in Pechstein et al. (2017), Article 101 AEUV para 1; Hatje, in Schwarze et al. (2019), Article 119 AEUV para 9.

[161] Hatje (2010), p. 594; according to Martucci, in Pingel (2010), Article 98 CE para 6, the provisions of Article 98 TEC, although favouring free market forces, do not prohibit interventionism, thus leaving the choice of economic conceptions underlying the European integration open, which may include extreme liberalism as well as indicative planning.

[162] Ohler, in Siekmann (2013), Article 120 AEUV para 22.

Article 120 [Conduction of Economic Policies]

List of Cases

ECJ/CJEU
ECJ 14.12.1991, Opinion 1/91, *European Economic Area*, ECLI:EU:C:1991:490 [cit. in para 34]
CJEU 03.10.2010, C-9/99, *Échirolles Distribution SA*, ECLI:EU:C:2000:532 [cit. in para 32, 43, 44]
CJEU 03.06.2010, C-484/08, *Caja de Ahorros*, ECLI:EU:C:2010:309 [cit. in para 32]
CJEU 26.10.2012, C-370/12, Opinion of AG Kokott, *Pringle*, ECLI:EU:C:2012:675 [cit. in para 29]
CJEU 27.11.2012, C-370/12, *Pringle*, ECLI:EU:C:2012:756 [cit. in para 4, 14, 15, 19, 21-23, 26]
CJEU 14.01.2015, C-62/14, Opinion of AG Cruz Villalón, *Gauweiler et al.*, ECLI:EU:C:2015:7 [cit. in para 15, 29]
CJEU 16.06.2015, C-62/14, *Gauweiler et al.*, ECLI:EU:C:2015:400 [cit. in para 15, 22-25, 27, 30]
CJEU 11.12.2018, C-493/17, *Weiss et al.*, ECLI:EU:C:2018:1000 [cit. in para 15, 21, 22, 27, 30]
CJEU 28.05.2020, C-597/18 P, Opinion of AG Pitruzella, *Chrysostomides et al.* ECLI:EU:C:2020:390 [cit. in para 2]

German Federal Constitutional Court
FCC 20.07.1954, 1 BvR 459/52 and others, *Investitionshilfe*, BVerfGE 4, 7-69 [cit. in para 34]
FCC 01.03.1979, 1 BvR 532, 533/77 and others, *Mitbestimmung*, BVerfGE 50, 290-340 [cit. in para 34]
FCC 12.10.1993, 2 BvR 2134/92 and 2 BvR 2159/922 BvE 2/08, *Maastricht*, BVerfGE 89, 155-213 [cit. in para 8]
FCC 14.01.2014, 2 BvR 2728/13, *Outright Monetary Transactions (OMT) – reference for preliminary ruling*, ECLI:DE:BVerfG:2014:rs20140114.2bvr272813 [cit. in para 23]
FCC 18.03.2014, 2 BvR 1390/12 and others, *European Stability Mechanism*, ECLI:DE:BVerfG:2014:rs20140318.2bvr139012 [cit. in para 23]
FCC 21.06.2016, 2 BvR 2728/13 and others, *Outright Monetary Transactions (OMT)*, ECLI:DE:BVerfG:2016:rs20160621.2bvr272813 [cit. in para 25, 26]
FCC 18.07.2017, 2 BvR 859/15 and others, *Weiss et al. – reference for preliminary ruling*, ECLI:DE:BVerfG:2017:rs20170718.2bvr085915 [cit. in para 15, 27]
FCC 05.05.2020, 2 BvR 859/15 and others, *PSPP*, ECLI:DE:BVerfG:2020:rs20200505.2bvr085915 [cit. in para 15, 26]

References[163]

Amtenbrink, F. (2008). Economic, monetary and social policy. In P. Kapteyn, A. McDonnell, K. Mortelmans, C. Timmermans, & L. Geelhoed (Eds.), *The law of the European Union and the European Communities with references to changes to be made by the Lisbon Treaty* (4th ed., pp. 881–989). Kluwer Law International.

Amtenbrink, F., & De Haan, J. (2003). Economic governance in the European Union – fiscal policy discipline versus flexibility. *Common Market Law Review, 40*(5), 1057–1106.

Badura, P. (1997). Staatsziele und Garantien der Wirtschaftsverfassung in Deutschland und Europa. In J. Burmeister et al. (Eds.), *Verfassungsstaatlichkeit. Festschrift für Klaus Stern zum 65. Geburtstag* (pp. 409–420). C.H. Beck.

Baum-Ceisig, A. (2002). *Lohnpolitik unter den Bedingungen der Europäischen Wirtschafts- und Währungsunion. Möglichkeiten und Grenzen europäischer Tarifverhandlungen*. PhD Thesis, Univ. Osnabrück / Fachbereich Sozialwissenschaften.

Bieber, R., Epiney, A., Haag, M., & Kotzur, M. (2020). *Die Europäische Union. Europarecht und Politik* (14th ed.).

Blanke, H.-J. (2011). The European Economic and Monetary Union – between vulnerability and reform. *International Journal of Public Law and Policy, 1*(4), 402–433.

Blanke, H.-J. (2012a). The economic constitution of the European Union. In H.-J. Blanke & S. Mangiameli (Eds.), *The European Union after Lisbon. Constitutional basis, economic order and external action* (pp. 369–419). Springer.

Blanke, H.-J. (2012b). Die Europäische Wirtschafts- und Währungsunion zwischen Krisenanfälligkeit und Reform. In A. Scherzberg et al. (Eds.), *Zehn Jahre Staatswissenschaften in Erfurt* (pp. 70–121). de Gruyter.

Blanke, H.-J., & Böttner, R. (2015). The democratic deficit in the (economic) governance of the European Union. In H.-J. Blanke et al. (Eds.), *Common European legal thinking. Essays in Honour of Albrecht Weber* (pp. 243–286). Springer.

Blanke, H.-J., & Böttner, R. (2020). § 13: Binnenmarkt, Rechtsangleichung, Grundfreiheiten. In M. Niedobitek (Ed.), *Grundlagen und Politiken der Union* (2nd ed., pp. 887–114). De Gruyter.

Bonn, U. (2007a). *Der Einfluss der monetären Integration auf wirtschaftliche Konvergenz in Europa*. PhD-Thesis: Oldenburg.

Bonn, U. (2007b). Theorie optimaler Währungsräume und ökonomische Konvergenz. In B. Graue, B. Mester, G. Siehlmann, & M. Westhaus (Eds.), *International, europäisch, regional* (pp. 227–246). BIS.

Borchardt, K.-D. (2020). *Die rechtlichen Grundlagen der Europäischen Union* (7th ed.). Facultas.

Calliess, C. (2012). Finanzkrisen als Herausforderung der internationalen, europäischen und nationalen Rechtsetzung. *Veröffentlichungen der Vereinigung der Deutschen Staatsrechtslehrer, 71*, 113–182.

Calliess, C., & Ruffert, M. (Eds.). (2022). *EUV/AEUV* (6th ed.). C. H. Beck.

De Grauwe, P. (2016). *Economics of the Monetary Union* (11th ed.). OUP.

Dietze, J., Kellerbauer, M., Klamert, M., Malferrari, L., Scharf, T., & Schnichels, D. (2020). Europa – Quo Vadis?: Ein kritischer Kommentar zum EZB-Urteil des BVerfG. *Europäische Zeitschrift für Wirtschaftsrecht, 31*(12), 525–530.

Flynn, L. (2021). Non fiscal surveillance of the Member States. In F. Amtenbrink & C. Herrmann (Eds.), *EU law of Economic & Monetary Union* (pp. 850–877). OUP.

Frenz, W., & Ehlenz, C. (2010). Europäische Wirtschaftspolitik nach Lissabon. *Gewerbearchiv*, 329–335.

Geiger, R., Khan, D.-E., & Kotzur, M. (Eds.). (2015). *European Union Treaties*. C.H. Beck.

Grabitz, E., Hilf, M., & Nettesheim, M. (Eds.) (2022). *Das Recht der Europäischen Union: EUV/AEUV. Kommentar*, loose leaf (last supplement: 75). C.H. Beck.

---

[163] All cited internet sources of this comment have been accessed on 6 June 2022.

Gramlich, L. (2020). § 15: Die Wirtschafts- und Währungspolitik der Union. In M. Niedobitek (Ed.), *Grundlagen und Politiken der Union* (2nd ed., pp. 1239–1331). de Gruyter.

Häde, U. (2012). Die Europäische Währungsunion in schwerer See: Ist der Euro noch zu retten? In T. Giegerich (Ed.), *Herausforderungen und Perspektiven der EU 60 Jahre nach dem Schuman-Plan* (pp. 35–49). Duncker & Humblot.

Hatje, A. (2010). The economic constitution within the internal market. In A. von Bogdandy & J. Bast (Eds.), *Principles of European constitutional law* (2nd ed., pp. 589–622). Hart Publishing.

Hellwig, H.-J. (2020). Die Verhältnismäßigkeit als Hebel gegen die Union: Ist die Ultra-vires-Kontrolle des BVerfG in der Sache Weiss noch mit dem Grundsatz der Gewaltenteilung vereinbar? *Neue Juristische Wochenschrift, 73*(35), 2497–2503.

Hentschelmann, K. (2011). Finanzhilfen im Lichte der No Bailout-Klausel – Eigenverantwortung und Solidarität in der Währungsunion. *Europarecht, 46*(2), 282–313.

Herrmann, C. (2010). Griechische Tragödie – der währungsverfassungsrechtliche Rahmen für die Rettung, den Austritt oder den Ausschluss von überschuldeten Staaten aus der Eurozone. *Europäische Zeitschrift für Wirtschaftsrecht, 21*(11), 413–418.

Herrmann, C. (2012a). Die Folgen der Finanzkrise für die europäische Wirtschafts- und Währungsunion. In S. Kadelbach (Ed.), *Nach der Finanzkrise. Rechtliche Rahmenbedingungen einer neuen Ordnung* (pp. 79–104). Nomos.

Herrmann, C. (2012b). Wirtschaftsverfassung und Wirtschaftsregierung in der Europäischen Union. In T. Giegerich (Ed.), *Herausforderungen und Perspektiven der EU 60 Jahre nach dem Schuman-Plan* (pp. 51–75). Duncker & Humblot.

Herzog, P., Campbell, C., Zagel, G., & (Eds.). (2019). *Smit & Herzog on the law of the European Union, loose-leaf*. LexisNexis.

Hilpold, P. (2021). So long *Solange*? The PSPP judgment of the German Constitutional Court and the conflict between the German and the European 'popular spirit'. *Cambridge Yearbook of European Legal Studies, 23*, 159–192. Retrieved from https://www.cambridge.org/core/journals/cambridge-yearbook-of-european-legal-studies/article/so-long-solange-the-psppjudgment-of-the-german-constitutional-court-and-the-conflict-between-the-german-and-the-european-popularspirit/F83C6DDF3516871E3377BD3E4B6EDB87

Horn, N. (2011). Die Reform der Europäischen Währungsunion und die Zukunft des Euro. *Neue Juristische Wochenschrift, 64*(20), 1398–1403.

Huber, P. M., & Voßkuhle, A. (Eds.). (2023). *Kommentar zum Grundgesetz: GG. Vol. 3: Art. 83–146* (8th ed.). C.H.Beck.

Hufeld, U. (2011). Zwischen Notrettung und Rütlischwur: der Umbau der Wirtschafts- und Währungsunion in der Krise. *integration, 34*(2), 117–131.

Jaeger, T., & Stöger, K. (Eds.). (2021). *Kommentar zu EUV und AEUV, loose-leaf (last supplement: 266)*. Manz.

Kahl, W., Waldhoff, C., & Walter, C. (Eds.). (2022). *Bonner Kommentar zum Grundgesetz (last supplement: 215)*. C.F. Müller.

Kenen, P. B. (1969). The theory of optimum currency areas: an eclectic view. In R. Mundell & A. Swoboda (Eds.), *Monetary problems of the international economy* (pp. 41–60). Chicago University Press.

Keppenne, J.-P. (2021). EU fiscal governance on the Member States. In F. Amtenbrink & C. Herrmann (Eds.), *EU law of Economic & Monetary Union* (pp. 813–849). OUP.

Kirchhof, P. (2012). *Deutschland im Schuldensog. Der Weg vom Bürger zurück zum Bürger*. C. H. Beck.

Kortz, H. (1996). *Die Entscheidung über den Übergang in die Endstufe der Wirtschafts- und Währungsunion*. Nomos.

Lasa López, A. (2013). El Impacto de la Nueva Gobernanza Económica Europea en la Estrategia hacia una Política de Empleo Mejorada. *Revista de Derecho Comunitario Europeo, 46*(17), 973–1006.

Lastra, R. M. (2006). *Legal foundations of international monetary stability*. OUP.

Lenaerts, K. (2014). EMU and the European Union's constitutional framework. *European Law Review*, *39*(6), 753–769.

Lipp, E. M., & Reichert, H. (1991). Konfliktfelder auf dem Weg zur Europäischen Währungsunion. In M. Weber (Ed.), *Europa auf dem Weg zur Währungsunion* (pp. 31–48). Wissenschaftliche Buchgesellschaft.

Lüttringhaus, J. D. (2018). *Vertragsfreiheit und ihre Materialisierung im Europäischen Binnenmarkt – Die Verbürgung und Materialisierung unionaler Vertragsfreiheit im Zusammenspiel von EU-Privatrecht, BGB und ZPO*. Mohr Siebeck.

McKinnon, R. L. (1963). Optimum currency areas. *The American Economic Review*, *53*(4), 717–725.

Mortensen, J. (2013). Economic policy coordination in the Economic and Monetary Union. From Maastricht via the SGP to the Fiscal Pact. *CEPS (Centre for European Policy Studies) Working Document*, *381*, 1–23.

Müller, T. (2014). *Wettbewerb und Unionsverfassung. Begründung und Begrenzung des Wettbewerbsprinzips in der europäischen Verfassung*. Mohr Siebeck.

Müller-Armack, A. (1956). Soziale Marktwirtschaft. In E. V. Beckeradt et al. (Eds.), *Handwörterbuch der Sozialwissenschaften* (Vol. 9, pp. 390–392). Fischer/Mohr/Vandenhoeck & Ruprecht.

Müller-Armack, A. (1966). *Wirtschaftsordnung und Wirtschaftspolitik*. Rombach.

Müller-Franken, S. (2014). Das Spannungsverhältnis zwischen Eigenverantwortlichkeit und Solidarität in einer Fiskalunion. In H.-J. Blanke & S. Pilz (Eds.), *Die "Fiskalunion". Voraussetzungen einer Vertiefung der politischen Integration im Währungsraum der Europäischen Union* (pp. 227–244). Mohr Siebeck.

Müller-Graff, P.-C. (1987). Privatrecht und Europäisches Gemeinschaftsrecht. In P.-C. Müller-Graff & M. Zuleeg (Eds.), *Staat und Wirtschaft in der EG* (pp. 17–52). Nomos.

Müller-Graff, P.-C. (2009). Das wirtschaftsverfassungsrechtliche Profil der EU nach Lissabon. In U. Fastenrath & C. Nowak (Eds.), *Der Lissabonner Reformvertrag. Änderungsimpulse in den einzelnen Rechts- und Politikbereichen* (pp. 173–186). Duncker & Humblot.

Mundell, R. A. (1961). A theory of optimum currency areas. *The American Economic Review*, *51*(4), 657–665.

Nettesheim, M. (2012). Der Umbau der europäischen Währungsunion. Politische Aktion und rechtliche Grenzen. In S. Kadelbach (Ed.), *Nach der Finanzkrise. Rechtliche Rahmenbedingungen einer neuen Ordnung* (pp. 31–78). Nomos.

Nettesheim, M. (2020). Das PSPP-Urteil des BVerfG – ein Angriff auf die EU? *Neue Juristische Wochenschrift*, *73*(23), 1631–1634.

Pechstein, M., Nowak, C., & Häde, U. (Eds.). (2017). *Frankfurter Kommentar zu EUV, GRC und AEUV*. Mohr Siebeck.

Pernice, I. (2020). Machtspruch aus Karlsruhe: "Nicht verhältnismäßig? – Nicht verbindlich? – Nicht zu fassen...": Zum PSPP-Urteil des BVerfG vom 5.5.2020. *Europäische Zeitschrift für Wirtschaftsrecht*, *31*(12), 508–519.

Pilz, S. (2012). Ein fiskalpolitischer Pakt als Brücke in die Stabilitätsunion? *Wirtschaftsdienst*, 457–464.

Pilz, S. (2016). *Der Europäische Stabilitätsmechanismus: eine neue Stufe der Integration*. Mohr Siebeck.

Pilz, S., & Dittmann, H. (2012). Perspektiven des Stabilitäts- und Wachstumspakts - Rechtliche und ökonomische Implikationen des Reformpakets "Economic Governance". *Zeitschrift für europarechtliche Studien*, *15*(1), 53–88.

Pingel, I. (Ed.). (2010). *De Rome à Lisbonne. Commentaire. Article par Article des Traités UE et CE* (2nd ed.). Helbing Lichtenhahn.

Ruffert, M. (2009). Zur Leistungsfähigkeit der Wirtschaftsverfassung. *Archiv des Öffentlichen Rechts*, *134*(2), 197–239.

Scharf, D. (2009). Die Kompetenzordnung im Vertrag von Lissabon – Zur Zukunft Europas: Die Europäische Union nach dem Vertrag von Lissabon. *Beiträge zum Europa- und Völkerrecht*,

5–29. Retrieved from https://opendata.unihalle.de/bitstream/1981185920/70942/1/iwr_276_1028.pdf.

Schoenfleisch, C. (2018). *Integration durch Koordinierung? Rechtsfragen der Politikkoordinierung am Beispiel der nationalen Wirtschaftspolitiken*, Mohr Siebeck.

Schorkopf, F. (2012). Finanzkrisen als Herausforderung der internationalen, europäischen und nationalen Rechtsetzung. *Veröffentlichungen der Vereinigung der Deutschen Staatsrechtslehrer, 71*, 113–182.

Schulze-Steinen, M. (1997). *Rechtsfragen zur Wirtschaftsunion: Möglichkeiten der gemeinschaftlichen Gestaltung mitgliedstaatlicher Wirtschaftspolitik nach dem EG-Vertrag*. Nomos.

Schütze, R. (2015). *European Union Law*. CUP.

Schwarze, J. (2007). *Europäisches Wirtschaftsrecht. Grundlagen, Gestaltungsformen, Grenzen*. Nomos.

Schwarze, J., Becker, U., Hatje, A., Schoo, J., & (Eds.). (2019). *EU-Kommentar* (4th ed.).

Seidel, M. (1992). Zur Verfassung der Europäischen Gemeinschaft nach Maastricht. *Europarecht*, 125–144.

Seidel, M. (1994). Verfassungsrechtliche Probleme der Wirtschafts- und Währungsunion. In R. Caesar & H.-E. Scharrer (Eds.), *Maastricht: Königsweg oder Irrweg zur Wirtschafts- und Währungsunion* (pp. 89–106). Europa Union Verlag.

Seidel, M. (1995). Probleme der Währungsunion der Europäischen Union. In J. Baur, R. Jacobs, M. Lieb, & P.-C. Müller-Graff (Eds.), *Festschrift für Ralf Vieregge zum 70. Geburtstag am 06. November 1994* (pp. 739–812). de Gruyter.

Seidel, M. (1998). Rechtliche Aspekte der Entscheidungsverfahren in der WWU. In R. Caesar & H. E. Scharrer (Eds.), *Die Europäische Wirtschafts- und Währungsunion. Regionale und globale Herausforderungen* (pp. 373–394). Europa Union Verlag.

Seidel, M. (2000). Konstitutionelle Schwächen der Währungsunion. *Europarecht*, 861–878.

Siekmann, H. (Ed.) (2013). *EWU: Kommentar zur Europäischen Währungsunion*. Mohr-Siebeck.

Siekmann, H. (2020). Gerichtliche Kontrolle der Käufe von Staatsanleihen durch das Eurosystem: Anmerkungen zum PSPP-Urteil des BVerfG vom 5.5.2020. *Europäische Zeitschrift für Wirtschaftsrecht, 31*(12), 491–500.

Städter, S. (2013). *Noch Hüter der Verfassung: Das Bundesverfassungsgericht und die europäische Integration*. Lucius & Lucius.

Streinz, R. (Ed.). (2018). *EUV/AEUV. Kommentar* (3rd ed.). C.H. Beck.

Tuori, K. (2021). Monetary policy (objectives and instruments). In F. Amtenbrink & C. Herrmann (Eds.), *EU law of Economic & Monetary Union* (pp. 615–698). OUP.

Vedder, C., & Heintschel von Heinegg, W. (Eds.). (2018). *Europäisches Unionsrecht. Handkommentar*. Nomos.

von Arnauld, A. (2013). Unions(ergänzungs)völkerrecht: Zur unions- und verfassungsrechtlichen Einbindung völkerrechtlicher Instrumente differenzierter Integration. In M. Breuer et al. (Eds.), *Der Staat im Recht. Festschrift für Eckart Klein (p. 509-527)*. Duncker & Humblot.

von der Groeben, H., Schwarze, J., & Hatje, A. (Eds.). (2015). *Europäisches Unionsrecht. Kommentar* (7th ed.). Nomos.

Weber, A. (1994). Die Wirtschafts- und Währungsunion nach dem Maastricht-Urteil des BVerfG. *JuristenZeitung*, 53–60.

Wendt, V. (2002). *Die Schaffung der Europäischen Wirtschafts- und Währungsunion: Spill-over und intentionale Entscheidung? Eine Analyse für Deutschland und Frankreich*. Ph.D Thesis, Univ. Passau/Philosophische Fakultät.

Yábar Sterling, A. (2004). La política económica de la Unión Europea. In E. Álvarez Calde & V. Garrido Mayol (Eds.), *Comentarios a la Constitución Europea* (Vol. III, pp. 665–684). Tirant Lo Blanch.

Article 121 [Coordination of Economic Policies]
(ex-Article 99 TEC)

1. Member States shall regard their economic policies as a matter of common concern[11–12] and shall coordinate them within the Council, in accordance with the provisions of Article 120.[8–10]
2. The Council shall, on a recommendation from the Commission, formulate a draft for the broad guidelines of the economic policies of the Member Statesand of the Union,[2, 12–13, 18–22] and shall report its findings to the European Council.[14–16]

    The European Council shall, acting on the basis of the report from the Council, discuss a conclusion[17] on the broad guidelines of the economic policies of the Member States and of the Union.[13]

    On the basis of this conclusion, the Council shall adopt a recommendation setting out these broad guidelines.[18–22] The Council shall inform the European Parliament of its recommendation.[18, 40–41]
3. In order to ensure closer coordination of economic policies and sustained convergence of the economic performances of the Member States, the Council shall, on the basis of reports submitted by the Commission, monitor economic developments in each of the Member States and in the Union as well as the consistency of economic policies with the broad guidelines referred to in paragraph 2, and regularly carry out an overall assessment.[26–30]

    For the purpose of this multilateral surveillance,[23–25] Member States shall forward information to the Commission about important measures taken by them in the field of their economic policy and such other information as they deem necessary.[27]
4. Where it is established, under the procedure referred to in paragraph 3, that the economic policies of a Member State are not consistent with the broad guidelines referred to in paragraph 2 or that they risk jeopardising the proper functioning of economic and monetary union,[36] the Commission may address a warning[34–35] to the Member State concerned. The Council, on a recommendation from the Commission, may address the necessary recommendations to the Member State concerned.[37–39] The Council may, on a proposal from the Commission, decide to make its recommendations public.[32, 38]

    Within the scope of this paragraph, the Council shall act without taking into account the vote of the member of the Council representing the Member State concerned.[32]

    A qualified majority of the other members of the Council shall be defined in accordance with Article 238(3)(a).[32]
5. The President of the Council and the Commission shall report to the European Parliament on the results of multilateral surveillance.[40] The President of the Council may be invited to appear before the competent

committee of the European Parliament if the Council has made its recommendations public.[41]

6. **The European Parliament and the Council, acting by means of regulations in accordance with the ordinary legislative procedure, may adopt detailed rules for the multilateral surveillance procedure referred to in paragraphs 3 and 4.**[43-70]

Contents

1. Aim, Scope and Context 1
2. Coordination of Economic Policies (Paragraph 1) 8
   - 2.1. Obligation of the Member States 9
   - 2.2. Matter of Common Concern 11
3. Coordination Through Broad Economic Policy Guidelines (Paragraph 2) 13
   - 3.1. The Procedure of the Council Recommendation's Adoption 14
     - 3.1.1. Phase I: A Recommendation Submitted by the Commission and Council Draft for Broad Guidelines 15
     - 3.1.2. Phase II: Conclusion of the European Council 17
     - 3.1.3. Phase III: Council Recommendation as a Legal Act Without a Legally Binding Effect 18
   - 3.2. Addressees of the Broad Guidelines 21
4. Multilateral Surveillance (Paragraphs 3 and 4) 23
   - 4.1. Purpose 23
   - 4.2. Monitoring and Assessment Procedure (Paragraph 3) 26
     - 4.2.1. Consequences of the Broad Scope of the Economic Policy Guidelines   26
     - 4.2.2. Reports of the Member States to the Commission 27
     - 4.2.3. Reactions of the Commission and Council 29
5. Sanctions (Paragraph 4) 31
   - 5.1. "Early Warning" of the Commission 34
   - 5.2. Risks Jeopardising the Proper Functioning of EMU 36
   - 5.3. Council Recommendations and Their Publication 37
6. The Role of the European Parliament in the Surveillance Procedure (Paragraph 5) 40
7. Regulations for the Multilateral Surveillance Procedure (Paragraph 6) 43
   - 7.1. Crisis-Driven Reform of the Multilateral Surveillance System Within the SGP Framework Since 2011 47
     - 7.1.1. Surveillance and Coordination Under the Maastricht Treaty: Regulation (EC) No 1466/97 53
     - 7.1.2. The "Six-Pack" 54
     - 7.1.3. The "Two-Pack" 63
     - 7.1.4. The European Fiscal Compact 66
   - 7.2. Assessing the Legislative Reforms 70
   - 7.3. Shifting EMU Reforms Through Union Law Towards International Public Law Instruments 71

List of Cases
References

1. Aim, Scope and Context

As a consequence of the MS retaining competence for their national economic policies (→ Article 119 TFEU para 7), the obligation to coordinate the national economic policies had already been laid down in Articles 6.1 and 103.1 TEEC. The Treaty of Maastricht introduced in Article 99.3 TEC the wording "closer coordination of economic policies and sustained convergence of the economic performances with the Council" with the effect that MS have to regard their economic policies as a matter of common concern. The wording has not been considerably amended since 1993. The failed Constitutional Treaty mentioned in Article I-15 TCE specifically the coordination of economic policies; Article III-179 TCE laid down the rules for the multilateral surveillance procedure. In the deliberations of the Constitutional Convention, the Commission's rights were strengthened in one crucial point: it was given the competence to issue the first warning, which had previously rested with the Council (Article III-179.4 TCE). Hence, the actual version of Article 121 TFEU follows from Article 99 TEC-Maastricht as adapted by the TCE. It contains the **legal basis for the coordination of economic policy between all MS** (inside or outside the euro area) and thus determines and structures the acting of a "*Gesamthandsgemeinschaft*" subject to joint coordination.[1]   1

Article 121 TFEU, as part of the chapter on EU economic policy, is tied to the **basic principles** of Article 119 TFEU already taken up in Article 120 sentence 2 TFEU, which comprise the essential and guiding principles of EMU, such as market openness, freedom of competition, price stability and sound public finances (→ Article 119 TFEU para 12, 40 et seq.; → Article 120 TFEU para 33 et seqq.).[2] They are indirectly pointed to by reference to Article 120 TFEU in the final words of Article 121.1 TFEU. This provision **combines**, via Article 120 TFEU, **the broad guidelines of the economic policies** (in the following: broad guidelines), to be established pursuant to Article 121.2 TFEU, **with the comprehensive, global and long-term objectives enshrined in Article 3 TEU and Article 119 TFEU**.[3] The broad guidelines are at the centre of the economic policy coordination process.   2

A significant **change in the coordination of economic policy** has been brought about by the introduction of a common currency, the euro. While its main objective was initially based on the intention to increase the convergence of economic development in order to achieve economic prosperity in EMU,[4] the objective **after the introduction of the euro** was of a macroeconomic nature. Thus, the   3

---

[1] Hufeld (2021), p. 1532; Ohler, in Siekmann (2013), Article 121 AEUV para 3; Pilz and Dittmann (2012), pp. 60 et seqq.

[2] Cf. Lasa López (2013), p. 992.

[3] Hufeld (2021), p. 1533.

[4] Economic policy coordination was given a formal framework for the first time in 1974 through Council Decision 74/120/EEC *on the attainment of a high degree of convergence of the economic policies of the Member States of the European Economic Community*, O.J. L 63/16 (1974), adopted in the—failed—process of establishing EMU in the 1970s; cf. Mortensen (2013), p. 13; on the history of economic policy coordination, see Smits (1997), pp. 42–43, 46–47 and 53–56.

achievement of the nominal convergence criteria of the Maastricht Treaty was implicitly expected to lead to greater synchronisation of the real economies.[5] The accession of 12 Central and Eastern European States to the EU in 2004 and 2007 brought sharply into focus the idea of convergence. The biggest impact on economic coordination clearly had the debt and economic crisis in the following years.[6]

4   In view of the threat to the cohesion of the euro area in connection with the sovereign debt crisis of some MS since 2010, there has been an intensification of economic policy coordination as a whole.[7] Under the impression of the crisis, the Union introduced a **policy change**, which not least also affected the rules on budgetary surveillance. Initially, three of the five regulations of the so-called Six-Pack as well as the Six-Pack Directive (2011), the Fiscal Compact (2012/2013) and the Two-Pack Regulations of 2013 led to a tightening of the Stability and Growth Pact (SGP) rules on budgetary surveillance (→ Supplement to Title VIII: Fiscal Union para 5). Economic governance is now characterised by a **higher degree of monitoring and enforceability**. More than in the years before the crisis, the MS have the obligation to coordinate their economic policies within the Council.[8] In recent years, budgetary stability has become an overarching principle in European constitutional law and, of course, in national law.[9] As a result, the wording of Article 121 TFEU remained, but the EU economic governance changed considerably.

5   These reforms only slightly affected European primary law (e.g. by inserting a third paragraph in Article 136 TFEU on the establishment of a stability mechanism) and, in addition to secondary legislation, also consist of international treaties concluded outside the Union legal order (Fiscal Compact and TESM). Although the **reforms are a no major step toward "European economic governance"**, they might be resumed as stimulation for an essential further development of EMU that

---

[5] See Council Decision 90/141/EEC *on the attainment of progressive convergence of economic policies and performance during stage one of economic and monetary union*, O.J. L 78/23 (1990), which, itself, was based upon, and expanded the 1974 Convergence Decision. Nicolaysen (1993), p. 32 describes the integration of national economic policies into the stability course at the European level as a "sprawling ensemble of arrangements, regulations and procedures". On the difficulties of coordination when MS have different market views, see Becker (2014), p. 5 who, on pp. 7 et seq., also sets out the necessity of coordination. See also Häde (2009), p. 201.

[6] On the development, cf. Amtenbrink (2008), pp. 910 et seq.; Yábar Sterling (2004), p. 666.; with regard to the Maastricht Treaty, see Martucci, in Pingel (2010), Article 99 CE para 3; Pipkorn (1994), pp. 263 et seqq.

[7] Cf. Schulte, in von der Groeben et al. (2015), Article 121 AEUV para 2; for further information, see Pilz (2016), pp. 42 et seqq.; Przesławska (2016), pp. 133 et seq.

[8] On the legal development in the wake of the crisis, cf. for example Antpöhler (2012), pp. 354 et seq.; Cremer (2016), pp. 267 et seq.; Nettesheim (2012), pp. 33 et seq.

[9] See Lasa López (2013), p. 977; also Gómez Urquijo (2012), p. 524.

puts the Treaty concept of coordination between MS on their economic policies into practice (→ para 71–73).[10]

In addition to Article 121 TFEU, **economic policy coordination is also included and specified in other parts of the Treaty**. In particular, there are provisions on the real economic basis of monetary union, the common market with a common external trade policy and the single market. Avoiding excessive government deficits is the subject of Articles 126 and 136 TFEU. With a view to the smooth functioning of economic and monetary union, they stipulate that special provisions on economic policy coordination apply to MS whose currency is the euro. As a result of the reform of the Treaty of Lisbon, Article 136.1 point (b) TFEU allows for the **elaboration of special broad guidelines for the MS of the euro area**. That provision refers to the procedures described in Articles 121 and 126.1 to 13 TFEU. On the basis of Article 136 TFEU, the **Eurogroup** as an informal group of the euro area's economics and finance ministers (Article 137 TFEU in conjunction with Protocol No 14) is involved in the coordination process on the draft of the broad guidelines for the euro area, so that this draft only needs to be formally adopted by the Council.[11] Article 148.2 TFEU provides for the **employment policy guidelines**. Whilst the broad economic policy guidelines remain **valid for an undetermined duration of time**, the employment guidelines need to be drawn up each year. Along with the broad economic policy guidelines, the employment guidelines are presented as a Council Decision on guidelines for the employment policies of the MS (Part II of the Integrated Guidelines) and provide the basis for country specific recommendations in the respective domains.[12] Together they form the Integrated Guidelines for the economic and employment policies of the MS.[13] The guidelines for employment must be consistent with the broad economic guidelines (Article 148.2 sentence 2 TFEU). 6

In addition to the exclusive and shared competences, the coordination of economic policies is a type of "non regulatory competence" enunciated in Article 2.3 TFEU and concretised with regard to the economic policies of the MS in Article 5.1 TFEU (→ para 10).[14] It is considered, **with regard to its methods and results**, a kind of **open coordination** characterised **by predominantly information and political consultation rather than legally binding agreements** at the intergovernmental level (→ para 8 et seqq.; → Article 120 TFEU para 6). Economic policy coordination aims to bring the policies of the MS closer together 7

---

[10] Herrmann (2012), pp. 92, 95; Pilz and Dittmann (2012), pp. 82 et seq.; see also Amtenbrink (2011), p. 429.

[11] Müller, in Jaeger and Stöger (2021), Article 121 AEUV para 20 (released in 2020).

[12] Most recently on 23 May 2022, the Commission submitted a proposal for a Council Decision on guidelines for employment policies of the MS; see COM(2022) 241 final.

[13] See European Commission, *Europe 2020 Integrated Guidelines* for the economic and employment policies of the Member States (Part I and II); available at https://ec.europa.eu/eu2020/pdf/Brochure%20Integrated%20Guidelines.pdf.

[14] Cf. Schoenfleisch (2018), p. 140 et seqq.: see also Lastra (2006), pp. 249 et seq.; Ohler, in Siekmann (2013), Article 121 AEUV para 6.

without giving the Union hard regulatory powers.[15] For this reason, the relevant Union institutions are mostly left with only politically, but not legally, binding means of action.[16] The MS willingness to follow suit can therefore only be achieved at the European level through the adoption of "framework rules" and "broad guidelines"[17] as well as "peer pressure".[18]

2. Coordination of Economic Policies (Paragraph 1)

8   The term "coordinate" or "coordination" is not defined in the Treaties. Economic policy coordination encompasses an entire spectrum of interactions between the MS and the relevant EU institutions. The **range of methods used for coordination** includes policy dialogue, exchange of information, identification of best practices through peer review and the use of benchmarking methodology, the latter in particular in an assessment of compliance with the so-called expenditure benchmark to fulfil the requirements of the preventive arm of the SGP[19] (→ para 3, 13 et seqq.). With a view to coordinate economic policies of the MS, a mutual exchange of information and communication on common economic measures between the MS, but also the adoption of the recommendation setting out the broad guidelines are required. This process of mutual concertation takes place first within the **Eurogroup** (Article 137 TFEU in conjunction with Article 1 of Protocol No 14),[20] an informal preparatory body for the ECOFIN Council (→ Article 137 TFEU para 11, 20, 29 et seqq.), than within the **ECOFIN**, where these decisions are adopted.[21] Substantial "coordination", however, goes beyond this process: it implies also **concerted actions** in the field of national economic policies, without prejudice to the fact that the provisions of Articles 121.2 to 121.5 TFEU

---

[15] Cf. Herrmann and Rosenfeldt, in Pechstein et al. (2017), Article 121 AEUV para 17 seq.; Lenaerts (2014), p. 755; Braams (2013), p. 181; see also Bavarian Higher Administrative Court (Bay. Verwaltungsgerichtshof), Order of 30 July 2012—Az. 22 ZB 11.1509 para 37.

[16] Herrmann and Rosenfeldt, in Pechstein et al. (2017), Article 121 AEUV para 17 seq.; Ohler, in Siekmann (2013), Article 121 AEUV para 6; Hattenberger, in Schwarze et al. (2019), Article 121 AEUV para 1; Thym (2011), p. 167; see in detail Braams (2013), pp. 237–240.

[17] Cf. Bieber (2011), p. 496; Seidel (1998), p. 169.

[18] Magiera (1998), p. 429; Italianer (1993), p. 77; Schoenfleisch (2018), pp. 20, 64 et seq.

[19] See Hagelstam et al. (2019), p. 27.

[20] The meetings of the Eurogroup are prepared by three preparatory bodies, the Economic and Financial Committee (EFC), the Economic Policy Committee (EPC) and the Eurogroup Working Group (EWG).

[21] Müller, in Jaeger and Stöger (2021), Article 121 AEUV para 19 (released in 2020). In the absence of an explicit provision in the Lisbon Treaty on the competence of ECOFIN in matters of economic policy coordination (see previously Declarations No 3 and 4 annexed to the Final Act of the Maastricht Treaty), its competence can be inferred indirectly from Article 134.1 TFEU on the EFC.

refer to a legally non-binding Council recommendation (Article 288 (5) TFEU).[22] Nonetheless, **any impact of the Union institutions on the economic policies** of the MS, as well as binding harmonisation or unification, is excluded.

2.1. Obligation of the Member States

In the Lisbon Treaty, the obligation to coordinate the national economic policies under the supervision of the Union was included in the general rules on competence in Articles 2.3 and 5.1 TFEU (→ para 7). These general provisions are further specified by Articles 120 TFEU et seqq., in particular Article 121 TFEU. **Coordination pursuant to Article 121 TFEU** is meant as a procedure **at the Union level** (→ Article 120 TFEU para 2, 9). While MS retain competence for their general economic policies as a whole, they must regard them at the same time as a matter of common concern (→ para 11) and submit the basic criteria for the orientation of these policies to the **Council**, which is the **place of coordination**. The Union has, under Article 121.3 TFEU, supervisory powers and, under Article 121.4 TFEU, sanctioning powers.

9

The role of the Union in the area of economic policy is limited to the adoption of coordinating measures.[23] Conducting their economic policies with a view to contributing to the achievement of the objectives set out in Articles 119 and 120 TFEU, Article 121 TFEU comprises a **legal obligation for the MS to participate actively in the coordination process and to implement the recommendation at their own discretion**.[24] So far, MS should regard the **coordination policy** as **a regulatory method which falls within the Union's sphere of competence,** [25] and is therefore also subject to the rules on the exercise of competences, i.e. the principles of subsidiarity and proportionality. The convergence of national economic policies is on a voluntary basis, but the objectives enshrined in Article 3 TEU are binding and to be considered guiding principles (→ Article 120 TFEU para 32 et seqq.). Long-term cooperation is provided for by the normative purpose of Article 121 TFEU. National economic policies that contradict the principles laid

10

---

[22] Cf. also similarly, Müller, in Jaeger and Stöger (2021), Article 121 AEUV para 8 (released in 2020), who speaks of an (ex-ante) coordination of national economic policies.

[23] Hattenberger, in Schwarze et al. (2019), Article 121 AEUV para 5 et seq.; Herrmann and Rosenfeldt, in Pechstein et al. (2017), Article 121 AEUV para 13; Richter, in Geiger et al. (2015), Article 121 TFEU para 2, 4; Rodi, in Vedder and Heintschel von Heinegg (2018), Article 121 AEUV para 4.

[24] Kempen, in Streinz (2018), Article 121 AEUV para 3 and 7; Schulte, in von der Groeben et al. (2015), Article 121 AEUV para 5.

[25] Cf. Schoenfleisch (2018), p. 139 et seqq., 142 et seq.; see also Smits (2005), pp. 430, 439, 450 who, referring to (now) Article 2.2 sentence 1 TFEU, considers the coordination of economic policies as a shared competence. This view was rejected in Case C-370/12, *Pringle* (Opinion of AG Kokott of 26 October 2012) para 93: "[. . .] Article 4 TFEU, which specifies the areas of shared competence, however presupposes in Article 4(1) the existence of a Union competence and does not in Article 4(2) establish any shared competence for economic policy."

down in Articles 119 and 120 TFEU or in the Council's recommendation do not only constitute a breach of the relevant rules or requirements, but they also signify violations of the coordination procedure.[26]

2.2. Matter of Common Concern

11   According to Article 121.1 TFEU, the MS have the obligation to regard their economic policies "as a matter of common concern". This wording illustrates the fundamental economic policy autonomy of the MS, which is subject to two constraints: on the one hand, national economic policy measures become a matter of common concern; on the other hand, the Council is responsible for the task of coordination.[27] As a result of this passage, the duty of coordination has a legal character under Union law.[28] It prevents the pursuit of solely self-serving interests in the framing of economic policy. The MS are bound by a **mutual consideration of the economic policy standpoints and measures**. This includes reciprocal consultations and exchange of information, coordination of the joint achievement of objectives and a ban on harming the interests of the other MS. Thus, the conduct of an MS which considers economic policy a *domaine réservé* of national sovereignty is contrary to the coordination obligation if other MS request economic policy information, make national economic policy processes the subject of a debate on Union level or even make economic policy proposals.[29]

12   The phrase "common concern" triggers various commitments: inter alia, to create the necessary **transparency** toward other MS in pursuit of an MS' own economic policy, to provide **information** on changes in economic policy at an early stage and to **take account of the economic policy of the other MS**.[30] A waiver of the obligation to coordinate is ruled out by the wording of Article 121.1 TFEU, which is formulated in the **imperative**.[31] At least in the event of a clear unwillingness to actively take part in the coordination procedure or of unjustifiable breaches of the broad guidelines on the part of one or more MS, this could authorise the Commission or another MS to initiate, as a last resort, an infringement procedure

---

[26] Kempen, in Streinz (2018), Article 121 AEUV para 7 et seq.; Ohler, in Siekmann (2013), Article 121 AEUV para 10.

[27] Hattenberger, in Schwarze et al. (2019), Article 121 AEUV para 4 et seqq.; Herrmann and Rosenfeldt, in Pechstein et al. (2017), Article 121 AEUV para 13; Rodi, in Vedder and Heintschel von Heinegg (2018), Article 121 AEUV para 2.

[28] Hufeld (2021), p. 1533; Ohler, in Siekmann (2013), Article 121 AEUV para 6.

[29] Kempen, in Streinz (2018), Article 121 AEUV para 6.

[30] Hattenberger, in Schwarze et al. (2019), Article 121 AEUV para 5; Herrmann and Rosenfeldt, in Pechstein et al. (2017), Article 121 AEUV para 14; Kempen, in Streinz (2018), Article 121 AEUV para 6; Rodi, in Vedder and Heintschel von Heinegg (2018), Article 121 AEUV para 7.

[31] Hufeld (2021), p. 1536.

(Articles 258 and 259 TFEU).[32] However, this involves only the duty to make every effort to meet the broad guidelines within the national margin of discretion[33] and does not apply to the budgetary behaviour of the MS (Article 126.10 TFEU). Apart from the view that the coordination obligation of the MS consists in the exchange of information and in the shaping of the baselines for their economic policies, there is also the view that Article 121 TFEU implies a first approach towards a mixed economic policy governance concept at the EU level.

3. Coordination Through Broad Economic Policy Guidelines (Paragraph 2)

Article 121.2 TFEU sets out the **procedure for the coordination of economic policies** by means of broad guidelines for the economic policies of the MS. It does not indicate any form, content or schedule with regard to the coordination or its results, namely the broad guidelines, with the consequence that this is left to the political discretion of the Union institutions. The same applies to the choice of methods and tools on which the coordination measures are based.[34] The term "broad guidelines" is not defined in primary law.[35] Systematically, little can be concluded about its use, in particular in view of the different wording in other Treaty versions (French: *grandes orientations*; German: *Leitlinien*).[36] The "broad guidelines" merely constitute the basic outlines, the orientation framework for economic policy action by the MS. The decisive factor is the **macroeconomic orientation of the Union as a whole**, as outlined by the broad guidelines, and, therefore, they include Union-wide as well as country-specific targets.[37] The content of the guidelines is marked by a functional conflict between the need for country-specific flexibility—namely, the necessary openness in terms of content—and their function as a yardstick for the peer review (multilateral surveillance) according to Article 121.3 to Article 121.5 TFEU, which requires clear assessment standards. In view of this conflict, **economic policy coordination has in practice developed into a preventive budgetary control**. This has led to a loss of focus on economic policy convergence.[38] The MS have a margin of discretion in

13

---

[32] Frenz and Ehlenz (2010), p. 331; Häde, in Calliess and Ruffert (2022), Article 121 AEUV para 15; Kempen, in Streinz (2018), Article 121 AEUV para 8 having regard to the absence of a general exclusion as provided for in Article 126.10 TFEU; Müller, in Jaeger and Stöger (2021), Article 121 AEUV para 12 (released in 2020); Rodi, in Vedder and Heintschel von Heinegg (2018), Article 121 para 8.

[33] Müller, in Jaeger and Stöger (2021), Article 121 AEUV para 12 (released in 2020).

[34] Schulte, in von der Groeben et al. (2015), Article 121 AEUV para 12.

[35] Cf. Amtenbrink (2008), pp. 915 et seq., who describes two different interpretive approaches to the term "broad guidelines".

[36] This view is shared by Herrmann and Rosenfeldt, in Pechstein et al. (2017), Article 121 AEUV para 26.

[37] Müller, in Jaeger and Stöger (2021), Article 121 AEUV para 11 (released in 2020).

[38] Schoenfleisch (2018), p. 251.

choosing the measures of action to implement the broad guidelines. Detailed requirements without a national scope for action and adjustment in the economies of the MS would be inadmissible unless they are oriented towards the economy as a whole.[39] Against this background, the concept of broad guidelines is based on the Union's objectives. In practice, they aim at **convergence and price stability** and therefore **budgetary discipline,** thus underpinning the importance of the principles laid down in Article 3.3 (1) TEU and highlighted in Article 120 sentence 1 TFEU (→ Article 119 TFEU para 15 et seqq.).

3.1. The Procedure of the Council Recommendation's Adoption

14 As a crucial outcome of that coordination, the broad economic policy guidelines are set out by a Council recommendation (Article 121.2 sentence 3 TFEU) in order to achieve the objectives laid down in Article 120 TFEU. The procedure for the adoption of the Council recommendation is only regulated in its main features; for example, there is no provision on the periodicity of the recommendation. Moreover, it is highly complex as it is supplemented by the provisions on the European Semester for economic policy coordination (→ para 57).[40] The Council's recommendation is **built up in three phases.**

3.1.1. Phase I: A Recommendation Submitted by the Commission and Council Draft for Broad Guidelines

15 According to Article 121.2 (1) TFEU, the procedure begins with **a "recommendation" submitted by the Commission to the Council**. The Commission, already in this procedural section, plays an important role since it drafts the first version of the broad economic guidelines eventually adopted as a Council "recommendation". Also in this non-binding preparatory measure,[41] within the area of European economic policy, the Commission "promotes the general interest of the Union", "[ensures] the application [in the sense of applicability] of the Treaties" (Article 17.1 sentences 1 and 2 TEU) and exercises a coordinating function (Article 17.1 sentence 4 TEU). Since the Treaty of Lisbon, it has fulfilled these tasks in the same context again when it performs a monitoring and warning function within the preventive framework under Article 121.4 TFEU, which is no longer the sole responsibility of the Council (→ para 31 et seqq.). Together with the Council, the Commission ensures that the principles set out in Article 119.3 TFEU, namely the "golden rule" of a balanced budget ("sound public finances"), are implemented and

---

[39] Hattenberger, in Schwarze et al. (2019), Article 121 AEUV para 12; Herrmann and Rosenfeldt, in Pechstein et al. (2017), Article 121 AEUV para 27; Martucci, in Pingel (2010), Article 99 CE para 6; Ohler, in Siekmann (2013), Article 121 AEUV para 11.

[40] Müller, in Jaeger and Stöger (2021), Article 121 AEUV para 13 (released in 2020).

[41] Hattenberger, in Schwarze et al. (2019), Article 121 AEUV para 8.

observed.[42] Against this background, its task in the procedure to submit an initial outline to the Council may also have a dissuasive effect with regard to MS that underestimate the **political binding effect and psychological importance** of the final recommendation (→ para 37).[43]

On this basis, the **Council (ECOFIN)**, following preparations carried out by the Eurogroup (→ para 8) and the COREPER (Article 240 TFEU) and with the technical assistance of the Economic and Financial Committee (Articles 134.1 and 134.2 third indent TFEU), **formulates a draft** for the broad guidelines. This draft is **adopted by a qualified majority** in accordance with Article 16.3 TEU.[44] Deviations from the Commission's recommendation are conceivable and possible but do not require unanimity as the Council does not act on a *proposal* from the Commission (Article 293.1 TFEU).[45] In practice, both the Commission and the Council require input from the MS for this type of **soft coordination**. Both sides rely on the principle of loyal cooperation under Article 4.3 TEU.[46]

16

3.1.2. Phase II: Conclusion of the European Council

According to Article 121.2 (2) TFEU, which follows Article 103.2 TEC-Maastricht, the European Council, in a second phase, shall "discuss" a conclusion on the upcoming broad guidelines to "define the general political directions and priorities" for the development of the Union (Article 15.1 sentence 1 TEU). This wording intends to avoid even the perception of a European Council's power to take a decision. Issuing conclusions is not part of its competence to take legally binding decisions under Article 15.4 TEU (→ Article 15 TEU para 49 et seq.).[47] However, the debate on the draft submitted by the Council is part of its duty to issue **political guidance**. Therefore, the **Council shall "report its findings" to the European Council**, which means all insights on the preparation, debates and preliminary results concerning the broad guidelines in order to make sure that they are in line with the common policy objectives defined by this high-ranking institution. In its **conclusion**, the European Council then refers to the findings reported by the Council, **without formally adopting as such the draft text**.[48] Once the European Council has endorsed the draft for the broad guidelines, the report, which is remitted to the Council, forms the basis for adopting the recommendation. The involvement of the European Council in the adoption procedure provides "political

17

---

[42] Borger and Cuyvers (2012), p. 382.
[43] Clerc and Kauffmann (2011), p. 594.
[44] Cf. Hattenberger, in Schwarze et al. (2019), Article 121 AEUV para 8 et seq.
[45] Bandilla, in Grabitz et al. (2021), Article 121 AEUV para 10 (released in 2021).
[46] Ohler, in Siekmann (2013), Article 121 AEUV para 13; Richter, in Geiger et al. (2015), Article 121 TFEU para 3.
[47] With regard to the genesis of Article 15.4 TFEU, see Bandilla, in Grabitz et al. (2021), Article 121 AEUV para 17 (released in 2021).
[48] Cf. Bandilla, in Grabitz et al. (2021), Article 121 AEUV para 11 (released in 2021); Häde, in Calliess and Ruffert (2022), Article 121 AEUV para 4.

authority" and also shall ensure a true and effective implementation of the recommendation on the basis of broad political consensus among all MS.[49]

3.1.3. Phase III: Council Recommendation as a Legal Act Without a Legally Binding Effect

18 On the basis of the conclusion of the European Council and without further involvement of the Commission, the **Council adopts a recommendation** setting out the broad guidelines.[50] They are **not legally binding** and therefore not enforceable (Article 288 (5) TFEU; → para 7, 17)[51] but may be considered European soft law.[52] Another consequence of their legal nature is that the European Parliament has merely a right to be informed by the Council of that recommendation (Article 121.2 (3) sentence 2 TFEU; → para 40 et seq.; → Article 120 TFEU para 11). This type of legal action reveals the weak, only coordinating, competence of the Union in the area of economic policy, but through its political bindingness, it also marks the **relevance of soft law** within EU policy.[53] The involvement of the European Council contributes significantly to the political binding effect of the broad guidelines (→ para 17; → Article 120 TFEU para 41),[54] which turns the recommendation into an **instrument for influencing the economic choices of the MS**, including the necessary structural reforms.[55] Hence, this "soft law" may have **"hard" consequences** (Article 121.4 TFEU).[56]

19 The wording of paragraph 2 leaves open the possibility that the Council may still decide on substantive amendments or clarifications, but these changes are likely to be limited to technical or editorial issues. In accordance with Article 16.3 TEU, the decision on the adoption is taken by a qualified majority of the Council members. According to Article 139.4 sentence 1 and Article 139.2 point (a) TFEU, the voting rights of the members of the Council who represent MS with a derogation are suspended when adopting parts of the broad guidelines that concern the **euro**

---

[49] Cf. Kempen, in Streinz (2018), Article 121 AEUV para 10; Müller, in Jaeger and Stöger (2021), Article 121 AEUV para 21 (released in 2020).

[50] Richter, in Geiger et al. (2015), Article 121 TFEU para 3.

[51] Ohler in Siekmann (2013), Article 121 AEUV para 13; Häde, in Calliess and Ruffert (2022), Article 121 AEUV para 5; Kempen, in Streinz (2018), Article 121 AEUV para 11; Hattenberger, in Schwarze et al. (2019), Article 121 AEUV para 11.

[52] Martucci, in Pingel (2010), Article 99 CE para 2 underlines the "soft-law" character of economic coordination. On the different forms of EU action, especially soft law, see also Ząbkowicz (2015), p. 106.

[53] Schoenfleisch (2018), p. 17 et seqq., 142, 155 et seqq.

[54] Hattenberger, in Schwarze et al. (2019), Article 121 AEUV para 10; Bandilla, in Grabitz et al. (2021), Article 121 AEUV para 9, 13 (released in 2021); Ohler, in Siekmann (2013), Article 121 AEUV para 13; Häde, in Calliess and Ruffert (2022), Article 121 AEUV para 4; Richter, in Geiger et al. (2015), Article 121 TFEU para 3, 8.

[55] Hufeld (2021), p. 1537.

[56] Richter, in Geiger et al. (2015), Article 121 TFEU para 3; Schütze (2015), p. 802.

area.[57] If necessary, the Union may review and amend an already adopted recommendation.[58] The broad guidelines thus drawn up define the common objectives of the MS and the EU in the field of economic policy enshrined in Articles 119.1 and 120 TFEU. Regardless of the nature of the Council recommendation as soft law, they provide the **framework for multilevel economic governance within the Union**.[59]

The broad guidelines have been strengthened since 1999 by the inclusion of **country-specific analyses with conclusions** and since 2005 by an increased focus on economic reforms and on increasing growth and employment in the Union and the MS within the framework of the Lisbon Strategy. Since then, under Article 121.2 TFEU and Regulation (EU) No 1176/2011 (in the case of the implementation of national stability and convergence programmes as part of multilateral surveillance also based on Council Regulation (EC) No 1466/97[60] as amended by No 1175/2011[61]), the Council gives a recommendation on the national reform programme of each MS and delivers an opinion on the country-specific convergence programme.[62] The latest Council Recommendation (EU) No 2015/1184 on broad guidelines for the economic policies of the MS and of the EU was adopted by the Council on 14 July 2015.[63] It refers to the "Europe 2020" strategy.[64] Generally, a recommendation shall be valid for an indefinite period of time (→ para 6). Meanwhile, contents partly overlapping with the broad guidelines are communicated within the overarching framework of the cyclical European Semester (country reports). 20

3.2. Addressees of the Broad Guidelines

The broad guidelines are **addressed to all MS and the Union**, while for those who have introduced the euro currency, Article 136 TFEU or enacted secondary legislation thereof may contain *further* obligations within a kind of enhanced cooperation in coordinating national economic policies.[65] In addition to the European Council, whose position has been further strengthened under the reformed macroeconomic 21

---

[57] In case the European Council accepts the Council's draft for the broad guidelines, its conclusion is worded in a brief manner: "The European Council endorses the draft Council recommendation on the economic policy of the euro area."
[58] Ohler, in Siekmann (2013), Article 121 AEUV para 13–14.
[59] Häde, in Calliess and Ruffert (2022), Article 121 AEUV para 5.
[60] O.J. L 209/1 (1997).
[61] O.J. L 306/12 (2011).
[62] See e.g. the Council Recommendations of 14 July 2015, O.J. L 192/1 et seqq. (2015).
[63] O.J. L 192/27 (2015). Regarding the euro area, see Council Recommendation *on the implementation of the broad guidelines for the economic policies of the Member States whose currency is the euro*, O.J. L 272/98 (2015).
[64] COM(2010) 2020 final.
[65] Cf. Müller, in Jaeger and Stöger (2021), Article 121 AEUV para 4, 9 (released in 2020).

peer review procedure (→ para 47 et seqq.), the Council and the Commission participate in the adoption of the recommendation. Pursuant to Article 134.2, second and third indent, TFEU, also the Economic and Financial Committee, a main discussant of the Commission, takes part in this procedure.[66]

22   Since the broad guidelines are also addressed to the Union, they can be applied to the **ESCB/ECB** as an institution of the Union.[67] This view is also supported by the double mandate given to the ESCB/ECB: maintaining price stability and supporting the general economic policies in the Union (Article 127.1 sentence 2 TFEU). The ECB/ESCB is even involved in the formulation of the broad guidelines within the framework of the preparatory committees (Economic and Financial Committee, Economic Policy Committee). In this context, the functional independence of the ESCB/ECB must be respected. However, as all the other addressees, the ECB/ESCB is only obliged to take the broad guidelines into account but is not bound by them. Nevertheless, the Union has so far given priority to the independence of the ECB/ESCB.[68] The broad guidelines therefore do not give any orientation for monetary policy.

4. Multilateral Surveillance (Paragraphs 3 and 4)

4.1. Purpose

23   Multilateral surveillance serves the economic policy objectives of the Union by establishing a two-stage procedure to ensure compliance with the broad guidelines and sound budgetary economic development in the MS (→ Article 120 TFEU para 11 et seqq.).[69] Since the primary law regulations were considered insufficient to guarantee the stability of the European single currency, on the occasion of the Amsterdam Treaty, they were **supplemented by the secondary law rules of the SGP**.[70] This Pact was created to act as a guardian of European public finances and not as a mechanism to foster European economic growth. According to paragraphs 3 through 6 of Article 121 TFEU, the purpose of multilateral surveillance is to combine economic policy coordination (Article 121.2 TFEU) with the effective enforcement of the prohibition of excessive deficits (→ Article 126 TFEU para 7 et seqq.). This is why multilateral surveillance is intended to ensure that the economic policies of the MS converge as permanently as possible, thereby guaranteeing the conditions for the existence of the EU not only as a convergence criterion upon

---

[66] Cf. Kempen, in Streinz (2018), Article 121 AEUV para 9; Martucci, in Pingel (2010), Article 99 CE para 4.
[67] Cf. Bandilla, in Grabitz et al. (2021), Article 121 AEUV para 22 (released in 2021).
[68] Müller, in Jaeger and Stöger (2021), Article 121 AEUV para 27 (released in 2020).
[69] Herrmann and Rosenfeldt, in Pechstein et al. (2017), Article 121 AEUV para 32.
[70] Cf. Pilz and Dittmann (2011), p. 150; on the legal situation before the SGP and further EU secondary legislation on economic and budgetary surveillance mechanisms, see Hentschelmann (2009), p. 287.

accession to the EU under Article 140 TFEU but also consistently and permanently.[71]

Economic policy convergence is **intended to achieve the uniformity of monetary policy** while also taking into account the different macroeconomic situations of the individual MS. They do not have to submit to a comprehensive economic policy control by the Union institutions; they only need to be monitored with regard to the aforementioned coordination and convergence. The closer coordination of economic policy thus automatically concerns national budgetary policy since the budgetary, economic and employment policies of the MS are closely intertwined and the European Semester (→ para 57) provides for their simultaneous review every year for a period of 6 months.[72]   24

A responsible budgetary policy is necessary and suitable to keep deficits and debt levels under control in the long term. The stabilisation of the single monetary policy is achieved through the instrument of a stable budget, which in turn is spelt out in the convergence criterion according to Article 140.1 TFEU and in the prohibition of excessive government deficits (Article 126 TFEU). Conversely, an unstable budgetary policy can be assumed if unsustainable government deficits or debt levels arise.[73] In the case of instability, a breach of **Article 123 TFEU** is likely to occur. According to this provision, overdraft or other credit facilities with the ECB or the central banks of the MS are ruled out. Similarly, Article 125 TFEU excludes the liability of the Union or other MS for the debts incurred by another MS. In order to avoid an excessive deficit under Article 126 TFEU and, as a result, measures of financial assistance or assumptions of liability ruled out by Articles 123 and 125 TFEU, the implementation of a system of preventive budgetary surveillance is required.[74]   25

4.2. Monitoring and Assessment Procedure (Paragraph 3)

4.2.1. Consequences of the Broad Scope of the Economic Policy Guidelines

The openness of the broad guidelines and their need to be filled in politically at the national level require the Commission and the Council to monitor, in a **staged procedure**, the economic developments in each of the MS and in the Union and to assess the consistency of national economic policies with the broad guidelines.   26

---

[71] Hattenberger, in Schwarze et al. (2019), Article 121 AEUV para 22; Ohler, in Siekmann (2013), Article 121 AEUV para 15.

[72] Herrmann and Rosenfeldt, in Pechstein et al. (2017), Article 121 AEUV para 34.

[73] See Lastra (2006), p. 252; Ohler, in Siekmann (2013), Article 121 AEUV para 15.

[74] Ohler, in Siekmann (2013), Article 121 AEUV para. 15.

4.2.2. Reports of the Member States to the Commission

27 In order to pursue coordinated economic policies and their objectives, MS shall forward to the Commission written **reports** "about important measures taken by them in the field of their economic policy and such other information as they deem necessary".[75] The information on economic and employment policies includes a medium-term macroeconomic scenario, national targets for growth and employment, the main obstacles to growth and short-term measures for growth-enhancing initiatives. The surveillance procedure was significantly concretised by Regulation (EC) No 1466/97, which is part of the SGP.[76] It was then **coordinated with the other economic policy tools** within the framework of the secondary legislation anchoring the "European Semester for economic policy coordination" according to Article 2-a of Regulation (EU) No 1175/2011 amending Council Regulation (EC) No 1466/97 on the strengthening of the surveillance of budgetary positions and the surveillance and coordination of economic policies (→ para 30 et seqq., 42).[77]

28 A distinction is also made here between MS whose currency is the euro and MS "with a derogation". Euro area MS submit **stability programmes** (Article 3 of Regulation 1466/97), while non-euro area MS submit **convergence programmes** (Article 7 of Regulation 1466/97). For all MS these programmes include medium-term budgetary objectives, the main assumptions about economic developments, a description of budgetary and economic policies and a cost-benefit analysis of how changes in assumptions may affect the budgetary and debt position. The information is crucial in terms of a stable national budgetary policy.[78] However, the nature and extent of the information are ultimately left to the discretion of the MS. Article 121.3 (2) TFEU provides for a **regular reporting system** but leaves the question of the exact time frame open. Articles 4 and 8 in conjunction with Article 11 of Regulation (EC) No 1466/97, set **30 April** as the ultimate annual deadline. The MS regularly publish their stability and convergence programmes (Articles 4.2 and 8.2 of Regulation (EC) No 1466/97).[79] In accordance with the principles of loyal cooperation, the MS must ensure the correctness and completeness of their reports; otherwise, they risk infringement proceedings under Article 258 TFEU.[80]

---

[75] See Hattenberger, in Schwarze et al. (2019), Article 121 AEUV para 31, for a critique of this wording.

[76] See Martucci, in Pingel (2010), Article 99 CE para 6.

[77] O.J. L 306/12 (2011); cf. Blanke (2012), pp. 83 et seqq.; Herrmann and Rosenfeldt, in Pechstein et al. (2017), Article 121 AEUV para 3, 36; for more details, see Pilz and Dittmann (2012), pp. 79 et seq.

[78] Clerc and Kauffmann (2011), p. 591; Häde, in Calliess and Ruffert (2022), Article 121 AEUV para 19 et seqq., 21 et seqq.; Bandilla in Grabitz et al. (2021), Article 121 AEUV para 24 et seqq. (released in 2021); Ohler, in Siekmann (2013), Article 121 AEUV para 15.

[79] Cf. Pilz and Dittmann (2012), p. 79.

[80] Cf. Ohler, in Siekmann (2013), Article 121 AEUV para 18.

4.2.3. Reactions of the Commission and Council

Based on the national reports, the **Commission** shall prepare an **independent** 29
analysis and inform the Council thereof in accordance with Article 121.3 TFEU.
Grounded in the Commission's reports, the Council shall monitor the economic
developments in each MS and in the Union as well as the consistency of economic
policies with the broad guidelines referred to in paragraph 2 and shall regularly
carry out an overall assessment.[81] The wording suggests an obligation of the
Council to **review the developments** of and (serious) divergences from the
broad guidelines in a kind of self-control exercised vis-à-vis the Union, which at
the same time extends to all MS, whether or not they participate in the final stage of
EMU.[82]

The broad guidelines are the yardstick for surveillance and overall assessment. 30
This results from a conclusion drawn from paragraph 4, which refers to paragraphs 3
and 2 and, alternatively, to the "risk jeopardising the proper functioning of economic and monetary union". Moreover, the assessment and surveillance procedure
is not subject to any content or time requirements. The **review of national economic policies** in the light of the broad guidelines, regulated with regard to their
coming into being in paragraph 2, **is conducted in an ex post control**. This shall
generate political pressure to make MS pay attention to and take seriously the
economic policy coordination activities.[83] However, the multilateral surveillance
procedure has been integrated into the **European Semester** for economic policy
coordination related to **ex ante coordination** and has thus been further elaborated
in secondary legislation by the legislative package on economic governance.
Article 2-a.1 of Regulation (EU) No 1175/2011 sets forth that "[i]n order to ensure
closer coordination of economic policies and sustained convergence of the economic performance of the Member States, the Council shall conduct multilateral
surveillance as an integral part of the European Semester in accordance with the
objectives and requirements set out in the Treaty on the Functioning of the
European Union [...]".[84]

5. Sanctions (Paragraph 4)

Paragraphs 2 through 4 of Article 121 TFEU urge the MS to understand the non- 31
binding nature of a recommendation as a (political) mandate to commit themselves.

---

[81] For more details on the role of the Commission, see Ząbkowicz (2015), pp. 97 et seq.; cf. also Heise (2015), pp. 166 et seq.

[82] Müller, in Jaeger and Stöger (2021), Article 121 AEUV para 28 (released in 2020).

[83] Cf. on this view Schulte, in von der Groeben et al. (2015), Article 121 AEUV para 42; Hattenberger, in Schwarze et al. (2019), Article 121 AEUV para 21; Ohler, in Siekmann (2013), Article 121 AEUV para 19.

[84] O.J. L 306/12 (2011).

Therefore, deficiencies in their implementation or non-observance cannot trigger infringement proceedings according to Articles 258 and 259 TFEU.[85] Article 121.4 TFEU provides for a **three-tier system of sanctions** (→ para 34 et seqq.). It ties in with the surveillance procedure under paragraph 3. The condition for this is that the economic policy of an MS is not consistent with the broad guidelines referred to in paragraph 2 or threatens to jeopardise the proper functioning of the EMU. In the latter case, it is irrelevant whether the MS has acted contrary to the broad guidelines or other Union law.

32   In the aforementioned constellations, the **Commission**, in a first step, **may address an early warning** to an MS if its economic policy is not consistent with the broad guidelines or it risks jeopardising the proper functioning of economic and monetary union (Article 121.4 sentence 1 TFEU) (→ para 34–35). In a second step, "the Council, on a recommendation from the Commission, may address the necessary recommendations to the Member State concerned" (Article 121.4 sentence 2 TFEU).[86] Given that the Council can act **without taking into account the vote of the member representing the MS concerned** (Article 121.4 (2) TFEU), its position so far is strong. On the occasion of voting for a recommendation, a qualified majority of the other members of the Council shall be defined in accordance with Article 238.3 point (a) TFEU (Article 121.4 (3) TFEU). This scheme involves a **special rule for the calculation of the qualified majority** based solely on the members of the Council (55% of the members) and the populations (65% of the population of these States) of the *participating* MS, i.e. without taking into account the MS concerned. Applying the same procedural rules, in a third step and on a proposal from the Commission, the Council may decide to make its recommendations public in order to increase or maintain public pressure on the country (Article 121.4 sentence 3 TFEU; → para 37–39).[87] The EU institutions' response options are **discretionary decisions**.[88]

33   In principle, according to the TFEU, the economic policies of the MS are subject to an efficient assessment by the financial markets, and unsound economic policies are to be sanctioned by an increase in financing costs in order to effect a redirection.

---

[85] Bandilla, in Grabitz et al. (2021), Article 121 AEUV para 13 (released in 2021); Frenz and Ehlenz (2010), p. 331; Hattenberger, in Schwarze et al. (2019), Article 121 AEUV para 11.

[86] Bandilla, in Grabitz et al. (2021), Article 121 AEUV para 12 et seqq. (released in 2021); Herrmann and Rosenfeldt, in Pechstein et al. (2017), Article 121 AEUV para 23.

[87] Cf. Amtenbrink (2011), p. 434; Borger and Cuyvers (2012), p. 382; Paz Ferreira, in Porto and Anastácio (2012), Article 121 TFUE p. 561; Schoenfleisch (2018), pp. 76 et seq. ("naming and shaming").

[88] Cf. Häde, in Calliess and Ruffert (2022), Article 121 AEUV para 13; Herrmann and Rosenfeldt, in Pechstein et al. (2017), Article 121 AEUV para 40; Kempen, in Streinz (2018) Article 121 AEUV para 20; Ohler, in Siekmann (2013), Article 121 AEUV para 21; Müller, in Jaeger and Stöger (2021), Article 121 AEUV para 34 et seq. (released in 2020).

But the legal framework looks much more nuanced and "soft".[89] Neither the Commission's warnings nor the Council's recommendations constitute legally binding measures vis-à-vis the MS. But pursuant to Article 288 (5) TFEU, the recommendations are regarded as legal acts.[90] This "soft" design of possible sanctions relies more on **political and public pressure** than on hard enforcement mechanisms.[91] The "political nature" of the multilateral surveillance system is made clear not least through the **intergovernmental structure of the surveillance procedure**.[92] According to some experts, under the conclusive provisions of Articles 121.3 and 121.4 TFEU, the introduction of tougher sanctions are precluded by the rules of this system.[93] Apart from this, however, also the sanctions are at the discretion of the respective organs.[94]

5.1. "Early Warning" of the Commission

Before the entry into force of the Lisbon Treaty, only the Council could react to deviations of national economic policy from the broad guidelines.[95] Article 121.4 (1) sentence 1 TFEU authorises the Commission to address a warning to such an MS.[96] It follows from the wording "may" that the warning is not a prerequisite for the following procedure. The warning triggers the **early warning mechanism** according to Article 6.2 of Regulation (EU) 1175/2011 in conjunction with Article 121.4 TFEU. This early warning mechanism has become even more important since the entry into force of the Six-Pack as it can now also trigger further steps, such as **financial sanctions** (→ para 61). If the Commission fails to issue a warning, the Council or an MS may request it under Article 135 TFEU to make a recommendation or a proposal, as appropriate. The Commission is obliged to examine this request and submit its conclusions to the Council without delay.

34

The **legal nature of the warning** is unclear. Following Article 6.2 and Article 10.2 of Regulation (EC) No 1466/97 (in the original version), which

35

---

[89] Nettesheim (2012), p. 47.

[90] Hattenberger, in Schwarze et al. (2019), Article 121 AEUV para 8; Hufeld (2021), p. 1538.

[91] Hattenberger, in Schwarze et al. (2019), Article 121 AEUV para 38; Herrmann and Rosenfeldt, in Pechstein et al. (2017), Article 121 AEUV para 40; Lenaerts (2014), p. 755; Rodi, in Vedder and Heintschel von Heinegg (2018), Article 121 AEUV para 12 seqq.; Clerc and Kauffmann (2011), p. 594, criticise the Commission's still too slow intervention in the sanctions procedure.

[92] Martucci, in Pingel (2010), Article 99 CE para 7.

[93] Herrmann and Rosenfeldt, in Pechstein et al. (2017), Article 121 AEUV para 40; Ohler, in: Siekmann (2016) Article 121 AEUV para 23.

[94] Cf. Häde, in Calliess and Ruffert (2022), Article 121 AEUV para 13; Herrmann and Rosenfeldt, in Pechstein et al. (2017), Article 121 AEUV para 40; Kempen, in: Streinz (2018) Article 121 AEUV para 20; Ohler, in Siekmann, (2013), Article 121 AEUV para 21.

[95] Häde, in Calliess and Ruffert (2022), Article 121 AEUV para 19; Bandilla, in Grabitz et al. (2021), Article 121 AEUV para 27 (released in 2021).

[96] Paz Ferreira, in Porto and Anastácio (2012), Article 121 TFUE p. 561.

provided for a "recommendation" by the Council, it is assumed that the warning issued by the Commission under Article 121.4 (1) TFEU also constitutes a recommendation to the MS concerned to "take the necessary measures".[97] However, within Article 121 TFEU, other monitoring instruments are explicitly marked as recommendations. Therefore, the Commission's warning is understood by other scholars as a declaration of knowledge and not of intent.[98] In any case, the warning does not have a legally binding meaning with regard to the soft sanction regime (→ para 33).[99] Its function is also regarded as sending an explicit signal to an MS that its national budgetary policy is outside the reference values of Article 126 TFEU.[100] Moreover, without a specific occasion of deviations from the adjustment path or of expenditure developments, the Commission, in a **"permanent dialogue"** with the MS, is entitled to "carry out missions for the purpose of the assessment of the economic situation" in all MS "and the identification of any risks or difficulties" in complying with the objectives of Regulation 1175/2011 (Article 11.1 of Regulation 1175/2011).

5.2. Risks Jeopardising the Proper Functioning of EMU

36   Besides inconsistency with the broad guidelines, also the situation that MS "risk jeopardising the proper functioning of economic and monetary union" can trigger an early warning of the Commission. This criterion can be substantiated by recourse to secondary law. Regulations (EU) No 1175/2011 and No 1176/2011 contain references to such risks, namely a **significant deviation from the path towards the medium-term budgetary objective** (Article 10.2 (1) in conjunction with Article 9.1 (3) of Regulation 1175/2011) and **an excessive macroeconomic imbalance** (Article 1 in conjunction with Articles 7 et seqq. of Regulation 1176/2011). For the assessment of whether the deviation is significant, Article 6.3 of Regulation 1175/2011 sets out the criteria. "Excessive imbalances" means severe imbalances, including imbalances that jeopardise or risk jeopardising the proper functioning of the economic and monetary union (Article 2.2 of Regulation 1176/2011). The Council and the Commission have a wide margin of appreciation in determining if a threat to the "proper functioning of the economic and monetary union" exists or

---

[97] Bandilla, in Grabitz et al. (2021), Article 121 AEUV para 28 (released in 2021); Müller, in Jaeger and Stöger (2021), Article 121 AEUV para 33 (released in 2020).

[98] Herrmann and Rosenfeldt, in Pechstein et al. (2017), Article 121 AEUV para 41; Ohler, in Siekmann (2013) Article 121 AEUV para 21.

[99] Müller, in Jaeger and Stöger (2021), Article 121 AEUV para 33 (released in 2020).

[100] Cf. Ohler, in Siekmann (2013), Article 121 AEUV para 21; Clerc and Kauffmann (2011), p. 594.

Article 121 [Coordination of Economic Policies]

is imminent.[101] Slight divergences between the Council and the Commission in the assessment of the respective economic situation of an MS are possible and deemed harmless.[102]

5.3. Council Recommendations and Their Publication

Since the Lisbon Treaty, the Commission has initiated a further procedure by means of a recommendation submitted to the Council. On the basis of this recommendation, it is possible for the Council to "address the necessary recommendations" to an MS if, in the course of the procedure according to paragraph 3, an inconsistency with the broad guidelines or a risk jeopardising the proper functioning of the EMU is identified. To that end, the Council shall, within 1 month of the date of adoption of the Commission's warning, "examine the situation and adopt a recommendation for the necessary policy measures" (Article 6.2 (2) or Article 10.2 (1) sentence 1 of Regulation 1175/2011). In accordance with the possible prior early warning of the Commission, the content of the Council recommendation can denounce the inconsistency with or the deviation from the broad guidelines and at the same time call on the MS to **dispel these discrepancies**. But the Council cannot adopt legally binding measures to overcome the situation. To date, the most significant case of an application of ex-Article 99 TEC has been the **Council Recommendation of 12 February 2001 with a view to ending the inconsistency with the broad guidelines of the economic policies in Ireland.**[103] The discretion of the Council as the last instance in the preventive procedure for multilateral surveillance to address the necessary recommendations to the MS concerned (→ para 29–30) is reduced to zero if otherwise the economic policy objectives are not met in a serious and evident manner.[104] The recommendation shall set a deadline of no more than 5 months for addressing the deviation. The deadline shall be reduced to three months if the Commission, in its warning, considers that the situation is particularly serious and warrants urgent action.[105]

37

As a third sanction option, the Council is entitled **to publish** the recommendation according to Article 121.4 (1) sentence 3 TFEU **"on a proposal from the**

38

---

[101] Hattenberger, in Schwarze et al. (2019), Article 121 AEUV para 34, 44, 49; Häde, in Calliess and Ruffert (2022), Article 121 AEUV para 13; Hentschelmann (2009), p. 344; Herrmann and Rosenfeldt, in Pechstein et al. (2017), Article 121 AEUV para 40; Ohler, in Siekmann (2013), Article 121 AEUV para 19; Kempen, in Streinz (2018), Article 121 AEUV para 20.

[102] Cf. Amtenbrink (2008), p. 929.

[103] O.J. L 69/22 (2001). In Recital 4 the Council points out: "Proper functioning of the coordination of economic policies in the euro area requires a timely use of instruments available under Article 99(4)."

[104] Müller, in Jaeger and Stöger (2021), Article 121 AEUV para 35 (released in 2020).

[105] Article 121.4 TFEU in conjunction with Article 6.2 (2) sentences 3 and 4 or, respectively, Article 10.2 (2) sentences 3 and 4 of Regulation (EU) No 1175/2011. See on this also Pilz and Dittmann (2012), p. 61.

Commission". The recommendations are also of relevance to the Commission, in particular when assessing the adjustment path towards the medium-term budgetary objective, thus making them part of the "peer pressure".[106] Additionally, the Commission may undertake **"enhanced surveillance missions"** in MS that are the subject of recommendations for the purposes of "on-site monitoring" (Article 11.2 of Regulation 1175/2011). These possibilities represent a significant strengthening of the Commission's role in the multilateral surveillance procedure following the adoption of Council recommendations.

39 **Other sanctions cannot be imposed** under primary law. Article 121.6 TFEU does not authorise measures or procedures that go beyond those exhaustively regulated in primary law.[107] Article 136 TFEU, which empowers the Council to adopt measures for the coordination and surveillance of budgetary discipline in accordance with the procedure referred to in Article 121 TFEU for the MS of the euro area with a view to the proper functioning of EMU, does not lead to an extension of the Union's powers within primary law.[108]

6. The Role of the European Parliament in the Surveillance Procedure (Paragraph 5)

40 Only after the adoption of the recommendation, the **Council "shall inform the European Parliament of its recommendation"** (Article 121.2 (3) sentence 2 TFEU). Hence, beyond its participation in the secondary legislation pursuant to

---

[106] Müller, in Jaeger and Stöger (2021), Article 121 AEUV para 36 (released in 2020).

[107] Insofar, some authors take a critical view of Article 6.2 (4 and 5) and Article 10.2 (4 and 5) of Regulation (EC) No 1466/97 as amended by Regulation (EU) No 1175/2011 which implies a legal fiction and therefore might go beyond Article 121 TFEU: "If the Member State concerned fails to take appropriate action within the deadline specified in a Council recommendation under the second subparagraph, the Commission shall immediately recommend to the Council to adopt, by qualified majority, a decision establishing that no effective action has been taken. [...] In the event that the Council does not adopt the decision on the Commission recommendation that no effective action has been taken, and failure to take appropriate action on the part of the Member State concerned persists, the Commission, after 1 month from its earlier recommendation, shall recommend to the Council to adopt the decision establishing that no effective action has been taken. *The decision shall be deemed to be adopted by the Council unless it decides, by simple majority, to reject the recommendation within 10 days of its adoption by the Commission.* [...]." (emphasis is mine); cf. Hattenberger, in Schwarze et al. (2019) Article 121 AEUV para 46; Müller, in Jaeger and Stöger (2021), Article 121 AEUV para 39 (released in 2020) who speaks of a "reverse majority" requirement; see with regard to the differences in the assessments concerning reverse majority voting under the Six-Pack, → Article 126 TFEU para 39 et seqq., 51, on the one hand, and → Article 136 TFEU para 15 et seqq., on the other; the use of "reverse majority voting" is also defended by Rodi, in Vedder and Heintschel von Heinegg (2018), Article 121 AEUV para 17.

[108] See Ohler, in Siekmann (2013), Article 121 AEUV para 23.

Article 121.6 TFEU as a result of the Treaty of Lisbon,[109] the EP cannot bring about any amendments to the draft broad guidelines and is not involved in the recommendations' adoption.[110] Its involvement aims to ensure "transparency and ownership of, and the accountability for the decisions taken, in particular by means of the economic dialogue" (Article 2-a.4 of Regulation (EC) No 1466/97).[111] Just as it is only informed about the drafting of a Council recommendation (→ para 18), it is also limited to a mere report by the President of the Council and the Commission "on the results of multilateral surveillance" without being able to participate actively in this procedure (Article 121.5 sentence 1 TFEU and Article 12 of Regulation (EC) No 1466/97).[112]

Although this weak position of the EP in economic policy is occasionally criticised, this situation consistently reflects the **enduring—albeit limited—national sovereignty reserve**[113] in this area. The very fact that the Council informs the EP emphasises that the **coordination of economic policy is not part of the Union legislation** but a specific expression of the limited economic policy competence of the Union, the exercise of which lies in the hands of the Council (ECO-FIN).[114] Obviously, to answer questions put by its members, the President of the Council may be invited to appear before the competent committee of the EP if the Council has made its recommendation public (Article 121.5 sentence 2 TFEU).[115]

41

Yet according to 121.6 TFEU, the **secondary legislation concretising Article 121 TFEU** is enacted in the ordinary legislative procedure (Article 121.6 TFEU). With the entry into force of the Lisbon Treaty, the EP is a co-legislator as regards the setting of rules for multilateral surveillance. This involves, in particular, the preventive arm of the SGP (→ para 44) as well as more diligent macroeconomic surveillance to prevent harmful imbalances following the fiscal crisis. The so-called

42

---

[109] Shortly after the coming into force of the Maastricht Treaty, the EP had described its role as in need of reform; cf. European Parliament, *Resolution on information and consultation of the European Parliament in relation to Articles 103, 103a, 104, 104a, 104b and 104c EC*, O.J. C 89/144 (1995).

[110] Häde, in Calliess and Ruffert (2022), Article 121 AEUV para 8 et seq.; Herrmann and Rosenfeldt, in Pechstein et al. (2017), Article 121 AEUV para 25; Hufeld (2021), p. 1533; Richter, in Geiger et al. (2015), Article 121 TFEU para 3.

[111] These expectations have been articulated by Bandilla, in Grabitz et al. (2021), Article 121 AEUV para 35 (released in 2021).

[112] Bandilla, in Grabitz et al. (2021), Article 121 AEUV para 34 (released in 2021); Herrmann and Rosenfeldt, in Pechstein et al. (2017), Article 121 AEUV para 46; Kempen, in Streinz (2018), Article 121 AEUV para 24; Rodi, in Vedder and Heintschel von Heinegg (2018), Article 121 AEUV para 15.

[113] See Hattenberger, in Schwarze et al. (2019), Article 121 AEUV para 2 who describes how the MS' autonomy in terms of the economic policy has been limited since the Maastricht Treaty.

[114] Amtenbrink and De Haan (2003), p. 1080; Häde, in Calliess and Ruffert (2022), Article 121 AEUV para 9; Bandilla, in Grabitz et al. (2021), Article 121 AEUV para 18 (released in 2021).

[115] Bandilla, in Grabitz et al. (2021), Article 121 AEUV para 34 (released in 2021); Häde, in Calliess and Ruffert (2022), Article 121 para 16; Kempen, in Streinz (2018), Article 121 AEUV para 23; Ohler, in Siekmann (2013), Article 121 AEUV para 24.

"Six-Pack" strengthens the EP's role in the EU's economic governance, especially through the introduction of the **European Semester**.

7. Regulations for the Multilateral Surveillance Procedure (Paragraph 6)

43 Article 121.6 TFEU empowers the EP and the Council to further **develop multilateral surveillance through the ordinary legislative procedure** (paragraphs 3 and 4 of Article 121 TFEU). For doing so, pursuant to Article 121.6 TFEU, regulations (Article 288 (2) TFEU) are the only applicable legislative tools. These regulations shall specify the "details" of the multilateral surveillance procedure. However, there is no obligation to put paragraphs 3 and 4 into more concrete terms. When it comes to the enactment of such legal acts, the Parliament at least gains some influence on the monitoring procedure.[116]

44 Articles 121 and 126 TFEU are the **legal bases for secondary legislation on** the **SGP**, a set of rules designed to ensure that the MS pursue sound public finances and coordinate their fiscal policies, including the so-called Six- and Two-Pack. MS with a derogation agreed that their national budgets should always be in balance. Eurozone MS agreed on stricter rules to ensure the stability of the euro. Some of the SGP's rules aim to prevent fiscal policies from heading in potentially problematic directions and to ensure sound budgetary policies over the medium term by setting parameters for MS' fiscal planning and policies "during normal economic time".[117] The **"preventive arm"**, which requires countries that are not in the corrective arm to improve their budget balance towards their medium-term objective, complements budgetary policy coordination, while other measures are meant to correct excessive budget deficits or excessive public debt burdens through the adoption of appropriate policy responses. The **"corrective arm"** is the basis for the so-called economic governance[118] (→ para 19). The "preventive arm" of the SGP is based on Article 121 TFEU,[119] whereas the "corrective arm" is based on Article 126 TFEU.[120] Regulation 1175/2011 contains provisions on the preventive part of the SGP, while Regulation (EU) No 1176/2011, in addition to preventive elements, is designed to correct excessive macroeconomic imbalances. Both regulations concern all MS. Both Regulation (EU) 1173/2011 on the effective enforcement of budgetary surveillance in the euro area[121] and Regulation (EU)

---

[116] Häde, in Calliess and Ruffert (2022), Article 121 AEUV para 17.

[117] See European Commission, Stability and Growth Pact—The preventive arm; available at https://ec.europa.eu/info/business-economy-euro/economic-and-fiscal-policy-coordination/eu-economic-governance-monitoring-prevention-correction/stability-and-growth-pact/preventive-arm_en.

[118] Cremer (2016), pp. 266 seq.; Herrmann and Rosenfeldt, in Pechstein et al. (2017), Article 121 AEUV para 1, 8.

[119] See Article 2 No 1 of Regulation (EU) No 1173/2011.

[120] See Article 2 No 2 of Regulation (EU) No 1173/2011.

[121] O.J. L 306/1 (2011).

No 1174/2011 on enforcement measures to correct excessive macroeconomic imbalances in the euro area,[122] based on Articles 121.6 and 136 TFEU, are pieces of the Six-Pack legislation designed to strengthen economic governance in the euro area and therefore refer to MS whose currency is the euro. The same applies to the so-called Two-Pack, which consists of Regulations (EU) No 472/2013[123] and No 473/2013.[124]

The interpretation of the **legislative framework that the TFEU provides to the EU institutions for coordinating the economic policies is disputed**. The regulations adopted on the basis of Article 121.6 TFEU fall within the scope of economic policy coordination according to Article 5.1 TFEU and therefore not within the scope of the exclusive or shared competence of the EU. This classification thus limits the subject matter of the regulations adopted on the basis of Article 121.6 TFEU to the details of the multilateral surveillance procedure. However, **unclear are the limits** on the Union legislator **when implementing its authorisation to issue these regulations**. In a literal interpretation of the provision, the Union is only entitled to concretise the multilateral surveillance procedure through secondary law. On the basis of this wording, it could be argued that shaping and defining substantive criteria for multilateral economic surveillance is reserved for the legislative bodies; on the other hand, Regulation (EU) No 1175/2011, which was adopted on the basis of Article 121 TFEU, contains precise and far-reaching substantive specifications for the surveillance procedure. Pursuant to Article 2-a of Section 1-A of this Regulation even country-specific medium-term budgetary objectives can be specified for an MS.[125] That indicates a detailed content-related regulatory density in the area of European economic policy, which finds no exact legal basis in the wording of the TFEU.[126] Article 10.4 (2) of Regulation (EC) No 1176/2011, which provides that in the event of non-compliance with the corrective action plan a new Council recommendation is deemed to have been adopted if the Council does not reject a corresponding recommendation of the Commission by a qualified majority within 10 days, is regarded as a deviation from the procedure provided for in Article 121 TFEU (→ Article 126 TFEU para 40 et

45

---

[122] O.J. L 306/8 (2011).

[123] Parliament/Council Regulation (EU) No 472/2013 *on the strengthening of economic and budgetary surveillance of Member States in the euro area experiencing or threatened with serious difficulties with respect to their financial stability*, O.J. L 140/1 (2013).

[124] Parliament/Council Regulation (EU) No 473/2013 *on common provisions for monitoring and assessing draft budgetary plans and ensuring the correction of excessive deficit of the Member States in the euro area*, O.J. L 140/11 (2013).

[125] See Article 2-a (2) of Regulation (EC) No 1466/97: "[...] the country-specific medium-term budgetary objectives shall be specified within a defined range between -1 % of GDP and balance or surplus, in cyclically adjusted terms, net of one-off and temporary measures."

[126] Cf. Herrmann and Rosenfeldt, in Pechstein et al. (2017), Article 121 AEUV para 48; Ohler, in Siekmann (2013), Article 121 AEUV para 25; see with regard to previous EU Treaties Louis (2004), pp. 575 seq.; Hatje (2006), p. 601.

seqq.).[127] This provision of primary law stipulates that the majority decisions of the Council are mandatory. However, taking into account the purpose of Article 121.6 TFEU, this regulatory technique, in principle, can be justified. So far, the decisive factor is the **task that has to be coped with when exercising the competence provided for in Article 121.6 TFEU**, namely to ensure the "proper functioning" of the EMU. According to Article 121.4 TFEU, the Council and the Commission are responsible for performing this task and have broad discretionary power in this regard. Consequently, the multilateral surveillance system can be dealt with effectively only if it does not remain vague in terms of content and substance.[128]

46   Similar formulations can be found in various places in the TFEU supporting the conclusion they stand for **references to a legal basis or** for the **Union's competence to define a term in need of concretisation**.[129] This also indicates that the surveillance procedure laid down in Articles 121.3 and 4 TFEU is conclusively regulated and that no stricter or additional surveillance mechanisms may be introduced by the EU legislator.[130]

7.1. Crisis-Driven Reform of the Multilateral Surveillance System Within the SGP Framework Since 2011

47   Already on the occasion of the conclusion of the SGP at the Amsterdam European Council in June 1997[131] but then drastically since the beginning of the financial and economic crisis (2008/2009), which all had repercussions on the national budgets of a whole series of MS, it became clear that the national obligations, anchored in primary law, to coordinate their economic policies are not sufficient to prevent a threat to the European currency and thus a destabilisation of the euro area. The coordination of the economic policies therefore required a far-reaching reform of primary law, which, however, shortly after the bumpy path of the Lisbon Treaty ratification process was not feasible in view of the lack of consensus to lead the Union to a higher level of integration. Hence, the **European legislator confined**

---

[127] See also Häde, in Calliess and Ruffert (2022), Article 121 AEUV para 23 with further references.

[128] Hatje (2006), p. 601; Ohler, in Siekmann (2013), Article 121 AEUV para 25.

[129] Cf. for example Article 120 sentence 1, Article 139.2 (2), Article 140.1 (1) sentence 3, second indent, or Article 144.1 sentence 1 TFEU.

[130] Cf. Herrmann and Rosenfeldt, in Pechstein et al. (2017), Article 121 AEUV para 18; Ohler, in Siekmann (2013), Article 121 AEUV para 23.

[131] In 1997, the intergovernmental agreement on SGP aimed to build an effective framework for the coordination and surveillance of national economic policies by requiring national governments to report their debt issuance programmes in advance to the Commission and Council of the European Union. As presented by the Commission's DG for Economic and Financial Affairs, SGP was the concrete EU answer to concerns on the continuation of budgetary discipline in EMU. See Mortensen (2013), p. 7.

itself to amending the secondary law on the EMU coordination and monitoring procedure, linking this reform to the SGP.[132]

In November 2011, the European Parliament and the Council, on the basis of proposals from the Commission and the European Council working group, adopted a legislative package consisting of six legal acts (so-called **Six-Pack**).[133] The key measures include a stronger focus on the long-term sustainability of public finances and the improvement of compliance by increasing the available instruments and enforcement measures as well as an expanding and automatic triggering of the sanction procedure. Further steps to deepen economic and financial integration were taken by the European Parliament and the Council in May 2013 by two other regulations, the so-called **Two-Pack**. Following on from the Six-Pack, these two Regulations (1) on the strengthening of the economic and budgetary surveillance of the MS experiencing or threatened with serious difficulties with respect to their financial stability[134] and (2) on the budgetary surveillance of the MS experiencing or threatened with severe difficulties with respect to their financial stability[135] were **intended to further tighten the theretofore existing control mechanisms in the euro area**. **48**

Reflecting the risks of explicit and implicit liabilities for public finance, as embodied in the aims of the SGP,[136] another significant reform is the intergovernmental **Treaty on Stability, Coordination and Governance** in the Economic and Monetary Union (2012/2013). It highlights again the need for major improvements to the fiscal policy framework. This Treaty contains common budgetary rules that are intended to help overcome the sovereign debt crisis and ensure sustainable and sound budgetary policies in the euro area (→ para 66; → Supplement to Title VIII: Fiscal Union para 16 et seqq., 34 et seqq., 41 et seqq.).[137] **49**

Since the **SGP** has come into force, it has never been a consensual instrument among the MS. It **has been criticised** by some **for imposing fiscal restraints during recessions and** by others **for a lack of compliance**. In 2003, when the big MS Germany and France, which represent the bulk of the economic activity **50**

---

[132] Cf. Kreilinger (2016), p. 1.

[133] The Six-Pack includes the following legal acts (partly already cited in full before): (1) Parliament/Council Regulation (EU) No 1173/2011, O.J. L 306/1 (2011); (2) Parliament/Council Regulation (EU) No 1174/2011, O.J. L 306/8 (2011); (3) Parliament/Council Regulation (EU) No 1175/2011, O.J. L 306/12 (2011); (4) Parliament/Council Regulation (EU) No 1176/2011, O.J. L 306/25 (2011); (5) Council Regulation (EU) No 1177/2011 amending Regulation (EC) No 1467/97 *on speeding up and clarifying the implementation of the excessive deficit procedure*, O.J. L 306/33 (2011); (6) Council Directive 2011/85/EU *on requirements for budgetary frameworks of the Member States*, O.J. L 306/41 (2011).

[134] O.J. L 140/1 (2013).

[135] O.J. L 140/11 (2013).

[136] Among various references made in the TSCG to the SGP, see Recital 12 TSCG.

[137] Cf. Blanke (2012), pp. 95 et seqq.; Pilz (2012), p. 460; Pilz (2016), p. 62.

in the eurozone, escaped punishment under the SGP for breaching its rules,[138] it has "lost its bite".[139] Its corrective arm is considered effective but procyclical; its preventive arm, in spite of the reforms in 2005, when medium-term objectives were first introduced,[140] and in 2011, when it became legally possible to sanction non-compliant MS,[141] is perceived as weak.[142] On 23 March 2020, the Ministers of Finance of the MS agreed with the Commission's assessment that in the light of the Covid-19 crisis, for the first time ever, the conditions for the **use of the general escape clause** of the EU fiscal framework—a severe economic downturn in the euro area or the Union as a whole[143]—were fulfilled.[144] A key legal impediment to the ability of national governments to support their economies by incurring for this purpose substantial deficits was removed.[145] Following a Commission assessement, as of March 2021, "current preliminary indications would suggest to continue applying the general escape clause in 2022 and to deactivate it as of 2023".[146] MS seem to be divided with regard to the return to the application of the SGP in in its current version. Here, roughly speaking, it is North against South. The main point of contention is the future applicability of the 60% rule for total debt, which has not been fulfilled by any of the MS since the Corona crisis. While France, as well as Italy and Spain, considers it obsolete,[147] Germany assumes

---

[138] On the non-application of the rules of the excessive deficit procedure and the Stability and Growth Pact in respect of France and Germany in November 2003, see the Court's Judgment of 13 July 2004 in Case C-27/04, *Commission v Council* (ECJ 13 July 2004) para 29 et seqq. See also Maher (2004), pp. 831 et seqq.

[139] Schäuble (2012); see also Blanke (2007), pp. 55 et seqq.

[140] Council Regulation (EC) No 1055/2005, O.J. L 174/1 (2005).

[141] Articles 6, 7, 8 and 12 of Regulation (EU) No 1175/2011, O.J. L 306/12 (2011).

[142] De Jong and Gilbert (2019).

[143] See Articles 5.1 (10), 6.3 (3), 9.1 (10) and 10.3 (3), of Regulation (EC) 1466/97 as amended by Regulation (EU) No 1175/2001 (in relation to the SGP's preventive arm): "In the case of an unusual event outside the control of the Member State concerned which has a major impact on the financial position of the general government or in periods of severe economic downturn for the euro area or the Union as a whole, Member States may be allowed temporarily to depart from the adjustment path towards the medium-term budgetary objective [...], provided that this does not endanger fiscal sustainability in the medium term."; Article 3.5 sentence 3 and Article 5.2 sentence 3 of Regulation (EC) No 1467/97 as amended by Regulation (EC) No 1177/2011 (in relation to the SGP's corrective arm).

[144] Cf. Commission Communication *on the activation of the general escape clause of the Stability and Growth Pact*, COM(2020) 123 final; Council of the EU, Statement of EU ministers of finance on the Stability and Growth Pact in light of the COVID-19 crisis, Press release 173/20 of 23 March 2020.

[145] Cf. Hadjiemmanuil (2020), pp. 188 et seq.

[146] Cf. European Commission, *One year since the outbreak of COVID-19: fiscal policy response*, COM(2021) 105 final, pp. 8, 14.

[147] See, e.g., French Finance Minister Le Maire (2021, 27 April): "[...] Our citizens are now waiting for more growth, more prosperity, more jobs. Looking beyond, we will need to draw lessons from the past and review when needed our common rules to ensure a better functioning of our common currency. One key question will be to take into account the very different situations in

that these rules will remain flexible enough to be applied also in the future.[148] Already in April 2019, the German Bundesbank suggested adding to the SGP **"national rainy day funds"** in order "not to undermine the necessarily strict limits by making numerous exceptions, on the one hand, and to allow flexibility on the other". The basic idea behind this type of fund is to build up a financial buffer in good times in order to prepare for the "rainy days" ahead.[149]

Since the activation of the general escape clause, the **debts of the MS have risen drastically**. By the end of 2021, the 19 euro MS owed an average of 102% of their GDP to the financial markets. The highest debt was accumulated by Greece with over 200% and Italy with 160%. Only five countries in the eurozone still complied with the maximum limit of 60% for national debt, and only one MS of the euro area, Luxembourg, respected the Maastricht criterion for annual new debt of a maximum of 3%.[150] In 2022, presumably, there will be just eight MS that respect the limit. 51

In its 2018 Annual Report, the **European Fiscal Board proposed a major overhaul of the EU fiscal framework**. The proposed new framework relies on a **single fiscal anchor: the 60% reference value for the debt ratio**. This shall be directly translated into a single operational target: a constant ceiling on the growth rate of the primary nominal expenditure net of discretionary revenue measures, ensuring that the debt ratio would reach 60% in about 15 years if the economy were at its potential and inflation at 2%. The expenditure ceiling thus shall include a built-in debt brake. The ceiling is fixed for a 3-year period to ensure a medium-term orientation of fiscal policies; at the end of the 3 years, it is re-calculated based on what is needed to reach the 60% reference value 15 years ahead. The debt reference value is, therefore, reached asymptotically. The Board also proposes to reform the overall governance of the rules by **assigning a greater role to independent institutions in assessing compliance**, particularly in relation to the use of the escape clause.[151] 52

---

which the member states will be in terms of debt." See Olaf Scholz and Bruno Le Maire in an interview with Die Zeit; available at https://www.bundesfinanzministerium.de/Content/EN/Interviews/2021/2021-04-27-interview-zeit.html. Already at the beginning of 2019, French President *E. Macron* has stigmatized the Maastricht convergence criteria as the result of "a debate of another century" (Le Monde, 13.04.2021).

[148] See e.g. former German Finance Minister Scholz (27 April 2021): "A common currency needs common rules. Our rules have recently proved to be very flexible. They work." See Olaf Scholz and Bruno Le Maire in an interview with Die Zeit; available at https://www.bundesfinanzministerium.de/Content/EN/Interviews/2021/2021-04-27-interview-zeit.html.

[149] Deutsche Bundesbank (2019), pp. 82, 87.

[150] Statista, National debt in EU countries in relation to GDP. In the fourth quarter of 2020, Greece's national debt was the highest in all of the European Union, amounting to 205.6% of Greece's gross domestic product.

[151] See European Fiscal Board, Annual Report 2018, in particular pp. 79 et seqq.; available at https://ec.europa.eu/info/sites/default/files/2018-efb-annual-report_en.pdf; for a short summary of the proposal, see Beetsma et al. (2018); with regard to five broad categories of reform proposals, see De Angelis and Mollet (2021), p. 3 et seq.

7.1.1. Surveillance and Coordination Under the Maastricht Treaty: Regulation (EC) No 1466/97

53 Already a few years after the entry into force of the Maastricht Treaty, the MS decided, at Germany's insistence, to fill the gaps left by the Treaty with regard to a procedure for economic and budgetary surveillance through rules intended to foster budgetary discipline by means of secondary legislation. Since then, failure during the **first stage**, the multilateral surveillance phase equipped with soft sanction measures, results in the introduction of the **second phase**, which is the excessive deficit procedure (→ para 67). In 1997, within the SGP framework,[152] the Council has adopted, on the basis of ex-Article 103.5 TEC (Article 121.6 TFEU), **Regulation (EC) No 1466/97** on the strengthening of the surveillance of budgetary positions and the surveillance and coordination of economic policies.[153] This Regulation concretises the rules on multilateral surveillance covering the content, submission, examination and monitoring of stability programmes and convergence programmes so as to prevent, at an early stage, the occurrence of excessive general government deficits and to promote the surveillance and coordination of economic policies (Article 1 of the Regulation). A distinction is made between the euro area and non-euro area countries. They link the coordination and multilateral surveillance of general economic policy with the supervision of budgetary discipline according to Article 126 TFEU.[154] These measures are enforced through the sanction mechanisms under Article 121.4 TFEU, in particular through warnings and recommendations.[155] In addition to ex-Article 103.4 TEC (Article 121.4 TFEU), the Regulation establishes another "early warning system". If the Council identified significant divergences of budgetary positions from the budgetary objectives of being close to balance or in surplus, it was enabled to give an early warning in order to prevent a government deficit in a MS from becoming excessive; in the event of persistent budgetary slippage, the Council can reinforce its recommendation and make it public (Articles 6.2 and 10.2 of the Regulation).

7.1.2. The "Six-Pack"

54 In the course of the economic and sovereign debt crisis, the EU decided to concentrate its economic policy instruments and means for crisis management. Since the numerous measures of the EU and its MS in the various policy areas were in danger of "running unconnectedly alongside each other" and thus losing impact and efficiency, the European Commission took up an older proposal, that is,

---

[152] With regard to the creation of the Pact, cf. Pilz and Dittmann (2011), pp. 150 et seq.

[153] O.J. L 209/1 (1997).

[154] Cf. Amtenbrink (2011), p. 434; Häde, in Calliess and Ruffert (2022), Article 121 AEUV para 18 et seqq.; Schütze (2015), p. 802.

[155] Cf. Heise (2015), pp. 161 et seq., who goes into more detail about the negotiations on the Regulation and the German government's position; Häde (2009), p. 203; Schütze (2015), p. 802.

of July 2003. In the "Sapir Report", a high-level group of experts recommended the **European coordination and national implementation processes to be deepened and more closely interlinked**.[156] Coordination and the requirement to avoid excessive deficits and to observe budgetary discipline (Article 126 TFEU) lead to a limit on the budgetary sovereignty of the national governments.[157]

The regulations that are part of the so-called Six-Pack were issued on the basis of Article 121.6 TFEU (→ Supplement to Title VIII: Fiscal Union para 5). Secondary Union law sets out in more detail how the regulations and procedures provided by the Treaty have to be implemented. The "Six-Pack" covered not only **fiscal surveillance** but also **macroeconomic surveillance** under the new Macroeconomic Imbalance Procedure.[158] Of crucial importance are the extension of economic policy coordination to macroeconomic imbalances as well as the possibility of issuing sanctions and their facilitated enforceability.[159]

Regulation No 1175/2011 amending Council Regulation (EC) No 1466/97 on the strengthening of the surveillance of budgetary positions and the surveillance and coordination of economic policies[160] aims to **strengthen** the preventive arm of the SGP. In particular, it fosters **the Commission's role in the enhanced surveillance procedure**, namely its responsibility to trigger the early warning mechanism (→ para 34–35),[161] **and gives the Council powers beyond its competence to address a recommendation** under Article 121 (4) TFEU to the MS concerned (→ para 37–39), for example by adopting, if necessary, **an opinion on the stability or convergence programme of an MS** and inviting it "to adjust its programme" in the case of deviations from the adjustment path towards the medium-term budgetary objective (Articles 5.2. and 9.2. of Regulation No 1175/2011).[162] In addition, Articles 2-a.4 and 2-ab of Regulation 1175/2011 institutionalise the so-called **Economic Dialogue**, which pursues, in particular, the early involvement of the European Parliament and the national parliaments.

The central pillar of economic policy coordination, however, is the **European Semester for economic policy coordination**, which is set forth in a prominent place in Section 1-A of Regulation (EU) No 1176/2011. The European Semester was adopted by ECOFIN on 7 September 2010 as a "code of conduct on implementation of the EU's stability and growth pact".[163] It was part of the "Europe 2020

---

[156] Sapir (2003), pp. 135 et seqq.

[157] Streinz (2015), pp. 1 et seqq.

[158] See with regard to the Six-Pack Gómez Urquijo (2012), p. 526; Schoenfleisch (2018), pp. 82 et seqq.

[159] Antpöhler (2012), p. 362.

[160] O.J. L 306/12 (2011).

[161] See Article 124.4 TFEU in conjunction with Articles 2-a.3 (3), 6.2 and 10.2 of Regulation (EU) No 1175/2011.

[162] See Article 6.2 of Regulation (EU) No 1175/201; Amtenbrink (2011), p. 433.

[163] 3030th Council meeting, Economic and Financial Affairs, Brussels, 7 September 2010, Press release, Council Doc. 13161/10, p. 6; cf. Schoenfleisch (2018), pp. 107 et seqq.

Strategy" to promote competitiveness[164] and applied for the first time in January 2011.[165] The procedure thus has a hinge function as it links multilateral surveillance within the SGP framework and the procedure for preventing and correcting macroeconomic imbalances. The European Semester is probably the most significant expression of the political will to interlink European coordination processes more closely, especially with a view to more effective implementation. It is the stated objective of the Commission that **in an ex ante coordination** of the national economic policies, the **individual economic policy plans shall be complementary** before the MS take final budget decisions.[166] In the first half of the year during the European Semester, the many economic policy steering and coordination processes are to be advanced and concretised at the European level, while in the second half of the year, the national Semester, the MS are to close their budgetary plans for the subsequent year. In stability or convergence programmes and in national reform programmes, the MS set out which economic policy and employment goals they want to achieve and which measures they will be pursuing. The European Commission then summarises the national reform programmes and assesses them in line with the broad economic policy and employment guidelines (Articles 121.2 and 148.2 TFEU) from a Union perspective.[167] Following the assessment of these programmes on the basis of recommendations from the Commission, the Council shall "address guidance" to the MS making full use of the legal instruments provided under Articles 121.4 and 148 TFEU and under Regulations (EU) No 1175/2011 and No 1176/2011. The scheme on surveillance is designed to **ensure compliance of the national economic policies with SGP and to prevent and correct macroeconomic imbalances** under Regulation (EU) No 1176/2011. It builds the main element within the preventive arm of the SGP. The budgetary surveillance framework of the Union for the individual MS is related to a synchronisation of the respective national stability or convergence programmes or national reform programmes (→ para 65).[168] All in all, **the surveillance processes fall**

---

[164] See European Commission, *Europe 2020: A strategy for smart, sustainable and inclusive growth*, COM(2010) 2020 final, p. 30.

[165] Pilz and Dittmann (2012), p. 78.

[166] Cf. Commission Communication, *Enhancing economic policy coordination for stability, growth and employment – tools for stronger EU economic governance*, COM(2010) 367; with regard to the coordination procedure within the European Semester, cf. Müller, in Jaeger and Stöger (2021), Article 121 AEUV para 30 (released in 2020).

[167] On the process of the European Semester for economic policy coordination, cf. Pilz and Dittmann (2012), pp. 79 et seq.

[168] On this objective, see COM(2010) 367 of 30 June 2010, pp. 11 et seq.: "Better integrated surveillance. The European Semester will cover all elements of economic surveillance, including policies to ensure fiscal discipline, macroeconomic stability, and to foster growth, in line with the Europe 2020 strategy. Existing processes—e.g. under the Stability and Growth Pact and the Broad Economic Policy Guidelines—*will be aligned in terms of timing while remaining legally separate*. Stability and Convergence Programmes (SCPs) and National Reform Programmes (NRPs) will be submitted by Member States at the same time and assessed simultaneously by the Commission." (emphasis is mine).

short of a substantial bundling of the national economic policy goals, which would, of course, exceed the mere EU coordination competence in this area. Further, such programmes on stability, convergence and national reforms lack a binding force; that is why they cannot be enforced by the Union.

Union coordination and the control of national economic policies beyond budgetary policy is strengthened by **Regulation (EU) No 1176/2011** on the prevention and correction of macroeconomic imbalances.[169] In addition to the Stability and Growth Pact, it sets rules for the early detection of emerging macroeconomic imbalances and the correction of excessive imbalances (Article 1 of Regulation (EU) No 1176/2011). In the course of the sovereign debt crisis, they affected namely Ireland and Spain in the form of speculative bubbles and distortions in the money and capital markets.[170] The **excessive imbalance procedure** shall include issuing recommendations to the MS concerned, enhanced surveillance and monitoring requirements and, in respect of the MS whose currency is the euro, the possibility of enforcement in accordance with Regulation (EU) No 1174/2011.[171] Through an alert mechanism, the early identification and monitoring of imbalances shall be facilitated (Article 3 of Regulation (EU) No 1176/2011) before they can affect the fiscal situation of an MS.[172] It requires enhanced surveillance tools based on those used in the multilateral surveillance procedure pursuant to Articles 121.3 and 121.4 TFEU.[173]

The monitoring and coordination of economic policies are based on the use of an indicative and transparent "scoreboard", comprised of indicative thresholds, combined with economic judgement. It consists of a limited set of economic, financial and structural indicators relevant to the detection of macroeconomic imbalances, with corresponding indicative thresholds. It comprises **indicators with a view to internal imbalances**, such as current account balances (large current-account deficits); financial and asset market developments, including housing; the evolution of private sector credit flow; the evolution of unemployment and **external imbalances** such as real effective exchange rates; export market shares; changes in price and cost developments; and non-price competitiveness (Article 4 of Regulation (EU) No 1176/2011). The scoreboard of indicators shall have upper and lower alert thresholds unless inappropriate.[174] The Commission's annual report, containing a qualitative economic and financial assessment based on that scoreboard, is made public (Article 3.1 of Regulation (EU) No 1176/2011).

If, on the basis of in-depth reviews (IDR), i.e. analytical documents prepared by the Commission and aimed at identifying and assessing the severity of

---

[169] Parliament/Council Regulation (EU) No 1176/2011, O.J. L 306/25 (2011).

[170] Pilz (2016), pp. 14 et seqq.

[171] Parliament/Council Regulation (EU) No 1174/2011, O.J. L 306/8 (2011).

[172] Kullas and Koch (2010), p. 6.

[173] For more information, see Pilz and Dittmann (2012), pp. 72 et seqq.

[174] Article 4.4 (3) of Regulation (EU) No 1176/2011.

macroeconomic imbalances (Article 5 of Regulation (EU) No 1176/2011),[175] the Commission considers that an MS is experiencing **imbalances**, the **Council**, on a recommendation from the Commission, may address the necessary **recommendations** to the MS concerned, in accordance with the procedure set out in Article 121.2 TFEU (Article 6 of Regulation (EU) No 1176/2011). In the **case of excessive imbalances**[176] **or even a "risk jeopardising the proper functioning of economic and monetary union"** (Article 121.4 (1) TFEU), the Council, upon a recommendation by the Commission, may, in accordance with Article 121.4 TFEU, adopt a recommendation establishing the existence of an excessive imbalance and recommending that the MS concerned takes corrective action (excessive imbalance procedure). The MS affected has to submit a corrective action plan to the Council and the Commission based on, and within a deadline to be defined in, the Council's recommendation. If, upon a Commission recommendation, the Council considers the actions or the timetable envisaged in the corrective action plan insufficient, it shall adopt a recommendation addressed to the MS to submit, within 2 months as a rule, a new corrective action plan.[177] During the implementation of corrective actions, Article 9.1 of Regulation (EU) No 1176/2011 requires the documentation of progress made by the MS ("regular intervals progress reports") to be presented to the Council and the Commission. If the MS affected has taken the corrective action recommended, the excessive imbalance procedure shall be "held in abeyance" (IDR: excessive imbalances with corrective action), or in the case of a full correction by the MS, it shall "abrogate recommendations issued under Articles 7, 8 or 10" of Regulation (EU) No 1176/2011 and thus close down the excessive imbalance procedure.[178] Where the Council considers that the **MS has not taken the recommended corrective action**, the Council, upon a recommendation from the Commission, shall adopt a decision establishing non-compliance, together with a recommendation setting new deadlines for taking corrective action. In this case, the Council, among other things, shall inform the European Council.[179] The procedure under Articles 6–11 of Regulation (EU) 1176/2011 is aligned with the procedure under Article 121 TFEU.[180]

61 **Regulation (EU) No 1174/2011** on enforcement measures to correct excessive macroeconomic imbalances in the euro area[181] provides for the imposition of sanctions in the form of interest-bearing deposits on the euro area countries that

---

[175] About the results of the in-depth review (IDR) for the MS the Commission last informed in 2022. The results of IDRs are available at https://economy-finance.ec.europa.eu/economic-and-fiscal-governance/macroeconomic-imbalances-procedure/depth-reviews_en#ref-2022-idrs.

[176] Article 7 of Regulation (EU) No 1176/2011.

[177] Article 8 of Regulation (EU) No 1176/2011.

[178] Article 10.5 and Article 11 of Regulation (EU) No 1176/2011.

[179] Article 10.4 of Regulation (EU) No 1176/2011.

[180] Cremer (2016), p. 276.

[181] O.J. L 306/8 (2011); with regard to this Regulation, see Cremer (2016), pp. 275 et seq.

have not taken the corrective action recommended by the Council.[182] An annual fine shall be imposed by a Council decision where (1) two successive Council recommendations in the same imbalance procedure are adopted and the Council considers that the MS has submitted an insufficient corrective action plan or (2) the MS affected has not taken the recommended corrective action and the Council had to adopt a second recommendation setting new deadlines for taking corrective action.[183] The amount of the fine shall be 0.1% of the preceding year's GDP of the MS concerned[184] and shall be assigned to the ESM.[185]

Some authors, particularly in Germany, argue that the **sanction regime enshrined** in **Regulation 1174/2011**, based in particular on Article 136, in combination with Article 121.6 TFEU, was **adopted in violation of EU competences**. In their opinion, these provisions, especially Article 136.1 point (b) TFEU, are not sufficient **legal bases** for enacting such provisions.[186]

7.1.3. The "Two-Pack"

On 21 May 2013, the European Parliament and the Council set the course for deepening economic and financial policy coordination by adopting **two regulations** based on Articles 36 and 121.6 TFEU (Two-Pack). The regulations following on from the Six-Pack are explicitly directed at the euro States and are intended to further strengthen the control mechanisms in the euro area.[187]

Regulation (EU) No 472/2013 provides for the enhanced surveillance procedure under which an MS may be placed by the Commission if it is experiencing, or is threatened with, serious difficulties with respect to its financial stability. These difficulties are likely to have adverse contagion effects on other MS in the euro area. The decision on this is taken by the Commission in accordance with Articles 2.1 and 2.2 of the Regulation. If a euro area MS receives financial assistance, it will be subject to the enhanced surveillance procedure under Articles 3–6 of the Regulation.

---

[182] Article 3.1 of Regulation (EU) No 1176/2011.

[183] Article 3.2 points (a) and (b) of Regulation (EU) No 1174/2011 in conjunction with Article 8.3 or Article 10.4 of Regulation (EU) No 1176/2011, respectively.

[184] Article 3.5 of Regulation (EU) No 1174/2011.

[185] Article 4 sentence 2 of Regulation (EU) No 1174/2011.

[186] Cf. on this debate: Häde, in Kahl et al. (2022), Article 88 of the German Basic Law para 512 et seqq.; Ohler (2010), p. 338; Pilz and Dittmann (2012), p. 69; Weber (2012), p. 802; Antpöhler (2012), p. 370; Martín y Pérez de Nanclares (2012), pp. 421 et seq. On the discussion of lawmaking as an emergency plan in the crisis, cf. Rodríguez (2016), pp. 268 et seq.; on the choice of Article 136 TFEU as the legal basis in the emergency crisis plan, cf. Ioannides (2016), pp. 1270 with further references and Häde (2011), p. 333.

[187] Cf. Gómez Urquijo (2012), pp. 525 et seqq.; Häde, in Calliess and Ruffert (2022), Article 121 AEUV para 26; Ioannides (2016), p. 1269; Weber (2014), pp. 7 et seq.; Pilz and Dittmann (2012), pp. 84 et seq.

65   A further strengthening of budgetary surveillance results for euro area States from **Regulation (EU) No 473/2013**.[188] This Regulation aims, in particular, at setting up a common **budgetary timeline to better synchronise the key steps in the preparation of national budgets**, thus contributing to the effectiveness of the SGP and the European Semester for economic policy coordination. This shall namely lead to stronger synergies by facilitating policy coordination among euro area States. That procedure shall be consistent with the economic policy guidance issued in the context of the SGP and the European Semester.[189] It does not impose on MS additional requirements or obligations with regard to country-specific numerical fiscal rules.[190]

7.1.4. The European Fiscal Compact

66   Finally, as part of the European stabilisation measures, the **Treaty on Stability, Coordination and Governance** (TSCG) was concluded on 2 December 2012. The Fiscal Compact is an international agreement concluded by 25 EU MS, except the United Kingdom (at the time still an EU MS), and the Czech Republic (→ Supplement to Title VIII: Fiscal Union para 5). Croatia, which joined the Union in 2013, did not sign the Fiscal Compact. Together with the "Treaty establishing the European Stability Mechanism" (ESM Treaty) of 2 February 2012, which is intended to ensure the solvency of the MS of the eurozone (→ Supplement to Title VIII: ESM para 2), the Fiscal Compact is considered the most important instrument for overcoming the financial and economic crisis of the European Union and preventing future crises.[191]

67   The core provisions of the Treaty can be found in **Part III of the TSCG**, i.e. in the real "Fiscal Compact". **Article 3 TSCG**, as its **centrepiece**, requests that a **balanced budget rule in structural terms should be applied, along with a correction mechanism in case of significant deviation**. For such purpose, the **Contracting Parties undertake within the framework of the TSCG**, in addition to their treaty obligations under primary law, to bring the budgetary position of the respective general government in a balance or in surplus (Article 3.1 point a); to follow a correction mechanism that shall be triggered automatically in the event of significant observed deviations from the medium-term objective or the adjustment path towards it (Article 3.1 point e); to transpose the "balanced budget rule" into their national legal systems through binding, permanent and preferably constitutional provisions, which shall be subject to the jurisdiction of the CJEU (Article 3.2); to reduce general government debt at an average rate of one twentieth per year as a benchmark, if its ratio to GDP exceeds the 60% reference value (Article 4);

---

[188] O.J. L 140/11 (2013).

[189] Cf. Recital 12 of Regulation (EU) No 473/2013.

[190] Cf. Herrmann and Rosenfeldt, in Pechstein et al. (2017), Article 121 AEUV para 55.

[191] Ohler, in Siekmann (2013), Article 121 AEUV para 35; Schorkopf (2012), p. 2; Wollenschläger (2012), p. 713.

to put in place a budgetary and economic partnership programme, including a detailed description of the structure to ensure an effective and durable correction of its excessive deficit, if a Contracting Party is subject to an excessive deficit procedure (→ Article 126 TFEU para 12 et seqq.); in the case of an excessive deficit procedure, to submit a detailed and comprehensive structural plan to the Council and the Commission for approval (Article 5); to report ex ante on public debt issuance plans to the Council and to the European Commission (Article 6); and to commit to supporting the proposals or recommendations submitted by the European Commission where it considers that an MS whose currency is the euro is in breach of the deficit criterion in the framework of an excessive deficit procedure (Article 7).[192]

The Fiscal Compact complements the comprehensive legal situation in the area of EMU. It has a **supplementary function to primary and secondary laws**. Some critics point out that for reasons of systematics and clarity, such legal obligations should be found in EU primary law. In the case of a general consensus among all MS, an amendment of the TFEU would have been possible since the subject matter of the TSCG concerns the coordination of the MS' economic policies.[193] But the **TSCG is the result of a political compromise**, which is considered a provisional and transitory **"emergency fix"**,[194] while an amendment of primary law could not find approval among all EU MS.[195] It was thus concluded outside the context of the procedure provided for in Article 48 TEU and does neither extend in any way the competences of the Union in the area of economic policy coordination nor amend the EU primary law.[196] Nevertheless, in Article 16 TSCG, the Contracting States commit themselves to take the necessary steps within 5 years, at most, of the date of entry into force of the TSCG "with the aim of incorporating the substance of this Treaty into the legal framework of the European Union". **68**

In December 2017, the Commission presented a package of measures towards completing the EMU. Besides the establishment of a European Monetary Fund anchored in the Union legal framework,[197] it suggests, i.a., the **incorporation of the TSCG into Union law**.[198] Greater synergies, streamlined procedures and the integration of intergovernmental arrangements within the EU legal framework would strengthen governance and decision-making.[199] The Commission's initiative **69**

---

[192] For more information, Blanke (2012), pp. 95 et seqq.; Pilz (2016), pp. 60 et seqq.; Pilz (2012), pp. 457 et seqq.

[193] Ohler, in Siekmann (2013), Article 121 AEUV para 36; see also Calliess and Schoenfleisch (2012), p. 481.

[194] Martín y Pérez de Nanclares (2012), pp. 426 et seqq.

[195] On the development history, see Schorkopf (2012), pp. 1–3.

[196] Ohler, in Siekmann (2013), Article 121 AEUV para 36; see also Calliess and Schoenfleisch (2012), p. 481.

[197] See on this Manger-Nestler and Böttner (2019).

[198] Cf. European Commission, *Further Steps towards completing Europe's Economic and Monetary Union: A Roadmap*, COM(2017) 821 final.

[199] COM(2017) 821 final, p. 3.

has taken the form of a proposal for a Council Directive.[200] Since some of the TSCG rules are already enshrined in EU law, the **proposed Directive integrates the essence of Article 3 TSCG**, the provisions of which meanwhile have been enacted into the MS' national laws (→ Supplement to Title VIII: Fiscal Union, para 25 et seqq.).

7.2. Assessing the Legislative Reforms

70 Despite the abundance of rules underlining the efforts of the Union regarding the "reform" of the coordination of the MS' economic policies, one cannot speak in a substantial sense of a step towards "European economic governance". Even if both the euro and non-euro MS are considered "already intertwined",[201] these dichotomous features of the EMU—although only factually, but not legally, conceived for the long term (Article 139.1 TFEU: "Member States with a derogation")—hinder the emergence of such "governance". The **strongly procedural content** that determines the **fragmented rules in matters of "economic and budgetary surveillance"** and the **exceptional character of enforceable measures or even sanctions** in this area gives more evidence of the vagueness of the concept of "governance" rather than of a "unitarisation of national economic policies".[202] Nevertheless, the regulations on economic policy coordination adopted since 2011 place the MS under pressure since they are accountable to the Council and Commission, namely, if they deviate from the adjustment path towards the medium-term budgetary objective. But all in all, these secondary law reforms could not amend the concept of the Treaty, which sets forth the coordination of the national economic policies "as a matter of common concern" (Article 121.1 TFEU), i.e. under the exclusion of legislative acts (arg. ex Article 5.1 TFEU).[203] If the Union shall have more power in the field of "common" economic policy, the MS would have to transfer a corresponding competence to it at the cost of losing their **budgetary sovereignty**.[204]

---

[200] Cf. European Commission, *Proposal for a Council Directive laying down provisions for strengthening fiscal responsibility and the medium-term budgetary orientation in the Member States*, COM(2017) 824 final.

[201] COM(2017) 821 final, p. 3.

[202] In favour of the pursuit of this (long-term) goal, Becker (2020), p. 31.

[203] See already Herrmann (2012), pp. 92, 95.

[204] Cf. Blanke and Pilz (2020), p. 287 who argue for a legally binding—i.e. not merely recommendatory—definition of the broad guidelines of a (then) "European economic policy" in order to reduce the imperfection of the institutional design of EMU and thus its susceptibility to crises.

7.3. Shifting EMU Reforms Through Union Law Towards International Public Law Instruments

EMU reforms affect European primary law only selectively, in particular by amending Article 136 TFEU with regard to a **stability mechanism** for the MS whose currency is the euro (→ Article 136 TFEU para 27 et seqq.).[205] As explained earlier, these reforms are implemented mainly by using **European secondary legislation but also public international law instruments** that fall outside the Union law framework (TSCG, TESM). These international law elements of the "new framework for fiscal policies and financial stability in the Union" have been characterised as legislation through international law instruments with legal effect only within the Union (*Binnenunionsvölkerrecht*),[206] acts of international law supplementing Union law (*Unions(ergänzungs)völkerrecht*)[207] or international law substituting Union law (*völkerrechtliches Ersatzunionsrecht*)[208]—thus following the designations given to the Schengen agreements by German scholars (→ Supplement to Title VIII: Introduction para 4).   71

Such "extensions" of Union law through public international law are not legally objectionable, provided that the **acts of international law supplementing Union law are bound back to the principles and standards of Union law**. Here, above all, the primacy of Union law and the principle of sincere cooperation between the MS and the Union (Article 4.3 TEU: "loyalty") secure the **link** between the European and the MS level. The apodictic statement of the ECJ in *Hurd*, according to which "[t]hose duties, which are derived from the Treaties [i.e. now Article 4.3 TEU], cannot be applied to agreements between the Member States which lie outside [the] framework [of the Treaties ...]",[209] may today be regarded as outdated in terms of coordination and integration policy.[210] According to the principle of sincere cooperation, the MS "refrain from any measure which could jeopardise the attainment of the Union's objectives" (Article 4.3 (3) TEU; → Article 4 TEU para 81 et seqq.). Following the **principles applicable to enhanced cooperation**,[211] which means   72

---

[205] European Council Decision 2011/199/EU, O.J. L 91/1 (2011).

[206] Cf. Weber (2014), p. 11.

[207] von Arnauld (2013), pp. 509 et seqq.

[208] Lorz and Sauer (2012), p. 575.

[209] Case C-44/84, *Hurd v Jones* (ECJ 15 January 1987) para 38.

[210] Case C-266/03, *Commission v Luxembourg* (ECJ 2 June 2005) para 61—international treaty concluded by an MS; Case C-105/03, *Pupino* (ECJ 16 June 2005) para 42—police and judicial cooperation in criminal matters; cf. von Arnauld (2013), p. 515 with further references in footnote 37.

[211] See in this regard Recital 22 TSCG: "NOTING, in particular, the wish of the Contracting Parties to make a more active use of enhanced cooperation, as provided for in Article 20 [TEU] and Articles 326 to 334 [TFEU], without undermining the internal market, and their wish to have full recourse to measures specific to the Member States whose currency is the euro pursuant to Article 136 [TFEU], and to a procedure for the ex ante discussion and coordination among the Contracting Parties whose currency is the euro of all major economic policy reforms planned by them, with a view to benchmarking best practices".

the requirements of subsidiarity, respect for Union law, responsibility towards other MS, openness towards non-participating MS and also institutional rules, could serve as reference points for the contracting parties when switching to instruments of public international law to be used in pursuit of the EU Treaties' objectives.[212]

73 Conflicts between Union law and the TSCG are minimised by exactly observing **Article 2 TSCG**, which, within Title II about "Consistency and Relationship with the Law of the Union", sets forth the following **compatibility rule**: "This Treaty shall apply insofar as it is compatible with the Treaties on which the European Union is founded and with European Union law. It shall not encroach upon the competence of the Union to act in the area of the economic union."

List of Cases

ECJ/CJEU

ECJ 15.01.1987, 44/84, *Hurd*, ECLI:EU:C:1986:2 [cit. in para 72]
ECJ 13.07.2004, C-27/04, *Commission v Council*, ECLI:EU:C:2004:436 [cit. in para 50]
ECJ 02.06.2005, C-266/03, *Commission v Luxembourg*, ECLI:EU:C:2005:341 [cit. in para 72]
ECJ 16.06.2005, C-105/03, *Pupino*, ECLI:EU:C:2005:386 [cit. in para 72]
CJEU 26.10.2012, C-370/12, Opinion of AG Kokott, *Pringle*, ECLI:EU:C:2012:675 [cit. in para 10]

References

Amtenbrink, F. (2008). Economic, monetary and social policy. In P. Kapteyn et al. (Eds.), *The law of the European Union and the European Communities with references to changes to be made by the Lisbon Treaty* (4th ed., pp. 881–989). Kluwer Law International.
Amtenbrink, F. (2011). Naar een effectievere economische governance in de Europese Unie. *SEW: tijdschrift voor Europese en economisch recht, 10*(154), 429–443.
Amtenbrink, F., & De Haan, J. (2003). Economic governance in the European Union – Fiscal policy discipline versus flexibility. *Common Market Law Review, 40*(5), 1057–1106.
Antpöhler, C. (2012). Emergenz der europäischen Wirtschaftsregierung – Das Six Pack als Zeichen supranationaler Leistungsfähigkeit. *Zeitschrift für ausländisches öffentliches Recht und Völkerrecht, 72*, 353–393.
Becker, P. (2014). Wirtschaftspolitische Koordinierung in der Europäischen Union. Europäisierung ohne Souveränitätsverlust. *SWP-Studie. Stiftung Wissenschaft und Politik.*
Becker, P. (2020). A European economic policy in the making. Success with modest means. *SWP Research Paper 13*. Stiftung Wissenschaft und Politik.

---

[212] Cf. von Arnauld (2013), pp. 516 et seqq.

Beetsma, R., et al. (2018). Reforming the EU fiscal framework: A proposal by the European Fiscal Board. *VoxEU*, 26 October. Retrieved from https://voxeu.org/article/reforming-eu-fiscal-framework-proposal-european-fiscal-board

Bieber, R. (2011). Kritik der "new economic governance" für die Europäische Union. In P.-C. Müller-Graff et al. (Eds.), *Europäisches Recht zwischen Bewährung und Wandel, Festschrift für Dieter H. Scheuing* (pp. 493–508). Nomos.

Blanke, H.-J. (2007). La Riforma del Patto di Stabilità e di Crescita. In M. Pagliarecci (Ed.), *Diritto, politica ed economia dell'Unione* (pp. 55 et seqq.). Giappichelli.

Blanke, H.-J. (2012). Die Europäische Wirtschafts- und Währungsunion zwischen Krisenanfälligkeit und Reform. In A. Scherzberg (Ed.), *10 Jahre Staatswissenschaften in Erfurt* (pp. 70–121). de Gruyter.

Blanke, H.-J., & Pilz, S. (2020). Europa 2019 bis 2024 – Wohin trägt uns der Stier? – Sieben Thesen zu den Herausforderungen der Europäischen Union. *Europarecht, 55*(3), 270–301.

Borger, V., & Cuyvers, A. (2012). Het Verdrag inzake Stabiliteit, Coördinatie en Bestuur in de Economische en Monetaire Unie: de juridische en constitutionele complicaties van de eurocrisis. *SEW: tijdschrift voor Europese en economisch recht, 60*(10), 370–390.

Braams, B. (2013). *Koordinierung als Kompetenzkategorie*. Mohr Siebeck.

Calliess, C., & Ruffert, M. (Eds.). (2022). *EUV/AEUV. Kommentar* (6th ed.). C.H. Beck.

Calliess, C., & Schoenfleisch, C. (2012). Auf dem Weg in die europäische "Fiskalunion"? – Europa- und verfassungsrechtliche Fragen einer Reform der Wirtschafts- und Währungsunion im Kontext des Fiskalvertrages. *JuristenZeitung, 67*(10), 477–487.

Clerc, O., & Kauffmann, P. (2011). Vers une nouvelle gouvernance macro-économique dans la Zone Euro. *Revue de l'Union Européenne, 11*(552), 589–596.

Cremer, W. (2016). Auf dem Weg zu einer Europäischen Wirtschaftsregierung? *Europarecht, 51*(3), 256–281.

De Angelis, F., & Mollet, F. (2021). *Rethinking EU economic governance: The Stability and Growth Pact*. European Policy Center. Retrieved from https://www.epc.eu/content/PDF/2021/Stability_and_Growth_Pact_PB_v4.pdf

De Jong, J., & Gilbert, N. (2019). *The mixed success of the Stability and Growth Pact*. Retrieved from https://voxeu.org/article/mixed-success-stability-and-growth-pact

Deutsche Bundesbank. (2019). European Stability and Growth Pact: individual reform options. *Monthly Report* (April 2019), 77–90.

Frenz, W., & Ehlenz, C. (2010). Europäische Wirtschaftspolitik nach Lissabon. *Gewerbearchiv, 9*(56), 329–335.

Geiger, R., Khan, D.-E., & Kotzur, M. (Eds.). (2015). *European Union Treaties*. C.H. Beck & Hart Publishing.

Gómez Urquijo, L. (2012). El Tratado de Estabilidad, Coordinación y Gobernanza dentro del nuevo marco condicional de cohesión social en la Unión Europea. *Revista de Derecho Comunitario Europeo, 16*(42), 521–541.

Grabitz, E., Hilf, M., & Nettesheim, M. (Eds.). (2021). *Das Recht der Europäischen Union: EUV/AEUV. Kommentar,* loose leaf (last supplement: 75). C. H. Beck.

Häde, U. (2009). Die Wirtschafts- und Währungsunion im Vertrag von Lissabon. *Europarecht, 44*(2), 200–218.

Häde, U. (2011). Art. 136 AEUV – eine neue Generalklausel für die Wirtschafts- und Währungsunion? *JuristenZeitung, 66*(7), 333–340.

Hadjiemmanuil, C. (2020). European economic governance and the pandemic: Fiscal crisis management under a flawed policy process. In C. V. Gortsos & W.-G. Ringe (Eds.), *Pandemic crisis and financial stability* (pp. 175–243). European Banking Institute.

Hagelstam, K., Dias, C., Angerer, J., & Zoppè, A. (2019). *The European Semester for economic policy coordination: A reflection paper*. Brussels: European Parliament – Directorate-General for Internal Policies. Retrieved from https://www.europarl.europa.eu/RegData/etudes/STUD/2019/624440/IPOL_STU(2019)624440_EN.pdf

Hatje, A. (2006). Die Reform des Stabilitäts- und Wachstumspaktes – Sieg der Politik über das Recht. *Die Öffentliche Verwaltung, 59*(14), 597–604.

Heise, A. (2015). Governance without government or: The Euro crisis and what went wrong with the European economic governance? In H. Brunkhorst, C. Gaitanides, & S. Panther (Eds.), *Europe at a crossroad. From currency union to political and economic governance?* (pp. 155–174). Nomos.

Hentschelmann, K. (2009). *Der Stabilitäts- und Wachstumspakt unter besonderer Berücksichtigung der norminterpretatorischen Leitfunktion der Paktbestimmungen für das Vertragsrecht.* Nomos.

Herrmann, C. (2012). Die Folgen der Finanzkrise für die europäische Wirtschafts- und Währungsunion. In S. Kadelbach (Ed.), *Nach der Finanzkrise. Rechtliche Rahmenbedingungen einer neuen Ordnung* (pp. 79–104). Nomos.

Hufeld, U. (2021). Das Recht der Europäischen Wirtschaftsunion. In P.-C. Müller-Graff (Ed.), *Enzyklopädie Europarecht. Europäisches Wirtschaftsordnungsrecht* (Vol. 4, 2nd ed., pp. 1513–1617). Nomos.

Ioannides, M. (2016). Europe's new transformations: How the EU economic constitution changed during the Eurozone Crisis. *Common Market Law Review, 53*(5), 1237–1282.

Italianer, A. (1993). Mastering Maastricht: EMU issues and how they were settled. In K. Gretschmann (Ed.), *Economic and Monetary Union: Implications for national policy-makers* (pp. 51–113). Nijhoff.

Jaeger, T., & Stöger, K. (Eds.) (2021). *Kommentar zu EUV und AEUV*, loose-leaf (last supplement: 266). Manz.

Kahl, W., Waldhoff, C., & Walter, C. (Eds.). (2022). *Bonner Kommentar zum Grundgesetz* (last supplement: 215). C.F. Müller.

Kreilinger, V. (2016). *Economic policy coordination in the EU: Linking national ownership and surveillance* (pp. 1–8). Jacques Delors Institut. Retrieved from https://institutdelors.eu/wp-content/uploads/2020/08/economicpolicycoordination-kreilinger-jdib-july16-4.pdf

Kullas, M., & Koch, J. (2010). *Fünf harte Regeln für einen harten Euro.* Centrum für Europäische Politik Freiburg (pp. 1–6). Retrieved from http://www.cep.eu/Studien/cepStandpunkt_Reform_SWP/cepStandpunkt_SWP.pdf

Lasa López, A. (2013). El Impacto de la Nueva Gobernanza Económica Europea en la Estrategia hacia una Política de Empleo Mejorada. *Revista de Derecho Comunitario Europeo, 17*(46), 973–1006.

Lastra, R. M. (2006). *Legal foundations of International Monetary Stability.* OUP.

Lenaerts, K. (2014). EMU and the European Union's constitutional framework. *European Law Review, 39*(6), 753–769.

Lorz, A., & Sauer, H. (2012). Ersatzunionsrecht und Grundgesetz. *Die Öffentliche Verwaltung, 65*(15), 573–581.

Louis, J.-V. (2004). The Economic and Monetary Union: Law and institutions. *Common Market Law Review, 41*(2), 575–608.

Magiera, S. (1998). Einführung und rechtliche Absicherung der einheitlichen europäischen Währung. In R. Caesar & H.-E. Scharrer (Eds.), *Die Europäische Wirtschafts- und Währungsunion. Regionale und globale Herausforderungen* (pp. 419–445). Europa Union Verlag.

Maher, I. (2004). Economic policy coordination and the European Court: Excessive deficits and ECOFIN discretion. *European Law Review, 29*(6), 831–841.

Manger-Nestler, C., & Böttner, R. (2019). Der Europäische Währungsfonds nach den Plänen der Kommission. *Zeitschrift für ausländisches öffentliches Recht und Völkerrecht*, 43–84.

Martín y Pérez de Nanclares, J. (2012). El nuevo Tratado de Estabilidad, Coordinación y Gobernanza de la UEM: Reflexiones a propósito de una peculiar reforma realizada fuera de los tratados constitutivos. *Revista de Derecho Comunitario Europeo, 16*(42), 397–431.

Mortensen, J. (2013). Economic policy coordination in the Economic and Monetary Union. From Maastricht via the SGP to the Fiscal Pact. *Centre for European Policy Studies, Working Document*, No 381, 1–23.

Nettesheim, M. (2012). *Der Umbau der europäischen Währungsunion. Politische Aktion und rechtliche Grenzen.* In S. Kadelbach (Ed.), *Nach der Finanzkrise. Rechtliche Rahmenbedingungen einer neuen Ordnung* (pp. 31–78) Nomos.
Nicolaysen, G. (1993). *Rechtsfragen der Währungsunion.* de Gruyter.
Ohler, C. (2010). Die zweite Reform des Stabilitäts- und Wachstumspakts. *Zeitschrift für Gesetzgebung, 25,* 330–345.
Pechstein, M., Nowak, C., & Häde, U. (Eds.). (2017). *Frankfurter Kommentar zum EUV und zum AEUV.* Mohr Siebeck.
Pilz, S. (2012). Ein fiskalpolitischer Pakt als Brücke in die Stabilitätsunion? *Wirtschaftsdienst,* 457–464.
Pilz, S. (2016). *Der Europäische Stabilitätsmechanismus: eine neue Stufe der Integration.* Mohr Siebeck.
Pilz, S., & Dittmann, H. (2011). Der europäische Stabilitäts- und Wachstumspakt – Quo vadis? *Zeitschrift für Rechtsvergleichung,* 149–159.
Pilz, S., & Dittmann, H. (2012). Perspektiven des Stabilitäts- und Wachstumspakts – Rechtliche und ökonomische Implikationen des Reformpakets "Economic Governance". *Zeitschrift für europarechtliche Studien,* 53–88.
Pingel, I. (Ed.). (2010). *De Rome à Lisbonne: Commentaire article par article des traités UE et CE* (2nd ed.). Helbing & Lichtenhahn.
Pipkorn, J. (1994). Legal arrangements in the Treaty of Maastricht for the effectiveness of the economic and monetary union. *Common Market Law Review, 31,* 263–291.
Porto, M., & Anastácio, G. (Eds.). (2012). *Tratado do Lisboa. Anotado e Comentado.* Almedina.
Przesławska, G. (2016). Rethinking economics in response to current crisis phenomena. *Ekonomia I Prawo. Economics and Law, 15*(1), 133–146.
Rodríguez, P. M. (2016). A missing piece of European emergency law: Legal certainty and individuals' expectations in the EU response to the crisis. *European Constitutional Law Review, 12*(2), 265–293.
Sapir, A. (2003). *An agenda for a growing Europe making the EU economic system deliver.* Report of an Independent High-Level Study Group established on the initiative of the President of the European Commission. Retrieved from http://cejm.univ-rennes.eu/digitalAssets/24/24407_sapirreport.pdf
Schäuble, W. (2012). *Economic and institutional perspectives.* Speech, Florence, 17 May.
Schoenfleisch, C. (2018). *Integration durch Koordinierung? Rechtsfragen der Politikkoordinierung am Beispiel der nationalen Wirtschaftspolitiken.* Mohr Siebeck.
Schorkopf, F. (2012). Europas Politische Verfasstheit im Lichte des Fiskalvertrages. *Zeitschrift für Staats- und Europawissenschaften, 10*(1), 1–29.
Schütze, R. (2015). *European Union Law.* CUP.
Schwarze, J., Becker, U., Hatje, A., & Schoo, J. (Eds.). (2019). *EU- Kommentar* (4th ed.). Nomos.
Seidel, M. (1998). Rechtliche und politische Probleme beim Übergang in die Endstufe der Wirtschafts- und Währungsunion. In H.-H. Francke et al. (Eds.), *Europäische Währungsunion: Von der Konzeption zur Gestaltung* (pp. 163–180). Duncker & Humblot.
Siekmann, H. (Ed.). (2013). *EWU. Kommentar zur Europäischen Währungsunion.* Mohr Siebeck.
Smits, R. (1997, 2000 reprint). *The European Central Bank: Institutional aspects.* Kluwer Law International.
Smits, R. (2005). The European Constitution and Emu: An appraisal. *Common Market Law Review, 42,* 425–468.
Streinz, R. (2015). *Reform der EU-Wirtschaftsverfassung: Kompetenzen und Institutionen.* Vortrag im Rahmen der 58. Bitburger Gespräche. Trier, 8.–9. Januar 2015 (p. 1–18). Retrieved from https://www.uni-trier.de/fileadmin/fb5/inst/IRP/BG_Einzeldokumente_ab_2010/BG_58/Streinz_Vorabversion_gesch%C3%BCtzt2.pdf
Streinz, R. (Ed.). (2018). *EUV/AEUV. Kommentar* (3rd ed.). C.H. Beck.
Thym, D. (2011). Euro-Rettungsschirm: zwischenstaatliche Rechtskonstruktion und verfassungsgerichtliche Kontrolle. *Europäische Zeitschrift für Wirtschaftsrecht, 31*(5), 167–171.

Vedder, C., & Heintschel von Heinegg, W. (Eds.). (2018). *Europäisches Unionsrecht. Handkommentar*. Nomos.
von Arnauld, A. (2013). Unions(ergänzungs)völkerrecht: Zur unions- und verfassungsrechtlichen Einbindung völkerrechtlicher Instrumente differenzierter Integration. In M. Breuer et al. (Eds.), *Der Staat im Recht, Festschrift für Eckart Klein* (pp. 509–526). Duncker & Humblot.
von der Groeben, H., Schwarze, J., & Hatje, A. (Eds.). (2015). *Europäisches Unionsrecht. Kommentar* (7th ed.). Nomos.
Weber, A. (2012). Die Europäische Union auf dem Wege zur Fiskalunion? *Deutsches Verwaltungsblatt, 127*, 801–806.
Weber, A. (2014). Grundzüge europa- und völkerrechtlich normierter Krisensteuerung zur Gewährleistung von Haushaltsdisziplin. In H.-J. Blanke & S. Pilz (Eds.), *Die "Fiskalunion" – Voraussetzungen einer Vertiefung der politischen Integration im Währungsraum der Europäischen Union* (pp. 3–23). Mohr Siebeck.
Wollenschläger, F. (2012). Völkerrechtliche Flankierung des EU-Integrationsprogramms als Herausforderung für den Europa-Artikel des Grundgesetzes (Art. 23 GG) am Beispiel von ESM-Vertrag und Fiskalpakt. *Neue Zeitschrift für Verwaltungsrecht, 31*(12), 713–719.
Yábar Sterling, A. (2004). La Política Económia de la Unión Europea. In E. Conde & V. Mayol (Eds.), *Políticas Comunitarias. Las Finanzas de la Unión. Libro III* (pp. 665–684). Tirant Lo Blanche.
Ząbkowicz, A. (2015). Governing economic interests by the European Commission. *Ekonomia I Prawo. Economics and Law, 14*(1), 95–111.

Article 122 [Solidarity]
(Ex-Article 100 TEC)

1. Without prejudice to any other procedures provided for in the Treaties,[5] the Council, on a proposal from the Commission, may decide, in a spirit of solidarity between Member States,[7] upon the measures appropriate to the economic situation, in particular if severe difficulties arise in the supply of certain products, notably in the area of energy.
2. Where a Member State is in difficulties or is seriously threatened with severe difficulties caused by natural disasters or exceptional occurrences[13–17] beyond its control,[1] the Council, on a proposal from the Commission, may grant, under certain conditions,[22] Union financial assistance[23–24] to the Member State concerned. The President of the Council shall inform the European Parliament of the decision taken.

Contents

1. Introduction: Genesis and Nature 1
2. Scope of Application of Article 122.1 TFEU 5
3. Financial Assistance (Article 122.2 TFEU) 12
   3.1. Normative Conditions 13
      3.1.1. "Natural Disasters or Exceptional Occurrences" (Causation) 13
      3.1.2. "Beyond Its Control" 18
      3.1.3. "In Difficulties or Seriously Threatened with Severe Difficulties" and Causality 20
      3.1.4. "Under Certain Conditions" (Conditionality) 22
   3.2. Granting of Financial Assistance 23
      3.2.1. Procedure 23
      3.2.2. Types of Assistance 24
   3.3. Article 125 TFEU (No Bail-Out Clause) in Relation to Temporary and Permanent Assistance Mechanisms 25
   3.4. Specific Agreements and Judicial Protection 30
4. Relationship to Articles 143 and 222 TFEU 34
5. Outlook 36
List of Cases
References

1. Introduction: Genesis and Nature

Article 122 TFEU is embedded in the first chapter of Title VIII under the heading "Economic Policy" after the complex regulation of the "Coordination of Economic Policies" contained in Article 121 TFEU enabling the preventive and corrective supervision and sanctioning of macroeconomic and budget imbalances. If this may be conceived as the core of "Economic Governance" implemented by EU

1

secondary law ("Six Pack" and "Two Pack") for all MS (→ Article 121 TFEU para 13 et seqq., 53 et seqq.),[1] Article 122 TFEU is an **emergency clause for temporary measures of the Union** if the normal regime of multilateral supervision cannot react adequately to exceptional and unforeseen severe difficulties.

2 A **similar safeguard clause** was inserted in the chapter "Policy on Economic Trends" in ex-Article 103.2 of the EEC Treaty, where the Council could decide "by means of unanimous vote on a proposal of the Commission on measures appropriate to the situation"; ex-Article 103.3 EEC Treaty enabled the Council to act by a qualified majority to issue any "requisite directives" concerning the application of paragraph 2, whereas paragraph 4 enabled the Council to act in the same procedure "in the event of difficulties arising in connection with the supply of certain products".

3 In the following treaty amendment, the scope of application was extended from conjunctural measures to all measures of economic policy (ex-Article 103a.2 TEC-Maastricht),[2] and the procedure was modified from unanimous vote to qualified majority in the case of natural disasters and after the **Nice Treaty** extended to all cases of emergencies (ex-Article 100 TEC-Nice).[3] The **Treaty of Lisbon** adds in Article 122.1 TFEU the intention of acting "in a spirit of solidarity" and for the supply of products "notably in the area of energy".[4]

4 Article 122 TFEU cannot be seen as the only enabling norm to act in the area of economic policy with legal effect on the conjunctural and budgetary policy of the MS[5] if one takes into consideration the potential of preventive and sanctioning measures laid down in paragraphs 6 to 14 of Article 126 TFEU, where decisions of the Council based on the preventive and corrective pillars of the "Six Pack" and "Two Pack" regulations have a direct impact on MS' economic policies. This view is based on the far-reaching competences for interferences of the Union organs into macroeconomic and budgetary policies having been concretised during the **financial crisis** since 2010 in secondary law and partially complemented by intergovernmental treaties like the "Treaty on Stability, Coordination and Governance" (**Fiscal Compact**; (→ Article 121 TFEU para 47 et seqq.).[6]

---

[1] On the extension of economic governance, cf. Pilz and Dittmann (2012), p. 60 et seqq.; Antpöhler (2012), p. 352 et seqq.; Ioannidis (2014), p. 61 et seqq. See also Herrmann-Rosenfeldt, in Pechstein et al. (2017), Article 121 AEUV para 1 et seqq.

[2] Kempen, in Streinz (2018), Article 122 AEUV para 1.

[3] Bandilla, in Grabitz et al. (2021), Article 122 AEUV para 3 (released in 2011).

[4] Hattenberger, in Schwarze (2019), Article 122 AEUV para 1.

[5] Thus Bandilla, in Grabitz et al. (2021), Article 122 AEUV para 5 (released in 2011); Hattenberger, in Schwarze (2019), Article 122 AEUV para 2.

[6] Treaty on Stability, Coordination and Governance in the Economic and Monetary Union of 2 March 2012; in force since 1 January 2013. Cf. Schorkopf (2012), p. 1 et seqq.; Pilz (2012), p. 457 et seqq.; Weber (2012), p. 801 et seqq.; Weber (2017), p. 743.

2. Scope of Application of Article 122.1 TFEU

As the wording of Article 122.1 TFEU makes clear, the measures taken may not collide with or infringe "other procedures provided for in the Treaties". This sounds almost self-evident with regard to Article 122 TFEU as an exceptional or **emergency clause** embedded **within the general economic policy framework** (Articles 120–126 TFEU). However, already the old "without prejudice" clause in ex-Article 103.2 EEC Treaty was controversial with regard to its application in other than conjunctural contexts.[7] The "without prejudice" clause, despite objections of a literal, systematic or teleological nature, does not preclude the applicability of more specialised safeguard clauses if the conditions of the latter are fulfilled and prevail as *leges speciales*.[8] This is true, for example, for safeguard clauses like Article 143 or 144 TFEU for non-euro MS in the case of difficulties of balance of payments, which, however, may not totally exclude measures of a more general economic nature; this leads to the assumption of "the priority of special causality" within concurrent emergency clauses.[9] The Council practice has so far interpreted ex-Article 103.2 EEC Treaty as a general safeguard clause, and the jurisprudence of the European Court of Justice (ECJ) largely followed this approach in the case law of *Balkan-Import-Export-GmbH*,[10] *Rewe*[11] and *Schlüter*.[12] The Court therefore accepted derogations from substantial treaty provisions under narrow conditions.[13] A **special relationship** exists **with** the **"no bail-out clause"** of Article 125 TFEU (→ para 25–29).

5

The Council may decide upon "measures appropriate to the economic situation". This wording amounts to a rather general safeguard clause, especially with regard to the modified and extended wording since Maastricht (Article 103a TEC-Maastricht). Taking into account the case law of the Luxembourg Court mentioned above, the Council may decide upon the proposal of the Commission on **all economic policy measures** of a **short-, medium- or long-term** nature.[14] Where special derogation clauses apply, these will prevail if the causation lies predominantly in the conditions of the latter (→ para 5).

6

The inserted wording "**in a spirit of solidarity**" in paragraph 1 reflects the value system of the Union, which is anchored in Articles 2 and 3.3 TEU for human relations, and also between MS (Article 3.3(3) TEU). Rightly so, Article 122.1

7

---

[7] See Weber (1982), p. 132 et seqq.
[8] Weber (1982), p. 134.
[9] Müller-Heidelberg (1970), p. 190 et seqq.
[10] Case 5/73, *Balkan-Import-Export-GmbH* (ECJ 24 October 1973).
[11] Case 10/73, *Rewe* (ECJ 24 October 1973).
[12] Case 9/73, *Schlüter* (ECJ 24 October 1973).
[13] Weber (1982), p. 136.
[14] Hattenberger, in Schwarze (2019), Article 122 AEUV para 3.

TFEU can be qualified as a "**direct result of the principle of solidarity**".[15] Other procedures in this common spirit are not substituted.[16]

8   A special example of temporary economic measures is the supply of products, especially in the area of energy, which apparently was the prior imagination for emergency situations.[17] The term "products" (*produits* in the French version) apparently is wider than the German wording (*Waren*) and may encompass all products, including financial services.[18] Directive 2006/67 of 24 July 2006 for the supply of mineral oil products was the only act based on Article 122.1 TFEU until 2016.[19]

9   The **humanitarian measures** taken by some MS as a result of the **migration and refugee crisis** required a second activation of Article 122.1 TFEU **in March 2016**. With Regulation (EU) No 2016/369 on the provision of emergency support within the Union,[20] the Union responded to a deterioration in the overall economic situation in some MS. The new Regulation on emergency support is intended for those MS whose own assistance capacities are overloaded by urgent needs and "exceptional circumstances", such as the sudden influx of refugees or other serious emergencies (Article 1.1 of Regulation (EU) No 2016/369). For example, Greece, already economically affected by the sovereign debt crisis, had to provide incoming refugees with food, emergency medical care, shelter, water and sanitation, as well as hygiene, protection and education. Regulation (EU) No 2016/369 provides for an emergency support instrument that is "appropriate to the economic situation" (Article 1.1) and is intended to enable more rapid, targeted support for national measures in the event of major crises (Article 1.2). The initiative requires funding in the range of EUR 700 million over three years: EUR 300 million in 2016, EUR 200 million in 2017, EUR 200 million in 2018.[21] Emergency aid will be provided in close cooperation with MS, UN agencies, non-governmental organisations (NGOs) and international organisations and will include basic food, shelter and medical supplies for the many refugees currently arriving in EU countries.[22]

10   A third activation of the solidarity clause of Article 122.1 TFEU took place in the course of the **COVID-19 pandemic crisis**. On 2 April 2020, the European Commission presented a **new solidarity instrument** called "SURE" (**Support mitigating Unemployment Risks in Emergency**). This is an instrument designed to provide temporary support to MS to finance national short-time work schemes

---

[15] Pilz (2016), p. 164.

[16] For a general survey on the principle of solidarity see Hilpold (2013).

[17] Häde, in Calliess and Ruffert (2022), Article 122 AEUV para 3.

[18] Bandilla, in Grabitz et al. (2021), Article 122 AEUV para 13 (released in 2011).

[19] Council Directive 2006/67/EC of 24 July 2006 *imposing an obligation on Member States to maintain minimum stocks of crude oil and/or petroleum products*, O.J. L 217/8 (2006).

[20] Council Regulation (EU) No 2016/369 of 15 March 2016 *on the provision of emergency support within the Union*, O.J. L 70/1 (2016).

[21] Proposal for a Council Regulation on the provision of emergency support within the Union, COM (2016) 115 final.

[22] Cf. 10th Recital of Regulation (EU) No 2016/369.

and similar measures during the crisis caused by the COVID-19 outbreak.[23] The temporary instrument proposed on the legal basis of Articles 122.1 and 122.2 TFEU allows for financial assistance of up to EUR 100 billion in the form of Union loans to the MS concerned. The Commission intends to raise the necessary funds by borrowing "on behalf of the Union" (Article 4 of the Regulation) on the capital markets or with financial institutions, which in turn will be covered "in a spirit of solidarity" by a guarantee scheme of the MS for an amount of EUR 25 billion. The construction of the guarantee system is based on voluntary contributions by the MS to the Union (Article 11 of Regulation (EU) No 2020/672). While the establishment of the MS guarantee system to secure the Union's financial assistance is based on Article 122.2 TFEU, the rules on the organisation and management of the SURE instrument are based on Article 122.2 TFEU (→ para 13 et seq.).

As to the procedure, the Council may act on the **proposal of the Commission** through all legal instruments, like regulations, directives, decisions or resolutions; the practice of the Council and the subsequent case law of the ECJ on ex-Article 103 TEC mentioned above justify this conclusion.[24]

11

3. Financial Assistance (Article 122.2 TFEU)

Article 122.2 TFEU enables the Union as such to grant financial assistance under certain conditions; financial assistance therefore is not obligatory ("the Council ... may grant...") and is narrowly linked to conditionality ("under certain conditions"). Article 122.2 TFEU leaves wide discretion for the proposal of the Commission and the Council for the type and means of financial assistance. The **conditionality** of financial assistance is an inherent element of financial assistance in Article 122.2 TFEU (→ para 22) and Article 136.3 TFEU ("under strict conditions"; → Article 136 TFEU para 36). One may even conceive conditionality as an emanation of the spirit of solidarity,[25] and conditional assistance may also be formulated for reasons of equality.[26]

12

---

[23] Council Regulation (EU) No 2020/672 *on the establishment of a European instrument for temporary support to mitigate unemployment risks in an emergency (SURE) following the COVID-19 outbreak*, O.J. L159/1 (2020).

[24] Case 5/73, *Balkan-Import-Export-GmbH* (ECJ 24 October 1973); Bandilla, in Grabitz et al. (2021), Article 122 AEUV para 15 (released in 2011).

[25] Rebhahn (2015), p. 134.

[26] Louis (2011), p. 120.

3.1. Normative Conditions

3.1.1. "Natural Disasters or Exceptional Occurrences" (Causation)

13 The provision of financial assistance by the EU shall initially be linked to a **triggering event**. Article 122.2 TFEU lists "exceptional occurrences" in addition to natural disasters as a specific requirement. Natural disasters include storms, floods, earthquakes and volcanic eruptions.[27] The undefined legal concept of extraordinary events is characterised in the literature as "unforeseen", "surprising" or "rapidly developing changes in the economic situation",[28] which manifest themselves in serious social problems, unrest, foreign policy or military entanglements, as well as a macroeconomic shock in foreign trade[29] or an imminent State bankruptcy.[30] As a consequence, these must be difficulties with "massively damaging effects on the economy" (→ para 9).[31] In the light of the above, the serious economic disruption caused by the COVID-19 outbreak is also a surprising and exceptional occurrence, which is having a serious impact on the economies of the MS and requires a collective response in a spirit of solidarity. If, on the other hand, other considerations are in the foreground, Article 122.2 TFEU is not applicable. It should be remembered here that financial interventions can also be made through the Union's Structural Funds as part of the policy to strengthen its economic, social and territorial cohesion.[32] On the basis of Article 175.3 TFEU, Regulation (EU) No 2012/2002 established a Solidarity Fund from which MS of the Union and candidate countries (third countries) can draw on financial resources if a major natural disaster has a serious impact on living conditions, the natural environment or the economy.[33]

14 Both forms of European solidarity were activated to deal with the serious consequences of the COVID-19 outbreak in Europe. First, the **EU Solidarity Fund** was extended to cover public health emergencies.[34] Until now, the Fund has been used to help MS cope with a wide range of natural disasters, such as floods, forest fires, earthquakes, storms and droughts. The amendment also included public health crises among the emergencies financed by the EU Solidarity Fund. The extension of the scope will thus allow the most affected MS to have access to

---

[27] Kämmerer, in Siekmann (2013), Article 122 AEUV para 26; Keller (2014), p. 211.

[28] Bandilla, in Grabitz et al. (2021), Article 122 AEUV para 16 (released in 2011).

[29] Kempen, in Streinz (2018), Article 122 AEUV para 9.

[30] Häde (2009), p. 401.

[31] Kempen, in Streinz (2018), Article 122 AEUV para 9; Lais (2007), p. 306 et seqq.

[32] Smulders and Keppenne, in von der Groeben et al. (2015), Article 122 AEUV para 11; Blanke and Pilz (2014), p. 269 et seq.

[33] Council Regulation (EC) No 2012/2002 *establishing the European Union Solidarity Fund*, O.J. L 311/3 (2002).

[34] Regulation (EU) No 2020/461 *amending Council Regulation (EC) No 2012/2002 in order to provide financial assistance to Member States and to countries negotiating their accession to the Union that are seriously affected by a major public health emergency*, O.J. L 99/9 (2020).

Article 122. [Solidarity]

financial assistance of up to EUR 800 million in 2020.[35] This is a clear sign of the Union's great solidarity with the MS in dealing with this crisis. The **SURE instrument**, which has its legal basis on Article 122.2 TFEU, is complementary to the regular grants made for similar purposes under the EU Solidarity Fund.[36] Both measures are designed to deal with major crises resulting from public health threats, with the EU Solidarity Fund being able to be used on a permanent basis, while the SURE instrument is limited to the specific case of the COVID-19 outbreak.[37]

Against this background, "exceptional occurrences" may—due to its wide formulation—also comprise a **severe financial and debt crisis of an MS**.[38] For example, in view of the threat of national bankruptcy of Greece, Ireland and Portugal, Regulation (EU) No 407/2010/EU establishing a **European Financial Stabilisation Mechanism** (EFSM) was formulated based on Article 122.2 TFEU.[39] With this instrument, the Union provides financial assistance to states threatened by serious financing problems.[40] However, it should be emphasised that, in the specific exceptional cases provided for in Article 122.2 TFEU, only the "Union" and not the MS may provide assistance. This is why it is difficult to derive from this provision a viable indication of a general solidarity obligation of the MS under Union law in the field of economic union.

15

The norm does not presuppose only external factors (e.g. a worldwide financial crisis) as causes for the difficulties but may encompass home-made macroeconomic and debt crisis management as well. Even if the context with the first alternative ("natural disasters") seems to favour the counter-argument of essential external causation, this differentiation would not go on much further as **external and internal factors** are most frequently linked together. As to the financial crisis in the EU since 2010, internal ("home-made") factors as well as external factors are closely linked together, which may have justified the wide interpretation of the

16

---

[35] European Commission 2020, IP/20/753.

[36] Council Regulation (EU) No 2020/672 *on the establishment of a European instrument for temporary support to mitigate unemployment risks in an emergency (SURE) following the COVID-19 outbreak*, O.J. L 159/1 (2020).

[37] For example, Portugal received loans of EUR 5.9 billion from the SURE instrument by Council decision to cope with sudden increases in public expenditure to preserve employment. Council Implementing Decision (EU) 2020/1354 *granting temporary support under Regulation (EU) 2020/672 to the Portuguese Republic to mitigate unemployment risks in the emergency following the COVID-19 outbreak*, O.J. L 314/49 (2020).

[38] Häde (2009), p. 401; Häde (2010), p. 858 et seq.; Frenz and Ehlenz (2010), p. 211 et seqq.; Herrmann (2010), p. 414; Louis (2010), p. 984.

[39] Council Regulation (EU) No 407/2010 *establishing a European financial stabilisation mechanism*, O.J. L 118/1 (2010). Cf. Martucci (2020), para 12.6 et seqq.

[40] This subsumption is not undisputed. In favour, for example, Calliess (2011), p. 247; with a sceptical view Frenz and Ehlenz (2010), p. 211 et seqq.; Potacs and Mayer (2011), p. 137 et seq.; against it Kube and Reimer (2010), p. 1914; Hentschelmann (2011), p. 282. The developments in May 2010 are documented in Tuori and Tuori (2014), p. 89 et seqq. and Borger (2020), para 32.4 et seqq.

normative element "beyond its control" for several countries receiving financial assistance. In general, the Commission and Council, while applying new instruments of financial assistance, strongly advocated the vulnerability of the eurozone as a whole and not only the financial and economic weaknesses of the members concerned to be decisive factors.

17 The **practice of financial assistance** based on Article 122.2 TFEU and later on Article 136.3 TFEU (ESM) during the financial crisis since 2010 and the CJEU judgment in *Pringle* (→ para 26–27) lastly confirm this evaluation. A closer look at the practice of the Union and the MS will elucidate this opinion.

3.1.2. "Beyond Its Control"

18 It is also necessary that the exceptional occurrence be outside the control of the MS. Since natural disasters such as volcanic eruptions or earthquakes[41] always fulfil this requirement, the second variant should be read as "other" exceptional events.[42] In view of the above-mentioned characteristics of exceptional events, they are beyond control if they are **an unforeseeable or infrequent or irregular deterioration of circumstances**.[43]

19 The recitals of Regulation (EU) No 407/2010 mention the "unprecedented global financial crisis", which has "seriously damaged economic growth and financial stability and provoked a strong deterioration in the deficit and debt positions of the Member States" (Recital 3). Moreover, the "deepening of the financial crisis has led to a severe deterioration of the borrowing conditions of several Member States" (Recital 4). In principle, the reaction of the financial markets is not an uncontrollable exceptional event in the sense of Article 122.2 TFEU but a consequence of the **high national debt of the individual MS**. However, due to misjudgements and inefficiencies in the financial markets in the run-up to the crisis, the situation must be assessed differently. The country-specific risk premiums for long-term government bonds were virtually eliminated by the single currency. It was not until the beginning of the **Greek crisis** that market confidence in the creditworthiness of the euro countries began to waver and country-specific creditworthiness again became the market's interest rate criterion.[44] Interest spreads between European government bonds diverged abruptly and without any objective change in the economic situation in the individual countries.[45] The result was a dangerous combination of high government debt and constantly rising risk premiums. As a result of the transition from eurozone to country-specific risk assessment, confidence in the debt of individual MS broke

---

[41] Keller (2014), p. 211.

[42] Kämmerer, in Siekmann (2013), Article 122 AEUV para 27.

[43] With a similar view Louis (2010), p. 984.

[44] Herrmann (2010), p. 314; de Gregorio Merino (2012), p. 1616.

[45] For an overview of the development of return of investment of ten-year government bonds, cf. Horn et al. (2011), p. 5.

down and became the basis for an acute debt crisis that "must be considered an uncontrollable and exceptional event".[46]

3.1.3. "In Difficulties or Seriously Threatened with Severe Difficulties" and Causality

The MS must be "in difficulties", which means actually **confronted with difficulties** or at least must be "threatened with severe difficulties". The norm clearly faces present and future dangers and has also, therefore, a preventive function. The difficulties will generally be of an economic nature (shocks) but are not limited to these circumstances, which may also comprise social unrest, external and military implications or insolvency.[47] Moreover, there must be causality between the natural disaster or exceptional occurrence and the difficulties.[48] Financial assistance must therefore always be an immediate response by the Union to the (imminent) consequences of a natural disaster or exceptional occurrence. 20

The crisis of confidence in the financial markets was accompanied by an unexpected deterioration in refinancing conditions, which did not correspond to fundamental economic data[49] and which pushed a large number of euro states to the brink of national bankruptcy.[50] The rising interest rates on government bonds and the need for refinancing on the markets triggered a spiral that would necessarily end in insolvency. The threat of national bankruptcy as a result of the financial and economic crisis thus presents an MS with serious difficulties that cannot be averted without Union assistance.[51] However, the wording of Article 122.2 TFEU does not presuppose that the MS has fallen into difficulties through **no fault of its own**.[52] Rather, it must be asked whether the crisis has left the MS in a position to react independently of the situation and initiate countermeasures.[53] Consequently, it is not the evolution towards the crisis that should be taken into account, but the position of the MS *in* the crisis.[54] The extreme volatility of risk premiums on 21

---

[46] Heinemann (1995), p. 609 (our translation). In the affirmative even before the Greek crisis Zehnpfund and Heimbach (2010), p. 6 et seq; with the same view Häde (2009), p. 401; Borger (2013), p. 28. Another view is expressed among others by Schwarz (2011), p. 709; Faßbender (2010), p. 801.

[47] Häde, in Calliess and Ruffert (2022), Article 122 AEUV para 8; Bandilla, in Grabitz et al. (2021), Article 122 AEUV para 16 (released in 2011).

[48] Kämmerer (2010), p. 164; Bandilla, in Grabitz et al. (2021), Article 122 AEUV para 17 (released in 2011).

[49] Fourth Recital of Regulation (EU) No 407/2010.

[50] Nettesheim (2012), p. 70.

[51] Häde (2011), p. 13.

[52] Häde (2009), p. 403; Bandilla, in Grabitz et al. (2021), Article 122 AEUV para 18 (released in 2011); Kempen, in Streinz (2018), Article 122 AEUV para 9.

[53] Nettesheim (2012), p. 70.

[54] Nettesheim (2012), p. 70; Hilpold (2015), p. 279 et seq.

government bonds meant that Portugal, Ireland, Italy, Greece and Spain had lost control over refinancing.[55]

3.1.4. "Under Certain Conditions" (Conditionality)

22 The contribution to the aggravation of its difficulties is irrelevant for the question of *whether* the MS will receive assistance. However, any possible fault on the part of its representatives will affect the *conditions* that the Council decides on and that are to be attached to the assistance.[56] This form of assistance, which is referred to as "conditionality", is intended to ensure that financial assistance is not granted without any requisites or conditions. This is explained by the close connection of Article 122.2 to Article 125 TFEU, according to which **a bail-out by the Union or the MS for national liabilities is excluded** (→ para 23–27). It is true that the conditions for financial assistance from the Union are not specified in Article 122.2 TFEU. However, in order not to override the principle of the MS' own economic responsibility through a bail-out, the conditions must contain concrete requirements for a change of economic policy direction.[57] Article 122.2 TFEU therefore does not constitute a legal basis for unconditional financial transfers by the Union to individual MS.[58] Assistance must therefore not be granted entirely without the addition of certain conditions, in particular without earmarking.[59] In the case of the SURE solidarity instrument, Article 3.2 of Regulation (EU) No 2020/672 provides that the beneficiary MS may only use Union loans "in support of national short-time work schemes or similar measures". In the case of the establishment of the EFSM, the Council limited itself to laying down guidelines for such conditions and obligations and instructed the Commission to specify the details of the negotiations with the recipient country (Article 3 of Regulation (EU) No 407/2010).[60] However, the conditions, which are essentially aimed at **austerity**, are not uncontested among economists.[61] In the case of an intergovernmental aid to Greece, strict austerity measures have not prevented the Greek economy from shrinking further.

---

[55] Cf. Louis (2010), p. 984, who affirmed that for "Greece, Ireland and potentially other States" in 2010. See also de Gregorio Merino (2012), p. 1618.

[56] Kämmerer, in Siekmann (2013), Article 122 AEUV para 34.

[57] Pilz (2016), p. 165; Bandilla, in Grabitz et al. (2021), Article 122 AEUV para 21 (released in 2011).

[58] Häde, in Calliess and Ruffert (2022), Article 122 AEUV para 14.

[59] Kempen, in Streinz (2018), Article 122 AEUV para 11.

[60] Borger (2013), p. 28.

[61] On the discussion, see the chapters in Corsetti (2012).

3.2. Granting of Financial Assistance

3.2.1. Procedure

If the conditions laid down in Article 122.2 TFEU are fulfilled, the Council, acting on a proposal from the Commission, may decide to grant financial assistance. The Council has a wide margin of discretion ("may") when making decisions, but this only concerns whether it grants support. Where financial assistance is granted, it must be subject to "certain conditions".[62] The Council decides by a qualified majority. The **European Parliament** (EP), on the other hand, is **not involved in decision-making**. However, Article 122.2 TFEU requires the President of the Council to inform the EP of the decision taken. In this respect, the EP's interests are taken more into account within the scope of application of paragraph 2 than within the framework of the first paragraph of Article 122 TFEU (→ para 10). Under paragraph 1, the Council also decides by a qualified majority on a proposal from the Commission, but it ultimately does so without involving the EP in any way.[63]

23

3.2.2. Types of Assistance

Article 122.2 TFEU provides for the granting of financial assistance. According to its wording, the provision is much more concrete than the provision in paragraph 1, which only considers "appropriate measures" (→ para 6). Financial assistance, on the other hand, covers **all forms of financial aid and support**.[64] In this context, loans (possibly on preferential terms), non-repayable grants or different types of guarantees are certainly conceivable.[65] All types have in common the fact that they are forms of support from which the recipient obtains an unrequited advantage that could not have been obtained under normal market conditions.[66] Consequently, loans on terms below the market level are also assistance under paragraph 2. The Union enables the beneficiary State to borrow at a favourable interest rate, which would otherwise be denied by the market mechanism. The financial assistance comes exclusively from the Union and must therefore be included in the Union budget.[67] Article 122.2 TFEU does not require MS to provide mutual financial

24

---

[62] Hattenberger, in Schwarze (2019), Article 122 AEUV para 7.

[63] Kämmerer, in Siekmann (2013), Article 122 AEUV para 54.

[64] Hattenberger, in Schwarze (2019), Article 122 AEUV para 8; Häde, in Calliess and Ruffert (2022), Article 122 AEUV para 9.

[65] Hattenberger, in Schwarze (2019), Article 122 AEUV para 8; Bandilla, in Grabitz et al. (2021), Article 122 AEUV para 19 (released in 2011); Smulders and Keppenne, in von der Groeben et al. (2015), Article 122 AEUV para 17.

[66] Kämmerer, in Siekmann (2013), Article 122 AEUV para 38.

[67] Häde, in Calliess and Ruffert (2022), Article 122 AEUV para 10; Smulders and Keppenne, in von der Groeben et al. (2015), Article 122 AEUV para 17.

assistance but does not exclude voluntary measures.[68] However, the CJEU has decided that **MS are free to establish a stability mechanism** such as the ESM, provided that it operates in accordance with Union law.[69]

3.3. Article 125 TFEU (No Bail-Out Clause) in Relation to Temporary and Permanent Assistance Mechanisms

25   The most interesting aspect, however, is the potential infringement of the "no bail-out" clause of Article 125 TFEU, which was largely voiced by a part of the literature in the case of assistance under Article 122.2 TFEU. If the no bail-out clause were interpreted as an overarching clause for prohibiting any assistance for MS in financial emergency situations[70] as provided, for example, by the EFSM and the European Financial Stability Facility (EFSF), then Article 122.2 TFEU would lose its practical relevance and also intergovernmental financial assistance mechanisms, like the ESM, might be prohibited. Therefore, Article 122.2 TFEU must be interpreted either as an exception to Article 125 TFEU[71] (*lex specialis*) or as "counterweight" to the latter,[72] or Article 125 TFEU must be reduced by teleological interpretation.[73]

26   The Court in **Pringle** unfolded its solution by applying all methods of interpretation, starting with the wording of the norm, which did not prohibit any financial assistance of an MS.[74]

27   Moreover, the Court supports this view by a contextual, systematic interpretation with regard to Articles 122 and 123 TFEU: if Article 125 TFEU had the intent to prohibit any financial assistance of the Union, this should have been clarified in Article 122 TFEU.[75] Finally, the Court applies the teleological interpretation linked to a historical argument of the genesis of Article 125 TFEU, aiming at the financial stability of the euro since Maastricht and the maintenance of a solid budgetary policy; financial assistance is only compatible with Article 125 TFEU if it is **"indispensable for the safeguarding of the financial stability of the euro area as a whole and subject to strict conditions"**.[76] The Court then elucidates that

---

[68] Häde, in Calliess and Ruffert (2022), Article 122 AEUV para 10.

[69] Case C-370/12, *Pringle* (CJEU 27 November 2012) para 121.

[70] In this sense Frenz and Ehlenz (2010), p. 212; Seidel (2011), p. 529; Faßbender (2010), p. 800.

[71] Weber (2011), p. 937; Hentschelmann (2011), p. 286; Häde (2011), p. 15.

[72] Louis (2010), p. 983.

[73] Häde (2010), p. 859.

[74] Case C-370/12, *Pringle* (CJEU 27 November 2012) para 130. Cf. Borger (2013), p. 7 (24 et seq.).

[75] Case C-370/12, *Pringle* (CJEU 27 November 2012) para 131. The argument is somehow redundant because Article 122 TFEU is a special clause following the multilateral supervision clause of Article 121 TFEU and even an express indication would not necessarily preclude any assistance outside the Treaty.

[76] Case C-370/12, *Pringle* (CJEU 27 November 2012) para 136.

assistance in the form of credit lines or loans (Articles 14–16 TESM) does not signify any liability of the ESM or the MS for a member's debts.[77]

From the comments above, it becomes clear that financial assistance based on Article 122.2 TFEU for temporary measures or a permanent financial mechanism based on Article 136.3 TFEU does not contradict Article 125 TFEU if the conditions of Article 122.2 TFEU are met and the permanent mechanism does not infringe the economic policy measures and price stability of the euro. An economic *and* monetary union cannot be built on the **principle of individual responsibility** alone. Within this form of organisation—as in all federal systems[78]—there is also a need for an **element of solidarity**, which accompanies this individual responsibility in order, for example, to allow members to help those affected in unforeseen emergencies, which cannot be controlled by the States. Article 122.2 TFEU normatively defines "solidarity" *de lege lata* as a motive for financial assistance from the Union. As a rule, Article 125 TFEU excludes solidarity measures of a financial nature. However, if in exceptional situations the members were not able to stand up for each other, there would be no basis for individual responsibility.[79] Both principles complement and alter each other. Thus, in the case of receiving solidarity assistance, the possibilities of independent decision-making for the recipient can naturally be reduced.[80] Within the scope of Article 122 TFEU, this can be done, for example, through economic policy conditions. In this way, the principle of the MS' individual economic responsibility is reduced but not invalidated by a bail-out.

28

It should be noted additionally that the German Federal Constitutional Court (FCC) in its ruling of 12 September 2012 has confirmed Article 136.3 TFEU as a legal basis for the ESM from a German constitutional point of view. It concerned the "eternity clause" of Article 79.3 of the German Basic Law (GG), the preciseness of Article 136.3 TFEU and the **budgetary responsibility of the German Parliament** (Bundestag) under certain conditions.[81] Furthermore, the Estonian Supreme Court, in its ruling of 12 July 2012 concerning the **compatibility of Article 4.4 TESM with the principle of democracy**,[82] found "that the economic and financial sustainability of the euro is contained in the constitutional values of Estonia as of the time Estonia became a euro member State".[83]

29

---

[77] Case C-370/12, *Pringle* (CJEU 27 November 2012) para 139–146.

[78] Pilz (2016), p. 131.

[79] Müller-Franken (2014), p. 232.

[80] U. Di Fabio, Interview, Der Spiegel Nr. 28/2012 of 9 July 2012, p. 23 (24); Calliess and Schoenfleisch (2012), p. 487.

[81] German Federal Constitutional Court, 2 BvR 130/12 (Judgment of 12 September 2012)—*ESM*, para 267 et seqq.

[82] Estonian Supreme Court, case 3-4-1-6-12 (Ruling of 12 July 2012); Estonia with its low voting percentage of 0,1855% in the Board of Governors could be overruled in the urgent voting procedure requiring only 85% of votes instead of unanimity.

[83] Estonian Supreme Court, case 3-4-1-6-12 (Ruling of 12 July 2012) para 163.

3.4. Specific Agreements and Judicial Protection

30 The conditionality of financial assistance is secured by so-called **Memoranda of Understanding** (MoUs), which under the EFSF regime were negotiated by the Commission with the respective MS based on the IMF model; under the ESM regime, the Board of Governors requests the Commission, upon the demand of the respective MS, to negotiate an "MoU". These "agreements" are specific forms of international treaties that are not enforceable.[84]

31 The austerity policy under a macroeconomic adjustment programme can lead to profound cuts in the fundamental social rights of citizens.[85] The **adjustment path** is paved with a rigid austerity programme and is characterised in the short term by a situation in which economic and social conditions are unfavourable and the standard of living of the population is falling.[86] Judicial protection at the EU level against **austerity measures** implied in the MoU is difficult to obtain because they normally have to be concretised by national measures of implementation. Actions for annulment did not succeed because "direct and individual concern" was missing (Article 263 TFEU);[87] similarly, the European Court of Human Rights (ECtHR) rejected individual complaints as manifestly ill-founded.[88]

32 However, it should be noted that the applicability of the Charter of Fundamental Rights of the European Union (EUCFR) cannot be completely discarded if the financial assistance is based on Article 122.2 TFEU and not on Article 136.3 TFEU.

33 The CJEU in **Pringle** only ruled that Article 51.1 EUCFR is not applicable when the Union is establishing a stability mechanism like the ESM but did not refer to short-term facilities like EFSF and EFSM.[89] Nevertheless, it is obvious that the standing of private citizens before the courts in Luxembourg and Strasbourg against national austerity measures agreed upon in bilateral MoUs will be difficult to assert.

4. Relationship to Articles 143 and 222 TFEU

34 The solidarity clause of Article 122 TFEU forms part of the economic and monetary policy provisions under Title VIII of Part Three of the TFEU. The provision applies "without exception"[90] and "indefinitely"[91] to all MS. However, Article 122 TFEU must be distinguished from **Articles 143–144 TFEU**. These allow MS whose currency is not the euro to receive financial assistance if they are experiencing or

---

[84] Portuguese Constitutional Tribunal, Acórdão 353/2012 (Ruling of 5 July 2012).
[85] Fisahn (2010), p. 248 et seqq.; Koursovitis (2012), p. 1 et seqq.
[86] On the term "austerity", cf. Drudy and Collins (2011), p. 339.
[87] Case T-541/10, *ADEDY et al. v Council* (CFI 27 November 2012) para 73 et seqq.
[88] Appl. No. No 57665/12 and 57657/12, *Koufaki and ADEDY v Greece* (ECtHR 7 May 2012).
[89] Case C-370/12, *Pringle* (CJEU 27 November 2012) para 180.
[90] Kämmerer, in Siekmann (2013), Article 122 AEUV para 66.
[91] Smulders and Keppenne, in von der Groeben et al. (2015), Article 122 AEUV para 2.

Article 122. [Solidarity]

are seriously threatened with difficulties as regards their balance of payments either as a result of an overall disequilibrium in their balance of payments or because of the type of currency at their disposal. In relation to Article 122 TFEU, Articles 143 and 144 TFEU are *leges speciales* in the case of **balance of payment difficulties**.[92] Accordingly, Article 122.2 TFEU applies only subsidiarily.[93] In the course of the sovereign debt crisis, Hungary,[94] Latvia[95] and Romania[96] relied on financial assistance based on Article 143.2 TFEU to avert imminent sovereign bankruptcy.[97]

The **solidarity clause** formulated in **Article 222 TFEU** is another specific form of the general principle of solidarity.[98] The provision is based on the preparatory work of the Constitutional Treaty (Articles I-43 and III-329) and has been incorporated into the Treaty of Lisbon with appropriate editorial amendments but without substantive changes.[99] Notwithstanding the general designation of the norm, this is not a general obligation of solidarity. Articles 222.1 and 222.2 TFEU limit the material scope of the solidarity clause to **sector-specific situations**. Only in the case of a terrorist attack, natural disaster or man-made disaster is the provision applicable. In view of the fact that the solidarity obligation has been specified, an extensive interpretation of the solidarity clause that goes beyond the groups of cases listed is not possible. For example, in the course of the emergency measures for Greece and the establishment of the temporary rescue mechanism, there were discussions about using the solidarity clause as a legal basis in view of the threat of national bankruptcy of individual States. Such considerations were rejected, however, since assistance provided by the MS or Union goes beyond the scope of Article 222 TFEU and is therefore illegal.[100] As a result, the MS established the EFSM umbrella on the basis of Article 122.2 TFEU (→ para 15, 19, 21). The provision in the area of economic policy is a *lex specialis* in relation to Article 222 TFEU. The reference to "exceptional events" includes a situation—albeit not

35

---

[92] Häde, in Calliess and Ruffert (2022), Article 122 AEUV para 7; Hufeld (2014), para 111; Herrmann, in Pechstein et al. (2017), Article 122 AEUV para 6. On the balance of payment assistance, see Pilz (2016), p. 165 et seqq.;, Keller (2014), p. 227 et seqq.

[93] Häde, in Calliess and Ruffert (2022), Article 122 AEUV para 7. Similarly, Kämmerer, in Siekmann (2013), Article 122 AEUV para 66.

[94] Council Decision 2009/102/EC *providing Community medium-term financial assistance for Hungary*, O.J. L 37/5 (2009).

[95] Council Decision 2009/289/EC *on granting mutual assistance for Latvia* and Council Decision 2009/290/EC *providing Community medium-term financial assistance for Latvia*, O.J. L 79/37 (2009).

[96] Council Decision 2013/532/EU *granting mutual assistance for Romania*, O.J. L 286/4 (2013).

[97] On the individual measures see Pilz (2016), p. 166 et seq. On the developments in Central and Eastern Europe in the global financial crisis, cf. Dietrich et al. (2011), p. 312. See also Hufeld (2014), para 110.

[98] Häde, in Calliess and Ruffert (2022), Article 222 AEUV para 10.

[99] On the structure and application of the solidarity clause, cf. Pilz (2016), p. 167 et seq.

[100] Häde, in Calliess and Ruffert (2022), Article 222 AEUV para 21.

undisputed—that legitimises solidarity-based aid measures by the Union in the event of budgetary emergencies.

5. Outlook

36   Since the outbreak of the financial, economic and sovereign debt crisis in 2008, the **mutual assistance clause in Article 122.2 TFEU has taken on a central role** that could not have been imagined earlier. Initially, it served as the legal basis to establish the EFSM and as an interpretative element for the overall structure of the provisions of EMU.[101] In the course of the migration and refugee crisis (2015) and with the introduction of the SURE solidarity mechanism to deal with the COVID-19 pandemic (2020), Article 122 TFEU once again became the legal basis for financial assistance. What all these measures have in common, however, is that they have only provided financial support to the Member States concerned for a short period. Thus, the EFSM, which was established in spring 2010 on the basis of Article 122.2 TFEU, was replaced by the European Stability Mechanism in September 2012. This is based on an international agreement under international law and has no reference to Article 122 TFEU. The period of application of Regulation (EU) No 2016/369, which was adopted in the migration and refugee crisis, was also limited to three years.

37   With the proposal of the so-called European Union Recovery Instrument, which was discussed in the course of the COVID-19 crisis, a **paradigm shift** is becoming apparent. On 27 May 2020, the European Commission presented an economic stimulus package with a total volume of EUR 750 billion under the title **"Next Generation EU"** to address the most urgent challenges in the management of the COVID-19 pandemic.[102] The Recovery Instrument will be set up for a limited period (2021–2024) and will be used exclusively for crisis response and reconstruction measures.[103] The instrument will support investments and reforms that are essential for a sustainable recovery, strengthening the economic and social resilience of Member States and supporting the green and digital transition. To this end, EUR 312 billion in financial aid can be drawn from the Member States in the form of grants. A further EUR 3600 billion will be made available as loans.[104]

38   The restructuring fund is divided into several legal acts (→ Supplement to Title VIII: Introduction para 55 et seqq.). The core element is the **European Union Recovery Instrument** adopted under Article 122.2 TFEU. However, this is essentially only a shell. Unlike previous measures that were based on Article 122 TFEU,

---

[101] Hilpold (2021), p. 55-64.

[102] Council Regulation (EU) 2020/2094 *establishing a European Union Recovery Instrument to support the recovery in the aftermath of the COVID-19 crisis*, O.J. L 433I/23 (2020).

[103] Council Regulation (EU) No 2020/2094 *establishing a European Union Recovery Instrument to support the recovery in the aftermath of the COVID-19 crisis* O.J. L 433I/23 (2020).

[104] Article 3.2 point (a, ii) and point (b) of Regulation 2020/2094.

the instrument does not authorise the Commission to borrow on the financial markets or determine how the money is to be disbursed. Rather, in order to allow for the borrowing, the Commission intends to amend the own resources ceiling of the EU's multiannual financial framework (Article 311.3 TFEU). The margin thus gained should be available as a guarantee for the bonds issued on the financial markets. To this end, the application of the emergency clause will be combined with the regular procedures of the Cohesion and Structural Funds (Article 175 et seqq. TFEU). In view of the financial and institutional design, this will create a hitherto unique **redistribution mechanism**. At some point, however, the courts will have to examine whether this legal construction is waterproof or ultra vires.

List of Cases

ECJ/CJEU

ECJ 24.10.1973, 5/73, *Balkan-Import-Export-GmbH*, ECLI:EU:C:1973:109 [cit. in para 10, 24]
ECJ 24.10.1973, 10/73, *Rewe*, ECLI:EU:C:1973:111 [cit. in para 11]
ECJ 24.10.1973, 9/73, *Schlüter*, ECLI:EU:C:1973:110 [cit. in para 12]
CJEU 27.11.2012, C-370/12, *Pringle*, ECLI:EU:C:2012:756 [cit. in para 70, 75–78, 90]

GC

GC 27.11.2012, T-451/10, *ADEDY et al. v Council*, ECLI:EU:T:2011:400 [cit. in para 88 et seq.]

National Constitutional Courts

Estonian Supreme Court 12.07.2012, case 3-4-1-6-12, ESM [cit. in para 29]
German Federal Constitutional Court 12.09.2012, 2 BvR 130/12, ESM, ECLI:DE: BVerfG:2012:rs20120912.2bvr139012 [cit. in para 29]
Portuguese Constitutional Tribunal 05.07.2012, Acórdão 353/2012, ESM [cit. in para 29]

References

Antpöhler, C. (2012). Emergenz der europäischen Wirtschaftsregierung – Das Six Pack als Zeichen supranationaler Leistungsfähigkeit. *Zeitschrift für ausländisches öffentliches Recht und Völkerrecht*, 353–393.

Blanke, H.-J., & Pilz, S. (2014). Solidarität in der "Schuldenunion". In H.-J. Blanke & S. Pilz (Eds.), *Die "Fiskalunion"* (pp. 245–296). Mohr Siebeck.

Borger, V. (2013). How the debt crisis exposes the development of solidarity in the Euro area. *European Constitutional Law Review*, 7–36.

Borger, V. (2020). EU financial assistance. In F. Amtenbrink & C. Herrmann (Eds.), *The EU law of Economic and Monetary Union (Chapter 12)*. OUP.

Calliess, C. (2011). Perspektiven des Euro zwischen Solidarität und Recht – Eine rechtliche Analyse der Griechenlandhilfe und des Rettungsschirms. *Zeitschrift für europarechtliche Studien*, 213–282.

Calliess, C., & Ruffert, M. (Eds.). (2022). *EUV/AEUV. Kommentar* (6th ed.). C. H. Beck.

Calliess, C., & Schoenfleisch, C. (2012). Auf dem Weg in die europäische "Fiskalunion"? – Europa- und verfassungsrechtliche Fragen einer Reform der Wirtschafts- und Währungsunion im Kontext des Fiskalvertrages. *JuristenZeitung*, 477–487.

Corsetti, G. (Ed.). (2012). *Austerity: Too much of a good thing?* Centre for Economic Policy Research.

de Gregorio Merino, A. (2012). Legal developments in the Economic and Monetary Union during the debt crisis: The mechanisms of financial assistance. *Common Market Law Review*, 1613–1646.

Dietrich, D., Knedlik, T., & Lindner, A. (2011). Mittel- und Osteuropa in der Weltfinanzkrise: Simultanes Auftreten von Banken- und Währungskrisen? In A. F. Michler & H.-D. Smeets (Eds.), *Die aktuelle Finanzkrise: Bestandsaufnahmen und Lehren für die Zukunft* (pp. 301–322). Lucius.

Drudy, P., & Collins, M. L. (2011). Ireland: From boom to austerity. *Cambridge Journal of Regions, Economy and Society*, 339–354.

Faßbender, K. (2010). Der europäische "Stabilitätsmechanismus" im Lichte von Unionsrecht und deutschem Verfassungsrecht. *Neue Zeitschrift für Verwaltungsrecht*, 799–803.

Fisahn, A. (2010). Griechenland und die Perspektiven. *Kritische Justiz*, 248–254.

Frenz, W., & Ehlenz, C. (2010). Schuldenkrise und Grenzen der europäischen Wirtschaftspolitik. *Europäisches Wirtschafts- und Steuerrecht*, 211–215.

Grabitz, E., Hilf, M., & Nettesheim, M. (Eds.). (2021). *Das Recht der Europäischen Union. Kommentar, loose-leaf (last supplement: 71)*. C.H. Beck.

Häde, U. (2009). Haushaltsdisziplin und Solidarität im Zeichen der Finanzkrise. *Europäische Zeitschrift für Wirtschaftsrecht*, 399–403.

Häde, U. (2010). Die europäische Währungsunion in der internationalen Finanzkrise – An den Grenzen europäischer Solidarität. *Europarecht*, 854–866.

Häde, U. (2011). Rechtsfragen der EU- Rettungsschirme. *Zeitschrift für Gesetzgebung*, 1–30.

Heinemann, F. (1995). Bailout- und Bonitätseffekte in der Wirtschafts- und Währungsunion. *Zeitschrift für Wirtschafts- und Sozialwissenschaften*, 605–622.

Hentschelmann, K. (2011). Finanzhilfen im Lichte der No Bailout-Klausel – Eigenverantwortung und Solidarität in der Währungsunion. *Europarecht*, 282–313.

Herrmann, C. (2010). Griechische Tragödie – der währungsverfassungsrechtliche Rahmen für die Rettung, den Austritt oder den Ausschluss von überschuldeten Staaten aus der Eurozone. *Europäische Zeitschrift für Wirtschaftsrecht*, 413–418.

Hilpold, P. (2013). Solidarität als Prinzip des Staatengemeinschaftsrechts. *Archiv für Völkerrecht*, 239–272.

Hilpold, P. (2015). Understanding solidarity within EU law: An analysis of the 'Islands of Solidarity' with particular regard to Monetary Union. *Yearbook of European Law, 34*, 257–285.

Hilpold, P. (2021). *Die Europäische Wirtschafts- und Währungsunion. Ihr Umbau im Zeichen der Solidarität*. Springer.

Horn, G. A., Lindner, F., Niechoj, T., et al. (2011). *Herausforderungen für die Wirtschaftspolitik 2011. Der Euroraum in Trümmern?.* (Report Nr. 59). Institut für Makroökonomie und Konjunkturforschung (Hans-Böckler-Stiftung).

Hufeld, U. (2014). Das Recht der Europäischen Wirtschaftsunion. In P.-C. Müller-Graff (Ed.), *Enzyklopädie Europarecht. Europäisches Wirtschaftsordnungsrecht.* (Vol. IV) (§ 22). Nomos.
Ioannidis, M. (2014). EU financial assistance conditionality after "Two Pack". *Zeitschrift für ausländisches öffentliches Recht und Völkerrecht,* 61–104.
Kämmerer, J. A. (2010). Insolvenz von EU-Mitgliedstaaten. *Wirtschaftsdienst,* 161–167.
Keller, A. (2014). *Vorgaben föderaler Ordnungen für das Ausmaß und die Grenzen finanzieller Solidarität in der Europäischen Union.* Duncker & Humblot.
Koursovitis, A. (2012). Griechenland: Keine Zukunft ohne Katharsis. *IBW Beiträge zur Wirtschaftspolitik,* 1–9.
Kube, H., & Reimer, E. (2010). Grenzen des Europäischen Stabilisierungsmechanismus. *Neue Juristische Wochenschrift,* 1911–1916.
Lais, M. (2007). *Das Solidaritätsprinzip im Europäischen Verfassungsverbund.* Nomos.
Louis, J. V. (2010). Guest editorial: The no-bailout clause and rescue packages. *Common Market Law Review,* 971–986.
Louis, J. V. (2011). Solidarité budgetaire et financière dans l'Union Européenne. In C. Boutayeb (Ed.), *La solidarité dans l'union Européenne* (pp. 107–124). Dalloz.
Martucci, F. (2020). Non-EU legal instruments (EFSF, ESM, and fiscal compact). In F. Amtenbrink & C. Herrmann (Eds.), *The EU law of Economic and Monetary Union (Chapter 12).* OUP.
Müller-Franken, S. (2014). Das Spannungsverhältnis zwischen Eigenverantwortlichkeit und Solidarität. In H.-J. Blanke & S. Pilz (Eds.), *Die "Fiskalunion"* (pp. 227–244). Mohr Siebeck.
Müller-Heidelberg, T. (1970). *Schutzklauseln im Europäischen Gemeinschaftsrecht.* Stiftung Europa-Kolleg.
Nettesheim, M. (2012). Der Umbau der europäischen Währungsunion: politische Aktion und rechtliche Grenzen. In S. Kadelbach (Ed.), *Nach der Finanzkrise: Politische und rechtliche Rahmenbedingungen einer neuen Ordnung* (pp. 31–78). Nomos.
Pechstein, M., Nowak, C., & Häde, U. (2017). *Frankfurter Kommentar zu EUV, GRC und AEUV.* Mohr Siebeck.
Pilz, S. (2012). Ein fiskalpolitischer Pakt als Brücke in die Stabilitätsunion? *Wirtschaftsdienst,* 457–464.
Pilz, S. (2016). *Der Europäische Stabilitätsmechanismus: eine neue Stufe der Integration.* Mohr Siebeck.
Pilz, S., & Dittmann, H. (2012). Perspektiven des Stabilitäts- und Wachstumspakts – Rechtliche und ökonomische Implikationen des Reformpakets "Economic Governance". *Zeitschrift für europarechtliche Studien,* 53–88.
Potacs, M., & Mayer, C. (2011). EU-rechtliche Rahmenbedingungen der Staateninsolvenz. In G. E. Kodek & A. Reinisch (Eds.), *Staateninsolvenz* (pp. 105–144). Linde.
Rebhahn, R. (2015). *Solidarität in der Wirtschafts- und Währungsunion.* Nomos.
Schorkopf, F. (2012). Europas politische Verfasstheit im Lichte des Fiskalvertrags. *Zeitschrift für Staats- und Europawissenschaften,* 1–29.
Schwarz, K.-A. (2011). Solidarität mit Griechenland – eine europäische Tragödie? In P.-C. Müller-Graff et al. (Eds.), *Europäisches Recht zwischen Bewährung und Wandel. Festschrift für Dieter H. Scheuing* (pp. 705–716). Nomos.
Schwarze, J. (Ed.). (2019). *EU-Kommentar* (4th ed.). Nomos.
Seidel, M. (2011). Die "No-Bail-Out"-Klausel des Art. 125 AEUV als Beistandsverbot. *Europäische Zeitschrift für Wirtschaftsrecht,* 529–530.
Siekmann, H. (2013). *EWU: Kommentar zur Europäischen Währungsunion.* Mohr Siebeck.
Streinz, R. (Ed.). (2018). *EUV/AEUV. Kommentar* (3rd ed.). C.H. Beck.
Tuori, K., & Tuori, K. (2014). *The Eurozone crisis: a constitutional analysis.* CUP.
von der Groeben, H., Schwarze, J., & Hatje, A. (2015). *Europäisches Unionsrecht. Kommentar* (7th ed.). Nomos.
Weber, A. (1982). *Schutznormen und Wirtschaftsintegration.* Nomos.

Weber, A. (2011). Die Reform der Wirtschafts- und Währungsunion in der Finanzkrise. *Europäische Zeitschrift für Wirtschaftsrecht*, 935–939.

Weber, A. (2012). Die Europäische Union auf dem Weg zur Fiskalunion? *Deutsches Verwaltungsblatt*, 801–806.

Weber, A. (2017). Europäisches Rechtsdenken in der Krise? *Die Öffentliche Verwaltung*, 741–748.

Zehnpfund, O., & Heimbach, M. (2010). *Finanzielle Hilfen für Mitgliedstaaten insbesondere nach Art. 122 des Vertrages über die Arbeitsweise der Europäischen Union*. Wissenschaftliche Dienste des Deutschen Bundestages, WD 11-3000-30/10.

Article 123 [Prohibition of Credit Facilities]
(ex-Article 101 TEC)

1. Overdraft facilities[15] or any other type of credit facility[16–25] with the European Central Bank or with the central banks of the Member States (hereinafter referred to as "national central banks") in favour of Union institutions, bodies, offices or agencies, central governments, regional, local or other public authorities, other bodies governed by public law, or public undertakings of Member States[7–11] shall be prohibited, as shall the purchase directly from them by the European Central Bank or national central banks of debt instruments.[26–50]
2. Paragraph 1 shall not apply to publicly owned credit institutions which, in the context of the supply of reserves by central banks, shall be given the same treatment by national central banks and the European Central Bank as private credit institutions.[11]

Contents

1. General Remarks 1
2. The Monetary Financing Prohibition: Scope *Ratione Personae* 7
3. The Monetary Financing Prohibition: Scope *Ratione Materiae* 12
   3.1. Forbidden Monetary Instruments 13
      3.1.1. Overdraft Facilities and Other Types of Credit Facilities 15
      3.1.2. Purchases of Public Debt Instruments in Primary Markets 26
   3.2. Allowed Monetary Instruments 39
      3.2.1. Management of Foreign Exchange Reserves 40
      3.2.2. Fiscal Agency Function 42
      3.2.3. IMF Contributions and Medium-Term Financial Assistance for Balances of Payments of the EU Member States Outside the Eurozone 47
List of Cases
References

1. General Remarks

The economic rationale behind the prohibition of monetary financing is the well-accepted idea that the public sector shall be financed in the same conditions applied to private investors and submitted to market discipline. History is littered with examples of governments using the central bank to finance public expenditure when they were unable or unwilling to raise the money on capital markets. The result was often spiralling inflation, and the literature has shown that high inflation, which can

1

The opinions expressed are strictly personal.

arise from such subordination of monetary policy to fiscal needs, is in turn detrimental for growth.[1] The application of **market discipline to the financing of States** and the **prohibition of central bank financing of public entities** prevent abuses of the central banks' ability to print money. Its purpose is to protect the central bank's independence and its ability to maintain price stability, which could be undermined if governments had direct access to central bank money. It helps to protect central banks from political pressures.

2   The advantages of this control of public financing by central banks were embraced by EU law, and it is a central idea to the Economic and Monetary Union (EMU). The TFEU includes **four rules of economic and budgetary discipline**, which limit Member States' (MS) competence on economic policy: **the no bail-out clause** (Article 125 TFEU), **the procedure to control excessive public deficit** (Article 126 TFEU) and the **two monetary financing prohibitions** laid down in Articles 123 and 124 TFEU. In spite of their common objective to submit State financing to market discipline,[2] the monetary financing prohibitions and the no bail-out obligations are rules with direct effect, but the interdiction of excessive public deficits has no direct effect because its enforcement needs the application of the Article 126 procedure.

3   Article 123 TFEU forbids the MS to be financed by the European Central Bank (ECB) or the national central banks (NCBs), and Article 124 TFEU prohibits the privileged access of MS public entities to financial institutions. This second ban complements the first one.

4   The **monetary financing prohibitions** have a **direct effect**, and consequently, there are a few cases resolved by the Court of Justice of the European Union (CJEU) that refer to them. However, the last economic crisis has compelled the ECB to adopt some non-conventional monetary measures, in particular the purchase of MS public debt on secondary markets. The compatibility of the latter with Article 123 TFEU was doubted strongly in Germany and gave rise to two relevant preliminary rulings from the German Constitutional Court. The **OMT case** was resolved by the CJEU in 2015,[3] and the **PSPP case** was brought before the CJEU in August 2017 and has now been resolved by the CJEU.[4] In addition, the ECB has developed a relevant doctrine on the prohibitions under Articles 123 and 124 TFEU within the framework of its advisory competence to review the compatibility of draft national legislation with the treaties and the European System of Central Banks (ESCB) Statute under Articles 131, 127.4 and 282.5 TFEU.[5]

---

[1] Fischer (1993), pp. 485–512; Mersch (2016), p. 3.

[2] Louis (2009), p. 95.

[3] Case C-62/14 *P. Gauweiler and others* (CJEU 16 June 2015).

[4] Case C-493/17, *Weiss et al.* (CJEU 11 December 2018).

[5] See also, Article 4 of the ESCB Statute and Council Decision 98/415/EC *on the consultation of the European Central Bank by national authorities regarding draft legislative provisions*, O.J L 189/42 (1998).

The monetary financing prohibition laid down in Article 123.1 TFEU and replicated in Article 21.1 of the ESCB Statute prohibits overdraft facilities or any other type of credit facility with the ECB or NCBs in favour of Union institutions, bodies, offices or agencies, central governments, regional, local or other public authorities, other bodies governed by public law, or public undertakings of the MS, as well as the purchase directly from these public sector entities by the ECB or NCBs of debt instruments.[6] The Treaty contains one exemption from the prohibition: it does not apply to publicly owned credit institutions that, in the context of the supply of reserves by central banks, must be given the same treatment as private credit institutions (Article 123.2 TFEU). Moreover, the ECB and NCBs may act as fiscal agents for the public sector bodies referred to above (Article 21.2 of the Statute). The precise scope of application of the monetary financing prohibition is further clarified by **Council Regulation (EC) No 3603/93**,[7] which makes it clear that the prohibition includes any financing of the public sector's obligations vis-à-vis third parties. 5

The **monetary financing prohibition** is of essential importance to **ensure price stability**, which is the primary objective of monetary policy. Furthermore, central bank financing of the public sector lessens the pressure for fiscal discipline. Consequently, the ECB has developed an extensive interpretation of this prohibition in order to ensure its strict application, subject only to certain limited exemptions contained in Article 123.2 TFEU and Regulation (EC) No 3603/93. The **ECB's doctrine** regarding the compatibility of national legislation with the prohibition has been primarily developed within the framework of consultations with the ECB by MS on draft national legislation. 6

2. The Monetary Financing Prohibition: Scope *Ratione Personae*

Article 123 TFEU applies to the relationship between the central banks and the public sector of the EU and the MS. The prohibition is compulsory for the ECB and the NCBs of all the MS, that is, all the components of the ESCB, even the NCBs of the countries outside the eurozone. The CJEU in *Pringle* clarified that the granting of financial assistance by one MS or by a group of MS to another MS is therefore not covered by that prohibition. Accordingly, even if the MS act via the European Stability Mechanism (ESM) to grant financial assistance to an ESM member, the MS are not derogating from the prohibition laid down in Article 123 TFEU since 7

---

[6] The CJEU said that "it is clear from its wording that Article 123(1) TFEU prohibits the ECB and the central banks of the Member States from granting overdraft facilities or any other type of credit facility to public authorities and bodies of the Union and of Member States and from purchasing directly from them their debt instruments"; Case C-370/12, *Pringle* (CJEU 27 November 2012) para 123, and Case C-62/14, *Gauweiler* (CJEU 16 December 2015) para 90.

[7] Council Regulation (EC) No 3603/93 *specifying definitions for the application of the prohibitions referred to in Articles 104* [Article 123 TFEU] and 104b(1) [Article 125 TFEU], O.J. L 332/1 (1993).

that article is not addressed to them.⁸ The ESM is not bound by Article 123 TFEU, and it can buy public debt instruments in the primary and secondary markets.

8   It is relevant to note that prohibitions of monetary financing (Article 123 TFEU) and privileged access (Article 124 TFEU) must be respected by the MS with a derogation as a **requirement to reach the final stage of EMU** and to integrate into the eurozone. In effect, Article 140.1 TFEU requires the ECB (and the Commission) to report, at least once every 2 years or at the request of an MS with a derogation, to the Council on the progress made by the MS with a derogation in fulfilling its obligations regarding the achievement of EMU. These reports must include an examination of the compatibility between the national legislation of each MS with a derogation, including the statutes of its NCB, and Articles 130 and 131 TFEU and the relevant articles of the Statute (legal convergence). To identify those areas where national legislation needs to be adapted, the ECB examines, among others, compatibility with the prohibitions on monetary financing (Article 123 TFEU) and privileged access (Article 124 TFEU).

9   According to Protocol No 15 annexed to the treaties, the United Kingdom was under no obligation to adopt the euro unless otherwise notified to the Council. On 30 October 1997, the **United Kingdom** notified the Council that it did not intend to adopt the euro on 1 January 1999, and this situation has not changed. Pursuant to this notification, certain provisions of the Treaty (including Articles 130 and 131 TFEU) and the Statute did not apply to the United Kingdom. Accordingly, there was no legal requirement to ensure the compatibility of its national legislation (including the Bank of England's statutes) with the Treaty and the Statute. This Protocol allowed the UK Government to maintain its "ways and means" facility with the Bank of England if and so long as the United Kingdom did not adopt the euro, notwithstanding Article 123 TFEU and Article 21.1 of the Statute.⁹ The United Kingdom withdrew from the EU (**Brexit**) in 2020, and consequently Articles 123 and 124 TFEU no longer apply to this country.

10   Article 3 of Regulation No 3603/93 defines "**public sector**" in a very broad way: EU institutions or bodies; central governments; regional, local or other public authorities; other bodies governed by public law; or public undertakings of MS. The ECB cannot finance any **EU institutions or bodies**, including the European Investment Bank (EIB), or international organisations close to the EU, like the ESM.

11   Monetary financing is forbidden in **all types of public institutions of the MS**. Neither central, regional or local authorities nor other public law bodies are able to obtain monetary financing from the ECB or NCBs. Also, "public undertaking", defined in Article 8.2 of Regulation No 3603/93 as "any undertaking over which the

---

⁸ Case C-370/12, *Pringle* (CJEU 27 November 2012) para 125–127.

⁹ The Protocol on Portugal to the Maastricht Treaty authorised Portugal to maintain the facility afforded to the Autonomous Regions of Azores and Madeira to benefit from an interest-free credit facility with the Banco de Portugal under the terms established by existing Portuguese law. Portugal committed itself to pursue its best endeavours in order to put an end to the above-mentioned facility as soon as possible and it disappeared in 2001.

State or other regional or local authorities may directly or indirectly exercise a dominant influence by virtue of their ownership of it, their financial participation therein or the rules which govern it," is covered by this prohibition. According to **Article 123.2 TFEU**, the prohibition does not apply to publicly owned credit institutions that, in the context of the supply of reserves by central banks, shall be given the same treatment by the ECB and NCBs as private credit institutions. This exception imposes the same treatment for public and private credit institutions.

3. The Monetary Financing Prohibition: Scope *Ratione Materiae*

Article 123.1 TFEU bans three monetary instruments, but Regulation No 3603/93 softens the prohibitions, allowing some financial services for public entities.

3.1. Forbidden Monetary Instruments

The ECB and NCBs cannot finance either the performance of functions by other public sector bodies or the **public sector's obligations vis-à-vis third parties**. In particular, national legislation may not confer on an NCB the task of financing the activities of third parties where such financing does not relate to any of the tasks and functions of the central bank but is a responsibility of the government.

Article 123 TFEU and Regulation No 3603/93 contain some explanations concerning overdraft facilities, other type of credit facilities and purchases of public debt instruments. The CJEU case law and the ECB doctrine have clarified these prohibitions.

3.1.1. Overdraft Facilities and Other Types of Credit Facilities

"**Overdraft facilities**" are defined by Article 1.1 point (a) of Regulation No 3603/93 in clear accountability terms and mean "any provision of funds to the public sector resulting or likely to result in a **debit balance**".

Article 1.1 point (b) of Regulation No 3603/93 defines "**other types of credit facility**" as:

1. any claim against the public sector existing at 1 January 1994, except for fixed-maturity claims acquired before that date;[10]
2. any financing of the public sector's obligations vis-a-vis third parties;
3. any transaction with the public sector resulting or likely to result in a claim against that sector.

---

[10] Before the accession, the new MS must transform their non-negotiable securities under non-market conditions into negotiable fixed-maturity securities under market conditions.

Article 1.2 prescribes that the following shall not be regarded as "**debt instruments**" within the meaning of Article 123 TFEU: securities acquired from the public sector to ensure the conversion into negotiable fixed-maturity securities under market conditions; fixed-maturity claims acquired before 1 January 1994 which are not negotiable or not under market conditions, provided that the maturity of the securities is not subsequent to that of the aforementioned claims; and the amount of the "ways and means" facility maintained by the United Kingdom Government with the Bank of England until the date, if any, on which the United Kingdom moves to stage three of EMU (with Brexit, this last provision has lost its meaning).

17   The **concept of "other types of credit facility"** includes any financing of the public sector's obligations vis-a-vis third parties, and the ECB has specified the field of application of this prohibition in relation to financing obligations imposed on NCBs but not related to any of the tasks and functions of the central bank. Therefore, the task of financing measures—which are usually the responsibility of the MS and financed from their budgetary sources rather than by the NCBs—must not be entrusted to NCBs. To decide what constitutes financing of the public sector's obligations vis-à-vis third parties, which can be interpreted as financing provided by an NCB outside the scope of central bank tasks, it is necessary to carry out an assessment, on a case-by-case basis, of whether the task to be undertaken by an NCB is a central bank task or a government task, i.e. a task within the responsibility of the MS. In other words, adequate safeguards must be in place to ensure there are no circumventions of the objective of the monetary financing prohibition that the Member States maintain to have a sound budgetary policy.[11]

18   The ECB Governing Council has endorsed safeguards in the form of criteria for determining what may be considered as falling within the scope of "the public sector's obligations vis-à-vis third parties" within the meaning of Article 1.1 point (b)(ii) of Regulation (EC) No 3603/93 or, in other words, what constitutes a government task.[12] First, central bank tasks are, in particular, those that have been conferred upon the ECB and NCBs by the Treaty and the Statute of the ESCB (Articles 127.2, 127.5, 127.6 and 28.1 of the Treaty, as well as Articles 22 and 25.1 of the ESCB Statute). Second, pursuant to Article 14.4 of the ESCB Statute, NCBs may perform "functions other than those specified in [the Statute of the ESCB]". However, the functions undertaken by an NCB and that are atypical of NCB activities or clearly discharged on behalf of, and in the exclusive interest of the government or other public sector entities, should be considered government tasks. Third, an important criterion for qualifying these functions as an atypical NCB task is their impact on the institutional, financial and personal independence

---

[11] ECB Opinion CON/2020/23 *on conferral of additional tasks related to the single euro payments area (SEPA) on the Bank of Greece as national competent authority* and ECB Opinion CON/2021/9 *on the reform of Latvijas Banka.*

[12] ECB Opinions CON/2020/23 and CON/2021/9.

of the NCB concerned. In particular, a task may be qualified as a **government task** if:

(a) it creates inadequately addressed conflicts of interests with existing central bank tasks;
(b) it is disproportionate to the NCB's financial or organisational capacity;
(c) it does not fit into the NCB's institutional set-up;
(d) it harbours substantial financial risks and
(e) it exposes the members of the NCB decision-making bodies to disproportionate political risks that may also negatively impact them in terms of their personal independence.[13]

In order to ensure compatibility with Article 123 TFEU, the ECB considers[14] that a **new task entrusted to an NCB** must be **fully and adequately remunerated** if it is (a) not a central bank task or an action that facilitates the performance of a central bank task or (b) linked to a government task and performed in the government's interest.[15]

Following the ECB doctrine, some **examples** of **new tasks conferred on NCBs** and **considered government tasks** by the ECB are the following: tasks relating to the establishment of a central register of bank account numbers;[16] tasks of a credit mediator[17] and those relating to financing resolution funds or financial arrangements, as well as those relating to deposit guarantee or investor compensation schemes;[18] tasks relating to the collection, maintenance and processing of data that support the calculation of insurance premium transfers; tasks relating to the protection of competition in the mortgage loan market; tasks relating to the provision of resources to bodies that are independent of the NCBs and operate as an extension of the government; tasks of an information authority for the purposes of facilitating cross-border debt recovery in civil and commercial matters; tasks relating to the establishment of an insurance claim database; and tasks relating to national defence preparedness going beyond the internal contingency planning tasks of a central bank.[19] These types of activities are government tasks, and they can only be entrusted to NCBs if enough financial or organisational resources are transferred to them, their independence is ensured and no substantial financial risks are taken by the NCBs.[20]

19

---

[13] ECB Opinions CON/2015/22, CON/2015/36 and CON/2015/46.
[14] ECB, *Convergence Report*, June 2016, pp. 30–31.
[15] ECB Opinions CON/2011/30, CON/2015/36 and CON/2015/46.
[16] ECB Opinions CON/2015/36 and CON/2015/46.
[17] ECB Opinion CON/2015/12.
[18] ECB Opinions CON/2011/103 and CON/2012/22.
[19] See ECB, *Convergence Report*, June 2020, p. 32 and ECB opinions cited.
[20] It is interesting to note that Article 14.4 of the ESCB Statute stipulates that "National central banks may perform functions other than those specified in this Statute unless the Governing Council finds, by a majority of two thirds of the votes cast, that these interfere with the objectives

20 However, the **supervisory and resolution tasks over financial institutions** lay out more difficulties in relation to the monetary financing prohibition. At first, supervisory tasks may be considered central bank tasks as well as tasks ancillary to them, such as those relating to consumer protection in the area of financial services, supervision over credit-acquiring companies or supervision of consumer credit providers and intermediaries.[21] Since resolution tasks over financial institutions and supervisory powers complement each other, tasks relating to the exercise of technical resolution powers and decision-making could also be considered central bank tasks, provided that they do not undermine the NCB's independence. Thus, the **financing by an NCB to a supervisory authority** does not breach Article 123 TFEU if the NCB will be financing the performance of a legitimate financial supervisory task under national law as part of its mandate or as long as the NCB can contribute to and have an influence on the decision-making of the supervisory authorities.[22] Therefore, it would be incompatible with the monetary financing prohibition to have national legislation that requires an NCB to take over the liabilities of a previously independent public resolution body without fully insulating the NCB from all financial obligations resulting from the prior activities of such a body.[23]

21 Along the same rationale, national legislation that requires an NCB to obtain approval from the government prior to taking resolution actions under a broad range of circumstances, but which does not limit the NCB's liability to its own administrative acts, would be incompatible with the monetary financing prohibition.[24] Furthermore, national legislation that requires an NCB to pay compensation for damages, to the extent that it results in that NCB assuming the liability of the State, would not be in line with the monetary financing prohibition.[25]

The **financing of any resolution fund or financial arrangement by NCBs** breaches the monetary financing prohibition. Where an NCB acts as a resolution authority, it should not, under any circumstances, assume or finance any obligation of either a bridge institution or an asset management vehicle.[26] Along the same lines, the financing by an NCB of a national deposit insurance scheme for credit

---

and tasks of the ESCB. Such functions shall be performed on the responsibility and liability of national central banks and shall not be regarded as being part of the functions of the ESCB".

[21] ECB Opinions CON/2007/29, CON/2015/45 and CON/2015/54.

[22] ECB Opinions CON/2015/22 and CON/2010/4. Also other activities such as those relating to licensing and supervision of microcredit providers, supervision of credit reference agencies, supervision of administrators of interest rate benchmarks, supervisory tasks to ensure compliance with Union legislation in the field of investment services and products, tasks relating to the oversight of payment schemes, tasks relating to the application and enforcement of Union legislation concerning payment accounts, administrative resolution tasks, or tasks relating to the operation and management of credit registers. See ECB, *Convergence Report*, June 2020, p. 32 and ECB opinions cited.

[23] ECB Opinion CON/2013/56.

[24] ECB Opinion CON/2015/22.

[25] ECB Opinion CON/2019/20.

[26] ECB Opinions CON/2011/103, CON/2012/99, CON/2015/3 and CON/2015/22.

institutions or a national investor compensation scheme for investment firms[27] is incompatible with the monetary financing prohibition, except if it were short term, it addressed urgent situations, systemic stability aspects were at stake, and decisions were at the NCB's discretion. In particular, central bank support for deposit guarantee schemes should not amount to a systematic pre-funding operation.[28]

The **support of insolvent credit and/or other financial institutions by the ECB or NCBs**, granted independently and at their full discretion, is incompatible with the monetary financing prohibition of Article 123 TFEU because it is a governmental task.[29] The same concerns apply to the Eurosystem financing of a credit institution that has been recapitalised to restore its solvency by way of direct placement of State-issued debt instruments where no alternative market-based funding sources exist (**recapitalisation bonds**) and where such bonds are to be used as collateral. In such a case, the subsequent use of the recapitalisation bonds as collateral in central bank liquidity operations raises monetary financing concerns.[30]

However, the NCBs can support solvent financial institutions that are facing temporary liquidity problems outside of normal Eurosystem monetary policy operations using the so-called **Emergency Liquidity Assistance** (ELA). It is a possibility founded on the basis of **Article 14.4 of the ESCB Statute**, and the rules governing this mechanism are compiled in the **ELA Agreement**[31] following a decision by the ECB Governing Council on 9 November 2020. In accordance with paragraph 1(2) of this Agreement, ELA occurs when a Eurosystem NCB provides central bank money and/or any other assistance that may lead to an increase in central bank money to a financial institution or a group of financial institutions facing liquidity problems, where, in either case, such an operation is not part of the single monetary policy. NCBs may provide ELA, but under the strict control of the ECB.[32] The main responsibility for the provision of ELA lies at the national level, and any costs and risks arising from the provision of ELA are incurred by the NCB concerned. The provision of ELA may only exceed 12 months following a non-objection by the Governing Council requested by the Governor of the NCB concerned at the latest once the provision of ELA exceeds ten months, and the NCBs will charge a penalty interest rate to the institution receiving ELA.

---

[27] Recital 27 of Parliament/Council Directive 2014/49/EU *on deposit guarantee schemes*, O.J. L 173/149 (2014) and Recital 23 of Parliament/Council Directive 97/9/EC *on investor-compensation schemes*, O.J. L 84/22 (1997) provides that the costs of financing deposit guarantee schemes and investor compensation schemes must be borne, respectively, by credit institutions and investment firms themselves.

[28] ECB Opinions CON/2015/40 and Opinion CON/2011/84.

[29] ECB Opinion CON/2013/5.

[30] ECB Opinions CON/2012/50, CON/2012/64, and CON/2012/71.

[31] *Agreement on emergency liquidity assistance*, 9 November 2020, available at https://www.ecb.europa.eu/pub/pdf/other/ecb.agreementemergencyliquidityassistance202012~ba7c45c170.en.pdf?dca797da3212289956ac24df607eb168.

[32] ELA is an element of the traditional central bank function of lender of last resort. See Lastra (2015), pp. 376 et seq.

24 NCBs may provide ELA unless the Governing Council finds, pursuant to Article 14.4 of the ESCB Statute, that the provision of ELA interferes with the objectives and tasks of the ESCB. In this case, the ECB can object to or restrict the provision of ELA, and paragraph 3 of the ELA Agreement subjects the NCB concerned and the institutions receiving ELA to a special information-sharing framework. Paragraph 5 of the ELA Agreement disciplines the compatibility of the ELA mechanism with the Article 123 TFEU prohibition. The provision of ELA is assessed *ex ante* as regards compliance with this ban. ELA transactions akin to an overdraft facility or any other type of credit facility for the State, in particular any financing of the public sector's obligations vis-à-vis third parties or the central bank de facto taking over a State task, violate the prohibition of monetary financing. **ELA provision to insolvent institutions and institutions** for which insolvency proceedings have been initiated according to national laws **is incompatible with the prohibition of monetary financing.**

25 The three main criteria endorsed by the ECB Governing Council in its opinions and convergence reports and used as a basis to determine whether the ELA operations of NCBs could breach the monetary financing prohibition are as follows:[33] (1) the solvency of the ELA recipient, (2) the independence of the NCB when providing ELA funding to its counterparty and (3) its temporary nature. Also, the ECB imposes that there must be no doubt as to the legal validity and enforceability of the State guarantee under applicable national law and no doubt as to the economic adequacy of the State guarantee, which should cover both the principal and interest on the loans.[34] **ELA is one of the most important tools of central banks in fighting financial distress and emergency situations** and was extensively used in the European financial crisis. During this crisis, several banks in Ireland, Portugal, Cyprus, and particularly in Greece were supported with ELA measures.[35] The restructuring of the Cypriot banking sector was very complex, and several individuals and companies introduced claims for compensation founded among other pleas on the application of ELA procedures by the ECB and the Cypriot central bank. The General Court (GC) rejected the claims, considering the condition relating to the unlawfulness of the EU's conduct that was complained about was not satisfied.[36] The GC considered that, under Article 14.4 of the ESCB Statute, the role of the Governing Council of the ECB is limited to verifying whether ELA interfered with the objectives and tasks of the ESCB. In particular, the Governing Council is required, for the purpose of ensuring compliance with the

---

[33] Scouteris and Athanassiou (2016), p. 15.
[34] ECB Opinion CON/2012/4.
[35] Dietz (2019), pp. 633–635.
[36] Case T-680/13, *K. Chrysostomides & Co. and Others v Council and Others* (GC 13 July 2018) and Case T-786/14, *Bourdouvali and Others v Council and Others* (GC 13 July 2018).

prohibition of monetary financing referred to in Article 123 TFEU and Article 21.1 of the ESCB Statute, to verify that ELA was not granted to an insolvent bank. Taking into account this power, the ECB correctly decided, as explained in the press release of 21 March 2013, "to maintain the current level of [ELA] until . . . 25 March 2013" and that "[t]hereafter, [ELA] could only be considered if an [EU or IMF] programme [was] in place that would ensure the solvency of the concerned banks". In the absence of such a programme, the ECB banned the Cypriot central bank from facilitating ELA to Cypriot banks.[37]

3.1.2. Purchases of Public Debt Instruments in Primary Markets

Article 123 TFEU prohibits the ECB and NCBs from purchasing public debt instruments directly on the primary market but allows **secondary market purchases of public debt instruments** as long as it is not used to circumvent the objectives of the prohibition on monetary financing, as clarified in Recital 7 of Regulation No 3603/93. **26**

The CJEU said that provision prohibits all financial assistance from the ESCB to an MS but does not preclude, generally, the possibility of the ESCB purchasing from the creditors of such State bonds previously issued by that State.[38] Furthermore, Article 18.1 of the ESCB Statute permits the ESCB, in order to achieve its objectives and carry out its tasks, to operate in the financial markets, inter alia, by buying and selling outright marketable instruments, which include government bonds. **27**

However, the Court has held that Article 123.1 TFEU imposes two further **limits** on the ESCB when it adopts a programme for purchasing bonds issued by the public authorities and bodies of the Union and MS: **28**

– The ESCB cannot validly purchase bonds on the secondary markets under conditions that would, in practice, mean that its intervention has an **effect equivalent to that of a direct purchase of bonds from the public authorities and bodies of the MS**.[39] In that regard, the Court observes that the ESCB's intervention could, in practice, have an effect equivalent to that of a direct purchase of government bonds if the potential purchasers of such bonds on the primary market knew for certain that the ESCB was going to purchase those bonds within a certain period and under conditions allowing those market

---

[37] Case T-786/14, *Bourdouvali and Others v Council and Others* (GC 13 July 2018) para 383 and 396, and Case T-680/13, *K. Chrysostomides & Co. and Others v Council and Others* (GC 13 July 2018) para 384 and 387. These judgments were confirmed on appeal in Cases C-597/18 P and C-603/18 P, *Council v K. Chrysostomides & Co. and Others* (CJEU 16 December 2020).

[38] See, to that effect, Case C-370/12, *Pringle* (CJEU 27 November 2012) para 132, and Case C-62/14, *Gauweiler* (CJEU 16 December 2015) para 95. See the comments on this last judgment by Borger (2016), Craig and Markakis (2016), Dawson and Bobic (2019), Hinarejos (2015), Hinarejos (2019), Martucci (2016), Sarmiento (2016) and Sáinz de Vicuña (2016).

[39] Case C-62/14, *Gauweiler* (CJEU 16 December 2015) para 97, and Case C-493/17, *Weiss* (CJEU 11 December 2018) para 106.

operators to act, de facto, as intermediaries for the ESCB for the direct purchase of those bonds from the public authorities and bodies of the MS concerned.
– The ESCB must build sufficient safeguards into its intervention to ensure that the latter does not fall foul of the prohibition of monetary financing in Article 123 TFEU by satisfying itself that the programme is **not** such as to **reduce the impetus** that the provision is intended to give the MS to follow a **sound budgetary policy**.[40] The safeguards will depend both on the particular features of the programme under consideration and on the economic context in which that programme is adopted and implemented.

29   The first preliminary reference of the German Constitutional Court (*Gauweiler* case) asked the CJEU, among other questions, about the compatibility with Article 123 TFEU of the press release of the ECB Governing Council on 5 and 6 September 2012, approving the main parameters of the **Outright Monetary Transactions Programme** (OMT). However, the adoption of the legal instruments regulating the programme was postponed, and those instruments have not been adopted. OMT was designed by the ECB as a non-standard monetary policy measure, considered as necessary to face the exceptional circumstances in EU financial markets in 2012. In order to respect Article 123 TFEU, the ECB subjects the OMT programme to certain **conditions for the purchase on secondary markets** of government bonds issued by euro area States:[41]

1. application only to MS which are subject to strict conditionality (States concerned with financial support programme of the EFSF or the ESM), provided that such a programme included the possibility of primary market purchases,
2. focus on purchases of government bonds with maturities of between one and three years,
3. full discretion of the ECB in deciding on the start, continuation and suspension of OMT in accordance with its monetary policy mandate, and
4. Eurosystem accepted the same (*pari passu*) treatment as private creditors, whilst an undertaking was given that liquidity created would be fully sterilised.

30   Taking into account these conditions, the CJEU considered that the Governing Council was to be responsible for deciding on the scope, the start, the continuation and the suspension of the intervention envisaged by the OMT Programme on the secondary market. Before the Court, the ECB has also explained that the ESCB intends to ensure that a minimum period is observed between the issue of a security on the primary market and its purchase on the secondary market and also to refrain from making any prior announcement concerning either its decision to carry out such purchases or the volume of purchases envisaged.[42]

31   Those safeguards prevent the distortion of the issue of government bonds with the certainty that those bonds will be purchased by the ESCB after their issue. The

---

[40] See, to that effect, Case C-62/14, *Gauweiler* (CJEU 16 December 2015) para 100–102 and 109.
[41] ECB, *Monthly Bulletin*, October 2012, pp. 8–9.
[42] Case C-62/14, *Gauweiler* (CJEU 16 December 2015) para 105 and 106.

CJEU concludes that they ensure that the implementation of the **OMT Programme will not, in practice, have an effect equivalent to a direct purchase of government bonds from public authorities and bodies of the MS**. The Court also pointed out that the features of the OMT Programme ensure the programme cannot be considered to be of such kind as to lessen the MS' impetus to follow a sound budgetary policy and thus to circumvent the objective pursued by the prohibition of monetary financing by the MS.[43]

The **GC in the *Accorinti* case** analyses the compatibility with the monetary financing prohibition of the exchange agreement of 15 February 2012 between the ECB and NCBs, on one part, and the Hellenic Republic, on the other part, with the aim of exchanging Greek bonds held by the ECB and NBCs for new Greek bonds having the same nominal values, interest rates, interest payment and repayment dates as the bonds to be exchanged but having different serial numbers and dates. Some days after, the Greek Ministry of Finance specified the conditions governing the voluntary bond exchange transaction involving private investors (private sector involvement), which become legally binding on the holders of all bonds governed by Greek law issued before 31 December 2011 when more than two thirds approved the proposed amendments on the application of the collective action clauses of the Greek bonds. The GC says that an **unconditional involvement of the ECB and NCBs in a restructuration of a public debt** can be classified as an **intervention having an effect equivalent to that of the direct purchase of State bonds by those central banks**, which is prohibited by Article 123 TFEU. Nevertheless, the ECB exchange agreement with Greece in this case was intended to prevent the involvement of the Eurosystem in the restructuring of the Greek public debt, which would mean sacrificing a part of the value of the Greek bonds held in their respective portfolios.[44]

32

After the announcement of the OMT Programme, the worse effects of the economic and financial crisis stopped and the path to economic recovery began. However, towards the middle of 2014, the momentum of the recovery was fading as weaker domestic demand, increased geopolitical tensions and insufficient implementation of structural reforms in some euro area countries negatively affected economic conditions. Against this background, the Governing Council has since mid-2014 adopted a package of new measures with the objective not only of enhancing the transmission of monetary policy but from now on of also reinforcing the accommodative monetary policy stance in light of a persistently weak inflation outlook, slowing growth momentum and subdued monetary and credit dynamics.[45] The main element of the package of measures was a large-scale purchase of private and public sector assets. Since 2014, the ECB Governing Council has adopted the **Expanded Asset Purchase Programme** (APP), a quantitative easing programme

33

---

[43] Case C-62/14, *Gauweiler* (CJEU 16 December 2015) para 121.

[44] Case T-79/13, *Accorinti and others v ECB* (GC 7 October 2015) para 93 and 114. See the comments by Grund and Grle (2016).

[45] Alvarez et al. (2017), p. 10.

that includes all purchase programmes under which private sector securities and public sector securities are purchased to address the risks of a too prolonged period of low inflation. It consists of three new private-sector purchase programmes: the **Covered Bond Purchase Programme** (CBPP3), the **Asset-Backed Securities Purchase Programme** (ABSPP) and the **Corporate Sector Purchase Programme** (CSPP). By these programmes, the ECB and NCBs buy private bonds in primary and secondary markets, and they have not raised concerns against Article 123 TFEU. The APP was completed by the **Public Sector Purchase Programme** (PSPP) announced in January 2015 as a forceful monetary policy response to the risks of deflation.

34   The **amounts of the purchases** of the APP programmes decided by the ECB were EUR 60 billion from March 2015 until March 2016, EUR 80 billion from April 2016 until March 2017, EUR 60 billion from April 2017 to December 2017, EUR 30 billion from January 2018 to September 2018 and EUR 15 billion from October 2018 to December 2018. The Governing Council decided on 25 October 2018 to stop the APP programmes at the end of December 2018, and it stated that it "intends to reinvest the principal payments from maturing securities purchased under the APP for an extended period of time after the end of the net asset purchases, and in any case for as long as necessary to maintain favourable liquidity conditions and an ample degree of monetary accommodation".[46]

35   The **PSPP** raised many concerns about its compatibility with the prohibition on monetary financing because the **purchases made are public sector assets although in the secondary markets**. Under the PSPP, the NCBs, in proportions reflecting their respective shares in the ECB's capital key, and the ECB itself may purchase outright eligible marketable debt securities from eligible counterparties on the secondary markets. Article 3.1 of this decision provides that "subject to the requirements laid down in Article 3, euro-denominated marketable debt securities issued by central, regional or local governments of a MS whose currency is the euro, recognised agencies located in the euro area, international organisations located in the euro area and multilateral development banks located in the euro area shall be eligible for purchases by the Eurosystem central banks under the PSPP". Article 3.2 says that in order to be eligible for purchase under the PSPP, marketable debt securities shall comply with the eligibility criteria for marketable assets for Eurosystem credit operations,[47] subject to some restrictive conditions.[48]

---

[46] See, the ECB press release available at https://www.ecb.europa.eu/press/pr/date/2018/html/ecb.mp181025.en.html.

[47] ECB Guideline (EU) 2015/510 *on the implementation of the Eurosystem monetary policy framework* (ECB/2014/60), O.J. L 91/3 (2015).

[48] These requirements were established by ECB Decision (EU) 2015/774 *on a secondary markets public sector asset purchase programme* (ECB/2015/10), O.J. L 121/20 (2015) as amended by ECB Decision (EU) 2017/100, O.J. L 16 (2017). This Decision was substituted by ECB Decision (EU) 2020/188 *on a secondary markets public sector asset purchase programme* (ECB/2020/9), O.J. L 39/12 (2020).

36 The German Federal Constitutional Court (FCC) once again asked the CJEU in *Weiss and Others*[49] to determine if the ECB Decision 2015/774[50] regulating the PSPP imposes safeguards to avoid the circumvention of Article 123 TFEU according to the *Gauweiler* conditions. In view of the Constitutional Court, significant reasons indicate that the ECB decisions governing the APP violate the prohibition of monetary financing and exceed the monetary policy mandate of the ECB, thus encroaching upon the competencies of the MS.[51]

Following the *Gauweiler* doctrine, the CJEU states in *Weiss* that the ECB's **PSPP** for the purchase of government bonds on secondary markets **does not infringe EU law** because it does not exceed the ECB's mandate and does not contravene the prohibition of monetary financing in Article 123 TFEU. After a detailed analysis,[52] the CJEU concludes that the implementation of the PSPP is not equivalent to a purchase of bonds on the primary markets and does not reduce the impetus of the MS to follow a sound budgetary policy.

First, the CJEU refuses the alleged equivalence of intervention under the PSPP and the purchase of bonds on the primary markets. It states that the ESCB's intervention would be incompatible with Article 123.1 TFEU if the potential purchasers of government bonds on the primary markets knew for certain that the ESCB was going to purchase those bonds within a certain period and under conditions allowing those market operators to act, de facto, as intermediaries for the ESCB for the direct purchase of those bonds from public authorities and bodies of the MS concerned.[53] However, the CJEU concludes that the fact that the PSPP procedures make it possible to foresee, at the macroeconomic level, that there will be a purchase of a significant volume of bonds issued by public authorities and

---

[49] German Federal Constitutional Court, 2 BvR 859/15 et al., *PSPP* (Order of 18 July 2017). The complainant's allegations are documented in Degenhart et al. (2021), p. 19 et seqq.

[50] ECB Decision (EU) 2015/774 *on a secondary markets public sector asset purchase programme* (ECB/2015/10), O.J. L 121/20 (2015), as amended by ECB Decision (EU) 2017/100, O.J. L 16 (2017).

[51] In the FCC's opinion, the PSPP does not provide sufficient guarantees to effectively ensure observance of the prohibition of monetary financing. Even though these public bonds are purchased exclusively on the secondary market, several factors indicate that the PSPP decision nevertheless violates Article 123 TFEU in the Federal Constitutional Court's opinion, namely: "(i) the fact that details of the purchases are announced in a manner that could create a de facto certainty on the markets that issued government bonds will, indeed, be purchased by the Eurosystem; (ii) that it is not possible to verify compliance with certain minimum periods between the issuing of debt securities on the primary market and the purchase of the relevant securities on the secondary market; (iii) that to date all purchased bonds were – without exception – held until maturity; and finally that (iv) the purchases include bonds that carry a negative yield from the outset."

The Federal Constitutional Court also has doubts about the compatibility with Article 123 TFEU of the unlimited distribution of risks between the NCBs of the Eurosystem regarding bonds in default where such bonds were issued by central governments or by issuers of equivalent status.

[52] Case C-493/17, *Weiss* (CJEU 11 December 2018) para 106–166.

[53] Case C-493/17, *Weiss* (CJEU 11 December 2018) para 110 and Case C-62/14, *Gauweiler* (CJEU 16 December 2015) para 104.

bodies of the MS does not afford a given private operator such certainty that he can act, de facto, as an intermediary of the ESCB for the direct purchase of bonds from an MS. Some **safeguards** built into the PSPP ensure that **a private operator cannot be certain**, when it purchases bonds issued by an MS, that those bonds will actually be bought by the ESCB in the foreseeable future:

1. a blackout period monitored by the ECB ensures that bonds issued by a MS cannot be purchased by the ESCB immediately after they are issued,
2. the ESCB discloses the total volume of projected purchases under the APP, but it does not disclose the volume of bonds issued by public authorities and bodies of a MS which will be purchased in a given month under the PSPP and it has laid down rules to difficult the determination of that volume in advance,
3. the volume set out therein applies for the whole of the APP and PSPP purchases may be made only up to the residual amount, which means that the volume of those purchases can vary from month to month depending on availability of bonds issued by private operators on the secondary markets,
4. the diversification of the securities purchased under the PSPP and,
5. purchase limits not allowing the ESCB to buy either all the bonds issued by such an issuer or the entirety of a given issue of those bonds.

Second, the CJEU rejects the allegation that the PSPP reduces an MS's impetus to conduct a sound budgetary policy[54] and concludes that the **MS cannot rely on the PSPP financing possibilities in order to abandon a sound budgetary policy**, without ultimately running the risk (1) of the bonds it issues being excluded from the PSPP because they have been downgraded or (2) of the ESCB selling the bonds that the MS had previously purchased. The PSPP has some limits to stop a possible relaxation of the MS budgetary policies: (1) the restriction of the total monthly volume of public sector asset purchases, (2) the subsidiary nature of the PSPP programme, (3) the distribution of purchases between the national central banks in accordance with the key for subscription of the ECB's capital, (4) purchase limits per issue and issuer (which means that only a minority of the bonds issued by an MS can be purchased by the ESCB under the PSPP) and (5) stringent eligibility criteria (based on a credit quality assessment). Accordingly, the CJEU concludes that Decision 2015/774 does not reduce the impetus of the MS concerned to conduct a sound budgetary policy.

---

[54] The CJEU stated that "in order to avoid a situation in which the Member States' impetus to pursue a sound budgetary policy is reduced, the adoption and implementation of such a programme may not create certainty regarding a future purchase of Member State bonds, in consequence of which Member States might adopt a budgetary policy that fails to take account of the fact that they will be compelled, in the event of a deficit, to seek financing on the markets, or in consequence of which they would be protected against the consequences which a change in their macroeconomic or budgetary situation may have in that regard", see Case C-62/14, *Gauweiler* (CJEU 16 December 2015) para 113 and 114, and Case C-493/17, *Weiss* (CJEU 11 December 2018) para 132.

Third, the CJEU also states that the **prohibition of monetary financing does not preclude either the holding of bonds until maturity or the purchase of bonds at a negative yield to maturity.**

37 The Second Senate of the Federal Constitutional Court (FCC) stated on 5 May 2020[55] that the CJEU judgment in *Weiss and Others* was rendered **ultra vires** because the application of the principle of proportionality to the ECB's decisions on the PSPP was not comprehensible (*nicht nachvollziehbar*). The FCC found that the Federal Government and the German Bundestag violated the complainants' rights under Article 38.1 first sentence in conjunction with Articles 20.1, 20.2 and 79.3 of the Basic Law by failing to take steps challenging that the ECB, in its decisions on the adoption and implementation of the PSPP, neither assessed nor substantiated that the measures provided for in these decisions satisfy the principle of proportionality.[56] Following this approach, the FCC clearly disregarded the authority of ECJ judgments and the primacy of EU law over national laws.

As regards the complainants' arguments that the PSPP effectively circumvents Article 123 TFEU, the FCC **did not find a violation of the prohibition of monetary financing** of MS budgets, and stated that his judgment does not concern any financial assistance measures taken by the EU or ECB in the context of the current coronavirus crisis.

The FCC considers[57] that the PSPP has significant economic policy effects, and it requires that the programme's monetary policy objective and economic policy effects be identified, weighed and balanced against one another. The ECB manifestly disregards the principle of **proportionality** by unconditionally pursuing the PSPP's monetary policy objective—to achieve inflation rates below, but close to, 2%—while ignoring its economic policy effects. Therefore, the ECB decision on **PSPP violates Article 5.1 second sentence and Article 5.4 TEU** and, in consequence, exceeds the monetary policy mandate of the ECB because it contains neither a prognosis as to the PSPP's economic policy effects nor an assessment of whether any such effects were proportionate to the intended advantages in the area of monetary policy.

The FCC notes the PSPP improves the refinancing conditions of the MS as it allows them to obtain financing on the capital markets at considerably better conditions than would otherwise be the case; it thus has a **significant impact on the fiscal policy terms** under which the MS operate. In particular, the PSPP could

---

[55] German FCC, Cases 2 BvR 859/15 et al., *Weiss et al.* (Judgment of 5 May 2020). Among other comments, see Martín Rodríguez (2020), Wendel (2020) and Simon and Rathke (2020).

[56] The FCC said that, by completely disregarding all economic policy effects arising from the programme, the Judgment of 11 December 2018 contradicts the methodological approach taken by the CJEU in virtually all other areas of EU law. It fails to give effect to the function of the principle of conferral as a key determinant in the division of competencies, and to the methodological consequences, this entails for the review as to whether that principle is observed.

[57] German FCC, Cases 2 BvR 859/15 et al., *Weiss et al.* (Judgment of 5 May 2020) para 116–221.

have the same effects as financial assistance instruments pursuant to Articles 12 et seq. of the ESM Treaty. The volume and duration of the PSPP may render the effects of the programme disproportionate, even where these effects are initially in conformity with primary law.[58]

It would have been incumbent upon the ECB to weigh these and other considerable economic policy effects and balance them, based on proportionality considerations, against the expected positive contributions to achieving the monetary policy objective the ECB itself has set. It is **not ascertainable that any such balancing was conducted**, neither when the programme was first launched nor at any point during its implementation. Unless the ECB provides documentation demonstrating that such balancing took place, and in what form, the FCC concludes that it is not possible to carry out an effective judicial review as to whether the ECB stayed within its mandate.

The FCC accepts the *Gauweiler* judgment on **"safeguards" to the application of Article 123.1 TFEU**, but in *Weiss and Others*, the ECJ did not apply it in an adequate manner. Nevertheless, the FCC accepts the CJEU's findings as binding in this respect, given the real possibility that the ECB observed the "safeguards" set out by the CJEU, which means that, for now, a manifest violation of Article 123.1 TFEU is not ascertainable. In the opinion of the FCC, the approach taken by the CJEU may render some of these "safeguards" largely ineffective in practice (for instance, the prohibition of prior announcements, the blackout period, the holding of bonds until maturity and the requirement to decide on an exit strategy). Nonetheless, the determination of whether a programme like the PSPP manifestly circumvents the prohibition in Article 123.1 TFEU is not contingent on a single criterion; rather, it requires an overall assessment and appraisal of the relevant circumstances. In the opinion of the FCC, a manifest circumvention of the prohibition of monetary financing is not ascertainable, especially because the volume of the purchases is limited from the outset, only aggregate information on the purchases carried out by the Eurosystem is published, the purchase limit of 33% per international securities identification number (ISIN) is observed, purchases are carried out according to the ECB's capital key, bonds of public authorities may only be purchased if the issuer has a minimum credit quality assessment that provides access to the bond markets, purchases must be restricted or discontinued, and

---

[58] The FCC indicates that the PSPP also affects the commercial banking sector by transferring large quantities of high-risk government bonds to the balance sheets of the Eurosystem, which significantly improves the economic situation of the relevant banks and increases their credit rating. The economic policy effects of the PSPP furthermore include its economic and social impact on virtually all citizens, who are at least indirectly affected, inter alia as shareholders, tenants, real estate owners, savers or insurance policyholders. For instance, there are considerable losses for private savings. Moreover, as the PSPP lowers general interest rates, it allows economically unviable companies to stay on the market. Finally, the longer the programme continues and the more its total volume increases, the greater the risk that the Eurosystem becomes dependent on Member State politics as it can no longer simply terminate and undo the programme without jeopardising the stability of the monetary union.

purchased securities are sold on the markets, if continuing the intervention on the markets is no longer necessary to achieve the inflation target.

The FCC orders that following a transitional period of no more than three months allowing for the necessary coordination with the Eurosystem, the *Bundesbank* may thus no longer participate in the implementation and execution of the ECB decisions at issue, unless the ECB Governing Council adopts a new decision that demonstrates in a comprehensible and substantiated manner that the monetary policy objectives pursued by the PSPP are not disproportionate to the economic and fiscal policy effects resulting from the programme. Following the FCC ruling, the Bundesbank has **fully explained the PSPP** to the *Bundestag*, the ECB has adopted a **new PSPP decision** with limited additional explanations, the *Bundesbank* continues to participate in the PSPP[59] and the *Bundesverfassungsgericht* has accepted the compatibility of the PSPP with the principle of proportionality and, therefore, the German constitutional law.

The coronavirus (COVID-19) outbreak posed serious risks to the monetary policy transmission mechanism and the outlook for the euro area. To counter the risk, the ECB adopted in March 2020 a non-standard monetary policy measure called **Pandemic Emergency Purchase Programme** (PEPP).[60] The PEPP is a temporary asset purchase programme of private and public sector securities. The Governing Council decided to increase the initial EUR 750 billion envelope for the PEPP by EUR 600 billion on 4 June 2020 and by EUR 500 billion on 10 December, for a new total of EUR 1850 billion. All the APP eligible assets are maintained under the new programme, in addition to the securities issued by the Greek Government. For the purchases of public sector securities under the PEPP, the benchmark allocation across jurisdictions will be the capital key of the national central banks. At the same time, purchases will be conducted in a flexible manner. This allows for fluctuations in the distribution of purchase flow over time, across asset classes and among jurisdictions.

38

The ECB will terminate net asset purchases under the PEPP once it judges that the COVID-19 crisis phase is over, but in any case not before the end of March 2022. **PEPP shares characteristics with OMT and APP**, and at first sight, this confirms the legality of PEPP since both measures were approved by the CJEU, but the merging of characteristics leads nonetheless to some legal issues.[61] As expected, the legality of the PEPP is questioned before the FCC,[62] and the answer could be as critical as the one given regarding the PSPP.

---

[59] Bundesbank Statement of 3 August 2020, "Bundesbank Will Continue Bond Buying as German Court Spat Ends", available at https://www.bloomberg.com/news/articles/2020-08-03/bundesbank-will-continue-bond-buying-as-german-court-spat-ends.

[60] ECB Decision (EU) 2020/440 *on a temporary pandemic emergency purchase programme* (ECB/2020/17), O.J. L 91/1 (2020).

[61] Van der Sluis (2020) and Smits (2020).

[62] German Federal Constitutional Court, Case 2 BvR 420/21, *PEPP*, pending.

3.2. Allowed Monetary Instruments

39 The prohibition of monetary financing aims to **submit MS's public loans to market conditions**. Therefore, **ECB and NCB operations related to the monetary policy and exchange rate policy are excluded from this prohibition**. Regulation No 3603/93 provides some specifications about controversial central bank activities in these fields.

3.2.1. Management of Foreign Exchange Reserves

40 Article 2.2 of Regulation No 3603/93 provides that it shall not be considered direct purchases within the meaning of Article 123 TFEU for the ECB or NCB of an MS participating in stage 3 of EMU to purchase, from the public sector of an MS not participating in stage 3, marketable debt instruments of the latter and vice versa if these purchases are conducted for the sole purpose of managing foreign exchange reserves.

41 These direct acquisitions of marketable debt instruments issued by the public sector of another MS do not help shield the public sector from the discipline of market mechanisms where such purchases are conducted for the sole purpose of managing foreign exchange reserves.

3.2.2. Fiscal Agency Function

42 **Article 21.2 of the ESCB Statute** establishes that the "ECB and the national central banks may act as fiscal agents" for "Union institutions, bodies, offices or agencies, central governments, regional local or other public authorities, other bodies governed by public law, or public undertakings of MS". The purpose of Article 21.2 of the Statute is to enable NCBs to continue to provide the fiscal agent service traditionally provided by central banks to governments and other public entities without automatically breaching the monetary financing prohibition.

43 **Regulation No 3603/93** specifies a number of explicit and narrowly drafted exemptions from the monetary financing prohibition relating to the fiscal agency function as follows:

1. **intra-day credits** to the public sector are permitted provided that they remain limited to the day and that no extension is possible (Article 4);
2. **crediting the public sector's account with cheques issued by third parties** before the drawee bank has been debited is permitted if a fixed period of time corresponding to the normal period for the collection of cheques by the NCB concerned has elapsed since receipt of the cheque, provided that any float which may arise is exceptional, is of a small amount and averages out in the short term (Article 5); and
3. the **holding of coins** issued by and credited to the public sector is permitted where the amount of such assets remains at less than 10% of coins in circulation (Article 6).

Article 123. [Prohibition of Credit Facilities]

Consequently, the provision by the ECB and NCBs of fiscal agency services complies with the prohibition on monetary financing, provided that such services remain within the field of the fiscal agency function and **do not constitute central bank financing of public sector obligations** vis-à-vis third parties or central bank crediting of the public sector outside the narrowly defined exceptions specified in Regulation No 3603/93.[63]

44

However, there would be a breach of the monetary financing prohibition if, for example, national legislation fixed a remuneration of deposits or current account balances above market rates because it constitutes a de facto credit, contrary to the objective of the prohibition on monetary financing. It is essential for any remuneration of an account to reflect market parameters, and it is particularly important to correlate the remuneration rate of the deposits with their maturity.[64] **ECB Decision 2014/8**[65] clarifies the criteria the ECB applies regarding the **remuneration of deposits held by governments and public authorities** with their central bank in relation to Article 123 TFEU, and it specifies the market rates that will operate as ceilings for the remuneration of these government deposits.

45

The ECB may act as a **fiscal agent for the ESM** pursuant to Article 21.2 of the Statute, in the same way the EFSM and EFSF do under the Union's Medium-Term Financial Assistance Facility, but Article 123 TFEU would not allow the ESM to become a counterparty of the Eurosystem under Article 18 of the ESCB Statute.[66]

46

3.2.3. IMF Contributions and Medium-Term Financial Assistance for Balances of Payments of the EU Member States Outside the Eurozone

Article 7 of Regulation No 3603/93 establishes an exemption for two kinds of financial instruments managed by NCBs: IMF contributions and medium-term financial assistance for balances of payments of the MS outside the eurozone. The rationale of these **two exemptions** is the character of these two instruments as reserve assets and not credit facilities.

47

Article 7 of Regulation No 3603/93 authorises the financing by the ECB or NCBs of **obligations falling upon the public sector vis-a-vis the IMF**, which shall not be regarded as a credit facility within the meaning of Article 123 TFEU. Recital 14 of Regulation No 3603/93 clarifies the rationale behind this exemption, stating that it is appropriate to authorise the financing by the NCBs of obligations falling upon the public sector vis-à-vis the IMF because such financing "results in foreign claims which have all the characteristics of reserve assets".

48

---

[63] See, ECB Opinions CON/2009/23, CON/2009/67 and CON/2012/9.

[64] See, among others, ECB Opinions CON/2010/54, CON/2010/55 and CON/2013/62.

[65] ECB Decision ECB/2014/8 *on the prohibition of monetary financing and the remuneration of government deposits by national central banks*, O.J. L 159/54 (2014), amended by ECB Decision (EU) 2015/1574, O.J. L 245/12 (2015).

[66] ECB Opinion CON/2011/24 *on a draft European Council Decision amending Article 136 [TFEU] with regard to a stability mechanism for Member States whose currency is the euro*, O.J. C 140/8 (2011).

49 Therefore, the ECB considers that the exemption in Article 7 of Regulation No 3603/93 must be interpreted in line with this rationale.[67] **Reserve assets** have been defined as those external assets that are readily available to and controlled by monetary authorities for meeting balance of payment financing needs, for interventions in exchange markets to affect the currency exchange rate and for other related purposes, such as maintaining confidence in the currency and the economy and serving as a basis for foreign borrowing. Under this definition, reserve assets must be foreign currency assets and, other than gold bullion, must be claims on non-residents. As a result, the ECB stated, for instance, that the Bank of Italy's transfer of Italy's contribution to the IMF's Poverty Reduction and Growth Trust (PRGT), its granting of loans under the New Arrangements to Borrow (NAB) and its bilateral agreements with the IMF on behalf of Italy fall within the exemption of Article 7 of Regulation No 3603/93 because this financing results in foreign currency (special drawing right (SDR))-denominated claims of the NCB against non-resident persons (the IMF and an IMF-administered trust) that have all the characteristics of reserve assets.[68] Based on the foregoing, the ECB considered that the Bank of Italy's transfer of Italy's contribution to the IMF's PRGT and grant of loans under the NAB and bilateral agreements with the IMF on behalf of Italy should not be regarded as a form of monetary financing prohibited under the Treaty.[69] However, the extension of a credit line to Lebanon by the *Banca d'Italia* to fulfil the Italian Prime Minister's commitment to provide EUR 200 million to support that country cannot be characterised as a financing of an obligation of the Italian State "vis-à-vis the IMF". It would not result in any claim on the IMF, and consequently the Article 7 exemption cannot be invoked to allow for *Banca d'Italia*'s proposed financing of Lebanon.[70]

50 In contrast, national legislation foreseeing the **financing by NCBs of an MS's financial commitments to international financial institutions (other than the IMF) or third countries** is incompatible with the monetary financing prohibition. For example, all commitments associated with EU MS membership in the World Bank should not be considered reserve assets and therefore are a form of monetary financing incompatible with Article 123 TFEU.

51 Article 7 of Regulation No 3603/93 also authorises the financing by the ECB or NCBs of obligations resulting from the implementation of the **medium-term**

---

[67] Consistent with this interpretation, see ECB Opinions CON/2005/29 and CON/2013/16. With regard to the issue of NCBs' financing of IMF quota increases, see ECB Opinions CON/2012/65 and CON/2011/97.

[68] Annex IV, Asset 2.1 of ECB Guideline (EU) 2016/2249/34 *on the legal framework for accounting and financial reporting in the European System of Central Banks*, O.J. L 347/37 (2016) lists "general arrangements to borrow, loans under special borrowing arrangements, deposits made to trusts under the management of the IMF" as "Receivables from the IMF".

[69] ECB Opinion CON/2017/4.

[70] ECB Opinion CON 2005/1.

Article 123. [Prohibition of Credit Facilities]

financial assistance facility for MS's balances of payments set up by **Regulation No 332/2002**,[71] which shall not be regarded as a credit facility within the meaning of Article 123 TFEU. The MS assisted shall open a special account with its NCB for the management of the EU medium-term financial assistance received. It shall also transfer the principal and interest due under the loan to an account with the ECB that will make the necessary arrangements for the administration of the loans.[72]

List of Cases

CJEU

CJEU 27.11.2012, C-370/12, *Pringle*, ECLI:EU:C:2012:756 [cit. in para 5, 7 and 27]
CJEU 16.06.2015, C-62/14, *P. Gauweiler and others* ECLI:EU:C:2015:400 [cit. in para 4]
CJEU 16.12.2015, C-62/14, *Gauweiler*, ECLI:EU:C:2015:400 [cit. in para 5, 27, 28, 30 and 31]
CJEU 11.12.2018, C-493/17, *Weiss and others*, ECLI:EU:C:2018:1000 [cit. in para 4, 28 and 36 et seq.]
CJEU 16.12.2020, C-597/18 P and C-603/18 P, *Council v K. Chrysostomides & Co. and others*, ECLI:EU:C:2020:1028 [cit. in para 25]

GC

GC 07.10. 2015, T-79/13, *Accorinti and others v ECB*, ECLI:EU:T:2015:756 [cit. in para 32]
GC 13.07.2018, T-680/13, *K. Chrysostomides & Co. and others v Council and others*, ECLI:EU:T:2018:486 [cit. in para 25]
GC 13.07.2018, T-786/14, *Bourdouvali and others v Council and others*, ECLI:EU:T:2018:487 [cit. in para 25]

German Federal Constitutional Court

German FCC 18.07.2017, 2 BvR 859/15, *Weiss et al., (PSPP) (reference for preliminary ruling)*, ECLI:DE:BVerfG:2017:rs20170718.2bvr085915 [cit. in para 35]

---

[71] Council Regulation (EC) No 332/2002 *establishing a facility providing medium-term financial assistance for Member States' balances of payments*, O.J. L 53/1 (2002), amended by Council Regulation (EC) No 431/2009, O.J. L 128/1 (2009).
[72] Articles 7.5 and 9 of Regulation (EC) No 332/2002.

German FCC 05.05.2020, 2 BvR 859/15, *Weiss et al.*, ECLI:DE:BVerfG:2020: rs20200505.2bvr085915 [cit. in para 35]

References[73]

Alvarez, I., et al. (2017). The use of the Eurosystem's monetary policy instruments and operational framework since 2012. *ECB Occasional Paper Series*, No 188/May 2017, 10–12.

Borger, V. (2016). Outright Monetary Transactions and the stability mandate of the ECB: Gauweiler. *Common Market Law Review*, 139–196.

Craig, P., & Markakis, M. (2016). Gauweiler and the legality of Outright Monetary Transactions. *European Law Review*, 4–24.

Dawson, M., & Bobic, A. (2019). Quantitative easing at the Court of Justice – Doing whatever it takes to save the euro: Weiss and Others. *Common Market Law Review*, 1005–1040.

Degenhart, C., et al. (2021). *Das Anleihekaufprogramm APP der Europäischen Zentralbank vor dem Bundesverfassungsgericht und dem Gerichtshof der Europäischen Union. Dokumentation der Verfahrensschriftsätze*. Nomos.

Dietz, S. E. (2019). The ECB as Lender of Last Resort in the eurozone? An analysis of an optimal institutional design of Emergency Liquidity Assistance competence within the context of the Banking Union. *Maastricht Journal of European and Comparative Law*, 628–668.

Fischer, S. (1993). The role of macroeconomic factors in growth. *Journal of Monetary Economics, 32*(3), 485–512.

Grund, S., & Grle, F. (2016). The European Central Banks's public sector purchase programme (PSPP), the prohibition of monetary financing and sovereign debt restructuring scenarios. *European Law Review*, 781–803.

Hinarejos, A. (2015). Gauweiler and the Outright Monetary Transactions Programme: The mandate of the European Central Bank and the changing nature of Economic and Monetary Union. *European Constitutional Law Review*, 563–576.

Hinarejos, A. (2019). On-going judicial dialogue and the powers of the European Central Bank: Weiss. *Revista de Derecho Comunitario Europeo*, 651–668.

Lastra, R. M. (2015). *International financial and monetary law*. OUP.

Louis, J.-V. (2009). *L'Union européenne et sa monnaie, Commentaire J. Mégret* (2nd edn). Brussels: Bruylant.

Martín Rodríguez, P. (2020). Y sonaron las trompetas a las puertas de Jericó… en forma de sentencia del Bundesverfassungsgericht. *Revista General de Derecho Europeo*, 2020, n° 52.

Martucci, F. (2016). La Cour de justice face à la politique monétaire en temps de crise de dettes souveraines: l'arrêt Gauweiler entre droit et marché. *Cahiers droit européen*, 493–534.

Mersch, Y. (2016). Scope and Limits of Monetary Policy. Introductory remarks. *Ambrosetti Conference on the Outlook for the Economy and Finance*, Villa d'Este, Cernobbio, 9 April 2016. Retrieved from https://www.ecb.europa.eu/press/key/date/2016/html/sp160409.en.html

Sáinz de Vicuña, A. (2016). La política monetaria del BCE ante el Tribunal Constitucional alemán: la sentencia de 21 de junio de 2016 en el caso OMT. *Revista de Derecho Comunitario Europeo*, 1067–1099.

Sarmiento, D. (2016). The Luxembourg 'Double Look': The Advocate General's opinion and the judgment in the Gauweiler Case. *Maastricht Journal of European and Comparative Law*, 40–54.

Scouteris, B., & Athanassiou, P. (2016). National Central Bank tasks and the boundaries of the ECB Governing Council's powers under Article 14.4 of the Statute: State of play and future prospects (November 16, 2015). In *Commemorative Volume in memory of Professor Dr.*

---

[73] All cited Internet sources of this comment have been accessed on 6 April 2021.

Leonidas Georgakopoulos, Bank of Greece's Center for Culture, Research and Documentation, 2016. Retrieved from https://ssrn.com/abstract=2691914

Simon, S., & Rathke, H. (2020). Simply not comprehensible. Why? *German Law Journal*, 950–955.

Smits, R. (2020). The European Central Bank's pandemic bazooka: Mandate fulfilment in extraordinary times. *EU Law Live*, 24 March 2020. Retrieved from https://eulawlive.com/op-ed-the-european-central-banks-pandemic-bazooka-mandate-fulfilment-in-extraordinary-times-by-rene-smits/

Van der Sluis, M. (2020). Fighting the fallout: The ECB adopts a purchase programme in response to the coronavirus. *EU Law Live*, 24 March 2020. Retrieved from https://eulawlive.com/analysis-fighting-the-fallout-the-ecb-adopts-a-purchase-programme-in-response-to-the-corona virus-by-marijn-van-der-sluis/

Wendel, M. (2020). Paradoxes of ultra-vires review: A critical review of the PSPP decision and its initial reception. *German Law Journal*, 979–994.

Article 124 [Prohibition of Privileged Access to Financial Institutions]
(ex-Article 102 TEC)

Any measure, not based on prudential considerations,[7,8] establishing privileged access[9–11] by Union institutions, bodies, offices or agencies, central governments, regional, local or other public authorities, other bodies governed by public law, or public undertakings of Member States to financial institutions,[4–6] shall be prohibited.

Contents

1. General Remarks 1
2. Scope of Prohibition *Ratione Personae* 4
3. Scope of Prohibition *Ratione Materiae* 9

List of Cases
References

1. General Remarks

Article 124 TFEU prohibits the privileged access of EU institutions and national public entities to financial institutions as a way to **complete the Article 123 TFEU prohibition**. The logic of these two rules is the same: forcing the MS to go to the capital markets to find funds for their financial needs. Market discipline compels the MS to apply orthodox budgetary policies that help the European Central Bank (ECB) to apply a monetary policy guided by its price stability objective. As with the monetary financing prohibition, the ban of privileged access aims to encourage the MS to follow a sound budgetary policy, not allowing the monetary financing of public deficits or the privileged access by public authorities to the financial markets to lead to excessively high levels of debts or excessive MS deficits.[1]

The Court of Justice declared that Article 124 TFEU prohibits any measure, not based on prudential considerations, granting MS, among others, privileged access to financial institutions so as to encourage the former to follow a sound budgetary policy, not allowing monetary financing of public deficits or privileged access by

---

The opinions expressed are strictly personal.

[1] See, to that effect, Case C-62/14, *Gauweiler* (CJEU 16 December 2015) para 100.

public authorities to the financial markets. This sound budgetary policy prevents an excessively high levels of debt or excessive MS deficits.[2]

2   Before the start of Economic and Monetary Union (EMU), it was a common practice in some MS to issue **public debt to finance public deficit** imposing the acquisition of an amount of its liabilities on private financial institutions. The treasuries offered preferential access to the private funds dismissing the competition of private clients for that capital. It was a way to have easy financing, which at the same time facilitates lax budgetary policies.

3   **Council Regulation No 3604/93**[3] provides some definitions, which help with the application of this prohibition by clarifying its personal and material scope.

2. Scope of Prohibition *Ratione Personae*

4   Article 124 TFEU prohibits the privileged access of public entities to "**financial institutions**", without any clarification of this large concept. Council Regulation No 3604/93 provided more details, distinguishing between covered and excluded financial institutions.[4]

5   Article 4.1 of Regulation No 3604/93 establishes a non-exhaustive enumeration of the **financial institutions covered** by Article 124 TFEU. This enumeration refers to the financial institutions regulated at the time by secondary EU rules, which have evolved since then. Now, these financial institutions are credit institutions,[5] insurance undertakings,[6] assurance undertakings, undertakings for collective investment in transferable securities (UCITS),[7] and investment firms.[8] Article 4.1 *in fine* adds "other undertakings the activities of which are like those of the undertakings

---

[2] Case C-201/14, *Bara and others* (CJEU 1 October 2015) para 22, and Case C-571/19, *EMB Consulting and others v ECB* (CJEU 12 March 2020) para 54.

[3] Council Regulation (EC) No 3604/93 *specifying definitions for the application of the prohibition of privileged access referred to in Article 104a of the* [EC] *Treaty*, O.J. L 332/4 (1993).

[4] Martucci, in Pingel (2010), p. 875.

[5] In accordance with Article 4.1 point (1) of Regulation (EU) No 575/2013, a credit institution is an undertaking the business of which is to take deposits or other repayable funds from the public and to grant credits for its own account.

[6] In the meaning of Directive 2009/138/EC, relevant insurance (and assurance) undertakings are those with self-employed activities of direct life and non-life insurance and reinsurance.

[7] According to Article 1.2 of Directive 2009/65/EC, UCITS means an undertaking (a) with the sole object of collective investment in transferable securities or in other liquid financial assets referred to in Article 50(1) of capital raised from the public and which operate on the principle of risk-spreading; and (b) with units which are, at the request of holders, repurchased or redeemed, directly or indirectly, out of those undertakings' assets. Action taken by a UCITS to ensure that the stock exchange value of its units does not significantly vary from their net asset value shall be regarded as equivalent to such repurchase or redemption.

[8] In accordance with Article 4.1(1) of Directive 2014/65/EU investment firm means any legal person whose regular occupation or business is the provision of one or more investment services to third parties and/or the performance of one or more investment activities on a professional basis.

Article 124.   [Prohibition of Privileged Access to Financial Institutions]

referred to in the previous indents or the principal activity of which is to acquire holdings of financial assets or to transform financial claims". This is a clause allowing the application of the Article 124 prohibition to financial institutions not yet covered by EU secondary rules and preventing the circumvention of this ban.

Article 4.2 of Regulation No 3604/93 identifies the **institutions that do not form part of** (i.e. that are excluded from) **the financial institutions** defined in paragraph 1: post-office financial services, when they form part of the general government sector defined in accordance with the European System of Integrated Economic Accounts or when their main activity is to act as the financial agent of the government; the institutions that are part of the general government sector defined in accordance with the European System of Integrated Economic Accounts or the liabilities of which correspond completely to a public debt; and the ECB and NCBs the relation of which with the public sector is regulated by Article 123 TFEU. The ECB and NCBs may not, as public authorities, take measures granting privileged access by the public sector to financial institutions if such measures are not based on prudential considerations. Furthermore, the rules on mobilisation or pledging of debt instruments enacted by the NCBs must not be used as a means of circumventing the prohibition on privileged access.

Article 124 TFEU applies to financial institutions unless the measures adopted by the public authorities are based on prudential considerations. Article 2 of Regulation No 3604/93 defines "**prudential considerations**" as those that underlie national laws, regulations or administrative actions based on, or consistent with, EU law and are designed to promote the soundness of financial institutions so as to strengthen the stability of the financial system as a whole and the protection of the customers of those institutions. Prudential considerations seek to ensure that banks remain solvent regarding their depositors. In the area of prudential supervision, EU secondary legislation has established a number of requirements to ensure the soundness of credit institutions,[9] and the most significant credit institutions of the eurozone are now submitted to the control of the Single Supervisory Mechanism (SSM) under the authority of the ECB.

For instance, the General Court stated that Greek Law No 4050/2012 was justified by prudential considerations as referred to in Article 124 TFEU and defined by Article 2 of Regulation No 3604/93. In fact, Greek Law No 4050/2012 introduced rules amending the terms applicable to marketable securities issued or guaranteed by the Greek State under agreements with their holders for the purpose of restructuring Greek public debt. Consequently, it contributed to preserving both Greek public finances and the stability of the financial system in the eurozone.[10]

The ECB requires credit institutions established in the euro area to hold the required **minimum reserves** (in the form of deposits) on accounts with their

---

[9] See Parliament/Council Regulation (EU) No 575/2013 *on prudential requirements for credit institutions and investment firms*, O.J. L 176/1 (2013); and Parliament/Council Directive 2013/36/EU *on access to the activity of credit institutions and the prudential supervision of credit institutions and investment firms*, O.J. L 176/338 (2013).

[10] Case T-107/17, *Steinhoff and Others v ECB* (GC 23 May 2019) para 138.

NCBs.[11] Although minimum reserves might be seen as privileged access to financial institutions, they are outside the Article 124 prohibition because they are part of the ECB operational framework and are used as a monetary policy tool.[12] This is supported by Article 3.2, which establishes that the ECB and NCBs "shall not, for the purposes of this Article, be considered as forming part of the public sector", and by Recital 9 of Regulation No 3604/93, which provides that "for reasons of monetary policy, financial institutions and, in particular, credit institutions may be obliged to hold claims" against the ECB and/or NCBs. As the ECB noted, the debt instruments issued by the ESCB as part of the implementation of the monetary policy are not classified as sovereign debt instruments, which would be contrary to the prohibition of the central bank financing of the public sector expressed in Article 123 TFEU.[13]

3. Scope of Prohibition *Ratione Materiae*

9   Article 124 TFEU is applicable to the **measures classifiable as "privileged access"** to the private financial institutions except if these measures are expressly excluded from the scope of this article.

10   Under Article 1.1 of Regulation No 3604/93, **privileged access** is understood as any law, regulation or other binding legal instruments adopted in the exercise of public authority that (a) obliges financial institutions to acquire or hold liabilities of EU institutions or bodies; central governments; regional, local or other public authorities; other bodies governed by public law; or public undertakings of MS or (b) confers tax advantages that only benefit financial institutions or financial advantages that do not comply with the principles of a market economy in order to encourage those institutions to acquire or hold such liabilities. It is necessary for privileged access to be imposed unilaterally by a compulsory legal act adopted by a public authority. By contrast, Article 124 TFEU allows financial entities to buy MS public debt on a voluntary basis. Article 124 TFEU forbids tax advantages that only benefit financial institutions and encourage them to acquire or hold liabilities (public bonds), but general fiscal advantages are allowed to promote popular saving systems.

11   In *Steinhoff and Others v ECB* (T-107/17), delivered on 23 May 2019, the General Court dismissed an action for damages seeking restitution of the loss allegedly suffered by private creditors, following the Opinion of the ECB on the

---

[11] See Article 19 of the Statute; Council Regulation (EC) No 2531/98 *concerning the application of minimum reserves by the European Central Bank*, O.J. L 318/1 (1998); ECB Regulation (EU) 2021/379 on *the balance sheet items of credit institutions and of the monetary financial institutions sector (recast)* (ECB/2021/2), O.J. L 73/16 (2021).

[12] ECB Guideline (EU) 2015/510 *on the implementation of the Eurosystem monetary policy framework (General Documentation Guideline)* (ECB/2014/60), O.J. L 91/3 (2015).

[13] ECB Opinion CON/2011/17 *on a proposal for a regulation of the European Parliament and of the Council on short selling and certain aspects of credit default swaps*, p. 2.

terms of securities issued or guaranteed by the Greek State. By their action, the applicants called into question the **liability of the ECB for the loss they allegedly suffered** due to the fact that the ECB failed, in its opinion, to draw the attention of the Hellenic Republic to the unlawful nature of the proposed restructuring of the Greek public debt by a mandatory exchange of bonds. The applicants invoked an infringement of Article 124 TFEU by the ECB.

On 2 February 2012, the Hellenic Republic submitted to the ECB, pursuant to Article 127.4 TFEU, read in conjunction with Article 282.5 TFEU, a request for an opinion on draft **Greek Law No 4050/2012** introducing rules amending the terms applicable to marketable securities issued or guaranteed by the Greek State under agreements with their holders for the purpose of restructuring the Greek public debt based, in particular, on the application of collective action clauses (CACs). Since the ECB delivered a positive opinion on the draft law, it was adopted, on 23 February 2012, by the Greek Parliament. Under the CACs mechanism, the proposed amendments would become legally binding on all holders of bonds governed by Greek law issued before 31 December 2011, as identified in the act of the Ministerial Council approving private sector involvement (PSI) invitations, if the modifications were approved by a quorum of bondholders representing at least two thirds of the face value of those bonds. Since the quorum and the majority required were reached, all holders, including those who opposed the deal, had their bonds exchanged pursuant to Law No 4050/2012, with the result that the value of those bonds fell. As a consequence, even the holders that had refused the exchange participated in the restructuring of the Greek public debt.

The General Court indicated that the applicants were wrong to invoke the existence of unlawfulness, rendering the ECB liable towards them based on the ECB's failure to draw attention to a breach of Article 124 TFEU. First, Law No 4050/2012 does not grant privileged access to financial institutions contrary to Article 124 TFEU, and its aim is not to increase the level of debt of the Hellenic Republic but rather to reduce it, due to its excessively high nature, by devaluing the bonds held by the applicants. In addition, Law No 4050/2012 was justified by prudential considerations and **contributed to preserving both Greek public finances and the stability of the financial system** in the euro area.[14]

Second, in any event, the General Court said that Article 124 TFEU is not designed to protect the applicants and does not confer rights on them. Article 124 TFEU is oriented to preserve the institutions of the EU and of the MS against the budgetary risks of privileged access to financial institutions. The prohibition set out in **Article 124 TFEU is therefore intended to protect not individuals and undertakings,** such as the applicants in the instant case, but the EU in itself, including MS, against conduct liable to undermine the economic and financial stability of the Union as a whole. Thus, Article 124 TFEU cannot be considered to be a provision conferring rights on the applicants, with the result that they cannot

12

---

[14] Case T-107/17, *Steinhoff and others v ECB* (GC 23 May 2019) para 135–137.

13 Article 1.2 of Regulation No 3604/93 provides three **exceptions to the privileged access interdiction** on a solidarity basis: (a) obligations for funding social housing under special terms, such as, inter alia, an obligation to centralise funds with public financial institutions; (b) obligation to centralise funds with a public credit institution in so far as such a constraint has been an integral part, as of 1 January 1994, of the organisation of a particular network of credit institutions or of specific savings arrangements designed for households and intended to provide the whole of the network or the specific arrangements with financial security; and (c) obligations to finance the repair of disaster damage. The application of these three exceptions is conditioned on the respect for market economy conditions (same treatment for public and private institutions). The ECB considers a breach of the prohibition on privileged access a national law containing tax advantages established for the benefit of persons that acquire savings certificates from or place term deposits with credit institutions with the effect of putting private and public institutions on an unequal footing, for instance by encouraging credit institutions to lend to public sector borrowers or buy public sector bonds.[17]

14 Central banks make providing credit to banks conditional on collateralisation, applying eligibility criteria for the collateral to be provided, and the ECB has developed the **Eurosystem Collateral Framework**. In line with its statutes, the Eurosystem provides credit only against adequate collateral, which refers to marketable financial securities such as bonds or other types of assets such as non-marketable assets or cash.[18] The term **"eligible asset"** is used for assets that are accepted as collateral by the ECB. Obviously, this obligation to provide eligible assets as collateral imposed on banks to have access to the ECB credits is compatible with the Article 124 prohibition.

List of Cases

CJEU
CJEU 01.10.2015, C-201/14, *Bara and others*, ECLI:EU:C:2015:638 [cit. in para 1]
CJEU 16.12.2015, C-62/14, *Gauweiler*, ECLI:EU:C:2015:400 [cit. in para 1]
CJEU 12.03.2020, C-571/19 P, *EMB Consulting and others v ECB*, ECLI:EU:C:2020:208 [cit. in para 1 and 11]

---

[15] Case T-107/17, *Steinhoff and others v ECB* (GC 23 May 2019) para 139–141.
[16] Case C-571/19, *EMB Consulting and others v ECB* (CJEU 12 March 2020) para 55.
[17] ECB Opinion CON/2013/55, *on measures to encourage long-term lending*.
[18] See ECB Guideline (EU) 2015/510 *on the implementation of the Eurosystem monetary policy framework*, O.J. L 91/3 (2015); Bindseil et al. (2017), p. 7.

CFI/GC
GC 23.05.2019, T-107/17, *Steinhoff and others v ECB*, ECLI:EU:T:2019:353 [cit. in para 7 and 11]

References

Bindseil, U., et al. (2017). *The Eurosystem collateral framework explained*, ECB Occasional Paper Series No 189/2017.

Pingel, I. (Ed.). (2010). *De Rome à Lisbonne: Commentaire article par article des traités UE et CE* (2nd ed.). Dalloz.

Article 125 ["No-Bail-Out" Clause]
(ex-Article 103 TEC)

1. The Union shall not be liable for or assume the commitments[24,25] of central governments, regional, local or other public authorities, other bodies governed by public law, or public undertakings of any Member State, without prejudice to mutual financial guarantees for the joint execution of a specific project.[21,22] A Member State shall not be liable for or assume the commitments of central governments, regional, local or other public authorities, other bodies governed by public law, or public undertakings of another Member State, without prejudice to mutual financial guarantees for the joint execution of a specific project.
2. The Council, on a proposal from the Commission and after consulting the European Parliament, may, as required, specify definitions[10–12] for the application of the prohibitions referred to in Articles 123 and 124 and in this Article.

Contents

1. The Historical Background to, and Grounds for, Article 125 TFEU 1
   1.1. Making the State Subject to Market Discipline 2
   1.2. The Need for Careful Wording 6
2. The Scope of the Bail-Out Prohibition 10
   2.1. The Prohibited Commitments 13
   2.2. Authorised Commitments 20
   2.3. Legal Subjects Prohibited to Bail Out 22
      2.3.1. The Union and the Member States 23
      2.3.2. The European Financial Stability Facility and the European Stability Mechanism 25
   2.4. Application *Ratione Temporis* 28
3. Authorised Financial Support 30
   3.1. Compatible Financial Operations 35
      3.1.1. The Purchase and Holding of Government Debt Instruments 36
      3.1.2. Loans 40
      3.1.3. Other Operations 43
   3.2. Financial Assistance Under Articles 122.2, 136.3 and 143.2 TFEU 44
   3.3. Restructuring of Public Debt 49
      3.3.1. Public Debt Restructuring 51
      3.3.2. Public Debt Rescheduling 61
4. Public Debt Pooling in Prospect 63

List of Cases
References

1. The Historical Background to, and Grounds for, Article 125 TFEU

1 Article 125 TFEU prohibits any transfer of debt from a MS to the EU or another MS. This prohibition applies without prejudice to the mutual guarantees set up for the purpose of financing joint transnational projects between a number of MS. This "no bail-out" rule supplements the prohibitions on monetary financing for the MS and their privileged access to the financial institutions defined in Articles 123 and 124 TFEU respectively. Together, these three rules make the **MS**, as issuers of debt, **subject to market discipline**. Articles 123 and 124 TFEU remove from the State its traditional means of financing, debt monetisation by the central bank or compulsory saving in order to force it to turn to the markets to meet its financing needs. Their purpose is to make sure that the MS follow a sound budgetary policy. In so doing, they contribute "at Union level to the attainment of a higher objective, namely maintaining the financial stability of the monetary union".[1]

1.1. Making the State Subject to Market Discipline

2 Article 125 TFEU completes the process of standardising the status of the State as an issuer of debt instruments. An **MS** is regarded as **bearing the sole responsibility for the financial commitments** it has taken on. The capacity of an MS to run its public finances soundly (→ Article 119 TFEU para 42, 44 et seq.) and service its debt (or credit risk) is assessed by investors and the Union's institutions (i.e. Commission, Ecofin Council and Eurogroup) in the light *solely* of its own economic, budgetary, fiscal or institutional performance.[2] Monetary union does away with the risk associated with currency exchange, and it means it is no longer possible to draw any distinctions between debts on that basis. The bail-out prohibition compensates for that change by guaranteeing that the other factors for making distinctions are effective. "Yield differentials would still exist if markets thought some governments could default on debt, but only if traders believed in a 'no bail-out' declaration", *Niels Thygesen* explained in 1990.[3]

3 The individual nature of the obligation of each State in relation to its creditors[4] forms **part of the broader system of economic and political accountability**, which underlies the **conduct of national economic policy** under Title VIII on economic and monetary policy. Under Articles 119 and 120 TFEU, each State keeps its sovereignty with respect to economic and budgetary policy, and they "remain responsible for their national budgetary policies, subject to the provisions

---

[1] Case C-370/12, *Pringle* (CJEU 27 November 2012) para 135.
[2] Report of the Monetary Committee of 19 July 1990, cited by Louis (2009), p. 97.
[3] Cited by Jukes (1990), also von Hagen and Eichengreen (1998), p. 150.
[4] Smits (1997), p. 77.

of the Treaty".[5] The Union for its part has the competence to coordinate economic policies, which include budgetary policies (→ Article 5 TFEU para 6 et seqq.).[6] That competence does not have the effect of substituting the Union's authority for that of the MS. To go into debt is a decision for an MS to make, the conditions of the indebtedness—particularly the risk premium required in the form of interest rate— are based essentially on its risk profile, and it is solely up to the MS to repay the debt. Freedom to go into debt entails responsibility for paying the debt off.

Article 125 TFEU has a radical sanctioning effect: it gives the markets the power to impose different terms and conditions on MS borrowing and, in the extreme case, refuse to lend.[7] As the ultimate sanction for budgetary indiscipline by the MS, it automatically makes all other forms of more binding regulations, as defended in 1991 by *Norman Lamont*, then Chancellor of the Exchequer, pointless.[8] This **repressive effect** makes the no bail-out clause the pivotal provision[9] in the economic pillar of the Economic and Monetary Union (EMU). Both literally and figuratively, this article sets up a **link between the system of market-imposed discipline** (Articles 123–125 TFEU) **and the system of discipline imposed by rules** (Article 126 TFEU). The threat of a loss of access to the financial markets and the prohibition on the covering of financial risks by the EU or another MS require the MS to formulate a cautious budgetary policy. Conversely, investors are asked to lend following a detailed assessment of the credit risk posed by the borrower country. Otherwise, they expose themselves to the risk of a default on the debt they hold, a risk that they would have to bear in full or in part.[10]

4

The same rigorous approach is called for on the part of the EU institutions in interpreting and applying the fiscal discipline procedure, whether in its preventive or corrective aspect (→ Article 126 TFEU para 4). Any laxity could lead to the

5

---

[5] Recital 6 of Council Regulation (EC) No 1467/97 *on speeding up and clarifying the implementation of the excessive deficit procedure*, O.J. L 209/6 (1997), as last amended by Regulation No 1177/2011, O.J. L 306/33 (2011). It is for the national governments to exercise that responsibility in accordance with Article 3 of Protocol (No 12) on the excessive deficit procedure. The MS' budgetary responsibility is one of the three pillars of the 2015 annual growth survey established by the Commission on 28 November 2014 (COM(2014) 902 final, particularly p. 5 and pp. 15–18) and approved by the European Council of 19 and 20 March 2015.

[6] Putting the coordination into practice is mainly the task of the Council (Article 16 TEU and Article 121.1 TFEU, and ex-Article 202 TEC, now repealed).

[7] Monetary Committee, *Monetary and fiscal policy in the EMU*. Contribution of the Italian Treasury to the debate in the Monetary Committee, Brussels, 1 March 1990. II/108/90-EN.

[8] Cited by Ubsborne (1991).

[9] Ruffert (2011), p. 1786.

[10] Drawing on the experience of the debt crisis in the Latin-American countries in the early 1980s, the Danish Ministry of Economic Affairs pointed out that "it can be argued that the financial system does not sufficiently evaluate the ability of public authorities to service their debt. This may be due to expectations that other countries will bail out a country with a debt problem." Reducing moral hazard makes market discipline effective. See Ministry of Economic Affairs of the Kingdom of Denmark, *Report on economic and monetary Union* [Unofficial translation by the European Commission], II/418/89-EN.1989 (1989), p. 4; also Palmstorfer (2012), p. 774.

encouragement of a situation where an MS became over-indebted. The financial stability of the euro area in its entirety could be affected. What particularly makes one expect a strict interpretation and effective application of Article 125 TFEU is that the purpose of the rule is to **limit the risks of moral hazard**[11] and, incidentally, the decrease of the likelihood of the solidarity mechanisms being activated. The bail-out prohibition defines the line of balance between market economy logic and the solidarity principle. In that context, the interpretation of the "no bail-out" clause has become a matter for legal discussion, giving rise to political, economic and legal developments and leaving its imprint on the economic governance reforms and the establishment of arrangements for financial assistance to the euro-area MS from spring 2010.

1.2. The Need for Careful Wording

6   Despite its importance for the proper functioning of EMU, the "no bail-out" clause in itself gave rise to **very little discussion during the preparatory work** for the Intergovernmental Conference (IGC) on EMU of 1990 and then during the negotiations on the Maastricht Treaty. Since the end of the 1970s, the MS had mostly turned to the financial markets to meet their financing needs and had standardised their issuer status by giving up some of their exorbitant powers.[12] For MS seeking to place their securities on the best available terms, the "no bail-out" rule made good sense.[13] The *Delors* Committee's Report on the establishment of EMU in the Community did not mention it when it set out the features of economic union. Conversely, it did mention the prohibition on monetary financing because of the immediate effect it would have on the conduct of the single monetary policy[14] and the fact that that form of financing was still common in many MS.[15] Another reason for the silence about the "no bail-out" clause in the *Delors* Report was the preference it gave to the coordination of budgetary policies on the basis of binding rules, as opposed to the market discipline that the bail-out prohibition favoured.[16]

---

[11] Fratianni et al. (1992), p. 39.

[12] Lemoine (2016); Pons (1988), p. 91.

[13] European Commission Press Release, Extracts from the speech by Sir Leon Brittan to the L'Expansion Conference, Salzburg, 10 November 1991, SPEECH-91-116.

[14] Committee for the Study of Economic and Monetary Union [Delors Committee], *Report on the establishment by stages of economic and monetary union in the Community* (1989), p. 20.

[15] At the beginning of 1990, six of the 12 Community MS still had automatic access to the credit operations of the national central banks or an obligation on the part of the banking system to buy sovereign instruments (these were Belgium, Greece, Spain, Ireland, Italy and Portugal). See Economic Policy Committee, *Requirements for the achievement of closer convergence of public finance in the Member States*, II/184/90-EN (22 May 1990), p. 3.

[16] Christophersen (1989).

Article 125. ["No-ail-ut" Clause]   655

7   The debate surrounding the "no bail-out" clause emerged at the same time as the choice of a **system for the coordination of economic policies**.[17] In spring 1990, although the demand for a management structure for budgetary policies was unanimously acknowledged by the various negotiators, the opinion was still deeply divided as to the practicalities of providing that management. The only matter on which there was a consensus was the inclusion of the "no monetary financing" and the "no bail-out" principles in future treaties.[18] Although the principle of prohibiting bail-outs was adopted, the precise wording to be used developed as the discussions progressed and became tougher.[19]

8   In the document submitted to the informal **Ecofin Council in Galway**, Ireland, on 31 March 1990, the Commission understood the "automatic" bail-out prohibition to mean that "the Community will have no obligation to go to the assistance of a Member State which is experiencing budgetary difficulties (no guarantee). This does not exclude ad hoc conditional assistance."[20] In the basic document for the IGC-EMU of 21 August[21] and in the draft treaty of 15 December 1990,[22] the Commission suggested prohibiting "the granting by the Community or the Member States of an unconditional guarantee in respect of the public debt of a Member State". *A contrario*, such a form of words allows for the *possibility* of assistance granted on *conditions*.

9   This statement regarding conditionality is absent from the draft treaties submitted by France.[23] Germany distanced itself from any reference to any kind of guarantee, laying down in its proposal that neither the Community nor the MS should be liable for another MS's commitments.[24] The rule was more carefully

---

[17] The coordination arrangement to be chosen was discussed at the informal Ecofin Council held in Antibes on 9 and 10 September 1989. It was also one of the points identified by the high-level EMU working party chaired by Elisabeth Guigou in autumn 1989. See Christophersen (1989); and General Secretariat of the Council, *Draft Report on the main questions raised by the establishment of an economic and monetary union*. Brussels, SN 3260/2/89 (EMU) (1989).

[18] Commission, *Economic and Monetary Union. Economic basis and design of the system*, in Europe Documents [Agence Europe] (23 April 1990), No. 1604/1605, p. 10; European Parliament, *Resolution on economic and monetary union* [Herman Report], A3-223/90, O.J. C 284/62 (1990).

[19] Smulders and Kepenne, in von der Groeben et al. (2016), Article 125 AEUV para 8–9.

[20] Commission, *Economic and Monetary Union. Economic basis and design of the system*, in Europe Documents [Agence Europe] (23 April 1990), No. 1604/1605, p. 10.

[21] Commission, *Report on Economic and Monetary Union for the intergovernmental conference*, 21 August 1990, in Europe Documents [Agence Europe] (27 September 1990), No 1650/1651, p. 11.

[22] Commission, *Commentaires au projet de traité pour l'Union économique et monétaire (Comments on the draft Treaty on Economic and Monetary Union)* in Europe Documents [Agence Europe] (27 December 1990), Nos 1678/1679, esp. Article 104A(1), also Parliament, [Herman Report] (1990), esp. Article 20.2.

[23] Government of the French Republic, *Projet de traité sur l'Union économique et monétaire*, in Europe Documents [Agence Europe] (31 January 1991), No 1686.

[24] Chancellery of the German Federal Republic, *Overall proposal for the intergovernmental conference*, in Europe Documents [Agence Europe] (20 March 1991), No 1700.

worded.²⁵ This wording largely inspired the wording used in the draft treaty of the Luxembourg Council Presidency on 20 June 1991.²⁶ The idea of a guarantee reappeared, however, under the heading "Mutual Financial Guarantees for Joint Projects". The point was to avoid any illegality in the financial packages for transnational projects or projects supported by the European Investment Bank (EIB). There were no further changes to the "no bail-out" clause during the later discussions leading up to the adoption of the **Maastricht Treaty**.

No proposal for an amendment was either planned or carried out during the later revisions of the Community treaties. Only the numbering of the article was changed: Article 104b TEC, which was brought in by the Maastricht Treaty and prohibited bail-outs, became Article 103 TEC as a result of the Amsterdam Treaty. The **wording in Article 125 TFEU has not changed**, except for some procedural rules laid down in paragraph 2.

2. The Scope of the Bail-Out Prohibition

10   Like Articles 123 and 124 TFEU, Article 125 TFEU has a **direct effect**.²⁷ It categorically imposes a prohibition in the form of a twofold obligation not to act, on the Union and on the MS: they must neither be liable for nor assume the financial commitments of another MS. The prohibition is clear and unconditional, and there is no associated reservation in the treaty to the effect that it depends for its application on secondary legislation or enactment in domestic law.²⁸

11   Article 125.2 TFEU provides at most that the Council "may, as required," specify definitions for the application of the prohibition.²⁹ It rules on a proposal from the Commission after consulting the Parliament. At the request of the Copenhagen European Council of 21 and 22 June 1993, the Commission, at the end of July 1993, put forward a series of informal legislative proposals³⁰ intended to **clarify the**

---

[25] Louis (2009), p. 97.

[26] Government of the Grand-Duchy of Luxembourg, *Projet de traité sur l'Union (Draft Treaty on the Union)* in Europe Documents [Agence Europe] (5 July 1991), Nos 1722/1723, esp. Article 104 (1)(b).

[27] Chemain (1996), p. 152; Louis (2010), p. 977; Smits (1997), p. 77; Bandilla, in Grabitz et al. (2021), Article 125 AEUV para 5 (released in 2011).

[28] Case 26-62, *Van Gend en Loos* (ECJ 5 February 1963); Commission, *Comment on the draft treaty* (1991), esp. Article 104A (budgetary rules), p. 5.

[29] Cloos et al. (1994), p. 247.

[30] Commission Communication *concerning secondary legislation for the second stage of Economic and Monetary Union*, COM(93) 371 final, p. 2. Following the second Danish referendum of 18 May 1993, the prospect of the entry into force of the Maastricht Treaty in the second half of 1993 came into view. The treaty laid down that stage two of EMU should begin automatically on 1 January 1994. The limited period of time between entry into force of the treaty and discussions on stage two meant that appropriate measures had to be prepared in advance. As Article 125 TFEU was not yet active, the legislative proposals were presented as "informal". They were a way of opening the discussions without launching legislative activity in the strict sense.

definitions in Article 104–104 C TEC [123 to 126 TFEU]. As the Brussels institution stated, **secondary legislation** relating to Article 104 B [125 TFEU] was not "obligatory". However, it deemed it advisable to clarify a number of issues, a viewpoint also supported by the Committee of Governors of the Central Banks.[31] The clarified points concern the concept of "public undertakings" referred to in Article 125.1 TFEU. Council Regulation (EC) No 3603/93[32] reproduced the definition laid down by Commission Directive No 80/723/EEC. No direct reference was made to the directive, owing to the exemptions that it provided for and that could have had the effect of reducing the effectiveness of the prohibition in Article 104 B TEC [125 TFEU].[33]

Compliance with Article 125 TFEU can be checked by the Commission and, where appropriate, give rise to the opening of an infringement procedure.[34] An infringement of the bail-out prohibition by an act of the EU or by a national law is open to an action for annulment under Article 263 TFEU[35] or domestic remedies.[36] In the event of a **breach of Article 125 TFEU**, any conflicting EU or national regulation must be left unapplied[37] by the judge and regarded as non-existent.[38] Guarantees given by the Union or an MS to another MS or any bail-out must be declared null and void.[39] If any debt has been paid off, the Union or the MS must be reimbursed by the beneficiary MS concerned.

12

---

[31] Committee of Governors of the Central Banks of the Member States of the EEC, *Annual Report 1992*, 1993, p. 84.

[32] Council Regulation (EC) No 3603/93 *specifying definitions for the application of the prohibitions referred to in Articles 104 and 104b (1) of the Treaty*, O.J. L 332/1 (1993).

[33] See above mentioned Commission Communication *concerning secondary legislation*, COM (93) 371 final, esp. comment on "Article 7 – Definition of the public sector", p. 9.

[34] Louis (1995), p. 35.

[35] Article 125 TFEU was invoked in support of an action for annulment brought by a German national against the ECB's decisions of 2010 and 2011 concerning temporary measures relating to the eligibility of marketable debt instruments issued or guaranteed by Greece, Ireland and Portugal, and against the ECB decision to establish a programme for the securities markets. The appeal was dismissed as it had not been lodged in time. See Case T-532/11, *Stefan Städter* (GC 16 December 2011).

[36] Breach of Article 125 TFEU was one of the means used before the national Supreme Court by Irish MP *Thomas Pringle* to contest the validity of ratification by the country of the ESM Treaty. The Court of Justice was asked to give a preliminary ruling. It confirmed that support granted by the ESM was compatible with Article 125 TFEU. See Supreme Court of Ireland, 339/2012, *Pringle v Government of Ireland* (Judgment of 31 July 2012); Case C-370/12, *Pringle* (ECJ 27 November 2012).

[37] Case 106/77, *Simmenthal SpA* (ECJ 9 March 1978) para 21-22; recently: Case C-173/09, *Elchinov* (ECJ 5 October 2010) para 25, 29.

[38] Barav (2015), p. 43.

[39] On this, see also: Smits (1997), pp. 292–293.

2.1. The Prohibited Commitments

13   The bail-out prohibition laid down in Article 125 TFEU is entirely centred on the notions of "**liability**" and "**commitment**"—the French version of the treaty uses the single term *engagement* and the German version *Verbindlichkeit*. The choice of these terms is a sign of the rejection of the terms "guarantee" and "public debt" proposed in the draft treaties by the Commission and France. The term "liability" entails the existence of a debt or pecuniary obligation for which a person or venture is liable. The word "commitment", on the other hand, points to the active nature of the undertaking given and is defined as "the action of committing". It expresses the principle of meeting the obligation by discharging it.[40] The first term refers to a particular type of financial instrument;[41] the second, which acts as the fulcrum on which the excessive deficit procedure hinges, refers back to an accounting concept and not to a particular *instrumentum*.[42]

14   In opting for general terms,[43] the authors of the treaty gave the prohibition the **widest scope possible** and, incidentally, prevented the treaty from becoming obsolete on account of developments in financial engineering. The outcome is that the commitment includes any official or unofficial act whereby the EU or the MS must, implicitly or explicitly,[44] discharge certain obligations (liabilities) contracted by another MS and whose effect is to entail a transfer of the financing costs of the initial debtor to the EU and/or the other MS.

15   The **commitment** is **prohibited on principle**. As Advocate General (AG) *Kokott* pointed out in the *Pringle* case, the "no-bail-out" clause refers to a "prohibition" that "prevents a Member State" from acting "either by discharging the commitment by making payment or by itself becoming the obligated party subject to the commitment, which it then has to discharge at a later date".[45] Article 125 TFEU uses two distinct verbs for this purpose to emphasise the prohibition on the liability itself ("shall not be liable for": *ne répond pas* in French, *haftet nicht* in German) and the prohibition on discharging it ("shall not [...] assume": *ne prend pas à sa charge* in French, *tritt nicht [...] ein* in German). The procedures for discharging an obligation are not explained in the Treaty, which means that discharging in any form is forbidden: payment or debt forgiveness where the authority that is bailing out writes off debts it holds against the MS that was bailed out. The point is to **prevent any arrangement that might modify the risk profile of an MS** irrespective of its own budgetary policy. This applies to both the MS

---

[40] See Oxford English Dictionary, Oxford University Press, 2nd edn., 1989; online version November 2016. See also for a discussion of these two terms: Steinbach (2016), pp. 227–228.

[41] Parliament/Council Directive 2002/47/EC *on financial collateral arrangements*, O.J. L 168/43 (2002), spec. Article 1.2.

[42] Allemand (2015), p. 247.

[43] Also pointed out in Case C-370/12, *Pringle* (Opinion of AG Kokott of 26 October 2012) para 120.

[44] Kepenne (2000), p. 982.

[45] Case C-370/12, *Pringle* (Opinion of AG Kokott of 26 October 2012) para 121.

Article 125. ["No-ail-ut" Clause]

bailed out and the EU or MS that performed the bail-out. The setting up of financial guarantees by the debtor for the benefit of the authority that undertakes to make reimbursement or assumes responsibility for the debt does not expunge the illegality of the liability or the commitment since the latter entails a future or immediate deterioration in the financial situation of the guarantor.

The identity of the authority that takes the initiative in conducting a bail-out (the EU, one or more MS or the MS in difficulty) is also not pertinent to the case: **neither a bail-out proposed by the EU or an MS nor one requested by an indebted MS is authorised.**[46] In the case of the EU, the bail-out prohibition is reinforced by the requirement to run a balanced budget (Article 310 TFEU). The EU may not adopt any act that is likely to have appreciable implications for the budget without providing guarantees that the expenditure arising from such an act is capable of being financed within the limit of the Union's own resources and in compliance with the multiannual financial framework. The limits on the level of own resources and the programmatic character of EU expenditure make it de facto impossible to assume liability for all or a part of an MS's public debts. **16**

Debts that it is forbidden to transfer are those entered into by central governments; regional, local or other public authorities; other bodies governed by public law; or public undertakings.[47] Because of the institutional autonomy of the MS, it is not possible to draw up an exhaustive list of all the forms of public entities under national law, as is shown by the use of the adjective "other" in Article 125 TFEU to refer to the public bodies covered by the prohibition. The deciding factor is **whether the entity concerned is or is not public**. Article 125 TFEU does not provide any definition or descriptive criteria by which the precise outlines of the public sector can be drawn. **17**

Article 2 of Protocol (No 12) on the excessive deficit procedure notes that the adjective "**public**" designates a "general government, that is central government, regional or local government and social security funds". Council Regulation (EC) No 479/2009 on the application of Protocol No 12[48] brings together the main elements in defining these concepts drawn from the European system of accounts for the purposes of properly applying the excessive deficit procedure. Methodological clarification is supplied by Eurostat in its *Manual on Government Deficit and* **18**

---

[46] Gnan, in von der Groeben and Schwarze (2003), Article 103 EGV para 22, 23; Ruffert (2011), p. 1785.

[47] The list of entities of MS concerned by the prohibition is the same as the one in Article 123.1 TFEU. See also Bandilla, in Grabitz et al. (2021) Article 125 AEUV para 7 (released in 2011) and → Article 123 TFEU para 10–11.

[48] Previously Council Regulation (EC) No 3605/93 *on the application of the Protocol on the excessive deficit procedure annexed to the Treaty establishing the European Community*, O.J. L 332/7 (1993), as codified by Council Regulation (EC) No 479/2009, O.J. L 145/1 (2009), last amended by Commission Regulation (EU) No 220/2014, O.J. L 69/101 (2014).

Allemand

Debt.[49] It relates in particular to the boundaries of the government units sector. Government units are understood as "**legal entities established by political process** which have legislative, judicial or executive **authority over other institutional units** within a given area. Their principal function is to **provide goods and services** to the community and to households **on a non-market basis** and to redistribute income and wealth."[50] Their public character is interpreted in the light of the purpose of the entity: the satisfaction of the need for public goods and services, i.e. the general interest and national solidarity. Depending on the circumstances, "defeasance structures" (bad banks) or market regulatory agencies can be regarded as being in the category of government units.[51] Thus, the concept is wider than that of the "general government" sector used in Protocol No 12. It makes it possible to take better account of the variety of arrangements for decentralised State organisation.

19 On the other hand, public **undertakings that basically engage in trading activities** and industrial and commercial public establishments are not classified as falling within the general government sector.[52] The public bail-out of these is outside the scope of the prohibition in Article 125 TFEU and is covered by the State aid regime.

2.2. Authorised Commitments

20 Article 125 TFEU prohibits the bail-out of government public bodies "without prejudice to **mutual financial guarantees for the joint execution of a specific project**". This is an exception to the rule. It has consistently been held in case law that it must be interpreted strictly.[53] When judging the legal compliance of a mutual financial guarantee with Article 125 TFEU, three cumulative criteria have to be considered:[54]

- (i) the **guarantee must be mutual**, which means that the participants (EU and/or MS) all contribute to the financing of the project as principal joint debtors and are bound to each other by a reciprocal guarantee obligation,
- (ii) the **project must be carried out jointly**, which suggests that project management is shared between the EU and/or the MS and there is shared responsibility

---

[49] Eurostat, *Manual on Government Deficit and Debt. Implementation of ESA 2010*, 2014 Edition.

[50] Parliament/Council Regulation (EU) No 549/2013 *on the European system of national and regional accounts in the European Union*, O.J. L174/1 (2013), esp. Annex A, para 20.06.

[51] For a presentation of the criteria applied for the purpose of classifying government administration units involved in the production of goods and services, see Regulation (EU) No 549/2013, Annex A, para 20.08 et seq.

[52] Morisset (1994).

[53] On that basis, it seems doubtful whether financial assistance provided under the EFSF and the EFSM can be tied to a "specific project", as suggested by Martucci (2011), pp. 256–257.

[54] Gnan, in von der Groeben and Schwarze (2003), Article 103 EGV para 25.

for defining the requirements, the objective pursued and the financing as well as in the event of failure, and

(iii) the **project must be specific**: the guarantee must not be constituted *in abstracto*, in a permanent manner and without limitation, but must be tied to the execution of one or more clearly identified projects.

On the other hand, nothing is said about the bilateral EU or international framework in which the project takes place. A failure to meet one or any of these criteria opens the way to an infringement procedure.

The implementation of mutual guarantees must also be looked at in the light of Article 170 TFEU. Under this article, **projects relating to transport, telecommunications or energy infrastructure** that are recognised as being in the common interest can be given assistance by the EU, particularly in the form of loan guarantees or an interest subsidy on loans granted by the EIB or other public or private financial institutions.[55] The subsidy is generally limited to 5 years.

21

2.3. Legal Subjects Prohibited to Bail Out

Article 125 TFEU places a bail-out prohibition on the EU and then each MS. Neither can commit itself, even freely, to covering or discharging the public debts of another MS. The order in which the EU and then the MS are presented in Article 125 TFEU corresponds to the traditional order of listing as laid down in the assistance arrangements defined in Articles 122 and 143 TFEU. By mentioning the Union first, the Article 125 TFEU prohibition highlights the fact "that **no implicit reciprocal guarantee of the Member States' commitments can be deduced from the existence of Monetary Union**".[56]

22

2.3.1. The Union and the Member States

Article 125 TFEU makes **no distinction as to whether the Union and an MS must act together or separately** or whether the commitment is accepted or assumed by a **single MS, several of them or all the MS**.[57] The prohibition applies to any MS, whether or not it belongs to the euro area. Article 125 TFEU is not mentioned as being among the provisions not applying to an MS with a derogation (Article 139.2 TFEU). The *ad hoc* derogation arrangement for Denmark specifies that that country

23

---

[55] Parliament/Council Regulation (EC) No 1316/2013 *establishing the Connecting Europe Facility*, O.J. L 348/129 (2013), as amended by Parliament/Council Regulation (EU) No 2015/1017, O. J. L 169/1 (2015).

[56] Case C-370/12, *Pringle* (Opinion of AG Kokott of 26 October 2012) para 114 (emphasis added).

[57] See also Smulders and Keppenne, in von der Groeben et al. (2016), Article 125 AEUV para 12.

is subject to the bail-out prohibition (Protocol No. 16).[58] The representatives of all the MS take part in the adoption of measures provided for in Article 125.2 TFEU.

24   If read *a contrario*, Article 125 TFEU authorises an **international body** other than the EU, a **third country** or a **private entity** to assume all or a part of the debt of an MS. The European Council of 24 and 25 March 2011 confirmed, in that sense, that participation by the private sector is one of the options open as a means of contributing to the financial stabilisation of an MS when it is clear that a macroeconomic adjustment programme would not by itself be enough to bring government debt down to tolerable levels.[59] A restructuring of Greek debt held by private investors took place on that basis in March 2012 under the heading *Private Sector Involvement* (→ para 51–53; →Supplement to Title VIII: TESM para 125). However, the MS could not contemplate the establishment of a joint undertaking or a new international body for the purpose of release from compliance with EU law in the field of economic policy.[60]

2.3.2. The European Financial Stability Facility and the European Stability Mechanism

25   It is important to describe the special position of the **European Financial Stability Facility** (EFSF), a special purpose vehicle created by the MS of the euro area in the spring of 2010 to provide financial assistance to Greece (→ Article 122 TFEU para 15, 25, 36).[61] The EFSF was set up as a limited company under Luxembourg law. Its capital is held by the MS of the euro area.[62] The EFSF is not regarded by Eurostat as capable of acting independently of its shareholders. The MS have been made liable for its debts in proportion to the level of the guarantees for the EFSF's operations that each participant assumes.[63] Any *ex ante* or *ex post* assumption of government debt of an MS by the EFSF would immediately be interpreted as a bail-out by the MS.[64]

---

[58] In a similar way, the special opting-out arrangement for the United Kingdom did not rule out the application of Article 125 TFEU either. Protocol (No 15) noted, in that connection, "the practice of the government of the United Kingdom to fund its borrowing requirement by the sale of debt to the private sector."

[59] European Council of 24–25 March 2011, Conclusions, EUCO 10/1/11 REV 1, p. 30.

[60] Case C-370/12, *Pringle* (CJEU 27 November 2012) para 68–69 and 109.

[61] Extraordinary Council Meeting. Economic and Financial Affairs, 9–10 May 2010, Doc. 9596/10 (Presse 108).

[62] Recueil des sociétés et associations. Mémorial C – No 1189, 8 June 2010, p. 57026.

[63] Eurostat, *Manual on Government Deficit and Debt. Implementation of ESA 2010*, 2014 Edition, pp. 63–64, para 9–11.

[64] For a similar conclusion: Smulders and Keppenne, in von der Groeben et al. (2016), Article 125 AEUV para 15.

The position of the **European Stability Mechanism** (ESM) is different from **26** that of the EFSF and also deserves comment. The ESM, which was set up by the MS of the euro area by international treaty, is an international financial institution.[65] It enjoys a level of institutional, functional and budgetary independence, which means that it can be regarded as being distinct from its MS. Debt entered into remains tied to it.[66] The ESM can grant financial assistance to an MS in the euro area on the condition that the MS "remains responsible for its commitments to its creditors and provided that the conditions attached to such assistance are such as to prompt that Member State to implement a sound budgetary policy".[67]

The **ESM is not subject to EU law**.[68] However, **its members**, on the other hand, **27** as MS of the EU, remain **bound by EU law**, including the no bail-out clause, when exercising their powers over economic policy.[69] They cannot approve any measure that, under the heading of the ESM, would be in breach of Article 125 TFEU. In a complementary sense, the new third paragraph of Article 136 TFEU requires the MS of the euro area to recognise that the granting of any financial assistance under the ESM should be subject to **strict conditionality** (→ Article 136 TFEU para 35; → Supplement to Title VIII: TESM para 62 et seq.). The conditionality is set in accordance with Article 121 TFEU[70] and in compliance with Article 125 TFEU, and the financial assistance may not be in the form of debt relief or transfer. Through the conditionality requirement imposed on the EU MS and the ESM members, the ESM in its operations will be in compliance with EU law:[71] the conditionality requirement shall ensure that the beneficiary MS is pursuing a sound

---

[65] The European Council of 24–25 March 2011 stated that the ESM is "an intergovernmental organisation under public international law." European Council of 24–25 March 2011, Conclusions, EUCO 10/1/11 REV 1, p. 22.

[66] Eurostat Decision of 31 January 2013 on the statistical classification of the European Stability Mechanism, Directorate D: Government Finance Statistics, Ref. Ares(2013)117666; Eurostat, *Manual on Government Deficit and Debt. Implementation of ESA 2010*, 2014 Edition, p. 64, para 12–13.

[67] Case C-370/12, *Pringle* (CJEU 27 November 2012) para 136–137.

[68] The Five Presidents' Report adopted in June 2015 called for the integration of the ESM into EU law. In December 2017, the Commission presented a proposal for a Council Regulation on the establishment of the European Monetary Fund (COM(2017) 827 final; see Manger-Nestler and Böttner (2019). Although the proposal has received positive support from the European Parliament, the Euro summit of December 2018, at the instigation of Germany and France, has dismissed such a prospect for the moment. According to the Franco-German statement made in Meseberg on 6 June 2018, "the incorporation of the ESM into EU Law, preserving the key features of its governance" will be ensured "in a second step".

[69] Case C-370/12, *Pringle* (CJEU 27 November 2012) para 69.

[70] Recital 3 of Parliament/Council Regulation (EU) No 472/2013 *on the strengthening of economic and budgetary surveillance of Member States in the euro area experiencing or threatened with serious difficulties with respect to their financial stability*, O.J. L 140/1 (2013).

[71] Case C-370/12, *Pringle* (CJEU 27 November 2012) para 69.

budgetary policy and that financial assistance is necessary to preserve financial stability in the euro area as a whole.[72]

2.4. Application *Ratione Temporis*

28   Article 125.1 TFEU, which lays down the bail-out prohibition, has been **applicable since** the European Community entered **stage two of establishing EMU on 1 January 1994**.[73] Paragraph 2 has been applicable since the entry into force of the Maastricht Treaty on 1 November 1993 in order to leave the Council time to adopt, as required, the definitions needed for the implementation of the ban.

29   Article 125 TFEU applies to every MS as from the date of its accession to the Union. This provision forms **part of the** *acquis* of the EU; it is part of the obligations every European country wishing to become a member of the EU must take on. Candidate countries have to align their legislation with EMU rules and procedures. The effectiveness of the prohibition is incompatible with expressing any reservation or allowing any temporary exemptions in the form of transitional measures or safeguard clauses.[74] Accession partnerships concluded by the EU with candidate countries assist such countries in the process of aligning their legislation to meet the requirements of EU law.[75] Candidate countries, on their side, adopt a national programme for the adoption of the *acquis*. Although compliance with the prohibition on monetary financing is regularly mentioned both in the accession partnerships and in the national programmes, there is no such reference to be found with respect to bringing national legislation in line with the bail-out prohibition. The chapter in the *acquis* relating to EMU is generally closed after six months, a sign that there are no major difficulties in the run-up to accession in this field.[76]

---

[72] Smulders and Keppenne, in von der Groeben et al. (2016), Article 125 AEUV para 15.

[73] In accordance with ex-Article 116 TEC, repealed by the Lisbon Treaty.

[74] Case C-179/00, *Gerald Weidacher v Bundesminister für Land- und Forstwirtschaft* (ECJ 5 July 2002) para 22, and recently in connection with the transitional measures in the sugar sector: Case T-324/05, *Estonia v Commission* (CFI 2 October 2009) para 163.

[75] For example, Council Regulation (EC) No 622/98 *on assistance to the applicant countries in the framework of the pre-accession strategy*, O.J. L 85/1 (1998); Council Regulation (EC) No 555/2000 *on the implementation of operations in the framework of the pre-accession strategy for the Republic of Cyprus and the Republic of Malta*, O.J. L 68/3 (2000); Council Regulation (EC) No 390/2001 *on assistance to Turkey in the framework of the pre-accession strategy, and in particular on the establishment of an Accession Partnership*, O.J. L 58/1 (2001).

[76] Glenn (2004), pp. 14–16, where the author points out that the negotiations with the Czech Republic and Poland lasted six months as opposed to just one month with Slovakia.

3. Authorised Financial Support

The fiscal discipline pursued by Article 125 TFEU does not have the effect of   **30**
prohibiting any solidarity towards an MS that is over-indebted and unable to honour its financial commitments.[77] **Solidarity** is at the very heart of the EU:[78] it is the driving force behind it as well as the reflection of it,[79] and it extends to the financial assistance mechanisms[80] provided for in Articles 122.2, 136.3 and 143 TFEU. Solidarity takes notice of the fact that however tough the discipline or good the will exercised by an MS is, it does not *per se* prevent the arising of an **unforeseeable crisis** that cannot be withstood and is not related to anything the national authorities have done. As *Bandilla* observes, "all these provisions have their place *next to* the no bail-out clause of Article 125 TFEU".[81] Moreover, the continuing deterioration in the level of indebtedness can be interpreted as an expression of both the manifest indiscipline by the MS concerned—which needs to be sanctioned— and the inefficiency and failure to adjust of the fiscal discipline mechanisms laid down by EU law.[82] Hence, the EU and the MS are all partly responsible for the financial difficulties facing one of the MS.

That responsibility is all the more pronounced within the **euro area** because of   **31**
the **close financial and banking interdependence of the various national economies**. In the end, there has to be solidarity because of the consequences that its absence would produce. A prohibition on all financial solidarity would open the door to the financial, economic, social and political collapse of the country that found itself unable to perform its basic governmental functions; the departure of the country in difficulty from the monetary union;[83] or the massive intervention by the Eurosystem to stabilise the debt market—given the destabilising effects on the financial market and, in particular, the banking market.[84] By stabilising the economic, social and, ultimately, political order of an MS in difficulty, the EU as a whole is thereby protected.[85]

Concurring with the view of the AG, the **Court of Justice**'s ruling in the *Pringle*   **32**
case is that Article 125 TFEU "is not intended to prohibit either the Union or the

---

[77] Athanassiou (2011); as opposed to Ruffert (2011).

[78] Calliess (2011).

[79] Monaco (1972), p. 318.

[80] Joined Cases 6 and 9/69, *Commission v France* (ECJ 10 December 1969) para 16.

[81] Bandilla, in Grabitz et al. (2021), Article 125 AEUV para 31 (released in 2011) (my translation).

[82] Council (2004). Press release. 2628th meeting of the Council, Economic and Financial Affairs. Brussels, 7 December 2004. 15150/04 (Press 339), esp. Stability and Growth Pact – Revisions of Greek budget data.

[83] Baroin (2012).

[84] von Hagen and Eichengreen (1998), p. 144.

[85] Or, to use the words of *Romano Prodi* 2000: "When a Member State is in difficulty so is the whole Union." (Prodi, *2000-2005: Shaping the New Europe*, Speech given at the European Parliament, Strasbourg, 15 February 2000, SPEECH/00/41).

Member States from granting any form of financial assistance whatever to another Member State".[86]

33   However, solidarity must not make the system of individual responsibility laid down by Articles 123 to 125 TFEU any less effective. Solidarity must be exercised within the limits laid down by those provisions. Thus, it would be contrary to Article 125 to make any grant of financial assistance "as a result of which the incentive of the recipient Member State to conduct a sound budgetary policy is diminished".[87] In other words, **solidarity is allowed only in so far as it maintains the responsibility of the indebted MS for meeting its commitments**. From that point of view, solidarity is not to be confused with generosity; it is not a willingness to give liberally and for free. To make sure that the country assisted does not lose a sense of its responsibilities, solidarity takes the form of *loans granted and released on certain conditions*. Paradoxically, an MS's solvency crisis is resolved by creating new debts for which the MS in receipt of assistance is liable.[88]

34   The characteristics of the loans and the conditions[89] attaching to the financial assistance, backed up by special surveillance procedures, are supposed to reproduce and supplement the discipline previously imposed by the markets and, in the end, ensure that the **financial support granted is reimbursed**.[90] In these circumstances, ongoing solidarity in the form of pooling of public-sector debt is ruled out.

However, the legality of other assistance arrangements such as **"perpetual" loans** could be open to discussion as, in such case, the debtor has not to redeem the principal while servicing its debt. One may consider that the debt is not a write-off, although it will never be reimbursed.[91] We are of the opinion that a moratorium and

---

[86] Case C-370/12, *Pringle* (CJEU 27 November 2012) para 130.

[87] Case C-370/12, *Pringle* (CJEU 27 November 2012) para 136.

[88] As of 31 December 2018, 80% of Greek public debt (EUR 292 billion) is made up of loans from the Bank of Greece, Special purpose and bilateral loans, Financial support Mechanism loans, Repos (Greek Public Debt Management Agency, 2019). The total outstanding public debt amounts to EUR 358 billion—an amount EUR 30 billion higher than that measured at the beginning of the debt crisis in spring 2010.

[89] The EUR 750 billion recovery plan for Europe approved by the European Council of 17–21 July 2020 clearly marks an evolution of this approach. EUR 390 billion is available to MS in the form of grants and the remaining EUR 360 billion in the form of loans. As criticised by several governments (Netherlands, Austria, Finland, Sweden, Denmark), this plan represents a kind of debt pooling, insofar as the financing of the grants is supported by the Union and, ultimately, by all the MS: almost 3/4 of the Union's own resources are currently consisting of national contributions. The political agreement of July 2020 and the legislation implementing it (Council Regulation 2020/2094/EU and Regulation 2021/241/EU) limit the availability of funds to a maximum period of 3 years (2021–2023) and make the payment of grants subject to strict conditionality monitored by the Commission and the Council. However, this plan should be seen above all as a deep criticism of the lack of flexibility in the European budget and the weakness of the Union's countercyclical budgetary capacity. See Allemand (2021).

[90] Allemand et al. (2016).

[91] The idea was defended by the Tsipras Government for a time in February 2015. See La technique de la Grèce pour réduire sa dette. *Le Figaro*, 3 February 2012. Since spring 2016, the Eurosystem has implemented several large-scale financial asset purchase programmes, including

bonds of that kind in fact lead to the payment of the debts due being "wiped out" since repayment will in theory never take place; they reduce the incentive to financial discipline and are thereby in breach of Article 125 TFEU. The quite long maturity of ESM loans granted to Greece—32 years on average, with amortisation from 2034 to 2060[92]—raised concerns about their future reimbursements. As the debate between the International Monetary Fund (IMF) and the European institutions has demonstrated all along the negotiations of the third Greek financial package in summer 2015, many doubted that Greece could keep its gross financing needs at a sustainable level[93] at long terms.[94] The Eurogroup agreed on debt relief for Greece in June 2018 ($\rightarrow$ para 60–61).

3.1. Compatible Financial Operations

Any financial operation not involving a debt transfer is authorised. The Union's economic policy, as defined by Article 119.1 TFEU, and the MS' economic policies have to be conducted in accordance with the principle of an open market economy with free competition ($\rightarrow$ Article 119 TFEU para 40 et seq.). The bail-out prohibition between MS is not one of the grounds for prohibiting or restricting the free movement of capital within the internal market. Since the repeal of Article 68.3 TEC by the Amsterdam Treaty, an MS can issue or place a government loan in another MS in order to attract local savings. Conversely, an MS can also purchase debt instruments issued by another MS. Thus, in 2008, the French government held EUR 6.2 billion worth of securities issued by other MS, including German

35

---

government debt instruments of euro area MS. The Covid-19 crisis has severely deteriorated the economic, financial and monetary situation in the euro area and has led the ECB to actively resume its purchases of government debt. The debate on the write-off of this debt held by the ECB and the Eurosystem central banks has gained renewed momentum since spring 2020. Beyond the outright write-off of MS' public debt (contrary to Article 123 TFEU), it has been proposed that the ECB should accept the exchange of current debt for zero-coupon perpetual debt. See Boonstra (2021); Piketty et al. (2020).

[92] ESM, ESM Disbursements to Greece, available at https://www.esm.europa.eu/assistance/greece. The average maturity of Greek government bonds is four times higher than that of bonds issued by other euro-area MS.

[93] The third financial assistance package is based on the hypothesis that Greece will maintain a primary surplus of 3.5% of GDP until 2022 and thereafter continue to ensure that its fiscal commitments are in line with the EU fiscal framework (i.e. a primary surplus of 2.2% of GDP on average from 2023 to 2060). This means also that gross financing needs "should remain below 15% of GDP in the medium term and below 20% of GDP thereafter while ensuring that debt remains on a sustained downward path". See Eurogroup, Statement on Greece, Brussels, 15 June 2015, and Eurogroup, Statement on Greece, Brussels, 22 June 2018.

[94] Wroughton et al. (2015). According to the IMF's debt sustainability analysis of July 2017, "Greece will not be able to restore debt sustainability and needs further debt relief from its European partners" (IMF, *Greece: Request for a stand-by arrangement*, IMF Staff Country Report No. 17/229).

sovereign instruments worth EUR 1.6 billion.[95] The financial stability of the euro area, lastly, constitutes a "higher objective" for economic policy. Financial support is deemed to be in accordance with Article 125 TFEU if it is indispensable to safeguard the stability of the euro area as a whole. The **granting of any required financial assistance** under the mechanism will be made **subject to strict conditionality** (Article 136.3 TFEU; Articles 3 and 12 TESM).[96]

3.1.1. The Purchase and Holding of Government Debt Instruments

36 The purchase on the primary and secondary markets of debt instruments of an MS in financial difficulty is one of the methods of financial support approved by the Court of Justice (CJEU). Indeed, it neither improves the financial position of the debtor State, which remains solely liable for its debt, nor worsens that of the investor. **Purchases must be made on market terms and conditions** and therefore not distort price formation mechanisms and reduce the incentive for fiscal discipline by borrowing States. As provided for in the ESM Guidelines, "Primary market purchases (PMP) shall, as a rule, be conducted at market price".[97] The fact that purchases of bonds or other debt securities issued by an MS on the secondary market are done at a price that is different from their face value is not seen as constituting support contrary to Article 125 TFEU as long as market prices result from the free play of market forces and are not distorted or altered by government intervention.

37 **Article 123 TFEU** on monetary financing (→ Article 123 TFEU para 1–6) **prohibits the purchase *directly* from MS by the ECB or national central banks (NCBs) of debt instruments**. Accordingly, Article 18 of the ESCB Statute permits the ESCB, in order to achieve its objectives and carry out its tasks, to operate in the financial markets, inter alia, "by buying and selling outright marketable instruments, which include government bonds, and does not make that authorisation subject to particular conditions as long as the nature of open market operations is not disregarded".[98]

As the Court stated in the **Gauweiler** case concerning a programme of outright monetary transactions (**OMT**) envisaged but never implemented by the ECB, it is important that such operations involving government debt instruments retain a **sufficient degree of uncertainty in keeping with market logic**. Such uncertainty is ensured when the purchaser retains full independence in decisions on implementing, renewing, suspending and halting financial operations. The particular issue of government bonds that will be purchased remains unknown to the issuer. The

---

[95] Natixis (2010).
[96] See also Case C-370/12, *Pringle* (CJEU 27 November 2012) para 136.
[97] ESM, *Guideline on the Primary Market Support Facility*, available at https://www.esm.europa.eu/sites/default/files/esm_guideline_on_the_primary_market_support_facility.pdf.
[98] Case C-62/14, *Gauweiler* (CJEU 16 June 2015) para 96; also Case C-493/17, *Weiss* (CJEU 11 December 2018) para 96.

Eurosystem is not permitted to buy either all the bonds issued by an issuer or the entirety of a given issue of those bonds. In addition, neither the time nor the volume of purchase or resale operations must be announced in advance. To limit the effects on the smooth operation of the debt market, there has to be a minimum period of time (so-called blackout period) between the issue of a security on the primary market and its purchase on the secondary market.[99] Otherwise, "purchasing government bonds on secondary markets [. . .] would, in practice, [have] an effect equivalent to that of a direct purchase of government bonds from the public authorities and bodies of the Member States, thereby undermining the effectiveness of the prohibition in Article 123.1 TFEU".[100]

In the **Weiss** case concerning the Public Sector Purchase Programme (**PSPP**) implemented by the Eurosystem from March 2015 to December 2018, the Court of Justice had to decide on the legality of **holding government bonds** by the central banks of the Eurosystem **until maturity** and **purchasing bonds at a negative yield to maturity**. In addition to other purchase programmes centred on corporate bonds, the monthly net purchase of public and private bonds on the secondary market could amount to up to EUR 60 billion.[101] The German Federal Constitutional Court (FCC), which referred the case to the CJEU, considered that the PSPP would diminish the impetus of euro-area MS to conduct sound budgetary policies. As of December 2018, the Eurosystem held around EUR 2.200 billion of government bonds. The CJEU recalled that "such a practice [massive bond purchase] is in no way precluded by Article 18.1 of the Protocol on the ESCB and the ECB and that it does not imply that the ESCB waives its right to payment of the debt, by the issuing Member State, once the bond matures". In addition, the Court made clear that the Eurosystem was entitled "to evaluate, on the basis of the objectives and characteristics of an open market operations programme, whether it is appropriate to envisage holding the bonds purchased under that programme; selling the bonds is not to be regarded as the rule and holding them as the exception to that rule".[102]

38

With regard to the PSPP's impact on the financing conditions of the euro-area MS and the impetus of the latter to conduct sound budgetary policies, the Court reaffirmed the requirement to preserve a state of uncertainty for issuers in line with market economy principles: "the adoption and implementation of such a

---

[99] Case C-493/17, *Weiss* (CJEU 11 December 2018) para 106–107.

[100] Case C-493/17, *Weiss* (CJEU 11 December 2018) para 97.

[101] The monthly net purchases were increased up to EUR 80 billion from mid-April 2016 to March 2017. From April 2017 to December 2018, the Eurosystem has gradually reduced its net purchases. Faced with a low inflation rate issue, the ECB decided to restart net purchases at a monthly pace of EUR 20 billion as from November 2019. In reaction to the economic and monetary effects of the "great lockdown" following the COVID-19 crisis, the ECB added a temporary envelope of additional net asset purchases of EUR 120 billion until the end of 2020. In the context of a stronger-than-expected economic downturn in the euro area, the ECB completed the PSPP with a temporary purchase programme, i.e. the pandemic emergency purchase programme (PEPP). The PEPP's initial envelope of EUR 600 billion was increased by EUR 750 billion in June 2020.

[102] Case C-493/17, *Weiss* (CJEU 11 December 2018) para 146–147.

programme may not create certainty regarding a future purchase of Member State bonds, in consequence of which Member States might adopt a budgetary policy that fails to take account of the fact that they will be compelled, in the event of a deficit, to seek financing on the markets, or in consequence of which they would be protected against the consequences which a change in their macroeconomic or budgetary situation may have in that regard".[103] From this perspective, a series of safeguards have to be complied with, ranging from the programme's temporary nature to the limitation of the volume of the MS bonds eligible to be purchased. **Three features of the programme are conducive to a self-restrained approach by the ECB** when purchasing MS bonds: the setting of a monthly purchase amount under the Asset Purchase Programme (APP),[104] the subsidiarity nature of the PSPP within the APP, the distribution of those purchases between NCBs in accordance with the key for the subscription of the ECB's capital, the compliance requirement with the eligible criteria for marketable assets for Eurosystem credit operations and, last but not least, the application of an issue share limit per international securities identification number.[105] In its critical assessment of the *Weiss* Judgment of 5 May 2020, the German FCC stated that "possible circumventions of the prohibition in Art. 123(1) TFEU are not sufficiently manifest for finding a violation" to the extent the ECB's purchase programmes respect these "crucial 'safeguards'".[106] Thus, any relaxation of these safeguards in future purchase programmes would infringe the prohibition of monetary financing.[107]

39   When transposed to the field of economic policy, the CJEU's interpretation means that the **MS** may buy, hold and sell government bonds issued by other MS. However, they **should not commit themselves to buying, holding and reselling government bonds issued by an MS without any limit** regarding a given issue, its volume and/or its amount. Mass purchases of government bonds that go beyond the mere dictates of treasury management must be undertaken for the purpose of preserving the financial stability of the euro area and must be decided on consistently and after the support operations carried out as part of the ESM. They must not be undertaken until the macroeconomic adjustment programme and strict conditions have been adopted with respect to the MS receiving financial assistance.

---

[103] Case C-493/17, *Weiss* (CJEU 11 December 2018) para 132.

[104] The APP is part of a package of non-standard monetary policy measures adopted by the ECB as from October 2014. It consists of four different purchase programmes—each targeting a specific category of financial assets: the corporate sector purchase programme, the public sector purchase programme, the asset-backed securities purchase programme and the 3rd covered bond purchase programme.

[105] Case C-493/17, *Weiss* (CJEU 11 December 2018) para 137–143.

[106] BVerfG, 2 BvR 859/15 (Judgment of 5 May 2020) para 213 and 216. For a discussion: Ipsen (2020), Storr (2020), and Wendel (2020). See also the testimony given before the European Affairs Committee of the German *Bundestag*, available at https://www.bundestag.de/ausschuesse/pe1_europaeischeunion/oeffentliche_anhoerungen.

[107] BVerfG, 2 BvR 859/15 (Judgment of 5 May 2020) para 217.

This guarantees that the MS follows a sound budgetary policy and will be able to repay its debts to the other MS.

3.1.2. Loans

The granting of loans between MS is not a commitment prohibited under Article 125 TFEU[108] either, even if it would be a way of covering a potential default of payment. "Loans [are] not grants," explained the Commission in the press release announcing the exceptional measures adopted on 10 May 2010 in response to the Greek debt crisis. "Loans have to be repaid with interest. As such it is compatible with Article 125 TFEU."[109] The application of an interest rate encourages the MS receiving assistance to implement a sound budgetary policy and is a factor when it comes to assessing whether the financial assistance is lawful. A zero- or negative-rated loan would be in direct breach of the bail-out prohibition. The Court of Justice therefore required that **the amount to be repaid should include an "appropriate margin"**.[110] **40**

As soon as Greece's financial difficulties first became apparent, the Heads of State or Government of the euro area announced that assistance would be in the form of "non-concessional" loans:[111] the State in receipt of aid must bear the actual costs of the financing supplied by the government investor, plus a margin corresponding to the risk premium normally required by the markets.[112] When they were first applied in Greece, the initial interest rates were set on the basis of the (Euribor) market rates, plus a risk premium imposed by the lending countries equal to 300 base points, plus 100 points for loans maturing in more than three years. A 50-base-point supplement was also applied to cover the operational management costs of the loans.[113] The **setting of the interest rates** was designed to give an incentive to conduct a sound budgetary policy. This requirement, however, had to be reconciled with the higher objective of re-establishing the sustainability of the assisted State's level of debt and the financial stability of the euro area as a whole. **41**

---

[108] Gnan, in von der Groeben and Schwarze (2003), Article 103, para 28; Rohleder et al. (2010). As opposed to Ruffert (2011). In our opinion, this author over-interprets the terms of Article 125 TFEU.

[109] Commission, *The European Stabilization Mechanism*, Press Release, 10 May 2010, MEMO/10/173.

[110] Case C-370/12, *Pringle* (CJEU 27 November 2012) para 139 (emphasis added).

[111] Statement by the Heads of State or Government of the euro area, Brussels, 25 March 2010; also Article 2(1) of the bilateral loans agreement concluded between the Member States of the euro area and Greece on 8 May 2010 (the "Loan Facility Agreement").

[112] Article 7, Council Regulation (EU) No 407/2010 *establishing a European financial stabilisation mechanism*, O.J. L 118/1 (2010); and for the implementation in respect of Ireland: Council Implementing Decision (2011/77/EU) *on granting Union financial assistance to Ireland*, O.J. L 30/34 (2011).

[113] Statement on the support to Greece by Euro Area Member States, Brussels, 11 April 2010. The method of calculation is based on the pricing formula applied by the IMF under its financial assistance programmes.

The version of the ESM Treaty, which was signed on 11 July 2011, provided for some adjustments to bring this about. In addition to the management costs, the customary interest rate had a 200-point premium added to it for the full duration of the loan and an additional premium of 100 points on the amount to be repaid beyond the first three years.[114]

42 The deteriorating financial situation in the autumn of 2011, coupled with the rising tension over Italian debt, led to a rethinking of the method for setting the interest rates on the loans granted. The final version of the ESM Treaty assigned the responsibility of determining the financial terms applicable to the financial assistance instruments to the Managing Director,[115] who had to act in accordance with the ESM pricing policy.[116] Under that policy, **a premium of 10 points is applied to loans,**[117] **plus the assumption of liability by the beneficiary State of the full costs of the financing** borne by the ESM as a result of the financial assistance. In the event of a delay in making repayments, **penalty interest charges** of 200 additional points are applied to the amounts still to be repaid to the ESM.[118]

3.1.3. Other Operations

43 There are some other financial operations that need to be mentioned, although nowadays they are marginal. **Sales of assets**[119] between MS are authorised, provided they are **carried out in accordance with market conditions**. A patently excessive purchasing price could be interpreted as a disguised bail-out between the transferor State and the assignee State. Debt buyback is a common debt management operation;[120] it is authorised when it is aimed at the Union's public creditors, provided the price applied[121] does not have the character of restructuring with a discount being applied. Lastly, debt compensatory arrangement seems to be allowed: it improves the financial situation of two debtor States in relation to each other, without involving any debt transfer. The compensation was defended

---

[114] Article 14 in conjunction with Annex III to the ESM Treaty (version of 11 July 2011).

[115] The Managing Director drafts the procedures and financial terms of the proposal for an agreement concerning the financial assistance facility: the proposal is approved by the Board of Governors of the ESM. The agreement is approved by the Board of Directors of the ESM and the agreement is signed by the Managing Director.

[116] See, in particular, Articles 16.4 and 20 of the ESM Treaty.

[117] Higher premiums are laid down for mobilising other financial assistance instruments.

[118] ESM, *ESM Pricing policy*, Luxembourg, 8 December 2014.

[119] As soon as the first financial assistance plan was adopted, Greece was asked to transfer some of its assets. In July 2011, the Hellenic Republic Asset Development Fund was set up as a limited company to manage the transfer of the assets. The third assistance plan targeted a EUR 50 billion privatisation programme.

[120] Medeiros et al. (2007); for a review in the OECD countries: Blommestein et al. (2012).

[121] There is no single methodology for determining the purchase price. For a discussion: Blommestein et al. (2012); Prokop and Wang (1997).

by the Greek authorities, who pointed to a German war debt to Greece that had not been paid. The current value of the debt was estimated at EUR 162 billion.[122]

Nor does **subrogation** by the Union or the MS (or the ESM) **of the rights of creditors of an MS in financial difficulties** have the effect of transferring debt from the debtor to the creditor, and it should be regarded as being compatible with Article 125 TFEU. Against the background of tension between the IMF and the euro area MS over Greece, the payment of loans due to the IMF by the ESM—which was subrogated to the latter's rights at the time—was raised.[123] Similarly, debt swaps are not banned provided they do not affect the nominal value of the debts, they continue to give the debtor an incentive to conduct a sound budgetary policy and they help strengthen the financial stability of both the State concerned and the euro area. This, for example, would be the case of an exchange of short-term securities for longer-term securities. The terms of the new issues should not be excessively long; otherwise, they would reduce the incentive to act with **fiscal discipline**. In their statement of 11 March 2011, the Heads of State or Government of the euro area called on the MS, in this connection, to "strive to lengthen the maturities of their new bond emissions *in the medium term* to avoid refinancing peaks".[124] However exceptional they may be, the moves to reschedule Greek debt were a sign that this request was being interpreted flexibly (→ para 60–61).

3.2. Financial Assistance Under Articles 122.2, 136.3 and 143.2 TFEU

In Articles 122.2, 136.3 and 143.2 TFEU, the Treaty provides for several arrangements designed to provide financial assistance to MS hit by specific difficulties. The oldest, which is a legacy from the EEC Treaty of 1957, relates to dealing with the balance of payment difficulties through the **granting of mutual assistance by the Council** (→ Article 143 TFEU para 22–32). The form of support is not laid down in definitive terms, and the treaty lists the most usual operations, including the granting of limited credits by other MS, subject to their agreement. Since 1 January 1999, the balance of payments has ceased to be relevant to the MS of the euro area, owing to the disappearance of the exchange-rate risk; financial assistance remains open only for MS that have not adopted the single currency. The twofold limitation, both material and personal, on the scope of Article 143 TFEU warranted the establishment of a supplementary financial assistance arrangement, which, in general terms, addressed the difficulties facing or threatening an MS.[125] **44**

The second arrangement, which is governed by Article 122.2 TFEU, forms "a system of **Community mutual aid**" for any MS that "is in difficulties or is seriously **45**

---

[122] Seelow (2012).
[123] Walker (2016).
[124] Conclusions of the Heads of State or Government of the euro area of 11 March 2011, Annex II, p. 14; also, for criticism of short-term issues on short terms: Dévoluy (2013), p. 201.
[125] Article 2, Council Regulation (EU) No 407/2010.

threatened with severe difficulties caused by natural disasters or exceptional occurrences beyond its control". Because of its general application, this provision, it has been said, constitutes "a true crisis clause"[126] (→ Article 122 TFEU para 12 et seqq.). The financial assistance is *from the Union*, which presupposes the mobilisation of the EU budget. No details of the form this financial assistance may take were given. Pursuant to the Nice Treaty, the unanimous vote of the Council required for granting this assistance was replaced by a qualified majority vote. This development gave grounds for hoping that a financial safety net for undisciplined MS could be provided. Declaration No. 6 on Article 100 TEC (now Article 122 TFEU), annexed to the Final Act adopting the Nice Treaty, took care to stress that the application of Article 122 TFEU **must be compatible with Article 125 TFEU**. The dropping of that declaration by the Lisbon Treaty did not alter the requirement for compatibility between Article 122 and Article 125 TFEU (→ Article 122 TFEU para 25 et seqq.).[127]

46   Additionally, the financial assistance that could be mobilised was confined within the limits of the EU budget: decisions on assistance had to be in accordance with the EU financial perspectives. The earmarking of expenditure and compliance with the balanced-budget requirement (Article 310.1 TFEU) reduced the volume of assistance. This kept the **moral hazard** within limits. At the same time, the budgetary limitation constituted a form of **rigidity,** which caused problems as soon as the requirements for financing in a spirit of solidarity exceeded the sub-ceiling margins available.[128] The question that then arose[129]—and that soon arose during the euro area crisis—is that of adopting other forms of financial assistance that could be implemented on the basis of it (or in conjunction with Article 352 TFEU), including the granting of credit by the MS or the purchasing of holdings in public undertakings.[130]

47   The third and last crisis solidarity scheme was the one provided for in Article 136.3 TFEU, which allows the MS of the euro area to "establish a **stability mechanism to be activated if indispensable to safeguard the stability of the euro area as a whole**". Without going into detail about the grounds for it (→ Article 136 TEU para 28 et seqq.), it should be pointed out that the paragraph in question springs from the first application of the simplified revision procedure

---

[126] Louis (2010), p. 983.

[127] Louis (2010), p. 983.

[128] All else being equal, incidentally, the economic costs of the destruction caused by the tsunami which struck Japan in March 2011 were estimated at more than USD 171 billion—including 50 billion just for the Fukushima nuclear power station. Although a tsunami on that scale is not very likely to strike the coasts of Europe, a major nuclear incident caused by an accident, whether a terrorist attack or something else, may still happen. Under the 2012 budget, the sub-ceiling margin on credit payments was set at EUR 20 billion.

[129] Martucci, in Pingel (2010), p. 860.

[130] Rohleder et al. (2010).

provided for in Article 48.6 TEU.[131] As the provision continues, the "granting of any required financial assistance under the mechanism will be made subject to strict conditionality". The possibility given to the MS of drawing up their own financial assistance instrument in the form of a European stability mechanism grounded in an international treaty[132] is not a way of circumventing the bail-out prohibition.[133] Financial assistance paid out through the ESM does not do away with the need to make the establishment of the financial assistance instrument, as well as the launching of that instrument, subject to compliance with Article 125 TFEU.[134]

Diverse though they are, these arrangements rely on a set of **common principles** that guarantee their conformity with Article 125 TFEU. In its decisions on financial assistance, the Council (or the Ministers for Finance of the euro area MS) must take the bail-out prohibition into account.[135] It means that any financial assistance has to be uncertain, temporary, financially limited, granted for consideration and subject to the implementation of an adjustment programme.[136] These precepts ensure that the principle of making the **MS individually financially liable remains fully relevant**. The uncertainty of the assistance lies in the fact that it is not automatic and requires the authorities responsible for granting it to decide whether it is expedient,[137] a decision over which the Court of Justice undertakes only a limited review.[138] The temporary nature of the assistance prevents it from being given without a specific term and renewed without particular grounds being stated. The conditionality also helps to place the assistance in a limited time frame. The duration of the assistance is closely tied to the timetable for taking corrective action, which is set up for each MS in difficulty as part of the excessive deficit procedure. Assistance is financially limited: it must not be an "on tap" system from which MS in need can refinance themselves without restriction. The ESM has a maximum lending capacity of EUR 500 billion.[139] As regards the actual amount of the assistance or guarantees, it must match, i.e. be in proportion to, the *estimated* financing needs—which does not rule out the amount of the assistance or the level

48

---

[131] European Council Decision 2011/199/EU *amending Article 136 of the Treaty on the Functioning of the European Union with regard to a stability mechanism for Member States whose currency is the euro*, O.J. L 91/1 (2011).

[132] Case C-370/12, *Pringle* (CJEU 27 November 2012) para 106.

[133] As opposed to de Sadeleer (2012), p. 3, also French Senate, Report No 395 (2011–2012) by Nicole Bricq on behalf of the Finance Committee on the draft law authorising ratification of the European Council Decision amending Article 136 TFEU, tabled on 21 February 2012.

[134] Allemand (2012), p. 586.

[135] Louis (2010), p. 984.

[136] Allemand (2012), p. 587.

[137] The Council in the case of Articles 143 and 122.2 TFEU; Eurogroup and Board of Governors of the ESM under Article 136 TFEU.

[138] Case 5-73, *Balkan-Import-Export* (ECJ 24 October 1973).

[139] As of February 2019, the ESM lending capacity stood at EUR 401 billion. See http://www.esm.europa.eu.

3.3. Restructuring of Public Debt

49 The restructuring of public debt is usually taken to mean "an exchange of outstanding sovereign debt instruments, such as loans or bonds, for new debt instruments or cash through a formal process".[140] Restructuring can consist in a **complete or partial cancellation of debt** by reducing the face (nominal) value of the outstanding debt. It can also be done with the object of **rescheduling the debt**, and in that case it centres on suspending the payment of the principal (a moratorium), extending the maturity of the securities and reducing the interest rates.[141] Article 125 TFEU prohibits any transfer of debt from an MS to the Union or to another MS. Within the limits set out in previous sections of this comment, it does not prevent either public debt rescheduling or the full or partial cancellation of the part of the public debt held by the private sector. Debt restructuring or even debt rescheduling could be criticised on grounds that make it easier for the MS concerned to make the financial efforts required of it, thereby reducing the incentives to follow sound budget policies. An MS with a high level of public debt may find itself unable to secure new financing from the markets if the latter consider the indebtedness situation of the country as unsustainable. However, market closing is the *ultimate* market sanction; in other words, it is the highest level of sanction and also the last that can be applied. Once exclusion has taken place, the markets have no further hold over the indebted State.

50 *J. Sperling* and *E.J. Kirchner*, among others, have pointed out that "a consequence of debt overhang is lower incentives to pursue economic reform by the fledgling democratic governments: the political costs of economic reform and servicing external debt are borne exclusively by the national governments, whereas the lion's share of the economic gains from economic reform are enjoyed by the creditor banks and governments".[142] In this respect, debt restructuring or debt rescheduling opens a new stage in negotiations between debtor and creditors and makes it possible to **re-establish the influence of the markets** over the MS.[143] These processes both guarantee debt sustainability and encourage the return of the MS to the markets; they gave an assurance to the investor that the MS will be capable of meeting its financial commitments in the future. This kind of improvement of the country debt profile is one thing; **supporting the structural and budgetary reforms** is another. They are nevertheless two sides of the same coin.

---

[140] Das et al. (2012), p. 4.

[141] Hereafter in this comment, debt restructuring will refer exclusively to the full or partial reduction (cancellation) of the face value of the debt.

[142] Sperling and Kirchner (1997), p. 164, also: Eaton and Gersovitz (1981); Rose (2005).

[143] For example, Prokop (2012).

On 26 October 2011, the details provided by the Heads of State or Government of the euro area concerning private-sector involvement go hand in hand in emphasising their full determination to continue with their policies of budgetary consolidation and structural reform,[144] the strengthening of the Stability and Growth Pact by the adoption of the "six-pack" and the opening of a round of thinking about further integration.

3.3.1. Public Debt Restructuring

Ontologically speaking, debt is a way of bringing two distinct parties, the debtor and the creditor, into contact with each other. In compliance with the principles of an open market economy with free competition (Articles 119.1, 120 TFEU), Article 125 TFEU leaves the debtor MS and its private creditors complete independence to alter the terms of their contractual relationships. The restructuring of the share of public debt that is held by the private sector is allowed and recognised as an **instrument for preventing or resolving an MS's financial difficulties and a financial stability crisis** in the euro area.[145] Throughout the debt crisis, there was strong support for this option from the German authorities, who were concerned about reducing their exposure to the public debt of other MS. The restructuring of the share of debt that is held by private investors improves the risk profile of the MS in debt and its ability to repay the financial assistance granted by the EU, the other MS directly or indirectly through the EFSF or the ESM.[146]

To make it easier for the private sector to be involved when there is a restructuring of the debt of a euro-area MS that has become insolvent, the Eurogroup agreed to the principle that a standardised, identical **collective action clause** (CAC) must be inserted into the contracts for the issue of any new debt with a maturity of more than one year as from 1 January 2013 (→ Supplement to Title VIII: TESM para 121 et seqq.).[147] The CAC was confirmed in principle by the summit of Heads of State or Government of the euro area on 11 March 2011 and drawn up in detail by the European Council of 24 and 25 March 2011.[148] The activation of the CAC is one of the "adequate and proportionate" forms of private-sector involvement; it can only be done in relation to MS receiving financial assistance whose level of indebtedness is unsustainable.[149] The requirement that the MS should include CACs in securities issued as from 1 January 2013 was laid down in Article 12.3 of the ESM Treaty in order to give it binding legal force. To ensure bond market liquidity and equal treatment between all-new securities, a model CAC (common terms of reference)

---

[144] Euro Summit Statement, 26 October 2011 (dated 8 November 2011), para 4 and 16.

[145] Eurogroup Statement, *Financial stability of the euro area*, 28 November 2010; Statement of the Heads of State or Government of the euro area, Annex II, 11 March 2011; Recital 12 TESM.

[146] Beesley (2010); Bradley and Gulati (2013), p. 1; Hofmann (2014), p. 393.

[147] Eurogroup Statement, *Financial stability of the euro area*, 28 November 2010.

[148] European Council of 24–25 March 2011, Conclusions, Annex II, EUCO 10/1/11 REV 1.

[149] European Council of 24–25 March 2011, Conclusions, Annex II, EUCO 10/1/11 REV 1.

was drawn up by the Economic and Financial Committee (EFC).[150] Explanatory notes are attached to it.[151] The model CAC, which is based on soft law, has no legal force whatsoever.[152] Each MS participating in the ESM has to adapt its domestic law.[153]

53 The worsening situation in Greece in summer 2011 and the threats to the financial stability of the euro area owing to the risks of its spreading to other MS made it necessary to depart from the general framework for private-sector involvement adopted a few months previously. An "exceptional and unique solution" was preferred by the Heads of State or Government of the euro area at the meeting of 26 October 2011: it was **private-sector involvement** (PSI).[154] The Greek authorities and private investors were asked to reach an agreement on the restructuring of the debt in the form of a voluntary[155] debt exchange.[156] The eligible securities, which came to a total value of EUR 206 billion, were discounted by 53.5% of their face value. The voluntary exchange concerned 85% of holders of government bonds issued under Greek law.[157] To organise the exchange with regard to the remaining bond holders, the Greek Parliament voted to include collective action clauses that would enable the discount terms to be applied to everyone holding local law bonds.[158] The exchange concerned almost 96% of the overall outstanding amount

---

[150] Economic and Financial Committee, Model CAC – Common Terms of Reference, 17 February 2012, available at http://europa.eu/efc/sub_committee/cac/cac_2012/index_en.htm.

[151] Economic and Financial Committee, Explanatory note. 26 July 2011; Supplemental Explanatory Note, 26 March 2011.

[152] Antonio Sainz de Vicuña (2011) points out that there is no legal basis in EU law for the adoption of a legal measure that, in a binding manner, defines the characteristics of CACs.

[153] For a presentation of the measures adopted: Economic and Financial Committee, *Report on the implementation of euro area model Collective Action Clauses. Brussels*, 8 December 2014. The requirement to include a CAC was enacted in French law in the Finance Law for 2013, No 2012-1509 of 29 December 2012. JORF (Official Journal of the French Republic) No 304, 30 December 2012, p. 20859; set out in detail in Order No 2012-1517 of 29 December 2012 concerning the CACs applicable to government securities. JORF No 304, 30 December 2012, p. 21021.

[154] Euro Summit Statement, 26 October 2011. Reproduced in General Secretariat of the Council, *Rules for the organisation of the proceedings of the Euro Summits*, Luxembourg, Publications Office of the European Union, March 2013, p. 13.

[155] As the swap is a voluntary one, the operation can avoid being described as constituting a credit accident.

[156] For a detailed description of the plan: Crédit Suisse, Greece's debt exchange. *Fixed Income Research*, 27 February 2012.

[157] The ECB, which holds the Greek debt instruments, particularly since the implementation of the Securities Market Programme, has a special exchange agreement that was signed with the Hellenic Republic on 15 February 2012. Its former securities were exchanged at par (same face value, same coupon, same maturity) for new securities. See Allemand (2016), p. 96; Case T-79/13, *Accorinti* (GC 7 October 2015). For a detailed presentation, see Reserve Bank of Australia, Statement on Monetary Policy. *Monthly Bulletin*, May 2012, p. 30, Box B: The Greek Private Sector Debt Swap.

[158] This alteration has, however, been described as a credit accident by ISDA. See ISDA, *News Release. ISDA EMEA Determinations committee: CDS Auction relating to The Hellenic Republic*, London, 19 March 2012.

of all PSI-eligible debt. Since the series of Greek bonds issued under foreign law (Swiss and English law) were not concerned by CACs introduced retroactively by the new law, they were fiercely targeted by Vulture funds. No amendment of the conditions of the bonds could be successfully agreed upon between the Greek government and the Vulture funds and other holdouts. Athens has no other choice but to pay in full these investors for a total of EUR 6.4 billion.[159]

The PSI applied to Greece excluded public-sector creditors. The application of any discount to public debt instruments held by the EU, or any other MS, was tantamount to a debt transfer, which is prohibited by Article 125 TFEU. With regard to Greek bonds held by the ECB, an *ad hoc* **exchange agreement** was reached **with the Hellenic Republic** on 15 February 2012. According to this agreement, the ECB secured a swap at par with the securities it held (same face value, same coupon, same maturity).[160] In its Judgment of 7 October 2015 in *Accorinti*, the General Court of the EU confirmed that the agreement was valid.[161] The exclusion of securities from the central banks in the Eurosystem was justified by the fact that they were held for public interest purposes—a situation considered as fundamentally different from that of the private investors "who purchased Greek bonds solely in their private pecuniary interest, whatever the precise reason for their investment decisions may have been".[162] This also obviates the risk of any legal inconsistency with Article 123 TFEU.[163] The argument can also be applied with regard to the ESM. The holding of public debt instruments takes place as part of financial assistance, whose primary purpose is to re-establish the financial stability of the MS being supported and of the euro area as a whole. However, the holding of securities for treasury management purposes, on the other hand, does not constitute a public interest objective but a way of optimising cash holdings. 54

Since 1 January 2013, the **requirement to include a CAC** in all-new debt issue contracts (Article 12.2 TESM) is **likely to call the current legal interpretation of the no-bail-out clause into question**. In agreement with the authorities of the MS, a qualified majority of creditors (i.e. holders of not less than 66 2/3% of the outstanding principal amount of the bonds represented at the meeting of 55

---

[159] Munevar (2017) and Zettelmeyer et al. (2013).

[160] The nominal value of the securities exchanged came to EUR 42.7 billion. The securities were mainly purchased under the SMP (Securities Markets Programme).

[161] The confidential nature of the agreement of 15 February 2012 and the ECB's refusal to allow access to a German pension fund were the subject of an action for annulment which was dismissed in its entirety by the Court. In confining itself to communicating a description of the content of the annexes, the ECB was considered to have fulfilled the requirements regarding access to documents. Its refusal to communicate the annexes was well-founded, having regard to the circumstances. See Case T-376/13, *Versorgungswerk der Zahnärtzekammer Schleswig-Holstein* (GC 4 June 2015).

[162] Case T-79/13, *Accorinti* (GC 7 October 2015) para 90–92; also Eurogroup Statement of 21 February 2012; and [Mario Draghi]. (2012). Interview with Frankfurter Allgemeine Zeitung. 24 February.

[163] Allemand (2016).

bondholders) acting on the basis of a CAC may adopt a decision authorising a legally binding amendment to the payment conditions (moratorium, repayment deferral, cut in interest rates and/or discount) should the debtor be unable to pay.[164] A lower level of bondholder consent is laid down in the model CAC for amending less important terms and conditions. The decision applies to all holders of the modified securities, including those opposed to the restructuring.[165]

56   This new **arrangement** is primarily intended to manage the relations between an issuing State that is in financial difficulties and the private sector. It helps to reduce public-sector involvement in resolving the difficulties of the debtor State.[166] Once included in the issue contract, it **is binding on any holder**, regardless of the holder's status. There is no provision for any derogation in that respect in the model CAC adopted by the Economic and Financial Committee in February 2012. When they buy debt instruments on the market, public authorities (MS, the ECB, the ESM) agree to be subject to the law of the market and the terms attaching to the securities they purchase.[167] The law that governs the parties is that of the issue contract.[168]

57   In its supplement explanatory note on the CACs, the EFC explicitly mentions the particular situation of the ECB and the national central banks in the ESCB in an ordered restructuring in accordance with the CAC. Consistent with the market practice, the model CAC disenfranchised government bonds held by the issuer or any agency or government-controlled legal entity that demonstrates no **autonomy of decisions**. Most of the national central banks being State-owned, some commentators questioned how much their interests were autonomous. Having regard to Article 130 TFEU and Article 7 of the ESCB Statute, the EFC concluded that "euro national central banks accordingly have autonomy of decision in deciding how to vote on the proposed modification of any euro area government securities so acquired, and their holdings of these securities will be enfranchised under the model CAC".[169]

58   The launch of the Public Sector Purchase Programme by the ECB in 2015 raised some concerns about the possible blocking minority that could result in the ECB and other national central banks implementing the programme under the CACs. It would go against the philosophy of Article 123 TFEU for the central banks to be able to vote for a restructuring that provided for a cut in face value.[170] This justifies the **limits on purchases of government securities** that the ECB imposes on

---

[164] Heads of State or Government of the euro area, Conclusions, 11 March 2011.

[165] Economic and Financial Committee, Model CAC – Common Terms of Reference, 17 February 2012, Article 2.10.

[166] Bradley and Gulati (2013), p. 5.

[167] Case C-370/12, *Pringle* (CJEU 27 November 2012) para 141.

[168] Hofmann (2014), p. 391.

[169] EFC Sub-committee on EU sovereign debt markets, Model collective action clause, Supplemental explanatory note, 26 March 2012, Article E.

[170] Hofmann (2015), pp. 418–419; Smits (2015).

itself.[171] In that sense, the public-sector programmes for asset purchases on the secondary markets place limits on purchases by the central banks in the Eurosystem in order to prevent them from holding a blocking minority for the various debt series during restructuring operations.[172] As the Court of Justice stated in its *Weiss* case, "the Eurosystem central banks cannot purchase more than 33% of a particular issue of bonds of a central government of a Member State or more than 33% of the outstanding securities of one of those governments".[173] The purchase programme is thus considered compatible with Article 123 TFEU since it may not create certainty regarding a future purchase of MS bonds, in consequence of which MS might adopt lax budgetary policies.[174]

Special transactions for the purchase of public debt on the primary and secondary markets by the ESM are also subject to a ceiling, with the **purchasing limit** set by the Board of Directors on a case-by-case basis (Article 5 TESM). For the same reasons, the creditor MS should not be allowed to enter into a mass purchase programme of bonds issued by another MS. In any case, the same purchase limits as those applied by the ECB should be considered, and any backing to a public debt restructuring would be incompatible with Article 125 TFEU. **59**

The Meseberg statement of June 2018 called for "the possible introduction of Euro CACs with single-limb aggregation [...] to improve the existing framework promoting debt sustainability and to improve their effectiveness". In short, such clauses make it easier for an MS to override holdouts: a single restructuring decision may encompass all bonds. In its Report to Leaders on EMU deepening, the Eurogroup backed the idea at its meeting of 3 December 2018 and proposed to the Euro Summit to introduce these CACs by 2022 and to include this commitment in the ESM Treaty. The Eurogroup also backed the Franco-German proposition of an **explicit involvement of the ESM in negotiations on debt restructuring** between an MS debtor and its creditors. The Finance Ministers made this involvement dependent upon a request by the MS debtor and organised "on a voluntary, informal, non-binding, temporary, and confidential basis".[175] One might question the appropriateness of such an approach in terms of democratic legitimacy and transparency.[176] **60**

---

[171] Mersch (2016).

[172] Article 5(1) of ECB Decision (EU) 2015/774 (ECB/2015/10) *on a secondary markets public sector asset purchase programme*, O.J. L 121/20 (2015), as last amended by ECB Decision (EU) 2015/2101 (ECB/2015/33), O.J. L 303/106 (2015).

[173] Case C-493/17, *Weiss* (CJEU 11 December 2018) para 124.

[174] Case C-493/17, *Weiss* (CJEU 11 December 2018) para 132.

[175] Report of the Eurogroup to Leaders on EMU deepening, Brussels, 3 December 2018.

[176] European Parliament resolution of 13 March 2014 *on the enquiry on the role and operations of the Troika (ECB, Commission and IMF) with regard to the euro area programme countries* (2013/2277/INI), para 66–68; also Transparency International (2017); Braun and Hübner (2019).

3.3.2. Public Debt Rescheduling

61 **Debt rescheduling** gives rise to less discussion as it **does not affect the amount owing to the principal**. Rescheduling has been carried out several times to the advantage of Greece since 2011. In July 2011, for example, the Heads of State or Government of the euro area and the Union institutions decided to extend the maturity of bilateral loans and loans granted by the EFSF: it was lengthened from 7.5 to a minimum of 15 years and up to 30 years. Greece was also given a grace period of 10 years with respect to interest payments on loans from the EFSF.[177] On 21 February 2012 and then 27 November 2012, a number of supplementary measures were adopted by the Eurogroup to improve the sustainability of Greece's public debt[178] and to run side by side with the effects of the PSI. The risk premium was lowered to 150 base points with a retroactive effect, then the interest rates were again reduced by 100 base points. It is hoped that this will lead to an overall reduction of EUR 1.9 billion in the financing costs borne by Greece up to 2016.[179] In June 2018, the Eurogroup addressed the Greek sustainability issue right before the country exits the rescue programme on 20 August 2018. A combination of deferred payments, cash buffers and buyback of loans was approved. Additional debt measures could be adopted at the end of the EFSF grace period in 2032 "to ensure the respect of the agreed gross financing needs targets, provided that the EU fiscal framework is respected, and take appropriate actions, if needed".[180]

62 However, does the **lowering of risk premiums** constitute concessional measures, or to put it another way, measures that subsidise the financial assistance to Greece? In EU law, public debt includes the principal and interest; cutting the interest rates on loans constitutes debt discounting. This literal interpretation has to be balanced against the objective pursued by financial assistance, which is to safeguard the financial stability of the euro area as a whole and of the participating MS (Article 12 TESM). Financial assistance is supposed to make it possible for the beneficiary State to meet its commitments and eventually refinance itself on the capital markets. Cutting the rates and risk premiums that apply is not the same thing as abolishing all rates and premiums. The ESM, like an MS, cannot give a loan at a rate lower than that it pays on the money it itself borrows on the markets. In general, all the financing and running costs on a financial assistance operation have to be covered, and there must be provision for an "**appropriate margin**" (Article 20 TESM).[181] Article 125 TFEU rules out concessional rates in that they are set at

---

[177] Statement by the Heads of State or Government of the euro area and the EU institutions, 21 July 2011, paragraph 3.

[178] Eurogroup Statement, 21 February 2012; Eurogroup Statement on Greece, 27 November 2012.

[179] EFSF (2014), *FAQ – New disbursement of financial assistance to Greece*.

[180] Eurogroup, Statement on Greece, 22 June 2018.

[181] See also Case C-370/12, *Pringle* (CJEU 27 November 2012) para 139.

below-the-market rates[182] at which the body providing the financial assistance borrows. On the other hand, Article 125 TFEU does not prohibit the implementation of "fair" financial arrangements.[183] When it comes to extending the maturity of EFSF loans or allowing a grace period for the payment of interest on them, the face value of the debt in circulation remains the same: only the **debt profile of the country is improved**, which helps to make a return to the markets easier.

4. Public Debt Pooling in Prospect

The task of managing the financial crisis that Greece ran into showed that it called for tougher coordination between the various parties involved: the euro-area Member States, the EU institutions and the financial assistance instruments. Should this "socialisation" of risk management and resolution go as far as sharing the financial risk? That was the main topic of the discussion that arose from the end of 2009 regarding the **pooling of public debt**. The idea was driven forward by economic doctrine and made great headway, being cited as one of the avenues for reflection being developed by the Commission, certain Foreign Ministries and the Four Presidents Group in their thinking about the attainment of a *genuine economic and monetary union*.[184] Besides the great variety of pooling arrangements proposed,[185] a group of experts set up by the European Commission in July 2013 focused its attention on two mechanisms, in particular the establishment of a **debt amortisation fund** and **eurobonds**. The report published on 31 March 2014 concluded, unsurprisingly, that putting them into effect in the short and medium terms would create legal and political difficulties.[186] Since then, the idea of debt pooling has been lying dormant. The June 2015 Five Presidents' Report does not mention it anymore as it favours another solution to make the euro area sustainable: the establishment of a genuine budget for the euro area supported by a European treasury office.

In the spring of 2020, the economic and budgetary difficulties caused by the **COVID-19 crisis** relaunched the debate on the establishment of public debt

63

64

---

[182] The policy followed is modelled on that of the IMF. See ECB, The European Stability Mechanism, Monthly Bulletin, July 2011, pp. 76–77.

[183] ECB, The European Stability Mechanism, Monthly Bulletin, July 2011, p. 74.

[184] See Commission Communication, *A blueprint for a deep and genuine economic and monetary union. Launching a European Debate*, COM(2012) 777 final; Final report of the think tank on the future of the European Union consisting of the German, Austrian, Belgian, Danish, Spanish, French, Italian, Luxembourg, Dutch, Polish and Portuguese Foreign Ministers, 17 September 2012; H. Van Rompuy, in collaboration with J. M. Barroso, J.-C. Juncker and M. Draghi, *Towards a genuine economic and monetary union* (Four Presidents' Report), 5 December 2012. A working version of the Four Presidents' Report was presented in June 2012 and an intermediate version in October 2012.

[185] For a discussion: Allemand (2012); Expert group on debt redemption fund and eurobills (2014).

[186] For a discussion of the setting up of the experts' group and its report: Allemand (2015).

pooling. The MS most affected by the epidemic (Italy, Spain, France) were also among those with high budgetary and economic risks.[187] Ensuring that euro-area MS maintain market access required the Eurogroup to agree on a new ESM financial instrument to "support domestic financing of direct and indirect healthcare, cure and prevention-related costs due to the COVID-19 crisis".[188] Although the conditionality requirement under Article 136.3 TFEU is relaxed in comparison with the other financial instruments of the ESM, the loan, if drawn by the MS having requested the pandemic emergency support, gives rise to the payment of a quite small margin and other related service fees. The risk of a long recession and slow economic recovery has called for a reconsideration of how to finance a fiscal stimulus.

65 Following a proposal made by the Italian Prime Minister, the idea of **coronabonds**, i.e. joint debt issued by a European institution to help finance the fight of MS against COVID-19, gained impetus among MS and was endorsed by the European Council at its extraordinary meeting of July 2020 in the form of an increase of the Union's borrowing capacity.[189] According to the new Own Resources Decision, the Commission is then empowered to **borrow funds on the capital markets on the behalf of the Union of up to EUR 750 billion**. The funds borrowed are to be used for loans to MS (up to EUR 360 billion) and for subsidies. Loans granted by the Union to the MS under this new specific scheme must be repaid by December 2058 at the latest. Allocating a loan to an MS is made conditional upon the submission of a national recovery and resilience plan and its approval by the European institutions. In parallel, the loan agreement to be concluded between the Commission and the MS concerned shall define the amount of the loan, the average maturity, the number of instalments and the repayment schedule, as well as the pricing formula.[190] As such, this scheme does not differ so much from the "Ortoli facility"—a Community instrument established in 1978 to finance investment projects, especially in the energy and infrastructure sectors[191]—or from the mutual assistance for the balance of payments difficulties.

66 The most innovative aspect of this new financial tool lies in the arrangements adopted to cover all **liabilities of the Union resulting from its borrowing**. Unlike the MS, the Union must have a balanced budget pursuant to Article 310.1 TFEU. Accordingly, the amounts of the traditional own resources, ceilings shall be temporarily increased by 0.6 percentage points. It is worth recalling that 72% of the

---

[187] Commission Staff Working Document, Country Report Italy 2020, SWD(2020)511 final.

[188] Eurogroup, Statement on the Pandemic Crisis Support, available at https://www.consilium.europa.eu/en/press/press-releases/2020/05/08/eurogroup-statement-on-the-pandemic-crisis-support/.

[189] Special meeting of the European Council (17–21 July 2020), Conclusions, EUCO 10/20, 21 July 2020.

[190] Parliament/Council Regulation (EU) No 2021/241 *establishing the Recovery and Resilience Facility*, O.J. L 57/17 (2021).

[191] Council Decision 78/870/EEC *empowering the Commission to contract loans for the purpose of promoting investment within the Community*, O.J. L 298/9 (1978).

budget's resources come from gross domestic product (GDP) national contributions. This means that MS will have to share the burden of the EU public debt and will be exposed to sovereign risks until the adoption of dedicated resources. In any case, Article 125 TFEU prohibits any transfer of debt from an MS to the EU or another MS, meaning the loan has to be reimbursed. In the event of financial difficulties, the MS will have to request financial assistance from the ESM, and the euro-area Member States themselves will have no other choice but to grant a loan to enable the repayment of the debt owed to the Union, opening the door to a never-ending debt rollover by public institutions.

List of Cases

ECJ/CJEU
ECJ 05.02.1963, 26/62, *Van Gend en Loos*, ECLI:EU:C:1963:1 [cit. in para 30]
ECJ 10.12.1969, 6 and 11/69, *Commission v France*, ECLI:EU:C:196:68 [cit. in para 31]
ECJ 24.10.1973, 5/73, *Balkan-Import-Export GmbH*, ECLI:EU:C:1973:109 [cit. in para 48]
ECJ 09.03.1978, 106/77, *Simmenthal*, ECLI:EU:C:1978:49 [cit. in para 12]
ECJ 15.01.2002, C-179/00, *Gerald Weidacher v Bundesminister für Land- und Forstwirtschaft*, ECLI:EU:C:2002:18 [cit. in para 30]
CJEU 05.10.2010, C-173/09, *Georgi Ivanov Elchinov v Natsionalna zdravnoosiguritelna kasa*, ECLI:EU:C:2010:581 [cit. in para 12]
CJEU 27.11.2012, C-370/12, *Pringle*, ECLI:EU:C:2012:756 [cit. in para 1, 12, 25, 27-28, 33-34, 36, 40, 47, 54, 56]
CJEU 16.06.2015, C-62/14, *Gauweiler*, ECLI:EU:C:2015:400 [cit. in para 38]
CJEU 11.12.2018, C-493/17, *Weiss*, ECLI:EU:C:2018:1000 [cit. in para 37]

CFI/GC
CFI 02.10.2009, T-324/05, *Estonia v Commission*, ECLI:EU:T:2009:381 [cit. in para 30]
GC 16.12.2011, T-532/11, *Stefan Städter*, ECLI:EU:T:2011:768 [cit. in para 12]
GC 04.06.2015, *Versorgungswerk der Zahnärtzekammer Schleswig-Holstein*, ECLI:EU:T:2015:361 [cit. in para 54]
GC 07.10.2015, T-79/13, *Accorinti*, ECLI:EU:T:2015:756 [cit. in para 53]

National Courts
Supreme Court of Ireland 19.12.2012, *Pringle v Government of Ireland*, 339/2012 IESC 47 [cit. in para 12]
German FCC 05.05.2020, 2 BvR 859/15, *PSPP* [cit. in para 38]

References[192]

Allemand, F. (2012). La faisabilité juridique des projets d'euro-obligations. *Revue trimestrielle de droit européen, 48*(3), 553–594.
Allemand, F. (2015). La dette en partage. Quelques réflexions juridiques sur le traitement de la dette publique en droit de l'Union européenne. *Cahiers de droit européen, 51*(1), 235–292.
Allemand, F. (2016). Crise des dettes souveraines: la contestation, par des particuliers, de certaines mesures adoptées par la B.C.E. *Journal de Droit européen, 227*, 90–98.
Allemand, F. (2021). Le pouvoir d'amendement budgétaire du Parlement européen: la démocratisation à petit pas de la fonction budgétaire dans l'Union. *Politeia, 38*(1), 333–369.
Allemand, F., Bion, M., & Sauron, J.-L. (2016). *Gouverner la zone euro après la crise: l'exigence d'intégration*. LexisNexis.
Athanassiou, P. (2011). Of past measures and future plans for Europe's exit from the sovereign debt crisis: What is legally possible (and what is not). *European Law Review, 36*(4), 558–575.
Barav, A. (2015). *L'application judiciaire du droit de l'Union européenne: Recueil d'études*. Bruylant.
Baroin, F. (2012). *Journal de crise*. J.-C. Lattès.
Beesley, A. (2010). EU moves to calm private sector fears of 'haircuts'. *Irish Times*, 29 November.
Blommestein, H. J., Elmadag, M., & Ejsing, J. W. (2012). Buyback and exchange operations: Policies, procedures and practices among OECD public debt managers. *OECD working papers on sovereign borrowing and public debt management*, (5).
Bradley, M., & Gulati, M. (2013). Collective action clauses for the eurozone. *Review of Finance, 18*(6), 1–58.
Braun, B., & Hübner, M. (2019). *Vanishing Act: The Eurogroup's accountability*. Transparency International.
Calliess, C. (2011). Das Europäische Solidaritätsprinzip und die Krise des Euro. Von der Rechtsgemeinschaft zur Solidaritätsgemeinschaft?. *Forum Constitutionis Europae* (FCE) 01/11.
Chemain, R. (1996). *L'Union économique et monétaire : aspects juridiques et institutionnels*. Pédone.
Christophersen, H. (1989). *Issues raised in the realization of economic and monetary union* (transmitted by H. Christophersen to the Presidency for the Antibes meeting). Brussels: Commission, p. 15. 9626/89.
Cloos, J., Reinesch, G., Vignes, D., & Weyland, J. (1994). *Le traité de Maastricht. Genèse, analyse, commentaires* (2nd ed.). Bruylant.
Das, U., Papaioannou, M., & Trebesch, C. (2012). *Restructuring sovereign debt: Lessons from recent history*. Contribution to the IMF seminar 'Financial Crises: Causes, Consequences, Policy Response', Washington D.C., 14 September 2012. Retrieved from https://www.imf.org/external/np/seminars/eng/2012/fincrises/pdf/ch19.pdf
de Sadeleer, N. (2012). La gouvernance économique européenne: Léviathan ou colosse aux pieds d'argile?. *Jean Monnet Working Paper Series*, 2012/4.
Dévoluy, M. (2013). Les dettes publiques sont-elles souveraines?. *L'Europe en formation*, (No. 368), 197–208.
Eaton, J., & Gersovitz, M. (1981). Debt with potential repudiation: Theoretical and empirical analysis. *The Review of Economic Studies, 48*(2), 289–309.
Expert group on debt redemption fund and eurobills. Chaired by G. Tumpel-Gugerell (2014). *Final Report*. Bruxelles: Commission. Retrieved from http://ec.europa.eu/economy_finance/articles/governance/pdf/20140331_report_en.pdf
Fratianni, M., von Hagen, J., & Waller, W. (1992). *The Maastricht way to EMU. Essays in International Finance*. Princeton University (No. 187).

---

[192] All cited Internet sources of this comment have been accessed on 6 April 2021.

Glenn, J. K. (2004). From Nation-States to Member States: Accession negotiations as an instrument of Europeanization. *Comparative European Politics, 2*, 3–28.
Grabitz, E., Hilf, M., & Nettesheim, M. (Eds.). (2021). *Das Recht der Europäischen Union: EUV/ AEUV. Kommentar*. Loose leaf. Beck.
Greek Public Debt Management Agency. (2019). Hellenic Republic Public Debt Bulletin (92). Retrieved from http://www.pdma.gr/en/quarterly-bulletin/2048-no92
Hofmann, C. (2014). Sovereign-debt restructuring in Europe under the new model collective action clauses. *Texas International Law Journal, 49*, 385–434.
Hofmann, H. (2015). *Gauweiler and OMT: Lessons for EU Public Law and the European Economic and Monetary Union*. University of Luxembourg, Working paper, 19 June.
Ipsen, J. (2020). Das Bundesverfassungsgericht ultra vires. Das Letztentscheidungsrecht im Spannungsfeld von Recht und Politik. *Recht und Politik, 56*(3), 344–364.
Jukes. (1990). EC split on how to impose budget discipline (2 of 2). *Reuters*, 28 March.
Kepenne, J.-P. (2000). Article 103. In P. Léger (Ed.), *Union européenne. Communauté européenne. Commentaire article par article des traités UE et CE*. Helbing & Lichtenhahn et al.
Lemoine, B. (2016). *L'ordre de la dette*. La Découverte.
Louis, J.-V. (1995). *Union économique et monétaire*. Coll. Commentaire J. Mégret (2nd ed.). Éditions de l'Université de Bruxelles.
Louis, J.-V. (2009). *L'Union européenne et sa monnaie*. Coll. Commentaire J. Mégret (3rd ed.). Éditions de l'Université de Bruxelles.
Louis, J.-V. (2010). Guest editorial: The no-bailout clause and rescue package. *Common Market Law Review, 47*(4), 971–986.
Manger-Nestler, C., & Böttner, R. (2019). Der Europäische Währungsfonds nach den Plänen der Kommission. *Zeitschrift für ausländisches öffentliches Recht und Völkerrecht, 43*–84.
Martucci, F. (2011). Le défaut souverain en droit de l'Union européenne. In M. Audit (Ed.), *Insolvabilité des États et dettes souveraines* (p. 233 et seqq). LGDJ.
Medeiros, C., Polan, M., & Ramlogan, P. (2007). A primer on sovereign debt buybacks and swaps. *IMF Working Paper*, WP/07/58. Retrieved from https://www.imf.org/external/pubs/ft/wp/2007/wp0758.pdf
Mersch, Y. (2016). *Monetary policy in the euro area: Scope, principles and limits*. Keynote speech, at the Natixis Meeting of Chief Economists, Paris, 23 June.
Monaco, R. (1972). Notes sur l'intégration juridique dans les Communautés européennes. In *Miscellanea W. J. Ganshof Van der Meersch. Studia ab discipulis amicisque in honorem egregii professoris édita* (tome II, p. 318 et seqq.). Bruylant.
Morisset, A. (1994). La procédure concernant les déficits excessifs. *Revue ECU*, (27). Retrieved from https://resume.uni.lu/story/la-procedure-concernant-les-deficits-excessifs
Munevar, D. (2017). Vulture funds: Lessons from Greece. *CATDM.org*. Retrieved from http://www.cadtm.org/spip.php?page=imprimer&id_article=14563
Natixis. (2010). Qui détient les dettes publiques européennes? *Flash Economie*, (124), 24 March.
Palmstorfer, R. (2012). To bail out or not to bail out? The current framework of financial assistance for euro area Member States measured against the requirements of EU primary law. *European Law Review, 37*(6), 771–784.
Pingel, I. (Ed.). (2010). *Commentaire article par article des traités UE et CE* (2nd ed.). Helbing Lichtenhahn.
Pons, J.-F. (1988). Réforme de la politique d'émission et de gestion de la dette publique en France (1985-1987). *Revue d'Économie financière, 4*, 88–99.
Prokop, J. (2012). Bargaining over debt rescheduling. *Munich Personal RePEc Archiv, Paper*. Retrieved from https://mpra.ub.uni-muenchen.de/44315/1/MPRA_paper_44315.pdf
Prokop, J., & Wang, R. (1997). Strategic buybacks of sovereign debt. *Queen's Economics Department Working Paper*. London: Queen's University, No. 957.
Rohleder, K., Zehnpfund, O., & Sinn, L. (2010). Bilaterale Finanzhilfen für Griechenland. *Wissenschaftliche Dienst, Info Brief*, WD 11 – 3000 – 103/10, 3 May. Berlin: Deutscher Bundestag.

Rose, A. (2005). One reason countries pay their debts: Renegotiation and international trade. *Journal of Development Economics, 77*, 189–206.

Ruffert, M. (2011). The European debt crisis and European Union law. *Common Market Law Review, 48*(6), 1777–1806.

Sainz de Vicuña, A. (2011). *Collective action clauses European model. Identical clauses, different legal systems*. Contribution presented at the Goethe-Universität Frankfurt – House of Finance, Frankfurt-am-Main, 27 October 2011. Retrieved from http://www.ilf.uni-frankfurt.de/uploads/media/Sanz_de_Vicuna_-_CAC_-_European_Model_03.pdf

Seelow, S. (2012). L'Allemagne a-t-elle une dette de guerre envers la Grèce? *LeMonde.fr*, 17 February.

Smits, R. (1997). *The European Central Bank*. Kluwer Law International.

Smits, R. (2015). *The European Central Bank's room for manoeuvre provisionally confirmed. 19 January*. Retrieved from https://acelg.blogactiv.eu/2015/01/19/european-central-bank%E2%80%99s-room-for-manoeuvre-provisionally-confirmed/

Sperling, J., & Kirchner, E. J. (1997). *Recasting the European Order: Security architectures and economic cooperation*. Manchester University Press.

Steinbach, A. (2016). The 'Haircut' of public creditors under EU law. *European Constitutional Law Review, 12*, 223–239.

Storr, S. (2020). Von der Kooperation zur Konfrontation: Das PSPP-Urteil des deutschen Bundesverfassungsgerichts vom 5. Mai 2020. *Journal für Rechtspolitik*, (2), 65–72.

Transparency International. (2017). *From crisis to stability. How to make the European Stability transparent and accountable*. Transparency International.

Ubsborne, D. (1991). Chancellor rejects EC plan to control economic policies. *The Independant*, 26 February.

von der Groeben, H., & Schwarze, J. (Eds.). (2003). *EUV/EGV. Kommentar*. (6th ed.). Nomos.

von der Groeben, H., Schwarze, J., & Hatje, A. (Eds.). (2016). *Europäisches Unionsrecht* (7th ed.). Nomos.

von Hagen, J., & Eichengreen, B. (1998). Politique budgétaire et union monétaire : existe-t-il un arbitrage entre fédéralisme et restrictions budgétaires? *Revue d'économie financière, 47*, 141–152.

Walker, M. (2016). IMF Proposal on Greece Sets Up Battle with Germany. *The Wall Street Journal*, 17 May.

Wendel, M. (2020). Paradoxes of ultra-vires review: A critical review of the PSPP decision and its initial reception. *German Law Journal, 21*(5), 979–994.

Wroughton, L., Schneider, L., & Kyriakidou, D. (2015). How the IMF's misadventure in Greece is changing the fund. *Reuters Investigates*, Reuter, 28 August. Retrieved from https://www.reuters.com/investigates/special-report/imf-greece/

Zettelmeyer, J., Trebesch, C., & Gulati, M. (2013). The Greek debt restructuring: An autopsy. *Economic Policy, 28*(75), 513–563.

Article 126 [Prohibition of Excessive Government Deficits]
(ex-Article 104 TEC)

1. Member States shall avoid excessive government deficits.[5]
2. The Commission[13] shall monitor the development of the budgetary situation and of the stock of government debt in the Member States with a view to identifying gross errors.[8] In particular it shall examine compliance with budgetary discipline[2] on the basis of the following two criteria:[7-11]
(a) whether the ratio of the planned or actual government deficit to gross domestic product exceeds a reference value, unless:
– either the ratio has declined substantially and continuously and reached a level that comes close to the reference value,
– or, alternatively, the excess over the reference value is only exceptional and temporary and the ratio remains close to the reference value;[9]
(b) whether the ratio of government debt to gross domestic product exceeds a reference value, unless the ratio is sufficiently diminishing and approaching the reference value at a satisfactory pace.[10]

The reference values are specified in the Protocol on the excessive deficit procedure annexed to the Treaties.[30]

3. If a Member State does not fulfil the requirements under one or both of these criteria, the Commission shall prepare a report.[17] The report of the Commission shall also take into account whether the government deficit exceeds government investment expenditure and take into account all other relevant factors, including the medium-term economic and budgetary position of the Member State.

The Commission may also prepare a report if, notwithstanding the fulfilment of the requirements under the criteria, it is of the opinion that there is a risk of an excessive deficit in a Member State.

4. The Economic and Financial Committee shall formulate an opinion on the report of the Commission.[18]
5. If the Commission considers that an excessive deficit in a Member State exists or may occur, it shall address an opinion to the Member State concerned and shall inform the Council accordingly.[19]
6. The Council[14-16] shall, on a proposal from the Commission, and having considered any observations which the Member State concerned may wish to make, decide after an overall assessment whether an excessive deficit exists.[20-21]
7. Where the Council decides, in accordance with paragraph 6, that an excessive deficit exists, it shall adopt, without undue delay, on a recommendation from the Commission, recommendations[22] addressed to the Member State concerned with a view to bringing that situation to an end within a given period. Subject to the provisions of paragraph 8, these recommendations shall not be made public.

8. Where it establishes that there has been no effective action in response to its recommendations within the period laid down, the Council may make its recommendations public.[23]
9. If a Member State persists in failing to put into practice the recommendations of the Council, the Council may decide to give notice[24] to the Member State to take, within a specified time limit, measures for the deficit reduction which is judged necessary by the Council in order to remedy the situation.

In such a case, the Council may request the Member State concerned to submit reports in accordance with a specific timetable in order to examine the adjustment efforts of that Member State.
10. The rights to bring actions provided for in Articles 258 and 259 may not be exercised within the framework of paragraphs 1 to 9 of this Article.[13]
11. As long as a Member State fails to comply with a decision taken in accordance with paragraph 9, the Council may decide to apply or, as the case may be, intensify one or more of the following measures:[25-26]
– to require the Member State concerned to publish additional information, to be specified by the Council, before issuing bonds and securities,
– to invite the European Investment Bank to reconsider its lending policy towards the Member State concerned,
– to require the Member State concerned to make a non-interest-bearing deposit of an appropriate size with the Union until the excessive deficit has, in the view of the Council, been corrected,
– to impose fines of an appropriate size.

The President of the Council shall inform the European Parliament of the decisions taken.[27]
12. The Council shall abrogate some or all of its decisions or recommendations referred to in paragraphs 6 to 9 and 11 to the extent that the excessive deficit in the Member State concerned has, in the view of the Council, been corrected.

If the Council has previously made public recommendations, it shall, as soon as the decision under paragraph 8 has been abrogated, make a public statement that an excessive deficit in the Member State concerned no longer exists.[28]
13. When taking the decisions or recommendations referred to in paragraphs 8, 9, 11 and 12, the Council shall act on a recommendation from the Commission.[20]

When the Council adopts the measures referred to in paragraphs 6 to 9, 11 and 12, it shall act without taking into account the vote of the member of the Council representing the Member State concerned.

A qualified majority of the other members of the Council shall be defined in accordance with Article 238(3)(a).
14. Further provisions relating to the implementation of the procedure described in this Article are set out in the Protocol on the excessive deficit procedure annexed to the Treaties.[29-31]

Article 126. [Prohibition of Excessive Government Deficits] 691

The Council shall, acting unanimously in accordance with a special legislative procedure and after consulting the European Parliament and the European Central Bank, adopt the appropriate provisions which shall then replace the said Protocol.[33-34, 36-37]

Subject to the other provisions of this paragraph, the Council shall, on a proposal from the Commission and after consulting the European Parliament, lay down detailed rules and definitions for the application of the provisions of the said Protocol.[35, 45-46]

Protocol (No 12)[29-31]
on the excessive deficit procedure

THE HIGH CONTRACTING PARTIES,

DESIRING TO lay down the details of the excessive deficit procedure referred to in Article 126 of the Treaty on the Functioning of the European Union,

HAVE AGREED upon the following provisions, which shall be annexed to the Treaty on European Union and to the Treaty on the Functioning of the European Union:

Article 1

The reference values[7-11, 30] referred to in Article 126(2) of the Treaty on the Functioning of the European Union are:

- 3% for the ratio of the planned or actual government deficit to gross domestic product at market prices;
- 60% for the ratio of government debt to gross domestic product at market prices.

Article 2

In Article 126 of the said Treaty and in this Protocol:

- "government" means general government, that is central government, regional or local government and social security funds, to the exclusion of commercial operations, as defined in the European System of Integrated Economic Accounts;
- "deficit" means net borrowing as defined in the European System of Integrated Economic Accounts;
- "investment" means gross fixed capital formation as defined in the European System of Integrated Economic Accounts;

– "debt" means total gross debt at nominal value outstanding at the end of the year and consolidated between and within the sectors of general government as defined in the first indent.[7, 30]

Article 3

In order to ensure the effectiveness of the excessive deficit procedure, the governments of the Member States shall be responsible under this procedure for the deficits of general government as defined in the first indent of Article 2. The Member States shall ensure that national procedures in the budgetary area enable them to meet their obligations in this area deriving from these Treaties. The Member States shall report their planned and actual deficits and the levels of their debt promptly and regularly to the Commission.[31]

Article 4

The statistical data to be used for the application of this Protocol shall be provided by the Commission.[32]

30. Declaration on Article 126 of the Treaty on the Functioning of the European Union[49]

With regard to Article 126, the Conference confirms that raising growth potential and securing sound budgetary positions are the two pillars of the economic and fiscal policy of the Union and the Member States. The Stability and Growth Pact is an important tool to achieve these goals.

The Conference reaffirms its commitment to the provisions concerning the Stability and Growth Pact as the framework for the coordination of budgetary policies in the Member States.

The Conference confirms that a rule-based system is the best guarantee for commitments to be enforced and for all Member States to be treated equally.

Within this framework, the Conference also reaffirms its commitment to the goals of the Lisbon Strategy: job creation, structural reforms, and social cohesion.

The Union aims at achieving balanced economic growth and price stability. Economic and budgetary policies thus need to set the right priorities towards economic reforms, innovation, competitiveness and strengthening of private investment and consumption in phases of weak economic growth. This should be reflected in the orientations of budgetary decisions at the national and Union level in particular through restructuring of public revenue and expenditure while respecting budgetary discipline in accordance with the Treaties and the Stability and Growth Pact.

Budgetary and economic challenges facing the Member States underline the importance of sound budgetary policy throughout the economic cycle.

The Conference agrees that Member States should use periods of economic recovery actively to consolidate public finances and improve their budgetary positions. The objective is to gradually achieve a budgetary surplus in good

Article 126. [Prohibition of Excessive Government Deficits]

times which creates the necessary room to accommodate economic downturns and thus contribute to the long-term sustainability of public finances.
The Member States look forward to possible proposals of the Commission as well as further contributions of Member States with regard to strengthening and clarifying the implementation of the Stability and Growth Pact. The Member States will take all necessary measures to raise the growth potential of their economies. Improved economic policy coordination could support this objective. This Declaration does not prejudge the future debate on the Stability and Growth Pact.

Contents

1. Overview 1
   1.1. Sound Public Finances of the Member States as Cornerstone Element of the EMU 1
   1.2. The Maastricht Treaty Framework 2
   1.3. Purpose and Structure of Article 126 TFEU 5
2. The Definition of Government Deficits 7
   2.1. The Two Reference Values 7
   2.2. The Deficit Criterion 9
   2.3. The Debt Criterion 10
   2.4. Assessment of the Reference Values 11
3. The Excessive Deficit Procedure 12
   3.1. Main Features 12
      3.1.1. Two Sections 12
      3.1.2. Role of the Commission 13
      3.1.3. Role of the Council 14
   3.2. Procedural Steps 17
      3.2.1. Commission Report 17
      3.2.2. Opinion of the Economic and Financial Committee 18
      3.2.3. Opinion of the Commission to the Member State Concerned 19
      3.2.4. The Council's Decision on the Existence of an Excessive Deficit 20
      3.2.5. Procedural Steps for All Member States 22
      3.2.6. Further Procedural Steps for Euro-Area Member States 24
4. The Excessive Deficit Protocol 29
5. Secondary Law 33
   5.1. The Legal Bases in Article 126.14 TFEU 33
      5.1.1. Article 126.14 (2) TFEU 33
      5.1.2. Article 126.14 (3) TFEU 35
   5.2. Regulation 1467/97 36
   5.3. Regulation 1173/2011 38
   5.4. The Budgetary Framework Directive 45
   5.5. The "Two Pack" 47
6. The Declaration on Article 126 TFEU 49
7. The Treaty on Stability, Coordination and Governance (TSCG) 50
8. Concluding Remarks 53

List of Cases
References

1. Overview

1.1. Sound Public Finances of the Member States as Cornerstone Element of the EMU

1 The authors of the Maastricht Treaty regarded **sound public finances** of the MS as the key element of a well-functioning Economic and Monetary Union (EMU) marked by **price stability**. This stance could already be found in the *Delors* Report (1989) written in preparation for the introduction of a single currency.[1] This means that an MS should not incur unsustainable public debts, for this could endanger the maintenance of price stability, which is the "primary objective" (Article 105.1 TEC-Maastricht, now Article 127.1 TFEU) of the ESCB. Under this logic, the nexus between sound public finances and price stability is as follows: an MS having joined the common currency has lost the competence to pursue a monetary policy tailored to its specific needs. Above all else, such an MS can no longer devaluate its currency, a useful tool to reduce sovereign debt provided that government bonds are not issued in a foreign currency. Against this background, an MS having piled up more and more debts may exert political pressure on the ECB to conduct an inflationary monetary policy running counter to price stability.[2] Furthermore, unsustainable public debts may also have negative spillover effects on other MS.[3]

1.2. The Maastricht Treaty Framework

2 To safeguard sound public finances, a series of provisions were included in Chapter 1, "Economic Policy", of Title VI, "Economic and Monetary Policy", of the TEC-Maastricht (Articles 102a–104c). Since then, this Treaty framework has been amended only insignificantly.[4] This is why the provisions of Chapter 1, "Economic Policy", of Title VIII TFEU (i.e. Articles 120–126 TFEU) are nearly identical with Articles 102a–104c TEC-Maastricht. Apart from Article 122 TFEU, all of these Treaty provisions—to a greater or lesser extent—aim at safeguarding sound public finances of the MS (Article 119.3 TFEU). This aim is also referred to by the term "**budgetary discipline**" (Article 126.2 TFEU) or "sound budgetary policy".[5] The prime importance of budgetary discipline for the EMU is reflected in the fact that Article 140.1 second indent TFEU defines the sustainability of the respective

---

[1] Committee for the Study of Economic and Monetary Union (1989), pp. 19, 20, 24, 36; also see Fratianni and von Hagen (1992), pp. 177 et seq.
[2] Baldwin and Wyplosz (2015), p. 426; Häde, in Calliess and Ruffert (2021), Article 126 AEUV para 2; Cf. Italianer (1997), p. 200.
[3] Baldwin and Wyplosz (2015), p. 426; De Grauwe (2016), p. 233.
[4] Häde (2012), p. 423; Palmstorfer (2014), p. 187.
[5] Case C-370/12, *Pringle* (CJEU 27 November 2012) para 135 et seq.

government financial position as one of the four convergence criteria for joining the common currency.

The approach to ensure sound public finances in the Chapter "Economic Policy" rests on **two pillars**:[6] the first pillar consists of a number of **prohibitions** on the forms of financial assistance to MS (Articles 123, 124, 125 TFEU).[7] This pillar should ensure that MS are on their own vis-à-vis the financial markets, the latter being regarded as actors to impose budgetary discipline on MS.[8] **3**

The second pillar consists of multi-stage **procedures** in the Council to make sure that MS follow a certain line of economic policy. Owing to the prominence of sound public finances, the focus is hereby laid on the expenditure and revenues of the MS, i.e. their budgetary policy.[9] These procedures are the **multilateral surveillance procedure** (MSP) and the **excessive deficit procedure** (EDP). Unlike the first pillar, it is the EU institutions, especially the Council, that are to impose budgetary discipline on the MS.[10] Both the MSP and the EDP serve the proper functioning of the EMU. The scope of the MSP, the purpose of which is to examine whether MS economic policies comply with the non-binding broad economic policy guidelines of the Council and whether they threaten the proper functioning of the EMU (Article 121.4 TFEU), is much broader than the one of the EDP. The MSP covers all fields of MS economic policies and not only their budgetary policies. And yet, compared with the EDP, the MSP is the "weaker" procedure as Article 121 TFEU does not contain legally binding sanctions to be imposed on deviant MS.[11] Nevertheless, there are close links between the MSP and the EDP as the former can be seen as a **preventive arm** to safeguard MS compliance with Article 126.1 TFEU.[12] By contrast, the EDP can be regarded as a **corrective arm**, that is, a procedure to remedy non-compliance with Article 126.1 TFEU.[13] **4**

---

[6] Cf. De Streel (2014), pp. 85 et seq.; Kempen, in Streinz (2018), Article 126 AEUV para 2.

[7] See Pilz (2016), p. 18.

[8] Concerning Article 125 TFEU see Case C-370/12, *Pringle* (CJEU 27 November 2012) para 135.

[9] Some authors also use the term "fiscal policy", see, e.g., Tuori and Tuori (2014), p. 31; van den Noord (2007), p. 36. These terms are often used interchangeably. However, "fiscal policy" is often used to designate a form of budgetary policy tailored to the economic cycle. Thus, public revenues and spending are used as tools to influence the economy.

[10] Cf. Van den Bogaert and Borger (2017), p. 216 who associate Articles 123–125 TFEU with "market discipline" and Article 126 TFEU with "public discipline". Also see De Streel (2013), p. 337.

[11] Amtenbrink and De Haan (2003), p. 1076.

[12] Ruffert (2011), p. 1798.

[13] Adamski (2012), p. 1322; Baldwin and Wyplosz (2015), pp. 433 et seqq.; Hinarejos (2013), p. 1625.

1.3. Purpose and Structure of Article 126 TFEU

5   In the Treaty framework to safeguard sound public finances of the MS, Article 126 TFEU is of prime importance.[14] The main purpose of Article 126 TFEU is to ensure price stability.[15] The function of Article 126 TFEU is to concretise and operationalise the ambiguous concept of sound public finances of the MS.[16] This is done through the concept of "excessive government deficits". Article 126.1 TFEU imposes a **legally binding obligation**[17] for MS to avoid such deficits.[18] This obligation applies to all MS, including the non-euro-area MS (Article 139.1 TFEU: "Member States with a derogation"). As regards the legal status of Denmark, the rules for non-euro MS apply (point 1 of Protocol No. 16 on Denmark).

6   This obligation and the EDP by which MS compliance can be examined are elaborated in Article 126.2–14 TFEU as well as in **Protocol (No 12) on the Excessive Deficit Procedure** (EDP Protocol) and in **secondary law**. According to Article 126.6 TFEU, the Council is competent to decide on the existence of an excessive deficit. Article 126.7–13 TFEU provide for corrective measures to remedy an excessive deficit. The need for a special Council procedure to establish and correct a violation of Article 126.1 TFEU is due to the fact that Article 126.10 TFEU excludes the right to bring an infringement action within the framework of Article 126.1–9 TFEU. Pursuant to Article 139.2 point (b) TFEU, the last two procedural steps of this corrective regime—Article 126.9 and Article 126.11 TFEU—do not apply to non-euro-area MS. Article 126.14 (2) and (3) TFEU serves as a legal basis for the adoption of legal acts to replace and, respectively, amplify the EDP Protocol. The following legal acts were adopted on these legal bases: Regulation 1467/97,[19] Regulation 1056/2005,[20] Regulation 479/2009,[21] Regulation 1177/2011[22] and Directive 2011/85.[23]

---

[14] Rebhahn (2015), p. 147.

[15] Kempen, in Streinz (2018), Article 126 AEUV para 29.

[16] It must be emphasised that there is still no consensus in the economic literature on the question of when public debts become unsustainable. See Klepzig (2015), p. 68.

[17] Häde, in Calliess and Ruffert (2021), Article 126 AEUV para 9; Hattenberger, in Schwarze et al. (2019), Article 126 AEUV para 15; Italianer (1997), p. 199; Kempen, in Streinz (2018), Article 126 AEUV para 4.

[18] Häde, in Calliess and Ruffert (2021), Article 126 AEUV para 9; Hattenberger, in Schwarze et al. (2019), Article 126 AEUV para 15; Italianer (1997), p. 199.

[19] Council Regulation (EC) No 1467/97 *on speeding up and clarifying the implementation of the excessive deficit procedure*, O.J. L 209/6 (1997).

[20] Council Regulation (EC) No 1056/2005 *amending Regulation (EC) No 1467/97*, O.J. L 174/5 (2005), legal base: Article 104.14 (2) TEC-Nice.

[21] Council Regulation (EU) No 479/2009 *on the application of the Protocol on the excessive deficit procedure annexed to the Treaty establishing the European Community*, O.J. L 145/1 (2009), legal base: Article 104.14 (3) TEC-Nice.

[22] Council Regulation (EU) No 1177/2011 *amending Regulation (EC) No 1467/97*, O.J. L 306/33 (2011), legal base: Article 126.14 (2) TFEU.

[23] Council Directive (EU) No 2011/85 *on requirements for budgetary frameworks of the Member States*, O.J. L 306/41 (2011), legal base: Article 126.14 (3) TFEU.

Article 126. [Prohibition of Excessive Government Deficits]

2. The Definition of Government Deficits

2.1. The Two Reference Values

In order to define the material scope of the obligation under Article 126.1 TFEU, it is necessary to define the concepts of "government" and "deficit". This is done in the **EDP Protocol**, which refers to the respective definitions in the European System of Integrated Economic Accounts (ESA). Consequently, "government" is to be understood as general government and comprises central government, regional or local government and social security funds, to the exclusion of commercial operations (Article 2 first indent of the EDP Protocol). "Deficit" means net borrowing as defined in ESA (Article 2 second indent of the EDP Protocol).

Article 126 TFEU is restricted to the avoidance of gross errors in terms of the budgetary situation and the stock of government debt in the MS (Article 126.2 sentence 1 TFEU). The reference to "gross errors" does not constitute a further yardstick for it can be assumed that the purpose of Article 126.2 TFEU is to operationalise the obligation of Article 126.1 TFEU. This is done by the two reference values listed in Article 126.2 points (a) and (b) TFEU, which are also considered to be examples of the gross errors mentioned in Article 126.1 TFEU. The wording of Article 126.2 sentence 2 TFEU ("in particular") indicates that gross errors can also exist even if neither of the **reference values** is fulfilled. Nevertheless, the next procedural stage (i.e. the Commission report under Article 126.3 sentence 1 TFEU, → para 17) requires that either one or both of these reference values are met. By means of these reference values, compliance with budgetary discipline shall be examined by the Commission. These reference values, which are further specified in the Deficit Protocol as well as in Regulation 479/2009, are commonly referred to as the **deficit criterion** (Article 126.2 point (a) TFEU) and the **debt criterion** (Article 126.2 point (b) TFEU).

2.2. The Deficit Criterion

Budgetary discipline is deemed to be not complied with if the ratio of the planned or actual government deficit to gross domestic product (GDP) exceeds the **reference value of 3%**, the latter value being laid down in Article 1 first indent of the EDP Protocol. However, the Treaty also introduces two alternative constellations in which a transgression of 3% is not tantamount to non-compliance with budgetary discipline: firstly, if "the ratio has declined substantially and continuously and reached a level that comes close" to 3% (Article 126.2 point (a) second indent TFEU) or, secondly and alternatively, if "the excess over the reference value is only exceptional and temporary and the ratio remains close to the reference value" (Article 126.2 point (a) second indent TFEU). Owing to this ambiguous wording,[24]

---

[24] Häde, in Calliess and Ruffert (2021), Article 126 AEUV para 28.

these exceptions were specified in Regulation 1467/97 as amended by Regulation 1177/2011, which defines "exceptional" (Article 126.2 point (a) second indent TFEU) as a state "resulting from an unusual event outside the control of the Member State concerned and with a major impact on the financial position of general government, or when resulting from a severe economic downturn" (Article 2.1). In a similar vein, "temporary" refers to a situation in which the "budgetary forecasts as provided by the Commission indicate that the deficit will fall below the reference value following the end of the unusual event or the severe economic downturn" (Article 2.1). The said reference to the exceptional circumstances also allows considering the economic disruptive effects caused by the **COVID-19 crisis**, which started to hit Europe in early 2020. Against this background, it has to be pointed out that Regulation 1467/97 refers to "unexpected adverse economic events with major unfavourable consequences for government finances" (Articles 3.5 and 5.2) as an element that needs to be taken into consideration in the EDP. Together with related provisions in Regulation 1467/96, this set of rules is also referred to as "general escape clause" by the Commission, which activated it on 20 March 2020 (→ Article 121 TFEU para 50 et seqq.).[25] However, unlike what this terminology might suggest, this activation results not in the non-application of Article 126 TFEU as such but in a departure from some of the secondary law rules that normally apply.[26]

2.3. The Debt Criterion

10 The debt criterion functions as the second yardstick for budgetary discipline, the question being whether or not the ratio of government debt to gross domestic product exceeds **the reference value of 60%** (Article 1 second indent of the EDP Protocol). The term "government debt" is specified in Article 1.5 of Regulation 479/2009 as amended by Regulation 220/2014 as the total gross debt at nominal value outstanding at the end of the year of the sector of general government (ESA) with the exception of those liabilities the corresponding financial assets of which are held by it. As with the deficit criterion, the Treaty in the same breath provides for an exception, for this transgression is not to be considered as a violation of budgetary discipline, if "the ratio is sufficiently diminishing and approaching the reference value at a satisfactory pace". Again, this exception is defined by secondary law. Pursuant to Article 2.1a of Regulation 1467/97 as amended by Regulation 1177/2011, such a sufficient diminishment is given "if the differential with respect to the reference value has decreased over the previous three years at an average rate of one twentieth per year as a benchmark, based on changes over the last three years for which the data is available". Moreover, the debt criterion is also

---

[25] Commission Communication *on the activation of the general escape clause of the Stability and Growth Pact*, COM(2020) 123 final.
[26] COM(2020) 123 final, p. 2.

deemed to be fulfilled if the budgetary forecasts of the Commission indicate that the required reduction in the differential will occur over the 3-year period encompassing the 2 years following the final year for which the data are available (Article 2.1a). These measures help to operationalise the debt criterion.[27]

2.4. Assessment of the Reference Values

As shown above, the clear numerical criteria are watered down by exceptions, which are vaguely formulated, leaving **considerable interpretative leeway**[28] to the Commission, which is in charge of monitoring the development of the budgetary situation and the stock of government debt in the MS (Article 126.2 (1) sentence 1 TFEU). The same is true for the Council, which is competent to decide upon the existence of an excessive deficit (Article 126.7 sentence 1 TFEU, → para 20 et seq.).[29] In brief, exceeding either one or both of these thresholds does not necessarily result in a violation of Article 126.1 TFEU.[30] The suitability of the reference values as yardsticks of budgetary discipline has been questioned and criticised by many authors.[31] It can be assumed that the specific values are not to be considered as established economic truths.[32] Rather, they are the product of political negotiation.[33] Given the fact that the creation of a single currency for a considerable number of European countries meant entering a new territory, the authors of the Maastricht Treaty inevitably had to experiment. The dilemma of the authors was that, on the one hand, they knew that unsustainable public finances were harmful to a well-functioning EMU; on the other hand, they did not really know when exactly public finances were on the brink of unsustainability. Be that as it may, it is undisputed that, in the longer run, a deficit of 3% can only go in hand with a debt of 60%[34] if there is economic growth of 5%, a rate that seems almost impossible to be reached in present-day Europe. What is more, the euro crisis has shown that complying with the two criteria is not a sufficient safeguard against the threat of sovereign default, like in the case of Ireland and Spain, both of which have relatively low deficit and debt levels before the outbreak of the crisis.[35] It is thus too

11

---

[27] Blanke (2011), p. 411.

[28] Lastra (2015), para 8.53; Herdegen (1998), pp. 27 et seq.

[29] Hattenberger, in Schwarze et al. (2019), Article 126 AEUV para 25.

[30] Häde, in Calliess and Ruffert (2021), Article 126 AEUV para 25.

[31] See, e.g., Adamski (2018), p. 42; De Grauwe (2016), p. 237; Ruiz Almendral (2017), p. 37; Stiglitz (2016), p. 346.

[32] Dittrich (2011), p. 578.

[33] Adamski (2012), p. 1322.

[34] Häde, in Calliess and Ruffert (2021), Article 126 AEUV para 24.

[35] Commission Reflection Paper *on the Deepening of the Economic and Monetary Union*, COM (2017) 291 final, p. 16.

simplistic to depict the euro crisis as being merely caused by the widespread violation of the values enshrined in Article 126.2 TFEU by the euro-area MS.[36]

3. The Excessive Deficit Procedure

3.1. Main Features

3.1.1. Two Sections

12   As mentioned above, the purpose of the EDP is to ensure MS compliance with their obligation under Article 126.1 TFEU, which is elaborated both by primary law and by secondary law. The EDP can be divided into two sections. The first section, governed by Article 126.3–5 TFEU, consists of rules for the Commission to assess whether or not an excessive deficit exists in a certain MS by means of a Commission opinion. Hereafter, the second section of the EDP, governed by Article 126.6–13 TFEU, sets in. While the first section only serves as a kind of preliminary investigation, the second section is construed as **main proceedings**, in which the existence of an excessive deficit is eventually established and remedied.

3.1.2. Role of the Commission

13   Article 126 TFEU ascribes different functions to the Commission and the Council: the Commission acts as the institution in charge of the investigation of possible violations of budgetary discipline, and thus, it takes over the typical role as watchdog. Consequently, the first section of the EDP clearly lies in the hands of the Commission. Also, the second section is pushed forward by the Commission. However, while the Commission has the **right of initiative**[37] in both sections, it lacks the key procedural instrument to safeguard MS compliance with EU law: the right to bring infringement actions under Article 258 TFEU (Article 126.10 TFEU). Simply put, in the EDP, the Commission as watchdog can only bark but not bite.

3.1.3. Role of the Council

14   However, the **decisive acts in this section are taken by the Council**, with the Commission acting as a mere initiator. Owing to the fact that in this system the "responsibility for making the Member States observe budgetary discipline lies essentially with the Council",[38] the well-functioning of the EDP heavily depends on

---

[36] Also see Lastra (2015), para 8.101.
[37] Richter, in Geiger et al. (2015), Article 126 TFEU para 14.
[38] Case C-27/04, *Commission v Council* (ECJ 13 July 2004) para 76.

a Council willing to take the necessary steps to pursue an MS violating Article 126.1 TFEU. Concerning the Council's room for manoeuvre, some authors take the view that this room is limited as the Council acts as a quasi-judicial actor.[39] It is true that the Council is legally bound by primary as well as secondary law, which means that the Council has to decide within the respective deadlines and, more importantly, that the Council—if it takes a decision on the respective Commission initiative—can only resort to criteria legally laid down by law. Yet it has to be stressed that the Council has discretion on whether it will adopt the acts recommended or proposed by the Commission.[40] Thus, the Council's non-adoption cannot be regarded as a violation of primary law.

To sum up, the EDP, as laid down in Article 126 TFEU, is based on the idea that **15** MS compliance with Article 126.1 TFEU can be safeguarded by **peer pressure**. This being said, a problem may arise if not only one MS but a group of MS faces an excessive deficit. In such a situation, there is a danger that measures will not be taken due to coalitions in the Council between MS that have not complied with Article 126.1 TFEU. Such a situation happened in 2003, when **EDP against Germany and France** were pending. Although the Council found an excessive deficit in both procedures,[41] the Council did not want to continue with the next procedural steps as recommended by the Commission. This did not come out of the blue, for commentators had already expressed their doubts concerning the credibility of an EDP being built on peer pressure.[42]

As if that were not enough, in its conclusions, the Council also decided to **16** suspend the EDP and prolong the periods laid down in the Council recommendations already adopted.[43] In the following **annulment procedure**, the ECJ annulled the Council Conclusions because such steps were not foreseen in the EDP as constituted by the Treaty and by Regulation 1467/1997.[44] Although this case made clear that the structure of the EDP is not at the discretion of the Council, it nevertheless showed that the Council has discretion whether or not to follow the Commission recommendations/proposals in this procedure. In brief, the Commission, wanting to press ahead with the EDP, cannot force the Council to adopt acts as recommended/proposed by the Commission. For the adoption of such measures, a qualified majority (QM) in the Council has to be reached.[45]

---

[39] See, e.g., Kempen, in Streinz (2018), Article 126 AEUV para 33, 36, 54.

[40] Case C-27/04, *Commission v Council* (ECJ 13 July 2004) para 80.

[41] Council Decision No. 2003/89/EC *on the existence of an excessive deficit in Germany*, O.J. L 34/16; Council Decision No. 2003/487/EC *on the existence of an excessive deficit in France*, O.J. L 165/29.

[42] Gros (1997), pp. 255 et seq.

[43] Council Conclusions of 25 November 2003, 14492/1/03 REV 1 (en) (Presse 320).

[44] Case C-27/04, *Commission v Council* (ECJ 13 July 2004) para 89 et seqq.

[45] Case C-27/04, *Commission v Council* (ECJ 13 July 2004) para 31.

3.2. Procedural Steps

3.2.1. Commission Report

17 If the Commission comes to the conclusion that an MS does not fulfil either or both of the two deficit criteria (Article 126.2 TFEU), it is obliged[46] ("shall") to prepare a **report** (Article 126.3 (1) sentence 1 TFEU). Article 126.3 sentence 2 TFEU gives interpretative leeway to the Commission, for, when preparing this report, the Commission is obliged to consider "all other relevant factors".[47] Thus, even if the government deficit exceeds the deficit criterion of Article 126.2 TFEU, the Commission can nevertheless arrive at the conclusion that budgetary discipline has not been infringed.[48] As regards these factors, the Treaty requires the Commission to look at the kind of expenditure financed by the government deficit in the respective MS. The Treaty suggests factoring out public debt used for government investment expenditure, which allows the Commission to take the golden rule into consideration.[49] Similarly, the Treaty requires the Commission to take an intertemporal perspective, that is, to look at the development of the medium-term economic and budgetary position of the MS. The relevant factors of Article 126.3 (1) TFEU are developed by secondary law (Article 2.3 of Regulation 1467/1997). In case of a non-violation of the criteria of Article 126.2 TFEU, the Commission can prepare a voluntary report if the Commission assumes a risk of an excessive deficit in a MS (Article 126.3 (2) TFEU).

3.2.2. Opinion of the Economic and Financial Committee

18 The Commission report is to be discussed by the Economic and Financial Committee (EFC), which formulates an opinion on the report (Article 126.4 TFEU) within two weeks of the adoption of the Commission report (Article 3.1 of Regulation 1467/1997). The EFC's opinion serves to safeguard objectivity in the procedure.[50] **The Commission is not bound by the EFC's opinion**, but it has to take the opinion fully into account (Article 3.2 of Regulation 1467/1997) when deciding upon whether or not to advance the procedure.

3.2.3. Opinion of the Commission to the Member State Concerned

19 If the Commission maintains the view that the MS has realised an excessive government deficit, it is obliged ("shall") to address an opinion to the MS concerned

---

[46] Kempen, in Streinz (2018), Article 126 AEUV para 30.
[47] Richter, in Geiger et al. (2015), Article 126 TFEU para 6.
[48] Kempen, in Streinz (2018), Article 126 AEUV para 30.
[49] Kempen, in Streinz (2018), Article 126 AEUV para 30.
[50] Häde, in Calliess and Ruffert (2021), Article 126 AEUV para 37; Kempen, in Streinz (2018), Article 126 AEUV para 31.

(Article 126.5 TFEU). This procedural step has been modified by the Lisbon Treaty, for previously the addressee of the Commission's opinion had been the Council (ex-Article 104.5 TEC). Along with other amendments, this amendment strengthened the position of the Commission at the expense of the Council,[51] which is merely informed of the Commission's opinion. Moreover, Article 126.5 TFEU also establishes a formal contact between the Commission and the MS concerned. This opinion can also be viewed as the **starting point of the EDP**.[52]

3.2.4. The Council's Decision on the Existence of an Excessive Deficit

The EDP lies in the hands of the Council, for it is the Council that decides whether or not an excessive deficit exists by means of a **decision having constitutive effect** (Article 288 (4) TFEU).[53] This is done "after an overall assessment" (Article 126.6 TFEU), a wording that clearly shows that the Council does not only examine MS compliance with the deficit criterion and the debt criterion.[54] Because of this vague terminology,[55] it is submitted that the Council has a considerable margin of appreciation.[56] The strong position of the Council has been slightly weakened by the Lisbon Treaty, for previously (cf. ex-Article 104.6 TEC) the Council acted upon a Commission recommendation and not upon a Commission proposal. As a consequence, the Council can amend a Commission proposal to establish an excessive deficit only by unanimity (Article 293.1 TFEU). However, this does not mean that the Council is obliged to follow such a proposal. In other words, it can still decide that there is no excessive deficit in a certain MS. This decision is to be taken as a rule within four months of the reporting dates for MS (i. e. 1 April and 1 October) (Article 3.3 of Regulation 1467/1997). Except for the decision under Article 126.6 TFEU, the Council acts upon a Commission recommendation (Article 126.13 TFEU).

20

The Council adopts this decision as well as the other acts in the EDP by a **qualified majority**, with the representative of the MS concerned having no right to take part in the voting (Article 126.13 (2) TFEU). This shows that the Treaty construes the EDP as a procedure that is carried out by a group of MS in the Council against a certain MS, which underlines the fact that the EDP functions as a substitute for the non-applicable infringement procedure. Moreover, the Treaty also differentiates between euro-area MS and non-euro-area MS. Pursuant to Article 139.4 point (b) TFEU, the voting rights of the members of the Council

21

---

[51] Häde, in Calliess and Ruffert (2021), Article 126 AEUV para 38.

[52] Häde, in Calliess and Ruffert (2021), Article 126 AEUV para 37. Of a different opinion: Richter, in Geiger et al. (2015), Article 126 TFEU para 9 who regards the preparation of the Commission report (→ para 17) as starting point of the EDP.

[53] Häde, in Calliess and Ruffert (2021), Article 126 AEUV para 41.

[54] Häde, in Calliess and Ruffert (2021), Article 126 AEUV para 40.

[55] See also Dawson (2015), p. 987.

[56] Harden (1999), p. 80; Leino-Sandberg and Salminen (2017), p. 75; of different view: Kempen, in Streinz (2018), Article 126 AEUV para 33.

representing a non-euro-area MS shall be suspended for the adoption of a decision under Article 126.6 TFEU addressed to a euro-area MS. The relevant majority is governed by Article 238.3 point (a) TFEU, according to which a qualified majority requires at least 55% of the members of the Council representing the participating MS, comprising at least 65% of the population of these States.

3.2.5. Procedural Steps for All Member States

22   If the Council has found that an excessive deficit exists, it is obliged ("shall") to make **recommendations to the MS concerned**. This recommendation is based on a Commission recommendation and aimed at remedying the excessive deficit (Article 126.7 sentence 1 TFEU). These recommendations can be qualified as acts under Article 288 (5) TFEU and, therefore, have no legally binding force.[57] As regards the content of these recommendations, it has been argued that they cannot be too detailed, considering that they concern a policy field (i.e. the budgetary policy of an MS) that still falls under MS competence.[58] Irrespective of the fact that such recommendations—lacking legal effects—cannot be the subject of an annulment procedure, there is no reason to assume that the content of such recommendations is limited. Given the fact that Article 126 TFEU refers to all aspects of public revenues and expenditure in the MS, such recommendations, precisely because they are non-binding, can concern all policy fields that have an impact on the public finances in the MS.

23   If there has been no effective action following these recommendations, a further step may be taken: the Council may make its recommendations public. It is believed that this public shaming might pressure the MS into following the Council's recommendation. This is why Article 126.8 TFEU empowers the Council to make its recommendations public if the MS concerned has not followed them within the prescribed period. As with Article 126.6 TFEU, the voting rights of non-euro-area MS are suspended for the Council acts concerning euro-area MS Article 126.7 and 126.8 TFEU (Article 139.4 TFEU). The reason for the **application of Article 126.1–8 TFEU for non-euro-area MS** is that the sustainability of the government financial position is listed as one of the four convergence criteria to be fulfilled before the introduction of the single currency (Article 140.1 second indent TFEU). Such sustainability is defined *ex negativo*, meaning that this criterion is met unless there exists an excessive deficit for this MS pursuant to Article 126.6 TFEU.[59] Article 126 TFEU can be seen as a gatekeeper concerning the accession to the third stage of EMU.[60]

---

[57] Häde, in Calliess and Ruffert (2021), Article 126 AEUV para 45.

[58] Kempen, in Streinz (2018), Article 126 AEUV para 36.

[59] Cf. Italianer (1997), p. 194.

[60] Kempen, in Streinz (2018), Article 126 AEUV para 35.

3.2.6. Further Procedural Steps for Euro-Area Member States

According to Article 139.2 point (b) TFEU, the further stages of the EDP—Article 126.9 and Article 126.11 TFEU—do not apply to non-euro-area MS. These provisions provide for "coercive means of remedying excessive deficits" (Article 139.2 point (b) TFEU). At a closer look, however, only Article 126.11 TFEU might qualify as an act marked by coercion. Article 126.9 (1) TFEU only provides that the Council, based on a Commission recommendation, has the discretion ("may") to give **notice** to the MS still not following the previous Council recommendations to take measures for the deficit reduction. Considering that the Council has already made recommendations aiming at the same objective under Article 126.7 TFEU, Article 126.9 TFEU is basically a mere repetition of the previous Council recommendation, the main difference being that the notice under Article 126.9 (1) TFEU takes the form of a legally binding decision (cf. Article 126.11 sentence 1 TFEU). Article 126.9 (2) TFEU enables the Council to request the MS to submit a report to examine its adjustment efforts.

The measures contained in Article 126.11 TFEU are the **first sanctions in the EDP** as laid down in the Treaty. These sanctions are triggered by an MS's non-compliance with the decision under Article 126.9 (1) TFEU. It must be stressed that it is not possible to change or rearrange the sequence of the steps in the EDP by means of secondary law, for example, by introducing new sanctions in an earlier stage of the EDP ($\rightarrow$ para 20 et seqq.). As regards the sanctions of Article 126.11 TFEU, the Treaty contains an exhaustive enumeration of four measures.[61] These measures do not have to be imposed in consecutive steps ("one or more of the following measures"); that is, the Council does not have to impose the lighter sanctions first before it may resort to the harder ones.[62] Such a decision is to be taken no later than four months after the Council decision under Article 126.9 TFEU (Article 6.2 of Regulation 1467/97).

Pursuant to Article 126.11 (1) first indent TFEU, the MS concerned can be obliged to publish additional information, to be specified by the Council, before issuing bonds and securities. The reasoning behind this measure is to inform the financial markets about the MS's non-compliance with budgetary discipline, hoping that the creditors of the MS concerned may increase the cost of borrowing for this MS. As with Article 125 TFEU, financial markets are considered a tool to enforce budgetary discipline. Similarly, Article 126.11 (1) second indent TFEU aims at a (potential) creditor of the MS concerned. Under this provision, the EIB may be asked by the Council to consider its lending policy concerning the MS concerned, that is, to toughen borrowing conditions. The EIB cannot be obliged to do so by the Council.[63] Article 126.11 (1) third indent TFEU provides for a non-

---

[61] Häde, in Calliess and Ruffert (2021), Article 126 AEUV para 48.

[62] The Council can, for example, also impose several sanctions at a time, see Kempen, in Streinz (2018), Article 126 AEUV para 44.

[63] Häde, in Calliess and Ruffert (2021), Article 126 AEUV para 50.

interest-bearing deposit of the MS concerned. This sum is to be paid back if the excessive deficit has been corrected. The most grievous sanctions are fines governed by Article 126.11 (1) fourth indent TFEU. Unlike deposits, fines imposed are not paid back even if the MS finally has complied with the decision under Article 126.9 (1) TFEU. Considering that fines will even worsen the financial situation of an MS, the efficiency of fines has often been questioned.[64] Being **decisions** under Article 288 (4) TFEU, the Council decisions can be the subject of an annulment procedure (Article 263 TFEU).[65] Unless the MS concerned complies with the sanction decisions, this can be a matter of an infringement procedure because the exception of Article 126.10 TFEU does not apply to Article 126.11 TFEU.[66]

27   Article 126.11 (2) TFEU obliges the President of the Council to **inform the European Parliament** (EP). As with many other provisions in the Chapter "Economic Policy", the EP is not involved in the actual decision-making process for it acts as an observer, which is to be informed only afterwards.

28   If the excessive deficit has ceased to exist, the Council is obliged ("shall") to abrogate the steps already taken, the most important step being the **abrogation** of the decision under Article 126.6 TFEU.

4. The Excessive Deficit Protocol

29   According to Article 126.14 (1) TFEU, further provisions for the implication of the EDP are governed by Protocol (No 12) on the EDP, having also the **rank of primary law** (Article 51 TEU).[67] As the wording of Article 126.14 (1) TFEU indicates, the function of the EDP Protocol is to complement Article 126 TFEU.

30   The EDP Protocol was developed with the Maastricht Treaty and was signed on the same day (7 February 1992). Since then, the EDP Protocol has not been amended. It consists of **four articles**. Interestingly enough, all of these articles deal with the subject of the MS obligations rather than the procedural aspects of the EDP: Article 1 of the EDP Protocol defines the reference values of Article 126.2 TFEU. Article 2 of the EDP Protocol provides for a definition of "government", "deficit", "investment" and "debt". Regarding the scope of the MS obligations under Article 126.1 TFEU, the EDP Protocol thus refers to the ESA. This scope makes it necessary to make sure that all of the general-government sector (ESA 2010), consisting of four subsectors (i.e. central government, regional or local government and social security funds, to the exclusion of commercial operations), complies with the obligations under Article 126 TFEU.

31   This issue is addressed by Article 3 first sentence of the EDP Protocol, which makes the **governments of the MS** responsible under the EDP for the deficits of the

---

[64] See, e.g., Amtenbrink and Repasi (2017), p. 177; De Streel (2014), p. 98.

[65] Kempen, in Streinz (2018), Article 126 AEUV para 56.

[66] Häde, in Calliess and Ruffert (2021), Article 126 AEUV para 59.

[67] Italianer (1997), p. 191; Kempen, in Streinz (2018), Article 126 AEUV para 7.

general-government sector. Considering that the Council, being the main institution for the control of compliance with Article 126.1 TFEU, is comprised of the ministers of the MS able to commit the government of that MS (Article 16.2 TEU), the provision highlights the MS's responsibility toward the complete general-government sector (ESA 2010).[68] Article 3 sentence 2 of the EDP Protocol imposes an obligation ("shall") on MS to have in place national procedures in the budgetary area that would enable them to meet their obligations in this area deriving from the Treaties. This obligation illustrates the regulatory approach followed by the treaties in the field of the budgetary policy of the MS. Although the budgetary discipline of the MS is considered to be of prime importance for the EMU, Article 3 sentence 2 of the EDP Protocol leaves this issue to the MS. Like the prominent role of the Council in the EDP in Articles 126.6 et seqq. TFEU, this shows that the MS have been and still are hesitant about having the Union control their budgetary policies. However, it would go too far to view Article 3 sentence 2 of the EDP Protocol as a shield of MS competencies in the field of budgetary policy against the adoption of EU rules. Pursuant to Article 3 sentence 3 of the EDP Protocol, the MS are subject to reporting requirements concerning their planned and actual deficits and the levels of their debt in order to make sure that the Commission is sufficiently informed about the budgetary situation in each MS.

As with Article 126 TFEU itself, the EDP Protocol positions the Commission as the institution in charge of collecting data relevant for the surveillance of budgetary discipline. For this reason, Article 4 of the EDP Protocol makes the Commission also competent to provide **statistical data** to be used for the application of the EDP Protocol. 32

5. Secondary Law

5.1. The Legal Bases in Article 126.14 TFEU

5.1.1. Article 126.14 (2) TFEU

The EDP Protocol and its content are closely linked to the **special legislative competence** of the Council enshrined in Article 126.14 (2) TFEU. According to this provision, the Council—after consulting the EP and ECB—is competent to "adopt the appropriate provisions which shall then replace the said Protocol". As regards the scope of this competence, it seems convincing that the Council may completely replace the EDP Protocol. In other words, the legislative competence is not limited to the replacement of individual provisions in the EDP Protocol.[69] It is true that Article 126.14 (2) TFEU makes the Council competent to amend primary 33

---

[68] Italianer (1997), p. 202.

[69] Herrmann (2017), p. 243; taking a different view: Häde, in Calliess and Ruffert (2021), Article 126 AEUV para 72.

law (i.e. the EDP Protocol) by secondary law.[70] However, this does not mean that the said competence has to be interpreted narrowly. The wording ("replace the said Protocol") clearly indicates that the whole EDP Protocol can be changed. Considering that Article 104c TEC-Maastricht (now Article 126 TFEU) and the EDP Protocol were drafted at the same time, one may come to the conclusion that the reason for placing some contents in the EDP Protocol was to simplify the amendment of the parts contained in the EDP Protocol.[71]

34   This being said, the purpose of Article 126.14 (2) TFEU is to **replace the EDP Protocol** completely with secondary law. Consequently, the competence contained in Article 126.14 (2) TFEU is a broad one. For example, it can be used to change the reference values in Article 1 of the EDP Protocol.[72] Doing so, the Council could increase the two values and mitigate the requirements of budgetary discipline. By contrast, Article 126.14 (2) TFEU cannot be used to amend Article 126 TFEU or any other Treaty provisions. Consequently, the Council cannot amend the procedural structure of the EDP as laid down in Articles 126.3 et seqq. TFEU, for example, by including new procedural steps or by amending the voting requirements in the Council.

5.1.2. Article 126.14 (3) TFEU

35   Another competence for the adoption of secondary law by the Council can be found in Article 126.14 (3) TFEU. Unlike Article 126.14 (2) TFEU, this provision **does not provide for the adoption of legislative acts**. This indicates that the scope of the competence is smaller than the one contained in the previous subparagraph: the Council is competent to elaborate on the EDP provisions. It is not competent to amend them. As with Article 126.14 (3) TFEU, the EP is only consulted before the adoption of the Council act.

5.2. Regulation 1467/97

36   This regulation was adopted on the basis of Article 104c.14 (2) TEC-Maastricht (now Article 126.14 (2) TFEU). However, Regulation 1467/97 did not replace the EDP Protocol. Containing further definitions and provisions to speed up (i.e. deadlines) the EDP, it can be regarded as an elaboration of Article 126 TFEU as well as the EDP Protocol. Together with Regulation 1466/1997[73] and a legally non-binding

---

[70] Hattenberger, in Schwarze et al. (2019), Article 126 AEUV para 66.

[71] Cf. Italianer (1997), p. 191; Kempen, in Streinz (2018), Article 126 AEUV para 57.

[72] Hattenberger, in Schwarze et al. (2019), Article 126 AEUV para 66; Kempen, in Streinz (2018), Article 126 AEUV para 57.

[73] Council Regulation (EC) No 1466/97 *on the strengthening of the surveillance of budgetary positions and the surveillance and coordination of economic policies*, O.J. L 209/1 (1997).

resolution of the European Council,[74] Regulation 1467/1997 forms the **Stability and Growth Pact** (SGP) (→ Article 121 TFEU para 47 et seqq.).[75] Unlike what its title ("Pact") suggests, the SGP is not an agreement between the MS, but it consists of secondary law. It was adopted before the third stage of the EMU (1 January 1999) on the initiative of Germany, which was having doubts as to the efficiency of the Treaty framework to avoid excessive deficits.[76]

After the events taking place in the EDPs against France and Germany in 2003, the requirements in Regulation 1467/1997 were watered down[77] by **Regulation 1056/2005**, which, above all else, extended the deadlines for the Council to decide upon the Commission initiatives.[78] It was only after the outbreak of the euro crisis in spring 2010 that the Council decided to amend Regulation 1467/1997 again. This was done in the context of the so-called **six pack**, which is a package of six Union acts[79] to strengthen the enforcement of the SGP or, better, to restore its effectiveness and credibility.[80] Against the background of the widespread non-observance of Article 126.1 TFEU, the six pack was also an attempt to address some of the design flaws of the EDP.[81] Whether the six pack will succeed to safeguard the budgetary discipline of the MS as well as its general objective of securing the proper functioning of the EMU remains to be seen. More than a few authors doubt that.[82]

One of these acts—Regulation 1177/2011—was adopted to amend Regulation 1467/97.[83] Although being based on Article 126.14 (2) TFEU, Regulation 1177/2011—like its forerunners—does not replace or even change the EDP Protocol but supplements it. Apart from building up the mentioned reference value, Regulation 1177/2011 introduces an **economic dialogue** between the Council, the

37

---

[74] European Council Resolution of 17 June 1997 *on the Stability and Growth Pact*, O.J. C 236/1 (1997).

[75] Kempen, in Streinz (2018), Article 126 AEUV para 9 et seq.

[76] Blanke (2011), p. 409.

[77] Blanke (2012), p. 399; Häde, in Calliess and Ruffert (2021), Article 126 AEUV para 90; Tuori and Tuori (2014), p. 107; Kempen, in Streinz (2018), Article 126 AEUV para 12.

[78] E.g. the deadline for the Council to decide upon sanctions pursuant to paragraph 11 was extended from 10 months to 16 months. See Article 7 of Regulation 1467/97 as amended by Regulation 1156/2005.

[79] Regulation (EU) No 1173/2011 *on the effective enforcement of budgetary surveillance in the euro area*, O.J. L 306/1 (2011); Regulation (EU) No 1174/2011 *on enforcement measures to correct excessive macroeconomic imbalances in the euro area*, O.J. L 306/8 (2011); Council Regulation (EU) No 1175/2011 *amending Council Regulation (EC) No 1466/97*, O.J. L 306/12; Regulation No 1176/2011 *on the prevention and correction of macroeconomic imbalances*, O.J. L 306/5; Council Regulation (EU) No 1177/2011 *amending Regulation (EC) No 1467/97*, O.J. L 306/33 and Council Directive (EU) No 2011/85 *on requirements for budgetary frameworks of the Member States*, O.J. L 306/41.

[80] Hinarejos (2013), p. 1626; Kempen, in Streinz (2018), Article 126 AEUV para 6.

[81] Fabbrini (2017), p. 123.

[82] See in particular Adamski (2018), pp. 59 et seqq.

[83] See Hattenberger, in Schwarze et al. (2019), Article 126 AEUV para 13.

Commission and the EP. This means that the competent committee in the EP may invite the President of the Council, the Commission and, where appropriate, the President of the European Council or the President of the Eurogroup to appear before the committee to discuss selected acts under Article 126 TFEU (e.g. the Council decision under Article 126.6 TFEU) (Article 2a of Regulation 1467/97). This economic dialogue aims at greater transparency and accountability of the steps taken in the EDP and other fields of economic governance.[84] It only brings about better information rights for the EP. Actual decision rights are not conferred on the EP.[85] Furthermore, Regulation 1177/2011 contains new reporting requirements for the MS in the EDP (Article 3.4a and Article 5.1a of Regulation 1467/97) and strengthens the powers of the Commission by introducing **enhanced surveillance missions**, by which the Commission assesses the actual economic situation in the MS (Article 10a.1 of Regulation 1467/97). Such missions can take place if the MS concerned is the subject of a recommendation or notice under Article 126.8 TFEU (Article 10a.2 of Regulation 1467/97). Another innovation can be seen in the involvement of the **European Council** in the EDP, which is to be informed of the Council decisions under Article 126.8 TFEU (Article 4.2 (2) of Regulation 1467/97).

5.3. Regulation 1173/2011

38   Also being a part of the six pack, Regulation 1173/2011 aims to strengthen budgetary surveillance in the euro area. As this purpose suggests, this Regulation only applies to MS whose currency is the euro. Based on **Article 136 TFEU in combination with Article 121.6 TFEU** and being adopted in the ordinary legislative procedure, this Regulation provides for new sanctions in both the MSP (→ Article 121 TFEU para 44 et seqq.) and the EDP.

39   Article 5.1 of Regulation 1173/2011 lays down a sanction foreseen neither in Article 126 TFEU nor in the EDP Protocol. If the Council decides that an excessive deficit exists in a euro-area MS and the Council has already imposed the sanction of a **non-interest-bearing deposit** on this MS in the MSP, the Commission shall recommend that the Council, by a further decision, shall require the MS concerned to lodge with the Commission a non-interest-bearing deposit amounting to 0.2% of its GDP in the preceding year. On top of that, this Council decision is adopted by means of **reverse majority voting** (RMV) in the Council; that is, the Commission recommendation is considered to be followed by the Council, unless the Council decides by a qualified majority not to do so. Pursuant to Article 5.2 of Regulation 1173/2011, the Council decision shall be deemed to be adopted by the Council unless it decides by a QM to reject the Commission's recommendation within ten days of the Commission's adoption thereof.

---

[84] De la Parra (2017), p. 118.
[85] Fasone (2014), p. 184.

Similarly, Article 6.1 of Regulation 1173/2011 lays down a **fine** amounting to 0.2% of the MS's GDP in the preceding year if the Council decides pursuant to Article 126.8 TFEU that no effective action has been taken. Again, this decision is based on a Commission recommendation and is to be taken by an RMV. That is, the decision shall be deemed to be adopted by the Council unless it decides by a qualified majority to reject the Commission's recommendation within ten days of the Commission's adoption thereof.[86]

40

Articles 5 and 6 of Regulation 1173/2011 **violate primary law**: as mentioned above, Regulation 1173/2011 is based on Article 136 TFEU in combination with Article 121.6 TFEU and not on Article 126.14 (2) or (3) TFEU, although Articles 5 and 6 of Regulation 1173/2011 contain provisions for the EDP. Against this background, it has to be pointed out that Article 136.1 TFEU, a provision by which measures to strengthen the budgetary discipline of euro-area MS can be adopted, cannot be combined with Article 126.14 TFEU. Owing to the clear wording of Article 136.1 TFEU ("with the exception of the procedure set out in Article 126 (14) [TFEU]"), the former legal basis cannot be used to adopt secondary legislative acts for the EDP.[87] However, this is done by Articles 5 and 6 of Regulation 1173/2011. In other words, the ordinary legislator resorted to Article 121.6 TFEU not only to adopt provisions for the procedure governed by Article 121 TFEU (i.e. the MSP) but also for the EDP, although the latter is governed by Article 126 TFEU and the EDP Protocol. Moreover, Articles 5 and 6 of Regulation 1173/2011 could not have been adopted on the basis of Article 126.14 (2) or (3) TFEU either. Article 126.14 (2) TFEU cannot be used to amend Article 126 TFEU and the procedural steps of the EDP laid down therein (→ para 34).[88]

41

As regards RMV, this voting mechanism, doubtlessly, will strengthen the position of the **Commission** at the expense of the Council's position.[89] This is also interpreted as a measure to promote the supranational element to the detriment of the intergovernmental element.[90]

42

It is recalled that already before the outbreak of the euro crisis, many commentators have championed a bigger say of the Commission in the EDP.[91] Yet it has been argued that **RMV conflicts with EU primary law**, the main reason being that Article 136 TFEU in combination with Article 121.6 TFEU does not confer the power to deviate from the general system for the voting in the Council, which does

43

---

[86] Article 6.2 of Regulation 1173/2011.

[87] Cf. Tuori and Tuori (2014), pp. 170 et seq.

[88] This is even more so with regard to Article 126.14 (3) TFEU.

[89] See, e.g., Blanke (2011), p. 412; Savage and Verdun (2016), pp. 114 et seq.; Smits (2017), pp. 53 et seqq.; De Streel (2014), p. 101.

[90] Armstrong (2014), p. 74.

[91] Louis (2007), p. 29.

44 not provide for RMV. The fact that RMV is only applicable to Council acts under secondary law does change this finding.[92]

44 The **efficiency of the EDP** is heavily dependent on the data reported by the MS. As the example of Greece shows, these data may not always be—to say the least—reliable. For this purpose, Article 8 of Regulation 1173/2011 introduces sanctions concerning the manipulation of statistics. These sanctions (i.e. fines of up to 0.2% of the GDP of the MS concerned)[93] are imposed by the Council on an MS intentionally or, by serious negligence, misrepresenting deficit and debt data relevant for the application of Articles 121 and 126 TFEU or the EDP Protocol. Article 8 of Regulation 1173/2011 does not introduce a new procedural step in the EDP or MSP, but the provision serves to safeguard these procedures, and unlike the new secondary sanctions for the EDP ($\rightarrow$ para 39 et seqq.), there have already been some incidents in which MS were sanctioned on the basis of Article 8 of Regulation 1173/2011.[94] Article 8 of Regulation 1173/2011 is compatible with primary law,[95] for by means of Article 136 TFEU in combination with Article 121.6 TFEU, the EP and Council can adopt legislation in order to elaborate on the information obligation of the MS under Article 121.4 (2) TFEU. Unlike Articles 5 et seqq. of Regulation 1173/2011, Article 8 of Regulation 1173/2011 does not supplement or, better, amend the EDP itself, a measure that is excluded from the scope of Article 136 TFEU, owing to the clear exemption of the procedure set out in Article 126 (14) TFEU.

5.4. The Budgetary Framework Directive

45 The Budgetary Framework Directive (i.e. Directive 2011/85) is the only directive in the six pack. As its legal form and title suggests, this Directive contains provisions to be transposed into the laws of the MS. Based on Article 126.14 (3) TFEU, the Budgetary Framework Directive is applicable to all MS (Article 8 of Directive 2011/85). The Directive follows a new approach as it lays down **rules for the budgetary framework within the MS** (Article 1 of Directive 2011/85). Therefore, the national ownership of compliance with budgetary discipline shall be strengthened.[96] Interestingly enough, it has hardly ever been questioned[97]

---

[92] Palmstorfer (2014), pp. 193 et seqq.

[93] Article 8.2 of Regulation 1173/2011.

[94] Council Implementing Decision (EU) No 2015/1289 *imposing a fine on Spain for the manipulation of deficit data in the Autonomous Community of Valencia*, O.J. L 198/19 (2015), confirmed by Case C-521/15, *Spain v Council* (CJEU 20 December 2017) para 165. Council Implementing Decision (EU) 2018/818 *imposing a fine on Austria for the manipulation of debt data in Land Salzburg*, O.J. L 137/23 (2018).

[95] Taking a different view: Grimm (2016), pp. 165 et seq.

[96] Recital 1 of Directive 2011/85; also see De Streel (2014), p. 97.

[97] See, however, Grimm (2016), pp. 171 et seq., who considers the Budgetary Framework Directive to be compatible with primary law. See also Keppenne (2014), p. 194.

whether or not the Council may use Article 126.14 (3) TFEU to adopt rules for the budgetary framework in the MS, for the EDP is a procedure taking place at the Union level in the Council. Nevertheless, it can be argued that the Budgetary Framework Directive can be based on Article 126.14 (3) TFEU as its content can be viewed as detailed rules for the MS obligation contained in Article 3 sentence 2 of the EDP Protocol. In other words, the budgetary framework aims to safeguard MS compliance with Article 126.1 TFEU and can, thus, be considered to be detailed rules for the application of Article 3 sentence 2 of the EDP Protocol (Article 126.14 (3) TFEU). This does not mean that the Council may adopt any rule as long as it serves MS compliance with Article 126.1 TFEU. Article 126.14 (3) TFEU relating to Article 3 sentence 2 of the EDP Protocol cannot be used to circumvent or, better, bypass the EDP as laid down in Article 126 TFEU. For this reason, the said legal competence only allows for the adoption of procedural rules in the MS.[98]

It has to be stressed that the Budgetary Framework Directive contains provisions for the elements under Article 121 TFEU, for the numerical rules in order to be put in place by the MS shall also contain a **multiannual fiscal planning horizon** that includes adherence to the MS' medium-term budgetary objective (MTO) (Article 5 point (b) of Directive 2011/85). However, owing to the fact that the MTO ultimately serves the prevention of excessive deficits, it is arguable that also rules concerning the procedural implementation of the MTO in the budgetary laws of the MS are covered by Article 126.14 (3) TFEU relating to Article 3 sentence 2 of the EDP Protocol. **46**

5.5. The "Two Pack"

In May 2013, the two pack, another legal package to reform the EMU, was enacted. It consists of two regulations,[99] both of which were adopted on the basis of Article 136 TFEU in combination with Article 121.6 TFEU (→ Article 121 TFEU para 63 et seqq.). This shows that these regulations only apply to euro-area MS. Regulation 472/2013 introduces a special procedure, i.e. the **enhanced surveillance procedure**.[100] The enhanced surveillance procedure applies to euro-area MS whose financial stability is threatened and/or that have requested or are receiving financial assistance from European (e.g. ESM) or other creditors (e.g. IMF) (Article 1.1 of Regulation 472/2013). The enhanced surveillance procedure is different from the EDP. That is why Regulation 472/2013 also prescribes that **47**

---

[98] See also De Streel (2014), p. 94.
[99] Parliament/Council Regulation (EU) No 472/2013 *on the strengthening of economic and budgetary surveillance of Member States in the euro area experiencing or threatened with serious difficulties with respect to their financial stability*, O.J. L 140/1 (2013); Parliament/Council Regulation (EU) No 473/2013 *on common provisions for monitoring and assessing draft budgetary plans and ensuring the correction of excessive deficit of the Member States in the euro area*, O.J. L 140/11 (2013).
[100] Also see Ioannidis (2016), pp. 1269 et seqq.

during the enhanced surveillance procedure, certain steps in the EDP foreseen in Regulation 1467/97 are not applicable (Article 10.2 of Regulation 472/2013). This raises the question of whether the Council and EP can derogate Regulation 1467/97 and introduce special provisions for euro-area MS by means of Article 136 TFEU in combination with Article 121.6 TFEU. Such a reading of the said competence clauses is to be rejected. As Article 136.1 TFEU clearly states that a combination with Article 126.14 TFEU is not possible, Article 136.1 TFEU combined with Article 121.6 TFEU can also not be used to derogate from provisions adopted under Article 126.14 (2) TFEU.

48   Regulation 473/2013 contains provisions for **monitoring and assessing draft budgetary plans** and ensuring the correction of an excessive deficit of euro-area MS. This suggests that Regulation 473/2013 also contains provisions relating to the EDP: if the Council establishes an excessive deficit (Article 126.6 TFEU), the MS concerned is obliged to present to the Commission and the Council an economic partnership programme describing the policy measures and structural reforms that are needed to ensure an effective and lasting correction of the excessive deficit (Article 9.1 of Regulation 473/2013). In the case of a finding under Article 126.6 TFEU, further reporting requirements become applicable to the MS concerned (Article 10.1 of Regulation 472/2013). As shown above, Article 136.1 TFEU cannot be used to adopt provisions that fall under Article 126.14 (2) or (3) TFEU. For this reason, one comes to the conclusion that the provisions on the economic partnership programme and the special reporting requirements could not have been adopted on the basis of Article 136 TFEU combined with Article 121.6 TFEU as these provisions concern details of the EDP and would have had to be based on Article 126.14 (2) TFEU. Be that as it may, these examples show that the Union legislator is willing to make use of Article 136 TFEU and Article 121.6 TFEU to enact provisions for the EDP, a tendency that leads to the fact that the difference between Article 121 TFEU and Article 126 TFEU becomes increasingly blurred.[101]

6. The Declaration on Article 126 TFEU

49   Declaration No. 30 **does not have a legally binding character**. It is only of importance when interpreting Article 126 TFEU.[102] Concerning its content, it is noticeable that the Declaration stresses the importance of economic growth and countercyclical budgetary policy. Therefore, the Declaration can be read as a counterweight to the austerity impetus of Article 126 TFEU and SGP. So far, this Declaration has not gained particular prominence.

---

[101] Armstrong (2013), p. 612; Hattenberger, in Schwarze et al. (2019), Article 126 AEUV para 68.
[102] Häde (2009), p. 205.

7. The Treaty on Stability, Coordination and Governance (TSCG)

The TSCG, often simply referred to as "**Fiscal Compact**",[103] is a treaty under public international law between 25 MS. Like the Treaty on the European Stability Mechanism (TESM), the TSCG is a measure "outside the framework of the Union" (→ Supplement to Title VIII: Fiscal Union para 11 et seqq.; Article 121 TFEU para 66 et seqq.).[104] Yet the TSCG has close links to Article 126 TFEU, for its purpose is to foster the budgetary discipline of the contracting parties (Article 1.1 TSCG). Like the TESM, the TSCG can be seen as a tool to complement EU law.[105] Owing to its strong links to fields covered by EU law, it is also referred to as "satellite treaty".[106] From the perspective of EU law, the MS can conclude such treaties provided that the respective issues fall under MS competencies and that the MS do not violate or disregard their duty to comply with EU law.[107]

50

Although the debt brake (Article 3 TSCG), the main provision of the TSCG, can be regarded as a stricter MTO and, therefore, as a provision closer to Article 121 TFEU than to Article 126 TFEU, the TFEU also contains a rule that obviously refers to Article 126 TFEU. Pursuant to **Article 7 TSCG**, the contracting parties belonging to the euro area commit themselves to supporting the Commission proposals/recommendation where it considers that such an MS is in breach of the deficit criterion in the EDP (→ Supplement to Title VIII: Fiscal Union para 45 et seqq.). Only if a QM in the Council is against this that this obligation shall not apply. At first sight, this provision seems like the above cases of RMV. On a closer look, there are two major differences: first, Article 7 TSCG does not alter the voting procedure in the Council. That is, the Council does not decide by an RMV, but a QM needs to be achieved if the Commission recommendation/proposal shall be adopted. However, when deciding in the Council, the euro-area MS are bound ("commit", "obligation") under public international law[108] to adopt the Commission recommendation/proposal unless a QM is reached not to do so. Unlike the RMV in the "six pack", there is no legal fiction that the Council has adopted an act.[109] Second, while RMV in the "six pack" refers to procedural steps introduced by secondary law, the obligation enshrined in Article 7 TSCG refers to Council steps contained in Article 126 TFEU itself, the most prominent being Article 126.6 TFEU. Whereas some authors[110] regard Article 7 TSCG to be compatible

51

---

[103] The Fiscal Compact, consisting of Articles 3–8 TSCG, contains the key provisions of the TSCG.

[104] Case C-370/12, *Pringle* (CJEU 27 November 2012) para 102.

[105] Fischer-Lescano and Oberndorfer (2013), p. 9.

[106] Thym (2017), p. 49.

[107] Case C-370/12, *Pringle* (CJEU 27 November 2012) para 69.

[108] Herrmann (2017), p. 246; Schorkopf (2012), p. 11.

[109] Ortmann (2015), p. 542.

[110] Calliess (2012), p. 108.

with primary law, others assume a violation.[111] Considering that pursuant to Article 126.6 TFEU the Council has discretion whether or not to follow the Commission proposal, a legally binding restriction of this discretion is contrary to the primary law.[112] The fact the contracting parties voluntarily bind themselves does not lead to the compatibility with the EU Treaties,[113] the key issue being that the contracting parties have made a provision that is tantamount to an amendment of Article 126 TFEU.[114] This being said, the salvation clause enshrined in Article 2.2 TSCG comes into play, according to which the TSCG shall apply insofar as it is compatible with the EU Treaties. For this reason, Article 7 TSCG has to be interpreted as a legally non-binding, political obligation. Interpreted as a political obligation, it can be argued that Article 7 TSCG does not infringe EU law.

52   Coming back to the debt brake of **Article 3 TSCG** (→ Supplement to Title VIII: Fiscal Union para 25 et seqq.), it has to be mentioned that in December 2017, the Commission submitted a proposal for a Council directive[115] containing an EU provision similar to Article 3 TSCG.[116] Based on Article 126.14 (2) TFEU, this proposal raises the question of its compatibility with the said competence clause. In principle, it can be argued that the proposed directive—being comparable to the Budgetary Framework Directive—can be based on Article 126.14 (2) TFEU in combination with Article 3 sentence 2 of the EDP Protocol, for this aims at safeguarding MS compliance with Article 126.1 TFEU without amending the ESP as laid down in Article 126 TFEU. As shown above, Article 126.14 (2) TFEU is a broad competence. As it allows for the replacement of the EDP Protocol, one may conclude that it also covers the (less far-reaching) supplementation of it. Furthermore, it can be induced from Article 126.14 (3) TFEU that Article 126.14 (2) TFEU allows for more than the adoption of mere details for the application of the EDP Protocol, for the latter measures are already covered by Article 126.14 (3) TFEU. However, given the fact that the proposed directive shall only be applicable to euro-area MS, with the non-euro-area MS having the right to participate voluntarily,[117] the Commission proposal de facto introduces the directive for euro area MS only. This is problematic from the perspective of Article 136 TFEU, for this provision has to be read in a way that Article 126.14 TFEU can be adopted not for euro-area MS alone but for all MS. Taking the systematic argument seriously, one has to arrive at the conclusion that the differentiation in the Commission proposal is in violation of Article 136.1 TFEU.

---

[111] See, e.g., Tuori and Tuori (2014), p. 177. Questioning the legality Keppenne (2014), p. 203.
[112] Ortmann (2015), pp. 543 et seq.
[113] See, however, Pilz (2012), p. 460.
[114] Cf. Ortmann (2015), pp. 543 et seq.
[115] Proposal for a Council Directive *laying down provisions for strengthening fiscal responsibility and the medium-term budgetary orientation in the Member States*, COM(2017) 824 final.
[116] Cf. COM(2017) 824 final, Article 3 point (a), according to which the MS have to set up a framework of binding and permanent fiscal rules including a medium-term objective in terms of structural balance.
[117] Cf. Article 4 of the proposed Directive.

Article 126. [Prohibition of Excessive Government Deficits]

8. Concluding Remarks

Without a doubt, the EDP as well as the Maastricht framework in general have undergone **considerable changes since 2010**.[118] The EDP has become stricter through the reforms in the course of the euro crisis. Nevertheless, the basic structure of the EDP has not been amended. And still, there is no consensus on the efficiency and necessity of the EDP as such. While some authors take the EDP seriously and regard it as too rigid,[119] others play down and marginalise its importance.[120] Empirical research has shown that the EDP does have significant effects on MS policies.[121] Therefore, it would go too far to simply ignore the EDP. What is more, from a legal point of view, the provisions on the EDP are in force and require compliance.

This being said, the EDP still is a **very lengthy procedure**,[122] which—after the reforms in the last decade—has become even more complicated. This and the fact that the rule of Article 126.1 TFEU contains a lot of ambiguous elements makes compliance to it difficult. This has not changed with the Commission's role having gained prominence.[123] All reforms aside, a sanction under Article 126.11 TFEU has not been imposed yet.[124] More importantly, the institutions have discretion when applying the EDP. Yet what is sure is that the Commission uses its new powers cautiously: in Summer 2016, sanctions on Spain and Portugal were imposed on the basis of Article 6.1 of Regulation 1173/2011. Although this issue was de facto in the hands of the Commission—the sanctions would have been imposed by RMV—the Commission, resorting to an exception enshrined in Article 6.4 of Regulation 1173/2011,[125] decided to recommend the Council to cancel the fine.[126] Again, this shows the discretion the institutions have when applying the EDP and their hesitance to impose sanctions.[127] Tellingly, the Commission has stressed that it will apply the

---

[118] Cf. Amtenbrink (2015), p. 740.

[119] De Grauwe (2016), p. 237.

[120] Adamski (2018), pp. 59 et seqq.

[121] De Jong and Gilbert (2018), pp. 3 et seq.

[122] Baldwin and Wyplosz (2015), p. 437.

[123] Leino and Saarenheimo (2017), p. 181.

[124] This does not necessarily indicate continuous non-compliance with Article 126.1 TFEU.

[125] This provision allows the Commission to reduce the amount of the fine or cancel it on grounds of exceptional economic circumstances or following a reasoned request by the MS concerned. In the case of Spain and Portugal, such requests were made.

[126] Commission press release—*Stability and Growth Pact: fiscal proposals for Spain and Portugal*, IP/16/2625. Council Implementing Decision No. 2017/2350/EU *on imposing a fine on Portugal for failure to take effective action to address an excessive deficit*, O.J. L 336/24 (2017); Council Implementing Decision No. 2017/2351/EU *on imposing a fine on Spain for failure to take effective action to address an excessive deficit*, O.J. L 336/27 (2017).

[127] Unsurprisingly, some authors regard the imposing of sanctions in the reformed SGP to be unlikely. See, e.g., Adamski (2016), p. 190; Moschella (2014), p. 1282.

SGP "not in a dogmatic manner, but with common sense and with the flexibility that we wisely built into the rules".[128]

List of Cases

ECJ 13.07.2004, C-27/04, *Commission v Council*, ECLI:EU:C:2004:436 [cit. in para 14; 16]
CJEU 27.11.2012, C-370/12, *Pringle*, ECLI:EU:C:2012:756 [cit. in para 3; 50]
CJEU 20.12.2017, C-521/15, *Spain v Council*, ECLI:EU:C:2017:982 [cit. in para 44]

References[129]

Adamski, D. (2012). National power games and structural failures in the European macroeconomic governance. *Common Market Law Review, 49*(4), 1319–1364.
Adamski, D. (2016). Economic policy coordination as a game involving economic stability and national sovereignty. *European Law Journal, 22*(2), 180–223.
Adamski, D. (2018). *Redefining European economic integration*. CUP.
Amtenbrink, F. (2015). The metamorphosis of European Economic and Monetary Union. In D. Chalmers & A. Arnull (Eds.), *The Oxford handbook of European Union law* (pp. 719–756). OUP.
Amtenbrink, F., & De Haan, J. (2003). Economic governance in the European Union - Fiscal policy discipline versus flexibility. *Common Market Law Review, 40*(5), 1075–1106.
Amtenbrink, F., & Repasi, R. (2017). Compliance and enforcement in economic policy coordination in EMU. In A. Jakab & D. Kochenov (Eds.), *The enforcement of EU law and values: Ensuring Member States' compliance* (pp. 145–181). OUP.
Armstrong, K. A. (2013). The new governance of EU fiscal discipline. *European Law Review, 38*(5), 601–617.
Armstrong, K. A. (2014). Differentiated economic governance and the reshaping of Dominium law. In M. Adams, F. Fabbrini, & P. Larouche (Eds.), *The constitutionalization of EU budgetary restraints* (pp. 65–83). Hart.
Baldwin, R., & Wyplosz, C. (2015). *The economics of European integration* (5th ed.). McGraw-Hill Education.
Blanke, H.-J. (2011). The European Economic and Monetary Union – Between vulnerability and reform. *International Journal of Public Law and Policy, 1*(4), 402–432.
Blanke, H.-J. (2012). The economic constitution of the European Union. In H.-J. Blanke & S. Mangiameli (Eds.), *The European Union after Lisbon: Constitutional basis, economic order and external action* (pp. 369–419). Springer.
Calliess, C. (2012). From fiscal compact to fiscal union? New rules for the Eurozone. In C. Barnard, M. Gehring, & I. Solanke (Eds.), *The Cambridge yearbook of European legal studies* (Vol. XIV, pp. 101–117). Hart.
Calliess, C., & Ruffert, M. (Eds.). (2021). *EUV/AEUV. Kommentar* (6th ed.). C. H. Beck.
Committee for the Study of Economic and Monetary Union. (1989). *Report on economic and monetary union in the European Economic Community*. Retrieved from http://aei.pitt.edu/1007/1/monetary_delors.pdf

---

[128] Commission speech, *State of the Union Address 2016: Towards a better Europe - a Europe that protects, empowers and defends*, SPEECH/16/3043.

[129] All cited Internet sources of this comment have been accessed on 6 April 2021.

Dawson, M. (2015). The legal and political accountability structure of 'Post-Crisis' EU economic governance. *Journal of Common Market Studies, 53*(5), 976–993.
De Grauwe, P. (2016). *Economics of Monetary Union* (11th ed.). OUP.
De Jong, J., & Gilbert, N. (2018). Fiscal discipline in EMU? Testing the effectiveness of the excessive deficit procedure. *De Nederlandsche Bank working paper*, 607. Retrieved from https://www.dnb.nl/binaries/Working%20paper%20No.%20607_tcm46-379142.pdf
De la Parra, S. (2017). The economic dialogue: An effective accountability mechanism? In L. Daniele, P. Simone, & R. Cisotta (Eds.), *Democracy in the EMU in the aftermath of the crisis* (pp. 101–120). Springer.
De Streel, A. (2013). The evolution of the EU economic governance since the Treaty of Maastricht: An unfinished task. *Maastricht Journal of European and Comparative Law, 20*(3), 336–362.
De Streel, A. (2014). EU fiscal governance and the effectiveness of its reform. In M. Adams, F. Fabbrini, & P. Larouche (Eds.), *The constitutionalization of European budgetary constraints* (pp. 85–104). Hart.
Dittrich, L. (2011). Die Defizitkriterien des Europäischen Primärrechts. *Zeitschrift für Staats- und Europawissenschaften, 9*(4), 574–585.
Fabbrini, F. (2017). The Euro-crisis, EMU and the perils of centralisation. In L. Daniele, P. Simone, & R. Cisotta (Eds.), *Democracy in the EMU in the aftermath of the crisis* (pp. 121–139). Springer.
Fasone, C. (2014). European economic governance and parliamentary representation. What place for the European Parliament? *European Law Journal, 20*(2), 164–185.
Fischer-Lescano, A., & Oberndorfer, L. (2013). Fiskalvertrag und Unionsrecht: Unionsrechtliche Grenzen völkervertraglicher Fiskalregulierung und Organleihe. *Neue Juristische Wochenschrift, 66*(1), 9–14.
Fratianni, M., & von Hagen, J. (1992). *The Monetary System and European Monetary Union*. Westview Press.
Geiger, R., Khan, D.-E., & Kotzur, M. (Eds.). (2015). *European Union Treaties: A Commentary*. C.H. Beck.
Grimm, B. H. (2016). *Zur Reform der Wirtschafts- und Währungsunion nach der Krise: Eine rechtliche Analyse von ESM, sixpack und Fiskalvertrag*. Nomos.
Gros, D. (1997). Towards a credible excessive deficit procedure. In M. Andenas et al. (Eds.), *European Economic and Monetary Union: The Institutional Framework* (pp. 241–256). Kluwer Law International.
Häde, U. (2009). Die Wirtschafts- und Währungsunion im Vertrag von Lissabon. *Europarecht, 44*(2), 200–219.
Häde, U. (2012). The Treaty of Lisbon and the Economic and Monetary Union. In H.-J. Blanke & S. Mangiameli (Eds.), *The European Union after Lisbon: Constitutional basis, economic order and external action* (pp. 421–441). Springer.
Harden, I. (1999). The fiscal constitution of EMU. In P. Beaumont & N. Walker (Eds.), *Legal framework of the single European currency* (pp. 71–93). Hart.
Herdegen, M. J. (1998). Price stability and budgetary restraints in the Economic and Monetary Union: The law as guardian of economic wisdom. *Common Market Law Review, 35*(1), 9–32.
Herrmann, C. (2017). Differentiated integration in the field of economic and monetary policy and the use of '(semi-)extra' Union legal instruments – The case for 'inter se Treaty amendments'. In B. De Witte, A. Ott, & E. Vos (Eds.), *Between flexibility and disintegration: The trajectory of differentiation in EU law* (pp. 237–251). Elgar.
Hinarejos, A. (2013). Fiscal federalism in the European Union: Evolution and future choices for EMU. *Common Market Law Review, 50*(6), 1621–1642.
Ioannidis, M. (2016). Europe's new transformations: How the EU economic constitution changed during the Eurozone crisis. *Common Market Law Review, 53*(5), 1237–1282.

Italianer, A. (1997). The excessive deficit procedure: A legal description. In M. Andenas et al. (Eds.), *European Economic and Monetary Union: The Institutional Framework* (pp. 191–237). Kluwer Law International.

Keppenne, J.-P. (2014). Institutional report. In U. Neergaard, C. Jacqueson, & J. H. Danielsen (Eds.), *The Economic and Monetary Union: Constitutional governance within the EU – The XXVI FIDE Congress in Copenhagen* (pp. 179–257). DJØF Publishing.

Klepzig, M. E. (2015). *Die "Schuldenbremse" im Grundgesetz – Ein Erfolgsmodell?* Duncker & Humblot.

Lastra, R. M. (2015). *International financial and monetary law* (2nd ed.). OUP.

Leino, P., & Saarenheimo, T. (2017). Sovereignty and subordination: On the limits of EU economic policy co-ordination. *European Law Review, 42*(2), 166–189.

Leino-Sandberg, P., & Salminen, J. (2017). A multi-level playing field for economic policy-making: Does EU economic governance have impact? In T. Beukers, B. De Witte, & C. Kilpatrick (Eds.), *Constitutional change through Euro-crisis law* (pp. 68–107). CUP.

Louis, J.-V. (2007). The legal foundations of the SGP in primary and secondary law. In F. Breuss (Ed.), *The stability and growth pact: Experiences and future aspects* (pp. 3–31). Springer.

Moschella, M. (2014). Monitoring macroeconomic imbalances: Is EU surveillance more effective than IMF surveillance? *Journal of Common Market Studies, 52*(6), 1273–1289.

Ortmann, A. (2015). Die Abstimmungsregel im Fiskalvertrag: Kollision von Völker- und Unionsrecht? *Europäische Zeitschrift für Wirtschaftsrecht, 26*(14), 539–543.

Palmstorfer, R. (2014). The reverse majority voting under the 'Six Pack': A bad turn for the Union? *European Law Journal, 20*(2), 186–203.

Pilz, S. (2012). Ein fiskalpolitischer Pakt als Brücke in die Stabilitätsunion? *Wirtschaftsdienst, 92*(7), 457–464.

Pilz, S. (2016). *Der Europäische Stabilitätsmechanismus: Eine neue Stufe der europäischen Integration*. Mohr Siebeck.

Rebhahn, R. (2015). *Solidarität in der Wirtschafts- und Währungsunion – Grundlagen und Grenzen*. Nomos.

Ruffert, M. (2011). The European Debt Crisis and European Union Law. *Common Market Law Review, 48*(6), 1777–1805.

Ruiz Almendral, V. (2017). The European Fiscal Consolidation Legal Framework: Its impact on national fiscal constitutions and parliamentary democracy. In T. Beukers, B. De Witte, & C. Kilpatrick (Eds.), *Constitutional change through Euro-crisis law* (pp. 27–67). CUP.

Savage, J. D., & Verdun, A. (2016). Strengthening the European Commission's budgetary and economic surveillance capacity since Greece and the euro area crisis: A study of five Directorates-General. *Journal of European Public Policy, 23*(1), 101–118.

Schorkopf, F. (2012). Europas politische Verfasstheit im Lichte des Fiskalvertrages. *Zeitschrift für Staats- und Europawissenschaften, 10*(1), 1–29.

Schwarze, J., et al. (Eds.). (2019). *EU-Kommentar* (4th ed.). Nomos.

Smits, R. (2017). From subordinated to prominent: The role of the European Commission in EMU. Reflections on Euro area democracy. In L. Daniele, P. Simone, & R. Cisotta (Eds.), *Democracy in the EMU in the aftermath of the crisis* (pp. 51–72). Springer.

Stiglitz, J. (2016). *The Euro: How a common currency threatens the future of Europe*. W.W. Norton & Company.

Streinz, R. (2018). *EUV/AEUV. Kommentar* (3rd ed.). Beck.

Thym, D. (2017). Competing models for understanding differentiated integration. In B. De Witte, A. Ott, & E. Vos (Eds.), *Between flexibility and disintegration* (pp. 28–75). Elgar.

Tuori, K., & Tuori, K. (2014). *The Eurozone crisis: A constitutional analysis*. CUP.

Van den Bogaert, S., & Borger, V. (2017). Differentiated integration in EMU. In B. De Witte, A. Ott, & E. Vos (Eds.), *Between flexibility and disintegration* (pp. 209–236). Elgar.

van den Noord, P. (2007). Fiscal policies in EMU at the crossroads. In F. Breuss (Ed.), *The stability and growth pact: Experiences and future aspects* (pp. 35–60). Springer.

Chapter 2
Monetary Policy

Article 127 [The European System of Central Banks]
(ex-Article 105 TEC)

1. The primary objective[4] of the European System of Central Banks (hereinafter referred to as "the ESCB") shall be to maintain price stability.[5–9] Without prejudice to the objective of price stability, the ESCB shall support the general economic policies in the Union with a view to contributing to the achievement of the objectives of the Union as laid down in Article 3 of the Treaty on European Union.[10, 11] The ESCB shall act in accordance with the principle of an open market economy with free competition, favouring an efficient allocation of resources, and in compliance with the principles set out in Article 119.[13]
2. The basic tasks[14, 15] to be carried out through the ESCB shall be:
   - to define and implement the monetary policy of the Union,[16–25]
   - to conduct foreign-exchange operations consistent with the provisions of Article 219,[26]
   - to hold and manage the official foreign reserves of the Member States,[27]
   - to promote the smooth operation of payment systems.[28]
3. The third indent of paragraph 2 shall be without prejudice to the holding and management by the governments of Member States of foreign-exchange working balances.
4. The European Central Bank shall be consulted:[40]
   - on any proposed Union act in its fields of competence,
   - by national authorities regarding any draft legislative provision in its fields of competence, but within the limits and under the conditions set out by the Council in accordance with the procedure laid down in Article 129(4).

   The European Central Bank may submit opinions to the appropriate Union institutions, bodies, offices or agencies or to national authorities on matters in its fields of competence.
5. The ESCB shall contribute[31] to the smooth conduct of policies pursued by the competent authorities relating to the prudential supervision of credit institutions and the stability of the financial system.[33]
6. The Council, acting by means of regulations in accordance with a special legislative procedure, may unanimously, and after consulting the European Parliament and the European Central Bank, confer specific tasks[35] upon the European Central Bank concerning policies relating to the prudential supervision of credit institutions and other financial institutions with the exception of insurance undertakings.[32–39]

Contents

1. Overview 1
2. Objectives of the ESCB 4
   - 2.1. Normative Function of Objectives 4
   - 2.2. Price Stability 5
   - 2.3. Support of the General Economic Policies in the Union 10
3. Guiding Principles for ESCB Measures 13
4. Tasks 14
   - 4.1. Normative Function of Tasks 14
   - 4.2. Monetary Policy of the Union 16
     - 4.2.1. Monetary Policy in the Broad Sense vs Monetary Policy in the Narrow Sense 16
     - 4.2.2. Monetary Policy in the Narrow Sense 18
   - 4.3. Foreign Exchange Operations 26
   - 4.4. Official Foreign Reserves of Member States 27
   - 4.5. Smooth Operation of Payment Systems 28
   - 4.6. Collection of Statistical Information 29
   - 4.7. International Cooperation 30
   - 4.8. Prudential Supervision of Credit Institutions 31
     - 4.8.1. Advisory Role 31
     - 4.8.2. Supervisory Role 32
   - 4.9. Advisory Functions 40

List of Cases
References

1. Overview

1 Article 127 TFEU is the **key provision** in Chapter 2, "Monetary Policy", of Title VIII TFEU (Economic and Monetary Policy) for it lays down the objectives (paragraph 1) and tasks (paragraphs 2, 3 and 5) of the European System of Central Banks (ESCB) and the supervisory role of the ECB (paragraph 6).

2 The provision was introduced in the Maastricht Treaty (Article 105.1 TEC-Maastricht). Since then, it has not been amended substantively. The content of Article 127 TFEU is reiterated and, respectively, specified in Protocol No. 4 on the Statute of the ESCB and the ECB (ESCB Statute). More importantly, Article 127 TFEU does not define the **instruments** of the ESCB to carry out its tasks and achieve its objectives. The instruments are contained in the ESCB Statute.

3 Pursuant to Article 139.2 point (c) TFEU, paragraphs 1, 2, 3 and 5 of Article 127 TFEU do not apply to "Member States with a derogation" (i.e. non-euro MS). As a consequence, the said paragraphs only apply to "Member States whose currency is the euro" (cf. Article 139.2 TFEU). Conversely, paragraphs 4 and 6 of Article 127 TFEU also apply to non-euro MS.

2. Objectives of the ESCB

2.1. Normative Function of Objectives

Article 127.1 TFEU defines the objectives to be reached by the actions of the ESCB. Article 127.1 TFEU does not list the measures by which these objectives shall be achieved. The normative function of the objectives is to **govern the use of the measures**, for the latter have to aim at the former being in conformity with Article 127.1 TFEU. In addition, the **proportionality principle** enshrined in Article 5.4 TEU requires that such measures may not exceed what is necessary to achieve the said objectives. However, the objectives as well as the proportionality principle leave a large room for manoeuvre to the Governing Council of the ECB as the relevant decision-making body for the ESCB (cf. Article 12.1 of the ESCB Statute). Inclined to regard unconventional monetary policy operations of the ESCB (→ para 21 et seqq.) as "choices of a technical nature" which involve "forecasts and complex assessments", the CJEU grants "broad discretion"[1] to the ESCB.

4

2.2. Price Stability

Article 127.1 TFEU as well as several other provisions of the Treaties (Articles 119.2, 219.2 and 282.2 TFEU; Article 2 of the ESCB Statute) refer to price stability as the "**primary objective**" of the ESCB. The paramount importance of price stability is due to Germany's position in the negotiations of the Maastricht Treaty, in which it championed an ECB that adopts the German *Bundesbank* model with its stability-oriented monetary policy.[2]

5

Despite its crucial importance, the term "price stability", unlike, for example, "excessive government deficits" (Article 126 TFEU), is defined neither in the TFEU nor in the ESCB Statute.[3] In 1998, the concept was defined by the Governing Council of the ECB as "a year-on-year increase in the Harmonised Index of Consumer Prices (HICP) for the euro area of below 2%. Price stability is to be maintained over the medium term."[4] In 2003, the Governing Council clarified that "it will aim to maintain **inflation rates close to 2% over the medium term**".[5] The

6

---

[1] Case C-62/14, *Gauweiler* (CJEU 16 June 2015) para 68; Case C-493/17, *Weiss* (CJEU 11 December 2018) para 73.
[2] Tuori and Tuori (2014), p. 45; Waldhoff, in Siekmann (2013), Artikel 127 AEUV para 7.
[3] Tuori (2020), para 22.7 et seq. Also see Case C-493/17, *Weiss* (CJEU 11 December 2018) para 55.
[4] ECB, *A stability-oriented monetary policy strategy for the ESCB*, ECB Press release of 13 October 1998.
[5] ECB, *The ECB's monetary policy strategy*, ECB Press release of 8 May 2003.

concept also has a temporal component ("medium term"), which indicates that price stability is achieved even if the HICP for some time exceeds 2%.

7 On 8 July 2021, the Governing Council[6] amended this definition in its new monetary policy strategy (→ Article 119 TFEU para 18). The amendment was twofold: first, by including the costs related to owner-occupied housing in the HICP and, second and even more importantly, by changing the definition of the price stability objective. This target is now to be understood as being symmetric, "meaning that **negative and positive deviations of inflation from the target are equally undesirable**".[7] Given the fact that the Treaty lacks a definition of price stability, one may assume that the Treaty confers on the ESCB some leeway for interpreting this objective, raising the question of where to draw a line for this assessment. The CJEU, drawing the line at a "manifest error of assessment",[8] considered the 2003 definition to be in conformity with the Treaties. Likewise, commentators consider the previous definition to be legal.[9]

8 Considering Article 127.1 TFEU a cornerstone element of the EMU constitution, it seems problematic that the Governing Council not only practically defines the objective to which it is legally committed but also amends a previously chosen definition. It goes without saying that the Governing Council inevitably has to base its measures on its interpretation of the term "price stability". The Treaties (Article 12.1 of the ESCB Statute) enable the Governing Council to "formulate the monetary policy of the Union including, as appropriate, decisions relating to intermediate monetary objectives". Yet this formulation implies that the prime objective as such may not be freely chosen or even amended by the Governing Council. That is, the price stability definition chosen by the Governing Council is only its interpretation of the term and has to be in conformity with primary law. Owing to the technical nature of the term, the expertise of the Governing Council and, more importantly, the fact that the Treaties make the Governing Council the main agent in this field, a **large margin of appreciation** for the latter is in conformity with primary law. But this does not mean that the Treaty allows for the assumption that the meaning of the term "price stability" can be considerably changed over time by the principal agent responsible to pursue this objective.

9 Statistical data reveal that the **ESCB was able to achieve price stability on the whole** since the introduction of the third stage of EMU (1 January 1999).[10] However, the second half of 2021 saw a sharp increase in the euro area's annual

---

[6] ECB, *ECB's Governing Council approves its new monetary policy strategy*, ECB Press release of 8 July 2021.

[7] ECB, *The ECB's monetary policy strategy statement*. Retrieved from https://www.ecb.europa.eu/home/search/review/html/ecb.strategyreview_monpol_strategy_statement.en.html.

[8] Case C-493/17, *Weiss* (CJEU 11 December 2018) para 56.

[9] Thiele (2013), p. 30; Tuori (2020), para 22.14; Waldhoff, in Siekmann (2013), Artikel 127 AEUV para 13; Case C-493/17, *Weiss* (CJEU 11 December 2018) para 56.

[10] See Tuori (2020), para 22.16 et seq.

inflation rate, which culminated with the rate of 4.9% in November 2021.[11] As the ESCB only has to reach its 2% objective over the medium term, this does not necessarily mean that the ESCB has not reached price stability. However, the longer such a situation persists, at some point, one has to come to the conclusion that price stability and, thus, the primary objective of the ESCB have not been realized. Against this background it has to be stressed that the Treaty does not make a difference between the causes of inflation, that is, even if inflation is imported by means of high energy prices, the ESCB has to pursue the objective of price stability, irrespective of the fact that this might have negative effects on other economic parameters. This issue could be brought to the CJEU either by a preliminary reference procedure or an action for failure to act. Hereby, the action for failure to act seems to be a more promising candidate.

2.3. Support of the General Economic Policies in the Union

From the fact that Article 127.1 first sentence TFEU refers to a "primary objective", it can be concluded that the provision also contains a **secondary objective**.[12] This secondary objective can be found in Article 127.1 second sentence TFEU. This sentence has to be read against the background of the first sentence of Article 127.1 TFEU. It acknowledges that—apart from price stability—there are also other objectives for ESCB measures. Making use of Article 127.1 sentence 2 TFEU, ESCB measures do not need to aim at price stability. However, the measures must not be detrimental to price stability ("without prejudice").[13]

10

The scope of Article 127.1 sentence 2 TFEU is broad.[14] As regards these objectives, the provision refers to Article 3 TEU, a provision that encompasses a large variety of EU objectives, that is, not only those with an economic background. As Article 127.1 TFEU is embedded in Title VIII TFEU (Economic and Monetary Policy) and refers to the "general economic policies in the Union" as the object of ESCB support, one may conclude that it may only support **objectives of an economic nature**. The term "general economic policies in the Union" is only used here in the Treaties. It does not inform about the actor(s) of such policies, which backs the argument that also MS' actions—if they are in conformity with EU measures—can be supported.[15] Owing to the fact that it does not expressly refer to Chapter 1 (Economic Policy) of Title VIII and does not contain the same wording, Article 127.1 sentence 2 TFEU is not limited to the support of actions taken under

11

---

[11] Eurostat, *Inflation in the euro area*. Retrieved from https://ec.europa.eu/eurostat/statistics-explained/index.php?title=Inflation_in_the_euro_area.

[12] Selmayr, in von der Groeben et al. (2015), Artikel 127 AEUV para 7.

[13] Häde, in Calliess and Ruffert (2022), Artikel 127 AEUV para 5.

[14] Amtenbrink (2019), p. 169.

[15] Häde, in Calliess and Ruffert (2022), Artikel 127 AEUV para 5.

Chapter 1. For example, also actions taken under Title XX of the TFEU (Environment) are covered, in so far as they refer to economic aspects.

12   According to the wording ("the ESCB shall support"), the provision confers a **supportive role** on the ESCB.[16] This does not mean that the ESCB is restricted to a mere advisory role for other actors (EU institutions and MS). Instead, the ESCB may make use of the instruments provided for in its Statute.[17] The supportive nature is expressed by the fact that the ECB itself does not define the respective EU policy. Therefore, the primary agent for the said policies is not the ECB and, respectively, the ESCB but a different EU institution or the MS (→ Article 119 TFEU para 28).

3. Guiding Principles for ESCB Measures

13   Article 127.1 sentence 3 TFEU commits the ESCB to a set of **substantive criteria** framed as principles (→ Article 119 para 39 et seqq.). These are the open-market economy principle (→ Article 120 para 37 et seq.) and the ones contained in Article 119 TFEU (i.e. stable prices, sound public finances and monetary conditions, and a sustainable balance of payments). Those criteria serve as guiding principles rather than objectives for ESCB actions. ESCB actions do not have to aim at those principles, but they have to comply with them. According to the CJEU, the application of the open-market economy principle "calls for complex economic assessments", which leads to a margin of appreciation for the ESCB, the borders of which have not been clarified yet.[18]

4. Tasks

4.1. Normative Function of Tasks

14   The term "tasks" of the **ESCB** describes its **fields of its activities**. Like objectives, the normative role of ESCB tasks is to define and delimit the use of the respective competences. For example, the use of the competence contained in Article 18.1., first indent, of the ESCB Statute is not only bound by the objectives of Article 127.1 TFEU but is also confined to the task or, better, field of "monetary policy of the Union" (Article 127.2, first indent, TFEU, Article 3.1, first indent, of the ESCB Statute; → para 18 set seqq.).

15   Article 127.2 TFEU only lists the most important ESCB tasks (basic tasks). Additional tasks of the ESCB can be found in Articles 127.3 and 127.5 TFEU (Article 9.2 of the ESCB Statute). Apart from that, the Treaties also list the **tasks of**

---

[16] Häde, in Calliess and Ruffert (2022), Artikel 127 AEUV para 5.
[17] Cf. Lamandini et al. (2016), p. 10.
[18] Ohler (2021), p. 66.

the ECB (e.g. Article 127.6 TFEU: prudential supervision of credit institutions and other financial institutions).

4.2. Monetary Policy of the Union

4.2.1. Monetary Policy in the Broad Sense vs Monetary Policy in the Narrow Sense

It is somewhat contradictory that Chapter 2 "Monetary Policy" contains "monetary policy of the Union" and other ESCB tasks. In this respect, the German language version of the Treaty is more nuanced as two different expressions are used (*Währungspolitik* vs *Geldpolitik*), which implies that also the other tasks listed in Article 127.2 TFEU are covered by the EU law concept of monetary policy. This being said, one may propose to differentiate between **monetary policy in the broad sense** (covering all issues contained in Chapter 2 "Monetary Policy") and **monetary policy in the narrow sense** (referring to the issues expressed by Article 127.2, first indent, TFEU). Monetary policy in the broad sense is thus a superordinate concept that includes, but is not limited to, monetary policy in the narrow sense. A similar differentiation can be found in a recent CJEU case, where AG *Pitruzella* considered Article 127.2, first indent, TFEU to be "monetary policy in the strict sense", which is a part of "monetary policy in the broad sense".[19] Though the CJEU has not adapted this terminology, it implicitly followed the opinion of the AG by holding that the monetary policy concept is not confined to Article 127.2, first indent, TFEU, a provision providing for the "operational implementation" of it, but "also entails a regulatory dimension intended to guarantee the status of the euro as the single currency". This finding was based on the wording of Article 119.2 TFEU.[20]

Monetary policy in the broad sense is not identical to the **monetary policy for the MS whose currency is the euro** (Article 3.1 point (c) TFEU). This is due to the fact that Article 139.2 TFEU, generally, makes Chapter 2, "Monetary Policy", also applicable to MS with a derogation (non-euro-area MS). However, by so doing, Article 139.2 TFEU excludes the most important provisions of Chapter 2 from their application to non-euro-area MS. As a result, the provisions on monetary policy in the narrow sense are not applicable to non-euro-area MS (Article 139.2 point (c) TFEU). As regards the category of EU competence for monetary policy not covered by Article 3.1 point (c) TFEU, it can be assumed that these fields fall into the domain of **shared competences**. This follows from Article 4.1 TFEU.[21]

16

17

---

[19] Joined Cases C-422/19 and C-423/19, *Hessischer Rundfunk* (Opinion of AG *Pitruzella* of 29 September 2020) para 57.

[20] Joined Cases C-422/19 and C-423/19, *Hessischer Rundfunk* (CJEU 26 January 2021) para 37 et seq.

[21] Also see Weismann (2021), p. 808.

4.2.2. Monetary Policy in the Narrow Sense

18 What is here referred to as "monetary policy in the narrow sense" is described by the ECB as "the decisions taken by central banks to influence the cost and availability of money in an economy".[22] In a similar vein, authors often describe the concept as the **control of supply and demand in the money market**.[23] This shows that the concept is a rather vague one. What is actually covered by it depends on the legal framework for the respective central bank.[24] Article 127.2, first indent, TFEU shows that the elements of monetary policy in the narrow sense are defined by the ESCB. Correspondingly, Article 12.1. of the ESCB Statute says that the "Governing Council shall formulate the monetary policy of the Union". This is done, in particular, by the **ECB's monetary policy strategy**, the latest version of which was published on 8 July 2021.[25]

19 A key element of monetary policy in the narrow sense is its **singleness**, an element expressed by the notions of "single monetary policy" (Article 119.2 TFEU) and "single currency" (Articles 119.2, 133, 140.3 TFEU; → Article 119 para 13 et seq.). Based on Article 119.2 TFEU, the CJEU has recently held that the concept of "monetary policy" is not confined to operational implementation, as expressed in Article 127.2, first indent, TFEU "but also entails a regulatory dimension intended to guarantee the status of the euro as the single currency".[26] The single currency status and also the price stability objective likewise rule out different rules in the euro-area MS but call for single rules.[27] The singleness element, however, does not require that ESCB government-purchase operations involve the bonds of all euro-area MS but allows for the selective nature of such operations.[28]

20 It is predominantly objectives and instruments that shape, concretize and ultimately define monetary policy in the narrow sense.[29] Talking of instruments, these can be found in Chapter IV of the ESCB Statute, which lists **open-market and credit operations** (Article 18 of the ESCB Statute) and **minimum reserves** (Article 19 of the ESCB Statute). Pursuant to Article 20 of the ESCB Statute, the Governing Council may also use "other operational methods of monetary control as

---

[22] ECB, *What is monetary policy?* Retrieved from https://www.ecb.europa.eu/ecb/educational/explainers/tell-me/html/what-is-monetary-policy.en.html.

[23] See, e.g., Selmayr, in von der Groeben et al. (2015), Artikel 127 AEUV para 12; Kempen, in Streinz (2018), Artikel 127 AEUV para 9. Also see the definition given by Tuori and Tuori (2014), p. 30: "policy conducted by a monetary authority and related to its monopolised right to issue the legal tender of state. Traditionally monetary policy has been conducted through controlling the supply of currency (legal tender)." Also see Ohler (2021), p. 42.

[24] Ohler (2021), p. 42.

[25] ECB, *The ECB's monetary policy strategy statement*, retrieved from https://www.ecb.europa.eu/home/search/review/html/ecb.strategyreview_monpol_strategy_statement.en.html.

[26] Joined Cases C-422/19 and C-423/19, *Hessischer Rundfunk* (CJEU 26 January 2021) para 38.

[27] Joined Cases C-422/19 and C-423/19, *Hessischer Rundfunk* (CJEU 26 January 2021) para 50.

[28] Implicitly held in Case C-62/14, *Gauweiler* (CJEU 16 June 2015) para 55, 89.

[29] Cf. Case C-62/14, *Gauweiler* (CJEU 16 June 2015) para 42.

it sees fit", which shows that the catalogue of instruments can also be expanded. Resorting to, amongst others, Articles 12.1 and 20 of the ESCB Statute, the Governing Council has adopted the ECB Guideline 2015/510[30] on the implementation of the Eurosystem monetary policy framework, which lists in its Article 3.1 the following instruments: open-market operations (point (a)), standing facilities (point (b)) and minimum reserve requirements (point (c)). The function of open-market operations is to steer interest rates, manage the liquidity situation in the financial market and signal the stance of monetary policy.[31] They may serve different functions and may be put into operation by different sub-instruments.[32] Unlike open-market operations, standing facilities can be resorted to on the initiative of the counterparties of the NCB.[33] Minimum reserve requirements for banks mean that they are obliged to hold reserves at accounts with the ECB and NCB.[34]

Starting with the financial crisis (2007), the Governing Council has been resorting more and more to monetary policy measures that differ from the measures used previously. These new and unorthodox measures are referred to as "**non-standard measures**"[35] (NSM) or "**unconventional monetary policy**".[36] NSM were taken in several stages,[37] the first stage being unlimited credit to banks at a fixed interest rate and the expansion of eligible assets qualifying as collateral during the financial crisis. The second stage consisted of the purchase of public bonds in the form of the securities markets programme (SMP) and outright monetary transactions (OMT) during what we may refer to as the "euro crisis". The third stage—addressing a credit crunch and the risk of deflation—consisted of a negative interest rate on the deposit facility, targeted longer term refinancing operations (TLTROs), an asset purchase programme (APP) and forward guidance. Like SMP and OMT, APP also allowed for the purchase of public bonds by means of the public sector purchase programme (PSPP). In 2020, the fourth stage set in. It was marked by the fight against the risks the coronavirus (**COVID-19**) outbreak posed to the monetary policy transmission mechanism and the outlook for the euro area. This is being done by means of the pandemic emergency purchase programme (PEPP). In July 2022, the Governing Council approved the creation of the transmission protection instrument (TPI). TPI was created against the background of the recent widening of euro area sovereign bond yield spreads. TPI means that the Eurosystem may make secondary market purchases of public sector securities issued by MS experiencing a

---

[30] ECB Guideline (EU) 2015/510 *on the implementation of the Eurosystem monetary policy framework* (ECB/2014/60), O.J. L 91/3 (2015).

[31] Article 5.1 of the ECB Guideline 2015/2010.

[32] Article 5.2 and 3 of the ECB Guideline 2015/2010. Cf Tuori (2020) para 22.40 et seqq.

[33] Article 17.1 of the ECB Guideline 2015/2010. Cf Tuori (2020) para 22.51 et seq.

[34] Article 19.1 of the ESCB Statute. Cf. Tuori (2020) para 22.36 et seqq.

[35] ECB, *Monetary policy decisions*. Retrieved from https://www.ecb.europa.eu/mopo/decisions/html/index.en.html.

[36] Tuori (2020) para 22.76 et seqq.

[37] See Ohler (2021), p. 127 et seqq.; Tuori (2020) para 22.76 et seqq.

deterioration in financing conditions not warranted by country-specific fundamentals. Again, this is done for the sake of the effective transmission of monetary policy. In order to be eligible for TPI, MS have to fulfil several criteria belonging to field of "Economic Policy" (Chapter 1): (i) They have to comply with the EU fiscal framework, which requires that they are not subject to an excessive deficit procedure (→ Article 126 TFEU para 12 et seqq.); (ii) they are not subject to a macroeconomic imbalance procedure; (iii) their public debt is sustainable (fiscal sustainability) and (iv) they have sound and sustainable macroeconomic policies, which requires compliance with the commitments submitted in the recovery and reslience plans for the Recovery and Resilience Facility and the Commission's country-specific recommendations in the fiscal sphere under the European Semester.[38] This development shows that we can no longer regard NSM as something temporary as they have been in place and diversified for a period of more than a decade. **NSM even seem to have become the new standard**.

22   Owing to their different features, NSM raise different questions as to their compatibility with the Treaties. So far, the legal debate has focused on the purchase of public bonds by means of SMP, OMT, APP (PSPP), PEPP and, most recently, TPI. The main argument for these measures on part of the ECB was that they were to safeguard **appropriate monetary policy transmission**.[39] This term describes "the assumed process through which monetary policy decisions affect the economy and particularly prices".[40] In brief, the transmission mechanism is the channel by which the ECB reaches the economy.

23   This debate also gave rise to two references from the German Federal Constitutional Court (FCC) to the CJEU for a preliminary ruling, one concerning OMT and the other one concerning PSPP. In *Gauweiler*, the CJEU found OMT to be compatible with the Treaties.[41] Likewise, in *Weiss*, the CJEU found PSPP to be in conformity with the Treaties.[42] Both cases raise the question of how to delimit monetary policy in the narrow sense from Chapter 1, "Economic Policy" (→ Article 120 TFEU para 21 et seqq.). To make this delimitation concerning a specific measure, the CJEU primarily focuses on the objectives of the measure and also on the instruments employed.[43] In both cases, the Court held that the respective measure was ultimately meant to aim at price stability and, thus, considered them to

---

[38] ECB, *The Transmission Protection Instrument*, ECB Press release of 21 July 2022.

[39] ECB, *Technical features of Outright Monetary Transactions*, retrieved from https://www.ecb.europa.eu/press/pr/date/2012/html/pr120906_1.en.html; ECB Decision (EU) 2015/774 *on a secondary markets public sector asset purchase programme* (ECB/2015/10), O.J. L 121/20 (2015).

[40] Tuori (2020) para 22.25.

[41] Case C-62/14, *Gauweiler* (CJEU 16 June 2015).

[42] Case C-493/17, *Weiss* (CJEU 11 December 2018).

[43] Case C-62/14, *Gauweiler* (CJEU 16 June 2015) para 46; Case C-493/17, *Weiss* (CJEU 11 December 2018) para 53.

be covered by Article 127.1 TFEU.[44] The fact that both measures have considerable positive effects on the stability of the euro area as a whole and the financing of the euro-area MS and, thus, on an issue falling under "Economic Policy" is downplayed by the CJEU, holding that such "indirect effects" do not change the monetary policy nature of the respective measure.[45] Therefore, the main issues were the objectives rather than the respective monetary policy instrument, which was in both cases open-market operations (Article 18.1 of the ESCB Statute).[46] Interestingly enough, the CJEU resorted to the **proportionality principle** to restrict the extent to which the ESCB may act to pursue its objectives through the above measures.[47] All in all, the Court is willing to grant "**broad discretion**"[48] to the decision-making bodies (i.e. the Governing Council) of the ECB leading the ESCB, which finds its boundaries in "a **manifest error of assessment**"[49] on part of the ECB.

The approach of the CJEU has been met with strong criticism from the German Federal Constitutional Court (FCC), finding that "the interpretation undertaken by the [CJEU] is not comprehensible from a methodological perspective".[50] The FCC declared the CJEU ruling to be "**simply not comprehensible**"[51] and declared it to be partly "an **ultra-vires act**".[52] The FCC's ruling triggered a fierce debate. As has been shown, the FCC's stance to use the proportionality principle to differentiate monetary policy in the narrow sense from economic policy is not convincing, the main reason being that the proportionality principle restricts the extent of the use of a certain competence, but it cannot be used to differentiate competences or policy areas from each other.[53] This shows that, in this respect, the main restriction for the ECB is to be found in Article 123 TFEU[54] rather than in Articles 127.1 et seq. and Article 18.1 of the ESCB Statute. The ruling of the FCC has led to an infringement

24

---

[44] Case C-62/14, *Gauweiler* (CJEU 16 June 2015) para 49 et seq.; C-493/17, *Weiss* (CJEU 11 December 2018) para 57.

[45] Case C-62/14, *Gauweiler* (CJEU 16 June 2015) para 51 et seq.; C-493/17, *Weiss* (CJEU 11 December 2018) para 59 et seqq.

[46] Case C-62/14, *Gauweiler* (CJEU 16 June 2015) para 54; C-493/17, *Weiss* (CJEU 11 December 2018) para 69.

[47] Case C-62/14, *Gauweiler* (CJEU 16 June 2015) para 66 et seqq.; C-493/17, *Weiss* (CJEU 11 December 2018) para 71 et seqq.

[48] Case C-62/14, *Gauweiler* (CJEU 16 June 2015) para 68; C-493/17, *Weiss* (CJEU 11 December 2018) para 24, 73 (emphasis added).

[49] Case C-62/14, *Gauweiler* (CJEU 16 June 2015) para 74; C-493/17, *Weiss* (CJEU 11 December 2018) para 24 (emphasis added).

[50] German FCC, 2 BvR 859/15 and others, *PSPP* (Judgment of 5 May 2020) para 153.

[51] German FCC, 2 BvR 859/15 and others, *PSPP* (Judgment of 5 May 2020) para 116 (emphasis added).

[52] German FCC, 2 BvR 859/15 and others, *PSPP* (Judgment of 5 May 2020) para 119 (emphasis added).

[53] See the discussion in Palmstorfer (2021), p. 272 et seqq; recently also see Häde, in Calliess and Ruffert (2022), Artikel 127 AEUV para 41.

[54] Also see Häde, in Calliess and Ruffert (2022), Artike 127 AEUV para 41.

procedure against Germany, which was closed by the Commission in December 2021 before reaching the CJEU because of Germany's commitments.[55]

25   Considering that also **PEPP** was adopted to safeguard the monetary policy transmission mechanism[56] and, basically, follows the design of previous ECB programmes, there is reason to believe that, measured by the standards of the CJEU, the programme does not violate the Treaties.[57] However, with the scale of the ECB's purchasing programmes, the question of how and where to set the legal boundaries for the ESCB, in particular how to demarcate the concept of monetary policy transmission mechanism, is becoming more and more pressing. Not least, TPI shows that the protection of the monetary policy transmission mechanism has become a magic word used to justify almost any measure, moving the ECB's actions closer to arbitrariness. Doing so, the ECB is also willing to ignore that Chapter 1 ("Economic Policy") provides for two elements to safeguard the budgetary discipline of the MS: Apart from the procedures provided for in Article 121 TFEU (multilateral surveillance procedure), Article 126 TFEU (EDP), it is the financial markets that shall safeguard the budgetary discipline of the MS by making public debts for less fiscally solvent States more expensive. With TPI, the ECB openly refuses to accept the role of financial markets in assessing the country-specific fundamentals. Under this logic, an MS having a policy in compliance with the procedures under Chapter 1 (i.e. EDP) also has sound public finances, irrespective of the markets' assessment. This logic, however, seems at odds with the open market principle (→ Article 120 TFEU para 37–38).

4.3. Foreign Exchange Operations

26   Article 127.2, second indent, TFEU is concretized by Article 23 of the ESCB Statute, pursuant to which the ECB and NCBs may carry out a **series of operations with foreign exchange assets**. The latter term is to be understood in a broad fashion, in particular covering—but not being restricted to—foreign currencies.[58] The scope of this competence may be confined by formal agreements on an exchange-rate system for the euro in relation to the currencies of third States concluded by the Council pursuant to Article 219 TFEU.

---

[55] Commission, *December infringements package: key decisions*, INF/21/6201.
[56] ECB Decision *(EU) 2020/440 on a temporary pandemic emergency purchase programme (ECB/2020/17)*, O.J. L 91/1 (2020), Recital 3.
[57] Mooij (2020), p. 716 et seqq; also see Palmstorfer (2021), p. 382 et seq.
[58] Thiele (2020) para 23.2.

4.4. Official Foreign Reserves of Member States

Article 127.2, third indent, TFEU ensures that the ESCB is able to carry out its exchange-rate policy, which requires the buying and selling of foreign reserves.[59] The term **"official foreign reserves of the Member States"** covers their gold reserves, foreign currency holdings and other reserve assets, such as special drawing rights (SDR) and IMF reserve positions.[60] Article 127.2, third indent, TFEU is concretised by Article 127.3 TFEU and Articles 30 et seq. of the ESCB Statute. The NCBs shall provide the ECB with foreign reserve assets (excluding IMF reserve positions and SDR) up to an amount equivalent to 50 billion euros (Article 30.1 of the ESCB Statute), depending on their shares in the ECB's subscribed capital (Article 30.2 of the ESCB Statute). As a result, foreign reserves boil down to foreign currencies and gold reserves.[61] The relevant provisions do not address the issue of who is the owner of the transferred assets. It is to be assumed that it is the MS that keep the ownership of them. This ownership, however, is legally seriously restricted by the ECB's "full right to hold and manage" them (Article 30.1 sentence 3 of the ESCB Statute).[62] The MS' power of disposal of their foreign reserve assets is also limited by Article 31 of the ESCB Statute, a provision dealing with those assets still held by the NCBs. Whilst NCB transactions to fulfil their obligations towards international organisations (e.g. IWF)[63] are allowed without restriction, other transactions above a certain threshold (laid down in the guidelines of the Governing Council, Article 31.3 of the ESCB Statute) need the prior approval of the ECB to ensure consistency with the exchange rate and monetary policies of the Union (Article 31.2 of the ESCB Statute).

4.5. Smooth Operation of Payment Systems

Payment systems can be regarded as a vital element of a single currency and the free movement of capital and payments (Articles 63 et seqq. TFEU).[64] Article 127.2, fourth indent, TFEU (reiterated in Article 3.1 of the ESCB Statute) speaks of the ESCB fostering such system, which implies that the ESCB acts mainly in a coordinative and surveillance function,[65] Article 22 of the ESCB Statute provides for the instruments to achieve this task. Firstly, the ECB and the NCBs may provide

---

[59] Selmayr, in von der Groeben et al. (2015), Artikel 127 AEUV para 21.
[60] Waldhoff, in Siekmann (2013), Artikel 127 AEUV para 49.
[61] Waldhoff, in Siekmann (2013), Artikel 127 AEUV para 50.
[62] Cf. Waldhoff, in Siekmann (2013), Artikel 127 AEUV para 55 et seq.; Kempen, in Streinz (2018), Artikel 127 AEUV para 16; Selmayr, in von der Groeben et al. (2015), Artikel 127 AEUV para 23.
[63] Keller, in Siekmann (2013), Artikel 31 ESZB/EZB-Satzung para 62.
[64] Kempen, in Streinz (2018), Artikel 127 AEUV para 17.
[65] Waldhoff, in Siekmann (2013), Artikel 127 AEUV para 57.

facilities, which can be seen as the basis[66] for **TARGET2** (Trans-European Automated Real-Time Gross Settlement Express Transfer System).[67] TARGET2, which replaced its predecessor system (i.e. TARGET) in 2007,[68] is a system to which NCBs and commercial banks can submit payment orders in euro, where they are processed and settled in central bank money.[69] Secondly, the ECB may adopt regulations to ensure efficient and sound clearing and payment systems within the Union and with other countries. As regards the scope of this competence, the General Court held that the term does not cover all kinds of clearing systems, including those relating to transactions in securities.[70]

4.6. Collection of Statistical Information

29 The task of the ECB to collect statistical information is contained in Article 5 of the ESCB Statute. The **necessary statistical information** shall be collected either from the competent national authorities or directly from economic agents (Article 5.1. of the ESCB Statute), which is to be carried out primarily by the national central banks (Article 5.2. of the ESCB Statute). This task has been specified by a Council Regulation[71] based on Article 5.4. of the ESCB Statute.

4.7. International Cooperation

30 In Articles 138 and 219 TFEU, the Treaty makes the Council the main institution to decide on issues regarding the external representation of the EU.[72] Pursuant to Article 6.2. of the ESCB Statute, the ECB—confined to tasks entrusted to the ESCB (e.g. external operations)—may decide how the ESCB is represented in the field of **international cooperation**.[73] This also includes the participation of the ECB and—with its approval—of the national central banks in international monetary organisations (Article 6.3. ESCB of the Statute).

---

[66] Keller, in Siekmann (2013), Artikel 22 ESZB/EZB-Satzung para 114.

[67] ECB Decision 2007/61/EC *concerning the terms and conditions of TARGET2-ECB (ECB/2007/7)*, O.J. L 237/71 (2007) most recently amended by ECB Decision (EU) 2021/1758 (ECB/2021/43), O.J. L 354/29 (2021).

[68] Kempen, in Streinz (2018), Artikel 127 AEUV para 17.

[69] Concerning the (decentralized) structure of TARGET2, see Athanassiou (2020), para 24.27 et seqq.

[70] T-496/11, *UK v ECB* (GC 4 March 2015) para 99.

[71] Council Regulation No 2533/98 *concerning the collection of statistical information by the European Central Bank*, O.J. L 318/8 (1998), most recently amended by Council Regulation (EU) 2015/373, O.J. L 64/6 (2015).

[72] Kempen, in Streinz (2018), Artikel 127 AEUV para 21.

[73] Kempen, in Streinz (2018), Artikel 127 AEUV para 21.

4.8. Prudential Supervision of Credit Institutions

4.8.1. Advisory Role

The task contained in **Article 127.5 TFEU** (reiterated in Article 3.3. of the ESCB Statute) can be described as a supportive one as the main political agent of the supervision of credit institutions are the MS' authorities.[74] This is also expressed by the instruments foreseen in Article 25.1. of the ESCB Statute, stating that the ECB may offer advice and be consulted on the scope and implementation of Union legislation relating to the prudential supervision of credit institutions and to the stability of the financial system. This clearly shows that the ECB only has an **advisory role**.[75] By means of a regulation adopted on the basis of Article 127.6 TFEU (Article 25.2. of the ESCB Statute), this role may be extended to a genuine supervisory role (→ para 32 et seqq.). As regards NCBs, they are not mentioned in Article 25.1. of the ESCB Statute. Article 127.5 TFEU rather deals with a **task of the ECB** than one of the ESCB.[76] If NCBs fulfil supervisory tasks under national law, they do not act as part of the ESCB, but this activity falls under Article 14.4. of the ESCB Statute.[77]

31

4.8.2. Supervisory Role

The reason for the ECB's advisory role in the domain of the supervision of credit institutions goes back to the drafting of the Maastricht Treaty, when the MS formed two opposing camps regarding the ECB's function in this field. Whilst one group of MS championed a bigger role, the others—fearing for the achievement of price stability—were in favour of a weaker role in this respect. The **political compromise** was that—under primary law—the ECB was confined to an advisory role, with the possibility that this role—by means of secondary law—could be upgraded to a supervisory role.[78] This may be done by means of the Council competence enshrined in Article 127.6 TFEU.

32

As regards the objective of this competence, it is noteworthy that Article 127.6 TFEU and, respectively, the ECB's supervisory role does not aim at price stability. Instead, it aims at the **stability of the financial system** (Article 127.5 TFEU).[79] These objectives may be congruent, but they may also conflict with each other.[80]

33

The political sensitivity of the ECB's supervisory role explains for some special thresholds in Article 127.6 TFEU: deviating from Article 16.3 TEU, the provision

34

---

[74] Kempen, in Streinz (2018), Artikel 127 AEUV para 18.
[75] Selmayr, in von der Groeben et al. (2015), Artikel 127 AEUV para 41.
[76] Weismann (2018), p. 313.
[77] Waldhoff, in Siekmann (2013), Artikel 127 AEUV para 67.
[78] Also see Selmayr, in von der Groeben et al. (2015), Artikel 127 AEUV para 41 et seqq.
[79] Wille, in Geiger et al. (2015), Article 127 TFEU para 11.
[80] Weismann (2018), p. 314; Häde, in Calliess and Ruffert (2022), Article 127 AEUV para 59.

requires **unanimity** in the Council. As Article 127.6 TFEU is not listed in Article 139.2 TFEU, also non-euro-area MS take part in the Council voting. However, ECB acts taken on the basis of such a regulation do not apply to non-euro-area MS because pursuant to Article 139.2 point (e) TFEU, Article 132 TFEU does not apply to them.[81] Owing to the involvement of non-euro-area MS, the competence contained in Article 127.6 TFEU falls not into the category of exclusive competences (Article 3.1 point (c) TFEU) but into one of **shared competences** (Article 4.1 TFEU).[82]

35 The core issue of Article 127.6 TFEU is the scope of the Council's competence. This boils down to the question of what is meant by the term "**specific tasks** (...) concerning policies relating to the prudential supervision". This issue should gain prominence with the emergence of the banking union ($\rightarrow$ para 37 et seq.). Considering that Article 127.5 TFEU, basically, leaves the competence for prudential supervision with the MS' authorities, the term "specific tasks" has to be interpreted in a narrow way. In any case, it **precludes general supervision** done by the ECB.[83] The key issue, however, is where to draw the line between general supervision and **specific supervision**.[84] It is clear that the threshold of general supervision can also be reached, that is, the scope of Article 127.6 TFEU transgressed, if after the regulation has been adopted some parts of supervision still remain with the MS' authorities.[85] The key element to draw this line seems to be the objective of the competence contained in Article 127.6 TFEU (i.e. the stability of the financial system). It can be argued that the Council may make the ECB competent for those aspects of supervision that are only relevant to the stability of the financial system.[86] For this sake, a respective Council regulation may confer the powers on the ECB necessary to fulfil this task. Considering that this objective is rather vague, the Council has a margin of appreciation. Using this competence, the Council has to respect the primary objective of the ESCB (i.e. price stability). The supervisory tasks of the ECB may therefore not impair this objective.

36 Prior to the financial crisis (from 2008 onwards), Article 127.6 TFEU had been a sleeping beauty. In 2010, the ECB was obliged to support the **European Systemic Risk Board** (ESRB) by means of a Secretariat.[87] The role of the ECB is to provide analytical, statistical, logistical and administrative support to the ESRB.[88] Doing so, the ECB itself does not act as a supervisory body.

---

[81] Waldhoff, in Siekmann (2013), Artikel 127 AEUV para 76.

[82] Also see Weismann (2021), p. 808 et seq.

[83] Kempen, in Streinz (2018), Artikel 127 AEUV para 31; Waldhoff, in Siekmann (2013), Artikel 127 AEUV para 72; Weismann (2014), p. 270 et seq.

[84] Also see Häde, in Calliess and Ruffert (2022), Article 127 AEUV para 66.

[85] See, e.g., Weismann (2014), p. 270 et seq.

[86] Also see Ohler (2020), para 37.27.

[87] Council Regulation (EU) No 1096/2010 *conferring specific tasks upon the European Central Bank concerning the functioning of the European Systemic Risk Board*, O.J. L 331/62 (2010).

[88] Article 2 of Council Regulation (EU) No 1096/2010. Cf. Häde, in Calliess and Ruffert (2022), Article 127 AEUV para 61.

With the project of an **EU banking union**, the role of the ECB was to become bigger. The EU banking union consists of three columns: the **single supervisory mechanism** (SSM),[89] the **single resolution mechanism** (SRM)[90] and the—yet not realized—**European deposit insurance scheme** (EDIS). Both the SSM and the SRM were created by a regulation, with the SSM being based on Article 127.6 TFEU and the SRM being based on Article 114 TFEU. 37

The SSM Regulation covers all credit institutions established in the euro-area MS and makes the ECB exclusively competent for the broad scope of supervisory tasks, ranging from the authorisation of these credit institutions to recovery plans.[91] Concerning non-euro-area MS, the SSM Regulation offers the possibility for an opt-in.[92] The SSM consists of the ECB and national competent authorities.[93] The SSM Regulation distinguishes between significant and less significant credit institutions, the supervision of the latter basically being implemented by national authorities.[94] In order to separate the supervisory function of the ECB from its "monetary policy function",[95] that is, monetary policy in the narrow sense, the SSM Regulation provides for a **supervisory board**.[96] 38

Owing to the large scope of tasks conferred upon the ECB by the SSM Regulation, many commentators convincingly take the view that the said regulation is not covered by Article 127.6 TFEU.[97] This is all the more true, considering that, according to the CJEU, also the tasks carried out by the national authorities in the SSM, ultimately, fall into the exclusive competence of the ECB, though being the subject of a "decentralised implementation".[98] 39

4.9. Advisory Functions

The advisory functions of the ECB (Article 4 of the ESCB Statute) are twofold: first, the Treaty provides for the **obligation** of EU institutions and the MS **to consult** 40

---

[89] Council Regulation (EU) No 1024/2013 *conferring specific tasks on the European Central Bank concerning policies relating to the prudential supervision of credit institutions*, O.J. L 287/63 (2013), hereafter referred to as "SSM Regulation".

[90] Parliament/Council Regulation (EU) No 806/2014 *establishing uniform rules and a uniform procedure for the resolution of credit institutions and certain investment firms in the framework of a Single Resolution Mechanism and a Single Resolution Fund*, O.J. L 225/1 (2014).

[91] See Article 1 point (a) through (i) of the SSM Regulation.

[92] Article 7 of the SSM Regulation.

[93] Article 6 of the SSM Regulation.

[94] Article 6.6 of the SSM Regulation; Ioannidis (2020), para 14.44.

[95] Article 25 of the SSM Regulation.

[96] Article 26 of the SSM Regulation.

[97] See, e.g., Kempen, in Streinz (2018), Artikel 127 AEUV para 31; Ohler (2020), para 37.29; Weismann (2014), p. 270 et seq.

[98] Case C-450/17 P, *Landeskreditbank Baden-Württemberg-Förderbank v ECB* (CJEU 8 May 2019) para 49. Also see Häde, in Calliess and Ruffert (2022), Artikel 127 AEUV para 64.

the **ECB** regarding prospective measures in the ECB's fields of competence (Article 127.4 (1) TFEU, Article 4 point (a) of the ESCB Statute); second, the ECB has the **right to submit opinions** to the Union institutions, bodies, offices or agencies or to national authorities on matters within its fields of competence (Article 127.4 (2) TFEU, Article 4 point (b) of the ESCB Statute). This serves to involve the special expertise of the ECB in the respective field.[99] Regarding the consultation obligations, these relate to areas in which the ECB has specific functions. By contrast, anti-fraud law does not belong to these fields.[100]

List of Cases

ECJ/CJEU
ECJ 10.07.2003, C-11/00, *Commission v ECB*, ECLI:EU:C:2003:395 [cit. in para 40]
CJEU 16.06.2015, C-62/14, *Gauweiler*, ECLI:EU:C:2015:400 [cit. in para 4, 19, 20, 23]
CJEU 11.12.2018, C-493/17, *Weiss*, ECLI:EU:C:2018:1000 [cit. in para 4, 6, 7, 23, 24]
CJEU 08.05.2019, C-450/17 P, *Landeskreditbank Baden-Württemberg-Förderbank*, ECLI:EU:C:2019:372 [cit. in para 38]
CJEU 26.06.2021, C-422/19 and C-423/19, *Hessischer Rundfunk*, ECLI:EU:C:2021:63 [cit. in para 16, 19]

GC
GC 15.03.2015, T-496/11, *UK v ECB*, ECLI:EU:T:2015:133 [cit. in para 28]

German Federal Constitutional Court
German FCC 05.05.2020, 2 BvR 859/15 et al., *PSPP* [cit. in para 24]

References[101]

Amtenbrink, F. (2019). The European Central Bank's intricate independence versus accountability conundrum in the post-crisis governance framework. *Maastricht Journal of European and Comparative Law, 26*(1), 165–179.

---

[99] Selmayr, in von der Groeben et al. (2015), Artikel 127 AEUV para 34 et seq.
[100] Case C-11/00, *Commission v ECB* (ECJ 10 July 2003) para 110 et seq.
[101] All Internet sources of this comment have been accessed on 17 August 2022.

Athanassiou, P. L. (2020). Payment systems. In F. Amtenbrink & C. Herrmann (Eds.), *The EU law of Economic and Monetary Union* (pp. 711–735). Oxford University Press.
Calliess, C., & Ruffert, M. (Eds.). (2022). *EUV/AEUV. Kommentar* (6th edn.). C. H. Beck.
Geiger, R., Khan, D.-E., & Kotzur, M. (2015). *European Union Treaties.* C. H. Beck.
Ioannidis, M. (2020). The European Central Bank. In F. Amtenbrink & C. Herrmann (Eds.), *The EU law of Economic and Monetary Union* (pp. 353–388). Oxford University Press.
Lamandini, M., Ramos, D., & Solana, J. (2016). The European Central Bank (ECB) as a catalyst for change in EU law. Part 1: The ECB's mandates. *The Columbia Journal of European Law, 23*(1), 1–53.
Mooij, A. A. M. (2020). The legality of the ECB responses to COVID-19. *European Law Review, 45*(5), 713–731.
Ohler, C. (2020). Banking supervision. In F. Amtenbrink & C. Herrmann (Eds.), *The EU law of Economic and Monetary Union* (pp. 1103–1144). Oxford University Press.
Ohler, C. (2021). *Unkonventionelle Geldpolitik.* Mohr Siebeck.
Palmstorfer, R. (2021). *Die WWU, ihre Krise und Reform: Eine Untersuchung ausgewählter unions- und bundesverfassungsrechtlicher Problemstellungen.* Verlag Österreich.
Siekmann, H. (Ed.). (2013). *EWU-Kommentar.* Mohr-Siebeck.
Streinz, R. (Ed.). (2018). *EUV/AEUV* (3rd ed.). C.H. Beck.
Thiele, A. (2013). *Das Mandat der EZB und die Krise des Euro.* Mohr-Siebeck.
Thiele, A. (2020). Foreign-exchange operations of the ECB and exchange-rate policy. In F. Amtenbrink & C. Herrmann (Eds.), *The EU law of Economic and Monetary Union* (pp. 699–710). Oxford University Press.
Tuori, K. (2020). Monetary policy (objectives and instruments). In F. Amtenbrink & C. Herrmann (Eds.), *The EU law of Economic and Monetary Union* (pp. 615–698). Oxford University Press.
Tuori, K., & Tuori, K. (2014). *The Eurozone crisis: A constitutional analysis.* Cambridge University Press.
von Groeben, H., Schwarze, J., & Hatje, A. (Eds.). (2015). *Europäisches Unionsrecht* (7th ed.). Nomos.
Weismann, P. (2014). Der einheitliche Bankaufsichtsmechanismus (SSM): ein rechtlich problematisches Konstrukt. *Österreichisches Bankarchiv, 62*(4), 265–272.
Weismann, P. (2018). The ECB's Supervisory Board under the Single Supervisory Mechanism (SSM): A comparison with European Agencies. *European Public Law, 24*(2), 311–334.
Weismann, P. (2021). Zur ebenenübergreifenden Verflechtung des Einheitlichen Aufsichtsmechanismus (SSM) aus Sicht des Unions- sowie des österreichischen Rechts. *Zeitschrift für öffentliches Recht, 76*(3), 799–839.

Article 128 [The Euro Currency]
(ex-Article 106 TEC)

1. The European Central Bank shall have the exclusive right to authorise the issue of euro banknotes within the Union.[1] The European Central Bank and the national central banks may issue such notes. The banknotes issued by the European Central Bank and the national central banks shall be the only such notes to have the status of legal tender[3-8] within the Union.[9]
2. Member States may issue[1,2] euro coins subject to approval by the European Central Bank of the volume of the issue.[11] The Council, on a proposal from the Commission and after consulting the European Parliament and the European Central Bank, may adopt measures to harmonise the denominations and technical specifications of all coins intended for circulation to the extent necessary to permit their smooth circulation within the Union.[11,12]

Contents

1. Overview 1
2. Scope 3
   2.1. Legal Tender 3
   2.2. Banknotes 9
   2.3. Coins 11
List of Cases
References

1. Overview

Article 128 TFEU goes back to Article 105a TEC-Maastricht and has not been amended since then. Like Article 133 TFEU (→ Article 133 TFEU para 8), Article 128 TFEU can be seen as a provision to serve the single-currency status of the euro and the singleness of monetary policy.[1] The provision deals with the **legal-tender status** within the Union, governs the **issue of the euro as cash** (i.e. **banknotes and coins**) and ascribes the competences for this issue. In this respect, the provision distinguishes between banknotes and coins. While the issue of banknotes is governed by Article 128.1 TFEU, the issue of coins falls under Article 128.2 TFEU. The issue of banknotes is also governed by Article 16 of the ESCB Statute, which supplements Article 128.1 TFEU. By contrast, the issue of coins is not dealt with in the Statute. Pursuant to Article 139.2 point (d) TFEU, Article 128 TFEU is not applicable to non-euro-area MS.

1

---

[1] Joined Cases C-422/19 and C-423/19, *Hessischer Rundfunk* (CJEU 26 January 2021) para 40, 43.

2   Article 128 TFEU falls into the exclusive competence of the Union (Article 3.1 point (c) TFEU). This qualification does not preclude MS' competences, as can be seen in Article 128.2 TFEU, which makes MS competent for the issue of coins.

2. Scope

2.1. Legal Tender

3   As with many other crucial terms in Chapter 2 (Monetary Policy), the Treaties lack a legal definition of the term **"legal tender"**. Resorting to the ordinary meaning of the term and Recommendation 2010/191,[2] the CJEU in its *Hessischer Rundfunk* ruling, recently followed the definition already proposed in academic literature.[3] The background for this case was a national provision that precluded the payment in cash of a radio and television licence fee to a regional public broadcasting body. Under the said recommendation, legal tender is marked by three elements: (1) mandatory acceptance (2) at full face value and (3) power to discharge from payment obligations.[4] The said CJEU ruling was about the aspect of mandatory acceptance. Concerning this, the CJEU held that currency units having the status of legal tender "cannot generally be refused in settlement of a debt denominated in the same currency unit, at its full face value, with the effect of discharging the debt". Therefore, the status entails "an **obligation in principle** to accept banknotes and coins denominated in euro for payment purposes".[5]

4   Since Article 128 TFEU does not lay down an absolute obligation to accept those banknotes as a means of payment, the MS are still competent to lay down details concerning the use of banknotes for specific payment relationships.[6] As a consequence, **MS may restrict the use of banknotes in payment relationships** as long as this principle obligation of acceptance is not impaired. In its *Hessischer Rundfunk* ruling, the CJEU held that Article 128.1 sentence 3 TFEU does not preclude MS from adopting such provisions provided that certain requirements are met.

5   First, those national provisions do not have "the object or effect of establishing legal rules governing the status of legal tender of such banknotes".[7] This means that the **MS are not allowed to adopt rules defining the elements of status** for the

---

[2] Commission Recommendation 2010/191/EU *on the scope and effects of legal tender of euro banknotes and coins*, O.J. L 83/70 (2010), point 1.
[3] See, e.g., Freimuth, in Siekmann (2013), Artikel 128 AEUV para 78.
[4] Joined Cases C-422/19 and C-423/19, *Hessischer Rundfunk* (CJEU 26 January 2021) para 49 referring to Commission Recommendation 2010/191/EU, point 1.
[5] Joined Cases C-422/19 and C-423/19, *Hessischer Rundfunk* (CJEU 26 January 2021) para 46, 49 (emphasis added).
[6] Joined Cases C-422/19 and C-423/19, *Hessischer Rundfunk* (CJEU 26 January 2021) para 56, 58.
[7] Joined Cases C-422/19 and C-423/19, *Hessischer Rundfunk* (CJEU 26 January 2021) para 78.

Article 128   [The Euro Currency]   745

term is an autonomous concept under EU law requiring a uniform interpretation.[8] Nor are they allowed to define a further currency as legal tender.

Second, MS' legislation may not lead, "in law or in fact, to abolition of those banknotes in particular by calling into question the possibility, as a general rule, of discharging a payment obligation in cash".[9] This pre-emption results from the concept of legal tender, having the inherent quality of discharging debts. 6

Third, such MS' legislation has to serve reasons of **public interest**, and it has to be in conformity with the principle of proportionality.[10] Regarding such reasons, the CJEU held that the provision at stake aims at the prevention of unreasonable expense of the public authorities that could prevent them from providing services cost-effectively, which is in the public interest.[11] 7

The CJEU's approach is to be welcome: at its core, Article 128 TFEU—and also Article 133 TFEU—deal with the issue of the euro banknotes and coins having the status of legal tender within the euro area. This normative concept refers to the **general use of a currency unit** in a currency area as such, and thus, it has legal effects primarily vis-à-vis the Union and the MS. However, it would go too far to assume that this status requires acceptance in all payment relationships for this would principally rule out non-cash payments. 8

2.2. Banknotes

Article 128.1 first sentence TFEU expresses that only the ECB ("exclusive right") is allowed to authorise **the issue of euro banknotes** within the Union. Those banknotes are issued both by the national central banks and the ECB, the latter issuing some 8% of them.[12] Pursuant to Article 128.1 sentence 3 TFEU and Article 16 sentence 3 of the ESCB Statute, only these banknotes have the status of **legal tender**. By contrast, other banknotes are precluded from having this status.[13] According to Article 16 last sentence of the ESCB Statute, the ECB shall respect, as far as possible, existing practices regarding the issue and design of banknotes. 9

In 2020, the ECB published a report about the creation of a **digital euro**. If this digital euro should serve as a kind of digital banknote having the status of legal tender, the report considers Article 128.1 TFEU in conjunction with Article 16 of the ESCB Statute as a possible legal basis.[14] Although this legal basis finds support 10

---

[8] Joined Cases C-422/19 and C-423/19, *Hessischer Rundfunk* (CJEU 26 January 2021) para 45.
[9] Joined Cases C-422/19 and C-423/19, *Hessischer Rundfunk* (CJEU 26 January 2021) para 78.
[10] Joined Cases C-422/19 and C-423/19, *Hessischer Rundfunk* (CJEU 26 January 2021) paras 69, 78.
[11] Joined Cases C-422/19 and C-423/19, *Hessischer Rundfunk* (CJEU 26 January 2021) para 73.
[12] Häde, in Calliess and Ruffert (2022), Artikel 128 AEUV para 6.
[13] Joined Cases C-422/19 and C-423/19, *Hessischer Rundfunk* (CJEU 26 January 2021) para 44. Cf. Wille, in Geiger et al. (2014), Article 128 TFEU para 3.
[14] ECB, *Report on a digital euro (October 2020)*, p. 24. Retrieved from https://www.ecb.europa.eu/pub/pdf/other/Report_on_a_digital_euro~4d7268b458.en.pdf.

in the academic literature,[15] it is nevertheless questionable whether such a digital banknote is covered by the concept of "euro banknotes" under Article 128.1 TFEU.

2.3. Coins

11   Pursuant to Article 128.2 sentence 1 TFEU, it is for the **MS** to **issue coins** provided that they have the approval of the ECB, which decides on the volume of the coin issuance.[16] This shows that MS have a right of coinage and are also competent to lay down rules for this coinage.[17] Making use of the competence contained in Article 128.2 sentence 2 TFEU, the Council created **eight denominations** ranging from 1 cent to 2 euro.[18]

12   This competence refers to all coins intended for circulation, excluding **collector coins**, the creation of the latter being possible though these coins only have the status of legal tender in the issuing MS.[19] By contrast, **circulation coins** (including **commemorative coins**) have the status of legal tender in all euro-area MS.[20]

List of Cases

CJEU 26.01.2021, C-422/19 and C-423/19, 26.6.2021, *Hessischer Rundfunk*, ECLI:EU:C:2021:63 [cit. in para 1, 3–9, 12]

References[21]

Calliess, C., & Ruffert, M. (Eds.). (2022). *EUV/AEUV. Kommentar* (6th ed.). C.H. Beck.
Geiger, R., Kahn, E., & Kotzur, M. (Eds.). (2014). *European Union Treaties: A Commentary*. C.H. Beck.

---

[15] Grünewald et al. (2021), p. 1033 et seqq.

[16] Most recently ECB Decision (EU) 2019/2231 *on the approval of the volume of coin issuance in 2020 (ECB/2019/40)*, O.J. L 333/149 (2019).

[17] Manger-Nestler, in Pechstein et al. (2017), Artikel 133 AEUV para 5; Häde, in Calliess and Ruffert (2022), Artikel 133 AEUV para 8; Griller, in Grabitz et al. (2021), Artikel 129 AEUV para 1 (released in 2013).

[18] Council Regulation (EU) No 729/2014 *on denominations and technical specifications of euro coins intended for circulation*, O.J. 194/1 (2014).

[19] Parliament/Council Regulation (EU) No 651/2012 *on the issuance of euro coins*, O.J. L 201/135 (2012), Article 5. Also see Häde, in Calliess and Ruffert (2022), Artikel 128 AEUV para 11; Papapaschalis, in von der Groeben et al. (2015), Artikel 128 AEUV para 32.

[20] Häde, in Calliess and Ruffert (2022), Artikel 128 AEUV para 12; Papapaschalis, in von der Groeben et al. (2015), Artikel 128 AEUV para 32; Wutscher, in Schwarze et al. (2019), Artikel 128 AEUV para 6. Council Regulation (EC) No 974/98 *on the introduction of the euro*, O.J. L 139/1 (1998), Article 11.

[21] All cited Internet sources have last been consulted on 6 September 2022.

Grabitz, E., Hilf, M., & Nettesheim, M. (Eds.). (2021). *Das Recht der Europäischen Union. Kommentar*, loose leaf (last supplement: 71). C.H. Beck.

Grünewald, S., Zellweger-Gutknecht, C., & Geva, B. (2021). Digital euro and ECB powers. *Common Market Law Review, 58*(4), 1029–1056.

Pechstein, M., Nowak, C., & Häde, U. (2017). *Frankfurter Kommentar zu EUV, GRC und AEUV*. Mohr Siebeck.

Schwarze, J., Becker, U., Hatje, A., & Schoo, J. (Eds.). (2019). *EU-Kommentar* (4th ed.). Nomos.

Siekmann, H. (2013). *EWU-Kommentar*. Mohr Siebeck.

von der Groeben, H., Schwarze, J., & Hatje, A. (Eds.). (2015). *Europäisches Unionsrecht. Kommentar* (7th ed.). Nomos.

Article 129 [Statute of the ESCB]
(ex-Article 107 TEC)

1. The ESCB shall be governed by the decision-making bodies of the European Central Bank which shall be the Governing Council and the Executive Board.[1,2]
2. The Statute of the European System of Central Banks and of the European Central Bank (hereinafter referred to as "the Statute of the ESCB and of the ECB") is laid down in a Protocol annexed to the Treaties.[3]
3. Articles 5.1, 5.2, 5.3, 17, 18, 19.1, 22, 23, 24, 26, 32.2, 32.3, 32.4, 32.6, 33.1(a) and 36 of the Statute of the ESCB and of the ECB may be amended by the European Parliament and the Council, acting in accordance with the ordinary legislative procedure. They shall act either on a recommendation from the European Central Bank and after consulting the Commission or on a proposal from the Commission and after consulting the European Central Bank.[4–7]
4. The Council, either on a proposal from the Commission and after consulting the European Parliament and the European Central Bank or on a recommendation from the European Central Bank and after consulting the European Parliament and the Commission, shall adopt the provisions referred to in Articles 4, 5.4, 19.2, 20, 28.1, 29.2, 30.4 and 34.3 of the Statute of the ESCB and of the ECB.[8,9]

Contents

1. General Issues 1
2. Governing Bodies of the ESCB 2
3. Statute of the ESCB 3
4. Simplified Amendments to the Statute 4
5. Adoption of Provisions Referred to in the Statute 8
References

1. General Issues

Article 129 TFEU is a duplication of provisions—while paragraph 1 is reflected in Article 282.1 and paragraph 2 is reflecting Article 51 TEU, paragraphs 3 and 4 have been mirrored in Articles 40 and 41 of the Statute. Paragraph 4 has been further reflected in substance in Article 282.5 TFEU.

2. Governing Bodies of the ESCB

See comments on Article 282 TFEU (→ Article 282 TFEU para 1 et seq.).

3. Statute of the ESCB

3 The Statute of the European System of Central Banks and of the European Central Bank (hereinafter 'the Statute') is laid down in a Protocol (No. 4) annexed to the Treaties. Under Article 51 TEU, protocols, such as the Statute, are an **integral part of the Treaties**. In addition, the internal organisation of the ECB and its decision-making bodies have been reflected in the ECB Rules of Procedure,[1] adopted by the ECB Governing Council under Article 12.3 of the Statute. The ECB Rules of Procedure are supplemented by the Executive Board Rules of Procedure,[2] the General Council Rules of Procedure,[3] as well as the Rules of Procedure of the Supervisory Board of the ECB,[4] and the rules for the Administrative Board of Review,[5] to name a few.

4. Simplified Amendments to the Statute

4 Under Article 129.3 TFEU, Articles 5.1, 5.2, 5.3, 17, 18, 19.1, 22, 23, 24, 26, 32.2, 32.3, 32.4, 32.6, 33.1(a) and 36 of this Statute may be **amended by the EP and the Council**, acting in accordance with the **ordinary legislative procedure** either on a recommendation[6] from the ECB and after consulting the Commission, or on a proposal from the Commission and after consulting the ECB.

5 In addition to the consultation requirement under Article 40.1 of the Statute, there is also a **consultation** requirement under **Article 40.2** if there is a

---

[1] Decision ECB/2004/2 *adopting the Rules of Procedure of the European Central Bank*, O.J. L 80/33 (2004), as amended.

[2] Decision ECB/1999/7 *concerning the Rules of Procedure of the Executive Board of the European Central Bank*, O.J. L 314/34 (1997).

[3] Decision ECB/2004/12 *adopting the Rules of Procedure of the General Council of the European Central Bank*, O.J. L 230/61 (2004).

[4] *Rules of procedure of the Supervisory Board of the European Central Bank*, O.J. L 182/56 (2014), as amended by *Amendment 1/2014 of 15 December 2014 to the Rules of Procedure of the Supervisory Board of the European Central Bank*, O.J. L 68/88 (2015).

[5] Decision ECB/2014/16 *concerning the establishment of an Administrative Board of Review and its Operating Rules*, O.J. L 175/47 (2014).

[6] A recommendation under Article 40 of the Statute requires a unanimous decision by the Governing Council. The ECB recommendations under the third indents of Article 132.1 TFEU and of Article 34.1 of the Statute are an instrument of legislative initiative which, pursuant to Article 288 TFEU, have no binding force. The use of ECB recommendations has been foreseen in Articles 129.3, 129.4, 289.4 and 292 TFEU as well as in Article 27.1 and Article 40 of the Statute. Pursuant to Article 17.4 of the ECB Rules of Procedure, ECB recommendations shall be adopted by the Governing Council or the Executive Board in their respective domain of competence and shall be signed by the President. It further specifies that the recommendations for secondary Union legislation under Article 41 shall be adopted by the Governing Council. The adoption of recommendations by the General Council is not foreseen in the ECB Rules of Procedure. The General Council can adopt recommendations under Article 43 of the Statute as further stipulated in Article 9.1 of the Rules of Procedure of the General Council, which shall then be signed by the President.

recommendation from the Commission to amend Article 10.2 of the Statute, which would then trigger consultations of the EP and the ECB.[7]

Alternatively, Article 40.2 of the Statute foresees amendment of Article 10.2 upon recommendation from the ECB. Both on the recommendation from the Commission or the ECB, the Council may amend Article 10.2 by acting unanimously, and such amendments shall not enter into force until they are **approved by the MS in accordance with their respective constitutional requirements**.

While both Article 129.3 TFEU and Article 40 of the Statute are silent on this, the Statute is a Protocol annexed to the Treaties and therefore further amendments are subject to the **treaty amendment procedure under Article 48 TEU**. Accordingly, an IGC, the purpose of which is to determine the amendments to be made to the Treaties, must be convened by the President of the Council. If institutional changes in the monetary area are foreseen, the ECB must be consulted. The amendments enter into force after being ratified by all MS in accordance with their respective constitutional requirements.

5. Adoption of Provisions Referred to in the Statute

Article 129.4 TFEU and Article 41 of the Statute provide that the **Council shall**, either on a proposal from the Commission and after consulting the EP and the ECB or on a recommendation from the ECB and after consulting the EP and the Commission, **adopt the provisions** referred to in Article 4 (consultation of the ECB by national authorities regarding any draft legislative provision in the ECB's field of competence), 5.4 (the definition of the natural and legal persons subject to reporting requirements, the confidentiality regime and the appropriate provisions for enforcement), 19.2 (the definition of the basis for minimum reserves required by the ECB and the maximum permissible ratios between those reserves and their basis, as well as the appropriate sanctions in cases of non-compliance), 20 (the scope of any other operational methods of monetary control if they impose obligations on third parties), 28.1 (the limits and conditions applicable to the increases in the ECB's capital), 29.2 (the rules applicable to the statistical data to be used for the application of the key for the ECB's capital subscription), 30.4 (the limits and the conditions applicable to further calls of foreign reserves by the ECB from the NCBs) and 34.3 (the imposition of fines or periodic penalty payments on undertakings for failure to comply with obligations under ECB regulations and decisions) of the Statute.[8]

---

[7] See ECB Opinion CON/00/30 *at the request of the Presidency of the Council of the European Union on a proposal to amend Article 10.2 of the Statute of the European System of Central Banks and of the European Central Bank*, O.J. C 362/13 (2000).

[8] See ECB Opinion CON/2003/5 at the request of the Council of the European Union *on a proposal for a Council decision on the statistical data to be used for the adjustment of the key for subscription to the capital of the European Central Bank*, O.J. C 102/11 (2003).

9   Under Article 127.4, Article 282.5 TFEU and Article 4 point (a) of the Statute, the **ECB can be consulted** on any proposed Union act in its fields of competence, and by national authorities regarding any draft legislative provision in its fields of competence, but within the limits and under the conditions set out by the Council in accordance with the procedure laid down in Article 129.4 TFEU and Article 41 of the Statute.[9] The sixth recital and Articles 3 and 4 of Council Decision 98/415/EC refer to ECB's opinion as a reply to the consultation by national authorities on national draft legislative provisions.

See further comments on Article 282.5 TFEU (→ Article 282 TFEU para 16-24). The consultation duty has been described in detail by *Lambrinoc*,[10] relying among others on the analyses by *Würtz*[11] and *Arda*.[12]

References

Arda, A. (2004). Consulting the European Central Bank. *Euredia*, 111–152.
Lambrinoc, S. E. (2009). The Legal Duty to Consult the European Central Bank - National and EU Consultations. *ECB Legal Working Paper No. 9*.
Würtz, K. (2005). The legal framework applicable to the ECB consultations on proposed Community acts. *Euredia*, 283–328.

---

[9] Such as Council Decision 98/415/EC *on the consultation of the European Central Bank by national authorities regarding draft legislative provisions*, O.J. L 189/42 (1998). Pursuant to Articles 4 and 7 of Protocol (No 15) on certain provisions relating to the United Kingdom of Great Britain and Northern Ireland (now obsolete), such duty of consultation did not apply to the United Kingdom.

[10] See Lambrinoc (2009).

[11] See Würtz (2005).

[12] See Arda (2004).

Article 130 [Independence of Central Banks]
(ex-Article 108 TEC)

When exercising the powers and carrying out the tasks and duties conferred upon them by the Treaties and the Statute of the ESCB and of the ECB,[61–63] neither the European Central Bank,[50,51] nor a national central bank,[52,53] nor any member of their decision-making bodies[54–56] shall seek or take instructions[16–21] from Union institutions, bodies, offices or agencies, from any government of a Member State or from any other body.[57–59] The Union institutions, bodies, offices or agencies and the governments of the Member States[57–59] undertake to respect this principle[4–10] and not to seek to influence[11–46] the members of the decision-making bodies of the European Central Bank or of the national central banks in the performance of their tasks.[61–63]

Contents

1. Overview 1
2. Principle of Independence 4
   2.1. Reasons for Central Bank Independence 7
   2.2. Typology of Central Bank Independence 11
      2.2.1. Institutional Independence 17
      2.2.2. Functional Independence 22
      2.2.3. Financial Independence 25
      2.2.4. Personal Independence 32
      2.2.5. Operational Independence 37
      2.2.6. De Facto Independence 41
3. Institutional Setup 47
   3.1. The ESCB and the Eurosystem 48
      3.1.1. The European Central Bank 50
      3.1.2. The National Central Banks 52
      3.1.3. Members of the Decision-Making Bodies of the ECB and NCBs .. 54
   3.2. Union Institutions, Bodies, Offices or Agencies, Governments of the Member States and Any Other Body 57
4. Limits 60
   4.1. Mandate of the ECB and NCBs 61
   4.2. External Controls 64
   4.3. Principle of Sincere Cooperation 72
5. Democratic Accountability and Transparency 75
List of Cases
References

1. Overview

1 In conjunction with Articles 282 et seq. TFEU and the ESCB Statute (Protocol No. 4), Article 130 TFEU forms the **legal basis for an institutional regime specific for the European Central Bank** (ECB) and the (currently) 27 national central banks (NCBs). Together they constitute the ESCB.

2 The first sentence of Article 130 TFEU defines the requirement, following the **principle of independence**, that neither the ECB, the NCBs, nor any member of their decision-making bodies shall seek or take instructions when exercising the powers and carrying out the tasks and duties conferred upon them by the Treaties and the ESCB Statute. Further, the provision enumerates institutions as well as authorities and refers generically to "any other body" from which they are not allowed to seek or take instructions. The second sentence enumerates the institutions and bodies that are not allowed to even try to influence any member of the decision-making bodies of the ECB or NCBs in the performance of their tasks. Article 130 TFEU determines a "right" and an obligation[1] at the same time: The central banks are first and foremost the guardians of their own independence. At the same time, there is an obligation for third parties, such as national governments, to respect the principle of independence.

3 **Historically**, central bank independence in EU law was—for the first time—introduced by the Maastricht Treaty in 1993[2] in Article 108 of the TEC.[3] The Maastricht Treaty established the ESCB and entrusted it with the task of defining and implementing the monetary policy of the Union, which had been transferred from national to supranational level under the guidance of the ECB. The 2009 Treaty of Lisbon replaced Article 108 TEC with Article 130 TFEU, which added minor updates taking into account the new institutional setting of the Union.

2. Principle of Independence

4 The principle of independence is not generally defined. Article 130 TFEU does not even mention the term "independence". Nevertheless, this article lays down the Union law principle of independence of central banks.[4] Article 7 of the ESCB

---

[1] Pingel (2010), p. 923.

[2] Some authors classify it as a form of constitutionalisation of central bank independence; see Zilioli (2016), p. 134.

[3] For a historical perspective see Snyder (2011), p. 688 et seq.

[4] Zilioli and Selmayr (2000), p. 592; Case C-11/00, *Commission v ECB* (Opinion of AG Jacobs of 3 October 2002) para 150; for the institutional independence regime in EU law, see Kröger (2020), p. 53 et seq.

Statute makes this clear because it repeats the substance of Article 130 TFEU under the heading "Independence". With regard to the ECB, Article 282 TFEU contains additional provisions on its independence.

Articles 130 and 282 TFEU are not the only provisions of the TFEU related to central bank independence. Although in their wording they are not about independence as such, there are TFEU provisions that give effect to or are relevant for the principle of independence. Article 127.1 TFEU and Article 2 of the ESCB Statute determine that the **maintenance of price stability** is the primary objective of the ESCB. This primary objective defines the scope of application of the independence of ESCB central banks. Another relevant provision for central bank independence is the **prohibition of monetary financing** laid down in Article 123 TFEU and Article 21 of the ESCB Statute. Further, Articles 11 and 14.2 of the ESCB Statute provide security of tenure to the members of the decision-making bodies of the ECB and NCBs with the aim of safeguarding their personal independence. All such provisions are tools designed to distance the central banks of the ESCB from undue influence.

The principle of independence is defined in the **Code of Conduct** for high-level ECB Officials[5] applicable to the members of the ECB's Governing Council, Executive Board and Supervisory Board and in the Conditions of Employment for the Staff of the ECB.[6] Furthermore, Part 0 of the ECB **Staff Rules**[7] as regards the ethics framework of the ECB[8] lays down—under the title "Independence" (Part 0.2)—the requirements for, inter alia, the avoidance of conflicts of interest and restrictions as regards receiving gifts or hospitality, restrictions on external activities or post-employment restrictions. In addition, the principle of independence appears in the statutes of the NCBs either by reference to Article 130 TFEU or on its own.

2.1. Reasons for Central Bank Independence

The MS, as the authors of the European Treaties, have chosen to endow the central banks of the ESCB with independence to achieve the goal of maintaining price stability (Article 127.1 TFEU). The Court of Justice of the European Union (CJEU) emphasised that Article 130 TFEU "**is intended to shield the ESCB from all political pressure** in order to enable it effectively to pursue the objectives attributed to its tasks, through the independent exercise of the specific powers conferred

---

[5] Code of Conduct for high-level ECB Officials, O. J. C 89/2 (2019).

[6] Published on the ECB's website, available at https://www.ecb.europa.eu/careers/pdf/conditions_of_employment.pdf.

[7] European Central Bank Staff Rules, available at https://www.ecb.europa.eu/careers/pdf/staff_rules_fixedterm.pdf.

[8] Amendment to the ethics framework of the ECB (This text replaces Part 0 of the ECB Staff Rules as regard the ethics framework of the text published in the Official Journal C 204 of 20 June 2015, p. 3) (2020/C 375/02) of 6 November 2020, O. J. C 375/25 (2020).

on it for that purpose by primary law".[9] This point of view is confirmed by historical documents which show that the mandate of the ECB as an institution with anti-inflationary goals[10] had been a central element in the negotiations of the Treaty of Maastricht.[11] Since Article 130 TFEU also applies to the NCBs, the same observation is true for them, too.

8   The goal of Article 130 TFEU is to protect the ESCB from **undue influence**, in particular by political players whose aims may be at variance from that of price stability.[12] The underlying assumption is that members of political institutions act within the logic of political systems.[13] It could be that their political aims have a higher value for them than price stability. In order to prevent political institutions from interfering with the goal of price stability, the MS decided to separate the central banks of the ESCB from the national governments' fiscal and structural policies, given the inherent **contradiction between government and central bank goals**. In addition, central bank independence is seen as being necessary in order to limit MS' activities that may conflict with the ESCB's aim of price stability.[14]

9   There is also the argument that the independence of central banks is justified by the complex and highly technical area for which they are competent.[15] According to this view, a **central bank's expertise** can only be safeguarded if it can act without being influenced by institutions that do not have such a high degree of expertise in the same area. However, expertise on its own cannot be a justification for central bank independence, in particular because experts can also be influenced in their decisions so-called "capture phenomenon". Expertise is necessary to formulate a decision but does not guarantee that the decision taken is without any undue influence.

10   The question of whether central bank independence is indeed necessary to achieve price stability has preoccupied many economists.[16] Most of them argue that there is a significant correlation between an independent central bank and price stability, while others doubt that an independent central bank is the key for price stability because they point to the fact that independence itself cannot guarantee

---

[9] Case C-62/14, *Gauweiler* (CJEU 16 June 2015) para 40; see, to that effect, Case C-11/00, *Commission v ECB* (CJEU 10 July 2003) para 134.

[10] For an overview of the, not entirely conclusive, empirical evidence on the impact of central bank independence on price stability, see Amtenbrink (1999), pp. 11–17 and 23–26.

[11] See Committee for the study of Economic and Monetary Union, Report on Economic and Monetary Union in the European Community (Delors Report), 17 April 1989, para 32; Ungerer (1997), p. 209 et seq.

[12] Kramer and Hinrichsen (2015), p. 674.

[13] Bini Smaghi (2008), p. 447.

[14] Zilioli, in von der Groeben et al. (2015), Article 130 AEUV para 2.

[15] Case C-62/14, *Gauweiler* (Opinion of AG Cruz Villalón of 14 January 2015) para 109.

[16] See the overview of empirical studies and theoretical approaches in Endler (1998), p. 214 et seq.; also see Thiele (2016), p. 196 et seq. with further references.

Article 130. [Independence of Central Banks]

price stability.[17] However, independence is at least **one major prerequisite to achieve price stability**.

2.2. Typology of Central Bank Independence

Article 130 TFEU encompasses more than a prohibition on various Union and national institutions and bodies to give instructions to or seek to influence an ESCB central bank. The provision establishes a **general Union law principle** of independence of ESCB central banks, which must be interpreted in light of its purpose as well as in conjunction with other provisions of the Treaties and the ESCB Statute. 11

Even though numerous **classifications of central bank independence** have been developed in the legal doctrine,[18] central bank independence may, in general, be subdivided into four different features: **functional, institutional and financial independence** of central banks, as well as **personal independence** of the members of their decision-making bodies. The European Monetary Institute (EMI)—the predecessor of the ECB—already distinguished between these four features.[19] Three of them (functional, institutional and financial independence) are derived from both a literal and a purposive interpretation of Article 130 TFEU and other relevant articles, while the fourth feature, namely personal independence, is mainly attributed to Article 11 and Article 14.2 of the ESCB Statute. 12

In addition, **operational independence** may be seen as a further and complementary characteristic of functional independence in that the central banks have the autonomy to conduct their operations as they see fit for the purpose.[20] The concept of operational independence is also used to designate the independence of central banks when carrying out their prudential supervisory tasks. This feature has become relevant for the ECB in the framework of its supervisory competencies within the Single Supervisory Mechanism (SSM).[21] 13

Regarding the **features of central bank independence**, the EMI made several basic assumptions, which are laid down in the EMI's "Progress Towards Conver- 14

---

[17] See for an overview of critical views on the correlation between independence and price stability Griller, in Grabitz et al. (2021), Article 130 AEUV para 32 et seq. (released in 2013); see also Eijffinger and de Haan (1996).

[18] For an extensive list of features and a combination of features or categories of independence, see Siekmann, in Siekmann (2013), Article 130 AEUV para 44–57.

[19] These features have been used by the EMI and thereafter by the ECB to assess the compatibility of national legislation of the MS with the Treaties and the ESCB Statute as regards central bank independence. They may be used to assess ECB's independence, too.

[20] Scheller (2004), p. 123 et seq.

[21] See Alexander (2016), p. 485 et seq.

gence 1996" Report[22] and the EMI Convergence Report of March 1998.[23] These assumptions were made in relation to the NCBs since they are part of the assessment of the convergence of the MS, but they also apply to the ECB. They are as follows:

- Central bank independence is required when exercising the powers and carrying out the tasks and duties conferred upon the ECB and the NCBs by the Treaties and the ESCB Statute; features of central bank independence should therefore be considered from that perspective.
- Such features should not be seen as a kind of secondary Union legislation going beyond the scope of the Treaties and the ESCB Statute, but as tools to facilitate an assessment of the independence of NCBs.
- Central bank independence is not a matter which can be expressed in arithmetical formulae or applied in a mechanical manner and the independence of individual NCBs should therefore be assessed on a case-by-case basis given that the institutional context in which NCBs operate differs from MS to MS.

15 Over the years, the ECB has refined the analysis of these features of central bank independence in ECB opinions and ECB's Convergence Reports.[24] They have been used as **criteria for the evaluation of central bank independence**.

16 Finally, *de jure* independence, which is the independence conferred on a central bank by law, is only an indication of the degree of independence of a central bank. It is complemented by **de facto independence**, which is equally important as the legal text itself.[25] *De facto* independence refers to circumstances and actions that are not mentioned in the legal text but have an impact on independence. It has been noted that non-legal indices of central bank independence are relevant since the actual degree of central bank independence may also depend on factual circumstances rather than only upon legal provisions.[26] A mismatch between *de facto* and *de jure* independence influences the overall degree of central bank independence, most likely by lowering the overall degree of independence.

---

[22] Published on the ECB's website, available at https://www.ecb.europa.eu/pub/pdf/conrep/cr1996en.pdf.

[23] Published on the ECB's website, available at https://www.ecb.europa.eu/pub/pdf/conrep/cr1998en.pdf.

[24] ECB's Convergence Reports analyse the degree of sustainable economic convergence among MS and include an examination of the compatibility between each MS's national legislation, including the statutes of its NCB, and Articles 130 and 131 TFEU and the ESCB Statute; the ECB regularly publishes opinions about amended legal provisions in the MS which interfere with central bank independence. Available at https://www.ecb.europa.eu/ecb/legal/opinions/html/index.en.html.

[25] Cukierman et al. (1992), p. 353 et seq.

[26] Amtenbrink (1999), pp. 22–23 with further references.

2.2.1. Institutional Independence

The **prohibition on seeking or taking instructions** as well as the prohibition on **17**
trying to influence the central banks of the ESCB when they take or implement decisions for the performance of the tasks conferred upon them by the Treaties are considered features of "institutional independence". Instructions and influence may take various forms. Institutional independence means that it is not possible for political authorities or any other body to approve, suspend, repeal or transfer a decision of a central bank to another institution. Any statutory duty of a central bank to discuss a decision related to its core task as a central bank of the ESCB with political authorities prior to its adoption is incompatible with the principle of institutional independence. Moreover, representatives of a national government or Union institution should not be allowed to vote in meetings of decision-making bodies of central banks of the ESCB on matters concerning the tasks conferred upon the central banks by the Treaties or the ESCB Statute.[27] Any national body should be prohibited from preventing central banks from taking decisions based on legal grounds.[28]

Central bank independence does not mean isolation or absence of cooperation. **18**
Article 130 TFEU does not prohibit the ECB or an NCB from **cooperating with third parties**. But it has to ensure that the decision-making process and the activities regarding monetary policy and the related **tasks entrusted to them are not unduly influenced** by other interests. The CJEU has accepted the idea proposed by Advocate General (AG) *Jacobs* that influence is permitted under specific provisions of the Treaties and prohibited only if it is undue influence. AG *Jacobs* has defined the concept of "undue influence" as an influence that is liable to undermine the ability of the ECB to carry out its tasks effectively with a view to price stability.[29] In this vein, the Treaties allow constructive dialogue with other institutions provided that the independence of the ESCB central banks is not affected by the dialogue. In the MS, the NCBs may carry on such a dialogue with the minister of finance, while at the Union level, the President of the ECB is invited to take part in the meetings of the ECOFIN Council when matters relating to the objectives and tasks of the ESCB are on the agenda (Article 284.2 TFEU). In turn, the President of the ECOFIN Council and also a member of the Commission may participate in the meetings of the Governing Council of the ECB (Article 284.1 TFEU).

The ECB and NCBs must not be incorporated into a hierarchical structure **19**
headed—for example—by a government official or an official of a Union institution. In order to prevent instructions or undue influence, the institutional structure must be separated from other Union institutions and bodies. The fact that central

---

[27] ECB Opinion CON/2014/25 *on the independence of Banka Slovenije*, para 3.

[28] ECB's Convergence Reports have consistently considered such powers of a national body as not compliant with the principle of institutional independence.

[29] Case C-11/00, *Commission v ECB* (Opinion of AG Jacobs of 3 October 2002) para 155; see also Case C-62/14, *Gauweiler* (CJEU 16 June 2015) para 40.

banks have their own **legal personality** is also a manifestation of their institutional independence. Article 35.6 of the ESCB Statute implies that NCBs have a legal personality as it provides that the NCBs can be subject to the jurisdiction of the CJEU.[30] NCBs may be organised in different legal forms. The choice between different forms of organisations, such as State-owned bodies, public institutions and public limited liability companies, is within the MS' competence in a way that is compatible with independence in the sense of Article 130 TFEU. The ECB is a Union institution (Article 13.1 TEU) and has a legal personality (Article 282.3 sentence 1 TFEU and Article 9.1 of the ESCB Statute).

20   **Public criticism and debate** about a central bank's decision is not prohibited under Article 130 TFEU.[31] Members of public institutions can—of course—criticise decisions of central banks as long as they do not put institutional pressure on them.[32] For example, the European Parliament (EP) is not prevented from discussing and assessing the ECB's reports and expressing its own views on the conduct of monetary policy and its relation with other policies. In turn, central banks may decide to react to criticism and publicly present their point of view.

21   Article 130 TFEU is not the only legal provision that safeguards the independence of the central banks of the ESCB. For the ECB, such further safeguards are laid down in **Article 282 TFEU**. For the NCBs, they are laid down in **national law**.

While an **amendment** to Article 282 TFEU would require an amendment to the Treaties, which is extremely difficult because approval by all MS would be necessary, an amendment to national law can be much easier to achieve. Their regulatory framework may be amended by the respective national parliament.[33] This differentiates the degree of the ECB's institutional independence from that of the NCBs'.[34] Since amending the national constitution requires—in general—a more complex and controversial procedure than amending statutory law, the degree of institutional independence is higher in those MS where independence is laid down in their constitution.[35] However, Article 130 TFEU does not require MS to include the independence of their central bank in a constitutional provision. Statutory law is sufficient.[36]

---

[30] Tupits (2012), pp. 20 and 63.

[31] Some authors argue that recommendations and non-binding statements do not infringe the independence of the ECB and the NCBs, see, for example, Häde, in Calliess and Ruffert (2022), Article 130 AEUV para 14.

[32] See also Wutscher, in Schwarze et al. (2019), Article 130 AEUV para 2.

[33] Case C-62/14, *Gauweiler* (Opinion of AG Cruz Villalón of 14 January 2015) para 108.

[34] Sparve (2005), p. 279 et seq.; Zilioli and Selmayr (2007), p. 370 et seq.; van der Sluis (2014), p. 113.

[35] In German law, it is disputed whether the independence of the Bundesbank is laid down in the Constitution because Article 88 of the Basic Law does not explicitly mention the Bundesbank, only the ECB; nonetheless, some authors argue that it is part of the Constitution; see, for example, Kämmerer, in von Münch and Kunig (2021), Article 88 Grundgesetz para 23.

[36] See, for example, Section 2.5 of the Austrian Nationalbankgesetz.

2.2.2. Functional Independence

Functional independence of central banks means the freedom to decide how to achieve the primary objective determined by the legislator. Central banks should have all the **powers, tasks and competencies, as well as the means and instruments** necessary to achieve their primary objective.[37] The ESCB central banks have functional independence; however, they do not have "goal independence" in that they cannot establish their own goal. Their goal is to maintain price stability as established in Article 127.1 TFEU and Article 2 of the ESCB Statute.[38]

The Governing Council of the ECB decides on the scope, timing and execution of the monetary policy operations. In October 1998, the ECB **defined price stability** as "a year-on-year increase in the Harmonised Index of Consumer Prices (HICP) for the euro area of below 2%" and added that price stability "was to be maintained over the medium term". In May 2003, the ECB specified that "in the pursuit of price stability, it aims to maintain inflation rates below but close to 2% over the medium term". In July 2021, following a new monetary policy strategy of the ECB's Governing Council, the ECB redefined price stability. In its monetary policy strategy statement the Governing Council of the ECB confirmed that HICP remains the appropriate price measure for assessing the achievement of the price stability objective, but it added that it considers that price stability is best maintained by aiming for two per cent inflation over the medium term, negative and positive deviations from this target being equally undesirable.[39]

The objectives of the NCBs that are laid down in national law provisions should be defined in a clear and legally certain manner. In the case of multiple objectives, it should be clear that **price stability prevails** over any other objective and that such objective may be pursued only to the extent that price stability is not endangered.[40]

2.2.3. Financial Independence

Financial independence is inherent to a central bank's independence. A financially independent central bank has sufficient financial and qualified human resources at its disposal in order to fulfil its mandate. Two types of financial independence may

---

[37] For example, the ECB has not only monetary policy instruments but also regulatory powers as laid down in Article 132.1 TFEU and Article 34 of the ESCB Statute in order to take the necessary steps for achieving the price stability objective.

[38] According to ECB (2020), p. 21, even though Article 127.1 TFEU is not applicable to MS with a derogation (Article 139.2 point (c) TFEU), Article 42.1 of the ESCB Statute declares that Article 2 of the ESCB Statute is also applicable to MS with a derogation. Moreover, in the view of the ECB, new MS have to comply with the objective of price stability on the day they enter the Union.

[39] ECB, New Monetary Policy Strategy Statement, available at https://www.ecb.europa.eu/home/search/review/html/ecb.strategyreview_monpol_strategy_statement.en.html.

[40] The ESCB central banks have a secondary objective which is set in Article 127.1 sentence 2 TFEU, namely to support the general economic policies in the Union with a view to contributing to the achievement of the objectives of the Union as laid down in Article 3 TEU.

be distinguished: **financing and staffing independence**. As regards financing, the central banks of the ESCB generate their own income through the performance of their monetary policy duties, the management of foreign reserves, fiscal agent services to the government or financial sanctions. The central banks' financial resources are their capital, reserves and profit. The financial resources of the ECB are derived exclusively from contributions of the NCBs and from profit realised out of operations performed by either the ECB or the NCBs. The ECB does not receive any resources from the Union budget. The ECB and NCBs have their own budget, which is separate from the Union and MS budgets, respectively. The budget of the ECB or an NCB should be determined by the central bank alone without interference from third parties and indeed in line with the accounting rules and standards and other applicable legal provisions. Any amendment of rules concerning an NCB's budget has to be initiated and decided in cooperation with the respective NCB.

26   The ECB's independence in the management of its finances is laid down in the third sentence of Article 282.3 TFEU. Further key requirements for the ECB's financial independence are laid down in Articles 28–30 of the ESCB Statute. The **NCBs' financial independence** is protected by provisions in national statutes[41] regarding their capital, accounting rules, independent external audit of their accounts, calculation and distribution of profits.

27   The NCBs are subscribers of the **ECB's capital**, and their monetary income derived from the performance of the ESCB's monetary policy function is allocated in proportion to their paid-up shares in the capital of the ECB at the end of each financial year (Article 32 of the ESCB Statute). The ECB's financial independence is emphasised by the power to draw up its annual accounts "in accordance with the principles established by the Governing Council" (Article 26.2 of the ESCB Statute).

28   Economic theory has not yet determined with precision what **level of central bank capital can be deemed adequate**. Central banks may function with low or negative capital in the short and medium term.[42] Nevertheless, the ECB is of the view that central bank independence would be infringed if the net equity of an NCB were below the level of its statutory capital or even negative for a prolonged period of time and the MS did not recapitalise the NCB.[43]

29   Article 28.1 of the ESCB Statute provides for a mechanism whereby the capital of the ECB may be increased by such amounts as may be decided by the Governing Council acting by the qualified majority provided for in Article 10.3 of the ESCB Statute, within the limits and under the conditions set by the Council under the procedure laid down in Article 41 of the ESCB Statute. Based on the authorisation

---

[41] According to Article 131 TFEU national law provisions must be in line with the financial provisions of the ESCB laid down in Chapter VI of the ESCB Statute. See, for example, Section 8 of the Austrian Nationalbankgesetz.

[42] See Stella (1997), who is of the opinion that central banks may function without capital, as conventionally defined.

[43] ECB (2020), p. 26 et seq.

provided for in Council Regulation (EC) No 1009/2000,[44] the Governing Council of the ECB **increased the ECB's capital in 2010**.[45] In addition, the ECB has the power to request the NCBs to equip the ECB with further financial means (Articles 28.1, 30.4 and 33.2 of the ESCB Statute). However, neither the Treaties nor the ESCB Statute includes the requirement for MS governments to recapitalise the NCBs, even if this were to be necessary for the NCBs to recapitalise the ECB.[46]

Financial independence is also safeguarded by the **prohibition of monetary financing** laid down in Article 123 TFEU (→ Article 123 TFEU para 5) and in Article 21 of the ESCB Statute.[47] These provisions contain the key rule concerning the prohibition on the financing of Union or national public authorities, bodies governed by public law or public undertakings of MS or the direct purchase of debt instruments. If the central banks were allowed to directly buy government bonds, it could not be discounted that governments would put pressure on the central banks to do so in order to receive new financial means. Euro and financial crisis programmes were contested also in this regard (→ para 62). 30

As regards **staffing**, an adequate allocation of human resources must be an element of a central bank's financial independence. Central banks must be able to employ and retain qualified staff in order to perform their complex central banking tasks, subject to a considerable degree of **discretion**, dependent on the national as well as international economic and financial environment. It is suggested that the autonomy of the central banks to manage their own staff is important to ensure that central banks can fulfil their tasks within the necessary time period and by relying on the expertise of their staff members.[48] 31

2.2.4. Personal Independence

The feature of personal independence encompasses rules to ensure that the members of the decision-making bodies of the ECB and NCBs who take decisions on behalf of a central bank, either alone or as part of a collegiate body, can **act without undue influence**. According to the second sentence of Article 130 TFEU, they are not allowed to seek or take instructions in the performance of their tasks. 32

Personal independence also covers the rules on the **term of office** and **removal from office** of members of the decision-making bodies of the ECB and NCBs. 33

---

[44] Council Regulation (EC) No 1009/2000 *concerning capital increases of the ECB*, O.J. L 115/1 (2000).

[45] Decision ECB/2010/26 *on the increase of the ECB's capital*, O.J. L 11/53 (2011).

[46] See also in Milton and Sinclair (2011) who, referring to the ECB's legal provisions on the increase of capital, plead that the national laws on the statutes of the NCBs should provide for a mechanism whereby national governments decide on the limits within which a central bank may decide on an actual increase of its capital.

[47] The avoidance of monetary financing is seen as a justification for central bank independence by Lastra (1997), p. 301.

[48] See ECB (2020), p. 29; ECB Opinion CON/2008/31 *on a legislative proposal amending Law No 312/2004 on the Statute of Banca Națională a României*.

Article 14.2 of the ESCB Statute determines the minimum term of office of a Governor, which is five years,[49] and the conditions for removing a Governor from office. An interpretation of this provision in light of Article 130 TFEU and Article 7 of the ESCB Statute speaks in favour of applying it to any other member of a decision-making body of an NCB involved in the performance of ESCB-related tasks since undue influence by the governments of an MS on any such member is contrary to the principle of independence laid down in Article 130 TFEU.[50]

A Governor can be **relieved from office** only in two possible cases: first, if he no longer fulfils the conditions required for the performance of his duties or, second, if he has been guilty of serious misconduct (Article 14 of the ESCB Statute). These requirements also apply to temporary measures.[51] Many national provisions simply reflect Article 14.2 of the ESCB Statute.[52] Since Article 14.2 of the ESCB Statute is directly applicable, national law can also opt not to include such a provision.

Further, Article 14.2 of the ESCB Statute establishes a unique competence of the CJEU to rule on a decision of an authority of an MS relieving a Governor from office based on a complaint that the Treaties have been infringed.[53] Both the limitation of the grounds for removal from office and the possibility of redress to the ECJ lead to **restrictive use of the power to relieve a Governor from office** by the authorities involved and therefore to additional safeguards for personal independence.

34 In addition, personal independence means that a **conflict of interest** must not arise. This is crucial to ensure that members of the decision-making bodies only act in the interest of the ESCB. The Code of Conduct for high-level ECB Officials contains rules on the avoidance of conflicts of interest and other ethical rules (→ para 6). Furthermore, members of the decision-making bodies of the ECB and NCBs of the Eurosystem are also subject to the internal rules adopted by the ECB and NCBs of the Eurosystem in the fulfilment of the provisions of the Eurosystem Ethics Framework.[54]

---

[49] Longer terms of offices are not precluded, see ECB (2020), p. 24; see, for example, Article 23.1 of the Belgian Law of 22 February 1998 establishing the organic statute of the National Bank of Belgium (the term of office is five years), Article 80.4 of the Croatian Act on the Croatian National Bank (the term of office is six years) or Section 7.3 of the German Bundesbank Act (the term of office is eight years).

[50] Smits (1997), p. 166 et seq.; Zilioli (2016), p. 146; see also ECB (2020), p. 25.

[51] Joined Cases C-202/18 and C-238/18, *Rimšēvičs v Latvia and ECB v Latvia* (CJEU 26 February 2019) para 55.

[52] See, for example, Article 23.1 of the Belgian Law of 22 February 1998 establishing the organic statute of the National Bank of Belgium; Article 81.1 of the Croatian Act on the Croatian National Bank; Article 12.3 of the Luxembourg Organic Law of the Central Bank of Luxembourg.

[53] The first two cases brought to the CJEU on this matter are Joined Cases C-202/18 and C-238/18, *Rimšēvičs v Latvia and ECB v Latvia* (CJEU 26 February 2019).

[54] Guideline (EU) 2015/855 of the ECB of 12 March 2015 *laying down the principles of a Eurosystem Ethics Framework and repealing Guideline ECB/2002/6 on minimum standards for the ECB and national central banks when conducting monetary policy operations, foreign exchange operations with the ECB's foreign reserves and managing the ECB's foreign reserve assets* of 2 June 2015, O. J. L 135/23 (2015).

The **procedure for appointing the Governors** and other members of the   35
decision-making bodies of the NCBs is not determined by any provision of the
Treaties or the ESCB Statute but is completely left to the law of each MS. This is
why there are several different appointment procedures for the Governors of the
NCBs. Even though appointment procedures could jeopardise personal independence,[55] the ECB has acknowledged that there is no obligation in Union law for MS
to structure the appointment procedure in a specific way.[56] However, the appointment procedure for members of the ECB's Executive Board is laid down in Article
11.2 of the ESCB Statute.

As regards the **members of the ECB's Executive Board**, their personal inde-   36
pendence is protected by Article 11 of the ESCB Statute, which provides for the
obligation to perform their duties on a full-time basis (Article 11.1), a limited and
non-renewable term of office of 8 years (Article 11.2), the requirement to have a
recognised standing and professional experience in monetary and banking matters
before being appointed, and limited cases for retirement.

2.2.5. Operational Independence

Operational independence is a concept typically applied to authorities competent at   37
banking supervision. Since the majority of the NCBs of the ESCB have full or
shared competencies in banking supervision, the concept of operational independence is relevant for the independence of an NCB. Operational independence is
relevant also for the ECB when exercising its supervisory tasks according to the
SSM Regulation.[57]

The attributes of operational independence have been developed in Principle   38
No 2 (i.e. regarding independence, accountability, resourcing and legal protection
for supervisors) of the **Basel Committee on Banking Supervision's Core Principles for Effective Banking Supervision**.[58] According to the Core Principles,
operational independence of banking supervisors means in essence discretion in
taking supervisory decisions or actions with regard to the supervised entities
without interference from a national government, an international organisation or
the private sector. Accordingly, operational independence of the supervisors is
necessary for effective banking supervision.

---

[55] Bini Smaghi (2008), p. 451 et seq.; Athanassiou (2014), p. 27 et seq.

[56] ECB Opinion CON/2009/13 *on a draft law supplementing the Law on Administration*, p. 3; ECB Opinion CON 2012/51 *on the Central Bank of Cyprus Laws of 2002 to 2007*, p. 2.

[57] See Recital 75 of Council Regulation (EU) No 1024/2013 *conferring specific tasks on the European Central Bank concerning policies relating to the prudential supervision of credit institutions*, O.J. L 287/63 (2013).

[58] The 29 Core Principles for Effective Banking Supervision are available on the Bank for International Settlement's website, available at http://www.bis.org/publ/bcbs230.pdf. The Core Principles serve as standards for the assessment of the independent status of banking supervisors.

39   The attributes of operational independence[59] of NCBs that are banking supervisors cannot be derived from Article 130 TFEU. Since Article 127.6 TFEU only entrusts the ECB, not the ESCB, with specific tasks, **prudential supervision of credit and financial institutions is not among the tasks attributed to the NCBs** under the TFEU. Therefore, it is clear that Article 130 TFEU does not apply to the NCBs when they act in their capacity as national competent authorities for prudential supervision of credit and financial institutions or in their capacity as resolution authorities. This may lead to differences in the degree of *de jure* and *de facto* independence in the NCBs' performance of their supervisory tasks compared to their independence in the performance of central banking tasks. Nevertheless, in some MS, the NCBs' independence in the exercise of national tasks is subject to the same legal basis as the one for the monetary policy and related tasks entrusted to them under the ESCB Statute.

40   It is not clear whether Article 130 TFEU also applies to the ECB in its role as a banking supervisor. On the one hand, it can be argued that supervisory tasks were conferred upon the ECB by Article 127.6 TFEU and Article 25.2 of the ESCB Statute. Accordingly, the Council has only activated these tasks by issuing the SSM Regulation and also defined their precise scope. This means that Article 130 TFEU also covers the independence of the ECB when acting as a banking supervisor. On the other hand, Article 1 of the SSM Regulation supports the understanding that supervisory tasks were conferred upon the ECB by the SSM Regulation. From this point of view, the **principle of independence in Article 130 TFEU does not apply to the ECB when exercising banking supervision tasks** because they are not conferred on it by the Treaties. This understanding would be in line with an interpretation of Article 19 of the SSM Regulation, which codifies a separate independence principle for the ECB and NCBs when acting as part of the SSM.[60]

2.2.6. De Facto Independence

41   In addition to strong *de jure* independence, *de facto* independence must be taken into account when measuring central bank independence. *De facto* independence means independence in practice, which may or may not be in line with the *de jure* independence laid down in Article 130 TFEU. In this regard, there may be **threats to central bank independence** that are not expressly prohibited by Article 130 TFEU but may have a negative impact on central bank independence. *De facto*

---

[59] For a comparison of the attributes of the operational independence of a central bank acting as a banking supervisor with the attributes of central bank independence, see Lambrinoc (2016), pp. 229–232.

[60] See also Article 4.4 of Directive 2013/36/EU *on access to the activity of credit institutions and the prudential supervision of credit institutions and investment firms*, O.J. L 176/338 (2013), which provides that "Member States shall ensure that the competent authorities have the expertise, resources, operational capacity, powers and independence necessary to carry out the functions relating to prudential supervision, investigations and penalties set out in this Directive and in Regulation (EU) No 575/2013".

independence is taken into account in the ECB Convergence Reports, which state that "the ECB is not limited to making a formal assessment of the letter of national legislation, but may also consider whether the implementation of the relevant provisions complies with the **spirit of the Treaties** and the Statute".[61]

The independence of a central bank may be put at risk if members of its decision-making bodies have a **political affiliation**, have played an active political role prior to their appointment or are expected to play such a role afterwards or have served in the government.[62] *De jure*, in such cases, there is no infringement of Article 130 TFEU because this provision applies only once appointment as a member of the Executive Board or Governor of an NCB has been made, and it ends with the termination of the term of office. However, there may be doubts that, *de facto*, these members of the decision-making bodies of the central banks of the ESCB are completely independent. In order to avoid such an impression, cooling-off periods between political and central bank appointments could be a solution.

Risks to the independence of an NCB may be brought about by **amendments to the national law governing the NCB**. Every time a provision is changed, there is a risk that central bank independence is affected either because the national legal provisions aimed at safeguarding the independence are amended without being contrary to Article 130 TFEU or new provisions that impede central bank independence are introduced.[63] Further, frequent amendments to the laws of an NCB often result in the NCB being overburdened with additional tasks that are outside the scope of core central banking tasks. The ECB consistently dissuades such frequent amendments because they may contribute to an unstable basis for an NCB's operation, thus adversely affecting its organisational and governance stability.[64]

It has also been suggested that central banks that are entrusted with the tasks of prudential supervision of credit institutions are, by the very nature of these tasks, exposed to political interests and therefore to increased risk of pressure regarding their financial and personal independence. The **transfer of government tasks** to the NCBs may also often conflict with the objective of central bank independence. The ECB has developed a standard test to assess whether new tasks conferred upon NCBs may conflict with the prohibition of monetary financing. Among the evaluation criteria is also the respect for the principle of central bank independence.[65]

---

[61] ECB (2020), p. 16.

[62] Bini Smaghi (2008), p. 450 et seq.

[63] In 2012 the Commission opened an infringement procedure against Hungary for an alleged breach of Article 130 TFEU based on concerns about national legislative amendments that provided for various possibilities to influence Hungary's NCB. The Hungarian legislation was amended, therefore the Commission closed the infringement procedure. See the European Commission Press Release of 17 January 2012, published under http://europa.eu/rapid/press-release_IP-12-24_en.htm?locale=fr.

[64] ECB Opinion CON/2011/104 *on the Magyar Nemzeti Bank*, p. 3 et seq.

[65] ECB Opinion CON/2016/54 *on the conferral of powers on the Central Bank of Ireland to assess competition in the market for mortgage loans and to issue lenders with directions on variable interest rates*, p. 7; ECB Opinion CON/2016/42 *on a central credit register*, p. 6 et seq.

45 The independent status of the ESCB central banks faced challenges during the financial crisis and euro crisis, in particular because the ECB became a key institution involved in the solution of the crises and their aftermath. During the global financial crisis, the ECB and other central banks have considerably expanded their balance sheets by conducting **non-standard monetary policy operations** (e.g. the Securities Markets Programme (SMP), the Asset-Backed Securities Purchase Programme (ABSPP), the Public Sector Purchase Programme (PSPP)). The securities held by the central banks in such programmes are associated with an **increased risk of incurring losses**. One could argue therefore that such programmes put at risk the financial independence of the ECB and Eurosystem NCBs. However, the aim of the central banks is not to make a profit or avoid losses. An infringement could only occur if there was negative capital in the long run.[66]

46 Participating in political negotiations for economic reforms could be seen as a further threat to the independence of the ECB, in particular when it comes to political trade-offs.[67] Another threat could be seen in the participation of the ECB during the negotiations with MS applying for financial assistance via the **European Stability Mechanism** (ESM). The ECB is indeed free to approve the results of the negotiations or to reject them. The fact that decisions in the framework of the **Outright Monetary Transactions** (OMT) **Programme** are bound to the obligations of the ESM is also not a violation of central bank independence[68] because it is the ECB itself that determines in this context whether an MS has fulfilled its obligation under the ESM. The ECB is not bound by the evaluations of MS or the ESM.

3. Institutional Setup

47 Central bank independence laid down in Article 130 TFEU is a **relative—not an absolute—principle** since it is specified in relation to for whom it exists, when it exists and how it is exercised.

3.1. The ESCB and the Eurosystem

48 The ESCB is a generic term for the **collaboration of the ECB and the NCBs**. Article 130 TFEU does not mention the ESCB because it is not a legal person that could benefit from the principle of independence. Only its constituents—the ECB

---

[66] Views about the capital of an NCB and the effects of negative capital have been expressed for example by Bindseil et al. (2004), p. 23 et seq. See also ECB (2020), p. 26; Archer and Moser-Boehm (2013), p. 3 ("losses or negative capital may raise doubts – however erroneous – about the central bank's ability to deliver on policy targets, and expose it to political pressure").

[67] Beukers (2013), p. 1618 et seq.

[68] Steinbach (2013), p. 920 et seq.; Nitze (2015), p. 205 et seq.

Article 130. [Independence of Central Banks]

and NCBs—are able to take legally valid actions. Within the ESCB, according to Article 9.2 of the ESCB Statute, the tasks of the ESCB are to be implemented either by the ECB's own activities or through the NCBs forming an integral part of the ESCB. In addition, the NCBs perform their specific national tasks in accordance with national legislation, which has to be compatible with the provisions of the Treaties and the ESCB Statute. NCBs act as national law bodies (the majority of the NCBs are public institutions).

The ESCB is a core feature of the **EMU** and a special model of the European administrative integration[69] within the Union institutional framework. The **Eurosystem** is part of the ESCB and comprises the ECB and NCBs of the euro area MS. Certain provisions of the Treaties only apply to the central banks of euro area MS. 49

3.1.1. The European Central Bank

The ECB is part of the EU's institutional setup. Since the Lisbon Treaty entered into force, Article 13.1 (2) TEU grants the ECB the status of a **Union institution** (→ Article 13 TEU paras 30 and 48 et seq.). In comparison to other Union institutions, such as the Commission, whose members are also independent (Article 17.3 TEU), the TFEU adds that Union institutions and MS' governments must respect the independence of the central banks and that any attempt to influence the members of the decision-making bodies of the ECB or NCBs in the performance of their tasks is prohibited. The ECB's independence is also different in that, unlike the Commission, the members of the ECB decision-making bodies are not subject to a motion of censure by the EP (Article 234 TFEU). Nonetheless, the independence of the ECB does not have the consequence of separating it entirely from the Union and exempting it from every rule of Union law.[70] 50

Whether the independence of the ECB makes it a **specialised organisation** connected with the Union but not classified as a typical Union institution was an important discussion at the beginning of ECB's existence.[71] This debate arose also because the ECB has a legal personality while other institutions, such as the Commission, do not. With the qualification of the ECB as a Union institution (Article 13.1 TEU), there is not much room to further argue that the ECB must be considered a specialised organisation. 51

3.1.2. The National Central Banks

The NCBs of the MS also benefit from the protection of Article 130 TFEU. In fact, NCBs of MS that have not adopted the euro are not yet responsible for implementing the Union monetary policy. Nonetheless, **Article 130 TFEU applies to them** to 52

---

[69] For details, see Everson and Rodrigues (2010), p. 15 et seq.
[70] Case C-11/00, *Commission v ECB* (ECJ 10 July 2003) para 135 et seq.
[71] Zilioli and Selmayr (2000), p. 598 et seq.; this point of view was criticised by Amtenbrink and de Haan (2002), p. 69 et seq., and by Häde (2006), p. 1611 et seq.

the extent they exercise powers and carry out tasks and duties conferred upon them by the Treaties and the ESCB Statute. In this regard, the objective of the NCBs of all MS (→ Article 127.1 TFEU para 21 et seq.) is to maintain price stability. The independence of an NCB can also be guaranteed under national law, provided the respective national law provisions are compatible with Article 130 TFEU.

53 A literal interpretation of Article 130 TFEU could lead to the view that the ECB belongs to the institutions that are not allowed to give instructions to NCBs because the ECB is also a Union institution. However, such an understanding would contradict other provisions of the Treaties. **NCBs cannot refuse to take instructions from the ECB** for ESCB tasks on grounds related to their independence, given that Article 14.3 of the ESCB Statute provides that the NCBs shall act in accordance with the guidelines and instructions of the ECB. In addition, within the ESCB, the ECB fulfils the function the Commission has in the infringement proceedings because the Governing Council of the ECB is the only institution that is allowed to bring an NCB to court on the basis of an alleged violation of the Treaties (Article 271 point (d) TFEU and Article 35.6 of the ESCB Statute). This is a further consequence of the principle of central bank independence, which would be violated if the Commission could initiate infringement proceedings against an NCB.

3.1.3. Members of the Decision-Making Bodies of the ECB and NCBs

54 Article 130 TFEU also applies to the members of the decision-making bodies of the ECB. The **ECB has three collegiate decision-making bodies**: the Governing Council as the supreme decision-making body (Article 283.1 TFEU and Article 10 of the ESCB Statute), the Executive Board (Article 283.2 TFEU and Article 11 of the ESCB Statute) and the (temporary) General Council (Article 141 TFEU and Article 44 of the ESCB Statute).

55 The **decision-making bodies of the NCBs** that are involved in the performance of ESCB tasks and related tasks are established under national legislation. The majority of the NCBs are governed by collegiate decision-making bodies, with only a few central banks, e.g. the central banks of Cyprus and Greece, having the Governor as the sole official responsible for taking decisions on monetary policies and related tasks.

56 In relation to the principle of independence, a collegiate decision-making body may **increase the independent position of a central bank** because it is likely that one person is more vulnerable to external influence than a group of persons. However, in determining the number of members of a decision-making body, the smooth functioning of that body has to be given considerable weight.

3.2. Union Institutions, Bodies, Offices or Agencies, Governments of the Member States and Any Other Body

The second sentence of Article 130 TFEU obliges Union institutions, bodies, 57
offices or agencies and the governments of the MS to respect the independence of the central banks and not seek to influence the members of the decision-making bodies of the ECB and NCBs. **Union institutions** are those enumerated in Article 13.1 TEU. Article 130 TFEU also refers to "bodies, offices or agencies" of the Union—an "umbrella term" that can also be found in other provisions of the Treaties (for example the second sentence of Article 263.1 TFEU).

Given that the aim of Article 130 TFEU is to protect the ESCB central banks 58
from any political influence,[72] the term "governments of the Member States" may be interpreted in a way that includes both the **executive and the legislative branches of an MS**.[73]

The first sentence of Article 130 TFEU also mentions "**any other body**" without 59
limitation. These bodies are not explicitly enumerated since the provision is meant to protect any body from undue influence, even if it has not been established yet. Therefore, it may be inferred that it includes national and Union executive and legislative institutions,[74] as well as private bodies as far as they execute public competencies. It includes, for example, **governments of state substructures in federal states, other central banks and international institutions**. Since there is a need for central banks of the ESCB also to be independent of commercially driven interests, **market participants** are also included among "any other bodies". In addition, we agree with those authors who consider that the provision protects the members of the decision-making bodies of the NCBs from internal influences, for example from other members of the same decision-making bodies who, however, are not involved in the performance of ESCB tasks and therefore are not subject to Article 130 TFEU.[75]

4. Limits

Central bank independence is not absolute. It is **relative to the purpose** determined 60
in the Treaties: primarily price stability. The precise parameters of independence of the central banks have been defined in relation to the powers that other institutions or bodies have towards an independent central bank, including the judicial control

---

[72] According to Case C-11/00, *Commission v ECB* (ECJ 10 July 2003) para 134 et seq. central bank independence protects the ECB from basically all political pressure so it can effectively pursue its monetary policy tasks.

[73] Van den Berg (2005), p. 27; also in this direction Smits (1997), p. 154.

[74] Häde, in Calliess and Ruffert (2022), Article 130 AEUV para 11 et seq.

[75] Manger-Nestler (2008), p. 165 et seq.; Selmayr (2002), p. 312; Griller, in Grabitz et al. (2021), Article 130 AEUV para 8 (released in 2013).

of central bank activities. ESCB central banks are also bound by the principle of sincere cooperation.

4.1. Mandate of the ECB and NCBs

61   The independence of the ESCB central banks is limited by its scope of application, which is confined to the limits of the ESCB central banks' mandate. The **independence of the ESCB central banks is a means to achieve the objectives** provided for in Article 127.1 TFEU and not an end in itself.[76] According to Article 127.1 TFEU, the ESCB shall primarily maintain price stability; the ESCB also supports the general economic policies of the Union with a view to contributing to the achievement of the objectives of the Union as laid down in Article 3 TEU as long as it does not interfere with the objective of price stability. Price stability can be achieved by various means.

62   In the framework of the euro and financial crises, the limits of the ESCB's means by which price stability can be achieved became subject to controversy,[77] in particular in relation to several crisis programmes, such as the **OMT** Programme[78] or the **PSPP**.[79] In particular, the German Federal Constitutional Court (FCC) raised doubts over the compatibility of these programmes with Union law, which is why the CJEU was requested to give preliminary rulings on the matter.[80] In those cases, the CJEU did not find any violation of the ECB's mandate or of the prohibition of monetary financing.[81]

63   Since 2014, the ECB has also been competent to do a further task, i.e. the **prudential supervision of credit institutions in accordance with the SSM**

---

[76] Case C-11/00, *Commission v ECB* (Opinion of AG Jacobs of 3 October 2002) para 149–150; Zahradnik, in Mayer and Stöger (2011), Article 130 AEUV para 1.

[77] Beukers (2013), p. 1579 et seq.; Wilsher (2013), p. 503 et seq.; Baroncelli (2014), p. 125 et seq.; Hinarejos (2015), p. 563 et seq.

[78] See the ECB press release from 6 September 2012, available at https://www.ecb.europa.eu/press/pr/date/2012/html/pr120906_1.en.html.

[79] ECB Decision (EU) 2020/188 *on a secondary markets public sector asset purchase programme* (ECB/2020/9), O.J. L 39/12 (2020); the prior ECB Decision (EU) 2015/774 *on a secondary markets public sector purchase programme* and its amendments were repealed by this Decision.

[80] In relation to the OMT programme, see German Federal Constitutional Court, 2 BvR 2728/13 et al. (Order of 14 January 2014), BVerfGE 134, 366, and German Federal Constitutional Court, 2 BvR 2728/13 et al. (Judgment of 21 June 2016), BVerfGE 142, 123; in relation to the PSPP, see German Federal Constitutional Court, 2 BvR 859/15 et al. (Order of 18 July 2017), BVerfGE 146, 216 and German Federal Constitutional Court, 2 BvR 859/15 et al. (Judgment of 5 May 2020), BVerfGE 154, 17.

[81] In relation to the OMT programme, see Case C-62/14, *Gauweiler* (CJEU 16 June 2015) para 46 et seq.; the delimitation of monetary policy from economic policy was already defined in an earlier decision of the CJEU, see Case C-370/12, *Pringle* (CJEU 27 November 2012) para 53 et seq.; in relation to the PSPP, see Case C-493/17, *Weiss* (CJEU 11 December 2018) para 45 et seq.; for an in-depth analysis of the Gauweiler judgment in relation to central bank independence, see Baroncelli (2016), p. 84 et seq.

Regulation.[82] The conferral of this additional task on the ECB has brought with it a different degree of *de jure* and *de facto* institutional and personal independence to the ECB compared to its independence in monetary policy. Article 19 of the SSM Regulation requires the ECB to act independently when supervising credit institutions on the basis of the SSM Regulation. However, the degree of independence laid down in Article 130 TFEU may vary in comparison to the independence laid down in Article 19 of the SSM Regulation[83] on several aspects.[84] First, while an amendment to Article 130 TFEU would require an amendment to the Treaties, which is extremely difficult to achieve, an amendment to the SSM Regulation requires acting in accordance with the legislative procedure. Further, unlike the ECB's policy-making powers in the area of monetary policy, when exercising supervisory tasks, the ECB is widely constrained by the policy-making powers of other Union institutions. In addition, Article 130 TFEU does not apply to the members of the Supervisory Board of the ECB when they carry out the ECB's tasks of prudential supervision of credit and financial institutions since the Supervisory Board is not a decision-making body of the ECB. In contrast, the independence requirement laid down in Article 19 of the SSM Regulation also covers the members of the Supervisory Board of the ECB when they carry out the ECB's tasks of prudential supervision of credit and financial institutions. Finally, the view that *de facto* independence does not apply to the ECB in its role as a banking supervisor as opposed to its role in the area of monetary policy materialised from the European Court of Auditors' demands for full scrutiny of its banking supervision.[85] The European Court of Auditors and the ECB have agreed on a Memorandum of Understanding[86] that establishes practical information-sharing arrangements between the two Union institutions.

4.2. External Controls

The ECB is subject to the control of other institutions and authorities, including the European Court of Auditors, the European Data Protection Supervisor, the European Ombudsman, the Union Anti-Fraud Office (OLAF) and the CJEU in their

64

---

[82] Council Regulation (EU) No 1024/2013 *conferring specific tasks on the European Central Bank concerning policies relating to the prudential supervision of credit institutions*, O.J. L 287/63 (2013).

[83] See for more details, Mersch (2017).

[84] Martucci (2019), p. 237 et seq.

[85] According to the press release of 14 January 2019 of the European Court of Auditors, "[t]he European Court of Auditors has called on the Union's legislators to intervene and ensure the European Central Bank allows full access to documents for audits related to banking supervision.", available at https://www.eca.europa.eu/Lists/News/NEWS1901_14/INPL19_ECB_EN.pdf.

[86] Memorandum of Understanding between the ECA and the ECB regarding audits on the ECB's supervisory tasks, 9 October 2019 (MOU/2019/10091), available at https://eur-lex.europa.eu/legal- content/EN/ALL/?uri=cellar:b44fbfa0-95f6-11ea-aac4-01aa75ed71a1.

respective fields of competence. Some authors see this control as part of the methods by which the ECB is held accountable.[87]

65   The competencies of **OLAF** were confirmed by the ECJ in a 2003 landmark decision: in the early times of the ECB, the ECB was of the opinion that OLAF could not investigate the ECB because any such investigation would infringe its independence. The ECJ rejected this argument because OLAF's powers were subject to legal guarantees intended to ensure its complete independence (in relation to the Commission), and its competencies were clearly described by law, among others by delineating the purpose for which the powers can be used. Since the ECB does not stand outside the Union legal order and is not exempted from any legislative action taken by the Union legislature,[88] other Union institutions or bodies can exercise competencies in relation to the ECB as long as there is no threat of **undue influence** in relation to the tasks entrusted to the ECB under the Treaties and the ESCB Statute.

66   Similarly, the **NCBs may be subject to investigations** in the exercise of their tasks as long as there is no spillover to ESCB-related tasks and the personal independence of their decision-making bodies is not impacted.

67   The **CJEU is competent to exercise judicial control over the ECB**. It is explicitly laid down in Article 35 of the ESCB Statute, which refers to the cases and conditions for such control laid down in the TFEU. The criteria for Union Courts' review are defined by the principle of conferral.[89] Therefore, one of the first questions in a review by the Court is whether the **ECB acts within its mandate** defined by the Treaties.

68   The ECB's independence does not exclude the fact that the acts or omissions of the ECB are subject to a review or interpretation by the CJEU.[90] The CJEU reviews the validity of the legally binding acts of the ECB pursuant to Article 263.1 TFEU.[91] The Court has jurisdiction in actions brought against the ECB for failure to act on the **infringement of the Treaties** pursuant to Article 265.1 TFEU as well as in **actions for damages** pursuant to Article 268 TFEU and Article 340 (2) to (3) TFEU in the case of the non-contractual liability of the ECB incurred by it or its servants in the performance of their duties, even outside the scope of the Union.[92] The ECB has to comply with the judgment of the CJEU in such instances as provided for in Article 266.1 TFEU.

---

[87] See, for example, Slot (1994), pp. 229 and 248; Zilioli (2016), p. 132.

[88] Case C-11/00, *Commission v ECB* (ECJ 10 July 2003) para 135.

[89] Case C-62/14, *Gauweiler* (CJEU 16 June 2015) para 41.

[90] Case C-11/00, *Commission v ECB* (ECJ 10 July 2003) para 135; Case C-62/14, *Gauweiler* (ECJ 16 June 2015) para 41.

[91] In the course of the euro crisis the ECB had to face several complaints before the CJEU based on this Article, see Case T-79/13, *Accorinti v ECB* (GC 7 October 2015); Case T-496/11, *United Kingdom v ECB* (GC 4 March 2015).

[92] Joined Cases C-8/15 P to C-10/15 P, *Ledra Advertising v Commission and ECB* (CJEU 20 September 2016) para 62 et seq.

The ECB and NCBs enjoy a considerable margin of **discretion** in taking 69
decisions that depend on the Union and international economic and financial
environment.[93] Their nature as expert bodies that make choices of a technical
nature and undertake economic forecasts and complex assessments has been an
argument for judicial restraint.[94] According to the CJEU judgment in *Gauweiler*,
central banks—when adopting ESCB monetary policy measures—have to act
within the limits of the powers conferred upon the ESCB by the TFEU, must
have a legitimate objective of monetary policy, and have to use their available
instruments for the purpose of implementing monetary policy. Any monetary policy
measure must be proportionate to the monetary policy objective and observe the
prohibition of monetary financing. This underlines the fact that **neither the ECB
nor the NCBs as part of the ESCB stand outside the Union legal order** when
they carry out tasks conferred upon them under the Treaties. Their acts are subject
to judicial review, which aims to ensure that the ESCB central banks do not take
arbitrary, unreasoned or inadequate measures or decisions.

In addition, pursuant to Article 271 point (d) TFEU, the CJEU has the power to 70
review acts of NCBs regarding compliance with their obligations under the
Treaties and the ESCB Statute. The European Commission can initiate an infringement procedure if an MS violates the independence of a central bank.[95]

The ECB and **NCBs can also protect their independent status by judicial** 71
means. If one of the members of the decision-making bodies violates the prohibition to accept instructions, the ECB can take judicial action against such behaviour
on the basis of Article 263 TFEU. Moreover, the ECB may also claim in court that a
legislative act of the EP and Council or any act by the Commission infringes the
independence of the ECB.

4.3. Principle of Sincere Cooperation

In accordance with Article 13.2 sentence 2 TEU, Union institutions are bound by 72
the obligation of mutual sincere cooperation, which could be seen as a potential
conflict with the principle of independence. **Duties to inform, consult and cooperate** can be established based on the principle of sincere cooperation.[96]

Mutual sincere cooperation between Union institutions had been acknowledged 73
by the ECJ before the ECB became a Union institution.[97] The principle aims at

---

[93] See Manger-Nestler, in Pechstein et al. (2017), Article 130 AEUV para 30.

[94] Case C-62/14, *Gauweiler* (Opinion of AG Cruz Villalón of 14 January 2015) para 111; Case C-62/14, *Gauweiler* (CJEU 16 June 2015) para 68; Case C-493/17, Weiss (ECJ 11 December 2018) para 73; Goldmann (2014), p. 269 et seq.; Hinarejos (2015), p. 575 and the references in footnote 32.

[95] Croonenborghs et al. (2016), p. 852.

[96] Selmayr, in von der Groeben et al. (2015), Article 282 AEUV para 108 et seq.

[97] Case 81/72, *Commission v Council* (ECJ 5 June 1973) para 13.

ensuring that none of the Union institutions uses its competencies with the sole aim of blocking other Union institutions. All Union institutions have to collaborate in order to serve the interests of the Union. This is also true for the ECB. It means that the ECB has to take into account the decisions taken by other Union institutions in their fields of competence, participate actively in discussions, support the **dialogue between the institutions** and not make abusive use of procedural regulations.[98] Therefore, the principle of sincere cooperation is a limitation on the ECB's independence, although a relatively flexible one, given that it is not circumscribed by explicit requirements and limitations.

74 The ECB and the NCBs also have to comply with the principle of sincere cooperation, which follows from Article 4.3 TEU (→ Article 4 TEU para 86 et seq.). Since **Article 4.3 TEU** obliges MS to observe the loyalty principle of Union law, this provision also **applies to the NCBs**.

5. Democratic Accountability and Transparency

75 MS have transferred decision-making powers concerning monetary policies to central banks. The ESCB central banks have been entrusted by the Treaties with the definition and **conduct of the monetary policy** of the Union. Such transfer **must not result in excluding democratic accountability**,[99] despite ESCB central banks being represented by independent, not directly elected, officials.

76 Articles 9 et seq. TEU binds Union institutions, including the ECB, to **democratic principles**. The Union law **principle of democracy** does not require all Union institutions to be bound by instructions issued by a national government or another Union institution. The ECJ applied such an interpretation when it decided that the independent status of data protection authorities does not violate the principle of democracy.[100] The Treaties make it clear that providing for independent central banks does not per se violate the principle of democracy in Union law.[101] NCBs are also bound by the principle of democracy laid down in the constitutions of the MS.

77 The German Federal Constitutional Court also ruled on the independence of the ECB[102] in that it emphasised the role of an independent central bank on the one hand and the principle of democracy on the other. An **independent ECB does not infringe the principle of democracy** as laid down in the German Constitution

---

[98] Hatje, in Schwarze et al. (2019), Article 13 EUV para 34.

[99] Amtenbrink (1999), pp. 27 and 33; also see European Parliament *Resolution on Democratic Accountability in the Third Phase of EMU* of 4 May 1998, O.J. C 138/177 (1998).

[100] Case C-518/07, *Commission v Germany* (CJEU 9 March 2010) para 23 et seq.; Case C-614/10, *Commission v Austria* (CJEU 16 October 2012) para 37 et seq.

[101] Kempen, in Streinz (2018), Article 130 AEUV para 5.

[102] German Federal Constitutional Court, 2 BvR 2134/92, 2 BvR 2159/92 (Judgment of 12 October 1993), BVerfGE 89, 155 (208 et seq.).

because it is an exceptional case in which the principle of democracy can be modified for the purpose of price stability.[103]

78 There is no general definition of the concept of "accountability" in either the Treaties or secondary Union law.[104] In relation to central banks, "accountability" implies an obligation to justify how they use the powers entrusted to them to achieve their primary objective.[105] **Accountability** is often seen as a limitation to central bank independence because means of democratic control may interfere with independent decision-making. In our view, it **complements the independence of central banks** in order to give legitimacy to independent decision-making.

79 Accountability is realised by different means. In the Treaties, the **important accountability rules** are as follows: the reporting required from the ECB by Article 284.3 TFEU and Article 15 of the ESCB Statute, the right of the President of the Council and the competent member of the Commission to participate in the meetings of the Governing Council of the ECB in accordance with Article 284.1 TFEU (→ Article 284 TFEU para 1) and the right of the EP to request the ECB President and other members of the Executive Board to be heard by the competent committees of the EP in accordance with Article 284.3 (2) TFEU (→ Article 284 TFEU para 3 et seqq.). In addition, the members of the EP may ask questions in writing, and the ECB is obliged to reply. Both questions and answers are made public, which contributes to the transparency of the ESCB's actions.

80 Moreover, under Article 20 of the SSM Regulation, the **ECB is accountable to the EP and the Council for the implementation of that Regulation**. The EP and the ECB concluded an interinstitutional agreement containing the modalities of democratic accountability with regard to the ECB's competencies related to the SSM.[106] The Council and the ECB concluded a Memorandum of Understanding on the cooperation on procedures related to the SSM. Further, for the supervisory tasks, the ECB is required to send its annual report on the execution of the tasks conferred upon it by the SSM Regulation to the national parliaments of the MS participating in the SSM (Article 21.1 (1) of the SSM Regulation), and the latter may address to the ECB their reasoned observations on that report. The ECB reports on not just its activities but also those of the ESCB. The statutes of the NCBs mostly require that the NCBs report at least annually to their national parliaments on their

---

[103] German Federal Constitutional Court, 2 BvR 2134/92, 2 BvR 2159/92 (Judgment of 12 October 1993), BVerfGE 89, 155 (208 et seq.); German Federal Constitutional Court, 2 BvR 2728/13 et al. (Judgment of 21 June 2016), BVerfGE 142, 123 para 131 (democratic accountability is realised by national and supranational "strands of legitimation").

[104] For a definition of the concept, see, for example, Zilioli (2016), p. 134 et seq. with further references.

[105] The ECB has defined the concept for itself: ECB, ECB's Monthly Bulletin of November 2002, p. 45 et seq.

[106] Interinstitutional Agreement between the European Parliament and the European Central Bank on the practical modalities of the exercise of democratic accountability and oversight over the exercise of the tasks conferred on the ECB within the framework of the Single Supervisory Mechanism, 2013/694/EU, O.J. L 320/1 (2013).

activities; however, they are only accountable to their national parliaments for the tasks conferred upon them under national law. Such national tasks are, according to Article 14.4 of the ESCB Statute, performed by the NCBs on their own responsibility. **National parliaments may hold NCBs accountable for the functions performed outside the ESCB**, whereas the ECB is accountable for the Eurosystem functions.[107] However, NCBs are not precluded from explaining the ECB's decisions and informing national policymakers of the conduct of the single monetary policy and the reasoning behind it.

81 **Transparency** is a **key element of the clarity and credibility** of the Union's monetary policy. It has become an important complement to accountability. It is realised in the information that the ECB makes public. The ECB consistently had to face criticism concerning its openness towards the public because it has not published the minutes of the Governing Council meetings.[108] The legal framework, namely Article 10.4 of the ESCB Statute, safeguards the confidentiality of both the **proceedings of the meetings of the Governing Council** and the outcome of its deliberations. The provision's aim is to protect the proceedings against the disclosure of individual positions and voting behaviours of the members of the Governing Council and of certain confidential matters specific to the performance of its tasks. This is essential for the personal independence of the Governors, who otherwise could be subject to national pressure, as well as for the independence of the Governing Council as a collegiate decision-making body.[109] The decisions, which are the outcome of the Governing Council deliberations, and their reasoning may be published without linking them to an individual member of the Governing Council, provided that the Governing Council has decided to make that outcome public in whole or in part.[110] The ECB started to publish accounts of the monetary policy meetings in 2015.[111]

List of Cases

ECJ/CJEU

ECJ 05.06.1973, 81/72, *Commission v Council*, ECLI:EU:C:1973:60 [cit. in para 73]

ECJ 10.07.2003, C-11/00, *Commission v ECB*, ECLI:EU:C:2003:395 [cit. in para 4, 7, 17, 50, 58, 61, 65, and 68]

---

[107] Scheller (2004), p. 127.

[108] See, for example, European Parliament resolution of 25 March 2010 on the ECB Annual Report 2008 (2009/2090(INI)), 2011/C 4 E/07, O.J. C 4 E/44 (2010), para 22.

[109] See also Van den Berg (2005), pp. 118–119.

[110] Case C-442/18 P, *ECB v Espírito Santo Financial (Portugal)* (ECJ 19 December 2019) para 43 and 56.

[111] The accounts can be found on the ECB website, available at http://www.ecb.europa.eu/press/accounts.

CJEU 09.03.2010, C-518/07, *Commission v Germany*, ECLI:EU:C:2010:125 [cit. in para 76]
CJEU 16.10.2012, C-614/10, *Commission v Austria*, ECLI:EU:C:2012:631 [cit. in para 76]
CJEU 27.11.2012, C-370/12, *Pringle*, ECLI:EU:C:2012:756 [cit. in para 62]
CJEU 16.06.2015, C-62/14, *Gauweiler*, ECLI:EU:C:2015:400 [cit. in para 7, 17, 21, 62, 67, 68, and 69]
CJEU 20.09.2016, C-8/15 P to C-10/15 P, *Ledra Advertising v Commission and ECB*, ECLI:EU:C:2016:701 [cit. in para 68]
CJEU 11.12.2018, C-493/17, *Weiss*, ECLI:EU:C:2018:1000 [cit. in para 62 and 68]
CJEU 26.02.2019, C-202/18 and C-238/18, *Rimšēvičs v Latvia and ECB v Latvia*, ECLI:EU:C:2019:139 [cit. in para 33]
CJEU 19.12.2019, C-442/18 P, *ECB v Espírito Santo Financial (Portugal)*, ECLI:EU:C:2019:1117 [cit. in para 81]

CFI/GC
GC 07.10.2015, T-79/13, *Accorinti v ECB*, ECLI:EU:T:2015:756 [cit. in para 68]
GC 04.03.2015, T-496/11, *United Kingdom v ECB*, ECLI:EU:T:2015:133 [cit. in para 68]

German Federal Constitutional Court
German FCC 12.10.1993, 2 BvR 2134/92, 2 BvR 2159/92, *Maastricht*, BVerfGE 89, 155 [cit. in para 77]
German FCC 14.01.2014, 2 BvR 2728/13 et al., *OMT (reference for preliminary ruling)*, ECLI:DE:BVerfG:2014:rs20140114.2bvr272813, BVerfGE 134, 366 [cit. in para 62]
German FCC 21.06.2016, 2 BvR 2728/13. *OMT*, ECLI:DE:BVerfG:2016:rs20160621.2bvr272813, BVerfGE 142, 123 [cit. in para 62 and 77]
German FCC 18.07.2017, 2 BvR 859/15 et al., *PSPP (reference for preliminary ruling)*, ECLI:DE:BVerfG:2017:rs20170718.2bvr085915, BVerfGE 146, 216 [cit. in para 62]
German FCC 05.05.2020, 2 BvR 859/15 et al., *PSPP*, ECLI:DE:BVerfG:2020:rs20200505.2bvr085915, BVerfGE 154, 17 [cit. in para 62]

References[112]

Alexander, K. (2016). The European Central Bank and banking supervision: The regulatory limits of the single supervisory mechanism. *European Company and Financial Law Review, 13*, 467–494.
Amtenbrink, F. (1999). *The democratic accountability of central banks: A comparative study of the European Central Bank*. Hart.

---

[112] All cited Internet sources of this comment have been accessed on 28 November 2021.

Amtenbrink, F., & de Haan, J. (2002). The European Central Bank: An independent specialized organization of community law – A comment. *Common Market Law Review, 39*, 65–76.

Archer, D., & Moser-Boehm, P. (2013). Central bank finances. *BIS Papers* No. 71.

Athanassiou, P. (2014). Reflections on the modalities for the appointment of national central bank governors. *European Law Review, 39*, 27–46.

Baroncelli, S. (2014). The independence of the ECB after the economic crisis. In M. Adams, F. Fabbrini, & P. Larouche (Eds.), *The constitutionalization of European budgetary constraints* (pp. 125–150). Hart Publishing.

Baroncelli, S. (2016). The Gauweiler judgment in view of the case law of the European Court of Justice on European central bank independence – Between substance and form. *Maastricht Journal of European and Comparative Law, 23*, 79–98.

Beukers, T. (2013). The new ECB and its relationship with the eurozone Member States: Between central bank independence and central bank intervention. *Common Market Law Review, 50*, 1579–1620.

Bindseil, U., Manzanares, A., & Weller, B. (2004). The role of central bank capital revisited. *ECB Working Paper Series*, 392.

Bini Smaghi, L. (2008). Central bank independence in the EU – From theory to practice. *European Law Journal, 14*, 446–460.

Calliess, C., & Ruffert, M. (Eds.). (2022). *EUV/AEUV. Kommentar.* (6th ed.). C.H. Beck.

Croonenborghs, K., Friebel, J., & Petocz, J. (2016). The principle of central bank independence and its monitoring by the European Commission. *Europäische Zeitschrift für Wirtschaftsrecht*, 849–855.

Cukierman, A., Webb, S. B., & Neyapti, B. (1992). Measuring the independence of central banks and its effect on policy outcomes. *The World Bank Economic Review, 6*, 353–398.

Eijffinger, S. C. W., & de Haan, J. (1996). *The political economy of central-bank independence*. Special Papers in International Economics No. 19.

Endler, J. (1998). *Europäische Zentralbank und Preisstabilität: eine juristische und ökonomische Untersuchung der institutionellen Vorkehrungen des Vertrages von Maastricht zur Gewährleistung der Preisstabilität*. Boorberg.

European Central Bank. (2020). *Convergence Report*.

Everson, M., & Rodrigues, F. (2010). *What can the law do for the European System of Central Banks? – Good governance and comitology 'within' the system*. ZERP Discussion Papers 3/2010.

Goldmann, M. (2014). Adjudicating economics? Central bank independence and the appropriate standard of judicial review. *German Law Journal, 15*, 265–280.

Grabitz, E., Hilf, M., & Nettesheim, M. (Eds.). (2021). *Das Recht der Europäischen Union*. (Loose leaf). Beck.

Häde, U. (2006). Zur rechtlichen Stellung der Europäischen Zentralbank. *Zeitschrift für Wirtschafts- und Bankrecht*, 1605–1613.

Hinarejos, A. (2015). Gauweiler and the Outright Monetary Transactions Programme: The mandate of the European Central Bank and the changing nature of economic and monetary union. *European Constitutional Law Review, 11*, 563–576.

Kramer, U., & Hinrichsen, T. (2015). Die Europäische Zentralbank. *Juristische Schulung*, 673–680.

Kröger, M. (2020). *Unabhängigkeitsregime im Europäischen Verwaltungsverbund – Eine europa- und verfassungsrechtliche Untersuchung unionsrechtlicher Organisationsregelungen für Mitgliedstaaten anhand von Regulierungsagenturen, Datenschutzbehörden sowie statistischen Ämtern*. Nomos.

Lambrinoc, S. (2016). Die Unabhängigkeit der Europäischen Zentralbank als Aufsichtsbehörde für Kreditinstitute. In M. Kröger & A. Pilniok (Eds.), *Unabhängiges Verwalten in der Europäischen Union* (pp. 221–238). Mohr Siebeck.

Lastra, R. M. (1997). Independence and accountability of the European Central Bank. In M. Andenas, L. Gormley, C. Hadjiuemmanuil, & I. Hardent (Eds.), *European economic and monetary union: The institutional framework* (pp. 289–329). Kluwer.

Manger-Nestler, C. (2008). *Par(s) inter pares? – Die Bundesbank als nationale Zentralbank im europäischen System der Zentralbanken*. Duncker & Humblot.

Martucci, F. (2019). Solving a "growing audit gap in banking supervision": The relationship between the ECA and the ECB. In ECB (Ed.), *Building bridges: Central banking law in an interconnected world*. Frankfurt. Retrieved from https://www.ecb.europa.eu/pub/pdf/other/ecb.ecblegalconferenceproceedings201912~9325c45957.en.pdf

Mayer, H., & Stöger, K. (2011). *Kommentar zu EUV und AEUV*. Manz.

Mersch, Y. (2017). *Central bank independence revisited - Keynote address*. Retrieved from https://www.ecb.europa.eu/press/key/date/2017/html/sp170330.en.html

Milton, S., & Sinclair, P. (2011). *The capital needs of central banks*. Routledge.

Nitze, K. (2015). *Finanzhilfen für Euro-Staaten in der Krise*. Duncker & Humblot.

Pechstein, M., Nowak, C., & Häde, U. (Eds.). (2017). *Frankfurter Kommentar EUV – GRC – AEUV*. Mohr Siebeck.

Pingel, I. (Ed.). (2010). *Commentaire article par article des traités UE et CE. De Rome à Lisbonne* (2nd ed.). Helbing & Lichtenhahn, Dalloz.

Scheller, H. K. (2004). *The European Central Bank. History, role and functions*. European Central Bank.

Schwarze, J., Becker, U., Hatje, A., & Schoo, J. (Eds.). (2019). *EU-Kommentar* (4th ed.). Nomos.

Selmayr, M. (2002). *Die Vergemeinschaftung der Währung*. Nomos.

Siekmann, H. (Ed.). (2013). *Kommentar zur Europäischen Währungsunion*. Mohr Siebeck.

Slot, P. J. (1994). The institutional provisions of the EMU. In D. Curtin & T. Heukels (Eds.), *Institutional dynamics of European Integration* (Vol. II, pp. 229–250). Kluwer Academic Publishers Group.

Smits, R. (1997). *The European Central Bank – Institutional aspects*. Kluwer Law International.

Snyder, F. (2011). EMU – Integration and differentiation: Metaphor for European Union. In P. Craig & G. de Búrca (Eds.), *The evolution of EU law* (2nd ed., pp. 687–716). OUP.

Sparve, R. (2005). Central bank independence under European and other international standards. In ECB (Ed.), *Legal aspects of the European System of Central Banks. Liber Amicorum Paolo Zamboni Garavelli* (pp. 271–285). European Central Bank.

Steinbach, A. (2013). Die Rechtmäßigkeit der Anleihekäufe der Europäischen Zentralbank. *Neue Zeitschrift für Verwaltungsrecht*, 918–921.

Stella, P. (1997). *Do Central Banks need capital?*. Working Paper of the International Monetary Fund, 83.

Streinz, R. (Ed.). (2018). *EUV/AEUV. Kommentar*. (3rd ed.). Beck.

Thiele, A. (2016). Die Unabhängigkeit der EZB. In M. Kröger & A. Pilniok (Eds.), *Unabhängiges Verwalten in der Europäischen Union* (pp. 195–219). Mohr Siebeck.

Tupits, A. (2012). *Legal framework for the Eurosystem national central bank – Analysis of the Eurosystem central bank statutes*. Lambert Academic Publishing.

Ungerer, H. (1997). *A concise history of European monetary integration: From EPU to EMU*. Quorum Books.

Van den Berg, C. C. A. (2005). *The making of the statute of the European System of Central Banks – An application of checks and balances*. Dutch University Press.

van der Sluis, M. (2014). Maastricht revisited: Economic constitutionalism, the ECB and the Bundesbank. In M. Adams, F. Fabbrini, & P. Larouche (Eds.), *The constitutionalization of European budgetary constraints* (pp. 105–123). Hart Publishing.

von der Groeben, H., Schwarze, J., & Hatje, A. (Eds.). (2015). *Europäisches Unionsrecht* (7th ed.). Nomos.

von Münch, I., & Kunig, P. (Eds.). (2021). *Grundgesetz-Kommentar* (7th ed.). Beck.

Wilsher, D. (2013). Ready to do whatever it takes? The legal mandate of the European Central Bank and the economic crisis. *Cambridge Yearbook of European Legal Studies*, 15, 503–536.

Zilioli, C. (2016). The independence of the European Central Bank and its new banking supervisory competences. In D. Ritleng (Ed.), *Independence and legitimacy in the institutional system of the EU* (pp. 125–179). OUP.

Zilioli, C., & Selmayr, M. (2000). The European Central Bank: An independent specialized organization of community law. *Common Market Law Review, 37*, 591–644.

Zilioli, C., & Selmayr, M. (2007). The constitutional status of the European Central Bank. *Common Market Law Review, 44*, 355–399.

Article 131 [Compatibility of National Legislation]
(ex-Article 109 TEC)

Each Member State[13–17] shall ensure that its national legislation,[6–12] including the statutes of its national central bank, is compatible[3,4] with the Treaties and the Statute of the ESCB and of the ECB.

Contents

1. Overview 1
2. "Compatibility" Versus "Harmonisation" 3
3. Scope of Application of the Provision 5
   3.1. Material Scope of Application 6
      3.1.1. Independence 7
      3.1.2. Confidentiality 8
      3.1.3. Monetary Financing and Privileged Access 9
      3.1.4. Legal Integration into the Eurosystem 10
   3.2. Personal Scope of Application 13
      3.2.1. Member States with a Derogation 14
      3.2.2. Member States with an "Opt-Out" 15
4. Monitoring and Compliance 19
   4.1. Convergence Reports 20
   4.2. Failure to Ensure Compatibility 22

List of Cases
References

1. Overview

This provision[1] deals with the requirement of the **legal compatibility of national legislation** with **central bank independence** (Article 130 TFEU and Article 7 of the ESCB Statute) and the provisions of the Treaties and the Statute. Underlying this obligation of the MS to ensure national legal compatibility with the Treaties and the Statute is the settled **case law of the European Court of Justice** (ECJ) stating that the Treaties and the law adopted by the EU on the basis of the Treaties have primacy over the law of MS, under the conditions laid down by the said case law,[2] as well as the **principle of sincere cooperation** (Article 4.3 TEU). 1

The views expressed in this commentary are those of the author and may not be attributed to the European Central Bank (ECB) or the Eurosystem.

[1] Also reproduced by Article 14.1 of Protocol (No 4) on the ESCB Statute.

[2] Case 26/62, *van Gend & Loos* (ECJ 5 February 1963) paras 79 and 81; Case 6/64, *Flaminio Costa v E.N.E.L.* (ECJ 15 July 1964) para 13; Case 106/77, *Simmenthal* (ECJ 9 March 1978) para 17.

[3] For further reading on the history of EMU see Smits (1997), pp. 37–147; Lastra and Louis (2013), pp. 1–17.

2   In order to prepare the integration of the national central banks (NCBs) into the European System of Central Banks (ESCB), as well as the transition to stage 3 of the Economic and Monetary Union (EMU), timely adaptation required the **legislative process to be initiated during stage 2 of EMU**. This would also allow the European Monetary Institute (EMI) and other Community institutions to assess the progress made towards the **fulfilment of the requirements for stage 3**.[3] As stated in ex-Article 109 TEC, MS (with the exception of the United Kingdom, → para 16) had to ensure, at the latest at the date of the establishment of the ESCB, that their national legislation, including the statutes of their NCBs, was compatible with the Treaty and the Statute. Taking into account the close link between the ECB and the NCBs, it was necessary to guarantee that the MS were effectively prevented from being tempted to interfere with the **primary objective of the ES**.

2. "Compatibility" Versus "Harmonisation"

3   This obligation of **legal convergence** does not require harmonisation of the NCBs' statutes, as the literal interpretation of the TFEU might suggest. In accordance with Article 14.4 of the Statute, **national particularities of the NCBs may be preserved** as long as they do **not impinge on the independence** of the NCBs or on their integration into the ESCB. The article instead implies that national legislation and the statutes of the NCBs need to be adapted in order to **eliminate inconsistencies** with the Treaties and the Statute. Such adjustments ensure the required compatibility and thus the NCBs' **coherent integration** into the ESCB.[4] Neither the supremacy of the Treaty and the Statute over national legislation nor the nature of the incompatibility affects this obligation.[5]

4   **No method is prescribed** by either the Treaties or the Statute for the adaptation of national legislation. However, the explicit obligation to ensure the compatibility of the national legislation implies that incompatibilities in national legislation should be avoided, amended or removed. The adaption by national legislation may be achieved by referring to the Treaties and the Statute, by incorporating the provisions thereof and referring to their provenance, by removing any incompatibility therewith or by a combination of these methods.[6]

---

[3] For further reading on the history of EMU see Smits (1997), pp. 37–147; Lastra and Louis (2013), pp. 1–17.

[4] Malatesta (2003), p. 88; Armati, in Curti Gialdino (2012), p. 1229.

[5] Dziechciarz, in von der Groeben et al. (2015), Article 131 AEUV para 16. See also ECB Convergence Report May 2002, p. 39. All ECB Convergence Reports are available on the ECB website at www.ecb.europa.eu.

[6] Arda, in Herzog et al. (2011), §131.4[1]; ECB Convergence Report June 2014 p. 20; for further reading cf. Steven, in Siekmann (2012), Article 131 AEUV para 35–52, with concrete examples, *inter alia*, of how the requirement of compatibility has been achieved in Germany.

3. Scope of Application of the Provision

The **compatibility requirements** of Article 131 TFEU needed to be met by the 5
establishment of the ESCB on 1 June 1998.[7] The United Kingdom and Denmark have been granted an **opt-out** (→ para 15–18), while Sweden does not currently seek to meet the requirements.[8] With the enlargement of the EU, the new MS have been obliged to fulfil the requirements when joining the EU, respectively on 1 May 2004,[9] 1 January 2007[10] and 1 July 2013.[11] From 4 November 2014, each MS whose derogation is abrogated will automatically join the **Single Supervisory Mechanism** (SSM) upon the adoption of the euro.[12]

3.1. Material Scope of Application

The wording of Article 131 TFEU **does not delineate** the material scope of 6
application as regards the Treaties and the Statute. Consequently, Article 131 TFEU might be understood as a general obligation of the MS; however, having regard to its **location** in the TFEU and the **purpose** of ensuring a **smooth and efficient operation of ESCB-related tasks**, the material scope of application is **restricted to the fields of competence of the ECB**.[13]

---

[7] Cf. ex-Article 109 TEC, although MS only moved to stage 3 of EMU on 1 January 1999. Greece was only able to fulfil the requirements on 1 January 2001. For further reading on the historical summary, see Smits (1997), p. 128.

[8] ECB Opinions CON/2008/34 and CON/2013/53 on the financial independence of the Sverige Riksbank. All ECB Opinions are available on the ECB website at www.ecb.europa.eu. For details on the Swedish convergence regarding the compatibility of national legislation, see ECB Convergence Report 2014, pp. 259–263.

[9] Cyprus, Czech Republic, Estonia, Hungary, Latvia, Lithuania, Malta, Poland, Slovak Republic and Slovenia.

[10] Bulgaria and Romania.

[11] Croatia.

[12] Cf. Article 33.2 of Council Regulation (EU) No 1024/2013 *conferring specific tasks on the European Central Bank concerning policies relating to the prudential supervision of credit institutions* (SSM Regulation), O.J. L 287/63 (2013); ECB Convergence Report 2014, pp. 5–6. In particular, see the compatibility requirements for the establishment of a close cooperation with the competent authorities of participating MS whose currency is not the euro laid down in Article 7.2 point (c) of the SSM Regulation and Article 3.2 of Decision ECB/2014/5 *on the close cooperation with the national competent authorities of participating Member States whose currency is not the euro*, O.J. L 198/7 (2014).

[13] The European Commission applies in its Convergence Reports a narrower approach than the ECB, see the Commission's Convergence Report 2014, pp. 30–31 (available at http://ec.europa.eu). For further reading, see Case C-11/00, *Commission v ECB* (Opinion of AG Jacobs of 3 October 2002) para 138. On the general obligation for the MS to comply with EU legislation see Case C-106/77, *Simmenthal* (ECJ 9 March 1978) para 7.

3.1.1. Independence

7 The NCBs must ensure their independence from Union institutions, bodies, offices or agencies; from any government of an MS; or from any other body (Article 130 TFEU and Article 7 of the Statute). The concept of **central bank independence comprises various types of independence, namely functional, institutional, personal** and **financial independence** (→ Article 130 TFEU para 11 et seqq.).[14] These aspects are also the basis for assessing the level of convergence between the national legislation of the MS with a derogation and the Treaties and the Statute.[15]

3.1.2. Confidentiality

8 The obligation of professional secrecy for ECB and NCB staff under Article 37 of the Statute may have an impact on similar provisions in NCB statutes or national legislation. The primacy of EU law and rules adopted thereunder also implies that national laws on the **access of third parties to documents** may not lead to infringements of the Statute.[16]

3.1.3. Monetary Financing and Privileged Access

9 The MS provisions regarding the **prohibition of monetary financing** (Article 123.1 TFEU) and the **prohibition on privileged access** (Article 124 TFEU) have to be adjusted where necessary.[17] The ECB's general stance regarding the compatibility of national legislation with the prohibition has been primarily developed within the framework of consultations of the ECB by MS on draft legislation under Article 127.4 TFEU and Article 282.5 TFEU.[18]

---

[14] ECB Convergence Report 1998, pp. 291–295; Arda, in Herzog et al. (2011), §131.04 (3a); Malatesta (2003), p. 81; Maçãs, in Anastácio and Lopes Porto (2012), Article 131 TFUE para 1–2; see CON/2015/9, for instance, on the progress regarding the personal independence of the Polish NCB.

[15] The ECB has introduced further refinement of the analysis of these aspects of central bank independence in several of its adopted opinions: on functional independence, see ECB Opinion CON/2012/44 subpara 2.2; on institutional independence, see ECB Opinion CON/2015/8 subpara 4.4; on personal independence, see both ECB Opinion CON/2014/25 para 3 and ECB Opinion CON/2011/6 para 3; on financial independence, see ECB Opinion CON/2008/34 para 1.2.

[16] Steven, in Siekmann (2012), Article 131 AEUV para 16; EMI, Progress towards convergence 1996, p. 100; ECB Convergence Report 2014, p. 27.

[17] European Commission Convergence Report 2014, p. 4; Dziechciarz, in von der Groeben et al. (2015), Article 131 AEUV para 8.

[18] Also under the third indent of Article 2.1 of Council Decision 98/415/EC *on the consultation of the ECB by national authorities*, O.J. L 189/42 (1998) and Article 34.1, third indent of the Statute; cf. Lambrinoc (2009), pp. 6–11. ECB Convergence Report 1998, p. 23 footnote 13 contains a list of formative EMI/ECB opinions in this area from May 1995 to March 1998. See also ECB Opinions CON/2008/46, CON/2009/59, CON/2011/9, CON/2010/4, CON/2012/44.

Article 131. [Compatibility of National Legislation]

3.1.4. Legal Integration into the Eurosystem

The **NCBs are an integral part of the ESCB** (Article 14.3 of the Statute). Provisions in national legislation and NCB statutes that would **prevent the implementation of ESCB-related tasks** or **compliance** with ECB decisions impede the smooth and efficient operation of the ESCB and therefore have to be considered **incompatible**.[19] **10**

The roles of the NCBs in relation to the ECB are subject to manifold discussions.[20] One view is that NCBs are **federal cosmetic**,[21] similar to the German *Landesbanken* within the **Bundesbank structure**.[22] This implies that the NCBs are mere **agents** of the ECB within the ESCB.[23] Another view holds that the NCBs still carry out **autonomous functions**, based on their legal personality, under national provisions (Article 14.4 of the Statute).[24] **11**

The criterion of **independence** serves as a **measure of integration into the ESCB**. With the fulfilment of the criteria of stage 3 of EMU and the independence criterion, there is an upward trend for the **autonomy of the NCBs from the MS while strengthening an already close link with the ECB** (Article 127.4 TFEU and Article 9.2 of the Statute). Instead of being under obligation to the national government or parliament that may exert influence, the NCBs are then under obligation to the ECB. This can be demonstrated by the NCBs having to adjust their statutes to comply with compatibility requirements,[25] the recognition of a specific legal remedy conferred on the Governor of an NCB before the ECJ against an MS's interference (Article 14.2 of the Statute[26]) and the subjection to the ECB's guidelines and instructions (Articles 12.1 and 14.3 of the Statute) at the risk of sanctions ($\rightarrow$ para 20–25). These are strong arguments in favour of categorising the **NCBs as agents of the ECB**, which is the **only truly independent institution**.[27] **12**

---

[19] See for instance ECB Convergence Report 2014, pp. 245–250 on the Hungarian convergence criteria and as an example for making the required adjustments, see pp. 240–244 on the Lithuanian convergence criteria.

[20] On the legal construction of the Eurosystem, see de Lhoneux (2005), pp. 161–178.

[21] Zilioli and Selmayr (2001), p. 73.

[22] For further reading concerning the Bundesbank system serving as a central bank role model, see Sparve (2005), p. 274.

[23] Zilioli and Selmayr (2001), pp. 73–80, deducting the argumentation from the ECJ Case C-165/84, *Krohn* (ECJ 12 December 1985) and the functional approach of the ECJ; Priego and Conlledo (2005), p. 193.

[24] Weber (1995), p. 53, although without specifying these autonomous functions.

[25] Cf. Lambrinoc (2009), p. 26; any amendment to NCB statutes is subject to consultation of the ECB.

[26] See the first judgments in Cases C-202/18 and C-238/18, *Rimšēvičs v Latvia and ECB v Latvia* (CJEU 26 February 2019).

[27] Cf. also Maçãs, in Anastácio and Lopes Porto (2012), Article 131 TFUE para 3–5.

3.2. Personal Scope of Application

13 This provision is applicable to all MS, with the exception of Denmark, by virtue of an "opt-out".[28]

3.2.1. Member States with a Derogation

14 MS that did **not fulfil the necessary conditions for the adoption** of the single currency became automatically "Member States with a derogation" pursuant to Article 139.1 TFEU.[29] Article 131 TFEU **is not subject to** the listed provisions that shall not apply to those MS (Article 139.2 TFEU and Artice 42 of the Statute). On the contrary, in Article 140.1 TFEU, the compatibility of national legislation and the statutes of the NCB are the subjects of **Convergence Reports** (→ para 20).

3.2.2. Member States with an "Opt-Out"

15 Denmark and the United Kingdom gave notification that they would not participate in stage 3 of EMU. As a consequence, the Convergence Reports only have to be provided for these two countries if they so request.

16 One of the conditions of the **United Kingdom** adopting the EC Treaty in 1992 was the **opt-out granted under** Protocol (No 25) annexed to the Treaty. The United Kingdom gave notice to the Council on 30 October 1997 saying that it did not intend to move to stage 3 of EMU and to adopt the single currency on 1 January 1999.[30] The opt-out has been annexed as Protocol (No 15)[31] to the current Treaties. In accordance with this Protocol, in contrast to the other MS, the United Kingdom was **not obliged to join the euro area**.[32]

17 On 23 June 2016, the United Kingdom held a referendum on whether it should remain in the EU (so-called **Brexit referendum**). On 29 March 2017, the United Kingdom notified the European Council of its intention to leave the EU, thus formally triggering the withdrawal procedure (→ Article 50 TEU para 26–27 and Article 26 TFEU para 67 et seqq.). On 17 October 2019, the European Council endorsed the UK's withdrawal from the EU and the European Atomic Energy Community (EAEC)[33] and the revised political declaration on the framework of the future EU-UK relationship. The entry into force of the **withdrawal**

---

[28] Together with Denmark, until its withdrawal from the EU on 1 February 2020, the United Kingdom also benefited from an exception by virtue of an "opt-out" granted under Protocol (No 15) annexed to the current Treaties.

[29] These are currently: Bulgaria, Czech Republic, Croatia, Hungary, Poland, Romania, Sweden.

[30] Recital 5 of Council Decision 98/317/EC *in accordance with Article 109j(4) of the Treaty*, O.J. L 139/30 (1998).

[31] Protocol (No 15) on certain provisions relating to the United Kingdom of Great Britain and Northern Ireland, annexed to the Treaties.

[32] Smits (1997), p. 138; Zilioli and Selmayr (2001), p. 137; Lastra and Louis (2013), p. 33.

[33] In accordance with Article 106a TEAEC, Article 50 TEU applies to Euratom as well.

agreement[34] marked the end of the period under Article 50 TEU and the start of a transition period until 31 December 2020, foreseen in the withdrawal agreement, aiming to provide more time for citizens and businesses to adapt.[35] During the transition period, the UK continued to apply Union law, but it would no longer benefit from the *opt-out* or be represented in the EU institutions (Article 126 of the Agreement). Although the withdrawal of the United Kingdom should be considered a failure for the European integration project, the remaining MS could interpret this event as an opportunity to engage in some significant legal and constitutional reforms in order to adapt the EU legal framework to the new Union of 27 MS.[36]

Following a negative outcome of a referendum in June 1992, **Denmark** was granted an opt-out during the Edinburgh Summit held in December 1992 in order to ratify the Treaties, subject to a national referendum.[37] Denmark has obtained a **special opt-out** as it is **treated as an MS with a derogation**, although it never joined stage 3 of EMU.[38] As Denmark bears the status of an MS with a derogation, theoretically it should be subject to the obligation of Article 131 TFEU. However, Denmark is not required to fulfil the convergence criteria, as in order to join the euro area, it **must request the removal of the special status**.[39]

18

4. Monitoring and Compliance

To ensure the fulfilment of the requirements, both the MS and the NCBs are monitored to ensure compliance.

19

4.1. Convergence Reports

The legal compatibility requirement is the subject of assessment in the Convergence Reports elaborated by the European Commission and the ECB as **reports to the Council** (Article 140.1 TFEU; → Article 140 TFEU para 7–9). These reports aim to provide an analysis and review concerning the **legal and economic convergence** the MS have to achieve in order to join the euro area. Article 140.1 TFEU

20

---

[34] Agreement on the withdrawal of the United Kingdom of Great Britain and Northern Ireland from the European Union and the European Atomic Energy Community, O.J. C 384I/1 (2019).

[35] Legal (2017), pp. 160–164.

[36] Fabbrini (2017), p. 181.

[37] In May 1993, Denmark accepted the Maastricht Treaty in a national referendum; cf. Zilioli and Selmayr (2001), p. 139; Saccomando (1994), p. 223.

[38] Recital 6 of Council Decision 98/317/EC.

[39] Protocol (No 16) on certain provisions relating to Denmark, annexed to the Treaties. Denmark is the subject of convergence assessment only as regards Article 130 TFEU. The Convergence Report 1998 stated that Denmark has achieved the central bank independence requirement of the Treaties and has since then not been the subject of Convergence Reports. For further reading on the special Danish status, see Zilioli and Selmayr (2001), pp. 137–142.

states explicitly that these reports shall contain an examination of the legal compatibility of each of the MS' national legislation, including the statute of their NCBs, with the Statute and Articles 130 and 131 TFEU.

21 Non-compliance by an MS may lead to **infringement procedures** pursuant to Articles 258 and 259 TFEU. Although the personal scope of application ($\rightarrow$ para 13–18) is addressed to the MS, it is also possible that an NCB fails to fulfil the requirements, especially when it has legislative competencies. In this case, the Governing Council has the same competencies with regard to the NCBs as those conferred upon the European Commission as concerns the MS (Article 258 in conjunction with Article 271 point (d) TFEU).

4.2. Failure to Ensure Compatibility

22 Whereas in ex-Article 109 TEC the time limit set was the date of the establishment of the ESCB, in the Treaties there is **no timetable**[40] defining the moment when an MS has failed to fulfil its obligations, that is, to reach stage 3 of EMU and consequently adopt the euro.

23 The Treaties remain unclear as regards the **timing for the adoption of the euro** by the MS with a derogation. The unlimited derogation option and the opt-outs must be considered politically motivated from the time of the Maastricht Treaty to ensure its ratification and therefore might be subject to adjustment in future treaties. However, also the Lisbon Treaty of 2007 did not introduce a time limit. Hence, it is difficult to say whether the procedures under Articles 258 and 259 TFEU are applicable as, on the one hand, the scope of application is restricted ($\rightarrow$ para 6–17) while, on the other, no time limit has been established.

24 Nonetheless, it is submitted that an **MS has to comply** with the compatibility requirements at **the latest upon the adoption of the euro**[41] based on Article 140.3 TFEU. It is an ongoing duty for the MS whose currency is the euro and MS with a derogation.[42]

25 The European Commission may bring a matter in which an MS has failed to fulfil its obligation before the ECJ (Articles 258 and 259 TFEU). Nonetheless, the Commission cannot take action against an MS to put an obligation on the NCB as this would impinge on the central bank's independence.[43] This kind of action can

---

[40] Cf. Steven, in Siekmann (2012), Article 131 AEUV para 1, mentions the time limit issue that is seldom addressed in the literature.

[41] Smits (1997), pp. 121–122; Steven, in Siekmann (2012), Article 131 AEUV para 11; EMI, Progress towards convergence 1996, p. 99.

[42] Cf. Dziechciarz, in von der Groeben et al. (2015), Article 131 AEUV para 20, infers from the change of the wording of ex-Article 109 TEC to Article 131 TFEU that it is an ongoing obligation for all the MS, although without stating a reason for the absence of any sanction for MS with no opt-out (e.g. Sweden) following non-compliance.

[43] Armati, in Curti Gialdino (2012), p. 1982; Castillo de la Torre, in Herzog et al. (2011), §271.04 [2].

only be based on **Article 258 in conjunction with Article 271 point (d) TFEU** as it is the sole provision specifying a measure against an NCB of an MS. The ECJ has jurisdiction in disputes concerning the fulfilment by an NCB of obligations under the Treaties and this Statute. If the Governing Council decides to take action against an NCB before the ECJ, the NCB will be obliged to comply with the judgment (Article 35.5 of the ESCB Statute). In case the ECB considers that an NCB has failed to fulfil an obligation under the Treaties and the Statute, it shall deliver a reasoned opinion on the matter after giving the NCB concerned the opportunity to submit its observations. If the NCB concerned does not comply with the opinion within the period laid down by the ECB, the matter may be brought before the ECJ by the ECB (Article 35.6 of the ESCB Statute).

In this connection, the powers of the Governing Council of the ECB in respect of the NCBs shall be the same as those conferred upon the Commission in respect of the MS by Article 258 TFEU. If the ECJ finds that an NCB has failed to fulfil an obligation under the Treaties, that NCB will have to take the necessary measures to comply with the judgment of the ECJ.

26

List of Cases

ECJ 05.02.1963, 26/62, *van Gend & Loos*, ECLI:EU:C:1963:1 [cit. in para 1]
ECJ 15.07.1964, 6/64, *Flaminio Costa v E.N.E.L.*, ECLI:EU:C:1964:66 [cit. in para 1]
ECJ 09.03.1978, 106/77, *Simmenthal*, ECLI:EU:C:1978:49 [cit. in para 1, 6]
ECJ 12.12.1985, 165/84, *Krohn v BALM*, ECLI:EU:C:1985:507 [cit. in para 11]
CJEU 26.02.2019, C-202/18 and C-238/18, *Rimšēvičs v Latvia and ECB v Latvia*, ECLI:EU:C:2019:139 [cit. in para 12]

References[44]

Anastácio, G., & Lopes Porto, M. (2012). *Tratado de Lisboa, Anotado e Comentado*. Almedina.
Curti Gialdino, C. (Ed.). (2012). *Codice Dell'Unione Europea operativo*. Simone.
de Lhoneux, E. (2005). The Eurosystem. In ECB (Ed.), *Legal aspects of the European System of Central Banks: Liber amicorum Paulo Zamboni Garavelli* (pp. 161–178). European Central Bank.
Fabbrini, F. (2017). Brexit and the future of Europe: Seizing the opportunity to complete the European Union. In ECB (Ed.), *ECB Legal Conference: Shaping a new legal order for Europe: a tale of crises and opportunities* (pp. 180–193) Available at https://www.ecb.europa.eu/pub/pdf/other/ecblegalconferenceproceedings201712.en.pdf
Herzog, P., Campbell, C., Zagel, G., & Smit, H. (Eds.). (2011). *On the law of the European Union*. LexisNexis Bender.

---

[44] All cited Internet sources of this comment have been accessed on 6 April 2021.

Lambrinoc, S. (2009). *The legal duty to consult the European Central Bank - National and EU consultations* (ECB Legal Working Paper No. 9). Retrieved from https://www.ecb.europa.eu/pub/pdf/scplps/ecblwp9.pdf

Lastra, R., & Louis, J.-V. (2013). European economic and Monetary Union: History, prospects and trends. *Yearbook of European Law*, 1–150.

Legal, H. (2017). The scope of transitional arrangements under Article 50 TEU. In ECB (Ed.), *ECB Legal Conference: Shaping a new legal order for Europe: A tale of crises and opportunities* (pp. 160–164). Available at https://www.ecb.europa.eu/pub/pdf/other/ecblegalconferenceproceedings201712.en.pdf

Malatesta, A. (2003). *La Banca Centrale Europea*. Giuffrè.

Priego, F.-J., & Conlledo, F. (2005). The role of the decentralisation principle in the legal construction of the European System of Central Banks. In ECB (Ed.), *Legal Aspects of the European System of Central Banks: Liber amicorum Paulo Zamboni Garavelli* (pp. 189–198). European Central Bank.

Saccomando, V. (1994). Maastricht's treaty's opt-out provisions for Denmark keep EC intact. *Boston College International & Comparative Law Review*, 223–232.

Siekmann, H. (Ed.). (2012). *Kommentar zur Europäischen Währungsunion*. Mohr Siebeck.

Smits, R. (1997). *The European Central Bank – Institutional aspects*. Kluwer Law International.

Sparve, R. (2005). Central bank independence under European Union and other international standards. In ECB (Ed.), *Legal aspects of the European System of Central Banks: Liber amicorum Paulo Zamboni Garavelli* (pp. 271–286). European Central Bank.

von der Groeben, H., Schwarze, J., & Hatje, A. (Eds.). (2015). *Europäisches Unionsrecht*. Nomos.

Weber, M. (1995). *Die Kompetenzverteilung im Europäischen System der Zentralbanken bei der Festlegung und Durchführung der Geldpolitik*. V. Florentz GmbH.

Zilioli, C., & Selmayr, M. (2001). *The law of the European Central Bank*. Hart Publishing.

Article 132 [Legal Acts of the ECB]
(ex-Article 110 TEC)

1. In order to carry out the tasks entrusted to the ESCB,[105–107] the European Central Bank shall, in accordance with the provisions of the Treaties and under the conditions laid down in the Statute of the ESCB and of the ECB:

 – make regulations[1–11, 38, 40–41, 80–83, 89, 95–98, 100–102] to the extent necessary to implement the tasks defined in Article 3.1, first indent, Articles 19.1, 22 and 25.2 of the Statute of the ESCB and of the ECB in cases which shall be laid down in the acts of the Council referred to in Article 129(4),
 – take decisions[1–5, 12, 40, 85–88] necessary for carrying out the tasks entrusted to the ESCB under the Treaties and the Statute of the ESCB and of the ECB,
 – make recommendations[1–5, 13–17, 40] and deliver opinions.[1–5, 18–21, 38, 40, 42, 54]

2. The European Central Bank may decide to publish[8, 44–46, 55] its decisions, recommendations and opinions.
3. Within the limits and under the conditions adopted by the Council under the procedure laid down in Article 129(4), the European Central Bank shall be entitled to impose fines or periodic penalty payments[40, 47–53, 91–93] on undertakings for failure to comply with obligations under its regulations and decisions.

Contents

1. Basic Provisions Regarding ECB Legal Acts 1
   1.1. Regulations 6
   1.2. Decisions 13
   1.3. Recommendations 14
   1.4. Opinions 19
   1.5. Legal Instruments Outside the Scope of Article 132 TFEU 23
         1.5.1. Guidelines 26
         1.5.2. Instructions 34
         1.5.3. Agreements 38
   1.6. Effects of the Legal Acts 39
   1.7. The Legislating Bodies and Their Competencies 41
   1.8. Relation to Legal Acts of Other Union Institutions 44
   1.9. Duty to State Reasons, Publication, Entry into Force and Enforcement 45
   1.10. Sanctioning Powers 48
   1.11. Remedies and Liability 55

The views expressed in this commentary are those of the author and may not be attributed to the ECB.

2.	Eurosystem	58
	2.1. Legal Acts on Monetary Policy	59
	2.2. Legal Acts on Banknotes	62
	2.3. Legal Acts on Reserve Requirements	64
	2.4. Legal Acts on Clearing and Payment Systems	67
	2.5. Legal Acts on Statistical Data Collection	71
	2.6. Legal Acts on the Capital of the ECB	73
3.	Banking Supervision	75
	3.1. Scope of the ECB's Competence to Issue Legal Acts	76
	3.2. Delimitation of Competencies Between the ECB and the EBA	81
	3.3. Specific Requirements for Banking Supervision Regulations	82
	3.3.1. Arrangements	84
	3.3.2. Need for a Regulation	85
	3.4. Regulations, Guidelines and General Instructions to National Competent Authorities	86
	3.5. Instructions to National Competent Authorities	87
	3.6. Supervisory Decisions	88
	3.7. Decision to Directly Supervise Less Significant Credit Institutions	90
	3.8. Decision to Classify a Bank That Fulfils the Significance Criteria as Less Significant	91
	3.9. Competencies and Procedures	92
	3.10. Sanctioning Powers	94
	3.11. Details Concerning Legal Acts in the Context of Prudential Supervision	97
	3.11.1. Framework on Practical Arrangements for Cooperation Within the SSM	98
	3.11.2. Legal Acts Based on the Framework for Close Cooperation	99
	3.11.3. Legal Acts Addressing Supervised Entities Regarding Prudential Tasks	102
	3.11.4. Legal Acts Regarding Less Significant Credit Institutions	104
	3.11.5. Legal Acts Relating to the Institutional Framework of the ECB for the SSM	105
	3.11.6. Instruments for the Effective and Consistent Functioning of the SSM	108

List of Cases
References

1. Basic Provisions Regarding ECB Legal Acts

1 Article 132.1 TFEU provides the ECB with the power to issue legal acts concerning any of its tasks. These are those of the European System of Central Banks (ESCB), i.e. **monetary policy, foreign exchange** transactions, the official **monetary reserves** of the MS and the smooth functioning of **payment systems**. In 2014, **banking supervision** was added as a reaction to the shortcomings of national approaches to limit the systemic risk produced by larger banks in the euro area.

2 The ECB's legislative competence is based on its **political, financial** and **operational independence** and legal personality, which also allows the ECB to adopt its own rules of procedure, enter into agreements with other institutions or States within and outside the Union and be a party to private law contracts.

Article 132. [Legal Acts of the ECB]

Moreover, the ECB may issue implementing regulations on the basis of a delegation from the Council pursuant to Article 127.6 TFEU.

Along with (the almost identical) Article 34 of the ESCB Statute, Article 132 TFEU is to be considered *lex specialis* with respect to Article 288 TFEU on the general competencies of the Union institutions to adopt legal acts. Article 132 TFEU does not provide the ECB with the power to issue **directives** as giving the MS discretion to implement them is incompatible with a single monetary policy. Regulations, decisions, recommendations and opinions are, however, part of the ECB's armoury of legal acts, as Article 132 TFEU explicitly states.

This list is, however, not exhaustive as Article 132.1 TFEU only specifies **public law acts addressed to third parties**, which exclude in particular the national central banks (NCBs) in the ESCB. The ECB may, however, issue **guidelines** and **instructions** to the NCBs, as for example the ECB Guideline on the implementation of the Eurosystem monetary policy framework.[1] The same applies as regards the national competent authorities (NCAs) in the field of **banking supervision** in the Single Supervisory Mechanism (SSM). Examples are the ECB Guidelines on the recording of certain data by NCAs in the register of institutions and affiliate data and on the approach for the recognition of institutional protection schemes for prudential purposes by NCAs pursuant to the Capital Requirements Regulation (CRR).[2]

The competence to issue legal acts on the prudential supervision of credit institutions is specified in Article 4.3 of the SSM Regulation,[3] empowering the ECB to "adopt **guidelines** and **recommendations**, and take **decisions** subject to and in compliance with the relevant Union law and in particular any legislative and non-legislative act, including those referred to in Article 290 and 291". The provision also provides a legal basis to adopt **regulations**, but "only to the extent necessary to organise or specify the arrangements for the carrying out of the tasks conferred on it by the SSM Regulation". This means that the ECB shall legislate only to the extent that the Union law framework for banking supervision, in particular the CRR, the national laws implementing the Capital Requirements Directive (CRD)[4] and the guidelines and regulatory or implementing technical standards of the European Banking Authority (EBA), is **incomplete**. The ECB

---

[1] ECB Guideline (EU) 2015/510 *on the implementation of the Eurosystem monetary policy framework*, O.J. L 116/22 (2015), last amended by ECB Guideline (EU) 2020/1690, O.J. L 379/77 (2020).

[2] Council Regulation (EU) No 575/2013 *on prudential requirements for credit institutions and investment firms*, O.J. L 176/1 (2013).

[3] Council Regulation (EU) 1024/2013 *conferring specific tasks on the European Central Bank concerning policies relating to the prudential supervision of credit institutions*, O.J. L 287/63 (2013).

[4] Council Directive 2013/36/EU *on access to the activity of credit institutions and the prudential supervision of credit institutions and investment firms*, O.J. L 176/338 (2013). This concept of a *European* institution applying *national* legislation is novel; see, in this regard, Witte (2014), pp. 89–109.

may not adopt legal acts in the areas of money laundering and consumer protection as these are outside its mandate.[5] Any such limitation does, however, not apply to ECB **opinions**, which the ECB may adopt regardless of whether or not it has been officially consulted by a national legislator or Union institution on a particular draft legal act.

1.1. Regulations

6   Regulations are adopted as **unilateral public law acts** of will by an agent exercising official powers (Article 288.2 TFEU). They generally create a system of Union law rights and obligations between the ECB and other legal entities outside the ESCB. However, an ECB regulation may also contain rights and obligations for the ECB, NCBs or NCAs, provided that this is justified within the specific context.

7   Regulations adopted by Union institutions, including the ECB, are of **general application** and are binding in their entirety and directly applicable in all MS without further implementing measures.

8   The regulation is the only legal act that must be **published** in the Official Journal of the EU. The publication of all other ECB legal acts is optional.

9   Provided that a **Union-wide harmonised provision** is necessary for the ECB in order to fulfil its tasks, an ECB regulation may be adopted in order to:

- Set and carry out the monetary policy of the Union
- Require credit institutions to hold minimum reserves on ECB accounts and calculate and determinate the required minimum reserves
- Ensure efficient and sound clearing and payment systems within the Union and with third countries
- Organise or specify the arrangements for carrying out the ECB's tasks related to banking supervision

10 The ECB's competence to adopt **implementing regulations**, which are provided for in the legal acts of the Council adopted pursuant to Article 129.4 TFEU, encompasses provisions on:

- The advisory role of the ECB (Article 4 of the Statute)

---

[5] After the number of cases in which the ECB's prudential mandate was concerned by money laundering had remarkably increased, as in particular in the areas of bank licence withdrawals and operational risk, and benefits of a stronger engagement of the ECB in the fight against money laundering had become more visible, a multilateral agreement on the practical modalities for exchange of information on money laundering and terror financing between the ECB and the competent authorities (CAs) was signed in 2019. The agreement is based on Article 57a.2 of Parliament/Council Directive (EU) 2015/849 *on the prevention of the use of the financial system for the purposes of money laundering or terrorist financing* (AMLD V), O.J. L 141/73 (2015) (as amended) which requires the European Supervisory Authorities (ESAs) to support the conclusion of an agreement on the practical modalities for exchange of information between the ECB and CAs.

- The collection of statistical data by the ECB and NCBs (Article 5.4 of the Statute)
- The basis for minimum reserves and the maximum permissible ratios between those reserves and their basis, as well as the appropriate sanctions in cases of non-compliance (Article 19.2 of the Statute)
- The Governing Council of the ECB's decisions on the use of "other operational methods of monetary control" (Article 20 of the Statute)
- The capital of the ECB (Article 28.1 of the Statute)
- The key for a capital subscription (Article 29.2 of the Statute)
- The transfer of foreign reserve assets (Article 30.4 of the Statute)
- The imposition of fines or periodic penalty payments (Article 34.3 of the Statute)

These competencies complement those set out in Article 132 TFEU in the areas of monetary policy, minimum reserves and monetary reserves.

The issuing of euro **banknotes** is part of the monetary policy tasks of the ECB. Even though it is not a monetary policy instrument in the strictest sense, it is one of the ECB's core central bank tasks and is thus covered by the ECB's competence to adopt regulations.

With blockchain or distributed ledger technology (DLT) gaining significance in the financial economy, most central banks, including the ECB, have announced that they are considering the issuance of a **central bank digital currency** (CBDC).[6] The basis for a legal act paving the way for a **digital euro** depends on the specific design, and there may be limitations excluding certain features. In essence, like a digital dollar or yen, a digital euro could be designed as a **wholesale** or **general-purpose** CBDC. A general purpose or wholesale could be **account** or **token based**, with the latter providing for a cash-like peer-to-peer exchange with or without anonymity towards the central bank.[7] While the ECB's monetary policy mandate or the (yet unapplied) provision in Article 20 of the Statute to use "other operational methods of monetary control" should provide sufficient legal basis for the issuance of most designs of a digital euro, an account-based general-purpose version with the ECB providing accounts for 300–500 million citizens or companies (instead of 10,000 as of now) might push the monetary policy mandate to its limit or beyond, given the large potential impact of such move on the financial economy.

---

[6] See "An ECB digital currency – a flight fancy of?" Speech by Yves Mersch, Member of the Executive Board of the ECB and Vice-Chair of the Supervisory Board of the ECB, at the Consensus 2020 virtual conference, 11 May 2020, available at ecb.europa.eu; Boar et al. (2020).
[7] BIS, Committee on Payments and Market Infrastructures (Markets Committee), Central bank digital currencies, (March 2018), available at bis.org.

1.2. Decisions

13 Decisions are also public legal acts that are adopted as unilateral acts by an agent exercising public power. They are typically used to handle **individual cases**, intended to create legal effects that are case-specific rather than applicable in general and are either generally binding or only binding on those to whom they are addressed (Article 288.4 TFEU). Potential addressees are the NCBs and NCAs, as well as credit institutions and the MS. In contrast to regulations, the areas in which the ECB may adopt decisions are not limited; there is simply a requirement that the decision must be necessary to fulfil the tasks of the ESCB or ECB, respectively, and (of course) be consistent with primary legislation.

1.3. Recommendations

14 Recommendations are adopted by the Union institutions if there is either **no competence** or **no need** to issue a **binding** legal act. They always target specific addressees, which can be legal or natural persons, Union institutions or MS, and always relate to a **concrete measure**. The material scope of recommendations is identical to that of regulations and decisions. Article 219 TFEU provides that the Council may adopt, based on a recommendation from the ECB or the Commission, formal agreements on an exchange rate system for the euro in relation to third-country currencies.

15 In contrast to regulations and decisions, recommendations are **non-binding** and thus not enforceable. However, despite their non-binding nature, all acts adopted by the institutions of the Union must, in their **explanatory memoranda**, refer to any recommendations that were adopted prior to the adoption of the legal act concerned (Article 296.2 TFEU).

16 Recommendations do not confer rights on the addressees that are enforceable before the **national courts**; this was clearly stated by the CJEU with regard to their lack of binding effect. The national courts are, however, required to take recommendations into account when ruling on disputes, in particular where they cast light on the interpretation of national legislation that implements Union law.[8] Any decision not to follow a recommendation should thus not be made *en passant* but should be explicitly justified.

17 Due to the specific expertise of the ECB, its recommendations have significant **political** and **psychological** importance, irrespective of their rather limited legal implications.

18 Article 132 TFEU provides the basis for ECB recommendations adopted within the general remit of the ECB's and ESCB's tasks. In addition, Article 129.3–4 TFEU provides the procedural basis for recommendations that are adopted in anticipation of the amendments of the articles of the Statute by the EP and Council,

---

[8] Case C-322/88, *Grimaldi* (ECJ 13 December 1989) para 18.

which are listed in Article 129.3 TFEU, or prior to the adoption of provisions by the Council on the basis of the articles of the Statute listed in Article 129.4 TFEU. Accordingly, the ECB may adopt recommendations in order to trigger a **simplified amendment procedure of the Statute**. Such recommendations must be adopted by the Governing Council acting unanimously (Article 40.3 of the Statute). The ECB has already adopted a number of recommendations that have resulted in such acts. These recommendations must be forwarded by the Council to national parliaments (Article 2.5 of Protocol No 1). If, as a result, an opinion is adopted, the Council will forward it to the ECB (Article 3.3 of Protocol No 1).

1.4. Opinions

As part of its **advisory role**, the ECB may, at its **own initiative**, issue opinions vis-à-vis the competent institutions and bodies of the Union. In addition, in its field of competence, the ECB must be **heard on** any proposed **Union legal act**. Furthermore, **national authorities** in all MS are obliged to consult the ECB on certain draft legislation.[9] The advisory role ensures that no legal act within the ECB's sphere of competence is adopted without its involvement. This function also underlines the ECB's special status as an independent entity within the Union with its own specific powers and emphasises the expertise and responsibility of the ECB with regard to price and financial stability within the Union's legal framework.

19

The ECB's **right to be heard** extends to the areas of currency, payments, NCBs, collection, compilation and the distribution of statistics in the subjects of currency, finance, banking, payment systems and balance of payments, as well as payment and clearing systems and rules on financial institutions in so far as they significantly affect the stability of the financial institutions and financial markets.[10] The Treaty specifically refers to the right to be heard in a number of instances. A hearing is required:

20

- When protective measures are imposed on third countries where there is a risk of serious difficulties for the operation of the Economic and Monetary Union (EMU) (Article 66 TFEU)
- When adopting measures for the use of the euro as a single currency (Article 133 TFEU)
- In relation to the composition of the Economic and Financial Committee (EFC) (Article 134.3 TFEU)

---

[9] This follows directly from Article 127.4 TFEU and Council Decision 98/415/EC *on the consultation of the ECB by national authorities regarding draft legislative provisions*, O.J. L 189/42 (1998). This short decision is complemented by the ECB's detailed guide on the matter: Guide to consultation of the ECB by national authorities regarding draft legislative provisions, available at www.ecb.europa.eu.

[10] Article 2 of Decision 98/415/EC, and Article 25.1 of the Statute.

- When deciding on a common position on matters of particular interest for EMU in order to secure the euro's place in the international monetary system within the competent international financial institutions and conferences (Article 138.1 TFEU)
- In relation to measures aimed at a ensuring a unified representation within the international financial institutions and conferences (Article 138.2 TFEU)
- When repealing derogations for an MS in respect of the adoption of the euro, in particular on the decision on the exchange rate at which the respective currency is replaced by the euro, and other measures for the introduction of the euro in that MS (Articles 139 and 140.3 TFEU),
- When replacing the protocol on the excessive deficit procedure (Article 126.14 TFEU)
- Regarding measures on the harmonisation of the denominations and technical specifications of all euro coins and in the context of the negotiation of monetary or foreign exchange regime matters with international organisations and/or third countries (Articles 218 and 219.3 TFEU).

The Governing Council has the right to submit opinions in the context of the staffing of the ECB's Executive Board (Article 283.2 TFEU). Furthermore, the ECB must be consulted on institutional changes in the monetary area.[11] The ECB was also consulted on the draft Treaty establishing a Constitution for Europe.[12]

21 ECB opinions are—like all opinions of Union institutions—**not binding** as they merely state the views of an external initiative within the ECB's consultative function (Article 4 of the Statute and Articles 127.4 and 282.5 TFEU). The exercise of this function relies heavily on the ECB's right to be heard. To omit consulting with the ECB on draft national legislation in its field of competence is an infringement of Decision 98/415/EC and may lead to an infringement procedure under the Treaty before the CJEU. The Union legislators are also obliged to refer to an ECB opinion in the explanatory memorandum of the legal act to be adopted (Article 296.2 TFEU).

22 The Commission is responsible for bringing any breach of the right to be heard in the context of **infringement proceedings against an MS** before the CJEU (Article 258 TFEU). Where an NCB with legislative competence does not consult the ECB in accordance with Decision 98/415/EC, the ECB itself can initiate infringement proceedings, provided that the ECB has adopted a reasoned opinion with which the NCB did not comply within a time limit set by the ECB.[13] In

---

[11] See ECB Opinion CON/00/30 at the request of the Presidency of the Council of the European Union on a proposal to amend Article 10.2 of the Statute of the European System of Central Banks and of the European Central Bank, O.J. C 362/13 (2000). All ECB opinions are available on the ECB website at www.ecb.europa.eu.

[12] The Council agreed, by written procedure on 10 July 2003, on the text of the draft letter to be sent to the ECB. See minutes of the 2520th meeting of the Council on 15 July 2003, available at www.europa.eu.

[13] Article 35.6 of the Statute and Article 271 point (d) TFEU.

addition, the consultation of the ECB is a precise and unconditional obligation, so that individuals before national courts may rely on this obligation. Without prejudice to the ECB's right to be heard, the CJEU ruled that a national provision adopted in breach of an essential procedural requirement is not enforceable against individuals.[14]

1.5. Legal Instruments Outside the Scope of Article 132 TFEU

As mentioned above, the ECB's power to adopt legal acts is not limited to the legal acts referred to in Article 132 TFEU; it may also adopt legislative instruments regarding the **internal affairs of the ESCB** and its management, in so far as these do not have immediate legal effects on third parties. In practice, the legal acts used for such decisions are guidelines and ESCB **internal decisions** that the Governing Council adopts to safeguard the performance of the tasks entrusted to the ESCB. This includes, in particular, decisions relating to intermediate monetary objectives, key interest rates and the supply of reserves in the ESCB (Article 12.1 (1) of the Statute). In turn, the Executive Board is responsible for implementing monetary policies in accordance with the guidelines and decisions that are laid down by the Governing Council and, in doing so, gives the necessary instructions to the NCBs (Article 12.1 (2) of the Statute). The Governing Council must take the necessary steps to ensure compliance with the guidelines and instructions of the ECB (Article 14.3 of the Statute). The need for these powers follows from the fact that both the ECB and the NCBs are distinct legal entities, while the ESCB has no legal personality of its own.[15] Taking into account this specific structure, the ECB must have the necessary internal legal instruments available to it in order to enable the system to work efficiently and speak with one voice and ensure that the objectives laid down in the Treaty are attained.

23

The direct obligation to act in accordance with the ECB's guidelines and instructions relates solely to the NCBs of the MS whose currency is the euro.[16] However, this purely internal right relating to the euro area may be extended to the MS that have not yet adopted the euro. In this respect, the ECB must conclude contracts with the NCBs.

24

Compliance with these intra-system acts is **enforceable** before the CJEU (Article 35.6 of the Statute). Admittedly, neither the Treaty nor the Statute defines

25

---

[14] See also the ECB's Guide to consultation of the ECB by national authorities regarding draft legislative provisions, p. 26.

[15] See ECB Monthly Bulletin, July 1999, pp. 59 et seq.

[16] See Article 14.3 in conjunction with Article 42.1 of the Statute. As such, it would have been an obvious step to add Article 14.3 to the list in Article 42.4. The failure to include such a list should not therefore be interpreted as meaning that Article 14.3 applies to all NCBs. This can be seen from a comparison with paragraph 8(2) of the Protocol on certain provisions relating to the United Kingdom of Great Britain and Northern Ireland. See also the comparison with Article 12.1 of the Statute. For Article 12.1, the same applies as for Article 14.3.

ECB guidelines and instructions. It follows, however, from the context that these terms also refer to instruments of a legal nature. Read in conjunction with the other relevant rules concerning the ESCB, and in particular Articles 8, 9.2, 12.1 and 14.3 of the Statute and Article 129.3 TFEU, it can be concluded that ECB guidelines and instructions are specific types of binding legal instruments whose introduction was necessary due to the specific structure of the ESCB. Both instruments are formal legal instruments and not just political orientations, which ensure that the tasks conferred upon the ESCB are implemented within the system and those tasks are implemented in accordance with the internal division of powers.[17] Since **guidelines and instructions are part of Union law**, they prevail, in the same way as regulations and decisions, over existing and subsequently adopted national legislation that falls within their scope.[18] The intra-system acts of the ECB are only binding within the ESCB; third parties may not rely on their rights and obligations. However, the NCBs' implementation of such acts may lead to an indirect effect on third parties. Whether such indirect effect is possible in the event of implementing errors is assessed differently.

1.5.1. Guidelines

26   On the basis of the provisions laid down in the Statute, guidelines are legal instruments with which the ECB's **Governing Council defines and implements the policies** of the ECB. To date, guidelines have been adopted in the areas of statistics, foreign exchange reserves, banknotes, monetary policy, payments and accounting, setting out the **general framework** and principal rules established by the ECB or NCBs of the euro area. Guidelines are often highly detailed. Unlike regulations, they are not subject to specific substantive restrictions but must, like all other ECB legal acts, be necessary for the performance of the tasks of the ESCB. This includes the need for them to comply with the principle of an open market economy with free competition and the principle of the efficient use of resources, as well as guiding principles such as price stability, sound public finances and a sustainable balance of payments (Article 127.1 TFEU).

27   The ECB may also issue guidelines to the NCAs of the MS participating in the SSM regarding the performance of **supervision of credit institutions** in general and the adoption of supervisory decisions in particular. The exercise of this competence is clearly defined by Article 6.5 point (a) of the SSM Regulation. In contrast to the traditional tasks of the ECB, guidelines on banking supervision must therefore be assessed solely against the criteria laid down by the SSM Regulation.

---

[17] Zilioli and Selmayr (2001), pp. 400 et seq.

[18] This fact is also highlighted in the final recital of all ECB guidelines: It states that, in accordance with Article 12.1 and Article 14.3 of the Statute, ECB guidelines form an integral part of Union law.

The NCBs and NCAs may refer the question of whether an ECB guideline was **28**
legally adopted to the CJEU (Article 35.1 of the Statute). In such cases, the crucial
point is the interpretation of the ECB's legislative discretion, which is rather broad.

In contrast to regulations and decisions, guidelines concern the internal affairs of **29**
the ESCB and relate exclusively to the ECB and NCBs or NCAs. Accordingly,
guidelines do **not** aim to **produce direct legal effects** vis-à-vis third parties and
require further **implementing measures** by the NCBs or NCAs to whom they are
addressed. Depending on the subject matter and the national law governing each
addressee, the implementation of guidelines takes place either by means of a
contract between the NCBs and their counterparties or through legal acts directly
addressed to these counterparties. Guidelines addressed to the NCAs are implemented by national supervisory decisions (Article 6.5 point (a) of the SSM Regulation).

As the legal instruments of the ECB do not give rise to rights and obligations for **30**
the NCBs of the MS that have not yet adopted the euro, the ECB may, where
necessary and appropriate, conclude **contracts** with these **NCBs** in order to make
the internal rules binding. This was done, for example, with regard to the TARGET
payment system ($\rightarrow$ para 66).

As regards the need for implementation, guidelines are similar to directives **31**
under Article 288.3 TFEU, except that **no formal implementing legislation is
required**.[19] It should be noted that within the ESCB, there is only one level of
decision-making, namely the ECB. The competencies of the ECB are exclusive in
nature and thus leave no room for manoeuvre to the national level as regards
implementation; however, for the implementation of directives, a second level of
competence at the level of the MS is needed. The fact that the ECB may not adopt
directives is therefore not a legislative gap but rather a conceptual expression of the
centralisation of decision-making and legislative competence at the ECB. A further
difference, compared to directives, is that guidelines do not set a time limit for
implementation, but they only establish an obligation for the NCBs to provide the
ECB with proof of implementation before a given date. In this respect, guidelines
generally contain a formula indicating that the NCBs must provide the ECB with
the texts and implementing measures by a specific date.[20]

It could be argued that, in certain constellations, the provisions of guidelines **32**
may have a **direct legal effect** on **third parties**. In support of this contention,
according to the settled case law of the CJEU when assessing whether such direct
legal effect exists, it is not the title of the legislative instrument that is essential but
rather the intended legal effect.[21] On the other hand, it is recalled that guidelines are
directly effective only within the Eurosystem. Only an implementing measure
could potentially create rights for third parties. Any erroneous implementing acts,

---

[19] See Zilioli and Selmayr (2001), p. 332.
[20] See, for example, Article 2 of Guideline ECB/2011/14 *on monetary policy instruments and procedures of the Eurosystem*, O.J. L 166/34 (2014).
[21] Case T-3/93, *Air France v Commission* (CFI 24 March 1994) para 154 et seq.

which would prevent the creation of such rights, would have to be repealed since a direct application would not be in line with Article 132 TFEU, which lays down the exhaustive rule for the external effects of the ECB's legal acts.[22]

However, the fact that guidelines are not addressed to third parties does **not prevent** them from being **directly applicable** in the same way as directives. In exceptional situations, inequalities or harm to third parties caused by a guideline (as from any unlawful administrative act by an EU institution) may even be resolved by the CJEU. The likelihood of such a procedure in relation to ECB Guidelines is, however, not high, although there are no legal obstacles to an analogy with the procedure for the direct application of directives. It should be acknowledged, however, that the ECB is not obliged to publish guidelines. In the absence of publication, it is not really possible for third parties to initiate proceedings regarding a direct application of a guideline.

33 It may be assumed that the ECB carries out sector-specific regulatory procedures in order to safeguard the **consistency** of the **implementing measures** taken by the NCBs or NCAs. In the event of ambiguities regarding interpretation, the implementing measures must be construed in compliance with the guidelines. Based on the number of ECB guidelines published, it can be concluded that in 2000, the ECB took a general decision in favour of more transparency.[23] It is therefore to be expected that only in those cases where there is a justifiable reason for confidentiality will a guideline, or other instruments whose publication is not legally binding, not be published.[24]

1.5.2. Instructions

34 Instructions are legal instruments of a **specific** and **individual** nature by which the ECB's Executive Board may give directions to the NCBs of the euro area in order to fulfil the obligation to carry out monetary policies according to the guidelines and decisions of the Governing Council (Article 12.1 (2) of the Statute). For the NCBs, these acts are binding and create a corresponding obligation to act accordingly (Article 14.3 of the Statute). Outside the field of monetary policy, the ECB may give instructions to the NCAs within the framework of the SSM. The ECB may also issue regulations, guidelines or **general instructions** with regard to the supervised credit institutions[25] and, in particular, adopt supervisory decisions. Such instructions may refer to the specific supervisory powers of the ECB (Article 16.2 of the

---

[22] Ohler and Schmidt-Wenzel, in Siekmann (2013), Article 132 AEUV para 61.

[23] With Decision ECB/2000/12 *on the publication of certain legal acts and instruments of the European Central Bank*, O.J. L 55/68 (2001), the ECB has published guidelines, which were not publicly available before.

[24] See also ECB Decision ECB/2004/3 *on public access to European Central Bank documents* (ECB/2004/3), O.J. L 80/42 (2004) and ECB Decision ECB/2015/1 *amending Decision ECB/2004/3 on public access to European Central Bank documents*, O.J. L 84/64 (2015).

[25] These tasks are listed in Article 4.1 of the SSM Regulation excluding the "common procedures" in points (a) and (c).

Article 132. [Legal Acts of the ECB]

SSM Regulation) and will ensure the consistency of the supervisory outcomes within the SSM (Article 6.5 point (a) of the SSM Regulation). Where necessary, the Governing Council must take measures to ensure compliance with an instruction.

Both an instruction and any implementation measure relating to it taken by the NCB are subject to judicial review by the CJEU (Article 35.1–6 of the Statute). With regard to instructions vis-á-vis the NCAs of the SSM, such review is not supported by the wording of the Statute. However, the Commission may launch an infringement procedure on the basis of Article 258 TFEU. If the respective MS does not remedy a Commission request regarding the implementation of an ECB instruction, the case may be brought before the CJEU under Article 260 TFEU. 35

As with guidelines, there are divided opinions as to whether **instructions** may have a **direct effect** vis-à-vis **third parties**. The mere fact that instructions are purely internal law that is subject to implementation is not necessarily an argument against such direct effect since this also applies to directives.[26] However, instructions and guidelines are different in other crucial aspects: most importantly, the very purpose of instructions is the implementation of guidelines and decisions. Should a need for direct third-party rights arise, these would thus have to be construed in view of the guideline or decision but not the implementing instruction. 36

Another area of contention is whether the ECB's Executive Board may, in addition to adopting specific and individual instructions, also use instructions to **interpret legal provisions**. This interpretation of the Board's powers is partly rejected on the basis of the risk of blurring the competencies of the Executive Board and the Governing Council. Furthermore, the existence of ECB guidelines means that interpretative instructions from the Executive Board are not necessary. It has also been argued that the Governing Council is competent and might delegate the power to issue instructions to the Executive Board.[27] However, it is not clear on what grounds such limitation of the Executive Board's competencies could be based. Moreover, in many cases, the interpretative character of instructions cannot be ruled out completely. A restriction of the Executive Board's power to use instructions that interpret legal provisions, in both material and practical terms, is thus not appropriate. It is sufficient to respect the focus of an instruction, particularly to implement a guideline or decision, including its specific and individual nature. It should also be noted that the SSM Regulation explicitly uses the term "general instructions" (Article 6.5 point (a)). Accordingly, it is correct to assume that the Executive Board may well adopt instructions that interpret legal provisions. 37

---

[26] See Ohler and Schmidt-Wenzel, in Siekmann (2013), Article 132 AEUV para 65, with reference to the second subparagraph of Article 12.1 of the Statute.
[27] See Ohler and Schmidt-Wenzel, in Siekmann (2013), Article 132 AEUV para 66.

1.5.3. Agreements

38 As the ECB has its own **legal personality** (Article 282.3 TFEU and Article 9.1 of the Statute) and **international competence**, it may therefore, within the sphere of its competence, conclude international treaties with other legal entities, including States or international organisations and other central banks both inside and outside the euro area or the Union (Articles 6.2 and 23 of the Statute). One example is the agreement between the ECB and NCBs of MS outside the euro area on the functioning of an exchange-rate mechanism in the third stage of EMU, which needs to be adapted each time the euro area is enlarged. Another example is the agreement between the ECB and the Government of the Federal Republic of Germany on the headquarters of the ECB, which covers issues such as the protection of the ECB's premises, communication and tax.

1.6. Effects of the Legal Acts

39 Similar to all other Union institutions, the effects of ECB legal acts are stipulated in **Article 288 TFEU**: regulations have general application and are binding in their entirety and directly applicable in all MS. The same applies to decisions except when they are exclusively addressed to a specific group of addressees. Recommendations and opinions have no binding force; it thus depends on the weight that each addressee gives to the ECB, either in its role as guardian of monetary policy and/or of monetary union or as the highest banking supervisor within the SSM. Since recommendations and opinions are not binding, it could even be questioned whether they should be considered to be legal acts. The simple reason for including them as legal acts is that the acts of other institutions may not be valid if the right of the ECB to deliver a recommendation or an opinion has been disregarded.

40 It should be noted that under the transitional provision of Article 139.2 point (e) TFEU, acts adopted by the ECB are applicable **only in the MS of the euro area**. Naturally, with the completion of EMU, this rule will become redundant.

1.7. The Legislating Bodies and Their Competencies

41 The internal competencies and procedures for the adoption of legal acts are stipulated in Article 17 of the ECB's Rules of Procedure.[28] Regulations and guidelines are adopted by the **Governing Council** as the primary legislative institution of the ECB and must be signed by the President. The same applies to opinions. Depending on the areas of competence, decisions and recommendations must be adopted by the Governing Council or the Executive Board. Instructions are also

---

[28] Decision ECB/2004/2 *adopting the Rules of Procedure of the European Central Bank*, O.J. L 80/33 (2004).

adopted by the **Executive Board** and are signed by the President or two members of the Executive Board. Decisions imposing sanctions on third parties must be signed by the President, the Vice-President or any two other members of the Executive Board.

The Governing Council may **delegate legislative powers** to the Executive Board for implementing its regulations and guidelines.[29] In the regulation or guideline concerned, the Governing Council must specify the measures to be implemented as well as the limits and scope of the delegated powers.[30] The Executive Board may then, taking into account the views of the Statistics Committee of the ESCB, implement technical amendments to the annexes to a guideline, provided that such amendments neither change the underlying conceptual framework nor affect the reporting burden of reporting agents in the MS.

42

Presumably, in the light of the political sensitivity of the matter, the Governing Council established **special requirements for the delegation of its competence to adopt opinions**.[31] The Executive Board may submit opinions in exceptional circumstances and unless at least three Governors object to the delegation. The opinion must be in line with the comments provided by the Governing Council and take into account the participation rights of the General Council, which are not at the disposal of the Governing Council (Articles 44.2 and 47.1 of the Statute). It is open to interpretation as to whether this approach is useful. However, since amendments to the Rules of Procedure may be adopted by a simple majority (Articles 12.3 and 10.2 (2) of the Statute), the Governing Council may, at any time, change the conditions for delegating its legislative competence to the Executive Board.

43

1.8. Relation to Legal Acts of Other Union Institutions

No hierarchical relationship exists between ECB legal acts and those of other Union institutions. This is not in conflict with the fact that the members of the ECB's decision-making bodies—unlike the members of the Parliament, the Council and the Commission—are not elected representatives.

44

However, the situation is different if the ECB adopts implementing regulations on the basis of the enabling regulations of the Council referred to in Article 129.4 TFEU: if the same subject matter is governed in both legal acts, the provisions in the enabling regulation will apply and take priority over those of the

---

[29] The delegation of legislative powers differs from the transfer of the general regulatory powers of the Governing Council to the Executive Board under the final sentence of Article 12.1 (2) of the Statute. See also Article 14.1 of the Statute.

[30] Article 17.3 of Decision ECB/2004/2. One example is Article 7 of Guideline ECB/2004/15 *on the statistical reporting requirements of the European Central Bank in the field of balance of payments and international investment position statistics, and the international reserves template*, O.J. L 354/34 (2004).

[31] Article 17.5 of Decision ECB/2004/2.

implementing regulation. This also applies to the regulations adopted by the ECB to fulfil the tasks conferred on it by the SSM Regulation: Here, too, the **enabling regulation takes priority over the implementing regulation**—which must be limited explicitly to the organisation or specification of the arrangements established by the enabling Regulation (Article 4.3 of the SSM Regulation).

1.9. Duty to State Reasons, Publication, Entry into Force and Enforcement

45   With regard to the formal conditions for the validity of ECB legal acts—justification, publication, entry into force and enforcement—the **general rules** in Articles 296, 297 and 299 TFEU apply. Exceptionally, the publication of decisions that are not addressed to a specified addressee is at the discretion of the ECB (Article 132.2 TFEU). This applies also to the publication of recommendations and opinions.

46   Additional rules on the formal requirements for ECB legal instruments are laid down in its Rules of Procedure. For example, regulations must be adopted by the Governing Council and signed on its behalf by the President.[32]

47   With regard to the **language regime**, the principles of Council Regulation No 1 determining the languages to be used by the European Economic Community[33] apply to the acts referred to in Article 34 of the Statute. In the Rules of Procedure, it is laid down that guidelines and instructions are adopted in one of the official languages of the EU and notified to the NCBs. Apparently in order to avoid language disputes, the Rules of Procedure do not specify which of the official languages this must be and provides therefore, at least from a legal point of view, for a number of options. The Rules of Procedure provide that legal instruments, if published, must be translated into the official languages of the EU. Unlike regulations, the publication of guidelines in the Official Journal is not a requirement for their effectiveness. This has consequences for the authenticity of the languages. In the case of guidelines, the only authentic language is the one in which the guideline has been adopted but not the languages in which the guideline is published in the Official Journal. The internal decisions of the ECB are not governed by the Rules of Procedure.

1.10. Sanctioning Powers

48   Article 132.3 TFEU empowers the ECB to sanction the **failure to comply** with its regulations and decisions by imposing **fines or periodic penalty payments**.[34] In

---

[32] Article 17.1 of Decision ECB/2004/2.

[33] O.J. 17/385 (1958).

[34] With regard to the ECB's sanctioning and enforcement powers in the context of the SSM, see Riso and Zagouras (2016), pp. 121 et seq.

view of its criminal law nature, the grounds on which a penalty is imposed must be clearly defined. To this end, the Council determines the limits and conditions for both the infringement and the amount of the fine. Against this background, the Council adopted Regulation (EC) No 2532/98.[35] The ECB's powers in this area include the right to adopt implementing regulations in order to **specify** the objectives endorsed by the Council.[36] Furthermore, the ECB may adopt guidelines on the coordination and harmonisation of the **infringement procedure**.[37] The limitation that the ECB may only adopt concretising provisions in implementing acts means that the nature and limits of sanctions must not go beyond the limits set by the Council regulations. The implementing regulation therefore specifies the various elements of the penalty procedure, which include, in particular, the right to a defence. It is also important to note that Regulation (EC) No 2157/1999 of the ECB (ECB/1999/4)[38] contains a simplified penalty procedure for minor infringements, with a view to reaching a final decision more quickly and efficiently.[39]

Both when initiating a sanctioning procedure and when imposing a specific sanction on the addressee, the ECB must take a **decision** under Article 132.1 TFEU, which is, since it refers to the imposition of a pecuniary obligation, enforceable (Article 299.1 TFEU).

The maximum amount that may be imposed as a penalty is **EUR 500,000**. Periodic penalty payments must not be higher than **EUR 10,000** per **day** and must not be imposed over a period of more than 6 months, starting from the date of notification to the credit institution concerned that an infringement procedure has been launched.[40] The determination of the penalty is subject to the proportionality principle and must take into account all the relevant circumstances of the case.

The **competence** to open a sanction procedure, the decision whether an **infringement** was committed and the determination of the **penalty amount** are regulated by Article 3 of Regulation (EC) No 2532/98. The ECB's Executive Board or the NCB of the MS where the infringement took place decides whether or not a sanction procedure should be initiated. However, in cases where the Executive Board alone decided on the application of a specific sanction, the concerned bank

---

[35] Council Regulation (EC) No 2532/98 *on the powers of the European Central Bank to impose sanctions*, O.J. L 318/4 (1998). See also Recommendation ECB/2014/19 *for a Council Regulation amending Regulation (EC) No 2532/98 concerning the powers of the European Central Bank to impose sanctions*, O.J. C 144/2 (2014). It recommends including specific procedural rules for sanctions in the framework of banking supervision.

[36] See ECB Regulation (EU) No 469/2014 *amending Regulation (EC) No 2157/1999 on the powers of the European Central Bank to impose sanctions*, O.J. L 141/51 (2014).

[37] These guidelines will be adopted as a communication. See, for example, the communication by the ECB on the imposition of sanctions for breaches of the obligation to hold minimum reserves.

[38] ECB Regulation (EC) No 2157/1999 *on the power of the European Central Bank to impose sanctions* (ECB/1999/4), O.J. L 264/21 (1999).

[39] See also Regulation No 469/2014 (ECB/1999/4), which established an independent investigating unit.

[40] Article 2.1 of Regulation (EC) No 2532/1998.

may request that the decision be reviewed by the Governing Council. If such a request is not made within the time limit, the decision will become final.[41] The credit institution concerned may bring an action for annulment before the CJEU in accordance with Article 263.4 TFEU. The CJEU has unlimited jurisdiction over the review of final decisions that impose a sanction.[42] In particular, the CJEU may **review the legality of the exercise of discretion**.

52 With regard to the issue of the impact that formal procedural breaches have on the sanctioning procedure, in particular where the right to be heard was not respected, it is partially presumed that, due to the applicability of the *ne bis in idem* principle, **formal irregularities** may lead to the exclusion of the specific penalty.[43] However, it appears preferable and advisable that the court-ordered remedy of procedural errors be regarded as part of the initial procedure. This approach does not hamper defence rights since the aim of the *ne bis in idem* principle is to avoid sanctioning the same infringement more than once. In any event, it would be difficult to explain why banks involved in sanction procedures for the breach of ECB stability requirements should be granted the same protection as an individual involved in criminal proceedings.

53 Due to its capital markets and monetary policy operations, the ECB also has *de facto* other means to sanction credit institutions than those laid down in Article 132.3 TFEU. These are, in particular, the levying of **penalty interests** and the **exclusion from ECB open market operations**. Such sanctioning right is stipulated with regard to the minimum reserve requirements:[44] if a bank fails to comply with the mandatory reserve requirement, the ECB may impose a payment of up to 5 percentage points above the ESCB's marginal lending rate or twice this interest rate, applied to the shortfall of the reserve requirement. Alternatively, the ECB may require the institution to hold non-interest-bearing deposits of up to three times the amount of the shortfall of the reserve requirement with the ECB or the NCBs of the participating MS. With regard to Article 132.3 TFEU, these sanctions may broadly be classified as fines.

54 In the absence of a clear contractual arrangement, there is disagreement as to whether the ECB, on the basis of Articles 19.1 and 5.4 of the Statute, must have **sanctioning powers outside the scope of Article 132 TFEU**, in particular exclusion from open market operations. This could be considered a result of non-compliance with minimum reserve requirements or statistical reporting requirements. However, according to Recital 7 of Regulation (EC) No 2531/98 and

---

[41] In accordance with ECB Recommendation ECB/2014/19, in the area of banking supervision, sanctioning decisions are subject to the non-objection procedure pursuant to Article 26.8 of the SSM Regulation and may be reviewed by the Administrative Board of Review (ABoR).

[42] Article 5 of Regulation (EC) No 2532/98.

[43] Ohler and Schmidt-Wenzel, in Siekmann (2013), Article 132 AEUV para 94 with reference to Recital 5 and Article 2.1 of Regulation (EC) No 2157/1999, under which no more than one infringement procedure shall be initiated against the same undertaking based on the same facts.

[44] Article 19.1 of the Statute and Article 7 of Council Regulation (EC) No 2531/98 *concerning the application of minimum reserves by the European Central Bank*, O.J. L 318/1 (1998).

Recital 13 of Council Regulation (EC) No 2533/98,[45] penalties must be without prejudice to the right of the ESCB to take appropriate measures vis-á-vis counterparties in the event of non-compliance with the obligations, including the partial or total exclusion of an institution from monetary policy operations in the case of serious infringements of the minimum reserve requirements or the statistical reporting requirements. However, it has been argued that the provision of central bank money is a basic prerequisite for the smooth functioning of credit institutions' business and that, in this respect, the ECB could be said to hold a monopoly in relation to a public task. Furthermore, consideration should be given to the fact that credit provided in open market transactions helps the banks meet their prudential liquidity standards.[46] However, the ECB is not under a duty of care with regard to banks' compliance with prudential requirements when carrying out monetary policy. On the contrary, according to the separation principle, the **ECB's monetary policy must not take prudential considerations into account**. The exclusion from open market operations is now explicitly foreseen in situations where the counterparty has not complied with its contractual or public law obligations to the NCBs or the ECB. These include certain offences in relation to the tender rules, for example if a counterparty in a liquidity-providing operation does not provide sufficient eligible collateral or liquid assets for the settlement of the operation or does not, upon the maturity date of the operation, secure it by means of corresponding margin calls or does not possess sufficient liquidity in a liquidity-absorbing operation. Breaches of the rules for bilateral transactions, for example the failure of a counterparty to transfer a sufficient amount of underlying assets or cash as agreed in a bilateral transaction or the failure of a counterparty to collateralise an outstanding bilateral transaction at any time prior to its maturity by means of corresponding margin calls, may lead to the exclusion of that counterparty from open market operations.[47] The ECB has already exercised this option on several occasions.

1.11. Remedies and Liability

Acts and omissions of the ECB may in principle be **challenged before the CJEU** (Article 35.1 of the Statute). The Court's competence includes, on the one hand, reviewing the legality of legislative acts other than recommendations or opinions (Article 263 TFEU) and, on the other hand, establishing the existence of a breach of the Treaty resulting from a failure to take a decision (Article 265 TFEU). This is in accordance with Article 256 TFEU on the jurisdiction of the General Court. Disputes on the fulfilment by NCBs of their obligations under the Treaties and

55

---

[45] Council Regulation (EC) No 2533/98 *concerning the collection of statistical information by the European Central Bank*, O.J. L 318/8 (1998).
[46] Ohler and Schmidt-Wenzel, in Siekmann (2013), Article 132 AEUV para 97, 98.
[47] See Article 158.1 of ECB Guideline (EU) 2015/510 *on the implementation of the Eurosystem monetary policy framework* (ECB/2014/60), O.J. L 91/3 (2015).

the Statute are subject to the jurisdiction of the CJEU (Article 35.6 of the Statute, Article 271 point (d) TFEU). Disputes between the ECB and its creditors, debtors or any other third party are subject to the jurisdiction of the competent **national courts** (Article 35.2 of the Statute).

56 Institutions that are directly and individually concerned with the internal legal acts of the ESCB may, in principle, bring a **direct action** in accordance with Article 263.4 TFEU. This requires, in particular, that the concern is not solely caused by an implementing legal act that has external effects. This is, in principle, the case where the NCBs have no discretionary powers. In addition, further reasons for an individual—not just a direct—concern must be stated.[48] Here, too, it should be kept in mind that internal legal acts do not have to be published.

57 From Article 340.3 TFEU, it can be deduced that the ECB is under an obligation, in accordance with the general principles common to the laws of the MS, to **make good any damage caused** by it or by its staff in the course of their duties.

2. Eurosystem

58 The ECB adopts internal and external legal acts on the stability of financial markets;[49] on employment conditions;[50] to combat fraud;[51] on accounting standards, reporting and auditing;[52] on data protection;[53] and on transparency.[54]

2.1. Legal Acts on Monetary Policy

59 The competence to define and implement the monetary policy of the Union in accordance with Article 3.1 of the Statute and Article 127.2 TFEU, as well as to

---

[48] See Case 25/62, *Plaumann & Co v Commission* (ECJ 15 July 1963) and Ohler and Schmidt-Wenzel, in Siekmann (2013), Article 132 AEUV para 100 and 101.

[49] In particular, the ECB regularly comments on the legislation of the MS, see, for instance, ECB Opinion CON/2014/39 *on public access to specific information regarding the non-performing loans of certain banks.*

[50] Decision ECB/1998/4 *on the adoption of the Conditions of Employment for Staff of the European Central Bank as amended on 31 March 1999*, O.J. L 125/32 (1999).

[51] Decision ECB/2004/11 *concerning the terms and conditions for European Anti-Fraud Office investigations of the ECB in relation to the prevention of fraud, corruption and any other illegal activities detrimental to the European Communities' financial interests*, O.J. L 230/56 (2004).

[52] Guideline ECB/2010/20 *on the legal framework for accounting and financial reporting in the European System of Central Banks*, O.J. L 35/31 (2011).

[53] Decision ECB/2007/1 *adopting implementing rules concerning data protection at the European Central Bank*, O.J. L 116/64 (2007); Decision ECB/2013/1 *laying down the framework for a public key infrastructure for the European System of Central Banks*, O.J. L 74/30 (2013).

[54] Decision ECB/2000/12 *on the publication of certain legal acts and instruments of the European Central Bank*, O.J. L 55/68 (2001) Decision ECB/2004/3 *on public access to European Central Bank documents*, O.J. L 80/42 (2004).

adopt legal acts on the application of other monetary instruments under Article 20 of the Statute is in principle very broad and thus partly considered a **blanket provision**.[55] The reason for such a broad competence is that the concept of monetary policy and, hence, also the range of associated measures are to be determined by the ECB itself. In principle, the monetary policy task should be understood as encompassing all actions required to control and steer the liquidity or amount of money within a currency area. The key instrument needed to accomplish this task is the supply of central bank money to commercial banks. When deciding on a monetary measure, the priority is the objective of maintaining price stability, and the second priority is the objective of preserving financial stability (also Article 2 of the Statute). However, Articles 17–19 and 23 of the Statute contain provisions that are relevant for determining the extent of the legislative competence regarding monetary policy, including the opening of accounts for the commercial banks with the ECB or NCBs, open market and credit operations, the establishment of minimum reserves and foreign exchange transactions with third countries and international organisations.

The legal **centrepiece of the ECB's monetary policy** is Guideline (EU) 2015/510 (ECB/2014/60),[56] which originally dates back to the year 2000 and was adjusted several times prior to its recast in 2011 and 2015. It lays down the fundamental principles (price stability and support of economic policies in the Union), the instruments (open market operations, standing facilities and reserves), the procedures for bilateral operations (tender and winding-up process) and the criteria for the single monetary policy, specifying, for example, what constitutes eligible collateral.[57] As the successful implementation of the single monetary policy requires a uniform approach, the ECB specifies the general principles to be followed by the NCBs when carrying out operations in assets and liabilities on their own initiative. This has been done in Guideline (EU) 2019/671, which stipulates, for example, that NCBs shall seek the ECB's prior approval if transactions conducted on an NCB's own initiative result in a net liquidity effect on the settlement date that is larger than EUR 500 million and before entering into bilateral liquidity arrangements because these transactions may have implications on the liquidity of the euro and consequently on the single monetary policy.[58] In order to ensure the integrity of the single monetary policy and create an incentive allowing deposits of public budgets to be placed on the market in a way that facilitates the Eurosystem's

60

---

[55] Ohler and Schmidt-Wenzel, in Siekmann (2013), Article 132 AEUV para 25.

[56] ECB Guideline (EU) 2015/510 *on the implementation of the Eurosystem monetary policy framework*, O.J. L 116/22 (2015), last amended by ECB Guideline (EU) 2020/1690, O.J. L 379/77 (2020).

[57] Council Decision 2013/169/EU *on the rules concerning the use of own-use uncovered government-guaranteed bank bonds as collateral for Eurosystem monetary policy operations*, O.J. L 95/22 (2013), and Guideline ECB/2012/25 *amending Guideline ECB/2011/14 on monetary policy instruments and procedures of the Eurosystem*, O.J. L 348/30 (2012).

[58] Guideline ECB/2019/7 *on domestic asset and liability management operations by the national central banks*, O.J. L 113 (2019).

61   Regulations in the field of monetary policy are rare. To date, there has only been one—ECB Regulation (EC) No 1053/2008 on temporary changes to the rules relating to the **eligibility of collateral** (ECB/2008/11).[60] Its aim was to improve the provision of liquidity to banks at risk in the context of open market operations at the outbreak of the financial crisis. To achieve this, the criteria for determining the eligibility of collateral provided by banks to the Eurosystem were extended. The near adoption of the Regulation to the insolvency of *Lehman Brothers Holdings Inc.* on 15 September 2008 demonstrates that the Regulation is a direct response by the ECB to insolvency, and the resulting lack of confidence between banks, which was threatening to dry out the money market. Because of the risks associated with this reduction of the quality standards for collateral, its application was limited to a period of a few weeks, which expired on 30 November 2008.

2.2. Legal Acts on Banknotes

62   The competence of the ECB to approve banknotes derives from Article 16 of the Statute, in conjunction with Article 128.1 TFEU. The central piece of legislation on the production of euro banknotes is Decision ECB/2010/29.[61] It implements the Eurosystem's competitive approach and aims to establish a **single Eurosystem tender procedure** with a level playing field for all printing companies participating in the tender process. In addition, there are a number of decisions concerning production and the corresponding quality assurance.[62] Finally, there is an ECB Guideline on the enforcement of measures to counter non-compliant reproductions of euro banknotes and on the exchange and withdrawal of euro banknotes, which contains measures protecting the integrity of euro banknotes and regulating their exchange and withdrawal.[63]

---

[59] See also Decision ECB/2014/8 *on the prohibition of monetary financing and the remuneration of government deposits in national central banks*, O.J. L 159/54 (2014).

[60] O.J. L 282/17 (2008).

[61] Decision ECB/2010/29 *on the issue of euro banknotes*, O.J. L 35/26 (2011).

[62] See, for example, Decision ECB/2013/54 *on the accreditation procedures for manufacturers of euro secure items and euro items*, O.J. L 57/29 (2014); and Decision ECB/2010/22 *on the quality accreditation procedure for manufacturers of euro banknotes*, O.J. L 330/14 (2010).

[63] See also Guideline ECB/2013/11 *amending Guideline ECB/2003/5 on the enforcement of measures to counter non-compliant reproductions of euro banknotes and on the exchange and withdrawal of euro banknotes*, O.J. L 118/43 (2013).

Article 132.   [Legal Acts of the ECB]   815

In relation to the **issue of euro banknotes**, Decision ECB/2013/6 is of particular   **63**
importance.[64] It contains provisions on the obligations of issuers and the allocation
of euro banknotes within the Eurosystem. In addition, Guideline ECB/2012/16[65]
defines the requirements that the NCBs must fulfil in relation to the use of the data
exchange for cash services. This exchange of data maximises the efficiency in the
supply and withdrawal of cash and the functioning of the cash cycle in the euro area.

2.3.   Legal Acts on Reserve Requirements

Pursuant to Article 19.2 of the Statute, the Governing Council of the ECB may   **64**
adopt regulations concerning the calculation and determination of the **minimum
reserves** that credit institutions are required to hold. This power complements the
ECB's power under Article 19.1 of the Statute to require the commercial banks of
the MS to hold minimum reserves on accounts with the NCBs and the ECB. This is
a tool for the **management of the money market** and to **control the money
supply**, which should enable the ECB to flexibly determine the reserve requirements, depending on the evolving economic and financial circumstances in the
participating MS.[66] This competence is accompanied by the possibility for the ECB
to impose penalties and comparable sanctions where the provisions on reserve
requirements are not complied with. According to Article 19.2 of the Statute,
ECB regulations with regard to reserve requirements must be adopted on the
basis of provisions from the Council defining the basis for minimum reserves and
the maximum permissible ratios between those reserves and their basis. Article 19.2
of the Statute also provides that the Council imposes sanctions for non-compliance
with the obligation to hold minimum reserves. The Council applied these competencies by adopting Regulation (EC) No 2531/98, which provides the basis for
minimum reserves and the maximum ratios between reserves and their basis. It also
lays down specific sanctions and refers (with regard to principles and procedures for
imposing sanctions) to Regulation (EC) No 2532/98, which provides for a **simplified procedure** for the imposition of sanctions in the event of certain types of
infringement. Should a conflict arise between the provisions of Regulation (EC)
No 2532/98 and Regulation (EC) No 2531/98, the provisions of Regulation (EC)
No 2531/98 prevail.[67]

---

[64] Decision ECB/2013/6 *amending Decision ECB/2010/29 on the issue of euro banknotes*, O.J. L 187/13 (2013). For further details see Zahradnik, in Jaeger and Stöger (2021), Article 128 AEUV para 1 et seq.
[65] Guideline ECB/2012/16 *on the Data Exchange for Cash Services*, O.J. L 245/3 (2012).
[66] See Recital 5 of Regulation (EC) No 2531/98.
[67] See Recital 3 of Regulation (EC) No 2531/98.

65   Article 30.4 of the Statute stipulates that the ECB may **call for further foreign reserves**, beyond the amount specified in Article 30.1 of the Statute. The limits and conditions are set out in Council Regulation (EC) No 1010/2000.[68]

66   Against this background, the ECB has a number of competencies, which provide for not only the adoption of regulations but also decisions. First, the ECB may determine **exceptional criteria** for the obligation to hold minimum reserves. While the basis for minimum reserves, which the ECB may require credit institutions to hold, is determined by the Council as liabilities of an institution resulting from the acceptance of funds and off-balance-sheet items, the ECB may determine certain parts of these liabilities *vis-à-vis* other institutions that are not to be taken into account for the calculation of minimum reserves. The ECB may also set the percentage of the minimum reserve at zero. In this area, the ECB has adopted Regulation (EC) No 1745/2003.[69]

2.4. Legal Acts on Clearing and Payment Systems

67   On the basis of Article 22 of the Statute and Article 132.2 TFEU, the ECB may adopt legal acts, including regulations, to provide for the efficient and sound clearing of payment systems within the Union and with third countries.[70] These legal acts principally relate to the Trans-European Automated Real-time Gross Settlement Express Transfer System (**TARGET2**) and the TARGET2-Securities platform (T2S) of the Eurosystem. They also encompass requirements for the supervision of systemically important payment systems. As regards TARGET2 and T2S, the ECB has adopted guidelines and decisions but not regulations.

68   TARGET2 is the **real-time gross settlement** (RTGS) **system** owned and operated by the Eurosystem for the **daily transfer of reserves between the affiliated banks**. Central bank operations, remittances between banks in large amount payment systems as well as other euro transfers have been settled in TARGET2 since 19 November 2007.[71] TARGET2 is legally structured as a multiplicity of RTGS systems. Guideline ECB/2012/27[72] sets out the basic legal framework under which the NCBs of the euro area organise their participation in TARGET2 within the framework of their national systems. The Guideline sets out the essential legal aspects of TARGET2, including governance, pricing and audit rules. Moreover, it

---

[68] Council Regulation (EC) No 1010/2000 *concerning further calls of foreign reserve assets by the European Central Bank*, O.J. L 115/2 (2000).

[69] ECB Regulation (EC) No 1745/2003 *on the application of minimum reserves*, O.J. L 250/10 (2003).

[70] See with regard to payment systems: Papathanassiou (2011), § 134, para 108 et seq.

[71] TARGET2 replaced the TARGET-system, which was established by Guideline ECB/2001/3 *on a Trans-European Automated Real-time Gross Settlement Express Transfer System (Target)*, O.J. L 140/72 (2001).

[72] Guideline ECB/2012/27 *on a Trans-European Automated Real-time Gross settlement Express Transfer system*, O.J. L 30/1 (2012).

contains harmonised conditions for participation in TARGET2 in order to achieve the broadest possible legal harmonisation of the mandatory rules for TARGET2 participants in all relevant jurisdictions. The ECB has also adopted Decision ECB/2007/7.[73] As payments have changed significantly in the meantime due to technological developments, regulatory requirements and changing consumer demands, the Eurosystem has launched a project to consolidate TARGET2 and T2S, in terms of both technical and functional aspects. The objective is to meet changing market demands by replacing TARGET2 with a new RTGS system and optimising liquidity management across all TARGET services.[74]

With the **Regulation on oversight requirements for systemically important payment systems** (SIPS Regulation),[75] the ECB used, for the first time, its competence under Article 132.1 TFEU in relation to Article 22 of the Statute to ensure the efficiency and robustness of systemically important payment systems (SIPS). More specifically, the Regulation implements the **CPSS-IOSCO Principles**,[76] established by the Committee on Payment and Settlement Systems (CPSS) of the Bank for International Settlements (BIS), as minimum requirements for SIPS. The Regulation concerns SIPS, including wholesale and retail payment systems of systemic importance, and applies to payment systems operated by central banks and private companies. It contains requirements with regard to governance, resolution plans, own funds and liquid assets, as well as collateral and investment risks. 69

T2S is a single technical platform for the clearing and settlement of securities on the internal market that is integrated into the central banks' real-time gross settlement systems. More specifically, it is a service of the Eurosystem for central securities depositories (CSD), providing for the **neutral cross-border settlement of securities transactions on a delivery-versus-payment basis in central bank money**. The cornerstone of the T2S legal framework is Guideline ECB/2012/13.[77] It provides the basis for all related legal agreements. It sets out a list of decisions to be taken by the Governing Council, provisions concerning the role and responsibility of the implementing bodies and relations with external stakeholders, principles for the financial regime, Eurosystem's rights regarding the T2S platform, access criteria for CSDs and eligibility conditions for the inclusion in T2S of European Economic Area currencies other than the euro-area MS.[78] 70

---

[73] Decision ECB/2007/7 *concerning the terms and conditions of TARGET2-EC*, O.J. L 237/71 (2007).

[74] The ECB has announced that the new consolidated platform will be launched in November 2021 but this is likely to be postponed due to the COVID-19 by one year.

[75] ECB Regulation (EU) No 795/2014 *on oversight requirements for systemically important payment systems* (ECB/2014/28), O.J. L 217/16 (2014).

[76] See the BIS report: Core principles for systemically important payment systems, January 2001, available on the BIS website at www.bis.org.

[77] Guideline ECB/2012/13 *on TARGET2-Securities*, O.J. L 215/19 (2012).

[78] See Decision ECB/2011/20 *establishing detailed rules and procedures for implementing the eligibility criteria for central securities depositories to access TARGET 2-Securities services*, O.J. L 319/117 (2011).

2.5. Legal Acts on Statistical Data Collection

71 To carry out the tasks of the ESCB and the European Systemic Risk Board (ESRB), the ECB collects the necessary statistical information either from competent national authorities or directly from economic agents. In doing so, the ECB is assisted by the NCBs and the **European Statistical System** (ESS), consisting of Eurostat and national statistical authorities. For these purposes, the ECB may adopt various types of legal acts provided for in Article 132 TFEU, including regulations. Their application is, in principle, extended to MS outside the euro area.[79] The purpose of these acts is to make the compilation and publication of statistics as effective as possible while ensuring that the reporting burden on reporting agents is reduced as much as possible and personal data and non-public information are treated in a confidential manner.

72 The main legal act is Council Regulation (EC) No 2533/98 of 23 November 1998 concerning the collection of statistical information by the ECB,[80] in conjunction with Article 5 of the Statute and Article 130 TFEU. Regulation (EC) No 2533/98 establishes the obligations of MS and the powers of the ECB and its right to **verify statistical information** or **carry out the compulsory collection** thereof. In addition, it provides an appropriate sanction regime and the rules on the confidentiality of data. On this basis, the ECB has adopted a significant number of legal acts in the areas of monetary statistics, statistics on financial institutions and markets,[81] financial accounts,[82] foreign trade,[83] and statistics on holdings of securities[84] and confidentiality.[85] In addition, there are over 100 opinions on national and European legislative initiatives in the field of statistics. Moreover, the data collected by the

---

[79] See for example the Recital 14 of ECB Regulation (EU) No 1071/2013 *concerning the balance sheet of the monetary financial institutions sector*, O.J. L 297/1 (2013).

[80] Council Regulation (EC) No 2533/98 *concerning the collection of statistical information by the European Central Bank*, O.J. L 318/8 (1998).

[81] For example, ECB Regulation (EU) No 1071/2013 *concerning the balance sheet of the monetary financial institutions sector (ECB/2013/33)*, O.J. L 297/1 (2013); ECB Regulation (EU) No 1409/2013 *on payment statistics*, O.J. L352/18 (2013); and Recommendation ECB/2014/27 *on the organisation of preparatory measures for the collection of granular credit data by the European System of Central Banks*, O.J. C 108/1 (2014).

[82] See, for example, Guideline ECB/2013/23 *on the government finance statistics*, O.J. L 57/12 (2014).

[83] Guideline ECB/2011/23 *on the statistical reporting requirements of the European Central Bank in the field of external statistics*, O.J. L 65/1 (2012).

[84] See, for example, ECB Regulation (EU) No 1011/2012 *concerning statistics on holdings of securities* (ECB/2012/24), O.J. L 305/6 (2012) and Guideline ECB/2013/7 *concerning statistics on holdings of securities*, O.J. L 125/17 (2013).

[85] Recommendation ECB/2014/14 *concerning the common rules and minimum standards to protect the confidentiality of the individual statistical information by the European Central Bank, assisted by the national central banks*, O.J. C 186/1 (2014).

Article 132. [Legal Acts of the ECB] 819

ECB are not limited to the statistical domain but may also be used in the context of the supervision of credit institutions within the SSM.[86]

2.6. Legal Acts on the Capital of the ECB

An appropriate level of continuously guaranteed capital is needed to support the operations of the ECB, especially in the event of an increase in the ECB's balance sheet. This is in particular the case when new MS join the Union as the ESCB will then also be enlarged by the addition of the central banks of the acceding MS. Acts adopted by the ECB in relation to its capital were mainly adopted in the form of decisions between 2010 and 2013. These were preceded by an ECB recommendation for a Council Regulation regarding the limits and conditions for capital increases of the ECB.[87] The recommendation refers to Article 28.1–2 of the Statute, which stipulates that the **NCBs must provide the ECB with a capital** of EUR 5 billion when taking up their duties. Technically, it is a recommendation to supplement certain articles of the Statute on the basis of Article 129.4 TFEU. In accordance with Article 28.1 of the Statute, the Governing Council must lay down the **conditions under which the ECB may increase its capital**. Accordingly, the fully implemented recommendation[88] aims to ensure that the Governing Council may increase the ECB's capital by an amount of up to EUR 5 billion.

73

An increase of the ECB's capital may lead to a decision requiring the **NCBs outside the euro area**, which, in principle, do not participate in the operational costs of the ECB, to make **payments on their subscribed capital**. Against this background, the ECB adopted Decision 2014/33/EU.[89] Formally, this requires the General Council to decide by a majority representing at least two thirds of the subscribed capital of the ECB and at least half of the shareholders that a minimal percentage must be paid up as a contribution to the operational costs of the ECB (Article 47 of the Statute). The precise amount is determined on the basis of the capital key weightings, which the ECB adjusts every 5 years by means of a decision (Article 29.3 of the Statute).[90]

74

---

[86] See Decision ECB/2014/29 *on the provision to the European Central Bank of supervisory data reported to the national competent authorities pursuant to Commission Implementing Regulation (EU) No 680/2014*, O.J. L 214/34 (2014).

[87] Recommendation ECB/1998/11 *for a Council Regulation (EC) concerning the limits and conditions for capital increases of the European Central Bank*, O.J. C 411/10 (1998).

[88] See Council Regulation (EC) No 1009/2000 *concerning capital increases of the European Central Bank*, O.J. L 115/1 (2000).

[89] Decision ECB/2013/31 *on the paying-up of the European Central Bank's capital by the non-euro area national central banks*, O.J. L 16/63 (2014).

[90] See also Decision ECB/2013/28 *on the national central banks' percentage shares in the key for subscription to the European Central Bank's capital*, O.J. L 16/53 (2014); Decision ECB/2013/29 *laying down the terms and conditions for transfers of the European Central Bank's capital shares between the national central banks and for the adjustment of the paid-up capital*, O.J. L 16/55 (2014); Decision ECB/2013/30 *on the paying-up of the capital of the European Central Bank by*

3. Banking Supervision

75 Until 2013, the ECB had adopted legal acts on banking supervision only in the context of its advisory function under Article 25.1 of the Statute, which vests the ECB with the right to be consulted by the Commission, the Council and the competent authorities of the MS and to issue opinions on the scope and implementation of legislation relating to the prudential supervision of credit institutions and the stability of the financial system in the Union.[91] With the adoption of the **SSM Regulation**,[92] the Council significantly **strengthened the legislative role of the ECB** in this field. Prior to the SSM Regulation, the Council had exercised this competence only through Council Regulation (EU) No 1096/2010,[93] which, however, only established the ESRB secretariat within the ECB, including the ECB's advisory support to the ESRB, but did not concern the ECB's legislative function.[94] The SSM Regulation provides the basis for the SSM and includes a number of provisions, which specify the general powers under Article 132 TFEU, on ECB legal acts in relation to its role as a European banking supervisory authority.

3.1. Scope of the ECB's Competence to Issue Legal Acts

76 The ECB's legislative powers with respect to prudential supervision are far narrower than those it possesses with regard to the ESCB tasks. This is due to the fact that the **ECB does not have exclusive competence** in this field. In principle, the ECB is directly responsible only for banks that are not "less significant" on a consolidated basis in accordance with Article 6.4 of the SSM Regulation. While the NCBs and the ECB form a common structure within the ESCB, there is no such link with the NCAs. Hence, it could be assumed that there might have been some

---

the national central banks of Member States whose currency is the euro, O.J. L 16/61 (2013); and Decision ECB/2013/31.

[91] See the ECB's Opinion CON/2009/94 *on the proposal for a Directive of the European Parliament and of the Council amending Directives 2006/48/EC and 2006/49/EC as regards capital requirements for the trading book and for re-securitisations, and the supervisory review of remuneration policies*, O.J. C 291/1 (2009).

[92] Council Regulation (EU) No 1024/2013 *conferring specific tasks on the European Central Bank concerning policies relating to the prudential supervision of credit institutions*, O.J. L 287/63 (2013).

[93] Council Regulation (EU) No 1096/2010 *conferring specific tasks upon the European Central Bank concerning the functioning of the European Systemic Risk Board*, O.J. L 331/162 (2010).

[94] The Regulation is based on Parliament/Council Regulation (EU) No 1092/2010 *on European Union macro-prudential oversight of the financial system and establishing a European Systemic Risk Board*, O.J. L 331/1 (2010). Given its expertise on macro-prudential issues, the ECB is entrusted with the task of ensuring that the Secretariat of the ESRB has sufficient human and financial resources to contribute to effective macro-prudential oversight of the financial system within the Union. See also Papathanassiou and Zagouras (2010), p. 1584.

Article 132. [Legal Acts of the ECB] 821

tense discussions when the specific scope of the ECB's competencies as the European supervisory authority for significant credit institutions was determined.

The ECB's **tasks as prudential supervisor** correspond with its legislative powers in this field. Article 4.1–3 of the SSM Regulation empowers the ECB to issue regulations, decisions, guidelines and recommendations in the following areas: **77**

- Conditions for granting or withdrawing credit institutions' banking licences (authorisations)
- Supervision of branches established in MS not participating in the SSM
- Assessing notifications of the acquisition and disposal of qualifying holdings in credit institutions
- Own fund requirements, securitisation, large exposure limits, liquidity, leverage, and reporting and the public disclosure of information on these matters
- Governance arrangements, including the fit and proper requirements for persons managing credit institutions, risk management processes, internal control mechanisms, remuneration policies and practices, and effective internal capital adequacy assessment processes, including internal-rating-based (IRB) models
- Supervisory reviews, stress tests and their publication
- Supervision on a consolidated basis
- Involvement of the ECB in the supplementary supervision of a financial conglomerate in relation to the credit institutions included in it
- Supervisory tasks in relation to recovery plans and early intervention where a credit institution or group for which the ECB is the consolidating supervisor is in a crisis situation

The legislative powers of the ECB in the supervisory field are rather limited. The **ECB cannot legislate beyond the "single rulebook"**, which—in terms of the *Lamfalussy* architecture—consists of the "level 1" texts adopted by the Parliament and Council, most importantly the Capital Requirements Directive (CRD),[95] the Bank Recovery and Resolution Directive (BRRD),[96] the Capital Requirements Regulation (CRR)[97] and the Single Resolution Mechanism Regulation (SRMR),[98] as well as the "level 2" texts consisting largely of regulatory technical standards (RTSs) drafted by the EBA on the basis of Article 10 of the EBA Regulation and subsequently adopted by the Commission on the basis of Article 290 TFEU, using empowerment included in a level 1 text and implementing technical standards **78**

---

[95] Parliament/Council Directive 2013/36/EU *on access to the activity of credit institutions and the prudential supervision of credit institutions and investment firms*, O.J. L 176/338 (2013).

[96] Parliament/Council Directive 2014/59/EU *establishing a framework for the recovery and resolution of credit institutions and investment firms*, O.J. L173/190 (2014).

[97] Parliament/Council Regulation (EU) No 575/2013 *on prudential requirements for credit institutions and investment firms*, O.J. L 176/1 (2013).

[98] Parliament/Council Regulation (EU) No 806/2014 *establishing uniform rules and a uniform procedure for the resolution of credit institutions and certain investment firms in the framework of a Single Resolution Mechanism and a Single Resolution Fund*, O.J. L 225/1 (2014).

(ITSs) drafted by the EBA on the basis of Article 15 of the EBA Regulation and subsequently adopted by the Commission on the basis of Article 291 TFEU, also using empowerment in a level 1 text.

In addition, there are cases where the Commission adopts delegated regulations in the area of banking supervision directly on the basis of Article 290 TFEU and empowerment in a level 1 text without the need for an EBA drafting procedure under Article 10 of the EBA Regulation.[99] One example is Commission Delegated Regulation (EU) 2015/61, which, on the basis of Article 291 TFEU and Article 460 CRR, defines the calculation of the liquidity coverage ratio (LCR). **RTSs, ITSs and Commission Delegated Regulations** make up the vast majority of "level 2" texts and are adopted in the form of regulations, ensuring their direct applicability throughout the Union. The ECB is mandated to apply these acts, and it may not amend or deviate from them or enact new legislation in the form of generally applicable Regulations not foreseen in the level 1 acts.[100]

79   The reason for strictly limiting the ECB's competencies under the SSM Regulation is that Article 127.6 TFEU, which provides the basis for the SSM Regulation, refers to the **ECB** having "**specific tasks** [...] concerning policies **relating to the prudential supervision of credit institutions** and other financial institutions with the exception of insurance undertakings". A more general drafted conferral of competencies could thus have been considered not being in compliance with the Treaty. The ECB's competence does not include the adoption of supervisory legal acts applicable to credit institutions that, according to their size, their relevance to the economy and the importance of their cross-border activity, are to be considered "**less significant**". It also has no (legislative) competence regarding the supervision of securities or derivatives trading activities, investment funds and insurance undertakings. Consumer protection and the prevention of money laundering are also excluded from the scope of the ECB's competencies (Article 6.4 of the SSM Regulation).

A **substantial part** of financial supervision thus remains within the remit of the **national supervisory authorities**.[101] Bearing in mind that a financial crisis is often linked to new financial instruments with an opaque risk profile, the success of the SSM depends to some extent on the efficient cooperation between the banking and the capital market supervisory authorities, in particular since exotic investment products are re-entering investor portfolios after a long period of near-zero interest rates and stimulus efforts from the ECB and central banks in Japan and the USA.

80   In contrast to its competence to adopt regulations, the ECB's competence to adopt guidelines, decisions and recommendations in the field of banking supervision is not limited to the **organisation or specification of the arrangements** for carrying out its tasks. With regard to guidelines, it can be assumed that their scope

---

[99] Parliament/Council Regulation (EU) No 1093/2010 *establishing a European Supervisory Authority (European Banking Authority)*, O.J. L 331/12 (2010).
[100] See Bax and Witte (2019).
[101] See Riso and Zagouras (2016), on the role of NCAs.

of application is confined to the national supervisory authorities, which are in many cases an NCB.

3.2. Delimitation of Competencies Between the ECB and the EBA

The EBA's mandate to draft technical standards, guidelines and recommendations to ensure supervisory convergence and the consistency of supervisory outcomes within the Union must not be undermined by the ECB's legal acts. In accordance with Article 4.3 and Recital 32 of the SSM Regulation, in order to avoid a potential collision of competencies, the **ECB must observe the binding RTSs and ITSs as well as the guidelines and recommendations** referred to in Article 16 of the EBA Regulation, which establishes consistent, efficient and effective supervisory practices to ensure a common, uniform and consistent application of Union law within the European system of financial supervision.[102]

81

3.3. Specific Requirements for Banking Supervision Regulations

Pursuant to Article 4.3 of the SSM Regulation, the ECB may **issue regulations** that specify the arrangements for carrying out its supervisory tasks, provided that the following conditions are met:

82

- At least one of the ECB's **supervisory tasks** listed in Article 4.1 of the SSM Regulation is affected.
- The envisaged provisions **only** relate to the **arrangements** for the performance of those tasks.
- In light of its general applicability, the regulation **organises** or **specifies** the arrangements for the performance of those tasks.

Otherwise, a regulation is not the appropriate legal act. The ECB may, however, choose a less intrusive instrument. The term "regulation" in Article 4.3 of the SSM Regulation is used in the same sense as in Articles 288.2 and 132.1 first indent TFEU and Article 34.1 first indent of the ESCB Statute. Regulations benefit from the supremacy of Union law and supersede the application of conflicting national legislation.[103]

One example of the **ECB's regulatory efforts** is Regulation 2016/445, in which the ECB exercised options and discretions available under Union law with direct applicability within the MS participating in the SSM, except those in close cooperation. The ECB could exercise these options and discretions only when they are entrusted not to the MS but to the competent authority—a role that, according to

83

---

[102] These standards are developed by EBA and adopted by the Commission in accordance with Articles 10–15 of the EBA Regulation.

[103] See Bax and Witte (2019).

Article 9.1 of the SSM Regulation, is now exercised by the ECB for significant institutions. Another example is Article 6.7, which enables the adoption of regulations establishing a framework to organise the practical arrangements for the implementation of the interaction between the ECB and the NCAs within the SSM and which has been used, most importantly, for the SSM Framework Regulation.[104] These examples show some parallels with the ECB's competence to adopt regulations within the area of monetary policy. The ECB may also only adopt regulations for specific fields of monetary policy, unlike the EU legislator, which, once it is conferred a competence, is normally granted the choice of the most appropriate legal instrument to adopt. In the case of ECB regulations, publication in the Official Journal of the EU is mandatory for them to enter into effect.[105]

3.3.1. Arrangements

84 In order to assess whether an envisaged ECB regulation addresses only the arrangements for the performance of a specific task under the SSM Regulation, it is first necessary to verify that it does **not amend Union law**. It is essential that ECB regulations are of a **specifying** or **organisational nature** in relation to the relevant task or its prudential supervisory role as a whole. The aim of a regulation must be **to adapt or adjust Union law** (essentially the single rulebook), while preserving its substance, to changing circumstances or new trends regarding supervisory practices. An ECB regulation may either aim to increase the efficiency of the implementation of prudential rules (organisational requirements) or further specify the substantive requirements of the single rulebook (specific requirements). Specific requirements may also relate to new risks in the banking sector. In spite of these systematic restrictions, it is necessary for the ECB to have ample scope for action in order to guarantee the financial stability of the Union.

3.3.2. Need for a Regulation

85 Among the legal instruments available to the ECB, regulations are the most extensive since they are directly applicable and often require more expensive implementation processes for the addressees than the other acts. Against this background, the ECB regulations can be considered to be the *ultima ratio* of its legal instruments in the field of banking supervision. The litmus test as regards the necessity of an ECB regulation in the field of supervision, therefore, is whether a decision or a recommendation would be equally efficient to achieve the desired aim of the legal act. Accordingly, there must be a **specific rationale** for implementing the proposed requirements in a **consistent manner** throughout the Union. The

---

[104] ECB Regulation (EU) No 468/2014 *establishing the framework for cooperation within the Single Supervisory Mechanism between the European Central Bank and national competent authorities and with national designated authorities (SSM Framework Regulation)* (ECB/2014/17), O.J. L 114/1 (2014).

[105] Article 297.2 TFEU and Article 17.7 of the ECB Rules of Procedure, see Bax and Witte (2019).

existence of such a rationale may be assumed if an inconsistent practice would cause specific disadvantages either for the exercise of supervisory activities or to the financial stability framework. In order for such an assumption to arise, it is sufficient if such friction cannot be ruled out. Any obligation to substantiate the need for a regulation more thoroughly, on the basis of empirical data, would constitute an undue restriction of the ECB's competencies with regard to its tasks and related responsibilities. Financial markets are not subject to clearly defined rules that can be easily anticipated; they rather tend to follow a complex combination of economic and psychological factors, which, in the context of efficient supervision, should be addressed in accordance with the **precautionary principle**. On the other hand, taking into account the proportionality principle, the level of additional implementation required should be compared to what would be required with respect to any less far-reaching legal measure that could be used to achieve the intended purpose.

3.4. Regulations, Guidelines and General Instructions to National Competent Authorities

In addition to the more general competence to adopt regulations and guidelines as referred to in Article 4.3 of the SSM Regulation, the power to adopt legal acts with regard to the national supervisory authorities is further specified in Article 6.5 point (a) of the SSM Regulation: the ECB has the power to adopt regulations and guidelines and issue general instructions, according to which the **NCAs carry out the tasks conferred on the ECB** by Article 4.1 of the SSM Regulation and adopt corresponding supervisory decisions, with the exception of the issue or withdrawal of banking licences and the assessment of the notifications of the acquisition and disposal of qualifying holdings in credit institutions. These so-called **common procedures** remain an exclusive ECB competence. General instructions may apply to specific groups or categories of credit institutions and should ensure the consistency of supervisory outcomes within the SSM in relation to the powers conferred on the ECB (also Article 16.2 SSM Regulation). In particular, on the basis of Article 16.2 SSM Regulation, the **ECB has the power to instruct the NCAs** to require the following measures from the supervised credit institutions:

86

(a) Holding own funds in excess of the statutory capital requirements related to the elements of risks and risks not covered by the relevant Union acts
(b) Reinforcement of the arrangements, processes, mechanisms and strategies
(c) Presentation and implementation of a plan to restore compliance with supervisory requirements pursuant to the acts of the ECB within a set deadline
(d) Implementation of a specific provisioning policy or treatment of assets in terms of own fund requirements
(e) Restriction or limitation of the business, operations or network of institutions or the divestment of activities that pose excessive risks to the soundness of an institution

(f) Reduction of the risk inherent in the activities, products and systems of institutions
(g) Limitation of variable remuneration as a percentage of net revenues when it is inconsistent with the maintenance of a sound capital base
(h) Use of net profits to strengthen own funds
(i) Restriction or prohibition of distributions by the NCAs to shareholders, members or holders of Additional Tier 1 instruments where the prohibition does not constitute an event of default of the institution
(j) Imposition of additional or more frequent reporting requirements, including reporting on capital and liquidity positions
(k) Imposition of specific liquidity requirements, including restrictions on maturity mismatches between assets and liabilities
(l) Provision of additional disclosures
(m) Dismissal of the members of the management body of credit institutions who do not comply with the laws forming the legal basis for the ECB's banking supervision

In these cases, the **ECB may deviate** from the otherwise mandatory, specific and individual nature of instructions to address groups or categories of credit institutions via the NCAs (Article 6.5 SSM Regulation).

3.5. Instructions to National Competent Authorities

87 For the preparation and implementation of its prudential supervisory legislation, the ECB has the power to issue instructions to the NCAs (Article 6.3 SSM Regulation). Instructions may be adopted to obtain **support for review activities**, especially stress tests. Moreover, in cases where the SSM Regulation does not confer the same powers on the ECB that the NCAs have under national law, the ECB may require the NCAs, by way of instructions, to **make use of their powers** under national law (Article 9.1 SSM Regulation). This competence also applies to national authorities in MS outside the euro area that have joined the SSM in the framework of close cooperation with non-euro-area MS (Article 7.1–4 SSM Regulation).

The instruction is in itself an act **subject to judicial review**. If, however, the NCA has already issued a measure under national law at implementing this instruction, then—depending on the national administrative legal framework—a parallel application to the national courts would be necessary from the supervised entity's point of view in order to prevent the national measure from achieving finality. In the context of this procedure, the national court might be required to refer the preliminary questions of European law to the CJEU under Article 267 TFEU.[106]

---

[106] For more detail on judicial review in the context of ECB instructions, see Witte (2015), p. 260.

Article 132. [Legal Acts of the ECB] 827

3.6. Supervisory Decisions

Of particular importance in the context of the SSM is the ECB supervisory decision, which is a legal act adopted by the ECB when performing the tasks and powers conferred on it by the SSM Regulation and which is not of general application: supervisory decisions are addressed to one or more supervised entities or supervised groups or one or more person(s) (Article 2.26 SSM Framework Regulation). A supervisory decision is preceded by a **supervisory procedure**, as specified in the SSM Framework Regulation.[107] In accordance with the general principle of administrative action restricting freedoms or rights, the addressed banks should be granted the **right to be heard** (Article 31 SSM Framework Regulation). The arguments put forward by the concerned party, unless irrelevant or incorrect, must be assessed in the rationale for the decision (also Article 33 SSM Framework Regulation). 88

At the request of the concerned parties, ECB supervisory decisions may be submitted to the ECB's **Administrative Board of Review** (ABoR), which is composed of five independent members who are staff of neither the ECB nor an NCA (Article 24 SSM Regulation). Specific details regarding the ABoR are laid down in the ABoR Decision.[108] The ABoR reviews supervisory decisions with regard to their procedural and substantive conformity with the SSM Regulation (Article 10 ABoR Decision).[109] 89

3.7. Decision to Directly Supervise Less Significant Credit Institutions

While, in principle, the ECB's supervisory competence is limited to significant credit institutions (SIs), leaving the supervision of less significant credit institutions (LSIs) to the NCAs, the ECB **may decide**, on its own initiative or at the request of the NCAs, to **directly supervise LSIs** under the conditions listed in Article 67.2 of the SSM Framework Regulation (Article 6.5 point (b) SSM Regulation).[110] For example, this could happen if a bank has indirectly received financial assistance from the European Financial Stability Facility (EFSF) or the European Stability Mechanism (ESM) (Article 67.2 point (f) SSM Framework Regulation). Prior to such a decision, a specific preparatory procedure must take place, which can be either requested by an NCA (Article 67 SSM Framework Regulation) or initiated by the ECB (Article 68 SSM Framework Regulation). However, direct supervision by the ECB must be necessary to ensure the **consistent application** of high supervisory standards and to avoid a glaring discrepancy between prudential standards in 90

---

[107] See the general provisions on due process for adopting supervisory decisions in Articles 25–35 SSM Framework Regulation.

[108] Decision ECB/2014/16 *concerning the establishment of an Administrative Board of Review and its Operating Rules*, O.J. L 175/47 (2014).

[109] See also Riso and Zagouras (2016), p. 148.

[110] The details regarding the direct supervision of LSIs by the ECB are set out in Articles 67–69 of the SSM Framework Regulation.

the Union. The objective behind granting direct supervision to the ECB in such situations is not so much to maintain financial stability – this is already safeguarded by the significance criteria in Article 6.4 SSM Regulation – but rather to guarantee the equal treatment of institutions.

3.8. Decision to Classify a Bank That Fulfils the Significance Criteria as Less Significant

91   The ECB's **competence** may not solely be extended; it may also be **limited** provided that the particular circumstances justify that a bank that otherwise fulfils the significance criteria is to be considered less significant.[111] Although this follows already from Article 297 TFEU, Article 71.3 SSM Framework Regulation states explicitly that an ECB decision must state the reasons leading to the conclusion that such particular circumstances exist. This emphasises the legislator's intention to interpret narrowly the term "particular circumstances". Consequently, such circumstances may only be assumed if the **risk profile** that follows from the bank's business model is **low** and also the business model, and all relevant circumstances, clearly indicate that the risk profile **cannot be increased** to an extent that would justify the consistent application of high supervisory standards that are required in Article 4.3 SSM Regulation. Considering how the financial crisis in connection with the collapse of *Lehman Brothers* on 15 September 2008 developed, it cannot safely be assumed that the business model of development, cooperative or savings banks would necessarily require lower standards of supervision. This is particularly true when one considers the fact that many of these banks were heavily affected by the financial crisis and were even wound up.[112] Since the concept of supervision provides a set of rules that prevent losses from not only transparent but also **opaque** yet unknown **risk structures** (such as, in the years preceding the financial crisis, the mortgage-based financial instruments that had undeservedly high ratings), it appears questionable whether the high standard of supervision was unnecessary for banks fulfilling the qualitative or quantitative significance criteria. Indeed, the materialisation of risk may quickly become a systemic problem if a bank has a large balance sheet, is largely interconnected or plays a dominant role in a particular economy. The assessment of whether a bank might be less vulnerable—as provided for under very narrow conditions by the SSM Regulation—and does therefore not require a higher standard of supervision is thus to be carried out with due care, and it is questionable whether this option should be available under the SSM Regulation, as is currently the case.

---

[111] Article 6.4 (2) of the SSM Regulation, Articles 70–72 of the SSM Framework Regulation.

[112] See Case T-122/15, *Landeskreditbank Baden-Württemberg v ECB* (GC 16 May 2017).

3.9. Competencies and Procedures

The allocation of competencies to adopt legal acts relating to the supervisory tasks of the ECB is laid down in Article 17a of the ECB's Rules of Procedure: for regulations, in principle, Article 17 of the Rules of Procedure applies, pursuant to which the **Governing Council** is competent. Guidelines, too, must be adopted by the Governing Council and thereafter signed on its behalf by the President. The same applies to instructions related to supervisory tasks and supervisory decisions.[113]

92

Legal acts applicable to credit institutions and adopted in the exercise of the ECB's supervisory powers, which have legal consequences for the addressees, are subject to the **non-objection procedure**.[114] Under this procedure, the **Supervisory Board** proposes a legal act in the form of a final decision to be adopted by the **Governing Council**. At the same time, these draft decisions are also sent to the NCAs. The core of the non-objection procedure is that a draft decision is deemed to be adopted unless the Governing Council objects within a period of a maximum of 10 days. In cases of particular urgency, the period is reduced to 48 h. An objection from the Governing Council must be justified in particular by any **monetary policy considerations**, which fall outside the competence of the Supervisory Board. The procedure also applies to acts relating to the NCAs in order to ensure consistency between supervisory practices relating to SIs and LSIs. However, the non-objection procedure does not apply to acts concerning the cooperation between the ECB and NCAs.[115]

93

3.10. Sanctioning Powers

Also within the framework of banking supervision, Article 34.3 of the Statute, Article 132.3 TFEU and Regulation (EC) No 2532/98 form the basis of the ECB's sanctioning powers.[116] Particularities and specificities are contained in Article 18 of the SSM Regulation and Part X of the SSM Framework Regulation: in order to carry out its prudential supervisory tasks, the ECB may issue administrative fines or penalties **where credit institutions**, either **intentionally** or **negligently**, **infringe requirements of ECB regulations** or decisions or of Union law. As regards breaches of national law in the context of the SSM, the **NCAs** remain responsible for imposing penalties. However, such penalties are imposed solely at the initiative of the ECB.

94

---

[113] Articles 4.1, 6.3, 7.5 point (a), 9.1 and 30.5 of the SSM Regulation.

[114] See Article 26.8 of the SSM Regulation, which lays down the procedure according to which the Supervisory Board takes a decision in accordance with Articles 26.6 and 26.7 of the SSM Regulation.

[115] This follows from Article 26.8 of the SSM Regulation according to which the procedure must be without prejudice to Article 6 of the SSM Regulation.

[116] See also Riso (2014).

95   Due to the possibility of **profit confiscation**, sanctions may go well beyond the traditional maximum ceiling of EUR 500,000 or EUR 10,000 per day. The ECB may impose administrative pecuniary penalties of up to **twice the amount of the profits** gained or losses avoided because of the infringement or of up to 10% of the total annual turnover, as defined in the relevant Union law, of a bank in the preceding business year (Article 18.1 SSM Regulation).

96   As any supervisory decision, sanctions are potentially **subject to review** by the ABoR (Article 24 SSM Regulation, → para 89).

3.11. Details Concerning Legal Acts in the Context of Prudential Supervision

97   The ECB may adopt different kinds of legal acts in the context of prudential banking supervision, depending on the specific task. Potential addressees of ECB legal acts are not only SIs but also LSIs and NCAs.

3.11.1. Framework on Practical Arrangements for Cooperation Within the SSM

98   Article 6.7 of the SSM Regulation contains precise requirements for a framework to organise the practical arrangements for implementing cooperation within the SSM; these are largely implemented by the SSM Framework Regulation. However, in some areas, the SSM Framework Regulation *de facto* goes beyond the mere establishment of arrangements and contains general provisions concerning the functioning of the SSM, which are not (or at least not directly) linked to cooperation with the NCAs. This includes, for example, the structuring of the ECB supervisory procedure (Articles 25–32 SSM Framework Regulation), which addresses the preparation of ECB supervisory decisions (Articles 33–35 SSM Framework Regulation). There are also provisions relating to **whistle-blowers** (Articles 36–38 SSM Framework Regulation: "Reporting of breaches") and the sanctioning regime (Articles 120–137 SSM Framework Regulation: "Administrative penalties"). With the entry into force of the SSM Framework Regulation, competence under Article 6.7 is, however, not exhausted, and further acts in this category may follow.

3.11.2. Legal Acts Based on the Framework for Close Cooperation

99   The SSM Framework Regulation clarifies the ECB's scope to adopt acts under the SSM Regulation. This clarification relates in particular to acts adopted in the context of the "close cooperation" mechanism, by which MS **outside** the **euro area** may become part of the **SSM**. It is triggered by the request that the ECB carries out prudential supervision and macro-prudential tasks as defined in Articles 4 and 5 of the SSM Regulation. Close cooperation requires an ECB decision before it can be entered into. Such decision is subject to certain conditions: there must be a cooperation request from an MS and a communication in which the MS concerned undertakes that its NCA will follow any guidelines or requests adopted

by the ECB and guarantees that the ECB will be provided with all the information necessary to assess the credit institutions in the MS concerned. Finally, the MS concerned must also have legal provisions in place according to which its NCA is required to comply with requests from the ECB made in relation to its supervisory powers (Article 7.2 SSM Regulation). Close cooperation is based on Article 7 of the SSM Regulation. An ECB decision specifies the relevant procedures.[117] A particular feature of close cooperation is that the ECB does not use its power directly, but only **indirectly**, acting through the NCAs that issue supervisory decisions (Article 107.2 SSM Framework Regulation).

The legal instruments available in the framework of close cooperation are **instructions**, **guidelines** and **requests** (Articles 107, 108 SSM Framework Regulation). The ECB may issue an NCA with general *and* specific instructions in relation to SIs and *only* with general instructions in relation to LSIs. This underlines the fundamental division of competencies, according to which the focus of the ECB's supervision lies with SIs and banking groups. The difference between a specific and a general instruction is that the former may refer to only one **specific SI**, whereas the latter must refer to a **number of LSIs**. **100**

It should be noted that the **request** and **specific instruction**, according to the wording of the SSM Framework Regulation, may only be applied to SIs (Article 108.2 point (a) SSM Framework Regulation). An ECB request to an NCA is only mentioned in the SSM Framework Regulation and is not further specified. Requests are to be understood as constituting specifications of instructions. As such, they will usually have a lighter impact, granting the addressee additional room for manoeuvre compared to a regular instruction. Requests are used particularly when the ECB requires support in performing its own measures rather than in situations where a measure is being requested from an NCA. **101**

3.11.3. Legal Acts Addressing Supervised Entities Regarding Prudential Tasks

Pursuant to Article 4.3 SSM Regulation, the ECB may issue legal acts related to its prudential supervision tasks[118] in connection with supervised entities. These are prepared by the Supervisory Board and transmitted to the Governing Council for adoption (Article 26.8 SSM Regulation). **102**

In accordance with Article 30 SSM Regulation, the ECB levies **fees** on supervised entities to cover the costs of carrying out its prudential tasks and determines the calculation methods for such fees. These are laid down in the ECB Regulation on supervisory fees,[119] which provides details on the **methodology** for the **103**

---

[117] Decision ECB/2014/5 *on the close cooperation with the national competent authorities of participating Member States whose currency is not the euro*, O.J. L 198/7 (2014).

[118] The ECB's prudential supervision tasks are listed in Article 4.1 of the SSM Regulation.

[119] ECB Regulation (EU) No 1163/2014 *on supervisory fees*, O.J. L 311/23 (2014).

calculation of the total annual supervisory fees, the **procedure** for the **recovery** of such fees and the rules on **cooperation** between the ECB and NCAs.

3.11.4. Legal Acts Regarding Less Significant Credit Institutions

104 With regard to LSIs, the ECB may adopt not only **regulations** but also **guidelines** or **general instructions** in accordance with which the NCAs must supervise banks and issue supervisory decisions. However, the authorisation of credit institutions and the withdrawal and assessment of the notifications of the acquisition and disposal of qualifying holdings in credit institutions remain as tasks exclusive to the ECB (Article 1.1 points (a) and (c) SSM Regulation).

3.11.5. Legal Acts Relating to the Institutional Framework of the ECB for the SSM

105 The Statute and the SSM Regulation together constitute the basis for the institutional framework of the SSM. The Governing Council, on a proposal from the Executive Board, will adopt these acts without prior public consultation.

106 The basic rule that adopts the ECB's institutional framework in the light of the establishment of the SSM is spelt out in the ECB Decision of 22 January 2014 amending its Rules of Procedure.[120] The key aspect of this Decision is to lay down detailed provisions on the **establishment** of the **Supervisory Board** (Article 26.1 SSM Regulation).[121] The Supervisory Board is an internal ECB body that performs its responsibilities under the SSM Regulation. It is supplemented by the Administrative Board of Review, whose operating rules are specified in the ABoR Decision, which covers the appointment of members of the ABoR and the formalities for the lodging and processing of applications for the review of a supervisory decision.

107 With a view to ensuring a separation between monetary policy and supervisory tasks, the ECB is mandated to set up a **mediation panel** for the settlement of differences of views between the competent authorities of the participating MS concerned regarding an objection of the Governing Council to a draft Supervisory Board decision (Article 25.5 SSM Regulation). The ECB exercised this mandate by adopting Regulation (EU) No 673/2014.[122] It provides that a representative from each MS participating in the SSM nominates a member to the panel. As part of its decision-making procedure, the mediation panel issues an opinion; the Supervisory

---

[120] Decision ECB/2014/1 *amending Decision ECB/2004/2 of 19 February 2004 adopting the Rules of Procedure of the European Central Bank*, O.J. L 95/56 (2014). See also Article 12.3 of the Statute and Articles 25.2 and 26.12 of the SSM Regulation.

[121] See also Decision ECB/2014/4 *on the appointment of representatives of the European Central Bank to the supervisory board*, O.J. L 196/38 (2014).

[122] ECB Regulation (EU) No 673/2014 *concerning the establishment of a Mediation Panel and its Rules of Procedure* (ECB/2014/26), O.J. L 179/72 (2014).

Article 132. [Legal Acts of the ECB] 833

Board must then submit, within a period of 10 working days, a new draft decision regarding this opinion to the Governing Council.

3.11.6. Instruments for the Effective and Consistent Functioning of the SSM

In the context of its overall responsibility, the ECB may adopt legal acts for the **108** effective and consistent functioning of the SSM.[123] This competence provides for the adoption of an **ethical framework** for ECB staff and management involved in banking supervision in the form of a Code of Conduct.[124]

The members of the **Supervisory Board** are subject to a **Code of Conduct**.[125] **109** The code includes the basic principles that members of the board are to abide by. This concerns, first and foremost, the creation of a comprehensive and formal procedure, including ethics procedures and proportionate periods, for the advance assessment and prevention of conflicts of interest, which could emerge in the context of subsequent employment within 2 years of membership in the Supervisory Board as well as rules on private financial transactions and wealth declarations. It is also intended to prevent conflicts of interest through the exchange of personnel between the ECB and national supervisors (Articles 31.3–4 SSM Regulation).

List of Cases

ECJ

ECJ 15.07.1962, 25/62, *Plaumann & Co v Commission*, ECLI:EU:C:1963:17 [cit. in para 56]
ECJ 13.12.1989, 322/88, *Grimaldi*, ECLI:EU:C:1989:646 [cit. in para 16]

CFI/GC

CFI 24.03.1994, T-3/93, *Air France v Commission*, ECLI:EU:T:1994:36 [cit. in para 32]
GC 08.05.2015, T-122/15, *Landeskreditbank Baden-Württemberg v ECB*, ECLI: EU:T:2017:337 [cit. in para 91]

---

[123] The legal basis is provided for in Articles 6.1 and 6.7 of the SSM Regulation.

[124] See Article 19.3 of the SSM Regulation and ECB Decision (EU) 2015/433 *concerning the establishment of an Ethics Committee and its Rules of Procedure*, O.J. L 70/58 (2015) as well as ECB Guideline (EU) 2015/856 *laying down the principles of an Ethics Framework for the Single Supervisory Mechanism*, O.J. L 135/29 (2015).

[125] *Code of Conduct for the Members of the Supervisory Board of the European Central Bank*, O.J. C 93/02 (2015).

References[126]

Bax, R., & Witte, A. (2019). *The taxonomy of ECB instruments available for banking supervision.* In: ECB Economic Bulletin, Issue 6/2019.

Boar, C., Holden, H., & Wadsworth, A. (2020). Impending arrival – A sequel to the survey on central bank digital currency. *BIS Paper, No 107*, Retrieved from bis.org

Jaeger, T., & Stöger, K. (Eds.) (2021). *Kommentar zu EUV und AEUV.* (loose-leaf). Manz.

Papathanassiou, C. (2011). Das Europäische System der Zentralbanken und die Europäische Zentralbank. In H. Schimansky, H.-J. Bunte, & H.-J. Lwowski (Eds.), *Bankrechts-Handbuch (§ 134).* C.H. Beck.

Papathanassiou, C., & Zagouras, G. (2010). Mehr Sicherheit für den Finanzsektor: der Europäische Ausschuss für Systemrisiken und die Rolle der EZB. *Wirtschafts- und Bankrecht,* 1584–1588.

Riso, A. L. (2014). The power of the ECB to impose sanctions in the context of the SSM. *Bančni vestnik,* 32–35.

Riso, A. L., & Zagouras, G. (2016). Single supervisory mechanism. In S. Grieser & M. Heemann (Eds.), *Europäisches Bankenaufsichtsrecht.* Frankfurt School Verlag.

Siekmann, H. (Ed.). (2013). *Kommentar zur Europäischen Währungsunion.* Mohr Siebeck.

Witte, A. (2014). The application of national banking supervision law by the ECB: Three parallel modes of executing EU law? *Maastricht Journal of European and Comparative Law, 21,* 89–109.

Witte, A. (2015). Standing and judicial review in the new EU financial markets architecture. *Journal of Financial Regulation,* 226–262.

Zilioli, C., & Selmayr, M. (2001). *The Law of the European Central Bank.* Hart.

---

[126] All cited Internet sources of this comment have been accessed on 6 April 2021.

Article 133 [Legal Acts Concerning the Euro]

Without prejudice to the powers of the European Central Bank,[6] the European Parliament and the Council, acting in accordance with the ordinary legislative procedure,[12] shall lay down the measures[4-6] necessary[7] for the use of the euro as the single currency[6, 8-10]. Such measures[11] shall be adopted after consultation of the European Central Bank.

Contents

1. Historical Background 1
2. Scope 4
   2.1. Opposing Views in the Academic Literature 4
   2.2. Author's Position 6
   2.3. Position of the CJEU 8
   2.4. Measures Adopted 11
3. Procedural Aspects 12

List of Cases
References

1. Historical Background

The provision dates back to Article 109.4l sentence 3 TEC-Maastricht.[1] In this provision, the Council was empowered to irrevocably fix both the conversion rates of the currencies of the participating MS and the rate at which these currencies shall be substituted by the ECU (European currency unit, now euro), making the latter a "currency in its own right" (Article 109.4l sentence 1 TEC-Maastricht). Whilst Article 109.4l sentence 2 TEC-Maastricht made clear that this measure does not by itself modify the external value of the ECU, Article 109.4l sentence 3 TEC-Maastricht enabled the Council, through the same procedure as that under Article 109.4l sentence 1 TEC-Maastricht, to "take the other measures necessary for the rapid introduction of the ECU as the single currency of those Member States". This context and the wording indicate that Article 109.4l sentence 3 TEC-Maastricht focused on the **introduction of the currency as such** at not on other aspects of the emerging EMU.

1

The material scope of Article 109.4l sentence 3 TEC-Maastricht was retained in later revisions of the TEC, with Article 123.5 TEC-Nice being its successor provision, which brought about a modification in the Council voting, replacing the unanimity requirement by a **qualified majority**.[2]

2

---

[1] Griller, in Grabitz et al. (2021), Artikel 133 AEUV para 1 (released in 2015).
[2] Also see Griller, in Grabitz et al. (2021), Artikel 133 AEUV para 2 (released in 2015).

3   The Lisbon Treaty moved the provision from Chapter 4 (Transitional Provisions), where it had been since the TEC-Maastricht, to Chapter 2 (Monetary Policy). Apart from that, the content of the provision has also been changed as regards both its procedural and its substantive aspects. Regarding the procedural aspects, measures under Article 133 TFEU are to be taken by means of the **ordinary legislative procedure**, making the provision one of the rare cases in Chapter 2 in which this procedure applies and, consequently, where a strong involvement of the EP is seen. Regarding the substantive aspects, the wording "measures necessary for the rapid introduction of the ECU as the single currency" has been replaced by "measures necessary for the use of the euro as the single currency".

2. Scope

2.1. Opposing Views in the Academic Literature

4   The wording of Article 133 TFEU ("measures necessary for the use of the euro as the single currency") is **broadly drafted** and ambiguous. Some authors advocate an extensive interpretation of Article 133 TFEU, according to which the provision—possibly in combination with other provisions—could have served to safeguard the stability of the euro area and, thus, create the European Stability Mechanism (ESM).[3] Others propose a narrower understanding of the provision.[4] For them, Article 133 TFEU is as a provision only allowing for measures that focus on the integrity and unity of the euro as a single currency.[5]

5   The issue of interpretation of Article 133 TFEU is important not only for the said provision but also for the demarcation of the competence contained therein and other subject matters, that is, Union and **MS' competences**.[6] This is all the more important against the background of Article 133 TFEU falling into the **exclusive competence** of the EU (Article 3.1 point (c) TFEU), which means that MS have lost their competence for the respective field regardless of whether or not the EU has adopted any measure.[7] In particular, this is of relevance to defining the remaining MS' competences concerning the forms in which payments may be settled.[8]

---

[3] Cf. Griller, in Grabitz et al. (2021), Artikel 133 AEUV para 18 set seqq. (released in 2015); Wutscher, in Schwarze et al. (2019), Artikel 133 AEUV para 5.

[4] Häde, in Calliess and Ruffert (2022), Artikel 133 AEUV para 2.

[5] Cf. Manger-Nestler, in Pechstein et al. (2017), Artikel 133 AEUV para 1; Selmayr, in von der Groeben et al. (2015), Artikel 133 AEUV para 7 et seqq.

[6] Cf. Häde, in Calliess and Ruffert (2022), Artikel 133 AEUV paras 4 et seqq.

[7] Joined Cases C-422/19 and C-423/19, *Hessischer Rundfunk* (CJEU 26 January 2021) para 53 et seq.

[8] See, e.g., Häde, in Calliess and Ruffert (2022), Artikel 133 AEUV para 11.

2.2. Author's Position

It seems convincing that Article 133 TFEU is to be interpreted narrowly[9] for the following reasons: first, the wording only refers to the "**use of the euro as the single currency**" (also see Article 139.2 point (f) TFEU). This precludes issues such as the general economic preconditions for the introduction of the single currency. Second, the finding that Article 133 TFEU does not concern issues such as sufficient economic and financial convergence among the participating MS in the euro area, in particular sound public finances and budgetary discipline, can also be derived from the fact that the Treaty frames those issues as ones falling under Chapter 1 (Economic Policy).[10] Third, the competence can only be used with respect to the ECB powers, which includes, among others, the ones contained in Articles 127 and 128 TFEU.[11] This shows that Article 133 TFEU has the function merely to supplement the repertoire of ECB measures in the field of monetary policy. Interpreting Article 133 TFEU broadly would distort the institutional set-up in Chapter 2 by laying large powers in the hands of the EP and the Council. To conclude, interpreting Article 133 TFEU as a far-reaching provision allowing steps necessary to achieve and safeguard the preconditions for the single currency and not only the ones necessary for the use of this currency would ignore not only the wording of Article 133 TFEU but also the systematic position of Article 133 TFEU vis-à-vis the structure both of Chapter 2 and 3 of Title VIII. For this reason, it is submitted that Article 133 TFEU covers issues related to the **general framework of the use of the euro as a currency and legal tender**. The safeguarding of this use can also be regarded as the **purpose** of the provision.

In addition, the competence of the EP and Council is so far restricted that only those measures that are **necessary** for the said purpose may be adopted, which as a result restricts the legislator's room for manoeuvre.[12] By contrast, measures that merely promote or foster the use are not covered by the provision.

2.3. Position of the CJEU

Only recently, in the *Hessischer Rundfunk* case (2021),[13] did the CJEU elaborate on the scope of the competence contained in Article 133 TFEU. This case dealt with the conformity with Article 133 TFEU of a national provision that precluded the payment in cash of a radio and television licence fee to a regional public

---

[9] Cf. Palmstorfer (2021), p. 349 et seq.

[10] Cf. Häde, in Calliess and Ruffert (2022), Artikel 133 AEUV para 2.

[11] Häde, in Calliess and Ruffert (2022), Artikel 133 AEUV para 3; Manger-Nestler, in Pechstein et al. (2017), Artikel 133 AEUV para 1.

[12] Also see Manger-Nestler, in Pechstein et al. (2017), Artikel 133 AEUV para 4; Wille, in Geiger et al. (2014), Article 133 TFEU para 2.

[13] Joined Cases C-422/19 and C-423/19, *Hessischer Rundfunk* (CJEU 26 January 2021).

broadcasting body. Like Article 128 TFEU (→ Article 128 TFEU para 1), the CJEU views Article 133 TFEU as a provision aimed to achieve the **single currency status of the euro** and underpins the **singleness of the euro**.[14] Accordingly, it was held to have the purpose of establishing "uniform principles (...) in order to safeguard the overall interests of the Economic and Monetary Union and of the euro as the single currency and (...) to contribute to the pursuit of the primary objective of the European Union's monetary policy, which is to maintain price stability".[15] Despite this broad wording, the CJEU convincingly does not interpret Article 133 TFEU extensively, for the Court found that the scope comprises "legal rules governing the status of legal tender (...) in so far that this is necessary for the use of the euro as single currency".[16] That is, Article 133 TFEU focusses on the aspects related to the legal tender status of the euro. This interpretation is to be welcome. It remains to be seen whether the CJEU—against the background of the Court's description of the purpose of the provision—will stick to this narrow interpretation in future cases.

9   In the *Hessischer Rundfunk* case, the CJEU based its finding on the definition of **legal tender**, which only entails a fundamental obligation and not an absolute obligation to accept banknotes in euro as a means of payment.[17] As a consequence, Article 133 TFEU does not confer on the EU and, respectively, the EP and the Council the competence to adopt provisions on any aspects of the use of banknotes and coins in euro as a means of payment, for this is not necessary for the use of the euro as a single currency. It is thus not necessary that "the EU legislature lay down exhaustively and uniformly the exceptions to that fundamental obligation, provided that every debtor is guaranteed to have the possibility, as a **general rule**, of discharging a payment obligation in cash".[18]

10 This finding is relevant for identifying the remaining **competences of the MS**. As a consequence, the definition of the specific constellations in which payment in cash may be excluded does not fall under the scope of Article 133 TFEU. Consequently, this issue does not fall not into the exclusive competence of the EU, and the MS are not precluded from adopting provisions requiring that public administration accept payment in cash for the pecuniary obligations imposed by the administration.[19] This, of course, also presupposes that such issues are not covered by other

---

[14] Joined Cases C-422/19 and C-423/19, *Hessischer Rundfunk* (CJEU 26 January 2021) paras 40, 43.
[15] Joined Cases C-422/19 and C-423/19, *Hessischer Rundfunk* (CJEU 26 January 2021) para 50.
[16] Joined Cases C-422/19 and C-423/19, *Hessischer Rundfunk* (CJEU 26 January 2021) para 51.
[17] Joined Cases C-422/19 and C-423/19, *Hessischer Rundfunk* (CJEU 26 January 2021) para 55.
[18] Joined Cases C-422/19 and C-423/19, *Hessischer Rundfunk* (CJEU 26 January 2021) para 55 (emphasis added).
[19] Joined Cases C-422/19 and C-423/19, *Hessischer Rundfunk* (CJEU 26 January 2021) para 56, 58.

fields of EU law. This is in line with some previous contributions holding that Article 133 TFEU does not govern issues such as indexation clauses.[20]

2.4. Measures Adopted

This narrow understanding is also mirrored in the **acts so far adopted** on the basis of Article 133 TFEU or its predecessor provisions. These acts dealt with details for conversion rates,[21] the substitution of the euro for the currencies of the participating MS,[22] the protection of the euro against forgery[23] and the authentication of euro coins and handling of euro coins unfit for circulation.[24] 11

3. Procedural Aspects

Measures under Article 133 TFEU are adopted in the **ordinary legislative procedure** (Article 294 TFEU). Article 133 TFEU does not apply to MS with a derogation (non-euro area MS; see Article 139.2 point (f) TFEU). Only representatives of MS whose currency is the euro are allowed to take part in the Council voting, for which a qualified majority is required (Article 16.3 TEU, Article 139.4 TFEU, Article 238.3 point (a) TFEU). By contrast, also MEPs from non-euro area MS are allowed to take part in the legislative procedure.[25] 12

List of Cases

CJEU 26.01.2021, C-422/19 and C-423/19, 26.6.2021, *Hessischer Rundfunk*, ECLI:EU:C:2021:63 [cit. in para 5, 8-10]

---

[20] See Manger-Nestler, in Pechstein et al. (2017), Artikel 133 AEUV para 6; Häde, in Calliess and Ruffert (2022), Artikel 133 AEUV para 12 et seq. implies that indexation clauses might be covered by Article 133 TFEU in so far as they are necessary for the use of the euro.

[21] Council Regulation (EC) No 1103/97 *on certain provisions relating to the introduction of the euro*, O.J. L 162/1 (1997) as amended by Council Regulation (EC) No 2595/2000, O.J. L 300/1 (2000).

[22] Council Regulation (EC) No 974/98 *on the introduction of the euro*, O.J. L 139/1 (1998) most recently amended by Council Regulation (EU) No 827/2014, O.J. L 228/3 (2014).

[23] Council Regulation (EC) No 1338/2001 *laying down measures necessary for the protection of the euro against counterfeiting*, O.J. L 181/6 (2001) as amended by Council Regulation (EC) No 44/2009, O.J. L 17/1 (2009).

[24] Parliament/Council Regulation (EU) No 1210/2010 *concerning authentication of euro coins and handling of euro coins unfit for circulation*, O.J. L 339/1 (2010).

[25] Manger-Nestler, in Pechstein et al. (2017), Artikel 133 AEUV para 2.

References

Calliess, C., & Ruffert, M. (Eds.). (2022). *EUV/AEUV. Kommentar* (6th ed.). C. H Beck.
Geiger, R., Kahn, E., & Kotzur, M. (Eds.). (2014). *European Union Treaties: A Commentary*. C.H. Beck.
Grabitz, E., Hilf, M., & Nettesheim, M. (Eds.). (2021). *Das Recht der Europäischen Union. Kommentar, loose leaf (last supplement: 71)*. C. H. Beck.
Palmstorfer, R. (2021). *Die WWU, ihre Krise und Reform: Eine Untersuchung ausgewählter unions- und bundesverfassungsrechtlicher Problemstellungen*. Verlag Österreich.
Pechstein, M., Nowak, C., & Häde, U. (2017). *Frankfurter Kommentar zu EUV, GRC und AEUV*. Mohr Siebeck.
Schwarze, J., Becker, U., Hatje, A., & Schoo, J. (Eds.). (2019). *EU-Kommentar* (4th ed.). Nomos.
von der Groeben, H., Schwarze, J., & Hatje, A. (Eds.). (2015). *Europäisches Unionsrecht. Kommentar* (7th ed.).

Chapter 3
Institutional Provisions

Article 134 [Economic and Financial Committee]
(ex-Article 114 TEC)

1. In order to promote coordination of the policies of Member States to the full extent needed for the functioning of the internal market, an Economic and Financial Committee is hereby set up.[1–2]
2. The Economic and Financial Committee shall have the following tasks:

    – to deliver opinions at the request of the Council or of the Commission, or on its own initiative for submission to those institutions,[8]
    – to keep under review the economic and financial situation of the Member States and of the Union and to report regularly thereon to the Council and to the Commission, in particular on financial relations with third countries and international institutions,[9–12]
    – without prejudice to Article 240, to contribute to the preparation of the work of the Council referred to in Articles 66, 75, 121(2), (3), (4) and (6), 122, 124, 125, 126, 127(6), 128(2), 129(3) and (4), 138, 140(2) and (3), 143, 144(2) and (3), and in Article 219, and to carry out other advisory and preparatory tasks assigned to it by the Council,[13–19]
    – to examine, at least once a year, the situation regarding the movement of capital and the freedom of payments, as they result from the application of the Treaties and of measures adopted by the Council; the examination shall cover all measures relating to capital movements and payments; the Committee shall report to the Commission and to the Council on the outcome of this examination.[10]

    The Member States, the Commission and the European Central Bank shall each appoint no more than two members of the Committee.[22–26]

3. The Council shall, on a proposal from the Commission and after consulting the European Central Bank and the Committee referred to in this Article, lay down detailed provisions concerning the composition of the Economic and Financial Committee.[6]

    The President of the Council shall inform the European Parliament of such a decision.

4. In addition to the tasks set out in paragraph 2, if and as long as there are Member States with a derogation as referred to in Article 139, the Committee shall keep under review the monetary and financial situation and the general payments system of those Member States and report regularly thereon to the Council and to the Commission.[17]

Contents

1. Overview 1
2. Origin of the Economic and Financial Committee 3
   2.1. The Monetary Committee 3
   2.2. Evolution into Economic and Financial Committee 4
   2.3. The Statutes and Their Amendments 6
3. Competencies and Tasks 8
   3.1. Overview of the Economic and Financial Situation in the Union and Coordination of the Member States' Policies 8
   3.2. The Preparation of the ECOFIN Council 13
   3.3. Dialogue Between the Council, the Commission and the ECB 20
   3.4. Division of Competence Between the Economic and Financial Committee and the Economic Policy Committee 21
4. Composition and Internal Organization 22
   4.1. The Members 22
   4.2. The President 27
   4.3. Subcommittees and Working Groups 30
   4.4. The Secretariat 37
5. Decisional Procedures 38
6. A Supranational or an Intergovernmental Body? 41
References

1. Overview

1   The Economic and Financial Committee (EFC) is an EU committee established by Article 134 TFEU to **monitor the economic and financial situation of the Union** and **promote policy coordination among the MS**. This body is a place for discussion and interaction between political and monetary institutions because (i) it has competence in monetary and financial policies, economic policies and the free circulation of capital, and the institutions represented here carry out various tasks; (ii) States with and without derogation are all represented, thus enjoying equal rights; (iii) each State is represented by a member of the government and one of the central bank (and the EU, too, is represented by the Commission and by the European Central Bank (ECB)).[1]

2   It provides opinions **at the request of the Council** or **the Commission** or **on its own initiative**. It is a **preparatory body for the** Economic and Financial Affairs **(ECOFIN)** Council, i.e. the Council sitting in the configuration of the economy and finance ministers. In this role, it provides assessments on the economic and financial situations of the Union and MS, the coordination of economic and fiscal policies, contributions on financial market matters, exchange rate policies, and relations with third countries and international institutions. The Committee also provides a

---
[1] Cafaro (2001), p. 225.

Article 134. [Economic and Financial Committee]

framework for preparing and pursuing a dialogue between the Council, the Commission and the ECB.

2. Origin of the Economic and Financial Committee

2.1. The Monetary Committee

Ex-Article 114 TEC regulated the advisory role of the Monetary Committee to promote the coordination of the MS' monetary policies to the extent needed for the functioning of the internal market. This was the only committee foreseen by the **EEC Treaty** since its origins for economic and monetary policy cooperation.

Other committees were added in the 1960s: the Short-Term Economic Policy Committee, the Budgetary Policy Committee, the Medium-Term Economic Policy Committee (all replaced in **1974** by the **Economic Policy Committee**) and the Committee of Governors of the central banks of the EEC, which ceased to exist during the second stage of the Economic and Monetary Union (EMU) (later to evolve into a body of the European Monetary Institute and, eventually, into the Governing and General Councils of the ECB).

2.2. Evolution into Economic and Financial Committee

The article establishing the Monetary Committee was amended to become Article 109C of the **Maastricht Treaty** (1992) to envisage the creation of the EFC on 1 January 1999, which was to replace the Monetary Committee.[2] The same article mandated the EFC to discuss the economic and financial issues arising during the third stage of the EMU.[3]

Several elements **differentiate the EFC from the previous Monetary Committee**—both preparatory bodies for the ECOFIN Council—as the Monetary Committee was intended for the coordination of the different monetary policies of the MS inside the EC, while the EFC was created to service the monetary union, to coordinate the euro area monetary policy with that of MS with derogation and with opting out and to allow a permanent dialogue between the Council, the Commission and the ECB.

2.3. The Statutes and Their Amendments

The Statutes of the Committee were defined by virtue of **Council Decision 1999/8/EC**,[4] following Council Decision 98/743/EC on detailed provisions concerning the

---

[2] Vassalli di Dachenhausen, in Tizzano (2014), Article 134 para 1.
[3] Among the first commentators, Díez Parra (1999), pp. 49–57.
[4] Council Decision 1999/8/EC *adopting the Statutes of the Economic and Financial Committee*, O. J. L 5/71 (1999).

composition of the Economic and Financial Committee.[5] They were amended by Council Decision 2003/476/EC[6] to prepare the body for enlargement to ten new MS, to happen in May 2004. A new revision was adopted through Council Decision 2012/245/EU.[7] It followed the decision of the Heads of State or Government of the Member States whose currency is the euro (Euro Summit), adopted on 26 October 2011, which stated that the Eurogroup Working Group (→ para 35) would be chaired by a full-time President. As a consequence, the person nominated for this post ceased to be an official in a national administration and became an official employed by the EU institutions.

7   Annexed to Decision 2012/245 are the **Statutes** currently in force: it is a synthetic text composed of 14 articles on the tasks and competencies as well as the internal organization of the Committee and a few procedural rules. It enables the EFC to adopt its own procedural arrangements (Article 14 of the Statutes).

3. Competencies and Tasks

3.1. Overview of the Economic and Financial Situation in the Union and Coordination of the Member States' Policies

8   Under Article 134 TFEU, the EFC has a broad competence, including the coordination of the policies of the MS to the full extent needed for the functioning of the internal market. To this aim, it carries a number of important tasks, all having an advisory nature, given that decisions are taken by other bodies, mostly the Council. According to Article 134.2 first indent TFEU, it may deliver opinions at the request of the Council or the Commission, or on its own initiative for submission to these institutions, but may as well produce reports or other atypical acts. Its activities and documents are also very useful to the Commission and the ECB in carrying out their tasks.

9   The Committee regularly reviews the economic and financial situations of the MS and the Union and submits reports to the Council and the Commission (Article 134.2 second indent TFEU). This activity is regulated specifically by the acts composing the Stability and Growth Pact and the other acts related to it. This activity is **preparatory to the relevant Council and Commission decisions** (→ para 15). The EFC opinions and acts are intended both for the internal use of the Union and for the conduct of external relations. In the field of financial relations with third countries and international institutions, its role is to coordinate the positions—inside the G7/8, the G20 and the International Monetary Fund (IMF)—of the MS of the EU as well as those in the eurozone.

---

[5] O.J. L 358/109 (1998).
[6] O.J. L 158/58 (2003).
[7] O.J. L 121/22 (2012).

A specific task envisaged by Article 134.2 fourth indent TFEU is to examine, at 10 least once a year, situations regarding the **movement of capital and freedom of payments** both inside the Union and across its borders. The outcome of this examination is then reported to the Commission and the Council.

The Committee is also at the service of the MS as it is aimed to **promote the** 11 **coordination** of State economic and financial policies necessary for the **functioning of the internal market**. This coordination takes place inside the Committee at the administration level, while at the governments' level, it occurs in the Council as well as in the European Council and—for the euro area—in the Eurogroup and the Euro Summit.

The relationships between the euro-area MS and the MS with a derogation—or 12 having a right of opting out (Denmark, formerly also the UK)—is a specific coordination task of the EFC, according to Article 134.4 TFEU. The Committee shall keep under review the monetary and financial situation and the general payments system of those MS and report regularly thereon to the Council and to the Commission. A number of Council decisions concerning those States are prepared by the EFC (→ para 17).

3.2. The Preparation of the ECOFIN Council

All the activities of the EFC are intended to support the Council (as well as the 13 Commission). Nonetheless, Article 134.2 third indent TFEU provides a list of specific legal bases in the TFEU for which the Council's decisions (sometimes adopted together with the Parliament) have to be specifically prepared by the EFC. These **legal bases cover a number of areas within the economic and monetary policy**.

A first block of acts falling within this provision regards the **free circulation of** 14 **capital**, as the adoption of safeguard measures to movements of capital to or from third countries in exceptional circumstances (Article 66 TFEU); or of measures such as the freezing of funds, financial assets or economic gains for preventing or combating terrorism (Article 75 TFEU).

A second group of decisions relates to **steering and monitoring economic** 15 **policy of the Union and MS** as drafting the broad economic policy guidelines (Article 121.2 TFEU); regulating and enforcing the preventive arm of the Stability and Growth Pact (Article 121.3, 4, 6 TFEU and legislation adopted on the basis of Article 121.6 TFEU → Article 121 TFEU para 47 et seqq.)[8] as well as the corrective arm of it, specifically focused on avoiding excessive deficits and debts of MS (Article 126 TFEU and legislation adopted on the basis of Article 126.14

---

[8] In the preventive arm of the Stability and Growth Pact, the role of the EFC is specified by Articles 2a, 5, 6, 9, 10 of Council Regulation (EC) No. 1466/97 *on the strengthening of the surveillance of budgetary positions and the surveillance and coordination of economic policies*, O.J. L 209/1 (1997), last amended by Parliament/Council Regulation (EU) No. 1175/2011, O.J. L 306/12 (2011).

TFEU).⁹ Further competencies in the monitoring of the MS' budgetary positions—specifically States under severe financial pressure—are envisaged in two Regulations, which entered into force on 30 May 2013 in the euro-area MS, the so-called Two-Pack,¹⁰ adopted on the basis of Article 136 TFEU.

Further preparatory work by the EFC is foreseen for interpreting and applying the prohibitions in Articles 124 and 125 TFEU and for adopting solidarity measures in case of severe difficulties in economic situations and implementing rules (Article 122 TFEU).

16   Some legal bases listed in Article 134.2 TFEU are more **specific to monetary policy** (or to the decisions that fall on one side or another of the thin line between economic and monetary policies). In this case, the role of the EFC is to provide a platform for an **open exchange of views among the Council, the Commission and the ECB** in order to build a shared position. Examples are:

- The conferral of tasks to the ECB in the field of prudential supervision—the legislation concerning the so-called banking union (Article 127.6 TFEU)
- The issuance of coins and the harmonization of their technical specifications (Article 128.2 TFEU)
- The preparation of acts by the European Parliament (EP) and the Council intended to amend the ESCB Statute to the extent envisaged by Article 129.3 TFEU and the preparation of acts of the Council envisaged by the ESCB Statute as listed in Article 129.4 TFEU
- The decisions—if any— adopted on Article 138 TFEU, establishing common positions or unified representation within the international financial institutions on matters of particular interest for EMU within international financial institutions and conferences, as IMF or G20.

17   Finally, some Council decisions **deal with the derogation status of some MS** concerning EMU, such as:

- Decisions abrogating a derogation and welcoming new members into the third phase of the monetary union (Article 140.2, 3 TFEU)
- Council decisions on mutual assistance or authorization to MS with a derogation to take protective measures in case of severe difficulties regarding balance of payments (Article 143 TFEU); or

---

⁹ In the corrective arm of the Stability and Growth Pact, the role of the EFC is specified by Article 3 of the Council Regulation (EC) No. 1467/97 *on speeding up and clarifying the implementation of the excessive deficit procedure*, O.J. L 209/6 (1997), last amended by Council Regulation (EU) No. 177/2011, O.J. L. 306/33 (2011).

¹⁰ These are the Parliament/Council Regulation (EU) 472/2013 *on the strengthening of economic and budgetary surveillance of Member States in the euro area experiencing or threatened with serious difficulties with respect to their financial stability*, O.J. L 140/1 (2013) and the Parliament/Council Regulation (EU) 473/2013 *on common provisions for monitoring and assessing draft budgetary plans and ensuring the correction of excessive deficit of the Member States in the euro area*, O.J. L 140/11 (2013). The role of the EFC is specified in the first act by Recital 5 of the preamble and in the second by Articles 10 and 11.

Article 134. [Economic and Financial Committee]

- When—in such a case—a Council decision is not immediately taken and an MS with a derogation takes a protective measure, the decision taken by the Council to amend, suspend or abolish it (Article 144 TFEU); and
- On the conclusion of agreements concerning exchange rates or monetary or foreign exchange regime matters (Article 219 TFEU)

The EFC may also carry out **other advisory and preparatory tasks** assigned to it by the Council.

As Article 134.2 third indent TFEU points out, all these tasks are carried out **"without prejudice to Article 240"**. As a consequence, the opinions and drafts by the EFC will go through the Committee of the Permanent Representatives of the Governments of the Member States to the European Union (**COREPER**), which is responsible for preparing the work of the Council (Article 240 TFEU) before arriving at the table of the Council. In particular, these documents will be sent to the configuration known as COREPER II, which consists of ambassadors of MS, who deal with economic matters and who are in charge of preparing the work of the ECOFIN Council (→ Article 240 TFEU paras 4 to 6).

3.3. Dialogue Between the Council, the Commission and the ECB

The EFC provides a framework within which a dialogue between the Council, the Commission and the ECB may be prepared, and so debates inside the EFC are an important step in negotiating and **building a consensus among the institutions**.[11]

It has been pointed out by the European Council of Luxembourg of 12–13 December 1997 in the Resolution on Economic Policy Coordination during stage 3 of the EMU that the EFC, "which will bring together senior officials from the national central banks and the ECB as well as from finance ministries, will provide the framework within which the dialogue can be prepared and continued at the level of senior officials" (→ para 12).

3.4. Division of Competence Between the Economic and Financial Committee and the Economic Policy Committee

The competence of the EFC may appear—as in fact is—partly overlapping with the competence of the Economic Policy Committee (EPC) established in 1974 (→ para 3).[12] Nonetheless, these **two bodies have different perspectives in their approach** to economic policy coordination among the MS. The EPC, too, is in charge of the preparation of the ECOFIN Council's decisions and especially of its task of coordinating the economic policies of the MS and the Union, but it works

---

[11] Di Preso, in Pocar and Baruffi (2014), Article 134 para III 2.

[12] A revised statute of the EPC was adopted by Council Decision 2003/475/EC, O.J. L 158/55 (2003).

specifically on two pillars: (1) an economic policy pillar, which essentially focuses on growth, globalisation, strengthening the single market and promoting greater coherence between macroeconomic, structural and employment policies, and (2) a public finance pillar, which is concerned about the quality and sustainability of States' public finances. The two committees **work in close relationship** with each other.

The different focus of **EPC** compared to the EFC is testified by its **membership**: it too comprises two delegates from each MS, the Commission and the ECB, but the two representatives from each MS are both senior officials coming from national authorities responsible for formulating economic and structural policy (usually economic ministries).

4. Composition and Internal Organization

4.1. The Members

22   The Council – on a proposal from the Commission and after consulting the ECB and Committee itself—adopts **detailed provisions concerning the composition of the EFC**. The EP is merely informed by the President of the Council of such a decision (Article 134.3 TFEU). The Council has exercised this power in Decision 98/743/EC and in the decisions adopting the Statutes ($\rightarrow$ para 6).

23   The MS, the Commission and the ECB shall each—according to Article 134.2 (2) TFEU—appoint no more than two members of the Committee and in fact—as for the Monetary Committee—**the MS, the ECB and the Commission appoint each two members.** They shall also appoint two alternate members (Article 1 of Council Decision 98/743). Members of the Committee and alternates shall be guided, in the performance of their duties, according to the general interests of the Union (Article 3 of the EFC Statutes).

Moreover, the members of the Committee and the alternates shall be selected from among **experts possessing outstanding competence in the economic and financial field** (Article 2 of Council Decision 98/743). The two members appointed by the MS shall be selected respectively from among senior officials from the administration and the national central bank. The alternates shall be selected under the same conditions (Article 3 of Council Decision 98/743).

No term of office for the members of the Committee was mentioned in either Decision 98/743/EC or the Statutes; this means that they are appointed for an indefinite period and that the appointing authorities may replace them.

24   The composition of the EFC would have become too large in the occasion of the 2004 enlargement of the EU to ten new MS. For this reason, the Decision 98/743 was revised by the Decision 2003/47. Since this amendment of the Statutes, the EFC may **meet in two different configurations,** i.e. with or without national central banks. The Committee in its full composition will regularly review the list of the issues on which the national central bank members attend the meetings (Article 4 of the EFC Statutes).

Article 134. [Economic and Financial Committee]

The EFC also meets in a euro-area configuration, the so-called **Eurogroup Working Group** (EWG), in which only the euro-area MS, the Commission and the ECB are represented (→ para 37; → Article 137 TFEU para 23 et seqq.). If the President of the EWG is not the President of the Committee, he may attend meetings of the Committee and take part in the discussions, unless the Committee decides otherwise (Article 8 (1) of the EFC Statutes). 25

Unless not permitted by the Committee, **alternates may attend its meetings**, though they shall not vote, and unless the Committee decides otherwise, they shall likewise not take part in the discussions (Article 8 (2) of the EFC Statutes). 26

A **member who is unable to attend** a meeting of the Committee **may delegate his functions** to one of the alternates or to another member. The Chairman and the Secretary of the Committee should be informed in writing before the meeting. In exceptional circumstances, the President may agree to alternative arrangements (Article 8 (3) of the EFC Statutes).

4.2. The President

The Committee is chaired by a President elected by a majority of its members for a renewable 2-year term. Those **eligible** for the Presidency shall be Committee members who are senior officials in national administrations or the President of the EWG (Article 6 of the EFC Statutes). 27

In the event of a failure to fulfill his duties, the President of the Committee shall be replaced by the Committee **Vice-President**. The Vice-President shall be elected for a term of two years by a vote of a majority of the Committee members. Similarly, those eligible for election as Vice-President shall be senior officials in national administrations or the President of the EWG, unless the latter has been appointed as President of the Committee (Article 7 of the EFC Statutes). 28

Among the **tasks of the President,** there is the duty to convene the Committee on his own initiative, at the request of the Council or the Commission or if at least four members of the Committee so request (Article 10 of the EFC Statutes), as well as the duty to represent the Committee (Article 11 sentence 1). He/she is in charge of making a report on the Committee discussions and delivering oral comments on the opinions and communications prepared by the Committee. The President has the responsibility of maintaining a good relationship with the EP (Article 11 sentence 2) and other Committees, especially the Economic Policy Committee (→ para 21). He is also a **non-voting member of the General Board of the ESRB** and **a member with full voting rights of the Steering Committee**.[13] 29

---

[13] Article 6.2 point (b) and Article 11.1 point (h), respectively, of Parliament/Council Regulation (EU) No. 1092/2010 *on European Union macro-prudential oversight of the financial system and establishing a European Systemic Risk Board*, O.J. L 331/1 (2010). See also Di Preso, in Pocar and Baruffi (2014), Article 134 TFEU para II 6.

4.3. Subcommittees and Working Groups

30   According to Article 9 of the Statutes, "[t]he **Committee may entrust the study of specific questions to its alternate members, to subcommittees or to working parties**. In these cases, the Presidency shall be assumed by a member or an alternate member of the Committee, appointed by the Committee. The members of the Committee, its alternates and its subcommittees or working parties may call upon experts to assist them." The EFC subcommittees cover a broad area of topics, mirroring all the tasks and competencies of the Committee itself.

31   The **Sub-Committee on EU Sovereign Debt Markets** was first established by the Monetary Committee as Subcommittee on EU Government Bills and Bonds Market in December 1997 to study the modalities of debt re-denomination in stage 3 of the EMU and other issues related to government bonds and bills markets in the context of a changeover to the euro and to further promote the integration and better functioning of EU government bond markets. Since then, the mandate was extended on several occasions: in 1999, to monitor the new euro-denominated bond market and discuss issues related to the efficient functioning of the EU's primary and secondary government debt markets and in 2010, for the preparation of EFC common positions and understandings in respect of changes in the financial architecture affecting sovereign debt markets (including technical issues such as collective action clauses and collateral swap agreements). The Sub-committee includes members from all 27 MS, the Commission and the ECB. The European Investment Bank (EIB) and the European Financial Stability Facility (EFSF) are also represented.

32   The Sub-Committee on International Monetary Fund and related issues (SCIMF) was established to interact directly with the EURIMF – the coordination group of European executive directors in the IMF. The regular communication and exchange of information between the working group in Brussels and EURIMF is given by the systematic involvement of the EURIMF President in the work of the SCIMF. The conclusions of the debates in the SCIMF are communicated to the European Executive Directors of the Fund, as an element to be considered in view of the decisions in the IMF Executive Board. The main issues raised by members of the SCIMF focus on the evolving role of the Fund, the periodical quota revisions and possible governance reforms, and the preparation of the meetings of the G20.

33   The **Joint EFC-EPC Working Group on the International Financial Aspects of Climate Change** has been established to bring together expertise in international climate finance and consider practical solutions to issues in this area, such as to mobilize long-term financing for climate change actions in developing countries, notably the potential sources of international climate finance; to assess potential international and national, public, private and innovative finance instruments; to propose methods to include public and private financing in agreed financial commitments, as well as in issues related to the design of the Green Climate Fund; and to contribute to the achievement of the goals set by the Conferences of the Parties (COPs) of the United Nations Framework Convention on Climate Change (UNFCCC). In addition, the group may address other issues within the competence

Article 134. [Economic and Financial Committee] 853

of the finance ministers concerning international negotiations, as may be necessary. The Working Group consists of two experts per MS: senior officials and climate experts from the finance or economics ministries.

Other subcommittees are the Circulation and Issuance of Euro Coins Subcommittee (Euro Coins Subcommittee), the Statistics Subcommittee and the *ad hoc* working groups and task forces that deal with financial stability and service issues. 34

The **Eurogroup Working Group** (EWG) is a preparatory body referred to in Article 1 of Protocol (No. 14) on the Eurogroup ($\rightarrow$ Article 137 TFEU para 18), which is composed of the representatives of the finance ministers of the MS whose currency is the euro, of the Commission and of the ECB. It provides assistance to the Eurogroup and its President, preparing discussions and providing opinions. It meets once a month, ahead of Eurogroup meetings. 35

The Heads of State or Government of the MS whose currency is the euro (Euro Summit) stated, on 26 October 2011, that the EWG will be chaired by a **full-time President**. As a consequence, he ceased to be an official in a national administration and is now an official employed by the EU institutions for a period of two years, which may be extended.

In addition, **a High-Level Expert Group (HLEG) on small and medium-sized enterprises (SMEs) and infrastructure financing** was established in May 2013. Its members, because of their specialized market expertise, have the specific task of following up on the European Commission's Green Paper on the long-term financing of the European economy[14] and making recommendations on increasing access to capital markets for SMEs and long-term infrastructure financing in Europe. 36

It published a final report in December 2013 called "Finance for Growth", which included a number of recommendations, some of which are addressed to the MS, the Commission, supervisory authorities and the private sector.[15]

4.4. The Secretariat

The **EFC and its President** are **assisted by a Secretariat**, which also provides support for the Economic Policy Committee and the Eurogroup. The Secretariat contributes to the formulation, coordination and surveillance of economic and financial policies in the EU via the smooth and efficient functioning of the EFC as well as its subcommittees, *ad hoc* working groups and task forces and, thus, contributes to efficiently preparing the Council and the Eurogroup. The committee is also assisted by experts (Article 9 of the EFC Statutes). 37

---

[14] Commission Green Paper, *Long-Term Financing of the European Economy*, COM(2013) 150 final.
[15] High Level Expert Group on SME and Infrastructure Financing, *Finance for Growth*, Report of 11 December 2013, available at http://www.cica.net/wp-content/uploads/2015/11/hleg_report_2013.pdf.

Article 13 of the Statutes provides that **the Secretary and the Secretariat's staff shall be supplied by the Commission**. The Secretary shall be appointed by the Commission after consultation with the Committee. The Secretary and his staff shall act on the instructions of the Committee when carrying out their responsibilities to the Committee. The expenses of the Committee shall be included in the budget of the Commission.

5. Decisional Procedures

38   Decisional procedures are set up by Article 5 of the Statutes: **all the acts are adopted by a majority of the members** if a vote is requested and each member has one vote. Nonetheless, when advice or an opinion is given on questions on which the Council will take a decision, members from central banks, if present, and the Commission shall participate fully in the discussions but shall not vote. The Committee shall also report on minority or dissenting views expressed in the course of the discussion.

39   A member who is **unable to attend** a meeting of the Committee may **delegate his/her right to vote** to one of the alternates or another member. Where alternates replace members, they have the right to vote. As a general rule, alternate members may attend committee meetings but do not get to vote or participate in discussions. However, the Committee may decide to amend this.

If the President of the EFC is a Committee member from a national administration, his/her voting right is delegated to the alternate (Article 6).

40   According to Article 12 of the Statutes, "the proceedings of the Committee shall be confidential. The same rule shall apply to the proceedings of its alternates, subcommittees or working parties." Because of this **confidentiality rule**, it is difficult to comment on the functioning of the EFC and its procedural practices.

6. A Supranational or an Intergovernmental Body?

41   The composition might suggest a kind of **"mixed" legal nature** as representatives of MS meet with officials from two supranational institutions, such as the ECB and Commission. Some considerations emphasize the supranational dimension over the intergovernmental one: the "one man/one vote" rule and also the provision in Article 3 of the Statutes stating that "[m]embers ... shall be guided, in their performance of duties, by the general interests of the Union".

However, Article 5 of the Statutes provides a **double-track decisional procedure** based on whether or not the Committee contributes to the preparation of the work of the Council. In the latter case, only the representatives of the States vote and the organ mirrors the decisional procedures of the Council's working groups. Interestingly enough, the Statutes are silent on the term of office of the members, except for the President. The secretariat of the EFC is exceptionally managed by the staff of the Commission and not by that of the General Secretariat of the Council, further confirmation of its hybrid legal nature.

References[16]

Cafaro, S. (2001). *Unione monetaria e coordinamento delle politiche economiche*. Giuffrè.

Díez Parra, I. (1999). El Comité económico y financiero. *Noticias de la Unión Europea*, n. 175/176.

Louis, J. V. (2009). *Commentaire J. Mégret L'Union européenne et sa monnaie*. Presses de l'ULB.

Pocar, F., & Baruffi, M. C. (Eds.). (2014). *Commentario breve ai Trattati dell'Unione europea* (2nd ed.). CEDAM.

Tizzano, A. (Ed.). (2014). *Trattati dell'Unione europea e della Comunità europea* (2nd ed.). Giuffrè.

---

[16] All cited Internet sources of this comment have been accessed on 6 April 2021.

Article 135 [Initiatives of the Council and the Member States]
(ex-Article 115 TEC)

For matters within the scope of Article s 121(4), 126 with the exception of paragraph 14, 138, 140(1), 140(2), first subparagraph, 140(3) and 219,[3–5] the Council or a Member State may request the Commission to make a recommendation or a proposal, as appropriate.[1] The Commission shall examine this request and submit its conclusions to the Council without delay.[2]

Contents

1. Scope of the Article 1
2. Fields of Application 3
3. Relation with Article 241 TFEU 6
4. Other Pre-initiative Procedures 8

1. Scope of the Article

The TEU/TFEU provide the **Commission** with an **almost exclusive right of initiative** (Article 17.2 TEU), which empowers and requires it to make proposals on the matters contained in the Treaty because either the Treaty explicitly provides for it or the Commission considers it necessary. This right is given in order to guarantee its role as guardian of the Treaties and as a defender of the general interest of the Union (→ Article 17 TEU para 2 et seq.).   **1**

Article 135 TFEU, like a few other provisions in the said Treaty, **limits somehow this exclusive right of initiative, allowing the Council or the MS** to exercise a (sort of) right of pre-initiative, i.e. to put pressure on the Commission in order to encourage the adoption of a recommendation or a proposal on some specific legal bases.

This request to the Commission is a **mere political pressure** as the Council or the States do not enjoy an autonomous right of initiative, as is the case, for instance, in Article 30.1 TEU. The Commission retains fully its right to adopt or not adopt any initiative, and its only duty is to examine the request and submit to the Council a conclusion, which motivates its choice to follow up on the request or to refuse it.   **2**

2. Fields of Application

This provision is specifically related to a few decisional procedures. The first two regard the **application of the so-called Stability and Growth Pact**. Article 121.4 TFEU regulates the enforcement of the broad economic policy guidelines and gives to   **3** the Commission the discretion to address a warning to the MS whose policies are not consistent and could jeopardise the proper functioning of the Economic and Monetary Union (EMU). Moreover, the Council, on a recommendation from the Commission, may address recommendations to the MS concerned and even decide to make them public. So the request to the Commission by the Council or an MS may be intended to encourage the Commission's warning as well as the Council's decision, as specified by the implementing rules.[1] Article 126 TFEU (with the exception of paragraph 14), instead, covers all the corrective measures that could be imposed upon an MS not fulfilling the criteria set for budgetary discipline, as specified by the article itself, paragraph 2; by the Protocol on the excessive deficit procedure annexed to the Treaties; and by the implementing regulation.[2]

4   A second area of application for Article 135 TFEU pertains to the external relations of the EMU. Article 138 TFEU is the key article relating to the **external representation of the euro**. According to the said article, the Council may decide on common positions on matters of particular interest for the EMU within the competent international financial institutions and conferences and on measures to ensure the unified representation within the area of international financial institutions and conferences (→ Article 138 TFEU para 20 et seqq., 27 et seqq.).

Article 219 TFEU concerns the exchange rate policy and specifically the decisions related to the conclusion of formal **agreements on an exchange-rate system** for the euro in relation to the currencies of third States (Article 219.1 (1) TFEU; → Article 219 TFEU paras 13–20); the adoption, adjustment or abandonment of the central rates of the euro within an exchange-rate system (Article 219.1 (2) TFEU; → Article 219 TFEU paras 21–22); the formulation of general orientations for an exchange-rate policy in relation to other currencies (Article 219.2 TFEU; → Article 219 TFEU paras 23–26); and arrangements for the negotiation and conclusion of such agreements (Article 219.3 TFEU; → Article 219 TFEU paras 27–31).

5   The third area of application of Article 135 TFEU is the **status of MS with a derogation** that are not yet in the third phase of the EMU. In fact, the Commission may be encouraged to report to the Council on the progress made by the MS with a derogation (something it should do once every two years or at the request of an MS with a derogation, according to Article 140.1; → Article 140 TFEU paras 3–4), to make a proposal to abrogate a derogation (Article 140.2 (1); → Article 140 TFEU paras 25–26) and—if this proposal is adopted—irrevocably fix the rate at which the euro shall be substituted for the currency of the MS concerned, and to take the other measures necessary for the introduction of the euro (Article 140.3; → Article 140 TFEU paras 27–37).

---

[1] Council Regulation (EC) No. 1466/97 *on the strengthening of the surveillance of budgetary positions and the surveillance and coordination of economic policies*, O.J. L 209/1 (1997), last amended by Parliament/Council Regulation (EU) No. 1175/2011, O.J. L 306/12 (2011).

[2] Council Regulation (EC) No. 1467/97 *on speeding up and clarifying the implementation of the excessive deficit procedure*, O.J. L 209/6 (1997), last amended by Council Regulation (EU) No. 177/2011, O.J. L. 306/33 (2011).

3. Relation with Article 241 TFEU

Article 135 TFEU may be considered some sort of **lex specialis compared to** **Article 241 TFEU**. According to the latter, "the Council, acting by a simple majority, may request the Commission to undertake any studies the Council considers desirable for the attainment of the common objectives, and to submit to it any appropriate proposals". The two provisions are very similar in nature and produce the same effects, with two differences. The first difference lies in the fact that Article 135 TFEU allows also MS to push for a Commission's proposal or recommendation, while Article 241 TFEU gives this option only to the Council; the second one relates to the wider scope of Article 241 TFEU, allowing the Council to put pressure on the Commission without any limitation or specification on legal bases, so it applies on any decisional procedure in the Treaty where the Commission enjoys its right of initiative.

The reason for granting the Council or individual MS a specific right to ask for a Commission's initiative on these specific legal bases may be questioned. It may reflect the **political nature** as well as the **economic implications of the related decisions**, and/or it could have the aim of improving the **dialogue among institutions and among States and institutions** on such sensitive decisions and of preventing a political impasse.

4. Other Pre-initiative Procedures

A similar pre-initiative procedure is envisaged by **Article 225 TFEU for the European Parliament** (EP), which can request the Commission "to submit any appropriate proposal on matters on which it considers that a Union act is required for the purpose of implementing the Treaties".

The latest pre-initiative was introduced by the Lisbon Treaty and is in **Article 11.4 TEU** (→ Article 11 TEU paras 27–30): the **European citizens' initiative**, which follows the collection of not less than one million signatures from citizens who are nationals of a significant number of MS. This case, too, is just an *invitation* to the European Commission, within the framework of its powers, "to submit any appropriate proposal on matters where citizens consider that a legal act of the Union is required for the purpose of implementing the Treaties".

Chapter 4
Provisions specific to Member States whose Currency is the Euro

Article 136 [Measures Specific to the Member States Whose Currency Is the Euro]

1. In order to ensure the proper functioning of economic and monetary union,[5] and in accordance with the relevant provisions of the Treaties, the Council shall, in accordance with the relevant procedure[22–26] from among those referred to in Articles 121 and 126, with the exception of the procedure set out in Article 126(14), adopt measures[5–8] specific to those Member States whose currency is the euro:

   (a) to strengthen the coordination and surveillance of their budgetary discipline;
   (b) to set out economic policy guidelines for them, while ensuring that they are compatible with those adopted for the whole of the Union and are kept under surveillance.

2. For those measures set out in paragraph 1, only members of the Council representing Member States whose currency is the euro shall take part in the vote.[27]
   A qualified majority of the said members shall be defined in accordance with Article 238(3)(a).

3. The Member States whose currency is the euro may establish a stability mechanism to be activated if indispensable to safeguard the stability of the euro area as a whole. The granting of any required financial assistance under the mechanism will be made subject to strict conditionality.[28–35]

Contents

1. Introduction 1
2. Measures Specific to the Member States of the Euro Area (Paragraphs 1 and 2) 4
   2.1. The Aims and Scope 5
   2.2. The Nature of Union Competence 9
   2.3. Use and Practice 12
   2.4. Procedural Aspects 22
3. Possibility to Establish a Stability Mechanism (Paragraph 3) 28
List of Cases
References

The views expressed by the author are strictly personal and do not engage the institution for which he works.

1. Introduction

1 Article 136 TFEU is part of Chapter 4 of Title VIII of the TFEU on Economic and Monetary Policy. That chapter establishes provisions specific to MS whose currency is the euro. Bearing in mind its objectives, scope and past use, Article 136 TFEU is the most prominent provision within that chapter. It allows for a **decision-making capacity specific to the euro area**, which has proven key in the adoption of legislative reforms of the economic governance of the Union during the economic and financial crisis.[1]

2 The **first two paragraphs** of Article 136 TFEU constitute a **genuine legal basis**, thus conferring the Union a power to act as well as the procedures to do so. In turn, the **third paragraph** of Article 136 TFEU is a **declaratory or recognitive provision**, which acknowledges the power of the MS whose currency is the euro to establish a stability mechanism if it is indispensable to safeguard the stability of the euro area as a whole.

3 This comment will examine in order the two different parts of Article 136 TFEU as identified above.

2. Measures Specific to the Member States of the Euro Area (Paragraphs 1 and 2)

4 Article 136.1–2 TFEU was **introduced by the Treaty of Lisbon**. A provision with almost identical drafting existed in the ill-fated Treaty establishing a Constitution for Europe (Article III-194 TCE), on whose content the Treaty of Lisbon largely builds upon. Article 136.1–2 TFEU is the result of a **joint Franco-German contribution** to the works of the Convention on the Future of Europe (the Convention), which proposed a number of measures to reinforce the cohesion and governance of the euro area. The contribution stated that "(...) because of a large number of Member States will not be members of the euro area for many years, France and Germany underline the necessity for Member States of the euro area to decide among themselves within the Council on issues arising out of the existence of their common currency (...)".[2]

---

[1] In this sense, Article 10 of the TSCG states that the Contracting Parties "stand ready to make active use, whenever appropriate and necessary, of measures specific to those Member States whose currency is the euro as provided for in Article 136 [TFEU]".

[2] See French-German contribution on economic governance, CONTRIB 180, CONV 470/02.

2.1. The Aims and Scope

The chapeau of Article 136.1 TFEU enounces its overarching objective, namely to   5
"ensure the proper functioning of the economic and monetary union". In order to achieve that objective, it confers upon the Council the **power to adopt measures specific to the euro-area MS**. These measures may consist of a) strengthening the coordination and surveillance of their budgetary discipline (on coordination → Article 119 TFEU para 11 et seq.; Article 120 TFEU para 6 et seq., 11 et seqq.) and b) setting out **economic policy guidelines** for them while ensuring that they are compatible with those adopted for the whole of the Union (→ Article 120 TFEU para 42; Article 121 TFEU para 13 et seqq.) and c) are **kept under surveillance** (Article 121.2 and 3 TFEU; → Article 121 TFEU para 23 et seqq., 31 et seqq.).

Specific action within the euro area provided for by Article 136.1 TFEU is hence   6
instrumental to the proper functioning of two policies: economic and monetary. By putting in connection those two policies, Article 136.1 TFEU makes evident their strong links and the fact that a performing monetary union requires **enhanced economic coordination** within the euro area. The achievement of the objective of **price stability** (Article 127.1 TFEU), to which monetary union is subdued, cannot be subtracted from the respect by the euro-area MS of their budgetary obligations under the Treaties as well as from the efficient coordination of their economic policies. The respect of **budgetary stability** by the euro-area MS is an underlying objective of Article 136.1–2 TFEU and is formulated by that provision in the wider context of price stability (monetary union). As will be shown (→ para 34), Article 136.3 TFEU introduces a third notion of stability, namely the stability of the euro area.

The two specific types of measures foreseen by Article 136.1 TFEU (i.e.,   7
strengthening the coordination and surveillance of the budgetary discipline and setting out economic policy guidelines) aim at reinforcing the current measures for economic coordination laid down by the Treaties. Measures under Article 136.1–2 TFEU may so supplement and enhance measures under the so-called **multilateral surveillance procedure**, which means the preventive arm of the Stability and Growth Pact laid down in Article 121 TFEU, which aims, notably, to prevent at an early stage the occurrence of excessive government deficits and promote the surveillance and coordination of economic policies, and the corrective arm, i.e. the excessive deficit procedure, laid down under Article 126.2–13 TFEU (→ Article 126 TFEU para 12 et seqq.; Supplement to Title VIII: Fiscal Union para 68 et seqq.). Their objective is to encourage and, if necessary, **compel the MS concerned to reduce a deficit** that might be identified.

The **supplementary nature of Article 136.1–2 TFEU** entails that measures   8
adopted under that basis must remain **consistent with the overall framework of economic governance** laid down by the Treaties. Article 136 TFEU cannot serve the purpose of establishing a parallel system of economic coordination that would break free, distort or be incompatible with the general means and procedures laid down in the Treaties in relation to economic policy.

2.2. The Nature of Union Competence

9   Because Article 136.1–2 TFEU is of a supplementary character, it is of an identical nature of the Union's competence to which it complements, i.e., the economic policy of the Union. The competence of the Union under that provision is therefore a **competence of coordination among the MS** "within arrangements as determined" by the Treaties (Article 2.3 TFEU). The coordinative nature of the competence, as opposed to the traditional competencies of "integration" as a par excellence internal market, means that **MS remain preponderantly sovereign over their economic and budgetary decisions** (Articles 2.3, 5.1 and 121.1 TFEU; → Article 120 TFEU para 4, 6 et seqq.). The preservation of the national budgetary and economic sovereignty is actually a "red line" for some Constitutional Courts, notably the German Federal Constitutional Court (FCC), beyond which the **principle of democracy** would be in danger.[3]

10   The coordinative nature of the competence means, first and foremost, that the **Commission** does not occupy the same executive and surveillance roles that it otherwise holds in the integration policies of the Union. It **shares with the Council the role of executing the economic policy of the Union** through the preventive and corrective procedures to which reference has been made previously, the Council remaining ultimately responsible to adopt the relevant decisions. The Commission does not have the competence to enforce the budgetary obligations incumbent upon the MS through the infringement procedure (Article 126.10 TFEU; → Article 126 TFEU para 13), and, accordingly, the CJEU has no jurisdiction to verify compliance by the MS with their budgetary obligations through that procedure. The **enforceability of economic and budgetary obligations** stemming from the Treaties is hence **very** much **limited** in comparison to obligations stemming from policies which are exclusive or shared competence of the Union. Economic policy is founded on the so-called peer review or control *inter pares*, where the MS are themselves the subjects and the objects of the procedures of economic coordination.

---

[3] See German Federal Constitutional Court, 2 BvE 2/08, *Treaty of Lisbon* (Judgment of 30 June 2009) para 256: "[a] transfer of the right of the Bundestag to adopt the budget and control its implementation by the government which would violate the principle of democracy and the right to elect the German Bundestag in its essential content would occur if the determination of the type and amount of the levies imposed on the citizen were supranationalised to a considerable extent. The German Bundestag must decide, in an accountable manner vis-à-vis the people, on the total amount of the burdens placed on citizens. The same applies correspondingly to essential state expenditure. [...] Budget sovereignty is where political decisions are planned to combine economic burdens with benefits granted by the state. Therefore the parliamentary debate on the budget, including the extent of public debt, is regarded as a general debate on policy. Not every European or international obligation that has an effect on the budget endangers the viability of the Bundestag as the legislature responsible for approving the budget. The openness to legal and social order and to European integration which the Basic Law calls for, includes an adaptation to parameters laid down and commitments made, which the legislature responsible for approving the budget must include in its own planning as factors which it cannot itself directly influence. What is decisive, however, is that the overall responsibility, with sufficient political discretion regarding revenue and expenditure, can still rest with the German Bundestag."

Accordingly, **measures** under Article 136.1–2 TFEU **must remain coordina-** 11
tive. They could not consist of measures that exceed the boundaries of economic coordination, such as the establishment of common euro-area funding means (a euro-area budget, a European Monetary Fund, a euro-area Treasury), effective powers of veto over the adoption of national budgets by the MS or obligations subject to enforceability means—such as the action for infringement—that go beyond those laid down in the Treaties for economic policy.

2.3. Use and Practice

As referred to previously, **recourse** to Article 136.1–2 TFEU **has been made often** 12
during the economic and financial crisis.

First, Article 136 TFEU has been the basis for **two Regulations of the so-called** 13
six-pack, composed of six legal acts adopted in 2011 with a view to improving the general economic governance of the Union (→ Article 121 TFEU para 54 et seqq.). These are Regulation 1173/2011[4] on the effective enforcement of budgetary surveillance in the euro area and Regulation 1174/2011[5] on enforcement measures to correct excessive macroeconomic imbalances in the euro area. The first Regulation lays down instruments to enforce the economic and budgetary measures addressed to the MS under the multilateral surveillance and excessive deficit procedures; the second one lays down measures for the effective correction of macroeconomic imbalances, for which a procedure is provided in Regulation 1176/2011[6] on the prevention and correction of macroeconomic imbalances.

Economic governance for the euro area is reinforced by the two Regulations 14
through two means: on the one hand, they establish a system of **pecuniary sanc-**
tions consisting of interest-bearing deposits, non-interest-bearing deposits and fines against the MS that fail to correct or take action in respect of deviations or breaches of their economic and budgetary obligations.[7] Article 8 of Regulation 1173/2011 also lays down a specific mechanism to sanction the manipulation of statistics.[8]

---

[4] O.J. L 306/1 (2011).

[5] O.J. L 306/8 (2011).

[6] O.J. L 306/25(2011).

[7] Pecuniary sanctions can go up to 0.2% of the GDP of the MS concerned. See Articles 4 to 6 of Regulation 1173/2011 and Article 3 of Regulation 1174/2011.

[8] Whereas sanctions in respect of breaches of the multilateral surveillance, excessive deficit and macroeconomic imbalances procedures have never been imposed by the date of publication of this commentary, the Council has imposed twice sanctions for manipulation of statistics, in respect of Spain and Austria: see Council Implementing Decision (EU) 2015/1289 *imposing a fine on Spain for the manipulation of deficit data in the Autonomous Community of Valencia*, O.J. L 198/19 (2015), and corrigendum at O.J. L 229/10 (2015), and Council Implementing Decision (EU) 2018/818 *imposing a fine on Austria for the manipulation of debt data in Land Salzburg*, O.J. L 137/23 (2018).

15 On the other hand, the two Regulations **reinforce the decision-making power of the Council** by rendering it semi-automatic through the so-called **reverse qualified majority voting**. Under that procedure, decisions on the imposition of sanctions (regarded by the Regulations as of an implementing nature) are deemed adopted by the Council unless rejected by that institution by a qualified majority within a period of time determined by the said Regulations. The introduction of a reverse qualified majority has been criticized by some legal literature on the ground that the Treaties do not provide for a reverse qualified majority, infringe institutional autonomy and violate the institutional balance of the Treaties.[9]

16 Yet in spite of the above criticism, it is possible for the legislator to define voting arrangements for the exercise by the Council of its implementing powers (as the ones to impose sanctions under the six-pack), which differ from the ones laid down in the Treaties for the adoption of the basic act, as long as the said arrangements do not undermine the balance of powers between institutions or modify the share of powers among members of the institutions or affect their fundamental prerogatives. This results from the fact that the Treaties do not prescribe voting rules for the exercise by the Council of its implementing powers. Article 16.3 TEU, according to which the Council shall act by a qualified majority "except where the Treaties provide otherwise", cannot be interpreted as meaning that all implementing acts of the Council have to be adopted by a qualified majority. The **legislator remains free to establish the procedural modalities for the implementing act** to be adopted by the Council, provided that the limitations referred to above are respected. Only when the legislator had not provided for such specific arrangements would Article 16.3 TEU apply.

17 It is true that the Court of Justice has not directly addressed the specific issue of establishing "reverse voting rules" in secondary legislation. However, in a case where the legality of the implementing powers of the Council was put into question, because they were exercised through a procedure different from that laid down in the Treaties for the adoption of the act granting such powers, the ECJ ruled that it is "sufficient for the purposes of that provision [namely, the relevant legal basis laid down in the Treaties] that the essential elements of the matter to be dealt with have been adopted in accordance with the procedure laid down by that provision, and the **provisions implementing the basic regulations or directives may be adopted according to a different procedure**, as provided for by those regulations or directives".[10] The practice of the co-legislators has confirmed in many instances

---

[9] See Palmstorfer (2014), p. 193; Fischer-Lescano and Oberndorfer (2013), p. 12 et seq.

[10] See Case C-303/94, *Parliament v Council* (ECJ 18 June 1996) para 23 (emphasis added). See also the underlying reasoning of the ECJ and the AG in Case C-133/06, *Parliament v Council* (ECJ 6 May 2008) para 43 to 51, (Opinion of AG Poiares Maduro of 27 September 2007) para 17. See in this respect, Case C-76/01P, *Eurocoton v Council* (ECJ 30 September 2003) para 65, where the Court of Justice, in the framework of an anti-dumping procedure based on a reversed simple majority, has already established that the failure of the Council to act by the deadline established in secondary legislation for the Council to exercise its implementing powers, amounts to an act of the Council with legal effects reviewable by the Court of Justice and which should be duly motivated.

Article 136. [Measures Specific to the Member States Whose Currency Is the Euro]

this approach, notably in the case of macroeconomic conditionality in the context of the current Common Provisions Regulation for Structural Funds.[11]

Second, Article 136 TFEU has been relied on as a legal basis for the **adoption of the "two-pack"**, two Regulations adopted in 2013 to further reinforce the economic coordination of the euro area (→ Article 121 TFEU para 63 et seqq.). These are Regulation 472/2013[12] on the strengthening of economic and budgetary surveillance of MS experiencing or threatened with serious difficulties with respect to their financial stability and Regulation 473/2013[13] on the common provisions for monitoring and assessing draft budgetary plans and ensuring the correction of excessive deficit of the MS of the euro area.

Regulation 472/2013 introduces **rules on enhanced budgetary surveillance by the Commission** on MS experiencing or threatened with serious difficulties with respect to their financial stability, which are likely to have adverse spillover effects on other euro-area MS (Articles 2 and 3). It also requires MS under the assistance of the European Financial Stability Facility (EFSF) or the European Stability Mechanism (ESM) to submit to the Council for its approval a so-called macro-economic adjustment programme (Article 7). The Council decision approving the adjustment programme aims at anchoring in the law of the Union the **conditionality measures** to be subsequently agreed upon by the MS concerned with the EFSF or ESM through the so-called Memoranda of Understanding (→ Supplement to Title VIII: TESM para 62, 69 et seqq.). The ultimate purpose of macroeconomic adjustment programmes is to ensure the correspondence and consistency between the intergovernmental (EFSF and ESM) and Union (economic policy) spheres of action so that the former does not interfere, prejudge or pre-empt actions under the latter.[14]

In that case the Court of Justice stated that "[...] the failure to adopt the proposal for a regulation imposing a definitive anti-dumping duty submitted by the Commission, together with the expiry of the 15-month period, determined definitively the Council's position in the final phase of the anti-dumping proceedings".

[11] See Article 23.10 of Regulation (EU) No 1303/2013 *laying down common provisions on the [Structural and Investment Funds]*, O.J. L 347/320 (2013). See also Articles 9.4, 12.3 and 14.4 of Regulation 1225/2009 *on protection against dumped imports from countries not members of the European Community*, O.J. L 343/51 (2009) (no longer in force), and Article 1.4 point (b) of Regulation 539/2001 *listing the third countries whose nationals must be in possession of visas when crossing the external borders and those whose nationals are exempt from that requirement*, O.J.L 81/1 (2001) (no longer in force).

[12] O.J. L 140/1 (2013).

[13] O.J. L 140/11(2013).

[14] See in this sense Recital 3 of Regulation 472/2013. Before the approval of the two-pack, a practice had developed whereby conditionality attached to assistance has been agreed with the beneficiary MS concurrently with Council decisions adopted on the basis of Article 136 TFEU. Memoranda of understanding, adopted outside the Treaties, mirror and expand the measures on budgetary discipline contained in the different Council Decisions. See, inter alia, Council Decision 2010/320/EU *addressed to Greece with a view to reinforcing and deepening fiscal surveillance and giving notice to Greece to take measures for the deficit reduction judged necessary to remedy the situation of excessive deficit*, O.J. L 145/6 (2010).

20   Under **Regulation 473/2013, the euro-area MS are held to submit draft budgetary plans** to the European Commission for the forthcoming year by 15 October (Articles 6 and 7). The Commission assesses the plans to ensure that economic policy among the countries sharing the euro is coordinated and that they all respect the economic governance rules. The draft budgetary plans are assessed as either compliant, broadly compliant or at risk of non-compliance on the basis of an opinion to be issued by the Commission for each euro-area MS and after a discussion has been held at the Eurogroup. Surveillance over draft budget plans is a clear example of peer review as well as of the coordinative nature of the competence, as explained above: although the opinion of the Commission was negative on the national draft budget, the euro-area MS remain ultimately free to adopt it in the form and manner they see fit. Yet the **effectiveness of peer pressure** undertaken through the review of national draft budgetary plans cannot be underestimated as the 2019 Italian experience (draft budget plan for 2019) testifies: the different Eurogroup discussions of November and December 2018 as well as the Commission opinions on the Italian 2019 draft budget plan and the perspective on the opening of an excessive deficit procedure led that country to substantial fiscal corrections, as finally acknowledged by the Commission.[15]

21   Third, **Article 136 TFEU** is the **legal basis of the yearly euro-area recommendations** adopted by the Council. These recommendations provide guidance to the euro-area MS on issues relevant to the functioning of the euro area as a whole. They are adopted at the beginning of the **European Semester**, typically in the month of March, to precede and inform the package of country-specific recommendations that are adopted in July of each year (→ Supplement to Title VIII: Fiscal Union para 62).

2.4. Procedural Aspects

22   According to Article 136.1 TFEU, the Council shall adopt measures specific to the euro-area MS "in accordance with the relevant procedure from among those referred to in Articles 121 and 126, with the exception of the procedure set out in Article 126(14)".

23   **Articles 121 and 126 TFEU contain a plethora of procedures that allow the adoption of heterogeneous acts**: two of those procedures aim at adopting regulatory acts of general application (such as regulations), i.e., the procedures laid down under Article 121.6–14 TFEU. The rest of the procedures allow for the adoption of individual acts, such as recommendations or decisions.

24   Now, how should *"relevant procedure* from among those referred to in Articles 121 and 126", to which Article 136.1 TFEU refers, be interpreted? When having recourse to that provision, **the Union holds a degree of discretion**. Yet the

---

[15] See letter from the Commission to Italy, available at https://ec.europa.eu/info/sites/info/files/economy-finance/7351969_letter_to_prime_minister_conte_and_minister_tria.pdf.

discretion for choosing the relevant procedure should rely not on reasons of political opportunity but on objective factors such as the content and objectives of the envisaged act—does action aim at supplementing or reinforcing the multilateral surveillance procedure under Article 121 TFEU or the obligation to avoid excessive deficits under Article 126 TFEU—or the nature of the envisaged act—does it consist of a regulatory norm of general application, or is it an individual act addressed to a MS? Is it a decision with a legally binding value, or is it a recommendation?

In practice, the adoption of regulatory Article 136 TFEU based acts referred to in the above section (the six-pack and two-pack Regulations) has relied on the **legislative procedure foreseen under Article 121.6 TFEU**, which as clarified allows for the adoption of regulations. One cannot forget that Article 136.1 TFEU expressly excludes recourse to the other procedures for the adoption of generally applicable rules, namely the one set out in Article 126.14 TFEU. The rationale of this exclusion is very clear: Article 126.14 TFEU is the legal basis for either "replacing" or laying down detailed rules and definitions on the application of Protocol (No 12) on the excessive deficit procedure. There is a clear will of the authors of the Treaties to avoid a differentiated action by the euro area that may lead to modifying or altering the rules fixed in primary law. **25**

An interesting issue that stems from the procedure referred to in Article 136.1 TFEU is the fact that it refers to the "**Council**" as the **institution in charge** of adopting the measures set out in that provision. However, the reference to the Council **should not be read as excluding the participation of the European Parliament** (EP) as a co-legislator when the "relevant" procedure in the sense clarified above so requires. The reference to the Council as the author of the acts under Article 136 TFEU should be subsumed within its role as a co-legislator where the ordinary legislative procedure constitutes a relevant one. **26**

Pursuant to Article 136.2 TFEU, for those measures set out in paragraph 1, "only members of the Council representing Member States whose currency is the euro shall take part in the vote". The **voting rights of the non-euro-area MS** are therefore **suspended**. However, this does not mean that they are not admitted to the Council deliberations on Article-136-based measures. Non-euro-area members of the Council cannot be excluded from taking part in the discussions, whether at the Council or any of its preparatory bodies. As a limitation of one of the rights inherent in the States' membership of the Union, the **suspension of voting rights must be interpreted restrictively** and may not affect any other rights inherent to that membership, such as expressing their views or actively participating in the discussions. The fact that other mechanisms of differentiated integration, such as enhanced cooperation, lay down guarantees for the non-participating MS would underpin by analogy this interpretation. Actually, the first subparagraph of Article 330 TFEU (on enhanced cooperation) sets out that all members of the Council may participate in its deliberations but only members of the Council representing the MS participating in enhanced cooperation shall take part in the vote. **27**

De Gregorio Merino

3. Possibility to Establish a Stability Mechanism (Paragraph 3)

28   **Article 136.3** TFEU was **introduced** in the Treaties by the European Council **through the simplified revision procedure** laid down in Article 48.6 TEU, whereby the Treaty can be amended by a decision of the European Council without having recourse to a Convention and an Intergovernmental Conference.[16]

29   The amendment took place in the context of a **debate on the compatibility of a permanent mechanism of financial assistance** (the ESM) with Article 125 TFEU, the no bail-out clause. The German participation in the 2010 Greek rescue package and in the EFSF had been the object of actions by German individuals before the German FCC. Among other arguments, the plaintiffs in these cases claimed that by granting loans to Greece and participating in the EFSF, Germany had breached the principles of monetary and price stability, on which the monetary union is based. For Germany, the respect of the principle of monetary stability, of which Article 125 TFEU is an evident expression, was an essential condition for its participation in the monetary union. The **monetary union should not become a "transfer union"** (→ Supplement to Title VIII: TESM para 4 et seqq.).[17]

30   In the midst of the political discussions on a permanent mechanism of assistance—which eventually became the ESM—the need to introduce a provision in the Treaties that guaranteed the **compatibility of such a mechanism with Article 125 TFEU** was especially felt. However, any such modification could not alter the scope and extent of the prohibition under that article. From a German legal and political perspective, Article 125 TFEU is an essential provision for the monetary union to exist, whose contours are accordingly rather untouchable.

31   The European Council of 16–17 December 2010 agreed on the establishment of the ESM together with an amendment to the Treaties, pursuant to the simplified amendment procedure.[18] The Decision was formally adopted by the European Council at its meeting of 24–25 March 2011. The entry into force of the European Council Decision was dependent on the **approval by all the 27 MS**.

---

[16] European Council Decision 2011/199/EU *amending Article 136 of the Treaty on the Functioning of the European Union with regard to a stability mechanism for Member States whose currency is the euro*, O.J. L 91/1 (2011).

[17] See German Federal Constitutional Court, 2 BvR 2134/92 & 2159/92, Treaty of Maastricht (Judgment of 12 October 1993), which stated at para 90 on the ratification of the Treaty of Maastricht by Germany that "this conception of the currency union as a community based on stability is the basis and subject-matter of the German Act of Accession. If the monetary union should not be able to develop on a continuing basis the stability present at the beginning of the third stage within the meaning of the agreed mandate for stabilization, it would be abandoning the Treaty conception".

[18] See Annex I of the conclusions of the European Council of 16–17 Dec. 2010, document EUCO 30/1/10, REV1.

The legality of the European Council Decision incorporating Article 136.3 **32** TFEU was **contested through a preliminary reference raised by the Supreme Court of Ireland** in the milestone case *Pringle*.[19] Eventually, the Court considered that the European Council Decision had been validly adopted since the conditions provided for its activation (i.e. that the revision concerns all or part of the provisions of Part Three of the TFEU and that it does not increase the competencies conferred on the Union in the Treaties) were respected.

Furthermore, in *Pringle*, the Court stated that Article 136.3 TFEU is neither a **33** new competence of the Union nor a legal basis or an authorization for the MS to establish mechanisms of financial assistance among themselves. From this point of view, the **ESM Treaty is founded not on Article 136.3 TFEU** but on the sovereign will of each Contracting Party expressed through the relevant instruments of ratification provided by domestic law (→ Supplement to Title VIII: TESM para 10).[20]

Article 136.3 TFEU has a declaratory value. It recognizes the power of MS **34** whose currency is the euro to establish *inter se* a mechanism of assistance, namely the ESM. Article 136.3 TFEU provides legal certainty as to the fact that **mechanisms of assistance** (i.e. the ESM) **are compatible with Article 125 TFEU** (→ Article 125 TFEU para 25 et seqq.) as all provisions of the Treaties must be consistent with each other.[21]

Article 136.3 TFEU may be regarded as **a provision of a fundamental inter- 35 pretative value** according to which mechanisms such **as the ESM do not run counter to the no-bailout clause** (→ Article 125 TFEU para 47). But Article 136.3 TFEU does not modify, restrict or deprive of sense Article 125 TFEU. Its two sentences build upon and reconcile two different concepts of stability: on the one hand, the stability of the euro area and, on the other hand, monetary stability—founded on budgetary discipline. While up to now the Treaties had used the concept of "stability" as exclusively linked to price, Article 136.3 TFEU introduces a **new meaning of "stability"**—"of the euro area as a whole"—linked then to the very existence of the monetary union whose establishment is an EU objective under Article 3.4 TEU. In fact, the first sentence of Article 136.3 TFEU refers to an *ultima ratio* instrument of financial assistance, "indispensable" to safeguard a greater good, the stability of the euro area as a whole. Preserving the **stability of the euro area cannot, however, be to the detriment of the monetary stability** enshrined at the core of the single currency project since its inception. In accordance with the second sentence of Article 136.3 TFEU, the activation of financial assistance is subject to "strict conditionality" (→ Supplement to Title VIII: TESM

---

[19] C-370/12, *Pringle* (CJEU 27 November 2012).

[20] See C-370/12, *Pringle* (CJEU 27 November 2012) para 73. According to the Court of Justice, the amendment "does not confer any new competence on the Union. The amendment of Article 136 TFEU [...] creates no legal basis for the Union to be able to undertake any action which was not possible before the entry into force of the amendment of the FEU Treaty."

[21] See C-370/12, *Pringle* (CJEU 27 November 2012) para 72.

para 62 et seqq.) in pursuance of the objective of budgetary discipline, intrinsically linked to the monetary stability that the no-bailout clause is intended to guarantee.

List of Cases

ECJ/CJEU
ECJ 18.6.1996, C-303/94, *Parliament v Council*, ECLI:EU:C:1996:238 [cit. in para 23]

ECJ 30.09.2003, C-76/01 P, *Eurocoton v Council*, ECLI:EU:C:2003:511 [cit. in para 17]

ECJ 27.09.2007, C-133/06, Opinion of AG Poiares Maduro, *Parliament v Council*, ECLI:EU:C:2007:551 [cit. in para 17]

ECJ 06.05.2008, C-133/06, *Parliament v Council*, ECLI:EU:C:2008:257 [cit. in para 43 to 51]

CJEU 27.11.2012, C-370/12, *Pringle,* ECLI:EU:C:2012:756 [cit. in para 32 to 34]

German Federal Constitutional Court
German FFC 12.10.1993, 2 BvR 2134 and 2159/92, *Treaty of Maastricht,* BVerfGE 89, 155-213 [cit. in para 29]

German FCC 30.06.2009, 2 BvE 2/08 and others, *Treaty of Lisbon,* BVerfGE 123, 267-436 [cit. in para 9]

References[22]

Fischer-Lescano, A., & Oberndorfer, L. (2013). Fiskalvertrag und Unionsrecht. *Neue Juristische Wochenschrift, 66*(1–2), 9–14.

Palmstorfer, R. (2014). The reverse majority voting under the 'six pack': A bad turn for the union? *European Law Journal, 20*, 186–203.

---

[22] All cited Internet sources of this comment have been accessed on 6 April 2021.

Article 137 [Eurogroup]

Arrangements for meetings between ministers[16] of those Member States whose currency is the euro are laid down by the Protocol on the Euro Group.

Protocol (No 14)
on the Euro Group

THE HIGH CONTRACTING PARTIES,

DESIRING to promote conditions for stronger economic growth in the European Union and, to that end, to develop ever-closer coordination of economic policies within the euro area,

CONSCIOUS of the need to lay down special provisions for enhanced dialogue between the Member States whose currency is the euro, pending the euro becoming the currency of all Member States of the Union,

HAVE AGREED UPON the following provisions, which shall be annexed to the Treaty on European Union and to the Treaty on the Functioning of the European Union:

Article 1

The Ministers of the Member States whose currency is the euro shall meet informally. Such meetings shall take place, when necessary, to discuss questions related to the specific responsibilities they share with regard to the single currency. The Commission shall take part in the meetings.[17] The European Central Bank shall be invited to take part in such meetings,[17] which shall be prepared by the representatives of the Ministers[23] with responsibility for finance of the Member States whose currency is the euro and of the Commission.[16]

Article 2

The Ministers of the Member States whose currency is the euro shall elect a president for two and a half years, by a majority of those Member States.[18,19]

Contents

1. Introduction 1
2. A Historic Outlook on the Eurogroup 3
   2.1. Birth of the Eurogroup 4

	2.2. Reinforcement of the Eurogroup	7
	2.3. Recognition of the Eurogroup	11
3.	The Eurogroup Composition	15
	3.1. The Eurogroup Itself	16
	3.2. The Eurogroup President	19
	3.3. The Eurogroup Working Group	23
4.	The Eurogroup Functions	26
	4.1. Economic Coordination	29
	4.2. Policy Mix	33
	4.3. Financial Assistance	34
	4.4. Preparatory Role	37
	4.5. Accountability	38
5.	The Eurogroup Legal Accountability	40
	5.1. Transparency	41
	5.2. Legal Responsibility	42

List of Cases
References

1. Introduction

1   Article 137 TFEU and Protocol No. 14 are **paradoxes**. They mention the Eurogroup[1] because according to the first sentence of the first article of the Protocol, the Ministers of the euro-area MS "shall meet informally". If this meeting is non-formal, laying down its existence in the Treaty seems paradoxical.

This paradox epitomises all the problems raised by the Eurogroup. It has **no real legal existence**, but it has **a major political role** in the economic union. In itself, every procedure and every institution of the economic union are paradoxes. Since Maastricht, and more recently since the sovereign debt crisis, the economic union has rested on complex legal procedures. However, they have never really been followed or enforced. For *P. Leino* and *T. Saarenheimo*, "EU co-ordination is fundamentally not about enforcing the rules, but rather about using various soft forms of soft power (advertising?, peer pressure, threats and incentives) to compel countries to follow the desired economic policies".[2] Despite its legal outfit, the economic union lies on a "**political constitution**"[3] that needs political institutions. The Eurogroup is the central institution of this political constitution.

2   As formal procedures, which do not really involve the Eurogroup, are "masks"[4] behind which political influence is exercised, the institution cannot have real legal existence. Nevertheless, it should have some kind of visibility to ensure that its influence is effective. This explains the fact that the Eurogroup needs some kind of

---

[1] The wording of the Treaty "Euro Group" is not the most common, so we will use "Eurogroup".
[2] Leino and Saarenheimo (2017), p. 184.
[3] Adamski (2013), p. 49.
[4] On the idea of law as a "mask" see Burley and Mattli (1993).

"constitutional" legitimacy, but **without** having **any real legal existence**.[5] Legal existence is a threat for the Eurogroup because it could entail/involve some kind of legal responsibility.

But as the political role of the Eurogroup has grown over the years, this situation has become unsustainable. This kind of disjunction between political and legal responsibilities poses major accountability issues. However, the wording of Article 137 TFEU and Protocol No. 14 still protects the Eurogroup while making it one of **the central organs of economic cooperation**. To understand it, the history of the Eurogroup needs to be recalled (2) before studying its composition (3), its functions (4) and, finally, its accountability (5).

2. A Historic Outlook on the Eurogroup

Initially, the "Euro Group" did not exist. All MS of the Union were supposed to participate in the Economic and Monetary Union (EMU). This was, of course, a myth because the United Kingdom always clearly refused to participate. Yet the institutions of the EMU are based on this myth, and in the Maastricht Treaty, there were no specific provisions concerning specific organs dedicated to the eurozone members. So the **articles on the economic union always mention the European Council**. Very quickly, the need for such organs emerged, and the Eurogroup was, informally, created. It was an informal creation because there was no real political consensus between the MS, especially France and Germany, on the form and role of this specific organ (→ para 4–6). Nevertheless, since its creation, the role and structure of the Eurogroup has been strengthened (→ para 7–10) before it was recognised in the Treaties (→ para 11–14).

3

2.1. Birth of the Eurogroup

The Maastricht Treaty created an **"asymmetry"**[6] **between the monetary and the economic pillars**: the first one is fully integrated,[7] and the second one remained mostly national and relied on cooperation rather than integration. Some considered this asymmetry unstable and wished for more integration on economic matters. In 1990, **French** President *François Mitterrand* called for an **"economic government of Europe"**.[8] Since then, there has been a paradigmatic opposition between the French stance (the economic government) and the **German** one (**rule-based**

4

---

[5] This will explain that one of the most "reliable" official sources of information on the Eurogroup is its website, on the Council website. Available at https://www.consilium.europa.eu/en/council-eu/eurogroup/. The website details the provisions of the Treaty and Protocol No. 14.

[6] Louis (1992), p. 254 ("asymétrie").

[7] See Adalid (2015).

[8] "[S]i la conférence intergouvernementale chargée de cette union économique et monétaire parvient à cette conclusion qu'il faut une monnaie, qu'il faut une banque, elle sera fatalement

economic constitution). The strangeness of the Eurogroup is the consequence of this opposition, and it represents a compromise.

The French proposition, made during the 1990s, always faced the British and German vetoes.[9] For Germany, an economic government represents a threat to the independence of the central bank and an expression of the specific French-planned economy (*dirigisme économique*). Both are considered unacceptable. Fortunately for Germany, the French vision of what an "economic government" could be was never really clear. So when Germany proposed the **Stability and Growth Pact** (SGP) in 1995, the French accepted it because the pact included a "**stability council**". The French saw it as their economic government, while the Germans considered it as a "budgetary government".[10] The Dublin European Council of December 1996 accepted the pact but rejected the "stability council".

5   However, the French are persistent. So in 1997, they began negotiating with Germany, and with the other MS as well, the creation of an informal group. By the **end of 1997**, an **agreement was reached**.[11] The asymmetry between monetary integration and economic coordination facilitated this agreement. It created the need, both for a closer coordination of economic policies between the States and for a forum of discussion with the European Central Bank (ECB), to sketch some kind of policy mix.[12]

The **Eurogroup** was **officially created by the Luxembourg European Council** of 12–13 December 1997. The way the presidency's conclusions are written reflects the negotiations and ambiguities of their outcome. It is worth fully reproducing it because Protocol No. 14 is largely inspired by it:[13]

> By virtue of the Treaty, the ECOFIN Council is the centre for the coordination of the Member States' economic policies and is empowered to act in the relevant areas. In particular, the ECOFIN Council is the only body empowered to formulate and adopt the broad economic policy guidelines which constitute the main instrument of economic coordination.
>
> The defining position of the ECOFIN Council at the centre of the economic coordination and decision-making process affirms the unity and cohesion of the Community.
>
> The Ministers of the States participating in the Euro Area may meet informally among themselves to discuss issues connected with their shared specific responsibilities for the

---

contrainte d'une conclure qu'il fait un gouvernement économique de l'Europe" (speech at Unesco for the French-Germano convention on Europe, see. Layer 2004, p. 805).

[9] On the birth of the Eurogroup, see Layer (2004), pp. 805–814.

[10] Layer (2004), p. 811.

[11] Layer (2004), pp. 812–814; Heintz and Hirsch (1998), pp. 32–39.

[12] During an informal Council of finance ministers in Mondorf-les-Bains (13 September 1997), *Jean-Claude Juncker* noted: "[...] tout le monde a admis qu'à partir de la troisième phase de l'UEM, il faudra davantage coordonner les politiques économiques; tout le monde est aussi d'accord pour que la Banque centrale européenne accomplisse sa mission en pleine indépendance; je suis certain que nous pourrons trouver une position commune avant la fin de l'année [...]"; cited by Heintz and Hirsch (1998), p. 33.

[13] Luxembourg European Council, 12–13 December 1997, Presidency Conclusions, para 44.

single currency. The Commission, and the European Central Bank when appropriate, will be invited to take part in the meetings.

Whenever matters of common interest are concerned they will be discussed by Ministers of all Member States.

Decisions will in all cases be taken by the ECOFIN Council in accordance with the procedures laid down in the Treaty.

At this point, three comments need to be made. First, the emphasis on the role of the Economic and Financial Affairs (ECOFIN) Council is logical but superfluous. The founding Treaties are not amended. Therefore, legally, **decisions can only be adopted by the ECOFIN** Council. Second, this emphasis and the fourth paragraph are the result of hard negotiations, especially with British Prime Minister *Tony Blair*. He asked for the non-participating members to be permanently invited.[14] This was, of course, unacceptable. So the conclusions had to insist on the **role of the common institutions**. Third, the conclusions are **deliberately vague on the status and role of this new group**. It is "informal" and deals with "issues connected with their shared specific responsibilities for the single currency", which does not really mean anything. This blur meant that the Eurogroup could become anything it wanted or what the circumstances wanted it to become. So it took more and more place in the economic union.

2.2. Reinforcement of the Eurogroup

At the beginning, the **official name of the Eurogroup** was "Euro 10" because in the Luxembourg Council, only ten States moved to the third stage. It became "Euro 11" when Greece was accepted. Because its name could not change every time a new State entered the euro area, in 2001, it was changed to "Eurogroup". This is not the only change the Eurogroup went through during these years.

The first reunion of the Eurogroup[15] laid down the **foundations of its working method**: one meeting per month, before the ECOFIN Council and an almost systematic invitation of the ECB's president, and the topics discussed are budgetary plans, wage policy, employment and competitiveness.[16] It also maintained the **ambiguity on its role**: exchange of information for the German and "important place of power" for the French.[17]

As usual, circumstances pushed aside these political differences. On 1 January 1999, EMU became a reality, and the need for closer economic cooperation became

---

[14] Heintz and Hirsch (1998), p. 37.

[15] In the Senning Castle, Luxembourg, 4 June 1998.

[16] Layer (2004), p. 815.

[17] For the German Finance Minister "the euro-11 will have nothing to decide, no statute, no formal existence. It wil be a place to exchange information", for the French Minister, "it is a 'place of power'"; cf. Quatremer and Klau (1999), p. 107, cited by Layer (2004), p. 815 (my translation).

obvious.[18] Therefore, the French and Belgian Presidents of the Eurogroup,[19] in 2000 and 2001,[20] proposed **reforms for its functioning**: a more stable presidency and the enlargement of the Eurogroup tasks. These ongoing efforts were supported by the successes achieved by the Eurogroup. Being a smaller group than the ECOFIN Council, where discussions are "boring and formal", the **Eurogroup enables interesting debates** to take place.[21] So the group decided to change its name, meet the day before the ECOFIN Council (and not hours before), discuss new subjects,[22] have an agenda for each meeting and hold a press conference led by its president and the European Commissioner for economic and financial affairs.[23]

9   The importance of the Eurogroup and its reforms was mentioned by the **European Council in Nice**. It welcomed "the improvements made to the workings of the Eurogroup and its visibility" and "the intention to extend the range of mainly structural matters dealt with in this forum, with due regard for the conclusions of the Luxembourg European Council meeting. These improvements intended to enhance the coordination of economic policies will help to boost the growth potential of the euro area."[24] J.-V. Louis observes that "the reference to the Luxembourg conclusions clearly indicates that the Group has to remain informal".[25]

However, one proposition made in early 2000 was accepted later, i.e., the **creation of a stable presidency for the Eurogroup**. In 2000, France proposed the creation of a "Mr. Euro"[26] and a troika presidency.[27] The decision to create a stable presidency was made only at the informal ECOFIN meeting in Scheveningen on 11 September 2004.[28] The rotating presidency posed two issues. First, it was too unstable. Second, the Eurogroup president was the Minister of Finance of the State presiding the EU. It became complicated when non-eurozone members assumed the presidency.

---

[18] This is outlined by the Report of the ECOFIN Council to the European Council on the coordination of economic policies ("Helsinki Report"), 29 November 1999, Doc. 13123/99, Rev. 1. The Report underlines the main features of economic coordination and it "observes that the recourse to a lot of procedures and possible overlapping have not allowed the public and the market to have a clear idea of the process of co-ordination (point 18)"; see Louis (2001–2002), p. 25.

[19] Which initially was rotating, mirroring the presidency of the Council.

[20] Layer (2004), pp. 817–821.

[21] Louis (2001–2002), p. 30.

[22] Notably, exchange rate policy, economic policy, structural policies, pensions funding, health care costs; cf. Fromont (2017), p. 201.

[23] Fromont (2017), p. 201.

[24] Nice European Council, 7–10 December 2000, Presidency Conclusions, para 31.

[25] Louis (2001–2002), p. 31.

[26] Like the High Representative for the Foreign Policy after the Amsterdam Treaty.

[27] Layer (2004), p. 818.

[28] Fromont (2017), pp. 200–201.

Article 137. [Eurogroup] 881

The decision to mention the Eurogroup in the Treaties was taken during the 10
negotiations on the **Constitutional Treaty**. Article III-195 TCE and Protocol No.
12 became the basis for what the Treaty of Lisbon accepted without further change
as Article 137 TFEU and Protocol No. 14.

2.3. Recognition of the Eurogroup

The role and place of the Eurogroup were discussed during the **Convention**. But, as 11
before, there was **no real consensus**. So the legal status of the Eurogroup evolved to
today's paradox, a paradox that got bigger with the crisis and all the economic
coordination reforms.

One idea was never seriously considered: transforming the Eurogroup into an
enhanced cooperation.[29] The important political place taken by the Eurogroup
rendered the *status quo* difficult. The Eurogroup needed to be recognised in some
way. This need is summarised by the preamble of Protocol No. 14, which reiterates
"the need to lay down special provisions for an enhanced dialogue between the
Member States whose currency is the euro". This dialogue is required following the
need "to promote conditions for stronger economic growth in the European Union
and, to that end, to develop ever-closer coordination of economic policies within
the euro area".

During the Convention, the **Commission** made a **suggestion**: the **creation** of a 12
"**Euro ECOFIN Council**" and the **preservation** of the **Eurogroup**.[30] The first
one should have decision-making powers over matters of common interest
for the euro-area MS. This would prevent the non-participating MS to vote on
such matters. The Commission kept the Eurogroup because of its advantages,
summarised by *J.-V. Louis*: "experience reveals that the Eurogroup is *de facto* a
place where in-depth discussions on any kind of subject related to EMU can take
place, precisely for the lack of formalism, the confidentiality of the debates, the
reduced numbers of participants (...). A kind of social integration is possible there
between the thirty or so persons attending the meeting."[31] The Constitutional
Treaty and later the Lisbon Treaty accepted this proposition. Article 137 TFEU
mentions the Eurogroup, and Article 136.2 TFEU allows for a voting procedure, in
the Council, of only "Member States whose currency is the euro" on specific matters,
i.e. the matter listed in Article 136.1 TFEU (→ Article 136 TFEU para 5 et seqq.).

During the **crisis**, two things happened: the **political role** of the Eurogroup **grew** 13
bigger, and **legal texts mentioned it** more and more frequently.

Because the Eurogroup is informal and opaque, it became the perfect place to
take the difficult decisions during the eurozone crisis. The first assistance granted to

---

[29] See Vigneron (2003); Martucci (2016), pp. 472–474. See now also Böttner (2020), p. 299 et seqq.
[30] See. Martucci (2016), pp. 474–476; Louis (2004), pp. 585–585.
[31] Louis (2004), p. 586.

Greece in 2010 is a perfect example.[32] On 25 March 2010, the Heads of States and Government of the eurozone members noted that "[a]s part of a package involving substantial International Monetary Fund financing and a majority of European financing, Euro area member states are ready to contribute to coordinated bilateral loans".[33] It is the Eurogroup that determined "the terms of the financial support that will be given to Greece".[34] The "stability support to Greece" was activated by the "euro area Ministers" on 2 May 2010.[35]

Since then, the Eurogroup has become central to the governance of the euro area (→ para 26 et seqq.). Consequently, **international and secondary law gave it some place**. For example, the Memorandum of Understanding (MoU) signed, as part of the European Financial Stability Facility (EFSF), needed to be approved by the Eurogroup Working Group.[36] European law did the same, and the new macroeconomic imbalance procedure mentions that reports concerning the euro-area MS are discussed by the Eurogroup.[37]

14 The **Eurogroup remained informal**. Nevertheless, "it is central to all major initiatives relating to the euro area, broadly conceived, which cover structural adjustment, macroeconomic planning, negotiations with states in receipt of aid from the ESM, and aspects of banking union".[38]

3. The Eurogroup Composition

15 Over the years, the **Eurogroup evolved into a complex structure**: it has its own president (→ para 19–22) and its own preparatory organ (→ para 23–25). But we should first study its composition (→ para 16–18). Details on the work and composition of the Eurogroup are laid down in its working methods.[39]

3.1. The Eurogroup Itself

16 Texts are deliberately vague on the Eurogroup's composition. They only talk about "Ministers", but they do not specify which ministers. Of course, it concerns only

---

[32] It is mentioned by Fromont (2017), pp. 204–205.

[33] Statement by the Head of States and Government of the Euro area, Brussels, 25 March 2010.

[34] Statement in the support to Greece by Euro Area Members States, Brussels, 11 April 2010.

[35] Statement by the Eurogroup, Brussels, 2 May 2010.

[36] Article 2.1 point (a) of the EFSF Framework Agreement, 10 October 2011.

[37] Article 3.5 of Regulation (EU) No. 1176/2011 *on the prevention and correction of macroeconomic imbalances*, O.J. L 306/25 (2011).

[38] Craig (2017), p. 235.

[39] Working Methods of the Eurogroup of 3 October 2008, ECFIN/CEFCPE(2008)REP/50842 rev 1.

ministers "of those Member States whose currency is the euro" (Article 1 of Protocol No. 14). So, in principle, it could be any minister.

Due to the specific tasks of the Eurogroup, only one kind of minister is concerned in practice, namely the **finance ministers**.[40] This is suggested by Article 1 of Protocol No. 14, according to which Eurogroup meetings "shall be prepared by the representatives of the Ministers with responsibility for finance". This provision deals only with the preparation of Eurogroup meetings and not the meetings *per se*. So other ministers of the eurozone members (agriculture, healthcare etc.) could gather informally as the Eurogroup, but this never happens in practice.

Ministers are not the only members. According to Article 1 of Protocol No. 14, "[t]he **Commission** shall take part in the meetings. The **European Central Bank** shall be invited to take part in such meetings." The difference of wording is linked to the ECB independence (cf. Article 130 TFEU). To preserve it, its members are only "invited", so that they are free to refuse. In practice, ECB members always take part in Eurogroup meetings. The only difference between the ECB and the Commission is that the latter is officially invited to the preparation of the Eurogroup meetings.

17

The Commission is represented by its president in addition to one other Commission member (usually the Commissioner responsible for economic and monetary affairs and the euro) and Commission official. The ECB is represented by its president as well as another member of the Executive Board or an ECB official.[41]

In fact, **attendance at the Eurogroup meetings**[42] exceeds its actual membership. Apart from the national ministers, the Commission and the ECB, a whole range of persons is present or may at least attend. This includes the members of the Eurogroup Working Group ($\rightarrow$ para 23) and their president, the secretary and a staff member of the Economic and Financial Committee, the Secretary-General of the Council, the Council Secretariat's Director General for ECOFIN matters and one member of the Council Secretariat staff. Moreover, whenever input from the Economic Policy Committee ($\rightarrow$ Article 134 TFEU para 3, 21) is needed, its president or a vice-president may attend the Eurogroup meeting.

18

3.2. The Eurogroup President

Created informally in 2004, the role of president of the Eurogroup was confirmed by the Constitutional Treaty[43] and Lisbon Treaty. Article 2 of Protocol No. 14 provides that the Eurogroup members shall elect a president for **two and a half years** by a vote of a majority of those MS. This term of office also detaches the

19

---

[40] "[...] the euro area ministers with responsibility for finance"; see Eurogroup website, available at https://www.consilium.europa.eu/en/council-eu/eurogroup/how-the-eurogroup-works/.

[41] Eurogroup Working Methods, point 2(ii).

[42] See Eurogroup Working Methods, point 2(ii).

[43] It was a French-German proposition, see Martucci (2016), p. 479.

president's office from the Council presidency.[44] According to the Eurogroup website, the election takes place by a simple majority. Formally, there is no vice-president. If the president is prevented from fulfilling his or her duties, he or she is replaced by the finance minister of the country that holds the presidency of the Council. In case the Council presidency rests with a non-euro State, the duties are fulfilled by the finance minister of the next euro-area country to hold the Council presidency.[45]

Jean-Claude Juncker was the first president, who served from 2005 to 2013. He was the most influential president, and he made this function a political one.[46] His successor was *Jeroen Dijsselbloem*, who served until 2018, when *Mário Centeno* took his place. Since 13 July 2020, *Paschal Donohoe*, Minister for Finance and Public Expenditure and Reform of Ireland, has been the president of the Eurogroup.

20 The **powers** assigned to the president are **classic**. He chairs and sets the agendas for the meetings, draws up the Eurogroup's long-term work programme, presents the conclusions of the Eurogroup discussions to the public and to the ministers of non-euro-area EU countries within the ECOFIN Council and represents the Eurogroup in international fora (e.g. G7)[47] Moreover, he regularly informs the European Parliament of the priorities of the Eurogroup work programme and reports on the progress achieved in the coordination of economic policies in the euro area.[48]

21 An important institutional upgrade exists with regard to the **European Stability Mechanism** (ESM). As Article 5.2 of the ESM Treaty (TESM) provides, the ESM's Boards of Governors, when deciding on its chair, may elect a person from among its members or appoint the president of the Eurogroup as its chair. In fact, the MS have decided to make use of the latter option (→ Supplement to Title VIII: TESM para 34). Thus, due to its personal identity, the ESM is *de facto* governed by the Eurogroup.[49]

22 In late 2018, the Commission presented a roadmap on the future of EMU.[50] As part of the comprehensive package, the Commission suggested the establishment of a **European Minister of Economy and Finance** (→ Supplement to Title VIII: TSCG para 109–110), which is supposed to lead to a consolidation of EMU's architecture.[51] The European Finance Minister shall be the Commissioner for Economic and Financial Affairs and a permanent vice-president of the Commission

---

[44] Eurogroup Working Methods, point 2(i).

[45] Eurogroup Working Methods, point 2(i).

[46] See Martucci (2016), pp. 466 & 480. He had frequent contacts with the press (mostly, but not only, via the press conference hold after each meeting), and he used his charisma to be an integral part of the EU public space.

[47] Eurogroup Working Methods, point 2(i).

[48] Eurogroup Working Methods, point 2(viii).

[49] Cf. also Manger-Nestler and Böttner (2019), p. 82.

[50] Commission Communication, *Further Steps towards completing Europe's Economic and Monetary Union: A Roadmap*, COM(2017) 821 final.

[51] COM(2017) 823 final. See in detail Böttner (2018).

(similar to the high representative for the Common Foreign and Security Policy (CFSP)). Moreover, he or she shall be the president of the Eurogroup. Article 2 of Protocol No. 14 does not oppose the possibility for the Eurogroup to elect someone who is not a national finance minister as its president, but this depends on the will of the euro-area MS.[52] Moreover, this accumulation of offices may lead to problems concerning the Commissioner's independence. As Article 17.3 (3) TEU and Article 245.1 TFEU provide, MS shall respect the Commission's independence and shall not seek to influence them in the performance of their tasks. It is hardly imaginable how the president of an MS body can act in full independence from these States.[53] In order to establish a legally binding link between the competent Commissioner and the office of the Eurogroup's president and to overcome the independence predicament, the Protocol needs to be amended, which may be possible in the simplified revision procedure under Article 48.6 TEU.[54]

3.3. The Eurogroup Working Group

The Eurogroup Working Group (EWG) is a **specific configuration of the Economic and Financial Committee** (EFC) foreseen by Article 134 TFEU (→ Article 134 TFEU para 25). In accordance with the EFC Statutes,[55] the EWG consists of representatives of the ministers with responsibility for the finance of the euro-area MS (i.e. the euro-area EFC members) and of the Commission. The Eurogroup Working Methods mention also the ECB. The EWG shall elect a president for a (renewable) two-year term. Since 1 April 2020, the EWG president has been *Tuomas Saarenheimo*, who succeeded *Hans Vijlbrief* (2018–2020) and *Thomas Wieser* (2011–2018).

As Article 1 of Protocol No. 14 provides, the Eurogroup meetings "shall be prepared by the representatives of the Ministers". Main assistance to the Eurogroup in **preparing and guiding the meetings** shall be provided by the EWG. On the basis of Commission analyses and contributions from the ECB and MS, the EWG shall prepare short discussion papers for ministers focussing on key policy issues, identify concrete policy implications and provide suggestions for the follow-up of discussions. The EWG shall also prepare short draft "terms of reference" or "common understandings", which are supposed to help in crystallising Eurogroup views.

The EWG is now an **integral part of the economic union**. It is mentioned not only by Article 1 of Protocol No. 14 but also by the EFSF Framework Agreement, which gave it numerous tasks. EFSF's replacement, the European Stability

23

24

25

---

[52] Böttner (2018), p. 78.
[53] See Böttner (2018), pp. 76–77.
[54] Böttner (2018), p. 78.
[55] Council Decision 1999/8/EC *adopting the Statutes of the Economic and Financial Committee*, O.J. L 5/71 (1999), as amended by Council Decision 2012/245/EU, O.J. L 121/22 (2012).

Mechanism,[56] does not mention the EWG explicitly. However, Article 6.1 TESM provides that the ESM governors, i.e. the euro-area finance ministers, shall each appoint one director (and alternate) to the ESM Board of Directors "from among people of high competence in economic and financial matters". In practice, "[t]he EWG members are also part of the European Stability Mechanism's board of directors".[57]

4. The Eurogroup Functions

26   Article 137 TFEU and Protocol No. 14 do not mention any specific task assigned to the Eurogroup. As it is informal, it has **no real legal powers**. According to the Working Methods of the Eurogroup and in line with the Luxembourg Resolution, Eurogroup meetings will discuss matters of key importance to fiscal, monetary and structural policies in the euro area and focus on themes of particular importance for the single currency. The Eurogroup has a role in defining the economic policy strategy for the euro area as a whole: to identify common challenges and formulate and agree on common approaches. On this basis and the Eurogroup's involvement in other areas of EMU (e.g., → Supplement to Title VIII: TSCG para 64), **discussions** shall be held primarily on the economic situation and outlook in the euro area, the budgetary policies of the euro-area MS, the macroeconomic situation in the euro area, structural reforms that have potential to increase growth, matters related to maintaining financial stability in the euro area, preparations for international meetings and euro area enlargement.

27   This could be misleading and support the view that the Eurogroup is simply a discussion forum. On the contrary, the Eurogroup has a **great "political power"**.[58] As of 2006, *J. Pisani-Ferry* noted that it "has gradually strengthened and has transformed from a mere talking shop into what increasingly looks like a policy-making institution".[59] Since then, with the crisis, its role extended. Between 2010 and 2017, the numbers of its reunion have boomed.[60] In 2016, the European Ombudsman expressed some concerns about the Eurogroup's transparency (→ para 42), largely because of "the economic, financial and societal impact of the decisions taken by" the Eurogroup.[61] In a nutshell, according to the best specialists, it is "an informal 'economic government' of the euro area".[62]

---

[56] Treaty establishing the European Stability Mechanism signed on 2 February 2012.

[57] https://www.consilium.europa.eu/en/council-eu/eurogroup/eurogroup-working-group/.

[58] Expression used by Craig (2017).

[59] Pisani-Ferry (2006), p. 840.

[60] 206 reunions of the Eurogroup and 264 of the EWG; cf. Sacriste and Vauchez (2019).

[61] European Ombudsman, *Recent initiative to improve Eurogroup transparency*, Letter to Mr. Jeroen Dijsselbloem, 14 March 2016.

[62] Louis and Lastra (2013), p. 93.

So there is a **gap between** the **lack of legal powers** of the Eurogroup and its **28** **huge political power**. Its powers mostly come from its absence of clear legal status, allowing it to be a "government of influence". But the recent reforms somehow recognise its powers, giving clues to its real influence. It has five main tasks, which, in chronological order, are economic coordination (→ para 29–31), policy mix (→ para 32), financial assistance (→ para 33–35), preparatory role (→ para 36) and democratic accountability (→ para 37–39). For the international role of the Eurogroup, see Article 138 TFEU.

4.1. Economic Coordination

Economic coordination is the core of the Eurogroup function. It was created for that **29** purpose. Yet its role was never clear. As it has no legal power, binding decisions are only taken by the ECOFIN Council. However, since its creation, the Eurogroup has been the **preparatory body for the ECOFIN Council** where the **eurozone members agree on their position**. So formal decisions are taken by the Council, but politically they are made in the Eurogroup. A few examples from before the crisis will show this. The reforms only confirmed this diagnosis.

During the 2003 crisis of the Stability and Growth Pact,[63] when the Council **30** refused to continue procedures against France and Germany, the Eurogroup played a central role. Indeed, the blocking minority was created inside the Eurogroup by the Italian presidency.[64] The same happened in 2007 when the Commission dropped its idea to use the "early warning" mechanism[65] against France. This State managed to get a favourable position inside the Eurogroup.[66] Finally, the 2005 reform of the SGP[67] was negotiated inside the Eurogroup and formally adopted by the ECOFIN Council.[68]

Since the eurozone crisis and the reforms of the economic governance, the **31** **formal role** of the Eurogroup has expanded, both inside and outside EU law.

Inside EU law, its role in the **macroeconomic imbalance procedure** has already been mentioned (→ para 13; → Supplement to Title VIII: TSCG para 63 et seqq.).[69] The more revealing text about the real power of the Eurogroup is **Regulation 473/2013**

---

[63] On this crisis see Louis and Lastra (2013), pp. 113–116.

[64] Martucci (2016), p. 501.

[65] Article 6 of Council Regulation (EC) No. 1466/97 of 7 July 1997 *on the strengthening of the surveillance of budgetary positions and the surveillance and coordination of economic policies*, O. J. L 209/1 (1997).

[66] Martucci (2016), p. 799.

[67] On this reform see Louis and Lastra (2013), pp. 116–120.

[68] Fromont (2017), p. 203.

[69] Fromont (2017), p. 208.

on common provisions for monitoring and assessing draft budgetary plans and ensuring the correction of excessive deficit of the MS in the euro area.[70] Following this Regulation, MS submit their "draft budgetary plans" to the Commission and the Eurogroup (Article 5.1). The Commission's opinion is presented to the Eurogroup, which discusses it (Article 7). Moreover, States should report "their national debt issues and plans" to the Commission and the Eurogroup (Article 8).

32   Outside EU law, according to **Article 7 TSCG** (→ Supplement to Title VIII: TSCG para 45 et seqq.), "the Contracting Parties whose currency is the euro commit to supporting the proposals or recommendations submitted by the European Commission where it considers that a Member State of the European Union whose currency is the euro is in breach of the deficit criterion in the framework of an excessive deficit procedure. This obligation shall not apply where it is established among the Contracting Parties whose currency is the euro that a qualified majority of them [...] is opposed to the decision proposed or recommended." This **reverse qualified majority** rule reinforces the Eurogroup. The discussion and negotiations of the eurozone MS can only happen inside the Eurogroup, and it makes the position found inside the Eurogroup mandatory for the eurozone MS inside the ECOFIN Council.

4.2. Policy Mix

33   Policy mix means the **coordination of monetary and economic policies**. The Treaties do not allow for any official policy mix in order to preserve the independence of the ECB. Notwithstanding this, many see the Eurogroup as an informal policy-mix forum because the president of the ECB is invited to its meetings, and he or she always participates.[71] However, there is no proof that real coordination takes place between the ECB and the eurozone MS inside the Eurogroup. The ECB does not even mention policy mix when it describes the Eurogroup.[72]

4.3. Financial Assistance

34   Financial assistance granted by the Union or other MS to one another was not planned by the Maastricht Treaty, which relied on market discipline to avoid this situation. But it happened, and the Union and the MS had to improvise, partly using the Eurogroup for this as the most flexible forum they had. Since then, **the role of the Eurogroup has formally declined but remained politically fundamental**.

---

[70] Regulation (EU) No 473/2013 *on common provisions for monitoring and assessing draft budgetary plans and ensuring the correction of excessive deficit of the Member States in the euro area*, O.J. L 140/11 (2013).

[71] Fromont (2017), pp. 202–203.

[72] ECB, *The ECB's relations with European Union institutions and bodies – Trends and Prospects*, Monthly Bulletin January 2010, pp. 78–79.

Article 137. [Eurogroup]

In 2010, the first assistance to Greece was granted via bilateral loans.[73] So the Union[74] and the MS[75] each created their own temporary mechanism before creating a stable one.[76] As seen before, the Eurogroup or the EWG played a central role in these mechanisms.[77] Assistance is granted via MoU, posing conditions—mostly national reforms—for the release of financial help. MoUs were **mostly negotiated inside the Eurogroup**.[78] During one of these negotiations about Greece, the European Commissioner for Economic and Financial Affairs declared: "we are deciding behind closed doors the fate of 11 million people".[79]

Now, two texts frame financial assistance, the **ESM Treaty** and Regulation 472/3013.[80] The first one does not mention the Eurogroup, but its main governing body is the Board of Governors. Each State appoints a governor and "[t]he Governor shall be a member of the government of that ESM Member who has responsibility for finance" (Article 5.1 TESM). Hence, the **Board of Governors and the Eurogroup are made up of the same persons**. Therefore, they can be seen as "one and the same body".[81] Moreover, the chair of the Board of Governors is the president of the Eurogroup (→ para 21). In a letter to the European Ombudsman, the president of the Eurogroup recognised that "the Members of the Eurogroup may meet in their capacity of Governors under the European Stability Mechanism Treaty".[82]

Regulation 472/2013 lays down some common features for the granting of financial help to the eurozone MS. In these procedures, the **EWG plays a central role**. When a MS intends to request financial assistance, it informs the president of the EWG (Article 5.1).[83] The Commission assesses the State's situation, and then "the EWG shall hold a discussion about the intended request" (Article 5.2). *In fine*,

35

36

---

[73] See Louis (2010).

[74] Council Regulation (EU) No. 407/2010 of 11 May 2010 *establishing a European financial stabilization mechanism*, O.J. L 118/1 (2010).

[75] See EFSF Framework Agreement.

[76] Treaty Establishing the European Stability Mechanism, signed on 2 February 2012.

[77] See Fromont (2017), pp. 204–206.

[78] See Sacriste and Vauchez (2019), pp. 15–16. Craig (2017), p. 237, calls the Eurogroup a "broker of agreements". The European Parliament reached the same conclusion: "the ultimate political responsibility for the design and approval of the macroeconomic adjustment programmes lies with EU finance ministers and their governments"; see European Parliament, *Report on the enquiry on the role and operations of the Troika (ECB, Commission and IMF) with regard to the euro area programme countries* (2013/2277(INI)", 28 February 2014, para 50.

[79] Sacriste and Vauchez (2019), p. 20.

[80] Regulation (EU) No. 472/2013 *on the strengthening of economic and budgetary surveillance of Member States in the euro area experiencing or threatened with serious difficulties with respect to their financial stability*, O.J. L 140/1 (2013).

[81] Fromont (2017), p. 207: "Un seul et même organe".

[82] Letter from the Eurogroup President to the European Ombudsman, *Recent initiatives to improve Eurogroup transparency*, The Hague, 16 May 2016.

[83] "A Member State intending to request financial (...), shall immediately inform the President of the Eurogroup Working Group, the member of the Commission responsible for Economic and

assistance is granted mostly by the ESM through its Board of Governors (i.e. the Eurogroup).

4.4. Preparatory Role

37 The Eurogroup always had a **preparatory role in the ECOFIN Council** meetings. But since the TSCG, the Eurogroup has been **formally responsible for the preparation of the Euro Summits** (Article 12 TSCG). These are the formation of the Eurogroup at the Head of States or Government level and the president of the Commission. The president of the ECB is invited to these summits. They were informally created in 2010.[84]

Like the Eurogroup, these summits "discuss questions relating to the specific responsibilities which the Contracting Parties whose currency is the euro share with regard to the single currency, other issues concerning the governance of the euro area and the rules that apply to it, and strategic orientations for the conduct of economic policies to increase convergence in the euro area" (Article 12.2 TSCG). These summits have no legal powers. They only constitute a discussion forum but at a higher political level than the Eurogroup.

4.5. Accountability

38 The role of the Eurogroup in accountability is dual: some organs are accountable to it, and it is accountable to the European Parliament. The Eurogroup guarantees part of the **accountability of the ECB as part of the banking union**.[85] Strangely, Article 20.1 of the SSM Regulation[86] states that "[t]he ECB shall be accountable to the European Parliament and to the Council" but mentions the Eurogroup in the next paragraphs. It requires the ECB to "submit on an annual basis to the European Parliament, to the Council, to the Commission and to the Euro Group a report on the execution of the tasks conferred on it by this Regulation" (Article 20.2). It authorises the Eurogroup to hear the chair of the Single Supervisory Board (Article 20.4) and to ask oral or written questions to the ECB (Article 20.6).

39 Since the adoption of the six pack, the **Eurogroup is accountable to the European Parliament**. It created the "economic dialogue", where the competent committee of the Parliament can invite "the President of the Council, the

---

Monetary Affairs and the President of the ECB of its intention". It should be noted that the President of the EWG is the first of the list, and the only one with no real legal status.

[84] Once before, in 2007, French President Nicolas Sarkozy came to the Eurogroup to defend its economic programme; cf Martucci (2016), p. 501.

[85] Craig (2017), pp. 237–238.

[86] Council Regulation (EU) No. 1024/2013 of 15 October 2013 *conferring specific tasks on the European Central Bank concerning policies relating to the prudential supervision of credit institutions*, O.J. L 287/63 (2013).

Article 137. [Eurogroup]

Commission and, where appropriate, the President of the European Council or the President of the Eurogroup to appear before the committee to discuss" matters relating to the economic union.[87] The inclusion of the Eurogroup inside the economic dialogue confirms its central political role, but it is not enough to ensure real democratic accountability of its activities,[88] especially when its legal accountability is very limited.

5. The Eurogroup Legal Accountability

The main quality of the Eurogroup is its informality. It does not take any formal decision. But, politically, the Eurogroup always took decisions, which were formally voted by the ECOFIN Council. Since the crisis, Eurogroup has taken decisions outside the Treaty, mostly concerning financial assistance. This raised the question of legal responsibility: **can the Eurogroup be held accountable for such decisions**? The Court of Justice delivered a very clear and simple opinion: the Eurogroup is not formal, it does not take decisions, so no annulment can be brought against its "decisions", and the Union is not responsible for the Eurogroup actions (→ para 42–45). This also brings attention to its activities, therefore questioning its transparency (→ para 41).

40

5.1. Transparency

The transparency of the Eurogroup activities was targeted by the **European Ombudsman**. The Eurogroup being informal, the democratic (Article 10 TEU) and transparency principles (Article 15 TFEU and Article 42 EUCFR) do not apply to it. This last principle applies only to "the Union's institutions, bodies, offices and agencies". The Eurogroup is none of the latter.

41

This was confirmed in the exchange of letters between the Ombudsman and the president of the Eurogroup. For the Ombudsman, the documents concerning the Eurogroup are held by the General Secretariat of the Council, so transparency legislation[89] applies to it.[90] In its first reply, the president of the Eurogroup stated that "the Eurogroup is an informal gathering of Finance Ministers", so the articles

---

[87] Article 14.1 of Regulation (EU) No. 1176/2011 *on the prevention and correction of macroeconomic imbalances*, O.J. L 306/25 (2011). Each regulation of the six-pack includes broadly the same article.

[88] On the democratic accountability of the Eurogroup, see Fromont (2017), pp. 217–219; Craig (2017), pp. 238–241.

[89] Mostly Regulation (EC) No. 1049/2001 *regarding public access to European Parliament, Council and Commission Documents*, O.J. L 145/43 (2001).

[90] European Ombudsman, *Recent initiative to improve Eurogroup transparency*, Letter to Mr. Jeroen Dijsselbloem, 14 March 2016.

of the Treaty and the Charter do not apply to it.[91] In its second reply, it argues that documents are "held only by the national delegations participating in the Eurogroup" and that "documents held by national delegations will have to be handled in accordance with the national legislation on transparency".[92]

However, its political role attracted public attention, and the transparency of its work was questioned. The **Eurogroup took some initiatives to improve its transparency**. Following an initiative of its president,[93] the Eurogroup decided, on 16 February 2016, "to publish Eurogroup agendas in a more detailed, annotated format, and to publish summing-up letters recapitulating the main conclusions from Eurogroup meetings".[94] One month later, it decided to publish "documents, final documents after Eurogroup meetings, unless there are well-founded objections coming from the authors".[95]

5.2. Legal Responsibility

42 When confronted with the question of the legal responsibility of the Eurogroup, the Court of Justice was very prudent. As in other cases concerning the economic union and financial assistance, the reasoning of the Court was strictly legal and **refused to take into account the political reality behind the facts of the case**. Its solutions can be summarised easily: the Eurogroup is informal, so no action can be brought against it.

The case of **Mallis** was simple. A group of Cypriot depositors lost part of their capital when the Cypriot banks were restructured. This restructuration was the principal condition laid down in exchange for financial assistance to the Cyprus Government.[96] This condition was, in particular, expressed in a **Eurogroup statement** of 25 March 2013, summed up by the General Court (GC): "the Euro Group stated that it had reached an agreement with the Cypriot authorities on the key elements necessary for a future macroeconomic adjustment programme that was supported by all euro area Member States and by the Commission, the ECB and the

---

[91] Letter from the Eurogroup President to the European Ombudsman, *Recent initiatives to improve Eurogroup transparency*, The Hague, 16 May 2016.

[92] Letter from the Eurogroup President to the European Ombudsman, *Initiatives to improve Eurogroup transparency*, The Hague, 25 November 2016.

[93] Letter from 17 December 2015; available on the Ombudsman's website at: https://www.ombudsman.europa.eu/en/correspondence/en/65359.

[94] Remarks by J. Dijsselbloem following the Eurogroup meeting of 11 February 2016.

[95] Remarks by J. Dijsselbloem following the Eurogroup meeting of 7 March 2016.

[96] For more details, see: Case T-327/13, *Mallis v Commission and ECB* (GC 16 October 2014) para 9–26; Cases C-105/15 P to C-109/15 P, *Mallis v Commission and ECB* (ECJ 20 September 2016) para 46 and 50.

Article 137. [Eurogroup] 893

IMF. Moreover, the Euro Group welcomed the plans for restructuring the financial sector specified in the annex to the statement."[97]

The applicants sought the **annulment of this statement**, or alternatively they asked this statement to be considered a joint decision of the ECB and the Commission and then to annul it. The first argument deals mainly with the Eurogroup; it implies that the Eurogroup can adopt legal acts and raises the issue of the legal status of the Eurogroup.

The General Court, Advocate General (AG) *Whatelet* and the Court of Justice reached the same conclusion and **dismissed the applicants' request**. The General Court held it inadmissible, and the Court of Justice dismissed the appeal. On the Eurogroup, the General Court simply quoted Protocol No. 14[98] and mostly focussed on the "informal" part. So it reached the logical conclusion: "the Euro Group is a forum for discussion, at ministerial level, between representatives of the Member States whose currency is the euro, and not a decision-making body".[99] The Court of Justice supported this conclusion.[100]

43

Later in the General Court judgment, this conclusion led to another one: that the **Eurogroup cannot adopt "legally binding measures"**.[101] Nevertheless, the General Court examined the content of the statement to demonstrate that "the contested statement is purely informative in nature".[102] This conclusion was not easily reached. Although the statement itself is very vague, its annex is very detailed. The General Court notes that it "listed the measures which, in its view, had been agreed within the Euro Group following the presentation by the Cypriot authorities of their plans".[103] The General Court infers from the content of the annex that it "contains statements which could be regarded as categorical".[104] However, the annex "must be read in their proper context, from which it is clear that the contested

---

[97] Cases C-105/15 P to C-109/15 P, *Mallis v Commission and ECB* (ECJ 20 September 2016) para 46 and 50.

[98] Cases C-105/15 P to C-109/15 P, *Mallis v Commission and ECB* (ECJ 20 September 2016) para 40.

[99] Cases C-105/15 P to C-109/15 P, *Mallis v Commission and ECB* (ECJ 20 September 2016) para 41.

[100] Cases C-105/15 P to C-109/15 P, *Mallis v Commission and ECB* (ECJ 20 September 2016) para 46 and 50.

[101] "As regards the substance of the contested statement, it is important to bear in mind that the Euro Group cannot be regarded as a decision-making body. Indeed, the provisions governing its operation do not empower it to adopt legally binding measures. In principle, a statement made by the Euro Group cannot, therefore, be regarded as a measure intended to produce legal effects with respect to third parties", Case T-327/13, *Mallis v Commission and ECB* (GC 16 October 2014) para 53.

[102] Case T-327/13, *Mallis v Commission and ECB* (GC 16 October 2014) para 61.

[103] Case T-327/13, *Mallis v Commission and ECB* (GC 16 October 2014) para 55.

[104] Case T-327/13, *Mallis v Commission and ECB* (GC 16 October 2014) para 61: "it is true that the annex to the contested statement contains statements which could be regarded as categorical, in particular the statement that Laïki was to be resolved immediately, with full contribution of equity shareholders, bond holders and uninsured depositors, and the statement that BoC was to be

statement is purely informative in nature".[105] Studying closely the wording of the statement, the General Court found that it "gave a very general account of certain policy measures which had been agreed with the Republic of Cyprus",[106] the Eurogroup only "welcomed the plans for restructuring the financial sector specified" and did not make it a condition for the granting of financial assistance[107] and the Eurogroup did not consider itself the deciding body on this matter, which falls within the competence of the ESM Board of Governors.[108]

The Court of Justice upheld this conclusion: "[...] that statement, of a purely informative nature, was intended to inform the general public of the existence of a political agreement between the Eurogroup and the Cypriot authorities reflecting a common intention to pursue the negotiations in accordance with the statement's terms".[109]

44   The **European Courts had very formal reasoning**. They did not take into account the political reality behind the statement. The AG had a look at it, but his opinion concurs with those of the Court. He only wrote: "It is true that that sequence of events shows that the Euro Group clearly carries considerable political weight and that the Member States feel bound by the agreements concluded within that forum. However, this is not sufficient to support the view that the contested statement produced binding legal effects with respect to third parties within the meaning of the Court's case-law."[110]

45   The GC tried, in two different cases, to push forward the idea that the **Union should be held liable for actions of the Eurogroup**.[111] The GC based its arguments on the different logic inherent to Articles 340 and 263 TFEU and the specific definition of "institutions" in non-contractual liability cases.[112] The Union should

---

recapitalised through a deposit/equity conversion of uninsured deposits with full contribution of equity shareholders and bond holders".

[105] Case T-327/13, *Mallis v Commission and ECB* (GC 16 October 2014) para 61.

[106] Case T-327/13, *Mallis v Commission and ECB* (GC 16 October 2014) para 56.

[107] Case T-327/13, *Mallis v Commission and ECB* (GC 16 October 2014) para 58, "it did not state that those plans were regarded as part of any macroeconomic adjustment programme that the Republic of Cyprus might be required to follow in order to receive financial assistance".

[108] Case T-327/13, *Mallis v Commission and ECB* (GC 16 October 2014) para 59: "Lastly, it follows implicitly but necessarily from the contested statement that, far from claiming any authority to grant or refuse the assistance requested, the Euro Group considered that such a decision fell not within the sphere of its own powers but within the competence of the Board of Governors of the ESM."

[109] Cases C-105/15 P to C-109/15 P, *Mallis v Commission and ECB* (ECJ 20 September 2016) para 46, 50 and 59.

[110] Cases C-105/15 P to C-109/15 P, *Mallis v Commission and ECB* (Opinion of AG Whatelet of 21 April 2016) para 132. He also wrote that "the language and content of the contested statement are not entirely consistent with the definition and tasks of the Euro Group as described in Protocol No 14" (para 126).

[111] Case T-680/13, *Dr. K. Chrysostomides & Co v Council and Others* (GC 13 July 2018) para 113 and Case T-786/14, *E.P. Bourdouvali v Council and Others* (GC 13 July 2018) para 109.

[112] Case C-370/89, *SGEEM & Roland Etroy v EIB* (ECJ 2 December 1992) para 16.

be liable for actions of bodies "established by the Treaties" and that "contribute to the achievement of the Union's objectives".[113] This leads the GC to the conclusion that "the acts and conduct of the Euro Group in the exercise of its powers under EU law are therefore attributable to the European Union".[114]

In the same proceedings, the **Court of Justice annulled** this part of the GC reasoning using three arguments. First, the formalisation of the existence of the Eurogroup by Articles 137 TFEU and Protocol No. 14 "did not alter its intergovernmental nature in the slightest". Second, the Eurogroup "is characterised by its informality" linked to its function of "intergovernmental coordination". Third, "it does not have any competence of its own in the EU legal order".[115]

This encapsulates the issues with the Eurogroup: although its political role is central, the language used by the Treaty makes it **legally intransparent**. This raises concerns with effective legal protection[116] and democratic accountability.

46

List of Cases

CJEU

CJEU 02.12.1992, C-379/98, *SGEEM & Roland Etroy v EIB*, ECLI:EU:C:1992:482 [cit. in para 45]

CJEU 20.09.2016, C-105/15 P to C-109/15 P, *Mallis v Commission and ECB*, ECLI:EU:C:2016:702 [cit. in para 42–44]

CJEU 16.12.2020, C-197/18 P to C-198/18 and C-603/18 P to C-604/18 P, *Council v K. Chrysostomides & Co. and Others*, ECLI:EU:C:2020:1028 [cit. in para 45]

---

[113] Case T-680/13, *Dr. K. Chrysostomides & Co v Council and Others* (GC 13 July 2018) para 112 and Case T-786/14, *E.P. Bourdouvali v Council and Others* (GC 13 July 2018) para 108.

[114] "Article 137 TFEU and Protocol No 14 ... make provision, inter alia, for the existence, the composition, the procedural rules and the functions of the Euro Group. In that last regard, Article 1 of that protocol provides that the Euro Group is to meet 'to discuss questions related to the specific responsibilities [the ministers composing it] share with regard to the single currency'. Those questions concern, under Article 119(2) TFEU, the activities of the European Union for the purposes of the objectives set out in Article 3 TEU, which include the establishment of an economic and monetary union whose currency is the Euro. It follows that the Euro Group is a body of the Union formally established by the Treaties and intended to contribute to achieving the objectives of the Union. The acts and conduct of the Euro Group in the exercise of its powers under EU law are therefore attributable to the European Union." Case T-680/13, *Dr. K. Chrysostomides & Co v Council and Others* (GC 13 July 2018) para 113 and Case T-786/14, *E.P. Bourdouvali v Council and Others* (GC 13 July 2018) para 109.

[115] Cases C-197/18 P to C-198/18 and C-603/18 P to C-604/18 P, *Council v K. Chrysostomides & Co. and Others* (ECJ 16 December 2020) para 87–89.

[116] See Craig (2017), pp. 246–249.

GC

GC 16.10.2014, T-327/13, *Mallis v Commission and ECB*, ECLI:EU:T:2014:909 [cit. in para 42–44]
GC 13.07.2018, T-680/13, *Dr. K. Chrysostomides & Co v Council and Others*, ECLI:EU:T:2018:486 [cit. in para 45]
GC 13.07.2018, T-786/14, *E.P. Bourdouvali v Council and Others*, ECLI:EU:T:2018:487 [cit. in para 45]

References[117]

Adalid, S. (2015). *La Banque centrale européenne et l'Eurosystème*. Bruylant.
Adamski, D. (2013). Europe's (misguided) constitution of economic prosperity. *Common Market Law Review, 50*(1), 47–86.
Böttner, R. (2018). Der Europäische Minister für Wirtschaft und Finanzen nach den Plänen der Kommission. *Zeitschrift für europarechtliche Studien*, 69–96.
Böttner, R. (2020). *The constitutional framework for enhanced cooperation in EU law*. Brill Nijhoff.
Burley, A.-M., & Mattli, W. (1993). Europe before the court: A political theory of legal integration. *International Organization, 47*(1), 41–76.
Craig, P. (2017). The Eurogroup, power and accountability. *European Law Journal, 23*(3/4), 234–249.
Fromont, L. (2017). L'Eurogroupe: le côté obscur de la gouvernance de la zone euro. *Revue de Droit de l'Union européenne, 2017*(4), 195–221.
Heintz, M., & Hirsch, M. (1998). L'Union européenne et la présidence luxembourgeoise (juillet-décembre 1997). *Courrier hebdomadaire du CRISP, 3*(1588–1589), 1–57.
Layer, F. (2004). Pour une constitutionnalisation du gouvernement économique européen. *Revue de la recherche juridique – Droit prospectif, 2004*(2), 803–844.
Leino, P., & Saarenheimo, T. (2017). Sovereignty and subordination: On the limits of EU economic policy co-ordination. *European Law Review, 42*(2), 166–189.
Louis, J.-V. (1992). L'union économique et monétaire. *Cahiers de Droit européen, 1992*(3–4), 251–305.
Louis, J.-V. (2001–2002). The Eurogroup and economic co-ordination. *Euredia*, 20–43.
Louis, J.-V. (2004). The economic and Monetary Union: Law and institution. *Common Market Law Review, 41*(2), 575–608.
Louis, J.-V. (2010). Guest Editorial: The no-bailout clause and rescue packages. *Common Market Law Review, 47*(4), 971–986.
Louis, J.-V., & Lastra, R.-M. (2013). European economic and Monetary Union: History, trends, and prospects. *Yearbook of European Law, 32*(1), 57–206.
Manger-Nestler, C., & Böttner, R. (2019). Der Europäische Währungsfonds nach den Plänen der Kommission. *Zeitschrift für ausländisches öffentliches Recht und Völkerrecht*, 43–84.
Martucci, F. (2016). *L'ordre économique et monétaire de l'Union européenne*. Bruylant.
Pisani-Ferry, J. (2006). Only one bed for two dreams: A critical retrospective on the debate over the economic governance of the Euro Area. *Journal of Common Market Studies, 44*(4), 823–844.
Quatremer, J., & Klau, T. (1999). *Ces hommes qui ont fait l'euro: querelles et ambitions européennes*. Plon.

---

[117] All cited Internet sources of this comment have been accessed on 6 April 2021.

Sacriste, G., & Vauchez, A. (2019). L'Euro-isation de l'Europe. Trajectoire historique d'une politique 'hors les murs' et nouvelle question démocratique. *Revue de l'OFCE, 165*, 1–42.

Vigneron, P. (2003). Instaurer une coopération renforcée pour l'Eurogroupe. In *Mélanges en hommage à Jean-Victor Louis* (pp. 377–394). Editions de l'Université Libre de Bruxelles.

Article 138 [Common Positions]
(ex-Article 111.4 TEC)

1. In order to secure the euro's place in the international monetary system, the Council,[17–18] on a proposal from the Commission,[15] shall adopt a decision[24–26] establishing common positions[20–22] on matters of particular interest for economic and monetary union[7,8] within the competent international financial institutions and conferences.[7–12] The Council shall act after consulting the European Central Bank.[17]
2. The Council,[17,18] on a proposal from the Commission,[15] may adopt appropriate measures to ensure unified representation[28–35] within the international financial institutions and conferences.[7,11,12] The Council shall act after consulting the European Central Bank.
3. For the measures referred to in paragraphs 1 and 2, only members of the Council representing Member States whose currency is the euro[10] shall take part in the vote.[18]

A qualified majority of the said members shall be defined in accordance with Article 238(3)(a).

Contents

1. Context and Meaning 1
2. Scope of Application 6
   2.1. Matters of Particular Interest for Economic and Monetary Union 7
   2.2. Euro Area Member States Only 10
   2.3. International and Financial Institutions and Conferences 11
3. Procedure 14
4. Common Positions 20
   4.1. The Concept of "Common Positions" 21
   4.2. The Legal Form 24
5. Unified Representation 27
   5.1. The Text 28
       5.1.1. The Principal 29
       5.1.2. The Agent 33
   5.2. The Practice 38
References

1. Context and Meaning

The Euro is a currency used internationally. In 2017, 20% of both "international reserves of foreign central banks" and "debt issuance on international markets" were denominated in euro, "36% of the value of international transactions were invoiced or settled in Euros" and 60 countries outside the EU used it or linked their currency to it.[1] However, **the euro area has no voice and no clear external politic**, thus affecting the international place of the Euro.[2] The Five Presidents' Report noted that: "This fragmented voice means the EU is punching below its political and economic weight as each euro area Member State speaks individually."[3]

2 The problem used to be tackled from an institutional perspective. The international weakness of the euro was the consequence of the **lack of uniformity in the international projection of the EU and the euro area institutions and organs**. For example, since the launch of the third phase, the main institutional and doctrinal issue was the representation of the euro area in the IMF.[4] Despite a legal basis in the Treaty (Articles 219 and 138 TFEU, before Article 111 TEC-Nice), MS' political will was always very modest (→ para 24 et seqq.). No decision was ever adopted based on this (these) article(s). The 2015 Commission proposal, for a unified representation in the IMF, went almost unnoticed by the Council.[5]

Recently, the Commission seems[6] to have changed its strategy. Instead of focusing on institutional and multilateral issues, the Commission proposed two other ways: strengthening the financial attractiveness of the euro area, mostly with a stronger and deeper financial sector; on the other hand, using "economic diplomacy by engaging with global partners to promote the use of the euro."[7]

3 Despite this recent turn, since the Treaty of Maastricht, primary law provides **procedures for the external relations of the euro area**. Laid down initially in Article 109 TEC-Maastricht, later Article 111 TEC-Nice, they were separated in two distinct articles by the Lisbon Treaty. The first three paragraphs of Article 111 TEC-Nice and the last one (the fifth) became Article 219 TFEU. The fourth paragraph became Article 138 TFEU, which was substantially amended.

Article 111 TEC, along with **Article 138 TFEU**, is the result of difficult negotiations, mostly about "the role of political authorities in the external aspect

---

[1] Commission Communication, *Towards a stronger international role of the Euro*, COM(2018) 796 final, p. 2.

[2] On the rationale for a better representation of the euro area, ECB, *The external representation of the EU and EMU*, Monthly Bulletin, May 2011, pp. 87–89.

[3] J.-C. Juncker, in close cooperation with D. Tusk, J. Dijsselbloem, M. Draghi, and M. Schulz (2015), The Five Presidents Report: Completing Europe's Economic and Monetary Union.

[4] For the former, see Commission Communication, *Proposal for a Council Decision laying down measures in view of progressively establishing unified representation of the euro area in the International Monetary Fund*, COM(2015) 603 final; for the latter on a prospective point of view, Lebullenger (1998) more precisely pp. 472–478 and on a retrospective one, Smits (2009).

[5] It was only mentioned by the Council, which did not seem to have discussed it during meeting on 10 November 2015 or later.

[6] This change is not explicit.

[7] Commission Communication, *Towards a stronger international role of the Euro*, COM(2018) 796 final, p. 11.

of monetary policy,"[8] some advocating for great involvement of government, others for total independence of the European Central Bank. The result **is a bad compromise**, a poorly written article.

The **effects are as disappointing** as the writing. No legal act has ever been adopted based on these articles. The separation made by the Lisbon Treaty tried to facilitate arrangements, by separating the question of exchange rates, Article 219 TFEU, and the other questions, Article 138 TFEU. Initially, Article 111 TEC was part of the Chapter 2 ("Monetary Policy") of Title VII ("Economic and Monetary Policy"), which was an odd choice because the fourth paragraph dealt with "issues of particular relevance to economic and monetary union," so not only monetary ones. After the Lisbon Treaty, Article 138 TFEU is part of Chapter 4 ("Provisions specific to Member States whose currency is the euro") of Title VIII ("Economic and Monetary Policy"). Article 219 TFEU is placed with other provisions on international agreements.

The actual wording makes the **distinction between two types of action** that can be done: the first paragraph concerns "common positions" and the second one "unified representation." This separation is useful. It allows for two different, albeit sometimes complementary, kinds of actions: a substantial one through common positions (paragraph 4) and a procedural one via a common representation (paragraph 5). These two paragraphs must be commented separately, after dealing with their common characteristics: their scope of application (paragraph 2) and the procedure (paragraph 3).

2. Scope of Application

The scope of application is the same for the first and the second paragraphs. It raises **three questions**: the identity of this scope for the two paragraphs, the fact that the article applies only to euro area MS and the notion of "international financial institutions and conferences."

2.1. Matters of Particular Interest for Economic and Monetary Union

The scope of application for the first paragraph is clearly mentioned: "matters or particular interest for economic and monetary union". But, the **second paragraph does not mention the field in which it is applicable**. This could mean that it is applicable to larger fields than only "matters of particular interest for economic and monetary union." This interpretation does not stand, for reasons. First, the article is part of the title on economic and monetary policy. Second, Article 220 TFEU is the general article on the cooperation of the EU with other international organizations. Thus, Article 138.2 TFEU can only be a specific clause, for a specific field. Third, Article 138 TFEU being only applicable to euro area MS, it can only deal with fields linked to the EMU. Fourth, both paragraphs mention, "international and financial

---

[8] Smits (1997), pp. 375–376.

institutions and conferences." The targeted institutions being the same, the field must be the same.

Hence, while the **wording** is different for the two paragraphs, the "matters of particular interest for economic and monetary union" **cover both paragraphs.**

8   This only shows how badly the article is written. Lousy phrasing is also remarkable for the expression: "matters for particular interest for economic and monetary union." This does not mean anything. Of course, "economic and monetary union" refers to fields covered by Chapter VIII: the "basic tasks" the ECB is entrusted[9] to ESCB are budgetary and economic policies (Article 127.2 TFEU; see Articles 126 and 121 TFEU).[10] But the meaning of "economic policies" is very wide and, potentially, every economic question can be a part of it. The imprecision is strengthened by the expression **"matters of particular interest,"** which **does not really mean anything** either and expands even for the potential scope of application. Fortunately, the Lisbon Treaty removed an even more confusing part of the article. The fourth paragraph of Article 111 TEC ended with the expression: "in compliance with the allocation of powers laid down in Articles 99 and 105."[11] This reference was "as useless as it is ambiguous."[12]

9   This **vagueness is deliberate**. It allows the Council to act freely and to adapt to different situations. Indeed, the institutions and conferences covered by the article have very different specialties, which does not fit with the repartition of competences in the EU ($\rightarrow$ para 11–13). Institutions must adapt their action to their interlocutors.

2.2. Euro Area Member States Only

10   The article applies only to euro area MS. This is not clearly stated by the article. However, these are the only States that can vote, and Article 138 TFEU is part of the chapter: "specific to Member States whose currency is the euro." Therefore, only them **can be the recipients of this article** and the actions taken on its basis. Non-euro area MS will not be bound by actions taken on the ground of Article 138 TFEU. However, the principle of loyal cooperation prevents them to undermine these actions.

2.3. International and Financial Institutions and Conferences

11   Here, again, the writing is deliberately vague. This is logical. **Different kinds of forums are competent in the field of economic and monetary policies.** Some are

---

[9] Smits (1997), p. 415 refers to "matters which may affect the monetary policy and ancillary policy areas for which the ESCB is competent."

[10] Smits (1997), p. 415 mentions "areas which are, or should have been, the subject matter of economic policy coordination within the Community."

[11] Respectively Articles 121 and 127 TFEU.

[12] See Martucci (2016), p. 143: "aussi inutile qu'ambigu."

Article 138. [Common Positions]

international organizations, such as the IMF or the OECD. Others are more informal gatherings, such as all the "Gs" (G7, G10, G20). "Institutions" refers to formal arrangements and especially international organizations, and "conferences" to informal ones. It is unfortunate that Article 138 TFEU does not use the same vocabulary as in the rest of the Treaty, especially in Article 219 TFEU. The last paragraph of the latter refers to "international bodies."[13] This last expression is vague enough to encompass every type of international gathering of states. Although "conference" is also vague, coherence of the Treaty should have been favored.

The institutions and conferences need to be international and to deal with financial questions. These two adjectives require some precision. "**International**" can either have a broad or a specific meaning. The former one refers to every actor, which gathers different States, the latter one refers to the universal organizations, as opposed to regional ones (such as the EU). The article uses the first one and encompasses regional organizations. This is coherent with the rest of the Treaty. Indeed, Article 220 TFEU mentions "other international organizations" after mentioning universal organizations (such as the UN) and regional organizations (such as the Council of Europe and the OECD).

Article 138 TFEU is about the EMU, but it refers to "financial institutions." Drafters of the Treaty did not want to tie their hand and thus favored vague language, more coherent with international practice than EU law. As mentioned before, international actors competent to deal with economic and monetary affairs often have a broader competence than this specific field. The **term "financial" is used here in its larger definition**. It does not refer specifically to the "financial sector" (often opposed to the banking and the insurance sector), but to "financial questions" from monetary to state debts, passing through economic policies, every field related to the finance of the State. With the recent enlargement of the EMU to banking and a finance union, this can also refer to the narrow definition.

3. Procedure

The procedure is the same for the first and the second paragraph. The **procedure** is quite simple, and it has been simplified by the Nice Treaty.

The **initiative** comes from the **Commission**. Without this reference, the Commission would not have a right of initiative, since its automatic "quasi-monopoly of initiative" applies only in case of Union legislative acts (Article 17.2, sentence 1, TEU). Since the legal acts in Article 138 TFEU are not legislative acts, but "other

---

[13] See also Articles 191.4 (2), 209.2 (2), 212.3 (2), and 214.4 (2) TFEU.

acts" (Article 17.2, sentence 2, TEU), the Commission needs to be mentioned explicitly. To this day, the Commission only made two propositions.[14]

16 It is only for the first paragraph of Article 138 TFEU that primary law specifies **the act to be adopted**, i.e., a Council Decision. In the case of the second paragraph, the Treaty refers to "appropriate measures" and could also take the form of a decision, but also another legal act, maybe even soft law measures such as a recommendation. This distinction is due to the fact that in the first case, a clear situation is envisaged, i.e., the definition of a common position to be represented within an international forum. The second situation is less specific, as "unified representation" could be achieved through different means and routes.

17 The **deciding institution is the Council**. The European Parliament is not consulted, only the ECB. The absence of the European Parliament is problematic, notably because under Article 219.1 TFEU its consultation is mandatory for the conclusion of "formal agreements on exchange rates" (→ Article 219 TFEU para 19–20). Also, for the conclusion of these types of agreements, **consultation of the ECB has a specific goal**: "reach a consensus consistent with the objective of price stability" (→ Article 219 TFEU para 17). This is not the case here; this is a simple consultation.

18 The Council votes in a specific formation, comprising only MS participating in the third stage of EMU, i.e., euro area states. This specific formation was formally recognized by the Lisbon Treaty, especially Article 136.2 TFEU. Since **not all the members of the Council participate in voting**, the default rule of Article 16.3 TEU for qualified majority voting is modified by Article 238.2 point (a) TFEU. Under this provision, a qualified majority shall be defined as at least 55% of the members of the Council representing the euro area states, comprising at least 65% of the population of these states. A blocking minority must include at least the minimum number of Council members representing more than 35% of the population of the participating MS, plus one member. These rules for counting and reaching the majority are flexible and allow easily for their adaptation to a more limited composition of the Council. It should be noted that the first version of this provision (from the Maastricht Treaty) used qualified majority only for common positions. Unified representation needed to be found via unanimity. The Treaty of Nice used qualified majority for both.

19 This last example is the illustration of the **difficulties of MS to relinquish their international powers**, in matters partially transferred to the European level, and their subsequent, but ineffective, efforts to simplify Treaty provisions to facilitate EU actions.

---

[14] Commission Communication, *Proposal for a Council Decision on the representation and position taking of the Community at international level in the context of Economic and Monetary Union*, COM(1998) 637 final, and Commission Communication, *Proposal for a Council Decision laying down measures in view of progressively establishing unified representation of the euro area in the International Monetary Fund*, COM(2015) 603 final.

Article 138. [Common Positions]

4. Common Positions

It seems odd that **Article 138 TFEU deals first with common positions and second with unified representation**.[15] The main goal of the EU, or the euro area, should be to achieve a unified representation or, if impossible, to define common positions. Therefore, unified representation should appear first. But MS prefer to reach common positions rather than unify the representation, which might require them to abandon their seats in some international organizations and it might prove complex to get these organizations to accept the EU. This is also reflected by the verbs used by the Treaty, on the "common positions," the first paragraph uses "shall," and on the "unified representation," the second one uses "may."[16] However, during the first twenty years of the Euro, states did not manage to adopt any single position. The Lisbon Treaty tried to encourage them by adding a goal to these positions, albeit a vague one. Indeed, "common positions" are adopted "in order to secure the euro's place in the international monetary system." Moreover, the Treaty is very vague on the concept of "common positions" and their legal form.

4.1. The Concept of "Common Positions"

The expression "common positions" is used only once in the Treaty. However, the meaning of this expression can be found through other provisions. Article 25 TEU, dealing with the CFSP, specifies that this policy shall be conducted by the adoption of "positions to be taken by the Union" (Article 25 point (b) (ii) TEU) and, before Lisbon, the Treaty mentioned "common position" (Article J.2 TEU-Maastricht). Drafters of the Maastricht Treaty were coherent in using the same expression; those of Lisbon forgot this point. "Common positions" were defined by the TEU as **"the approach** of the Union **to a particular matter of a geographical or thematic nature"** (Article 15 TEU-Nice). Moreover, in the TFEU, this word is used in different contexts, the most relevant one being "positions" taken by the European Parliament and the Council during the legislative procedure (Article 294 TFEU). Adding to these two occurrences of the term its common meaning, a position, and moreover, a "common position" refers to the position that MS have adopted on a specific issue that they want to uphold at the international level. It is the opinion that the euro area, as a whole, has agreed upon, the common interest states share.

The question left unanswered by the first paragraph is the identity of the **agent which will be expressing and upholding this position** in international financial

---

[15] Article 111.4 TEC used the same order of matters.

[16] See Louis and Lastra (2013), p. 184: "This difference surely reflects the more delicate feature of the theme of 'a unified representation' which requires a political decision in conformity with its charter from the part of the institution or conference concerned."

institutions and conferences. Two possibilities need to be distinguished. In both cases, the **position will be constraining**, because it will be adopted as a decision.

23 First, **where there is an already unified representation**, the measures taken to ensure this representation will mention the person(s) or the organ(s) entrusted with such representation. They will be the one expressing the common position. In this case, for each question, a common position can be voted by the Council to guide its representative.

Second, and conversely, where there is an **absence of unified representation**. It will be up to the States as members of the organizations and conferences, to be the voice of the euro area. EU institutions and organs, the Commission and the ECB, can also express it, but they often only have the status of observer (→ para 38 et seqq.).

4.2. The Legal Form

24 Article 138.1 TFEU seems clear, the Council "shall adopt a decision." However, the word **decision is twofold**. It could either mean a decision in the formal sense of Article 288 (4) TFEU. Yet it could also, more largely, refer to a decision in the common sense, which means the fact that the Council has reached an agreement, whatever the form it takes.

25 The logical interpretation is the first one. Decisions in the formal sense are binding either in general or, when it specifies those to whom it is addressed, only on the addressees. This way, **"common positions" bind MS, the person, or the organ responsible** for the unified representation. This is the best way to ensure that "common positions" are effective.

26 However, in the field of **EMU**, states are reluctant to bind themselves (→ para 38 et seqq.). Thus, it might be possible that **MS prefer to adopt non-formal acts**, such as simple conclusions of the Council. This is the most likely outcome, although it will weaken the position of the euro area as a whole.

5. Unified Representation

27 The external representation of the EU in economic and monetary matters is a complex one.[17] Article 136.2 TFEU lays down the procedure to establish a "unified representation." As no decision has ever been taken, the practice for the first twenty years needs to be studied.

---

[17] See Hervé (2012).

Article 138. [Common Positions]

5.1. The Text

The text is deliberately vague. Apart from the procedure, it does not indicate what form a "unified representation" could take. The concept of "representation" needs to be understood in its classical sense in international law, which means the **person** (the agent) **is able to speak for the entity that enabled him** (the principal). The TEU used it in this sense, when it mentions "the Union's external representation" (Article 17.1 TEU). This raises two questions: the identity of the principal and of the agent. These questions will be answered using the only text proposed by the Commission, the unified representation in the IMF.[18]

28

5.1.1. The Principal

Classically, to delegate power, a person needs to be entrusted with this power, in the EU language, a competence. The problem here is dual, there is a **question of competence** (between the States and the Union) and if the competence is transferred to the Union there is an additional question of allocation of power between the institutions and organs of the EU.[19] Moreover, in the EMU, repartition of competences is different between the monetary and the economic matter. They need to be dealt with separately.

29

The interpretation of the Treaty needs to be completed by some basic notions of the case law. The Treaty is often silent about the external competence. The Court always deduced **external competence by studying the internal** one (cf. Article 3.2 TEU).

Monetary policy is an exclusive competence of the Union; logically this encompasses the external dimension. This is confirmed by Article 219 TFEU and Article 6 of the ESCB Statute. These two articles raise the issue of the repartition of this competence between the Council and the ECB/ESCB.[20] The former is competent in exchange-rate policy and the latter in all fields "involving the tasks entrusted to the ESCB" (Article 6.1 ESCB Statute), and therefore "may participate in international monetary institutions" (Article 6.2 ESCB Statute). However, this last article clearly states that the ECB should exercise its powers "without prejudice to Article 138" (Article 6.3 ESCB Statute). Thus, the Council can act in matters related to the tasks entrusted to the ESCB, as long as it does not interfere with the conduct of monetary policy. Therefore, **the principal can only be the Council**, acting on behalf of the euro area in the field of exchange-rate policy.

30

---

[18] Commission Communication, *Proposal for a Council Decision laying down measures in view of progressively establishing unified representation of the euro area in the International Monetary Fund*, COM(2015) 603 final.

[19] The Commission takes this into account; see, COM(1998) 637 final, p. 3.

[20] On the delicate question, see Hervé (2012).

31   The nature of the **economic policy competence** always raised questions. The writing of the Treaty is very opaque. Article 5.1 TFEU seems to indicate that the EU has no proper competence and is used as a forum towards which MS—which remain competent—coordinate their economic policies. Thus, in this area, the Council, when creating a unified representation, is not doing it on behalf of the EU rather the MS. The European Council of Luxembourg recognized that: "On elements of economic policy other than monetary and exchange-rate policy, **the Member States should continue to present their policies outside the Community framework**, while taking full account of the Community interest."[21]

32   This presentation needs to be nuanced, because the repartition of competence among the EU and the MS, and among the EU institutions, does not perfectly reflect the structure and competences of international institutions and conferences. For example, the IFM deals with monetary as well as economic questions. The unified representation needs to consider this by sometimes interfering in the area entrusted to the ECB or to MS. Briefly, **principals are the Union, its institutions, and the MS acting through those institutions**.[22] The best solution to this problem is to have **multiple agents responsible for the unified representation**.

5.1.2. The Agent

33   As the article does not specify anything about the agent, it **can be anything or anyone**: an MS, an EU institution (speaking, for example, through its President) even an informal body as the Eurogroup (Article 137 TFEU) or its President. MS could represent the euro area in conferences where they are not all represented, such as the G7; it could also be the Union, which is a member of the G20.

34   The two proposals of the European Commission reflect this diversity. In its first **proposal** of 1998, the Commission proposed that "the Community shall be represented at international level by the Council with the Commission, and by the ECB."[23] This **representation** would have been made "**through the office of President of the Council**."[24] The ECB would have participated in the G10 Ministerial meetings.[25] Of course, when rules of the organization would not allow for this

---

[21] Luxembourg European Council, 12–13 December 1997, Presidency Conclusions, Annex 1: "Resolution of the European Council of Economic Policy co-ordination in stage 3 of EMU and on Treaty articles 109 and 109b," para 10 (emphasis added).

[22] For Smits (1997), p. 414, Article 111.4 TEC encompassed "both the Community (including the separate legal entities comprising the ESCB) and its Member States, with the Council to respect the privileges attributed to the monetary authority."

[23] COM(1998) 637 final, Article 1. It should be noted that the writing is misleading; it is not the Community that would have been represented, but only the euro area.

[24] COM(1998) 637 final, Article 2. That article provides for the case where the President is not from a euro area MS.

[25] COM(1998) 637 final, Article 3.

kind of representation, the states and the institutions should have adopted temporary arrangements.[26] This proposition was never adopted.

More than 15 years later, the Commission tried again, with a less ambitious **proposal, concerning** only the **IMF**. This proposition is more acceptable. The President of the Eurogroup would represent the euro area in the Board of Governors of the IMF.[27] The euro area should then be represented by an "Executive Director" on the IMF's Executive Board.[28] He or she would be elected following the procedure used for the President of the Eurogroup (Article 2 of Protocol No. 14; → Article 137 TFEU para 19). 35

In 2018, the Commission added to this with its proposal on a **European Minister of Economy and Finance** (→ Supplement to Title VIII: TSCG para 109–110).[29] Based on this proposal, the competent Commissioner should also become the President of the Eurogroup and would thus, based on the 2015 proposal, be responsible for the euro area's unified representation. The detachment of the Eurogroup presidency from national governments could lead to a better consolidation of national positions and reinforce the representation of the interests of the euro area and of the Union as a whole.[30] 36

None of the proposals so far have been adopted. Instead, since 1998, **external representation is based on a simple "report"**. 37

5.2. The Practice

Ground rules for the external representation of the euro area were laid down by the European Council of Luxembourg in December 1997. After that, the European Commission adopted the proposition mentioned before. However, the Council and the European Council preferred more flexible rules laid down in a report of the Council of the European Council of Vienna (11 and 12 December 1998). 38

The **resolution adopted in Luxembourg** simply **underlines the central role given to the Council** by Article 109 TEC-Maastricht (Article 111 TEC-Nice), and the subsidiary role of the ECB and the respective allocation of powers: "The Council and the European Central Bank will carry out their tasks in representing the Community at international level in an efficient manner and in compliance with the allocation of powers laid down in the Treaty."[31] 39

---

[26] COM(1998) 637 final, Article 4.
[27] COM(2015) 603 final and COM(1998) 637 final, Article 3.
[28] COM(2015) 603 final, Article 3: "direct representation of the euro area by the Executive Director of a euro area constituency, following the establishment of one or several constituencies composed only of euro area Member States."
[29] COM(2017) 823 final. See in detail Böttner (2018).
[30] Böttner (2018), p. 84 et seqq.
[31] Luxembourg European Council, 12–13 December 1997, Presidency Conclusions, Annex 1: "Resolution of the European Council of Economic Policy co-ordination in stage 3 of EMU and on Treaty articles 109 and 109b", para 10.

The **Vienna Report** is very slim. It first acknowledges the difficulties of achieving a unified representation, mostly because "third countries and institutions will need to be persuaded to accept the solutions proposed by the European Union."[32] It underlines that "the Community shall be represented at the Council/ministerial level and at the central banking level."[33] After that, the Report only deals with the G7 Finance Minister's and Governors' Group and the IMF. For the first one, the President of the ECB can attend "meetings of the Group for the discussions which relate to EMU,"[34] and the President of the Eurogroup to be "at the table."[35] For the IMF, the ECB should be granted the status of observer and "the views of the European Community/EMU would be presented at the IMF Board by the relevant member of the Executive Director's office of the Member State holding the Euro 11 Presidency."[36]

40   Since then, those rules have been applied. Two examples will be developed: IMF and the G20 as well as the G7.[37] Concerning the **IMF**, the main problem is that only countries can be part of the Fund and that the EU is not a country or, if it could somehow be considered as one,[38] it is doubtful that other members will share this point of view.[39] Thus, the **ECB** has been granted the **observer status**, its President and the Commissioner for Economic and Monetary Affairs "attend the meetings of the International Monetary and Financial Committee (IMFC) twice a year in the context of the IMF's Spring and Annual Meetings."[40] Moreover, EU States coordinate their positions inside the IMF via a sub-committee of the Economic and Financial Committee: the "sub-committee on IMF related issues (SCIMF)" in Brussels, which gathers ten times per year,[41] or via the "EURIMF group" a Washington-based group of EU MS representatives,[42] who meet on a weekly

---

[32] Vienna European Council, 11–12 December 1998, Presidency Conclusions, Annex II: "Report to the European Council on the state of preparation for Stage 3 of EMU, in particular the external representation of the Community," para 3.

[33] Presidency Conclusions, Annex II, para 5.

[34] Presidency Conclusions, Annex II, para 7.

[35] Presidency Conclusions, Annex II, para 8.

[36] Presidency Conclusions, Annex II, para 13.

[37] For the OECD, see, ECB, *The external representation of the EU and EMU*, Monthly Bulletin, May 2011, pp. 92–93.

[38] See the "out-of-the-box thinking" of *René Smits*, for who the EU can be seen as a country in the IMF, cf. Smits (2009), pp. 319–322.

[39] There is a very legitimate concern of "over-representation" of the EU, moreover in 1998 the Chairman of the IFM reaffirmed the "country-based status of the organization"; see Smits (2009), p. 308 and p. 311.

[40] ECB, *The external representation of the EU and EMU*, Monthly Bulletin, May 2011, p. 91.

[41] Hervé (2012), p. 158.

[42] ECB, *The external representation of the EU and EMU*, Monthly Bulletin, May 2011, p. 92.

Article 138. [Common Positions]

basis.[43] When these groups arrive at a common position,[44] it is expressed by the Council presidency, and in monetary matters by the ECB.[45]

The different "G"-combinations are more flexible arenas, so adapting to the specificity of the EU is easier, notwithstanding the difficulties of having the other participants' consent.[46] The EU is a member of the **G20**, and it is represented here by the Presidents of the Commission and the European Council. When it gathers at the level of finance ministers and central bank governors, the EU is "represented by the ECB, the rotating EU Council Presidency and the European Commission."[47]

At the **G7** finance minister and central bank governors, the Presidents of the ECB and the Eurogroup are "invited to all parts of the meetings (...) whereas the European Commissioner for Economic and Monetary Affairs only participates in certain parts of the meetings."[48] Partners of the EU accepted this solution, yet with difficulties, mostly because of the important weight all these representatives give to the EU.[49]

41

References

Böttner, R. (2018). Der Europäische Minister für Wirtschaft und Finanzen nach den Plänen der Kommission. *Zeitschrift für europarechtliche Studien*, 69–96.

Hervé, A. (2012). The participation of the European Union in global economic governance fora. *European Law Journal, 18*(1), 143–161.

Lebullenger, J. (1998). La projection externe de la zone euro. *Revue Trimestrielle de Droit européen, 34*(4), 458–478.

Lopez Escudero, M. (2011). La politique de change de l'Euro. *Cahiers de Droit européen, 47*, 369–432.

Louis, J.-V. (2000). Les relations internationales de l'union économique et monétaire. In Société française pour le droit international (Ed.), *Droit international et droit communautaire – Perspectives actuelles (Colloque de Bordeaux)* (pp. 387–413). Pedone.

Louis, J.-V., & Lastra, R.-M. (2013). European economic and Monetary Union: History, trends, and prospects. *Yearbook of European Law, 1*(32), 57–206.

Martucci, F. (2016). *L'ordre économique et monétaire de l'Union européenne*. Bruylant.

Smits, R. (1997). *The European Central Bank – Institutional aspects*. Kluwer Law International.

Smits, R. (2009). International representation of Europe in the Area of Economic and Monetary union and practice in the first ten years of the Euro. *Euredia, 2009*(2), 297–333.

---

[43] Hervé (2012), p. 158.

[44] But these positions are never expressed through a formal decision in the sense of Article 138.1 TFEU.

[45] ECB, *The external representation of the EU and EMU*, Monthly Bulletin, May 2011.

[46] See Lopez Escudero (2011), pp. 418–422.

[47] ECB, *The external representation of the EU and EMU*, Monthly Bulletin, May 2011, p. 93 (emphasis added).

[48] ECB, *The external representation of the EU and EMU*, Monthly Bulletin, May 2011, p. 93.

[49] See Louis (2000), pp. 401–402.

Chapter 5
Transitional Provisions

Article 139 [Member States with a Derogation]

1. Member States in respect of which the Council has not decided that they fulfil the necessary conditions for the adoption of the euro shall hereinafter be referred to as "Member States with a derogation".[7–20]
2. The following provisions of the Treaties shall not apply to Member States with a derogation:

    (a) adoption of the parts of the broad economic policy guidelines which concern the euro area generally (Article 121(2));[23–28]
    (b) coercive means of remedying excessive deficits (Article 126(9) and (11));[29–32]
    (c) the objectives and tasks of the ESCB (Article 127(1) to (3) and (5));[33–40]
    (d) issue of the euro (Article 128);[41–44]
    (e) acts of the European Central Bank (Article 132);[45–48]
    (f) measures governing the use of the euro (Article 133);[49–51]
    (g) monetary agreements and other measures relating to exchange-rate policy (Article 219);[52,53]
    (h) appointment of members of the Executive Board of the European Central Bank (Article 283(2));[54–58]
    (i) decisions establishing common positions on issues of particular relevance for economic and monetary union within the competent international financial institutions and conferences (Article 138(1));[59,60]
    (j) measures to ensure unified representation within the international financial institutions and conferences (Article 138(2)).[59,60]

    In the Articles referred to in points (a) to (j), "Member States" shall therefore mean Member States whose currency is the euro.

3. Under Chapter IX of the Statute of the ESCB and of the ECB, Member States with a derogation and their national central banks are excluded from rights and obligations within the ESCB.[63–65]
4. The voting rights of members of the Council representing Member States with a derogation shall be suspended for the adoption by the Council of the measures referred to in the Articles listed in paragraph 2, and in the following instances:

    (a) recommendations made to those Member States whose currency is the euro in the framework of multilateral surveillance, including on stability programmes and warnings (Article 121(4));[69–71]
    (b) measures relating to excessive deficits concerning those Member States whose currency is the euro (Article 126(6), (7), (8), (12) and (13)).[72–74]

A qualified majority of the other members of the Council shall be defined in accordance with Article 238(3) (a).[67]

Protocol (No 16)[14,15]
on Certain Provisions Relating to Denmark

THE HIGH CONTRACTING PARTIES,

TAKING INTO ACCOUNT that the Danish Constitution contains provisions which may imply a referendum in Denmark prior to Denmark renouncing its exemption,

GIVEN THAT, on 3 November 1993, the Danish Government notified the Council of its intention not to participate in the third stage of economic and monetary union,

HAVE AGREED UPON the following provisions, which shall be annexed to the Treaty on European Union and to the Treaty on the Functioning of the European Union:

1. In view of the notice given to the Council by the Danish Government on 3 November 1993, Denmark shall have an exemption. The effect of the exemption shall be that all Articles and provisions of the Treaties and the Statute of the ESCB referring to a derogation shall be applicable to Denmark.
2. As for the abrogation of the exemption, the procedure referred to in Article 140 shall only be initiated at the request of Denmark.
3. In the event of abrogation of the exemption status, the provisions of this Protocol shall cease to apply.

Contents

1.	Genesis and Overview	1
2.	Member States with a Derogation (Paragraph 1)	7
	2.1. Notion	7
	2.2. Opt-Out in Favour of Denmark (and the United Kingdom)	11
	2.3. Sweden: Member State with a Derogation	17
3.	Rules Inapplicable to Member States with a Derogation (Paragraph 2)	21
	3.1. Economic Policy	23
	3.1.1. Economic Policy Coordination (Point a)	23
	3.1.2. Excessive Deficits (Point b)	29
	3.2. Monetary Policy (Point c)	33
	3.2.1. Overview	33
	3.2.2. Objectives and Tasks of the European System of Central Banks	34
	3.2.3. Prudential Supervision of Credit Institutions	36
	3.3. Issue of the Euro (Point d)	41
	3.4. Acts of the ECB (Point e)	45
	3.5. Measures Governing the Use of the Euro (Point f)	49
	3.6. Monetary Agreements Relating to Exchange-Rate Policy (Point g)	52
	3.7. Appointments of Members of the Executive Board of the ECB (Point h)	54
	3.8. Relations with International Financial Institutions (Points i and j)	59
	3.9. European Stability Mechanism and Fiscal Compact	61

Seyad

4. Rights and Obligations Within the ESCB (Paragraph 3)	63
5. Suspension of Voting Rights of Member States with a Derogation (Paragraph 4)	66
5.1. Framework of Multilateral Surveillance	69
5.2. Measures Relating to Excessive Deficits	72
References	

1. Genesis and Overview

Article 3.4 TEU provides one of the EU's objectives, i.e. the Union shall establish **1** an economic and monetary union whose currency is the euro. The **legal foundation of the EMU** was constructed step-by-step in three distinct stages. The initial phase of this process began on 1 July 1990, which also marks the date on which the Directive 88/361 was adopted to liberalise free movement of capital between the MS.[1] The ratification of the Maastricht Treaty (1993) provides the legal basis of the second stage of the EMU project. It provides two alternative dates for the launching of the third and final stage of EMU. If a majority of the MS fulfil the convergence criteria, the EMU was to be launched on 1 January 1998. If the MS missed this deadline, the Treaty provides that the third stage shall be launched on 1 January 1999 even if the required majority is not fulfilled.

To consider the transitory nature of (full) EMU membership, transitional provi- **2** sions were introduced into primary law. The **Treaty of Maastricht** included Article 109k TEC dealing with the MS with a derogation. As the third stage of EMU (single currency) had not yet begun, the Council must decide by qualified majority (and on a recommendation from the Commission) which MS shall have a derogation in the future. The **Treaty of Amsterdam** renumbered the provision to Article 122 TEC but left its content unchanged. Despite its confusing technique of references to other Treaty provisions (paragraph 2), Article 139 TFEU facilitates comprehension compared to its predecessor (third paragraph of Article 109k TEC-Maastricht) and removes some ambiguities, e.g. on what should apply if the Council does not decide on a derogation for an MS that does not yet meet the convergence criteria (paragraph 1 of Article 119k TEC-Maastricht). Because almost one-third of the current MS are still outside the euro area, this treaty provision will not become obsolete in the near future.

Since there was no clear majority of MS that fulfilled the entry requirements, the **3** EU thus missed the first deadline, but launched the **third stage on 1 January 1999** as stipulated in the Treaty. This was a significant date in the history of the EU when the euro, the **single currency,** became the legal tender of 11 of the 15 MS. Since then, the membership of the EU has expanded to 27 with the accession of Croatia on 1 July 2013 and at the same time the monetary union also grew to 19 with the

---

[1] Seyad (1996), p. 273. Council Directive 88/361/*EEC for the implementation of Article 67 of the Treaty*, O.J. L 178/5 (1988).

accession of Lithuania on 1 January 2015[2] and the withdrawal of the United Kingdom on 31 January 2020. Apart from Denmark and formerly the United Kingdom with their special status as MS with an EMU opt-out (→ para 11–16) and others who joined the euro area, the rest of the MS have a derogation (→ para 7–10).

4 A significant feature in the **Lisbon Treaty** is that it simplifies the Treaties by abolishing redundant provisions on the EMU as their legal and practical value diminished with each stage of the construction of the monetary project.[3] Since the third stage of EMU had already started, the Treaty of Lisbon takes the logical procedural adaptation and assumes that any (new) MS outside the single currency is an MS with a derogation, i.e. there is no longer a Council decision determining this status.[4] A decision is only required to abrogate this treaty-based status. Another distinct feature in this Treaty is that it clarifies the relations between the MS of the euro area and outside what is known as MS with a derogation. It clearly demarcates the rules that are applicable to MS of the euro and non-euro area. A positive outcome of making such a precise and clear distinction is that it has facilitated to provide legal clarity on the application of various rules governing the EMU.

5 The title of Chapter 5 of Title VIII of the TFEU ('Transitional Provisions') suggests the relevant **legal provisions may cease to exist if and when all MS adopt the euro as their single currency**. This statement however must be qualified in the light of Article 49 TEU, which declares that '[a]ny European State which respects the values referred to in Article 2 TEU and is committed to promoting them may apply to become a member of the Union'. In other words, one may declare with certainty that this chapter will survive until all the countries located within the geographical limits of the European continent not only join the EU, but also adopt the euro as their single currency. It may be said that this chapter will exist for quite an indefinite period.

6 Within the framework of EMU, Article 139 TFEU reveals its status as a case of primary-law based **differentiated integration**.[5] In the light of Article 139 TFEU, it shows that participation in the third stage of EMU (i.e. the abrogation of the derogatory status) is the aim and duty of every MS. So long as this has not happened, they are—temporarily—granted derogations. Therefore, certain provisions of the Treaty which are relevant to the euro area shall not apply to those

---

[2] As of 1 January 2015, the Eurozone consists of: Austria, Belgium, Cyprus, Estonia, Finland, France, Germany, Greece, Ireland, Italy, Latvia, Lithuania, Luxembourg, Malta, the Netherlands, Portugal, Slovakia, Slovenia, and Spain.

[3] Seyad (2008).

[4] Frankly, the language versions of Article 109k TEC-Maastricht or 122 TEC-Amsterdam were misleading. While the French ('*le Conseil ...décide si des États membres font l'objet d'une dérogation*') and the English version ('the Council shall ... decide whether any ... Member States shall have a derogation') implied that the Council determined the situation, the German version ('*entscheidet der Rat ... ob ... Mitgliedstaaten eine Ausnahmeregelung ... gewährt wird*') suggested that the Council actually *granted* the derogatory status.

[5] Cf. inter alia Böttner (2021), p. 26 et seqq.

Article 139. [Member States with a Derogation] 919

States. Chapter 5 (Articles 139 to 144 TFEU) and Articles 42 to 50 of the ESCB Statute lay down the transitional provisions that characterise this form of flexible integration. Similar to the rules on enhanced cooperation (Article 20 TEU), MS shall not have rights and obligations from legal acts on whose adoption they did not participate.

2. Member States with a Derogation (Paragraph 1)

2.1. Notion

The phrase 'Member States with a derogation' is a complex expression which needs to be briefly elaborated. The EMU is one of the most prominent flagships of the EU in which all MS participate to varying degrees. The requirement to liberalise the free movement of capital (Articles 63 et seqq. TFEU) and the duty to coordinate the economic policies (Articles 120, 121 TFEU) are obligations imposed on all MS, irrespective of whether they join the euro area or not (→ Article 119 TFEU para 87 et seqq. → Article 120 TFEU para 6 et seqq., 11 et seqq.). The free movement of capital is part of the single market with no permanent exceptions granted in favour of any MS. The liberalisation of the **free movement of capital** is an indispensable requirement for the construction of the EMU. This linkage between the single market and the EMU based on the free movement of capital makes it abundantly clear that no MS is completely outside the EMU.[6]

All non-participating MS of the euro project except Denmark (→ para 14–15) are treated as MS with a derogation. An **MS with a derogation means** that it has **not fulfilled the convergence requirements for the adoption of the euro**. They are exempt from some of the provisions which otherwise apply from the beginning of third stage of EMU as laid down in Chapter 5. The MS without an opt-out are legally bound to fulfil the EMU entry conditions and once they do so, their status as MS with a derogation shall be abrogated by a Council decision. Therefore, it would be appropriate to label these States as 'pre-ins' (instead of 'outs'). The first two countries to be labelled as MS with a derogation were Greece and Sweden as they did not fulfil the EMU entry requirements when its founder members were initially selected in 1998.[7] On 1 January 2001, Greece joined the third stage of the EMU without fulfilling the necessary requirements in substance.

The number of MS with a derogation had been gradually shrinking ever since the euro was introduced on 1 January 1999 in 11 countries. **Since the withdrawal of the UK** on 31 January 2020, **there are only eight countries that qualify as MS**

7

8

9

---

[6] Seyad (1995).

[7] Seyad (2002), p. 191.

with a derogation. Any MS joining the Union will have the same status as MS with derogation unless they secure a primary-law based opt-out.[8]

The 2008 global financial crisis and the 2011 fiscal crisis had slowed down the process of enlargement of the euro area.[9] During the fiscal crisis the worst affected were the countries within the Eurozone. The MS outside the Eurozone were relatively less affected by the fiscal crisis, but it has sent a negative message to such countries about the euro project. Consequently, most of the MS with a derogation adopt a **wait and see** attitude to join the Eurozone or not.

10 Based on Article 140.2 (1) TFEU, the **status of MS with a derogation will end** once the Council decides by qualified majority and on a proposal from the Commission that an MS in question fulfils the necessary conditions for participation in the third stage of EMU based on the convergence criteria in Article 140.1 TFEU (→ Article 140 TFEU para 8 et seqq.). While the Council acts in full composition, it can do so only on a recommendation from a qualified majority of the euro area members (Article 140.2 (2) TFEU; → Article 140 TFEU para 29).

2.2. Opt-Out in Favour of Denmark (and the United Kingdom)

11 Any Treaty amendment needs to be ratified by all MS in accordance with their constitutional requirements (Article 48.4 (2) TEU), i.e. by national parliaments, referendum or both as required by the national constitutional requirements. As such, even a single MS had and has the **power to veto** any **changes to the Treaty**.

12 The ratification of the Maastricht Treaty was the most difficult and cumbersome process as some MS considered it to be too intrusive and undermined their sovereignty. The speed and direction of the EU was accelerated by the **Maastricht Treaty** to the extent that it departed from its traditional competence in the field of single market in economic activities to more contentious areas such as EMU, European citizenship, Justice and Home Affairs, CFSP, etc.[10] Such an expansion of the competences of the EU was too much to swallow for certain MS.[11] Not surprisingly, the legality of the Maastricht Treaty was thus challenged in some of the highest constitutional courts as an undue encroachment of national sovereignty.[12] The MS

---

[8] See, most recently, Article 5 of the Act of Accession of Croatia, O.J. L 112/21 (2012): 'Croatia shall participate in the Economic and Monetary Union from the date of accession as a Member State with a derogation within the meaning of Article 139 of the TFEU'.
[9] Allam (2009).
[10] Laurent and Maresceau (1998).
[11] MacCorwick (1995).
[12] Boom (1995), p. 177.

Article 139.   [Member States with a Derogation]

which had a referendum on the Maastricht Treaty were Denmark, Ireland[13] and France.[14]

The Maastricht Treaty was thus a product of **compromise** to ensure that all MS shall ratify it, giving Denmark and the United Kingdom a special status reserving the right to adopt or not the euro as their single currency. There are **two protocols annexed to the Maastricht Treaty** whereby they were granted the right to choose whether to participate in the final stage of EMU.[15] Just before the selection of the founder MS of the Eurozone, Denmark and the United Kingdom notified the Council of the EU that they did not intend to move to third stage of EMU and therefore do not form part of the euro area.

Unlike in Ireland and France, the outcome at the Danish referendum on the Maastricht Treaty was negative.[16] Thus, a second referendum was held with some concessions made to **Denmark** such as an opt-out from the EMU, and with these guarantees the Danes approved it.[17] The special status of Denmark is laid down in **Protocol No. 16** annexed to the Treaties.

According to this Protocol, Denmark is granted an 'exemption'. Technically speaking, Denmark does not count as an MS with a derogation, but it is 'treated as such' under Article 1 of said Protocol.[18] Article 2 modifies Article 140 TFEU in that the procedure abrogating Denmark's exemption can only be initiated by that MS itself. In contrast to other MS with a derogation, while it is still the Council (and the Commission) deciding on the abrogation, they cannot do so without Denmark's explicit consent. This means that Denmark—as opposed the other MS with a derogation—is not obliged to introduce the euro. Under Article 3 of the Protocol, in the event of abrogation of the exemption status, the provisions of Protocol No. 16 shall cease to apply. From a technical point of view, this is a form of simplified treaty amendment (though not set out specifically in Article 48 TEU).

As far as the monetary policy area is concerned, the United Kingdom from the very outset had raised and registered its objection. To secure its consent for the ratification of the Maastricht Treaty, the **United Kingdom** was given an opt-out

---

[13] At the referendum on the Eleventh Amendment of the Constitution of Ireland, held in Ireland on 18 June 1992, a majority of 68.7% voted in favour. The turnout at the referendum was around 57.31%.

[14] At the French Maastricht Treaty referendum, held on 20 September 1992, the yes side won with a small margin of 51.1%, but the turnout was higher than in Ireland, around 69.7%.

[15] See now Protocol No. 15 on certain provisions relating to the United Kingdom and Northern Ireland and Protocol No. 16 on certain provisions relating to Denmark respectively.

[16] The first referendum was held on 2 June 1992 and had a turnout of 82.9%, but failed to secure the required majority to ratify the Maastricht Treaty.

[17] A second referendum was held on 18 May 1993 where 56.8% voted in favour of the renegotiated treaty. A further referendum held on 28 September 2000 rejected a Danish membership of the eurozone: 46.8% voted in favour and 53.2% rejected joining the euro (turnout 87.6%).

[18] Interestingly, English ('exemption' instead of 'derogation') and German ('*Freistellung*' instead of '*Ausnahmeregelung*') use different terms, while French ('*dérogation*') uses the same term for Denmark's status and the MS with a derogation.

allowing it to decide on a later date to join or not the EMU. The status was secured by Protocol No. 15 annexed to the Treaties.

With the dawn of the **Brexit Day** on 31 January 2020, the UK withdrew from the EU. Since the end of the transition period on 31 December 2020, it is treated as a **third country**. The current relationship is governed by the EU-UK Trade and Cooperation Agreement (→ Article 26 TFEU para 87 et seqq.).[19]

2.3. Sweden: Member State with a Derogation

17 Sweden joined the EU together with Finland and Austria in 1995, but unlike the other two countries, it is still not part of the euro area.[20] When the EMU was launched in 1999, Sweden had **not made the necessary changes to its laws on national bank legislation** (*Sveriges Riksbank* Act) as required by EU law and also failed to link its currency, the Swedish *krona*, to the ERM for a period of two years, another EMU entry requirement. Sweden is therefore labelled as an MS with a derogation.[21]

18 In the accession agreement to the EU, Sweden did not have any reservations in relation to joining EMU. When Sweden joined the EU in 1995, it also signed up to become a full member of EMU as soon as it fulfilled the convergence rules.[22] Any such referendum on the issue of EMU legally would be rather superfluous.[23] Since **Sweden did not secure an opt-out** in its accession agreement to remain out of the euro area, it held a **non-binding referendum** on 14 September 2003, asking the Swedes 'Do you think that Sweden should introduce the euro as currency?' A majority of the voters clearly expressed their disapproval to exchange their national currency with the euro. From a legal perspective, there is in fact no requirement for Sweden to seek a fresh mandate from its people to join EMU.

19 If Sweden is to hold another euro referendum, it is better not to formulate the question asking the voters whether they wish to join the EMU or not. The question that should be put to the voter is 'Should Sweden opt-out from participation in the euro area?' If the outcome of the referendum were in favour of such an opt-out, then it would become necessary to negotiate another **Treaty amendment in order to grant a specific derogation to Sweden from EMU**. There is no such precedent set in the EU, but such a drastic decision to hold a referendum would be greeted with relief or regret by other MS and the Swedish people at large.

20 Sweden had many opportunities to secure an opt-out from EMU after joining the EU, e.g. during the IGCs which culminated in the Treaties of Amsterdam, Nice and

---

[19] Seyad (2020), p. 182.
[20] Seyad (1995), p. 288.
[21] Seyad (1997a), p. 1.
[22] Treaty concerning the accession of the Kingdom of Norway, the Republic of Austria, the Republic of Finland and the Kingdom of Sweden to the European Union, O.J. C 241/9.
[23] Taggart (2005).

Article 139. [Member States with a Derogation]

Lisbon, respectively. Since the adoption of the Maastricht Treaty, it is almost a precedent for various MS to demand an opt-out from some policy area as a precondition to ratify such treaty amendments. During these negotiations there is no evidence to suggest Sweden raised the issue of its future membership in the euro area. As such the presumption is that Sweden is **still politically committed to join the euro** area and until then to remain an MS with a derogation.

3. Rules Inapplicable to Member States with a Derogation (Paragraph 2)

There are a host of exclusionary rules set out in Chapter 5. They all apply to MS with a derogation. These rules have a bearing on the chapter on economic policy (Articles 120 to 126 TFEU), monetary policy (Articles 127 to 133 TFEU), institutional provisions (Articles 134 and 135 TFEU) and provisions specific to MS whose currency is the euro (Articles 136 to 138 TFEU) respectively. Article 139.2 (1) TFEU provides that certain of these provisions shall not apply to MS with a derogation and consequently Article 139.2 (2) TFEU provides that in those provisions, 'Member States' shall be read as 'Member States whose currency is the euro'. Moreover, voting rights of MS with a derogation are suspended for the cases listed in paragraphs 2 and 4 (Article 139.4 TFEU; → para 54 et seqq.). The rules applicable to euro area or non-euro area members thus must be determined on a **combined reading of the provisions on (exclusive) applicability of rules 'to Member States whose currency is the euro' and exemption of rules to non-euro area States**, either by referring to 'Member States with a derogation' or by excluding the applicability of rules to those States, as does Article 139 TFEU. The following comments will be limited to highlight the significance of exclusionary rules in the non-exhaustive list of Article 139 TFEU.

21

Non-applicability means that MS with a derogation are not entitled or obliged by acts on whose adoption they have not participated. This is similar to the rule of Article 327 TFEU in the context of enhanced cooperation that participating and non-participating States may not impede each other.[24] In a more general way, since all MS—regardless of their participation in the euro—are bound by the duty to **sincere cooperation** (Article 4.3 TEU), MS may not act against legal acts or prevent their effective application although they are not bound by them.

22

3.1. Economic Policy

3.1.1. Economic Policy Coordination (Point a)

There are comprehensive and binding rules in the Lisbon Treaty for the establishment of a monetary union, but no such corresponding rules are found in the field of

23

---

[24] Cf. Böttner (2021), p. 196 et seqq.

economic policy. However, to facilitate the proper functioning of the monetary union, the Treaty lays down a set of less-binding rules to facilitate the **monitoring and surveillance of the economic policies of the MS,** but applying more strictly to euro countries (→ Article 120 TFEU para 18 → Article 121 TFEU para 23 et seqq., 26 et seqq.).

24 The MS are required to conduct their economic policies in a manner that will promote a wide range of objectives as set out in Article 3 TEU, which includes the establishment of EMU (Article 3.4 TEU; → Article 3 TEU para 48-50). Even if an MS is not part of the euro area, it is required to pursue its **economic policies which will not be detrimental to the proper functioning of the EMU**. The aim of this objective is quite obvious as it is a mandatory requirement for all MS to fully participate in its internal market except in the case of an MS which has secured a transitional arrangement in some policy areas in its accession agreement.

25 The EMU and the internal market cannot be viewed in isolation as both are inter-related. Their stability can only be guaranteed if both function harmoniously. A simple illustration of this **inter-dependence** is in the field of free movement of capital, which forms an indispensable foundation of both the EMU and internal market (→ para 7).

26 Although all MS are required to regard their economic policies as a **matter of common concern** (Article 121.1 TFEU;→ Article 121 TFEU para 11 et seq.), the non-euro States are less susceptible to pressure from the Commission and Council. To effectively coordinate the economic policies of the MS, the Council on a recommendation from the Commission shall formulate a draft for the broad guidelines of the economic policies of the MS and the Union (Article 121.1 TFEU; → Article 121 TFEU para 15 et seq.).

27 This must be read in conjunction with Article 136.1 point (b) TFEU, which allows the Council to set out **economic policy guidelines for the euro area MS**, while ensuring that they are compatible with those adopted for the whole of the Union. These euro-area specific guidelines are adopted by the Council members of the euro area (Article 136.2 TFEU). Therefore, while the overall competence in the field of economic policy is with the MS (arg.: Article 5.1 TFEU), specific measures shall apply to the euro area. Since **those guidelines do not apply to MS with a derogation**, those MS shall not take part in their adoption (Article 139.2 point (a) TFEU).[25]

28 Such exclusion may be justified as evidenced by the successive fiscal crises; **closer economic coordination** is of paramount importance particularly within the Eurozone. Evidently, most of the legal measures adopted in the light of the fiscal crisis were specifically directed towards the MS of the Eurozone.

---

[25] Louis and Lastra (2013), p. 57.

3.1.2. Excessive Deficits (Point b)

Similar to the provisions on economic policy, there are also **rules on fiscal matters** 29
applicable to all MS, again with more stringent rules applicable to the euro area.
Article 126 TFEU dealing with fiscal policy is one of the comprehensive provisions in the Lisbon Treaty. The procedural framework of this Treaty provision was further clarified and elaborated by the adoption of the SGP as amended in 2005 and 2011 (→ Supplement to Title VIII: Fiscal Union para 2, 5; → Article 121 TFEU para 47 et seqq.).

Article 126 TFEU aims to **prevent MS from pursuing expansive fiscal policies** 30 **which may damage the stability and proper functioning of the EMU**. A control mechanism is put in place where the Commission plays a major role as enforcer of fiscal discipline in the MS. It provides for naming and shaming of the habitual offenders of the fiscal rules allowing the Commission to make public the names of MS which have an excessive deficit.

The next stage after disclosing to the public the name of MS who have breached 31 the fiscal rules is for the Commission to recommend to the Council to take further measures to **impose sanctions** (Articles 126.9 and 126.11 TFEU) such as to invite the EIB to reconsider its lending policy towards the MS concerned, to require the MS to make a non-interest bearing deposit and if still in breach as last resort to convert such deposit into a fine. The **deterrent and punitive measures** adopted beyond naming and shaming of an MS for violating the fiscal rules **do not apply to MS with a derogation** (Article 139.2 point (b) TFEU). The exclusion of the imposition of sanctions on MS outside the Eurozone is justifiable as the level of fiscal discipline required is less rigid than those applied to the euro countries.

This derogation does not cover the entire excessive deficit procedure, but only 32 the imposition of sanctions on an MS. The **basic obligation to avoid an excessive deficit** (Articles 126.1 and 126.2 TFEU) also **binds** unreservedly **any MS** with a derogation. This is confirmed by Article 140.1 (1), second indent, TFEU, which requires MS with a derogation to show a sustainable government financial position in the form of non-existence of an excessive deficit under Article 126.6 TFEU (→ Article 140 TFEU para 17–20).

3.2. Monetary Policy (Point c)

3.2.1. Overview

The main actor in the formulation and implementation of the monetary policy 33 within the Eurozone is the **ECB** (Article 127.2 TFEU).[26] The ECB has a legal personality (Article 282.3 sentence 1 TFEU; → Article 282 TFEU para 10) with power to sue and liable to be sued. It is the legal (and meanwhile also economic)

---

[26] Cf. Berger and de Haan (2010), p. 1 et seqq.

guardian of the euro and the powerful monetary authority of the euro area. Since all matters relating to monetary policy within the euro area are formulated, adopted and implemented by the ECB, such **policy measures also have repercussions beyond its territorial limits** especially in the MS outside the euro area. Hence, there are various mechanisms created for the purpose of coordination and cooperation between the ECB and its counterparts in the non-euro countries.

3.2.2. Objectives and Tasks of the European System of Central Banks

34   Article 127 TFEU assigns a long list of powers and functions to the ESCB. The primary task is to keep in check the inflation within the euro area and thereby **maintain price stability**. Apart from its main task to ensure the stability of the euro, some of the other tasks of the ECB are to define and implement monetary policy, to conduct foreign exchange operations, to hold and manage the foreign reserves of the MS, the operation of euro payment systems, known as the **TARGET** (Trans-European Automated Real-time Gross Settlement Express Transfer System).

35   Article 282.1 TFEU states that the ECB and all national central banks form the European System of Central Banks, but only the ECB and the euro area NCBs form the Eurosystem. Moreover, Article 139.3 TFEU in combination with Chapter IX of the ESCB Statute render most of the substantial provisions inapplicable to non-euro area NCBs. Moreover, Article 282.4, sentence 2, TFEU now explicitly underlines that MS whose currency is not the euro, and their NCBs, shall retain their powers in monetary matters.[27] Therefore, generally speaking, monetary policy by the ESCB is monetary policy by the Eurosystem. Since the ECB is the **monetary authority of the euro area**, its powers and functions are limited to this monetary area (EMU) and not apply to MS with a derogation.

3.2.3. Prudential Supervision of Credit Institutions

36   The Lisbon Treaty gives competence to the ECB in the field of prudential supervision of credit institutions and the **stability of the financial system**. Article 127.5 TFEU provides that the ECB shall contribute to the smooth conduct of policies by the competent authorities relating to **prudential supervision**. Such a competence can be exercised by the ECB only in relation to the activities of the competent authorities located within the euro area.

37   One of the factors that contributed to the 2008 financial crisis and the 2011 fiscal crisis was the shortcomings in the **supervisory mechanism of the EU's banking market**.[28] The laws adopted to liberalise the banking market focus only on the

---

[27] See already before: Article 43.2 of the ESCB Statute-Maastricht (now: Article 42.2 of the ESCB Statute-Lisbon).

[28] European Commission, DG Economic and Financial Affairs, *Economic Crisis in Europe: Causes, Consequences and Responses*, European Economy 7/2009. See Seyad (2015).

deregulation and integration of the market by allowing the banks to provide financial services across the Union either directly or through the establishment of branches in other MS.[29] They provided for home country control whereby banks operating in other MS were subject to supervision by the home state banking regulators. Although the banking law provides for **closer cooperation between the supervisory authorities of the MS**, the financial crisis exposed the lack of such cooperation. The problem associated with supervisory deficiency either due to lack of expertise or non-willingness to cooperate could have been rectified if the relevant laws had provided for a pan-European banking regulator.[30]

After the fiscal crisis, this deficiency was identified and to some extent rectified by launching the **Banking Union** (→ Supplement to Title VIII: Fiscal Union para 13).[31] The fiscal crisis exposed the insidious nexus between the unmanageable sovereign debts of the MS and the stability of the banking market. To prevent another financial crisis developing within the euro area, the EU decided to establish the Banking Union, which consists of three distinct but inter-related pillars (→ Supplement to Title VIII: Banking Union para 2 to 10). It provides for a Single Supervisory Mechanism, a Single Resolution Fund (IGA on the SRF of 2014, as amended in 2021[32]) and to finally elevate the national deposit guarantee scheme to a pan-European model.[33] **38**

The **Single Supervisory Mechanism** to supervise the banks applies not only within the euro area, but also to non-euro countries provided they expressly make a declaration to that effect (Article 7 of Council Regulation 1024/2013; Articles 13 and 14.3 IGA on the SRF; → Supplement to Title VIII: Banking Union para 174 et seqq.).[34] Bulgaria and Croatia joined European banking supervision through close cooperation in October 2020. For members of the euro area, the EU adopted a Council Regulation to give effect to the objectives of Article 127.6 TFEU.[35] This Treaty provision provides that such an act could only be adopted by special legislative procedure and unanimity in Council. The Regulation confers wide **39**

---

[29] Seyad (1997b), p. 67.

[30] Seyad (2001), p. 203; see, in general, Lannoo (2003).

[31] Seyad (2013); for an overview, see also the contributions in Beck (Ed.) (2012).

[32] Cf. the Intergovernmental Agreement *on the transfer and mutualisation of contributions to the Single Resolution Fund* of 21 May 2014 (IGA on the SRF, available at https://data.consilium.europa.eu/doc/document/ST-8457-2014-INIT/en/pdf) as amended by the Agreement *amending the Agreement on the transfer and mutualisation of contributions to the Single Resolution Fund* of 27 January 2021 (available at https://www.consilium.europa.eu/media/48068/agreement-amending-the-intergovernmental-agreement-on-the-transfer-and-mutualisation-of-contributions-to-the-single-resolution-fund-27-january-2021_en.pdf).

[33] Niknejad (2014).

[34] See ECB Decision 2014/434/EU *on the close cooperation with the national competent authorities of participating Member States whose currency is not the euro* (ECB/2014/5), O.J. 198/7 (2014).

[35] Council Regulation (EU) No. 1024/2013 *conferring specific tasks on the European Central Bank concerning policies relating to the prudential supervision of credit institutions*, O.J. L 287/63 (2013), O.J. L 287/63 (2013).

powers and functions (SSM) to the ECB such as issuing and withdrawal of banking authorisation, monitor own funds requirements, large exposure limits, etc. The ECB to start in capitals or the SSM will be the supervisor for all banks (especially the significant banks) within the euro area. Even MS outside the euro area can sign up for the SSM and in that case their banks too will be subject to supervision by the ECB.

40 Since point (c) of Article 139.2 TFEU does not exclude paragraph 6 of Article 127 TFEU (and neither is the latter restricted to the euro area), one may wonder why the general application of the SSM has been restricted to euro area MS (with the option of close cooperation). This may be explained by the fact that under point (e) of Article 139.2 TFEU, acts of the ECB shall not apply to MS with a derogation and that paragraph 5 of Article 127 TFEU, which provides that the ESCB shall contribute to the smooth conduct of policies pursued by the competent authorities, is not applied to non-euro area MS either. Thus, **ECB supervision over national competent authorities could not be effective in MS with a derogation.**[36]

3.3. Issue of the Euro (Point d)

41 As the monetary authority of the euro area, the **ECB** has the **exclusive right to authorise the issue of the euro bank notes** (Article 128.1 TFEU). Once printed, such banknotes are put into circulation by the ECB and the national central banks of the euro area. The **national central banks** of the MS of the euro area may issue **euro coins with the permission of the ECB** (Article 128.2 TFEU). The volume of euro coins that a national central bank proposed to put into the market should be approved in advance by the ECB.

42 There is no prohibition on the MS outside the euro area to freely use the euro, but the ECB shall not take any responsibility for any loss or otherwise caused by such usage. There are **four entities or principalities which are not part of the EU** but have special relations with some MS of the euro area. These entities or principalities had been using the currency of such MS before they adopted the euro. Hence, special agreements had to be signed by the relevant parties to enable such entities and principalities to use the euro. Four such entities have adopted the euro as their official currency: the Principality of Monaco,[37] the Republic of San Marino,[38] the

---

[36] Cf. Kämmerer (2013), p. 835; Wymeersch (2014), p. 18.

[37] Commission Decision 2012/23/EU of 28 November 2011 *on the conclusion, on behalf of the European Union of the Monetary Agreement between the European Union and the Principality of Monaco*, O.J. C 23/1 (2012).

[38] Monetary Agreement between the European Union and the Republic of San Marino, O.J. C 121/1 (2012).

Vatican City State[39] and the Principality of Andorra.[40] Before the introduction of the euro, Monaco used the French franc and San Marino and the Vatican used the Italian lira. Andorra, which is a principality located on the French-Spanish border, was using the Spanish peseta and the French franc.

Some of the MS of the euro area have certain colonial possessions which were using their replaced national currencies. Examples are certain French **overseas territories**, which are in fact not part of the EU. They are however authorised to use the euro as their official currency through special monetary agreements with the EU such as Saint-Pierre-et-Miquelon islands close to the eastern coast of Canada and the island of Mayotte in the Indian Ocean.[41]

Depending on the nature of each agreement, some entities and principalities are authorised to mint and issue limited amounts of euro coins with their own design on the national side but prohibited from issuing bank notes. There are some newly independent States such as **Kosovo and Montenegro** which previously used the German mark and now use the euro. They use the **euro as a de facto domestic currency** as they have no specific agreements with the EU.

43

44

3.4. Acts of the ECB (Point e)

The Lisbon Treaty gave birth to two more Union institutions to the existing five institutions and one of them is the ECB (Article 13.2 TEU; → Article 13 TEU para 30). As the sole authority responsible for the monetary policy of the euro area and the guardian of the euro currency (→ para 26), it was essential that, with the entry into force of the Lisbon Treaty, the **legal standing of the ECB** has been elevated to that of an **institution of the EU**.

The ECB also acts as a legislator with power to adopt different kinds of laws to carry out its functions as the monetary authority of the euro area.[42] To carry out its multitude of tasks, the **ECB is empowered to adopt legal acts** such as regulations, decisions or issue opinion or recommendations (Article 132.1 TFEU). The first two categories of legal acts are hard laws and strictly binding whereas the other two legal acts are soft laws having only persuasive value (→ Article 132 TFEU para 1 et seqq.).

During the height of the 2008 financial crisis and 2011 fiscal crisis, the ECB adopted several legal acts both hard and soft laws to contain such crises. Apart from the power to adopt such legal acts, the ECB also has the power to **impose sanctions**

45

46

47

---

[39] Commission Decision 2012/355/EU of 2 July 2012 *updating the Annex to the Monetary Agreement between the European Union and the Vatican City State*, O.J. L 174/24 (2012).

[40] Council Decision 2004/548/EC of 11 May 2004 *on the position to be taken by the Community regarding an agreement concerning the monetary relations with the Principality of Andorra*, O.J. L 244/24 (2004).

[41] Council Decision 1999/95/EC of 31 December 1998 *concerning the monetary arrangements in the French territorial communities of Saint-Pierre-et-Miquelon and Mayotte*, O.J. L 30/29 (1999).

[42] Smits (2003).

on any entity if they breach them (Article 132.3 TFEU; → Article 132 TFEU para 48 et seqq.).[43]

48   Any hard or soft law adopted by the ECB does not apply to MS with a derogation. Since the national central banks of **MS with a derogation are responsible for their own monetary policy**, they are not obliged to comply with any decisions issued by the ECB.

3.5. Measures Governing the Use of the Euro (Point f)

49   There was no specific legal basis in the Maastricht Treaty to adopt measures to facilitate the use of the euro. One of the legal uncertainties in the introduction of the euro was the **impact** it might have **on the financial contracts denominated in the national currencies** which were also replaced by the euro.[44]

50   There was an appeal from the financial market to have more specific and clearer set of legal rules to guarantee the **continuity of contracts** after the changeover to EMU. Such a demand for legal certainty was justified in view of the sensitiveness of the market.[45] The market concern was that the new currency may be potentially raised as an excuse to invoke the principle of frustration to get out of loss-making financial contracts, thereby igniting a flood of litigation. Since there was no specific legal basis in the Maastricht Treaty for the adoption of such a legal act, it had to be invoked under ex-Article 235 TEC (Article 352 TFEU).[46]

51   The Lisbon Treaty rectified this legal vacuum by **incorporating Article 133 TFEU to adopt legal measures for the use of the euro**. The Council and the EP shall use the ordinary legislative procedure to adopt such legislation, but in the Council the voting rights will be limited to MS of the euro area. There are several legal acts adopted based on this Treaty provision ranging from cross-border transport of euro cash,[47] issuing of euro coins[48] to authentication of euro coins.[49] Since these legal measures are based on Article 133 TFEU, they are inapplicable to MS with a derogation.

---

[43] Regulation ECB/1999/4 of 23 September 1999 *on the powers of the European Central Bank to impose sanctions*, O.J. L 264/21 (1999).

[44] Wölker (1996), p. 1126.

[45] Seyad (1997b), p. 67.

[46] Council Regulation (EC) No. 1103/97 *on certain provisions relating to the introduction of the euro. It is the first regulation adopted dealing with the euro*, O.J. L 131/1 (1998).

[47] Parliament/Council Regulation (EU) No. 1214/2011 *on the professional cross-border transport of euro cash by road between euro-area Member States*, O.J. L 316/1 (2001).

[48] Parliament/Council Regulation (EU) No. 651/2012 *on the issuance of euro coins*, O.J. L 201/135 (2012).

[49] Parliament/Council Regulation (EU) No. 1210/2010 *concerning authentication of euro coins and handling of euro coins unfit for circulation*, O.J. L 339/1 (2010).

Article 139. [Member States with a Derogation]

3.6. Monetary Agreements Relating to Exchange-Rate Policy (Point g)

There are several kinds of **international agreements** which the EU may conclude based on Article 219.3 TFEU with third countries, regional organisations or international financial institutions.[50] In agreements such as to adopt a common commercial policy in relation to third countries, the EU would seek to speak with one voice on behalf of its MS. There are different procedures and decision-making process prescribed to enter into different kinds of international agreements such as ordinary legislative procedure to conclude trade agreements or special legislative procedure in the field of trade in cultural and audio-visual services. 52

In the field of monetary agreements and other measures relating to exchange-rate policy, the overall competence to enter into related international agreements are vested on the **Council representing MS of the euro area** (Article 219 TFEU). The Ministers representing the MS with a derogation have no voting rights if the agreement involves for example agreements on an exchange rate system for the euro in relation to the currencies of third states. Such agreements are concluded by the Council when they are initiated either on a recommendation from the ECB or on a recommendation of the Commission after consulting the ECB. There is no binding effect of such agreements for MS with a derogation. 53

3.7. Appointments of Members of the Executive Board of the ECB (Point h)

The ESCB is governed by the **decision-making bodies of the ECB**, i.e. the Governing Council, the Executive Board and the General Council. The Governing Council is composed of the governors of the national central banks of the euro area countries whereas the governors of the national central banks of all MS of the EU are represented in the General Council. They are not appointed by the Union or MS, but occupy the seat by virtue of their position as members of the national central banks. 54

In both the Governing and General Council, some or all the six members of the Executive Board are represented. However, the President, Vice President and the four **members of the Executive Board are appointed by the European Council** acting by a qualified majority (Article 283.2 (2) TFEU). Before the Lisbon Treaty they were appointed by consensus. 55

The Executive Board of the ESCB is responsible for the effective enforcement of the monetary policy formulated by the Governing Council (Article 12.2 of the ESCB Statute). Since the ambit of such **monetary policy is limited to the euro area**, the MS with a derogation do not have a say in the appointment of the 56

---

[50] Under Article 219.3 TFEU, 'the Council, on a recommendation from the Commission and after consulting the European Central Bank, shall decide the arrangements for the negotiation and for the conclusion of [...] agreements [...] concerning monetary or foreign exchange regime matters [...] to be negotiated by the Union with one or more third States or international organisations'. This procedure derogates the rules set out in Article 218 TFEU.

members of the powerful Executive Board (Article 42.3 in conjunction with Article 11.2 (3) of the ESCB Statute). It is the European Council in the composition of the **Heads of State and Government of the euro area** who appoint the members of the Executive Board (Article 283.2 TFEU in conjunction with Article 11.2 of the ESCB Statute).

57 Article 283.2 TFEU specifically declares that persons of recognised standing and professional experience in monetary or banking matters are eligible for appointment as members of the Executive Board. It further declares that only nationals of MS may be members of the Executive Board. Moreover, in the light of Article 42.3 of the ESCB Statute, Article 11.2 (3) of the ESCB Statute provides that **only nationals of 'Member States whose currency is the euro' may be members of the Executive Board**.

58 In contrast, the Governors or their representatives of the national central banks of *all* MS of the EU occupy a seat in the **General Council** of the ECB (Article 141 TFEU and Article 44 of the ESCB Statute). In other words, the General Council as a body of the ECB includes representatives of the 19 euro area NCBs and the 8 non-euro area NCBs as part of the ESCB (Article 282.1 sentence 1 TFEU), but the MS with a derogation do not participate in the desisions on the monetary union within the Eurosystem (Article 282.1 sentence 2 TFEU). It is designated as 'a third decision-making body of the European Central Bank' without having substantial decision-making powers (Article 141 TFEU; → Article 141 TFEU para 16 et seqq.) and as such conceived to be of a transitional character ('as long as there are Member States with a derogation') (→ Article 141 TFEU para 9).

3.8. Relations with International Financial Institutions (Points i and j)

59 The EU aims not only to make the euro as its single currency, but also to make it freely convertible and internationally competitive currency. To promote and secure a strong and firm stand in the **international monetary system**, the Council representing the MS whose currency is the euro shall take necessary measures especially to effectively interact with international financial institutions such as the IMF or the World Bank.

60 There are two additional areas included in Article 138 TFEU which were not found in the previous treaties. One of the additional features relates to decisions establishing **common positions on matters of particular interest for the EMU** within the competent international financial institutions and conferences (Article 138.1 TFEU). The other innovative feature relates to adoption of measures to ensure **unified representation within international financial institutions and conferences** (Article 138.2 TFEU). Any such decision either to ensure a uniform representation in an international financial institution or conference shall be adopted by the Council on a proposal from the European Commission after consulting the ECB. In such a decision-making process, the Ministers representing the MS outside the euro area shall have no voting rights.

Article 139. [Member States with a Derogation]

3.9. European Stability Mechanism and Fiscal Compact

In addition to the architecture provided for by the Treaties, the EMU has been supplemented by international treaties concluded between parts of the Union's MS. One of these elements is the **European Stability Mechanism** (ESM). It is established by an international treaty concluded between the euro area MS. To this end, Article 136 TFEU has been amended by adding a new paragraph 3.[51] In the eyes of the CJEU, however, this amendment, which allows 'the Member States whose currency is the euro' to 'establish a stability mechanism to be activated if indispensable to safeguard the stability of the euro area as a whole', is only of declaratory nature ($\rightarrow$ Supplement to Title VIII: TESM para 6).[52] In line with the explicit wording of Article 136.3 TFEU, membership in the ESM is restricted to euro area MS. Based on Article 2.1 TESM, any EU State can become a member once the Council has abrogated its derogation in line with Article 140.2 TFEU. In December 2018, the European Commission proposed transferring the ESM into EU law ($\rightarrow$ Supplement to Title VIII: TESM para 145 et seqq.).[53] While Article 8 of the proposed Regulation provides that the Regulation 'shall be binding in its entirety and directly applicable in *all* Member States',[54] Article 2.1 of the proposed EMF Statute restricts *membership* in the EMF to the euro area MS. Under Article 2.2 of the EMF Statute, any MS (with a derogation) whose derogation has been abrogated shall become an EMF member as from the date of entry into force of the respective decision. Thus, as opposed to the current ESM, membership in the proposed EMF would be *automatic* upon adoption of the single currency.[55]

61

As a second new architectural element, 25 EU Member States (all but Czechia and Croatia) are Contracting Parties to the **Treaty on Stability, Coordination and Governance** in the Economic and Monetary Union (TSCG). This treaty intends to foster budgetary discipline and is open for participation by all EU States. However, many of its provisions repeat what is already stipulated in EU law ($\rightarrow$ Supplement to Title VIII: Fiscal Union para 5). Under Article 14.5 TSCG, the Treaty shall apply to MS with a derogation or Denmark, respectively, if they have signed up to the Treaty, once their derogation has been abrogated, unless the Contracting Party concerned declares its intention to be bound at an earlier date by all or part of the provisions in Titles III and IV of the Treaty. Only then can a State be subject to proceedings before the CJEU for failure to implement a debt brake into national law, including the imposition of financial sanctions. Title V of that Treaty on the

62

---

[51] European Council Decision 2011/199/EU, O.J. L 91 (2011).

[52] Case C-370/12, *Pringle* (CJEU 27 November 2012) para 184.

[53] European Commission, *Proposal for a Council Regulation on the establishment of the European Monetary Fund*, COM(2017) 827 final and Annex to the Proposal for a Council Regulation on the establishment of the European Monetary Fund, COM(2017) 827 final Annex.

[54] Emphasis added.

[55] Manger-Nestler and Böttner (2019), p. 49 et seq.

Euro Summit (Article 12) and the Interparliamentary Conference (Article 13) will apply directly upon membership, irrespective of the status as euro area MS.

4. Rights and Obligations Within the ESCB (Paragraph 3)

63   The Treaties together with the ESCB Statute provide the legal framework of the ESCB and the ECB (Article 129.2 TFEU). As mentioned above (→ para 35), Article 282.1 TFEU distinguishes between the ESCB (ECB and *all* NCBs) and the Eurosystem (ECB and euro area NCBs). The rights and obligations of the MS of the euro area and outside it within the framework of the ESCB are obviously not the same. Under Article 139.3 TFEU, **MS with a derogation** and their NCBs are **excluded from certain rights and obligations within the ESCB** under Chapter IX of the Statute (Articles 42 to 50) entitled 'Transitional and other provisions for the ESCB'.

64   More precisely, Article 42.1 of the Statute lists a number of provisions of the Statute which shall not apply to MS with a derogation. **Some of these exclusions mirror exceptions under Article 139.2 TFEU.** For example, in the field of international cooperation, the ECB shall decide how the ESCB shall be represented, and the ECB may participate in international monetary institutions (Article 6 of the ESCB Statute), but this international cooperation shall not bind the MS with a derogation and their NCBs. Under Article 14.3 (in conjunction with Article 42.1), NCBs from non-euro area MS are not bound by guidelines and instructions of the ECB. NCBs from MS with a derogation are not entitled to issue euro banknotes (Article 16 in conjunction with Article 42.1). The rules relating to the allocation of monetary income of national central banks, the allocation of net profits and losses of the ECB are inapplicable to MS with a derogation (Articles 32 and 33 in conjunction with Article 42.1).

65   Furthermore, the remaining articles of that Chapter deal with the special status of those MS, especially via the **General Council** (Articles 44 et seqq. of the ESCB Statute). As mentioned (→ para 58), Article 141 TFEU and the ESCB Statute establish the General Council as a third decision-making body of the ECB as long as there are MS with a derogation. It shall facilitate the transition of MS with a derogation to the third stage of EMU.

5. Suspension of Voting Rights of Member States with a Derogation (Paragraph 4)

66   Article 139.4 TFEU declares that the **voting rights of MS with a derogation shall be suspended in the Council** in relation to decision making in areas covered under Article 139.2 TFEU (→ para 17 et seqq.). It further **suspends their voting rights in relation to multilateral surveillance** (→ para 57–59) and excessive deficit procedure (→ para 60–62). The distortion created in the Council in relation to the system of decision making and voting rights is a **by-product of the multi-speed Europe**, a

precedent set by the Maastricht Treaty. With the launching of EMU in 1999, the uniform method of voting in the Council in monetary matters, too, was sacrificed. MS which are not affected by a measure (because the underlying rules are inapplicable to them) should not be entitled to vote on these very issues. However, the fact that MS with a derogation are deprived of the voting rights does not necessarily mean they will be barred from taking part in the proceedings of the Council unless it sits as a Eurogroup meeting within the meaning of Articles 136 to 138 TFEU respectively.

All legal acts which deal with the EMU are adopted in the Council **without counting the votes of the non-euro countries** as specifically set out in Articles 139.2, 3 and 4 (2) respectively. Similar to differentiated integration through enhanced cooperation (Article 330 TFEU), all members of the Council may take part in its deliberations, but only euro area MS shall be eligible to vote. The voting rights of an MS with a derogation is *suspended* until its derogation is abrogated. Accordingly, the **qualified majority** in the Council is calculated based on Article 238.3 point (a) TFEU, according to which a qualified majority shall be defined as at least 55% of the members of the Council representing the participating MS, comprising at least 65% of the population of these States. This corresponds to the ordinary requirement for a qualified majority in the Council (see Article 16.3 TEU), but limited to the participating MS.

67

However, there are certain provisions in the Treaty that touch upon the EMU which specifically require that all MS of the EU should adopt the relevant act. For example, legal acts adopted under Article 127.6 TFEU conferring specific tasks to the ECB in relation to the prudential supervision of credit institutions and the stability of the financial system were adopted unanimously by all MS of the EU.[56]

68

5.1. Framework of Multilateral Surveillance

Although Article 121 TFEU generally refers to the economic policies of the MS and of the Union, its scope of application should be restricted to MS within the Eurozone under Article 139.2 TFEU. Article 121.1 TFEU requires MS of the EU to regard their economic policies as a matter of common concern and coordinate them within the Council. A procedural mechanism is devised to monitor economic developments in all the MS and in the Union by way of adoption of Council guidelines. A multilateral surveillance mechanism is put in place to achieve this objective. It is essential to highlight that the Council shall formulate a draft for the **broad guidelines of the economic policies** which are addressed to all MS and the Union, while for those which have introduced the Euro currency Article 136 TFEU or secondary legislation enacted thereof may contain further obligations

69

---

[56] Council Regulation (EU) No. 1024/2013 *conferring specific tasks on the European Central Bank concerning policies relating to the prudential supervision of credit institutions*, O.J. L 287/63 (2013).

(Article 139.1 point (a) TFEU; → para 18–21; → Article 121 TFEU para 6, 21). It shall thereafter report its findings to the European Council.

70   Under Article 121.3 TFEU, to ensure closer coordination of economic policies and sustained **convergence of the economic performances of the MS**, the Council shall, based on reports submitted by the Commission, **monitor economic developments in each of the MS** (i.e. also non-euro MS) and in the Union as well as the consistency of economic policies with the broad guidelines referred to in paragraph 2, and regularly carry out an overall assessment.

71   If the economic policy pursued by an MS is not consistent with economic guidelines set by the Council or risk jeopardising the proper functioning of EMU, an **early warning system** will be alerted at an early stage so it could take immediate corrective action to prevent the budget deficit becoming excessive. As for the recommendations issued under Article 121.4 TFEU, MS with a derogation shall only be excluded from voting in the Council insofar as the vote concerns an MS whose currency is the euro. If an MS with a derogation is subject of a vote, all MS, including those with a derogation, are eligible to vote. The same result can be derived from Articles 136.1 point (b) and 136.2 TFEU, according to which the Council, by vote of the euro area members, shall adopt measures specific to those MS whose currency is the euro in the field of economic surveillance under Article 121 TFEU.

5.2. Measures Relating to Excessive Deficits

72   Article 126.1 TFEU expressly prohibits all MS to have excessive deficit. The competence to **monitor the budget deficit** of the MS is assigned to the Commission and the Council. If an MS runs an excessive deficit, the Lisbon Treaty supported by the relevant legal instruments in the SGP provides a procedural mechanism to rectify it. The excessive deficit rules apply to MS with a derogation to the point where the Council is authorised to make an assessment whether there in fact exists an excessive deficit or not. If it decides that an excessive deficit exists or may occur, the Council can merely issue an opinion under Article 126.5 TFEU or a recommendation under Articles 126.7 and 8 TFEU to that effect. The procedure prescribed in Article 126 TFEU beyond this point such as making public the existence of excessive deficits or the prescribed sanction mechanism do not apply to MS with a derogation. Correspondingly, the MS with a derogation also lose their voting rights when such corrective measures are to be adopted or in the enforcement of the sanction mechanism.

73   Under Article 139.2 point (b) TFEU, the **coercive measures** enshrined in Article 126, paragraphs 9 and 11 TFEU **shall not apply to MS with a derogation** (→ para 23–25) and that they do not take part in the respective Council votes under Article 139.4 TFEU. All other paragraphs of Article 126 TFEU shall apply to all MS, including MS with a derogation.

74   The further reference to Article 126 TFEU contained in Article 139.4 TFEU merely states that if any of the **votes according to Article 126 TFEU** (particularly

Article 139. [Member States with a Derogation] 937

paragraphs 6, 7, 8, 12 and 13) **concern an MS whose currency is the euro**, the MS with a derogation may not take part in the vote. If an MS with a derogation is subject to a Council vote under Article 126 TFEU, all MS, including those with a derogation, are eligible to vote.

References[57]

Allam, M. (2009). The adoption of the euro in the EU Member States: Repercussions of the financial crisis. *EIPA Scope, 1*, 27–34.
Beck, T. (Ed.). (2012). *Banking Union for Europe - risks and challenges*. Centre for Economic Policy Research.
Berger, H., & de Haan, J. (2010). Introduction. In J. de Haan & H. Berger (Eds.), *The European Central Bank at ten* (pp. 1–10). Springer.
Boom, S. J. (1995). The European Union after the Maastricht decision: Will Germany be the Virginia of Europe? *American Journal of Comparative Law, 43*(2), 177–226.
Böttner, R. (2021). *The constitutional framework for enhanced cooperation in EU law*. Brill Nijhoff.
Kämmerer, J. A. (2013). Bahn frei der Bankenunion? Die neuen Aufsichtsbefugnisse der EZB im Lichte der EU-Kompetenzordnung. *Neue Zeitschrift für Verwaltungsrecht*, 830–836.
Lannoo, K. (2003). Supervising the European financial system. In F. Cecchini, M. J. Heinemann, & M. Joop (Eds.), *The incomplete European market for financial services* (pp. 231–255). Springer.
Laurent, P., & Marescau, M. (1998). *The State of the European Union (Vol. IV): Deepening and widening*. Lynne Rienner Publishers.
Louis, J.-V., & Lastra, R. (2013). European economic and Monetary Union: History, trends, and prospects. *Yearbook of European Law, 32*(1), 1–150.
MacCorwick, N. (1995). The Maastricht-Urteil: Sovereignty now. *European Law Journal, 1*(3), 259–266.
Manger-Nestler, C., & Böttner, R. (2019). Der Europäische Währungsfonds nach den Plänen der Kommission. *Zeitschrift für ausländisches öffentliches Recht und Völkerrecht*, 43–84.
Niknejad, M. (2014). European Union towards the Banking Union, single supervisory mechanism and challenges on the road ahead. *European Journal of Legal Studies, 7*(1), 92–124.
Seyad, S. (1995). Sweden and European economic and monetary union. *European Financial Services Law, 2*, 288–295.
Seyad, S. (1996). Legal and judicial developments in the field of capital movements. *European Business Law Review, 7*, 273–279.
Seyad, S. (1997a). A critical interpretation of the EMU convergence rules. *Legal Issues of Economic Integration*, 1–16.
Seyad, S. (1997b). Limitations to the free movement of banking services. *Journal of International Banking Law & Regulation*, 67–73.
Seyad, S. (2001). A single regulator for the EC financial market. *Journal of International Banking Law & Regulation, 16*, 203–212.
Seyad, S. (2002). Swedish accession to the Euroland. *Europarättslig tidskrift, 2*, 191–211.
Seyad, S. (2008). *The Lisbon Treaty and the Economic and Monetary Union. European Policy Report (4)*. Swedish Institute for European Policy Studies.
Seyad, S. (2013). The impact of the proposed Banking Union on the unity and integrity of the EU's single market. *Journal of International Banking Law & Regulation*, 49–58.

---

[57] All cited Internet sources in this comment have been accessed on 6 April 2021.

Seyad, S. (2015). The impact of the financial and fiscal crisis on regional integration within and outside EU. *Chinese Journal of International Law*, 35–50.

Seyad, S. (2020). Legal implications of Brexit on the free movement of capital. *Journal of International Banking Law & Regulation, 35*, 182–195.

Smits, R. (2003). *The European Central Bank in the European constitutional order*. Eleven International Publishing.

Taggart, T. (2005). *EU enlargement and referendums*. Routledge.

Wölker, U. (1996). The continuity of contracts in the transition to the third stage of Economic and Monetary Union. *Common Market Law Review, 33*, 1117–1132.

Wymeersch, E. (2014). The single supervisory mechanism or "SSM," part one of the Banking Union. *National Bank of Belgium Working Paper Research*, April 2014.

Article 140 [Progress Reports and Abrogation of Derogations]
(ex-Articles 121.11, 122.2 Sentence 2, and 123.5 TEC)

1. At least once every two years, or at the request of a Member State with a derogation, the Commission and the European Central Bank shall report to the Council on the progress made by the Member States with a derogation in fulfilling their obligations regarding the achievement of economic and monetary union.[3–5] These reports shall include an examination of the compatibility between the national legislation of each of these Member States, including the statutes of its national central bank,[10–12] and Articles 130 and 131 and the Statute of the ESCB and of the ECB. The reports shall also examine the achievement of a high degree of sustainable convergence by reference to the fulfilment by each Member State of the following criteria:

   - the achievement of a high degree of price stability; this will be apparent from a rate of inflation which is close to that of, at most, the three best performing Member States in terms of price stability,[13–16]
   - the sustainability of the government financial position; this will be apparent from having achieved a government budgetary position without a deficit that is excessive as determined in accordance with Article 126(6),[17–20]
   - the observance of the normal fluctuation margins provided for by the exchange-rate mechanism of the European Monetary System, for at least 2 years, without devaluing against the euro,[21–25]
   - the durability of convergence achieved by the Member State with a derogation and of its participation in the exchange-rate mechanism being reflected in the long-term interest-rate levels.[26,27]

   The four criteria mentioned in this paragraph and the relevant periods over which they are to be respected are developed further in a Protocol annexed to the Treaties. The reports of the Commission and the European Central Bank shall also take account of the results of the integration of markets, the situation and development of the balances of payments on current account and an examination of the development of unit labour costs and other price indices.

2. After consulting the European Parliament and after discussion in the European Council, the Council shall, on a proposal from the Commission, decide which Member States with a derogation fulfil the necessary conditions on the basis of the criteria set out in paragraph 1, and abrogate the derogations of the Member States concerned.[28]

   The Council shall act having received a recommendation of a qualified majority of those among its members representing Member States whose currency is the euro. These members shall act within six months of the Council receiving the Commission's proposal.[29]

The qualified majority of the said members, as referred to in the second subparagraph, shall be defined in accordance with Article 238(3)(a).

3. If it is decided, in accordance with the procedure set out in paragraph 2, to abrogate a derogation, the Council shall, acting with the unanimity of the Member States whose currency is the euro and the Member State concerned, on a proposal from the Commission and after consulting the European Central Bank, irrevocably fix the rate at which the euro shall be substituted for the currency of the Member State concerned, and take the other measures necessary for the introduction of the euro as the single currency in the Member State concerned.[32–42]

Protocol (No. 13)

on the Convergence Criteria

THE HIGH CONTRACTING PARTIES,

DESIRING to lay down the details of the convergence criteria which shall guide the Union in taking decisions to end the derogations of those Member States with a derogation, referred to in Article 140 of the Treaty on the Functioning of the European Union,

HAVE AGREED upon the following provisions, which shall be annexed to the Treaty on European Union and to the Treaty on the Functioning of the European Union:

Article 1[13–16]

The criterion on price stability referred to in the first indent of Article 140(1) of the Treaty on the Functioning of the European Union shall mean that a Member State has a price performance that is sustainable and an average rate of inflation, observed over a period of one year before the examination, that does not exceed by more than 1 ½ percentage points that of, at most, the three best performing Member States in terms of price stability. Inflation shall be measured by means of the consumer price index on a comparable basis taking into account differences in national definitions.

Article 2[17–20]

The criterion on the government budgetary position referred to in the second indent of Article 140(1) of the said Treaty shall mean that at the time of the

Article 140.   [Progress Reports and Abrogation of Derogations]   941

examination the Member State is not the subject of a Council decision under Article 126(6) of the said Treaty that an excessive deficit exists.

Article 3[21–25]

The criterion on participation in the Exchange Rate mechanism of the European Monetary System referred to in the third indent of Article 140(1) of the said Treaty shall mean that a Member State has respected the normal fluctuation margins provided for by the exchange-rate mechanism on the European Monetary System without severe tensions for at least the last two years before the examination. In particular, the Member State shall not have devalued its currency's bilateral central rate against the euro on its own initiative for the same period.

Article 4[26–27]

The criterion on the convergence of interest rates referred to in the fourth indent of Article 140(1) of the said Treaty shall mean that, observed over a period of one year before the examination, a Member State has had an average nominal long-term interest rate that does not exceed by more than two percentage points that of, at most, the three best performing Member States in terms of price stability. Interest rates shall be measured on the basis of long-term government bonds or comparable securities, taking into account differences in national definitions.

Article 5[7]

The statistical data to be used for the application of this Protocol shall be provided by the Commission.

Article 6[4]

The Council shall, acting unanimously on a proposal from the Commission and after consulting the European Parliament, the ECB and the Economic and Financial Committee, adopt appropriate provisions to lay down the details of the convergence criteria referred to in Article 140(1) of the said Treaty, which shall then replace this Protocol.

Contents

1. Overview 1
2. Two Year Rule to Review the Status of the Derogation 5
3. Convergence Criteria on EMU 8
   3.1. Independence of the National Central Banks 10

	3.2. Price Stability	13
	3.3. Fiscal Rules	17
	3.4. Exchange Stability Rule	21
	3.5. Low Interest Rates	26
4.	Abrogation of Derogation	28
5.	Final Measures	32
	5.1. Irrevocably Fixing the Conversion Rate	32
	5.2. Adoption of Measures for the Introduction of the Euro	38

List of Cases
References

1. Overview

1   The establishment of the EMU is one of the main objectives of the Union (Article 3.4 TEU) and includes 'a single and stable currency' which is connected with 'the strengthening and the convergence' of the national economies (Recital 8 of the TEU Preamble). Convergence as a prerequisite for entry into the third stage of EMU serves the purpose of securing price stability (Article 127.1 TFEU). For this reason, the introduction of EMU with the Treaty of Maastricht also brought along rules on convergene and the transition to the third stage,[1] whose content was kept throughout the Treaty revisions. Article 140 TFEU in its current version is based on different **predecessors** in the previous Treaties. Paragraphs 1 and 2 in essence take up the contents of Articles 121.1 and 122.2 TEC-Nice, but subparagraphs 2 and 3 of paragraph 2 are new. The third paragraph of Article 140 TFEU goes back to Article 123.5 TEC-Nice.

2   All MS which are outside the euro area and have secured no specific opt-out of EMU are under a legal **obligation to fulfil the convergence rules** prescribed in the Treaty.[2] In other words, when an MS fails to fulfil the convergence rules and thereby assumes the status as an MS with a derogation, it is only of a transitional value. They must continue to do their utmost to put their economies in order to meet the convergence criteria and join the euro area. Article 140 TFEU lays down the necessary substantial requirements and the procedural steps for the entry into the third stage of EMU. Once the single currency is adopted, MS are primarily bound by the fiscal rules of Article 126 TFEU and the Stability and Growth Pact (→ Article 126 TFEU para 12 et seqq.; → Supplement to Title VIII: Fiscal Union para 16 et seqq.).

3   Article 140 TFEU should be read together with **Protocol (No. 13) on the convergence criteria,** which sheds more light to the extent to which MS should fulfil the convergence rules on inflation, fiscal discipline, currency stability and

---

[1] See especially Articles 109j, 109k.2 and 109l.5 TEC-Maastricht.
[2] Seyad (1995).

interest rates. As Article 51 TEU declares, Protocols annexed to the Treaty are an integral part thereof and therefore constitute primary law.

The laying down of specific criteria in primary law for the adoption of the euro makes it predictable which conditions an MS must fulfil. Although a Council decision is necessary for the abrogation of the derogation, Article 140 TFEU and the Protocol decrease the political discretion of the Council. Moreover, a set of predefined rules helps ensure that **MS are treated equally** (Article 4.2, sentence 1, TEU) with regard to euro area membership.[3] However, under Article 6 of the Protocol, the Protocol could be replaced by the Council acting unanimously on a proposal from the Commission and after consulting the EP, the ECB and the Economic and Financial Committee. Hence, this is a form of (simple) Treaty amendment apart from Article 48 TEU.

2. Two Year Rule to Review the Status of the Derogation

Under Articles 7 and 8 of the preventive arm of the SGP,[4] MS with a derogation are required to submit a yearly report on variables related to convergence for multilateral surveillance under Article 121 TFEU (→ Supplement to Title VIII: Fiscal Union para 60 et seqq.). For the transition to the third stage of EMU under Article 140 TFEU, the Treaty mandates the European Commission and the ECB to submit a **report** to the Council based on the convergence report submitted by an MS with a derogation.[5] Such reports shall be published at least once every two years or at the request of an MS seeking entry to the euro area, independently of potentially ongoing euro-area accessions.

The general rule is to wait for at least two years after an MS is disqualified to join the euro area, but it is not a hard and fast rule. Article 140I.1 TFEU provides that the **MS concerned can submit a request**. Additionally, under Article 135 TFEU, the Council or an MS may request the Commission to make a proposal. The Commission shall examine this request and submit its conclusions to the Council without delay. For example, when Greece failed to join the euro area in 1999, it prepared and submitted another convergence report and made an application to the EU to secure membership in the euro area even before the expiry of the said two years.

Article 5 of Protocol No. 13 sets forth that the Commission shall provide **the statistical data** to be used for the evaluation of compliance with the convergence criteria. The wording is the same in Article 4 of the excessive deficit Protocol No. 12 and specifies the Commission's power under Article 337 TFEU to 'collect

---

[3] Cf. Allemand (2005), p. 590.

[4] Council Regulation (EC) No 1466/97 *on the strengthening of the surveillance of budgetary positions and the surveillance and coordination of economic policies*, O.J. L 209/1 (1997), as amended by Parliament/Council Regulation (EU) No 1175/2011, O.J. L 306/12 (2011).

[5] The report 2020 covered the seven non-euro area MS that are legally committed to adopting the euro: Bulgaria, Czechia, Croatia, Hungary, Poland, Romania, and Sweden.

3. Convergence Criteria on EMU

8   Unlike the MS within the euro area, which are required to submit a stability report, MS with a derogation are required to submit **convergence reports** to the Commission and the ECB. They should fulfil all the rules on convergence criteria, which is a set of macroeconomic indicators that was laid down in the Maastricht Treaty as a precondition to join the euro area. The **economic rational of these accession criteria is still disputed** today, particularly the equalisation of the lowest values with the best values within the first and fourth convergence criterion (Article 140.1 TFEU).[6] Overall, they are criticised for being political instruments, not economically vital measures.[7] There are all in all five convergence rules that an MS with a derogation should fulfil for the Council to adopt a decision to abrogate it. Lithuania is the last country that joined the euro area on 1 January 2015. The manner in which an MS with a derogation is required to fulfil the convergence rules can be explained more clearly and precisely by reference to the Commission convergence report on Lithuania.[8]

9   When a country joins the EU as a new member, it is normally referred to in the **accession** agreement as an **MS with a derogation** for the purposes of EMU.[9] Since acceding MS assume the obligation to join the third stage of EMU eventually (→ para 1), the primary-law based status as MS with a derogation is the default rule, but is supposed to be only temporary, unless the MS concerned secures an opt-out upon accession as Denmark did, for example (→ Article 139 TFEU paras 8–9, 11 et seqq.). However, since Article 140 TFEU is hardly enforceable, an MS may retain its derogatory status even without explicit exemption, as the example of Sweden illustrates (→ Article 139 TFEU para 17 et seqq.)

3.1. Independence of the National Central Banks

10 The Commission and the ECB shall check the **compatibility** of an MS's national legislation, including the statute of its national central bank, **with the Treaties and the ESCB Statut**e (Article 140.1, sentence 2, TFEU).[10] This comprises not only central bank independence, but also adapting rules for the national central bank to ensure that they can fulfil their tasks in the ESCB, especially as (future) part of the

---

[6] Ishikawa (1999), p. 21 et seqq.; auf dem Brinke et al. (2015), pp. 14–15.
[7] De Grauwe (1996).
[8] European Commission, Convergence Report 2014, European Economy 4/2014.
[9] For Lithuania, see Article 4 of the 2003 Act of Accession, O.J. C. 236/1 (2003).
[10] Amtenbrink (1999).

Eurosystem. For example, national legislation must ensure that the NCB will act in accordance with the guidelines and instructions of the ECB as foreseen by Article 14.3 of the ESCB Statute.

The core element of this legal convergence is the **independence of the national central bank**.[11] It works in two ways. First, it also prohibits NCBs and the members of their decision-making bodies from seeking or taking instructions from any MS government or from any other national body when exercising the powers and carrying out the tasks and duties conferred upon them by the national constitutions and the EU Treaties. Second, the nature and level of independence expected of the national central bank is that they should have the ability to take all decisions on monetary and financial matters without any interference emanating not only from their respective MS, but also any institutions, bodies, offices or agencies of the Union. Since the ESCB is conferred with the exclusive competence to formulate an independent monetary policy for the entire euro area, it is particularly important to ensure that they are **immune** not only **from political pressures** both **at national and Union level**, but also guarantee their **personal and functional independence** (→ Article 130 TFEU para 4 et seqq.). The Treaty therefore imposes an express prohibition on the members of the central bank's decision-making bodies to seek or take instructions from Union institutions or any national government. 11

Lithuania made the necessary amendments to the law pertaining to the independence of the national central bank. It was made immune from political control. The method of dismissal of the Governor of the Bank of Lithuania was amended to comply with Article 130 TFEU and Article 14.2 of the ESCB Statute. In addition, the Lithuanian law relating to prohibition of monetary financing and privileged access was declared compatible with Articles 123 and 124 TFEU, respectively. 12

3.2. Price Stability

The general rule on price stability as enunciated in Article 140.1 (1), first indent, TFEU provides that the **rate of inflation should be close to that of the three best performing MS of the EU** (not only the euro area) in terms of price stability. For example, the 2014 Commission report on convergence criteria on price stability relating to Croatia was calculated by reference to the average of the 12-month average inflation rates in Latvia, Portugal and Ireland plus 1.5 percentage points. 13

The Treaty does not give a precise definition of what constitutes price stability (→ Article 127 TFEU para 5 et seqq.). It does not provide any clear indication on the extent to which inflation is tolerable to guarantee that the euro will be a stable 14

---

[11] Cf. Neyer (2019), p. 3 et seqq.

currency. This legal vacuum was rectified in Protocol No. 13 which declares in clear terms that inflation should **not be more than 1.5 per cent above those in the three countries with the lowest inflation rates** to secure admission to the euro area (Article 1 of the Protocol).[12] It is guaranteed when the average of all prices of goods and services, i.e. the price level, remains stable overall,[13] which the ECB measures by using a harmonised index of consumer prices. Price stability is achieved when the increase in consumer prices in the euro area as a whole is below, but close to, 2% per annum over the medium term (**relative price stability**).[14] Additionally, a **reference period** for price stability is not specified in the Treaty, but Article 1, first sentence, of the Protocol mentions 'that a Member State has a price performance that is **sustainable**'. However, in practice the sustainable nature of price stability is reduced to a corrective for cases in which an MS with high inflation rates moves exceptionally within the reference values in the year of the test.

15   The rate of inflation not to exceed 1.5% above the average of the best performing MS imposed by the Protocol **cannot be treated as an absolute margin**. It should accommodate an inflation rate, which is close to that of the EU average.[15] This line of interpretation may be supported by reference to the wording of Article 140 TFEU, which declares that the rate of inflation 'is close to that of the three best performing Member States'. MS whose inflation rates cannot be seen as 'a meaningful benchmark' are excluded from the best performers, e.g. if the inflation rate and profile deviate by a wide margin from the euro area average or if deflation occurs in a country.[16]

16   To determine whether **Lithuania** fulfilled the inflation rule, the Commission had to examine three countries within the euro area which have the lowest rate of inflation, namely Latvia, Portugal and Ireland. It found the reference value as 1.7% calculated as the average of the 12-month average inflation rates in these three countries plus 1.5 percentage points below the reference value. The corresponding inflation rate in Lithuania was 0.6%, which was 1.1% below the reference value, and was therefore declared as fulfilling the price stability rule.

---

[12] On the consumer price index referred to in Article 1 of the Protocol, see Parliament/Council Regulation (EU) 2016/792 *on harmonised indices of consumer prices and the house price index*, O.J. L 135/11 (2016).

[13] Häde, in Calliess and Ruffert (2022), Article 119 AEUV para 22.

[14] Cf. ECB, Monthly Bulletin, January 1999, p. 46.

[15] In the first round of selection to euro area, Austria had the lowest inflation rate of 1.1% and highest figure was 5.2% in Greece. The EU average was 2.7%, Sweden 1.9% and all the MS except Greece fulfilled this requirement.

[16] Cf., inter alia, the Commission's Convergence Report 2013 on Latvia, p. 3, and Recital 8 of Council Decision 2014/509/EU *on the adoption by Lithuania of the euro on 1 January 2015*, O.J. L 228/29 (2014).

3.3. Fiscal Rules

An MS with a derogation should ensure **sound and sustainable public finances** if it is to join the euro area (Article 140.1 (1), second indent, TFEU and Article 2 of Protocol No. 13). Before the launching of the third stage of EMU, it was found that the rules on fiscal discipline were the most difficult criteria to be satisfied by the MS. The relevant fiscal convergence rules enunciated in Article 140 TFEU which an MS with a derogation is required to fulfil should be read together with Article 126 TFEU and the Protocol (No. 12) on the excessive deficit procedure. In terms of the fiscal rule, such an MS should keep its **budget deficit and national debts below 3% and 60% of their respective GDP** (Article 1 of Protocol No. 12; → Article 126 TFEU para 9 et seq.)

A closer examination of the wording of convergence rules, however, indicates they appear to be more tolerant when it comes to the determination of the fiscal criteria. The relevant test is whether the **deficit has declined substantially and continuously and has reached a level which comes close to the reference value**. An MS should also be assumed to have satisfied this requirement if the excess deficit is only exceptional and temporary and the ratio remains close to the reference value (Article 126.2 point (a) TFEU; → Article 126 TFEU para 9). The public debt criterion may be deemed met if the ratio is sufficiently diminishing and approaching the reference value at a satisfactory pace (Article 126.2 point (b) TFEU; → Article 126 TFEU para 10).

When selecting the **founder MS of the euro area**, the manner in which the Commission evaluated the fiscal rules of some MS attracted much criticism. France and Italy were able to fulfil the budget deficit rule of not more than 3% of the GDP on technical grounds. France had a deficit of exactly 3% and the method of computing the figures by France to reach this margin had been disputed and criticised by various EU institutions and MS. Only France, Luxembourg, Finland and the UK fulfilled the reduction of the national debts to 60% of GDP. Even Germany, the economic superpower of the EU, failed to fulfil this criterion.[17] Some countries such as Belgium and Italy had debts of over 120%, which is double the rate stipulated in the Maastricht Treaty.

Lithuania was subject to excessive deficit procedure based on a Council decision as its budget deficit had exceeded the EU ceiling. It later rectified the deficit, and in July 2013 the Council abrogated the said decision.[18] According to the European Commission assessment of the budget deficit in Lithuania, its forecast is around 2.1% of GDP in 2014 and the Lithuanian government forecast to have a surplus of 0.1% of GDP for 2016. The debt level of Lithuania is also below the EU threshold and the Commission forecast is to be around 39.4% of GDP in 2014.

---

[17] Its debt was 61.3% of GDP, slightly higher than the EC ratio of 60%.
[18] Council Decision 2013/316/EU *abrogating Decision 2009/588/EC on the existence of an excessive deficit in Lithuania*, O.J. L173/46 (2013).

Lithuania is part of the euro area since 1 January 2015. In 2017 Lithuania had a budget surplus of 0.5%, the gross debt was around 40% of GDP.

3.4. Exchange Stability Rule

21 The exchange stability rule provides that the **exchange rate should be held within the normal fluctuation margins of the ERM II** of the European Monetary System for at least the previous two years without devaluing against the euro (Article 140.1(1), third indent, TFEU and Article 3 of Protocol No. 13). It was set up on 1 January 1999[19] (successor to the orginal exchange-rate mechanism and the ECU) to ensure that exchange rate fluctuations between the euro and other EU currencies do not disrupt economic stability within the single market. Currently, Denmark,[20] Bulgaria,[21] and Croatia[22] are the only non-euro area countries that participate in the ERM II.[23]

22 The rule on exchange stability is formulated in a flexible but imprecise manner.[24] It provides that the MS should maintain the stability of their currencies within the normal fluctuation margins and **without severe tensions for at least the last two years** before the examination. The standard fluctuation band around the central rates was originally ± 2.25%, but was later widened to ± 15%. These two margins are still in use as the 'standard' (15%) and the 'narrow' (2.25%) fluctuation band.[25] The criterion also stipulates that an MS should not devalue its currency's bilateral central rate against any other MS's currency on its own initiative. This rule implies that if a currency fluctuates in a manner which is not severe enough to disrupt the exchange-rate mechanism, it does not offend the rules of exchange stability. Since it **prohibits only unilateral devaluation** of the currency, devaluation caused by external factors should not breach the exchange rule.

23 It is not precisely clear whether it is a mandatory requirement for a currency to be pegged to the ERM for at least two years before seeking membership in the euro area.[26] While Article 140.1 TFEU only mentions the 'observance' of the fluctuation margins, Article 3 of Protocol No. 13 mentions 'participation' in the ERM.

---

[19] See the Resolution of the European Council *on the establishment of an exchange rate mechanism in the Third Stage of Economic and Monetary Union*, O.J. C 236/5 (1997) and the Agreement of 16 March 2006 between the ECB and the national central banks of the Member States outside the euro area laying down the operating procedures for an exchange rate mechanism in stage three of Economic and Monetary Union, O.J. C 73/21 (2006), as amended by Agreement of 22 January 2020, O.J. C 32I/1 (2020). See on this Rohde Jensen (2005).

[20] The central rate is 1 EUR = 7.46038 Danish Kroner.

[21] The central rate is 1 EUR = 1.95583 Lev.

[22] The central rate is 1 EUR = 7.53450 Kuna.

[23] See recently Dorrucci et al. (2020).

[24] Seyad (1999).

[25] Cf. Rohde Jensen (2005), p. 142.

[26] Schioppa (2003).

Article 140.   [Progress Reports and Abrogation of Derogations]

Moreover, the fourth convergence criterion speaks of the durability of participation in the ERM. However, the **ERM**, which was originally based on secondary legislation, **does not impose a legal obligation on MS to link their currencies** to this mechanism. Otherwise, since participation in the ERM II is voluntary, a participation requirement would amount to an opportunity to opt-out from EMU. Therefore, even if a currency remains outside the ERM, but behaves stably against the other currencies during the relevant period, it should be assumed to be in sufficient compliance of the convergence rules.[27]

The general political stand taken in **Sweden** is not to link its currency to the ERM II.[28] From a legal point of view, this requirement is not precisely clear nor is it free from ambiguity. It is ambiguous as neither the Treaty nor the relevant secondary law[29] specifies a clear margin within which a currency should fluctuate to fulfil the exchange stability rule. The widening of the ERM margin following the currency crisis in August 1993 from 2.25 to 15% have fuelled more ambiguity to the interpretation of this rule, leaving no guidelines to MS which margin their currencies should follow.[30] This uncertainty has still not been resolved as evidenced by ERM II to which Denmark and Greece before joining the euro area fixed their currencies to fluctuate against the euro at different margins.

Lithuania had pegged its currency, *litas*, to the ERM II in June 2004, and has never withdrawn from this mechanism. The central rate was set at 1 EUR = 3.45280 *litas*. The rate of fluctuation of *lita* to euro was fixed at the margin of plus/minus 15%. Until 2014 there had been no evidence of any deviation, and its currency was fluctuating within this margin.

24

25

3.5. Low Interest Rates

An MS with a derogation should keep its long-term interest rates under control to qualify for admission to the third stage of EMU (Article 140.1 (1), fourth indent, TFEU). The Treaty is not precisely clear how low the long-term interest should be, but Protocol No. 13 gives more flesh and blood to this rule. It declares that **interest rate should not be more than 2% above those in the three countries with the lowest interest rate** (Article 4 of Protocol No. 13). The convergence rule on interest rates is formulated in a flexible manner in the Protocol itself. It declares

26

---

[27] The United Kingdom and Sweden strongly support this view. For the view that two years membership in the ERM is mandatory, see, Randzio-Plath (1996).

[28] See also Bernitz (2001), p. 931 et seqq.; Louis (2004), p. 603 et seqq.

[29] Resolution of the Amsterdam European Council of 16 June 1997 *on the establishment of an exchange rate mechanism in the third stage of economic and monetary union*; O.J. C 236/5 (1997).

[30] Bordes (1995).

that an MS should be deemed to have satisfied the convergence requirement if interest rate is approaching that of best-performing States.[31]

27   To determine whether **Lithuania** fulfils this rule, the Commission examined the secondary market yield on a single benchmark government bond with a residual maturity of around nine years. It compared the figures in Lithuania with three countries having lowest rate of interest, which were again Latvia, Portugal and Ireland. The EU reference value on long term interest rate was found to be 6.2%. The Lithuanian benchmark bond stood at 3.6%, which was much below the reference value, and thus qualified this convergence test.

4. Abrogation of Derogation

28   The Treaty prescribes a specific procedure for the adoption of a Council decision to abrogate derogation if such an **MS fulfils the convergence rules**. There are different institutions of the EU that are involved in this process.

29   The Commission should submit a proposal to the Council to abrogate derogation, as it did in the case of Lithuania.[32] The **Council** shall thereafter consult the EP and after discussions at the level of Heads of State and Government in the European Council, it shall adopt the proposal of the Commission to grant membership to the relevant MS in the euro area.[33] A **double qualified majority** scenario is envisaged in this context. Primarily, it requires a recommendation from a qualified majority of the euro area MS. The qualified majority is calculated based on Article 238.3 point (a) TFEU. It requires the same majorities as under Article 16.3 TEU, but only as regards the euro area MS. From this recommendation, a qualified majority of *all* Council members as envisaged in Article 16.3 TFEU is necessary to adopt the decision abrogating the derogation. Technically, the recommendation of the euro area States does not bind the Council at large, but considering that these States make up the majority of the Council members, it is hardly imaginable that the Council would act against a recommendation.

30   As regards **Denmark**, under Protocol No. 16, the procedure is modified in that the procedure abrogating Denmark's exemption can only be initiated by that MS itself (→ Article 139 TFEU para 15).

31   During the 2011 fiscal crisis, discussions arose on the possibility to withdraw from the eurozone or to be expelled.[34] However, the derogatory status before the introduction of the single currency is supposed to be of a transitional nature. Once

---

[31] France and the Netherlands had the lowest long-term interest rates of 5.5%, and the highest was 9.8% in Greece. The EU average was fixed at 7.8%, Sweden 6.5%, and only Greece failed to satisfy this rule.

[32] Proposal for a Council Decision *on the adoption by Lithuania of the euro on 1 January 2015*, COM(2014) 324 final.

[33] Council Decision 2014/509/EU *on the adoption by Lithuania of the euro on 1 January 2015*, O. J. L 228/29 (2014).

[34] Cf. inter alia, Siekmann (2017).

Article 140. [Progress Reports and Abrogation of Derogations]

convergence has been reached and the derogation is abrogated, there are Treaty provisions in place (notably Article 126 TFEU) that shall prevent economic difficulties that would warrant a leaving of the euro area. **Participation in the third stage of EMU is** thus **irreversible** (Protocol No. 24 on the Transition to the Third Stage of Economic and Monetary Union), and can be terminated only by leaving the EU at large (Article 50 TEU).[35]

5. Final Measures

5.1. Irrevocably Fixing the Conversion Rate

Once a decision is taken in Council to abrogate a derogation, the next step would be to fix a **rate at which the euro shall be substituted for the relevant national currency**. The conversion rate is irrevocably fixed by the Council acting unanimously based on a Commission proposal and after consulting the ECB. The General Council of the ECB shall contribute to the necessary preparations for irrevocably fixing the exchange rates (Article 46.3 of the ESCB Statute). Similar to the decision on abrogation of a derogation, only the MS of the euro area plus the MS concerned vote in the Council on the decision to fix the conversion rates. Under Article 49 of the ESCB Statute, following the fixing of the exchange rate, the ECB's Governing Council shall take the necessary measures to ensure that banknotes denominated in that currency are exchanged by the national central banks at their respective par values.

32

---

[35] When reviewing the constitutionality of the Maastricht Treaty, the German Federal Constitutional Court has held the following view to preserve in particular the parliamentary rights of scrutiny of the German *Bundestag*: '[...] the Federal Republic of Germany is not, by ratifying the Maastricht Treaty, subjecting itself to an uncontrollable, unforeseeable process which will lead inexorably towards monetary union; the Maastricht Treaty simply paves the way for gradual further integration of the European Community as a community of laws. Every further step along this way is dependent either upon conditions being fulfilled by the parliament which can already be foreseen, or upon further consent from the Federal Government, which consent is subject to parliamentary influence. [...] Even after transition to the third stage, development of the monetary union is subject to foreseeable standards and thus to parliamentary accountability. [...] The Maastricht Treaty sets long-term standards which establish the goal of stability as the yardstick by which the monetary union is to be measured, which endeavour, by institutional provisions, to ensure that these objectives are fulfilled, and which finally do not stand in the way of withdrawal from the Community as a last resort if it proves impossible to achieve the stability sought [...].' See German Federal Constitutional Court (Bundesverfassungsgericht), 2 BvR 2134/92, 2 BvR 2159/92, *Maastricht* (Judgment of 12 October 1993), para 145 et seq.

33   The Maastricht Treaty was not precisely clear on the timetable or the method of adoption of a single currency such as fixing the conversion rates. It merely provided in ex-Article 109.1 (4) TEC for the adoption 'of the other measures necessary for the rapid introduction of the ECU' as the single currency. The European Council at the **Madrid** summit meeting held on 15-16 December 1995 identified these problems and laid down certain **guidelines** based on the reports of the Commission[36] and the EMI[37] as to when and how to introduce a single currency in Europe.[38]

34   All matters relating to fixing conversion rates, introduction of the euro, etc. are provided by **EU secondary legislation**. The manner in which the conversion rates must be expressed and applied is laid down in Council Regulation 974/98[39] read together with Council Regulation 2866/98[40] on the conversion rates between the euro and the currencies of the MS adopting the euro. The aim of this Regulation is to ensure fairness and continuity of contracts during the changeover from national to euro currency.[41]

35   The conversion rate from national currency to the euro is expressed with **six significant figures**. Once the conversion from the national currency has been made, the euro amount is rounded up or down to the nearest euro cent. If the number in the third decimal place is less than 5, the second decimal remains unchanged (for example EUR 1.264 becomes EUR 1.26), but if the third decimal is 5 or above, then the second decimal must be rounded up (for example EUR 1.265 becomes EUR 1.27).

36   The law dealing with the conversion rates must be amended when a new MS joins the euro area. When **Lithuania** joined the euro area, the relevant regulation had to be amended to make it adaptable to the date of the adoption of the euro, the date of the cash changeover, etc. The irrevocable conversion rate is usually set at the central rate observed by the national currency within the ERM II. Since participation in ERM II for at least two years without severe tensions is one of the preconditions an MS must meet for adopting the euro, it provides the best reference for the fixing of the conversion rate. Lithuania joined ERM II on 28 June 2004 and since then *lita*, the Lithuanian currency, was pegged to ERM II one euro at the rate of 3.4528.

---

[36] The Green Paper on the Practical Arrangements for the Introduction of a Single Currency (May 1995) sets out a three-phase plan.

[37] Memorandum by the EMI Council on the changeover to the single currency (19 June 1995) provides for a four-phase plan.

[38] 'The scenario for the Change-over to the Single Currency', Annex 1 to the Conclusions of the European Council, O.J. C 22/2 (1996).

[39] Council Regulation (EC) No 974/98 *on the introduction of the euro*, O.J. L 139/1 (1998).

[40] Council Regulation (EC) No 2866/98 *on the conversion rates between the euro and the currencies of the Member States adopting the euro*, O.J. L 359/1 (1998).

[41] Wölker (1996); Dunnett (1996).

The irrevocably **fixed conversion rate** of the *lita* to the euro was officially set by amending Council Regulation 2866/98.[42] The *lita* which was the official Lithuanian currency until 31 December 2014 was replaced by the euro as the official currency of Lithuania effective from 1 January 2015, and the conversion rate was irrevocably fixed at 3.45280 *litas*/EUR.

5.2. Adoption of Measures for the Introduction of the Euro

Apart from fixing the conversion rate, there are many other **measures** that an MS with a derogation must adopt **to facilitate the smooth and harmonious change over from the national to euro currency**. When an MS with a derogation is to join the euro area, it should set out a road map for the introduction of the euro as its single currency. It is not practicable for any country to withdraw and replace its currency with the euro overnight.[43] It needs time to print and put into circulation the new money and to withdraw its national currency from the market.

Council Regulation 1103/97 on certain provisions relating to the introduction of the euro[44] forms the legal basis for the introduction of the euro. It deals with issues such as the continuity of contracts, conversion rules, rounding rules, etc. The **Council Regulation 974/98** on the introduction of the euro[45] provides the mechanism for the replacement of the national currency with the euro, the method of substitution of banknotes, etc. The time framework set out in the Regulation applies only to the founder euro MS. These Regulations should therefore be applied to new MS with necessary adaptations

The founder MS of the eurozone were selected in 1998, and the euro became their official currency the following year. It was only in January 2002 that the euro bank notes and coins were introduced into the market and became the sole legal tender after the expiry of further two months. It will also be necessary for new MS to have a **transitional period for the final introduction of the euro** as its single currency. The length of the transitional process would however depend very much on the level of preparation of such countries to introduce the euro.

It is inevitable to escape from having a dual circulation period of the euro and national currency. It is left to the relevant MS and the EU institutions to decide on the length of the dual circulation period. Originally it was decided that founder euro States shall have a six-month dual circulation period from 1 January 2002, but this period was subsequently reduced to two months. During this period, **national currency will be withdrawn** as means of payment, and shall be **replaced by the euro bank notes and coins**. However, both euro and national currency will be legal

---

[42] Council Regulation 851/2014 *amending Regulation 2866/98 as regards the conversion rate to the euro for Lithuania*, O.J. L 233/21 (2014).
[43] Seyad (1997).
[44] O.J. L 162/1 (1997).
[45] O.J. L 139/1 (1998).

tender during this period. Once the transitional period expires, euro will be the sole legal tender.

42 In the case of **Lithuania**, the country followed a big bang changeover scenario with a dual circulation period of 15 calendar days. The euro banknotes and coins were introduced on 1 January 2015, the same day the euro became its legal currency.[46] This method had been used in all MS which joined the euro area after 2002.

List of Cases

German FCC 12.10.1993, 2 BvR 2134/92, 2 BvR 2159/92, *Maastricht* [cit. in para 31]

References

Allemand, F. (2005). The impact of the EU enlargement on economic and Monetary Union: What lessons can be learnt from the differentiated integration mechanisms in an enlarged Europe? *European Law Journal, 11*(5), 568–617.
Amtenbrink, F. (1999). *The democratic accountability of central banks: A comparative study of the European Central Bank*. Hart Publishing.
Auf dem Brinke, A., Enderlein, H., & Fritz-Vannahme, J. (2015). *What kind of convergence does the euro area need?* Bertelsmann Stiftung.
Bernitz, U. (2001). Sweden and the European Union: on Sweden's implementation and application of European law. *Common Market Law Review, 38*(4), 903–934.
Bordes, C. (Ed.). (1995). *European currency crisis and after*. Manchester University Press.
Calliess, C., & Ruffert, M. (Eds.). (2022). *EUV/AEUV. Kommentar* (6th ed.). C. H. Beck.
De Grauwe, P. (1996). The economics of convergence: Towards Monetary Union in Europe. *Weltwirtschaftliches Archiv, 132*(1), 1–27.
Dorrucci, E., Fidora, M., Gartner, C., & Zumer, T. (2020). The European Exchange Rate Mechanism (ERM II) as a preparatory phase on the path towards euro adoption – the cases of Bulgaria and Croatia. *ECB Economic Bulletin, 8/2020*.
Dunnett, D. (1996). Some legal principles applicable to the transition to the single currency. *Common Market Law Review, 33*, 1133–1167.
Ishikawa, J. (1999). *A critique of the Maastricht road to European Monetary Union: Bringing labour market analysis back in*. ProQuest.
Louis, J.-V. (2004). The economic and Monetary Union: Law and institutions. *Common Market Law Review, 41*(2), 575–608.
Neyer, U. (2019). The independence of the European Central Bank. *Volkswirtschaft, Finanzen, Betriebswirtschaft und Management, 52*(1), 35–68.
Randzio-Plath, C. (1996). A new exchange rate mechanism for the euro age? *Inter-Economist, 31*, 277–281.
Rohde Jensen, K. (2005). Inside EU, outside EMU: Institutional and legal aspects of the Exchange Rate Mechanism II. In European Central Bank (Ed.), *Legal aspects of the European system of central banks* (pp. 135–146). Frankfurt/Main.

---

[46] Lithuania introduced 132 million euro banknotes and 370 million euro coins to replace the *litas* coins and banknotes.

Schioppa, P. (2003). Trajectories towards the euro and the role of ERM II. *International Finance*, 6(1), 129–144.

Seyad, S. (1995). Sweden and European Economic and Monetary Union. *European Financial Servcies Law, 2*, 288–295.

Seyad, S. (1997). A legal analysis of the Euro Regulations. *European Business Law Review, 8*, 166–169.

Seyad, S. (1999). *European Community law on the free movement of capital and the EMU*. Kluwer Law International.

Siekmann, H. (2017). Exit, exclusion, and parallel currencies in the euro area. In T. Massart & A. Mbotaingar (Eds.), *Liber Amicorum en l'honneur du Professeur Joël Monéger* (pp. 773–796). LexisNexis.

Wölker, U. (1996). The continuity of contracts in the transition to the third stage of Economic and Monetary Union. *Common Market Law Review, 33*, 1117–1132.

Article 141 [General Council of the ECB]
(ex-Articles 123.3 and 117.2 First Five Indents, TEC)

1. If and as long as there are Member States with a derogation,[1] and without prejudice to Article 129(1), the General Council of the European Central Bank referred to in Article 44 of the Statute of the ESCB and of the ECB shall be constituted as a third decision-making body of the European Central Bank.[6–18]
2. If and as long as there are Member States with a derogation, the European Central Bank shall, as regards those Member States:[19–22]

    - strengthen cooperation between the national central banks,[23]
    - strengthen the coordination of the monetary policies of the Member States, with the aim of ensuring price stability,[24]
    - monitor the functioning of the exchange-rate mechanism,[25]
    - hold consultations concerning issues falling within the competence of the national central banks and affecting the stability of financial institutions and markets,[26]
    - carry out the former tasks of the European Monetary Cooperation Fund which had subsequently been taken over by the European Monetary Institute.[27]

Contents

1. Overview 1
2. Organisational Structure of the ESCB 2
    2.1. Governing Council 4
    2.2. Executive Board 5
3. General Council of the ECB 6
    3.1. Composition of the General Council 8
    3.2. Responsibilities of the General Council 12
4. Transitory Functions of the European Central Bank 19

1. Overview

The heading of Chapter 5 of Title VIII of the TFEU ('transitional provisions') insinuates that within an (undefined) period, all MS will adopt the single currency. Indeed, MS are obliged to adopt the euro unless they have secured an opt-out. However, this obligation is hardly enforceable so that in the near future there will be 'Member States with a derogation' (→ Article 139 TFEU para 7 et seqq.). The **central banks of MS with a derogation** as specified in Article 139.1 TFEU **shall retain their powers in the field of monetary policy** according to national law (Article 282.4, sentence 2, TFEU and Article 42.2 of the ESCB Statute).

Nevertheless, all NCBs are part of the ESCB, but only euro area NCBs are part of the Eurosystem (Article 282.1 TFEU). Article 141 TFEU (in conjunction with Article 44 of the ESCB Statute) considers this situation by establishing the General Council as a third decision-making body of the ECB. The **General Council** provides a link between the MS inside and those outside the Eurosystem. This body is charged with **tasks regarding the MS currently not participating in the euro**. In addition, if and as long as there are MS with a derogation, the General Council is entrusted with additional tasks.

2. Organisational Structure of the ESCB

2   The organisational structure of the ESCB is quite complex. It is designed to reflect the **lack of unity in the framework of the EMU**. All MS of the EU participate at different levels of EMU. Every MS even with a derogation should take part in the first stage of EMU as they are legally required to completely liberalise the free movement of capital which is one of the fundamental freedoms in the internal market (Article 63 et seqq. TFEU). Such liberalisation also forms part of the first stage of EMU. It is only the MS which fully comply with the convergence rules that qualify to enter the third stage of EMU.

3   Since only the MS which fulfil the convergence rules adopt the euro as their currency, the decision-making system within the framework of the ESCB reflects this **asymmetrical structure** of the EMU. In many countries the organisational structure of their national central banks has a two-tier decision-making bodies, but in the context of the ESCB there are three such tiers. Under Article 11 of the ESCB Statute, 'the ESCB shall be governed by the decision-making bodies of the ECB'. These are the Governing Council, the Executive Board and the General Council.

2.1. Governing Council

4   The Governing Council (Articles 129.1 and 283.1 TFEU read together with Article 10 of the ESCB Statute) is the **main decision-making body of the ESCB**. It consists of the six members of the Executive Board, plus the governors of the national central banks of the 19 euro area countries. Its primarily responsibility is to formulate monetary policy for the euro area. It is also responsible to adopt the guidelines and take the decisions necessary to ensure the performance of the tasks entrusted to the ECB and the Eurosystem which includes decisions relating to monetary objectives, key interest rates, etc. ($\rightarrow$ Article 283 TFEU para 2 et seqq.).

2.2. Executive Board

5   The second tier in the ESCB is the Executive Board (Articles 129.1 and 283.2 TFEU read together with Article 11 of the ESCB Statute), which consists of the

Article 141. [General Council of the ECB] 959

President, Vice-President and four other members. All members are appointed by the European Council, acting by a qualified majority. The main responsibility of the Executive Board is to **implement the monetary policy for the euro area** in accordance with the decisions taken by the Governing Council. It also prepares the meetings of the Governing Council, gives the necessary instructions to the national central banks of the euro area to manage the day-to-day business of the ECB, etc. ($\rightarrow$ Article 283 TFEU para 15 et seqq.). Generally, the Executive Board shall act by a **simple majority** of the votes cast (Article 11.5 of the ESCB Statute).

3. General Council of the ECB

The General Council (Article 141 TFEU read together with Articles 44 to 46 of the 6 ESCB Statute) is the third tier in the overall structure of the ESCB. Although the General Council forms part of the ECB (Article 141.1 TFEU) and is referred to as a decision-making body of the ECB, the Lisbon Treaty does not guarantee its perpetual existence. The longevity of this body is guaranteed **only if and as long as there are MS with a derogation**.

There is no clear and definite deadline fixed in the Treaty on which the General 7 Council of the ESCB shall cease to exist. It will certainly exist so long as there are still MS of the EU which will not adopt the euro as their single currency. There are also so-called candidate countries waiting to join the EU and if and when they join the EU, they will automatically secure membership in the General Council of the ESCB. Hence, the General Council, although often referred to as a transitional body, **may continue to exist for an unpredictable period**.

3.1. Composition of the General Council

The Governing Council comprises the **President of the ECB**, the **Vice-President** 8 **of the ECB** and the **governors of the NCBs of the MS**. In other words, the General Council includes representatives of the (actually) 19 euro area countries and the 8 non-euro area countries, the last-mentioned however are without voting rights in relation to decision making in areas covered under Article 139.2 TFEU (Article 139.4 TFEU; $\rightarrow$ Article 139 para 23 et seqq., 69 et seqq.). Even other members of the Executive Board may participate in meetings of the General Council but without voting rights (Article 44.2 of the ESCB Statute). The President of the Council of the EU and one member of the European Commission may also attend the meetings of the General Council, but do not have the right to vote. For the General Council to vote, there shall be a quorum of two-thirds of the members or their alternates. Generally, decisions are taken by simple majority (Article 10.2 (2) of the ESCB Statute).

Before the Lisbon Treaty, the President, Vice-President and the members of the 9 Executive Board of the ECB were **appointed by** common accord of **the European Council** on a recommendation from the Council in consultation with the EP and the

Governing Council of the ECB. Under Article 283.2 (2) TFEU, the unanimity procedure in the European Council has been replaced by a qualified majority system (→ Article 283 TFEU para 18–19). This Treaty provision refers to the European Council as a whole, which would mean in the composition of both euro and non-euro MS. On the other hand, it is required to consult not the ESCB, but the Eurosystem which excludes the Governors of MS that have not adopted the euro.

10 The date of **meetings** of the General Council shall be decided itself on a proposal from the President of the ECB. The latter shall chair the meetings and in his absence the Vice-President of the ECB. Such meetings shall be convened if at least three members of the General Council so request, or the President deems it necessary. The President shall prepare the meetings of the General Council.

11 It is the General Council which **adopts its own Rules of Procedure** under Article 45.4 of the ESCB Statute. The **Secretariat** of the General Council is provided by the ECB.

3.2. Responsibilities of the General Council

12 During its interim period of existence there are **several functions** allocated to the General Council (Article 46 of the ESCB Statute). It is required to contribute to the ECB's advisory functions, collect statistical information, prepare the ECB's annual report, establish the necessary rules for standardising the accounting and reporting of operations undertaken by the national central banks, lay down the conditions of employment of the members of staff of the ECB.

13 The General Council **does not have competence to formulate or implement monetary policy** except as a meeting point of the Governors of both euro and non-euro MS.

14 An important advisory function relates to the **abrogation of the derogations** specified in Article 140 TFEU. There are several MS of the EU which were not the founding members of the eurozone as most of them failed to fulfil the EMU convergence criteria. Such countries classified as MS with a derogation (→ Article 139 TFEU para 7 et seqq.) should fulfil the relevant convergence rules to abrogate such derogation (→ Article 140 TFEU para 28-29).

15 The General Council under Article 127.4 TFEU may be **consulted** whenever the EU is to adopt any legal acts touching upon monetary matters. Even national authorities may consult the General Council on any draft legislative provision in its field of competence.

16 The General Council shall contribute to the **collection of statistical information** either from the national authorities or directly from economic agents. To carry out this function, the General Council as part of the ESCB shall cooperate with the Union institutions, bodies, offices or agencies and with the competent authorities of the MS or third countries and with international organisations.

17 There are various reporting commitments that are assigned to the General Council. As part of the ESCB, the General Council shall contribute to **draw up and publish reports** on its activities at least quarterly. It shall contribute to prepare

an annual report to the European Parliament, the Council, the Commission and the European Council on matters relating to monetary policy.

It is the Governing Council on a proposal from the Executive Board shall lay down the **conditions of employment of the staff of the ECB**. Under Article 46 of the ESCB Statute, the General Council shall contribute to the laying down of such conditions of employment. **18**

4. Transitory Functions of the European Central Bank

Cooperation between the monetary authorities of the MS may be traced back to the establishment of the **Committee of the Governors of the Central Banks**. It was established on 8 May **1964** by the Council of Ministers. The Committee was composed of the Governors of the *Banque Nationale de Belgique*, the *Deutsche Bundesbank*, the *Banque de France*, the *Banca d'Italia* and the *Nederlandsche Bank*. **19**

The aim of this committee was to provide a platform for the monetary authorities of the MS to **exchange their views on monetary policy**. It was a forum for pure exchange of ideas on monetary matters with no competence whatsoever to recommend or formulate monetary policies. **20**

This Committee was replaced by the **European Monetary Cooperation Fund** (EMCF).[1] The EMCF is an institution and a fund established in **1973** by the MS to stabilise exchange rates in the single market. The EMCF was replaced by the **European Monetary Institute** on 1 January **1994** after the Maastricht Treaty came into force. Article 109f TEC-Maastricht entrusted the EMI with two strands of tasks. Under the paragraph 2 of that provision, the EMI was in essence to strengthen the cooperation between the national central banks, while paragraph 3 charged the EMI with preparatory tasks for the third stage of EMU. **21**

The EMI was subsequently replaced by the **ECB** with effect from 1 July **1998**. Since EMU has entered the third stage, the tasks laid down in ex-Article 109f.3 TEC-Maastricht have been abolished. Due to the continued existence of non-euro area States, the tasks of former Article 109f.2 TEC-Maastricht are nonetheless relevant. Except for the task to 'facilitate the use of the ECU', these tasks are now contained in Article 141.2 TFEU. Article 43 (1) of the ESCB Statute reiterates this assignment, paraphrasing them as 'tasks of the EMI ... which, because of the derogations of one or more Member States, still have to be performed after the introduction of the euro'. Under Article 46.1, first indent, and Article 43 (1) of the ESCB Statute, the **General Council** shall perform these tasks. **22**

Under the first indent of Article 141.2 TFEU, the ECB shall **strengthen cooperation between the NCBs**. In essence, this paraphrases the overall mission of the General Council as forum for cooperation and coordination between the NCBs, **23**

---

[1] Council Regulation (EEC) No. 907/73 *establishing a European Monetary Cooperation Fund*, O.J. L 89/2 (1973).

especially those within and outside the Eurosystem. It does not confer specific tasks on the General Council.

24   Second, the ECB shall **strengthen the coordination of the monetary policies of the MS** (Article 141.2, second indent, TFEU). This task aims at ensuring price stability, which is, according to Article 127.1 TFEU, the primary objective of the ESCB for the euro area MS (Article 139.2 point (c) TFEU). The same is reiterated by Article 16.1 of the ERM II Agreement.[2] A high degree of price stability is one precondition for accession to the third stage of EMU (→ Article 140 TFEU para 13–16). This does not, however, entail any decision-making competences of the General Council as non-euro area NCBs retain their powers in the field of monetary policy (Article 282.4, sentence 2, TFEU and Article 42.2 of the ESCB Statute).

25   Furthermore, the General Council shall, under the third indent, **monitor the functioning of the exchange-rate mechanism**. This is in line with the task prescribed by Article 16.1 of the ERM II Agreement, according to which the General Council shall monitor the functioning of ERM II and serve as the forum for exchange-rate policy coordination. This enables the General Council to fulfil its advisory role for preparing the abrogation of the derogations (Article 140.3 TFEU read together with Article 46.3 of the ESCB Protocol). Observance of fluctuation margins provided for by the ERM II are part of the convergence criteria to be fulfilled for the adoption of the euro (→ Article 140 TFEU para 32 et seqq.).

26   Fourth, the ECB (through the General Council) shall **hold consultations concerning issues** falling within the competence of the national central banks and **affecting the stability of financial institutions and markets** (Article 141.2, fourth indent, TFEU). In 2010 the Union established the European Systemic Risk Board[3] for macro-prudential oversight of the financial system within the Union to contribute to the prevention or mitigation of systemic risks to financial stability in the Union that arise from developments within the financial system (Article 3.1 of Regulation 1092/2010). The President and Vice-President of the ESB and the Governors of the NCBs form the majority of voting members of the ESRB's General Board (Article 6.1 of Regulation 1092/2010).[4]

27   Finally, under the fifth indent of Article 141.2 TFEU, the General Council shall **carry out the former tasks of the EMI** (successor to the EMCF → para 21) which the ECB is required to perform in stage three of EMU because not all MS have

---

[2] Agreement of 16 March 2006 *between the European Central Bank and the national central banks of the Member States outside the euro area laying down the operating procedures for an exchange rate mechanism in stage three of Economic and Monetary Union*, O.J. C 73/21 (2006), as amended by Agreement of 22 January 2020, O.J. C 32I/1 (2020).

[3] Parliament/Council Regulation (EU) No 1092/2010 *on European Union macro-prudential oversight of the financial system and establishing a European Systemic Risk Board*, O.J. L 331/1 (2010), as amended by Parliament/Council Regulation (EU) No 2019/2176, O.J. L 334/126 (2019).

[4] Article 6.1 point (b) of Regulation 1092/2010 specificies that, if the NCB is not the designated authority for prudential supervision of credit institutions, the MS concerned shall nominate a representative from the competent authority.

adopted the euro (Article 46.1, first indent, in conjunction with Article 43 (1) of the ESCB Statute). Disregarding the redundancy with Article 43 (1) of the ESCB Statute, this task includes the administration of financing operations under Articles 6 et seqq. of the ERM II Agreement on a 'very short-term financing facility'. These correspond, in essence, to the administration of financial operations under the Regulation on medium-term financial assistance.[5]

---

[5] Council Regulation (EC) No 332/2002 *establishing a facility providing medium-term financial assistance for Member States' balances of payments*, O.J. L 53/1 (2002), as amended by Council Regulation (EC) No 431/2009, O.J. L 128/1 (2009).

Article 142 [Exchange-Rate Policy]
(ex-Article 124 (1) TEC)

Each Member State with a derogation shall treat its exchange-rate policy as a matter of common interest.[8–13] In so doing, Member States shall take account of the experience acquired in cooperation within the framework of the exchange-rate mechanism.[14–38]

Contents

1. General Remarks 1
2. Exchange-Rate Policy as a Matter of Common Interest 8
3. Experience in the Exchange-Rate Mechanism 14
4. Exchange-Rate Mechanism II 18
   4.1. Operation of ERM II 25
   4.2. Monitoring the Functioning of ERM II 28
   4.3. Amendments to the Agreement on ERM II 29
   4.4. EU Currencies in the ERM II Basket 30
   4.5. Participation in ERM II: Voluntary or Mandatory? 33
   4.6. Non-EU Currencies and ERM II 35
References

1. General Remarks

Before the launching of the third stage of EMU, all MS were required under ex-Article 124 (1) TEC to treat their exchange-rate policy as a matter of common interest. This Treaty provision further declared that until the beginning of the third stage of EMU, MS shall consider the experience acquired in cooperation within the framework of the **European Monetary System** (EMS) and in developing the **European currency unit** (ECU). It further declared that from the beginning of the third stage of EMU and as long as an MS has a derogation, such countries shall treat their exchange-rate policy as a matter of common interest. They need to consult each other and, where necessary, coordinate their action. **1**

With the adoption of the euro replacing 19 different currencies and conferring the monetary competence to the ECB, there was **no need to adopt a common exchange-rate policy within the euro area**. When the euro was adopted, it also replaced the national exchange-rate policies of the MS within the euro area. **2**

However, **outside the euro area** there are currently eight **MS retaining** their own currency pursuing an **independent monetary and exchange-rate policy**. The current Article 142 TFEU takes up the content of ex-Article 124 TEC and applies to the MS with a derogation. **3**

4 After the launching of the **third stage of EMU**, the MS that adopted the euro as their single currency had to surrender their monetary competence to the ECB. The EU thus assumed full competence in the field of monetary policy within the eurozone. On the other hand, countries such as Sweden, which have their own national currencies continue to retain, maintain and formulate their independent monetary policies.

5 Apart from coordinating the currency cooperation between the euro and the national currencies within the EU, there are also other **legal mechanisms** put in place to facilitate and pursue the external exchange-rate policy of the euro area.

6 Under Article 138 TFEU, to secure the euro's place in the international monetary system, the Council, on a proposal from the Commission, shall adopt a decision establishing **common positions** on matters of particular interest for EMU **within the competent international financial institutions and conferences** (→ Article 138 TFEU para 20 et seq.).

7 Under Article 219.1 TFEU the Council, in an endeavour to reach a consensus consistent with the objective of price stability, may **conclude formal agreements on an exchange-rate system** for the euro in relation to the currencies of third states (→ Article 219 TFEU para 13 et seq.).

2. Exchange-Rate Policy as a Matter of Common Interest

8 Before the introduction of the euro, all MS were required to treat their exchange rate as a matter of common interest. There were fifteen MS when the third stage of EMU was launched in 1999 and before this date all the MS had a common obligation to pursue a **national exchange-rate policy, which aimed to facilitate the smooth launching of the third stage of EMU.**

9 With the launching of the third stage of EMU, the question arises whether the aim of Article 142 TFEU is to require only the **MS with a derogation** to **develop their respective exchange-rate policy** as a matter of common interest. In other words: whether such an obligation should be limited to states outside the euro area.

10 The Lisbon Treaty requires MS to attain a **certain degree of exchange and currency stability as precondition to join the third stage of EMU** (Article 140.1 (1), fourth indent, TFEU; → Article 140 TFEU para 26–27). To reach this goal, the Treaty mandates the currencies of MS with a derogation to link their currencies to ERM II, in which the euro is the anchor currency. To that extent, the obligation to treat the exchange-rate policy as a matter of common interest should not be interpreted as applicable only to the MS with a derogation, but also to the euro area as a whole.

11 Although Article 142 TFEU is confined to the chapter on transitional provisions, its scope of application is **not limited to the MS with a derogation**. It also applies to MS located within the euro area. Therefore, it is not only the authorities of MS with a derogation, but also the ECB as the sole monetary authority of the euro area that are collectively obliged to pursue their exchange-rate policy as a matter of concern covering the entire Union.

Article 142. [Exchange-Rate Policy]   967

Finland, a member of the euro area, expressed its concern regarding the negative   **12**
attitude of Sweden to adopt the euro. These Nordic countries have large companies that compete in the paper industry. Both countries are major exporters of this product. Since Finland is part of the euro area, it lost its competence to manipulate its exchange-rate policy whereas Sweden may still do so as it retains competence in this policy area. It is partly to **prevent the development of** such potential **unfair competition by exchange-rate manipulation** that it is preferable to broadly construe the obligation emerging from Article 142 TFEU to treat the exchange-rate policy as a matter concerning all MS.

The Treaty does not specifically stipulate that the obligation imposed on the MS   **13**
outside the eurozone to treat their exchange-rate policy vis-a-vis the euro as a matter of common interest as a legally binding obligation, similar to the imprecise requirement to peg the currencies of the MS outside the eurozone to ERM II. Such an obligation may be treated as legally binding if we are to stretch that obligation by reference to the **principle of solidarity** or **loyalty**.

On the other hand, hierarchy of obligation imposed on the ECB as guardian of the euro to treat its exchange-rate policy vis-a-vis the non-euro currencies as a matter of common interest is made clear in Article 127 TFEU, which should be without prejudice to its **primary objective of maintaining price stability**.

3. Experience in the Exchange-Rate Mechanism

When the **third stage of EMU was launched in 1999** with eleven MS as its   **14**
founding members, Denmark and the United Kingdom had opt-outs, and it was only Greece and Sweden which failed to meet all the economic convergence requirements.[1] Nevertheless, these countries however had been part of the European exchange-rate mechanism at least for some time.[2]

The objective to develop the MS exchange-rate policy as a matter of common   **15**
interest was to a great extent achieved by the establishment of the **EMS** in 1979. The two pillars of the EMS were the exchange-rate mechanism and the ECU. The EMS based on a fixed but adjustable exchange rate was devised to limit fluctuations among the participating currencies. The currencies pegged to the ERM had a permissible fluctuation of ± 2.25% except for the Spanish *peseta* and Italian *lira*, which were allowed to fluctuate 6% either side for a prescribed period.

The currency crisis of 1992 seriously undermined the credibility of this mecha-   **16**
nism leading to the ejection of several currencies from the system.[3] Sweden, which only became an MS of the EU in 1995 but had voluntarily tied its currency to the ERM, was also caught in the midst of this **financial crisis**. The Swedish Central Bank (*Riksbank*) made a futile attempt to protect its currency by raising its lending

---

[1] Seyad (2000).
[2] For the UK, see No. 5, sentence 2, of Protocol No. 15; for Denmark, see No. 1 of Protocol No. 16.
[3] Seyad (1996).

rates to an incredible figure of 500%. When all efforts to withstand the speculative attacks on their currencies proved ineffective, the Community authorities decided to stretch the fluctuation margin to 15% to restore confidence and maintain the stability of the ERM.[4] Soon after this crisis, **many currencies** such as the Spanish *peseta*, Italian *lira*, Finnish *markka*, British *sterling pound*, and Swedish *krona* **left the exchange-rate mechanism**. Swedish *krona* is not linked to ERM II.

17   After launching of the third stage of EMU, thirteen countries joined the EU. Some of these countries have joined the euro area after experiencing a minimum of two years in pegging their currencies to ERM II. Of these newly acceded countries it is only Bulgaria, Croatia, the Czech Republic, Hungary, Poland and Romania which are outside the euro area and designated as MS with a derogation. Meanwhile, in July 2020, Croatia[5] and Bulgaria[6] have pegged their currencies to the ERM II.[7] Since the introduction of the euro in 1999, Denmark,[8] as a non-euro area MS, joined the ERM II.

4. Exchange-Rate Mechanism II

18   The first reference to the **EMS** in the **Treaty of Rome** was made after its first amendment by the Single European Act in 1987. This amendment introduced a new chapter on EMU and its sole provision, Article 102a TEEC. It provided that the MS shall consider the experience acquired in co-operation within the framework of the EMS. With the Treaty of Maastricht, the content of that provision was transferred to Article 109m TEC, which eventually became Article 124 TEC.

19   There were detailed rules in the **Maastricht Treaty** for the establishment of EMU, but it contained hardly any provisions on the legal status and structure of the EMS. Even after the Amsterdam Treaty, the legal status of the EMS, particularly ERM II, which replaced the original ERM, continued to be based on a European Council Resolution,[9] a legal instrument which belongs to the branch of the soft law of the Union's Community's legal order.

20   The exchange-rate mechanism aims to reduce exchange-rate variability and achieve **monetary stability** in the Union as a prelude to the launching of the third stage of EMU with a single currency.

21   After launching the euro, one of the important functions assigned to the General Council of the ESCB is to make the necessary preparations **for irrevocably fixing**

---

[4] On 2 August 1993, the Ministers of Finance and central bank Governors jointly took the decision to widen the ERM fluctuation margin.

[5] The central rate is 1 EUR = 7.53450 Kuna.

[6] The central rate is 1 EUR = 1.95583 Lev.

[7] See recently Dorrucci et al. (2020).

[8] The central rate is 1 EUR = 7.46038 Danish Kroner.

[9] Resolution of the Amsterdam European Council of 16 June 1997 *on the establishment of an exchange-rate mechanism in the third stage of economic and monetary union*, O.J. C 236/5 (1997).

Article 142. [Exchange-Rate Policy]

the exchange rates of the currencies of the MS with a derogation against the euro. To achieve this objective, the original mechanism was replaced by the ERM II on 1 January 1999, euro replacing ECU as the anchor currency.[10] Thus, a new Agreement was adopted which establishes an exchange-rate mechanism to replace the old EMS as the latter became obsolete with the introduction of the euro. This Agreement replaces the previous Agreement concluded in September 1998[11] and amended on several occasions for technical reasons. ERM II is based on an agreement between the ministers and central bank governors of the non-euro area MS and the euro-area MS, and the ECB. On 22 January 2020, the Agreement on the ERM II had to be amended because of the withdrawal of the UK from the EU.[12]

One of the objectives of this mechanism is to ensure that **exchange-rate fluctuations** between the euro and other EU currencies **do not disrupt economic stability within the single market**.[13] The aim of this monetary arrangement and cooperation is based on the assumption that it will contribute to the smooth operation of the single market. The stability and harmonious functioning of the single market should not be endangered by exchange-rate misalignments or fluctuations between the euro and the other Union currencies. Such potential disruption may disrupt trade flows between the MS, which is not consistent with the primary Treaty objective to develop a uniform and distortion-free single market. The ERM therefore aims to ensure a stable economic environment by establishing an exchange-rate mechanism between the euro and the participating national currencies.

Another reason to create this mechanism is to help non-euro area countries prepare themselves for participation in the euro area. The **convergence criterion on exchange-rate stability** (Article 140.1 (1), fourth indent, TFEU; → Article 140 TFEU para 26–27) requires participation in ERM II. Therefore, the currency linkage is an essential part of the preparations for entry to the euro area by MS with a derogation.

Within the euro area, there are nineteen MS that use one currency, the euro. The other MS outside the euro area have their own currencies such as Swedish *krona*,

---

[10] Resolution of the European Council of 16 June 1997 *on the exchange rate mechanism* ('ERM II') when the third stage of Economic and Monetary Union began on 1 January 1999.

[11] Agreement of 1 September 1998 *between the European Central Bank and the national central banks of the Member States outside the euro area laying down the operating procedures for an exchange rate mechanism in stage three of Economic and Monetary Union*, O.J. C 345/6 (1998).

[12] Agreement of 22 January 2020 *between the European Central Bank and the national central banks of the Member States outside the euro area amending the Agreement of 16 March 2006 between the European Central Bank and the national central banks of the Member States outside the euro area laying down the operating procedures for an exchange rate mechanism in stage three of Economic and Monetary Union*, O.J. C 32 I/1 (2020).

[13] Agreement of 16 March 2006 *between the European Central Bank and the national central banks of the Member States outside the euro area laying down the operating procedures for an exchange rate mechanism in stage three of Economic and Monetary Union*, O.J. L 73/11 (2006), as amended by Agreement of 13 November 2014, O.J. C 64/1 (2015).

Danish *krona*, etc. The ERM II aims to **prevent excessive fluctuations in the exchange rates between the euro and other Union currencies**.

4.1. Operation of ERM II

25 The exchange rate of a non-euro area MS is fixed against the euro, and is allowed to fluctuate within set limits. Any such entry to ERM II is based on an **agreement between the ministers and central bank governors of the euro and non-euro area MS and the ECB**. Under this arrangement, a central exchange rate between the euro and the relevant MS should be first agreed. The relevant currency is allowed to fluctuate by 2.5% above or below the central rate.[14] After the monetary crisis, the margin of fluctuation was widened to 15% except Germany and The Netherlands, which entered into a separate agreement to limit the fluctuation margin to 2.25%.[15]

26 Whenever it is necessary, the **currency** will be **supported by way of intervention**, either buying or selling to keep the exchange rate against the euro within the 15% fluctuation margin. Such intervention is coordinated by the ECB and the central banks of the MS of the non-euro area.

27 The MS outside the euro area that have signed up to ERM II can decide to maintain an even narrower fluctuation band as once decided by Germany and The Netherlands. Such a decision will have no impact on the **officially fixed 15% fluctuation margin**. For example, Denmark has no such special agreement like Germany and The Netherlands, but the Danish *krona* is pegged to ERM II to fluctuate within the narrow margin of 2.25%.

4.2. Monitoring the Functioning of ERM II

28 Since the exchange-rate mechanism aims to prevent major fluctuations between the euro and the national currencies of the MS outside the eurozone, it is essential that the competence to monitor the movements between these currencies is given to a body representing the monetary authorities of all MS of the EU. As such, the competence to monitor the proper functioning of the ERM II is assigned to the **General Council of the ECB** (Article 46.1, first indent, and Article 43 of the ESCB Statute in connection with Article 141.2, third indent, TFEU). It shall ensure the co-ordination of monetary and exchange-rate policies of the parties to ERM II (→ Article 141 TFEU para 24 et seq.). The General Council also administers the intervention mechanisms together with the central banks of the MS outside the euro area.

---

[14] Cf. Rohde Jensen (2005), p. 142.
[15] Seyad (1996).

Article 142. [Exchange-Rate Policy]

4.3. Amendments to the Agreement on ERM II

The Agreement on ERM II must be amended each time a new **national central bank becomes party** to it. It is also amended whenever a **national central bank ceases to be party** to the Agreement, specifically when an MS adopts the euro as its single currency. The Agreement on ERM II was amended for example to consider the **joining of the euro area** by Slovenia, Cyprus, Malta, Slovakia, Estonia[16] and Lithuania.[17] Similar amendments to the Agreement were made when Romania and Bulgaria joined the Union. Like any other new MS, they are designated in their accession agreement as MS with a derogation.

29

4.4. EU Currencies in the ERM II Basket

One of the two grounds on which **Sweden** was disqualified to enter euro area as its founding member was its failure to maintain the stability of its currency by reference to the exchange-rate mechanism of the EMS. Swedish *kronor* were pegged to the ERM until 1992/93 when a monetary turbulence wreak havoc on several European currencies and almost destroyed the entire structure of the ERM.[18] After failing to protect the stability of the *krona* even after raising the interest to 500%, Sweden decided to depart from the ERM. Since then, Sweden has kept away from the ERM.

30

Denmark is not an MS with a derogation, but it has an opt-out from the third stage of EMU. The Danish *kroner* joined ERM II on 1 January 1999, and it observes a central rate of 7.46038 to the euro with a narrow fluctuation band of $\pm$ 2.25%. Denmark held a referendum to join the eurozone, but the Danes rejected it.[19]

31

Besides Denmark, **Bulgaria** and **Croatia** have joined ERM II. Bulgarian *lev* (2020) and the Croatian *kuna* (2020) are pegged to the euro and fluctuate within the wider margin of 15%. The other MS with a derogation, Czechia, Hungary, Poland and Romania have not linked their national currencies to ERM II, but substantially their currencies keep within the standard fluctuation band. There are different legal opinions on whether the currency must be pegged to ERM II for a minimum period of two years as a precondition to join the third stage of EMU ($\rightarrow$ Article 140 TFEU para 23).[20]

32

---

[16] Agreement of 13 December 2010, O.J. C 5/04 (2011).

[17] Agreement of 13 November 2014, O.J. C 64/1 (2015).

[18] Seyad (1996).

[19] A referendum on joining the euro was held in Denmark on 28 September 2000, but it was rejected by 53.2% of voters with a turnout of 87.6%.

[20] Seyad (2000).

4.5. Participation in ERM II: Voluntary or Mandatory?

33 It is not precisely clear from a legal perspective whether participation in ERM II by an MS with a derogation is mandatory or voluntary. As **one of the convergence criteria** for entry to the eurozone, an MS must participate in the ERM II without severe tensions for at least two years before it can qualify to adopt the euro.

34 There are several MS with a derogation such as Sweden which have not linked their currencies to ERM II. Hence, the nature of the obligation imposed on MS with a derogation to link their respective currencies to ERM II is apparently more of a **political nature rather than a legal issue** in the final determination on this entry requirement to EMU.

4.6. Non-EU Currencies and ERM II

35 **EU law does not prohibit currencies from outside its territory from being linked to the exchange-rate mechanism.** Even countries such as Sweden and Finland had linked their currencies to the ERM before joining the EU. The ECB or the euro area, however, has no agreements or obligations to support such non-EU currencies. Some external currencies are linked to ERM II voluntarily and others through bilateral agreements.

36 There are several countries and territories outside the EU which have linked their currencies to the euro for various reasons. Before the introduction of the euro, American dollar had been viewed as the hard currency to anchor other less strong currencies. One reason is the perceived stability of the monetary system behind the euro, and this makes it an attractive anchor currency for them. Sometimes countries with weak **economies may consider linking their currency to ERM II supported by euro as a safety measure.** Such linkages with hard currencies may also bring more certainty and stability to their national economies. If two currencies are linked to each other with the objective of avoiding strong exchange-rate fluctuations, such a monetary arrangement may also strengthen and enhance their trade relations.

37 There are **some currencies which are linked to the euro by bilateral agreements**. The third countries behind such monetary arrangements are largely former colonies of some of the MS. The *CFA francs* used in French overseas territories in the Pacific region (French Polynesia, New Caledonia and Wallis and Futuna Islands) have historical relations with France.[21] These currencies had earlier been pegged to the French *franc* and now pegged to the euro through bilateral agreements with France. Thus, the euro area has no obligation to support the exchange rate with the *CFP franc*.

---

[21] The Comorian *franc* [O.J. L 320/58 (1998)] and the Cape Verde *escudo* [O.J. L 358/11 (1998)] which was previously linked to the French *franc* and Portuguese *escudo* are now linked to the euro through bilateral agreements.

There are also **external currencies which are linked unilaterally to the euro.** 38
This is achieved through supporting an exchange rate against the euro which is only allowed to fluctuate within defined limits. The monetary authorities of such third country currencies support the exchange-rate peg on their own by intervening in currency markets. Neither the ECB nor the governments of the MS of the euro area have an obligation to do so.[22]

References

Dorrucci, E., Fidora, M., Gartner, C., & Zumer, T. (2020). The European exchange rate mechanism (ERM II) as a preparatory phase on the path towards euro adoption – the cases of Bulgaria and Croatia. *ECB Economic Bulletin*, 8/2020.
Rohde Jensen, K. (2005). Inside EU, outside EMU: Institutional and legal aspects of the exchange rate mechanism II. In European Central Bank (Ed.), *Legal aspects of the European System of Central Banks* (pp. 135–146). European Central Bank.
Seyad, S. (1996). Capital movements and the currency crisis in the European Union. *European Financial Services Law*, 193–200.
Seyad, S. (2000). Is the purported exclusion of Sweden from the Euro land Justified? *European Business Law Review*, 363–372.

---

[22] A few examples of such unilateral links with the euro are the former Yugoslav Republic of Macedonia, Serbia and Tunisia.

Article 143 [Mutual Assistance]
(ex-Article 119 TEC)

1. Where a Member State with a derogation[5–8] is in difficulties or is seriously threatened with difficulties as regards its balance of payments[9–12] either as a result of an overall disequilibrium in its balance of payments, or as a result of the type of currency at its disposal, and where such difficulties are liable in particular to jeopardise the functioning of the internal market[13–15] or the implementation of the common commercial policy,[16–21] the Commission shall immediately investigate the position of the State in question and the action which, making use of all the means at its disposal, that State has taken or may take in accordance with the provisions of the Treaties. The Commission shall state what measures it recommends the State concerned to take.

   If the action taken by a Member State with a derogation and the measures suggested by the Commission do not prove sufficient to overcome the difficulties which have arisen or which threaten, the Commission shall, after consulting the Economic and Financial Committee, recommend to the Council the granting of mutual assistance and appropriate methods therefor.[22–32]

   The Commission shall keep the Council regularly informed of the situation and of how it is developing.

2. The Council shall grant such mutual assistance;[22–32] it shall adopt directives or decisions laying down the conditions and details of such assistance, which may take such forms as:

   (a) a concerted approach to or within any other international organisations to which Member States with a derogation may have recourse;
   (b) measures needed to avoid deflection of trade where the Member State with a derogation which is in difficulties maintains or reintroduces quantitative restrictions against third countries;
   (c) the granting of limited credits by other Member States, subject to their agreement.

3. If the mutual assistance recommended by the Commission is not granted by the Council or if the mutual assistance granted and the measures taken are insufficient, the Commission shall authorise the Member State with a derogation which is in difficulties to take protective measures, the conditions and details of which the Commission shall determine.[33,34]

   Such authorisation may be revoked and such conditions and details may be changed by the Council.

Contents

1. Overview 1
2. Conditions to Invoke Article 143 TFEU 4
   2.1. Restriction to Member States Outside the Euro Area 5
   2.2. Balance of Payment Difficulties 9
   2.3. Jeopardising the Functioning of the Internal Market 13
   2.4. Jeopardising the Implementation of the Common Commercial Policy 16
3. Mutual Assistance 22
   3.1. Mutual Assistance in General 22
   3.2. Council Regulation 332/2002 on Medium Term Financial Assistance 23
4. Protective Measures 33
5. Impact of COVID-19 on Article 143 TFEU 35
List of Cases
References

1. Overview

1   Articles 143 and 144 TFEU contain the safeguard clauses which can be invoked to adopt balance of payments measures. A country's balance of payments is the difference between all money flowing into the country and money flowing out of the country in a particular period (usually as receipts and payments by natural and legal persons for goods and services). Since 1 January 1999, which marks the beginning of the third stage of EMU, the **safeguard clause to remedy crises in the balance of payments** is only applicable to those MS outside the euro area.

2   Article 143 TFEU **applies to MS with a derogation** when they are confronted with balance of payments difficulties. This legal provision authorises the EU institutions to borrow money from the financial market on behalf of the MS to offer them financial assistance.[1] The aim of providing financial assistance to MS outside the euro area suffering from balance of payments difficulties is essentially to help them ease their external financing constraints. Article 66 TFEU may serve as a legal basis for temporary safeguard measures where movements of capital to or from third countries cause, or threaten to cause, serious difficulties for the operation of EMU.

3   The criteria to provide such assistance are that they should be confronted with a **critical balance of payments crisis**. It is the Commission which is authorised to contract borrowings on the capital market or with financial institutions. The wording of this Treaty provision declares that it only applies to MS that are suffering from a balance of payments crisis, but also if there is a risk or potential to develop such a crisis.

---

[1] In 2008 and 2009, the EU lent EUR 6.5 billion to Hungary, EUR 3.1 billion to Latvia and EUR 6 billion to Romania as part of wider assistance plans funded together with the IMF and World Bank.

2. Conditions to Invoke Article 143 TFEU

There are certain conditions stipulated to invoke this legal provision.[2] Primarily, there must be evidence to show that the MS with a derogation (→ para 5–8) is in difficulties or seriously threatened with difficulties concerning its balance of payments (→ para 9–12). Such difficulty must have been caused by disequilibrium of its balance of payments or because of the type of currency which it uses. The MS seeking assistance must also show that the potential balance of payment difficulties will have a negative impact on the functioning of the internal market (→ para 13–15) or the implementation of the common commercial policy (→ para 16–21).

2.1. Restriction to Member States Outside the Euro Area

Article 143 TFEU specifically contemplates balance of payments **support only for MS with a derogation**. By virtue of No. 1 of Protocol No. 16, it also applies to Denmark, which is technically not an MS with a derogation (→ Article 139 TFEU para 14–15). The 2008 global financial crisis seriously affected most of the MS, both inside and outside the euro area. This crisis was immediately followed by the fiscal crisis in 2011, which contributed to further deteriorate the economic conditions of some MS especially within the euro area.[3] The MS within the euro area which were affected by these twin crises could not have access to any Union financial assistance since the benefit of this Treaty provision is limited to MS outside the euro area.

There is no clear explanation for this legal contradiction whereby it allows one category of MS to have access to financial assistance whereas the other category is completely prohibited from accessing it. The financial rescue provision may have been formulated that way based on the assumption that at the time of negotiating the Maastricht Treaty, the MS would not have contemplated the insolvency of a country within the euro area.[4] Another reason for limiting the scope of application of Article 143 TFEU may have been to avoid contradictions with the **no-bail out rule in Article 125 TFEU**. Once all MS of the EU have joined the euro area, Article 143 TFEU will automatically cease to be operative.

To rescue financially some of the MS' economies collapsing from the debt crisis, beginning at the end of 2009, the immediate dilemma for the EU was to find the proper legal basis for the creation of a bailout fund. Article 125 TFEU declares unambiguously that the Union shall not be liable for or assume the commitments of central governments, regional, local or other public authorities, other bodies governed by public law, or public undertakings of any MS. Since this Treaty provision

---

[2] Zander (2010).
[3] Seyad (2015).
[4] Seyad (2011), p. 421.

expressly prohibits the bail-out of an MS, the EU had to look for other legal avenues to achieve the same goal.

The legal framework for the **loan package to Greece, Ireland and Portugal** was thus shifted to **Article 122.2 TFEU**[5] which is designed to provide financial aid to MS experiencing serious difficulties (→ Article 122 TFEU para 18–22). However, it is problematic from a legal point of view to justify the invocation of Article 122 TFEU to grant financial assistance to Greece, Ireland and Portugal on the legal basis foreseen for natural disasters such as an earth quake or tsunami. The serious debt crisis in these countries was a man-made financial disaster as a consequence of the failure to restructure state (e.g. concerning high state expenditure relative to GDP with a decline in public revenue) and economy (excessive wages and low productivity). Not least, the crisis was created by their failure to respect the Stability and Growth Pact adopted to ensure fiscal discipline amongst all MS, particularly the euroland countries.[6] As a result of the economic and financial crisis in 2008/2009, the Irish financial sector collapsed. The Irish government saw the need to spend billions to recapitalise its distressed banks and thus public finances deteriorated rapidly. It was pure **fiscal mismanagement** which culminated in the debt crisis in these countries. The ECJ however in *Pringle* declared that in particular 'Articles [...] 119 TFEU to 123 TFEU and 125 TFEU to 127 TFEU, and the general principle of effective judicial protection do not preclude the conclusion between the Member States whose currency is the euro of an agreement such as the Treaty establishing the European stability mechanism'.[7]

8   Nonetheless, the **serious deterioration in the international economic and financial environment** in the relevant period may be **treated as an 'exceptional occurrence'** to justify the invocation of this Treaty provision.[8] Although the debt crisis was generated by the failure to respect the rules on fiscal discipline, the crisis was further aggravated by the global financial meltdown. There were many countries both inside and outside the EU which had to seek financial assistance from the IMF due to balance of payments difficulties generated by the global financial crisis. The difficulties confronted by Greece, Ireland and later Portugal may thus be treated as exceptional circumstances outside their control (→ Article 122 para 15 et seqq.).

---

[5] See Council Regulation (EU) No. 407/2010 *establishing a European financial stabilisation mechanism*, O.J. L 118/1 (2010), which was based on Article 122 TFEU. Cf. Martucci (2020), para 12.6 et seqq.
[6] Seyad (2012).
[7] Case C-370/12, *Pringle* (ECJ 27 November 2012) para 182: cf. Borger (2013), p. 7 (24 et seq.).
[8] Seyad (2011).

2.2. Balance of Payment Difficulties

A balance of payments difficulty is a situation where **sufficient financing on** 9
reasonable and affordable terms cannot be obtained by an MS to meet international payment obligations and the best example is the case of Greece, although being a eurozone MS and not an MS with a derogation. In an extreme worst-case scenario as in Greece, such balance of payments difficulties may even develop into a serious crisis.

A balance of payment difficulty may arise because of **exceptional circum-** 10
stances such as a natural disaster or from the **adoption of inappropriate economic and financial policies** in an MS or a combination of both as in the case of Greece.

When an MS is in difficulties or seriously threatened with difficulties such as 11
disequilibrium in its balance of payments, the **Commission** may investigate and recommend what measures the state should take to overcome the crisis. If the measures suggested by the Commission do not prove sufficient to overcome the difficulties, it shall recommend to the Council, after consulting the Economic and Financial Committee (Article 134 TFEU), to grant mutual assistance. It is also possible for an MS suffering from a balance of payments crisis to seek credit directly from other MS as well.

It is possible for the Commission to approach any **international financial** 12
institutions to mobilise the financial resources necessary to fulfil its mandate. Since Article 143 TFEU provides only a general framework to assist MS with a derogation, further implementing measures have to be adopted.

2.3. Jeopardising the Functioning of the Internal Market

Article 143 TFEU is concerned with the adverse repercussions a balance of pay- 13
ments difficulties may have on the proper functioning of the internal market. If the balance of payments difficulties in an MS develop into a crisis as in the case of Greece, it can have a **negative impact on the currency** as it did with the **stability of the euro**. Any such disruption to the economy or the financial system suffering from balance of payments difficulties could infect other countries especially within the integrated and inter-dependent internal market of the EU.

One of the fundamental objectives of the EU is not only to establish an internal 14
market in goods, persons, services and capital, but also to ensure that it functions smoothly, uniformly and harmoniously. Any kind of undue advantage unilaterally exercised or conferred upon an MS of the Union will **disrupt the level playing field in the internal market**. Some new economically less developed MS joining the Union may secure certain derogations in the internal market, but they are subject to strict conditions and such benefits are always only for a limited period (e.g. Article 27 TFEU).

Any financial measures, adopted or proposed to be adopted by an MS, should not 15
directly or indirectly jeopardise the proper functioning of the internal market. There are strict rules in the Treaty to ensure the smooth functioning of the internal market.

There are comprehensive and detailed rules in the Treaty such as on competition rules (Articles 101–106 TFEU), state aid rules (Articles 107–109 TFEU), etc. which are incorporated to prevent causing any disturbance or distortion to the internal market. Any MS with a derogation, which benefits from Article 143 TFEU, must ensure the **measures it adopted** or seeks to adopt to deal with a potential balance of payments strictly **comply with the rules on competition and state aid**.

2.4. Jeopardising the Implementation of the Common Commercial Policy

16   Article 143 TFEU is not only concerned with the impact the balance of payments difficulties may have on the internal market, but also in relation to the common commercial policy (Articles 206, 207 TFEU). The EU is one of the largest blocs in the global **trading system**. Its trading partners are not just the other major countries such as the USA, China and Japan, but also almost all the economies across the globe are exposed to it.

17   There are special legal instruments for the EU to develop a commercial policy common towards third countries. It uses such instruments not only to **liberalise international trade**, but also as an **instrument of foreign policy** in its international relations. As a founding member of the WTO, the EU is also subject to a host of rights and obligations flowing from this international organisation.

18   One of the objectives of the Lisbon Treaty in relation to external trade is to develop a commercial policy common to all MS. Such a policy evolved as the EU established a dynamic **customs union** for the benefit of all its MS.[9] The Treaty declares that customs duties on imports and exports shall be abolished between MS (Article 30 TFEU). At the same time, the Lisbon Treaty declares quantitative restrictions on imports shall be prohibited between MS (Article 34 TFEU). To preserve the stability and homogeneity of the customs union, the EU has also adopted a **common commercial policy towards third countries**.[10] Since the Treaty of Lisbon, this is part of the exclusive competences of the Union (Article 3.1 point (e) TFEU). Already before, there have been clear judicial pronouncements to the effect that in the realm of common commercial policy MS cannot take any unilateral action which 'would [...] distort competition between [national] undertakings [...] in external markets'.[11]

19   The EU shall enter into **international agreements** to pursue and give effect to develop and enforce the common commercial policy (Article 216–219 TFEU).[12]

---

[9] There are several publications dealing with the customs union of the EU. See for example, Lasok (1998).

[10] Elsig (2002).

[11] Opinion 1/75, *EC competence for commercial policy* (ECJ 11 November 1975) point B.2 on the exclusive nature of the Community's powers.

[12] Martines (2014).

Article 143. [Mutual Assistance]

Such agreements are negotiated by the Commission, and, with the consent of the EP, the Council by qualified majority shall conclude such agreements (Article 218 TFEU). Such agreements relate to trade protection generalised system of preferences, anti-dumping and rules of origin.[13]

To develop and sustain this policy, the **Commission** is given wide powers both within and outside the Union. It has the duty to **ensure the MS fully comply with this policy** in all international forums such as the WTO, where the Commission represents the Union and its MS. This unified representation aims to ensure that all MS of the Union speak with one voice in such international trade forums.[14] 20

Since the EU is trading not just within its geographical limits but increasingly dependent on international trade, any **balance of payment difficulties developing within the Union will have its repercussions beyond its boundaries**. If an MS with a derogation is threatened with balance of payments, and if it risks the implementation of the common commercial policy, it may take necessary measures to deal with the situation. If such unilateral measures did not produce any positive results, the EU may consider granting such an MS mutual assistance. 21

3. Mutual Assistance

3.1. Mutual Assistance in General

The issue of the provision of mutual assistance to a fellow MS arises only **after it has exhausted all national means at its disposal in accordance with EU law** and with support of the Commission, and if these measures have proven insufficient. The involvement of the Commission is to investigate the balance of payment situation in a given MS even without a formal request from the latter. It is useful to highlight that the Commission can only suggest or recommend the granting of mutual assistance to the MS concerned after consulting the Economic and Financial Committee (Article 134 TFEU). 22

3.2. Council Regulation 332/2002 on Medium Term Financial Assistance

The facility to provide financial assistance as contemplated in Article 143 TFEU was established by Council Regulation 332/2002,[15] which was, however, **based on ex-Article 308 TEC (= Article 352 TFEU)** and *not* on ex-Article 119 TEC (= Article 143 TFEU). Although Article 143 TFEU authorises the Council to 23

---

[13] Meunier (2005).

[14] Kuijper et al. (2013).

[15] Council Regulation No. 332/2002 *establishing a facility providing medium-term financial assistance for Member States' balances of payments*, O.J. L 53/1 (2002), as amended by Council Regulation (EC) No. 431/2009, O.J. L 128/1 (2009).

grant mutual assistance to MS suffering from balance of payments difficulties, it does not give any indication as to what kind of instrument should be employed to provide such mutual assistance. This legal vacuum was filled by the Regulation.

24   The Regulation provides for the establishment of a **medium-term financial assistance facility**. If an MS with a derogation is confronted with serious market turbulences or difficulties in refinancing its external debt, it can seek medium financial assistance from the Union. After the launching of the third stage of EMU, the number of MS with a derogation reduced drastically. As such, the **number of potential recipients** of such financial assistance also dropped correspondingly.

25   The original volume of the facility which stood at EUR 16 billion was reduced to EUR 12 billion after the launching of the euro. The reason is obvious as there were fewer MS outside the euro area that are entitled to seek such financial assistance in the event of a balance of payment crisis. It was later increased again to now EUR 50 billion (Article 1.1 of Regulation No. 332/2002). It is the **ECB** which is responsible for **administering the loans** granted under this facility.[16] This function was earlier assigned to the European Monetary Cooperation Fund, which was later succeeded by the European Monetary Institute.

26   An MS facing balance of payments difficulties may secure a loan from this facility. The granting of such loans shall be **subject to conditions** imposed by the Council. An important condition is that the recipient MS should adopt economic policy measures to move towards a sustainable balance of payments situation (Article 3.2 of Regulation No. 332/2002).

27   The Union shall raise the loan on behalf of its MS. Since creditworthiness of the EU as an international organisation is generally viewed by the credit rating agencies in a positive light, it could normally borrow from the financial market at concessionary rates of interest. Such **borrowings** from the capital markets or the financial institutions should be in the euro currency. This is because all EU institutions use the euro and it is also the currency used by the borrower, which is the European Commission.

28   It is the **Council** which **decides** on such application for financial relief. The legal construction is interesting to note: The Council first takes a decision, based on Article 143 TFEU, to grant mutual assistance to the MS concerned.[17] This is followed by a second Council decision (based on the first decision taken) to make available the mutual financial assistance under Regulation No. 332/2002. Hungary, Latvia, and Romania have secured such medium-term financial assistance from the

---

[16] ECB Decision 2003/797/EC *concerning the administration of the borrowing-and-lending operations concluded by the European Community under the medium-term financial assistance facility* (ECB/2003/14), O.J. L 297/35 (2003).

[17] See Council Decision 2009/103/EC *granting mutual assistance for Hungary*, O.J. L 37/7 (2009); Council Decision 2009/289/EC *granting mutual assistance for Latvia*, O.J. L 79/37 (2009); Council Decision 2009/458/EC *granting mutual assistance for Romania*, O.J. L 150/6 (2009); Council Decision 2013/532/EU *granting mutual assistance for Romania*, O.J. L 286/4 (2013).

Article 143. [Mutual Assistance] 983

Union supported by other international financial agencies such as the IMF and World Bank.[18]

Article 3 of the Regulation stipulates that it is for the Council to implement the **medium-term financial assistance facility** on the initiative of the Commission. The Council shall decide whether to grant a loan and if so the amount and its average duration. To this end, the Commission and the MS concerned shall conclude a **Memorandum of Understanding** (MoU) and the **Loan Agreement** setting out in detail the conditions laid down by the Council pursuant to Article 3. The Commission shall communicate the MoU to the EP and the Council (Article 3a). The MoU will set out the economic policy conditions for the loan and the Loan Agreement will incorporate the technicalities of the borrowing process and the detailed financial conditions of the loan. They give concrete form to an agreement between the EU and the MS on an economic programme enabling the latter to benefit from medium-term financial assistance referred to in Article 143 TFEU and specified in Regulation No. 332/2002. **29**

The volume of the loan, its duration and the quantum of instalments to repay the loan are all matters decided by the Council. The type of interest rate on the loan is however subject to an agreement between the recipient MS and the Commission. Such an agreement is indispensable as it is the Commission which is authorised to contract on behalf of the Union borrowings on capital markets or from financial institutions. As the CJEU has ruled, the MoU between the Commission and the MS in question constitutes an act of an EU institution within the meaning of Article 267 point (b) TFEU, thus opening the scope of application of the Union's Charter of Fundamental Rights.[19]

It is the responsibility of the Commission under Article 5 of the Regulation to take the necessary measures to **verify** at regular intervals that the economic policy of the recipient **MS accords with the adjustment programme** as laid down by the Council pursuant to Article 3 of the Regulation. It is only after the completion of the verification procedure and after the delivery of the opinion of the Economic and Financial Committee that the Commission shall decide on the release of future instalments. **30**

In addition, the **European Court of Auditors** shall have the right to carry out, in the MS receiving financial assistance, any financial controls or audits that it considers necessary in relation to the management of that assistance. The Commission (including OLAF) shall have the right to send its officials or duly authorised representatives to carry out any necessary technical or financial controls or audits in the MS concerned (Article 9a). **31**

---

[18] Council Decision 2009/102/EC *on Community medium-term financial assistance for Hungary*, O.J. L 37/5 (2009); Council Decision 2009/290/EC *providing Community medium-term financial assistance for Latvia*, O.J. L 79/39 (2009); Council Decision 2009/459/EC *providing Community medium-term financial assistance for Romania*, O.J. L 150/8 (2009); Council Decision 2013/531/EU *providing precautionary Union medium-term financial assistance to Romania*, O.J. L 286/1 (2013).

[19] Case C-258/14, *Florescu* (CJEU 13 June 2017) para 35, 48.

32　It is also possible for an MS to look for **financing outside the Union**. It should, however, first consult the Commission and the other MS. Such consultations are held in the forum of the Economic and Financial Committee of the Union.[20]

4. Protective Measures

33　In the event of mutual assistance not being granted or if such assistance given and the measures adopted prove insufficient, the Commission may authorise the MS to take **unilateral protective measures (Article 143.3 TFEU)**. Such protective measures are subject to an ex post review by the Council. The Council has the power to revoke the authorisation given by the Commission or alternatively to revise the terms and conditions on which such authorisation was issued by the Commission. These protective measures may deviate from the provisions of the Treaties.

34　If a decision within the meaning of Article 143.2 TFEU is not immediately taken, an MS with a derogation may, as a precaution, take the necessary protective measures without Council or Commission authorisation by virtue of **Article 144 TFEU**. These measures shall be replaced by Union measures as soon as possible (→ Article 144 TFEU para 9). In practice, however, the Regulation 332/2002 has diminished the relevance of Articles 143 and 144 TFEU.

5. Impact of COVID-19 on Article 143 TFEU

35　The EU since its inception in 1958 has never confronted a collective human, economic and financial crisis similar to the threat posed by the COVID-19 pandemic in 2020. COVID-19 first appeared in Europe in France and then spread across the entire continent without discriminating between the euro and non-euro MS. However, the initial indications are that the **economic impact of the crisis** across the Union **appears to be asymmetric**, impacting during the first wave of the pandemic some countries such as Italy and Spain harder than others both in terms of human costs and economic losses.

36　The mixed and complex crises confronted especially by the non-euro MS will have a direct bearing on the operation of Article 143 TFEU. The **impact of COVID-19 on the non-euro MS** are already felt in their balance of payments positions, the stress on their respective national currencies and these factors will have adverse consequences on the proper functioning of the single market.

37　Apart from the unimaginable human costs, the economies and financial systems of all the MS both within and outside the euro area are under stress and strain because of the devastating impact of this invisible but deadly and infectious virus.

---

[20] See Grosche and Puetter (2008).

There are **mixed responses** activated or likely to be activated by the EU collectively and the MS unilaterally to confront the COVID-19 crisis.

Amid the crisis, the European Commission triggered the '**general escape clause**' in the EMU treaty provisions allowing MS to increase emergency spending without regard to limits imposed by the **Stability and Growth Pact**. The relaxation of the fiscal rules aims to allow the MS to borrow and spend more on their own that could potentially add to their existing debt burdens (→ Art. 121 TFEU para 50 et seqq.). **38**

MS have unilaterally committed billions of euro for their own countries. In addition, they have also adopted various other **preventive and remedial measures** to prevent the virus from infecting their economies such as deferred tax payments, emergency loans and paid job furloughs. **39**

There are other options that the EU may trigger in response to the crisis. One such option discussed by the EU leaders is the creation of a Corona Fund with the issuance of corona bonds. The MS agreed on a comprehensive recovery programme for Europe with vast spending of (new) EU resources. This comprises a development instrument called '**Next Generation EU**' (NGEU) based on Article 122 TFEU (budget: EUR 750 billion) and a recovery instrument based on Article 175 (3) TFEU, the '**Recovery and Resilience Facility**' (→ Supplement to Title VIII: Introduction para 54 et seqq.). Clearly, the situation that these instruments tackle is not a typical situation envisaged by Articles 143 (and 144) TFEU. It shows, however, that the Union and the MS can take a comprehensive approach beyond the (certainly valid) distinction of euro and non-euro area MS and the instruments available, thus further diminishing the practical relevance of Article 143 TFEU. **40**

List of Cases

CJEU 11.11.1975, Opinion 1/75, *EC competence for commercial policy*, ECLI:EU:C:1975:145 [cit. in para 18]
CJEU 27.11.2012, C-370/12, *Pringle*, ECLI:EU:C:2012:756 [cit. in para 7]
CJEU 13.06.2017, C-258/14, *Florescu*, ECLI:EU:C:2017:448 [cit. in para 29]

References

Borger, V. (2013). How the debt crisis exposes the development of solidarity in the euro area. *European Constitutional Law Review*, 7–36.
Elsig, M. (2002). *The EU's common commercial policy: Institutions, interests and ideas*. Ashgate.
Grosche, G., & Puetter, U. (2008). Preparing the Economic and Financial Committee and the Economic Policy Committee for enlargement. *Journal of European Integration, 30*(4), 527–543.
Kuijper, P. J., Wouters, J., Hoffmeister, F., de Baere, G., & Ramopoulos, T. (2013). *The law of EU external relations: Cases, materials, and commentary*. OUP.
Lasok, D. (1998). *The trade and customs law of the European Union*. Kluwer Law International.

Martines, F. (2014). Direct effect of international agreements of the European Union. *European Journal of International Law, 25*(1), 129–147.

Martucci, F. (2020). Non-EU legal instruments (EFSF, ESM, and Fiscal Compact). In F. Amtenbrink & C. Herrmann (Eds.), *The EU law of economic and monetary union* (Chapter 12). OUP.

Meunier, S. (2005). *Trading voices: The European Union in international commercial negotiations*. Princeton University Press.

Seyad, S. (2012). A critical evaluation of the revised and enlarged European stability and growth pact. *Journal of International Banking Law and Regulation*, 202–211.

Seyad, S. (2015). The impact of the financial and fiscal crisis on regional integration within and outside EU. *Chinese Journal of International Law*, 35–50.

Seyad, S. (2011). A legal analysis of the European financial stability mechanism. *Journal of International Banking Law and Regulation*, 421–433.

Zander, J. (2010). *The application of the precautionary principle in practice*. CUP.

Article 144 [Protective Measures]
(ex-Article 120 TEC)

1. Where a sudden crisis in the balance of payments[6] occurs and a decision within the meaning of Article 143(2) is not immediately taken,[7] a Member State with a derogation may, as a precaution, take the necessary protective measures.[8-10] Such measures must cause the least possible disturbance in the functioning of the internal market and must not be wider in scope than is strictly necessary to remedy the sudden difficulties which have arisen.
2. The Commission and the other Member States shall be informed of such protective measures not later than when they enter into force. The Commission may recommend to the Council the granting of mutual assistance under Article 143.
3. After the Commission has delivered a recommendation and the Economic and Financial Committee has been consulted, the Council may decide that the Member State concerned shall amend, suspend or abolish the protective measures referred to above.[11,12]

Contents

1. Overview 1
2. Balance of Payments Crisis 6
3. Adoption of Necessary Protective Measures 7
4. Amendment, Suspension or Abolishment of the Protective Measures ... 11
5. European Solidarity in Situations of Distress Beyond Article 144 TFEU in the Light of the COVID-19 Crisis 13

List of Cases
References

1. Overview

Article 144 TFEU, which is part of EU law from the outset (ex-Article 109 TEEC), should be read together with Article 143 TFEU. Article 144 TFEU also **applies only to MS with a derogation**. It is activated when an MS outside the euro area is confronted with a balance of payments crisis and financial assistance under Article 143 TFEU is not available in time. Article 144 TFEU therefore must be understood as an **exception to the procedure of Article 143 TFEU**. A reading of Articles 143 and 144 TFEU clearly indicates they are closely inter-connected. When the balance of payments difficulties in an MS with a derogation explode suddenly and not least on a wider scale, Article 144 TFEU will be activated. Once the protective measures are adopted under Article 144 TFEU, the procedure prescribed in Article 143 TFEU to access financial facility and related matters will apply ($\rightarrow$ Article 143 TFEU para 23–32).

1

2   Although not explicitly mentioned in either Article 143 or Article 144 TFEU, **mutual financial assistance** would presumably refer to the **medium-term financial assistance facility** (→ Article 143 TFEU para 24). A loan to an MS experiencing balance of payments difficulties will fit into this expression.[1]

3   If an MS is confronted with real and serious balance of payments difficulties, its negative impact will not be limited to this MS. All MS with a derogation are active participants in the single market of the EU. The negative consequences produced by any serious balance of payments difficulties in an MS will quickly **spill over** to other MS, which are part of the integrated internal market.

4   Since the launch of the euro on 1 January 1999, which also marks the date on which a new category of MS known as MS with a derogation was born, there is no evidence of an invocation of Article 144 TFEU to confront a balance of payment crisis in such countries. After the fiscal crisis, beginning at the end of 2009, it is even more **unlikely that this Treaty provision will be invoked**. This assumption is based on the fact that the Stability and Growth Pact had been further strengthened by the so-called two-pack and six-pack legal instruments with the objective of further strengthening the multilateral economic surveillance in the EU (→ Supplement to Title VIII: Fiscal Union para 5).

5   The aim of the relevant Treaty provisions providing for the Union financial intervention in response to the exceptional circumstances developing in MS with a derogation is an extension of the **principle of solidarity**, which had been developing slowly but surely between all the MS of the EU.[2] For example, Article 222 TFEU provides that MS should assist if an MS is subject to a terrorist attack or victim of a natural or man-made disaster (→ Article 222 TFEU para 20). Likewise, based on Article 122 TFEU the Council may extend assistance to an MS which is in difficulties or seriously threatened with severe difficulties caused by natural disasters or exceptional occurrences (Article 122 TFEU; → Article 122 TFEU para 13–17).

2. Balance of Payments Crisis

6   The wording of this Treaty provision is different from the preceding article. Article 143 TFEU deals with a potential development of balance of payments difficulties in MS with a derogation (→ Article 143 TFEU para 9–12). On the other hand, Article 144 TFEU would apply to a more **acute situation** where there is a sudden crisis in the balance of payments of an MS. In view of the serious nature of the balance of payments crisis faced by an MS, it is authorised to take immediate protective measures. Article 143 TFEU regards a potential threat with difficulties as regards the balance of payments of MS with a derogation. On the other hand, Article 144 TFEU would be applicable in a situation when balance of payments difficulties

---

[1] Seyad (2011).
[2] For the impact of the principle of solidarity on EMU, see Hilpold (2015).

Article 144. [Protective Measures] 989

occur suddenly and in an acute manner, thereby **justifying the adoption of unilateral measures** by MS with a derogation.

3. Adoption of Necessary Protective Measures

If an MS with a derogation is seriously threatened with balance of payments problems, it may adopt **immediate measures to remedy the situation**. There are certain conditions that should be satisfied to adopt such emergency measures. Primarily, it must be established that there was insufficient time to secure assistance from the Union under Article 143 TFEU because of the seriousness and urgency of the balance of the payments crisis. As highlighted before, it is time consuming to secure financial assistance or guarantee from the Union.

An MS which proposes to adopt emergency measures should be conscious of the fact that such measures should cause the least possible disturbance in the functioning of the internal market. The emergency measures must also respect the **principle of proportionality** as such remedy must not be wider than is strictly necessary to remedy the sudden balance of payments difficulties.

It is the duty of this MS to **inform the Commission** and **other MS** on or before the adoption of such urgent measures ('immediately or not later than when such measures enter into force'[3]). Although Articles 143 and 144 TFEU expressly link the balance of payment difficulties and crisis to its potential adverse impact on the proper functioning of the internal market and the implementation of the common commercial policy, it must be borne in mind that the underlying objective of these provisions is to **facilitate the smooth and harmonious accession of the MS with a derogation to the eurozone**.

In the light of this objective and the multitude of legal measures adopted at the Union level in the wake of the fiscal crisis in relation to multilateral economic surveillance, it is predictable that at the proper time the **national approach** in dealing with balance of payment difficulties and crisis may be **replaced by Union action**.

4. Amendment, Suspension or Abolishment of the Protective Measures

Once the **Commission** is informed of the emergency measures adopted, it shall investigate and issue **recommendations** to the relevant MS. If the measures adopted are insufficient, the Commission can recommend that the Council grants mutual assistance to the MS in difficulties based on Article 143 TFEU.

Although an MS is empowered to invoke the emergency measures unilaterally, the final authority to determine the legality, sufficiency or insufficiency of such measures is the Council. Once the Commission has delivered its recommendation

---

[3] Joined Cases 6 and 11/69, *Commission v France* (ECJ 10 December 1969) para 30–31.

after consulting the **Economic and Financial Committee**, the Council has a wide range of options such as to **amend, suspend or abolish** the protective measures adopted by the MS with a derogation.

5. European Solidarity in Situations of Distress Beyond Article 144 TFEU in the Light of the COVID-19 Crisis

13 Any MS outside the euro area could have relied on Article 144 TFEU if a serious balance of payments crisis had developed that could be attributable to COVID-19. Such an MS could have unilaterally taken protective measures appropriate to counter the sudden crisis triggered by this virus if assistance under Article 143 TFEU would have been untimely.

14 Similar to Article 143 TFEU, even Article 144 TFEU provides for the granting of mutual financial assistance to the affected MS. Any MS within the euro area could have access to the **European Stability Mechanism** (ESM).[4] In April 2020, the euro area MS decided to create within the ESM a EUR 540 billion **Pandemic Crisis Support** instrument for sovereigns.[5] The ECB established a new EUR 750 billion **Pandemic Emergency Purchase Programme** (PEPP) allowing the ECB to purchase large amounts of private and public sector securities to ensure that weaker countries' costs of borrowing remain low and stable.[6]

15 Since the non-euro MS have no access to the ESM, an option for them is to secure a soft **loan from the European Investment Bank** (EIB). The EU have also decided to increase funding for EIB to support especially the small and medium businesses across the Union, and grant loans on favourable terms, specially to protect employment.

16 As the COVID-19 virus began to spread violently across the Union, the President of the European Commission declared that they would do 'whatever is necessary to support the Europeans and the European economy' (13 March 2020). In keeping with this promise, in April 2020 the Commission launched two packages of measures: the Coronavirus **Response Investment Initiative** (CRII) and the Coronavirus **Response Investment Initiative Plus** (CRII+). Existing funds have been re-oriented and unspent **cash reserves from the EU funds** have been mobilised. This provided immediate liquidity to MS' budgets, and helped to frontload the yet unallocated EUR 37 billion of cohesion policy funding within the 2014 to 2020 cohesion policy programmes, thus fostering crisis repair facilities as well as investments. The Commission also made **all Coronavirus crisis related expenditure** since 1 February 2020 **eligible under cohesion policy rules**. The rules for cohesion

---

[4] Seyad (2011).

[5] The Pandemic Crisis Support is based on current ESM legal framework, notably Article 14 of the ESM Treaty, the ESM Guideline on Precautionary Financial Assistance and the ESM lending documents (General Terms and Facility Specific Terms). See the term sheet at https://www.esm.europa.eu/sites/default/files/20200508-pcs-term-sheet-final.pdf.

[6] The PEPP is based on ECB Decision 2020/440 of 24 March 2020, O.J. L 91/1 (2020).

Article 144. [Protective Measures]

spending are applied with maximum flexibility, thus enabling MS to use the funds to finance crisis-related action. The **Recovery Assistance for Cohesion and the Territories of Europe (REACT)** extended the crisis response and crisis repair measures delivered through the CRII and the CRII+, and provided a bridge to the long-term recovery plan (EUR 47 billion).

The **EU Solidarity Fund** provided an additional assistance of up to EUR 800 million to the worst affected countries to alleviate the financial burden of the immediate response measures.[7] Under Article 2 of the Regulation on the Solidarity Fund, 'at the request of a Member State or of a country involved in accession negotiations with the Union, [...], assistance from the Fund may be mobilised when **serious repercussions on** living conditions, human health, the natural environment or **the economy occur** in one or more regions of that [...] State **as a consequence of** a major or regional natural disaster having taken place on the territory of the same [...] State or of a neighbouring [...] State or **a major public health emergency** having taken place on the territory of the same [...] State [...]'. 17

List of Cases

ECJ 10.12.1969, 6 and 11/69, *Commission v France*, ECLI:EU:C:1969:68 [cit. in para 9]

References[8]

Hilpold, P. (2015). Understanding solidarity within EU law: An analysis of the 'Islands of Solidarity' with particular regard to Monetary Union. *Yearbook of European Law, 34*, 257–285.

Seyad, S. (2011). A legal analysis of the European financial stability mechanism. *Journal of International Banking Law and Regulation,* 421–433.

---

[7] See EP/Council Regulation (EC) No. 2012/2002 of 11 November 2002 *establishing the European Union Solidarity Fund*, O.J. L 311/3 (2002), as amended by Regulation 2020/461 of 30 March 2020 *in order to provide financial assistance to Member States and to countries negotiating their accession to the Union that are seriously affected by a major public health emergency*, O.J. L. 99/9 (2020).

[8] The cited Internet source in this comment has been accessed on 6 April 2021.

Supplement to Title VIII

Reforms and Perspectives of the Economic and Monetary Union: An Introduction

Contents

1. The Reorganization of Economic and Monetary Union Marked by the Crisis 1
2. Crisis Management by Means of "Escaping into International Law" 3
3. Treaties for the "Transfer," "Fiscal," and "Banking Union" as a New Framework for the Economic and Monetary Union 5
   - 3.1. Elements of the Three Pillars 6
     - 3.1.1. Treaty on Stability, Coordination and Governance in the Economic and Monetary Union 6
     - 3.1.2. Treaty Establishing the European Stability Mechanism 10
     - 3.1.3. Agreement on the Transfer and Mutualization of Contributions to the Single Resolution Fund 13
   - 3.2. Ownership and Solidarity as Characterizing Stress Ratio 19
     - 3.2.1. The Relationship of Ownership and Solidarity in EMU 19
     - 3.2.2. Ownership and Solidarity in the International Treaties 22
4. Objectives, Principles, and Interfaces of the Three Pillars 26
   - 4.1. Objectives 27
     - 4.1.1. "Ensuring the Financial Stability" as a Cross-Pillar Objective 27
     - 4.1.2. Further Objectives 31
   - 4.2. Principles 34
     - 4.2.1. Conditionality 34
     - 4.2.2. The Magical Triangle of Price Stability, Economic Growth and Full Employment 36
   - 4.3. Interfaces 40
     - 4.3.1. Repatriation of Intergovernmental Instruments Within the Ambit of Union Law 40
     - 4.3.2. Consistency and Coherence of Union Law 42
     - 4.3.3. Institutional Links 44
     - 4.3.4. Accession of New Members 46
5. Further Development of the Three Pillars: An Outlook 47

List of Cases
References

1. The Reorganization of Economic and Monetary Union Marked by the Crisis

The financial and sovereign debt crisis (2008) exposed the weaknesses of the European financial architecture and encouraged a debate on reforms to improve the economic policy framework.[1] Reform steps beyond the granting of financial assistance, reorganising the economic pillar of the EMU, have been evoked and are still being continued, independent of the political will of the actors. In addition to temporary *ad hoc* measures (Greece Package, EFSM → Article 122 TFEU para 15

1

---

[1] Cf. the genesis of the crisis in Martucci (2020), para 12.3 et seqq.

et seqq.), extensive reforms were gradually developed and implemented, aiming to preserve the single currency. The political aspirations initially rested on a reform of the primary law architecture. Article 121 TFEU, together with Article 126 and Article 136.1 TFEU, formed the (controversial[2]) legal basis for an extensive reform of economic policy coordination and a tightening of fiscal surveillance. From six legislative acts (Six-Pack), adopted in November 2011, the Member States formed the basis for the so-called **Economic Governance**, which was supplemented by two further regulations in May 2013 (Two-Pack) (→ Supplement to Title VIII: Fiscal Union para 5 et seqq.).[3]

2 In addition to the Economic Governance reform package, which was implemented in secondary legislation, the **Treaty on Stability, Coordination and Governance in the Economic and Monetary Union** adopted economic and budgetary agreements outside the Union law in spring 2012, that complemented and intensified the SGP (→ Supplement to Title VIII: Fiscal Union para 25 et seqq.).[4] Together with the **Treaty establishing the European Stability Mechanism**,[5] which aims to ensure the solvency of EA Member States (→ Supplement to Title VIII: TESM para 19), the SCG Treaty is seen as the most important tool to tackle the sovereign debt crisis in the EU and prevent future crises. By means of the TSCG, an approach is taken to strengthen the stability regime of the EA, in the form of a system of rule-based monitoring budgetary imbalances (**Fiscal Union**). The Member States' compliance with it as well as its application is yet a mandatory requirement for receiving the ESM financial assistance (**Transfer Union**). The Fiscal and Transfer Union is flanked by a **Banking Union**. The Banking Union was created on the legal basis of Article 114 TFEU and Article 127.6 TFEU and currently has two elements,

---

[2] Häde, in Kahl et al. (2017), Article 88 GG para 512 seqq.; Häde (2013), p. 196; similar also Frenz and Ehlenz (2010), p. 212.

[3] Economic Governance consists of the following secondary legal acts: (1) Parliament/Council Regulation (EU) No. 1173/2011 *on the effective enforcement of budgetary surveillance in the euro-area*; (2) Parliament/Council Regulation (EU) No. 1174/2011 *on enforcement measures to correct excessive macroeconomic imbalances in the euro-area*; (3) Parliament/Council Regulation (EU) No. 1175/2011 amending Council Regulation (EC) No. 1466/97 *on the strengthening of the surveillance of budgetary positions and the surveillance and coordination of economic policies*; (4) Parliament/Council Regulation (EU) No. 1176/2011 *on the prevention and correction of macroeconomic imbalances*; (5) Council Regulation (EU) No. 1177/2011 amending Regulation (EC) No. 1467/97 *on speeding up and clarifying the implementation of the excessive deficit procedure*; (6) Council Directive 2011/85/EU *on requirements for budgetary frameworks of the Member States*, O.J. L 306/1 (2011) and (7) Parliament/Council Regulation (EU) No. 472/2013 *on the strengthening of economic and budgetary surveillance of Member States in the euro-area experiencing or threatened with serious difficulties with respect to their financial stability*; (8) Parliament/Council Regulation (EU) No. 473/2013 *on common provisions for monitoring and assessing draft budgetary plans and ensuring the correction of excessive deficit of the Member States in the euro-area*, O.J. L 140/1 (2013). On the Economic Governance reform package, see Pilz and Dittmann (2012), p. 53 et seqq.; Blanke (2011), p. 402 et seqq.; Weber (2011), p. 935 et seqq.; De Gregorio Merino (2012), p. 1613 et seqq.

[4] Statement by the Euro-area Heads of State or Government, 9 December 2011, No. 1, 4 et seqq.

[5] See also Ruffert (2011), p. 1783; Thym (2011), p. 167 et seq.

the Single Supervisory Mechanism (SSM) and the Single Resolution Mechanism (SRM). The secondary legislation aligns responsibility for supervision, resolution and funding at the EU level and force banks throughout the EA to abide by the same rules (→ Supplement to Title VIII: Banking Union para 11 et seqq.). The relationship between the Banking Union and the Fiscal Treaty stems from the fact that the centralization of the banks' supervision and its resolution by means of a resolution fund is intended to protect Member States from further debt burdens because of bank bailouts. *Chiti* and *Teixeira* concluded, that "at the institutional level, the economic governance of the EU now relies on a complex of multiple institutions, both internal and external to the EU framework, partially overlapping and acting in different compositions."[6]

2. Crisis Management by Means of "Escaping into International Law"

One characteristic that forms the basis of all measures establishing the Transfer, Fiscal and Banking Union, is the use of international treaties.[7] In addition to the establishment of a SRF as the only international legal element of the Banking Union (→ para 17), the conclusion of the ESM Treaty and the SCG Treaty was also based on international law. In view of the intensified use of international treaties, terms such as **"flight into international law"** or "intergovernmental pacts" were used in the legal literature.[8]

However, international law agreements, concluded by individual MS to supplement European integration, are not new in EU law. As an example reference can be made to the **Schengen Convention** (1986/1990).[9] With the renaissance of this intergovernmental integration method during the sovereign debt crisis, new terminology emerged to characterize the use of authentic international instruments in a close relationship to EU law.[10] The conclusion of these so-called "satellite

---

[6] Chiti and Teixeira (2013), p. 692. Cf. Ioannidis (2016), p. 1237 et seqq.

[7] Schorkopf (2012a), p. 209 et seq. speaks of an intergovernmental transformation ("intergouvernementale Transformation"). Cf. Dimopoulos (2014), p. 41 et seqq; de Witte (2015), pp. 437 et seqq., 448 et seqq.

[8] Kau (2016), p. 707; Pilz (2016), p. 63; Thym (2014), para 84 (translated by the author).

[9] Agreement between the Governments of the States of the Benelux Economic Union, the Federal Republic of Germany and the French Republic on the gradual abolition of checks at their common borders, ("Schengen I"), 14 June 1985, O.J. L 239/13 (2000); Convention implementing the Schengen Agreement of 14 June 1985 between the Governments of the States of the Benelux Economic Union, the Federal Republic of Germany and the French Republic on the gradual abolition of checks at their common borders, O.J. L 239/19 (2000).

[10] Hence Weber (2014), pp. 9, 11 speaks of an "internal union instrument under international law" (*"binnenunionsvölkerrechtliches Instrumentarium,"* translated by the author), von Arnauld (2013), p. 511 speaks of a "union (supplementing) international law" (*"Unions(ergänzungs)völkerrecht"* translated by the author), Lorz and Sauer (2012), p. 575 of a "substitutional Union law under international law" (*"völkerrechtliches Ersatzunionsrecht,"* translated by the author), Keppenne

treaties"[11] between MS is more effective than the rather time-consuming and politically challenging process of amending the primary Union law.[12] Hence, a pan-European ratification procedure for amending treaties at the peak of crisis would have had little chance of success. In particular, the transfer of further competencies to the Union, aiming to strengthen budgetary surveillance by the Commission, would have created a negative attitude in many MS.[13] Failing to make comprehensive changes in primary law would thus very likely have led to integration backlogs.[14] Compared with this, the intergovernmental conclusion of the Treaty enabled the EU States to undertake a **reactive crisis management without the participation of Parliament or the Commission**[15] and prepared a new consolidating step by means of differentiated integration.[16] The international treaties are not part of **supranational Union law**. The vertical control by the primacy of Union law is replaced by a horizontal coordination between MS amongst themselves.[17] This approach raises no objections in principle, especially since, strictly speaking, the MS are not allowed to question the unity of EU law.[18]

3. Treaties for the "Transfer," "Fiscal," and "Banking Union" as a New Framework for the Economic and Monetary Union

5   From the experiences gained in the tedious process of the Treaty reform of Lisbon, the MS knew that the consolidation of EMU by means of a comprehensive restructuring of the treaties would not find a majority of votes. Intergovernmental solutions were required to shape a stable EMU in the long-term. For this purpose, the MS first established the ESM as an "international financial institution" (Article 1.1 TESM) to assist individual States during the crisis through solidarity transfer payments (**Transfer Union**). The ESM Treaty is flanked by the Treaty on Stability, Coordination and Governance in the Economic and Monetary Union as a tool to strengthen the stability regime of the eurozone (**Fiscal Union**). As a fiscal sustainability element, the Banking Union forms the third pillar supplementing TESM and TSCG. An integral part of the **Banking Union** is the SRM (→ para 15), which is to be financed by the financial industry through the SRF. This approach ensures that

---

(2014), p. 203 of "semi-intergovernmental method" and Lenaerts (2014), p. 756 of "semi-intergovernmentalism."

[11] Thym (2014), para 82 (our translation).
[12] Schorkopf (2012a), p. 208.
[13] Franzius (2014), p. 45; Thym (2014), para 84.
[14] Kau (2016), p. 707.
[15] Thym (2011), p. 171.
[16] Schorkopf (2012a), p. 210; Chiti and Teixeira (2013), p. 686 et seq.
[17] Franzius (2014), p. 45.
[18] Classen (2014), para 49; Thym (2014), para 83.

banks at risk of payment default are not being settled at the expense of taxpayers or the real economy.[19]

3.1. Elements of the Three Pillars

3.1.1. Treaty on Stability, Coordination and Governance in the Economic and Monetary Union

After the UK and the Czech Republic rejected an inclusion of fiscal rules in Union law as part of a treaty amendment,[20] the remaining 25 MS signed the TSCG on 2 March 2012. The intergovernmental agreement provides for the establishment of a Fiscal Stability Union by means of binding and firm rules for sound financial management. The SCG Treaty aims to improve the **economic convergence** within the EA as well as the **fiscal discipline** of its MS. It furthermore aims to strengthen the existing primary and secondary law of the **Stability and Growth Pact** and to add further measures to it.[21] In substance, the Contracting Parties have established a Fiscal Union by means of the SCG Treaty.[22]

6

At the heart of the Fiscal Treaty is the **Fiscal Compact**, regulated under Title III, which contains provisions to strengthen the MS' budgetary discipline. To achieve this objective, Article 3.1 point (a) TSCG enacts the (close to) balanced budget rule of Article 2a of Regulation (EU) No. 1175/2011.[23] However, with the establishment of a **close to balance or in surplus target**, the fiscal agreement goes beyond the secondary legislation. Furthermore, Article 3.1 point (a) TSCG limits the MS' flexibility in pursuit of the medium-term budgetary objective by reducing the annual structural deficit threshold to 0.5% of the nominal GDP ($\rightarrow$ Supplement to Title VIII: Fiscal Union para 25 et seq., 30). The Maastricht debt criterion is taken up in Article 4 TSCG ($\rightarrow$ Supplement to Title VIII: Fiscal Union para 23). Both the threshold of 0.5% for the structural deficit and the 1:20-rule of Article 4 TSCG, which are to be transposed into national law, are interpreted as **debt brakes**.[24]

7

A central new regulation, on the other hand, is Article 3.2 sentence 1 TSCG. According to it, the Contracting States must **enshrine the stability criteria** contained in Article 3.1 TSCG **in their domestic law** by means of "preferably constitutional" provisions or sub-constitutional regulations. As soon as a MS deviates "significantly" from the medium-term objective or the adjustment path, a

8

---

[19] Wojcik (2016), p. 102 et seq.

[20] Cf. Craig (2012), p. 232 et seq.

[21] Peers (2012), p. 441.

[22] The terminology "Fiscal Union" was used by the then German Minister of Finance *W. Schäuble* during the first consultation about the German implementation act of the TSCG and the TESM in the 172nd Meeting of the 17th German Bundestag on 29 March 2012, plenary protocol 17/172, p. 20210.

[23] Article 2a of Regulation (EU) No. 1175/2011. Cf. Pilz and Dittmann (2012), p. 60 et seqq.

[24] Cf. also Blanke (2012), p. 96.

correction mechanism is "automatically" triggered under Article 3.1 point (e) TSCG. The introduction and application of this instrument is regulated in Article 3.2 sentence 2 TSCG (→ Supplement to Title VIII: Fiscal Union para 32). If a MS that has agreed to the Fiscal Compact fails to comply with the provisions of Article 3.2 TSCG, the other Contracting States may appeal to the CJEU. The Court's right of inspection extends only to the establishment of the debt brake. The Contracting States' right of action neither aims towards the actual national enforcement of the rule nor does it provide for a sanction for any behaviour of the Contracting Parties in breach of the treaty.[25]

9 To promote the budgetary discipline of the MS, the Contracting States commit themselves to assisting the Commission in launching a deficit procedure, without affecting the voting rules of Article 126 TFEU.[26] Instead, the parties agree in Article 7 TSCG on an unjustifiable voluntary restriction of their discretions in the vote on the existence of an excessive deficit (→ Supplement to Title VIII: Fiscal Union para 45 et seqq.). Accordingly, the deficit procedure will be launched as soon as the Commission finds that a MS has exceeded the 3% threshold. The procedure can only be stopped if the EA Member States vote against it by qualified majority, excluding the MS concerned (**reverse qualified majority voting**, → Supplement to Title VIII: Fiscal Union para 42 et seq.).

3.1.2. Treaty Establishing the European Stability Mechanism

10 The establishment and organization of the ESM as an international financial institution takes place outside the legal and institutional framework of the Union by means of an international treaty, constituting the ESM as an "intergovernmental organisation under international law."[27] The ESM has a subscribed authorized capital **totalling EUR 700 billion,**[28] of which MS provide EUR 620 billion only through a combination of committed callable capital and guarantees. The sum of the capital actually paid by the euro States amounts to EUR 80 billion. The decision-making bodies and their powers, particularly regarding the financial structure arrangement of the mechanism and the granting of stability support, are regulated over eight chapters of the ESM Treaty (→ Supplement to Title VIII: TESM para 19–120).

---

[25] Pilz (2012), p. 460.

[26] Cf. Calliess and Schoenfleisch (2012), p. 482 et seq., who are in favor of an interpretation of the Article 7 TSCG in accordance with the procedure steps of the deficit procedure. Similar also Häde, in Kahl et al. (2017), Article 88 GG para 532; Schorkopf (2012b), p. 11. Other opinion Ortmann (2015), p. 540 et seqq.

[27] Treaty establishing the European Stability Mechanism, 2 February 2012. An amendment to Article 136 TFEU preceded the establishment of the ESM (→ Supplement to Title VIII: TESM para 4 et seqq.). See also Häde (2011a), p. 333 et seqq.

[28] Articles 8.1, 8, 22 TESM. Including the pending EFSF stability support amounting to EUR 200 billion. Cf. Statement by the Eurogroup (30 March 2012).

As measures for stability support, **five financial assistance instruments** were established in Articles 14 to 18 TESM. Specifically, these are the instruments of the consolidated EFSF,[29] namely the provision of precautionary financial assistance (Article 14 TESM), the granting of loans to non-programme countries for the recapitalization of financial institutions (Article 15 TESM), ESM loans (Article 16 TESM), the purchase of a State's government bonds on the secondary market (Article 18 TESM) and the direct purchase of a Member State's bonds on the primary market (Article 17 TESM).[30] Following a decision by the ESM Board of Governors according to Article 19 TESM, concerning the **extension of the range of instruments**, grants may also be given out directly by the ESM to a financial institution (direct bank recapitalization) under narrow conditions.[31] The individual instruments are described in the ESM Guidelines, which contain binding conditional and procedural requirements for the application of those instruments (→ Supplement to Title VIII: TESM para 77–116).

In addition to structural and fiscal requirements, the use of ESM funds is linked to the **prior ratification of the TSCG**.[32] This conjunction underlines the **reserve function of the ESM**, which is available if the fiscal rules of the Fiscal Compact fail to prevent a sovereign debt crisis (→ Supplement to Title VIII: TESM para 62). The TESM and the TSCG establish a "support and austerity responsibility,"[33] which binds the ESM States, but is economically controversial in view of the extent and the form of the austerity policy.[34]

11

12

3.1.3. Agreement on the Transfer and Mutualization of Contributions to the Single Resolution Fund

The Single Resolution Fund (SRF) is an integral part of the **Banking Union**. This major project of the European Commission essentially consists of **three pillars**: A Single Supervisory Mechanism, a framework for orderly resolution of failing banks, and a European Deposit Insurance (→ Supplement to Title VIII: Banking

13

---

[29] European Stability Mechanism (2019), p. 144 et seq.

[30] Conclusions of the Heads of State and Government of the Member States of the euro area, 11 March 2011, No. 5; Declaration by the Heads of State and Government of the Member States and the EU Institutions, 21 July 2011, No. 8.

[31] ESM Board of Governors Resolution, Meeting of 8 December 2014, Establishment of the instrument for the Direct Recapitalization of Institutions.

[32] Preamble to the SCG Treaty, 25th Recital: "the granting of assistance in the framework of new programmes under the European Stability Mechanism will be conditional [...] on the ratification of this Treaty."

[33] Hufeld (2014), para 172.

[34] Cf. also Corsetti (Ed.) (2012), passim.

Union para 284 et seqq.).[35] Based on Article 127.6 TFEU, the Banking Union brings together the supervisory structures and powers, spread at national level and at supranational level, at Union level to support the reliability and soundness of credit institutions as well as the stability of the financial system.[36] The objective is to ensure that the banking sector in the EA as well as in the EU as a whole is stable and reliable and that the resolution of banks at risk of insolvency is not at the expense of the taxpayer and furthermore has as little impact on the real economy as possible.

14   In November 2014, the **Single Supervisory Mechanism (SSM)** was launched and has taken over the supervision of EA banks through a supervisory board affiliated to the ECB (→ Supplement to Title VIII: Banking Union para 14 et seqq).[37] Under Article 4 of Regulation (EU) No. 1024/2013, the supervisory tasks include, amongst others, ensuring compliance with own funds requirements and conducting supervisory reviews and stress tests.[38] The Governing Council of the ECB is entitled to the supervisory power of last decision, though.[39]

15   The European Banking Supervision is supplemented by a **Single Resolution Mechanism** as the second pillar of the Banking Union (→ Supplement to Title VIII: Banking Union para 125 et seqq.). A consistent resolution regime should ensure an efficient and low-cost settlement of distressed banks. Against this

---

[35] The Banking Union consists of three pillars: (1) The Single Supervisory Mechanism (SSM), established by Council Regulation (EU) No. 1024/2013 *conferring specific tasks on the European Central Bank supervision of credit institutions*, O.J. L 287/63 (2013); (2) The Single Resolution Mechanism (SRM), established by Parliament/Council Directive 2014/59/EU *establishing a framework for the recovery and resolution of credit institutions and investment firms*, O.J. L 173/190 (2014); Parliament/Council Regulation (EU) No. 806/2014 *establishing uniform rules and a uniform procedure for the resolution of credit institutions and certain investment firms in the framework of a Single Resolution Mechanism and a Single Resolution Fund*, O.J. L 225/1 (2014) and the Single Resolution Fund (SRF) established by the Intergovernmental Agreement *on the Transfer and Mutualisation of Contributions to the Single Resolution Fund* of 21 May 2014 (IGA on the SRF) as amended by the Agreement amending the Agreement *on the transfer and mutualisation of contributions to the Single Resolution Fund* of 27 January 2021 (available at https://www.consilium.europa.eu/media/48068/agreement-amending-the-intergovernmental-agreement-on-the-transfer-and-mutualisation-of-contributions-to-the-single-resolution-fund-27-january-2021_en.pdf); (3) European Deposit Guarantee Scheme (EDIS), Proposal for a Parliament/Council Regulation *amending Regulation (EU) 806/2014 in order to establish a European Deposit Insurance Scheme*, COM(2015) 586. Cf. Hinarejos (2015), p. 45 et seqq.

[36] Article 1 of Regulation (EU) No. 1024/2013. See also Binder (2013), p. 297 et seqq.; Kämmerer (2013), p. 830 et seqq.; Lehmann and Manger-Nestler (2014), p. 2 et seqq.

[37] Preamble to Regulation (EU) No. 1024/2013, 67th Recital. For details Ohler (2020), para 37.25 et seqq. See also Manger-Nestler (2014), p. 319.

[38] Article 4.1 point (f) of Regulation (EU) No. 1024/2013.

[39] Article 26.8 sentence 1 of Regulation (EU) No. 1024/2013. Manger-Nestler (2014), p. 320. But see also the reading of the German Federal Constitutional Court, 2 BvR 1685/14 (Judgment of 30 July 2019) – *Banking Union*, which seems to contradict the exclusive competence of the ECB in banking supervision.

background, the SRM was established in 2014 based on Article 114 TFEU.[40] The standardized resolution mechanism at the heart of the European Banking Union consists of a Single Resolution Board (SRB) at Union level and a SRF financed by the banking sector.[41] The regulations of the Banking Union were the subject of a constitutional complaint before the German FCC. The Court concluded that the EU did not exceed the competences conferred on it by the Treaties when adopting the legislative framework regarding the European Banking Union, including the SSM and the SRM, if this framework is interpreted strictly. Neither the SSM Regulation nor the SRM Regulation encroach on the constitutional identity of the German Basic Law.[42]

The SRM came through its baptism of fire in the summer of 2017 when **"Banco Popular Español"** was sent to liquidation for its toxic property loans.[43] Previously, the ECB had classified Spain's sixth-largest bank at the time with its 1800 branches and almost 12,000 employees as not viable in June after a massive capital flight. The *Banco Popular* case has shown that the single legal framework can work if implemented efficiently. Thus, the taxpayer did not have to pay a cent to save the bank.

An intergovernmental **Agreement on the Transfer and Mutualisation of Contributions to the Single Resolution Fund** (TMCA) outside the Union's legal framework completes the SRM.[44] This Agreement, concluded on 21 May 2014 between the EU Member States (with the exception of the UK and Sweden), sets out, among others, the transfer of contributions at the national level in accordance with the BRRD and the SRM Regulation to national compartments related to the progressive development of the SRF (→ Supplement to Title VIII: Banking Union para 133). The SRF is aimed at providing the resolution financing within the SRM. The fund is financed, under SSM supervision, by a "bank levy" amounting to 1% of the deposit guaranteed by the deposit guarantee schemes of banks. This ensures that banks at risk of payment default cannot be settled at the expense of taxpayers or the real economy.[45] Since the SRF has only been set up since 2016 and

---

[40] Parliament/Council Regulation (EU) No. 806/2014 *establishing uniform rules and a uniform procedure for the resolution of credit institutions and certain investment firms in the framework of a Single Resolution Mechanism and a Single Resolution Fund*, O.J. L 225/1 (2014). Cf. Jimenez-Blanco (2014), p. 365; Wojcik (2016), p. 100 et seqq.

[41] Cf. Adamski (2020), para 9.115.

[42] German Federal Constitutional Court, 2 BvR 1685/14 (Judgment of 30 July 2019) – *Banking Union*.

[43] See Quaglia and Royo (2015), p. 491 et seqq for details about the Spanish banking crisis.

[44] Intergovernmental Agreement *on the Transfer and Mutualisation of Contributions to the Single Resolution Fund* of 21 May 2014 (IGA on the SRF) as amended by the Agreement amending the Agreement *on the transfer and mutualisation of contributions to the Single Resolution Fund* of 27 January 2021 (available at https://www.consilium.europa.eu/media/48068/agreement-amending-the-intergovernmental-agreement-on-the-transfer-and-mutualisation-of-contributions-to-the-single-resolution-fund-27-january-2021_en.pdf). For a detailed analysis of the TMC Agreement, see Zavvos and Kaltsouni (2015), p. 117 et seq.

[45] Jimenez-Blanco (2014), p. 364.

will only reach a volume of approximately EUR 55 billion after a pay-in period of eight years, the Banking Union relies on a "fiscal backstop"[46] of the ESM during this period (→ Supplement to Title VIII: TESM para 107, 148).[47] Until the SRF is fully activated, the ESM can provide financial assistance for the resolution of banks on a subsidiary basis and as a last resort (*ultima ratio*).[48]

18 So far, however, there is no agreement among the EU countries about the **European Deposit Insurance System (EDIS)** as the third element of the Banking Union (→ Supplement to Title VIII: Banking Union para 288 et seqq.).[49] The Deposit Guarantee Schemes Directive (DGSD) established in 2014 has already led to a wide harmonization of national deposit guarantee schemes but has not yet been implemented by many MS. According to the Directive, all depositors—even larger companies—have a legal right to compensation for their covered deposits up to EUR 100.000.[50] A further reform of the national deposit guarantee schemes is meant to complete the Banking Union.[51] On 24 November 2015, the European Commission presented a draft regulation establishing EDIS, which provides for a communitarization of deposit insurances by 2024 in three steps.[52] However, economists, the German Federal Bank, and the German Banking Industry Committee see the risk that the measure of communitarization sets wrong incentives and creates a gateway for lasting transfer achievements. Further, countries such as Germany and The Netherlands reject the proposal so far. They call for risk minimization in the banking system, especially in Italy, to avoid large redistributions in the event of a potential imbalance of large and systemically important banks.[53] On the other hand, the EP on 19 June 2020 urged the Council to resume negotiations on EDIS as soon as possible, while ensuring a coherent framework with the DGSD to deliver on the objective of enhancing financial stability. The completion of the third pillar is necessary to protect depositors against banking disruptions, ensure confidence among depositors and investors across the Banking Union, and reinforce the stability of the EA as a whole.[54]

---

[46] Towards a Genuine Economic and Monetary Union, Report by President of the European Council Herman Van Rompuy, 26 June 2012, EUCO 120/12, p. 5.

[47] Critical towards the financial volume of the SRF, Gordon and Ringe (2015), p. 1354 et seqq.

[48] Euro Summit meeting (29 June 2018), EURO 502/18, p. 1.

[49] The Euro Summit meeting from 29 June 2018 called for negotiations regarding the creation of a European Deposit Guarantee Scheme (EDIS) to be launched by the end of 2018. Cf. Euro Summit meeting (29 June 2018), EURO 502/18, p. 1. Cf. Adamski (2020), para 9.118.

[50] Parliament/Council Directive 2014/49/EU *on deposit guarantee schemes*, O.J. L 1173/149 (2014). Cf. Jimenez-Blanco (2014), p. 361 et seqq.

[51] Cf. Commission Communication, *Towards the completion of the Banking Union*, COM(2015) 587.

[52] Proposal for a Parliament/Council Regulation *amending Regulation (EU) 806/2014 in order to establish a European Deposit Insurance Scheme*, COM(2015) 586.

[53] As examples: Demary et al. (2018), p. 3; Deutsche Bundesbank (2015), p. 63; Dombret (2016).

[54] Resolution of the European Parliament of 19 June 2020 on Banking Union – annual report 2019, P9_TA-PROV(2020)0165, No. 53 et seq.

3.2. Ownership and Solidarity as Characterizing Stress Ratio

3.2.1. The Relationship of Ownership and Solidarity in EMU

The principles of ownership and solidarity are central, but in their dominance **unequal characteristics of the asymmetric structure of EMU**. The principle of the Member States' national responsibility is mainly expressed in economic policy (Articles 121 et seqq. TFEU; → Article 121 TFEU para xx), which in contrast to monetary policy (Articles 127 et seqq. TFEU) was not communitarized. Member States themselves are responsible for their autonomous economic, fiscal and budgetary policies. The individual MS' ownership is mirrored in Articles 123 to 125 TFEU, which stipulate the autonomy of all EU MS and exclude guarantees of solidarity by the Union and between the Member States.[55]

In contrast to federal fiscal constitutions, which oscillate between autonomy and solidarity,[56] EA Member States rely on a sound loan financing that is in line with Article 126 TFEU. Consequently, Article 125 TFEU categorically excludes the assumption of liability by the Union or MS (**no bail-out**).[57] The central importance of ownership is demonstrated by the negotiations in the *Delors* Committee (1988/89), which discussed the possibility of granting a "cash credit" as a monetary policy instrument to the national governments but eventually refused it point-blank.[58]

On the other hand, it must be said that an Economic and Monetary Union cannot be based solely on the principle of ownership. Within this form of organization—as in all federal orders—a solidarity element is required, which flanks the individual responsibility to allow assistance of the members to those affected, for example, in unforeseen situations which cannot be controlled by the States. In Article 122.2 TFEU alone, the "solidarity" *de lege lata* is normatively substantiated by the Union as a motive for financial assistance (→ Article 122 TFEU para 26). This standard justifies such assistance in the event "where a Member State is in difficulties or is seriously threatened with severe difficulties caused by natural disasters or exceptional occurrences beyond its control." Generally, Article 125 TFEU excludes solidarity measures of any financial nature. However, if the members were not able to assist each other in exceptional situations, the principle of ownership would lack a basis.[59] Both principles complement and transform each other. Thus, in the case of receiving solidary help, the possibilities of self-responsible decision-making for the recipient could naturally be reduced.[60] This way, the principle of economic

---

[55] Hahn and Häde (2010), § 27 para 19.
[56] Pilz (2016), p. 144.
[57] Ohler, in Siekmann (2013), Article 125 TFEU para 2.
[58] H. Schlesinger, "Differing opinions must be tolerable" (translated by the author), Handelsblatt of 23 May 2014, p. 56.
[59] Müller-Franken (2014), p. 232.
[60] Calliess and Schoenfleisch (2012), p. 487.

ownership of the MS is curtailed but not overridden by a bail-out. An overdose of solidarity would eventually weaken ownership as well as encouragement for MS to implement economic policy reforms.[61] This would rather lead to incentive problems, which were already attested as a consequence to the federal redistribution mechanisms.[62] Solidarity must, therefore, be proportionate to ownership in order to **not undermine the objective of sustainable and long-term stabilization of the currency area**.

3.2.2. Ownership and Solidarity in the International Treaties

22 The **SCG Treaty** aims to strengthen the **budgetary discipline of the MS** and, for that purpose, emphasizes compliance with the budget rules and the Member States' budgetary autonomy. The international TSCG strengthens the **principle of national ownership,** by confirming both Maastricht criteria in Article 3.1 point (b) and Article 4 TSCG and thus commits the MS on budgetary guidelines, limiting their national budgetary policies (→ Supplement to Title VIII: Fiscal Union para 26 et seqq.). The binding and permanent incorporation into national law of the debt rules closes the door for the MS to the political retraction of Article 126 TFEU and breaks the political dominance of the Council regarding the Union law deficit control. Instead of politicized negotiations in the Council, which in the past have always been dominated by the personal interests of the members and rarely led to sanctions in case of deviations from the budgetary objective,[63] deviations now "automatically" trigger a correction mechanism (Article 3.1 point (e) TSCG). The fiscal rules contained in the Fiscal Compact reaffirm and reinforce the determination in Union law that each Member State must take responsibility for "sound public finances (Article 119.3 TFEU) on its own responsibility."[64]

23 The **ESM Treaty**, on the other hand, expresses the idea of solidarity, regarding the **granting of financial assistance** ("stability support") to a crisis State, which can only be expected of the other ESM States under strict conditionality and in compliance with the requirements of the TSCG (Article 12.1 TESM, Preamble to the ESM Treaty, 5th Recital). The ESM States form a **supportive community** that seeks to tackle fiscal risks together.

24 The **TMC Agreement** is aimed finance resolution within the SRM. The main objective of the intergovernmental agreement is to regulate the way in which the establishment of national compartments will be progressively mutualized over a transitional period of eight years to give full financial capacity to the SRF

---

[61] Sinn (2012), p. 214.
[62] Pilz (2016), p. 146 et seq.; Peffekoven (1992), p. 349 et seqq. Critically also Kirchhof (2012), p. 143.
[63] Pilz and Dittmann (2011), p. 153.
[64] Hufeld (2014), para 147.

(→ Supplement to Title VIII: Banking Union para 178). This ensures that an effective **backstop provision** is in place for the resolution of financial institutions, which is **financed by contributions from the financial sector**.[65] By offsetting public support through subsequent levies from the financial sector, the backstop affects the budgets in a neutral way in the medium term. This burden sharing, implemented by SRM/SRF, means a break through the vicious circle between banks and sovereign bonds and implicitly ensures **national ownership** and **fiscal sustainability** of public finances.

TESM, TSCG, and TMCA appear to be governed by **different principles**. While the solidarity[66] embodied in the ESM is focused solely on the stability of the EA as a whole (Article 3 sentence 1 TESM), the TSCG and the TMCA are meant to strengthen the ownership of the Member States' fiscal policies. It is also in the face of this dichotomy, that economists have called for the ESM crisis management mechanism to be used as a tool to restore fiscal ownership.[67] Only in this way it can be avoided that the ESM leads to an equalization of financial resources over the individual responsibility of the Member States or even to the recognition of "emergency compensation claims" of the crisis countries, thereby superimposing the "core area of the economic policy competence of the MS."[68] 25

4. Objectives, Principles, and Interfaces of the Three Pillars

The TESM, the TSCG, and the TMCA are inseparable in the light of the underlying objectives and defining principles. At the same time, several factors point to a strong link and even interdependence with Union law. 26

4.1. Objectives

4.1.1. "Ensuring the Financial Stability" as a Cross-Pillar Objective

Financial stability is the ability of a financial system to smoothly perform its central macroeconomic functions at any time, especially during stressful situations and periods of upheaval. The term refers to a situation in which the various parts of the financial system can perform their tasks without major disruptions in the financial system or the economy in general.[69] A stable financial system is the prerequisite for 27

---

[65] Preamble to the TMC Agreement, 6th Recital.
[66] Pernice (2013), p. 49.
[67] Cf. Fahrholz et al. (2012), pp. 3, 28, 33 et seqq.
[68] German Federal Constitutional Court, 2 BvR 2728/13 (Judgment of 14 January 2014), para 40 – *OMT-Order for reference* (in BVerfGE 134, 366 [393]).
[69] Tuori and Tuori (2014), p. 58. Similar also Selmayr, in von der Groeben et al. (2015), Article 127 TFEU para 38.

direct financing through the capital markets and indirect financing by financial intermediaries to channel funds between providers and buyers in a rational manner. In this sense, **financial stability** is understood as **a comprehensive concept**[70] that, in the name of the banking system's stability, focuses on both governments and private financial institutions and seeks to integrate cross-border financial markets.[71] Ensuring the financial stability in the EA combines, as a cross-pillar objective, the measures of the MS to establish a "Transfer," "Fiscal," and "Banking Union." This is normatively compressed in the three agreements to a varying degree.[72]

28   This objective is expressed most clearly within the **ESM Treaty**. Given the strong interdependencies within the EA, serious risks to the financial stability of one EA Member State could jeopardize the financial stability of the EA as a whole.[73] In that case, the ESM Treaty raises the maintenance of the EA's financial stability as a whole, as well as its MS, in Article 3.1, Article 12.1 TESM as a condition for providing stability support to ESM members. The ESM Treaty thus repeats the basic condition, which is also contained in the enabling provision of **Article 136.3 TFEU**, and thus expresses its far-reaching significance under European law (→ Supplement to Title VIII: TESM para 4).

29   In contrast to the ESM Treaty, the **SCG Treaty** primarily aims to strengthen economic policy coordination and to foster the budgetary discipline of the MS (Article 1.1 TSCG). However, in the third Recital of the Preamble, the Contracting Parties emphasize the "essential importance" of sound public finances to "safeguard the stability of the euro area as a whole." The maintenance of financial stability is therefore also the **overarching objective** of this Fiscal Compact (→ Supplement to Title VIII: Fiscal Union para 5).

30   A similar target constellation is also laid down in the **TMC Agreement**. In Article 1.1 TMCA, the Contracting Parties commit to transfer to the SRF the contributions raised at national level. However, this measure too is "essential [...] for guaranteeing the financial stability of the EA."[74] Maintaining financial stability is the basic idea that links the TMCA with the TSCG and the TESM. Thus, the already well-established nexus between States and banks implies that the financial stability of the EA and of the single currency itself depend crucially on the financial solidity of not only governments but also systemically important banks.[75] It seems only logical that after the Commission has planned to reform the ESM, it is being considered to extend its tasks. The ESM, as a European Monetary Fund, is meant to assist the SRB in providing its services through the provision of credit lines or guarantees, thereby ensuring the **backstop for the**

---

[70] Tuori and Tuori (2014), p. 58.

[71] Cf. Pilz (2016), p. 66, Blanke and Pilz, in von Mangoldt et al. (2018), Article 88 para 69.

[72] Preamble to the TMC Agreement, 1st Recital.

[73] In the same way Preamble to the ESM Treaty, 6th Recital.

[74] Preamble to the TMC Agreement, 1st Recital.

[75] Proposal for a Council Regulation *on the establishment of the European Monetary Fund*, COM (2017) 827, p. 4.

European Banking System (→ Supplement to Title VIII: TESM para 104, 107, 148).

4.1.2. Further Objectives

The Contracting States commit themselves in Article 1.1 TSCG to **foster fiscal discipline** through a Fiscal Compact. The Fiscal Compact (Article 3–8 TSCG) thus builds on the prohibition of an excessive deficits (Article 126.1 TFEU) and aims to ensure "sound public finances" in the MS (→ Supplement to Title VIII: Fiscal Union para 5). By means of sound public finances, MS help to support the ECB's price stability-oriented monetary policy.[76]   31

Another objective of the SCG Treaty is to **intensify the economic policy coordination** to which the MS commit in Article 9 TSCG. The objective above all should be help strengthen the competitiveness and market flexibility of the EA countries through coordinated measures, as well as curbing new private and public debt crises.   32

In June 2012, the presidents of the European Council, the Commission, the ECB and the Eurogroup proposed an **integrated financial framework**, a set of common European banking supervision and a common framework for deposit protection and bank restructuring (→ Supplement to Title VIII: Banking Union para 132).[77] The TMC Agreement is intended to complement the Union's banking resolution legislation. It is rather designed as supportive and intrinsically linked to the achievement of Union policies, particularly the **establishment of an internal market in the field of financial services**.   33

4.2. Principles

4.2.1. Conditionality

The principle of conditionality, which was raised to a guiding theme in the wake of the sovereign debt crisis, links the granting of stability support to the **fulfilment of conditions** imposed on the recipient State, such as restructuring the budget and initiating economic reform measures.[78] The principle of conditionality aims primarily to counteract the confidence of MS in a *bail-out* and to use the limited resources of the ESM in an economically sensible way (→ Supplement to Title   34

---

[76] Selmayr (2014), para 104; Pilz (2016), p. 24 et seq.

[77] Towards a Genuine Economic and Monetary Union, Interim Report by President of the European Council Herman Van Rompuy, 12 October 2012, p. 4 et seq.; Towards a Genuine Economic and Monetary Union, Final Report by President of the European Council Herman Van Rompuy, 5 December 2012.

[78] In the TESM this is laid down within the 2nd, 6th, and 12th Recital of the Preamble as well as in Articles 3, 12 and 13 TESM, where it is stated normatively, and in Article 136.3 TFEU, where it is being flanked by Union law.

VIII: TESM para 61 et seq.).⁷⁹ If the recipient States violate these conditions, no further assistance loans will be granted.⁸⁰ It is this economic logic that constitutes the essential purpose of conditionality. In *Pringle*—among others—the CJEU declared the stability support to be compatible with the prohibition of assuming liability if it is subject to conditionality.⁸¹

35   Another condition for granting stability support from the ESM is the prior **ratification of the TSCG**.⁸² This link emphasizes the reserve function of the ESM, which is available in case the budget rules of the Fiscal Compact cannot prevent a public debt crisis. By means of the **package deal clause**, both agreements ensure compliance with the normative purpose of Article 125 TFEU, meaning the safeguarding of a stability-oriented national budgetary policy and the maintenance of the financial stability of the common currency (→ Supplement to Title VIII: Fiscal Union, para 35; → Supplement to Title VIII: TESM para 62). Thus, the package deal between the two treaties aims to ensure that "the anomaly of assistance in an emergency" ends as soon as possible and "the normality of ownership and self-financing" is restored.⁸³

4.2.2. The Magical Triangle of Price Stability, Economic Growth and Full Employment

36   A stability-oriented economic and monetary policy is a permanent yardstick for the Union and its MS. Sound public finances are indispensable for the maintenance of stable economic conditions in the MS and within the Union. They are essential to promote a sustainable development of Europe based on balanced economic growth and price stability, a highly competitive social market economy, aiming at full employment and social progress.⁸⁴ Within the scope of application of the TESM, TSCG, and TMCA, the Contracting Parties are also obliged to comply with the magical triangle of price stability, economic growth and full employment contained in Article 3.3 TEU.⁸⁵

37   To emphasize the stability-oriented nature of the EMU, European primary law stipulates the primacy of **price stability**. As a key point of reference, this should be considered in the interpretation and application of the Treaty provisions on the

---

⁷⁹ Ohler (2013), p. 289 et seq.; Schoenfleisch (2018), p. 104.

⁸⁰ Pilz (2016), p. 71.

⁸¹ Case C-370/12, *Pringle* (CJEU 27 November 2012) para 130. See also Adamski (2020), para 9.73 et seqq.

⁸² Preamble to the TESM, 5th Recital in conjunction with Preamble to the SCG Treaty, 25th Recital: "the granting of assistance in the framework of new programmes under the European Stability Mechanism will be conditional [...] on the ratification of this Treaty."

⁸³ Pilz (2016), p. 199 (our translation); Hufeld (2014), para 160.

⁸⁴ European Commission, *Proposal for a Council Regulation on the establishment of the European Monetary Fund*, 8th Recital of the Preamble, COM(2017) 827.

⁸⁵ On the consistency and coherence of Union Law → Supplement to Title VIII: TESM para 14 et seqq.

EMU by the competent institutions of the Union and the MS.[86] The term price stability refers to the internal value and thus the purchasing power of a currency.[87] Price stability exists when the average of all prices for goods and services, in other words, the price level, remains stable overall.[88] The indicator of this economic policy objective is the **inflation rate**. The ECB measures price stability on the Harmonized Index of Consumer Prices (HICP). Price stability is best maintained by **aiming for two per cent inflation over the medium term** (→ Article 119 TFEU para 17).[89] However, to ensure price stability, it is not enough that monetary and exchange rate policy alone are primarily committed to maintaining low inflation rates. Price stability is threatened above all by the authorities of the MS responsible for economic and financial policy decisions. Those states that conclude international treaties establishing the "Transfer," "Fiscal," and "Banking Union" consider price stability in the EA by adhering to the cross-pillar objective of maintaining financial stability. The concept of financial stability is not the same as price stability.[90] However, financial stability is an implicit requirement of price stability, since the latter can only be secured in an environment where the transmission of monetary policy signals runs smoothly. This, in turn, requires a stable financial system (→ Supplement to Title VIII: TESM para 58).[91]

The objective of price stability is inextricably linked to the goal of **"balanced economic growth."** The term implies a long-term continuity of economic growth. It is about initiating a slowly but steadily growing economy, indicated by the GDP. The GDP summarizes the value of all goods and services generated in one year and gives an indication of the economic growth of a State. Long-term sound economic fundamentals are therefore an **indispensable requirement of measures within the scope of the TESM and TSCG**. Admittedly, the adjustment programmes linked to an ESM financial assistance are primarily aimed at restoring the sustainability of public debt and thus at enabling refinancing of the MS on the capital markets.

38

---

[86] Häde, in Calliess and Ruffert (2021), Article 119 TFEU para 28. Yoo, in von der Groeben et al. (2015), Article 119 TFEU para 15.

[87] Potacs, in Schwarze (2012), Article 127 TFEU para 2.

[88] Häde, in Calliess and Ruffert (2021), Article 119 TFEU para 22.

[89] For the quantitative definition of price stability in the Eurosystem cf. European Central Bank, Monetary policy strategy statement of 8 July 2021 (available at https://www.ecb.europa.eu/home/search/review/html/ecb.strategyreview_monpol_strategy_statement.en.html). Thereby the ECB relinquished the previous target (2003) of "below, but close to, 2%, over the medium term." Underlying, this is an absolute concept of stability. A more flexible understanding of stability, on the other hand, would call into question the credibility of the ECB; cf. with regard to the previous inflation target (2003): Manger-Nestler (2008), p. 176; in further detail, also Blanke and Pilz, in von Mangoldt et al. (2018), Article 88 GG para 65 et seqq.; Adamski (2020), para 9.21; Thiele (2019), p. 74.

[90] Case C-370/12, *Pringle* (CJEU 27 November 2012) para 56. The AGs in *Pringle* and *Gauweiler* also do not attempt to further define the concept of financial stability. Cf. also Case C-370/12, *Pringle* (Opinion of AG Kokott of 26 October 2012) as well as Case C-62/14, *Gauweiler* (Opinion of AG Cruz Villalón of 14 January 2015) para 143.

[91] Selmayr, in von der Groeben et al. (2015), Article 282 TFEU para 61.

However, a sustainable return is only possible if the adjustment programme is based on a long-term plan that focuses on reducing public debt but also provides options for action on how to create sustainable economic conditions (→ Supplement to Title VIII: TESM para 68 et seqq., 81). Likewise, under Article 5.1 TSCG, a Contracting Party that is also subject to an excessive deficit procedure must submit a budgetary and economic partnership programme detailing the necessary structural reforms. The reform measures aim at improving competitiveness and long-term sustainable growth and addressing structural weaknesses in the MS concerned (→ Supplement to Title VIII: Fiscal Union para 49 et seqq.). The Banking Union and the associated deeper integration of the financial markets also are meant to give new impulses for investment and stronger economic growth.

39 Another element of the magic triangle is **full employment**. This is a condition that is rarely achieved but is yet an objective that the Union pursues, as stated by Article 3.3 TEU, by appropriate means and in accordance with its competences. Full employment occurs usually when the unemployment rate is less than 3%.[92] This is because a certain percentage of unemployment cannot be avoided, even under optimal economic conditions. The State's objective is always to achieve the lowest possible unemployment rate, since in that case, fewer social benefits (such as unemployment benefits) must be paid and in return, the State budget is rehabilitated by tax revenues and social security contributions.

4.3. Interfaces

4.3.1. Repatriation of Intergovernmental Instruments Within the Ambit of Union Law

40 The international treaties do not exclude the possibility of a future supranationalization of their regulatory content. On the contrary, the parties expressly state in Article 16 TSCG and Article 16.2 TMCA that they will take the necessary steps within five (TSCG) or ten (TMCA) years with the aim of **incorporating the substance** of the respective treaty **into the legal framework of the EU** (→ Supplement to Title VIII: Fiscal Union para 15). The SCG Treaty and the TMC Agreement thus gain a temporary character.[93] By contrast, the ESM Treaty does not contain any comparable wording, but does not explicitly exclude supranationalization either.[94] Instead, as early as 2012, the Commission proposed attaining a deep and genuine EMU by the integration of the ESM into the EU Treaty framework.[95]

---

[92] Woll (2011), p. 342; Ruffert, in Calliess and Ruffert (2021), Article 3 TEU para 29.

[93] The temporary nature of the intergovernmental treaties is confirmed by the seventh Recital of the TSCG and the 25th Recital of the TMCA. Cf. Lenaerts (2014), p. 758 et seq.; Keppenne (2014), p. 204 et seq.

[94] Cf. Lenaerts (2014), p. 758.

[95] Commission Communication, *A blueprint for a deep and genuine economic and monetary union Launching a European Debate*, COM (2012) 777 final, p. 33. For details Martucci (2020), para 12.57 et seqq.

41 The political declarations of intent of the Contracting States do not contain any further details regarding the transfer into the Union's legal framework. Therefore, this can be done by means of primary and secondary law.[96] In view of the circumstances which led to the drafting of the SCG Treaty, it seems obvious that Article 16 TSCG provides for an amendment of EU primary law.[97] However, it remains doubtful whether the approval of all MS, required under Article 48 TEU for treaty amendments, can be achieved. Therefore, it is not surprising that the **Roadmap for Deepening Europe's Economic and Monetary Union** presented by the European Commission in December 2017 includes four main initiatives (→ para 47 et seqq.), each of which is to be implemented by means of secondary legislation.[98] In addition to the transformation of the ESM into a European Monetary Fund and its transfer into the institutional framework of the Union (→ Supplement to Title VIII: TESM para 145 et seqq.), the measures include the incorporation of the provisions of the SCG Treaty into Union law (→ Supplement to Title VIII: Fiscal Union para 38).[99]

4.3.2. Consistency and Coherence of Union Law

42 To avoid conflicts between Union law and international treaties, the Contracting States use corresponding **compatibility rules**. The parties expressly affirm in Article 2.1 TSCG and in Article 2.1 TMCA that the Agreements shall be applied and interpreted in conformity with EU law, including procedural law. In addition to the commitment made in Article 13.3 TESM to the TFEU's economic policy coordination guidelines, the TESM also contains in the fourth Recital of the Preamble the commitment of the Contracting States to "strict observance to the European Union framework," particularly to the provisions of the Stability and Growth Pact.[100] The so-called **clauses of coherence** confirm the primacy of EU law[101] and the consistency with Union policy. This primacy of EU law over agreements between Member States derives both from Union law itself and from principles of international law (Article 26 VCLT).[102]

43 Consistency means avoiding the creation of a parallel legal regime outside Union law that could overrule, for example, the regulations on economic policy

---

[96] Cf. Messina (2014), p. 413 et seq.

[97] Cf. Peers (2012), p. 440 et seq.

[98] European Commission, *Commission sets out Roadmap for deepening Europe's Economic and Monetary Union*, IP 17/5005, 6 December 2017.

[99] Cf. European Commission, *Proposal for a Council Regulation on the establishment of the European Monetary Fund*, 6 December 2017, COM(2017) 827 final; European Commission, *Proposal for a Council Directive laying down provisions for strengthening fiscal responsibility and the medium-term budgetary orientation in the Member States*, 6 December 2017, COM(2017) 824 final.

[100] Preamble to the ESM Treaty, 4th Recital.

[101] Case 6/64, *Flaminio Costa v E.N.E.L.* (ECJ 3 June 1964), p. 1270.

[102] Cf. Keppenne (2014), p. 203.

coordination. The overlapping between the two spheres should not lead to inconsistencies or conflicts of legal provisions, impede the exercise of the EU competences, or render it inefficient or superfluous, nor should it amount to a circumvention of the obligations of MS under the Treaties or of the procedures laid down therein.[103] For that reason, Article 2.2 of both the SCG Treaty and the TMC Agreement provide that both international agreements are compatible with Union law. The **requirement of compatibility**, in effect gives **primacy to Union law** in the event of any conflict. In case of contradictions between the two levels which cannot be resolved by means of consistent interpretation the relevant provision of the SCG Treaty or the TMC Agreement are left unconsidered.[104] After all, the objectives and spirit of the Treaties can only be realized if the common agreements cannot be undermined by unilateral regulations.[105] The effectiveness and actual implementation of Union law, as well as the achievement of the objectives of Article 3 TEU, would be called into question if it were possible for individual MS to create sources of law prior to the Union law.

4.3.3. Institutional Links

44 For the performance of individual operational tasks, the parties to the SCG Treaty, the ESM Treaty, and the TMC Agreement also include supranational institutions, particularly the European Commission, the ECB, and the CJEU. The **delegation of tasks** to the European Commission and the ECB does not take place based on an international treaty. Although the three treaties stand in a particular proximity to EU law,[106] they are still not an integral part of primary law and therefore cannot justify the competences of an EU institution.[107]

45 The involvement of the Commission and the ECB in the ESM Treaty (→ Supplement to Title VIII: TESM para 42 et seqq.), respectively the Commission in the SCG Treaty (→ Supplement to Title VIII: Fiscal Union para 53 et seqq.) and the TMC Agreement (→ Supplement to Title VIII: Banking Union para 194 et seqq.) is carried out through a so-called "**borrowed administration arrangement.**" By means of the borrowed administration arrangement, functional parts of the Union's institutional framework are transferred to an intergovernmental cooperation, consisting of a group of MS organized in accordance with international law. This action is taken to achieve those objectives which the Union's Member States as a whole could not agree on.[108] The application of this measure is a recognized practice which has been confirmed on several occasions by the case law of the

---

[103] De Gregorio Merino (2012), p. 1635 et seq.

[104] Cf. Peers (2012), p. 409 et seq.

[105] Case 6/64, *Flaminio Costa v E.N.E.L.* (ECJ 3 June 1964), p. 1269.

[106] German Federal Constitutional Court, 2 BvE 4/11 (Judgment of 19 June 2012), para 100 – *obligatory notifications* (in BVerfGE 131, 152 [199 et seq.]).

[107] Thym (2004), p. 315.

[108] Fischer-Lescano and Oberndorfer (2013), p. 9; Thym (2004), p. 317.

CJEU.[109] The jurisdiction of the CJEU within the scope of the ESM Treaty (→ Supplement to Title VIII: TESM para 49 et seqq.), the SCG Treaty[110] (→ Supplement to Title VIII: Fiscal Union para 53 et seqq.) and the TMC Agreement results from an intergovernmental arbitration agreement under Article 273 TFEU, which is legally established in Article 37.3 TESM, Article 8 TSCG and Article 14.2 TMCA.[111]

4.3.4. Accession of New Members

Under Article 44 in conjunction with Article 2 TESM, an EU Member State may also join the ESM Treaty—as a Treaty of the EMU States—after the introduction of the euro. Moreover, the TMC Agreement and the SCG Treaty are open for accession, too. Croatia and the Czech Republic, countries that refrained from the treaty, can join the TSCG by means of Article 15 TSCG. A similar provision is laid down in Article 13 TMCA. This openness to the accession of other MS as Contracting Parties strengthens the compatibility of international treaties with Union law.

5. Further Development of the Three Pillars: An Outlook

More than ten years after the onset of the financial, economic, and sovereign debt crisis, the broad reform of the EMU remains the "**core of the European project**" (*J.-C. Juncker*).[112] During the term of office of the *Juncker* Commission (2014–2019), the Member States not only had to preserve the stability and integrity of the Eurozone, but also to remedy the weaknesses in the architecture of the single currency area. Against this background, the five Presidents launched the agenda for **Deepening the Economic and Monetary Union** in June 2015[113] and on 6 December 2017 the Commission presented a whole package of proposals to deepen EMU.

The proposals of the so-called **Saint Nicholas Package**[114] aim to bring the international legal institutions and mechanisms, created in response to the financial

---

[109] Joined Cases C-181/91 and C-248/91, *Parliament v Council and Commission* (ECJ 30 June 1993) para 20; Case C-316/91, *Parliament v Council* (ECJ 2 March 1994) para 41. Cf. De Gregorio Merino (2012), p. 1638; Peers (2013), p. 44 et seq.

[110] Critically Craig (2012), p. 245 et seqq.; Peers (2012), p. 417 et seqq.

[111] Cf. Peers (2013), p. 61 et seq.; Craig (2012), p. 245 et seq. See also Lenaerts et al. (2006), p. 502 et seq.

[112] Commission Communication, *Deepening Europe's Economic and Monetary Union: Taking stock four years after the Five Presidents' Report European Commission's contribution to the Euro Summit on 21 June 2019*, COM(2019) 279 final.

[113] *J.-C. Juncker*, in close cooperation with *D. Tusk, J. Dijsselbloem, M. Draghi, and M. Schulz* (2015), The five Presidents Report: Completing Europe's Economic and Monetary Union.

[114] Commission Communication, *Further Steps towards completing Europe's Economic and Monetary Union: A Roadmap*, COM(2017) 821 final.

and sovereign debt crisis, into the EU legal framework, and to supplement them with further elements. The end of the coexistence of supranational and intergovernmental organs and processes are meant to make the procedures of economic policy coordination more efficient and integrated in European law as well as strengthen overall economic integration. Thus, the package is supposed to lay the foundation to complete the EMU by 2025.[115]

49 The Commission focused on the transfer of the ESM into Union law. To this end, the Commission presented a draft Regulation establishing a European Monetary Fund, which aims to establish a legal framework by secondary legislation for the existing financial and institutional structures of the ESM, and furthermore aims to complement the provision of credit lines or guarantees for the Single Resolution Fund as a new task (→ Supplement to Title VIII: TESM para 145–148).[116] By drafting a directive on the **incorporation of the substance of the Fiscal Compact**, the Commission complies with the declaration of intent by the Contracting States in Article 16 TSCG to transfer the SCG Treaty into the EU's legal framework.[117] As some of the rules are already included in Union law and others are beyond the scope of secondary legislation, the draft directive's focus lies on the budgetary rules of Article 3 TSCG (→ Supplement to Title VIII: Fiscal Union para 25 et seqq.).

50 In addition to the transfer of the international treaties into Union law, the Commission presented a Communication on the creation of a **European Minister for Economic and Financial Affairs**.[118] Accordingly, the Commissioner for Economic and Financial Affairs, as Vice-President of the Commission, will be merged with the President of the Eurogroup to increase the coherence and efficiency of managing the economic policies of all MS. As long as there is no upgrading of the existing Commissioner's competences with the introduction of this office, such a nominal distinction seems questionable. For even if a European Finance Minister were appointed Chairman of the Eurogroup and of the Board of Governors of a future EMF, he would not receive the competences of a national Minister of Finance. In particular, he would not have a veto on budgetary matters.

51 Even after several years, no agreement could be reached on all these proposals. The **EMU remains incomplete**. Despite significant reforms over the last two decades, the EA remains divided, politically, and financially. The completion of

---

[115] European Commission, *Communication to the European Parliament, the European Council, the Council and the European Central Bank. Further Steps towards completing Europe's Economic and Monetary Union: A Roadmap*, COM(2017) 821 final.

[116] European Commission, *Proposal for a Council Regulation on the establishment of the European Monetary Fund*, COM(2017) 827 final and *Annex to the Proposal for a Council Regulation on the establishment of the European Monetary Fund*, COM(2017) 827 final Annex.

[117] "[...] incorporating the substance of this Treaty into the legal framework of the European Union." (Article 16 TSCG). Cf. European Commission, *Proposal for a Council Directive laying down provisions for strengthening fiscal responsibility and the medium-term budgetary orientation in the Member States*, COM(2017) 824 final.

[118] Commission Communication, *A European Minister for Economy and Finance*, COM(2017) 823 final.

the EMU is thus also one of the major challenges which the *von der Leyen* Commission will have to face.[119] In addition to the above-mentioned measures, it is essential to tackle the completion of the Banking Union and to implement EDIS. The work of the ESM/EMF would be easier with a complete Banking Union. With a deposit guarantee scheme for depositors throughout the EA and a weaker link between banks and governments, financial fragmentation would be prevented and the risk of a bank going into crisis would be reduced. The volume of all previous ESM programmes would have been lower if there had already been EDIS in the previous crisis.

Following years of sustained growth, policymakers in Europe—and beyond— have been unexpectedly confronted with the largest health, economic and social challenges since World War II, as the corona pandemic spreads to Europe in February 2020. Due to COVID-19 and the far-reaching public health measures taken to contain it, the economies of all EA Member States are experiencing a simultaneous symmetric external shock. Unlike those experienced during the European banking and sovereign debt crisis, this is not caused by the banking or public sector but by the real economy. It does not only affect certain Member States but has a more or less equal impact on all of them within a certain corridor. The **COVID-19 crisis** was a severe test for the EA with extremely serious socio-economic consequences. The EA fell into a deep recession at the end of 2020, with the southern European MS, as the most vulnerable economies, being hit the hardest by the onset of the crisis.[120] The global economy is projected to grow by 4.9% in 2022. The distortion caused by COVID-19 appears to become entrenched in 2022—short-term divergences are likely to have a lasting impact on medium-term development. The EA economy is recovering swiftly despite continued uncertainty related to the COVID-19 pandemic and supply bottlenecks. Real GDP is expected to grow by 4.6% in 2022 and by 2.1% in 2023.[121]

The crisis caused by the COVID-19 pandemic has required rapid and strong action. As in the sovereign debt crisis, it was again the ECB that was the first to react decisively, announcing on 18 March 2020 the launch of a **Pandemic Emergency Purchase Programme (PEPP)** and promising to invest up to EUR 750

---

[119] Cf. Blanke and Pilz (2020), p. 285.

[120] In its latest World Economic Outlook, the IMF concludes that the global economy is facing the biggest economic downturn since the Great Depression: "It is very likely that this year the global economy will experience its worst recession since the Great Depression, surpassing that seen during the global financial crisis a decade ago. The Great Lockdown, as one might call it, is projected to shrink global growth dramatically." International Monetary Funds, World Economic Outlook, April 2020: Chapter 1, p. v (foreword). Available at: https://www.imf.org/~/media/Files/Publications/WEO/2020/April/English/text.ashx?la=en.

[121] European Central Bank (2021), ECB staff macroeconomic projections for the euro area, September 2021. Available at: https://www.ecb.europa.eu/pub/projections/html/ecb.projections202109_ecbstaff~1f59a501e2.en.html.

billion in EA assets and debt securities.[122] Together with the support measures adopted by the Commission, the ESM and the EIB on 9 April 2020 in a spirit of solidarity, a financial safeguard of almost EUR 1.3 billion has been put in place to cushion the fall of Member States' economies into recession.[123] The new solidarity instrument called SURE ("**Support mitigating Unemployment Risks in Emergency**"), set up by the Commission based on Article 122 TFEU (→ Article 122 TFEU para 10, 14, 36), provides loans of up to EUR 100 billion to finance national short-time work schemes,[124] as well as a pandemic credit line of EUR 240 billion provided by the ESM (→ Supplement to Title VIII: TESM para 91) and loans from the EIB for companies of up to EUR 200 billion to complete the rescue package.[125] In addition, the Commission and the Council have agreed to activate the **general escape clause** of the Stability and Growth Pact and to make full use of the flexibility offered by the legal framework of EU state aid rules.[126]

54 The above measures are complemented by a comprehensive European Economic Recovery Plan, which the European Commission proposed in late May 2020.[127] At the heart of this plan is a new development instrument called the "**Next Generation EU**" (NGEU), with a budget of EUR 750 billion to stimulate the economy.[128] The legal basis for the new instrument is Article 122 TFEU, which allows assistance to Member States in exceptional occurrences. An essential component of the recovery instrument is a new "**Recovery and Resilience Facility**"

---

[122] ECB Decision (EU) 2020/440 *on a temporary pandemic emergency purchase programme* (ECB/2020/17), O.J. L 91/1 (2020). ECB Press Release 18 March 2020, ECB announces EUR 750 billion Pandemic Emergency Purchase Programme (PEPP).

[123] Council of the EU (Eurogroup), Report on the comprehensive economic policy response to the COVID-19 pandemic, Press Release 223/20, 9 April 2020.

[124] Council Regulation (EU) 2020/672 *on the establishment of a European instrument for temporary support to mitigate unemployment risks in an emergency (SURE) following the COVID-19 outbreak*, O.J. L 159/1 (2020).

[125] Conclusions of the President of the European Council following the video conference of the members of the European Council, 23 April 2020, Press 251/20.

[126] Commission Communication *on the activation of the general escape clause of the Stability and Growth Pact*, COM(2020) 123 final; ECOFIN Press Release 173/20, 23 March 2020; Commission Communication, *Temporary Framework for State aid measures to support the economy in the current COVID-19 outbreak*, 19 March 2020, C(2020) 1863, O.J. C 91I/1 (2020) and Commission Communication, *Amendment to the Temporary Framework for State aid measures to support the economy in the current COVID-19 outbreak*, 3 April 2020, C(2020) 2215, O.J. C 112I/1 (2020).

[127] The project will be legally incorporated into several legislative acts. The following legal acts are to be mentioned as the main pillars of the recovery plan: (1) European Commission, *Proposal for a Council Regulation establishing a European Union Recovery Instrument to support the recovery in the aftermath of the COVID-19 pandemic*, COM(2020) 441 final; (2) European Commission, *Proposal for a Regulation of the European Parliament and of the Council establishing a European Recovery and Resilience Facility*, COM(2020) 408 final; European Commission, *Amended proposal for a Council Decision on the system of Own Resources of the European Union*, COM(2020) 445 final.

[128] Council Regulation (EU) No. 2020/2094 *establishing a European Union Recovery Instrument to support the recovery in the aftermath of the COVID-19 crisis*, O.J. LI 433/23 (2020).

based on Article 175 (3) TFEU.[129] NGEU is **embedded in the revised MFF 2021–2027** and financed by the Commission's issuance of large volumes of debt on international capital markets under the empowerment granted by the Own Resources Decision.[130] At its meeting on 17 to 21 July 2020, the European Council modified and clarified the recovery plan while maintaining its basic orientation.[131] Following the European Parliament's consent, on 17 December 2020 the Council adopted the Regulation laying down the EU's MFF 2021–2027. This Regulation provides for a long-term EU budget of EUR 1 074.3 billion for the EU27 in 2018 prices, including the integration of the European Development Fund. Together with the NGEU recovery instrument of EUR 750 billion, it will allow the EU to provide an unprecedented EUR 1.8 trillion of funding over the coming years to support recovery from the COVID-19 pandemic and the EU's long-term priorities across different policy areas.[132]

To provide the financing of the recovery instrument, the Commission plans to raise up to **EUR 750 billion** on the capital markets on behalf of the EU. The Commission wants to make this possible through a new Own Resources Decision to apply from the next MFF 2021–2027.[133] The Commission had already presented a proposal for a new Own Resources Decision in 2018[134] to replace the current Own Resources Decision of 2014.[135] The Commission now intends to amend its 2018 proposal by the amended proposal for a Council Decision on the system of own resources of the EU.[136] The amended proposal includes an authorization for the Commission to **raise funds on the capital markets** and an additional **increase of the own resources ceiling**. The legal basis for this proposal should be Article 311 TFEU, according to which the EU shall provide itself with the means necessary to attain its objectives and carry through its policies. By Decision of 14 December 2020, the Council adopted the Commission's proposal.[137] The Council has received formal notifications about the approval of the Own Resources Decision from all 27

55

---

[129] Parliament/Council Regulation (EU) 2021/241 *establishing the Recovery and Resilience Facility*, O.J. L 57/17 (2021).

[130] Commission Communication, *Europe's moment: Repair and Prepare for the Next Generation*, COM(2020) 456 final, p. 5.

[131] European Council of 17–21 July 2020, Conclusions, Doc. EUCO 10/20.

[132] Council Press Release 969/20, 17 December 2020.

[133] According to the compromise negotiated between the European Council and the Commission, the overall amount for commitments in MFF 2021–2027 is EUR 1074.3 billion. European Council of 17–21 July 2020, Conclusions, Doc. EUCO 10/20, A23.

[134] European Commission, *Proposal for a Council Decision on the system of Own Resources of the European Union*, COM(2018) 325 final.

[135] Council Decision of 26 May 2014 *on the system of own resources of the European Union*, O.J. L 168/105 (2014).

[136] European Commission, *Amended proposal for a Council Decision on the system of Own Resources of the European Union*, COM(2020) 445 final.

[137] Council Decision (EU, Euratom) 2020/2053 *on the system of own resources of the European Union*, O.J. L 424/1 (2020).

MS on 31 May 2021. National ratifications being completed, the EU can now start making available funds under the Recovery and Resilience Facility.[138]

56 The EU Recovery Plan aims "to prevent a further deterioration of the economy, employment and social cohesion and to boost a sustainable and resilient recovery of the economic activity [. . .]."[139] According to the Commission's initial proposal, the recovery instrument was to comprise **EUR 750 billion** to be provided **in the form of grants** (EUR 310 billion) via Union programmes **and loans** (EUR 250 billion) to the MS. Although the European Council left the total volume of EUR 750 billion untouched, the relationship between non-repayable support and loans has shifted considerably. The funds raised on the capital markets may be used for loans of up to EUR 360 billion and non-repayable grants of up to EUR 390 billion.[140] EUR 312.5 billion of the grants and the total of EUR 360 billion of the loans to MS will be channelled into a newly created Recovery and Resilience Facility ($\rightarrow$ para 57).[141] The funds mobilized as grants are partly provided through EU programmes in the field of cohesion and structural policy (Articles 174 to 178 TFEU), industrial policy (Article 173 TFEU), and civil protection policy (Article 196 TFEU) to **support the immediate measures needed to secure livelihoods, boost the economy and strengthen sustainable and robust growth**. The European Council has also made some considerable shifts in the allocation of funds to the various EU programmes compared to the original Commission proposal. Some programmes are not intended to obtain any (e.g., EU solvency instrument and EU Health) or only receive significantly lower additional funds (e.g., InvestEU EUR 5.6 billion instead of EUR 30.3 billion).[142]

57 At the heart of the recovery instrument is the **Recovery and Resilience Facility**, which is specifically designed to finance investments and reforms in line with European priorities.[143] The facility is designed to support investments and reforms that are essential for a sustainable recovery, strengthening the economic and social resilience of the MS and supporting the green and digital transition.[144] To fulfil these tasks, the Recovery and Resilience Facility has EUR 612.5 billion at its disposal from the instrument's total budget.[145] To be able to draw on funds from this facility, MS must draw up so-called "**recovery and resilience plans**," which

---

[138] Council of the EU, Green light from all member states for EU recovery spending, Press Release 425/21, 31 May 2021.

[139] European Commission, *Proposal for a Council Regulation establishing a European Union Recovery Instrument to support the recovery in the aftermath of the COVID-19 pandemic*, COM (2020) 441 final, 5th Recital.

[140] European Council of 17–21 July 2020, Conclusions, Doc. EUCO 10/20, A6.

[141] European Council of 17–21 July 2020, Conclusions, Doc. EUCO 10/20, A14.

[142] European Council of 17–21 July 2020, Conclusions, Doc. EUCO 10/20, A14.

[143] Parliament/Council Regulation (EU) 2021/241 *establishing the Recovery and Resilience Facility*, O.J. L 57/17 (2021).

[144] COM(2020) 408 final, 6th Recital.

[145] European Council of 17–21 July 2020, Conclusions, Doc. EUCO 10/20, A14.

will be defined **in line with the priorities identified in the European Semester**, including with regard to environmental and digital change and the resilience of economies.[146] Therefore, MS submit draft recovery and resilience plans from 15 October 2020. The Commission discusses plans with each MS. MS submit official plans by 30 April 2021.[147] The plans can be amended at a later stage. Commission assesses plans and transmits to Parliament and Council. The Council assesses and adopts plans based on the Commission proposal. Once these plans have been approved, they will be eligible for financial assistance from the facility to implement the reforms and investments foreseen in the plans. The Council can suspend adoption or payments in case of significant non-compliance.[148] MS report on progress twice a year within the European Semester. Commission reports on implementation to Parliament and Council every year. Independent evaluations are due in 2023 and, ex post, by 2029.[149]

Many legal questions arise regarding the **recovery instrument**. The complexity and nesting of the instrument means that its legal assessment is extremely demanding. The recovery instrument is based on several components, each of which is regulated by a separate legal act.[150] These legal acts in turn have different legal bases in the EU Treaties. Whether this construction is a convincing way of circumventing the EU's no bail-out clause (Article 125 TFEU) requires intensive examination.

The choice of Article 122 TFEU as the legal basis for the recovery instrument appears to be legally problematic. Financial support cannot be based on Article 122.1 TFEU but at best on Article 122.2 TFEU. However, the requirements of Article 122.2 TFEU are stretched very far in several respects—apart from the additional problematic question of whether the EU may actually raise the envisaged funds of EUR 750 billion on the capital markets. Thus, the wording of Article 122.2 TFEU explicitly does not include either a multi-level solution or such a complex construct according to which further instruments and regulations are interposed when assistance is granted. Even if one assumes that Article 122.2 TFEU can be interpreted in a correspondingly broad way and allows such constructions, adjustments to the recovery instrument are necessary. Finally, the planned **use and distribution of the funds** as grants and loans to finance the eligible measures

---

[146] COM(2020) 408 final, Article 14.2.
[147] European Commission, *Commission Staff Working Document. Guidance to Member States Recovery and Resilience Plans.* SWD(2020) 205 final, Part 1/2, p. 2.
[148] SWD(2020) 205 final, Part 1/2, p. 37.
[149] SWD(2020) 205 final, Part 1/2, p. 28.
[150] The following legal acts are the main pillars of the recovery plan: (1) Council Regulation (EU) No. 2020/2094 *establishing a European Union Recovery Instrument to support the recovery in the aftermath of the COVID-19 crisis*, O.J. LI 433/23 (2020); (2) Parliament/Council Regulation (EU) No. 2021/241 *establishing a European Recovery and Resilience Facility*, O.J. L 57/17 (2021); (3) Council Decision (EU, Euratom) 2020/2053 *on the system of Own Resources of the European Union*, O.J. L 424/1 (2020).

does not fully comply with the exceptional nature of Article 122.2 TFEU (→ Article 122 TFEU para 13), which is limited to financial assistance in the event of a crisis. The allocation of the funds must be more closely linked to the actual need to cope with the negative consequences of the COVID-19 crisis.[151]

60 The Commission's empowerment in the Own Resources Decision to borrow funds from the capital markets, on behalf of the Union, is also legally problematic. Article 311.3 TFEU is not an appropriate legal basis for this approach. The provision allows the Council to lay down the rules relating to the system of the EU's own resources. According to the proposals for the recovery instrument, however, funds generated from bonds should not constitute own resources, although this is widely accepted in the literature.[152] However, neither the original proposal for a new Own Resources Decision of 2018[153] nor the amended proposal of 28 May 2020[154] provides for this. Rather, the proceeds of the **EU bonds** used to finance the recovery instrument are explicitly defined as "external assigned revenue"[155] and are therefore not treated as own resources. This is **a new category of "other" revenue**.[156] Both the Commission and the Council's Legal Service consider it legally problematic to qualify the proceeds of borrowings as a new category of own resources.[157] This revenue cannot be definitively allocated to the EU—as is required for own resources—because the EU must repay the loans and thus incur liabilities.

61 Neither can the empowerment to issue bonds be included in the Own Resources Decision as an annex to the increase in the own resources ceiling, as it is not merely a secondary element compared to the latter. It seems artificial to regard a borrowing authorization from the EU—specially to take on debt in immense, never before known amounts—as a subordinate component and to include it in the Own Resources Decision. Rather, the **complete financing and** thus the **feasibility of the recovery instrument** depends on the bond issue by the EU. Since the bond issue is to take place outside the EU budget, the increase in the own resources

---

[151] Opinion of the Council Legal Service, *Proposals of Next Generation EU*, Council Doc. 9062/20, para 126.

[152] Häde (2011b), p. 297; Bieber, in von der Groeben et al. (2015), Article 311 TFEU para 43; Rossi, in Vedder and Heintschel von Heinegg (2018), Article 311 TFEU para 8; Storr (2001), p. 866.

[153] European Commission, *Proposal for a Council Decision on the system of Own Resources of the European Union*, COM(2018) 325 final.

[154] European Commission, *Amended proposal for a Council Decision on the system of Own Resources of the European Union*, COM(2020) 445 final.

[155] In any event, to the extent that these amounts are to be paid to the Member States in the form of grants. See Article 4.1 of the proposal for a Council Regulation establishing a European Union Recovery Instrument to support the recovery in the aftermath of the COVID-19 pandemic, COM (2020) 441, cf. 9th Recital.

[156] "The borrowed funds will not constitute own resources but a new category of 'other revenue'(...)," European Commission, QANDA/20/1024.

[157] European Commission, QANDA/20/1024; Opinion of the Council Legal Service, *Proposals of Next Generation EU*, Council Doc. 9062/20, para 57.

ceiling is conversely a means to an end, so that the funds raised can be repaid from the EU budget and the AAA rating of the EU for the bond issue can be maintained.[158]

Thus, **raising the own resources ceiling** is rather the logical consequence of raising the ceiling to comply with the requirement of Article 310.4 TFEU, according to which the EU may not adopt any act with potentially significant budgetary implications without ensuring that the expenditure involved can be financed within the limit of the EU's own resources. Without the empowerment to issue bonds, there would be no borrowing, no liabilities of the EU and therefore no need to allow for their settlement through the EU budget and to raise the own resources ceiling for that purpose. All this argues against considering the bond authorization as subordinate to the increase in the own resources ceiling. **62**

The national parliaments, which must agree to the increase of the own resources ceiling, and the EP should press for the EU to have a fast-acting economic recovery plan, but to invest much more in an **innovative industrial policy** that counteracts the macro-economic imbalance between the North and the South in Europe. These efforts will only be meaningful if, in the long term, all Member States are enabled to implement social programmes under their own steam. Europeans will only be able to restore **global competitiveness in the industries** of the future with major, truly European projects. However, these must not follow an intergovernmental logic of decision-making, but must be in the **pan-European interest** and should be initiated by the EP. **63**

List of Cases

ECJ/CJEU
ECJ 03.06.1964, 6/64, *Flaminio Costa v E.N.E.L.*, ECLI:EU:C:1964:66 [cit. in para 42 et seq.]
ECJ 30.06.1993, C-181/91 and C-248/91, *Parliament v Council and Commission*, ECLI:EU:C:1993:271 [cit. in para 45]
ECJ 02.03.1994, C-316/91, *Parliament v Council*, ECLI:EU:C:1994:76 [cit. in para 45]
CJEU 26.10.2012, C-370/12, Opinion of AG Kokott, *Pringle*, ECLI:EU:C:2012:675 [cit. in para 37]
CJEU 27.11.2012, C-370/12, *Pringle*, ECLI:EU:C:2012:756 [cit. in para 34, 37]
CJEU 14.01.2015, C-62/14, Opinion of AG Cruz Villalón, *Gauweiler*, ECLI:EU:C:2015:7 [cit. in para 37]

---

[158] "This temporary increase enables the Commission to borrow on a much larger scale than in the past, and aims to preserve the Union's AAA credit rating." Thus, the Research Service of the European Parliament, Future financing of the Union: MFF, Own Resources and Next Generation EU, PE 652.023 – July 2020, p. 1.

German Federal Constitutional Court

German FCC 19.06.2012, 2 BvE 4/11, *Obligatory notifications*, ECLI:DE:BVerfG:2012:es20120619.2bve000411 [cit. in para 44]

German FCC 14.01.2014, 2 BvR 2728/13, *OMT (reference for preliminary ruling)*, ECLI:DE:BVerfG:2014:rs20140114.2bvr272813 [cit. in para 25]

German FCC 30.07.2019, 2 BvR 1685/14, *Banking Union*, ECLI:DE:BVerfG:2019:rs20190730.2bvr168514 [cit. in para 14, 15]

References[159]

Adamski, D. (2020). Objectives of EMU. In F. Amtenbrink & C. Herrmann (Eds.), *The EU law of Economic and Monetary Union* (Chapter 9). OUP.

Binder, J.-H. (2013). Auf dem Weg zu einer europäischen Bankenunion? Erreichtes, Unerreichtes, offene Fragen. *Zeitschrift für Bankrecht und Bankwirtschaft*, 297–312.

Blanke, H.-J. (2011). The European Economic and Monetary Union – between vulnerability and reform. *International Journal of Public Law and Policy*, 402–433.

Blanke, H.-J. (2012). Die Europäische Wirtschafts- und Währungsunion zwischen Krisenanfälligkeit und Reform. In A. Scherzberg et al. (Eds.), *Zehn Jahre Staatswissenschaften in Erfurt* (pp. 70–121). De Gruyter.

Blanke, H.-J., & Pilz, S. (2020). Europa 2019 bis 2024 – Wohin trägt uns der Stier? Sieben Thesen zu den Herausforderungen der Europäischen Union. *Europarecht*, 270–301.

Calliess, C., & Ruffert, M. (2021). *EUV/AEUV Kommentar* (6th ed.). C.H. Beck.

Calliess, C., & Schoenfleisch, C. (2012). Auf dem Weg in die europäische "Fiskalunion"? – Europa- und verfassungsrechtliche Fragen einer Reform der Wirtschafts- und Währungsunion im Kontext des Fiskalvertrages. *JuristenZeitung*, 477–487.

Chiti, E., & Teixeira, P. D. (2013). The constitutional implication of the European response to the financial and public debt crisis. *Common Market Law Review, 50*, 683–708.

Classen, C. D. (2014). Zur offenen Finalität der europäischen Integration. In A. Hatje & P.-C. Müller-Graff (Eds.), *Enzyklopädie Europarecht: Europäische Organisations- und Verfassungsrecht*. (Vol. I) (§ 37). Nomos.

Corsetti, G. (Ed.). (2012). *Austerity: Too much of a good thing?* Centre for Economic Policy Research.

Craig, P. (2012). The stability, coordination and governance treaty: Principle, politics and pragmatism. *European Law Review, 37*, 231–248.

De Gregorio Merino, A. (2012). Legal developments in the economic and monetary union during the debt crisis: The mechanisms of financial assistance. *Common Market Law Review, 49*, 1613–1646.

Demary, M., Diermeier, M., Hüther, M., Jung, M., & Matthes, J. (2018). *Schriftliche Stellungnahme zu einer öffentlichen Anhörung des Bundestagsausschusses für die Angelegenheiten der Europäischen Union*. IW-Report 20/2018.

de Witte, B. (2015). Euro crisis responses and the EU legal order: Increased institutional variation or constitutional mutation? *European Constitutional Law Review*, 434–457.

Deutsche Bundesbank. (2015). *Pläne der Europäischen Kommission für ein European Deposit Insurance Scheme*. Monthly Report December 2015 (p. 63). Frankfurt.

Dimopoulos, A. (2014). The use of international law as a tool for enhancing governance in the Eurozone and its impact on EU institutional integrity. In M. Adams, F. Fabbrini, & P. Larouche (Eds.), *The constitutionalization of European budgetary constraints* (pp. 41–63). Hart.

---

[159] All cited Internet sources of this comment have been accessed on 6 April 2021.

Dombret, A. (2016). *Baustelle europäische Bankenunion – Gemeinsame Aufsicht, gemeinsame Abwicklung, gemeinsame Einlagensicherung? Vortrag beim Bundesbank-Symposium "Bankenaufsicht im Dialog"*. Retrieved from: https://www.bundesbank.de/Redaktion/DE/Reden/2016/2016_06_01_dombret.html

European Stability Mechanism. (2019). *Safeguarding the Euro in times of crisis. The inside story of the ESM*. Publications Office of the European Union.

Fahrholz, C., Freytag, A., & Ohler, C. (2012). *Ein Rahmen für die Europäische Wirtschafts- und Währungsunion*. Texte zur sozialen Marktwirtschaft 9. Retrieved from: https://www.aicgs.org/site/wp-content/uploads/2012/07/Text-zur-Sozialen-Marktwirtschaft.pdf

Fischer-Lescano, A., & Oberndorfer, L. (2013). Unionsrechtliche Grenzen völkervertraglicher Fiskalregulierung und Organleihe. *Neue Juristische Wochenschrift*, 9–14.

Franzius, C. (2014). *Recht und Politik in der transnationalen Konstellation*. Campus.

Frenz, W., & Ehlenz, C. (2010). Schuldenkrise und Grenzen der europäischen Wirtschaftspolitik. *Europäisches Wirtschafts- und Steuerrecht*, 211–215.

Gordon, J. N., & Ringe, W.-G. (2015). Bank resolution in the European Banking Union: A Transatlantic perspective on what it would take. *Columbia Law Review*, 1297–1369.

Häde, U. (2011a). Art. 136 AEUV – eine neue Generalklausel für die Wirtschafts- und Währungsunion? *JuristenZeitung*, 333–340.

Häde, U. (2011b). Neue Entwicklungen bei den Finanzierungsformen der Europäischen Union. In M. Junkernheinrich et al. (Eds.), *Jahrbuch für öffentliche Finanzen 2011* (pp. 293–308). Berliner Wissenschaftsverlag.

Häde, U. (2013). Rechtliche Bewertungen der Maßnahmen im Hinblick auf eine "Fiskalunion". In C. Calliess (Ed.), *Europäische Solidarität und nationale Identität: Überlegungen im Kontext der Krise im Euroraum* (pp. 193–206). Mohr Siebeck.

Hahn, H. J., & Häde, U. (2010). *Währungsrecht* (2nd ed.). C.H. Beck.

Hinarejos, A. (2015). *The euro-area crisis in constitutional perspective*. OUP.

Hufeld, U. (2014). Das Recht der Europäischen Wirtschaftsunion. In P.-C. Müller-Graff (Ed.), *Enzyklopädie Europarecht. Europäisches Wirtschaftsordnungsrecht* (Vol. IV) (§ 22). Nomos.

Ioannidis, M. (2016). Europe's new transformations: How the EU economic constitution changed during the Eurozone crisis. *Common Market Law Review*, 1237–1282.

Jimenez-Blanco, A. (2014). Die Bankenunion aus rechtsvergleichender und internationaler Sicht: eine spanische Perspektive. In H.-J. Blanke & S. Pilz (Eds.), *Die "Fiskalunion" – Voraussetzungen einer Vertiefung der politischen Integration im Währungsraum der Europäischen Union* (pp. 347–369). Mohr Siebeck.

Kahl, W., Waldhoff, C., & Walter, C. (Eds.) (2017). *Bonner Kommentar zum Grundgesetz*. Loose leaf. C.F. Müller.

Kämmerer, J. A. (2013). Bahn frei der Bankenunion? *Neue Zeitschrift für Verwaltungsrecht*, 830–836.

Kau, M. (2016). *Rechtsharmonisierung*. Mohr Siebeck.

Keppenne, J.-P. (2014). Institutional report. In U. Neergaard, C. Jacqueson, & J. Danielsen (Eds.), *The Economic and Monetary Union: Constitutional and institutional aspects of the economic governance within the EU. The XXVI FIDES Congress in Copenhagen. Congress Publication* (Vol. 1, pp. 179–257). DJOF Publishing.

Kirchhof, P. (2012). *Deutschland im Schuldensog: Der Weg vom Bürgen zurück zum Bürger*. C.H. Beck.

Lehmann, M., & Manger-Nestler, C. (2014). Einheitlicher Europäischer Aufsichtsmechanismus: Bankenaufsicht durch die EZB. *Zeitschrift für Bankrecht und Bankwirtschaft*, 2–21.

Lenaerts, K. (2014). EMU and the European Union's Constitutional Framework. *European Law Review*, 753–769.

Lenaerts, K., Arts, D., & Maselis, I. (2006). *Procedural law of the European Union*. Sweet & Maxwell.

Lorz, A., & Sauer, H. (2012). Ersatzunionsrecht und Grundgesetz. *Die Öffentliche Verwaltung*, 573–582.

Manger-Nestler, C. (2008). *Par(s) inter pares? Die Bundesbank als nationale Zentralbank im Europäischen System der Zentralbanken*. Duncker & Humblot.

Manger-Nestler, C. (2014). Die Bankenunion: Gemeinsame Mechanismen zur Bankensicherung und –überwachung. In H.-J. Blanke & S. Pilz (Eds.), *Die "Fiskalunion" – Voraussetzungen einer Vertiefung der politischen Integration im Währungsraum der Europäischen Union* (pp. 299–345). Mohr Siebeck.

Martucci, F. (2020). Non-EU legal instruments (EFSF, ESM, and Fiscal Compact). In F. Amtenbrink & C. Herrmann (Eds.), *The EU law of Economic and Monetary Union* (Chapter 12). OUP.

Messina, M. (2014). Strengthening economic governance of the European Union through enhanced cooperation: A still possible, but already missed, opportunity. *European Law Review*, 404–417.

Müller-Franken, S. (2014). Das Spannungsverhältnis zwischen Eigenverantwortlichkeit und Solidarität in einer Fiskalunion. In H.-J. Blanke & S. Pilz (Eds.), *Die "Fiskalunion" – Voraussetzungen einer Vertiefung der politischen Integration im Währungsraum der Europäischen Union* (pp. 227–244). Mohr Siebeck.

Ohler, C. (2013). Gemeinschaftssolidarität und finanzpolitische Eigenverantwortung. In T. M. J. Möllers & F.-C. Zeitler (Eds.), *Europa als Rechtsgemeinschaft – Währungsunion und Schuldenkrise* (pp. 277–293). Mohr Siebeck.

Ohler, C. (2020). Banking supervision. In F. Amtenbrink & C. Herrmann (Eds.), *The EU law of Economic and Monetary Union* (Chapter 37). OUP.

Ortmann, A. (2015). Die Abstimmungsregel im Fiskalvertrag: Kollision von Völker- und Unionsrecht? *Europäische Zeitschrift für Wirtschaftsrecht*, 539–544.

Peers, S. (2012). The stability treaty: Permanent austerity or gesture politics? *European Constitutional Law Review*, 404–441.

Peers, S. (2013). The use of EU institutions outside the EU legal framework. *European Constitutional Law Review*, 37–72.

Peffekoven, R. (1992). Das Urteil des Bundesverfassungsgerichts zum Länderfinanzausgleich. *Wirtschaftsdienst*, 349–354.

Pernice, I. (2013). Solidarität in Europa: Eine Ortsbestimmung im Verhältnis zwischen Bürger, Staat und Europäischer Union. In C. Calliess (Ed.), *Europäische Solidarität und nationale Identität: Überlegungen im Kontext der Krise im Euroraum* (pp. 25–56). Mohr Siebeck.

Pilz, S. (2012). Ein fiskalpolitischer Pakt als Brücke in die Stabilitätsunion? *Wirtschaftsdienst*, 457–464.

Pilz, S. (2016). *Der Europäische Stabilitätsmechanismus: eine neue Stufe der Integration*. Mohr Siebeck.

Pilz, S., & Dittmann, H. (2011). Der europäische Stabilitäts- und Wachstumspakt – Quo vadis? *Zeitschrift für Europarecht, internationales Privatrecht und Rechtsvergleichung*, 149–159.

Pilz, S., & Dittmann, H. (2012). Perspektiven des Stabilitäts- und Wachstumspakts - Rechtliche und ökonomische Implikationen des Reformpakets "Economic Governance". *Zeitschrift für europarechtliche Studien*, 53–88.

Quaglia, L., & Royo, S. (2015). Banks and the political economy of the sovereign debt crisis in Italy and Spain. *Review of International Political Economy*, 485–507.

Ruffert, M. (2011). The European debt crisis and European Union law. *Common Market Law Review, 48*, 1777–1805.

Schoenfleisch, C. (2018). *Integration durch Koordinierung? Rechtsfragen der Politikkoordinierung am Beispiel der nationalen Wirtschaftspolitiken*. Mohr Siebeck.

Schorkopf, F. (2012a). Finanzkrisen als Herausforderung der internationalen, europäischen und nationalen Rechtsetzung. In G. Lienbacher, B. Grzeszick, & C. Calliess (Eds.), *Grundsatzfragen der Rechtsetzung und Rechtsfindung. Vereinigung der Deutschen Staatsrechtslehrer (VVdStRL 71)* (pp. 183–220). De Gruyter.

Schorkopf, F. (2012b). Europas politische Verfasstheit im Lichte des Fiskalvertrags. *Zeitschrift für Staats- und Europawissenschaften*, 1–29.

Schwarze, J. (Ed.). (2012). *EU-Kommentar* (3rd ed.). Nomos.

Selmayr, M. (2014). Das Recht der Europäischen Währungsunion. In Hatje & Müller-Graff (Eds.), *Enzyklopädie Europarecht: Europäische Organisations- und Verfassungsrecht*. (Vol. IV) (§ 23). Nomos.
Siekmann, H. (2013). *EWU: Kommentar zur Europäischen Währungsunion*. Mohr Siebeck.
Sinn, H.-W. (2012). *Die Target-Falle. Gefahren für unser Geld und unsere Kinder*. Hanser.
Storr, S. (2001). Die Bewältigung defizitärer Haushaltslagen in der EU. *Europarecht*, 846–871.
Thiele, A. (2019). *Die Europäische Zentralbank. Von technokratischer Behörde zu politischem Akteur?* Mohr Siebeck.
Thym, D. (2004). *Ungleichzeitigkeit und europäisches Verfassungsrecht*. Nomos.
Thym, D. (2011). Euro-Rettungsschirm: zwischenstaatliche Rechtskonstruktion und verfassungsgerichtliche Kontrolle. *Europäische Zeitschrift für Wirtschaftsrecht*, 167–171.
Thym, D. (2014). Einheit in Vielfalt: Binnendifferenzierung der EU-Integration. In A. Hatje & P.-C. Müller-Graff (Eds.), *Enzyklopädie Europarecht: Europäische Organisations- und Verfassungsrecht*. (Vol. 1) (§ 5). Nomos.
Tuori, K., & Tuori, K. (2014). *The Eurozone crisis: A constitutional analysis*. CUP.
Vedder, C., & Heintschel von Heinegg, W. (2018). *Europäisches Unionsrecht* (2nd ed.). C.H. Beck.
von Arnauld, A. (2013). Unions(ergänzungs)völkerrecht: Zur unions- und verfassungsrechtlichen Einbindung völkerrechtlicher Instrumente differenzierter Integration. In M. Breuer et al. (Eds.), *Der Staat im Recht, Festschrift für Eckart Klein* (pp. 509–526). Duncker & Humblot.
von der Groeben, H., Schwarze, J., & Hatje, A. (2015). *Europäisches Unionsrecht. Kommentar*. (7th ed.). Nomos.
von Mangoldt, H., Klein, F., & Starck, C. (2018). *Kommentar zum Grundgesetz*. Bd. II (7th ed.). Franz Vahlen.
Weber, A. (2011). Die Reform der Wirtschafts- und Währungsunion in der Finanzkrise. *Europäische Zeitschrift für Wirtschaftsrecht*, 935–939.
Weber, A. (2014). Grundzüge europa- und völkerrechtlich normierter Krisensteuerung zur Gewährleistung von Haushaltsdisziplin. In H.-J. Blanke & S. Pilz (Eds.), *Die "Fiskalunion" – Voraussetzungen einer Vertiefung der politischen Integration im Währungsraum der Europäischen Union* (pp. 3–23). Mohr Siebeck.
Wojcik, K. P. (2016). Bail-in in the Banking Union. *Common Market Law Review*, 91–138.
Woll, A. (2011). *Allgemeine Volkswirtschaftslehre* (16th ed.). Franz Vahlen.
Zavvos, G. S., & Kaltsouni, S. (2015). The single resolution mechanism in the European Banking Union. In M. Haentjens & B. Wesens (Eds.), *Research handbook on crisis management in the banking sector* (pp. 117–149). Elgar.

Treaty Establishing the European Stability Mechanism (TESM)

Contents

1. Genesis and Nature of the European Stability Mechanism 1
    1.1. Genesis 1
    1.2. Legal Basis for the Establishing of the ESM 4
    1.3. Legal Status, Privileges and Immunities 10
    1.4. Consistency and Coherence of Union Law 14
    1.5. Duration and Termination 17
2. Purpose, Governance and Voting Conditions 19
    2.1. Purpose (Article 3 TESM) 19
    2.2. Capital and Liability 20
        2.2.1. Authorised Capital Stock (Article 8 TESM) 20
        2.2.2. Capital Calls (Article 9 TESM) and Coverage of Losses
               (Article 25 TESM) 25
        2.2.3. Funding 27
    2.3. Institutional Structure (Articles 4 et seqq. TESM) 32
        2.3.1. Board of Governors (Article 5 TESM) 34
        2.3.2. Board of Directors (Article 6 TESM) 37
        2.3.3. Managing Director (Article 7 TESM) 40
        2.3.4. The Involvement of Other EU Institutions 42
        2.3.5. The Cooperation with the International Monetary Fund 53
3. Financial Assistance Operations (Articles 12 et seqq. TESM) 58
    3.1. Normative Conditions (Article 12 TESM) 59
        3.1.1. Safeguarding Financial Stability as a Triggering Event 59
        3.1.2. Indispensable Nature 61
        3.1.3. Strict Conditionality 62
    3.2. Procedure for Granting Stability Support (Article 13 TESM) 64
        3.2.1. Request for Stability Support 64
        3.2.2. Debt Sustainability Analysis 65
        3.2.3. Voting Rules 67
        3.2.4. Memorandum of Understanding 69
        3.2.5. Guidelines on the Modalities for Implementing Stability Support 78
    3.3. Numerus Clausus of the Financial Assistance Instruments
         (Articles 14–18 TESM) 79
        3.3.1. ESM-Loans (Article 16 TESM) 80
        3.3.2. Precautionary Financial Assistance (Article 14 TESM) 86
        3.3.3. Financial Assistance for the Recapitalisation of Financial Institutions
               of an ESM Member (Article 15 TESM) 94
        3.3.4. Financial Assistance for the Direct Recapitalisation of Institutions .. 101
        3.3.5. Secondary Market Support Facility (Article 18 TESM) 108
        3.3.6. Primary Market Support Facility (Article 17 TESM) 115
        3.3.7. Review of the List of Financial Assistance Instruments
               (Article 19 TESM) 118
    3.4. Private Sector Participation (Article 12.3 TESM: Collective Action Clauses) .. 121
    3.5. The ECB's Relationship with the ESM 126
4. Ensuring the Democratic Legitimacy of the ESM 128
    4.1. The European Principle of Democracy (Article 10 TEU) 129
    4.2. A Member State's Democratic Deficit? 130

© Springer Nature Switzerland AG 2021
R. Böttner, H.-J. Blanke (eds.), *Treaty on the Functioning of the European Union – A Commentary*, Springer Commentaries on International and European Law,
https://doi.org/10.1007/16559_2021_21

4.3. Technocratic Expertise as a Compensation for Direct Legitimation? 139
4.4. Conclusion 142
5. Outlook: The Development of the ESM to a European Monetary Fund 145
List of Cases
References

1. Genesis and Nature of the European Stability Mechanism

1.1. Genesis

1   To ensure the continued existence of the EMU against the ever-present threat of an economic and financial crisis, as well as to secure the long-term stability of the common currency, the European Council on 28–29 October 2010 agreed to establish a robust framework for crisis management within the euro area (EA) in the medium term. The agreement was based on the task force report on **'Strengthening Economic Governance in the EU'** and was intended to help overcome financial difficulties as well as prevent them from spreading.[1] At the Brussels Summit on 17 December 2010, the Heads of State and Government agreed to establish a permanent crisis mechanism that would replace the EFSF and the EFSM, aiming to safeguard the financial stability of the EA as a whole.[2]

2   The TESM was originally signed on 11 July 2011 by the finance ministers of the (then) 17 EA countries. A **modified version of the Treaty**, aimed at improving the effectiveness of the mechanism, was signed in Brussels on 2 February 2012. The TESM entered into force on 27 September 2012 and the ESM was inaugurated on 8 October 2012, following ratification by all (then) 17 EA Member States.[3] The current version of the Treaty, amended following the accession of Latvia and Lithuania to the ESM, entered into force on 3 February 2015.[4] The consolidation of the EFSF in the ESM is going hand in hand with a continuity of the IMF's active involvement in the ESM's actions, both at technical and financial level.[5] In 2018, intensive efforts began to reform the ESM (→ para 145–151). The direct integration of the ESM into Union law has not yet been successful, but the amendment of the ESM Treaty has further strengthened the de facto intertwining of the ESM and EU

---

[1] European Council of 28–29 October 2010, Conclusions, Doc. EUCO 25/1/10 REV 1, para 2. First key points of the crisis mechanism were subsequently defined by the Eurogroup on 28 November 2010. Cf. European Council of 16–17 December 2010, Conclusions, Doc. EUCO 30/1/10 REV 1, Annex II. Concerning the outlines of such a mechanism, see already Pilz and Dittmann (2011), pp. 438 et seqq.

[2] European Council of December 2010, Conclusions, Doc. EUCO 30/1/10 REV 1, para 1.

[3] EFSF Press Release, European Stability Mechanism (ESM) is inaugurated, 8 October 2012.

[4] ESM Press Release, Joint Statement: Andris Vilks and Klaus Regling hail Latvia's accession to ESM, 3 March 2014; ESM Press Release, Joint Statement by Finance Minister of Lithuania and ESM Managing Director, 3 February 2015.

[5] Preamble to the ESM Treaty, Recital 8.

law. The reformed Treaty was signed by the ESM members on 27 January 2021 and is pending ratification.

The ESM is a central element of the EA's coping strategy concerning sovereign debt crisis. It includes the euro rescue packages, economic reforms in the respective MS, strengthened economic policy coordination within the EA (→ Article 121 TFEU para 13 et seqq.), the tightening of the SGP (→ Supplement to Title VIII: Fiscal Union para 5) as well as the financial market policy reforms.

3

1.2. Legal Basis for the Establishing of the ESM

On 25 March 2011 the European Council adopted the **Decision 2011/199/EU amending Article 136 TFEU** (→ Article 136 TFEU para 28), based on Article 48.6 TEU, to set up the ESM.[6] In context of the simplified revision procedure, a paragraph 3 was added to Article 136 TFEU, stating that 'the Member States whose currency is the euro may establish a stability mechanism to be activated if indispensable to safeguard the stability of the euro area as a whole. The granting of any required financial assistance under the mechanism will be made subject to strict conditionality' (→ para 62 et seq.).[7]

4

By means of this amendment the European Council aimed to ensure that the **no-bail-out clause** (Article 125 TFEU) remained untouched.[8] Therefore, the purpose of Article 136.3 TFEU is to declare stability support granted in connection with an established stability mechanism as legally justified under EU law.[9] The introduction of Article 136.3 TFEU has no impact on other obligations arising from the EMU. The provision does not release the recipient States from the economic policy conditions in Article 121 TFEU and Article 126 TFEU.[10] The principle of ownership for national budgetary policy remains normatively untouched.[11] It only ceases to apply if indispensable to achieve stability in the EA, which the principle itself serves.[12]

5

In the case of **Pringle**, the CJEU raised no objection to the European Council Decision amending Article 136 TFEU and the ESM Treaty.[13] In course of a reference for a preliminary ruling from the Supreme Court of Ireland,[14] the Court

6

---

[6] European Council Decision 2011/199/EU, O.J. L 91 (2011).

[7] Cf. European Council of 16–17 December 2010, Conclusions, Doc. EUCO 30/1/10 REV 1, Annex I, p. 6. Cf. Häde (2014), para 148; Hufeld (2014), para 106 et seqq.

[8] European Stability Mechanism (2019), pp. 134 et seq.

[9] Palm, in Grabitz et al. (2021), Article 136 AEUV para 43 (released in 2014); Smulders and Keppenne, in von der Groeben et al. (2015), Article 136 AEUV para 14; Hofmann and Konow (2012), p. 155; De Gregorio Merino (2012), pp. 1625 et seqq.; Messina (2014), pp. 406 et seqq.

[10] Ohler, in Siekmann (2013), Article 136 AEUV para 25.

[11] Hofmann and Konow (2012), p. 155.

[12] Palm, in Grabitz et al. (2021), Article 136 AEUV para 48 (released in 2014).

[13] On this case Adam and Mena Parras (2013), pp. 848 et seqq.; Borger (2013), pp. 113 et seqq.; de Witte and Beukers (2013), pp. 805 et seqq.; van Malleghem (2013), pp. 141 et seqq.

[14] The Supreme Court of Ireland, Rec. No. 339/2012, *Pringle v The Government of Ireland*, 2012 IESC 47.

classified activities of the **ESM as an economic policy measure by the Member States** that does not conflict with the Union's exclusive competence in the field of monetary policy (→ para 7).[15] The Court did not find a violation of Article 122.2 TFEU and Article 125 TFEU (→ para 9), however.[16] Against this background, legal protection against **Article 136.3 TFEU** would have not been necessary in the opinion of the CJEU.[17] Therefore, the provision is only of **declaratory nature**.[18]

7   Allocating the ESM to the field of economic policy, the CJEU, given the absence of a treaty-level definition of monetary policy,[19] relies on the Treaty's objective and instruments of the monetary policy.[20] In doing so, the Court misjudges the **connection between economic and monetary policy**, in consideration of which a different classification should have been the result.[21] Preceding the economic and monetary policy provisions listed in Title VIII of the TFEU's third part ('Union policies and internal actions'), Article 119.3 TFEU designates four guiding principles that are supposed to govern the activities of the MS and the EU within the EMU. These include 'stable prices, sound public finances and monetary conditions and a sustainable balance of payments' (→ Article 119 TFEU para 42 et seqq.).[22] The aggregation of stable prices and public finances evidences that **both policy areas are closely linked**.[23] This link is also reflected at institutional level, namely in the form of the Economic and Financial Committee (Article 134 TFEU) and the Economic Policy Committee. Both committees are expert advisory panels, composed of Member State representatives, the Commission and the ECB, focusing on economic and financial matters.[24] The ESM's purpose (→ para 19) also reveals a monetary dimension, as 'to safeguard the financial stability' (Article 3 TESM) is attributable to monetary policy under Article 127.5 TFEU.

8   A similar blur of boundaries is evident in the announced implementation of the OMT, which links measures of the ECB to an ongoing ESM programme.[25] Lastly, the monetary component of the ESM is underlined by the involvement of the IMF,

---

[15] Case C-370/12, *Pringle* (CJEU 27 November 2012) para 57–63, 93–98. Cf. Hentschelmann (2011), p. 290.

[16] Case C-370/12, *Pringle* (CJEU 27 November 2012) para 105, 147.

[17] Selmayr (2013), pp. 259 et seqq.; different opinion Glaser (2012), pp. 906 et seq.

[18] Case C-370/12, *Pringle* (CJEU 27 November 2012) para 184. The German FCC is of a different opinion as it interprets the introduction of Article 136.3 TFEU as a 'fundamental transformation' of the former EMU. Accordingly, the provision would have constitutive significance. German Federal Constitutional Court, 2 BvR 1390/12 et al. (Judgment of 12 September 2012) para 128, 132—*ESM* (in BVerfGE 132, 195 [247 et seqq.]). See also Ohler, in Siekmann (2013), Article 136 AEUV para 15; Ketterer (2016), pp. 213 et seqq.

[19] Case C-370/12, *Pringle* (CJEU 27 November 2012) para 53.

[20] Case C-370/12, *Pringle* (CJEU 27 November 2012) para 56 et seq.

[21] In addition, Städter (2013), pp. 148 et seqq.

[22] Cf. Adamski (2020), para 9.21 et seqq.

[23] Simon (2015), pp. 114 et seq.

[24] Cf. also Blanke and Böttner (2020), § 13 para 101.

[25] Pilz (2016), p. 36.

which, under Article I i), iii), v) of the IMF Agreement, aims to support international cooperation in monetary policy matters.[26] In the end, the **ESM's hybrid nature, as mosaic of economic and monetary policy elements,** does not correspond to the Court's initial interpretation. In fact, *U. Hufeld*'s legal evaluation deserves approval. He identifies the ESM as a functional building that pushes itself into the asymmetric statics of EMU with national fiscal and supranational monetary policy.[27]

On Article 122.2 TFEU, the CJEU concludes that the provision does not assign specific power to the Union for the ESM's establishment. Therefore, Member States could take action and establish a permanent stability mechanism.[28] Likewise, the ESM Treaty would not conflict with the **no bail-out clause** of Article 125.2 TFEU. The rationale of the Court's analysis enquires about the purpose of the liability exclusion. Thus, the Court follows the prevailing opinion in literature,[29] which recognises the *telos* of the provision, i.e. to submit MS to market logic to give them an incentive to preserve budgetary discipline. 'The prohibition laid down in Article 125 TFEU ensures that they remain subject to the logic of the market when they enter into debt, since that ought to prompt them to maintain budgetary discipline. Compliance with such budgetary discipline contributes at Union level to the attainment of a higher objective, namely maintaining the financial stability of the monetary union'.[30] Against this background, it is not intended to prohibit either the Union or the MS from granting any form of financial assistance whatsoever to another MS in general. 'Given that that is the objective pursued by Article 125 TFEU, it must be held that that provision prohibits the Union and the MS from granting financial assistance as a result of which the incentive of the recipient MS to conduct a sound budgetary policy is diminished'.[31] By implication, this interpretation allows **all measures that have the same disciplinary effect on the MS as does the market mechanism.** Article 125 TFEU is not violated because the ESM provides financial assistance only in cases where it is indispensable to maintain financial stability within the euro area, underlying strict conditionality at the same time and not standing surety for the recipient State's debts by means of the instrument.[32]

9

---

[26] Städter (2013), pp. 151 et seq.

[27] Hufeld (2011), p. 120 (translated by the author).

[28] Case C-370/12, *Pringle* (CJEU 27 November 2012) para 105, 121.

[29] Hentschelmann (2011), pp. 290 et seqq.; Hattenberger, in Schwarze (2019), Article 125 AEUV para 5; Khan, in Geiger et al. (2010), Article 125 AEUV para 5.

[30] Case C-370/12, *Pringle* (CJEU 27 November 2012) para 135.

[31] Case C-370/12, *Pringle* (CJEU 27 November 2012) para 130, 136 et seq.

[32] Case C-370/12, *Pringle* (CJEU 27 November 2012) para 138, 142, 147. Cf. also Lengauer (2013), pp. 7 et seq.; Lenaerts (2014), p. 757; Ioannidis (2016), pp. 1263 et seqq.; Forsthoff and Lauer (2020), para 30.20 et seqq. Similar also AG *Kokott,* who states that it 'would be incompatible with the concept of solidarity', if Article 125 TFEU would prohibit MS from awarding financial aid; cf. Case C-370/12, *Pringle* (Opinion of AG Kokott of 26 October 2012) para 142 et seq.

1.3. Legal Status, Privileges and Immunities

10 The establishment and organisation of the ESM as an 'international financial institution' (Article 1.1 TESM) takes place outside the legal and institutional framework of the Union by means of an international treaty, constituting the ESM in the form of an **'intergovernmental organisation under international law'**.[33] The Treaty establishes the ESM as an institution with full legal personality (Article 32.2 TESM), that has its seat and principle office in Luxembourg (Article 31.1 TESM). In contrast to the initial temporary rescue fund—the EFSF—a special purpose vehicle under private (Luxembourgian) law, the ESM is a **legal entity of international law**. The institutional structure and powers granted (→ para 32 et seqq.), particularly on the mechanism's financial arrangement (→ para 20 et seqq.) and the granting of stability support (→ para 64 et seqq.), is spelled out in eight chapters of the TESM.

11 In fulfilling its duties, the ESM and its staff have extensive privileges set out in the 'General Provisions' in Chapter 6 TESM. It is not possible to take legal proceedings against the ESM before any national court, as the ESM, its property, funding and assets, wherever located and by whomsoever held, enjoy **immunity** from every form of judicial process (Article 32.3 TESM). Furthermore, the property, funding and assets of the ESM also enjoy immunity from search, requisition, confiscation, expropriation or any other form of seizure, taking or foreclosure by executive, judicial, administrative or legislative action (Article 32.4 TESM). The archives of the ESM and all documents belonging to the ESM or held by it, shall be inviolable (Article 32.5 TESM). In addition, the ESM is not subject to 'restrictions, regulations, controls and moratoria of any nature [... as well as] any requirements to be authorised or licensed as a credit institution, investment services provider or other authorised licensed or regulated entity under the laws of each ESM Member' (Articles 32.8, 32.9 TESM).

12 The members (or former members) of the Board of Governors and of the Board of Directors, including all **203 employees** of the ESM (as of December 2020),[34] are **subject to professional secrecy**, which also applies after the end of their employment (Article 34 TESM). All staff members enjoy immunity from legal proceedings with respect to acts performed by them in their official capacity as well as inviolability in respect to their official papers and documents (Article 35.1 TESM). Under Article 35.2 TESM, the Board of Governors may waive any of the immunities conferred to individual officials, however this may only happen 'to such extent and upon such conditions as it determines'. Within the scope of its official activities, the ESM, its assets, income, property and its operations and transactions authorised by the Treaty shall be exempt from all direct taxes (Article 36.1 TESM). This also

---

[33] Treaty Establishing the European Stability Mechanism, 2 February 2012. Cf. Ruffert (2011), p. 1783; Thym (2011), pp. 167 et seq.; Müller-Graff (2011), p. 299.

[34] In 2020, the ESM reached a total of 203 staff, secondees, trainees and interims at year-end. ESM staff will continue to perform tasks for the EFSF. Cf. ESM Annual Report 2020, p. 109.

applies to the salaries of ESM staff. Under Article 36.5 sentence 1 TESM, the salaries and other benefits paid by the ESM shall be subject to an internal tax for the benefit of the ESM. From the date on which this tax is applied, such salaries and emoluments shall be exempt from national income tax.

However, on the immunity clauses in Articles 32.5, 34 and 35.1 TESM, concerns arose in Germany regarding the **assurance of information and data** being provided to the German *Bundestag*, which would be relevant for parliamentary control.[35] Information obligations vis-à-vis the national parliaments are not provided by the Treaty. It merely states that the Board of Governors is obliged to make the annual audit report of financial accounting that is prepared by an audit committee, accessible to national parliaments and supreme audit institutions of the ESM members and to the European Court of Auditors (Article 30.5 TESM). Against this background, the inviolability of archives and the absolute and continued professional secrecy, that acting individuals, bodies and employees of the ESM are subject to, both depict the border of a largely impermeable area, free of control, which is subject neither to democratic-parliamentary nor to constitutional-judicial control.[36] In the view of the German FCC, the obligation to give the German *Bundestag* comprehensive information must not be ruled out though (→ para 131 et seqq.).[37] If domestic provisions concerning the ESM require not only handling at government level, where relevant information is always accessible, but also discussion and approval in parliamentary bodies, it is inevitable that these entities are being informed, too. The fact that the mention of national parliaments in Article 30.5 TESM does not justify the conclusion that in other cases their notification is excluded, may as well be substantiated by the purpose and objective set out in Articles 32.5, 34 and 35.1 TESM. There are plenty of indications for the fact that these regulations primarily aim to prevent information flows to unauthorised third parties, such as those involved in the capital market. However, they may not prevent the information flow to the bearers of the ESM itself.[38] The MS' parliaments as bearers of budget autonomy, having to justify bonds based on the ESM Treaty in the further execution of the Treaty towards their citizens,[39] are not among the third parties to be excluded from the information flow. Corresponding with this

13

---

[35] German Federal Constitutional Court, 2 BvE 4/11 (Judgment of 19 June 2012)—*Obligatory notifications* (in BVerfGE 131, 152). Cf. Austrian Constitutional Court SV2/12–18 (16 March 2013), para 91 et seqq. Detailed discussion and procession by the German FCC, cf. Grimm (2016), pp. 98 et seqq., 204 et seqq.; Ketterer (2016), pp. 106 et seqq.

[36] Critically Ketterer (2016), pp. 325 et seqq.

[37] German Federal Constitutional Court, 2 BvE 4/11 (Judgment of 19 June 2012), para 99 et seqq.—*Obligatory notifications* (in BVerfGE 131, 152 [199 et seqq.]). In depth to the jurisdiction by the FCC in the participation and information of the German *Bundestag*, cf. Pilz (2016), pp. 103 et seqq.

[38] German Federal Constitutional Court, 2 BvR 1390/12 et al. (Judgment of 12 September 2012), para 151 et seqq.—*European Stability Mechanism* (in BVerfGE 132, 195 [258 et seq.]).

[39] German Federal Constitutional Court, 2 BvE 6/99 (Judgment of 22 November 2001), para 152—*NATO-Concept* (in BVerfGE 104, 151 [209]); German Federal Constitutional Court, 2 BvE 2/08 et al. (Judgment of 30 June 2009), para 256—*Lisbon* (in BVerfGE 123, 267 [361 et seq.]).

interpretation is the stronger role of national parliaments in the EU's institutional structure by means of Article 12 TEU. Against this background, this is even more important, as the chosen form of international treaty as supplement of the Union's integration programme enables no control by the European Parliament (→ para 129). It is therefore a necessity of the national democratic principle that national parliaments make the decisive contribution of legitimacy. The joint declaration of the euro area States (→ para 26) ensures that the professional secrecy for members of the ESM bodies, as set out in Articles 32.5, 34 and 35.1 TESM, as well as the immunity rules, do not oppose the comprehensive information of national parliaments in accordance with national regulations.[40]

1.4. Consistency and Coherence of Union Law

14 The intergovernmental treaty is concluded under Article 6 VCLT and is thus **standing outside the scope of Union law** (→ Supplement to Title VIII: Introduction para 3 et seq.).[41] Nevertheless, ESM measures are interdependent with EU law so that, in the field of ESM application, the unity and coherence of EU law must be ensured. While, for example, Contracting States explicitly affirm that the Agreements are 'applied and interpreted [...] in conformity with the Treaties on which the European Union is founded and with European Union law' in Article 2.1 TSCG (→ Supplement to Title VIII: Fiscal Union para 15) or Article 2.1 TMCA[42] (→ Supplement to Title VIII: Banking Union para 176 et seqq.), the TESM does not contain a comparable coherence clause. It is only in the fourth Recital of the Preamble that ESM members commit themselves to 'strict observance of the European Union framework', particularly the rules concerning the SGP.

15 Meanwhile, Contracting States are bound to the principles of unity and coherence of Union law even without any explicit clause. Both principles are manifested not only in the contractual foundations of the EU (Article 7 TFEU, Articles 256.2, 256.3 TFEU), but also in settled case law by the CJEU, in which judges emphasize the fundamental importance of common Union law and stress the need to safeguard its uniform validity and primary application in all MS.[43] Hence, the ECJ

---

[40] German Federal Law Gazette 2012 part II, pp. 1086 et seq. This observation was also made by the Austrian Constitutional Court SV2/12–18 (16 March 2013), para 91–96.

[41] In literature, the outsourcing of EU law to international law has been described with many different terminologies. Lorz and Sauer (2012), p. 575 describe the phenomenon as 'substitutional Union law under international law' ('*völkerrechtliches Ersatzunionsrecht*') (translated by the author). Weber (2014), p. 11, cites the TESM as a prime example of an 'internal Union instrument under international law' ('*binnenunionsvölkerrechtliches Instrumentarium*'). Likewise, he speaks of 'Union law under international law' ('*Unionsvölkervertragsrecht*', p. 6, 11, translation by the author). By contrast, von Arnauld (2013), pp. 509 et seqq. speaks of a 'union (supplementary) international law' ('*Unions(ergänzungs)völkerrecht*', translation by the author).

[42] Council of the European Union, Agreement on the transfer and mutualization of contributions to the single resolution fund, 8457/14 (ECOFIN 342).

[43] Case 235/87, *Matteucci* (ECJ 27 September 1988), pp. 5611 et seq.

urges Member States to comply with the **'unity principle'**[44] in its decision *Costa/E.N.E.L.*, as the European legislation otherwise would be 'deprived of its character as Community law and the legal basis of the Community itself [would be] called into question' by unilateral and subsequent derogations.[45] The unity of law is **an identity-forming characteristic** of the European Community of law.[46] It ensures the consistency and inner coherence of Union law[47] and forms the basis for proper functioning of its institutions. Preserving it requires MS to respect the primacy of EU law when international treaties affect EU affairs.[48]

Closely related to the unity principle of law is the requirement of **coherence** (Article 7 TFEU), that encompasses the whole Union law and is based on a consistent realisation of objectives and the resolution of conflicting goals.[49] It primarily binds the Union institutions.[50] In the field of coordinated policies, it also obliges MS to refrain from uncoordinated or contradictory measures and to ensure the coherence of Union policy.[51] MS cannot escape this obligation, even if they conclude international agreements outside the Union law. The Treaty's spirit and objectives can only be realised if the common rules cannot be undermined again by unilateral measures.[52] In its argument, the ECJ relies on Article 4.3 TEU and derives the so-called efficiency requirement (*'effet utile'*) from the duty of loyalty by the Member States. The essential meaning of the efficiency principle is that the standards of Union law must be interpreted and applied in such manner that they may fulfil their practical purpose and have an effective impact.[53] The efficiency and effective implementation of Union law as well as the achievement of the objectives set out in Article 3 TEU would be called into question if it were possible for individual MS to create sources of law, prior in relation to EU law. If, therefore, a MS's measure takes on the tasks and objectives of the EU Treaties (the so-called **contractual accessoriness**), the loyalty requirement must be obeyed

16

---

[44] Thym (2006), p. 637 (translated by the author).

[45] Case 6/64, *Flaminio Costa v E.N.E.L.* (ECJ 3 June 1964), p. 1270.

[46] Thym (2006), p. 637.

[47] Schmidt-Aßmann (2015), p. 91.

[48] Opinion 1/91, *European Economic Area I* (ECJ 14 December 1991).

[49] Lippert (2012), p. 90; Schorkopf, in Grabitz et al. (2021), Article 7 AEUV para 11 (released in 2019); Ruffert, in Calliess and Ruffert (2021), Article 7 AEUV para 3.

[50] Ruffert, in Calliess and Ruffert (2021), Article 7 AEUV para 3.

[51] Case C-370/12, *Pringle* (CJEU 27 November 2012) para 158; Case 208/80, *Lord Bruce of Donington v Aspden* (ECJ 15 September 1981) para 14; Case 230/81, *Luxembourg v Parliament* (ECJ 10 February 1983) para 37; Case 44/84, *Hurd v Jones* (ECJ 15 January 1986) para 39; Joined Cases C-181/91 and C-248/91, *Parliament v Council and Commission* (ECJ 30 June 1993) para 16, 20, 22; Case C-316/91, *Parliament v Council* (ECJ 2 March 1994) para 26, 34, 41; Opinion 1/91, *European Economic Area I* (ECJ 10 April 1992), para 32, 41; Case C-1/00, *European Common Aviation Area* (ECJ 18 April 2002), para 20; Case C-1/09, *European and Community Patents Court* (ECJ 8 March 2011) para 75. Cf. Obwexer, in von der Groeben et al. (2015), Article 7 AEUV para 11.

[52] Case 6/64, *Flaminio Costa v E.N.E.L.* (ECJ 3 June 1964), p. 1269.

[53] Härtel (2012), § 82 para 217.

(→ Article 4 TEU para 82).⁵⁴ Both TSCG and TESM are directly linked to EMU rules. Therefore, the Contracting States are also obliged within the scope of the TESM, to facilitate the application of Union law by means of an interpretation consistent with EU law.⁵⁵ Otherwise, the momentum arising from within the Treaties that established the Fiscal Union, holds the threat of gradually decoupling the Contracting States from the European Community of law.⁵⁶

1.5. Duration and Termination

17   The TESM does not contain any explicit rule on the treaty's duration. Rather, the members of the EA have established the ESM as a **'permanent crisis mechanism'**, in contrast to the temporary rescue fund.⁵⁷ This classification corresponds with Article 44 in conjunction with Article 2 TESM, according to which the ESM is open to the **accession of new members**. Under Article 44 in conjunction with Article 5.6 point (k) TESM, the Board of Governors, adopting a decision by mutual agreement, approves a MS's request to join the ESM Treaty once the MS has joined the EA. The link between ESM membership and participation in the monetary union is reinforced by the seventh Recital of the TESM Preamble, which states that all euro countries will become members of the ESM.

18   However, there is no explicit possibility for the **termination** of and hence the **withdrawal of a MS** from the ESM. In contrast to EU law (Article 50 TEU), there is no corresponding provision in the TESM. Other long-term international organisations also typically include rules on the exit of a Contracting Party.⁵⁸ Nonetheless, even without an explicit provision, the Contracting States of the ESM **did not enter into an irreversible commitment**. After all, even for international treaties which do not contain a withdrawal clause, it is considered international customary law that parties can unilaterally terminate the treaty under certain conditions. For example, in the event of a fundamental change in the circumstances relevant to the conclusion of contract, the Contracting States may rely on Article 62 VCLT (*clausula rebus sic stantibus*) and unilaterally disassociate themselves from the TESM.⁵⁹ Article 62 VCLT could be applied, for example, if the TESM was applied differing from the common interpretative declaration of the euro countries in respect to the

---

⁵⁴ Kahl, in Calliess and Ruffert (2021), Article 4 AEUV para 47.

⁵⁵ In reference to Case 235/87, *Matteucci* (ECJ 27 September 1988), p. 5611; see also German Federal Constitutional Court, 2 BvR 1390/12 et al. (Judgment of 12 September 2012), para 172—*European Stability Mechanism* (in BVerfGE 132, 195 [267]).

⁵⁶ In view of this threat, von Ondarza (2014), p. 166 claims the application of subcontracts under international law only as a *measure of last resort*.

⁵⁷ European Council of 28–29 October 2010, Conclusions, Doc. EUCO 25/1/10 REV 1, para 2.

⁵⁸ Cf. Article XXVI Section 1 of the IMF Agreement, Article 58.1 ECHR, Article 317.1 UNCLOS.

⁵⁹ Pilz (2012), p. 911; Weber (2014), p. 15.

information rights of national parliaments and the absolute liability (→ para 26).[60] On the Fiscal Compact, the German FCC refers to Germany's EU membership as well as the affiliation to a common currency as a prerequisite for the bond to the TSCG's reciprocal obligations.[61] This finding also applies to the membership in the ESM.[62] An exit from the EU under Article 50 TEU or a withdrawal from the eurozone would eliminate the basis for the TESM. According to the case law of the German FCC, a failure of the stability community, which is established by the Treaties, justifies a withdrawal from the community itself. Therefore, if the institutions no longer followed the enforcement of the EMU's fundamental principles and thus left the contractual conception, the Federal Republic of Germany could, as a consequence, not only back out of the EMU, but also withdraw from the ESM.[63]

2. Purpose, Governance and Voting Conditions

2.1. Purpose (Article 3 TESM)

Under Article 3 sentence 1 TESM, the purpose of the ESM is to mobilise funding and to provide stability support to ESM members which are facing severe financing problems or which are threatened by such problems, if this is indispensable to safeguard the financial stability of the EA as a whole or of its MS. The granting of such support is subject to **strict conditionality appropriate to the selected financial assistance instrument** (→ para 62 et seq.). With the establishment of the ESM, the signatories respond to the risks, both for the financial stability of the EA countries individually and for the eurozone as a whole, posed by the interdependencies within the EA.[64] In addition to the definition of a specific purpose, the provision already contains specific conditions that must be met for the granting of stability support. These conditions must be *indispensable* to safeguard the financial stability of the EA and its MS (→ para 61). The provision thus repeats the basic conditions, which are also mentioned in the enabling rule for the establishment of the ESM in Article 136.3 TFEU (→ para 4), and thus expresses their far-reaching significance under European law.

19

---

[60] Ketterer (2016), pp. 336 et seq.

[61] German Federal Constitutional Court, 2 BvR 1390/12 et al. (Judgment of 12 September 2012) para 215—*European Stability Mechanism* (in BVerfGE 132, 195 [286 et seq.]).

[62] Ohler, in Siekmann (2013), Article 136 AEUV para 16.

[63] German Federal Constitutional Court, 2 BvR 2134, 2159/92 (Judgment of 12 October 1993) para 147—*Maastricht* (in BVerfGE 89, 155 [204 et seqq.]).

[64] Preamble to the ESM Treaty, sixth Recital.

2.2. Capital and Liability

2.2.1. Authorised Capital Stock (Article 8 TESM)

20 Under Articles 8.1 and 8.2 TESM, the ESM has an authorised capital stock of EUR 704.8 billion,[65] of which MS provide only EUR 624.3 billion financed by a combination of **committed callable capital and guarantees**. The total for **capital actually paid** by the euro States amounts to EUR 80.5 billion.[66] Each MS is obliged under Article 8.4 TESM to make an irrevocable and full contribution to the authorised capital stock. The payment of contributions assured by each MS is paid in five annual instalments of 20% of the total amount. Under Article 41.1 TESM, the first instalment was due within 15 days after the ESM Treaty came into force. The first two instalments were paid in 2012 and two more followed in 2013. Including the payment of the last instalment on 30 April 2014, the ESM commands approximately EUR 80 billion of capital, thus reaching a **minimum lending capacity of EUR 500 billion**. By their payment, MS have acquired a share in the ESM. States such as Latvia (2014) and Lithuania (2015), which have joined the EA and thus the ESM after the founding of the ESM, are also meant to transfer their share of the paid-in capital in five annual tranches.

21 The member's financial contribution to the ESM is measured by its economic performance. The amount of the contribution is based on the **capital key of the ECB** (Article 11 in conjunction with Annex I TESM). It is measured proportional to the relation of a MS's size in comparison to the entire EU, which in turn is determined halfway by the population and halfway by the GDP in each case. A country's economic fundamental data becomes the reference point for the assessment of the respective contribution. The social dimension of the respective economy's individual performance sets the benchmark for determining the capital contribution.[67] The temporary final adjustment of the contribution key took place with the accession of Lithuania in 2015 (Annex I TESM). The largest number of shares are held by Germany (1.9 billion, representing EUR 1.9 billion of subscribed capital), France (1.42 billion) and Italy (1.25 billion) (Annex II TESM).

22 In addition to the authorised capital stock, the Board of Governors established a **reserve fund**, which includes both net income from ESM operations and the proceeds of the financial sanctions received from ESM members for excessive deficits or macroeconomic imbalances under the TFEU procedures (Articles 24.1, 24.2 TESM). On 11 June 2020, the Board of Governors decided at their annual general meeting to appropriate the net result of 2019 amounting to EUR 289.7 million to the reserve fund. Consequently, the outstanding balance of the reserve fund

---

[65] Including the pending EFSF stability aid amounting to EUR 200 billion. Cf. Statement by the Eurogroup (30 March 2012).

[66] Cf. ESM Annual Report 2019, p. 110.

[67] Pilz (2016), p. 105.

as of 31 December 2020 is EUR 2.6 billion (31 December 2019: EUR 2.3 billion).[68] Losses of the ESM are first paid out of this reserve fund (Article 25.1 point (c) TESM). The paid-in capital and, lastly, the committed, callable capital is only used subsidiarily to settle possible losses arising in ESM operations. The resulting liability cascade attracts problem-causing States more than solid States to funding the ESM. However, the existence of this reserve fund does not strengthen the incentives for States to respect the deficit limits and economic surveillance rules, as the use of the penalties for political willingness to behave in an irregular manner is irrelevant.

Because of the MS' obligation to pay in a cash deposit and to provide callable capital, the euro rescue fund for the **first time** has its **own capital base**. Opposed to previous practice (EFSF), the ESM's liquidity is decoupled from the guarantees of its MS. This means that the creditworthiness of the ESM is no longer determined directly by the creditworthiness of the guarantors. Hence, the capital markets' confidence in the liquidity of the mechanism and the MS' willingness to use capital effectively is strengthened and the highest solvency rating is ensured by the rating agencies.[69] The paid-in capital of the authorised capital stock is not available for stability support to ESM members but rather ensure the high creditworthiness of the ESM as an issuer.[70] Raising capital in the capital markets of banks, financial institutions or other persons and institutions requires a top credit rating (Article 21.1 TESM, → para 27 et seq.). To facilitate refinancing at low interest rates, the ESM has over EUR 200 billion more capital than it is allowed to lend ('**overcollateralisation**'). On the other hand, the Board of Directors may call for committed but unpaid capital at any time to restore the amount of paid-in capital, if the latter is reduced by the absorption of losses (Articles 9.1, 9.2, 9.3 TESM; → para 25 et seqq.).

23

Due to the ESM's capital structure, the **TESM makes arrangements for a possible dividend distribution**. Under Article 23.1 sentence 1 TESM, the distribution is to be made when the paid-in capital and the reserve fund exceed the amount required to maintain the minimum lending capacity of EUR 500 billion and the funds are not available to prevent possible default on creditors. The Dividend Policy Guideline provides the details of a possible distribution of dividends to ESM members and assigns authority to the ESM Board of Directors following the Executive Director's proposal. However, up to the payment of the share capital's last tranche, a distribution is excluded.[71] To enable a transparent profit and loss account, the ESM is obligated, under Article 27.2 TESM, to publish an annual report with externally audited financial statements (Article 29 TESM) and to

24

---

[68] ESM Annual Report 2020, p. 108.
[69] Also Bark and Gilles (2013), p. 367.
[70] The investment guidelines set out the framework for that prudent investment policy aimed at ensuring the high creditworthiness for the ESM, the liquidity of investments, and the constant availability of the ESM's lending capacity, while also maximising the ability to absorb potential losses.
[71] ESM Guideline on Dividend Policy, pp. 1 et seq. Cf. Bark and Gilles (2013), p. 371.

provide information on the quarterly results. In addition, an inspection by the Board of Auditors (Article 30.3 TESM) is prescribed.[72] Amongst the deciding five-member body, a member of the European Court of Auditors is represented (Article 30.1 TESM). The committee independently examines the ESM's accounts and the regularity of the profit and loss statement as well as the balance sheet (Article 30.3 TESM).

2.2.2. Capital Calls (Article 9 TESM) and Coverage of Losses (Article 25 TESM)

25 Article 8.5 sentence 1 TESM limits the liability of each ESM member 'in all circumstances' to its portion of the authorised capital stock. The obligation of the ESM members to pay capital contributions to the authorised capital stock remains unaffected if an ESM member receives financial support from the ESM or fulfils the conditions for this (Article 8.5 sentence 3 TESM). However, the principle of liability limitation is contrary to the provisions on **capital calls** and **loss compensation** (Article 9.2, 3 in conjunction with Article 25.2 TESM), which impose an obligation to make additional payments on the MS and thus counteract the liability cap. Under Article 9.2 TESM, the Board of Directors may call in authorised but unpaid capital from ESM members to restore the level of paid-in capital (Article 8.2 TESM), if the latter has sunk below the specified amount by means of covering losses. In this respect no member possesses a veto right. The amount of the capital call-up depends on the amount of settled losses with paid-in capital. Under Article 9.3 sentence 1 TESM, the Managing Director issues authorised but unpaid capital in the event of risk of defaulting on ESM creditors. However, no specific upper limit is provided for this case so that the liability cap (Article 8.5 sentence 1 TESM) could in principle be broken. The same result would come from a revised increased capital call under Article 25.2 sentence 1 TESM. Thereafter, an increased capital call will be issued to all MS if one ESM member is late in payment, to ensure that the ESM receives the full amount of the capital injection. In this case, a capital call would be equivalent to a 'communitarisation' of public debt, as the remaining, solvent ESM members must raise funds that would otherwise be made available by other MS.

26 The **German FCC considered both scenarios in its case law to be compatible with the act of assent to the TESM.**[73] Within the scope of Articles 9.2, 9.3 TESM, the Board of Directors may, according to the wording of the provision, at all times only call up shares of *authorised* capital. In this respect, a breach of the liability cap is not possible.[74] Further, on the revised capital call under Articles 9.2, 9.3 in

---

[72] Cf. Bark and Gilles (2013), p. 371.

[73] German Federal Constitutional Court, 2 BvR 1390/12 et al. (Judgment of 12 September 2012)—*European Stability Mechanism* (in BVerfGE 132, 195). Cf. Pilz (2012), p. 909; Schorkopf (2012), p. 1273; Tomuschat (2012), p. 1431; Ukrow (2012), p. 417; Weiß (2014), pp. 113 et seqq.

[74] German Federal Constitutional Court, 2 BvR 1390/12 et al. (Judgment of 12 September 2012), para 145—*European Stability Mechanism* (in BVerfGE 132, 195 [254 et seq.]).

conjunction with Article 25.2 TESM, the German FCC concludes that, in view of the default of individual Member States, it is possible to charge the other ESM States beyond the upper limit. In this case, the inclusion of a ceiling of liability in Article 8.5 sentence 1 TESM would serve no purpose.[75] Nevertheless, the Second Senate admits that, considering the systematic and teleological arguments, an interpretation is also possible which precludes a clear and conclusive amount of budgetary burdens.[76] Against this background, the German FCC considers it necessary to ensure that dynamic treaty provisions, allowing for various interpretations, are safeguarded by appropriate precautions. 'The Federal Republic of Germany must clearly express that it cannot be bound by the Treaty establishing the European Stability Mechanism in its entirety if the reservation made by it should prove to be ineffective'.[77] Conformity with the relevant legislation and the interpretation of the relevant provisions regarding the budget and the responsibility for integration of the German *Bundestag* must be ensured by the act of assent and accompanying legislation or in the form of the declarations under international law for the relevant treaties. For this purpose and as result of the judgment and instigation of the German Federal Government, interpretative statements have been added to the ESM Treaty to consider the requirements of the Second Senate.[78]

The joint declaration by the ESM members became binding under international law, after being adopted by the Contracting States' Ambassadors and deposited with the Council Secretariat. The unanimous declaration adopted by the Contracting States is an 'agreement' within the meaning of Article 31.2 point (a) VCLT, which is relevant for the interpretation of the Treaty.[79] In this way, the German FCC has succeeded at this point in making a final binding decision on the interpretation and application of the Treaty. The German Court has thus replaced the CJEU in this

---

[75] German Federal Constitutional Court, 2 BvR 1390/12 et al. (Judgment of 12 September 2012), para 146—*European Stability Mechanism* (in BVerfGE 132, 195 [255]). Cf. Häde (2014), para 148; Hufeld (2014), para 26.

[76] German Federal Constitutional Court, 2 BvR 1390/12 et al. (Judgment of 12 September 2012), para 148—*European Stability Mechanism* (in BVerfGE 132, 195 [256]). The Austrian Constitutional Court SV2/12-18 (16 March 2013), para 83 also followed this interpretation.

[77] German Federal Constitutional Court, 2 BvR 1390/12 et al. (Judgment of 12 September 2012), para 149—*European Stability Mechanism* (in BVerfGE 132, 195 [257]). See also Austrian Constitutional Court SV2/12-18 (16 March 2013), para 82 et seq., 95, 104.

[78] 'Article 8(5) [...] limits all payment liabilities of the ESM Members under the Treaty in the sense that no provision of the Treaty may be interpreted as leading to payment obligations higher than the portion of the authorised capital stock corresponding to each ESM Member, as specified in Annex II of the Treaty, without prior agreement of each member's representative and due regard to national procedures. Article 32(5), Article 34 and Article 35(1) of the Treaty do not prevent providing comprehensive information to the national parliaments, as foreseen by national regulation. The above-mentioned elements constitute an essential basis for the consent of the Contracting States to be bound by the provisions of the Treaty'. Cf. German Federal Law Gazette 2012 part II, pp. 1086 et seq.

[79] Similar also Schorkopf (2012), p. 1275, who is basing his argument on Article 31.2 point (b) VCLT, however.

question with its interpretation of the Treaty, which, under Article 37.3 TESM, makes the final binding decision on the interpretation and application of the Treaty.

2.2.3. Funding

27 To refinance the loans granted by the ESM to the States participating in the programme the ESM itself raises funds by issuing bonds on the capital markets, without encumbering or pledging share capital (Article 21.1 TESM). However, neither Article 136.3 TFEU nor the TESM contains concrete requirements and limits which the acting parties must consider regarding their investment policy.[80] Legal precautions used in the ESM's investment policy are rather vague and indeterminate in their content. Thus, the ESM seeks a 'prudent investment policy' (Article 22.1 TESM) that ensures access to a broad spectrum of funding sources. Only the **Guidelines on Borrowing Operations** specify and describe the main elements and scope of the ESM's lending activities. The paid-in capital is invested in high-quality and liquid assets in accordance with the ESM Investment Guidelines. In doing so, the ESM can access a variety of capital market as well as money market instruments and furthermore create variable terms.[81] Thereby, the ESM pursues a 'diversified financing strategy', according to which investments are spread and not invested in bonds to a particular country.[82] Emissions have a term of up to 29 years.[83]

28 In this context, it was discussed under the heading **'carry trade'**, whether the ESM may issue low-yielding Yen-bonds to make a higher-yielding investment in another currency.[84] Such carry trades are suitable for an **expansive refinancing policy**, since using large sums of money can create a leverage effect that, consequently, generates huge profits solely from its interest margin. However, this form of investment, which is mainly used by institutional investors, is **highly speculative**, given the uncertainty concerning the exchange rate. To prevent the exchange rate risk from becoming too determinative, the holding period of such a trade is relatively short and requires a high investment volume. The ESM Treaty and the Guidelines on Borrowing Operations do not exclude risky carry trades per se, as long as they are part of a diversified financing strategy. Thereby, the extent to which carry trades are proportionate to the rest of the ESM's investment strategy is likely to be the decisive factor. It makes sense that only highly speculative foreign exchange speculations are incompatible with a prudent investment policy (Article 22.1 TESM) and are therefore not covered by the ESM mandate.

---

[80] Ohler, in Siekmann (2013), Article 136 AEUV para 24.
[81] ESM Guideline on Borrowing Operations, pp. 2 et seq.
[82] ESM Annual Report 2012, p. 13. Cf. European Stability Mechanism (2019), p. 159; Forsthoff and Aerts (2020), para 33.133.
[83] ESM Annual Report 2019, p. 98; Zoppè and Dias (2019), pp. 5 et seq.
[84] Kerber (2017), p. 250; Flassbeck (2007), pp. 1 et seq.

The ESM's legal framework on the question of whether the ESM can manage 29
government deficits not only via the capital market, but also via the ECB or the
national central banks, remains largely undetermined. The wording of Article 21.1 TESM—much like Article 18.1 ESCB Statute—does not exclude financing
the euro rescue fund via the ECB.[85] The latter permits the ECB to grant credit to the
ESM as 'other market participants' against adequate collaterals. However, the
ESM's refinancing via the European Central Bank is precluded by Article 123 TFEU and Article 21.1 ESCB, both prohibiting monetary State financing.
If the ESM passes on ECB bonds to distressed states, this would, for all intends,
represent an unlawful monetary public financing by the ECB.[86] In this sense, the
German FCC affirms the principle of refinancing public deficits via the capital
market by confirming the incompatibility of the ESM's financing via the ECB with
Article 123 TFEU (→ Article 123 TFEU para 10, 46).[87]

The costs incurred in financing the ESM are not borne by the ESM States but are 30
passed on to the members using the stability support. Accordingly, when granting
stability support, the ESM considers an appropriate margin which, while below the
level of interest rates on the capital market, nevertheless ensures full coverage of
the financing and operating costs of the ESM (Article 20.1 TESM). In the ESM
Pricing Policy Guideline, this is substantiated by the fact that refinancing costs are
passed on to States using the stability support.[88] In addition to a general processing
fee and a margin that depends on the relevant financing instrument, the beneficiary
States therefore also bear the risk of potential interest mark-ups for the instrument's
refinancing.[89] Those restrictive interest rates largely correspond to the principles of
the IMF and are intended to counteract the attractiveness of financial assistance and
thus potential moral hazard problems. This means that the minimum interest rate
must be higher than the historical average rate, charged on the markets under
'normal conditions'. This minimum interest rate is also required to provide adequate compensation for the risk taken by members of the ESM.[90]

Limiting the liability risk for each MS to their share of the ESM's capital (pro 31
rata) excludes the communitisation of public debts. Thus, the issue of ESM bonds is
not comparable to the introduction of Eurobonds that was considered during the
euro crisis[91] (and later in the wake of the COVID-19 pandemic[92]). The latter would

---

[85] Häde (2014), para 36.

[86] Kube (2012), pp. 13 seqq.

[87] German Federal Constitutional Court, 2 BvR 1390/12 et al. (Judgment of 12 September 2012), para 172 seqq.—*European Stability Mechanism* (in BVerfGE 132, 195 [266]).

[88] For details Forsthoff and Aerts (2020), para 33.137 et seqq.

[89] ESM Guideline on Pricing Policy, pp. 2 et seqq.

[90] ECB, The European Stability Mechanism, Monthly Bulletin 7/2011, p. 76.

[91] European Commission, *Green Paper on the feasibility of introducing Stability Bonds*, COM (2011) 818 final; Delpla and von Weizsäcker (2010); Delpla and von Weizsäcker (2011); De Gregorio Merino (2012), pp. 1630 et seqq.

[92] Giavazzi and Tabellini (2020); Pröbstl (2020), pp. 309 et seqq.

have involved the joint borrowing of all euro States by issuing bonds on the capital market, which would lead to a common liability for the debts of all euro states.

2.3. Institutional Structure (Articles 4 et seqq. TESM)

32   Article 4.1 TESM designates the Board of Governors, the Board of Directors and a Managing Director as bodies of the ESM; details are provided in Articles 5–7 TESM (→ para 34–41). The intergovernmental nature of the ESM ensures that the **States** financing the institution **retain the full rights of influence and control**. All management and decision-making bodies are staffed by representatives of the national governments. Nevertheless, like its predecessor, the EFSF, the ESM is a hybrid construct that integrates supranational elements at an operational level (→ para 42–52). This also includes the ECB (Article 13 TESM) and the CJEU (Article 37.3 TESM) next to the European Commission.

33   The ESM's institutional structure **resembles that of the IMF**. In Article XII Section 1 of the IMF Agreement, a Board of Governors, an Executive Board and a Managing Director are designated as main bodies.[93] It thus becomes clear that, in addition to financial and technical support, the IMF also acts as a trusted partner for the ESM at institutional level, since the institutions of both organisations have considerable parallels in aspects concerning structure and competences (→ para 53–57).

2.3.1. Board of Governors (Article 5 TESM)

34   Under Article 5 TESM, the Board of Governors consists of one Governor and one deputy from the government of each Member State. Under Article 5.1 sentence 3 TESM, the **Minister of Finance** should be appointed as the representative of the national governments. The Board then appoints a chairman. Concerning the election, Article 5.2 TESM sets out two options: The members of the Board of Governors may decide whether to elect the Chairman from their midst or to be chaired by the **President of the Eurogroup**. In practice, the Board of Governors chose the second option and elected the Irish Minister of Finance and Chairman of the Eurogroup, *Paschal Donohoe*, as Chairman of the Board of Governors on 9 July 2020.[94] In this capacity *Donohoe* succeeds *Mário Centeno*, who had served as Chairman since 21 December 2017. *Centeno* has taken over from *Jeroen Dijsselbloem*, who succeeds *Jean-Claude Juncker*, the former president of the Eurogroup, who was elected first chairman of the Board of Governors on 8 October 2012. The Commissioner for Economic and Monetary Affairs and the President of the ECB

---

[93] The IMF Agreement contains only one derogation on the possibility of establishing a Council at ministerial level. However, IMF members have not yet made use of this possibility, cf. Krajewski (2006), § 4 para 748.

[94] ESM Press Release, ESM Board of Governors appoints Paschal Donohoe as its Chairman, 20 July 2020.

may participate as observers in the meetings of the Board of Governors (Article 5.3 TESM).

The Board of Governors meets at least once a year and whenever the affairs of the ESM so require. The **most important decisions** taken by the Board of Governors **require mutual agreement** (Article 5.6 TESM). These include decisions to provide stability support to an ESM member and the choice of instruments and the financial terms and conditions (Article 5.6 point (f) TESM), to change the list of financial assistance instruments that may be used by the ESM (point (i)), to change the authorised capital stock and adapt the maximum lending volume of the ESM (point (d)) as well as to delegate tasks to the Board of Directors (point (m)). In several areas, the Board of Governors takes decisions by qualified majority (Article 5.7 TESM). These areas include setting out the detailed technical terms of accession of a new member to the ESM (Article 5.7 point (a) TESM), appointing the Managing Director (point (e)), establishing other funds (point (f)), approving the annual accounts of the ESM (point (h)), appointing the members of the Board of Auditors (point (i)) and waiving the immunity of any board official or the Managing Director (point (k)). Under Article 4.5 TESM, 80% of the votes cast are required for the adoption of a qualified majority decision. Due to its extensive responsibilities, the Board of Governors can be described as the **main body of the ESM**.[95]

35

A similar arrangement was made by the States of the IMF in Article XII Section 2 of the IMF Agreement on the organisation and tasks of the IMF Board of Governors. Only in the decision making did the **IMF Agreement** deviate from the ESM Treaty by weighting the votes depending on the amount of the quota.[96]

36

2.3.2. Board of Directors (Article 6 TESM)

Each Governor appoints one member and one alternate member to the Board of Directors (Article 6.1 TESM). The task of the Board of Directors is to ensure that the ESM is managed in accordance with the TESM and the by-laws, adopted by the Board of Governors, as well as ensuring the exercise of powers conferred by the Board of Governors (Article 6.6 TESM). Directors should have 'a high competence in economic and financial matters'. For the most part, the role is therefore taken by a **State Secretary or a Senior Official** from the respective national Ministry of Finance.[97]

37

The Board of Directors' meetings are chaired by the ESM Managing Director (→ para 40 et seq.). As a rule, the Board of Directors takes decisions by qualified majority under Article 6.5 sentence 1 TESM. An exception is made, however, if the decisions are based on powers delegated by the Board of Governors. In this case,

38

---

[95] In terms of its organisation and competencies, Heß (2011), p. 208 also calls the committee an 'administrative board' (translation by the author). Likewise: Ketterer (2016), p. 66.
[96] Article XII Section 2 point (e) of the IMF Agreement.
[97] Häde (2014), para 13, translation by the author.

the relevant contractual voting rules apply.[98] The Board of Directors is primarily charged with **operational business**, e.g. the adoption of detailed guidelines for the implementation modalities of the instruments for stability support, the decision on the disbursement of the tranches of the financial assistance, the initiation of a primary market or secondary market operation and decisions on the rules and conditions for capital calls, under Article 9 TESM. In addition, the Board of Governors can, under Article 5.6 point (m) TESM, delegate all tasks to the Board of Directors by mutual agreement. There are no exemptions to this for budgetary powers or contract modification powers of the Board of Governors.[99] In view of the far-reaching tasks exercised by the Board of Directors, this qualifies as a so-called 'shadow government' of the ESM.[100] This configuration is not without risk with respect to the democratic legitimacy and control of the ESM's decisions (→ para 128–144).

39   The **IMF's Board of Directors** has a **similar organisational structure**. The Executive Board consists of 24 directors and deputies appointed or elected by members of the Board of Governors.[101] However, the configuration of the TESM has a much higher degree of autonomy. While the IMF's Board of Governors may only delegate the exercise of power to the Board of Directors, and, under Article XII Section 3 point (b) of the IMF Agreement, not the power as such, the ESM's Board of Governors in contrast may decide to delegate all the functions and powers assigned to the Board of Governors in Article 5 TESM and other Treaty provisions to its Board of Directors.[102]

2.3.3. Managing Director (Article 7 TESM)

40   The Managing Director is appointed by the Board of Governors from among candidates who are nationals of any ESM member with relevant international experience and a high level of competence in economic and financial matters (Article 7.1 TESM). The **term of office** is **five years**; a single re-appointment is possible. The Managing Director **chairs the meetings of the Board of Directors and**, as a legal representative of the ESM, **is responsible for managing day-to-day business** in accordance with the directives by the Board (Article 7.3, 7.5 TESM). As the supervisor of all ESM staff, he is responsible for the organisation, appointment and dismissal of staff in accordance with staff regulations, determined by the Board of Directors (Article 7.4 TESM). On 8 October 2012, the Board of Governors

---

[98] Article 6.5 sentence 2 TESM in conjunction with Articles 5.6, 5.7 TESM.

[99] Ketterer (2016), p. 324.

[100] Pilz (2016), p. 97 (translated by the author).

[101] Article XII Section 3 point (b); Annex E of the IMF Agreement.

[102] Cf. Ketterer (2016), pp. 324 et seqq. Quite rightfully, Häde (2014), para 12, emphasises that such a transfer should not lead to a complete disposition of the Board of Governors' tasks.

appointed *Klaus Regling* (Germany) as the first Managing Director, under Article 7.1 TESM.[103]

A similar institutional structure exists at the level of the **IMF** in the position of the IMFs Executive Director, who is appointed by the Executive Board.[104] He is head of the Fund's staff and carries out the ordinary business of the Fund according to the directives of the Executive Board.[105]

2.3.4. The Involvement of Other EU Institutions

European Commission

Expressing its role as an 'honest broker' and born negotiator of the Union,[106] the Commission, joined by ECB and the IMF, is conducting a rigorous debt sustainability analysis within the ESM, which forms the basis for the Board of Directors' decision whether to provide stability support or not (Articles 13.1, 13.2 TESM).[107] The adjustment programme's configuration and the monitoring of its implementation and compliance also take place under supervision of the European Commission (Articles 13.3, 13.7 TESM).[108] Even the final signing of the agreement between the Member State and the ESM is carried out by the Commission on behalf of the ESM's Member States (Article 13.4 TESM). However, the delegation of tasks to the European Commission does not take place based on the ESM Treaty, since despite a special closeness to the EU law,[109] it is not a component of primary law and, therefore, cannot establish the competence of an EU institution.[110] Furthermore, the competence of the Commission cannot be based on Article 136.3 TFEU either, which only has a 'declaratory value' for the establishment of the ESM (→ para 6).[111] Instead, the involvement of the Union institution takes place by means of a **'borrowed administration arrangement'** (*Organleihe*) based on an authorisation by the representatives of all EU Member States.

By means of the borrowed administration arrangement, functional parts of the Union's institutional framework are transferred to an intergovernmental cooperation, consisting of a group of MS organised in accordance with international law.

---

[103] ESM, Annual Report 2012, p. 24.
[104] Article XII Section 4 point (a) of the IMF Agreement.
[105] Article XII Section 4 point (b) of the IMF Agreement.
[106] Hallstein (1973), p. 58 (translated by the author).
[107] About the procedure of granting stability support → para 63 et seqq.
[108] Cf. Craig (2013), pp. 265 et seq.; van Duin (2020), para 18.33 et seq.
[109] German Federal Constitutional Court, 2 BvE 4/11 (Judgment of 19 June 2012), para 100— *Obligatory notifications* (in BVerfGE 131, 152 [199 et seq.]).
[110] Thym (2004), p. 315.
[111] Nettesheim (2013a), p. 15 (translated by the author).

This action is taken to achieve those objectives which the Union's MS jointly could not agree on.[112] It is a legally recognised practice which has been confirmed on several occasions by the ECJ.[113] In its judgment on the Fourth ACP-EEC Convention signed at Lomé, the Court observes that 'no provision of the Treaty prevents Member States from using, outside its framework, procedural steps drawing on the rules applicable to Community Expenditure and from associating the Community institutions with the procedure thus set up'.[114] However, the utilisation of the Union institutions is permitted only if primary law allows it or if all 27 MS agree to the borrowed administration arrangement within the scope of an international agreement.[115] The Schengen Agreements (1986/1990)[116] and the European Social Agreement of 1991[117] exemplify **international agreements** on the acquisition of tasks initially assigned by the EU institutions based on international treaties. The delegation of the Commission (and the ECB) and the takeover of tasks listed in the TESM was approved in the decision of the representatives of the MS' governments on 20 June 2011.[118] Although the decision on the borrowed administration arrangement was taken eight months before the conclusion of the TESM, the procedure is permissible, since on the one hand, the essential features of the ESM were already approved by the European Council at the time of the decision.[119] On the other hand, all government members of the (then) 27 Member States have given their approval.[120]

---

[112] Fischer-Lescano and Oberndorfer (2013), p. 9; Thym (2004), p. 317.

[113] Cases C-181/91 and C-248/91, *Parliament v Council and Commission* (ECJ 30 June 1993) para 20; Case C-316/91, *Parliament v Council* (ECJ 2 March 1994) para 41.

[114] Case C-316/91, *Parliament v Council* (ECJ 2 March 1994) para 41.

[115] Thym (2004), p. 317.

[116] Agreement *between the Governments of the States of the Benelux Economic Union, the Federal Republic of Germany and the French Republic on the gradual abolition of checks at their common borders* ('Schengen I', 14 June 1985), O.J. L 239/13 (2000); Convention *implementing the Schengen Agreement of 14 June 1985 between the Governments of the States of the Benelux Economic Union, the Federal Republic of Germany and the French Republic on the gradual abolition of checks at their common borders* ('Schengen II', 19 June 1990), O.J. L 239/19 (2000). On the Schengen Agreement as a 'lesson of differentiated integration', cf. Schauer (2000), pp. 194 et seqq.

[117] Agreement *on social policy concluded between the Member States of the European Community except for the United Kingdom of Great Britain and Northern Ireland*, O.J. C 191/91 (1992), although the utilisation of the Community institutions was accepted by all Member States in the Protocol on Social Policy in the Treaty of Maastricht, O.J. C 191/90 (1992). Cf. Coen (1995), pp. 50 et seqq.; McGlynn (1999), pp. 85 et seqq.

[118] 'The Representatives of the Governments of the Member States of the European Union agree that the ESM Treaty include provisions for the European Commission and the European Central Bank to carry out the tasks as set out in that Treaty', cf. Decision of the Representatives of the Governments of the Member States of the European Union (12114/11), 24 June 2011. The reference to this decision is also made in the Preamble to the ESM Treaty, tenth Recital.

[119] European Council of 24–25 March 2011, Conclusions, Doc. EUCO 10/11, para 17, Annex II.

[120] Case C-370/12, *Pringle* (Opinion of AG Kokott of 26 October 2012) para 173.

In addition to the requirement for an approval by all MS regarding a borrowed administration arrangement, the action of the Commission is subject to certain requirements. **Compliance with EU law** must always be ensured (→ Supplement to Title VIII: Introduction para 42 et seq.). Against this background, the European Commission may only assume those tasks outside EU law that are in accordance with the competences provided for in Article 13.2 sentence 1 TEU.[121] The Union's institutions are still bound by the principle of conferral (Article 5.1 sentence 1, Article 5.2 sentence 1 TEU) and the prohibition on granting them own competences (the so-called '*Kompetenz-Kompetenz*') in the case of a borrowed administration arrangement.[122] Meanwhile, the assumption of tasks by the European Commission within the framework of the ESM is not contrary to the EU law, as the TESM does not assign to the Commission any tasks leading to an extension of competences outside the treaty revision procedure under Article 48 TEU. The CJEU in *Pringle* underlines this finding. In the Court's view, the European Commission's exercise of tasks within the framework of the ESM is helping to safeguard the financial stability of the EA. Hence, it is contributing to promoting the general interests of the Union in line with Article 17.1 TEU. The tasks set out in the TESM and the guidelines (→ para 78) are therefore not an extension of the Commission's competences, but are similar to the tasks governed by primary and secondary Union law.[123] Tasks such as the assessment of a country's economic and fiscal fundamentals, the agreement on conditions to address budgetary imbalances as well as the monitoring of compliance with these conditions, using on-the-spot monitoring where appropriate, are rated among the tasks that the Commission is already carrying out under the Stability and Growth Pact (→ Supplement to Title VIII: Fiscal Union para 63 et seqq.).[124]

44

In April 2018, the Commission and the ESM supplemented the cooperation and working relationship with a **Memorandum of Understanding**.[125] It emphasises the common objectives and the joint performance of tasks in relation to financial assistance programmes for the EA Member States. It does not change the applicable legal rules in any way and does not create any obligations under EU or international

45

---

[121] Peers (2013), p. 45.

[122] German Federal Constitutional Court, 2 BvE 4/11 (Judgment of 19 June 2012), para 140—*Obligatory notifications* (in BVerfGE 131, 152 [217]). Corresponding: Case C-370/12, *Pringle* (CJEU 27 November 2012) para 158, that is based on the fact that tasks allocated by international law do not alter the essential character of the powers conferred on those institutions by the TEU/TFEU.

[123] Case C-370/12, *Pringle* (CJEU 27 November 2012) para 164.

[124] Article 6.1, 11 of Regulation (EU) No 1175/2011; Article 121.4 TFEU in conjunction with Article 6.2 (5) of Regulation (EU) No 1175/2011; Article 126.2 TFEU; Article 7 of Regulation 472/2013.

[125] Memorandum of Understanding on the working relations between the Commission and the European Stability Mechanism, 27 April 2018, available at https://www.esm.europa.eu/sites/default/files/20180427_esm_ec_mou.pdf.

law. It aims at facilitating cooperation between the parties, inter alia, in the context of budgetary surveillance of the euro area Member States.

46 In the light of the Commission's experience in the EU deficit procedure it is doubtful, however, whether the Commission has a sufficient arsenal of surveillance and intervention powers to support the compliance, monitoring and implementation of the relevant conditions regarding the adjustment programme, to ensure readiness to comply by the recipient country. Similar to its deficit procedure competencies, which are limited to monitoring tasks and recommendations, the Commission also merely plays a subordinate role in the ESM. This is because the ESM—and its dominating Board of Directors (→ para 37 et seq.)—**does not provide for compulsory elements** and instead seeks support of the Contracting States, counting on their will to reform and innovate. The intergovernmental approach of **cooperation** thus takes place **at eye level**. By contrast, the Commission, summoned as 'guardian of the treaties', is pushed back to the function of a secretary's office and 'the duties conferred on the Commission and ECB do [...] not entail any power to make decisions of their own'.[126] The mere status as an observer in the Board of Governors underlines this finding (Article 5.3 TESM).

European Central Bank

47 To secure the financial stability of the EA (→ para 58), the ESM relies on the **expertise** of the European Central Bank; and to avert threats to the economic and financial stability of the EA, the ECB has a **separate audit competence** based on Article 4.4 (1) sentence 1 and Article 18.2 TESM. Thus, the Board of Governors and the Board of Directors have the right to introduce an emergency procedure (→ para 68) or a secondary market operation (→ para 108 et seqq.).[127] In addition to exercising its own tasks, the ECB supports the European Commission in the procedure of granting stability support under Article 13 TESM (→ para 64 et seqq.) and Article 14.6 TESM by means of reviewing the actual or potential financing requirements under a precautionary credit line (→ para 85 et seqq.).

48 The ECB's involvement in the institutional framework of the ESM is carried out by means of a borrowed administration arrangement in accordance with the requirements for transferring tasks to the European Commission (→ para 42 et seqq.). The legal basis for this arrangement is the Decision of the representatives of the governments of the MS dating on 20 June 2011, which requests the ECB to fulfil the tasks provided by the TESM.[128] The wording 'to request' used in the Decision and in the tenth Recital of the Preamble to the TESM underlines the independence

---

[126] Case C-370/12, *Pringle* (CJEU 27 November 2012) para 161.

[127] The compatibility of the emergency procedure with the principle of democracy, the rule of law and sovereignty was raised before the Supreme Court of Estonia, Case No. 3-4-1-6-12, 12 July 2012, available at https://www.riigikohus.ee/en/constitutional-judgment-3-4-1-6-12. Cf. Ginter (2013), pp. 335 et seqq.

[128] Decision of the Representatives of the Governments of the Member States of the European Union (12114/11), 24 June 2011; Preamble to the ESM Treaty, tenth Recital.

of the ECB under Article 130 TFEU, which must be observed even outside EU law.[129] The Decision therefore has merely an **appellative character,** which expresses the MS' wish for a corresponding act of the ECB. The ECB is neither obliged to assume the tasks within the scope of the ESM, nor to be influenced by the ESM's institutions or the Member States behind it.

The ECB's participation in measures of the ESM must **comply with Union law.** This also forms the base for the jurisdiction by the CJEU in the *Pringle* case, where the Court requires that the exercise of tasks regulated outside EU law is permitted, 'provided, that those tasks do not alter the essential character of the powers conferred on those institutions' by the TEU/TFEU.[130] Against the background of the ESM's qualification as a measure of economic policy by the CJEU (→ para 6 et seq.),[131] the tasks are in accordance with Articles 282.1, 282.2 sentence 3 TFEU, according to which the support of general economic policy belongs to the tasks of the ECB. The tasks foreseen in the TESM therefore are within the competence of the ECB. The assessment of a request for stability support (Articles 4.4, 13.1 TESM) and the monitoring of compliance with the conditions attached to financial assistance (Article 13.7 TESM) are in line with the ECB's primary objective of ensuring price stability (Article 127.1 TFEU) and its fundamental task of safeguarding the smooth operation of payment systems (Article 127.2, fourth indent TFEU). Even the ECB's participation in secondary market interventions is fundamentally compatible with its mandate, as it has already implemented them in 2010 in support of its economic policy as part of its open market operations on the one hand,[132] and on the other hand has no decision-making powers in the ESM.[133] Instead, the initiation and activation of the secondary market intervention is carried out by the ESM's Board of Governors and the Board of Directors (Articles 18.1, 18.6 TESM). The activities of the ECB within the framework of the TESM only obliges the ESM.[134] In addition, the MS' relinquishment, during the formation of the ESM rules, to involve the ECB in the preparation and implementation of primary market interventions, which would have constituted a manifest breach of Article 123.1 TFEU (prohibition of immediate acquisition of government debt securities), speaks for compliance with the ECB's provisions on responsibility and against a distortion of EU law. **49**

European Court of Justice

The CJEU makes an important contribution to resolving conflicts within the ESM. Under Article 37.2 sentence 1 TESM, the Board of Governors decides 'on any **50**

---

[129] Case C-370/12, *Pringle* (Opinion of AG Kokott of 26 October 2012) para 181.
[130] Case C-370/12, *Pringle* (CJEU 27 November 2012) para 158.
[131] Case C-370/12, *Pringle* (CJEU 27 November 2012) para 57, 93–98.
[132] ECB Decision ECB/2010/5 *establishing a securities markets programme*, O.J. L 124/8 (2010).
[133] Keppenne (2014), pp. 243 et seq.
[134] Case C-370/12, *Pringle* (CJEU 27 November 2012) para 161. Cf. Craig (2013), p. 266.

dispute arising between an ESM Member and the ESM, or between ESM Members, in connection with the interpretation and application of this Treaty, including any dispute about the compatibility of the decisions adopted by the ESM with this Treaty'. If a member of the ESM challenges the decision of the Board of Governors, the **CJEU is responsible for the settlement of disputes** by Article 37.3 TESM **as first and final instance**.

51 The jurisdiction of the CJEU is based on Article 273 TFEU, as Recital 16 of the TESM Preamble points out. The Contracting Parties thereby deviate from the borrowed administration arrangement, practiced in the case of the Commission's and the ECB's involvement, and by means of an arbitration agreement, create jurisdiction of the CJEU within the scope of the TESM.[135] The instrument of arbitration agreement makes it possible to **transfer responsibilities to the CJEU based on an agreement concluded between the MS**.[136] The effectiveness of the arbitration agreement depends on the existence of connection between the presented dispute and EU law.[137] Thereby, it is not necessary for the legal disputes to be related to the Union Treaties. The respective disagreement may as well arise from the protocols or from secondary Union law.[138]

52 **Article 37.3 TESM** constitutes an **arbitration agreement** in line with Article 273 TFEU. Under Article 273 TFEU, the Court shall have jurisdiction over disputes between MS which relates to the subject-matter of the Treaties, if that dispute is submitted to it under a special agreement. Such agreement can be given in advance, with reference to a whole class of pre-defined disputes, by virtue of a clause like Article 37.3 TESM. As the CJEU holds, the disputes to be submitted to its jurisdiction are related to the subject-matter of the Treaties.[139] The CJEU refers in an exemplary way to the conditions laid down in a Memorandum of Understanding, which always 'must be fully consistent with European Union law and, in particular, with the measures taken by the Union in the area of coordination of the economic policies of the Member States'.[140] Whether the parties to the dispute are MS of the ESM and/or the Board of Governors as an institution of an International Organisation is irrelevant concerning the question of the Court's jurisdiction. After all, signatories to the ESM are also MS of the EA, who, represented by government representatives, take the central decisions jointly in the Board of Governors. A dispute involving the ESM can therefore be considered as a dispute between MS within the meaning of Article 273 TFEU.[141]

---

[135] de Gregorio Merino (2012), pp. 1639 et seqq.

[136] Cremer, in Calliess and Ruffert (2021), Article 273 AEUV para 2.

[137] Karpenstein, in Grabitz et al. (2021), Article 273 AEUV para 1 (released in 2020).

[138] Karpenstein, in Grabitz et al. (2021), Article 273 AEUV para 13 (released in 2020).

[139] Case C-370/12, *Pringle* (CJEU 27 November 2012) para 170–173. See also Peers (2013), pp. 62 et seqq.

[140] Case C-370/12, *Pringle* (CJEU 27 November 2012) para 174.

[141] Case C-370/12, *Pringle* (CJEU 27 November 2012) para 175.

2.3.5. The Cooperation with the International Monetary Fund

Financial and Technical Participation

To help MS in financial difficulty, the ESM is working 'very closely' with the IMF to provide stability support. Additional funds and expertise about the debt sustainability of a country can be acquired with the help of the IMF (Articles 13.1, 13.3 TESM, → para 65 et seq.). To this end, the Member State requesting stability support from the ESM will submit a similar request to the IMF that will participate in the financial assistance within the EA whenever possible.[142] At the same time, the Fund's financial resources are only granted under **strict compliance to given conditions**. Thus, the IMF is only concerned with the granting of a precautionary financial assistance (Article 14 TESM, → para 85 et seqq.) to MS that are not yet threatened with financial difficulties, as well as a lending facility (Article 16 TESM, → para 79 et seqq.). The receipt of a lending facility involves the implementation of a rigorous macroeconomic adjustment programme. If the specified conditions are not met, no additional payments will be provided (→ para 69 et seqq.). 53

In addition to a monetary contribution, the IMF supports the ESM at a technical level. This is demonstrated by the nature of the lending facility for Greece,[143] which was used as a pattern of action for the EFSF and the ESM interventions by the MS.[144] The intention of the financial assistance, 'ensuring the financial stability in the euro area' (Section 1.1 WFStG),[145] already reminds of the wording in Article I Section v) in conjunction with Article V Section 3 of the IMF Agreement on balance of payments support. The purpose of this assistance is to prevent States from covering up any **balance of payments problems** with an inflationary budgetary policy, thus jeopardising national and international prosperity. Instead, MS shall be provided with temporary general fund resources to settle balance of payment difficulties. At this point, the influence of the IMF's set of rules on the EA crisis management becomes clear. The MS' lending facility in favour of Greece and the financing of the IMF were granted by means of a **stand-by arrangement**.[146] Therefore, the EA countries have used the IMF practice as a blueprint to the 54

---

[142] Preamble to the ESM Treaty, eighth Recital.

[143] For details Martucci (2020), para 12.10 et seq.

[144] For the first Greek programme, the IMF brought crisis management expertise that, at the time, was in short supply at the EU level. Cf. de Gregorio Merino (2012), pp. 1616 et seqq.; Martucci (2020), para 12.14 et seq.; European Stability Mechanism (2019), p. 79.

[145] Law *on the giving of guarantees to maintain the Hellenic Republic's ability to pay which is required for financial stability in the monetary union* (Gesetz zur Übernahme von Gewährleistungen zum Erhalt der für die Finanzstabilität in der Währungsunion erforderlichen Zahlungsunfähigkeit der Hellenischen Republik, WFStG), German Federal Law Gazette 2010 part I, p. 537.

[146] Third Recital of the Loan Facility Agreement (8 May 2010).

modalities of financial support by the EFSF.[147] This standby credit or so-called stand-by arrangement is the most common form of credit intervention by the Funds.[148]

Normative Basis of the Mandate in the Euro Area

55 The involvement of the IMF in ESM matters of intervention is in line with the statutes of the Fund, whose overarching goal is to promote economic policy cooperation and the stability of currencies.[149] For this purpose, members of the Fund may temporarily and 'with appropriate security' access the general fund resources to settle 'imbalances in their balance of payments' under Article I points (v) and (vi) of the IMF Agreement. Legal basis of an 'IMF Funding' is Article V Section 3 of the IMF Agreement, which authorises the purchase of funds. The choice of term is based on the nature of the fund's way to raise capital, which is defined by the quota of members. The quotas are determined according to the member's economic data and define the amount of deposit obligation, the extent of loan demands and the weighting of votes within the institutions.[150] By paying the quota, the MS acquires the right to receive funding in the event of an external imbalance.[151] The conditions for the utilisation of general fund resources are set out in Article V Section 3 points (b)(ii) and (iii) of the IMF Agreement, and are substantiated by the IMF's business principles (so-called 'Guidelines').

56 IMF interventions within the EA do not deviate from these objectives and procedures. Thus, the 'cooperation' with the ESM takes place within the scope of the Fund's responsibilities. As the eighth Recital in the TESM Preamble points out, the **mandate of the IMF** is not granted by the TESM, but by the IMF's Statute itself. As Member States of the EA, requesting financial assistance from the ESM, 'are expected' to address a similar request to the IMF, the IMF Statute will be relevant upon receipt of this request. Hence, not the ESM's Board of Governors but the IMF Statute gets to decide on the possibility and appropriateness of cooperation with the IMF in the framework of a debt sustainability analysis under Article 13.1 point (b) TESM. If a MS's request is approved by the IMF, the institution acts within its field of competence. Given the duplication of instruments and procedures for providing financial assistance, a cooperation between the IMF on the one hand and the European Commission and the ECB on the other hand is

---

[147] Forsthoff and Lauer (2020), para 30.42.

[148] Krajewski (2006), p. 242 para 771.

[149] Article I points (ii) and (iii) of the IMF Agreement.

[150] Krajewski (2006), p. 235 para 743.

[151] As the balance of payments assistance cannot be financed exclusively through the subscription payments by members, the IMF may additionally take out bilateral loans from strong countries in regard to balance-of-payments and reserves (G20). It was only in 2009 that the G20 decided to triple the IMF's financial clout, raising its bilateral loans from EUR 250 billion to EUR 750 billion. It is from this fund that Member States may receive up to 200% of their quota as balance of payments assistance (Article V, section 3 point (b)(iii) of the IMF Agreement).

possible and, in view of the experience that the IMF gained in dealing with sovereign debt for many years, even seems to be appropriate. However, this also forms the foundation of the TESM's interpretation of the relationship, which grants the stability mechanism in Article 38 the right to cooperate with the IMF within the framework of its 'specialised responsibilities in related fields'.

Since the outbreak of the sovereign debt crisis, the IMF has acted as a trusted partner to the members of the EA. The agreements that have been made so far regarding Greece, Ireland, Portugal, and Cyprus, in which the IMF is involved with EUR 100 billion[152] for financial support, confirm this finding. However, although the ESM Contracting States work very closely with the IMF, both professionally and financially[153] the ESM seems emancipating itself from its big brother in Washington. There are many indications that in future the ESM will autonomously secure financial stability in the EA as the **European Monetary Fund** (→ para 146 et seqq.). Thus, the IMF made its participation in a third rescue package for Greece dependent on the condition that the creditors agreed to a debt relief so that the country's finances would be sustainable in the long term. By contrast, the ESM countries are refusing a debt restructuring for Greece and are financing the third assistance programme with the IMF only formally participating. Special drawing rights are not provided by the IMF. The proposals for a European Monetary Fund presented by the European Parliament and the European Commission in spring 2017 are further indications of a **withdrawal of the IMF** from the EA.[154]

3. Financial Assistance Operations (Articles 12 et seqq. TESM)

The activation and use of stability support from the ESM is, under Article 136.3 TFEU, only eligible if the measure seems indispensable to safeguard the financial stability of the EA. In that case, an ESM member may receive stability assistance under appropriate conditions. However, the actual terms and procedures concerning the support are not regulated by the TFEU. Instead, they are specified by the ESM Treaty (Articles 12 et seqq.) and the **guidelines on the modalities of the specific financial assistance instrument**.

---

[152] Greece I: EUR 20.2 billion, Greece II: EUR 28.9 billion, Ireland: EUR 22.6 billion, Portugal: EUR 27.4 billion, Cyprus (2013): EUR 1.0 billion, Greece III (2015): formal participation. See: German Federal Ministry for Finance, Overview of European financial aid (State: 30 June 2020). Available at http://www.bundesfinanzministerium.de/Content/DE/Standardartikel/Themen/Europa/Stabilisierung_des_Euro/europaeische-finanzhilfen-im-ueberblick-pdf.pdf?__blob=publicationFile&v=23.

[153] Preamble to the ESM Treaty, eighth Recital.

[154] European Parliament resolution of 16 February 2017 on budgetary capacity for the euro area, P8_TA(2017)0050; European Commission, *Reflection Paper on the deepening of the Economic and Monetary Union*, 31 May 2017, COM(2017) 291, 28 et seq.; European Commission, *Proposal for a Council Regulation on the establishment of the European Monetary Fund*, 6 December 2017, COM(2017) 827 final.

3.1. Normative Conditions (Article 12 TESM)

3.1.1. Safeguarding Financial Stability as a Triggering Event

59 To preserve the financial stability of the EA, the ESM can grant loans amounting up to EUR 500 billion (→ para 20). As fundamental condition for initiating the procedure for granting stability support in line with Article 13 TESM, there must be **a severe situation for the 'stability of the euro area as a whole'** (Article 136.3 TFEU). The term 'stability of the euro area' is used throughout the ESM Treaty under the more precise term 'financial stability'. Article 12.1 sentence 1 TESM, which has adopted its wording from Article 136.3 TFEU, explains the risk to financial stability as *the* **triggering event**. However, it is by no means clear what the term 'financial stability' that is standardised in Articles 127.5, 127.6 and 136.3 TFEU in conjunction with Article 12.1 TESM precisely means and how it relates to the maintenance of price stability.[155] In the regulations governing the various instruments of the ESM, respectively of its predecessor institution EFSF, which have been activated due to a threat to financial stability, there is no indication as to what is meant by the term 'financial stability'. The variety of measures to maintain financial stability rather testifies to the **vagueness of the term**.[156] The opinions of the Advocates General in *Pringle*[157] and *Gauweiler*[158] do not attempt to further define the term either.[159] Solely in the *Pringle* decision, the CJEU stated that the concept of financial stability was not to be equated with the objective of price stability, but rather goes beyond this objective.[160] Thus, financial stability is rather an implicit requirement for price stability, as the latter can only be secured in an environment where the transmission of monetary policy signals is running smoothly. This, in turn, requires a stable financial system.[161] The ECB defines financial stability as 'a state whereby the build-up of systemic risk is prevented. Systemic risk can best be described as the risk that the provision of necessary financial products and services by the financial system will be impaired to a point

---

[155] Also, Nettesheim (2013a), p. 16, misses an independent subsumption of the term in the jurisdiction of the CJEU. Thiele (2014a), pp. 256 et seq., however, cannot identify normative bases in German constitutional law ('The terminology of financial market stability is not used within the German Basic Law [...]'. (translated by the author). On the concept of financial stability, cf. Pilz (2016), pp. 65 et seqq.

[156] Tuori and Tuori (2014), p. 133.

[157] Case C-370/12, *Pringle* (Opinion of AG Kokott of 26 October 2012).

[158] Case C-62/14, *Gauweiler* (Opinion of AG Cruz Villalón of 14 January 2015) para 143.

[159] Nettesheim (2013a), p. 16.

[160] Case C-370/12, *Pringle* (CJEU 27 November 2012) para 56.

[161] Selmayr, in von der Groeben et al. (2015), Article 282 AEUV para 61.

where economic growth and welfare may be materially affected'.[162] If one focuses on the use and scope of financial stability including the 'stability of the financial system' (Articles 127.5, 127.6 TFEU), the term refers to a situation in which the various parts of the financial system are able to perform their tasks without major disruption to the financial system or the economy in general.[163] A stable financial system is the prerequisite for direct financing through capital markets and indirect funding by financial intermediaries to channel funds between the supplier and the buyer in a rational manner. In this sense, **stability of the financial system** is seen as a more comprehensive approach[164] that is focusing on both State and financial institutions, striving for cross-border integration of financial markets to secure the banking system's stability. In this concept, actors of both sides only remain unconsidered if actions taken by MS and banks have no relevant consequences on the (financial) system.[165]

This interpretation of the concept of financial stability is in line with the principles of EMU as laid down in Article 119.3 TFEU. Due to the systematic positioning of Article 136.3 TFEU in Title VIII of the TFEUs third part, **'financial stability'** is to be understood in the **economic and monetary sense** and follows the principles and systematics of this area. Accordingly, financial stability can be classified in the principles of stability under Article 119.3 TFEU.[166] The objective of this article in particular is to ensure price stability. However, this also includes the preservation of well-functioning public finances and monetary conditions, as well as securing a permanently sustainable balance of payments. They form sub-objectives to the actual financial stability, whose cumulative realisation is a precondition for a stable financial system. Thereby, **regarding its conceptual basis, financial stability is much more complex than price stability**, as the latter can be measured by a single index, namely the index of consumer prices.

3.1.2. Indispensable Nature

The utilisation of ESM stability support requires that measures to safeguard the financial stability of the EA under Article 12.1 sentence 1 TESM must be

---

[162] European Central Bank, Financial Stability Review, May 2016, p. 3. The German Bundesbank shares a similar understanding: financial stability is the financial system's ability to smoothly perform key macroeconomic functions at all times, especially in periods of stress and upheaval, German Bundesbank, Financial Stability Report 2012, p. 5 (translated by the author). See also Danzmann (2015), p. 94; Freedman and Goodlet (2007), p. 3.

[163] Tuori and Tuori (2014), p. 58. Similar also Selmayr, in von der Groeben et al. (2015), Article 127 AEUV para 38.

[164] Tuori and Tuori (2014), p. 58.

[165] The terms' vagueness suggests, according to Tuori and Tuori (2014), p. 133, a conscious approach by the institutions to avoid *moral hazard* on the part of recipient countries in the scope of financial rescue measures. Otherwise, a state could take fiscal decisions that jeopardise the financial stability of the euro area as a whole to obtain stability assistance.

[166] Palm, in Grabitz et al. (2021), Article 136 AEUV para 55 (released in 2014).

indispensable. On the principle of independence regarding the MS' budgetary policy, this condition must be understood as **last resort**.[167] Therefore, a threat of an emerging or amplifying financial crisis, affecting the entire EA, would be present if stability support was denied. Thus, only crises that threaten to affect the real economy within the eurozone in a serious and persistently harmful way are defined as relevant.[168] In fact, experiences during the sovereign debt crisis have shown that a MS' financial difficulties can spread over various transmission channels and become a threat to the EU's overall macroeconomic stability (**'contagion risk'**).[169] Whether an actual risk exists, however, will depend on the reaction of the international financial markets in each case. Here, the case of Greece can serve as a reference: At first, financial markets reacted by downgrading Greece's creditworthiness and raising interest rates on Greek government bonds. Later, the country was denied new loans and the opportunity to refinance expiring liabilities by capital markets. Shortly thereafter, confidence in the heavily indebted euro crisis States as a whole declined.[170] Consequently, Portugal and Ireland were no longer able to finance maturing government bonds by means of new loans, either.[171] Therefore, a hazardous situation can most likely be assumed in the individual cases, given the close interdependence of the economies, particularly the financial sectors.[172]

3.1.3. Strict Conditionality

62 The use of ESM funds goes hand in hand with the obligation to debtor States to remedy their national budget. **Conditions** vary based on the case and are *adequately* adjusted to the granted instrument of financial assistance (Article 12.1 sentence 1 TESM; → para 79 et seqq.). Thus, the granting of 'financial assistance through loans to an ESM member for the specific purpose of recapitalising the financial institutions of that ESM Member' (Article 15.1 TESM, → para 94) is linked to restructuring the financial sector. According to ESM Guidelines, the restructuring can take place by means of various institutional, sectoral or macroeconomic reform requirements that are in line with TFEU rules concerning State aid.[173] In this case, a macroeconomic adjustment programme is not intended. However, in case of a loan within the meaning of Article 16 TESM (→ para 80),

---

[167] Bark and Gilles (2013), pp. 368 et seq.; Palm, in Grabitz et al. (2021), Article 136 AEUV para 57 (released in 2014).

[168] Ohler, in Siekmann (2013), Article 136 AEUV para 20.

[169] Preamble to the ESM Treaty, third Recital.

[170] On the economic development in the PIIGS States during the crisis, cf. Schefold (2014), pp. 22 et seq.

[171] On the economic developments in the three States since 1990, cf. Tuori and Tuori (2014), pp. 78 et seqq.

[172] Pilz (2016), pp. 14 et seqq.; Morwinsky (2014), pp. 42 et seqq.

[173] Article 4.5 point (a) ESM Guideline on Financial Assistance for the Recapitalisation of Financial Institutions.

the granting of stability support is linked to the implementation of a macroeconomic adjustment programme.[174] The conditions are set out in a **Memorandum of Understanding** by the debtor State and the European Commission 'in liaison with the ECB' (Article 13.3 sentence 1 TESM) and include modalities concerning budget restructuring as well as economic policy guidelines (→ para 69). If the debtor States violate the conditions, further assistance loans will be denied and the case of insolvency that governments actually tried to avoid will occur.[175]

In addition to structural and fiscal requirements, the use of the ESM funds is linked to the prior **ratification of the TSCG**.[176] This link highlights the special function of the ESM as a reserve capacity, which becomes available if the budgetary rules of the Fiscal Compact could not prevent a public debt crisis. Thus, the TESM and the TSCG substantiate a **'support- and austerity responsibility'**[177] that binds the ESM States, which, however, is controversial both economically and on the extent and form of the austerity policy (→ para 77).[178]

63

3.2. Procedure for Granting Stability Support (Article 13 TESM)

3.2.1. Request for Stability Support

The procedural framework for granting stability support is enshrined in Article 13 TESM. If a Member State encounters difficulties in payment or already entered insolvency, the debtor State may address a request for stability support to the Chairperson of the ESM's Board of Governors, indicating the required financial assistance instrument (Article 13.1 TESM). Therefore, the procedure can only be initiated by means of a request from the affected Member State in distress (**'application principle'**).[179] An ex officio initiation of the procedure by the donor countries represented in the Board of Governors is excluded.

64

---

[174] Article 13.3 TESM in conjunction with Article 2.3 point (a) of the ESM Guidelines on Loans.

[175] Regular monitoring of the conditions' implementation, which are defined by the *Troika*, is an indispensable prerequisite to receive further tranches of the financial assistance, cf. in general Article 13.7 TESM, for each individual instrument Articles 14.5, 15.5, 16.5 and Article 17.7 TESM.

[176] Preamble to the TSCG, Recital 25: 'the granting of assistance in the framework of new programmes under the European Stability Mechanism will be conditional [...] on the ratification of this Treaty'.

[177] Hufeld (2014), para 172 (translated by the author).

[178] Cf. the contributions in Corsetti (2012a); Pilz (2016), pp. 211 et seqq.

[179] European Council of 24–25 March 2011, Conclusions, Doc. EUCO 10/11, p. 27. See also Heß (2011), p. 208.

3.2.2. Debt Sustainability Analysis

65 The provision of stability support is linked to the existence of a threat to financial stability in the EA and a rigorous analysis of debt sustainability. A debt sustainability analysis is a standard instrument of fiscal surveillance, but it is also a tool for taking decisions about the provision of financial support.[180] The assessment of a risk situation and the identification of the actual or potential financing requirements are carried out by the European Commission accompanied by the ECB and, 'wherever appropriate and possible', together with the IMF (Article 13.1 point (b) TESM). The **complex forecasting and assessment** in evaluating the situation require a **special economic expertise** contributed by the ECB and the IMF. The debt sustainability assessment will be done on a transparent and predictable basis, while allowing sufficient margin of judgement.[181] The analysis is largely based on a practical definition of sustainability. One such definition, as proposed by the IMF, includes debt dynamics, the level of debt, and the feasibility to achieve or maintain primary balance surpluses, as follows: 'In general terms, public debt can be regarded as sustainable when the primary balance needed to at least stabilise debt under both the baseline and realistic shock scenarios is economically and politically feasible, such that the level of debt is consistent with an acceptably low rollover risk and with preserving potential growth at a satisfactory level [...] The higher the level of public debt, the more likely it is that fiscal policy and public debt are unsustainable [...]'.[182] The ESM does not publish its own framework for the analysis of debt sustainability, and unlike the ECB, no methodological framework has ever been published.[183] The role of the ESM is at present in flux. With the transformation into the European Monetary Fund, the Fund could engage in the process of debt sustainability surveillance and directly produce the debt sustainability analysis for the financial assistance programmes.[184]

66 The fulfilment of tasks, however, takes place exclusively 'in liaison with the ECB' (Article 13.1 sentence 3 TESM). This concept, borrowed from German general administrative law, expresses a weaker form of participation. If the administrative law requires cooperation 'in liaison', the authority eligible to take part in the proceeding may submit its own opinion on the measure in question, by means of a non-binding statement.[185] Yet, it is denied the right to consent.[186] This form of participation is also referred to as 'official consultation' or 'institutional hearing' in

---

[180] Alcidi and Gros (2018), p. 5.

[181] ESM Annual Report 2018, p. 20.

[182] IMF (2013), pp. 4 et seq.

[183] European Central Bank (2017).

[184] Alcidi and Gros (2018), p. 14.

[185] Badura (2019), pp. 261 et seq.

[186] German Federal Administrative Court, IV C 184/65 (Judgment of 19 November 1965) = NJW 1966, pp. 513 et seq.; German Federal Administrative Court, 1 C 28.81 (Judgment of 16 May 1983) = DVBl 1983, pp. 1002 et seq.; Bredemeier (2007), pp. 161 et seq.; Fengler (2003), p. 21; Zeitler (1979), pp. 61 et seq.

the literature.[187] The wording 'in liaison' also indicates that the ECB is only to be involved in a consulting manner. Accordingly, the institutions do not have to reach an agreement regarding their conceptions. The **European Commission, as the decisive authority**, merely is required to assess the ECB's position in its own decision and to examine its factual and legal considerations carefully. For the purpose of decision, **an agreement with the ECB is not required.** It is, however, aspired to for the final evaluation in the light of the complex macroeconomic issues.

3.2.3. Voting Rules

Based on the request for stability support as well as the evaluation of the European Commission in liaison with the ECB and, wherever possible, together with the IMF (the so called *Troika*), the Board of Governors decides **by mutual agreement** on the granting of financial assistance including the conditions under which the assistance will be made available (Article 13.2 TESM in conjunction with Article 5.6 point (f) TESM). If the Board of Governors has adopted the programme, the Commission will sign the agreement on behalf of the ESM's Member States (Article 13.4 TESM). Subsequently, the Board then approves a financial facility agreement proposed by the Managing Director and decides on the disbursement of the first tranche of the assistance (Article 13.3, 13.5 TESM). The **decision of the Board of Governors** is **justiciable only in a limited way**, which can be explained by the complexity of macroeconomic issues and the need for wide discretion in such an emergency situation.[188] In this respect, the involvement of ECB and IMF is essential, as only their expertise can ensure a proper functioning of financial markets and assess serious dangers to national economies. The Board of Governors must be able to rely on the accuracy of the ECB's and the IMF's expertise with its decision. In view of the institutions' **discretion and prerogative of evaluation**, the decisions by the Board of Governors are permissible.[189] Whether they are economically viable or politically correct, however, cannot be guaranteed ex ante. When thinking about **judicial control** of the decisions based on the ECB's and IMF's expertise, judicial restraint is advisable, given the ECB's independence.[190] The courts may indeed provide **legal protection**,[191] however the result may turn out rather unsatisfactory in view of the wider discretion. Additionally, it seems inappropriate to question the ECB's sound economic decisions by 'at best, amateurishly interested judges', limited in their expertise for this situation.[192]

---

[187] Fengler (2003), p. 21 (translated by the author).

[188] The CJEU grants the ECB 'a broad discretion' on its margin of judgement in exercising its open-market policy. Case C-62/14, *Gauweiler* (CJEU 16 June 2015) para 68.

[189] Pilz (2016), p. 70.

[190] Herrmann (2012), p. 811; Thiele (2014b), p. 696.

[191] On legal remedies against EU economic and monetary policy measures, cf. Gramlich (2020), para 162 et seqq.

[192] Herrmann (2012), p. 811 (translated by the author).

68 In urgent cases, the Treaty allows a deviation from the voting requirements of Article 5.6 point (f) TESM. Under Article 4.4 sentence 2 TESM, the Board of Governors may take decisions on whether financial assistance is granted and the modalities that go with it by a **qualified majority of 85% of the votes cast**. On the application of an **emergency procedure**, the European Commission and the ECB decide without participation of the MS. This takes place provided the institutions consider it to be an urgent decision that is deemed necessary to avoid jeopardising the economic and financial stability of the EA (Article 4.4 sentence 1 TESM). Moving away from the unanimity principle means that in future, individual ESM members will have to take responsibility for stabilisation measures in favour of other Contracting States, even against their will. Only Germany, Italy and France have a **blocking minority** with a voting share of more than 15%. Since the voting shares are based on the scales of contribution ($\rightarrow$ para 21), it is possible that a shift of voting shares and thus the loss of the blocking minority may occur, particularly if other MS are joining in (Article 44 TESM, $\rightarrow$ para 17).

3.2.4. Memorandum of Understanding

Establishment and Content

69 The disbursement of the individual tranches of financial assistance is linked to the implementation of an adjustment programme. The latter is negotiated in a Memorandum of Understanding by the *Troika,* with the ESM member concerned (Article 13.3 TESM). The content of the MoU reflects the degree of severity of the weaknesses to be addressed and the financial assistance instrument of choice ($\rightarrow$ para 79 et seqq.). The measures to be agreed on may vary from mere political commitments regarding the future securing of Maastricht criteria, over economic and fiscal reforms that behove the Member State's assessment, up to a specific **macroeconomic adjustment programme** (conditionality, $\rightarrow$ para 62 et seq.).

70 Several measures can be considered to restructure the national budget. First, the MS could reduce its government spending to reduce public debt (**spending cut**).[193] In the political process, however, this is difficult to put into practice. Therefore, it is usually done in the form of a linear spending cut. In doing so, each ministerial department's spending is cut by the same percentage.[194] The method offers the advantage that a detailed examination and evaluation of each individual case becomes unnecessary. However, this may lead to non-fulfilment of certain tasks previously performed by the State so that in many cases a linear reduction in public expenditure would equal the cessation of public services.[195]

---

[193] Otte (2010), p. 150. About the scope of cutting competencies, cf. Kratzmann (1982), p. 323.
[194] This procedure is referred to as 'cuts across the board'; cf. Kotler and Caslione (2009), p. 63.
[195] Pilz and Dittmann (2011), p. 444.

Another possibility to restructure government debt is to repay it by liquidating state assets by means of **privatisation**.[196] In the case of asset privatisation, State and municipal assets are sold to private economic entities.[197] Selling real estate and holdings in commercial enterprises lies within the focus of asset privatisation. In addition to rebalancing the budget, asset privatisation is also used to reduce overstaffing in the public sector. This reduction of staff can be done faster and more efficient within the private sector than in the public sector. Furthermore, the effectiveness of competition is also enhanced by the State's withdrawal from business enterprises.[198] On fiscal policy, the liquidation of State assets is a suitable means of generating capital in the short term while reducing government spending at the same time.[199] On the other hand, however, the selling of state and municipal property also leads to a gradual erosion of public resources.[200]

The recovery of public finances can also be achieved through the element of **taxation**. Due to its tax sovereignty, the government can increase its taxes domestically and thereby contribute to the repayment of debts.[201] However, tax increases are critical during times of economic crisis, as they weaken the incentives for economic performance as well as international competitiveness. This would in turn have a negative impact on potential economic growth.[202] At the same time, high tax rates represent a potential disadvantage in international tax competition and can lower the attractiveness as business location, as companies in principle focus on minimising the tax burden to be paid. Short-term benefits of a tax rate increase could therefore be offset by long-term economic disadvantages.[203]

To prevent a complete payment default of creditors and to achieve a reduction in the government debt ratio, the instrument of **debt restructuring** is cited. In the event of debt restructuring, creditors and representatives of the debtor country come together to agree on a modification in the terms of payment (private sector participation, → para 121 et seqq.).

In the **cases of Greece, Portugal and Ireland**, the various measures have been applied to different degrees to deal with the sovereign debt crisis. To rehabilitate the national budgets, it was necessary to reduce public spending and to raise public revenues at first. To this end, the three States cut public sector salaries and employee benefits, reduced jobs, cancelled special payments, set aside tax exemptions, cut pensions in payment to beneficiaries and raised the legal retirement age, abolished special payments to pensioners, cut the spending on educational policy,

71

---

[196] Otte (2010), p. 150.
[197] Lee (1997), p. 158.
[198] Cf. Möschel (1988), pp. 887 et seq.
[199] Pilz and Dittmann (2011), p. 445.
[200] Beck and Wentzel (2010), p. 169.
[201] *Kratzmann*'s statement is corresponding to this, as he excludes the insolvency of a state if not all sources of tax have been made use of, cf. Kratzmann (1982), p. 323.
[202] Glomb (2010), p. 187.
[203] Pilz and Dittmann (2011), p. 445. In detail Blanke and Böttner (2020), § 13 para 168 et seqq.

reduced public subsidies to private companies, reduced public investment and services, privatised government property (ports, airports, energy, real estate), cut spending in social protection systems and in contrast to that introduced extensive tax increases in VAT, CAT, capital gains-, land-, sales-, environmental-, excise- and wealth taxes, introduced a progressive tax rate for all types of income and took measures to ensure effective tax collection.[204] In addition, Ireland also had to take measures to restructure and consolidate its oversized financial sector, as the cause of the Irish sovereign debt crisis rooted in the very same.[205]

72   The **adjustment programme**, drawn up by the *Troika*, forms the basis of the whole procedure, since it specifies all the restructuring measures. Without strict implementation of the qualitatively and quantitatively well-defined conditions, no further rescue measures will be taken. The coordination between the ESM and the EU rules relevant for the MoU is addressed in the ESM Treaty as well as in EU law. Under Article 13.3 TESM, 'the MoU shall be fully consistent with the measures of economic policy coordination provided for in the TFEU, in particular with any act of European Union law, including any opinion, warning, recommendation or decision addressed to the ESM Member concerned'. Likewise the Commission shall ensure, under Articles 7.2 and 7.12 of Regulation 472/2013,[206] that the MoU is 'fully consistent with the macroeconomic adjustment programme approved by the Council' in case such programme is prescribed by the applicable ESM rules or, otherwise, that the MoU is fully consistent with the Council decision approving the main policy requirements, which the ESM plans to include in conditionality for its financial support, to the extent the content of these measures falls within the competence of the Union.[207]

Accountability

73   Concerns about the loss of State autonomy due to the establishment of substantive interferences in national budgetary sovereignty are justified, but nevertheless inevitable, to restore the State's ability to act. The granting of stability support to individual MS to maintain financial stability does not take place based on a sovereignty-preserving procedure. It rather is the result of a set of measures

---

[204] The measures listed were taken from the adjustment programmes of the PIIGS States. Cf. European Commission, The Economic Adjustment Programme for Greece, Occasional Papers 61, 2010; European Commission, The Economic Adjustment Programme for Ireland, Occasional Papers 76, 2011; European Commission, The Economic Adjustment Programme for Portugal, Occasional Papers 79, 2011; European Commission, The Second Economic Adjustment Programme for Greece, Occasional Papers 94, 2012. Available at http://ec.europa.eu/economy_finance/publications/occasional_paper/index_en.htm.

[205] For a presentation of the cornerstones of the Irish austerity programme, cf. Drudy and Collins (2011), pp. 345 et seq. See also European Stability Mechanism (2019), pp. 91 et seqq.

[206] Parliament/Council Regulation (EU) No 472/2013 *on the strengthening of economic and budgetary surveillance of Member States in the euro-area experiencing or threatened with serious difficulties with respect to their financial stability*, O.J. L 140/1 (2013).

[207] Cf. Forsthoff and Lauer (2020), para 30.49.

imposed and monitored by the public creditors. However, to ensure the MS's acceptance of the implementation of austerity measures, the **country should not be placed under the foreign rule of its creditors**. Both the representatives of MS in the Board of Governors as well as the European institutions (the Commission and the ECB) and the IMF are actors,[208] guided by interest, that have indirect democratic legitimisation at best.[209] These institutions are the operational arm of the ESM in the form of *Troika* and are entrusted with the arrangement, implementation and surveillance of the macroeconomic adjustment programmes. A connection to the MS is provided via Article 13.3 TESM, according to which the ministers of finance (the Eurogroup), meeting within the Board of Governors, entrust the European Commission with the task to negotiate a MoU with the corresponding ESM Member State, in liaison with the ECB and, if possible, including the IMF. Because of the government representatives on the Board of Governors who have been confirmed by the national parliaments, the *Troika* is at least indirectly democratically legitimised.

Nonetheless, the negotiation and implementation of the macroeconomic adjustment programmes in the so-called crisis countries threatens the **budget autonomy of national parliaments**.[210] Given the specific circumstances of the *Troika*, the Greek, Irish or Portuguese parliaments have virtually no say for example. At most, during the negotiation and adoption of a MoU (Article 13.3 TESM) the national parliament's approval is obtained. In this respect, the agreement between the ESM and the respecting MS is democratically legitimised.[211] However, the influence of the national parliament is low, since the *Troika* specifies the key points of the adjustment programme for the most part. Admittedly, the adjustment programme is not adopted by the *Troika*, but unanimously by the finance ministers in the Board of Governors. In the implementation phase, however, the national parliament is effectively overruled. Hence, to name an example, the adjustment programme in Greece includes detailed saving targets for each quarter that must be achieved through measures such as tax increases or the removal of public service conditions. The *Troika* monitors the implementation of measures agreed upon by means of on-the-spot checks. Furthermore, its final report is a major contributor to the Board of Governors decision to disburse further tranches. Notwithstanding the importance of its tasks, the work of the *Troika* has no impact on the national parliament's participation rights. The programme's implementation or non-implementation is the responsibility of the parliament and government of the Member State concerned, which also reflects the respective political priorities. Whether the respective parliament is intensively involved from the beginning to

---

[208] Paulus (2012), p. 22.

[209] Pilz (2016), pp. 101 et seqq.

[210] Different opinion: Calliess (2013), p. 789, who denies an intervention by the adjustment programmes in the budgetary sovereignty, since in view of the impending state bankruptcy no budgetary autonomy can exist in which the measures could intervene.

[211] Ohler, in Siekmann (2013), Article 136 AEUV para 22.

the conclusion of a programme depends on the countries' constitution and its strength (→ para 128 et seqq.).

74 From the perspective of the **indebted State's citizens**, the MoU agreed upon—and democratically legitimised by the national parliaments—is a democratically unjustified rule of foreign governments, which is only accepted reluctantly and with angry sentiments amongst various sections of the public.[212] Citizens seem to find it too difficult to understand the responsibilities behind the *Troika*: although the Board of Governors, and thus the finance ministers of the EA countries, holds the power to decide on the conditions, in the eyes of citizens the *Troika* takes the decisions on its own authority.[213] This finding is confirmed by the Greek tragedy: Since May 2010, the EU's weakest economy has been granted large sums of new debt by means of rescue packages, while at the same time a rigid austerity policy was decreed. The citizen's **discontent** manifested itself in the political instability of the country.[214] Hence, several parliamentary and presidential elections had to be held since the outbreak of the crisis, as a stable environment for implementing the necessary reforms was missing. The Greek crisis peaked in January 2015, when the newly elected Greek government broke off the cooperation with the *Troika* and expelled the institution's representatives.[215]

Social Rights

75 The austerity policy under a macroeconomic adjustment programme can lead to profound cuts in fundamental social rights of citizens.[216] The adjustment path within the austerity policy is paved with a rigid austerity programme by the government and in the short term by a State in which the economic and social conditions are unfavourable and the population's standard of living decreases.[217] However, the interventions linked to fiscal consolidation are unavoidable and must be supported by the citizens of the MS reliant on the solidarity of its partner countries. For the State is not only in a budgetary emergency but also has to reduce its previous socio-political guarantees.[218] The interventions, in accordance to the *Troika*, vault national constitutional law by means of **limiting the national**

---

[212] Scharpf (2014), p. 37.

[213] Antpöhler (2015).

[214] An overview of the juxtaposition of elections and new governments in Greece since 2010 is presented by Wiesner (2016), p. 241.

[215] Rickens, 'Troika-Aus in Athen: Ein Abschied, bei dem keiner weint', Spiegel Online 31 January 2015.

[216] Fisahn (2010), pp. 248 et seqq.; Schrader and Laaser (2012).

[217] On the terminology of austerity, cf. Drudy and Collins (2011), p. 339: 'A situation in which economic and social conditions are unfavorable and living standards fall, possibly but not necessarily, due to government policies'.

[218] M. J. *Neumann* (German Central Bank) compares the rehabilitation of the State budget with a drug withdrawal, which, while dangerous 'in one stroke', can very possibly be successful and sustainable. Cf. Neumann (2012), p. 66.

parliament's autonomy by reducing its budgetary rights.[219] Interventions in the citizens' fundamental social rights are inevitable for the rehabilitation of the national budget.[220] In this context the guarantee of the core content of fundamental rights (*Wesensgehaltsgarantie*) is essential, especially in cases of bankruptcy or a serious State crisis, in the case of which, the assessment of counter-limits (*Schranken-Schranken*) does not dominate, as would be the case in a standard situation, examining the proportionality under consideration of public interests and a fundamental right.[221] The principle of proportionality for all governmental actions, including a rigid austerity policy, naturally also applies during the event of crisis. However, due to the balance between the fundamental right affected and the goal to restore the national budget, which must be established in the light of *appropriateness*, legislature and government are forced into a trade-off. This cannot be captured by means of the usual categories of appropriate State intervention during a normal situation. Thus, the adequacy of austerity policy is not justiciable in a comprehensive manner either. The guarantee of the core content thus rises to the decisive counter-limit of government austerity policy on the brink of bankruptcy. An interference with fundamental social rights of the Charter of Fundamental Rights cannot solely be regarded as proportionate in narrowly defined exceptional cases.[222] Ultimately, in times of severe crisis, a minimum level of social guarantees for the benefit of Union citizens should be guaranteed, without losing sight of the need for a rigid reform and austerity policy. Moreover, the longer the saving process lasts, the more public support for saving efforts will decrease.[223] Social advantages counteract the austerity efforts and deprives the state of the fruits of its previously introduced austerity measures. The rehabilitation of the national budget would thus become a Sisyphean task.

The fact that the reasons causing the **lack of convergence between Member States** were partially self-imposed, must not be ignored with these considerations. Thus, in some cases the lack of convergence was caused due to the failure to exhaust all national sources of income and to reduce expenditure. As examples, the crisis countries Greece, Ireland and Portugal must be mentioned due to their failure to exhaust the tax potential, the inefficient administrative structures and the social

---

[219] Hufeld (2014), para 174.

[220] Application No. 75916/13, *Danutė Mockiene v Lithuania* (ECtHR 4 July 2017) para 43–49; Applications No. 62235/12 and 57725/12, *Da Conceição Mateus and Santos Januário v Portugal* (ECtHR 8 October 2013) para 29; Applications No. 57665/12 and 57657/12, *Koufaki and ADEDY v Greece* (ECtHR 7 May 2013) para 36–41.

[221] Other opinion represented by Fischer-Lescano (2013), who, referring to the principle of proportionality, bemoans a violation of fundamental rights from the Charter of Fundamental Rights in the wake of the sovereign debt crisis.

[222] Application No. 75916/13, *Danutė Mockiene v Lithuania* (ECtHR 4 July 2017) para 48; Applications No. 62235/12 and 57725/12, *Da Conceição Mateus and Santos Januário v Portugal* (ECtHR 8 October 2013) para 29; Applications No. 57665/12 and 57657/12, *Koufaki and ADEDY v Greece* (ECtHR 7 May 2013) para 44. Cf. Fischer-Lescano (2013), pp. 49 et seqq.

[223] Neumann (2012), p. 66.

benefits of disproportional extend. Thus, all national sources of revenue within the national budgetary policy must first be exhausted (→ para 70 et seqq.), before the solidary community is asked to pay.[224] Only if the State can no longer take control of the situation, e.g. in the event of an occurring confidence crisis on the capital markets despite a State's compliance with the TSCG's requirements, the community has the duty to take care of the weaker.

Economic Rationality

77 Meanwhile, economists controversially discuss the economic sense of austerity programmes.[225] G. *Corsetti* refers to the declining economic growth because of austerity measures. According to him, this is particularly problematic in States with high government debts, as the pace of economic growth is closely linked to the evolution of yields on the market for government bonds. A dilemma as a Keynesian macroeconomic policy[226] is also not a stabilising modus operandi, given the high public debt.[227] However, rising unemployment and burgeoning economic growth cannot necessarily be indicators against austerity policy. Hence, **streamlining fiscal policy** is rather an important building block to curb macroeconomic instability and lower government bond yields.[228]

3.2.5. Guidelines on the Modalities for Implementing Stability Support

78 The general procedure is substantiated by special regulations concerning the individual financial assistance instruments in the ESM Treaty (Articles 14 et seqq., TESM). In addition, further **specification by the Guidelines** of the ESM's Board of Directors is repeatedly needed, due to the vagueness of some Treaty arrangements. In particular, arrangements concerning the provision of an ESM precautionary financial assistance (Article 14.4 TESM), a financial assistance for the recapitalisation of financial institutions (Article 15.4 TESM), an ESM loan (Article 16.4 TESM) as well as a primary market or secondary market support facility (Articles 17.4, 18.5 TESM) have to be further defined by 'detailed guidelines'. This nested arrangement does not provide a lean and transparent collection of regulations. It rather depicts an interaction of different levels of regulations, which can only be understood by specialists.

---

[224] Kirchhof (2012a), p. 92 points out that autonomous reductions and increases in expenditure must be considered when granting solidarity.

[225] Concerning the state of discussion, cf. the individual contributions in Corsetti (2012b).

[226] Keynes (1936).

[227] Corsetti (2012b), p. 108.

[228] Corsetti (2012b), p. 110.

3.3. Numerus Clausus of the Financial Assistance Instruments (Articles 14–18 TESM)

Five financial assistance instruments are foreseen as measures for stability support in Articles 14–18 TESM. Specifically, these are the instruments of the consolidated EFSF (→ Supplement to Title VIII: Introduction para 11), namely the provision of precautionary conditioned credit lines (Article 14 TESM), the granting of loans to non-programme States for the recapitalisation of financial institutions (Article 15 TESM), ESM loans (Article 16 TESM), the buying-up of government bonds on secondary market (Article 18 TESM) and the direct purchase of a MS's bonds on the primary market (Article 17 TESM).[229] The individual instruments are defined within the ESM Guidelines, which contain binding conditional and procedural requirements for the use of those instruments. In the course of the sovereign debt crisis, the Heads of State and Government of the EA decided in their summit declaration of 29 June 2012 that the ESM would have the option of directly intervening the recapitalisation of banks after a resolution is given by the Board of Governors.[230] To comply with the Summit Declaration, the Board of Governors decided to make a corresponding amendment to the ESM toolbox set out in Article 19 TESM, on 8 December 2014 (→ para 97 et seqq.).[231]

79

3.3.1. ESM-Loans (Article 16 TESM)

The ESM may provide stability support in the form of a loan to a MS whose regular access to market funding is threatened or likely to be affected.[232] In the event of a threat to the financial stability of the EA (→ para 59 et seq.),[233] the ESM's Board of Governors decides to **grant stability support** to the ESM member **in the form of a loan**, based on a debt **sustainability analyses** by the *Troika* (Article 13.2 TESM in conjunction with Article 2.2 of the ESM Guideline on Loans).[234]

80

The lending facility of the MS is granted under a **financial assistance facility agreement** similar to a stand-by arrangement of the IMF (Article 16.1, 16.3 TESM). Therefore, the EA countries have used the practice of the IMF for orientation regarding the modalities of financial support from the ESM. The stand-by arrangement is thus the most commonly used form of loan interventions by the

81

---

[229] Conclusions of the Heads of State and Government of the Member States of the euro area, 11 March 2011, No. 5; Declaration by the Heads of State and Government of the Member States and the EU Institutions, 21 July 2011, No. 8.

[230] Euro Area Summit Statement of 29 June 2012. Available at https://www.consilium.europa.eu/media/21400/20120629-euro-area-summit-statement-en.pdf.

[231] ESM Press Release of 8 December 2014, ESM direct bank recapitalisation instrument adopted.

[232] Article 1 sentence 1 of the ESM Guidelines on Loans; ESM Annual Report 2014, p. 64.

[233] Article 13.1 point (a) TESM in conjunction with Article 2.1 point (a) of the ESM Guideline on Loans.

[234] Article 13.1 point (b) TESM in conjunction with Article 2.1 point (b) of the ESM Guideline on Loans.

fund.[235] The loan conditions and the requirements for granting the ESM loan are—as in the case of Greece[236]—established by a stand-by arrangement.

82   To restore capital market refinancing and to ensure a sustainable economic and financial environment, the loan facility is linked to a **macroeconomic adjustment programme**. The latter is passed by the MS in agreement with the Commission in liaison with the ECB and, if possible, involving the IMF.[237] The disbursement of individual loan tranches will be linked to the adjustment programme's implementation, which was agreed upon in a MoU.[238]

83   **Monitoring compliance** is carried out by the European Commission in cooperation with the ECB and, if possible, together with the IMF.[239] The ESM member is required **to cooperate with the Troika** and to enable the ESM to analyse financial developments. If the country deviates significantly from the macroeconomic adjustment programme, the Board of Governors may decide at proposal of the European Commission, to **temporarily** suspend the **disbursement** of further tranches.[240] A new authorisation of disbursement is made by the Board of Governors, which activates the standard procedure under Article 3.3 of the ESM Guideline on Loans.

84   As first Member State, the Board of Governors on **8 May 2013** granted an assistance programme **amounting to EUR 9 billion** to the **Republic of Cyprus**.[241] The IMF contributed by committing to a loan of EUR 1 billion.[242] However, the financial requirements of Cyprus up to the year 2016 were significantly higher than the amount granted by ESM and the IMF. The country had to raise EUR 13 billion independently, among other things by cuts in the budget, tax increases and privatisations.[243] Out of the total of EUR 10 billion financial assistance, EUR 4.1 billion were intended to be used for the repayment of loans and the repayment of expiring government bonds. EUR 3.4 billion were reserved to close the gaps in the budget of the Republic of Cyprus in the coming years. The remaining EUR 2.5 billion were meant to serve to equip the banking sector beyond the two largest institutions—the Bank of Cyprus and Laiki Bank—with new capital.[244] It was explicitly stated that the loans were not to be used as financial support for Laiki Bank and the Bank of Cyprus. The money, required for the conversion of these two banks, had to be paid

---

[235] Krajewski (2006), p. 242 para 771.

[236] Loan Facility Agreement of 8 May 2010.

[237] Article 1 sentence 2 of the ESM Guidelines on Loans in conjunction with Article 7.2 of Regulation 472/2013.

[238] Article 13.3 TESM in conjunction with Article 2.3 point (a) of the ESM Guidelines on Loans.

[239] Article 13.7 TESM in conjunction with Article 4.1 of the ESM Guideline on Loans.

[240] Article 13.7 TESM in conjunction with Articles 4.2 and 4.3 of the ESM Guideline on Loans.

[241] For a presentation of the cornerstones of the Cypriot programme, see European Stability Mechanism (2019), pp. 261 et seqq.

[242] German Federal Ministry for Finance, BT-Drs. 17/13060, p. 6. See also Ketterer (2016), pp. 112 et seqq.

[243] German Federal Ministry for Finance, BT-Drs. 17/13060, pp. 4 et seq.

[244] German Federal Ministry for Finance, BT-Drs. 17/13060, p. 4.

by their shareholders and creditors instead.[245] The ESM programme for the Republic of Cyprus ended on 31 March 2016. In total, ESM disbursed EUR 6.3 billion in loans. The country is obliged to pay off these loans by the year 2031. The IMF programme for the Republic of Cyprus has ended on 7 March 2016.[246]

Following the expiry of the second EFSF-funded rescue package for **Greece** on 30 June 2015, the Hellenic Republic applied for stability assistance from the ESM on 8 July 2015.[247] The subsequently negotiated assistance programme ran for three years until 20 August 2018. In return for implementing a macroeconomic adjustment programme, Greece received loans of up **to EUR 86 billion**.[248] The first instalment of **EUR 26 billion** was given out one day after several national parliaments had ratified the package and the Board of Governors had formally approved on 19 August 2015. Out of this first tranche, EUR 16 billion were earmarked exclusively for Greece's short-term repayment obligations towards external creditors. Furthermore EUR 10 billion were intended for capital grants to Greek banks or for costs arising from possible winding-up of institutions.[249] The second tranche with a volume of EUR 10.3 billion was released in June 2016.[250] The maximum term of the loan is 32.5 years.[251]

85

For the time being, an **involvement of the IMF** in the third rescue package was not intended. The Washington institution rejected a swift decision on the participation and did not want to make a final decision until after the implementation of important reforms in Greece. At an early stage, IMF officials pointed out that the agreement between Greece and the ESM was too ambitious and the saving criteria were not realistic. The country's debt sustainability could only be achieved through further debt relief measures.[252] The willingness of the Europeans to debt restructuring thus becomes the basic condition for further involvement of the IMF (→ para 57).

---

[245] German Federal Ministry for Finance, BT-Drs. 17/13060, pp. 3, 9 et seqq., 43 et seq., 59 et seqq.

[246] German Federal Ministry for Finance, Overview of European financial assistance (30 June 2020), p. 14. Available at http://www.bundesfinanzministerium.de/Content/DE/Standardartikel/Themen/Europa/Stabilisierung_des_Euro/europaeische-finanzhilfen-im-ueberblick-pdf.pdf?__blob=publicationFile&v=23.

[247] German Federal Ministry for Finance, Overview of European financial assistance (30 June 2020), p. 15.

[248] Assessment of Greece's financing needs, BT-Drs. 18/5780, Annex 5.

[249] German Federal Ministry for Finance, BT-Drs. 18/5780, p. 5.

[250] German Federal Ministry for Finance, Overview of European financial assistance (30 June 2020), p. 15.

[251] German Federal Ministry for Finance, BT-Drs. 18/5780, p. 5.

[252] German Federal Ministry for Finance, BT-Drs. 18/5590, p. 6; German Federal Ministry for Finance, BT-Drs. 18/5780, p. 6. On the possibility of a debt restructuring under EU law, see Steinbach (2016), pp. 223 et seqq.

3.3.2. Precautionary Financial Assistance (Article 14 TESM)

86 To increase the effectiveness of the crisis mechanism and to ensure efficient operation, Member States have implemented **additional preventive measures** in the context of the EFSF's revision, which have been included in the ESM toolbox and can be applied in support of a sound budgetary policy.

87 Following the IMF's approach,[253] MS exposed to pressure by risk surcharges on the financial markets can obtain a flexible credit line even **before financial difficulties arise** (precautionary financial assistance).[254] The instrument is intended primarily to support MS with sound economic and fiscal policies that are **not ESM programme States** but are threatened by the contagion effects of the financial crisis in other MS. In this way, countries with sound fundamentals can continue to refinance in the capital markets as the country's credibility is strengthened by 'ensuring an adequate safety-net'.[255]

88 Due to a **Precautionary Conditioned Credit Line** (PCCL) and an **Enhanced Conditions Credit Line** (ECCL) the preventive granting of credit can take place in two ways.[256] The allocation of a credit line and the conditions attached to it depend on a State's economic fundamentals. MS receiving a PCCL already have sound fundamentals. Assignment criteria include compliance with the requirements of the SGP, sustainable general governmental debt, compliance with the EIP, access to capital markets on reasonable terms, a sustainable external balance and a stable banking system.[257] The reform of the ESM Treaty (2021) aims to make precautionary assistance more accessible and transparent. To make the conditions for the approval of a PCCL more transparent, the MS have substantiated these provisions through quantitative figures.[258] Accordingly, the applicant MS must prove that it has complied with the 1:20 rule of the Fiscal Treaty in the previous two years in addition to the Maastricht criteria.[259] Under this regime, once an ESM member meets the eligibility criteria, it is no longer required to conclude a MoU. Strict conditionality is thereby replaced by a simplified conditionality, documented in a Letter of Intent, instead of a MoU. If these parameters are met, it will be sufficient if the beneficiary MS agrees to continue ensuring these relevant criteria in the future.[260] ECCL, on the other hand, is available to MS whose overall economic fundamentals remain solid, but who are nevertheless unable to meet some PCCL

---

[253] German Central Bank, Worldwide Organizations and Committees in the Field of Currency and Economy, 2003, p. 37.

[254] Article 14.1 TESM in conjunction with Article 1 of the ESM Guideline on Precautionary Financial Assistance.

[255] Article 1 of the ESM Guideline on Precautionary Financial Assistance.

[256] Article 2.1 of the ESM Guideline on Precautionary Financial Assistance.

[257] Article 2.2 points (a)–(f) of the ESM Guideline on Precautionary Financial Assistance.

[258] Article 14 in conjunction with Annex III TESM (Draft 2021).

[259] Annex III TESM (Draft 2021).

[260] Article 2.3 of the ESM Guideline on Precautionary Financial Assistance.

access criteria. Accordingly, the MS concerned commits itself in a MoU, to take corrective actions to address the deficits identified as well as to further complying in those criteria that were fulfilled when the credit line was granted.[261] Those corrective actions are not the same as a detailed macroeconomic adjustment programme negotiated with the *Troika*, but rather a sectoral related measure left to the MS's assessment.[262] It is not to be expected that the new regulation will lead to greater use of the PCCL in the future, now that the existing conditions have not only been adopted, but have been made much more restrictive by the quantitative requirements. At the same time, the practical consequences of issuing a Letter of Intent are not yet foreseeable. Even without signing a MoU, the Commission checks whether the policy intentions are fully consistent with the economic policy coordination measures provided for in the TFEU.

89 To get access to a credit line, the MS concerned must already fulfil certain criteria ex ante, the compliance to which is examined by the European Commission in cooperation with the ECB. From this analysis, the Board of Governors decides unanimously on type (PCCL or ECCL), quantity (amount and number of tranches) and duration of a credit line.[263] The **duration of the credit line** is initially one year. This period can be extended twice for six months each. A **credit limit** is not provided for by the statutes of the ESM. The conditions for the call of a credit line, namely the corrective actions to be taken, are set out in a MoU and monitored by the Commission in cooperation with the ECB, ESA, the ESRB and, if possible, the IMF.[264] The scope of **monitoring** depends on the nature of risks to the financial stability within the EA. To ensure the objective of a sound budgetary policy, a lack of willingness to follow-up on the implementation of corrective actions threatens to result in a reassessment or a complete renegotiation of corrective measures in a new MoU.[265] In this case, the MS can only apply for a loan facility under a full macroeconomic adjustment programme.

90 On 15 May 2020, the Board of Governors approved the establishment of **Pandemic Crisis Support** as part of a coordinated and joint response to the symmetric shock caused by the COVID-19 crisis (→ Supplement to Title VIII: Introduction para 52 et seqq.).[266] As a result of the pandemic and the unprecedented economic downturn, governments have increased spending to address their urgent health care needs. The Pandemic Crisis Support, which is based on the existing ESM precautionary credit line, the ECCL, will be available to all ESM members to **support domestic financing of direct and indirect healthcare, cure, and**

---

[261] Article 2.4 of the ESM Guideline on Precautionary Financial Assistance.
[262] 'The beneficiary ESM Member *shall*, after consultation of the European Commission and of the ECB, adopt corrective measures aimed at addressing the above-mentioned weaknesses [...].' Cf. Article 2.4 of the ESM Guideline on Precautionary Financial Assistance.
[263] Article 13.2 TESM in conjunction with Article 3.2 of the ESM Guideline on Precautionary Financial Assistance.
[264] Article 5.1 of the ESM Guideline on Precautionary Financial Assistance.
[265] Article 7.2 of the ESM Guideline on Precautionary Financial Assistance.
[266] ESM Press Release of 15 May 2020, ESM Board of Governors backs Pandemic Crisis Support.

prevention-related costs due to the COVID-19 crisis. The Board of Governors deliberated based on the preliminary assessments provided by the European Commission, in liaison with the ECB and in collaboration with the ESM, in relation to the financial stability risks, debt sustainability, financing needs and eligibility criteria of each ESM member. These preliminary assessments confirm that each Member State is eligible for receiving Pandemic Crisis Support.[267]

91 An MS can access the ESM's Pandemic Crisis Support by sending a request to the chairperson of the ESM Board of Governors until 31 December 2022. Individual requests for Pandemic Crisis Support must be approved by a unanimous vote of the ESM Board of Governors. For a requesting ESM member, the available amount will be 2% of its GDP as of end-2019, as a benchmark. Should all 19 countries draw from the credit line, this would amount to around **EUR 240 billion**.[268] Once a facility is signed, the ESM can disburse money under the credit line over a period of twelve months, which can be extended twice for 6 months (→ para 89).

92 The ESM members benefitting from Pandemic Crisis Support will be subject to **enhanced surveillance by the European Commission**. According to the Commission, the monitoring and the reporting requirements will focus on the actual use of the funds to cover direct and indirect healthcare costs. For this purpose, the Commission will not perform ad-hoc missions in addition to the standard ones that take place within the European Semester.[269] Given the history of the ESM, it is unlikely that the countries most affected by the crisis will make use of the Pandemic Crisis Support, even if the instrument's conditions of application are limited. In line with its application during the European banking and sovereign debt crisis, some MS are reluctant to use it in the current situation. They fear the stigmatisation that would accompany it and probably also the resistance of their own populations. Italy's then Prime Minister *Giuseppe Conte*, for example, made it clear in April 2020 that he did not want the approximately EUR 37 billion that Italy could call up from the ESM.

---

[267] European Commission, Pandemic Crisis Support: Eligibility assessment conducted by the Commission services in preparation of any evaluation pursuant to Article 6 of Regulation (EU) No 472/13, Article 13(1) ESM Treaty and Article 3 of ESM Guideline on Precautionary Financial Assistance, 6 May 2020, available at https://ec.europa.eu/info/sites/info/files/economy-finance/20-05-04_pre_eligibility.pdf.

[268] Proposal from the Managing Director for financial assistance in the form of a Pandemic Crisis Support, 8 May 2020, available at https://www.esm.europa.eu/sites/default/files/20200515_-_esm_bog_-_md_proposal_for_financial_assistance_-_draft.pdf. See also ESM, Meeting of the Board of Governors 15 May 2020, Summary of decisions, available at: https://www.esm.europa.eu/sites/default/files/2020-05-15-bog-summary_of_decisions.pdf.

[269] European Commission, Letter from Executive Vice-President Dombrovskis and Commissioner Gentiloni to Eurogroup President Centeno clarifying how the Commission intends to carry out surveillance in the framework of ESM's Pandemic Crisis Support, 7 May 2020, available at https://ec.europa.eu/info/sites/info/files/economy-finance/letter_to_peg.pdf.

However, the granting of a precautionary credit line is different from 'using' the financial assistance. The credit line is activated on the initiative of the beneficiary MS.[270] The latter may draw down the credit line within the appropriation period, considering the implementation of the agreed corrective measures. This possibility of short-term capital is meant to already strengthen confidence of private creditors.[271] It gives financial markets a positive outlook on the medium-term development of the MS. With the decision of the ESM, in the role of a credit rating agency that positively values a country's fundamental data, the State is given the time to prevent potential inflationary effects and quickly avert the spread of the crisis. Against this background, it is clear that a 'precautionary programme' is always a **short-term agreement** that has the most effect if it is not needed.

3.3.3. Financial Assistance for the Recapitalisation of Financial Institutions of an ESM Member (Article 15 TESM)

During the sovereign debt crisis, it became apparent that the violation of the Maastricht criteria and the pursuit of a credit-financed consumption policy cannot be described as the root of this crisis in all States. With Ireland and Spain, States that formerly were regarded as model pupil of the EMU for a long time were also caught up in the turmoil of crisis. In both countries, the causes of **emergency laid in the financial sector**, which had to be saved from collapse by State rescue packages. However, **the increase in public debt** because of the applied relief efforts put the financial stability of the EA at risk.[272] Moreover, due to the close interconnection of the financial markets, contagion risks emerged from the banking sector, which could also force the governments of other MS to recapitalise their national banks.[273]

To prevent the dangers of another banking crisis, the ESM may, under Article 15.1 TESM, provide loans to MS to recapitalise their banks. The scope of this instrument initially includes MS that do not participate in an ESM programme and whose **financial difficulties are solely in the financial sector** and not directly linked to the country's fiscal and structural framework.[274] In addition, the instrument is also available to MS that already have taken up a loan facility under a macroeconomic adjustment programme.[275]

The ESM is not qualified to address the refinancing problems of European banks by 'communitising' the burden on the EA countries. Instead, shareholders initially

---

[270] Article 4.1 of the ESM Guideline on Precautionary Financial Assistance.

[271] Nettesheim (2012), p. 43.

[272] Pilz (2016), pp. 14 et seqq.; Tuori and Tuori (2014), pp. 78 et seqq. In view of Spain: Jimenez-Blanco (2014), pp. 347 et seqq.

[273] Article 2.2 of the ESM Guideline on Financial Assistance for the Recapitalisation of Financial Institutions.

[274] Article 15.1 TESM in conjunction with Article 1.3 of the ESM Guideline on Financial Assistance for the Recapitalisation of Financial Institutions.

[275] Article 15.1 TESM in conjunction with Article 1.4 of the ESM Guideline on Financial Assistance for the Recapitalisation of Financial Institutions.

need to be consulted as owners of the financial institution and as the main responsible persons for past recapitalisation decisions. If banks cannot rely on private sources of capital, national governments need to provide support to preserve financial stability and contain contagion risk.[276] In this context, legal measures for the implementation of deposit insurance schemes or the establishment of a *Bad Bank* for the processing of ailing financial institutions are just as conceivable as the monetary support of those banks. However, the Irish banking crisis has shown that due to its size, the financial sector requires support that pushes the economy to its limits. If, in this exceptional case, the State cannot fulfil its task, the recapitalisation is made possible by means of a loan from the ESM.[277] The granting of loans to governments for the recapitalisation of financial institutions is therefore **generally subsidiary**.

97 To obtain a loan to recapitalise national banks, the MS must first address a **request to the Board of Governors**.[278] An independent assessment of the eligibility criteria will then be carried out by the European Commission in cooperation with the ECB and, where appropriate, with the relevant European Supervisory Authorities (EBA, ESMA, EIOPA). The assistance provided by the ESM is tied to the proof of systemic relevance of the financial institution concerned. The systemic dimension is assessed ex ante on the scale of capital shortfalls, the resilience of the financial institution and the extent of the threat to the financial stability of the EA, as well as the contagion risk.[279] In addition, the beneficiary MS must have a sound fiscal policy, must comply with the rules of the SGP and have a sufficient financial stability, in order to not be endangered if the recapitalisation fails.[280]

98 Support by the ESM includes the restructuring of the financial sector as *conditio sine qua non*. The restructuring may take place through various institutional, sectoral or macroeconomic reform requirements in line with the rules of the TFEU on State aid. The policy conditions about the financial assistance will be prepared and defined by the European Commission in cooperation with the ECB and, where appropriate, including the relevant European Supervisory Authorities.[281] The final decision on the loan granting is made by the Board of Governors

---

[276] Article 3.1 of the ESM Guideline on Financial Assistance for the Recapitalisation of Financial Institutions.

[277] Declaration by the Heads of State and Government of the euro area, 26 October 2011, Annex II, No. 5 ('bank liquidity and capitalization').

[278] Article 4.1 of the ESM Guideline on Financial Assistance for the Recapitalisation of Financial Institutions.

[279] Article 4.2 in conjunction with Article 3.2 of the ESM Guideline on Financial Assistance for the Recapitalisation of Financial Institutions.

[280] Article 3.1 of the ESM Guideline on Financial Assistance for the Recapitalisation of Financial Institutions.

[281] Article 4.5 point (a) of the ESM Guideline on Financial Assistance for the Recapitalisation of Financial Institutions.

Treaty Establishing the European Stability Mechanism (TESM)

based on a proposal by the ESM's Managing Director.[282] Due to the enormous **contagion risk** on financial markets, the eligibility conditions must be assessed within a short period and a swift completion of the decision-making process must be secured to ensure the effectiveness of the instrument.

All financial and contractual aspects are documented and **monitored under the special direction of the ESM**, which covers both the monitoring of the funds' use and the disbursement of individual tranches, as well as the monitoring of the specific conditions' implementation. Thereby, the ESM relies on the technical expertise and reports of the European Commission, the ECB and, where appropriate, the European Supervisory Authorities.[283] Monitoring by these institutions includes their right to carry out **on-site inspections** to ensure the implementation of conditions and to inform the ESM, as a lender, of any relevant credit-related developments.[284] **99**

As a first Member State, Spain submitted an official request for financial assistance for the recapitalisation of Spanish banks on 24 June 2012.[285] After the former Spanish saving banks that already receive government grants as commercial banks had triggered a mortgage-financed construction boom over the years, banks were threatened by a real estate bubble by spring 2012.[286] The Spanish State, on the other hand, was no longer able to carry out the required recapitalisation of its banks by means of its own funds, as the refinancing of Spain on capital markets had also become more expensive during the sovereign debt crisis.[287] Thereupon, Spain requested a loan from the ESM to support its banks. After an analysis carried out by the European Commission, the ECB and EBA, the Eurogroup agreed to an **18-month financial assistance programme** with a maximum programme volume of up to **EUR 100 billion**. In return, Spain committed to reform the labour market and the financial sector as well as to submit redevelopment plans for the ailing financial institutions.[288] After all the implementation reports of the European Commission and the ECB confirmed the timely implementation of the programme requirements, a total of around EUR 41.3 billion of ESM assistance were issued to the Spanish bank restructuring fund FROB (*Fondo de Restructuración Ordenada Bancaria*). Thereby, the possible total amount of up to EUR 100.0 billion until the end of the **100**

---

[282] Article 4.3 of the ESM Guideline on Financial Assistance for the Recapitalisation of Financial Institutions.

[283] Articles 5, 6 of the ESM Guideline on Financial Assistance for the Recapitalisation of Financial Institutions.

[284] Article 5.2 of the ESM Guideline on Financial Assistance for the Recapitalisation of Financial Institutions.

[285] German Federal Ministry of Finance, BT-Drs. 17/10320, Annex 1 and 1a, pp. 7 et seqq. The development of the Banking Crisis in Spain, Quaglia and Royo (2015), pp. 491 et seqq. For a presentation of the cornerstones of the Spanish programme see also European Stability Mechanism (2019), pp. 213 et seqq.

[286] Jimenez-Blanco (2014), pp. 348 et seq.

[287] Ketterer (2016), p. 110.

[288] German Federal Ministry of Finance, BT-Drs. 17/10320, Annex 3 and 3a, pp. 35 et seqq.

programme on 23 January 2014 was significantly undercut.[289] According to the programme, Spain would have to reimburse from 2022 onward. However, as the ESM has received an early partial repayment of the financial assistance amounting to EUR 17.6 billion, the annual repayments during the years 2022–2027 will be correspondingly lower.[290]

3.3.4. Financial Assistance for the Direct Recapitalisation of Institutions

101 As part of the sovereign debt crisis management, it has been revealed that the crisis in public finances of individual ESM Member States is closely linked to the crisis in their respective financial sector. Thus, it may occur that an ESM Member State is not able to provide the necessary financial assistance to its financial institutions, without significantly endangering its fiscal sustainability due to a severe risk of contagion from the financial sector to the sovereign or without endangering its long-term access to the capital markets.[291] This would necessitate financing the State's financial requirements depending on ESM funds. To counteract the effects of the vicious circle between a fragile financial sector and a deteriorating creditworthiness of the sovereign, the Heads of State and Government of the EA Member States decided in their summit declaration of 29 June 2012 that the ESM would have the option of directly intervening the **recapitalisation of banks** after a resolution is given by the Board of Governors.[292]

102 To comply with the Summit Declaration, the Board of Governors decided to make a corresponding amendment to the ESM toolbox set out in Article 19 TESM, on 8 December 2014.[293] An implementation of national procedures preceded this decision. In Germany, this required authorisation by federal law, which was approved by the *Bundestag* and *Bundesrat* in November 2014.[294] Necessary conditions for this new instrument were the establishment of a **Single Supervisory Mechanism** (→ Supplement to Title VIII: Banking Union para 14 et seqq.)[295] by

---

[289] German Federal Ministry for Finance, Overview of European financial assistance (30 June 2020), p. 13.

[290] Spanish Loan Repayments, available at https://www.esm.europa.eu/assistance/spain#spain:_a_fast_and_effective_programme.

[291] Article 2.1 of the ESM Guideline on Financial Assistance for the Direct Recapitalisation of Institutions.

[292] Declaration by the Heads of State and Government of the euro area Member States, 29 June 2012.

[293] ESM Board of Governors Resolution, Meeting of 8 December 2014, Establishment of the instrument for the direct recapitalisation of institutions (SG/BoG/2014/05/04).

[294] See also Ketterer (2016), pp. 99 et seqq.

[295] Declaration by the Heads of State and Government of the euro area Member States, 29 June 2012.

Regulation 1024/2013[296] and the **strict maintenance of a liability cascade**, according to which the financial responsibility was rather embedded 'at the source' instead of basically burdening the ESM community.

With the establishment of a **Single Supervisory Mechanism** under a European 'roof', local expertise and experience—including language skills—can be combined with the advantages of centralisation.[297] In addition, the ECB collects and aggregates important micro-prudential data as part of its statistical surveys (Article 5 ESCB Statute) and thus has a significant informational advantage in systemically relevant developments.[298] Identifying these developments is important because only systemically relevant institutions that violate or, in future, will violate the capital requirements set by the ECB as supervisor, can be supported *de lege lata* via direct recapitalisation.[299] However, whether the **systemic relevance** is actually a decision-relevant dimension on the use of this instrument can only be shown by the application in individual cases. The wording in Article 3.1 point (b) of the ESM Guideline ('*should* have a systemic relevance') indicates that this is not a mandatory but only **a recommended requirement**. With such a weakened formulation, the systemic relevance is not made a legal requirement, but a condition to be observed as far as possible. That way, financial assistance can be provided although the conditions are not fully met, given the fact, however, that the provision is deemed politically reasonable by the Board of Governors.[300]

103

The direct recapitalisation of financial institutions marks the end of a **liability cascade**, which succeeds a previous phase of involving private shareholders and creditors ('bail in') and the SRF (→ Supplement to Title VIII: Banking Union para 176 et seqq.).[301] Thus, this instrument may only be used as an **ultima ratio**. This corresponds to the specification in Articles 2.1, 3.2 point (a) ESM Guideline, according to which a direct recapitalisation of banks is only to be applied **subsidiary** to indirect recapitalisation under Article 15 TESM (→ para 94 et seqq.). In addition, the requesting MS must also contribute a level of capital to the recapitalisation operation.[302] If the institution does not have sufficient equity capital to achieve the specified minimum capital ratio of 4.5%, the ESM Member State must

104

---

[296] Council Regulation (EU) No 1024/2013 of 15 October 2013 *conferring specific tasks on the European Central Bank concerning policies relating to the prudential supervision of credit institutions*, O.J. L 287/63 (2013).

[297] Cf. German Central Bank, Monthly Bulletin 7/2013, p. 19; Ferran and Babis (2013), p. 9.

[298] Manger-Nestler (2014), pp. 324 et seq.

[299] Article 3.1 of the ESM Guideline on Financial Assistance for the Direct Recapitalisation of Institutions.

[300] Critically Murswiek (2014), p. 11.

[301] Articles 3.1 point (a), and 8 of the ESM Guideline on Financial Assistance for the Direct Recapitalisation of Institutions.

[302] Article 9 of the ESM Guideline on Financial Assistance for the Direct Recapitalisation of Institutions.

implement a one-off capital injection to reach this capital ratio.[303] Under Article 2.3 ESM Guideline, the instrument of direct bank recapitalisation is explicitly not to be used for bank resolutions. It should rather be used only in circumstances when it comes to preventing future **contagion risks** of a crisis in the private banking market for the public sector. Therein lies not only the economic logic of the instrument on financial market stability, but also its *ultima ratio* characteristic.

105 The use of the instrument of direct bank recapitalisation requires a **request from the ESM Member State concerned**.[304] The further procedure follows the procedure prescribed in Article 13 TESM (→ para 64 et seqq.). In addition to the **conditions** attached to a stability support, institution-specific, sector-specific or macroeconomic conditions are established regarding the direct recapitalisation. Those conditions will be captured in an institution-specific agreement between the ESM, the MS and the institution concerned.[305] It is the responsibility of the ESM member as contractor to ensure compliance with the requirements.[306] This conditionality-mediated influence on the ESM Member State and the bank is supplemented by **the control by the European Banking Authority**.[307] For, as long as the institution concerned is not already subject to the single banking supervision within the framework of the SSM due to its systemic importance, the supervisory authority must be taken by the ECB in the event of a direct bank recapitalisation, under Article 4.2 ESM Guideline. This eventually norms the politically formulated link between direct bank recapitalisation and uniform European supervision.[308]

106 The volume available to the ESM for direct bank **recapitalisation is limited to a total of EUR 60 billion** by a resolution of the Board of Governors.[309] This does not increase the upper liability cap of Article 8.5 TESM (→ para 25 et seq.), but rather limits the volume of instruments to a share of the total lending volume available. In

---

[303] Article 9.1 point (a) of the ESM Guideline on Financial Assistance for the Direct Recapitalisation of Institutions.

[304] Article 4.1 of the ESM Guideline on Financial Assistance for the Direct Recapitalisation of Institutions.

[305] Articles 1.4, 4.7 point (b) of the ESM Guideline on Financial Assistance for the Direct Recapitalisation of Institutions.

[306] Articles 4.5, 6.1 of the ESM Guideline on Financial Assistance for the Direct Recapitalisation of Institutions.

[307] Article 4.2 of the ESM Guideline on Financial Assistance for the Direct Recapitalisation of Institutions.

[308] Calliess, Written Submission in the context of the public consultation of the budget committee of the German Bundestag, 6 October 2014, Committee Bulletin 18/0944, Annex to stenographic protocol of the budget committee of the German Bundestag 18/21, p. 7.

[309] ESM Board of Governors Resolution, Meeting of 8 December 2014, Establishment of the instrument for the direct recapitalisation of institutions.

doing so, the banking risks, which the ESM assumes by means of the instrument for direct bank recapitalisation, are nominally limited at the same time.[310]

In December 2018, the Heads of State or Government endorsed a package of reforms to reinforce the resilience of the EA.[311] The ESM will provide a **backstop for the SRF** (→ Supplement to Title VIII: Introduction para 30).[312] On 30 November 2020, the Eurogroup has agreed to proceed with the reform of the ESM, to sign the revised Treaty in January 2021 and launch the ratification process (→ para 151). The Treaty reform also establishes a common backstop to the SRF (→ Supplement to Title VIII: Banking Union para 179 et seq.) in the form of a revolving credit line from the ESM.[313] The nominal cap for ESM loans to the SRF is set at EUR 68 billion.[314] If the credit line is used, the SRF will pay back the ESM loan with money from bank contributions within three years, although this period can be extended so that the total maturity is up to five years. Thus, it will be fiscally neutral over the medium term. The backstop will be used only as a last resort, in the situation that the SRF is depleted, and the SRB is not able to raise sufficient contributions or borrow funds from other sources at acceptable rates.[315] The SRF should be able to access the backstop for banks of all participating MS. The Eurogroup have also agreed to advance the entry into force of the common backstop to the SRF by the beginning of 2022.[316] The Direct Recapitalisation Instrument will be replaced by the common backstop at the time it is introduced.

3.3.5. Secondary Market Support Facility (Article 18 TESM)

The purchase of government bonds on the secondary market is another instrument in the context of a **preventive strategy** supporting the financial stability of the eurozone. The inclusion of this instrument (Article 18 TESM) in the toolbox of the ESM became necessary after the financial markets encountered an unexpected

---

[310] Calliess, Written Submission in the context of the public consultation of the budget committee of the German Bundestag, 6 October 2014, Committee Bulletin 18/0944, Annex to stenographic protocol of the budget committee of the German Bundestag 18/21, p. 7.

[311] Euro Area Summit Statement of 14 December 2018, available at https://www.consilium.europa.eu/media/37563/20181214-euro-summit-statement.pdf. Cf. Term sheet on the European Stability Mechanism reform, available at: https://www.consilium.europa.eu/media/37267/esm-term-sheet-041218_final_clean.pdf.

[312] Draft Guideline on the backstop facility to the SRB for the SRF, available at https://www.consilium.europa.eu/media/41668/20191206-draft-backstop-guideline.pdf.

[313] Article 18.2 TESM (Draft 2021).

[314] ESM Draft resolution granting the backstop facility and determining the key financial terms and conditions thereof and for the termination of the backstop facility. Available at https://www.consilium.europa.eu/media/41670/20191206-draft-bog-resolution-2-key-financial-terms.pdf.

[315] Article 12.1a TESM (Draft 2021), Article 1.2 Draft Guideline on the backstop facility to the SRB for the SRF, available at https://www.consilium.europa.eu/media/41668/20191206-draft-backstop-guideline.pdf.

[316] Council of the EU, Statement of the Eurogroup in inclusive format on the ESM reform and the early introduction of the backstop to the Single Resolution Fund, Press Release 839/20.

deterioration of the refinancing conditions that did not correspond to economic fundamentals and brought a large number of states within the EA to the brink of bankruptcy.[317] The interventions are meant to support the elimination of transmission disruptions on sovereign debt markets and to support appropriate pricing.[318] As part of the sovereign debt crisis, this instrument (**Securities Markets Programme**) has been used by the ECB since May 2010 to overcome transmission disruptions on sovereign debt markets.[319] Furthermore, with the **Outright Monetary Transactions** another programme has been initiated by the ECB in September 2012 under President Mario Draghi, allowing unlimited purchase of government bonds on the secondary market.[320]

109 However, in contrast to the ECB, which is primarily committed to maintaining the price stability,[321] the ESM interventions have **another objective**. For one thing, the purchase of secondary securities by the ESM is meant to provide **liquidity in the markets** and furthermore provide incentives for investors to participate in the financing of ESM Member States.[322] Growing uncertainty on the capital markets had made it difficult to refinance many countries of the EA and had also created refinancing problems for the banking system,[323] which are to be combated by the intervention of the ESM. This goal cannot be met within the mandate of the ECB. However, an exclusive right of the ESM to intervene in the secondary market is neither provided for in the ESM Treaty nor in the Guidelines of the Mechanism. This arrangement underlines the fact that the ESM would reach its financial limits in a liquidity crisis in France, Italy and Spain. Since the rescue package is missing the financial resources as a 'second barrier' against confidence crisis, in the case of an emergency only the **ECB** could fill in as **lender of last resort** and prevent a collapse of the EA.

110 The potential purchase of government bonds allows the ESM to intervene in the markets at an early stage. This is not unobjectionable however, since secondary market purchases only lead to a relief for investors—namely the banks—from the liability for default risk. Therefore, the **existence of exceptional circumstances** is

---

[317] Pilz (2016), pp. 14 et seqq. On the development of yield gaps of European government bonds after the outbreak of the sovereign debt crisis, cf. Bernoth and Erdogan (2010), pp. 12 et seqq.

[318] Article 18.1 TESM in conjunction with Article 1 of the ESM Guideline on Secondary Market Support Facility.

[319] ECB Decision ECB/2010/5 *establishing a securities markets programme*, O.J. L 124/8 (2010). On the role of the ECB in tackling the financial and sovereign debt crisis, cf. Pilz (2016), pp. 33 et seqq., 54 et seqq.; Morwinsky (2014), pp. 45 et seqq.; Thiele (2013), pp. 26 et seqq. For additional information on a corresponding economic analysis of the measures taken by the ECB, cf. Neyer (2010), pp. 504 et seqq.

[320] European Central Bank, Press Release: Technical features of Outright Monetary Transactions, 6 September 2012. See also Pilz (2016), p. 36.

[321] Blanke and Pilz, in von Mangoldt, Klein, and Starck (2018), Article 88 GG para 65 et seq.

[322] Article 1 of the ESM Guideline on Secondary Market Support Facility.

[323] Pilz (2016), pp. 11 et seqq.

absolutely necessary to prevent the danger of 'moral hazard'. In this respect, the ECB's expertise is of tremendous importance for the stabilisation of the EA.

The decision to buy up government bonds by the ESM is based on an analysis by the ECB that aims to reveal the existence of **'exceptional financial market circumstances and risks to financial stability [of the EA]'**.[324] For this purpose, the ECB will analyse disruptions in the financial markets and assess potential contagion risks. The ECB's report to the Board of Directors and the Managing Director, which follows the analysis, then makes recommendations on the nature and volume of assets to be acquired.[325] To receive support from the ESM, the MS concerned must take appropriate efforts, which are set out in a MoU. The content of the MoU reflects the severity of the weaknesses to be addressed. In cooperation with the ECB, the Commission then prepares the Memorandum on the duration and the necessary adjustments to be made within the timeframe of one or two days.[326] 111

An ESM intervention on the secondary markets may be in favour of MS, taking part in a **macroeconomic adjustment programme**. As long as the countries comply with the conditions attached to the loan granted, buying up bonds on the secondary markets is an additional option of intervention.[327] However, secondary market support can also be granted to MS that do not participate in any macroeconomic adjustment programme. Therefore, the respective State only must comply ex ante with the requirements of the SGP and the EIP. However, if a State is in an excessive deficit or excessive imbalance procedure, it may still receive Secondary Market Support if it complies with the Council's recommendation on the elimination of excessive deficits and macroeconomic imbalances. In addition, the MS must show sustainable general government debt, steady access to international capital markets on reasonable terms, a sustainable external position and a stable banking system.[328] 112

The MS's further **compliance** with these criteria and the fulfilment of the requirements, contained in the MoU, are indispensable conditions for the implementation of secondary market interventions. The Commission, in liaison with the ECB, is monitoring the compliance with the policy conditions and reports regularly to the Board of Directors.[329] If the MS deviates from its obligations, the arrangements may be revised, the conditions may be strengthened or even terminated.[330] 113

The **operational implementation** of the interventions is carried out by the ESCB, which can acquire all marketable debt securities listed in Euro on the 114

---

[324] Article 18.2 TESM in conjunction with Article 3.1 point (a) of the ESM Guideline on Secondary Market Support Facility.

[325] Articles 3.2, 3.3 of the ESM Guideline on Secondary Market Support Facility.

[326] Articles 18.3, 13.3 TESM in conjunction with Article 4.3 point (a) of the ESM Guideline on Secondary Market Support Facility.

[327] Articles 2.1, 3 of the ESM Guideline on Secondary Market Support Facility.

[328] Articles 2.2, 4 of the ESM Guideline on Secondary Market Support Facility.

[329] Article 6.1 of the ESM Guideline on Secondary Market Support Facility.

[330] Article 6.5 of the ESM Guideline on Secondary Market Support Facility.

secondary market. After the purchased bonds are booked in the ESM's deposit, the bonds can be held to maturity, sold back to the beneficiary ESM member or used for repos with commercial banks to support the liquidity management of the ESM.[331]

3.3.6. Primary Market Support Facility (Article 17 TESM)

115 To maximise the cost-efficiency of the financial assistance under other programmes, the ESM may decide to arrange for the purchase of bonds of an ESM member under strict conditions in the primary market.[332] Main instruments remain the regular ESM loan under a macroeconomic adjustment programme (→ para 69 et seqq.) and precautionary credit lines (→ para 86 et seqq.).[333] However, the financial assistance will only have an effective impact if the concerned MS is able to incur new debts on reasonable terms on the capital markets. Therefore, in parallel with an on-going loan facility, the ESM can also become active through **purchases on the primary market** to give the beneficiary MS time to regain the confidence of the capital markets. ESM's interventions in the primary market for government bonds allow the respective State to continue placing government bonds on the primary market and trade them at reasonable rates. The price adjustment on the secondary markets will thus be avoided, giving this country the opportunity to incur new debts at the lowest possible cost.

116 The financial support to a MS by means of an intervention on the primary market is usually supplemented by an on-going assistance programme. The Board of Directors unanimously approves the use of the support facility on primary markets, based on the Managing Director's proposal.[334] The Board of Directors decision is based on a report by the European Commission in liaison with the ECB on the compliance by the beneficiary state with the policy conditionality attached to the assistance facility.[335] In the context of **the prohibition of direct purchase of government bonds by the ECB**, as set out in Article 123.1 TFEU, the Contracting States have waived to base the primary market support on ECB participation, analogically to the case of participation in secondary market intervention (→ para 104 et seqq.).

117 To maximise the cost-effectiveness of ESM funds, the measure of primary market purchases should only be taken at the end of a loan facility, when a MS would be ready to return to the capital markets. However, a Primary Market Support Facility can also be carried out at an earlier stage, as interest rate spreads often have risen even further, after a country has applied for financial assistance.

---

[331] Article 7.1 of the ESM Guideline on Secondary Market Support Facility.

[332] Cf. Conclusions of the Heads of State and Government of the Member States of the euro area, 11 March 2011, No. 5; Article 17.1 TESM in conjunction with Article 1 of the ESM Guideline on the Primary Market Support Facility.

[333] Article 1 of the ESM Guideline on the Primary Market Support Facility.

[334] Article 3.1 of the ESM Guideline on the Primary Market Support Facility.

[335] Articles 17.5, 13.7 TESM in conjunction with Article 2.3 of the ESM Guideline on the Primary Market Support Facility.

Nevertheless, it is advisable to see the purchase of government bonds on primary markets only as a supplement to an on-going assistance programme. It is only in this way that it corresponds to the **exceptional nature** of the instrument and thus can contribute to the development of highest possible cost-efficiency of ESM funds already being used.

3.3.7. Review of the List of Financial Assistance Instruments (Article 19 TESM)

118 The Board of Governors may review, amend and supplement the list of financial assistance instruments **by mutual agreement**.[336] In doing so, the ESM Treaty itself sets legal limits with regard to the introduction of new financial assistance instruments. Thus, decisions by the Board of Governors must not contradict the ESM Treaty, which may only be amended in a formal agreement by all MS. Otherwise, the Board of Governors could become 'Master of the Treaty' and take away the MS' chance to contribute to the further development of the Treaty. In this respect, the TESM establishes a **hierarchy of norms**, similar to the one between primary and secondary Union law.

119 As the TESM is an international treaty of some EU Member States in the normative environment of EMU,[337] the EU law furthermore sets legal limits in this regard. This applies to both, the provisions of the treaty itself as well as decisions based on the treaty. This particularly means that the introduction of additional instruments must **comply with Article 136.3 TFEU**, which determines the ESM under EU law (→ para 4 et seqq.). The principles laid down in Articles 3, 12, 13 TESM determine the content of the provisions under Article 136.3 TFEU and draft the same conditions for granting stability support in this regard. Consequently, the general rules on the principles of granting stability support, namely the definition of purpose under Article 3 TESM (→ para 19), the general principles of Article 12 TESM (→ para 58 et seqq.) and the procedural requirements under Article 13 TESM (→ para 64 et seqq.) form the **benchmark for amendments** in the list of financial assistance instruments.

120 So far, the Board of Governors has only resorted to the option provided in Article 19 TESM when introducing **direct bank recapitalisation** and decided to change the ESM toolset accordingly on 8 December 2014 (→ para 95 et seqq.).[338]

---

[336] Article 19 TESM in conjunction with Article 5.6 point (i) TESM.
[337] German Federal Constitutional Court, 2 BvE 4/11 (Judgment of 19 June 2012), para 100—*Obligatory notifications* (in BVerfGE 131, 152 [199 et seq.]). Pilz (2016), p. 103.
[338] ESM Board of Governors Resolution, Meeting of 8 December 2014, Establishment of the instrument for the Direct Recapitalisation of Institutions.

3.4. Private Sector Participation (Article 12.3 TESM: Collective Action Clauses)

121 As a building block for a permanent response to crisis, the Eurogroup discussed standardised **collective action clauses** for the first time on 28 November 2010.[339] Preceding this discussion was the fundamental decision to establish a permanent crisis mechanism in October 2010 (→ para 1). The clauses are intended to be consistent with those that are common in both British and US law, according to the G10 report about CACs. Furthermore, the CACs are intended to include aggregation clauses, by means of which all debt instruments of a MS can be cumulated during negotiations.[340] Aggregation clauses are supposed to allow an overarching majority decision on multiple bond issues within an applicable jurisdiction. Further announced are also an 'appropriate representation', 'appropriate quorum requirements' and eventually an 'appropriate disenfranchisement clause [that will] ensure a proper voting process'.[341] In the event of a crisis in capital markets, CACs may allow **private sector participation** by facilitating an agreement between creditors on a comprehensive restructuring plan.[342]

122 Since June 2013, the terms and conditions of all new sovereign bonds in the EA, that include a maturity of more than one year, have been extended with standardised and identical CACs (→ Article 125 TFEU para 52). This way, an identical legal implication in all jurisdictions within the EA is ensured. Thus, a consistent internal framework for all MS of the EA is created.[343] In the event of a debtor's insolvency, creditors can thus take a decision by **qualified majority** which makes legally binding changes in the conditions of payment possible.[344] The clause allows the issuing state to either change its payment obligations partially, or rather completely suspend them. However, it is a precondition that at least 75% of the creditors agree or more than two thirds agree in writing. The proposed amendment to the ESM Treaty attempts to introduce 'single limb' Collective Action Clauses that would allow creditors to reach a single-layered majority to have the possibility to introduce a debt restructuring within the bond.[345]

123 Arrangements for a restructuring within the framework of an ESM stability support are not included in primary law under Article 136.3 TFEU.[346] The ESM

---

[339] Cf. European Council of 16–17 December 2010, Conclusions, Doc. EUCO 30/1/10 REV 1, Annex II (Declaration by the Eurogroup, 28 November 2010). For additional information on the political processes and motivations in the background that took place before this determination, cf. Gelpern and Gulati (2013), pp. 374 et seqq.

[340] European Council of 16–17 December 2010, Conclusions, Doc. EUCO 30/1/10 REV 1, Annex II, p. 9.

[341] European Council of 24–25 March 2011, Conclusions, Doc. EUCO 10/1/11, pp. 31 et seq. See also Seitz (2014), pp. 102 et seq. (translated by the author).

[342] Pilz and Dittmann (2011), p. 440.

[343] European Council of 24–25 March 2011, Conclusions, Doc. EUCO 10/1/11, p. 32.

[344] European Council of 24–25 March 2011, Conclusions, Doc. EUCO 10/1/11, p. 9.

[345] Article 12.4 TESM (Draft 2021).

[346] Ohler, in Siekmann (2013), Article 136 AEUV para 23.

Treaty does not focus on participation of capital market creditors either. Therefore, the ESM Treaty only mentions the **inclusion of debt restructuring clauses** in Recital 11 of the Preamble and in Article 12.3 TESM. Concerning the concrete arrangements, Recital 11 of the Preamble refers to the Economic and Financial Committee. The Economic and Financial Committee (Article 134 TFEU) is an expert advisory committee that is composed of two representatives of each MS, the Commission and the ECB, and that focuses on economic and financial matters.[347] According to the conclusions of the European Council from 24–25 March 2011, the Subcommittee to the **Economic and Financial Committee** is assigned to develop concrete clauses for the government securities market, after consultation with market participants and other interested parties.[348] The final version of the clause was adopted by the Economic and Financial Committee on 18 November 2011.[349] By contrast, Article 12.3 TESM only contains the core statement that from 1 January 2013 all new government debt instruments of the EA, including a maturity of more than one year, will have to be amended with restructuring clauses.[350] Thereby, the Contracting States specify the international legal requirement for the use of debt restructuring clauses within the MS of the EA. The actual implementation of the clauses into national law and in the borrowing agreements is, on the other hand, a responsibility of each country.[351]

The provision, arranged within the TESM, reflects a **contractual approach** to ensure the smoothest debt restructuring possible, meaning without first having to implement a specific Union or international law rule of procedure within the framework of the ESM Treaty. The basic assumption is rather that this problem can be solved solely on the level of bond conditions by means of appropriate arrangements. Thus, everything depends on the civil law arrangement of the legal relationship between the creditor and the debtor State, without legal intervention from outside.[352] However, this position is **not an undisputed fact**. Hence, there is an increase of voices calling for the introduction of so-called **State resolvency in the form of a procedural and institutional procedure**[353] that enables the indebted State to restore its budget on the 'course of law'[354] and return to the capital markets. Such a procedure offers the possibility of involving the indebted State's creditors in the consolidation of budget or allowing a fresh start in hopeless or unwilling

124

---

[347] Palm, in Grabitz et al. (2021), Article 134 AEUV para 4 (released in 2017).

[348] European Council of 24–25 March 2011, Conclusions, Doc. EUCO 10/1/11, p. 32.

[349] Subcommittee of the Economic and Financial Committee for government bond markets, Model Collective Action Clause Supplemental Explanatory Note, 18 November 2011, p. 10.

[350] Seitz (2014), pp. 102 et seq.; Ohler, in Siekmann (2013), Article 136 AEUV para 23.

[351] Seitz (2014), pp. 104 et seq.

[352] Seitz (2014), pp. 105 et seq.

[353] During the Greek crisis, there was a call for a bankruptcy procedure for states, cf. Aden (2010), pp. 191 et seqq.; Beck and Wentzel (2010), pp. 167 et seqq.; Belke (2010), pp. 152 et seqq.; Boysen-Hogrefe (2011), pp. 452 et seqq.; Kämmerer (2010), pp. 164 et seqq.; Pilz (2016), pp. 207 et seqq.

[354] Kirchhof (2012a), p. 150 (translated by the author).

restructuring cases by means of a resolvency procedure.[355] So far, a State's bankruptcy is not yet fundamentally regulated due to the dogma of a sovereign's inability to reach the status of insolvency. The internal self-determination of the constitutive people that enables the decision on economic, social and cultural matters of State development forbids transferring principles of civil law, on insolvency of private individuals, to the States. Otherwise, the underperforming State would have to be broken up and dissolved, in the event of impending bankruptcy. In view of its sovereignty, however, a State cannot be made liquid, but must be set for further development.[356] In contradiction to private insolvency proceedings, the management of government debt problems is not aiming to satisfy the creditors, but to reach a 'resolvency'[357] of the State. This way, the State is supposed to regain liquidity to shape its social and political life as well as to secure peace in the future. Against this background, *A. O. Krueger*, in those days Managing Director of the IMF, proposed the introduction of a transparent and predictable procedure for situations of **'unsustainability of debts'** in 2002. This procedure aims at restructuring the debtor state. In other words, it aims to lead the sovereign State back to solvency ('resolvency') within the framework of a court-like, expert-supervised procedure (Sovereign Debt Tribunal).[358] However, 'a new approach to Sovereign Debt Restructuring' has never been put into practice. The proposal failed as many members saw a threat to their state autonomy in the assumption of a restructuring mechanism.

125 During the sovereign debt crisis, the use of CACs facilitated **a debt relief** in Greece. On 26 October 2011, the EU Heads of State and Government agreed on a debt relief amounting to 50% as well as an exchange of Greek bonds into securities with longer terms and reduced interest level (→ Article 125 TFEU para 53 et seq.). These measures were meant to reduce the country's deficit ratio to 120% by 2020.[359] The exchange of Greek bonds counting a volume of EUR 197 billion was completed on 9 March 2012. In the process, 95% of private creditors agreed to voluntarily waive 53.5% of their claims value and exchange the remaining 46.5% of their claims against new Greek bonds and bonds issued by the EFSF. The banks' losses from depreciation are even greater, due to the average annual interest rate of 3.65% on the new Greek securities, which was well below the risk premium back then. Consequently, the actual debt reduction amounted to 75% of the claims. To achieve the highest possible participation, the Greek government announced to enforce the exchange, if necessary. For this purpose, a law was adopted which subsequently introduced restructuring clauses for bonds issued under Greek law.

---

[355] Pilz (2016), pp. 207 et seqq.

[356] Kirchhof (2012b), § 214 para 111; Kirchhof (2012a), p. 150; von Lewinsky (2012), § 217 para 61.

[357] The original term '*Resolvenz*', as publicised by *C. G. Paulus*, has its origin with *P. Kirchhof*. Cf. Paulus (2012), p. 14 (footnote 9).

[358] Krueger (2002).

[359] Declaration by the Heads of State and Government of the euro area, 26 October 2011, No. 12.

With the help of these CACs, unwilling holders of Greek bonds are obliged to exchange their claims by a determination of the body of creditors.[360] Although retrospectively, the Greek debt relief was completely inadequate and could hardly reduce the debt burden. Thus, the euro countries will probably have to carry out another debt restructuring in the foreseeable future.[361] However, a large amount of the Greek debt has now been passed on to government creditors, meaning that a debt relief would hit public budgets and thus national taxpayers.[362]

With the reform of the ESM (→ para 145–151), the euro States have considerably extended the use of collective action clauses. With regard to sovereign bond issues, a uniform debt restructuring vote is envisaged from 2022 (single limb CACs), which makes it impossible for individual creditors to pursue a holdout strategy with regard to individual issues.[363]

3.5. The ECB's Relationship with the ESM

The ECB's role in the institutional and procedural set up of the ESM, raises the question whether its actions seem compatible on the base of primary law. In addition to its active involvement in the process of granting stability support in line with Article 13 TESM (→ para 64 et seqq.), the ECB holds an **observer status** at meetings of the Board of Governors under Article 5.3 TESM. While participation as an observer is not linked to any legally binding decision-making powers, the ECB is responsible, within the scope of Article 13.1 TESM, **for assessing a threat to financial stability**, carrying out a **debt sustainability analysis** and determining a **MS's actual funding needs**. These far-reaching powers of the ECB contradict the institution's mere role as observer under Article 5.3 TESM and raise the question of compatibility with primary law requirements. **126**

The ECB is bound by Article 127.1 sentence 1 TFEU to the primary objective of price stability. Only subordinately, without affecting this primary objective, the ECB may support the **general economic policies** in the Union (Article 127.1 sentence 2 TFEU). The ECB's engagement is furthermore to be seen critically in regard to its compatibility with another 'pillar of the monetary union':[364] the independence of the Central Bank in performing its duties, as documented in Articles 130 and 282.3 sentence 3 TFEU. The ECB's participation as an observer in meetings of the Board of Governors threatens its monetary independence, as in doing so, the institution is clearly involved in a MS's macroeconomic policies.[365] **127**

---

[360] Paulus (2011), p. 140.

[361] About the Greek debt relief, cf. Pilz (2016), pp. 205 et seqq.

[362] Häde (2014), para 37.

[363] Cf. Hilpold (2021), p. 109 et seq.

[364] Zilioli, in von der Groeben et al. (2015), Article 130 AEUV para 1 (translated by the author).

[365] Mayer (2015), p. 2001, already foresees the ECB being deprived of its independence.

However, within the Treaty, provision is made only for a supportive role in economic policy. The economic policy guidelines, also applicable to a crisis State, must come from the European Council or ECOFIN and not from the ECB.[366] Although the wording of the ESM Treaty indicates an action compatible with primary law, the risks are virulent.[367] This presumption is underlined by the legal constraint of AG *Pedro Cruz Villalón* in his Opinion on the ECB's OMT programme (*Gauweiler*). According to him, the ECB plays a 'crucial role' in the preparation, approval and regular monitoring of financial assistance programmes, which in turn has significant macroeconomic effects on the economies of the countries concerned.[368] Therefore, implementing the OMT programme, as a measure of monetary policy, would require a **'functional distance'** between participation in a financial assistance programme and the OMT programme.[369] Otherwise, given the **'double role'** of the ECB, it would be likely that the OMT programme produces effects that go beyond its monetary function.[370] So far, the CJEU has had no objections to the functions of the ECB within the ESM. Measures taken by the ECB under Article 13.1 points (a)–(c) TESM are not in conflict with their monetary policy mandate, as those measures do not constitute a form of active economic policy. The ECB's participation in 'safeguarding financial stability' within the framework of the ESM rather contributes to ensuring the consistency of monetary policy and thus the maintenance of price stability.[371] The ECB's measures derived from the TESM support the Union's general economic policy in line with Article 282.2 TFEU.[372]

4. Ensuring the Democratic Legitimacy of the ESM

128 The international ESM Treaty establishes a legal regime that enables representatives of the MS to make extensive decisions of economic and budgetary relevance. The decision-makers in the ESM exercise sovereignty without being accountable by parliamentary means. This independence allows the Board of Governors and the

---

[366] Similar also Ohler (2015), p. 1005.

[367] Economists seem to consider that the involvement of the ECB in designing and monitoring financial assistance programmes is a 'dangerous liaison'. Cf. Darvas and Merler (2013); Pisany-Ferry et al. (2013).

[368] Case C-62/14, *Gauweiler* (Opinion of AG Cruz Villalón of 14 January 2015) para 143. In its decision, the CJEU dispenses to raise the issue of compatibility with Articles 130 and 282.3 sentence 3 TFEU. This is critically commented by Mayer (2015), p. 2001.

[369] Case C-62/14, *Gauweiler* (Opinion of AG Cruz Villalón of 14 January 2015) para 150.

[370] Case C-62/14, *Gauweiler* (Opinion of AG Cruz Villalón of 14 January 2015) para 145. The concerns expressed by the AG about the ECB's role in the *Troika* were also not considered in the ECJ's *Gauweiler* judgment.

[371] Selmayr, in von der Groeben et al. (2015), Article 282 AEUV para 61, 63.

[372] Case C-370/12, *Pringle* (CJEU 27 November 2012) para 165. Manger-Nestler and Böttner (2014), p. 634.

Board of Directors to take all necessary measures to maintain the financial stability of the EA independently and without external interference. It is decisively based on an institutionally secured decision-making process resting on expertise. The *exemptio partialis*, opened from the perspective of the national legislature, allows the institutions of the ESM effective **governance beyond the parliamentary control of a nation State**. This fact is remarkable from a constitutional perspective, as the consequences of the ESM's decisions are of utmost social and economic importance. Hence, this raises the question of democratic legitimacy of the international financial institution from the European law and national constitutional law perspective.

4.1. The European Principle of Democracy (Article 10 TEU)

One of the fundamental values contained in Article 2 TEU, on which the EU is founded, is the principle of representative democracy. Article 10.1 TEU substantiates the principle of democracy and takes it as structural principle of the Union's functioning.[373] Representative democracy finds its specific embodiment in the **concept of the Union's dual legitimacy** that provides the connection of the civic moment (European Parliament) on the one hand, with the Member States' strands of legitimacy (government representative in the Council) on the other hand.[374] The scope of legitimacy and the control function of the European Parliament is set '**as laid down in the Treaties**' (Article 14.1 sentence 2 TEU). The involvement of the EP is, therefore, also limited by the principle of conferral (Articles 5.1, 5.2 TEU).[375] Against this background, the question of the democratic legitimacy of the ESM must first be answered as to who must democratically legitimise the ESM. The ESM is an international organisation established by an international treaty between the, at that time, 17 members[376] of the eurozone. According to the CJEU's case law, it is a measure affecting the area of economic policy[377] that not all EU Member States are participating in. Consequently, the **involvement of the European Parliament** in ESM measures by means of Article 10.2 (1) TEU, is **excluded under primary**

129

---

[373] Haag, in von der Groeben et al. (2015), Article 10 EUV para 3.

[374] Gerkrath (2006), pp. 376 et seqq.

[375] Cf. Repasi (2020), para 17.36, 17.38; Forsthoff and Lauer (2020), para 30.133.

[376] In 2014 respectively 2015, Latvia and Lithuania joined the euro and thus also the ESM Treaty.

[377] Case C-370/12, *Pringle* (CJEU 27 November 2012) para 57, 93–98. Confirmed by the German Federal Constitutional Court, 2 BvR 2728/13 (Judgment of 14 January 2014)—*OMT-Beschluss* (in BVerfGE 134, 366 [393]). Cf. Pilz (2016), pp. 197 et seq.

law.[378] It is rather a necessity of the national democracy principle that national parliaments make the decisive contribution to legitimisation.

4.2. A Member State's Democratic Deficit?

130   In view of the classification of the TESM as an international treaty, the national parliaments must ensure the democratic legitimacy of the ESM. The **ratification of the ESM Treaty** takes place in accordance with the legal requirements of the respective MS.

131   In **Germany**, the *Bundestag* is to be informed in all EU affairs 'comprehensively and at the earliest possible date' (Article 23.2 sentence 2 of the German Basic Law). To this end, the Federal Government continuously transmits 'updated information on the course of discussions (...)' (Section 8.1 EUZBBG).[379] According to the case law of the German FCC, the wording 'European Union matters' also includes agreements under international law 'if they supplement, or stand in another particular proximity to, the law of the European Union'.[380] This way, the German Parliament is able to give its opinion in the phase of the **initiation of an international treaty** such as the TESM. In this case, the Federal Government bases its negotiations on this opinion under Section 8.2 EUZBBG.[381]

132   In addition to the participation of the German *Bundestag* in the initiation of international treaties, Section 5.3 EUZBBG clarifies the relationship to the ESM Financing Act. The ESM Financing Act regulates the participation rights of the *Bundestag* within the framework of the ESM.[382] Under Section 5.3 EUZBBG, 'the provisions of the ESM-Financing Act (...) [apply to ESM matters] notwithstanding the provisions of Sections 1–4 [EUZBBG]'. The detailed information obligation of the EUZBBG thus remains within the scope of the ESM. Concerning the specific rights of participation, however, the ESM Financing Act precedes the EUZBBG as *lex specialis*.[383] The **ESM Financing Act** proves to be the 'crux of the

---

[378] Therefore, the Committee on Economic and Monetary Affairs demands that the ESM be integrated in the Union's legal framework and evolve towards a Community-based mechanism, as provided for in the ESM Treaty; demands further that it be made accountable to the EP and the European Council; cf. Motion for an EP resolution on the enquiry on the role and operations of the Troika (ECB, Commission and IMF) with regard to the euro area programme countries (2013/2277 (INI)), point 106. In addition, cf. Ohler, in Siekmann (2013), Article 136 AEUV para 18; Häde (2014), para 39.

[379] EUZBBG: Act on Cooperation between the Federal Government and the German *Bundestag* in Matters concerning the European Union.

[380] German Federal Constitutional Court, 2 BvE 4/11 (Judgment of 19 June 2012), para 144—*Obligatory notifications* (in BVerfGE 131, 152 [219]).

[381] Pilz (2016), p. 104.

[382] Act on financial participation in the European Stability Mechanism (ESM Financing Act), 13 September 2012 (available German Federal Law Gazette 2012 part I 2012, p. 1918).

[383] Schäfer and Schulz (2013), pp. 204 et seq.

reparlamentarisation' by providing a concept in Sections 4, 5, 6, which ensures the budget responsibility of the German *Bundestag* within the scope of the ESM Treaty.[384]

Central to the Financing Act's conception is a **requirement of parliamentary approval** for decisions in the ESM (Sections 4.1, 4.2 of the ESM Financing Act). Because of the non-exhaustive list ('in particular') of the matters that impact on the **'overall budgetary responsibility'** of the German *Bundestag*, all important decisions within the ESM are linked to a decision in the plenary of the *Bundestag*. The areas of application include, for example, the principle decision of the Board of Governors on the granting of stability assistance (Article 13.2 TESM) or the approval of a MoU with the requesting ESM Member State (Article 13.3 sentence 3 TESM). All 'other matters (...)' affecting the budgetary responsibility' shall require the prior approval of the Budget Committee of the German *Bundestag* (Sections 5.1, 5.2 of the ESM Financing Act). These include, for example, decisions on the provision of additional instruments without changing the total funding volume of an existing financial assistance facility, or decisions on capital calls under Article 9.1 TESM. The Budget Committee, therefore, decides on 'the way things go' within the framework of a previous principle decision of the plenary. Its involvement ensures the continued influence of the *Bundestag*. At the same time, the competence of the Budget Committee, which results from the responsibility for the national budget, is included in the decision-making process.

133

The constitutionally guaranteed participation rights of the German *Bundestag* and the additional 'firewalls' established by the FCC ensure the compatibility of the ESM Treaty with the democratic principle of the Basic Law.[385] If the Federal Republic of Germany did not have the *Bundestag* involved in full as a parliament, the FCC would have to declare the construction under international law as incompatible with the democratic principle of the Basic Law. From a German perspective, the **ESM is sufficiently democratically legitimised in its present form**.

134

However, a democratic deficit appears in MS where the participation of national parliaments in the negotiation and ratification of the ESM Treaty is not intended for. In fact, the problem lies in the overall consideration of all 19 ESM Contracting States, many of whom make the government act on their behalf—without any parliamentary backing and thus accept a considerable legitimation deficit. This is also confirmed by an analysis of national regulations used to ratify the ESM Treaty. Given its classification as an international treaty, the national parliaments have only **limited scope of action and influence**. Several parliaments have no means of influence on the content **such a treaty is drawn up**. On the contrary, the parliamentary approval is exclusively used ex post to implement the international treaty. The quorum, which is necessary for this purpose, further underlines the low

135

---

[384] Hufeld (2012), p. 143 (translated by the author).

[385] Blanke and Pilz (2014), p. 248.

requirements imposed on the ratification of international treaties: the parliaments of all MS have agreed on the Treaty with a simple majority.[386] The concerned parliaments solely decided upon acceptance or rejection of respective ratification laws, without having the possibility to influence the content.

136   Hence, the question arises as to how the foreign-policy **preponderance of the executive** branch, which has always existed, can be subjected to a stronger democratic legitimation.[387] Nonetheless, as 'masters of the Treaties', the MS must ensure the democratic legitimacy of the Union; especially in case of acting outside the core area of competences conferred on the Union. From a constitutional perspective, it thus can only be a question of whether national parliaments must mandatorily be involved beyond the ratification act.

137   **National legislative bodies** assume the **primary democratic legitimacy** of the ESM. They are responsible to reconnect the executive decisions in the Board of Governors to central issues of budget. The ESM Treaty is directly democratically legitimised by its ratification in the MS. Then again, the functioning of the institutions of the ESM seems problematic. The Board of Governors and the Board of Directors are only indirectly democratically legitimised. As government representatives, confirmed by the national parliament, members of the Board of Governors are democratically legitimised in personnel matters. The sending of a Secretary of State to the Board of Directors and the appointment of a ministerial official as his representative also does not seem objectionable. With a view to personnel matters, they too are democratically legitimised by an unbroken chain of individual acts of appointment. However, there is a legitimacy deficit in the substantive-contextual democratic legitimation. On the ESM, the national parliaments are only involved in the Treaty's ratification by an act of approval. Participation rights exceeding ratification are only established in Germany, Estonia, Finland, The Netherlands and Austria.[388] In other countries, no other accompanying laws, such as the ESM Financing Act in Germany or the Austrian ESM Accompanying Amendment (*ESM*

---

[386] A simple parliamentary majority sufficed in Belgium (Article 167 of the Constitution), Estonia (Article 121 of the Constitution), Finland (Article 94 of the Basic Law), France (Article 53 of the Constitution), Greece (Article 36 of the Constitution, Article 112 of the Parliament's Rules of Procedure), Ireland (Articles 29, 15 of the Constitution), Italy (Article 80 of the Constitution), Latvia (Article 68 of the Constitution), Lithuania (Article 138 of the Constitution), Luxembourg (Articles 37, 62 of the Constitution), Malta (Article 71 of the Constitution), The Netherlands (Article 91 of the Constitution), Austria (Article 50 B-VG), Portugal (Articles 116, 161 of the Constitution), Slovakia (Article 84 of the Constitution), Slovenia (Article 86 of the Constitution), Spain (Article 93 of the Constitution) and Cyprus (Articles 50, 169 of the Constitution). Cf. European Parliament, Article 136 TFEU, ESM, Fiscal Stability Treaty Ratification requirements and present situation in the Member States, 2013, pp. 5 et seqq.; Kirch and Schwarzer (2012).

[387] Blanke and Böttner (2016), p. 253 et seqq., 263 et seqq.

[388] Cf. also Ismayer (2008); Ismayer (2009); Ismayer (2010).

Begleitnovelle)³⁸⁹ exist, which would bind the national representatives in the institutions of the ESM to the resolution of their national parliament. This is because several States, such as Italy (Article 80 of the Italian Constitution) and Spain (Article 93 seq. of the Spanish Constitution), see all obligations to cooperate satisfied by the authorisation in the form of international treaty. Thus, it becomes clear that those States with a **strong parliamentary participation culture** are the northern European shareholders.

However, a stronger parliamentary participation would also be excluded if the MS ratified the ESM Treaty according to the respective national rules and procedures applied in EU matters. The differences in national constitutions on the parliamentary function of control towards governmental representatives are getting in the way of some MS' active participation in European policy.³⁹⁰ This is also the result of three individual studies which systematise the political actions of national parliaments in European affairs.³⁹¹ The studies concluded that the **strongest parliaments in European policy are found in Denmark, Finland, Sweden and Austria**.³⁹² These parliaments are followed closely by the German *Bundestag* and the *Tweede Kamer*, the Second Chamber of The Netherlands.³⁹³ As **weak parliamentary controllers**, however, the studies identify the parliaments in the southern European MS, namely **Spain, Portugal and Greece**.

138

4.3. Technocratic Expertise as a Compensation for Direct Legitimation?

To justify political rule, the outdated concepts of normative democratic legitimacy must be extended; and to legitimise the ESM, it is recommended to use the **democracy model of input and output legitimation**³⁹⁴ based on *F. W. Scharpf*. The legitimation by means of *input* is based on the direct and indirect influence from the people, hence political decisions are legitimate when they reflect the will of the people (**rule *by* the people**). In contrast to this approach, the *output*-oriented perspective measures the legitimacy with view to the results and outcome of the political process (**rule *for* the people**).³⁹⁵ Thereby it is necessary at first, to standardise a desirable quality of political performance and, from this point, to

139

---

³⁸⁹ 65th Federal Act, amending the Federal Constitutional Law and the Balance of Payments Stabilization Act, in conjunction with the 66th Federal Act, amending the Federal Act on the Rules of Procedure of the National Council (Rules of Procedure 1975). Cf. Austrian Federal Law Gazette of 25 July 2012 part I, no. 65, 66.

³⁹⁰ Franzius and Preuß (2012), p. 144; Blanke and Böttner (2016), p. 268 et seqq.

³⁹¹ Bergmann (2000), p. 418; Maurer and Wessels (2001), pp. 425 et seqq.; Raunio (2005), pp. 319 et seqq. This investigation took place before the eastward enlargement and thus solely includes 15 Member States.

³⁹² This conclusion is also reached by Kiiver (2006), p. 54; Buche (2013), p. 368.

³⁹³ Kiiver (2006), p. 54.

³⁹⁴ Cf. Scharpf (1970); Scharpf (1999), pp. 16 et seqq.

³⁹⁵ Scharpf (1999), p. 16.

determine further requirements for the structures of the political system.[396] On the ESM, the question arises whether the level of input legitimation is sufficient to democratically legitimise the international financial institution.

140 The answer to the question of whether an *output*-oriented understanding of democracy can compensate for less *input* legitimacy, depends crucially on the nature and extent of competences assigned to the ESM. It would be conceivable to qualify the ESM as an **special-purpose compound of functional integration** ('*Zweckverband funktionaler Integration*'). In this case, the requirements of legitimation standards for the ESM would be low. The theory of a 'special-purpose compound of functional integration' goes back to *H.P. Ipsen*, the doyen of German doctrine of European law, who unfolded this concept during the qualification of the three European Communities in the mid-1960s.[397] By the term 'special-purpose compound', *Ipsen* identifies the 'relevance [of] tasks' for its communities.[398] The tasks to be carried out, which have previously been fulfilled by the MS, were 'assigned in a process of "functional unbundling" of joint completion'.[399] The functionally oriented action scope of a special-purpose compound does not require any legitimation of its own, since 'all perception of community power is ex ante tied to its realisation by community institutions'.[400] The acting bodies are bound by tasks and objectives defined in the Treaties, and thus are not authorised to enhance or vary these provisions autonomously.[401] Since the tasks to be performed are depoliticised tasks, the 'technical realisation'[402] of which is carried out within a supranational bureaucracy, the **technocratic rationality** of a community is emphasised and, at the same time, restricted in its sphere of action. In this manner, in regard to kind and perceptibility of the tasks of the special-purpose compound, a democratic legitimation beyond the association's foundation is not needed.[403] The theory of the special-purpose compound thus ties up to the model of output legitimation, since the association's competencies are exercised by experts and limited to specific tasks.

141 When looking more closely at the institutional structure of the ESM and its procedures for granting stability assistance,[404] an expert-based, **technocratic, output-oriented regime** becomes visible, the aim of which is to handle transnational problems by the force of acknowledged experts.[405] This arrangement reflects

---

[396] Cf. Scharpf (1970); Scharpf (1999), pp. 16 et seqq.
[397] Ipsen (1972), pp. 196 et seqq. (translated by the author).
[398] Ipsen (1972), p. 197 (translated by the author).
[399] Ipsen (1972), p. 199 (translated by the author).
[400] Ipsen (1972), p. 163 (emphasis in original), translated by the author.
[401] Ipsen (1972), p. 163.
[402] Ipsen (1972), pp. 1011 et seq. (translated by the author).
[403] Ipsen (1972), p. 1044.
[404] Pilz (2016), pp. 67 et seqq.
[405] Scharpf (1997), p. 29.

a long-held concept of a depoliticised policy[406] in the EU, which sees 'the functional detachment of European officials and their dismissal into expertocratic independence' as a necessary and justified approach to enable the EU to achieve its tasks.[407] This view seems to be confirmed in regard to the ESM, which has benefited greatly from expertocratic dealing with the financial crisis of its MS under international law. The focus of interest for the ESM Member States is on the effectiveness and efficiency of problem-solving (output) by independent experts, who are to ensure the financial stability in the EA in an effective manner. Certainly, the international ESM Treaty establishes a legal regime that exercises autonomous and independent public authority within its bodies. The democratically legitimised national legislator thus loses decisive configuration options to the supranational executive. However, does the delegation of subject-specific decision-making competences to an international organisation necessarily require a stronger input-legitimation to control the integration process? The measures taken by the ESM are not an expression of a redistributive policy. Redistribution, as occurs in the context of the fiscal equalisation in federal States, is excluded by the conditionality of the measures.[408] The policy of rescue packages is rather a regulative policy, run by experts. The procedures and financial resources available are defined based on a treaty as well as limited and have been legitimised by the national parliaments (→ para 130). A legitimation which goes beyond the existing level is neither possible nor necessary. The highly complex decisions, taken by technocrats, are in the interest of public welfare and aim to achieve 'good' results. It remains questionable, though, whether national parliaments would have the ability to ensure public decision-making regarding the lack of expertise of the parliaments' elected members and the mechanisms of party competition for electoral votes.[409]

4.4. Conclusion

ESM measures must be democratically legitimised. However, the peculiarities of political rule in the multi-level system make it impossible to transfer the understanding of national democracy to the EU. The legitimation of political decisions within the ESM is achieved through the MS' ratification laws, which have been created in accordance with the constitutional requirements. In doing so, national parliaments solely have limited scope for action and influence, which results into a parliamentary participation in establishing the integration programme that is extremely concerning in some MS. The confidence of citizens in a European-led consolidation policy can only be strengthened if democratic control takes place at

142

---

[406] Neyer (2014), p. 139.

[407] Nettesheim (2005), p. 181 (translated by the author).

[408] Pilz (2016), pp. 71, 149 et seqq.

[409] Scharpf (1999), pp. 24 et seq. In this respect, even the involvement of the European Parliament, demanded by *Kingreen*, would bring no added value. See Kingreen (2015), pp. 2 et seq.

MS level. However, national parliaments must also be willing to control the behaviour of their governments at European level.[410] **Reporting and consultation obligations** of the government towards the parliament, as well as opportunities for participation and approval requirements can provide very effective institutional mechanisms.[411] However, such levers have not yet been established in all EU MS.

143   In Germany, Estonia, Finland and The Netherlands, the national representative on the Board of Governors must obtain a parliamentary authorisation before any decision affecting budgetary sovereignty is made. This concept must be seen as a **blueprint for all MS**. They all have an interest to retain their sovereignty and remain masters of the Treaties even in a system of intergovernmental governance. All of them included the principle of democracy in their constitutional law and thus follow the principle of popular sovereignty. It is therefore the task of the national parliaments to get involved and to provide for appropriate participation in their national area.[412] This means for the parliaments of southern European countries, especially in the recipient countries, that they themselves hold their fate, for example, in regard to deliberations on the adjustment programmes, negotiated by the government with the *Troika*. The parliaments are not obliged to accept the measures proposed by the *Troika*. National parliaments can still act themselves and submit their own reform proposals that help to make the necessary savings in a more effective and socially acceptable way.

144   Looking at the result, however, the indirect democratic legitimacy is sufficient, as the ESM is a special-purpose compound of functional integration. The ESM Treaty establishes an expert-driven, technocratic output-oriented regime that seeks to tackle transnational issues with the help of competent experts. The European officials, released into expertocratic independence, move within a treaty-based framework of action. The ESM Treaty limits the purpose and scope of operations as well as the equity, and excludes the dangers of an extension of powers in a reliable and procedural manner. The ESM's delegation of technical decision-making competencies serves as an expert-driven regulatory policy that does not require further input legitimation to steer the course of integration. Democratisation at all costs, on the other hand, would risk creating a '**parliamentarism without substantive democratic rooting**'.[413] Eventually, parliamentarians in the MS without the necessary expertise could only accompany executive acts as notaries.[414] In addition, the finding that the ESM needs a stronger parliamentary legitimacy than the EEC at the time of its perception of mere functionalist integration tasks would not go without consequences. In this case, the legitimacy level of the IMF or the ECB would also have to be called into question. After all, the ESM cannot be more

---

[410] Patzelt (2014), p. 72.

[411] Patzelt (2014), p. 77.

[412] Pilz (2016), p. 122; Forsthoff and Lauer (2020), para 30.144.

[413] Nettesheim (2013b), p. 49 (translated by the author).

[414] Thus, with a view to the German *Bundestag,* Nettesheim (2013b), p. 50, speaks of 'executive parliamentarianism' ('Exekutivparlamentarismus') (translated by the author).

or less valid than other international organisations or institutions of international organisations.[415] Everything else would create special criterions for the ESM.

5. Outlook: The Development of the ESM to a European Monetary Fund

Since the outbreak of the sovereign debt crisis, the MS and the EU have sought to safeguard the stability of the single currency through Union law under international law acquisitions and secondary legislation. First experiences show that the recent reforms in the EMU have significantly strengthened the budgetary discipline of its MS and banished the threat of insolvency of individual States. Nevertheless, the **vulnerability of the eurozone** and its dependence on external partners is still present. In his State of the Union Address in the European Parliament on 9 September 2015, European Commission President *J.-C.* Juncker made the case for completing EMU to create the conditions for a lasting recovery.[416] To strengthen the path to convergence of national economies, 'The Five President's Report'[417] initiated a fundamental reform of the EMU. **145**

The European Commission presented concrete proposals in December 2017, aiming to further deepen the EMU (→ Supplement to Title VIII: Introduction para 47 et seqq.). This included transforming the European Stability Mechanism into a **European Monetary Fund** and incorporating it into EU law based on Article 352 TFEU.[418] **146**

According to the will of the Commission, the establishment of the EMF is to be carried out by means of a **regulation**. The regulation introduces the EMF into the Union framework (Articles 1 and 2 of the EMF Regulation) and links the governance structures of the EMF with the Council that is meant to approve the discretionary decisions of the Board of Governors and the Board of Directors to strengthen democratic accountability in the future (Articles 3 and 4 of the EMF Regulation). The secondary legal framework is backed up by the **EMF Statute**, which has adopted the provisions of the ESM Treaty largely unchanged. The Statute is annexed to the EMF Regulation and is 'an integral part [of the regulation]' (Article 1.2 of the EMF Regulation). Due to the vagueness of some statutes, there is also the need for **further specification** by means of guidelines. In particular, the modalities of providing stability support should be specified by 'detailed **147**

---

[415] Pilz (2016), pp. 116 et seqq.

[416] Commission, SPEECH/15/5614.

[417] Juncker/Tusk/Dijsselbloem/Draghi/Schulz, The Five Presidents' Report: Completing Europe's Economic and Monetary Union, 22 June 2015.

[418] European Commission, *Proposal for a Council Regulation on the establishment of the European Monetary Fund*, COM(2017) 827 final and Annex to the Proposal for a Council Regulation on the establishment of the European Monetary Fund, COM(2017) 827 final Annex. Cf. Manger-Nestler and Böttner (2019), pp. 43 et seqq.; Zoppè and Dias (2019), pp. 13 et seq.

guidelines'.[419] The Commission thus adheres to the established practices of the ESM and the IMF.[420]

148 The EMF, as **legal successor to the ESM**, is meant to ensure financial stability in the EA. Given the expertise acquired by the ESM over the past few years in coping with the sovereign debt crisis, the EMF should build on the well-established structure of the ESM. The current financial and institutional structures of the ESM would be maintained and enshrined in the Union's legal framework. According to the Commission, **the main task** of the EMF will continue to be granting of financial assistance to struggling MS, which will be linked to reform requirements. In addition to this purpose that was already assigned to the ESM, the EMF also receives **a new task** in Article 3.2 point (b) EMF Statute. According to the draft regulation, the EMF is to assist the SRB (→ Supplement to Title VIII: Banking Union para 301) in its duties by granting credit lines or guarantees and, in doing so, ensuring the **backstop for the European banking system** (Article 22 of the EMF Statute).

149 The choice of **Article 352 TFEU as the legal basis for the proposed EMF Regulation** is not as obvious as the—admittedly short—explanatory memorandum of the Commission would have us believe. A closer look reveals that the flexibility clause can barely support the incorporation of the ESM into Union law.[421] It is undoubtedly at the limits of what can be justified under current primary law.

150 The Commission's **plan to establish an EMF** has so far lacked the necessary political support from the EU Member States. Some (southern) MS want to use the reform as an opportunity to abolish or at least reduce the conditionality attached to stability support. In addition to the loss of State autonomy through the specification of substantial interventions in national budgetary sovereignty, the stigma attached to the use of a stability instrument is also cited as a rationale for the reform. However, this demand cannot be followed within the existing legal framework of the EMU. Stability, conditionality and solidarity are the guiding principles of the ESM, which are also reflected in the construction of the EMU established by the Maastricht Treaty. Every reform must be oriented towards the guiding principles of the Treaty (→ Supplement to Title VIII: Introduction para 19 et seqq.). Overcoming this paradigm therefore presupposes a change in the Treaty basis (Articles 122–125, 136.3 TFEU). Secondary legislation alone cannot create a different balance between conditionality and solidarity.[422]

151 To escape this deadlock, the Eurogroup has been discussing another reform proposal since December 2018, which provides for a selective revision of the ESM Treaty without affecting the status of the ESM as an intergovernmental organisation

---

[419] Serving as an example: Articles 14.4, 15.4, 16.4, 17.4, 18.4 of the EMF Statute.

[420] In depth, Pilz (2016), pp. 69, 149 et seqq.

[421] Martucci (2020), para 12.61; Manger-Nestler and Böttner (2019), pp. 66 et seqq.

[422] To escape the strict conditionality, Italian Prime Minister *G. Conte* called in March 2020 for the issuance of European Bonds (Corona Bonds) that could be used by any Member State under the same conditions. Even the mild form of *ex ante* conditionality attached to the precautionary credit lines was rejected by Italy.

under international law.[423] After the Eurogroup was able to reach an agreement in principle on a reform of the ESM in December 2019, the adoption in January 2020 was blocked by Italy for domestic political reasons. It was only due to the deterioration of the economic situation in Europe in the wake of the COVID-19 pandemic that the Heads of State and Government of the EA Member States agreed on 11 December 2020 to adopt the **revised ESM Treaty** in January 2021 and to initiate the complex ratification process in the MS.[424] The **key points** of the reform are the introduction of a backstop to the Single Resolution Fund (→ para 107), new conditions for the precautionary financial assistance (→ para 88) and a simplified application of collective action clauses (→ para 122). The result of this reform, however, can only be an interim solution. A sustainable situation can only be achieved by amending primary legislation, which is certainly difficult to implement at present. However, the integration of the EMF into EU law and the parliamentary and audit control possibilities deserve unreserved approval on the substance.

List of Cases

ECJ/CJEU

ECJ 03.06.1964, 6/64, *Flaminio Costa v E.N.E.L.*, ECLI:EU:C:1964:66 [cit. in para 15 et seq.]
ECJ 15.09.1981, 208/80, *Lord Bruce of Donington v Aspden*, ECLI:EU:C:1981:194 [cit. in para 16]
ECJ 10.02.1983, 230/81, *Luxembourg v Parliament*, ECLI:EU:C:1983:32 [cit. in para 16]
ECJ 15.01.1986, 44/84, *Hurd v Jones*, ECLI:EU:C:1986:2 [cit. in para 16]
ECJ 27.09.1988, 235/87, *Matteucci*, ECLI:EU:C:1988:460 [cit. in para 15 et seq.]
ECJ 10.04.1992, Opinion 1/91, *European Economic Area II*, ECLI:EU:C:1991:490 [cit. in para 15 et seq.]
ECJ 30.06.1993, C-181/91 and C-248/91, *Parliament v Council and Commission*, ECLI:EU:C:1993:271 [cit. in para 16, 43]
ECJ 02.03.1994, C-316/91, *Parliament v Council*, ECLI:EU:C:1994:76 [cit. in para 16, 43]
ECJ 18.04.2002, Opinion 1/00, *European Common Aviation Area*, ECLI:EU:C:2002:231 [cit. in para 16]
CJEU 08.03.2011, Opinion 1/09, *European and Community Patents Court*, ECLI:EU:C:2011:123 [cit. in para 16]

---

[423] Term sheet on the European Stability Mechanism reform, which was already established on 4 December 2018. Available at https://www.consilium.europa.eu/media/37267/esm-term-sheet-041218_final_clean.pdf.
[424] Statement of the Euro Summit in inclusive format, EURO 502/20, 11 December 2020, p. 1.

CJEU 26.10.2012, C-370/12, Opinion of AG Kokott, *Pringle*, ECLI:EU:C:2012:675 [cit. in para 9, 43, 48, 59]
CJEU 27.11.2012, C-370/12, *Pringle*, ECLI:EU:C:2012:756 [cit. in para 6 et seq., 9, 16, 44, 46, 49, 52, 59, 127, 129]
CJEU 14.01.2015, C-62/14, Opinion of AG Cruz Villalón, *Gauweiler*, ECLI:EU:C:2015:7 [cit. in para 59, 127]
CJEU 16.06.2015, C-62/14, *Gauweiler*, ECLI:EU:C:2015:400 [cit. in para 67]

Austrian Constitutional Court

Austrian Constitutional Court 16.03.2013, SV 2/12–18, *ESM Treaty* [cit. in para 13, 26]

German Federal Constitutional Court

German FCC 12.10.1993, 2 BvR 2134, 2159/92, *Maastricht*, BVerfGE 89, 155 [cit. in para 18]
German FCC 22.11.2001, 2 BvE 6/99, *NATO-Concept*, ECLI:DE:BVerfG:2001:es20011122.2bve000699 [cit. in para 13]
German FCC 30.06.2009, 2 BvE 2/08 et al., *Lisbon*, ECLI:DE:BVerfG:2009:es20090630.2bve000208 [cit. in para 13]
German FCC 19.06.2012, 2 BvE 4/11, *Obligatory notifications*, ECLI:DE:BVerfG:2012:es20120619.2bve000411 [cit. in para 13, 42, 44, 119, 131]
German FCC 12.09.2012, 2 BvR 1390/12 et al., *ESM*, ECLI:DE:BVerfG:2012:rs20120912.2bvr139012[cit. in para 6, 13, 16, 18, 26, 29]
German FCC 14.01.2014, 2 BvR 2728/13 et al., *OMT*, ECLI:DE:BVerfG:2014:rs20140114.2bvr272813 [cit. in para 129]

References[425]

Adam, S., & Mena Parras, F. J. (2013). The European Stability Mechanism through the legal meanderings of the Union's constitutionalism: Comment on *Pringle*. *European Law Review*, 848–865.
Adamski, D. (2020). Objectives of EMU. In F. Amtenbrink & C. Herrmann (Eds.), *The EU Law of Economic and Monetary Union (Chapter 9)*. OUP.
Aden, M. (2010). Insolvenzverfahren über Fiskalvermögen eines Staates. *Zeitschrift für Rechtspolitik*, 191–193.
Alcidi, C., & Gros, D. (2018). *Debt sustainability assessments: The state of the art*. European Parliament Economic Governance Support Unit, PE 624.426 – November 2018. Retrieved from http://www.europarl.europa.eu/RegData/etudes/IDAN/2018/624426/IPOL_IDA(2018) 624426_EN.pdf

---

[425] All cited Internet sources of this comment have been accessed on 6 April 2021.

Antpöhler, C. (2015). *Die OMT-Schlussanträge als Anfang vom Ende der Troika?* Verfassungsblog, 2015/1/16. Retrieved from http://www.verfassungsblog.de/die-omt-schlussantraege-als-anfang-vom-ende-der-troika/

Badura, P. (2019). Das Verwaltungsverfahren. In H.-U. Erichsen & P. Badura (Eds.), *Allgemeines Verwaltungsrecht* (pp. 233–298). De Gruyter.

Bark, F., & Gilles, A. (2013). Der ESM in der Praxis: Rechtsgrundlagen und Funktionsweisen. *Europäische Zeitschrift für Wirtschaftsrecht*, 367–371.

Beck, H., & Wentzel, D. (2010). Eine Insolvenzordnung für Staaten. *Wirtschaftsdienst*, 167–171.

Belke, A. (2010). Lernen aus der Griechenland-Krise – Europa braucht mehr Governance. *Wirtschaftsdienst*, 152–157.

Bergmann, T. (2000). The European Union as the next step of delegation and accountability. *European Journal of Political Research*, 415–429.

Bernoth, K., & Erdogan, B. (2010). Zinsspreads auf europäische Anleihen: Finanzmärkte verstärken Druck zu mehr Haushaltsdisziplin. *Deutsches Institut für Wirtschaftsforschung. Wochenbericht* No. 51–52, 12–18.

Blanke, H.-J., & Böttner, R. (2020). Binnenmarkt, Rechtsangleichung, Grundfreiheiten. In M. Niedobitek (Ed.), *Europarecht – Grundlagen und Politiken der Union (§ 13)* (2nd ed.). De Gruyter.

Blanke, H.-J., & Böttner, R. (2016). The democratic deficit in the (economic) governance of the European Union. In H.-J. Blanke, P. Cruz Villalón, T. Klein & J. Ziller (Eds.), *Common European legal thinking. Essays in honour of Albrecht Weber* (pp. 243–286). Springer.

Blanke, H.-J., & Pilz, S. (2014). Solidarität in der "Schuldenunion"? In H.-J. Blanke & S. Pilz (Eds.), *Die "Fiskalunion" – Voraussetzungen einer Vertiefung der politischen Integration im Währungsraum der Europäischen Union* (pp. 245–297). Mohr Siebeck.

Borger, V. (2013). The ESM and the European Court's predicament in Pringle. *German Law Journal*, 113–140.

Boysen-Hogrefe, J. (2011). Für einen Schuldenschnitt und gegen den Rettungsschirm? *Wirtschaftsdienst*, 452–456.

Bredemeier, B. (2007). *Kommunikative Verfahrenshandlungen im deutschen und europäischen Verwaltungsrecht*. Mohr Siebeck.

Buche, J. (2013). Europäisierung parlamentarischer Kontrolle im Norden Europas: Dänemark, Finnland und Schweden im Vergleich. In B. Eberbach-Born, S. Kropp, A. Stuchlik, & W. Zeh (Eds.), *Parlamentarische Kontrolle und Europäische Union* (pp. 367–396). Nomos.

Calliess, C. (2013). Die Reform der Wirtschafts- und Währungsunion. *Die Öffentliche Verwaltung*, 785–795.

Calliess, C., & Ruffert, M. (2021). *EUV/AEUV Kommentar* (6th ed.). C.H. Beck.

Coen, M. (1995). Abgestufte soziale Integration nach Maastricht. *Europäische Zeitschrift für Wirtschaftsrecht*, 50–52.

Corsetti, G. (Ed.). (2012a). *Austerity: Too much of a good thing?* Centre for Economic Policy Research.

Corsetti, G. (2012b). Has austerity gone too far? In G. Corsetti (Ed.), *Austerity: Too much of a good thing?* (pp. 103–113). Centre for Economic Policy Research.

Craig, P. (2013). Pringle and the use of EU institutions outside the EU Legal Framework: Foundations, procedure and substance. *European Constitutional Law Review*, 263–284.

Danzmann, M. (2015). *Das Verhältnis von Geldpolitik, Fiskalpolitik und Finanzstabilitätspolitik*. Duncker & Humblot.

Darvas, Z., & Merler, S. (2013). *The European Central Bank in the age of banking union*. Bruegel Policy Contribution 2013/13. Retrieved from http://bruegel.org/wp-content/uploads/imported/publications/pc_2013_13_ECB.pdf

De Gregorio Merino, A. (2012). Legal developments in the Economic and Monetary Union during the debt crisis: The mechanisms of financial assistance. *Common Market Law Review, 49*, 1613–1646.

de Witte, B., & Beukers, T. (2013). The Court of Justice approves the creation of the European Stability Mechanism outside the EU legal order: Pringle. *Common Market Law Review*, 805–848.

Delpla, J., & von Weizsäcker, J. (2010). *The Blue Bond Proposal*. Bruegel Policy Brief 2010/03. Retrieved from http://aei.pitt.edu/13911/1/1005%2DPB%2DBlue_Bonds.pdf

Delpla, J., & von Weizsäcker, J. (2011). *Eurobonds: Das Blue Bond-Konzept und seine Implikationen*. FES Perspektiven. Retrieved from https://library.fes.de/pdf-files/id/ipa/08209.pdf

Drudy, P. J., & Collins, M. L. (2011). Ireland: From Boom to Austerity. *Cambridge Journal of Regions, Economy and Society*, 339–354.

European Central Bank. (2017). *Debt sustainability analysis for Euro area sovereigns: A methodological framework*. Occasional Paper Series No. 185. Frankfurt am Main.

European Stability Mechanism. (2019). *Safeguarding the Euro in times of crisis. The inside story of the ESM*. Publications Office of the European Union.

Fengler, N. (2003). *Die Anhörung im europäischen Gemeinschaftsrecht und deutschen Verwaltungsverfahrensrecht*. Lang.

Ferran, E., & Babis, V. (2013). *The European single supervisory mechanism*. Cambridge Legal Studies Research Paper Series, No. 10/2013.

Fisahn, A. (2010). Griechenland und die Perspektiven. *Kritische Justiz*, 248–254.

Fischer-Lescano, A. (2013). *Austeritätspolitik und Menschenrechte, Rechtspflichten der Unionsorgane beim Abschluss von Memoranda of Understanding*. Rechtsgutachten im Auftrag der Kammer für Arbeiter/innen und Angestellte für Wien. Wien.

Fischer-Lescano, A., & Oberndorfer, L. (2013). Fiskalvertrag und Unionsrecht: Unionsrechtliche Grenzen völkervertraglicher Fiskalregulierung und Organleihe. *Neue Juristische Wochenschrift*, 9–14.

Flassbeck, H. (2007). *Carry Trade – Der Devisenmarkt führt die Ökonomie ad absurdum und die Ökonomen schweigen*. Retrieved from http://www.flassbeck.de/pdf/2007/28.2.07/Carry%20Trade.pdf

Forsthoff, U., & Aerts, J. (2020). Financial assistance to Euro Area Members (EFSF and ESM). In F. Amtenbrink & C. Herrmann (Eds.), *The EU Law of Economic and Monetary Union (Chapter 33)*. OUP.

Forsthoff, U., & Lauer, N. (2020). Policy conditionality attached to ESM financial assistance. In F. Amtenbrink & C. Herrmann (Eds.), *The EU Law of Economic and Monetary Union (Chapter 30)*. OUP.

Franzius, C., & Preuß, U. K. (2012). Die Zukunft der Europäischen Demokratie. In *Heinrich Böll – Schriften zu Europa, Bd. 7*. Heinrich-Böll-Stiftung.

Freedman, C., & Goodlet, C. (2007). *Financial stability*. In C.D. Howe Institute Commentary, Issue 256.

Geiger, R., Khan, D.-E., & Kotzur, M. (2010). *EUV/AEUV. Kommentar* (5th ed.). C.H. Beck.

Gelpern, A., & Gulati, M. (2013). The wonder-clause. *Journal of Comparative Economics*, 367–385.

Gerkrath, J. (2006). Die Bedingungen der Demokratie in der Europäischen Union: Ein französischer Standpunkt. *Europäische Grundrecht-Zeitschrift*, 371–384.

Giavazzi, F., & Tabellini, G. (2020). Covid perpetual Eurobonds: Jointly guaranteed and supported by the ECB. *VOX*: CEPR's Policy Portal.

Ginter, C. (2013). Constitutionality of the European Stability Mechanism in Estonia: Applying proportionality to sovereignty. *European Constitutional Law Review*, 335–354.

Glaser, A. (2012). Die Neuausrichtung der EU-Finanzverfassung durch den Europäischen Stabilitätsmechanismus. *Die Öffentliche Verwaltung*, 901–908.

Glomb, W. (2010). Exitstrategien aus den Staatsschulden. *Wirtschaftsdienst*, 187–191.

Grabitz, E., Hilf, M., & Nettesheim, M. (Eds.). (2021). *Das Recht der Europäischen Union. Kommentar, loose-leaf (last supplement: 71)*. C.H. Beck.

Gramlich, L. (2020). Die Wirtschafts- und Währungspolitik der Union. In M. Niedobitek (Ed.), *Europarecht – Grundlagen und Politiken der Union (§ 15)*. De Gruyter.

Grimm, B. H. (2016). *Zur Reform der Wirtschafts- und Währungsunion nach der Krise: eine rechtliche Analyse von ESM, sixpack und Fiskalvertrag*. Nomos.
Häde, U. (2014). Der Europäische Stabilitätsmechanismus (ESM). In P.-C. Müller-Graff, et al. (Eds.), *Enzyklopädie Europarecht. Europäisches Organisations- und Verfassungsrecht* (Vol. I) (§ 17). Nomos.
Hallstein, W. (1973). *Die Europäische Gemeinschaft*. Econ-Verlag.
Härtel, I. (2012). Kohäsion durch föderale Selbstbindung – Gemeinwohl und die Rechtsprinzipien Loyalität, Solidarität und Subsidiarität in der Europäischen Union. In I. Härtel (Ed.), *Handbuch Föderalismus. Föderalismus in Europa und der Welt* (Vol. IV) (§ 82). Springer.
Hentschelmann, K. (2011). Finanzhilfen im Lichte der No Bailout-Klausel – Eigenverantwortung und Solidarität in der Währungsunion. *Europarecht*, 282–313.
Herrmann, C. (2012). Die Bewältigung der Euro-Staatsschulden-Krise an den Grenzen des deutschen und europäischen Währungsverfassungsrechts. *Europäische Zeitschrift für Wirtschaftsrecht*, 805–812.
Heß, J. (2011). Der Europäische Stabilitätsmechanismus: Eine Analyse der Regelungen und ihrer Vereinbarkeit mit Europarecht. *Zeitschrift für das juristische Studium*, 207–215.
Hilpold, P. (2021). *Die Europäische Wirtschafts- und Währungsunion. Ihr Umbau im Zeichen der Solidarität*. Springer.
Hofmann, H., & Konow, C. (2012). Die neue Stabilitätsarchitektur der Europäischen Union. *Zeitschrift für Gesetzgebung*, 138–163.
Hufeld, U. (2011). Zwischen Not-Rettung und Rütlischwur: der Umbau der Wirtschafts- und Währungsunion in der Krise. *Integration*, 117–131.
Hufeld, U. (2012). ESM und Fiskalpakt: Staatsressourcenpolitik für die Europäische Union. In D. Meyer (Ed.), *Die Zukunft der Währungsunion* (pp. 135–156). LIT.
Hufeld, U. (2014). Das Recht der Europäischen Wirtschaftsunion. In P.-C. Müller-Graff, et al. (Eds.), *Enzyklopädie Europarecht. Europäisches Wirtschaftsordnungsrecht* (Vol. IV) (§ 22). Nomos.
International Monetary Fund. (2013). *Staff guidance note for public debt sustainability analysis in market-access countries*. May, Washington DC.
Ioannidis, M. (2016). Europe's new transformations: How the EU Economic Constitution changed during the Eurozone crisis. *Common Market Law Review*, 1237–1282.
Ipsen, H. P. (1972). *Europäisches Gemeinschaftsrecht*. Mohr Siebeck.
Ismayer, W. (2008). *Gesetzgebung in Westeuropa. EU-Staaten und Europäische Union*. Springer VS.
Ismayer, W. (2009). *Die politischen Systeme Westeuropas* (4th ed.). Springer VS.
Ismayer, W. (2010). *Die politischen Systeme Osteuropas* (3rd ed.). Springer VS.
Jimenez-Blanco, A. (2014). Die Bankenunion aus rechtsvergleichender und internationaler Sicht: eine spanische Perspektive. In H.-J. Blanke & S. Pilz (Eds.), *Die "Fiskalunion" – Voraussetzungen einer Vertiefung der politischen Integration im Währungsraum der Europäischen Union* (pp. 347–369). Mohr Siebeck.
Kämmerer, J. A. (2010). Insolvenz von EU-Mitgliedstaaten. *Wirtschaftsdienst*, 161–167.
Keppenne, J.-P. (2014). Institutional Report. In U. Neergaard, C. Jacqueson & J. Hartig Danielsen (Eds.), *The Economic and Monetary Union: Constitutional and institutional aspects of the economic governance within the EU* (pp. 179–257). The XXVI FIDE Congress in Copenhagen 2014 Congress Publications Vol. 1. DJØF Publishing.
Kerber, M. C. (2017). Buchbesprechung zu Pilz, Der Europäische Stabilitätsmechanismus. *Recht und Politik*, 248–250.
Ketterer, L. (2016). *Zustimmungserfordernis beim Europäischen Stabilitätsmechanismus*. Mohr Siebeck.
Keynes, J. M. (1936). *The general theory of employment, interest and money*. Macmillan.
Kiiver, P. (2006). *The national Parliaments in the European Union – A critical view on EU constitution building*. Kluwer Law International.

Kingreen, T. (2015). *Die Stunde der europäischen Legislative*. Berliner Online-Beiträge zum Europarecht Nr. 100.

Kirch, A.-L., & Schwarzer, D. (2012). *Die Ratifizierung des Fiskalpakts und des ESM in den Ländern der Eurozone – rechtliche und politische Rahmenbedingungen*. Arbeitspapier No. 02. Stiftung Wissenschaft und Politik.

Kirchhof, P. (2012a). *Deutschland im Schuldensog: Der Weg vom Bürgen zurück zum Bürger*. C. H. Beck.

Kirchhof, P. (2012b). Der deutsche Staat im Prozeß der europäischen Integration. In J. Isensee & P. Kirchhof (Eds.), *Handbuch des Staatsrechts der Bundesrepublik Deutschland (§ 214)* (Vol. X, 3rd ed.). C.F. Müller.

Kotler, P., & Caslione, J. A. (2009). *Chaotics: Management und Marketing für turbulente Zeiten*. FinanzBuch-Verl.

Krajewski, M. (2006). *Wirtschaftsvölkerrecht*. C.-F. Müller.

Kratzmann, H. (1982). Der Staatsbankrott. *JuristenZeitung*, 319–325.

Krueger, A. O. (2002). *A new approach to sovereign debt restructuring*. International Monetary Fund.

Kube, H. (2012). *Refinanzierung des ESM bei der EZB – Welche Grenzen setzt das Recht? Rechtsgutachten vom 29.8.2012*. Berlin.

Lee, W.-W. (1997). *Privatisierung als Rechtsproblem*. Heymanns.

Lenaerts, K. (2014). EMU and the European Union's constitutional framework. *European Law Review*, 753–769.

Lengauer, A. (2013). Neue Grundlagen der Währungsunion. *Zeitschrift für Europarecht, internationales Privatrecht und Rechtsvergleichung*, 4–8.

Lippert, A. (2012). Das Kohärenzerfordernis des EuGH. *Europarecht*, 90–99.

Lorz, A., & Sauer, H. (2012). Ersatzunionsrecht und Grundgesetz. *Die Öffentliche Verwaltung*, 573–581.

Manger-Nestler, C. (2014). Die Bankenunion: Gemeinsame Mechanismen zur Banken sicherung und –überwachung. In H.-J. Blanke & S. Pilz (Eds.), *Die "Fiskalunion" – Voraussetzungen einer Vertiefung der politischen Integration im Währungsraum der Europäischen Union* (pp. 299–345). Mohr Siebeck.

Manger-Nestler, C., & Böttner, R. (2014). Ménage à trois? Zur gewandelten Rolle der EZB im Spannungsfeld zwischen Geldpolitik, Finanzaufsicht und Fiskalpolitik. *Europarecht*, 621–638.

Manger-Nestler, C., & Böttner, R. (2019). Der Europäische Währungsfonds nach den Plänen der Kommission. *Zeitschrift für ausländisches öffentliches Recht und Völkerrecht*, 43–84.

Martucci, F. (2020). Non-EU Legal Instruments (EFSF, ESM, and Fiscal Compact). In F. Amtenbrink & C. Herrmann (Eds.), *The EU Law of Economic and Monetary Union (Chapter 12)*. OUP.

Maurer, A., & Wessels, W. (2001). National Parliaments after Amsterdam: From slow adapters to national players. In A. Maurer & W. Wessels (Eds.), *National Parliaments on their ways to Europe: Losers or latecomers?* (pp. 425–475). Nomos.

Mayer, F. C. (2015). Zurück zur Rechtsgemeinschaft: Das OMT-Urteil des EuGH. *Neue Juristische Wochenschrift*, 1999–2003.

McGlynn, C. (1999). Opting-out of Community Social Policy: Some legal, practical and political consequences. In C. D. Ehlermann (Ed.), *Der rechtliche Rahmen eines Europas in mehreren Geschwindigkeiten und unterschiedlichen Gruppierungen* (pp. 85–100). Bundesanzeiger.

Messina, M. (2014). Strengthening economic governance of the European Union through enhanced cooperation: A still possible, but already missed, opportunity. *European Law Review*, 404–417.

Morwinsky, O. (2014). Die Rolle der EZB in der Staatsschuldenkrise. In H.-J. Blanke & S. Pilz (Eds.), *Die "Fiskalunion" – Voraussetzungen einer Vertiefung der politischen Integration im Währungsraum der Europäischen Union* (pp. 39–89). Mohr Siebeck.

Möschel, W. (1988). Privatisierung, Deregulierung und Wettbewerbsordnung. *JuristenZeitung*, 885–893.

Müller-Graff, P.-C. (2011). Euroraum-Budgethilfenpolitik im rechtlichen Neuland. *Integration*, 289–307.

Murswiek, D. (2014). *Die direkte Bankenrekapitalisierung durch den ESM. Sind die geplante Schaffung eines neuen Finanzhilfeinstruments des Europäischen Stabilitätsmechanismus (ESM) sowie die Änderung des ESM-Finanzierungsgesetz mit Europarecht, mit dem ESM-Vertrag und mit dem Grundgesetz vereinbar?* Stiftung Familienunternehmen.

Nettesheim, M. (2005). Demokratisierung der Europäischen Union und Europäisierung der Demokratietheorie. In H. Bauer, P. M. Huber, & K.-P. Sommermann (Eds.), *Demokratie in Europa* (pp. 143–189). Mohr Siebeck.

Nettesheim, M. (2012). Der Umbau der europäischen Währungsunion: politische Aktion und rechtliche Grenzen. In S. Kadelbach (Ed.), *Nach der Finanzkrise: Politische und rechtliche Rahmenbedingungen einer neuen Ordnung* (pp. 31–77). Nomos.

Nettesheim, M. (2013a). Europarechtskonformität des Europäischen Stabilitätsmechanismus. *Neue Juristische Wochenschrift*, 14–16.

Nettesheim, M. (2013b). Demokratische Legitimation und Vertrauenskultur: zu den Grenzen majoritären Entscheidens in der EU. In M. Niedobitek & K.-P. Sommermann (Eds.), *Die Europäische Union als Wertegemeinschaft* (pp. 39–56). Duncker & Humblot.

Neumann, M. J. (2012). Too early to sound the alarm. In G. Corsetti (Ed.), *Austerity: Too much of a good thing?* (pp. 65–69). Centre for Economic Policy Research.

Neyer, J. (2014). Deutsche Europapolitik als Demokratiepolitik. Implikationen für die europäische Finanzkrise. In H.-J. Blanke & S. Pilz (Eds.), *Die "Fiskalunion" – Voraussetzungen einer Vertiefung der politischen Integration im Währungsraum der Europäischen Union* (pp. 133–148). Mohr Siebeck.

Neyer, U. (2010). Unkonventionelle Maßnahmen der EZB im Zuge der Finanzkrise. *Wirtschaftsdienst*, 503–507.

Ohler, C. (2015). Rechtliche Maßstäbe der Geldpolitik nach dem Gauweiler-Urteil des EuGH. *Neue Zeitschrift für Verwaltungsrecht*, 1001–1007.

Otte, M. (2010). Möglichkeiten zum Umgang mit der Schuldenkrise Griechenlands und anderer Mitgliedstaaten. *Wirtschaftsdienst*, 147–152.

Patzelt, W. J. (2014). Zur Lage der Parlamente in der Europäischen Union. *Zeitschrift für Staats- und Europawissenschaften*, 68–95.

Paulus, C. G. (2011). Lehren aus den vergangenen Krisen und neue Ansätze zur Staatenresolvenz. In C. Giegerich (Ed.), *Internationales Wirtschafts- und Finanzrecht in der Krise* (pp. 135–153). Duncker & Humblot.

Paulus, C. G. (2012). Die Eurozone und das größere Thema eines Staateninsolvenzrechts. In G. E. Kodek & A. Reinisch (Eds.), *Staateninsolvenz* (2nd ed., pp. 9–32). Bank-Verl.

Peers, S. (2013). The use of EU institutions outside the EU Legal Framework. *European Constitutional Law Review*, 37–72.

Pilz, S. (2012). Europa auf dem Weg zur Stabilitätsunion? Der Fiskalvertrag im Lichte der Entscheidung des Bundesverfassungsgerichts. *Die Öffentliche Verwaltung*, 909–916.

Pilz, S. (2016). *Der Europäische Stabilitätsmechanismus: eine neue Stufe der Integration*. Mohr Siebeck.

Pilz, S., & Dittmann, H. (2011). Die Europäische Wirtschafts- und Währungsunion am Scheideweg – Essentialia eines ständigen robusten Krisenmechanismus. *Die Öffentliche Verwaltung*, 438–447.

Pisany-Ferry, J., Sapir, A., & Wolff, G. B. (2013). *EU-IMF assistance to euro-area countries: an early assessment*. Bruegel Blueprint Vol. XIX. Retrieved from http://bruegel.org/wp-content/uploads/imported/publications/1869_Blueprint_XIX_-_web__.pdf

Pröbstl, J. (2020). Unions- und verfassungsrechtliche Zulässigkeit einer gemeinsamen fiskalischen Antwort der Eurozonen-Mitgliedstaaten auf COVID-19. *Europäische Zeitschrift für Wirtschaftsrecht*, 305–311.

Quaglia, L., & Royo, S. (2015). Banks and the political economy of the sovereign debt crisis in Italy and Spain. *Review of International Political Economy*, 485–507.

Raunio, T. (2005). Holding governments accountable in European affairs: Explaining cross-national variation. *Journal of Legislative Studies*, 319–342.

Repasi, R. (2020). European Parliament and National Parliaments. In F. Amtenbrink & C. Herrmann (Eds.), *The EU Law of Economic and Monetary Union (Chapter 17)*. University Press.

Ruffert, M. (2011). The European debt crisis and European Union law. *Common Market Law Review, 48*, 1777–1805.

Schäfer, A., & Schulz, F. (2013). Der Bundestag wird europäisch – zur Reform des Begleitgesetzes EUZBBG. *Integration*, 199-212.

Scharpf, F. W. (1970). *Demokratietheorie zwischen Utopie und Anpassung*. Univ.-Verlag.

Scharpf, F. W. (1997). Economic integration, democracy and the welfare state. *Journal of European Public Policy, 4*, 18–36.

Scharpf, F. W. (1999). *Regieren in Europa. Effektiv und demokratisch?* Campus.

Scharpf, F. W. (2014). Legitimierung, oder das demokratische Dilemma der Euro-Rettungspolitik. *Wirtschaftsdienst, Sonderheft*, 35–41.

Schauer, M. (2000). *Schengen – Maastricht – Amsterdam: auf dem Weg zu einer flexiblen Union*. Verlag Österreich.

Schefold, B. (2014). In Krisen verändert sich unser Wirtschaftssystem. Wohin führt uns diese? In S. Kadelbach & K. Günther (Eds.), *Europa: Krise, Umbruch und neue Ordnung* (pp. 17–60). Nomos.

Schmidt-Aßmann, E. (2015). *Kohärenz und Konsistenz des Verwaltungsrechtsschutzes*. Mohr Siebeck.

Schorkopf, F. (2012). "Startet die Maschinen" – Das ESM-Urteil des BVerfG vom 12. 9. 2012. *Neue Zeitschrift für Verwaltungsrecht*, 1273–1276.

Schrader, K., & Laaser, C.-F. (2012). Die Angst in Südeuropa oder die Angst vor dem Dominoeffekt. Griechenland, Portugal und Spanien im Krisentest. *Kieler Diskussionsbeiträge* No. 500/501.

Schwarze, J. (Ed.). (2019). *EU-Kommentar* (4th ed.). Nomos.

Seitz, G. (2014). *Umschuldungsklauseln (Collective Action Clauses) in Staatsanleihen des europäischen Währungsraumes*. Driesen.

Selmayr, M. (2013). Die "Euro-Rettung" und das Unionsprimärrecht. *Zeitschrift für öffentliches Recht*, 259–318.

Siekmann, H. (2013). *EWU: Kommentar zur Europäischen Währungsunion*. Mohr Siebeck.

Simon, S. (2015). "Whatever it takes": Selbsterfüllende Prophezeiung am Rande des Unionsrechts? *Europarecht*, 107–130.

Städter, S. (2013). *Noch Hüter der Verfassung? Das Bundesverfassungsgericht und die europäische Integration*. Lucius & Lucius.

Steinbach, A. (2016). The 'Haircut' of public creditors under EU Law. *European Constitutional Law Review*, 223–239.

Thiele, A. (2013). *Das Mandat der EZB und die Krise des Euro*. Mohr Siebeck.

Thiele, A. (2014a). *Finanzaufsicht: der Staat und die Finanzmärkte*. Mohr Siebeck.

Thiele, A. (2014b). Die EZB als fiskal- und wirtschaftspolitischer Akteur? *Europäische Zeitschrift für Wirtschaftsrecht*, 694–698.

Thym, D. (2004). *Ungleichzeitigkeit und europäisches Verfassungsrecht*. Nomos.

Thym, D. (2006). Supranationale Ungleichzeitigkeit im Recht der europäischen Integration. *Europarecht*, 637–655.

Thym, D. (2011). Euro-Rettungsschirm: zwischenstaatliche Rechtskonstruktion und verfassungsgerichtliche Kontrolle. *Europäische Zeitschrift für Wirtschaftsrecht*, 167–171.

Tomuschat, C. (2012). Anmerkung zum Urteil des BVerfG vom 12.09.2012 - BvR 1390/22 u.a. - Verhinderung der Ratifikation von ESM-Vertrag und Fiskalpakt überwiegend erfolglos. *Deutsches Verwaltungsblatt*, 1431–1434.

Tuori, K., & Tuori, K. (2014). *The Eurozone crisis: A constitutional analysis*. Cambridge University Press.

Ukrow, J. (2012). Ein Rettungsschirm für das BVerfG? - Zum Urteil vom 12. September 2012. *Zeitschrift für europarechtliche Studien*, 417–444.

van Duin, K. (2020). The European Commission. In F. Amtenbrink & C. Herrmann (Eds.), *The EU Law of Economic and Monetary Union (Chapter 18)*. OUP.

van Malleghem, P.-A. (2013). Pringle: A paradigm shift in the European Union's monetary constitution. *German Law Journal*, 141–168.

von Arnauld, A. (2013). Unions(ergänzungs)völkerrecht: Zur unions- und verfassungsrechtlichen Einbindung völkerrechtlicher Instrumente differenzierter Integration. In M. Breuer et al. (Eds.), *Der Staat im Recht, Festschrift für Eckart Klein* (pp. 509–526). Duncker & Humblot.

von der Groeben, H., Schwarze, J., & Hatje, A. (2015). *Europäisches Unionsrecht. Kommentar* (7th ed.). Nomos.

von Lewinsky, K. (2012). Nationale und internationale Staatsverschuldung. In J. Isensee & P. Kirchhof (Eds.), *Handbuch des Staatsrechts der Bundesrepublik Deutschland (§ 217)* (Vol. X, 3rd ed.). C.F. Müller.

von Mangoldt, H., Klein, F., & Starck, C. (2018). *Kommentar zum Grundgesetz. Bd. II* (7th ed.). Franz Vahlen.

von Ondarza, N. (2014). Die vertragliche und außervertragliche verstärkte Zusammenarbeit als Katalysator einer engeren Integrationsgemeinschaft. In H.-J. Blanke & S. Pilz (Eds.), *Die "Fiskalunion" – Voraussetzungen einer Vertiefung der politischen Integration im Währungsraum der Europäischen Union* (pp. 149–169). Mohr Siebeck.

Weber, A. (2014). Grundzüge europa- und völkerrechtlich normierter Krisensteuerung zur Gewährleistung von Haushaltsdisziplin. In H.-J. Blanke & S. Pilz (Eds.), *Die "Fiskalunion" – Voraussetzungen einer Vertiefung der politischen Integration im Währungsraum der Europäischen Union* (pp. 3–23). Mohr Siebeck.

Weiß, W. (2014). Das deutsche Bundesverfassungsgericht und der ESM: Verfassungsjustiz an den Grenzen der Justiziabilität. In P. Hilpold & W. Steinmair (Eds.), *Neue europäische Finanzarchitektur: Die Reform der WWU* (pp. 113–142). Springer.

Wiesner, C. (2016). Demokratie- und Gewaltenteilung in der Euro-Finanzhilfenpolitik. *Zeitschrift für Politikwissenschaft, Sonderheft, 1*, 231–247.

Zeitler, H. (1979). Einvernehmen und Benehmen im Bauplanungsrecht. In T. Maunz (Ed.), *Verwaltung und Rechtsbindung, Festschrift zum hundertjährigen Bestehen des Bayerischen Verwaltungsgerichtshofs* (pp. 51–64). Boorberg.

Zoppè, A., & Dias, C. (2019). *The European Stability Mechanism: Main Features, Instruments and Accountability*. European Parliament Economic Governance Support Unit (EGOV), PE 497.755 - 14 February 2019. Retrieved from http://www.europarl.europa.eu/RegData/etudes/BRIE/2014/497755/IPOL-ECON_NT(2014)497755_EN.pdf

Fiscal Union

Contents

1. On the Term 'Fiscal Union' and the Scope of this Contribution 1
2. Primary Law Prerequisites 7
   2.1. EU Competence for Budgetary Surveillance 7
   2.2. Member States' Competence to Conclude the TSCG 11
3. The Obligation to Avoid Excessive Deficits After the Fiscal Compact 16
   3.1. Reference Criteria 16
   3.2. Exemptions from the Reference Criteria 19
   3.3. Balanced Budget Rule, Medium-Term Objective, Automatic Correction Mechanism 25
   3.4. Obligations to Implement Rules in National Law 34
   3.5. Deficit Procedure 40
        3.5.1. New Sanctions and Reverse Qualified Majority Voting 41
        3.5.2. Article 7 TSCG 45
        3.5.3. Economic Partnership Programmes and Reporting Requirements 49
   3.6. ECJ and Commission's Competences Under the TSCG 53
4. Multilateral Surveillance 60
   4.1. The 'Surveillance-Cycle' 60
        4.1.1. European Semester: Economic Policy Coordination 60
        4.1.2. 'National Semester': Monitoring of Budgetary Policies 63
   4.2. Multilateral Surveillance Procedure 68
        4.2.1. New Sanctions and Reverse Qualified Majority Voting 70
        4.2.2. Enhanced Surveillance 74
   4.3. Coordination by Coercion 79
        4.3.1. The Legal Status of the European Semester Instruments 79
        4.3.2. Consequences of Non-Compliance 86
   4.4. European Fiscal Board 91
5. The Way Forward: Completing EMU? 92
   5.1. State of Debate and 'Constitutional' Limits 92
   5.2. Selected Proposals 100
        5.2.1. European Safe Asset 101
        5.2.2. Macroeconomic Stabilisation Function 106
        5.2.3. EA Treasury and Finance Minister 109
6. Concluding Remarks 111

List of Cases
References

1. On the Term 'Fiscal Union' and the Scope of this Contribution

When commenting on the 'Fiscal Union' in the context of EU law, one needs to start by explaining what is meant by this notion, since the chosen definition will determine what is (and, consequently, what is not) discussed in the following chapter. On a very general level, the term 'Fiscal Union' refers to the integration of fiscal policies, i.e. the **decisions taken both regarding the collection as well as the expenditure of public resources** (most notably, taxes) to influence the

1

economy. Interpretations, however, range 'from a set of common fiscal rules to the creation of a fully federal government with tax and spending authority'.[1] In the EU context, proposals on both ends of this spectrum are not new.

2   Even before the establishment of the Economic and Monetary Union (EMU) under the Treaty of Maastricht 1992, many scholars claimed that since individual exchange rate adjustments would no longer be possible, a monetary union needed to be complemented by some kind of fiscal union to ensure its stability over a longer period.[2] However, despite such claims, the Treaties only placed monetary policy in the exclusive competence of the Union (Article 3.1 point (c) TFEU) but left economic, including budgetary and fiscal policy making largely in the hands of the MS, thereby enshrining what is commonly referred to as the **constitutional 'asymmetry'**[3] **of EMU**.[4] Fiscal policy integration was thus limited to obligations for budgetary discipline (Article 126 TFEU and Protocol (No. 12) on the Excessive Deficit Procedure) and a rather vague duty to cooperate in a multilateral surveillance exercise (Article 121 TFEU), both of which were fleshed out on the level of secondary law by the so-called **Stability and Growth Pact** (SGP) in 1997. These rules were complemented by a prohibition of monetary financing and bail-out (Articles 123 and 125 TFEU). There was, however, 'no centralised fiscal policy function and no centralised exercise of fiscal power',[5] creating only an 'extremely decentralized system of fiscal governance, where the units maintain[ed] full fiscal sovereignty'.[6]

3   The primary motive for the conclusion of the SGP in 1997 was to enable the ECB **to pursue price stability, achieve stable and low inflation**,[7] and **fight the trend of accumulating government debt**, which was perceived as a threat to the new currency.[8] While it might be slightly exaggerated to describe it as 'one of the most remarkable pieces of policy coordination in world history',[9] the **SGP still**

---

[1] Thirion (2017), p. 3.

[2] E.g. Artis and Winkler (1999), p. 183. Cf. also Selmayr (2015), para 17; Masson (1996), p. 1002 et seqq.; Häde (1996a), p. 505.

[3] E.g. Amtenbrink and De Haan (2003), p. 1078; Lenaerts (2014), p. 754; Hinarejos (2012), p. 248; Manger-Nestler (2020), para 8.11 et seqq.

[4] On the history and evolution of EMU see, e.g. Schlosser (2019), p. 21 et seqq. Interestingly, the Werner Report 1980 still foresaw more centralisation as opposed to the provisions later adopted (and modelled after the Delors Report); see Amtenbrink and De Haan (2003), p. 1078.

[5] Lenaerts (2014), p. 754.

[6] Hinarejos (2013), p. 1625.

[7] Artis and Winkler (1999), p. 169. See the monetary policy strategy statement of the ECB's Governing Council of 8 May 2021: 'The Governing Council considers that price stability is best maintained by aiming for two per cent inflation over the medium term'. Available at https://www.ecb.europa.eu/home/search/review/html/ecb.strategyreview_monpol_strategy_statement.en.html (→ Article 119 TFEU para 17).

[8] Amtenbrink and De Haan (2003), p. 1076. On the history of the SGP, including the far-reaching first proposal of November 1995 by Germany, Hahn (1997), p. 1134 et seqq.; Hahn (1998), p. 80 et seqq.

[9] Artis (2002), p. 101.

forms the heart of the EU's 'fiscal governance framework' more than twenty years after its establishment. Based on what are now Articles 121 and 126 TFEU, the original SGP consisted of a European Council Resolution and two Council Regulations,[10] which substantiated said rules in the Treaties. The idea behind the SGP as the framework for the coordination of national budgetary policies is that MS should apply anti-cyclical policies, using periods of economic recovery actively to consolidate public finances and improve their budgetary positions. When an excessive deficit occurs, the SGP aims to ensure a swift recovery.

To this end, the SGP contains a '**preventive**' and a '**corrective**' **arm**, building upon Articles 121 and 126 TFEU, respectively. The preventive arm, established by Regulation (EC) No. 1466/97, concerns the 'strengthening of the surveillance of budgetary positions and the surveillance and coordination of economic policies'. Within the multilateral surveillance framework established by this Regulation, MS are obliged to annually submit and make public[11] 'stability'[12] or, with a slightly different terminology for non-participating MS, 'convergence programmes',[13] in which they are to present, inter alia, a county-specific medium-term budgetary objective (MTO) and the adjustment path towards that objective.[14] The 'corrective' arm of the SGP, as established by Regulation (EC) No. 1467/97, contains specifications on speeding up and clarifying the implementation of the excessive deficit procedure (EDP). Specifically, it stipulates time limits for each step of the procedure and clarifies the scope of the exceptional circumstances in which it is permissible to exceed the reference values of Protocol (No. 12). The two Regulations were first amended in 2005[15] following ultimately fruitless EDPs against Germany and France, and a judgment by the ECJ.[16] This amendment introduced more flexibility at the price of weakening initial commitments.[17]

Ultimately, however, the **sovereign debt crisis** confirmed initial concerns that the rules in the Treaties and the SGP would not be able to ensure sound public finances in the eurozone and, thus, the stability of the Euro.[18] Even more so, the

---

[10] European Council Resolution *on the Stability and Growth Pact*, O.J. C 236/1 (1997); Council Regulation (EC) No. 1466/97 *on the strengthening of the surveillance of budgetary positions and the surveillance and coordination of economic policies*, O.J. L 209/1 (1997), and Council Regulation (EC) No. 1467/97 *on speeding up and clarifying the implementation of the excessive deficit procedure*, O.J. L 209/6 (1997).

[11] See Article 4 and Article 8 of Regulation (EC) No. 1466/97.

[12] See Articles 3 et seqq. of Regulation (EC) No. 1466/97.

[13] See Articles 7 et seqq. of Regulation (EC) No. 1466/97.

[14] Article 3.1 point (a) of Regulation (EC) No. 1466/97.

[15] Council Regulation (EC) No. 1055/2005, O.J. L 174/1 (2005), amending Regulation (EC) No. 1466/97 and Council Regulation (EC) No. 1056/2005, O.J. L 174/5 (2005), amending Regulation (EC) No. 1467/97.

[16] Case C-27/04, *Commission v Council* (ECJ 13 July 2004).

[17] Cf. e.g. Calliess (2012), p. 102.

[18] Cf. Gröpl (2013), p. 1.

institutional and legal design of EMU has been viewed as part of the cause of said crisis.[19] While leaving the Treaties (largely[20]) unchanged, the crisis thus led to what has been described as a '**dramatic overhaul**'[21] substantially modifying the law of EMU. The overriding objective of these measures was to ensure financial stability (→ Supplement to Title VIII: Introduction para 19, 59 et seqq.). On the one hand, with the establishment of a permanent European Stability Mechanism as an international financial institution, financial solidarity in the EMU was institutionalised (→ Supplement to Title VIII: TESM para 10 et seqq.), calling the market-based paradigm of State financing into question.[22] On the other hand, a comprehensive reform of the EU economic governance framework introduced, along with new measures of macroeconomic surveillance and socio-economic coordination, **further elements towards a 'Fiscal Union'**, namely regarding **budgetary surveillance**:[23]

- Starting with the first half of 2011 and initially based on an agreement in the European Council,[24] MS committed to an institutionalised 'surveillance cycle', the so-called **European Semester,** which for the first time allowed for the collective evaluation and comparison of MS' fiscal policies.[25] It has since been 'the main mechanism through which they discuss their economic and fiscal policy'.[26]
- The **Euro Plus Pact**[27] concluded in March 2011 aims to improve socio-economic coordination.[28] To this end, it focuses on four priority areas, namely competitiveness and employment, sustainability of public finances, and

---

[19] E.g. Fabbrini (2014), p. 64; Fabbrini (2013), p. 5; Hinarejos (2013), p. 1621; Hinarejos (2012), p. 244, 250; Sadeleer (2012), p. 355.

[20] The one exception being the introduction of paragraph 3 in Article 136 TFEU. According to the ECJ in *Pringle*, this provision, however, only has declaratory character confirming the existence of a power possessed by the Member States without conferring any new power on the Union, see Case C-370/12, *Pringle* (ECJ 27 November 2012) para 184.

[21] Lenaerts (2014), p. 753. Cf. Leino and Saarenheimo (2017), p. 171; Amtenbrink (2014), p. 74; Fabbrini (2014), p. 64; De Streel (2013), p. 456; Ruffert (2011), p. 1788; and many further references at Ioannidis (2016), p. 1238 et seq.

[22] Ioannidis (2016), p. 1249.

[23] De Streel (2013), p. 456, 460 et seqq., thus distinguishes four pillars of economic governance: budgetary surveillance, macroeconomic surveillance, socio-economic coordination and financial solidarity. For an analysis of the negotiations of the Six-Pack, the TSCG, and the Two-Pack see Schlosser (2019), p. 45 et seqq.

[24] European Council Conclusions of 17 June 2010, EUCO 13/10.

[25] Cf. Cloos (2011), p. 47 et seq.

[26] Commission Reflection Paper *on the deepening of the economic and monetary union*, COM (2017) 291, p. 10.

[27] Annex I to the European Council Conclusions of 24–25 March 2011, EUCO 10/11. The Euro Plus Pact was concluded between all seventeen EA members as signatories as well as (hence the 'Plus' in the name) Bulgaria, Denmark, Latvia, Lithuania, Poland, and Romania. Latvia and Lithuania have since become members of the EA.

[28] Lenaerts (2014), p. 756.

reinforcing financial stability, where it seeks to create incentives for MS to undertake reforms. However, the Pact is of an intergovernmental non-binding nature[29] and has, as a mere political declaration of intent, which therefore, if at all, possesses only soft law character, not gained much importance.

- Five Regulations and one Directive[30] enacted in 2011 and commonly referred to as the '**Six-Pack**', considerably increased the EU's capacity to exert influence over MS' budgetary and economic policies, laying the foundations of a European Economic Government.[31] On the one hand, some of these acts **updated the SGP:**[32] Both the preventive and the corrective arm were amended and complemented,[33] notably making it more flexible through the possibility to adapt the pace of fiscal consolidation to consider, e.g. structural reforms. In addition, the surveillance cycle of the European Semester was codified in secondary law with this SGP reform. Moreover, enforcement of both the preventive and corrective arm of the SGP was considerably strengthened for members of the euro area (EA) with the introduction of a system of additional sanctions for enhancing the enforcement of the SGP by Regulation (EU) No. 1173/2011. These new rules were flanked by Directive 2011/85/EU on requirements for budgetary frameworks of the MS. On the other hand, the SGP was complemented by a **Macroeconomic Imbalance Procedure** (MIP)[34] which aims to identify, prevent and address the emergence of potentially harmful macroeconomic imbalances that could adversely affect economic stability in a particular EU country, the EA, or the EU as a whole. When a MS is affected by excessive imbalances, which is assessed by using a Scoreboard of macroeconomic and macrofinancial indicators, it is subject to enhanced monitoring known as the **Excessive Imbalance Procedure** (EIP).

- Outside the EU legal order, 25 EU MS concluded the **Treaty on Stability, Coordination and Governance** in the Economic and Monetary Union (TSCG) as an international treaty, which contains 'a set of rules intended to foster budgetary discipline through a fiscal compact, to strengthen the coordination of their economic policies and to improve the governance of the euro area'

---

[29] Gröpl (2013), p. 19. Cf. also Hinarejos (2012), p. 253.

[30] Regulations (EU) No. 1173/2011 *on the effective enforcement of budgetary surveillance in the euro area*, O.J. L 306/1 (2011); No. 1174/2011 *on enforcement measures to correct excessive macroeconomic imbalances in the euro area*, O.J. L 306/8 (2011); No. 1175/2011 *amending Council Regulation (EC) No. 1466/97 on the strengthening of the surveillance of budgetary positions and the surveillance and coordination of economic policies*, O.J. L 306/12 (2011); No. 1176/2011 *on the prevention and correction of macroeconomic imbalances*, O.J. L 306/25 (2011); Council Regulation (EU) No. 1177/2011 *amending Regulation (EC) No. 1467/97 on speeding up and clarifying the implementation of the excessive deficit procedure*, O.J. L 306/33 (2011); Council Directive 2011/85/EU *on requirements for budgetary frameworks of the Member States*, O.J. L 306/41 (2011).

[31] Antpöhler (2012), p. 356.

[32] See Regulation (EU) No. 1175/2011 and Council Regulation (EU) No. 1177/2011.

[33] De Streel (2013), p. 457.

[34] See Regulation (EU) No. 1176/2011 and Regulation (EU) No. 1174/2011.

(Article 1.1). Whereas the TSCG has gained much scholarly attention, its legal significance seems limited[35] given that many of its provisions repeat what is already stipulated in EU law,[36] particularly in the Six-Pack and as far as the provisions on 'coordination' are concerned. On 'governance', the TSCG institutionalises the Euro Summit (Article 12), but retains its informal character.[37] The 'stability' commitments in the provisions on the '**Fiscal Compact**' (Articles 3 to 8) reinforce and complement existing EU rules. In particular, considering that sound and sustainable public finances are seen as essential to safeguard the stability of the euro area as a whole (Recital 3), they contain strict budget rules and the obligation to introduce an 'automatic' debt correction mechanism into national law (→ para 25 et seqq., 34 et seqq.).

- These commitments were partly integrated into and reinforced by EU law with the subsequent '**Two-Pack**'[38] of 2013, which is applicable only to EA Member States.[39] The two Regulations build on and complement the SGP, but also integrate several elements of the TSCG into the EU legal order.[40] Thus, Regulation (EU) No. 473/2013 introduced common budgetary rules and a common budgetary timeline as a 'National Semester' (→ para 63 et seqq.) complementing the European Semester for economic policy coordination, which takes place in the first half of the year under Article 2a of Regulation (EC) No. 1466/97 (→ para 60 et seqq.). The common budgetary rules require the setting up of an independent body to monitor compliance with the budgetary rules at national level.[41] More stringent reporting requirements for MS in EDPs allow enhanced monitoring, particularly through the obligation to submit an economic partnership programme (EPP) describing the structural reforms to ensure the correction of the excessive deficit. Regulation (EU) No. 472/2013 goes another step further and foresees even stricter budgetary surveillance and monitoring procedures for MS experiencing or threatened with serious difficulties with respect to their financial stability, including those that receive(d) financial assistance.

---

[35] Hinarejos (2012), p. 256; Calliess (2012), p. 114.

[36] Cf. also Gröpl (2013), p. 21; Repasi (2013), p. 68; Calliess and Schoenfleisch (2012), p. 486; Antpöhler (2012), p. 382.

[37] Calliess and Schoenfleisch (2012), p. 483; Calliess (2012), p. 109. Of course, agreements within the Euro Summit must also respect Article 4.3 TEU. Cf., however, Fischer-Lescano and Oberndorfer (2013), p. 13 on possible effects of Article 12 TSCG on the EU's institutional set-up.

[38] Regulation (EU) No. 472/2013 *on the strengthening of economic and budgetary surveillance of Member States in the euro area experiencing or threatened with serious difficulties with respect to their financial stability*, O.J. L 140/1 (2013); Regulation (EU) No. 473/2013 *on common provisions for monitoring and assessing draft budgetary plans and ensuring the correction of excessive deficit of the Member States in the euro area*, O.J. L 140/11 (2013).

[39] See Article 1.3 of Regulation (EU) No. 472/2013 and Article 1.3 of Regulation (EU) No. 473/2013. Cf. also Lenaerts (2014), p. 758; De Streel (2013), p. 459.

[40] Cf. Two Pack Code of Conduct (*Specifications on the implementation of the Two Pack and Guidelines on the format and content of draft budgetary plans, economic partnership programmes and debt issuance reports*, as of 30 September 2016, 13045/16) p. 3.

[41] Cf. Article 5.1 of Regulation (EU) No. 473/2013.

Thus, the current fiscal governance framework consists of highly intertwined and partly overlapping instruments of different legal nature (soft law measures, international and intergovernmental treaties, EU secondary legislation), which create a rather complex framework of budgetary surveillance.[42] While the TSCG might have been an important addition, this framework can only be understood when taking this interplay into consideration. Thus, the following chapter will aim to unravel the tangle by analysing the **EU fiscal governance framework** as it stands today, taking note of the unprecedented challenges posed by the COVID-19 pandemic, as well as the review of the framework currently underway, where appropriate. Starting by briefly recapitulating the primary law (i.e. 'constitutional'[43]) prerequisites for the steps so far taken towards a 'Fiscal Union' both in secondary legislation and on the international and intergovernmental level (→ para 7 et seqq.), we will continue by analysing the obligation to avoid excessive deficits after the recent reforms, notably by the TSCG (→ para 16 et seqq.).

The second focal point will be the multilateral coordination under the SGP and the rules in the TSCG (→ para 60 et seqq.), particularly considering the '**surveillance-cycle**' and its implications on MS' budgetary autonomy, as well as the consequences of non-compliance by MS with the Union's recommendations. Whereas these measures are extensive when compared to the status quo ante (and the primary law prerequisites), they are still far from creating a European 'super State' with a central budget and comprehensive tax competences.[44] Rather, 'spending, taxing and borrowing remain primarily the responsibility of the Member States'.[45] Thus, the last section will comment on selected proposals for further fiscal integration (→ para 92 et seqq.) before concluding with a few final remarks (→ para 111 et seqq.).

2. Primary Law Prerequisites

2.1. EU Competence for Budgetary Surveillance

According to the **principle of conferral** (Article 5.2 TEU), the Union shall act only within the limits of the competences conferred upon it by the MS in the Treaties to attain the objectives set out therein. Thus, competences not conferred upon the

---

[42] This new framework was complemented by an update of the European system of national and regional accounts (ESA), according to which MS submit their data. Cf. now Regulation (EU) No. 549/2013 (ESA 2010), O.J. L 174/1 (2013), which replaced Regulation (EC) No. 2223/96 (ESA 95), O.J. L 310/1 (1996).

[43] Cf. Opinion 2/13, *Accession to the ECHR* (ECJ 18 December 2014) para 158; Joined Cases C-402/05 P and C-415/05 P, *Kadi* (ECJ 3 September 2008) para 281 et seqq.; Opinion 1/91, *EEA I* (ECJ 14 December 1991) para 21; Case 294/83, *Les Verts* (ECJ 23 April 1986) para 23. Cf also De Witte (2020).

[44] Cf. Häde (2013), p. 193.

[45] Harden et al. (1997), p. 143.

Union in the Treaties remain with the MS (Article 4.1 TEU). With the Treaties thus determining the limits for exercising Union competences, all measures taken by Union institutions need an appropriate legal basis in the Treaties, in absence of which they may be annulled by the ECJ under Article 263.2 TFEU ('lack of competence'). For the budgetary surveillance framework, such a legal basis may be found in Article 5.1 TFEU in conjunction with Articles 121, 126 and 136 TFEU.[46]

8   Under Article 5.1 TFEU, the **MS shall coordinate their economic policies** within the Union. According to what is arguably the prevailing view, economic policy coordination, together with employment and social policies which are also mentioned in Article 5 TFEU, thus falls in a *sui generis* type of competence category, neither complementary nor shared (→ Article 5 TFEU para 1 et seqq.).[47] Another view uses the wording of Article 4.1 TFEU to argue that the coordination of economic and employment policy may rather be qualified as a shared competence, where, under Article 2.2 TFEU, the Union also has powers to adopt binding legal acts, which possibly create a barring effect.[48]

Both views, however, agree that responsibility for economic policy decisions taken must essentially remain with the MS.[49] Irrespective of the competence category, the Union competences are to be delineated based on the respective (substantive) provisions in the Treaties. Thus, under Article 121 TFEU, MS shall regard '**their economic policies**' as a '**matter of common concern**', which they shall coordinate within the Council. To do so, Article 121 TFEU sets up the main features of a multilateral surveillance procedure. This procedure facilitates the coordination of economic policies on national level without altering the national character of these policies.[50] Arguably, the wording and structure of Article 121 TFEU also excludes any barring effect which may otherwise be associated with shared competences. Article 126 TFEU, on the other hand, contains the obligation to avoid excessive deficits as well as the EDP. Both Article 121 and Article 126 TFEU grant the Council an important role, highlighting the political character of the decisions taken in these procedures.

9   Apart from the 'broad economic policy guidelines which concern the euro area generally' (Article 121.2 TFEU and Article 139.2 point (a) TFEU) and the 'coercive means of remedying excessive deficits' (Articles 126.9 and 11 TFEU) in the EDP, both Article 121 and Article 126 TFEU apply to all EU Member States (Article 139.2 points (a) and (b) TFEU; → Article 139 TFEU para 18–25). However, some of the most controversial measures taken in the sovereign debt

---

[46] The entry into force of the Treaty of Lisbon saw the introduction of several provisions on different categories of competences divided between the EU and its MS in Articles 2 to 6 TFEU. These different categories only clarify the consequences of a competence being in any one category, but do not themselves grant new competences.
[47] Cf. e.g. Hinarejos (2012), p. 260, Braams (2013), p. 232.
[48] E.g. Palmstorfer (2014), p. 95.
[49] Krebber (2004), p. 595.
[50] Cf. e.g. Hinarejos (2012), p. 259 et seq.

crisis apply only to the EA and, thus, also cite **Article 136 TFEU** as their legal basis. The Treaty of Lisbon introduced this provision to consider the increased coordination and control needs of EA countries (→ Article 136 TFEU para 5 et seqq.). Its paragraph 1 allows the introduction of additional measures for those MS whose currency is the euro in the areas of economic policy coordination as well as the coordination and monitoring of budgetary discipline.

Owing to its rather ambiguous wording, however, the **scope of this new competence is disputed**. Arguably the prevailing opinion[51] does not see Article 136 TFEU as an additional competence, but interprets the wording 'in accordance with the relevant provisions of the Treaties' and 'in accordance with the relevant procedure from among those referred to in Articles 121 and 126, with the exception of the procedure set out in Article 126 (14)' as limiting its possible field of application to measures, which substantially and formally correspond to Articles 121 and 126 TFEU while being limited to the EA (or individual EA members).[52]

Understanding Article 136 TFEU in such a manner, however, makes it largely dispensable, as such measures could also be taken based on Articles 121 and 126 TFEU (in conjunction with Article 139 TFEU) alone.[53] I have, therefore, argued elsewhere[54] that Article 136.1 TFEU can indeed be used as a legal basis for **additional or complementing measures** (i.e. the introduction of additional sanctions), provided they do not contravene the wording and *telos* of Articles 121 and 126 TFEU. This also seems to have been the view taken by the European legislator when it based Six Pack-Regulations (EU) No. 1173 and 1174/2011 as well as Two-Pack Regulations (EU) No. 472 and 473/2013 on said competence.[55] However, given that Article 136 TFEU can only be used in combination with Articles 121 and 126 TFEU, the competence is linked to the competences under said Articles (→ Article 136 TFEU para 9). Article 136 TFEU is, therefore, 'no basis allowing the Union to exercise its own economic policy'.[56]

10

2.2. Member States' Competence to Conclude the TSCG

As opposed to the other binding measures taken in response to the sovereign debt crisis, the TSCG was **concluded as an international treaty** by 25 EU Member States and, thus, outside the EU legal order. Original plans to include its contents in

11

---

[51] Cf. e.g. Häde, in Calliess and Ruffert (2021), Article 136 AEUV para 4, 6; Kempen, in Streinz (2018), Article 136 AEUV para 2. Cf. also Ruffert (2011), p. 1800 f.

[52] Häde (2013), p. 193, 196 with further references; Häde (2011), p. 333, 334 et seqq.; see also the references at Antpöhler (2012), p. 369 fn. 59, and p. 371 fn. 68.

[53] Cf. e.g. Schoenfleisch (2018), p. 170.

[54] Wutscher, in Schwarze et al. (2018), Article 136 AEUV para 3 et seqq.

[55] Cf. also Article 10 TSCG according to which Member States commit to make active use, whenever appropriate and necessary, of Article 136 TFEU as well as enhanced cooperation under Article 20 TEU.

[56] Keppenne (2014), p. 213.

the framework of the Treaties had to be dismissed given the UK's and ultimately also the Czech Republic's opposition.[57] However, while '[t]echnically drafted as an international treaty'[58] outside the EU legal order and (unlike the ESM → Supplement to Title VIII: TESM para 4 et seqq.; → Article 136 TFEU para 28 et seqq.) without a particular indication in the Treaties, it is nonetheless '**intrinsically linked to EU law**',[59] comprising tasks for CJEU and EU Commission as well as numerous cross-references to provisions of EU law. One could, therefore, question whether the conclusion of the TSCG as an international treaty was compatible with EU law.[60]

12 While Sovereign States' capacity to conclude treaties as expressed in Article 6 VCLT[61] is limited from an EU law perspective (however, arguably not from the perspective of public international law[62]) by the division of competences contained in the Treaties (→ para 7, → Article 2 TFEU para 41, Article 216 TFEU),[63] MS are not legally precluded from taking measures under international law in areas in which the subject matter of the measure does not fall within a specific Union competence but remains a national competence under EU law (→ Supplement to Title VIII: Introduction para 3 et seq.).[64] In principle, the ECJ clarified in *Pringle* that this also holds true for international treaties concluded only among a group of EU Member States with no third countries involved.[65] As the Union's competence for economic policy is limited to coordination, **Member States** otherwise **retain the capacity to act** on matters of economic and budgetary policy also **by means of public international law**.[66]

13 However, even where MS are, in principle, competent to act, they 'may not disregard their duty to comply with European Union law when exercising their

---

[57] Cf. Hinarejos (2012), p. 254; Calliess (2012), p. 101.

[58] Fabbrini (2013), p. 2.

[59] Lenaerts (2014), p. 757. Cf. also Gröpl (2013), p. 7 et seqq.; Martucci (2020), para 12.63 et seqq., who speaks of a 'legal hybridity' of the TSCG.

[60] This issue was already discussed in the wake of the introduction of the SGP 1997, where the original German proposal foresaw the conclusion of an international treaty, see Häde (1996b), p. 140 et seq.; Hahn (1997), p. 1135.

[61] UN Treaty Series vol 1155, p. 331.

[62] Cf. Repasi (2013), p. 47 et seqq.; Kort (1997), p. 640. According to the so-called 'competence theory', on the contrary, the EU division of competences is also applicable under public international law, limiting MS capacity to act also from the point of view of public international law, see Thym (2004), p. 298 para 8 with further references.

[63] Cf. Article 3.2, Article 216.1 TFEU. Cf. also Opinion 1/76, *European laying-up fund for inland waterway vessels* (ECJ 26 April 1977); Joined Cases 3/76, 4/78, 6/76, *Kramer* (ECJ 14 July 1976) para 30/33; Case 22/70, *AETR* (ECJ 31 March 1971) para 16.

[64] E.g. Joined Cases C-181/91 and C-248/91, *Parliament v Council and Commission* (ECJ 30 June 1993) para 16; cf. also Calliess and Schoenfleisch (2012), p. 481; Kort (1997), p. 642; Häde (1996b), p. 141.

[65] Case C-370/12, *Pringle* (ECJ 27 November 2012) para 68.

[66] Repasi (2013), p. 66; Calliess (2012), p. 105.

competences'.[67] Thus, even when acting outside the scope of EU law, MS are bound by the Treaties, which can only be modified by means of the amendment procedure in Article 48 TEU,[68] as well as by obligations stemming from secondary law.[69] It already follows from the **principle of loyal cooperation** (Article 4.3 TEU) that a measure taken to implement an agreement concluded between the MS outside the scope of the Treaties violates this principle if the implementation of a provision of the Treaties or of secondary EU law or the functioning of the Community institutions were impeded by it.[70] Hence, the aims and objectives of the Treaties must be respected.[71] While deeper integration among a group of MS may therefore be possible by means of international law, international treaties cannot take back what has been agreed upon in the EU Treaties[72] or on their basis.

While it would perhaps have been possible (and given the legally questionable use of Union institutions by the TSCG maybe even somewhat easier to justify → para 53 et seqq.) to use the **enhanced cooperation** procedure instead of an international treaty for most[73] of the TSCG's content, the wording and context of the provisions on enhanced cooperation (Article 20 TEU and Articles 326 et seqq.) suggests that the MS may make use of them at their own discretion, while continuing to allow other forms of intergovernmental cooperation.[74] The enhanced cooperation procedure thus constitutes an optional instrument of closer cooperation between several MS, which generally does not preclude the conclusion of an international treaty between a group of MS on the same subject matter (provided, of course, it respects the limits of the Treaties[75]). Although this interpretation arguably comes with risks of bypassing the democratic EU decision-making **14**

---

[67] Case C-370/12, *Pringle* (ECJ 27 November 2012) para 69.

[68] Case 43/75, *Defrenne II* (ECJ 8 April 1976) para 58. Article 48 TEU thus supersedes Articles 39 et seqq. VCLT (cf. Article 5 VCLT).

[69] Cf. Case C-55/00, *Gottardo* (ECJ 15 January 2002) para 33. Cf. also Schoenfleisch (2018), p. 179 et seqq.

[70] Case 44/84, *Hurd* (ECJ 15 January 1986) para 39; cf. also the decision in Case C-284/16, *Achmea* (ECJ 6 March 2018) para 34, 58, according to which provisions in intra-EU BITs enabling investors to bring proceedings before arbitral tribunals are incompatible with EU law and violate the principle of loyal cooperation.

[71] Cf. Kort (1997), p. 645.

[72] Repasi (2013), p. 74.

[73] While most, if not all, of the substantive provisions could have been, and some of them even have since been, introduced by way of secondary law, institutionalising the Euro Summit would arguably only be possible by Treaty amendment. Thus, it is also not foreseen in the Commission's Proposal COM(2017) 824 final, proposing to integrate the 'substance' of the TSCG into Union law.

[74] Hatje, in Schwarze et al. (2018), Article 20 EUV para 36; Ruffert, in Calliess and Ruffert (2021), Article 20 EUV para 22; Mayer (2012), p. 131; Blanke, in Grabitz et al. (2021), Article 20 EUV para 26 (released in 2016); Thym (2004), p. 305 et seqq. Claiming, on the contrary, that whenever enhanced cooperation is possible it has to be used: Repasi (2013), p. 59 et seq.; Martenczuk (1998), p. 464; Constantinesco (1997), p. 47.

[75] Hinarejos (2012), p. 260; Böttner (2021), p. 67 et seqq.

process (and thus marginalising not only political control by the European Parliament[76] and, by way of subsidiarity control,[77] national Parliaments[78] but also 'weaker' societal interests[79]), it respects the MS' role as 'Masters of the Treaties'.

15   Under Article 16 as well as its Preamble, the substance of the TSCG shall be **incorporated as soon as possible into the Treaties**, with the necessary steps to be taken within five years of its entry into force (i.e. until 1 January 2018). At the time of completion of this chapter (December 2021), such incorporation has not yet taken place and negotiations on the respective proposal presented by the Commission in late 2017 for an incorporation by way of a Directive[80] seem to have stalled even before the COVID-19 pandemic somewhat shifted priorities from consolidating public finances to dealing with health emergency needs, and supporting economic activity and recovery. Until an eventual integration into the EU legal order takes place, Article 2 TSCG stipulates not only that the TSCG should be applied and interpreted in conformity with the EU Treaties, particularly Article 4.3 TEU. This so-called '**coherence clause**' also confirms the primacy of EU law[81] when it states that the TSCG shall only 'apply insofar as it is compatible with the Treaties on which the European Union is founded and with European Union law [...] shall not encroach upon the competence of the Union to act in the area of the economic union' (Article 2.2).[82]

3. The Obligation to Avoid Excessive Deficits After the Fiscal Compact

3.1. Reference Criteria

16   Based on the assumption that financial stability is an implicit prerequisite for price stability,[83] the obligation to avoid excessive government deficits under Article 126 TFEU limits the freedom of MS to pursue independent fiscal policies[84] as well as their options to absorb shocks.[85] To ensure the observance of this obligation, the

---

[76] See Keppenne (2014) p. 220. Cf. also Ioannidis (2016), p. 1276; Chiti and Teixeira (2013), p. 705; Armstrong (2013), p. 604; Thym (2004), p. 299 et seqq.

[77] Article 5.2 TEU in combination with Protocol (No. 2) on the application of the principles of subsidiarity and proportionality.

[78] Cf. Ioannidis (2016), p. 1276.

[79] Cf. Dawson and De Witte (2013), p. 827.

[80] Commission, *Proposal for a Council Directive laying down provisions for strengthening fiscal responsibility and the medium-term budgetary orientation in the Member States*, COM(2017) 824 final.

[81] Cf. Case 6/64, *Costa v ENEL* (ECJ 15 July 1964).

[82] Cf. also Calliess (2012), p. 105. This rule takes precedence over Article 30 VCLT, cf. Thym (2004), p. 311 et seq.

[83] Pilz (2016), p. 66.

[84] Andersen and Dogonowski (1999), p. 83 et seqq.; Taylor (1997), p. 172.

[85] Andersen and Dogonowski (1999), p. 88.

Commission monitors the development of the budgetary situation and of the stock of government debt in the MS based on two so-called '**reference criteria**', namely the ratio of the planned or actual government deficit to GDP and the ratio of government debt to GDP (→ Article 126 TFEU para 7 et seqq.). These criteria (which, given their introduction with the Treaty of Maastricht, are also referred to as 'Maastricht criteria') are contained in Protocol No. 12 to the TFEU on the EDP. Protocol No. 12 sets the reference value for the deficit criterion at 3% of GDP and the reference value for the debt criterion at 60% of GDP.

17 Compliance with these criteria was (and still is) not only a prerequisite for joining stage three of the EMU (→ Article 140 TFEU para 8 et seqq.),[86] but remains a constant legal duty for all MS.[87] Contrary to popular belief and despite their having been exceeded regularly even before the COVID-19 pandemic further expanded public spending, however, the reference criteria are not meant as target values, but as ceilings.[88] However, economically, there is no compelling reason for taking exactly these reference values as criteria to monitor excessive deficits.[89] The **meaningfulness of the Maastricht criteria**, therefore, has always been questioned from an economic point of view, also because they were deemed too inflexible.[90] However, one explanation may be that at a deficit level of around 3% and a nominal growth of about 5%, debt levels seem to stabilise at around 60% of GDP.[91] Therefore, in an economic situation with adequate growth the selected criteria are not particularly ambitious.[92]

18 Whereas Article 126 TFEU does not differentiate between the two criteria, both the SGP and political practice accorded a **higher legal and political weight** to the deficit criterion. This left the debt criterion, which given its impact on interests and future room for budgetary manoeuvre arguably is the more important criterion from the point of view of economics,[93] rather marginalised.[94] While the revised SGP

---

[86] Article 140.1 (2) 2nd indent TFEU; Protocol (No. 13) on the convergence criteria.

[87] Hahn (1998), p. 77; Hahn (1997), p. 1133.

[88] Gröpl (2013), p. 3; Häde (2009), p. 399. Cf. Leino and Saarenheimo (2017), p. 171.

[89] Häde (2009), p. 399; Artis and Winkler (1999), p. 159; Harden et al. (1997), p. 160.

[90] E.g. Andersen and Dogonowski (1999), p. 88 et seq. Recent events have arguably rather added to these doubts. Given this primary law situation, even the activation of the general escape clauses of the SGP in the COVID-19 pandemic in principle fails to remedy the non-compliance with the deficit criterion as both exemptions under Article 126.2 point (a) TFEU only apply if the ratio remains 'close to the reference value'; see → para 19 et seqq. Of course, the Council has a wide margin of discretion in determining whether an excessive government deficit exists under Article 126.6 TFEU; see → para 40 et seqq. on the EDP.

[91] Häde (2009), p. 399; Artis and Winkler (1999), p. 159.

[92] Masson (1996), p. 997.

[93] Calliess and Schoenfleisch (2012), p. 479; Häde (2009), p. 399. Cf. Ohler (1997), p. 260.

[94] Amtenbrink and De Haan (2003), p. 1100; Hahn (1998), p. 78; Hahn (1997), p. 1134.

somewhat redeemed this imbalance,[95] and also the TSCG and the Two-Pack now contain an obligation for the ex-ante coordination of MS' debt issuance plans,[96] it is still reflected in Article 7 TSCG, which contains rules on the use of voting rights within the Council (→ para 45) only applicable to breaches of the deficit criterion. Rather than serving as a definition of the term 'excessive government deficit', the reference criteria are, however, merely the criteria according to which the Commission monitors compliance with budgetary discipline.[97]

3.2. Exemptions from the Reference Criteria

19 The Union institutions have a rather broad discretion in the EDP, especially since Article 126 TFEU already contains exemptions from the reference criteria. Thus, the reference criteria do not serve as absolute ceilings.[98] Rather, when the reference criteria are exceeded, the Commission only instigates an EDP if no exemption is relevant. For the violation of the **deficit criterion**, Article 126.1 point (a) TFEU contains exemptions for when 'the ratio has declined substantially and continuously and reached a level that comes close to the reference value' or 'the excess over the reference value is only exceptional and temporary and the ratio remains close to the reference value'. It is not further substantiated in primary law when these conditions are met, leaving them rather unspecific.[99] Thus, it remains open and ultimately to be decided by Commission and Council in the EDP, if a value remained 'close to the reference value', if excess is only 'exceptional and temporary' or if the 'ratio has declined substantially and continuously' (→ Article 126 TFEU para 9). From an economic point of view, this flexibility may be useful to have the necessary room for manoeuvre for an adequate reaction (especially in times of crises).[100]

20 Only the second exemption, namely the exceptional and temporary excess of the deficit criterion, was fleshed out in the now revised SGP. Accordingly, the reference criterion is deemed only 'exceptionally' exceeded within the meaning of Article 126.1 point (a) TFEU, 'when resulting from an unusual event outside the control of the Member State concerned and with a major impact on the financial position of general government, or when resulting from a severe economic downturn'.[101] This wording bears similarities with Article 122.2 TFEU on temporary financial support

---

[95] Cf. Article 2.4 sentence 1 of Regulation (EC) No. 1467/97 as amended by Regulation (EU) No. 1177/2011. Under Recital 12 of Regulation (EU) No. 1177/2011, the reform of the SGP by the Six-Pack intended to give 'a more prominent role to the level and evolution of debt and to overall sustainability'.
[96] Article 6 TSCG, Article 8 of Regulation (EU) No. 473/2013.
[97] Harden et al. (1997), p. 157.
[98] Cf. Ohler (1997), p. 261.
[99] Gröpl (2013), p. 3.
[100] Cf. Häde (1996b), p. 139.
[101] Article 2.1 (1) of Regulation (EC) No. 1467/97 as amended.

of the Union.[102] In the wake of the financial and sovereign debt crisis it was, thus, discussed whether such a crisis might justify the **application of an exemption from the reference criteria**. While a high government deficit can arguably never be an exceptional event in itself,[103] an economic and financial crisis, which goes hand in hand with low GDP growth, may fall under the exemption as a severe economic downturn.[104] The nature of the COVID-19 pandemic as an 'exceptional event' is unlikely to be called into question.

Even in case of a violation of the deficit criterion because of a severe economic downturn, a MS's violation is only 'exceptional' 'if the excess over the reference value results from a negative annual GDP volume growth rate or from an accumulated loss of output during a protracted period of very low annual GDP volume growth relative to its potential'.[105] While it remains open whether the assessment of the (potential) GDP volume growth rate is made according to annual data or to twelve-months comparisons of quarterly data throughout the year,[106] again there is **a clear similarity to Article 122.2 TFEU** insofar as the MS concerned has no control and an 'exceptional' excess is one which would not occur in the course of 'normal' economic policy under good economic conditions. 21

To fall under the exemption, the excess not only has to be 'exceptional' but also needs to be 'temporary'. Both criteria must be fulfilled cumulatively. An excess is 'temporary' within the meaning of Article 126.1 point (a) TFEU 'if budgetary forecasts as provided by the Commission indicate that the deficit will fall below the reference value following the end of the unusual event or the severe economic downturn'.[107] Moreover, both exemptions mentioned under Article 126.1 point (a) TFEU only apply when the ratio stays '**close to the reference value**'. Therefore, if the deficit criterion is considerably exceeded,[108] an application of the exception is not possible even when the override is only 'exceptional and temporary' in the meaning of the provisions of secondary law illustrated above.[109] Given these primary law prerequisites, the activation of the general escape clauses of the SGP (→ para 31) in the COVID-19 pandemic will not be able to remedy breaches of the deficit criterion when the ratio has not remained 'close to the reference value'. Considering the political nature of the EDP, such a "breach" of the reference criteria does not, however, necessarily lead to a decision that an excessive deficit exists (Article 126 TFEU; cf., on the EDP, → also para 40 et seqq.). 22

---

[102] Cf. Häde (2009), p. 400.

[103] Häde (2009), p. 401.

[104] Cf. Häde (2009), p. 401.

[105] Article 2.2 of Regulation (EC) No. 1467/97 as amended.

[106] Artis and Winkler (1999), p. 167.

[107] Article 2.1 (2) of Regulation (EC) No. 1467/97 as amended.

[108] As was the case, e.g. in Greece in the years after 2009 and in most Member States in light of the measures taken in response to the COVID-19 pandemic and the economic downturn following it.

[109] Häde (2009), p. 400.

23 Article 126.1 point (b) TFEU provides an exemption to the **debt criterion** when 'the ratio is sufficiently diminishing and approaching the reference value at a satisfactory pace'. Under the revised SGP, this is deemed to be the case 'if the differential with respect to the reference value has decreased over the previous three years at an average rate of one twentieth per year as a benchmark, based on changes over the last three years for which the data is available'[110] or 'if the budgetary forecasts of the Commission indicate that the required reduction in the differential will occur over the three-year period encompassing the two years following the final year for which the data is available'.[111] This so-called '**1/20 rule**' is reiterated in Article 4 TSCG.[112]

24 Under the SGP, the Council and the Commission, in their assessment of compliance with the reference criteria, **exercise their discretion by means of a balanced overall assessment of all relevant factors**[113] and with due regard for the implementation of pension reforms[114] and the cost of such reforms.[115] Those criteria, which are to be considered under Article 2.3 of Regulation (EC) No. 1467/97 in the preparation of a report under Article 126.3 TFEU, therefore also play a role in the interpretation of the exemptions under Article 126.1 TFEU. In addition to medium-term economic development and developments in the medium-term budgetary positions and government debt, other factors may also be relevant from the point of view of the MS concerned. In particular, 'consideration shall be given to financial contributions to fostering international solidarity and achieving the policy goals of the Union, the debt incurred in the form of bilateral and multilateral support between MS in the context of safeguarding financial stability, and the debt related to financial stabilisation operations during major financial disturbances'.

---

[110] Article 2.1a of Regulation (EC) No. 1467/97 as amended.

[111] Article 2.1a of Regulation (EC) No. 1467/97 as amended. Under Article 2.1a (3), in implementing the debt ratio adjustment benchmark, account is to be taken of the influence of the cycle on the pace of debt reduction. There was a transition scheme for MS that were subject to an EDP on 8 November 2011 according to which, for a period of three years from the correction of the excessive deficit, the requirement under the debt criterion was considered fulfilled if the Member State concerned made sufficient progress towards compliance.

[112] Given the explicit reference and despite its ambiguous wording, Article 4 TSCG is to be interpreted in conformity with Article 2 of Regulation (EC) No. 1467/97 (as amended); see Repasi (2013), p. 70 et seq.

[113] Article 2.4 of Regulation (EC) No. 1467/97 as amended.

[114] Article 2.5 of Regulation (EC) No. 1467/97 as amended.

[115] Article 2.7 of Regulation (EC) No. 1467/97 as amended.

3.3. Balanced Budget Rule, Medium-Term Objective, Automatic Correction Mechanism

Under Article 3.1 TSCG, 'the budgetary position of the general government of a Contracting Party shall be balanced or in surplus'. This so-called **'golden rule'**[116] is not new. Already in the original SGP 1997 MS politically committed 'to respect the medium-term budgetary objective of positions close to balance or in surplus'.[117] However, the TSCG introduced a definition of when such a balanced budgetary position is deemed to be respected and linked it to the country-specific MTO of the SGP, now laid down in Article 2a of Regulation (EC) No. 1466/97 (as amended).

25

Under Article 3.1 point (b) TSCG, the golden rule is respected when 'the annual structural balance of the general government is at its country-specific medium-term objective, as defined in the revised Stability and Growth Pact, with a lower limit of a **structural deficit of 0.5%** of the gross domestic product at market prices'. This lower limit is slightly higher, namely at 1.0%, where government debt to GDP is significantly below 60% and risks to long-term sustainability are low (Article 3.1 point (d) TSCG). Article 3.1 TSCG was modelled after Article 115.2 of the German Basic Law (*Grundgesetz*),[118] which provides for an even stricter limit, according to which revenue obtained by the borrowing of funds at Federal government level may, in principle, not exceed 0.35%.[119]

26

Article 2a of the revised Regulation (EC) No. 1466/97, to which the TSCG refers, requires all MS to have 'a differentiated **medium-term objective** (MTO) for its budgetary position'. The obligation to achieve and maintain a county-specific MTO applies to all MS. The MTO is defined in cyclically adjusted terms, net of one-off and other temporary measures and aims to provide a safety margin with respect to the 3% deficit limit or ensure rapid progress towards sustainability, while allowing room for budgetary manoeuvre.[120] MTOs are revised every three years or in the event of the implementation of a structural reform with a major impact on the sustainability of public finances.[121]

27

Sufficient progress towards the MTO is evaluated based on an overall assessment with the annual structural balance as a reference, understood as the balance in

28

---

[116] E.g. Fabbrini (2013), p. 3.

[117] European Council Resolution *on the Stability and Growth Pact*, O.J. C 236/1 (1997). Cf. also Article 109.3 of the German Basic Law which was amended in 2009 to stipulate that the budgets of the Federation and the *Länder* 'shall in principle be balanced without revenue from credits'.

[118] Federal Law Gazette Part III, No. 100-1, as amended by Article 1 of the Act of 23 December 2014 (Federal Law Gazette I p. 2438).

[119] Cf. Fabbrini (2013), p. 11.

[120] See Code of Conduct of the Stability and Growth Pact (*Specifications on the implementation of the Stability and Growth Pact and Guidelines on the format and content of Stability and Convergence Programmes*), p. 4.

[121] Article 2a.3 of Regulation (EC) No. 1466/97.

cyclically adjusted terms, net of one-off and temporary measures.[122] The MTO 'shall ensure the sustainability of public finances or a rapid progress towards such sustainability while allowing room for budgetary manoeuvre, considering in particular the need for public investment'.[123] MS, which have not yet reached their MTO, should take steps to achieve it over the cycle according to an **adjustment path**. Their adjustment effort should be higher in good times and can be more limited in bad times, with an annual adjustment in cyclically adjusted terms, net of one-off and other temporary measures, of 0.5% of GDP as a benchmark.[124] The Code of Conduct on the SGP and the Communication on the use of flexibility in the SGP contain more detailed specifications in this regard, including a matrix specifying the necessary budgetary adjustments for different scenarios. For this assessment, annual **expenditure growth** is set in relation to a medium-term reference rate of potential GDP growth (potential growth rate) to be notified to the MS by the Commission. According to this '**expenditure brake**', annual expenditure shall, in principle, remain below the potential growth rate.[125]

29 The county-specific MTO may 'diverge from the requirement of a close to balance or in surplus position', while respecting a safety margin with respect to the 3% deficit criterion, which remains in place as the upper limit for the assessment of excessive government deficits. To substantiate this rule, Regulation (EC) No. 1466/97 provides that the country-specific MTO for EA Member States and for Member States participating in the ERM2 must range '**between -1% of GDP and balance or surplus**, in cyclically adjusted terms, net of one-off and temporary measures'.[126]

30 While it is evident that with a lower limit of 0.5% the TSCG insofar sets a **stricter target** for the structural deficit,[127] Article 2a of Regulation (EC) No. 1466/97 and Article 3.1 point (b) TSCG are, however, fully compatible with one another. Whereas Article 3.1 TSCG defines the circumstances of when the requirement of a close to balance or in surplus position 'shall be deemed to be respected', Article 2a of Regulation (EC) No. 1466/97 allows MS to 'diverge from' this requirement when setting their county-specific MTO. Thus, it makes sense that the relevant threshold might be less strict in the second case. Both rules complement the primary law reference criteria,[128] aiming to set targets for the structural deficit in such a way as to ultimately ensure adherence to the 3% criterion. The Commission Proposal for a Directive to integrate the substance of the TSCG into the EU legal order explicitly

---

[122] Article 5.1 of Regulation (EC) No. 1466/97 as amended; Article 3.1 point (b), and Article 3.3 point (a) TSCG.

[123] Article 2a.1 of Regulation (EC) No. 1466/97 as amended.

[124] Article 5.1 (2) of Regulation (EC) No. 1466/97 as amended. See also Code of Conduct of the Stability and Growth Pact (*Specifications on the implementation of the Stability and Growth Pact and Guidelines on the format and content of Stability and Convergence Programmes*), p. 6).

[125] See Article 5.1 and Article 9.1 of Regulation (EC) No. 1466/97 as amended.

[126] Articles 2a.2 and 2a.3 of Regulation (EC) No. 1466/97 as amended.

[127] E.g. Calliess (2012), p. 106.

[128] De Streel (2013), p. 460.

includes this goal in its Article 1, while (perhaps rather surprisingly) neither maintaining the target of a close to balance or in surplus position nor the lower limit for the structural deficit of 0.5%.[129] Rather, it simply requires the MTO to be specified in such a way as to ensure that the reference value is respected.

Under Article 3.1 point (c) TSCG, the Contracting Parties may temporarily deviate from the MTO or the adjustment path towards the MTO in exceptional circumstances. **Exceptional circumstances** are defined as an 'unusual event outside the control of the Contracting Party which has a major impact on the financial position of the general government or to periods of severe economic downturn as set out in the revised Stability and Growth Pact, provided that the temporary deviation of the Contracting Party concerned does not endanger fiscal sustainability in the medium-term' (Article 3.3 point (b) TSCG). With this rule, the TSCG repeats what is stipulated in Article 5 of Regulation (EC) No. 1466/97, which additionally clarifies that a deviation from the adjustment path to the MTO or the MTO itself may be allowed when MS implement pension reforms introducing a multi-pillar system that includes a mandatory, fully funded pillar.[130] For the corrective arm it is similarly specified that in the event of a severe economic downturn in the euro area or in the Union as a whole, the Council may decide, on a recommendation from the Commission, to adopt a revised budgetary stance.[131] These general **escape clauses** of the SGP were first applied in spring 2020 in the context of the COVID-19 pandemic.[132] The parallel to the permissible deviations from the reference criteria is no coincidence, since the concretisation of the primary law provisions in the SGP serves to ensure compliance with precisely these criteria.[133]

In addition to the 'golden rule' and its specifications (and limitations) in Article 3.1, Article 3.1 point (e) TSCG requires the introduction of an **automatic correction mechanism** for 'significant observed deviations' from the MTO or the adjustment path towards it. This **debt brake** 'shall be triggered automatically' and 'include the obligation of the Contracting Party concerned to implement measures to correct the deviations over a defined period of time'. Given the context, it is obvious that the mechanism shall only be triggered for deviations which do not fall under the escape clause of Article 3.1 point (c) or within the higher threshold of Article 3.1 point (d) TSCG.

Under Article 3.2 TSCG, the automatic correction mechanism, put in place at the national level, must be based on **common principles**, to be proposed by the

---

[129] COM(2017) 824 final.

[130] Article 5.1 (8) of Regulation (EC) No. 1466/97 as amended.

[131] Articles 3.5 and 5.2 of Regulation (EC) No. 1467/97 as amended.

[132] Cf. Commission Communication *on the activation of the general escape clause of the Stability and Growth Pact*, COM(2020) 123 final. In its Communication, Economic policy coordination in 2021: overcoming COVID-19, supporting the recovery and modernising our economy, COM (2021) 500 final, the Commission assumes that the escape clauses will be continue to be applied for 2022, while a deactivation is envisaged for 2023.

[133] What is not quite clear, however, is why a severe economic downturn 'in the euro area' is a relevant reason for deviation even for countries that do not belong to the euro area.

Commission 'concerning in particular the nature, size and time-frame of the corrective action to be undertaken, also in the case of exceptional circumstances, and the role and independence of the institutions responsible at national level for monitoring compliance'. The Commission, thus, set out **seven** principles on national fiscal correction mechanisms in a Communication of 20 June 2012.[134] Under those principles it is, inter alia, necessary that the correction, in terms of size and timeline, shall be made consistent with possible recommendations under the SGP (2), that the activation triggers may comprise EU-driven or country-specific criteria, with both ex ante and ex post mechanisms possibly fulfilling the requirements (3), that MS adopt a corrective plan which is binding over the budgets covered by the correction period at the onset of the correction (4), or that independent bodies conforming to certain criteria shall support the credibility and transparency of the correction mechanism (7).

3.4. Obligations to Implement Rules in National Law

34   While purportedly 'fully respect[ing] the prerogatives of national Parliaments', Article 3.2 TSCG obliges the Contracting Parties to implement the rules in paragraph 1, comprising the 'golden rule' but also its definition and exemptions as well as the automatic correction mechanism and requirement to establish an independent monitoring institution in their national law 'through **provisions of binding force and permanent character**, preferably constitutional, or otherwise guaranteed to be fully respected and adhered to throughout the national budgetary processes'.[135] Thus, the Contracting Parties of the TSCG commit to institutionalise, and 'preferably' even constitutionalise the fiscal rules.[136]

35   However, an implementation below constitutional rank can also fulfil the obligation under Article 3.2 TSCG. Thus, it was possible to implement Article 3 TSCG, e.g. in France by Organic Law ('*loi organique*')[137] or in Austria through an Agreement between the federal level, the federal states and the municipalities.[138] As the systems of constitutional review within the EU differ greatly, it also seems, contrary to what *Fabbrini* argues, not indispensable that such rules 'can work as

---

[134] Commission Communication, *Common principles on national fiscal correction mechanisms*, COM(2012) 342 final.

[135] In contrast, the first draft of the TSCG still stipulated that the debt brake was to be introduced into national law 'in constitutional or equal rank', Antpöhler (2012), p. 383.

[136] Cf. Armstrong (2013), p. 604.

[137] Loi organique n° 2012-1403 du 17 décembre 2012 relative à la programmation et à la gouvernance des finances publiques (Organic Law No. 2012-1403 of 17 December 2012 on the Programming and Governance of the Public Finances). Cf. French *Conseil Constitutionnel*, Décision n° 2012-653 DC (9 August 2012) and Décision n° 2012-658 DC (13 December 2012).

[138] Österreichischer Stabilitätspakt 2012, Federal Law Gazette I 30/2013 (Austrian Internal Stability Pact 2012). Cf. Austrian Constitutional Court, SV1/2013 (3 October 2013).

benchmarks for the constitutional review of budgetary laws',[139] so long as their **observance in the budgetary process is** otherwise **ensured**.[140] The actual implications of the TSCG on MS's national laws therefore depend, to some extent, on the respective budgetary law as well as the system of constitutional review.[141] Notably, it remains with national (constitutional) courts to reconcile conflicts between the fiscal rules and substantive (constitutional) guarantees.[142] However, under the Preamble to the ESM Treaty, ESM support is also conditional upon the ratification of the TSCG and the effective implementation of the balanced budget rule.[143]

Under Article 8.1 TSCG, the **Commission** is invited to **report** in due time on the provisions adopted in the Contracting Parties to comply with the obligations in Article 3.2 TSCG. Thus, in its report of 22 February 2017, the Commission concluded that 'the substance of the Fiscal Compact has been introduced in the national fiscal frameworks of all Contracting Parties'.[144] However, the Commission seems to have been rather lenient, accepting formal commitments by the national authorities to apply the rules in conformity with the TSCG or pledges to still carry out certain necessary steps.[145] Should it have found that a Contracting Party had failed to comply with Article 3.2 TSCG, the matter would have had to be brought to the CJEU by the Council Trio Presidency (Article 16.9 TEU) under Article 8.1 TSCG in conjunction with a Protocol to the TSCG (→ para 55 et seqq.) within three months after the Commission's report.

In addition to these international law commitments in the TSCG, **Chapter IV of Directive 2011/85/EU** requires each Member State to put in place '**numerical fiscal rules**, which are specific to it and which effectively promote compliance with its obligations deriving from the TFEU in the area of budgetary policy over a multiannual horizon for the general government as a whole' (Article 5), and to ensure that their annual budget legislation reflects these country-specific numerical fiscal rules (Article 7). In particular, such rules shall promote compliance with the reference criteria as well as the adoption of a multiannual fiscal planning horizon, including the adherence to the country-specific MTO (Article 5), by specifying the

36

37

---

[139] Fabbrini (2013), p. 7.

[140] This will normally require norms of a higher status than budget laws, although 'weaknesses in their legal status could be offset by the presence of strong national independent institutions monitoring compliance with the rules', see Commission Report of 22 February 2017 *presented under Article 8 of the Treaty on Stability, Coordination and Governance in the Economic and Monetary Union*, C(2017) 1201 final.

[141] Cf. Fabbrini (2013), p. 24.

[142] Armstrong (2013), p. 604 et seq.; cf. e.g. on the review of austerity measures in Portugal by the Portuguese Constitutional Tribunal (Tribunal Constitucional) Fabbrini (2014), p. 100 with further references.

[143] Arguably, this also follows from Article 125 TFEU, cf. Calliess (2012), p. 115.

[144] Commission Report of 22 February 2017 *presented under Article 8 of the Treaty on Stability, Coordination and Governance in the Economic and Monetary Union*, C(2017) 1201 final. Appendix III to this Communication contains a list of national provisions considered in the assessment.

[145] Such necessary steps could be the appointment of members of the monitoring body or the adoption of provisions regulating access to information for the monitoring institution.

target definition and scope of the rules, effective and timely monitoring of compliance by independent bodies or bodies endowed with functional autonomy, the consequences in case of non-compliance, as well as specific circumstances and stringent procedures for when temporary non-compliance with the rule is permitted (Article 6). Thus, Directive 2011/85/EU also requires the introduction of a correction mechanism. Article 2a of Regulation (EC) No. 1466/97 complements this framework by stipulating that MS shall include the respect of the MTO in their national medium-term budgetary frameworks.

38   For EA Member States (only), **Two-Pack Regulation (EU) 473/2013** reiterates in Article 5.1 that independent bodies shall monitor the compliance with the fiscal rules enacted under Directive 2011/85/EU and Regulation (EC) No. 1466/97. Moreover, those bodies shall, inter alia, provide public assessments on the occurrence of circumstances leading to the activation of the correction mechanism (Article 5.2 point a). Integrating the specifications of the Commission's Common principles to Article 3.2 TSCG into Union law, Article 2.1 point (a) of Regulation (EU) No. 473/2013 now clarifies that 'independent bodies' means structurally independent bodies or bodies endowed with functional autonomy *vis-à-vis* the budgetary authorities of the MS. Accordingly, for monitoring bodies to fulfil their mandate effectively, national legal provisions must ensure a high degree of functional autonomy and accountability.[146] These obligations led to the setting up of National Independent Fiscal Councils in the MS.

39   With reference to Opinion 2/94[147] and the respect for MS' national identities under Article 4.2 TEU (→ Article 4 TEU para 8 et seqq.), it has been questioned whether secondary law can legitimately be used as a means of seeking change in national law when this has institutional and constitutional implications for the MS.[148] However, while there may indeed be **limits to the capacity of the EU to induce constitutional change** in the MS by way of secondary law, the provisions introduced by the Six-Pack and the Two-Pack arguably do not transgress these limits. For one, they do not expressly require the introduction of constitutional provisions but leave the decisions on the means of implementation with the MS. Moreover, it would certainly not be the first time that national constitutional orders have to be amended to comply with secondary law obligations.[149] Thus, the implementation of Article 3 TSCG into the EU legal framework[150] would also be possible by means of secondary law.

---

[146] See, in detail, Article 2.1 point (a) of Regulation (EU) No. 473/2013. Cf. also Recital 17 of Regulation (EU) No. 473/2013 and Principle (7) in the Annex to the Commission Communication, *Common principles on national fiscal correction mechanisms*, COM(2012) 342 final.

[147] Opinion 2/94, *Accession by the Community to the ECHR* (ECJ 28 March 1996) para 35.

[148] Armstrong (2013), p. 604.

[149] Dimopoulos (2014), p. 61.

[150] Cf. Article 16.2 as well as the Preamble to the TSCG.

Fiscal Union

The Commission **Proposal for a Directive to integrate the substance of the TSCG into the EU legal order,**[151] however, goes much less far and no longer contains the strict 0.5% target for the structural deficit or the obligation to implement the rules by way of constitutional law or otherwise guaranteed to be fully respected and adhered to throughout the national budgetary processes.[152] Therefore, it seems to respect primary law limits, although, by leaving these key elements of the Fiscal Compact out, the Commission Proposal arguably dilutes its substance rather than integrating it into EU law.[153]

3.5. Deficit Procedure

Article 126 TFEU contains the EDP. While this provision is rather detailed at first, the Council has a considerable margin of discretion at each stage of the procedure. The 'corrective' arm of the SGP, as established by Regulation (EC) No. 1467/97 (last amended by Regulation (EU) No. 1177/2011) limits this discretion. It contains specifications on speeding up and clarifying the implementation of the EDP. Specifically, it stipulates **time limits for each step of the procedure** and clarifies the scope of the exceptional circumstances in which it is permissible to exceed the reference values ($\rightarrow$ para 19 et seqq.). Since the 2011 reform, it also contains a rule for when the debt ratio shall be considered sufficiently diminishing, and annual nominal and structural deficit targets for the duration of the EDP. Overall, the procedure under Article 126 TFEU is quite complex and consists of several stages which shall not be repeated in detail here ($\rightarrow$ Article 126 TFEU paras. 17 to 28). However, three issues relating to the measures taken to combat the sovereign debt crisis, notably the Six-Pack, the TSCG, and the Two-Pack, will be addressed in turn. **40**

3.5.1. New Sanctions and Reverse Qualified Majority Voting

With Regulation (EU) No. 1173/2011, the Six-Pack introduced **new sanctions** of an administrative nature (Article 9) in the corrective part of the SGP for members of the EA (only).[154] Under Article 5 of that Regulation, a **non-interest-bearing deposit** amounting to[155] 0.2% of the Member State's GDP in the preceding year **41**

---

[151] COM(2017) 824 final.

[152] Cf., however, Recital 13 to Proposal COM(2017) 824 final.

[153] According to *J. Graf von Luckner* on europeanlawblog.eu, *Bruno De Witte* therefore spoke of a 'Fake Repatriation' in this context, available at http://europeanlawblog.eu/2018/04/09/how-to-bring-it-home-the-eus-options-for-incorporating-the-fiscal-compact-into-eu-law/.

[154] Cf. Article 1.2 of Regulation (EU) No. 1173/2011. This follows from the Regulation being based on Article 136 TFEU.

[155] The non-interest-bearing deposit may be reduced or cancelled on grounds of exceptional economic circumstances or following a reasoned request under Article 5.4 of Regulation (EU) No. 1173/2011.

may be imposed on a MS with an excessive deficit which has lodged an interest-bearing deposit with the Commission in the preventive part of the SGP (→ para 68) or in case of particularly serious non-compliance with the budgetary policy obligations of the SGP. Moreover, a **fine**, amounting to 0.2% of the national GDP in the preceding year,[156] may be imposed under Article 6 of the Regulation if the Council, acting under Article 126.8 TFEU, decides that a MS has not taken effective action to correct its excessive deficit.

42   In both instances, the decision 'shall be deemed to be adopted by the Council unless it decides by a qualified majority to reject the Commission's recommendation within ten days of the Commission's adoption thereof' (Articles 5.2 and 6.2). This so called **reverse qualified majority voting** (RQMV) was introduced for the additional sanctions now available at earlier stages of the EDP to enhance enforcement of the obligation to avoid excessive deficits and to 'de-politicise' the procedure.[157] Decisions which are not rejected by a qualified majority are, therefore, attributed to the Council, even if it refrains from acting at all or only a simple majority rejects the Commission's recommendation.[158]

43   However, there are several **doubts as to the legality** of the additional sanctions in general and the RQMV procedure in particular. Primarily, it must be pointed out that the legality of the additional sanctions and the RQMV procedure depends on the understanding of **Article 136 TFEU** (→ para 9 et seq.). Seeing it (as proposed here) as a real additional competence for the EA which allows complementary measures, as long as they are not in conflict with Article 121 or 126 TFEU, the introduction of sanctions following decisions taken by the Council at earlier stages of the EDP is generally possible. While it is true that the EDP is characterised by a strong position of the Council enjoying wide discretionary powers, these powers remain untouched in the new system, since the automatism generated by the RQMV procedure does not include the actual Council decisions under Article 126.6 or Article 126.8 TFEU. Rather, the decisions under Article 126.6 or Article 126.8 TFEU are still taken according to the **political discretion of the Council**.

44   On the other hand, it has been argued that the RQMV procedure was incompatible with **Article 16.3 TEU** according to which the Council 'shall act by a qualified majority except where the Treaties provide otherwise' (→ Article 16 TEU para 86 et seqq.) and with Article 240.3 TFEU (→ Article 240 TFEU para34 et seqq.)

---

[156] The fine may be reduced or cancelled on grounds of exceptional economic circumstances or following a reasoned request under Article 6.4 of Regulation (EU) No. 1173/2011.

[157] Piecha (2016), p. 273; Herzmann (2012), p. 171. Before the Six-Pack, despite the possibility of the Council to impose sanctions under Article 126.11 TFEU, none of the around 60 EDPs initiated between 1997 and 2012 actually led to the imposition of sanctions; see Weber (2013), p. 377. So far, the objective to enhance enforcement has not been reached. Rather, in conferring highly political decisions upon it, the *Commission* might have been further politicised. This is illustrated by the EDPs against Portugal and Spain, where the Commission proposed a cancellation of the sanctions, which was then 'accepted' by the Council by RQMV; cf. Leino and Saarenheimo (2017), p. 181 et seq., as well as para 90.

[158] Cf. Bast and Rödl (2012), p. 275.

according to which the Council adopts its Rules of Procedure by a simple majority.[159] Regulation (EU) No. 1173/2011 was passed in accordance with the ordinary legislative procedure, in which the Council decides by qualified majority. The procedures foreseen in this Regulation, however, are not provided for in the Treaties at all. Considering its wording, it seems then that Article 16.3 TEU is not applicable to such procedures established by secondary law (→ Article 136 TFEU para 16 et seq.).[160] This is confirmed by the fact that the decisions foreseen in Article 126.6 and Article 126.8 TFEU remain decisions which the Council has to take with qualified majority.[161] If and *only if* they are taken, the Commission will impose sanctions to which the Council can only object by RQMV. The RQMV procedure for the imposition of sanctions is, therefore, not in conflict with Article 16.3 TEU or Article 126 TFEU.

3.5.2. Article 7 TSCG

Article 7 TSCG contains a mechanism which, at first glance, seems similar to the described RQMV (→ para 42). Under this provision, 'the Contracting Parties whose currency is the euro commit to supporting the proposals or recommendations submitted by the European Commission' in the framework of an EDP where the Commission considers that an EA member is in breach of the deficit criterion. This obligation does not apply 'where it is established among the Contracting Parties whose currency is the euro that a qualified majority of them [...] is opposed to the decision proposed or recommended'. The qualified majority is calculated 'by analogy with the relevant provisions of the Treaties on which the European Union is founded', i.e. Article 16.4 TEU and Article 238 TFEU, but 'without taking into account the position of the Contracting Party concerned'. 45

Evidently, Article 7 TSCG aims to strengthen the Commission's position in the EDP, which is otherwise characterised by a strong position of the Council. However, the scope and compatibility with primary law of this commitment to support the Commission's proposals or recommendations has been highly disputed.[162] Thus, it is clear that despite other efforts to strengthen the debt criterion (→ para 18), Article 7 TSCG is only applicable to cases in which the **deficit criterion** is violated.[163] It is less clear, however, how the mechanism functions and what stages 46

---

[159] Cf. Bast and Rödl (2012), p. 276 et seq.

[160] Cf. Antpöhler (2012), p. 380 et seq., who sees Article 136 TFEU as an implicit exception to Article 16.3 TEU and suggests applying Article 333.1 TFEU by analogy. However, because it is based on Article 136 TFEU, this solution (while legitimising the RQMV in Regulation (EU) No. 1173/2011) has to declare illegal the introduction of RQMV in measures applicable also outside the EA, as foreseen, e.g. in Article 10.4 of Regulation (EU) No. 1176/2011 on the prevention and correction of macroeconomic imbalances.

[161] The qualified majority is determined under Article 16.4 TEU and Article 238 TFEU.

[162] Arguing against its legality, e.g. Weber (2013), p. 380; Fischer-Lescano and Oberndorfer (2013), p. 13.

[163] Cf. Calliess and Schoenfleisch (2012), p. 482 et seq.; Calliess (2012), p. 108.

of the EDP it applies to. Given its nature as an international treaty and the coherence clause in Article 2.2, the TSCG cannot be interpreted in a way incompatible with EU primary law. Therefore, the procedures of Article 126 TFEU must remain unchanged. Accordingly, all decisions foreseen in this provision are still to be taken by (normal) qualified majority.

47 Hence, Article 7 TSCG does not create an automatism in the strict sense.[164] Rather, it intends to streamline the EDP[165] by ex-ante coordinating votes in the Council. The commitment to support the Commission's proposals or recommendations submitted within the framework of the EDP, therefore, only creates an obligation to cast the vote in the Council accordingly, without changing the modus in the Council.[166] While it is true that MS of the EA already **coordinated** their **behaviour in the Council** (also with regard to the EDP) within the informal Euro Group meetings (Article 137 TFEU and Protocol No. 14) before the TSCG, Article 7 TSCG seems to go at least two steps further: First, it creates an **international law obligation** to support the Commission, while the coordination within the Euro Group was only politically binding.[167] Second, and above all, this obligation may (and for the mechanism to have any added value *must* be able to) arise against the will of a Contracting Party.

48 However, the scope of Article 7 TSCG is also disputed. According to its wording, it is possible to understand it in a way that *all* decisions in an EDP in which the deficit criterion is violated are subject to this quasi-automatism created by Article 7 TSCG. The *telos* supports this reading. However, given the obvious implications on the institutional balance (Article 13.2 TEU)[168] of reducing the vote in the Council to a mere formality, it is preferable to interpret Article 7 TSCG in such a way that it only applies to the (constitutive) **decision** (→ Article 126 TFEU para 20–21) of '**whether an excessive deficit exists**' under Article 126.6 TFEU.[169] In any case, the obligation to support the Commission under Article 7 TSCG is (merely) an obligation under public international law. Hence, an enforcement of the obligation is accordingly limited to public international law, and, therefore, to retaliation measures. From the point of view of EU law, however, it can be assumed that the MS in the Council may continue to **vote freely**.

---

[164] Weber (2013), p. 379.

[165] Calliess and Schoenfleisch (2012), p. 480.

[166] Calliess and Schoenfleisch (2012), p. 482; Bast and Rödl (2012), p. 276; Calliess (2012), p. 108. According to Weber (2013), p. 379, on the contrary, the decision-making rules are altered by Article 7 TSCG.

[167] Repasi (2013), p. 70, on the other hand, argues that Article 7 TSCG is merely politically binding.

[168] On the principle of institutional balance see, e.g. Jacqué (2004), p. 383; Dawson and De Witte (2013), p. 828 et seqq.

[169] Similarly Calliess (2012), p. 108, who seems to want to limit the application of Article 7 TSCG to those steps of the EDP preceding the decision on the excessive deficit under Article 126.6 TFEU.

3.5.3. Economic Partnership Programmes and Reporting Requirements

Article 5 TSCG introduced the obligation for Contracting Parties subject to an EDP to submit a budgetary and **economic partnership programme** (EPP) to the Council and the Commission, which endorses and monitors adherence to it within the context of the existing surveillance procedures under the SGP. With the Two-Pack, this obligation to provide a 'roadmap for structural reforms'[170] was integrated into EU law. Regulation (EU) No. 473/2013 thus stipulates that when the Council decides (under Article 126.6 TFEU) that an excessive deficit exists in an MS,[171] the respective State shall, together with the report on actions taken provided for in Article 3.4a of Regulation (EC) No. 1467/97 'present to the Commission and to the Council an economic partnership programme describing the policy measures and structural reforms that are needed to ensure an effective and lasting correction of the excessive deficit'.[172] Subsequently, the Council, acting on a proposal from the Commission, will adopt an opinion on the EPP and monitor its implementation within the context of the European Semester and based on MS reporting in national reform programmes or stability programmes.[173] **49**

Under Regulation (EU) No. 473/2013, an EPP 'shall identify and select a number of specific priorities aiming to enhance competitiveness and long-term sustainable growth and addressing structural weaknesses in the Member State concerned' (Article 9.2). Further specifications on the content and format of EPP, including a model structure, were provided in the so-called '**Two-Pack Code of Conduct**'.[174] The EPP builds upon the national reform programmes and stability programmes (Article 9.1). Thus, it may be considered 'a focused update' of the stability programme and the national reform programme, considering the respective MS's country-specific recommendations (CSR) from the European Semester ($\rightarrow$ para 60 et seqq.). **50**

Moreover, the Two-Pack introduced **more stringent reporting requirements** for all EA Member States under an EDP, complementing the reporting obligations under the revised SGP as set out in Article 3.4a and Article 5.1 point (a) of Regulation (EC) No. 1467/97. Thus, Article 10 of Regulation (EU) No. 473/2013 **51**

---

[170] Two Pack Code of Conduct (*Specifications on the implementation of the Two Pack and Guidelines on the format and content of draft budgetary plans, economic partnership programmes and debt issuance reports*, as of 30 September 2016, 13045/16), p. 18.

[171] Consequently, EDPs, commenced after the entry into force of the Two-Pack, must comply with this requirement. However, under Article 17.2 of Regulation (EU) No. 473/2013, new steps in existing EDPs are also included.

[172] Article 9.1 and Article 9.3 of Regulation (EU) No. 473/2013. Cf. also Article 11 TSCG which contains a general duty to ex ante discuss all major economic policy reforms and coordinate them where appropriate.

[173] Article 9.4 and Article 9.6 of Regulation (EU) No. 473/2013. Cf. also Article 4.2 TSCG.

[174] *Specifications on the implementation of the Two Pack and Guidelines on the format and content of draft budgetary plans, economic partnership programmes and debt issuance reports*, as of 30 September 2016, 13045/16. Cf. also Article 5 TSCG, where it is anticipated that the content and format of the economic partnership programmes shall be defined in EU law.

allows the Commission to request the activation of additional reporting requirements, when recommending to the Council to place a MS under an EDP. These additional reporting requirements aim at ensuring prevention and early correction of any deviations from the Council recommendations or decisions to give notice to correct the excessive deficit by requiring a more frequent reporting[175] from EA Member States under an EDP.[176] The reports, which are made public, shall contain, for the general government and its subsectors, the in-year budgetary execution, the budgetary impact of discretionary measures taken on both the expenditure and the revenue side, targets for the government expenditure and revenues, and information on the measures adopted and the nature of those measures envisaged to achieve the targets (Article 10.3). Further specifications concerning the content and structure of the reports are laid down in a Commission Delegated Regulation.[177]

52 For MS subject to a macroeconomic adjustment programme ($\rightarrow$ para 74 et seqq.; $\rightarrow$ Supplement to Title VIII: TESM para 68 et seqq.), the **enhanced surveillance** under Regulation (EU) No. 472/2013 **takes priority over the other procedures of economic and budgetary surveillance**, thus substituting the EPP[178] as well as the additional reporting requirements of Regulation (EU) No. 473/2013, the EIP, and the monitoring and assessment of the European Semester.[179] In case enhanced surveillance does not apply but the respective MS is already subject to an EIP, the provisions of Regulation (EU) No. 1176/2011 will take precedence over the rules of Regulation (EU) No. 473/2013 on the EPP, with the Corrective Action Plan replacing or standing for the EPP.[180]

3.6. ECJ and Commission's Competences Under the TSCG

53 The **TSCG is closely linked to EU law**, not only because it refers to, duplicates or complements EU rules on substance, but also because it makes use of Union institutions to attain its objectives. Under Article 8 TSCG, the ECJ is competent to assess compliance of the Contracting Parties with their international law

---

[175] An EA Member State under an EDP thus must report to the Commission and to the Economic and Financial Committee (EFC) every six months if subject to a Council recommendation under Article 126.7 TFEU and every three months if subject to a Council decision under Article 126.9 TFEU; cf. Article 10.4 and Article 10.5 of Regulation (EU) No. 473/2013.

[176] Cf. Recitals 1 and 4 of Commission Delegated Regulation (EU) No. 877/2013.

[177] Commission Delegated Regulation (EU) No. 877/2013 *supplementing Regulation (EU) No. 473/2013 of the European Parliament and of the Council on common provisions for monitoring and assessing draft budgetary plans and ensuring the correction of excessive deficit of the Member States in the euro area*, O.J. L 244/23 (2013).

[178] Articles 7.1 and 13 of Regulation (EU) No. 472/2013, and Article 13 of Regulation (EU) No. 473/2013.

[179] Cf. Recital 7 of Regulation (EU) No. 472/2013.

[180] Article 9.5 of Regulation (EU) No. 473/2013.

obligation[181] to implement the rules of Article 3.1 TSCG into national law. If a Contracting Party fails to take the necessary measures to comply with a judgment of the CJEU, the matter may be referred to the CJEU again, which may impose a lump-sum or a penalty payment of up to 0.1% of the respective country's GDP. In a Protocol to the TSCG, which may be seen as an integral part of the Treaty,[182] MS committed to bringing a case to the CJEU through the Council Trio Presidency within three months after the Commission's report under Article 8.1 TSCG. The Commission, on the other hand, is responsible to propose the common principles the national implementing provisions must be based on (Article 3.1) and to endorse and monitor the budgetary and economic partnership programmes (Article 5), and it is 'invited' to present a report on the provisions adopted by the Contracting Parties (Article 8).

However, given its nature as an international treaty (→ para 11), it is disputed whether entrusting the CJEU and the Commission with these tasks under the TSCG is compatible with EU law. In that regard, the ECJ clarified in *Pringle*[183] that MS are indeed 'entitled, in areas which do not fall under the exclusive competence of the Union, to entrust tasks to the institutions, outside the framework of the Union', provided that those tasks 'do not alter the essential character of the powers conferred on those institutions by the EU and FEU Treaties'. Since Union institutions may only act 'within the limits of the powers conferred on it in the Treaties, and in conformity with the procedures, conditions and objectives set out in them',[184] the **use of Union institutions** is only be permitted under the Treaties, if it is explicitly or implicitly allowed therein.

Concerning the **CJEU** competence under Article 8 TSCG, the legal basis mentioned in the Preamble is **Article 273 TFEU**. Under this provision, the CJEU 'shall have jurisdiction in any dispute between MS which relates to the subject matter of the Treaties if the dispute is submitted to it under a special agreement between the parties'. While it is undisputed that the TSCG 'relates to the subject matter of the Treaties' and that a clause such as Article 8 TSCG is generally suitable to establish the competence under Article 273 TFEU, it is less clear whether the mechanism foreseen in the Protocol to the TSCG according to which matters are brought before the CJEU complies with the Treaties.

Thus, it was viewed as problematic that the Contracting Parties committed to bringing a case before the CJEU through the Council Trio Presidency within three months after the Commission's report under Article 8.1 TSCG. While the wording of the Protocol suggests that in case of a finding of non-compliance in the Commission's report, the Council Presidency would indeed be obliged to initiate proceed-

---

[181] Cf. Fabbrini (2013), p. 6.
[182] Calliess (2012), p. 111.
[183] Case C-370/12, *Pringle* (ECJ 27 November 2012) para 158.
[184] Article 13.2 TEU. Cf. also Article 5.2 TEU.

ings (contrary to the initiation of the second proceedings regarding sanctions[185]), Article 273 TFEU only allows **claims brought by MS**. It could be argued that involving the Commission beforehand and binding MS to a certain extent to its findings unduly circumvents this limitation.[186] Moreover, with the possibility to decide on a **period** within which the respective MS shall take the necessary measures to comply with the judgment, Article 8 TSCG goes beyond Articles 258 et seqq. TFEU. However, since Article 273 TFEU does not specify which disputes the Court may decide on (and how), it is arguably possible to let it set a time limit under Article 273 TFEU.[187]

57 However, Article 126.10 TFEU **excludes** the **infringement procedure**[188] under Articles 259, 260 TFEU as regards compliance with the obligation to avoid excessive deficits. It might be argued that the purpose of the exclusion of the CJEU's jurisdiction in Article 126.10 TFEU is to ensure that politically and economically sensitive questions are not left to be decided by lawyers but remain in the hands of the MS (in the Council). Against the background of Article 344 TFEU, which provides that 'Member States undertake not to submit a dispute concerning the interpretation or application of the Treaties to any method of settlement other than those provided for therein', Article 8 TSCG could be seen as problematic. However, although the TSCG is closely linked to the EDP, the jurisdiction of the ECJ under Article 8 TSCG concerns merely the monitoring of the implementation of the rules of Article 3.1 TSCG into national law and does not include the competence of the ECJ to determine whether an excessive deficit exists in a particular case. This decision remains with the Council in the EDP.

58 As regards the tasks conferred upon the **Commission**, there is no legal basis mentioned in the TSCG. According to the ECJ, however, the Treaties do not prevent the MS from entrusting the Commission with tasks concerning actions undertaken by them outside the EU legal order under international law.[189] However, with reference to Article 35 VCLT[190] it can generally be assumed that such a transfer of tasks by way of international law needs the (express) consent of all MS.[191] Contrary to the ESM, where the delegation of powers to the Commission

---

[185] This is criticised by Calliess (2012), p. 111, who claims that a legally binding provision 'would have been particularly necessary' for the second proceedings on the imposition of sanctions.

[186] E.g. Fischer-Lescano and Oberndorfer (2013), p. 10 et seqq.; Antpöhler (2012), p. 385.

[187] Calliess (2012), p. 111 et seq.

[188] Actions for annulment (Article 263 TFEU) or for failure to act (Article 265 TFEU) are, however, still permissible.

[189] Joined Cases C-181/91 and C-248/91, *Parliament v Council and Commission* (ECJ 30 June 1993) para 20; Case C-316/91, *Parliament v Council* (ECJ 2 March 1994) para 41.

[190] Article 35 VCLT reads: 'An obligation arises for a third State from a provision of a treaty if the parties to the treaty intend the provision to be the means of establishing the obligation and the third State expressly accepts that obligation in writing'.

[191] Repasi (2013), p. 57; Schoenfleisch (2018), p. 182 ff.

was expressly agreed upon by all MS,[192] no such decision exists with regard to the TSCG.[193] Moreover, according to the ECJ in *Pringle*[194] it is important for their being compatible with EU law that the tasks conferred upon Union institutions 'do not entail any power to make decisions of their own'. With the power to decide on common principles for the implementation of the Fiscal Compact into national law as well as the responsibility to report on this implementation with the consequence of MS being bound to bring the case before the CJEU, it is highly questionable whether this requirement is fulfilled here.

The introduction of several elements of the TSCG into Union law with the Two-Pack, including the requirement for ex-ante coordination of MS' debt issuance plans,[195] the requirement for MS in EDP to prepare economic partnership programmes[196] (→ para 49), as well as the existence of independent bodies monitoring compliance with national fiscal rules,[197] rectifies these problems to a certain extent.[198] They might eventually be solved with the **integration of the TSCG into the Treaties**, as foreseen in Article 16.2 and the Preamble to the TSCG. Thus, the Commission Proposal for a Council Directive incorporating the substance of the TSCG into the EU legal order[199] includes a competence of the Commission to report on the implementation of the Directive in the MS.[200] Negotiations on this proposal are still pending, but they are obviously (and not surprisingly in view of the COVID-19 pandemic) not a priority at present and it is not foreseeable at present whether the integration of the TSCG into the Union legal framework will take place procedure referred to in Article 121.

59

---

[192] On 20 June 2011, the representatives of the Governments of the Member States of the European Union authorised the Contracting Parties to request the Commission and the ECB to perform the tasks provided for in the ESM Treaty, cf. Recital 10 of the ESM Treaty.

[193] Claiming that the delegation of powers to the Commission was, thus, illegal, e.g. Calliess (2012), p. 113; Fischer-Lescano and Oberndorfer (2013), p. 10 et seqq.; more nuanced Antpöhler (2012), p. 389 et seq.

[194] Case C-370/12, *Pringle* (ECJ 27 November 2012) para 161.

[195] Article 8 of Regulation (EU) No. 473/2013.

[196] Article 9 of Regulation (EU) No. 473/2013.

[197] Article 5 of Regulation (EU) No. 473/2013.

[198] However, it could also give rise to additional problems considering that when violations of EU law (and not just the TSCG) are concerned, the ECJ could no longer be competent under Article 273 TFEU; cf. Calliess (2012), p. 112.

[199] COM(2017) 824 final.

[200] Cf. Article 5 of the proposal for a Council Directive laying down provisions for strengthening fiscal responsibility and the medium-term budgetary orientation in the Member States, COM (2017) 824 final. The competences of the CJEU would, then, follow directly from Articles 258 et seqq. TFEU.

4. Multilateral Surveillance

4.1. The 'Surveillance-Cycle'

4.1.1. European Semester: Economic Policy Coordination

60 The European Semester coordinates coordination.[201] As a 'yearly cycle of economic policy coordination', it thus allows for the collective evaluation and comparison of Member States' fiscal and macroeconomic policies, providing a framework and (tight[202]) timetable, inter alia, for the multilateral surveillance procedure referred to in Article 121 TFEU ($\rightarrow$ Article 121 TFEU para 23 et seqq.). Ever since its introduction in the first half of 2011, the **European Semester for economic policy coordination** has been 'the main mechanism through which Member States discuss their economic and fiscal policy'.[203] With the Six-Pack, the European Semester was institutionalised in secondary law and is now anchored in Article 2-a of Regulation (EC) No. 1466/97. Thus, it includes the formulation of the broad economic policy guidelines under Article 121.2 TFEU and of the employment guidelines under Article 148.2 TFEU, and the surveillance of their implementation, the submission and assessment of MS' stability or convergence programmes, of their national reform programmes, as well as the surveillance to prevent and correct macroeconomic imbalances under Regulation (EU) No. 1176/2011.[204] In the future, MS' compliance with their 'recovery and resilience plans', submitted as part of their national reform programmes in the context of the 'Recovery and Resilience Facility'[205] providing financial support to MS as part of the EU's response to the COVID-19 crisis, will also be monitored within the European Semester.

61 The name 'European Semester' suggests that the cycle lasts about half a year. However, while it is true that most documents are produced in spring, the cycle already starts with the autumn economic forecast conducted by the Commission in November,[206] which ultimately leads to the adoption of **euro area recommendations**, conclusions on the **Annual Growth Survey** (AGS), and the **Alert Mechanism Report** (AMR) by the Council in December/January. While the AGS sets out

---

[201] Hufeld (2015), para 40; Armstrong (2013), p. 613.

[202] The time constraints imposed by the European Semester make it difficult for national parliaments to control their executives, see Dawson and De Witte (2013), p. 834 with further references.

[203] Commission Reflection Paper *on the deepening of the economic and monetary union*, COM (2017) 291, p. 10.

[204] Article 2-a.2 of Regulation (EC) No. 1466/97 as amended.

[205] Parliament/Council Regulation (EU) 2021/241 *establishing the Recovery and Resilience Facility*, O.J. L 57/17 (2021). See also the European Council Conclusions, 17–21 July 2020, on the recovery plan and multiannual financial framework for 2021–2027, EUCO 10/20.

[206] For EA Member States, the Commission's opinions on national budgets will also be published by the end of November and discussed in the Council, linking the European with the 'National Semester' ($\rightarrow$ para 63 et seqq.).

general economic priorities for the EU, provides MS with policy guidance for the following year and is accompanied by a set of euro area recommendations reinforcing these policy priorities[207] as well as by the Joint Employment Report and the employment guidelines of the Social Pillar,[208] the AMR identifies the MS for which an in-depth review is necessary to decide whether an imbalance in need of policy action exists.[209]

The European Semester continues with the Commission's **country reports**[210] in February, which assess the overall economic and social developments[211] in each MS and the progress made in addressing the issues identified in the CSR of the preceding year. In March, the European Council adopts economic priorities based on the AGS, and in April MS present **national reform programmes** for economic policies,[212] outlining the respective strategy for sustainable, smart and inclusive growth in the sense of the Europe 2020 strategy,[213] as well as **stability or convergence programmes** for their budgetary policies.[214] In May, the European Commission proposes the **new CSR**. Following a detailed analysis of MS' plans for macroeconomic, budgetary and structural reforms, these individual recommendations set out the policy guidance for each MS for the next 12 to 18 months. The Semester ends in July, when the CSR proposed by the Commission are endorsed by the European Council and formally adopted by the Council. The European Parliament also issues a resolution on the CSR in September. Given the severe deterioration of the economic situation because of the COVID-19 pandemic and the activation of the escape clauses of the SGP, the requirements for MS' reports in the 2020 European Semester were simplified and the 2021 cycle saw the temporary adaption of the Semester in order to coordinate it with the Recovery and Resilience Facility.[215]

62

---

[207] Cf. Articles 121.3 and 136.2 point (b) TFEU.

[208] Cf. Article 148 TFEU. According to a 'Social Scoreboard' presented in April 2017, the Joint Employment Report also contains an analysis of several indicators, which feeds into the preparation of the Country Reports alongside the indicators of the MIP.

[209] Article 3.1 of Regulation (EU) No. 1176/2011.

[210] Before 2015, instead of the Country Reports, the Commission adopted staff working documents on the CSR and in-depth reports in the MIP.

[211] Based on the Scoreboard of macroeconomic imbalances and the 'Social Scoreboard' in the 'European Pillar of Social Rights'.

[212] Cf. Article 2-a.2 point (d) of Regulation (EC) No. 1466/97 as amended.

[213] Commission Communication, *EUROPE 2020, A strategy for smart, sustainable and inclusive growth*, COM(2010) 2020 final.

[214] Cf. Article 2-a.2 point (c), Articles 3 et seqq. and 7 et seqq. of Regulation (EC) No. 1466/97 as last amended by Regulation (EU) No. 1175/2011.

[215] Thus, Member States were encouraged to submit national reform programmes and recovery and resilience plans in a single integrated document, which the Commission evaluated. CSR were limited to the budgetary situation for those Member States who submitted recovery and resilience plans.

4.1.2. 'National Semester': Monitoring of Budgetary Policies

63 MS which are also members of the EA are also included in a **surveillance cycle** during the second half of the year. It is in this second half of the year which is sometimes referred to as the '**national semester**' that MS prepare their national budgets for the forthcoming year. In this context, the Two-Pack Regulation (EU) No. 473/2013, which, as it is based on Article 136 TFEU, is applicable only to EA Member States (Article 1.3), prescribes a synchronised monitoring of budgetary policies (cf. Recital 11). Accordingly, the 'draft budget for the forthcoming year for the central government and the main parameters of the draft budgets for all the other subsectors of the general government', as well as the independent macroeconomic forecasts they are based on, shall be made public each year no later than 15 October (Articles 4.2 and 4.4).[216]

64 By the same annual deadline MS must also submit to the Commission and to the Euro Group a '**draft budgetary plan**' for the forthcoming year, which must contain certain minimum information (Article 6).[217] In this context, it is worth noting that the draft budgetary plan must be consistent with the recommendations issued in the context of the SGP and the annual cycle of surveillance, including the macroeconomic imbalances procedure, and with opinions on the EPP. Additionally, MS must also ensure that their national budgetary *procedure* is consistent with these prescriptions (Article 3). Regulation (EU) No. 473/2013 thus renders the recommendations and opinions issued within the multilateral surveillance of EA members binding targets for their budgetary planning (→ para 86 et seqq.).

65 The draft budgetary plans are subsequently made public (Article 6.2) and the Commission adopts an opinion on them 'as soon as possible and in any event by 30 November' (Article 7.1).[218] The Commission's opinion is also made public and presented to the Euro Group, as well as, at request, to the parliament of the MS concerned or to the EP (Article 7.3). This way, the **Commission can be directly involved in the national budgetary debates**.[219] If, after the submission of the draft budgetary plan, the Commission identifies particularly serious non-compliance with the budgetary policy obligations laid down in the SGP, it requests, in an

---

[216] Under the Recitals, these parameters 'include, in particular, the projected budgetary outcomes of the other subsectors, the main assumptions underlying those projections and the reasons for expected changes with respect to the stability programme assumptions'; see Recital 14 of Regulation (EU) No. 473/2013.

[217] Under Article 6.5, the Commission had to establish a harmonised framework in cooperation with the MS setting out the specification of the content of the draft budgetary plan. This has been done by the Commission Communication *replacing the Communication from the Commission on Harmonized framework for draft budgetary plans and debt issuance reports within the euro area (COM(2013) 490 final)*, COM(2014) 675 final.

[218] Under Recital 21, the Commission's opinion should 'tak[e] into account, to the extent possible, the specific national fiscal schedule and parliamentary procedures, in order to ensure that Union's policy guidance in the budgetary area can be appropriately integrated in the national budgetary preparations'.

[219] Cf. Budgetdienst des Parlamentes (2013), p. 12.

opinion to be adopted within twwo weeks of submission of the draft budgetary plan, that a revised draft budgetary plan be submitted (Article 7.2 (1)).[220] On this revised draft budgetary plan, the Commission adopts a new opinion (Article 7.2 (3)).[221]

Moreover, the Commission, based on the national budgetary prospects and their interaction across the area, undertakes an **overall assessment** of the budgetary situation and prospects in the euro area as a whole, including sensitivity analyses that provide an indication of the risks to public finance sustainability in the event of adverse economic, financial or budgetary developments and, where appropriate, measures to reinforce the coordination of budgetary and macroeconomic policy at the euro area level (Article 7.4). This overall assessment is made public and considered in the annual general guidance[222] to MS issued by the Commission. Both the country-specific opinions of the Commission on the draft budgetary plans as well as the overall assessment are subsequently discussed in the Euro Group.[223]

Ultimately, the **budget** for the central government as well as the updated main budgetary parameters for the other sub-sectors of the general government are to be **adopted** or fixed upon and made public annually **not later than 31 December** (Article 4.3). If, for objective reasons beyond the control of the government, the budget is not adopted or fixed upon and made public by 31 December, MS shall, under Article 4.3 of Regulation (EU) No. 473/2013, 'have in place reversionary budget procedures to be applied'. While this requires national provisions on the provisional budget to be available, it leaves the decision on the means to the MS. Accordingly, '[s]uch arrangements could include the implementation of the government's draft budget, of the preceding year's approved budget, or of specific parliament-approved measures' (Recital 15).

4.2. Multilateral Surveillance Procedure

Under Article 121.3 TFEU, 'the Council shall, on the basis of reports submitted by the Commission, monitor economic developments in each of the MS and in the Union as well as the consistency of economic policies with the broad guidelines [of Article 121.2 TFEU] and regularly carry out an overall assessment'. If a MS's economic policies are not consistent with the broad economic guidelines or risk jeopardising the proper functioning of EMU, the Commission may first issue a warning to the MS, which is then addressed by the Council with the necessary recommendations. Article 121.6 TFEU stipulates that 'detailed rules for the multilateral surveillance procedure' may be adopted by means of regulations in

---

[220] The revised draft budgetary plan must be submitted as soon as possible and in any event within three weeks of the date of the Commission's opinion.

[221] The Commission's new opinion shall be adopted 'as soon as possible and in any event within three weeks of submission of the revised draft budgetary plan'.

[222] Supposedly, this particularly refers to the AGS and the recommendations for the euro.

[223] The results of those discussions of the Euro Group shall be made public where appropriate; see Article 7.5 of Regulation (EU) No. 473/2013.

accordance with the ordinary legislative procedure. Consequently, the **multilateral surveillance procedure** is essentially laid down in what is referred to as the 'preventive' arm of the SGP, namely Regulation (EC) No. 1466/97 as last revised and significantly tightened[224] by Six-Pack Regulation (EU) No. 1175/2011, setting out the rules on the content, the submission, the examination and the monitoring of stability programmes and convergence programmes to achieve the MTO (Article 1).

69 However, the MIP and EIP[225] as well as the measures taken only for the EA, namely the introduction of sanctions also for the 'preventive' arm with Six-Pack Regulation (EU) No. 1173/2011 and the enhanced surveillance under the Two-Pack Regulations (EU) No. 472 and 473/2013 were also based on (Article 136 in conjunction with) **Article 121.6 TFEU**. As far as the surveillance cycle is concerned, the rules on the European Semester and on the monitoring of budgetary policies in Two-Pack Regulation (EU) No. 473/2013 have been described above (→ para 60 et seqq., 63 et seqq.). Further, the multilateral surveillance procedure under Regulation (EC) No. 1466/97 as such as well as MIP and EIP shall not be repeated here (→ Article 121 TFEU para 23 et seqq., 58). However, as with the EDP (para 40 et seqq.), certain specific issues will briefly be addressed.

4.2.1. New Sanctions and Reverse Qualified Majority Voting

70 In the revised multilateral surveillance procedure, the Council is now 'expected to, as a rule, follow the recommendations and proposals of the Commission or explain its position publicly' (Article 2-ab.2 of Regulation (EC) No. 1466/97). Most notably, this general **comply-or-explain obligation** applies to the CSR. However, Six-Pack Regulation (EU) No. 1173/2011 for the first time also introduced **sanctions** of an administrative nature (Article 9) in the **preventive arm of the SGP**. As said Regulation is based on Article 136 TFEU (in combination with Article 121.6 TFEU), it applies to EA members only (Article 1.2). Under its Article 4, an **interest-bearing deposit**[226] amounting to 0.2%[227] of the Member State's GDP in the preceding year may be imposed on a MS which failed to take action in response to the Council recommendation under Article 6.2 (2) of Regulation (EC) No. 1466/97 setting a deadline for the necessary policy measures following a significant observed deviation from the adjustment path towards the MTO.

71 Similarly, Article 3 of Regulation (EU) No. 1174/2011 introduced sanctions in the **MIP**, which also constitutes a form of multilateral surveillance under Article 121 TFEU. Under this provision, an **interest-bearing deposit** amounting

---

[224] Cf. Weber (2013), p. 379.

[225] Cf. Regulations (EU) No. 1175/2011 and No. 1176/2011.

[226] Under Article 4.5 of Regulation (EU) No. 1173/2011, the interest-bearing deposit shall bear an interest rate reflecting the Commission's credit risk and the relevant investment period.

[227] The sanctions may be reduced or cancelled on grounds of exceptional economic circumstances or following a reasoned request under Article 4.4 of Regulation (EU) No. 1173/2011.

to 0.1%[228] of the Member State's GDP in the preceding year (Article 3.5) may be imposed where a Council decision establishing non-compliance is adopted under Article 10.4 of Regulation (EU) No. 1176/2011 and the Council concludes that the MS concerned has not taken the corrective action recommended by the Council. Moreover, an annual fine amounting to 0.1%[229] of the Member State's GDP in the preceding year (Article 3.5) may be imposed when two successive Council recommendations in the same MIP are adopted under Article 8.3 of Regulation (EU) No. 1176/2011 and the MS has submitted an insufficient Corrective Action Plan. Likewise, an annual fine of 0.1% may be imposed by means of converting the interest-bearing deposit into an annual fine in cases where two successive Council decisions in the same MIP are adopted establishing non-compliance under Article 10.4 of Regulation (EU) No. 1176/2011.

Corresponding to the sanctions in the corrective arm of the SGP, the decision on the sanctions in the preventive arm of the SGP and the MIP 'shall [also] be deemed to be adopted by the Council unless it decides by a qualified majority to reject the Commission's recommendation within ten days of the Commission's adoption thereof'.[230] Consequently, the legality of the additional sanctions as well as the **RQMV** has been highly disputed in the preventive arm of the SGP as well. While with Article 126.11 TFEU the Council had sanctioning powers in the EDP even before the adoption of the Six-Pack, the multilateral surveillance procedure did not know sanctions at all until the Six-Pack. However, given that all sanctioning powers are based on the **same legal basis**, namely Article 136 TFEU in combination with Article 121.6 TFEU, the conclusions as to their **legality** must be the same. **72**

Therefore, they shall not be repeated here (→ para 41 et seqq.). Suffice it to say that Article 136 TFEU is seen as a proper additional competence and that also in the multilateral surveillance procedure, the decisions on sanctions taken by RQMV are tied to decisions taken with qualified majority, namely the decisions under Article 6.2 (2) of Regulation (EC) No. 1466/97 as well as under Articles 8.3 and 10.4 of Regulation (EU) No. 1176/2011, thus largely leaving the institutional balance intact. However, the fact that EA Member States now face **sanctions in the multilateral surveillance procedure**, especially when considered together with the rules on the national budgetary policies of the Two-Pack, significantly **changed the nature of the coordination of economic policies**, creating a system of 'coordination by coercion', the legality of which is at least questionable (→ para 86 et seqq.). **73**

---

[228] The sanctions may be reduced or cancelled on grounds of exceptional economic circumstances or following a reasoned request under Article 3.6 of Regulation (EU) No. 1174/2011.

[229] The sanctions may be reduced or cancelled on grounds of exceptional economic circumstances or following a reasoned request under Article 3.6 of Regulation (EU) No. 1174/2011.

[230] Article 4.2 of Regulation (EU) No. 1173/2011; Article 3.3 of Regulation (EU) No. 1174/2011.

4.2.2. Enhanced Surveillance

74 Aside from the strengthening of the preventive arm of the SGP and the establishment of the MIP, the (sovereign debt crisis) induced changes to economic governance also introduced a new system of **enhanced economic and budgetary surveillance** for EA members experiencing or threatened with serious difficulties with respect to their financial stability. For these Member States, Two-Pack Regulation (EU) No. 472/2013 provides rules on enhanced surveillance, which complement and partly take priority over other surveillance procedures. Thus, while recommendations in the SGP and MIP must be considered when preparing a macroeconomic adjustment programme, once a MS is subject to such a macroeconomic adjustment programme, the provisions on the EPP[231] as well as the additional reporting requirements of Regulation (EU) No. 473/2013 (→ para 51), the MIP, as well the monitoring and assessment of the European Semester (→ para 60 et seqq.) no longer apply.[232]

75 Initially, however, the procedure is interlinked with the multilateral surveillance framework. Thus, the **Commission** may, after a comprehensive assessment considering, inter alia, the alert mechanism under Article 3.1 of Regulation (EU) No. 1176/2011 and available in-depth reviews, **decide to subject to enhanced surveillance** a MS **experiencing or threatened with serious difficulties** with respect to its financial stability which are likely to have adverse spill-over effects on other Member States in the EA (Article 2.1 of Regulation 472/2013). It is bound to do so, where a MS is in receipt of **financial assistance** on a precautionary basis from one or several other MS or third countries, the EFSM, the ESM, the EFSF, or another relevant international financial institution such as the IMF (Article 2.3 of Regulation 472/2013).

76 Under Article 3.1 of Regulation (EU) No. 473/2013, MS subject to enhanced surveillance shall adopt measures aimed at addressing the sources or potential **sources of difficulties**, thereby considering any recommendations under the SGP or the MIP. Regular review missions are made by the Commission, in liaison with the ECB and with the relevant ESAs and, where appropriate, with the IMF in the MS to verify the progress made in the implementation of these measures (Article 3.5 of Regulation No. 472/2013). Upon request from the Commission, the respective MS must also provide necessary information, carry out stress-tests, and submit to regular assessments (Article 3.3 of Regulation No. 472/2013). The enhanced surveillance, generally, includes wider access to the information needed for a close monitoring of the economic, fiscal and financial situation and a regular reporting to the competent EP committee of the European Parliament and to the Economic and Financial Committee (Article 134 TFEU).

---

[231] Articles 7.1 and 13 of Regulation (EU) No. 472/2013, Article 13 of Regulation (EU) No. 473/2013.
[232] Cf. Recital 7 of Regulation (EU) No. 472/2013.

If further measures are needed and the financial and economic situation of the MS concerned has significant adverse effects on the financial stability of the euro area or of its MS, however, the Council may recommend to the MS concerned to adopt precautionary corrective measures or to prepare a draft **macroeconomic adjustment programme**. This recommendation may be made public. This decision, as well as the decision to place a MS under the obligation to adopt precautionary corrective measures or to prepare a draft macroeconomic adjustment programme is a discretionary decision of the Council. By contrast, when a MS requests financial assistance from one or several other MS or third countries, the EFSM, the ESM, the EFSF or the IMF, it is *always* bound to prepare a draft macroeconomic adjustment programme. 77

The macroeconomic adjustment programme, which is subsequently **approved** by the Council upon proposal from the Commission (Article 7.2 of Regulation 472/2013), addresses 'the specific risks emanating from that MS for the financial stability in the euro area and [aims] at rapidly re-establishing a sound and sustainable economic and financial situation and restoring the MS's capacity to finance itself fully on the financial markets' (Article 7.1 (2)). It includes annual budgetary targets (Article 7.1) and must be fully consistent with the Memorandum of Understanding (MoU) concluded between the MS and the ESM or the EFSF (Article 7.2 (2)) (→ Supplement to Title VIII: TESM para 69 et seqq.). The progress made in the implementation of its macroeconomic adjustment programme is **monitored by the Commission**, where appropriate with the IMF (Article 7.4). The respective MS is obliged to fully cooperate and to provide the Commission and the ECB with all information that they consider necessary (Article 7.4). These provisions on enhanced surveillance grant the Commission and the ECB (acting as part of what used to be called 'Troika') rather far-reaching powers and seem to institutionalise the politics of austerity practiced in the sovereign debt crisis.[233] 78

4.3. Coordination by Coercion[234]

4.3.1. The Legal Status of the European Semester Instruments

The elements of economic and budgetary surveillance introduced in the wake of the sovereign debt crisis significantly changed the procedure of multilateral surveillance. Thus, while it evolved from the so-called open method of coordination (OMC),[235] the 'European Semester' now brings together a wide range of EU governance instruments with **different legal bases**, such as the SGP, the MIP, the 79

---

[233] Therefore, they are condemned, e.g. by Fischer-Lescano and Oberndorfer (2013), p. 12. Criticising the priority of austerity see also Dawson and De Witte (2013), p. 826 et seq.

[234] This section builds on my habilitation thesis (Wutscher 2020).

[235] Amtenbrink and De Haan (2003), p. 1079.

TSCG, the Europe 2020 Strategy and the Integrated Economic and Employment Policy Guidelines. Similarly, a **range of instruments** is produced during the Semester, namely the AGS, the AMR, the Joint Employment Report, the recommendations for the euro area, the Country Reports, and perhaps most importantly, the CSR.

80   Designed as a policy coordination mechanism, AGS, AMR, recommendations for the euro area, Joint Employment Report, Country Reports, as well as CSR adopted in the context of the European Semester are generally classified as '**soft law**' measures. However, the term 'soft law' is ambiguous.[236] Generally speaking, it may be said that 'soft law' instruments are instruments, which are (i) either not legally binding and/or (ii) not enforceable in a court of law, but may, aside from the practical effects they are aimed at, nonetheless have certain (possibly only indirect) legal effects.[237] However, not only is there no definition in primary law, EU law practice also developed various manifestations of such instruments with different functions, ranging from recommendations and opinions to guidelines, communications, handbooks, green books, white books, and so on. Regarding 'recommendations', Article 288 TFEU explicitly states that they shall have 'no binding force', but also communications from the Commission and Council conclusions are deemed not to be binding in nature but mere policy documents. However, it already follows from their being mentioned in Article 288 TFEU that the Treaties embrace a wide notion of law, with soft law instruments forming part of the EU legal order.[238] Thus, soft law instruments are also 'valid' when they comply with the prerequisites of primary and secondary law, without being legally binding as such.

81   Of the many possible classifications of soft law adopted by European institutions, *Senden* distinguishes **three main functions of soft law instruments**, namely preparatory and informative instruments, formal an informal steering instruments, and interpretative and decisional instruments, also referred to as 'European administrative soft law'.[239] To the extent that they originate from European institutions, the European Semester instruments can thus be regarded in part as steering instruments, and in part as administrative soft law since they have as their goal to guide and facilitate the interpretation and implementation of European hard law,[240] especially the obligations anchored in primary and secondary law to coordinate

---

[236] See, e.g. Terpan (2015), p. 70 et seqq.; Senden (2004), p. 111 et seqq.; Knauff (2010), p. 214 et seqq.

[237] Cf. e.g. Senden (2004), p. 112. Terpan (2015), p. 76 et seq., proposes a typology of soft and hard law combining the criteria 'obligation' and 'enforcement'.

[238] von Bogdandy et al. (2002), p. 114. Cf. also Schoenfleisch (2018), p. 17 with further references.

[239] Senden (2004), pp. 119–120.

[240] See, e.g. Luijendijk and Senden (2011), p. 316.

economic policy[241] and to avoid excessive public deficits[242] (and macroeconomic imbalances[243]).

By way of the **principle of loyal cooperation** under Article 4.3 TEU, which applies to the whole EU legal order including its 'non-binding' instruments, such European soft law is vested with a limited degree of normativity, in that this principle would be violated if MS deliberately disregarded existing soft law.[244] At least[245] where the respective EU institutions are also competent for the oversight of the relevant area of EU law, soft law instruments from those institutions serve as a **yardstick for the interpretation** of the 'hard' norms concerned and are, in this sense and despite Article 288 TFEU, indeed binding for national courts and authorities.[246] Thus, European Semester instruments, which are connected to the procedures under Articles 121 and 126 TFEU and originate from the same institutions acting in these procedures (as a general rule that is the Council upon recommendation by the Commission), must already be considered by MS because of their obligation under Article 4.3 TEU. **82**

Moreover, additional legal effects may be conferred by secondary law. Technically speaking, in such cases the **source of normativity** remains the respective act of secondary law. However, through reference to what would otherwise be 'mere policy documents', taking such documents into consideration is turned into an (enforceable) legal obligation, which at least requires increased justification by a national authority where it deviates from such an act. Regarding the European Semester instruments, the interlinkage with both the SGP and the MIP effectively creates such enforceable obligations. For example, being identified in the AMR as one of the MS for which an in-depth review will be carried out,[247] has concrete consequences for the MS concerned, not only because it may lead to the opening of an MIP, but also because it gives rise to obligations to facilitate this review.[248] **83**

Moreover, **Article 2-a.3 of Regulation (EC) No. 1466/97** explicitly states that 'Member States **shall take due account of the guidance** addressed to them in the development of their economic, employment and budgetary policies before taking **84**

---

[241] As specified in Articles 5.1 and 121 TFEU, and Regulation (EC) No. 1466/97 as last amended by Regulation (EU) No. 1175/2011.

[242] As specified in Article 126 TFEU, Protocol (No. 12), and Regulation (EC) No. 1467/97 as amended.

[243] As specified in Regulations (EU) No. 1174/2011 and No. 1176/2011.

[244] Cf. already Case C-322/88, *Grimaldi* (ECJ 13 December 1989).

[245] It is less apparent if such an obligation to consider soft law measures also persists where the EU either has no legislative competence at all or when such acts originate from an institution which has no powers in the relevant area of EU law. In both cases there is the inherent danger of a 'competence creep', be it towards the Union as a whole or to the detriment of the institutional balance.

[246] Cf. Ruffert, in Calliess and Ruffert (2021), Article 288 AEUV para 95.

[247] Article 3 of Regulation (EU) No. 1176/2011.

[248] Cf. Recital 15, Articles 5, 13 of Regulation (EU) No. 1176/2011.

key decisions on their national budgets for the succeeding years'.[249] The 'guidance' referred to in this provision is addressed to MS by the Council making full use of the legal instruments provided under Articles 121 and 148 TFEU, the preventive arm of the SGP, and the MIP.[250] Thus, it particularly refers not only to the CSR, but also to the euro area recommendations. Already this obligation 'to take due account of the guidance' goes beyond what is generally required by the principle of loyal cooperation.

85   With the entry into force of the Two-Pack, this obligation is repeated and strengthened in the respective Regulations (EU) No. 472/2013 and No. 473/2013. While Regulation (EU) No. 472/2013 only reiterates that a MS subject to enhanced surveillances shall consider any recommendations addressed to it under the SGP or MIP (Article 3.1), Article 3 of Regulation (EU) No. 473/2013 requires that MS' budgetary procedure **'shall be consistent with' the general guidance and the recommendations** issued in the context of the annual cycle of surveillance, including the MIP. Article 6 of the same Regulation stipulates that draft budgetary plans **'shall be consistent with' the recommendations** issued in the context of the SGP and the annual cycle of surveillance, including the MIP. The formulation of these provisions leaves no room for disregarding the instruments and, thus, seems to go even further than the obligation to take due account of the guidance under Article 2-a of Regulation (EC) No. 1466/97. These provisions, however, apply only to the EA.

4.3.2. Consequences of Non-Compliance

86   Non-compliance with European Semester instruments is also followed by **hard enforcement**, creating 'a hybrid framework that combines rules-based and co-ordination based forms of governance'.[251] Under the MIP and revised SGP, a MS potentially faces financial sanctions by the Council if it violates the fiscal rules or faces excessive macroeconomic imbalances that are insufficiently addressed (→ para 41 et seqq., 70 et seqq.).[252] However, violations of these stability obligations are indeed identified by monitoring the adherence to the European Semester instruments, particularly the CSR. Consequently, it is the progress made in addressing the issues identified in last year's CSR which is assessed in the country reports. Thus, and as stipulated in Article 2-a of Regulation (EC) No. 1466/97, potential consequences of the failure to 'take due account' of the 'guidance' by the Council reach from further recommendations to warnings or 'measures', i.e. ultimately **sanctions**, under the SGP or the MIP.

87   Moreover, non-compliance with European Semester instruments may also be penalised on other accounts. Thus, when deciding on the support through

---

[249] Emphasis added.
[250] See Article 2-a of Regulation (EC) No. 1466/97 as amended.
[251] Armstrong (2013), p. 616.
[252] See, e.g. De Streel (2015), p. 84.

programmes of the European Structural and Investment Funds (**ESI Funds**)[253] account is taken, inter alia, of the relevant CSR adopted under Articles 121.2 and 148.4 TFEU, and of the national reform programme.[254] Support may, therefore, be suspended or withdrawn when European Semester instruments are not adhered to.[255] Similarly, the MoU, which is negotiated with a EA Member State requesting stability support by the ESM 'must be fully consistent with European Union law and, in particular, with the measures taken by the Union in the area of coordination of the economic policies of the Member States'.[256] Arguably, this makes compliance with the CSR obligatory for such MS.

Thus, not only the SGP and the MIP but also the financial support through the ESI Funds and the ESM are closely interlinked with the European Semester instruments. Through the Two-Pack, the instruments are also binding for MS' budgetary *procedures*. It may, therefore, be said that at least far as **EA Member States** are concerned, the coordination under the European Semester is in effect built on coercion, where seemingly 'soft' measures are declared binding in secondary law and followed by hard enforcement. The legitimacy of this '**coordination by coercion**' is at least questionable, not only since the CSR deal with a wide range of national policy areas, some of which are excluded from EU legislative competence (social security, taxation, health care, labour markets), but also because the new multilateral surveillance system stretches the limits of the coordination competence of Article 5 TFEU, thus undermining the system of competence division of the Lisbon Treaty (→ Article 2 TFEU para 1 et seqq.) and raising concerns for the constitutional balance[257] of the Union.

88

This is especially problematic since direct **legal protection** against CSR seems difficult, as Article 263 TFEU explicitly excludes the possibility to challenge 'recommendations and opinions' of the Council and the Commission before the ECJ. Taking this literally, MS could thus not directly challenge CSR but would be limited to bringing an action of annulment against the subsequent Council decision

89

---

[253] ESI Funds are the European Regional Development Fund, the European Social Fund, the Cohesion Fund, the European Agricultural Fund for Rural Development and the European Maritime and Fisheries Fund; cf. Article 1 of Regulation (EU) No. 1303/2013 *laying down common provisions on the European Regional Development Fund, the European Social Fund, the Cohesion Fund, the European Agricultural Fund for Rural Development and the European Maritime and Fisheries Fund and laying down general provisions on the European Regional Development Fund, the European Social Fund, the Cohesion Fund and the European Maritime and Fisheries Fund and repealing Council Regulation (EC) No. 1083/2006*, O.J. L 347/320 (2013).

[254] Article 4.1 of Regulation (EU) No. 1303/2013.

[255] Cf. Leino and Saarenheimo (2017), p. 179. As regards the 'Recovery and Resilience Facility', providing financial support in the (aftermath of the) COVID-19 crisis, the Commission shall examine the disbursement of tranches based on the 'national recovery and resilience plans' forming part of the national reform programmes; cf. Articles 17 et seqq. of Regulation (EU) 2021/241.

[256] Case C-370/12, *Pringle* (ECJ 27 November 2012) para 174.

[257] Cf. Dawson and De Witte (2013), p. 817 et seqq.

imposing sanctions under the SGP or MIP. Case law of the ECJ, however, suggests that as far as recommendations create binding legal effects, they may be challenged before the Court.[258] In the light of the effects of CSR under the current system of fiscal and economic policy governance, it would therefore be sensible to allow a direct review of CSR by the ECJ. The same holds true for the identification as one of the MS for which an in-depth review will be carried out in the AMR.

90   In **practice**, however, despite the EU's strong coercive powers against EA Member States, implementation continues to be based less on coercion than on negotiation, cooperation and persuasion, taking political considerations into account.[259] Moreover, the obligations of the SGP continue to be broken on a regular basis.[260] Thus, the rules on sanctions have been especially criticised as toothless, a critique that seems to have been confirmed by relatively recent decisions on sanctions, proposed by the Commission and not reversed by the Council, in which the fines for failure to take effective action to address an excessive deficit against Spain and Portugal were fully cancelled.[261] So far, there has, thus, never been a sanction imposed within the multilateral surveillance procedure or the EDP. In contrast, the new sanctioning powers concerning the manipulation of statistics, which were also introduced by the Six-Pack,[262] have already led to decisions on sanctions, namely against Spain for the manipulation of deficit data in the Autonomous Community of Valencia[263] as well as against Austria for misreporting debt data in the *Land* of Salzburg.[264] Moreover, in autumn 2018, the Commission for the first time requested the presentation of a revised draft budgetary plan under the Two-Pack Regulation (EU) No. 473/2013 after identifying in Italy's draft budgetary plan for 2019 a particularly serious non-compliance with the fiscal CSR.[265]

---

[258] Cf. e.g. Case C-31/13 P, *Hungary v Commission* (ECJ 13 February 2014) para 54 with further references; Case C-27/04, *Commission v Council* (ECJ 13 July 2004) para 50, where Council conclusions modifying recommendations under Article 126.7 TFEU in the course of the EDP were seen as a legitimate subject-matter of an annulment action. Cf., however, Joined Cases C-593/15 P and C-594/15P, *Slovakia v Commission*, and C-599/15 P, *Romania v Commission* (ECJ 25 October 2017) para 46 et seqq.

[259] Leino and Saarenheimo (2017), p. 169.

[260] Cf. e.g. the references at Leino and Saarenheimo (2017), p. 167.

[261] Council Implementing Decision of 5 August 2016 *on imposing a fine on Spain for failure to take effective action to address an excessive deficit*, 11554/16, and Council Implementing Decision of 5 August 2016 on *imposing a fine on Portugal for failure to take effective action to address an excessive deficit*, Doc. 11554/16.

[262] See Chapter V of Regulation (EU) No. 1173/2011.

[263] See Council Decision (EU) 2015/1289 *imposing a fine on Spain for the manipulation of deficit data in the Autonomous Community of Valencia*, O.J. L 198/19 (2015); see also Case C-521/15, *Spain v Council* (ECJ 20 December 2017).

[264] See Council Implementing Decision (EU) 2018/818 *imposing a fine on Austria for the manipulation of debt data in Land Salzburg*, O.J. L 137/23 (2018).

[265] See Press Release of 23 October 2018, IP/18/6174.

4.4. European Fiscal Board

Following the Five Presidents' Report of 22 June 2015 on completing Europe's Economic and Monetary Union (→ para 92 et seqq.), the Commission set up a **European Fiscal Board** (EFB) whose mandate is to contribute in an advisory capacity to the exercise of the Commission's functions in the multilateral fiscal surveillance of the EA.[266] Accordingly, it evaluates the implementation of the Union fiscal framework and the appropriateness of the actual fiscal stance at EA and national level, makes suggestions for the future evolution of the Union fiscal framework (also in the ongoing review of the fiscal governance framework), assesses the prospective fiscal stance appropriate for the EA and the national level under the SGP, cooperates with the National Independent Fiscal Councils,[267] and provides ad-hoc advice to the Commission President.[268] The EFB is composed of a Chair and four members and acts independently without instructions from the Union's institutions or bodies, from any government of a MS or from any other public or private body.[269] Arguably, it may thus be qualified as a structurally independent agency albeit one for which the requirements of the updated *Meroni* doctrine[270] are met, as no decision making-powers are transferred and the Commission's responsibility for the oversight of MS' fiscal policies in the multilateral surveillance exercise remains unaltered.

91

5. The Way Forward: Completing EMU?[271]

5.1. State of Debate and 'Constitutional' Limits

While the reforms implemented in the wake of the sovereign debt crisis were significant, they have not changed the general structure of EMU provided for in the Treaties.[272] However, since this asymmetrical structure of EMU (→ para 2) was identified as one of the causes of the crisis, on-going reform discussions under the headline of 'completing EMU' have revolved around **proposals for further fiscal integration** and the question of whether the EMU should, at least in the long run,

92

---

[266] Article 2.1 of the Commission Decision (EU) 2015/1937 *establishing an independent advisory European Fiscal Board*, O.J. L 282/37 (2015), as amended by Commission Decision (EU) 2016/221, O.J. L 40/15 (2016).

[267] These were set up as 'independent bodies' in accordance with the obligations to implement rules in national law as described under → para 34 et seqq.

[268] Article 2.2 of the Commission Decision (EU) 2015/1937.

[269] Cf. Articles 3 and 4 of the Commission Decision (EU) 2015/1937.

[270] Cf. Case 9/56, *Meroni* (ECJ 15 June 1958); Case C-270/12, *Short-Selling* (ECJ 22 January 2014).

[271] This section builds on my habilitation thesis (Wutscher 2020).

[272] Leino and Saarenheimo (2017), p. 166.

become a fully integrated fiscal and economic union to safeguard long-term stability.[273] These reform discussions have been shaped and guided by a **series of policy documents** produced at EU level, which essentially aim at bringing national economic policies further under EU control.[274] Of course, these proposals were accompanied and followed by a large number of alternative proposals from academia and civil society.[275]

93 The kick-off may be seen in the Commission's 'Blueprint for a deep and genuine EMU'[276] of 28 November 2012, which has been followed by the so-called Four Presidents' Report[277] of 5 December 2012 by the Presidents of the European Council, the Commission, the Euro Group, and the ECB, and the Five Presidents' Report[278] of 22 June 2015 adding to the four the President of the European Parliament. After the 2016 Brexit referendum, the debate gained new momentum. With the '**White Paper on the future of Europe and the way forward**'[279] of 1 March 2017, marking the 60th anniversary of the signing of the Treaty of Rome, the Commission proposed several possible scenarios for how Europe could evolve by 2025, ranging from carrying on with 'the status quo, to a change of scope and priorities, to a partial or collective leap forward'.[280] This White Paper was followed by several reflection papers on particular areas, notably also on the deepening of the EMU[281] and on EU finances.[282] A large package of initiatives was presented by the Commission on 6 December 2017, with several proposals for the next 18 months.[283] At the time of completion of this contribution (December 2021), however, only limited progress had been made, partly because reform discussions

---

[273] Cf. Calliess and Schoenfleisch (2012), p. 483.

[274] Leino and Saarenheimo (2017), p. 168.

[275] It is not possible to provide an even near comprehensive list here. However, as a starting point reference shall be made to the 2016 VoxEU.org eBook by Baldwin and Giavazzi (eds.) (2016), as well as the list of main references in the European Parliamentary Research Service's In-Depth Analysis *European Economic Governance. State of play and reform proposals*, November 2015, PE 571.319, p. 26.

[276] Commission Communication, *A Blueprint for a deep and genuine EMU – Launching a European Debate*, COM(2012) 777 final/2.

[277] Four Presidents' Report of 5 December 2012, *Towards a Genuine Economic and Monetary Union*.

[278] Five Presidents' Report of 22 June 2015 *on completing Europe's Economic and Monetary Union*.

[279] Commission White Paper *on the future of Europe and the way forward*, COM(2017) 2025.

[280] See Commission White Paper *on the future of Europe and the way forward*, p. 15 et seqq. The White paper distinguishes five possible scenarios, namely 'Carrying on', 'Nothing but the single market', 'Those who want more do more', 'Doing less more efficiently' as well as 'Doing much more together'.

[281] Commission Reflection Paper *on the deepening of the economic and monetary union*, COM (2017) 291.

[282] Commission Reflection Paper *on the future of EU finances*, COM(2017) 358.

[283] Cf., in particular, Commission Communication, *Further Steps Towards Completing Europe's Economic and Monetary Union: A Roadmap*, COM(2017) 821 final.

were overshadowed by the difficult Brexit negotiations and were then on hold for the benefit of immediate management of the COVID-19 crisis. A public debate on the review of the EU's economic governance framework, which was first initiated by the Commission in early 2020 and suspended due to the COVID-19 pandemic, was relaunched in October 2021 and is currently ongoing.

Hardly surprising, the proposals regarding fiscal integration in virtually all of the documents mentioned aim at achieving a **more integrated Economic and Fiscal Union**, both on an institutional and a substantive level. These proposals include, but are not limited to, stronger economic policy coordination and simpler fiscal rules, a macroeconomic stabilisation function ('fiscal capacity') for the EA, decision making powers for the Euro Group, the issuance of 'Eurobonds', the establishment of a EA Finance Minister[284] or a Treasury for the EA, a separate EA budget, as well as a European Monetary Fund (EMF)[285] or a European Debt Restructuring Regime. Some proposals, such as the establishment of an independent advisory European Fiscal Board (EFB), which was envisaged in the Five Presidents' Report,[286] have already been implemented.[287] Others, such as the formalisation of the regular dialogue with the European Parliament in EA matters, including matters related to the European Semester and the SGP,[288] the proposal to integrate the Fiscal Compact into the EU legal framework,[289] or a simplification of fiscal rules[290] could arguably be realised relatively swiftly. **94**

However, since the new economic and budgetary surveillance framework already pushes the limits of what is legally possible under the primary law prerequisites (→ para 87), several of the more ambitious proposals could only by implemented after **an amendment of the Treaties** in accordance with the procedures prescribed in Article 48 TEU, e.g. because they lack a sufficient competence base at EU level and/or affect the current institutional balance. Thus, the 'EU constitutional framework' would need to be adapted by unanimous agreement of all MS to accommodate such proposals for fiscal integration. Since substantive rules on taxation or allocation of resources would not be covered by Article 5.1 **95**

---

[284] Commission Communication, *A European Minister of Economy and Finance*, COM(2017) 823 final. See Böttner (2018).

[285] Cf. e.g. Commission, *Proposal for a Council Regulation on the establishment of the European Monetary Fund*, COM(2017) 827 final. See, inter alia, Manger-Nestler and Böttner (2019).

[286] Five Presidents' Report, p. 14.

[287] See → para 91 and Commission Decision (EU) 2015/1937 *establishing an independent advisory European Fiscal Board*, O.J. L 282/37 (2015), as amended by Commission Decision (EU) 2016/221, O.J. L 40/15 (2016).

[288] Commission Reflection Paper *on the deepening of the economic and monetary union*, p. 27 et seq.

[289] Cf. Commission, *Proposal for a Council Directive laying down provisions for strengthening fiscal responsibility and the medium-term budgetary orientation in the Member States*, COM(2017) 824 final.

[290] Cf. Commission Reflection Paper *on the deepening of the economic and monetary union*, p. 28. On the possibilities of reforming the fiscal rules without Treaty change cf. e.g. Dullien et al. (2021).

TFEU,[291] this is certainly true for any **fully-fledged fiscal competence**. Such broad decision-making powers regarding the collection as well as the expenditure of public resources at EU level would, to a certain extent, mean the abandoning of the principle of conferral and arguably require a higher degree of democratic legitimacy and financial solidarity among citizens at EU level than is currently foreseen.[292]

96 However, because budgetary policy 'is a core State function going to the heart of the political self-determination',[293] even less far-reaching Treaty amendments aiming at further fiscal integration would have to reassess the democratic system, ensuring further powers transferred to the EU level are accompanied by increased **mechanisms of democratic legitimization and accountability**.[294] At present (December 2021) it is unclear whether the political environment will allow any ambitious reform agenda to succeed within the next few years or whether pragmatism will limit changes to what is possible under existing primary law.[295] The COVID-19 pandemic could, however, have the potential to also trigger major upheavals.

97 On the other hand, **national constitutional law** may prove an obstacle to more ambitious proposals in fiscal integration. Various MS argue that there are constitutional barriers to European integration in certain areas, and notably in matters of fiscal integration and as far as the budgetary sovereignty of national parliaments as 'their most traditional and symbolic prerogative'[296] is concerned.[297] Thus, a further transfer of fiscal policy competences to the EU may also be subject to national constitutional limits, which (given ratification of the Treaty amendment 'in accordance with the respective constitutional requirements' is required by Article 48.4 TEU) may mean that such reforms would, in some Member States, require constitutional amendments or may not be realised at all under the current constitutional regime. Since Article 48 TEU requires unanimous agreement of all MS, constitutional barriers in only one of them may hinder the entry into force of any Treaty amendment.

98 Regarding, for example, the German legal order, the existence of such inviolable barriers has repeatedly been voiced by the **German Federal Constitutional Court** (FCC). In its famous *Lisbon* Decision, the FCC held that there are certain areas where the principle of democracy as well as the principle of subsidiarity require factually to restrict the transfer and exercise of sovereign powers to the EU in a

---

[291] Hinarejos (2012), p. 260.

[292] Hinarejos (2012), p. 262 et seqq. Cf. also Keppenne (2014), p. 213.

[293] Keppenne (2014), p. 221. Cf. also Chiti and Teixeira (2013), p. 706; Dawson and De Witte (2013), p. 835.

[294] Cf. Fabbrini (2014), p. 121.

[295] Cf. for the possibilities without a change of primary law e.g. the Study for the EESC by Dullien et al. (2021).

[296] Dawson and De Witte (2013), p. 827.

[297] E.g. Leino and Saarenheimo (2017), p. 170; cf. also Grewe and Rideau (2010), p. 325 et seqq. on the positions of the constitutional courts of several MS.

predictable manner. Among these areas are the 'fundamental fiscal decisions on public revenue and public expenditures'.[298] Thus, the protection of the principle of democracy in the German Basic Law includes a protection of parliamentary budgetary sovereignty as a key prerogative of any parliament. Accordingly, it would constitute a transfer of the right of the German *Bundestag* to adopt the budget and control its implementation and, thus, violate the **principle of democracy** and the right to elect the German *Bundestag* in its 'essential content' as protected by Article 79.3 of the German Basic Law if 'the determination of the type and amount of the levies imposed on the citizen were supranationalised to a considerable extent'.[299]

Therefore, under the German Basic Law, the overall budgetary responsibility, 'with sufficient political discretion regarding revenue and expenditure'[300] is seen as part of the **constitutional identity** of the Basic Law[301] which must always remain with the German *Bundestag*. At present, it is highly improbable that the German public would agree to enact a new constitution[302] to overcome these obstacles. Thus, such national constitutional limits further restrict the room for manoeuvre for potential Treaty reforms and, accordingly, for the establishment of a genuine 'Fiscal Union'. **99**

5.2. Selected Proposals

Considering the twofold 'constitutional' limits described above (→ para 95 et seqq.) the **political constraints facing any reform discussion**, and the variety of proposals on the table, this contribution cannot analyse their legal implications in detail. However, three key proposals for the medium-term, taken from the Commission's Reflection Paper on deepening the EMU, shall briefly be outlined and commented on.[303] **100**

5.2.1. European Safe Asset

For the period of 2020–2025, the Commission's Reflection Paper on deepening the EMU proposes to develop a so-called '**European safe asset**' as a new financial **101**

---

[298] German Federal Constitutional Court, 2 BvE 2/08 (30 June 2009) - *Lisbon* (BVerfGE 123, 267), para 251.
[299] German Federal Constitutional Court, 2 BvE 2/08 (30 June 2009), *Lisbon* (BVerfGE 123, 267), para 256.
[300] German Federal Constitutional Court, 2 BvE 2/08 (30 June 2009), *Lisbon* (BVerfGE 123, 267), para 256.
[301] German Federal Constitutional Court, 2 BvR 2728/13 (21 June 2016), *OMT* (BVerfGE 134, 366), para 210. Cf. Article 79.3 of the German Basic Law.
[302] Cf. Article 146 of the German Basic Law.
[303] For a commentary on the Proposal to establish a European Monetary Fund → Supplement to Title VIII: TESM para 145 et seqq. and Manger-Nestler and Böttner (2019).

instrument for the common issuance of (national government)[304] debt.[305] According to the Reflection Paper, such a European safe asset could be comparable to the US Treasury bond and become the benchmark for European financial markets. The Reflection Paper does not provide any further details but refers to necessary further reflections on the 'design features' of the European safe asset, namely the questions of full or partial common issuance, mutualisation or joint liabilities.

102 Despite the new name, which is arguably an attempt to evoke positive associations for the concept, the proposal thus refers to the extensive discussions on **'Eurobonds'**, which have been going on for almost two decades. Recently, the discussion about the introduction of common bonds has again gained momentum under the label of 'corona bonds' in the context of the COVID-19 pandemic.[306] With first 'official' assessments of the feasibility of instruments for the common issuance of debt in the late 1990s/early 2000s,[307] the idea was first revived in the wake of the sovereign debt crisis, when in 2010 high EU and MS representatives proposed the issuance of Eurobonds by a 'European Debt Agency' to combat the sovereign debt crisis.[308] Similar ideas were advocated by academics, financial analysts and policy-makers.[309] Those ideas were reflected on and considered by the Commission in its **Green paper on Stability Bonds.**[310]

103 The Green paper distinguished between **three broad approaches**, based on the degree of substitution of national issuance (full or partial) and the nature of the underlying guarantee (joint and several or several). The most far-reaching option presented was a full substitution of national debt issuance by Stability Bonds, with joint and several guarantees. Obviously, this approach poses a high risk of moral hazard[311] since it abolishes all market or interest rate pressure on MS. The second approach went a little less far, constituting only in the partial substitution of

---

[304] In connection with the Europe 2020 agenda, the Commission and the EIB also launched the Project Bond initiative. With this initiative, Commission and EIB wanted to attract institutional private investors to issue private bonds for the financing of infrastructure projects by involving the EIB in the financing of the projects with a subordinated debt portion and providing a cushion, where the EU budget absorbs the first potential losses that occur on portfolio operations up to an agreed level, while losses above this level are absorbed by the EIB contribution. Cf. Commission Report, *Interim Report on the Pilot Phase of the Europe 2020 Project Bond Initiative*, COM(2013) 929 final.

[305] Commission Reflection Paper *on the deepening of the economic and monetary union*, p. 22.

[306] Cf. e.g. Goldmann (2020).

[307] Cf. e.g. Giovannini Group, Report of 8 November 2000 *on co-ordinated issuance of public debt in the euro area*, available at http://ec.europa.eu/economy_finance/publications/pages/publication6372_en.pdf.

[308] Cf. Athanassiou (2011), p. 571 et seq. with further references.

[309] E.g. by Delpla and von Weizsäcker (2010). For further references cf. Annex 2 of the Commission Green Paper *on the feasibility of introducing Stability Bonds*, COM(2011) 818 final.

[310] Commission Green Paper *on the feasibility of introducing Stability Bonds*, COM(2011) 818 final. A broad public consultation was planned, but ultimately failed; see Dawson and De Witte (2013), p. 831.

[311] On this concept see, e.g. Ioannidis (2016), p. 1245 et seq.

national issuance by Stability Bonds, but still with joint and several guarantees. The third approach, the partial substitution by Stability Bond issuance of national issuance, with several but not joint guarantees, was the most limited one proposed. Thus, it is also the one with the least risk of moral hazard for the conduct of economic and fiscal policies in MS.

The three approaches as well as the remarks on the European safe asset in the Commission's Reflection Paper seem to suggest that MS, not the Union budget, would in some form be liable for the debt issuance under this regime, either directly or by guaranteeing the debt issued via an agency set up specifically for this purpose[312] or an existing facility such as the ESM. By contrast, funds of up to EUR 750 billion for the 'Recovery Instrument'[313] to combat the effects of the COVID-19 crisis shall be raised by way of bonds issued by the Union itself, for which (assuming the continued existence of the Union) only the **Union** is liable. Although the financial resources are passed on to the MS in the form of direct grants and loans, from a legal point of view, it is the Union, which is indebted on the capital markets. Although the legality of this construction (based on Article 122 TFEU) is disputed and while it could serve as a template e.g. for a future green investment fund, it must, thus, be distinguished from the introduction of common bonds with a liability of the MS. For such common issuance of national debt, however, it is not clear what competence it could be based on. One possibility might prima facie be Article 136 in combination with Article 352 TFEU.[314] Nonetheless, any proposal implying a joint and several liability by MS would need a formal amendment of the Treaties, most notably of the **no-bail-out clause** of **Article 125 TFEU**.[315] Eurobonds with only a several but not joint liability, on the contrary, may be possible without a Treaty change.[316]

However, since it is based on **economic risk sharing**, any form of common issuance of debt would also need to build upon the mechanisms of control established by the fiscal surveillance framework to make it a credible instrument.[317] This is problematic not least because of the weak enforcement of this framework so far (→ para 90).[318] Moreover, the relationship to the obligation to avoid excessive

---

[312] Cf. Athanassiou (2011), p. 572.

[313] 'Next Generation EU'. See Council Regulation (EU) 2020/2094 *establishing a European Union Recovery Instrument to support the recovery in the aftermath of the COVID-19 crisis*, O. J. L 433I/23 (2020), and the European Council conclusions, 17-21 July 2020, on the recovery plan and multiannual financial framework for 2021-2027, EUCO 10/20.

[314] Cf. Mayer and Heidfeld (2012), p. 129.

[315] Cf. e.g. Keppenne (2014), p. 213; Heun and Thiele (2012), p. 982; Mayer and Heidfeld (2012), p. 130.

[316] Cf. Athanassiou (2011), p. 572, who suggests, however, that the establishment of a European Debt Agency would only be possible following a Treaty change.

[317] Cf. Athanassiou (2011), p. 573.

[318] Cf. Leino and Saarenheimo (2017), p. 188.

government deficits under Article 126 TFEU (→ para 16 et seqq.) would have to be clarified, possibly by limiting the availability of Eurobonds (European safe assets). Depending on the chosen approach, possible national constitutional limits (→ para 97 et seqq.) must be considered as well. As these constraints stand in the way of swift implementation, the Commission has, under Article 114 TFEU, additionally proposed a regulation for so-called sovereign bond-backed securities (SBBS), defined as low-risk liquid assets backed by a pre-defined pool of euro-area central government bonds.[319] Other than Eurobonds, SBBS would, however, be created by the private sector and not involve any mutualisation of risks and losses among MS.[320]

5.2.2. Macroeconomic Stabilisation Function

106 Because of its limited volume, the EU budget and ESI Funds currently only fulfil a limited stabilisation role. Since individual exchange rate adjustments at national level are no longer possible in a monetary union,[321] economic shocks[322] may thus cause a threat to the stability of the monetary union as a whole. National budget stabilisers may dampen the effects of an economic downturn, but they generally aggravate the debt situation. Hence, if economic growth falls, the deficit automatically rises, since less revenue from taxes is generated but higher expenditure (e.g. for unemployment benefits) accrues. The danger is that MS then apply pro-cyclical measures to avoid violating the Maastricht criteria, thereby further aggravating the situation.[323] Thus, to complement the national budget stabilisers in the event of severe economic shocks, the Five Presidents' Report envisaged the creation of a **macroeconomic stabilisation function**,[324] a proposal which was taken up as well in the Commission's Reflection Paper on deepening the EMU.[325]

107 According to the Reflection Paper, a macroeconomic stabilisation function **open to all MS** could be introduced within the EU framework **until 2025**. Various

---

[319] Cf. Commission Proposal for a Regulation on *sovereign bond-backed securities*, COM(2018) 339 final. According to the Commission, such SBBS may lead to a greater diversification of banks' sovereign exposures.

[320] Negotiations on this proposal have not been concluded at the time of completion of this contribution (December 2021).

[321] Cf. Andersen and Dogonowski (1999), p. 71; Artis and Winkler (1999), p. 162; Masson (1996), p. 1000; Hinarejos (2012), p. 250; Ruffert (2011), p. 1793.

[322] Economists distinguish between asymmetric and symmetric shocks, whereas a shock is asymmetric if an economic event affects one economy more than another.

[323] Artis and Winkler (1999), p. 166.

[324] Five Presidents' Report, p. 14 et seq. Cf. Masson (1996), p. 1001 on early proposals for a larger fiscal capacity of the Union.

[325] Commission Reflection Paper *on the deepening of the economic and monetary union*, p. 25 et seq.

configurations are conceivable.[326] In designing a macroeconomic stabilisation function, however, the Commission considers that several principles should be respected, namely that it does not lead to permanent transfers, minimises moral hazard, and does not duplicate the role of the ESM as crisis management tool, while nonetheless (and arguably in that respect similar to the ESM) being strictly conditional on clear criteria and continuous sound policies, including compliance with EU fiscal rules and the economic surveillance framework. Depending on the approach followed, such a macroeconomic stabilisation function may take the form of a fiscal capacity,[327] e.g. as a European Investment Protection Scheme, a European Unemployment (Re-)Insurance[328] or a rainy-day fund, possibly equipped with the capacity to borrow. More concrete plans to create a European Investment Stabilisation Function[329] were dropped in favour of the recovery instrument 'Next Generation EU' to combat the COVID-19 crisis. With this temporary recovery instrument which has the aforementioned "Recovery and Resilience Facility" as its centrepiece, more than EUR 800 billion will be made available. In addition, the Union has decided on temporary emergency measures in the form of loans totalling up to EUR 100 billion as temporary support to reduce the risk of unemployment ('SURE instrument'),[330] with which national short-time work schemes can particularly be financed. Both Next Generation EU and the SURE instrument are financed by the EU issuing bonds on the capital markets.

The consideration of a European Investment Protection Scheme or a European Unemployment (Re-)Insurance show that, while permanent transfers may not be intended, a permanent **fiscal capacity** would arguably nonetheless constitute another foray into redistributive matters. If limited to the EA, it could possibly be combined with ideas to establish a separate EA budget,[331] arguably requiring an amendment of the budgetary rights of the EP under Articles 310 et seqq. TFEU.[332] However, based on solidarity and similar to the European safe asset, it presupposes the control established by the fiscal surveillance framework, which is equally problematic given the lax enforcement of these parts of the framework so far **108**

---

[326] Cf. Weber (2013), p. 386. The Four Presidents' Report of 2012 had also considered that such a fiscal capacity could, in the longer term, be able to issue debt.

[327] Cf. on the economic discussion about the feasibility of a fiscal capacity already Masson (1996), p. 1002 et seq.

[328] For a discussion on design options for a European Unemployment Insurance cf. Koester and Sondermann (2018), especially p. 18 et seqq.

[329] Commission, *Proposal for a Regulation on the establishment of a European Investment Stabilisation Function*, COM(2018) 387 final.

[330] Council Regulation (EU) 2020/672 *on the establishment of a European instrument for temporary support to mitigate unemployment risks in an emergency (SURE) following the COVID-19 outbreak*, O.J. L 159/1 (2020).

[331] Cf. e.g. European Parliament resolution of 16 February 2017 *on the budgetary capacity for the euro area*, CJ16/8/05365, 2015/2344(INI).

[332] Repasi (2013), p. 74.

(→ para 90).³³³ In order not to duplicate the ESM, it could be used as a stabilisation tool for medium-sized asymmetrical shocks, while the ESM would be used for bigger crises.³³⁴ If the ESM should some day be replaced by an EMF as had been proposed by the Commission³³⁵ (→ Supplement to Title VIII: TESM para 145 et seqq.), a future EMF might also perform functions in the implementation of a stabilisation function, e.g. by organising and making available any necessary market financing associated with the triggering of the function.³³⁶

5.2.3. EA Treasury and Finance Minister

109 On the institutional side, the Commission, inter alia, proposed in its Reflection Paper on the deepening of the EMU the setting up of a **EA Treasury** under the responsibility of an **EU Finance Minister**, who would also be Chair of the Euro Group/ECOFIN.³³⁷ According to the Commission, the Treasury could be entrusted with the economic and fiscal surveillance of the EA and its MS with the support of the European Fiscal Board, the coordination of issuing a possible European safe asset, and the management of the macroeconomic stabilisation function. It is envisaged that decision-making powers could be attributed to the Euro Group, while the Treasury would prepare and execute these decisions. Possibly, the Treasury could also become responsible for the ESM after its integration into the EU legal framework or for a possible EMF.

110 In this sense, a Commission Communication specifies possible 'key functions' of a European Minister of Economics and Finance.³³⁸ In any case, far-reaching institutional changes would require Treaty amendments, e.g. of Article 16 TEU and Protocol (No. 14) on the Euro Group for the introduction of decision-making powers to the Euro Group. Considering that already under the current system of 'coordination by coercion', Union institutions possess significant discretionary

---

³³³ Cf. Leino and Saarenheimo (2017), p. 188.

³³⁴ Cf. Weder di Mauro (2015), p. 70 et seq., who considers such a stabilisation tool for medium-sized asymmetrical shocks not to be a priority. Rather, he suggests strengthening the instruments designed for larger shocks, notably ESM and Single Resolution Fund (SRF).

³³⁵ Commission, *Proposal for a Council Regulation on the establishment of the European Monetary Fund*, COM(2017) 827 final. The ESM has since undergone a reform, but retained not only its name but also its intergovernmental character.

³³⁶ Cf. Recital 71 COM(2017) 827 final.

³³⁷ Commission Reflection Paper *on the deepening of the economic and monetary union*, p. 28. Already in his 2015 'State of the Union' speech, Commission President *J.-C. Juncker* announced the longer term aim of setting up a euro area Treasury.

³³⁸ Commission Communication, *A European Minister of Economy and Finance*, COM(2017) 823 final. According to this Communication, the European Minister of Economy and Finance shall be both Vice-President of the Commission and Chairman of the Euro Group and, in particular, have powers to monitor compliance with the economic, fiscal and financial rules outlined above, and to monitor the use of EU budgetary instruments. In addition, the Minister shall also monitor the EMF that is to be set up. See Böttner (2018).

powers[339] when assessing MS' economic and fiscal policies, **accountability and ownership** of decisions would be key issues for such a reform. Despite Euro Group members and national finance ministers remaining accountable to national parliaments, the Commission rightly points out that it is 'essential to ensure greater parliamentary control of common economic, fiscal and financial instruments and policies'.[340] After all, it is the citizens affected by decision on the collection and allocation of resources who legitimise the political decision-making process.[341]

6. Concluding Remarks

A main lesson of the sovereign debt crisis was that responsible fiscal policies are 111 essential to ensure not only price stability but also financial stability in the EMU.[342] However, while the reforms implemented in the wake of the crisis to some extent only unleashed the potential held ready by the primary law prerequisites, they arguably also stretched their limits. While there is still neither a common European fiscal policy[343] nor a real 'Fiscal Union' in the strict sense,[344] the reforms of the past decade introduced a comprehensive scrutiny of EA Member States' fiscal and economic policies. While fiscal policy-making is still done at MS level, the new surveillance framework has had significant effects on national fiscal and budgetary processes, with considerable rights of EU institutions to interfere in these policies,[345] thus creating a **complex system** of 'coordination by coercion'. Paradoxically, in view of the declared objective of avoiding a federal system to protect national autonomy, these coercive rights seem to already go beyond what is provided for, e.g. in the US,[346] and grant considerable discretion to the Union institutions involved.[347]

Moreover, with **important parts of the reforms only applicable to EA Mem-** 112 **ber States**, they aggravate the differentiation between EMU and the rest of the EU, posing the question of the finality of the Union and challenging its legal and institutional unity.[348] Ultimately, introducing further elements of a 'Fiscal Union', such as entailed, inter alia, by the proposals for a European safe asset, a macroeconomic stabilisation function or a EA Treasury and Finance Minister, and abolishing the constitutional asymmetry of the EMU might need an amendment of

---

[339] Cf. Leino and Saarenheimo (2017), p. 174.

[340] Commission Reflection Paper *on the deepening of the economic and monetary union*, p. 28.

[341] Cf. Jančić (2016), p. 227 on national parliaments' key role as a source of input legitimacy.

[342] Five Presidents' Report, p. 13.

[343] Hinarejos (2012), p. 248.

[344] Cf Calliess and Schoenfleisch (2012), p. 485; Calliess (2012), p. 115.

[345] Cf. Leino and Saarenheimo (2017), p. 172.

[346] Fabbrini (2013), p. 32 et seqq.

[347] Cf. Leino and Saarenheimo (2017), p. 174.

[348] Chiti and Teixeira (2013), p. 695 et seq.

the Treaties. Such an amendment, however, requires unanimity of all MS and faces considerable limits through Member States' constitutions, which aim to ensure that the budgetary and fiscal autonomy of national parliaments is not limited further. Ultimately, the decisions on the way forward are inherently political[349] and hard to predict. However, whether key **redistributive choices** will in the future be taken at the EU level or remain with the MS is indeed a political matter to be determined by the citizens affected by these choices.

List of Cases

ECJ/CJEU

ECJ 13.06.1958, 9/56, *Meroni*, ECLI:EU:C:1958:7 [cit. in para 91]
ECJ 15.07.1964, 6/64, *Costa v ENEL*, ECLI:EU:C:1964:66 [cit. in para 15]
ECJ 31.03.1971, 22/70, *AETR*, ECLI:EU:C:1971:32 [cit. in para 12]
ECJ 08.04.1976, 43/75, *Defrenne II*, ECLI:EU:C:1976:56 [cit. in para 13]
ECJ 14.07.1976, 3/76, 4/78, 6/76, *Kramer*, ECLI:EU:C:1976:114 [cit. in para 12]
ECJ 26.04.1977, Opinion 1/76, *European laying-up fund for inland waterway vessels*, ECLI:EU:C:1977:63 [cit. in para 12]
ECJ 15.01.1986, 44/84, *Hurd*, ECLI:EU:C:1986:2 [cit. in para 13]
ECJ 23.04.1986, 294/83, *Les Verts*, ECLI:EU:C:1986:166 [cit. in para 6]
ECJ 13.12.1989, C-322/88, *Grimaldi*, ECLI:EU:C:1989:646 [cit. in para 82]
ECJ 14.12.1991, Opinion 1/91, *EEA I*, ECLI:EU:C:1991:490 [cit. in para 6]
ECJ 30.06.1993, C-181/91 and C-248/91, *Parliament v Council and Commission*, ECLI:EU:C:1993:271 [cit. in para 12, 58]
ECJ 02.03.1994, C-316/91, *Parliament v Council*, ECLI:EU:C:1994:76 [cit. in para 58]
ECJ 28.03.1996, Opinion 2/94, *Accession by the Community to the ECHR*, ECLI:EU:C:1996:140 [cit. in para 39]
ECJ 15.01.2002, C-55/00, *Gottardo*, ECLI:EU:C:2002:16 [cit. in para 13]
ECJ 13.07.2004, C-27/04, *Commission v Council*, ECLI:EU:C:2004:436 [cit. in para 4, 89]
ECJ 03.09.2008, C-402/05 P and C-415/05 P, *Kadi*, ECLI:EU:C:2008:461 [cit. in para 6]
CJEU 27.11.2012, C-370/12, *Pringle*, ECLI:EU:C:2012:756 [cit. in para 5, 12, 13, 54, 58, 87]
CJEU 22.01.2014, C-270/12, *Short-Selling*, ECLI:EU:C:2014:18 [cit. in para 91]
CJEU 13.02.2014, C-31/13 P, *Hungary v Commission*, ECLI:EU:C:2014:70 [cit. in para 89]
CJEU 18.12.2014, Opinion 2/13, *Accession to the ECHR*, ECLI:EU:C:2014:2454 [cit. in para 6]

---

[349] Chiti and Teixeira (2013), p. 683.

CJEU 25.10.2017, C-593/15 P and C-594/15 P, *Slovakia v Commission*, ECLI:EU: C:2017:800 [cit. in para 89]
CJEU 25.10.2017, C-599/15 P, *Romania v Commission*, ECLI:EU:C:2017:801 [cit. in para 89]
CJEU 20.12.2017, C-521/15, *Spain v Council*, ECLI:EU:C:2017:982 [cit. in para 90]
CJEU 06.03.2018, C-284/16, *Achmea*, ECLI:EU:C:2018:158 [cit. in para 14]

National Constitutional Courts

Austrian CC 03.10.2013, SV 1/2013, *TSCG* [cit. in para 35]
French CC 09.08.2012, Décision n° 2012-653 DC, *TSCG* [cit. in para 35]
French CC 13.12.2012, Décision n° 2012-658 DC, *Loi organique relative à la programmation et à la gouvernance des finances publiques* [cit. in para 35]
German FCC 30.06.2009, 2 BvE 2/08, *Lisbon* [cit. in para 98, 99]
German FCC 21.06.2016, 2 BvR 2728/13, *OMT* [cit. in para 99]

References[350]

Amtenbrink, F. (2014). General report. In U. Neergaard, C. Jacqueson, & J. H. Danielsen (Eds.), *The Economic and Monetary Union: Constitutional and institutional aspects of the economic governance within the EU. XXVI FIDE Congress Publications Vol. 1* (pp. 73–178). DJØF Publishing.
Amtenbrink, F., & De Haan, J. (2003). Economic governance in the European Union: Fiscal policy discipline versus flexibility. *Common Market Law Review, 40*(5), 1075–1106.
Andersen, T., & Dogonowski, R. R. (1999). EMU and budget norms. In H. Hallett, M. Hutchinson, & S. Jensen (Eds.), *Fiscal aspects of European monetary integration* (pp. 69–95). CUP.
Antpöhler, C. (2012). Emergenz der europäischen Wirtschaftsregierung. Das Six-Pack als Zeichen supranationaler Leistungsfähigkeit. *Zeitschrift für ausländisches öffentliches Recht und Völker-recht, 72*(2), 353–393.
Armstrong, K. A. (2013). The new governance of EU fiscal discipline. *European Law Review, 38*, 601–617.
Artis, M. J. (2002). Stability and Growth Pact. In F. Breuss, G. Fink, & S. Griller (Eds.), *Institutional, legal and economic aspects of the EMU* (pp. 101–115). Springer.
Artis, M. J., & Winkler, B. (1999). The stability pact: Trading off flexibility for credibility? In H. Hallett, M. Hutchinson, & S. Jensen (Eds.), *Fiscal aspects of European monetary integration* (pp. 157–188). CUP.
Athanassiou, P. (2011). Of past measures and future plans for Europe's exit from the sovereign debt crisis. what is legally possible (and what is not). *European Law Review, 36*, 558–575.
Baldwin, R., & Giavazzi, F. (Eds.). (2016). *How to fix Europe's monetary union: Views of leading economists*. CEPR Press. (available at http://voxeu.org/sites/default/files/file/epub/rebooting2_upload.pdf)
Bast, J., & Rödl, F. (2012). Jenseits der Koordinierung? Zu den Grenzen der EU-Verträge für eine Europäische Wirtschaftsregierung. *Europäische Grundrechte-Zeitschrift, 39*(10–12), 269–278.

---

[350] All cited Internet sources of this comment have been accessed on 13 December 2021.

Böttner, R. (2018). Der Europäische Minister für Wirtschaft und Finanzen nach den Plänen der Kommission. *Zeitschrift für europarechtliche Studien*, 69–96.

Böttner, R. (2021). *The constitutional framework for enhanced cooperation in EU law*. Brill Nijhoff.

Braams, B. (2013). *Koordinierung als Kompetenzkategorie*. Mohr Siebeck.

Budgetdienst des Parlamentes. (2013). *Europäisches Semester. Die Rolle der Nationalen Parlamente in den Mitgliedstaaten*. Retrieved from https://www.parlament.gv.at/ZUSD/BUDGET/2012u2013/BD-Anfragebeantwortung_Europaeisches_Semester.pdf

Calliess, C. (2012). From fiscal compact to fiscal union? New rules for the Eurozone. In C. Barnard & M. W. Gehring (Eds.), *Cambridge Yearbook of European legal studies* (Vol. 14, pp. 101–117). Cambridge: Hart.

Calliess, C., & Ruffert, M. (Eds.). (2021). *EUV/AEUV. Kommentar*. (6th ed.). C.H. Beck.

Calliess, C., & Schoenfleisch, C. (2012). Auf dem Weg in die europäische "Fiskalunion"? – Europa- und verfassungsrechtliche Fragen einer Reform der Wirtschafts- und Währungsunion im Kontext des Fiskalvertrages. *JuristenZeitung, 67*(10), 477–478.

Chiti, E., & Teixeira, P. G. (2013). The constitutional implications of the European responses to the financial and public debt crisis. *Common Market Law Review, 50*, 683–708.

Cloos, J. (2011). "Incentive" governance: A key component of a future European economic government. *Studia Diplomatica, LXIV-4*, 41–54.

Constantinesco, V. (1997). Les clauses de « coopération renforcée ». Le protocole sur l'application des principes de subsidiarité et de proportionnalité. *Revue trimestrielle de droit européen, 33*, 43–59.

Dawson, M., & De Witte, F. (2013). Constitutional balance in the EU after the Euro-Crisis. *The Modern Law Review, 76*(5), 817–844.

De Streel, A. (2013). La gouvernance économique européenne réformée. *Revue trimestrielle de droit européen, 49*(3), 455–481.

De Streel, A. (2015). The confusion of tasks in the decision-making process of the European economic governance. In F. Fabbrini, E. H. Ballin, & H. Somsen (Eds.), *What form of government for the European Union and the Eurozone?* (pp. 79–94). Hart Publishing.

De Witte, B. (2020). EMU as constitutional law. In F. Amtenbrink & C. Herrmann (Eds.), *The EU law of economic and Monetary Union*. (ch. 11). OUP.

Delpla, J., & von Weizsäcker, J. (2010). The Blue Bond Proposal. *Bruegel Policy Briefs*, Issue 2010/03. Retrieved from http://bruegel.org/wp-content/uploads/imported/publications/1005-PB-Blue_Bonds.pdf

Dimopoulos, A. (2014). The use of international law as a tool for enhancing governance in the Eurozone and its impact on EU institutional integrity. In M. Adams, F. Fabbrini, & P. Larouche (Eds.), *The constitutionalization of European budgetary constraints*. Hart Publishing.

Dullien, S., Paetz, C., Repasi, R., Watt, A., & Watzka, S. (2021). *Between high ambition and pragmatism: Proposals for a reform of fiscal rules without treaty change*. Study for the EESC. Retrieved from https://www.eesc.europa.eu/en/our-work/publications-other-work/publications/between-high-ambition-and-pragmatism-proposals-reform-fiscal-rules-without-treaty-change

Fabbrini, F. (2013). The fiscal compact, the "golden rule," and the paradox of European federalism. *Boston College International & Comparative Law Review, 36*(1), 1–38.

Fabbrini, F. (2014). The Euro-Crisis and the courts: Judicial review and the political process in comparative perspective. *Berkeley Journal of International Law, 32*(1), 64–123.

Fischer-Lescano, A., & Oberndorfer, L. (2013). Fiskalvertrag und Unionsrecht. Unionsrechtliche grenzen völkervertraglicher Fiskalregulierung und Organleihe. *Neue Juristische Wochenschrift, 66*(1–2), 9–14.

Goldmann, M. (2020). The case for corona bonds: A proposal by a group of European lawyers, *Verfassungsblog*, 2020/4/05.

Grabitz, E., Hilf, M., & Nettesheim, M. (Eds.). (2021). *Das Recht der Europäischen Union, looseleaf*. C.H. Beck.

Grewe, C., & Rideau, J. (2010). L'identité constitutionnelle des états membres de l'Union européenne. Flash back sur le coming-out d'un concept ambigu. In *Chemins d'Europe. Mélanges en l'honneur de Jean Paul Jacqué* (pp. 319–345). Dalloz.

Gröpl, C. (2013). Schritte zur Europäisierung des Haushaltsrechts. *Der Staat, 52*(1), 1–25.

Häde, U. (1996a). *Finanzausgleich. Die Verteilung der Aufgaben, Ausgaben und Einnahmen im Recht der Bundesrepublik Deutschland und der Europäischen Union.* Mohr Siebeck.

Häde, U. (1996b). Ein Stabilitätspakt für Europa? Zur Zulässigkeit völkerrechtlicher Verträge zwischen den Mitgliedstaaten der EU. *Europäische Zeitschrift für Wirtschaftsrecht, 7*(5), 138–143.

Häde, U. (2009). Haushaltsdisziplin und Solidarität im Zeichen der Finanzkrise. *Europäische Zeitschrift für Wirtschaftsrecht, 20*(12), 399–403.

Häde, U. (2011). Article 136 AEUV – eine neue Generalklausel für die Wirtschafts- und Währungsunion? *JuristenZeitung, 66*(7), 333–340.

Häde, U. (2013). Rechtliche Bewertung der Maßnahmen im Hinblick auf eine "Fiskalunion". In C. Calliess (Ed.), *Europäische Solidarität und nationale Identität. Überlegungen im Kontext der Krise im Euroraum* (pp. 193–206). Mohr Siebeck.

Hahn, H. J. (1997). Der Stabilitätspakt für die Europäische Währungsunion. Das Einhalten der Defizitobergrenze als stete Rechtspflicht. *JuristenZeitung*, 1133–1141.

Hahn, H. J. (1998). The stability pact for the European Monetary Union: Compliance with deficit limit as a constant legal duty. *Common Market Law Review, 35*(1), 77–100.

Harden, I., von Hagen, J., & Brookes, R. (1997). The European constitutional framework for Member States' public finances. In M. Andenas et al. (Eds.), *European Economic and Monetary Union: the institutional framework* (pp. 141–167). Kluwer.

Herzmann, K. (2012). Europäische Währungsstabilität über Bande gespielt. Ein Überblick über den Fiskalpakt. *Zeitschrift für das Juristische Studium, 5*(2), 168–174.

Heun, W., & Thiele, A. (2012). Verfassungs- und europarechtliche Zulässigkeit von Eurobonds. *JuristenZeitung, 67*(20), 973–982.

Hinarejos, A. (2012). The euro area crisis and constitutional limits to fiscal integration. In C. Barnard & M. W. Gehring (Eds.), *Cambridge Yearbook of European legal studies Vol. 14 2011/12* (pp. 243–268). Hart Publishing.

Hinarejos, A. (2013). Fiscal federalism in the European Union. Evolution and future choices for EMU. *Common Market Law Review, 50*(6), 1621–1642.

Hufeld, U. (2015). Das Recht der Europäischen Wirtschaftsunion. In P.-C. Müller-Graff (Ed.), *Europäisches Wirtschaftsordnungsrecht. Enzyklopädie Europarecht* (Vol. 4, pp. 1301–1385). Nomos.

Ioannidis, M. (2016). Europe's new transformations: How the EU economic constitution changed during the Eurozone crisis. *Common Market Law Review, 53*, 1237–1282.

Jacqué, J.-P. (2004). The principle of institutional balance. *Common Market Law Review, 41*(2), 383–391.

Jančić, D. (2016). National parliaments and EU fiscal integration. *European Law Journal, 22*(2), 225–249.

Keppenne, J.-P. (2014). Institutional report. In U. Neergaard, C. Jacqueson, & J. H. Danielsen (Eds.), *The Economic and Monetary Union: Constitutional and institutional aspects of the economic governance within the EU. XXVI FIDE Congress Publications Vol. 1* (pp. 179–257). DJØF Publishing.

Knauff, M. (2010). *Der Regelungsverbund: Recht und Soft Law im Mehrebenensystem.* Mohr Siebeck.

Koester, G., & Sondermann, D. (2018). A euro area macroeconomic stabilisation function: assessing options in view of their redistribution and stabilisation properties, *ECB Occasional Paper No 216 / October 2018*

Kort, M. (1997). Zur europarechtlichen Zulässigkeit von Abkommen der Mitgliedstaaten untereinander. *JuristenZeitung, 52*(13), 640–647.

Krebber, S. (2004). Die Koordinierung als Kompetenzkategorie im EU-Verfassungsentwurf aus dogmatischer Sicht. *Europäische Grundrechte-Zeitschrift*, 592–596.

Leino, P., & Saarenheimo, T. (2017). Sovereignty and subordination: On the limits of EU economic policy co-ordination. *European Law Review, 42*, 166–189.

Lenaerts, K. (2014). EMU and the European Union's constitutional framework. *European Law Review, 39*(6), 753–769.

Luijendijk, H., & Senden, L. (2011). De gelaagde doorwerking van Europese administratieve soft law in de nationale rechtsorde. *SEW, tijdschrift voor Europees en economisch recht, 59*(7-8), 312–353.

Manger-Nestler, C. (2020). The architecture of EMU. In F. Amtenbrink & C. Herrmann (Eds.), *The EU law of economic and Monetary Union (ch. 8)*. OUP.

Manger-Nestler, C., & Böttner, R. (2019). Der Europäische Währungsfonds nach den Plänen der Kommission. *Zeitschrift für ausländisches öffentliches Recht und Völkerrecht*, 43–84.

Martenczuk, B. (1998). Die differenzierte Integration nach dem Vertrag von Amsterdam. *Zeitschrift für europarechtliche Studien, 1*(4), 447–474.

Martucci, F. (2020). Non-EU legal instruments (EFSF, ESM, and Fiscal Compact). In F. Amtenbrink & C. Herrmann (Eds.), *The EU law of Economic and Monetary Union*. (ch. 12). OUP.

Masson, P. R. (1996). Fiscal dimensions of EMU. *The Economic Journal, 106*(437), 996–1004.

Mayer, C. (2012). Vertrag über Stabilität, Koordinierung und Steuerung in der WWU und Europäischer Stabilitätsmechanismus. Ausgewählte Fragen. *Journal für Rechtspolitik, 20*(2), 124–136.

Mayer, F. C., & Heidfeld, C. (2012). Eurobonds, Schuldentilgungsfonds und Projektbonds – Eine dunkle Bedrohung? *Zeitschrift für Rechtspolitik*, 129–133.

Ohler, C. (1997). *Die fiskalische Integration in der Europäischen Gemeinschaft*. Nomos.

Palmstorfer, R. (2014). Die "Koordinationskompetenz" der EU im Bereich der Fiskalpolitiken der MS: Das unbekannte Wesen. In K. Gotthard et al. (Eds.), *Kooperation und Koordination als Rechtsentwicklungstrends* (pp. 89–106). Jan Sramek.

Piecha, S. (2016). *Die Rettungsmaßnahmen zugunsten zahlungsunfähiger EU-Mitgliedstaaten. Eine unions- und verfassungsrechtliche Analyse*. Peter Lang.

Pilz, S. (2016). *Der Europäische Stabilitätsmechanismus. Eine neue Stufe der europäischen Integration*. Mohr Siebeck.

Repasi, R. (2013). Völkervertragliche Freiräume für EU-Mitgliedstaaten. *Europarecht, 48*(1), 45–75.

Ruffert, M. (2011). The European debt crisis and European Union law. *Common Market Law Review, 48*, 1777–1805.

Sadeleer, N. (2012). The new architecture of the European economic governance: A Leviathan or a flat-footed Colossus? *Maastricht Journal, 19*(3), 354–382.

Schlosser, P. (2019). *Europe's new fiscal Union*. Palgrave Macmillan.

Schoenfleisch, C. (2018). *Integration durch Koordinierung? Rechtsfragen der Politikkoordinierung am Beispiel der nationalen Wirtschaftspolitiken*. Mohr Siebeck.

Schwarze, J., Becker, U., Hatje, A., & Schoo, J. (Eds.). (2018). *EU-Kommentar*. Nomos.

Selmayr, M. (2015). Das Recht der Europäischen Währungsunion. In P.-C. Müller-Graff (Ed.), *Europäisches Wirtschaftsordnungsrecht. Enzyklopädie Europarecht Vol. 4* (pp. 1387–1623). Nomos.

Senden, L. (2004). *Soft law in European community law*. Hart Publishing.

Streinz, R. (Ed.). (2018). *EUV/AEUV. Kommentar* (3rd ed.). C.H. Beck.

Taylor, C. (1997). The separation of monetary and fiscal policy in stage three of EMU. In M. Andenas et al. (Eds.), *European Economic and Monetary Union: The institutional framework* (pp. 171–188). Kluwer.

Terpan, F. (2015). Soft law in the European Union – The changing nature of EU law. *European Law Journal, 21*(1), 68–96.

Thirion, G. (2017). *European fiscal union: Economic rationale and design challenges* (CEPS Working Document No 01-2017). Retrieved from https://www.ceps.eu/system/files/WD2017-01GT%20FiscalUnion.pdf.

Thym, D. (2004). *Ungleichzeitigkeit und europäisches Verfassungsrecht*. Nomos.

von Bogdandy, A., Bast, J., & Arndt, F. (2002). Handlungsformen im Unionsrecht – Empirische Analysen und dogmatische Strukturen in einem vermeintlichen Dschungel. *Zeitschrift für ausländisches öffentliches Recht und Völkerrecht*, 77–161.

Weber, A. (2013). Europa- und völkerrechtliche Elemente der Gewährleistung von Haushaltsdisziplin in der Währungsunion. *Europarecht, 48*(4), 375–389.

Weder di Mauro, B. (2015). Braucht die Eurozone eine Fiscal Capacity? In S. Kadelbach (Ed.), *Die Europäische Union am Scheideweg: mehr oder weniger Europa?* (pp. 67–72). Nomos.

Wutscher, C. (2020). *Budgethoheit. Eine systematische Untersuchung der verfassungsrechtlichen Grundlagen des Budgetrechts des Bundes unter Berücksichtigung des Völker- und Europarechts*. Unpublished habilitation thesis, Wirtschaftsuniversität Wien.

The European Banking Union

Contents

1. General Introduction on the Banking Union 1
    1.1. Genesis 2
    1.2. General Overview 11
2. The Single Supervisory Mechanism (SSM) 14
    2.1. Rationale 14
    2.2. Creation 18
    2.3. Legal Basis 25
    2.4. Institutional Structure 31
        2.4.1. The Creation and Functions of the Supervisory Board of the ECB 33
        2.4.2. The SSM Decision-Making Procedures 36
        2.4.3. Independence and Accountability of the ECB in the Exercise of Supervisory Tasks 40
        2.4.4. The Separation of Supervisory Tasks and Monetary Policy in the ECB ... 45
        2.4.5. The Relationship of the ECB with the European Supervisory Authorities, the Single Resolution Board and the European Systemic Risk Board .. 49
        2.4.6. Close Cooperation with Non-Euro Area Member States 59
    2.5. Substantive Rules in the SSM 64
        2.5.1. The Determination of the 'Significance' of Supervised Entities 65
        2.5.2. Tasks of the ECB 67
        2.5.3. The Applicable Law by the ECB in the Exercise of Its Tasks 82
        2.5.4. The Allocation of Competences Between the ECB and the National Competent Authorities 88
        2.5.5. Powers of the ECB 95
    2.6. Procedural Safeguards in the SSM 114
        2.6.1. Right to be Heard 115
        2.6.2. Motivation 118
        2.6.3. Access to the File 119
        2.6.4. Administrative and Judicial Review 121
3. The Single Resolution Mechanism (SRM) 123
    3.1. Rationale 123
    3.2. Creation 125
    3.3. Legal Basis of the SRM (and the Bank Recovery and Resolution Directive) ... 132
    3.4. Institutional Structure 139
        3.4.1. The Role of the Single Resolution Board 139
        3.4.2. The Composition and Functions 144
        3.4.3. Accountability and Independence in the Exercise of Resolution Tasks 146
        3.4.4. The Decision-Making Procedure for Resolution in the SRM 151
    3.5. Substantive Rules 155
        3.5.1. Scope 155
        3.5.2. Tasks and Powers of the SRB 157
        3.5.3. Recovery and Resolution Planning in the SRM 161
        3.5.4. Resolution Tools in the SRM 167
    3.6. Resolution Funding in the SRM 174
    3.7. The SRM and State Aid 182
        3.7.1. Extra-Resolution Extraordinary Public Financial Support 186
        3.7.2. Resolution Financing Arrangements as State Aid in the SRM 192
        3.7.3. Government Financial Stabilisation Tools 195
    3.8. Procedural Safeguards in the SRM 197

		3.8.1.	Right to be Heard	198
		3.8.2.	Access to the File	199
		3.8.3.	Administrative and Judicial Review	201
4.	The Main Substantial Rules of the European Banking Union			204
	4.1.	The Capital Requirements Regulation and the Capital Requirements Directive		206
		4.1.1.	The Capital Requirements Regulation	208
		4.1.2.	The Capital Requirements Directive	217
		4.1.3.	Assessment	234
	4.2.	The Bank Recovery and Resolution Directive		242
	4.3.	The Deposit Guarantee Scheme Directive		254
	4.4.	The Other Substantive Sources of EU Legal Acts in the European Banking Union		260
		4.4.1.	Delegated and Implementing EU Acts	262
		4.4.2.	Guidelines, Recommendations and Other Acts	266
5.	The Unfinished Agenda of the European Banking Union			268
	5.1.	Reviewing Substantive EU Banking Regulation		270
	5.2.	The Reforms to the EU Banking Resolution and Insolvency Regime		279
	5.3.	The European Deposit Insurance Scheme as the Missing Third Pillar of the European Banking Union		284
	5.4.	The Creation of a Common Fiscal Backstop for the European Banking Union		294
6.	Conclusions			300
List of Cases				
References				

1. General Introduction on the Banking Union

1 The economic and financial crisis has had a great impact on regulation and prudential supervision of credit institutions in Europe. The creation of a single currency and the conferral of exclusive monetary tasks to the ECB in the Economic and Monetary Union (EMU) did not correspond to the creation of a centralised level of a supranational regulation and supervision of the banking sector. After the outbreak of the financial crisis in Europe, **the European Banking Union** (EBU) **is an unprecedented reform on institutional and substantive rules on banking regulation and supervision**.[1] This section briefly looks at the genesis and the general framework of the EBU.

The views expressed in this commentary are purely personal and in no way intended to represent those of the European Central Bank. All errors and omissions remain my own. The chapter take regulatory developments until 31 January 2021. Subsequent developments could not be taken into account.

[1] On the EBU from the legal perspective see, among others, Busch and Ferrarini (2020), Lastra (2015), Moloney (2014), Alexander (2015), Castañeda et al. (2015), Hinojosa-Martínez and María Beneyto (2015).

1.1. Genesis

The creation of the EBU has been triggered by the deepening of the financial crisis in 2012 when systemic problems arose both in the banking system and in fiscal and economic sustainability of sovereigns.[2] In particular, the euro area revealed costs of public bank rescues and the vicious circle between the banking system and sovereigns brought to a euro-area sovereign debt crisis.[3] The main reasons for the establishment of the EBU may be summarised as follows: **reduce the fiscal cost of bank bailouts; achieve a higher level of supervisory convergence and integration in the internal market; breaking the vicious circle between the financial risks in the bank and sovereign sectors.**

While the ECB announced the OMT programme in July 2012 and the financial assistance programme was agreed for Spain in June 2012, the European Council and the Eurogroup formation agreed in June 2012 to establish a centralised system of banking supervision and resolution that would break the vicious circle between ailing banks and sovereigns and the euro in general.[4] Subsequently, the **European Commission** published a **'Roadmap towards a Banking Union'** in September 2012 on the reform agenda to establish the EBU as a new institutional and substantive framework with a single supervisory mechanism, a common system of deposit guarantees and an integrated crisis management framework.[5]

Together with this Roadmap, the Commission proposed two regulations in September 2012[6] aiming at establishing a Single Supervisory Mechanism (SSM) by conferring new direct supervisory tasks to the ECB and by revising the decision-making procedures of the European Banking Authority (EBA). In the words of *Barroso*, a single system of banking supervision would create a 'new system, with the European Central Bank at the core and involving national supervisors (...) [to] restore confidence in the supervision of all banks in the Euro area (...)'.[7]

---

[2] Goyal et al. (2013), p. 7. On the role of the ECB to pursue its monetary policy objectives and the public purchase programmes see the CJEU case law on the matter: case C-493/17, *Weiss and Others* (CJEU 11 December 2018). The CJEU in this case accepted as a compatible measure the purchase on secondary markets of public sector government bonds by the ECB.

[3] Moloney (2014), p. 1622.

[4] Euro area summit and European Council statement of 29 June 2012.

[5] Commission Communication, *A roadmap towards a Banking Union*, COM(2012) 510.

[6] COM(2012) 511 final and COM(2012) 512 final.

[7] Commission Press Release of 12 September 2012, *Commission proposes new ECB powers for banking supervision as part of a banking union*, IP/12/953.

5   The process of adoption of the SSM founding regulations was completed in October 2013 when the Council agreed on the **adoption of the two SSM founding Regulations**.[8]

6   Meanwhile, the Commission published a proposal for a Bank Recovery and Resolution Directive (BRRD) in June 2012[9] as a proposal for **a directive on the recovery and resolution of credit institutions and other financial institutions**. The BRRD has been adopted in April 2014[10] after a legislative process of almost two years. Furthermore, the Commission presented a proposal to establish a **Single Resolution Mechanism** (SRM) **as the supranational institutional system of banking resolution**.[11] The proposal was eventually adopted in 2014.[12] A legal challenge on the legal basis and existence of the EBU brought before the German FCC was rejected in July 2019.[13] The judgment particularly considered that the legal basis and structure of the SSM and the SRM comply with the German constitutional requirements.[14]

7   In November 2015, the Commission adopted a **Communication on the completion of the EBU**.[15] Furthermore, it unveiled a plan for the completion of the EBU particularly with the proposal to **create the European Deposit Insurance Scheme** (EDIS) as a supranational deposit guarantee scheme arrangement and urging the establishment of bridge-financing measures for resolution and a common fiscal backstop as last resort.[16]

8   As put by *Moloney*, the EBU framework is **a legal matrix, 'which is composed of multiple interlinked components** which have different Treaty bases and which operate in the internal market and the euro area to differing extents'.[17]

---

[8] Parliament/Council Regulation (EU) No. 1022/2013 *amending Regulation (EU) No. 1093/2010 establishing a European Supervisory Authority (European Banking Authority) as regards the conferral of specific tasks on the European Central Bank pursuant to Council Regulation (EU) No. 1024/2013*, O.J. L 287/5 (2013); Council Regulation (EU) No. 1024/2013 *conferring specific tasks on the European Central Bank concerning policies relating to the prudential supervision of credit institutions*, O.J. L 287/63 (2013) (hereinafter the 'SSM Regulation'). See generally Moloney (2014), p. 1630.

[9] COM(2012) 280 final.

[10] Parliament/Council Directive 2014/59/EU *establishing a framework for the recovery and resolution of credit institutions and investment firms*, O.J. L 173/190 (2014).

[11] COM(2013) 520 final.

[12] Parliament/Council Regulation (EU) No. 806/2014 *establishing uniform rules and a uniform procedure for the resolution of credit institutions and certain investment firms in the framework of a Single Resolution Mechanism and a Single Resolution Fund*, O.J. L 225/1 (2014).

[13] See German FCC, 2 BvR 1685/14, *SSM Regulation and SRM Regulation* (Judgment of 30 July 2019).

[14] German FCC, 2 BvR 1685/14, *SSM Regulation and SRM Regulation* (Judgment of 30 July 2019) para 197, 204, 212 for the SSM; para 246, 247, 252, 253 and 265 for the SRM.

[15] European Commission, *Towards the completion of the Banking Union*, COM(2015) 587.

[16] European Commission, *Proposal for a Regulation amending Regulation (EU) No. 806/2014 in order to establish a European Deposit Insurance Scheme*, COM(2015) 586 final.

[17] Moloney (2014), p. 1625 (emphasis added).

The **existing legal acts are of diverse nature and content**. It is clear that the building block of the EBU is composed of the SSM, the SRM and their founding legal instruments, and the proposed EDIS. However, the single rulebook on banking regulation and the substantial rules on deposit guarantee schemes complement the EBU. All these parts of the EBU reforms express to various degrees a (r)evolutionary reform to the pre-crisis system of banking regulation and supervision. The main drivers of the EBU reform are 'the degree of mutualisation of losses achieved under the SRM, the cession of supervisory sovereignty under the SSM, and the development of legal technology to grapple with the complex euro area/internal market asymmetry'.[18]

While the presence of some risks inherent in the project to create and complete the EBU, **the EBU is now firmly established in the European system**. The existence of the two EBU pillars reveals that the main drivers of the EBU are to centralise banking supervision at the European level and to establish a supranational system of orderly resolution of credit institutions.

1.2. General Overview

The EBU is a **structured and complex system of legal provisions, institutional structures and substantive rules**. The identification of the EBU is not straightforward but requires some clarifications. In general terms, it can be said that the EBU is a supranational governance structure composed of **three ideal pillars, the SSM, the SRM and the EDIS** (Fig. 1). Only the first two pillars have been established to date, while the third is still under political negotiations following the publication of the Commission's proposals in 2015.

At the same time, together with the existence of pillars, the EBU is grounded on **substantive rules that constitute the basis of the three pillars** (Fig. 1). In other words, the substantive rules are the essential components allowing the functioning of the pillars. The substantive rules compose the **Single Rulebook** that sets out all the applicable rules on substantive banking regulation, supervision and resolution. These are Level 1 legislative acts, which are mainly the Capital Requirements Regulation, the Capital Requirement Directive, the BRRD and the Deposit Guarantee Scheme Directive (DGSD). Furthermore, the Single Rulebook is composed of Level 2 and Level 3 measures such as delegated or implementing Commission acts or EU agencies' guidelines, opinions as well as national rules implementing or supplementing the EU rules.

In this chapter, **the EBU is examined in detail**. The first section looks at the SSM as the centralised system of prudential supervision at the European level with particular focus on the role of the ECB therein. After that, the SRM is assessed, and in particular the tasks, powers and functions of the Single Resolution Board (SRB). Then, the analysis moves to the substantive rules on banking regulation, supervision

---

[18] Moloney (2014), p. 1629.

Fig. 1 The EBU structure (own creation)

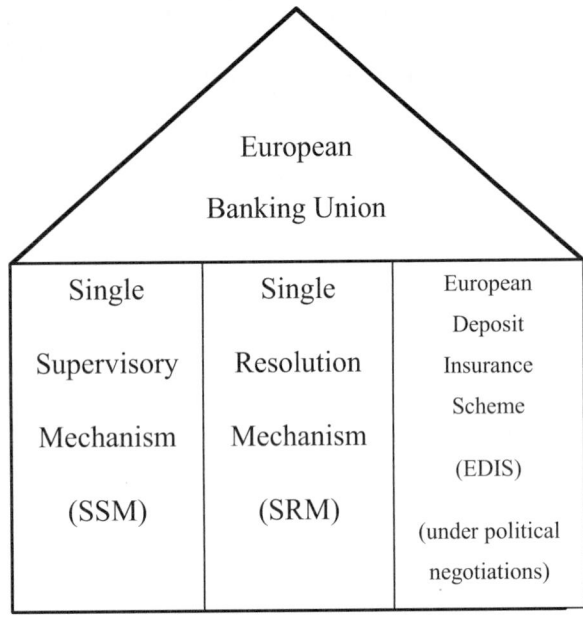

and resolution. Finally, the chapter will engage on the prospects of reform to the EBU, also taking into account the 2020 Commission's initiatives in this area.

2. The Single Supervisory Mechanism (SSM)

2.1. Rationale

14 In 2014, the European institutions succeeded in adopting a new institutional set-up for banking supervision in the euro area: the SSM. **The SSM is the first pillar of**

the EBU and has been set up with the SSM Regulation that has conferred supervisory tasks to the ECB.[19]

The financial and sovereign debt crisis has shown that the European banking system is vulnerable (→ para 2). The liquidity and solvability of credit institutions are still at risk and contagion effects can spread to other banks and to the real economy in Europe. This has generated many difficulties for the single currency and the transmission of the monetary stimulus of the single monetary policy, for market integration in Europe as well as for the overall financial stability of Europe. One of the reasons for the establishment of the SSM was the **conduct of banking supervision at the national level**.

The SSM Regulation refers to the impact of the financial crisis and the need to adopt an integrated system of banking supervision. Recital 2 of the SSM Regulation clearly shows the rationale that has driven the SSM: 'The present financial and economic crisis has shown that the integrity of the single currency and the internal market may be threatened by the fragmentation of the financial sector. It is therefore essential to **intensify the integration of banking supervision in order to bolster the Union, restore financial stability and lay the basis for economic recovery'**.[20]

This recital is noteworthy in affirming the main **rationale** of the SSM, namely intensifying the integration of banking supervision in Europe, restoring financial stability and ensuring economic recovery. These three points are the essential policy objectives that have driven the creation of the SSM. Moreover, other aspects relate to the need to sever the nexus between banking and sovereign debt crises, foster a European level-playing field in banking supervision, and ensure fair and non-discriminatory supervision over credit institutions in Europe.

2.2. Creation

Before creating the SSM, there were some regulatory efforts before and during the financial crisis to harmonise banking supervision in Europe. Before the financial crisis, **the main actors for banking supervision were National Competent Authorities** (NCAs). Central banks or other supervisory entities at the national level exercised tasks and powers for micro-prudential and macro-prudential supervision in Europe.[21] Even after the creation of the ESCB and the conferral of exclusive monetary policy to the ECB, prudential supervision remained at the national level.[22] MS conducted banking supervision based on the principle of **home country control** and mutual recognition in the EU internal market.[23]

---

[19] On the SSM in general see Moloney (2014), p. 1630 et seqq.; Ferran and Babis (2013), Lo Schiavo (2014a), Tröger (2014).

[20] Emphasis added.

[21] Dragomir (2009), p. 238.

[22] See Pisani-Ferry et al. (2012), p. 6.

[23] See Walker (2004), p. 305.

Home country control became an essential aspect in the internal market for credit institutions and has contributed to foster cross-border mobility and ultimately market integration. However, the home country principle is not absolute, but some powers or areas of action generally remain in the hands of the host state supervisors, especially when the public good derogation is invoked to restrict market integration.[24] At the same time, the conduct of day-to-day supervision with powers of imposing prudential requirements, inspections and authorisations in prudential matters were exercised by home state NCAs.

19 The establishment of a supranational system of **banking supervision did not constitute a reform priority in Europe after the adoption of the Lisbon Treaty**.[25] Before the SSM, scholarship promoted the creation of a new system of financial supervision through reinforced coordination and cooperation between national authorities in network-based structures or committees at the European level. In 2001, the *Lamfalussy* Report addressed the issue of who should provide the law-making competence for financial regulation by proposing the establishment of a committee structure.[26] The Committee on European Banking Supervisors (CEBS) was established as an advisory regulatory body aimed at providing adequate supervisory convergence in law-making and implementation of supervisory functions. However, no clear European mandate for supranational banking supervision was proposed.

20 The impact of the financial crisis in the EU led the EU institutions to respond quickly to market pressure to reform and **reinforce the system of prudential supervision**. When in February 2009 the *de Larosière* Report was published, the need to put forward a reform of the system of financial—and thus banking—supervision was envisaged.[27] The findings of the *de Larosière* Report were important grounds that prompted a change at regulatory level in the approach to be taken at supervisory level with the creation of the European System of Financial Supervision (ESFS).[28] However, the report did not envisage the centralisation of supervisory functions at European level and rejected the use of the existing EU Treaty legal basis to confer direct prudential supervisory powers to the ECB.[29]

21 Nevertheless, the *de Larosière* Report promoted some reform measures at prudential level that were followed-up by the Commission. First, the Commission promoted the creation of the European Systemic Risk Board (ESRB) as a new

---

[24] See Dragomir (2009), p. 165.

[25] See Lastra (2003), p. 55.

[26] Lamfalussy, *Final Report of the Committee of Wise Men*, (2001) 6, available at http://ec.europa.eu/internal_market/securities/docs/lamfalussy/wisemen/final-report-wise-men_en.pdf.

[27] Report by the High-Level Group on Financial Supervision in the EU of 25 February 2009 (de Larosière Report), p. 38.

[28] See Ferran (2012), p. 132.

[29] de Larosiere (2009), p. 43.

European macro-prudential body.[30] Second, the Commission proposed the creation of European Supervisory Authorities (ESAs). In particular, the **European Banking Authority was established** as the authority that would be part of 'an integrated network of national and Union supervisory authorities, leaving day-to-day supervision to the national level'[31] at banking level.

The Commission proposed a Council Regulation on the creation of the SSM in September 2012. Most importantly, the European Council conclusions of 14 December 2012 changed the content of the proposal, especially on the scope of application of the ECB direct supervision. After the adoption of the **SSM Regulation**[32] in October 2013, the ECB conducted extensive preparatory work to exercise its new supervisory tasks. 22

As from **4 November 2014, the SSM formally entered into force** as in that date the ECB started exercising its new supervisory tasks. 23

Shortly after the entry into force of the SSM Regulation, the ECB adopted a regulation specifying the cooperation between the ECB and the NCAs, the **SSM Framework Regulation**.[33] Together with the SSM Regulation, the SSM Framework Regulation is a key legal act, which sets out the main rules on cooperation between the ECB and the NCAs as well as procedural rules on the exercises of prudential supervision by the ECB. 24

2.3. Legal Basis

Both the TFEU and the ESCB Statute refer to the possibility of enabling the ECB to have supervisory functions in prudential supervision. The SSM Regulation is based on **Article 127.6 TFEU**. This is the essential legal basis conferring prudential tasks to the ECB and envisages the possibility to centralise supervisory functions within the ECB. 25

Article 127.6 TFEU provides for a special legislative procedure in which the **Council**, acting by means of regulations, may **unanimously**, and after consulting the EP and the ECB, confer specific tasks upon the ECB as regards policies relating to the prudential supervision of credit institutions and other financial institutions except for insurance undertakings.[34] 26

---

[30] Parliament/Council Regulation (EU) No. 1092/2010 *on European Union macro-prudential oversight of the financial system and establishing a European Systemic Risk Board*, O.J. L 331/1 (2010).

[31] Parliament/Council Regulation (EU) No. 1093/2010 *establishing a European Supervisory Authority (European Banking Authority)*, O.J. L 331/12 (2010), Recital 9.

[32] Council Regulation (EU) No. 1024/2013, O.J. L 287/63 (2013).

[33] ECB Regulation (EU) No. 468/2014 *establishing the framework for cooperation within the Single Supervisory Mechanism between the European Central Bank and national competent authorities and with national designated authorities* (ECB/2014/17), O.J. L 141/1 (2014), Articles 20, 21.

[34] See Smits (1997), p. 356.

27   The European Council mandate to explore fully Article 127.6 TFEU led the Commission to make the appropriate use of this article with a view to create the SSM. Scholarship argued that the limits of this legal basis are not circumvented to confer an extensive mandate to the ECB.[35] This is the correct reading as Article 127.6 TFEU provides for **extensive grounds to centralise supervisory functions** even beyond the current SSM Regulation.[36] Other legal bases such as Article 352 TFEU, the flexibility clause,[37] or Article 114 TFEU would not be sufficiently grounded. Similarly, the centralisation of prudential supervision by the implied powers doctrine,[38] through an extensive reading of Article 127.5 TFEU, cannot be upheld.

28   The existence of Article 127.6 TFEU is important for a number of reasons. First, the **addressee of the 'tasks' is the ECB**, an **EU institution which is not limited in its decision-making powers** by the restrictive interpretation held **by the CJEU in *Meroni*.**[39] EBA's rules show that the Commission put some limits on the decision-making and the EBA enforcement powers. On the contrary, the ECB is an EU institution that can exercise full decision-making powers. No limitations on the scope of supervisory powers are contained in Article 127.6 TFEU apart from the supervision on insurance undertakings. Correctly, it was submitted that the expression 'conferring tasks (...) concerning policies relating to prudential supervision (...)' does not create limits for the legislator.[40] The rather open expression in the Treaty article suggests that extensive supervisory tasks and powers can be conferred to the ECB. The term 'policies' is broad enough to confer day-to-day supervision of credit institutions. This legal basis clearly indicates that EU institutions may be granted powers that are necessary to ensure the practical effect of a Treaty provision, while being respectful of the principle of **conferral of powers and institutional balance.**[41]

29   Second, Article 127.6 TFEU places the ECB as the **best EU institution to exercise banking supervision** without concerns on the problem of delegation of powers or legitimacy.[42] Three arguments support this. First, under Article 25.1 ESCB Statute, the ECB also enjoys wide advisory competence in banking matters.[43] Second, the ECB plays an important role in contributing to the regulatory

---

[35] Wymeersch (2014), pp. 18–19. See also Tridimas (2019), pp. 36–38.

[36] Another open legal problem is whether the use of Article 127.6 TFEU could be extended to non-euro area MS. Article 139.2 point (c) TFEU (→ Article 139 TFEU para 33) extends Article 127 TFEU also to MS with a derogation. However, Article 139.2 point (e) TFEU (→ Article 139 TFEU para 45) excludes acts of the ECB from applying to non-euro area MS.

[37] Smits (1997), p. 356.

[38] Panourgias (2005), p. 173.

[39] Cases 9/56 and 10/56, *Meroni v High Authority* (ECJ 13 June 1958).

[40] Wymeersch (2014), p. 19.

[41] Cases 9/56 and 10/56, *Meroni v High Authority* (ECJ 13 June 1958) para 105.

[42] See Pisani-Ferry et al. (2012), p. 11. See also the German FCC, 2 BvR 1685/14, *SSM Regulation and SRM Regulation* (Judgment of 30 July 2019).

[43] See Dragomir (2009), pp. 226–230.

activities of establishing the financial market and the stability of the financial system. This takes place through the consultative task that the ECB can exercise when EU or national banking regulation is adopted (Article 25 of the ESCB Statute). It has been suggested that this is already well established in ECB practice.[44] Third, the ECB has explicit regulatory powers as stated in Article 132.1 TFEU which do not explicitly include prudential functions of supervision, but which do not exclude them either. These arguments indicate that the ECB has already been given some regulatory powers in the Treaty and the ESCB Statute. The ECB can thus enjoy full prudential powers under Article 127.6 TFEU.

Therefore, the use of Article 127.6 TFEU is the **appropriate legal basis** to confer prudential tasks and powers to the ECB. This legal basis creates the required legal certainty on the conferral of prudential functions to the ECB and establishes an adequate level of legitimacy for the SSM.

30

2.4. Institutional Structure

The SSM Regulation is the essential legislative act that established the SSM. It is divided into **five chapters**: subject matter and definitions (Chapter I), cooperation and tasks (Chapter II), powers of the ECB (Chapter III), organisational principles (Chapter IV), general and final provisions (Chapter V).

31

The **role of the ECB is essential in the SSM**.[45] The main aspect is that the ECB is competent to directly supervise credit institutions, financial holdings and mixed financial holdings. The SSM Regulation makes clear that the ECB is responsible primarily to conduct direct supervision especially in cross-border situations at the European level. The ECB cooperation and tasks chapter in the SSM Regulation contains the most important aspects to establish the institutional system of ECB supervision.

32

2.4.1. The Creation and Functions of the Supervisory Board of the ECB

The creation of the SSM in the context of the EBU has completely changed banking supervision in Europe by **centralising it at ECB level for MS participating in the SSM** (participating MS) and upgrading the level-playing field in prudential supervision. This is done with the establishment of a new internal body, the **Supervisory Board**, which exercises the prudential tasks in the SSM at the ECB level.

33

Article 26 of the SSM Regulation creates the Supervisory Board as an **independent internal body** undertaking the ECB supervisory tasks. This body carries out the required supervisory functions established in the regulation. The Supervisory Board is composed of a Chair, a Vice Chair, four representatives of the ECB

34

---

[44] Dragomir (2009), pp. 232–234.

[45] This has been confirmed by the CJEU in Case C-450/17 P, *Landeskreditbank Baden-Württemberg v ECB* (CJEU 8 May 2019) para 39–41.

and one representative of the NCA of each participating MS. It shall undertake the planning and the execution of the supervisory tasks conferred on the ECB (→ para 69).

35   The Supervisory Board meets at regular intervals, **approves supervisory decisions** and discusses issues related to the exercise of ECB prudential tasks under Article 26 of the SSM Regulation. In particular, Article 26.8 of the SSM Regulation provides that the Supervisory Board still carries out all **preparatory work** for the ECB's Governing Council regarding the supervisory tasks conferred on the ECB and proposes to the Governing Council complete draft decisions to be adopted by the latter.

2.4.2. The SSM Decision-Making Procedures

36   The SSM involves the exercise of **considerable decision-making powers** in the hands of the ECB. The SSM Regulation makes clear that the ECB has wide decision-making powers. Under Article 4.3 of the SSM Regulation, the ECB can adopt guidelines, recommendations and decisions to exercise the tasks conferred by the regulation, as well as adopt regulations to the extent necessary to organise or specify the arrangements for the carrying out of the tasks conferred on it by the SSM Regulation. Furthermore, Recital 34 of the SSM Regulation makes clear that the ECB 'will apply the material rules relating to the prudential supervision of credit institutions'. This means that the ECB can apply national legislation based on EU regulation giving national options or national legislation transposing EU directives (→ para 84).

37   Article 26.6 and 26.7 of the SSM Regulation detail the **decision-making procedure** for the exercise of supervisory tasks by the ECB. The Supervisory Board approves draft supervisory decisions by **simple majority** (paragraph 6). The draft ECB decisions are then submitted to the Governing Council, which adopts the draft supervisory decisions approved by the Supervisory Board with a non-objection procedure. The approval by the Supervisory Board does not confer legal effects to the decisions of the ECB in the exercise of prudential tasks. It is necessary to have the formal adoption of the decision by the Governing Council, which is the main decision-making body of the ECB, under a non-objection procedure.

38   The **non-objection procedure** consists in the adoption of a decision by the Governing Council through the absence of objections expressed by the members of the Governing Council. This means that the Governing Council still has the final say on prudential decisions following a procedure of non-opposition to the draft decision prepared by the Supervisory Board. The non-objection procedure does not apply to ECB regulations in prudential matters that the ECB might adopt under Article 4.3. ECB regulations in the exercise of supervisory tasks are adopted by qualified majority in the Supervisory Board and then are adopted by the Governing Council following the normal ECB decision-making procedure.

Appropriate independence safeguards have been included, especially to **39**
ensure separation of the monetary policy and supervisory tasks (Article 19 of the
SSM Regulation; → para 47) Furthermore, the ECB has developed a system of
delegation of decision-making in certain areas such as certain fit and proper
decisions, significance decisions or own funds decisions, which allows reducing
approvals of decisions at Supervisory Board and Governing Council level.[46]

2.4.3. Independence and Accountability of the ECB in the Exercise of Supervisory Tasks

Chapter IV of the SSM Regulation deals with the organisational principles in **40**
carrying out the supervisory functions conferred to the ECB. The ECB's strong
form of independence as set forth in the TFEU raises important issues regarding the
extent to which the ECB is accountable for the exercise of its supervisory tasks. The
relationship between accountability and independence is a long-standing debate
in central banking. The conferral of supervisory tasks to the ECB also extends this
debate to the supervisory realm.[47]

Article 19 of the SSM Regulation states that the ECB and the NCAs acting **41**
within the SSM '**shall act independently**'. This requires that the members of the
Supervisory Board and the steering committee 'act independently and objectively
in the interest of the Union as a whole' and 'neither seek nor take instructions from
the institutions or bodies of the Union, from any government of a MS or from any
other public or private body'. To respect the independence principle, the ECB has
adopted a Code of Conduct that particularly addresses conflicts of interest situations.

At the same time, Article 20 of the SSM Regulation establishes that the ECB is **42**
directly **accountable to the EP and Council** for carrying out its supervisory role.
Under the SSM Regulation, the Chair of the Single Supervisory Board is required to
present an annual report in public to the EP (Article 20.3). There are also additional
channels of accountability such as meetings between the Chair of the Supervisory
Board and members of the EP or the Council or replies to written requests.
Moreover, Article 21 of the SSM Regulation, which was included as part of the
Parliament-Council compromise, includes a reporting obligation for the ECB in the
exercise of supervisory tasks towards national parliaments (Article 21.1). These are
similar in content to the SSB's reporting obligation to the EP and Council under
Article 20.[48]

---

[46] See the general framework decision: ECB Decision (EU) 2017/933 *on a general framework for delegating decision-making powers for legal instruments related to supervisory tasks* (ECB/2016/40), O.J. L 141/14 (2017). See, further, ECB, Annual Report on supervisory activities, March 2018, pp. 86–89. See also German FCC, 2 BvR 1685/14, *SSM Regulation and SRM Regulation* (Judgment of 30 July 2019).

[47] See generally, Ter Kuile et al. (2015).

[48] See further Ter Kuile et al. (2015).

43   The degree of independence and accountability in the exercise of supervisory tasks is further detailed in an **inter-institutional agreement between the ECB and the EP**.[49] It contains provisions on the ways in which the ECB complies with independence and accountability as well as on the separation of monetary and supervisory policy and cooperation with parliamentary investigations.

44   Furthermore, the **appointment of the Supervisory Board's Chair and Vice-Chair** requires the EP to approve an ECB proposal. This is a dimension of accountability similar to the ECB monetary policy one.

2.4.4. The Separation of Supervisory Tasks and Monetary Policy in the ECB

45   The organisational structure of the ECB also raises the question of the **relationship between the exercise of monetary policy and supervisory tasks**. The SSM Regulation envisages a separation principle between monetary policy and prudential tasks of the ECB. The relationship between monetary policy and supervisory tasks is well analysed in scholarship especially at the national level.

46   Article 25 provides that the ECB separates between the monetary and the supervision functions. The degree of separation between the two functions is a crucial principle that shall be respected to conduct a sound monetary policy and an effectively independent supervision.[50] This obligation directly derives from the overall ECB tasks as framed in the TFEU. While under Article 127.1 TFEU monetary policy functions are aimed at maintaining price stability as the overarching objective of the ECB, the exercise of prudential supervision has objectives to 'protect the safety and the soundness of credit institutions and the stability of the financial system' (Recital 65 of the SSM Regulation). Correctly, *Goodhart* and *Schoenmaker* argued that this is mainly **to avoid conflicts of interest in conducting different functions**. Therefore, this important aspect needs to be considered in the exercise of monetary policy powers. The SSM Regulation thus requires that separation exists in exercising each function.

47   The degree of **separation** between supervisory and monetary policy functions to conduct a sound monetary policy and to achieve an effectively independent prudential supervision is an important aspect in the exercise of the ECB tasks. The submission of the Supervisory Board's preparatory work to the Governing Council may question the real effectiveness of the regulatory arrangements to separate monetary and supervisory functions (→ para 68).

48   Overall, the SSM **governance structure** is in line with the need for an institutional mandate on the exercise of prudential supervision at supranational level. It establishes a Supervisory Board to carry out supervisory tasks, while preserving the ECB Governing Council as the final decision-maker (→ para 39). Thus far, the

---

[49] Interinstitutional Agreement 2013/694/EU between the European Parliament and the European Central Bank *on the practical modalities of the exercise of democratic accountability and oversight over the exercise of the tasks conferred on the ECB within the framework of the Single Supervisory Mechanism*, O.J. L 320/1 (2013).

[50] See Goodhart and Schoenmaker (1995), p. 539.

internal place of the Supervisory Board in the ECB institutional structure and the dual separate functions of the Governing Council have reached an appropriate level of decision-making efficiency, as shown by the lack of objections to ECB supervisory acts by the Governing Council members.[51]

2.4.5. The Relationship of the ECB with the European Supervisory Authorities, the Single Resolution Board and the European Systemic Risk Board

The Relationship with the European Supervisory Authorities and the Single Resolution Board

The relationship between the ECB and EU agencies or organs is an important issue in the context of the SSM. The ECB relationship with EU agencies, particularly the European Banking Authority (EBA) and the Single Resolution Board (SRB) (→ para 139 et seqq.) poses questions in relation to the level of **coordination between supranational regulation, standard-setting, supervision and resolution of credit institutions**. These two EU agencies have different tasks. EBA does not supervise credit institutions on a day-to-day basis, but has mainly the mandate to develop guidelines and recommendations as well as to draft delegated or implemented technical standards to be adopted by the Commission in EU banking regulation (Recital 32 of the SSM Regulation). The SRB has the tasks to prepare and manage resolutions as well as prepare documents ensuring orderly resolutions. These two agencies question the balancing of horizontal competences between the ECB and the EU agencies.   **49**

The ECB relationship with EBA and the SRB shows that the conferral of supervisory powers to the ECB has necessarily changed the established set of rules as regards regulation and supervision in the euro area. As regards EBA, the need to adopt Regulation No. 1022/2013 proved to be essential for a correct **rebalancing of powers** between EBA and the ECB, especially to ensure participation and involvement of non-SSM competent authorities in banking regulation and standard setting.   **50**

The SSM Regulation provides for a degree of **close cooperation between the ECB and ESAs as well as the SRB**. Recital 32 addresses the issue of the relationship between the ECB and ESAs and affirms that the ECB should carry out its tasks in compliance with relevant Union law. This means that the ECB should not exercise its powers in a way that compromises ESA's role in 'developing draft technical standards and guidelines and recommendations ensuring supervisory convergence and consistency of supervisory outcomes within the Union'. Furthermore, the relationship between the ECB and the SRB as the resolution authority require close cooperation and close participation to each other.   **51**

---

[51] ECB, Annual Report on supervisory activities, March 2018, p. 83.

52 However, the degree of cooperation is relevant for the ECB exercise of prudential tasks as **the ECB disposes the power to adopt regulations and decisions** under Article 132 TFEU as well as the power to adopt regulations in supervisory tasks under Article 4.3 of the SSM Regulation. The ECB may adopt (regulatory) measures in supervisory matters, which not only cover its supervisory task, but which may impact EBA's or SRB's tasks.

53 It has been argued that the level of regulatory functions that EBA, SRB and the ECB exercise may be a source of **inter-institutional concern**.[52] However, apart from Recital 31 in the SSM Regulation, there is no clear prohibition on the part of the ECB to adopt an act which has some indirect impact on the EBA or SRB sphere. At the same time, to counterbalance this potential problem of legitimacy of EBA, Article 44.1(2) of Regulation No. 1093/2010 provides that a double simple majority (qualified majority) of MS participating in the SSM, and non-participating MS is needed for deliberations of the EBA Board of Supervisors, both in its regulatory and enforcement/conflict resolution tasks. At the same time, the intention to modify the voting modalities is tempered by the provision stating that the board of supervisors of EBA shall 'strive for consensus' when taking decisions (Article 44.1(4)). These voting modalities have the aim to **safeguard the consistency of EBA's rulemaking**. Similarly, the explicit **exclusion of resolution tasks** to the ECB under Article 4 of the SSM Regulation as well as the guarantees in ensuring the participation of the SRB in ECB tasks indicate that the ECB does not encroach with the tasks and powers of the SRB.

54 Scholarship held that the ECB-EU agencies arrangements may be problematic from a practical perspective as it is not clear to what extent the ECB and the EU agencies will follow similar policies or contrast with each other.[53] The ECB may provide indications to the regulator in the exercise of supervision of credit institutions established in the SSM. Nevertheless, EBA remains responsible to adopt such documents if so provided in Level 1 regulation and the SRB is in charge of resolution planning and management. EBA has been mainly created to draft measures in the banking field, both in the form of hard law and soft law to the benefit of the EU as a whole, and the SRB to prepare and manage resolution.

55 Overall, it can be concluded that the ECB-EU agencies relationship shows a positive degree of **coordination and balance** for the correct functioning of the EBU. The ECB, EBA and the SRB are strongly linked with each other while keeping their own competences. It can be said that these EU agencies **are not undermined under the SSM structure**[54] because there are safeguards in ensuring their good relationship such as cooperation arrangements, Memoranda of

---

[52] Moloney (2014), pp. 1667–1668.
[53] Moloney (2014), pp. 1668–1669. See also Wojcik (2016), p. 115.
[54] See Ferran and Babis (2013), p. 277.

Understanding[55] and (in)formal high-level contacts. So far, the relationship between the ECB, EBA and the SRB has proved to work well in practice with an important level of synergy, cooperation and communication. The 2019 ESAs review Regulation[56] strengthens inter-institutional coordination between the ECB and EBA.

The Relationship with the ESRB

The exercise of **macro-prudential supervision** remains a controversial aspect in Europe. The *de Larosière* Report stressed that there should be a European macro-prudential policy.[57] As a result, the ESRB was established in 2011 (→ para 21). However, the regulatory reforms on banking law implemented so far show that the focus of supranational banking supervision is mainly at micro-prudential level. Europe still lacks a European institution or agency exclusively and strongly dealing with macro-prudential regulation from both the institutional as well as the substantial dimension. 56

At present, the **ESRB is the soft-law European macro-prudential 'supervisor'** in Europe. It is responsible for the macro-prudential oversight of the EU financial system to contribute to the prevention or mitigation of systemic risks to financial stability (Article 3.1 of Regulation No. 1092/2010). The ESRB has no legal personality, cannot adopt legally binding acts and its instruments are limited to warnings of systemic risks and recommendations for remedial action that should be taken to address the risk identified (Article 16). These limitations have questioned the real effectiveness of the ESRB to conduct macro-prudential supervision.[58] At the same time, the ECB has been conferred some macro-prudential tasks and tools within the SSM under Article 5.2 of the SSM Regulation. These particularly consist of applying 'higher requirements for capital buffers than applied by the national competent authorities or national designated authorities of participating MS' (→ para 80). 57

While the ESRB has developed a 'soft' European dimension for macro-prudential policy, there is **not a truly supranational exercise of macro-prudential policy** at present. Even if the ECB has been conferred some macro-prudential tasks, national regulators and supervisors remain substantially competent as regards macro-prudential decisions, especially those concerned with borrowed-based instruments. The ESRB is not sufficiently resilient to perform the function of supranational macro-prudential supervisor in Europe. Some reforms are needed to strengthen the European macro-prudential policy either by establishing a stronger 58

---

[55] See for the SRB: Memorandum of Understanding between the Single Resolution Board and the ECB on cooperation and information exchange, 23 December 2015, available at https://www.bankingsupervision.europa.eu/ecb/legal/pdf/en_mou_ecb_srb_cooperation_information_exchange_f_sign_.pdf.
[56] Parliament/Council Regulation (EU) No. 2019/2175, O.J. L 334/1 (2019).
[57] de Larosiere (2009), p. 44.
[58] Ferran and Alexander (2010), p. 760.

agency regulator for macro-prudential purposes or by letting the ECB exercise further macro-prudential tools.

2.4.6. Close Cooperation with Non-Euro Area Member States

59   The creation of the SSM as a system for euro area MS questions whether there exist forms of **integration with non-euro area MS**. This level of integration is achieved primarily with two means.

60   First, the SSM Regulation provides that the non-participating MS shall conclude **MoUs with the ECB** and exercise their supervisory activities in colleges of supervisors together with the ECB (Recital 14). While these instruments establish the background for cooperation between non-SSM supervisory authorities and the ECB, the SSM Regulation recognises that the responsibility of non-participating MS shall be fully respected (Recital 44). The content of the MoU shall be in line with the established practice of providing detailed provisions on information sharing and supervision coordination. The degree of consistency in MoU would reinforce the argument that non-euro area membership does not (dis-)integrate the established legal order.

61   Second, the SSM Regulation provides in Article 7 that non-euro area MS might join the SSM through **'close cooperation' agreements**. The close cooperation arrangement subjects the non-euro area MS' credit institutions to the SSM framework and requires that their NCAs respects guidelines or requests issued by the ECB and follow instructions issued by the ECB (paragraphs 1, 2, and 4). ECB supervisory governance is adjusted to reflect the exclusion of close cooperation Member States' authorities from the Governing Council as they would be represented in the Supervisory Board. This is made by means of an objection mechanism that applies to Governing Council decisions and to Supervisory Board decisions. Furthermore, the NCA of the close-cooperation Member State receives instructions by the ECB and needs to adopt national decisions closely based on ECB instructions. At the same time, the ECB retains the power to suspend or terminate a close cooperation arrangement where NCAs do not comply with Article 7 of the SSM Regulation, while the 'close cooperation' participating MS have the right to request termination (paragraphs 5 through 7).

62   In cases of **disagreement**, a procedure is available which allows in close cooperation MS not to follow a Governing Council decision although such an action may lead to the suspension or removal of the MS from the SSM close-cooperation arrangement (paragraphs 7 and 8). In particular, non-euro area NCAs are empowered to notify the Governing Council of their disagreement with a draft Supervisory Board decision, following which the Governing Council is to explain its decision to the MS concerned. The non-euro area MS may subsequently request termination of close cooperation (paragraph 8).

63   Even if scholarship has questioned its legal and policy strength,[59] it is argued that the inclusion of this level of cooperation is **beneficial for consistent**

---

[59] Ferran and Babis (2013), p. 280.

The European Banking Union

supranational supervision in Europe.[60] The SSM Regulation is favourable to the position of non-euro area members as the non-euro area MS are in a position comparable to the euro area members as regards the exercise of supervisory tasks. Within a close cooperation under the SSM, problems of differential conditions are not entirely solved in the SSM Regulation. Most importantly, non-euro area members cannot be represented in the Governing Council. While the participating non-euro area MS would be represented in the Supervisory Board, their position cannot be equal in the Governing Council. This is because the Treaties and the ESCB Statute do not allow the non-euro area members to participate in the Governing Council (Article 10 ESCB Statute). The SSM Regulation attempts to solve this legacy of the ESCB Statute by giving the participating MS the possibility to express disagreement on the Supervisory Board's draft decision (Article 7.8 SSM Regulation),[61] and to terminate the close cooperation. Equally, the SSM Regulation states that the participating non-euro area MS are invited to express their disagreement with the draft decision of the Supervisory Board to the Governing Council (Recital 72). However, it remains clear that the impossibility for the non-euro area NCAs to participate in the Governing Council is an open problem that can be solved only with an amendment of the Treaty and the ESCB Statute. At present, two non-euro area Member States (Bulgaria and Croatia) have officially entered into close cooperation.

2.5. Substantive Rules in the SSM

The ECB is now fully competent to exercise supervisory tasks and powers vis-à-vis credit institutions, financial holding companies and mixed financial holding companies. This requires an analysis of the main **substantive rules** in the exercise of the ECB banking supervision in the SSM Regulation.   **64**

2.5.1. The Determination of the 'Significance' of Supervised Entities

Article 6 on cooperation within the SSM contains the most important paragraph on the scope of application of the ECB direct supervision. In fact, under Article 6.4 the term '**significance**' provides the yardsticks for the exercise of ECB or NCAs supervision. The credit institution is not 'less significant' under subparagraphs 1 and 2 when: **65**

(i) the total value of its assets exceeds EUR 30 billion;
(ii) the ratio of its total assets over the GDP of the participating MS of establishment exceeds 20%, unless the total value of its assets is below EUR 5 billion;
(iii) following a notification by its NCA that it considers such an institution of significant relevance with regard to the domestic economy, the ECB takes a

---

[60] Moloney (2014), p. 1663.
[61] See Moloney (2014), p. 1663.

66 These combined criteria of 'significance' are not exhaustive. Other circumstances may justify exclusive ECB supervision. First, the ECB can also consider an institution of 'significant relevance' if 'it has established **banking subsidiaries in more than one participating MS and its cross-border assets or liabilities represent a significant part** of its total assets or liabilities' (subparagraph 3). Second, the ECB exclusive supervision also includes the banks that have received **direct financial assistance** from the EFSF or the ESM (→ Supplement to Title VIII: ESM para 101 et seqq.), as those institutions cannot be considered 'less significant' (subparagraph 4). Third, subparagraph 5 states that the ECB is also competent to exercise its tasks for the **three most significant credit institutions** in each of the participating MS, unless justified by particular circumstances. Finally, the ECB may also decide to **exercise directly by itself all the relevant powers** for one or more credit institutions regardless of their significance but based on high supervisory standards (Article 6.5 SSM Regulation). Therefore, Article 6 of the SSM Regulation sets out the main difference in scope between significance and less significant prudential supervision.

2.5.2. Tasks of the ECB

67 The tasks of the ECB are **essential to exercise prudential functions** in the SSM. The SSM Regulation includes a list of micro-prudential tasks in Article 4 and confers macro-prudential tasks to the ECB under Article 5.

Micro-Prudential Tasks

68 **Article 4** SSM Regulation is the **key provision** setting out the micro-prudential supervisory tasks of the ECB in the SSM. It provides that the ECB shall be exclusively competent to carry out the following tasks in relation to credit institutions established in the participating MS:

(a) to authorise credit institutions and to withdraw authorisations of credit institutions;
(b) for credit institutions established in a participating MS, which wish to establish a branch or provide cross-border services in a non-participating MS, to carry out the tasks which the competent authority of the home MS shall have under the relevant Union law;
(c) to assess notifications of the acquisition and disposal of qualifying holdings in credit institutions;
(d) to ensure compliance with the acts which impose prudential requirements on credit institutions in the areas of own funds requirements, securitisation, large exposure limits, liquidity, leverage, and reporting and public disclosure of information on those matters;

(e) to ensure compliance with the acts which impose requirements on credit institutions to have in place robust governance arrangements;
(f) to carry out supervisory reviews, including where appropriate in coordination with EBA, stress tests and their possible publication;
(g) to carry out supervision on a consolidated basis over credit institutions' parents established in one of the participating MS;
(h) to participate in supplementary supervision of a financial conglomerate in relation to the credit institutions included in it and to assume the tasks of a coordinator where the ECB is appointed as the coordinator for a financial conglomerate in accordance with the criteria set out in relevant Union law;
(i) to carry out supervisory tasks in relation to recovery plans, and early intervention.

This provision is **very wide** and confers the ECB **appropriate tasks** to carry out comprehensive micro-prudential supervision. **69**

Point (a) confers the task of essential importance to **authorise or withdraw the authorisations of the credit institutions**. This task is exercised regardless of the 'significance' of the institutions as Article 6(4) of the SSM Regulation excludes point (a) from the distinction between significant and less significant institutions. Therefore, in applying Article 14 of the SSM Regulation and the rules in the SSM Framework Regulation, the ECB authorises and withdraws the licenses of credit institutions in the SSM. **70**

Point (b) gives the task to the ECB to exercise the role of the home competent authority whenever an institution established in the SSM and is qualified as significant exercises the **freedom of establishment or carries out services in non-participating MS**. In other words, the ECB also exercises prudential tasks related to passporting when the single passport rules are exercised outside the SSM, but within the EU and the EEA. **71**

Point (c) gives a key task to the ECB to authorise the **acquisition of qualifying holdings in a credit institution established in the SSM MS**. Similar to task (a), this task is exercised exclusively by the ECB regardless of the significance or less significance of the credit institution. Specific rules on the procedure and the acquisitions of qualifying holding are provided in the Article 15 of the SSM Regulation and in the SSM Framework Regulation. **72**

Point (d) deals with the core prudential supervision and confers to the ECB the task to supervise the respect of **own funds requirements, securitisation, limits to exposures, liquidity, financial leverage and transparency**. This task empowers the ECB to assess the prudential situation of significant credit institutions in compliance with the rules provided in Union law, the CRR and the CRD as well as in national laws implementing Union law on the matter. **73**

Point (e) deals with the corporate **governance requirements**, including fit and proper requirements of senior management, risk management, internal controls, remuneration practices. This task has the main objective of ensuring the correct management of corporate governance in credit institutions. This is exercised with **74** the assessment of corporate governance and follows the rules provided in the CRR, CRD and national law on these matters.

75 Point (f) gives the ECB the task to exercise more general micro-prudential assessment on the situation of credit institutions established in the SSM as well as to impose **specific measures on credit institutions that are not fully complying** with prudential requirements. In particular, this task may allow the conduct of stress test exercises, impose additional capital or liquidity measures or require ad hoc disclosures.

76 Point (g) also extends consolidated supervision on mother companies with the nature of **financial holdings or mixed financial holdings**. These entities other than credit institutions in the banking group are subject to prudential supervision of the banking supervisor.

77 Point (h) gives the task to the ECB to exercise supplementary supervision in the context of **financial conglomerates**. In particular, the ECB participates as the consolidating supervisor when the conglomerate is controlled by a bank established in the SSM.

78 Finally, point (i) provides for the tasks of applying prudential powers in cases when credit institutions do not respect or risk not respecting the supervisory measures imposed by the ECB. In particular, these may take the form of the **early intervention** powers set out in the BRRD or the power to **trigger resolution** under the SRM Regulation with the **failing or likely to fail determination**. Moreover, the ECB is competent to approve recovery plans. Conversely, the ECB is not competent to exercise resolution powers as provided in the BRRD/SRM Regulation.

79 Outside the micro-prudential tasks provided in Article 4 of the SSM Regulation, the NCAs remain responsible to exercise their tasks, while the ECB cannot exercise any supervisory power, except for adopting instructions under Article 9(1) indent 3 of the SSM Regulation (→ para 88 et seqq.). Recital 28 of the SSM Regulation **excludes ECB tasks** for the supervision of payments services, carrying out the function of competent authorities over credit institutions in relation to markets in financial instruments, the prevention of the use of the financial system for money laundering and terrorist financing and consumer protection.

Macro-Prudential Tasks

80 Article 5 of the SSM Regulation introduces **supranational macro-prudential tasks** that the ECB may exercise under particular conditions. If deemed necessary, the ECB can in fact 'apply higher requirements for capital buffers' instead of national authorities or national designated authorities of the participating MS and 'apply more stringent measures aimed at addressing systemic or macro-prudential risks at the level of credit institutions' (Article 5.2). These requirements would be higher than the ones applied by the national authorities of the participating MS where the credit institutions are established. If any of the NCAs or national designated authorities object, the ECB can exercise such macro-prudential tasks and tools by providing its statement of reasons within the very short timeframe of five working days. Furthermore, Article 102 of the SSM Framework Regulation

provides that the ECB may also set a buffer requirement in cases where the national authority does not set a buffer rate. This suggests that the ECB may also apply macro-prudential tools even regardless of whether the national authorities have set them.

The SSM may change European macro-prudential policy as the ECB is now vested with a **new macro-prudential competence under Article 5**. The establishment of the SSM has certainly increased the ECB's role while the role of the ESRB as a stand-alone body. A full macro-prudential supervisor does not exist at European level (→ para 58). At the same time, some reforms are needed to strengthen the European macro-prudential policy either by establishing a stronger agency regulator for macro-prudential purposes or by letting the ECB exercise further macro-prudential tools. 81

2.5.3. The Applicable Law by the ECB in the Exercise of Its Tasks

The applicable law by the ECB is a key aspect in understanding how the ECB can carry out its supervisory tasks. **Article 4.3 of the SSM Regulation** sets out the general rule on the applicable law by specifying that the ECB can apply EU directly applicable law and national law implementing the EU law within its supervisory tasks. 82

The ECB applies **directly applicable EU law**. Article 4.3 states that '[w]here the relevant Union law is composed of Regulations and where currently those Regulations explicitly grant options for Member States, the ECB shall apply also the national legislation exercising those options'. This provision covers both rules in EU regulations such as the CRR, delegated or implementing regulations as well as provisions in decisions as EU legal acts. 83

For the first time in European integration, the ECB as an EU institution can also **directly apply national law**.[62] Article 4.3 of the SSM Regulation provides that the ECB shall apply: 'where (...) Union law is composed of Directives, the national legislation transposing those Directives. (...)'. This provision therefore includes all the **rules under national law transposing EU Directives** such as the CRD, the BRRD or the FICOD. Furthermore, Article 4.3 of the SSM Regulation also includes the case of **national options provided in national law resulting from EU regulations**. This means that whenever an option results from an EU regulation in national law, the ECB can directly apply this national option. 84

Article 4.3 has a **very wide scope** as it includes all provisions in national law regardless of their nature (primary, secondary, administrative) in whatever forms they are. In the absence of a truly harmonised single rulebook in Europe, this provision in the SSM Regulation is extremely important as it allows the ECB to directly apply national laws, without having to instruct the NCAs or to let them adopt decisions at the national level. 85

---

[62] See Lo Schiavo (2019), p. 177.

86 However, the determination of what constitute transposition of EU directives, the different degree of implementing measures under national law and the existence of specific supervisory powers under national law remains a **challenge to integrated financial European banking supervision**.[63] In certain areas, the national transposition of the CRD shows different legal regimes in participating MS. Explicit supranational banking law provisions in EU regulations and directives, which give scope to ECB powers under Article 4.3 of the SSM Regulation, are not sufficiently detailed and comprehensive to include all supervisory powers provided in national law.

87 Furthermore, Article 9.1 indent 3 of the SSM Regulation states that 'the ECB may require, by way of **instructions**, those national authorities to make use of their powers (...) where this Regulation does not confer such powers on the ECB'. This provision does not make it clear to what extent the ECB has the supervisory tasks but not the direct supervisory power. It seems that Article 9.1 indent 3 of the SSM Regulation should be interpreted as giving the ECB the opportunity to instruct the NCAs whenever some national provisions outside the ECB supervisory tasks may have an impact on the ECB supervisory tasks.

2.5.4. The Allocation of Competences Between the ECB and the National Competent Authorities

88 The **allocation of supervisory responsibilities** in the form of tasks and powers between the ECB and the NCAs is an essential component in the SSM. The ECB/NCAs' allocation of responsibilities is an essential aspect of the SSM. The SSM creates a cooperative and integrated supervisory framework with the exercise of prudential tasks and powers by the ECB and the NCAs.

89 Although the SSM establishes a centralised level of prudential supervision, there is still considerable **scope for supervisory intervention of NCAs** as provided in the SSM Regulation and under national laws. The Commission proposal gave full supervisory tasks to the ECB over all participating MS' banks.[64] After the December 2012 Council conclusions, the scope of ECB supervision has been considerably reduced, mainly for political reasons.

90 The SSM Regulation establishes that only banks that are considered as 'significant' (→ para 65) are directly supervised by the ECB. **'Less significant'** banks are **supervised by NCAs** except for licenses, withdrawal of licenses and qualifying holdings in credit institutions.[65] The main aspect is that the ECB is responsible to conduct all the day-to-day assessment of prudential requirements for 'significant'

---

[63] ECB, *Annual Report on supervisory activities*, March 2018, pp. 13–14.
[64] COM(2012) 511, Article 4.
[65] See Ferran and Babis (2013), p. 270.

institutions, while the NCAs are responsible for the day-to-day supervision of 'less significant' institutions.[66]

The SSM Regulation provides that the NCAs supervise less significant credit institutions, and prepare and implement guidance on the ECB's supervision. First, the SSM Regulation is designed to create an integrated framework of activities between the ECB and NCAs. This indicates that a **duty to cooperate in good faith and exchanges of information** between the ECB and NCAs are key aspects. The SSM Framework Regulation establishes the main modalities to achieve cooperation in supervising 'significant' banks: the Joint Supervisory Teams (JST) composed of ECB and national officials with an ECB JST coordinator. These are internal administrative structures shared between the ECB and the NCAs that conduct the day-to-day supervision of 'significant' institutions. The coordinator of the JST is an ECB official, while the sub-coordinator of the JST is an NCA official. 91

Second, the SSM Regulation contains important clauses that provide that the ECB is responsible of prudential supervision beyond the notion of 'significant' credit institutions under specific circumstances. These may be helpful to avoid risks of national fragmentation in the conduct of supervision in participating MS. In fact, the ECB might **develop standards, policy stances and methodologies** for supervised entities regardless of their 'significance'.[67] The NCAs are expected to provide all the information necessary as well as assist the preparation and implementation of ECB direct supervision. Furthermore, the ECB may even take upon itself direct supervision of banks established in participating MS, even if they are not 'significant' under the SSM Regulation. 92

At the same time, NCAs are the **entry points** for notifications for some authorisation decisions under the SSM Regulation and the SSM Framework Regulation, and notifications from credit institutions to NCAs will continue to apply. Moreover, the NCAs under Article 6.6 of the SSM Regulation may still conduct **inspections and request of information** activities in parallel with the ECB. 93

Therefore, the ECB exercises **full prudential supervision on significant institutions as well as key prudential tasks in the SSM banking sector**, such as having the final say on authorisation, licensing, withdrawal of authorisation and the day-to-day supervision on significant banks. At the same time, NCAs conduct certain activities in the exercise of the exclusive ECB competence in banking supervision, i.e. preparatory supervisory activities, participation in JST, monitoring 94

---

[66] On the distinction between 'significant' and 'less significant' institutions see Case T-122/15, *Landeskreditbank Baden-Württemberg v ECB* (GC 16 May 2017) upheld by the CJEU in C-450/17 P, *Landeskreditbank Baden-Württemberg v ECB* (CJEU 8 May 2019), in which the General Court dismissed an action brought by a significant German institution to claim that, despite being significant in terms of assets, there were particular circumstances justifying it being 'less significant'. But see also the reading of the German FCC, 2 BvR 1685/14, *SSM Regulation and SRM Regulation* (Judgment of 30 July 2019), which seems to contradict the exclusive competence of the ECB in banking supervision.

[67] See ECB, Annual Report on supervisory activities, March 2018, 84.

tasks and participation in the Supervisory Board, as well as day-to-day responsibilities over 'less-significant' institutions.

2.5.5. Powers of the ECB

95 The use of a wide array of ECB supervisory powers is one of the most remarkable aspects of the SSM. Articles 9 et seqq. of the SSM Regulation provide for ECB **supervisory and investigatory powers**. Article 9 of the SSM Regulation sets out the general notion of supervisory and investigatory powers in affirming that the ECB exercises the powers that it has been conferred based on the ECB tasks under Article 4 of the SSM Regulation (→ para 68). Furthermore, Recital 35 of the SSM Regulation states that the ECB can require national authorities to make use of their own powers where the SSM Regulation does not confer such powers to the ECB.

Supervisory Powers

96 Chapter III section 2 of the SSM Regulation deals with ECB **specific supervisory powers**. In general terms, the SSM Regulation is more stringent on the role of the ECB as compared with the initial Commission's proposal of the SSM Regulation. Articles 14 and 15 of the SSM Regulation deal with licences and qualifying holdings.

97 Article 16 of the SSM Regulation sets out specific supervisory powers that the ECB enjoys in **controlling a credit institution, financial holding company or mixed financial holding company** in participating MS. Among others, Article 16.2 of the SSM Regulation allows the ECB:

(a) to require institutions to hold own funds in excess of the capital requirements;
(b) to require the reinforcement of the arrangements, processes, mechanisms and strategies;
(c) to require institutions to present a plan to restore compliance with supervisory requirements;
(d) to require institutions to apply a specific provisioning policy or treatment of assets in terms of own funds requirements;
(e) to restrict or limit the business, operations or network of institutions or to request the divestment of activities that pose excessive risks to the soundness of an institution;
(f) to require the reduction of the risk inherent in the activities, products and systems of institutions;
(g) to require institutions to limit variable remuneration;
(h) to require institutions to use net profits to strengthen own funds;
(i) to restrict or prohibit distributions by the institution to shareholders, members or holders of Additional Tier 1 instruments where the prohibition does not constitute an event of default of the institution;
(j) to impose additional or more frequent reporting requirements;
(k) to impose specific liquidity requirements;

(l) to remove at any time members from the management body of credit institutions.

These supervisory powers are **in line with the wide ECB supervisory mandate** and are essential to exercise an intrusive and fair supervision over significant supervised entities. (→ para 90) The fact that these are only some and not all supervisory powers suggests that the ECB may also exercise other supervisory powers beyond the non-exhaustive list provided in Article 16 of the SSM Regulation. 98

Three main ECB supervisory powers, reflecting ECB tasks, are analysed below: Supervisory Review and Evaluation Process (SREP), the authorisation powers and early intervention measures. 99

The ECB has the task and power to adopt supervisory decisions imposing significant institutions to hold own funds beyond the CRR Pillar 1 regulatory requirements as well as impose additional qualitative measures through the **SREP** power. This is meant to be a supervisory review process as a core supervisory decision and is defined as the SREP. This is the most important power based on Article 16 of the SSM Regulation. It allows the ECB to impose capital requirements and other additional quantitative and qualitative measures to supervised entities on top of Pillar 1 requirements and is called Pillar 2.[68] 100

The ECB can also exercise a **wide array of authorisation powers**. These are provided in directly applicable Union law and national law implementing Union law. A general categorisation, based on the SSM Framework Regulation, may be the following: common procedures, fit and proper and other authorisation procedures. Common procedures are those applying to all credit institutions established in the SSM and are the licensing, withdrawal of license and qualifying holding authorisations. As to the **licensing** power, the ECB has the exclusive task and power to confer and withdraw banking licenses in the SSM (Article 4.1 point (a) in conjunction with Article 6.4 SSM Regulation). Article 14 of the SSM Regulation establishes for a bottom-up administrative procedure where the NCAs analyse the application for an authorisation on the part of the credit institution. The NCA will issue a draft decision for the ECB to assess. Only when the draft decision does not comply with the conditions for authorisation, the ECB will object to the authorisation (Article 14.2). The role of the national authority is quite important, as the authorisation will be first assessed at national level and, only once the draft decision is submitted to the ECB, the ECB will conduct its assessment. The licence application is assessed based on the criteria contained in Articles 8–16 CRD and national law. In case the ECB does not object the draft decision, this is deemed to be adopted as a positive silence (Article 14.5–6 SSM Regulation). Withdrawals of licences are subject to a similar procedure, with the notable difference that the ECB shall adopt an explicit decision withdrawing the licence without the possibility of a silent decision. The ECB assesses the withdrawal of license in light of the criteria established in the CRD and in national law (Article 18 CRD). 101

---

[68] Article 16.2 SSM Regulation in conjunction with Article 97 CRD.

102 As to the **qualifying holding power**, the ECB has the exclusive task and power of authorising qualifying holdings in credit institutions established in the SSM (Article 4 point (c) in conjunction with Article 6.4 of the SSM Regulation). Article 15 of the SSM Regulation provides for the supervisory power for such authorisation. The procedure is based on the assessment criteria contained in Article 23 CRD as implemented in national law and follows a bottom-up administrative procedure where the NCA issues the draft decision to the ECB that ultimately adopts a decision within the timeframe provided in Article 22 CRD.[69]

103 The **fit and proper assessment and procedure** is provided in the SSM Framework Regulation as a 'quasi' common procedure as the entry point of notification of the intention to appointee a member of the management body is made at the NCA level, but the exercise of ECB authorisation is only made for significant institutions. Furthermore, the ECB is the final decision maker and adopts the final decisions in accordance with national law procedural rules.

104 The **other authorisation procedures** are those that apply with a direct notification to the ECB and which follow the rules of Article 95 of the SSM Framework Regulation. These are generally provided in Union directly applicable law, such as authorisation for internal models, waivers and options in direct applicable Union law or national laws directly or indirectly implementing EU directives such as requests, authorisations or notifications concerning mergers, qualifying holdings in non-banks, outsourcing or statutes amendments.

105 **Early intervention** measures are provided in the BRRD and in the national law implementing the BRRD. These powers are exercised when there is a situation of deterioration of the financial situation of a supervised entity and a swift and intrusive action on the part of the ECB as the competent authority needs to be taken. The objective of early intervention is to remedy the situation before triggering the resolution of the institution (Recital 23 BRRD). In particular, under Article 27 BRRD, early intervention powers should be taken when the institution does not meet or is likely to breach the prudential requirements provided in the Capital Requirement Regulation/Capital Requirement Directive (CRR/CRD).[70] The competent supervisory authorities shall be empowered to exercise the prerogatives indicated under Article 104 CRR and those set out in Article 23.1 BRRD (→ para 249). Among other early intervention powers, the management body can be required to implement the measures indicated in the recovery plan; examine the problem situation, identify the measures to overcome the problem and draw up an action plan to resolve the problem; convene shareholders' meetings; remove and replace board members and managing directors; draw up debt restructuring plans. If

---

[69] On the exclusive scope of competence of the ECB in the matter, see Case C-219/17, *Berlusconi and Fininvest* (CJEU 19 December 2018).

[70] EBA has adopted guidelines determining further the conditions for early intervention measures: EBA, *Guidelines on triggers for use of early intervention measures pursuant to Article 27(4) of Directive 2014/59/EU* EBA/GL/2015/03 (2015), available at http://www.eba.europa.eu/documents/10180/1151520/EBA-GL-2015-03_EN+Guidelines+on+early+intervention+measures.pdf/9d796302-bbea-4869-bd2c-642d3d817966.

these early intervention measures are insufficient, the BRRD allows the competent authorities to also appoint a temporary administrator. The role of early intervention measures under the existing recovery and resolution regime remains doubtful. These measures are intended to prevent the use of resolution, but they may still generate problems on the institution. This is because the public impact of using early intervention measures may go against the purpose of avoiding the resolution of the institution and could deteriorate the situation of the institution further. Furthermore, it is not clear whether early intervention measures have a purely supervisory nature, and they are already covered under Article 16 SSM Regulation powers or whether they are intended to have other purposes. Moreover, the fact that they are in the BRRD makes them subject to national law implementation.

As regards **investigatory powers**, the ECB can request information and conduct on-site inspections. The scope of the power to request information is **quite wide** as the requests span from credit institutions established in the participating MS up to third parties where supervised entities have outsourced functions or activities (Article 10.1 of the SSM Regulation).

In this context the ECB has a **wide spectrum of powers**. Under Article 11 of the SSM Regulation, the ECB can:

(a) require the submission of documents;
(b) examine the books and records of the persons indicated in Article 10 and take copies or extracts from such books and records;
(c) obtain written or oral explanations from any person referred to in Article 10(1) or their representatives or staff;
(d) interview any other person who consents to be interviewed for the purpose of collecting information relating to the subject matter of an investigation; interview any other person who consents to be interviewed.

Furthermore, under Article 12 of the SSM Regulation, the ECB can conduct **on-site inspections** at the business premises to both the legal persons indicated under Article 10 and to any other undertaking included in supervision. The power of on-site inspection might also extend to the sealing of any business premises and of books and records. The investigatory powers draw extensively from the Commission's enforcement in antitrust.

Enforcement and Sanctioning Powers

Article 18 of the SSM Regulation provides for '**administrative penalties**' that the ECB can impose in cases of breaches of supervised entities. The SSM Regulation states that the ECB can impose administrative pecuniary sanctions of up to twice the amount of the profits gained or losses avoided, or up to 10% of the total annual turnover (paragraph 1). The scope of direct ECB sanctioning powers is limited to credit institutions, financial holding companies, or mixed financial holding companies within the SSM scope that breached directly applicable EU law.

In cases where breaches have occurred in accordance with national law implementing EU directives or any relevant national legislation conferring specific powers that are currently not required by Union law, the ECB may require NCAs to open the proceedings based on an ECB instruction (Article 18.4 SSM Regulation). Accordingly, Recital 53 stresses that the ECB cannot impose penalties on natural or legal persons other than credit institutions, financial holding companies or mixed financial holding companies. The ECB sanctioning powers mark a **new stage in sanctioning credit institutions in the euro area** when breaches of prudential requirements have occurred.

111   Furthermore, the ECB may adopt **administrative penalties** in case a supervised entity breaches an ECB decision under Article 18.7 of the SSM Regulation.

Regulatory Powers

112 The ECB as the prudential supervisory authority may also exercise **regulatory powers** in the exercise of its tasks to certain extent. At European level, the Commission, the Council, the EP and the EBA have regulatory tasks at different levels (→ para 262). Differently from these institutions and the EBA, the ECB has not been conferred a general regulatory power in prudential matters. Therefore, it is essential to understand to what extent the ECB can exercise such powers. In the SSM Regulation, Article 4.3 indent 2 specifies that the ECB 'may adopt guidelines and recommendations, and take decisions. The ECB may also adopt regulations only to the extent necessary to organise or specify the arrangements for the carrying out of the tasks conferred on it by this Regulation'. This provision gives the power to the ECB to also adopt recommendations, guidelines as non-binding instruments as well as regulations. The adoption of ECB regulations is subject to the limitation that these shall be necessary to organise or specify the tasks conferred on the ECB in prudential matters.

113   In practice, the ECB has adopted **two main regulations**: the SSM Framework Regulation, which sets out the cooperation arrangements between the ECB and the NCAs, and the Regulation addressing certain options and discretions contained in the CRR. Both these instruments are in line with Article 4.3 of the SSM Regulation: the former concerns the organisation of the exercise of supervisory tasks, while the latter specifies how the ECB will exercise its prudential tasks when it applies certain options or discretions. There are also other ECB regulations that concern the way in which the ECB exercises a specific power provided in the EU law.

2.6. Procedural Safeguards in the SSM

114 Procedural safeguards are an important aspect to ensure the respect of the **fundamental right of defence** in the exercise of supervisory tasks by the ECB. The SSM Regulation and the SSM Framework Regulation set out rules on the right to be heard, motivation, access to the file, administrative review of supervisory decisions. In doing so, the SSM Regulation specifies requirements enshrined in Article 41 EUCFR that covers the 'right to good administration'.

2.6.1. Right to be Heard

Article 22 of the SSM Regulation states that the 'ECB shall give the persons who are the subject of the proceedings the opportunity of being heard' before a final supervisory decision is adopted. This provision is further detailed in Article 31 of the SSM Framework Regulation which sets out the rules on the **right to be heard**. In particular, the ECB shall give the opportunity of commenting in writing to the ECB on the facts, objections and legal grounds relevant to the ECB supervisory decision to 'a party which would adversely affect the rights of such party'. This opportunity is usually given for two weeks when the ECB intends to adversely affect the position of such party. There may also be the opportunity to comment at a meeting. This right is more generally framed in the EU constitutional framework as expression of the right to be heard recognised in the EUCFR provision on the right to good administration (Article 41.2 point (a) EUCFR).

The SSM Framework Regulation provides that the right to be heard **does not apply** to request for information and on-site inspections. Furthermore, the right to be heard does not apply when an ECB decision affecting the rights of a party has been adopted following explicit written commitments from the said party and when the ECB adopts statutory provisions not leaving any discretion to exercise supervisory powers.

There are some **exceptions to the two-weeks rule**. There may be a need to adopt a decision without the right to be heard before notification of the final decision if this is necessary to prevent a significant damage to the financial system. Furthermore, for licensing, withdrawal of licenses and qualifying holding the timeline of two weeks is reduced to three working days.

2.6.2. Motivation

The right of motivation is an essential guarantee to **motivate the factual background and the legal grounds** for the adoption of an ECB decision. Article 21.2 of the SSM Regulation states that the ECB decision 'shall state reasons on which they are based'. This is also provided in Article 33 of the SSM Framework Regulation, which states that the ECB decision shall provide a statement of reasons which contains 'the material facts and legal reasons on which the ECB supervisory decision is based'. The right to state reasons particularly applies in cases where the ECB intends to adopt a decision adversely affecting the rights of a party to a supervisory procedure. The right to have a motivated decision is recognised in the EUCFR provision to good administration (Article 41.2 point (c) EUCFR).

2.6.3. Access to the File

Access to the file is a procedural guarantee to ensure that the party to a supervisory procedure can **get access to the documentation** that led to the adoption of the ECB decision. The right to have access to the file is recognised in the EUCFR provision to good administration (Article 41.2 point (b) EUCFR). The access to the file is provided in Article 22 of the SSM Regulation as an essential guarantee to 'access to the ECB's file, subject to the legitimate interest of other persons in the protection of their business secrets. The right of access to the file shall not extend to confidential information'.

120   Article 32 of the SSM Framework Regulation further states that 'the parties shall be entitled to have access to the ECB's file, subject to the legitimate interest of legal and natural persons other than the relevant party, in the protection of their business secrets'. The assessment of the **grounds to get access to the file** requires balancing the right to get access to the documents with the right to protect confidential information and business secrets. Confidential information may include business secrets of the party or other persons, internal documents of the ECB and the NCAs as well as internal correspondence between the NCAs and the ECB and between NCAs.

2.6.4. Administrative and Judicial Review

121   Administrative review is a ground to review a decision through administrative bodies. The SSM Regulation establishes in Article 24 an **Administrative Board of Review (ABoR)** as an independent body for the review of supervisory decisions. This is an internal body of the ECB, which acts as an independent body for administrative review of supervisory decisions. The body is composed of a Chair, Vice-Chair, three members and two alternate members. Within one month after notification of the supervisory decision, the applicant may challenge the ECB decision before the ABoR. The ABoR can only adopt an opinion transmitted to the Supervisory Board. The ABoR opinion may propose to revoke, reform or confirm the contested ECB decision. However, the Supervisory Board is not obliged to follow the opinion of the ABoR and the ABoR request for review is not a condition to challenge an ECB decision before the CJEU. The ABoR has therefore the nature of an internal administrative body with soft law powers to adopt opinions suggesting the review of the ECB supervisory decisions.

122   Finally, **judicial review** is the opportunity given to the addressee of a supervisory decision or to other directly and individually concerned parties to contest the decision before the CJEU. This may take place in accordance with the general two-months rule to challenge the contested decision before the CJEU.

3. The Single Resolution Mechanism (SRM)

3.1. Rationale

123   The rationale to create the SRM lies in the need to have an appropriate European system of common **resolution powers with tools and instruments** framed at supranational level.[71] This means that there is an institutional framework for the

---

[71] On the SRM in general, see Moloney (2014), p. 1638 et seqq.; Alexander (2015), p. 176 et seqq.; Ferran (2015); Zavvos and Kaltsouni (2015).

recovery and resolution of credit institutions. While the BRRD empowers national authorities with resolution tasks and establishes financing arrangements with the conferral of substantive powers to resolve credit and financial institutions, the SRM creates a supranational institutional framework at European level to resolve credit institutions. The SRM is essential to reach effective decisions to resolve credit institutions within participating MS. Four main reasons are in favour of a single system for resolution in Europe: the presence of a single authority can facilitate timely and cross-border resolutions; it provides a mechanism to internalise home-host concerns and reach agreement on recovery, resolution planning, resolution procedures and burden sharing; it aligns incentives for least cost resolution; it may achieve economies of scale, avoid administrative confusion and duplication.[72]

In this context, the SRM is an **institutional development** to enhance enforcement of cross-border crisis management situations in Europe by conferring the power to exercise banking resolution at the European level. However, the SRM institutional complexity, the political dimension of orderly resolutions in MS, the SRB extent of discretionary powers and the role of the National Regulatory Authorities (NRAs) in implementing resolutions may impact resolution objectives, administrative efficiency, property rights and broader economic rights.[73] This may question the SRM effectiveness and role in the EU law and policy. Furthermore, the BRRD provides for a minimum harmonisation framework where MS and NRAs still retain considerable powers on the ways in which they can configure the national resolution framework as well as in conducting normal insolvency proceedings. This is especially true for the non-participating MS that could still adopt divergent rules than euro area MS. An aspect to be explored in future is the reinforcement of existing substantive framework providing for EU rules going beyond a minimum harmonisation approach and look at centralised substantive instruments to deal with bank recovery and resolution.

3.2. Creation

The **special supervisory treatment of credit institutions** requires particular attention especially as a consequence of the financial crisis in Europe. This is because 'the distress of Systemically Important Financial Institutions (SIFIs) and its subsequent disorderly liquidation can create risks to overall financial stability'.[74] Until the outbreak of the financial crisis, the European legal system **did not provide** for harmonised and cross-border **rules on resolution or winding down of credit institutions**. At the international level, soft law measures have been adopted to

---

[72] See Goyal et al. (2013), p. 16.
[73] See also Alexander (2015), p. 184.
[74] Zhou et al. (2012), p. 4.

frame the debate on orderly procedures for cross-border insolvencies for non-banking companies and for banks.[75]

126 As of 2009, the Commission proposed a **new statutory framework for banking recovery and resolution** throughout the financial crisis in order to allow administrative authorities to effectively deal with ailing financial institutions.[76] This regulatory framework at European level aims to provide early intervention, prevention of resolutions and resolution measures for financial institutions in Europe.[77] This is because an orderly liquidation of financial institutions may jeopardise financial stability in the system.

127 While in 1999 the Financial Services Action Plan (FSA Plan)[78] intended to set up a minimum European regime for the orderly winding-down of credit institutions in Europe, it **did not establish a regulatory European regime to resolve credit institutions** in Europe. The result of this process was the adoption of Directive 2001/24/EC on the reorganisation and winding-up of credit institutions.[79] This Directive, which had an extremely long negotiation process for adoption, included general principles applicable to the single market for credit institutions and in particular the home country control.[80]

128 The need to develop a **new regulatory framework was envisaged in the de Larosière Report** where a chapter was dedicated to crisis management and resolution. The report stressed that '[t]he lack of consistent crisis management and resolution tools across the Single Market places Europe at a disadvantage vis-à-vis the US and these issues should be addressed by the adoption at EU level of adequate measures'.[81] However, the *de Larosière* Report did not go as far as to provide specific regulatory proposals for the creation of a new European resolution or insolvency regime for credit institutions. The problem of too-big-to-fail remained unresolved and required a solution in the short-term. In the meantime, the Commission exercised an increasingly important role as to determine the compatibility of State aid measures to financial institutions in the context of State aid control.[82]

129 Before the outbreak of the financial crisis, no common European regulatory framework existed for the recovery and resolution for credit institutions and more generally for financial institutions. The EU law did not regulate on resolution and

---

[75] See among others Haentjens (2014), p. 255.

[76] Commission Communication, *An EU framework for crisis management in the financial sector*, COM(2010) 579 final.

[77] See Hüpkes and Devos (2010), p. 359.

[78] European Commission, *Financial Services Action Plan*, COM(1999) 232.

[79] O.J. L 125/15 (2001).

[80] See Peters (2011), p. 128.

[81] de Larosiere (2009), p. 32.

[82] See Lo Schiavo (2014b).

winding-down of financial institutions.[83] After the outbreak of the financial crisis in Europe, the Commission issued a number of communications **proposing the creation of a new European architecture for the resolution** of individual financial institutions and EU-based financial groups.[84] It also launched a consultation on a new framework for recovery and resolution of financial institutions and published a Communication on an EU Framework for Cross-border Crisis Management in the banking sector.[85] It emphasised the gaps and limits of the resolution regime for early intervention, bank resolution and insolvency framework and, accordingly, proposed a wide-ranging reform.[86]

130 In 2012 the Commission published a discussion paper on the bail-in instrument as a major tool in the context of resolution.[87] After a public consultation on resolution regimes, the Commission published the **BRRD** proposal in June 2012, which was eventually **adopted in 2014**. In December 2012, the Four Presidents' Report stressed that an integrated financial framework would require the establishment of the SRM for the euro area. This would complement the set-up of the SSM as the SRM would be based on 'robust governance arrangements, including adequate provisions on independence and accountability, as well as an effective common backstop'.[88]

131 EU Regulation No. 806/2014 (the SRM Regulation)[89] is the main legal instrument for the **establishment and functioning of the SRM**. This Regulation was adopted in April 2014 by the European legislators under the legal basis of Article 114 TFEU. In parallel to the adoption of the SRM Regulation, MS in the Council resorted to the adoption of an Intergovernmental Agreement outside the EU legal framework.[90] This Agreement, concluded on 21 May 2014 between the EU Member States with the exception of the UK and Sweden and amended on 27 January 2021, sets out, among others, the transfer of contributions raised at national

---

[83] See Hüpkes and Devos (2010), p. 374.

[84] See Avgouleas (2012), p. 394.

[85] COM(2009) 561 final.

[86] COM(2009) 561 final, 2–3.

[87] European Commission, *Discussion paper on the debt write-down tool – bail-in*, available at http://ec.europa.eu/internal_market/bank/docs/crisis-management/discussion_paper_bail_in_en.pdf.

[88] Four Presidents' Report, 5 December 2012, p. 7, available at http://www.consilium.europa.eu/uedocs/cms_Data/docs/pressdata/en/ec/134069.pdf.

[89] Parliament/Council Regulation (EU) No. 806/2014 *establishing uniform rules and a uniform procedure for the resolution of credit institutions and certain investment firms in the framework of a Single Resolution Mechanism and a Single Resolution Fund*, O.J. L 225/1 (2014).

[90] Cf. the Intergovernmental Agreement *on the transfer and mutualisation of contributions to the Single Resolution Fund* of 21 May 2014 (IGA on the SRF, available at https://data.consilium.europa.eu/doc/document/ST-8457-2014-INIT/en/pdf) as amended by the Agreement amending the Agreement *on the transfer and mutualisation of contributions to the Single Resolution Fund* of 27 January 2021 (available at https://www.consilium.europa.eu/media/48068/agreement-amending-the-intergovernmental-agreement-on-the-transfer-and-mutualisation-of-contributions-to-the-single-resolution-fund-27-january-2021_en.pdf).

level in accordance with the BRRD and the SRM Regulation to national compartments related to the progressive development of the SRF (→ para 174 et seqq., 178).

3.3. Legal Basis of the SRM (and the Bank Recovery and Resolution Directive)

132 **The BRRD and the SRM establish tasks and powers on the recovery and resolution of credit institutions and financial firms** in Europe. The development of a common system of resolution procedures in Europe faces a basic problem: the choice of the appropriate legal basis in the EU law and policy. The conferral of resolution tasks and powers required a sound and effective legal basis for such purposes. Differently from the SSM (→ para 27), the legal basis used to adopt the BRRD and to create the SRM was Article 114 TFEU. This Treaty provision allows for the adoption of measures for the approximation of the provisions laid down by law, regulation or administrative action in MS that have as their object the establishment and functioning of the internal market. However, it may be questioned whether the legal basis of Article 114 TFEU is sufficiently broad to establish a fully-fledged substantial and institutional resolution regime.[91]

133 Banking crisis management has been indicated as the main reason for further **harmonisation of the internal market** and, thus, for the use of Article 114 TFEU. The use of Article 114 TFEU could be questioned as its use may be seen as overcoming the legal limitations contained in that provision.

134 The CJEU favours a **wide interpretation on the use of Article 114 TFEU**. The CJEU held in the *ESMA* case that Article 114 TFEU gives grounds to attribute wide powers to EU agencies—in the specific case to ESMA to prohibit short selling under specific conditions. The expression 'measure for the approximation' in Article 114 TFEU is broad enough to also include measures adopted by EU agencies in the context of banking regulation and supervision. Furthermore, the CJEU held that the measure assessed in the *ESMA* case reduces the obstacles to the proper functioning of the internal market.[92] Therefore, the CJEU concluded that the European legislator enjoys a certain level of discretion in adopting measures to reduce obstacles to the internal market, such as the one scrutinised in the *ESMA* case. This questions whether the BRRD and the SRM respect this interpretation.

135 As regards the BRRD, the choice of Article 114 TFEU for the resolution of credit institutions is compliant with the scope of Article 114 TFEU as it **generally improves the functioning of the internal market** by creating common resolution powers in all MS as regards resolution procedures. This is an important point as the BRRD provides a minimum harmonisation framework for the creation of a European-wide system of resolution to be implemented into national law. The scope of Article 114 TFEU is respected, and its use reveals that the attempt to

---

[91] See Zavvos and Kaltsouni (2015), p. 123. See also the German FCC, 2 BvR 1685/14, *SSM Regulation and SRM Regulation* (Judgment of 30 July 2019).

[92] Case C-270/12, *United Kingdom v Parliament and Council (ESMA)* (CJEU 22 January 2014).

harmonise resolution substantive rules aims to crisis prevention and crisis management. Therefore, the use of Article 114 TFEU fills the gap in dealing with banking resolution from a regulatory point of view. Its use shows that a resolution regime can be well established to harmonise the internal market. This is also justified by the need to move from the unconventional use of the de facto recovery and resolution with an assessment on the compatibility of State aid under Article 107.3 TFEU to a new harmonised regulatory regime to deal with banking recovery and resolution.

As regards the SRM, there are a number of **arguments in favour of the use of Article 114 TFEU** to establish a supranational institutional framework for banking resolution. First, the proper functioning of the single market is highly dependent on the level of integration of MS that share the single currency. This justifies the use of Article 114 TFEU for the establishment of a system that applies to euro area MS, and is ideally open to all the Member States. Second, the use of Article 114 TFEU is the most practical legal basis to the integration of financial markets. The effectiveness of the EBU is subject to the appropriate use of the legal tools to establish an integrated financial market. This explains the creation of a euro area system for resolution that aims to reduce the obstacles that can arise in the context of market integration where certain MS have opted for further integration. Third, it is essential that resolution authorities do not create obstacles to the cross-border resolution arrangements and be able to act swiftly and effectively for crisis management. A fragmented and lengthy national decision-making framework has shown evident problems in the recent past, especially on cross-border recovery and resolution measures.[93] This suggests that Article 114 TFEU reduces obstacles and promotes harmonisation to 'ensure a coherent and uniform approach' for resolutions in the internal market, including in case of the SRM. **136**

In terms of institutional framework, it may be questioned whether Article 114 TFEU embraces the **possibility to adopt the SRM agency structure** for supranational European resolution regime. However, Article 114 TFEU has been used extensively, especially during the financial crisis to establish new EU agencies. The CJEU upheld almost all EU legislation that relies on Article 114 TFEU as a legal basis to establish EU agencies when the agencies' responsibilities derive from its founding regulation and supported the argument that the EU agency improves the conditions for the establishment and functioning of the internal market. The CJEU also held that the legislator enjoys a wide margin of discretion in adopting legal acts under Article 114 TFEU. In this respect, Article 114 TFEU is fully respected in reinforcing the institutional framework for banking recovery and resolution. In particular, the conferral of resolution powers to the SRB as well as the introduction of a supranational procedure for the resolution of credit institutions subject to SRM resolution is compliant with the purpose of reducing obstacles to the functioning of the internal market as well distortions of competition. Furthermore, it has also been argued that the need to avoid divergent solutions followed for the ad hoc resolution **137**

---

[93] See Moloney (2014), p. 1617.

or the bailout of credit institutions are sufficient grounds to make use of Article 114 TFEU to establish a new institutional framework.⁹⁴

138   Overall, these reasons suggest that the use of Article 114 TFEU is the **appropriate legal basis** for the creation of a European or euro area substantial and institutional system of bank recovery and resolution.

3.4. Institutional Structure

3.4.1. The Role of the Single Resolution Board

139   The SRM Regulation establishes the SRB as an **EU agency** with legal personality (Article 42) and seat in Brussels (Article 48).

140   The role of the SRB is **central for the correct functioning of the SRM**. As argued above, the use of Article 114 TFEU also allows for the establishment of EU agencies for cross-border resolution purposes. The detailed technical area of banking resolution led to the establishment of an ad hoc EU agency for such purposes rather than conferring resolution powers to an already established EU agency or to an EU institution such as the Commission or the ECB. The establishment of a new agency in banking resolution is an important development that nonetheless needs to be framed in the context of the existing constitutional constraints to the establishment of EU agency in the EU law. The power to establish an EU agency through Article 114 TFEU is legally possible. However, it is open to question **whether and to what extent an EU agency might be empowered to deal effectively with resolution**. The EU legislator possesses discretion on the 'harmonisation technique most appropriate for achieving the desired result',⁹⁵ and it can achieve this result by establishing a new agency for such purposes. The establishment of a new EU agency for the exercise of resolution powers to ensure a coherent and uniform approach to bank resolution within the SRM is feasible, although open to competence and powers challenges.⁹⁶

141   A major issue is the **extent of powers that have been conferred to the SRB**. This was a source of contention for the adoption of the SRM Regulation. The CJEU provided for the limitation to the delegation of powers with the (in-)famous *Meroni* doctrine (→ para 28). With the *ESMA* ruling, it appears that the *Meroni* doctrine has been downgraded to some extent.⁹⁷ EU agencies can be empowered so long as a clear delegation framework is established for the EU agencies and appropriate safeguards are provided to that effect. The CJEU judgment plays an important role to support the legitimate use of agency-making and to improve the decision-making powers conferred to the SRB for future revisions. While the *Meroni*

---

⁹⁴ See Ferran (2015), pp. 79–80.

⁹⁵ Case C-217/04, *United Kingdom v Council and Parliament (ENISA)* (ECJ 2 May 2006) para 43.

⁹⁶ See Moloney (2014), p. 1657.

⁹⁷ See Lo Schiavo (2015), p. 315.

doctrine is inadequate to the current constitutional challenges arising from the financial crisis especially with a view to integrate financial markets further, it still prevents the SRB to possess full-decision making discretionary powers to deal with resolutions. In looking at the provision of the SRM Regulation, the extent of the SRB powers has been restrained as compared with the initial Commission's Regulation proposal.

The analysis of the SRB powers shows that the SRB possesses **much discretion in the realm of resolution planning but limited powers in resolution taking**. For instance, it may require banks or banking groups to change their organisational structure if the SRB determines that the bank or banking group's organisational structure is a substantial impediment to a feasible and credible resolution of the bank or group (Article 17.5 BRRD). Furthermore, if it determines that there are substantial impediments to the implementation of the resolution plan, it may order the institution to remove the impediments, including changing its organisational structure or business activities (Articles 15 and 16 BRRD and SRM Regulation). Moreover, the SRM Regulation provides that if the firm's or group's proposals are considered inadequate, the resolution authority will have the power to take specific actions that address or remove the impediments to resolvability (Article 17.5 BRRD and Article 10.11 of the SRM Regulation). This selection of provisions shows that the SRB can exercise wide discretion to choose a measure based on the nature of the impediment. This goes beyond the simple technical analysis. It can imply a substantial degree of discretionary decision-making based on criteria that belong to an assessment made by the SRB.

However, **the Meroni doctrine is reflected in the resolution decision-making**. The SRB's resolution scheme shall be endorsed by the Commission and—in certain circumstances—by the Council. This was justified by the need to have a *Meroni*-compliant agency and perhaps the need not to dissociate the SRB too much from other EU political institutions such as the Commission and the Council. In particular, resolution powers are subject at least to the Commission's scrutiny. Furthermore, the NRAs are responsible for the implementation of the resolution scheme agreed at the supranational level in the SRM. These arrangements in the SRM Regulation question whether the SRB is such an effective entity in exercising its resolution mandate, as the limited degree of discretion remains an essential limitation in delegating powers to EU agencies.[98] In practice, such limitations may considerably restrict the SRB's powers to play a primary and decisive role in the resolution procedure. Recent cases brought to the attention of the SRB have revealed the political interests in executing resolution actions.

3.4.2. The Composition and Functions

The SRB is composed of an **Executive Director, four full-time members** and **a member appointed by each MS representing the NRAs** (Article 43 SRM

---

[98] Moloney (2014), p. 1661.

Regulation). The Commission and the ECB are permanent observers in plenary and executive sessions. The SRB convenes in plenary and executive sessions (Article 49 SRM Regulation).

Among other functions, the **plenary sessions** comprise the power to adopt the annual work programme, the annual budget and annual activity report (Article 50 SRM Regulation). Importantly, the plenary session is convened when the action to be taken requires more than EUR 5 billion in capital from the SRF. The plenary session shall also evaluate the application of resolution tools, including the use of the SRF, in case EUR 5 billion or more have been used throughout the calendar year. Moreover, the plenary session is convened to decide the necessity to raise extraordinary ex post contributions, borrowing of the SRF and financing arrangements in case the resolution of a group with entities in participating and non-participating MS is above the EUR 5 billion threshold.

Conversely, the **executive session** takes all decisions to implement the SRM Regulation (Article 53 of the SRM Regulation). The executive session takes specific decisions relating to single credit institutions or a banking group. Importantly, the executive session is represented only by the Executive Director, the permanent members and the responsible NRA and not by all the NRAs.

145 Article 51 of the SRM Regulation regulates the **decision-making** of the SRB. Both in cases of a deliberation on an individual entity or on a cross-border group, the SRB in executive session requires consensus among the SRB's members. If this is not possible, then the SRM Regulation provides that the SRB members shall take decision by **simple majority**. Similarly, decisions in the executive session are to be taken by consensus, but if this is not possible, the Chair and the executive members take decision by simple majority. No member has a veto power.

3.4.3. Accountability and Independence in the Exercise of Resolution Tasks

146 Similar to the SSM, the SRM includes several accountability provisions in the SRM Regulation. These have the objective to ensure that the **activities of the SRB are shared with a number of external actors** and to let EU institutions and national parliaments scrutinise the work of the SRB.

147 Article 45 of the SRM Regulation deals with the **accountability provisions of the SRB**. The SRB is accountable to the EP, the Council and the Commission. The relationship with each institution varies. The SRB presents an annual report not only to the EP, but also to the Council, the Commission and the European Court of Auditors. The Chair of the SRB may participate in a hearing of the competent committee of the EP to discuss the performance of resolution tasks by the SRB. Furthermore, the Chair can have hearings before the Council. The SRB shall reply orally or in writing to questions addressed by the EP or by the Council. Furthermore, the Chair shall hold confidential oral discussion with the Chair and Vice-Chair of the competent committees of the EP.

In December 2015, the SRB concluded an **agreement with the EP** detailing the modalities of **exercise of democratic accountability**.[99] The Agreement contains several provisions on reports, public hearings and ad hoc exchanges of views and special confidential meeting. The Agreement has the purpose to reinforce the cooperation on accountability between the SRB and the EP.

Similar to the SSM, the **accountability provisions at the national level** are also present in the SRM Regulation. The SRB, under Article 46, is accountable before the national parliaments. These accountability requirements state that the national parliaments may formulate questions to the SRB and the SRB shall reply in writing. Furthermore, the annual report is also sent to all the national parliaments of participating MS. There may be questions and observations from national parliaments to which the SRB shall reply. The national parliaments may also invite the Chair of the SRB to participate in exchanges of views in relation to resolutions of entities. The national accountability provisions of national resolution authorities remain without prejudice.

Similar to the SSM, the SRM Regulation sets an **independence principle** for the SRB and the national authorities in the performance of their tasks. These require that the SRB and its members shall act in the interest of the EU and shall neither seek nor take instructions from the EU's institutions or bodies or any government of an MS or any other public or private body. Also, internally at the SRB, independence means that the SRB members shall not influence the Chair, the Vice-Chair or the other SRB members.

3.4.4. The Decision-Making Procedure for Resolution in the SRM

The **resolution procedure under the SRM Regulation** is set out in Article 18 of the SRM Regulation. This is the most important provision on the decision-making process in the SRM. First, the ECB or the national supervisory authority signals when a credit institution or group in a participating MS is failing or likely to fail. This first appraisal can also come by the SRB that, under particular conditions, can trigger the process on its own initiative. Second, the SRB determines that there is no reasonable prospect of a timely private sector rescue and that a resolution action is in the public interest. Third, the SRB, with the support of the relevant NRAs, prepares and adopts the resolution scheme. The adoption of a resolution scheme somehow involves a margin of discretion. The arrangement finally adopted in Article 18 is that the assessment of discretion is attributed to the Commission's responsibility. However, the Commission simply endorses the resolution scheme or may object to its discretionary aspects. In addition, the Council has a right to object, but only on a proposal from the Commission and on a limited number of matters

---

[99] See Interinstitutional Agreement between the European Parliament and the Single Resolution Board *on the practical modalities of the exercise of democratic accountability and oversight over the exercise of the tasks conferred on the Single Resolution Board within the framework of the Single Resolution Mechanism*, O.J. L 339/58 (2015). See also the German FCC, 2 BvR 1685/14, *SSM Regulation and SRM Regulation* (Judgment of 30 July 2019).

(the existence of a public interest or a material modification of the amount of SRF to be used in a specific resolution action). The Commission and the Council have only twenty-four hours from adoption of the resolution scheme by the SRB in which they can object. Once adopted, the resolution decision is implemented by the responsible NRA. The procedure should take place within twenty-four hours or, at most, thirty-two hours (eight hours being the period for the SRB to modify the scheme in response to Commission or Council objections). The Commission is empowered to adopt delegated acts to further specify the criteria or conditions to be taken by the SRB in the exercise of its tasks (Article 93 SRM Regulation). The SRM Regulation expressly limits the power of intervention of the Council and the SRB on the impact over MS' budgetary sovereignty. It states that neither the SRB nor the Council can require participating MS to provide extraordinary financial support or impinge on budgetary or fiscal responsibilities (Article 6.6 of the SRM Regulation).

152   While the **problem of the creation of a fully-fledged EU agency** to deal with a European-wide resolution regime has been discussed, some reflections on the resolution procedure in the SRM are needed. As discussed earlier, the SRM Regulation does not provide for a European resolution procedure regarding all credit institutions established in participating MS. Rather, NRAs remain responsible to deal with the resolution procedures as regards 'less significant' non-cross-border institutions and execute resolution measures. This limitation restricts the procedures subject to the SRM Regulation. However, the use of the resolution procedure established in the SRM Regulation is critical as the resolved institution may be of significant relevance for the euro area and the internal market.

153   The existing SRM procedural decision-making does not fulfil the objective of achieving an effective resolution. Rather, **it may generate a conundrum.**[100] This is for a number of reasons. First, the resolution procedure is cumbersome. Even if the SRM Regulation sets a strict timing, the different steps of the procedure put several stakeholders under stress for a quick decision. The solution found sets several steps that put at risk the urgency of coming up with a fast resolution in a very short time. Second, the procedure involves many political interests that may lead to the adoption of political decisions to place or not an institution under resolution. The criterion of **public interest** in the SRB assessment proves to be **vague and politically sensitive**, especially when the use of public funds may determine the alternative between insolvency proceedings and resolution.[101] Third, the procedure involves too many political actors. Apart from the Commission, which shall approve, under a silent procedure, the resolution scheme due to the *Meroni* doctrine constraints, the procedure might also involve the Council under specific

---

[100] See Ferran (2015), p. 76.

[101] See the different SRB decisions taken in 2017: SRB Decision SRB/EES/2017/08 of 7 June 2017 *concerning the adoption of a resolution scheme in respect of Banco Popular Español, S.A.*, and, on the other hand, SRB Decision SRB/EES/2017/11 of 23 June 2017 *concerning the assessment of the conditions for resolution in respect of Veneto Banca S.p.A.* and SRB Decision SRB/EES/2017/12 of 23 June 2017 *concerning the assessment of the conditions for resolution in respect of Banca Popolare di Vicenza S.p.A.*

circumstances. This does not really make the resolution procedure viable for an effective and truly *European* solution as the Council may express its dissent to the adoption of the resolution decision and will reflect, by its very nature, national rather than European interests. It is not excluded that other institutions and national authorities are also heavily involved in the final resolution decision. Fourth, the resolution procedure is highly **technical and complex**. The resolution scheme may be amended several times, and several bodies and organs are involved with its drafting at an informal level. This indicates that the resolution procedure is politically negotiated and the result is a political compromise rather than a purely technical decision. Furthermore, the SRM Regulation is extremely complex and detailed on the matter. This hardly contributes to the efficiency of the SRM procedure.

The assessment of the resolution procedure in the SRM shows that determining and executing the resolution of a big banking group may be **difficult** to achieve in practice and is subject to political considerations. **154**

3.5. Substantive Rules

3.5.1. Scope

The first articles of the SRM Regulation provide for the **scope of application of the SRM**. The SRM Regulation identifies as a subject matter of the mechanism 'uniform rules and a uniform procedure for the resolution of credit institutions'. Article 1 of the SRM Regulation stresses that uniform rules will be applied by the Council, the SRB and the national resolution authorities of the participating MS. The resolution mechanism will be supported by the SRF that has been created upon the entry into force of the Intergovernmental Agreement among the participating MS to transfer the funds raised at national level (→ para 131, 174 et seqq.). The SRM applies to (a) credit institutions established in participating MS; (b) parent undertakings established in one of the participating MS, including financial holding companies and mixed financial holding companies; (c) investment firms and financial institutions established in participating MS when they are covered by the consolidated supervision of the parent undertaking. Hence, the SRM applies to participating MS of the SSM (Article 4 SRM Regulation). Similar to the SSM, there may also be the conclusion of a close cooperation agreement with non-euro area MS that will give the status of participating MS to the one joining close cooperation (Articles 2 and 7 of the SSM Regulation). **155**

The SRM division of tasks reflects the **differentiation between significant and less significant entities under the SSM** (→ para 65).[102] Article 7 of the SRM Regulation provides for an explicit division of tasks between the SRB as the EU **156**

---

[102] Article 4 of the SRM Regulation refers to the distinction between 'significant' and 'less significant' credit institutions in the SSM Regulation.

agency responsible for banking resolution and the NRAs. The SRB is responsible to draw up the resolution plans and to adopt all schemes related to the possible resolution of significant credit institutions in compliance with the SSM Regulation, of those in relation to which the ECB is the competent supervisor as well as of other cross-border groups.[103] Interestingly, the SRM Regulation also includes under the tasks of the SRB cross-border groups not qualified as 'significant' institutions. Conversely, Article 7.3 of the SRM Regulation attributes the resolution planning and functions of the other institutions to the NRAs. These are responsible for executing bank resolution schemes under the SRB's instructions (Article 28 of the SRM Regulation). Nonetheless, if a resolution action requires the use of the SRF, then the SRB is responsible to conduct the resolution regardless of the significance of the credit institutions (Article 7.3 sentence 2 of the SRM Regulation). This is an important exception that also confers resolution powers to the SRB for 'less significant' or non-cross border entities under the SRM.

3.5.2. Tasks and Powers of the SRB

157 The **main tasks of the SRB** are provided in Articles 50 et seq. of the SRM Regulation. These are framed in the context of the activities of the SRB sessions. The SRB acts in two types of sessions: plenary and executive.

158 The **plenary session** is in charge of the most important tasks: approve the annual plan and report, decide on the use of the SRF if support is above 5 billion euro, the decision on raising ex-post contributions, voluntary borrowing between financing arrangements, alternative financing means, and the mutualisation of national financing arrangements.

159 The **executive session** has all other powers provided in the SRM Regulation, save as otherwise provided. In particular, the executive session prepares, assesses and approves the resolution plans, determines the Minimum Requirements for own funds and Eligible Liabilities (MREL) for each institution, determines the situation of failing or likely to fail and provides the resolution scheme to the Commission.

160 The **distinction between plenary and executive section** and the different composition of the SRB members in the two sessions ensures that all the NRA members approve only the most important tasks of the SRB. This separation may prove useful when a swift agreement for an individual institution needs to be taken at the SRB level and majority shall be reached among the SRB members.

3.5.3. Recovery and Resolution Planning in the SRM

161 The idea to establish a European resolution regime reveals that recovery and resolution tools are of critical importance for the functioning of the European

---

[103] It shall be noted that in the SSM not all cross-border supervised groups are directly supervised by the ECB as they may not meet the 'significance' criteria.

financial system, particularly in case of cross-border activities.[104] **Crisis prevention** is one of the main aspects that the SRM (and the BRRD) intends to address by avoiding the recourse to resolution. Substantive rules in the SRM (and in the BRRD) are intended to prepare to the earliest phase the financial recovery of ailing institutions at the preventive stage. Furthermore, before resolution is triggered early intervention measures may apply.

In view of avoiding the trigger of resolution, Articles 10 et seqq. of the SRM Regulation (and BRRD Title II) require MS to ensure that each institution draws up and maintain **recovery and resolution plans**. These are two essential documents ensuring that the institutions within the scope of the BRRD have in place robust resolution planning. Competent authorities are entrusted to assess recovery and resolution plans. **162**

Recovery and resolution planning are expected to significantly improve supervision, especially with regard to systemically important institutions and groups.[105] The assessment of the recovery plans is detailed in Article 6 BRRD. The **recovery plans** are prepared by the financial institutions to set out how to restore their financial position in case of a significant deterioration. These plans are then submitted to the financial institution's relevant supervisor, hence for significant institutions to the ECB. First, these plans are required to evaluate whether the implementation of the arrangements is reasonably likely to maintain or restore the viability of the institution and the financial position of the institution. Second, they need to assess whether the plan and the specific options envisaged in it are likely to be implemented quickly and effectively in case of financial stress while avoiding any significant adverse effect in the financial system. In the SRM the SRB is consulted on the recovery plans for significant and cross-border institutions (Article 10.2 SRM Regulation). In case the recovery plan is not submitted, or it does not adequately respect the established requirements of the supervisor, the competent authority may already require at this state the institution to reduce its risk profile, enable recapitalisation measures, change institution's strategy and structure, review the funding strategy, make changes to the governance structure. **163**

Resolution authorities, hence the SRB for significant and cross-border institutions, shall prepare **resolution plans** for each institution with a view to provide the resolution actions that the resolution authority may take, particularly the resolution tools and powers. Article 8 of the SRM Regulation (Article 9 BRRD) indicate the elements of the resolution plans. These articles make clear that the resolution plan shall demonstrate, among others, how critical functions and core business activities could be separated from other functions. **164**

The SRB shall assess the extent to which the institutions are **'resolvable'** (→ para 251). This is made by an assessment to determine how feasible and credible it is that the resolution authority can either liquidate the institution under normal insolvency proceedings or resolve it by applying the resolution tools and **165**

---

[104] See Avgouleas and Goodhart (2015), p. 15.
[105] Avgouleas (2012), p. 425.

powers (Article 10 of the SRM Regulation, Article 13 BRRD). It could be that the assessment of 'resolvability' shows that there are potential impediments for the institutions. In case the measures proposed by the institution do not reduce or remove its resolvability,[106] the competent authority will have, among others, certain powers such as limit exposures, request additional information, divest specific assets, limit or cease specific activities (Article 10 of the SRM Regulation, Article 14.4 BRRD). In the SRM the SRB is competent to assess and decide on the impediments on resolvability (Article 10.3 through 10.10 of the SRM Regulation). The NRA will implement the SRB decision (Article 10.10 SRM Regulation; → para 151).

166   Overall, the **preventive phase is essential** in the context of the new resolution regime in the SRM as it intends to prevent and anticipate to the extent possible the trigger of resolution. The preparation of recovery plans and the approval of resolution plans make clear that financial institutions shall be prepared to take preventive measures to avoid deterioration of their financial situation and bear the burden to avoid resolution in any possible way. The interaction between the financial institutions, the competent supervisors and the resolution authorities remains an important paradigm in this sense.[107] At the same time, awareness of the solvency problems of financial institutions together with an appropriate planning of the actions to take in case of the deterioration of the situation are key elements to avoid the trigger of resolution. This is also important from the perspective of banks and their investors. Furthermore, recovery planning allows the appropriate consideration of measures to recover to the extent possible ailing institutions and may enhance transparency and awareness of banking problems.

3.5.4. Resolution Tools in the SRM

167   Resolution tools are provided in Articles 22–27 of the SRM Regulation (Articles 37 to 58 BRRD). These are analysed from the softer to the harder tool. The **sale of business** is aimed to achieve an efficient and easy transfer of the shares, the assets, the rights or the liabilities to a purchaser (Article 24.1 of the SRM Regulation, Article 38.1 BRRD). This means that resolution authorities have the power to sell the business without requesting the consent of the shareholders, the institution or other third parties. The transfer needs to be made **on commercial terms** with due attention to the circumstances of the case (Article 38.3 BRRD). Resolution authorities shall find ways to comply with commercial conditions for the sale. Procedural requirements establish that the sale of business shall be transparent, fair and effective, and it shall aim to maximise the sale price for the instruments involved (Article 39 BRRD). In case the sale of business to a private party is not possible, resolution authorities may make use of the bridge institution tool.

---

[106] These are not mandatory as indicated under Recital 10 BRRD.

[107] See Binder (2015), p. 145.

The **bridge institution tool** consists in the set-up of a legal entity to which **168** shares, instrument of ownership, assets, rights or liabilities are transferred (Article 25 of the SRM Regulation, Article 40.1 BRRD). The bridge institution is wholly or partially owned by public authorities and is created for the purpose of receiving and holding the shares or the instruments, or the assets, rights and liabilities (Article 40.2 BRRD). The resolution authority exercises considerable powers on the bridge institution. In particular, it appoints the bridge institution's board of directors. The main objective of the bridge institution is to sell its business to a private sector buyer when market conditions are appropriate (Article 40.5 BRRD).

The **asset separation tool** aims to transfer assets, rights and liabilities to an asset **169** management vehicle, which is a legal entity wholly owned by public authorities (Article 26 of the SRM Regulation, Article 42 BRRD). This is a special resolution tool which aims at transferring assets, rights or liabilities only when normal insolvency procedures would have adverse effects on the market. It can be used only in conjunction with other resolution tools (Article 42.4 BRRD).

The **bail-in instrument** is the most intrusive and important tool under the new **170** European resolution regime (Article 27 of the SRM Regulation, Article 43 BRRD).[108] The BRRD puts a great emphasis on the role of the bail-in tool for an appropriate resolution of credit institutions. Article 2 defines bail-in as 'the mechanism for effecting the exercise by a resolution authority of the write-down and conversion powers in relation to liabilities of an institution under resolution'.

The bail-in is a **statutory enforcement mechanism** for shareholders and private **171** sector creditors of the costs of a bank rescue/recapitalisation. Its objective is to ensure that 'shareholders and creditors of the failing institution **suffer appropriate losses and bear an appropriate part of those costs arising from the failure of the institution**' (Recital 44 BRRD). According to the Commission, bail-in shall serve as an instrument to resolve large and complex financial institutions when other resolution tools are not sufficient.[109] In other words, the bail-in instrument 'punishes' shareholders, creditors, bondholders and uncovered depositors for the losses that the institution suffers by their conversion into equity or their reduction and avoids bailouts funded by taxpayers. Article 27 of the SRM Regulation and Article 44 BRRD specify the scope and conditions of application of the bail-in tool. They provide that the bail-in applies to all liabilities of an institution save as the general exclusions contained under Article 27.3 of the SRM Regulation and Article 44.2 BRRD. Furthermore, Article 27.5 of the SRM Regulation and Article 44.3 BRRD contain other exceptions that apply in exceptional circumstances by the resolution authority.

The SRM Regulation and the BRRD require some **minimum conditions to** **172** **trigger the bail-in tool** ($\rightarrow$ para 170). The resolution authority may decide whether

---

[108] On the bail-in instrument, see further Wojcik (2016), p. 120; Avgouleas and Goodhart (2015), p. 3; Clifford Chance (2011).

[109] Commission Communication, *An EU framework for crisis management in the financial sector*, COM(2010) 579 final, p. 5.

to apply the bail-in tool or not and shall provide that the institutions maintain a sufficient aggregate amount of own funds and eligible liabilities (Article 45 BRRD). The implementation of the bail-in tool requires that the resolution authorities establish the aggregate amount by which eligible liabilities must be written down (Article 27.13 of the SRM Regulation and Article 46.1 BRRD). This assessment will allow for the establishment of the amount of eligible liabilities that need to be written down or converted (Article 48.2 BRRD). Most importantly, Article 17 of the SRM Regulation (Article 48 BRRD) contain the hierarchy in the exercise of the bail-in tool. Common Equity Tier 1 (CET1) instruments are reduced first, then, if, and only if, the CET1 is not sufficient, Additional Tier 1 (AT1) instruments are reduced. Further, the other aggregates that should be reduced are in turn and one following the other AT1, Tier 2, and senior eligible debt (Article 18 of the SRM Regulation and Article 48.1 BRRD).

173 To ensure that sufficient resources are present to allow a workable bail-in, the BRRD establishes that institutions shall meet the **Minimum Requirements for own funds and Eligible Liabilities** (MREL) ($\rightarrow$ para 282). This allows that 'losses could be absorbed and the Common Equity Tier 1 ratio of the bank could be restored at a level necessary to enable it to continue to comply with the conditions for authorization' (Article 12 of the SRM Regulation and Article 45.6 BRRD). Determining an appropriate level of MREL and the interactions between resolution objectives and prudential requirements established in the CRR/CRD are essential aspects for a workable and effective bail-in instrument.[110] The Commission has adopted a delegated Regulation specifying the criteria related to the methodology to set the MREL.[111] The SRB has published an MREL policy, which considers the recent changes in the European Banking Package.[112] The issuance of MREL will take some years, especially for those institutions with only a limited amount of bailinable instruments.

3.6. Resolution Funding in the SRM

174 In the context of the SRM, there are certain **financial arrangements** to fund resolution under specific circumstances. This is the case of the **Single Resolution Fund** (SRF) which may be used in favour of the participating MS in the SRM (Articles 67 to 79 of the SRM Regulation) as a tool of last resort among the resolution tools.

---

[110] Wojcik (2016), pp. 114–115.

[111] Commission Delegated Regulation (EU) No. 2016/1450 *supplementing Directive 2014/59/EU of the European Parliament and of the Council with regard to regulatory technical standards specifying the criteria relating to the methodology for setting the minimum requirement for own funds and eligible liabilities*, O.J. L 237/1 (2016).

[112] SRB, *MREL Policy under the banking Package*, 2020, available at https://srb.europa.eu/sites/srbsite/files/srb_mrel_policy_2020.pdf.

The BRRD also sets out national financing arrangements that together form a **175** European System of Financing Arrangements (Articles 99 to 100 BRRD). The objective of such financing arrangements is to ensure the **effective application of the resolution tools and powers by the resolution authorities**. Article 101 BRRD contains an exhaustive list of authorised uses of financing arrangements, avoiding thus the risks of an inappropriate use of the funds. Even if the financing arrangements are publicly managed, the financial means originate exclusively from contributions paid by the banks.[113] The creation of financing arrangements aims to let the banking sector pay the costs of resolving ailing banks. Each national financing arrangement needs to attain a target level of at least 1% of covered deposits of all banks authorised in the relevant territory by 2024 (Article 102.1 BRRD). Should national financing arrangements be insufficient in an MS, the BRRD allows borrowing between national financial arrangements (Article 106 BRRD).

The SRF is the essential, although not exclusive, financial arrangement provided **176** in the SRM. The Fund is the property of the Single Resolution Board (SRB). Its creation is mandated by the need to 'ensure a uniform administrative practice in the financing of resolution and to avoid the creation of obstacles for the exercise of fundamental freedoms or the distortion of competition in the internal market due to divergent national practices' (Recital 19 of the SRM Regulation). This means that the SRF will be a European fund to assist the competent resolution authority in exercising resolution tools. This will ensure the availability of medium-term funding support while a credit institution is being restructured. The SRF will **take over national resolution financing arrangements and will constitute the main financing arrangement** to deal with resolution expenses within the SRM once it is fully mutualised. The target level for the SRF is indicated as at least 1% of the amount of deposits of all credit institutions authorised in the participating MS (Article 69 of the SRM Regulation). The resources are taken directly by covered entities. The individual contribution to create the SRF shall not exceed 12.5% of the target level each year. The calculation of the contribution of each individual institution consists of a flat contribution based on the institution's pro rata share of the liabilities of all institutions in the participating MS and a risk-adjusted contribution based on the institution's own risk profile (Article 70 of the SRM Regulation). The **target level** will be achieved in a period no longer than eight years since the entry into force of the provision on the constitution of the SRF, hence by 31 December 2023 (Article 77 of the SRM Regulation). Upon completion of the ex ante contributions, this level is expected to be between EUR 70 billion and EUR 75 billion. Similar to the financing arrangements provided in the BRRD, the SRF can be used for a range of purposes, including providing guarantees, making loans, purchasing assets and providing compensation to shareholders or creditors. It can be used to provide capital to a bridge bank or asset management vehicle, but it must

---

[113] See Commission Delegated Regulation (EU) No. 2015/63 *supplementing Directive 2014/59/EU of the European Parliament and of the Council with regard to ex ante contributions to resolution financing arrangements*, O.J. L 11/44 (2014).

not be used directly to absorb the losses of a failing institution or for direct recapitalisation (Article 76 of the SRM Regulation).

177 At the same time, **extraordinary ex post contributions** can be raised to cover shortfalls and the SRB may borrow or arrange other means of support to increase the funding available to the SRF (Article 71 of the SRM Regulation). Finally, alternative funding means may be **borrowings or other forms of support from institutions, financial institutions or other third parties** in case the amount raised with ex ante, ex post contributions and voluntary arrangements are not sufficient (Article 73 of the SRM Regulation). To increase the financing arrangements in the SRM, in December 2015, the SRM Member States agreed on a Loan Facility Agreement with the SRB, providing national credit lines to the SRB to support the national compartments of the Fund in case of possible funding shortfalls in that compartment following resolution cases of banks during the transition period.[114]

178 As a result, the SRF is aimed to provide the resolution financing within the SRM. As indicated above ($\rightarrow$ para 131, 155), the Council was involved in the adoption of the SRM and framed in 2014 a separate **Intergovernmental Agreement to mutualise progressively the individual national compartments** of the SRF.[115] The Fund can be used to enable the SRB to apply its resolution tools and powers effectively and efficiently. The SRF is intended to ensure that the financial industry makes a financial contribution to the stabilisation of the financial system. It will be funded by national compartments to be merged over time during the transitional period. These national financing structures collect ex ante contributions from covered entities each year (Article 5 of the SRM Regulation). The functioning of the compartments is to provide the collection of national resources for financing arrangements before the SRF is fully capitalised. The main objective of the Intergovernmental Agreement is to regulate the way in which the establishment of national compartments will be progressively mutualised over a transitional period of eight years to give full financial capacity to the SRF.

179 The **creation of the SRF** as the new pan-SRM bank resolution fund is a **positive development** to provide financial funds to resolution procedures if necessary at the European level. The SRF is a statutory European fund managed by the SRB and may be used to manage bank resolutions if financial resources are needed. The SRF should help ensuring a uniform resolution financing practice and avoiding national obstacles to resolution measures or distortions of competition in the internal market due to divergent national practices.

---

[114] SRB Press Release, December 2015, available at https://srb.europa.eu/sites/srbsite/files/20151208-press-release_en.pdf.

[115] Cf. the Intergovernmental Agreement *on the transfer and mutualisation of contributions to the Single Resolution Fund* of 21 May 2014 (IGA on the SRF, available at https://data.consilium.europa.eu/doc/document/ST-8457-2014-INIT/en/pdf) as amended by the Agreement of 27 January 2021, concluded between 26 MS (except Estonia), available at https://www.consilium.europa.eu/media/48068/agreement-amending-the-intergovernmental-agreement-on-the-transfer-and-mutualisation-of-contributions-to-the-single-resolution-fund-27-january-2021_en.pdf.

There are also **some limitations downsizing the SRF**.[116] First, the full mutualisation and transfer of resources to the SRF is phased-in over a long period—eight years—hence by 2024. Furthermore, it is also arguable whether the overall amount of financial resources once the SRF is fully mutualised—EUR 55 billion—is sufficient to achieve its purposes. Second, the SRM is also based on the Intergovernmental Agreement that sets the rules for the pooling together of the financial resources from the NRAs to the SRB and for the transfer of these resources from the national compartments to the SRF. The pooling and mutualisation of financial resources should have taken place as part of the SRM Regulation, an EU law instrument, and not with an intergovernmental instrument (→ para 296).[117] Third, the actual use of the SRF may be politically controversial when there are other national public resources available to be used by the MS where the resolving institution is established. Furthermore, the SRF does not address the need to find liquidity in the context of resolution. 180

To conclude, the SRF is a **welcome development for resolution financing**. This is because the MS have agreed on the creation of a common fund with financial resources levied from credit institutions intended to provide funding to credit institutions under resolution. However, some limitations exist as to its effective structure and use. 181

3.7. The SRM and State Aid

This section looks at the relationship between the SRM and the State aid framework. This is an important **aspect** in the on-going discussion **to complete the EBU** as under certain conditions an entity to be resolved or under resolution in the SRM may receive State aid. 182

The EBU has the purpose of breaking the malicious link between the banks and the sovereigns. One of the objectives of the EBU is to reduce to the extent possible State aids to credit institutions (→ para 2; Recitals 6 and 19 of the SRM Regulation). The EBU should **reduce the likelihood of public rescues in the banking sector** to the extent possible. Moreover, public funds should be protected as much as possible by minimising reliance on extraordinary public financial support (Article 14.2 point (c) of the SRM Regulation). 183

Notwithstanding the limitations of State aids to the banking sector, certain measures can be **treated as compatible State aid under certain conditions**. These are provided in the SRM Regulation and the BRRD. In particular, the BRRD sets out situations where, regardless of the financial deterioration of credit institutions or the exercise of resolution tools, the State can grant still financial support in the form of guarantees or capital injections in compliance with the European State aid law framework. The BRRD defines in fact 'extraordinary public 184

---

[116] See Fabbrini (2014), p. 444.
[117] Fabbrini (2014), p. 456.

support' as 'State aid within the meaning of Article 107(1) TFEU or any other public financial support at supranational level which, if provided for at national level, would constitute State aid, that is provided in order to preserve or restore the viability, liquidity or solvency of an institution or entity (...) or of a group of which such an institution or entity forms part' (Article 2.28 BRRD). This definition is broad enough to include all measures that are defined as State aid and serve the purpose to preserve or restore the financial situation of a financial entity.

185 Under the SRM Regulation and the BRRD, **there are mainly three situations** when public support measures can be granted: one is before the resolution is triggered (extra-resolution extraordinary public financial support) and two after resolution is triggered (financing arrangement tools and government financial stabilisation tools).

3.7.1. Extra-Resolution Extraordinary Public Financial Support

186 First, Article 32.4 point (d) BRRD lists three situations that give grounds to an extra-resolution extraordinary public financial support (→ para 253). These are intended to be State aid instruments aimed at **safeguarding the ailing institution in order to prevent serious disturbances** to the economy of an MS and financial stability. The normal scenario is that if State aid is required, then the ailing institution would go under resolution or liquidation. However, the BRRD lists situations constituting the exception to this rule.

187 The first are **State guarantees to 'back liquidity facilities provided by central banks** according to the central banks' conditions'. These are State guarantees intended to provide financial support in case the national central bank granted emergency liquidity assistance (ELA).[118]

188 The second are **State guarantees of newly issued liabilities**. These are intended to be newly issued liability instruments of the credit institutions that have guarantees of the MS serving the purpose to remedy a serious disturbance to its economy. These instruments are limited to guarantees on liability instruments and are not to be made on equity. Furthermore, this instrument should be limited in time and not be part of a large aid package (Recital 41 BRRD).

189 The third instrument is **precautionary recapitalisation**. This is of particular interest as State support outside the resolution of a credit institution may be granted in the form of a direct recapitalisation, hence conferring direct capital instruments to the ailing entity. Under Article 32.4 (4) point (d)(iii) BRRD, precautionary recapitalisation may take place if certain conditions are fulfilled.

---

[118] ELA is not considered State aid in accordance with the State aid framework if four cumulative conditions are met: (a) the credit institution is temporarily illiquid but solvent at the moment of the liquidity provision which occurs in exceptional circumstances and is not part of a larger aid package; (b) the facility is fully secured by collateral to which appropriate haircuts are applied, in function of its quality and market value; (c) the central bank charges a penal interest rate to the beneficiary; (d) the measure is taken at the central bank's own initiative, and in particular is not backed by any counter-guarantee of the State. On ELA and State aid, see Steinbach (2016), p. 375.

The analysis above suggests that **before granting precautionary recapitalisa- 190 tion some strict conditions shall be respected**. First, these State Support measures shall be granted to a solvent institution. The definition of solvency is a key aspect in banking supervision as it provides the limitation of a viable, going-concern credit institution respecting the prudential regulatory requirements that, if it becomes insolvent, would be considered likely to fail. Second, these measures are precautionary and temporary in nature. The MS shall provide for specific rules justifying their precautionary nature and, more importantly, limit them in time. Third, they shall have the purpose to 'remedy the consequences of the serious disturbance and shall not be used to offset losses that the institution has incurred or is likely to incur in the near future'. This means that they need to be grounded on the seriousness of the situation while avoiding a forward-looking perspective. In particular, State aid shall be used to cover the losses detected from the adverse scenario of a stress test and not those stemming from an Asset Quality Review (AQR) or the baseline scenario of a stress test. Therefore, it is argued that such losses are limited to those resulting from the adverse scenario in a stress test situation and not the historical losses or those to be incurred in the near future.[119]

Overall, the role of the MS for the **public bail out** of an ailing credit institution **191 also remains an option** before and against any resolution is triggered.

3.7.2. Resolution Financing Arrangements as State Aid in the SRM

In the context of a resolution, the use of resolution financing may be used. These are **192 financial resources collected among the banking sector**, but under control of the resolution authority. The nature of this financial contribution is considered State aid that needs to be authorised by the Commission (Article 19 of the SRM Regulation). Therefore, the burden-sharing arrangements under State aid rules also apply in this case. In particular, the progressive creation of the SRF is a notable development of this process. The SRF is qualified as State aid in the form of **Fund Aid in the SRM Regulation** (Article 19 of the SRM Regulation). This means that whenever the SRF contributions are sought, the Commission shall approve them and submit to the SRB the clearance of measures.

First, the SRB can make use of such funding **only to make the resolution tools 193 effective instruments**. The SRM Regulation mentions certain purposes on the use of resolution funding (Article 76.1 of the SRM Regulation). When resolution funding takes place, this requires that the Commission approves the use of Fund aid (Recitals 30 and 75 of the SRM Regulation). Nevertheless, the SRF cannot be used to absorb losses of an entity or to recapitalise the entity. At the same time, it can happen that certain losses are transferred to the SRB. In this case it may be that the contribution of the SRF is made to cover losses not absorbed by bail-inable debt and/or to purchase instruments of ownership or capital instruments in the institution under resolution to recapitalise the institution (Article 27.6 of the SRM Regulation).

---

[119] Gardella (2015), p. 383.

194 Nevertheless, **two conditions** must be applied to make such contribution. First, there shall be an own contribution of shareholders and holders of other eligible liabilities through write-down, conversion or otherwise to loss absorption and recapitalisation is equal to an amount not less than 8% of the total liabilities of the institution under resolution. Second, the contribution of the SRF shall not exceed 5% of the total liabilities, including own funds of the institution under resolution (Article 27.7 of the SRM Regulation).

3.7.3. Government Financial Stabilisation Tools

195 Finally, in case resolution is triggered and the ailing credit institution undergoes resolution, the State may still grant support measures in the form of **government financial stabilisation tools** (Articles 56 to 58 BRRD). These instruments are granted when the resolution tools are not sufficient to prevent adverse effects on the financial system or to protect the public interest (Article 56.4 BRRD). These tools can be used only if the conditions provided in Article 37.10 BRRD are met.

196 Overall, government stabilisation tools are State aid measures that can be provided in a resolution scenario **under strict conditions** and respecting a certain level of burden-sharing.

3.8. Procedural Safeguards in the SRM

197 Procedural safeguards are an important aspect to ensure the respect of the **fundamental right of defence** in the exercise of resolution tasks by the SRB. Further, the procedural safeguards in the SRM are generally framed in the EU constitutional framework in the EUCFR provision on the right to good administration (Article 41.2 EUCFR; → para 114 et seqq.). The SRM Regulation sets out rules on access to the file, administrative review of resolution decisions.

3.8.1. Right to be Heard

198 A general right to be heard is **not expressly provided in the SRM Regulation**. However, when the SRB applies penalties to credit institutions in the context of the exercise of SRB investigatory powers under Articles 38 et seqq. of the SRM Regulation it shall grant the right to be heard. Article 40 of the SRM Regulation sets out the right to be heard on the decisions setting penalties, which the SRB shall fully comply with. The respect of the right to be heard does apply in other cases where the SRB adopts decisions, such as the decisions setting out the MREL or the expenses for the activities of the SRM.

3.8.2. Access to the File

199 Access to the file is a procedural guarantee to ensure that the party or other persons to a resolution procedure **can get access to the documentation** that led to the

adoption of an SRB decision. Article 90 of the SRM Regulation provides for the access to the files. Access to the file is generally subject to the general EU access to documents regime under EU Regulation No. 1049/2001.[120] The SRB takes a decision on the request in line with Article 8 of Regulation No. 1049/2001.

Article 90 of the SRM Regulation sets out that the persons subject of the SRB's **200** decision can have access to the SRB file. This right is subject to the **legitimate interest** of other persons in the protection of their business secrets as well as to confidential information or internal preparatory documents of the SRB.

3.8.3. Administrative and Judicial Review

Administrative review is a ground to review a decision through **administrative** **201** **bodies**. The SRM Regulation established an **Appeal Panel** deciding on appeals submitted under Article 85 of the SRM Regulation. The Appeal Panel is composed of five individuals and two alternates. Article 85.3 of the SRM Regulation sets out the challenges that can be brought before the Appeal Panel. The scope of the Appeal Panel review comprises the following acts: the act determining the impediments to resolvability of the institution in the resolution plan (Article 10.10), the resolution plan adopted following simplified obligations (Article 11), the decision setting out the MREL (Article 12.1), decisions on penalties (Articles 38 to 41), the decision on contributions to the administrative expenditures of the SRB (Article 65.3), the decision on extraordinary contributions (Article 71) and decisions on access to documents (Article 90.3). These decisions of the SRB can be challenged by the addressee or by persons of direct and individual concern. The appeal is filed within six weeks after the notification of the decision to the person concerned, or, in the absence of a notification, on the day in which the decision came to the knowledge of the person concerned. The Appeal Panel shall decide in one month after the appeal is lodged.

The **decision** adopted by the Appeal Panel **is binding on the SRB**. Therefore, **202** the SRB shall follow the decision adopted the Appeal Panel, which can confirm the contested decision or amend the contested decision.

Finally, **judicial review** is the opportunity given to the addressee of a decision **203** adopted by the SRB or the resolution decision proposed by the SRB and approved by the Commission, and possibly by the Council, may be challenged by the addressee or any other directly and individually concerned parties before the CJEU. Most importantly, the resolution decision and the application of the resolution tools taken under Article 18 of the SRM Regulation can only be contested before the CJEU and not before the Appeal Panel. The challenges before the CJEU may take place in accordance with the general rules of two months to challenge the contested decision. The Appeal Body decision may be challenged as well before the CJEU.

---

[120] Parliament/Council Regulation (EC) No. 1049/2001 *regarding public access to European Parliament, Council and Commission documents*, O.J. L 145/43 (2001).

4. The Main Substantial Rules of the European Banking Union

204 After assessing the SSM and the SRM, this section looks at the main aspects of **banking regulation, supervision and resolution as provided in the Single Rulebook** for banks in the EU. The creation of a single regulatory market for banks is a project that has been conceived as part of the creation of the EU and that, as part of the regulatory effort to counteract the financial crisis, has been substantially reinforced in the last decade. In recent times, banking regulation is a field that has been subject to extensive regulatory reforms due to the topical role and functions of banks in society. This is particularly due to the strong impact of the financial crisis on credit institutions' capital, activities and business models.

205 The creation of a 'Single Rulebook' for banks in Europe was first coined in the Council conclusions in 2009 by affirming that a single rulebook should be established to provide '**a core set of EU-wide rules and standards** directly applicable to all financial institutions active in the Single Market, so that key differences in national legislations are identified and removed'.[121] So far, the objective to create a single rulebook for banks has been a remarkable result for the reinforcement of banking regulation in Europe. However, there are still areas of banking rules that are not fully harmonised in Europe.

4.1. The Capital Requirements Regulation and the Capital Requirements Directive

206 The CRR and the CRD constitute the essential **substantive framework for banking regulation** in Europe as of 2013. They are the currently applicable Level 1 rules on banking regulation that set out the provisions on the conduct of banking business and the respect of prudential requirements in Europe. The CRR and the CRD are pieces of legislation that reflect previous Level 1 rules already adopted before the financial crisis and consolidated in an EU regulation and an EU directive.

207 On 26 February 2010, the Commission launched public consultations on possible **further amendments of the CRD, CRD II and CRD III**.[122] These consultations were focused on the question of how the financial soundness of banks and investment firms could be assured and thus on how the minimum capital requirements for credit institutions in the EU should be revised. The amendments were substantially aligned with the amendments to the Basel III Framework.[123] The

---

[121] Council of the EU, *Conclusions on strengthening EU financial supervision*, 10 June 2009, available at http://register.consilium.europa.eu/doc/srv?l=EN&f=ST%2010862%202009%20INIT. See also European Council, *Conclusions*, 18 and 19 June 2009, para 20 (emphasis added).

[122] Before that, the existing EU regulatory regimes contained rules on capital adequacy and solvency requirements. For extensive analysis of these developments, see Dragomir (2009), p. 65 et seqq.

[123] The Basel Framework on banking supervision is an international standard-setting framework for banking supervision in Basel. See further Brummer (2015), p. 77 et seqq.

regulatory package that was eventually adopted consists of the CRR as Regulation No. 575/2013[124] and the CRD IV as Directive 2013/36/EU. MS needed to apply the new rules from 1 January 2014, with full implementation by 1 January 2019. Following the Commission's proposal to reform the CRR/CRD IV package, the CRR II[125] and CRD V[126] have entered into force in 2020. As of 2021, discussions are ongoing on a new CRR III / CRD VI package.

4.1.1. The Capital Requirements Regulation

The CRR is the first EU Regulation that introduces **directly applicable capital requirements in the internal market for credit institutions**. It aims to realise a single rulebook for credit institutions and investment firms in Europe. The CRR comprises more than 500 articles. This section aims to show what the most important aspects are in the CRR including the CRR II.

The CRR is intended to **provide uniform rules on the general prudential requirements** that supervised institutions need to respect. In this sense, Recital 7 indicates that the main purpose of the Regulation is to include prudential requirements for credit institutions that are meant to ensure financial stability of the operators on financial markets as well as a high level of protection of investors and depositors. This particularly applies to own funds, requirement to limit large exposures, liquidity risks, reporting requirements and public disclosure requirements (Article 1 CRR).

Capital Adequacy

The first important element in banking regulation is **sound capital adequacy**. The authorisation of a business activity of credit institutions presupposes that an initial capital is present and that the institution respects the capital adequacy requirements. The CRR sets own funds requirements (Pillar 1 requirements) as the required holding ratio of capital in percentage to Risk Weighted Assets (RWAs).

The CRR identifies how to **weigh the institution's assets according to their risks**. In this sense, the RWA amount is reflected in the recognition and amount of capital and the calculation of RWAs. Capital ratios are calculated on Tier 1 and

---

[124] Parliament/Council Regulation (EU) No. 575/2013 *on prudential requirements for credit institutions and investment firms*, O.J. L 176/1 (2013) (CRR).

[125] Parliament/Council Regulation (EU) No. 2019/876 *amending Regulation (EU) No. 575/2013 as regards the leverage ratio, the net stable funding ratio, requirements for own funds and eligible liabilities, counterparty credit risk, market risk, exposures to central counterparties, exposures to collective investment undertakings, large exposures, reporting and disclosure requirements*, O.J. L 150/1 (2019).

[126] Parliament/Council Directive (EU) 2019/878 *amending Directive 2013/36/EU as regards exempted entities, financial holding companies, mixed financial holding companies, remuneration, supervisory measures and powers and capital conservation measures*, O.J. L 150/253 (2019).

Tier 2 own funds instruments. The former consists mainly in shareholder's equity and disclosed reserves, while the latter corresponds to hybrid capital and subordinated debt. The CRR reproduces an 8% rule of minimum own funds requirements as developed in the Basel standards and requires that credit institutions have 4.5% of CET1 on RWAs (Article 92.1 CRR). CET1 is the purest form of capital which needs to respect the capital ratio rule of 4.5% as provided in the CRR. Furthermore, in the 8% rule, the CET1 and AT1 as additional capital instruments shall be at least 6% on RWAs and form Tier 1 capital. Tier 2 capital is the other component of the own funds. Tier 2 comprises capital instruments that are not sufficiently reliable to constitute Tier 1 capital instruments. Tier 2 capital instruments have less qualitative criteria to be Tier 1, but are still an important part for loss absorption for a credit institution. The CRR requires that Tier 2 amounts to 2%. RWAs are calculated either through a standardised method provided in the CRR or through internal calculations made by the banks through internal models. RWAs are usually assessed with risk levels that are calculated looking at the type of exposure that the bank has.

Large Exposure Limits

212 An important set of regulatory requirements imposed on credit institutions is the **limit on certain large exposures** that credit institutions may incur. The harmonised rules require that credit institutions avoid being excessively exposed to a single client. The CRR provides a general prohibition for credit institutions to incur an exposure to one client or a group of connected clients the value of which amounts to more than 25% of its own funds (Article 395 CRR). The CRR introduces a definition of large exposure as where 'its value is equal to or exceeds 10%' of the own funds of the credit institution (Article 392 CRR). Several exemptions to such rules are notably calculated based on RWAs. For instance, some exposures to central governments, central banks or public sector entities which, unsecured, would be assigned a 0% risk-weight are exempted from the calculation of large exposures (Article 400 CRR).

The Liquidity Ratios

213 An important aspect of the financial crisis has been to reinforce **liquidity requirements** to allow a number of liquid financial resources to withstand financial crises. Following the Basel III, the CRR has introduced two liquidity ratios: the liquidity coverage ratio (LCR) and the net stable funding ratio (NSFR).

214 The LCR consists in a requirement to **hold liquid assets** in order to ensure that institutions maintain a certain level of liquidity in case of liquidity shortage. The LCR is meant to withstand the crisis over a period of thirty days by holding some liquid assets covering the liquidity outflows less the liquidity inflows in stressed conditions (Article 412 CRR). The LCR has been object of fierce negotiations as a

high level of liquidity buffer might have an adverse impact on the real economy.[127] In theory, an excessively high LCR would promote the shift from lending to liquid assets. In 2015, the Commission adopted a delegated Regulation setting a binding LCR.[128] This instrument introduces a high-quality liquid assets ratio to cover the difference between the expected cash outflows and the expected capped cash inflows over a thirty-day stressed period. The LCR is set at 100% of high-quality liquid assets.

Furthermore, the CRR II introduces the NSFR as the second liquidity ratio requiring an **acceptable amount of stable funding** to support the institutions assets and activities **over the medium term**. This is a complementary liquidity instrument that envisages holding funding instrument over a longer period. NSFR is calculated by assessing the amount of available stable funding minus the amount of required stable funding. **215**

The Definition and Role of the Leverage Ratio

The CRR II also includes the leverage ratio as a new binding requirement for the safeguarding of risks associated with risk models. The leverage ratio is calculated as **Tier 1 capital divided by a measure of non-risk weighted on- and off-balance sheet items** (Article 429 CRR). The leverage ratio is a new regulatory tool introduced in the CRR II (Article 430 CRR). **216**

4.1.2. The Capital Requirements Directive

While the CRR intends to achieve full harmonisation on capital requirements, relevant prudential sectors are subject to national implementation of the CRD. Differently from the CRR, the CRD **needs to be implemented by the MS into national law** and in general gives certain discretionary powers to the MS to regulate national law. **217**

The CRD includes rules for access to taking up/pursuit of banking business, exercise of freedom of establishment and free movement of services, prudential supervision, capital buffers, corporate governance and sanctions. While the CRD has a maximum harmonisation approach at least in some areas, the CRD provisions as such are **not directly prescriptive and enforceable, but shall be implemented in national law**. **218**

---

[127] The issue was also discussed at Basel Committee Level which decided to adopt a standard on liquidity ratio in January 2013, see Basel Committee on Banking Supervision, Liquidity Coverage Ratio and Liquidity Risk Monitoring Tools, January 2013, available at www.bis.org/publ/bcbs238.pdf.

[128] Commission Delegated Regulation (EU) No. 2015/61 *to supplement Regulation (EU) No. 575/2013 of the European Parliament and the Council with regard to liquidity coverage requirement for Credit Institutions*, O.J. L 11/1 (2015).

Rules on the Taking Up the Business of Credit Institutions

219 The criteria for taking up the business of credit institutions are the first essential condition to the exercise of banking activities. Article 5 CRD provides for the **authorisation procedure** and requires that national authorities decide in their own procedures whether to authorise an institution so to allow the fulfilment of some **minimum requirements**. The initial requirement for the pursuit of the banking business is that the credit institution shall have separate own funds and have an initial capital of EUR 5 million. Furthermore, other conditions need to be complied with to be granted authorisation. First, the Directive stipulates that competent authorities require an application of authorisation to the institution with a programme of operations indicating among other aspects the type of business envisaged and the structural organisation of the credit institution. Second, competent authorities are not allowed to authorise entities in light of economic needs (Article 11 CRD). Third, the competent authorities shall grant authorisation only to credit institution which are effectively directed by at least two persons of sufficiently good repute and with sufficient expertise to perform such duties. Fourth, the competent authorities shall consider the characteristics of the important shareholders of the credit institution.

220 As for the credit institution, **the authorisation may be withdrawn** in case the said institution does not fulfil some requirements. Article 18 lists the cases in which withdrawal of authorisation may take place. Among other situations, two are the most relevant ones.

Point (c) prescribes the withdrawal of authorisation in case the **institution does not respect the conditions for authorisation** as granted under the conditions examined earlier. This means that the requirements for the initial authorisation are not fulfilled any longer. This applies for the initial capital condition of EUR 5 million, for the requirement that at least two persons direct the institution, for the required robust governance arrangements, risk management processes or internal control mechanisms, remuneration policies.

Point (d) lists a series of situations that would lead to the withdrawal of authorisation. First, withdrawal would apply when the credit institution **no longer meets the prudential requirements** provided in the CRR.[129] Second, withdrawal would apply when the **specific capital requirements** on additional own funds or on specific liquidity imposed by competent authorities are **not fulfilled**. Finally, the withdrawal would apply if the institution can no longer be relied on to fulfil its obligations towards its creditors with particular attention to the fact that it 'no longer provides security for the assets entrusted to it by depositors'.

---

[129] This particularly applies to Part Three (Capital Requirements), Four (Large Exposures) and Six (Liquidity) of the CRR.

Rules on the Exercise of the Business of Credit Institutions

The CRD also harmonises to a certain extent the **requirement on credit institu-** 221
tions for the pursuit of their business activities. This has a dual dimension, as
both the MS and the authorised institutions need to fulfil some requirements.

As for the MS, once the conditions for authorisation have been complied with, 222
the CRD allows the authorised institution to benefit from the '**single passport**'.
This means that each MS needs to comply with the home country principle that
provides that credit institutions may establish branches or provide services without
any other authorisation (Article 33 CRD).

The conduct of business also requires that competent authorities monitor the 223
changes in qualifying holdings in the credit institution. It requires that the
changes in such holdings need to be notified in writing to the competent authorities
in case the holding increases by reaching or exceeding 20%, 30% or 50% or so that
the credit institution would become a subsidiary (Article 22.1 CRD). The CRD
contains rules on the approval of the acquisition of qualifying holdings, setting out
the requirement and the procedure to be followed for such acquisitions (Articles 22
et seq. CRD). Qualifying holding is defined in the CRR as a 'direct or indirect
holding in an undertaking which represents 10% or more of the capital or of the
voting rights or which makes possible to exercise a significant influence over the
management of that undertaking' (Article 4.1 point (36) CRR).

Furthermore, the CRD contains rules on **Pillar 2 measures as additional** 224
capital requirements imposed by the competent supervisor on credit institutions.
While Pillar 1 measures are those imposed in the CRR as minimum own funds
requirements, Pillar 2 requirements are additional institution-specific measures that
could be used to address risks to which an institution is exposed. The competent
supervisory authorities perform the SREP as an assessment and review of risks of
supervised entities ($\rightarrow$ para 100). This includes an assessment of: '(a) risks to which
the institutions are or might be exposed; (b) risks that an institution poses to the
financial system (...); and (c) risks revealed by stress testing (...)' (Article 97.1
CRD).

Corporate Governance

The CRD also contains rules on the **harmonisation of corporate governance of** 225
credit institutions. The CRD requires that the credit institutions have robust
corporate arrangements in place, adequate internal control mechanisms and remuneration policy and practice consistent with and promote sound and effective risk
management (Article 74.1 CRD).

As regards corporate governance rules, the CRD contains rules that concern the 226
composition of boards, their functioning and their role in risk oversight and
strategy. The CRD provides that MS introduce principles and standards to ensure
effective oversight to monitor the adequacy of internal governance arrangements
(Recital 54 CRD). The regulatory framework introduces rules on diversity in the
management board composition to avoid the effect of 'groupthink' according to

which board decisions are taken by a group and not by each member individually because of the lack in diversity (Recital 60 CRD). Furthermore, the CRD contains rules on transparency and reporting as regards the disclosure of important information on turnover, profits, taxes and public subsidies as well as the return on assets (Articles 89 and 90 CRD).

227 These are in particular rules on organisational structures, personal requirements for board members and board members' duties and responsibilities.

The first group consists of **rules imposing requirements on banks' corporate structures**. The CRD contains rules that concern the composition of boards, their functioning and their role in risk supervision and strategy. The CRD provides that MS introduce principles and standards to ensure effective supervision to monitor the adequacy of internal governance arrangements such as maximum numbers of directorships by managers (Recital 54 CRD). The new regulatory framework introduces rules on diversity in the management board composition to avoid the process of 'groupthink' according to which board decisions are taken by a group and not by each because of the lack in diversity (Recital 60 CRD). First, the chairman of the management body in its supervisory function shall not hold simultaneously the function of chief executive officer within the same institutions, unless justified by the institution and authorised by the competent supervisory authority (Article 88.1 point (e) CRD). Second, the CRD contains rules on the establishment of special committees. These are the risk committee, the remuneration committee, the nomination committee as well as the audit committee.

The second group establishes **fit and proper rules both for executive and non-executive members of the board** and its committees (Article 91 CRD). The CRD includes provisions on individual and collective qualities of executive and non-executive board members, limitations on directorships as well as rules on board diversity.

The third group includes **rules on how the management body defines, oversees and is accountable for the implementation of governance arrangements** that ensure effective and prudent management of the institution (Articles 88, 92 and 94 CRD). The board is particularly responsible for the implementation of sound remuneration policies and efficient risk governance. On risk governance, the CRD devotes some provisions on the role of the management body to approve and review the strategies and policies for taking up, managing, monitoring and mitigating risks (Article 76 CRD). The focus of these provisions is to ensure that risks are controlled and managed, and that an appropriate institutional structure for risk control is in place.

As regards remuneration, the CRD lists a series of **standards on remuneration policies**. These deal with the governance, but most importantly, the design of remuneration. It contains technical criteria on the total remuneration policies of staff of credit institutions whose professional activities have an impact on the institution risk profile. The CRD introduces two new main remuneration rules. First, it increases transparency and disclosure requirements by requiring disclosure on remuneration policies for the number of natural persons in each institution that are remunerated EUR 1 million or more each year (Article 75.3 CRD). Second, it strengthens the essential conditions for the relationship between the variable component (the bonus) and the fixed component of remuneration (the salary) (Article 94.1 point (g), Article 94.2 CRD). In particular, the CRD sets a cap on bonuses whereby the variable component shall not exceed 100% of the fixed component of the total remuneration for each individual.[130] Therefore, there is a need for balancing the fixed and variable component of the executive pay.

Capital Buffers

The CRD contains provisions on the introduction of capital buffers that may **complement the existing basic capital requirements** as contained in the CRR. The CRD introduces the capital conservation buffer, the counter-cyclical capital buffer, the global systemic institution buffer, the other systemically important institutions buffer and the systemic risk institution buffer. **228**

The **capital conservation buffer** is a prudential tool that consists of total exposures of a bank that needs to be met in common tier equity Tier 1 capital equal to 2.5% of the institution total exposure. The CRD stipulates that MS require credit institutions to adopt this buffer. The objective of this instrument is to conserve a bank's capital and to allow automatic safeguards to apply in order to limit the amount of dividend and bonus payments the credit institution can make. **229**

The second instrument is the **counter cyclical buffer** whose purpose is to counteract the effects of the economy cycle. By accumulating capital resources during economic growth, the capital buffer is used in case of a countercyclical situation and provides additional capital resources. **230**

Furthermore, the CRD introduces a **mandatory systemic risk buffer**, the global Systemic Institution Buffer **for credit institutions considered as being systemically important**. The identification of globally important institutions is based on the size, cross-border activity and interconnectedness. The Global Systemically Important Institutions (G-SIIs) need to apply a mandatory surcharge which is between 1% and 3.5% of CET1 of RWAs. As clearly indicated in the CRD, the main reason for the introduction of the G-SII buffer is 'to compensate for the higher risk that G-SIIs represent for the financial system and the potential impact of their failure on taxpayers' (Recital 90 CRD). **231**

The CRD also introduces the option for MS to require other systemically important institutions to maintain **other systemically important institution buffers**. This would apply to domestically important as well as other institutions that are considered as such according to their size, cross-border activities and interconnectedness. The inclusion of this instrument requires that the competent authorities notify the justification, the likely positive and/or negative impact and the buffer rate **232**

---

[130] It should be noted that the new provisions on transparency and bonus cap were contested by the United Kingdom and brought to the CJEU. The AG delivered the opinion in Case C-507/13, *United Kingdom v Parliament and Council* (Opinion of AG Jääskinen of 20 November 2014). In November 2014 the UK withdrew its challenge; see the Order of the President of the Court of 9 December 2014.

to establish (Article 128.7 CRD). These safeguards are introduced to avoid disproportionate adverse effects for the integrity of the internal market (Article 128.6 CRD).

233   Finally, the **systemic risk buffer** is the last category of buffers introduced in the CRD. Each MS may introduce this buffer as corresponding to CET1 for the financial sector or one specific sub-sector. This instrument serves to '**prevent and mitigate long-term non-cyclical systemic or macroprudential risks**' (Recital 85 CRD). In other words, the systemic risk buffer is an additional tool that MS could introduce to avoid potential disruptions to the financial system. In case the proposed systemic risk buffer rate is between 3% and 5%, its introduction is subject to a procedure whereby the MS notifies the proposed measure to the Commission, the EBA and the ESRB (Article 133.14 CRD). The Commission provides an opinion and, if this is negative, the MS will need to follow a 'comply or explain' procedure. In case the proposed systemic risk buffer rate is above 5%, the Commission needs to adopt it with an implementing act (Article 133.13 last indent CRD).

4.1.3. Assessment

234   This subsection intends to summarise and assess the main regulatory trends on prudential requirements for banks as stemming from the CRR/CRD regulatory package. These concentrate on the **degree of harmonisation** reached with the CRR/CRD, the level of **options and discretions** contained in the existing CRR/CRD and the level of **complexity** of Level 1 regulation.

235   The **increased level of harmonisation** in capital requirements is a positive development as compared to the previous EU legislation. The first and most evident improvement is the fact that the minimum capital requirements are now contained in an EU regulation rather than an EU directive. The *de Larosière* Report already held that Europe suffers from 'the lack of a consistent set of rules'[131] and invited EU institutions to use regulations rather than directives (→ para 20).[132] As emphasised by the Report, the lack of harmonised rules creates market distortions, and, by creating regulatory inconsistencies, threatens financial stability.[133] This point suggests that directly applicable regulations shall be adopted whenever possible as they constitute directly applicable obligations while MS are not allowed to impose any stricter requirements than those laid down in the instrument itself, and not even further options ('maximum harmonisation'). The outcome of the reform efforts was to introduce the CRR while retaining less harmonised rules in the CRD.

236   Second, the **overall general harmonised approach** followed in the reform package is intended to set a European regulatory regime on capital requirements and the limitations to large exposures. Similarly, there is a general legal limit to large exposures of credit institutions to 25% of their capital. These two regulatory

---

[131] de Larosiere (2009), p. 27.
[132] de Larosiere (2009), p. 29.
[133] de Larosiere (2009), p. 29.

developments are the most important changes as compared with the previous framework. The EU attempt has been to reduce the number of national options and, thus, uncertainties.

Third, the European approach to prudential regulation is **very comprehensive**, as the EU has followed the 'one-size-fits-all' approach. The CRR and the CRD substantive rules apply to all credit institutions. This is an important requirement to ensure that business models in Europe follow certain rules and ensure an adequate **level-playing field** in the banking sector. Conversely, it may still be argued whether the application of the same rules for big and small credit institutions or different business models is justifiable from the perspective of the impact on banking business. While big banks may well develop their own internal models, small banks may not have enough resources to 'personalise' their models and need to make use of the standardised model. **237**

If the CRR intends to achieve maximum harmonisation on capital requirements, many prudential elements are **still subject to national implementation in the CRD**, an EU directive. Differently from the CRR, the CRD includes provisions that require MS' implementation in national law, and which may differ considerably from jurisdiction to jurisdiction. EU directives in general are not directly prescriptive but need to be implemented in national provisions possibly leaving MS marge of manoeuvre to adopt different rules. There may be exceptions where the directive sets maximum harmonisation rules and MS are not allowed to deviate from these rules. Nonetheless, they may still retain some discretion on how to implement procedural aspects. There may also be the risk of 'gold-plating' measures (→ para 276). **238**

Furthermore, the CRR/CRD contains a **large number of options and discretions in the regulatory framework** that limits the adoption of a completely harmonised approach in Europe and does not contribute to achieve supranational financial integration. At the same time, the increasing complexity of the European rules transposing the Basel III standards and the approach of Level 1 regulation shows that finding an appropriate balance between what needs to be regulated at Level 1 and what can be delegated or implemented at Level 2 or Level 3 remains an open question (→ para 262). **239**

The general capital requirements package **appears extremely complex** and may be considered itself a source of concern as there are intricate rules that may raise difficult interpretations. A number of examples show the above-mentioned problematic aspects in the CRR/CRD package. **240**

First, the definitions of capital and capital instruments might lead to **divergences** as MS may choose to introduce additional buffers going beyond the capital requirements, leverage and liquidity ratios. The latter are still not fully harmonised and give broad spaces for divergent approaches.

Second, MS can adopt **exemptions** to a list of exposures fully or partially exempted from the large exposure rules (Article 395.1 and 5 CRD). These may be problematic as divergences can lead to fragmented approaches between regulators.

Third, the introduction of capital buffers in the CRD is **not yet fully harmonised** as Member States may adjust the level of buffers over time, and there is not yet a supranational level playing field for capital buffers.

Fourth, the CRD includes **rules** for access to taking up/pursuit of banking business, exercise of freedom of establishment and free movement of services, prudential supervision and supervisory powers, capital buffers, corporate governance and sanctions which **may vary considerably in national laws**. Similarly, the rules on supervisory powers provided in Europe are still not supranational as their national implementation can lead to different provisions. This is the case for Article 104 of the CRD which lists only certain supervisory powers but does not set an exhaustive list of supervisory powers, and MS can still introduce further national provisions.

Fifth, CRR/CRD, in their revised versions, also contain **no certain explicit provisions or minimum requirements on important banking operations** or activities and this remains an unsolved problem. This is the case of mergers, acquisitions—apart from qualifying holding in credit institutions—asset transfer and divestments, covered bond issuance, corporate structures of credit institutions, activities of credit institutions in third countries. The lack of EU law on such topics remains an open problem.

241 The above analysis reveals that there are still **supranational regulatory limits leading to divergences—or even fragmentations—in MS** as regards banking rules. These are mainly national laws implementing the EU law, the absence of EU rules in certain banking fields, as well as options and discretions contained in EU secondary law. As supranational regulation still requires that directly applicable EU rules supersede national laws in many areas, supranational banking regulation still does not fully contribute to achieve market integration and equally sound supervisory treatment of credit institutions across Europe.[134]

4.2. The Bank Recovery and Resolution Directive

242 The BRRD has been adopted in April 2014[135] after a legislative process of almost two years. The BRRD contains many **technical provisions setting out the substantive powers of resolution** that MS should implement into national law as a minimum harmonisation approach. The analysis here will only concentrate on aspects not yet covered in the previous section on the SRM, where the main aspects of the resolution framework were examined. While the BRRD contains similar rules to the SRM Regulation, the main difference between the two is that the SRM Regulation is intended to establish the supranational institutional resolution framework that are already contained in the BRRD (→ para 123).

---

[134] See also Angeloni (2018).

[135] Parliament/Council Directive 2014/59/EU *establishing a framework for the recovery and resolution of credit institutions and investment firms*, O.J. L 173/190 (2014).

243 The **definition and scope of the resolution regime** are the first important element to analyse. The expression 'resolution' is different from insolvency or bankruptcy procedure. 'Resolution' is a special regulatory procedure for credit institutions in distress. It considers the special role of credit institutions by providing the means to deal with banking failure outside the ordinary bankruptcy legislation.[136] This excludes the situation whereby normal bankruptcy procedures are triggered leading to the immediate cessation of banking activities. However, the BRRD does not provide for a clear definition of what resolution is, but it specifies that resolution is different from normal insolvency proceedings (Article 2.1 point (49) BRRD).[137] The BRRD could have contained a general definition of what a 'resolution' is.

244 The BRRD has a **minimum harmonisation approach**. Emphatically, it indicates that: 'Member States may adopt or maintain stricter or additional rules to those laid down in the Directive and in the delegated and implementing acts adopted on the basis of the Directive' (Article 1.2 BRRD). The minimum harmonisation approach is a welcome development as compared with the absence of a resolution regime in MS. However, it may generate regulatory divergences among them, especially between those that participate in the SRM and those that do not.

245 Article 1.1 affirms that the BRRD **lays down rules and procedures relating to the recovery and resolution of a number of entities**. These rules apply not only to credit institutions, but also to financial institutions, financial holding companies, parent financial holding companies, branches of institutions established outside the Union according to the specific conditions of the BRRD (Articles 1.2 and 2.1). Its scope is wide as there is no certainty on which entities could create a systemic crisis, and a widespread failure of a number of smaller firms may cause devastating effects to the economy.[138] The resolution regime applies to all covered institutions regardless of their size.

246 As regards the **statutory institutions** in charge of resolution, the BRRD provides that MS design the resolution authorities (Article 3.1 BRRD). So long as the resolution authorities are public administrative authorities, the Member States are free to designate the resolution authority (Article 3.2 BRRD). The BRRD envisages that the supervisory authorities or the central banks may also be entrusted with resolution tools, provided that a structural separation between the functions is in place (Article 3.3 BRRD). In practice, in most MS the competent supervisory authority has also been entrusted with resolution powers. However, as shown below, at the European level the entrustment to the competent resolution authority has been given to the SRB and not to the ECB as the competent supervisory authority.

---

[136] See Grünewald (2014), pp. 13–15.

[137] Normal insolvency proceedings are defined as 'proceedings which entail the partial or total divestment of a debtor and the appointment of a liquidator or an administrator normally applicable to institutions under national law and either specific to those institutions or generally applicable to any natural or legal person'.

[138] COM(2012) 28, Explanatory Memorandum 4.3.

247 While planning and early intervention measures aim to prevent resolution from taking place,[139] the case may be that the institution(s) may be resolved. It is essential to outline the **definition, conditions, principles and conditions of resolution set out in the BRRD.**

248 **Resolution may be defined** as the restructuring of one or more financial institutions with the resolution tools implemented under the BRRD with the aim to ensure the continuity of critical functions, to avoid adverse impact on financial stability, to minimise reliance on public funds, to protect depositors and to protect client funds and client assets (Article 31 BRRD). It appears that what identifies resolution is the use of statutory measures to ensure the continuity of function of the institution.

249 Under Article 31.2 BRRD, resolution has the following **main objectives**:

(a) to ensure the continuity of critical functions;
(b) to avoid a significant adverse effect on the financial system, particularly by preventing contagion, including to market infrastructures, and by maintaining market discipline;
(c) to protect public funds by minimising reliance on extraordinary public financial support;
(d) to protect depositors covered by Directive 2014/49/EU and investors covered by Directive 97/9/EC;
(e) to protect client funds and client assets.

250 The BRRD indicates that the **objectives of resolution are of equal importance** and resolution authorities 'need to balance them as appropriate to the nature and circumstances of each case' (Article 31.3 BRRD). Arguably, it does not appear possible that all these objectives are treated at the same level, but a certain level of prioritisation will take place in practice.

251 Article 32 BRRD contains the fundamental provision to determine whether an institution needs to be resolved. There are **three cumulative conditions to put an institution under resolution** (paragraph 1): (a) that the institution is failing or likely to fail; (b) that there are no other possible alternatives, which would prevent the failure of the institution within a reasonable timeframe; (c) that a resolution action is necessary under the public interest.

Condition (a) is the key prudential requirement as it is necessary to identify the situation of failure (or likeliness to failure) to apply resolution. Thus, the **failing or the likeliness to fail** is defined under Article 32.4 BRRD as when one or more of the circumstances indicated below are fulfilled. These are: (a) that the institution breaches or is likely to breach the requirements for the authorisation and licensing of its activity; (b) that the assets are or will be less than the liabilities; (c) that the

---

[139] See → para 155 et seqq. for the assessment of recovery and resolution planning.

institution is or will be unable to pay its debts or other liabilities; (d) that extraordinary public financial support is required.[140]

Public interest under condition (c) is defined as a situation where a resolution action achieves and is proportionate to one or more of the resolution objectives, while the winding up of the institution pursuant to normal insolvency proceedings would not meet the same resolution objectives (Article 32.5 BRRD).

The BRRD conditions to initiate resolution show that the **competent authority** has much **discretion** in assessing whether an institution shall be resolved or be subject to other measures. This is particularly the case of the second and third criteria. At the same time, the formulation of the resolution conditions may generate regulatory competition between competent authorities and increase legal uncertainties among market operators as to whether resolution will apply in the specific case.[141] The interpretation of conditions (c) on public interest gives ground to political discretion as to the impact of such concept for the credit institutions and the affected MS.

Article 34 BRRD contains a cumulative list of **general principles governing resolution**: 252

(a) The shareholders of the institution under resolution bear first losses.
(b) Creditors of the institution under resolution bear losses after the shareholders in accordance with the order of priority of their claims under normal insolvency proceedings, save as expressly provided otherwise in the BRRD. Points (a) and (b) are intended to indicate rules regarding the order of losses that resolution tools will entail. This clarifies that **shareholders and creditors will be involved** when resolution powers are exercised.
(c) Management body and senior management of the institution under resolution are replaced, except in those cases when the retention of the management body and senior management, in whole or in part, as appropriate to the circumstances, is considered necessary to achieve the resolution objectives. Point (c) involves a **change in the management bodies** of the institution under resolution. This means that those involved in the management activity of the institution under resolution will be excluded from the activities of management of the institution under resolution.
(d) Management body and senior management of the institution under resolution shall provide all **necessary assistance** to achieve the resolution objectives.
(e) Natural and legal persons are **made liable**, subject to national law, under civil or criminal law for their responsibility for the failure of the institution.

---

[140] See further EBA Guidelines EBA/GL/2015/07 of 26 May 2015 *on the interpretation of the different circumstances when an institution shall be considered as failing or likely to fail under Article 32(6) of Directive 2014/59/EU*, available at http://www.eba.europa.eu/documents/10180/1156219/EBA-GL-2015-07_EN_GL+on+failing+or+likely+to+fail.pdf/9c8ac238-4882-4a08-a940-7bc6d76397b6.

[141] Grünewald (2014), p. 89.

(f) Except where otherwise provided in the BRRD, **creditors of the same class are treated in an equitable manner**.

(g) No creditor shall incur greater losses than would have been incurred if the institution or entity had been wound up under normal insolvency proceedings. Point (g) refers to the '**no creditor worse off principle**' which indicates that if a proper evaluation of bank assets and liabilities establishes a difference between the treatment that shareholders and creditors are actually afforded and the treatment they would have received under normal insolvency proceedings, they are entitled to compensation (Recital 50 BRRD).[142]

(h) **Covered deposits are fully protected**. This is to guarantee that covered deposits are always protected whenever resolution takes place. Deposit Guarantee Schemes (DGS) ensure that covered deposits are protected.[143]

(i) Resolution action is taken in accordance with the safeguards in the BRRD.

253 Furthermore, the BRRD sets out a new European framework for the resolution of financial institutions with **resolution tools** conferred on resolution authorities (→ para 167 et seqq.). Finally, the BRRD contains rules on **resolution financing** as the ways to ensure that financial assistance is provided to the entities going under resolution (→ para 174 et seqq.).

4.3. The Deposit Guarantee Scheme Directive

254 Substantive rules on banking in the EBU also include the degree of European harmonisation of deposit insurance. In banking theory, deposit insurances serve as an **instrument for the protection of depositor's assets held by credit institutions**.[144] Without going into the details of deposit insurance theory, many authors have assessed the importance of deposit insurance as a source of stability for the financial system and as a system for the protection for medium and small depositors, predominantly the retail ones.[145] The main objectives of deposit insurance schemes are to avoid deposits' run from an ailing bank and to allow a third-party guarantee on bank deposits.

255 Together with the progressive harmonisation of capital requirements rules for credit institutions, the EU has **legislated also in the field of deposit insurance**. Already in 1994, the Deposit Guarantee Schemes Directive was adopted.[146] This Directive provided for the harmonisation of deposit insurance policies across the EU with the fourfold aims of boosting the freedom of establishment and of provision of services as well as assuring the stability of the banking system and the protection of savers (Recital 1 DGSD 94/19). The Directive followed a

---

[142] On this principle, see further Wojcik (2016), p. 120.

[143] For discussions on the institutional reform on deposit guarantee schemes → para 284 et seqq.

[144] See Blair et al. (2007), p. 73.

[145] See Kleftouri (2015), p. 3; Payne (2015), p. 540.

[146] Parliament/Council Directive 94/19/EC *on deposit guarantee schemes*, O.J. L 135/5 (1994).

minimum harmonisation approach and set a minimum level of deposit protection as well as the maximum pay-out time (Articles 7 and 10).

Following the financial crisis, a new wave of reforms for the **harmonisation** of the DGSs in Europe has taken place. The new Recast DGS Directive 2014/49 was adopted in April 2014.[147] It does not create a single pan-European DGS. Rather, it aims to **strengthen the network of national DGS regimes**, and to deal with some of the pitfalls of national DGS systems in an internal market. In particular, the Directive provides for substantive improvements as regards the applicability of rules for DGS. First, it reproduces the covered deposit agreed in the 2009 Directive[148] for an amount up to EUR 100,000 (Article 6.1 of Directive 2014/49). Second, it strengthens the level of protection by progressively reducing the repayment days from twenty working days up to seven working days in 2024 (Article 8 of Directive 2014/49). Third, it improves the overall level of protection of covered depositors in the context of resolution or insolvency proceedings. The Directive provides a rule on creditor preference for all deposits below EUR 100,000 as well as for deposits held by natural persons and small and medium enterprises (SMEs) above the coverage of EUR 100,000. Finally, funding depositor guarantee schemes is, to some extent, harmonised as the credit institutions will have to pay ex ante as well as ex post contributions. The Directive introduces an obligation to reach a target level of 0.8% of the amount of the covered deposits to be reached by 3 July 2024, so ten years after the entry into force of the Directive. However, MS retain discretion as to the possible target funding levels for DGS by allowing MS to raise the available financial means above the target level set in the Directive (Article 10.4 of Directive 2014/49). **256**

The European approach towards DGS has been **improved as compared with the 2009 rules**. Two developments are welcome: first, the introduction of priority rules in DGS resolution or insolvency proceedings is a welcome development considering the risks that depositors face during the financial crisis; second, the requirement to establish DGS in national law with ex ante contributions to reach certain funded levels over time. **257**

Although these two main developments are surely an improvement to protect further depositors and assist them in case a credit institution needs to be resolved or fails, European attempts to create a reinforced system for depositor protection **fall short both from a substantive and institutional** point of view. The existing supranational law on DGS is still not a sufficient safeguard against national divergences in the application of DGS rules that may lead to regulatory divergences and fragmentation. There is still scope for national choices in the context of deposit guarantees as MS might set higher targets for guaranteeing the DGS system. Furthermore, while the 2014 Directive proposes a new role for deposit insurers in **258**

---

[147] Parliament/Council Directive 2014/49/EU *on deposit guarantee schemes*, O.J. L 173/149 (2014).

[148] Parliament/Council Directive 2009/14/EC *amending Directive 94/19/EC on deposit guarantee schemes as regards the coverage level and the payout delay*, O.J. L 68/3 (2009).

the context of cross-border issues, i.e. to provide a single point of contact for depositors and banks, and the coordination of reimbursement procedures, it does not provide sufficient clarity as to the way to deal with home/host issues, especially in a crisis situation. Furthermore, at present, a common supranational framework for deposit insurance does not exist. Its creation allows a harmonised deposit insurance system where the same level of protection of depositors is guaranteed at European level (→ para 285).

259 Overall, the current European regulatory environment on DGSs still **lacks a system of fully harmonised and institutional rules** affording the same degree of depositor protection throughout Europe. This is a major limitation to build a truly effective EBU.

4.4. The Other Substantive Sources of EU Legal Acts in the European Banking Union

260 Together with the main legal instruments examined above, the EBU is also composed of **other legal sources** that are adopted and applied by the competent authorities.

261 Without being exhaustive, the SSM Regulation, the SRM Regulation, the CRR, the CRD and the BRRD empower the Commission, the ECB, the EBA, the SRB to adopt a **number of acts within their scope of competences**. These are for example delegated and implementing EU acts or guidelines and recommendations.

4.4.1. Delegated and Implementing EU Acts

262 Delegated and implementing EU acts are Level 2 acts that the Commission is given the power to adopt based on Level 1 legislative acts adopted by the EU legislators. According to the new legislative and non-legislative distinction introduced in the Lisbon Treaty, the Commission can adopt delegated and implementing acts under **Articles 290 and 291 TFEU**. The co-legislators (the EP and the Council) adopt the general rules in banking regulation after the Commission has proposed them.

263 The EU co-legislators are also empowered to **delegate to the Commission** the power to amend or supplement primary legislation with delegated or implementing acts (Article 290 TFEU).[149] In general terms, the Commission's delegated powers are subject to scrutiny provided in the legislative act and to control mechanisms for the delegated and implementing acts.[150] It is important to note that the power of delegation to the Commission is constrained by a number of conditions.[151]

---

[149] For a full list of EU Level 2 provisions adopted in Europe, available at http://ec.europa.eu/info/sites/info/files/overview-table-level-2-measures_en.pdf.

[150] Bast (2012), p. 918.

[151] See Schütze (2010), p. 1399.

The category of **implementing acts** empowers the Commission to adopt acts 264
relating to the implementation policies adopted by the legislative authorities. As
provided in Article 291 TFEU, implementing acts remain a subsidiary form of
regulation to the implementation in MS. Thus, the Commission shall adopt implementing acts only as much as 'uniform conditions for implementing legally binding
Union acts are needed' (Article 291.2 TFEU).

Furthermore, EU **agencies**, particularly EBA, can also adopt **draft** regulatory 265
and implementing **technical standards** that are then 'transformed' into delegated
or implementing regulations or directives. These are preparatory acts that, based on
a specific empowerment in Level 1 regulation, allow EU agencies to prepare the
technical document that is then formally approved by the Commission.

4.4.2. Guidelines, Recommendations and Other Acts

Guidelines, recommendations and other soft law acts constitute **Level 3 provisions** 266
that can be adopted by the above institutions and agencies in the context of their
competences. These contribute to shape the Single Rulebook and to delineate the
scope of regulation, supervision and resolution in the EBU.

Finally, **the NCAs and the NRAs** may still adopt acts that **implement or** 267
complement the existing body of EU rules in the EBU. These are subordinated
rules but can still play a role in the Single Rulebook. This is the case, for instance, of
national law implementing EU directives or options and discretions set out in EU
regulations.

5. The Unfinished Agenda of the European Banking Union

The assessment of the main reforms on banking regulation suggests that the EBU is 268
still an unfinished institutional and substantive reform to strengthen the banking
sector, to integrate financial markets and ultimately to complete the EMU. However, the above analysis has also shown that certain improvements have been made
in banking regulation at European level. On 31 May 2017 the EU Commission
published a paper on the completion of the EMU.[152] A certain attention is given to
the **completion of the EBU as a key factor in improving the EMU**. The proposals
of the Commission in the financial sector focus on two aspects, namely a political
agreement on the EDIS and on the creation of a common fiscal backstop for the
Banking Union through a credit line of the ESM to the SRF.[153] In October 2017, the
Commission published a Communication on the completion of the Banking
Union.[154]

---

[152] Commission, *Reflection Paper on the deepening of the Economy and Monetary Union*, COM (2017) 291.

[153] COM(2017) 291, pp. 19–20.

[154] Commission Communication, *completing the Banking Union*, COM(2017) 592 final.

269 Against this background, this section covers **four main reform projects**. First, it looks at the main improvements to the CRR/CRD in light of the CRR II and CRD V legislation. Second, it examines the main amendments in the BRRD II and the resolution regime. Third, it looks at the EDIS as the essential, although missing, third pillar of the EBU. Finally, it discusses the development of a public backstop for the EBU to make it more resilient to shocks and risks arising in financial markets.

5.1. Reviewing Substantive EU Banking Regulation

270 **Revisions in the CRR II/CRD V** are the first, and most important, area that have improved banking regulation in Europe (→ para 234). As examined above, the European regulatory framework established in banking regulation still suffers from considerable divergences and national implementations that do not contribute to a truly supranational regulatory framework. Even if prudential supervision and resolution have to a certain extent be transferred to the supranational level, EU banking regulation still suffers from relevant banking rules being national and divergent in MS. The review of the CRR/CRD IV has been finalised in 2019 as a new Banking Package together with the BRRD II.

271 First, among others, the new Banking Package includes **new binding prudential ratios**: the leverage ratio and the net stable funding ratio (NSFR). As mentioned earlier (→ para 216), the leverage ratio binds credit institutions with a certain percentage of capital measures divided by the credit institution's total exposures. The CRR text introduces a binding leverage ratio of at least 3% for systemic banks. The leverage ratio would enhance financial stability by determining capital requirements based on non-RWAs and would avoid building excessive leverage. As for the NSFR, this is considered a liquidity-based ratio stable calculating the funding profile of a credit institution in relation to its on- and off-balance sheet activities. The NSFR will allow credit institutions to finance their long-term activities (assets and off-balance sheet items) with stable sources of funding (liabilities). The NSFR binding ratio is expressed as a minimum level of 100% of stable funding ratio.

272 Second, the new CRD introduces a **regulatory distinction in the SREP assessment** between additional Pillar 2 requirements and Pillar 2 guidance in the CRD. The former are the mandatory requirements imposed by supervisors. The latter refers instead to the possibility for competent authorities to communicate expectations to supervised entities to hold capital in excess of Pillar 1 capital requirement, Pillar 2 capital requirements and combined buffers requirements to cope with certain situations.

273 Third, the new CRD introduces **additional authorisation requirements** for financial holdings, mixed financial holdings for credit institutions established in Europe. The text also requires for third country banks to have an intermediate EU parent undertaking (IPU) where two or more institutions established in the EU have the same ultimate parent undertaking in a third country.

Other changes in the new Banking Package relate to a reform of trading books 274
for calculations of capital requirements for market risk, exemptions from the
prudential rules to certain categories of credit institutions, reinforcements to the
prudential rules on large exposures.

However, the Package **falls short on some aspects** that could be included in the 275
next amendments. First, options and discretions provided to MS should be reduced
considerably in the CRR/CRD. These are provisions in the CRD that mainly grant
discretions or options directly to a MS. The use of such discretions or options may
generate an uneven playing field with differential rules in Member States. Furthermore, an important aspect that remains open in the new Banking Package is the
treatment of sovereign exposures of credit institutions. At present, the Basel
Committee is still developing its stance on the prudential treatment of such exposures on banks.[155]

Moreover, **the CRR/CRD would have benefitted from other regulatory** 276
amendments. These particularly concern the content of the CRD as it has provisions that have led to considerable divergences at the national level. For instance, fit
and proper requirements as well as governance arrangements stemming from the
CRD are still subject to divergent degrees of national implementation. Furthermore,
other regulatory provisions should be included at the EU level. This is the case of
merger by or concerning credit institutions, activities of credit institutions in third
countries with an impact on prudential requirements, specific banking authorisations such as covered bonds issuance.

The new Banking Package is a **welcome development** to improve the existing 277
rules on prudential requirements, especially three years after the establishment of
the first pillar of the EBU. However, the still existing **different rules at the**
national level and single supervisory and resolution authorities for significant
credit institutions—the ECB and the SRB—**will require further harmonisation**
efforts to avoid a differential application of rules.[156]

Without analysing them in details, other recent initiatives of the Commission to 278
also improve the EU banking substantial framework are the following:

– **Review of prudential rules for investment firms**:[157] this review aims to
 include in the scope of credit institutions certain investment firms of a specific
 size. The main impact of this reform is that the ECB and SRB will also extend
 their scope of supervision and resolution to some of these entities in the Banking
 Union.

---

[155] See Basel Committee on Banking Supervision, *The Basel Committee's work programme for 2015 and 2016*, 2016, available at http://www.bis.org/bcbs/about/work_programme.htm.

[156] See also Angeloni (2016).

[157] Parliament/Council Directive (EU) 2019/2034 *on the prudential supervision of investment firms*, O.J. L 314/64 (2019).

- **EU framework on covered bonds**:[158] the directive aims to harmonise at a minimum the supervision of covered bonds by credit institutions in Europe and create an EU label for covered bonds with specific features.
- **Measures address risks related to Non-Performing Loans (NPLs)**:[159] these measures aim to establish Pillar 1 prudential backstops for loans that will serve to regulate provisioning of NPLs by credit institutions.

5.2. The Reforms to the EU Banking Resolution and Insolvency Regime

279 The second ground of reforms relate to **improve the bank recovery and resolution regime** in Europe or to extend the scope of EU law and policy in other resolution or insolvency fields. Without being complete, some reflections are made on possible reforms to the existing EU banking resolution/insolvency regime.

280 The adoption of a directive or even a regulation harmonising insolvency rules, or setting the creditor hierarchy in banking insolvency as well as a provision establishing a moratorium tool at European level, would be welcome additions in the current regulatory regime. The new Banking Package has included some changes to the BRRD[160] and the SRM Regulation. At present, **the BRRD and the SRM Regulation do not harmonise insolvency rules** for banks but establish a European framework for orderly resolution. These rules do not set harmonised insolvency regimes for credit institutions in Europe. A new harmonising EU instrument on banking insolvency and restructuring proceedings could be developed in future.

281 Article 108 BRRD harmonises partially the **order of priority of claims in insolvency proceedings**. This provision requires that the part of eligible deposits from natural persons and micro, small and medium enterprises (SMEs) exceeding EUR 100,000 and that deposits which would be eligible deposits from natural persons, micro enterprises and SMEs have the same priority ranking, which is higher than the ranking provided for the claims of ordinary unsecured, non-preferred creditors. Similarly, covered deposits and DGSs subrogating to the rights and obligations of covered depositors in insolvency shall have the same priority ranking, to be higher than the ranking for the claims mentioned before. This is a welcome regulatory development, which, however, does not harmonise generally creditor hierarchy in insolvency.

282 Furthermore, the adoption of the MREL at European level requires that **certain liabilities are 'bail-inable' instruments** to ensure that losses are absorbed, and credit institutions are recapitalised if they get into financial difficulties and are

---

[158] Parliament/Council Directive (EU) 2019/2162 *on the issue of covered bonds and covered bond public supervision*, O.J. L 328/29 (2019).

[159] Parliament/Council Regulation (EU) 2019/630 *amending Regulation (EU) No. 575/2013 as regards minimum loss coverage for non-performing exposures*, O.J. L 111/4 (2019).

[160] Parliament/Council Directive (EU) 2019/879 *amending Directive 2014/59/EU as regards the loss-absorbing and recapitalisation capacity of credit institutions and investment firms*, O.J. L 150/296 (2019).

subsequently placed in a resolution. The Financial Stability Board (FSB) adopted the Total-Loss Absorption Capacity (TLAC) standard applying only to global systemically important institutions. The new Banking Package contains revised rules on **calibration of MREL, issuance of bail-inable instruments and compliance with MREL**.[161] These establish a system of MREL requirements, which is higher for globally systemically important institutions, and MREL requirements for all credit institutions. This is a Pillar 2 add on MREL requirement. Furthermore, resolution authorities may introduce additional MREL guidance to credit institutions (→ para 173).

Finally, the introduction of a **moratorium tool** at European level ensures that resolution authorities have an adequate instrument to intervene and avoid the trigger of resolution. Moratorium tools are intended to 'freeze transfers out of a failing bank to prevent it haemorrhaging cash before authorities can intervene'.[162] In other words, a moratorium tool is a regulatory power to suspend the payments to be made by an ailing institution under specific circumstances and with specific exceptions in cases of major risks to financial stability. The new BRRD rules introduce the possibility for the resolution authority under certain conditions to suspend certain obligations when an entity is under resolution (Article 33a BRRD). However, the new BRRD does not harmonise rules on moratorium before resolution and does not create a general moratorium tool for supervisory authorities, such as the ECB in the SSM.

283

5.3. The European Deposit Insurance Scheme as the Missing Third Pillar of the European Banking Union

The creation of a **supranational system of deposit insurance** is a key reform to complete the EBU. This section intends to briefly analyse the Commission's EDIS proposal as a supranational attempt to enhance risk sharing with the creation of a single deposit insurance scheme in Europe (→ para 259).

284

The EDIS is conceived as a supranational system of deposit insurance where a **single authority is in charge of protecting covered depositors of credit institutions in case of an ailing credit institution**. This would allow deposit insurance to be exercised at supranational level through a mutualised fund for deposit insurance purposes. The EDIS goes beyond the established system of European harmonisation of DGS, which was improved with the 2014 Directive. In November 2015, the Commission put forward a proposal for a regulation setting up of such a system. This would be the third pillar of the EBU and would consist in a new supranational framework for deposit insurance that would apply to deposits below EUR 100,000

285

---

[161] See European Commission, *Frequently Asked Questions: Capital requirements (CRR/CRD IV) and resolution framework (BRRD/SRM) amendments.*

[162] EU weighs guillotine powers to freeze transfers. *Financial Times*, 15 May 2016 (available at https://www.ft.com/content/fe11824e-1914-11e6-bb7d-ee563a5a1cc1).

of credit institutions in the euro area.[163] The Commission Communication of 2015 on completing the EBU states that a common deposit insurance scheme would be an essential measure to reduce risks and shocks and to improve financial stability.[164] This would be the case as large local shocks may justify the use of a supranational deposit insurance system in case the national DGS is insufficient.

286   Without going into too many details, the EDIS would include DGSs established in euro area MS and in those of them willing to enter into a close cooperation. The scope provided by the EDIS would be limited to the mandatory part of participating DGSs under the DGS directive.[165] The EDIS would be based on the **pooling together of financial resources levied by the banking sector in a form of an EDIS Fund**. The Commission's proposal envisages three consecutive phases: re-insurance, co-insurance and full insurance to be developed over a certain number of years.

287   The **reinsurance phase** would allow that the EDIS Fund resources are used only when the resources of the participating DGSs have already been exhausted.[166] When a bank faces liquidity crisis or is placed in resolution and it is necessary to pay out deposits or to finance their transfer to another bank, the national DGSs and EDIS will intervene.[167]

288   Subsequently, in the **co-insurance phase**, the participating DGS contributions would be combined with the Fund. The contribution from the Fund to depositor payouts would progressively increase to 100%. This phase would allow that participating DGSs may request both funding and loss cover directly to the EDIS Fund.[168]

289   Finally, a third phase of **full insurance** would provide that only the European Fund insures participating DGSs. In this final stage of the EDIS set-up, which is envisaged in a transitional phase until 2024, the protection of covered deposits will be fully financed by EDIS and supported in a close cooperation between EDIS and national DGSs.

290   In the EDIS the **SRB** (→ para 139 et seqq.) **would be entrusted with the administration of this Fund**. In case circumstances resulting in a payout event or a request to contribute for resolution purposes arise, the participating DGSs would inform the SRB immediately of these situations and the need to make use of the EDIS Fund.[169] Once detailed information is received,[170] the SRB would determine

---

[163] Commission, *Proposal for a Regulation of the European Parliament and of the Council amending Regulation (EU) No. 806/2014 in order to establish a European Deposit Insurance Scheme*, COM(2015) 586 final.

[164] Commission Communication, *Towards the completion of the Banking Union*, COM(2015) 587 final.

[165] COM(2015) 586 final, Article 1.2.
[166] COM(2015) 586 final, Article 9.2.
[167] COM(2015) 586 final, Article 41a.
[168] COM(2015) 586 final, Article 41d.
[169] COM(2015) 586 final, Article 41i.
[170] COM(2015) 586 final, Article 41k.

within twenty-four hours whether the conditions for an EDIS intervention are met and, in a positive case, would specify the amount of funding to be provided to the participating DGS. EDIS funding would then be given immediately after in cash to the participating DGSs.

The EDIS Fund would be **financed by ex ante contributions** owed and paid directly **by the banking sector** to the SRB. As of the co-insurance phase, the SRB may also claim extraordinary ex post contributions from the banks when the available means are insufficient for funding and loss cover. As regards decision-making, the EDIS would be administered by the SRB in its executive and plenary sessions. Decisions involving both SRM and EDIS matters would be taken by a joint plenary session.

The establishment of the EDIS would be a **very welcome reform for the completion of the EBU** as it would constitute its missing third pillar. The creation of a truly European system of deposit insurance would ensure that local shocks and risks related to deposits in credit institutions are solved at the European level. This would both avoid that depositors generate bank runs to withdraw their deposits as a crisis prevention measure, or that DGS would face risks of insufficient resources to repay covered depositors as a crisis management measure. National DGSs still remain vulnerable to large local shocks. EDIS would ensure equal deposit protection within the EBU regardless of the MS where the deposit is located. Furthermore, it would guarantee that the decision to pay out depositors is taken at the European level, with less risks of national political or local influence. Moreover, it would deal adequately with cross-border issues of banking groups and limit problems related to the home/host regime.

Nevertheless, the proposed EDIS Regulation is still **under political discussions** by the EU legislators, and it is far from clear whether it will be eventually adopted. Political negotiations on the EDIS design seem to have reached a deadlock.

5.4. The Creation of a Common Fiscal Backstop for the European Banking Union

Finally, the creation of a common fiscal backstop in the euro area and the EBU remains an open issue. A common fiscal backstop is considered as a **supranational public intervention assistance measure** to provide public funding to enhance the financial capacity of resolution funds. The Commission states that '[s]uch a backstop would imply a temporary mutualisation of possible fiscal risk related to bank resolutions across the EBU. However, use of the backstop would be fiscally neutral in the medium term, as any public funds used would be reimbursed over time by the banks (via ex-post contributions to the SRF)'.[171]

---

[171] Commission Communication, *Towards the completion of the Banking Union*, COM(2015) 587 final, p. 5.

295 These considerations reveal that a common fiscal backstop would serve the purpose to **mutualise fiscal risks and to ensure further risk reduction measures**. However, before the creation of a fiscal backstop, in case of financing need, further financial resources to finance resolution would be taken only through available resolution financing arrangements beyond the SRF, the national financing arrangement or through compatible state aids. At the same time, the problematic set-up of the SRF shows that a pan-euro area and public supranational backstop to finance resolutions beyond the pooling of financial resources raised from private operators is needed.

296 While a common fiscal backstop has not been established yet in Europe, the **European Stability Mechanism** (ESM) will serve that function. The ESM may be involved with either an indirect or a direct instrument for bank recapitalisation, which may be granted under specific circumstances and which may constitute credit lines to finance resolutions (→ Supplement to Title VIII: TESM para 94 et seqq., 101 et seqq.). In this context, the ESM Guideline on direct recapitalisation has been adopted in December 2014 for an amount of up to EUR 60 billion.[172] It provides for very strict conditions for activation to recapitalise ailing credit institutions. Thus far, the direct recapitalisation instrument has never been used and it will be repealed once the ESM fiscal backstop enters into force.[173]

297 In December 2018, a term of reference on the creation of the ESM common backstop to the SRF was published (→ Supplement to Title VIII: TESM para107).[174] It outlines the main terms for the **creation of a common backstop to support the SRF**. In 2021 the ESM Amending Agreement has been signed by the participating MS. Among other changes, the ESM Treaty contains a new Article 18a on the backstop facility to the SRB and a new Annex IV detailing the conditions for loans and disbursements under this backstop facility.

298 Meanwhile, in December 2017, the Commission has published a Communication outlining how the suggested new **European Monetary Fund** (EMF)[175] would replace the ESM and would also serve as a public fiscal backstop for the SRM (→ Supplement to Title VIII: TESM para 145 et seqq.). In particular, the EMF would provide credit lines or set guarantees in support of the SRB under Articles 3 and 22 of the proposed Council Regulation.[176]

---

[172] ESM, *Guideline on Financial Assistance for the Direct Recapitalisation of Institutions*, available at https://www.esm.europa.eu/sites/default/files/20141208_guideline_on_financial_assistance_for_the_direct_recapitalisation_of_institutions.pdf.

[173] See the Agreement *Amending the Treaty Establishing the ESM*, signed on 27 January 2021 (available at https://www.esm.europa.eu/about-esm/esm-reform-documents).

[174] Term of Reference of the common backstop to the Single Resolution Fund, 4 December 2018 available at https://www.consilium.europa.eu/media/37268/tor-backstop_041218_final_clean.pdf

[175] Commission, *Proposal for a Council Regulation on the establishment of the European Monetary Fund*, COM(2017) 827. On the proposal see Manger-Nestler and Böttner (2019) and Zoppè and Dias (2019).

[176] Annex to COM(2017) 827.

The ESM backstop will grant further credibility to the EBU for the safeguard of 299
credit institutions, should the resolution tools at disposal not be sufficient. Furthermore, it would contribute to justify the progressive integration of the ESM into the EU legal order. A common fiscal backstop in the euro area as an EU law tool should be established in the medium-term.

6. Conclusions

This study has demonstrated that the EBU is a **major reform in the EU** as a new 300 paradigm for supranational supervision and resolution of credit institutions in Europe. As regards the SSM, the powers conferred to the ECB in the SSM for the supervision of credit institutions established in participating MS are unprecedented and contribute to achieve a new stage of integration and resilience of the banking sector in Europe. The tasks and powers conferred to the ECB in the SSM for the supervision of credit institutions established in participating MS will—hopefully—contribute to establish a **better model framework for top-down supervisory governance, supervisory convergence, supervisory transparency, regulatory harmonisation and lead to a strengthened model of bank supervision** in participating MS. In the words of *Draghi*, the 'SSM offers a tremendous opportunity to move from different national approaches to the treatment of banks to a genuinely European perspective'.[177] The SSM is a critical evolutionary reform and has been described as 'the most ambitious and encompassing reform of the EU architecture since the institution of the single currency'.[178]

As regards the SRM and the resolution framework, this study has examined the 301 reforms to establish a new European framework for bank resolution in Europe. The creation of a European-wide substantive and institutional framework for the resolution of credit institutions is an important evolution in the EU law and policy. After fierce negotiations among key political players the SRM has been established. It is a welcome development in European banking regulation as it sets a supranational institutional framework for the orderly resolution of credit institutions in participating MS. The SRM will hopefully establish '**a credible mechanism to proceed swiftly, orderly and efficiently in the resolution of banks that have attained the point of non-viability**'.[179] This may be achieved in a system where there four main constituents are present: '(a) a single system, (b) a single authority with efficient decision-making procedures (c) a single fund and (d) a backstop facility for bridge financing'.[180] Furthermore, the BRRD sets a new regime in banking crisis management as it provides new statutory resolution tools to address privately ailing credit

---

[177] Draghi (2013).
[178] Praet (2014).
[179] Praet (2014) (emphasis added).
[180] Praet (2014).

institutions in Europe. As *Constâncio* indicated, the BRRD is 'the most crucial regulatory change in Europe in relation to breaking the bank-sovereign nexus. It represents a true paradigm change, ending the culture of bail-out and ushering in a culture of bail-in'.[181] The establishment of resolution tools marks a new era for in banking legislation as resolution aims to break the vicious circle between the sovereign and the banks and to avoid taxpayers' bail-outs.

302 At the same time, **many questions are still open** to debate as regards the EBU as an unprecedented project of European integration. Future practice will tell whether the BRRD will be effective in addressing the orderly resolution of credit institutions from a European perspective. Some recent examples of banking crises (Banco Popular, Banca Popolare di Vicenza/Veneto Banca, ABLV) have shown that there is still margin of manoeuvre to improve the existing regulatory framework, especially to avoid national bias in the application or non-application of the EU resolution framework. Furthermore, future will show whether the SRM will work as a centralised and swift system for the resolution of credit institutions in participating MS. As demonstrated in this study, some key challenges are present in the EBU and some regulatory reforms are still needed to reinforce the regulatory, supervisory and resolution regime for credit institutions in Europe. The 2019 Banking Package is a welcome development in the field but falls short of some key improvements. Furthermore, the adoption of the EDIS as the missing third pillar of the EBU would be an essential step to move forward with the EBU and allow a truly supranational level of deposit insurance.

List of Cases

ECJ/CJEU

ECJ 13.06.1958, 9/56 and 10/56, *Meroni v High Authority*, ECLI:EU:C:1958:7 and ECLI:EU:C:1958:8 [cit. in para 28, 141, 143, 153]

ECJ 02.06.2006, C-217/04, *United Kingdom v Council and Parliament (ENISA)*, ECLI:EU:C:2006:279 [cit. in para 140]

CJEU 22.01.2014, C-270/12, *United Kingdom v Parliament and Council (ESMA)*, ECLI:EU:C:2014:18 [cit. in para 134]

CJEU 20.11.2014, C-507/13, Opinion of AG Jääskinen, *United Kingdom v Parliament and Council*, ECLI:EU:C:2014:2394 [cit. in para 227]

CJEU 11.12.2018, C-493/17, *Weiss and Others*, ECLI:EU:C:2018:1000 [cit. in para 2]

CJEU 19.12.2018, C-219/17, *Berlusconi and Fininvest*, ECLI:EU:C:2018:1023 [cit. in para 102]

CJEU 08.05.2019, C-450/17 P, *Landeskreditbank Baden-Württemberg v ECB*, ECLI:EU:C:2019:372 [cit. in paras 32, 90]

---

[181] Constâncio (2014).

GC

GC 16.05.2017, T-122/15, *Landeskreditbank Baden-Württemberg v ECB*, ECLI: EU:T:2017:337 [cit. in para 90]

German Federal Constitutional Court

German FCC 30.07.2019, 2 BvR 1685/14, *SSM Regulation and SRM Regulation* [cit. in para 90, 132, 148]

References[182]

Alexander, K. (2015). European Banking Union: A legal and institutional analysis of the single supervisory mechanism and the single resolution mechanism. *European Law Review, 40*, 154–187.
Angeloni, I. (2016, October 6). *Challenges facing the single supervisory mechanism*. Speech. Retrieved from https://www.bankingsupervision.europa.eu/press/speeches/date/2016/html/se161006.en.html
Angeloni, I. (2018, May 2). *ECB supervision at five: Re-charting the route*. Speech. Retrieved from https://www.bankingsupervision.europa.eu/press/speeches/date/2018/html/ssm.sp180502.en.html
Avgouleas, E. (2012). *Governance of global financial markets*. CUP.
Avgouleas, E., & Goodhart, C. (2015). Critical reflections on Bank Bail-ins. *Journal of Financial Regulation, 2*, 3–29.
Bast, J. (2012). New categories of acts after the Lisbon reform: Dynamics of parlamentarization in EU law. *Common Market Law Review, 49*, 885–927.
Binder, J.-H. (2015). Resolution planning and structural bank reform within the Banking Union. In J. Castañeda, D. Mayes, & G. G. Wood (Eds.), *European Banking Union (Chapter 7)*. Routledge.
Blair, C., Carns, F., & Kushmeider, R. (2007). Instituting a deposit insurance system: Why? How? In A. Campbell, J. La Brosse, D. Mayes, & D. Singh (Eds.), *Deposit insurance (ch. 3)*. Palgrave MacMillan.
Brummer, C. (2015). *Soft law and the global financial system*. CUP.
Busch, D., & Ferrarini, G. (2020). *European Banking Union*. OUP.
Castañeda, J., Mayes, D., & Geoffrey Wood, G. (Eds.). (2015). *European Banking Union*. Routledge.
Clifford Chance. (2011). *Legal Aspects of Bank Bail-ins*. Retrieved from http://www.cliffordchance.com/publicationviews/publications/2011/05/legal_aspects_ofbankbail-ins.htm
Constâncio, V. (2014, April 24). *Banking Union: meaning and implications for the future of banking*. Retrieved from https://www.ecb.europa.eu/press/key/date/2014/html/sp140424_1.en.html
de Larosiere, J. (2009). *The high level group on financial supervision in the EU*. Retrieved from https://ec.europa.eu/economy_finance/publications/pages/publication14527_en.pdf
Draghi, D. (2013, November 22). *Opening speech at the European Banking Congress The future of Europe*. Retrieved from https://www.ecb.europa.eu/press/key/date/2013/html/sp131122.en.html

---

[182] All cited Internet sources in this Chapter have been accessed on 6 April 2021.

Dragomir, L. (2009). *European prudential banking regulation and supervision: The legal dimension*. Routledge.

Fabbrini, F. (2014). On banks, courts and international law. The intergovernmental agreement on the single resolution fund in context. *Maastricht Journal of European and Comparative Law, 21*, 444–463.

Ferran, E. (2015). European Banking Union: Imperfect but it can still work. In D. Busch & G. Ferrarini (Eds.), *European Banking Union (ch. 3)*. OUP.

Ferran, E., & Alexander, K. (2010). Can soft law bodies be effective? The special case of the European systemic risk board. *European Law Review, 35*, 751–777.

Ferran, E., & Babis, V. (2013). The single supervisory mechanism. *Journal of Corporate Law Studies, 13*, 255–285.

Ferran, EF. (2012). Understanding the new institutional architecture of EU financial market supervision. In E. Wymeersch, K. Hopt, & F. Ferrarini (Eds.), *Financial regulation and supervision. A post-crisis analysis (ch. 5)*. OUP.

Gardella, A. (2015). Bail-in and the financing of the SRM. In D. Busch & G. Ferrarini (Eds.), *European Banking Union (ch. 11)*. OUP.

Goodhart, C., & Schoenmaker, D. (1995). Should the functions of monetary policy and banking supervision be separated?. *Oxford Economic Papers, 47*.

Goyal, R., et al. (2013). *A Banking Union for the Euro Area*. IMF Staff Discussion Note SDN/13/01.

Grünewald, S. (2014). *The resolution of cross-border banking crises in the European Union*. Kluwer.

Haentjens, M. (2014). Bank recovery and resolution: An overview of international initiatives. *International Insolvency Law Review, 3*, 255–270.

Hinojosa-Martínez, L. M., & María Beneyto, J. (2015). *European Banking Union: The new regime*. Kluwer.

Hüpkes, E., & Devos, D. (2010). Cross-border bank resolution: A reform Agenda. In M. Giovanoli & D. Devos (Eds.), *International Monetary and financial law (ch. 17)*. OUP.

Kleftouri, N. (2015). *Deposit protection and bank resolution*. OUP.

Lastra, R. (2003). The governance structure for financial regulation and supervision in Europe. *Columbia Journal of European Law, 10*, 49–68.

Lastra, R. (2015). *International financial and Monetary law*. OUP.

Lo Schiavo, G. (2014a). From national banking supervision to a centralized model of prudential supervision in Europe? The stability function of the single supervisory mechanism. *Maastricht Journal of European and Comparative Law, 21*, 110–140.

Lo Schiavo, G. (2014b). State aids and credit institutions in Europe: What way forward? *European Business Law Review, 25*, 427–457.

Lo Schiavo, G. (2015). A Judicial re-thinking on the delegation of powers to European agencies under EU law? Comment on Case C-270/12 UK v. Council and Parliament. *German Law Journal, 16*, 315–336.

Lo Schiavo, G. (2019). The ECB and its application of national law. In G. Lo Schiavo (Ed.), *The European Banking Union and the role of law (ch. 9)*. Edward Elgar.

Manger-Nestler, C., & Böttner, R. (2019). Der Europäische Währungsfonds nach den Plänen der Kommission. *Zeitschrift für ausländisches öffentliches Recht und Völkerrecht*, 43–84.

Moloney, N. (2014). European Banking Union: Assessing its risks and resilience. *Common Market Law Review, 51*, 1609–1670.

Panourgias, L. (2005). *Banking regulation and World Trade law: GATS, EU and prudential institution building*. Hart Publishing.

Payne, J. (2015). The reform of deposit guarantee schemes in Europe. *European Company Financial Law Review, 12*, 539–562.

Peters, G. (2011). Developments in the EU. In R. Lastra (Ed.), *Cross-border bank insolvency (ch. 6)*. OUP.

Pisani-Ferry, J., et al. (2012). *What kind of European Banking Union?* Bruegel Policy Contribution 2012/12.
Praet, P. (2014). *Fixing finance* Panel intervention 18 February 2014. Retrieved from http://www.ecb.europa.eu/press/key/date/2014/html/sp140218.en.html
Schütze, R. (2010). From Rome to Lisbon: "Executive federalism" in the (new) European Union. *Common Market Law Review, 47*, 1385–1427.
Smits, R. (1997). *The European Central Bank.* Alphen aan den Rijn.
Steinbach, A. (2016). The lender of last resort in the Eurozone. *Common Market Law Review, 53*, 361–383.
Ter Kuile, G., Wissink, L., & Bovenschen, W. (2015). Tailor-made accountability within the single supervisory mechanism. *Common Market Law Review, 52*, 155–189.
Tridimas, T. (2019). The constitutional dimension of Banking Union. In S. Grundmann & H. Micklitz (Eds.), *The European Banking Union and constitution: Beacon for advanced integration or death-knell for democracy (ch. 2).* Bloomsbury.
Tröger, T. (2014). The single supervisory mechanism – Panacea or Quack banking regulation? *European Business Organization Law Review, 15*, 449–497.
Walker, G. (2004). European financial programme: Content, structure and completion. *European Business Law Review, 15*, 305–345.
Wojcik, K.-P. (2016). Bail in the Banking Union. *Common Market Law Review, 53*, 90–138.
Wymeersch, E. (2014). *The single supervisory mechanism or "SSM," part one of the Banking Union.* NBB/BNB Working Paper No. 255.
Zavvos, G., & Kaltsouni, S. (2015). The single resolution mechanism in the European Banking Union: Legal foundation, governance structure and financing. In M. Haentjens & B. Wessel (Eds.), *Research handbook on crisis management in the banking sector (ch. 7).* Edward Elgar.
Zhou, J., et al. (2012). *From Bail-out to Bail-in: Mandatory Debt Restructuring of Systemic Financial Institutions Paper on Bail in.* IMF Staff Discussion Note SDN/12/03.
Zoppè, A., & Dias, C. (2019). *The European Stability Mechanism: Main Features, Instruments and Accountability.* European Parliament Economic Governance Support Unit (EGOV), PE 497.755 - 14 February 2019. Retrieved from http://www.europarl.europa.eu/RegData/etudes/BRIE/2014/497755/IPOL-ECON_NT(2014)497755_EN.pdf

Title IX
Employment

Article 145 [Coordinated Strategy for Employment]
(ex-Article 125 TEC)

Member States and the Union shall, in accordance with this Title,[1–29] work towards developing a coordinated strategy for employment[30–38] and particularly for promoting a skilled,[39,40] trained[41,42] and adaptable workforce[43] and labour markets responsive to economic change[44,45] with a view to achieving the objectives defined in Article 3 of the Treaty on European Union.[46–51]

Contents

1. Title IX. Conceptual Development 1
   1.1. First Concerns on Employment 1
   1.2. Inclusion of an Employment Title 8
   1.3. Lisbon and Later 14
   1.4. New Concerns in the Aftermath of COVID-19 26
2. European Employment Strategy 30
3. Skilled, Trained and Adaptable Workforce 39
4. Responsive Labour Markets 44
5. Objectives 46
References

1. Title IX. Conceptual Development

1.1. First Concerns on Employment

Title IX TFEU is the outcome of a long process of development, marked by periods of excitement and also by moments of stagnation. As it has been shown, "there is an ongoing learning process at European level about what is working and not working",[1] especially in a permanently changing economic and social environment. Promoting employment is one of the objectives of the EU's social policy (Article 151.1 TFEU). However, the **interdependence between employment and social policy** is not a novelty of TFEU; historically, it is revealed in the manner European documents have been drafted, at first hesitantly, and then increasingly firm.

2 Concerns about employment can be traced back to the foundation of the EU. They can be found within the **Treaty of Rome**, which aimed at the "close cooperation between national employment services", as well as the creation of a European Social Fund to improve employment opportunities for workers. And the idea that the human capital was the vital resource of any advanced economy was promoted by the economists of the early European construction. However, the foundation of Europe started with a limited and weak social component.

3 With the creation of the **Standing Committee on Employment** in 1970,[2] made up of government representatives of the MS and of the organisations on the two sides of industry, employment policy was to prove its importance for the EEC. A number of directives on labour relations were adopted, such as the directives on collective redundancies (Council Directive 75/129/EEC[3]), on the transfer of enterprises (Acquired Rights Directive, Council Directive 77/187/ECC[4]) or on employee protection in case of employer insolvency (Council Directive 80/987/EEC[5])—relevant in terms of the social policy of the Union, and with certain impact on employment. Unemployment, however, continued to be regarded as a national, rather than a European, issue.

4 Subsequently, the **Maastricht Treaty** included significant references to employment,[6] for example in its Article 2: "The Community shall have as its task [...] a high level of employment and of social protection", and in 1991 the **Protocol on Social Policy** was included, aimed at establishing the objectives of social policy (prefigured in the Social Charter). Among them were the same as today: promoting employment. The protocol was subsequently to be incorporated into chapter IX of the Amsterdam Treaty.

---

[1] Pochet (2005), p. 38.

[2] Set up by Council Decision No. 70/532/EEC *setting up the Standing Committee on Employment in the European Communities*, O.J. L 273/25 (1970). In 1999, the Committee was restructured, and in 2003 it was replaced by the Tripartite Social Summit for Growth and Employment (→ para 16).

[3] Subsequently replaced by Council Directive 98/59/EC *on the approximation of the laws of the Member States relating to collective redundancies*, O.J. L 225/16 (1998).

[4] Subsequently replaced by Council Directive 2001/23/EC *on the approximation of the laws of the Member States relating to the safeguarding of employees' rights in the event of transfers of undertakings, businesses or parts of undertakings or businesses*, O.J. L 82/16 (2001).

[5] Amended by Council Directive 2002/74/EC, O.J. L 270/10 (2002) and repealed by Council Directive 2008/94/EC *on the protection of employees in the event of the insolvency of their employer*, O.J. L 283/36 (2008).

[6] But, as it has been shown, "on the other hand, Article 3 lists 20 different policies and actions which the EU should pursue but omits reference to employment". See Goetschy (1999), p. 119.

Article 145 [Coordinated Strategy for Employment]

In 1993, **Delors White Paper** on growth, competitiveness and employment, was elaborated against noticing the reality that the "unemployment has been steadily rising from cycle to cycle". This White Paper was instrumental in determining the future evolution of the European approach on employment, especially as it chose to adopt a holistic approach on European strategies. It emphasised the need for capacity-building state interventions, social partnership, and the proliferation of a "sustainable developmental model".[7]

Recognising the existence of a long-term structural unemployment, the **Essen European Council** set five key objectives to which the MS have committed themselves: the development of human resources through vocational training; the promotion of productive investments through moderate wage policies; the improvement of the efficiency of labour market institutions; the identification of new sources of jobs through local initiatives; and promotion of access to the world of work for some specific target groups such as young people, long-term unemployed and women.[8] It was a moment of debate because, on the one hand, the European response in relation to unemployment seemed legitimate, but, on the other hand, it was considered that, given that jobs were created by private entrepreneurs, the employment strategies cannot be decided at the European level.[9]

The year 1996 marked the starting point for a new initiative: the **European Confidence Pact for Employment**. The idea was, inter alia, to harmonise monetary stability and budgetary discipline with higher levels of employment. Unemployment continued to remain at the heart of all attempts to add a social dimension to the single market.[10]

1.2. Inclusion of an Employment Title

In 1997, the **Treaty of Amsterdam** introduced a special chapter on employment into a Community already familiar with the "four freedoms" (the free movement of goods, services, people and capital), but which had not yet been enlarged to the East.[11] At the time of the TEU-Amsterdam, the inclusion of the chapter dedicated to

---

[7] Weishaupt (2011), p. 157.

[8] Publications Office of the EU 1997, *The birth of the European Employment Strategy: the Luxembourg process*. Available at http://eur-lex.europa.eu/legal-content/EN/TXT/?uri=URISERV:c11318.

[9] Pochet (2005), p. 47. The author adds that "the proposal to add an employment dimension to the European project lacked a legal base, a sistematised methodology, a strong permanent structure, a long term vision and a control process".

[10] Goetschy (1999), p. 122.

[11] During the adoption of Article 125 TEC, the MS were: Austria, Belgium, Denmark, Finland, France, Germany, Greece, Ireland, Italy, Luxembourg, the Netherlands, Portugal, Spain, Sweden and the United Kingdom. Their employment strategies did not have significant disparities, which led to optimism on the part of European decision makers in terms of the coordination of these strategies.

employment was also a response to increasing levels of unemployment, leading to the need for the European decision makers to find solutions also by using the mechanisms for the coordination of national strategies. These strategies were considered insufficient on their own for a balanced approach to combating European unemployment. The inclusion in the Treaty of a special title on employment signalled recognition of a greater interdependence of economic, social and employment policies than had been perceived until that moment. The inclusion of a section on employment in the TEU-Amsterdam sought to strike a balance between the economic and the social, without, however, turning the issue of the European unemployment into "hard law".[12] In fact, the TEU-Amsterdam marked the transition from the hard law type of regulatory regime to the most subtle soft law that would define and establish the **Open Method of Coordination**.

9   Employment has thus become an explicit EU priority.[13] But the EU's competence was mainly limited to the adoption of guidelines, making recommendations and coordination of national policies on employment. Indeed, employment policy remained at the national level, the EU's role being confined to the coordination of national strategies. In addition, the budgetary aspects of the employment policies at the European level remained a constant concern of the MS, so much so that they might have hold back some initiatives in the field.

10 The inclusion of an employment title was followed immediately, at the **Luxembourg Summit**, by the elaboration of the first **European Employment Strategy** (EES), with a view to coordinate national strategies in the field for the first time at the European level, on four pillars: employability, entrepreneurship, adaptability and equal opportunities. In this context, the first pillar, which concerns the activation of labour market policies, is the most important, emphasising preventive actions and strategies aimed at employability.[14] The intervention aimed at mitigating unemployment is individualised, centred on individual capacities and their enhancement through training, with an important preventive component. It encouraged the participation of social partners, who are "urged, at their various levels of responsibility and action, to conclude as soon as possible agreements with a view to increasing the possibilities for training, work experience, traineeships or other measures likely to promote employability".[15]

---

[12] Hence the idea "to develop a method which would borrow its vocabulary and its instruments from the EMU (common objectives, criteria, peer control), without however resorting to the threat of exclusion that turned Maastricht into a rigorous framework", Dehousse (2003), p. 8.

[13] It is considered that the issue of employment "reached the EU agenda as a result of a complex mixture of intergovernmentalist and supranational forces as well as over effects"; see Goetschy (1999), p. 117. On the "spill-over effect", it must be noted that, indeed, integration in other areas also fostered increased preoccupation for the coordination of employment strategies. Other authors use the concept of "cross-pollination"; see, for instance, Mavrommati and Papathanassiou (2006), p. 1639.

[14] For an analysis of the four pillars, see Weishaupt and Lack (2011), p. 12.

[15] European Commission 1997, Extraordinary European Council Meeting on Employment, Presidency Conclusions. Available at http://europa.eu/rapid/press-release_PRES-97-300_en.htm?locale=en.

11 The Luxembourg Process (1997) was followed by the Cardiff Process (1998), then the Cologne Process (1999)—the three meetings considered decisive for the development of the European policies on three levels:

- labour market policies (the Luxembourg process)
- microeconomic and structural reforms (the Cardiff process)
- macroeconomic and budgetary measures (the Cologne process)

12 Inspired by the pressing need for macro-economic coordination between EU MS,[16] the adoption of the **European Employment Pact** represented acknowledgement of the need to coordinate economic and employment policies, the so-called "EU macro-dialogue".[17] It thus provided a macroeconomic dialogue involving representatives of the Council, European Commission, ECB and of the social partners.

13 In 1998, "Promoting employment, economic growth and stability" was included as an element of the Vienna Strategy for Europe.[18] **National Action Plans** were analysed to evaluate the reaction of the states to the paradigm shift in matters of employment. A series of innovations on working methods have now been introduced: comparable statistics, benchmarks, standards, evaluation methods.

1.3. Lisbon and Later

14 The **Lisbon Strategy**—developed in 2000 during the Portuguese presidency—set out the EU's 10-year objective: "to transform the EU into the most competitive and dynamic knowledge-based economy in the world, capable of sustainable economic growth with more and better jobs and greater social cohesion". The document outlined the strategy designed to achieve it, considering almost all economic, social and environmental aspects of the EU.

15 Economic performance was thus correlated with the creation of more and better jobs in a **knowledge-based society**. The targets and goals set for 2010 could not be achieved due to the 2008 economic crisis,[19] but would be reaffirmed in a new form in the Europe 2020 Strategy (→ para 20).

16 Council Decision No. 2003/174/EC[20] established the **Tripartite Social Summit for Growth and Employment**. Under Article 2 of Council Decision No. 2003/174/EC, the task of the Summit is to ensure continuous concertation between the Council, the Commission, and the social partners (→ Article 150 TFEU para 7).

---

[16] Nedergaard (2006), p. 312.
[17] Heise (2002), p. 89.
[18] Vienna European Council 1998, Presidency Conclusions; available at http://www.europarl.europa.eu/summits/wie1_en.htm.
[19] Kotzur, in Geiger et al. (2015), Article 145 TFEU para 4.
[20] Council Decision No. 2003/174/EC, O.J. L 70/31 (2003), repealed by Council Decision No. 2016/1859/EU *on the Tripartite Social Summit for Growth and Employment*, O.J. L 284/27 (2016).

The Employment Guidelines 2003[21] set out the priorities for structural reforms to be implemented to achieve the main economic objectives of the EU:

- to increase employment and participation rates ("more jobs")
- to raise quality and productivity at work ("better jobs")
- to promote an inclusive labour market ("jobs for all")

17   To achieve these objectives, **ten policy priorities** are formulated: active and preventive measures for unemployed and inactive people; job creation and entrepreneurship; addressing change and promoting adaptability and mobility in the labour market; development of human capital and lifelong learning; labour supply and active ageing; gender equality; integrating and combating discrimination against disadvantaged people; making work pay; undeclared work; regional employment disparities.

18   The 2004 Report of the High Level Group chaired by *Wim Kok*, "Facing the challenge. The Lisbon strategy for growth and employment" identifies four reasons why the ambitious objectives of Lisbon Strategy are unlikely to be reached: overloaded agenda, poor coordination, conflicting priorities and lack of determined political action.[22] The report recommended the translation into National Reform Programmes, a European budget adequate for the objectives and benchmarking as a coercion mechanism for poor performance.[23] Partly acknowledging the conclusions of the report in the mid-term evaluation of the Lisbon Strategy, the Commission finds the results to date "somewhat disappointing", so that it was decided at the 2005 European Council "to give the strategy some fresh momentum". The number of objectives, sub-objectives, indicators and reports that the MS were required to produce was very high; simplification was deemed necessary.[24] The Lisbon Strategy is launched, integrating the EES.[25] Thus a simplified coordination procedure focusing on results is designed, and guidelines for employment and the broad economic policy guidelines merge into a single set of 24 **Integrated Guidelines for Growth and Jobs**,[26] addressing in an integrated approach economic policies, employment policies and structural reforms. National Action Plans become National Reform Programmes (→ Article 148 TFEU para 20).

19   The economic crisis brought with it the need to rethink some of the systems that had been functional up to that time. In 2008, the initiative "New Skills for New

---

[21] Council Decision No. 2003/578/EC *on guidelines for the employment policies of the Member States*, O.J. L 197/13 (2003).

[22] Publications Office of the EU 2004, *Facing The Challenge. The Lisbon strategy for growth and employment*. Report from the High Level Group chaired by Wim Kok. Available at https://op.europa.eu/s/odyN. See also, Bongardt and Torres (2012), p. 475.

[23] Bongardt and Torres (2012), p. 476.

[24] For further details, see Barnard (2012), p. 102.

[25] Communication to the Spring European Council, *Working together for growth and jobs - A new start for the Lisbon strategy*, COM(2005) 24.

[26] Council Decision No. 2005/600/EC *on Guidelines for the employment policies of the Member States*, O.J. L 215/26 (2006).

Jobs. Anticipating and matching labour market and skills needs"[27] was put forward—including ways of action and expected results, the reconfiguration of the concept of flexicurity, the need to identify and develop the "right skills for the jobs of today and tomorrow", improving job quality and conditions for creating new jobs. The initiative is part of the **European Economic Recovery Plan** adopted in December 2008, aimed at reducing the impact of the economic crisis on the labour market. In reality, the effects of the economic crisis on unemployment were so dramatic that they jeopardised reaching the targets initially set. It seemed necessary to use adaptive strategies for the post-crisis period, allowing the adoption of a new view on employment.

Thus, the **Europe 2020 Strategy** was adopted by the European Council of 17 June 2010, against the backdrop of increased long-term challenges such as globalisation, pressure on resources and ageing of the population. It identifies the source of certain economic difficulties, lack of competitiveness and unemployment—in some European regions—and proposes a new economic vision, one that would build a smart, sustainable and inclusive economy, delivering high levels of employment, productivity and social cohesion.

In November 2017, at the Gothenburg Social Summit for Fair Jobs and Growth, the European Parliament, the European Council, and the European Commission adopted the **European Pillar of Social Rights** (EPSR) to advance the social dimension of European integration. The EPSR sets out 20 essential principles and rights in the areas of equal opportunities and access to the labour market; fair working conditions; and social protection and inclusion.[28] The EPSR constitutes a reference framework to monitor the employment and social performance of MS, to drive reforms at the national level and to serve as a compass for a renewed process of convergence across Europe.[29] MS have a major responsibility in implementation of the EPSR, and the Commission monitors their involvement "by reflecting the priorities of the EPSR in the analysis of measures taken and progress made at national level, by providing technical assistance, supporting benchmarking and promoting the exchange of good practices among MS and stakeholders".[30] On 8 May 2021, at the Porto Social Summit, the EPSR has been recognised as a fundamental element of the recovery, after the pandemic crisis.

The EPSR can be seen as a game changer; it created the proper context for further involvement of the social actors in the governance of the European Semester and to "socialise" the next EU strategy.[31] Particularly, the **Social Scoreboard** has

---

[27] Commission Communication, *New Skills for New Jobs Anticipating and matching labour market and skills needs*, COM(2008) 868/3.

[28] https://ec.europa.eu/info/sites/default/files/social-summit-european-pillar-social-rights-booklet_en.pdf.

[29] Council Decision No. 2019/1181/EU *on Guidelines for the Employment Policies of the Member States*, O.J. L 185/44 (2019).

[30] Commission Communication, *Monitoring the implementation of the European Pillar of Social Rights*, COM(2018)130.

[31] Vanhercke et al. (2020).

23 The EPSR has already proved to be an important element in the process of convergence of social policies and even a paradigm shift in the economic and social relationship within the EU, concertising the Commission's aim to earn a **"social triple A"** for Europe. EPSR not only develops existing rights, but also extends their applicability and goes beyond pre-existing limits. The **Action Plan** to implement the principles of the EPSR (adopted in March 2021) includes among the targets to be reached by 2030 that at least 78% of the population aged 20 to 64 to be in employment by 2030.

24 Indeed, the EPSR has begun to be considered in most of the European initiatives in the field. Notably, for example, it was followed by the Directive on transparent and predictable working conditions in the European Union[32] or by the Directive on work-life balance for parents and carers.[33] Also, in October 2020, the Commission published its proposal for a directive on adequate minimum wages in the European Union, seeking to ensure that minimum wages are set at an adequate level and every worker can earn a decent living.[34]

25 The **Social Fairness Package**, adopted by the Commission on March 2018 provides several measures, including establishing of a **European Labour Authority** (ELA), complementing previous initiatives to improve the rules for the posting of workers and the coordination of social security systems. ELA[35] is primarily aimed at supporting fair labour mobility within the EU, by facilitating access to information, carry out inspections and even mediating cross-border disputes between national authorities. Based on this initiative, ELA has been established as a permanent structure on 31 July 2019.

1.4. New Concerns in the Aftermath of COVID-19

26 The health crisis and the economic crisis that followed it, as well as the multiple political crises experienced in recent years did not reduce the concern for a coordinated strategy on employment. On the contrary, new instruments have been adopted, aimed at enabling the economic recovery of the MS, also with an important component related to employment. In response to the COVID-19 outbreak, a

---

[32] Council Directive (EU) 2019/1152 *on transparent and predictable working conditions in the European Union*, O.J. L 186/105 (2019).

[33] Council Directive (EU) 2019/1158 *on work-life balance for parents and carers*, O.J. L 188/79 (2019).

[34] *Proposal for a Directive of the European Parliament and of the Council on adequate minimum wages in the European Union*, COM(2020) 682.

[35] Parliament/Council Regulation No. 2019/1149/EU *establishing a European Labour Authority*, O.J. L 186/21 (2019).

temporary European support instrument was established: **Support to mitigate Unemployment Risks in an Emergency** (SURE), providing financial assistance for MS to protect jobs and workers through short-time work schemes or similar measures.

Moreover, the **Next Generation EU** (NGEU) fund of more than EUR 800 billion temporary recovery instrument was put in place a as one of the strongest community reactions in economic terms, but also in terms of employment.

The main component of the NGEU is the **Recovery and Resilience Facility** (RRF),[36] meant to mitigate the economic and social impact of the COVID-19 crisis. One of the general objectives of this facility is "fostering high quality employment creation" (Article 4).

Given the fact that "attention should be given to the risks of phasing out emergency measures without effective new policies in place to support workers and firms during the recovery", the **Commission** issued a **recommendation on an effective active support** to employment following the COVID-19 crisis.[37] The Recommendation includes measures to support job creation and employment that may be subsidised by the RRF as part of coherent packages of reforms and investments. It should be noted how the social component, initially a Cinderella of European policies, acquired a central place within them; even in periods of prolonged crisis a European recovery strategy is currently inconceivable without including references to employment and the quality of jobs.

2. European Employment Strategy

The idea of a strategy in the field of employment took shape in the Delors White Paper (→ para 5), which for the first time marked a concerted approach at the EU level to employment issues. It emerged even more clearly during the Essen European Council (→ para 6), but it was formalised only in the TEU-Amsterdam. Inspired by measures for economic convergence, the **European Employment Strategy** (EES) was implemented even before ratification of the Treaty. Thus, the first strategy was developed during the 1997 Summit in Luxembourg (→ para 10). It was essentially geared towards young people, with a view to reduce unemployment through training and participation in specific employment schemes. On this occasion, the concept of **employability** was introduced as a new human characteristic consisting of the ability to be employed, a trait of the person looking for a job, obtained through training and adaptive policies.

The EES made substantial progress in the fight against unemployment in Europe. The strategy was designed as a primary tool for setting and coordinating European priorities in this area, **priorities that will be addressed by each MS**.

---

[36] Parliament/Council Regulation (EU) 2021/241 *establishing the Recovery and Resilience Facility*, O.J. L 57/17 (2021).
[37] O.J. L 80/1 (2021).

Originally a response to EMU,[38] the EES gradually became autonomous and gained a voice of its own. As shown,[39] the EES marked an important paradigm shift: shifting the focus from the protection of employees, namely those formally integrated into the labour market, to employment creation ("getting people into employment"). This was also a reaction to the increasingly expensive social protection programmes in the context of low employment levels, especially given that the traditional instruments used to fight unemployment—for example, those of fiscal nature—could no longer be used because of the constraints imposed by the Stability and Growth Pact.[40] Fundamental to the EES is the use of a specific method (although it was subsequently largely imported into other sectors), namely the Open Method of Coordination (→ Article 146 TFEU para 9–21), as a voluntary form of governance.

32   The EES led to an increase in the legitimacy of European action in the field and of the concerted action to align national policies, while respecting the principle of **subsidiarity** (→ Article 149 TFEU para 15–17). The responsibility for the adoption and implementation of employment policies was not transferred from MS to the EU, but the approach had become multi-level. First, the goals are defined at the European level, then they are implemented in the MS, and then the results are monitored—back at the European level. MS may choose different methods, from the legislative to the contractual ones, with the contribution of the social partners, which would negotiate sector-level collective agreements with solutions for employment, but the results are correlated. National policies are thus subject to comparison, capable of putting pressure on decision-makers in the MS and facilitating the exchange of best practices. As it has been shown, "despite the role of the Commission in shaping the employment guidelines, the Member States dominate the EES. Subsidiarity plays a key role".[41]

33   **Active labour market policies,** which are emphasised more and more clearly, also play a major part in elaborating the EES. The EES has the following **components,** which are currently aligned to the European Pillar of Social Rights:

- Employment Guidelines reflecting common priorities for MS' employment policies (→ Article 148 TFEU para 11–19)
- National Reform Programmes (→ Article 148 TFEU para 20–22), which MS draw up to implement these Guidelines into national policy
- Joint Employment Reports (→ Article 148 TFEU para 30–32), adopted by the Commission and Council, which review the progress made at both national and community levels in response to the Employment Guidelines
- Country Specific Recommendations (→ Article 148 TFEU para 23–29)

---

[38] Pochet (2005), p. 46.
[39] Barnard (2012), p. 22.
[40] Barnard (2012), p. 22.
[41] Anderson (2015), p. 118.

Article 145 [Coordinated Strategy for Employment]

Another strategy that has been elaborated since 1992 is the **OECD Jobs Strategy**, which involves, as the EES, a type of cooperation and mutual monitoring based on a somewhat similar circular procedure. As noted, however,[42] the approach of the OECD Jobs Strategy is more academic, with a more pronounced neo-liberal view that differs to some extent from the EES, as the latter values social solidarity more highly, in conjunction with the efficiency of the market economy. 34

It has been said that the EES was "a way to 'depoliticize' the unemployment problem from its immediate national contingencies and to address it in a longer-term perspective".[43] According to various authors, the EES "is a political compromise aiming to exclude pure neo-liberal and social democratic approaches".[44] The fact is that the viability of the EES is the result of a **trans-political approach**, designed to release employment objectives from the contingency of purely political decision. 35

The aim is to create a new culture of entrepreneurship, social partners are encouraged to negotiate sectoral collective agreements to increase the adaptability of companies and, the necessity of a correlation between flexibility and security is gradually emerging (an idea that would generate the composite concept of flexicurity). It was the occasion for asserting one of the principles that would guide European policies from then on, namely **lifelong learning** as a formula for maintaining competitiveness on the labour market. 36

It has been remarked that one of the difficulties is the accurate assessment of the effectiveness of the strategy, as national and European strategy may not always be clearly distinguishable.[45] 37

The application of the EES entails the judicious use of the **European Social Fund** (ESF—established in 1958), under Articles 162–164 TFEU. Based on the EES, the ESF funding is implemented by the MS to support the National Reform Programmes (→ Article 148 TFEU para 20–22). And even if it is sometimes considered that the target groups and priorities of the ESF do not correspond exactly to those of the EES,[46] the EU's crusade through the most diverse instruments to boost employment and mitigate imbalances becomes sustainable only in the context in which EES can rely on a wise tailored ESF. Moreover, starting with 2021, the Commission proposed a new instrument, European Social Fund Plus (ESF+), merging a number of existing funds and programmes (→ Article 149 TFEU para 7). 38

---

[42] Velluti (2010), pp. 118–119.
[43] Goetschy (1999), p. 132.
[44] Pochet (2005), p. 58.
[45] Pochet (2005), p. 56.
[46] Casey (2009), p. 41.

3. Skilled, Trained and Adaptable Workforce

39 Under Article 145 TFEU, MS and the Union shall work together for promoting a "skilled, trained and adaptable workforce and labour markets responsive to economic change". This marks a new paradigm of employment in the EU, a new way to understand the effects of a changing society on employment. The issue of training and promoting a **skilled workforce** has not ceased to be among the constant concerns of European decision-makers, since the adoption of the title on employment.

40 This is even more true now, after the end of the COVID-19 crisis. Some studies show that once the economy recovers, Europe may have a shortage of skilled workers, particularly because there is a shrinking labor supply: Europe's working-age population is likely to shrink by 13.5 million (or 4%) due to aging by 2030.[47]

41 As a result, one of the integrated guidelines adopted for 2018[48] and maintained for the following years[49] is "Enhancing labour supply and improving access to employment, skills and competences", which notably includes addressing structural weaknesses in education and training systems, and providing quality and **inclusive education, training and life-long learning**. This is in fact an expression of the Principle 1 of the EPSR: "Everyone has the right to quality and inclusive education, training and life-long learning in order to maintain and acquire skills that enable them to participate fully in society and manage successfully transitions in the labour market". Consequently, according to the **Action plan on the implementation of the EPSR** of 4 March 2021, by 2030 at least 60% of all adults should participate in training every year.

42 In July 2020, the Commission presented a new plan to help individuals and businesses develop more and better skills, built upon the ten actions of the Commission's 2016 Skills Agenda. It contains **12 actions** focused on skills for jobs to ensure that the right to training and lifelong learning becomes a reality across Europe. The European Skills Agenda sets objectives to be achieved by 2025 (a so-called "skills revolution" facilitated by the opportunities offered by Next Generation EU → para 27).

43 **Adaptability** is a trait of the working individual that requires in itself an entrepreneurial attitude,[50] with respect to their careers. Like any entrepreneur faced with the imperatives of the new economy, the worker is able to adapt to changes in the market. Although there is support from the state, adaptability is

---

[47] Smit (2020), p. iv.

[48] Council Decision No. 2018/1215/EU *on Guidelines for the employment policies of the Member States*, O.J. L 224/4 (2018).

[49] Council Decision No. 2019/1181/EU *on Guidelines for the employment policies of the Member States*, O.J. L 185/44 (2019); Council Decision No. 2021/1868 *on Guidelines for the employment policies of the Member States*, O.J. L 379/1 (2021).

[50] The phrase "entrepreneurial employee" belongs to Klare (2004), p. 16.

primarily a matter of self-responsibility. The culture of adaptability and performance involves enhanced flexibility both for those who already have the status of employees and for those who are seeking employment. As a consequence, contractual flexibility is encouraged, but also that regarding organisation—for example, working time—in direct relation to employability.

4. Responsive Labour Markets

As MS began to turn their attention "from employment protection to employment promotion", the need to create labour markets responsive to economic change was reflected in an exemplary way by the creation and strategic taking on of the concept of **flexicurity**.[51] It was brought to the attention of analysts and policymakers by the Dutch sociologist *Ton Wilthagen* in the late 1990s. In spring 2006, the concept of flexicurity was put on the European agenda for the first time, and from then on it ceased to be a simple matter of academic discussion, becoming a strategy to reform the European labour market. Four mutually reinforcing principles were introduced: flexible and reliable work contracts, in accordance with labour laws, collective agreements and modern work organisation principles; the introduction of lifelong learning strategies, support for the continual adaptability of employees, particularly the most vulnerable in the labour market; effective active labour market policies to help employees find employment again after a period out of work; the modernisation of social security systems, to provide financial support which encourages employment and facilitates labour market mobility. Flexicurity became part of the European Employment Strategy.

Even thou the notion of flexicurity survived the economic crisis, flexicurity gradually slipped down the European agenda. From 2017, it disappeared as an explicit reference, the emphasis going on the EPSR principles (→ para 21), but the idea of a good balance between flexibility and security is not abandoned, both in theory and as a political decision.

44

45

5. Objectives

Article 145 TFEU aims to promote a skilled, trained and adaptable workforce and labour markets capable to respond to the economic changes of our time. Finally, these strategies on employment are aimed at achieving the objectives provided in Article 3.3, second sentence, TEU, especially the goal of **full employment** (which becomes a "high level of employment" in Article 147.1 sentence 1 TFEU) and social cohesion. MS are called upon to act alongside the EU as a whole to achieve the ambitious employment goals. Indeed, the employment chapter of the TFEU was

46

---

[51] Bekker and Mailand (2019). 142 et seqq.; Madsen (2014); Nardo and Rossetti (2013); Tangian (2010).

introduced and applied against the background of a disturbing unemployment rate, which has not decreased even in recent years.

The means to achieve these goals is the **coordination of employment strategies**, an attribute of the EU as defined by Article 5.2 TFEU, which provides that the Union shall take measures to ensure coordination of the employment policies of the MS, particularly by defining guidelines for these policies.[52] It does not imply that the policies have to be identical or even similar from one MS to another, but by using indicators that allow comparisons, it enables the identification of medium and long-term goals—common throughout the EU.

47   The need for concerted action to reduce the unemployment rate arises from the demographic evolution in Europe. Late access of youth to the labour market, low population growth and increased life expectancy of Europeans have led to concerns about the sustainability of national pension systems and the high risks of unemployment, challenging the entire **European Social Model**. This has been reaffirmed in respect of the new forms of work, Guidelines for the employment policies of the MS emphasising that "MS should ensure that employment relationships stemming from new forms of work maintain and strengthen Europe's social model".[53]

48   By setting a smaller number of objectives, the 2020 strategy managed to set priorities to eliminate the criticisms that had been raised regarding the heterogeneity of strategies. Naturally, coordinating strategies for employment is difficult, and even within each MS **controversies on the model to be followed** are extremely vivid. Therefore, achieving such goals is possible by the use of soft law methods, such as the Open Method of Coordination.

49   Creating jobs, however, is not sufficient in itself. Although the main focus of employment strategies is not on the protection of employees, but on conferring the status of employee to as many as possible, the objective of employment policies is also linked to the **quality of new jobs**. Especially as part-time work, fixed-term contracts or contracts not governed by labour law multiplied, the mere focus on creating jobs can lead to an increase in precarious work. The Lisbon Strategy in 2000 was meant to emphasise this idea. One step further, the 2020 Strategy has established the objective of creating an economy "based on knowledge, research and innovation, the promotion of more resource-efficient, greener and competitive markets, job creation and poverty reduction". In this context, the creation of green jobs against the general flexicurity background may be regarded as an imperative for the immediate future.

50   Job quality is not easy to measure. Several attempts to produce statistical indicators for monitoring of job quality have been made. However, as noted, "the progress observed thus far in developing job quality indicators at policy level has

---

[52] Article 5 TEU sets out the principles of conferral, subsidiarity and proportionality with respect to the limits of its powers. As noted, Article 3.1 point (i) TEC used the concept of "employment strategy" explicitly, as opposed to the current Article 5.2 TFEU, which only refers to the coordination capacity. See Kotzur, in Geiger et al. (2015), Article 145 TFEU para 3.

[53] Council Decision No. 2018/1215 *on Guidelines for the employment policies of the Member States*, O.J. L 224/4 (2018).

been hindered by conceptual confusion, the lack of a shared definition and disagreement on how to mold a multitude of work dimensions into a coherent comparative framework of indicators".[54]

Yet, the concern for creating jobs, especially in the difficult context that we are going through at present, and for reaching high standards in terms of their quality, is here to stay. The new technologies used in the performance of work and the challenges they bring are the starting point for many new initiatives, among which the Proposal for a Directive on improving working conditions in platform work[55] or the European Parliament resolution in favour of the right to disconnect.[56]

51

References[57]

Anderson, K. M. (2015). *Social policy in European Union.* Palgrave Macmillan.
Barnard, C. (2012). *EU employment law* (4th ed.). OUP.
Bekker, S., & Mailand, M. (2019). The European flexicurity concept and the Dutch and Danish flexicurity models: How have they managed the Great Recession? *Social Policy Administration, 53*(1), 142–155.
Bongardt, A., & Torres, F. (2012). Lisbon Strategy. In E. Jones, A. Menon, & S. Weatherill (Eds.), *The Oxford handbook of the European Union* (pp. 469–482). OUP.
Casey, B. (2009). Employment promotion. In M. Gold (Ed.), *Employment policy in the European Union. Origins, theories and prospects* (pp. 27–43). Palgrave Macmillan.
Dehousse, R. (2003). The open method of coordination: A new policy paradigm? *Les Cahiers européens de Sciences Po*, n° 03. Centre d'études européennes at Sciences Po.
Geiger, R., Khan, D.-E., & Kotzur, M. (Eds.). (2015). *European Union Treaties.* C.H. Beck/Hart.
Goetschy, J. (1999). The European Employment Strategy: Genesis and development. *European Journal of Industrial Relations, 5*(2), 117–137.
Heise, A. (2002). The 'Cologne process': A neglected aspect of European employment policy. *International Politics and Society, 2*(10), 88–102.
Klare, K. (2004). The horizons of transformative labour and employment law. In J. Conaghan, R. M. Fischl, & K. Klare (Eds.), *Labour law in an era of globalization. Transformative practices & possibilities* (pp. 3–30). OUP.
Madsen, P. K. (2014). *Danish flexicurity – Still a beautiful swan? Peer review on adjustments in the Danish flexicurity model in response to the crisis.* Publications Office of the European Union.
Mavrommati, S., & Papathanassiou, C. (2006). A modified open method of coordination in corporate governance. *European Business Law Review, 17*(6), 1637–1649.
Nardo, M., & Rossetti, F. (2013). *Flexicurity in Europe. Administrative agreement. JRC N°31962-2010-11 NFP ISP - Flexicurity 2. Final Report.* Publications Office of the European Union.
Nedergaard, P. (2006). Policy learning in the European Union: The case of the European Employment Strategy. *Policy Studies, 27*(4), 311–323.
Piasna, A., Burchell, B., & Sehnbruch, K. (2019). Job quality in European employment policy: One step forward, two steps back? *European Review of Labour and Research, 25*(2), 165–180.

---

[54] Piasna et al. (2019), p. 12.
[55] COM(2021) 762 final.
[56] 2019/2181(INL).
[57] All cited Internet sources in this comment have been accessed on 15 August 2022.

Pochet, P. (2005). The open method of co-ordination and the construction of social Europe. A historical perspective. In J. Zeitlin & P. Pochet (Eds.), *The open method of co-ordination in action. The European employment and social inclusion strategies* (pp. 37–82). Peter Lang.

Smit, S., Tacke, T., Lund, S., Manyika, J., & Thiel, L. (2020). *The future of work in Europe: Automation, workforce transitions, and the shifting geography of employment.* McKinsey Global Institute.

Tangian, A. (2010). Not for bad weather: Flexicurity challenged by the crisis. *ETUI Policy Brief – European Economic and Employment Policy*, Issue 3. ETUI.

Vanhercke, B., Ghailani, D., Spasova, S., & Pochet, P. (2020). *Social policy in European Union 1999-2019: The long an winding road.* ETUI.

Velluti, S. (2010). *New governance and the European Employment Strategy*. Routledge.

Weishaupt, J. T. (2011). *From the manpower revolution to the activation paradigm. Explaining institutional continuity and change in an integrating Europe.* Amsterdam University Press.

Weishaupt, J. T., & Lack, K. (2011). The European Employment Strategy: Assessing the status quo. *German Policy Studies, 7*(1), 9–44.

Article 146 [Promoting Employment]
(ex-Article 126 TEC)

1. Member States, through their employment policies, shall contribute to the achievement of the objectives referred to in Article 145[1, 2] in a way consistent with the broad guidelines of the economic policies of the Member States and of the Union adopted pursuant to Article 121(2).[3, 4]
2. Member States, having regard to national practices related to the responsibilities of management and labour,[5–7] shall regard promoting employment as a matter of common concern[8] and shall coordinate their action in this respect within the Council, in accordance with the provisions of Article 148.[9–21]

Contents

1. Role of the Member States 1
2. Broad Economic Policy Guidelines 3
3. Social Partners 6
4. "Common Concerns" 8
5. Open Method of Coordination 9
   5.1. The Open Method of Coordination as an Instrument of Soft Law 9
   5.2. Constituent Elements and Characteristics 14
   5.3. OMC Beyond Employment 17
   5.4. Advantages and Limitations 18
List of Cases
References

1. Role of the Member States

The aim of Article 146 TFEU is to determine the role of MS in terms of employment, and the relationship between national and European objectives. Indeed, MS are the main actors in employment policies,[1] policies in the field belong to them ("their employment policies"[2]) in the context of the **principle of subsidiarity**. The object of coordination is not necessarily institutions, but ideas, views, concepts, knowledge.[3] Not least, the role of MS has to be integrated into the full array of responsibilities for employment policies. As a result, Article 146.2 TFEU also imposes obligations: they "shall contribute", "shall regard", "shall coordinate". However, the requirement for MS to contribute to the objective of full employment does not give rise to a subjective position under public law of an individual person

---

[1] Barnard (2012), p. 22.
[2] See also Kotzur, in Geiger et al. (2015), Article 146 TFEU para 1.
[3] Pochet (2005), p. 42.

seeking employment.[4] Although free to organise their own policies, their approach is geared towards a common goal—enshrined in Article 145 TFEU, which in turn refers to Article 3 TEU. This normative ambivalence has led some authors to assert that the chapter on employment "sends mixed messages".[5]

2   This is precisely why the method of soft law, especially the OMC (→ para 9–13)—used to coordinate their policies—is best suited to maintain this balance of forces. Thus, employment policies are no less national, but they go hand in hand to achieve the objectives set at European level. The very concept of a **mutual learning programme** (→ Article 149 TFEU para 8–14) is centred on MS as key actors capable of providing and receiving knowledge. And the monitoring is arranged in such a way to enable mutual assessment rather than being carried out by supranational entities. MS shall evaluate each other, and the Commission's role is only one of surveillance.[6]

2. Broad Economic Policy Guidelines

3   The aim of the broad economic policy guidelines (BEPG) is to coordinate the economic policies of MS. They also aim at creating **smart, sustainable and inclusive growth** throughout the EU.[7] They cover macroeconomic developments and are adopted as recommendations according to a procedure established in Article 121.2 TFEU (→ Article 121 TFEU para 14–20).

In the context of the BEPG, specific employment guidelines are drawn up each year[8] (→ Article 148 TFEU para 11–19).

4   Based on these guidelines, MS develop their own policies and a number of country-specific recommendations may be addressed to them at the **European Semester**, which also have an integrated character. Therefore, the employment guidelines must be fully compatible with the broad economic guidelines addressed

---

[4] See Case C-233/12, *Gardella* (CJEU 4 July 2013) para 40, stating that Articles 145 TFEU to 147 TFEU lay down the objectives of and general measures for EU employment policy. The right asserted by the applicant in the main proceedings or the obligation for a MS to guarantee such a right cannot be inferred from those provisions.

[5] Kenner (2000), p. 123.

[6] See also Bongardt and Torres (2012), p. 475.

[7] Council Recommendation 2010/410/EU *on broad guidelines for the economic policies of the Member States and of the Union*, O.J. L 191/28 (2010).

[8] In 2018, the employment guidelines were aligned with the principles of the EPSR; in 2020, they integrated elements related to the consequences of the COVID-19 crisis, the green and digital transitions, and the UN Sustainable Development Goals; in 2021, they reflected the outcomes of the Porto Social Summit and the EPSR Action Plan; in 2022, they have been amended in the context of the post-COVID 19 environment, also reflecting recent policy elements in the context of the Russian invasion of Ukraine. See the *Explanatory Memorandum of the Proposal on guidelines for the employment policies of the Member States*, COM (2022) 241 final.

to MS; for some authors this may lead to the idea that the EU's economic and monetary objectives retain precedence over employment considerations.[9]

However, a change in the Commission's position needs to be emphasised. Since the adoption of the European Pillar of Social Rights (EPSR), currently the Commission is putting "greater focus on social priorities and put them on a par with economic objectives at the core of the annual cycle of economic governance".[10]

As an expression of the symmetric regulation of economic policies/employment strategies both Article 121.1 TFEU and Article 146.2 TFEU use the concept of "common concerns" (→ para 8; → Article 121 TFEU para 8 et seqq.). The need for **consistency with BGEP** is further be reiterated in Article 148.2, second sentence, TFEU (→ Article 148 TFEU para 19), and "the synergy between the EES, macroeconomic policy coordination and the process of economic reform" will be one of the constant concerns of the whole mechanism, as well as of some of its actors such as the Employment Committee.[11]

3. Social Partners

National practices are considered with respect to the distribution of responsibilities for employment policies between the government and the social partners. As regards terminology, it should be noted that in recent EU legislation the term "management and labour" is no longer used in favour of the more explicit "social partners". For example, Council Decision (EU) No. 2015/772 establishing the Employment Committee[12] specifically refers to the "social partners" in its Article 6, unlike the previous Council Decision No. 2000/98/EC,[13] which in its Article 5 was referring to "management and labour" (→ Article 150 TFEU para 9). Even more so, the **European Pillar of Social Rights** repeatedly refers to "social partners", notably in Principle 8 regarding social dialogue and involvement of workers: "The social partners shall be consulted on the design and implementation of economic, employment and social policies according to national practices."

Promoting employment is consistent with the rules and traditions of each MS and the involvement of the social partners emphasises the **decentralised nature of the OMC** in this field—at national, sub-national, cross-sectoral, and sectoral level. The procedure is bottom-up, and the social partners have not only the right but also the responsibility to engage in employment policies.

---

[9] Goetschy (1999), p. 125.

[10] Commission Communication, *Monitoring the implementation of the European Pillar of Social Rights*, COM(2018) 130 final, p. 4.

[11] Article 2.2 point (b) of Council Decision No. 2015/772/EU.

[12] Council Decision No. 2015/772/EU *establishing the Employment Committee and repealing Decision 2000/98/EC*, O.J. L 121/12 (2015).

[13] Council Decision No. 2000/98/EC *establishing the Employment Committee*, O.J. L 29/21 (2000).

At the beginning, some authors pointed out that although "the role of the social partners has been institutionalized, analysis has shown that the social partners have not been integrated fully into the decision-making processes."[14] The EES was subject to debate at European level, but less so at national level,[15] playing an even smaller role in negotiations between local social partners. The reference to the social partners was viewed as "rather vague"[16] and "the participation of labour and management in the EES has been widely recognized as one of its weakest parts."[17] It was considered that the mechanism by which the ambitious objective of "full employment" could be achieved is "extraordinarily fragile" in the absence of a solid social partnership to ensure a European social consensus on employment.[18]

However, since 2015, "steps towards a **more structured and timely involvement** of social partners in the compilation of key Semester documents have been taken",[19] since new procedural elements have been added to the process (such as the ex-ante consultation on the Annual Growth Survey). Since 2017, these developments took place especially in the light of the Principle 8 of the EPSR, on improving social dialogue and the involvement of workers. Currently, especially in the context of the prolonged crises that Europe is facing, the involvement of the social partners is even more accentuated. For instance, the 2022 Annual Sustainable Growth Survey notes that the systematic involvement of social partners is key for the success of the economic and employment policy coordination and implementation at all steps of the Semester cycle.[20]

4. "Common Concerns"

8 The idea of "common concerns" allows for cooperation and consensus-building, starting with the setting of goals to ways to achieve them. In the past, the OMC policies could be either national or union wide. By including the concept of "common concerns", an intermediate register is configured through which **national policies** that remain national are **subject to common goals**, allowing for European correlation of strategies. In the OMC, based on the objectives identified as "common concerns", MS use standard indicators and develop National Reform Programmes (→ Article 148 TFEU para 20–22). The concept of common concern is also used in Article 121.1 TFEU, referring to economic policies (→ Article 121

---

[14] Szyszczak (2006), p. 499.

[15] Casey (2009), p. 42.

[16] Rhodes (2005), p. 295.

[17] Rhodes (2005), p. 299.

[18] Veneziani (2012), p. 140.

[19] Sabato et al. (2017), p. 14.

[20] European Commission (2021), *2022 European Semester: Annual sustainable growth survey*, p. 16.

TFEU para 11–12). Thus, the employment strategies shall be correlated to the economic ones.

5. Open Method of Coordination

5.1. The Open Method of Coordination as an Instrument of Soft Law

Once it was acknowledged that there are common goals in terms of employment at European level, the identification of the suitable methods for achieving them required fine-tuning between the need for convergence and the need to maintain policies in the area at national level. When originally released, the EES was regarded rather as a complement to the EMU; lacking a **method to ensure its implementation**, it remained largely an aspiration. Only after the emergence of the OMC had the EES become a topic of intense interest.[21] Although not named as such, the OMC (→ Article 5 TEU para 31) was substantively introduced into employment by the chapter on this subject in the TEU-Amsterdam. The name itself was only established at the 2000 Lisbon Council.

The use of OMC marked a certain shift from the traditional approach to an alternative one, especially in areas where regulatory intervention at European level seems necessary but where it is difficult to reach a consensus on its content. The OMC was thus considered a "part of the inherent ability of the EU integration process to constantly reinvent itself as part of an evolutionary process of political and economic survival."[22] This method, which never takes the form of directives or regulations and is rather a form of **soft law**, is characterised by flexibility and by the ability to involve not only the government and Union actors, but also private actors within the civil society. As noted, the OMC is mainly based on the willingness of participants to learn from other participants and from their own failures.[23] In terms of regulation, soft law is preferable to hard law methods when objectives tend to change from period to period and centralised regulatory mechanisms do not acquire full legitimacy.[24]

The concept of "open" itself triggered a series of debates due to its ambivalence. OMC is "open" in the sense of being open to a **broad range of actors**, being transparent or maybe even implying that it is open to different ways of achieving common goals. In any way, the open character of the method requires **coordination across sectors** of employment policies, both at national and at European level, and emphasises the participation of social actors in order to enhance the quality of deliberative and mutual learning processes. Also, the very idea of "coordination"

---

[21] Rhodes (2005), p. 292.
[22] Szyszczak (2006), p. 487.
[23] Assinger (2020), p. 53.
[24] Hodson (2015), p. 185.

may not be very easy to apply among all MS. "The coordination must be seen, then, as a process rather than a stable framework".[25]

12   The method has proved to be effective in avoiding blockages in European decision-making, especially in matters such as employment, tending to cause controversy and lack of consensus. Since MS largely regard the issue of job creation to be a domestic issue that falls within national competence, the use of this instrument of soft law is particularly useful in **preserving the national character of employment policies**. OMC opens the way for mutual learning and exchange of best practices based on the use of indicators that allow for comparisons. Its starting point is the acceptance of the existence of a common problem, but with solutions that may differ at the national level; their repeated application may lead to the convergence of these solutions, especially under the impact of the exchange of best practices.

13   The OMC is seen as a **"third way of governance"** (not simple intergovernmental cooperation, not adoption of supranational policies, not fragmentation, not uniformity, not traditional policy-making at EU level, not intergovernmental diplomatic approach, not centralised regulation through binding legal instruments—regulations and directives, not solutions negotiated through collective bargaining agreements), adaptable in areas where MS would be reluctant to accept greater European intervention, "used in cases where EU institutions have limited power to develop community policies or resistance(s) from MS to EU policies".[26] It is not a legislative process, but rather is capable of generating, through the joint will of the MS, structural changes in employment policy.

5.2. Constituent Elements and Characteristics

14   Technically, the OMC led to the introduction of a common language and to effective steps taken on the ground through **comparable indicators** and **methods of statistical analysis**. Such assessments initially led to the development of comparative tables to show the performance and failures of each national policy on employment; at present, open criticism of a MS is avoided (among other things, amidst great disparities between the performance of each MS), but the comparison remains open to academic review.

15   At the 2000 Lisbon Council, the following **elements of the OMC** were identified:[27]

(a) fixing guidelines for the Union combined with specific timetables for achieving the goals which they set in the short, medium and long terms;

---

[25] Léonard et al. (2012), p. 57.

[26] Aliu (2022), p. 29.

[27] Lisbon European Council 2000, Presidency Conclusions, point 37. Available at https://www.europarl.europa.eu/summits/lis1_en.htm.

(b) establishing, where appropriate, quantitative and qualitative indicators and benchmarks against the best in the world and tailored to the needs of different MS and sectors as a means of comparing best practice;
(c) translating these European guidelines into national and regional policies by setting specific targets and adopting measures, taking into account national and regional differences;
(d) periodic monitoring, evaluation and peer review organised as mutual learning processes.

In order to achieve these objectives, the OMC has a range of features, including: **16**

- Respecting the **principle of subsidiarity** and its correlation with the **principle of convergence**, which consists in pursuing common objectives through inter-related actions without prejudice to the competences of the MS. Expectations for convergence are, however, long-term;
- Involving a **multitude of actors** at the regional and sub-regional level, interacting horizontally rather than vertically (NGOs, social partners, academic experts, etc.);
- **Transparency**, which enables benchmarking of performance and learning through comparison, as well as the wide dissemination of relevant information among all stakeholders.[28] However, there is a reverse proportionality between the degree of complexity of a mechanism—such as the OMC—due, inter alia, to the involvement of a very large number of actors and its availability, which may reduce the degree of transparency;
- **Flexibility**, adaptability according to the particularities and traditions of each MS, allowing specific diversity to be respected and considered,[29] without (necessarily) aiming at institutional and procedural uniformity. The direction is the same, speeds may vary;[30]
- The decentralised nature and **multi-level integration**—at least in intention, because there are opinions arguing that argue that the process is rather centralist and elitist;[31]
- The use of **statistics** and common and measurable indicators to compare national performance both between countries and from period to period. More and more indicators are being used in the OMC, which is becoming increasingly accurate, "suited to stimulate learning processes through reflexive self-evaluation".[32] OMC aims to improve the analytical capacities of MS, which is itself a method to stimulate performance. New indicators are used from year to year, such as, for example, the Social Scoreboard which accompanies the EPSR. It

---

[28] Hartlapp (2009), p. 11.
[29] "Diversity is here to stay, and it needs to be responded to adequately": see Scott and Trubek (2002), pp. 6–7; Pochet (2005), p. 52.
[30] Mosher (2000), p. 7.
[31] Rhodes (2005), pp. 299–300.
[32] Hartlapp (2009), p. 10.

includes headline indicators, used to compare MS' performance, based on two criteria: the level of the indicator itself, and the progress made in one year;
- **Cooperation, exchanges of information and best practices**. Best practices are defined, for example, in the context of MLP as specific policies "that have proven to be effective and sustainable in the field of employment, demonstrated by evaluation evidence and/or monitoring and assessment methods using process data and showing the potential for replication";[33]
- The **innovative character**, the ability to encourage MS to reassess already established national **strategies through the solutions chosen by other MS;**
- **The voluntary nature;**
- **Use of specific tools** (peer review, joint reports, benchmarking, good practices, transfer of know-how, action plans, monitoring, exchange projects etc.) that outline a multifaceted and flexible working method;
- **Absence of sanction mechanisms** (a feature of soft law). The Council may issue recommendations to MS if it deems necessary, but non-compliance is not subject to sanctions. It may not even be possible because of the lack of Union jurisdiction in this matter, but the absence of sanctions is sometimes considered to go hand in hand with a certain lack of efficiency. On the other hand, since the performance of each MS is public, and this is based on indicators which allow comparison with the other MS, such advertising can itself be considered as a type of "sanction", at least in terms of public image;
- Use of **management by objectives**, which refers to the monitoring and evaluation of progress by establishing common indicators for all MS.

5.3. OMC Beyond Employment

17   Due to the way it works, the OMC may also be used in other areas where the EU has no or only limited competence. It can be seen as an effective working method in different areas of European interest, such as culture, the fight against poverty, education, training, social protection and social inclusion, pensions, consumer care, research and innovation, enterprise promotion, information society, immigration etc. In each case, the procedure has some **specific elements** ranging from procedural steps to deadlines. Sometimes the OMC is used as an additional method designed to complement European legislative instruments in areas where they cannot be used. Although OMC pattern is employment, some successes in this area have made it possible and desirable to **transfer the method** in various fields, from tourism to immigration policies.

However, the particularity of OMC in the field of employment remains to be formally rooted in the TFEU itself; for this reason and due to the longer period during which the OMC has been used in this area, the method has become more

---

[33] European Commission, Database of national practices on European employment policies and measures; available at http://ec.europa.eu/social/main.jsp?langId=en&catId=1080.

Article 146 [Promoting Employment]

articulated in employment, than in any other field. As has already been said, "the EES tends to dominate OMC processes".[34] In terms of procedure, OMC is the only one in the EES which allows the use of **recommendations**. Inspired by this mechanism, the European social partners also use their own OMC,[35] identifying their most urgent priorities for action and a common framework for action.

5.4. Advantages and Limitations

Much has been written in the legal literature about the advantages of the OMC compared to regulation through "hard law" (centralised, through binding rules sanctioning non-application). Such analyses are carried out especially in the context of assessing the **overall effectiveness of "soft law" in employment policies**.[36] However, according to *Goetschy*, the search for more "porous frontiers" between the study of hard and soft law may be welcomed.[37]   18

Apart from the indisputable advantages of using the OMC, which is considered "a new mode of governance"[38] in such national-sensitive areas as employment, the mechanisms for effectively controlling the implementation of the "Guidelines" remain fragile. In any case, they fall outside the legal perimeter (conduct inconsistent with the established objectives may not be sanctioned). The Commission proposes, and the Council only draws up "recommendations" for MS in the specific field. The **voluntary character** of the method involves the initial will, but also the permanent reiteration of the will of MS to collaborate and to correlate their actions in the field of employment, even though a target set generally for the EU may be further away for some MS than for others. Therefore, OMC has often been regarded (because of its "soft law" nature) as a way of working, leaving much to be desired in terms of **efficiency**, with practically no real impact on MS.[39]   19

In reality, **evaluating the effectiveness of the OMC** itself poses considerable difficulties,[40] as it is not always easy to identify a causal link between the OMC and the progress made by a given MS in the field of employment. In addition, it is sometimes difficult to estimate "how far policy coordination and policy transfer can be attributed to OMC processes, and how far it can be attributed to other externalities",[41] as it is also difficult to isolate the determining cause in the case of a set of policies and European processes, influences from a number of international bodies   20

---

[34] Szyszczak (2006), p. 494.
[35] Müllensiefen (2012), p. 27.
[36] Trubek and Trubek (2005), pp. 343–364.
[37] Goetschy (2012), p. 191.
[38] Scott and Trubek (2002), p. 1.
[39] For a discussion of the pros and cons of the OMC, see Zeitlin (2005), pp. 23–24; Armstrong (2018), pp. 58–60.
[40] Zeitlin (2005), p. 27.
[41] Szyszczak (2006), p. 497.

(such as the ILO or the IMF) or other national political events, such as a change of government.[42] On the contrary, some authors question the **legitimacy of the OMC** in relation to the proclaimed competence of the MS in developing employment policies.

21 The method has thus been subject to various **criticisms**, ranging from lack of effectiveness to lack of legitimacy. Most of the features listed above (→ para 16) are often questioned: compliance with the principle of subsidiarity, decentralisation, transparency—one by one the subject of critical analysis. The fact is that OMC has ceased to be a simple experimental method and by being applied for 20 years has become a classic. A number of empirical studies have proved that the OMC, especially in employment, is likely to cause or facilitate a number of cognitive or programmatic mutations.[43] Open to experimental approaches, the OMC is better shielded against risks than traditional methods and may have the ability to stimulate national creativity.

List of Cases

CJEU 04.07.2013, C-233/12, *Gardella*, ECLI:EU:C:2013:449 [cit. in para 1]

References[44]

Aliu, Y. (2022). New governance in the European Union: OMC. *Mediterranean Journal of Social Sciences, 13*(1), 25–31.
Armstrong, K. A. (2018). The open method of coordination: Obstinate or obsolete? In R. Schütze & T. Tridimas (Eds.), *Oxford principles of European Union law: The European Union legal order* (Vol. I, pp. 777–807). OUP.
Assinger, P. (2020). *Education and training politics in Europe: A historical analysis with special emphasis on adult and continuing education.* LIT Verlag.
Barnard, C. (2012). *EU employment law* (4th ed.). OUP.
Bongardt, A., & Torres, F. (2012). Lisbon strategy. In E. Jones, A. Menon, & S. Weatherill (Eds.), *The Oxford handbook of the European Union* (pp. 469–482). OUP.
Casey, B. (2009). Employment promotion. In M. Gold (Ed.), *Employment policy in the European Union. Origins, theories and prospects* (pp. 27–43). Palgrave Macmillan.
Geiger, R., Khan, D.-E., & Kotzur, M. (Eds.). (2015). *European Union Treaties.* C.H. Beck/Hart.
Goetschy, J. (1999). The European employment strategy: Genesis and development. *European Journal of Industrial Relations, 5*(2), 117–137.
Goetschy, J. (2012). The Lisbon Strategy, industrial relations and social Europe: An assessment of theoretical frameworks and policy developments. In S. Smismans (Ed.), *The European Union and industrial relations. New procedures, new context* (pp. 190–205). Manchester University Press.

---

[42] Zeitlin (2009), p. 242.

[43] Zeitlin (2009), p. 217. The author also notes the mobilisation of statistical capacities at the national level.

[44] All cited Internet sources in this comment have been accessed on 15 August 2022.

Hartlapp, M. (2009). Learning about policy learning. Reflections on the European employment strategy. In S. Kröger (Ed.), *What we have learnt: Advances, pitfalls and remaining questions in OMC research. European Integration online Papers (EIoP)*, Special Issue 1(13).

Hodson, D. (2015). Policy-making under economic and monetary union: Crisis, change, and continuity. In H. Wallace, M. A. Pollack, & A. R. Young (Eds.), *Policy–making in the European Union* (7th ed., pp. 166–195). OUP.

Kenner, J. (2000). The paradox of social dimension. In P. Lynch, N. Neuwahl, & W. Reed (Eds.), *Reforming the European Union from Maastricht to Amsterdam* (pp. 108–129). Longman.

Léonard, E., Parin, E., & Pochet, P. (2012). The European sectoral social dialogue as a tool for the coordination across Europe? In S. Smismans (Ed.), *The European Union and industrial relations. New procedures, new context* (pp. 56–78). Manchester University Press.

Mosher, J. (2000). Open method of co-ordination: Functional and political origins. *ECSA Review, 13*(3), 2–7.

Müllensiefen, T. (2012). The European cross-sectoral social dialogue between autonomous action and regulatory involvement. In S. Smismans (Ed.), *The European Union and industrial relations. New procedures, new context* (pp. 25–40). Manchester University Press.

Pochet, P. (2005). The open method of co-ordination and the construction of social Europe. A historical perspective. In J. Zeitlin & P. Pochet (Eds.), *The open method of co-ordination in action. The European employment and social inclusion strategies* (pp. 37–82). Peter Lang.

Rhodes, M. (2005). In H. Wallace, M. A. Pollack, & A. R. Young (Eds.), *Employment policy: Between efficacy and experimentation* (5th ed., pp. 279–304). Policy–making in the European Union, OUP.

Sabato, S., Vanhercke, B., & Spasova, S. (2017). *Listened to, but not heard? Social partners' multilevel involvement in the European Semester*. OSE research paper; Brussels.

Scott, J., & Trubek, D. M. (2002). Mind the gap: Law and new approaches to governance in the European Union. *European Law Journal*, 1–18.

Szyszczak, E. (2006). Experimental governance: The open method of coordination. *European Law Journal*, 486–502.

Trubek, D. M., & Trubek, L. G. (2005). Hard and soft law in the construction of social Europe: The role of the open method of co-ordination. *European Law Journal*, 343–364.

Veneziani, B. (2012). The role of social partners in the Lisbon strategy. In N. Brunn, K. Lörcher, & I. Schömann (Eds.), *The Lisbon strategy and social Europe*. Hart Publishing.

Zeitlin, J. (2005). The open method of co-ordination in question. In J. Zeitlin & P. Pochet (Eds.), *The open method of co-ordination in action. The European employment and social inclusion strategies* (pp. 19–35). Peter Lang.

Zeitlin, J. (2009). The open method of coordination and reform of national social and employment policies: Influences, mechanisms, effects. In J. Zeitlin & M. Heidenreich (Eds.), *Changing European employment and welfare regimes: The influence of the open method of coordination on national reforms* (pp. 214–244). Routledge.

Article 147 [High Level of Employment]
(ex-Article 127 TEC)

1. The Union shall contribute to a high level of employment by encouraging cooperation between Member States and by supporting and, if necessary, complementing their action.[1–3] In doing so, the competences of the Member States shall be respected.[4–6]
2. The objective of a high level of employment shall be taken into consideration in the formulation and implementation of Union policies and activities.[7–11]

Contents

1. Role of the European Union 1
2. Competences of the Member States 4
3. High Level of Employment 7

List of Cases
References

1. Role of the European Union

While Article 146 TFEU defines the role of MS in reaching employment objectives, Article 147.1 TFEU provides the general role of the Union in this respect. Thus, the EU shall "actively encourage, facilitate, and implement policy coordination and transfer."[1] Article 147.1 TFEU is programmatic,[2] proposing a high level of employment with the **contribution of the Union**; it has a supporting role, which cannot jeopardise the **primary role of MS**. Indeed, the EU would contribute to a high level of employment by encouraging cooperation between MS and by supporting and, if necessary, complementing their action. The objective of a high level of employment is to be considered in the formulation and implementation of EU's policies and activities.[3] The concrete way in which the role of the Union can be fulfilled is to be detailed in the subsequent articles.

For now, the focus is on the adjacent nature of the role of the Union; it "encourages", "supports" or "complements". The question of the relation between the competence of the Union and that of the MS is crucial in such sensitive areas as employment, so that the **principle of subsidiarity** should be established as a starting point. Developing common European strategies must therefore be achieved without questioning the competence of MS to develop their own policies in this area.

1

2

---

[1] Szyszczak (2006), p. 490.
[2] Kotzur, in Geiger et al. (2015), Article 147 TFEU para 1.
[3] Case C-110/03, *Belgium v Commission* (ECJ 14 April 2005) para 65.

© Springer Nature Switzerland AG 2022
R. Böttner, H.-J. Blanke (eds.), *Treaty on the Functioning of the European Union – A Commentary*, Springer Commentaries on International and European Law, https://doi.org/10.1007/16559_2022_52

3   Such a balance between the participants can be established in terms of procedure by the **Open Method of Cooperation (OMC)**, which, on a voluntary basis, respecting diversity and subsidiarity, allows MS to be the main actors in employment (→Article 146 TFEU para 9–13). A concrete way to encourage cooperation among MS involves the use of **incentive measures** (→ Article 149 TFEU para 5–7): exchanges of information and best practices, providing comparative analyses, promoting innovative approaches and evaluating experiences accumulated by each MS, using budgetary resources provided by the European Social Fund, and since 2021, the European Social Fund Plus (→ Article 149 TFEU para 7).

2. Competences of the Member States

4   Concerns about preserving the limits of competence and the principle of subsidiarity run through the entire Title IX TFEU. More specifically, the idea of **respecting MS' competence** is reiterated in Article 146.1 TFEU ("*their* employment policies"), Article 147.1, second sentence, TFEU ("the competence of the Member States shall be respected"), Article 150.2 TFEU ("those measures shall not include harmonisation of laws and regulations of the Member States")—to mention only provisions directly referring to these competences. And the terminology used in Title IX leads to the same conclusion: MS "shall coordinate their action" (Article 146.2 TFEU), and the EU "shall contribute", "by encouraging", "by supporting", "by complementing" (Article 147.1, first sentence, TFEU), the Council may "make recommendations to Member States" (Article 148.4, second sentence, TFEU), the European Parliament and the Council "may adopt incentive measures designed to encourage" and "to support" (Article 149.1 TFEU).

5   However, this somewhat redundant emphasis on the limits of the Union's prerogatives failed to protect the mechanism for **cooperation in employment**, the European Employment Strategy and OMC from criticism and fears. Thus, some authors saw the OMC as a discreet but determined way for the Union to interfere in matters that would otherwise fall within the exclusive competence of the MS. The OMC has sometimes been perceived as a potential threat to the Community Method, a subversive means of affecting national sovereignty and enforcing the limits of jurisdiction assigned to the EU, which may affect the very legitimacy of the procedure. For example, the Report on institutional and legal implications of the use of "soft law" instruments,[4] drafted by the EP's Committee on Legal Affairs, has shown that "whereas no procedure is laid down for consulting Parliament on the proposed use of soft-law instruments, such as recommendations and interpretative communications" might be considered "the open method of coordination to be legally dubious, as it operates without sufficient parliamentary participation and judicial review; believes that it should therefore be employed only

---

[4] Report *on institutional and legal implications of the use of 'soft law' instruments*, 2007/2028(INI) (2007).

in exceptional cases and that it would be desirable to consider how Parliament might become involved in the procedure."

In the 20 years of its application, the OMC does not seem to confirm these fears. On the contrary, as we have shown (→ Article 146 TFEU para 17), the **system of coordinating national strategies has been exported to many other areas**, and measures of support and encouragement by the EU and its bodies have not been perceived (or only rarely) as aggressively intrusive by MS. Today's scholars affirm, "policy coordination is alive and well in the form of the European Semester".[5] As for the effectiveness of these methods and whether they have really led to a reduction in unemployment, this is a different matter.

3. High Level of Employment

While Article 3.3 TEU refers to "full employment" (→ Article 3 TEU para 38), the text of Article 147 TFEU enshrines a more realistic objective[6]—that of "high level of employment". The objective of "high level of employment" is also found in **Article 9 TFEU**, which establishes a **horizontal clause** able to substantiate (although without forming a legal basis as such) the social perspective for developing and implementing EU policies (→ Article 9 TFEU para 7).[7] But how high must the employment rate be to be (considered) high?

The concrete objectives of the European employment strategies have fluctuated, being partly compromised by the **economic crisis**. Thus, the target for 2010 was to achieve an overall employment rate of 70%, an employment rate of 60% for women and an employment rate of 50% for those aged between 55 and 64. However, the employment trends have reversed as a result of the economic crisis on the European labour market. In 2009, the employment rate fell to 69.0%.

Overcoming the economic crisis has allowed the setting of higher objectives in terms of the employment rate. One of the key targets of the Europe 2020 strategy concerning employment was to have at least 75% of the active population (20–64 year olds) in work, a goal which again could not be reached, this time by the COVID-19 crisis.

Later, the European Pillar of Social Rights Action Plan brought with it a new target, and also a precise deadline: at least 78% of the population aged 20 to 64 should be in employment by 2030. Reaching an employment rate of 78% is an ambitious plan, but it seems feasible considering the current recovery, after the

---

[5] Armstrong (2018), p. 836.
[6] Kotzur, in Geiger et al. (2015), Article 147 TFEU para 3.
[7] Although the horizontal application of this objective "is to be welcomed", some scholars consider that "it is less clear how it can be ensured in practice and what type of results can be expected as well as problems of how to measure them". See, Velluti (2018), p. 138.

decrease recorded during the COVID-19 crisis. Thus, the EU employment rate (for people aged 20–64) reached in 2021 at 73.5%, surpassing pre-pandemic levels.

11   The active support for employment constitutes Principle 4 of the **European Pillar of Social Rights**, which affirms that "Everyone has the right to timely and tailor-made assistance to improve employment or self-employment prospects".

List of Cases

ECJ 04.04.2005, C-110/03, *Belgium v Commission*, ECLI:EU:C:2005:223 [cit. in para 1]

References[8]

Armstrong, K. A. (2018). The open method of coordination: Obstinate or obsolete? In R. Schütze & T. Tridimas (Eds.), *Oxford principles of European Union law: The European Union legal order* (Vol. I, pp. 777–807). OUP.
Geiger, R., Khan, D.-E., & Kotzur, M. (Eds.). (2015). *European Union Treaties*. C.H. Beck/Hart.
Szyszczak, E. (2006). Experimental governance: The open method of coordination. *European Law Journal, 12*(4), 486–502.
Velluti, S. (2018). Article 147 TFEU. In E. Ales, M. Bell, O. Deinert, & S. Robin-Olivier (Eds.), *International and European labour law: Article-by-article commentary* (pp. 136–138). Nomos/Beck/Hart.

---

[8] All cited Internet sources in this comment have been accessed on 15 August 2022.

Article 148 [Employment Guidelines]
(ex-Article 128 TEC)

1. The European Council shall each year consider the employment situation in the Union and adopt conclusions thereon,[1] on the basis of a joint annual report by the Council[2] and the Commission.[3]
2. On the basis of the conclusions of the European Council, the Council, on a proposal from the Commission and after consulting the European Parliament, the Economic and Social Committee, the Committee of the Regions and the Employment Committee referred to in Article 150, shall each year draw up guidelines[4–10] which the Member States shall take into account in their employment policies.[11–18] These guidelines shall be consistent with the broad guidelines adopted pursuant to Article 121(2).[19]
3. Each Member State shall provide the Council and the Commission with an annual report on the principal measures taken to implement its employment policy in the light of the guidelines for employment as referred to in paragraph 2.[20–22]
4. The Council, on the basis of the reports referred to in paragraph 3 and having received the views of the Employment Committee, shall each year carry out an examination of the implementation of the employment policies of the Member States in the light of the guidelines for employment. The Council, on a recommendation from the Commission, may, if it considers it appropriate in the light of that examination, make recommendations to Member States.[23–29]
5. On the basis of the results of that examination, the Council and the Commission shall make a joint annual report to the European Council on the employment situation in the Union and on the implementation of the guidelines for employment.[30–32]

Contents

1.	Preliminary Considerations	1
2.	Procedure	4
3.	Employment Guidelines	11
4.	National Reform Programmes	20
5.	Country-Specific Recommendations	23
6.	Joint Employment Report	30

References

1. Preliminary Considerations

The deliberative process specific to the OMC is cyclical and iterative. The role of Article 148 TFEU is to determine the **procedure for coordinating national**

1

strategies at Union level as well as to outline the mode of cooperation between the MS and the EU in implementing these strategies. It comprises a division of roles between European institutions and a description of the procedural steps that the TFEU provides for to achieve the objectives under Article 3 TEU.

2   The **Council**, composed of one representative of each MS at ministerial level (Article 16.2 TEU), is the body competent to develop guidelines consistent with the broad guidelines adopted under Article 121.2 TFEU. The implementation of the guidelines is also examined by the Council, which is also the body that, on the recommendation of the Commission, may adopt recommendations to MS. Under Article 16.3 TEU, the Council shall act by qualified majority voting. Since the development of guidelines is carried out on a Commission's proposal, Article 293.1 TFEU becomes applicable, according to which the Commission's proposal can only be amended by the Council acting unanimously. This makes it more difficult for the ministers of the MS to overturn the Commission's proposals (→ Article 293 TFEU para 11).

3   The role of the **Commission** is not as important as in adopting hard law, but it can hardly be overlooked. The Commission monitors the National Reform Programmes and elaborates reports at European level.

2. Procedure

4   The procedure described is **circular,** meaning that the results declared by the MS and analysed based on the common reference indicators influence the goals set for the next cycle. Due to its circular nature, virtually "there is no clear demarcation between rule-making and rule-implementation".[1] Once the process is complete, it starts all over again, seeking to draw on past experience.

5   The procedure corresponds to the **European Semester** in an annual cyclic process of economic and budgetary coordination, intended to reveal the progress made in achieving the Europe 2020 objectives. Introduced in 2011, the European Semester includes a six-month period in which MS' budgetary policies are examined. Indeed, under Article 2-a of Council Regulation (EC) No. 1466/97,[2] the European Semester includes:

(a) the formulation, and the surveillance of the implementation, of the broad guidelines of the economic policies of the MS and of the Union (broad economic policy guidelines) under Article 121.2 TFEU;
(b) the formulation, and the examination of the implementation, of the employment guidelines that must be considered by MS under Article 148.2 TFEU (employment guidelines);

---

[1] Szyszczak (2006), p. 495.
[2] As amended by Council Regulation (EU) No. 1175/2011 *amending Council Regulation (EC) No. 1466/97 on the strengthening of the surveillance of budgetary positions and the surveillance and coordination of economic policies*, O.J. L 306/12 (2011).

Article 148 [Employment Guidelines]

(c) the submission and assessment of MS' stability or convergence programmes under this Regulation;
(d) the submission and assessment of MS' national reform programmes supporting the Union's strategy for growth and jobs and established in line with the guidelines and with the general guidance to MS issued by the Commission and the European Council at the beginning of the annual cycle of surveillance;
(e) the surveillance to prevent and correct macroeconomic imbalances under Regulation (EU) No. 1176/2011.[3]

The European Semester starts each year with the publication of the Annual Growth Survey, setting out the broader EU objectives for the year to come.[4] The Commission also issues an **Alert Mechanism Report**, identifying countries that may be affected by economic imbalances.

It should be stressed that the European Semester has undergone a progressive socialisation process. As a series of studies attest, "this shift was visible at the level of substantive policy orientations, in terms of a growing emphasis on social objectives in the Annual Growth Survey and especially the Countries Specific Recommendations".[5] This trend is amplified after the adoption of European Pillar of Social Rights (EPSR), whose implementation is being analysed through the Social Scoreboard,[6] currently incorporated in the European Semester policy cycle.

Indeed, according to the Commission Communication entitles "Monitoring the implementation of the European Pillar of Social Rights"[7] the Commission "has mainstreamed social priorities across the board, fully acknowledging the social dimension of everything it does". This includes the European Semester of policy coordination, where the "Commission has put greater focus on social priorities and put them on a par with economic objectives at the core of the annual cycle of economic governance", reflecting the priorities of the European Pillar of Social Rights.

With the adoption of the **Recovery and Resilience Facility**,[8] the importance of the European semester has grown immensely, as today the Semester constitutes a governance framework for the RRF. Even though some hesitations have been expressed about the extent to which the European Semester is appropriate for

---

[3] Parliament/Council Regulation (EU) No. 1176/2011 *on the prevention and correction of macroeconomic imbalances*, O.J. L 306/25 (2011).

[4] Notably, the current Annual Survey considers "the need to adapt to the processes under the Recovery and Resilience Facility"; European Commission, *2022 European Semester: Annual sustainable growth survey*, COM(2021) 740 final.

[5] Zeitlin and Vanhercke (2018), p. 167.

[6] The Social Scoreboard is considered a "key tool for informing and reinforcing the social dimension of the European Semester process, mainly by providing clear social indicators and data". See Ryszka (2021), p. 139.

[7] Commission Communication, *Monitoring the Implementation of the European Pillar of Social Rights*, COM(2018) 130 final.

[8] Parliament/Council Regulation (EU) 2021/241 *establishing the Recovery and Resilience Facility*, O.J. L 57/17 (2021).

managing the RRF,[9] the incorporation of the RRF and the Semester gives rise to "important synergies between the new Facility and the established economic governance framework".[10]

8   The **procedural phases** are the following:

(a) The European Council, which under Article 15.1 TEU has been given the power to set "general political directions and priorities" for the Union, periodically (annually) reviews the employment situation in the MS.
(b) The Council and the European Commission prepare a joint annual report.
(c) The Council adopts conclusions based on this joint report.
(d) The European Commission proposes policy guidelines.
(e) The European Council consults the EP, the Economic and Social Committee, the Committee of the Regions and the Employment Committee (Article 150 TFEU) on the future employment guidelines.
(f) The Council elaborates the employment guidelines, correlated with the broad economic policy guidelines (Article 121.2 TFEU).
(g) MS develop national policies on employment taking into account these guidelines.
(h) MS provide the Council and the Commission with an annual report on measures taken to implement their employment policies, taking into account the guidelines (Article 148.3 TFEU).
(i) The Employment Committee issues an opinion, forwarding it to the Council (Article 148.4 TFEU).
(j) The Council examines the implementation of the national employment policies.
(k) The Commission recommends to the Council to make recommendations country-specific recommendations (CSR) to MS.
(l) The Council makes recommendations to MS if they are considered necessary.
(m) The Council and the Commission draw up a joint annual report on employment in the EU and the implementation of the guidelines (Article 148.5 TFEU).
(n) The report is presented to the European Council.

9   As it has been shown, "the emphasis in open co-ordination is on process, not on substance".[11] The **process is iterative**: setting the objectives—elaborating the guidelines—identifying measurable indicators—preparing National Reform Programmes—their monitoring and evaluation—adopting recommendations—elaborating the guidelines for the next phase.

10   We may now note that the type of documents produced during this process belongs to what is known as **soft law**: "Presidency conclusions, Commission communications, annual reports, Employment guidance - all fall into the category

---

[9] See, for instance, D'Erman and Verdun (2022), pp. 3–20; Creel et al. (2021), pp. 1–8.
[10] Moschella (2020), p. 8.
[11] Tsakatika (2004), p. 94.

of soft law: they are no more than methods of Union guidance or rules which create an expectation that the conduct of Member States will be in conformity with them, but without any accompanying legal obligation".[12]

3. Employment Guidelines

With employment now enshrined in a separate title since the TEU-Amsterdam, mechanisms for coordinating these national strategies are defined according to a model similar to that established in the field of economic policies. In legal terms, non-compliance with these guidelines does not entail sanctions. The MS "**shall take into account**" the guidelines; the verb, although lacking normative or imperative value, establishes a certain obligation to align national policies with European guidelines. It is also worth mentioning that the Employment Guidelines include quantitative targets, most of which are precise, concrete and measurable objectives, which usually makes them more useful than if they consisted of mere employment aspirations. 11

Starting with 2018, the guidelines were aligned with the principles of the **European Pillar of Social Rights**. 12

Employment guidelines are **specific documents** which "cannot be assigned clearly to a specific act of legislation".[13] Indeed, they are neither recommendations (specific recommendations may be issued based on the report on the application of the guidelines into national policies,) nor, naturally, directives as they are not binding. 13

The guidelines are also the result of a **consultation procedure** involving the EP, the Economic and Social Committee, the Committee of Regions and the Employment Committee. By incorporating them into the NRPs, the guidelines should be subject of a wider consultation process involving national experts, local representatives of the social partners and the civil society, local authorities, depending on the particularities of each MS. 14

However, some authors highlight an absence of reference to **the role of subnational public policies or the social partners** in preparing the annual report. This report remains essentially a work of government.[14] Currently however, the Guidelines for the employment policies of the MS expressly provide that "while the Integrated Guidelines are addressed to Member States and the Union, they should be implemented in partnership with all national, regional and local authorities, closely involving parliaments, as well as the social partners and representatives of civil society".[15] 15

---

[12] Barnard (2012), p. 63.
[13] Kotzur, in Geiger et al. (2015), Article 148 TFEU para 2.
[14] Borragán and Smismans (2012), p. 126.
[15] European Commission, *Proposal for a Council Decision on guidelines for the employment policies of the Member States*, COM (2022) 241 final Recital 12.

16 The number of the guidelines has been limited, with a view to ensure **increased clarity**. The current (revised) set of integrated guidelines include:

- Guideline 5: Boosting the demand for labour
- Guideline 6: Enhancing labour supply: access to employment, skills and competences[16]
- Guideline 7: Enhancing the functioning of labour markets and the effectiveness of social dialogue
- Guideline 8: Promoting equal opportunities for all, fostering social inclusion and combatting poverty

These guidelines for the employment policies of the MS reflects the sinusoid of periods of stability and crisis. It currently includes references to climate change and environment-related challenges, globalisation, digitalisation, artificial intelligence, teleworking, the platform economy and demographic change, but also COVID-19 crisis (in 2020 and 2021)[17] or post-COVID-19 environment or elements of particular relevance in the context of the Russian invasion of Ukraine (in 2022).[18]

17 Implementing Integrated Guidelines is facilitated by the **European Social Fund Plus** (ESF+),[19] established for the period of 2021–2027 and by the **Recovery and Resilience Facility** promoting the Union's economic, social and territorial cohesion by improving the resilience, crisis preparedness, adjustment capacity and growth potential of the MS.[20]

18 The MS consider these guidelines in their employment policies and reform programmes, then report them in line with Article 148.3 TFEU.

19 The Employment guidelines are in line with the **broad economic policy guidelines** (BEPG), which deal with macroeconomic and structural policies for the EU and each MS (→ Article 120 para 11 et seqq., 42; → Article 121 TFEU para 13–22; → Article 146 TFEU para 3–4). The BEPG of the MS and of the Union set out in Council Recommendation (EU) 2015/1184[21] and the Guidelines for the Employment Policies of the Member States form the Integrated Guidelines for Implementing the Europe 2020 Strategy.

---

[16] For an analysis of Guideline 6 on the adapted work environment for people with disabilities, see Vanhegen and Hendrickx (2020), p. 161.

[17] Council Decision (EU) 2020/1512 *on guidelines for the employment policies of the Member States*, O.J. L 344/22 (2020) and Council Decision (EU) 2021/1868 *on guidelines for the employment policies of the Member States*, O.J. L 379/1 (2021).

[18] European Commission, *Proposal for a Council Decision on guidelines for the employment policies of the Member States*, COM (2022) 241 final, Recital 9.

[19] Parliament/Council Regulation (EU) 2021/1057 *establishing the European Social Fund Plus (ESF+)*, O.J. L 231/21 (2021).

[20] *Joint Employment Report 2022* as adopted by the EPSCO Council on 14 March 2022.

[21] Council Recommendation (EU) 2015/1184, *on broad guidelines for the economic policies of the Member States and of the European Union*, O.J. L 192/27 (2015).

4. National Reform Programmes

In April, in the light of the Employment Guidelines received, MS submit their policy plans to be assessed at the EU level. Such policy plans were originally called National Action Plans; at the 2005 European Council, their transformation into National Reform Programmes (NRPs) (appreciated as "much broader and less explicit"[22]) was decided. Currently, the NRP includes **reports on developments in the field of employment**, but also concerning the micro and macro-economic situation. NRP are accompanied by a stability programme (for euro area countries) or a convergence programme (for non-euro area countries). 20

Initially, some authors signalled the lack of involvement of the **social partners** in drafting NRPs. NRPs were considered to involve a very small number of actors: "responsibility for preparing NRPs is often entrusted to departments specialised in international policies".[23] 21

Since 2014, however, the Commission creates new procedures for the involvement of EU social partners. Besides, important changes in the **Semester timeline** left the social partners the necessary time to intervene with their own input. It appears that the procedures for adopting the plans at national level are in the process of reaching their full potential, allowing the transformation of NRPs into the expected strategic documents. 22

5. Country-Specific Recommendations

In May each year, the European Commission assesses the stability or convergence programmes and the National Reform Programmes and proposes country-specific recommendations (CSRs) to each MS. The CSRs are discussed, and in July of each year the **European Council endorses the CSRs**, thus formally closing the "European" cycle of the Semester. The implementation phase then starts in MS. Recommendations are sent to MS before they draw up their national budget. 23

Recommendations are an important tool in the process of adopting the European Employment Strategy (→ Article 145 TFEU para 30–38). They differ substantively from the recommendations made, for instance, for an excessive deficit based on Article 126.7 TFEU, which may lead to sanctions under Article 126.11 TFEU in case of non-compliance.[24] The recommendations issued by the Council based on Article 148.4 TFEU cannot lead to sanctions, at least not legal sanctions. Sanctions usually come from the public opinion, given that each MS's performance in a particular area is public and is also presented by means of a set of indicators that allow comparison with the other MS (the so-called "**name and shame mechanisms**"). 24

---

[22] Weishaupt and Lack (2011), p. 18.
[23] Hartlapp (2009), p. 7.
[24] See Barnard (2012), p. 94.

25 In the legal literature, various types of doubts have been raised concerning these recommendations: from the questions on their **legitimacy**—since the recommendations contain references not only to the goals that each MS should achieve, but also to the way in which it should do that—to questions on their **effectiveness** in the absence of a sanctioning mechanism.

26 National governments may feel pressured to act in a certain way, which, according to some authors, would risk European intervention in areas that would otherwise fall within the exclusive competence of the MS. In addition, some authors are of the opinion that the system of "shaming" the MS that do not perform well enough could undermine the very **architecture of mutual trust** that the Open Method of Coordination (OMC) and the procedures of mutual learning presuppose.[25] Without doubt, there are some consequences to these recommendations, which, although not binding, do raise certain issues in public opinion and the media in that country.

27 In contrast, other authors complain about the non-binding nature of the recommendations and associate them with a certain degree of inefficiency. However, this **does not necessarily imply a lack of effectiveness**: even in the absence of sanctions, MS do not want to obtain indicators certifying poor performance in comparison with all other MS. Moreover, reiteration of recommendations for a given country from year to year may in itself be a way of putting pressure on that country.

28 Before the economic crisis, economic, employment and budgetary policies were governed by independent processes. With the adoption of the European Semester, these policies are coordinated, and the strategies are developed in an **integrated project**, communicated in time to the MS, who in turn will consider the European objectives when preparing national policies. Macroeconomic, structural, competitiveness developments and overall financial stability are thus jointly examined.[26] This approach has a number of advantages in terms of employment analysis in **interaction** with economic indicators. For example, excessive structural unemployment can be an indicator of the existence of difficulties at macro-economic level.

29 Today, CSRs are aimed to become "one of the main vehicles for implementing the 20 principles enshrined in the EPSR"[27] with "no less than 63% of the recommendations are to be situated in or contain an element related to the social field, this being the highest percentage since the start of the European Semester".[28]

---

[25] Hartlapp (2009), p. 8.

[26] Council Recommendation of 27 April 2010 *on broad guidelines for the economic policies of the Member States and of the Union. Part I of the Europe 2020 Integrated Guidelines*, SEC(2010) 488 final.

[27] Clauwaert (2018), p. 6.

[28] Clauwaert (2018), p. 11.

Article 148 [Employment Guidelines]

6. Joint Employment Report

The Joint Employment Report (JER) is **part of the Annual Growth Survey**. It is meant to assess the progress made each year by the MS on employment policies and their implementation. The report includes comparisons of MS performance and examples of best practice; it identifies patterns and may lead to recalibration of targets for the next period.

One of the concerns in the elaboration of the JER is the **comparability** of the indicators used, so that the employment situation and the social trends could be determined for each MS. In fact, as we have shown (→ Article 146 TFEU para 14), the indicators and their analysis are means of encouraging performance. For this purpose, more indicators are used with greater accuracy, allowing comparisons to be made:

— between each MS and the European average;
— for each MS, compared to the previous period;
— for each MS, by comparing the evolution over the previous period with the evolution of other MS (relative dynamics).

Since 2017, the JER **monitors MS' performance in relation to the Social Scoreboard** which accompanies the European Pillar of Social Rights. For example, the JER for 2022 "has a stronger focus on the implementation of the European Pillar of Social Rights, in line with the Action Plan of March 2021 and the commitments of the EU leaders in the 8 May Porto Declaration".[29] It integrates the three new 2030 EU headline targets of the Pillar Action Plan:

— at least 78% of the 20–64 population should be in employment;
— at least 60% of people aged 25–64 should participate in learning activities each year;
— the number of people at risk of poverty or social exclusion should decrease by at least 15 million compared to 2019.

References[30]

Barnard, C. (2012). *EU employment law* (4th ed.). OUP.
Borragán, N. P.-S., & Smismans, S. (2012). The EU and institutional change in industrial relations in the new member states. In S. Smismans (Ed.), *The European Union and industrial relations. New procedures, new context* (pp. 116–138). Manchester University Press.
Clauwaert, S., (2018). *The country-specific recommendations (CSRs) in the social field.*, ETUC.
Creel, J., Leron, N., Ragot, X., & Saraceno, F. (2021). *Embedding the recovery and resilience facility into the European Semester.* ETUI.

---

[29] *Joint Employment Report 2022* as adopted by the EPSCO Council on 14 March 2022.
[30] All cited Internet sources in this comment have been accessed on 15 August 2022.

D'Erman, V., & Verdun, A. (2022). An introduction: Macroeconomic policy coordination and domestic politics: Policy coordination in the EU from the European semester to the Covid-19 crisis. *Journal of Common Market Studies, 60*, 3–20.

Geiger, R., Khan, D.-E., & Kotzur, M. (Eds.). (2015). *European Union Treaties*. C.H. Beck/Hart.

Hartlapp, M. (2009). Learning about policy learning. Reflections on the European employment strategy. In S. Kröger (Ed.), What we have learnt: Advances, pitfalls and remaining questions in OMC research. *European Integration online Papers (EIoP)*, Special Issue 1 (13).

Moschella, M. (2020). *What role for the European Semester in the recovery plan?*. Brussels, European Parliament.

Ryszka, J. (2021). Protection of social rights as a permanent challenge for the European Union. *Review of European and Comparative Law, 46*(3), 109–143.

Szyszczak, E. (2006). Experimental governance: The open method of coordination. *European Law Journal, 12*(4), 486–502.

Tsakatika, M. (2004). The open method of co-ordination in the European convention: An opportunity lost? *Political Theory and the European Constitution*, 91–102.

Vanhegen, M., & Hendrickx, F. (2020). Disability in EU labour law beyond non-discrimination. In D. Ferri & A. Broderick (Eds.), *Research handbook on EU disability law* (pp. 146–163). Edward Elgar.

Weishaupt, J. T., & Lack, K. (2011). The European employment strategy: Assessing the status quo. *German Policy Studies, 7*(1), 9–44.

Zeitlin, J., & Vanhercke, B. (2018). Socializing the European semester: EU social and economic policy co-ordination in crisis and beyond. *Journal of European Public Policy, 25*(2), 149–174.

Article 149 [Incentive Measures]

(ex-Article 129 TEC)

The European Parliament and the Council, acting in accordance with the ordinary legislative procedure[1, 2] and after consulting the Economic and Social Committee[3] and the Committee of the Regions,[4] may adopt incentive measures[5–7] designed to encourage cooperation between Member States and to support their action in the field of employment through initiatives aimed at developing exchanges of information and best practices, providing comparative analysis and advice as well as promoting innovative approaches and evaluating experiences, in particular by recourse to pilot projects.[8–14]

Those measures shall not include harmonisation of the laws and regulations of the Member States.[15–17]

Contents

1. Procedure 1
2. Incentive Measures 5
3. Mutual Learning Programme 8
4. The Principle of Subsidiarity 15

References

1. Procedure

Article 149 TFEU provides the EP and the Council with the right to adopt incentive measures to encourage cooperation between MS and to support their actions in developing their own employment policies. The EP and the Council act in accordance with the **ordinary legislative procedure**, i.e. in accordance with the provisions of Article 294 TFEU.

The adoption of incentive measures is preceded by a **consultation** phase, involving the Economic and Social Committee and the Committee of the Regions.

The **Economic and Social Committee** is established and operates under Article 13.4 TEU and Articles 301–304 TFEU, acting in an advisory capacity in many areas. The consultation is mandatory in the procedure for adopting incentives in the field of employment.[1]

4   Consultation of the **Committee of the Regions** is necessary (→ Article 307 TFEU para 3), especially as the guidelines must be implemented at the local or regional level, so that the views of local representatives on employment are relevant.[2] Founded in 1992/1993 by the Maastricht Treaty, the Committee of Regions expresses its views on the employment guidelines (→ Article 148 TFEU para 11–19), and is concerned about some specific issues such as the role of the "green economy" in creating jobs. However, the legal literature sometimes deplores the absence of involvement of local authorities, as they are usually directly responsible for the development, and if not, then at least for the implementation of employment policies.

2. Incentive Measures

5   Measures may be taken to (1) develop exchanges of information and best practices, (2) deliver comparative analyses and advice, (3) support innovative initiatives and (4) evaluate experiences.

6   Two **declarations** issued as annexes to the Treaty of Amsterdam aimed to define the role of incentive measures in a somehow restrictive way. According to Declaration No. 23, the Conference agrees that the incentive measures should always specify the following:

- the grounds for their adoption based on an objective assessment of their necessity and the existence of an added value at Community level;
- their duration, which should not exceed five years;
- the maximum amount of their financing, which should reflect the incentive nature of such measures.

7   Despite these limitations, a number of such programmes have been developed in recent years. Most notably, the **Recovery and Resilience Facility**[3] (→ Article 148 TFEU para 7) is a temporary recovery instrument, allowing the Commission to raise funds to help MS to implement reforms and investments, in the European Semester framework. Other examples include the Programme for Employment and

---

[1] See, for example, Proposal for a Council Decision *on guidelines for the employment policies of the Member States*, COM(2011) 813 final - 2011/0390 (CNS).

[2] *On the* mandatory consultation required by the Treaty in policies that have direct 'territorial' relevance, see Nicolosi and Mustert (2020), p. 289.

[3] Parliament/Council Regulation (EU) 2021/241 *establishing the Recovery and Resilience Facility*, O.J. L 57/17 (2021).

Social Innovation (EaSI),[4] or the European Social Fund Plus (ESF+),[5] directly referring to the European Pillar of Social Rights.

3. Mutual Learning Programme

The Mutual Learning Programme (MLP) is one of the main tools of the Social Open Method of Coordination (OMC, → Article 146 TFEU para 9–21), one of the ways to develop exchanges of information and **best practice**. It allows MS to learn from each other's experience and is particularly relevant in the context of the current configuration of the EU, including MS with a different background and an unequal pace in the implementation of the employment policies. Indeed, differences can sometimes be significant, both in terms of the size of the problem itself—namely the unemployment rate—and in terms of legal traditions, the choice of legislation, the degree of participation of the social partners in identifying solutions and national employment options. MLP enables the results of MS to be extended and multiplied—by transferring and creatively implementing them into the policies of another MS. By familiarising themselves with the problems faced by other MS, and even more so with the solutions identified, decision-makers at the national level can expand their field of knowledge and decision. As it has been shown, "such processes often take an analogic rather than a directly mimetic form".[6]

MLP encompasses a multitude of tasks such as developing databases, peer reviews, learning exchanges, European thematic and dissemination events, as well as various policy-related publications.

For example, **peer review** activities are tools for the evaluation and dissemination of already implemented employment policies and for the exchange of views among MS on how to achieve certain performances effectively. They have been conducted since 1999 and involve meetings between representatives of a "host country" and those of the "peer countries", covering selected employment policy practices perceived to be effective. As has been shown, "given the variety of participants, these meetings are privileged venues for observing how multi-level and multi-stakeholder interactions and mutual learning dynamics develop in the context of 'soft' governance mechanisms such as the Social OMC and for exploring the outcomes of such interactions", peer reviews representing "an element of continuity between the overarching EU strategies, the Lisbon strategy and Europe 2020".[7]

---

[4] Parliament/Council Regulation (EU) No. 1296/2013 *on a European Union Programme for Employment and Social Innovation ("EaSI")*, O.J., L 347/238 (2013).

[5] Parliament/Council Regulation (EU) 2021/1057 *establishing the European Social Fund Plus (ESF+)*, O.J. L 231/21 (2021).

[6] See Zeitlin (2009), p. 216 and the bibliography cited by the author.

[7] Sabato (2018), p. 203.

Peer countries have committed themselves to **learning from the host country**, providing useful feedback and information about their own experiences in the field. Such meetings involve the participation of a limited number of peer countries through government representatives and independent experts and representatives of the European Commission. Transfer of practice is not a straightforward uncritical process. Rather, it involves adjusting the results and the experience of other countries to their own normative particularities (i.e., size of the country, level of economic development, labour law based primarily on legislation or collective agreements, a system of civil law or common law, etc.).

11   Over time, MLP was not immune to **criticism**, since "learning is difficult to define, isolate, operationalise and thus measure empirically".[8] MS may resist the assimilation of policies that are not consistent with their own normative traditions, their representatives may feel awkward with the very idea of learning (especially when the mutual character is not particularly visible) or may consider that the labour market in their own country constitutes a "special and unique case". In addition, some policies are not easily transferable. Essentially, **MLP works best among MS that are similar** in terms of regulatory framework, infrastructure, political options or regulation of industrial relations.[9]

12   **Learning** is a mutual relation, but representatives of MS that have had some success in their employment policies tend to have a certain authority over those that have suffered setbacks and have a high rate of unemployment.[10] One example is the case of Denmark within the MLP regarding flexicurity. Who learns from whom is therefore a separate issue; the process is influenced by the results and the policies considered exemplary, and also by the degree of similarity of the normative systems (in the sense that the transfer of knowledge between systems that have certain common elements or deal with similar problems of employment is achieved more easily). Learning is a conscious, voluntary, and sometimes experimental process[11]—meant to change the traditional paradigm of developing employment policies.

13   Without going into detail about the **learning process** itself, we merely note that in the context of the OMC it is believed to take place **at various levels**: Inspiration—an MS draws inspiration from the policies applied in another country; combined inspiration—an MS combines different sources of inspiration from other MS; reflexive policy learning—when adjustments are made with specific elements of originality, based on a reflective process at political level.[12] The literature also

---

[8] Nedergaard (2006), p. 312.

[9] Hartlapp (2009), p. 9. See also, Curry (2016), p. 178.

[10] For further details, see Nedergaard (2006), p. 319.

[11] Weishaupt and Lack (2011), p. 29.

[12] For further details, see Office for Official Publications of the European Communities 2009, *The Open Method of Coordination in Research Policy: Assessment and Recommendations. A report from the Expert Group for the follow-up of the research aspects of the revised Lisbon strategy*, p. 14. Available at https://op.europa.eu/s/odUp.

Article 149 [Incentive Measures] 1309

distinguishes between political calculation, coercion, learning, and other transfer mechanisms such as imitation or copying.[13]

Policy learning is not an end in itself,[14] but an **instrument at the service of MS** **14** **to improve their policies and programmes**, in the least invasive manner possible, without manifestations of dirigisme from European organisations, which have a rather support role. The reflexive nature of the transfers from one country to another makes the evaluation of the results of the MLP difficult since the effects do not occur immediately or in the expected form. However, learning, understood in a broad sense as a complex process capable of influencing employment policies, even if there is no faithful transfer of policies from one MS to another, has proven to be one of the most tempting levers for progress in the field of employment.

4. The Principle of Subsidiarity

Article 149.2 TFEU explicitly **prohibits harmonisation** of the laws and regula- **15** tions of the MS, similar to Article 150.2 TFEU. Indeed, the role of the above-mentioned programmes is rather to support and supplement the MS's action, than to replace national measures.[15] The MS retain their competence of action, although in doing so they may not act in contradiction to the EU law, under the principle of sincere cooperation.[16]

Indeed, Article 149.2 TFEU constitutes an explicit expression of the principle of **16** subsidiarity enshrined in Article 5.3 TEU, consisting in establishing/dividing responsibilities between the European and the national level by setting European objectives and the responsibility of the MS for implementing measures adopted at the national level to achieve them. The field of employment is among the special powers of the Union which, acting under Article 5.2 TFEU, is responsible for **coordinating employment policies of the MS** in the field of labour force without acting further than that (→ Article 5 TFEU para 17). This is in fact the best area for applying the concept of "active subsidiarity".[17]

The **EU** has therefore a **limited role** in imposing, coercing or correcting the MS **17** opting for a particular employment policy rather than another (→ Article 147 TFEU para 2).

---

[13] Hartlapp (2009), p. 5.
[14] Hartlapp (2009), p. 3.
[15] See also Velluti (2018), p. 142.
[16] Sjaak (2011), p. 15.
[17] Calame (2001), p. 227: "'Active subsidiarity' is a practical approach to governance which starts from a realisation that one of the most important needs of the modern world is to reconcile unity and diversity".

References[18]

Calame, P. (2001). Active subsidiarity: Reconciling unity and diversity. In O. de Schutter, N. Lebessis, & J. Paterson (Eds.), *Governance in the European Union* (pp. 227–240). Office for Official Publication of the European Commission.

Curry, D. (2016). The question of EU legitimacy in the social OMC peer review process. *Journal of European Social Policy, 26*(2), 168–182.

Hartlapp, M. (2009). Learning about policy learning. Reflections on the European employment strategy. In S. Kröger (Ed.), What we have learnt: Advances, pitfalls and remaining questions in OMC research. *European Integration online Papers (EIoP),* Special Issue 1(13).

Nedergaard, P. (2006). Policy learning in the European Union: The case of the European employment strategy. *Policy Studies, 27*(4), 311–323.

Nicolosi, S. F., & Mustert, L. (2020). The European Committee of the Regions as a watchdog of the principle of subsidiarity. *Maastricht Journal of European and Comparative Law, 27*(3), 284–301.

Sabato, S. (2018). Linking Lisbon and Europe 2020: the 'peer reviews' in the social OMC. In M. Jessoula & I. Madama (Eds.), *Fighting poverty and social exclusion in the EU. A chance in Europe 2020* (pp. 203–225). Routledge.

Sjaak, J. (2011). *Fiscal sovereignty of the member states in an internal market: Past and future.* Kluwer Law International.

Velluti, S. (2018). Article 148 TFEU. In E. Ales, M. Bell, O. Deinert, & S. Robin-Olivier (Eds.), *International and European labour law: Article-by-article commentary* (pp. 138–141). Nomos/Beck/Hart.

Weishaupt, J. T., & Lack, K. (2011). The European employment strategy: Assessing the status quo. *German Policy Studies, 7*(1), 9–44.

Zeitlin, J. (2009). The open method of coordination and reform of national social and employment policies: Influences, mechanisms, effects. In J. Zeitlin & M. Heidenreich (Eds.), *Changing European employment and welfare regimes: The influence of the open method of coordination on national reforms* (pp. 214–244). Routledge.

---

[18] All cited Internet sources in this comment have been accessed on 15 August 2022.

Article 150 [Employment Committee]
(ex-Article 130 TEC)

The Council, acting by a simple majority after consulting the European Parliament, shall establish an Employment Committee with advisory status to promote coordination between Member States on employment and labour market policies.[1] The tasks of the Committee shall be:[2–5]

- to monitor the employment situation and employment policies in the Member States and the Union,
- without prejudice to Article 240, to formulate opinions at the request of either the Council or the Commission or on its own initiative, and to contribute to the preparation of the Council proceedings referred to in Article 148.

In fulfilling its mandate, the Committee shall consult management and labour.[7–9]

Each Member State and the Commission shall appoint two members of the Committee.[10]

Contents

1. Employment Committee 1
2. Tasks 2
3. Consultation of Social Partners 7
4. Membership 10

References

1. Employment Committee

The initiative of establishing an Employment Committee (EMCO) had been formulated by the Council in December 1996; it had been formally enshrined in the Treaty of Amsterdam (ex-Article 130 TEC). It currently operates under Council [1]

Decision (EU) No. 2015/772 of 11 May 2015,¹ which repealed Council Decision No. 2000/98/EC. The latter had repealed, in turn, Council Decision No. 97/16/EC,² whereby the Council had set up an Employment and Labour Market Committee based on ex-Article 145 TEC, the provision giving the Council the power to ensure coordination of the general economic policies of the MS and adopt decisions to that end. Like the Economic and Social Committee, the EMCO has only **advisory status**,³ a position reiterated by the recent Council Decision. Its role is to promote coordination of MS's employment and labour market policies, in full compliance with the Treaty and with due regard for the powers of the Union institutions and bodies.

2. Tasks

2   The EMCO is an involved **observer of the labour market and employment situation** in the MS and throughout the EU. From this perspective, its main objective is the monitoring, as it is often closer to the reality of the labour market relations than the high European policymakers. The EMCO can do even more than that: it either formulates a position on specific issues upon request of the Council or the Commission or express its position on its own initiative, without prejudice to the powers of COREPER provided under Article 240 TFEU. Similarly, under Article 148.2 TFEU, the Employment Committee is consulted in the elaboration of the Employment Guidelines (→ Article 148 TFEU para 14) and, under Article 148.4 TFEU, expresses its views on their implementation. Although the EMCO opinions have no binding force, in fulfilling its tasks, it "should contribute to ensuring that the European Employment Strategy (EES), macroeconomic policy coordination and the process of economic reform are formulated and implemented in a consistent and mutually supportive way".⁴

3   EMCO has a rather important role in the socialisation process of the **European Semester** (→ Article 148 TFEU para 5), a process often seen as "a product of reflexive learning and creative adaptation on the part of EU social and employment actors to the new institutional conditions of the European Semester".⁵

4   Article 150.1 TFEU is the only provision in Title IX that does not relate exclusively to employment, but also introduces the concept of **labour market**. Indeed, the role of the Employment Committee exceeds the scope of employment, and its powers are not only inter-governmental but also cross-sectoral.

---

¹ Council Decision No. 2015/772/EU *establishing the Employment Committee*, O.J. L 121/12 (2015).
² Council Decision No. 97/16/EC *setting up an Employment and Labour Market Committee*, O.J. L 6/32 (1997).
³ Kotzur, in Geiger et al. (2015), Article 150 TFEU para 2; Velluti (2018), p. 143.
⁴ Recital 3 of Council Decision No. 2015/772/EU.
⁵ Zeitlin and Vanhercke (2015), p. 91.

To achieve the **objective** set out in Article 150 TFEU, under Article 2.2 of 5
Council Decision No. 2015/772/EU, the EMCO shall, in particular, endeavour:

(a) to promote the consideration of the objective of a high level of employment in the formulation and implementation of Union policies and activities;
(b) to contribute to the procedure leading to the adoption of the broad economic guidelines in order to ensure consistency between the employment guidelines and those guidelines and contribute to the synergy between the EES, macroeconomic policy coordination and the process of economic reform in a mutually supportive way;
(c) to participate actively in the macroeconomic dialogue at Union level;
(d) to contribute to all aspects of the European Semester within its mandate and report on them to the Council. This competence was newly introduced in 2015;
(e) to promote exchanges of information and experience between MS and with the Commission.

In performing its tasks, the **EMCO collaborates with other committees**, 6
notably with the Social Protection Committee (Article 160 TFEU), and this collaboration has been gradually intensified to counterbalance the power of more "economic oriented" actors.[6] EMCO not only collaborates with the Economic and Financial Committee (Article 134 TFEU), the Economic Policy Committee,[7] the Education Committee (the Council working group that prepares the items for decision by EU education ministers) and the governing board of the European Network of Public Employment Services,[8] but also with other European bodies relevant to the activity of coordinating the economic and employment policies.

3. Consultation of Social Partners

The Employment Committee regularly consults the social partners concerning 7
every stage of the European Semester.[9] Meetings take place on several levels, especially with social partners represented in the **Tripartite Social Summit for Growth and Employment** (Article 152 TFEU). The latter had been established by Council Decision of 6 March 2003,[10] which institutionalised the practice since 1997 of organising informal high-level meetings under the European Employment Strategy and subsequently under the Lisbon Strategy. As a result, the previous Standing Committee on Employment was dissolved.

---

[6] Vanhercke (2013), p. 181.

[7] Council Decision 2000/604/EC *on the composition and the statutes of the Economic Policy Committee*, O.J. L 257/28 (2000).

[8] Parliament/Council Decision No. 573/2014/EU *on enhanced cooperation between Public Employment Services (PES)*, O.J. L 159/32 (2014).

[9] See also *Kšiňan* (2021), p. 174.

[10] Council Decision No. 2003/174/, O.J. L 70/31 (2003), repealed by Council Decision (EU) 2016/1859 *on the Tripartite Social Summit for Growth and Employment*, O.J. L 284/27 (2016).

8   The role of social partners in the Tripartite Summit has been considered for a while as not being sufficiently accentuated.[11] But their involvement seems to be revived. And, indeed, this intent to **increase involvement** accompanies every Tripartite Social Summit in recent years. The main theme of the Tripartite Social Summit in October 2018 was, for instance, reinforcing competitiveness, sustainable job creation and social fairness in the EU, discussions being focused on the implementation of the European Pillar of Social Rights. Today, aiming to increase Europe's capacity to overcome the pandemic's fallout, the topic of the Tripartite Social Summit of October 2020 was "Implementing together an inclusive economic and social recovery in Europe".

9   Concerning terminology, Article 150.2 TFEU (English version) as well as Article 146.2 TFEU use the notion of "**management and labour**", while Article 152 TFEU and Declaration No. 31 to Article 156 TFEU refer to the "social partners". More recently, regulating the advisory role of the Employment Committee, Article 6 of Council Decision (EU) No. 2015/772 establishing the Employment Committee ceases to use the phrase "management and labour" (used in Article 5 of the previous Council Decision No. 2000/98/EC) in favour of the more explicit one of "social partners". Moreover, the other language versions of Article 150.2 TFEU use the phrase "social partners", e.g. German (*Sozialpartner*), French (*les partenaires sociaux*) or Italian (*le parti sociali*).

4. Membership

10   Concerning organisation, the EMCO consists of two members appointed by each MS and by the Commission. They may also appoint two alternate members.[12] They are elected from among the officials and experts with experience in the field of employment and labour market policy from each MS,[13] respecting, as far as possible, a gender balance.[14] The participation of representatives from all MS emphasises the inter-governmental role of the EMCO, which had already been laid out in Article 150.1 TFEU, by determining the role of the EMCO in promoting coordination between MS.

11   **Working groups** may be set up—on specific issues that benefit from an adequate organisational and analytical support from the Commission.[15] Furthermore, the EMCO is supported by **two sub-groups**: the policy analysis group, promoting coordination between MS, and the indicators group, which carries out technical work related to the indicators which are used to monitor EU employment strategy

---

[11] Goetschy (2012), p. 201.
[12] Article 3.1 of Council Decision No. 2015/772/EU.
[13] Article 3.2 of Council Decision No. 2015/772/EU.
[14] Article 3.3 of Council Decision No. 2015/772/EU.
[15] Article 5 of Council Decision No. 2015/772/EU.

implementation. The Committee may also establish joint working groups with other committees or bodies.

The changes in 2015 have operational purposes. Thus, the **chairperson is elected from the members of the Employment Committee**, with a mandate that (unlike the previous regulation) may be renewed. Overall, the chairperson may serve up to a total of four years and eight months.[16] He/she is assisted by four vice presidents: two are elected by the EMCO from among its members, one represents the MS holding the Presidency of the Council and one is from the MS that will hold the next Council Presidency.[17]

12

References

Geiger, R., Khan, D.-E., & Kotzur, M. (Eds.). (2015). *European Union Treaties. Treaty on European Union, Treaty on the Function of the European Union. A commentary*. C.H. Beck/Hart.

Goetschy, J. (2012). The Lisbon strategy, industrial relations and social Europe: An assessment of theoretical frameworks and policy developments. In S. Smismans (Ed.), *The European Union and industrial relations. New procedures, new context* (pp. 190–205). Manchester University Press.

Kšiňan, J. (2021). EU issues on tripartism. In B. ter Haar & A. Kun (Eds.), *EU collective labour law* (pp. 163–177). Edward Elgar.

Vanhercke, B. (2013). Under the radar? EU social policy in times of austerity. In D. Natali & B. Vanhercke (Eds.), *Social developments in the European Union 2012* (pp. 91–121). OSE, ETUI.

Velluti, S. (2018). Article 147 TFEU. In E. Ales, M. Bell, O. Deinert, & S. Robin-Olivier (Eds.), *International and European labour law: Article-by-article commentary* (pp. 136–138). Nomos/Beck/Hart.

Zeitlin, J., & Vanhercke, B. (2015). Economic governance in Europe 2020: Socialising the European Semester against the odds? In D. Natali & B. Vanhercke (Eds.), *Social policy in the European Union: State of play 2015* (pp. 65–95). European Trade Union Institute and European Social Observatory.

---

[16] Article 4.1 of Council Decision No. 2015/772/EU.

[17] Article 4.2 of Council Decision No. 2015/772/EU.

Title X
Social Policy

Title X
Social Policy

Article 151 [Objectives]
(ex-Article 136 TEC)

The Union and the Member States, having in mind fundamental social rights such as those set out in the European Social Charter signed at Turin on 18 October 1961 and in the 1989 Community Charter of the Fundamental Social Rights of Workers, shall have as their objectives the promotion of employment, improved living and working conditions, so as to make possible their harmonisation while the improvement is being maintained, proper social protection, dialogue between management and labour, the development of human resources with a view to lasting high employment and the combating of exclusion.

To this end the Union and the Member States shall implement measures which take account of the diverse forms of national practices, in particular in the field of contractual relations, and the need to maintain the competitiveness of the Union economy.

They believe that such a development will ensue not only from the functioning of the internal market, which will favour the harmonisation of social systems, but also from the procedures provided for in the Treaties and from the approximation of provisions laid down by law, regulation or administrative action.

Contents

1. Introduction: The Social Policy as Part of the Objectives of the European Construction 1
2. Balancing European and National Parameters to Achieve the Transversal Social Policy 11
3. The Concrete Social Objectives and the Counterweight of the Competitiveness of the Union Economy 18
4. Challenges: Balancing Different Speeds in a Broader Social Europe 27

List of Cases
References

1. Introduction: The Social Policy as Part of the Objectives of the European Construction

Article 151 TFEU, and in particular its last paragraph (harmonisation of social systems), has its precedent in the opening provision of Chapter 1 ("Social Provisions") of Title III ("Social Policy") of the EEC Treaty, that is, Article 117 TEEC. Indeed, the 1957 EEC Treaty contained a few provisions on social policy, which was conceived closely related to two important goals: **free competition** and   1

© Springer Nature Switzerland AG 2023
R. Böttner, H.-J. Blanke (eds.), *Treaty on the Functioning of the European Union – A Commentary*, Springer Commentaries on International and European Law, https://doi.org/10.1007/16559_2023_70

worker mobility. In this regard, it has been noted that **economic integration** was the primary objective of the EEC and its predecessor, the European Coal and Steel Community (ECSC), and the founding Treaties reflected this.[1] In this sense, even the Treaties establishing the ECSC in 1952 and the European Atomic Energy Community (EAEC) in 1957 emphasised social policy more than the Treaty of Rome did. The reason for this is that because they referred to specific industries (coal, steel, nuclear energy), the ECSC and EAEC had fairly strong social policy mandates in order to deal with the employment and health effects of these rapidly changing industries. The ECSC had funds to deal with redundant workers, and the EAEC was empowered to set health and safety standards.[2]

2   The adoption of the **Single European Act** (SEA) in 1986 gave a new impetus to several areas of social policy, especially in the working environment (as regards the health and safety of workers) and in the social dialogue (new Articles 118a and 118b TEEC). The SEA also introduced in its preamble the first reference to the 1961 European Social Charter in the founding treaties.

According to the **Preamble** of the SEA, MS were "determined to promote democracy on the basis of the fundamental rights recognized in the constitutions and laws of the Member States, in the [ECHR] and the European Social Charter, notably freedom, equality and social justice". This reference to the main social rights treaty of the Council of Europe acquired binding value with the 1997 Amsterdam Treaty through its inclusion in the former Article 117 TEEC, which became Article 136 TEC, whose content has remained identical in Article 151 TFEU, with the exception of the updated notions of "Union" (instead of "Community") and "internal market" (instead of "common market").

3   In real terms, like the EEC Treaty, a first approach to "social policy" in the **Lisbon Treaty** shows that Article 151 TFEU, serving as a basis for or an introduction to the new Title X ("Social Policy"), introduces an apparent prevalence of commercial objectives over the Union's social objectives. In particular, Article 151 TFEU, while it explicitly mentions "the European Social Charter signed at Turin on 18 October 1961" (together with the 1989 Community Charter of the Fundamental Social Rights of Workers), makes it clear that the social dimension must take into account "the need to maintain the competitiveness of the Union economy". This reference once again highlights the **close link between economic and social policies**, pointing out that social policy measures, especially from a cost point of view, are submitted to the pressure deriving from the economy, which contrasts with the Commission's repeated argument that competitiveness, economic growth and social security are not contradictory but complementary.[3]

In parallel, in the **Preamble of the TEU**, the MS confirm "their attachment to fundamental social rights as defined in the European Social Charter signed at Turin on 18 October 1961 and in the 1989 Community Charter of the Fundamental Social

---

[1] Anderson (2015), pp. 52–54.
[2] Anderson (2015), pp. 52–54.
[3] Langer, in von der Groeben et al. (2015), Article 151 AEUV para 88.

Rights of Workers" (→ Preamble TEU para 5), whereas Article 3.3 TEU declares that "the Union shall establish an internal market. It shall work for the sustainable development of Europe based on balanced economic growth and price stability, a highly competitive social market economy, aiming at full employment and social progress, and a high level of protection and improvement of the quality of the environment" (→ Article 3 TEU para 31 et seqq.).

From a formal point of view, the contribution of the Lisbon Treaty to the social policy seems merely terminological. Indeed, apart from including the area of "social policy" in the scope of **shared competence** between the Union and the MS (Article 4.2 point (b) TFEU), the Lisbon Treaty states that the EC Treaty's heading of Title XI of "social policy, education, vocational training and youth" shall be replaced by the heading "social policy" with new renumbering (Title X) in the TFEU.

In this context, the adjective "social" accompanies the principle of the "market economy" only once in the Lisbon Treaty (in the above-mentioned Article 3.3 TEU), and therefore, it can also be maintained that the adjective "social" has less weight than the adjective "economic". From this perspective, while in the economic sphere advances in the EU have been occurring evenly, social progress has been introduced "asymmetrically" (according to the dynamic of the "**Europe of different speeds**"). In truth, the adjective "social" as an element associated with the "market economy" is merely incidental. Ultimately, the idea of a "**European social and economic constitution**" projects not a balance between social and economic but rather an imbalance clearly in favour of economic issues rather than social concerns.

Thus, in 1989, the United Kingdom was the only one of the then 12 MS that did not sign the Community Charter of the Fundamental Social Rights of Workers, even though this was conceived as a mere policy document with no compulsory value. In 1992, it was also necessary to include the nucleus of social policy as a Protocol attached to the Maastricht Treaty to make an opting-out clause possible, once again for the United Kingdom. For their part, the 1997 Amsterdam Treaty improved the extent of the anti-discriminatory clause (new Article 13 TEC), while the 2001 Nice Treaty created the new Social Protection Committee and tried to better implement the "**open method of co-ordination**", compensating the achievement of the market with the protection of social rights.

By recalling the origins of Title X TFEU and the **weak status of social policy**, it has been stated that debates about the relationship between social and economic policies in the Treaty of Rome negotiations presaged the debates that would shape EU social policy for the next 55 years. Indeed, the Treaty left a partial vacuum in terms of social policy because goals were not matched with effective instruments.[4]

The context of the **economic and financial crisis** since 2008 (aggravated by the **coronavirus crisis** since 2020 in the context of a multi-dimensional crisis or

---

[4] Anderson (2015), pp. 52–54.

polycrisis faced by the EU) has even weakened those social policy instruments[5] since the development of such a policy has been consolidated not in accordance with "the procedures provided for in the Treaties" but following new controversial procedures under the dynamics of the **Troika**. In this respect, the adoption of **austerity measures**, as such, is neither positive nor negative. The problem lies in their conception in an unbalanced manner by forgetting that the goal of economics (like law) should be at the service of people. Unfortunately, the concept of austerity measures (in economic and legal terms) appears to have asymmetrically transmitted a legacy of shared debt, instead of producing a common heritage of prosperity and solidarity.

8   Nevertheless, when reading the major texts of the Council of Europe and the EU, one may find this common idea of achieving greater unity through economic and social progress based on the observation of minimum standards in the field of human rights. Moreover, the objective set out in the EEC Treaty of 1957 according to which "the removal of existing obstacles calls for concerted action in order to guarantee a steady expansion a balanced trade and fair competition" is not necessarily contradictory to the dynamics of the **international social concertation** that (to avoid the loss of external competitiveness of a country) guides the introduction of all social progress and, consequently, also inspired the adoption of the European Social Charter in 1961.

9   As indicated above, the adjective "social" was explicitly added to the definition of the **European economic model** late in the primary law of the EU, particularly in the Lisbon Treaty. Nonetheless, the European Social Charter, which reflects largely the **European social model**, has been ratified by MS of the EU (in most cases even before EU membership). For this reason, it is incomprehensible that some MS did not accept at first a non-binding instrument, such as the Community Charter of the Fundamental Social Rights of Workers of 1989 (which does not compete with the 1961 Social Charter but is rather based on it),[6] or that they have also articulated a confusing opt-out clause from the EU Charter of Fundamental Rights (EUCFR) (whose catalogue of social rights—especially those under the heading "Solidarity"[7]—has been based precisely on the Revised Social Charter of the

---

[5] Cf. García Ninet (2014); cf. also Jimena Quesada (2009), pp. 455–456.

[6] Clapham (1992), pp. 189–198.

[7] For example, Protocol (No 30) on the application of the EUCFR to Poland (and formerly the United Kingdom), restricts its interpretation by the Court of Justice and the domestic courts, in particular concerning the rights of "Solidarity". Indeed the CJEU has activated a restricted approach to the EU Charter, as illustrated by Case C-176/12, *Association de médiation sociale* (CJEU 15 January 2014) para 51: "Art. 27 [EUCFR], by itself or in conjunction with the provisions of Directive 2002/14/EC, must be interpreted to the effect that, where a national provision implementing that directive, such as Art. L. 1111-3 of the [French] Labour Code, is incompatible with European Union law, *that article of the Charter cannot be invoked in a dispute between individuals in order to disapply that national provision*" (emphasis added). See also, in the same restrictive direction (concerning Article 20 EUCFR), Case C-198/13, *Julián Hernández* (CJEU 10 July 2014) para 49. On the contrary, a more recent broader approach (in terms of direct applicability of some provisions of the EUCFR—Articles 21 and 31—in a dispute between individuals) in

Article 151. [Objectives]

Council of Europe).[8] From this perspective, the Preamble of the Interinstitutional Proclamation on the **European Pillar of Social Rights**[9] (EPSR) highlights that the EUCFR, "first proclaimed at the Nice European Council on 7 December 2000, safeguards and promotes a number of fundamental principles that are essential for the **European social model**" (fifth recital of the preamble to the EPSR).

The Covid-19 pandemic has exposed the social objectives of the European construction to further challenges, which are changing our daily lives. In response to such challenges, the European Commission launched on 4 March 2021 the **Action Plan on the EPSR**,[10] which presents three targets to be achieved by 2030 (towards updating the goals of the Europe 2020 Strategy and meeting the Sustainable Development Goals **2030 Agenda**): equal opportunities and access to the labour market, fair working conditions, and social protection and inclusion. Crucial support to the 2021 EPSR Action Plan was given by the Porto Social Summit on 7–8 May 2021 under the Portuguese Presidency of the Council of the EU, including the **Porto Social Commitment** subscribed by the EU institutions, social partners and the Social Platform.

10

---

the following cases: Case C-414/16, *Egenberger* (CJEU 17 April 2018) para 82; Case C-68/17, *IR* (CJEU 11 September 2018) para 71; Joined Cases C-569/16 and C-570/16, *Bauer* (CJEU 6 November 2018) para 92; Case C-684/16, *Max-Planck-Gesellschaft zur Förderung der Wissenschaften* (CJEU 6 November 2018) para 81; Case C-193/17, *Cresco Investigation* (CJEU 22 January 2019) para 77; Case C-243/19, *Veselības ministrija* (CJEU 29 October 2020) para 36; Case C-824/19, *Komisia za zashtita ot diskriminatsia* (CJEU 21 October 2021) para 32, and Case C-485/20, *HR Rail* (CJEU 10 February 2022) para 42.

[8] The Explanations of the following provisions of the EUCFR mention the provisions of the European Social Charter as a source of law: Explanations on Article 14 (the right to education: Article 10 of the Social Charter), on Article 15 (freedom to choose an occupation and right to engage in work: Article 1 point 2 of the Social Charter), on Article 23 (equality between men and women: Article 20 of the Social Charter), on Article 25 (the rights of the elderly: Article 23 of the Social Charter), on Article 26 (integration of persons with disabilities: Article 15 of the Social Charter), on Article 27 (workers' right to information and consultation within the undertaking: Article 21 of the Social Charter), on Article 28 (right of collective bargaining and action: Article 6 of the Social Charter), on Article 29 (right of access to placement services: Article 1 point 3 of the Social Charter), on Article 30 (protection in the event of unjustified dismissal: Article 24 of the Social Charter), on Article 31 (fair and just working conditions: Article 3 of the Social Charter concerning Article 31 EUCFR and Article 2 of the Social Charter concerning Article 31.2 EUCFR), on Article 32 (prohibition of child labour and protection of young people at work: Article 7 of the Social Charter), on Article 3 (family and professional life: Articles 8 and 27 of the Social Charter) on Article 34 (social security and social assistance: Article 12 of the Social Charter concerning Article 34.1 EUCFR, Article 12 point 4 and Article 13 point 4 of the Social Charter concerning Article 34.2 EUCFR and Article 13 of the Social Charter concerning Article 34.3 EUCFR) and on Article 35 (health care: Articles 11 and 13 of the Social Charter).

[9] See *Interinstitutional Proclamation on the European Pillar of Social Rights*, O.J. C 428/09 (2017).

[10] COM(2021) 102 final.

2. Balancing European and National Parameters to Achieve the Transversal Social Policy

11 Indeed, in spite of the explicit distribution of competences between the EU and MS through the Lisbon Treaty, it is true that a certain degree of ambiguity still appears when facing the concrete delimitation between European and national parameters to achieve the transversal social policy, insofar as the distinction between objective, competence and other related notions remains complex. In particular, Article 151 TFEU details the EU's **social policy objectives**, which are primarily the responsibility of the MS. However, certain aspects are **shared competence** with the EU (Article 4.2 point (b) TFEU), without prejudice to the possibility for the EP and the Council to adopt incentive **measures to support and complement** the actions of the MS in certain areas (Article 153 TFEU) as well as to the Commission's role to "encourage **cooperation** between the Member States and facilitate the **coordination** of their action in all social policy fields" (Article 156 TFEU).[11] In addition, Article 6 TEU gives **binding force to the social rights** set forth in the EUCFR, whereas a **horizontal social clause** is introduced by Article 9 TFEU. Furthermore, the implementation of these measures may be carried out by **social partners**,[12] whose major role is recognised in Article 152 TFEU (in connection with Articles 153 and 154 TFEU).[13] In practice, although the primary responsibility for social policies lies with the MS, Articles 151 et seqq. TFEU do allow the EU to develop its own social policy, thus enabling the further **development of a European social model**.

12 As an example of this complexity deriving from the ambiguous nature of competences in the social field (shared competence versus coordinating competence),[14] in his Opinion in *Trijber* and *Harmsen*, AG *Szpunar* considered that it is "otiose to establish a difference between the terms '**coordination**', '**approximation**' and '**harmonisation**'. [These] terms are used interchangeably. It should be borne in mind in this context that the term 'harmonisation' was used in the Treaty of Rome in one instance only [Article 117.2 TEEC, now Article 151 TFEU:

---

[11] Such coordinated strategy between MS and the EU also inspires Title IX of the TFEU in the field of employment. Although harmonisation of the laws and regulations of the MS cannot be extended to this field, it is true that EU institutions have adopted relevant legal acts in the material scope of workers' rights (to limit working hours, tackle workplace discrimination, make working conditions safer and ensure employees receive compensation for work injuries).

[12] See Benecke (2021), p. 214.

[13] See also the Preamble of the Interinstitutional Proclamation on the EPSR: "Delivering on the European Pillar of Social Rights is a shared political commitment and responsibility. The European Pillar of Social Rights should be implemented at both the Union level and the Member State level within their respective competences, taking due account of different socioeconomic environments and the diversity of national systems, including the role of social partners, and in accordance with the principles of subsidiarity and proportionality" (para 17).

[14] It should be taken into account that the Union's competences in this area derive not from Article 151 but from Articles 153, 157.3, 46 and 48 TFEU.

'harmonisation of social systems'], before it was gradually resorted to across the whole FEU Treaty."[15]

Another example of such complexity is provided by the Opinion of AG *Jääskinen* in the Case of *Jansen* in the context of a preliminary ruling from the Higher Labour Court of Cologne (Germany) concerning the interpretation of clause 5.1 and clause 8.3 of the framework agreement on fixed-term work concluded by the Union of Industrial and Employers' Confederations of Europe (UNICE), the European Centre of Enterprises with Public Participation (CEEP) and the European Trade Union Confederation (ETUC) on 18 March 1999 (annexed to Council Directive 1999/70/EC). It is recalled that "in matters of social policy, the Member States have retained a certain degree of legislative competence". From this perspective, AG *Jääskinen* agreed that under Article 151 TFEU, the measures adopted by the EU and the MS in that domain "must **take account of the varied national practices**. Accordingly, Directive 1999/70 provides that the Member States have a wide discretion, with regard to the choice of form and methods, in adopting the measures to be taken in order to implement the framework agreement annexed thereto, and points out that that agreement lays down only minimum requirements and general principles in respect of fixed-term work."[16]

However, AG *Jääskinen* adds that "it is not disputed that even in the spheres of competence which they have retained, the **Member States must act in a way which respects the wording and objectives of European Union law**, as is apparent inter alia from [Article 288.3 TFEU]. As regards the terms used in the framework agreement but not specifically defined therein, Directive 1999/70 and the aforementioned agreement allow Member States to define such terms in conformity with national law or practice, provided that the definitions adopted at national level respect the content of the framework agreement and do not undermine its purpose, its aims or its effectiveness. In particular, clause 5(1)(a) of the framework agreement does not define what is meant by 'objective reasons' within the meaning of that provision. The lack of guidance from the authors of the framework agreement has created uncertainties as to the meaning and scope of that term. The Court has held that the term must be interpreted taking account of the objectives pursued by the framework agreement and of the context of that clause."[17] As a result, he concluded that "Clause 5(1) of the framework agreement is to be interpreted as precluding legislation such as that at issue in the main proceedings which is based on budgetary reasons that are too general to satisfy the requirements of the Court's case law concerning the objective reasons justifying the renewal of fixed-term

---

[15] Joined Cases C-340/14 and C-341/14, *Trijber and Harmsen* (Opinion of AG Szpunar of 16 July 2015) para 52.

[16] Case C-313/10, *Jansen* (Opinion of AG Jääskinen of 15 September 2011) para 30 (emphasis added).

[17] Case C-313/10, *Jansen* (Opinion of AG Jääskinen of 15 September 2011) para 31–32.

contracts within the meaning of that provision", in order to prevent the abusive use of successive fixed-term contracts.[18]

15   These requirements established by the CJEU (well-founded reasons based on **budgetary rules**) in the field of social policy when consolidating European parameters deriving from EU law (Council Directive 1999/70/EC) have nonetheless been counterbalanced by conferring a more important weight to national parameters (or, more exactly, to a **State margin of discretion**) based on anti-crisis legislation incorporating austerity measures deriving from the operations of the Troika. An illustration of this approach is offered by the case *Nisttahuz Poclava*, concerning an employment contract of indefinite duration to support entrepreneurs introduced by Law 3/2012 of 6 July 2012 on urgent measures for labour market reform, which amended the employment legislation because of the economic crisis that Spain was undergoing. According to the referring court, this new employment contract (entailing a one-year probationary period during which the employer might freely terminate the contract without notice or compensation) infringed Article 30 EUCFR, Council Directive 1999/70/EC, Articles 2.2 point (b) and 4 of the 1982 ILO Convention No 158 concerning the Termination of Employment at the Initiative of the Employer and the 1961 European Social Charter 1961 (in relation to a decision of the European Committee of Social Rights (ECSR) of 23 May 2012 on a similar Greek contract).

16   Nevertheless, on the one hand, the CJEU validates this "diverse national solution" by holding that Article 151 TFEU "does not impose any specific obligation with respect to probationary periods in employment contracts. The same is true for the guidelines and recommendations in the field of employment policy adopted by the Council" under Article 148 TFEU.[19] On the other hand, the CJEU states that Article 30 EUCFR is not at stake since "the fact that the employment contract of indefinite duration to support entrepreneurs may be financed by structural funds is not sufficient, in itself, to support the conclusion that the situation at issue in the main proceedings involves the implementation of EU law for the purposes of Article 51(1) of the Charter".[20] In addition, for the CJEU, the external international sources that are invoked by the referring court (including those explicitly mentioned in Article 151 TFEU, such as the European Social Charter) would not have any impact due to the fact that "**the Court has no jurisdiction** under Article 267 TFEU to rule on the interpretation of **provisions of international law which bind Member States outside the framework of EU law**".[21] For these reasons, the Court

---

[18] Case C-313/10, *Jansen* (Opinion of AG Jääskinen of 15 September 2011) para 98 point 3. This conclusion has not had any substantial follow-up before the CJEU, since the case was removed from the Register by Order of 25 October 2011.

[19] Case C-117/14, *Nisttahuz Poclava* (CJEU 5 February 2015) para 40 and 41 with reference to Case C-361/07, *Polier* (ECJ Order of 16 January 2008) para 13, regarding the French "new recruitment contract".

[20] Case C-117/14, *Nisttahuz Poclava* (CJEU 5 February 2015) para 42.

[21] Case C-117/14, *Nisttahuz Poclava* (CJEU 5 February 2015) para 43 with reference to Case 130/73, *Vandeweghe and Others* (ECJ 27 November 1973) para 2; C-533/08, *TNT Express*

concluded that the situation at issue in the main proceedings did not fall within the scope of EU law.

The final solution reached in Luxembourg is perhaps not so deceiving if we take into account the fact that, this way, a **potential contradiction between the CJEU and the previous decision by the ECSR has been avoided**. In particular, in its decision, the Committee of Strasbourg declared that the 2010 Greek legislation (imposed by the Troika) allowing a dismissal without notice or the compensation of employees in an open-ended contract during an initial period of 12 months is incompatible with Article 4 point 4 of the 1961 Charter as it excessively destabilises the situation of those enjoying the rights enshrined in the Charter.[22] Among others, in its legal reasoning, the Committee did not accept the observation made by the Government to the effect that the rights safeguarded under the European Social Charter had been restricted pursuant to the Government's other international obligations, namely those it had under the loan arrangement with the EU institutions (Commission and ECB) and the IMF within the "Troika"; in other words, these obligations did not absolve the Government from their obligations under the Social Charter. This position has been reiterated and validated by the ECSR in a more recent decision against Greece.[23] 17

3. The Concrete Social Objectives and the Counterweight of the Competitiveness of the Union Economy

The promotion of employment (the first objective mentioned in Article 151 TFEU) has been, in the atmosphere of the crisis practically coinciding with the entry into force of the Lisbon Treaty, one of the most precarious social objectives and a pilot area to check the balance with EU economic priorities. In practical terms, the objectives set out in Article 151 TFEU are **primarily programmatic in nature** and serve to interpret other provisions of the Treaty, in particular the competences set out in Article 153 TFEU, and the secondary legislation adopted on this basis.[24] 18

Nederland (CJEU 4 May 2010) para 61; C-134/12, *Corpul Naţional al Poliţiştilor* (CJEU Order of 10 May 2012) para 14; C-481/13, *Qurbani* (CJEU 17 July 2014) para 22.

[22] Complaint No. 65/2011, *General federation of employees of the national electric power corporation and Confederation of Greek Civil Servants' Trade Unions v Greece* (ECSR 23 May 2012) para 17–18.

[23] Complaint No. 111/2014, *Greek General Confederation of Labour (GSEE) v Greece* (ECSR 23 March 2017) para 86–88. See, in contrast, Complaint No. 165/2018, *Panhellenic Association of Pensioners of the OTE Group Telecommunications (PAP-OTE) v Greece* (ECSR 17 May 2022) para 63–66.

[24] See [*mutatis mutandis* in relation to Article 117 TEEC] Case C-126/86, *Giménez Zaera* (ECJ 29 September 1987) para 13 et seq., and Joined Cases C-72/91 and C-73/91, *Sloman Neptun* (ECJ 17 March 1993) para 25 et seq.

On the other hand, no **subjective rights** may arise from the objectives listed in Article 151 TFEU.[25] Such rights may derive only from Articles 45 and 157.1 TFEU and the fundamental rights listed in Articles 27 et seq. EUCFR. Subjective rights may, however, arise insofar as secondary legislation serves to achieve the objectives.

19   Indeed, in contrast to the early 1990s, where the **White Paper *Growth, Competitiveness, Employment*** drafted by the European Commission in **1993** adopted an integrated perspective emphasising the need for the EU to pursue policies that promoted not only economic growth but also employment, the starting point of the twenty-first century reduced expectations for social goals within the EU.[26] Even before the Lisbon Treaty and in spite of the completion of the internal market, the beginning of the new millennium was marked by difficult negotiations concerning the delicate balance between growth, competitiveness and employment.

This was the background against which the Lisbon European Council in March **2000** decided to adopt a strategy to meet the challenges posed by globalisation and create a new knowledge-driven economy. The new growth strategy (the **Lisbon Strategy**) was aimed at making the EU the most competitive economy in the world by 2010. The centrepiece of the Lisbon Strategy was the use of soft law (embodied by the Open Method of Coordination (OMC)) rather than hard law, to pursue a modernisation agenda.[27]

20   The launch of the Lisbon Strategy marks the first time that the EU formulated an integrated, long-term policy for social and economic (as well as environmental) modernisation. Despite slow progress in achieving the Lisbon goals, the strategy was revised and relaunched in 2005 and replaced by a new growth strategy, **Europe 2020**, in March 2010. Europe 2020, the new growth strategy, is designed to overcome Lisbon's weaknesses by creating stronger governance structures that support simpler goals ("smart" growth, "sustainable" growth and "inclusive" growth). The governance architecture of Europe 2020 is complex, although it is based on soft governance instruments similar to those of the Lisbon Strategy. Like Lisbon, Europe 2020 integrates social, economic and employment goals into one strategy; the MS then formulate National Reform Programmes annually, which lay out national strategies for achieving Europe 2020 goals and targets (currently updated by the 2021 Action Plan on the EPSR, which is expected to be reviewed in 2025). However, the economic crisis and sovereign debt crisis have overwhelmed the new strategy and prompted changes in its governance structure.[28]

---

[25] See Case C-126/86, *Giménez Zaera* (ECJ 29 September 1987) para 11.
[26] Anderson (2015), p. 66.
[27] Anderson (2015), p. 66.
[28] Anderson (2015), p. 66.

In such direction, the legal instruments and mechanisms for economic stability **21**
(namely the ESM),[29] as well as the influence of the "Fiscal Compact" of 2013,[30]
have paradoxically provoked a component of legal instability and legitimacy within
the EU.[31] In addition, the difficulties of the judicial dialogue at the European level
have become even more complex in terms of stability and legitimacy when classic
misgivings are promoted by constitutional courts[32] due to the classic reluctance
concerning sovereignty.[33] Certainly, the new unprecedented fiscal package adopted
by the European Council in the summer of 2020 (**NextGenerationEU**) has been
vital for the recovery of the euro area from the pandemic shock,[34] but at the same
time, it adds a new dimension to our Social Europe (to build a new greener, more
digital and more resilient future) and has to be vital for the implementation of the
EPSR.[35]

Under these conditions and taking into account the unambitious as well as non- **22**
binding character of the 1989 Community Charter,[36] it is worth reflecting on the
potential impact of the explicit reference to the European Social Charter in the first
paragraph of Article 151 TFEU. From this perspective, the **European Social
Charter** may be conceived as a complementary "**European Pact for Social
Stability**" (alongside the above-mentioned instruments of economic stability) in
order to balance the concrete social objectives and the competitiveness of the Union

---

[29] In August 2015, the European Commission signed the Memorandum of Understanding (MoU) with Greece for a new stability support programme. The ESM will be able to disburse up to EUR 86 billion in loans over the next three years, provided that Greek authorities implement reforms to address fundamental economic and social challenges, as specified in the MoU. Following months of intense negotiations, the programme aims at helping to lift uncertainty, stabilise the economic and financial situation and will assist Greece in its return to sustainable growth based on sound public finances, enhanced competitiveness, a functioning financial sector, job creation and social cohesion. As provided in Article 13 of the ESM Treaty, the MoU details the reform targets and commitments needed to unlock ESM financing.

[30] Anderson (2015), p. 71.

[31] In this sense, Schwarz (2014), p. 389.

[32] For example, the request for a preliminary ruling from the German FCC lodged on 10 February 2014: Case C-62/14, *Gauweiler and Others* (CJEU 16 June 2015). On this point, see more extensively Panzera (2009) and Vidal Prado (2004).

[33] Czaplinski (2013), pp. 124–125. A more extensive comparative approach in Tajadura Tejada and De Miguel Bárcena (2008). As a recent illustration of this difficult judicial dialogue, see the press release issued by the ECJ following the judgment of the German FCC of 5 May 2020 regarding the ECB's PSPP programme, where the Court of Luxembourg recalled that "Divergences between courts of the Member States as to the validity of such acts would indeed be liable to place in jeopardy the unity of the EU legal order and to detract from legal certainty. Like other authorities of the Member States, national courts are required to ensure that EU law takes full effect. That is the only way of ensuring the equality of Member States in the Union they created" (Press Release No. 58/20, Luxembourg, 8 May 2020: https://curia.europa.eu/jcms/upload/docs/application/pdf/2020-05/cp200058en.pdf). See Häde (2020), p. 177.

[34] Codogno and van der Noord (2022), p. 59.

[35] Corti (2022), p. 7.

[36] See Anderson (2015), pp. 62–63.

economy. With such philosophy, it has been highlighted that the ECSR, "acting under the European Social Charter adopted in the framework of the Council of Europe, as well as various human rights treaty bodies, have made clear their expectations that greater attention should be paid to the social rights impacts of fiscal consolidation and structural adjustment measures adopted by the EU member States either in order to conform themselves to the requirements of the European Semester, or to comply with the Fiscal Compact, or because they have been receiving financial support and are subject to enhanced forms of surveillance or have agreed to certain conditionalities".[37]

23 In this sense, like the 1950 ECHR, the 1961 European Social Charter derives from the Universal Declaration of Human Rights. Both the Convention and the Charter were adopted within the **Council of Europe** (currently composed of 46 members) in order to effectively guarantee both civil and political as well as social rights. Both the Convention and the Charter are international treaties, and obviously, they are legally binding. They both also established specific monitoring bodies (the ECtHR and the ECSR) to ensure the compulsory character and effectiveness of the rights.

24 The **Social Charter of 1961** recognised a first list of social rights related to work and non-discrimination, social protection and vulnerable people, as well as the so-called reporting system as a mandatory monitoring mechanism. The Charter evolved and was improved: in 1988, a first Protocol extended the range of protected social rights; in 1995, another Protocol provided for a judicial procedure of collective complaints; and in 1996, the revised Charter added other important rights,[38] and it also established a consolidated version of the Charter, including the whole catalogue of rights and the clauses incorporating the two mechanisms (national reports and collective complaints).[39]

25 In spite of the diversity of commitments made by each EU MS under the Social Charter "system" on the basis of its sovereign will,[40] **normative interactions between the Social Charter and EU law** are explicit. Firstly, references to the Social Charter have been confirmed by the current sources of EU primary law after the entry into force of the Treaty of Lisbon (Recital 5 of the TEU Preamble and

---

[37] De Schutter and Dermine (2016), p. 17.

[38] In some cases as a result of the positive influence of international NGOs, for example in the elaboration of Articles 30 and 31 on the protection against poverty and social exclusion as well as the right to housing.

[39] At present, among the 46 members of the Council of Europe, 42 (with the exception of Liechtenstein, Monaco, San Marino and Switzerland) have ratified the Social Charter, 7 are bound by the 1961 original Charter and 35 by the 1996 revised Charter. And 16 have accepted the collective complaints procedure.

[40] Indeed, the current 27 MS are part of the Charter "system" (Charter of 1961, Additional Protocol of 1988, Additional Protocol of 1995, Revised Charter), with differences as to the commitments made: 7 MS are bound by the 1961 Charter (3 of which are also bound by the 1988 Protocol) and 19 by the Revised Charter. The 15 MS that have accepted the 1995 Protocol providing for a collective complaints system comprise the great majority of Contracting Parties that have accepted this Protocol (the remaining party is Norway).

Article 151 TFEU), including the EUCFR (Preamble and Explanations). Secondly, the links between the Social Charter and the sources of EU secondary law are also important in both directions as well.[41] Finally, the Social Charter is also presented in significant non-binding instruments of the EU, precisely related to legal synergies between the Council of Europe and the EU and the debate on austerity measures.[42]

Nevertheless, these normative links appear to be more complex in practice. On the one hand, in contrast to the "Bosphorus doctrine",[43] the **ECSR has not accepted a general presumption of compatibility between the social standards of EU law and the Social Charter**. Such issue has been held by the Committee in controversial areas, such as the organisation of working time,[44] the delocalisation of undertakings and social dumping,[45] or in the field of restrictions (controversial also under competition law) concerning collective agreements setting out minimum rates of pay and other working conditions,[46] without forgetting anti-crisis legislation and austerity measures (→ para 16).

26

This lack of presumption is very significant "in view of the overlapping membership of the European Union and the Council of Europe, and the far-reaching impact of EU law on domestic law",[47] which is admittedly notorious in the field of social legislation.[48] From this point of view, the complexities of the judicial dialogue are accentuated since the ECSR is increasingly occupying a place next to the two European Courts (CJEU and the ECtHR) in this area.[49]

---

[41] As it is well known, the Community Charter of the Fundamental Social Rights of Workers (a declaration adopted in 1989 by eleven Heads of State and Government) was explicitly inspired by the Charter of 1961. On the basis of this declaration, the Community institutions then adopted a series of directives on labour law. On the other hand, the Explanatory Report of the Revised Social Charter makes clear that some of its provisions were inspired by those directives.

[42] For example, European Parliament Resolution of 27 February 2014 *on the situation of fundamental rights in the European Union* (2012): "The European Parliament, [...] – having regard to the European Social Charter, as revised in 1996, and the case law of the European Committee of Social Rights [...]."

[43] Appl. No. 45036/98, *Bosphorus Hava Yollari Tutizim ve Ticaret Anoniom Sirketi v Ireland* (ECtHR 30 June 2005) para 156.

[44] For example, Complaint No. 55/2009, *Confédération Générale du Travail v France* (ECSR 23 June 2010) para 31–42.

[45] For example, Complaint No. 85/2012, *Swedish Trade Union Confederation (LO) and Swedish Confederation of Professional Employees (TCO) v Sweden* (ECSR 19 July 2013) para 72–74.

[46] See Complaint No. 123/2016, *Irish Congress of Trade Unions (ICTU) v Ireland* (ECSR 12 September 2018) para 114.

[47] Ryngaert (2014), p. 191.

[48] See further developments in Stangos (2013).

[49] See Douglas-Scott (2006), p. 629.

4. Challenges: Balancing Different Speeds in a Broader Social Europe

27 Since its origins, the EU's negotiations and strategies have been focusing on the combat against **distortion of competition** and against **social dumping** associated with worker mobility. More recently, other types of migration within the common territory, including the current **crisis of refugees** in Europe, are dealt with through the **Asylum, Migration and Integration Fund** (AMIF),[50] which also supports the **European Migration Network**, the **Union Resettlement Programme** and the transfer of beneficiaries of international protection from an EU State with high migratory pressure to another.

28 Taking into account the idea of a broader Social Europe, it must be recalled that in the Preamble of the 1996 Revised European Social Charter, the signatories expressed their wish "to update and adapt the substantive contents of the Charter in order to take account in particular of the **fundamental social changes** which have occurred since the text was adopted", as well as their will to progressively replace the 1961 Charter. The economic and financial crisis has actually consolidated the place of the Revised Charter as one essential instrument to face and manage these fundamental social changes by balancing different speeds.

29 Indeed, the configuration of the Revised Social Charter as a kind of "**European Pact for Social Democracy**", which allows for improving social standards at the European level, remains obvious from both the Council of Europe and the EU perspectives. Within the framework of the Council of Europe, the Committee of Ministers adopted an important political Declaration on the occasion of the 50th anniversary of the 1961 Charter, in October 2011, in which all MS were invited to accept both the collective complaint procedure and the Revised Charter. This is consistent with the "social version" of the three pillars of the Council of Europe, that is to say, Democracy, Human Rights and the Rule of Law and, therefore, Social Democracy, Social Rights and Social State.

30 As far as the EU is concerned, such configuration seems clear from the substantive and formal **synergies between the EUCFR** (legally binding since December 2009 with the entry into force of the Lisbon Treaty) and **the Revised Charter** (in particular, the set of social rights, especially under the title "Solidarity").

31 In this sense, it appears that there is a manifest **lack of consistency** between the fact of being an **EU MS** and, at the same time, the fact of **not having accepted the**

---

[50] The AMIF was set up for the period 2014–20, with a total of EUR 3.137 billion for the seven years. For the period 2021–2027, it has a budget of around EUR 10 billion. The Fund promotes the efficient management of migration flows and the implementation, strengthening and development of a common Union approach to asylum and immigration. It contributes to the achievement of four specific objectives: 1. **Asylum**: strengthening and developing the Common European Asylum System by ensuring that EU legislation in this field is efficiently and uniformly applied; 2. **Legal migration and integration**: supporting legal migration to EU States in line with the labour market needs and promoting the effective integration of non-EU nationals; 3. **Return**: enhancing fair and effective return strategies, which contribute to combating irregular migration, with an emphasis on sustainability and effectiveness of the return process; 4. **Solidarity**: making sure that EU States that are most affected by migration and asylum flows can count on solidarity from other EU States.

Article 151. [Objectives]

Revised Charter. In practice, both the EUCFR and the Revised Social Charter aim at improving the social standards at a European level. Accordingly, when adopting secondary legislation (directives and regulations), EU institutions must take the EUCFR directly and the Revised Social Charter indirectly into account. In parallel, when transposing or incorporating this secondary legislation, EU MS also must take the EUCFR directly and the Revised Social Charter indirectly into consideration.

This is the best way, at the stage of drafting, to "favour the harmonization of social systems" (as foreseen in Article 151 TFEU), to keep a convergence between the EU and the Council of Europe and, by extension, to avoid subsequent interpretative or jurisdictional divergences. The high-level Conference was organised in Turin from 17 to 18 October 2014 (launching the above-mentioned "**Turin process**"), bringing together political personalities from the Council of Europe and the EU, in order to hold an exchange of views and find political solutions to meet the challenge of enforcing human rights in times of austerity, and with a view to reinforcing the synergies between EU legislation and the Charter. **32**

With the same spirit, it has been illustrated (specific case law of the "anti-crisis" legislation in Greece, → para 15) that the collective complaint procedure before the ECSR is an adequate mechanism for giving more **visibility and effectiveness** to the rights recognized in the European Social Charter. It is worthwhile to note that the main virtue of the 1950 ECHR was not its set or catalogue of human rights but its monitoring mechanism (the ECtHR). Indeed, the ECHR aimed at ensuring only some of the rights recognised within the Universal Declaration, being that the right to formulate individual applications before the ECtHR was initially conceived as optional but has logically become mandatory for all MS since 1981. Anyway, such individual mechanism of action has appeared to be rather limited to challenging austerity measures implemented by States Parties in response to both the **economic crisis**[51] and the **pandemic crisis**.[52] **33**

At the universal level, the Optional Protocol to the International Covenant on Economic, Social and Cultural Rights providing for a system of individual communication was hopefully adopted on 10 December 2008 at the beginning of the crisis. Of course, there appears a clear lack of consistency for some European countries having accepted this Protocol (Luxembourg, Slovakia or Spain) and not having accepted the European collective complaints procedure. Accepting both procedures is a good example of international commitment to the idea of **indivisibility** (of guarantees). We all know that the key element is not the level of formal recognition of human rights but the establishment of effective remedies. Definitely, both universal and European Protocols, respectively providing for individual and collective remedies, represent the best opportunity to protect social rights in times of economic crisis. **34**

---

[51] See ECtHR (Press Unit/Unité de la Presse), *Factsheet – Austerity Measures*, February 2023 (https://www.echr.coe.int/Documents/FS_Austerity_measures_ENG.pdf).

[52] See ECtHR (Press Unit/Unité de la Presse), Factsheet – Covid-19 health crisis, January 2023 (https://www.echr.coe.int/Documents/FS_Covid_ENG.pdf).

35   Last but not least, regarding the establishment of coherent and harmonious relationships between the two normative systems (EU and Council of Europe) in favour of the **harmonization of the social models** and in order to avoid the kind of controversies analysed above, it appears essential not to forget the **EU accession to the European Social Charter**[53] as a further step to complete the parallel accession to the ECHR.[54] In any case, the current synergies must be inspired by the so-called *favor libertatis* or *pro personae* principle, as foreseen in the Preamble of the Interinstitutional Proclamation on the EPSR: this one "shall not prevent Member States or their social partners from establishing more ambitious social standards. In particular, nothing in the European Pillar of Social Rights shall be interpreted as restricting or adversely affecting rights and principles as recognised, in their respective fields of application, by Union law or international law and by international agreements to which the Union or all the Member States are a party, including the European Social Charter signed at Turin on 18 October 1961 and the relevant Conventions and Recommendations of the International Labour Organisation" (recital 16 of the Preamble to the EPSR).[55]

36   In this context, it has been held that the EPSR is neither a legislative instrument nor a binding catalogue of rights. It is, rather, a set of principles that shall lead to measures of implementation at EU and MS levels, in the form of legislative and policy initiatives,[56] and it is already ensuring that social rights are taken more systematically into consideration in the social and economic governance of the EU. As such, thanks to the flexible nature of the implementation measures that could be considered, the **EPSR** provides a **unique opportunity to improve the synergies**

---

[53] See De Schutter (2014): The report recalls the reasons why the dossier now deserves to be revisited. It examines the main legal arguments in favour of accession (and its modalities): accession, it shows, will contribute to reducing the risk of conflicts between the duties that are imposed under the (Revised) European Social Charter and EU law; and it will ensure the uniformity of application of EU law throughout all the EU MS. The report also examines whether the EU has the required international competence to accede to the (Revised) European Social Charter. It answers the question in the affirmative, based on Article 216 TFEU which codifies the implicit external powers that the EU may exercise. The report also questions whether the classical approach of the CJEU to the question of implicit external powers is well-suited to the specific nature of human rights treaties. The report considers, finally, the consequences that will follow from the accession of the EU to the (Revised) European Social Charter, taking into account the conditions under which the CJEU recognizes that international agreements concluded by the EU may be invoked.

[54] See the European Parliament Resolution of 19 May 2010 *on the institutional aspects of the accession of the EU to the ECHR*, 2009/2241(INI) para 30–31. On this point, see Gragl (2014), p. 58: in emphasising the synergies, the author concludes that "these courts must bear in mind that the purpose and objective of the accession is not to distinguish themselves in judicial battles with their respective counterpart, but to cooperate in order to improve the protection of human rights for individuals in Europe."

[55] Stangos (2018), p. 146 (footnote 31).

[56] It has been stated that the EPSR has allowed a revival of social dynamics aiming at adopting social directives. However, this social policy is still fragile: Mazuyer (2022), p. 73.

Article 151. [Objectives] 1335

with the ESC and to make progress towards overcoming the deficits of Social Europe. Six proposals are made in order to ensure that this opportunity is seized:[57]

- Proposal No. 1: To the extent that there is an overlap between the EUCFR and the EPSR, **strengthening the references to the ESC in the commentary to the EPSR** could help compensate, in part at least, for the paucity of references to the ESC in the Explanations appended to the EUCFR, which serve as an authoritative guide to its interpretation.
- Proposal No. 2: The references in the EPSR to the corresponding provisions of the ESC should be accompanied by a recommendation to take into **account their interpretation by the ECSR**.
- Proposal No. 3: The references to the ESC and to its interpretation by the ECSR shall constitute a strong encouragement to **the CJEU to align the status of the ESC** with that of other international human rights instruments ratified by all the EU members and to treat as authoritative its interpretation by the ECSR.
- Proposal No. 4: In the current situation, the **budgetary discipline** imposed under the "Fiscal Compact" may lead the EU MS parties to the 2012 Treaty on Stability, Coordination and Governance within the Economic and Monetary Union (TSCG) to adopt measures that lead to **violations of the ESC**. Article 3.3 point (b) of the TSCG allows for certain deviations from budgetary commitments in the presence of "exceptional circumstances", defined as "an unusual event outside the control of the Contracting Party concerned". In the future, a finding by the ECSR that a particular measure, made in the name of fiscal consolidation, leads to a situation that is not in conformity with the ESC should be treated as an "exceptional circumstance".
- Proposal No 5: **Impact Assessments** (IAs) are currently prepared to accompany the legislative proposals filed by the Commission as well as its major policy initiatives. The fundamental rights component of such IAs has been made more visible since 2005, by reference to the EUCFR. The adoption of the EPSR provides an opportunity to **further strengthen the social rights component of** such **IAs**. This could be achieved not only by reference to the EPSR but also **by an explicit reference to the ESC**.
- Proposal No. 6: Most of the provisions of the EPSR require to be implemented not (only) by the EU but (also) by its MS. The process of convergence encouraged by the EPSR would be significantly facilitated if all EU MS ratified the most recent version of ESC and accepted all its provisions or, if that cannot be achieved, if they agreed on a number of key paragraphs that they all accept as binding. Indeed, the Commission has already noted that **the ratification by the EU MS of relevant international instruments** figures among the tools that could support the **implementation of the principles of the EPSR**.

---

[57] De Schutter (2018), pp. 47–49.

List of Cases

ECJ/CJEU

ECJ 29.09.1987, 126/86, *Giménez Zaera*, ECLI:EU:C:1987:395 [cit. in para 18]
ECJ 17.03.1993, C-72/91 and C-73/91, *Sloman Neptun*, ECLI:EU:C:1993:97 [cit. in para 18]
CJEU 04.05.2010, C-533/08, *TNT Express Nederland*, ECLI:EU:C:2010:243 [cit. in para 16]
CJEU 15.09.2011, C-313/10, Opinion of AG Jääskinen, *Jansen*, ECLI:EU:C:2011:593 [cit. in para 13–14]
CJEU 15.01.2014, C-176/12, *Association de médiation sociale*, ECLI:EU:C:2014:2 [cit. in para 9]
CJEU 10.07.2014, C-198/13, *Julián Hernández*, ECLI:EU:C:2014:2055 [cit. in para 9]
CJEU17.07.2014, C-481/13, *Qurbani*, ECLI:EU:C:2014:2101 [cit. in para 16]
CJEU 05.02.2015, C-117/14, *Nisttahuz Poclava*, ECLI:EU:C:2015:60 [cit. in para 16]
CJEU 16.07.2015, C-340/14 and C-341/14, Opinion of AG Szpunar, *Trijber and Harmsen*, ECLI:EU:C:2015:505 [cit. in para 12]
CJEU 17.04.2018, C-414/16, *Egenberger*, ECLI:EU:C:2018:257 [cit. in para 9]
CJEU 11.09.2018, C-68/17, *IR*, ECLI:EU:C:2018:696 [cit. in para 9]
CJEU 06.11.2018, C-569/16 and C-570/16, *Bauer*, ECLI:EU:C:2018:871 [cit. in para 9]
CJEU 06.11.2018, C-684/16, *Max-Planck-Gesellschaft zur Förderung der Wissenschaften*, ECLI:EU:C:2018:874 [cit. in para 9]
CJEU 22.01.2019, C-193/17, *Cresco Investigation*, ECLI:EU:C:2019:43 [cit. in para 9]
CJEU 29.10.2020, C-243/19, *Veselības ministrija*, ECLI:EU:C:2020:872 [cit. in para 9]
CJEU 21.10.2021, C-824/19, *Komisia za zashtita ot diskriminatsia*, ECLI:EU:C:2021:862 [cit. in para 9]
CJEU 10.02.2022, C-485/20, *HR Rail*, ECLI:EU:C:2022:85 [cit. in para 9]

ECtHR

ECtHR 30.06.2005, 45036/98, *Bosphorus Hava Yollari Tutizim ve Ticaret Anoniom Sirketi v Ireland* [cit. in para 26]

ECSR

ECSR 23.06.2010, 55/2009, *Confédération Générale du Travail v France* [cit. in para 26]

ECSR 23.05.2012, 65/2011, *General federation of employees of the national electric power corporation and Confederation of Greek Civil Servants' Trade Unions v. Greece* [cit. in para 17]
ECSR 19.07.2013, 85/2012, *Swedish Trade Union Confederation (LO) and Swedish Confederation of Professional Employees (TCO) v Sweden* [cit. in para 26]
ECSR 23.03.2017, 111/2014, *Greek General Confederation of Labour (GSEE) v. Greece* [cit. in para 17]
ECSR 12.09.2018, 123/2016, *Irish Congress of Trade Unions (ICTU) v Ireland (TCO) v Sweden* [cit. in para 26]
ECSR 17.05.2022, 165/2018, *Panhellenic Association of Pensioners of the OTE Group Telecommunications (PAP-OTE) v Greece* [cit. in para 17]

References[58]

Anderson, K. M. (2015). *Social policy in the European Union*. Palgrave Macmillan.
Benecke, M. (2021). Zum Gewicht der Sozialpartner bei der Rechtsetzung durch sozialen Dialog. *Europäische Zeitschrift für Arbeitsrecht*, 214–222.
Clapham, A. (1992). Is there any competition between the two social charters? *Affari sociali internazionali, 1*, 189–198.
Codogno, L., & van der Noord, P. (2022). Assessing next generation EU. In L. Paganetto (Ed.), *Economic challenges for Europe after the pandemic* (pp. 59–82). Springer.
Corti, M. (2022). Un Pilastro vitale. In M. Corti (Ed.), *Il Pilastro europeo dei diritti social e il rilancio della politica sociale dell'UE* (pp. 7–11). Vita e Pensiero.
Czaplinski, W. (2013). European Union law and the laws of the member states. Sources of EU law. In D. Milczarek, A. Adamczyk, & K. Zajaczkowski (Eds.), *Introduction to European studies: A new approach to uniting Europe* (pp. 117–145). Centre for Europe/University of Warsaw.
De Schutter, O. (2014). *L'adhésion de l'Union européenne à la Charte sociale européenne*. Université Catholique de Louvain. Retrieved from https://cadmus.eui.eu/bitstream/handle/1814/2826/law04-11.pdf?sequence=1
De Schutter, O. (2018). *The European Pillar of Social Rights and the role of the European Social Charter in the EU legal order*. Council of Europe. Retrieved from https://rm.coe.int/study-on-the-european-pillar-of-social-rights-and-the-role-of-the-esc-/1680903132
De Schutter, O., & Dermine, P. (2016). The two constitutions of Europe: Integrating social rights in the new economic architecture of the Union. *CRIDHO Working Paper, 2*, 1–40.
Douglas-Scott, S. (2006). A tale of two courts: Luxembourg, Strasbourg and the growing European human rights acquis. *Common Market Law Review., 43*(3), 629–665.
García Ninet, J. I. (Ed.). (2014). *El impacto de la gran crisis mundial sobre el Derecho del Trabajo y de la Seguridad Social. Su incidencia en España, Europa y Brasil, 2008-2014*. Ariel.
Gragl, P. (2014). A giant leap for European human rights? The final agreement on the European Union's accession to the European Convention on Human Rights. *Common Market Law Review, 51*(1), 13–58.
Häde, U. (2020). Europäischer Gerichtshof und Bundesverfassungsgericht im Spannungsfeld zwischen Selbstbehauptung und Kooperation: Die Judikatur zu den Anleihekaufprogrammen der EZN. In M. Ludwigs & S. Schmahl (Eds.), *Die EU zwischen Niedergang und Neugründung. Wege aus der Polykrise* (pp. 177–194). Nomos.

---

[58] All cited internet sources in this comment have been accessed on 17.02.2023.

Jimena Quesada, L. (2009). The social policy in the light of the Lisbon Treaty. In *Studia z zakresu prawa pracy/Studies on labour law and social policy (in honour of Andrej M. Swiatkowski)*. Uniwersytetu Jagiellonskiego.

Mazuyer, E. (2022). Une Europe sociale qui protège? *Revue de l'Union Européenne, 655*, 73–77.

Panzera, C. (2009). Il bello dell'essere diversi. Corte costituzionale e Corti europee ad una svolta. *Rivista Trimestrale di Diritto Pubblico, Anno LIX, Fasc, 1*, 1–43.

Ryngaert, C. (2014). Oscillating between embracing and avoiding *Bosphorus*: The European Court of Human Rights on member state responsibility for acts of international organisations and the case of the European Union. *European Law Review, 39*(2), 176–192.

Schwarz, M. (2014). Memorandum of misunderstanding – The doomed road of the European Stability Mechanism and a possible way out: Enhanced cooperation. *Common Market Law Review, 51*(1), 389–424.

Stangos, P. (2013). Les rapports entre la Charte sociale européenne et le droit de l'Union européenne: le rôle singulier du Comité européen des Droits Sociaux et de sa jurisprudence. *Cahiers de droit européen, 49*, 319–393.

Stangos, P. (2018). Sinergias entre la Unión Europea y la Carta Social Europea, en la hora del Pilar Europeo de Derechos Sociales. *Revista del Ministerio de Trabajo, Migraciones y Seguridad Social, 137*, 139–164.

Tajadura Tejada, J., & De Miguel Bárcena, J. (Eds.). (2008). *Justicia constitucional y Unión Europea*. Centro de Estudios Políticos y Constitucionales.

Vidal Prado, C. (2004). *El impacto del nuevo derecho europeo en los tribunales constitucionales*. Colex.

von der Groeben, H., Schwarze, J., & Hatje, A. (Eds.). (2015). *Europäisches Unionsrecht*. Nomos.

Article 152 [Social Dialogue]

The Union recognises and promotes the role of the social partners at its level, taking into account the diversity of national systems. It shall facilitate dialogue between the social partners, respecting their autonomy.

The Tripartite Social Summit for Growth and Employment shall contribute to social dialogue.[11–19]

Contents

1. Introductory Remarks: Recognition of the Role of the Social Partners in the European Construction 1
2. The Aim and the Tools to Encourage Social Dialogue: Focus on the Tripartite Social Summit for Growth and Employment 11
3. Balancing National Diversity and European Unity 20
4. Challenges: Dynamics of the Social Dialogue in a Broader Social Europe 29

List of Cases
References

1. Introductory Remarks: Recognition of the Role of the Social Partners in the European Construction

Article 152 TFEU has its precedent in **Article 118b TEEC** (introduced by the 1986 SEA): 'The Commission shall endeavour to develop the dialogue between management and labour at European level which could, if the two sides consider it desirable, lead to relations based on agreement'. From this new legal basis and in contrast to the Treaty of Rome (which included labour and management only via the Economic and Social Committee), it has been held that the SEA **resurrected the social dialogue process**. The drafting of Article 118b TEEC itself was an example of the fruits of social dialogue in the framework of the *Delors* Commission.[1]

As is well known, the 1992 **Maastricht Treaty** focused on the EMU and, therefore, neglected the development of the social dimension. In effect, MS failed to introduce new social policy provisions within the Treaty and, as a result, they agreed on a new Social Chapter of the EEC Treaty through a **Protocol on Social Policy** (the UK was not signatory of this Protocol). In this Protocol, the other 11 MS

---

[1] Anderson (2015), p. 62.

expressed that they 'wish to continue along the path laid down in the 1989 Social Charter; that they have adopted among themselves an Agreement to this end; that this Agreement is annexed to this Protocol; that this Protocol and the said Agreement are without prejudice to the provisions of this Treaty, particularly those relating to social policy which constitute an integral part of the *acquis communautaire*'.

3   The Agreement, which actually contained most of the current profiles of the **social policy chapter** in the TFEU (with the exception of the reference to the European Social Charter of the Council of Europe, which was a novelty introduced by the 1997 Amsterdam Treaty), emphasised the importance of the social dialogue and the role of social partners. It must be pointed out that that Agreement was also negotiated by European-level unions and employer organisations (ETUC, CEEP and UNICE) during the IGC in December 1991 with the support of the European Commission encouraging these European social partners to formulate an agreement concerning the role of the social partners in European social policy-making. This was considered a major step forward for **euro-corporatism**, because the existing institution for social partner involvement in policy-making, the Economic and Social Committee, was weak and only played a consultative role.[2]

4   Indeed, the Protocol on Social Policy expanded the policy-making influence of **trade unions and employers' organisations** at the EU level. It required the European Commission to facilitate the dialogue between labour and management 'by ensuring balanced support for the parties', as well as to consult them before submitting proposals in the social field on the possible direction of the EU. Most important, social partners could also submit to the Commission proposals for EU action and conclude agreements at the European level leading to EU legal acts.

5   These provisions went 'a long way towards establishing **corporatist policy practices** at EU level'[3] and constituted the basis for four important directives in which the role of social partners is underlined: 1) the introduction of a **European Works Council;**[4] 2) a **framework agreement** on parental leave;[5]

---

[2] Anderson (2015), p. 64.

[3] Anderson (2015), p. 65.

[4] See Council Directive 94/45/EC, O.J. L 254/64 (1994), repealed by Council Directive 2009/38/EC *on the establishment of a European Works Council or a procedure in Community-scale undertakings and Community-scale groups of undertakings for the purposes of informing and consulting employees (Recast)*, O.J. L 122/28 (2009). On 14 May 2018, the Commission published a REFIT (European Commission's regulatory fitness and performance programme) evaluation of the European Works Council Directive and concluded that information for workers has improved in terms of quality and scope, but the directive has not increased the rate at which new EWCs are set up. The Commission proposed to draw up a practical handbook for EWC practitioners and provide funding to social partners to support the implementation and effectiveness of EWCs.

[5] Council Directive 96/34/EC, O.J. L 145/4 (1996), repealed by Council Directive 2010/18/EU *implementing the revised Framework Agreement on parental leave concluded by BUSINESSEUROPE, UEAPME, CEEP and ETUC*, O.J. L 68/1 (2010). The status of the three social partners that concluded the original framework agreement on parental leave (UNICE, CEEP and the ETUC) was challenged by the UEAPME (Union Européenne de l'Artisanat et des Petites et Moyennes

3) gender discrimination;[6] and 4) the framework agreement on part-time work.[7]

As indicated above, the Agreement appended to the Protocol on Social Policy incorporated into the Maastricht Treaty has constituted the substantial basis for the current Title X of the TFEU. Moreover, the Lisbon Treaty has further strengthened the role of social partners at the EU level,[8] insofar as Article 152 TFEU now provides that the Union as a whole – and not only the Commission – is committed to promoting social dialogue, what is consistent with the new **horizontal clause** (Article 9 TFEU), which stipulates that the EU shall consider the **social dimension** in defining and implementing its policies.[9] Indeed, Article 152 TFEU is a novelty introduced in the Lisbon Treaty and raises to an institutional level the dynamics of social dialogue which characterised the style, as well as the practice, of the policies inspired by Jacques Delors in the 1980s.[10] Moreover, Article 152 TFEU has also institutionalised the Tripartite Social Summit for Growth and Employment.

Article 152 TFEU is closely connected with other provisions within the Title on social policy as well. Particularly at the Union level, **social partners** are to be consulted under Article 154 TFEU on possible initiatives based on Article 153 TFEU, and may sign agreements, which may be implemented at the Union level at their request under Article 155 TFEU. Of course, social partners may also collect and exchange good practices across the Union. At national level, social partners may support the implementation of social policy through their involvement in the design and implementation of relevant policies as well as via **collective bargaining**, in conformity with Articles 27 and 28 EUCFR. These two provisions refer to 'national laws and practices'.

To summarised, it can be held that today the role of European social dialogue is fully recognised across the EU and its institutions. With such spirit, the 2017 **Interinstitutional Proclamation on the European Pillar of Social Rights** has put the emphasis on this important role (recitals 4 and 20 of the Preamble to the EPSR, and principle 8 on 'social dialogue and involvement of workers'). However, Article 152 TFEU does not refer specifically to the industrial democracy model, but

---

Entreprises) by submitting an application for annulment of Council Directive 96/34/EC: see Case T-135/96, *UEAPME v Council* (CFI 17 June 1998) para 110–112. The CFI dismissed the application as inadmissible. In doctrine, see Moreau (1999), p. 53 et seqq, and more extensively Adinolfi, in Tizzano (2014), p. 1427 et seqq.

[6] Council Directive 97/80/EC, O.J. L 14/6 (1997), repealed by Council Directive 2006/54/EC *on the implementation of the principle of equal opportunities and equal treatment of men and women in matters of employment and occupation (recast)*, O.J. L 204/23 (2006).

[7] Annexed to Council Directive 97/81/EC *concerning the Framework Agreement on part-time work concluded by UNICE, CEEP and the ETUC*, O.J. L 14/9 (1997).

[8] Veneziani (2012), p. 123.

[9] See Schmitt (2014), pp. 743–744.

[10] Sciarra (2020), p. 1.

9   With this regard, the Commission announced in the **EPSR Action Plan** of 4 March 2021[12] that it would present an initiative to support national and EU social dialogue following consultations with the social partners. Strengthened social dialogue at all levels was also urged at the highest political level with the **Porto Social Commitment** signed on 7 May 2021 by the Portuguese Presidency of the Council of the EU, the European Parliament, the European Commission, social partners, and the Social Platform. The social dialogue initiative, also mentioned in the Commission Communication 'Conference on the Future of Europe, Putting Vision into Concrete Action' of 17 June 2022, made a significant contribution to the follow-up to the Conference.[13]

10   Finally, the **social dialogue initiative** was made more concrete throughout the Commission Communication 'Strengthening social dialogue in the European Union: harnessing its full potential for managing fair transitions' of 25 January 2023,[14] by including: the launch of a new award for innovative social dialogue practices; an information and visiting programme for young future social partner leaders; the review of sectoral social dialogue at the EU level; and a new supporting frame for social partner agreements at the EU level. In the context of the recent changes affecting the world of work such as climate change, digitalisation and demographic trends (accelerated by the COVID-19 pandemic), the Communication recalls that social dialogue is a cornerstone of the European Social Model[15] and that strong social partners are essential for effective and balanced change management.

2. The Aim and the Tools to Encourage Social Dialogue: Focus on the Tripartite Social Summit for Growth and Employment

11   The main tool to encourage social dialogue is **Tripartite Social Summit for Growth and Employment** institutionalised in Article 152.2 TFEU.[16] Its main aim is to ensure that there is a continuous concertation between EU institutions (mainly, the Council and the Commission) and the social partners, that is to say, without prejudice of electoral interests or strategies.[17] From this point of view, it

---

[11] Veneziani (2017), p. 385.

[12] COM(2021) 102 final.

[13] COM(2022) 404 final, Annex.

[14] COM(2023) 40 final.

[15] Brieger (2022), p. 816.

[16] See originally Council Decision No. 2003/174/EC, O.J. L 70/31 (2003), repealed by Council Decision (EU) 2016/1859 *on the Tripartite Social Summit for Growth and Employment*, O.J. L 284/27 (2016).

[17] For further critical reflection on this point, see Alfonso (2013). On one hand, the author shows that the involvement of trade unions and employers in policymaking is a strategy of compromise-building used by governments to insulate policies from electoral dynamics when they are faced

has been found a positive trend that tripartism is becoming more prominent at the EU level.[18]

The Tripartite Social Summit for Growth and Employment has is precedent in the Standing Committee on Employment.[19] Within the action of that Committee, the Luxembourg European Council of 20–21 November 1997 decided to associate social partners in the implementation of the coordinated **employment strategy**. Then, the Cologne European Council of 3–4 June 1999 set up a **macroeconomic dialogue** with the participation of representatives from the Council, the Commission, the ECB and the social partners. The follow-up of this **concertation** was ensured by the Lisbon European Council of 23–24 March 2000, which set a new strategic goal for the next decade and agreed that achievement of that goal required an overall strategy designed to integrate structural reforms, a **coordinated European employment strategy**, social protection and macroeconomic policies in the context of coordination of the general economic policies of the MS.

In its Communication of 26 June 2002 entitled 'The European social dialogue, a force for innovation and change,'[20] the Commission stressed that the Tripartite Social Summit could contribute to the debate on these topics by strengthening the social dialogue, in other words, the **social partners' contribution to the work of the public institutions**, 'to improve public governance and economic and social reform within the EU'. According to the Commission, the three main aspects to be improved by a greater involvement of social partners are:

(A) **Developing the social dialogue within the EU**: The purpose is to increase the **consultation of the social partners** in the drafting of European legislation (since consulting the social partners is compulsory in the areas of employment and social policy but optional concerning sectoral issues with social repercussions) and the transposition of European legislation at national level. In this respect, the effectiveness of the social dialogue is linked to the **representativeness of the social partners** at European level and, consequently, the co-operation between national organisations and the improvement of their internal governance are relevant aspects. In addition, the social partners are also encouraged to **broaden and enhance the social dialogue** by concluding more agreements to be integrated into European law and by developing the processes for sectoral and intersectoral dialogue.

---

with partisan divisions, or to pre-empt mass protest when unpopular reforms are likely to have risky electoral consequences. On the other hand, he suggests that European integration is somehow undermining the patterns of 'social concertation' by illustrating the political underpinnings of social concertation with a focus on the regulation of labour mobility and unemployment protection in Austria and Switzerland, as well as empirical examples from other European countries.

[18] Kšiňan (2021), p. 176.

[19] Council Decision No. 70/532/EEC *setting up the Standing Committee on Employment of the European Communities*, O.J. L 273/25 (1970).

[20] COM(2002) 341 final. See also Commission Communication adapting and promoting the social dialogue at Community level, COM(98) 322 final, Commission Communication concerning the Development of the Social Dialogue at Community level, COM(96) 448 final and Commission Communication concerning the application of the Agreement on social policy, COM(93) 600 final.

15 **(B) Contribution to growth and employment**: Having in mind that the actions of the social partners may contribute to the attainment of the growth and employment goals set by the **Lisbon Strategy** (adopted at the Lisbon European Council of March 2000, then replaced by the EU 2020 strategy), their role is particularly associated with the management of change in the organisation of work, employee training, the promotion of equal opportunities and active ageing policies.[21]

16 **(C) International co-operation:** The European social partners may collaborate in the EU enlargement process (by improving the structure and the capacities of labour and management in countries which are candidates to accede to the EU), in the EU foreign policy (the social partners of the EU and non-MS may exchange experience and best practice, particularly concerning the countries of the Euro-Mediterranean Partnership, the EU Partnership with Latin America, with the African, Caribbean and Pacific countries, and with the United States and Japan), and in the context of multilateral negotiations, particularly within international organisations (by playing a role as experts).

17 Afterwards, in their joint contribution to the **Laeken European Council** of 14–15 December 2001, the social partners pointed out that the Standing Committee on Employment had not led to such an integration of concertation and that it did not meet the need for coherence and synergy between the various processes in which they were involved. They therefore proposed that it should be abolished and that a new form of **tripartite consultation** should be established. In that joint contribution, the social partners proposed to formalise their meetings with the Troika at the level of Heads of State or Government and the Commission which, in the context of the Luxembourg process, have been held since 1997 on the eve of European Councils.

18 Since December 2000, these meetings have been known as Social Summits and they are attended by the President of the Commission and the Troika of Heads of State or Government together with the Ministers for Labour and Social Affairs and the social partners[22] (comprising 10 workers' representatives and 10 employers' representatives). The concrete membership within the Tripartite Social Summit for Growth and Employment is set out in Article 2 of Council Decision (EU) 2016/1859, taking into account the necessity of enlargement and development of an **autonomous social dialogue**,[23] the widest possible **representativeness** as well

---

[21] Cf. Pochet (2010), p. 6: In the field of employment policies there is a need for an agenda that focuses on quality jobs, social security, social rights, social dialogue, public services, etc., an agenda that has to be debated with the aim of achieving a fair transition through participation of the collective actors in the steps required to achieve this radical change in social and economic model.

[22] The social partners have been represented by the Union of Industrial Employers' Confederations of Europe (UNICE), the European Centre of Enterprises with Public Participation and of Enterprises of General Economic Interest (CEEP), the European Association of Craft, Small and Medium-sized Enterprises (UEAPME), the European Trade Union Confederation (ETUC), Eurocadres and the Confédération européenne des cadres (CEC).

[23] See Bogoni (2015), p. 242 et seqq.

as the **legitimacy** and **effectiveness** of the consultation of social partners[24] are of the highest importance.[25]

The **functioning of the Tripartite Social Summit** is foreseen in Article 3 **19** (preparation of the agenda by the Council meeting in its Employment, Social Policy, Health and Consumer Affairs configuration and, then, determination of such agenda jointly by the Council Presidency, the Commission and the workers' and employers' cross-industry organisations), Article 4 (operation of the Summit based on a meeting at least once a year) and Article 6 (summary of the Summit's discussions to inform the relevant Council configurations, the European Parliament and the general public) of Council Decision (EU) 2016/1859. Indeed, the Tripartite Social Summit operates with other fora which enable a comprehensive bipartite and tripartite EU dialogue (the macroeconomic dialogue, the Employment Committee, the Social Protection Committee or the Social Dialogue Committee) to develop better tools to deal with rapid labour market and social changes caused by COVID-19 pandemic and other recent crises (e.g. the energy crisis due to the war in Ukraine).[26] In this context of **polycrisis**, there is an increasing dissensus and politicisation of Social Europe which does not only apply to social and employment issues but grasps a broader dynamic that unfolds from a broader tension between the dynamics of EU-building and the preservation of the cultural, redistributive and political capacities of national governments.[27]

3. Balancing National Diversity and European Unity

In practice, the national diversity and the autonomy of social partners at a domestic **20** level which is recognised by the EU in Article 152 TFEU[28] has been counterbalanced by the European unity, at least in the name of two **European standards**,

---

[24] To that end, the Commission verifies the representativeness of the social partners and the revised list of organisations involved in all dimensions of social dialogue at European level, and that list should be updated.

[25] Baylos Grau (2001), pp. 84–85.

[26] At the Tripartite Social Summit held on 19 October 2022 EU leaders and social partners discussed on 'Tackling the energy crisis and the cost of living crisis: How to protect the economy, businesses and workers'.

[27] Corti (2022), p. 10.

[28] This is seen as a respect for national sovereignty and the peculiarity of national industrial relations system in line with the 'diverse forms of national practices' (Article 151.2 TFEU) and the idea of national reservation deriving from Article 153.5 TFEU (the powers given by Article 153 TFEU do not apply to pay, the right of association, the right to strike or the right to impose lock-out).

Generally, the MS and, where appropriate, the social partners at national level enjoy broad discretion in their choice, not only to pursue a particular aim in the field of social and employment policy, but also in the definition of measures capable of achieving it. See Case C-411/05, *Palacios de la Villa* (ECJ 16 October 2007) para 68.

21   The first modulation to this autonomy is illustrated by judgment of 28 June 2012 in the case of *Erny* concerning free movement for workers under Council Regulation (EEC) No. 1612/68.[29] Mr Erny, a French national residing in France and working in Germany, submitted that the top-up amount that was payable to him under a scheme of 'part-time working for older employees prior to retirement' was subject to income tax in France and that the de facto double taxation resulting from the disputed method of calculation resulted in discrimination inasmuch as different situations were treated in the same way.

22   The Court found those clauses, in collective and individual agreements, to be incompatible with EU primary and secondary law.[30] The CJEU's decision was mainly founded on the principle of **non-discrimination** and the **disadvantaged position** (as **cross-border worker**) suffered from Mr Erny (subject to income tax in the MS of residence as well as to tax on wages of the MS of employment). In this line of reasoning, the CJEU held that the prohibition of discrimination laid down in Article 45.2 TFEU 'applies not only to the actions of public authorities, but also to all agreements intended to regulate paid labour collectively, as well as to contracts between individuals'. Moreover, 'Article 7(4) of Regulation No. 1612/68, which clarifies and gives effect to certain rights conferred on migrant workers by Article 45 TFEU, provides that any clause of a collective or individual agreement concerning, inter alia, remuneration and other conditions of work or dismissal is null and void in so far as it lays down discriminatory conditions in respect of workers who are nationals of the other Member States'.[31]

23   Furthermore, in connection with this substantial ground, on the one hand, the CJEU did not accept the argument based on the administrative difficulties provided by Daimler to justify the application of that method of calculation to cross-border workers.[32] On the other hand, the CJEU rejected the other argument from Daimler invoking 'the autonomy which the social partners should enjoy in developing working conditions', since although the EU respects the autonomy of the social partners, 'the fact none the less remains, as is stated in Article 28 [EUCFR], that the right of workers and employers, or their respective organisations, to negotiate and conclude collective agreements at the appropriate levels must be exercised in accordance with European Union law and, consequently, with the principle of non-discrimination'.[33]

---

[29] Council Regulation (EEC) No. 1612/68, O.J. L 257/2 (1968), repealed and replaced by Parliament/Council Regulation (EU) No. 492/2011 *on freedom of movement for workers within the Union*, O.J. L 141/ (2011).

[30] Case C-172/11, *Erny* (CJEU 28 June 2012) para 54.

[31] Case C-172/11, *Erny* (CJEU 28 June 2012) para 36–37.

[32] Case C-172/11, *Erny* (CJEU 28 June 2012) para 48.

[33] Case C-172/11, *Erny* (CJEU 28 June 2012) para 50.

Article 152. [Social Dialogue]

24 The second restriction to this **autonomy of the social partners** is exemplified by Case C-271/08, *Commission v Germany*, where the CJEU declared that **direct award of contracts** (in respect of occupational old-age pensions for local authority employees), without a call for tenders at the EU level, to pension providers designated in a collective agreement concluded between management and labour, was in breach of freedom of establishment and freedom to provide services.[34] Particularly, this direct award referred to the Collective agreement on the conversion, for local authority employees, of earnings into pension savings.[35]

25 In the pre-litigation procedure, the German Government reacted to the formal letter from the Commission that application of public procurement law to the award of the contracts at issue would be contrary to the autonomy of management and labour protected in Article 9.3 of the German Basic Law. Then, before the CJEU, Germany was supported by the Governments of Denmark and Sweden by arguing that those awards implemented a **collective agreement** negotiated between management and labour. As it is known, within these two other countries, the weight of collective bargaining and the importance of trade unionist culture are strongly emphasised.

26 The starting point of the legal reasoning from the CJEU also consisted of highlighting the fundamental character of the right to collective bargaining in different human rights instruments (including the European Social Charter) signed by EU MS.[36] In addition, the CJEU underlines the conjunction between Article 28 and Article 52.6 EUCFR by recalling that 'protection of the **fundamental right to bargain collectively** must take full account, in particular, of national laws and practices' as well as that 'by virtue of Article 152 TFEU the European Union recognises and promotes the role of the social partners at its level, taking into account the diversity of national systems'. The CJEU accepts likewise that the collective agreement 'meets, in a general way, a social objective'.[37]

27 However, these premises find a prominent fluctuation when the CJEU holds that 'the fact that the right to bargain collectively is a fundamental right, and the [collective agreement]'s social objective perceived as a whole, cannot, in

---

[34] See also Case C-410/14, *Falk Pharma* (CJEU 2 June 2016) para 24 and Case C-9/17, *Tirkkonen* (CJEU 1 March 2018) para 29–35.

[35] *Tarifvertrag zur Entgeltumwandlung für Arbeitnehmer im kommunalen öffentlichen Dienst (TV-EUmw/VKA)*.

[36] See para 37: 'the right to bargain collectively, which the signatories of the TV-EUmw/VKA have exercised in the present case, is recognised both by the provisions of various international instruments which the Member States have cooperated in or signed, such as Article 6 of the European Social Charter, signed at Turin on 18 October 1961 and revised at Strasbourg on 3 May 1996, and by the provisions of instruments drawn up by the Member States at Community level or in the context of the European Union, such as Article 12 of the Community Charter of the Fundamental Social Rights of Workers adopted at the meeting of the European Council held in Strasbourg on 9 December 1989, and Article 28 of the Charter of Fundamental Rights of the European Union ("the Charter"), an instrument to which Article 6 TEU accords the same legal value as the Treaties'.

[37] Case C-271/08, *Commission v Germany* (CJEU 15 July 2010) para 38–40.

themselves, mean that local authority employers are automatically excluded from the obligation to comply with the requirements stemming from Directives 92/50 and 2004/18, which implement freedom of establishment and the freedom to provide services in the field of public procurement'.[38] In fact, this is the final outcome of the case and seems to be the current position of the CJEU,[39] which intends to show in the following paragraphs of its ruling an apparent and **difficult balancing between 'secondary fundamental rights' and 'prevalent economic freedoms'**. From this perspective, it mentions the *Viking* and *Laval* cases[40] to contrast them with previous judgments more sensitive to fundamental social rights[41] and, finally, to emphasise the difficult 'equilibrium'[42] which is solved giving priority to economic aims over to social goals.[43]

28   With such parameters, the diversity of the national social system in the MS would be inherent to respect for their '**national identity**' under Article 4.2 TEU.[44] From this perspective, the main challenge is making compatible such '**social identity**' with the construction of a 'European social reality' founded on MS' common values contributing to the modernisation of **social protection systems**.[45] Otherwise, the Europeanisation of social policies will appear fragmented.[46]

4. Challenges: Dynamics of the Social Dialogue in a Broader Social Europe

29   In the above-mentioned Commission Communication of 26 June 2002, 'The European social dialogue, a force for innovation and change', the European Commission explicitly supported 'the improvement of **social dialogue at all levels of governance**' by proposing, particularly, to improve training for the European social partners and representatives of national authorities. The Commission also puts the accent in the international co-operation, by emphasising the collaboration of European social partners in the EU enlargement process. By contrast, the British

---

[38] Case C-271/08, *Commission v Germany* (CJEU 15 July 2010) para 41.

[39] Case C-699/17, *Allianz Vorsorgekasse* (CJUE 4 April 2019) para 56–58.

[40] See Case C-271/08, *Commission v Germany* (CJEU 15 July 2010) para 42–43.

[41] See Case C-271/08, *Commission v Germany* (CJEU 15 July 2010) para 45 and, by contrast, para 46.

[42] See Case C-271/08, *Commission v Germany* (CJEU 15 July 2010) para 49–52. Indeed, in *Schmidberger* and *Omega* the ECJ made apparently prevail fundamental rights over classical economic freedoms: see Morijn (2006).

[43] On the conflict between the judgment in Case C-341/05, *Laval* (ECJ 18 December 2007) para 90–91 and Complaint No. 85/2012, *Swedish Trade Union Confederation (LO) and Swedish Confederation of Professional Employees (TCO) v Sweden* (ECSR 3 July 2013) para 73–74, see Salcedo Beltrán (2014), as well as, under the principle of proportionality perspective, Llobera Vila (2013). See also Case C-438/05, *Viking* (ECJ 11 December 2007) para 43–44.

[44] Lamblin-Gourdin (2013), p. 420.

[45] Favarel-Dapas and Quintin (2007), pp. 15–16.

[46] Pochet (2019), p. 236.

withdrawal from the EU ('**Brexit**') implied a major challenge in terms of possible negative impact on worker's rights (including working conditions for workers in the UK, implications for migrant workers and students working in or from the UK, or the future preservation of the single market with freedom of movement for workers).[47] Indeed, framework agreements reached between social partners on a raft of social measures further complicated a dichotomous UK-EU view.[48]

From these considerations, it is obvious that the **dynamics of the social dialogue** in a broader Social Europe implies the optimisation of the **synergies between the EU and the Council of Europe**. With such a spirit, both national and European social partners have a major role to play in achieving social goals, since the input (strengthening social dialogue) will logically optimise the output (the protection of social rights). 30

In this context, it is regrettable that the same actors are less active within the Council of Europe than within the EU. For example, apart from the national social partners (employers' organisations and trade unions in the country concerned), the two more representative European social partners (European Trade Union Confederation, ETUC, and BUSINESSEUROPE, formerly UNICE), should be more proactive as organisations entitled to submit **collective complaints** on human rights violations linked to social objectives before the European Committee of Social Rights (ECSR). Such new dynamics would also imply that the social dialogue is associated with the transition from a **culture of conflict** to a **culture of partnership** within a broader process of 'social cooperation'.[49] 31

On the other hand, national and European social partners may also formulate observations or comments as 'amici curiae' (third-party intervention) in the framework of a collective complaint already submitted before the ECSR by NGOs entitled to do so. We must consider that most of the NGOs with this '**participatory status**' and entitlement to lodge complaints with the ECSR[50] also take part (as 'participant organisation') in the network composing the **Fundamental Rights Platform** (FRP) of the EU.[51] This implies that the FRP, within the Fundamental Rights Agency (FRA), is a unique forum allowing a truly European debate on the protection of social rights. In other words, with regard to the synergies of both organisations (the Council of Europe and the EU) at NGOs level, there is a direct connection between FRP and the complaints submitted to the Committee. With such spirit, it has been suggested further involvement of **non-governmental organisations** in the social dialogue[52] to avoid the predominance of 32

---

[47] Ellison (2017), pp. 275–277.

[48] Plomien (2018), p. 261.

[49] Hurbean (2016), p. 26.

[50] As of January 2023, there are 60 organisations entitled to submit complaints. Available at https://rm.coe.int/gc-2022-26-bil-list-ingos-01-01-2023/1680a99bfc.

[51] Currently, the network of civil society organisations within the FRP is composed of over 500 member organisations from the civil society at local, regional/national and EU level.

[52] Rust, in von der Groeben et al. (2015), Article 152 AEUV para 52.

intergovernmentalism as main approach in the development of the European social dimension (as shown by consultations leading to the adoption of the EPSR).[53]

33   Furthermore, if we consider that FRP helps to better tailor the Agency's work to the genuine needs of European citizens (e.g. by providing feedback and suggestions for the agency's Annual Work Programme and Annual Report, or participating as stakeholders at different stages of FRA thematic projects) and, in addition, that FRA provides valuable input into the Committee's judicial work (findings from FRA are important as a factual source in the Committee's assessment, when taking decisions on the merits in the collective complaints procedure),[54] there is also an indirect connection between FRP and complaints before the Committee to be exploited.

34   Indeed, if we specifically tackle the protection of social rights in Europe, this complementarity is clearly illustrated by the EUCFR,[55] the catalogue of social rights of which has been elaborated following the model of the European Social Charter (as explicitly indicated in the Appendix of the EU Charter). In the same vein, it has been reflected on what is called the 'living interpretation' of both the ECHR and the revised European Social Charter in relation to other social rights rules of international law, by putting the accent on the synergies with the EU and the ILO.[56]

List of Cases

ECJ/CJEU

ECJ 16.10.2007, C-411/05, *Palacios de la Villa*, ECLI:EU:C:2007:604 [cit. in para 20]

ECJ 11.11.2007, C-438/05, *Viking*, ECLI:EU:C:2007:772 [cit. in para 27]

ECJ 18.12.2007, C-341/05, *Laval*, ECLI:EU:C:2007:809 [cit. in para 27]

CJEU 15.07.2010, C-271/08, *Commission v Germany*, ECLI:EU:C:2010:426 [cit. in para 26–27]

CJEU 28.06.2012, C-172/11, *Erny*, ECLI:EU:C:2012:399 [cit. in para 22–23]

CJEU 02.06.2016, C-410/14, *Falk Pharma*, ECLI:EU:C:2016:399 [cit. in para 24]

CJEU 01.03.2018, C-9/17, *Tirkkonen*, ECLI:EU:C:2018:142 [cit. in para 24]

CJEU 04.04.2019, C-699/17, *Allianz Vorsorgekasse*, ECLI:EU:C:2019:290 [cit. in para 27]

---

[53] Carella and Graziano (2022), p. 390.

[54] See, for example, Complaint No. 151/2017, *European Roma Rights Centre (ERRC) v Bulgaria* (ECSR 5 December 2018) para 77 and 83, Complaint No. 62/2010, *FIDH v Belgium* (ECSR 21 March 2012) para 117 and Complaint No. 49/2008, *INTERIGHTS v Greece* (ECSR 11 December 2009) para 39.

[55] Kollonay-Lehoczky et al. (2012), p. 61 et seqq.

[56] Gerasimova and Sychenko (2021), p. 114.

CFI
CFI 17.06.1998, T-135/96, *UEAPME v Council*, ECLI:EU:T:1998:128 [cit. in para 5]

ECSR
ECSR 11.12.2009, 49/2008, *INTERIGHTS v Greece* [cit. in para 33]
ECSR 21.03.2012, 62/2010, *FIDH v Belgium* [cit. in para 33]
ECSR 03.07.2013, 85/2012, *Swedish Trade Union Confederation (LO) and Swedish Confederation of Professional Employees (TCO) v Sweden* [cit. in para 27]
ECSR 05.12.2018, 151/2017, *European Roma Rights Centre (ERRC) v Bulgaria* [cit. in para 33]

References[57]

Alfonso, A. (2013). *Social concertation in times of austerity. European integration and the politics of labour market reforms in Austria and Switzerland.* Amsterdam University Press.
Anderson, K. M. (2015). *Social policy in the European Union.* Palgrave Macmillan.
Baylos Grau, A. (2001). Representación y representatividad sindical en la globalización. *Cuadernos de Relaciones Laborales, 19,* 69–94.
Bogoni, M. (2015). *El espacio europeo de negociación colectiva.* Bomarzo.
Brieger, A. (2022). Sozialer Dialog. In *Fachlexikon der Sozialen Arbeit* (pp. 816–816). Nomos.
Carella, B., & Graziano, P. (2022). Back to the future in EU social policy? Endogenous critical junctures and the case of the European Pillar of Social Rights. *Journal of Common Market Studies, 60*(2), 374–390.
Corti, F. (2022). *The politicisation of social Europe: Conflict dynamics and welfare integration.* Elgar.
Ellison, M. (2017). Through the looking glass: young people, work and the transition between education and employment in a post-Brexit UK. *Journal of Social Policy, 46*(4), 675–698.
Favarel-Dapas, B., & Quintin, O. (2007). *L'Europe sociale, enjeux et réalités* (2nd ed.). La documentation française.
Gerasimova, E., & Sychenko, E. (2021). Council of Europe: European Social Charter and European Convention on Human Rights. In B. ter Haar & A. Kun (Eds.), *EU collective labour law* (pp. 102–114). Elgar.
Hurbean, A. (2016). Some aspects regarding the European Social Dialogue. *AGORA International Journal of Juridical Sciences, 10*(2), 26–33.
Kollonay-Lehoczky, C., Lörcher, K., & Schöman, I. (2012). The Lisbon treaty and the charter of fundamental rights of the European Union. In I. Schöman, K. Lörcher, & N. Bruun (Eds.), *The Lisbon treaty and social Europe* (pp. 61–103). Hart Publishing.
Kšiňan, J. (2021). EU issues on tripartism. In B. ter Haar & A. Kun (Eds.), *EU collective labour law* (pp. 165–176). Elgar.
Lamblin-Gourdin, A. S. (2013). In J. M. Thouvenin & A. Trebilcock (Eds.), *Droit international social.* Vol. I. (pp. 418–446). Bruylant.
Llobera Vila, M. (2013). *El desplazamiento transnacional de trabajadores. Libre prestación de servicios, Constitución económica y principio de proporcionalidad.* Tirant lo Blanch.
Moreau, M. A. (1999). Sur la représentativité des partenaires sociaux européens. *Droit Social, 1,* 53–63.

---

[57] All cited Internet sources in this comment have been accessed on 17.02.2023.

Morijn, J. (2006). Balancing fundamental rights and common market freedoms in Union Law: Schmidberger and the Omega in the light of the European Constitution. *European Law Journal, 12*(1), 15–40.

Plomien, A. (2018). UK's membership of the EU: Brexit and the gains, losses and dilemmas for social policy. *Social Policy and Society, 17*(2), 259–264.

Pochet, P. (2010). *What is wrong with Europe 2020*. Brussels: ETUI (Policy Brief/European Social Policy, Issue 2).

Pochet, P. (2019). *À la recherche de l'Europe sociale*. PUF.

Salcedo Beltrán, C. (2014). *Negociación colectiva, conflicto laboral y Carta Social Europea*. Bomarzo.

Schmitt, M. (2014). Le rôle des partenaires sociaux dans la gestion de la crise économique et financière: prendre le Traité de Lisbonne au sérieux. *Le travail humain au Carrefour du droit et de la sociologie. Hommage au Professeur Nikitas Aliprantis*. Presses universitaires de Strasbourg.

Sciarra, S. (2020). Eppur si muove? La strategia della Commissione per rilanciare l'Europa sociale. *Freedom, Security & Justice: European Legal Studies, 1*, 1–9.

Tizzano, A. (Ed.). (2014). *Trattati dell'Unione Europea* (2nd ed.). Giuffrè.

Veneziani, B. (2012). The role of social partners in the Lisbon treaty. In I. Schöman, K. Lörcher, & N. Bruun (Eds.), *The Lisbon treaty and social Europe* (pp. 123–159). Hart Publishing.

Veneziani, B. (2017). Article 21. The right to information and consultation. In N. Bruun, K. Lorcher, I. Schömann, & S. Clauwaert (Eds.), *The European social charter and the employment relation* (pp. 381–403). Hart Publishing.

von der Groeben, H., Schwarze, J., & Hatje, A. (Eds.). (2015). *Europäisches Unionsrecht*. Nomos.

Article 153 [Union Action]
(ex-Article 137 TEC)

1. With a view to achieving the objectives of Article 151, the Union shall support and complement the activities of the Member States in the following fields:

   (a) improvement in particular of the working environment to protect workers' health and safety;[23–25]
   (b) working conditions;[26–28]
   (c) social security and social protection of workers;[29–31]
   (d) protection of workers where their employment contract is terminated;[32–34]
   (e) the information and consultation of workers;[35,36]
   (f) representation and collective defence of the interests of workers and employers, including co-determination, subject to paragraph 5;[37,38]
   (g) conditions of employment for third-country nationals legally residing in Union territory;[39,40]
   (h) the integration of persons excluded from the labour market, without prejudice to Article 166;[41–43]
   (i) equality between men and women with regard to labour market opportunities and treatment at work;[44–47]
   (j) the combating of social exclusion;[48–50]
   (k) the modernisation of social protection systems without prejudice to point (c).[51–53]

2. To this end, the European Parliament and the Council:

   (a) may adopt measures designed to encourage cooperation between Member States through initiatives aimed at improving knowledge, developing exchanges of information and best practices, promoting innovative approaches and evaluating experiences, excluding any harmonisation of the laws and regulations of the Member States;
   (b) may adopt, in the fields referred to in paragraph 1(a) to (i), by means of directives, minimum requirements for gradual implementation, having regard to the conditions and technical rules obtaining in each of the Member States. Such directives shall avoid imposing administrative, financial and legal constraints in a way which would hold back the creation and development of small and medium-sized undertakings.

   The European Parliament and the Council shall act in accordance with the ordinary legislative procedure after consulting the Economic and Social Committee and the Committee of the Regions.[21]
   In the fields referred to in paragraph 1(c), (d), (f) and (g), the Council shall act unanimously, in accordance with a special legislative procedure, after consulting the European Parliament and the said Committees.[21]

The Council, acting unanimously on a proposal from the Commission, after consulting the European Parliament, may decide to render the ordinary legislative procedure applicable to paragraph 1(d), (f) and (g).[22]

3. A Member State may entrust management and labour, at their joint request, with the implementation of directives adopted pursuant to paragraph 2, or, where appropriate, with the implementation of a Council decision adopted in accordance with Article 155.

In this case, it shall ensure that, no later than the date on which a directive or a decision must be transposed or implemented, management and labour have introduced the necessary measures by agreement, the Member State concerned being required to take any necessary measure enabling it at any time to be in a position to guarantee the results imposed by that directive or that decision.

4. The provisions adopted pursuant to this Article:

– shall not affect the right of Member States to define the fundamental principles of their social security systems and must not significantly affect the financial equilibrium thereof,
– shall not prevent any Member State from maintaining or introducing more stringent protective measures compatible with the Treaties.

5. The provisions of this Article shall not apply to pay, the right of association, the right to strike or the right to impose lock-outs.[54-62]

Contents

1.	First Approach to Article 153 TFEU: The Progressive Extension of the Explicit Union's Powers in the Social Field and the Horizontal Social Clause	1
2.	Balancing the Supplementary Union's Actions and the Principles of European Union Social Law (Paragraphs 1 Through 3)	15
	2.1. Introduction	15
	2.2. Specific Fields	21
	2.2.1. Improvement in Particular of the Working Environment to Protect Workers' Health and Safety	23
	2.2.2. Working Conditions	26
	2.2.3. Social Security and Social Protection of Workers	29
	2.2.4. Protection of Workers Where Their Employment Contract Is Terminated	32
	2.2.5. The Information and Consultation of Workers	35
	2.2.6. Representation and Collective Defence of the Interests of Workers and Employers, Including Co-Determination, Subject to Paragraph 5	37
	2.2.7. Conditions of Employment for Third-Country Nationals Legally Residing in Union Territory	39
	2.2.8. The Integration of Persons Excluded from the Labour Market, Without Prejudice to Article 166	41
	2.2.9. Equality Between Men and Women on Labour Market Opportunities and Treatment at Work	44
	2.2.10. The Combating of Social Exclusion	48

Jimena Quesada

	2.2.11. The Modernisation of Social Protection Systems Without Prejudice to Point (c)	51
3.	Balancing the Union's Powers and the Substantial Exclusions: A Difficult Tension Between State Margin and European Action (Paragraphs 4 and 5)	54
4.	Challenges: A Complex Approach to Social Policy and Fundamental Rights in a Broader Social Europe	63

List of Cases
References

1. First Approach to Article 153 TFEU: The Progressive Extension of the Explicit Union's Powers in the Social Field and the Horizontal Social Clause

In the original provision (ex-Article 118 TEEC) the Commission had very limited powers.[1] In other words, in the founding Treaties the Community action was not supported by any explicit **competence in the social fields**. For this reason, the secondary legislation on social matters adopted within the original European Communities was based on the doctrine of '**implied powers**' deriving from ex-Article 235 TEEC[2] (now Article 352 TFEU, the so called '**flexibility clause**'), in conjunction with the aim of harmonising the MS's laws concerning the internal market (ex-Article 100 TEEC = Article 115 TFEU).[3] Such legal basis implied putting into practice the unanimity rule.

Later on, the SEA conferred **explicit powers** to European institutions by moving from unanimity to **qualified majority** rule in relation to the working environment, as regards the health and safety of workers (Article 118a TEEC), what coincides with current Article 153.1 point (a) TFEU. Then, the Maastricht Treaty extended (only through the Agreement appended to Protocol on Social Policy with the opt-

---

[1] Under ex-Article 118 TEEC, for this purpose 'the Commission shall act in close contact with Member States by means of studies, the issuing of opinions, and the organising of consultations both on problems arising at the national level and on those of concern to international organisations [...]'.

[2] See also Opinion 2/94 of the Court, *Accession to the ECHR* (ECJ 28 March 1996), particularly para 29–30.

[3] See, for example, Council Directive 75/129/EEC *on the approximation of the laws of the Member States relating to collective redundancies,* O.J. L 47/29 (1975): 'Having regard to [Article 100 EEC]; Whereas it is important that greater protection should be afforded to workers in the event of collective redundancies while taking into account the need for balanced economic and social development within the Community; Whereas, despite increasing convergence, differences still remain between the provisions in force in the Member States of the Community concerning the practical arrangements and procedures for such redundancies and the measures designed to alleviate the consequences of redundancy for workers; Whereas these differences can have a direct effect on the functioning of the common market [...]'.

out from the UK) qualified majority voting to several areas: working conditions (Article 153.1 point (b) TFEU and Article 31 EUCFR), the information and consultation of workers (Article 153.1 point (e) TFEU and Article 27 EUCFR), equality between men and women with regard to labour market opportunities and treatment at work (Article 153.1 point (i) TFEU and Article 23 EUCFR), and the integration of persons excluded from the labour market (Article 153.1 point (h) TFEU).

3   However, that Protocol on Social Policy incorporated in the Maastricht Treaty kept the **unanimity rule for other areas**: social security and social protection of workers (Article 153.1 point (c) TFEU and Article 34 EUCFR), protection of workers where their employment contract is terminated (Article 153.1 point (d) TFEU and Article 30 EUCFR), representation and collective defence of the interests of workers and employers (Article 153.1 point (f) TFEU), conditions of employment for third-country nationals legally residing in Community territory (Article 153.1 point (g) and Article 179.2 point (b) TFEU and Article 15 EUCFR) and financial contributions for promotion of employment and job-creation. On the other hand, that Protocol did not apply to pay, the right of association, the right to strike or the right to impose lockouts; similarly, Article 153.5 TFEU keeps such exclusion.

4   The **Amsterdam Treaty** incorporated the Protocol on Social Policy to the provisions of the EC Treaty (Article 137 TEC). The new version of Article 137 TEC-Nice (2001) added two other social fields: the combating of social exclusion (paragraph 1 point (j)) and the modernisation of social protection systems (paragraph 1 point (k)), which also exactly coincide (like the whole list) with the same paragraphs in current Article 153.1 TFEU. Apart from this, both the **Nice Treaty** and the Lisbon Treaty have kept the unanimity rule in relation to social security and social protection of workers, protection of workers where their employment contract is terminated; representation and collective defence of the interests of workers and employers, and conditions of employment for third-country nationals legally residing in Union territory. From this perspective, the main qualitative difference between the **Lisbon Treaty** and the previous revisions (mainly, the Amsterdam Treaty and the Nice Treaty) is that the TFEU has extended the ordinary legislative procedure (former co-decision procedure) to those social fields.

5   In any case, putting into practice the Union action in these fields is very complex (including the use of the adjective 'social'[4]), not only because of the existence of potential and different procedures and actors foreseen in Article 153 TFEU (MS, European institutions and bodies as well as European social partners), but also because the boundary problems concerning the distributions of competences are

---

[4] In the EU language, 'social' also relates to employment policy, working conditions and labour law. From this point of view, the adjective 'social' may be applied not only to the specific Title X of the TFEU on social policy, but also to Titles IX (employment), XII (education, vocational training, youth and sport) and XVIII (economic, social and territorial cohesion). It must also be recalled that, before the Lisbon Treaty, social policy was included into a broader Title on 'Social Policy, Education, Vocational Training and Youth' (Title VIII in the Maastricht Treaty and Title XI in both the Amsterdam and the Nice Treaties).

evident in relation to **social policy**.⁵ On the other hand, it should be observed that Article 153 TFEU does not establish **subjective rights**.⁶

In this regard, it has been noted that 'the difficulties in this area are especially marked, since certain aspects of social policy fall within shared competence, although it is not clear which; other aspects appear to fall within the category of supporting, coordinating, and supplementary action, even though they are not within the relevant list, ant there is in addition separate provision for social policy in the category being considered here'.⁷

Indeed, Article 4.2 point (b) TFEU labels as **shared competence** between the EU and the MS 'social policy, for the aspects defined in this Treaty'. In addition, Article 5.3 TFEU provides that 'the Union may take initiatives to ensure coordination of Member States' social policies'. Furthermore, Article 9 TFEU contains the so-called 'horizontal social clause', which is an important new feature of the Lisbon Treaty and requires social concerns to be considered in all EU activities.

In contrast to the areas associated with the single European market where instruments for harmonisation are extensively used, the EU assigns social policy largely only a supporting, supplementing and coordinating function. The subsidiarity principle (Article 5.3 TEU) is the EU's legally binding guide when framing legislation in the social policy field as well.⁸ In cases where the EU has authority (Article 5.2 TEU) in the social policy field, it must first be determined whether the proposed activity could be performed better by the MS. As a last resort, the **boundaries of competences** are subject to interpretation by the ECJ.⁹ Additionally, a comprehensive impact assessment must be conducted, particularly on the social consequences of the activity (Article 5 of Protocol No. 2). Once again, it must be kept in mind the difficult balance between social, economic, and employment policy at the European level.

As is well known, the 2000 '**Lisbon Strategy**'¹⁰ (targeting the year 2010) included, in the framework of a comprehensive approach, the promotion of the inclusion of people who suffer from poverty or social exclusion. Similarly, the **Europe 2020 Strategy** (as the follow-up strategy to the Lisbon Strategy) has outlined, among the five strategic headline targets, two which are directly related to labour market and social policies, namely: the EU is to raise employment rates among men and women to 75% and reduce the number of persons at risk of poverty and social exclusion by 20 million by the year 2020.

---

⁵ Lörcher (2012), p. 165.

⁶ Rights of individuals may, however, arise from the directives issued based on the provision. See Case C-126/86, *Giménez Zaera* (ECJ 29 September 1987) para 11.

⁷ Craig (2010), p. 180.

⁸ See Blanke (2012), p. 235 et seqq. According to this author, the Union is strictly bound by fundamental rights and cannot avoid this obligation by reference to the principle of subsidiarity.

⁹ In addition, the context of the regulation and the pursued objectives must also be considered. See, for example, Case C-268/06, *Impact* (ECJ 15 April 2008) para 110; Joined Cases C-395/08 and C-396/08, *Bruno and Others* (CJEU 10 June 2010) para 28.

¹⁰ Lisbon European Council, 23–24 March 2000, Presidency Conclusions.

9   In this last regard, while Article 153.1 point (j) TFEU includes 'the combating of social exclusion', Article 153.2 (1) TFEU does not even mention this field among the **potential actions and procedures to be undertaken**. How to compensate this intentional omission? Of course, based on Article 153.1 TFEU, the Union is empowered to support and complement the activities of the MS in the field of combating social exclusion and, from this perspective, the Union can act under Article 153.2 (1) point (a), TFEU.[11] Furthermore, on the one hand, it is clear that in compliance with the principle of subsidiarity, MS' local, regional and national authorities have a primary and major role to play in adopting initiatives to combat poverty and social exclusion. On the other hand, it is also evident that the combating of exclusion is not only one of the Union's social objectives under Article 151 TFEU (in conjunction with Article 153 TFEU),[12] but also one of the Union's main and general objectives set forth in Article 3.3 TEU, which refers to 'a highly competitive social market economy, aiming at full employment and social progress' by adding that the EU 'shall combat social exclusion and discrimination, and shall promote social justice and protection, equality between women and men, solidarity between generations and protection of the rights of the child'.

10   In the same vein, this general objective established in Article 3 TEU is closely related to the values referred to in Article 2 TEU. As a result, **Article 34 EUCFR** must also be considered by 'institutions, bodies, offices and agencies of the Union with due regard for the principle of subsidiarity' and by 'Member States' when they are implementing EU law (under Article 51 EUCFR). Particularly, Article 34.3 EUCFR states that 'in order to combat social exclusion and poverty, the Union recognises and respects the right to social and housing assistance so as to ensure a decent existence for all those who lack sufficient resources, in accordance with the rules laid down by Union law and national laws and practices'.

11   The **explanation on Article 34 EUCFR** explicitly refers to Article 13 (the right to social and medical assistance), Article 30 (the right to protection against poverty and social exclusion) and Article 31 (the right to housing) of the 1996 Revised European Social Charter as well as, above all, to Article 153 TFEU by somehow compensating the above mentioned omission. This explanation furthermore holds: 'The Union must respect [Article 34.3 EUCFR] it in the context of policies based on [Article 153 TFEU]'.

12   In this sense, some authors have proposed a '**human-developmental interpretation**' of the EU's economic constitution, which should lead to the systematic promotion of social goals enshrined in the Treaty in connection with the EUCFR. Their premise is that the EU is not based solely on objectives, and the notion of

---

[11] See Langer, in von der Groeben et al. (2015), Article 153 AEUV para 41.

[12] Indeed, Article 151 TFEU must be considered as the basis of interpretation for other provisions of the Treaties and secondary legislation in the field of social policy: See Benecke, in Grabitz et al. (2022), Article 153 AEUV para 31 (released in 2022).

values appeared in the European discourse with the conclusion of the Constitutional Treaty,[13] which has been 'substantially rescued' on these matters by the Lisbon Treaty.[14] From this perspective, those authors develop an evaluation of the EUCFR looking at the constitutional values underlying the Charter with the purpose of strengthening the social dimension vis-à-vis the conflicting economic objectives. Nonetheless, these authors seem to be much more in favour of another instrument (instead of EU law and the CJEU's case law): the ECHR supported by the ECtHR.[15]

In my view, despite the self-restraint exercised by the CJEU in some social fields (and, especially, its reluctance to exploit the social rights recognised in the EUCFR under the heading of 'solidarity'), the importance of the **social case law of the ECtHR** cannot be exaggerated. Indeed, in the field of combating poverty and social exclusion, without prejudice of several interesting judgments from Strasbourg,[16] the specific case law on this topic is being elaborated by the **European Committee of Social Rights** (ECSR), precisely under Articles 13, 30 and 31 of the European Social Charter.[17]

In any case, it seems that the most important issue regarding social policy is how fundamental **social rights** are **balanced towards economic freedoms** and also how social policy considerations and national traditions are considered within other policy areas of the EU. The debate on EU competences in the social field is strongly polarised. This complex equilibrium is still present after the adoption of the European Pillar of Social Rights (EPSR) and its 2021 Action Plan.[18] Some researchers see strong national competences as the only way of protecting national systems, while others argue that only a strong EU social policy can end the present process of indirect undermining national social systems through market regulation.[19]

---

[13] See Deakin (2012), p. 19 et seqq.

[14] Aldecoa Luzarraga and Guinea Llorente (2008). See also Ziller (2007).

[15] Particularly, Dorssemont (2012), p. 45 et seqq.

[16] For example, Appl. No. 30696/09, *M.S.S. v Belgium and Greece* (ECtHR 21 January 2011) para 254, Appl. No. 27013/07, *Winterstein and Others v France* (ECtHR 17 October 2013) para 155–158, Appl. No. 24720/13, *Hirtu and Others v France* (ECtHR 14 May 2020) para 70–76, and Appl. No. 17808/19 and 36972/19, *Paketova and Others v Bulgaria* (ECtHR 4 October 2022) para 148–152.

[17] Among others, Complaint No. 58/2009, *COHRE v Italy* (ECSR 25 June 2010) para 96–110; Complaint No. 63/2010, *COHRE v France* (ECSR 28 June 2011) para 41–45; Complaint No.110/2014, *FIDH v Ireland* (ECSR 12 May 2017) para 162–171; Complaint No. 151/2017, *ERRC v Bulgaria* (ECSR 5 December 2018) para 75, and Complaint No. 173/2018, *ICJ and ECRE v Greece* (ECSR January 2021) para 135.

[18] On the three EU headline targets to be achieved according to the 2021 Action Plan on the EPSR (in the areas of employment, skills, and social protection), it its stated that 'while the majority of the instruments for achieving them are competence of the Member States, the EU targets reflect a common ambition by 2030 to which this Action Plan offers an important contribution'.

[19] To approach this doctrinal debate in considering the impact of the EPSR in light of Article 153 TFEU, see Lasa López (2019), p. 143, and Mülder (2020), p. 103.

2. Balancing the Supplementary Union's Actions and the Principles of European Union Social Law (Paragraphs 1 Through 3)

2.1. Introduction

15 The supporting and complementary Union's actions with a view to achieving the social objectives of Article 151 TFEU, in conformity with Article 153.1 TFEU, have been more significant in several fields (e.g., improvement of the working environment to protect workers' health and safety or working conditions) than in others (e.g., protection of workers in the event of termination of employment or the information and consultation of workers). Such significance derives not only from specific legislative acts, but also from the case law of the CJEU. In effect, the **choice of the legal basis** must be based on objective factors, which are amenable to **judicial review** and particularly include the aim and content of the measure.[20]

16 From this perspective, European **secondary law** has been developed in the field of **safety and health at work** on the explicit basis of Article 118a TEEC (introduced in the primary law through the SEA), to which Article 153 TFEU corresponds. This is the case and objective of Council Directive 92/85/EEC on the introduction of measures to encourage improvements in the safety and health at work of pregnant workers and workers who have recently given birth or are breastfeeding.[21] The eighth recital in the preamble to that directive states that those workers must be considered a specific risk group, and measures must be taken with regard to their safety and health.

17 In the same vein, according to the case law of the ECJ, the right to **maternity leave** granted to pregnant workers must be regarded as a particularly important mechanism of protection under employment law. The EU legislature thus considered that the fundamental changes to the living conditions of the persons concerned during the period of at least 14 weeks preceding and after childbirth constituted a legitimate ground on which they could suspend their employment, without the public authorities or employers being allowed in any way to call the legitimacy of that ground into question.[22]

The scope of this protection has been **nuanced by the CJEU** in other cases, such as an employer's refusal to provide maternity leave to a commissioning mother who

---

[20] See, for instance, Case C-94/03, *Commission v Council* (ECJ 10 January 2006) para 34–37. Of course, if the content or objective of a measure affects several of the areas mentioned in Article 153.1 TFEU, they are to be based on respective competencies, provided that they can be separated from each other.

[21] Council Directive 92/85/EEC *on the introduction of measures to encourage improvements in the safety and health at work of pregnant workers and workers who have recently given birth or are breastfeeding (tenth individual Directive within the meaning of Article 16 (1) of Directive 89/391/EEC)*, O.J. L 348/1 (1992). See Case C-460/06, *Paquay* (ECJ 11 October 2007) para 27, and Case C-232/09, *Danosa* (CJEU 11 November 2010) para 58.

[22] See Case C-116/06, *Kiiski* (ECJ 20 September 2007) para 49, and Case C-5/12, *Betriu Montull* (CJEU 19 September 2013) para 48.

Article 153. [Union Action]

has had a baby through a surrogacy arrangement, which has not been considered discriminatory on grounds of sex in light of the above mentioned Council Directive 92/85/EEC read in conjunction with Parliament/Council Directive 2006/54/EC on the implementation of the principle of equal opportunities and equal treatment of men and women in matters of employment and occupation.[23] Indeed, both directives do not preclude MS from applying or introducing laws, regulations or administrative provisions more favourable to the protection of the safety and health of commissioning mothers who have had babies through a surrogacy arrangement by allowing them to take maternity leave as a result of the birth of the child.[24]

18 Such interpretation, consisting of guaranteeing a better level of protection of the safety and health of workers, seems also confirmed by Article 153 TFEU, which provides in paragraph 2 for the adoption (in the fields referred to in paragraph 1 point (a) to point (i)) of '*minimum requirements* for **gradual implementation**', and in its fourth paragraph that 'the provisions adopted pursuant to this Article [...] shall not prevent any Member State from maintaining or introducing *more stringent protective measures* compatible with the Treaties'. That approach, as the Court held in *United Kingdom v Council*,[25] is also in accordance with the legislative responsibility imposed by the enabling legal basis in the Treaty, which authorised the EU legislature only to adopt minimum requirements so as to contribute, through harmonisation, to achieving the objective of raising the level of health and safety protection of workers, which is primarily the MS' responsibility.[26] Furthermore, Article 153.1 point (i) TFEU also refers to 'equality between men and women with regard to labour market opportunities and treatment at work', which has to be read conjunction with Articles 3.3 TEU, 157 TFEU and 23 EUCFR ('equality between women and men must be ensured in all areas, including employment, work and pay').[27]

19 On working conditions, in the case of *Strack*, dealing with the interpretation of Article 7 of Council Directive 2003/88/EC on certain aspects of the organisation of working time[28] in relation to the right to **paid annual leave**, the Court recalled its settled case law according to which: first, the entitlement of every worker to paid annual leave must be regarded as 'a particularly important principle of European Union social law, affirmed by Article 31(2) of the Charter, which the first subparagraph of Article 6(1) TEU recognises as having the same legal value as the

---

[23] Parliament/Council Directive 2006/54/EC *on the implementation of the principle of equal opportunities and equal treatment of men and women in matters of employment and occupation*, O.J. L 204/23 (2006).

[24] Case C-167/12, *C. D.* (CJEU 18 March 2014) para 42.

[25] Case C-84/94, *United Kingdom* v *Council* (ECJ 12 November 1996) para 47.

[26] Case C-155/10, *Williams and Others* (Opinion of AG Trstenjak of 16 June 2011) para 35.

[27] See Case C-624/19, *Tesco Stores* (CJEU 3 June 2021) para 33 and 34, and Case C-405/20, *BVAEB* (CJEU 2 May 2022) para 39.

[28] Council Directive 2003/88/EC *concerning certain aspects of the organisation of working time*, O.J. L 299/9 (2003).

Treaties'.[29] In addition, the CJEU highlighted the sources of inspiration of this provision of the EUCFR, including the European Social Charter.[30] And second, 'the right to paid annual leave cannot be interpreted restrictively', which means that Article 7.1 of Council Directive 2003/88/EC 'precludes national legislation or practices which provide that the right to paid annual leave is extinguished at the end of the leave year and/or of a carry-over period laid down by national law even where the worker has been on sick leave for the whole year and where his incapacity for work persisted until the end of his employment relationship, which was the reason why he could not exercise his right to paid annual leave'.[31]

20 Moreover, the CJEU also recalled its previous case law, in which it was held 'that the measures on the **organisation of working time** which form the subject-matter of Directive 93/104, particularly those contained in Article 7 of that directive, contribute directly to the improvement of health and safety protection for workers within the meaning of [Article 153 TFEU] and the evolution of social legislation at both national and international levels confirms the existence of a link between measures relating to working time and the health and safety of workers'. The Court pointed out that 'such an interpretation of the words "safety" and "health" derives support in particular from the preamble to the Constitution of the World Health Organisation to which all the Member States belong'.[32]

2.2. Specific Fields

21 As a premise, it should be noted that EU policies and legislation on Article 153 TFEU can be developed following the two different legislative procedures, namely the **ordinary legislative procedure** under Article 294 TFEU on the competences of Article 153.1 points (a), (b), (e), (h) and (i) TFEU, and the **special legislative procedure** on the competences of Article 153.1 points (c), (d), (f) and (g) TFEU.

22 Subparagraph 4 of contains a **special passerelle clause**.[33] Under this provision, the Council, acting unanimously on a proposal from the Commission, after consulting the European Parliament, may decide to render the ordinary legislative procedure applicable to some of the cases where a special procedure applies. Social security and social protection of workers in point (c), however, is not included in the enumeration. This is due to the fact that social security is still a sensitive area for the MS for which they are reluctant to transfer sovereign rights to the EU. A transition

---

[29] Case C-579/12 RX-II, *Commission v Strack* (CJEU 19 September 2013) para 26 with references to further case law.

[30] Case C-579/12 RX-II, *Commission v Strack* (CJEU 19 September 2013) para 27.

[31] Case C-579/12 RX-II, *Commission v Strack* (CJEU 19 September 2013) para 29, 31.

[32] Case C-579/12 RX-II, *Commission v Strack* (CJEU 19 September 2013) para 4 with reference to Case C-84/94, *United Kingdom v Council* (ECJ 12 November 1996) para 36 to 39 and 59.

[33] Böttner and Grinc (2018), p. 37–38.

to the ordinary legislative procedure would require a decision in accordance with the general passerelle of Article 48(7) TEU.

2.2.1. Improvement in Particular of the Working Environment to Protect Workers' Health and Safety

Specifically, Article 153.1 point (a) TFEU (alongside a mainstreaming approach, e.g. Article 168 TFEU)[34] is closely connected with Article 31.1 EUCFR, which gives every worker the **right to working conditions which respect his or her health, safety and dignity**.[35] In addition, Principle 10 of the EPSR has highlighted the **importance of protection of personal data for workers**[36] in consistency with Article 8 EUCFR and Article 16 TFEU. This new approach shows that 'in particular' under Article 153.1 point (a) is not restricted to 'working environment'.[37] In this particular field,[38] the synergies between the EU and the Council of Europe must be emphasised both at normative and judicial level[39] to harmonise their respective new legal developments (mainly the 2016 EU General Data Protection Regulation[40] and

23

---

[34] Article 168.1 TFEU states that 'a high level of human health protection shall be ensured in the definition and implementation of all Union policies and activities'.

[35] This is without prejudice to other specific rules set forth in the TFEU, such as Article 91.1 point (c) and Article 100 TFEU concerning 'measures to improve transport safety', which may be considered as *lex specialis* to Article 153.1 point (a).

[36] The heading of Principle 10 of the EPSR is 'healthy, safe and well-adapted work environment and data protection'. Principle 10b introduces two inter-related rights: first, it goes beyond the protection of health and safety by affording workers the right to a working environment adapted to their specific occupational circumstances. Second, in accordance also with the principle of active ageing, it recognises the need to adapt the working environment to enable workers to have sustainable and longer working careers. Certain adaptations, such as for example better lighting for carrying out clerical work, may be necessary due to the worker's age. In addition, adjustments, such as more flexible working hours, may be necessary to maintain older workers' health and well-being.

[37] In the same vein, in Commission Communication, *Safer and Healthier Work for All*, COM (2017) 12 final, the Commission emphasises the need to refocus efforts on ensuring better and broader protection, compliance and enforcement of occupational safety and health standards on the ground. It announces a number of legislative actions to step up fight against occupational cancer, as well as initiatives to support effective implementation of the rules, notably in micro-enterprises and SMEs. The Commission invites Member States and social partners to work together to modernise occupational safety and health legislation at the EU and national level, while maintaining or improving workers' protection.

[38] See Martínez López-Sáez (2018), pp. 146–152.

[39] The processing of personal data by the employer has always to be based on a legal ground, normally performance of a contract, compliance with a legal obligation or for the purposes of the legitimate interest pursued by the employer, except where such interest is overridden by the interest or fundamental rights of the worker: See Commission Staff Working Document, SWD (2017) 201 final.

[40] Council Regulation (EU) 2016/679 *on the protection of natural persons with regard to the processing of personal data and on the free movement of such data*, O.J. L 119/1 (2016).

24 the 2018 Council of Europe Convention 108+[41]) and recent case law (from the CJEU[42] and the ECtHR[43]). More generally, we must consider the specific case law from the ECSR in this field.[44]

At the level of EU secondary law, some significant legal acts concerning improvement of the working environment have already been adopted, such as Council Framework Directive 89/391/EEC[45] and more than twenty related directives setting minimum requirements for the **prevention of occupational risks**, the **protection of safety and health** and the **elimination of risks and accident factors**.[46] The Framework Directive establishes the general principles for a proper management of safety and health, such as the responsibility of the employer, rights and duties of workers, risk assessment as an instrument to continuously improve company processes, or workers' representation. The related directives tailor these main principles to some specific workplaces and sectors, specific risks, tasks or categories of workers. They define how to assess these risks and, in some cases, set limit exposure values for certain substances and agents.[47]

25 In this framework, for example, Council Directive 92/85/EEC introduced measures to encourage improvements in the safety and health at work of pregnant workers and workers who have recently given birth or are breastfeeding. To this end, Council Directive 2004/37/EC (the Carcinogens and Mutagens Directive)[48] has been amended several times with the aim of improving protection for millions of workers by revising or establishing binding occupational exposure limit values for a number of dangerous chemical agents.[49] The Commission, in consultation with the social partners, shall continue to propose further updates of these directives and to support the implementation of the acquis by improving compliance with the

---

[41] Protocol *amending the Convention for the Protection of Individuals with regard to Automatic Processing of Personal Data*, CETS No.223 (2018).

[42] E.g. Case C-434/16, *Novak* (CJEU 20 December 2017) para 61.

[43] E.g. Appl. No. 61496/08, *Bărbulescu v Romania* (ECtHR 5 September 2017) para 50–51 and Appl. No. 1874/13 and 8567/13, *López Ribalda and Others v Spain* (ECtHR 17 October 2019) para 63–66.

[44] For example, Complaint No. 10/2000, *Tehy ry and STTK v Finland* (ECSR 17 October 2001) para 25–27: Violation of Article 2§4 ESC (elimination of risks for workers in dangerous or unhealthy occupations). See also Article 3 ESC (right to safe and healthy working conditions).

[45] Council Directive 89/391/EEC *on the introduction of measures to encourage improvements in the safety and health of workers at work*, O.J. L 183/1 (1989), amended by Parliament/Council Regulation (EC) No. 1137/2008, O.J. L 311/1 (2008).

[46] See, for example, Council Directive 90/270/EEC of 29 May 1990 *on the minimum safety and health requirements for work with display screen equipment*, O.J. L 156/14 (1990). On this directive, see Case C-392/21, *Inspectoratul General pentru Imigrări* (CJEU 22 December 2022) para 60.

[47] See SWD(2017) 201 final, p. 41.

[48] Council Directive 2004/37/EC *on the protection of workers from the risks related to exposure to carcinogens or mutagens at work*, O.J. L158/50 (2004).

[49] Last amendment by Parliament/Council Directive (EU) 2022/431, O.J. L 88/1 (2022).

rules.⁵⁰ The Commission acts also in cooperation with the **European Agency for Safety and Health at Work** (EU-OSHA),⁵¹ which plays a key role in collecting and disseminating good practice through inter alia healthy workplaces campaigns.

2.2.2. Working Conditions

Article 153.1 point (b) TFEU is also linked to Article 31 EUCFR (entitled 'fair and just working conditions') as well as partly to Article 34 EUCFR in that it affirms respect for the entitlement to social security benefits and social services providing protection in cases such as maternity, illness, industrial accidents, dependency or old age, and in the case of loss of employment, in accordance with the rules laid down by Union law and national laws and practices. It is also related to Principle 5 of the new EPSR ('**secure and adaptable employment**'). Under Article 153.2 TFEU, directives adopted based on Article 153.2 TFEU to support and complement the activities of MS in the field of working conditions shall avoid imposing administrative, financial and legal constraints in a way which would hold back the creation and development of small and medium-sized undertakings. In addition, Article 162 TFEU enables the **European Social Fund** to **increase the geographical and occupational mobility of workers** within the Union, and to facilitate their **adaptation to industrial changes and to changes in production systems**,⁵² whereas Article 166 TFEU mandates the Union to implement a **vocational training policy**, which shall support and supplement the action of MS.

In this framework, three main directives have already been enacted to protect workers working under non-standard employment relationships:

- The Framework Agreement on part-time work concluded by social partners (annexed to Council Directive 97/81/EC)⁵³ protects **part-time workers** from being treated less favourably than comparable full-time workers and provides that employers should give consideration to requests by workers to transfer from full-time to part-time work or vice-versa.

26

27

---

⁵⁰ As known, at Union level social partners are to be consulted (Article 154 TFEU) on possible initiatives based on Article 153 TFEU and may request their agreements to be implemented at Union level (Article 155 TFEU). For example, European social partners signed on 8 March 2017 an autonomous agreement on active ageing and intergenerational approach also covering health and safety.

⁵¹ It is one of the EU's decentralised agencies, originally established by Council Regulation (EC) No. 2062/94 (however, based on what is now Article 352 TFEU), O.J. L 216/1 (1994). The Regulation has been replaced by Parliament/Council Regulation (EU) 2019/126, O.J. L 30/58 (2019), based now on Article 152.3 point (a) TFEU. See also Council Decision of 22 July 2003 *setting up an Advisory Committee on Safety and Health at Work*, O.J. C 218/1 (2003).

⁵² On the fiscal regime of a study grant co-financed by the ESF, see Case C-667/17, *Cadeddu* (CJEU 19 December 2018) para 15–21.

⁵³ Council Directive 97/81/EC *concerning the Framework Agreement on part-time work concluded by UNICE, CEEP and the ETUC*, O.J. L 14/9 (1998).

- The Framework Agreement on fixed-term work also concluded by social partners (annexed to Council Directive 1999/70/EC)[54] protects **fixed-term workers** from being treated less favourably than comparable permanent workers and requires MS to take measures to prevent abuse arising from the use of successive fixed-term contracts.
- Council Directive 2008/104/EC on temporary agency work[55] establishes equal treatment regarding the essential conditions of work and of employment between **temporary agency workers** and workers who are directly recruited by the user company.[56]

In addition, Directive (EU) 2019/1152[57] gives workers the right to be informed of the essential aspects of their employment relationship at the latest one week (or one month, respectively) after the employment started. Furthermore, the Commission supports **innovative business models** that create opportunities for EU citizens in terms of facilitating entry into employment, work flexibility and new sources of income.[58] In any case, the Commission proceeds at regular intervals to a REFIT (Regulatory Fitness and Performance programme) evaluation of these directives, with the support of **Eurofound** (the European Foundation for the Improvement of Living and Working Conditions), which deals with **working conditions and sustainable work**, **industrial relations**, **monitoring structural change** and **managing restructuring**, focusing as well on **opportunities and challenges in the digital age**.

28   To face these challenges (including a difficult **balance between security and flexibility**, the emergence of **new forms of work** or the **transferability of social protection and training entitlements** in view of facilitating occupational mobility), some initiatives at the EU level are taken, among others: the Entrepreneurship 2020 Action Plan sets out a vision and concrete measures to reignite the **entrepreneurial spirit** in Europe;[59] measures to support self-employment at the EU level also aim to reach those segments of the population whose **entrepreneurial potential** is not yet fully exploited, particularly for **women** (who represent only 29% of

---

[54] Council Directive 1999/70/EC *concerning the Framework Agreement on fixed-term work concluded by UNICE, CEEP and the ETUC*, O.J. L 175/43 (1999).

[55] Council Directive 2008/104/EC *on temporary agency work*, O.J. L 327/9 (2008).

[56] In this respect, see Case C-311/21, *TimePartner Personalmanagement* (CJEU 15 December 2022) para 79: the CJEU concluded that Article 5(3) of Directive 2008/14 'must be interpreted as meaning that collective agreements which authorise, under that provision, differences in treatment with regard to basic working and employment conditions to the detriment of temporary agency workers must be amenable to effective judicial review in order to determine whether the social partners have complied with their obligation to respect the overall protection of those workers'. See also Case C-681/18, *JH v KG* (CJEU 14 October 2020) para 72.

[57] Parliament/Council Directive (EU) 2019/1152 *on transparent and predictable working conditions in the European Union*, O.J. L 186/105 (2019).

[58] See in this respect the Commission Communication, *A European agenda for the collaborative economy*, COM(2016) 356 final.

[59] Commission Communication *Entrepreneurship 2020 Action Plan*, COM(2012) 795 final.

Article 153. [Union Action] 1367

entrepreneurs in Europe); and dedicated actions to develop **social entrepreneurship** were proposed by a group of experts in 2016.[60]

2.2.3. Social Security and Social Protection of Workers

It is evident that the material scope and impact of Article 153.1 point (c) TFEU is 29 clearly determined by both Article 153.2 TFEU (which enables the EU to set 'minimum requirements' in the field of social security and social protection of workers) and Article 153.4 TFEU (which prevents the EU from affecting the right of MS to define the fundamental principles of their social security systems and manage their public finances). Consequently, the margin of manoeuvre left to the EU is foreseen, on the one hand on Article 16 TFEU (which tasks the Commission to **encourage cooperation** between the MS and **facilitate coordination** of their action in all social policy fields under Title X of the TFEU) and, on the other hand, on Article 48 TFEU (which requires the Union legislature to adopt such measures in the field of social security as are necessary to provide **freedom of movement for workers and the self-employed** between the MS).[61] Of course, the EU actions must be also inspired by Article 34 (**social security and social assistance**) and Article 35 (**health care**) of the EUCFR. Particularly, this fundamental rights approach connected with freedom of movement is reinforced by the non-discrimination principle, as demonstrated by the ECJ case law,[62] without forgetting leading cases from the ECtHR (based on Article 14 ECHR in conjunction with Article 1 of Protocol No. 1 [63] as well as Article 14 in conjunction with Article 8

---

[60] Expert Group on Social Economic and Social Enterprises (GECES), available at http://ec.europa.eu/growth/sectors/social-economy/enterprises/expert-groups_en.

[61] See Parliament/Council Regulation (EU) No. 492/2011 *on freedom of movement for workers within the Union*, O.J. L 141/1 (2011). On the interpretation of this regulation, see Case C-328/20, *Commission v Austria (Indexation des prestations familiales)* (CJEU 16 June 2022) para 113.

[62] E.g. Case C-312/17, *Bedi* (CJEU 19 September 2018) para 28 and 44–50 and Case C-451/17, *Walltopia* (CJEU 25 October 2018) para 46–49.

[63] For example, Appl. No. 55707/00, *Andrejeva v Latvia* (ECtHR 18 February 2009) para 87–89. Cf. Appl. No. 49270/11, *Savickis and Others v Latvia* (ECtHR 9 June 2022) para 209–210: Case distinguished from *Andrejeva v. Latvia* in so far as it concerns employment periods completed outside, and before establishing any link with, Latvia; and weight given to applicants' personal choice to remain 'permanently resident non-citizens' while acceding to citizenship was open to them). See also, on refusal by domestic authorities to grant survivor's pensions (in violation with Article 1 of Protocol 1 to the ECHR) Appl. No. 46141/07, *Muñoz Díaz v Spain* (ECtHR 8 December 2009) para 47–50 and 63–71, as well as Appl. No. 32667/19 and No. 30807/20, *Doménech Aradilla and Rodríguez González v Spain* (ECtHR 19 January 2023) para 112.

ECHR[64]) and from the ECSR (concerning the specific provisions on social protection of the ESC, Articles 12, 13 and 14[65]).

30   Thus, the diversity and intensity of the **EU secondary legal acts** in this field are in consistency with the diversity and intensity of the actions and inspirations deriving from the above-mentioned legal provisions of EU primary law. In this regard, it is worth to mention the following existing measures:

- Recommendation 92/442/EEC on the convergence of social protection objectives and policies covers social insurance for workers in relation to sickness, maternity, unemployment, incapacity for work, the elderly and family;[66]
- Directive 2010/41/EU on the application of the principle of equal treatment between men and women engaged in self-employed activity grants access to maternity leave and benefits for at least 14 weeks. It does not cover access to any other social insurance risks;[67]
- Regulation (EC) No. 883/2004 coordinates the social security rules of the Member States as regards persons in cross-border situations;[68]
- Regulation (EU) No. 1231/2010 coordinates social security systems in the case of third country nationals and their family members legally residing in the territory of the Union who have moved between MS.[69]

31   Finally, the new EPSR states in Principle 12 that 'regardless of the type and duration of their employment relationship, workers, and, under comparable conditions, the self-employed, have the **right to adequate social protection**'. In doing so, the pillar not only covers the whole range of non-standard contracts for the provision of work, which are increasingly prevalent in today's labour market, but also transforms the call for a replacement income, which will maintain the workers' standard of living in the 1992 Recommendation into a right. In guaranteeing also to the self-employed access to social protection under comparable conditions, the Principle goes beyond Directive 2010/41/EU, which dealt only with maternity leave.

---

[64] See the new case law settled by the ECtHR's Grand-Chamber in Appl. No. 78630/12, *Beeler v Switzerland* (ECtHR 11 October 2022) para 50–65 (development and current state of case law on social welfare benefits).

[65] Among others, Complaint No. 108/2014, *Finnish Society of Social Rights v. Finland* (ECSR 8 December 2016) para 47–55 and: no violation of Article 12§3 (the right to social security—development of the social security system); violation of Article 13§1 (the right to social and medical assistance—adequate assistance for every person in need).

[66] Council Recommendation 92/442/EEC *on the convergence of social protection objectives and policies*, O.J. L 245/49 (1992).

[67] Council Directive 2010/41/EU *on the application of the Principle of equal treatment between men and women engaged in an activity in a self-employed capacity*, O.J. L 180/1 (2010).

[68] Council Regulation (EC) No. 883/2004 *on the coordination of social security systems*, O.J. L 166/1 (2004).

[69] Council Regulation (EU) No. 1231/2010 *extending Regulation (EC) No. 883/2004 and Regulation (EC) No. 987/2009 to nationals of third countries who are not already covered by these Regulations solely on the ground of their nationality*, O.J. L 344/1 (2010).

2.2.4. Protection of Workers Where Their Employment Contract Is Terminated

The material scope of Article 153.1 point (d) TFEU is also covered by Article 30 EUCFR, which protects every worker against unjustified dismissal.[70] In addition, such protection is strengthened by Article 27 (which gives every worker the right to be guaranteed information and consultation in good time and at the appropriate levels, in the cases and under the conditions provided for by Union law and national laws and practices) and Article 47 (right to an effective remedy and to a fair trial) of the EUCFR. Principle 7 of the EPSR (information about employment conditions and protection in case of dismissals) reflects such approach.[71]

32

The relevant legal acts of EU secondary law in this field are the following:

33

- Directive (EU) 2019/1152[72] gives workers the **right to be notified in writing** of the essential aspects of their employment relationship, at the latest one week (or one month, respectively) after the employment started. It does not contain specific obligations in relation to **probation periods**. The Written Statement Directive requires an employer to notify an employee of the length of the periods of notice to be observed should their contract or employment relationship be terminated or, where this cannot be indicated at the time when the information is given, the method for determining such periods of notice.
- Directive 98/59/EC on collective redundancies requires employers to inform and consult workers' representatives and to notify public authorities prior to collective redundancies.[73]
- Directive 2001/23/EC regulates workers' rights in the case of **transfer of undertakings**. It stipulates that the transfer of an undertaking does not in itself constitute valid grounds for dismissal.[74]

---

[70] See also Article 24 of the Revised European Social Charter.

[71] Under the Principle 7 EPSR: 'a. Workers have the right to be informed in writing at the start of employment about their rights and obligations resulting from the employment relationship, including on probation period. b. Prior to any dismissal, workers have the right to be informed of the reasons and be granted a reasonable period of notice. They have the right to access to effective and impartial dispute resolution and, in case of unjustified dismissal, a right to redress, including adequate compensation'.

[72] Parliament/Council Directive (EU) 2019/1152 *on transparent and predictable working conditions in the European Union*, O.J. L 186/105 (2019).

[73] Council Directive 98/59/EC *on the approximation of the laws of the Member States relating to collective redundancies*, O.J. L 225/16 (1998).

[74] Council Directive 2001/23/EC *on the approximation of the laws of the Member States relating to the safeguarding of employees' rights in the event of transfers of undertakings, businesses or parts of undertakings or businesses*, O.J. L 82/6 (2001).

- Directive 92/85/EEC on maternity protection[75] and Directive (EU) 2019/1158[76] provide, respectively, specific protection against dismissal for women during their **pregnancy** and for parents taking **paternity or adoption leave**.
- Directive 2000/78/EC (the Employment Equality Directive)[77] on equal treatment in employment and occupation protects workers against dismissal where there is **discrimination** on a prohibited ground, including **victimisation**. On the other hand, protection against dismissal and unfavourable treatment is also provided under the EU anti-discrimination law through the Part-time Work Directive,[78] the Gender Equality Directive,[79] the Directive on equal treatment between men and women engaged in an activity in a self-employed capacity[80] and the Work-Life Balance Directive (EU) 2019/1158.[81] Such protection has been reinforced by the case law of the Court of Justice.[82]

34 As far as the novelties introduced by the EPSR are concerned, it requires for example written information to be provided to the worker about his or her working conditions at the start of the employment relationship, rather than within the two months under the former Written Statement Directive. The EPSR also goes beyond the existing acquis by introducing procedural and substantive safeguards for workers in case of dismissals. Adequate reasoning should be provided, and a reasonable period of notice be respected. Moreover, it provides that workers should have access to **effective and impartial dispute-resolution procedures** (arbitration, mediation or conciliation). Finally, in the framework of the EPSR, MS are in charge of transposing and enforcing rules adopted at Union level. Given that the Union measures set out above contain minimum standards, MS are invited to go beyond these rules to give effect to the Pillar. Furthermore, MS may ratify, if not yet done

---

[75] Council Directive 92/85/EEC *on the introduction of measures to encourage improvements in the safety and health at work of pregnant workers and workers who have recently given birth or are breastfeeding*, O.J. L 348/1 (1992).

[76] Parliament/Council Directive (EU) 2019/1158 *on work-life balance for parents and carers*, O.J. L 188/79 (2019).

[77] Council Directive 2000/78/EC *establishing a general framework for equal treatment in employment and occupation*, O.J. L 303/16 (2000).

[78] Council Directive 97/81/EC *concerning the Framework Agreement on part-time work concluded by UNICE, CEEP and the ETUC*, O.J. L 14/9 (1998).

[79] Council Directive 2006/54/EC *on the implementation of the principle of equal opportunities and equal treatment of men and women in matters of employment and occupation* (recast) O.J. L 204/23 (2006).

[80] Council Directive 2010/41/EU *on the application of the Principle of equal treatment between men and women engaged in an activity in a self-employed capacity*, O.J. L 180/1 (2010).

[81] A first critical approach has led to argue that, while some progress has been made towards the recognition of 'non-standard' families, many non-standard workers may still fall outside the scope of the Directive, or may not meet the eligibility criteria to access Work-Life Balance measures, with detrimental effects in terms of equality: Chieregato (2020), p. 80.

[82] For example, Case C-41/17, *González Castro* (CJEU 19 September 2018) para 52–53 and 83, and Case C-129/20, *Caisse pour l'avenir des enfants (Emploi à la naissance)* (CJEU 25 February 2021) para 42.

so, and apply relevant ILO Conventions such as No. 122 on Employment Policy (1964), No. 135 on Workers' Representatives (1971), No. 144 on Tripartite Consultations (1976) and No. 154 on Promotion of Collective Bargaining (1981). [83]

2.2.5. The Information and Consultation of Workers

Article 153.1 point (e) TFEU is also in connection with Article 27 EUCFR (workers' right to information and consultation within the undertaking).[84] Its main legal framework is established by Directive 2002/14/EC on informing and consulting workers (the Information and Consultation Directive),[85] which aims at ensuring workers' involvement ahead of decision-making by management, notably where restructuring is envisaged. On the other hand, Directive 2009/38/EC on the establishment of a European Works Council[86] addresses the need for proper information and consultation processes in the case of EU-scale companies through the setting up of European Works Councils to deal with transnational issues that could affect workers, whereas Directive 98/59/EC on collective redundancies[87] and Directive 2001/23/EC on the transfer of undertakings[88] go beyond **ensuring the information and consultation of workers' representatives**.[89] 35

In the context of Principle 8 of the EPSR (social dialogue and involvement of workers) social partners shall be consulted on the design and implementation of economic, employment and social policies. The EPSR entitles **all workers in all sectors to be informed and consulted** directly or through their representatives on matters relevant to them such as the transfer, restructuring and merger of undertakings and collective redundancies. It looks beyond the current Union acquis given that: it applies regardless of the staff numbers involved; its material scope encompasses both the restructuring and merger of companies; and the right is not just to receive information but also to be consulted about any such corporate action, which implies an exchange of views and the establishment of a consistent dialogue with the employer. Moreover, Principle 8b covers any issues that concern workers, 36

---

[83] See Commission Staff Working Document *accompanying the Communication establishing a European Pillar of Social Rights*, SWD(2017) 201 final, p. 31.

[84] See also Article 21 ESC.

[85] Parliament/Council Directive 2002/14/EC *establishing a general framework for informing and consulting employees in the European Community*, O.J. L 80/29 (2002).

[86] Parliament/Council Directive 2009/38/EC *on the establishment of a European Works Council or a procedure in Community-scale undertakings and Community-scale groups of undertakings for the purposes of informing and consulting employees*, O.J. L 122/28 (2009).

[87] Council Directive 98/59/EC *on the approximation of the laws of the Member States relating to collective redundancies*, O.J. L 225/16 (1998).

[88] Council Directive 2001/23/EC *on the approximation of the laws of the Member States relating to the safeguarding of employees' rights in the event of transfers of undertakings, businesses or parts of undertakings or businesses*, O.J. L 82/16 (2001).

[89] See also Parliament/Council Directive (EU) 2015/1794 *as regards seafarers*, O.J. L 263/1 (2015).

whereas existing Directives contain a limited list of topics for engaging in information and consultation processes.[90]

2.2.6. Representation and Collective Defence of the Interests of Workers and Employers, Including Co-Determination, Subject to Paragraph 5

37 Article 153.1 point (f) TFEU is related to Article 28 EUCFR (right of collective bargaining and action)[91] and implies a logical *continuum* in relation to Article 153.1 point (e) TFEU, since information and consultation of workers constitute somehow a *prius* of successful negotiations and agreements. From this perspective, Principle 8 of the EPSR gives a clear role to social partners not only in consultation and preparation of relevant legislation and policies, but also in **negotiation and conclusion of collective agreements** in matter relevant to them. In this context, without prejudice to the Tripartite Social Summit for Growth and Employment and of the macroeconomic dialogue (which remain the crucial fora to discuss with social partner representatives at political level under Article 152 TFEU), the powers and measures under Articles 153, 154 and 155 TFEU do not apply to **pay**,[92] the right of **association**, the right to **strike** or the right to impose **lock-outs** (Article 153.5 TFEU). As far as EU secondary law under Article 153.1 point (f) TFEU is concerned, two legal acts are relevant: on the one hand, Directive 2001/86/EC supplementing the Statute for a **European company** with regard to the involvement of employees[93] and, on the other hand, Directive (EU) 2017/1132 relating to certain **aspects of company law**.[94]

38 Principle 8c EPSR states also that 'support for increased capacity of social partners to promote social dialogue shall be encouraged'. Particularly, the EU Quality Framework for anticipation of change and restructuring[95] promotes principles and good practices addressed to employers, employees, social partners and public authorities with regard to the anticipation of change and the management of

---

[90] By referring to 'matters relevant to them, in particular (...) the transfer, restructuring and merger of undertakings and (...) collective redundancies', it goes further than Article 27 EUCFR, which provides for a right to information and consultation 'in the cases and under the conditions provided for by Union law and national laws and practices'. On the other hand, it is true that the effectiveness of information and consultation mechanisms might be hampered by the Consultation Framework Directive 2002/14/EC's vague legal framework: Brameshuber (2021), p. 254.

[91] See also Articles 5 and 6 ESC.

[92] Such exception is explained by the fact that fixing the level of pay falls within the contractual freedom of the social partners at national level and within the relevant MS competence: Joined Cases C-257/21 and C-258/21, *Coca-Cola European Partners Deutschland GmbH* (CJEU 7 July 2022) para 47.

[93] Council Directive 2001/86/EC *supplementing the Statute for a European company with regard to the involvement of employees*, O.J. L 294/22 (2001). Council Regulation (EC) No. 2157/2001 *on the Statute for a European company (SE)*, O.J. L 294/1 (2001).

[94] Parliament/Council Directive (EU) 2017/1132 *relating to certain aspects of company law*, O.J. L 169/46 (2017).

[95] Commission Communication, *EU Quality Framework for anticipation of change and restructuring*, COM(2013) 882 final.

the restructuring processes. In addition, the Joint Statement signed by the Presidency of the Council of the European Union, the European Commission and the European Social Partners on 'A New Start for Social Dialogue'[96] emphasises the importance of **capacity building** of national social partners, the strengthened involvement of social partners in EU policy and law-making and the commitment to promote cross-industry and sectoral social dialogue, including their outcomes at all levels.

2.2.7. Conditions of Employment for Third-Country Nationals Legally Residing in Union Territory

In principle, the '**working conditions**' prescribed by Article 153.1 point (b) TFEU apply on an equal footing to all workers (**citizens of the Union and third-country nationals**) when referring to the fundamental worker's rights and duties in the context of a concrete employment relationship.[97] In this respect, the CJEU 'has repeatedly held that migrant workers contribute to the financing of the social policies of the host Member State through the tax and social security contributions which they pay in that State by virtue of their employment there. They must therefore be able to profit from them under the same conditions as national workers (...). Accordingly, that factor reinforces the importance of the approach whereby migrant workers must enjoy equal treatment as regards family benefits and tax and social advantages'.[98] From this perspective, 'the principles enshrined in the European Pillar of Social Rights concern Union citizens and third-country nationals with legal residence. Where a principle refers to workers, it concerns all persons in employment, regardless of their employment status, modality and duration' (recital 5 of the Preamble to the EPSR).

39

However, the '**conditions of employment**' under Article 153.1 point (g) TFEU have a broader meaning, since they also refer to the rules on the access of third-country nationals to national labour markets in the framework of measures on **immigration policy** relating to conditions of entry and residence, standards on procedures for the issue by MS of long-term visas and residence permits, and measures defining the rights and conditions under which nationals of third-countries who are legally resident in an MS may reside in other MS. Moreover, the enjoyment of **freedom of movement** without 'any discrimination based on nationality between workers of the Member States as regards employment, remuneration and other conditions of work and employment' is 'subject to **limitations**

---

[96] Statement of the Presidency of the Council of the European Union, the European Commission and the European Social Partners 2016, A new start for Social Dialogue. Available at https://www.businesseurope.eu/sites/buseur/files/media/position_papers/social/2016-06-27_quadri-partite_statement_signed_on_a_new_start_for_social_dialogue.pdf.

[97] See also Article 19 ESC (the right of migrant workers and their families to protection and assistance).

[98] Case C-328/20, *Commission v Austria (Indexation des prestations familiales)* (CJEU 16 June 2022) para 109.

justified on grounds of **public policy, public security** or **public health**;[99] such limitations are also applied to employment in the **public service** (Article 45 TFEU). The ECJ has consistently held that freedom of movement for workers forms one of the foundations of the Union and, consequently, that the provisions laying down that freedom must be given a broad interpretation.[100]

40   In any case, the **increased voluntary geographical and occupational mobility of workers** on a fair basis are included in the objectives of both the European Network of Public Employment Services (PES), established through Decision No. 573/2014/EU,[101] and of the European Network of Employment Services (EURES), established through Regulation (EU) 2016/589.[102] For highly qualified third country nationals, Directive 2009/50/EC limits, however, their occupational mobility for the first two years of legal employment in an MS.[103] In addition, Directive 2003/109/EC concerning the status of third-country nationals who are long-term residents,[104] together with a number of other Union directives concerning legal migration of third country nationals in the Union,[105] confer

---

[99] See, *mutatis mutandis*, Appl. No. 31039/11, 48511/11, 76810/12, 14618/13 and 13817/14, *Novruk and Others v Russia* (ECtHR 16 March 2016): violation of Article 14 (prohibition of discrimination) read together with Article 8 ECHR (right to private life and family) due to the legislation aimed at preventing HIV transmission, which was used in a discriminatory way to exclude the applicants from entry or residence on account of their health status.

[100] See, particularly, Case 139/85, *Kempf v Staatssecretaris van Justitie* (ECJ 13 June 1986) para 13. The ECJ has held that the freedom of movement of workers contained in Article 45 TFEU also entails certain rights for nationals of MS moving within the Union for the purposes of seeking employment, see Case C-292/89, *The Queen v Immigration Appeal Tribunal, ex parte Antonissen* (ECJ 26 February 1991) para 13. Furthermore, the concept of 'worker' has been considered to include, in certain circumstances, persons undertaking an apprenticeship, see Case C-188/00, *Bülent Kurz, né Yüce v Land Baden-Württemberg* (ECJ 19 November 2002) para 33 or a traineeship, see e.g. Case C-109/04, *Kranemann* (ECJ 17 March 2005) para 21 and 36.

[101] Parliament/Council Decision No. 573/2014/EU *on enhanced cooperation between Public Employment Services (PES)*, O.J. L 159/32 (2014).

[102] Parliament/Council Regulation (EU) 2016/589 *on a European network of employment services (EURES), workers' access to mobility services and the further integration of labour markets*, O.J. L 107/1 (2016).

[103] Council Directive 2009/50/EC *on the conditions of entry and residence of third-country nationals for the purposes of highly qualified employment*, O.J. L 155/17 (2009).

[104] Council Directive 2003/109/EC *concerning the status of third-country nationals who are long-term residents*, O.J. L 16/44 (2004), amended by Parliament/Council Directive 2011/51/EU, O.J. L 132/1. See also, for example, Parliament/Council Directive 2011/98/EU *on a single application procedure for a single permit for third-country nationals to reside and work in the territory of a Member State and on a common set of rights for third-country workers legally residing in a Member State*, O.J. L 343/1 (2011).

[105] Directives on family reunification, see Council Directive 2003/86/EC *on the right to family reunification*, O.J. L 251/12 (2003), on Blue Card, see Council Directive 2009/50/EC *on the conditions of entry and residence of third-country nationals for the purposes of highly qualified employment*, O.J. L 155/17 (2009), on Single Permit, see Parliament/Council Directive 2011/98/EU *on a single application procedure for a single permit for third-country nationals to reside and work in the territory of a Member State and on a common set of rights for third-country workers*

them equal treatment rights with host country's nationals in relation to social protection and social security.

2.2.8. The Integration of Persons Excluded from the Labour Market, Without Prejudice to Article 166

Although connected with the combating of social exclusion (Article 153.1 point (j), *infra*), Article 153.1 point (h) TFEU relates more specifically to the combating **in-work exclusion** factors. In this respect, the above-mentioned Regulation (EU) 2016/589 highlights that 'the free movement of workers is one of the key elements in the development of a more integrated Union labour market, including in cross-border regions, which allows higher worker mobility, thereby increasing diversity and contributing to Union-wide social inclusion and integration of persons excluded from the labour market. It also contributes to finding the right skills for vacant positions and overcoming bottlenecks in the labour market' (recital 2). **41**

With such spirit, the Preamble of the EPSR refers to the objectives of 'the promotion of employment, improved living and working conditions' under Article 151 TFEU to ensure 'the development of human resources with a view to lasting high employment and the combating of exclusion' (recital 3 of the Preamble to the EPSR). With this in mind, some Principles of the EPSR are related to Article 153.1 point (h) TFEU, particularly Principles 13 (**unemployment benefits**), 14 (**minimum income**) and 17 (**inclusion of people with disabilities**), which also reflect several fundamental rights recognised in the EUCFR, such as the right of access to a free placement service (Article 29), the right to social security benefits and social services providing protection inter alia in the case of loss of employment (Article 34), or the right of persons with disabilities to benefit from measures designed to ensure their social and occupational integration and that enable them to participate in the labour market. From this perspective, in the 2021 Action Plan on the EPSR the Commission encouraged companies 'to put in place mechanism to combat discriminatory practices in recruitment, selection and promotion, and promote diversity in the workplace'. **42**

---

legally residing in a Member State, O.J. L 343/1 (2011), on researchers and students, see Parliament/Council Directive (EU) 2016/801 *on the conditions of entry and residence of third-country nationals for the purposes of research, studies, training, voluntary service, pupil exchange schemes or educational projects and au pairing*, O.J. L 132/21 (2016), on qualification as a beneficiary of international protection, see Parliament/Council Directive 2011/95/EU *on standards for the qualification of third-country nationals or stateless persons as beneficiaries of international protection, for a uniform status for refugees or for persons eligible for subsidiary protection, and for the content of the protection granted*, O.J. L 337/9 (2011), on seasonal workers, see Parliament/Council Directive 2014/36/EU *on the conditions of entry and stay of third-country nationals for the purpose of employment as seasonal workers*, O.J. L 94/375 (2014) and on intra-corporate transferees, see Parliament/Council Directive 2014/66/EU *on the conditions of entry and residence of third-country nationals in the framework of an intra-corporate transfer*, O.J. L 157/1 (2014).

43   The EU has adopted relevant **secondary legislation** in this field under Articles 153 and 166.4 TFEU (implementation of a vocational training policy to facilitate vocational integration and reintegration into the labour market), among others:

- Council Recommendation 92/441/EEC on common criteria concerning sufficient resources and social assistance in social protection systems (commonly known as the 'Minimum Income Recommendation') calls on MS to recognise the right to social assistance and sets out principles and guidelines to implement this right.[106] Indeed, the efficient set up of minimum income schemes at national level is encouraged in Country Specific Recommendations within the **European Semester** process of economic policy coordination, to which the **Social Protection Committee** contributes. The **Open Method of Coordination** in the Social Protection Committee ensures policy coordination and monitors the progress of the MS. The EU financial instruments, particularly the **European Social Fund** play an important role supporting the development of minimum income benefits. Lastly, **NextGenerationEU Funds** (mainly, the **Recovery and Resilience Facility**) aim at providing the Union with the necessary means to address the challenges posed by the Covid-19 pandemic.[107] In comparing the 2008 world economic and financial crisis with the 2020 coronavirus crisis it has been held that, although the rules on liability sharing for NextGenerationEU prevent a significant mutualisation of the debt, European leaders have taken the long-recognised significant first step towards European financial and political unification that stands in stark contrast to the misguided austerity programmes during the European sovereign debt crisis.[108]
- Regulation (EC) No. 883/2004 on the coordination of social security systems[109] provides the right to retain the entitlement to unemployment benefits in cash for a period of up to three months, with a possibility of extension up to six months, for a wholly unemployed person who satisfies the conditions for entitlement to unemployment benefits and who goes to another MS to **seek work**.

---

[106] Council Recommendation 92/441/EEC *on common criteria concerning sufficient resources and social assistance in social protection systems*, O.J. L 245/46 (1992). See also the Council Conclusions of 9 October 2020 *on strengthening minimum income protection to combat poverty and social exclusion in the COVID-19 pandemic and beyond* (11721/2/20).

[107] See the Conclusions adopted by the European Council at its special meeting in summer 2020 (17–21 July 2020): EUCO 10/20, CO EUR 8 CONCL 4, https://www.consilium.europa.eu/media/45109/210720-euco-final-conclusions-en.pdf. The new 2021–2027 Multiannual Financial Framework (MFF), reinforced by NextGeneratio EU (NGEU), will be the main European tool to invest, create jobs and build a green and digital future.

[108] Picek (2020), p. 325.

[109] Parliament/Council Regulation (EC) No. 883/2004 *on the coordination of social security systems*, O.J. L 166/1 (2004).

- Commission Recommendation 2008/867/EC on the active inclusion of people excluded from the labour market[110] calls for an integrated comprehensive strategy for the active inclusion of people excluded from the labour market, combining **adequate income support, inclusive labour markets** and **access to quality services**.[111]
- Decision No. 573/2014/EU on enhanced **cooperation between Public Employment Services** (PES)[112] provides a platform to compare PES performance at European level, identify good practice and foster mutual learning to strengthen the active support services.[113]
- Council Decision (EU) 2019/1181,[114] particularly guideline 6, calls upon the MS to continue to address youth unemployment and the issue of young people not in employment, education or training ('**NEETs**') through prevention of early school leaving and structural improvement in the school-to-work transition, including through the full implementation of the **Youth Guarantee**.
- Council Recommendation of 30 October 2020 on A Bridge to Jobs – Reinforcing the Youth Guarantee[115] invites MS, in the context of the Covid-19 crisis, to ensure that all **young people** under 30 years of age receive a good quality offer of employment, continued education, an apprenticeship or a traineeship within a period of four months of becoming unemployed or leaving formal education, in line with Principle 4 of the EPSR.
- Directive 2000/78/EC (the Employment Equality Directive) prohibits discrimination on the ground of inter alia **disability** as regards **access to employment, self-employment, occupation and vocational training**.[116] It requires employers to provide reasonable accommodation, which means to take appropriate measures, where needed in a particular case, to enable a person with a disability to have access to, participate in, or advance in employment, or to undergo training, unless such measures would impose a disproportionate burden on the employer. Directive (EU) 2019/882 (the European Accessibility Act) aims at ensuring accessibility of certain products and services in the internal market,

---

[110] Commission Recommendation 2008/867/EC *on the active inclusion of people excluded from the labour market*, O.J. L 307/11 (2008).

[111] This call to the MS was reiterated in Council Recommendation *on the integration of the long-term unemployed into the labour market*, O.J. C 67/1 (2016).

[112] Parliament/Council Decision No. 573/2014/EU *on enhanced cooperation between Public Employment Services (PES)*, O.J. L 159/32 (2014).

[113] The European Network of Employment Services (PES Network) is implementing the *Bench-learning project* aiming to improve the PES' performance, linking indicator-based benchmarking with mutual learning to better address the active support to job seekers.

[114] Council Decision (EU) 2019/1181 of 8 July 2019 *on guidelines for the employment policies of the Member States*, O.J. L 185/44 (2019).

[115] Council Recommendation of 30 October 2020 *on A Bridge to Jobs – Reinforcing the Youth Guarantee* and replacing the Council Recommendation of 22 April 2013 on establishing a Youth Guarantee (2020/C 372/01).

[116] Council Directive 2000/78/EC *establishing a general framework for equal treatment in employment and occupation*, O.J. L 303/16 (2000).

thus facilitating people with disabilities' employment and participation in society on an equal basis with others.[117] In addition, the Union is a party to the UN Convention on the Rights of Persons with Disabilities (UNCRPD),[118] which requires its parties to adopt all appropriate measures for the implementation of the rights recognised therein,[119] including persons with disabilities' right to work on an equal basis with others.[120] All Union MS are also parties to the Convention.

2.2.9. Equality Between Men and Women on Labour Market Opportunities and Treatment at Work

44 Article 153.1 point (i) TFEU is connected with both a broader general basis (Article 8 TFEU)[121] and another more specific provision on 'equal pay for male and female workers for equal work or work of equal value' (Article 157 TFEU). In addition, Article 21 EUCFR prohibits any discrimination based on any ground such as sex. Article 23 EUCFR provides that equality between men and women must be ensured in all areas (including employment, work and pay, as well as the adoption of measures providing for **specific advantages in favour of the underrepresented sex**). Finally, Article 33.2 EUCFR stipulates that to reconcile family and professional life, everyone shall have the right to protection from dismissal for a reason

---

[117] Parliament/Council Directive (EU) 2019/882 *on the accessibility requirements for products and services*, O.J. L 151/70 (2019).

[118] Council Decision of 26 November 2009 *concerning the conclusion, by the European Community, of the United Nations Convention on the Rights of Persons with Disabilities*, O.J. L 23/35 (2010).

[119] In its recent case law, the CJEU has reaffirmed its interpretation of the concept 'reasonable accommodation' in light of the UNCRPD: see Case C-397/18, *Nobel Plastiques Ibérica* (CJEU 11 September 2019) para 40, and Case C-795/19, *Tartu Vangla* (CJEU 15 July 2021) para 48–49. Indeed, the UNCRPD so far had and is having an impact on EU legislation and EU jurisprudence: Degener (2020), p. 349.

[120] The core elements of the UNCRPD are reflected in the European Disability Strategy 2010–2020, see Commission Communication, *European Disability Strategy 2010-2020: A Renewed Commitment to a Barrier-Free Europe*, COM(2010) 636 final. The new Disability Rights Strategy (*Union of Equality: Strategy for the Rights of Persons with Disabilities 2021-2030*, COM(2021) 101 final) sets out key initiatives in three main areas: (1) EU rights: This is based on the simple fact that persons with disabilities enjoy the same rights as any EU citizen. Against this background, the Commission wants to introduce a European Disability Card for all EU countries that will facilitate mutual recognition of disability status. (2) Independent living and autonomy: The Commission wants to develop guidance and launch an initiative to improve social services for persons with disabilities to guarantee that persons with disabilities can enjoy and independent and self-determined living situation. (3) Non-discrimination and equal opportunities: Any form of discrimination against persons with disabilities is to be abolished. The strategy aims to ensure equal opportunities in and access to justice, education, culture, sport, tourism, health services, and employment.

[121] Article 8 TFEU illustrates a clear mainstreaming approach by affirming that 'in all its activities, the Union shall aim to eliminate inequalities, and to promote equality, between men and women'. See also Article 19 TFEU (EU 'appropriate action to combat discrimination based on sex').

connected with maternity and the right to paid maternity leave and to parental leave following the birth or adoption of a child.

The new EPSR approaches also the 'gender equality' under the **mainstreaming approach** (Principle 2) by emphasising 'participation in the labour market, terms and conditions of employment and career progression' and 'the right to equal pay for work of equal value'; Principles 3 ('equal opportunities',[122] regardless of gender), 9 (**'work-life balance'**[123]) and 15 ('old-age pensions'[124]). Particularly, alongside the 2021 Action Plan on the EPSR, the Commission has proposed a Directive to strengthen the application of the principle of equal pay for equal work or work of equal value between men and women through **pay transparency measures and enforcement mechanisms.**[125]

Without prejudice of other legal acts prohibiting various forms of discrimination on access to employment, self-employment, occupation and vocational training,[126] the existing EU secondary law under Article 157.1 point (i) TFEU is mainly contained in the Work-Life Balance Directive (EU) 2019/1158,[127] which gives male and female workers an individual right to parental leave of at least four months and requires MS to take measures to ensure that workers may request a change to their working hours and/or patterns when returning from parental leave,

---

[122] 'Regardless of gender, (...), everyone has the right to equal treatment and opportunities regarding employment, social protection, education, and access to goods and services available to the public'. In doing so, the EPSR extends the prohibition of discrimination based on gender to the area of education, which is not covered by the current acquis.

[123] 'Women and men shall have equal access to special leaves of absence in order to fulfil their caring responsibilities and be encouraged to use them in a balanced way'.

[124] 'a. Workers and the self-employed in retirement have the right to a pension commensurate to their contributions and ensuring an adequate income. Women and men shall have equal opportunities to acquire pension rights. b. Everyone in old age has the right to resources that ensure living in dignity'. Concerning the existing measures of EU secondary law, see Council Directive 98/49/EC *on safeguarding the supplementary pension rights of employed and self-employed persons moving within the Community*, O.J. L 209/46 (1998); Parliament/Council Directive 2014/50/EU *on minimum requirements for enhancing worker mobility between Member States by improving the acquisition and preservation of supplementary pension rights*, O.J. L 128/1 (2014); Parliament/Council Directive (EU) 2016/2341 *on the activities and supervision of institutions for occupational retirement provision (IORPs)*, O.J. L 354/37 (2016).

[125] COM(2021) 93 of 4 March 2021.

[126] For example, Council Directive 2000/78/EC *establishing a general framework for equal treatment in employment and occupation*, O.J. L 303/16 (2000), as well as other EU directives (already mentioned) covering legally residing third-country nationals that are long-term residents on: Family reunification, Blue Card, Single Permit, Researchers, Students, Qualification as a beneficiary of international protection, seasonal workers and intra-corporate transferees. See also Council Recommendation of 9 December 2013 *on effective Roma integration measures in the Member States*, O.J. C 378/1 (2013); such Recommendation has been renewed throughout Council Recommendation of 12 March 2021 *on Roma equality, inclusion and participation*, O.J. C 93/1 (2021).

[127] O.J. L 188/79 (2019).

for a set period of time. On the other hand, the Framework Agreement on part-time work concluded by social partners (implemented by Directive 97/81/EC)[128] protects **part-time workers** from being treated less favourably than **full-time workers** and provides that employers should consider requests by workers to switch from full-time to part-time work or vice-versa.[129]

47 In this context, the EPSR highlights the importance of work-life balance for all people with caring responsibilities and confers rights that are essential to attain this balance in today's working environment, such as the right to access childcare or long-term care. The Principle goes beyond the current acquis by providing rights for all people in employment with caring responsibilities. It will hence also apply to people in employment who are not parents, but who may, for example, care for elderly or disabled family members. Furthermore, the EPSR confers a right to **flexible working arrangements** such as teleworking, adaptation of working schedules or switching between full-time and part-time work. That right currently exists in Union legislation only when a worker returns to work following parental leave. On gender equality, the EPSR sets a new focus on ensuring equal access for women and men to special leave arrangements.[130] With such spirit, the Commission presented together with the EPSR the 'New start to support Work-Life Balance for parents and carers' initiative.[131] Of course, some EU's decentralised agencies (such as Eurofound or the European Institute for Gender Equality) and the FRA are supporting the work of the Commission, MS and social partners in this area.

2.2.10. The Combating of Social Exclusion

48 The objective of 'combating the social exclusion' established in Article 153.1 point (j) TFEU is above all a projection of the values set forth in Article 3.3 (2) TEU, according to which the Union 'shall **combat social exclusion and discrimination**, and shall promote social justice and protection, equality between women and men, solidarity between generations and protection of the rights of the child'. From this perspective, in all its activities and policies, the EU 'shall eliminate inequalities' (Article 8 TFEU), 'combat discrimination' (Article 19 TFEU) and 'fight against social exclusion' (Article 9 TFEU). In addition, under Article 145 TFEU, the Union and the MS shall work towards developing a **coordinated**

---

[128] O.J. L 14/9 (1998).

[129] See also Council Directive 92/85/EEC *on the introduction of measures to encourage improvements in the safety and health at work of pregnant workers and workers who have recently given birth or are breastfeeding*, O.J. L 348/1 (1992), and the above mentioned Council Directive 2010/41/EU *on the application of the Principle of equal treatment between men and women engaged in an activity in a self-employed capacity*, O.J. L 180/1 (2010).

[130] The EPSR also encourages the balanced use of these arrangements by men and women, for instance by adjusting the level of payment, or conditions related to flexibility and non-transferability.

[131] Commission Communication, *An Initiative to support work-life balance for working parents and carers*, COM(2017) 252 final.

Article 153. [Union Action]

strategy for employment and under Article 147 TFEU, the Union shall contribute to a **high level of employment** by encouraging cooperation between MS and by supporting and, if necessary, complementing their action. Furthermore, 'in order to combat social exclusion and poverty, the Union recognises and respects the right to social and housing assistance so as to ensure a decent existence for all those who lack sufficient resources, in accordance with the rules laid down by Union law and national laws and practices' (Article 34.3 EUCFR[132]). Moreover, the Preamble of the EPSR mentions also the combating of social exclusion by referring to Articles 3 TEU and 9 TFEU (Recitals 1 and 2 of the Preamble EPSR).[133] By contrast, the Principles of the EPSR do not refer to the combating of social exclusion, but to the fight against poverty: particularly, Principle 6 (wages) holds that '**in-work poverty** shall be prevented' and Principle 11 (childcare and support to children) states that 'children have the right to protection from poverty. Children from disadvantaged backgrounds have the right to specific measures to enhance equal opportunities', whereas Principles 19 (housing and assistance for the homeless) and 20 (access to essential services 'of good quality, including water, sanitation, energy, transport, financial services and digital communications') reflect a clear parallelism with Article 34 EUCFR.

As far as EU **secondary law** is concerned, apart from some relevant provisions aimed at combating discrimination,[134] other important legal acts must be taken into consideration: **49**

- The above-mentioned Council Recommendation 92/441/EEC of 24 June 1992 ('Minimum Income Recommendation'). The EPSR goes beyond this Recommendation by explicitly stating the right to a minimum income that ensures a life in dignity. The concept of 'minimum income', pointing to a specific form of benefit, is used explicitly for the first time, replacing the more generic terms such as 'social assistance' or 'sufficient resources'.[135] In effect, the expansion of the

---

[132] See also Articles 30 (protection against poverty and social exclusion) and 31 (right to housing) of the 1996 Revised European Social Charter.

[133] See also para 7, which refers to 'a Union which fights unemployment, discrimination, social exclusion and poverty'.

[134] For example, Council Directive 2000/43/EC *implementing the principle of equal treatment between persons irrespective of racial or ethnic origin*, O.J. L 180/22 (2000), and the above mentioned Council Directive 2000/78/EC *establishing a general framework for equal treatment in employment and occupation*, O.J. L 303/16 (2000).

[135] Minimum income aims at preventing destitution of people who are not eligible for social insurance benefits, or whose entitlement to such benefits has expired, thus combating poverty and social exclusion. Such benefits should also ensure a life in dignity at all stages of life combined with effective access to enabling services. They are non-contributory, universal and means-tested. They require people to be available for work or participate in community activities, if the individuals are capable. In the framework of the Council of Europe, see Parliamentary Assembly Resolution 2197(2018), *The case for a basic citizenship income*. According to the report of the Committee on Social Affairs, Health and Sustainable Development accompanying Resolution 2197 (2018), the European guaranteed minimum income is a corollary obligation under Articles 13 and 14 of the European Social Charter (Doc. 14462, p. 12).

EU has given significant impetus to the analysis of non-monetary indicators to propose a rationale for developing measures of deprivation that focus on not only the limitations of income measurement but also the relative nature of **at-risk-poverty indicators** in a context where living standards now vary widely across the MS.[136]
- The also already cited Commission Recommendation 2008/867/EC of 3 October 2008 on the active inclusion of people excluded from the labour market[137] calls for an integrated comprehensive strategy for the active inclusion of people excluded from the labour market, view to preventing in-work poverty.[138]
- On **access to shelter**,[139] Union legislation lays down specific protection for particularly **vulnerable people** such as unaccompanied children, asylum-seekers and refugees. For example, Council Directive 2012/29/EU establishing minimum standards on the rights, support and protection of victims of crime provides for the provision of shelter or any other appropriate interim accommodation.[140]
- Commission Recommendation 2013/112/EU of 20 February 2013 entitled 'Investing in children: breaking the cycle of disadvantage'[141] calls on all MS to step up their investment in children to address **child poverty**, as part of an

---

[136] Nolan and Whelan (2018), p. 101.

[137] Commission Recommendation 2008/867/EC *on the active inclusion of people excluded from the labour market*, O.J. L 307/11 (2008).

[138] Minimum wages and other measures to address in-work poverty, as well as more general issues related to wage developments are addressed in Country Specific Recommendations within the European Semester process.

[139] The reform of social housing, the accessibility and affordability of housing, as well as the effectiveness of housing allowances are monitored and assessed within the European Semester process. The Open Method of Coordination in the Social Protection Committee ensures policy coordination and monitors the progress of the Member States. The implementation of this policy may be supported by Union Funds, including the European Fund for Strategic Investments for social housing investments, the European Regional Development Fund for housing infrastructure, the European Social Fund for social services and the Fund for European Aid for the Most Deprived for food assistance to homeless persons. The European Union also supports financially a number of civil society organisations active in the promotion of social inclusion and poverty reduction, including organisations working on homelessness.

[140] Parliament/Council Directive 2012/29/EU *establishing minimum standards on the rights, support and protection of victims of crime*, O.J. L 315/57 (2012).

[141] Commission Recommendation 2013/112/EU, *Investing in children: breaking the cycle of disadvantage*, O.J. L 59/5 (2013). Principle 11b of the EPSR gives children from disadvantaged backgrounds (such as Roma children, some migrant or ethnic minority children, children with special needs or disabilities, children in alternative care and street children, children of imprisoned parents, as well as children within households at particular risk of poverty) the right to specific measures—namely reinforced and targeted support—with a view to ensure their equitable access to and enjoyment of social rights.

integrated child-rights based package of policy measures to improve outcomes for children and break intergenerational cycles of disadvantage.[142]
- The sectorial legislation adopted at the Union level has considered the need to increase competition and the use of market mechanisms as well as the need to guarantee that every citizen continues to have access to essential services of high quality at prices that they can afford. This has been the case, for instance, in the **energy sector**,[143] of the 2019 Electricity Directive, whose implementation has raised new serious concerns after the Russia's February 2022 invasion of Ukraine.[144] On the other hand, Union water policy is based on the principle that affordability of water services is critical and, therefore, it is important safeguarding disadvantaged people and tackling **water-poverty** issues.[145] Indeed, the principle that essential services should be available to all may be considered as 'the core of the European social model',[146] which is to be developed in the context of one of the greatest challenges of the twenty-first century: the climate change.[147]

---

[142] On 16 June 2016, Council Conclusions on *Combating Poverty and Social Exclusion: An Integrated Approach*, encouraged the MS to address child poverty and promote children's well-being through multi-dimensional and integrated strategies, in accordance with the Commission Recommendation on investing in children.

[143] The Commission set up in December 2016 the EU Energy Poverty Observatory (predecessor of the current project of the Energy Poverty Advisory Hub) to provide better data on the problem and its solutions as well as to help MS in their efforts to combat energy poverty (https://energy-poverty.ec.europa.eu/observing-energy-poverty_en).

[144] Parliament/Council Directive (EU) 2019/944 *on common rules for the internal market for electricity*, O.J. L 158/125 (2019). An energy transition will have to take place, in which renewable energy must replace fossil-based energy, and energy efficiency policy and measures should be implemented. Such need for transition, accelerated by the war in Ukraine, is also raising tension between the growing demand for consumer data under EU energy law and the need to limit the processing of personal data under data protection law: see Hirth (2020), p. 10.

[145] See the 'Drinking Water Directive': Parliament/Council Directive (EU) 2020/2184 *on the quality of water intended for human consumption*, O.J. L 435/1 (2020). It has repealed the former Council Directive 98/83/EC, O.J. L 330/32 (1998). Of course, General comment no. 15 (2002), *The right to water* (Articles 11 and 12 of the International Covenant on Economic, Social and Cultural Rights) has to be considered. Unfortunately, the significant number of disease outbreaks (and of other suspected/potential health effects) related to DW, even in developed countries, attests to the fact that these issues require vigilance and continuous re-appraisal, particularly considering the assorted emerging contaminants and the ever-improving technological tools to cope with them: Tsaridou and Karabelas (2021), p. 21.

[146] See Commission Staff Working Document *accompanying the Communication on establishing a European Pillar of Social Rights*, SWD(2017) 201 final, p. 75.

[147] Lastly, on accelerating clean energy supply, momentum behind nuclear electricity has increased. The inclusion of nuclear (and gas) in the EU's 'green taxonomy' marks a policy departure. In March 2022, a Commission delegated act argued that nuclear energy does qualify for investment if there is no technologically and economically feasible alternative to move to decarbonisation. The European Parliament voted in favour of the amendment in July 2022, despite opposition from the Environmental Committee of the European Parliament, Germany and various groups of European lawmakers. However, it has been criticized that nuclear remains environmentally controversial: it produces toxic waste, little is known about where waste will be stored long-

50 More recently, as reminded in the Commission Staff Working Document accompanying the Communication establishing the EPSR, 'the adoption of the UN **Sustainable Development Goals for 2030** has provided a new agenda to address poverty eradication and the economic, social, solidarity and environmental dimensions of sustainable development in a balanced and integrated manner'.[148]

2.2.11. The Modernisation of Social Protection Systems Without Prejudice to Point (c)

51 Apart from the more specific social protection of workers set forth in Article 153.1 point (c) TFEU, a **broader social protection** is a major objective established in Article 153.1 point (k) TFEU which relates to the general material scope of Article 34 EUCFR,[149] without forgetting health protection under Article 35 EUCFR. The Preamble of the EPSR generally refers to social protection (Recitals 2, 3 and 8 of the Preamble EPSR) whereas Principle 12 (social protection), alongside Principles 3 (equal opportunities), 4 (active support to employment) and 5 (secure and adaptable employment) have an employment relationship dimension (similar to Article 153.1 point (c) TFEU).

52 The main existing **measures** relating to Article 153.1 point (k) TFEU are the following:

- Council Recommendation 92/442/EEC on the convergence of social protection objectives and policies[150] covers social insurance for workers in relation to sickness, maternity, unemployment, incapacity for work, the elderly and family.
- Council Recommendation 92/441/EEC on common criteria concerning sufficient resources and social assistance in social protection systems;[151]
- Council Regulation (EC) No. 883/2004[152] coordinates the social security rules of the Member States as regards persons in cross-border situations. Indeed, the material scope of the right to social protection covers both social assistance and

---

term, the mining of uranium can be environmentally and socially damaging, whilst it does not operate well when water levels are low and under extreme heat. Indeed, it can only be considered environmentally sustainable under energy policymaking conditions, which have been encouraged by the crisis, where sustainability is judged narrowly, according to GHG emissions: Kuzemko et al. (2022), p. 3.

[148] SWD(2017) 201 final, p. 2.

[149] Article 34 EUCFR affirms respect for the entitlement to social security benefits and social services providing protection in cases such as maternity, illness, industrial accidents, dependency or old age, and in the case of loss of employment. According to the Explanation on Article 34 EUCFR, this provision has been inspired by Articles 12, 13, 14, 30 and 31 of the European Social Charter.

[150] Council Recommendation 92/442/EEC *on the convergence of social protection objectives and policies*, O.J. L 245/49 (1992).

[151] Council Recommendation 92/441/EEC *on common criteria concerning sufficient resources and social assistance in social protection systems*, O.J. L 245/46 (1992).

[152] Council Regulation (EC) No. 883/2004 *on the coordination of social security systems*, O.J. L 166/1 (2004).

social security. The latter, which includes both contributory and non-contributory schemes, is defined in Council Regulation (EC) No. 883/2004 to include the following branches: (a) sickness benefits; (b) maternity and equivalent paternity benefits; (c) invalidity benefits; (d) old-age benefits; (e) survivors' benefits; (f) benefits in respect of accidents at work and occupational diseases; (g) death grants; (h) unemployment benefits; (i) pre-retirement benefits; (j) family benefits. The Regulation applies also to special non-contributory cash benefits which display characteristics of both social security and social assistance.

- Council Directive 2003/109/EC concerning the status of third-country nationals who are long-term residents,[153] together with a number of other Union directives concerning legal migration of third country nationals in the Union,[154] confer them equal treatment rights with host country's nationals in relation to social protection and social security.
- Council Directive 2010/41/EU on the application of the principle of equal treatment between men and women engaged in self-employed activity[155] grants access to maternity leave and benefits for at least 14 weeks. It does not cover access to any other social insurance risks.
- Council Regulation (EU) No. 1231/2010[156] coordinates social security systems in the case of third country nationals and their family members legally residing in the territory of the Union who have moved between MS.

Finally, concerning the **modernisation of social protection systems**, on the one hand, the Commission presented together with the EPSR a first-stage consultation of the social partners on an initiative concerning 'Access to Social Protection' to address varying access to social protection by workers in standard employment and people employed on non-standard contracts and in various forms of self-employment.[157] On the other hand, the Commission Staff Working Document

53

---

[153] Council Directive 2003/109/EC *concerning the status of third-country nationals who are long-term residents*, O.J. L 16/44 (2004). See also, for example, Parliament/Council Directive 2011/98/EU *on a single application procedure for a single permit for third-country nationals to reside and work in the territory of a Member State and on a common set of rights for third-country workers legally residing in a Member State*, O.J. L 343/1 (2011).

[154] The above mentioned directives on: family reunification, Blue Card, Single Permit, researchers, students, qualification as a beneficiary of international protection, seasonal workers and intra-corporate transferees.

[155] Parliament/Council Directive 2010/41/EU *on the application of the Principle of equal treatment between men and women engaged in an activity in a self-employed capacity*, O.J. L 180/1 (2010).

[156] Parliament/Council Regulation (EU) No. 1231/2010 *extending Regulation (EC) No. 883/2004 and Regulation (EC) No. 987/2009 to nationals of third countries who are not already covered by these Regulations solely on the ground of their nationality*, O.J. L 344/1 (2010).

[157] Consultation Document, *First phase consultation of Social Partners under Article 154 TFEU on a possible action addressing the challenges of access to social protection for people in all forms of employment in the framework of the European Pillar of Social Rights*, C(2017) 2610 final. In guaranteeing also to the self-employed access to social protection under comparable conditions,

accompanying the Communication establishing the EPSR, invites MS 'to adapt their rules in order to give effect to the Pillar provisions on social protection, in addition to transposing and enforcing rules adopted at Union level. Furthermore, MS may ratify, if not done so, and apply the relevant ILO conventions on social security, the European Code of Social Security and the Revised European Social Charter, and may review the reservations made for some Articles of the revised European Social Charter'.[158] Obviously, this invitation has to do with the exceptions or exclusions foreseen in paragraphs 4 and 5 of Article 153 TFEU. Anyway, the Covid-19 crisis has highlighted old and new types of inequalities that are related to structural weaknesses in the labour market and welfare states.[159]

3. Balancing the Union's Powers and the Substantial Exclusions: A Difficult Tension Between State Margin and European Action (Paragraphs 4 and 5)

54   Article 153 TFEU, which authorises the EU institutions to enact legislation relating to working conditions (paragraph 1), expressly excludes pay alongside the right of association, the right to strike or the right to impose lock-outs from its scope (paragraph 5).[160] Apart from these last material exclusions set forth in paragraph 5, whereas Article 153.1 point (c) TFEU refers to 'social security and social protection of workers', paragraph 4 adds a further limitation stating that 'the provisions adopted pursuant to this Article shall not affect the **right of MS to define the fundamental principles of their social security systems** and must not significantly affect the financial equilibrium thereof'.

55   In relation to pay, in *Del Cerro Alonso*, after pointing out that **the principle of non-discrimination cannot be interpreted restrictively**, the Court stated that, as paragraph 5 of Article 153 TFEU derogates from paragraphs 1 to 4, the matters reserved by paragraph 5 must be narrowly construed so as not to affect unduly the scope of paragraphs 1 to 4, nor to call into question the aims pursued by Article 151 TFEU.[161] The Court also held that, more specifically, the exception relating to 'pay' set out in Article 153.5 TFEU is explained by the fact that fixing the level of wages falls within the contractual freedom of the social partners at national level and

---

Principle 12 of the EPSR goes beyond Directive 2010/41/EU, which dealt only with maternity leave. Taken together, part one and part two of the provision on social protection ensure that comparable access to social protection is made available to people employed as workers and people working as self-employed.

[158] Commission Staff Working Document *accompanying the Communication on establishing a European Pillar of Social* Rights, SWD(2017) 201 final, p. 50.

[159] Eichhorst et al. (2020), p. 380.

[160] Despite the exception of Article 153.5 TFEU, the influence of European law on the right of association of MS is considerable: Benecke, in Grabitz et al. (2022), Article 153 AEUV para 102 (released in 2022).

[161] Case C-307/05, *Del Cerro Alonso* (ECJ 13 September 2007) para 37–39.

within the relevant competence of MS. In those circumstances, it was considered appropriate, as EU law currently stood, to exclude determination of the level of wages from harmonisation under Article 151 et seqq. TFEU.[162]

According to this criterion, the Court has held that Article 153.5 TFEU stands for the rule that the establishment of the level of the various constituent parts of pay of a worker 'is still unquestionably a matter for the **competent bodies in the various Member States**',[163] and that the exception contained in Article 153.5 'must therefore be interpreted as covering measures – such as the equivalence of all or some of the constituent parts of pay and/or the level of pay in the Member States, or the setting of a minimum guaranteed Community wage – which amount to direct interference by Community law in the determination of pay within the Community'.[164]

With this in mind, it has been pointed out that Article 153.5 TFEU aims to **prevent EU wide standardisation by the EU legislature of the wage levels** applicable in each of the MS, since such a levelling would represent significant interference in competition between undertakings operating in the internal market.[165] From this point of view, the prohibition in Article 153.5 TFEU would apply only to the determination of the 'level' of pay[166] and, therefore, the EU would not have competence, for example to 'introduce an upper limit for annual pay increases or regulate the amount of pay for overtime or for shift-work, public holiday overtime or night work'.[167]

On the contrary, the Court has approved the compatibility with Article 153.5 TFEU of EU actions that have only an **indirect link with the level of pay**, such as those measures relating to working time, posted workers and, of course, anti-discrimination,[168] since pay constitutes an essential element of employment conditions,[169]

---

[162] Case C-307/05, *Del Cerro Alonso* (ECJ 13 September 2007) para 40. See also Case C-268/06, *Impact* (ECJ 15 April 2008) para 123 and Joined Cases C-395/08 and C-396/08, *Bruno and Pettini* (CJEU 10 June 2010) para 36.

[163] Case C-307/05, *Del Cerro Alonso* (ECJ 13 September 2007) para 46.

[164] Case C-268/06, *Impact* (ECJ 15 April 2008) para 124.

[165] Case C-268/06, *Impact* (Opinion of AG Kokott of 9 January 2008) para 173.

[166] E.g., Case C-268/06, *Impact* (ECJ 15 April 2008) para 123–124, 130 and Joined Cases C-395/08 and C-396/08, *Bruno and Pettini* (CJEU 10 June 2010) para 36–37.

[167] Case C-268/06, *Impact* (Opinion of AG Kokott of 9 January 2008) para 174.

[168] Cf. the position of the ECSR concerning organisation of working time, for example, Complaint No. 55/2009, *Confédération Générale du Travail v France* (ECSR 23 June 2010) para 31–42; or delocalisation of undertakings and social dumping, for example, Complaint No. 85/2012, *Swedish Trade Union Confederation (LO) and Swedish Confederation of Professional Employees (TCO) v Sweden* (ECSR 3 July 2013) para 72–74.

[169] The ECJ highlighted the importance of remuneration in Case C-425/02, *Delahaye* (ECJ 11 November 2004) para 33.

perhaps even the most important and the most open to discrimination.[170] Consequently, if pay conditions were to be included in the exception under Article 153.5 TFEU, that would render Article 19 TFEU—which seeks to combat discrimination—largely meaningless.

59 In any case, the **frontier between the Union's powers and the substantial exclusions** set forth in Article 153.5 TFEU is very thin. The Opinion of AG *Sharpston* delivered in *Epitropos tou Elegktikou Synedriou*[171] shows this complexity, since remuneration and the other substantial exclusions (particularly the right of association) are closely related to the principle of non-discrimination in the enjoyment of working conditions (Article 153.1 point (a) TFEU). In the context of the proceeding before the Court, the Greek Elegktiko Sinedrio (Court of Auditors) intended to seek answers to several questions concerning the compatibility with EU law of national rules as a result of which, where public sector employees are entitled to leave for trade union business, that leave is paid or not paid according to the classification of the employment relationship, particularly on whether it is of indefinite duration or for a fixed term.

60 In AG *Sharpston*'s view, 'a rule that remuneration is, or is not, to be paid in respect of leave which is accorded by law to employees who are trade union officials for absence from work on trade union business is, *prima facie* and on a straightforward interpretation of the terms, an employment or working condition for such employees'. On the other hand, it is true that Articles 153, 155 and 159 TFEU, read together, do not authorise the Union to take action in the fields of, inter alia, pay or the right of association. However, 'that limitation concerns **only direct intervention** in those matters. It does not preclude measures which affect them only indirectly'.[172]

61 With reference to Clause 4.1 of the framework agreement on fixed-term work concluded on 18 March 1999 by three European cross-industry organisations (ETUC, UNICE and CEEP),[173] the conclusion would be that such provision does not purport to regulate pay or the right of association in any substantive way. It merely requires that whatever rules govern employment conditions in the MS must be applied without discrimination as between fixed-term and permanent workers.[174]

---

[170] See the Proposal for a Council Directive *establishing a general framework for equal treatment in employment and occupation*, COM(1999) 565 final. In the 2021 Action Plan on the EPSR, the Commission continues to encourage MS to advance and conclude the negotiations in Council on the Commission proposal for a horizontal Equal Treatment Directive (COM(2008)426 final of 2 July 2008).

[171] Case C-363/11, *Epitropos tou Elegktikou Synedriou* (Opinion of AG Sharpston of 20 September 2012).

[172] Case C-363/11, *Epitropos tou Elegktikou Synedriou* (Opinion of AG Sharpston of 20 September 2012) para 67 to 71.

[173] The framework agreement formed the annex to Council Directive 1999/70/EC *concerning the framework agreement on fixed-term work concluded by ETUC, UNICE and CEEP*, O.J. L 175/43 (1999), which was adopted based on ex-Article 139.2 TEC (now Article 155.2 TFEU).

[174] Clause 4.1 of the framework agreement provides: 'In respect of employment conditions, fixed-term workers shall not be treated in a less favourable manner than comparable permanent workers

The Court has made it clear that Article 153.5 TFEU, which must be interpreted strictly, cannot prevent a fixed-term worker from **relying on the requirement of non-discrimination** in Clause 4.1 of the framework agreement to seek the benefit of an employment condition reserved for permanent workers, even where it concerns pay.[175] The same conclusion must apply by analogy in so far as the disputed difference in treatment relates to the exercise of the right of association. Consequently, according to AG *Sharpston*, the treatment at issue in the proceedings before the Elegktiko Sinedrio must be regarded as falling within the concept of 'employment conditions' in Clause 4.1 of the framework agreement, and as not being concerned by the limitation in Article 153.5 TFEU.

Finally, since the EU does not have the competence to create legally binding social security standards under Article 153.4 TFEU, it has been argued that the conventions signed within the framework of the ILO and the Council of Europe are of central importance to the development of international social security standards.[176] With this in mind, it has also been advocated a more active role for the CJEU in constitutionalising the European social model, by proposing that the CJEU should consider the ILO standards when interpreting the EU primary and secondary law.[177] From this point of view, it has been suggested that **restrictions and exclusions** established in Article 153.3-153.5 TFEU are **not** inspired by the **broad interpretation** of limits associated to sovereignty under Public International Law, **but** they have been approached by the CJEU as exceptions to be **interpreted in a restricted way** according to the **useful effect** doctrine.[178] The same should be applied, *a fortiori*, to the relevant assumption by the CJEU of the case law from the ECSR interpreting the fundamental right to social security set forth in Article 12 of the European Social Charter.[179]

62

---

solely because they have a fixed-term contract or relation unless different treatment is justified on objective grounds'.

[175] See Case C-307/05, *Del Cerro Alonso* (ECJ 13 September 2007) para 33 et seq. See also, in this field, Complaint No. 144/2017, *CGS v Italy* (ECSR 9 September 2020), where the ECSR concluded that 'there is a violation of Article 1§2 of the Charter in respect of public education staff not registered in the ERE lists ['eligibility ranking lists to be drawn upon exhaustion'] and recruited under successive contracts with interruptions for an overall length of more than 36 months', after citing the relevant EU law (EU Council Directive 1999/70/EC of 28 June 1999 concerning the framework agreement on fixed-term work concluded by ETUC, UNICE and CEEP) and CJEU's case law (para 41–42).

[176] Korda and Pennings (2008), p. 132.

[177] Bercusson (2008), p. 58 et seqq.

[178] Mirando Boto (2018), p. 75.

[179] See Jimena Quesada (2014).

4. Challenges: A Complex Approach to Social Policy and Fundamental Rights in a Broader Social Europe

63 In light of the previous reference to the ILO Conventions[180] but, especially, to the European Social Charter, it must be said that not only substantial exclusions and limitations affecting EU law, but also social policy aspects covered by EU legal provisions, cannot avoid a human rights approach in a broader Social Europe which necessarily must consider the synergies between the EU and the Council of Europe.

64 Such dynamics has been recently promoted by the Council of Europe in the framework of the so-called new 'Turin process for the European Social Charter'. Particularly, the '**Turin process**' was launched by the Secretary General of the Council of Europe at the High-Level Conference on the European Social Charter organised in Turin on 17-18 October 2014 by the Council of Europe in co-operation with Italian Presidency of the Council of the EU and the Turin municipality. This process aims at **reinforcing the normative system of the Charter within the Council of Europe and in its relationship with the law of the EU**. Its key objective is to improve the implementation of social and economic rights at the continental level, in parallel to the civil and political rights guaranteed by the ECHR.[181]

65 Of course, as commented in the previous section, the 'social case law' from the ECJ has evolved and is undoubtedly valuable. In contrast, as also announced before, the ECJ's case law has known a recent restrictive evolution in other fields covered by Article 153 TFEU, such as the workers' right to information and consultation within the undertaking (Article 27 EUCFR) or the protection in the event of unjustified dismissal (Article 30 EUCFR). Furthermore, these two aspects have been assessed without considering the European Social Charter (and the interpretation by the ECSR) and, therefore, both have raised the issue of real **potential divergent views between the ECJ and the ECSR**.

66 Particularly, concerning the **right to information and consultation within the undertaking**, the recent restricted approach (restriction contrary to the Opinion of AG *Cruz Villalón*[182]) is illustrated by *Association de médiation sociale*, in which the Court found that Article 27 EUCFR must be interpreted to the effect that, where a national provision implementing that directive (such as Article L. 1111-3 of the French Labour Code), is incompatible with EU law, Article 27 EUCFR cannot be invoked in a dispute between individuals to disapply that national provision.[183] By

---

[180] See Wendeling-Schröder (2014), pp. 799–810.

[181] All relevant documents available at https://www.coe.int/en/web/turin-process.

[182] Case C-176/12, *Association de médiation sociale* (Opinion of AG Cruz Villalón of 18 July 2013) para 80.

[183] Case C-176/12, *Association de médiation sociale* (CJEU 15 January 2014) para 51. See also, in the same restrictive direction (concerning Article 20 EUCFR on equality before the law), Case C-198/13, *Julián Hernández* (CJEU 10 July 2014) para 49. Such restrictive approach has been also adopted by the CIEU, when hearing a dispute which is exclusively between private individuals, in relation to the principle of the primacy of EU law (specifically,

contrast, the same situation was analysed by the ECSR under Article 21 of the Revised Social Charter and, also by considering EU law (even in the light of the above mentioned judgment of the CJEU, which is explicitly cited), it concluded that there was a breach of such provision.[184]

In relation to the protection in case of **termination of employment**, in *Nisttahuz Poclava*[185] the ECJ decided not to tackle the impact[186] of a new employment contract to support entrepreneurs (entailing a one-year probationary period during which the employer might freely terminate the contract without notice or compensation) introduced in Spain by Law 3/2012 of 6 July 2012 on urgent measures for labour market reform to face the economic crisis. For the Court, despite Article 30 EUCFR, the situation at issue paradoxically did not fall within the scope of EU law.[187] In real terms, according to the Explanation relating to Article 30 EUCFR, this provision draws on Article 24 of the 1996 Revised ECS so that it should be interpreted in light of the ECSR requirements and case law. The critical issue lies in 'the limited scope' of Article 30 EUCFR 'due to the absence of any general directive regulating the termination of employment, although "protection of workers where their employment contract is terminated" falls under EU competence under Article 153 TFEU. However, Member States must respect the Charter "only

67

---

with regard to directives): 'the principle that national law must be interpreted in conformity with EU law has certain limits. Thus, the obligation on a national court to refer to the content of a directive when interpreting and applying the relevant rules of domestic law is limited by general principles of law and it cannot serve as the basis for a *contra legem* interpretation of national law'; Case C-261/20, *Thelen Technopark Berlin* (CJEU 18 January 2022) para 28.

[184] See European Committee of Social Rights *Conclusions 2014*, Article 21, France. Available at https://www.coe.int/en/web/european-social-charter). For the ECSR: 'The minimum framework which the Committee has adopted for Article 21 of the Charter is Directive 2002/14/EC of the European Parliament and of the Council of 11 March 2002. In this context, the Committee points out that all categories of worker (all employees holding an employment contract with the company regardless of their status, length of service or place of work) must be included in the calculation of the number of employees enjoying the right to information and consultation (Case C-385/05, *Confédération générale du travail and Others* (ECJ 18 January 2007) and Case C-176/12, *Association de médiation sociale* (CJEU 15 January 2014). It considers therefore that the exclusion, provided for in Article L. 1111-3 of the Code of workers on state-subsidised contracts from the calculation of companies' staff numbers – a calculation which is necessary to determine the minimum thresholds beyond which staff representative bodies ensuring the information and consultation of workers must be set up – is not in conformity with the Charter'.

[185] Case C-117/14, *Nisttahuz Poclava* (CJEU 5 February 2015) para 40–44.

[186] Under Article 30 EUCFR, Council Directive 1999/70/EC, 1982 ILO Convention No. 158 concerning the Termination of Employment at the Initiative of the Employer and the 1961 European Social Charter—in relation to the decision of the ECSR on a similar Greek contract: Complaint No. 65/2011, *General federation of employees of the national electric power corporation and Confederation of Greek Civil Servants' Trade Unions v Greece* (ECSR 23 May 2012) para 25–28.

[187] See Case C-32/20, *Balga* (CJEU Order of 4 June 2020) para 16, 18, 24–25 and 33–35. Cf. Complaint No. 158/2017, *CGIL v Italy* (ECSR 11 September 2019) para 35–28 and 96–105.

when they are implementing Union law," this wording being interpreted restrictively by the CJEU'.[188]

68   Recently, it is true that the CJEU's case law has experienced an evolution in terms of **direct applicability of some provisions of the EUCFR** in a dispute between individuals (*Drittwirkung*), particularly to ensure the judicial protection deriving for individuals from Article 21 (non-discrimination)[189] or from Article 31 (fair and just working conditions)[190] and to guarantee the full effectiveness of those articles by disapplying if need be any contrary provision of national law.[191]

List of Cases

ECJ/CJEU

ECJ 13.06.1986, 139/85, *Kempf v Staatssecretaris van Justitie*, ECLI:EU:C:1986:223 [cit. in para 39]

ECJ 29.09.1987, 126/86, *Giménez Zaera*, ECLI:EU:C:1987:395 [cit. in para 5]

ECJ 26.02.1991, C-292/89, *The Queen v Immigration Appeal Tribunal, ex parte Antonissen*, ECLI:EU:C:1991:80 [cit. in para 39]

ECJ 28.03.1996, Opinion 2/94, *Accession to the ECHR*, ECLI:EU:C:1996:140 [cit. in para 1]

ECJ 12.12.1996, C-84/94, *United Kingdom v Council*, ECLI:EU:C:1996:431 [cit. in para 18, 20]

ECJ 19.11.2002, C-188/00, *Bülent Kurz, né Yüce v Land Baden-Württemberg*, ECLI:EU:C:2002:694 [cit. in para 39]

ECJ 11.11.2004, C-425/02, *Delahaye*, ECLI:EU:C:2004:706 [cit. in para 58]

ECJ 17.03.2005, C-109/04, *Kranemann*, ECLI:EU:C:2005:187 [cit. in para 39]

ECJ 10.01.2006, C-94/03, *Commission v Council*, ECLI:EU:C:2006:2 [cit. in para 15]

ECJ 13.09.2007, C-307/05, *Del Cerro Alonso*, ECLI:EU:C:2007:509 [cit. in para 55, 56, 61]

ECJ 20.09.2007, C-116/06, *Kiiski*, ECLI:EU:C:2007:536 [cit. in para 17]

ECJ 11.10.2007, C-460/06, *Paquay*, ECLI:EU:C:2007:601 [cit. in para 16]

ECJ 09.01.2008, C-268/06, *Impact*, Opinion of AG Kokott, ECLI:EU:C:2008:2 [cit. in para 57]

ECJ 15.04.2008, C-268/06, *Impact*, ECLI:EU:C:2008:223 [cit. in para 7, 55-57]

---

[188] Schmitt (2017), p. 418.

[189] See Case C-414/16, *Egenberger* (CJEU 17 April 2018) para 82 and Case C-68/17, *IR* (CJEU 11 September 2018) para 71.

[190] See Joined Cases C-569/16 and C-570/16, *Bauer/Willmeroth* (CJEU 6 November 2018) para 92, Case C-684/16, *Max-Planck-Gesellschaft zur Förderung der Wissenschaften* (CJEU 6 November 2018) para 81, Case C-193/17, *Cresco Investigation* (CJEU 22 January 2019) para 77 and Case C-243/19, *Veselības ministrija* (CJEU 29 October 2020) para 36.

[191] See recent developments in Tomás Mallén (2022), pp. 225–228.

Article 153. [Union Action]

CJEU 10.06.2010, C-395/08 and C-396/08, *Bruno and Pettini*, ECLI:EU:C:2010:329 [cit. in para 7, 55, 57]
CJEU 11.11.2010, C-232/09, *Danosa*, ECLI:EU:C:2010:674 [cit. in para 16]
CJEU 16.06.2011, C-155/10, Opinion of AG Trstenjak, *Williams and Others*, ECLI:EU:C:2011:403 [cit. in para 18]
CJEU 20.09.2012, C-363/11, Opinion of AG Sharpston, *Epitropos tou Elegktikou Synedriou*, ECLI:EU:C:2012:584 [cit. in para 59-60]
CJEU 19.09.2013, C-5/12, *Betriu Montull*, ECLI:EU:C:2013:571 [cit. in para 17]
CJEU 19.09.2013, C-579/12 RX-II, *Commission v Strack*, ECLI:EU:C:2013:570 [cit. in para 19-20]
CJEU 18.07.2013, C-176/12, Opinion of AG Cruz Villalón, *Association de médiation sociale*, ECLI:EU:C:2013:491 [cit. in para 66]
CJEU 15.01.2014, C-176/12, *Association de médiation sociale*, ECLI:EU:C:2014:2 [cit. in para 66]
CJEU 18.03.2014, C-167/12, *C. D.*, ECLI:EU:C:2014:169 [cit. in para 17]
CJEU 10.07.2014, C-198/13, *Julián Hernández*, ECLI:EU:C:2014:2055 [cit. in para 66]
CJEU 05.02.2015, C-117/14, *Nisttahuz Poclava*, ECLI:EU:C:2015:60 [cit. in para 67]
CJEU 20.12.2017, C-434/16, *Novak*, ECLI:EU:C:2017:994 [cit. in para 23]
CJEU 17.04.2018, C-414/16, *Egenberger*, ECLI:EU:C:2018:257 [cit. in para 68]
CJEU 11.09.2018, C-68/17, *IR*, ECLI:EU:C:2018:696 [cit. in para 68]
CJEU 19.09.2018, C-41/17, *González Castro*, ECLI:EU:C:2018:736 [cit. in para 33]
CJEU 19.09.2018, C-312/17, *Bedi*, ECLI:EU:C:2018:734 [cit. in para 29]
CJEU 25.10.2018, C-451/17, *Walltopia*, ECLI:EU:C:2018:861 [cit. in para 29]
CJEU 06.11.2018, C-569/16 and C-570/16, *Bauer/Willmeroth*, ECLI:EU:C:2018:871 [cit. in para 68]
CJEU 06.11.2018, C-684/16, *Max-Planck-Gesellschaft zur Förderung der Wissenschaften*, ECLI:EU:C:2018:874 [cit. in para 68]
CJEU 19.12.2018, C-667/17, *Cadeddu*, ECLI:EU:C:2018:1036 [cit. in para 26]
CJEU 22.01.2019, C-193/17, *Cresco Investigation*, ECLI:EU:C:2019:43 [cit. in para 68]
CJEU 11.09.2019, C-397/18, *Nobel Plastiques Ibérica*, ECLI:EU:C:2019:703, [cit. in para 43]
CJEU 14.10.2020, C-681/18, *JH v KG*, ECLI:EU:C:2020:823 [cit. in para 27]
CJEU 29.10.2020, C-243/19, *Veselības ministrija*, ECLI:EU:C:2020:872 [cit. in para 68]
CJEU 25.02.2021, C-129/20, *Caisse pour l'avenir des enfants (Emploi à la naissance)*, ECLI:EU:C:2021:140 [cit. in para 33]
CJEU 03.06.2021, C-624/19, *Tesco Stores*, ECLI:EU:C:2021:429 [cit. in para 18]
CJEU 15.07.2021, C-795/19, *Tartu Vangla*, ECLI:EU:C:2021:606 [cit. in para 43]
CJEU 18.01.2022, C-261/20, *Thelen Technopark Berlin*, ECLI:EU:C:2022:33 [cit. in para 66]
CJEU 02.05.2022, C-405/20, *BVAEB*, ECLI:EU:C:2022:347 [cit. in para 18]

CJEU 16.06.2022, C-328/20, *Commission v Austria (Indexation des prestations familiales)*, ECLI:EU:C:2022:468 [cit. in para 29, 39]

CJEU 07.07.2022, C-257/21 and C-258/21, *Coca-Cola European Partners Deutschland GmbH*, ECLI:EU:C:2022:529 [cit. in para 37]

CJEU 15.12.2022, C-311/21, *TimePartner Personalmanagement*, ECLI:EU:C:2022:983 [cit. in para 27]

CJEU 22.12.2022, C-392/21, *Inspectoratul General pentru Imigrări*, ECLI:EU:C:2022:1020 [cit. in para 24]

ECtHR

ECtHR 18.02.2009, 55707/00, *Andrejeva v Latvia* [cit. in para 29]

ECtHR 08.12.2009, 46141/07, *Muñoz Díaz v Spain* [cit. in para 29]

ECtHR 21.01.2011, 30696/09, *M.S.S. v Belgium and Greece* [cit. in para 13]

ECtHR 17.10.2013, 27013/07, *Winterstein and Others v France* [cit. in para 13]

ECtHR 05.09.2017, 61496/08, *Bărbulescu v Romania* [cit. in para 23]

ECtHR 17.10.2019, 1874/13 and 8567/13, *López Ribalda and Others v Spain* [cit. in para 23]

ECtHR 14.05.2020, 24720/13, *Hirtu and Others v France* [cit. in para 13]

ECtHR 04.10.2021, 17808/19 and 36972/19, *Paketova and Others v Bulgaria* [cit. in para 13]

EctHR 09.06.2022, 49270/11, *Savickis and Others v Latvia* [cit. in para 29]

ECtHR 11.10.2022, 78630/12, *Beeler v Switzerland* [cit. in para 29]

ECtHR 19.01.2023, 32667/19 and 30807/20, *Doménech Aradilla and Rodríguez González v Spain* [cit. in para 29]

ECSR

ECSR 17.10.2001, 10/2000, *Tehy ry and STTK v. Finland* [cit. in para 23]

ECSR 23.06.2010, 55/2009, *Confédération Générale du Travail v France* [cit. in para 56]

ECSR 25.06.2010, 58/2009, *COHRE v Italy* [cit. in para 13]

ECSR 28.06.2011, 63/2010, *COHRE v France* [cit. in para 13]

ECSR 23.05.2012, 65/2011, *General federation of employees of the national electric power corporation and Confederation of Greek Civil Servants' Trade Unions v Greece* [cit. in para 65]

ECSR 03.07.2013, 85/2012, *Swedish Trade Union Confederation (LO) and Swedish Confederation of Professional Employees (TCO) v Sweden* [cit. in para 56]

ECSR 08.12.2016, 108/2014, *Finnish Society of Social Rights v. Finland* [cit. in para 29]

ECSR 12.05.2017, 110/2014, *FIDH v Ireland* [cit. in para 13]

ECSR 05.12.2018, 151/2017, *ERRC v Bulgaria* [cit. in para 13]

ECSR 11.09.2019, 158/2017, *CGIL v Italy* [cit. in para 65]

ECSR 09.09.2020, 144/2017, *CGS v Italy* [cit. in para 61]

ECSR 26.01.2021, 173/2018, *ICJ and ECRE v Greece* [cit. in para 13].

References[192]

Aldecoa Luzarraga, F., & Guinea Llorente, M. (2008). *El rescate sustancial de la Constitución Europea a través del Tratado de Lisboa: la salida del laberinto*. Real Instituto Elcano (Working Paper No. 9).

Bercusson, B. (2008). The European Court of Justice, labour law and ILO standards. In F. Müntefering & U. Becker (Eds.), *50 Jahre EU – 50 Jahre Rechtsprechung des Europäischen Gerichtshofs zum Arbeits- und Sozialrecht* (pp. 41–54). Nomos.

Blanke, T. (2012). The principle of subsidiarity in the Lisbon Treaty. In I. Schöman, K. Lörcher, & N. Bruun (Eds.), *The Lisbon Treaty and social Europe* (pp. 235–260). Hart Publishing.

Böttner, R., & Grinc, J. (2018). *Bridging clauses in European constitutional law*. Springer.

Brameshuber, E. (2021). Information and consultation rights. In B. ter Haar & A. Kun (Eds.), *EU collective labour law* (pp. 239–254). Elgar.

Chieregato, E. (2020). A work–life balance for all? Assessing the inclusiveness of EU Directive 2019/1158. *International Journal of Comparative Labour Law and Industrial Relations, 36*(1), 59–80.

Craig, P. (2010). *The Lisbon Treaty: Law, politics, and treaty reform*. OUP.

Deakin, S. (2012). The Lisbon Treaty, the Viking and Laval judgments and the financial crisis: In search of new foundations for Europe's 'social market economy'. In I. Schöman, K. Lörcher, & N. Bruun (Eds.), *The Lisbon Treaty and social Europe* (pp. 19–43). Hart Publishing.

Degener, T. (2020). The impact of the UN Convention on the Rights of Persons with Disabilities on EU anti-discrimination law. In T. Giegerich (Ed.), *The European Union as protector and promoter of equality* (pp. 349–362). Springer.

Dorssemont, P. (2012). Values and objectives. In I. Schöman, K. Lörcher, & N. Bruun (Eds.), *The Lisbon Treaty and social Europe* (pp. 45–59). Hart Publishing.

Eichhorst, W., Paul Marx, P., & Rinne, U. (2020). Manoeuvring through the crisis: Labour market and social policies during the COVID-19 pandemic. *Intereconomics, 6*, 375–380.

Grabitz, E., Hilf, M., & Nettesheim, M. (Eds.). (2022). *Das Recht der Europäischen Union: EUV/ AEUV*. C.H. Beck.

Hirth, L. (2020). Open data for electricity modelling: Legal aspects. *Energy Strategy Reviews, 27*, 1–11.

Jimena Quesada, L. (2014). Adoption and rejection of austerity measures: Current controversies under European law (focus on the role of the European Committee of Social Rights). *Revista Catalana de Dret Públic, 49*, 41–59.

Korda, M., & Pennings, F. (2008). The legal character of international social security standards. *European Journal of Social Security, 10*(2), 131–158.

Kuzemko, C., et al. (2022). Russia's war on Ukraine, European energy policy responses & implications for sustainable transformations. *Energy Research & Social Science, 93*, 1–8.

Lasa López, A. (2019). El Pilar Europeo de Derechos Sociales: un análisis desde las coordenadas del constitucionalismo de mercado europeo. *Revista de Derecho Comunitario Europeo, 62*, 117–154.

Lörcher, K. (2012). Social competences. In I. Schöman, K. Lörcher, & N. Bruun (Eds.), *The Lisbon Treaty and social Europe* (pp. 165–233). Hart Publishing.

Martínez López-Sáez, M. (2018). *Una revisión del derecho fundamental a la protección de datos de carácter personal. Un reto en clave de diálogo judicial y constitucionalismo multinivel en la Unión Europea*. Tirant lo Blanch.

Mirando Boto, J. M. (2018). Competencias, fuentes y papel de las instituciones de la UE en materia social. In *Derecho Social de la Unión Europea. Aplicación por el Tribunal de Justicia* (pp. 71–90). Francis Lefebvre.

---

[192] All cited internet sources have been accessed on 17 February 2023.

Mülder, M. (2020). Stütze für Europa? Die Europäische Säule sozialer Rechte. In S. Martini & H. Rathke (Eds.), *Zehn Jahre Vertrag von Lissabon. Reflexionen zur Zukunft der europäischen Integration* (pp. 103–116). Nomos.

Nolan, B., & Whelan, C. T. (2018). Poverty and social exclusion indicators in the European Union. The role of non-monetary deprivation indicators. In R. M. Carmo, C. Rio, & M. Medgyesi (Eds.), *Reducing inequalities: A challenge for the European Union?* (pp. 97–114). Palgrave Macmillan.

Picek, O. (2020). Spillover effects from NextGenerationEU. *Intereconomics, 55*, 325–331.

Schmitt, M. (2017). Article 24. The right to protection in cases of termination of employment. In N. Bruun, K. Lorcher, I. Schömann, & S. Clauwaert (Eds.), *The European social charter and the employment relation* (pp. 412–438). Hart Publishing.

Tomás Mallén, B. (2022). Derechos fundamentales y *Drittwirkung* en perspectiva multinivel: desarrollos recientes en el Derecho europeo. *Revista de Derecho Político, 115*, 207–235.

Tsaridou, C., & Karabelas, A. (2021). Drinking water standards and their implementation – a critical assessment. *Water, 13*, 1–33.

von der Groeben, H., Schwarze, J., & Hatje, A. (Eds.). (2015). *Europäisches Unionsrecht*. Nomos.

Wendeling-Schröder, U. (2014). Die ILO und ihre arbeitsrechtlichen Standards – was leisten sie in der Krise der EU? In C. Mestre, C. Sachs-Durand, & M. Storck (Eds.), *Le travail humain au Carrefour du droit et de la sociologie. Hommage au Professeur Nikitas Aliprantis* (pp. 799–810). Presses universitaires de Strasbourg.

Ziller, J. (2007). Il Trattato modificativo del 2007: sostanza salvata e forma cambiata del Trattto costituzionale de 2004. *Quaderni costituzionali, 4*, 875–892.

Article 154 [Participation of the Social Partners]
(ex-Article 138 TEC)

1. The Commission shall have the task of promoting the consultation of management and labour at Union level and shall take any relevant measure to facilitate their dialogue by ensuring balanced support for the parties.
2. To this end, before submitting proposals in the social policy field, the Commission shall consult management and labour on the possible direction of Union action.[9]
3. If, after such consultation, the Commission considers Union action advisable, it shall consult management and labour on the content of the envisaged proposal. Management and labour shall forward to the Commission an opinion or, where appropriate, a recommendation.[10–11]
4. On the occasion of the consultation referred to in paragraphs 2 and 3, management and labour may inform the Commission of their wish to initiate the process provided for in Article 155. The duration of this process shall not exceed nine months, unless the management and labour concerned and the Commission decide jointly to extend it.[28–30]

Contents

1. Preliminary Remarks: Social Partners' Views Crucial to Building a Social Europe 1
2. Modalities of Consultation Under Article 154 TFEU 6
3. A Broader Framework of Social Consultation: Other Structures in Support of the Social Policy 14
4. Challenges: European Social Partners' Contribution to Actions and Legal Acts of the European Union in the Social Area 19

List of Cases
References

1. Preliminary Remarks: Social Partners' Views Crucial to Building a Social Europe

Article 154 TFEU (ex-Article 138 TEC) has its origin (like Article 155 TFEU) in Articles 3 and 4 of the Social Policy Agreement included into the Social Policy Protocol appended to the 1992 **Maastricht Treaty**. The content of current Article 154 TFEU is exactly the same as the one of Article 3 of that Agreement, with logical adaptations.[1]

Apart from this novelty introduced by the Maastricht Treaty, the **consultation of social partners** has been developed since the EC's origins within their representatives in the European Economic and Social Committee. From this point of view,

1

---

[1] 'Union' instead of 'Community' and internal reference to Article 155 TFEU instead of to Article 4 of the Agreement.

since the beginning of European integration, the European social partners have played an important and ever-increasing role in the field of social policy. European social partners have been consulted by the Commission prior to legislative proposals on social matters. As a result, the European social partners have in a number of cases influenced the shaping of European social policy legislation and contributed significantly to the **definition of European social standards** as well as to the **modernisation of labour markets**.

2   In this context, **formal consultations** play a key role in the regulatory processes of EU decision-making. Since 1995, the European social partners have been formally consulted by the Commission many times. Their views have enabled the Commission to assess its various legislative options and to prepare its suggestions for the future.[2] This way, the Commission put into practice its main institutional mission in promoting the general interest of the EU, what 'preserves a proactive potential in it such as to place the Commission – thanks to the institutional instruments it can make use of in the European decisional proceedings – in the role of protagonist in the definition of decision-making policies' (→ Article 17 TEU para 4).

3   Moreover, the Lisbon Treaty further strengthened the role of the social partners at the EU level by providing in Article 152 TFEU that now the Union as a whole (and not only the Commission) must promote **social dialogue**, which is consistent with the new 'horizontal social clause' (Article 9 TFEU). Article 152 TFEU has also institutionalised the Tripartite Social Summit for Growth and Employment (→ Article 152 TFEU para 9 et seqq.). Of course, the Commission is the 'motor of European integration' and, therefore, the role of social partners is more visible in relation to it, as specifically foreseen in Article 154 TFEU.

4   From this last perspective, social partners (either at European or at national level) may also take part in any **public consultation on non-legislative initiatives** (e.g. Green papers, White papers, Communications, Staff Working Documents, etc.) launched by the Commission, which give all relevant stakeholders the opportunity to express their views.

---

[2] As examples, European social partners have had a considerable influence on the preparation of the following Commission proposals: (a) Revamping the rules to protect EU workers from harmful electromagnetic fields (Council Directive 2013/35/EU *on the minimum health and safety requirements regarding the exposure of workers to the risks arising from physical agents (electromagnetic fields) (20th individual Directive within the meaning of Article 16(1) of Directive 89/391/EEC)*, O.J. L 179/1 (2013)); (b) The new framework Directive 2009/38/EC *on the establishment of a European Works Council or a procedure in Community-scale undertakings and Community-scale groups of undertakings for the purposes of informing and consulting employees*, O.J. L 122/28 (2009); (c) The Council Directive 2010/18/EU *implementing the revised Framework Agreement on parental leave concluded by BUSINESSEUROPE, UEAPME, CEEP and ETUC and repealing Directive 96/34/EC*, O.J. L 68/13 (2010), now replaced by Parliament/Council Directive (EU) 2019/1158 *on work-life balance for parents and carers*, O.J. L 188/79 (2019); (d) Council Recommendation *on a smoke-free environment*, O.J. C 296/4 (2009).

Article 154. [Participation of the Social Partners]

In any case, considering the **complexity of consultation mechanisms** and the **increasing number of consultations**,[3] 'it is a major challenge for European social partners to contribute in a timely manner and develop qualitative expertise on the issues that concern them. Accordingly, the Commission may support the efforts of European social partners in strengthening their administrative capacity'.[4] Nevertheless, it has been argued that the decision-making processes of the social partners, unlike the legislative procedure, reflect the outcome of negotiation processes which are not so transparent.[5]

2. Modalities of Consultation Under Article 154 TFEU

The **types of consultation social partners** are entitled to participate in under Article 154 TFEU deal not only with the elaboration and implementation of EU law, but also with the interpretation of it in controversial cases. Indeed, **European social partners** are not only consulted prior to the adoption of **new EU initiatives**; they are also consulted during the **implementation phase of EU law**, for instance when preparing implementation reports. European social partners may also be consulted by the European Commission on the occasion of litigations brought before the ECJ concerning the interpretation of social dialogue agreements implemented by means of directives.

All these modalities are consistent with the social partners' rights as recognised in Article 28 EUCFR and Article 155 TFEU. From this same perspective, these provisions reinforce the role of social partners as a special **'expression of subsidiarity'** in the functioning of the Union, in addition to the general principle of subsidiarity under Article 5 TEU.[6] Particularly, the first two types of consultations (adoption and implementation) have to do with the phases *ex ante* and *ex post facto* of the drafting of EU legislation and they are also consistent with the feed-back from management and labour on any new European initiative relating to the policy fields as set out in Article 153 TFEU. As far as the third type of consultation is concerned, the role and views of management and labour in relation to the interpretation of an agreement are often reflected in the text of the agreement itself.[7]

Under Article 154 TFEU only the European **organisations representing employers and workers at EU level** who are **recognised as 'European social**

---

[3] See Laborde (2014).

[4] Publications Office of the European Union (2011), p. 5.

[5] Rust, in von der Groeben et al. (2015), Article 154 AEUV para 67.

[6] Benecke, in Grabitz et al. (2022), Article 154 AEUV para 2 (released in 2022).

[7] See, for example, Council Directive 97/81/EC *concerning the Framework Agreement on part-time work concluded by UNICE, CEEP and the ETUC*, O.J. L 14/9 (1998). It provides as follows in this respect: 'Without prejudice to the respective role of the Commission, national courts and the Court of Justice, any matter relating to the interpretation of this agreement at European level should, in the first instance, be referred by the Commission to the signatory parties who will give an opinion'.

partners' can be consulted by the Commission.[8] To this end, the Commission regularly updates its list of consulted organisations (almost one hundred)[9] based on representativeness studies carried out by Eurofound.[10] All European social partners (whether they are sectoral or cross-industry organisations) are on an equal footing. However, the Commission may limit the number of organisations which are consulted according to the specific nature of the topic to collect only relevant contributions. Obviously, the Commission does not enjoy any unlimited power in this field, since its refusal to include an organisation in the Commission's list or to proceed to a relevant consultation under Article 154 TFEU may be challenged before the CJEU to have such infringements established. On the other hand, as an alternative legal remedy to this action for annulment or for failure to act lodged at first instance with the General Court (Article 265 TFEU in conjunction with Article 256 TFEU), it would be possible to submit the issue before the European Ombudsperson as a case of maladministration (Article 228 TFEU in conjunction with Article 43 EUCFR).

9   Article 154 TFEU, in establishing an 'original procedure of law making',[11] provides for a formal **two-stage consultation procedure**. In the first stage, the Commission consults the European social partners on the possible direction of a new legislative proposal in the social policy field.[12] In this context, the Commission notifies to the European social partners a **first phase** consultation document setting

---

[8] More specifically, Commission Communication *concerning the application of the Agreement on social policy presented by the Commission to the Council and the European Parliament*, COM(93) 600 final set out some criteria to define the organisations which are potentially eligible to be consulted: (1) be cross-industry or relate to specific sectors or categories and be organised at European level; (2) consist of organisations which are themselves an integral and recognised as part of Member State social partner structures, have the capacity to negotiate agreements and are representative of all Member States, as far as possible; (3) have adequate structures to ensure their effective participation in the consultation process (point 7).

[9] See the list of European social partners' organisations consulted under Article 154 TFEU. Available at http://ec.europa.eu/social/BlobServlet?docId=2154&langId=en. See also Annex 1 (List of European social-partner organisations consulted under ex Article 138 TEC) of Commission Communication, *The European social dialogue, a force for innovation and change. Proposal for a Council Decision establishing a Tripartite Social Summit for Growth and Employment*, COM (2002) 341 final.

[10] The European Foundation for the Improvement of Living and Working Conditions (Eurofound) is a tripartite EU agency, whose role is to provide knowledge in the area of social and work-related policies. Eurofound was established in 1975 by Council Regulation (EEC) No. 1365/75, O.J. L 139/1 (1975), now replaced by Parliament/Council Regulation (EU) 2019/127, O.J. L 30/74 82019), to contribute to the planning and design of better living and working conditions in Europe. Eurofound's role is to provide information, advice and expertise—on living and working conditions, industrial relations and managing change in Europe—for key actors in the field of EU social policy on the basis of comparative information, research and analysis. More information available at https://www.eurofound.europa.eu/.

[11] Sciarra (2020), p. 6.

[12] As a recent example, see the Consultation Document, *First phase consultation of Social Partners under Article 154 TFEU on a consolidation of the EU Directives on information and consultation of workers*, C(2015) 2303 final.

Article 154. [Participation of the Social Partners] 1401

out the **framework of a possible initiative**. The aim is to obtain the opinion of the European social partners on the need for such an initiative, its direction and the type of legislative instrument (regulation, directive or decision). The Commission collects their individual or joint opinions within a period of 6 weeks.[13]

After having collected the contributions from the European social partners, the Commission services summarise them in a **second-phase** consultation document, which is also notified to the European social partners. This time, the Commission indicates the **possible scope and content of the envisaged legislative proposal**. The consultation process enables the European social partners to directly influence the drafting of new legislative initiatives. Social partners may decide to open negotiations and to deal with a specific issue through bipartite social dialogue at any stage during the two consultation phases. Consequently, the Commission initiative is suspended. However, if the European social partners do not come to a conclusion and the Commission considers that Union action is desirable, it will continue preparing its legislative proposal.[14]

10

In any case, the prerequisites for launching a **formal consultation** under Article 154 TFEU (which, from this perspective, imposes on the Commission a duty to consult European social partners) are the following: first, the formal consultation is limited to **legislative proposals** (regulations, directives, decisions); second, the formal consultation has to focus on the **social policy area** (Title X of the TFEU); third, EU legislative proposals may only be undertaken in the fields as defined by Article 153.1 TFEU. During the consultation process, the European social partners may inform the Commission of their intention to enter into contractual relations, including with a view to concluding agreements.[15] In this respect, the consequences of a **lack of consultation** are to be considered. In any case, in the event of a **qualified infringement of the consultation requirement** (e.g. exclusion of social partner from some important negotiation processes or obviously inadequate procedure), the legal act in question may have to be annulled if the lack of consultation has not been remedied.[16]

11

---

[13] Example of questions raised by the Commission during the first consultation phase: '– Do you consider it advisable to take an initiative in this area? – Should this initiative be taken at Union level, if appropriate? – If so, do you share the Commission's view as to how the Union should approach the problem, namely by initially encouraging Member States to take the necessary measures on a voluntary basis, or do you consider that a binding instrument is called for from the outset?'

[14] Example of questions raised by the Commission during the second consultation phase: 'The Commission invites the social partners to: – forward an opinion or, where appropriate, a recommendation on the content of the envisaged regulatory and non-regulatory initiatives; – inform the Commission of their readiness to start a negotiation process on the basis of the proposals described in this document'.

[15] For an overview of some formal consultations leading to negotiations, see Publications Office of the European Union (2011), p. 12.

[16] Such lack of consultation can be approached as an infringement of the rights to information and consultation as enshrined in Articles 27 and 28 EUCFR and Article 154 TFEU. More specifically, 'failure to comply with the procedural rules relating to the adoption of an EU act, established by

12   In addition to the contributions received via the consultation process, the Commission considers the work of European social partners in its legislative proposals for social policies, and particularly their outcomes, such as recommendations (codes of conduct, guidelines, etc.), declarations, joint opinions or tools (studies, handbooks, etc.).

13   Ultimately, it is clear that **permanent feed-back from European social partners** will help the Commission to identify the areas where an update or new provisions are needed to address the concerns of the social partners. For instance, guidance from European social partners could help the Commission to improve the balance between ensuring adequate protection of the workers' interests and minimising the burden on enterprises.

3. A Broader Framework of Social Consultation: Other Structures in Support of the Social Policy

14   As already mentioned, apart from the Tripartite Social Summit for Growth and Employment (Article 152 TFEU), other important complementary structures in support of the social policy are the **Social Dialogue Committees** (SDCs). In this regard, the SDC itself, which was set up in 1992, is the main body for bipartite autonomous (between trade unions and employers) cross-industry social dialogue at European level. It meets 3–4 times a year to discuss the views of social partners on various topics. The SDC consists of maximum 66 representatives of the social partners, equally divided between the employers' and the workers' representative organisations and including the EU Secretariats of the cross-industry social partners, as well as representatives from the national member organisations on each side. It can set up technical working groups to discuss various issues like labour market challenges, reconciliation of working and family life, flexicurity, etc. The SDC adopts and proceeds to follow up the results of negotiations between employers and workers' representative bodies and takes part in social dialogue summits (high-level meetings chaired by the president of the Commission).

15   Alongside the SDC, the **European Sectoral Social Dialogue Committees** are the fora where representatives from European social partners can discuss all matters related to their specific sectoral activities (agriculture, audiovisual, banking, catering, chemical industry, etc.). They are also the instrument for consultations, autonomous social dialogue, joint actions or negotiations on issues of common interest, thereby directly contributing to the shaping of EU standards, legislation and policies. The work of the 40 sectoral Committees is coordinated by the Liaison

---

the competent institutions themselves, [...] may constitute] an infringement of essential procedural requirements for the purposes of the second paragraph of Article 263 TFEU, which the Union judicature may examine of its own motion'. See Case T-456/14, *TAO-AFI and SFIE-PE v Parliament and Council* (GC 15 September 2016) para 51.

Forum. In line with the 1998 Commission Decision setting up these committees,[17] the Commission consults the European social partners on the orientations of policies which directly concern their sector, and which may have employment and social implications.

Continuing with this sectoral approach, several EU policies are backed by the establishment of **advisory committees**. These are laid down either by Treaty provisions (e.g. the European Social Fund Committee, Article 163 TFEU) or by legislative acts (e.g. the Advisory Committee on Safety, Hygiene and Health at Work[18]). Although they vary considerably in terms of their functions, some advisory committees have a tripartite structure and bring together representatives from the MS and social partners appointed at national level. In this way, European social partners can play an informal coordination role.[19]

On the other hand, European social partners may be invited to participate on an *ad hoc* basis in meetings of **permanent structures** for concertation between EU institutions and MS, such as the Employment Committee (Article 150 TFEU) and the Social Protection Committee (Article 160 TFEU). In addition, European social partners are represented on the management boards of the following **European agencies** and therefore contribute directly to the governance of the following bodies: (a) the European Foundation for the Improvement of Living and Working Conditions (Eurofound)[20] (Dublin, Ireland); (b) the European Agency for Safety and Health at Work (EU-OSHA)[21] (Bilbao, Spain); and (c) the European Centre for the Development of Vocational Training (Cedefop)[22] (Thessaloniki, Greece).

This broader European framework of social dialogue and consultation has led to both **intersectoral and sectoral European collective agreements**. Its outcomes are modest if compared to national systems of collective bargaining and social

---

[17] Commission Decision 98/500/EC *on the establishment of Sectoral Dialogue Committees promoting the Dialogue between the social partners at European level*, O.J. L 225/27 (1998). This Decision refers to point 12 of the Community Charter of the Fundamental Social Rights of Workers, which states that employers or employers' organisations, on the one hand, and workers' organisations, on the other, should have the right to negotiate and conclude collective agreements under the conditions laid down by national legislation and practice.

[18] See Council Decision 74/325/EEC *on the setting up of an Advisory Committee on Safety, Hygiene and Health Protection at Work*, O.J. L 185/15 (1974), repealed by Council Decision of 22 July 2003, O.J. L 218/1 (2003). The Committee's remit covers all sectors of the economy (except the extractive industries) and the protection of workers' health against the dangers arising from ionising radiation.

[19] Other examples of advisory committees of the DG for Employment, Social Affairs and Inclusion are: the Scientific Committee on Occupational Exposure, the Advisory Committee on Freedom of Movement for Workers and the Advisory Committee on Social Security for Migrant Workers.

[20] Article 4 of Parliament/Council Regulation (EU) 2019/127 *establishing the European Foundation for the improvement of living and working conditions (Eurofound)*, O.J. L 30/74 (2019).

[21] Article 4 of Parliament/Council Regulation (EU) 2019/126 *establishing the European Agency for Safety and Health at Work (EU-OSHA)*, O.J. L 30/58 (2019).

[22] Article 4 of Parliament/Council Regulation (EU) 2019/128 *establishing a European Centre for the Development of Vocational Training (Cedefop)*, O.J. L 30/90 (2019).

dialogue. Yet, the European social dialogue is a process that stipulates a relationship between collective bargaining and law specific to the EU that cannot simply be equated with such systems at the national level. First, it implies a **flexible relationship** between social dialogue at all levels and is contingent upon national traditions of social dialogue within the MS. Second, collective bargaining and social dialogue within MS is regarded as reflecting a balance of power between labour and capital, exercised traditionally through industrial conflict. The Treaty does not address even the possibility of industrial conflict at the EU level. Indeed, Article 153.5 TFEU seems explicitly to exclude regulatory competences on the right to strike, which would be most relevant.[23]

4. Challenges: European Social Partners' Contribution to Actions and Legal Acts of the European Union in the Social Area

19 Before the Commission proposes new initiatives, it assesses their potential economic, social and environmental consequences. To that end, the **Commission** has rolled out a comprehensive **Impact Assessment** system based on an integrated approach, which analyses both benefits and costs. Such Impact Assessments are carried out for all initiatives which define future policies, including legislative proposals, non-legislative initiatives (white papers, action plans, financial programmes or negotiating guidelines for international agreements) and implementing and delegated acts (Article 5 of Protocol (No 2); → Protocol (No 2) para 47 et seqq.).

20 The views and inputs of European social partners can be a key element for the Commission's impact assessment process.[24] The Commission's Impact Assessment Guidelines include standards for consulting European social partners. Particularly, the latest **Better Regulation Guidelines** (November 2021)[25] contain guidance on how Commission services conduct impact assessments. An approach to such guidelines suggests that several proposals have great potential to simplify the better regulation process and make it more transparent. By contrast, the envisaged simplification of the public consultation process may jeopardise its effectiveness and should be carefully reconsidered. In addition, a more cautious, stepwise approach to introducing, testing and adjusting the new EU one-in, one-out system is certainly needed.[26]

21 On the other hand, these guidelines are accompanied by a toolbox which provides complementary guidance for Commission staff on specific impact

---

[23] Eurofund (2018).

[24] Information on upcoming impact assessments is available on the Commission's website.

[25] See Better regulation: guidelines and toolbox. Available at https://ec.europa.eu/info/law/law-making-process/planning-and-proposing-law/better-regulation-why-and-how/better-regulation-guidelines-and-toolbox_en.

[26] Simonelli and Iacob (2021), p. 849.

assessment elements. All draft impact assessment reports have to be submitted for quality scrutiny to the **Regulatory Scrutiny Board** (RSB) (which replaced the Impact Assessment Board on 1 July 2015).[27] A positive opinion is in principle needed from the Board for an initiative accompanied by an impact assessment to proceed. RSB opinions are published alongside the final impact assessment report and proposal at the time of adoption.

They point out that consultation must comply with the Commission's **general principles and minimum standards for consultation** (for example, regarding minimum response times, sufficient publicity and outreach to all relevant target groups, or the need to provide feedback on the outcomes of the consultation). They also highlight the obligation to consult European sectoral social dialogue committees in cases where the Commission initiative could be expected to have social implications for the sector(s) concerned. 22

Consultation of European Sectoral Social Dialogue Committees is complementary to other forms of consultation, particularly public consultations which are launched prior to the preparation of impact assessment. A **possible joint position of the European social partners** can therefore provide a strong and representative indication of realistic policies and their impacts and implementation, which should be considered in the impact assessment. European social partners are particularly well placed to provide detailed evidence and expertise for their sector, including data and other technical input, thereby contributing to the quality of both the impact assessment and decision-making. 23

When planning the impact assessment work, the Commission departments in charge **coordinate the organisation of consultations** with sectoral social dialogue committees in response to their interests, in close cooperation with the Social Dialogue and Industrial Relations Unit of DG Employment, Social Affairs and Inclusion. It is important that the results of consultations with Sectoral Social Dialogue Committees should be clearly summarised in the draft Impact Assessment report. 24

In this context and considering that the greatest inflation of regulations concerning the secondary EU law occurs in the area of competition rules and consolidation of the internal market, the 'balancing' views from the European social partners have a **major value**. In fact, apart from the implementation of the 25

---

[27] Decision of the President of the European Commission *on the establishment of an independent Regulatory Scrutiny Board*, C(2015) 3263 final. The Board examines and issues opinions on all the Commission's draft impact assessments and of major evaluations and 'fitness checks' of existing legislation. The Board is independent of the policy making departments. It is chaired at Director General level. In addition to the Chair, the Board consists of three high-level Commission officials and three members who are recruited from outside the Commission, selected on the basis of their expertise. All members work for the Board full time, with no other policy responsibilities.

principle of legal certainty,[28] the directives on legislative technique[29] given within the EU (that is, the rules on drawing up or writing European law) have as two of their main concerns: (a) the *ex-ante* analysis of the economic impact of the European regulations on the operation of the internal market;[30] (b) the encouragement of the establishment of regulations by private agents (**co-regulation** and **self-regulation**).[31]

26 Indeed, in spite the still current use of co-regulation and self-regulation in the decision-making process at the EU level,[32] the current 2016 Interinstitutional Agreement on **Better Law-Making**[33] has replaced such notions by a broader approach to 'stakeholder consultation' or 'stakeholder feedback': particularly, the three institutions 'consider that public and stakeholder consultation, ex-post

---

[28] The Interinstitutional Agreement of 22 December 1998 *on common guidelines for the quality of drafting of Community legislation*, O.J. C/73/1 (1999), pointed out that 'according to the case-law of the Court of Justice, the principle of legal certainty, which is part of the Community legal order, requires that Community legislation must be clear and precise and its application foreseeable by individuals. That requirement must be observed all the more strictly in the case of an act liable to have financial consequences and imposing obligations on individuals in order that those concerned may know precisely the extent of the obligations which it imposes on them'.

[29] See Pagano (1997).

[30] See the Interinstitutional Agreement of 16 December 2003 *on better law-making*, O.J. C 321/1 (2003), point 25 et seqq., replaced by Interinstitutional Agreement between the European Parliament, the Council of the European Union and the European Commission *on Better Law-Making*, O.J. L 123/1 (2016).

[31] In the former 2003 IIA on better law-making, co-regulation meant the mechanism whereby a Community legislative act entrusts the attainment of the objectives defined by the legislative authority to parties which are recognised in the field (such as economic operators, the social partners, NGOs, or associations): point 18 et seqq.; see also Kriele (2000). This mechanism might be used based on the criteria defined in the legislative act to enable the legislation to be adapted to the problems and sectors concerned, to reduce the legislative burden by concentrating on essential aspects and to draw on the experience of the parties concerned: an interdisciplinary approach has been highlighted by Recchia (1998), p. 7. On the other hand, self-regulation was defined as the possibility for economic operators, the social partners, NGOs or associations to adopt amongst themselves and for themselves common guidelines at European level (particularly codes of practice or sectoral agreements): point 22 et seqq. Generally, this type of voluntary initiative did not imply that the institutions had adopted any particular stance, particularly where such initiatives were undertaken in areas which were not covered by the Treaties or in which the Union had not hitherto legislated. As one of its responsibilities, the Commission had to scrutinise self-regulation practices to verify that they comply with the provisions of the European Treaties.

[32] See, for example, in the field of Data Protection Law, von Grafenstein (2022), pp. 402–432.

[33] This Agreement complements the following agreements and declarations on Better Law-Making: Interinstitutional Agreement of 20 December 1994—*Accelerated working method for official codification of legislative texts*, O.J. C 102/2 (1996); Interinstitutional Agreement of 22 December 1998 *on common guidelines for the quality of drafting of Community legislation*, O.J. C 73/1 (1999); Interinstitutional Agreement of 28 November 2001 *on a more structured use of the recasting technique for legal acts*, O.J. C 77/1 (2002); Joint Declaration of 13 June 2007 *on practical arrangements for the codecision procedure*, O.J. C 145/5 (2007), and Joint Political Declaration of 27 October 2011 of the European Parliament, the Council and the Commission *on explanatory documents*, O.J. C 369/15 (2011).

evaluation of existing legislation and impact assessments of new initiatives will help achieve the objective of Better Law-Making' (recital 6).[34]

In the field of ex-post evaluation of existing legislation, the **Regulatory Fitness and Performance programme (REFIT)** is an important specific part of the Better Regulation process. The REFIT programme began in 2010 when the European Commission announced that it would be reviewing EU legislation in selected policy areas through 'fitness checks' to keep current regulation 'fit for purpose'. This included identifying excessive regulatory burdens, overlaps, gaps, inconsistencies and/or obsolete measures which may have appeared over time. Pilot exercises began in 2010 in four areas: employment and social policy, environment, transport and industrial policy. From this perspective, the focus of the REFIT Programme on the **social acquis** has permitted to identify some gaps which have shown, to some extent, the European Commission's lack of action in fulfilling its social agenda.[35] Consequently, further participation of the social partners under Article 154 TFEU is also needed.

27

In light of this, the aim of Article 154 TFEU is closely related to the idea of making compatible the conflicting interests at stake (economic and social ones) within the formula 'social market economy' (Article 3.3 (1) TEU)[36] as well as to the idea of establishing **common minimum social standards** to avoid **social dumping**.[37] With this major aim in mind,[38] there is a strong **connection and complementarity between the consultation** under Article 154 TFEU **and the potential**

28

---

[34] See also points 19, 20–24, 25, 28, 32 and 48 of the 2016 IIA, as well as 6 of its Annex (Common Understanding between the European Parliament, the Council and the Commission on Delegated Acts).

[35] Laulom (2018), p. 22.

[36] From this perspective, the 2016 IIA on Better Law-Making emphasises that 'Impact assessments should cover the existence, scale and consequences of a problem and the question whether or not Union action is needed. They should map out alternative solutions and, where possible, potential short and long-term costs and benefits, assessing the economic, environmental and social impacts in an integrated and balanced way and using both qualitative and quantitative analyses. The principles of subsidiarity and proportionality should be fully respected, as should fundamental rights. Impact assessments should also address, whenever possible, the "cost of non-Europe" and the impact on competitiveness and the administrative burdens of the different options, having particular regard to SMEs ("Think Small First"), digital aspects and territorial impact. Impact assessments should be based on accurate, objective and complete information and should be proportionate as regards their scope and focus' (Point 12).

[37] This wordplay has been analysed by Astola Madariaga (2009), pp. 378–379: particularly, the author criticises that there is somehow a manipulation of definition of the services of general economic interest. More extensively, see Karayigit (2009), pp. 576–577; Jacobs (2012), pp. 277 et seqq.

[38] In fact, the envisaged social dimension is a safeguard against social dumping: see Vandenbroucke (2012), p. 7.

social dialogue under Article 155 TFEU,[39] as also highlighted in the 2016 IIA on Better Law-Making.[40]

29   However, the interplay of these two provisions (Articles 154 and 155 TFEU) has been overshadowed by the Commission's general power of initiative laid down in Article 17 TEU. This interpretation has been established by the CJEU in an important judgment where the main controversial issue at stake was the Commission's refusal to submit to the Council of the EU a proposal for a decision implementing at the EU level an agreement between the social partners on information and consultation involving civil servants and employees of central government administrations: *EPSU v. Commission*,[41] which has been criticised as a missed

---

[39] See the Consultation Document *First phase consultation of Social Partners under Article 154 TFEU on a consolidation of the EU Directives on information and consultation of workers*, C(2015) 2303 final: 'Under Article 154(2) TFEU, before submitting proposals in the Social Policy field, the Commission must consult management and labour on the possible direction of Union action [...]'.

The questions on which the Commission consults the social partners are: 'Do you consider the description of the issues in this paper correct and sufficient?'; 'Do you think that the Commission should launch an initiative to revise or recast the three Directives on I&C of workers at national level? If so, what should be its scope?'; '*Would you consider initiating a dialogue under Article 155 TFEU on any of the issues identified in this consultation?*' (emphasis added). The follow-up of this procedure is summarised in Case C-928/19 P, *EPSU v Commission* (CJEU 2 September 2021) para 8–18.

[40] Point 19: 'Public and stakeholder consultation is integral to well-informed decision-making and to improving the quality of law-making. Without prejudice to the specific arrangements applying to the Commission's proposals under Article 155(2) of the Treaty on the Functioning of the European Union, the Commission will, before adopting a proposal, conduct public consultations in an open and transparent way, ensuring that the modalities and time-limits of those public consultations allow for the widest possible participation. The Commission will in particular encourage the direct participation of SMEs [small and medium-sized enterprises] and other end-users in the consultations. This will include public internet-based consultations. The results of public and stakeholder consultations shall be communicated without delay to both co-legislators and made public'.

[41] Case C-928/19 P, *EPSU v Commission* (CJEU 2 September 2021) para 46–47: 'In the specific field of social policy, one of the aims ... is to promote the role of the social partners and to facilitate dialogue between them, while respecting their autonomy, and Article 154(1) TFEU provides that the Commission is to have inter alia the task of promoting the consultation of management and labour at EU level. Furthermore, in the specific context of implementation of agreements concluded between management and labour at EU level, Article 155(2) TFEU has conferred on management and labour a right comparable to that possessed more generally, under Articles 225 and 241 TFEU respectively, by the Parliament and the Council to request the Commission to submit appropriate proposals for the purpose of implementing the Treaties. ... However, by the words 'on a proposal from the Commission', Article 155(2) TFEU confers on that institution a specific power which, although it can be exercised only following a joint request by management and labour, is, once such a request has been made, similar to the general power of initiative laid down in Article 17(2) TEU for the adoption of legislative acts, since the existence of a Commission proposal is a precondition for the adoption of a decision by the Council under that provision. That specific power falls within the scope of the role assigned to the Commission in Article 17(1) TEU, which consists in the present context in determining, in the light of the general interest of the European Union, whether it is appropriate to submit a proposal to the Council on the

opportunity for the European social dialogue to be strengthened.[42] In the same way, it can be argued that this case has implied putting into question social democracy standards, as well as putting an end to horizontal subsidiarity in the social field.[43]

Finally, it is true that the CJEU has validated the parallelism established, in paragraph 112 of the judgment under appeal,[44] between the procedure laid down in Articles 154 and 155 TFEU and the European citizens' initiative procedure.[45] From this point of view, the CJEU dismissed EPSU's submissions according to which: first, the European citizens' initiative procedure constitutes neither a process of collective bargaining nor the exercise of a fundamental right enshrined in Article 28 of the Charter of Fundamental Rights and, second, the instigators of such a procedure do not participate in the drawing up of the text of the legislative proposal.[46] Nevertheless, in understanding logical EPSU's reluctance to extend the Commission's broad margin of discretion in blocking European citizens' initiatives or participation of social partners under Articles 154 and 155 TFEU, it is also true that the problem does not derive from that parallelism, but rather from the restrictive approach by the GC and the CJEU to both indivisible dimensions (civil and social ones) of democracy.

List of Cases

CJEU

CJEU 02.09.2021, C-928/19 P, *EPSU v Commission*, ECLI:EU:C:2021:656 [cit. in para 28-30]

GC

GC 15.09.2016, T-456/14, *TAO-AFI and SFIE-PE v Parliament and Council*, ECLI:EU:T:2016:493 [cit. in para 11]

---

basis of an agreement between management and labour, for the purpose of its implementation at EU level'.

[42] Thomas (2022), p. 115.

[43] Miranda Boto (2020), p. 757.

[44] Case T-310/18, *EPSU and Goudriaan v Commission* (GC 24 October 2019), by which the GC dismissed the action for annulment of the decision of the European Commission of 5 March 2018 refusing to submit to the Council of the EU a proposal for a decision implementing at the EU level the agreement entitled 'General framework for informing and consulting civil servants and employees of central government administrations [of the Member States]', concluded between the Trade Unions' National and European Administration Delegation (TUNED) and European Public Administration Employers (EUPAE).

[45] By referring to Case T-561/14, *One of Us and Others v Commission* (GC 23 April 2018) para 169, delivered in relation to European citizens' initiatives.

[46] Case C-928/19 P, *EPSU v Commission* (CJEU 2 September 2021) para 92 and 99.

GC 23.04.2018, T-561/14, *One of Us and Others v Commission*, ECLI:EU:T:2018:210 [cit. in para 30]
GC 24.10.2019, T-310/18, *EPSU and Goudriaan v Commission*, ECLI:EU:T:2019:757 [cit. in para 30]

References[47]

Astola Madariaga, J. (2009). Lo social y lo económico en los Tratados de la Unión y en la jurisprudencia del Tribunal de Justicia. *Revista Europea de Derechos Fundamentales, 13*, 351–387.
Eurofund. (2018). *European social dialogue*. https://www.eurofound.europa.eu/observatories/eurwork/industrial-relations-dictionary/european-social-dialogue
Grabitz, E., Hilf, M., & Nettesheim, M. (Eds.). (2022). *Das Recht der Europäischen Union: EUV/AEUV*. C.H. Beck.
Jacobs, A. (2012). Services of general interest and the Treaty of Lisbon. In I. Schöman, K. Lörcher, & N. Bruun (Eds.), *The Lisbon Treaty and social Europe* (pp. 277–301). Hart Publishing.
Karayigit, M. T. (2009). The notion of services of general interest revisited. *European Public Law, 15*(4), 575–595.
Kriele, M. (2000). Máximas para el arte de legislar. In *La función legislativa de los parlamentos y la técnica de legislar* (pp. 19–42). Congreso de los Diputados.
Laborde, J. P. (2014). Sur ce que consulter veut dire. À propos notamment du droit d'information et de consultation du comité d'entreprise. In C. Mestre, C. Sachs-Durand, & M. Storck (Eds.), *Le travail humain au Carrefour du droit et de la sociologie. Hommage au Professeur Nikitas Aliprantis* (pp. 209–220). Presses universitaires de Strasbourg.
Laulom, S. (2018). Better regulation and the social acquis: Is the REFIT fit for purpose? *European Labour Law Journal, 9*(1), 7–23.
Miranda Boto, J. M. (2020). ¿El fin de la subsidiariedad horizontal? *Derecho de las Relaciones Laborales, 5*, 745–758.
Pagano, R. (Ed.). (1997). *Le direttive di tecnica legislativa in Europa*. Camera dei Deputati-Quaderni di documentazione.
Publications Office of the European Union. (2011). *Consulting European social partners: Understanding how it works*. http://erc-online.eu/wp-content/uploads/2014/04/2012-00292-E.pdf
Recchia, G. (1998). La qualità della legge. *Nomos. Le attualità del diritto, 1*, 7–22.
Sciarra, S. (2020). Eppur si muove? La strategia della Commissione per rilanciare l'Europa sociale. *Freedom, Security & Justice: European Legal Studies, 1*, 1–9.
Simonelli, F., & Iacob, N. (2021). Can we better the European Union better regulation agenda? *European Journal of Risk Regulation, 12*(4), 849–860.
Thomas, L. (2022). La mise en œuvre des accords européens: une autonomie *a minima* des partenaires sociaux. *Revue de droit comparé du travail et de la sécurité sociale, 2*, 106–115.
Vandenbroucke, F. (2012). Europe: the social challenge. OSE Paper series (No. 11).
von der Groeben, H., Schwarze, J., & Hatje, A. (Eds.). (2015). *Europäisches Unionsrecht*. Nomos.
von Grafenstein, M. (2022). Co-regulation and the competitive advantage in the GDPR: Data protection certification mechanisms, codes of conduct and the 'state of the art' of data protection-by-design. In G. González & R. Van Brakel (Eds.), *Research handbook on privacy and data protection law* (pp. 402–432). Elgar.

---

[47] All cited internet sources have been accessed on 17 February 2023.

Article 155 [Agreements at Union Level]
(ex-Article 139 TEC)

1. Should management and labour so desire, the dialogue between them at Union level may lead to contractual relations, including agreements.
2. Agreements concluded at Union level shall be implemented either in accordance with the procedures and practices specific to management and labour and the Member States or, in matters covered by Article 153, at the joint request of the signatory parties, by a Council decision on a proposal from the Commission. The European Parliament shall be informed.
   The Council shall act unanimously where the agreement in question contains one or more provisions relating to one of the areas for which unanimity is required pursuant to Article 153(2).

Contents

1. Preliminary Remarks: The Increasing Legal Value of Agreements Concluded Between Management and Labour in the EU Law 1
2. Adoption and Implementation of Such European Agreements 12
3. Procedural and Substantial Rights at Stake 19
4. Challenges: The Impact of European Agreements in a Broader Social Europe 24

List of Cases
References

1. Preliminary Remarks: The Increasing Legal Value of Agreements Concluded Between Management and Labour in the EU Law

First, it must be highlighted that the value of the **dialogue between management and labour** at Union level under Article 155 TFEU concerns precisely one of the main topics and objectives of 'social policy' which is also listed in the opening provision (Article 151 TFEU) of Title X of the TFEU on social policy. Such premise has to be read not only in terms of European 'public policy' as well as under the perspective of the **increasing role of social partners at European level**, but also in terms of their real impact in **developing the EU system of law sources**[1] as well as under a **human rights approach**, since the **rights to organise and to collective bargaining** are recognised in the EUCFR and the most emblematic universal (ILO Conventions) and Council of Europe standards (Article 11 ECHR as well as Articles 5 and 6 of the European Social Charter).[2]

1

---

[1] Such pluralism of law sources has been emphasised by Nadalet (2005). See also, more extensively, Lo Faro (1999).
[2] See the overview in Papadakis (2011).

© Springer Nature Switzerland AG 2023
R. Böttner, H.-J. Blanke (eds.), *Treaty on the Functioning of the European Union – A Commentary*, Springer Commentaries on International and European Law,
https://doi.org/10.1007/16559_2023_74

2 From this point of view, it must also be recalled that ex-Article 139 TEC (based on Article 4 of the Social Policy Agreement appended to the Social Policy Protocol annexed to the 1992 Maastricht Treaty), the provision which preceded Article 155 TFEU, made it possible to adopt directives for the purpose of implementing European agreements concluded between management and labour. In truth, as pointed out in the doctrine, such agreements do not yet have any legislative effect in themselves,[3] but need to be implemented in conformity with Article 155.2 TFEU, that is to say, through national *measures* (including **collective agreements** as an **essential source of labour law**) or by means of EU legal acts becoming a direct part of EU secondary law and subject to the interpretation by the ECJ.

3 In the same vein, despite the outcome of the case,[4] in *EPSU v Commission* the CJEU highlighted that in the specific context of implementation of agreements concluded between management and labour at the EU level, Article 155.2 TFEU 'has conferred on management and labour a right comparable to that possessed more generally, under Articles 225 and 241 TFEU respectively, by the Parliament and the Council to **request the Commission to submit appropriate proposals** for the purpose of implementing the Treaties'.[5] As recalled in the Opinion of AG *Pikamäe*,[6] although this is not the first time that the Commission has opposed an agreement negotiated by management and labour,[7] it is the first time that such opposition has been brought before the CJEU and that the CJEU has had the opportunity to consider the powers and obligations of the Commission in the procedure for implementing agreements concluded by management and labour under Article 155.2 TFEU.[8]

4 Indeed, the CJEU has validated a broad interpretation of Article 155.2 TFEU giving priority of a comfortable **discretionary power** (to assess the appropriateness of a legislative measure) in the hands of the **Commission** over the **crucial role** conferred to **the social partners** under the TFEU itself and, thus, opening a breach in the **European social concertation model** that appears totally out of place in the current political phase of rebuilding the EU's social dimension.[9] In this sense, as

---

[3] Egger (2010), p. 223.

[4] Such outcome has been criticised as implying social democratic deficit, since 'in acting as the watchdog of the Commission's prerogatives, the Court of Justice is taking a political position: that of not trusting a social democracy which has great difficulty in emerging in Europe, even though it is explicitly enshrined in the Treaties': Pataut (2022), p. 349.

[5] Case C-928/19 P, *EPSU v Commission* (CJEU 2 September 2021) para 46.

[6] Case C-928/19 P, *EPSU v Commission* (Opinion of AG Pikamäe of 20 January 2021) para 2.

[7] On 26 April 2012, the Commission opposed a European framework agreement on the protection of occupational health and safety in the hairdressing sector signed by Coiffure EU and UNI Europa Hair & Beauty. No action was brought at that time and a new version of the agreement was proposed by the social partners. Some authors have suggested that the Commission's refusal was contrary to the formal obligation enshrined in Article 155.2 TFEU: Dorssemont et al. (2019), pp. 571–603.

[8] See Schmitt et al. (2020), p. 297.

[9] Guarriello (2021), p. 703.

Article 155. [Agreements at Union Level]

suggested by AG *Pikamäe*, the CJEU has determined that the Commission may, in addition to reviewing the legality of the agreement negotiated by the social partners and the social partners' representativeness, conduct a review as to whether it is appropriate to implement that agreement.[10]

In light of these considerations, in *Konstantinos Maïstrellis*, in which the scope of Council Directive 96/34/EC on the Framework Agreement on parental leave concluded by UNICE, CEEP and the ETUC[11] was at stake, the CJEU recalled its settled case law according to which 'in interpreting a provision of EU law, it is necessary to consider not only its wording, but also the context in which it occurs, and the objectives pursued by the rules of which it is part'.[12]

The **framework agreement** deals, as foreseen by Article 155.2 TFEU, with one of the important 'matters covered by Article 153', particularly 'equality between men and women with regard to labour market opportunities and treatment at work' (Article 153.1 point (i) TFEU). The other relevant social matter covered by Article 153 TFEU, which led to the conclusion of another significant framework agreement, is referred to in its paragraph 1 point (b), that is 'working conditions', particularly the Framework Agreement on fixed-term work concluded by the above-mentioned social partners on 18 March 1999, which is set out in the Annex to Council Directive 1999/70/EC.[13]

Generally, the recent CJEU's case law shows that both framework agreements have been interpreted in a favourable direction **compensating the social restrictions** deriving from the **economic and financial crisis**.[14] On the one hand, such favourable interpretation of the Framework Agreement on parental leave (making effective its main purpose of compatibility between occupational and family obligations[15]) is illustrated by the above mentioned judgment in *Konstantinos*

---

[10] Case C-928/19 P, *EPSU v Commission* (Opinion of AG Pikamäe of 20 January 2021) para 3 and 44.

[11] Council Directive 96/34/EC *on the framework agreement on parental leave concluded by UNICE, CEEP and the ETUC*, O.J. L 145/4 (1996); read in conjunction with Parliament/Council Directive 2006/54/EC *on the implementation of the principle of equal opportunities and equal treatment of men and women in matters of employment and occupation*, O.J. L 204/23 (2006). Council Directive 96/34/EC has been replaced by what is now Parliament/Council Directive (EU) 2019/1158 *on work-life balance for parents and carers*, O.J. L 188/79 (2019).

[12] Case C-222/14, *Konstantinos Maïstrellis* (CJEU 16 July 2015) para 30.

[13] Council Directive 1999/70/EC *concerning the framework agreement on fixed-term work concluded by ETUC, UNICE and CEEP*, O.J. L 175/43 (1999).

[14] Cf. Bruun (2012), pp. 261 et seqq. In addition, such interpretation appears to be very significant in compensating the decline in the numbers of companies and workers covered by a collective agreement, insofar as collective bargaining systems, frameworks and practices in the EU have come under some pressure in recent years since the 2008 crisis when a number of EU Member States, in response to high unemployment rates, implemented labour reforms aimed at increasing competitiveness, productivity and job creation, see Eurofound (2015), p. 1.

[15] The preamble to the Framework Agreement stated that it 'represents an undertaking by UNICE, CEEP and the ETUC to set out minimum requirements on parental leave [...], as an important means of reconciling work and family life and promoting equal opportunities and treatment between men and women'.

Maïstrellis,[16] in which the Court concluded that Council Directives 96/34/EC and 2006/54/EC preclude national provisions under which a civil servant is not entitled to parental leave in a situation where his wife does not work or exercise any profession, unless it is considered that due to a serious illness or injury the wife is unable to meet the needs related to the upbringing of the child.

8   A **more restrictive and nuanced interpretation** was held in the previous case of *Chatzi*.[17] Here, the CJEU concluded that the framework agreement is not to be interpreted as requiring the birth of twins to confer entitlement to a number of periods of parental leave equal to the number of children born. However, read in the light of the principle of equal treatment, the national legislature is obliged to establish a parental leave regime which, according to the situation obtaining in the MS concerned, ensures that the parents of twins receive treatment that takes due account of their particular needs.[18]

9   On the other hand, illustrations of **favourable interpretation** of the Framework Agreement on fixed-term work are provided in *Commission v Luxembourg*, on clause 5.1 concerning measures to prevent abusive use of successive fixed-term relationships or contracts in relation to greater flexibility,[19] or in *Regojo Dans*,[20] which underlines 'the importance of the principles of equal treatment and non-discrimination, which are among the general principles of EU law' and, consequently, 'the provisions set out in that regard by Directive 1999/70 and the framework agreement for the purpose of ensuring that fixed-term workers enjoy the same benefits as those enjoyed by comparable permanent workers, except where a difference in treatment is justified on objective grounds, [...] since they are rules of EU social law of particular importance, from which each employee should benefit as a minimum protective requirement'.[21]

---

[16] In Case C-222/14, *Konstantinos Maïstrellis* (CJEU 16 July 2015), the Court concluded that 'the provisions of Council Directive 96/34/EC [...] and Directive 2006/54/EC [...], must be interpreted as precluding national provisions under which a civil servant is not entitled to parental leave in a situation where his wife does not work or exercise any profession, unless it is considered that due to a serious illness or injury the wife is unable to meet the needs related to the upbringing of the child'.

[17] Case C-149/10, *Chatzi* (CJEU 16 September 2010) para 39–40.

[18] On the contrary, the Opinion of AG Kokott of 7 July 2010 proposed to conclude that this clause 2.1 of the framework agreement 'is to be interpreted as meaning that men and women workers have an individual entitlement to parental leave of at least three months for each twin'.

[19] Case C-238/14, *Commission v Luxembourg* (CJEU 26 February 2015). See also Case C-109/09, *Deutsche Lufthansa* (CJEU 10 March 2011) para 32.

[20] Case-177/14, *Regojo Dans* (CEU 9 July 2015) para 62. The ECJ concluded that 'Clause 4(1) of the framework agreement on fixed-term work must be interpreted as precluding national legislation [...], which excludes, without justification on objective grounds, non-permanent staff from the right to receive a three-yearly length-of-service increment granted, inter alia, to career civil servants when, as regards the receipt of that increment, those two categories of workers are in comparable situations, a matter which is for the referring court to ascertain'.

[21] Case-177/14, *Regojo Dans* (CJEU 9 July 2015) para 32. See also Case C-307/05, *Del Cerro Alonso* (ECJ 13 September 2007) para 37; Joined Cases C-444/09 and C-456/09, *Gavieiro Gavieiro and Iglesias Torres* (CJEU 22 December 2010) para 48; and C-38/13, *Nierodzik*

Article 155. [Agreements at Union Level]

In other cases, a general framework in the social field is not established by means of an agreement concluded by social partners, but directly by a **legal act**, such as the Council Directive 93/104/EC concerning certain aspects of the organisation of working time.[22] In such cases, the willingness of social partners is expressed to develop specific aspects in certain economic sectors or fields of activity, for instance in the area of civil aviation.[23]

10

In connection with this last example, it is interesting to refer to the Opinion of AG *Trstenjak* in *Williams and Others*, who expresses that 'Article 14 of each of the aforementioned two directives makes it possible for the EU legislature to adopt more specific provisions for certain occupations or professional activities which take precedence over the provisions of the Working Time Directives, in accordance with a legal rule of primacy. Directive 2000/79, which, in this regard, contains more specific provisions on the organisation of working time of mobile staff in civil aviation, falls into that category of provisions, as Clause 1(2) of the European Agreement expressly indicates'.[24]

11

2. Adoption and Implementation of Such European Agreements

As foreseen in Article 154 TFEU, prior to taking action in the social field, the European Commission must consult the social partners. Then, in conformity with Article 155 TFEU, the partners can negotiate agreements that may be implemented independently according to their **national practices** through the MS directly or through the social partners by '**autonomous agreements**'[25]

12

(CJEU 13 March 2014) para 23; and orders in Case C-273/10, *Montoya Medina* (CJEU 18 March 2011) para 30, and in Case C-556/11, *Lorenzo Martínez* (CJEU 9 February 2012) para 35.

[22] O.J. L 307/18 (1993), replaced by Parliament/Council Directive 2003/88/EC *concerning certain aspects of the organisation of working time*, O.J. L 299/9 (2003).

[23] See Council Directive 2000/79/EC *concerning the European Agreement on the Organisation of Working Time of Mobile Workers in Civil Aviation concluded by the Association of European Airlines (AEA), the European Transport Workers' Federation (ETF), the European Cockpit Association (ECA), the European Regions Airline Association (ERA) and the International Air Carrier Association (IACA)*, O.J. L 302/57 (2000).

[24] Case C-155/10, *Williams and Others* (Opinion of AG Trstenjak of 16 June 2011) para 33.

[25] Some examples of 'autonomous' agreements implemented by social partners: Framework agreement on telework (16 July 2002); Framework agreement on work-related stress (8 October 2004); Framework agreement on harassment and violence at work (26 April 2007), and Framework agreement on inclusive labour markets (25 March 2010). In addition, European social partners are obliged to ensure that their national members ensure that the rules agreed in the Euro-agreement are implemented into the individual employment relationship. A basic agreement for autonomous implementation of European Social Partner Agreements could expand on this or establish additional procedural rules for the protection of individual employees' and employers' interests in the matter: Schiek (2005), p. 55.

(Article 153.3 (1) TFEU), or request their implementation through a Council decision (Article 153.3 (2) TFEU).[26] Indeed European-level social partners should be consulted and allowed to play, if they so wish, their role of co-legislators in relation to all matters of immediate or less direct relevance to workers, according to the spirit and the letter of Article 152 TFEU.[27]

13   With these premises, it is worth emphasising the relationship between Article 154.4 and Article 155 TFEU[28] to reflect on a possible refusal by the Commission to propose that the Council implements an agreement by decision. Such possibility has been **challenged by social partners** for the first time **before the Court** in July 2018:[29] the applicants asked the GC to annul the defendant's decision of 5 March 2018 not to propose to the Council that the EU Social Partners' Agreement of 21 December 2015 on rights of information and consultation for civil servants and employees of central government administrations enter into force under Article 155.1 TFEU, be implemented by a directive by means of a Council decision under Article 155.2 TFEU. Particularly, the applicants argued that the Commission's decision not to propose to the Council that the Agreement be implemented by Council decision is in breach of Article 155.2 TFEU, and contrary to the requirement for respect for the autonomy of the social partners as enshrined in Article 152 TFEU. As mentioned, and following the AG's Opinion in the case,[30] the appeal was dismissed by the CJEU.[31]

14   As a matter of principle, the **adoption and implementation of European Agreements** can be seen as covered by **loyalty obligations, sincere cooperation, good faith and *effet utile*** ($\rightarrow$ Article 4 TEU para 81 et seqq.). On the other hand, the adoption and implementation of those Agreements must logically consider the **will of management and labour** (including the possibility of establishing a **legal European framework for transnational collective bargaining**),[32] what is

---

[26] Some examples of agreements implemented by the Council: Framework agreement on parental leave (Directive 96/34/EC of 3 June 1996); Framework agreement on part-time work (Directive 97/81/EC of 15 December 1997); Framework agreement on fixed-term contracts (Directive 99/70/EC of 28 June 1979), and Framework agreement on parental leave (now replaced by Parliament/Council Directive (EU) 2019/1158 *on work-life balance for parents and carers*, O.J. L 188/79 (2019)).

[27] Clauwaert (2012), p. 144.

[28] Even more, there would be a previous *continuum* between social dialogue (consultation under Article 154.3 TFEU) and collective bargaining (agreements under Article 154.4 TFEU) at Union level: García-Muñoz Alhambra (2018), pp. 1116–1117.

[29] Through an action for annulment or for failure to act lodged at first instance with the General Court (Article 265 TFEU in conjunction with Article 256 TFEU). See Case T-310/18, *EPSU and Willem Goudriaan v Commission* (GC 24 October 2019).

[30] Case C-928/19 P, *EPSU v Commission* (Opinion of AG Pikamäe of 20 January 2021) para 129.

[31] Case C-928/19 P, *EPSU v Commission* (CJEU 2 September 2021) para 132.

[32] Especially, see Commission Communication *on the Social Agenda*, COM(2005) 33 final, p. 8: 'Providing an optional framework for transnational collective bargaining at either enterprise level or sectoral level could support companies and sectors to handle challenges dealing with issues such as work organisation, employment, working conditions, training. It will give the social partners a

consistent with their rights as recognised in Article 28 EUCFR and Article 155 TFEU. From this point of view, the role and views of management and labour when interpreting an agreement are often reflected in the text of the agreement itself. For example, clause 4.6 of the above-mentioned Framework Agreement on parental leave provides as follows in respect of **interpretation of the framework agreement**: 'Without prejudice to the respective role of the Commission, national courts and the Court of Justice, any matter relating to the interpretation of this agreement at European level should, in the first instance, be referred by the Commission to the signatory parties who will give an opinion'.

It cannot, however, be inferred from this that the CJEU's interpretative jurisdiction is restricted if there is no such opinion of the agreement's signatory parties. As expressed by AG *Kokott* in *Chatzi*,[33] under Article 267 TFEU, the CJEU has the task of interpreting directives when references are made for a preliminary ruling. Whilst it is true that the framework agreement set out in the annex to Council Directive 96/34/EC was negotiated between management and labour, it became, however, by virtue of Article 1 of Council Directive 96/34/EC, an integral part of that directive and shares its legal status. Clause 4.6 of the Framework Agreement thus also explicitly states that the provisions of that clause apply 'without prejudice to the role of the Court of Justice'. The extent of the **CJEU's jurisdiction** to interpret the Framework Agreement therefore **does not differ from its comprehensive jurisdiction to interpret other provisions** of directives. Nor could this interpretative jurisdiction of the Court, which results from primary law, be restricted anyway by a provision contained in a directive such as clause 4.6 of the Framework Agreement.

15

In other words, when the EU adopts a legislative act to implement a European agreement, it proceeds in exercise of the regulatory powers conferred on it by Article 155.2 TFEU. By virtue of its inclusion in it, the **Europe agreement becomes an integral part of the corresponding directive**, which, like any directive, is **subject to the interpretative jurisdiction of the CJEU**. In this regard, in the framework of the procedure under Article 155.2 TFEU, instead of a co-decision (ordinary procedure), the European Parliament is only informed, what is somehow controversial in terms of legitimacy and respect for the principle of democracy.[34] On the contrary, the question is that mitigating the major role of social partners

16

---

basis for increasing their capacity to act at transnational level. It will provide an innovative tool to adapt to changing circumstances, and provide cost-effective transnational responses. Such an approach is firmly anchored in the partnership for change priority advocated by the Lisbon strategy'. See also European Parliament Resolution of 12 September 2013 *on cross-border collective bargaining and transnational social dialogue* (2012/2292(INI)). With this in mind, it is true that EMU has created additional challenges for the European social dialogue, particularly by sharpening conflicts of interest—or the perception of such conflicts—between the labour movements of different MS: Dukes and Cannon (2016), p. 113.

[33] Case C-149/10, *Chatzi* (Opinion of AG Kokott of 7 July 2010) para 19.

[34] Kocher (2016), p. 64, and Kocher, in Pechstein et al. (2017), Article 155 AEUV para 1031.

would also imply a clear deficit in terms of **social democracy**.³⁵ Furthermore, as a matter of transparency during the negotiations of the entire legislative process, the social partners might be interested in accessing relevant information, invoking the connection of Article 155 TFEU with the right of access to documents recognised in Article 42 EUCFR.³⁶

17 On the other hand, it is also logical that both the adoption and implementation of European agreements must logically consider the **principles of subsidiarity and proportionality**. The above mentioned Council Directive 2000/79/EC implementing the European Agreement on the Organisation of Working Time of Mobile Workers in Civil Aviation states in recital 11 of its preamble that, in view of the highly integrated nature of the civil aviation sector and the conditions of competition prevailing in it, the objectives of this Directive to protect workers' health and safety cannot be sufficiently achieved by the MS and, therefore, EU action is required and necessary to achieve those objectives in accordance with the principles of subsidiarity and proportionality laid down in Article 5 TEU.

18 In this context, the exercise by the CJEU of its interpretative jurisdiction in relation to European agreements is not easy at all due to, at least, a double interplay of weights and counterweights between the various competences attributed to the EU to achieve the social policy objectives:³⁷ first, the very formula 'highly competitive social market economy' (Article 3.3 (1) TEU) projects a clear **dialectic tension between the dictates of social progress and the imperatives of economic development**;³⁸ and second, the governing principles of conferral, subsidiarity and proportionality imply that the EU action, in the exercise of its regulatory powers (through directives and European agreements), combines a **certain homogeneity and degree of harmonisation at EU level** with a **certain flexibility and margin of discretion at domestic level** (→ Article 2 TEU para 53). This last aspect has been compared in doctrine with the use in the ILO conventions of so-called '**flexibility clauses**'.³⁹

---

[35] Mathieu and Sterdyniak (2008), p. 80.

[36] See Case C-560/18 P, *Izba Gospodarcza Producentów i Operatorów Urządzeń Rozrywkowych v Commission* (CJEU 30 April 2020) para 57.

[37] See, for example, the differences between, on the one hand, the development of the economic activities carried out by the self-employed (which falls within the EU's competences in the field of industrial policy, as provided for in Article 173 TFEU) and, on the other hand, the TFEU's provisions on employment and social policy. From this perspective, Article 173 TFEU, unlike Articles 151 and 155 TFEU, does not encourage the self-employed to conclude collective agreements with a view to improving their working conditions: Case C-413/13, *FNV Kunsten Informatie en Media v Staat der Nederlanden* (Opinion of AG Wahl of 11 September 2014) para 41–42, and Case C-413/13, *FNV Kunsten Informatie en Media v Staat der Nederlanden* (CJEU 4 December 2014) para 29.

[38] Jimena Quesada (2005), p. 108.

[39] According to Böhnert (2002), p. 100, the use of such 'flexibility clauses' refers to a variety of measures, including the use of generic terms and the conferral of broad discretion in the discharge of obligations and the setting of the objectives to be achieved.

3. Procedural and Substantial Rights at Stake

Undoubtedly the primary procedural right leading to conclude European agreements and, consequently, to regulate the exercise of a set of substantial social rights, is the **right to bargain collectively** itself. Particularly, under Article 28 EUCFR, 'workers and employers [have] the right to negotiate and conclude collective agreements at the appropriate levels and, in cases of conflicts of interest, to take collective action to defend their interests, including strike action'. Similarly, both the 1961 European Social Charter and the 1996 Revised Charter establish in their Article 6 that the effective exercise of the right to bargain collectively oblige the parties 'to promote, where necessary and appropriate, machinery for voluntary negotiations between employers or employers' organisations and workers' organisations, with a view to the regulation of terms and conditions of employment by means of collective agreements'. In the same vein, point 12 of the Community Charter of the Fundamental Social Rights of Workers states that employers or employers' organisations, on the one hand, and workers' organisations, on the other, are to have the right to negotiate and conclude collective agreements under the conditions laid down by **national legislation and practice**. 19

In this framework,[40] it is worth pointing out that the elaboration of Article 28 EUCFR was inspired in Article 6 of the Social Charter and point 12 of the Community Charter, as explicitly expressed in the Explanations appended to the EUCFR. Moreover, the Preamble of the EUCFR also refers to 'the Social Charters adopted by the Union and by the Council of Europe'. Third, and above all, Article 151 TFEU states that both the Social Charter of the Council of Europe and the 1989 Community Charter are the essential standards of '**fundamental social rights**' to be **taken into account** by the Union and the MS to develop as their social objectives 'the promotion of employment, improved living and working conditions, so as to make possible their harmonisation while the improvement is being maintained, proper social protection, dialogue between management and labour, the development of human resources with a view to lasting high employment and the combating of exclusion'. 20

The previous example concerning the European Agreement on the Organisation of Working Time of Mobile Workers in Civil Aviation, in conjunction with the two Working Time Directives (Council Directives 93/104/EC and 2003/88/EC), shows the **balancing game between the EU and the MS** in delimitating the different substantial rights by means of such agreement. In her Opinion in *Williams and Others*, AG *Trstenjak* recalled that the EU legislature, which is bound by the principle of subsidiarity in the exercise of its regulatory powers, confined itself to laying down rules governing certain essential matters such as the minimum period of annual leave, whereas, in relation to the conditions for entitlement to, and granting of, such leave, it referred to the '**national legislation and/or practice**'.[41] 21

---

[40] See Drouin (2010).
[41] Case C-155/10, *Williams and Others* (Opinion of AG Trstenjak of 16 June 2011) para 35.

22   In relation to the level of protection affecting this set of substantial social rights, it is also important to note that 'a **minimum degree of harmonisation**', as sought by, *inter alia*, the European Agreement pursuant to Article 2.1 of Directive 2000/79/EC in the area of aviation, does **not** mean that the action taken by the EU is confined to the **lowest common denominator**. It does not therefore by any means equate to minimal harmonisation. Its aim is not to extend across the EU the lowest level of protection in place in a particular MS but to formulate the basic protection necessary for the EU policy in question. Anything else would be incompatible with the objectives laid down in Article 151 TFEU, of '[improving] living and working conditions' to 'make possible their harmonisation while the improvement is being maintained' and to provide 'proper social protection'. A provision which lays down minimum standards for the safety and health of workers must be objectively and clearly formulated to ensure that it is effectively and uniformly implemented throughout the territory of the EU.[42]

23   Finally, it should likewise be pointed out that, despite the fact that they have different legal bases in the Treaty, the purpose both of the Working Time Directives and of Council Directive 2000/79/EC is to organise working time in such a way as to impose certain limits on it in the interests of the **safety and health of workers**.[43] As a part of these limits, some substantial rights cannot be derogated when it comes to implementing the EU law at MS level, unless this is expressly provided for by the Working Time Directives. In this regard, Article 7 of Council Directive 2003/88/EC (right to the payment of holiday pay) is not one of the provisions from which that directive expressly permits derogation. In other words, that provision must not be derogated from to the detriment of the worker either in law or in contract and, therefore, the payment of holiday pay is mandatory in character and implies the exercise of a fundamental right which cannot be subject to relinquishment or renunciation.[44]

4. Challenges: The Impact of European Agreements in a Broader Social Europe

24   In light of the previous considerations, the issue of the extent of the interpretative jurisdiction of the CJEU in relation to European Agreements in the field of the social policy must be emphasised in accordance with a clear fundamental rights

---

[42] Case C-155/10, *Williams and Others* (Opinion of AG Trstenjak of 16 June 2011) para 54.

[43] This follows, for example, from recital 11 in the preamble to Council Directive 2000/79/EC and from recital 11 in the preamble to Directive 2003/88/EC. Moreover, the wording of clause 3 is almost identical to that of Article 7 of the Working Time Directive.

[44] The same conclusion has been highlighted in doctrine, *mutatis mutandis*, in relation to Article 12 of ILO Convention No. 132, which states that agreements to relinquish the right to the minimum annual holiday with pay prescribed in Article 3.3 of that Convention or to forgo such a holiday, for compensation or otherwise, must, as appropriate to national conditions, be null and void or be prohibited. See Blanpain (2000), p. 364.

approach. Indeed, the mainly political perspective dealing with the **governing principles of the distribution of competences between the EU and the MS** when tackling the implementation of European Agreements must be *prima facie* re-orientated by putting the accent in the potential impact of the essential legal focus on the fundamental social rights, especially after the entry into force of the Lisbon Treaty and, consequently, of the EUCFR. In doing so, the AGs play a major role within the CJEU.[45]

With such a spirit, in Opinions in *Schultz-Hoff*[46] and in *Williams and Others*,[47] AG *Trstenjak* highlighted the fact that the right of every worker to paid annual leave is included in the EUCFR 'provides the most reliable and definitive confirmation that it constitutes a **fundamental right**'. As the Charter acquired the definitive status of EU primary law (Article 6.1 TEU), by virtue of the commitment to fundamental rights laid down in Article 51.1 EUCFR, legislative acts adopted by the EU institutions in this sphere must now be assessed by reference to that provision. The MS are henceforth also bound by that provision in so far as they implement the EU law.[48]

In addition, both opinions underlined that Article 31.2 EUCFR, according to the Explanations relating to the Charter, is based on Council Directive 93/104/EC and point 8 of the 1989 Community Charter on the rights of workers, but above all in Article 2 of the European Social Charter of the Council of Europe. As stated above, the Social Charter is also mentioned in the Preamble of the EUCFR and in Article 151 TFEU. Such vision of a broader social Europe taking into account the **synergies between the EU and the Council of Europe** is necessary to optimise the achievement of social policy and the respect for social rights, insofar as one condition is not forgotten: the European Social Charter must be located at the centre of the reflection on an equal footing in respect of the ECHR (indivisibility and inter-dependence), without exaggerating the social dimension (perhaps irrelevant) of the latter and, at the same time, without neglecting the parallel accession of the EU to the Social Charter.[49]

---

[45] See Case C-155/10, *Williams and Others* (Opinion of AG Trstenjak of 16 June 2011) para 65.

[46] Joined Cases C-350/06 and C-520/06, *Schultz-Hoff and Stringer and Others* (Opinion of AG Trstenjak of 24 January 2008) para 38.

[47] Case C-155/10, *Williams and Others* (Opinion of AG Trstenjak of 16 June 2011) para 31 et seqq.

[48] See Jarass (2021), Article 51 EUCFR para 15 et seqq.

[49] According to Case C-282/10, *Dominguez* (Opinion of AG Trstenjak of 8 September 2011) para 85, on the interpretation of Article 7 of Council Directive 2003/88/EC should be *mutatis mutandis* applied to the Social Charter: 'Although the ECHR admittedly does not provide for a right to annual leave comparable with that in Article 31(2) of the Charter it should nevertheless be borne in mind that under Articles 52(3) and 53 of the Charter the level of protection of fundamental rights contained in the ECHR is decisive for the EU legal system. These provisions, according to their spirit and purpose, are to be interpreted as meaning that the level of protection of fundamental rights guaranteed in the Charter must not lag behind the minimum standards in the ECHR. For that reason [...] it would appear essential to take account of approaches to the solution afforded by this pan-European system of protection of fundamental rights'.

27 In this context of broader social Europe, the ECSR has recently dealt with the legislative framework in France concerning the limits of the social partners' ability to use collective bargaining to conclude agreements on complementary social protection at the branch level, particularly the impossibility to use designation clauses, and that in relation to **competition rules**. Indeed, in its complaint the *Confédération Générale du Travail Force Ouvrière* alleged a violation of Article 6.2 of the 1996 Revised ECS with respect to the conditions under the French legislation concerning complementary social protection of employees with regard to the choice of an insurer.[50] The ECSR adopted its decision on the merits on 3 July 2018 and concluded unanimously that there was a violation of Article 6.2 ESC (right to bargain collectively) on the issue of prohibiting designation clauses.[51]

28 In conclusion, the need for exploiting those synergies (at an interpretative level until the moment of the actual EU's accession to the Social Charter) is not merely theoretical, since the parallel solutions have already emerged on several occasions. In some cases, convergence has been the final solution (e.g. in relation to on 'on-call duty' periods and working time/periods of rest),[52] while in other cases divergence has been the outcome (e.g. concerning collective action and protection of posted workers with regard to the Case *Laval*).[53] In my view, in case of different solutions, all these human rights treaties contain specific *favor libertatis* **clauses**, such as Article 53 EUCFR, Article 32 of the European Social Charter (Article H of the Revised Charter) and Article 53 ECHR.[54] In addition, those **synergies** constitute a clear expression of *inter-textuality* as a hermeneutical tool for courts and academia.[55]

List of Cases

ECJ/CJEU

ECJ 01.12.2005, C-14/04, *Abdelkader Dellas*, ECLI:EU:C:2005:728 [cit. in para 26]

ECJ 13.09.2007, C-307/05, *Del Cerro Alonso*, ECLI:EU:C:2007:509 [cit. in para 7]

---

[50] Particularly, Article L. 912-1 of the Social Security Code as amended by Law No. 2013-1203 of 23 December 2013 on social security financing for 2014 and implementing decrees.

[51] Complaint No. 118/2015, *Confédération Générale du Travail Force Ouvrière* (FO) v France (ECSR 3 July 2018) para 70–77.

[52] Complaint No. 16/2003, *Confédération Française de l'Encadrement v France* (ECSR 12 October 2004) para 52 and Case C-14/04, *Abdelkader Dellas* (ECJ 1 December 2005) para 63.

[53] Cf. Case C-341/05, *Laval* (ECJ 18 December 2007) and Complaint No. 85/2012, *Swedish Trade Union Confederation and Swedish Confederation of Professional Employees v Sweden* (ECSR 3 July 2013).

[54] This view is also suggested by Becker, in Schwarze et al. (2019), Article 53 EUCFR para 4–5. The same favourable interpretation under Article 53 EUCFR, in Mikkola (2010), p. 95.

[55] Dorssemont and Lörcher (2013), p. 423.

ECJ 18.12.2007, C-341/05, *Laval*, ECLI:EU:C:2007:809 [cit. in para 26]
ECJ 24.01.2008, C-350/06 and C-520/06, Opinion of AG Trstenjak, *Schultz-Hoff and Stringer and Others*, ECLI:EU:C:2008:37 [cit. in para 23]
CJEU 07.07.2010, C-149/10, Opinion of AG Kokott, *Chatzi*, ECLI:EU:C:2010:407 [cit. in para 13]
CJEU 16.09.2010, C-149/10, *Chatzi*, ECLI:EU:C:2010:534 [cit. in para 6]
CJEU 22.12.2010, C-444/09 and C-456/09, *Gavieiro Gavieiro and Iglesias Torres*, ECLI:EU:C:2010:819 [cit. in para 7]
CJEU 10.03.2011, C-109/09, *Deutsche Lufthansa*, ECLI:EU:C:2011:129 [cit. in para 7]
CJEU 16.06.2011, C-155/10, Opinion of AG Trstenjak, *Williams and Others*, ECLI:EU:C:2011:403 [cit. in para 9, 19–20, 22–23]
CJEU 08.09.2011, C-282/10, Opinion of AG Trstenjak, *Dominguez*, ECLI:EU:C:2011:559 [cit. in para 24]
CJEU 13.03.2014, C-38/13, *Nierodzik*, ECLI:EU:C:2014:152 [cit. in para 7]
CJEU 11.09.2014, C-413/13, Opinion of AG Wahl, *FNV Kunsten Informatie en Media v Staat der Nederlanden*, ECLI:EU:C:2014:2215 [cit. in para 18]
CJEU 04.12.2014, C-413/13, *FNV Kunsten Informatie en Media v Staat der Nederlanden*, ECLI:EU:C:2014:2411 [cit. in para 18]
CJEU 26.02.2015, C-238/14, *Commission v Luxembourg*, ECLI:EU:C:2015:128 [cit. in para 7]
CJEU 09.07.2015, C-177/14, *Regojo Dans*, ECLI:EU:C:2015:450 [cit. in para 7]
CJEU 16.07.2015, C-222/14, *Konstantinos Maïstrellis*, ECLI:EU:C:2015:473 [cit. in para 3, 5]
CJEU 20.04.2020, C-560/18 P, *Izba Gospodarcza Producentów i Operatorów Urządzeń Rozrywkowych v Commission*, ECLI:EU:C:2020:330 [cit. in para 16]
CJEU 20.01.2021, C-928/19 P, Opinion of AG Pikamäe, *EPSU v Commission*, ECLI:EU:C:2021:38 [cit. in para 3–4, 13]
CJEU 02.09.2021, C-928/19 P, *EPSU v Commission*, ECLI:EU:C:2021:656 [cit. in para 3, 13]

CFI/GC

GC 24 October 2019, T-310/18, *EPSU and Willem Goudriaan v Commission*, ECLI:EU:T:2019:757 [cit. in para 11]

ECSR

ECSR 12.10.2004, 16/2003, *Confédération Française de l'Encadrement v France* [cit. in para 26]
ECSR 03.07.2013, 85/2012, *Swedish Trade Union Confederation and Swedish Confederation of Professional Employees v Sweden* [cit. in para 26]

ECSR 03.07.2018, 118/2015, *Confédération Générale du Travail Force Ouvrière (FO) v France* [cit. in para 25]

References

Blanpain, R. (2000). The holidays with pay convention of the ILO (No 132): A commentary. *The International Journal of Comparative Labour Law and Industrial Relations, 16*(4), 359–385.

Böhnert, S. (2002). *Das Recht der ILO und sein Einfluss auf das deutsche Arbeitsrecht im Zeichen der europäischen Integration*. Nomos.

Bruun, N. (2012). Economic governance of the EU crisis and its social policy implications. In I. Schöman, K. Lörcher, & N. Bruun (Eds.), *The Lisbon Treaty and social Europe* (pp. 261–276). Hart Publishing.

Clauwaert, S. (2012). European framework agreements: 'nomina nuda tenemus' or what's in a name? Experiences of the European social dialogue. In I. Schöman et al. (Eds.), *Transnational collective bargaining at company level. A new component of European industrial relations?* (pp. 117–155). European Trade Union Institute.

Dorssemont, F., Lörcher, K., & Schmitt, M. (2019). On the duty to implement European framework agreements: Lessons to be learned from the hairdressers case. *Industrial Law Journal, 48*(4), 571–603.

Dorssemont, P., & Lörcher, K. (2013). The ECHR and the employment relation. In P. Dorssemont, K. Lörcher, & I. Schömann (Eds.), *The European Convention on Human Rights and the employment relation* (pp. 417–429). Hart Publishing.

Drouin, R. C. (2010). Promoting fundamental labor rights through international framework agreements: Practical outcomes and present challenges. *Comparative Labor Law & Policy Journal, 31*, 591–636.

Dukes, R., & Cannon, C. (2016). The role of social partners. In A. Bogg, C. Costello, & A. C. L. Davies (Eds.), *Research handbook on EU labour law* (pp. 89–113). Elgar.

Egger, J. (2010). Rechtswirkungen von Rahmenvereinbarungen im Sozialbereich. In W. Hummer (Ed.), *Neueste Entwicklungen im Zusammenspiel von Europarecht und nationalem Recht der Mitgliedstaaten* (pp. 187–224). Springer.

Eurofound. (2015). *Collective bargaining in Europe in the 21st century*. Publications Office of the European Union.

García-Muñoz Alhambra, M. A. (2018). Diálogo social y negociación colectiva. *Derecho Social de la Unión Europea*. In *Aplicación por el Tribunal de Justicia* (pp. 1111–1140). Francis Lefebvre.

Guarriello, F. (2021). La concertazione: prospettive euro-unitarie. *Giornale di diritto del lavoro e di relazioni industriali, 172*(4), 703–718.

Jarass, H. D. (2021). *Charta der Grundrechte der Europäischen Union – Kommentar* (4th ed.). C. H. Beck.

Jimena Quesada, L. (2005). *European constitution and competition policy. Focus on conflicts between freedom of enterprise and other fundamental rights*. Philos Edizioni.

Kocher, E. (2016). *Europäisches Arbeitsrecht*. Nomos.

Lo Faro, A. (1999). *Funzioni e finzioni della contrattazione collettiva comunitaria. La contrattazione colettiva come risorsa dell'ordinamento giuridico comunitario*. Giuffrè.

Mathieu, C., & Sterdyniak, H. (2008). Le modèle social européen et l'Europe sociale. *Revue de l'OFCE, Presses de Sciences Po*, 43–104.

Mikkola, M. (2010). *Social human rights in Europe*. Karelactio.

Nadalet, S. (2005). Le dinamiche delle fonti nella globalizzazione: ipotesi per un diritto transnazionale del lavoro. *Lavoro e Diritto, 4*, 671–706.

Papadakis, K. (2011). Globalizing industrial relations: That role for international framework agreements? In S. Hayter (Ed.), *The role of collective bargaining in the global economy* (pp. 277–304). Edward Elgar.

Pataut, E. (2022). Les limites de l'accord collectif européen: À propos de l'affaire EPSU. In G. Loiseau et al. (Eds.), *Mélanges en l'honneur de Pierre-Yves Verkindt* (pp. 327–339). LGDJ.

Pechstein, M., Nowak, C., & Häde, U. (Eds.). (2017). *Frankfurter Kommentar zu EUV, GRC und AEUV*. Mohr Siebeck.

Schiek, D. (2005). Autonomous collective agreements as a regulatory device in European labour law: How to read article 139 EC. *Industrial Law Journal, 34*(1), 23–56.

Schmitt, M., Moizard, N., & Frapard, M. (2020). Droit social européen. *Journal de Droit Européen, 270*, 286–301.

Schwarze, J., et al. (Eds.). (2019). *EU-Kommentar* (4th ed.). Nomos.

Article 156 [Inter-State Cooperation]
(ex-Article 140 TEC)

With a view to achieving the objectives of Article 151 and without prejudice to the other provisions of the Treaties, the Commission shall encourage cooperation between the Member States and facilitate the coordination of their action in all social policy fields under this Chapter, particularly in matters relating to:

- employment,
- labour law and working conditions,
- basic and advanced vocational training,
- social security,
- prevention of occupational accidents and diseases,
- occupational hygiene,
- the right of association and collective bargaining between employers and workers.

To this end, the Commission shall act in close contact with Member States by making studies, delivering opinions and arranging consultations both on problems arising at national level and on those of concern to international organisations, in particular initiatives aiming at the establishment of guidelines and indicators, the organisation of exchange of best practice, and the preparation of the necessary elements for periodic monitoring and evaluation. The European Parliament shall be kept fully informed.

Before delivering the opinions provided for in this Article, the Commission shall consult the Economic and Social Committee.

Declaration No. 31 on Article 156 of the Treaty on the Functioning of the European Union[7]

The Conference confirms that the policies described in Article 156 fall essentially within the competence of the Member States. Measures to provide encouragement and promote coordination to be taken at Union level in accordance with this Article shall be of a complementary nature. They shall serve to strengthen cooperation between Member States and not to harmonise national systems. The guarantees and practices existing in each Member State as regards the responsibility of the social partners will not be affected.

This Declaration is without prejudice to the provisions of the Treaties conferring competence on the Union, including in social matters.

Contents

1. Introduction: The Complexity of the Inter-State Cooperation on Social Policy Since the Origins of the European Construction 1
2. From a Difficult Harmonisation to an Open Method of Coordination in the Social Field 15

3. The Impact of European Soft-Law and the Real Weight of the Goals
   in the Social Field 23
4. Challenges: The Social Dimension as a Necessary Feature of the
   Integrated Vision of Post-Europe 2020 Strategy 27

List of Cases

References

1. Introduction: The Complexity of the Inter-State Cooperation on Social Policy Since the Origins of the European Construction

1 The genesis of Article 156 TFEU shows the original and current reluctances of the MS to assume **social commitments**, not only based on the **dynamics of integration** but even on the **softer cooperation**, since the social policy (like employment and fiscal policy) 'form part of the core of the sovereign powers of the Member States and can thus be shaped supranationally only with regard to their budgetary components' (→ Article 1 TEU para 41). At first glance, if we consider that the first version of Article 156 TFEU appeared in the Social Policy Protocol annexed to the 1992 Maastricht Treaty, it could be seen as paradoxical that the pan-European organisation of cooperation *par excellence* (the Council of Europe) preceded the organisational model of integration (the European Communities) in tackling under the form of fundamental rights (both in the ECHR[1] and especially in the 1961 European Social Charter[2]) the social matters referred to in the TFEU as a mere potential source of cooperation.

2 More specifically, Article 156 TFEU has its **origin** in ex-Article 118 TEEC, whose wording has almost remained unchanged after the adoption of the Lisbon Treaty with the exception of some terminological adjustments and adaptations. With the 1992 Maastricht Treaty, Article 5 of the Maastricht Agreement on Social Policy strangely limited the content of the former Article 118 TEEC to the current equivalence first sentence of Article 156 TFEU. Nonetheless, the 'Maastricht' approach articulated through this Social Protocol 'can be regarded as a manifestation of a flexible integration anticipating basic structures of enhanced cooperation' (→ Article 20 TEU para 8).

3 Then, the 1997 Amsterdam Treaty (Article 140 TEC) added as novelty the **'coordination'** of MS' action to their **'cooperation'**. The current version of Article 156 TFEU is practically identical to ex-Article 140 TEC-Amsterdam, with the addition of the second paragraph of Article 156 TFEU: 'in particular initiatives aiming at the establishment of guidelines and indicators, the organisation of exchange of best practice, and the preparation of the necessary elements for periodic monitoring and evaluation. The European Parliament shall be kept fully

---

[1] For example, Article 11 ECHR.

[2] See Articles 1, 2, 3, 4, 5, 6, 9, 10 and 12 of the European Social Charter.

Article 156. [Inter-State Cooperation]

informed'. In other words, the only novelty introduced by the Lisbon Treaty consisted of, on the one hand, specifying the material scope of the possible **studies, opinions and consultations** made by the Commission and, on the other hand, giving a certain role to the EP in terms of **information**.

To sum up, the real source of inspiration of current Article 156 TFEU seems still to be former Article 118 TEEC in terms of unambitious promotional efforts (of collaboration, cooperation or coordination),[3] what suggests that both provisions are characterised by **soft-nature**. Such soft nature of ex-Article 118 TEEC (and, as a result, still of Article 156 TFEU) is explained when considering the two essential documents drafted in 1956 (the Spaak Report, together with the Ohlin Report) which provided the basis for the 1957 EEC Treaty.

Particularly, the **Ohlin Report**, prepared by ILO experts who advocated a minimal role for the EEC in social policy, had a certain influence in the Spaak Report, which argued that **harmonisation** would follow naturally from the development of a common market. From this perspective, the **Spaak Report** accepted the key element of the Ohlin Report (that the common market did not presuppose a harmonised level of labour standards) in two specific areas that might distort competition such as equal pay and paid holidays.[4] For this reason, even with a limited scope, ex-Article 119 TEEC (equal pay for men and women—now Article 157 TFEU) and ex-Article 120 TEEC (paid holiday schemes—now Article 158 TFEU) were conceived as having a harder nature than ex-Article 120 TEEC (now Article 156 TFEU).

In the context of this complex inter-State **cooperation on social policy**, what is striking is the tension between ambitious but rather **vague goals** and the relative **absence of potent instruments** to pursue them. Article 156 TFEU is still clearly affected by this tension. Indeed, 'the preamble and the social policies articles refer several times to the goals of raising living standards, improving working conditions and promoting social progress. However, [Articles 151–164 TFEU] provided little in the way to forceful, binding instruments. The two exceptions to this are [Article 157 TFEU] on equal pay and [Articles 162–164 TFEU] concerning the European Social Fund (ESF). Even these exceptions are somewhat deceiving'.[5]

In any case, inter-State cooperation on social policy is still difficult nowadays as shown by the reluctant position expressed by MS in their **Declaration (No 31)** on Article 156 TFEU. First of all, the declaration makes clear that is without prejudice to the provisions of the Treaties conferring competence on the Union, including in

4

5

6

7

---

[3] Ex-Article 118 TEEC referred to 'the aim of the Commission to *promote close collaboration* between Member States in the social field', whereas current Article 156 TFEU states that 'the Commission shall *encourage cooperation* between the Member States and *facilitate the coordination* of their action in all social policy fields'.

[4] In Chapter 2 ('Correction of Distortions and Harmonization of National Legislation') of the Spaak Report, it is stated that 'even if the existing disparities should not imply any distortion, it would be necessary for the Governments to make a special effort to harmonise progressively the national regimes affecting the equality of salaries for men and women, the length of the work week and the length of paid holidays'.

[5] See Anderson (2015), pp. 56–57.

social matters. This s in line with its legal status as interpretative declaration (→ Article 51 TEU para 12 et seqq.). In this Declaration, the Conference confirms that the policies described in Article 156 TFEU 'fall essentially within the competence of the Member States'. Nonetheless, it also emphasises that measures 'to provide encouragement and promote coordination to be taken at Union level' under Article 156 TFEU shall be 'of a complementary nature'. Under Article 5.3 TFEU (→ Article 5 TFEU para 22–24), these measures shall serve to strengthen cooperation between Member States while, under Article 2.5 (2) TFEU (→ Article 2 TFEU para 72–73), they shall not entail harmonisation of national systems. Finally, 'the guarantees and practices existing in each Member State as regards the responsibility of the social partners will not be affected'.

8   On this last point, if we consider the list of specific social matters referred to in Article 156 TFEU, it is possible to verify the following connections: in the field of employment, Article 9 TFEU included into the 'horizontal social clause' the 'promotion of a high level of employment', what is developed in Title IX on employment (Articles 145–150 TFEU); on labour law and working conditions, several provisions of the TFEU (Articles 45 TFEU, freedom of movement for workers and Articles 56 TFEU, freedom to provide services) are linked with two Articles of the EUCFR (Articles 15 EUCFR on freedom to choose an occupation and right to engage in work and Article 31 EUCFR on fair and just working conditions);[6] in relation to vocational training, Articles 6, 9, 41, 162, 166 and 180 TFEU are also relevant (e.g. the **Youth Guarantee**[7]); social security issues are likewise covered by Articles 21.3 and 48 TFEU as well as Article 34 EUCFR;[8]

---

[6] On the connection between Articles 31 EUCFR and 156 TFEU, see Case C-681/18, *KG (Missions successives dans le cadre du travail intérimaire)* (CJEU 14 October 2020) para 54: The Explanations relating to Article 31 EUCFR 'indicate, in that regard, that the expression "working conditions" is to be understood in accordance with Article 156 TFEU. However, that provision merely refers, without any further definition, to "working conditions" as being one of the areas of the European Union's social policy in which the Commission may intervene to encourage cooperation between Member States and facilitate the coordination of their action. In the light of the objective of Directive 2008/104 to protect the rights of temporary agency workers, that lack of precision supports a broad interpretation of the concept of "working conditions"'. See also Case C-232/20, *Daimler* (Opinion of AG Tanchev of 9 September 2021), para 66, note 57: The reference in the Explanations to Article 31 EUCFR 'to Article 156 TFEU with regard to "working conditions" provides no further precision'.

[7] See Proposal for a Council Recommendation of 30 October 2020 *on A Bridge to Jobs— Reinforcing the Youth Guarantee and replacing Council Recommendation of 22 April 2013 on establishing a Youth Guarantee*, O.J. C 372/1 (2020). On the other hand, on the assessment of possible practices of unpaid internships affecting young workers and apprentices, and the lack of enforcement of provisions in the national legislation regulating internships, see Complaint No. 150/2017, *European Youth Forum (YFJ) v Belgium* (ECSR 8 September 2021) para 156–164.

[8] On the link between Articles 34 EUCFR and 156 TFEU, see Case C-647/13, *Melchior* (Opinion of AG Mengozzi of 16 October 2014) para 60: 'Under Article 34(1) of the Charter, "[t]he Union recognises and respects the entitlement to social security benefits and social services providing protection ... in the case of loss of employment, in accordance with the rules laid down by Union law and national laws and practices." As is clear from its wording and from the Explanations relating to the Charter ("the Explanations"), that provision sets out a "principle" based on

with regard to prevention of occupational accidents and diseases as well as occupational hygiene, Articles 31 and 34 EUCFR are also at stake when referring to workers' health and safety and to 'industrial accidents', respectively; finally, Article 28 EUCFR covers the right of collective bargaining and action.[9] In any case, the list of areas established in Article 156 TFEU is not exhaustive and, therefore, the Commission can also carry out its functions in other areas which, however, must be directly related to social policy issues.[10]

Among these fields, **employment** plays the role of a **'pilot' source of cooperation**, especially since the 1992 Treaty included the promotion of a 'high level of employment' (alongside a high level of 'social protection') as a transversal task of the EU in Article 2 TEC (= Article 9 TFEU) and, with the same spirit, the 1997 Amsterdam Treaty incorporated a separate Title (VIII) on employment. From this perspective, that new Title (now Title IX of the TFEU) was considered a 'compromise' being compensated with the goal of a **'high degree of competitiveness'** which 'was inserted into the treaty to balance the emphasis on employment'.[11]

For this reason, it is not strange that the new **European Pillar of Social Rights** (EPSR) has mainly put the accent, 'to a large extent', on 'the **employment and social challenges** facing Europe', since 'economic and social progress are intertwined' and the establishment of a EPSR 'should be part of wider efforts to build a more inclusive and sustainable growth model by improving Europe's competitiveness and making it a better place to invest, create jobs and foster social cohesion'. The aim of the EPSR 'is to serve as a guide towards efficient employment and social outcomes when responding to current and future challenges which are directly aimed at fulfilling people's essential needs, and towards ensuring better enactment and implementation of social rights', 'is particularly important to increase resilience and deepen the Economic and Monetary Union' and 'expresses principles and rights essential for fair and well-functioning labour markets and welfare systems in 21st century Europe. It reaffirms some of the rights already present in the Union

---

Articles 153 TFEU and 156 TFEU, Article 12 of the European Social Charter and point 10 of the Community Charter of Fundamental Social Rights of Workers. In accordance with Articles 51(2) and 52(5) of the Charter, the provisions of the Charter which contain principles are addressed first and foremost to public authorities, have merely programmatic character (as opposed to the prescriptive character of the provisions setting out "rights") and require "implementing acts." With regard to their enforceability, they do not create, at least in the absence of "legislative implementation," rights to positive action by the Member States' authorities and may be invoked in law only as interpretative references or as parameters for the ruling on the legality of the acts for their implementation'.

[9] On the link between Articles 28 EUCFR and 156 TFEU, see Case C-561/19, *Consorzio Italian Management e Catania Multiservizi* (CJEU 6 October 2021) para 67.

[10] Benecke, in Grabitz et al. (2022), Article 156 AEUV para 4 (released in 2022).

[11] Anderson (2015), p. 68: 'the new employment policy would not require new financial resources, and as the treaty states: "the competences of the Member States shall be respected" [Article 147 TFEU]. This social policy innovation is thus a compromise between Member State autonomy and union competence. While the EU began to play a more important role in supporting the coordination of national employment policies, the Member States appeared to remain more or less in control'.

acquis. It adds new principles which address the challenges arising from societal, technological and economic developments. For them to be legally enforceable, the principles and rights first require dedicated measures or legislation to be adopted at the appropriate level' (Recitals 10 through 14 of the Preamble EPSR). In this sense, ten of the twenty principles that make up the EPSR are devoted to 'equal opportunities and access to the labour market' (Chapter I, principles 1–4) and to 'fair working conditions' (Chapter II, principles 5–10).[12] In any case, the COVID-19 crisis has demonstrated that the EPSR should be linked to better socio-economic policy coordination and further socialisation of the European Semester.[13]

11 Eventually, it is very complicated to understand the impact of the inter-State cooperation on social policy in the framework of the categories and areas of EU competences, especially in light of Article 2.3 and Article 5.2 and 5.3 TFEU. From this point of view, the reach of Article 5.3 TFEU and its relationship with more detailed Treaty provisions on social policy is not clear. The most natural 'linkage' would seem to be Article 156 TFEU, which empowers the Commission to encourage **cooperation between MS** and facilitate **coordination of their action** in all fields of social policy, albeit through soft law measures. Assuming this to be so, the wording of the respective provision does not fit, since Article 5.3 TFEU is framed in discretionary terms ('the Union may take initiatives'), while Article 156 TFEU is drafted in mandatory language (to the effect that the 'Commission shall encourage the relevant cooperation and coordination').[14]

12 From this last perspective, it could be considered that the social policy objectives imply a '**promotional obligation** [which] also extends to the adoption of **positive measures** but leaves the final decision up to the competent organs as long as they recognise their obligation to consider the objectives and as long as they act according to priorities justifiable under the Treaty law. A substantial **margin of appreciation** of the Union and of the MS, especially when pursuing competing Union principles, has to be respected' (→ Article 3 TEU para 20). To sum up, Article 156 TFEU continues to give the Union limited powers in the field of social policy, since the only institution mentioned therein is the Commission, whose role is limited to promoting close cooperation between the MS on social matters.[15]

---

[12] The heading of Chapter III is 'Social protection and inclusion' (Principles 11–20).

[13] Vesan et al. (2021), p. 277, in having an optimistic approach to the EPSR, consider that it has left a legacy to improve the Commission's social agenda and the EU responses to the COVID-19 pandemic.

[14] Craig (2010), pp. 180–181: dealing with 'Economic employment and social policy: category and consequence', this author holds that 'the Treaty schema for competence in Article 2 TFEU is in general premised on the ascription of legal consequence for EU and Member State power as the result of coming within a particular category. [...] Legal consequences are also spelt for the category of supporting, coordination and supplementary action. Article 5 TFEU is an exception in this respect, since Article 2(3) TFEU does not spell out the legal consequences of inclusion within this category. [...] The legal consequences of inclusion within this category can therefore only be divined by considering the language of Article 5 TFEU, which is couched largely in terms of coordination, and by considering the detailed provisions that apply to these areas'.

[15] Langer, in von der Groeben et al. (2015), Article 156 AEUV para 3.

Article 156. [Inter-State Cooperation]

In the same vein, the EPSR is conceived as 'a shared political commitment and responsibility' which 'should be implemented at both Union level and MS level within their respective competences, taking due account of different socioeconomic environments and the diversity of national systems, including the role of social partners, and in accordance with the principles of subsidiarity and proportionality'. At Union level, it 'does not entail an extension of the Union's powers and tasks as conferred by the Treaties' and 'respects the diversity of the cultures and traditions of the peoples of Europe, as well as the national identities of the Member States and the organisation of their public authorities at national, regional and local levels. Particularly, the establishment of the EPSR does not affect the right of Member States to define the fundamental principles of their **social security systems** and manage their public finances, and must not significantly affect the financial equilibrium thereof' (Recitals 17 through 19 of the Preamble EPSR).

13

Lastly, the COVID-19 outbreak led the European Commission to launch a **temporary framework for State aid measures to support the economy** in march 2020.[16] This soft-law legal instrument was adopted based on rules on competition and State aids set forth in the TFEU (mainly, Article 107) and could be review 'on the basis of important competition policy or economic considerations' (point 39); in addition, the Commission, 'in close cooperation with the Member States concerned, ensures swift adoption of decisions upon clear and complete notification of measures covered by this Communication' (point 42). It is obvious that this framework does not directly refer to the cooperation and coordination which aim at satisfying the objectives of Article 151 TFEU or the social policy matters listed in Article 156 TFEU. However, this can be seen as a good exercise of **indirect social inter-State cooperation** under Article 156,[17] as also shown by the different amendments to the Temporary Framework since its adoption on 19 March 2020 to cope with post-pandemic repercussions[18] (aggravated in the context of Russia's war against Ukraine).[19]

14

---

[16] Commission Communication, *Temporary Framework to support the economy in the context of the coronavirus outbreak* (2020/C 91 I/01), O.J. C 91/1, 20 March 2020.

[17] In effect, the Temporary Framework tackled measures which 'have an immediate impact on both demand and supply, and hit undertakings and employees, especially in the health, tourism, culture, retail and transport sectors. Beyond the immediate effects on mobility and trade, the COVID-19 outbreak is also increasingly affecting undertakings in all sectors and of all kinds, small and medium enterprises ("SMEs") as well as large undertakings' (point 3); 'if the flow of credit is severely constrained, economic activity will decelerate sharply, as undertakings struggle to pay their suppliers and employees' (point 4). Thus, the social dimension or impact of such measures is evident.

[18] See the amendments to the State Aid Temporary Framework in: https://competition-policy.ec.europa.eu/state-aid/coronavirus/temporary-framework/amendments_en.

[19] See the Commission Communication, *Temporary Crisis Framework for State Aid measures to support the economy following the aggression against Ukraine by Russia* (2022/C 131 I/01), O.J. C 131/1, 24 March 2022: 'A coordinated economic response of MS and EU institutions is crucial to mitigate the immediate social and economic negative repercussions in the EU, to preserve

2. From a Difficult Harmonisation to an Open Method of Coordination in the Social Field

15 The above-mentioned Declaration (No 31) on Article 156 TFEU confirms that the measures aiming at **coordinating social matters** at Union level are 'of a complementary nature' and *softly* consist of just encouraging and promoting coordination and, therefore, such measures shall serve 'to strengthen cooperation' between MS and 'not to harmonise' national systems. In other words, while emphasising the protection of free movement of people, priority has been given to coordination over harmonisation within the EU, thus preventing from the **creation of a common system of social security**.[20] Under these conditions, the **'Open Method of Coordination'** (OMC), which was launched by the European Council of Lisbon in March 2000 to help MS progress jointly in the reforms they needed to undertake to reach the Lisbon goals,[21] is a light but structured way MS use to cooperate at European level, especially (but not only) in the social fields. The OMC process is structured as 3-year cycles, leading to national reports which are synthesised by the Commission and the Council in a joint report. The proper conduct of the process is reviewed periodically by the Social Protection Committee (Article 160 TFEU) in partnership with representatives of civil society and the social partners.

16 The OMC creates a common understanding of problems and helps to **build consensus on solutions and their practical implementation**. Through an **exchange of good practice between EU countries**, it contributes to improving the design and implementation of social policies, without regulatory instruments. In other words, the main idea is that MS learn from sharing their experience of national policies in areas of common interest, what can help them to improve the design and implementation of their own policies, to develop coordinated or joint initiatives on issues of transnational interest, and to identify areas where Union initiatives could reinforce national actions.

17 Initially, the **OMC** was only applied to **employment and economic policy** and included the following elements: (a) Fixing **guidelines and timetables** for achieving short, medium and long-term goals; (b) Establishing quantitative and qualitative **indicators and benchmarks**, tailored to the needs of MS and sectors involved, as a means of comparing best practices; (c) Translating European guidelines into **national and regional policies**, by setting specific measures and targets; and (d) Periodic **monitoring** of the progress achieved to put in place **mutual learning** processes between MS.

---

economic activities and jobs, and to facilitate the structural adjustments needed in response to the new economic situation created by the Russian military aggression against Ukraine' (point 7).

[20] Carrascosa Bermejo (2018), p. 512.

[21] The term was coined in 2000, but the method dates back somewhat further to the 1992 Maastricht Treaty where a similar type of governance was used in economic coordination (with the Broad Economic Policy Guidelines, or BEPGs), and to the 1997 Amsterdam Treaty where it was used in employment policy (the so-called Luxembourg process or European Employment Strategy—EES).

The single **social OMC established in 2005** applied to three specific areas, particularly the eradication of poverty and social exclusion, guaranteeing adequate and sustainable pension systems and providing accessible, high-quality and sustainable health care and long-term care.[22] Then, in 2008 the Commission proposed a reinforcement of the single social OMC in accordance with the objectives of the **Renewed Social Agenda** and the Council's conclusions of March 2008 for improved integration of economic, social and employment policies.[23] That reform conceived the OMC as an essential instrument in the development of the **European social model** concerning certain sectors (particularly, child poverty, in-work poverty and poverty of older people), insofar as it should make it possible to consolidate the OMC and to exploit its potential more fully to increase social cohesion and solidarity in the EU.[24]

Then, the OMC was located in the framework of the EU 2020 Strategy[25] as the successor of the Lisbon Strategy aiming at facing the reduction of social standards which has been provoked by the global economic and financial crisis that started in 2008.[26] In this atmosphere, the OMC could be understood as **a new form of EU governance** which might be seen in an optimistic manner, although there were also pessimistic authors who doubted about the suitable character of this instrument to balance the potential and real negative consequences deriving from the prevalent economic integration.[27]

OMC's future, in light of the post-pandemic repercussions, is thus at this point uncertain. Recent criticisms point to its abandonment in the future, but it may be too early to make such a sweeping prognosis, especially because OMC is applied in different policy areas; although it is more probable that it will survive in those policy areas where it does not threaten the community method and after improvements have been made to those elements construed as problematic. From this perspective, it has been noted that only as an integral part of the **post-Europe 2020 Strategy** can the social OMC maintain its influence: promoting upward social convergence and ultimately supplementing and counterbalancing budgetary and macro-economic coordination.[28]

---

[22] See Commission Communication, *A new framework for the open coordination of social protection and inclusion policies*, COM(2005) 706.

[23] Commission Communication, *A renewed commitment to social Europe: Reinforcing the Open Method of Coordination for Social Protection and Social Inclusion*, COM(2008) 418 final.

[24] On the importance of solidarity as European constitutional value, see Torres del Moral (2009), p. 63; see also Tajadura Tejada (2014), p. 110. The idea of 'transnational solidarity' has also been highlighted by Salazar (2015), p. 119.

[25] Of course, after 2010, the EU's role was expanded because MS were then required to report on their progress in achieving Europe 2020's social goals, and because the Commission and the Council now have the competence within the European Semester to make country-specific recommendations to individual MS' governments.

[26] Cf. Ferrera (2010), p. 65. See also Zietlin (2010).

[27] For a summary of both contradictory positions, see Hatzopoulos (2007).

[28] Vanhercke (2020), p. 118.

21   In real terms, the OMC has not been established as a universal method of coordination in the Treaties, but several provisions in the TFEU refer to it in substance, without naming it as such: for example Article 149 TFEU (employment), Articles 153 and 156 TFEU (social policy), Article 168 TFEU (health), Article 173 TFEU (industry) and Article 181 TFEU (research and technology). In such framework, it has been criticised the current 'spread' of the OMC by offering proposals on how to neutralise some of the identified shortfalls of the OMC. As a result, the conclusion is not opting for the demise of the OMC, but rather for its 'communautarisation'. The conclusion which follows is both that the **application and the effects of the OMC** should be **more clearly defined** and better integrated with the other pre-existing forms of cooperation, in accordance with basic requirements stemming from the EU legal order.

22   In addition, as a complement to this concern for properly expressing the powers of the European authorities and the MS as regards achieving the **model of 'social market economy'**, it should be mentioned that there is an equally strong concern to implement the OMC **compensating the achievement of the market with the protection of social rights**. For this purpose, the legally binding character of the EUCFR is a key element.[29] On the other hand, the EPSR has been seen as both a political strategy seeking a renewed consensus on the EU and a policy initiative serving 'to restate certain principles and rights already enshrined in the EU Treaties and secondary legislation, update the so-called "social acquis," reinforce the monitoring and coordination of social and employment issues in the context of the European Semester and strengthen the redistributive dimension of the EU budget'.[30]

3. The Impact of European Soft-Law and the Real Weight of the Goals in the Social Field

23   In light of the foregoing considerations, the OMC somehow constitutes a procedure of producing EU soft-law, which does not lead to binding EU legal acts, but just requires MS to spread best practices and achieve greater convergence in the social field.[31] It is evident that the current economic crisis has amplified the importance of the OMC and the soft-law dimension. The EP had alerted, even before the 2008 financial crisis, on the abusive use of **soft-law instruments**.[32] Unfortunately, it can

---

[29] In this field, see De Schutter (2004) and De la Rosa (2007).

[30] Corti (2022), p. 27.

[31] See Trubek (2005).

[32] See European Parliament Resolution *on institutional and legal implications of the use of 'soft law' instruments*, 2007/2028(INI) point 18–19, where the EP reiterates 'the importance of Parliament's participating, as the main representative of the interests of EU citizens, in all decision-making processes, in order to help reduce their current mistrust in European integration and values' and stresses 'that the expression of soft law, as well as its invocation, should be avoided at all times in any official documents of the European institutions'.

be argued that history is repeating itself in the COVID-19 crisis,[33] although the recourse to soft law in a time of crisis might be understandable, given its flexibility and speedy adoption processes.[34] Despite this, the social provisions of the Treaties (alongside the potential impact of the social rights recognised in the EUCFR), including those having a more modest character, must be exploited in a good direction through positive political and judicial willingness.[35]

Indeed, the energy crisis of the early 1970s also raised problematic questions which unfortunately are not currently unknown and which were likewise analysed under the European Social Charter by the European Committee of Social Rights (ECSR), i.e. housing crisis[36] or high rate of unemployment.[37] In any case, the Committee has proceeded to a balanced assessment between the possible restrictions and the necessity of respecting the **positive obligations imposed by the Social Charter**.[38]

In the framework of the EU, the petrol crisis in the 1970s, alongside the accession of five new MS in the 1970s and 1980s (Greece, Spain, Portugal, the UK, Ireland and Denmark) which increased **social policy diversity among European territories**, led in the early 1980s to decade of stagnation for EC social policy.[39] Nonetheless, the June 1984 Fontainebleau European Council and the 1985 appointment of *Jacques Delors* as president of the European Commission

---

[33] In identifying almost 200 EU soft law instruments which were issued to deal with the COVID-19 crisis, and analysed the procedures for their adoption, it has been found little evidence of parliamentary involvement or stakeholder consultation, with COVID-19 soft law replicating decision-making patterns which have been constantly criticised in the literature as illegitimate and opaque. For these reason, it has been highlighted the importance of reflecting on some quick fixes which might increase, ex post factum, the legitimacy of these instruments: Eliantonio and Stefan (2021), p. 159.

[34] Ştefan (2020), p. 329.

[35] See Fontana (2015).

[36] Conclusions IV, 1975, United Kingdom: 'The Committee fully appreciated the difficulties arising from the housing crisis, but it could not retain this fact as valid argument for not taking appropriate steps in accordance with the Charter'.

[37] Conclusions IV, 1975, Germany: the Committee welcomes 'the fact that the ban on the recruitment of foreign workers issued by the Federal Republic following the petrol crisis did not apply to nationals of the Contracting Parties to the Charter'. See also Conclusions IV, 1975, Italy: 'the effects of the oil crisis seemed to have affected the employment situation in Italy in 1974 much less than in other Western European countries. [It] seemed at least to prove that Italy had made a considerable effort to honour the undertaking arising out of [the Social Charter]. The report admittedly remained rather vague as to specific measures - both short and medium-term - which are claimed to have been taken in order to maintain, and indeed improve the employment situation in the different categories of the working population, especially among young people, women, and elderly workers, and to remove certain cases of regional imbalance'.

[38] See on this point Jimena Quesada (2014), pp. 429–443.

[39] Similarly, it has been noted by Lelie and Vanhercke (2013), p. 13, that 'his proliferation of soft law tools did not come as a great surprise. In view of the 2004 and 2007 EU enlargements, and with further enlargements ahead, very few EU initiatives have been taken with a view to finding agreement on EU social legislation, and it seems highly unlikely that the amount of legislation in the social sphere will increase substantially in the next few years'.

strengthened the social dimension and resulted in 'a new Social Action Plan, with the aim of introducing a balance between the social and economic goals of the EU. National trade unions and the European Trade Union Confederation (ETUC) also lobbied for a strong social dimension to the SEA, particularly after the publication of the Commission's 1985 White Paper titled *Completing the Internal Market*. The ratification of the SEA was thus based on renewed attempts to strengthen the social aspects of the next phase of European integration. These efforts were only partially successful, because the SEA contained only limited innovations in the field of social policy'.[40]

26   With these parameters, it is important to emphasise the social goals established in the European Treaties. Despite the weakness of its social policy provisions, it has been argued that the original EEC Treaty provided legal openings for the Commission to take a positive social policy stance. Otherwise said, the Treaty of Rome's provisions concerning social policy were thus an invitation to **institutional innovation and expansion**. Early analyses of EU social policy demonstrate that the Commission did not view social policy integration as something subordinate to economic integration. Even if the Treaty of Rome was given a limited view of social policy, included ambiguity and left uncertainties for future resolution, in the following decades the Commission was able to exploit these openings to expand its social policy competence. Such approach must *mutatis mutandis* be applied to the current TFEU,[41] since the social dimension does not imply a danger for the market economy.[42]

4. Challenges: The Social Dimension as a Necessary Feature of the Integrated Vision of Post-Europe 2020 Strategy

27   Currently, the inter-State cooperation seems to be the prevalent EU dynamics aiming at tackling the social challenges in the coming years.[43] At the same time, the EU social dimension has been also marked in the recent years by the 'Troika method', which suggests that 'the traditional institutional structure, and the so called classic Monnet method, the Community method has not been adequately

---

[40] Anderson (2015), pp. 58–61.

[41] Anderson (2015), pp. 58–61. Indeed, in the White Paper, *Completing the Internal Market*, 1985, the Commission saw in Articles 155, 156 TFEU the rationale for an active Commission role in EU social policy, arguing that 'the sphere of action of the institutions and social matters has no strict limits, the problems listed in [Article 156 TFEU] being in no way exclusive' (para 103). The Commission also stated that 'it is clear that the objectives of social character are placed on the same footing as those of economic character; it is from this standpoint that the future of the community in the social field will have to be conceived and judged' (para 102).

[42] Rodríguez-Piñero Bravo-Ferrer (2014), pp. 513–514.

[43] See Wallace (2001), p. 33: 'policy co-ordination and benchmarking [would be] a typical mode in future EU policy-making, as an alternative to the formal reassignment of policy powers from national to EU level'.

Article 156. [Inter-State Cooperation] 1439

equipped to deal with the challenges presented by globalisation'.[44] In effect, the major challenge face by the European social dimension is also fully overcoming the 2020 COVID-19 world crisis, which has accentuated the 2008 financial world crisis. For this purpose, the relevant EU institutional and legal instruments put into practice, although different in nature in responding to Eurozone (e.g. Troika memoranda as atypical legal acts) and COVID-19 (e.g. abuse of soft-law instruments) crises, have demonstrated that the EU democratic deficit remains.[45]

In this sense, the inter-State cooperation, and especially the OMC, must be approached under an integrated vision of the **post-Europe 2020 Strategy** that considers the social objectives of the TFEU, particularly the horizontal social clause (Article 9 TFEU).[46] In addition, the Europe 2020 social goals and targets have currently been updated by the 2021 Action Plan on the EPSR,[47] which is expected to be reviewed in 2025.   **28**

With the same philosophy, in several resolutions since 2012, the European Parliament criticises the fact that the full potential of the Lisbon Treaty on employment and social policies has remained untapped. It calls for the introduction of social and economic benchmarks with minimum standards to be applied.[48] Other recent resolutions express EP's concerns that the EU is a long way from achieving the **employment and social targets**, particularly the poverty target. The EP calls for a growth-friendly and differentiated fiscal consolidation which would allow MS also to tackle unemployment.[49] On social scoreboard, it calls for the inclusion of additional indicators, such as child poverty levels and homelessness. The scoreboard should have a real influence on the whole European semester process. In such direction, the EP insists in calling on the Commission to continue developing the social dimension and to make greater use of the social scoreboard in policy   **29**

---

[44] Villiers (2006), p. 89.

[45] Sebastião (2021), p. 253.

[46] See Opinion of the European Economic and Social Committee *The open method of coordination and the social clause in the context of Europe 2020*, 2011/C 44/04: 'The EESC gives its full support to setting up the "European Platform against Poverty," making it an instrument that will boost the commitment of businesses, workers and the general public to reduce social exclusion through practical measures. The Platform and the OMC will mutually benefit each other. However, the EESC considers that the OMC can also help develop other flagship initiatives, particularly if supported by the social impact assessments of the horizontal clause'.

[47] See Kubera and Morozowski (2020), pp. 20–21.

[48] For example, European Parliament Resolution of 20 November 2012, *Towards a genuine Economic and Monetary Union*, Resolution of 21 November 2013, *Strengthening the social dimension of the EMU*.

[49] European Parliament Resolution of 22 October 2014, *The European Semester for economic and policy coordination: implementation of 2014 priorities*, Resolution of 25 November 2014, *Employment and social aspects of the Europe 2020 strategy*.

formulation, since the follow-up of the EU 2020 Strategy should consider the urgent need to make more progress towards poverty reduction and other social targets.[50] Ultimately, the EP also calls for a 'more democratic European Semester', which is a well-established framework for MS to coordinate their fiscal, economic, social and employment policies, as well as to implement the digital and environmental transitions.[51]

30   On the other hand, such integrated vision of the **post-Europe 2020 Strategy** and the precedent 'Troika method' experience have highlighted the necessity of considering not only the **globalisation challenges**, but also the **synergies between EU and Council of Europe's social standards** within a broader Europe, as imposed by Article 151 TFEU and the EUCFR. From this point of view, the ECSR has assessed the 'anti-crisis' legislation adopted in Greece in 2010 following the operations of the Troika in the field of **flexicurity and labour market policy** as well as **flexicurity and pensions**. In both areas, **labour rights**[52] and social security

---

[50] European Parliament Resolution of 11 March 2015, *The European Semester for economic and policy coordination: employment and social aspects in the Annual Growth Survey 2015*.

[51] See European Parliament Resolution of 10 March 2022 *on the European Semester for economic policy coordination: annual sustainable growth survey 2022* (2022/2006(INI)). Particularly, under the heading '*A more democratic European Semester*', the EP: '21. Highlights the importance of engaging in a full debate and properly involving both the national parliaments and the European Parliament in the European Semester process; reiterates its call to strengthen Parliament's democratic role in the economic governance framework and calls on the Council and Commission to take due account of its resolutions. 22. Invites the Commission to keep both Parliament and the Council, as co-legislators, equally well informed on all aspects relating to the application of the EU economic governance framework, including on the preparatory stages; 23. Notes that the Commission, the Council and the President of the Eurogroup should appear regularly before the competent Parliament committee in order to provide information and exchange views on the latest economic and political events; 24. Calls for committed coordination with social partners and other relevant stakeholders at both national and European levels in order to strengthen democratic accountability and transparency'.

[52] In Complaint No. 65/2011 and No. 66/2011, *GENOP-DEI and ADEDY v Greece* (ECSR 23 May 2012), the ECSR declared that the 2010 Greek legislation allowing dismissal without notice or compensation of employees in an open-ended contract during an initial period of 12 months is incompatible with Article 4.4 of the 1961 Social Charter (Complaint No. 65/2011, para 26–28). The Committee also found several violations of the European Social Charter (Articles 4.1, 7.7, 10.2, 12.3) in relation to the domestic provisions (on 'special apprenticeship contracts' for employees aged between 15–18 years) on entitlement to annual holiday with pay, systematic arrangements for apprenticeships and training, as well as social security coverage (Complaint No. 66/2011, para 31, 40, 48, 54, 65 and 69). See also Complaint No. 111/2014, *Greek General Confederation of Labour (GSEE) v Greece* (ECSR 23 March 2017) para 135, 159, 192, 197, 204, 221, 227, 244.

system,⁵³ the Committee found that Greece had violated the European Social Charter.⁵⁴

It appears interesting to add that these decisions of the ECSR on Greek 'anti- 31
crisis legislation' (particularly the five decisions of 7 December 2012 on social cuts affecting pension schemes) have been explicitly applauded by the EP in a Resolution of 13 March 2014,⁵⁵ in which it has strongly criticised the '**Troika method**' on **austerity measures** (which, by the way, is not even so consistent with the recent political-strategic documents concerning the **economic governance** of the EU)⁵⁶ and calls for compliance with these European social legal standards.

Particularly, the criticism from the EP addresses two connecting aspects: Firstly, 32
from a substantial point of view, the Resolution underlines the **synergies between the Council of Europe and EU human rights instruments** (European Social Charter and EU Charter of Fundamental Rights) in terms of *social acquis*.⁵⁷

---

⁵³ In this field, the ECSR adopted on 7 December 2012 five decisions on the merits against Greece [*IKA-ETAM v Greece* (Complaint No. 76/2012) para 78–83, *POPS v Greece* (Complaint No. 77/2012) para 73–78, *I.S.A.P v Greece* (Complaint No. 78/2012) para 73–78, *POS-DEI v Greece* (Complaint No. 79/2012) para 73–78 and *ATE v Greece* (Complaint No. 80/2012) para 73–78] where it considered that although restrictions to the benefits available in a national social security system do not under certain conditions breach the Social Charter, the cumulative effect of restrictions introduced as 'austerity measures', together with the procedures applied to put them into place, amounted to a violation of Article 12.3 (right to social security) of the Charter, by developing the idea of progressiveness and non-regression. Indeed, in spite of the absence of a general clause of progressiveness within the European Social Charter, the case law of the Committee has covered such an absence, see Chatton (2013), pp. 184–185.

⁵⁴ Critical comments about these decisions in Deliyanni-Dimitrakou (2013), Guiglia (2013), Salcedo Beltrán (2013) and Yannaakourou and Tsimpoukis (2014).

⁵⁵ European Parliament Resolution of 13 March 2014 *Employment and social aspects of the role and operations of the Troika (ECB, Commission and IMF) with regard to euro area programme countries*, 2014/2007(INI).

⁵⁶ An interesting approach to the reforms made in the economic governance of the EU by means of both political-strategic documents (such as the Stability and Growth Pact, Europe 2020, the Euro Plus Pact) and the legal provisions of Article 126 TFEU and the excessive deficit procedure; the amendment of Article 136 TFEU and the European Stability Mechanism; the set of six legal instruments commonly known as 'The Six Pack', and the new reinforcing set of two legal instruments commonly known as 'The Two Pack', in Bar Cendón (2012).

⁵⁷ The EP states on this issue: 'having regard to the five decisions of the Council of Europe's European Committee on Social Rights [...] concerning pension schemes in Greece; [...] 26. Recalls that the Council of Europe has already condemned the cuts in the Greek public pension system, considering them to be a violation of Article 12 of the 1961 European Social Charter and of Article 4 of the Protocol thereto, stating that "the fact that the contested provisions of domestic law seek to fulfil the requirements of other legal obligations does not remove them from the ambit of the Charter"; notes that this doctrine of maintaining the pension system at a satisfactory level to allow pensioners a decent life is generally applicable in all four countries (Greece, Portugal, Ireland and Cyprus) and should have been taken into consideration; [...] 39. Calls for compliance with aforementioned legal obligations laid down in the Treaties, and in the Charter of Fundamental Rights, as failure to comply constitutes an infringement of EU primary law; calls on the European Union Agency for Fundamental Rights to assess thoroughly the impact of the measures on human rights and to issue recommendations in case of breaches of the Charter'.

Secondly, from an institutional point of view, the EP expresses once again deep concern on the democratic deficit within the EU.[58] To sum up, apart from the impact on the enjoyment of social rights, the acts adopted by the Troika (alongside the controversial nature and extent of the Stability Pacts[59]) go beyond a mere semantic confusion existing between **openness and transparency in EU Law**, insofar as they challenge the foundations of participation and democracy of the Union.[60]

33 A final conclusion arises, under Article 156 TFEU, from the foregoing considerations. On the one hand, even the obligation according to which the EP 'shall be kept fully informed' is not always respected. On the other hand, especially in the context of the current economic and financial crisis, the weakness of such mere information is parallel to **the weakness of the whole inter-State cooperation**. From this last perspective, developments of Article 156 TFEU are closer to the dynamics of cooperation governing the functioning of the Council of Europe than to the 'typical' EU dynamics of integration. As a result, the **potential equalisation of social standards** will come more **via European jurisprudence**[61] (from the ECJ and the ECtHR, but also and above all, the specific one from the ECSR)[62] **than through European legislative harmonisation**. Ultimately, the **synergies between the EU and the Council of Europe in this social field** are consistent with the so-called '**Turin Process for the European Social Charter**' launched by the Council of Europe in October 2014[63] and, of course, with the reference in Article 156 TFEU to the 'problems arising at national level and on those of concern to international organisations', the pan-European organisation *par excellence* being the Council of Europe.

---

[58] '40. Calls on the Troika and the Member States concerned to end the programmes as soon as possible and to put in place crisis management mechanisms enabling all EU institutions, including Parliament, to achieve the social goals and policies – also those relating to the individual and collective rights of those at greatest risk of social exclusion – set out in the Treaties, in European social partner agreements and in other international obligations (ILO Conventions, the European Social Charter and the European Convention of Human Rights); calls for increased transparency and political ownership in the design and implementation of the adjustment programmes'.

[59] See Kochenov (2014).

[60] Alemanno (2014), p. 75.

[61] Cf. Semmelmann (2010).

[62] See Panzera (2015) and more extensively, Alfonso Mellado et al. (2014).

[63] See Council for Europe, The Turin process for the European Social Charter. Available at http://www.coe.int/en/web/turin-process.

List of Cases

CJEU

CJEU 16.10.2014, C-647/13, Opinion of AG Mengozzi, *Melchior*, ECLI:EU:C:2014:2301 [cit. in para 8]
CJEU 14.10.2020, C-681/18, *KG (Missions successives dans le cadre du travail intérimaire)*, ECLI:EU:C:2020:823 [cit. in para 8]
CJEU 06.10.2021, C-561/19, *Consorzio Italian Management e Catania Multiservizi*, ECLI:EU:C:2021:799 [cit. in para 8]
CJEU 09.09.2021, C-232/20, Opinion of AG Tanchev, *Daimler*, ECLI:EU:C:2021:727 [cit. in para 66, note 8]

ECSR

ECSR 23.05.2012, 65/2011, *General federation of employees of the national electric power corporation and Confederation of Greek Civil Servants' Trade Unions v Greece* [cit. in para 30]
ECSR 23.05.2012, 66/2011, *GENOP-DEI and ADEDY v Greece* [cit. in para 30]
ECSR 07.12.2012, 76/2012, *IKA-ETAM v Greece* [cit. in para 30]
ECSR 07.12.2012, 77/2012, *POPS v Greece* [cit. in para 30]
ECSR 07.12.2012, 78/2012, *I.S.A.P v Greece* [cit. in para 30]
ECSR 07.12.2012, 79/2012, *POS-DEI v Greece* [cit. in para 30]
ECSR 07.12.2012, 80/2012, *ATE v Greece* [cit. in para 30]
ECSR 23.03.2017, 111/2014, *Greek General Confederation of Labour (GSEE) v. Greece* [cit. in para 30]
ECSR 08.09.2021, 150/2017, *European Youth Forum (YFJ) v Belgium* [cit. in para 8]

References[64]

Alemanno, A. (2014). Unpacking the principle of openness in EU Law: Transparency, participation and democracy. *European Law Review, 39*(1), 72–90.
Alfonso Mellado, C. A., Jimena Quesada, L., & Salcedo Beltrán, C. (2014). *La Jurisprudencia del Comité Europeo de Derechos Sociales frente a la crisis económica*. Bomarzo.
Anderson, K. M. (2015). *Social policy in the European Union*. Palgrave Macmillan.
Bar Cendón, A. (2012). La reforma constitucional y la gobernanza económica de la Unión Europea. *Teoría y Realidad Constitucional, 30*, 59–87.
Carrascosa Bermejo, D. (2018). Coordinación de los sistemas nacionales de Seguridad Social. In *Derecho Social de la Unión Europea. Aplicación por el Tribunal de Justicia* (pp. 509–556). Francis Lefebvre.

---

[64] All cited Internet sources have been accessed on 17 February 2023.

Chatton, G. T. (2013). *Vers la pleine reconnaissance des droits économiques, sociaux et culturels.* Schulthess Médias Juridiques/LGDJ.
Corti, F. (2022). *The politicisation of social Europe: Conflict dynamics and welfare integration.* Elgar.
Craig, P. (2010). *The Lisbon Treaty: Law, politics, and treaty reform.* OUP.
De la Rosa, S. (2007). *La méthode ouverte de coordination dans le système juridique communautaire.* Bruylant.
De Schutter, O. (2004). *The implementation of the EU Charter of Fundamental Rights through the open method of coordination.* New York University School of Law, Jean Monnet Working Paper 07/04.
Deliyanni-Dimitrakou, C. (2013). La Charte sociale européenne et les mesures d'austérité grecques: à propos décisions n° 65 et 66/2012 du Comité européen des droits sociaux fondamentaux. *Revue de Droit du Travail, 7*(8), 457–470.
Eliantonio, M., & Stefan, O. (2021). The elusive legitimacy of EU soft law: An analysis of consultation and participation in the process of adopting COVID-19 soft law in the EU. *European Journal of Risk Regulation, 12*(1), 159–175.
Ferrera, M. (2010). Mapping the components of social EU: A critical analysis of the current institutional patchwork. In E. Marlier & D. Natali (Eds.), *Europe 2020. Towards a more social EU?* (pp. 45–64). PIE-Peter Lang.
Fontana, G. (2015). I giudici europei di fronte alla crisi economica. In B. Carusso & G. Fontana (Eds.), *Lavoro e diritti sociali nella crisi europea* (pp. 131–167). Il Mulino.
Grabitz, E., Hilf, M., & Nettesheim, M. (Eds.). (2022). *Das Recht der Europäischen Union: EUV/AEUV.* C.H. Beck.
Guiglia, G. (2013). Il diritto alla sicurezza sociale in tempo di crisi: la Grecia di fronte al Comitato Europeo dei Diritti Sociali. *Diritto Pubblico Comparato et Europeo, IV,* 1414–1416.
Hatzopoulos, V. (2007). Why the open method of coordination is bad for you: A letter to the EU. *European Law Journal, 13*(3), 309–342.
Jimena Quesada, L. (2014). Les obligations positives dans la jurisprudence du Comité européen des Droits sociaux. In *L'homme et le droit. Mélanges en hommage au Professeur Jean-François Flauss* (pp. 429–443). Pedone.
Kochenov, D. (2014). Europe's crisis of values. *Revista catalana de dret públic, 48,* 106–118.
Kubera, J., & Morozowski, T. (2020). The social turn and the potential to reconstruct the social dimension of the European Union. In J. Kubera & T. Morozowski (Eds.), *A 'social turn' in the European Union? New trends and ideas about social convergence in Europe* (pp. 3–29). Routledge.
Lelie, P., & Vanhercke, B. (2013). *Inside the social OMC's learning tools: How "benchmarking social Europe" really worked.* OSE Paper Series, Research Paper No. 10.
Panzera, G. (2015). La 'voce' del Comitato europeo dei diritti sociali. In B. Carusso & G. Fontana (Eds.), *Lavoro e diritti sociali nella crisi europea* (pp. 253–270). Il Mulino.
Rodríguez-Piñero Bravo-Ferrer, M. (2014). Droits sociaux et crise. In *Le travail humain au Carrefour du droit et de la sociologie. Hommage au Professeur Nikitas Aliprantis* (pp. 511–518). Presses universitaires de Strasbourg.
Salazar, C. (2015). La Costituzione, I diritti fondamentali, la crisi: 'Qualcosa di nuovo, anzi d'antico'? In B. Carusso & G. Fontana (Eds.), *Lavoro e diritti sociali nella crisi europea* (pp. 95–129). Il Mulino.
Salcedo Beltrán, C. (2013). Crisis económica, medidas laborales y vulneración de la Carta Social Europea. *Revista Europea de Derechos Fundamentales, 22,* 81–135.
Sebastião, D. (2021). Covid-19: A different economic crisis but the same paradigm of democratic deficit in the EU. *Politics and Governance, 9*(2), 252–264.
Semmelmann, C. (2010). The EU's economic constitution under the Lisbon Treaty: Soul-searching shifts the focus to procedure. *European Law Review, 35*(4), 516–542.
Ştefan, O. (2020). The future of European Union soft law: A research and policy agenda for the aftermath of COVID-19. *Journal of International and Comparative Law, 7*(2), 329–350.

Tajadura Tejada, J. (2014). El principio de solidaridad como fundamento común de los Estados sociales europeos. In M. J. Terol Becerra & L. Jimena Quesada (Eds.), *Tratado sobre Protección de Derechos Sociales* (pp. 89–116). Tirant lo Blanch.

Torres del Moral, A. (2009). Constitucionalización del Estado social. *Revista Europea de Derechos Fundamentales, 13*, 19–65.

Trubek, D. (2005). Hard law and soft law in the construction of social Europe: The role of the open method of co-ordination. *European Law Journal, 11*(3), 343–364.

Vanhercke, B. (2020). From the Lisbon strategy to the European Pillar of Social Rights: The many lives of the Social Open Method of Coordination. In B. Vanhercke et al. (Eds.), *Social policy in the European Union 1999–2019: The long and winding road* (pp. 99–123). OSE ETUI.

Vesan, P., Corti, F., & Sabato, S. (2021). The European Commission's entrepreneurship and the social dimension of the European semester: From the European Pillar of Social Rights to the Covid-19 pandemic. *Comparative European Politics, 19*, 277–295.

Villiers, C. (2006). European integration and globalisation. The experience of financial reporting regulation. In S. MacLeod (Ed.), *Global governance and the quest for justice, Volume II: Corporate governance* (pp. 73–92). Hart Publishing.

von der Groeben, H., Schwarze, J., & Hatje, A. (Eds.). (2015). *Europäisches Unionsrecht* (pp. 1619–1622). Nomos.

Wallace, H. (2001). The institutional setting. Five variations on a theme. In H. Wallace & W. Wallace (Eds.), *Policy making in the European Union* (pp. 3–38). OUP.

Yannaakourou, M., & Tsimpoukis, C. T. (2014). Flexibility without security and deconstruction of collective bargaining: The new paradigm of labour law in Greece. *Comparative Labor Law & Policy Journal, 35*(3), 331–370.

Zietlin, J. (2010). Towards a stronger OMC in a more social Europe 2020: A new governance architecture for EU policy coordination. In E. Marlier & D. Natali (Eds.), *Europe 2020. Towards a more social EU?* (pp. 253–273). PIE-Peter Lang.

Jimena Quesada

Article 157 [Equal Pay Between Men and Women]
(ex-Article 141 TEC)

1. Each Member State shall ensure that the principle of equal pay for male and female workers for equal work or work of equal value is applied.
2. For the purpose of this Article, "pay"[16] means the ordinary basic or minimum wage or salary and any other consideration, whether in cash or in kind, which the worker receives directly or indirectly, in respect of his employment, from his employer.
   Equal pay without discrimination based on sex means:
   (a) that pay for the same work at piece rates shall be calculated on the basis of the same unit of measurement;
   (b) that pay for work at time rates shall be the same for the same job.
3. The European Parliament and the Council, acting in accordance with the ordinary legislative procedure, and after consulting the Economic and Social Committee, shall adopt measures to ensure the application of the principle of equal opportunities and equal treatment of men and women in matters of employment and occupation, including the principle of equal pay for equal work or work of equal value.[4]
4. With a view to ensuring full equality in practice between men and women in working life, the principle of equal treatment shall not prevent any Member State from maintaining or adopting measures providing for specific advantages in order to make it easier for the underrepresented sex to pursue a vocational activity or to prevent or compensate for disadvantages in professional careers.

Protocol (No 33)
concerning Article 157 of the Treaty on the Functioning of the European Union
THE HIGH CONTRACTING PARTIES,
HAVE AGREED upon the following provision, which shall be annexed to the Treaty on European Union and to the Treaty on the Functioning of the European Union:
For the purposes of Article 157 of the Treaty on the Functioning of the European Union, benefits under occupational social security schemes shall not be considered as remuneration if and in so far as they are attributable to periods of employment prior to 17 May 1990, except in the case of workers or those claiming under them who have before that date initiated legal proceedings or introduced an equivalent claim under the applicable national law.

Contents

1. Introduction: The Increasing Interest in Combating the Gender Pay Gap in the European Construction 1
2. The Specific Principle of Equal Pay in a Broader Framework of Tension Between Economic and Social Goals 10
3. Equal Pay for Male and Female Workers as Both a Principle of EU Social Law and a Fundamental Right 22
4. New Challenges in a Broader Social Europe 28

List of Cases
References

1. Introduction: The Increasing Interest in Combating the Gender Pay Gap in the European Construction

1 The current EU has, from its **origins**, put the emphasis on the protection against non-discrimination on grounds of sex in the field of wages. Ex-Article 119 TEEC included likewise the meaning of 'remuneration' (now 'pay'), as well as of the principle of 'equal remuneration without discrimination based on sex'. The **content has practically remained unchanged** in the first two paragraphs of Article 157 TFEU. Then, the 1997 Amsterdam Treaty (Article 141 TEC) added two other paragraphs on legislative procedure and positive measures, which also practically coincide with current paragraphs 3 and 4 of Article 157 TFEU after the entry into force of the Treaty of Lisbon. That new approach introduced by the 1997 Amsterdam Treaty has been of course maintained in Article 23 EUCFR. Finally, a Protocol on Article 157 TFEU has been annexed to the Treaties.

2 The **evolved gender perspective**[1] was a novelty introduced by the Amsterdam Treaty to provide a specific legal basis in the European Treaties in this field, which also aimed at overcoming the restrictive approach established by the ECJ in

---

[1] Cruz Villalón (2018), p. 236: That represents an evolution from a non-discrimination perspective to a positive action approach, in other words, a metamorphosis of gender equality in EU law, see Wobbe (2010), p. 69. In truth, it can be argued that establishing the direct application of equal pay was the first metamorphosis of equality law, see Rust, in von der Groeben et al. (2015), Article 157 AEUV para 169.

Article 157. [Equal Pay Between Men and Women]

Kalanke,[2] which started to be reviewed in *Marschall*[3] concerning a provision similar to that in *Kalanke* but containing a 'saving clause'.[4] Before the *Kalanke* case, the case law of the ECJ was founded in two directives adopted based on ex-Article 119 TEEC,[5] Both directives[6] were then repealed by Directive 2006/54/EC,[7] which consolidates the reaction against the *Kalanke* doctrine.[8]

Indeed, **EU directives prohibit discrimination and promote gender equality** in employment and occupation, in self-employment, in the access to and supply of goods and services and in social security, and lay down rights related to maternity and parental leave. Particularly, the above-mentioned Directive 2006/54/EC guarantees **equal treatment of men and women in access to employment**, including promotion, and to vocational training; working conditions, including pay,[9] and occupational social security schemes. In addition, Commission Recommendation 2014/124/EU aims to strengthen the principle of equal pay between men and women through transparency.[10] In this respect, it is worth mentioning that, in   3

---

[2] Case C-450/93, *Kalanke* (ECJ 17 October 1995) para 17–24: 'Article 2(1) and (4) of Council Directive 76/207/EEC [...] precludes national rules [...] which, where candidates of different sexes shortlisted for promotion are equally qualified, automatically give priority to women in sectors where they are underrepresented, under-representation being deemed to exist when women do not make up at least half of the staff in the individual pay brackets in the relevant personnel group or in the function levels provided for in the organization chart'.

[3] Case C-409/95, *Marschall* (ECJ 11 November 1997) para 30–35: 'A national rule which [...] requires that priority be given to the promotion of female candidates unless reasons specific to an individual male candidate tilt the balance in his favour is not precluded by Article 2(1) and (4) of Council Directive 76/207/EEC [...], provided that: in each individual case the rule provides for male candidates who are equally as qualified as the female candidates a guarantee that the candidatures will be the subject of an objective assessment which will take account of all criteria specific to the candidates and will override the priority accorded to female candidates where one or more of those criteria tilts the balance in favour of the male candidate, and such criteria are not such as to discriminate against the female candidates'.

[4] Hinton (1997), pp. 238–239.

[5] Council Directive 75/117/EEC *on the approximation of the laws of the Member States relating to the application of the principle of equal pay for men and women*, O.J. L 45/19 (1975) as well as Council Directive 76/207/EEC *on the implementation of the principle of equal treatment for men and women as regards access to employment, vocational training and promotion, and working conditions*, O.J. L 39/40 (1976).

[6] A connecting legal act is Council Directive 79/7/EEC *on the progressive implementation of the principle of equal treatment for men and women in matters of social security*, O.J. L 6/24 (1979). In this respect, see Case C-137/94, *Richardson* (ECJ 19 October 1995) para 24–29.

[7] Parliament/Council Directive 2006/54/EC *on the implementation of the principle of equal opportunities and equal treatment of men and women in matters of employment and occupation*, O.J. L 204/23 (2006).

[8] Rodríguez Escanciano (2018), p. 268.

[9] See Case C-335/15, *Ornano* (CJEU 14 July 2016) para 40 and 44.

[10] Commission Recommendation 2014/124/EU *on strengthening the principle of equal pay between men and women through transparency*, O.J. L 69/112 (2014).

March 2021, alongside the Action Plan on the EPSR,[11] the European Commission proposed a new directive on pay transparency and enforcement mechanisms.[12]

4 On the other hand, EU **secondary legislation** in this field includes the following other important directives:

- Directive 79/7/EEC provides for equal treatment of men and women in matters of social security such as statutory social security schemes that provide protection against sickness, invalidity, accidents at work and occupational diseases, unemployment and risks related to old age; and social assistance that supplements or replaces the basic schemes.[13]
- Directive 2004/113/EC guarantees equal treatment between men and women in access to and supply of goods and services.[14]
- Directive 2010/41/EU clarifies that the principle of equal treatment between men and women applies to self-employed workers and where spouses or life partners of a self-employed worker participate in his or her activities.[15]
- Directive 92/85/EEC contains measures to encourage improvements in the safety and health at work of pregnant workers and workers who have recently given birth or who are breastfeeding and establishes the right to maternity leave for the duration of 14 weeks and guarantees protection against dismissal during the period from the beginning of pregnancy to the end of the maternity leave.[16]
- Directive (EU) 2019/1158 establishes the right to parental leave and sets out minimum requirements for that leave (4 months for each parent, at least 1 month of which cannot be transferred to the other parent) as well as protection of

---

[11] In the 2021 Action Plan on the EPSR, it is emphasised that adequate work-life balance policies facilitate conciliation of work and private life. Particularly, the provision of paid leave 'can contribute to reducing the gender employment gap. The level and design of parental benefits, and the possibility to share the leave equally between men and women are also important in this context. In line with the Work-Life Balance Directive, the EU will continue to promote equal sharing of care and work responsibilities. The availability of affordable and high-quality early childhood education and care (ECEC) as well as long-term care of good quality have strong positive impact on the employment situation of parents and in particular women and is an important determinant of the gender pay and pension gap'.

[12] Proposal for a Directive *to strengthen the application of the principle of equal pay for equal work or work of equal value between men and women through pay transparency and enforcement mechanisms*, COM(2021) 93 final.

[13] Council Directive 79/7/EEC *on the progressive implementation of the principle of equal treatment for men and women in matters of social security*, O.J. L 6/24 (1979).

[14] Council Directive 2004/113/EC *implementing the principle of equal treatment between men and women in the access to and supply of goods and services*, O.J. L 373/37 (2004).

[15] Parliament/Council Directive 2010/41/EU *on the application of the principle of equal treatment between men and women engaged in an activity in a self-employed capacity*, O.J. L 180/1 (2010).

[16] Council Directive 92/85/EEC *on the introduction of measures to encourage improvements in the safety and health at work of pregnant workers and workers who have recently given birth or are breastfeeding (tenth individual Directive within the meaning of Article 16 (1) of Directive 89/391/EEC)*, O.J. L 348/1 (1992).

employment rights and when returning to work and the right to leave from work on grounds of force majeure.[17]

Article 2.1 point (b) of the Equal Treatment Directive 2006/54/EC defines **indirect discrimination** as a situation 'where an apparently neutral provision, criterion or practice would put persons of one sex at a particular disadvantage compared with persons of the other sex, unless that provision, criterion or practice is objectively justified by a legitimate aim, and the means of achieving that aim are appropriate and necessary'. Indeed, the delimitation between direct and indirect discrimination is legally significant above all because the possibilities of justification differ according to whether unequal treatment is directly or indirectly linked to sex.

The ECJ has held that there is **direct**—and not only indirect **discrimination— based on sex** where an employer's actions are linked to the existence or absence of a pregnancy, as pregnancy is inseparably linked to a female employee's sex.[18] In this regard, as highlighted by AG *Kokott* in her Opinion in *Kleist*, '[Article 2.1 point (b) of the Equal Treatment Directive 2006/54/EC] sets out in a very general manner the possibilities of justifying *indirect unequal treatment* on the grounds of sex ("objectively justified by a legitimate aim"), whereas *direct unequal treatment* on the grounds of sex can be **justified** only by special requirements specific to one sex – for example as regards pregnancy and maternity [Article 2.2 of Directive 2006/54/EC] – or by the objective of **assisting the underrepresented sex** [Article 3 of Directive 2006/54/EC in conjunction with now Article 157.4 TFEU]'.[19]

In any case, the *Kalanke* judgment gave rise to a great deal of controversy throughout Europe because of the uncertainty it created in respect of the **legitimacy of quotas** and other **forms of positive action** aimed at increasing the number of women employed in certain sectors or at certain levels where they were underrepresented. In this context, the Commission[20] took the view that the Court had only condemned the special feature of the Bremen law which automatically gave women an absolute and unconditional right to appointment or promotion over men in sectors where they were under-represented provided their qualifications were the same. The Commission considered that the only type of quota system which was unlawful was one which is completely rigid and does not leave open any possibility to take account of individual circumstances. MS and employers would be thus free to have recourse to all other forms of positive action, including flexible quotas.

---

[17] Parliament/Council Directive (EU) 2019/1158 *on work-life balance for parents and carers*, O.J. L 188/79 (2019).

[18] See Case C-177/88, *Dekker* (ECJ 8 November 1990) para 12 and 17; Case C-179/88, *Handelsog Kontorfunktionærernes Forbund* (ECJ 8 November 1990) para 13; Case C-320/01, *Busch* (ECJ 27 February 2003) para 39; and Case C-116/06, *Kiiski* (ECJ 20 September 2007) para 55.

[19] Case C-356/09, *Kleist* (Opinion of AG Kokott of 16 September 2010) para 33 (emphasis in the original).

[20] Commission Communication *on the interpretation of the Judgment of the Court of Justice on 17 October 1995 in Case C-450/93, Kalanke v Freie Hansestadt Bremen*, COM(96) 88 final.

8   The Commission proposed to amend Article 2.4 of Council Directive 76/207/EEC, which specified that the measures envisaged by this provision included actions favouring the recruitment or promotion of one sex in circumstances where the latter were under-represented, on condition that the employer always had the possibility of taking account of the particular circumstances of a given case to specifically permit the kinds of positive action which remained untouched by *Kalanke*. In the Commission's view, 'such an amendment would make it clear that positive action measures short of rigid quotas are permitted by Community law and would ensure that the text of the Directive reflects more clearly the true legal position which results from the judgement of the Court'.

9   On the other hand, in the annex to this Communication, the Commission included examples of the type of **positive action measures** which (according to it) remained untouched by the *Kalanke* judgement:

- Quotas linked to the qualifications required for the job, as long as they allow account to be taken of particular circumstances which might, in a given case, justify an exception to the principle of giving preference to the under-represented sex;
- Plans for promoting women, prescribing the proportions and the time limits within which the number of women should be increased but without imposing an automatic preference rule when individual decisions on recruitment and promotion are taken;
- An obligation of principle for an employer to recruit or promote by preference a person belonging to the under-represented sex; in such a case, no individual right to be preferred is conferred on any person;
- Reductions of social security contributions which are granted to firms when they recruit women who return to the labour market, to perform tasks in sectors where women are under-represented;
- State subventions granted to employers who recruit women in sectors where they are under-represented;
- Other positive action measures focusing on training, professional orientation, the reorganisation of working time, child-care and so on.

2. The Specific Principle of Equal Pay in a Broader Framework of Tension Between Economic and Social Goals

10   It is obvious that the principle of equal pay is a specific manifestation of the principle of **equal treatment between women and men** and, more generally, of the principle of equality, which is always subject to the broad category of 'objective justification'.[21] At the same time, in the famous judgment in *Defrenne*, in which the

---

[21] See for example Case C-236/09, *Association belge des Consommateurs Test-Achats and Others* (CJEU 1 March 2011) para 28.

application of the principle of equal pay for men and women was at stake,[22] the ECJ held that this provision pursued 'a double aim, which is at once economic and social': first, 'in the light of the different stages of the development of social legislation in the various Member States, the aim of [Article 157 TFEU] is to avoid a situation in which undertakings established in states which have actually implemented the principle of equal pay suffer a **competitive disadvantage** in intra-community competition as compared with undertakings established in states which have not yet eliminated discrimination against women workers as regards pay'; and second, 'this provision forms part of the social objectives of the community, which is not merely an economic union, but is at the same time intended, by common action, to ensure **social progress** and seek the constant improvement of the living and working conditions of their peoples, as is emphasized by the Preamble to the Treaty', and accentuated by the insertion of ex-Article 119 TEEC (Article 157 TFEU) into the block devoted to social policy.[23]

In addition, the ECJ already held in *Defrenne* that ex-Article 119 TEEC was of such a character as to have not only **vertical effect** (enforceable not merely between individuals and public authorities), but also a **horizontal effect** (between individuals, *Drittwirkung* approach).[24] This case law has been recently confirmed by the CJEU in relation to Article 157 TFEU, which 'must be interpreted as having direct effect in proceedings between individuals in which failure to observe the principle of equal pay for male and female workers for work of equal value'.[25] Of course, the EU's action has also focused on the application of the principle of equal treatment between men and women engaged in a self-employed capacity, including the main original economic sector (agriculture);[26] consequently, 'it is beyond question that Member States are bound by the principle of equal treatment in the application and implementation of EU agricultural law'.[27]   11

On the other hand, the tension between economic and social goals within the EU cannot be an obstacle to the collaboration of the MS with the social partners to continue to address the problem of the continuing gender-based wage differentials and marked gender segregation on the labour market by means of flexible working   12

---

[22] Under Belgian law, female flight attendants were obliged to retire at the age of 40, unlike their male counterparts. Mrs Defrenne complained that the lower pension rights this entailed violated her right to equal treatment on grounds of gender under Article 119 TEEC.

[23] Case-43/75, *Defrenne II* (ECJ 8 April 1976) para 9–12.

[24] Case-43/75, *Defrenne II* (ECJ 8 April 1976) para 39. See the case law of the ECJ in De Mol (2011). The author focused on the 'sensitive issue' of the application of the EU principle of non-discrimination in private disputes in the light of recent cases, especially, Case C-144/04, *Mangold* (ECJ 22 November 2005) para 65 and 77, and Case C-555/07, *Kücükdeveci* (CJEU 19 January 2010) para 28 and 43.

[25] Case C-624/19, *Tesco Stores* (CJEU 3 June 2021) para 39.

[26] See now Article 17 of Parliament/Council Directive 2010/41/EU *on the application of the principle of equal treatment between men and women engaged in an activity in a self-employed capacity*, O.J. L 180/1 (2010).

[27] Case C-401/11, *Blanka Soukupová* (Opinion of AG Jääskinen of 23 October 2012) para 54.

time arrangements which enable both men and women to **combine family and work commitments** more successfully, also in conformity with Article 33 EUCFR (family and professional life). In this sense, **part-time work** constitutes a kind of a **pilot situation** in order to verify, as foreseen in Article 157.2 TFEU, not only the specific 'principle of equal pay for equal work or work of equal value' and, as a result, the combat against gender pay gap, but also a broader framework ensuring 'the application of the principle of equal opportunities and equal treatment of men and women in matters of employment and occupation, including the principle of equal pay for equal work or work of equal value'.

13   In addition, the Covid-19 pandemic has accentuated the evolution of work from the traditional platform to the **digital platform** and has called for a diversification in the EU legislation to adjust the labour and social protection for **gig economy workers**. A recent EU directive in this field focuses on providing minimum rights to platform workers, zero-hour contract workers and vouchers, as a first step towards ensuring a balance between flexibility and security for workers in the digital economy.[28] The 2021 Action Plan on the EPSR has also paid attention to this challenge.[29] However, social protection in most of the EU MS focuses primarily on fulltime workers or full-time open-ended contracts. Therefore, when it comes to the social protection of women in the labour market, they end up facing 'a three-layered discrimination based on gender, race and the precarious nature of their work', including the gender pay gap in the gig economy.[30]

14   At the same time, alongside the **accelerated digitalisation of workplaces** and the related challenges of algorithmic decision-making (notably the use of **artificial intelligence** and the risks of biased decisions, discrimination and lack of transparency), the 2021 Action Plan on the EPSR has also put the accent in **telework** as the

---

[28] Parliament/Council Directive (EU) 2019/1152 *on transparent and predictable working conditions in the European Union*, O.J. L 186/105 (2019).

[29] The 2021 Action Plan recalls that a case in point is the emergence of vulnerable self-employed working through platforms and operating under precarious conditions. The pandemic has highlighted this for delivery workers, particularly on their access to social protection, and health and safety risks. The Commission is therefore gathering evidence on the working conditions particularly of people working through platforms. In June 2020, the Commission also launched an initiative to ensure that EU competition law does not stand in the way of improving working conditions through collective agreements for the self-employed who need it: https://ec.europa.eu/commission/presscorner/detail/en/IP_20_1237 and https://ec.europa.eu/commission/presscorner/detail/en/mex_21_23. On the other hand, in line with Article 154 TFEU, in February 2021, the Commission launched a social partners' consultation on the possible direction of EU action 32: C (2021) 1127 final of 24 February 2021.

[30] Vyas (2021), pp. 39–40. From this point of view, 'the question of the gender pay gap is still an issue even in the traditional labour market and will now have to be addressed in respect of digital platforms as well. There is a possibility that female workers can fare better on digital platforms but the profiling of the workers takes into consideration the gender and age of workers, which might lead to inherent gender discrimination. Despite anonymity, there are certain male-dominated and advanced technological roles for which women are not preferred. This leads to discrimination on digital platforms and makes women vulnerable, thereby resulting in stagnation of the position of women when it comes to the gender pay gap' (Vyas (2021), p. 48).

norm for many because of the pandemic. Telework has been crucial for **business continuity** as well as for a more flexible organisation of **professional and private life**. From this last perspective, telework offers efficiencies on work-life balance, but generalised teleworking raises the need to reflect on the boundaries of contractual working time in conjunction with other pressing social needs, such as protecting the **right to disconnect** and safeguarding equal pay between women and men.[31]

In this framework, the ECJ's case law has dealt with specific controversies concerning the interpretation and application of the European **Framework Agreement on part-time work** concluded by UNICE, CEEP and the ETUC on 6 June 1997.[32] Particularly, one of the objectives of the agreement is 'to provide for the removal of discrimination against part-time workers and to improve the quality of part-time work' [Clause 1 point (a)] and, consequently, it provides that 'in respect of employment conditions, part-time workers shall not be treated in a less favourable manner than comparable full-time workers solely because they work part time unless different treatment is justified on objective grounds. Where appropriate, the principle of *pro rata temporis* shall apply' (Clause 4).[33] Such application of different treatments implies to assess whether they take the form of 'pay' or not and, on the other hand, they are justified or not under a non-discriminatory and gender perspective.

15

Concerning the first criterion, according to settled ECJ's case law, under Article 157.2 TFEU **'pay'** means the **ordinary basic or minimum wage or salary and any other consideration**, whether in cash or in kind, which the worker receives directly or indirectly, in respect of his employment, from his employer. That concept covers any consideration, whether immediate or future, which the worker receives it, albeit indirectly, in respect of his employment, from his employer.[34] In that context, the ECJ has explained that the legal nature of that consideration is not important for the purposes of the application of Article 157 TFEU provided that it is granted in respect of the employment.[35] The ECJ has also held that, although it is true that many advantages granted by an employer also reflect considerations of social policy, the fact that a benefit is in the nature of pay cannot be called in question where the worker is entitled to receive the benefit in question from his employer by reason of the existence of the employment relationship.[36] By contrast,

16

---

[31] The 2021 Action Plan on the EPSR mentions several initiatives in this field, such as European Parliament Resolution of 21 January 2021 with recommendations to the Commission *on the right to disconnect* (2019/2181(INL)).

[32] Annexed to Council Directive 97/81/EC *concerning the Framework Agreement on part-time work concluded by UNICE, CEEP and the ETUC*, O.J. L 14/9 (1998).

[33] See Case C-354/16, *Kleinsteuber* (CJEU 13 July 2017) para 47 and 66.

[34] Joined Cases C-216/12 and C-217/12, *Hliddal and Bornand* (CJEU 19 September 2013) para 41 and the case law cited therein.

[35] Case C-281/97, *Krüger* (ECJ 9 September 1999) para 16.

[36] Case C-262/88, *Barber* (ECJ 17 May 1990) para 18.

17 in other cases, the ECJ has classified other concepts not as 'pay' but as 'social security benefits' outside the scope of Article 157 TFEU.[37]

In respect of the second criterion, the ECJ has already applied the principle of *pro rata temporis* to other benefits payable by the employer and related to a part-time employment relationship. Thus, the ECJ has considered that, in the case of **part-time employment**, EU law does not preclude a retirement pension being calculated *pro rata temporis* in the case of part-time employment,[38] nor does it preclude paid annual leave from being calculated in accordance with the same principle.[39] In the cases giving rise to those judgments, taking account of the reduced working time as compared with that of a full-time worker constituted an objective criterion **allowing a proportionate reduction** of the rights of the workers concerned.[40]

18 On the contrary, the ECJ has considered in breach of EU law the legislation of an MS which requires a **proportionally greater contribution period from part-time workers**, the vast majority of whom are women, than from full-time workers for the former to qualify, if appropriate, for a contributory retirement pension in an amount reduced in proportion to the part-time nature of their work. Particularly, in *Elbal Moreno* the Court concluded that there was an **indirect discrimination** on grounds of sex, since the national measure at issue, albeit formulated in neutral terms, worked to the disadvantage of far more women than men.[41] In such circumstances, it was an indisputable statistical fact that legislation such as that at issue affected women far more than men, given that, in Spain, at least 80% of part-time workers were women.

---

[37] Specifically, in relation to a career break allowance granted, subject to certain conditions, to a worker taking a break from his or her career using parental leave, the ECJ has held that that type of benefit must be treated as a family benefit: Case C-469/02, *Commission v Belgium* (ECJ 7 September 2004) para 16. Similarly, a parental leave allowance has not been classified as 'pay' within the meaning of Article 157 TFEU, but as a social security benefit with the characteristics of a 'family benefit' within the meaning of Parliament/Council Regulation (EC) No. 883/2004 *on the coordination of social security systems*, O.J. L 166/1 (2004): Joined Cases C-216/12 and C-217/12, *Hliddal* (CJEU 19 September 2013) para 59. See also (as excluding social security or social protection schemes, the benefits of which are not equivalent to 'pay' within the meaning given to that term for the application of Article 157(2) TFEU) Case C-312/17, *Bedi* (CJEU 19 September 2018) para 30.

[38] Joined Cases C-4/02 and C-5/02, *Schönheit and Becker* (ECJ 23 October 2003) para 90 and 91.

[39] See, to that effect, Case C-486/08, *Zentralbetriebsrat der Landeskrankenhäuser Tirols* (CJEU 22 April 2010) para 33, and Case C-229/11, *Heimann and Toltschin* (CJEU 8 November 2012) para 36.

[40] See also Case C-476/12, *Österreichischer Gewerkschaftsbund* (CJEU 5 November 2014) para 21–25, concerning the justification of a dependent child allowance paid based on the collective agreement applicable to bank staff and bankers being calculated to part-time workers in accordance with the principle of *pro rata temporis*.

[41] Case C-385/11, *Elbal Moreno* (CJEU 22 November 2012) para 29–30. See also Case C-527/13, *Cachaldora Fernández* (CJEU 14 April 2015) para 28, Case C-98/15, *Espadas Recio* (CJEU 9 November 2017) para 38, and Case 486/18, *Praxair MRC* (CJEU 8 May 2019) para 79–87.

Only in **exceptional cases**, the principle of equal pay for male and female workers has been unduly broken **in favour of women**. This situation is illustrated by the Case *Leone* concerning the interpretation of Article 157 TFEU in relation to a claim for compensation for the loss incurred by them as a result of the refusal by the CNRACL[42] to grant Mr Leone early retirement with immediate payment of pension and a service credit for the purposes of calculating his pension. The fact is that the apparent neutrality of the national measures at stake implied an indirect discrimination, since there were in practice advantages benefiting mainly female civil servants.[43]

From this point of view, in the 2021 Action Plan on the EPSR[44] it is announced that the Commission will also map best practices in providing **pension rights for care-related career breaks** in pension schemes and promote the exchange of practices among MS, social partners and pension stakeholders.[45] Such practices become even more important when the CJEU's case law excludes from the current stage of EU law certain controversial issues raised by national legislation. Among these issues, it is worth noticing:

- the employer's refusal to grant an employee the right to work at a fixed schedule to care for his or her children in the framework of an employment relationship where the employer uses a shift work system;[46]
- the annual adjustment of retirement pensions of civil servants in the light of Protocol No. 33 concerning Article 157 TFEU;[47]

---

[42] Caisse nationale de retraite des agents des collectivités locales (National pension fund for local community civil servants).

[43] Case C-173/13, *Leone* (CJEU 17 July 2014) para 44–47.

[44] COM(2021) 102 final of 4 March 2021.

[45] The Commission has also put forward ambitious strategies for a *Union of Equality*, with which synergies will be created to give equal opportunities to all: among others, the EU Anti-racism Action Plan 2020–2025, COM (2020) 565 final; the EU Roma strategic framework for equality, inclusion and participation for 2020–2030, COM(2020) 620 final; the Action Plan on Integration and Inclusion, COM(2020) 758 final; the LGBTIQ Equality Strategy, COM(2020) 698 final.

[46] See Case C-366/18, *Ortiz Mesonero* (CJEU 18 September 2019) para 39–40 and 48. The national legislation at dispute made the granting of parental leave conditional on a reduction in working time, with a proportional reduction in pay. The referring court suggested (referring in its question to Articles 8, 10 and 157 TFEU and Article 3 TEU, as well as Directive 2010/18 and Articles 23 and 33.2 EUCFR) that such national rule implied indirect discrimination against female workers, However, the CJEU noted that 'neither Directive 2010/18 nor the Framework Agreement on parental leave contain any provision which would require Member States, in the context of a request for parental leave, to grant the applicant the right to work a fixed working time when his usual pattern of work is shift work with variable hours' (para 48) and concluded that 'Council Directive 2010/18/EU of 8 March 2010 implementing the revised Framework Agreement on parental leave concluded by BUSINESSEUROPE, UEAPME, CEEP and ETUC and repealing Directive 96/34/EC must be interpreted as not applying to national legislation, such as that at issue in the main proceedings, (...)'. The same conclusion seems to be extended to the current Directive (EU) 2019/1158 in light of its Articles 3(2) *in fine* and 9 (flexible working arrangements).

[47] Case C-405/20, *BVAEB* (CJEU 5 May 2022) para 69.

- a national collective agreement which reserves to female workers who bring up their child on their own the right to leave after the expiry of the statutory maternity leave, provided that such leave is intended to protect workers in connection with the effects of pregnancy and motherhood.[48]

21 Finally, it must be added that, under Article 157(4) TFEU, to ensure **full equality in practice** between men and women in working life, the principle of equal treatment must not prevent any MS from maintaining or adopting measures providing for specific advantages to make it easier for the **under-represented** sex to pursue a vocational activity or to **prevent or compensate for disadvantages** in professional careers. However, that provision cannot be applied to national legislation which makes provision for the right to a pension supplement for women who have had at least two biological or adopted children and who are in receipt of contributory permanent incapacity pensions under a scheme within the national social security system, while men in an identical situation do not have a right to such a pension supplement. In other words, such difference constitutes **direct discrimination** on grounds of sex and is, therefore, prohibited by EU law.[49] The CJEU had also found direct discrimination on grounds of sex and contrary to Article 157 TFEU as regards the Polish legislation establishing different retirement ages for men and women holding the position of judge of the ordinary courts or of the Supreme Court or that of the public prosecutor in Poland.[50] The same can be said in relation to national legislation which treats differently persons who have changed gender after marrying and persons who have kept their birth gender and are married, with regard to the age of entitlement to a state retirement pension.[51]

3. Equal Pay for Male and Female Workers as Both a Principle of EU Social Law and a Fundamental Right

22 In light of the precedent considerations, it is obvious that equal pay for male and female workers is **a principle of European social law** which is set out in Article 157 TFEU as one that 'forms part of the foundations of the Community'[52] and it is actually the key employment law provision on equal treatment.[53] On the other hand, such particular principle is consistent with the general one established in Article 8 TFEU as well as with the powers conferred to EU institutions 'to combat discrimination based on sex' (Article 19 TFEU). In parallel, it has been confirmed

---

[48] Case C-463/19, *Syndicat CFTC* (CJEU 18 November 2020) para 74.

[49] Case C-450/18, *Instituto Nacional de la Seguridad Social* (CJEU 12 December 2019) para 64–67.

[50] Case C-192/18, *Commission v Poland* (CJEU 5 November 2019) para 77–78.

[51] Case C-451/16, *MB* (CJEU 28 June 2018) para 50–53.

[52] Case 43/75, *Defrenne II* (ECJ 8 April 1976) para 12 and, more recently, Case C-624/19, *Tesco Stores* (CJEU 3 June 2021) para 33–39, and Case C-405/20, *BVAEB* (CJEU 5 May 2022) para 39.

[53] Krebber, in Calliess and Ruffert (2022), Article 157 AEUV para 1.

by Article 23 EUCFR, in the form of the right not to be discriminated against on grounds of sex in the area of pay, which makes more concrete the general **fundamental right** not to be discriminated against set forth in Article 21 EUCFR. Lastly, the adoption of **compensatory measures** reinstating equal treatment throughout **retroactive levelling down** (e.g. retroactive equalisation of retirement pension benefits for the male and female members of a private occupational retirement pension scheme to the normal pension age of the persons previously disadvantaged) can be interpreted, in the absence of an objective justification, as contrary to Article 157 TFEU.[54] Otherwise said, **levelling up** is to be considered more consistent with the *favor libertatis* **principle**.

From this double perspective (principle and fundamental right), the issue of indirect discrimination has improved the assessment of controversial situations under the '**test of equality**'. The ECJ's case law may be summarised by referring to *Margaret Kenny and Others*.[55] According to this ruling, the main interpretative criteria dealing with the principle of equal pay for men and women are the following:

– employees perform the same work or work to which equal value can be attributed if, taking account of a number of factors such as the nature of the work, the training requirements and the working conditions, those persons can be considered to be in a **comparable situation**, which it is a matter for the national court to ascertain;
– in relation to indirect pay discrimination, it is for the employer to establish **objective justification for the difference** in pay between the workers who consider that they have been discriminated against and the comparators;
– the employer's justification for the difference in pay, which is evidence of a prima facie case of gender discrimination, must relate to the **comparators** who, on account of the fact that their situation is described by **valid statistics** which cover enough individuals, do not illustrate purely fortuitous or short-term phenomena, and which, generally appear to be significant, have been considered by the referring court in establishing that difference, and
– the interests of good industrial relations may be taken into consideration by the national court as one factor among others in its assessment of whether differences between the pay of two groups of workers are due to objective factors unrelated to any discrimination on grounds of sex and are compatible with the **principle of proportionality**.

In any case, one of the main difficulties in this field has to do, not only with the evidential value of statistics adduced in proceedings to demonstrate the existence of discrimination or the burden of persuasion that a discriminatory situation exists

---

[54] Case C-171/18, *Safeway* (CJEU 7 October 2019) para 45.
[55] Case C-427/11, *Margaret Kenny and Others* (CJEU 28 February 2013) para 19–20 and 52.

(within a complex structure of alternating the **burden of proof**),[56] but above all with the identification of a valid comparator demonstrating the existence of a group of persons who, in an equivalent situation, receive different treatment in terms of their rates of pay.

25   With such parameters and in accordance with the ECJ's case law, it is true that these are questions that fall to the domestic courts to resolve. In other words, it is *prima facie* for domestic jurisdictions to assess the **weight of statistics**, the alternative articulation of shifts of a proof burden from one party to the other and the **weight of the comparator** to determine whether the principle of equal pay for male and female workers has been infringed.[57]

26   Nonetheless, these European criteria are still not sufficient to palliate gender discrimination in pay, since from the **ECJ's case law** the **comparator** seems to be **circumscribed to the same undertaking,** as confirmed in June 2021 in the case of *Tesco Stores Ltd*.[58] With such a limit, it will be difficult for the national court to reach the firm conviction that, in accordance with the applicable rules of evidence under national procedural law and in the light of the European case law, there is an unequivocally representative number of male workers who perform (within the same undertaking) the same tasks as female workers and, nevertheless, the latter are paid at a lower rate.

27   For these reasons, one of the main challenges in this field is, from the European case law perspective, to provide the national courts with more elements and tools to give full effect to the principle of equal pay for male and female workers. To this purpose, the impact of the '**horizontal social clause**' (Article 9 TFEU) must be considered.[59] With such a philosophy, the solution to the problematic gender inequality situation may be improved by adopting a broader social Europe approach, as analysed in the following section. On the other hand, the synergies of European law with other possibly more favourable international standards cannot be underestimated, mainly the recent General Comment No. 23 (2015) on the right to just and favourable conditions of work (Article 7 of the International Covenant

---

[56] Cf. Case C-427/11, *Margaret Kenny and Others* (Opinion of AG Cruz Villalón of 29 November 2012) para 47, 51, in which the AG recalls this complex structure according to which the burden of proof remains in principle on the worker as regards liability, but it would be reasonable to shift the burden back to the employer once liability has been established.

[57] On the obligations incumbent of MS, including their courts, where discrimination infringing EU law has been found, see for example Case C-399/09, *Landtová* (CJEU 22 June 2011) para 51 and the case law cited therein. See also Joined Cases C-231/06 to C-233/06, *Jonkman and Others* (ECJ 21 June 2007) para 36–40.

[58] Case C-624/19, *Tesco Stores* (CJEU 3 June 2021) para 37: 'it must be held that Article 157 TFEU may be relied upon before national courts in proceedings concerning work of equal value carried out by workers of different sex having the same employer and in different establishments of that employer, provided that the latter constitutes such a single source'.

[59] According to Vielle (2012), p. 105, there will be numerous and regular opportunities to invoke the new horizontal social clause in the national courts and the ECJ to reiterate the social aims of the Treaty, including on those occasions when economic freedoms enshrined in this same Treaty are subject to examination.

on Economic, Social and Cultural Rights),[60] where it is recalled that 'the level of wages in many parts of the world remains low and the gender pay gap is a persistent and global problem', as well as that 'progress on the three key interrelated indicator for gender equality in the context of labour rights – the "glass ceiling," the "gender pay gap" and the "sticky floor" remains far from satisfactory'.[61]

4. New Challenges in a Broader Social Europe

Alongside the major substantial challenge (the 'traditional' existence of gender wage gap), it is necessary to face it—in conjunction—with other **two important procedural challenges**: first, the role of social partners and relevant organisations of civil society in salary negotiations; and second, the extension of the scope of the valid comparator beyond the same undertaking to make easier the protective role of national judges. In both aspects, the synergies between the EU and the Council of Europe in a broader social Europe are essential.[62]

28

Concerning the first aspect, it implies **greater involvement of social partners**, since several studies have revealed the persistent **disadvantage that women have at the bargaining table**.[63] In this sense, as argued by AG *Cruz Villalón* in *Prigge and Others*[64] and recalled in his Opinion in *Margaret Kenny and Others*, 'autonomy in collective bargaining deserves proper protection at the EU level' and, 'evidently, part of ensuring the proper levels of protection is respect for the principle of equality [and] the right not to be discriminated against on grounds of sex in the area of pay'. In addition, he pointed out that 'extensive case-law has held that collective agreements are not excluded from the scope of the provisions relating to the freedoms protected under the Treaty and, in particular, that the principle of non-discrimination between male and female workers in terms of pay, as set out in the Treaties [Article 157 TFEU] and in secondary legislation, applies to collective agreements because it is mandatory'.[65]

29

---

[60] De Schutter and Jimena Quesada (2019), p. 210.

[61] Committee on Economic, Social and Cultural Rights, General Comment No. 23 (E/C.12/GC/23, 27 April 2016) para 2 and 47. See also para 62.

[62] From another perspective, the Commission is stepping up its efforts to combat violence against women and is working towards the EU's accession to the Council of Europe Convention on preventing and combating violence against women (the 2011 Istanbul Convention) based on its proposal for a Council Decision *on the signing, on behalf of the European Union, of the Council of Europe Convention on preventing and combating violence against women and domestic violence*, COM(2016) 111. The signature of this Convention by the EU (on 13 June 2017) has not yet been followed by ratification.

[63] Another interesting issue under the gender perspective in Romero Rodenas and Bogoni (2009).

[64] Case C-447/09, *Prigge and Others* (Opinion of AG Cruz Villalón of 19 May 2011) para 41–46.

[65] Case C-427/11, *Margaret Kenny and Others* (Opinion of AG Cruz Villalón of 29 November 2012) para 64–65.

30 From this perspective, it has been criticised in doctrine that the European regulatory landscape has changed to one relying heavily on **soft law approaches** and with more limited ambitions in the field of gender equality than at the creation of the European Employment Strategy in 1997. In this environment the European Commission has placed greater emphasis on the role of social partners in addressing the gender pay gap.[66] However, at the same time, the tensions within the EU's 'governance architecture' concerning pay equality have shown, on the one hand, the inconsistencies between the architecture of the antidiscrimination framework (established following the EU's old governance-by-law approach) and the assessment of equal pay public policy measures (in the context of the EU's new governance-by-numbers approach). On the other hand, a second empirical field enables an assessment of the tensions within the EU's new governance system itself, specifically between the approach in the area of equal pay and in the area of economic policy, with specific regard to the participatory role of the social partners in tackling the gender pay gap.[67]

31 In the same vein, such a perception is also somehow confirmed in the context of the **Council of Europe** if we consider that the so-called '**participatory status**' (not a mere 'consultative' one) of the organisations (**social partners and NGOs**)[68] entitled to submit complaints collective complaints before the ECSR has been very recently activated in cases of a gender pay gap.[69] Particularly, fifteen complaints (No. 124/2016 to No. 138/2016) were registered by 'University Women of Europe' (UWE) on 24 August 2016 (respectively, against Belgium, Bulgaria, Croatia, Cyprus, Czech Republic, Finland, France, Greece, Ireland, Italy, the Netherlands, Norway, Portugal, Slovenia and Sweden). The complaints related to Articles 1 (right to work), 4(3) (right to a fair remuneration—non-discrimination between women and men with respect to remuneration) and 20 (right to equal opportunities and treatment in employment and occupation without sex discrimination) in conjunction with Article E (non-discrimination) of the 1996 Revised ESC

---

[66] Smith (2012) and Deakin et al. (2015).

[67] Peruzzi (2015), pp. 441–465, if the role of the social partners is emphasised in several policy documents, the potentialities of their action are seriously jeopardised by the push for decentralisation of collective bargaining, aimed at anchoring wages to productivity, fostered by the EU's governance reforms responding to the crisis, particularly by the Euro Plus Pact and by the 'six-pack' regulations of 2011. He confirms a narrowing down of pay equality in the context of an EU flexibility-centred and neoliberalist political perspective.

[68] It is also important that the Union supports intermediary players such as NGOs, social partners and equality bodies to improve their capacity to combat discrimination.

[69] See the list of the collective complaints and of the organisations entitle to submit them on the official website of the Council of Europe. Available at https://www.coe.int/en/web/european-social-charter.

(or equivalent provisions of the 1961 ESC).[70] The decisions on the merits were adopted by the ECSR on 5 and 6 December 2019.[71]

In these decisions, the ECSR emphasises the need to recognise **the right to equal pay in national legislation**, the **right to an adequate and effective remedy** in case of alleged wage discrimination, the **obligation to ensure wage transparency** and the **possibility of making job comparisons**. States must also promote the establishment of **independent equality bodies with adequate resources and a strong mandate**. To ensure and promote equal pay, the ECSR finds that the **collection of high-quality pay statistics** broken down by gender as well as statistics on the number and type of pay discrimination cases are crucial. The collection of such data increases **pay transparency** at aggregate levels and ultimately uncovers the cases of unequal pay and therefore the gender pay gap. Other measures, such as adoption and implementation of **national action plans** for employment which effectively ensure equality between women and men, including pay, or to require individual undertakings to draw up **enterprise or company plans** to secure equal pay or the **inclusion of equality issues in collective agreements**, are also mentioned among the criteria. The ECSR also points out the importance of taking measures to ensure a **balanced representation of women in decision-making positions in private companies**. **32**

It must be recalled that the UWE decisions were adopted in December 2019, before the outbreak of Covid-19 pandemic and were made public just between the **33**

---

[70] See Kollonay-Lehoczky (2017), p. 510: Although not mentioned in the EUCFR Explanations, Article E of the Revised ESC can play an important role in interpreting the anti-discrimination content of the provisions in Articles 21–26 EUCFR, not all of them worded as an equal treatment rule, and clearly treated as such under the ESC.

[71] Particularly, 14 out of the 15 states (the exception was Sweden) were found to be in violation of one or more of the above-mentioned aspects of the obligation to guarantee the right to equal pay and the right to equal opportunities in the workplace. More specifically, see 126/2016, *University Women of Europe (UWE) v Croatia* (ECSR 5 December 2019) para 131–134, 137–140, 146–150, 158–160, 187–193 and 204; 127/2016, *UWE v Cyprus* (ECSR 5 December 2019) para 132–135, 138–141, 148–152, 158–160, 185–191 and 206; 128/2016, *UWE v Czech Republic* (ECSR 5 December 2019) para 142–145, 148–151, 172–175, 210–216 and 235; 129/2016, *UWE v Finland* (ECSR 5 December 2019) para 144–147, 150–153, 160–164, 173–176, 206–212 and 228; 130/2016, *UWE v France* (ECSR 5 December 2019) para 163–166, 169–172, 179–183, 189–192, 218–224 and 241; 131/2016, *UWE v Greece* (ECSR 5 December 2019) para 143–146, 149–152, 159–163, 172–175, 212–218 and 230; 132/2016, *UWE v Ireland* (ECSR 5 December 2019) para 133–136, 139–142, 148–152, 161–166, 185–191 and 203; 135/2016, *UWE v Norway* (ECSR 5 December 2019) para 113–116, 119–122, 129–133, 143–146, 181–187 and 205; 136/2016, *UWE v Portugal* (ECSR 5 December 2019) para 129–132, 135–138, 143–147, 154–157, 188–194 and 214; 137/2016, *UWE v Slovenia* (ECSR 5 December 2019) para 123–126, 129–132, 138–142, 152–155, 188–194 and 210; 124/2016, *UWE v Belgium* (ECSR 6 December 2019) para 139–141, 145–148, 154–158, 167–169, 202–208 and 218; 125/2016, *UWE v Bulgaria* (ECSR 6 December 2019) para 128–131, 135–138, 143–147, 154–157, 180–186 and 196; 133/2016, *UWE v Italy* (ECSR 6 December 2019) para 122–125, 128–131, 141–145, 153–156, 178–184 and 206; 134/2016, *UWE v the Netherlands* (ECSR 6 December 2019) para 135–138, 141–144, 151–155, 163–166, 192–198 and 222, and 138/2016, *UWE v Sweden* (ECSR 6 December 2019) para 125–128, 131–134, 141–145, 152–155, 181–187 and 204.

'waives' in June 2020. With this in mind, it can be expected that Covid-19 situation could have a negative impact on gender equality in general and within this on equal pay as well. For this reason, it can be argued that such ECSR's decisions could serve as a strong argument for keeping equal pay in the heart of political and legal debates, already during the Covid-19 pandemic and also in the post-pandemic times, and for confirming that the right to equal pay is a human rights and, therefore, it must be recognised as such, respected, enforced and promoted.[72] Delving into the impact of these decisions, it should be added that for the first time the ECSR has systematised a list of obligation on the state both in terms of remuneration and women's access to decision-making positions. However, the notion of **'measurable progress'**, which is essential to the reasoning on social rights, has a heterogeneous weight depending on the aspect analysed. If it is not rigorously applied, the ECSR risks giving a wide berth to those who still defend the **non-justiciability of social rights** as an intrinsic characteristic.[73]

34   Indeed, the Committee had publicly developed (in December 2012)[74] a **new case law** in this field in the framework of the reporting system which affects the 43 State Parties to the **European Social Charter**. Particularly, it adopted a new interpretation under Article 20 of the 1996 Revised Social Charter (equivalent to Article 1 of the 1988 Additional Protocol) which enables national courts to make comparisons outside the same undertaking. According to this interpretation: 'equal treatment between women and men includes the issue of equal pay for work of equal value. Usually, pay comparisons are made between persons within the same undertaking/company. However, there may be situations where, to be meaningful, this comparison can only be made across companies/undertakings. Therefore, the Committee requires that it be **possible to make pay comparisons across companies**. It notes that at the very least, legislation should require pay comparisons across companies in one or more of the following situations:

- cases in which statutory rules apply to the working and pay conditions in more than one company;
- cases in which several companies are covered by a collective works agreement or regulations governing the terms and conditions of employment;
- cases in which the terms and conditions of employment are laid down centrally for more than one company within a holding [company] or conglomerate'.

35   Of course, a positive *judicial will* in this direction from the ECJ[75] would also be desirable in assuming these **more favourable standards deriving from the European Social Charter**,[76] in consistency with the explicit reference, to this

---

[72] Kresal (2021), p. 324.
[73] Brillat (2021), p. 297.
[74] Statement of interpretation of Article 20 of the 1996 Revised Social Charter/Article 1 of the 1988 Additional Protocol: equal pay comparisons, Conclusions 2012 (published in January 2013).
[75] Kocher (2016), para 219.
[76] Jimena Quesada (2017), p. 13.

emblematic social rights treaty of the Council of Europe, in Article 151 TFEU as well as in the Preamble and Explanations to the EUCFR.[77] It is worth recalling that the ECJ held a vanguard position in this field (since the famous case *Defrenne I*[78]), while the ECtHR proceeded to a 'belated recognition' of gender equality issues.[79]

In any case, without prejudice of 'judicial solutions' (and non-judicial ones having a preventive nature), it is important to put the accent in the protection of equal pay for women and men as a transversal principle of EU law imposing a positive obligation to promote it in all EU's activities in systematic accordance with other significant provisions of the Treaties and, as a result, as a *leitmotiv* **of all EU's actions** and resources (including financial ones). From this point of view, Article 157 TFEU is not only in close connection with the values and aims of respect for non-discrimination and equality between women and men set out in Article 2 TEU and Article 3.3 TEU (in conjunction with the EU's competence established in Article 153.1 point (i) TFEU), but also with the existence of the European Social Fund (Title XI of TFEU) and the other European Structural and Investment Funds (ESI Funds),[80] the EIB and the other existing Financial Instruments (Title XVII of TFEU on 'Economic, Social and Territorial Cohesion').[81]

Finally, the European Pillar of Social Rights (EPSR) emphasises the need to foster proactively equality between women and men through **positive action in all areas**. By extending equality to all areas, the EPSR goes beyond the existing acquis. The provisions on gender equality focus particularly on **participation in the labour market** (as reflected by the gap in employment between women and men), **terms and conditions of employment** (e.g. the gap in the use of part-time employment between women and men) and on **career progression** (e.g. the share of women in management positions and the low numbers of women entrepreneurs),

---

[77] Spadaro (2015), pp. 28–29.

[78] Case 80/70, *Defrenne I* (ECJ 25 May 1971) para 5–6.

[79] Carmona Cuenca (2015), p. 299. See 30078/06, *Konstantin Markin v Russia* (ECtHR 22 March 2012) para 127: 'The advancement of gender equality is today a major goal in the Member States of the Council of Europe and very weighty reasons would have to be put forward before such a difference of treatment could be regarded as compatible with the Convention ... In particular, references to traditions, general assumptions or prevailing social attitudes in a particular country are insufficient justification for a difference in treatment on grounds of sex'.

[80] The ESI Funds include the European Regional Development Fund (ERDF), the European Social Fund (ESF) and the Cohesion Fund, with the Fund for rural development, namely the European Agricultural Fund for Rural Development (EAFRD), and for the maritime and fisheries sector, namely measures financed under shared management in the European Maritime and Fisheries Fund (EMFF).

[81] Particularly, Articles 175 and 177 TFEU. See also, in this regard, Article 4.2 of Parliament/Council Regulation (EU) No. 1303/2013 *laying down common provisions on the [ESI Funds]*, O.J. L 347/320 (2013), which provides that the Commission and the Member States shall ensure 'that support from the ESI Funds is consistent with the relevant policies, horizontal principles referred to in Articles 5, 7 and 8 and priorities of the Union, and that it is complementary to other instruments of the Union', whereas Article 7 requires promotion of equality between men and women and non-discrimination. Moreover, Article 6 states that 'operations supported by the ESI Funds shall comply with applicable Union law and the national law relating to its application'.

all areas where further progress needs to be made. Principle 2b (Gender Equality) of the EPSR addresses the specific challenge of the gender pay gap, which persists despite the existing legislation.[82]

38   As far as recent and ongoing initiatives at the EU level are concerned, the Commission has implemented the **Strategic Engagement for Gender Equality 2016–2019**,[83] which set out the main priorities in this area, and outlined the use of existing tools such as the European Semester, the Union Funds and enforcement of legislation. A follow-up is ensured by the **Gender Equality Strategy 2020–2025**,[84] according to which the EU will continue to combat gender-based violence, counter gender stereotypes, to promote women's participation in decision-making and work to close gender gaps in the labour market, pay and pensions.[85]

39   On the other hand, in November 2017, the Commission adopted the **EU Action Plan 2017–2019, tackling the gender pay gap**.[86] Furthermore, the Commission presented together with the EPSR the **New start to support Work-Life Balance for parents and carers** initiative:[87] it proposed legislative and policy actions aiming to facilitate the uptake of parental leave by both women and men, to

---

[82] According to Principle 2 of the EPSR: 'a. Equality of treatment and opportunities between women and men must be ensured and fostered in all areas, including regarding participation in the labour market, terms and conditions of employment and career progression. b. Women and men have the right to equal pay for work of equal value'.

[83] Commission Staff Working Document *Strategic engagement for gender equality 2016–2019*, SWD (2015)278.

[84] COM(2020) 152 final of 5 March 2020.

[85] It is also worth mentioning the EU's new *EU Gender Action Plan (GAP) II – An Ambitious Agenda for Gender Equality and Women's Empowerment in EU External Action 2021–2025* (GAP III), which was launched on 25 November 2020 by the European Commission and the High Representative, JOIN(2020) 17 final. Drawing from the EU gender equality strategy 2020–2025, which calls for a gender-equal Europe, this new EU gender action plan for 2021–2025 (GAP III) calls for a gender-equal world and is complementary to the LGBTIQ equality strategy for 2020–2025. The Gender Action Plan III provides the EU with a policy framework with five pillars of action for accelerating progress towards meeting international commitments and a world in which everyone has space to thrive. It makes the promotion of gender equality a priority of all external policies and actions; offers a roadmap for working together with stakeholders at national, regional and multilateral levels; steps up action in strategic thematic areas; calls for the institutions to lead by example, and; ensures the transparency of the results.

[86] See Commission Communication, *EU Action Plan 2017–2019—Tackling the gender pay gap*, COM(2017) 678 final. The Action Plan presents ongoing and upcoming measures taken by the Commission to combat the gender pay gap in 2018–2019. It identifies eight areas for Action, namely: (1) improving the application of the equal pay principle; (2) combating segregation in occupations and sectors; (3) breaking the ceiling: initiatives to combat vertical segregation; (4) tackling the care penalty; (5) better valorising women's skills, efforts and responsibilities; (6) fighting the fog: unveiling inequalities and stereotypes; (7) alerting and informing about the gender pay gap, and (8) enhancing partnerships to tackle the gender pay gap.

The Commission published a Report on the implementation of such Action Plan in March 2020 (available at https://ec.europa.eu/info/sites/info/files/com-2020-101_en.pdf).

[87] Parliament/Council Directive (EU) 2019/1158 *on work-life balance for parents and carers*, O.J. L 188/79 (2019).

introduce the paternity leave and the carers' leave, to promote the use of flexible working arrangements, as well as to provide more and better child and other care facilities and remove economic disincentives such as tax-benefit disincentives, which discourage second-earners, often women, from entering the labour market.[88] Moreover, the Commission had proposed in 2012 a Directive aimed at further ensuring greater equality (**gender quotas**) among management positions in the corporate sphere (**Directive on women on boards**).[89] In this respect, in the **2021 Action Plan on the EPSR**, it is emphasised that 'efforts are particularly urgent to address gender-based stereotypes and discrimination. Despite progress in the last decade, the employment rate and pay levels of women still lag behind those of men. Women continue to be seriously underrepresented in decision-making positions, especially in senior management functions and in corporate boardrooms'.

In this context, it has been argued that the success of the EU's gender quality policy appears to be relative, since its overall impact 'remains unclear when viewed in the light of is problematic interpretation in MS. Moreover, the strength of this social policy, which has developed endosymbiotically with the single market, has also been its weakness: it was first and foremost designed for the market, which automatically limits its scope. Although a "militant elite" have endeavoured to move the policy beyond the confines of its strict labour market framework, their actions have carried out under cover of the ambiguous nature of the policy's status, that is, the policy is subordinated to employment objectives'.[90]

40

List of Cases

ECJ/CJEU

ECJ 25.05.1971, 80/70, *Defrenne I*, ECLI:EU:C:1971:55 [cit. in para 35]
ECJ 08.04.1976, 43/75, *Defrenne II*, ECLI:EU:C:1976:56 [cit. in para 10–11, 22]
ECJ 17.05.1990, C-262/88, *Barber*, ECLI:EU:C:1990:209 [cit. in para 16]
ECJ 08.11.1990, C-177/88, *Dekker*, ECLI:EU:C:1990:383 [cit. in para 6]
ECJ 08.11.1990, C-179/88, *Handels- og Kontorfunktionærernes Forbund*, ECLI:EU:C:1990:384 [cit. in para 6]
ECJ 17.10.1995, C-450/93, *Kalanke*, ECLI:EU:C:1995:322 [cit. in para 2, 7]
ECJ 19.10.1995, C-137/94, *Richardson*, ECLI:EU:C:1995:342 [cit. in para 2]

---

[88] The European Institute for Gender Equality, one of the EU's decentralised agencies, is supporting the work of the Commission, Member States and social partners in the area of work-life balance.

[89] Proposal for a Parliament/Council Directive *on improving the gender balance among non-executive directors of companies listed on stock exchanges and related measures*, COM(2012) 614 final of 14 November 2012. Although the Directive has not yet successfully gone through the legislative procedure, it has already evoked intense political and legal debate: Leszczyńska (2018), p. 36.

[90] Perrier (2018), pp. 156–157.

ECJ 11.11.1997, C-409/95, *Marschall*, ECLI:EU:C:1997:533 [cit. in para 2]
ECJ 09.09.1999, C-281/97, *Krüger*, ECLI:EU:C:1999:396 [cit. in para 16]
ECJ 27.02.2003, C-320/01, *Busch*, ECLI:EU:C:2003:114 [cit. in para 6]
ECJ 23.10.2003, C-4/02 and C-5/02, *Schönheit and Becker*, ECLI:EU:C:2003:583 [cit. in para 17]
ECJ 07.09.2004, C-469/02, *Commission v Belgium*, ECLI:EU:C:2004:489 [cit. in para 16]
ECJ 22.11.2005, C-144/04, *Mangold*, ECLI:EU:C:2005:709 [cit. in para 11]
ECJ 21.06.2007, C-231/06 to C-233/06, *Jonkman and Others*, ECLI:EU:C:2007:373 [cit. in para 25]
ECJ 20.09.2007, C-116/06, *Kiiski*, ECLI:EU:C:2007:536 [cit. in para 6]
CJEU 19.01.2010, C-555/07, *Kücükdeveci*, ECLI:EU:C:2010:21 [cit. in para 11]
CJEU 22.04.2010, C-486/08, *Zentralbetriebsrat der Landeskrankenhäuser Tirols*, ECLI:EU:C:2010:215 [cit. in para 17]
CJEU 16.09.2010, C-356/09, Opinion of AG Kokott, *Kleist*, ECLI:EU:C:2010:532 [cit. in para 6]
CJEU 01.03.2011, C-236/09, *Association belge des Consommateurs Test-Achats and Others*, ECLI:EU:C:2011:100 [cit. in para 10]
CJEU 19.05.2011, C-447/09, Opinion of AG Cruz Villalón, *Prigge and Others*, ECLI:EU:C:2011:321 [cit. in para 29]
CJEU 22.06.2011, C-399/09, *Landtová*, ECLI:EU:C:2011:415 [cit. in para 25]
CJEU 23.10.2012, C-401/11, Opinion of AG Jääskinen, *Blanka Soukupová*, ECLI:EU:C:2012:658 [cit. in para 11]
CJEU 08.11.2012, C-229/11, *Heimann and Toltschin*, ECLI:EU:C:2012:693 [cit. in para 17]
CJEU 22.11.2012, C-385/11, *Elbal Moreno*, ECLI:EU:C:2012:746 [cit. in para 18]
CJEU 29.11.2012, C-427/11, Opinion of AG Cruz Villalón, *Margaret Kenny and Others*, ECLI:EU:C:2012:762 [cit. in para 23, 29]
CJEU 28.02.2013, C-427/11, *Margaret Kenny and Others*, ECLI:EU:C:2013:122 [cit. in para 23]
CJEU 19.09.2013, C-216/12 and C-217/12, *Hliddal and Bornand*, ECLI:EU:C:2013:568 [cit. in para 14]
CJEU 17.07.2014, C-173/13, *Leone*, ECLI:EU:C:2014:2090 [cit. in para 19]
CJEU 05.11.2014, C-476/12, *Österreichischer Gewerkschaftsbund*, ECLI:EU:C:2014:2332 [cit. in para 17]
CJEU 14.04.2015, C-527/13, *Cachaldora Fernández*, ECLI:EU:C:2015:215 [cit. in para 18]
CJEU 14.07.2016, C-335/15, *Ornano*, ECLI:EU:C:2016:564 [cit. in para 3]
CJEU 13.07.2017, C-354/16, *Kleinsteuber*, ECLI:EU:C:2017:539 [cit. in para 15]
CJEU 09.11.2017, C-98/15, *Espadas Recio*, ECLI:EU:C:2017:833 [cit. in para 18]
CJEU 28.06.2018, C-451/16, *MB*, ECLI:EU:C:2018:492 [cit. in para 21]
CJEU 19.09.2018, C-312/17, *Bedi*, ECLI:EU:C:2018:734 [cit. in para 16]
CJEU 08.05.2019, C-486/18, *Praxair MRC*, ECLI:EU:C:2019:379 [cit. in para 18]
CJEU 18.09.2019, C-366/18, *Ortiz Mesonero*, ECLI:EU:C:2019:757 [cit. in para 20]

Article 157. [Equal Pay Between Men and Women] 1469

CJEU 07.10.2019, C-171/18, *Safeway*, ECLI:EU:C:2019:839 [cit. in para 22]
CJEU 05.11.2019, C-192/18, *Commission v Poland*, ECLI:EU:C:2019:924 [cit. in para 21]
CJEU 12.12.2019, C-450/18, *Instituto Nacional de la Seguridad Social*, ECLI:EU:C:2019:1075 [cit. in para 21]
CJEU 18.11.2020, C-463/19, *Syndicat CFTC*, ECLI:EU:C:2020:932 [cit. in para 20]
CJEU 03.06.2021, C-624/19, *Tesco Stores*, ECLI:EU:C:2021:429 [cit. in para 11, 22, 26]
CJEU 05.05.2022, C-405/20, *BVAEB*, ECLI:EU:C:2022:347 [cit. in para 20, 22]

ECtHR

ECtHR 33.04.2023, 30078/06, *Konstantin Markin v Russia* [cit. in para 30]

ECSR

ECSR 05.12.2019, 126/2016, *University Women of Europe (UWE) v Croatia* [cit. in para 30]
ECSR 05.12.2019, 127/2016, *UWE v Cyprus* [cit. in para 31]
ECSR 05.12.2019, 128/2016, *UWE v Czech Republic* [cit. in para 31]
ECSR 05.12.2019, 129/2016, *UWE v Finland* [cit. in para 31]
ECSR 05.12.2019, 130/2016, *UWE v France* [cit. in para 31]
ECSR 05.12.2019, 131/2016, *UWE v Greece* [cit. in para 31]
ECSR 05.12.2019, 132/2016, *UWE v Ireland* [cit. in para 31]
ECSR 05.12.2019, 135/2016, *UWE v Norway* [cit. in para 31]
ECSR 05.12.2019, 136/2016, *UWE v Portugal* [cit. in para 31]
ECSR 05.12.2019, 137/2016, *UWE v Slovenia* [cit. in para 31]
ECSR 06.12.2019, 124/2016, *UWE v Belgium* [cit. in para 31]
ECSR 06.12.2019, 125/2016, *UWE v Bulgaria* [cit. in para 31]
ECSR 06.12.2019, 133/2016, *UWE v Italy* [cit. in para 31]
ECSR 06.12.2019, 134/2016, *UWE v the Netherlands* [cit. in para 31]
ECSR 06.12.2019, 138/2016, *UWE v Sweden* [cit. in para 31]

References[91]

Brillat, M. (2021). UWE c. Europe: Marie Curie s'en va-t-en guerre! *Lex Social: Revista De Derechos Sociales, 11*(1), 284–297.
Calliess, C., & Ruffert, M. (Eds.). (2022). *EUV, AEUV. Kommentar* (6th ed.). C.H. Beck.

---

[91] All cited internet sources have been accessed on 17 February 2023.

Carmona Cuenca, E. (2015). La igualdad de género en el Tribunal Europeo de Derechos Humanos: un reconocimiento tardío con relación al Tribunal de Justicia de la Unión Europea. *Revista Española de Derecho Constitucional, 104*, 381–403.

Cruz Villalón, J. (2018). Las medidas de acción positiva. In *Derecho Social de la Unión Europea. Aplicación por el Tribunal de Justicia* (pp. 231–253). Francis Lefebvre.

De Mol, M. (2011). The novel approach of the CJEU on the horizontal direct effect of the EU principle of non-discrimination: (Unbridled) expansionism of EU law. *Maastricht Journal of European and Comparative Law, 18*, 109–135.

De Schutter, O., & Jimena Quesada, L. (2019). Article 7. In E. Decaux & O. De Schutter (Eds.), *Le Pacte international relatif aux droits économiques, sociaux et culturels – Commentaire article par article* (pp. 206–234). Éditions Economica.

Deakin, S., Fraser Butlin, S., McLaughlin, C., & Polanska, A. (2015). Are litigation and collective bargaining complements or substitutes for achieving gender equality? A study of the British Equal Pay Act. *Cambridge Journal of Economics, 39*(2), 381–403.

Hinton, E. F. (1997). The limits of affirmative action in the European Union: Eckhard Kalanke v. Freie Hansestadt Bremen. *Texas Journal of Women and the Law, 6*, 215–239.

Jimena Quesada, L. (2017). Combating the gender pay gap in European social law. *Citecma (Ciencia, Técnica y Mainstreaming social), 1*, 5–15.

Kocher, E. (2016). Arbeitsrechtlicher Diskriminierungsschutz. In M. Schlachter & H. M. Heinig (Eds.), *Europäisches Arbeits- und Sozialrecht. Enzyklopädie Europarecht.* (para 219–292. Nomos.

Kollonay-Lehoczky, C. (2017). Article E. Non-discrimination. In N. Bruun, K. Lorcher, I. Schömann, & S. Clauwaert (Eds.), *The European Social Charter and the Employment Relation* (pp. 493–511). Hart Publishing.

Kresal, B. (2021). Gender pay gap and under-representation of women in decision-making positions: UWE decisions of the European Committee of Social Rights. *ERA Forum, 22*, 311–325.

Leszczyńska, M. (2018). Mandatory quotas for women on boards of directors in the European Union: Harmful to or good for company performance? *European Business Organization Law Review, 19*(1), 35–61.

Perrier, G. (2018). European Union policy on gender equality: The scope and limits of equality in the single market. In R. M. Carmo, C. Rio, & M. Medgyesi (Eds.), *Reducing inequalities: A challenge for the European Union?* (pp. 149–159). Palgrave Macmillan.

Peruzzi, M. (2015). Contradictions and misalignments in the EU approach towards the gender pay gap. *Cambridge Journal of Economics, 39*(2), 441–465.

Rodríguez Escanciano, S. (2018). Condiciones de trabajo y discriminación salarial por razón de sexo. In *Derecho Social de la Unión Europea. Aplicación por el Tribunal de Justicia* (pp. 255–291). Francis Lefebvre.

Romero Rodenas, M. J., & Bogoni, M. (2009). La negociación colectiva europea a través del Acuerdo marco europeo sobre la violencia de género. *Revista de Derecho Social, 47*, 209–230.

Smith, M. (2012). Social regulation of the gender pay gap in the EU. *European Journal of Industrial Relations, 18*(4), 365–380.

Spadaro, A. (2015). *La crisi, i diritti sociali e le risposte dell'Europa*. In B. Carusso & G. Fontana (Eds.), *Lavoro e diritti sociali nella crisi europea* (pp. 15–55). Il Mulino.

Vielle, P. (2012). How the horizontal social clause can be made to work: The lessons of gender mainstreaming. In I. Schöman, K. Lörcher, & N. Bruun (Eds.), *The Lisbon Treaty and social Europe* (pp. 105–122). Hart Publishing.

von der Groeben, H., Schwarze, J., & Hatje, A. (Eds.). (2015). *Europäisches Unionsrecht*. Nomos.

Vyas, N. (2021). Gender inequality-now available on digital platform: An interplay between gender equality and the gig economy in the European Union. *European Labour Law Journal, 12*(1), 37–51.

Wobbe, T. (2010). The metamorphosis of gender equality in the European Community: Shifting forms of social inclusion from the nation-building to the market-building frame. In S. Niccolai & I. Ruggiu (Eds.), *Dignity in change. Exploring the constitutional potential of EU gender and anti-discrimination law* (pp. 69–87). European Press Academic Publishing.

Jimena Quesada

Article 158 [Paid Holiday Schemes]
(ex-Article 142 TEC)

Member States shall endeavour to maintain the existing equivalence between paid holiday schemes.[2–5]

Contents

1. Overview 1
2. Scope and Resulting Obligations 2
3. Obsolete and Unnecessary Provision? 6

List of Cases
References

1. Overview

Article 158 TFEU repeats in an identical manner the wordings of ex-Article 142 TEC and ex-Article 119a TEEC and establishes the maintenance of any pre-existing national systems relating to paid holiday schemes. The **content of the provision has remained static**[1] since 1957 when it was introduced for the purpose of safeguarding the French concerns about social dumping[2] that could result from diverging systems and especially from national systems offering a lower standard of protection for workers, thus being in a position to attract capital[3] and to gain a competitive advantage.[4] Therefore, the inception of the wording pursued two objectives of 'interventionist Member States':[5] (a) the **greater harmonisation** through the protection of already granted benefits under national law in order to permanently entrench the social policy choices contained therein, and, (b) the prevention of a **distortion in competition**. The key in understanding the historical background of the provision is the existence of French legislation entitling workers to longer paid leave than other MS.[6]

1

---

[1] Ioannidou, in Skouris (2003), Article 142 EC para 1.
[2] Banard and Deakin (2012), p. 543.
[3] Banard and Deakin (2012), p. 543.
[4] Ellis and Watson (2012), p. 23.
[5] Falkner (2003a), p. 186; Falkner (2003b), p. 57.
[6] Sitz, in Smit et al. (2005), Article 158 TFEU para 3.

© Springer Nature Switzerland AG 2023
R. Böttner, H.-J. Blanke (eds.), *Treaty on the Functioning of the European Union – A Commentary*, Springer Commentaries on International and European Law, https://doi.org/10.1007/16559_2023_77

2. Scope and Resulting Obligations

2   The provision on paid holiday schemes was **declaratory**[7] in nature and had a **programmatic scope** aiming to declare the intention to endeavour[8] to maintain the status quo.[9] As a corollary, the provision is characterised by **vagueness of duty** and lacks the necessary detail, preciseness and clarity required for a provision to have direct effect.[10] Therefore, the provision cannot be considered a *lex perfecta* and cannot be directly relied upon by individuals, yet serves the purpose of stating in ambitious terms the vague goal of advancing social policy[11] as well as an interpreting tool of Union law, particularly with regard to Article 7 of the Working Time Directive[12] as well as for Article 31.2 EUCFR. Nonetheless, it must be clarified that the **social policy dimension** in this context also has a close connection with maximum working time and in a consequential bearing on **employment and social rights**.[13] Furthermore, the substance of the maximum working time entitlement remains unaffected by Article 158 TFEU due to its 'non-committal wording'.[14] That is also the outcome because national holiday schemes are not any longer characterised by noticeable divergence.[15]

3   The addressee of the provision, beyond the MS, is also the Union as an entity responsible with the task of harmonisation. In that context, the actions of the Union have reflected the programmatic nature of Article 158 TFEU. Specifically, the Council proceeded to adopt **Recommendation 75/457/EEC**[16] encouraging the MS to regulate national schemes on the basis of the 40 h week and the 4 weeks annual paid leave[17] either through introducing legislation or through collective agreements.[18] In addition, point 8 of the non-binding[19] and strictly declaratory[20] **Community Charter on Basic Social Rights for Workers 1989** provides that 'Every worker of the European Community shall have a right to a weekly rest

---

[7] Kotzur and Lichtblau, in Geiger et al. (2015), Article 158 TFEU para 1.

[8] The same term has been held to be too general in Case 203/80, *Casati* (ECJ 11 November 1981) para 19.

[9] Ioannidou, in Skouris (2003), Article 142 EC para 1.

[10] As established in the jurisprudence of the ECJ, see Case 26/62, *Van Gend en Loos* (ECJ 5 February 1963) p. 13.

[11] Anderson (2015), p. 56.

[12] Parliament/Council Directive 2003/88/EC *concerning certain aspects of the organisation of working time*, O.J. L 299/9 (2003).

[13] Ioannidou, in Skouris (2003), Article 142 EC para 2.

[14] Sitz, in Smit et al. (2005), Article 158 TFEU para 4.

[15] Potočnjak et al. (2014), p. 163.

[16] Council Recommendation 75/457/EEC *on the principle of the 40-hour week and the principle of four weeks' annual paid holiday*, O.J. L 199/32 (1975).

[17] Kotzur and Lichtblau, in Geiger et al. (2015), Article 158 TFEU para 1.

[18] Ioannidou, in Skouris (2003), Article 142 EC para 2.

[19] Sitz, in Smit et al. (2005), Article 158 TFEU para 4.

[20] Bercusson (1990).

period and to annual paid leave, the duration of which must be progressively harmonized in accordance with national practices'.[21]

However, the declaratory nature of Article 158 TFEU has been indirectly supplemented by the introduction of the **Working Time Directive**[22] that imposes at least 4 weeks of annual paid leave[23] (Article 7.1) and which may not be replaced by an allowance in lieu, except where the employment relationship is terminated (Article 7.2). As different facts may require different application of that latter provision of Article 7, the Court held that it is in any case an obligation of the national court to interpret the national legislation in a consistent way with Article 7 of the Directive and if this is not possible then the national provision should be set aside in order for the right of the individual to paid annual leave entitled to him under EU law, to be ensured.[24] It must be clarified that the legal basis for the preceding secondary act was not Article 158 TFEU but ex-Article 118a TEEC (now Article 153 TFEU). The Court examined the selection of that provision as legal basis and it was held that the appropriate legal basis was used because the Directive in question had as its aim the protection of the health and safety of the workers.[25]

4

The content of the provision has been intended to prevent distortion of competition (→ para 1) but the overlap with the protection for workers seems to have overshadowed the scope and application of Article 158 TFEU. The Court has held that 'with regard to both the objective of Directive 93/104 and to its scheme, paid annual leave of a minimum duration of three weeks during the transitional period provided for in Article 18(1)(b)(ii) and four weeks after the expiry of that period *constitutes a **social right*** directly conferred by that directive on every worker as the minimum requirement necessary to ensure protection of his health and safety'.[26]

5

---

[21] Community Charter on Basic Social Rights for Workers 1989, COM(89) 568 final.

[22] Originally Council Directive 93/104/EC, now Parliament/Council Directive 2003/88/EC *concerning certain aspects of the organisation of working time*, O.J. L 299/9 (2003). This Directive was created in order to lay down minimum requirements intended to improve the living and working conditions of workers through the approximation of national provisions concerning, in particular, the duration of working time, see to that effect, Case C-147/17, *Sindicatul Familia Constanţa and Others* (ECJ 20 November 2018) para 39; Joined Cases C-257/21 and C-258/21, *Coca-Cola European Partners Deutschland GmbH* (ECJ 7 July 2022) para 46.

[23] This is the minimum requirement and any legislation over and above the minimum standard provided by Article 7.1 of the Directive, does not disregard the 'nature and purpose of the fundamental right to an annual period of paid leave that is laid down by Article 31(2) of the Charter', see Joined Cases C-119/19 P and C-126/19 P, *Commission and Council v Francisco Carreras Sequeros and Others* (ECJ 8 September 2020) para 133.

[24] Case C-684/16, *Max-Planck-Gesellschaft zur Förderung der Wissenschaften* (ECJ 6 November 2018) para 62 et seqq.

[25] Case C-84/94, *United Kingdom v Council* (ECJ 12 November 1996) para 11-49; the aim of the Directive, i.e. to protect the health and safety of the workers, was also confirmed in the Court's judgment in Joined Cases C-257/21 and C-258/21, *Coca-Cola European Partners Deutschland GmbH* (ECJ 7 July 2022) para 45-46.

[26] Case C-173/99, *BECTU* (ECJ 26 June 2001) para 47.

That approach was more limited than the approach adopted by AG *Tizzano*,[27] which emphasised the inclusion of paid annual leave in Article 31.2 EUCFR.

3. Obsolete and Unnecessary Provision?

6 It can be argued[28] that since the provision has a programmatic nature ($\rightarrow$ para 2) and because the Union has since adopted binding measures implementing and applying ($\rightarrow$ para 4) the content of the provision, as a result Article 158 TFEU has limited use. Moreover, the issue is now perceived as coming within the **protection of the social rights** of the workers and as such within the regulatory scope of **Article 153 TFEU** ($\rightarrow$ Article 153 TFEU para 2 et seqq.).

However, the argument can be challenged, at least in *formal terms*, by highlighting the differences between Article 158 and Article 153 TFEU. The distinguishing factor is that under the latter only the minimum level protection is required to be observed, thus allowing the MS to apply higher standards. Article 158 TFEU remains the *benchmark* for such varying standards based on the **principle of equivalence** as a voluntary yardstick against distortion of competition.[29] In *actual terms*, the non-binding nature of Article 158 TFEU makes any such assessment merely voluntary and a mere expression of endeavoured regulatory self-restraint on behalf of the MS.

List of Cases

ECJ

ECJ 05.02.1963, 26/62, *Van Gend en Loos*, ECLI:EU:C:1963:1 [cit. in para 2]
ECJ 11.11.1981, 203/80, *Casati*, ECLI:EU:C:1981:261 [cit. in para 2]
ECJ 12.11.1996, C-84/94, *United Kingdom v Council*, ECLI:EU:C:1996:431 [cit. in para 4]
ECJ 08.02.2001, C-173/99, Opinion of AG Tizzano, *BECTU*, ECLI:EU:C:2001:81 [cit. in para 5]
ECJ 26.06.2001, C-173/99, *BECTU*, ECLI:EU:C:2001:356 [cit. in para 5]
ECJ 06.11.2018, C-684/16, *Max-Planck-Gesellschaft zur Förderung der Wissenschaften*, ECLI:EU:C:2018:874 [cit. in para 5]
ECJ 20.11.2018, C-147/17, *Sindicatul Familia Constanţa and Others*, ECLI:EU:C:2018:926 [cit. in para 4]
ECJ 08.09.2020, C-119/19 P and C-126/19 P, *Commission and Council v Francisco Carreras Sequeros and Others*, ECLI:EU:C:2020:676 [cit. in para 4]

---

[27] Case C-173/99, *BECTU* (Opinion of AG Tizzano of 8 February 2001) para 26.
[28] Sitz, in Smit et al. (2005), Article 158 TFEU para 4.
[29] Ioannidou, in Skouris (2003), Article 142 EC para 2.

ECJ 07.07.2022, Joined Cases C-257/21 and C-258/21, *Coca-Cola European Partners Deutschland GmbH*, ECLI:EU:C:2022:529 [cit. in para 4]

References

Anderson, K. (2015). *Social policy in the European Union*. Palgrave Macmillan.
Banard, C., & Deakin, S. (2012). Social policy and labor market regulation. In E. Jones, A. Menon, & S. Weatherill (Eds.), *The Oxford handbook of the European Union* (pp. 542–555). OUP.
Bercusson, B. (1990). The European Community's Charter of fundamental social rights of workers. *The Modern Law Review, 53*(5), 624–642.
Ellis, E., & Watson, P. (2012). *EU anti-discrimination law*. OUP.
Falkner, G. (2003a). The Treaty on European Union and its revision: Sea change or empty shell for European social policies? In S. Kuhnle (Ed.), *The survival of the European welfare state* (pp. 185–201). Routledge.
Falkner, G. (2003b). *EU social policy in the 1990s. Towards a corporatist policy community*. Routledge.
Geiger, R., Khan, D-E., & Kotzur, M. (Eds.) (2015). *European Union treaties*. Beck/Hart/Nomos
Potočnjak, Z., Grgić, A., & Čatipović, I. (2014). The right to annual leave: The implications of accession. *Croatian Yearbook of European Law and Policy, 10*, 159–187.
Skouris, V. (Ed.) (2003). *Commentary of EU and EC treaties*. Sakkoulas. (in Greek).
Smit, H., Herzog, P., Campbell, C., & Zagel, G. (Eds.). (2005). *On the law of the European Union*. LexisNexis Bender.

Article 159 [Report on the Social and Demographic Situation]
(ex-Article 143 TEC)

The Commission shall draw up a report each year on progress in achieving the objectives of Article 151, including the demographic situation in the Union. It shall forward the report to the European Parliament, the Council and the Economic and Social Committee.[2–4]

Contents

1. Overview 1
2. Scope and Resulting Obligations 2
References

1. Overview

The provision has its **origins** in ex-Article 143 TEC, which was introduced by the Treaty of Amsterdam.[1] The foundation[2] for that article was Article 7 of the Agreement on Social Policy[3] that became effective with the entry into force of the Treaty of Maastricht. Article 7.1 provided that 'The Commission shall draw up a report each year on progress in achieving the objectives of Article 1, including the demographic situation in the Community. It shall forward the report to the European Parliament, the Council and the Economic and Social Committee'. The **nature of the obligation** is essentially a **reporting** one, whereby the European Commission is tasked with providing annually a report on the **progress of attaining the objectives** of the Union in the field of **social policy**, including specifically the demographic situation. The intention behind the provision is to ensure that the progress of implementation of the social policies of the Union is **monitored** and that the Union institutions are **informed** about that progress.

2. Scope and Resulting Obligations

Article 159 TFEU establishes a reporting obligation for the European Commission in two ways: (1) with direct reference to Article 151 TFEU, (2) with direct reference to the demographic situation in the Union. On the former and in effect the content of the reporting obligation, the task is about the **general social policy objectives of the Union**. Those are broad and include the promotion of employment, improved

---

[1] Ioannidou, in Skouris (2003), Article 143 EC para 1.

[2] Sitz, in Smit et al. (2005), Article 159 TFEU para 3; Kotzur and Lichtblau, in Geiger et al. (2015), Article 159 TFEU para 1.

[3] Protocol *on Social Policy and Agreement on Social Policy* (with the exception of the United Kingdom), O.J. C 224/1 (1992), p. 126.

living and working conditions, proper social protection, the dialogue between management and labour, the development of human resources and the combating of exclusion. It is evident that the emphasis is placed on the employment relationship, yet with the strong possibility of expanding into all other areas that can be construed as coming within social cohesion and protection of the vulnerable groups (e.g. combating exclusion, improved living conditions). Therefore, it can be argued that the reference in Article 159 TFEU to the objectives listed in Article 151 TFEU (→ Article 151 TFEU para 3, 17) renders the scope of the reporting obligation under the former broader[4] and general to the extent that the European Commission wants to define its task.[5] Moreover, the two provisions are complementing each other. Article 159 TFEU is also connected with Article 161 TFEU (→ Article 161 TFEU para 2) with both provisions imposing specific reporting obligations on the European Commission that are in effect identical, hence the maintenance of both provisions is perhaps and in terms of structural coherence a duplication.

3   The reporting obligation was originally complied with through the Special Situation Report that the European Commission drafted **annually** and in close cooperation with Eurostat since 2000.[6] The annual report was comparable[7] in style, structure and approach with the report on employment in the Union (Article 148.5 TFEU; → Article 148 TFEU para 6). In fact, after the entry into force of the Lisbon Treaty, the Commission publishes a joint annual review on '**Employment and Social Developments** in Europe' with a section on the social situation.[8] The report offers a description of the social tendencies in the Union by composing and analysing special social parameters and based on national experiences and statistics.[9] In 2016 and 2020, the Commission has published an EU regional Social Progress Index, which aims to measure social progress for each EU region.[10]

4   The recipients of the report include the EP, the Council and the Economic and Social Committee. The **obligation to report** is annual and permanent and before the entry into force of the Treaty of Lisbon it was possible for the EP to invite the Commission to prepare reports on specific problems concerning the social situation (ex-Article 143.2 TEC). That provision has been repealed. Nonetheless, it must be clarified that under Article 161.2 TFEU the EP has the same and exact power (→ Article 161 TFEU para 3); hence the latitude of its powers remains unaffected.

---

[4] Sitz, in Smit et al. (2005), Article 159 TFEU para 4.

[5] Ioannidou, in Skouris (2003), Article 143 EC para 1.

[6] Kotzur and Lichtblau, in Geiger et al. (2015), Article 159 TFEU para 2.

[7] Ioannidou, in Skouris (2003), Article 143 EC para 1.

[8] See the most recent report of 2022, entitled 'Young Europeans: employment and social challenges ahead'.

[9] Kotzur and Lichtblau, in Geiger et al. (2015), Article 159 TFEU para 2.

[10] Available at https://ec.europa.eu/regional_policy/en/information/maps/social_progress.

References[11]

Geiger, R., Khan, D-E., & Kotzur, M. (Eds.) (2015). *European Union treaties*. Beck/Hart/Nomos.
Skouris, V. (Ed.). (2003). *Commentary of EU and EC treaties*. Sakkoulas. (in Greek).
Smit, H., Herzog, P., Campbell, C., & Zagel, G. (Eds.). (2005). *On the law of the European Union*. LexisNexis Bender.

---

[11] All cited internet sources in this comment have been accessed on 20 July 2022.

Article 160 [Social Protection Committee]
(ex-Article 144 TEC)

The Council, acting by a simple majority after consulting the European Parliament, shall establish a Social Protection Committee with advisory status to promote cooperation on social protection policies between Member States and with the Commission.[2, 3] The tasks of the Committee shall be:

- to monitor the social situation and the development of social protection policies in the Member States and the Union,
- to promote exchanges of information, experience and good practice between Member States and with the Commission,
- without prejudice to Article 240, to prepare reports, formulate opinions or undertake other work within its fields of competence, at the request of either the Council or the Commission or on its own initiative.

In fulfilling its mandate, the Committee shall establish appropriate contacts with management and labour.[6]

Each Member State and the Commission shall appoint two members of the Committee.[4]

Contents

1. Overview 1
2. Scope and Tasks 2
References

1. Overview

Article 160 TFEU replaces ex-Article 144 TEC. The provision has its origins in the Treaty of Nice and the therein introduction established the explicit legal basis for the **Social Protection Committee**. As a result, the Social Protection Committee acquired institutional status after 2003 and that status was originating directly from the Treaties.[1] It must be noted that prior to the entry into force of the Treaty of Nice, the Council had proceeded to establish the Social Protection Committee through secondary legislation.[2] The legal basis that was used at that time was ex-Article 202 TEC (repealed and in effect replaced now by Article 16.1 TEU and Articles 290 and 291 TFEU). After the creation of an express legal basis in ex- 1

---

[1] Kotzur and Lichtblau, in Geiger et al. (2015), Article 160 TFEU para 3.
[2] Council Decision No. 2000/436/EC *setting up a Social Protection Committee*, O.J. L 712/26 (2000).

© Springer Nature Switzerland AG 2023
R. Böttner, H.-J. Blanke (eds.), *Treaty on the Functioning of the European Union – A Commentary*, Springer Commentaries on International and European Law,
https://doi.org/10.1007/16559_2023_79

Article 144 TEC, the relevant secondary act was replaced[3] and recently a new and more elaborate legal basis has been introduced.[4]

2. Scope and Tasks

2 The Social Protection Committee is a purely **advisory body** and has as its mission the promotion of cooperation on social protection policies between MS and with the Commission. That purpose is to be attained through the establishment of contacts within the various social partners that include employers and workers (Article 160.2 TFEU). However, the definition of 'social partners' remains vague in relation to whether the term can include national associations or only actors operating at the union level.[5] The tasks of the Social Protection Committee include monitoring functions regarding the progression of social policies, facilitating the promotion of communication between the MS and the Commission and reporting obligations and/or initiatives for the improvement of the progression of the implementation of social policies.

3 The provision runs in parallel with Article 150 TFEU on the Employment Committee with advisory status (→ Article 150 TFEU para 1) and Article 153.1 point (k) TFEU (→ Article 153 TFEU para 32). Nonetheless, the ambit of the tasks of the Social Protection Committee is **broader** and covers the full scope of social situations in the MS and the Union level.[6] That conclusion can be reached if the emphasis is placed on the reporting capacity of the Social Protection Committee at its own initiative, which enables it to 'undertake other work within its fields of competence' (Article 160.1 TFEU). Given that the tasks entrusted to the Social Protection Committee are phrased in general terms (→ para 2), then it is reasonable to argue that the Social Protection Committee has **wide discretion when defining its own competence**. Nonetheless, that must always be remembered that the Social Protection Committee is an advisory body.

4 The Social Protection Committee consists of **two members** for **each MS** and two additional members of the **Commission** (Article 160.3 TFEU). They may also appoint two alternates (Article 3.1 of Decision 2015/773/EU). In the composition of the Committee, the MS and the Commission 'shall use their best endeavours' to achieve a gender balance (Article 3.2 of Decision 2015/773/EU). The Committee shall elect its Chairperson from among the members appointed by the MS for a term of 2 years (renewable once) (Article 4.1 of Decision 2015/773/EU).

---

[3] Council Decision No. 2004/689/EC *establishing a Social Protection Committee*, O.J. L 314/8 (2004).

[4] Council Decision No. 2015/773/EU e*stablishing the Social Protection Committee*, O.J. L 121/16 (2015).

[5] Kotzur and Lichtblau, in Geiger et al. (2015), Article 160 TFEU para 4.

[6] Sitz, in Smit et al. (2005), Article 160 TFEU para 4.

The function of the Social Protection Committee is carried out in direct compliance with the **open method of coordination**[7] that aims to promote the further convergence between MS in relation to the promotion of the Union's objectives.[8] In its work, the SPC is being assisted in developing and defining the EU social indicators on MS's progress by its permanent sub-group namely the Indicators' sub group (ISG).[9] Under certain circumstances, the Committee has the discretion to create ad hoc working groups.[10] The role of the Social Protection Committee is now defined in detail through the new secondary legal basis, that states that the Social Protection Committee actively participates in the European Semester process of policy coordination for employment, social affairs and health.[11] The Committee carries out that task by relying on the social open method of coordination as the main policy framework, including all major social policy strands: social inclusion, pensions, health and long-term care.[12] The foundation for that is to be found in the recognition that the social dimension of the EMU should be strengthened through enhanced monitoring and consideration of the social and labour market situation within the EMU.[13] That task should be carried out by using appropriate social and employment indicators within the European Semester, by ensuring better coordination of employment and social policies between MS, while at the same time respecting national competences.[14] Therefore, the Decision reflects the development of the European Semester and regulates the role of the Committee in this process. The European Semester provisions required that the Committee is involved through a duty of consultation[15] and is tasked with conducting in-depth reviews on the prevention and correction of macroeconomic imbalances taking into account Council recommendations or invitations addressed to MS. The Committee was also tasked with drafting corrective action plans for any MS for which an excessive imbalance procedure is opened by considering the economic and social impact of the policy actions and by ensuring consistency with the broad economic policy guidelines and the employment guidelines.[16]

Moreover, the Committee shall establish **appropriate contacts with the social partners** (Article 160.2 TFEU, Article 2.4 of Decision 2015/773/EU) represented

---

[7] Commission Communication *A renewed commitment to social Europe: Reinforcing the Open Method of Coordination for Social Protection and Social Inclusion*, COM(2008) 418 final.

[8] Sitz, in Smit et al. (2005), Article 160 TFEU para 4.

[9] https://ec.europa.eu/social/main.jsp?catId=830&langId=en.

[10] Ibid. https://ec.europa.eu/social/main.jsp?catId=758.

[11] Article 2.2 point (b) of Council Decision No. 2015/773/EU.

[12] Social Protection Committee 2016, Work Programme for 2016. Available at http://ec.europa.eu/social/main.jsp?catId=758&langId=en&moreDocuments=yes.

[13] Preamble of Council Decision No. 2015/773/EU.

[14] Preamble of Council Decision No. 2015/773/EU.

[15] Council Regulation (EC) No 1466/97 *on the strengthening of the surveillance of budgetary positions and the surveillance and coordination of economic policies*, O.J. L 209/97 (1997).

[16] Parliament/Council Regulation (EU) No 1176/2011 *on the prevention and correction of macroeconomic imbalances*, O.J. L 306/11 (2011).

at the Tripartite Social Summit for Growth and Employment[17] as well as with social non-governmental organisations, account being taken of their respective roles and responsibilities in the social protection sphere. The provision attempts to clarify whether the duty to establish contacts applies to actors operating at the EU level and/or to national social partners. The previous Decision[18] made only a general statement about social partners while in the new setting an additional direct reference is being made to the Tripartite Social Summit for Growth and Employment. Therefore, the primary task is to establish contacts with social partners at the EU level with direct reference to the European Trade Union Confederation (ETUC) and for the employers' delegation by the Union of Industrial and Employers' Confederations of Europe (UNICE).

References[19]

Geiger, R., Khan, D-E., & Kotzur, M. (Eds.) (2015). *European Union treaties*. Beck/Hart/Nomos.
Smit, H., Herzog, P., Campbell, C., & Zagel, G. (Eds.). (2005). *On the law of the European Union*. LexisNexis Bender.

---

[17] Council Decision No. 2016/1859/EC *on the Tripartite Social Summit for Growth and Employment*, O.J. L 284/16 (2016).

[18] Council Decision No. 2004/689/EC.

[19] All cited internet sources in this comment have been accessed on 20 July 2022.

Article 161 [Annual Report on Social Development]
(ex-Article 145 TEC)

The Commission shall include a separate chapter on social developments within the Union in its annual report to the European Parliament.
The European Parliament may invite the Commission to draw up reports on any particular problems concerning social conditions.

Contents

1. Overview 1
2. Scope 2
Reference

1. Overview

The provision adopts the same phraseology as ex-Article 145 TEC and has as its objective the maintenance of the reporting obligation of the European Commission towards the EP on matters of social development and policy. The **obligation to report to the EP** ensures that the only directly elected body in the Union is specifically informed on matters of social development and is thus in a better position to debate about the selection and the progress of specific social policy choices. 1

2. Scope

Article 161 TFEU remains in a complementary relationship with Article 159 TFEU (→ Article 159 TFEU para 1–4) with both provisions imposing specific reporting obligations on the European Commission that are in effect notably similar. Therefore, the maintenance of both provisions is perhaps and in terms of structural coherence unjustifiable.[1] 2

In the provision, the specific reporting obligation of the Commission is exclusively towards the EP, in contrast to Article 159 TFEU (→ Article 159 TFEU para 4). The **obligation to report** is annual and permanent. Under Article 161 TFEU, the EP can invite the Commission to prepare reports on specific problems concerning the social situation. Prior to the entry into force of the Treaty of Lisbon, the same wording was used and in effect that specific power was duplicated (ex-Article 143.2 TEC). That provision has been **repealed** and the 3

---

[1] Kotzur and Lichtblau, in Geiger et al. (2015), Article 161 TFEU para 2.

power of the EP to **request special reports on problematic social matters** now is to be found exclusively in Article 161.2 TFEU.

Reference

Geiger, R., Khan, D-E., & Kotzur, M. (Eds.) (2015). *European Union treaties*. Beck/Hart/Nomos.

Title XI
The European Social Fund

Article 162 [Aims of the ESF]
(ex-Article 146 TEC)

In order to improve employment opportunities for workers in the internal market and to contribute thereby to raising the standard of living, a European Social Fund is hereby established in accordance with the provisions set out below; it shall aim to render the employment of workers easier and to increase their geographical and occupational mobility within the Union, and to facilitate their adaptation to industrial changes and to changes in production systems, in particular through vocational training and retraining.

Contents

1. ESF Establishment and First Period 1
2. The First Reform of the ESF in 1971 5
3. Enlargement: United Kingdom, Denmark and Ireland 7
4. The Second ESF Reform in 1977 8
5. Second and Third Enlargement and Changes Introduced in the 1983–1988 Funding Period 9
6. The Fourth Reform of the ESF in 1988 12
7. A Further Reform of the Structural Funds in 1993 13
8. Enlargement: Finland and Sweden 16
9. Enlargement: Ten New Member States 20
10. The ESF Reform for the 2007–2013 Programming Period 22
11. ESF for the 2014–2020 Period 26
12. ESF+ for the 2021–2027 Period 30
References

1. ESF Establishment and First Period

The provision was originally Article 123 TEEC, then Article 146 TEC, and the Lisbon Treaty changed it to Article 162 TFEU. Its content was modified by Article G of the Maastricht Treaty. 1

The ESF is a **financial item in the multiannual financial framework** within the meaning of Article 312 TFEU and one of the so-called European Structural and Investment Funds (ESIF) financing EU cohesion policy. The foundations of the ESIF are laid down in the TFEU, namely 2

- Article 175.1, third sentence, TFEU in general;
- for agriculture and fisheries, Articles 42 and 43.2 TFEU;
- for the European Social Fund in Articles 162 et seq. TFEU;
- Articles 174 and 176 TFEU on regional policy and territorial cooperation;
- for the Cohesion Fund, Article 177.2 TFEU.

3   In 1957, the **Treaty of Rome established** the EEC and with it **the European Social Fund** (Article 123 TEEC). It is part of the structural funds system, which serves the EU's economic and social cohesion policy.[1] From the outset, the ESF has been an integral part of the European vision and was set up to improve employment opportunities in the Community by **promoting employment and increasing the geographical and occupational mobility** of workers. The ESF provided **short-term retraining support** for workers in sectors that were modernising production or moving to new types of production. It also provided **relocation support** for unemployed people looking for work elsewhere in their region. The ESF had a wider scope than the European Coal and Steel Community Fund because it covered all sectors except agriculture.

4   For the first time, the so-called **additionality rule** for Community funding was applied to the use of the Fund's resources, and it still applies today: ESF support had to be complemented by national funding. In the 1960s, ESF funding was a quasi-normative system, i.e. it did not support projects but undertook to co-fund mobility and training programmes ex post. Until the end of the 1960s, the ESF was financed entirely by contributions from the MS, the amount of which was fixed in agreements. The grant acted as an **intergovernmental transfer of funds, reimbursing once a year 50% of the cost of the tasks identified in the target areas**. This was a slow, bureaucratic process which hindered monitoring and accountability for the quality of training. Once approved, the funding was channelled into public sector-led retraining and resettlement projects. In this early period, private companies did not receive ESF support.

2. The First Reform of the ESF in 1971

5   As part of their efforts to coordinate their own social policies, the governments of the EEC members expressed the need to reform the ESF at the Hague Conference in 1969. The aim of the 1971 ESF reform[2] was to **strengthen the Community dimension over national interests and to increase the effectiveness and flexibility of the ESF**. The reform was based on Council Decision 71/66/EEC[3] which converted the previous normative funding system into a project-based programme. In addition, the ESF resources were no longer generated by MS' contributions but were allocated from the Community budget (the new Fund's budget in 1972 and 1973 exceeded the total of the previous 12 years), thus increasing the role of the Community institutions and the award of grants was no longer automatic.

6   The ESF was opened to a wider range of workers. As agriculture was in transition, farmers and farm workers leaving **agriculture** needed support; they

---

[1] Hajdu et al. (2017).

[2] The legal basis for the first reform was Article 126 TEEC, which gave the Council the power to make changes to make it work more efficiently.

[3] O.J. L 28/15 (1971).

became eligible in 1972. Similarly in the textile sector, early global trade patterns transformed the sector from labour-intensive to capital-intensive. Textile workers had to learn new skills, whether they wanted to stay in the industry or move to other jobs. The ESF was therefore opened to the **textile industry** in 1975. The ESF had already provided resettlement support for migrants in earlier decades, but in the 1970s this was extended to help people with the practical problems they faced when finding work in another EEC country. Workers were helped with the costs of **learning the local language** and given advice to help them and their families adjust to new living and working conditions. The ESF was also extended to support **preparatory studies and innovative pilot schemes** to test new ideas and practices.

3. Enlargement: United Kingdom, Denmark and Ireland

In 1973 the United Kingdom, Denmark and Ireland joined the EEC in the **first** 7 **enlargement**. The leaders of the nine countries met in Paris in October 1972 and agreed to tackle regional and structural disparities in economic development. Three years later, in 1975, the European Regional Development Fund (ERDF) was created to support regions facing difficulties resulting from restructuring or industrial conversion. The idea was that the two funds should have worked hand in hand: the ESF focused on helping people to acquire new skills and the ERDF on improving infrastructure in regions lagging behind. Together, the two funds were called 'Structural Funds'.

4. The Second ESF Reform in 1977

Even so, the system was not perfect: the problem was that, as the number of 8 programmes increased, the administrative work did not improve. A further reform of the system seemed inevitable. The second ESF reform was carried out in 1977, marking the beginning of the third period of the ESF. The overall change was forced by the **deepening employment crisis and administrative problems**. New groups were added to the previous target group system. Addressing the problems of **young unemployed people** (target group under 25) has been a priority of the ESF since that time; the ESF has increasingly taken account of the problems arising from the growing role of women in the workplace and has provided **support for women**, whether they have lost their jobs, are entering the labour market for the first time or returning to work after a break. The Fund also targeted other specific social groups, such as people with disabilities and older workers (aged 50 and over).

5. Second and Third Enlargement and Changes Introduced in the 1983–1988 Funding Period

9   A major change introduced in the 1983–1988 funding period removed the requirement that the retrained person had to work in a job related to his training for at least six months after his training. This reflected the reality of a changing labour market and opened up the Fund to provide training in all areas of the economy. The two priorities of the ESF were **vocational training** (half of which was work experience) and training in the use of new technologies. In 1983, it was decided that ESF funding should be channelled to regions in particular need. This led to an increase in applications for support and in 1988 the ESF was reformed to better **support the most deprived regions** (thus reducing the imbalance between rich and poor) and to cope with the increased number of applications.

10   Greece joined the European Community in 1981, followed by Spain and Portugal in 1986. Since the early 1980s, the ESF has been used for **training in emerging technologies**. In fact, more than half of ESF funding has been allocated to programmes to boost employment in poorer regions and countries such as Greece, the French overseas departments, Ireland, the Mezzogiorno in southern Italy, and Northern Ireland. When Spain and Portugal joined the EC in 1986, regions such as Andalusia and the Canary Islands, as well as Portugal as a whole, also joined the programme.

11   The implementation of the **single market** significantly increased the size of the ESF; but also the administrative workload it entailed. The Fund has received thousands of individual applications in all the languages of the Community and has found it very difficult to select the best projects. For each ESF project, the MS had to submit an application to the Commission; the Commission then had to evaluate each application and approve the successful ones. This made the management of the ESF increasingly difficult for both MS and the Commission.

6. The Fourth Reform of the ESF in 1988

12   The reform of the ESF (the fourth in succession) was launched in 1988, which marked **a shift from (individual) projects** implemented in a national context **to multi-annual programming** agreed in partnership between the MS and the Commission. The new rules[4] laid down four principles: concentration (the narrowing down of the objectives of aid), programming (multiannual planning), partnership (cooperation between Member States), and additionality (complementary function of aid). With the reform, the ESF has better **focused its efforts on those most in need**, whether regions or population groups. The reform has also reinforced the principle that Community funding goes hand in hand with national action. Finally,

---

[4] Two new articles were introduced into the Rome Treaty and the new rules for the Funds were contained in Council Regulation (EEC) No. 4255/88, O.J. L 374/21 (1988).

the ESF was given greater financial weight. The ESF has played an important role in cushioning the negative impact of change on individuals and helping them adapt to a changing world.

7. A Further Reform of the Structural Funds in 1993

A further reform of the Structural Funds was forced by the massive increase in unemployment in 1993. The basis for the reform was the **TEU**, which made **economic and social cohesion a fundamental objective of the EU**, with education and vocational training being the first of the instruments to be included. This means that the whole EU must show solidarity with the poorest countries and regions. An important innovation was the introduction of the NUTS (*Nomenclature des Unités Territoriales Statistiques*) system, which grouped MS into five categories based on eligibility for aid. The reform was accompanied by the creation of two new funds, the Financial Instrument for Fisheries Guidance and the Cohesion Fund.

In 1994, EU governments adopted an employment strategy aimed at improving the competitiveness of the European economy. In 1997, with the approval of the Amsterdam Treaty, MS agreed on a framework of employment guidelines and a common strategy. In line with the guidelines and the common strategy, the ESF **shifted the focus from unemployment to employment**. Better training to obtain recognised and relevant professional qualifications, job creation and improved employment advice and guidance were at the focus of the Fund. While the priority has shifted to people in work, helping them to stay in and progress in their jobs, the ESF has not forgotten the most vulnerable in society. The Fund continued to target training for young people, the unemployed and those excluded from the labour market. The social partners, NGOs and others, such as charities and the voluntary sector, have played a particularly important role in achieving the ESF's objectives.

A total of 5% of the ESF budget has been earmarked to finance **innovative instruments** (including pilot actions and studies, transfer and dissemination of good practices), to assess the effectiveness of ESF-funded projects and to promote exchanges of experience between MS. These ESF initiatives have led to the creation of three major Community programmes: EUROFORM, which experimented with new ways of training and employment; HORIZON, which dealt with training for people with disabilities; and NOW (New Opportunities for Women), which looked at how to help women enter or re-enter the labour market. Building on the success of these Community initiatives, a series of new programmes were soon launched to address specific labour market problems and to further stimulate the pan-European, transnational exchange of ideas and approaches. YOUTH-START helped young people with no qualifications to get their first job; INTEGRA helped groups such as single parents, homeless people, refugees, prisoners and ex-prisoners to secure employment and to combat racial or other discrimination in training or employment; and ADAPT, which helped people adapt to business and industrial change, for example through IT training.

8. Enlargement: Finland and Sweden

16 When Finland and Sweden joined the EU in 1995, the new objective of the Structural Funds became to **support the development of sparsely populated regions** (those with eight or fewer inhabitants per square kilometre). The ESF has responded to the need to attract more workers into the market by allocating resources to **on-the-job training for older people** to enable them to stay in work longer or return to the labour market. The ESF has also supported initiatives to provide care for older people to enable family members to stay in or return to work. The ESF contributed by subsidising **childcare facilities**, for example, if a mother had to attend a training course three days a week, the ESF paid the fees. The reform of the ESF in 1993 ensured that support was not only available to **women** returning to work after childbirth, but also to low-skilled and under-skilled women at risk of unemployment or social exclusion. It also helped women to become entrepreneurs.

17 The ESF was designed to support the **European Employment Strategy**[5] in the context of the **Lisbon Strategy**.[6] One of the priorities of the ESF was to increase the flexibility of the workforce by **developing skills** and introducing new forms of work organisation. The ESF has contributed to improving education systems to make them more responsive to labour market needs. It has focused on **lifelong learning and continuous training**. Entrepreneurship—the development of **new businesses** and the **growth of small and medium-sized enterprises** (SMEs)—has also become a priority to unlock the full employment potential of the services and industry-related services sector, particularly the information society and the environment sector. The ESF has continued to **promote equal opportunities in access to the labour market** and the prevention of social exclusion.

18 The main objective of the common EU immigration policy, defined in 1999 and 2004, was to better manage migration flows through a coordinated approach that considers the economic and demographic situation in the EU. The ESF supports the **integration of migrants**, including asylum seekers, through specific measures to increase their participation in employment, improve their language skills and prevent discrimination in the labour market, thus strengthening their social inclusion.

19 The **EQUAL initiative** was launched in 2000 to develop new ways of tackling discrimination and inequalities in the labour market and to promote a more inclusive working life by combating discrimination and exclusion. EQUAL's principles and structure (empowering partnership, transnationality, mainstreaming,

---

[5] The European Employment Strategy (EES) dates back to 1997, when the EU MS undertook to establish a set of common objectives and targets for employment policy. Its main aim is the creation of more and better jobs throughout the EU.

[6] Lisbon European Council, 23–24 March 2000, Presidency Conclusions. The Lisbon Strategy focused on innovation and the internal market, and on employment and labour market reform, by incorporating the major elements of the former EES. Among its aims were for the EU's overall employment rate to reach 70% and the female employment rate to reach more than 60%. Subsequently an additional target was added: to raise the employment rate for older workers to 50% by 2010.

innovation and thematic approach) have proved effective in addressing disadvantage and discrimination in a comprehensive way. These tools have now become the EU's approach and solutions.

9. Enlargement: Ten New Member States

In 2004, with the accession of ten new MS, the ESF faced new demands: most of the new MS faced major **challenges in transforming their societies and economies into market economies**, in defining employment policies and in aligning institutions and policies with the European Employment Strategy. The ESF has supported the new MS in addressing disparities and setting employment policy priorities when they joined the EU.[7]

The scope of the ESF has been extended to 'combating all forms of discrimination and inequalities in the labour market' and new tools have been developed to help employers comply with the equity directives.[8] **New types of employment services and roles** were also promoted, as well as personalised training,[9] communication as an integral part of the integration process.

10. The ESF Reform for the 2007–2013 Programming Period

The ESF has been reformed again for the 2007–2013 programming period to **support a strategic approach to growth and jobs**. ESF support was focused on areas where it could have the greatest impact in achieving the objectives agreed between MS and the Commission. The rules of the ESF have been simplified to clarify the responsibilities of MS and regions, as well as those of the Commission.

In the 2007–2013 period, the aim was to increase the **adaptability of workers**, businesses and entrepreneurs in the context of creating a flexible labour market. Under this priority, the ESF supported the modernisation and strengthening of labour market institutions, active labour market measures and lifelong learning activities. In addition, the Fund also sought to prevent social exclusion and combat discrimination.

From 2007, a new area of the Fund was the strengthening of the **capacity of public institutions** at all levels of government (national, regional and local) to develop and implement policies and services. The ESF has also supported partnerships between employers, trade unions, NGOs and public administrations to

---

[7] Musiałkowska et al. (2020).

[8] Parliament/Council Directive 2006/54/EC *on the implementation of the principle of equal opportunities and equal treatment of men and women in matters of employment and occupation (recast)*, O.J. L 204/23 (2006), has brought together some older directives. This directive requires the implementation of the prohibition of direct and indirect sex discrimination, harassment and sexual harassment in pay, (access to) employment and in occupational social security schemes.

[9] Pelucha et al. (2019).

promote reforms in the field of employment and social inclusion. Transnational cooperation is an integral part of all ESF actions and has become part of all innovation activities.

25   In 2014, the **European Social Policy Network** (ESPN) was established to provide the European Commission with independent information, analysis and expertise on social policies and to help monitor progress towards the EU's social protection and social inclusion objectives set out in the Europe 2020 strategy. According to the report "Social Investment in Europe" drawn-up by ESPN experts, only a few EU MS maintain a social investment approach in a number of social policy areas, while the majority have not made much progress and have yet to develop one.[10]

11. ESF for the 2014–2020 Period

26   For the period of 2014–2020, the ESF covered the following four **main areas of investment**: employment, particularly youth employment; social inclusion; education; and good governance (i.e. better public administration).[11] The ESF also focuses on several **key themes**, such as promoting employment and labour mobility; promoting social inclusion and combating poverty; investing in education, skills development and lifelong learning; and improving institutional capacity and the efficiency of public administration. The new instrument of **thematic concentration and ring-fencing** is introduced in the cohesion policy, which is reflected in the ESF area by introducing a minimum share of ESF 23.1% of total cohesion resources and by requiring MS to allocate at least 20% of these ESF funds to social inclusion and poverty reduction.

27   To address persistent high youth unemployment at the EU level, the initial prefinancing rate for operational programmes supported by the **Youth Employment Initiative** will increase from 1% to 30% in 2015.[12]

28   The **European Pillar of Social Rights**[13] sets out 20 key principles and rights as strategic objectives covering three themes:

---

[10] Bouget et al. (2015).

[11] Parliament/Council Regulation (EU) No. 1304/2013 *on the European Social Fund*, O.J. L 347/470 (2013).

[12] Regulation (EU) 2015/779 of the European Parliament and of the Council of 20 May 2015 amending Regulation (EU) No. 1304/2013, as regards an additional initial prefinancing amount paid to operational programmes supported by the Youth Employment Initiative.

[13] President Juncker spoke of an EPSR for the first time in his State of the Union speech of 2015. In April 2017, the Pillar was the subject of a Commission Recommendation, later jointly signed by the European Parliament, the Council and the Commission. https://ec.europa.eu/info/strategy/priorities-2019-2024/economy-works-people/jobs-growth-and-investment/european-pillar-social-rights/european-pillar-social-rights-20-principles_en.

- equal opportunities and access to the labour market (e.g. skills, education and lifelong learning, equal opportunities, gender equality and active support for employment);
- fair working conditions (e.g. safe and adaptable employment, wages, information on employment conditions and protection in the event of dismissal, social dialogue and work-life balance);
- social protection and social inclusion (e.g. childcare, minimum income, unemployment benefits, inclusion of people with disabilities, assistance to the homeless, access to basic services, health and long-term care).

The **Action Plan of the European Pillar of Social Rights**[14] outlines three priority objectives and a set of actions which form the basis for the programmes to be implemented with the resources used in this area.

12. ESF+ for the 2021–2027 Period

In 2018, the Commission proposed a regulation for the ESF+, which was then amended in May 2020 to address the economic and social damage caused by the pandemic of the coronavirus.[15] The ESF+[16] supports the **implementation of the EPSR**, particularly investment in youth, support for people in vulnerable situations after job or income loss, food and basic material assistance for the most deprived (the European Fund for Aid to the Most Deprived (FEAD)[17] has been integrated into the ESF+), investment in children, and support for social innovation and entrepreneurship through the new Employment and Social Innovation (EaSI) funds.[18]

As a response to the COVID-19 crisis, regulations were amended[19] to allow for more flexibility in the implementation of operational programmes supported by the European Regional Development Fund, the European Social Fund and the

---

[14] https://op.europa.eu/webpub/empl/european-pillar-of-social-rights/en/.

[15] COM(2020) 447.

[16] Parliament/Council Regulation (EU) 2021/1057 *establishing the European Social Fund Plus (ESF+)*, O.J. L 231/21 (2021).

[17] Parliament/Council Regulation (EU) No. 223/2014 *on the Fund for European Aid to the Most Deprived*, O.J. L 72/1 (2014).

[18] Parliament/Council Regulation (EU) No. 1296/2013 *on a European Union Programme for Employment and Social Innovation ("EaSI")*, O. J. L 347/238 (2013).

[19] Parliament/Council Regulation (EU) No. 1301/2013 *on the European Regional Development Fund and on specific provisions concerning the Investment for growth and jobs goal*, O.J. L 347/289 (2013) and Parliament/Council Regulation (EU) No. 1303/2013 *laying down common provisions on the [ESI Funds]*, O.J. L 347/320 (2013) were amended by Parliament/Council Regulation (EU) No. 2020/460 *amending Regulations (EU) No. 1301/2013, (EU) No. 1303/2013 and (EU) No. 508/2014 as regards specific measures to mobilise investments in the healthcare systems of Member States and in other sectors of their economies in response to the COVID-19 outbreak (Coronavirus Response Investment Initiative)*, O.J. L 99/5 (2020).

Cohesion Fund and by the European Maritime and Fisheries Fund. However, as the serious negative effects on Union economies and societies worsened, both Regulations were amended again by Regulation (EU) 2020/558.[20] Those amendments have provided **additional flexibility to mobilise non-utilised support** from the Funds for the necessary response to the crises and by simplifying procedural requirements linked to programme implementation and audits.

32 The so-called **REACT-EU** (Recovery Assistance for Cohesion and the Territories of Europe)[21] is one of the largest programmes set up under the NextGenerationEU instrument. This new funding will complement the 2014–2020 programmes and top up cohesion allocations for 2021–2027, bringing the total envelope for structural and investment funds to above current levels and making it the highest single policy support instrument in the EU budget. These additional resources will be used for projects to support crisis recovery capacities in the context of the crisis and for investments in operations contributing to the preparation of a green, digital and resilient recovery of the economy.

33 The EU introduced a new instrument for temporary **Support to mitigate Unemployment Risks in an Emergency** (SURE),[22] which provides low-interest loans of up to EUR 100 billion to MS to finance short-time work schemes. In supporting national unemployment[23] benefit schemes in the EU, SURE has the potential of substantially keeping down the number of unemployed.

34 The need for a larger European Social Fund would demonstrate a stronger commitment to social policy through the ESF+ designation.[24] However, the larger numbers are largely the result of tracking inflation and incorporating some instruments into ESF+ that were not previously included. At the same time, a larger share of the ESF is dedicated to social inclusion.

---

[20] Parliament/Council Regulation (EU) 2020/558 *amending Regulations (EU) No. 1301/2013 and (EU) No. 1303/2013 as regards specific measures to provide exceptional flexibility for the use of the European Structural and Investments Funds in response to the COVID-19 outbreak*, O.J. L 130/1 (2020).

[21] Parliament/Council Regulation (EU) 2020/2221 *amending Regulation (EU) No. 1303/2013 as regards additional resources and implementing arrangements to provide assistance for fostering crisis repair in the context of the COVID-19 pandemic and its social consequences and for preparing a green, digital and resilient recovery of the economy (REACT-EU)*, O.J. L 437/30 (2020).

[22] Council Regulation (EU) 2020/672 *on the establishment of a European instrument for temporary support to mitigate unemployment risks in an emergency (SURE) following the COVID-19 outbreak*, O.J. L 159/1 (2020). SURE is based on Article 122 TFEU and funded as a European instrument backed by EUR 25 billion guarantees committed by MS to the EU budget to leverage its financial power.

[23] Lichner et al. (2022).

[24] Lecerf (2019).

References[25]

Bouget, D., Frazer, H., Marlier, E., Sabato, S., & Vanhercke, B. (2015). Social Investment in Europe, a Study of National Policies, Post-Print hal-03038843, HAL. https://ideas.repec.org/p/hal/journl/hal-03038843.html

Hajdu, S., Kondor, Z., Kondrik, K., Miklós-Molnár, M., Nyikos, G., & Sódar, G. (2017). *Kohéziós Politika 2014–2020*. Dialóg Campus Kiadó.

Lecerf, M. (2019). *European Social Fund Plus (ESF+) 2021-2027*, EPRS: European Parliamentary Research Service. Retrieved June 26, 2022, from https://policycommons.net/artifacts/1335100/european-social-fund-plus-esf-2021-2027/1941340/. CID: 20.500.12592/wmj4s9.

Lichner, I., Lyócsa, Š., & Výrostová, E. (2022). Nominal and discretionary household income convergence: The effect of a crisis in a small open economy. *Structural Change and Economic Dynamics, 61*, 18–31. https://doi.org/10.1016/j.strueco.2022.02.004

Musiałkowska, I., Idczak, P., & Potluka, O. (2020). Successes & failures in EU cohesion policy: An introduction to EU cohesion policy in Eastern, Central, and Southern Europe. *De Gruyter Open Poland*, 119–142.

Pelucha, M., Kveton, V., & Potluka, O. (2019). Using mixed method approach in measuring effects of training in firms: Case study of the European Social Fund support. *Evaluation and Program Planning, 73*, 146–155. https://doi.org/10.1016/j.evalprogplan.2018.12.008

---

[25] All cited internet sources have last been consulted on 28 June 2022.

References

Article 163 [Administration]
(ex-Article 147 TEC)

The Fund shall be administered by the Commission.
The Commission shall be assisted in this task by a Committee presided over by a Member of the Commission and composed of representatives of governments, trade unions and employers' organisations.

Contents

1. Origin and the First Period 1
2. Changes Related to the Transition from the Annual Budget to the Multiannual Financial Framework 5
3. Roles and Responsibilities in Shared Management 7
References

1. Origin and the First Period

The article was originally numbered Article 124 TEEC, then Article 147 TEC, and the Lisbon Treaty changed the numbering to Article 163 TFEU. The content has not been changed. **1**

The ESF is the longest-established structural fund, initially seen as a form of support for the practicalities of free movement of workers. The **ESF was managed by the Commission, assisted by the ESF Committee**. The ESF Committee was and still is composed of an equal number of members representing governments, trade unions and employers. **2**

In the early years, the fund was used by EEC governments to tackle problems at the national level. There were a number of difficulties, the main one being the division of responsibilities between the Community institutions and the MS. In the early days, the ESF was used to 'compensate' for job losses. Support was a slow and bureaucratic process, operating as an '**intergovernmental transfer of funds**', which hindered the monitoring and accountability of the quality of training. Applications were **automatically** accepted by the Commission. In the absence of an overall European strategy, the funds were not used for strategic purposes but were **allocated to** a wide range of **ad hoc projects**. The problems increasingly supported reform of the ESF system. **3**

The growing administrative burden continued to be a problem for the ESF, and experience led to the conclusion that the Fund should be based on a **bottom-up approach**. A major change in financial management was introduced by Council **4**

Regulation (EEC) No. 1787/84 on the European Regional Development Fund.[1] It also set a minimum and a maximum for the ESF, instead of the previous quota, which determined the framework within which each MS could receive aid.

2. Changes Related to the Transition from the Annual Budget to the Multiannual Financial Framework

5   The initiative for longer-term planning for the ESF and MS' employment policies was aligned with the process of moving from an annual budget to a multiannual financial framework (1989–1993). This meant that the Commission and MS could be confident that resources would be available for the whole period and that multi-annual programmes could be launched safely. The **MS and the Commission coordinate and plan together** for spending from the European Funds. MS have agreed to exchange employment data and strategies to better integrate the ESF into MS' labour market policies. The reform has brought the ESF closer to the needs of regions and MS.

6   The ESF is guided by three principles: partnership, co-financing and shared management. **Partnership** requires the ESF to be designed, implemented and monitored in cooperation between the Commission, regional authorities and other partners such as NGOs and trade unions. **Co-financing** requires national and regional authorities to take ownership of the programme by funding part of it. Co-financing for grants may be provided from beneficiaries' own resources, income generated by the project or financial or in-kind contributions from third parties.[2] **Shared management** requires that on-the-spot implementation is managed by national authorities, following European rules and guidelines and under the control of national authorities.

3. Roles and Responsibilities in Shared Management

7   To adequately ensure the protection of the EU's financial interests, Union secondary legislation provides for different methods of **budget implementation**. Accordingly, the Commission implements the budget either 'directly' through its departments and executive agencies[3] or by way of 'shared management'.[4] In this case, the Commission delegates budget implementation tasks to the MS. The Commission and the MS are required to observe the principles of sound financial

---

[1] O.J. L 169/1 (1984).

[2] Parliament/Council Regulation (EU, Euratom) 2018/1046 (the 'Financial Regulation'), O.J. L 193/1 (2018), lays down rules on the implementation of the general budget of the Union (Union budget), including the rules on grants, prizes, procurement, indirect management, financial instruments, budgetary guarantees, financial assistance and the reimbursement of external experts.

[3] Article 62.1 point (a) of the Financial Regulation.

[4] Article 62.1 point (b) of the Financial Regulation.

management, transparency and non-discrimination.[5] They are also required to ensure 'adequate visibility of the Union's action'.[6]

The **Commission is responsible** for the management of the ESF, including its administration and decisions on the use of the funds.[7] The Commission also controls the use of the funds. The Commission keeps the European Parliament and the Council regularly informed of developments concerning the ESF+. This ensures the Commission's overall accountability.

To carry out its tasks more effectively, the Commission is assisted by a committee (the **European Social Fund+ Committee**[8]), which is made up of representatives of the EU, the MS (government), trade unions and employers. The MS are represented as follows: one government representative, one representative of the workers' organisations, one representative of the employers' organisations and one alternate for each member. The Committee shall also include one representative of each of the organisations representing workers' and employers' organisations at the EU level. Depending on the issues to be discussed, the Committee may invite other non-voting representatives of stakeholders to its meetings (e.g. acceding, candidate or potential candidate countries, the European Investment Bank and the European Investment Fund, and relevant civil society organisations).

Following the reorganisation of the ESF+, the ESF Committee has been maintained, but with expanded tasks to cover the new areas of the ESF+ Regulation. The ESF+ Committee **shall be consulted** on the planned use of technical assistance in the case of support from the ESF+ area under shared management,[9] as well as on other issues having an impact on the implementation of EU-level strategies relevant to ESF+. The ESF+ Committee may **give an opinion** on issues related to the ESF+ contribution to the implementation of the European Pillar of Social Rights, including country-specific recommendations and priorities related to the European Semester, such as the National Reform Programmes and issues relevant to ESF+. The European Commission is not legally bound by the resolutions but must inform the committee of the extent to which its position has been considered or disregarded.

The Commission should also set up **working groups** for each area of ESF+ to provide an appropriate forum for discussing the implementation of ESF+. Under Article 163 TFEU and Article 40 of the ESF+ Regulation, two working groups have been set up to deal with the technical aspects of the implementation of ESF+ programmes.

Each **MS**, after approval by the Commission, implements one or more **Operational Programmes** (OPs) financed by the ESF over a seven-year period. OPs set

---

[5] Article 63.1 sentence 2 of the Financial Regulation.
[6] Fiebelkorn and Petzold (2020).
[7] Hajdu et al. (2017).
[8] Article 39 of the Parliament/Council Regulation (EU) 2021/1057 *establishing the European Social Fund Plus (ESF+)*, O.J. L 231/21(2021).
[9] Article 35 of Regulation (EU) 2021/1060.

priorities and objectives for employment-related projects, which are then managed by public and private organisations. These projects are usually implemented with the involvement of individuals, companies or organisations.

13   MS are responsible for **managing the programmes**. This includes project selection, control and monitoring—to prevent, detect and correct irregularities—and evaluation of the projects implemented. The MS must also ensure that rules in other areas of Community law, such as public procurement, state aid rules and environmental protection, are properly applied.[10] The Commission must satisfy itself that the MS has set up and maintains an implementation and control system which is in conformity with the rules and which functions properly and effectively (Article 317 TFEU).

References[11]

Fiebelkorn, V., & Petzold, H. A. (2020). EU-Förderung in geteilter Verwaltung – am Beispiel der Europäischen Struktur- und Investitionsfonds. *Europarecht*, 536–553.

Hajdu, S., Kondor, Z., Kondrik, K., Miklós-Molnár, M., Nyikos, G., & Sódar, G. (2017). *Kohéziós Politika 2014–2020*. Dialóg Campus Kiadó.

Nyikos, G. (2012). Végrehajtási intézményrendszer a kohéziós politikában [Implementing institutions in cohesion policy]. *Polgári Szemle: Gazdasági És Társadalmi Folyóirat* (1786-6553 1786-8823): 8 3-6, 40-164.

---

[10] Nyikos (2012).

[11] All cited internet sources have last been consulted on 28 June 2022.

Article 164 [Implementation]
(ex-Article 148 TEC)

The European Parliament and the Council, acting in accordance with the ordinary legislative procedure and after consulting the Economic and Social Committee and the Committee of the Regions, shall adopt implementing regulations relating to the European Social Fund.

Contents

1. Origin and Legal Bases 1
2. Priority Areas and Policy Objectives 5
3. Thematic Concentration and Ring-Fencing 7
4. Co-Financing Benefit 11
5. Enabling Conditions 14

1. Origin and Legal Bases

The article was originally numbered as Article 125 TEEC, then Article 148 TEC, and following the Lisbon Treaty it was renumbered as Article 164 TFEU. Its content has been modified due to the change of the co-decision procedure introduced by the Maastricht Treaty into an ordinary legislative procedure by the Lisbon Treaty but has not been substantially changed.

Under Article 178 TFEU, the European Parliament and the Council, acting in accordance with the ordinary legislative procedure, shall adopt the implementing regulations for the European Regional Development Fund, but Article 164 TFEU shall continue to apply to the European Social Fund. It follows from the above that the **general regulations for the Funds** are adopted by the EP and the Council based on **Article 177 TFEU**, while the **implementing regulation** for the ESF is adopted based on **Article 164 TFEU**.

The Treaties give the Union the power to establish and implement regulations on the European Social Fund (Article 164 TFEU), which aims to improve employment opportunities for workers in the internal market and thereby contribute to the **EU's standard of living** (Article 162 TFEU). The ESF is tasked with improving employment opportunities, strengthening social inclusion, fighting poverty, promoting education, skills and life-long learning, and developing active, comprehensive and sustainable inclusion policies in accordance with the missions entrusted to the ESF under Article 162 TFEU and thereby to contribute to **economic, social and territorial cohesion** (Article 174 TFEU).

© Springer Nature Switzerland AG 2023
R. Böttner, H.-J. Blanke (eds.), *Treaty on the Functioning of the European Union – A Commentary*, Springer Commentaries on International and European Law, https://doi.org/10.1007/16559_2022_64

4   In terms of competences and **legal bases**, in the 2021–2027 programming period the ESF+[1] brings together different competences by creating a single overarching instrument. The combination of powers and provisions can be divided into two strands. On the one hand, the common management objectives for the former **ESF** (Articles 162 and 164 TFEU) and **Youth Employment Initiative**, on the other hand, the basic material **support for the most deprived persons** (Article 175 TFEU), which also covers the specificities of the outermost regions through Article 349 TFEU. On the other hand, there are the areas of direct and indirect management, which mediate **measures to promote social innovation** (EaSI, Articles 46 point (d), 149 and 153.2 point (a) TFEU). The regulation thus combines the competences and sources of free movement of workers, employment, social policy, ESF and social cohesion to address the different social objectives in a comprehensive way through funding.

2. Priority Areas and Policy Objectives

5   ESF+ focuses on a number of **priority areas** (Article 4 of the Regulation), including: improving access to employment and activation measures for all jobseekers; modernising labour market institutions and services; promoting a gender-balanced labour market participation, equal working conditions, the adaptation of workers; improving the quality, inclusiveness, effectiveness and labour market relevance of education and training systems; promoting equal access to and completion of quality and inclusive education and training, lifelong learning and equal opportunities; enhancing equal and timely access to quality, sustainable and affordable services and promoting social innovation and social integration in the EU.

6   The ESF+ under shared management supports the **'smarter Europe'** and the **'greener, low carbon Europe'** policy objectives as defined in the Common Provisions Regulation.[2]

3. Thematic Concentration and Ring-Fencing

7   In line with the **principle of thematic concentration** introduced in cohesion policy in the previous programming period and continued in the current period, the ESF+ Regulation also provides for a **minimum level of shared management of ESF+**

---

[1] Parliament/Council Regulation (EU) 2021/1057 establishing the European Social Fund Plus (ESF+), O.J. L 231/21 (2021).

[2] Parliament/Council Regulation (EU) 2021/1060 *laying down common provisions on the [ESI Funds]*, O.J. L 231/159 (2021), establishes the operational framework for the different funds and sets out, in particular, the policy objectives and rules for programming, monitoring and evaluation, management and control of EU funds implemented under shared management. It defines the general objectives of the ESF+ and the specific provisions concerning the type of actions that may be financed by the ESF+.

resources by MS for certain areas for the period 2021–2027: at least 25% of the resources to promote social inclusion (Article 7.4); at least 3% to support the most deprived (Article 7.5); MS with an average proportion of children at risk of poverty or social exclusion above the EU average for the period 2017–2019 should allocate at least 5% of their resources to addressing child poverty (Article 7.3). MS with an average share of young people aged 15–29 not in employment, education or training above the EU average for the period 2017–2019[3] should allocate at least 12.5% of their ESF+ resources to targeted measures and structural reforms in this area (Article 7.6).

The link between European economic governance and cohesion policy is also strongly reflected in the ESF+ Regulation: programming of shared management funds should reflect interventions addressing the challenges identified in the **National Reform Programmes** and relevant **country-specific recommendations** in the context of the European Semester (Article 7.1).

The implementation of the ESF+ shall respect the principles and rights set out in the **European Pillar of Social Rights** and **the EU Charter of Fundamental Rights**. MS should pay particular attention to ensuring that complaints are examined effectively. If the Commission finds that the Charter has been breached, it will decide on the corrective measures to be taken.

Under the **partnership principle** of cohesion policy, each programme is developed through a collective process involving public authorities at European, regional and local level, social partners and civil society organisations. This partnership applies to all stages of the programming process, from programming, through management and implementation, to monitoring and evaluation. MS should ensure the meaningful participation of social partners and civil society organisations in this process, for which the ESF+ under shared management will provide support for **capacity building of social partners and civil society organisations**, including through training, networking measures and strengthening social dialogue, as well as for activities jointly undertaken by the social partners. Where capacity-building of social partners and civil society organisations is identified in a country-specific recommendation, the MS concerned shall allocate an amount equivalent to **at least 0.25% of the resources of the ESF+ shared management area** for this purpose (ring-fencing).

4. Co-Financing Benefit

Additionality is a fundamental principle of the cohesion policy. This means that contributions from the funds must not replace structural or equivalent public expenditure in the regions covered by the principle but must complement it. For the programming period 2021–2027, the **co-financing rates** are 85–15% in less developed regions (GDP per capita < 75% EU-27 average), 60–40% in transition

---

[3] Ten eligible MS: BG, HR, CY, FR, EL, HU, IT, RO, SK and ES.

regions (GDP per capita between 75% and 100% EU-27 average) and 40–60% in more developed regions (GDP per capita > 100% EU-27 average).

12 **Support for the most deprived is encouraged** by the ESF+ Regulation in such a way that if the Member State allocates the funds under a specific priority or programme, the EU co-financing rate is **90%**, which is higher than the rates presented above.

13 If MS dedicate at least one priority to implementing **social innovation and social experimentation activities** or **innovative approaches** developed under the EaSI and other EU programmes, or both, the maximum co-financing rate for such priorities may be increased to **95%** up to a maximum of 5% of the national resources of the ESF+ area under shared management.

5. Enabling Conditions

14 Enabling conditions (the successors of the so-called ex-ante conditions) are listed in the legislation. Each permit condition is **linked to a specific objective** and applies automatically for the whole period. In the event of non-compliance, the expenditure concerned may be included in payment claims but will not be reimbursed by the Commission.

15 The enabling condition for ESF+ investment in **youth employment** is a strategic policy framework for active labour market policies, including youth employment interventions: pathways to young people not in employment, education or training, including catch-up measures, based on quality criteria, taking into account the criteria for quality vocational education and training, including in the framework of the Youth Guarantee.

16 The investment of the ESF+ in **active inclusion** is conditional on a national strategic policy framework for social inclusion and poverty reduction, including an evidence-based diagnosis of poverty and social exclusion, including child poverty, with a particular focus on equal access to quality services for vulnerable children, homelessness, spatial and educational segregation, limited access to basic services and infrastructure, and the specific needs of vulnerable people of all ages.

17 The **shared management** strand of the ESF+ will continue to be part of cohesion policy and it will mainly be regulated by the Common Provisions Regulation. As such, the same rules on management, programming, monitoring, auditing, etc. will apply as for most of the other Funds under shared management. Programmes in MS can continue to combine European Regional Development Fund (ERDF) funding and ESF+ funding through multi-fund programmes.

Index

The references printed in bold refer to the provision (Article; Pre.: Preamble), the regular numbers refer to the margin number in the respective comment. The entries for "144 post ..." refer to the Supplement to Title VIII on the reform of EMU: Introduction (a), the ESM Treaty (b), the Fiscal Compact (c) and the Banking Union (d).

A
Abuse of dominance **102**, 40-88, **106** 19, 20, 36, 38
   bundling **102** 74
   essential facilities **102** 71
   exclusionary abuse **102** 60-88
   exclusive dealing **102** 78
   exploitative abuse **102** 53-58
   margin squeeze **102** 65
   predatory pricing **102** 62
   price discrimination **102** 61
   rebates **102** 81
   refusal to deal **102** 68
   self-preferencing **102** 88
   tying **102** 74
   unfair excessive prices **102** 54
Accession agreement **139** 13, 14, 19; **140** 6
Access to documents **155** 16
Access to the occupation **90** 15
Accident investigation **91** 20
Acquis communautaire
   and enhanced cooperation **118** 20
   and intellectual property **118** 7-10
Acute situation **144** 6
Adjustment Programme
   accountability **144 post b** 73, 74
   debt restructuring **144 post b** 70
   European Stability Mechanism **144 post b** 69-72
   privatisation **144 post b** 70
   social rights **144 post b** 75-77
   spending cuts **144 post b** 70
Administrative cooperation **113** 35
Advisory Committee on Restrictive Practices and Dominant Positions **103** 12, 31
Agreement on the Transfer and Mutualization of Contributions to the Single Resolution Fund **139** 31
Arbitration Clause **144 post a** 45
Backstop **144 post a** 24
Borrowed administration arrangement **144 post a** 45
Clause of Coherence **144 post a** 42
financial stability **144 post a** 30
integrated financial framework **144 post a** 33
legal nature **144 post a** 17
primacy of EU law **144 post a** 43
Purpose **144 post a** 24
SRF financing volume **144 post a** 17
Agreement with a third country **91** 4
Agriculture **103** 46
Altmark test **93** 6, 20; **107** 49-53
Animal wellbeing **91** 23
Annual paid leave **158** 2-5
Antitrust law
   abuse of dominance (*see* Abuse of dominance)
   association of undertakings **101** 17
   cartel facilitators **101** 16
   concerted practice **101** 18
   coordination **101** 13-22

Antitrust law (*cont.*)
   dominance **102** 10-36
   dominant undertakings **102** 1
   effect on trade **101** 59
   essential facilities **102** 71
   evidence of concertation **101** 20
   hard core restrictions **101** 1
   horizontal restrictions **101** 15
   hypothetical monopolist test **101** 32
   intellectual property rights **102** 20
   interbrand competition **101** 48
   intrabrand competition **101** 48
   legal monopoly **102** 19
   market definition **101** 31-38
   monopoly **102** 19
   oligopolistic interdependence **101** 19
   oligopolistic markets **101** 19
   prohibited agreements **101** 12-66
   relevant market **101** 31-38
   restrictions **101** 27-29
   Sherman Act **101** 49
   SSNIP test **101** 32
   State action defence **102** 19
   State prerogatives **101** 25
   undertaking **101** 23-26
   US antitrust **101** 3
   vertical cooperation **101** 14
   Wouters exception **101** 50
Approximation of laws **90** 14; **144 post d** 124, 133, 217, 218, 234, 235, 244, 254-256, 277, 300
   ex-ante approximation **117** 7, 13, 17
   ex-post approximation **117** 7, 9, 13, 14, 17, 18
   consumer protection **114** 57, 60
   delegated acts **114** 50
   directives **114** 46
   direct taxes **115** 3
   environmental protection **114** 56, 60
   exceptions **114** 51-73
   fiscal provisions **114** 42
   flexibility clause **114** 13
   free movement of persons **114** 43
   full harmonisation **114** 23
   goal-driven approximation **116** 4, 7, 10, 24
   high level of protection **114** 37
   implementing acts **114** 50
   infringement procedure **114** 75
   in intellectual property **118** 8
   indirect approximation **117** 2, 5
   minimum harmonisation **114** 22
   national opt-outs **114** 51-73
   necessary measures **114** 25
   non-harmonised field **92** 2
   optional harmonisation **114** 21
   precautionary principle **114** 39
   proportionality **114** 32
   preventive approximation **116** 4, 7, 24
   protection of the working environment **114** 56, 60
   public health **114** 62
   regulations **114** 47
   rights and interests of employed persons **114** 44
   Single European Act **114** 5
   social policy **151** 12
   soft law **114** 49
Area of freedom, security and justice
   border checks, asylum and immigration **116** 17
   judicial cooperation **116** 17
   police cooperation **117** 17
Article 98 TFEU
   addressee **98** 7
   and secondary law **98** 5, 16
   and State aid provisions **98** 2
   and Title "Transport" **98** 5
   as a legal basis for secondary law **98** 16
   beneficiary **98** 7
   interpretation **98** 9
   jurisprudence of the ECJ **98** 3
   obsolescence **98** 13, 14
   principle of proportionality **98** 11
   relevance **98** 12-14, 17
   repeal **98** 1, 17
   retention **98** 2
Article 136 TFEU
   and Article 122 TFEU **122** 29-33
Artificial intelligence **157** 14
Artificial Intelligence Act **114** 83
Asset purchase programme **127** 21
Association of undertakings **101** 17
Asylum, Migration and Integration Fund **151** 27
Asylum Policy **151** 27
Austerity **144 post b** 63, 75; **151** 7
Autonomous treaty amendment
   Article 98 TFEU **98** 17

B

Bad Bank **144 post b** 96
Balance of payment **119** 35, 42, 45; **120** 41; **143** 9-12
   disequilibrium **143** 4, 11
   difficulties **122** 5, 34, 35
Balanced budget **144 post a** 7

Balanced budget rule
  implementation **144 post c** 34
  Stability and Growth Pact **144 post c** 25
  Treaty on Stability, Coordination and Governance **144 post c** 25
Balanced economic growth **144 post a** 38
Bank notes **139** 33, 36
  as legal tender **128** 9
  issue of **128** 9
  restriction of use **128** 4
Bank Recovery and Resolution Directive **144 post d** 6, 78, 105, 123, 124, 130-135, 161-176, 184-186, 195, 242-253, 269, 270, 280, 281, 283, 301, 302
  bail-in **144 post d** 170-173, 301
  bank insolvency **144 post d** 243, 251, 252, 256, 257, 279-281
  bridge institution tool **144 post d** 167, 168
  early intervention **144 post d** 105, 126, 129, 161, 247
  government financial stabilisation tools **144 post d** 195
  legal basis **144 post d** 132-138
  precautionary recapitalisation **144 post d** 189, 190
  resolution objectives **144 post d** 252
  resolvability **144 post d** 165, 252
Banking regulators **139** 30
Banking Union **139** 31; **144 post a** 2
  Agreement on the Transfer and Mutualization of Contributions to the Single Resolution Fund (*see* Agreement on the Transfer and Mutualization of Contributions to the Single Resolution Fund)
  Banco Popular Español **144 post a** 16
  competences **144 post d** 49, 55, 88, 261
  components **127** 37
  European Deposit Insurance System **144 post a** 18; **144 post d** 7, 11, 268, 269, 284-293
  extraordinary public financial support **144 post d** 183-186
  fiscal discipline **139** 24, 25; **140** 2, 16
  governance **144 post d** 11, 48
  guidelines **144 post d** 266
  legal basis **144 post d** 6
  price stability **144 post a** 37
  qualifying holdings **144 post d** 72, 90, 102, 223
  Single Resolution Board **144 post d** 49, 139-165, 177, 193, 197-203, 290, 291

  Single Resolution Fund **144 post a** 3, 5; **144 post d** 144, 158, 174-181, 192-194, 295-297
    liquidity **144 post d** 144
  Single Resolution Mechanism (*see* SRM)
  Single Supervisory Mechanism (*see* SSM)
Banknotes **132** 11, 25, 61, 62
Banks *see* Financial Institutions
Blockchain technology **132** 11a
Block exemption *see at* Competition law ~exemptions
Border adjustment **111** 3
Borrowed administration agreement **144 post a** 45
Brexit **123** 9; **131** 16; **152** 29
Bridging Clause
  social policy **153** 22
Budget deficit **139** 59, 60; **140** 16-19
Budgetary discipline **126** 2; **144 post a** 31
  conditionality **136** 19
  coordination and surveillance **136** 5
  COVID-19 **126** 9
Budgetary Framework Directive **126** 45
Bundling **102** 74

C

Cabotage **90** 29; **91** 10
Capital duty **113** 33
Capital market **143** 3, 27, 29
Capital Requirements Directive **144 post d** 73, 74, 105, 173, 206, 207, 217-240
  accountability **144 post d** 227
  capital buffers **144 post d** 218, 228-233, 240
  Liquidity Coverage Ratio **144 post d** 213, 214
  Net Stable Funding Ratio **144 post d** 213, 215
Capital Requirements Regulation **144 post d** 73, 74, 100, 105, 113, 173, 206-216, 234-240, 269-271, 275, 276
Care-related career breaks **157** 20
Carriage of goods **95** 2, 11
Carrier **94** 11
Cartel **101** 1, 15
Cartel facilitators **101** 16
Cedefop **154** 17
Central bank digital currency **132** 11a
Central securities depositaries **132** 69
Certification **90** 14
Charges and dues
  reasonable level **97** 1, 3 et seq.

Charges with equivalent effect to customs
    duties **106** 3; **110** 15
Child poverty **153** 49
Circulation of money **140** 33, 36, 37
Citizenship of the EU **106** 45; **139** 6
Close cooperation **144 post d** 51, 61-63, 155,
    168
Co-decision **91** 1
Cohesion
    economic **164** 4
    ESF **162** 2
    social and territorial **106** 9, 44, 45; **164** 4
Coins
    as legal tender **128** 1
    issue of **128** 11
Collective agreements **101** 9
Collective bargaining **153** 37; **155** 19
Collective dominance **102**33
Collective redress **103** 35
Commission *see* European Commission
Committee of the Regions **149** 2, 4
Common Agricultural Policy **101** 9
Common commercial policy **139** 44
Common concerns **146** 8
Common transport policy **90** 7, 9 et seq., 12,
    17, 22 et seq., 39 et seq.
    scope **100** 5
    implementation **100** 9
    requirement of positive action by Council
        100 3
Community Charter of the Fundamental Social
    Rights of Workers **151** 6, 9
Community design **118** 8, 9, 25
Community trade-mark **118** 8, 9, 25, 35, 36, 48
Compensation test **107** 49-53
Competences
    of the EU
        exclusive **113** 2, 3; **128** 2
        monetary policy **120** 15, 21-30; **127** 23;
            132 58
        priority **90** 36
        residual **90** 6, 36; **91** 12
        shared **90** 30, 36; **91** 12; **113** 2, 3; **118**
            19-21; **151** 4; **153** 6
        treaty-making power **90** 36; **91** 4
    of the Member States **147** 5
    parallel competences **91** 12
    parallel enforcement competence **103** 20
Competing products **110** 23, 43-45
Competition
    autonomy of undertakings **101** 26
    competitive tendering **93** 19
    distortion **90** 14, 17, 29; **91** 9

excessive **90** 15
general provisions **93** 2
restrictions **101** 27-29
tariff fixed to meet **96** 16 et seq.
Treaty rules **100** 14
Competition culture **103 6**
Competition Law **106** 6, 9, 18, 41, 47, 48, 52,
    54, 56, 62, 63, 87; **143** 15
    abuse of dominance (*see* Abuse of
        dominance)
    abuse model **103** 1
    administration **103** 4, 16, 19
    association of undertakings **101** 17
    authorisation **103** 1, 6, 7, 17, 20, 40
    cartel **101** 15
    cartel facilitators **101** 16
    cartel settlement **103** 24
    case allocation **103** 13, 29
    commitment decisions **103** 23, 28, 40
    concerted practice **101** 18
    coordination **101** 13-22
    de minimis doctrine **101** 44; **103** 17
    direct enforcement **101** 10
    dominance **102** 10-36
    dominant undertakings **102** 1
    effect on trade **101** 31, 59; **103** 1, 38
    effective supervision **103** 16
    enabling regulations **103** 42, 43 (*see also*
        Enabling Regulation 2015/1588)
    enforcement **103** 1, 2, 5-8, 10-16, 18, 20-22,
        28, 30, 32, 33, 35, 38, 40, 43-47
        appropriate regulations or directives
            103 2
        decentralisation **103** 18, 20, 27, 32, 40
        Directive 2019/1 **103** 1, 3, 41
        increase **103** 32
        parallel competence **103** 20
        private **103** 15, 34
        sector specific legislation **103** 5
        transitional arrangements **103** 1; **104** 4,
            8; **105** 2, 4-6
    essential facilities **102** 71
    European Competition Network **103** 29, 31
    evidence of concertation **101** 20
    ex ante control **103** 20, 42
    exemptions **103** 1, 6-8, 12, 14, 16, 27, 42-
        44, 46
        Article 101(3) TFEU exemptions **104** 1
        block exemption **90** 11; **103** 14, 31, 42,
            44
    findings of inapplicability **103** 25
    General Enforcement Regulations **103** 5-40
    hard core restrictions **101** 1

Index

horizontal restrictions **101** 15
hypothetical monopolist test **101** 32
inspections **103** 7, 21, 23, 28, 30
intellectual property rights **102** 20
interbrand competition **101** 48
interim measures **103** 14, 24, 27, 31
intrabrand competition **101** 48
justifications **101** 67-71
legal exceptions **103** 1, 20, 40, 44
legal monopoly **102** 19
leniency **103** 24, 28, 40
market definition **101** 31-38
merger control **103** 47
Merger Regulation **103** 1, 3, 10
monopoly **102** 19
national competition authorities (*see* National competition authorities)
national competition law **103** 10, 38
national procedural law **103** 12; **104** 7
negative clearance **103** 12, 25
network effects **102** 29
Notice on cooperation between national competition authorities and the Commission **103** 10, 13; **104** 6
Notice on cooperation between national courts and the Commission **103** 10, 15; **104** 6
notification **103** 1, 6, 12, 16, 19, 20, 40
 comfort letter **103** 16
oligopolistic interdependence **101** 19
oligopolistic markets **101** 19
powers of investigation and enforcement **103** 7
Private Action Directive (*see* Private Action Directive)
prohibition model **103** 1
prohibition regime **103** 6
prohibited agreements **101** 12-66
relationship between national and EU competition law **103** 38
relevant markets **101** 31-38; **102** 12
restrictions **101** 27-29
role of national courts **103** 14, 33
role of the Commission **116** 7
role of the ECJ **103** 27
role of the EP **103** 3
sanctions
 criminal sanctions **103** 27, 30
 fines **103** 7, 9, 22, 31, 37
 periodic penalty payments **103** 7, 9, 19, 22, 31, 37, 39
sector enquiries **103** 7, 24
Sherman Act **101** 49

SSNIP test **101** 32
State action defence **102** 19
State prerogatives **101** 25
structural remedies **103** 22, 28
substantive rules (*see* Substantive competition law rules)
sunk cost investments **102** 26
technological lead **102** 22
undertaking **101** 23-26
US antitrust **101** 3
uniform application **103** 6, 10
vertical cooperation **101** 14
vertical integration **102** 22
White Paper on the modernisation of the implementing rules of Article 81 and 82 of the EC Treaty **103** 18
Wouters exception **101** 50
Competition policy
 Common Agricultural Policy **101** 9
 internal market **101** 6, 8
 loyalty **101** 7
Competitive markets **106** 9
Competitive neutrality **106** 6
Concertation
 autonomy of undertakings **101** 26
 evidence **101** 20
 forms **101** 13-22
Concerted practice **101** 18
Conditionality **122** 12, 22; **136** 19; **144** post a 34
Constitution for Europe **139** 22
 Article 98 TFEU, development **98** 1
Consumer harm **106** 37
Consumer protection **90** 17; **91** 23
 harmonisation **114** 57, 63
Consumer Rights Directive **114** 80
Consumer welfare **101** 43
Continuity of contracts **140** 29, 34
Continuity of supply **106** 13
Convention on the future of Europe **137** 11, 12
Cooperation in employment **147** 6
Coordination
 across sectors **146** 11
 competition law **101** 13-22
 concerted practice **101** 18
 decision of an association of undertakings **101** 17
 effects **101** 42
 evidence of concertation **101** 20
 horizontal **101** 15
 oligopolistic interdependence **101** 19
 oligopolistic markets **101** 19
 vertical **101** 14

Copyright **118** 5, 10, 14, 15, 29, 37, 45
COREPER
    Economic and Financial Committee **134** 19
Core provision **91** 1
Coronabonds **125** 65
Council of the EU **148** 2
    COREPER (*see* COREPER)
    ECOFIN **134** 13-19; **137** 3, 5, 6, 8, 9, 12, 22-24, 29, 33
    Economic and Financial Committee **134** 13-19 (*see also* Economic and Financial Committee)
    Employment Committee **146** 4, 5 (*see also* Employment Committee)
    excessive spending procedure **126** 14 (*see also* Excessive deficit procedure)
    qualified majority voting (*see* Qualified majority voting)
    right of initiative **135** 1
    unanimity (*see* Unanimity)
    voting rights in Euro Area matters **136** 27
Court of Justice of the European Union *see* European Court of Justice
COVID-19 **122** 10, 13, 37; **125** 64; **143** 35-41; **144** 13-16; **144 post a** 52; **144 post b** 90; **151** 7, 10; **156** 14
    budgetary discipline **126** 9
    State aid **107** 75, 81
    See also PEPP
Credit facilities **123** 16, 17
Credit institutions *see* Financial institutions
Credit rating agencies **143** 27
Creditworthiness **143** 27
Cross-border transport *see at* Transport
Cross-subsidization **91** 16; **93** 19
Culture
    State aid **107** 83
Currency crisis **142** 16
    See also Euro crisis
Customs duties **106** 3; **110** 1, 15; **113** 9
Customs Union **143** 18
Cyprus
    financial assistance **144 post b** 84

D

Damages
    State aid **108** 48
Dangerous goods **91** 19
Debt break **126** 51
Debt relief
    Greece **144 post b** 125
Debt restructuring **144 post b** 70
Declaration No. 28

    Article 98 TFEU **98** 3
Declaratory effect **158** 2-4
Delegated acts **144 post d** 151, 261, 262-265
    approximation of laws **114** 50
Demand-side substitution **101** 33
De minimis aid **107** 69
Democracy
    dual legitimacy **144 post b** 129
    EU law **144 post b** 129
    input legitimation **144 post b** 139
    output legitimation **144 post b** 139
Demographic situation **159** 1, 2
Denmark **131** 5, 13, 15, 18
Deposition guarantee schemes **139** 31; **144 post d** 12, 252-259, 281-292
Deregulation **90** 15
Destination-state taxation **113** 14
Development of trade **106** 6, 41, 49, 71, 74, 76
Dialogue between management and labour **155** passim
Digital Euro **128** 10
Digitalization of workplaces **157** 14
Digital Markets Act **102** 5; **114** 83
Digital Services Act **114** 83
Digital services tax **113** 37
Digital single market **114** 83
Direct discrimination *see sub* Discrimination
Direct enforcement **101** 4
    competition law **101** 10
Direct taxes **112** 1; **113** 2; **115** 3
Discrimination **91** 9; **92** 1; **95** 2, 5; **106** 21; **153** 48-50
    based on sex **157** passim
    direct **110** 28-32
    indirect **110** 33-36
    reverse **92** 2; **110** 6
Discriminatory and protectionist internal taxation **106** 3; **110** 1
Dismissal
    protection against unjustified~ **153** 32-24
Distortion of competition **107** 70 et seq.; **111** 1; **158** 1, 5, 6
    concerted practice **116** 12, 15
    elimination of distortion **116** 5-29; **117** 5
    existence of a distortion **116** 12, 13
    limited effect of distortion **117** 18
    need for elimination **116** 14, 15
    reasonable risk of distortion **117** 6
    See also Competition law
Division of Germany **98** 1
Domaine réservé of the MS **118** 3-6
Domestic market **110** 4
Domestic producers **110** 14

Index   1517

Domestic products **110** 2, 8, 14, 15, 28
Dominance **102** 10-136
   abuse (*see* Abuse of dominance)
   burden of proof **102** 15
   collective **102** 33
   economics of scale **102** 28
   exclusive rights **102** 19
   independence from customers and consumers **102** 31
   intellectual property rights **102** 20
   legal regime **102** 19
   market shares **102** 14
   market shares of close competitors **102** 16
   network effects **102** 29
   sunk cost investments **102** 26
   technological lead **102** 23
   vertical integration **102** 22
Dominant undertakings **102** 1
Draft budgetary plan **144 post c** 64
Driver's licence **91** 19
Driving time limitation **91** 19
Driving time restriction **91** 19
Duty to cooperate **103** 30, 36

E
EBU *see* Banking Union
ECB**119** 13; **131** 1, 2, 6, 8-12, 20; **137** 5, 8, 16, 17, 25, 29, 30, 35; **144 post b** 47-49, 66, 67, 126; **144 post d** 4, 24, 25, 28-61, 64-121, 300
   access to the file **144 post d** 119, 120
   accountability **130** 38, 75, 78-81; **144 post d** 40-44
   accounting **141** 16
   advisory function **127** 40
   as Legislator **139** 38
   as monetary authority **139** 26, 28, 33, 38
   banking supervision **130** 37, 38, 40, 63
   bodies
      Administrative Board of Review **132** 86; **144 post d** 121
      any other body **130** 2, 16, 59
      decision making bodies **130** 2, 5, 12, 16, 32-35, 42, 50, 54, 55, 57, 59, 66, 71
      Executive Board **130** 6, 35, 36, 42, 54, 79; **132** 33, 36, 41, 42
      Governing Council **131** 21, 25, 26; **132** 10, 17, 19, 21, 22, 25, 33, 36, 40-42, 45, 69, 89, 90
      President **132** 45, 89
      Supervisory Board **130** 6, 63; **132** 90, 106; **144 post d** 33-35, 37-39, 41-44, 47, 48, 61-63, 121
   borrowed administration agreement **144 post a** 45

Code of Conduct **132** 106
competences **144 post d** 49, 55, 88, 261
compliance **131** 10, 19, 21
confidentiality **131** 8
discretion **130** 31, 38, 69
early intervention **144 post d** 68, 78, 99
ethical framework **132** 105
European Stability Mechanism (*see* ESM)
fit and proper decisions **144 post d** 39, 101, 103
guidelines **144 post d** 112
independence **144 post d** 39-43
   de facto **130** 15, 39, 41, 63
   financial **130** 25-27, 30, 31, 45
   functional **130** 13, 22
   institutional **130** 16, 18, 21
   operational **130** 13, 37-39
   personal **130** 5, 12, 32-36, 44, 63, 66, 81
   undue influence **130** 5, 17, 18, 32, 59, 65
inspection powers **144 post d** 106-108
instructions **130** 2, 11, 16, 18, 32, 53, 71, 76
international cooperation **127** 30
investigatory powers **144 post d** 95, 106-108
judicial control **130** 60, 67
legal personality **139** 26
macro-prudential supervision **139** 29-32, 56; **144 post d** 57
mandate **130** 7, 25, 61, 62, 67
micro-prudential supervision **139** 29-32, 56; **144 post d** 68-79
monetary policy **130** 3, 17, 19, 23, 45, 63, 80, 81; **132** 25, 59, 60, 90; **141** 3
   territorial limits **139** 27
observer status in the IMF **138** 40
Pandemic Emergency Purchase Programme (*see* PEPP)
price stability **131** 2
prohibition of monetary financing **131** 9
prohibition of privileged access **131** 9
qualifying holdings **132** 83; **144 post d** 72, 90, 102
recovery plan **144 post d** 105
sanctioning power **139** 25, 39; **144 post d** 109, 110
single rulebook **132** 77, 81
statistics **127** 29; **132** 25
Statute **129** 3
   amendments **129** 4-7
supervision of credit and financial institutions **127** 31-39; **130** 39, 63
Supervisory Review and Evaluation Process **144 post d** 99, 100
ECJ *see* European Court of Justice
Economics of scale **102** 28

ECN *see sub* Competition Law
Economic activity **106** 11, 14, 15, 54, 56
Economic advantage **107** 33-35
Economic and Financial Committee **132** 19; **143** 11, 22, 30, 32; **144 post b** 7, 123 **150** 5
  competences **134** 8-12
  composition **134** 22-37
  COREPER **134** 19
  decision making **134** 38-40
  ECOFIN **134** 13-19
  economic policy coordination **134** 8-12
  Economic Policy Committee **134** 21; **144 post b** 7
  Eurogroup Working Group **134** 25, 35
  European Stability Mechanism **134** passim; **144 post b** 7
  excessive deficit procedure **126** 18 (*see also* Excessive deficit procedure)
  High Level Expert Group on SME and infrastructure financing **134** 36
  Joint EFC-EPC Working Group on International Financial Aspects of Climate Change **134** 33
  President **134** 27
  Secretariat **134** 37
  Statute **134** 6
  Sub-Committee on EU Sovereign Debt Markets **134** 31
  Sub-Committee on IMF and related issues **134** 32; **138** 40
  tasks **134** 8-21
Economic and Monetary Union *see* EMU
Economic and Social Committee **149** 2, 3
Economic backwardness of the new *Länder* **98** 10
Economic circumstances
  of carriers **94** 1
  taking account of **94** 1
Economic crisis **145** 19, 39
  financial crisis (*see* Financial crisis)
Economic dialogue **126** 37
Economic disadvantages
  Article 98 TFEU **98** 10
Economic Governance
  Six-Pack **119** 10; **120** 5; **121** 4, 34, 42, 44, 54-62; **126** 36; **136** 13 **144 post a** 1; **144 post c** 5, 70

Two-Pack **120** 5; **121** 4, 44, 63-65; **126** 47; **136** 18; **144 post a** 1; **144 post c** 5, 38, 74
Economic partnership programme **126** 48; **144 post c** 49
Economic Policy **119** 7, 9, 11 et seq.; **120** 4 et seqq., 15-19; **134** 8-12; **137** 4, 22
  broad guidelines **120** 11, 14, 42-44; **146** 3
  coordination **120** 1, 3-5, 6-13, 15-20; **139** 18-22, 58
    conditionality **136** 19
    multilateral surveillance **136** 7
    Six-Pack (*see at* Economic Governance)
    Two-Pack (*see at* Economic Governance)
  distinction between economic policies and monetary policy **120** 21-30; **127** 23 (*see also at* Competences ~of the EU)
  efficient allocation of resources **120** 39, 40
  free competition **120** 34
  guidelines **126** 5
  liberal order **120** 35
  open market with free competition **119** 12, 40 et seq.; **120** 16, 19, 33-34, 37-41, 44
  relationship between economic policies and EMU **120** 2, 14
  social market economy **120** 34-36
Economic Recovery Plan *see* European Economic Recovery Plan
ECSC Treaty
  and Article 98 TFEU **98** 4
ECU **133** 1; **142** 1, 15
EEA Agreement
  Article 98 TFEU, development **98** 2
EEC Treaty
  Article 98 TFEU, development **98** 1
Effective control **91** 17
Effect on trade **101** 31, 59
EFSF **137** 13, 18
EMCF **143** 25
Emergency Liquidity Assistance **123** 23-25; **144 post d** 187
EMI **143** 25
Employment Committee **146** 4, 5; **150** 1, 2, 4, 5, 10
  chairperson **150** 11
  membership **150** 9
  objectives **150** 4
  working groups **150** 9

Index

Employment policy **91** 24; **145** 9, passim
  active ageing **145** 17
  Active Labour Market Policies **145** 26
  Annual Progress Report **148** 21
  Cardiff Process **145** 11
  Cologne Process **145** 11
  conditions for third-country nationals **153** 39
  contractual flexibility **145** 34
  Delors White Paper **145** 5, 23
  employability **145** 23
  employment strategy **152** 12
  Employment Package **145** 22
  European Confidence Pact for Employment **145** 7
  European Employment Pact **145** 12
  European Employment Strategy **145** 10, 23, 28, 30; **147** 9; **162** 17
    country-specific recommendations **148** 17-19
  fight against unemployment **147** 12
  full employment **145** 43
  Guidelines **145** 32, 40; **148** 6, 11, 12
    European Employment Guidelines 2015 **148** 16
  high level of employment **147** 8; **150** 4
  Integrated Guidelines for Growth and Jobs **145** 18, 26
  Interdependence between employment and social policy **145** 1
  Job creation **145** 17
  Joint Employment Report **145** 33; **147** 11; **148** 6, 24, 25
    for 2015 **148** 15, 26
  labour and management **146** 5, 7
  labour market **150** 3
  lifelong learning **145** 17, 29, 35, 40
  National Action Plans **145** 13
  Programme for Employment and Social Innovation **149** 7
  Standing Committee on Employment **145** 3
  Tripartite Social Summit for Growth and Employment (*see* Tripartite Social Summit for Growth and Employment)
  undeclared work **145** 17
EMS **141** 7; **142** 1, 15, 18, 19, 30
EMU
  and Article 3 TEU **119** 39; **120** 22 et seq., 32 et seqq., 36 et seqq. (*see also* Principles)
  and differentiated integration **119** 6
  and European Parliament **121** 40-42
  and EU objectives **119** 39 st seq., 21, 33 et seqq.
  and internal market **119** 11, 39; **120** 14 et seq., 23, 33 et seq., 43, 45
  Asymmetry **141** 2; **144 post a** 19; **144 post c** 2
  balanced economic growth **144 post a** 38
  Banking Union **119** 10
  broad guidelines **120** 11, 13 et seq., 37, 42; **121** 2, 29-31
  Budgetary Framework Directive **126** 45
  common provisions **138** 1-5, 20-26
  Convergence **121** 28; **141** 1, 2, 6, 18
    Criteria **140** 1, 2, 5, 10
    Reports **131** 14, 15, 20
  Conversion rates **140** 27-31
  coordination of economic policies **119** 8, 11 et seq.; **120** 1-6, 9-14, 20; **121** 8-10, 58
  Delors Report **120** 7
  early warning **121** 32, 34 et seq., 37-53, 56
  excessive deficits **120** 8
  excessive imbalances **121** 36, 58, 60
  monitoring and assessment **121** 26-30
  risks jeopardizing the proper functioning of EMU **121** 36, 60
  recommendations **121** 32 et seq., 37-39, 56, 60
  sanctions **120** 20; **121** 31, 33 et seq., 38 et seq., 48, 50, 53, 61 et seq.
  scoreboard **121** 59
  surveillance procedure **121** 1, 4, 23, 27, 29 et seq., 34-39, 43-46, 53, 57-69
COVID-19 **144 post a** 52
Crisis Management **144 post a** 1
delimitation of economic and monetary policy **120** 15, 21-30; **127** 23
Devaluation **140** 21
Economic and Financial Committee **134** passim; **144 post b** 7
economic dialogue **126** 37
economic governance **120** 20
economic policy/policies (*see* Economic Policy)
economic policy convergence **121** 24
Economic Policy Committee **134** 3, 21; **144 post b** 7
Economic Recovery Plan **144 post a** 54
enhanced surveillance procedure **126** 47
European Finance Minister **144 post a** 50
European Minister for Economic and Financial Affairs **138** 36; **144 post a** 50

EMU (*cont.*)
- European Monetary Fund (*see at* Treaty Establishing the European Stability Mechanism)
- European Semester (*see* European Semester)
- Euro Plus Pact **119** 10; **120** 5
- excessive deficit procedure **126** 4, 12-28 (*see also* Excessive deficit procedure)
- exchange-rate policy (*see at* Exchange Rates)
- external dimension **135** 4; **138** 1-5
- financial soundness **119** 42, 44 et seq.
- financial stability (*see* Financial stability)
- full employment **144 post a** 39
- history **119** 2-5
- international relations **138** 1-5
- legal tender **119** 5
- macroeconomic indicators **140** 5
- Member States with a derogation **127** 3, 17; **131** 14, 18, 23; **135** 5; **144** 1-7, 9, 12 (*see also at* Member States)
- Monetary Committee **134** 3
- monetary policy **119** 3, 5, 8 et seq., 13-16, 17 et seqq., 21, 26, 28; **120** 2, 15, 24; **121** 22, 24 et seq.
  - strategy **119** 16, 18
- multilateral surveillance procedure **121** 23-30, 43-46; **126** 4; **136** 7
- Next Generation EU **122** 37; **144 post a** 54
- No-Bail-out **120** 7; **144 post a** 20
- opt-out **131** 5, 13, 15
- Ownership and Solidarity **144 post a** 19
- Pact for Growth and Employment (*see* Pact for Growth and Employment)
- Pandemic Emergency Purchase Programme (*see* PEPP)
- price stability **126** 1; **144 post a** 37
- principles
  - ecological market economy **120** 36
  - guiding **119** 39 et seqq., 42-45; **120** 41
  - liberal order **120** 35
  - margin of appreciation/discretion of MS **119** 12, 42 et seq.; **120** 12, 23 32
  - open market with free competition **119** 12, 40 et seq.; **120** 16, 19, 33 et seq., 37-41, 44
  - price stability (*see* Price stability)
  - social market economy **120** 34, 36
  - sound monetary conditions **119** 35, 42, 45
  - sound public finances **119** 35, 42, 44
  - sustainable balance of payments **119** 35, 42, 45; **120** 41
- Recovery and Resilience Fund **144 post a** 54, 57
- reform proposals **144 post c** 92
- representation **138**, 1-5
  - in the G20 **138** 41
  - in the G7 **138** 41
  - in the IMF **138** 40
  - unified ~ **138** 27-41
- role of EP **121** 40-43
  - Economic Dialogue **121** 56
- single currency **119** 1, 4, 5, 13 (*see also at* Euro)
- Single Resolution Fund **119** 10; **144 post a** 3, 5, 13, 17; **144 post d** 144, 158, 174-181, 192-194, 295-297
  - liquidity **144 post d** 144
- Six-Pack (*see at* Economic Governance)
- sound public finances **126** 1
- Stability and Growth Pact **119** 10, 44; **120** 5; **121** 23, 27, 44, 47 et seq., 50-52; **126** 36; **135** 3
  - general escape clause **121** 50 et seq.
- stability programmes **121** 28
- stable prices **119** 42
- Stage Three **131** 2, 12, 15, 16, 18, 22
- Stage Two **131** 2
- support of general economic policies **119** 28 et seqq., 38; **127** 10-12
- transfer union **136** 29
- Two-Pack (*see at* Economic Governance)
- two-pillar structure **119** 7-9
- warning system **139** 59
- *See also* Fiscal Union

Enabling Regulation 2015/1588 *see* Regulation 2015/1588

Enhanced cooperation **113** 7, 36; **144 post c** 14
- and implementation of Patent's Regulation **118** 18, 51
- authorisation **118** 39

Enhanced surveillance procedure **126** 47

Environmental protection **90** 17, 19, 29, 33; **91** 23
- approximation of laws **114** 56, 60

Equal pay **153** 45

Equal treatment *see* Non-discrimination

Equality between men and women **153** 44-47

Equality of opportunity **106** 19, 25, 36

ESCB **119** 14; **131** 2, 3, 5, 6, 10-12, 22
- financial stability (*see at* EMU)
- foreign-exchange operations **127** 26
- guiding principles **119** 39 et seqq., 42 et seqq.; **120** 41; **127** 13
- independence **119** 19-27; **120** 2
- instruments **127** 2
- monetary policy **130** 3, 25, 27, 39, 45, 69, 75, 80, 81; **132** 1

Index   1521

National Central Banks as integral part **131** 10
official foreign reserves of the Member States **127** 27
primary objective **127** 5
Statute **129** 3; **131** 20
    amendments **129** 4-7
    simplified amendment **129** 4-7
smooth operation of payment systems **127** 28
support of general economic policies **119** 28 et seqq., 38; **127** 10-12
supportive role **127** 12
tasks **127** 14 et seq.
undue influence **130** 5, 8, 33, 59
ESF **145** 31; **147** 4; **153** 26, 43
    budget implementation **163** 7
    ~ Committee **163** 2
    ESF+ **162** 30-34
    establishment **162** 3
    European Pillar of Social Rights **162** 28
    implementation **164** 3
    multiannual financial framework **162** 2; **163** 5
    Next Generation EU **162** 32
    REACT-EU **162** 32
    shared management **163** 7-13
    SURE **162** 33
ESM **130** 46; **136** 28-35 **137** 17, 28; **144** 14, 15; **144 post b** passim; **144 post d** 66, 296-299
    See also Treaty Establishing the European Stability Mechanism
Essential facilities **102** 71
Essential service **91** 6
EU bonds **144 post a** 60
EUCFR
    social policy **153** 10
EU Finance Minister **144 post c** 109
EU interests **106** 6, 41, 71-74, 76
EU medium-term financial assistance **123** 49
EU-OSHA **153** 25; **154** 17
EU Recovery Instrument **122** 37, 38
EURATOM Treaty
    and Article 98 TFEU **98** 4
Euro
    common positions **138** 1-5, 20-26
    digital (*see* Digital Euro)
    singleness of **133** 8
    use of as the single currency **133** 6
    See also EMU
Euro area
    conditionality **136** 19
    coordination and surveillance **136** 5
    economic policy guidelines **136** 5

European Semester **136** 21
measures specific to Euro Area members **136** 4-27
recommendations **136** 21
voting rights **136** 27
Euro area Treasury **144 post c** 109
Euro crisis **126** 36 **130** 45
Euro Plus Pact **144 post c** 5
Euro System **130** 34, 45, 49, 80
Eurobonds **125** 63, 65; **144 post a** 60; **144 post c** 102
    European safe asset **144 post c** 101
    Greenpaper **144 post c** 102, 103
Eurofound **153** 27; **154** 17
Eurogroup
    ESM **144 post b** 34
    European Finance Minister **144 post a** 50
    European Minister for Economic and Financial Affairs **144 post a** 50
    President **137** 9, 17
Europe 2020 Strategy **145** 15, 20, 42; **147** 10; **151** 20; **153** 8
European Anti-Fraud Office *see* OLAF
European Agency for Safety and Health at Work *see* EU-OSHA
European Banking Authority **114** 82; **144 post d** 4, 21, 28, 49-55, 112, 265
European Banking Union *see* Banking Union
European Central Bank *see* ECB
European Centre for the Development of Vocational Training *see* Cedefop
European Commission **131** 20, 21, 25; **137** 12, 16, 23, 24, 28-31, 35; **143** 29, 30, 33, 34; **144 post b** 42-46; **148** 3
    authorisation **103** 1, 6, 7, 17, 20, 40
    borrowed administration agreement **144 post a** 45
    Economic Recovery Plan **144 post a** 54
    European Finance Minister **144 post a** 50
    European Minister for Economic and Financial Affairs **144 post a** 50
    European Stability Mechanism (*see* ESM)
    excessive deficit procedure **126** 13 (*see also* Excessive deficit procedure)
    Fiscal Compact **122** 4; **144 post a** 45
    implementing acts **144 post d** 262-265
    non-compliance of a Member State **117** 16
    recommendation of the Commission **117** 13-14
    right of initiative **135** 1
    role in the law approximation **116** 7, 12, 14, 18-24; **117** 4, 6, 11, 9-18
    role in the enforcement of competition law **116** 7
    TMC Agreement **144 post a** 45

European Committee of Social Rights **153** 13
European Competition Network **101** 60
European Council
　Essen European Council **145** 6, 23
European Court of Justice **131** 25; **144 post b**
　　50-52
　amicus curiae briefs **103** 36
　ESM **144 post b** 50-52
　exhaustion doctrine **118** 5
　infringement procedure **131** 1, 21
　Meroni doctrine **144 post d** 28, 141, 143, 153
　OMT **127** 23
　Pringle decision **144 post b** 6
　role in competition law **103** 37
　Weiss ruling **127** 23 et seq.
European Deposit Insurance **144 post a** 13
European Deposit Insurance Scheme **127** 37;
　　144 post a 18
European economic model **151** 9
European Economic Recovery Plan **144 post a**
　　54; **145** 19
European Employment Strategy *see at*
　　Employment policy
European Energy and Transport Forum **99** 4
European Finance Minister **144 post a** 50
European Fiscal Board **144 post c** 91
European Foundation for the Improvement of
　　Living and Working Conditions *see*
　　Eurofound
European Insurance and Occupational
　　Pensions Authority **114** 82
European Investment Bank **139** 25
　Pandemic Emergency Purchase Programme
　　(*see* PEPP)
European Law
　approximation of laws (*see* Approximation
　　of laws)
　coherence **144 post a** 42; **144 post b** 14-16
　consistency **144 post a** 42
　democracy **144 post b** 129
　directly applicable EU law **144 post d** 82,
　　83, 101, 104, 109, 208, 235, 241
　European administrative soft law **144 post c**
　　81
　general principles **106** 88
　hard law **146** 18
　implementing acts **144 post d** 262-265
　Intergovernmental Agreements (*see*
　　Intergovernmental Agreement)
　primacy (*see* Primacy of EU law)
　recommendations **146** 17
　representative democracy **144 post b** 129
　soft law (*see* Soft law)

　supremacy (*see* Primacy of EU law)
European Media Freedom Act **114** 84
European Migration Network **151** 27
European Minister for Economic and Financial
　　Affairs **138** 36; **144 post a** 50
European Monetary and Cooperation Fund *see*
　　EMCF
European Monetary Fund *see at* Treaty
　　Establishing the European Stability
　　Mechanism
European Monetary Institute *see* EMI
European Pact for Social Democracy **151** 29
European Pact for Social Stability **151** 22
European Parliament **137** 31
　right of initiative **135** 8
　role in competition law **103** 3
　veto right **91** 4
European Patent
　and language arrangements **118** 43, 44, 49,
　　50
　Office **118** 40, 42
　Organisation **118** 16
　institutional framework **118** 39
　unitary effect **118** 41-44
European Pillar of Social Rights **151** 9 et seq.,
　　21, 35; **152** 8; **153** 14; **156** 10; **164** 9
　ESF **162** 28
European Regional Development Fund **162** 7
European safe asset *see* Eurobonds
European Securities and Markets Authority
　　114 82
European semester **121** 27, 30, 42, 57; **136** 21;
　　144 post c 5; **145** 21; **148** 5, 23; **153** 43;
　　156 10
　Annual Growth Survey **144 post c** 61; **148**
　　5, 23, 24
　coordination by coercion **144 post c** 88
　Country Reports **144 post c** 62
　Country-specific recommendations **144**
　　post c 62; **148** 17-19
　enforcement **144 post c** 86
　Euro Area recommendation **144 post c** 61
　instruments **144 post c** 81
　legal protection **144 post c** 89
　National Reform Programmes **144 post c**
　　62; **148** 7, 9, 10
　Stability and Convergence Programmes
　　144 post c 62
　surveillance-cycle **144 post c** 6, 60
European Social Charter **151** 22, 24, 29, 35;
　　157 35
　1961 **151** 22, 24
　1996 **151** 24, 29

European Social Fund *see* ESF
European Social Fund (Plus) *see at* ESF
European Social Model **145** 44; **151** 9
European Social Partners **146** 7
European Social Policy Network **162** 25
European Stability Mechanism *see* ESM
European Statistical System **132** 70
European Structural and Investment Funds **157** 36; **162** 2
European Supervisory Authorities **114** 82
European System of Central Banks *see* ESCB
European Systemic Risk Board **114** 82; **132** 70 **144 post d** 21, 56-58
   macro-prudential supervision **144 post d** 56-58
European Works Council **152** 5
Eurosystem Collateral Framework **124** 12
Eurosystem tender procedure **132** 61
Euro-vignette **92** 4
Eurozone **139** 9, 12, 21
   backstop **144 post b** 107
Evidence of concertation **101** 20
Exceptional occurrences **122** 13
   COVID-19 **122** 13
   financial and debt crisis **122** 15
   humanitarian measures **122** 9
Excessive deficit procedure **139** 54, 60-62
   Budgetary Framework Directive **126** 45
   Council **126** 14
   debt criterion **126** 10
   deficit criterion **126** 9
   Economic and Financial Committee **126** 18
   Economic partnership programme **126** 48; **144 post c** 49
   enhanced surveillance procedure **126** 47
   European Commission **126** 13
   Maastricht criteria **144 post c** 16
   new sanctions **144 post c** 41
   procedure **126** 17-28
   Protocol on the ~ **126** 6, 29-32
   reference criteria **126** 8; **144 post c** 16
   reporting requirements **144 post c** 51
   reverse qualified majority voting **144 post c** 42
   sanctions **126** 25; **139** 25
   Six-Pack **126** 36
   Stability and Growth Pact **126** 36
   Two-Pack **126** 47
Exchange Rates **141** 15
   policy **119** 15
Excise duties **113** 29-31
Exclusionary abuse **102** 60-88
Exclusive dealing **102** 78

Exclusive rights **91** 15
Exemption **92** 3
   See also Block Exemption; General Block Exemption Regulation; *and at* Competition law; Reference criteria; State aid; Tax advantages
Exploitative abuse **102** 53-59
Export of products **111** 1
External debt **143** 24
Externalities **91** 23
External trade **143** 18

F

Financial assistance
   collective action clause **144 post b** 121-125
   conditionality **122** 12, 22; **144 post b** 62
   COVID-19 **144 post b** 90
   Cyprus **144 post b** 84
   debt restructuring clause **144 post b** 123
   direct recapitalisation of financial institutions **144 post b** 101-107
   enhanced conditioned credit line **144 post b** 88, 89
   European Stability Mechanism **144 post b** 58-127
   Greece **144 post b** 85
   loans **144 post b** 80-85
   pandemic crisis support **144 post b** 90
   precautionary **144 post b** 86-93
   precautionary conditioned credit line **144 post b** 88, 89
   Primary Market Support Facility **144 post b** 115
   private sector participation **144 post b** 121-125
   procedure **144 post b** 64-78
   recapitalisation of financial institutions **144 post b** 94-107
   Secondary Market Support Facility **144 post b** 108-114
   Spain **144 post b** 100
   See also EU medium-term financial assistance; Medium-term financial assistance facility
Financial contracts **139** 41, 42
Financial crisis **122** 4; **139** 12, 30, 31, 39; **143** 5, 8, 41
   Euro crisis (*see* Euro crisis)
Financial institutions **124** 5, 6
   authorisation **144 post d** 210, 219, 220, 222, 273
   bail-in **144 post d** 130, 170-173, 193, 301
   banking licence **132** 83

Financial institutions **124 5** (*cont.*)
  capital buffers **144 post d** 218, 228-233, 240
  direct recapitalisation of **144 post b** 101-107
  failing or likely to fail **144 post d** 151, 159, 190
  fit and proper **144 post d** 74, 227, 276
  governance **144 post d** 74, 225-227
  home country control **139** 30
  insolvency **144 post d** 124, 128, 129, 165, 169, 243, 251, 252, 256, 257, 279-281
  liquidity **144 post d** 15, 220-240
  own funds **139** 32
  recapitalisation **144 post b** 94-107
  recovery plans **144 post d** 105, 163, 166
  resolvability **144 post d** 165, 251
Financial market **143** 2, 27
Financial resources **143** 12
Financial services **139** 30
Financial solvency **90** 16
Financial stability **119** 32 et seqq. ; **132** 87; **144 post a** 28; **144 post b** 59
  Agreement on the Transfer and Mutualization of Contributions to the Single Resolution Fund **144 post a** 30
  European Financial Stability Facility **144 post b** 1
  European Financial Stability Mechanism **122** 15; **144 post b** 1
  European Stability Mechanism **144 post a** 28
  Fiscal Compact **122** 4; **144 post a** 29
  Price Stability **144 post a** 37
  SSM (*see* SSM)
  SURE **122** 10; **144 post a** 53
  Term **144 post a** 27
  Treaty Establishing the European Stability Mechanism **144 post a** 28
Financial transaction tax **113** 36
Fiscal agent functions **123** 40-44
Fiscal Compact *see* Treaty on Stability, Coordination and Governance in the Economic and Monetary Union
Fiscal crisis **139** 12, 21, 30, 31, 39; **143** 5, 41
Fiscal, customs or statistical classification **110** 24
Fiscal governance **144 post c** 6; **144 post d** 11, 48
Fiscality **91** 23
Fiscal rules **140** 16-18
Fiscal Union **119** 10, 44; **144 post a** 2, 6
  constitutional law limits **144 post c** 97
  EU law limits **144 post c** 95
  proposals for further integration **144 post c** 92
Fixed-term workers **153** 27
Flag state control **90** 14
Flexibility clause
  and creation of intellectual property titles **118** 24, 26
  approximation of laws **114** 13
Fluctuation (of money) **142** 15, 16, 24-28
  fluctuation margin **140** 20, 21
Foreign exchange reserves **132** 25
  management **123** 38, 39
Foreign exchange transactions **132** 1
Foreign reserves **132** 64
France **137** 4, 5, 7
Free circulation **110** 11
Free movement of goods **106** 15, 61; **110** 1, 11, 44; **113** 10
Free movement of workers **106** 18, 24
Free trade
  barriers **97** 2
Freedom of establishment **106** 18
Freedom of services **90** 6 et seq., 13, 17, 41; **106** 18; **113** 10
Full employment **144 post a** 39; **147** 8
Functional dissociation **91** 16
Fundamental Freedoms **141** 1
Fundamental Rights Platform **152** 32

G
G20
  representation of the Euro **138** 41
G7
  representation of the Euro **138** 41
GATT **110** 12
GBER *see* General Block Exemption Regulation
Gender equality **153** 44-47; **157** passim
  Gender Equality Strategy **157** 38
Gender pay gap **153** 45; **157** passim
Gender quotas **157** 39
General Block Exemption Regulation **107** 85; **108** 7, 33
Genuine link **91** 17
Geographical indications and appellation of origin **118** 9, 36
Geographical market **101** 37
Germany **137** 4, 5
  Constitutional identity **144 post c** 99
  Federal Constitutional Court
    PSPP decision **127** 24
  unification **98** 1, 9; **107** 76

Index

Golden rule **126** 17
Government bonds **130** 30; **140** 15
Greece
  debt relief **144 post b** 125
  financial assistance **144 post b** 85

H

Hard core cartels **101** 52
Harmonisation *see* Approximation of laws
High level of employment **91** 24; **147** 8
High level of protection **114** 37
Home country control **90** 14
Horizontal restrictions **101** 15
Hybrid mail **106** 14, 37, 68
Hypothetical monopolist test **101** 32

I

IMF **139** 50; **143** 8, 28
  and ESM **144 post b** 36, 39, 41, 53-57
  Committee **138** 40
  contributions by EU Member States **123** 45-48
  EU representatives to the ~ **138** 40
  observer status of the ECB **138** 40
  representation of the Euro **138** 11-13, 40
Implementing acts
  approximation of laws **114** 50
Imported products **110** 2, 4, 8, 19, 28
  use **110** 8, 19
Important projects of common EU interest **107** 81
Indirect discrimination *see sub* Discrimination
Indirect taxes **113** 1, 5
Information and consultation of workers **153** 25
Infringement procedure
  approximation of laws **114** 75
Intellectual property rights **102** 20; **116** 4; **117** 2
  and fundamental rights **118** 22
  Community titles **118** 9, 25
  exhaustion doctrine **118** 5
  harmonisation competence **118** 8, 27-30
  "optional instruments" **118** 35
  supplementary protection certificates **118** 8
  titles and rights **118** 45
Integrated project **148** 22
Interbrand competition **101** 48

Intergovernmental Agreement **144 post d** 131, 158, 178, 180
Interinstitutional Agreement on Better Law-Making **154** 26
Intermodality **91** 23
Internal market **106** 2, 9, 13, 48, 54, 56, 75; **139** 19, 20; **141** 1; **144** 3, 8, 9
  approximation of laws **114** 1-17
  competition policy **101** 6, 8
  Digital Markets Act **114** 83
  Digital Services Act **114** 83
  digital single market **114** 83
  disturbance to the functioning **144** 8
  Office for Harmonization in the Internal Market **114** 81
  secure the establishment and functioning of **113** 14; **118** 19, 20-22, 28, 29
  transport services **90** 3, 11 et seq., 13 et seq., 17, 39, 41
Internal taxation **110** 1, 2, 4, 15-20
  complete neutrality **110** 4
  imposing **110** 7
  new internal taxes **110** 6
  protective **110** 50
  repayment **110** 38; **111** 1, 3
  system **110** 32, 48, 49
International agreements **139** 44, 45; **143** 7, 18, 19
International Monetary Fund *see* IMF
Interoperability **91** 23
Interpretation
  narrow **98** 9, 10
Interventionist State **158** 1
Intrabrand competition **101** 48
InvestEU EUR **144 post a** 56
Investment firm **144 post d** 155, 207, 208, 278
In-work exclusion
  Combatting **152´3** 41-43

J

Joint legal basis **103** 1, 3
Judicial review **103** 9; **144 post d** 122, 203

K

Knowledge-based society **145** 15

1525

L

Lamfalussy architecture **132** 77
Large exposure **139** 32; **144 post d** 68, 209, 212, 236, 274
Legal basis
   joint **103** 1, 3
   sole **103** 1
Legal certainty **139** 42
Legal compatibility of national legislation **131** 1, 3
Legal monopoly **102** 19
Legal tender **133** 9; **140** 35, 36
   banknotes **128** 9
   coins **128** 1
   definition **128** 3
Legislative procedure
   citizens' initiative **135** 9
   consultation procedure **148** 13; **149** 2
   ordinary legislative procedure **90** 33; **91** 3; **100** 6; **103** 3, 46; **106** 1, 78; **113** 23, 24; **129** 2; **149** 1
   right of initiative **135** 1
   special legislation procedure **103** 3
Legitimate expectation
   State aid **108** 41
Level playing field **106** 6
Liberalisation **90** 11, 15, 17; **91** 21; **106** 2, 4, 5, 34, 67, 82, 85, 86; **141** 1
Licensing **90** 16; **91** 17
   operator **91** 14
Lisbon Strategy **151** 19
   social policy **153** 8
Loyalty **101** 48
Luxemburg Process *see* Luxemburg Summit
Luxemburg Summit **145** 10, 11

M

Macro-prudential supervision **139** 29-32, 56; **144 post d** 18, 56-58, 81
Macroeconomic adjustment programme **144 post c** 77
Macroeconomic dialogue **152** 12
Macroeconomic imbalance procedure
   sanctions **144 post c** 71
Macroeconomic stabilisation function **144 post c** 106-108
Margin squeeze **102** 65
Market access **90** 1, 15, 17, 33; **91** 8
Market definition **101** 31-38; **102** 12
   demand-side substitution **101** 33
   geographic **101** 37
   substitution **101** 32
   supply-side substitution **101** 35

Market economy investor test **107** 39-41
Market economy operator test **107** 36-38
Market integration **106** 2, 3
Market services **106** 55, 56
Market structure **106** 36, 37
Maternity leave **153** 17
Measures with equivalent effect **106** 3, 18
   to subsidies **107** 4
Medium-term budgetary objective **144 post c** 27
   adjustment path **144 post c** 28
   expenditure brake **144 post c** 28
   limits **144 post c** 29
Medium-term financial assistance facility **143** 24, 29; **144** 2, 16
   loan agreement **143** 29
   Memorandum of Understanding **143** 29
Member States
   administration **110** 37
   competences **147** 5
   domaine réservé (*see* Domaine réservé)
   employment policies **148** 6
   insolvency **143** 6
   mandatory requirements **139** 19; **140** 22
   right of initiative **135** 1
   social parameters **159** 3
   state authorities **110** 5
   with derogation from the EMU **127** 3, 17; **131** 14, 18, 23; **135** 5; **144** 1-7, 9, 12
   abrogation **140** 5, 25-27
   disqualification **140** 4
   exclusionary rules **139** 17
Micro-prudential supervision **139** 29-32, 56; **144 post d** 18, 68-79
Minimum reserves **124** 8; **132** 63
Minimum Requirement for Eligible Liabilities **144 post d** 173, 282
   bail-in **144 post d** 282
Monetary Committee **134** 3
Monetary financing prohibition **123** 2, 4, 6, 8; **130** 5, 30, 44, 62, 69
Monetary policy
   COVID-19 **127** 21
   delimitation from economic policy **120** 15, 21-30 **127** 23
   guiding principles **127** 13
   in a broad sense **127** 16
   in a narrow sense **127** 18
   instruments **127** 20
   margin of appreciation **127** 8
   new strategy **127** 7
   non-standard measures **127** 21
   primary objective **127** 5

Index 1527

principle of proportionality **127** 4, 23 et seq.
secondary objective **127** 10
singleness **127** 19
transmission mechanism **127** 22
unconventional **127** 21
See also at EMU; National Central Banks; Treaty Establishing the European Stability Mechanism; Competences
Monetary reserves **132** 1
Money supply **132** 63
Monopoly **102** 19; **106** 12, 14, 21, 22, 25, 26, 30, 33, 37, 49, 65, 84
economic viability **106** 37, 65
natural **91** 6, 15
public **91** 6, 15
revenue producing monopolies **106** 1, 6, 41-43, 49, 50, 61, 62
Moratorium tool **144 post d** 280, 283
Multiannual financial framework
ESF **162** 2; **163** 5
Multilateral surveillance procedure **126** 4; **136** 7; **139** 57-59; **144 post c** 68
enhanced surveillance (two pack) **126** 47; **144 post c** 74-78
new sanctions **144 post c** 70
reverse qualified majority voting **144 post c** 72
Multimodal **91** 23
Mutual assistance **144**, 11
financial **144** 2, 14
Mutual Learning Programme **146** 2; **149** 9, 10, 12
learning **149** 13
Peer Review **149** 11
policy learning **149** 15
Mutual recognition **90** 14; **114** 14

N
National Competent Authorities **144 post d** 18, 61-63, 88, 94, 120, 267
inspection powers **144 post d** 18, 93
macro-prudential supervision **139** 29-32, 56; **144 post d** 18
micro-prudential supervision **139** 29-32, 56; **144 post d** 18
National Central Banks **131** 3, 8, 10-12, 14, 20, 21, 25; **139** 7-9
agents **131** 12
autonomous functions **131** 11
banking supervision **130** 38
compliance **131** 10, 19, 21
confidentiality **131** 8
federal cosmetic **131** 11

financing resolution funds **123** 21
guidelines and instructions **131** 12
independence **131** 1, 3, 7, 12, 23; **140** 7-9; **144 post d** 150
functional, institutional, personal and financial independence **131** 7
integral part of the ESCB **131** 10
monetary policy **130** 17, 25, 27, 39, 45, 52, 55, 75, 80; **142** 16
Riksbank (Sweden) **142** 16
support of insolvent credit institutions **123** 22
undue influence **130** 5, 8, 9, 18, 32, 33, 59
National competition authorities **103** 11-14, 16, 18, 20, 27, 30, 31-33, 36, 38-40, 44; **104** 1-3, 5-7
National courts **103** 14, 27, 38
constitutional courts **139** 6
role in competition law **103** 14, 33; **104** 5
National debt **140** 16, 18
National employment policies **148** 6
National Resolution Authorities **144 post d** 124, 144, 156, 267
Nationalisation **106** 2, 4
Natural disasters **122** 13
State aid **107** 75
New internal taxes **110** 6
Next Generation EU **122** 37 **144 post a** 54; **151** 21; **153** 43; **162** 32
NGEU *see* Next Generation EU
"no bail-out" clause **122** 5, 25-29; **125** 7, 12, 15, passim; **144 post a** 20; **144 post b** 5, 9
Non-discrimination **106** 3, 18, 46, 54, 57; **110** 2, 8
of women and men **157** 10
Non-harmonised field *see at* Approximation of laws
Non-Performing Loans **144 post d** 278
Nordic States **142** 12
Normal conditions of competition **110** 1
Numerical fiscal rules **144 post c** 37
NUTS **162** 13

O
Obstacles
arising from Titel VI (Transport) **98** 6
OECD
Jobs Strategy **145** 27
Office for Harmonization in the Internal Market **114** 81
Ohlin Report **156** 5
OLAF **130** 64, 65; **143** 31

Oligopolistic interdependence **101** 19
Oligopolistic markets **101** 19
Ombudsman **137** 34
OMT **123** 29-31; **130** 46, 62
   concept **127** 21
   objective **127** 22
   view of the ECJ **127** 23
Open ended provision **91** 7
Open market economy **106** 9; **120** 37, 38, 41
Open market operations **132** 52
Open Method of Coordination **145** 8, 24, 45; **146** 9, 12, 16; **148** 20; **149** 14; **156** 15-22 **160** 4
   comparable indicators **146** 14
   cooperation **146** 16; **148** 1
   decentralized nature **146** 6
   elements **146** 15
   evaluating the effectiveness **146** 20
   incentive measures **147** 3; **149** 5
   legitimacy **146** 21
   social policy **151** 6
   soft law **146** 2, 10, 16
   statistics **146** 16
Outright Monthly Transactions **144 post b** 108
Overdraft facilities **123** 15
Own resources of the EU **144 post a** 60-63
Own Resources Decision **144 post a** 60-63

P

Pact for Growth and Employment **120** 5
Paid annual leave **153** 19
Paid holiday Schemes **158** 1, 2
Pandemic Crisis Support **144 post b** 90
Pandemic Emergency Purchase Programme *see* PEPP
Paper Industry **142** 12
Parental leave **153** 46
Part-time workers **153** 27; **157** 17
Passenger rights **90** 17
Passerelle Clause *see* Bridging Clause
"Passing on defence" **108** 41
Pegging **142** 17
PEPP **123** 35; **144 post a** 53
   concept **127** 21
   legal assessment **127** 25
   objective **127** 22
Personal data protection
   social policy **153** 23
Ports
   and maritime infrastructure **100** 21
   services **100** 22
      liberalisation **100** 23
Port state control **90** 14

Postal Directive **106** 37, 68
Postal Notice **106** 68
Poverty **147** 12
Predatory pricing **102** 62
Precautionary principle **114** 39
Price and cost factors **110** 34
Price discrimination **102** 61
Price regulation **90** 15, 17; **91** 9, 17
Price Stability **119** 16-18, 28-31, 35-37, 42 et seq.; **120** 2, 30, 33, 37 et seq.; **130** 5, 7, 8, 10, 17, 22-24, 52, 60-62, 77; **132** 59; **140** 10-13
   definition **127** 6
   financial assistance **122** 28
   financial stability **144 post a** 37
   primary objective of the ESCB **127** 5
   Term **144 post a** 37
Primacy of EU law **104** 6; **144 post a** 43
Principles
   of conferral **113** 1
   of equivalence **158** 6
   of frustration **139** 42
   of ne bis in idem **132** 51
   of precaution **114** 39
   of proportionality **90** 31; **98** 11; **106** 47, 62, 64, 69, 74, 76; **118** 47; **127** 4, 23 et seq.; **144** 8
      less restrictive alternative **106** 62, 69
   of sincere cooperation **101** 7; **106** 9; **130** 60, 72-74; **144 post c** 82 (*see also* Duty to cooperate
      competition law **102** 9
   of solidarity **106** 11; **122** 3
   of subsidiarity **90** 31; **118** 46; **146** 1, 16; **147** 2; **149** 16, 17
Priority competence *see at* Competences ~of the EU
Private Action Directive **103** 1, 3, 34, 35
Private creditor test **107** 42-45
Private investor test **107** 39-41
Private Sector Involvement **123** 32
Private vendor test **107** 46-48
Privatisation **106** 4; **144 post b** 70
Privileged access **124** 9-11
   interdictions
      exceptions **124** 11
Privileged undertakings **106** 1, 4-9, 81-83, 87
   See also Public and privileged undertakings
Procedural Regulation 2015/1589 *see* Regulation 2015/1589
Producer **111** 6
Products from other Member States **110** 1, 2, 9, 10
Products from third countries **110** 9, 10

Programmatic provision **158** 2, 3, 6
Professional competence **90** 16
Property ownership **106** 4, 9-11, 23-25, 30, 63, 67
   public and private ownership **106** 4
   public ownership **106** 5, 7, 9
   state ownership **91** 15; **106** 4, 7
   substantive ownership **91** 17
Property regime
   EU competence **118** 4, 14
Protectionism **90** 1, 8, 39
Protocol No. 4
   simplified amendment **129** 4-7
Protocol No. 26 **106** 44, 46-48, 53, 57
Protocol No. 27 **106** 9
Protocol on Social Rights **152** 2
Prudential considerations **124** 7
PSPP **123** 33-36; **130** 45, 62
   concept **127** 21
   objective **127** 22
   view of the ECJ **127** 23
   view of the German Federal Constitutional Court **127** 24
Public and privileged undertakings
   absolute competition approach **106** 7
   absolute sovereignty approach **106** 7
   accumulation of rights **106** 23
   advantageous position **106** 35
   anti-competitive consequence **106** 20, 36-38
   causal link **106** 21, 27
   conflict of interest **106** 21, 23, 25, 32
   contrary to Treaty rules **106** 10, 16-38, 41
   discrimination **106** 21
   dominant influence **106** 12
   dominant position **106** 6, 21, 22, 25, 27-32, 35-37, 42, 66
      led to abuse **106** 28-31
   effectiveness **106** 13, 26
   efficiency **106** 13
   exclusive rights **106** 12-14, 22-31, 33, 36, 37, 82
   inability to meet demand **106** 21-24
   induced abuse **106** 24
   inequality of opportunity **106** 21, 32, 34-38
   liability to result in an abuse **106** 26, 31
   potential for abuse **106** 23, 25
   privileged status **106** 4, 19
   regulatory function **106** 25
   regulatory powers **106** 42
   risk of abuse **106** 32, 37
   unavoidable abuse **106** 21, 24
   unavoidable infringement **106** 22, 23

Public authorities **106** 12, 29, 54, 55
Public finances **140** 16
Public health
   approximation of laws **114** 62
Public procurement **93** 19
Public resources **93** 19
Public service compensation **93** 7
Public service **106** 11, 47, 89
Public service obligation **91** 6, 15; **93** 18; **106** 4, 51, 54, 59
Public undertakings **106** 1, 3-6, 9-13, 33, 37, 50, 61, 81
   See also Public and privileged undertakings
Purchase of public debt
   in primary markets **123** 26
   in secondary markets **123** 27-36
   by financial entities on a voluntary basis **124** 11

Q

Qualified majority voting **100** 4; **103** 2, 3; **113** 16
Quality control **90** 15 et seq.
Quality of jobs **145** 46
Quantitative restrictions **90** 15, 17; **91** 9; **106** 3, 18

R

REACT-EU **162** 32
Rebates **102** 81
Reciprocal recognition *see* Mutual recognition
Recovery and Resilience Facility **144 post a** 54, 57; **153** 43
Recovery Assistance for Cohesion and the Territories of Europe *see* REACT-EU
Reference criteria **144 post c** 16
   exemptions **144 post c** 19, 23
REFIT **154** 27
Refusal to deal **102** 68
Regional organisations **139** 44
Regulation 2015/1588 **108** 7; **109** 4
Regulation 2015/1589 **108** 5; **109** 7
Regulatory Fitness and Perand Performance Programme *see* REFIT
Relevant market **101** 31-38
   definition **102** 12
   demand-side substitution **101** 33
   geographic **101** 37
   supply-side substitution **101** 35
Reliability **90** 16
Reporting obligation **159** passim; **161** passim
Resettlement Programme **151** 27
Resolution objectives **144 post d** 124, 252

Resolution plan **144 post d** 142, 156, 162-166
Restrictions
　　ancillary restraints **101** 48
　　appreciability **101** 44
　　by effect **101** 30
　　by object **101** 29
　　by object or by effect **101** 27
　　context analysis **101** 54
　　counterfactual analysis **101** 30
　　cumulative effect **101** 47
　　de minimis **101** 44
　　hard core restrictions **101** 1, 52
　　qualitative analysis **101** 46
　　quantitative analysis **101** 45
　　rule of reason analysis **101** 49
　　Wouters exception **101** 50
Reverse qualified majority voting **126** 39; **136** 15; **144 post a** 9; **144 post c** 42, 72
Right to disconnect **157** 14
Right to be heard **132** 19, 85; **144 post d** 115-117, 198
Risk Weighted Assets **144 post d** 210, 212
Roadworthiness **91** 19
Rounding rules **140** 34

S
Safeguard clause **143** 1
Safety and health at work **153** 16, 23-25
Schengen Convention **144 post a** 4
S-C-P paradigm
　　conduct **101** 40
　　consumer welfare **101** 43
　　structure **101** 39
Secondary legislation **90** 9, 24, 32; **93** 13
Security **90** 4, 9, 17; **91** 18
Selectivity
　　State aid **107** 54-66
Self-preferencing **102** 88
Services of general economic interest **93** 6, 17; **106** 1, 6, 28, 41-76, 79; **107** 50
　　affordability **106** 46, 54, 57
　　development of trade **106** 6, 41, 49, 71, 74, 76
　　economically acceptable conditions **106** 64, 65, 67-69
　　efficiency **106** 57, 75
　　equal treatment **106** 46, 54, 57
　　exclusive rights **106** 64, 66, 68
　　financial balance **106** 65
　　financial equilibrium **106** 67
　　market services **106** 55, 56
　　obstruct the performance **106** 49, 62, 63, 71, 76
　　political tension **106** 47
　　State aid **107** 87-91
Services of general interest **106** 44, 46, 48, 53, 54, 57
Sherman Act **101** 49
Similar domestic products **110** 4
Similar products **110** 21-28, 42
　　method of manufacture **110** 25
　　needs from the point of view of consumers **110** 25
　　organoleptic properties **110** 25
　　test of similarity **110** 27
Simplified revision procedure **136** 28
Sincere cooperation *see* Principle of sincere cooperation
Single European Act **100** 4
Single European Sky *see at* Transport
Single Market **97** 8; **139** 6, 10; **141** 15
Single Resolution Fund *see at* EMU
Skilled workforce **145** 32
Smart, sustainable and inclusive growth **146** 3
SMP **127** 21
Social and territorial cohesion *see* Cohesion
Social dialogue **152** passim
　　committees **154** 14
　　Fundamental Rights Platform **152** 32
　　origin **152** 1 et seqq.
　　initiative **152** 10
Social exclusion **153** 48-50
Social functions **106** 11, 48
Social market economy **106** 9; **120** 34-36
Social parameters **159** 3
Social partners **151** 11
Social Policy **159** 1, 2
　　approximation **151** 12
　　austerity **151** 7
　　bridging clause **153** 22
　　Cedefop (*see* Cedefop)
　　care-related career breaks (*see* Care-related career breaks)
　　collective bargaining (*see* Collective bargaining)
　　combatting in-work exclusion **153** 41-43
　　conditions of employment for third-country nationals **153** 39
　　consultation of social partners **154** passim
　　coordination **151** 11, 12
　　COVID-19 **156** 14
　　dialogue between management and labour (*see* Dialogue between management and labour)
　　discrimination **153** 48-50
　　based on sex **157** passim

Index 1531

equal pay **153** 45; **157** passim
equality between women and men **153** 44-47; **157** 10
EUCFR **153** 10
EU-OSHA (*see* EU-OSHA)
Eurofund (*see* Eurofund)
Europe 2020 **153** 8
European Agency for Safety and Health at Work **153** 25
European Committee of Social Rights **153** 13
European Pact for Social Stability **151** 22
European Pillar of Social Rights (*see* European Pillar of Social Rights)
European Social Charter **151** 22
fixed-term workers **153** 27
Fundamental Rights Platform **152** 32
gender equality (*see* Gender equality)
improvement of the working environment **153** 23-25
information and consultation of workers **153** 25
inter-state cooperation **156** passim
Lisbon Strategy **151** 19; **153** 8
maternity leave **153** 17
modernisation of social protection systems **153** 53
open method of cooperation **151** 6; **156** 15-22
origin **151** 1 et seqq.
paid annual leave **153** 46
parental leave **153** 46
part-time workers **153** 27; **157** 17
protection of personal data **153** 23
protection of workers against unjustified dismissal **153** 32-34
Protocol **152** 2
REFIT (*see* REFIT)
safety and health at work **153** 16, 23-25
shared competence **151** 4, 11; **153** 6
social dialogue (*see* Social dialogue)
social exclusion **153** 48-50
social protection **153** 51-53
social security **153** 29-31
soft law **156** 23-26; **157** 30
temporary agency workers **153** 27
Tripartite Social Summit for Growth and Employment **152** 11-19

Union action **153** 15-20
Universal Declaration of Human Rights **151** 23
working conditions **153** 26-28
working time **153** 20
work-life balance **153** 45
Social problems **161** 3
Social protection **153** 51-53
of workers **153** 29-31
Social Protection Committee **150** 5; **160** 1-4
advisory body **160** 2, 3
new secondary legal basis **160** 4, 5
Social protection systems
modernisation **153** 53
Social rights **144 post b** 75-77; **158** 2, 3, 5, 6
Social security **106** 11, 14, 54; **153** 29-31
Soft law **106** 48, 52, 53, 57; **144 post c** 80; **146** 2, 10, 16; **148** 8
approximation of laws **114** 49
social policy **156** 23-26; **157** 30
Sole legal basis **103** 1
Solidarity clause **122** 34, 35
Solidarity fund **122** 14
Sound public finances **126** 1
Sovereignty **139** 6
budget sovereignty **144 post c** 98
tax sovereignty **113** 4
Spaak Report **156** 5
Spain
financial assistance **144 post b** 100
recapitalisation of financial institutions **144 post b** 100
Special or exclusive rights **106** 1, 4, 10, 13-15, 19-21, 26, 32, 36, 37, 68, 82
Special rights **106** 13, 15, 83, 84
Speculative attacks **142** 16
SRM **127** 37; **144 post a** 5, 15
access to the file **144 post d** 199, 200
Appeal Panel **144 post d** 201-203
asset separation tool **144 post d** 169
bail-in **144 post d** 193
bank insolvency **144 post d** 165, 169, 279-281
early intervention **144 post d** 161
investigatory powers **144 post d** 198
legal basis **144 post d** 131-138
right to be heard **144 post d** 198

SSM **119** 32, 38; **127** 37 et seq.; **130** 13, 37, 40, 63, 80; **131** 6; **139** 31, 32; **144 post a** 13, 14; **144 post b** 102; **144 post d** 4-6, 14-122, 156, 300
   close cooperation **132** 96
   legal assessment **127** 39
   legal basis **144 post d** 25-30
   macro-prudential supervision **144 post d** 81
   Memorandums of Understanding **144 post d** 55, 60
   motivation **144 post d** 118
   non-objection procedure **144 post d** 37, 38
   qualifying holdings **132** 83; **144 post d** 72, 90, 102
   right to be heard **132** 85; **144 post d** 115-117
   structure **127** 37 et seq.
   supervisory board **127** 38
   supervisory fees **132** 100
SSNIP test **101** 32
Stability and Growth Pact **126** 36 **135** 3; **144 post a** 6
   escape clauses **144 post c** 31
   new sanctions **144 post c** 41, 70
   reverse qualified majority voting **144 post c** 42, 72
Stability support **144 post b** 64-78
   collective action clause **144 post b** 121-125
   debt restructuring clause **144 post b** 123
   debt sustainability clause **144 post b** 65, 66
   direct recapitalisation of financial institutions **144 post b** 101-107
   implementation **144 post b** 78
   loans **144 post b** 80-85
   Memorandum of Understanding **144 post b** 69-72
   precautionary financial assistance **144 post b** 86-93
   Primary Market Support Facility **144 post b** 115
   private sector participation **144 post b** 121-125
   recapitalisation of financial institutions **144 post b** 94-107
   request **144 post b** 64
   Secondary Market Support Facility **144 post b** 108-114
   SURE **122** 10; **144 post a** 53
   voting rules **144 post b** 67, 68
Staged integration **90** 38
Standard of living **91** 24
Standstill provision **90** 1, 38; **92** 1
State action defence **102** 19

State aid **90** 7; **91** 6; **93** 3, 7; **96** 11; **106** 3, 6, 18, 75, 81, 89; **144 post d** 128, 182-186, 192, 196, 295
   advantage **107** 33-53
   adverse effects on trade and competition **107** 13
   Altmark test **93** 6, 20; **107** 49-53
   compatibility **107** 15, 72-93; **108** 3
   compensation for disasters **107** 75
   compensation test **107** 49-53
   concept of "State" **107** 16
   COVID-19 **107** 75, 81; **156** 14
   cultural interests **107** 83
   damages **108** 48
   de minimis aid **93** 11; **107** 69
   differentiation **107** 18
   distortion of competition **107** 70 et seq.
   economic advantage **107** 12
   economic projects **107** 82
   effect of inter-State trade **107** 67-69
   Enabling Regulation 2015/1588 **108** 5; **109** 4
   exclusive rights **93** 19
   exemptions **93** 12; **107** 72-93
   existing aid **108** 13, 21
   formal investigation procedure **108** 28-32
   General Block Exemption Regulation **107** 85; **108** 7, 33
   German unification **107** 76
   important projects of common EU interest **107** 81
   imputability **107** 10, 26-32
   judicial review **108** 8
   legitimate expectation **108** 41
   manual of procedures **108** 11
   market economy investor test **93** 5; **107** 39-41
   market economy operator test **93** 5; **107** 36-38
   measures with equivalent effect to subsidies **107** 4
   new aid **108** 14, 22-32
   notion of **107** 2
   "passing on defence" **108** 41
   preliminary examination **108** 24
   private creditor test **107** 42-45
   private enforcement **108** 44
   private investor test **107** 39-41
   private vendor test **107** 46-48
   Procedural Regulation 2015/1589 **108** 5; **109** 7
   recovery of unlawful aid **108** 35-43
   review by national courts **108** 44-51

review by Union courts **108** 52-56
rules **98** 2; **143** 15; **144 post d** 192
selectivity **107** 11, 54-66
services of general economic interest **107** 50, 87-91
social aid **93** 14; **107** 74
standstill obligation **108** 3, 9
State resources **107** 20-32
Subsidies **93** 1, 8; **107** 4
tax policy **107** 19
transport **107** 92 et seq.
underdeveloped areas **107** 80
Union aid **107** 7
unlawful aid **108** 19
State intervention **91** 6; **106** 3, 5
State measure **106** 8, 19, 21, -23, 25-27, 29-31, 34-37, 41, 66, 83, 87
State monopolies **102** 9
State-of-origin taxation **113** 14
State prerogatives **101** 25
State resolvency **144 post b** 124
Statistical analysis **146** 14
Structural deficit **144 post c** 26
Sub-national public policies **148** 14
Subsidies **107** 4
Substantive competition law rules **103** 1
Sudden crisis **144** 6, 13
Sunk cost investment **102** 26
Supervisory and resolution tasks over financial institutions **123** 20
Supremacy of EU law *see* Primacy of EU law
Support to Mitigate Unemployment Risks in an Emergency *see* SURE
SURE **122** 10; **144 post a** 53; **162** 33
Surveillance cycle **144 post c** 6
European Semester (*see* European Semester)
national semester **144 post c** 63
Sustainability **143** 26
mobility **91** 23
System of open and competitive markets **106** 9
System of taxation **110** 32, 48, 49
Systemically Important Payment Systems **132** 68

T
TARGET2 **132** 66, 67
securities platform (T2S) **132** 66, 69
Tax advantages **110** 20
exemptions **110** 20, 28
reductions **110** 20
Tax arrangements **110** 35, 48
Tax policy
State aid **107** 19
Tax provisions **113** 6, 9, 19, 28

Technical characteristics **91** 19
Technical lead **102** 23
Technological developments **91** 23
Telecommunications Equipment Directive **106** 82, 84
Telecommunications Services Directive **106** 82, 84
Temporary agency workers **153** 27
Third way of governance **146** 13
TMC Agreement *see* Agreement on the Transfer and Mutualization of Contributions to the Single Resolution Fund
Trade protection **143** 19
Traffic congestion **91** 23
Traffic rights **91** 10
Traffic safety **90** 33; **91**, 18–20
Trans European Network **91** 23
Trans-European Transport Network *see at* Transport
Transfer Union **136** 29; **144 post a** 2
Transparency **130** 79, 81
Transparency Directive **106** 12-15, 81
Transport **98** 5, 15; **103** 21, 45
Advisory Committee **99** 1 et seq.
cabotage (*see* Cabotage)
conditions **94** 8-10; **95** 6; **96** 7
coordination **93** 17
cross-border **90** 27, 29; **91** 8
extra-union **90** 6, 23, 28, 36; **91** 11
inbound **91** 10
intra-union **90** 27
licensing **90** 16; **91** 14, 17
links **95** 2
modal split **91** 6
network **100** 2
operations **96** 8
outbound **91** 10
rates **94** 8-10; **95** 6; **96** 7
residual external competence **90** 6, 36
road, rail and inland waterway transport **100** 1, 7
scope of Transport Title 9 **100** 9 et seq.
sea and air transport
and general rules of the Treaties **100** 12 et seq.
and Transport Title 9 **100** 9
control **100** 3
Single European Sky **100** 17-20
State aid **107** 92 et seq.
Trans-European Transport Network **100** 21, 23
Transboundery **91** 6
Transport intermediary **90** 20

Transport facility **91** 24
Transport mode **90** 13, 23
Transit **90** 37; **91** 10
Transitional rules **90** 41
Transition period **90** 38
Treaty Establishing the European Stability Mechanism **119** 10
   accession of new Members **144 post b** 17
   accountability **144 post b** 73, 74, 128-144
   amendments to Article 136 TFEU **144 post b** 4
   adjustment programme **144 post b** 69-72 (*see also* Adjustment Programme)
   Arbitration Clause **144 post a** 45; **144 post b** 51,52
   austerity **144 post b** 63, 75
   Authorised Capital Stock **144 post b** 20
   backstop **144 post b** 107; **144 post d** 297
   blocking minority **144 post b** 68
   Board of Directors **144 post b** 37-39
   Board of Governors **144 post b** 34-36
   borrowed administration arrangement **144 post a** 45; **144 post b** 42, 48, 51
   capital **144 post a** 10
   capital calls **144 post b** 25
   carry trade **144 post b** 28
   Clause of Coherence **144 post a** 42; **144 post b** 14, 16
   Clausula rebus sic stantibus **144 post b** 18
   Collective Action Clauses **144 post b** 121, 123
   conditionality **144 post a** 34; **144 post b** 62
   Contribution Key **144 post b** 21
   Cyprus **144 post b** 84
   Debt Restructuring Clause **144 post b** 123
   debt sustainability analysis **144 post b** 65, 66
   democratic legitimacy **144 post b** 73, 74, 128-144
   dividend distribution **144 post b** 24
   duration **144 post b** 17
   dynamic treaty provisions **144 post b** 26
   Economic and Monetary Policy **144 post b** 7
   emergency procedure **144 post b** 68
   European Central Bank **144 post b** 47-49, 66
   European Commission **144 post b** 42-46
   European Monetary Fund **144 post a** 49; **144 post b** 53-57, 145-151
   financial assistance operations **144 post b** 58
   financial stability (*see* Financial stability)
   funding **144 post b** 27
   genesis **144 post b** 1
   Greece **144 post b** 84, 85
   Guidelines **144 post b** 78
   indispensable nature **144 post b** 61
   institutional structure **144 post b** 32
   instruments **144 post a** 11; **144 post b** 79-117
      Direct Recapitalisation of Financial Institutions **144 post b** 101-107
      Enhanced Conditioned Credit Line **144 post b** 88, 89
      loans **144 post b** 80-85
      Precautionary Conditioned Credit Line **144 post b** 88, 89
      Precautionary Financial Assistance **144 post b** 86-93
      Primary Market Support Facility **144 post b** 115
      Recapitalisation of Financial Institutions **144 post b** 94-107
      Secondary Market Support Facility **144 post b** 108-114
   Joint Declaration by the ESM Members **144 post b** 26
   legal basis **144 post b** 4
   legal personality **144 post b** 10
   lending capacity **144 post b** 20
   liability cap **144 post b** 25
   liability cascade **144 post b** 104
   Managing Director **144 post b** 40, 41
   Memorandum of Understanding **144 post b** 62, 69-77
   moral hazard **144 post b** 30
   no-bail-out **136** 35; **144 post b** 5, 9
   Package Deal Clause **144 post a** 35
   pandemic crisis support **144 post b** 90
   parliamentary control **144 post b** 13
   pricing policy **144 post b** 30
   primacy of EU law **144 post a** 43
   Pringle decision **144 post b** 6
   Private Sector Participation **144 post b** 121-125
   privileges and immunities **144 post b** 11, 12
   procedure for granting stability support **144 post b** 59, 64-78
   purpose **144 post a** 2, 23; **144 post b** 7, 19
   Reserve Fund **144 post b** 22
   Resolvency Procedure **144 post b** 124
   seat **144 post b** 10
   Single Supervisory Mechanism (*see* SSM)
   social rights **144 post b** 75-77
   Spain **144 post b** 100

special-purpose compound of functional integration **144 post b** 140
Staff of the ESM **144 post b** 12
professional secrecy **144 post b** 12
termination **144 post b** 18
Troika **144 post b** 67, 68, 73, 74
voting rules **144 post b** 67, 68
Withdrawal of a Member State **144 post b** 18
Treaty-making power **90** 36; **91** 4
Treaty of Amsterdam
Article 98 TFEU, development **98** 1
declarations **149** 6
Treaty of Maastricht **131** 23
Protocol No. 25 **131** 16
Protocol on Social Policy **152** 1
Treaty on Stability, Coordination and Governance in the Economic and Monetary Union **119** 10; **120** 5, 12, 49, 66-69, 73; **121** 49, 66; **122** 4; **126** 50 **144 post a** 6; **144 post b** 63; **144 post c** 5
1/20 Rule **144 post a** 7; **144 post c** 23
Arbitration Clause **144 post a** 45
Balanced Budget Rules **144 post a** 7; **144 post c** 25
borrowed administration arrangement **144 post a** 45
Commission's tasks **144 post c** 58
ECJ competence **144 post c** 55
Budgetary Discipline **144 post a** 31
Clause of Coherence **144 post a** 42; **144 post c** 15
correction mechanism **144 post c** 32
debt brakes **144 post a** 7, 22; **144 post c** 32
financial stability **144 post a** 29
Genesis **144 post a** 6
legal nature **144 post c** 11
national implementation **144 post c** 34
Package Deal Clause **144 post a** 35
primacy of EU law **144 post a** 43
purpose **144 post a** 2
Treaty revision **144 post c** 95
autonomous **98** 17
national parliaments **139** 5
simplified revision procedure **136** 28
veto power **139** 5
Tripartite Social Summit for Growth and Employment **145** 16; **150** 6, 7; **152** 11-19

Turnover taxes **113** 22-28
Tying **102** 74

U
Ultra vires act
PSPP ruling (German Federal Constitutional Court) **127** 24
Weiss ruling (ECJ) **127** 23 et seq.
Unanimity **103** 2; **113** 12
Unbundling **91** 16
Undertaking **101** 23-26; **106** 1, 3-15, 17, 19-23, 26-27, 29, 31-33, 35-38, 41-43, 49-52, 55, 56, 61-65, 70, 71, 73, 76, 81-83, 85, 87
autonomous conduct **101** 26
functional concept **101** 26
social functions **106** 11, 48
solidarity activities **101** 24
State prerogatives **101** 25
Undistorted competition **106** 19, 25, 36, 37
system ensuring undistorted competition **106** 9
Unfair competition **142** 12
Unfair excessive prices **102** 54
Unilateral protective measures authorisation **143** 33, 34
Union aid **107** 7
Uniform application
of competition law **103** 6, 10
United Kingdom **131** 2, 5, 15-17
withdrawal from the EU (*see* Brexit)
Universal Declaration of Human Rights **151** 23
Universal rights **106** 46
Universal service **91** 6; **106** 13, 37, 46, 57, 59, 66, 68
obligation **106** 4, 54, 64, 68
provision **106** 13
US antitrust **101** 3, 51

V
Value added tax **113** 22-28
single area **113** 27
Vertical cooperation **101** 14
Vertical integration **102** 22
Vocational training **162** 9
Voluntarism **146** 19
Voluntary cooperation **147** 3

W

Ways and means facility **123** 9
Whistle-blower **132** 95
White Paper
    Delors White Paper **145** 5, 23
    on the modernisation of the implementing rules of Article 81 and 82 of the EC Treaty **103** 18
World Bank **139** 50; **143** 28
Working conditions **153** 26-28
Working environment **153** 23-25
Working time **153** 20
Work-life balance **153** 45
Wouters exception **101** 50
WTO **143** 17, 21

Y

Youth Employment Initiative **164** 4
Youth Guarantee **153** 43

Printed by Printforce, the Netherlands